The
Oxford Dictionary of
Quotations

THIRD EDITION

Oxford   New York   Toronto   Melbourne

OXFORD UNIVERSITY PRESS

PREFACE TO THE THIRD EDITION

Many a home and library in the English-speaking world has a copy of the *Oxford Dictionary of Quotations* in the first or, more frequently, second edition. Those should not be dispensed with nor superseded; but need will be found to make room for this new, third edition. For over a quarter of a century has passed since the publication of the last revision, and much that is quoted or quotable has been said or written or simply come into wider cognizance during this period. Add that the second edition, published in 1953, was about 95% the same in content as the first edition of 1941 — the differences consisting then chiefly of the addition of Second World War quotations (essentially of course those of Winston Churchill),[1] correction of errors, rearrangement of certain sections, and much more full and precise indexing — and it will be seen that this volume presents the first substantial revision of the *Dictionary* since its original compilation.

To have simply incorporated modern and freshly recognized quotations into the preceding edition in like measure to its ingredients would have resulted in a volume which, on account of the present costs of producing so bulky a work, must have been priced beyond the book-purchasing powers of all but the wealthier owners of libraries, private or even public. To have published a separate supplement to the second edition would have been unfair to those (mostly younger) readers and writers who did not already possess a copy of a previous edition, and might reasonably seek a single-volume coverage of what they heard or saw quoted from all periods and places that impinged on their own conversation or culture. It was resolved therefore that space must be made for new inclusions by considerable cutting of the contents of the second edition.

Besides, there were positive reasons for omitting parts of the earlier selection of quotations in fairly extensive quantity. The first edition was compiled within the Oxford University Press in the decade of the 1930s by men and women imbued with the history and politics, the culture whether educated or popular, of the first quarter of the twentieth century in Britain, and especially the literature of the ancient and the English-speaking worlds that was then read and studied at home, school, and university. They had mostly been to Oxford or Cambridge and before that to schools where learning poetry (and even prose) by heart for repetition was regular. Some had served in the First World War and the songs they knew were those of marching soldiers or of the music-hall; drawing-room ballads too were not forgotten. Hymns, though, when church-going was still the rule, were probably the most widely known forms of song for the compilers of the first edition; and constant acquaintance with

---

[1] The first edition contained only the one 'terminological inexactitude' part-sentence; the second edition added another 25 quotations from the then Prime Minister; in this new edition appear 41 Churchill items, including enough context for the original one to explain its sense and correct those who often misuse 'terminological inexactitude'.

the Bible and the Book of Common Prayer enabled them to assume that 'five smooth stones out of the brook' or ' sat in the seat of the scornful' needed no context for their recognition and the understanding of their significance. The Greek and Latin classics were still then drawn on for quotations by Members of Parliament, or elsewhere in debating or after-dinner speeches. Dr. Johnson's observation in the first sentence of the prefatory pages of 'The Compilers to the Reader' of this *Dictionary* in 1941 — see p. x — was still, if not strictly, true.

Much of that lettered world of reference has disappeared. The *Dictionary* was claimed to be one of *familiar* quotations. But take now any page that has two or more authors represented on it, in the second edition, and ask someone of great general knowledge and wide reading, someone even of an older generation, and they will find several quotations quite unknown to them. Every generation, every decade perhaps, needs its new *Dictionary of Quotations.*

In order to select and accommodate the desired new quotations, a team of revisers consisting of a few members of the Press, together with a greater number of alert, enthusiastic, and variously interested members of the public, was asked during 1975—7 to suggest cuts to be made from the contents of the second edition and additions to be inserted in the third. Apart from the publishing editors, they included a former literary editor and other active or retired journalists, writers, and representatives of Parliament and the professions, the universities, the Church, Whitehall and the City, the British Museum, and even another publishing house. No definition of what constitutes a quotation was imposed; we suggest that a quotation is what is recognized for one (even without quotation marks) by some at least of its hearers or readers, or else what is welcomed as quotable, and then probably quoted. The claim that this is a dictionary of *familiar* quotations is, moreover, hereby dropped. (It would have been unkind to set a ban on the 'innocent vanity' Bernard Darwin refers to in the first paragraph of his Introduction, of those who know a quotation that may be unfamiliar to others.)[1] But neither is it simply an anthology displaying the choice and taste of one man, or even of a small committee of the Press such as compiled the first edition of the *Dictionary. Popularity,* rather, is the word (not eschewed even by the original compilers — see p. x): every quotation or passage excluded had been marked for omission by a majority of those who read right through the second edition, and all quotations added have likewise had a majority vote in favour of them.

The method of revision was, first, to issue some ten copies of the second edition, interleaved with blank pages, to the core of the revision team, each of whom read through every single quotation and marked their recommended deletions, corrections, or additions; these were then collated and the balance of opinion calculated by the editors in the Press. Secondly, suggestions for quotations to be added were sought on specially prepared forms, with a voting box for each item; the suggestions lists were then photocopied and distributed to the full team of revisers,

[1] Bernard Darwin in his second paragraph used a quotation from Charles Lamb that has never been included in this *Dictionary;* his quotation from *The Wrecker* (p.xvii) was inserted in the second edition, but not in the first; nor in this.

about twenty in all, whose votes in favour or against each provided the editors, when the forms were returned to them, with at least a sample poll for that popularity which had seemed the only valid criterion. A twenty-five years' accumulation of correspondence from readers of the second edition had also brought to the Press a small harvest of quotations offered by members of the public in general; these were likewise given the suggestions-list treatment and voted on.

Public opinion and discussion within the Press had helped to evolve too some new principles for whole classes of 'quotations' to be excluded. The original compilers of the *Dictionary* had claimed — see p. xi — that 'proverbs and phrases are not included, since these have been dealt with fully in the *Oxford Dictionary of English Proverbs*'; this was not altogether true, and several so-called quotations have been removed because they are found in proverbial form much earlier than the authors to whom they were attributed.

Nursery rhymes, as a section, have been ousted. In the second edition reference was made to the *Oxford Dictionary of Nursery Rhymes,* edited by Iona and Peter Opie, as having provided the sources for many rhymes. Since these rarely have a named author, and the sources given were those of earliest written or published appearance, the information the *Dictionary of Quotations* supplied was not only largely drawn from but duplicated the Opies' *Dictionary of Nursery Rhymes,* to which masterly work the reader is commended.

Songs, with some regret, have also been excluded. The writers of the words of music-hall or popular songs identified in the preceding editions were often so obscure that the reader was informed of no more than their names, not even their dates. To have extended the citing of snatches of song on the scale of the earlier editions would have been a boundless venture: if 'my dear old Dutch' had been kept to the credit of Albert Chevalier, why not 'We'll gather lilacs...' added to Ivor Novello's or 'It's been a hard day's night' to the Beatles'? And how could justice be done then to the galaxy of shining, singing phrases, from the Gershwins to Cole Porter to Bob Dylan, in America's greatest contribution to Western civilization? The reader will look in vain to know who 'had plenty of privilege' — or was it 'twenty years' privilege'? — 'taken away from him' or when and where; and if authors and sources of popular songs had been given, why should the reader not also have expected to be told who wrote, 'How beautiful they are, the lordly ones', or even *'Che gelida manina'* ? No: the rule of thumb, given to the revision team and followed by the editors, has been that if the words cannot be said without the tune (*a* tune, in the case of many hymns) coming to mind, they are *not* quotations in the same sense as the others. Try 'Night and Day'.... This rule has not prevented the inclusion of poems that have subsequently been set to music; nor verses which, though written for musical setting, such as John Gay's, W. S. Gilbert's, or Noël Coward's, may now be quoted without a tune in the mental background.

Broadcasting and other mass-media have, in the past forty years, vastly multiplied the use and recognition and even therefore the 'quoting' of advertisements, slogans, and other catch-phrases. It would have been an equally vast and pointless task to try to record even the most familiar of them, apart from the near impossibility of ascribing each to the actual copywriter, speechwriter, or scriptwriter. This applies as much to the cinema and popular theatre as to radio and television. 'After you, Claude!' 'A funny thing happened on the way...'; yes, but not in the *O.D.Q.,* for lack of space and time.

Titles of books, films, and plays have been excised for similar reasons. Two or three exceptions may be found, where a title has come to be used in quotation often by people with no inkling that it was a title. (But no one would ever say, for example, *'Mourning Becomes Electra'* without that awareness.)

There will indeed probably be found places where all these guide-lines for the revisers have been departed from. One principle, however, of exclusion was not formulated or imposed but does seem to have emerged from the collective spirit of all the revisers: much that was sententious moralizing, homely wisdom, or merely uplifting reflection has been omitted.

But what of what remains? About 60% of the contents of the second edition is retained, not surprisingly. Well-known passages of the drama and literature of the past, from the Authorized Version of the Bible and from Shakespeare, together naturally with many famous historical *mots,* dicta, quips, and other utterances, still form the solid core of the universe of discourse in quotations, and the major part of this *Dictionary.*

Readers acquainted with the earlier editions may be interested (as the original compilers expected they would be) in the most quoted writers: they are still largely the same as those listed for the first edition on p. xi in alphabetical order before the Bible and the Book of Common Prayer. Less is quoted in this edition than in its predecessors in the case of every author in that list. But there are very nearly the same number of quotations from the two leading prose-writers, Dr. Johnson and Dickens. Wordsworth has suffered most; one of the revisers wrote of the 'huge snowdrifts of Wordsworth' that needed to be cleared, and indeed there were: beautiful, but not useful, and in the way! Cowper is the other poet who has (to change the metaphor) taken the biggest tumble. Both these illustrate certainly the decline in learning of English verse by heart. Cowper actually had no more space given to him in the second edition than Keats or Pope, though they are not listed by the first edition compilers; those two are well ahead of him in this new edition. The order of most quoted writers (the Bible and Prayer Book apart) is: Shakespeare, Tennyson, Milton, Johnson, Browning, Kipling, Dickens, Byron, Wordsworth, Pope, Keats, and Shelley. There are recent poets with more space given to them here than Cowper. The four novelists mentioned by the compilers of the first edition — Trollope, Henry James, Jane Austen and P. G. Wodehouse — all have more quotations in this third one (in each case continuing the trend of the second).

If proportionately more space has been given here to passages from the Bible of 1611 and the Prayer Book of 1662 (in which quotations from the Psalms appear) that is because English speaking and English writing are both shot through with phrases that derive from those books, still used, often unwittingly, even though the amount of church-going or Bible-reading has certainly diminished; indeed, for that very reason, as has been implied, more of the context of a biblical phrase, or one, say, from the Collects, has now been provided. It is no longer true, as the compilers were able to claim in 1941, that, in great part, both books are familiar to most people.

Not many concessions have been made, however, to the fact that the Greek and Latin classics are less studied in the original than they were; it is likely that rather more people are acquainted now, through translation, with Homer and Plato, Catullus and Martial, for example, and for the sake of those who do know the original languages they are for the most part quoted in Greek or Latin (with a translation supplied). Horace still has the 'array of columns' Bernard Darwin refers to, though half are English-made. Many more quotations from other modern European languages have been included. In all cases where a translator has not been named, the translation has in this edition been newly supplied by the publishing editors, in it is hoped a livelier rendering than earlier versions (but a close one).

In general it has been thought helpful in many instances to give more context to a quotation retained from the previous edition consisting only of a phrase or fragment of words; and the same principle has been applied to the few thousand newly added quotations. The length of the average quotation will thus probably be greater than in the earlier editions.

Beneath each quotation its source is given or is deducible from those immediately above it, and it has proved possible often to supply a better source reference than before. But in many cases (many more than for earlier editions) this annotation also includes some explanation of circumstances, a cross-reference to a related quotation, or some added point of quirky interest.

Throughout, the editors have endeavoured to correct errors perpetrated in the preceding editions. Many have been pointed out by members of the public since the last corrected impression of the second edition, and many discovered by the revisers in preparing this one. Others have doubtless lurked, or even slipped in; and for these the editors only are to blame, not the contributory revisers from outside the Press. The attempt was made to check the texts and verify the references of all new quotations elected for inclusion. The *Dictionary,* however, cannot aspire to be a work of scholarship in the strictest sense; no claim is made that the best or most authoritative text has been sought out and used in each case. It is a general work of reference, and normally a standard twentieth-century text, such as a World's Classics or an Oxford Classical Texts edition, has been followed. The editors will of course welcome corrections of their errors.

In the interests of book-production economy the index is neither as intensive nor as extensive as in the second edition, but it still occupies over a third of the volume and contains nearly 70,000 entries. The selection of words to be indexed has been made more after careful consideration of the salient word likely to be recalled in any quotation, and less at the mechanical rate of about two words per line. The actual process of printing and numbering the index has, moreover, been ingeniously achieved by computer; and a new attempt to assist the user of the index has also thus been contrived by the printing, before each page and quotation number reference, of the first few letters of the author's name. Thus a search under 'hill' to discover what manner of man Stevenson described as being 'home from the hill' will be promptly ended by the letters 'STEV' and sight of the 'hunter'.

But it will inevitably be upon the quotations newly chosen for inclusion that attention will be principally focused. Whether they are drawn from authors and works that have appeared in the last forty years or so, from the political and social memorabilia of the last quarter-century, or from areas neglected in preceding editions (writers now more widely known, foreign literature and drama, passages earlier evidently considered indelicate), it is hoped that for their familiarity or relevance or sheer appeal they resonate a bell in the memory, or carry a ring of aptness and truth, or just simply entertain and amuse.

It remains to record and renew the thanks of the Press to the team of scrutineers and contributors who agreed to take part in the process of revision described above, naming first the one who first took up the challenge and undertaking, and who by his example and zest influenced the whole new edition; the other names follow, in reverse alphabetical order:

the late Mr. T. C. Worsley; Mr. John Sparrow; Mr. Alan Ryan; the Hon. Sir Steven Runciman; Mrs. M. C. Rintoul; Mr. John Rayner; Mr. Charles Monteith; Mr. Colin Leach; Miss Marghanita Laski; Mr. Antony Jay; the Revd. Gerard Irvine; Miss Phyllis Hartnoll; Mr. John Gere; Miss Bertha Gaster; the late Lord Bradwell (Tom Driberg); Mr. Richard Boston; and Lord Annan.

As has been mentioned, many members of the public have contributed some few or more quotations or corrections, and the editors have not been without recourse to other published collections of quotations; it would be invidious to name some and not all, but the Press is grateful to all who have helped, and (it is expected and hoped) will continue to help the *Dictionary* in this way. But special thanks are due to the following who, at the editors' request, sought sources or supplied quotations in particular sections or otherwise made this a more accurate reference book:

Dr. Raymond Tyner; the late Mr. Oliver Stallybrass; Professor Richard Ellmann; Lady Donaldson; Mr Nevill Coghill; Mr. George Chowdharay-Best; and Professor Mortimer Chambers.

There has proved no need to reprint the 'Note to the Second Edition' (1953), but thanks were there recorded to two distinguished officers of the Press, Dr. R. W. Chapman and Sir Humphrey Milford, for their help in preparing that edition; also to Mr. S. H. Moore for French, German, and Spanish quotations. Much of their work probably survives in this third edition. The members of the past or present staff of the Press who have been principally concerned in the preparation of this edition are Andrew Thomson, Ena Sheen, Richard Sabido (and the Computer Department), Betty Palmer, Christina Lacey, Bob Knowles, Derek Hudson, Judy Gough, Roy Girling (and the Computer Typesetting Unit), and Richard Brain.

March 1979   R.T.B.

CONTENTS

THE COMPILERS TO THE READER
(1941)

'Classical quotation', said Johnson, 'is the *parole* of literary men all over the world.' Although this is no longer strictly true the habit of quoting, both in speech and writing, has steadily increased since his day, and Johnson would undoubtedly be surprised to find here eight and a half pages of his own work that have become part of the *parole* of the reading public. Small dictionaries of quotations have been published for many years — in 1799 D. E. Macdonnel brought out a *Dictionary of Quotations chiefly from Latin and French translated into English* — and during comparatively recent years several large works of American editorship have been produced. In this book the Oxford Press publishes what it is hoped will be a valuable addition to the Oxford Books of Reference already in existence.

The work remained in contemplation for some time before it first began to take shape under the general editorship of Miss Alice Mary Smyth, who worked, for purposes of selection, with a small committee formed of members of the Press itself. The existing dictionaries were taken as a foundation and the entries, pasted on separate cards, considered individually for rejection or inclusion. With these as a basis the most important authors were again dealt with either by the expert, or in committee, or by both. The Press is indebted for a great deal of work to the late Charles Fletcher, who among others made the original selections from Shakespeare, Milton, Pope, Tennyson, and Dryden: among those who dealt with single authors were Lady Charnwood and Mr. Bernard Darwin, who did the Dickens entries, Professor Dewar the Burns, Professor Ernest de Selincourt the Wordsworth: Mr. Colin Ellis did the Surtees, Sterne, and Whyte-Melville, Mr. E. Latham contributed the French quotations, and Mr. Harold Child made many valuable suggestions. A great many people, whom it is impossible to name individually, sent in one or more quotations.

During the whole work of selection a great effort was made to restrict the entries to actual current quotations and not to include phrases which the various editors or contributors believed to be quotable or wanted to be quoted: the work is primarily intended to be a dictionary of *familiar* quotations and not an anthology of every author good and bad; popularity and not merit being the password to inclusion. The selections from the Bible and Shakespeare were the most difficult because a great part of both are familiar to most people; but as concordances of both the Bible and Shakespeare are in print the quotations here included are meant to be the most well known where all is well known.

It has been found very difficult to put into precise words the standard of familiarity that has been aimed at or to imagine one man who might be asked whether or not the particular words were known to him. But it is believed that any of the quotations here printed might be found at some time in one or other of the leading articles of the daily and weekly papers with their wide range of matter — political, literary, descriptive, humorous, &c. So much for the very elastic standard to which the quotations conform. No one person having been imagined to whom everything included in this book would be familiar, the committee have tried to keep in mind that a number of different kinds of readers would be likely to use the book: these are the 'professionals', such as journalists, writers, public speakers, &c.; the cross-word devotee, since this form of intellectual amusement appears to have come to stay; the man who has in his mind either a few or many half-completed or unidentified quotations which he would like to complete or verify; and (since, as Emerson wrote — 'By necessity, by proclivity — and by delight, we all quote') everyone who has found joy and beauty in the words of the writers and wishes to renew that pleasure by using the words again — he whom perhaps Johnson meant by 'the literary man'. The book is not intended as a substitute for the complete works nor as an excuse to anyone not to drink deep of the Pierian spring. But it *is* hoped that the lover of Dickens, for instance, may find pleasure in reading through his entries and that even his detractors will have to admit how good he is in quotation: that the man who has always regarded Milton as a heavy and dull poet may here come across some lovely line and be inclined to read *Paradise Lost.* If the book serves to start people reading the poets it will have accomplished a great deal besides being a work of reference.

It is interesting to observe that the following are the most quoted writers (arranged in the order in which they appear here): Browning, Byron, Cowper, Dickens, Johnson, Kipling, Milton, Shakespeare, Shelley, Tennyson, Wordsworth, the Bible, and the Book of Common Prayer. On the other hand, certain authors of accepted merit or favour such as Trollope, Henry James, Jane Austen, and P. G. Wodehouse have none of them as much as one page to their credit: it would seem that their charm depends on character and atmosphere and that quotability is no real criterion of either popularity or merit in a writer.[1]

The arrangement of authors is alphabetical and not chronological. Under each author the arrangement of the extracts is alphabetical according to the title of the poem or work from which the quotation is taken. The text is, wherever possible, the acknowledged authoritative text and the source of the quotation is always given as fully as possible. Some quotations have had to be omitted because every effort to trace their source has failed — e.g. 'Home, James, and don't spare the horses'. Proverbs and phrases are not included, since these have been dealt with fully in the *Oxford Dictionary of English Proverbs.*

It is to be expected that almost every reader will be shocked by what he considers obvious omissions. Should the reader's indignation be strong enough to prompt him to write pointing these out it is to be hoped that he will give the source of all his suggestions. It is not possible to give all the quotations familiar to every reader;

[1] But see p. vi for a change now (3rd edn.).

almost all households have favourite books and authors from whom they frequently quote: to one family Stevenson is known and quoted by heart, to another the whole of the *Beggar's Opera* is as familiar as the extracts given here. Nor must the user expect to find here every quotation given in cross-word puzzles: compilers of these often seek to be obscure rather than familiar.

Latin is no longer a normal part of the language of educated people as it was in the eighteenth century; but from that age certain classical phrases have survived to become part of contemporary speech and writing. It is these 'survivals' that have been included here together with a few of the sayings or writings of the Schoolmen and early theologians. In many places more of the context of the actual familiar phrase has been given than is strictly necessary; but this has been a practice throughout the book, and one which it was thought would add to its value and charm. The translations are usually taken from the works of the better-known translators. Some one or two of the Greek quotations may be known to the general reader in their English version — e.g. 'The half is better than the whole' or 'Call no man happy till he dies'; but no apology is needed for the inclusion of two pages of matter most of which cannot pretend to be familiar to any but classical scholars.

The foreign quotations are not intended to satisfy the foreigner: they include such things as have become part of the speech and writings of English-speaking people either in their own language, such as 'les enfants terribles', or in an English translation, such as 'We will not go to Canossa'. As hardly any Spanish and no Russian or Swedish quotations are familiar to English readers most of these have been given only in translation.[1]

The index occupies approximately one-third of the total bulk of the book. A separate note will be found at the beginning of the index explaining the arrangement that has been adopted. Of the Latin quotations only those phrases that are familiar to the reader have been indexed; the unfamiliar context has not. In the English translations much the same principle has been followed: where the quotation is known to the reader in its English equivalent it has been indexed; where only the Latin is familiar and a translation is merely supplied to assist the reader it is left unindexed. A great deal of care has been spent on the index and the compilers look at it with some pride, believing that unless the searcher has to say 'Iddy tiddity' for every important word in the quotation he is looking for he will be able to find it; if, like Pig-wig (in Beatrix Potter's *Pigling Bland*), he has only forgotten some of the words, the index is full enough for him to trace it.

[1] At least for Spanish, there are more English readers now, and they have been honoured accordingly (3rd edn.).

INTRODUCTION
By Bernard Darwin

Quotation brings to many people one of the intensest joys of living. If they need any encouragement they have lately received it from the most distinguished quarters. Mr. Roosevelt quoted Longfellow to Mr. Churchill; Mr. Churchill passed on the quotation to us and subsequently quoted Clough on his own account. Thousands of listeners to that broadcast speech must have experienced the same series of emotions. When the Prime Minister said that there were some lines that he deemed appropriate we sat up rigid, waiting in mingled pleasure and apprehension. How agreeable it would be if we were acquainted with them and approved the choice! How flat and disappointing should they be unknown to us! A moment later we heard 'For while the tired waves, vainly breaking' and sank back in a pleasant agony of relief. We whispered the lines affectionately to ourselves, following the speaker, or even kept a word or two ahead of him in order to show our familiarity with the text. We were if possible more sure than ever that Mr. Churchill was the man for our money. He had given his ultimate proofs by flattering our vanity. He had chosen what we knew and what, if we had thought of it, we could have quoted ourselves. This innocent vanity often helps us over the hard places in life; it gives us a warm little glow against the coldness of the world and keeps us snug and happy. It certainly does its full share in the matter of quotations. We are puffed up with pride over those that we know and, a little illogically, we think that everyone else must know them too. As to those which lie outside our line of country we say, with Jowett as pictured by some anonymous genius[1] at Balliol, 'What I don't know isn't knowledge.' Yet here again we are illogical and unreasonable, for we allow ourselves to be annoyed by those who quote from outside our own small preserves. We accuse them in our hearts, as we do other people's children at a party, of 'showing off'. There are some departments of life in which we are ready to strike a bargain of mutual accommodation. The golfer is prepared to listen to his friend's story of missed putts, in which he takes no faintest interest, on the understanding that he may in turn impart his own heart-rending tale, and the bargain is honourably kept by both parties. The same rule does not apply to other people's quotations, which are not merely tedious but wound us in our tenderest spot. And the part played by vanity is perhaps worth pointing out because everybody, when he first plunges adventurously into this great work, ought in justice to the compilers to bear it in mind.

It is safe to say that there is no single reader who will not have a mild grievance or two, both as to what has been put in and what has been left out. In particular he will 'murmur a little sadly' over some favourite that is not there. I, for instance, have a

[1] Since identified as H. C. Beeching.

small grievance. William Hepworth Thompson, sometime Master of Trinity, the author of many famous and mordant sayings on which I have been brought up, is represented by but a single one.[1] Can it be, I ask myself, that this is due to the fact that an Oxford Scholar put several of the Master's sayings into his Greek exercise book but attributed them to one Talirantes? Down, base thought! I only mention this momentary and most unworthy suspicion to show other readers the sort of thing they should avoid as they would the very devil. It is not that of which any one of us is fondest that is entitled as of right to a place. As often as he feels ever so slightly aggrieved, the reader should say to himself, if need be over and over again, that this is not a private anthology, but a collection of the quotations which the public knows best. In this fact, moreover, if properly appreciated, there ought to be much comfort. 'My head', said Charles Lamb, 'has not many mansions nor spacious',[2] and is that not true of most of us? If in this book there are a great many quotations that we do not know, there are also a great many that we do. There is that example of Clough with which I began. We may have to admit under cross-examination that we have only a rather vague acquaintance with Clough's poems, but we do know 'Say not the struggle'; and there on page so-and-so it is. Both we and the dictionary's compilers are thereupon seen to be persons of taste and discrimination.

If I may be allowed to harp a little longer on this string of vanity, it is rather amusing to fancy the varied reception given to the book by those who are quoted in it. They will consist largely of more or less illustrious shades, and we may picture them looking over one another's pale shoulders at the first copy of the dictionary to reach the asphodel. What jealousies there will be as they compare the number of pages respectively allotted to them! What indignation at finding themselves in such mixed company! Alphabetical order makes strange bedfellows. Dickens and Dibdin must get on capitally and convivially together, but what an ill-assorted couple are Mrs. Humphry Ward and the beloved Artemus of the same name![3] George Borrow may ask, 'Pray, who is this John Collins Bossidy?'[4] Many readers may incidentally echo his question, and yet no man better merits his niche, for Mr. Bossidy wrote the lines ending 'And the Cabots talk only to God', which have told the whole world of the blue blood of Boston. John Hookham Frere, singing of the mailed lobster clapping his broad wings, must feel his frivolity uncomfortably hushed for a moment by his next-door neighbour, Charles Frohman, on the point of going down with the *Lusitania*.[5] And apropos of Frere, there rises before me the portentous figure of my great-great-grandfather, Erasmus Darwin. He was thought a vastly fine poet in his day and there is a family legend that he was paid a guinea a line for his too fluent verses. And yet he is deservedly forgotten, while those who parodied him in the

---

[1] Two in the 2nd edn., three in this 3rd.
[2] *The Essays of Elia* (1820-23), 'The Old and the New Schoolmaster'.
[3] 'Propinquity does it, indeed.
[4] These two were already separated in the 2nd edn. by the admission of foreign quotations among the English and thus by Maréchal Bosquet's magnificent put-down of the Light Brigade.
[5] For this pathetic juxtaposition readers must refer to the 1st or 2nd edn.

Anti-Jacobin attain an equally well-deserved immortality. He was a formidable old gentleman, with something of the Johnson touch, but not without a sense of humour, and I do not think he will be greatly hurt.

The most famous poets must be presumed to be above these petty vanities, though it would be agreeable to think of Horace contemplating his array of columns and saying, 'I told you so — Exegi monumentum'. In any case the number of columns or pages does not constitute the only test. Another is the number of words in each line by which any particular quotation can be identified, and this gives me a chance of making my compliments to the ingenuity and fullness of the index. The searcher need never despair and should he draw blank under 'swings' he is pretty sure to find what he wants under 'roundabouts'. There is a little game to be played (one of the many fascinating games which the reader can devise for himself) by counting the number of 'key words' in each line and working out the average of fame to which any passage is entitled. Even a short time so spent shows unexpected results, likely to spread envy and malice among the shades. It might be imagined that Shakespeare would be an easy winner. It has been said that every drop of the Thames is liquid history and almost every line of certain passages in Shakespeare is solid quotation. Let us fancy that his pre-eminence is challenged, that a sweepstake is suggested, and that he agrees to be judged by 'To be or not to be'. It seems a sufficiently sound choice and is found to produce fifty-five key words[1] in thirty-three lines. All the other poets are ready to give in at once; they cannot stand against such scoring as that and Shakespeare is about to pocket the money when up sidles Mr. Alexander Pope. What, he asks, about that bitter little thing of his which he sent to Mr. Addison? And he proves to be right, for in those two and twenty lines to Atticus there are fifty-two key words.[2] I have not played this game nearly long enough to pronounce Pope the winner. Very likely Shakespeare or someone else can produce a passage with a still higher average, but here at any rate is enough to show that it is a good game and as full of uncertainties as cricket itself.

Though the great poets may wrangle a little amongst themselves, they do not stand in need of anything that the dictionary can do for them. Very different is the case of the small ones, whose whole fame depends upon a single happy line or even a single absurd one. To them exclusion from these pages may virtually mean annihilation, while inclusion makes them only a little lower than the angels. Their anxiety therefore must be pitiful and their joy when they find themselves safe in the haven proportionately great. Sometimes that joy may be short-lived. Think of Mr. Robert Montgomery, who was highly esteemed till the ruthless Macaulay fell upon him. With trembling hand he turns the pages and finds no less than four extracts from 'The Omnipresence of the Deity'.[3] Alas! under his own letter M the traducer is waiting for him, and by a peculiar refinement of cruelty there are quoted no less than five[4] of Lord Macaulay's criticisms on that very poem. This is a sad case; let us take a

[1] Now only forty-one since many fewer phrases have had words indexed (3rd edn.).
[2] In this 3rd edn. thirty-one in only twenty of those lines.
[3] *The...Deity* now (3rd edn.) virtually annihilated.   [4] Reduced to three (3rd edn.).

more cheerful one and still among the M's. Thomas Osbert Mordaunt has full recognition as the author of 'Sound, sound the clarion, fill the fife', after having for years had to endure the attribution of his lines to Sir Walter Scott, who in pure innocency put them at the head of a chapter. This to be sure was known already, but whoever heard before the name of the author of 'We don't want to fight', the man who gave the word 'Jingo' to the world? We know that the Great McDermott sang it, but even he may not have known who wrote it, just as Miss Fotheringay did not know who wrote 'The Stranger'. Now G. W. Hunt comes into his kingdom and with him another who helped many thousands of soldiers on their way during the last war. Mr. George H. Powell[1] is fortunately still alive to enjoy the celebrity of 'Pack up your troubles in your old kit bag'. How many thousands, too, have sung 'Wrap me up in my tarpaulin jacket' without realizing that it was by Whyte-Melville?[2] To him, however, recognition is of less account. His place was already secure.

Among the utterers of famous sayings some seem to have been more fortunate than others. Lord Westbury, for instance, has always had the rather brutal credit of telling some wretched little attorney to turn the matter over 'in what you are pleased to call your mind'; but how many of us knew who first spoke of a 'blazing indiscretion' or called the parks 'the lungs of London'? We may rejoice with all these who, having for years been wronged, have come into their rights at last, but there are others with whom we can only sympathize. They must be contented with the fact that their sayings or their verses have been deemed worth recording, even though their names 'shall be lost for evermore'. The Rugby boy who called his headmaster 'a beast but a just beast' sleeps unknown, while through him Temple lives. He can only enjoy what the dynamiter Zero called 'an anonymous infernal glory'. So do the authors of many admirable limericks, though some of the best are attributed to a living divine of great distinction, who has not disclaimed such juvenile frolics.[3] So again do those who have given us many household words from the advertisement hoardings, the beloved old jingle of 'the Pickwick, the Owl, and the Waverley pen', the alluring alliteration of 'Pink Pills for Pale People'.[4] Let us hope that it is enough for them that they did their duty and sent the sales leaping upward.

So much for the authors without whom this book could never have been. Now for the readers and some of the happy uses to which they will put it. 'Hand me over the Burton's *Anatomy* ', said Captain Shandon, 'and leave me to my abominable devices.' It was Greek and Latin quotations that he sought for his article, but fashion has changed and today it would rather be English ones. Here is one of the most obvious purposes for which the dictionary will be used. It cannot accomplish impossibilities. It will not prevent many an honest journalist from referring to 'fresh fields and pastures new' nor from describing a cup-tie as an example of 'Greek meeting Greek'. There is a fine old crusted tradition of misquoting not lightly to be

[1] Georg Asaf.

[2] Both these verses are omitted from this 3rd edn. as songs: see p. v.

[3] The late Mgr. Ronald Knox (1888-1957).

[4] The latter, like most advertising (see p. v), has been excluded from the 3rd edn.

broken and it might almost seem pedantry to deck these ancient friends in their true but unfamiliar colours. Misquoting may even be deemed an amiable weakness, since Dickens in one of his letters misquoted Sam Weller; but here at least is a good chance of avoiding it. There is likewise a chance of replenishing a stock grown somewhat threadbare. 'Well, you're a boss word', exclaimed Jim Pinkerton,[1] when he lighted on 'Hebdomadary' in a dictionary. 'Before you're very much older I'll have you in type as long as yourself.' So the hard-pressed writer in turning over these pages may find and note many excellent phrases against future contingencies, whether to give a pleasing touch of erudition or to save the trouble of thinking for himself. These, however, are sordid considerations, and the mind loves rather to dwell on fireside quoting-matches between two friends, each of whom thinks his own visual memory the more accurate. There are certain writers well adapted to this form of contest and among the moderns Conan Doyle must, with all respect to Mr. Wodehouse, be assigned the first place. Sherlock Holmes scholars are both numerous and formidable; they set themselves and demand of others a high standard. It is one very difficult to attain since there often seems no reason why any particular remark should have been made on any particular occasion. This is especially true of Dr. Watson. He was constantly saying that his practice was not very absorbing or that he had an accommodating neighbour, but when did he say which? Even the most learned might by a momentary blunder confuse 'A Case of Identity' with 'The Final Problem'. It would be dry work to plough through all the stories, even though the supreme satisfaction of being right should reward the search. Now a glance at the dictionary will dispose of an argument which would otherwise 'end only with the visit'.

It is incidentally curious and interesting to observe that two authors may each have the same power of inspiring devotion and the competitive spirit, and yet one may be, from the dictionary point of view, infinitely more quotable than the other. Hardly any prose writer, for instance, produces a more fanatical adoration than Miss Austen, and there are doubtless those who can recite pages of her with scarce a slip; but it is perhaps pages rather than sentences that they quote. Mr. Bennet provides an exception, but generally speaking she is not very amenable to the treatment by scissors and paste. George Eliot, if we leave out Mrs. Poyser, a professed wit and coiner of aphorisms, is in much poorer case. Another and a very different writer, Borrow, can rouse us to a frantic pitch of romantic excitement, but it is the whole scene and atmosphere that possess this magic and we cannot take atmosphere to pieces. These are but three examples of writers who do not seem to lend themselves to brief and familiar quotations.[2] They have jewels in plenty, but these form part of a piece of elaborate ornament from which they cannot be detached without irreparable damage. The works of some other writers may by contrast be said to consist of separate stones, each of which needs no setting and can sparkle on its own account.

[1] Robert Louis Stevenson (with Lloyd Osbourne), *The Wrecker* (1892), ch. 7.
[2] A good many more quotations from both Jane Austen and George Eliot are included in this 3rd than in the preceding editions.

Dickens is an obvious and unique instance. Stevenson, too, has the gift of producing characters such as Prince Florizel and Alan Breck, John Silver and Michael Finsbury, whose words can stand memorable by themselves, apart from context or atmosphere. Those who share my love for Florizel will rejoice to observe that he has had some faithful friend among the compilers. As for Michael I cannot help feeling that he has been rather scurvily used, for *The Wrong Box* is admirably suited to competition and even learned Judges of the Court of Appeal have been known, all unsuspected by their ignorant auditors, to bandy quotations from it on the Bench. Here, however, I take leave to give any indignant reader a hint. Let him not cry too loudly before he is hurt! It is true that 'nothing like a little judicious levity' is not in the main body of the dictionary, but someone awoke just in time and it is among the addenda.[1]

To return to those friends by the fireside whom I pictured indulging in a heated quoting-match, it may be that they will presently become allies and unite to use the dictionary over a cross-word puzzle. It is hardly too much to say that the setters of these problems should not use a quotation unless it is to be found in the dictionary. A cross-word quotation should not be too simple, but it should be such that that hypothetical personage, the reasonable man, might have heard of it. The solver demands fair play, and the setter who takes a volume of verse at haphazard, finds a word that fits, and substitutes a blank for it, is not playing the game. There are solvers whose standard of sportsmanship is so high that they would as soon allow themselves to cheat at patience as have recourse to a book. We may admire though we cannot emulate this fine austere arrogance. It is the best fun to win unaided, but there is good fun too in ferreting out a quotation. It well repays the ardours of the chase. Moreover a setter of puzzles who oversteps honourable limits should be fought with his own weapons. He has palpably used books and this is an epoch of reprisals. Then let us use books too and hoist him with his own petard.

It is difficult today not to deal in warlike metaphors, but perhaps the truest and most perfect use of the dictionary is essentially peaceful. Reviewers are apt to say of a detective story that it is 'impossible to lay it down till the last page is reached'. It is rather for books of reference that such praise should be reserved. No others are comparable with them for the purposes of eternal browsing. They suggest all manner of lovely, lazy things, in particular the watching of a cricket match on a sunshiny day. We have only dropped in for half an hour, but the temptation to see just one more over before we go is irresistible. Evening draws on, the shadows of the fielders lengthen on the grass, nothing much is happening, a draw becomes every minute more inevitable, and still we cannot tear ourselves away. So it is with works of reference, even with the most arid, even with Bradshaw, whose vocabulary, as Sherlock Holmes remarked, is 'nervous and terse but limited'. Over the very next page of Bradshaw there may be hidden a Framlingham Admiral; adventure may always be in wait a little farther down the line. So, but a thousand times more so, is

---

[1] In the main body all right in the 2nd edn., and further amends have been made to *The Wrong Box* in this new edn.

some exciting treasure-trove awaiting us over the next page of this dictionary. What it is we cannot guess, but it is for ever calling in our ears to turn over just one more. We have only taken down the book to look up one special passage, but it is likely enough that we shall never get so far. Long before we have reached the appropriate letter we shall have been waylaid by an earlier one, and shall have clean forgotton our original quest. Nor is this all, for, if our mood changes as we browse, it is so fatally, beautifully easy to change our pasture. We can play a game akin to that 'dabbing' cricket, so popular in private-school days, in which the batsman's destiny depended or was supposed to depend — for we were not always honest — on a pencil delivered with eyes tightly shut. We can close the book and open it again at random, sure of something that shall set us off again on a fresh and enchanting voyage of not too strenuous discovery.

Under this enchantment I have fallen deep. I have pored over the proofs so that only by a supreme effort of will could I lay them down and embark on the impertinent task of trying to write about them. I now send them back to their home with a sense of privation and loneliness. Here seems to me a great book. Then

Deem it not all a too presumptuous folly,

this humble tribute to Oxford from another establishment over the way.

B.D.

May 1941

HOW TO USE THE DICTIONARY

The arrangement is alphabetical by the names of authors; their surnames mostly, but sometimes their titles, monarchs by their imperial or royal titles, writers sometimes by their pseudonyms. In general the best-known names are given, and usually in the form most used: T. S. (rather than Thomas Stearns) Eliot and no Fingal O'Flahertie Wills for Oscar. Sections such as the Anonymous one, Ballads, the Bible, the Mass in Latin, etc., are included in the alphabetical order.

Under each author, quotations are arranged by the alphabetical order of the titles of the works from which they come: books, plays, poems. These are printed in bold italic type. Titles of pieces (e.g., articles, essays, short stories) that constitute part of a published volume are in bold roman (the volume title having been given in bold italic). Quotations from diaries, letters, speeches, etc., however, are given in chronological order, and normally follow the literary works quoted. Poetry quotations precede prose ones for poets; and vice versa for writers most of whose work was in prose. Quotations cited from biographies or other writers' works are kept to the end under each author; sources are then given conventionally with titles of books or plays in italic (not bold) type.

Numerical source references are given for the first line of each quotation, by, e.g., act, scene, and, if appropriate, line number; by chapter or by page or section or verse number. But references are not repeated for every single quotation. The use of *'Ib.'* — ubiquitous in the earlier editions — has been avoided. Each quotation without a full source given depends from its immediate predecessor. If no source reference is given at all, that is an invisible *'Ib.'*: the quotation is from the same poem or chapter or whatever as the last preceding named or numbered one.

A date in brackets is of the first performance or publication of the work cited.

Italic has been used for all quotations in foreign languages and Latin. Throughout, spelling and capitalization have been modernized, except in English writers of the Middle Ages.

Running headlines give the names of the first and last authors *starting* a section on each page (not usually of the author of the first quotation on a page).

Sub-headings have been used under Dickens with the titles of novels, under the Bible with the books named — kept in canonical order, not alphabetically — followed by the Vulgate, and under Shakespeare with the titles of plays and poems.

QUOTATIONS

PETER ABELARD 1079–1142

1 *O quanta qualia sunt illa sabbata,*
Quae semper celebrat superna curia.
O how great and glorious are those sabbaths which the heavenly court for ever celebrates!
Hymnus Paraclitensis

2 *Quis rex, quae curia, quale palatium,*
Quae pax, quae requies, quod illud gaudium.
What a king, what a court, how fine a palace, what peace, what rest, what rejoicing is there!

ACCIUS 170–c.90 B.C.

3 *Oderint, dum metuant.*
Let them hate, so long as they fear.
Atreus. Seneca, *De Ira*, I, 20, 4

DEAN ACHESON 1893–1971

4 Great Britain has lost an Empire and has not yet found a role.
Speech at the Military Academy, West Point, 5 Dec. 1962

LORD ACTON 1834–1902

5 Power tends to corrupt and absolute power corrupts absolutely.
Letter to Bishop Mandell Creighton, 3 Apr. 1887. See *Life and Letters of Mandell Creighton* (1904), i.372. See 373:23

CHARLES FRANCIS ADAMS 1807–1886

6 It would be superfluous in me to point out to your lordship that this is war.
Dispatch to Earl Russell, 5 Sept. 1863. C.F. Adams, *Charles Francis Adams*, p.342

HENRY ADAMS 1838–1918

7 A friend in power is a friend lost.
The Education of Henry Adams, ch.7

PRESIDENT JOHN QUINCY ADAMS 1767–1848

8 Think of your forefathers! Think of your posterity!
Speech, 22 Dec. 1802

SAMUEL ADAMS 1722–1803

9 A nation of shop-keepers are very seldom so disinterested.
Oration said to have been delivered at Philadelphia, 1 Aug. 1776. See 359:15, 509:12

SARAH F. ADAMS 1805–1848

10 Nearer, my God, to thee,
Nearer to thee!
Nearer My God to Thee

JOSEPH ADDISON 1672–1719

11 Pray consider what a figure a man would make in the republic of letters.
Ancient Medals, 1

12 There is nothing more requisite in business than dispatch.
5

13 'Twas then great Marlbro's mighty soul was prov'd.
The Campaign, l.279

14 And, pleas'd th' Almighty's orders to perform,
Rides in the whirl-wind, and directs the storm.
l.291

15 And those who paint 'em truest praise 'em most.
l.476

16 'Tis not in mortals to command success,
But we'll do more, Sempronius; we'll deserve it.
Cato, I.ii.43

17 Blesses his stars, and thinks it luxury.
iv.70

18 'Tis pride, rank pride, and haughtiness of soul;
I think the Romans call it stoicism.
82

19 Were you with these, my prince, you'd soon forget
The pale, unripened beauties of the north.
134

20 The woman that deliberates is lost.
IV.i.31

21 Curse on his virtues! they've undone his country.
Such popular humanity is treason.
iv.35

22   What pity is it
That we can die but once to serve our country!
81

23 Content thyself to be obscurely good.
When vice prevails, and impious men bear sway,
The post of honour is a private station.
139

24 It must be so—Plato, thou reason'st well!—
Else whence this pleasing hope, this fond desire,
This longing after immortality?
Or whence this secret dread, and inward horror,
Of falling into naught? Why shrinks the soul
Back on herself, and startles at destruction?
'Tis the divinity that stirs within us;
'Tis heaven itself, that points out an hereafter,
And intimates eternity to man.
Eternity! thou pleasing, dreadful thought!
V.i.1

25 From hence, let fierce contending nations know
What dire effects from civil discord flow.
iv.111

1 Round-heads and Wooden-shoes are standing jokes.
The Drummer, Prologue

2 I should think my self a very bad woman, if I had done what I do, for a farthing less.
I

3 He more had pleas'd us, had he pleas'd us less.
English Poets. Of Cowley

4 For wheresoe'er I turn my ravished eyes,
Gay gilded scenes and shining prospects rise,
Poetic fields encompass me around,
And still I seem to tread on classic ground.
Letter from Italy

5 A painted meadow, or a purling stream.

6 Music, the greatest good that mortals know,
   And all of heaven we have below.
A Song for St. Cecilia's Day, st. 3

7 A reader seldom peruses a book with pleasure until he knows whether the writer of it be a black man or a fair man, of a mild or choleric disposition, married or a bachelor.
The Spectator, 1

8 Thus I live in the world rather as a spectator of mankind than as one of the species.

9 As a perfect tragedy is the noblest production of human nature, so it is capable of giving the mind one of the most delightful and most improving entertainments.
39

10 In all thy humours, whether grave or mellow,
Thou'rt such a touchy, testy, pleasant fellow;
Hast so much wit, and mirth, and spleen about thee,
There is no living with thee, nor without thee.
68. See 331:13

11 The infusion of a China plant sweetened with the pith of an Indian cane.
69

12 As Sir Roger is landlord to the whole congregation, he keeps them in very good order, and will suffer nobody to sleep in it [the church] besides himself; for if by chance he has been surprised into a short nap at sermon, upon recovering out of it, he stands up, and looks about him; and if he sees anybody else nodding, either wakes them himself, or sends his servant to them.
112

13 Sir Roger told them, with the air of a man who would not give his judgment rashly, that much might be said on both sides.
122

14 My friends Sir Roger de Coverley and Sir Andrew Freeport are of different principles, the first of them inclined to the *landed* and the other to the *monied* interest.
126

15 It was a saying of an ancient philosopher, which I find some of our writers have ascribed to Queen Elizabeth, who perhaps might have taken occasion to repeat it, that a good face is a letter of recommendation.
221. See 402:4

16 I have often thought, says Sir Roger, it happens very

well that Christmas should fall out in the Middle of Winter.
269

17 Dr Busby, a great man! he whipped my grandfather; a very great man! I should have gone to him myself, if I had not been a blockhead; a very great man!
329

18 These widows, Sir, are the most perverse creatures in the world.
335

19 The Knight in the triumph of his heart made several reflections on the greatness of the *British* Nation; as, that one *Englishman* could beat three *Frenchmen;* that we cou'd never be in danger of Popery so long as we took care of our fleet; that the *Thames* was the noblest river in *Europe;* that *London Bridge* was a greater piece of work than any of the Seven Wonders of the World; with many other honest prejudices which naturally cleave to the heart of a true *Englishman.*
383

20 Through all Eternity to Thee
A joyful Song I'll raise,
For oh! Eternity's too short
To utter all thy Praise.
453

21 We have in England a particular bashfulness in every thing that regards religion.
458

22 The spacious firmament on high,
With all the blue ethereal sky.
465

23 A woman seldom asks advice before she has bought her wedding clothes.
475

24 Our disputants put me in mind of the skuttle fish, that when he is unable to extricate himself, blackens all the water about him, till he becomes invisible.
476

25 I value my garden more for being full of blackbirds than of cherries, and very frankly give them fruit for their songs.
477

26 If we may believe our logicians, man is distinguished from all other creatures by the faculty of laughter.
494

27 'We are always doing', says he, 'something for Posterity, but I would fain see Posterity do something for us.'
583

28 I remember when our whole island was shaken with an earthquake some years ago, there was an impudent mountebank who sold pills which (as he told the country people) were very good against an earthquake.
The Tatler, 240

29 See in what peace a Christian can die.
Dying words to his stepson Lord Warwick. Young, *Conjectures on Original Composition,* 1759

30 Should the whole frame of nature round him break,
In ruin and confusion hurled,
He, unconcerned, would hear the mighty crack,
And stand secure amidst a falling world.
Translation of Horace, Odes, III.iii. See 260:18, 376:21

AESCHYLUS 525/4–456 B.C.

1 ἐλέναυς ἔλανδρος ἐλέπτολις.
Hell to ships, hell to men, hell to cities.
Agamemnon, 689. Of Helen; literally 'Ship-destroyer, (etc.)'.

2 ὤμοι, πέπληγμαι καιρίαν πληγὴν ἔσω.
Oh me, I have been struck a mortal blow right inside.
1343

3 ποντίων τε κυμάτων ἀνήριθμον γέλασμα.
Innumerable twinkling of the waves of the sea.
Prometheus Bound, 89

AGATHON 446?–c.401 B.C.

4 Even God cannot change the past.
Aristotle, *Nicomachean Ethics*, VI.2.1139b

MARIA, MARCHIONESS OF AILESBURY
d.1902

5 My dear, my dear, you never know when any
beautiful young lady may not blossom into a Duchess!
Duke of Portland, *Men, Women, and Things*, ch.3

CANON AINGER 1837–1904

6 No flowers, by request.
Speech, 8 July 1897. *D.N.B.* Summary of principle of
conciseness for its contributors.

ALBERT, PRINCE CONSORT 1819–1861

7 The works of art, by being publicly exhibited and
offered for sale, are becoming articles of trade,
following as such the unreasoning laws of markets and
fashion; and public and even private patronage is
swayed by their tyrannical influence.
Speech at the Royal Academy Dinner, 3 May 1851

SCIPIONE ALBERTI fl. 1550–1590

8 *I pensieri stretti ed il viso sciolto* will go safely over
the whole world.
Secret thoughts and open countenance...
On being asked how to behave in Rome. Sir Henry Wotton, letter
to Milton, 13 Apr. 1638, prefixed to *Comus*.

ALCUIN c.735–804

9 *Nec audiendi qui solent dicere, Vox populi, vox Dei,
quum tumultuositas vulgi semper insaniae proxima sit.*
And those people should not be listened to who keep
saying the voice of the people is the voice of God,
since the riotousness of the crowd is always very close
to madness.
Letter to Charlemagne, A.D.800. *Works*, Epist.127

DEAN ALDRICH 1647–1710

10 If all be true that I do think,
There are five reasons we should drink;
Good wine—a friend—or being dry—
Or lest we should be by and by—
Or any other reason why.
Reasons for Drinking

THOMAS BAILEY ALDRICH 1836–1907

11   The fair, frail palaces,
The fading alps and archipelagoes,
And great cloud-continents of sunset-seas.
Sonnet: Miracles

ALEXANDER THE GREAT 356–323 B.C.

12 εἰ μὴ ᾽Αλέξανδρος ἤμην, Διογένης ἄν ἤμην.
If I were not Alexander, I would be Diogenes.
Plutarch, *Life of Alexander*, xiv.3

MRS. ALEXANDER 1818–1895

13 All things bright and beautiful,
    All creatures great and small,
All things wise and wonderful,
    The Lord God made them all.
All Things Bright and Beautiful (1848)

14 The rich man in his castle,
    The poor man at his gate,
God made them, high or lowly,
    And order'd their estate.

SIR WILLIAM ALEXANDER, EARL OF STIRLING 1567?–1640

15 The weaker sex, to piety more prone.
Doomsday, Hour v, lv

ALFONSO THE WISE, KING OF CASTILE
1221–1284

16 Had I been present at the Creation, I would have given
some useful hints for the better ordering of the
universe.
Said after studying the Ptolemaic system. Attr.

KING ALFRED 849–901

17 Then began I...to turn into English the book that is
named in Latin *Pastoralis*...one-while word for word,
another-while meaning for meaning.
Whole Works (*Jubilee Edition*, 1852), vol.III, p.64. Preface to
the Anglo-Saxon version of Gregory's *Pastoral Care*.

RICHARD ALISON fl. c.1606

18 There cherries grow, that none can buy
Till cherry ripe themselves do cry.
An Hour's Recreation in Music. See 129:22, 248:21

ABBÉ D'ALLAINVAL 1700–1753

19 *L'embarras des richesses.*
The more alternatives, the more difficult the choice.
Title of comedy, 1726

WILLIAM ALLINGHAM 1828–1889

20 Up the airy mountain,
Down the rushy glen,
We daren't go a-hunting,
For fear of little men.
The Fairies

21 Four ducks on a pond,
A grass-bank beyond,

A blue sky of spring,
White clouds on the wing:
What a little thing
To remember for years—
To remember with tears!
A Memory

ST. AMBROSE c.339–397

1 *Ubi Petrus, ibi ergo ecclesia.*
Where Peter is, there must be the Church.
Explanatio psalmi 40, 30. *Corpus Scriptorum Ecclesiasticorum Latinorum* 64, 250

2 *Si fueris Romae, Romano vivito more;*
Si fueris alibi, vivito sicut ibi.
If you are at Rome live in the Roman style; if you are elsewhere live as they live elsewhere.
Jeremy Taylor, *Ductor Dubitantium*, I.i.5. Usually quoted as 'When in Rome, do as the Romans do.'

FISHER AMES 1758–1808

3 A monarchy is a merchantman which sails well, but will sometimes strike on a rock, and go to the bottom; a republic is a raft which will never sink, but then your feet are always in the water.
House of Representatives, 1795

KINGSLEY AMIS 1922–

4 More will mean worse.
Encounter, July 1960

HANS CHRISTIAN ANDERSEN 1805–1875

5 'But the Emperor has nothing on at all!' cried a little child.
The Emperor's New Clothes

BISHOP LANCELOT ANDREWES 1555–1626

6 But we are not so much to regard the *Ecce,* how great it is, as *Gaudium,* what joy is in it; that is the point we are to speak to.
Sermon 5, Of the Nativity (1610)

7 It was no summer progress. A cold coming they had of it, at this time of the year; just, the worst time of the year, to take a journey, and specially a long journey, in. The ways deep, the weather sharp, the days short, the sun farthest off *in solstitio brumali,* the very dead of Winter.
Sermon 15, Of the Nativity (1622)

8 The nearer the Church the further from God.

ANONYMOUS

ENGLISH

9 A beast, but a just beast.
Of Dr. Temple, Headmaster of Rugby, 1857-69

10 Absence makes the heart grow fonder.
Davison, *Poetical Rhapsody,* 1602

11 A Company for carrying on an undertaking of Great Advantage, but no one to know what it is.
The South Sea Company Prospectus, 1711. Cowles, *The Great Swindle* (1963), ch.5

12 Adam

Had 'em.
On the antiquity of Microbes. (Claimed as the shortest poem.)

13 A gentleman haranguing on the perfection of our law, and that it was equally open to the poor and the rich, was answered by another, 'So is the London Tavern'.
Tom Paine's Jests... (1794), 23. Also attr. to John Horne Tooke (1736–1812) in W. Hazlitt, *The Spirit of the Age* (1825), 'Mr. Horne Tooke'.

14 All human beings are born free and equal in dignity and rights.
Universal Declaration of Human Rights (1948), Article 1

15 All present and correct.
King's Regulations (Army). Report of the Orderly Sergeant to the Officer of the Day

16 All this buttoning and unbuttoning.
18th Century suicide note

17 Along the electric wire the message came:
He is not better—he is much the same.
Said to be from a poem on the illness of the Prince of Wales, afterwards Edward VII, often attr. to Alfred Austin (1835–1913), Poet Laureate. Gribble, *Romance of the Cambridge Colleges* (1913), p.226

18 An abomination unto the Lord, but a very present help in time of trouble. [A lie.]
(Cf. Proverbs 12:22; Psalms 46:1)

19 An old song made by an aged old pate,
Of an old worshipful gentleman who had a great
    estate.
The Old Courtier

20 Any officer who shall behave in a scandalous manner, unbecoming the character of an officer and a gentleman shall...be CASHIERED.
Articles of War (1872), *Disgraceful Conduct,* 79. The Naval Discipline Act (10 Aug. 1860), Article 24, contained the words 'conduct unbecoming the character of an Officer'.

21 A place within the meaning of the Act.
Betting Act

22 Appeal from Philip drunk to Philip sober.
Valerius Maximus, *Facta ac Dicta Memorabilia* (c. A.D. 32), VI, ii

23 Are we downhearted? No!
Expression much used by British soldiers in 1914-18, probably based on 139:7

24 A sympathetic Scot summed it all up very neatly in the remark, 'You should make a point of trying every experience once, excepting incest and folk-dancing'.
Sir Arnold Bax (1883–1953), *Farewell My Youth* (1943), 'Cecil Sharp'

25 A was an apple-pie;
B bit it;
C cut it.
John Eachard, *Some Observations* (1671)

26 A willing foe and sea room.
Naval toast in the time of Nelson. Beckett, *A Few Naval Customs, Expressions, Traditions, and Superstitions* (1931)

27 Be happy while y'er leevin,
For y'er a lang time deid.
Scottish motto for a house. N. & Q. 7 Dec. 1901, 469

28 Conduct...to the prejudice of good order and military discipline.
Army Act, 40

29 Dear Sir, Your astonishment's odd:
I am always about in the Quad.
    And that's why the tree
    Will continue to be,

Since observed by Yours faithfully, God.
Reply to limerick on idealism. See 305:22

1 Defence, not defiance.
Motto of the Volunteers Movement, 1859

2 Dollar Diplomacy.
Term applied to Secretary Knox's activities in securing opportunities for the investment of American capital abroad, particularly in Latin America and China. *Harper's Weekly*, 23 Apr. 1910, 8

3 Early one morning, just as the sun was rising,
I heard a maid sing in the valley below:
'Oh, don't deceive me; Oh, never leave me!
How could you use a poor maiden so?'
Early One Morning

4 Earned a precarious living by taking in one another's washing.
Attr. Mark Twain by William Morris in *The Commonweal*, 6 Aug. 1887

5 An intelligent Russian once remarked to us, 'Every country has its own constitution; ours is absolutism moderated by assassination.'
Georg Herbert, Count Münster, *Political Sketches of the State of Europe, 1814–1867* (1868), 19

6 *Knowledge:* Everyman, I will go with thee, and be thy guide.
In thy most need to go by thy side.
Everyman (c.500), l.522

7 Father of his Country. [George Washington.]
Francis Bailey, *Nord Americanische Kalender*, 1779

8 From ghoulies and ghosties and long-leggety beasties
And things that go bump in the night,
      Good Lord, deliver us!
Cornish

9 God be in my head,
And in my understanding;

God be in my eyes,
And in my looking;

God be in my mouth,
And in my speaking;

God be in my heart,
And in my thinking;

God be at my end,
And at my departing.
Sarum Missal

10 Great Chatham with his sabre drawn
Stood waiting for Sir Richard Strachan;
Sir Richard, longing to be at 'em,
Stood waiting for the Earl of Chatham.
At Walcheren, 1809

11 Greensleeves was all my joy,
    Greensleeves was my delight,
Greensleeves was my heart of gold,
    And who but Lady Greensleeves?
A new Courtly Sonnet of the Lady Greensleeves, to the new tune of 'Greensleeves'. From *A Handful of Pleasant Delites* (1584)

12 Happy is that city which in time of peace thinks of war. (Inscription in the armoury of Venice.)
Burton, *Anatomy of Melancholy*, pt.ii, 3, memb.6. See 556:3

13 Here lies a poor woman who always was tired,
For she lived in a place where help wasn't hired.
Her last words on earth were, Dear friends I am going
Where washing ain't done nor sweeping nor sewing,
And everything there is exact to my wishes,
For there they don't eat and there's no washing of
    dishes...
Don't mourn for me now, don't mourn for me never,
For I'm going to do nothing for ever and ever.
Epitaph in Bushey churchyard, before 1860, destroyed by 1916. Quoted in a letter to the *Spectator*, 2 Sept. 1922

14 Here lies a valiant warrior
Who never drew a sword;
Here lies a noble courtier
Who never kept his word;
Here lies the Earl of Leicester
Who governed the estates
Whom the earth could never living love,
And the just heaven now hates.
Attr. Ben Jonson in Tissington, *Collection of Epitaphs* (1857), p.377

15 Here lies Fred,
Who was alive and is dead:
Had it been his father,
I had much rather;
Had it been his brother,
Still better than another;
Had it been his sister,
No one would have missed her;
Had it been the whole generation,
Still better for the nation:
But since 'tis only Fred,
Who was alive and is dead,—
There's no more to be said.
Horace Walpole, *Memoirs of George II* (1847), I, 436

16 Here's tae us; wha's like us?
Gey few, and they're a' deid.
Scottish Toast, probably of nineteenth-century origin. The first line appears in Crosland, *The Unspeakable Scot* (1902), p.24n. Various versions of the second line are current.

17 He talked shop like a tenth muse.
Of Gladstone's Budget speeches. G.W.E. Russell, *Collections and Recollections*, ch.12

18   He tickles this age that can
Call Tullia's ape a marmasyte
   And Leda's goose a swan.
Fara diddle dyno, from Thomas Weelkes, *Airs or Fantastic Spirits* (1608). See N. Ault, *Elizabethan Lyrics*

19 Hierusalem, my happy home
   When shall I come to thee?
When shall my sorrows have an end,
   Thy joys when shall I see?
Hierusalem. See *Songs of Praise Discussed*

20 'How different, how very different from the home life of our own dear Queen!'
Irvin S. Cobb, *A Laugh a Day*. Comment by a middle-aged British matron at a performance of Cleopatra by Sarah Bernhardt. The story is probably apocryphal.

21 I can not eat but little meat,
   My stomach is not good:
But sure I think, that I can drink
   With him that wears a hood.
Though I go bare, take ye no care,
   I am nothing acold;
I stuff my skin, so full within,
   Of jolly good ale and old,
Back and side go bare, go bare,
   Both foot and hand go cold:
But belly God send thee good ale enough,

Whether it be new or old.
Song from *Gammer Gurton's Needle* (acted 1566, printed 1575), Act II. The play has been attr. to William Stevenson (1530?–1575) and to John Still (1543–1608); the song may be earlier in origin.

1 I feel no pain dear mother now
But oh, I am so dry!
O take me to a brewery
And leave me there to die.
Parody of \209:21

2 If God were to take one or other of us, I should go and live in Paris.
Reported in S. Butler, *Notebooks*, ed. G. Keynes and B. Hill, 1951, p.193

3 If he only knew a little of law, he would know a little of everything.
Of Lord Brougham. Emerson, *Quotation and Originality* (1877)

4 I'm arm'd with more than complete steel—The justice of my quarrel.
Lust's Dominion (1657), IV.iii

5 I'll sing you twelve O.
Green grow the rushes O.
What is your twelve O?
Twelve for the twelve apostles,
Eleven for the eleven who went to heaven,
Ten for the ten commandments,
Nine for the nine bright shiners,
Eight for the eight bold rangers,
Seven for the seven stars in the sky,
Six for the six proud walkers,
Five for the symbol at your door,
Four for the Gospel makers,
Three for the rivals,
Two, two, the lily-white boys,
Clothed all in green O,
One is one and all alone
And ever more shall be so.
The Dilly Song. See G. Grigson, *The Faber Book of Popular Verse*; see also Revd. S. Baring-Gould and Revd. H. Fleetwood Sheppard, *Songs and Ballads of the West* (1891), no.78, for a variant version.

6 I met wid Napper Tandy, and he took me by the hand,
And he said, 'How's poor ould Ireland, and how does she stand?'
She's the most disthressful country that iver yet was seen,
For they're hangin' men an' women there for the wearin' o' the Green.
The Wearin' o' the Green. (Famous street ballad, later added to by Boucicault.)

7   I saw my lady weep,
And Sorrow proud to be exalted so
In those fair eyes where all perfections keep.
     Her face was full of woe;
But such a woe, believe me, as wins more hearts,
Than Mirth can do with her enticing parts.
Songs set by John Dowland, *Oxford Book of 16th Cent. Verse*

8 It is positively dangerous to sit to Sargent. It's taking your face in your hands.
W. Graham Robertson, *Time Was* (1931), ch.21

9 The children of Lord Lytton organized a charade. The scene displayed a Crusader knight returning from the wars. At his gate he was welcomed by his wife to whom he recounted his triumphs and the number of heathen he had slain. His wife, pointing to a row of dolls of various sizes, replied with pride, 'And I too, my lord, have not been idle'.
G.W.E. Russell, *Collections and Recollections*, ch.31

10 Like a fine old English gentleman,
All of the olden time.
The Fine Old English Gentleman. Oxford Song Book

11 The newly-elected mayor who...said that during his year of office he should lay aside all his political prepossessions and be 'like Caesar's wife, all things to all men'.
G.W.E. Russell, *Collections and Recollections*, ch.30

12 Lizzie Borden took an axe
And gave her mother forty whacks;
When she saw what she had done
She gave her father forty-one!
Lizzie Borden was acquitted of murdering her father and stepmother on 4 Aug. 1892 in Fall River, Massachusetts

13 Love me little, love me long,
Is the burden of my song.
Love me Little, Love me Long (1569–70)

14 *Child:* Mamma, are Tories born wicked, or do they grow wicked afterwards?
Mother: They are born wicked, and grow worse.
G.W.E. Russell, *Collections and Recollections*, ch.10

15 Matthew, Mark, Luke, and John,
The Bed be blest that I lie on.
Four angels to my bed,
Four angels round my head,
One to watch, and one to pray,
And two to bear my soul away.
Thomas Ady, *A Candle in the Dark* (1656)

16 Miss Buss and Miss Beale
Cupid's darts do not feel.
How different from us,
Miss Beale and Miss Buss.
Of the Headmistress of the North London Collegiate School and the Principal of the Ladies' College, Cheltenham, c. 1884

17 Most Gracious Queen, we thee implore
To go away and sin no more,
But if that effort be too great,
To go away at any rate.
Epigram on Queen Caroline, quoted in Lord Colchester's Diary, 15 Nov. 1820

18 Multiplication is vexation,
Division is as bad;
The Rule of three doth puzzle me,
And Practice drives me mad.
Elizabethan MS. dated 1570

19 My sledge and anvil lie declined
My bellows too have lost their wind
My fire's extinct, my forge decayed,
And in the Dust my Vice is laid
My coals are spent, my iron's gone
My Nails are Drove, My Work is done.
Epitaph in Nettlebed churchyard on William Strange, d. 6 June 1746, and used similarly for other blacksmiths.

20 My Love in her attire doth show her wit,
     It doth so well become her:
For every season she hath dressings fit,
     For winter, spring, and summer.
No beauty she doth miss,
     When all her robes are on;
But beauty's self she is,
     When all her robes are gone.
Madrigal

1 My name is George Nathaniel Curzon,
I am a most superior person.
The Masque of Balliol, composed by and current among members of Balliol College in the late 1870's. See 37:8, 517:11–12

2 My face is pink, my hair is sleek,
I dine at Blenheim once a week.
(A later addition.)

3 Now I lay me down to sleep;
I pray the Lord my soul to keep.
If I should die before I wake,
I pray the Lord my soul to take.
First printed in a late edition of the *New England Primer,* 1781

4 O Death, where is thy sting-a-ling-a-ling,
O Grave, thy victoree?
The bells of Hell go ting-a-ling-a-ling
For you but not for me.
Song popular in the British Army, 1914–18

5 O God, if there be a God, save my soul, if I have a soul!
Prayer of a common soldier before the battle of Blenheim (see N. & Q., clxxiii.264). Quoted in Newman's *Apologia*

6 Oh my dear fellow, the noise…and the people!
Of the Battle of Bastogne. Attr. to a Captain Strahan. See Griffin, 'Dialogue with W.H. Auden', *Hudson Review* III, iv, Winter 51, p.583

7 One Cartwright brought a Slave from Russia, and would scourge him, for which he was questioned: and it was resolved, That England was too pure an Air for Slaves to breathe in.
'In the 11th of Elizabeth' (17 Nov. 1568–16 Nov. 1569). Rushworth, *Historical Collections* (1680–1722), II, p.468

8 On Waterloo's ensanguined plain
Full many a gallant man was slain,
But none, by sabre or by shot,
Fell half so flat as Walter Scott.
On Scott's *Field of Waterloo. 1815*

9 Please do not shoot the pianist. He is doing his best.
Oscar Wilde, *Impressions of America.* 'Leadville'

10 Please to remember the Fifth of November,
Gunpowder Treason and Plot.
We know no reason why gunpowder treason
Should ever be forgot.
Traditional since 17th cent.

11 Raise the stone, and there thou shalt find me, cleave the wood and there am I.
Oxyrhynchus Papyri, B.P. Grenfell and A.S. Hunt (eds.) *Sayings of Our Lord* (1897) Logion 5, l.23

12 Says Tweed to Till—
'What gars ye rin sae still?'
Says Till to Tweed—
'Though ye rin with speed
And I rin slaw,
For ae man that ye droon
I droon twa'.
Two Rivers, Oxford Book of English Verse

13 See the happy moron,
He doesn't give a damn.
I wish I were a moron,
My God! Perhaps I am!
Eugenics Review, July 1929, 86/2

14 Seven wealthy Towns contend for HOMER Dead
Through which the Living HOMER begged his Bread.
Epilogue to *Aesop at Tunbridge; or, a Few Selected Fables in Verse.* By No Person of Quality, 1698. See 250:22

15 Since first I saw your face, I resolved to honour and renown ye;
If now I be disdained, I wish my heart had never known ye.
What? I that loved and you that liked, shall we begin to wrangle?
No, no, no, my heart is fast, and cannot disentangle.
Music of Sundry Kinds (1607)

16 Since wars begin in the minds of men, it is in the minds of men that the defences of peace must be constructed.
Constitution of the United Nations Educational, Scientific and Cultural Organisation (1946)

17 Spheres of influence.
Hertslet, *Map of Africa by Treaty,* 3rd edn., 868. See 234:10

18 Sumer is icumen in,
Lhude sing cuccu!
Groweth sed, and bloweth med,
And springth the wude nu.
Cuckoo Song, c. 1250, sung annually at Reading Abbey gateway. First recorded by John Fornset, a monk of Reading Abbey

19 That this house will in no circumstances fight for its King and country.
Motion passed at the Oxford Union, 9 Feb. 1933

20 That we spent, we had:
That we gave, we have:
That we left, we lost.
Epitaph of the Earl of Devonshire, as quoted by Spenser in *The Shepherd's Calendar,* May, l.70. See 8:17

21 The almighty dollar is the only object of worship.
Philadelphia Public Ledger, 2 Dec. 1836

22 The children in Holland take pleasure in making
What the children in England take pleasure in breaking.
Nursery Rhyme

23 The eternal triangle.
Book review in the *Daily Chronicle,* 5 Dec. 1907

24 The fault is great in man or woman
Who steals a goose from off a common;
But what can plead that man's excuse
Who steals a common from a goose?
The Tickler Magazine, 1 Feb. 1821

25 The King over the Water.
Jacobite Toast, 18th cent.

26 The ministry of all the talents.
A name given ironically to Grenville's coalition of 1806; also applied to later coalitions

27 The nature of God is a circle of which the centre is everywhere and the circumference is nowhere.
Said to have been traced to a lost treatise of Empedocles. Quoted in the *Roman de la Rose,* and by S. Bonaventura in *Itinerarius Mentis in Deum,* cap.v, *ad fin.*

28 Therefore let us sing and dance a galliard,
To the remembrance of the mallard:
And as the mallard dives in pool,
Let us dabble, dive, and duck in Bowl.
Oh! by the blood of King Edward,
Oh! by the blood of King Edward,
It was a swapping, swapping mallard.
All Souls College, Oxford, song (perhaps of Tudor date). See *The Oxford Sausage* (1764), pp.83–84. Manuscript sources suggest

that the song was first printed in 1752. Hearne's Diaries, 17, p.46, May 1708 (see *Collections*, ed. C.E. Doble, ii, O.H.S. vii, 1886, p.111), have the order 'duck and dive' in the last line of the verse.

1 There is a lady sweet and kind,
  Was never face so pleased my mind;
  I did but see her passing by,
  And yet I love her till I die.
  Found on back of leaf 53 of 'Popish Kingdome or reigne of Antichrist', in Latin verse by Thomas Naogeorgus, and Englished by Barnabe Googe. Printed 1570. See N. & Q., 9th series, x.427

2 There is so much good in the worst of us,
  And so much bad in the best of us,
  That it hardly becomes any of us
  To talk about the rest of us.
  Good and Bad. Attr. to Edward Wallis Hoch (1849–1925) but disclaimed by him; and to many others.

3 There's nae luck about the house,
    There's nae luck at a',
  There's nae luck about the house
    When our gudeman's awa'.
  The Mariner's Wife

4 The Sun himself cannot forget
  His fellow traveller.
  On Sir Francis Drake. *Wit's Recreations* (1640), Epigrams, No.146

5 They come as a boon and a blessing to men,
  The Pickwick, the Owl, and the Waverley pen.
  Advertisement by MacNiven and Cameron Ltd, Edinburgh and Birmingham

6 Thirty days hath September,
  April, June, and November;
  All the rest have thirty-one,
  Excepting February alone,
  And that has twenty-eight days clear
  And twenty-nine in each leap year.
  Stevins MS. (c.1555)

7 The singer not the song.
  From a West Indian calypso and used as the title of a novel (1959) by Audrey Erskine Lindop

8 This is a rotten argument, but it should be good enough for their lordships on a hot summer afternoon.
  Annotation to ministerial brief, said to have been read inadvertently in the House of Lords. Lord Home, *The Way the Wind Blows* (1976), p.204

9 Thought shall be the harder, heart the keener, courage the greater, as our might lessens.
  The Battle of Maldon. Tr. R.K. Gordon (1926) from Anglo-Saxon.

10 To many people Victorian wit and humour is summed up by *Punch*, when every joke is supposed to end with 'Collapse of Stout Party', though this phrase tends to be as elusive as 'Elementary, my dear Watson' in the Sherlock Holmes sagas.
  R. Pearsall, *Collapse of Stout Party* (1975), Introduction

11 Too small to live in and too large to hang on a watch-chain. [Of Chiswick House.]
  Cecil Roberts, *And so to Bath* (1940), ch.4. 'By Way of Chiswick', attr. to 'one guest'

12 Two men wrote a lexicon, Liddell and Scott;
  Some parts were clever, but some parts were not.
  Hear, all ye learned, and read me this riddle,
  How the wrong part wrote Scott, and the right part
    wrote Liddell.
  On Henry Liddell (1811–98) and Robert Scott (1811–87), co-authors of the Greek Lexicon, 1843

13 Weep you no more, sad fountains;
    What need you flow so fast?
  Songs set by John Dowland, *Oxford Book of 16th Cent. Verse*

14 We hold these truths to be self-evident, that all men are created equal, that they are endowed by their Creator with certain unalienable rights, that among these are life, liberty and the pursuit of happiness.
  The American Declaration of Independence, 4 July 1776. See 272:6

15 'Well, what sort of sport has Lord — had?'
  'Oh, the young Sahib shot divinely, but God was very merciful to the birds.'
  G.W.E. Russell, *Collections and Recollections*, ch.30

16 Western wind, when wilt thou blow,
    The small rain down can rain?
  Christ, if my love were in my arms
    And I in my bed again!
  Oxford Book of 16th Cent. Verse

17 What wee gave, wee have;
  What wee spent, wee had;
  What wee kept, wee lost.
  Epitaph on Edward Courtenay, Earl of Devonshire (d. 1419), and his wife, at Tiverton. See 7:20

18 When Israel was in Egypt land,
  Let my people go,
  Oppressed so hard they could not stand,
  Let my people go.
    Go down, Moses,
    Way-down in Egypt land,
    Tell old Pharaoh
    To let my people go.
  Negro Spiritual. See 47:13

19 When I was a little boy, I had but a little wit,
  'Tis a long time ago, and I have no more yet;
  Nor ever ever shall, until that I die,
  For the longer I live the more fool am I.
  Wit and Mirth, an Antidote against Melancholy (1684)

20 Where is the man who has the power and skill
  To stem the torrent of a woman's will?
  For if she will, she will, you may depend on't;
  And if she won't, she won't; so there's an end on't.
  From the Pillar Erected on the Mount in the Dane John Field, Canterbury *Examiner*, 31 May 1829

21 Whilst Adam slept, Eve from his side arose:
  Strange his first sleep should be his last repose.
  The Consequence

22 Whose Finger do you want on the Trigger When the World Situation Is So Delicate?
  Headline in the *Daily Mirror*, see H. Cudlipp, *Publish and Be Damned* (1953), p.263

23 Would you like to sin
  With Elinor Glyn
  On a tiger-skin?
  Or would you prefer
  to err
  with her
  on some other fur?
  c. 1907. A. Glyn, *Elinor Glyn* (1955), pt.II.30

24 Yet, if his majesty our sovereign lord
  Should of his own accord
  Friendly himself invite,
  And say 'I'll be your guest tomorrow night',
  How should we stir ourselves, call and command

All hands to work!
From Christ Church MS.

1 But at the coming of the King of Heaven
All's set at six and seven:
We wallow in our sin.
Christ cannot find a chamber in the inn.
We entertain Him always like a stranger,
And as at first still lodge Him in the manger.

2 You pays your money and you takes your choice.
From a peepshow rhyme. See V.S. Lean, *Collectanea* (1902-4)

FRENCH

3 An army marches on its stomach.
Attr. Napoleon in, e.g., *Windsor Magazine*, 1904, p.268.
Probably condensed from a long passage in Las Cases, *Mémorial de Ste-Hélène* (Nov. 1816)

4 *Cet animal est très méchant,*
Quand on l'attaque il se défend.
This animal is very bad; when attacked it defends itself.
La Ménagerie, by Théodore P.K., 1828

5 *Chevalier sans peur et sans reproche.*
Knight without fear and without blemish.
Description in contemporary chronicles of Pierre Bayard, 1476-1524

6 *Honi soit qui mal y pense.*
Evil be to him who evil thinks [of it].
Motto of the Order of the Garter, originated by Edward III probably on 23 Apr. of 1348 or 1349.

7 *Il y avait un jeune homme de Dijon,*
Qui n'avait que peu de religion.
Il dit: 'Quant à moi,
Je déteste tous les trois,
Le Père, et le Fils, et le Pigeon.'
The Norman Douglas limerick book (1969, first privately printed in 1928 under the title *Some Limericks*), introduction.

8 *Je suis le capitaine de vingt-quatre soldats, et sans moi Paris serait pris?* [Answer:] *A.*
Hugh Rowley, *Puniana: or thoughts wise and otherwise a new collection of the best* (1867), p.42. The saying 'With twenty-six lead soldiers [the characters of the alphabet set up for printing] I can conquer the world' may be derived from this riddle, but probably arose independently.

9 *La grande phrase reçue, c'est* qu'il ne faut pas être plus royaliste que le roi. *Cette phrase n'est pas du moment; elle fut inventée sous Louis XVI: elle enchaîna les mains des fidèles, pour ne laisser libre que le bras du bourreau.*
The big catch-phrase is *that you mustn't be more of a royalist than His Royal Highness.* This expression is not new; it was coined under the reign of Louis XVI: it chained up the hands of the loyal, leaving free only the arm of the hangman.
Chateaubriand, *De La Monarchie selon la Charte*, II, xli

10 *Laisser-nous-faire.*
M. Colbert assembla plusieurs Deputés de commerce chez lui pour leur demander ce qu'il pourroit faire pour le commerce; le plus raisonnable et le moins flatteur d'entre eux, lui dit ce seul mot: 'Laissez-nous-faire.' *Journal Oeconomique*, Paris, Apr. 1751

11 *L'amour est aveugle; l'amitié ferme les yeux.*
Love is blind; friendship closes its eyes.
See 11:25, 402:22

12 *Le monde est plein de fous, et qui n'en veut pas voir*
Doit se tenir tout seul, et casser son miroir.
The world is full of fools, and he who would not see it should live alone and smash his mirror.
An adaptation from an original form attr. to Claude Le Petit (1640–1665) in *Discours Satiriques*, 1686

13 *Liberté! Égalité! Fraternité!*
Freedom! Equality! Brotherhood!
Motto of the French Revolution, but of earlier origin. The Club des Cordeliers passed a motion, 30 June 1793, ' *que les propriétaires seront invités,…de faire peindre sur la façade de leurs maisons, en gros caractères, ces mots: Unité, indivisibilité de la République, Liberté, Égalité, Fraternité ou la mort':Journal de Paris*, 182. From 1795 the words '*ou la mort*' were dropped from this prescription. See 139:18

14 *L'ordre règne à Varsovie.*
Order reigns in Warsaw.
After the brutal suppression of an uprising, the newspaper *Moniteur* reported (16 Sept. 1831) '*L'ordre et la tranquillité sont entièrement rétablis dans la capitale.*' On the same day Count Sebastiani, minister of foreign affairs said '*La tranquillité règne à Varsovie.*'

15 *Nous n'irons plus aux bois, les lauriers sont coupés.*
We'll to the woods no more,
The laurels all are cut.
Old nursery rhyme quoted by Banville in *Les Cariatides, les stalactites*. Tr. Housman, *Last Poems*, introductory

16 *Revenons à ces moutons.*
Let us return to our sheep. (Let us get back to the subject.)
Maistre Pierre Pathelin (line 1191). Often quoted as '*Retournons à nos moutons*'

17 *Si le Roi m'avait donné,*
Paris, sa grand'ville,
Et qu'il me fallût quitter
L'amour de ma mie,
Je dirais au roi Henri:
'Reprenez votre Paris:
J'aime mieux ma mie, au gué,
J'aime mieux ma mie.'
If the king had given me Paris, his great city, and if I were required to give up my darling's love, I would say to King Henry: 'Take your Paris back; I prefer my darling, by the ford, I prefer my darling'.
Popular song, attr. Antoine de Bourbon (1518–1562), father of Henri IV; see Ampère, *Instructions relatives aux poésies populaires de la France.* Quoted in this form in Molière, *Le Misanthrope*, I.ii

18 *Taisez-vous! Méfiez-vous! Les oreilles ennemies vous écoutent.*
Keep your mouth shut! Be on your guard! Enemy ears are listening to you.
Official Notice in France in 1915

19 *Toujours perdrix!*
Always partridge!
Said to originate in a story of Henri IV's having ordered that nothing but partridge should be served to his confessor, who had rebuked the king for his liaisons.

20 *Tout passe, tout casse, tout lasse.*
Everything passes, everthing perishes, everthing palls.
Cahier, *Quelques six mille proverbes*

GREEK

21 γνῶθι σεαυτόν.
Know thyself.
Inscribed on the temple of Apollo at Delphi. Plato, *Protagoras*, 343 b, ascribes the saying to the Seven Wise Men.

22 μηδὲν ἄγαν.
Nothing in excess.

1 ὅταν δ' ὁ δαίμων ἀνδρὶ πορσύνῃ κακά,
τὸν νοῦν ἔβλαψε πρῶτον, ᾧ βουλεύεται.
Whenever God prepares evil for a man, He first
damages his mind.
Scholiast on Sophocles, *Antigone*, 622 ff. See R.C. Jebb's edn.
(1906), Appendix, pp.255-6. Perhaps best known in Latin
translation. See 199:15

2 ἀγεωμέτρητος μηδεὶς εἰσίτω.
Let no one enter who does not know geometry
[mathematics].
Inscription on Plato's door, probably at the Academy at Athens.
Elias Philosophus, *In Aristotelis Categorias Commentaria*, 118.18
(A. Busse ed., *Comm. in Arist. Graeca*, Berlin, 1900, XVIII, i.)

ITALIAN

3 *Se non è vero, è molto ben trovato.*
If it is not true, it is a happy invention.
Apparently a common saying in the sixteenth century. Found in
Giordano Bruno (1585) in the above form, and in Antonio Doni
(1552) as '*Se non è vero, egli è stato un bel trovato.*'

LATIN

4   *Adeste, fideles,*
      Laeti triumphantes;
Venite, venite in Bethlehem.
      O come, all ye faithful,
      Joyful and triumphant,
O come, ye, O come ye to Bethlehem.
French or German hymn of 18th Cent. Trans. F. Oakeley in
Murray's Hymnal, 1852. See *Songs of Praise Discussed*

5 *Venite adoremus, venite adoremus,*
Venite adoremus Dominum.
O come, let us adore him! O come, let us adore him!
O come, let us adore him, Christ the Lord!

6 *Ad majorem Dei gloriam.*
To the greater glory of God.
Motto of the Society of Jesus

7 *Ave Caesar, morituri te salutant.*
Hail Caesar; those who are about to die salute you.
Gladiators saluting the Roman Emperor. See Suetonius, *Claudius*,
21

8 *Ave Maria, gratia plena, Dominus tecum: Benedicta
tu in mulieribus, et benedictus fructus ventris tui,
Jesus.*
Hail Mary, full of grace, the Lord is with thee: Blessed
art thou among women, and blessed is the fruit of thy
womb, Jesus.
Ave Maria, also known as *The Angelic Salutation*, dating from
the 11th cent.

9 *Ave verum corpus,*
Natum Ex Maria Virgine.
Hail the true body, born of the Virgin Mary.
Eucharistic hymn, dating probably from the 14th cent.

10 *Caveant consules ne quid res publica detrimenti
caperet.*
Let the consuls see to it that no harm come to the
state.
Senatorial 'ultimate decree' in the Roman Republic. See, e.g.,
Cicero, *Pro Milone*, 26, 70

11 *Cras amet qui nunquam amavit, quique amavit cras
amet!*
Let those love now, who never lov'd before:
Let those who always lov'd, now love the more.
Pervigilium Veneris, 1. Tr. Parnell

12 *Et in Arcadia ego.*
And I too in Arcadia.
Tomb inscription often depicted in classical paintings. The
meaning is disputed.

13 *Gaudeamus igitur,*
Juvenes dum sumus
Post jucundam juventutem,
Post molestam senectutem,
Nos habebit humus.
Let us then rejoice,
While we are young.
After the pleasures of youth
And the tiresomeness of old age
Earth will hold us.
Medieval students' song, traced to 1267, but revised in the 18th
cent.

14 *Meum est propositum*
   In taberna mori,
Ut sint vina proxima
   Morientis ori.
Tunc cantabunt laetius
   Angelorum chori:
'*Sit Deus propitius*
   Huic potatori!'
I desire to end my days in a tavern drinking,
May some Christian hold for me the glass when I am
   shrinking;
That the Cherubim may cry, when they see me
   sinking,
'God be merciful to a soul of this gentleman's way of
   thinking.'
'The Archpoet' (fl. 1159-67), *Estuans intrinsecus ira vehementi*.
Tr. Leigh Hunt.

15 *Nemo me impune lacessit.*
No one provokes me with impunity.
Motto of the Crown of Scotland and of all Scottish regiments

16 *Per ardua ad astra.*
Hard and high to the stars!
Motto of the Mulvany family, quoted in Rider Haggard, *The
People of the Mist* (1894), ch.1, proposed by J.S. Yule in 1912,
adopted as official motto of the Royal Flying Corps and approved
by King George V in 1913, still in use as motto of the R.A.F. See
P.G. Hering, *Customs and Traditions of the Royal Air Force*
(1961). Rider Haggard's rendering was 'Through Struggle to the
Stars'.

17 *Post coitum omne animal triste.*
After coition every animal is sad.
Post-classical

18 *Quidquid agas, prudenter agas, et respice finem.*
Whatever you do, do cautiously, and look to the end.
Gesta Romanorum, 103

19 *Salve, regina, mater misericordiae,*
Vita, dulcedo et spes nostra, salve!
Ad te clamamus exsules filii Evae,
Ad te suspiramus gementes et flentes
In hac lacrimarum valle.
Eia ergo, advocata nostra,
Illos tuos misericordes oculos ad nos converte.
Et Iesum, benedictum fructum ventris tui,
Nobis post hoc exsilium ostende,
O clemens, o pia,
O dulcis virgo Maria.
Hail holy queen, mother of mercy, hail our life, our
   sweetness, and our hope! To thee do we cry, poor
   banished children of Eve; to thee do we send up our
   sighs, mourning and weeping in this vale of tears.

Turn then, most gracious advocate, thine eyes of
mercy towards us; and after this our exile show unto
us the blessed fruit of thy womb, Jesus, O clement,
O loving, O sweet virgin Mary.
Attr. to various eleventh-century authors. See *Analecta Hymnica...*
vol.50 (1907), p.318.

1 *Sic transit gloria mundi.*
Thus passes the glory of the world.
Spoken during the coronation of a new Pope, while flax is burned
to represent the transitoriness of earthly glory. Used at the
coronation of Alexander V, Pisa, 7 July 1409, but earlier in
origin. See 546:7

2 *Si monumentum requiris, circumspice.*
If you seek for a monument, gaze around.
Inscription in St. Paul's Cathedral, London, attr. to the son of the
architect, Sir Christopher Wren.

3 *Te Deum laudamus: Te Dominum confitemur.*
We praise thee, God: we own thee Lord.
Te Deum. Hymn traditionally ascribed to St. Ambrose and St.
Augustine in 387, but some modern scholars attribute it to St.
Niceta (d.c.414). See 384:16

4 *In te Domine, speravi: non confundar in aeternum.*
Lord, I have set my hopes in thee, I shall not be
destroyed for ever.
See 384:18

5 *Tempora mutantur, et nos mutamur in illis.*
Times change, and we change with them.
Harrison, *Description of Britain* (1577), III, iii, 99. Attributed to
the Emperor Lothar I (795-855) in the form *Omnia mutantur, nos
et mutamur in illis*

6 *Vox et praeterea nihil.*
A voice and nothing more.
Of a nightingale. See also Plutarch, *Moralia,* 'Sayings of
Spartans', 233a

CHRISTOPHER ANSTEY 1724–1805

7 If ever I ate a good supper at night,
I dream'd of the devil, and wak'd in a fright.
**The New Bath Guide. Letter 4. A Consultation of the
Physicians**

8 You may go to Carlisle's, and to Almack's too;
And I'll give you my head if you find such a host,
For coffee, tea, chocolate, butter, and toast:
How he welcomes at once all the world and his wife,
And how civil to folk he ne'er saw in his life.
Letter 13. A Public Breakfast

F. ANSTEY 1856–1934

9 Drastic measures is Latin for a whopping.
Vice Versa, ch.7

GUILLAUME APOLLINAIRE 1880–1918

10 *Les souvenirs sont cors de chasse
Dont meurt le bruit parmi le vent.*
Memories are hunting horns whose sound dies on the
wind.
Cors de Chasse

11 *Sous le pont Mirabeau coule la Seine
    Et nos amours
        Faut-il qu'il m'en souvienne
La joie venait toujours après la peine*

*Vienne nuit sonne l'heure
Les jours s'en vont je demeure.*

Under Mirabeau Bridge flows the Seine.

Why must I be reminded again
    Of our love?
Doesn't happiness issue from pain?

Bring on the night, ring out the hour.
The days wear on but I endure.
Le Pont Mirabeau, tr. William Meredith

THOMAS GOLD APPLETON 1812–1884

12 A Boston man is the east wind made flesh.
Attr.

13 Good Americans, when they die, go to Paris.
O.W. Holmes, *Autocrat of the Breakfast Table,* 6

ARABIAN NIGHTS

14 Who will change old lamps for new ones?...new
lamps for old ones?
The History of Aladdin

15 Open Sesame!
The History of Ali Baba

WILLIAM ARABIN 1773–1841

16 If ever there was a case of clearer evidence than this
of persons acting in concert together, this case is that
case.
Sir R. Megarry, *Arabinesque at Law* (1969)

17 They will steal the very teeth out of your mouth as you
walk through the streets. I know it from experience.
[The citizens of Uxbridge.]

18 Prisoner, God has given you good abilities, instead of
which you go about the country stealing ducks.
See N. & Q., clxx.310

DR. ARBUTHNOT 1667–1735

19 He warns the heads of parties against believing their
own lies.
The Art of Political Lying (1712)

20 Law is a bottomless pit.
The History of John Bull (1712), ch.24

21 Here continueth to rot the body of Francis Chartres.
See A. Pope, note to l.20 of *Epistles to Several Persons,* iii. 'To
Lord Bathhurst' (1733)

ARCHILOCHUS fl. c.650 B.C.

22 πολλ᾽ οἶδ᾽ ἀλώπηξ, ἀλλ᾽ ἐχῖνος ἓν μέγα.
The fox knows many things—the hedgehog one *big*
one.
E. Diehl (ed.), *Anth. Lyr. Gr.,* I, p.241, no.103

ARCHIMEDES 287–212 B.C.

23 εὕρηκα.
Eureka! (I've got it!)
Vitruvius Pollio, *De Architectura,* ix.215

24 δός μοι ποῦ στῶ καὶ κινῶ τὴν γῆν.
Give me somewhere to stand, and I will move the
earth.
Pappus, *Synagoge,* ed. F. Hultsch, Berlin, 1876-8, VIII, 10, xi

COMTE D'ARGENSON 1652–1721

25 *Laisser-faire.*

No interference.
Mémoires, vol.5, p.364. See 9:10, 403:22

1 Abbé Guyot Desfontaines: *Il faut que je vive.*
D'Argenson: *Je n'en vois pas la nécessité.*
Desfontaines: I must live.
D'Argenson: I do not see the necessity.
Voltaire, *Alzire, Discours Préliminaire*

LUDOVICO ARIOSTO 1474–1533

2 *Natura il fece, e poi roppe la stampa.*
Nature made him, and then broke the mould.
Orlando Furioso, x.84

ARISTOPHANES c.444–c.380 B.C.

3 βούλει Νεφελοκοκκυγίαν;
How about 'Cloudcuckooland'?
Birds, 819. Naming the capital city of the Birds.

4 ὁ δ' εὔκολος μὲν ἐνθάδ', εὔκολος δ' ἐκεῖ.
But he was contented there, is contented here.
(Sophocles)
Frogs, 82

5 βρεκεκεκὲξ κοὰξ κοάξ.
Brekekekex koax koax.
209 and elsewhere. Cry of the Frogs.

ARISTOTLE 384–322 B.C.

6 διὸ καλῶς ἀπεφήναντο τἀγαθόν, οὗ πάντ' ἐφίεται.
So the good has been well explained as that at which
all things aim.
Nicomachean Ethics, I.1.1094a

7 ἄνθρωπος φύσει πολιτικὸν ζῷον.
Man is by nature a political animal.
Politics, i.2.1253a

8 Where some people are very wealthy and others have
nothing, the result will be either extreme democracy or
absolute oligarchy, or despotism will come from either
of those excesses.
4.1296a

9 ἔστιν οὖν τραγῳδία μίμησις πράξεως σπουδαίας
καὶ τελείας μέγεθος ἐχούσης ... δι' ἐλέου καὶ
φόβου περαίνουσα τὴν τῶν τοιούτων παθημάτων
κάθαρσιν.
Tragedy is thus a representation of an action that is
worth serious attention, complete in itself and of some
amplitude...by means of pity and fear bringing about
the purgation of such emotions.
Poetics, 6.1449b

10 διὸ καὶ φιλοσοφώτερον καὶ σπουδαιότερον ποίησις
ἱστορίας ἐστίν.
For this reason poetry is something more philosophical
and more worthy of serious attention than history.
9.1451b

11 προαιρεῖσθαί τε δεῖ ἀδύνατα εἰκότα μᾶλλον ἢ
δυνατὰ ἀπίθανα.
Probable impossibilities are to be preferred to
improbable possibilites.
24.1460a

12 *Amicus Plato, sed magis amica veritas.*
Plato is dear to me, but dearer still is truth.
Greek original ascribed to Aristotle

LEWIS ADDISON ARMISTEAD 1817–1863

13 Give them the cold steel, boys!
Attr. during Amer. Civil War, 1863

DR. JOHN ARMSTRONG 1709–1779

14 Virtuous and wise he was, but not severe;
He still remember'd that he once was young.
Art of Preserving Health (1744), bk.iv, l.226

15   Much had he read,
Much more had seen; he studied from the life,
And in th'original perus'd mankind.
l.231

16 Of right and wrong he taught
Truths as refin'd as ever Athens heard;
And (strange to tell!) he practis'd what he preach'd.
l.303

17 'Tis not too late to-morrow to be brave.
l.460

NEIL A. ARMSTRONG 1930–

18 That's one small step for a man, one giant leap for
mankind.
On landing on the moon, 21 July 1969. First reported without the
word 'a'.

SIR EDWIN ARNOLD 1832–1904

19   Nor ever once ashamed
     So we be named
Press-men; Slaves of the Lamp; Servants of Light.
The Tenth Muse (1895), st.18

GEORGE ARNOLD 1834–1865

20 The living need charity more than the dead.
The Jolly Old Pedagogue

MATTHEW ARNOLD 1822–1888

21 And we forget because we must
And not because we will.
Absence

22 A bolt is shot back somewhere in our breast,
And a lost pulse of feeling stirs again.
The eye sinks inward, and the heart lies plain,
And what we mean, we say, and what we would, we
     know.
A man becomes aware of his life's flow,
And hears its winding murmur; and he sees
The meadows where it glides, the sun, the breeze.

And there arrives a lull in the hot race
Wherein he doth forever chase
That flying and elusive shadow, rest.
An air of coolness plays upon his face,
And an unwonted calm pervades his breast.
And then he thinks he knows
The hills where his life rose,
And the sea where it goes.
The Buried Life, l.84

23 The Sea of Faith
Was once, too, at the full, and round earth's shore
Lay like the folds of a bright girdle furl'd.
But now I only hear
Its melancholy, long, withdrawing roar,
Retreating, to the breath
Of the night-wind, down the vast edges drear
And naked shingles of the world.

Ah, love, let us be true
To one another! for the world, which seems
To lie before us like a land of dreams,
So various, so beautiful, so new,
Hath really neither joy, nor love, nor light,
Nor certitude, nor peace, nor help for pain;
And we are here as on a darkling plain
Swept with confused alarms of struggle and flight,
Where ignorant armies clash by night.
Dover Beach, l.21

1 Be neither saint nor sophist-led, but be a man.
Empedocles on Etna (1852), I.ii.136

2 Not here, O Apollo!
Are haunts meet for thee.
But, where Helicon breaks down
In cliff to the sea.
II.421

3 'Tis Apollo comes leading
His choir, the Nine.
—The leader is fairest,
But all are divine.
445

4 Let beam upon my inward view
Those eyes of deep, soft, lucent hue—
Eyes too expressive to be blue,
Too lovely to be grey.
Faded Leaves, 4. **On the Rhine**

5 Now the great winds shoreward blow;
Now the salt tides seaward flow;
Now the wild white horses play,
Champ and chafe and toss in the spray.
The Forsaken Merman, l.4

6 Sand-strewn caverns, cool and deep,
Where the winds are all asleep;
Where the spent lights quiver and gleam;
Where the salt weed sways in the stream;
Where the sea-beasts rang'd all round
Feed in the ooze of their pasture-ground...
Where great whales come sailing by,
Sail and sail, with unshut eye,
Round the world for ever and aye.
l.35

7 She will start from her slumber
When gusts shake the door;
She will hear the winds howling,
Will hear the waves roar.
We shall see, while above us
The waves roar and whirl,
A ceiling of amber,
A pavement of pearl.
Singing, 'Here came a mortal,
But faithless was she!
And alone dwell for ever
The kings of the sea.'
l.112

8 Not as their friend or child I speak!
But as on some far northern strand,
Thinking of his own Gods, a Greek
In pity and mournful awe might stand
Before some fallen Runic stone—
For both were faiths, and both are gone.

Wandering between two worlds, one dead,
The other powerless to be born,
With nowhere yet to rest my head,

Like these, on earth I wait forlorn.
The Grande Chartreuse, l.79

9 What helps it now, that Byron bore,
With haughty scorn which mock'd the smart,
Through Europe to the Aetolian shore
The pageant of his bleeding heart?
That thousands counted every groan,
And Europe made his woe her own?
l.133

10 What shelter to grow ripe is ours?
What leisure to grow wise?
In Memory of the Author of Obermann, l.71

11 This truth—to prove, and make thine own:
'Thou hast been, shalt be, art, alone.'
Isolation. To Marguerite, l.29

12 Yes! in the sea of life enisled,
With echoing straits between us thrown,
Dotting the shoreless watery wild,
We mortal millions live *alone*.
To Marguerite—Continued, l.1

13 A God, a God their severance ruled!
And bade betwixt their shores to be
The unplumb'd, salt, estranging sea.
l.22

14 Creep into thy narrow bed,
Creep, and let no more be said!
Vain thy onset! all stands fast.
Thou thyself must break at last.

Let the long contention cease!
Geese are swans, and swans are geese.
Let them have it how they will!
Thou art tired; best be still.
The Last Word

15 Let the victors, when they come,
When the forts of folly fall,
Find thy body by the wall.

16 When Byron's eyes were shut in death,
We bow'd our head and held our breath.
He taught us little: but our soul
Had *felt* him like the thunder's roll.
Memorial Verses, l.6

17 He spoke, and loos'd our heart in tears.
He laid us as we lay at birth
On the cool flowery lap of earth. [Wordsworth.]
l.47

18 Time may restore us in his course
Goethe's sage mind and Byron's force:
But where will Europe's latter hour
Again find Wordsworth's healing power?
l.60

19 Ere the parting hour go by,
Quick, thy tablets, Memory!
A Memory Picture

20 With women the heart argues, not the mind.
Merope (1858), l.341

21 He bears the seed of ruin in himself.
l.856

22 For this is the true strength of guilty kings,
When they corrupt the souls of those they rule.
l.1436

23 With aching hands and bleeding feet
    We dig and heap, lay stone on stone;

We bear the burden and the heat
  Of the long day, and wish 'twere done.
Not till the hours of light return,
All we have built do we discern.
Morality, st.2. See 67:15

1 Say, has some wet bird-haunted English lawn
  Lent it the music of its trees at dawn?
  Parting, l.19

2 Hark! ah, the Nightingale!
  The tawny-throated!
  Hark! from that moonlit cedar what a burst!
  What triumph! hark—what pain!
  Philomela, l.1

3 Listen, Eugenia—
  How thick the bursts come crowding through the
      leaves!
  Again—thou hearest!
  Eternal Passion!
  Eternal Pain!
  l.28

4 Cruel, but composed and bland,
  Dumb, inscrutable and grand,
  So Tiberius might have sat,
  Had Tiberius been a cat.
  Poor Matthias, l.40

5 Strew on her roses, roses,
    And never a spray of yew.
  In quiet she reposes:
    Ah! would that I did too.
  Requiescat

6 Her cabin'd ample Spirit,
    It flutter'd and fail'd for breath.
  To-night it doth inherit
    The vasty hall of death.

7 Not deep the Poet sees, but wide.
  Resignation, l.214

8 Coldly, sadly descends
  The autumn evening. The Field
  Strewn with its dank yellow drifts
  Of wither'd leaves, and the elms,
  Fade into dimness apace,
  Silent.
  Rugby Chapel, l.1

9 Friends who set forth at our side,
  Falter, are lost in the storm.
  We, we only, are left!
  l.102

10 Go, for they call you, Shepherd, from the hill.
  The Scholar-Gipsy (1853), l.1

11 All the live murmur of a summer's day.
  l.20

12 Tired of knocking at Preferment's door.
  l.35

13 In hat of antique shape, and cloak of grey,
  The same the Gipsies wore.
  l.55

14 Crossing the stripling Thames at Bab-lock-hithe,
    Trailing in the cool stream thy fingers wet,
      As the slow punt swings round.
  l.74

15 Rapt, twirling in thy hand a wither'd spray,
    And waiting for the spark from heaven to fall.
  l.119

16 The line of festal light in Christ-Church hall.
  l.129

17 Thou waitest for the spark from heaven! and we,
  Light half-believers in our casual creeds...
  Who hesitate and falter life away,
  And lose to-morrow the ground won to-day—
    Ah, do not we, Wanderer, await it too?
  l.171

18 With close-lipp'd Patience for our only friend,
    Sad Patience, too near neighbour to Despair.
  l.194

19 This strange disease of modern life.
  l.203

20 Still nursing the unconquerable hope,
    Still clutching the inviolable shade.
  l.211

21 As some grave Tyrian trader, from the sea,
    Descried at sunrise an emerging prow
  Lifting the cool-hair'd creepers stealthily,
    The fringes of a southward-facing brow
      Among the Aegean isles;
  And saw the merry Grecian coaster come,
  Freighted with amber grapes, and Chian wine,
  Green bursting figs, and tunnies steep'd in brine;
    And knew the intruders on his ancient home,

  The young light-hearted Masters of the waves;
    And snatch'd his rudder, and shook out more sail,
    And day and night held on indignantly
  O'er the blue Midland waters with the gale,
    Betwixt the Syrtes and soft Sicily,
      To where the Atlantic raves
  Outside the Western Straits, and unbent sails
    There, where down cloudy cliffs, through sheets
      of foam,
    Shy traffickers, the dark Iberians come;
      And on the beach undid his corded bales.
  l.232

22 Resolve to be thyself: and know, that he
  Who finds himself, loses his misery.
  Self-Dependence, l.31

23 Others abide our question. Thou art free.
  We ask and ask: Thou smilest and art still,
  Out-topping knowledge.
  Shakespeare

24 And thou, who didst the stars and sunbeams know,
  Self-school'd, self-scann'd, self-honour'd, self-secure,
  Didst tread on Earth unguess'd at.—Better so!
  All pains the immortal spirit must endure,
  All weakness which impairs, all griefs which bow,
  Find their sole speech in that victorious brow.

25 Curl'd minion, dancer, coiner of sweet words!
  Sohrab and Rustum (1853), l.458

26   And Ruksh, the horse,
  Who stood at hand, utter'd a dreadful cry:
  No horse's cry was that, most like the roar
  Of some pain'd desert lion, who all day
  Hath trail'd the hunter's javelin in his side,
  And comes at night to die upon the sand.
  l.501

27 Truth sits upon the lips of dying men.
  l.656

28 But the majestic River floated on,
  Out of the mist and hum of that low land,

Into the frosty starlight.
1.875

1 Oxus, forgetting the bright speed he had
In his high mountain cradle in Pamere,
A foil'd circuitous wanderer—till at last
The long'd-for dash of waves is heard, and wide
His luminous home of waters opens, bright
And tranquil, from whose floor the new-bathed stars
Emerge, and shine upon the Aral Sea.
1.886

2 Still bent to make some port he knows not where,
Still standing for some false impossible shore.
A Summer Night, 1.68

3 The signal-elm, that looks on Ilsley downs,
The Vale, the three lone weirs, the youthful
Thames.
Thyrsis, 1.14

4 And that sweet City with her dreaming spires,
She needs not June for beauty's heightening.
1.19

5 So have I heard the cuckoo's parting cry,
From the wet field, through the vext garden-trees,
Come with the volleying rain and tossing breeze:
'The bloom is gone, and with the bloom go I.'
1.57

6 Too quick despairer, wherefore wilt thou go?
Soon will the high Midsummer pomps come on,
Soon will the musk carnations break and swell,
Soon shall we have gold-dusted snapdragon,
Sweet-William with his homely cottage-smell,
And stocks in fragrant blow.
1.61

7 For Time, not Corydon, hath conquer'd thee.
1.80

8 I know what white, what purple fritillaries
The grassy harvest of the river-fields,
Above by Ensham, down by Sandford, yields,
And what sedg'd brooks are Thames's tributaries.
1.107

9 The foot less prompt to meet the morning dew,
The heart less bounding at emotion new,
And hope, once crushed, less quick to spring again.
1.138

10 Who saw life steadily, and saw it whole:
The mellow glory of the Attic stage;
Singer of sweet Colonus, and its child. [Sophocles.]
To a Friend

11 France, fam'd in all great arts, in none supreme.
To a Republican Friend. Continued.

12 Nor bring, to see me cease to live,
Some doctor full of phrase and fame,
To shake his sapient head and give
The ill he cannot cure a name.
A Wish

13 And sigh that one thing only has been lent
To youth and age in common—discontent.
Youth's Agitations

14 Our society distributes itself into Barbarians,
Philistines, and Populace; and America is just
ourselves, with the Barbarians quite left out, and the
Populace nearly.
Culture and Anarchy (1869), preface

15 The pursuit of perfection, then, is the pursuit of
sweetness and light…He who works for sweetness and
light united, works to make reason and the will of God
prevail.
i. See 525:33

16 The men of culture are the true apostles of equality.

17 One has often wondered whether upon the whole earth
there is anything so unintelligent, so unapt to perceive
how the world is really going, as an ordinary young
Englishman of our upper class.
ii

18 For this [Middle] class we have a designation which
now has become pretty well known, and which we
may as well still keep for them, the designation of
Philistines.
iii

19 I often, therefore, when I want to distinguish clearly
the aristocratic class from the Philistines proper, or
middle class, name the former, in my own mind *the
Barbarians.*

20 But that vast portion, lastly, of the working-class
which, raw and half-developed, has long lain
half-hidden amidst its poverty and squalor, and is now
issuing from its hiding-place to assert an Englishman's
heaven-born privilege of doing as he likes, and is
beginning to perplex us by marching where it likes,
meeting where it likes, bawling what it likes, breaking
what it likes—to this vast residuum we may with great
propriety give the name of Populace.

21 Hebraism and Hellenism—between these two points
of influence moves our World…they are, each of
them, contributions to human development.
iv

22 'He knows' says Hebraism, 'his Bible!'—whenever
we hear this said, we may, without any elaborate
defence of culture, content ourselves with answering
simply: 'No man, who knows nothing else, knows
even his Bible.'

23 The magnificent roaring of the young lions of the
Daily Telegraph.
Essays in Criticism, First Series (1865), preface

24 Passionate, absorbing, almost blood-thirsty clinging to
life.

25 Beautiful city! so venerable, so lovely, so unravaged
by the fierce intellectual life of our century, so
serene!…whispering from her towers the last
enchantments of the Middle Age…Home of lost
causes, and forsaken beliefs, and unpopular names,
and impossible loyalties! [Oxford.]

26 What a touch of grossness in our race, what an
original shortcoming in the more delicate spiritual
perceptions, is shown by the natural growth amongst
us of such hideous names as Higginbottom, Stiggins,
Bugg!
The Function of Criticism at the Present Time

27 'Our unrivalled happiness';—what an element of
grimness, bareness, and hideousness mixes with it and
blurs it; the workhouse, the dismal Mapperly
Hills,—how dismal those who have seen them will
remember;—the gloom, the smoke, the cold, the
strangled illegitimate child!…And the final
touch,—short, bleak and inhuman: *Wragg is in
custody.* The sex lost in the confusion of our unrivalled

happiness; or (shall I say?) the superfluous Christian name lopped off by the straightforward vigour of our old Anglo-Saxon breed!
Prompted by a newspaper report of the murder of her illegitimate child by a girl named Wragg.

1 I am bound by my own definition of criticism: a disinterested endeavour to learn and propagate the best that is known and thought in the world.

2 It always seems to me that the right sphere for Shelley's genius was the sphere of music, not of poetry.
Maurice de Guérin, footnote

3 Philistine must have originally meant, in the mind of those who invented the nickname, a strong, dogged, unenlightened opponent of the chosen people, of the children of the light.
Heinrich Heine

4 Philistinism!—We have not the expression in English. Perhaps we have not the word because we have so much of the thing.

5 The absence, in this country, of any force of educated literary and scientific opinion.
Literary Influence of Academies

6 The great apostle of the Philistines, Lord Macaulay.
Joubert

7 His expression may often be called bald...but it is bald as the bare mountain tops are bald, with a baldness full of grandeur.
Second Series (1888), preface to Poems of Wordsworth

8 Nature herself seems, I say, to take the pen out of his hand, and to write for him with her own bare, sheer, penetrating power.

9 The difference between genuine poetry and the poetry of Dryden, Pope, and all their school, is briefly this: their poetry is conceived and composed in their wits, genuine poetry is conceived and composed in the soul.
Thomas Gray

10 In poetry, no less than in life, he is 'a beautiful and ineffectual angel, beating in the void his luminous wings in vain'.
Shelley. (Quoting his own sentence in his essay on Byron, Essays on Criticism, Second Series)

11 The translator of Homer should above all be penetrated by a sense of four qualities of his author:—that he is eminently rapid; that he is eminently plain and direct both in the evolution of his thought and in the expression of it, that is, both in his syntax and in his words; that he is eminently plain and direct in the substance of his thought, that is, in his matter and ideas; and, finally, that he is eminently noble.
On Translating Homer (1861), i

12 Wordsworth says somewhere that wherever Virgil seems to have composed 'with his eye on the object', Dryden fails to render him. Homer invariably composes 'with his eye on the object', whether the object be a moral or a material one: Pope composes with his eye on his style, into which he translates his object, whatever it is.

13 He [the translator] will find one English book and one only, where, as in the Iliad itself, perfect plainness of speech is allied with perfect nobleness; and that book is the Bible.
iii

14 Nothing has raised more questioning among my critics than these words—noble, the grand style....I think it will be found that the grand style arises in poetry, when a noble nature, poetically gifted, treats with simplicity or with severity a serious subject.
Final words

15 The theatre is irresistible; organise the theatre!
Irish Essays. The French Play in London

16 Miracles do not happen.
Literature and Dogma, preface to 1883 edition, last words

17 Culture, the acquainting ourselves with the best that has been known and said in the world, and thus with the history of the human spirit.
Preface to 1873 edition

18 Terms like grace, new birth, justification...terms, in short, which with St Paul are literary terms, theologians have employed as if they were scientific terms.
i, 1

19 When we are asked further, what is conduct?—let us answer: Three-fourths of life.

20 The true meaning of religion is thus not simply morality, but morality touched by emotion.
2

21 Conduct is three-fourths of our life and its largest concern.
3

22 But there remains the question: what righteousness really is. The method and secret and sweet reasonableness of Jesus.
xii, 2

23 So we have the Philistine of genius in religion—Luther; the Philistine of genius in politics—Cromwell; the Philistine of genius in literature—Bunyan.
Mixed Essays, Lord Falkland

24 I am past thirty, and three parts iced over.
Letter to A.H. Clough, 12 Feb. 1853

25 People think that I can teach them style. What stuff it all is! Have something to say, and say it as clearly as you can. That is the only secret of style.
G.W.E. Russell, Collections and Recollections, ch.13

DR. THOMAS ARNOLD 1795–1842

26 What we must look for here is, 1st, religious and moral principles: 2ndly, gentlemanly conduct: 3rdly, intellectual ability.
Arnold of Rugby (ed. J.J. Findlay), p.65

27 My object will be, if possible, to form Christian men, for Christian boys I can scarcely hope to make.
Letter, in 1828, on appointment to Headmastership of Rugby

28 As for rioting, the old Roman way of dealing with that is always the right one; flog the rank and file, and fling the ringleaders from the Tarpeian rock.
From an unpublished letter written before 1828, quoted by M. Arnold, Cornhill Magazine, Aug. 1868

ANTONIN ARTAUD 1896–1948

29 Il faut nous laver de la littérature. Nous voulons être hommes avant tout, être humains.
We must wash literature off ourselves. We want to be

men first of all; to be human.
Les Oeuvres et les Hommes, unpublished ms., 17 May 1922

ROGER ASCHAM 1515–1568

1 I said...how, and why, young children, were sooner allured by love, than driven by beating, to attain good learning.
The Schoolmaster (1570), preface

2 There is no such whetstone, to sharpen a good wit and encourage a will to learning, as is praise.
1

3 *Inglese Italianato, è un diavolo incarnato,* that is to say, you remain men in shape and fashion, but become devils in life and condition.
Of Englishmen travelling in Italy

4 He that will write well in any tongue, must follow this counsel of Aristotle, to speak as the common people do, to think as wise men do; and so should every man understand him, and the judgment of wise men allow him.
Toxophilus (1545), **To all gentlemen and yeomen of England**

DAISY ASHFORD 1881-1972

5 Mr Salteena was an elderly man of 42 and was fond of asking peaple to stay with him.
The Young Visiters (1919), ch.1

6 I do hope I shall enjoy myself with you...I am parshial to ladies if they are nice I suppose it is my nature. I am not quite a gentleman but you would hardly notice it.

7 You look rather rash my dear your colors dont quite match your face.
ch.2

8 My own room is next the bath room said Bernard it is decerated dark red as I have somber tastes. The bath room has got a tip up bason and a hose thing for washing your head.

9 Bernard always had a few prayers in the hall and some whiskey afterwards as he was rarther pious but Mr Salteena was not very addicted to prayers so he marched up to bed.
ch.3

10 It was a sumpshous spot all done up in gold with plenty of looking glasses.
ch.5

11 Oh I see said the Earl but my own idear is that these things are as piffle before the wind.

12 My dear Clincham, The bearer of this letter is an old friend of mine not quite the right side of the blanket as they say in fact he is the son of a first rate butcher but his mother was a decent family called Hyssopps of the Glen so you see he is not so bad and is desireus of being the correct article.

13 Ethel patted her hair and looked very sneery.
ch.8

14 My life will be sour grapes and ashes without you.

15 Take me back to the Gaierty hotel.
ch.9

H.H. ASQUITH 1852–1928

16 We had better wait and see.

Phrase used repeatedly in speeches in 1910, referring to the rumour that the House of Lords was to be flooded with new Liberal peers to ensure the passage of the Finance Bill. R.Jenkins, *Asquith,* ch.14

17 We shall never sheathe the sword which we have not lightly drawn until Belgium receives in full measure all and more than all that she has sacrificed, until France is adequately secured against the menace of aggression, until the rights of the smaller nationalities of Europe are placed upon an unassailable foundation, and until the military domination of Prussia is wholly and finally destroyed.
Guildhall, 9 Nov. 1914

MARGOT ASQUITH 1865–1945

18 Ettie has told enough white lies to ice a cake.
Nicholas Mosley, *Julian Grenfell* (1976), ch.3. Of Lady Desborough (1867–1952)

19 Mrs Asquith remarked indiscreetly that if Kitchener was not a great man, he was, at least, a great poster.
Said in 1914. Sir Philip Magnus, *Kitchener: Portrait of an Imperialist* (1958), ch.14

SIR JACOB ASTLEY 1579–1652

20 O Lord! thou knowest how busy I must be this day: if I forget thee, do not thou forget me.
Prayer before the Battle of Edgehill. Sir Philip Warwick, *Memoires,* 1701, p.229

SURGEON-CAPTAIN E.L. ATKINSON 1882–1929
and APSLEY CHERRY-GARRARD 1882–1959

21 Hereabouts died a very gallant gentleman, Captain L.E.G. Oates of the Inniskilling Dragoons. In March 1912, returning from the Pole, he walked willingly to his death in a blizzard, to try and save his comrades, beset by hardships.
Epitaph on a cairn and cross erected in the Antarctic, November 1912

JOHN AUBREY 1626–1697

22 How these curiosities would be quite forgot, did not such idle fellows as I am put them down.
Brief Lives. **Venetia Digby**

23 The parliament intended to have hanged him; and he expected no less, but resolved to be hanged with the Bible under one arm and Magna Carta under the other.
David Jenkins

24 He was so fair that they called him *the lady of* Christ's College.
John Milton

25 Sciatica: he cured it, by boiling his buttock.
Sir Jonas Moore

26 Sir Walter, being strangely surprised and put out of his countenance at so great a table, gives his son a damned blow over the face. His son, as rude as he was, would not strike his father, but strikes over the face the gentleman that sat next to him and said 'Box about: 'twill come to my father anon'.
Sir Walter Raleigh

27 When he killed a calf he would do it in a high style, and make a speech.
William Shakespeare

1 He was a handsome, well-shaped man: very good
   company, and of a very ready and pleasant smooth
   wit.

2 Anno 1670, not far from Cirencester, was an
   apparition; being demanded whether a good spirit or a
   bad? returned no answer, but disappeared with a
   curious perfume and most melodious twang. Mr W.
   Lilly believes it was a fairy.
   Miscellanies. Apparitions (1696)

W.H. AUDEN 1907–1973

3 In a garden shady this holy lady
   With reverent cadence and subtle psalm,
   Like a black swan as death came on
   Poured forth her song in perfect calm:
   And by ocean's margin this innocent virgin
   Constructed an organ to enlarge her prayer,
   And notes tremendous from her great engine
   Thundered out on the Roman air.

   Blonde Aphrodite rose up excited,
   Moved to delight by the melody,
   White as an orchid she rode quite naked
   In an oyster shell on top of the sea.
   Anthem for St. Cecilia's Day, I. Dedicated to Benjamin Britten,
   and set to music by Britten as *Hymn to St. Cecilia,* op.27 (1942)

4 *Blessed Cecilia, appear in visions*
   To all musicians, appear and inspire:
   Translated Daughter, come down and startle
   Composing mortals with immortal fire.

5 *O dear white children casual as birds,*
   Playing among the ruined languages,
   So small beside their large confusing words,
   So gay against the greater silences
   Of dreadful things you did.
   III

6 *Weep for the lives your wishes never led.*

7 Reindeer are coming to drive you away
   Over the snow on an ebony sleigh,
   Over the mountains and over the sea
   You shall go happy and handsome and free.
   The Ascent of F.6 (with Christopher Isherwood) (1936), II.v

8 *Mother:* Over the green pastures there
   You shall go hunting the beautiful deer,
   You shall pick flowers, the white and the blue,
   Shepherds shall flute their sweetest for you.
   Chorus: True, Love finally is great,
   Greater than all; but large the hate,
   Far larger than Man can ever estimate.

9 I'll love you, dear, I'll love you
        Till China and Africa meet,
   And the river jumps over the mountain
        And the salmon sing in the street.

   I'll love you till the ocean
        Is folded and hung up to dry
   And the seven stars go squawking
        Like geese about the sky.
   As I Walked Out One Evening

10 O let not Time deceive you,
        You cannot conquer Time.

   In the burrows of the Nightmare
        Where Justice naked is,
   Time watches from the shadow

And coughs when you would kiss.

In headaches and in worry
     Vaguely life leaks away,
And Time will have his fancy
     To-morrow or today.

Into many a green valley
     Drifts the appalling snow;
Time breaks the threaded dances
     And the diver's brilliant bow.

O plunge your hands in water,
     Plunge them in up to the wrist;
Stare, stare in the basin
     And wonder what you've missed.

The glacier knocks in the cupboard,
     The desert sighs in the bed,
And the crack in the tea-cup opens
     A lane to the land of the dead.

11 O stand, stand at the window
        As the tears scald and start;
   You shall love your crooked neighbour
        With your crooked heart.

12 August for the people and their favourite islands.
   Birthday Poem

13 The desires of the heart are as crooked as corkscrews,
        Not to be born is the best for man;
   The second-best is a formal order,
        The dance's pattern; dance while you can.
   Dance, dance, for the figure is easy,
        The tune is catching and will not stop;
   Dance till the stars come down from the rafters;
        Dance, dance, dance till you drop.
   Death's Echo

14 Happy the hare at morning, for she cannot read
   The Hunter's waking thoughts.
   The Dog Beneath the Skin (with Christopher Isherwood) (1935),
   Chorus following II.ii

15 Perfection, of a kind, was what he was after,
   And the poetry he invented was easy to understand;
   He knew human folly like the back of his hand,
   And was greatly interested in armies and fleets;
   When he laughed, respectable senators burst with
        laughter,
   And when he cried the little children died in the
        streets.
   Epitaph on a Tyrant. See 358:20

16 Altogether elsewhere, vast
   Herds of reindeer move across
   Miles and miles of golden moss,
   Silently and very fast.
   The Fall of Rome

17 'O where are you going?' said reader to rider,
   'That valley is fatal where furnaces burn,
   Yonder's the midden whose odours will madden,
   That gap is the grave where the tall return.'
   Five Songs, V

18 Behind you swiftly the figure comes softly,
   The spot on your skin is a shocking disease.

19   Clutching a little case,
   He walks out briskly to infect a city
   Whose terrible future may have just arrived.
   Gare du Midi

20 Lawrence was brought down by smut-hounds, Blake

went dotty as he sang,
Homer Lane was killed in action by the Twickenham
    Baptist gang.
Get there if you can and see the land

1 As it is, plenty.
  His Excellency

2 He disappeared in the dead of winter:
The brooks were frozen, the airports almost deserted,
And snow disfigured the public statues;
The mercury sank in the mouth of the dying day.
What instruments we have agree
The day of his death was a dark cold day.
  In Memory of W.B. Yeats, I

3 The provinces of his body revolted,
The squares of his mind were empty,
Silence invaded the suburbs,
The current of his feeling failed; he became his
    admirers.

4 The words of a dead man
Are modified in the guts of the living.

5 You were silly like us; your gift survived it all:
The parish of rich women, physical decay,
Yourself.
  II

6   Now Ireland has her madness and her weather still,
For poetry makes nothing happen.

7 Earth, receive an honoured guest:
William Yeats is laid to rest.
Let the Irish vessel lie
Emptied of its poetry.

Time that is intolerant
Of the brave and innocent,
And indifferent in a week
To a beautiful physique,

Worships language and forgives
Everyone by whom it lives.
  III

8 Time that with this strange excuse
Pardoned Kipling and his views,
And will pardon Paul Claudel,
Pardons him for writing well.

9 In the deserts of the heart
Let the healing fountain start,
In the prison of his days
Teach the free man how to praise.

10 Certainly the growth of the fore-brain has been a
    success:
He has not got lost in a backwater like the lampshell
Or the limpet; he has not died out like the
    super-lizards.

His boneless worm-like ancestors would be amazed
At the upright position, the breasts, the
    four-chambered heart,
The clandestine evolution in the mother's shadow.
  In Time of War, Commentary, from *Journey to a War* (1939)

11 By wire and wireless, in a score of bad translations,
They give their simple message to the world of man:
'Man can have Unity if Man will give up Freedom.

The State is real, the Individual is wicked;
Violence shall synchronize your movements like a
  tune,

And Terror like a frost shall halt the flood of thinking.

Barrack and bivouac shall be your friendly refuge,
And racial pride shall tower like a public column
And confiscate for safety every private sorrow.'

12 'Leave Truth to the police and us; we know the Good;
We build the Perfect City time shall never alter;
Our Law shall guard you always like a cirque of
  mountains,

Your Ignorance keep off evil like a dangerous sea;
You shall be consummated in the General Will,
Your children innocent and charming as the beasts.'

13 And, if we care to listen, we can always hear them:
'Men are not innocent as beasts and never can be,
Man can improve himself but never will himself be
  perfect,

Only the free have disposition to be truthful,
Only the truthful have the interest to be just,
Only the just possess the will-power to be free.'

14 It's no use raising a shout.
No, Honey, you can cut that right out.
I don't want any more hugs;
Make me some fresh tea, fetch me some rugs.
Here am I, here are you:
But what does it mean? What are we going to do?
  It's no use raising a Shout

15 It wasn't always like this?
Perhaps it wasn't, but it is.
Put the car away; when life fails,
What's the good of going to Wales?

16   To me Art's subject is the human clay,
And landscape but a background to a torso;
    All Cézanne's apples I would give away
    For one small Goya or a Daumier.
  Letter to Lord Byron, III

17 Lay your sleeping head, my love,
Human on my faithless arm;
Time and fevers burn away
Individual beauty from
Thoughtful children, and the grave
Proves the child ephemeral:
But in my arms till break of day
Let the living creature lie,
Mortal, guilty, but to me
The entirely beautiful.
  Lullaby

18 About suffering they were never wrong,
The Old Masters: how well they understood
Its human position; how it takes place
While someone else is eating or opening a window or
    just walking dully along.
  Musée des Beaux Arts

19 They never forgot
That even the dreadful martyrdom must run its course
Anyhow in a corner, some untidy spot
Where the dogs go on with their doggy life and the
    torturer's horse
Scratches its innocent behind on a tree.

20 Only God can tell the saintly from the suburban,
Counterfeit values always resemble the true;
Neither in Life nor Art is honesty bohemian,
The free behave much as the respectable do.
  New Year Letter (1941), note to line 1277

1 This is the Night Mail crossing the Border
   Bringing the cheque and the postal order.

   Letters for the rich, letters for the poor,
   The shop at the corner, the girl next door.

   Pulling up Beattock, a steady climb:
   The gradient's against her, but she's on time.

   Past cotton-grass and moorland border,
   Shovelling white steam over her shoulder.
   Night Mail, I

2 Letters of thanks, letters from banks,
   Letters of joy from girl and boy,
   Receipted bills and invitations
   To inspect new stock or to visit relations,
   And applications for situations,
   And timid lovers' declarations,
   And gossip, gossip from all the nations.
   III

3 Look, stranger, on this island now
   The leaping light for you discovers,
   Stand stable here
   And silent be,
   That through the channels of the ear
   May wander like a river
   The swaying sound of the sea.
   On This Island

4 O what is that sound which so thrills the ear
      Down in the valley drumming, drumming?
   Only the scarlet soldiers, dear,
      The soldiers coming.
   O What is That Sound

5 O it's broken the lock and splintered the door,
      O it's the gate where they're turning, turning;
   Their boots are heavy on the floor
      And their eyes are burning.

6 O Love, the interest itself in thoughtless Heaven,
   Make simpler daily the beating of man's heart; within,
   There in the ring where name and image meet,

   Inspire them with such a longing as will make his
      thought
   Alive like patterns a murmuration of starlings,
   Rising in joy over wolds, unwittingly weave.
   Perhaps (Prologue from **On This Island)**

7 Send to us power and light…
   Harrow the house of the dead; look shining at
   New styles of architecture, a change of heart.
   Petition

8 It's not only this we praise, it's the general love:
   Let cat's mew rise to a scream on the tool-shed roof.
   Prothalamion

9 Hunger allows no choice
   To the citizen or the police;
   We must love one another or die.
   September 1, 1939

10 Out of the air a voice without a face
      Proved by statistics that some cause was just
   In tones as dry and level as the place.
   The Shield of Achilles

11 Let us honour if we can
   The vertical man,
   Though we value none
   But the horizontal one.
   Collected Poems, II *1927–1932, Shorts*

12 Private faces in public places
   Are wiser and nicer
   Than public faces in private places.

13 To the man-in-the-street, who, I'm sorry to say,
      Is a keen observer of life,
   The word 'Intellectual' suggests straight away
      A man who's untrue to his wife.
   IV *1939-47, Shorts*

14 A poet's hope: to be,
   like some valley cheese,
   local, but prized elsewhere.
   XII *1958–1971, Shorts II*

15 And the poor in their fireless lodgings, dropping the
      sheets
   Of the evening paper: 'Our day is our loss, O show us
      History the operator, the
   Organizer, Time the refreshing river.'

   And the nations combine each cry, invoking the life
   That shapes the individual belly and orders
      The private nocturnal terror:
   'Did you not found once the city state of the sponge,

   'Raise the vast military empires of the shark
   And the tiger, establish the robin's plucky canton?
      Intervene. O descend as a dove or
   A furious papa or a mild engineer, but descend.'
   Spain 1937

16 Tomorrow for the young the poets exploding like
      bombs,
   The walks by the lake, the weeks of perfect
      communion;
   Tomorrow the bicycle races
   Through the suburbs on summer evenings. But to-day
      the struggle.

17 The stars are dead. The animals will not look.
   We are left alone with our day, and the time is short,
      and
         History to the defeated
   May say Alas but cannot help nor pardon.

18 Out on the lawn I lie in bed,
   Vega conspicuous overhead.
   A Summer Night

19 That later we, though parted then,
   May still recall those evenings when
      Fear gave his watch no look;
   The lion griefs loped from the shade
   And on our knees their muzzles laid,
      And Death put down his book.

20 He still loves life
   But O O O O how he wishes
   The good Lord would take him.
   Thank You, Fog (1974), in introductory Note

21 Let a florid music praise,
      The flute and the trumpet,
   Beauty's conquest of your face:
   In that land of flesh and bone,
   Where from citadels on high
   Her imperial standards fly
      Let the hot sun
      Shine on, shine on.
   Twelve Songs, III

22 At last the secret is out, as it always must come in the
      end,

The delicious story is ripe to tell to the intimate friend;
Over the tea-cups and in the square the tongue has its
    desire;
Still waters run deep, my dear, there's never smoke
    without fire.
VIII

1 For the clear voice suddenly singing, high up in the
    convent wall,
The scent of elder bushes, the sporting prints in the
    hall,
The croquet matches in summer, the handshake, the
    cough, the kiss,
There is always a wicked secret, a private reason for
    this.

2 When it comes, will it come without warning
    Just as I'm picking my nose?
Will it knock on my door in the morning,
    Or tread in the bus on my toes?
Will it come like a change in the weather?
    Will its greeting be courteous or rough?
Will it alter my life altogether?
    O tell me the truth about love.
XII

3 Nerves that steeled themselves for slaughter
Are shot to pieces by the shorter
    Poems of Donne.
Under Which Lyre

4 Thou shalt not do as the dean pleases,
Thou shalt not write thy doctor's thesis
    On education.

5   Thou shalt not sit
With statisticians nor commit
    A social science.

6 Thou shalt not live within thy means
Nor on plain water and raw greens.
    If thou must choose
Between the chances, choose the odd:
Read *The New Yorker*, trust in God;
    And take short views.
See 510:31

7 He stood there above the body,
    He stood there holding the knife;
And the blood ran down the stairs and sang:
    'I'm the Resurrection and the Life'.

They tapped Victor on the shoulder,
    They took him away in a van;
He sat as quiet as a lump of moss
    Saying, 'I am the Son of Man'.

Victor sat in a corner
    Making a woman of clay;
Saying: 'I am Alpha and Omega, I shall come
    To judge the earth one day.'
Victor

8 A shilling life will give you all the facts.
Who's Who

9 Some of the last researchers even write
Love made him weep his pints like you and me.

With all his honours on, he sighed for one
Who, say astonished critics, lived at home;
Did little jobs about the house with skill
And nothing else; could whistle; would sit still
Or potter round the garden; answered some

Of his long marvellous letters but kept none.

10 The sky is darkening like a stain;
Something is going to fall like rain,
    And it won't be flowers.
The Witnesses (1932 poem)

ÉMILE AUGIER 1820–1889

11 Marquis: *Mettez un canard sur un lac au milieu des
cygnes, vous verrez qu'il regrettera sa mare et finira
par y retourner.*
Montrichard: *La nostalgie de la boue!*
Marquis: Put a duck on a lake in the midst of some
swans, and you'll see he'll miss his pond and
eventually return to it.
Montrichard: Longing to be back in the mud!
Le Mariage d'Olympe, I.i

ST. AUGUSTINE 354–430

12 *Nondum amabam, et amare amabam…quaerebam
quid amarem, amans amare.*
I loved not yet, yet I loved to love…I sought what I
might love, in love with loving.
Confessions, bk.iii, ch.1

13 *Et illa erant fercula, in quibus mihi esurienti te
inferebatur sol et luna.*
And these were the dishes wherein to me,
hunger-starven for thee, they served up the sun and
moon.
ch.6

14 *Da mihi castitatem et continentiam, sed noli modo.*
Give me chastity and continency—but not yet!
bk.viii, ch.7

15 *Tolle lege, tolle lege.*
Take up and read, take up and read.
ch.12

16 *Sero te amavi, pulchritudo tam antiqua et tam nova,
sero te amavi! et ecce intus eras et ego foris, et ibi te
quaerebam.*
Too late came I to love thee, O thou Beauty both so
ancient and so fresh, yea too late came I to love thee.
And behold, thou wert within me, and I out of myself,
where I made search for thee.
bk.x, ch.27

17 *Da quod iubes et iube quod vis. Imperas nobis
continentiam.*
Give what you command, and command what you
will. You impose continency upon us.
ch.29

18 *Securus iudicat orbis terrarum.*
The verdict of the world is conclusive.
Contra Epist. Parmen., iii.24

19 *Salus extra ecclesiam non est.*
There is no salvation outside the church.
De Bapt. IV, c.xvii.24. See 170:19

20 *Audi partem alteram.*
Hear the other side.
De Duabus Animabus, XIV.ii

21 *Dilige et quod vis fac.*
Love and do what you will.
(Often quoted as *Ama et fac quod vis*.)
In Epist. Joann. Tractatus, vii, 8

22 *Multi quidem facilius se abstinent ut non utantur, quam*

temperent ut bene utantur.
To many, total abstinence is easier than perfect moderation.
On the Good of Marriage, xxi

1 *Cum dilectione hominum et odio vitiorum.*
With love for mankind and hatred of sins.
Often quoted in the form: Love the sinner but hate the sin. **Opera Omnia,** vol.II. col.962, letter 211. Migne's *Patrologiae* (1845), vol.XXXIII

2 *Roma locuta est; causa finita est.*
Rome has spoken; the case is concluded.
Sermons, bk.i

3 We make ourselves a ladder out of our vices if we trample the vices themselves underfoot.
iii. **De Ascensione**

EMPEROR AUGUSTUS 63 B.C.–A.D. 14

4 Quintilius Varus, give me back my legions.
Suetonius, *Divus Augustus,* 23

5 I inherited it brick and left it marble.
(Of the city of Rome.) 28

6 It will be paid at the Greek Kalends.
(Meaning, Never.) 87

JANE AUSTEN 1775–1817

7 An egg boiled very soft is not unwholesome. [Mr. Woodhouse.]
Emma, ch.3

8 One half of the world cannot understand the pleasures of the other. [Emma.]
ch.9

9 With men he can be rational and unaffected, but when he has ladies to please, every feature works. [Mr. John Knightley of Mr. Elton.]
ch.13

10 A man...must have a very good opinion of himself when he asks people to leave their own fireside, and encounter such a day as this, for the sake of coming to see him. He must think himself a most agreeable fellow. [Mr. John Knightley.]

11 She believed he had been drinking too much of Mr Weston's good wine.
ch.15

12 My mother's deafness is very trifling, you see, just nothing at all. By only raising my voice, and saying anything two or three times over, she is sure to hear. [Miss Bates.]
ch.19

13 The sooner every party breaks up the better. [Mr. Woodhouse.]
ch.25

14 That young man...is very thoughtless. Do not tell his father, but that young man is not quite the thing. He has been opening the doors very often this evening and keeping them open very inconsiderately. He does not think of the draught. I do not mean to set you against him, but indeed he is not quite the thing. [Mr. Woodhouse.]
ch.29

15 Open the windows! But, surely Mr Churchill, nobody would think of opening the windows at Randalls. Nobody could be so imprudent. [Mr. Woodhouse.]

16 They will have their barouche-landau, of course. [Mrs. Elton.]
ch.32

17 Young ladies should take care of themselves. Young ladies are delicate plants. They should take care of their health and their complexion. My dear, did you change your stockings? [Mr. Woodhouse.]
ch.34

18 One has no great hopes from Birmingham. I always say there is something direful in the sound. [Mrs. Elton.]
ch.36

19 N.B. There will be very few Dates in this History.
The History of England (1791)

20 Henry the 4th ascended the throne of England much to his own satisfaction in the year 1399.

21 One of Edward's Mistresses was Jane Shore, who has had a play written about her, but it is a tragedy and therefore not worth reading.

22 Nothing can be said in his vindication, but that his abolishing Religious Houses and leaving them to the ruinous depredations of time has been of infinite use to the landscape of England in general.

23 Lady Jane Grey, who has been already mentioned as reading Greek.

24 It was too pathetic for the feelings of Sophia and myself—we fainted Alternately on a Sofa.
Love and Freindship. Letter the 8th

25 She was nothing more than a mere good-tempered, civil and obliging young woman; as such we could scarcely dislike her—she was only an Object of Contempt.
Letter the 13th

26 There certainly are not so many men of large fortune in the world, as there are pretty women to deserve them.
Mansfield Park, ch.1

27 You must give my compliments to him. Yes—I think it must be compliments. Is there not a something wanted, Miss Price, in our language—a something between compliments and—and love—to suit the sort of friendly acquaintance we have had together? [Mary Crawford.]
ch.11

28 A large income is the best recipe for happiness I ever heard of. It certainly may secure all the myrtle and turkey part of it.
ch.22

29 Let other pens dwell on guilt and misery.
ch.48

30 She was of course only too good for him; but as nobody minds having what is too good for them, he was very steadily earnest in the pursuit of the blessing.

31 'And what are you reading, Miss —?' 'Oh! it is only a novel!' replies the young lady: while she lays down her book with affected indifference, or momentary shame.—'It is only Cecilia, or Camilla, or Belinda:' or, in short, only some work in which the most thorough knowledge of human nature, the happiest delineation of its varieties, the liveliest effusions of wit and humour are conveyed to the world in the best

chosen language.
Northanger Abbey, ch.5

1 But are they all horrid, are you sure they are all horrid? [Catherine.]
ch.6

2 Oh, Lord! not I; I never read much; I have something else to do. [John Thorpe.]
ch.7

3 Oh! who can ever be tired of Bath?
ch.10

4 Real solemn history, I cannot be interested in...The quarrels of popes and kings, with wars or pestilences, in every page; the men all so good for nothing, and hardly any women at all.
ch.14

5 Where people wish to attach, they should always be ignorant. To come with a well-informed mind, is to come with an inability of administering to the vanity of others, which a sensible person would always wish to avoid. A woman especially, if she have the misfortune of knowing any thing, should conceal it as well as she can.

6 From politics, it was an easy step to silence.

7 Sir Walter Elliot, of Kellynch-hall, in Somersetshire, was a man who, for his own amusement, never took up any book but the Baronetage; there he found occupation for an idle hour, and consolation in a distressed one;...this was the page at which the favourite volume always opened: ELLIOT OF KELLYNCH-HALL.
Persuasion, ch.1

8 'My idea of good company, Mr Elliot, is the company of clever, well-informed people, who have a great deal of conversation; that is what I call good company.'
'You are mistaken,' said he gently, 'that is not good company, that is the best.'
ch.16

9 My sore throats are always worse than anyone's. [Mary Musgrove.]
ch.18

10 All the privilege I claim for my own sex...is that of loving longest, when existence or when hope is gone. [Anne.]
ch.23

11 It is a truth universally acknowledged, that a single man in possession of a good fortune, must be in want of a wife.
Pride and Prejudice, ch.1

12 'Kitty has no discretion in her coughs,' said her father: 'she times them ill.'
'I do not cough for my own amusement,' replied Kitty fretfully.
ch.2

13 May I ask whether these pleasing attentions proceed from the impulse of the moment, or are the result of previous study? [Mr. Bennet.]
ch.14

14 You have delighted us long enough. [Mr. Bennet.]
ch.18

15 An unhappy alternative is before you, Elizabeth. From this day you must be a stranger to one of your parents.—Your mother will never see you again if you do *not* marry Mr Collins, and I will never see you

again if you *do*. [Mr. Bennet.]
ch.20

16 Nobody is on my side, nobody takes part with me: I am cruelly used, nobody feels for my poor nerves. [Mrs. Bennet.]
ch.20

17 'It is very hard to think that Charlotte Lucas should ever be mistress of this house, that *I* should be forced to make way for *her*, and live to see her take my place in it.'
'My dear, do not give way to such gloomy thoughts. Let us hope for better things. Let us flatter ourselves that *I* may be the survivor.'
ch.23

18 No arguments shall be wanting on my part, that can alleviate so severe a misfortune: or that may comfort you, under a circumstance that must be of all others most afflicting to a parent's mind. The death of your daughter would have been a blessing in comparison of this. [Mr. Collins.]
ch.48

19 You ought certainly to forgive them as a christian, but never to admit them in your sight, or allow their names to be mentioned in your hearing. [Mr. Collins.]
ch.57

20 For what do we live, but to make sport for our neighbours, and laugh at them in our turn? [Mr. Bennet.]

21 I have been a selfish being all my life, in practice, though not in principle. [Mr. Darcy.]
ch.58

22 If any young men come for Mary or Kitty, send them in, for I am quite at leisure. [Mr. Bennet.]
ch.59

23 Dear, dear Lizzy. A house in town! Every thing that is charming! Three daughters married! Ten thousand a year! Oh, Lord! What will become of me? I shall go distracted. [Mrs. Bennet.]

24 An annuity is a very serious business. [Mrs. Dashwood.]
Sense and Sensibility, ch.2

25 'I am afraid,' replied Elinor, 'that the pleasantness of an employment does not always evince its propriety.'
ch.13

26 Lady Middleton...exerted herself to ask Mr Palmer if there was any news in the paper.
'No, none at all,' he replied, and read on.
ch.19

27 Where so many hours have been spent in convincing myself that I am right, is there not some reason to fear I may be wrong?
ch.31

28 A person and face, of strong, natural, sterling insignificance, though adorned in the first style of fashion.
ch.33

29 We met...Dr Hall in such very deep mourning that either his mother, his wife, or himself must be dead.
Letter to Cassandra Austen, 17 May 1799

30 I am proud to say that I have a very good eye at an Adultress, for tho' repeatedly assured that another in the same party was the *She,* I fixed upon the right one

from the first.
12 May 1801

1 How horrible it is to have so many people
killed!—And what a blessing that one cares for none
of them!
31 May 1811, after the battle of Albuera, 16 May 1811

2 I think I may boast myself to be, with all possible
vanity, the most unlearned and uninformed female who
ever dared to be an authoress.
Letter to James Stanier Clarke. 11 Dec. 1815

3 The little bit (two inches wide) of ivory on which I
work with so fine a brush as produces little effect after
much labour.
Letter, 16 Dec. 1816

SIR ROBERT AYTOUN 1570–1638

4 I loved thee once. I'll love no more,
    Thine be the grief, as is the blame;
Thou art not what thou wast before,
    What reason I should be the same?
To an Inconstant Mistress

W.E. AYTOUN 1813–1865

5 They bore within their breasts the grief
    That fame can never heal—
The deep, unutterable woe
    Which none save exiles feel.
The Island of the Scots, xii

6 Fhairshon swore a feud
    Against the clan M'Tavish;
Marched into their land
    To murder and to rafish;
For he did resolve
    To extirpate the vipers,
With four-and-twenty men
    And five-and-thirty pipers.
The Massacre of the Macpherson, i

7 Fhairshon had a son,
    Who married Noah's daughter,
And nearly spoiled ta Flood,
    By trinking up ta water:

Which he would have done,
    I at least pelieve it,
Had the mixture peen
    Only half Glenlivet.
vii

8 And some that came to scoff at him
    Now turned aside and wept.
The Execution of Montrose, vi

9 'He is coming! he is coming!'
    Like a bridegroom from his room,
Came the hero from his prison
    To the scaffold and the doom.
xiv

10 The grim Geneva ministers
    With anxious scowl drew near,
As you have seen the ravens flock
    Around the dying deer.
xvii

11 Like a brave old Scottish Cavalier,
    All of the olden time!
The Old Scottish Cavalier. See 6:10

12 The earth is all the home I have,
    The heavens my wide roof-tree.
The Wandering Jew, l.49

CHARLES BABBAGE 1792–1871

13 Every moment dies a man,
    Every moment $1\frac{1}{16}$ is born.
See *New Scientist*, 4 Dec. 1958, p.1428. Unpublished letter to
Tennyson, whose *Vision of Sin* this parodies. See 544:8

FRANCIS BACON 1561–1626

14 For all knowledge and wonder (which is the seed of
knowledge) is an impression of pleasure in itself.
Advancement of Learning, I.i.3

15 So let great authors have their due, as time, which is
the author of authors, be not deprived of his due,
which is further and further to discover truth.
iv.12

16 If a man will begin with certainties, he shall end in
doubts; but if he will be content to begin with doubts,
he shall end in certainties.
v.8

17 [Knowledge is] a rich storehouse for the glory of the
Creator and the relief of man's estate.
11

18 Antiquities are history defaced, or some remnants of
history which have casually escaped the shipwreck of
time.
II.ii.1

19 Poesy was ever thought to have some participation of
divineness, because it doth raise and erect the mind, by
submitting the shows of things to the desires of the
mind; whereas reason doth buckle and bow the mind
unto the nature of things.
iv.2

20 The knowledge of man is as the waters, some
descending from above, and some springing from
beneath; the one informed by the light of nature, the
other inspired by divine revelation.
v.1

21 They are ill discoverers that think there is no land,
when they can see nothing but sea.
vii.5

22 Words are the tokens current and accepted for
conceits, as moneys are for values.
xvi.3

23 A dance is a measured pace, as a verse is a measured
speech.
5

24 But men must know, that in this theatre of man's life
it is reserved only for God and angels to be lookers on.
xx.8

25 We are much beholden to Machiavel and others, that
write what men do, and not what they ought to do.
xxi.9

26 Men must pursue things which are just in present, and
leave the future to the divine Providence.
11

27 Did not one of the fathers in great indignation call
poesy *vinum daemonum*?
xxii.13

28 All good moral philosophy is but an handmaid to

religion.
14

1 Man seeketh in society comfort, use, and protection.
xxiii.2

2 A man must make his opportunity, as oft as find it.
3

3 Fortunes...come tumbling into some men's laps.
43

4 It is in life as it is in ways, the shortest way is commonly the foulest, and surely the fairer way is not much about.
45

5 The inseparable propriety of time, which is ever more and more to disclose truth.
xxiv

6 Books must follow sciences, and not sciences books.
Proposition touching Amendment of Laws

7 Wise nature did never put her precious jewels into a garret four stories high: and therefore...exceeding tall men had ever very empty heads.
Apophthegms, 17

8 Hope is a good breakfast, but it is a bad supper.
36

9 Riches are a good handmaid, but the worst mistress.
De Dignitate et Augmentis Scientiarum, I, vi, 3. Antitheta, 6 (ed. 1640, tr. Gilbert Watts)

10 *Antiquitas saeculi juventus mundi.*
Ancient times were the youth of the world.
vii, 81

11 The voice of the people hath some divineness in it, else how should so many men agree to be of one mind?
9

12 No terms of moderation takes place with the vulgar.
30

13 Silence is the virtue of fools.
31

14 The worst solitude is to be destitute of sincere friendship.
37

15 It is sufficiently agreed that all things change, and that nothing really disappears, but that the sum of matter remains exactly the same.
Cogitationes de Natura Rerum, 5; translated from the Latin.

16 I hold every man a debtor to his profession.
The Elements of the Common Law, preface

17 My essays, which of all my other works have been most current; for that, as it seems, they come home, to men's business, and bosoms.
Essays. Dedication of 1625 edition

18 Prosperity is the blessing of the Old Testament, adversity is the blessing of the New.
5. **Of Adversity**

19 The pencil of the Holy Ghost hath laboured more in describing the afflictions of Job than the felicities of Solomon.

20 Prosperity is not without many fears and distastes; and adversity is not without comforts and hopes.

21 Prosperity doth best discover vice, but adversity doth best discover virtue.

22 I had rather believe all the fables in the legend, and the

Talmud, and the Alcoran, than that this universal frame is without a mind.
16. **Atheism**

23 God never wrought miracle to convince atheism, because his ordinary works convince it.

24 A little philosophy inclineth man's mind to atheism, but depth in philosophy bringeth men's minds about to religion.

25 They that deny a God destroy man's nobility; for certainly man is of kin to the beasts by his body; and, if he be not of kin to God by his spirit, he is a base and ignoble creature.

26 Virtue is like a rich stone, best plain set.
43. **Of Beauty**

27 That is the best part of beauty, which a picture cannot express.

28 There is no excellent beauty that hath not some strangeness in the proportion.

29 There is in human nature generally more of the fool than of the wise.
12. **Boldness**

30 He said it that knew it best. (Demosthenes)

31 In civil business; what first? boldness; what second and third? boldness: and yet boldness is a child of ignorance and baseness.

32 Boldness is an ill keeper of promise.

33 Mahomet made the people believe that he would call a hill to him, and from the top of it offer up his prayers for the observers of his law. The people assembled: Mahomet called the hill to come to him again and again; and when the hill stood still, he was never a whit abashed, but said, 'If the hill will not come to Mahomet, Mahomet will go to the hill.' (Proverbially, 'If the mountain will not...')

34 Houses are built to live in and not to look on; therefore let use be preferred before uniformity, except where both may be had.
45. **Of Building**

35 Light gains make heavy purses.
52. **Of Ceremonies and Respects**

36 Small matters win great commendation.

37 He that is too much in anything, so that he giveth another occasion of satiety, maketh himself cheap.

38 A wise man will make more opportunities than he finds.

39 Books will speak plain when counsellors blanch.
20. **Of Counsel**

40 There be that can pack the cards and yet cannot play well; so there are some that are good in canvasses and factions, that are otherwise weak men.
22. **Of Cunning**

41 In things that are tender and unpleasing, it is good to break the ice by some whose words are of less weight, and to reserve the more weighty voice to come in as by chance.

42 I knew one that when he wrote a letter he would put that which was most material in the postscript, as if it had been a bymatter.

43 Nothing doth more hurt in a state than that cunning

men pass for wise.

1 Men fear death as children fear to go in the dark; and as that natural fear in children is increased with tales, so is the other.
2. **Of Death**

2 There is no passion in the mind of man so weak, but it mates and masters the fear of death. And therefore death is no such terrible enemy, when a man hath so many attendants about him that can win the combat of him. Revenge triumphs over death; love slights it; honour aspireth to it; grief flieth to it.

3 It is as natural to die as to be born; and to a little infant, perhaps, the one is as painful as the other.

4 Above all, believe it, the sweetest canticle is *Nunc dimittis*, when a man hath obtained worthy ends and expectations. Death hath this also, that it openeth the gate to good fame, and extinguisheth envy.

5 If you dissemble sometimes your knowledge of that you are thought to know, you shall be thought, another time, to know that you know not.
32. **Of Discourse**

6 I knew a wise man that had it for a by-word, when he saw men hasten to a conclusion. 'Stay a little, that we may make an end the sooner.'
25. **Of Dispatch**

7 To choose time is to save time.

8 It is a miserable state of mind to have few things to desire and many things to fear.
19. **Of Empire**

9 Riches are for spending.
28. **Of Expense**

10 A man ought warily to begin charges which once begun will continue.

11 There is little friendship in the world, and least of all between equals.
48. **Of Followers and Friends**

12 Chiefly the mould of a man's fortune is in his own hands.
40. **Of Fortune**

13 If a man look sharply, and attentively, he shall see Fortune: for though she be blind, yet she is not invisible.

14 It had been hard for him that spake it to have put more truth and untruth together, in a few words, than in that speech: 'Whosoever is delighted in solitude is either a wild beast, or a god.'
27. **Of Friendship**. See Aristotle, *Politics*, i, 14, 1253a

15 A crowd is not company, and faces are but a gallery of pictures, and talk but a tinkling cymbal, where there is no love.

16 It [friendship] redoubleth joys, and cutteth griefs in halves.

17 As if you would call a physician, that is thought good for the cure of the disease you complain of but is unacquainted with your body, and therefore may put you in the way for a present cure but overthroweth your health in some other kind; and so cure the disease and kill the patient.

18 God Almighty first planted a garden; and, indeed, it is the purest of human pleasures.
46. **Of Gardens**

19 The inclination to goodness is imprinted deeply in the nature of man: insomuch, that if it issue not towards men, it will take unto other living creatures.
13. **Goodness, and Goodness of Nature**

20 If a man be gracious and courteous to strangers, it shows he is a citizen of the world.

21 Men in great place are thrice servants: servants of the sovereign or state, servants of fame, and servants of business.
11. **Of Great Place**

22 It is a strange desire to seek power and to lose liberty.

23 The rising unto place is laborious, and by pains men come to greater pains; and it is sometimes base, and by indignities men come to dignities. The standing is slippery, and the regress is either a downfall, or at least an eclipse.

24 Set it down to thyself, as well to create good precedents as to follow them.

25 Severity breedeth fear, but roughness breedeth hate. Even reproofs from authority ought to be grave, and not taunting.

26 All rising to great place is by a winding stair.

27 As the births of living creatures at first are ill-shapen, so are all innovations, which are the births of time.
24. **Of Innovations**

28 He that will not apply new remedies must expect new evils; for time is the greatest innovator.

29 The speaking in a perpetual hyperbole is comely in nothing but in love.
10. **Of Love**

30 It has been well said that 'the arch-flatterer with whom all the petty flatterers have intelligence is a man's self.'

31 He that hath wife and children hath given hostages to fortune; for they are impediments to great enterprises, either of virtue or mischief.
8. **Of Marriage and Single Life.** See 319:25

32 There are some other that account wife and children but as bills of charges.

33 A single life doth well with churchmen, for charity will hardly water the ground where it must first fill a pool.

34 Wives are young men's mistresses, companions for middle age, and old men's nurses.

35 He was reputed one of the wise men that made answer to the question when a man should marry? 'A young man not yet, an elder man not at all.'

36 Nature is often hidden, sometimes overcome, seldom extinguished.
38. **Of Nature in Men**

37 It is generally better to deal by speech than by letter.
47. **Of Negotiating**

38 It is a reverend thing to see an ancient castle or building not in decay.
14. **Of Nobility**

39 New nobility is but the act of power, but ancient nobility is the act of time.

1 Nobility of birth commonly abateth industry.

2 The joys of parents are secret, and so are their griefs and fears.
   7. **Of Parents and Children**

3 Children sweeten labours, but they make misfortunes more bitter.

4 The noblest works and foundations have proceeded from childless men, which have sought to express the images of their minds where those of their bodies have failed.

5 Fame is like a river, that beareth up things light and swollen, and drowns things weighty and solid.
   53. **Of Praise**

6 Age will not be defied.
   30. **Of Regimen of Health**

7 Revenge is a kind of wild justice, which the more man's nature runs to, the more ought law to weed it out.
   4. **Of Revenge**

8 Why should I be angry with a man for loving himself better than me?

9 A man that studieth revenge keeps his own wounds green.

10 The four pillars of government...(which are religion, justice, counsel, and treasure).
   15. **Of Seditions and Troubles**

11 The surest way to prevent seditions (if the times do bear it) is to take away the matter of them.

12 Money is like muck, not good except it be spread.

13 The remedy is worse than the disease.

14 The French are wiser than they seem, and the Spaniards seem wiser than they are.
   26. **Of Seeming Wise**

15 Studies serve for delight, for ornament, and for ability.
   50. **Of Studies**

16 To spend too much time in studies is sloth.

17 They perfect nature and are perfected by experience.

18 Read not to contradict and confute, nor to believe and take for granted, nor to find talk and discourse, but to weigh and consider.

19 Some books are to be tasted, others to be swallowed, and some few to be chewed and digested; that is, some books are to be read only in parts; others to be read but not curiously; and some few to be read wholly, and with diligence and attention. Some books also may be read by deputy, and extracts made of them by others.

20 Reading maketh a full man; conference a ready man; and writing an exact man.

21 Histories make men wise; poets, witty; the mathematics, subtile; natural philosophy, deep; moral, grave; logic and rhetoric, able to contend.

22 There is a superstition in avoiding superstition.
   17. **Of Superstition**

23 Suspicions amongst thoughts are like bats amongst birds, they ever fly by twilight.
   31. **Of Suspicion**

24 There is nothing makes a man suspect much, more than to know little.

25 Neither is money the sinews of war (as it is trivially said).
   29. **Of the True Greatness of Kingdoms.** See 151:30

26 Neither will it be, that a people overlaid with taxes should ever become valiant and martial.

27 Travel, in the younger sort, is a part of education; in the elder, a part of experience. He that travelleth into a country before he hath some entrance into the language, goeth to school, and not to travel.
   18. **Of Travel**

28 What is truth? said jesting Pilate; and would not stay for an answer.
   1. **Of Truth.** See 72:44

29 A mixture of a lie doth ever add pleasure.

30 It is not the lie that passeth through the mind, but the lie that sinketh in, and settleth in it, that doth the hurt.

31 The inquiry of truth, which is the love-making, or wooing of it, the knowledge of truth, which is the presence of it, and the belief of truth, which is the enjoying of it, is the sovereign good of human nature.

32 All colours will agree in the dark.
   3. **Of Unity in Religion**

33 It was prettily devised of Aesop, 'The fly sat upon the axletree of the chariot-wheel and said, what a dust do I raise.'
   54. **Of Vain-Glory**

34 In the youth of a state arms do flourish; in the middle age of a state, learning; and then both of them together for a time; in the declining age of a state, mechanical arts and merchandise.
   58. **Of Vicissitude of Things**

35 Be so true to thyself as thou be not false to others.
   23. **Of Wisdom for a Man's Self**

36 It is a poor centre of a man's actions, himself.

37 It is the nature of extreme self-lovers, as they will set a house on fire, and it were but to roast their eggs.

38 It is the wisdom of the crocodiles, that shed tears when they would devour.

39 Young men are fitter to invent than to judge, fitter for execution than for counsel, and fitter for new projects than for settled business.
   42. **Of Youth and Age**

40 I have often thought upon death, and I find it the least of all evils.
   An Essay on Death, 1

41 I do not believe that any man fears to be dead, but only the stroke of death.
   3

42 Why should a man be in love with his fetters, though of gold?
   4

43 He is the fountain of honour.
   Essay of a King

44 For they thought generally that he was a Prince as ordained, and sent down from heaven to unite and put to an end the long dissensions of the two houses; which although they had had, in the times of Henry the Fourth, Henry the Fifth, and a part of Henry the Sixth on the one side, and the times of Edward the Fourth on the other, lucid intervals and happy pauses; yet they did ever hang over the kingdom, ready to break forth

in new perturbations and calamities.
History of King Henry VII, par.3

1 I have taken all knowledge to be my province.
Letter to Lord Burleigh, 1592

2 Opportunity makes a thief.
Letter to the Earl of Essex, 1598

3 I am too old, and the seas are too long, for me to double the Cape of Good Hope.
Memorial of Access

4 I would live to study, and not study to live.

5 God's first Creature, which was Light.
New Atlantis (1627)

6 The end of our foundation is the knowledge of causes, and secret motions of things; and the enlarging of the bounds of human Empire, to the effecting of all things possible.

7 *Quod enim mavult homo verum esse, id potius credit.*
For what a man would like to be true, that he more readily believes.
Novum Oganum, bk.I, Aphor.49. See 126:27

8 *Magna ista scientiarum mater.*
That great mother of sciences.
80. [Of natural philosophy]

9 *Vim et virtutem et consequentias rerum inventarum notare juvat; quae non in aliis manifestius occurrunt, quae in illis tribus quae antiquis incognitae, et quarum primordia, licet recentia, obscura et ingloria sunt: Artis nimirum Imprimendi, Pulveris Tormentarii, et Acus Nauticae.*
It is well to observe the force and virtue and consequence of discoveries, and these are to be seen nowhere more conspicuously than in those three which were unknown to the ancients, and of which the origin, though recent, is obscure and inglorious; namely, printing, gunpowder and the magnet [i.e. Mariner's Needle]. For these three have changed the whole face and state of things throughout the world.
129, tr. Spedding. See 131:3

10 *Naturae enim non imperatur, nisi parendo.*
Nature cannot be ordered about, except by obeying her.

11 *Nam et ipsa scientia potestas est.*
Knowledge itself is power.
Religious Meditations. Of Heresies

12 Universities incline wits to sophistry and affectation.
Valerius Terminus of the Interpretation of Nature, ch.26

13 I have rather studied books than men.
Works, ed. 1765, II, 258

14 For my name and memory, I leave it to men's charitable speeches, and to foreign nations, and the next ages.
III, 677. Last Will (19 Dec. 1625)

15 The world's a bubble; and the life of man
    Less than a span.
The World

16 Who then to frail mortality shall trust,
But limns the water, or but writes in dust.

17 What is it then to have or have no wife,
But single thraldom, or a double strife?

18 What then remains, but that we still should cry,
Not to be born, or being born, to die?

KARL BAEDEKER 1801–1859

19 Oxford is on the whole more attractive than Cambridge to the ordinary visitor; and the traveller is therefore recommended to visit Cambridge first, or to omit it altogether if he cannot visit both.
Baedeker's Great Britain (1887), 30. **From London to Oxford**

WALTER BAGEHOT 1826–1877

20 There is a glare in some men's eyes which seems to say, 'Beware, I am dangerous; *Noli me tangere.*' Lord Brougham's face has this. A mischievous excitability is the most obvious expression of it. If he were a horse, nobody would buy him; with that eye no one could answer for his temper.
Biographical Studies. Essay II, **Lord Brougham**

21 The mystic reverence, the religious allegiance, which are essential to a true monarchy, are imaginative sentiments that no legislature can manufacture in any people.
The English Constitution (1867), 1. **The Cabinet**

22 The Crown is according to the saying, the 'fountain of honour'; but the Treasury is the spring of business.
See 27:43

23 It has been said that England invented the phrase, 'Her Majesty's Opposition'; that it was the first government which made a criticism of administration as much a part of the polity as administration itself. This critical opposition is the consequence of cabinet government.

24 The *Times* has made many ministries.

25 The great qualities, the imperious will, the rapid energy, the eager nature fit for a great crisis are not required—are impediments—in common times. A Lord Liverpool is better in everyday politics than a Chatham—a Louis Philippe far better than a Napoleon.

26 We turned out the Quaker (Lord Aberdeen), and put in the pugilist (Lord Palmerston). (Change of Ministry, 1855).

27 The best reason why Monarchy is a strong government is, that it is an intelligible government. The mass of mankind understand it, and they hardly anywhere in the world understand any other.
2. **The Monarchy**

28 The characteristic of the English Monarchy is that it retains the feelings by which the heroic kings governed their rude age, and has added the feeling by which the constitutions of later Greece ruled in more refined ages.

29 Women—one half the human race at least—care fifty times more for a marriage than a ministry.

30 Royalty is a government in which the attention of the nation is concentrated on one person doing interesting actions. A Republic is a government in which that attention is divided between many, who are all doing uninteresting actions. Accordingly, so long as the human heart is strong and the human reason weak, Royalty will be strong because it appeals to diffused feeling, and Republics weak because they appeal to the understanding.

31 An Englishman whose heart is in a matter is not easily baffled.

1 Throughout the greater part of his life George III was a kind of 'consecrated obstruction'.

2 But of all nations in the world the English are perhaps the least a nation of pure philosophers.

3 The Sovereign has, under a constitutional monarchy such as ours, three rights—the right to be consulted, the right to encourage, the right to warn.
3. **The Monarchy** (continued)

4 The order of nobility is of great use, too, not only in what it creates, but in what it prevents. It prevents the rule of wealth—the religion of gold. This is the obvious and natural idol of the Anglo-Saxon.
4. **The House of Lords**

5 The House of Peers has never been a House where the most important peers were most important.

6 A severe though not unfriendly critic of our institutions said that 'the cure for admiring the House of Lords was to go and look at it.'

7 Nations touch at their summits.

8 Years ago Mr Disraeli called Sir Robert Peel's Ministry—the last Conservative Ministry that had real power—'an organized hypocrisy', so much did the ideas of its 'head' differ from the sensations of its 'tail'.
See 184:16

9 It has been said, not truly, but with a possible approximation to truth, 'that in 1802 every hereditary monarch was insane.'

10 Queen Anne was one of the smallest people ever set in a great place.
7. **Checks and Balances**

11 The soldier—that is, the great soldier—of to-day is not a romantic animal, dashing at forlorn hopes, animated by frantic sentiment, full of fancies as to a love-lady or a sovereign; but a quiet, grave man, busied in charts, exact in sums, master of the art of tactics, occupied in trivial detail; thinking, as the Duke of Wellington was said to do, *most* of the shoes of his soldiers; despising all manner of *éclat* and eloquence; perhaps, like Count Moltke, 'silent in seven languages'.

12 No real English gentleman, in his secret soul, was ever sorry for the death of a political economist.
Estimates of some Englishmen and Scotchmen (1858), **The First Edinburgh Reviewers**

13 Writers, like teeth, are divided into incisors and grinders.

14 To a great experience one thing is essential, an experiencing nature.
Shakespeare—The Individual

15 A constitutional statesman is in general a man of common opinion and uncommon abilities.
Historical Essays. **The Character of Sir Robert Peel**

16 No man [Sir R. Peel] has come so near our definition of a constitutional statesman—the powers of a first-rate man and the creed of a second-rate man.

17 He believes, with all his heart and soul and strength, that there *is* such a thing as truth; he has the soul of a martyr with the intellect of an advocate.
Mr. Gladstone

18 The most melancholy of human reflections, perhaps, is that, on the whole, it is a question whether the benevolence of mankind does most good or harm.
Physics and Politics, No.v

19 One of the greatest pains to human nature is the pain of a new idea.

20 Wordsworth, Tennyson and Browning; or, Pure, Ornate, and Grotesque Art in English Poetry.
Essay, *National Review,* Nov. 1864

PHILIP JAMES BAILEY 1816–1902

21 We should count time by heart-throbs.
Festus (1839), v

22 America, thou half-brother of the world;
With something good and bad of every land.
x

BRUCE BAIRNSFATHER 1888–1959

23 Well, if you knows of a better 'ole, go to it.
Fragments from France, No.1 (1915)

MICHAEL BAKUNIN 1814–1876

24 *Die Lust der Zerstörung ist zugleich eine schaffende Lust!*
The urge for destruction is also a creative urge!
'Die Reaktion in Deutschland' in *Jahrbuch für Wissenschaft und Kunst* (1842), under the pseudonym 'Jules Elysard'

25 We wish, in a word, equality—equality in fact as corollary, or rather, as primordial condition of liberty. From each according to his faculties, to each according to his needs; that is what we wish sincerely and energetically.
Declaration signed by forty-seven anarchists on trial after the failure of their uprising at Lyons in 1870. See J. Morrison Davidson, *The Old Order and the New*, 1890. See 333:5

STANLEY BALDWIN 1867–1947

26 A lot of hard-faced men who look as if they had done very well out of the war.
Of the House of Commons returned after the election of 1918. J.M. Keynes, *Economic Consequences of the Peace*, ch.5; and see Middlemass and Barnes, *Baldwin* p.72n.

27 I think it is well also for the man in the street to realise that there is no power on earth that can protect him from being bombed. Whatever people may tell him, the bomber will always get through, and it is very easy to understand that, if you realise the area of space.
House of Commons, 10 Nov. 1932. A reference to the effectiveness of air power in modern warfare.

28 When you think about the defence of England you no longer think of the chalk cliffs of Dover. You think of the Rhine. That is where our frontier lies to-day.
30 July 1934

29 I shall be but a short time to-night. I have seldom spoken with greater regret, for my lips are not yet unsealed. Were these troubles over I would make a case, and I guarantee that not a man would go into the Lobby against us.
10 Dec. 1935, speech on the Abyssinian crisis. Usually quoted as 'My lips are sealed.'

A.J. BALFOUR 1848–1930

1 Do not hesitate to shoot.

Attr. to Balfour, actually part of a telegram sent by the Divisional Magistrate for Cork district in 1888: 'Deal very summarily with any organized resistance to lawful authority. If necessary do not hesitate to shoot. Plunkett.'

2 I thought he was a young man of promise; but it appears he was a young man of promises. (Said of Winston Churchill in 1899.)

R.S. Churchill, *Winston Churchill* (1966), I, 449

3 The energies of our system will decay, the glory of the sun will be dimmed, and the earth, tideless and inert, will no longer tolerate the race which has for a moment disturbed its solitude. Man will go down into the pit, and all his thoughts will perish.

The Foundations of Belief, I, 1

4 It is unfortunate, considering that enthusiasm moves the world, that so few enthusiasts can be trusted to speak the truth.

Letter to Mrs. Drew, 1918

5 Frank Harris...said...: 'The fact is, Mr Balfour, all the faults of the age come from Christianity and journalism.' 'Christianity, of course but why journalism?'

Margot Asquith, *Autobiography,* I, 10

6 This is a singularly ill-contrived world, but not so ill-contrived as all that.

W.S. Churchill, *Into Battle* (1941), p. 123

BALLADS

7 There was a youth, and a well-beloved youth,
  And he was an esquire's son,
He loved the bailiff's daughter dear,
  That lived in Islington.

The Bailiff's Daughter of Islington

8 But when his friends did understand
  His fond and foolish mind,
They sent him up to fair London,
  An apprentice for to bind.

9 She stept to him, as red as any rose,
  And took him by the bridle-ring:
'I pray you, kind sir, give me one penny,
  To ease my weary limb.'

'I prithee, sweetheart, canst thou tell me,
  Where thou wast born?'
'At Islington, kind sir,' said she,
  'Where I have had many a scorn.'

'I prithee, sweetheart, canst thou tell me
  Whether thou dost know
The bailiff's daughter of Islington?'
  'She's dead, sir, long ago.'

'Then will I sell my goodly steed,
  My saddle and my bow;
I will into some far countrey,
  Where no man doth me know.'

'O stay, O stay, thou goodly youth!
  She's alive, she is not dead;
Here she standeth by thy side,
  And is ready to be thy bride.'

10 In Scarlet town, where I was born,
There was a fair maid dwellin',
Made every youth cry *Well-a-way!*

Her name was Barbara Allen.

All in the merry month of May,
When green buds they were swellin',
Young Jemmy Grove on his death-bed lay,
For love of Barbara Allen.

Barbara Allen's Cruelty

11 So slowly, slowly rase she up,
And slowly she came nigh him,
And when she drew the curtain by—
'Young man, I think you're dyin'!'.

12 'O mother, mother, make my bed,
O make it saft and narrow:
My love has died for me to-day,
I'll die for him to-morrow.'

13 'Farewell,' she said, 'ye virgins all,
And shun the fault I fell in:
Henceforth take warning by the fall
Of cruel Barbara Allen.'

14 There were twa sisters sat in a bour;
  Binnorie, O Binnorie!
There came a knight to be their wooer,
  By the bonnie milldams o' Binnorie.
Binnorie

15 Ye Highlands and ye Lawlands,
  O where hae ye been?
They hae slain the Earl of Murray,
  And hae laid him on the green.
The Bonny Earl of Murray

16 He was a braw gallant,
  And he rid at the ring;
And the bonny Earl of Murray,
  O he might hae been a king!

17 He was a braw gallant,
  And he play'd at the gluve;
And the bonny Earl of Murray,
  O he was the Queen's luve!

O lang will his Lady
  Look owre the Castle Downe,
Ere she see the Earl of Murray
  Come sounding through the town!

18 She hadna sail'd a league, a league,
  A league but barely three,
Till grim, grim grew his countenance
  And gurly grew the sea.

'What hills are yon, yon pleasant hills,
  The sun shines sweetly on?'—
'O yon are the hills o' Heaven,' he said,
  'Where you will never won.'
The Daemon Lover

19 He strack the top-mast wi' his hand,
  The fore-mast wi' his knee;
And he brake that gallant ship in twain,
  And sank her in the sea.

20 O well's me o' my gay goss-hawk,
  That he can speak and flee!
He'll carry a letter to my love,
  Bring another back to me.
The Gay Gosshawk

21 But ne'er a word wad ane o' them speak,
  For barring of the door.
Get Up and Bar the Door

1 Goodman, you've spoken the foremost word!
  Get up and bar the door.

2 A ship I have got in the North Country
  And she goes by the name of the *Golden Vanity*,
  O I fear she will be taken by a Spanish Ga-la-lee,
  As she sails by the Low-lands low.
  The Golden Vanity

3 He bored with his augur, he bored once and twice,
  And some were playing cards, and some were playing
      dice,
  When the water flowed in it dazzled their eyes,
  And she sank by the Low-lands low.

  So the Cabin-boy did swim all to the larboard side,
  Saying 'Captain! take me in, I am drifting with the
      tide!'
  'I will shoot you! I will kill you!' the cruel Captain
      cried,
  'You may sink by the Low-lands low.'

4 I wish I were where Helen lies,
  Night and day on me she cries;
  O that I were where Helen lies,
      On fair Kirkconnell lea!

  Curst be the heart that thought the thought,
  And curst the hand that fired the shot,
  When in my arms burd Helen dropt,
      And died to succour me!
  Helen of Kirkconnell

5 'What gat ye to your dinner, Lord Randal, my Son?
      What gat ye to your dinner, my handsome young
          man?'
  'I gat eels boil'd in broo'; mother, make my bed soon,
      For I'm weary wi' hunting, and fain wald lie down.'
  Lord Randal

6 This ae nighte, this ae nighte,
      —*Every nighte and alle,*
  Fire and fleet and candle-lighte,
      And Christe receive thy saule.
  Lyke-Wake Dirge

      fleet;floor. Other readings are 'sleet' and 'salt'

7 From Brig o' Dread when thou may'st pass,
      —*Every nighte and alle,*
  To Purgatory fire thou com'st at last;
      And Christe receive thy saule.

  If ever thou gavest meat or drink,
      —*Every nighte and alle,*
  The fire sall never make thee shrink
      And Christe receive thy saule.

  wap;wrap.

8 When captains couragious whom death could not
      daunte,
  Did march to the seige of the city of Gaunt,
  They mustered their soldiers by two and by three,
  And the foremost in battle was Mary Ambree.
  Mary Ambree

9 For in my mind, of all mankind
      I love but you alone.
  The Nut Brown Maid

10 For I must to the greenwood go
       Alone, a banished man.

11 Marie Hamilton's to the kirk gane
       Wi' ribbons on her breast;
   The King thought mair o' Marie Hamilton

Than he listen'd to the priest.
The Queen's Maries

12 Yestreen the Queen had four Maries,
       The night she'll hae but three;
   There was Marie Seaton, and Marie Beaton,
       And Marie Carmichael, and me.

13 There are twelve months in all the year,
       As I hear many men say,
   But the merriest month in all the year
       Is the merry month of May.
   Robin Hood and the Widow's Three Sons

14 'Let me have length and breadth enough,
       And under my head a sod;
   That they may say when I am dead,
       —*Here lies bold Robin Hood!*'
   The Death of Robin Hood

15 Fight on, my men, sayes Sir Andrew Bartton,
   I am hurt but I am not slain;
   Ile lay mee downe and bleed a while
   And then Ile rise and fight againe.
   Sir Andrew Bartton

16 The king sits in Dunfermline town
       Drinking the blude-red wine.
   Sir Patrick Spens

17 Our king has written a braid letter,
       And seal'd it with his hand,
   And sent it to Sir Patrick Spens,
       Was walking on the strand.

   'To Noroway, to Noroway,
       To Noroway o'er the faem;
   The king's daughter o' Noroway,
       'Tis thou must bring her hame.'

   The first word that Sir Patrick read
       So loud, loud laughed he;
   The neist word that Sir Patrick read
       The tear blinded his e'e.

18 'I saw the new moon late yestreen
       Wi' the auld moon in her arm;
   And if we gang to sea master,
       I fear we'll come to harm.'

   Go fetch a web o' the silken claith,
       Another o' the twine,
   And wap them into our ship's side,
       And let nae the sea come in.

19 O laith, laith were our gude Scots lords
       To wat their cork-heel'd shoon;
   But lang or a' the play was play'd
       They wat their hats aboon.

20 O lang, lang may the ladies sit,
       Wi' their fans into their hand,
   Before they see Sir Patrick Spens
       Come sailing to the strand!

   And lang, lang may the maidens sit
       Wi' their gowd kames in their hair,
   A-waiting for their ain dear loves!
       For them they'll see nae mair.

   Half-owre, half-owre to Aberdour,
       'Tis fifty fathoms deep;
   And there lies good Sir Patrick Spens,
       Wi' the Scots lords at his feet!

1 And she has kilted her green kirtle
   A little abune her knee;
And she has braided her yellow hair
   A little abune her bree.
Tam Lin, v

2 About the dead hour of the night
   She heard the bridles ring;
And Janet was as glad at that
   As any earthly thing.
   xli

3 'But what I ken this night, Tam Lin,
   Gin I had kent yestreen,
I wad ta'en out thy heart o' flesh,
   And put in a heart o' stane.'
   l

4 She's mounted on her milk-white steed,
   She's ta'en true Thomas up behind.
Thomas the Rhymer, viii

5 'And see ye not yon braid, braid road,
   That lies across the lily leven?
That is the Path of Wickedness,
   Though some call it the Road to Heaven.'
   xii

6 It was mirk, mirk night, there was nae starlight,
   They waded thro' red blude to the knee;
For a' the blude that's shed on the earth
   Rins through the springs o' that countrie.
   xvi

7 There were three ravens sat on a tree,
They were as black as they might be.
The one of them said to his make,
'Where shall we our breakfast take?'
The Three Ravens

8 As I was walking all alane,
I heard twa corbies making a mane:
The tane unto the tither did say,
'Where sall we gang and dine the day?'

'—In behint yon auld fail dyke
I wot there lies a new-slain knight;
And naebody kens that he lies there
But his hawk, his hound, and his lady fair.

'His hound is to the hunting gane,
His hawk to fetch the wild-fowl hame,
His lady's ta'en anither mate,
So we may make our dinner sweet.

'Ye'll sit on his white hause-bane,
And I'll pike out his bonny blue e'en:
Wi' ae lock o' his gowden hair
We'll theek our nest when it grows bare.'
The Twa Corbies

corbies; ravens. fail; turf. hause; neck. theek; thatch.

9 'The wind doth blow to-day, my love,
   And a few small drops of rain;
I never had but one true love;
   In cold grave she was lain.

'I'll do as much for my true-love
   As any young man may;
I'll sit and mourn all at her grave
   For a twelvemonth and a day.'
The Unquiet Grave

10 O waly, waly, up the bank,
   And waly, waly, doun the brae,
And waly, waly, yon burn-side,
   Where I and my Love wont to gae!

I lean'd my back unto an aik,
   I thocht it was a trustie tree;
But first it bow'd and syne it brake—
   Sae my true love did lichtlie me.

O waly, waly, gin love be bonnie
   A little time while it is new!
But when 'tis auld it waxeth cauld,
   And fades awa' like morning dew.

O wherefore should I busk my heid,
   Or wherefore should I kame my hair?
For my true Love has me forsook,
   And says he'll never lo'e me mair.
Waly, Waly

11 But had I wist, before I kist,
   That love had been sae ill to win,
I had lock'd my heart in a case o' gowd,
   And pinn'd it wi' a siller pin.

And O! if my young babe were born,
   And set upon the nurse's knee;
And I mysel' were dead and gane,
   And the green grass growing over me!

12 'Tom Pearse, Tom Pearse, lend me your grey mare,
All along, down along, out along, lee.
For I want for to go to Widdicombe Fair,
Wi' Bill Brewer, Jan Stewer, Peter Gurney, Peter
   Davey, Dan'l Whiddon, Harry Hawk,
   Old Uncle Tom Cobbleigh and all.
   Old Uncle Tom Cobbleigh and all.'
Widdicombe Fair

GEORGE BANCROFT 1800–1891

13 It [Calvinism in Switzerland] established a religion
without a prelate, a government without a king.
History of the United States (1834–40), vol.iii, ch.6

RICHARD BANCROFT 1544–1610

14 Where Christ erecteth his Church, the devil in the
same churchyard will have his chapel.
Sermon at Paul's Cross, 9 Feb. 1588

EDWARD BANGS fl. 1775

15 Yankee Doodle keep it up,
   Yankee Doodle dandy;
Mind the music and the step,
   And with the girls be handy.
Yankee Doodle; or Father's Return to Camp. See Nicholas
Smith, *Stories of Great National Songs*

16 Yankee Doodle came to town
   Riding on a pony;
Stuck a feather in his cap
   And called it Macaroni.

THÉODORE FAULLAIN DE BANVILLE
1823–1891

1 *Jeune homme sans mélancolie,*
Blond comme un soleil d'Italie,
Garde bien ta belle folie.
Young man untroubled by melancholy, fair as an
    Italian sun, take good care of your fine carelessness.
A Adolphe Gaïffe

2 Licences poétiques. *Il n'y en a pas.*
Poetic licence. There's no such thing.
Petit traité de poésie française (1872)

JOHN BARBOUR 1316?–1395

3 Storys to rede ar delitabill,
Suppos that thai be nocht bot fabill.
The Bruce (1375), I, l.1

4 A! fredome is a noble thing!
Fredome mayse man to haiff liking.
l.225

REVD. R.H. BARHAM 1788–1845

5 Like a blue-bottle fly on a rather large scale,
With a rather large corking-pin stuck through his tail.
The Ingoldsby Legends. The Auto-da-Fé

6 She help'd him to lean, and she help'd him to fat,
And it look'd like hare—but it might have been cat.
The Bagman's Dog

7 Though I've always considered Sir Christopher Wren,
As an architect, one of the greatest of men;
And, talking of Epitaphs,—much I admire his,
'Circumspice, si Monumentum requiris';
Which an erudite Verger translated to me,
'If you ask for his Monument, Sir-come-spy-see!'
The Cynotaph. See 11:2

8 What Horace says is,
Eheu fugaces
Anni labuntur, Postume, Postume!
Years glide away, and are lost to me, lost to me!
Epigram: Eheu fugaces. See 260:10

9 What *was* to be done?—'twas perfectly plain
That they could not well hang the man over again;
What *was* to be done?—The man was dead!
Nought *could* be done—nought could be said;
So—my Lord Tomnoddy went home to bed!
Hon. Mr. Sucklethumbkin's Story

10 A servant's too often a negligent elf;
—If it's business of consequence, do it yourself!
The Ingoldsby Penance. Moral

11 The Jackdaw sat on the Cardinal's chair!
Bishop, and abbot, and prior were there;
    Many a monk, and many a friar,
    Many a knight, and many a squire,
With a great many more of lesser degree,—
In sooth a goodly company;
And they served the Lord Primate on bended knee.
        Never, I ween,
        Was a prouder seen,
Read of in books, or dreamt of in dreams,
Than the Cardinal Lord Archbishop of Rheims!
The Jackdaw of Rheims

12 And six little Singing-boys,—dear little souls!
In nice clean faces, and nice white stoles.

13 He cursed him in sleeping, that every night
He should dream of the devil, and wake in a fright.

14 Never was heard such a terrible curse!
    But what gave rise to no little surprise,
Nobody seem'd one penny the worse!

15 Heedless of grammar, they all cried, 'That's him!'

16 Here's a corpse in the case with a sad swell'd face,
And a Medical Crowner's a queer sort of thing!
A Lay of St. Gengulphus

17   A German,
Who smoked like a chimney.
Lay of St. Odille

18 So put that in your pipe, my Lord Otto, and smoke it!

19 'Twas in Margate last July, I walk'd upon the pier,
I saw a little vulgar Boy—I said, 'What make you
        here?'
Misadventures at Margate

20 And now I'm here, from this here pier it is my fixed
        intent
To jump, as Mr Levi did from off the Monu-ment!

21 I could not see my little friend—because he was not
        there!

22 But when the Crier cried, 'O Yes!' the people cried, 'O
        No!'

23 It's very odd that Sailor-men should talk so very
        queer—
And then he hitch'd his trousers up, as is, I'm told,
        their use,
It's very odd that Sailor-men should wear those things
        so loose.

24 He smiled and said, 'Sir, does your mother know that
        you are out?'

25 They were a little less than 'kin', and rather more than
        'kind'.
Nell Cook. See 429:21

26 She drank Prussic acid without any water,
And died like a Duke-and-a-Duchess's daughter!
The Tragedy

BARNABE BARNES 1569?–1609

27 Ah, sweet Content! where doth thine harbour hold?
Parthenophil and Parthenophe (1593), Sonnet lxvi

WILLIAM BARNES 1801–1886

28 An' there vor me the apple tree
Do leän down low in Linden Lea.
My Orcha'd in Linden Lea

29 But still the neäme do bide the seäme—
'Tis Pentridge—Pentridge by the river.
Pentridge by the River

30 My love is the maïd ov all maïdens,
Though all mid be comely.
In the Spring

31 Since I noo mwore do zee your feäce.
The Wife A-Lost

RICHARD BARNFIELD 1574–1627

32 As it fell upon a day
In the merry month of May,

Sitting in a pleasant shade,
Which a grove of myrtles made.
Beasts did leap and birds did sing,
Trees did grow and plants did spring,
Everything did banish moan,
Save the nightingale alone.
She, poor bird, as all forlorn,
Lean'd her breast up-till a thorn,
And there sung the dolefull'st ditty
That to hear it was great pity.
Fie, fie, fie, now would she cry;
Tereu, Tereu, by and by.
An Ode. Also attr. Shakespeare

1 King Pandion, he is dead,
All thy friends are lapp'd in lead.

2 If Music and sweet Poetry agree,
As they must needs (the Sister and the Brother)
Then must the love be great, 'twixt thee and me,
Because thou lov'st the one, and I the other.
Sonnet

3 Nothing more certain than incertainties;
Fortune is full of fresh variety:
Constant in nothing but inconstancy.
The Shepherd's Content, xi

4 My flocks feed not,
My ewes breed not,
My rams speed not,
        All is amiss.
Love is dying,
Faith's defying,
Heart's denying,
        Causer of this.
A Shepherd's Complaint

5 The waters were his winding sheet, the sea was made
his tomb;
Yet for his fame the ocean sea, was not sufficient
room.
(On the death of Hawkins.) **Encomion of Lady Pecunia. To the
Gentlemen Readers**

PHINEAS T. BARNUM 1810–1891

6 There's a sucker born every minute.
Attr.

J.M. BARRIE 1860–1937

7 His Lordship may compel us to be equal upstairs, but
there will never be equality in the servants' hall.
The Admirable Crichton, I

8 I'm a second eleven sort of chap.
III

9 Never ascribe to an opponent motives meaner than
your own.
'Courage', Rectorial Address, St. Andrews, 3 May 1922

10 Courage is the thing. All goes if courage goes.

11 Facts were never pleasing to him. He acquired them
with reluctance and got rid of them with relief. He was
never on terms with them until he had stood them on
their heads.
Love Me Never or For Ever

12 I do loathe explanations.
My Lady Nicotine, 16

13 When the first baby laughed for the first time, the

laugh broke into a thousand pieces and they all went
skipping about, and that was the beginning of fairies.
Peter Pan, I

14 Every time a child says 'I don't believe in fairies'
there is a little fairy somewhere that falls down dead.

15 To die will be an awfully big adventure.
III

16 Do you believe in fairies?…If you believe, clap your
hands!
IV

17 Oh the gladness of her gladness when she's glad,
And the sadness of her sadness when she's sad,
But the gladness of her gladness
And the sadness of her sadness
Are as nothing, Charles,
To the badness of her badness when she's bad.
Rosalind

18 It's a sort of bloom on a woman. If you have it
[charm], you don't need to have anything else; and if
you don't have it, it doesn't much matter what else you
have.
What Every Woman Knows, I

19 A young Scotsman of your ability let loose upon the
world with £300, what could he not do? It's almost
appalling to think of; especially if he went among the
English.

20 You've forgotten the grandest moral attribute of a
Scotsman, Maggie, that he'll do nothing which might
damage his career.
II

21 There are few more impressive sights in the world than
a Scotsman on the make.

22 Every man who is high up loves to think that he has
done it all himself; and the wife smiles, and lets it go
at that. It's our only joke. Every woman knows that.
IV

GEORGE BARRINGTON b. 1755

23 From distant climes, o'er widespread seas we come,
Though not with much *éclat* or beat of drum;
True patriots we; for be it understood,
We left our country for our country's good.
No private views disgraced our generous zeal,
What urged our travels was our country's weal;
And none will doubt but that our emigration
Has proved most useful to the British nation.
D.N.B. Prologue for the opening of the Playhouse, Sydney, New
South Wales, 16 Jan. 1796, when the actors were principally
convicts. Also attr. Henry Carter (d. 1806): see *Annual Register,*
1801. See 212:4

CHARLES BARTLETT 1921–

24 The hawks favoured an air strike to eliminate the
Cuban missile bases…. The doves opposed the air
strike and favoured a blockade.
Saturday Evening Post, 8 Dec. 1962

BERNARD M. BARUCH 1870–1965

25 Let us not be deceived—we are today in the midst of a
cold war.
Speech before South Carolina Legislature, 16 Apr. 1947. Mr.
Baruch said the expression 'cold war' was suggested to him by
H.B. Swope, former editor of the New York *World.*

WILLIAM BASSE d. 1653?

1 Renowned Spenser, lie a thought more nigh
   To learned Chaucer, and rare Beaumont lie,
   A little nearer Spenser, to make more room
   For Shakespeare, in your threefold, fourfold tomb.
   On Shakespeare

THOMAS BASTARD 1566–1618

2 Age is deformed, youth unkind,
   We scorn their bodies, they our mind.
   Chrestoleros (1598), Bk.7, Epigram 9

EDGAR BATEMAN nineteenth century

3 Wiv a ladder and some glasses,
   You could see to 'Ackney Marshes,
   If it wasn't for the 'ouses in between.
   If it wasn't for the 'Ouses in between

KATHERINE LEE BATES 1859–1929

4 America! America!
      God shed His grace on thee
   And crown thy good with brotherhood
      From sea to shining sea!
   America the Beautiful

CHARLES BAUDELAIRE 1821–1867

5 *Hypocrite lecteur,—mon semblable,—mon frère.*
   Hypocrite reader—my likeness—my brother.
   Les Fleurs du Mal, Préface

6 *Le poète est semblable au prince des nuées*
   Qui haute la tempète et se rit de l'archer;
   Exilé sur le sol, au milieu des huées,
   Ses ailes de géant l'empêchent de marcher.
   The poet is like the prince of the clouds, who rides out
      the tempest and laughs at the archer. But when he is
      exiled on the ground, amidst the clamour, his
      giant's wings prevent him from walking.
   ii, **L'Albatros**

7 *Là, tout n'est qu'ordre et beauté,*
   Luxe, calme et volupté.
   Everything there is simply order and beauty, luxury,
      peace and sensual indulgence.
   liii, **L'Invitation au Voyage**

8 *Quelle est cette île triste et noire? C'est Cythère,*
   Nous dit-on, un pays fameux dans les chansons,
   Eldorado banal de tous les vieux garçons.
   Regardez, après tout, c'est un pauvre terre.
   What sad, black isle is that? It's Cythera, so they say,
      a land celebrated in song, the banal Eldorado of all
      the old fools. Look, after all, it's a land of poverty.
   cxvi, **Un Voyage à Cythère**

LILIAN BAYLIS 1874–1937

9 I do like to see the Jews coming, don't you dear? Even
   if they aren't Christians, it must do them good, but I
   wish we didn't have to give them *The Merchant of
   Venice,* the Christians all behave so badly.
   Richard Findlater, *Lilian Baylis: The Lady of the Old Vic* (1975)

THOMAS HAYNES BAYLY 1797–1839

10 Oh! no! we never mention her,

Her name is never heard;
My lips are now forbid to speak
That once familiar word.
Oh! No! We Never Mention Her

AUBREY BEARDSLEY 1872–1898

11 Really I believe I'm so affected, even my lungs are
   affected.
   O. Sitwell, *Noble Essences* (1950, vol.5 of *Left Hand, Right
   Hand!*), 6

EARL BEATTY 1871–1936

12 There's something wrong with our bloody ships
   to-day, Chatfield.
   Remark during the Battle of Jutland, 1916: Winston Churchill,
   The World Crisis (1927), I, 129. The additional words commonly
   attributed: 'Steer two points nearer the enemy' are denied by Lord
   Chatfield

TOPHAM BEAUCLERK 1739–1780

13 [On Boswell saying that a certain man had good
   principles.] Then he does not wear them out in
   practice.
   Boswell, *Life of Johnson*, 14 Apr. 1778

PIERRE-AUGUSTIN CARON DE
BEAUMARCHAIS 1732–1799

14 *Aujourd'hui ce qui ne vaut pas la peine d'être dit, on
   le chante.*
   Today if something is not worth saying, people sing it.
   Le Barbier de Séville, I.ii

15 *Je me presse de rire de tout, de peur d'être obligé d'en
   pleurer.*
   I make myself laugh at everything, for fear of having
   to weep.

16 *Est-ce qu'un homme comme vous ignore quelque
   chose?*
   Can anything be beyond the knowledge of a man like
   you?
   (Figaro to Count Almaviva.)
   vi

17 *Boire sans soif et faire l'amour en tout temps,
   madame, il n'y a que ça qui nous distingue des autres
   bêtes.*
   Drinking when we are not thirsty and making love all
   year round, madam; that is all there is to distinguish us
   from other animals.
   Le Mariage de Figaro, II.xxi

18 *Parce que vous êtes un grand seigneur, vous vous
   croyez un grand génie!...Vous vous êtes donné la
   peine de naître, et rien de plus.*
   Because you are a great lord, you believe yourself to
   be a great genius!...You took the trouble to be born,
   but no more.

FRANCIS BEAUMONT 1584–1616

19   What things have we seen,
   Done at the Mermaid! heard words that have been
   So nimble, and so full of subtil flame,
   As if that every one from whence they came,
   Had meant to put his whole wit in a jest,
   And had resolv'd to live a fool, the rest

Of his dull life.
Letter to Ben Jonson

1 Here are sands, ignoble things,
Dropt from the ruin'd sides of Kings;
Here's a world of pomp and state,
Buried in dust, once dead by fate.
On the Tombs in Westminster Abbey

FRANCIS BEAUMONT 1584–1616
and
JOHN FLETCHER 1579–1625
(see also under FLETCHER)

2 You are no better than you should be.
The Coxcomb, IV.iii

3 I care not two-pence.

4 It is always good
When a man has two irons in the fire.
The Faithful Friends, I.ii (attr.)

5 Nose, nose, jolly red nose,
Who gave thee this jolly red nose?…
Nutmegs and ginger, cinnamon and cloves,
And they gave me this jolly red nose.
The Knight of the Burning Pestle, I, l.334

6 This is a pretty flim-flam.
II.iii

7 The sturdy steed now goes to grass and up they hang
his saddle.
IV, interlude

8 Upon my buried body lay
Lightly gently earth.
The Maid's Tragedy, II.i

9 Those have most power to hurt us, that we love.
V.iv

10 *Philaster:* Oh, but thou dost not know
What 'tis to die.
Bellario: Yes, I do know, my Lord:
'Tis less than to be born; a lasting sleep;
A quiet resting from all jealousy,
A thing we all pursue; I know besides,
It is but giving over of a game,
That must be lost.
Philaster, III.i

11 Kiss till the cow comes home.
The Scornful Lady, II.ii

12 There is no other purgatory but a woman.
III.i

13 It would talk:
Lord how it talk't!
IV.i

LORD BEAVERBROOK 1879–1964

14 Our cock won't fight.
Said to W.S. Churchill during the abdication crisis, 1936. Frances
Donaldson, *Edward VIII,* ch.22

SAMUEL BECKETT 1906–

15 *Estragon:* Let's go.
Vladimir: We can't.
Estragon: Why not?
Vladimir: We're waiting for Godot.
Waiting for Godot (1954), I

16 We always find something, eh, Didi, to give us the

impression that we exist?
II

17 If I had the use of my body I would throw it out of the
window.
Malone Dies, English version (1956), p.44

PETER BECKFORD 1740–1811

18 The colour I think of little moment; and am of opinion
with our friend Foote, respecting his negro friend, that
a good dog, like a good candidate, cannot be of a bad
colour.
Thoughts upon Hare and Fox Hunting (1781), letter 3

WILLIAM BECKFORD 1759–1844

19 When he was angry, one of his eyes became so
terrible, that no person could bear to behold it; and the
wretch upon whom it was fixed, instantly fell
backward, and sometimes expired. For fear, however,
of depopulating his dominions and making his palace
desolate, he but rarely gave way to his anger.
Vathek (1782, 3rd edn. 1816), 1st para.

20 He did not think, with the Caliph Omar Ben Adalaziz,
that it was necessary to make a hell of this world to
enjoy paradise in the next.
2nd para.

21 Your presence I condescend to accept; but beg you
will let me be quiet; for, I am not over-fond of
resisting temptation.
215th para.

THOMAS BECON 1512–1567

22 For when the wine is in, the wit is out.
Catechism, 375

THOMAS LOVELL BEDDOES 1803–1849

23 If thou wilt ease thine heart
Of love and all its smart,
Then sleep, dear, sleep.
Death's Jest Book, II.ii

24 But wilt thou cure thine heart
Of love and all its smart,
Then die, dear, die.

25 I have a bit of FIAT in my soul,
And can myself create my little world.
V.i

26 Old Adam, the carrion crow.
iv

27 King Death hath asses' ears.

28 If there were dreams to sell,
What would you buy?
Some cost a passing bell;
Some a light sigh,
That shakes from Life's fresh crown
Only a roseleaf down.
If there were dreams to sell,
Merry and sad to tell,
And the crier rung the bell,
What would you buy?
Dream-Pedlary

THE VENERABLE BEDE c.673–735

1 The present life of men on earth, O king, as compared with the whole length of time which is unknowable to us, seems to me to be like this: as if, when you are sitting at dinner with your chiefs and ministers in wintertime,...one of the sparrows from outside flew very quickly through the hall; as if it came in one door and soon went out through another. In that actual time it is indoors it is not touched by the winter's storm; but yet the tiny period of calm is over in a moment, and having come out of the winter it soon returns to the winter and slips out of your sight. Man's life appears to be more or less like this; and of what may follow it, or what preceded it, we are absolutely ignorant.
Ecclesiastical History (completed 731), 2, 13

2 *'Magister dilecte, restat adhuc una sententia non descripta.' At ille inquit 'Scribe.' Et post modicum dixit puer: 'Modo descripta est.' At ille 'Bene' inquit, 'consummatum est; veritatem dixisti.'*
'There is still one sentence, dear master, that we haven't written down.' And he said, 'Write it.' After a little while the boy said, 'There, now it is written.' 'Good' he replied, 'It is finished, you have spoken the truth.'
Cuthbert's letter to Cuthwin on the death of Bede, A.D.735. See *Ecclesiastical History*, Colgrave and Mynors (eds) (1969), p.579 ff.

BARNARD ELLIOTT BEE 1823–1861

3 Let us determine to die here, and we will conquer. There is Jackson standing like a stone wall. Rally behind the Virginians.
First Battle of Bull Run, 1861. Poore, *Reminiscences of Metropolis,* II.85

SIR THOMAS BEECHAM 1879–1961

4 Too much counterpoint; what is worse, Protestant counterpoint. [Of Bach.]
Neville Cardus, *Guardian*, 8 Mar. 1971

5 When the history of the first half of this century comes to be written—properly written—it will be acknowledged the most stupid and brutal in the history of civilisation.
H. Proctor-Gregg, *Beecham Remembered* (1976), p.153

6 A musicologist is a man who can read music but can't hear it.
p.154

7 In the first movement alone, I took note of six pregnancies and at least four miscarriages. [Of Bruckner's 7th Symphony.]
Oral trad.

REVD. H.C. BEECHING 1859–1919

8 First come I; my name is Jowett.
There's no knowledge but I know it.
I am Master of this college:
What I don't know isn't knowledge.
The Masque of Balliol, composed by and current among members of Balliol College in the late 1870's. See 7:1, 517:11–12

9 Not when the sense is dim,
But now from the heart of joy,
I would remember Him:

Take the thanks of a boy.
Prayers

MAX BEERBOHM 1872–1956

10 Most women are not so young as they are painted.
A Defence of Cosmetics

11 I belong to the Beardsley period.
Diminuendo

12 There is always something rather absurd about the past.
1880

13 To give an accurate and exhaustive account of that period would need a far less brilliant pen than mine.

14 She swam to the bell-rope and grasped it for a tinkle.
(Parody of Meredith.) *Euphemia Clashthought*

15 A swear-word in a rustic slum
A simple swear-word is to some,
To Masefield something more.
(Caption to a cartoon) *Fifty Caricatures*, 1913. See 579:19

16 None, it is said, of all who revelled with the Regent, was half so wicked as Lord George Hell.
The Happy Hypocrite, ch.1

17 Mankind is divisible into two great classes: hosts and guests.
Hosts and Guests

18 I maintain that though you would often in the fifteenth century have heard the snobbish Roman say, in a would-be off-hand tone, 'I am dining with the Borgias to-night,' no Roman ever was able to say, 'I dined last night with the Borgias.'

19 The Nonconformist Conscience makes cowards of us all.
King George the Fourth. See 573:12

20 Fate wrote her [Queen Caroline] a most tremendous tragedy, and she played it in tights.

21 Not that I had any special reason for hating school. Strange as it may seem to my readers, I was not unpopular there. I was a modest, good-humoured boy. It is Oxford that has made me insufferable.
More. Going back to School

22 Undergraduates owe their happiness chiefly to the fact that they are no longer at school...The nonsense which was knocked out of them at school is all put gently back at Oxford or Cambridge.

23 They so very indubitably *are*, you know!
(Parody of Henry James.) *Mote in the Middle Distance*

24 'After all', as a pretty girl once said to me, 'women are a sex by themselves, so to speak'.
The Pervasion of Rouge

25 Enter Michael Angelo. Andrea del Sarto apears for a moment at a window. Pippa passes.
Savonarola Brown, III

26 The fading signals and grey eternal walls of that antique station, which, familiar to them and insignificant, does yet whisper to the tourist the last enchantment of the Middle Age.
Zuleika Dobson, ch.1

27 Zuleika, on a desert island, would have spent most of her time in looking for a man's foot-print.
ch.2

28 The dullard's envy of brilliant men is always assuaged

by the suspicion that they will come to a bad end.
ch.4

1 Your mentality, too, is bully, as we all predicate.
ch.8

2 Deeply regret inform your grace last night two black
owls came and perched on battlements remained there
through night hooting at dawn flew away none knows
whither awaiting instructions Jellings.
ch.14

3 Prepare vault for funeral Monday Dorset.

4 The Socratic manner is not a game at which two can
play.
ch.15

5 'Ah, say that again,' she murmured. 'Your voice is
music.'
He repeated his question.
'Music!' she said dreamily; and such is the force of
habit that 'I don't', she added, 'know anything about
music, really. But I know what I like.'
ch.16

6 Of course he was a wonderful all-round man, but the
act of walking round him has always tired me.
Of William Morris. S.N. Behrman, *Conversations with Max*, ch.2

7 Only the insane take themselves quite seriously.
Lord David Cecil, *Max* (1964), ch.2

ETHEL LYNN BEERS 1827–1879

8 All quiet along the Potomac to-night,
    No sound save the rush of the river,
While soft falls the dew on the face of the dead—
    The picket's off duty forever.
The Picket Guard. See 324:29

LUDWIG VAN BEETHOVEN 1770–1827

9 *Muss es sein? Es muss sein.*
Must it be? It must be.
Epigraph to String Quartet in F Major, Opus 135

MRS. APHRA BEHN 1640–1689

10 Oh, what a dear ravishing thing is the beginning of an
Amour!
The Emperor of the Moon, I.i

11 Of all that writ, he was the wisest bard, who spoke
this mighty truth—
He that knew all that ever learning writ,
Knew only this—that he knew nothing yet.
iii

12 Love ceases to be a pleasure, when it ceases to be a
secret.
The Lover's Watch, Four o'clock

13 Faith, Sir, we are here to-day, and gone to-morrow.
The Lucky Chance, IV

14 I owe a duty, where I cannot love.
The Moor's Revenge, III.iii

15 A brave world, Sir, full of religion, knavery, and
change: we shall shortly see better days.
The Roundheads, I.i

16 Variety is the soul of pleasure.
The Rover, Part II, Act I

17 Come away; poverty's catching.

18 Money speaks sense in a language all nations

understand.
III.i

19 Beauty unadorn'd.
IV.ii

20 'Sure, I rose the wrong way to-day, I have had such
damn'd ill luck every way'.
The Town Fop, V.i

21 The soft, unhappy sex.
The Wandering Beauty

W.H. BELLAMY nineteenth century

22 Old Simon the Cellarer keeps a rare store
    Of Malmsey and Malvoisie.
Song: *Simon the Cellarer*

HILAIRE BELLOC 1870–1953

23 Child! do not throw this book about;
Refrain from the unholy pleasure
Of cutting all the pictures out!
Preserve it as your chiefest treasure.
Bad Child's Book of Beasts, dedication

24 Your little hands were made to take
The better things and leave the worse ones:
They also may be used to shake
The massive paws of elder persons.

25 A manner rude and wild
Is common at your age.
introduction

26 Who take their manners from the Ape,
Their habits from the Bear,
Indulge the loud unseemly jape,
And never brush their hair.

27 The Dromedary is a cheerful bird:
I cannot say the same about the Kurd.
The Dromedary

28 When people call this beast to mind,
They marvel more and more
At such a little tail behind,
So large a trunk before.
The Elephant

29 The Frog is justly sensitive
    To epithets like these.
The Frog

30 I shoot the Hippopotamus
With bullets made of platinum,
Because if I use leaden ones
His hide is sure to flatten 'em.
The Hippopotamus

31 Mothers of large families (who claim to common
    sense)
Will find a Tiger well repay the trouble and expense.
The Tiger

32 The nicest child I ever knew
Was Charles Augustus Fortescue.
Cautionary Tales. **Charles Augustus Fortescue**

33 Godolphin Horne was nobly born;
He held the human race in scorn.
Godolphin Horne

34 The chief defect of Henry King
Was chewing little bits of string.
Henry King

1   Physicians of the utmost fame
    Were called at once, but when they came
    They answered, as they took their fees,
    'There is no cure for this disease.'

2   'Oh, my friends, be warned by me,
    That breakfast, dinner, lunch, and tea
    Are all the human frame requires...'
    With that the wretched child expires.

3   And always keep a hold of Nurse
    For fear of finding something worse.
    Jim

4   In my opinion Butlers ought
    To know their place, and not to play
    The Old Retainer night and day.
    Lord Lundy

5   Towards the age of twenty-six,
    They shoved him into politics.

6   We had intended you to be
    The next Prime Minister but three:
    The stocks were sold; the Press was squared;
    The Middle Class was quite prepared.
    But as it is!...My language fails!
    Go out and govern New South Wales!

7   Matilda told such Dreadful Lies,
    It made one Gasp and Stretch one's Eyes;
    Her Aunt, who, from her Earliest Youth,
    Had kept a Strict Regard for Truth,
    Attempted to Believe Matilda:
    The effort very nearly killed her.
    Matilda

8   Summoned the Immediate Aid
    Of London's Noble Fire Brigade.

9   Until Matilda's Aunt succeeded
    In showing them they were not needed;
    And even then she had to pay
    To get the Men to go away!

10 It happened that a few Weeks later
    Her Aunt was off to the Theatre
    To see that Interesting Play
    The Second Mrs Tanqueray.

11 For every time she shouted 'Fire!'
    They only answered 'Little Liar!'

12 She was not really bad at heart,
    But only rather rude and wild;
    She was an aggravating child.
    Rebecca

13 Her funeral sermon (which was long
    And followed by a sacred song)
    Mentioned her virtues, it is true,
    But dwelt upon her vices too.

14 Of Courtesy—it is much less
    Than courage of heart or holiness;
    Yet in my walks it seems to me
    That the Grace of God is in Courtesy.
    Courtesy

15 From quiet homes and first beginning,
        Out to the undiscovered ends,
    There's nothing worth the wear of winning,
        But laughter and the love of friends.
    Dedicatory Ode

16 The moon on the one hand, the dawn on the other:
    The moon is my sister, the dawn is my brother.
    The moon on my left and the dawn on my right.
    My brother, good morning: my sister, good night.
    The Early Morning

17 I said to Heart, 'How goes it?' Heart replied:
    'Right as a Ribstone Pippin!' But it lied.
    Epigrams. The False Heart

18 I'm tired of Love: I'm still more tired of Rhyme.
    But Money gives me pleasure all the time.
    Fatigue

19 When I am dead, I hope it may be said:
    'His sins were scarlet, but his books were read.'
    On his Books

20 Of this bad world the loveliest and the best
    Has smiled and said 'Good Night,' and gone to rest.
    On a Dead Hostess

21 The accursed power which stands on Privilege
    (And goes with Women, and Champagne, and Bridge)
    Broke—and Democracy resumed her reign:
    (Which goes with Bridge, and Women and
        Champagne).
    On a Great Election

22 Sleep your fill—but when you wake
    Dawn shall over Lethe break.
    On a Sleeping Friend

23 I am a sundial, and I make a botch
    Of what is done far better by a watch.
    On a Sundial

24 The Devil, having nothing else to do,
    Went off to tempt my Lady Poltagrue.
    My Lady, tempted by a private whim,
    To his extreme annoyance, tempted him.
    On Lady Poltagrue, a Public Peril

25 Pale Ebenezer thought it wrong to fight,
    But Roaring Bill (who killed him) thought it right.
    The Pacifist

26 Sally is gone that was so kindly,
    Sally is gone from Ha'nacker Hill.
    Ha'nacker Mill

27 Remote and ineffectual Don
    That dared attack my Chesterton.
    Lines to a Don

28 Don different from those regal Dons!
    With hearts of gold and lungs of bronze,
    Who shout and bang and roar and bawl
    The Absolute across the hall,
    Or sail in amply billowing gown,
    Enormous through the Sacred Town.

29 Lord Finchley tried to mend the Electric Light
    Himself. It struck him dead: and serve him right!
    It is the business of the wealthy man
    To give employment to the artisan.
    Lord Finchley

30 Lord Heygate had a troubled face,
    His furniture was commonplace—
    The sort of Peer who well might pass
    For someone of the middle class.
    I do not think you want to hear
    About this unimportant Peer.
    Lord Heygate

31 The nuisance of the tropics is
    The sheer necessity of fizz.
    The Modern Traveller (1898), iv

1 Whatever happens, we have got
The Maxim Gun, and they have not.
vi

2 The Llama is a woolly sort of fleecy hairy goat,
With an indolent expression and an undulating throat
Like an unsuccessful literary man.
More Beasts for Worse Children. **The Llama**

3 Oh! let us never, never doubt
What nobody is sure about!
The Microbe

4 I had an aunt in Yucatan
Who bought a Python from a man
And kept it for a pet.
She died, because she never knew
These simple little rules and few;—
The Snake is living yet.
The Python

5 Like many of the upper class
He liked the sound of broken glass.
New Cautionary Tales. **About John**

6 Birds in their little nests agree
With Chinamen, but not with me.
On Food. See 565:20

7 A smell of burning fills the startled air—
The Electrician is no longer there!
Newdigate Poem

8 Strong Brother in God, and last Companion: Wine.
Short Talks with the Dead, The Good Poet and the Bad Poet.
Heroic Poem on Wine. (An adaptation from the Heroic Poem in
Praise of Wine.)

9 When I am living in the Midlands
That are sodden and unkind...
The great hills of the South Country
Come back into my mind.
The South Country

10 A lost thing could I never find,
Nor a broken thing mend.

11 If I ever become a rich man,
Or if ever I grow to be old,
I will build a house with deep thatch
To shelter me from the cold,
And there shall the Sussex songs be sung
And the story of Sussex told.
I will hold my house in the high wood
Within a walk of the sea,
And the men that were boys when I was a boy
Shall sit and drink with me.

12 Do you remember an Inn,
Miranda?
Tarantella

13 The fleas that tease in the high Pyrenees.

14 Balliol made me, Balliol fed me,
Whatever I had she gave me again;
And the best of Balliol loved and led me,
God be with you, Balliol men.
To the Balliol men still in Africa

15 It is the best of all trades, to make songs, and the
second best to sing them.
On Everything. **On Song**

16 From the towns all Inns have been driven: from the
villages most...Change your hearts or you will lose
your Inns and you will deserve to have lost them. But
when you have lost your Inns drown your empty

selves, for you will have lost the last of England.
This and That. **On Inns**

P.-L. B. DU BELLOY 1725–1775

17 *Plus je vis d'étrangers, plus j'aimai ma patrie.*
The more foreigners I saw, the more I loved my
homeland.
Le Siège de Calais (1765), II.iii

JULIEN BENDA 1868–1956

18 *La trahison des clercs.*
The intellectuals' betrayal.
Title of book (1927)

STEPHEN VINCENT BENÉT 1898–1943

19 I have fallen in love with American names,
The sharp names that never get fat,
The snakeskin-titles of mining-claims,
The plumed war-bonnet of Medicine Hat,
Tucson and Deadwood and Lost Mule Flat.
American Names

20 I shall not rest quiet in Montparnasse.
I shall not lie easy at Winchelsea.
You may bury my body in Sussex grass,
You may bury my tongue at Champmédy.
I shall not be there, I shall rise and pass.
Bury my heart at Wounded Knee.

ARNOLD BENNETT 1867-1931

21 'Ye can call it influenza if ye like,' said Mrs Machin.
'There was no influenza in my young days. We called
a cold a cold.'
The Card, ch.8

22 Being a husband is a whole-time job.
The Title, Act I

23 Journalists say a thing that they know isn't true, in
that hope that if they keep on saying it long enough it
will be true.
Act II

A.C. BENSON 1862–1925

24 Land of Hope and Glory, Mother of the Free,
How shall we extol thee, who are born of thee?
Wider still and wider shall thy bounds be set;
God who made thee mighty, make thee mightier yet.
Words written to be sung as the Finale of Elgar's *Coronation Ode*
(1902) to music derived from the *Pomp and Circumstance March*,
op.39, No.1 in D major

JEREMY BENTHAM 1748–1832

25 The greatest happiness of the greatest number is the
foundation of morals and legislation.
The Commonplace Book (*Works*, x.142). See 268:20

26 The Fool had stuck himself up one day, with great
gravity, in the King's throne; with a stick, by way of a
sceptre, in one hand, and a ball in the other: being
asked what he was doing? he answered *'reigning'*.
Much of the same sort of reign, I take it would be that
of our Author's [Blackstone's] Democracy.
Fragment on Government (1776), ch.2, note to sect. 34

27 All punishment is mischief: all punishment in itself is

evil.
Principles of Morals and Legislation, ch.13, 2

1 He rather hated the ruling few than loved the suffering many.
Of James Mill. *Journals of Caroline Fox,* 17 Aug. 1840

2 Prose is when all the lines except the last go on to the end. Poetry is when some of them fall short of it.
M. St.J. Packe, *Life of John Stuart Mill*, bk.I, ch.ii

EDMUND CLERIHEW BENTLEY 1875–1956

3 The art of Biography
Is different from Geography.
Geography is about maps,
But Biography is about chaps.
Biography for Beginners

4 Chapman and Hall
Swore not at all.
Mr Chapman's yea was yea,
And Mr Hall's nay was nay.

5 What I like about Clive
Is that he is no longer alive.
There is a great deal to be said
For being dead.

6 Sir Humphrey Davy
Abominated gravy.
He lived in the odium
Of having discovered Sodium.

7 Edward the Confessor
Slept under the dresser.
When that began to pall
He slept in the hall.

8 John Stuart Mill
By a mighty effort of will
Overcame his natural bonhomie
And wrote 'Principles of Political Economy'

9 Sir Christopher Wren
Said, 'I am going to dine with some men.
If anybody calls
Say I am designing St Paul's.'

10 George the Third
Ought never to have occurred.
One can only wonder
At so grotesque a blunder.
More Biographies

RICHARD BENTLEY 1662–1742

11 He is believed to have liked port, but to have said of claret that 'it would be port if it could'.
R.C. Jebb, *Bentley,* p.200

12 It is a pretty poem, Mr Pope, but you must not call it Homer.
Johnson, *Life of Pope*

13 I hold it as certain, that no man was ever written out of reputation but by himself.
William Warburton, *The Works of Alexander Pope,* iv.159

PIERRE-JEAN DE BÉRANGER 1780–1857

14 *Il était un roi d'Yvetot*
Peu connu dans l'histoire.
There was a king of Yvetot

Little known to history.
Le Roi d'Yvetot (1815)

15 *Nos amis, les ennemis.*
Our friends, the enemy.
L'Opinion de ces demoiselles

LORD CHARLES BERESFORD 1846–1919

16 The idea of a Commercial Alliance with England based on the integrity of China and the open door for all nations' trade.
The Break-Up of China (1899)

17 Very sorry can't come. Lie follows by post.
Telegram to the Prince of Wales after an eleventh-hour summons to dine. R. Nevill, *The World of Fashion 1837–1922* (1923), ch 5. See 401:24

BISHOP BERKELEY 1685–1753

18 We have first raised a dust and then complain we cannot see.
Principles of Human Knowledge, introduction, 3

19 All the choir of heaven and furniture of earth—in a word, all those bodies which compose the mighty frame of the world—have not any subsistence without a mind.
Principles of Human Knowledge

20 Westward the course of empire takes its way;
    The first four acts already past,
A fifth shall close the drama with the day:
    Time's noblest offspring is the last.
On the Prospect of Planting Arts and Learning in America

21 [Tar water] is of a nature so mild and benign and proportioned to the human constitution, as to warm without heating, to cheer but not inebriate.
Siris, par.217

22 Truth is the cry of all, but the game of the few.
par.368

SIR ISAIAH BERLIN 1909–

23 Injustice, poverty, slavery, ignorance—these may be cured by reform or revolution. But men do not live only by fighting evils. They live by positive goals, individual and collective, a vast variety of them, seldom predictable, at times incompatible.
Four Essays on Liberty, **Political Ideas in the Twentieth Century**

ST. BERNARD 1091–1153

24 *Liberavi animam meam.*
I have freed my soul.
Epistle 371

BERNARD OF CHARTRES d. c.1130

25 Bernard of Chartres used to say that we are like dwarfs on the shoulders of giants, so that we can see more than they, and things at a greater distance, not by virtue of any sharpness of sight on our part, or any physical distinction, but because we are carried high and raised up by their giant size.
John of Salisbury, *Metalogicon* (1159), bk.III.ch.iv. See also R.K. Merton, *On the Shoulders of Giants* (1965)

LORD BERNERS 1883–1950

1 He's always backing into the limelight.
Oral tradition, of T.E. Lawrence

CHARLES BEST fl. 1602

2 Look how the pale Queen of the silent night
Doth cause the Ocean to attend upon her,
And he, as long as she is in his sight,
With his full tide is ready her to honour.
A Sonnet of the Moon

THEOBALD VON BETHMANN HOLLWEG 1856–1921

3 Just for a word—'neutrality', a word which in wartime
has so often been disregarded, just for a scrap of
paper—Great Britain is going to make war.
To Sir Edward Goschen, 4 Aug. 1914

SIR JOHN BETJEMAN 1906–

4 He sipped at a weak hock and seltzer,
  As he gazed at the London skies
Through the Nottingham lace of the curtains
  Or was it his bees-winged eyes?
The Arrest of Oscar Wilde at the Cadogan Hotel

5 Green Shutters, shut your shutters! Windyridge,
Let winds unnoticed whistle round your hill!
Beside the Seaside

6 From the geyser ventilators
  Autumn winds are blowing down
On a thousand business women
  Having baths in Camden Town.
Business Girls

7 Rest you there, poor unbelov'd ones,
  Lap your loneliness in heat.
All too soon the tiny breakfast,
  Trolley-bus and windy street!

8 And girls in slacks remember Dad,
  And oafish louts remember Mum,
And sleepless children's hearts are glad,
  And Christmas morning bells say 'Come!'
Even to shining ones who dwell
Safe in the Dorchester Hotel.

And is it true? And is it true,
This most tremendous tale of all,
  Seen in a stained-glass window's hue,
  A Baby in an ox's stall?
Christmas

9 And Nurse came in with the tea-things
  Breast high 'mid the stands and chairs—
But Nurse was alone with her own little soul,
  And the things were alone with theirs.
Death in Leamington

10 Oh! chintzy, chintzy cheeriness,
  Half dead and half alive!

11 Spirits of well-shot woodcock, partridge, snipe
Flutter and bear him up the Norfolk sky.
Death of King George V

12 Old men in country houses hear clocks ticking
  Over thick carpets with a deadened force;

Old men who never cheated, never doubted,
Communicated monthly, sit and stare

At the new suburb stretched beyond the run-way
Where a young man lands hatless from the air.

13 Rime Intrinsica, Fontmell Magna, Sturminster Newton
  and Melbury Bubb,
Whist upon whist upon whist upon whist drive, in
  Institute, Legion and Social Club.
Horny hands that hold the aces which this morning
  held the plough—
While Tranter Reuben, T.S. Eliot, H.G. Wells and
  Edith Sitwell lie in Mellstock churchyard now.
Dorset. See 239:17

14 You ask me what it is I do. Well actually, you know,
I'm partly a liaison man and partly P.R.O.
Essentially I integrate the current export drive
And basically I'm viable from ten o'clock till five.
Executive

15 Glow, white lily in London,
  You are high in our hearts today!
14 November, 1973. On Princess Anne's wedding

16 When melancholy Autumn comes to Wembley
  And electric trains are lighted after tea
The poplars near the Stadium are trembly
  With their tap and tap and whispering to me,
    Like the sound of little breakers
    Spreading out along the surf-line
When the estuary's filling
    With the sea.

Then Harrow-on-the-Hill's a rocky island
  And Harrow churchyard full of sailors' graves
And the constant click and kissing of the trolley buses
  hissing
    Is the level to the Wealdstone turned to waves.
Harrow-on-the-Hill

17 There's a storm cloud to the westward over Kenton,
  There's a line of harbour lights at Perivale,
Is it rounding rough Pentire in a flood of sunset fire
  The little fleet of trawlers under sail?

18 When shall I see the Thames again?
The prow-promoted gems again,
    As beefy ATS
    Without their hats
Come shooting through the bridge?
  And 'cheerioh' and 'cheeri-bye'
Across the waste of waters lie
And lightly skims the midge.
Henley-on-Thames

19 Phone for the fish-knives, Norman,
  As Cook is a little unnerved;
You kiddies have crumpled the serviettes
  And I must have things daintily served.
How to Get On in Society

20 Milk and then just as it comes dear?
  I'm afraid the preserve's full of stones;
Beg pardon, I'm soiling the doileys
  With afternoon tea-cakes and scones.

21 It's awf'lly bad luck on Diana,
  Her ponies have swallowed their bits;
She fished down their throats with a spanner
  And frightened them all into fits.
Hunter Trials

22 Oh wasn't it naughty of Smudges?
  Oh, Mummy, I'm sick with disgust.
She threw me in front of the judges

And my silly old collarbone's bust.

1 In the Garden City Café with its murals on the wall
Before a talk on 'Sex and Civics' I meditated on the
Fall.
Huxley Hall

2 The Church's Restoration
In eighteen-eighty-three
Has left for contemplation
Not what there used to be.
Hymn

3 Sing on, with hymns uproarious,
Ye humble and aloof,
Look up! and oh how glorious
He has restored the roof!

4 'Let us not speak, for the love we bear one another—
Let us hold hands and look.'
She, such a very ordinary little woman;
He, such a thumping crook;
But both, for a moment, little lower than the angels
In the.teashop's ingle-nook.
In a Bath Teashop. See 244:10

5 Gracious Lord, oh bomb the Germans.
Spare their women for Thy Sake,
And if that is not too easy
We will pardon Thy Mistake.
But, gracious Lord, whate'er shall be,
Don't let anyone bomb me.
In Westminster Abbey

6 Think of what our Nation stands for,
Books from Boots' and country lanes,
Free speech, free passes, class distinction,
Democracy and proper drains.
Lord, put beneath Thy special care
One-eighty-nine Cadogan Square.

7 Bells are booming down the bohreens,
White the mist along the grass.
Now the Julias, Maeves and Maureens
Move between the fields to Mass.
Twisted trees of small green apple
Guard the decent whitewashed chapel.
Ireland with Emily

8 Where a Stone Age people breeds
The last of Europe's stone age race.

9 There in pinnacled protection,
One extinguished family waits
A Church of Ireland resurrection
By the broken, rusty gates.
Sheepswool, straw and droppings cover,
Graves of spinster, rake and lover,
Whose fantastic mausoleum
Sings its own seablown Te Deum,
In and out the slipping slates.

10 I made hay while the sun shone.
My work sold.
Now, if the harvest is over
And the world cold,
Give me the bonus of laughter
As I lose hold.
The Last Laugh

11 Take me, Lieutenant, to that Surrey homestead!
Love in a Valley

12 Belbroughton Road is bonny, and pinkly bursts the
spray

Of prunus and forsythia across the public way,
For a full spring-tide of blossom seethed and departed
hence,
Leaving land-locked pools of jonquils by sunny garden
fence.

And a constant sound of flushing runneth from
windows where
The toothbrush too is airing in this new North Oxford
air.
May-Day Song for North Oxford

13 Gaily into Ruislip Gardens
Runs the red electric train,
With a thousand Ta's and Pardon's
Daintily alights Elaine.
Middlesex

14 Well-cut Windsmoor flapping lightly,
Jacqmar scarf of mauve and green
Hiding hair which, Friday nightly,
Delicately drowns in Drene.

15 Dear Mary,
Yes, it will be bliss
To go with you by train to Diss,
Your walking shoes upon your feet;
We'll meet, my sweet, at Liverpool Street.
A Mind's Journey to Diss. Addressed to Mrs. Harold Wilson
(Lady Wilson)

16 Pink may, double may, dead laburnum
Shedding an Anglo-Jackson shade,
Shall we ever, my staunch Myfanwy,
Bicycle down to North Parade?
Kant on the handle-bars, Marx in the saddlebag,
Light my touch on your shoulder-blade.
Myfanwy at Oxford

17 Rumbling under blackened girders, Midland, bound
for Cricklewood,
Puffed its sulphur to the sunset where the Land of
Laundries stood.
Rumble under, thunder over, train and tram alternate
go.
Parliament Hill Fields

18 Outside Charrington's we waited, by the 'STOP HERE
IF REQUIRED',
Launched aboard the shopping basket, sat precipitately
down,
Rocked past Zwanziger the baker's, and the terrace
blackish-brown,
And the curious Anglo-Norman parish church of
Kentish Town.

19 Oh the after-tram-ride quiet, when we heard a mile
beyond,
Silver music from the bandstand, barking dogs by
Highgate Pond;
Up the hill where stucco houses in Virginia creeper
drown—
And my childish wave of pity, seeing children carrying
down
Sheaves of drooping dandelions to the courts of
Kentish Town.

20 Pam, I adore you, Pam, you great big mountainous
sports girl,
Whizzing them over the net, full of the strength of
five.
Pot Pourri from a Surrey Garden

1 Oh would I could subdue the flesh
    Which sadly troubles me!
And then perhaps could view the flesh
As though I never knew the flesh
And merry misery.
Senex

2 The gas was on in the Institute,
    The flare was up in the gym,
A man was running a mineral line,
    A lass was singing a hymn,
When Captain Webb the Dawley man,
    Captain Webb from Dawley,
Came swimming along the old canal
    That carried the bricks to Lawley.
A Shropshire Lad

3 We saw the ghost of Captain Webb,
    Webb in a water sheeting,
Come dripping along in a bathing dress
    To the Saturday evening meeting.
        Dripping along—
        Dripping along—
        To the Congregational Hall;
Dripping and still he rose over the sill and faded away
    in a wall.

4 Come, friendly bombs, and fall on Slough
It isn't fit for humans now,
There isn't grass to graze a cow
    Swarm over, Death!
Slough

5 Come, friendly bombs, and fall on Slough
To get it ready for the plough.
The cabbages are coming now:
    The earth exhales.

6 Miss J. Hunter Dunn, Miss J. Hunter Dunn,
Furnish'd and burnish'd by Aldershot sun,
What strenuous singles we played after tea
We in the tournament—you against me!

Love-thirty, love-forty, oh! weakness of joy,
The speed of a swallow, the grace of a boy,
With carefullest carelessness, gaily you won,
I am weak from your loveliness, Joan Hunter Dunn.

Miss Joan Hunter Dunn, Miss Joan Hunter Dunn,
How mad I am, sad I am, glad that you won.
The warm-handled racket is back in its press,
But my shock-headed victor, she loves me no less.
A Subaltern's Love Song

7 Her father's euonymus shines as we walk.

8 By roads 'not adopted', by woodlanded ways,
She drove to the club in the late summer haze,
Into nine-o'clock Camberley, heavy with bells
And mushroomy, pine-woody, evergreen smells.

Miss Joan Hunter Dunn, Miss Joan Hunter Dunn,
I can hear from the car-park the dance has begun.
Oh! full Surrey twilight! importunate band!
Oh! strongly adorable tennis-girl's hand!

9 I heard the church bells hollowing out the sky,
Deep beyond deep, like never-ending stars,
And turned to Archibald, my safe old bear,
Whose woollen eyes looked sad or glad at me.
Summoned by Bells, ch.I, l.37

10 Balkan Sobranies in a wooden box,
The college arms upon the lid; Tokay

And sherry in the cupboard; on the shelves
The University Statutes bound in blue,
Crome Yellow, Prancing Nigger, Blunden, Keats.
ch.IX, l.1

11 While Sandy Lindsay from his lodge looks down
    Dreaming of Adult Education where
        The pottery chimneys flare
On lost potential firsts in some less favoured town.
Oxford Ode, l.41. Of A.D. Lindsay

12 Lunching with poets, dining late with peers,
    I felt that I had come into my own.
l.96

13 There was sun enough for lazing upon beaches,
    There was fun enough for far into the night.
But I'm dying now and done for,
What on earth was all the fun for?
    For I'm old and ill and terrified and tight.
Sun and Fun

14 Broad of Church and broad of mind,
Broad before and broad behind,
A keen ecclesiologist,
A rather dirty Wykehamist.
The Wykehamist

15 *Ghastly Good Taste,* or *A Depressing Story of the Rise and Fall of English Architecture.*
Book title (1933)

ANEURIN BEVAN 1897–1960

16 No amount of cajolery, and no attempts at ethical and social seduction, can eradicate from my heart a deep burning hatred for the Tory Party…So far as I am concerned they are lower than vermin.
Speech at Manchester, 4 July 1948

17 If you carry this resolution and follow out all its implications and do not run away from it you will send a Foreign Minister, whoever he may be, naked into the conference chamber.
M. Foot, *Aneurin Bevan,* vol. ii (1973), ch 15. Speech at Labour Party Conference, 3 Oct. 1957, against motion proposing unilateral nuclear disarmament by the U.K.

ERNEST BEVIN 1881–1951

18 My [foreign] policy is to be able to take a ticket at Victoria Station and go anywhere I damn well please.
Spectator, 20 Apr. 1951

19 If you open that Pandora's Box you never know what Trojan 'orses will jump out.
On the Council of Europe. Sir Roderick Barclay, *Ernest Bevin and the Foreign Office* (1975), p.67

THE BIBLE

20 Upon the setting of that bright *Occidental Star*, Queen *Elizabeth* of most happy memory.
Authorized Version, Epistle Dedicatory

21 The appearance of Your Majesty, as of the Sun in his strength.

OLD TESTAMENT. GENESIS

22 In the beginning God created the heaven and the earth. And the earth was without form, and void; and darkness was upon the face of the deep. And the Spirit of God moved upon the face of the waters.

And God said, Let there be light: and there was light.
1:1

1 And the evening and the morning were the first day.
5

2 And God saw that it was good.
10

3 And God made two great lights; the greater light to rule the day, and the lesser light to rule the night: he made the stars also.
16

4 And God said, Let us make man in our image, after our likeness: and let them have dominion over the fish of the sea, and over the fowl of the air, and over the cattle, and over all the earth and over every creeping thing that creepeth upon the earth.
26

5 Male and female created he them.
27

6 Be fruitful, and multiply, and replenish the earth, and subdue it.
28

7 And the Lord God formed man of the dust of the ground, and breathed into his nostrils the breath of life; and man became a living soul.
And the Lord God planted a garden eastward in Eden.
2:7

8 And out of the ground made the Lord God to grow every tree that is pleasant to the sight, and good for food; the tree of life also in the midst of the garden, and the tree of knowledge of good and evil.
9

9 But of the tree of the knowledge of good and evil, thou shalt not eat of it: for in the day that thou eatest thereof thou shalt surely die.
17

10 It is not good that the man should be alone; I will make him an help meet for him.
18

11 And the Lord God caused a deep sleep to fall upon Adam, and he slept: and he took one of his ribs, and closed up the flesh instead thereof;
And the rib, which the Lord God had taken from man, made he a woman.
21

12 This is now bone of my bones, and flesh of my flesh: she shall be called Woman, because she was taken out of Man.
23

13 Therefore shall a man leave his father and his mother, and shall cleave unto his wife: and they shall be one flesh.
24

14 Now the serpent was more subtil than any beast of the field.
3:1

15 Ye shall be as gods, knowing good and evil.
5

16 And they sewed fig leaves together, and made themselves aprons [breeches in Genevan Bible, 1560].
And they heard the voice of the Lord God walking in the garden in the cool of the day.
7

17 The woman whom thou gavest to be with me, she

gave me of the tree, and I did eat.
12

18 What is this that thou hast done?
13

19 The serpent beguiled me, and I did eat.
20

20 It shall bruise thy head, and thou shalt bruise his heel.
15

21 In sorrow thou shalt bring forth children.
16

22 In the sweat of thy face shalt thou eat bread.
19

23 For dust thou art, and unto dust shalt thou return.

24 The mother of all living.
20

25 Am I my brother's keeper?
4:9

26 The voice of thy brother's blood crieth unto me from the ground.
10

27 My punishment is greater than I can bear.
13

28 And the Lord set a mark upon Cain.
15

29 And Cain went out from the presence of the Lord, and dwelt in the land of Nod, on the east of Eden.
16

30 And Enoch walked with God: and he was not; for God took him.
5:24

31 And all the days of Methuselah were nine hundred sixty and nine years: and he died.
27

32 And Noah begat Shem, Ham, and Japheth.
32

33 There were giants in the earth in those days; and also after that, when the sons of God came in unto the daughters of men, and they bare children to them, the same became mighty men which were of old, men of renown.
6:4

34 There went in two and two unto Noah into the Ark, the male and the female.
7:9

35 But the dove found no rest for the sole of her foot.
8:9

36 For the imagination of man's heart is evil from his youth.
21

37 While the earth remaineth, seedtime and harvest, and cold and heat, and summer and winter, and day and night shall not cease.
22

38 At the hand of every man's brother will I require the life of man.
9:5

39 Whoso sheddeth man's blood, by man shall his blood be shed.
6

40 I do set my bow in the cloud, and it shall be for a token of a covenant between me and the earth. And it shall come to pass, when I bring a cloud over the

earth, that the bow shall be seen in the cloud.
13

1 Even as Nimrod the mighty hunter before the Lord.
10:9

2 Let there be no strife, I pray thee, between thee and
me…for we be brethren.
13:8

3 An horror of great darkness fell upon him.
15:12

4 Thou shalt be buried in a good old age.
15

5 His [Ishmael's] hand will be against every man, and
every man's hand against him.
16:12

6 Now Abraham and Sarah were old and well stricken in
age; and it ceased to be with Sarah after the manner of
women.
18:11

7 Shall not the Judge of all the earth do right.
25

8 But his wife looked back from behind him, and she
became a pillar of salt.
19:26

9 Take now thy son, thine only son Isaac, whom thou
lovest.
22:2

10 My son, God will provide himself a lamb.
8

11 Behold behind him a ram caught in a thicket by his
horns.
13

12 Esau selleth his birthright for a mess of potage.
Heading to chapter 25 in Genevan Bible

13 Esau was a cunning hunter, a man of the field; and
Jacob was a plain man, dwelling in tents.
25:27

14 And he sold his birthright unto Jacob.
33

15 Behold, Esau my brother is a hairy man, and I am a
smooth man.
27:11

16 The voice is Jacob's voice, but the hands are the hands
of Esau.
22

17 Thy brother came with subtilty, and hath taken away
thy blessing.
35

18 And he dreamed, and behold a ladder set up on the
earth, and the top of it reached to heaven: and behold
the angels of God ascending and descending on it.
28:12

19 Surely the Lord is in this place; and I knew it not.
16

20 This is none other but the house of God, and this is the
gate of heaven.
17

21 And Jacob served seven years for Rachel; and they
seemed unto him but a few days, for the love he had to
her.
29:20

22 Mizpah; for he said, The Lord watch between me and

thee, when we are absent one from another.
31:49

23 There wrestled a man with him until the breaking of
the day.
And when he saw that he prevailed not against him, he
touched the hollow of his thigh; and the hollow of
Jacob's thigh was out of joint, as he wrestled with
him.
32:24

24 I will not let thee go, except thou bless me.
26

25 For I have seen God face to face, and my life is
preserved.
30

26 Now Israel loved Joseph more than all his children,
because he was the son of his old age; and he made him
a coat of many colours.
37:3

27 Behold, your sheaves stood round about, and made
obeisance to my sheaf.
7

28 Behold, this dreamer cometh.
19

29 Some evil beast hath devoured him.
20

30 And she caught him by his garment, saying, Lie with
me; and he left his garment in her hand, and fled.
39:12

31 And the lean and the ill favoured kine did eat up the
first seven fat kine.
41:20

32 And the thin ears devoured the seven good ears.
24

33 Jacob saw that there was corn in Egypt.
42:1

34 Ye are spies; to see the nakedness of the land ye are
come.
9

35 My son shall not go down with you; for his brother is
dead, and he is left alone: if mischief befell him by the
way in which ye go, then shall ye bring down my gray
hairs with sorrow to the grave. [Jacob, of Benjamin.]
38

36 Ye shall eat the fat of the land.
45:18

37 See that ye fall not out by the way.
24

38 Few and evil have the days of the years of my life
been.
47:9

39 Unstable as water, thou shalt not excel.
49:4

EXODUS

40 Now there arose up a new king over Egypt, which
knew not Joseph.
1:8

41 She took for him an ark of bulrushes, and daubed it
with slime.
2:3

1 Who made thee a prince and a judge over us?
14

2 I have been a stranger in a strange land.
22. See Exodus 18:3

3 Behold, the bush burned with fire, and the bush was not consumed.
3:2

4 Put off thy shoes from off thy feet, for the place whereon thou standest is holy ground.
5

5 And Moses hid his face; for he was afraid to look upon God.
6

6 A land flowing with milk and honey; unto the place of the Canaanites, and the Hittites, and the Amorites, and the Perizzites, and the Hivites, and the Jebusites.
8

7 I AM THAT I AM.
14

8 The Lord God of your fathers, the God of Abraham, the God of Isaac, and the God of Jacob.
15

9 But I am slow of speech, and of a slow tongue.
4:10

10 I know not the Lord, neither will I let Israel go.
5:2

11 And I will harden Pharaoh's heart, and multiply my signs and my wonders in the land of Egypt.
7:3

12 Aaron's rod swallowed up their rods.
And he hardened Pharaoh's heart, that he hearkened not.
12

13 Let my people go.
7:16

14 A boil breaking forth with blains.
9:10

15 Stretch out thine hand toward heaven, that there may be darkness over the land of Egypt, even darkness which may be felt.
10:21

16 Your lamb shall be without blemish.
12:5

17 And they shall eat the flesh in that night, roast with fire, and unleavened bread; and with bitter herbs they shall eat it.
Eat not of it raw, nor sodden at all with water, but roast with fire; his head with his legs, and with the purtenance thereof.
8

18 With your loins girded, your shoes on your feet, and your staff in your hand; and ye shall eat it in haste; it is the Lord's passover.
For I will pass through the land of Egypt this night, and will smite all the firstborn in the land of Egypt, both man and beast.
11

19 And Pharaoh rose up in the night, he, and all his servants, and all the Egyptians; and there was a great cry in Egypt; for there was not a house where there was not one dead.
30

20 And they spoiled the Egyptians.
36

21 And the Lord went before them by day in a pillar of a cloud, to lead them the way; and by night in a pillar of fire, to give them light.
13:21

22 The Lord is a man of war.
15:3

23 Would to God we had died by the hand of the Lord in the land of Egypt, when we sat by the flesh pots, and when we did eat bread to the full.
16:3

24 And God spake all these words, saying,
I am the Lord thy God, which have brought thee out of the land of Egypt, out of the house of bondage.
Thou shalt have no other gods before me.
Thou shalt not make unto thee any graven image, or any likeness of any thing that is in heaven above, or that is in the earth beneath, or that is in the water under the earth:
Thou shalt not bow down thyself to them, nor serve them: for I the Lord thy God am a jealous God, visiting the iniquity of the fathers upon the children unto the third and fourth generation of them that hate me;
And showing mercy unto thousands of them that love me, and keep my commandments.
Thou shalt not take the name of the Lord thy God in vain; for the Lord will not hold him guiltless that taketh his name in vain.
Remember the sabbath day, to keep it holy.
Six days shalt thou labour, and do all thy work:
But the seventh day is the sabbath of the Lord thy God: in it thou shalt not do any work, thou, nor thy son, nor thy daughter, thy manservant, nor thy maidservant, nor thy cattle, nor thy stranger that is within thy gates:
For in six days the Lord made heaven and earth, the sea, and all that in them is, and rested the seventh day: wherefore the Lord blest the sabbath day, and hallowed it.
Honour thy father and thy mother: that thy days may be long upon the land which the Lord thy God giveth thee.
Thou shalt not kill.
Thou shalt not commit adultery.
Thou shalt not steal.
Thou shalt not bear false witness against thy neighbour.
Thou shalt not covet thy neighbour's house, thou shalt not covet thy neighbour's wife, nor his manservant, nor his maidservant, nor his ox, nor his ass, nor any thing that is thy neighbour's.
20:1

25 Life for life,
Eye for eye, tooth for tooth, hand for hand, foot for foot,
Burning for burning, wound for wound, stripe for stripe.
21:23

26 Thou shalt not suffer a witch to live.
22:18

27 Thou shalt not seethe a kid in his mother's milk.
23:19

1 And thou shalt put in the breastplate of judgment the
   Urim and the Thummin. [Sacred symbols worn on the
   breastplate of the high priest.]
   28:30

2 These be thy gods, O Israel.
   32:4

3 And the people sat down to eat and to drink, and rose
   up to play.
   6

4 I will not go up in the midst of thee; for thou art a
   stiffnecked people: lest I consume thee in the way.
   33:3

5 There shall no man see me and live.
   20

LEVITICUS

6 And the swine, though he divide the hoof, and be
   cloven-footed, yet he cheweth not the cud; he is
   unclean to you.
   11:7

7 Let him go for a scapegoat into the wilderness.
   16:10

8 Thou shalt love thy neighbour as thyself.
   19:18. See Matt. 19:19

NUMBERS

9 The Lord bless thee, and keep thee:
   The Lord make his face shine upon thee, and be
   gracious unto thee:
   The Lord lift up his countenance upon thee, and give
   thee peace.
   6:24

10 These are the names of the men which Moses sent to
   spy out the land.
   13:16

11 And there we saw the giants, the sons of Anak, which
   come of the giants: and we were in our own sight as
   grasshoppers, and so we were in their sight.
   33

12 And Israel smote him with the edge of the sword, and
   possessed his land.
   21:24

13 He whom thou blessest is blessed, and he whom thou
   cursest is cursed.
   22:6

14 God is not a man, that he should lie.
   23:19

15 What hath God wrought!
   23. Quoted by Samuel Morse in the first electric telegraph
   message, Washington, 24 May 1844

16 I called thee to curse mine enemies, and, behold, thou
   hast altogether blessed them these three times.
   24:10

17 Be sure your sin will find you out.
   32:23

DEUTERONOMY

18 I call heaven and earth to witness against you this day.
   4:26

19 Remember that thou wast a servant in the land of
   Egypt, and that the Lord thy God brought thee out

thence through a mighty hand and by a stretched out
arm.
5:15

20 Hear, O Israel: The Lord our God is one Lord.
   6:4

21 For the Lord thy God is a jealous God.
   15

22 Man doth not live by bread only, but by every word
   that proceedeth out of the mouth of the Lord doth man
   live.
   8:3. See 64:1

23 If there arise among you a prophet, or a dreamer of
   dreams...Thou shalt not hearken.
   13:1

24 If thy brother, the son of thy mother, or thy son, or thy
   daughter, or the wife of thy bosom, or thy friend,
   which is as thine own soul, entice thee secretly...Thou
   shalt not consent.
   6

25 Thou shalt not muzzle the ox when he treadeth out the
   corn.
   25:4

26 Cursed be he that removeth his neighbour's landmark.
   27:17

27 In the morning thou shalt say, Would God it were
   even! and at even thou shalt say, Would God it were
   morning!
   28:67

28 The secret things belong unto the Lord our God.
   29:29

29 I have set before you life and death, blessing and
   cursing: therefore choose life that both thou and thy
   seed may live.
   30:19

30 He found him in a desert land, and in the waste
   howling wilderness; he led him about, he kept him as
   the apple of his eye.
   32:10

31 For they are a very froward generation, children in
   whom is no faith.
   20

32 I will heap mischiefs upon them; I will spend mine
   arrows upon them.
   23

33 The eternal God is thy refuge, and underneath are the
   everlasting arms.
   33:27

34 No man knoweth of his [Moses'] sepulchre unto this
   day.
   34:6

JOSHUA

35 As I was with Moses, so I will be with thee: I will not
   fail thee, nor forsake thee.
   1:5

36 Be strong and of a good courage; be not afraid,
   neither be thou dismayed: for the Lord thy God is with
   thee, whithersoever thou goest.
   9

37 This line of scarlet thread.
   2:18

1 All the Israelites passed over on dry ground.
3:17

2 When the people heard the sound of the trumpet, and the people shouted with a great shout, that the wall fell down flat, so that the people went up into the city.
6:20

3 Let them live; but let them be hewers of wood and drawers of water unto all the congregation.
9:21

4 Sun, stand thou still upon Gibeon; and thou, Moon, in the valley of Ajalon.
10:12

5 I am going the way of all the earth.
13:14

JUDGES

6 He delivered them into the hands of spoilers.
2:14

7 Then Jael Heber's wife took a nail of the tent, and took an hammer in her hand, and went softly unto him, and smote the nail into his temples, and fastened it into the ground: for he was fast asleep and weary.
4:21

8 I arose a mother in Israel.
5:7

9 The stars in their courses fought against Sisera.
20

10 He asked water, and she gave him milk; she brought forth butter in a lordly dish. [Jael.]
25

11 At her feet he bowed, he fell, he lay down.
27

12 The mother of Sisera looked out at a window, and cried through the lattice, Why is his chariot so long in coming? why tarry the wheels of his chariots?
28

13 Have they not divided the prey; to every man a damsel or two?
30

14 The Lord is with thee, thou mighty man of valour.
6:12

15 The Spirit of the Lord came upon Gideon, and he blew a trumpet.
34

16 The host of Midian was beneath him in the valley.
7:8

17 Is not the gleaning of the grapes of Ephraim better than the vintage of Abi-ezer?
8:2

18 Faint, yet pursuing.
4

19 Let fire come out of the bramble and devour the cedars of Lebanon.
9:15

20 Then said they unto him, Say now Shibboleth: and he said Sibboleth: for he could not frame to pronounce it right. Then they took him, and slew him.
12:6

21 Out of the eater came forth meat, and out of the strong came forth sweetness.
14:14

22 If ye had not plowed with my heifer, ye had not found out my riddle.
18

23 He smote them hip and thigh.
15:8

24 With the jawbone of an ass, heaps upon heaps, with the jaw of an ass have I slain a thousand men.
16

25 The Philistines be upon thee, Samson.
16:9

26 He wist not that the Lord was departed from him.
20

27 He did grind in the prison house.
21

28 The dead which he slew at his death were more than they which he slew in his life.
30

29 In those days there was no king in Israel, but every man did that which was right in his own eyes.
17:6

30 From Dan even to Beer-sheba.
20:1

31 The people arose as one man.
8

RUTH

32 Intreat me not to leave thee, or to return from following after thee: for whither thou goest, I will go; and where thou lodgest, I will lodge: thy people shall be my people, and thy God my God:
Where thou diest, will I die, and there will I be buried: the Lord do so to me, and more also, if ought but death part thee and me.
1:16

1 SAMUEL

33 All the increase of thy house shall die in the flower of their age.
2:33

34 The Lord called Samuel: and he answered, Here am I.
3:4

35 Here am I; for thou calledst me. And he said, I called not; lie down again.
5

36 Speak, Lord; for thy servant heareth.
9

37 The ears of every one that heareth it shall tingle.
11

38 Quit yourselves like men, and fight.
4:9

39 He fell from off the seat backward by the side of the gate, and his neck brake.
18

40 And she named the child I-chabod, saying, The glory is departed from Israel.
21

41 Is Saul also among the prophets?
10:11

42 God save the king.
24

1 A man after his own heart.
13:14

2 Come up to us and we will shew you a thing.
14:12

3 I did but taste a little honey with the end of the rod that was in mine hand, and, lo, I must die.
43

4 To obey is better than sacrifice, and to hearken than the fat of rams.
For rebellion is as the sin of witchcraft.
15:22

5 Agag came unto him delicately. And Agag said, Surely the bitterness of death is past.
32

6 For the Lord seeth not as man seeth: for man looketh on the outward appearance, but the Lord looketh on the heart.
16:7

7 Now he was ruddy, and withal of a beautiful countenance, and goodly to look to.
12

8 I know thy pride, and the naughtiness of thine heart.
17:28

9 Let no man's heart fail because of him [Goliath].
32

10 Go, and the Lord be with thee.
37

11 And he took his staff in his hand and chose him five smooth stones out of the brook. [David.]
40

12 Am I a dog, that thou comest to me with staves?
43

13 Saul hath slain his thousands, and David his ten thousands.
18:7

14 And Saul said, God hath delivered him into mine hand.
23:7

15 Behold, I have played the fool, and have erred exceedingly. [Saul.]
26:21

2 SAMUEL

16 The beauty of Israel is slain upon thy high places: how are the mighty fallen!
Tell it not in Gath, publish it not in the streets of Askelon; lest the daughters of the Philistines rejoice, lest the daughters of the uncircumcised triumph.
Ye mountains of Gilboa, let there be no dew, neither let there be rain, upon you, nor fields of offerings: for there the shield of the mighty is vilely cast away.
1:19

17 Saul and Jonathan were lovely and pleasant in their lives, and in their death they were not divided: they were swifter than eagles, they were stronger than lions.
Ye daughters of Israel, weep over Saul, who clothed you in scarlet, with other delights, who put on ornaments of gold upon your apparel.
How are the mighty fallen in the midst of the battle! O Jonathan, thou wast slain in thine high places.
I am distressed for thee, my brother Jonathan: very

pleasant hast thou been unto me: thy love to me was wonderful, passing the love of women.
How are the mighty fallen, and the weapons of war perished!
23

18 And David danced before the Lord with all his might.
6:14

19 Set ye Uriah in the forefront of the hottest battle, and retire ye from him, that he may be smitten, and die.
11:15

20 The poor man had nothing, save one little ewe lamb.
12:3

21 Thou art the man.
7

22 While the child was yet alive, I fasted and wept... But now he is dead, wherefore should I fast? can I bring him back again? I shall go to him but he shall not return to me.
22

23 For we needs must die, and are as water spilt on the ground, which cannot be gathered up again; neither doth God respect any person.
14:14

24 Come out, come out, thou bloody man, thou son of Belial.
16:7

25 And when Ahithophel saw that his counsel was not followed, he saddled his ass, and arose, and gat him home to his house, to his city, and put his household in order, and hanged himself.
17:23

26 And the king was much moved, and went up to the chamber above the gate, and wept: and as he went, thus he said, O my son Absalom, my son, my son Absalom! would God I had died for thee, O Absalom, my son, my son!
18:33

27 By my God have I leaped over a wall.
22:30

28 David...the sweet psalmist of Israel.
23:1

29 Went in jeopardy of their lives.
17

1 KINGS

30 And Zadok the priest took an horn of oil out of the tabernacle, and anointed Solomon. And they blew the trumpet; and all the people said, God save king Solomon.
1:39

31 Then will I cut off Israel out of the land which I have given them; and this house, which I have hallowed for my name, will I cast out of my sight; and Israel shall be a proverb and a byword among all people.
9:7

32 And when the queen of Sheba had seen all Solomon's wisdom...there was no more spirit in her.
10:4

33 Behold, the half was not told me.
7

34 Once in three years came the navy of Tharshish, bringing gold, and silver, ivory, and apes, and

peacocks.
22

1 But king Solomon loved many strange women.
11:1

2 My little finger shall be thicker than my father's loins.
12:10

3 My father hath chastised you with whips, but I will chastise you with scorpions.
11

4 To your tents, O Israel: now see to thine own house, David.
16

5 He slept with his fathers.
14:20

6 He went and dwelt by the brook Cherith, that is before Jordan.
And the ravens brought him bread and flesh in the morning, and bread and flesh in the evening; and he drank of the brook.
17:5

7 An handful of meal in a barrel, and a little oil in a cruse.
12

8 How long halt ye between two opinions?
18:21

9 He is talking, or he is pursuing, or he is in a journey, or peradventure he sleepeth, and must be awaked.
27

10 There is a sound of abundance of rain.
41

11 There ariseth a little cloud out of the sea, like a man's hand.
44

12 He girded up his loins, and ran before Ahab.
46

13 He himself went a day's journey into the wilderness, and came and sat down under a juniper tree.
19:4

14 But the Lord was not in the wind: and after the wind an earthquake; but the Lord was not in the earthquake: And after the earthquake a fire: but the Lord was not in the fire: and after the fire a still small voice.
11

15 Elijah passed by him, and cast his mantle upon him.
19

16 Let not him that girdeth on his harness boast himself as he that putteth it off.
20:11

17 Naboth the Jezreelite had a vineyard, which was in Jezreel, hard by the palace of Ahab King of Samaria.
And Ahab spake unto Naboth, saying, Give me thy vineyard, that I may have it for a garden of herbs, because it is near unto my house.
21:1

18 Hast thou found me, O mine enemy?
20

19 I saw all Israel scattered upon the hills, as sheep that have not a shepherd.
22:17

20 Feed him with bread of affliction and with water of affliction, until I come in peace.
And Micaiah said, If thou return at all in peace, the

Lord hath not spoken by me.
27

21 And a certain man drew a bow at a venture, and smote the king of Israel between the joints of the harness.
34

2 KINGS

22 Elijah went up by a whirlwind into heaven.
And Elisha saw it, and he cried, My father, my father, the chariot of Israel, and the horsemen thereof.
2:11

23 The spirit of Elijah doth rest on Elisha.
15

24 Go up, thou bald head.
23

25 Is it well with the child? And she answered, It is well.
4:26

26 There is death in the pot.
40

27 He shall know that there is a prophet in Israel.
5:8

28 Are not Abana and Pharpar, rivers of Damascus, better than all the waters of Israel?
12

29 I bow myself in the house of Rimmon.
18

30 Whence comest thou, Gehazi?
25

31 Is thy servant a dog, that he should do this great thing?
8:13

32 Is it peace? And Jehu said, What hast thou to do with peace? turn thee behind me.
9:18

33 The driving is like the driving of Jehu, the son of Nimshi; for he driveth furiously.
20

34 She painted her face, and tired her head, and looked out at a window.
30

35 Had Zimri peace, who slew his master?
31

36 Who is on my side? who?
32

37 They found no more of her than the skull, and the feet, and the palms of her hands.
35

38 Thou trustest upon the staff of this bruised reed, even upon Egypt, on which if a man lean, it will go into his hand, and pierce it.
18:21

1 CHRONICLES

39 For we are strangers before thee, and sojourners, as were all our fathers: our days on the earth are as a shadow, and there is none abiding.
29:15

40 He died in a good old age, full of days, riches, and honour.
28

NEHEMIAH

1 Every one with one of his hands wrought in the work, and with the other hand held a weapon.
4:17

ESTHER

2 And if I perish, I perish.
4:16

3 Thus shall it be done to the man whom the king delighteth to honour.
6:6

4 Behold also, the gallows fifty cubits high.
7:9

JOB

5 The sons of God came to present themselves before the Lord, and Satan came also among them.
And the Lord said unto Satan, Whence comest thou? Then Satan answered the Lord, and said, From going to and fro in the earth, and from walking up and down in it.
1:6

6 Doth Job fear God for naught?
9

7 The Lord gave, and the Lord hath taken away; blessed be the name of the Lord.
21

8 All that a man hath will he give for his life.
2:4

9 And he took him a potsherd to scrape himself withal.
8

10 Curse God, and die.
9

11 Let the day perish wherein I was born, and the night in which it was said, There is a man child conceived.
3:3

12 For now should I have lain still and been quiet, I should have slept: then had I been at rest,
With kings and counsellors of the earth, which built desolate places for themselves.
13

13 There the wicked cease from troubling, and there the weary be at rest.
17

14 Wherefore is light given to him that is in misery, and life unto the bitter in soul?
20

15 Then a spirit passed before my face; the hair of my flesh stood up.
4:15

16 Shall mortal man be more just than God? shall a man be more pure than his maker?
17

17 Man is born unto trouble, as the sparks fly upward.
5:7

18 My days are swifter than a weaver's shuttle.
7:6

19 He shall return no more to his house, neither shall his place know him any more.
10

20 Let me alone, that I may take comfort a little,

Before I go whence I shall not return, even to the land of darkness and the shadow of death.
10:20

21 A land...where the light is as darkness.
22

22 Canst thou by searching find out God?
11:7

23 No doubt but ye are the people, and wisdom shall die with you.
12:2

24 With the ancient is wisdom; and in length of days understanding.
12

25 Though he slay me, yet will I trust in him: but I will maintain mine own ways before him.
13:15

26 Man that is born of a woman is of few days, and full of trouble.
He cometh forth like a flower, and is cut down: he fleeth also as a shadow, and continueth not.
14:1. See 389:11

27 Miserable comforters are ye all.
16:2

28 I also could speak as ye do: if your soul were in my soul's stead.
4

29 I am escaped with the skin of my teeth.
19:20

30 Oh that my words were now written! oh that they were printed in a book!
23

31 I know that my redeemer liveth, and that he shall stand at the latter day upon the earth:
And though after my skin worms destroy this body, yet in my flesh shall I see God.
25

32 Ye should say, Why persecute we him, seeing the root of the matter is found in me?
28

33 But where shall wisdom be found? and where is the place of understanding?
28:12

34 The price of wisdom is above rubies.
18

35 I was eyes to the blind, and feet was I to the lame.
29:15

36 For I know that thou wilt bring me to death, and to the house appointed for all living.
30:23

37 I am a brother to dragons, and a companion to owls.
29

38 My desire is...that mine adversary had written a book.
31:35

39 Great men are not always wise.
32:9

40 He multiplieth words without knowledge.
35:16

41 Who is this that darkeneth counsel by words without knowledge?
38:2

1 Gird up now thy loins like a man.
3

2 Where wast thou when I laid the foundations of the earth? declare, if thou hast understanding.
4

3 When the morning stars sang together, and all the sons of God shouted for joy.
7

4 Hath the rain a father? or who hath begotten the drops of dew?
28

5 Canst thou bind the sweet influences of Pleiades, or loose the bands of Orion?
31

6 He paweth in the valley, and rejoiceth in his strength: he goeth on to meet the armed men.
39:21

7 He swalloweth the ground with fierceness and rage: neither believeth he that it is the sound of the trumpet. He saith among the trumpets, Ha, ha; and he smelleth the battle afar off, the thunder of the captains, and the shouting.
24

8 Behold now behemoth. which I made with thee; he eateth grass as an ox.
40:15

9 He is the chief of the ways of God: he that made him can make his sword to approach unto him.
19

10 He lieth under the shady trees, in the covert of the reed, and fens.
The shady trees cover him with their shadow; the willows of the brook compass him about.
Behold, he drinketh up a river, and hasteth not.
21

11 Canst thou draw out leviathan with an hook?
41:1

12 I have heard of thee by the hearing of the ear: but now mine eye seeth thee.
42:5

13 So the Lord blessed the latter end of Job more than his beginning.
12

For psalms in the Book of Common Prayer see PRAYER BOOK.

PROVERBS

14 Surely in vain the net is spread in the sight of any bird.
1:17

15 For whom the Lord loveth he correcteth.
3:12

16 Length of days is in her right hand; and in her left hand riches and honour.
16

17 Her ways are ways of pleasantness, and all her paths are peace.
17

18 Wisdom is the principal thing; therefore get wisdom: and with all thy getting get understanding.
4:7

19 The path of the just is as the shining light, that shineth

more and more unto the perfect day.
18

20 For the lips of a strange woman drop as an honeycomb, and her mouth is smoother than oil:
But her end is bitter as wormwood, sharp as a twoedged sword.
Her feet go down to death; her steps take hold on hell.
5:3

21 Go to the ant thou sluggard; consider her ways, and be wise.
6:6

22 How long wilt thou sleep, O sluggard? When wilt thou arise out of thy sleep?
Yet a little sleep, a little slumber, a little folding of the hands to sleep:
So shall thy poverty come as one that travelleth, and thy want as an armed man.
9. See Prov. 24:33

23 Can a man take fire in his bosom, and his clothes not be burned?
27

24 Come, let us take our fill of love until the morning: let us solace ourselves with loves.
For the goodman is not at home, he is gone a long journey.
7:18

25 He goeth after her straightway, as an ox goeth to the slaughter.
22

26 Wisdom is better than rubies.
8:11

27 Wisdom hath builded her house, she hath hewn out her seven pillars.
9:1

28 Stolen waters are sweet, and bread eaten in secret is pleasant.
17

29 A wise son maketh a glad father: but a foolish son is the heaviness of his mother.
10:1

30 The destruction of the poor is their poverty.
15

31 He that is surety for a stranger shall smart for it.
11:15

32 As a jewel of gold in a swine's snout, so is a fair woman which is without discretion.
22

33 A virtuous woman is a crown to her husband.
12:4

34 A righteous man regardeth the life of his beast: but the tender mercies of the wicked are cruel.
10

35 Hope deferred maketh the heart sick: but when the desire cometh, it is a tree of life.
13:12

36 The way of transgressors is hard.
15

37 The desire accomplished is sweet to the soul.
19

38 He that spareth his rod hateth his son.
24

1 Even in laughter the heart is sorrowful.
14:13

2 In all labour there is profit.
23

3 Righteousness exalteth a nation.
34

4 A soft answer turneth away wrath.
15:1

5 A merry heart maketh a cheerful countenance.
13

6 Better is a dinner of herbs where love is, than a stalled ox and hatred therewith.
17. Better is a mess of pottage with love, than a fat ox with evil will. (Matthew's Bible, 1535)

7 A word spoken in due season, how good is it!
23

8 Pride goeth before destruction, and an haughty spirit before a fall.
16:18

9 He that is slow to anger is better than the mighty; and he that ruleth his spirit than he that taketh a city.
32

10 He that repeateth a matter separateth very friends.
17:9

11 A friend loveth at all times, and a brother is born for adversity.
17

12 A merry heart doeth good like a medicine.
22

13 A wounded spirit who can bear?
18:14

14 There is a friend that sticketh closer than a brother.
24

15 Wine is a mocker, strong drink is raging.
20:1

16 Every fool will be meddling.
3

17 Even a child is known by his doings.
11

18 The hearing ear, and the seeing eye, the Lord hath made even both of them.
12

19 It is naught, it is naught, saith the buyer: but when he is gone his way, then he boasteth.
14

20 It is better to dwell in a corner of the housetop, than with a brawling woman in a wide house.
21:9

21 A good name is rather to be chosen than great riches.
22:1

22 Train up a child in the way he should go: and when he is old, he will not depart from it.
6

23 Remove not the ancient landmark, which thy fathers have set.
28

24 Look not thou upon the wine when it is red, when it giveth his colour in the cup,...
At the last it biteth like a serpent, and stingeth like an adder.
23:31

25 The heart of kings is unsearchable.
25:3

26 A word fitly spoken is like apples of gold in pictures of silver.
11

27 Whoso boasteth himself of a false gift is like clouds and wind without rain.
14

28 Withdraw thy foot from thy neighbour's house; lest he be weary of thee, and so hate thee.
17

29 If thine enemy be hungry, give him bread to eat; and if he be thirsty, give him water to drink.
For thou shalt heap coals of fire upon his head, and the Lord shall reward thee.
21

30 As cold waters to a thirsty soul, so is good news from a far country.
25

31 Answer not a fool according to his folly, lest thou also be like unto him.
Answer a fool according to his folly, lest he be wise in his own conceit.
26:4

32 As a dog returneth to his vomit, so a fool returneth to his folly.
11

33 Seest thou a man wise in his own conceit? There is more hope of a fool than of him.
12

34 The slothful man saith, There is a lion in the way: a lion is in the streets.
13

35 The sluggard is wiser in his own conceit than seven men that can render a reason.
16

36 Boast not thyself of to morrow; for thou knowest not what a day may bring forth.
27:1

37 Open rebuke is better than secret love.
5

38 Faithful are the wounds of a friend.
6

39 A continual dropping in a very rainy day and a contentious woman are alike.
15

40 Iron sharpeneth iron; so a man sharpeneth the countenance of his friend.
17

41 The wicked flee when no man pursueth: but the righteous are bold as a lion.
28:1

42 He that maketh haste to be rich shall not be innocent.
20

43 A fool uttereth all his mind.
29:11

44 Where there is no vision, the people perish.
18

45 Give me neither poverty nor riches; feed me with food convenient for me.
30:8

46 There are three things that are never satisfied, yea,

four things say not, It is enough:
The grave; and the barren womb; the earth that is not filled with water; and the fire that saith not, It is enough.
15

1 There be three things which are too wonderful for me, yea, four which I know not:
The way of an eagle in the air; the way of a serpent upon a rock; the way of a ship in the midst of the sea; and the way of a man with a maid.
18

2 It is not for kings, O Lemuel, it is not for kings to drink wine; nor for princes strong drink:
Lest they drink and forget the law, and pervert the judgment of any of the afflicted.
Give strong drink unto him that is ready to perish, and wine unto those that be of heavy hearts.
Let him drink, and forget his poverty, and remember his misery no more.
31:4

3 Who can find a virtuous woman? for her price is far above rubies.
10

4 Her children arise up, and call her blessed.
28

ECCLESIASTES

5 Vanity of vanities, saith the Preacher, vanity of vanities; all is vanity.
What profit hath a man of all his labour which he taketh under the sun?
One generation passeth away, and another generation cometh.
1:2. See 83:14

6 All the rivers run into the sea; yet the sea is not full.
7

7 All things are full of labour; man cannot utter it: the eye is not satisfied with seeing, nor the ear filled with hearing.
The thing that hath been, it is that which shall be; and that which is done is that which shall be done: and there is no new thing under the sun.
8

8 All is vanity and vexation of spirit.
14

9 He that increaseth knowledge increaseth sorrow.
18

10 Wisdom excelleth folly, as far as light excelleth darkness.
2:13

11 One event happeneth to them all.
14

12 To every thing there is a season, and a time to every purpose under the heaven:
A time to be born, and a time to die; a time to plant, and a time to pluck up that which is planted;
A time to kill, and a time to heal; a time to break down, and a time to build up;
A time to weep, and a time to laugh; a time to mourn, and a time to dance;
A time to cast away stones, and a time to gather stones together; a time to embrace, and a time to refrain from embracing;

A time to get, and a time to lose; a time to keep, and a time to cast away;
A time to rend, and a time to sew; a time to keep silence, and a time to speak;
A time to love, and a time to hate; a time of war, and a time of peace.
3:1

13 For that which befalleth the sons of men befalleth beasts; even one thing befalleth them: as the one dieth, so dieth the other; yea, they have all one breath; so that a man hath no preeminence above a beast: for all is vanity.
19

14 Wherefore I praised the dead which are already dead more than the living which are yet alive.
4:2

15 A threefold cord is not quickly broken.
12

16 God is in heaven, and thou upon earth: therefore let thy words be few.
5:2

17 The sleep of a labouring man is sweet.
12

18 As the crackling of thorns under a pot, so is the laughter of a fool.
7:6

19 Better is the end of a thing than the beginning thereof.
8

20 Say not thou, What is the cause that the former days were better than these? for thou dost not enquire wisely concerning this.
10

21 In the day of prosperity be joyful, but in the day of adversity consider.
14

22 Be not righteous over much.
16

23 One man among a thousand have I found; but a woman among all those have I not found.
28

24 God hath made man upright; but they have sought out many inventions.
29

25 There is no man that hath power over the spirit to retain the spirit; neither hath he power in the day of death; there is no discharge in that war.
8:8

26 A man hath no better thing under the sun, than to eat, and to drink, and to be merry.
15. See 58:15, 70:4, 76:24

27 A living dog is better than a dead lion.
9:4

28 Go thy way, eat thy bread with joy, and drink thy wine with a merry heart; for God now accepteth thy works.
7

29 Whatsoever thy hand findeth to do, do it with thy might; for there is no work, nor device, nor knowledge, nor wisdom, in the grave, whither thou goest.
10

30 The race is not to the swift, nor the battle to the strong.
11

1 Dead flies cause the ointment of the apothecary to send forth a stinking savour.
10:1

2 He that diggeth a pit shall fall into it.
8

3 Woe to thee, O land, when thy king is a child, and thy princes eat in the morning!
16

4 Wine maketh merry: but money answereth all things.
19

5 Cast thy bread upon the waters: for thou shalt find it after many days.
11:1

6 In the place where the tree falleth, there it shall be.
3

7 He that observeth the wind shall not sow; and he that regardeth the clouds shall not reap.
4

8 In the morning sow thy seed, and in the evening withhold not thine hand.
6

9 Truly the light is sweet, and a pleasant thing it is for the eyes to behold the sun.
7

10 Rejoice, O young man, in thy youth; and let thy heart cheer thee in the days of thy youth.
9

11 Remember now thy Creator in the days of thy youth, while the evil days come not, nor the years draw nigh, when thou shalt say, I have no pleasure in them;
While the sun, or the light, or the moon, or the stars, be not darkened, nor the clouds return after the rain:
In the day when the keepers of the house shall tremble, and the strong men shall bow themselves, and the grinders cease because they are few, and those that look out of the windows be darkened,
And the doors shall be shut in the streets, when the sound of the grinding is low, and he shall rise up at the voice of the bird, and all the daughters of musick shall be brought low;
Also when they shall be afraid of that which is high, and fears shall be in the way, and the almond tree shall flourish, and the grasshopper shall be a burden, and desire shall fail: because man goeth to his long home, and the mourners go about the streets:
Or ever the silver cord be loosed, or the golden bowl be broken, or the pitcher be broken at the fountain, or the wheel broken at the cistern.
Then shall the dust return to the earth as it was: and the spirit shall return unto God who gave it.
12:1

12 The words of the wise are as goads.
11

13 Of making many books there is no end; and much study is a weariness of the flesh.
12

14 Fear God, and keep his commandments: for this is the whole duty of man.
For God shall bring every work into judgment, with every secret thing, whether it be good, or whether it be evil.
13

SONG OF SOLOMON

15 The song of songs, which is Solomon's.
Let him kiss me with the kisses of his mouth: for thy love is better than wine.
1:1

16 I am black, but comely, O ye daughters of Jerusalem, as the tents of Kedar, as the curtains of Solomon.
5

17 O thou fairest among women.
8

18 A bundle of myrrh is my wellbeloved unto me; he shall lie all night betwixt my breasts.
13

19 I am the rose of Sharon, and the lily of the valleys.
2:1

20 His banner over me was love.
4

21 Stay me with flagons, comfort me with apples: for I am sick of love.
His left hand is under my head, and his right hand doth embrace me.
5

22 Rise up, my love, my fair one, and come away.
For, lo, the winter is past, the rain is over and gone;
The flowers appear on the earth; the time of the singing of birds is come, and the voice of the turtle is heard in our land.
2:10

23 Take us the foxes, the little foxes, that spoil the vines.
15

24 My beloved is mine, and I am his: he feedeth among the lilies.
Until the day break, and the shadows flee away.
16

25 By night on my bed I sought him whom my soul loveth.
3:1

26 Behold, thou art fair, my love; behold, thou art fair; thou hast doves' eyes within thy locks: thy hair is as a flock of goats, that appear from mount Gilead.
Thy teeth are like a flock of sheep that are even shorn, which came up from the washing; whereof every one bear twins, and none is barren among them.
Thy lips are like a thread of scarlet, and thy speech is comely: thy temples are like a piece of a pomegranate within thy locks.
Thy neck is like the tower of David builded for an armoury, whereon there hang a thousand bucklers, all shields of mighty men.
Thy breasts are like two young roes that are twins, which feed among the lilies.
4:1

27 Thou art all fair, my love; there is no spot in thee.
7

28 A garden inclosed is my sister, my spouse; a spring shut up, a fountain sealed.
12

29 Awake, O north wind; and come, thou south; blow upon my garden, that the spices thereof may flow out.

Let my beloved come into his garden, and eat his pleasant fruits.
16

1 I sleep, but my heart waketh: it is the voice of my beloved that knocketh, saying, Open to me, my sister, my love, my dove, my undefiled.
5:2

2 The watchmen that went about the city found me, they smote me, they wounded me; the keepers of the walls took away my veil from me.
I charge you, O daughters of Jerusalem, if ye find my beloved, that ye tell him, that I am sick of love.
What is thy beloved more than another beloved, O thou fairest among women?
7

3 My beloved is white and ruddy, the chiefest among ten thousand.
10

4 His hands are as gold rings set with the beryl: his belly is as bright ivory overlaid with sapphires.
His legs are as pillars of marble, set upon sockets of fine gold: his countenance is as Lebanon, excellent as the cedars.
His mouth is most sweet: yea, he is altogether lovely. This is my beloved, and this is my friend, O daughters of Jerusalem.
14

5 Who is she that looketh forth as the morning, fair as the moon, clear as the sun, and terrible as an army with banners?
6:10

6 Return, return, O Shulamite; return, return, that we may look upon thee.
13

7 How beautiful are thy feet with shoes, O prince's daughter!
7:1

8 Thy navel is like a round goblet, which wanteth not liquor: thy belly is like an heap of wheat set about with lilies.
2

9 Thy neck is as a tower of ivory; thine eyes like the fishpools in Heshbon, by the gate of Bath-rabbim: thy nose is as the tower of Lebanon which looketh toward Damascus.
4

10 Like the best wine, for my beloved, that goeth down sweetly, causing the lips of those that are asleep to speak.
9

11 Set me as a seal upon thine heart, as a seal upon thine arm: for love is strong as death; jealousy is cruel as the grave.
8:6

12 Many waters cannot quench love, neither can the floods drown it: if a man would give all the substance of his house for love, it would utterly be contemned.
7

13 We have a little sister, and she hath no breasts.
8

14 Make haste, my beloved, and be thou like to a roe or to a young hart upon the mountain of spices.
14

ISAIAH

15 The ox knoweth his owner, and the ass his master's crib.
1:3

16 The daughter of Zion is left as a cottage in a vineyard, as a lodge in a garden of cucumbers, as a besieged city.
8

17 Bring no more vain oblations; incense is an abomination unto me; the new moons and sabbaths, the calling of assemblies, I cannot away with.
13

18 Though your sins be as scarlet, they shall be as white as snow.
18

19 They shall beat their swords into plowshares, and their spears into pruninghooks: nation shall not lift up sword against nation, neither shall they learn war any more.
2:4

20 What mean ye that ye beat my people to pieces, and grind the faces of the poor?
3:15

21 My wellbeloved hath a vineyard in a very fruitful hill.
5:1

22 And he looked that it should bring forth grapes, and it brought forth wild grapes.
2

23 And he looked for judgment, but behold oppression; for righteousness, but behold a cry.
7

24 Woe unto them that join house to house, that lay field to field, till there be no place.
8

25 Woe unto them that rise up early in the morning, that they may follow strong drink.
11

26 Woe unto them that call evil good, and good evil.
20

27 For all this his anger is not turned away, but his hand is stretched out still.
25

28 In the year that king Uzziah died I saw also the Lord sitting upon a throne, high and lifted up, and his train filled the temple.
Above it stood the seraphims: each one had six wings; with twain he covered his face, and with twain he covered his feet, and with twain he did fly.
And one cried unto another, and said, Holy, holy, holy, is the Lord of hosts: the whole earth is full of his glory.
6:1

29 Then said I, Woe is me! for I am undone; because I am a man of unclean lips, and I dwell in the midst of a people of unclean lips.
5

30 Then flew one of the seraphims unto me, having a live coal in his hand...And he laid it upon my mouth, and said, Lo, this hath touched thy lips.
6

1 Whom shall I send, and who will go for us? Then said I, Here am I; send me.
8

2 Then said I, Lord, how long?
11

3 Behold, a virgin shall conceive, and bear a son, and shall call his name Immanuel.
Butter and honey shall he eat, that he may know to refuse the evil, and choose the good.
7:14

4 Sanctify the Lord of hosts himself; and let him be your fear, and let him be your dread.
And he shall be for a sanctuary; but for a stone of stumbling and for a rock of offence to both the houses of Israel.
8:13

5 Wizards that peep and that mutter.
19

6 The people that walked in darkness have seen a great light: they that dwell in the land of the shadow of death, upon them hath the light shined.
Thou hast multiplied the nation, and not increased the joy: they joy before thee according to the joy in harvest, and as men rejoice when they divide the spoil.
9:2

7 For unto us a child is born, unto us a son is given: and the government shall be upon his shoulder: and his name shall be called Wonderful, Counsellor, The mighty God, The everlasting Father, The Prince of Peace.
Of the increase of his government and peace there shall be no end.
6

8 The zeal of the Lord of hosts will perform this.
7

9 And there shall come forth a rod out of the stem of Jesse, and a Branch shall grow out of his roots:
And the spirit of the Lord shall rest upon him, the spirit of wisdom and understanding, the spirit of counsel and might, the spirit of knowledge and of the fear of the Lord.
11:1

10 The wolf also shall dwell with the lamb, and the leopard shall lie down with the kid; and the calf and the young lion and the fatling together; and a little child shall lead them.
6

11 And the lion shall eat straw like the ox.
And the sucking child shall play on the hole of the asp, and the weaned child shall put his hand on the cockatrice' den.
They shall not hurt nor destroy in all my holy mountain: for the earth shall be full of the knowledge of the Lord, as the waters cover the sea.
7

12 Dragons in their pleasant palaces.
13:22

13 How art thou fallen from heaven, O Lucifer, son of the morning!
14:12

14 Watchman, what of the night? Watchman, what of the night?
The watchman said, The morning cometh, and also the night.
21:11

15 Let us eat and drink; for to morrow we shall die.
22:13. See 55:26, 70:4, 76:24

16 Tyre, the crowning city, whose merchants are princes.
23:8

17 Howl, ye ships of Tarshish.
14

18 In this mountain shall the Lord of hosts make unto all people a feast of fat things, a feast of wine on the lees, of fat things full of marrow, of wine on the lees well refined.
25:6

19 He will swallow up death in victory; and the Lord God will wipe away tears from off all faces.
8

20 We have as it were brought forth wind.
26:18

21 For precept must be upon precept, precept upon precept; line upon line, line upon line; here a little, and there a little.
28:10

22 We have made a covenant with death, and with hell are we at agreement.
15

23 They are drunken, but not with wine.
29:9

24 Their strength is to sit still.
30:7

25 Now go, write it before them in a table, and note it in a book.
8

26 Speak unto us smooth things, prophesy deceits.
10

27 In quietness and in confidence shall be your strength.
15

28 The bread of adversity, and the waters of affliction.
20

29 This is the way, walk ye in it.
21

30 And a man shall be as an hiding place from the wind, and a covert from the tempest; as rivers of water in a dry place, as the shadow of a great rock in a weary land.
32:2

31 And thorns shall come up in her palaces, nettles and brambles in the fortresses thereof: and it shall be an habitation of dragons, and a court for owls.
34:13

32 The wilderness and the solitary place shall be glad for them; and the desert shall rejoice, and blossom as the rose.
35:1

33 Strengthen ye the weak hands, and confirm the feeble knees.
3

34 Then shall the lame man leap as an hart, and the tongue of the dumb sing: for in the wilderness shall waters break out, and streams in the desert.
6

35 The wayfaring men, though fools, shall not err

therein.
8

1 They shall obtain joy and gladness, and sorrow and sighing shall flee away.
10

2 Set thine house in order: for thou shalt die, and not live.
38:1

3 I shall go softly all my years in the bitterness of my soul.
15

4 Comfort ye, comfort ye my people, saith your God. Speak ye comfortably to Jerusalem, and cry unto her, that her warfare is accomplished.
40:1

5 The voice of him that crieth in the wilderness, Prepare ye the way of the Lord, make straight in the desert a highway for our God.
Every valley shall be exalted, and every mountain and hill shall be made low: and the crooked shall be made straight, and the rough places plain:
And the glory of the Lord shall be revealed, and all flesh shall see it together: for the mouth of the Lord hath spoken it.
3. See 63:36 ·

6 The voice said, Cry. And he said, What shall I cry?
All flesh is grass, and all the goodliness thereof is as the flower of the field:
The grass withereth, the flower fadeth: because the spirit of the Lord bloweth upon it: surely the people is grass.
6. See 80:21

7 He shall feed his flock like a shepherd: he shall gather the lambs with his arm, and carry them in his bosom, and shall gently lead those that are with young.
11

8 The nations are as a drop of a bucket, and are counted as the small dust of the balance: behold, he taketh up the isles as a very little thing.
15

9 Have ye not known? have ye not heard? hath it not been told you from the beginning?
21

10 But they that wait upon the Lord shall renew their strength: they shall mount up with wings as eagles; they shall run, and not be weary; and they shall walk, and not faint.
31

11 A bruised reed shall he not break, and the smoking flax shall he not quench.
42:3

12 He warmeth himself, and saith, Aha, I am warm, I have seen the fire.
44:16

13 Woe unto him that striveth with his maker! Let the potsherd strive with the potsherds of the earth. Shall the clay say to him that fashioneth it, What makest thou?
45:9

14 I have chosen thee in the furnace of affliction.
48:10

15 O that thou hadst hearkened to my commandments! then had thy peace been as a river, and thy

righteousness as the waves of the sea.
18

16 There is no peace, saith the Lord, unto the wicked.
22

17 Can a woman forget her sucking child, that she should not have compassion on the son of her womb? yea, they may forget, yet will I not forget thee.
49:15

18 How beautiful upon the mountains are the feet of him that bringeth good tidings, that publisheth peace; that bringeth good tidings of good, that publisheth salvation; that saith unto Zion, Thy God reigneth!
52:7

19 For they shall see eye to eye, when the Lord shall bring again Zion.
Break forth into joy, sing together, ye waste places of Jerusalem: for the Lord hath comforted his people, he hath redeemed Jerusalem.
8

20 Who hath believed our report? and to whom is the arm of the Lord revealed?
53:1

21 He hath no form nor comeliness; and when we shall see him there is no beauty that we should desire him.
He is despised and rejected of men; a man of sorrows, and acquainted with grief: and we hid as it were our faces from him; he was despised, and we esteemed him not.
Surely he hath borne our griefs, and carried our sorrows.
2

22 But he was wounded for our transgressions, he was bruised for our iniquities: the chastisement of our peace was upon him; and with his stripes we are healed.
All we like sheep have gone astray; we have turned every one to his own way; and the Lord hath laid on him the iniquity of us all.
He was oppressed, and he was afflicted, yet he opened not his mouth: he is brought as a lamb to the slaughter, and as a sheep before her shearers is dumb, so he openeth not his mouth.
5

23 He was cut off out of the land of the living.
8

24 He was numbered with the transgressors; and he bare the sin of many, and made intercession for the transgressors.
12

25 Ho, every one that thirsteth, come ye to the waters, and he that hath no money; come ye, buy, and eat; yea, come, buy wine and milk without money and without price.
Wherefore do ye spend money for that which is not bread? and your labour for that which satisfieth not?
55:1

26 Seek ye the Lord while he may be found, call ye upon him while he is near.
6

27 For my thoughts are not your thoughts, neither are your ways my ways, saith the Lord.
8

28 Instead of the thorn shall come up the fir tree, and

instead of the brier shall come up the myrtle tree.
13

1 I will give them an everlasting name, that shall not be cut off.
56:5

2 The righteous perisheth, and no man layeth it to heart.
57:1

3 Peace to him that is far off, and to him that is near.
19

4 Is not this the fast that I have chosen? to loose the bands of wickedness, to undo the heavy burdens, and to let the oppressed go free, and that ye break every yoke?
58:6

5 Then shall thy light break forth as the morning, and thine health shall spring forth speedily.
8

6 They make haste to shed innocent blood.
59:7

7 Arise, shine; for thy light is come, and the glory of the Lord is risen upon thee.
60:1

8 The Spirit of the Lord God is upon me...
To bind up the brokenhearted, to proclaim liberty to the captives, and the opening of the prison to them that are bound;
To proclaim the acceptable year of the Lord, and the day of vengeance of our God; to comfort all that mourn.
61:1

9 To give unto them beauty for ashes, the oil of joy for mourning, the garment of praise for the spirit of heaviness.
3

10 Who is this that cometh from Edom, with dyed garments from Bozrah?
63:1

11 I have trodden the winepress alone.
3

12 All our righteousnesses are as filthy rags; and we all do fade as a leaf.
64:6

13 [A people] Which say, Stand by thyself, come not near to me; for I am holier than thou.
65:5

14 For, behold, I create new heavens and a new earth.
17

JEREMIAH

15 Can a maid forget her ornaments, or a bride her attire?
2:32

16 They were as fed horses in the morning: every one neighed after his neighbour's wife.
5:8

17 This people hath a revolting and a rebellious heart.
23

18 The prophets prophesy falsely, and the priests bear rule by their means; and my people love to have it so: and what will ye do in the end thereof?
31

19 They have healed also the hurt of the daughter of my people slightly, saying, Peace, peace; when there is no peace.
6:14

20 The harvest is past, the summer is ended, and we are not saved.
8:20

21 Is there no balm in Gilead?
22

22 Can the Ethiopian change his skin, or the leopard his spots?
13:23

23 Woe is me, my mother, that thou hast borne me a man of strife and a man of contention to the whole earth!
15:10

24 The heart is deceitful above all things, and desperately wicked.
17:9

25 As the partridge sitteth on eggs, and hatcheth them not; so he that getteth riches, and not by right, shall leave them in the midst of his days.
11

26 Behold, I will make thee a terror to thyself, and to all thy friends.
20:4

LAMENTATIONS

27 How doth the city sit solitary, that was full of people!
1:1

28 Is it nothing to you, all ye that pass by? behold, and see if there be any sorrow like unto my sorrow.
12

29 And I said, My strength and my hope is perished from the Lord:
Remembering mine affliction and my misery, the wormwood and the gall.
3:18

30 It is good for a man that he bear the yoke in his youth.
27

31 He giveth his cheek to him that smiteth him.
30

32 O Lord, thou hast seen my wrong: judge thou my cause.
4:59

EZEKIEL

33 As is the mother, so is her daughter.
16:44

34 The fathers have eaten sour grapes, and the children's teeth are set on edge.
18:2

35 When the wicked man turneth away from his wickedness that he hath committed, and doeth that which is lawful and right, he shall save his soul alive.
27

36 The king of Babylon stood at the parting of the ways.
21:21

37 She doted upon the Assyrians her neighbours, captains and rulers clothed most gorgeously, horsemen riding upon horses, all of them desirable young men.
23:12

38 The hand of the Lord was upon me, and carried me out in the spirit of the Lord, and set me down in the

midst of the valley which was full of bones.
37:1

1 Can these bones live?
3

2 Again he said unto me, Prophesy upon these bones, and say unto them, O ye dry bones, hear the word of the Lord.
4

DANIEL

3 To you it is commanded, O peoples, nations, and languages,
That at what time ye hear the sound of the cornet, flute, harp, sackbut, psaltery, dulcimer, and all kinds of musick, ye fall down and worship the golden image that Nebuchadnezzar the king hath set up:
And whoso falleth not down and worshippeth shall the same hour be cast into the middle of a burning fiery furnace.
3:4

4 Shadrach, Meshach, and Abed-nego, ye servants of the most high God, come forth and come hither.
26

5 In the same hour came forth fingers of a man's hand, and wrote over against the candlestick upon the plaister of the wall of the king's palace.
5:5

6 And this is the writing that was written, MENE, MENE, TEKEL, UPHARSIN.
This is the interpretation of the thing: MENE; God hath numbered thy kingdom, and finished it.
TEKEL; Thou art weighed in the balances and art found wanting.
PERES; Thy kingdom is divided, and given to the Medes and Persians.
25

7 Now, O king, establish the decree, and sign the writing, that it be not changed, according to the law of the Medes and Persians, which altereth not.
6:8

8 The Ancient of days did sit, whose garment was white as snow, and the hair of his head like the pure wool: his throne was like the fiery flame, and his wheels as burning fire.
A fiery steam issued and came forth from behind him: thousand thousands ministered unto him, and ten thousand times ten thousand stood before him: the judgment was set, and the books were opened.
7:9

9 O Daniel, a man greatly beloved.
10:11

10 Many shall run to and fro, and knowledge shall be increased.
12:4

HOSEA

11 They have sown the wind, and they shall reap the whirlwind.
8:7

12 I drew them...with bands of love.
11:4

JOEL

13 That which the palmerworm hath left hath the locust eaten.
1:4

14 I will restore to you the years that the locust hath eaten, the cankerworm, and the caterpillar, and the palmerworm, my great army which I sent among you.
2:25

15 And it shall come to pass afterward, that I will pour out my spirit upon all flesh; and your sons and your daughters shall prophesy, your old men shall dream dreams, your young men shall see visions.
28

16 Beat your plowshares into swords, and your pruninghooks into spears.
3:10

17 Multitudes, multitudes in the valley of decision: for the day of the Lord is near in the valley of decision.
14

AMOS

18 Can two walk together, except they be agreed?
3:3

19 Shall there be evil in a city, and the Lord hath not done it?
6

20 I have overthrown some of you, as God overthrew Sodom and Gomorrah, and ye were as a firebrand plucked out of the burning.
4:11

JONAH

21 Come, and let us cast lots, that we may know for whose cause this evil is upon us. So they cast lots, and the lot fell upon Jonah.
1:7

22 Jonah was in the belly of the fish three days and three nights.
17

MICAH

23 They shall sit every man under his vine, and under his fig tree.
4:4

24 But thou, Beth-lehem Ephratah, though thou be little among the thousands of Judah, yet out of thee shall he come forth unto me that is to be ruler in Israel.
5:2

25 What doth the Lord require of thee, but to do justly, and to love mercy, and to walk humbly with thy God?
6:8

NAHUM

26 Woe to the bloody city! it is all full of lies and robbery; the prey departeth not.
3:1

ZEPHANIAH

27 Woe to her that is filthy and polluted, to the

oppressing city!
3:1

HABAKKUK

1 Write the vision, and make it plain upon tables, that he may run that readeth it.
2:2

HAGGAI

2 Ye have sown much, and bring in little; ye eat but ye have not enough…and he that earneth wages earneth wages to put it into a bag with holes.
1:6

MALACHI

3 But unto you that fear my name shall the Sun of righteousness arise with healing in his wings.
4:2

APOCRYPHA. 1 ESDRAS

4 The first wrote, Wine is the strongest.
The second wrote, The king is strongest.
The third wrote, Women are strongest: but above all things Truth beareth away the victory.
3:10

5 Great is Truth, and mighty above all things.
4:41

2 ESDRAS

6 Nourish thy children, O thou good nurse; stablish their feet.
2:25

7 For the world has lost his youth, and the times begin to wax old.
14:10

8 I shall light a candle of understanding in thine heart, which shall not be put out.
25

TOBIT

9 So they went forth both, and the young man's dog with them.
5:16

WISDOM OF SOLOMON

10 The ear of jealousy heareth all things.
1:10

11 Let us crown ourselves with rosebuds, before they be withered.
2:8

12 Through envy of the devil came death into the world.
24

13 But the souls of the righteous are in the hand of God, and there shall no torment touch them.
In the sight of the unwise they seemed to die: and their departure is taken for misery,
And their going from us to be utter destruction: but they are in peace.
For though they be punished in the sight of men, yet is their hope full of immortality.

And having been a little chastised, they shall be greatly rewarded: for God proved them, and found them worthy for himself.
3:1

14 And in the time of their visitation they shall shine, and run to and fro like sparks among the stubble.
7

15 He, being made perfect in a short time, fulfilled a long time.
4:13

16 We fools accounted his life madness, and his end to be without honour:
How is he numbered among the children of God, and his lot is among the saints!
5:4

17 Even so we in like manner, as soon as we were born, began to draw to our end.
13

18 For the hope of the ungodly…passeth away as the remembrance of a guest that tarrieth but a day.
14

19 And love is the keeping of her laws; and the giving heed unto her laws is the assurance of incorruption.
6:18

ECCLESIASTICUS

20 For the same things uttered in Hebrew, and translated into another tongue, have not the same force in them: and not only these things, but the law itself, and the prophets, and the rest of the books, have no small difference, when they are spoken in their own language.
The Prologue

21 For the Lord is full of compassion and mercy, long-suffering, and very pitiful, and forgiveth sins, and saveth in time of affliction.
2:11

22 We will fall into the hands of the Lord, and not into the hands of men: for as his majesty is, so is his mercy.
18

23 Be not curious in unnecessary matters: for more things are shewed unto thee than men understand.
3:23

24 Be not ignorant of any thing in a great matter or a small.
5:15

25 A faithful friend is the medicine of life.
6:16

26 Laugh no man to scorn in the bitterness of his soul.
7:11

27 Miss not the discourse of the elders.
8:9

28 Open not thine heart to every man.
19

29 Give not thy soul unto a woman.
9:2

30 Forsake not an old friend; for the new is not comparable to him; a new friend is as new wine; when it is old, thou shalt drink it with pleasure.
10

31 Many kings have sat down upon the ground; and one

that was never thought of hath worn the crown.
11:5

1 Judge none blessed before his death.
28

2 He that toucheth pitch shall be defiled therewith.
13:1

3 For how agree the kettle and the earthen pot together?
2

4 When a rich man is fallen, he hath many helpers: he speaketh things not to be spoken, and yet men justify him: the poor man slipped, and yet they rebuked him too; he spake wisely, and could have no place.
14:22

5 When thou hast enough, remember the time of hunger.
18:25

6 Be not made a beggar by banqueting upon borrowing.
33

7 He that contemneth small things shall fall by little and little.
19:1

8 All wickedness is but little to the wickedness of a woman.
25:19

9 Neither [give] a wicked woman liberty to gad abroad.
25

10 A merchant shall hardly keep himself from doing wrong.
26:29

11 Many have fallen by the edge of the sword: but not so many as have fallen by the tongue.
28:18

12 And weigh thy words in a balance, and make a door and bar for thy mouth.
25

13 Envy and wrath shorten the life.
30:24

14 Leave off first for manners' sake.
31:17

15 Wine is as good as life to a man, if it be drunk moderately: what life is then to a man that is without wine? for it was made to make men glad.
27

16 Leave not a stain in thine honour.
33:22

17 Honour a physician with the honour due unto him for the uses which ye may have of him: for the Lord hath created him.
38:1

18 He that sinneth before his Maker, Let him fall into the hand of the physician.
15

19 The wisdom of a learned man cometh by opportunity of leisure: and he that hath little business shall become wise.
24

20 How can he get wisdom...whose talk is of bullocks?
25

21 Let us now praise famous men, and our fathers that begat us.
44:1

22 Such as did bear rule in their kingdoms.
3

23 Such as found out musical tunes, and recited verses in writing:
Rich men furnished with ability, living peaceably in their habitations.
5

24 There be of them, that have left a name behind them.
8

25 And some there be, which have no memorial.
9

26 Their bodies are buried in peace; but their name liveth for evermore.
14

27 As the flower of roses in the spring of the year, as lilies by the rivers of waters, and as the branches of the frankincense tree in the time of summer.
50:8

28 Get learning with a great sum of money, and get much gold by her.
51:28

2 MACCABEES

29 It is a foolish thing to make a long prologue, and to be short in the story itself.
2:32

30 When he was at the last gasp.
7:9

NEW TESTAMENT. ST. MATTHEW

31 There came wise men from the east to Jerusalem, Saying, Where is he that is born King of the Jews? for we have seen his star in the east, and are come to worship him.
2:1

32 They presented unto him gifts; gold, and frankincense, and myrrh.
11

33 They departed into their own country another way.
12

34 In Rama was there a voice heard, lamentation, and weeping, and great mourning, Rachel weeping for her children, and would not be comforted, because they are not.
18 and Jer. 31:15

35 Repent ye: for the kingdom of heaven is at hand.
3:2

36 The voice of one crying in the wilderness, Prepare ye the way of the Lord, make his paths straight.
3. See 59:5

37 John had his raiment of camel's hair, and a leathern girdle about his loins; and his meat was locusts and wild honey.
4

38 O generation of vipers, who hath warned you to flee from the wrath to come?
7

39 And now also the axe is laid unto the root of the trees.
10

40 This is my beloved Son, in whom I am well pleased.
17

1 Man shall not live by bread alone, but by every word that proceedeth out of the mouth of God.
4:4. See 48:22

2 Thou shalt not tempt the Lord thy God.
7 and Deut. 6:16

3 The devil taketh him up into an exceeding high mountain, and sheweth him all the kingdoms of the world, and the glory of them.
8

4 Angels came and ministered unto him.
11

5 [Jesus] saith unto them, Follow me, and I will make you fishers of men.
19

6 Blessed are the poor in spirit: for theirs is the kingdom of heaven.
Blessed are they that mourn: for they shall be comforted.
Blessed are the meek: for they shall inherit the earth.
Blessed are they which do hunger and thirst after righteousness: for they shall be filled.
Blessed are the merciful: for they shall obtain mercy.
Blessed are the pure in heart: for they shall see God.
Blessed are the peacemakers: for they shall be called the children of God.
5:3

7 Ye are the salt of the earth: but if the salt have lost his savour, wherewith shall it be salted?
13

8 Ye are the light of the world. A city that is set on an hill cannot be hid.
14

9 Let your light so shine before men, that they may see your good works.
16

10 Think not that I am come to destroy the law, or the prophets: I am come not to destroy, but to fulfil.
17

11 Except your righteousness shall exceed the righteousness of the scribes and Pharisees, ye shall in no case enter into the kingdom of heaven.
20

12 Whosoever shall say, Thou fool, shall be in danger of hell fire.
22

13 Agree with thine adversary quickly, whiles thou art in the way with him.
25

14 Till thou hast paid the uttermost farthing.
26

15 Swear not at all; neither by heaven; for it is God's throne:
Nor by the earth; for it is his footstool.
34

16 Let your communication be Yea, yea; Nay, nay.
37

17 Resist not evil: but whosoever shall smite thee on thy right cheek, turn to him the other also.
39

18 Whosoever shall compel thee to go a mile, go with him twain.
41

19 He maketh his sun to rise on the evil and on the good, and sendeth rain on the just and on the unjust.
45

20 For if ye love them which love you, what reward have ye? do not even the publicans the same?
46

21 Be ye therefore perfect, even as your Father which is in heaven is perfect.
48

22 When thou doest alms, let not thy left hand know what thy right hand doeth.
That thine alms may be in secret: and thy Father which seeth in secret himself shall reward you openly.
6:3

23 Use not vain repetitions, as the heathen do: for they think that they shall be heard for their much speaking.
7

24 After this manner therefore pray ye: Our Father which art in heaven, Hallowed be thy name.
Thy kingdom come. Thy will be done in earth, as it is in heaven.
Give us this day our daily bread.
And forgive us our debts, as we forgive our debtors.
And lead us not into temptation, but deliver us from evil: For thine is the kingdom, and the power, and the glory, for ever. Amen.
9 and Luke 11:2

25 Lay not up for yourselves treasures upon earth, where moth and rust doth corrupt, and where thieves break through and steal:
But lay up for yourselves treasures in heaven.
19

26 Where your treasure is, there will your heart be also.
21

27 No man can serve two masters…Ye cannot serve God and mammon.
24

28 Is not the life more than meat, and the body than raiment?
Behold the fowls of the air: for they sow not, neither do they reap, nor gather into barns.
25

29 Which of you by taking thought can add one cubit unto his stature?
27

30 Consider the lilies of the field, how they grow; they toil not, neither do they spin:
And yet I say unto you, That even Solomon in all his glory was not arrayed like one of these.
28

31 Seek ye first the kingdom of God, and his righteousness; and all these things shall be added unto you.
33

32 Take therefore no thought for the morrow: for the morrow shall take thought for the things of itself.
Sufficient unto the day is the evil thereof.
34

33 Judge not, that ye be not judged.
7:1. See 69:22

34 Why beholdest thou the mote that is in thy brother's eye, but considerest not the beam that is in thine own

eye?
3

1 Neither cast ye your pearls before swine.
6

2 Ask, and it shall be given you; seek, and ye shall find; knock, and it shall be opened unto you.
7

3 Every one that asketh receiveth; and he that seeketh findeth.
8

4 Or what man is there of you, whom if his son ask bread, will he give him a stone?
9

5 Therefore all things whatsoever ye would that men should do to you, do ye even so to them: for this is the law and the prophets.
12

6 Wide is the gate, and broad is the way, that leadeth to destruction, and many there be that go in thereat.
13

7 Strait is the gate, and narrow is the way, which leadeth unto life, and few there be that find it.
14

8 Beware of false prophets, which come to you in sheep's clothing, but inwardly they are ravening wolves.
15

9 Do men gather grapes of thorns, or figs of thistles?
16

10 By their fruits ye shall know them.
20

11 The winds blew, and beat upon that house; and it fell not: for it was founded upon a rock.
25

12 Every one that heareth these sayings of mine, and doeth them not, shall be likened unto a foolish man, which built his house upon the sand:
And the rain descended, and the floods came, and the winds blew, and beat upon that house; and it fell: and great was the fall of it.
27

13 For he taught them as one having authority, and not as the scribes.
29

14 Lord I am not worthy that thou shouldest come under my roof.
8:8

15 I am a man under authority, having soldiers under me: and I say to this man, Go, and he goeth; and to another, Come, and he cometh; and to my servant, Do this, and he doeth it.
9

16 I have not found so great faith, no, not in Israel.
10

17 But the children of the kingdom shall be cast out into outer darkness: there shall be weeping and gnashing of teeth.
12

18 The foxes have holes, and the birds of the air have nests; but the Son of man hath not where to lay his head.
20

19 Let the dead bury their dead.
22

20 The whole herd of swine ran violently down a steep place into the sea, and perished in the waters.
32

21 He saw a man, named Matthew, sitting at the receipt of custom: and he saith unto him, Follow me. And he arose and followed him.
9:9

22 Why eateth your Master with publicans and sinners?
11

23 They that be whole need not a physician, but they that are sick.
12

24 I am not come to call the righteous, but sinners to repentance.
13

25 Neither do men put new wine into old bottles.
17

26 Thy faith hath made thee whole.
22

27 The maid is not dead, but sleepeth.
24

28 He casteth out devils through the prince of the devils.
34

29 The harvest truly is plenteous, but the labourers are few.
37

30 Go rather to the lost sheep of the house of Israel.
10:6

31 Freely ye have received, freely give.
8

32 When ye depart out of that house or city, shake off the dust of your feet.
14

33 Be ye therefore wise as serpents, and harmless as doves.
16

34 The disciple is not above his master, nor the servant above his lord.
24

35 Are not two sparrows sold for a farthing? and one of them shall not fall on the ground without your Father.
29. See 70:3

36 The very hairs of your head are all numbered.
30

37 Fear ye not therefore, ye are of more value than many sparrows.
31

38 I came not to send peace, but a sword.
34

39 A man's foes shall be they of his own household.
36

40 He that findeth his life shall lose it: and he that loseth his life for my sake shall find it.
39

41 Whosoever shall give to drink unto one of these little ones a cup of cold water only in the name of a disciple, verily I say unto you, he shall in no wise lose his reward.
42

1 Art thou he that should come, or do we look for another?
11:3

2 What went ye out into the wilderness to see? A reed shaken with the wind?
But what went ye out for to see? A man clothed in soft raiment?...
But what went ye out for to see? A prophet? yea, I say unto you, and more than a prophet.
7

3 We have piped unto you, and ye have not danced; we have mourned unto you, and ye have not lamented.
17

4 Wisdom is justified of her children.
19

5 Come unto me, all ye that labour and are heavy laden, and I will give you rest.
Take my yoke upon you, and learn of me; for I am meek and lowly in heart: and ye shall find rest unto your souls.
For my yoke is easy, and my burden is light.
28

6 He that is not with me is against me.
12:30 and Luke 11:23

7 The blasphemy against the Holy Ghost shall not be forgiven unto men.
31

8 The tree is known by his fruit.
33

9 Out of the abundance of the heart the mouth speaketh.
34

10 Every idle word that men shall speak, they shall give account thereof in the day of judgment.
36

11 An evil and adulterous generation seeketh after a sign.
39

12 Behold, a greater than Solomon is here.
42

13 When the unclean spirit is gone out of a man, he walketh through dry places, seeking rest, and findeth none.
Then he saith, I will return into my house from whence I came out; and when he is come, he findeth it empty, swept, and garnished.
43

14 Then goeth he, and taketh with himself seven other spirits more wicked than himself, and they enter in and dwell there: and the last state of that man is worse than the first.
45

15 Behold my mother and my brethren!
49

16 Behold, a sower went forth to sow;
And when he sowed, some seeds fell by the wayside, and the fowls came and devoured them up:
Some fell upon stony places, where they had not much earth: and forthwith they sprung up, because they had no deepness of earth:
And when the sun was up, they were scorched; and because they had no root, they withered away.
And some fell among thorns; and the thorns sprang up and choked them:
But other fell into good ground, and brought forth

fruit, some an hundredfold, some sixtyfold, some thirtyfold.
13:3

17 He also that received the seed among the thorns is he that heareth the word; and the care of this world, and the deceitfulness of riches, choke the word, and he becometh unfruitful.
22

18 His enemy came and sowed tares.
25

19 An enemy hath done this.
28

20 The kingdom of heaven is like to a grain of mustard seed, which a man took, and sowed in his field:
Which indeed is the least of all seeds: but when it is grown, it is the greatest among herbs, and becometh a tree, so that the birds of the air come and lodge in the branches thereof.
31

21 The kingdom of heaven is like unto a merchant man, seeking goodly pearls:
Who, when he had found one pearl of great price, went and sold all that he had, and bought it.
45

22 Is not this the carpenter's son?
55

23 A prophet is not without honour, save in his own country, and in his own house.
57

24 They took up of the fragments that remained twelve baskets full.
14:20

25 In the fourth watch of the night Jesus went unto them, walking on the sea.
25

26 Be of good cheer; it is I; be not afraid.
27

27 O thou of little faith, wherefore didst thou doubt?
31

28 Not that which goeth into the mouth defileth a man; but that which cometh out of the mouth, this defileth a man.
15:11

29 They be blind leaders of the blind. And if the blind lead the blind, both shall fall into the ditch.
14

30 Truth, Lord: yet the dogs eat of the crumbs which fall from their masters' table.
27

31 When it is evening, ye say, It will be fair weather: for the sky is red.
16:2

32 Ye can discern the face of the sky; but can ye not discern the signs of the times?
3

33 Thou art Peter, and upon this rock I will build my church; and the gates of hell shall not prevail against it.
18

34 Get thee behind me, Satan.
23

35 What is a man profited, if he shall gain the whole

world, and lose his own soul?
26. See 68:34

1 If ye have faith as a grain of mustard seed, ye shall say unto this mountain, Remove hence to yonder place; and it shall remove.
17:20

2 Except ye be converted, and become as little children, ye shall not enter into the kingdom of heaven.
18:3

3 Whoso shall receive one such little child in my name receiveth me.
But whoso shall offend one of these little ones which believe in me, it were better for him that a millstone were hanged abut his neck, and that he were drowned in the depth of the sea.
5

4 It must needs be that offences come; but woe to that man by whom the offence cometh!
7

5 If thine eye offend thee, pluck it out, and cast it from thee: it is better for thee to enter into life with one eye, rather than having two eyes to be cast into hell fire.
9

6 For where two or three are gathered together in my name, there am I in the midst of them.
20

7 Lord, how oft shall my brother sin against me, and I forgive him? till seven times?
Jesus saith unto him I say not unto thee, Until seven times: but Until seventy times seven. [To Peter.]
21

8 What therefore God hath joined together, let not man put asunder.
19:6

9 If thou wilt be perfect, go and sell that thou hast, and give to the poor, and thou shalt have treasure in heaven.
21

10 He went away sorrowful: for he had great possessions.
22

11 It is easier for a camel to go through the eye of a needle, than for a rich man to enter into the kingdom of God.
24

12 With men this is impossible; but with God all things are possible.
26

13 But many that are first shall be last; and the last shall be first.
30

14 Why stand ye here all the day idle?
20:6

15 These last have wrought but one hour, and thou hast made them equal unto us, which have borne the burden and heat of the day.
12

16 I will give unto this last, even as unto thee.
Is it not lawful for me to do what I will with mine own?
14

17 It is written, My house shall be called the house of prayer; but ye have made it a den of thieves.
21:13 and Is. 56:7

18 For many are called, but few are chosen.
22:14

19 Whose is this image and superscription?
20

20 Render therefore unto Caesar the things which are Caesar's; and unto God the things that are God's.
21

21 For in the resurrection they neither marry, nor are given in marriage.
30

22 They make broad their phylacteries, and enlarge the borders of their garments,
And love the uppermost rooms at feasts, and the chief seats in the synagogues.
23:5

23 Whosoever shall exalt himself shall be abased; and he that shall humble himself shall be exalted.
12. See 70:9

24 Woe unto you, scribes, and Pharisees, hypocrites! for ye pay tithe of mint and anise and cummin, and have omitted the weightier matters of the law, judgment, mercy, and faith: these ought ye to have done, and not to leave the other undone.
Ye blind guides, which strain at a gnat, and swallow a camel.
23

25 Ye are like unto whited sepulchres, which indeed appear beautiful outward, but are within full of dead men's bones, and of all uncleanness.
27

26 O Jerusalem, Jerusalem, thou that killest the prophets, and stonest them which are sent unto thee, how often would I have gathered thy children together, even as a hen gathereth her chickens under her wings, and ye would not!
37

27 Ye shall hear of wars and rumours of wars: see that ye be not troubled: for all these things must come to pass but the end is not yet.
24:6

28 For nation shall rise against nation, and kingdom against kingdom.
7

29 When ye therefore shall see the abomination of desolation, spoken of by Daniel the prophet, stand in the holy place, (whoso readeth, let him understand:).
15 and Dan. 12:11

30 Wheresoever the carcase is, there will the eagles be gathered together.
28

31 Heaven and earth shall pass away, but my words shall not pass away.
35

32 For as in the days that were before the flood they were eating and drinking, marrying and giving in marriage, until the day that Noe entered into the ark,
And knew not until the flood came, and took them all away; so shall also the coming of the Son of Man be.
38

33 One shall be taken, and the other left.
40

1 Watch therefore: for ye know not what hour your Lord doth come.
42

2 Well done, thou good and faithful servant: thou hast been faithful over a few things, I will make thee a ruler over many things: enter thou into the joy of thy lord.
25:21

3 Lord, I knew thee that thou art an hard man, reaping where thou hast not sown, and gathering where thou hast not strawed.
24

4 Unto every one that hath shall be given, and he shall have abundance: but from him that hath not shall be taken away even that which he hath.
29

5 And he shall set the sheep on his right hand, but the goats on the left.
33

6 For I was an hungred, and ye gave me meat: I was thirsty and ye gave me drink: I was a stranger, and ye took me in:
Naked, and ye clothed me: I was sick, and ye visited me: I was in prison, and ye came unto me.
35

7 Inasmuch as ye have done it unto one of the least of these my brethren, ye have done it unto me.
40

8 There came unto him a woman having an alabaster box of very precious ointment, and poured it on his head, as he sat at meat.
But when his disciples saw it, they had indignation saying, To what purpose is this waste?
For this ointment might have been sold for much, and given to the poor.
26:7

9 What will ye give me, and I will deliver him unto you? And they covenanted with him for thirty pieces of silver.
15

10 It had been good for that man if he had not been born.
24

11 Jesus took bread, and blessed it, and brake it, and gave it to the disciples, and said, Take, eat; this is my body.
26

12 This night, before the cock crow, thou shalt deny me thrice.
34

13 Though I should die with thee, yet will I not deny thee.
35

14 If it be possible, let this cup pass from me.
39

15 What, could ye not watch with me one hour?
40

16 Watch and pray, that ye enter not into temptation: the spirit indeed is willing but the flesh is weak.
41

17 Friend, wherefore art thou come?
50

18 All they that take the sword shall perish with the sword.
52

19 Thy speech bewrayeth thee.
Then began he to curse and to swear, saying, I know not the man. And immediately the cock crew.
73

20 Have thou nothing to do with that just man.
27:19

21 He took water, and washed his hands before the multitude, saying, I am innocent of the blood of this just person: see ye to it.
24

22 His blood be on us, and on our children.
25

23 He saved others; himself he cannot save.
42

24 Eli, Eli, lama sabachthani?...My God, my God, why hast thou forsaken me?
46. See 390:16

25 And, lo, I am with you alway, even unto the end of the world.
28:20

ST. MARK

26 The sabbath was made for man, and not man for the sabbath.
2:27

27 If a house be divided against itself, that house cannot stand.
3:25

28 He that hath ears to hear, let him hear.
4:9

29 With what measure ye mete, it shall be measured to you.
24

30 My name is Legion: for we are many.
5:9

31 Clothed, and in his right mind.
15

32 Jesus, immediately knowing in himself that virtue had gone out of him, turned him about in the press, and said, Who touched my clothes?
30

33 I see men as trees, walking.
8:24

34 For what shall it profit a man, if he shall gain the whole world, and lose his own soul?
36. See 66:35

35 Lord, I believe; help thou mine unbelief.
9:24

36 Suffer the little children to come unto me, and forbid them not: for of such is the kingdom of God.
10:14

37 Beware of the scribes, which love to go in long clothing, and love salutations in the marketplaces,
And the chief seats in the synagogues, and the uppermost rooms at feasts:
Which devour widows' houses, and for a pretence make long prayers.
12:38

38 And there came a certain poor widow, and she threw

in two mites.
42

1 Watch ye therefore: for ye know not when the master of the house cometh...
Lest coming suddenly he find you sleeping.
13:35

2 Go ye into all the world, and preach the gospel to every creature.
16:15

ST. LUKE

3 It seemed good to me also...to write unto thee...most excellent Theophilus.
1:3

4 Hail, thou art highly favoured, the Lord is with thee: blessed art thou among women.
28

5 My soul doth magnify the Lord,
And my spirit hath rejoiced in God my Saviour.
For he hath regarded the low estate of his handmaiden: for, behold, from henceforth all generations shall call me blessed.
46

6 He hath shewed strength with his arm; he hath scattered the proud in the imagination of their hearts.
He hath put down the mighty from their seats, and exalted them of low degree.
He hath filled the hungry with good things; and the rich he hath sent empty away.
51

7 To give light to them that sit in darkness and in the shadow of death, to guide our feet into the way of peace.
79

8 And it came to pass in those days, that there went out a decree from Caesar Augustus, that all the world should be taxed.
2:1

9 She brought forth her firstborn son, and wrapped him in swaddling clothes, and laid him in a manger; because there was no room for them in the inn.
And there were in the same country shepherds abiding in the field, keeping watch over their flock by night.
And, lo, the angel of the Lord came upon them, and the glory of the Lord shone round about them: and they were sore afraid.
7

10 Behold, I bring you good tidings of great joy.
10

11 Glory to God in the highest, and on earth peace, good will toward men.
14

12 Lord, now lettest thou thy servant depart in peace, according to thy word.
29

13 Wist ye not that I must be about my Father's business?
49

14 Jesus increased in wisdom and stature, and in favour with God and man.
52

15 Be content with your wages.
3:14

16 And the devil, taking him up into a high mountain, shewed unto him all the kingdoms of the world in a moment of time.
4:5

17 Physician, heal thyself.
23

18 Master, we have toiled all the night, and have taken nothing: nevertheless at thy word I will let down the net.
5:5

19 No man...having drunk old wine straightway desireth new: for he saith, The old is better.
39

20 Woe unto you, when all men shall speak well of you!
6:26

21 Love your enemies, do good to them which hate you.
27

22 Judge not, and ye shall not be judged.
37. See 64:33

23 Give, and it shall be given unto you; good measure, pressed down, and shaken together, and running over, shall men give into your bosom.
38

24 Her sins, which are many, are forgiven; for she loved much.
7:47

25 No man, having put his hand to the plough, and looking back, is fit for the kingdom of God.
9:62

26 Peace be to this house.
10:5

27 For the labourer is worthy of his hire.
7

28 I beheld Satan as lightning fall from heaven.
18

29 Blessed are the eyes which see the things which ye see:
For I tell you, that many prophets and kings have desired to see those things which ye see, and have not seen them; and to hear those things which ye hear, and have not heard them.
23

30 A certain man went down from Jerusalem to Jericho, and fell among thieves.
30

31 He passed by on the other side.
31

32 He took out two pence, and gave them to the host...whatsoever thou spendeth more, when I come again, I will repay thee.
35

33 Go, and do thou likewise.
37

34 But Martha was cumbered about much serving, and came to him, and said, Lord, dost thou not care that my sister hath left me to serve alone? bid her therefore that she help me.
40

35 But one thing is needful: and Mary hath chosen that good part, which shall not be taken away from her.
42

36 When a strong man armed keepeth his palace, his

goods are in peace,
But when a stronger than he shall come upon him, and overcome him, he taketh from him all his armour wherein he trusted, and divideth his spoils.
11:21

1 No man, when he hath lighted a candle, putteth it in a secret place, neither under a bushel, but on a candlestick, that they which come in may see the light.
33

2 Woe unto you, lawyers! for ye have taken away the key of knowledge.
52

3 Are not five sparrows sold for two farthings, and not one of them is forgotten before God?
12:6. See 65:35

4 Soul, thou hast much goods laid up for many years; take thine ease, eat, drink, and be merry.
19. See 55:26, 58:15, 76:24

5 Thou fool, this night thy soul shall be required of thee.
20

6 Let your loins be girded about, and your lights burning.
35

7 When thou art bidden of any man to a wedding, sit not down in the highest room; lest a more honourable man than thou be bidden of him;
And he that bade thee and him come and say to thee, Give this man place; and thou begin with shame to take the lowest room.
14:8

8 Friend, go up higher.
10

9 For whosoever exalteth himself shall be abased; and he that humbleth himself shall be exalted.
11. See 67:23

10 They all with one consent began to make excuse...I pray thee have me excused.
18

11 I have married a wife, and therefore I cannot come.
20

12 Go out quickly into the streets and lanes of the city, and bring in hither the poor, and the maimed, and the halt, and the blind.
21

13 Go out into the highways and hedges, and compel them to come in.
23

14 For which of you, intending to build a tower, sitteth not down first, and counteth the cost, whether he have sufficient to finish it?
28

15 Leave the ninety and nine in the wilderness.
15:4

16 Rejoice with me; for I have found my sheep which was lost.
6

17 Joy shall be in heaven over one sinner that repenteth, more than over ninety and nine just persons, which need no repentance.
7

18 The younger son gathered all together, and took his journey into a far country, and there wasted his substance with riotous living.
13

19 He would fain have filled his belly with the husks that the swine did eat: and no man gave unto him.
And when he came to himself, he said, How many hired servants of my father's have bread enough and to spare, and I perish with hunger!
I will arise and go to my father, and will say unto him, Father, I have sinned against heaven, and before thee,
And am no more worthy to be called thy son: make me as one of thy hired servants.
16

20 Bring hither the fatted calf, and kill it.
23

21 This my son was dead, and is alive again; he was lost, and is found.
24

22 Which hath devoured thy living with harlots.
30

23 I cannot dig; to beg I am ashamed.
16:3

24 Take thy bill, and sit down quickly, and write fifty.
6

25 And the Lord commended the unjust steward, because he had done wisely: for the children of this world are in their generation wiser than the children of light.
8

26 Make to yourselves friends of the mammon of unrighteousness; that, when ye fail, they may receive you into everlasting habitations.
9

27 He that is faithful in that which is least is faithful also in much.
10

28 There was a certain rich man, which was clothed in purple and fine linen, and fared sumptuously every day:
And there was a certain beggar named Lazarus, which was laid at his gate, full of sores,
And desiring to be fed with the crumbs which fell from the rich man's table: moreover the dogs licked his sores.
And it came to pass that the beggar died, and was carried by the angels into Abraham's bosom.
19

29 Between us and you there is a great gulf fixed.
26

30 It were better for him that a millstone were hanged about his neck, and he cast into the sea.
17:2

31 The kingdom of God is within you.
21

32 Remember Lot's wife.
32

33 Men ought always to pray, and not to faint.
18:1

34 God, I thank thee, that I am not as other men are.
11

35 God be merciful to me a sinner.
13

36 How hardly shall they that have riches enter into the

kingdom of God!
24

1 Out of thine own mouth will I judge thee...Thou knewest that I was an austere man.
19:22

2 If these should hold their peace, the stones would immediately cry out.
40

3 If thou hadst known, even thou, at least in this thy day, the things which belong unto thy peace! but now they are hid from thy eyes.
42

4 And when they heard it, they said, God forbid.
20:16

5 In your patience possess ye your souls.
21:19

6 He shall shew you a large upper room furnished.
22:12

7 I am among you as he that serveth.
27

8 Nevertheless, not my will, but thine, be done.
42

9 And the Lord turned, and looked upon Peter.
61

10 For if they do these things in a green tree, what shall be done in the dry.
23:31

11 Father, forgive them: for they know not what they do.
34

12 Lord, remember me when thou comest into thy kingdom.
42

13 To day shalt thou be with me in paradise.
43

14 Father, into thy hands I commend my spirit.
46. See 391:15

15 He was a good man, and a just.
50

16 Why seek ye the living among the dead?
24:5

17 Their words seemed to them as idle tales.
11

18 Did not our heart burn within us, while he talked with us by the way?
32

19 He was known of them in breaking of bread.
35

20 A piece of a broiled fish, and of an honeycomb.
42

ST. JOHN

21 In the beginning was the Word, and the Word was with God, and the Word was God.
1:1

22 All things were made by him; and without him was not any thing made that was made.
3

23 And the light shineth in darkness; and the darkness comprehended it not.
5

24 There was a man sent from God, whose name was John.
6

25 He was not that Light, but was sent to bear witness of that Light.
That was the true Light, which lighteth every man that cometh into the world.
8

26 He was in the world, and the world was made by him, and the world knew him not.
He came unto his own, and his own received him not.
10

27 And the Word was made flesh, and dwelt among us, (and we beheld his glory, the glory as of the only begotten of the Father,) full of grace and truth.
14

28 No man hath seen God at any time.
18. See 1 John 4:12

29 I baptize with water: but there standeth one among you, whom ye know not;
He it is, who coming after me is preferred before me, whose shoe's latchet I am not worthy to unloose.
26

30 Behold the Lamb of God, which taketh away the sin of the world.
29

31 Can there any good thing come out of Nazareth?
46

32 Behold an Israelite indeed, in whom is no guile!
47

33 Woman, what have I to do with thee? mine hour is not yet come.
2:4

34 Every man at the beginning doth set forth good wine; and when men have well drunk, then that which is worse: but thou hast kept the good wine until now.
10

35 When he had made a scourge of small cords, he drove them all out of the temple.
15

36 The wind bloweth where it listeth, and thou hearest the sound thereof, but canst not tell whence it cometh, and whither it goeth.
3:8

37 How can these things be?
9

38 God so loved the world, that he gave his only begotten Son, that whosoever believeth in him should not perish, but have everlasting life.
16

39 Men loved darkness rather than light, because their deeds were evil.
19

40 God is a Spirit: and they that worship him must worship him in spirit and in truth.
4:24

41 They are white already to harvest.
35

42 Other men laboured, and ye are entered into their labours.
38

43 Except ye see signs and wonders, ye will not believe.
48

1 Rise, take up thy bed, and walk.
5:8

2 He was a burning and a shining light.
35

3 Search the scriptures; for in them ye think ye have eternal life: and they are which testify of me.
39

4 What are they among so many?
6:9

5 Gather up the fragments that remain, that nothing be lost.
12

6 Him that cometh to me I will in no wise cast out.
37

7 Verily, verily, I say unto you, He that believeth on me hath everlasting life.
47

8 It is the spirit that quickeneth.
63

9 And the scribes and the Pharisees brought unto him a woman taken in adultery.
8:3

10 He that is without sin among you, let him first cast a stone at her.
7

11 Neither do I condemn thee: go, and sin no more.
11

12 And ye shall know the truth, and the truth shall make you free.
32

13 Ye are of your father the devil, and the lusts of your father ye will do. He was a murderer from the beginning, and abode not in the truth, because there is no truth in him. When he speaketh a lie, he speaketh of his own: for he is a liar, and the father of it.
44

14 The night cometh, when no man can work.
9:4

15 He is of age; ask him: he shall speak for himself.
21

16 One thing I know, that, whereas I was blind, now I see.
25

17 I am the door.
10:9

18 I am the good shepherd: the good shepherd giveth his life for the sheep.
11

19 The hireling fleeth, because he is an hireling, and careth not for the sheep.
13

20 Other sheep I have, which are not of this fold.
16

21 Though ye believe not me, believe the works.
38

22 I am the resurrection, and the life.
11:25

23 Jesus wept.
35

24 Ye know nothing at all,
Nor consider that it is expedient for us, that one man

should die for the people, and that the whole nation perish not.
49

25 Why was not this ointment sold for three hundred pence, and given to the poor?
12:5

26 The poor always ye have with you.
8

27 Lord, dost thou wash my feet?
13:6

28 Now there was leaning on Jesus' bosom one of his disciples, whom Jesus loved.
23

29 That thou doest, do quickly.
27

30 Let not your heart be troubled: ye believe in God, believe also in me.
14:1

31 In my Father's house are many mansions...I go to prepare a place for you.
2

32 I am the way, the truth, and the life: no man cometh unto the Father, but by me.
6

33 Have I been so long time with you, and yet hast thou not known me, Philip?
9

34 Judas saith unto him, not Iscariot.
22

35 Peace I leave with you, my peace I give unto you: not as the world giveth, give I unto you.
27

36 Greater love hath no man than this, that a man lay down his life for his friends.
15:13

37 Ye have not chosen me, but I have chosen you.
16

38 It is expedient for you that I go away: for if I go not away, the Comforter will not come unto you.
16:7

39 I have yet many things to say unto you, but ye cannot bear them now.
12

40 A little while, and ye shall not see me: and again, a little while, and ye shall see me, because I go to the Father.
16

41 In the world ye shall have tribulation: but be of good cheer; I have overcome the world.
33

42 While I was with them in the world, I kept them in thy name: those that thou gavest me I have kept, and none of them is lost but the son of perdition.
17:12

43 Put up thy sword into the sheath.
18:11

44 Pilate saith unto him, What is truth?
38

45 Now Barabbas was a robber.
40

1 What I have written I have written.
19:22

2 Woman, behold thy son!...
Behold thy mother!
26

3 I thirst.
28

4 It is finished.
30

5 The first day of the week cometh Mary Magdalene
early, when it was yet dark, unto the sepulchre, and
seeth the stone taken away from the sepulchre.
20:1

6 So they ran both together: and the other disciple did
outrun Peter, and came first to the sepulchre.
4

7 They have taken away my Lord, and I know not where
they have laid him.
13

8 Jesus saith unto her, Woman, why weepest thou?
whom seekest thou? She supposing him to be the
gardener saith unto him, Sir, if thou have borne him
hence, tell me where thou hast laid him, and I will take
him away. [Mary Magdalene.]
15

9 Touch me not.
17. See 83:24

10 Except I shall see in his hands the print of the nails,
and put my finger into the print of the nails, and thrust
my hand into his side, I will not believe.
25

11 Be not faithless, but believing.
27

12 Thomas, because thou hast seen me, thou hast
believed: blessed are they that have not seen, and yet
have believed.
29

13 Simon Peter saith unto them, I go a fishing.
21:3

14 Simon, son of Jonas, lovest thou me more that
these?...Feed my lambs.
15

15 Feed my sheep.
16

16 Lord, thou knowest all things; thou knowest that I love
thee.
17

17 When thou wast young, thou girdedst thyself, and
walkedst whither thou wouldest: but when thou shalt
be old, thou shalt stretch forth thy hands, and another
shall gird thee, and carry thee whither thou wouldest
not.
18

18 Peter, turning about, seeth the disciple whom Jesus
loved following; which also leaned on his breast at
supper, and said Lord, which is he that betrayeth thee?
20

19 What shall this man do?
Jesus saith unto him, If I will that he tarry till I come,
what is that to thee?
21

ACTS OF THE APOSTLES

20 The former treatise have I made, O Theophilus, of all
that Jesus began both to do and teach,
Until the day in which he was taken up.
1:1

21 Ye men of Galilee, why stand ye gazing up into
heaven?
11

22 And suddenly there came a sound from heaven as of a
rushing mighty wind, and it filled all the house where
they were sitting.
And there appeared unto them cloven tongues like as
of fire.
2:2

23 Parthians, and Medes, and Elamites, and the dwellers
in Mesopotamia, and in Judaea, and Cappadocia, in
Pontus, and Asia.
Phrygia, and Pamphylia, in Egypt, and in the parts of
Libya about Cyrene, and strangers of Rome, Jews and
proselytes,
Cretes and Arabians, we do hear them speak in our
tongues the wonderful works of God.
9

24 And all that believed were together, and had all things
common.
44

25 Silver and gold have I none; but such as I have give I
thee.
3:6

26 Walking, and leaping, and praising God
8

27 It is not reason that we should leave the word of God,
and serve tables.
6:2

28 The witnesses laid down their clothes at a young
man's feet, whose name was Saul.
7:58

29 Saul was consenting unto his death.
8:1

30 Thy money perish with thee, because thou hast
thought that the gift of God may be purchased with
money.
20

31 Thou hast neither part nor lot in this matter.
21

32 Breathing out threatenings and slaughter.
9:1

33 Saul, Saul, why persecutest thou me?
4

34 It is hard for thee to kick against the pricks.
5

35 The street which is called Straight.
11

36 Dorcas: this woman was full of good works.
36

37 He fell into a trance,
And saw heaven opened, and a certain vessel
descending unto him, as it had been a great sheet knit
at the four corners, and let down to the earth:
Wherein were all manner of four-footed beasts of the
earth, and wild beasts, and creeping things, and fowls

of the air.
10:10

1 What God hath cleansed, that call not thou common.
15

2 God is no respecter of persons.
34. See 74:34

3 He was eaten of worms, and gave up the ghost. [Herod Agrippa I.]
23

4 The gods are come down to us in the likeness of men.
14:11

5 We also are men of like passions with you.
15

6 Come over into Macedonia, and help us.
16:9

7 What must I do to be saved?
30

8 The Jews which believed not, moved with envy, took unto them certain lewd fellows of the baser sort, and gathered a company, and set all the city on an uproar.
17:5

9 Those that have turned the world upside down are come hither also;
Whom Jason hath received: and these all do contrary to the decrees of Caesar, saying that there is another king, one Jesus.
6

10 What will this babbler say?
18

11 For all the Athenians and strangers which were there spent their time in nothing else, but either to tell, or to hear some new thing.
21

12 Ye men of Athens, I perceive that in all things ye are too superstitious.
For as I passed by, and beheld your devotions, I found an altar with this inscription, TO THE UNKNOWN GOD. Whom therefore ye ignorantly worship, him declare I unto you.
22

13 God that made the world and all things therein, seeing that he is Lord of Heaven and earth, dwelleth not in temples made with hands.
24

14 For in him we live, and move, and have our being.
28

15 Gallio cared for none of those things.
18:17

16 We have not so much as heard whether there be any Holy Ghost.
19:2

17 All with one voice about the space of two hours cried out, Great is Diana of the Ephesians.
34

18 I go bound in the spirit unto Jerusalem.
20:22

19 It is more blessed to give than to receive.
35

20 But Paul said, I am a man which am a Jew of Tarsus, a city in Cilicia, a citizen of no mean city.
21:39

21 And the chief captain answered, With a great sum

obtained I this freedom. And Paul said, But I was free born.
22:28

22 A conscience void of offence toward God, and toward men.
24:16

23 I appeal unto Caesar.
25:11

24 Hast thou appealed unto Caesar? unto Caesar shalt thou go.
12

25 Paul, thou art beside thyself; much learning doth make thee mad.
26:24

26 For this thing was not done in a corner.
26

27 Almost thou persuadest me to be a Christian.
28

28 I would to God, that not only thou, but also all that hear me this day, were both almost, and altogether such as I am, except these bonds.
29

ROMANS

29 Without ceasing I make mention of you always in my prayers.
1:9

30 I am debtor both to the Greeks, and to the Barbarians; both to the wise, and to the unwise.
14

31 The just shall live by faith.
17

32 Worshipped and served the creature more than the Creator.
25

33 Patient continuance in well doing.
2:7

34 For there is no respect of persons with God.
11. See 74:2

35 These...are a law unto themselves.
14

36 Let God be true, but every man a liar.
3:4

37 Let us do evil, that good may come.
8

38 For all have sinned, and come short of the glory of God.
23

39 For where no law is, there is no transgression.
4:15

40 Who against hope believed in hope, that he might become the father of many nations. [Abraham.]
18

41 Hope maketh not ashamed; because the love of God is shed abroad in our hearts by the Holy Ghost which is given unto us.
5:5

42 Where sin abounded, grace did much more abound.
20

43 Shall we continue in sin, that grace may abound? God forbid. How shall we, that are dead to sin, live

any longer in sin?
6:1

1 We also should walk in newness of life.
4

2 Christ being raised from the dead dieth no more; death hath no more dominion over him.
For in that he died, he died unto sin once: but in that he liveth, he liveth unto God.
9

3 The wages of sin is death.
23

4 Is the law sin? God forbid. Nay, I had not known sin, but by the law.
7:7

5 For the good that I would I do not: but the evil which I would not, that I do.
19. See 366:17

6 O wretched man that I am! who shall deliver me from the body of this death?
24

7 They that are after the flesh do mind the things of the flesh; but they that are after the Spirit the things of the Spirit.
For to be carnally minded is death.
8:5

8 For ye have not received the spirit of bondage again to fear; but ye have received the Spirit of adoption, whereby we cry, Abba, Father.
15

9 We are the children of God:
And if the children, then heirs; heirs of God, and joint-heirs with Christ.
16

10 For we know that the whole creation groaneth and travaileth in pain together until now.
22

11 All things work for good to them that love God.
28

12 If God be for us, who can be against us?
31

13 For I am persuaded, that neither death, nor life, nor angels, nor principalities, nor powers, nor things present, nor things to come,
Nor height, nor depth, nor any other creature, shall be able to separate us from the love of God, which is in Christ Jesus our Lord.
38

14 Shall the thing formed say to him that formed it, Why hast thou made me thus?
Hath not the potter power over the clay, of the same lump to make one vessel unto honour, and another unto dishonour?
9:20

15 I beseech you therefore, brethren, by the mercies of God, that ye present your bodies a living sacrifice, holy, acceptable unto God.
12:1

16 Rejoice with them that do rejoice, and weep with them that weep.
15

17 Mind not high things, but condescend to men of low

estate. Be not wise in you own conceits.
16

18 Vengeance is mine; I will repay, saith the Lord.
19

19 Be not overcome of evil, but overcome evil with good.
21

20 Let every soul be subject unto the higher powers...the powers that be are ordained of God.
13:1

21 For rulers are not a terror to good works, but to the evil.
3

22 Render therefore to all their dues: tribute to whom tribute is due; custom to whom custom; fear to whom fear; honour to whom honour.
Owe no man anything, but to love one another: for he that loveth another hath fulfilled the law.
7

23 Love is the fulfilling of the law.
10

24 Now it is high time to awake out of sleep: for now is our salvation nearer than when we believed.
The night is far spent, the day is at hand: let us therefore cast off the works of darkness, and let us put on the armour of light.
11

25 Make not provision for the flesh, to fulfil the lusts thereof.
14

26 Doubtful disputations.
14:1

27 Let every man be fully persuaded in his own mind.
5

28 Salute one another with an holy kiss.
16:16

1 CORINTHIANS

29 The foolishness of preaching to save them that believe.
1:21

30 God hath chosen the foolish things of the world to confound the wise; and God hath chosen the weak things of the world to confound the things which are mighty.
27

31 I have planted, Apollos watered; but God gave the increase.
3:6

32 Stewards of the mysteries of God.
4:1

33 A spectacle unto the world, and to angels.
9

34 Absent in body, but present in spirit.
5:3

35 Know ye not that a little leaven leaveneth the whole lump?
6

36 Christ our passover is sacrificed for us:
Therefore let us keep the feast, not with the old leaven, neither with the leaven of malice and wickedness; but with the unleavened bread of sincerity

and truth.
7

1 Your body is the temple of the Holy Ghost.
6:19

2 It is better to marry than to burn.
7:9

3 The unbelieving husband is sanctified by the wife.
14

4 The fashion of this world passeth away.
31

5 Knowledge puffeth up, but charity edifieth.
8:1

6 Who goeth a warfare any time at his own charges?
who planteth a vineyard, and eateth not of the fruit
thereof?
9:7

7 I am made all things to all men.
22

8 Know ye not that they which run in a race run all, but
one receiveth the prize?
24

9 Now they do it to obtain a corruptible crown; but we
an incorruptible.
I therefore so run, not as uncertainly; so fight I, not as
one that beateth the air:
But I keep under my body, and bring it into
subjection: lest that by any means, when I have
preached to others, I myself should be a castaway.
25

10 All things are lawful for me, but all things are not
expedient.
10:23

11 For the earth is the Lord's, and the fulness thereof.
26. See Ps. 24:1

12 Doth not even nature itself teach you, that, if, a man
have long hair, it is a shame unto him?
But if a woman have long hair, it is a glory to her.
11:14

13 Now there are diversities of gifts, but the same Spirit.
12:4

14 Though I speak with the tongues of men and of
angels, and have not charity, I am become as sounding
brass, or a tinkling cymbal.
And though I have the gift of prophecy, and
understand all mysteries, and all knowledge; and
though I have all faith, so that I could remove
mountains, and have not charity, I am nothing.
And though I bestow all my goods to feed the poor,
and though I give my body to be burned, and have not
charity, it profiteth me nothing.
Charity suffereth long, and is kind; charity envieth
not; charity vaunteth not itself, is not puffed up,
Doth not behave itself unseemly, seeketh not her own,
is not easily provoked, thinketh no evil;
Rejoiceth not in iniquity, but rejoiceth in the truth;
Beareth all things, believeth all things, hopeth all
things, endureth all things.
Charity never faileth: but whether there be prophecies,
they shall fail; whether there be tongues, they shall
cease; whether there be knowledge, it shall vanish
away.
For we know in part, and we prophesy in part.
But when that which is perfect is come, then that

which is in part shall be done away.
When I was a child, I spake as a child, I understood as
a child, I thought as a child: but when I became a
man, I put away childish things.
For now we see through a glass, darkly; but then face
to face: now I know in part; but then shall I know even
as also I am known.
And now abideth faith, hope, charity, these three; but
the greatest of these is charity.
13:1

15 If the trumpet give an uncertain sound, who shall
prepare himself to the battle?
14:8

16 Let your women keep silence in the churches: for it is
not permitted unto them to speak.
34

17 If they will learn any thing, let them ask their
husbands at home: for it is a shame for women to
speak in the church.
35

18 Let all things be done decently and in order.
40

19 Last of all he was seen of me also, as of one born out
of due time.
For I am the least of the apostles, that am not meet to
be called an apostle, because I persecuted the church
of God.
But by the grace of God I am what I am.
15:8

20 I laboured more abundantly than they all: yet not I,
but the grace of God which was with me
10

21 If in this life only we have hope in Christ, we are of
all men most miserable.
19

22 But now is Christ risen from the dead, and become the
firstfruits of them that slept.
For since by man came death, by man came also the
resurrection of the dead.
For as in Adam all die, even so in Christ shall all be
made alive.
20

23 The last enemy that shall be destroyed is death.
26

24 If after the manner of men I have fought with beasts at
Ephesus, what advantageth it me, if the dead rise not?
let us eat and drink; for to morrow we die.
32. See 55:26, 58:15, 70:4

25 Evil communications corrupt good manners.
33

26 One star differeth from another star in glory.
41

27 So also is the resurrection of the dead. It is sown in
corruption; it is raised in incorruption.
42

28 The first man is of the earth, earthy.
47

29 Behold, I shew you a mystery; We shall not all sleep,
but we shall all be changed,
In a moment, in the twinkling of an eye, at the last
trump: for the trumpet shall sound, and the dead shall
be raised incorruptible, and we shall be changed.
For this corruptible must put on incorruption, and this

mortal must put on immortality.
51

1 O death, where is thy sting? O grave, where is thy victory?
55

2 Quit you like men, be strong.
16:13

3 Let him be Anathema Maran-atha.
22

2 CORINTHIANS

4 Our sufficiency is of God;
Who also hath made us able ministers of the new testament; not of the letter, but of the spirit: for the letter killeth, but the spirit giveth life.
3:5

5 We have this treasure in earthen vessels.
4:7

6 We know that if our earthly tabernacle of this house were dissolved, we have a building of God, an house not made with hands, eternal in the heavens.
5:1

7 Now is the accepted time.
6:2

8 As having nothing, and yet possessing all things.
10

9 God loveth a cheerful giver.
9:7

10 For ye suffer fools gladly, seeing ye yourselves are wise.
19

11 Are they Hebrews? so am I. Are they Israelites? so am I. Are they the seed of Abraham? so am I.
Are they ministers of Christ? (I speak as a fool) I am more.
11:22

12 Of the Jews five times received I forty stripes save one.
Thrice was I beaten with rods, once was I stoned, thrice I suffered shipwreck, a night and a day have I been in the deep;
In journeyings often, in perils of waters, in perils of robbers, in perils by mine own countrymen, in perils by the heathen, in perils of the city, in perils in the wilderness, in perils in the sea, in perils among false brethren;
In weariness and painfulness, in watchings often, in hunger and thirst, in fastings often, in cold and nakedness.
Beside those things that are without, that which cometh upon me daily, the care of all the churches.
24

13 There was given to me a thorn in the flesh, the messenger of Satan to buffet me.
12:7

14 My strength is made perfect in weakness.
9

GALATIANS

15 The right hands of fellowship.
2:9

16 It is written, that Abraham had two sons, the one by a

bondmaid, the other by a freewoman.
But he who was of the bondwoman was born after the flesh; but he of the freewoman was by promise.
Which things are an allegory.
4:22

17 Ye are fallen from grace.
5:4

18 But the fruit of the Spirit is love, joy, peace, longsuffering, gentleness, goodness, faith,
Meekness, temperance.
22

19 Be not deceived; God is not mocked: for whatsoever a man soweth, that shall he also reap.
6:7

20 Let us not be weary in well doing: for in due season we shall reap, if we faint not.
9. See 2 Thess. 3:13

21 Ye see how large a letter I have written unto you with mine own hand.
11

EPHESIANS

22 Christ came and preached peace to you which were afar off, and to them that were nigh.
2:17

23 Unto me, who am less than the least of all saints, is this grace given, that I should preach among the Gentiles the unsearchable riches of Christ.
3:8

24 I bow my knees unto the Father of our Lord Jesus Christ,
Of whom the whole family in heaven and earth is named,
That he would grant you, according to the riches of his glory, to be strengthened with might by his Spirit in the inner man.
14

25 The love of Christ, which passeth knowledge.
19

26 Now unto him that is able to do exceeding abundantly above all that we ask or think, according to the power that worketh in us,
Unto him be glory in the church by Christ Jesus throughout all ages, world without end. Amen.
20

27 I therefore, the prisoner of the Lord, beseech you that ye walk worthy of the vocation wherewith ye are called.
4:1

28 He gave some, apostles; and some, prophets; and some, evangelists; and some, pastors and teachers;
For the perfecting of the saints, for the work of the ministry, for the edifying of the body of Christ:
Till we all come in the unity of the faith, and of the knowledge of the Son of God, unto a perfect man, unto the measure of the stature of the fulness of Christ:
That we henceforth be no more carried about with every wind of doctrine, by the sleight of men, and cunning craftiness, whereby they lie in wait to deceive.
11

29 We are members one of another.
25

1 Be ye angry and sin not: let not the sun go down upon your wrath.
26

2 Fornication, and all uncleanness, or covetousness, let it not once be named among you, as becometh saints;
Neither filthiness, nor foolish talking, nor jesting, which are not convenient.
5:3

3 Let no man deceive you with vain words: for because of these things cometh the wrath of God upon the children of disobedience.
6

4 See then that ye walk circumspectly, not as fools, but as wise,
Redeeming the time, because the days are evil.
15

5 Be not drunk with wine, wherein is excess; but be filled with the Spirit;
Speaking to yourselves in psalms and hymns and spiritual songs, singing and making melody in your heart to the Lord.
18

6 Wives, submit yourselves to your own husbands, as unto the Lord.
22

7 Ye fathers, provoke not your children to wrath.
6:4

8 Not with eyeservice, as menpleasers.
6

9 Put on the whole armour of God.
11

10 For we wrestle not against flesh and blood, but against principalities, against powers, against the rulers of the darkness of this world, against spiritual wickedness in high places.
Wherefore take unto you the whole armour of God, that ye may be able to withstand in the evil day, and having done all, to stand.
Stand therefore, having your loins girt about with truth, and having on the breastplate of righteousness;
And your feet shod with the preparation of the gospel of peace;
Above all, taking the shield of faith, wherewith ye shall be able to quench all the fiery darts of the wicked.
12

PHILIPPIANS

11 For me to live is Christ, and to die is gain.
1:21

12 Having a desire to depart, and to be with Christ; which is far better.
23

13 Let this mind be in you, which was also in Christ Jesus:
Who, being in the form of God, thought it not robbery to be equal with God:
But made himself of no reputation, and took upon him the form of a servant and was made in the likeness of men.
2:5

14 God hath also highly exalted him, and given him a name which is above every name:

That at the name of Jesus every knee should bow, of things in heaven, and things in earth, and things under the earth.
9

15 Work out your own salvation with fear and trembling.
12

16 If any other man thinketh that he hath whereof he might trust in the flesh, I more:
Circumcised the eighth day, of the stock of Israel, of the tribe of Benjamin, an Hebrew of the Hebrews; as touching the law, a Pharisee.
3:4

17 But what things were gain to me, those I counted loss for Christ.
7

18 Forgetting those things which are behind, and reaching forth unto those things which are before,
I press toward the mark.
13

19 Whose God is their belly, and whose glory is their shame.
19

20 Rejoice in the Lord alway: and again I say, Rejoice.
4:4

21 The peace of God, which passeth all understanding, shall keep your hearts and minds through Christ Jesus.
7

22 Whatsoever things are true, whatsoever things are honest, whatsoever things are just, whatsoever things are pure, whatsoever things are lovely, whatsoever things are of good report; if there be any virtue and if there be any praise, think on these things.
8

23 I can do all things through Christ which strengtheneth me.
13

COLOSSIANS

24 Touch not; taste not; handle not.
2:21

25 Set your affection on things above, not on things on the earth.
3:2

26 Ye have put off the old man with his deeds:
And have put on the new man, which is renewed in knowledge after the image of him that created him:
Where there is neither Greek nor Jew, circumcision nor uncircumcision, Barbarian, Scythian, bond nor free: but Christ is all, and in all.
9

27 Husbands, love your wives, and be not bitter against them.
19

28 Let your speech be alway with grace, seasoned with salt.
4:6

29 Luke, the beloved physician, and Demas, greet you.
14

1 THESSALONIANS

30 We give thanks to God always for you all, making mention of you in our prayers;

Remembering without ceasing your work of faith and labour of love, and patience of hope in our Lord Jesus Christ.
1:2

1 Study to be quiet, and to do your own business.
4:11

2 But let us, who are of the day, be sober, putting on the breastplate of faith and love; and for an helmet, the hope of salvation.
5:8

3 Pray without ceasing.
17

4 Prove all things; hold fast that which is good.
21

2 THESSALONIANS

5 If any would not work, neither should he eat.
3:10

1 TIMOTHY

6 Fables and endless genealogies.
1:4

7 I did it ignorantly in unbelief.
13

8 Sinners; of whom I am chief.
15

9 Let the woman learn in silence with all subjection. But I suffer not a woman to teach, nor to usurp authority over the man, but to be in silence.
2:11

10 And Adam was not deceived, but the woman being deceived was in the transgression.
14

11 If a man desire the office of a bishop, he desireth a good work.
3:1

12 A bishop then must be blameless, the husband of one wife, vigilant, sober, of good behaviour, given to hospitality, apt to teach;
Not given to wine, no striker, not greedy of filthy lucre; but patient, not a brawler, not covetous.
2

13 Giving heed to seducing spirits, and doctrines of devils.
4:1

14 Refuse profane and old wives' fables, and exercise thyself rather unto godliness.
7

15 But the younger widows refuse: for when they have begun to wax wanton against Christ, they will marry; Having damnation, because they have cast off their first faith.
5:11

16 Drink no longer water, but use a little wine for thy stomach's sake and thine often infirmities.
23

17 For we brought nothing into this world, and it is certain we can carry nothing out.
6:7

18 The love of money is the root of all evil.
10

19 Fight the good fight of faith, lay hold on eternal life.
12

20 Rich in good works.
18

21 Science falsely so called.
20

2 TIMOTHY

22 For God hath not given us the spirit of fear; but of power, and of love, and of a sound mind.
1:7

23 Hold fast the form of sound words.
13

24 Silly women laden with sins, led away with divers lusts.
3:6

25 Be instant in season, out of season.
4:2

26 I have fought a good fight, I have finished my course, I have kept the faith.
7

TITUS

27 Unto the pure all things are pure.
1:15

HEBREWS

28 God, who at sundry times and in divers manners spake in time past unto the fathers by the prophets,
Hath in these last days spoken unto us by his Son, whom he hath appointed heir of all things, by whom he also made the worlds:
Who being the brightness of his glory, and the express image of his person, and upholding all things by the word of his power, when he had by himself purged our sins, sat down on the right hand of the Majesty on high.
1:1

29 Without shedding of blood is no remission.
9:22

30 It is a fearful thing to fall into the hands of the living God.
10:31

31 Faith is the substance of things hoped for, the evidence of things not seen.
11:1

32 For he looked for a city which hath foundations, whose maker and builder is God.
10

33 These all died in faith, not having received the promises, but having seen them afar off, and were persuaded of them, and embraced them, and confessed that they were strangers and pilgrims on the earth.
13

34 Of whom the world was not worthy.
38

35 Wherefore seeing we also are compassed about with so great a cloud of witnesses, let us lay aside every weight, and the sin which doth so easily beset us, and let us run with patience the race that is set before us, Looking unto Jesus the author and finisher of our

faith; who for the joy that was set before him endured the cross, despising the shame, and is set down at the right hand of God.
12:1

1 Whom the Lord loveth he chasteneth.
6

2 The spirits of just men made perfect.
23

3 Let brotherly love continue.
Be not forgetful to entertain strangers: for thereby some have entertained angels unawares.
13:1

4 Jesus Christ the same yesterday, and to day, and for ever.
8

5 For here have we no continuing city, but we seek one to come.
14

6 To do good and to communicate forget not.
16

JAMES

7 Let patience have her perfect work.
1:4

8 Blessed is the man that endureth temptation: for when he is tried, he shall receive the crown of life.
12

9 Every good gift and every perfect gift is from above, and cometh down from the Father of lights, with whom is no variableness, neither shadow of turning.
.17

10 Be swift to hear, slow to speak, slow to wrath:
For the wrath of man worketh not the righteousness of God.
Wherefore lay apart all filthiness and superfluity of naughtiness, and receive with meekness the engrafted word, which is able to save your souls,
But be ye doers of the word, and not hearers only, deceiving your own selves.
For if any be a hearer of the word, and not a doer, he is like unto a man beholding his natural face in a glass:
For he beholdeth himself, and goeth his way, and straightway forgetteth what manner of man he was.
19

11 If any man among you seem to be religious, and bridleth not his tongue, but deceiveth his own heart, this man's religion is vain.
Pure religion and undefiled before God and the Father is this, To visit the fatherless and widows in their affliction, and to keep himself unspotted from the world.
26

12 Faith without works is dead.
2:20

13 How great a matter a little fire kindleth.
3:5

14 The tongue can no man tame; it is an unruly evil.
8

15 Doth a fountain send forth at the same place sweet water and bitter?
11

16 For what is your life? It is even a vapour, that

appeareth for a little time, and then vanisheth away.
4:14

17 Ye have heard of the patience of Job.
5:11

18 Let your yea be yea; and your nay, nay.
12

19 The effectual fervent prayer of a righteous man availeth much.
16

1 PETER

20 Jesus Christ:
Whom having not seen, ye love; in whom, though now ye see him not, yet believing, ye rejoice with joy unspeakable and full of glory.
1:7

21 All flesh is as grass, and all the glory of man as the flower of grass. The grass withereth, and the flower thereof falleth away.
24. See 59:6

22 As newborn babes, desire the sincere milk of the word, that ye may grow thereby:
If so be ye have tasted that the Lord is gracious.
2:2

23 But ye are a chosen generation, a royal priesthood, an holy nation, a peculiar people.
9

24 Abstain from fleshly lusts, which war against the soul.
11

25 Honour all men. Love the brotherhood. Fear God. Honour the king.
17

26 For what glory is it, if, when ye be buffeted for your faults, ye shall take it patiently? but if, when ye do well, and suffer for it, ye take it patiently, this is acceptable with God.
20

27 Ye were as sheep going astray; but are now returned unto the Shepherd and Bishop of your souls.
25

28 Ornament of a meek and quiet spirit.
3:4

29 Giving honour unto the wife, as unto the weaker vessel.
7

30 Not rendering evil for evil, or railing for railing: but contrariwise blessing.
9

31 The end of all things is at hand.
4:7

32 Charity shall cover the multitude of sins.
8

33 Be sober, be vigilant; because your adversary the devil, as a roaring lion, walketh about, seeking whom he may devour.
5:8

2 PETER

34 And the day star arise in your hearts.
1:19

1 Not afraid to speak evil of dignities.
2:10

2 The dog is turned to his own vomit again.
22

1 JOHN

3 If we say that we have no sin, we deceive ourselves, and the truth is not in us.
1:8

4 But whoso hath this world's good, and seeth his brother have need, and shutteth up his bowels of compassion from him, how dwelleth the love of God in him?
3:17

5 He that loveth not knoweth not God; for God is love.
4:8

6 There is no fear in love; but perfect love casteth out fear.
18

7 If a man say, I love God, and hateth his brother, he is a liar: for he that loveth not his brother whom he hath seen, how can he love God whom he hath not seen?
20

3 JOHN

8 He that doeth good is of God: but he that doeth evil hath not seen God.
11

REVELATION

9 John to the seven churches which are in Asia: Grace be unto you, and peace, from him which is, and which was, and which is to come.
1:4

10 Behold, he cometh with clouds; and every eye shall see him, and they also which pierced him: and all kindreds of the earth shall wail because of him. Even so, Amen.
I am Alpha and Omega, the beginning and the ending, saith the Lord.
7

11 I was in the Spirit on the Lord's day, and heard behind me a great voice as of a trumpet.
10

12 What thou seest, write in a book, and send it unto the seven churches which are in Asia.
11

13 Being turned, I saw seven golden candlesticks.
12

14 His head and his hairs were white like wool, as white as snow; and his eyes were as a flame of fire;
And his feet like unto fine brass, as if they burned in a furnace; and his voice as the sound of many waters.
And he had in his right hand seven stars: and out of his mouth went a sharp twoedged sword: and his countenance was as the sun shineth in his strength.
And when I saw him, I fell at his feet as dead.
14

15 I am he that liveth, and was dead; and, behold, I am alive for evermore, Amen; and have the keys of hell and of death.
18

16 I have somewhat against thee, because thou hast left thy first love.
2:4

17 Be thou faithful unto death, and I will give thee a crown of life.
10

18 I will not blot out his name out of the book of life.
3:5

19 I will write upon him my new name.
12

20 I know thy works, that thou art neither cold nor hot: I would thou wert cold or hot.
So then because thou art lukewarm, and neither cold nor hot, I will spue thee out of my mouth.
15

21 Behold, I stand at the door, and knock.
20

22 And he that sat was to look upon like a jasper and a sardine stone: and there was a rainbow round about the throne, in sight like unto an emerald.
4:3

23 And before the throne there was a sea of glass like unto crystal: and in the midst of the throne, and round about the throne, were four beasts full of eyes before and behind.
6

24 They were full of eyes within: and they rest not day and night, saying, Holy, holy, holy, Lord God Almighty, which was, and is, and is to come.
8

25 Thou hast created all things, and for thy pleasure they are and were created.
11

26 Who is worthy to open the book, and to loose the seals thereof?
5:2

27 The four beasts and four and twenty elders fell down before the Lamb, having every one of them harps, and golden vials full of odours, which are the prayers of saints.
8

28 He went forth conquering, and to conquer.
6:2

29 And I looked, and behold a pale horse: and his name that sat on him was Death.
8

30 The kings of the earth, and the great men, and the rich men, and the chief captains, and the mighty men, and every bondman, and every free man, hid themselves in the dens and in the rocks of the mountains;
And said to the mountains and rocks, Fall on us, and hide us from the face of him that sitteth upon the throne, and from the wrath of the Lamb:
For the great day of his wrath is come; and who shall be able to stand?
15

31 A great multitude, which no man could number, of all nations, and kindreds, and people, and tongues, stood before the throne, and before the Lamb.
7:9

32 And all the angels stood round about the throne, and about the elders and the four beasts, and fell before the

throne on their faces, and worshipped God.
11

1 And one of the elders answered, saying unto me,
What are these which are arrayed in white robes? and
whence came they?
13

2 These are they which came out of great tribulation,
and have washed their robes, and made them white in
the blood of the Lamb.
14

3 They shall hunger no more, neither thirst any more;
neither shall the sun light on them, nor any heat.
16

4 God shall wipe away all tears from their eyes.
17

5 And when he had opened the seventh seal, there was
silence in heaven about the space of half an hour.
8:1

6 And the name of the star is called Wormwood.
11

7 And in those days shall men seek death, and shall not
find it; and shall desire to die, and death shall flee from
them.
9:6

8 And there were stings in their tails.
10

9 It was in my mouth sweet as honey: and as soon as I
had eaten it, my belly was bitter.
10:10

10 And there appeared a great wonder in heaven; a
woman clothed with the sun, and the moon under her
feet, and upon her head a crown of twelve stars.
12:1

11 And there was war in heaven: Michael and his angels
fought against the dragon; and the dragon fought and
his angels.
7

12 Who is like unto the beast? who is able to make war
with him?
13:4

13 And that no man might buy or sell, save he that had
the mark, or the name of the beast, or the number of
his name.
17

14 Let him that hath understanding count the number of
the beast: for it is the number of a man; and his
number is Six hundred threescore and six.
18

15 And I heard a voice from heaven, as the voice of many
waters, and as the voice of a great thunder: and I heard
the voice of harpers harping with their harps:
And they sung as it were a new song...and no man
could learn that song but the hundred and forty and
four thousand, which were redeemed from the earth.
14:2

16 Babylon is fallen, is fallen, that great city.
8

17 And the smoke of their torment ascendeth up for ever
and ever: and they have no rest day or night, who
worship the beast and his image.
11

18 Blessed are the dead which die in the Lord from

henceforth: Yea, saith the Spirit, that they may rest
from their labours; and their works do follow them.
13

19 And I saw as it were a sea of glass mingled with fire.
15:2

20 Behold, I come as a thief.
16:15

21 And he gathered them together into a place called in
the Hebrew tongue Armageddon.
16

22 I will shew unto thee the judgment of the great whore
that sitteth upon many waters.
17:1

23 MYSTERY, BABYLON THE GREAT, THE
MOTHER OF HARLOTS AND ABOMINATIONS
OF THE EARTH.
5

24 And a mighty angel took up a stone like a great
millstone, and cast it into the sea, saying, Thus with
violence shall that great city Babylon be thrown down,
and shall be found no more at all.
18:21

25 And I saw heaven opened, and behold a white horse;
and he that sat upon him was called Faithful and True.
19:11

26 And he hath on his vesture and on his thigh a name
written, KING OF KINGS, AND LORD OF LORDS.
16

27 And he laid hold on the dragon, that old serpent,
which is the Devil, and Satan, and bound him a
thousand years.
20:2

28 And I saw a great white throne.
11

29 And the sea gave up the dead which were in it; and
death and hell delivered up the dead which were in
them: and they were judged every man according to
their works.
13

30 And I saw a new heaven and a new earth: for the first
heaven and the first earth were passed away; and there
was no more sea.
And I John saw the holy city, new Jerusalem, coming
down from God out of heaven, prepared as a bride
adorned for her husband.
21:1

31 And God shall wipe away all tears from their eyes; and
there shall be no more death, neither sorrow, nor
crying, neither shall there be any more pain: for the
former things are passed away.
And he that sat upon the throne said, Behold, I make
all things new. And he said unto me, Write: for these
words are true and faithful.
4

32 I will give unto him that is athirst of the fountain of
the water of life freely.
6

33 The street of the city was pure gold.
21

34 And the gates of it shall not be shut at all by day: for
there shall be no night there.
25

35 And he shewed me a pure river of water of life, clear

as crystal, proceeding out of the throne of God and of the Lamb.
22:1

1 And the leaves of the tree were for the healing of the nations.
2

2 And, behold, I come quickly.
12

3 For without are dogs, and sorcerers, and whoremongers, and murderers, and idolaters, and whosoever loveth and maketh a lie.
15

4 Amen. Even so, come, Lord Jesus.
20

VULGATE

5 *Dominus illuminatio mea, et salus mea, quem timebo?*
The Lord is the source of my light and my safety, so whom shall I fear?
Psalm 26:1. See 391:7

6 *Asperges me hyssopo, et mundabor; lavabis me, et super nivem dealbabor.*
You will sprinkle me with hyssop, and I shall be made clean; you will wash me and I shall be made whiter than snow.
50:9 (A.V. Psalm 51:7)

7 *Cantate Domino canticum novum, quia mirabilia fecit.*
Sing to the Lord a new song, because he has done marvellous things.
97:1. See 396:7

8 *Jubilate Deo, omnis terra; servite Domino in laetitia.*
Sing joyfully to God, all the earth; serve the Lord with gladness.
99:2. See 396:11

9 *Beatus vir qui timet Dominum, in mandatis ejus volet nimis!*
Happy is the man who fears the Lord, who is only too willing to follow his orders.
111:1 (A.V. Psalm 112:1)

10 *Non nobis, Domine, non nobis; sed nomini tuo da gloriam.*
Not unto us, Lord, not unto us; but to thy name give glory.
113:(9). See 397:17

11 *Laudate Dominum, omnes gentes; laudate eum, omnes populi.*
Praise the Lord, all nations; praise him, all people.
116:1 (A.V. Psalm 117:1)

12 *Nisi Dominus aedificaverit domum, in vanum laboraverunt qui aedificant eam.*
Nisi Dominus custodierit civitatem, frustra vigilat qui custodit eam.
Unless the Lord has built the house, its builders have laboured in vain. Unless the Lord guards the city, it's no use its guard staying awake.
126:1. See 398:18 [Shortened to *Nisi Dominus frustra* as the motto of the city of Edinburgh.]

13 *De profundis clamavi ad te, Domine;*
Domine, exaudi vocem meam.
Up from the depths I have cried to thee, Lord; Lord, hear my voice.
129:1. See 398:23

14 *Vanitas vanitatum, dixit Ecclesiastes; vanitas vanitatum, et omnia vanitas.*
Vanity of vanities, said the preacher; vanity of vanities, and everything is vanity.
Ecclesiastes 1:2. See 55:5

15 *Rorate, coeli, desuper, et nubes pluant Justum; aperiatur terra, et germinet Salvatorem.*
Drop down dew, heavens, from above, and let the clouds rain down righteousness; let the earth be opened, and a saviour spring to life.
Is. 45:8

16 *Benedicite, omnia opera Domini, Domino; laudate et superexaltate eum in secula.*
Bless the Lord, all the works of the Lord; praise him and exalt him above all things for ever.
Dan. 3:57. See 384:19

17 *Magnificat anima mea Dominum;*
Et exsultavit spiritus meus in Deo salutari meo.
My soul doth magnify the Lord: and my spirit hath rejoiced in God my Saviour. [Tr. Book of Common Prayer]
Ev. S. Luc. 1:46

18 *Esurientes implevit bonis, et divites dimisit inanes.*
He hath filled the hungry with good things: and the rich he hath sent empty away. [Tr. Book of Common Prayer]
53

19 *Nunc dimittis servum tuum, Domine, secundum verbum tuum in pace.*
Lord, now lettest thou thy servant depart in peace: according to thy word. [Tr. Book of Common Prayer]
2:29

20 *Pax Vobis.*
Peace be unto you.
24:36

21 *Quo vadis?*
Where are you going?
Ev. S. Joann. 16:5

22 *Ecce homo.*
Behold the man.
19:5

23 *Consummatum est.*
It is achieved.
30

24 *Noli me tangere.*
Do not touch me.
20:17. See 73:9

25 *Sicut modo geniti infantes, rationabile, sine dolo lac concupiscite.*
After the fashion of newborn babes, desire the sincere milk of the word.
1 Pet. 2:2

26 *Magna est veritas, et praevalet.*
Great is truth, and it prevails.
3 Esdr. 4:41

ISAAC BICKERSTAFFE 1735?–1812?

27 Perhaps it was right to dissemble your love,
But—why did you kick me downstairs?
An Expostulation

28 There was a jolly miller once,
    Lived on the river Dee;
He worked and sang from morn till night;

No lark more blithe than he.
Love in a Village (1762), I.v

1 And this the burthen of his song,
For ever us'd to be,
I care for nobody, not I,
If no one cares for me.

2 We all love a pretty girl—under the rose.
II.ii

3 In every port he finds a wife.
Thomas and Sally (1761), ii

REVD. E.H. BICKERSTETH 1825–1906

4 Peace, perfect peace, in this dark world of sin?
The Blood of Jesus whispers peace within.
Songs in the House of Pilgrimage (1875)

ROGER BIGOD, EARL OF NORFOLK 1245-1306

5 By God, O King, I will neither go nor hang!
Reply to King Edward I's expostulation, 'By God, earl, you shall
either go or hang', 24 Feb. 1297, when Edward required the
barons to invade France through Gascony while he took command
in Flanders. *Hemingburgh's Chronicle*, ii.121

JOSH BILLINGS (HENRY WHEELER SHAW) 1818–1885

6 Thrice is he armed that hath his quarrel just,
But four times he who gets his blow in fust.
Josh Billings, his Sayings (1865). See 446:6

7 The trouble with people is not that they don't know
but that they know so much that ain't so.
Josh Billings' Encyclopedia of Wit and Wisdom (1874)

LAURENCE BINYON 1869–1943

8 Now is the time for the burning of the leaves.
The Burning of the Leaves

9 With proud thanksgiving, a mother for her children,
England mourns for her dead across the sea.
Poems For the Fallen

10 They shall grow not old, as we that are left grow old:
Age shall not weary them, nor the years condemn.
At the going down of the sun and in the morning
We will remember them.

NIGEL BIRCH 1906–

11 For the second time the Prime Minister has got rid of a
Chancellor of the Exchequer who tried to get
expenditure under control.
Once is more than enough.
Letter, *The Times*, 14 July 1962

EARL OF BIRKENHEAD (F.E. SMITH) 1872–1930

12 We have the highest authority for believing that the
meek shall inherit the Earth; though I have never found
any particular corroboration of this aphorism in the
records of Somerset House.
Contemporary Personalities (1924). **Marquess Curzon**

13 Nature has no cure for this sort of madness
[Bolshevism], though I have known a legacy from a
rich relative work wonders.
Law, Life and Letters (1927), ii. ch.19

14 The world continues to offer glittering prizes to those
who have stout hearts and sharp swords.
Rectorial Address, Glasgow University, 7 Nov. 1923

15 *Judge Willis:* You are extremely offensive, young
man.
F.E. Smith: As a matter of fact, we both are, and the
only difference between us is that I am trying to be,
and you can't help it.
Birkenhead, *Frederick Elwin, Earl of Birkenhead* (1933), vol.I,
ch.9

16 *Judge Willis:* What do you suppose I am on the Bench
for, Mr Smith?
Smith: It is not for me to attempt to fathom the
inscrutable workings of Providence.

AUGUSTINE BIRRELL 1850–1933

17 That great dust-heap called 'history'
Obiter Dicta. **Carlyle**

18 In the name of the Bodleian.
Dr. Johnson

PRINCE BISMARCK 1815–1898

19 *Die Politik ist keine exakte Wissenschaft.*
Politics is not an exact science.
Prussian Chamber, 18 Dec. 1863

20 *Die Politik ist die Lehre von Möglichen.*
Politics is the art of the possible.
In conversation with Meyer von Waldeck, 11 Aug. 1867

21 *Nach Canossa gehen wir nicht.*
We will not go to Canossa.
Reichstag, 14 May 1872

22 *Die gesunden Knochen eines einzigen pommerschen
Musketiers.*
The healthy bones of a single Pomeranian grenadier.
5 Dec. 1876

23 *Ehrlicher Makler.*
An honest broker.
19 Feb. 1878

24 *Die Politik ist keine Wissenschaft...sondern eine
Kunst.*
Politics is not a science...but an art.
15 Mar. 1884

25 *Legt eine möglichst starke militärische Kraft...in die
Hand des Königs von Preussen, dann wird er die
Politik machen können, die Ihr wünscht; mit Reden
und Schützenfesten und Liedern macht sie sich nicht,
sie macht sich nur durch Blut und Eisen.*
Place in the hands of the King of Prussia the strongest
possible military power, then he will be able to carry
out the policy you wish; this policy cannot succeed
through speeches, and shooting-matches, and songs; it
can only be carried out through blood and iron.
Prussian House of Deputies, 28 Jan. 1886. Used by Bismarck in
the form *Eisen und Blut*, 30 Sept. 1862

26 If there is ever another war in Europe, it will come out
of some damned silly thing in the Balkans.
Said to Herr Ballen 'towards the end of [Bismarck's] life', and
related by Ballen to Winston S. Churchill a fortnight before World
War I. See *Hansard*, Vol.413, col.84

27 I may avail myself of the opportunity of denying once
more the truth of the story that Prince Bismarck had
ever likened Lord Salisbury to a lath of wood painted

to look like iron.
Sidney Whitman, *Personal Reminiscences of Prince Bismarck*
(1902), p.252

SIR WILLIAM BLACKSTONE 1723–1780

1 Man was formed for society.
Commentaries on the Laws of England, introd. 2

2 Mankind will not be reasoned out of the feelings of
humanity.
bk.i.5

3 The king never dies.
7

4 The royal navy of England hath ever been its greatest
defence and ornament; it is its ancient and natural
strength; the floating bulwark of the island.
13

5 That the king can do no wrong, is a necessary and
fundamental principle of the English constitution.
iii.17

6 It is better that ten guilty persons escape than one
innocent suffer.
iv.27

WILLIAM BLAKE 1757–1827

7 When Sir Joshua Reynolds died
All Nature was degraded:
The King dropped a tear into the Queen's ear,
And all his pictures faded.
Annotations to Reynolds, *Discourses,* p.109

8 To see a World in a Grain of Sand,
    And a Heaven in a Wild Flower,
Hold Infinity in the palm of your hand,
    And Eternity in an hour.
Auguries of Innocence, 1

9 A Robin Redbreast in a Cage
Puts all Heaven in a Rage.
5

10 A dog starv'd at his master's gate
Predicts the ruin of the State,
A horse misus'd upon the road
Calls to Heaven for human blood.
Each outcry of the hunted hare
A fibre from the brain does tear,
A skylark wounded in the wing,
A cherubim does cease to sing.
9

11 The bat that flits at close of eve
Has left the brain that won't believe.
25

12 He who shall hurt the little wren
Shall never be belov'd by men.
He who the ox to wrath has mov'd
Shall never be by woman lov'd.
29

13 The caterpillar on the leaf
Repeats to thee thy mother's grief.
Kill not the moth nor butterfly,
For the Last Judgement draweth nigh.
37

14 A truth that's told with bad intent
Beats all the lies you can invent.
It is right it should be so;

Man was made for Joy and Woe;
And when this we rightly know,
Thro' the World we safely go,
Joy and woe are woven fine,
A clothing for the soul divine.
53

15 The bleat, the bark, bellow, and roar
Are waves that beat on Heaven's shore.
71

16 The strongest poison ever known
Came from Caesar's laurel crown.
97

17 He who doubts from what he sees
Will ne'er believe, do what you please.
If the Sun and Moon should doubt,
They'd immediately go out.
To be in a passion you good may do,
But no good if a passion is in you.
The whore and gambler, by the state
Licensed, build that nation's fate.
The harlot's cry from street to street
Shall weave old England's winding sheet.
107

18 God appears, and God is Light,
To those poor souls who dwell in Night;
But does a Human Form display
To those who dwell in realms of Day.
129

19 Does the Eagle know what is in the pit
Or wilt thou go ask the Mole?
Can Wisdom be put in a silver rod,
Or Love in a golden bowl?
The Book of Thel, Thel's motto

20   Everything that lives,
Lives not alone, nor for itself.
xi.26

21 The Vision of Christ that thou dost see
Is my vision's greatest enemy.
Thine has a great hook nose like thine,
Mine has a snub nose like to mine.
The Everlasting Gospel, a, 1.1

22 Both read the Bible day and night,
But thou read'st black where I read white.
1.13

23 This life's five windows of the soul
Distorts the Heavens from pole to pole,
And leads you to believe a lie
When you see with, not thro', the eye.
d, 1.103

24 Jesus was sitting in Moses' chair.
They brought the trembling woman there.
Moses commands she be ston'd to death.
What was the sound of Jesus' breath?
He laid His hand on Moses' law;
The ancient Heavens, in silent awe,
Writ with curses from pole to pole,
All away began to roll.
e, 1.7

25 I am sure this Jesus will not do,
Either for Englishman or Jew.
f

26 Mutual Forgiveness of each vice,

Such are the Gates of Paradise.
The Gates of Paradise, prologue

1 Truly, my Satan, thou art but a dunce,
And dost not know the garment from the man;
Every harlot was a virgin once,
Nor canst thou ever change Kate into Nan.

Tho' thou art worshipp'd by the names divine
Of Jesus and Jehovah, thou art still
The Son of Morn in weary Night's decline,
The lost traveller's dream under the hill.
epilogue

2 I must Create a System, or be enslav'd by another
Man's;
I will not Reason and Compare: my business is to
Create.
Jerusalem, pl.10, 1.20

3   Near mournful
Ever-weeping Paddington.
pl.12, 1.27

4 The fields from Islington to Marybone,
To Primrose Hill and Saint John's Wood,
Were builded over with pillars of gold;
And there Jerusalem's pillars stood.
pl.27, 1.1

5 Pancras and Kentish Town repose
Among her golden pillars high,
Among her golden arches which
Shine upon the starry sky.
1.9

6 For a tear is an intellectual thing,
And a sigh is the sword of an Angel King,
And the bitter groan of the martyr's woe
Is an arrow from the Almighty's bow.
pl.52, 1.25

7 He who would do good to another must do it in
Minute Particulars.
General Good is the plea of the scoundrel, hypocrite,
and flatterer;
For Art and Science cannot exist but in minutely
organized Particulars.
pl.55, 1.60

8 I give you the end of a golden string;
Only wind it into a ball,
It will lead you in at Heaven's gate,
Built in Jerusalem's wall.
pl.77

9 O ye Religious, discountenance every one among you
who shall pretend to despise Art and Science!

10 Let every Christian, as much as in him lies, engage
himself openly and publicly, before all the World, in
some mental pursuit for the Building up of Jerusalem.

11 England! awake! awake! awake!
Jerusalem thy sister calls!
Why wilt thou sleep the sleep of death,
And close her from thy ancient walls?

12 And now the time returns again:
Our souls exult, and London's towers
Receive the Lamb of God to dwell
In England's green and pleasant bowers.

13 I care not whether a man is Good or Evil; all that I
care
Is whether he is a Wise man or a Fool. Go! put off

Holiness,
And put on Intellect.
pl.91, 1.55

14 For double the vision my eyes do see,
And a double vision is always with me.
With my inward eye 'tis an old Man grey,
With my outward, a Thistle across my way.
Letter to Thomas Butts, 22 Nov. 1802, 1.27

15 O why was I born with a different face?
Why was I not born like the rest of my race?
Letter to Thomas Butts, 16 Aug. 1803

16 And did those feet in ancient time
Walk upon England's mountains green?
And was the holy Lamb of God
On England's pleasant pastures seen?

And did the Countenance Divine
Shine forth upon our clouded hills?
And was Jerusalem builded here
Amoung these dark Satanic mills?

Bring me my bow of burning gold!
Bring me my arrows of desire!
Bring me my spear! O clouds, unfold!
Bring me my chariot of fire!

I will not cease from Mental Fight,
Nor shall my Sword sleep in my hand,
Till we have built Jerusalem,
In England's green & pleasant Land.
Milton, preface

17 What is it men in women do require?
The lineaments of gratified desire.
What is it women do in men require?
The lineaments of gratified desire.
MS. Notebooks, 1793, p.99

18 He who binds to himself a Joy
Doth the winged life destroy;
But he who kisses the Joy as it flies
Lives in Eternity's sunrise.

19 The sword sung on the barren heath,
The sickle in the fruitful field:
The sword he sung a song of death,
But could not make the sickle yield.
p.105

20 Abstinence sows sand all over
The ruddy limbs and flaming hair,
But Desire gratified
Plants fruits of life and beauty there.

21 Never pain to tell thy love,
Love that never told can be;
For the gentle wind does move
Silently, invisibly.
p.115

22 Soon as she was gone from me,
A traveller came by,
Silently, invisibly:
He took her with a sigh.

23 Mock on, mock on, Voltaire, Rousseau;
Mock on, mock on, 'tis all in vain!
You throw the sand against the wind,
And the wind blows it back again.
1800-03, p.7

24 The Atoms of Democritus
And Newtons Particles of Light

Are sands upon the Red sea shore
Where Israel's tents do shine so bright.

1 [On William Haines]
  The Sussex men are noted fools,
  And weak is their brain-pan;
  I wonder if H— the painter
  Is not a Sussex man?
  1808-11, p.24

2 [Of Hayley's birth]
  Of H—'s birth this was the happy lot:
  His mother on his father him begot.
  p.27

3 [On Cromek]
  A petty sneaking knave I knew—
  O! Mr Cr—, how do ye do?
  p.29

4 He has observ'd the golden rule,
  Till he's become the golden fool.
  p.30

5 [On Hayley]
  To forgive enemies H— does pretend,
  Who never in his life forgave a friend.
  p.34

6 On H[ayle]y's Friendship.
  When H—y finds out what you cannot do,
  This is the very thing he'll set you to.
  p.35

7 To H[ayley]
  Thy friendship oft has made my heart to ache:
  Do be my enemy—for friendship's sake.
  p.37

8 I understood Christ was a carpenter
  And not a brewer's servant, my good Sir.
  p.38

9 The errors of a wise man make your rule,
  Rather than the perfections of a fool.
  p.42

10 Great things are done when men and mountains meet;
   This is not done by jostling in the street.
   p.43

11 When I tell any Truth it is not for the sake of
   convincing those who do not know it, but for the sake
   of defending those who do.
   Public Address

12 O Rose, thou art sick!
   The invisible worm
   That flies in the night,
   In the howling storm,

   Has found out thy bed
   Of crimson joy:
   And his dark secret love
   Does thy life destroy.
   The Sick Rose

13 Hear the voice of the Bard!
   Who present, past, and future sees.
   Songs of Experience, introduction

14 Tyger! Tyger! burning bright
   In the forests of the night,
   What immortal hand or eye
   Could frame thy fearful symmetry?
   The Tyger

15 What the hand dare seize the fire?

And what shoulder, and what art,
Could twist the sinews of thy heart?
And when thy heart began to beat,
What dread hand? and what dread feet?

16 When the stars threw down their spears,
   And water'd heaven with their tears,
   Did he smile his work to see?
   Did he who made the Lamb make thee?

17 Children of the future age,
   Reading this indignant page,
   Know that in a former time,
   Love, sweet love, was thought a crime.
   A Little Girl Lost

18 Love seeketh not itself to please,
   Nor for itself hath any care,
   But for another gives its ease,
   And builds a Heaven in Hell's despair.
   The Clod and the Pebble

19 Love seeketh only Self to please,
   To bind another to its delight,
   Joys in another's loss of ease,
   And builds a Hell in Heaven's despite.

20 Then the Parson might preach, and drink, and sing,
   And we'd be as happy as birds in the spring;
   And modest Dame Lurch, who is always at church,
   Would not have bandy children, nor fasting, nor birch.
   The Little Vagabond

21 I was angry with my friend
   I told my wrath, my wrath did end.
   I was angry with my foe:
   I told it not, my wrath did grow.
   A Poison Tree

22 Ah, Sun-flower! weary of time,
   Who countest the steps of the Sun;
   Seeking after that sweet golden clime,
   Where the traveller's journey is done;

   Where the Youth pined away with desire,
   And the pale Virgin shrouded in snow,
   Arise from their graves and aspire
   Where my Sun-flower wishes to go.
   Ah, Sun-Flower!

23 My mother groan'd, my father wept,
   Into the dangerous world I leapt;
   Helpless, naked, piping loud,
   Like a fiend hid in a cloud.
   Infant Sorrow

24 Piping down the valleys wild,
   Piping songs of pleasant glee,
   On a cloud I saw a child,
   And he laughing said to me:

   'Pipe a song about a Lamb!'
   So I piped with merry cheer.
   'Piper, pipe that song again;'
   So I piped: he wept to hear.

   'Drop thy pipe, thy happy pipe;
   Sing thy songs of happy cheer:'
   So I sang the same again,
   While he wept with joy to hear.
   Songs of Innocence, introduction

25 And I wrote my happy songs
   Every child may joy to hear.

26 Little Lamb, who made thee?

Dost thou know who made thee?
Gave thee life, and bid thee feed,
By the stream and o'er the mead;
Gave thee clothing of delight,
Softest clothing, woolly, bright;
Gave thee such a tender voice,
Making all the vales rejoice?
The Lamb

1 'I have no name;
I am but two days old.'
What shall I call thee?
'I happy am,
Joy is my name.'
Sweet joy befall thee!
Infant Joy

2 My mother bore me in the southern wild,
And I am black, but O! my soul is white;
White as an angel is the English child,
But I am black, as if bereav'd of light.
The Little Black Boy

3 When the voices of children are heard on the green,
And laughing is heard on the hill.
Nurse's Song

4 Then cherish pity, lest you drive an angel from your
door.
Holy Thursday

5 When my mother died I was very young,
And my father sold me while yet my tongue
Could scarcely cry, ''weep! 'weep! 'weep! 'weep!'
So your chimneys I sweep, and in soot I sleep.
The Chimney Sweeper

6 To Mercy, Pity, Peace, and Love
All pray in their distress.
The Divine Image

7 For Mercy has a human heart.
Pity a human face,
And Love, the human form divine,
And Peace, the human dress.

8 Can I see another's woe,
And not be in sorrow too?
Can I see another's grief,
And not seek for kind relief?
On Another's Sorrow

9 Cruelty has a human heart,
And Jealousy a human face;
Terror the human form divine,
And Secrecy the human dress.
Appendix to **Songs of Innocence and of Experience. A Divine
Image**

10 Whether on Ida's shady brow,
Or in the chambers of the East,
The chambers of the sun, that now
From ancient melody have ceas'd...
How have you left the ancient love
That bards of old enjoy'd in you!
The languid strings do scarcely move!
The sound is forc'd, the notes are few!
To the Muses

11 Energy is Eternal Delight.
The Marriage of Heaven and Hell: The Voice of the Devil

12 The reason Milton wrote in fetters when he wrote of
Angels and God, and at liberty when of Devils and
Hell, is because he was a true Poet, and of the Devil's

party without knowing it.
(note)

13 The road of excess leads to the palace of wisdom.
Proverbs of Hell

14 Prudence is a rich, ugly, old maid courted by
Incapacity.

15 He who desires but acts not, breeds pestilence.

16 A fool sees not the same tree that a wise man sees.

17 Eternity is in love with the productions of time.

18 Bring out number, weight, and measure in a year of
dearth.

19 If the fool would persist in his folly he would become
wise.

20 Prisons are built with stones of Law, brothels with
bricks of Religion.

21 The pride of the peacock is the glory of God.
The lust of the goat is the bounty of God.
The wrath of the lion is the wisdom of God.
The nakedness of woman is the work of God.

22 The tigers of wrath are wiser than the horses of
instruction.

23 Damn braces. Bless relaxes.

24 Sooner murder an infant in its cradle than nurse
unacted desires.

25 Truth can never be told so as to be understood, and
not be believ'd.

26 Then I asked: 'Does a firm persuasion that a thing is
so, make it so?'
He replied: 'All Poets believe that it does, and in ages
of imagination this firm persuasion removed
mountains; but many are not capable of a firm
persuasion of anything.'
A Memorable Fancy, pl.12-13

27 I was in a printing house in Hell, and saw the method
in which knowledge is transmitted from generation to
generation.

28 If the doors of perception were cleansed everthing
would appear as it is, infinite.
pl.14

29 'What,' it will be questioned, 'when the sun rises, do
you not see a round disc of fire somewhat like a
guinea?' 'O no, no, I see an innumerable company of
the heavenly host crying, ''Holy, Holy, Holy is the
Lord God Almighty.'''
A Vision of the Last Judgement, Descriptive Catalogue (1810)

LESLEY BLANCH 1907–

30 She was an Amazon. Her whole life was spent riding
at breakneck speed along the wilder shores of love.
The Wilder Shores of Love, 2. Jane Digby El Mezrab

PHILIP PAUL BLISS 1838–1876

31 Hold the fort, for I am coming.
The Charm. Ho, My Comrades, See the Signal!

PRINCE BLÜCHER 1742–1819

32 *Was für plunder!*

What rubbish!
Of London seen from the Monument, June 1814. Often misquoted
as *'Was für plündern!'* (What a place to plunder!) Prince Gebhard
Lebrecht Blücher, *Memoirs* (1932), p. 33

1 Blücher and I met near La Belle Alliance; we were
both on horseback; but he embraced and kissed me
exclaiming *Mein lieber Kamerad,* and then *quelle
affaire!* which was pretty much all he knew of French.
Stanhope, *Conversations with the Duke of Wellington,* 4 Nov.
1840. (In 1816 Wellington said the meeting took place at
Genappe.)

EDMUND BLUNDEN 1896–1974

2 All things they have in common being so poor,
And their one fear, Death's shadow at the door.
Each sundown makes them mournful, each sunrise
Brings back the brightness in their failing eyes.
Almswomen

3 I have been young, and now am not too old;
And I have seen the righteous forsaken,
His health, his honour and his quality taken.
    This is not what we formerly were told.
Report on Experience. See 391:28

WILFRID SCAWEN BLUNT 1840–1922

4 I like the hunting of the hare
Better than that of the fox.
The Old Squire

5 I like to be as my fathers were,
In the days ere I was born.

BOETHIUS c.480–c.524

6 *Nam in omni adversitate fortunae infelicissimum
genus est infortunii, fuisse felicem.*
For in every ill-turn of fortune the most unhappy sort
of misfortune is to have been happy.
Consolation of Philosophy, bk.ii, prose 4

HUMPHREY BOGART 1899–1957

7 If she can stand it I can. Play it!
Casablanca (1942), script by Julius J. Epstein, Philip G. Epstein,
Howard Koch. Often quoted as 'Play it again, Sam.'

8 Here's looking at you, kid.

JOHN B. BOGART 1845–1921

9 When a dog bites a man that is not news, but when a
man bites a dog that is news.
Oral tradition: also attr. Charles Dana and Amos Cummings

NICOLAS BOILEAU 1636–1711

10 *Enfin Malherbe vint, et, le premier en France,
Fit sentir dans ses vers une juste cadence.*
At last came Malherbe, and, first ever in France, made
a proper flow felt in verse.
L'Art Poétique, i.131

11 *Qu'en un lieu, qu'en un jour, un seul fait accompli
Tienne jusqu'à la fin le théâtre rempli.*
Let a single completed action, all in one place, all in
one day, keep the theatre packed to the end of your
play.
iii.45

12 *Si j'écris quatre mots, j'en effacerai trois.*
Of every four words I write, I strike out three.
Satires, ii

HENRY ST. JOHN, VISCOUNT BOLINGBROKE
1678–1751

13 What a world is this, and how does fortune banter us!
Letter, 3 Aug. 1714

14 Pests of society; because their endeavours are directed
to loosen the bands of it, and to take at least one curb
out of the mouth of that wild beast man.
12 Sept. 1724

15 Truth lies within a little and certain compass, but error
is immense.
Reflections upon Exile

16 They make truth serve as a stalking-horse to error.
On the Study of History, letter 1

17 Nations, like men, have their infancy.
letter 4

18 They [Thucydides and Xenophon] maintained the
dignity of history.
letter 5

SIR DAVID BONE 1874–1959

19 It's 'Damn you, Jack—I'm all right!' with you chaps.
The Brassbounder (1910), ch.3

DANIEL J. BOORSTIN 1914–

20 The celebrity is a person who is known for his
well-knownness.
The Image (1961), ch.2, **From Hero to Celebrity: The Human
Pseudo-event,** pt.iii

21 A best-seller was a book which somehow sold well
simply because it was selling well.
ch.4, **From Shapes to Shadows: Dissolving Forms,** pt.viii

GENERAL WILLIAM BOOTH 1829–1912

22 This Submerged Tenth—is it, then, beyond the reach
of the nine-tenths in the midst of whom they live.
In Darkest England (1890), I.ii.23

JORGE LUIS BORGES 1899–

23 *Que el cielo exista, aunque nuestro lugar sea el
infierno.*
Let heaven exist, even though our estate be hell.
La Biblioteca de Babel

24 *El original es infiel a la traducción.*
The original is unfaithful to the translation (Henley's
translation of Beckford's *Vathek*).
Sobre el 'Vathek' de William Beckford

CESARE BORGIA 1476–1507

25 *Aut Caesar, aut nihil.*
Caesar or nothing.
Motto

GEORGE BORROW 1803–1881

26 The author of 'Amelia', the most singular genius
which their island ever produced, whose works it has
long been the fashion to abuse in public and to read in
secret.
The Bible in Spain, ch.1

1 My favourite, I might say, my only study, is man.
ch.5

2 The poor Ferrolese, with the genuine spirit of localism
so prevalent in Spain, boast that their town contains a
better public walk than Madrid.
ch.31

3 There are no countries in the world less known by the
British than these selfsame British Islands.
Lavengro, preface

4 There's night and day, brother, both sweet things;
sun, moon, and stars, brother, all sweet things; there's
likewise a wind on the heath. Life is very sweet,
brother; who would wish to die?
ch.25

5 There's the wind on the heath, brother; if I could only
feel that, I would gladly live for ever.

6 Let no one sneer at the bruisers of England. What
were the gladiators of Rome, or the bull-fighters of
Spain, in its palmiest days, compared to England's
bruisers?
ch.26

7 A losing trade, I assure you, sir: literature is a drug.
ch.30

8 Good ale, the true and proper drink of Englishmen. He
is not deserving of the name of Englishman who
speaketh against ale, that is good ale.
ch.48

9 Youth will be served, every dog has his day, and mine
has been a fine one.
ch.92

10 Fear God, and take your own part.
The Romany Rye, ch.16

11 So when folks are disposed to ill-treat you, young
man, say, 'Lord have mercy upon me!' and then tip
them to Long Melford, which, as the saying goes,
there is nothing comparable for shortness all the world
over.

MARÉCHAL BOSQUET 1810–1861

12 *C'est magnifique, mais ce n'est pas la guerre.*
It is magnificent, but it is not war.
Remark on the charge of the Light Brigade, 1854

JOHN COLLINS BOSSIDY 1860–1928

13 And this is good old Boston,
    The home of the bean and the cod,
Where the Lowells talk only to Cabots,
    And the Cabots talk only to God.
Toast at Holy Cross Alumni dinner, 1910

JACQUES-BÉNIGNE BOSSUET 1627–1704

14 *L'Angleterre, ah, la perfide Angleterre, que le
rempart de ses mers rendoit inaccessible aux
Romains, la foi du Sauveur y est abordée.*
England, ah, faithless England, which the protection
afforded by its seas rendered inaccessible to the
Romans, the faith of the Saviour spread even there.
*Premier Sermon pour La Fête de la Circoncision de Notre
Seigneur*

JAMES BOSWELL 1740–1795

15 *Johnson:* Well, we had a good talk.
Boswell: Yes, Sir; you tossed and gored several
persons.
Life of Johnson, vol.ii, p.66. 1769

16 A man, indeed, is not genteel when he gets drunk; but
most vices may be committed very genteelly: a man
may debauch his friend's wife genteelly: he may cheat
at cards genteelly.
p.340. 6 Apr. 1775

GORDON BOTTOMLEY 1874–1948

17 When you destroy a blade of grass
You poison England at her roots:
Remember no man's foot can pass
Where evermore no green life shoots.
To Ironfounders and Others

DION BOUCICAULT 1820?–1890

18 Men talk of killing time, while time quietly kills them.
London Assurance (1841), II.i

ANTOINE BOULAY DE LA MEURTHE
1761–1840

19 *C'est pire qu'un crime, c'est une faute.*
It is worse than a crime, it is a blunder.
On hearing of the execution of the Duc d'Enghien, 1804

MATTHEW BOULTON 1728–1809

20 I sell here, Sir, what all the world desires to
have—POWER.
[To Boswell, of his engineering works.]
Boswell, *Life of Johnson,* vol.ii, p.459. 22 Mar. 1776

F.W. BOURDILLON 1852–1921

21 The night has a thousand eyes,
    And the day but one;
Yet the light of the bright world dies,
    With the dying sun.

The mind has a thousand eyes,
    And the heart but one;
Yet the light of a whole life dies,
    When love is done.
Light. See 321:15

LORD BOWEN 1835–1894

22 The rain it raineth on the just
    And also on the unjust fella:
But chiefly on the just, because
    The unjust steals the just's umbrella.
Walter Sichel, *Sands of Time*

23 On a metaphysician: A blind man in a dark
room—looking for a black hat—which isn't there.
Attr. See N. & Q., clxxxii.153

E.E. BOWEN 1836–1901

24 Forty years on, when afar and asunder
Parted are those who are singing to-day.
Forty Years On. Harrow School Song

25 Follow up! Follow up! Follow up! Follow up! Follow
up!

Till the field ring again and again,
With the tramp of the twenty-two men,
Follow up!

ELIZABETH BOWEN 1899–1973

1 One can live in the shadow of an idea without grasping it.
The Heat of the Day (1949), ch.10

2 Art is the only thing that can go on mattering once it has stopped hurting.
ch.16

3 There is no end to the violations committed by children on children, quietly talking alone.
The House in Paris (1935), pt.I, ch.2

4 Nobody speaks the truth when there's something they must have.
ch.5

5 Fate is not an eagle, it creeps like a rat.
pt.II, ch.2

6 No, it is not only our fate but our business to lose innocence, and once we have lost that, it is futile to attempt a picnic in Eden.
'Out of a Book', *Orion III* (1946), eds. R. Lehmann and others

REVD. WILLIAM LISLE BOWLES 1762–1850

7 The cause of Freedom is the cause of God!
Edmund Burke, l.78

REVD. E.E. BRADFORD 1860–1944

8 I walked with Will through bracken turning brown,
    Pale yellow, orange, dun and golden-red.
'God made the country and man made the town—
    And woman made Society,' he said.
Society. See 166:31

JOHN BRADFORD 1510?–1555

9 But for the grace of God there goes John Bradford.
D.N.B. Exclamation on seeing some criminals taken to execution.

F.H. BRADLEY 1846–1924

10 Unearthly ballet of bloodless categories.
The Principles of Logic, vol.III, ch.2, iv

11 The secret of happiness is to admire without desiring. And that is not happiness.
Aphorisms (1930), 33

JOHN BRADSHAW 1602–1659

12 Rebellion to tyrants is obedience to God.
Supposititious epitaph. Randall, *Life of Jefferson,* vol.III, appendix IV, p.585

ANNE BRADSTREET 1612–1672

13 I am obnoxious to each carping tongue,
Who sayes my hand a needle better fits,
A Poet's Pen, all scorne, I should thus wrong;
For such despight they cast on female wits:
If what I doe prove well, it won't advance,
They'l say it's stolne, or else, it was by chance.
The Prologue

14 Let *Greeks* be *Greeks,* and Women what they are,
Men have precedency, and still excell.

15 This meane and unrefined stuffe of mine,
Will make your glistering gold but more to shine.

JOHN BRAHAM 1774?–1856

16 England, home and beauty.
The Americans (1811). Song, The Death of Nelson

HARRY BRAISTED nineteenth century

17   If you want to win her hand,
    Let the maiden understand
That she's not the only pebble on the beach.
You're Not the Only Pebble on the Beach

ERNEST BRAMAH 1868–1942

18 It is a mark of insincerity of purpose to spend one's time in looking for the sacred Emperor in the low-class tea-shops.
The Wallet of Kai Lung. Transmutation of Ling

19 An expression of no-encouragement.
Confession of Kai Lung

20 The whole narrative is permeated with the odour of joss-sticks and honourable high-mindedness.
Kin Yen

21 It has been said…that there are few situations in life that cannot be honourably settled, and without loss of time, either by suicide, a bag of gold, or by thrusting a despised antagonist over the edge of a precipice upon a dark night.
Kai Lung's Golden Hours. The Incredible Obtuseness…

22 However entrancing it is to wander unchecked through a garden of bright images, are we not enticing your mind from another subject of almost equal importance?
Story of Hien

REVD. JAMES BRAMSTON 1694?–1744

23 What's not destroy'd by Time's devouring hand?
Where's Troy, and where's the Maypole in the Strand?
The Art of Politicks (1729), l.71

RICHARD BRATHWAITE 1588?–1673

24 To Banbury came I, O profane one!
Where I saw a Puritane-one
Hanging of his cat on Monday
For killing of a mouse on Sunday.
Barnabee's Journal (1638), pt.i

BERTOLT BRECHT 1898–1956

25 *Erst kommt das Fressen, dann kommt die Moral.*
First comes fodder, then comes morality.
Die Dreigroschenoper, II, finale

26 *Ich will mit ihm gehen, den ich liebe.*
Ich will nicht ausrechnen, was es kostet.
Ich will nicht nachdenken, ob es gut ist.
Ich will nicht wissen, ob er mich liebt.
Ich will mit ihm gehen, den ich liebe.
It is my will to go with the man I love. I do not wish to count the cost. I do not wish to consider whether it is good. I do not wish to know whether he loves

me. It is my will to go with him whom I love.
Der gute Mensch von Sezuan, V

1 Andrea: *Unglücklich das Land, das keine Helden hat!...*
Galileo: *Nein, unglücklich das Land, das Helden nötig hat.*
Andrea: Unhappy the land that has no heroes.
Galileo: No, unhappy the land that needs heroes.
Leben des Galilei, sc.13

NICHOLAS BRETON 1545?–1626?

2 We rise with the lark and go to bed with the lamb.
The Court and Country, par.8

3 I wish my deadly foe, no worse
Than want of friends, and empty purse.
A Farewell to Town

4 He is as deaf as a door.
Miseries of Mavillia, v

5 In the merry month of May,
In a morn by break of day,
Forth I walked by the wood side,
Whenas May was in his pride:
There I spied all alone,
Phillida and Coridon.
Phillida and Coridon

6 Come little babe, come silly soul,
Thy father's shame, thy mother's grief,
Born as I doubt to all our dole,
And to thy self unhappy chief:
  Sing lullaby and lap it warm,
  Poor soul that thinks no creature harm.
A Sweet Lullaby

ROBERT BRIDGES 1844–1930

7 Awake, my heart, to be loved, awake, awake!
Awake, My Heart, To be Loved

8 Awake, the land is scattered with light, and see,
Uncanopied sleep is flying from field and tree:
And blossoming boughs of April in laughter shake.

9 Thus may I think the adopting Muses chose
Their sons by name, knowing none would be heard
Or writ so oft in all the world as those,—
Dan Chaucer, mighty Shakespeare, then for third
The classic Milton, and to us arose
Shelley with liquid music in the word.
Growth of Love, 4

10 I love all beauteous things,
I seek and adore them;
God hath no better praise,
And man in his hasty days
  Is honoured for them.

I too will something make
And joy in the making;
Altho' to-morrow it seem
Like the empty words of a dream
  Remembered on waking.
I Love All Beauteous Things

11 I will not let thee go.
Ends all our month-long love in this?
Can it be summed up so,
Quit in a single kiss?

I will not let thee go.
I Will Not Let Thee Go

12 When men were all asleep the snow came flying,
In large white flakes falling on the city brown,
Stealthily and perpetually settling and loosely lying,
  Hushing the latest traffic of the drowsy town.
London Snow

13 All night it fell, and when full inches seven
It lay in the depth of its uncompacted lightness,
The clouds blew off from a high and frosty heaven;
  And all woke earlier for the unaccustomed brightness
Of the winter dawning, the strange unheavenly glare.

14 Or peering up from under the white-mossed wonder,
'O look at the trees!' they cried, 'O look at the trees!'

15   The daily word is unspoken,
The daily thoughts of labour and sorrow slumber
At the sight of the beauty that greets them, for the charm they have broken.

16 My delight and thy delight
Walking, like two angels white,
In the gardens of the night.
My Delight and Thy Delight

17 Beautiful must be the mountains whence ye come,
And bright in the fruitful valleys the streams, wherefrom
    Ye learn your song:
Where are those starry woods? O might I wander there,
Among the flowers, which in that heavenly air
    Bloom the year long!
Nightingales

18 Rejoice ye dead, where'er your spirits dwell,
Rejoice that yet on earth your fame is bright,
And that your names, remembered day and night,
Live on the lips of those who love you well.
Ode to Music

19 Whither, O splendid ship, thy white sails crowding,
Leaning across the bosom of the urgent West,
That fearest nor sea rising, nor sky clouding,
Whither away, fair rover, and what thy quest?
A Passer-By

20 So sweet love seemed that April morn,
When first we kissed beside the thorn,
So strangely sweet, it was not strange
We thought that love could never change.

But I can tell—let truth be told—
That love will change in growing old;
Though day by day is nought to see,
So delicate his motions be.
So Sweet Love Seemed

21 When Death to either shall come,—
    I pray it be first to me,—
Be happy as ever at home,
    If so, as I wish, it be.
Possess thy heart, my own;
    And sing to the child on thy knee
Or read to thyself alone
    The songs that I made for thee.
When Death to Either Shall Come

22 When first we met we did not guess
That Love would prove so hard a master;
Of more than common friendliness

When first we met we did not guess.
Who could foretell this sore distress,
This irretrievable disaster
When first we met?—We did not guess
That Love would prove so hard a master.
Triolet

JOHN BRIGHT 1811–1889

1 The angel of death has been abroad throughout the
land; you may almost hear the beating of his wings.
House of Commons, 23 Feb. 1855

2 I am for 'Peace, retrenchment, and reform', the
watchword of the great Liberal party 30 years ago.
Birmingham, 28 Apr. 1859

3 My opinion is that the Northern States will manage
somehow to muddle through.
During the American Civil War. Justin McCarthy, *Reminiscences*
(1899)

4 England is the mother of Parliaments.
Birmingham, 18 Jan. 1865

5 The right hon Gentleman...has retired into what may
be called his political Cave of Adullam—and he has
called about him every one that was in distress and
every one that was discontented.
House of Commons, 13 Mar. 1866

6 This party of two is like the Scotch terrier that was so
covered with hair that you could not tell which was the
head and which was the tail.

7 Force is not a remedy.
Birmingham, 16 Nov. 1880

8 The knowledge of the ancient languages is mainly a
luxury.
Letter in *Pall Mall Gazette*, 30 Nov. 1886

ANTHELME BRILLAT-SAVARIN 1755–1826

9 *Dis-moi ce que tu manges, je te dirai ce que tu es.*
Tell me what you eat and I will tell you what you are.
Physiologie du Goût (1825), **Aphorismes...pour servir de
prolégomènes...** iv. See 210:35

ALEXANDER BROME 1620–1666

10 I have been in love, and in debt, and in drink,
This many and many a year.
The Mad Lover, 1.1

RICHARD BROME d. 1652?

11 You rose o' the wrong side to-day.
The Court Beggar (1632), Act II

12 I am a gentleman, though spoiled i' the breeding. The
Buzzards are all gentlemen. We came in with the
Conqueror.
English Moor, III.ii

ANNE BRONTË 1820–1849

13 Because the road is rough and long,
Shall we despise the skylark's song?
Views of Life

CHARLOTTE BRONTË 1816–1855

14 Conventionality is not morality. Self-righteousness is
not religion. To attack the first is not to assail the last.

To pluck the mask from the face of the Pharisee, is not
to lift an impious hand to the Crown of Thorns.
Jane Eyre. Preface to 2nd edition, 1847

15 Reader, I married him.
ch.38

16 Of late years an abundant shower of curates has fallen
upon the North of England.
Shirley, ch.1, opening words

17 One day, in the autumn of 1845, I accidentally lighted
on a MS volume of verse in my sister Emily's
handwriting...I looked it over, and something more
than surprise seized me,—a deep conviction that these
were not common effusions, nor at all like the poetry
women generally write. I thought them condensed and
terse, vigorous and genuine. To my ear, they had also
a peculiar music—wild, melancholy, and elevating.
Biographical Notice of Ellis and Acton Bell by Currer Bell.
Published in the 1850 reprint of *Wuthering Heights* and *Agnes
Grey.*

EMILY BRONTË 1818–1848

18 No coward soul is mine,
No trembler in the world's storm-troubled sphere:
    I see Heaven's glories shine,
And faith shines equal, arming me from fear.
Last Lines

19 O God within my breast,
Almighty! ever-present Deity!
    Life—that in me has rest,
As I—undying Life—have power in Thee!

20 Vain are the thousand creeds
That move men's hearts: unutterably vain;
    Worthless as withered weeds,
Or idlest froth amid the boundless main.

21 Oh! dreadful is the check—intense the agony—
When the ear begins to hear, and the eye begins to
    see;
When the pulse begins to throb, the brain to think
    again;
The soul to feel the flesh, and the flesh to feel the
    chain.
The Prisoner

22 Cold in the earth—and fifteen wild Decembers,
From those brown hills, have melted into spring.
Remembrance

23 Sweet Love of youth, forgive, if I forget thee,
While the world's tide is bearing me along;
Other desires and other hopes beset me,
Hopes which obscure, but cannot do thee wrong!

24 But when the days of golden dreams had perished,
And even Despair was powerless to destroy,
Then did I learn how existence could be cherished,
Strengthened, and fed without the aid of joy.

25 If all else perished, and he remained, I should still
continue to be; and if all else remained, and he were
annihilated, the universe would turn to a mighty
stranger: I should not seem a part of it. My love for
Linton is like the foliage in the woods; time will
change it, I'm well aware, as winter changes the
trees—My love for Heathcliff resembles the eternal
rocks beneath:—a source of little visible delight, but
necessary.
Wuthering Heights, ch.9

1 I lingered round them, under that benign sky: watched
the moths fluttering among the heath and hare-bells;
listened to the soft wind breathing through the grass;
and wondered how any one could ever imagine
unquiet slumbers for the sleepers in that quiet earth.
last words

REVD. PATRICK BRONTË 1777–1861

2 Girls, do you know Charlotte has been writing a book,
and it is much better than likely?
Elizabeth Gaskell, *Life of Charlotte Brontë*, ch.16

3 No quailing, Mrs Gaskell! no drawing back!
About her undertaking to write the life of Charlotte Brontë.
Elizabeth Gaskell, letter to Ellen Nussey, 24 July 1855

HENRY BROOKE 1703?–1783

4 For righteous monarchs,
Justly to judge, with their own eyes should see;
To rule o'er freemen, should themselves be free.
Earl of Essex (1749), I

RUPERT BROOKE 1887–1915

5 The hawthorn hedge puts forth its buds,
And my heart puts forth its pain.
All Suddenly the Spring Comes Soft

6 Now that we've done our best and worst, and parted.
The Busy Heart

7 Blow out, you bugles, over the rich Dead!
    There's none of these so lonely and poor of old,
    But, dying, has made us rarer gifts than gold.
These laid the world away; poured out the red
Sweet wine of youth; gave up the years to be
    Of work and joy, and that unhoped serene,
    That men call age; and those who would have been,
Their sons, they gave, their immortality.
The Dead

8 The cool kindliness of sheets, that soon
Smooth away trouble; and the rough male kiss of
    blankets.
The Great Lover

9 The benison of hot water.

10 Fish say, they have their stream and pond;
But is there anything beyond?
Heaven

11 One may not doubt that, somehow, good
Shall come of water and of mud;
And, sure, the reverent eye must see
A purpose in liquidity.

12 But somewhere, beyond space and time,
Is wetter water, slimier slime!

13 Immense, of fishy form and mind,
Squamous, omnipotent, and kind;
And under that Almighty Fin,
The littlest fish may enter in.
Oh! never fly conceals a hook,
Fish say, in the Eternal Brook,
But more than mundane weeds are there,
And mud, celestially fair.

14 Unfading moths, immortal flies,
And the worm that never dies.
And in that Heaven of all their wish,

There shall be no more land, say fish.

15 Breathless, we flung us on the windy hill,
Laughed in the sun, and kissed the lovely grass.
The Hill

16 With snuffle and sniff and handkerchief,
    And dim and decorous mirth,
With ham and sherry, they'll meet to bury
    The lordliest lass of earth.
**Lines Written in the Belief that the Ancient Roman Festival of
the Dead was called Ambarvalia**

17 Oh! there the chestnuts, summer through,
Beside the river make for you
A tunnel of green gloom, and sleep
Deeply above.
The Old Vicarage, Grantchester

18 Here tulips bloom as they are told;
Unkempt about those hedges blows
An English unofficial rose.

19 And there the unregulated sun
Slopes down to rest when day is done,
And wakes a vague unpunctual star,
A slippered Hesper.

20 εἴθε γενοίμην …would I were
In Grantchester, in Grantchester!

21 Curates, long dust, will come and go
On lissom, clerical, printless toe;
And oft between the boughs is seen
The sly shade of a Rural Dean.

22 God! I will pack, and take a train,
And get me to England once again!

23 For Cambridge people rarely smile,
Being urban, squat, and packed with guile.

24 They love the Good; they worship Truth;
They laugh uproariously in youth;
(And when they get to feeling old,
They up and shoot themselves, I'm told.)

25 Stands the Church clock at ten to three?
And is there honey still for tea?

26 Now, God be thanked Who has matched us with His
    hour,
And caught our youth, and wakened us from sleeping.
Peace

27 Leave the sick hearts that honour could not move,
And half-men, and their dirty songs and dreary,
And all the little emptiness of love.

28 Naught broken save this body, lost but breath;
Nothing to shake the laughing heart's long peace there
But only agony, and that has ending;
And the worst friend and enemy is but Death.

29 Some white tremendous daybreak.
Second Best

30 If I should die, think only this of me:
That there's some corner of a foreign field
That is for ever England. There shall be
In that rich earth a richer dust concealed;
A dust whom England bore, shaped, made aware,
Gave, once, her flowers to love, her ways to roam,
A body of England's, breathing English air,
Washed by the rivers, blest by suns of home.
And think, this heart, all evil shed away,
A pulse in the eternal mind, no less

Gives somewhere back the thoughts by England given.
Her sights and sounds; dreams happy as her day;
And laughter, learnt of friends; and gentleness,
In hearts at peace, under an English heaven.
The Soldier

1 And there's an end, I think, of kissing,
When our mouths are one with Mouth.
Tiare Tahiti

THOMAS BROOKS 1608–1680

2 For (magna est veritas et praevalebit) great is truth,
and shall prevail.
The Crown and Glory of Christianity (1662), p.407. See 83:26

ROBERT BARNABAS BROUGH 1828–1860

3 My Lord Tomnoddy is thirty-four;
The Earl can last but a few years more.
My Lord in the Peers will take his place:
Her Majesty's councils his words will grace.
Office he'll hold and patronage sway;
Fortunes and lives he will vote away;
And what are his qualifications?—ONE!
He's the Earl of Fitzdotterel's eldest son.
My Lord Tomnoddy

LORD BROUGHAM 1778–1868

4 In my mind, he was guilty of no error,—he was
chargeable with no exaggeration,—he was betrayed by
his fancy into no metaphor, who once said, that all we
see about us, Kings, Lords, and Commons, the whole
machinery of the State, all the apparatus of the system,
and its varied workings, end in simply bringing twelve
good men into a box.
Speech on the Present State of the Law, 7 Feb. 1828

5 Look out, gentlemen, the schoolmaster is abroad!
Speech, London Mechanics' Institute, 1825

6 Education makes a people easy to lead, but difficult to
drive; easy to govern, but impossible to enslave.
Attr.

JOHN BROWN 1715–1766

7 Altogether upon the high horse.
Letter to Garrick, 27 Oct. 1765

THOMAS BROWN 1663–1704

8 In the reign of King Charles the Second, a certain
worthy Divine at Whitehall, thus address'd himself to
the auditory at the conclusion of his sermon: 'In short,
if you don't live up to the precepts of the Gospel, but
abandon your selves to your irregular appetites, you
must expect to receive your reward in a certain place,
which 'tis not good manners to mention here.'
Laconics

9 A little before you made a leap into the dark.
Letters from the Dead. See 251:24

10 I do not love you, Dr Fell,
But why I cannot tell;
But this I know full well,
I do not love you, Dr Fell.
Works (1719), vol.IV, p.113. See 331:9

T.E. BROWN 1830–1897

11 O blackbird, what a boy you are!
How you do go it.
The Blackbird

12 A garden is a lovesome thing, God wot!
My Garden

CECIL BROWNE

13 But not so odd
As those who choose
A Jewish God,
But spurn the Jews.
Reply to 209:13

SIR THOMAS BROWNE 1605–1682

14 Oblivion is a kind of Annihilation.
Christian Morals, pt.i, xxi

15 He who discommendeth others obliquely commendeth
himself.
xxxiv

16 As for that famous network of Vulcan, which enclosed
Mars and Venus, and caused that unextinguishable
laugh in heaven, since the gods themselves could not
discern it, we shall not pry into it.
The Garden of Cyrus (1658), ch.2

17 Life itself is but the shadow of death, and souls
departed but the shadows of the living. All things fall
under this name. The sun itself is but the dark
simulacrum, and light but the shadow of God.
ch.4

18 Flat and flexible truths are beat out by every hammer;
but Vulcan and his whole forge sweat to work out
Achilles his armour.
ch.5

19 But the quincunx of heaven runs low, and 'tis time to
close the five ports of knowledge.

20 All things began in order, so shall they end, and so
shall they begin again; according to the ordainer of
order and mystical mathematics of the city of heaven.

21 Nor will the sweetest delight of gardens afford much
comfort in sleep; wherein the dullness of that sense
shakes hands with delectable odours; and though in the
bed of Cleopatra, can hardly with any delight raise up
the ghost of a rose.

22 Though Somnus in Homer be sent to rouse up
Agamemnon, I find no such effects in these drowsy
approaches of sleep. To keep our eyes open longer
were but to act our Antipodes. The huntsmen are up in
America, and they are already past their first sleep in
Persia. But who can be drowsy at that hour which
freed us from everlasting sleep? or have slumbering
thoughts at that time, when sleep itself must end, and,
as some conjecture, all shall awake again?

23 That children dream not in the first half year, that men
dream not in some countries, are to me sick men's
dreams, dreams out of the ivory gate, and visions
before midnight.
On Dreams

24 Half our days we pass in the shadow of the earth; and
the brother of death exacteth a third part of our lives.

25 That the Jews stink naturally...is a received opinion

we know not how to admit.
Pseudodoxia Epidemica, Bk.4, 10

1 Half our days we pass in the shadow of the earth; and the brother of death exacteth a third part of our lives.

2 I dare, without usurpation, assume the honourable style of a Christian.
Religio Medici (1643), pt.i, 1

3 At my devotion I love to use the civility of my knee, my hat, and hand.
3

4 I could never divide my self from any man upon the difference of an opinion, or be angry with his judgment for not agreeing with me in that, from which perhaps within a few days I should dissent my self.
6

5 Many...have too rashly charged the troops of error, and remain as trophies unto the enemies of truth.

6 A man may be in as just possession of truth as of a city, and yet be forced to surrender.

7 There is another man within me, that's angry with me, rebukes, commands, and dastards me.
7

8 As for those wingy mysteries in divinity, and airy subtleties in religion, which have unhinged the brains of better heads, they never stretched the *pia mater* of mine. Methinks there be not impossibilities enough in Religion for an active faith.
9

9 I love to lose myself in a mystery; to pursue my reason to an *O altitudo!*
10

10 Who can speak of eternity without a solecism, or think thereof without an ecstasy? Time we may comprehend, 'tis but five days elder than ourselves.
11

11 I have often admired the mystical way of Pythagoras, and the secret magic of numbers.
12

12 We carry within us the wonders we seek without us: There is all Africa and her prodigies in us.
15

13 All things are artificial, for nature is the art of God.
16

14 'Twill be hard to find one that deserves to carry the buckler unto Samson.
21

15 Obstinacy in a bad cause, is but constancy in a good.
25

16 Persecution is a bad and indirect way to plant religion.

17 There are many (questionless) canonized on earth, that shall never be Saints in Heaven.
26

18 Not wrung from speculations and subtleties, but from common sense and observation—not pickt from the leaves of any author, but bred amongst the weeds and tares of mine own brain.
36

19 When I take a full view and circle of myself, without this reasonable moderator and equal piece of justice, Death, I do conceive myself the miserablest person extant.
38

20 I am not so much afraid of death, as ashamed thereof; 'tis the very disgrace and ignominy of our natures, that in a moment can so disfigure us that our nearest friends, wife, and children, stand afraid and start at us.
40

21 Certainly there is no happiness within this circle of flesh, nor is it in the optics of these eyes to behold felicity; the first day of our Jubilee is death.
44

22 He forgets that he can die who complains of misery—we are in the power of no calamity while death is in our own.

23 I have tried if I could reach that great resolution...to be honest without a thought of Heaven or Hell.
47

24 To believe only possibilities, is not faith, but mere Philosophy.
48

25 There is no road or ready way to virtue.
55

26 My desires only are, and I shall be happy therein, to be but the last man, and bring up the rear in heaven.
57

27 I am of a constitution so general, that it consorts and sympathiseth with all things. I have no antipathy, or rather idiosyncrasy, in diet, humour, air, any thing.
pt.ii, 1

28 I feel not in myself those common antipathies that I can discover in others; those national repugnances do not touch me, nor do I behold with prejudice the French, Italian, Spaniard, or Dutch; but where I find their actions in balance with my countrymen's, I honour, love and embrace them in the same degree.

29 All places, all airs make unto me one country; I am in England, everywhere, and under any meridian.

30 If there be any among those common objects of hatred I do contemn and laugh at, it is that great enemy of reason, virtue, and religion, the multitude; that numerous piece of monstrosity, which, taken asunder, seem men, and the reasonable creatures of God, but, confused together, make but one great beast, and a monstrosity more prodigious than Hydra.

31 It is the common wonder of all men, how among so many millions of faces, there should be none alike.
2

32 No man can justly censure or condemn another, because indeed no man truly knows another.
4

33 I could be content that we might procreate like trees, without conjunction, or that there were any way to perpetuate the World without this trivial and vulgar way of coition: it is the foolishest act a wise man commits in all his life; nor is there any thing that will more deject his cool'd imagination, when he shall consider what an odd and unworthy piece of folly he hath committed.
9

34 Sure there is music even in the beauty, and the silent note which Cupid strikes, far sweeter than the sound of an instrument. For there is a music wherever there is a harmony, order or proportion; and thus far we may maintain the music of the spheres; for those well ordered motions, and regular paces, though they give no sound unto the ear, yet to the understanding they strike a note most full of harmony.

1 For even that vulgar and tavern music, which makes one man merry, another mad, strikes in me a deep fit of devotion, and a profound contemplation of the first Composer, there is something in it of divinity more than the ear discovers.

2 We all labour against our own cure, for death is the cure of all diseases.

3 For the world, I count it not an inn, but an hospital, and a place, not to live, but to die in.
11

4 There is surely a piece of divinity in us, something that was before the elements, and owes no homage unto the sun.

5 [Sleep is] in fine, so like death, I dare not trust it without my prayers.
12

6 Sleep is a death, O make me try,
By sleeping what it is to die.
And as gently lay my head
On my grave, as now my bed.

7 Old mortality, the ruins of forgotten times.
Urn Burial (1658), Epistle Dedicatory

8 With rich flames, and hired tears, they solemnized their obsequies.
ch.3

9 Men have lost their reason in nothing so much as their religion, wherein stones and clouts make martyrs.
ch.4

10 They carried them out of the world with their feet forward.

11 Were the happiness of the next world as closely apprehended as the felicities of this, it were a martyrdom to live.

12 Time, which antiquates antiquities, and hath an art to make dust of all things, hath yet spared these minor monuments.
ch.5

13 The long habit of living indisposeth us for dying.

14 What song the Syrens sang, or what name Achilles assumed when he hid himself among women, though puzzling questions, are not beyond all conjecture.

15 But to subsist in bones, and be but pyramidally extant, is a fallacy in duration.

16 Generations pass while some tree stands, and old families last not three oaks.

17 To be nameless in worthy deeds exceeds an infamous history.

18 But the iniquity of oblivion blindly scattereth her poppy, and deals with the memory of men without distinction to merit of perpetuity.

19 Herostatus lives that burnt the Temple of Diana—he is almost lost that built it.

20 The night of time far surpasseth the day, and who knows when was the equinox?

21 Diuturnity is a dream and a folly of expectation.

22 Mummy is become merchandise, Mizraim cures wounds, and Pharaoh is sold for balsams.

23 Man is a noble animal, splendid in ashes, and pompous in the grave.

24 Ready to be any thing, in the ecstasy of being ever, and as content with six foot as the *moles* of Adrianus.

WILLIAM BROWNE 1591–1643

25 Underneath this sable hearse
Lies the subject of all verse,
Sidney's sister, Pembroke's mother;
Death! ere thou hast slain another,
Fair and learn'd, and good as she,
Time shall throw a dart at thee.
Epitaph. On the Countess of Pembroke

SIR WILLIAM BROWNE 1692–1774

26 The King to Oxford sent a troop of horse,
For Tories own no argument but force:
With equal skill to Cambridge books he sent,
For Whigs admit no force but argument.
Reply to Trapp's epigram See 552:5. Nichols' *Literary Anecdotes*, vol.III, p.330

ELIZABETH BARRETT BROWNING 1806–1861

27   Near all the birds
Will sing at dawn,—and yet we do not take
The chaffering swallow for the holy lark.
Aurora Leigh (1857), bk.i

28 God answers sharp and sudden on some prayers,
And thrusts the thing we have prayed for in our face,
A gauntlet with a gift in't.
bk.ii

29 The music soars within the little lark,
And the lark soars.
bk.iii

30 I think it frets the saints in heaven to see
How many desolate creatures on the earth
Have learnt the simple dues of fellowship
And social comfort, in a hospital.

31 Since when was genius found respectable?
bk.vi

32 The devil's most devilish when respectable.
bk.vii

33   Earth's crammed with heaven,
And every common bush afire with God;
But only he who sees, takes off his shoes,
The rest sit round it and pluck blackberries,
And daub their natural faces unaware
More and more from the first similitude.

34   'Jasper first,' I said,
'And second sapphire; third chalcedony;
The rest in order,—last an amethyst.'
bk.ix

35 And kings crept out again to feel the sun.
Crowned and Buried

36 But the young, young children, O my brothers,
They are weeping bitterly!
They are weeping in the playtime of the others,

In the country of the free.
The Cry of the Children (1843)

1 And lips say, 'God be pitiful,'
Who ne'er said, 'God be praised.'
Cry of the Human

2 And that dismal cry rose slowly
And sank slowly through the air,
Full of spirit's melancholy
And eternity's despair!
And they heard the words it said—
Pan is dead! great Pan is dead!
Pan, Pan is dead!
The Dead Pan

3 Or from Browning some 'Pomegranate', which, if cut
    deep down the middle,
Shows a heart within blood-tinctured, of a veined
    humanity.
Lady Geraldine's Courtship, xli

4 By thunders of white silence, overthrown.
Hiram Power's Greek Slave

5 'Yes,' I answered you last night;
    'No,' this morning, sir, I say.
Colours seen by candle-light
Will not look the same by day.
The Lady's Yes

6 What was he doing, the great god Pan,
    Down in the reeds by the river?
Spreading ruin and scattering ban,
Splashing and paddling with hoofs of a goat,
And breaking the golden lilies afloat
    With the dragon-fly on the river.
A Musical Instrument

7 I tell you, hopeless grief is passionless.
Sonnets. Grief

8   Deep-hearted man, express
Grief for thy dead in silence like to death;
Most like a monumental statue set
In everlasting watch and moveless woe,
Till itself crumble to the dust beneath.
Touch it: the marble eyelids are not wet—
If it could weep, it could arise and go.

9   Straightway I was 'ware,
So weeping, how a mystic shape did move
Behind me, and drew me backward by the hair
And a voice said in mastery while I strove...
'Guess now who holds thee?'—'Death', I said, but
    there
The silver answer rang...'Not Death, but Love.'
Sonnets from the Portuguese, 1

10   For frequent tears have run
The colours from my life.
8

11 If thou must love me, let it be for naught
Except for love's sake only.
14

12 First time he kissed me, he but only kissed
The fingers of this hand wherewith I write;
And, ever since, it grew more clean and white.
38

13 How do I love thee? Let me count the ways.
43

14   If God choose,
I shall but love thee better after death.

15 Thou large-brained woman and large-hearted man.
To George Sand. A Desire

16 And the rolling anapaestic
Curled like vapour over shrines!
Wine of Cyprus, x

ROBERT BROWNING 1812–1889

17 Burrow awhile and build, broad on the roots of things.
Abt Vogler, ii

18 On the earth the broken arcs; in the heaven, a perfect
    round.
ix

19 All we have willed or hoped or dreamed of good shall
    exist.
x

20 The high that proved too high, the heroic for earth too
    hard,
The passion that left the ground to lose itself in the
    sky,
Are music sent up to God by the lover and the bard;
Enough that he heard it once: we shall hear it by and
    by.

21 But God has a few of us whom he whispers in the ear;
The rest may reason and welcome; 'tis we musicians
    know.
xi

22   I feel for the common chord again...
The C Major of this life.
xii

23 So free we seem, so fettered fast we are!
Andrea del Sarto, l.51

24 Ah, but a man's reach should exceed his grasp,
Or what's a heaven for?
l.97

25 It all comes to the same thing at the end.
Any Wife to Any Husband, xvi

26 Why need the other women know so much?
xvii

27 A minute's success pays the failure of years.
Apollo and the Fates, prologue

28 But, thanks to wine-lees and democracy,
We've still our stage where truth calls spade a spade!
Aristophanes' Apology, l.392

29 But flame? The Bush is bare.
Asolando, Prologue

30 All the breath and the bloom of the year in the bag of
    one bee.
Summum Bonum

31 At the midnight in the silence of the sleep-time,
When you set your fancies free.
Epilogue

32 One who never turned his back but marched breast
    forward,
    Never doubted clouds would break,
Never dreamed, though right were worsted, wrong
    would triumph,
    Held we fall to rise, are baffled to fight better,
        Sleep to wake.

33 Greet the unseen with a cheer.

34   I find earth not grey but rosy,
Heaven not grim but fair of hue.

Do I stoop? I pluck a posy.
Do I stand and stare? All's blue.
At the 'Mermaid'

1   There up spoke a brisk little somebody,
Critic and whippersnapper, in a rage
    To set things right.
Balaustion's Adventure, pt.i, l.308

2   Don't you know,
I promised, if you'd watch a dinner out,
We'd see truth dawn together?—truth that peeps
Over the glass's edge when dinner's done,
And body gets its sop and holds its noise
And leaves soul free a little.
Bishop Blougram's Apology, l.15

3   A piano-forte is a fine resource,
All Balzac's novels occupy one shelf,
The new edition fifty volumes long.
l.107

4   Just when we're safest, there's a sunset-touch,
A fancy from a flower-bell, some one's death,
A chorus-ending from Euripides,—
And that's enough for fifty hopes and fears
As old and new at once as nature's self,
To rap and knock and enter in our soul,
Take hands and dance there, a fantastic ring,
Round the ancient idol, on his base again,—
The grand Perhaps.
l.182

5   All we have gained then by our unbelief
Is a life of doubt diversified by faith,
For one of faith diversified by doubt:
We called the chess-board white—we call it black.
l.209

6   Demirep
That loves and saves her soul in new French books.
l.397

7   You, for example, clever to a fault,
The rough and ready man who write apace,
Read somewhat seldomer, think perhaps even less.
l.420

8   And that's what all the blessed Evil's for.
l.655

9   How you'd exult if I could put you back
Six hundred years, blot out cosmogeny,
Geology, ethnology, what not...
And set you square with Genesis again.
l.678

10 No, when the fight begins within himself,
A man's worth something.
l.693

11 He said true things, but called them by wrong names.
l.996

12 Saint Praxed's ever was the church for peace.
The Bishop Orders His Tomb at Saint Praxed's Church, l.14

13 And have I not Saint Praxed's ear to pray
Horses for ye, and brown Greek manuscripts,
And mistresses with great smooth marbly limbs?
—That's if ye carve my epitaph aright.
l.73

14 And then how I shall lie through centuries,
And hear the blessed mutter of the mass,
And see God made and eaten all day long,
And feel the steady candle-flame, and taste

Good strong thick stupefying incense-smoke!
l.80

15 Aha, ELUCESCEBAT quoth our friend?
No Tully, said I, Ulpian at the best.
l.99

16 I was so young, I loved him so, I had
No mother, God forgot me, and I fell.
A Blot in the 'Scutcheon (1843), I.iii.l.508

17 How well I know what I mean to do
    When the long dark autumn-evenings come.
By the Fireside, i

18 I shall be found by the fire, suppose,
    O'er a great wise book as beseemeth age,
While the shutters flap as the cross-wind blows
    And I turn the page, and I turn the page,
Not verse now, only prose!
ii

19   That great brow
And the spirit-small hand propping it.
xxiii

20 When earth breaks up and heaven expands,
How will the change strike me and you
In the house not made with hands?
xxvii. See 77:6

21 We two stood there with never a third.
xxxviii

22 Oh, the little more, and how much it is!
    And the little less, and what worlds away!
xxxix

23 If two lives join, there is oft a scar.
    They are one and one, with a shadowy third;
One near one is too far.
xlvi

24 Letting the rank tongue blossom into speech.
Setebos, Setebos, and Setebos!
'Thinketh, He dwelleth i' the cold o' the moon.
'Thinketh He made it, with the sun to match,
But not the stars; the stars came otherwise.
Caliban upon Setebos, l.24

25 'Let twenty pass, and stone the twenty-first.
Loving not, hating not, just choosing so.
l.103

26 Kentish Sir Byng stood for his King,
Bidding the crop-headed Parliament swing:
And, pressing a troop unable to stoop
And see the rogues flourish and honest folk droop,
Marched them along, fifty-score strong,
Great-hearted gentlemen, singing this song.

God for King Charles! Pym and such carles
To the Devil that prompts 'em their treasonous parles!
Cavalier Tunes, 1. **Marching Along**

27 Boot, saddle, to horse, and away!
3. **Boot and Saddle**

28 One stiff blind horse, his every bone a-stare.
Childe Roland to the Dark Tower Came, xiii

29 I never saw a brute I hated so;
He must be wicked to deserve such pain.
xiv

30 Dauntless the slug-horn to my lips I set,
And blew. '*Childe Roland to the Dark Tower came.*'
xxxiv. See 454:27

1 In the natural fog of the good man's mind.
Christmas Eve, l.226

2 Some thrilling view of the surplice-question.
l.839

3 The raree-show of Peter's successor.
l.1242

4   For the preacher's merit or demerit,
   It were to be wished the flaws were fewer
     In the earthen vessel, holding treasure,
   Which lies as safe in a golden ewer;
     But the main thing is, does it hold good measure?
   Heaven soon sets right all other matters!
   l.1311

5 I have written three books on the soul,
   Proving absurd all written hitherto,
   And putting us to ignorance again.
   Cleon, l.57

6 What is he buzzing in my ears?
   'Now that I come to die,
   Do I view the world as a vale of tears?'
     Ah, reverend sir, not I!
   Confessions

7 To mine, it serves for the old June weather
     Blue above lane and wall;
   And that farthest bottle labelled 'Ether'
     Is the house o'ertopping all.

8   We loved, sir—used to meet:
   How sad and bad and mad it was—
     But then, how it was sweet!

9 Stung by the splendour of a sudden thought.
   A Death in the Desert, l.59

10 For I say, this is death and the sole death,
   When a man's loss comes to him from his gain,
   Darkness from light, from knowledge ignorance,
   And lack of love from love made manifest.
   l.482

11 Progress, man's distinctive mark alone,
   Not God's, and not the beasts': God is, they are,
   Man partly is and wholly hopes to be.
   l.586

12 Your ghost will walk, you lover of trees,
     (If our loves remain)
   In an English lane.
   De Gustibus

13 The bean-flowers' boon,
   And the blackbird's tune,
   And May, and June!

14 Italy, my Italy!
   Queen Mary's saying serves for me—
     (When fortune's malice
     Lost her—Calais)—
   Open my heart and you will see
   Graved inside of it, 'Italy'.

15 Reads verse and thinks she understands.
   Dis aliter visum, iv

16 Schumann's our music-maker now.
   viii

17 Ingres's the modern man who paints.

18 Heine for songs; for kisses, how?

19 Sure of the Fortieth spare Arm-chair

When gout and glory seat me there.
xii

20 Here comes my husband from his whist.
xxx

21   'Tis well averred,
   A scientific faith's absurd.
   Easter Day, vi

22 At last awake
   From life, that insane dream we take
   For waking now.
   xiv

23 A fierce vindictive scribble of red.
   xv

24 Karshish, the picker-up of learning's crumbs,
   The not-incurious in God's handiwork.
   An Epistle

25 Beautiful Evelyn Hope is dead!
   Evelyn Hope

26 You will wake, and remember, and understand.

27 Truth never hurts the teller.
   Fifine at the Fair, xxxii

28 I must learn Spanish, one of these days,
     Only for that slow sweet name's sake.
   The Flower's Name

29 If you get simple beauty and nought else,
   You get about the best thing God invents.
   Fra Lippo Lippi, l.217

30 You should not take a fellow eight years old
   And make him swear to never kiss the girls.
   l.224

31   This world's no blot for us,
   Nor blank; it means intensely, and means good:
   To find its meaning is my meat and drink.
   l.313

32 Let us begin and carry up this corpse,
     Singing together.
   A Grammarian's Funeral, l.1

33 Our low life was the level's and the night's;
     He's for the morning.
   l.23

34 This is our master, famous, calm, and dead,
     Born on our shoulders.
   l.27

35 Yea, but we found him bald too, eyes like lead,
     Accents uncertain:
   'Time to taste life,' another would have said,
     'Up with the curtain!'
   l.53

36 Yea, this in him was the peculiar grace...
   Still before living he'd learn how to live.
   l.75

37 He said, 'What's time? Leave Now for dogs and apes!
     Man has Forever.'
   l.83

38 That low man seeks a little thing to do,
     Sees it and does it:
   This high man, with a great thing to pursue,
     Dies ere he knows it:
   That low man goes on adding one to one,
     His hundred's soon hit;
   This high man, aiming at a million,
     Misses an unit.

That, has the world here—should he need the next,
  Let the world mind him!
This, throws himself on God, and unperplext
  Seeking shall find Him.
1.113

1 He settled *Hoti's* business—let it be!--
  Properly based *Oun*—
Gave us the doctrine of the enclitic *De*,
  Dead from the waist down.
1.129

2 Lofty designs must close in like effects:
  Loftily lying,
Leave him—still loftier than the world suspects,
  Living and dying.
1.145

3 The Lord will have mercy on Jacob yet,
And again in his border see Israel set.
Holy-Cross Day, xiii

4 We withstood Christ then? Be mindful how
At least we withstand Barabbas now!
xviii

5 Oh, to be in England
Now that April's there,
And whoever wakes in England
Sees, some morning, unaware,
That the lowest boughs and the brushwood sheaf
Round the elm-tree bole are in tiny leaf,
While the chaffinch sings on the orchard bough
In England—now!
Home-Thoughts, from Abroad

6 That's the wise thrush; he sings each song twice over,
Lest you should think he never could recapture
The first fine careless rapture!

7 All will be gay when noontide wakes anew
The buttercups, the little children's dower
—Far brighter than this gaudy melon-flower!

8 Nobly, nobly Cape St Vincent to the North-west died
    away;
Sunset ran, one glorious blood-red, reeking into Cadiz
    Bay.
Home-Thoughts, from the Sea

9 'Here and here did England help me: how can I help
    England?'—say,
Whoso turns as I, this evening, turn to God to praise
    and pray,
While Jove's planet rises yonder, silent over Africa.

10   'With this same key
Shakespeare unlocked his heart' once more!
Did Shakespeare? If so, the less Shakespeare he!
House, x. See 582:14

11 He took such cognizance of men and things.
How it Strikes a Contemporary, 1.30

12 I sprang to the stirrup, and Joris, and he;
I galloped, Dirck galloped, we galloped all three.
How they brought the Good News from Ghent to Aix

13 A man can have but one life and one death,
One heaven, one hell.
In a Balcony, 1.13

14   I count life just a stuff
To try the soul's strength on.
1.651

15 The moth's kiss, first!

Kiss me as if you made believe
You were not sure, this eve,
How my face, your flower, had pursed
Its petals up...
The bee's kiss, now!
Kiss me as if you entered gay
My heart at some noonday.
In a Gondola

16 'You're wounded!' 'Nay,' the soldier's pride
  Touched to the quick, he said:
'I'm killed, Sire!' And his chief beside
  Smiling the boy fell dead.
Incident of the French Camp

17 Ignorance is not innocence but sin.
The Inn Album, v

18 Just my vengeance complete,
The man sprang to his feet,
Stood erect, caught at God's skirts, and prayed!
—So, *I* was afraid!
Instans Tyrannus

19 The swallow has set her six young on the rail,
  And looks seaward.
James Lee's Wife, III.i

20 Oh, good gigantic smile o' the brown old earth,
  This autumn morning!
VII.i

21 I should be dead of joy, James Lee.
IX.viii

22 I said—Then, dearest, since 'tis so,
Since now at length my fate I know,
Since nothing all my love avails,
Since all, my life seemed meant for, fails,
  Since this was written and needs must be—
My whole heart rises up to bless
Your name in pride and thankfulness!
Take back the hope you gave,—I claim
Only a memory of the same.
The Last Ride Together, i

23 Who knows but the world may end to-night?
ii

24   My soul
Smoothed itself out, a long-cramped scroll
Freshening and fluttering in the wind...
Had I said that, had I done this,
So might I gain, so might I miss.
Might she have loved me? just as well
She might have hated, who can tell!
iv

25 Look at the end of work, contrast
The petty done, the undone vast,
This present of theirs with the hopeful past!
v

26 What hand and brain went ever paired?
vi

27 They scratch his name on the Abbey-stones.
My riding is better, by their leave.

28 Sing, riding's a joy! For me, I ride.
vii

29 Ride, ride together, for ever ride?
x

30 Escape me?
Never—

Beloved!
Life in a Love

1 But what if I fail of my purpose here?
It is but to keep the nerves at strain,
    To dry one's eyes and laugh at a fall,
And, baffled, get up and begin again.

2 So, I gave her eyes my own eyes to take,
    My hand sought hers as in earnest need,
And round she turned for my noble sake,
    And gave me herself indeed.
A Light Woman

3 'Tis an awkward thing to play with souls,
And matter enough to save one's own.

4 Just for a handful of silver he left us,
    Just for a riband to stick in his coat.
The Lost Leader

5 We that had loved him so, followed him, honoured
    him,
    Lived in his mild and magnificent eye,
Learned his great language, caught his clear accents,
    Made him our pattern to live and to die!
Shakespeare was of us, Milton was for us,
Burns, Shelley, were with us—they watch from their
    graves!

6 We shall march prospering,—not thro' his presence;
    Songs may inspirit us,—not from his lyre;
Deeds will be done,—while he boasts his quiescence,
    Still bidding crouch whom the rest bade aspire.

7 One more devils'-triumph and sorrow for angels,
One wrong more to man, one more insult to God!

8 Never glad confident morning again!

9 All's over, then; does truth sound bitter
    As one at first believes?
The Lost Mistress

10 Oppression makes the wise man mad.
Luria, iv

11 Argument's hot to the close.
Master Hugues of Saxe-Gotha, xiii

12 One dissertates, he is candid;
    Two must discept,—has distinguished.
xiv

13 And find a poor devil has ended his cares
At the foot of your rotten-runged rat-riddled stairs?
    Do I carry the moon in my pocket?
xxix

14 As I gain the cove with pushing prow,
And quench its speed i' the slushy sand.

Then a mile of warm sea-scented beach;
Three fields to cross till a farm appears;
A tap at the pane, the quick sharp scratch
And blue spurt of a lighted match,
And a voice less loud, thro' its joys and fears,
Than the two hearts beating each to each!
Meeting at Night

15 Ah, did you once see Shelley plain,
    And did he stop and speak to you
And did you speak to him again?
    How strange it seems, and new!
Memorabilia

16 A moulted feather, an eagle-feather!
Well, I forget the rest.

17 If such as came for wool, sir, went home shorn,
Where is the wrong I did them?
Mr. Sludge, 'The Medium', l.630

18   Solomon of saloons
And philosophic diner-out.
l.773

19 This trade of mine—I don't know, can't be sure
But there was something in it, tricks and all!
Really, I want to light up my own mind.
l.809

20 Boston's a hole, the herring-pond is wide,
V-notes are something, liberty still more.
Beside, is he the only fool in the world?
l.1523

21 That's my last Duchess painted on the wall,
Looking as if she were alive.
My Last Duchess, l.1

22   She had
A heart—how shall I say?—too soon made glad,
Too easily impressed; she liked whate'er
She looked on, and her looks went everywhere.
l.21

23 All I can say is—I saw it!
Natural Magic

24 Never the time and the place
    And the loved one all together!
Never the Time and the Place

25   A lion who dies of an ass's kick,
The wronged great soul of an ancient Master.
Old Pictures in Florence, vi

26   What's come to perfection perishes.
Things learned on earth, we shall practise in heaven.
    Works done least rapidly, Art most cherishes.
xvii

27 Lose who may—I still can say,
Those who win heaven, blest are they!
One Way of Love

28 Rafael made a century of sonnets,
Made and wrote them in a certain volume
Dinted with the silver-pointed pencil
Else he only used to draw Madonnas.
One Word More, ii

29 Suddenly, as rare things will, it vanished.
iv

30 Dante once prepared to paint an angel:
Whom to please? You whisper 'Beatrice'.
v

31 Dante, who loved well because he hated,
Hated wickedness that hinders loving.

32 Does he paint? he fain would write a poem,—
Does he write? he fain would paint a picture.
viii

33 Never dares the man put off the prophet.
x

34 Where my heart lies, let my brain lie also.
xiv

35 Blank to Zoroaster on his terrace,
Blind to Galileo on his turret,
Dumb to Homer, dumb to Keats—him, even!
xvi

36 God be thanked, the meanest of his creatures
Boasts two soul-sides, one to face the world with,

One to show a woman when he loves her!
xvii

1 Oh, their Rafael of the dear Madonnas,
Oh, their Dante of the dread Inferno,
Wrote one song—and in my brain I sing it,
Drew one angel—borne, see, on my bosom!
xix

2 Truth is within ourselves.
Paracelsus, pt.I, l.726

3 *Paracelsus:*
    I am he that aspired to KNOW: and thou?
Aprile:
    I would LOVE infinitely, and be loved!
pt.II, l.384

4   God is the perfect poet,
Who in his person acts his own creations.
l.648

5 Measure your mind's height by the shade it casts!
pt.III, l.821

6 I give the fight up: let there be an end,
A privacy, an obscure nook for me.
I want to be forgotten even by God.
pt.V, l.363

7 Like plants in mines which never saw the sun,
But dream of him, and guess where he may be,
And do their best to climb and get to him.
l.882

8   If I stoop
Into a dark tremendous sea of cloud,
It is but for a time; I press God's lamp
Close to my breast; its splendour, soon or late,
Will pierce the gloom: I shall emerge one day.
l.899

9 Round the cape of a sudden came the sea,
And the sun looked over the mountain's rim;
And straight was a path of gold for him,
And the need of a world of men for me.
Parting at Morning

10 It was roses, roses, all the way.
The Patriot

11 The air broke into a mist with bells.

12 Sun-treader, life and light be thine for ever!
(Shelley) *Pauline*, l.151

13 Ah, thought which saddens while it soothes!
Pictor Ignotus

14 Hamelin Town's in Brunswick,
    By famous Hanover city;
The river Weser, deep and wide,
    Washes its walls on the southern side.
The Pied Piper of Hamelin, st.i

15 Rats!
They fought the dogs and killed the cats,
    And bit the babies in the cradles,
And ate the cheeses out of the vats,
    And licked the soup from the cooks' own ladles,
Split open the kegs of salted sprats,
Made nests inside men's Sunday hats,
And even spoiled the women's chats
        By drowning their speaking
        With shrieking and squeaking
In fifty different sharps and flats.
ii

16 A plate of turtle green and glutinous.
iv

17 Anything like the sound of a rat
Makes my heart go pit-a-pat!

18 'Come in!'—the Mayor cried, looking bigger:
And in did come the strangest figure!
v

19 So munch on, crunch on, take your nuncheon,
Breakfast, supper, dinner, luncheon.
vii

20 So, Willy, let me and you be wipers
Of scores out with all men, especially pipers!
xv

21 The year's at the spring
And day's at the morn;
Morning's at seven;
The hill-side's dew-pearled;
The lark's on the wing;
The snail's on the thorn:
God's in his heaven,
All's right with the world!
Pippa Passes, pt.I, l.222

22 God must be glad one loves His world so much!
pt.III, l.73

23 No need that sort of king should ever die!
l.178

24 You'll look at least on love's remains,
    A grave's one violet:
Your look?—that pays a thousand pains.
    What's death? You'll love me yet!
l.314

25 All service ranks the same with God—
With God, whose puppets, best and worst,
Are we; there is no last nor first.
pt.IV, l.113

26 Stand still, true poet that you are!
    I know you; let me try and draw you.
Some night you'll fail us: when afar
    You rise, remember one man saw you,
Knew you, and named a star!
Popularity

27 Hobbs hints blue,—straight he turtle eats:
    Nobbs prints blue,—claret crowns his cup:
Nokes outdares Stokes in azure feats,—
    Both gorge. Who fished the murex up?
What porridge had John Keats?

28 The rain set early in to-night.
Porphyria's Lover

29   All her hair
In one long yellow string I wound
Three times her little throat around,
And strangled her. No pain felt she;
I am quite sure she felt no pain.

30 And all night long we have not stirred,
And yet God has not said a word!

31 Fear death?—to feel the fog in my throat,
    The mist in my face.
Prospice

32 I was ever a fighter, so—one fight more,
    The best and the last!
I would hate that death bandaged my eyes, and
    forbore,

And bade me creep past.

1 No! let me taste the whole of it, fare like my peers
   The heroes of old,
   Bear the brunt, in a minute pay glad life's arrears
   Of pain, darkness and cold.

2 Grow old along with me!
   The best is yet to be,
   The last of life, for which the first was made:
   Our times are in His hand
   Who saith, 'A whole I planned,
   Youth shows but half; trust God: see all, nor be
   afraid!'
   Rabbi ben Ezra, i

3 Irks care the crop-full bird? Frets doubt the
   maw-crammed beast?
   iv

4 For thence,—a paradox
   Which comforts while it mocks,—
   Shall life succeed in that it seems to fail:
   What I aspired to be,
   And was not, comforts me:
   A brute I might have been, but would not sink i' the
   scale.
   vii

5 Once more on my adventure brave and new.
   xiv

6   When evening shuts,
   A certain moment cuts
   The deed off, calls the glory from the grey.
   xvi

7   Now, who shall arbitrate?
   Ten men love what I hate.
   Shun what I follow, slight what I receive;
   Ten, who in ears and eyes
   Match me: we all surmise,
   They this thing, and I that: whom shall my soul
   believe?
   xxii

8 Fancies that broke through language and escaped.
   xxv

9   All that is, at all,
   Lasts ever, past recall;
   Earth changes, but thy soul and God stand sure.
   xxvii

10 Time's wheel runs back or stops: Potter and clay
   endure.

11 He fixed thee mid this dance
   Of plastic circumstance.
   xxviii

12 Look not thou down but up!
   To uses of a cup.
   xxx

13 My times be in Thy hand!
   Perfect the cup as planned!
   Let age approve of youth, and death complete the
   same!
   xxxii

14 Do you see this square old yellow Book, I toss
   I' the air, and catch again.
   The Ring and the Book, bk.i, l.33

15 The Life, Death, Miracles of Saint Somebody,

Saint Somebody Else, his Miracles, Death and Life.
l.80

16 Well, British Public, ye who like me not,
   (God love you!).
   l.410

17 'Go get you manned by Manning and new-manned
   By Newman and, mayhap, wise-manned to boot
   By Wiseman.'
   l.444

18   Youth means love,
   Vows can't change nature, priests are only men.
   l.1056

19 O lyric Love, half-angel and half-bird
   And all a wonder and a wild desire.
   l.1391

20 The story always old and always new.
   bk.ii, l.214

21 But facts are facts and flinch not.
   l.1049

22   Go practise if you please
   With men and women: leave a child alone
   For Christ's particular love's sake!—so I say.
   bk.iii, l.88

23 In the great right of an excessive wrong.
   l.1055

24 Everyone soon or late comes round by Rome.
   bk.v, l.296

25 'T was a thief said the last kind word to Christ:
   Christ took the kindness and forgave the theft.
   bk.vi, l.869

26 The uncomfortableness of it all.
   bk.vii, l.400

27   Through such souls alone
   God stooping shows sufficient of His light
   For us i' the dark to rise by. And I rise.
   l.1843

28 Faultless to a fault.
   bk.ix, l.1175

29   Of what I call God,
   And fools call Nature.
   bk.x, l.1072

30 Why comes temptation but for man to meet
   And master and make crouch beneath his foot,
   And so be pedestalled in triumph?
   l.1184

31 White shall not neutralize the black, nor good
   Compensate bad in man, absolve him so:
   Life's business being just the terrible choice.
   l.1235

32   There's a new tribunal now
   Higher than God's—the educated man's!
   l.1975

33   That sad obscure sequestered state
   Where God unmakes but to remake the soul
   He else made first in vain; which must not be.
   l.2129

34   It is the glory and good of Art,
   That Art remains the one way possible
   Of speaking truth, to mouths like mine at least.
   bk.xii, l.838

35 Good, to forgive;
      Best, to forget!

Living, we fret;
Dying, we live.
La Saisiaz, dedication

1 How good is man's life, the mere living! how fit to
employ
All the heart and the soul and the senses, for ever in
joy!
Saul, ix

2 'Tis not what man Does which exalts him, but what
man Would do!
xviii

3 Because a man has shop to mind
In time and place, since flesh must live,
Needs spirit lack all life behind,
All stray thoughts, fancies fugitive,
All loves except what trade can give?
Shop, xx

4 I want to know a butcher paints,
A baker rhymes for his pursuit,
Candlestick-maker much acquaints
His soul with song, or, haply mute,
Blows out his brains upon the flute.
xxi

5 Gr-r-r- there go, my heart's abhorrence!
Water your damned flower-pots, do!
Soliloquy of the Spanish Cloister

6 I the Trinity illustrate,
Drinking watered orange-pulp—
In three sips the Arian frustrate;
While he drains his at one gulp.

7 There's a great text in Galatians,
Once you trip on it, entails
Twenty-nine distinct damnations,
One sure, if another fails.

8 My scrofulous French novel
On grey paper with blunt type!

9 'St, there's Vespers! *Plena gratiâ
Ave, Virgo!* Gr-r-r—you swine!

10 Nay but you, who do not love her,
Is she not pure gold, my mistress?
Song

11 Who will, may hear Sordello's story told.
Sordello, bk.i, l.1

12 Sidney's self, the starry paladin.
l.69

13 Still more labyrinthine buds the rose.
l.476

14   A touch divine—
And the scaled eyeball owns the mystic rod;
Visibly through his garden walketh God.
l.502

15   Any nose
May ravage with impunity a rose.
bk.vi, l.881

16 Who would has heard Sordello's story told.
l.886

17 You are not going to marry your old friend's love,
after all?
A Soul's Tragedy, Act II

18 The world and its ways have a certain worth.
The Statue and the Bust, l.138

19 The glory dropped from their youth and love,
And both perceived they had dreamed a dream.
l.152

20 The soldier-saints, who row on row,
Burn upward each to his point of bliss.
l.222

21 The sin I impute to each frustrate ghost
Is—the unlit lamp and the ungirt loin,
Though the end in sight was a vice, I say.
l.246

22 As I ride, as I ride.
Through the Metidja to Abd-el-kadr

23 There may be heaven; there must be hell;
Meantime, there is our earth here—well!
Time's Revenges

24 Hark, the dominant's persistence till it must be
answered to!
A Toccata of Galuppi's, viii

25 What of soul was left, I wonder, when the kissing had
to stop?
xiv

26 Dear dead women, with such hair, too—what's
become of all the gold
Used to hang and brush their bosoms? I feel chilly and
grown old.
xv

27 Grand rough old Martin Luther
Bloomed fables—flowers on furze,
The better the uncouther:
Do roses stick like burrs?
The Twins

28 I would that you were all to me,
You that are just so much, no more.
Two in the Campagna, 8

29   I pluck the rose
And love it more than tongue can speak—
Then the good minute goes.
10

30   Only I discern—
Infinite passion, and the pain
Of finite hearts that yearn.
12

31 *Bang-whang-whang* goes the drum, *tootle-te-tootle* the
fife.
Oh, a day in the city-square, there is no such pleasure
in life!
Up at a Villa—Down in the City

32 What's become of Waring
Since he gave us all the slip?
Waring, I.i

33 In Vishnu-land what Avatar?
vi

34 'When I last saw Waring...'
(How all turned to him who spoke!
You saw Waring? Truth or joke?
In land-travel or sea-faring?)
II.i

35 Let's contend no more, Love,
Strive nor weep:
All be as before, Love,
—Only sleep!
A Woman's Last Word

36 I knew you once: but in Paradise,

If we meet, I will pass nor turn my face.
The Worst of It, xix

1 I chanced upon a new book yesterday:
I opened it, and where my finger lay
'Twixt page and uncut page those words I read,
Some six or seven at most, and learned thereby
That you, FitzGerald, whom by ear and eye
She never knew, 'thanked God my wife was dead.'
Ay, dead! and were yourself alive, good Fitz,
How to return your thanks would pass my wits.
Kicking you seems the common lot of curs—
While more appropriate greeting lends you grace:
Surely to spit there glorifies your face—
Spitting from lips once sanctified by Hers.
Rejoinder to 213:19. *Athenaeum,* 13 July 1889

ROBERT BRUCE 1274–1329

2 Now, God be with you, my dear children: I have
breakfasted with you and shall sup with my Lord Jesus
Christ.
Oral tradition

BEAU BRUMMELL 1778–1840

3 Who's your fat friend? (Of the Prince of Wales.)
Gronow, *Reminiscences* (1862), p.63

4 I always like to have the morning well-aired before I
get up.
Charles Macfarlane, *Reminiscences of a Literary Life,* 27

5 No perfumes, but very fine linen, plenty of it, and
country washing.
Harriette Wilson, *Memoirs,* ch.2

6 Shut the door, Wales.
(To the Prince.) Attr.

WILLIAM JENNINGS BRYAN 1860–1925

7 The humblest citizen of all the land, when clad in the
armor of a righteous cause, is stronger than all the
hosts of error.
National Democratic Convention, Chicago, 1896

8 You shall not press down upon the brow of labour this
crown of thorns, you shall not crucify mankind upon a
cross of gold.

WILLIAM CULLEN BRYANT 1794–1878

9   They seemed
Like old companions in adversity.
A Winter Piece, l.26

ROBERT BUCHANAN 1841–1901

10   She just wore
Enough for modesty—no more.
White Rose and Red, I, v, l.60

11 The sweet post-prandial cigar.
De Berny

GEORGE VILLIERS, SECOND DUKE OF
BUCKINGHAM 1628–1687

12 The world is made up for the most part of fools and
knaves.
To Mr. Clifford, on his Humane Reason

13 What the devil does the plot signify, except to bring in

fine things?
The Rehearsal (1671), III.i

14 Ay, now the plot thickens very much upon us.
ii

JOHN SHEFFIELD, FIRST DUKE OF
BUCKINGHAM AND NORMANBY 1648–1721

15 Learn to write well, or not to write at all.
Essay on Satire, l.281

H. J. BUCKOLL 1803–1871

16 Lord, behold us with Thy blessing
    Once again assembled here.
**Psalms and Hymns for the Use of Rugby School Chapel. Lord,
Behold us with Thy Blessing**

17 Lord, dismiss us with Thy blessing,
    Thanks for mercies past receive.
Lord, Dismiss us with Thy Blessing

J. B. BUCKSTONE 1802–1879

18 On such an occasion as this,
    All time and nonsense scorning,
Nothing shall come amiss,
    And we won't go home till morning.
Billy Taylor, I.ii

EUSTACE BUDGELL 1686–1737

19 What Cato did, and Addison approved
Cannot be wrong.
Lines found on his desk after his suicide, 4 May 1737

COMTE DE BUFFON 1707–1788

20 *Ces choses sont hors de l'homme, le style est l'homme
même.*
These things [subject matter] are external to the man;
style is the man.
Discours sur le Style, address given to the Académie française, 25
Aug. 1753

21 *Le génie n'est qu'une plus grande aptitude à la
patience.*
Genius is only a greater aptitude for patience.
Hérault de Séchelles, *Voyage à Montbar* (1803), p.15

PROF. ARTHUR BULLER 1874–1944

22 There was a young lady named Bright,
Whose speed was far faster than light;
    She set out one day
    In a relative way,
And returned home the previous night.
Punch, 19 Dec. 1923

COUNT VON BÜLOW 1849–1929

23 *Mit einem Worte: wir wollen niemand in den Schatten
stellen aber wir verlangen auch unseren Platz an der
Sonne.*
In a word, we desire to throw no one into the shade [in
East Asia], but we also demand our own place in the
sun.
Reichstag, 6 Dec. 1897

EDWARD GEORGE BULWER-LYTTON, BARON LYTTON 1803–1873

1 Ah, never can fall from the days that have been
A gleam on the years that shall be!
A Lament

2 Here Stanley meets,—how Stanley scorns, the glance!
The brilliant chief, irregularly great,
Frank, haughty, rash,—the Rupert of Debate.
Of Edward Stanley, 14th Earl of Derby. **The New Timon**
(1845-7), pt.I.vi. See 184:13

3 Out-babying Wordsworth and out-glittering Keats.
(Tennyson.)

4 Beneath the rule of men entirely great
The pen is mightier than the sword.
Richelieu (1838), II.ii

5 In the lexicon of youth, which Fate reserves
For a bright manhood, there is no such word
As—*fail*!

6 Poverty has strange bedfellows.
The Caxtons (1850), pt.iv, ch.4

7 There is no man so friendless but what he can find a
friend sincere enough to tell him disagreeable truths.
What Will He Do With It? (1858), bk.iii, ch.15 (heading)

EDWARD ROBERT BULWER, EARL OF LYTTON
see OWEN MEREDITH

ALFRED BUNN 1796?–1860

8 Alice, where art thou?
Song

9 I dreamt that I dwelt in marble halls,
With vassals and serfs at my side.
The Bohemian Girl, Act II

JOHN BUNYAN 1628–1688

10 As I walk'd through the wilderness of this world.
The Pilgrim's Progress (1678), pt.i

11 The name of the slough was Despond.

12 *Christian:* Gentlemen, Whence came you, and whither
do you go?
Formalist and *Hypocrisy:* We were born in the land of
Vainglory, and we are going for praise to Mount Sion.

13 The valley of Humiliation.

14 A foul Fiend coming over the field to meet him; his
name is Apollyon.

15 Then Apollyon straddled quite over the whole breadth
of the way.

16 It beareth the name of Vanity-Fair, because the town
where 'tis kept, is lighter than vanity.
See 393:20

17 Hanging is too good for him, said Mr Cruelty.

18 Yet my great-grandfather was but a water-man,
looking one way, and rowing another: and I got most
of my estate by the same occupation. [Mr. By-Ends.]
See 116:15

19 They are for religion when in rags and contempt; but I
am for him when he walks in his golden slippers, in
the sunshine and with applause.

20 A castle, called Doubting-Castle, the owner whereof
was Giant Despair.

21 Now Giant Despair had a wife, and her name was
Diffidence.

22 A grievous crab-tree cudgel.

23 They came to the Delectable Mountains.

24 Sleep is sweet to the labouring man.
See 55:17

25 A great horror and darkness fell upon Christian.

26 Then I saw that there was a way to Hell, even from the
gates of heaven.

27 So I awoke, and behold it was a dream.

28 A man that could look no way but downwards, with a
muckrake in his hand.
pt.ii

29 One leak will sink a ship, and one sin will destroy a
sinner.

30 A young Woman her name was Dull.

31 One Great-heart.

32 He that is down needs fear no fall,
He that is low no pride.
He that is humble ever shall
Have God to be his guide.
Shepherd Boy's Song

33 A very zealous man...Difficulties, Lions, or
Vanity-Fair he feared not at all; 'Twas only Sin,
Death, and Hell that was to him a terror. [Mr.
Fearing.]

34 A man there was, tho' some did count him mad,
The more he cast away, the more he had.

35 An ornament to her profession.

36 Who would true valour see,
Let him come hither;
One here will constant be,
Come wind, come weather.
There's no discouragement
Shall make him once relent
His first avow'd intent
To be a pilgrim.

Who so beset him round
With dismal stories,
Do but themselves confound—
His strength the more is.

37 The last words of Mr Despondency were, Farewell
night, welcome day. His daughter went through the
river singing, but none could understand what she
said.

38 Though with great difficulty I am got hither, yet now I
do not repent me of all the trouble I have been at to
arrive where I am. My sword, I give to him that shall
succeed me in my pilgrimage, and my courage and
skill to him that can get it. My marks and scars I carry
with me, to be a witness for me, that I have fought his
battles, who will now be my rewarder...So he passed
over, and the trumpets sounded for him on the other
side. [Mr. Valiant-for-Truth.]

39 I have formerly lived by hearsay, and faith, but now I
go where I shall live by sight, and shall be with Him in
whose company I delight myself. [Mr. Standfast.]

REVD. SAMUEL DICKINSON BURCHARD
1812–1891

1 We are Republicans and don't propose to leave our party and identify ourselves with the party whose antecedents are rum, Romanism, and rebellion.
Speech, New York City, 29 Oct. 1884

GELETT BURGESS 1866–1951

2 I never saw a Purple Cow,
  I never hope to see one;
But I can tell you, anyhow,
  I'd rather see than be one!
Burgess Nonsense Book. The Purple Cow

3 Ah, yes! I wrote the 'Purple Cow'—
  I'm sorry, now, I wrote it!
But I can tell you anyhow,
  I'll kill you if you quote it!

DEAN BURGON 1813–1888

4 Match me such marvel save in Eastern clime,
A rose-red city 'half as old as Time'!
Petra (1845). See 407:9

GENERAL BURGOYNE 1722–1792

5 You have only, when before your glass, to keep pronouncing to yourself nimini-pimini—the lips cannot fail of taking their plie.
The Heiress (1786), III.ii

EDMUND BURKE 1729–1797

6 I would rather sleep in the southern corner of a little country church-yard, than in the tomb of the Capulets. I should like, however, that my dust should mingle with kindred dust.
Letter to Matthew Smith, 1750

7 There are others so continually in the agitation of gross and merely sensual pleasures, or so occupied in the low drudgery of avarice, or so heated in the chase of honours and distinction, that their minds, which had been used continually to the storms of these violent and tempestuous passions, can hardly be put in motion by the delicate and refined play of the imagination.
On the Sublime and Beautiful (1756), introduction

8 I am convinced that we have a degree of delight, and that no small one, in the real misfortunes and pains of others.
pt.i, xiv

9 No passion so effectually robs the mind of all its powers of acting and reasoning as fear.
pt.ii, ii

10 Custom reconciles us to everything.
pt.iv, xviii

11 The fabric of superstition has in our age and nation received much ruder shocks than it had ever felt before; and through the chinks and breaches of our prison we see such glimmerings of light, and feel such refreshing airs of liberty, as daily raise our ardour for more.
A Vindication of Natural Society (1756)

12 A good parson once said, that where mystery begins, religion ends. Cannot I say, as truly at least, of human laws, that where mystery begins, justice ends? It is hard to say whether the doctors of law or divinity have made the greater advance in the lucrative business of mystery.

13 There is, however, a limit at which forbearance ceases to be a virtue.
Observations on a Publication, 'The present state of the nation' (1769)

14 It is piteously doleful, nodding every now and then towards dulness; well stored with pious frauds, and, like most discourses of the sort, much better calculated for the private advantage of the preacher than the edification of the hearers.

15 It is a general popular error to imagine the loudest complainers for the public to be the most anxious for its welfare.

16 People not very well grounded in the principles of public morality find a set of maxims in office ready made for them, which they assume as naturally and inevitably as any of the insignia or instruments of the situation. A certain tone of the solid and practical is immediately acquired. Every former profession of public spirit is to be considered as a debauch of youth, or, at best, as a visionary scheme of unattainable perfection. The very idea of consistency is exploded. The convenience of the business of the day is to furnish the principle for doing it.

17 To complain of the age we live in, to murmur at the present possessors of power, to lament the past, to conceive extravagant hopes of the future, are the common dispositions of the greatest part of mankind.
Thoughts on the Cause of the Present Discontents (1770)

18 I am not one of those who think that the people are never in the wrong. They have been so, frequently and outrageously, both in other countries and in this. But I do say, that in all disputes between them and their rulers, the presumption is at least upon a par in favour of the people.

19 The power of the crown, almost dead and rotten as Prerogative, has grown up anew, with much more strength, and far less odium, under the name of Influence.

20 We must soften into a credulity below the milkiness of infancy to think all men virtuous. We must be tainted with a malignity truly diabolical, to believe all the world to be equally wicked and corrupt.

21 The circumstances are in a great measure new. We have hardly any landmarks from the wisdom of our ancestors to guide us.

22 When bad men combine, the good must associate; else they will fall, one by one, an unpitied sacrifice in a contemptible struggle.

23 Of this stamp is the cant of *Not men, but measures;* a sort of charm by which many people get loose from every honourable engagement.

24 It is therefore our business carefully to cultivate in our minds, to rear to the most perfect vigour and maturity, every sort of generous and honest feeling that belongs to our nature. To bring the dispositions that are lovely in private life into the service and conduct of the commonwealth; so to be patriots, as not to forget we are gentlemen.

1 The greater the power, the more dangerous the abuse.
Speech on the Middlesex Election, 7 Feb. 1771

2 Would twenty shillings have ruined Mr Hampden's fortune? No! but the payment of half twenty shillings, on the principle it was demanded, would have made him a slave.
Speech on American Taxation (1774)

3 It is the nature of all greatness not to be exact, and great trade will always be attended with considerable abuses.

4 Falsehood has a perennial spring.

5 Sir, the venerable age of this great man, his merited rank, his superior eloquence, his splendid qualities, his eminent services, the vast space he fills in the eye of mankind, and, more than all the rest, his fall from power, which like death canonizes and sanctifies a great character, will not suffer me to censure any part of his conduct. I am afraid to flatter him; I am sure I am not disposed to blame him. Let those who have betrayed him by their adulation insult him with their malevolence. But what I do not presume to censure I may have leave to lament. For a wise man, he seemed to me at that time to be governed too much by general maxims. I speak with the freedom of history, and I hope without offence.
(Of Lord Chatham.)

6 For even then, sir, even before this splendid orb was entirely set, and while the western horizon was in a blaze with his descending glory, on the opposite quarter of the heavens arose another luminary, and, for his hour, became lord of the ascendant.
(Of Lord Chatham and Charles Townshend.)

7 Great men are the guide-posts and landmarks in the state.

8 He had no failings which were not owing to a noble cause; to an ardent, generous, perhaps an immoderate passion for fame; a passion which is the instinct of all great souls.
(Of Charles Townshend.)

9 To tax and to please, no more than to love and to be wise, is not given to men.

10 The only liberty I mean, is a liberty connected with order; that not only exists along with order and virtue, but which cannot exist at all without them.
Speech at his arrival at Bristol, 13 Oct. 1774

11 Your representative owes you, not his industry only, but his judgement; and he betrays, instead of serving you, if he sacrifices it to your opinion.
Speech to the Electors of Bristol, 3 Nov. 1774

12 Parliament is not a *congress* of ambassadors from different and hostile interests; which interests each must maintain, as an agent and advocate, against other agents and advocates; but parliament is a *deliberative* assembly of *one* nation, with *one* interest, that of the whole; where, not local purposes, not local prejudices ought to guide, but the general good, resulting from the general reason of the whole. You choose a member indeed; but when you have chosen him, he is not member of Bristol, but he is a member of *parliament*.

13 I have in general no very exalted opinion of the virtue of paper government.
Speech on Conciliation with America, (22 Mar. 1775)

14 The concessions of the weak are the concessions of fear.

15 Young man, there is America—which at this day serves for little more than to amuse you with stories of savage men, and uncouth manners; yet shall, before you taste of death, show itself equal to the whole of that commerce which now attracts the envy of the world.

16 When we speak of the commerce with our colonies, fiction lags after truth; invention is unfruitful, and imagination cold and barren.

17 Neither the perseverance of Holland, nor the activity of France, nor the dexterous and firm sagacity of English enterprise, ever carried this most perilous mode of hard industry to the extent to which it has been pushed by this recent people; a people who are still, as it were, but in the gristle and not yet hardened into the bone of manhood.
(Of Americans and their fishing industry.)

18 Through a wise and salutary neglect [of the colonies], a generous nature has been suffered to take her own way to perfection; when I reflect upon these effects, when I see how profitable they have been to us, I feel all the pride of power sink and all presumption in the wisdom of human contrivances melt and die away within me. My rigour relents, I pardon something to the spirit of liberty.

19 The use of force alone is but *temporary.* It may subdue for a moment; but it does not remove the necessity of subduing again; and a nation is not governed, which is perpetually to be conquered.

20 Nothing less will content me, than *whole America.*

21 Abstract liberty, like other mere abstractions, is not to be found.

22 All protestantism, even the most cold and passive, is a sort of dissent. But the religion most prevalent in our northern colonies is a refinement on the principle of resistance; it is the dissidence of dissent, and the protestantism of the Protestant religion.

23 In no country perhaps in the world is the law so general a study...This study renders men acute, inquisitive, dexterous, prompt in attack, ready in defence, full of resources...They augur misgovernment at a distance, and snuff the approach of tyranny in every tainted breeze.

24 The mysterious virtue of wax and parchment.

25 I do not know the method of drawing up an indictment against an whole people.

26 It is not, what a lawyer tells me I *may* do; but what humanity, reason, and justice, tell me I ought to do.

27 Govern two millions of men, impatient of servitude, on the principles of freedom.

28 I am not determining a point of law; I am restoring tranquillity.

29 The march of the human mind is slow.

30 Freedom and not servitude is the cure of anarchy; as religion, and not atheism, is the true remedy for superstition.

31 Instead of a standing revenue, you will have therefore a perpetual quarrel.

1 Parties must ever exist in a free country.

2 My hold of the colonies is in the close affection which grows from common names, from kindred blood, from similar privileges, and equal protection. These are ties which, though light as air, are as strong as links of iron.

3 Slavery they can have anywhere. It is a weed that grows in every soil.

4 Deny them this participation of freedom, and you break that sole bond, which originally made, and must still preserve the unity of the empire.

5 It is the love of the people; it is their attachment to their government, from the sense of the deep stake they have in such a glorious institution, which gives you your army and your navy, and infuses into both that liberal obedience, without which your army would be a base rabble, and your navy nothing but rotten timber.

6 Magnanimity in politics is not seldom the truest wisdom; and a great empire and little minds go ill together.

7 By adverting to the dignity of this high calling, our ancestors have turned a savage wilderness into a glorious empire: and have made the most extensive, and the only honourable conquests, not by destroying, but by promoting the wealth, the number, the happiness of the human race.

8 People crushed by law have no hopes but from power. If laws are their enemies, they will be enemies to laws; and those, who have much to hope and nothing to lose, will always be dangerous, more or less.
Letter to the Hon. C.J. Fox, 8 Oct. 1777

9 I know many have been taught to think that moderation, in a case like this, is a sort of treason.
Letter to the Sheriffs of Bristol (1777)

10 Between craft and credulity, the voice of reason is stifled.

11 If any ask me what a free government is, I answer, that for any practical purpose, it is what the people think so.

12 Liberty, too, must be limited in order to be possessed.

13 Nothing in progression can rest on its original plan. We may as well think of rocking a grown man in the cradle of an infant.

14 Among a people generally corrupt, liberty cannot long exist.

15 The coquetry of public opinion, which has her caprices, and must have her way.
Letter to Thos. Burgh, New Year's Day, 1780

16 Corrupt influence, which is itself the perennial spring of all prodigality, and of all disorder; which loads us, more than millions of debt; which takes away vigour from our arms, wisdom from our councils, and every shadow of authority and credit from the most venerable parts of our constitution.
Speech on the Economical Reform, 11 Feb. 1780

17 Individuals pass like shadows; but the commonwealth is fixed and stable.

18 The people are the masters.

19 Applaud us when we run; console us when we fall; cheer us when we recover; but let us pass on—for God's sake, let us pass on!
Speech at Bristol previous to the Election, 1780

20 Bad laws are the worst sort of tyranny.

21 The worthy gentleman [Mr. Coombe], who has been snatched from us at the moment of the election, and in the middle of the contest, whilst his desires were as warm, and his hopes as eager as ours, has feelingly told us, what shadows we are, and what shadows we pursue.
Speech at Bristol on Declining the Poll, 1780

22 Not merely a chip of the old 'block', but the old block itself.
On Pitt's First Speech, 1781

23 The arrogance of age must submit to be taught by youth.
Letter to Fanny Burney, 29 July, 1782

24 Every other conqueror of every other description has left some monument, either of state or beneficence, behind him. Were we to be driven out of India this day, nothing would remain to tell that it had been possessed, during the inglorious period of our dominion, by anything better than the orang-outang or the tiger.
Speech on Fox's East India Bill, 1 Dec. 1783

25 Your governor stimulates a rapacious and licentious soldiery to the personal search of women, lest these unhappy creatures should avail themselves of the protection of their sex to secure any supply for their necessities.
(Of Warren Hastings in India).

26 He has put to hazard his ease, his security, his interest, his power, even his darling popularity, for the benefit of a people whom he has never seen.

27 The people never give up their liberties but under some delusion.
Speech at County Meeting of Buckinghamshire, 1784

28 What the greatest inquest of the nation has begun, its highest Tribunal [the British House of Commons] will accomplish.
Impeachment of Warren Hastings, 15 Feb. 1788

29 Religious persecution may shield itself under the guise of a mistaken and over-zealous piety.
17 Feb. 1788

30 An event has happened, upon which it is difficult to speak, and impossible to be silent.
5 May 1789

31 Resolved to die in the last dyke of prevarication.
7 May 1789

32 There is but one law for all, namely, that law which governs all law, the law of our Creator, the law of humanity, justice, equity—the law of nature, and of nations.
28 May 1794

33 I impeach him in the name of the people of India, whose rights he has trodden under foot, and whose country he has turned into a desert. Lastly, in the name of human nature itself, in the name of both sexes, in the name of every age, in the name of every rank, I impeach the common enemy and oppressor of all!
Impeachment of Warren Hastings, as recorded by Macaulay in his essay on Warren Hastings

34 I flatter myself that I love a manly, moral, regulated

liberty as well as any gentleman.
Reflections on the Revolution in France (1790)

1 Whenever our neighbour's house is on fire, it cannot be amiss for the engines to play a little on our own.

2 Politics and the pulpit are terms that have little agreement. No sound ought to be heard in the church but the healing voice of Christian charity.

3 Surely the church is a place where one day's truce ought to be allowed to the dissensions and animosities of mankind.

4 A state without the means of some change is without the means of its conservation.

5 Make the Revolution a parent of settlement, and not a nursery of future revolutions.

6 We, on our parts, have learned to speak only the primitive language of the law, and not the confused jargon of their Babylonian pulpits.

7 People will not look forward to posterity, who never look backward to their ancestors.

8 Government is a contrivance of human wisdom to provide for human *wants*. Men have a right that these wants should be provided for by this wisdom.

9 It is now sixteen or seventeen years since I saw the Queen of France, then the Dauphiness, at Versailles; and surely never lighted on this orb, which she hardly seemed to touch, a more delightful vision. I saw her just above the horizon, decorating and cheering the elevated sphere she just began to move in,—glittering like the morning star, full of life, and splendour, and joy. Oh! what a revolution! and what a heart I must have, to comtemplate without emotion that elevation and that fall! Little did I dream when she added titles of veneration to those of enthusiastic, distant, respectful love, that she should ever be obliged to carry the sharp antidote against disgrace concealed in that bosom; little did I dream that I should have lived to see disasters fallen upon her in a nation of gallant men, in a nation of men of honour, and of cavaliers. I thought ten thousand swords must have leaped from their scabbards to avenge even a look that threatened her with insult. But the age of chivalry is gone. That of sophisters, economists, and calculators, has succeeded; and the glory of Europe is extinguished for ever.

10 The unbought grace of life, the cheap defence of nations, the nurse of manly sentiment and heroic enterprise is gone! It is gone, that sensibility of principle, that chastity of honour, which felt a stain like a wound, which inspired courage whilst it mitigated ferocity, which ennobled whatever it touched, and under which vice itself lost half its evil, by losing all its grossness.

11 This barbarous philosophy, which is the offspring of cold hearts and muddy understandings.

12 In the groves of *their* academy, at the end of every vista, you see nothing but the gallows.

13 Kings will be tyrants from policy, when subjects are rebels from principle.

14 Learning will be cast into the mire, and trodden down under the hoofs of a swinish multitude.

15 France has always more or less influenced manners in England; and when your fountain is choked up and polluted, the stream will not run long, or will not run clear with us, or perhaps with any nation.

16 Because half a dozen grasshoppers under a fern make the field ring with their importunate chink, whilst thousands of great cattle, reposed beneath the shadow of the British oak, chew the cud and are silent, pray do not imagine that those who make the noise are the only inhabitants of the field; that, of course, they are many in number; or that, after all, they are other than the little, shrivelled, meagre, hopping, though loud and troublesome *insects* of the hour.

17 Who now reads Bolingbroke? Who ever read him through? Ask the booksellers of London what is become of all these lights of the world.

18 Man is by his constitution a religious animal.

19 A perfect democracy is therefore the most shameless thing in the world.

20 The men of England, the men, I mean, of light and leading in England, whose wisdom (if they have any) is open and direct, would be ashamed, as of a silly, deceitful trick, to profess any religion in name, which, by their proceedings, they appear to contemn.
See 352:7

21 Nobility is a graceful ornament to the civil order. It is the Corinthian capital of polished society.

22 Superstition is the religion of feeble minds.

23 He that wrestles with us strengthens our nerves, and sharpens our skill. Our antagonist is our helper.

24 Our patience will achieve more than our force.

25 Good order is the foundation of all good things.

26 Every politician ought to sacrifice to the graces; and to join compliance with reason.

27 The conduct of a losing party never appears right: at least it never can possess the only infallible criterion of wisdom to vulgar judgments—success.
Letter to a Member of the National Assembly (1791)

28 Those who have been once intoxicated with power, and have derived any kind of emolument from it, even though but for one year, can never willingly abandon it.

29 Cromwell was a man in whom ambition had not wholly suppressed, but only suspended the sentiments of religion.

30 Tyrants seldom want pretexts.

31 You can never plan the future by the past.

32 Old religious factions are volcanoes burnt out.
Speech on the Petition of the Unitarians, 11 May 1792

33 Dangers by being despised grow great.

34 The cold neutrality of an impartial judge.
Preface to the Address of M. Brissot, 1794

35 Nothing is so fatal to religion as indifference, which is, at least, half infidelity.
Letter to Wm. Smith, 29 Jan. 1795

36 The silent touches of time.

37 Somebody had said, that a king may make a nobleman, but he cannot make a gentleman.

1 The grand Instructor, Time.
Letter to Sir H. Langrishe, 26 May 1795

2 To innovate is not to reform.
A Letter to a Noble Lord (1796)

3 These gentle historians, on the contrary, dip their pens in nothing but the milk of human kindness.

4 The storm has gone over me; and I lie like one of those old oaks which the late hurricane has scattered about me. I am stripped of all my honours; I am torn up by the roots, and lie prostrate on the earth!

5 The king, and his faithful subjects, the lords and commons of this realm,—the triple cord, which no man can break.
See 55:15

6 All men that are ruined are ruined on the side of their natural propensities.
Letters on a Regicide Peace, letter 1 (1796)

7 Example is the school of mankind, and they will learn at no other.

8 Never, no never, did Nature say one thing and Wisdom say another.
No.3 (1797)

9 Well is it known that ambition can creep as well as soar.

10 And having looked to government for bread, on the very first scarcity they will turn and bite the hand that fed them.
Thoughts and Details on Scarcity (1797)

11 Laws, like houses, lean on one another.
Tracts on the Popery Laws, ch.3, pt.i

12 In all forms of Government the people is the true legislator.

13 His virtues were his arts.
Inscription on the statue of the Marquis of Rockingham in Wentworth Park

14 'No,no', said he, 'it is not a good imitation of Johnson; it has all his pomp, without his force; it has all the nodosities of the oak without its strength; it has all the contortions of the Sibyl without the inspiration.'
Remark to Boswell who had spoken of Croft's *Life of Dr. Young* as a good imitation of Johnson's style. Boswell, *Life of Johnson,* vol.iv, p.59

WILLIAM CECIL, LORD BURLEIGH 1520–1598

15 What! all this for a song?
To Queen Elizabeth, when ordered to give a pension of £100 to Spenser. Birch, *Life of Spenser,* p.xiii

FANNY BURNEY 1752–1840

16 In the bosom of her respectable family resided Camilla.
Camilla (1796), bk.i, ch.1

17 Travelling is the ruin of all happiness! There's no looking at a building here after seeing Italy. [Mr. Meadows.]
Cecilia (1782), bk.iv, ch.2

18 'True, very true, ma'am,' said he [Mr. Meadows], yawning, 'one really lives no where; one does but vegetate, and wish it all at an end.'
bk.vii, ch.5

19 'The whole of this unfortunate business,' said Dr Lyster, 'has been the result of PRIDE AND PREJUDICE.'
bk.x, ch.10

20 Indeed, the freedom with which Dr Johnson condemns whatever he disapproves is astonishing.
Diary, 23 Aug. 1778

21 All the delusive seduction of martial music.
5-6 May, 1802

22 'Do you come to the play without knowing what it is?' 'O yes, Sir, yes, very frequently: I have no time to read play-bills; one merely comes to meet one's friends, and show that one's alive.'
Evelina, letter 20

JOHN BURNS 1858–1943

23 I have seen the Mississippi. That is muddy water. I have seen the St Lawrence. That is crystal water. But the Thames is liquid history.
Oral trad.

ROBERT BURNS 1759–1796

24 O thou! whatever title suit thee,
Auld Hornie, Satan, Nick, or Clootie.
Address to the Devil

25 Then gently scan your brother man,
   Still gentler sister woman;
Tho' they may gang a kennin wrang,
   To step aside is human.
Address to the Unco Guid

26 Then at the balance let's be mute,
   We never can adjust it;
What's done we partly may compute,
   But know not what's resisted.

27 Ae fond kiss, and then we sever;
Ae fareweel, and then for ever!
Ae Fond Kiss

28 But to see her was to love her,
Love but her, and love for ever.

29 Had we never lov'd sae kindly,
Had we never lov'd sae blindly,
Never met—or never parted,
We had ne'er been broken-hearted.

30 Should auld acquaintance be forgot,
   And never brought to mind?
Auld Lang Syne

31 We'll tak' a right gude-willie waught
   For auld lang syne.

32 We'll tak a cup o' kindness yet,
   For auld lang syne.

33 And there's a hand, my trusty fiere,
   And gie's a hand o'thine.

34 But tell me whisky's name in Greek,
   I'll tell the reason.
The Author's Earnest Cry and Prayer, xxx

35 Freedom and Whisky gang thegither!
xxxi

36 Sleep I can get nane
   For thinking on my dearie.
Ay Waukin O

37 O saw ye bonnie Lesley

As she gaed o'er the border?
She's gane, like Alexander,
  To spread her conquests farther.
To see her is to love her,
  And love but her for ever,
For Nature made her what she is,
  And ne'er made anither!
Bonnie Lesley

1 Bonnie wee thing, cannie wee thing,
    Lovely wee thing, wert thou mine,
  I wad wear thee in my bosom,
    Lest my jewel I should tine.
  The Bonnie Wee Thing

2 She draiglet a' her petticoatie,
    Coming through the rye.
  Coming Through the Rye (taken from an old song, *The Bob-tailed Lass*).

3 Gin a body meet a body
    Coming through the rye;
  Gin a body kiss a body,
    Need a body cry?

4 Contented wi' little and cantie wi' mair,
  Whene'er I forgather wi' Sorrow and Care,
  I gie them a skelp, as they're creeping alang,
  Wi' a cog o' gude swats and an auld Scotish sang.
  Contented wi' Little

5 Th' expectant wee-things, toddlin', stacher through
    To meet their Dad, wi' flichterin' noise an' glee.
  His wee bit ingle, blinkin bonnilie,
    His clean hearth-stane, his thrifty wifie's smile,
  The lisping infant prattling on his knee,
    Does a' his weary kiaugh and care beguile,
  An' makes him quite forget his labour an' his toil.
  The Cotter's Saturday Night, iii

6 They never sought in vain that sought the Lord aright!
  vi

7 Is there, in human-form, that bears a heart—
    A wretch! a villain! lost to love and truth!
  That can, with studied, sly, ensnaring art,
    Betray sweet Jenny's unsuspecting youth?
  x

8 The halesome parritch, chief of Scotia's food.
  xi

9 The sire turns o'er, wi' patriarchal grace,
    The big ha'-Bible, ance his father's pride.
  xii

10 From scenes like these old Scotia's grandeur springs,
     That makes her loved at home, revered abroad:
   Princes and Lords are but the breath of kings,
     'An honest man's the noblest work of God.'
   xix. See 379:24

11 I wasna fou, but just had plenty.
   Death and Dr. Hornbook, iii

12 On ev'ry hand it will allow'd be,
   He's just—nae better than he should be.
   A Dedication to Gavin Hamilton, l.25

13 There's threesome reels, there's foursome reels,
     There's hornpipes and strathspeys, man,
   But the ae best dance e'er cam to the Land
     Was, the de'il's awa wi' th'Exciseman.
   The De'il's awa wi' th'Exciseman

14 But Facts are chiels that winna ding,

An' downa be disputed.
A Dream

15 A Gentleman who held the patent for his honours
   immediately from Almighty God.
   Elegy on Capt. Matthew Henderson: from the title

16 Perhaps it may turn out a sang,
     Perhaps turn out a sermon.
   Epistle to a Young Friend, 1786

17 I wave the quantum o'the sin,
     The hazard of concealing;
   But och; it hardens a' within,
     And petrifies the feeling!

18 An atheist-laugh's a poor exchange
     For Deity offended.

19 What's a' your jargon o' your schools,
   Your Latin names for horns and stools;
   If honest Nature made you fools,
       What sairs your grammars?
   First Epistle to John Lapraik

20 Gie me ae spark o' Nature's fire,
   That's a' the learning I desire.

21 For thus the royal mandate ran,
   When first the human race began,
   'The social friendly, honest man,
       Whate'er he be,
   'Tis he fulfils great Nature's plan,
       And none but he!'
   Second Epistle to Lapraik

22 A Workhouse! ah, that sound awakes my woes,
   And pillows on the thorn my racked repose!
   In durance vile here must I wake and weep,
   And all my frowzy couch in sorrow steep.
   Epistle from Esopus to Maria, l.57

23 Just now I've taen the fit o' rhyme,
   My barmie noddle's working prime.
   Epistle to James Smith

24 Some rhyme a neebor's name to lash;
   Some rhyme (vain thought!) for needfu' cash;
   Some rhyme to court the country clash,
       An' raise a din;
   For me, an aim I never fash;
       I rhyme for fun.

25 Farewell dear, deluding Woman,
   The joy of joys!

26 If there's another world, he lives in bliss;
   If there is none, he made the best of this.
   Epitaph on Wm. Muir

27 Flow gently, sweet Afton, among thy green braes,
   Flow gently, I'll sing thee a song in thy praise.
   My Mary's asleep by thy murmuring stream,
   Flow gently, sweet Afton, disturb not her dream.
   Flow gently, sweet Afton

28 The rank is but the guinea's stamp,
     The man's the gowd for a' that!
   For a' that and a' that

29 A man's a man for a' that.

30 There's Death in the cup—so beware!
   On a Goblet

31 Go fetch to me a pint o' wine,
   An' fill it in a silver tassie.
   Go Fetch to Me a Pint

1 Green grow the rashes O,
   Green grow the rashes O;
The sweetest hours that e'er I spend,
Are spent among the lasses O!
Green Grow the Rashes

2 But gie me a canny hour at e'en,
   My arms about my dearie O;
An' warly cares, an' warly men,
May a' gae tapsalteerie O!

3 The wisest man the warl' saw,
   He dearly lov'd the lasses O.

4 Auld nature swears, the lovely dears
   Her noblest work she classes O;
Her prentice han' she tried on man,
   An' then she made the lasses O.

5 It's guid to be merry and wise,
   It's guid to be honest and true,
It's guid to support Caledonia's cause,
   And bide by the buff and the blue.
Here's a Health to Them that's Awa'

6 O, gie me the lass that has acres o' charms,
O, gie me the lass wi' the weel-stockit farms.
Hey for a Lass wi' a Tocher

7 Here some are thinkin' on their sins,
   An' some upo' their claes.
The Holy Fair, x

8 Leeze me on drink! it gi'es us mair
   Than either school or college.
xix

9 There's some are fou o' love divine,
   There's some are fou o' brandy.
xxvii

10 It was a' for our rightfu' King
   We left fair Scotland's strand.
It was a' for our Rightfu' King

11 The soger frae the wars returns,
   The sailor frae the main,
But I hae parted frae my Love,
   Never to meet again, my dear,
   Never to meet again.

12 John Anderson my jo, John,
   When we were first acquent,
Your locks were like the raven,
   Your bonny brow was brent.
John Anderson My Jo

13 There were three kings into the east,
Three kings both great and high;
And they hae sworn a solemn oath
John Barleycorn should die.
John Barleycorn

14 Some have meat and cannot eat,
   Some cannot eat that want it:
But we have meat and we can eat,
   Sae let the Lord be thankit.
The Kirkudbright Grace. (Also known as the Selkirk Grace.)

15 I've seen sae mony changefu' years,
   On earth I am a stranger grown;
I wander in the ways of men,
   Alike unknowing and unknown.
Lament for James, Earl of Glencairn

16 Cease, ye prudes, your envious railing,
   Lovely Burns has charms—*confess;*

True it is, she had one failing,
   Had ae woman ever less?
Lines written under the Picture of Miss Burns

17 I once was a maid, tho' I cannot tell when,
   And still my delight is in proper young men.
Love and Liberty—A Cantata, 1.57

18 Partly wi' love o'ercome sae sair,
   And partly she was drunk.
1.183

19 A fig for those by law protected!
   Liberty's a glorious feast!
Courts for cowards were erected,
   Churches built to please the priest.
1.254

20 Life is all a variorum,
   We regard not how it goes;
Let them cant about decorum
   Who have characters to lose.
1.270

21 May coward shame distain his name,
   The wretch that dares not die!
Macpherson's Farewell

22   Nature's law,
That man was made to mourn!
Man was made to Mourn

23 Man's inhumanity to man
   Makes countless thousands mourn!

24 O Death, the poor man's dearest friend,
   The kindest and the best!

25 My heart's in the Highlands, my heart is not here;
My heart's in the Highlands a-chasing the deer;
Chasing the wild deer, and following the roe,
My heart's in the Highlands, wherever I go.
My Heart's in the Highlands

26 Farewell to the Highlands, farewell to the North,
The birth-place of valour, the country of worth.

27 O, my Luve's like a red red rose
   That's newly sprung in June:
O my Luve's like the melodie
   That's sweetly play'd in tune.
My Love is like a Red Red Rose

28 The minister kiss'd the fiddler's wife,
   An' could na preach for thinkin' o't.
My Love she's but a Lassie yet

29 An idiot race to honour lost,
   Who know them best, despise them most.
On Seeing Stirling Palace in Ruins

30 The wan moon sets behind the white wave,
   And time is setting with me, Oh.
Open the door to me, Oh

31 Or were I in the wildest waste,
   Sae black and bare, sae black and bare,
The desert were a paradise,
   If thou wert there, if thou wert there.
O, Wert Thou in the Could Blast

32 The mair they talk I'm kent the better.
The Poet's Welcome (to his bastard child)

33 O Luve will venture in, where it daur na weel be seen.
The Posie

34 Scots, wha hae wi' Wallace bled,
Scots, wham Bruce has aften led,
Welcome to your gory bed,

Or to victorie.
Now's the day, and now's the hour;
See the front o' battle lour!
See approach proud Edward's power—
        Chains and slaverie!
Scots, Wha Hae (Robert Bruce's March to Bannockburn)

1 Liberty's in every blow!
        Let us do or die!

2 Good Lord, what is man! for as simple he looks,
Do but try to develop his hooks and his crooks,
With his depths and his shallows, his good and his
    evil,
All in all, he's a problem must puzzle the devil.
Sketch: inscribed to C.J. Fox

3 While we sit bousing at the nappy,
And getting fou and unco happy,
We think na on the lang Scots miles,
The mosses, waters, staps, and styles,
That lie between us and our hame,
Whare sits our sulky sullen dame,
Gathering her brows like gathering storm,
Nursing her wrath to keep it warm.
Tam o' Shanter, l.10

4 Auld Ayr, wham ne'er a town surpasses
For honest men and bonnie lasses.
l.15

5 His ancient, trusty, drouthy crony;
Tam lo'ed him like a vera brither;
They had been fou for weeks thegither.
l.43

6 Kings may be blest, but Tam was glorious,
O'er a' the ills o' life victorious!
l.57

7 But pleasures are like poppies spread—
You seize the flow'r, its bloom is shed;
Or like the snow falls in the river—
A moment white—then melts for ever.
l.59

8 Nae man can tether time or tide.
l.67

9 Inspiring bold John Barleycorn!
What dangers thou canst make us scorn!
Wi' tippenny, we fear nae evil;
Wi' usquebae, we'll face the devil!
l.105

10 As Tammie glowr'd, amaz'd, and curious,
The mirth and fun grew fast and furious.
l.143

11 Ev'n Satan glowr'd, and fidg'd fu' fain,
An' hotched an' blew wi' might an' main:
Till first ae caper, syne anither,
Tam tint his reason a' thegither,
And roars out, 'Weel done, Cutty-sark!'
l.185

12 Ah, Tam! ah, Tam! thou'll get thy fairin'!
In hell they'll roast thee like a herrin'!
l.201

13 A man may drink and no be drunk;
    A man may fight and no be slain;
A man may kiss a bonnie lass,
    And aye be welcome back again.
There was a Lass, they ca'd her Meg

14 Come, Firm Resolve, take thou the van,

Thou stalk o' carl-hemp in man!
And let us mind, faint heart ne'er wan
A lady fair;
Wha does the utmost that he can,
Will whyles do mair.
To Dr. Blacklock

15 To make a happy fire-side clime
    To weans and wife,
That's the true pathos and sublime
    Of human life.

16 Fair fa' your honest sonsie face,
Great chieftain o' the puddin'-race!
Aboon them a' ye tak your place,
           Painch, tripe, or thairm:
Weel are ye wordy o' a grace
           As lang's my arm.
To a Haggis

17 His spindle shank a guid whip-lash,
        His nieve a nit.

18 O wad some Pow'r the giftie gie us
To see oursels as others see us!
It wad frae mony a blunder free us,
        And foolish notion.
To a Louse

19 Ev'n thou who mourn'st the Daisy's fate,
That fate is thine—no distant date;
Stern Ruin's ploughshare drives elate
    Full on thy bloom,
Till crush'd beneath the furrow's weight
    Shall be thy doom!
To a Mountain Daisy

20 Wee, sleekit, cow'rin', tim'rous beastie,
O what a panic's in thy breastie!
Thou need na start awa sae hasty,
        Wi' bickering brattle!
I wad be laith to rin an' chase thee,
        Wi' murd'ring pattle!
To a Mouse

21 I'm truly sorry Man's dominion
Has broken Nature's social union,
An' justifies th' ill opinion
    Which makes thee startle
At me, thy poor, earth-born companion
An' fellow-mortal!

22 The best laid schemes o' mice an' men
    Gang aft a-gley.

23 Their sighin', cantin', grace-proud faces,
Their three-mile prayers, and half-mile graces.
To the Rev. John M'Math

24 We labour soon, we labour late,
    To feed the titled knave, man,
And a' the comfort we're to get,
    Is that ayont the grave, man.
The Tree of Liberty

25 His lockèd, lettered, braw brass collar,
Shew'd him the gentleman and scholar.
The Twa Dogs, l.13

26 And there began a lang digression
About the lords of the creation.
l.45

27 But human bodies are sic fools,
For a' their colleges and schools,
That when nae real ills perplex them,

They mak enow themsels to vex them.
1.195

1 Rejoiced they were na men but dogs.
1.236

2 Up in the morning's no' for me,
Up in the morning early.
Up in the Morning

3 What can a young lassie, what shall a young lassie,
What can a young lassie do wi' an auld man?
What can a Young Lassie

4 O whistle, and I'll come to you, my lad:
O whistle, and I'll come to you, my lad:
Tho' father and mither and a' should gae mad,
O whistle, and I'll come to you, my lad.
Whistle, and I'll come to you, my Lad

5 It is the moon, I ken her horn,
    That's blinkin' in the lift sae hie;
She shines sae bright to wyle us hame,
    But, by my sooth! she'll wait a wee.
Willie Brewed a Peck o' Maut

6 Ye banks and braes o' bonny Doon,
    How can ye bloom sae fresh and fair?
How can ye chant, ye little birds,
    And I sae weary fu' o' care?
Ye Banks and Braes o' Bonny Doon

7 Thou minds me o' departed joys,
Departed never to return.

8 And my fause lover stole my rose,
But ah! he left the thorn wi' me.

9 Don't let the awkward squad fire over me.
A. Cunningham, *Works of Burns; with his Life*, 1834, vol.i,
p.344

SIR FRED BURROWS 1887–1973

10 Unlike my predecessors, I have devoted more of my
life to shunting and hooting than to hunting and
shooting.
Speech as last Governor of undivided Bengal (1946-7), having
been President of the National Union of Railwaymen. Obituary,
Daily Telegraph, 24 Apr. 1973

SIR RICHARD BURTON 1821–1890

11 Don't be frightened; I am recalled. Pay, pack, and
follow at convenience.
Note to Isabel Burton, 19 August 1871 on being replaced as
Consul to Damascus. Isabel Burton, *Life of Sir Richard Burton*,
ch.21

ROBERT BURTON 1577–1640

12 All my joys to this are folly,
Naught so sweet as Melancholy.
Anatomy of Melancholy. **Author's Abstract of Melancholy**

13 They lard their lean books with the fat of others'
works.
Democritus to the Reader

14 I had no time to lick it into form, as she [a bear] doth
her young ones.

15 Like watermen, that row one way and look another.

16 Him that makes shoes go barefoot himself.

17 All poets are mad.

18 A loose, plain, rude writer.

19 Cookery is become an art, a noble science: cooks are
gentlemen.
pt.i, 2, memb.2, subsect.2

20 Die to save charges.
memb.3, subsect.12

21 I may not here omit those two main plagues, and
common dotages of human kind, wine and women,
which have infatuated and besotted myriads of people.
They go commonly together.
subsect.13

22 *Hinc quam sit calamus saevior ense patet.*
From this it is clear how much the pen is worse than
the sword.
memb.4, subsect.4

23 One was never married, and that's his hell; another is,
and that's his plague.
subsect.7

24 Seneca thinks he takes delight in seeing thee. The
gods are well pleased when they see great men
contending with adversity.
pt.ii, 3, memb.1, subsect.1

25 Every thing, saith Epictetus, hath two handles, the one
to be held by, the other not.
memb.3

26 Who cannot give good counsel? 'tis cheap, it costs
them nothing.

27 What is a ship but a prison?
memb.4

28 All places are distant from Heaven alike.

29 Tobacco, divine, rare, superexcellent tobacco, which
goes far beyond all their panaceas, potable gold, and
philosopher's stones, a sovereign remedy to all
diseases...But, as it is commonly abused by most
men, which take it as tinkers do ale, 'tis a plague, a
mischief, a violent purger of goods, lands, health,
hellish, devilish, and damned tobacco, the ruin and
overthrow of body and soul.
4, memb.2, subsect.1

30 Let me not live, saith Aretine's Antonia, if I had not
rather hear thy discourse than see a play!
pt.iii, 1, memb.1, subsect.1

31 And this is that Homer's golden chain, which reacheth
down from Heaven to earth, by which every creature is
annexed, and depends on his Creator.
subsect.2

32 To enlarge or illustrate this—is to set a candle in the
sun.
2, memb.1, subsect.2

33 No chord, nor cable can so forcibly draw, or hold so
fast, as love can do with a twined thread.

34 Cornelia kept her in talk till her children came from
school, and these, said she, are my jewels.
memb.2, subsect.3

35 To these crocodile's tears, they will add sobs, fiery
sighs, and sorrowful countenance.
subsect.4

36 Diogenes struck the father when the son swore.

37 England is a paradise for women, and hell for horses:
Italy a paradise for horses, hell for women, as the
diverb goes.
3, memb.1, subsect.2

1 The fear of some divine and supreme powers, keeps men in obedience.
4, memb.1, subsect.2

2 One religion is as true as another.
memb.2, subsect.1

3 Be not solitary, be not idle.
final words

HERMANN BUSENBAUM 1600–1668

4 *Cum finis est licitus, etiam media sunt licita.*
The end justifies the means.
Medulla Theologiae Moralis (1650)

COMTE DE BUSSY-RABUTIN 1618–1693

5 *L'amour vient de l'aveuglement,*
L'amitié de la connaissance.
Love comes from blindness, friendship from knowledge.
Histoire Amoureuse des Gaules. Maximes d'Amour, pt.I

6 *L'absence est à l'amour ce qu'est au feu le vent;*
Il éteint le petit, il allume le grand.
Absence is to love what wind is to fire; it extinguishes the small, it enkindles the great.
pt.II. See 218:2, 310:15

7 *Comme vous savez, Dieu est d'ordinaire pour les gros escadrons contre les petits.*
As you know, God is usually on the side of the big squadrons against the small.
Letter to the Comte de Limoges, 18 Oct. 1677

BISHOP BUTLER 1692–1752

8 It has come, I know not how, to be taken for granted, by many persons, that Christianity is not so much as a subject of inquiry; but that it is, now at length, discovered to be fictitious.
The Analogy of Religion (1756), Advertisement

9 But to *us*, probability is the very guide of life.
Introduction

10 Things and actions are what they are, and the consequences of them will be what they will be: why then should we desire to be deceived?
Fifteen Sermons. No.7, 16

11 Sir, the pretending to extraordinary revelations and gifts of the Holy Ghost is a horrid thing, a very horrid thing. [To John Wesley.]
Wesley, *Works*, xiii.449

NICHOLAS MURRAY BUTLER 1862–1947

12 ...a society like ours [U.S.A.] of which it is truly said to be often but three generations 'from shirt-sleeves to shirt-sleeves'.
True and False Democracy

13 An expert is one who knows more and more about less and less.
attr. to a Commencement Address. Columbia University

SAMUEL BUTLER 1612–1680

14 He'd run in debt by disputation,
And pay with ratiocination.
Hudibras, pt.I, c.1, l.77

15 For rhetoric he could not ope

His mouth, but out there flew a trope.
l.81

16 For all a rhetorician's rules'
Teach nothing but to name his tools.
l.89

17 A Babylonish dialect
Which learned pedants much affect.
l.93

18 Beside, he was a shrewd philosopher,
And had read ev'ry text and gloss over.
l.127

19 What ever sceptic could inquire for;
For every why he had a wherefore.
l.131

20 He knew what's what, and that's as high
As metaphysic wit can fly.
l.149

21 Such as take lodgings in a head
That's to be let unfurnished.
l.160

22 And still be doing, never done:
As if Religion were intended
For nothing else but to be mended.
l.202

23 Compound for sins, they are inclin'd to
By damning those they have no mind to.
l.213

24 The trenchant blade, Toledo trusty,
For want of fighting was grown rusty,
And eat into it self, for lack
Of some body to hew and hack.
l.357

25 For rhyme the rudder is of verses,
With which like ships they steer their courses.
l.457

26 For what is Worth in anything,
But so much Money as 'twill bring.
l.465

27 He ne'er consider'd it, as loth
To look a gift-horse in the mouth.
l.483

28 Great actions are not always true sons
Of great and mighty resolutions.
l.885

29 Ay me! what perils do environ
The man that meddles with cold iron!
c.3, l.1

30 I'll make the fur
Fly 'bout the ears of the old cur.
l.277

31 Cheer'd up himself with ends of verse,
And sayings of philosophers.
l.1011

32 Cleric before, and Lay behind;
A lawless linsy-woolsy brother,
Half of one order, half another.
l.1226

33 Learning, that cobweb of the brain,
Profane, erroneous, and vain.
l.1339

34 For nothing goes for sense, or light,
That will not with old rules jump right;

As if rules were not in the schools
Derived from truth, but truth from rules.
l.1353

1 She that with poetry is won
Is but a desk to write upon.
pt.II, c.1, l.591

2 Love is a boy, by poets styl'd,
Then spare the rod, and spoil the child.
l.844

3 The sun had long since in the lap
Of Thetis, taken out his nap,
And like a lobster boil'd, the morn
From black to red began to turn.
c.2, l.29

4 Oaths are but words, and words but wind.
l.107

5 For saints may do the same things by
The Spirit, in sincerity,
Which other men are tempted to.
l.235

6 Doubtless the pleasure is as great
Of being cheated, as to cheat.
As lookers-on feel most delight,
That least perceive a juggler's sleight,
And still the less they understand,
The more th' admire his sleight of hand.
c.3, l.1

7 Still amorous, and fond, and billing,
Like Philip and Mary on a shilling.
pt.III, c.1, l.687

8 For in what stupid age or nation
Was marriage ever out of fashion?
l.817

9 Discords make the sweetest airs.
l.919

10 What makes all doctrines plain and clear?
About two hundred pounds a year.
And that which was prov'd true before,
Prove false again? Two hundred more.
l.1277

11 For if it be but half denied,
'Tis half as good as justified.
c.2, l.803

12 For, those that fly, may fight again,
Which he can never do that's slain.
c.3, l.243

13 He that complies against his will,
Is of his own opinion still.
l.547

14 For Justice, though she's painted blind,
Is to the weaker side inclin'd.
l.709

15 For money has a power above
The stars and fate, to manage love.
l.1279

16 The best of all our actions tend
To the preposterousest end.
Genuine Remains: Satire upon the Weakness and Misery of Man, l.41

17 All love at first, like generous wine,
Ferments and frets until 'tis fine;
But when 'tis settled on the lee,
And from th' impurer matter free,

Becomes the richer still the older,
And proves the pleasanter the colder.
Miscellaneous Thoughts

18 The souls of women are so small,
That some believe they've none at all.

19 The law can take a purse in open court,
While it condemns a less delinquent for't.

20 For trouts are tickled best in muddy water.
On a Hypocritical Nonconformist, iv

SAMUEL BUTLER 1835–1902

21 It has been said that though God cannot alter the past, historians can; it is perhaps because they can be useful to Him in this respect that He tolerates their existence.
Erewhon Revisited, ch.14

22 I keep my books at the British Museum and at Mudie's.
The Humour of Homer. Ramblings in Cheapside

23 The most perfect humour and irony is generally quite unconscious.
Life and Habit, ch.2

24 It has, I believe, been often remarked, that a hen is only an egg's way of making another egg.
ch.8

25 Life is one long process of getting tired.
Note Books, selected and edited by H. Festing Jones (1912), ch.I

26 Life is the art of drawing sufficient conclusions from insufficient premises.

27 All progress is based upon a universal innate desire on the part of every organism to live beyond its income.

28 When the righteous man turneth away from his righteousness that he hath committed and doeth that which is neither lawful nor quite right, he will generally be found to have gained in amiability what he has lost in holiness.
ch.II

29 I believe that more unhappiness comes from this source than from any other—I mean from the attempt to prolong family connection unduly and to make people hang together artificially who would never naturally do so. The mischief among the lower classes is not so great, but among the middle and upper classes it is killing a large number daily. And the old people do not really like it much better than the young.

30 It costs a lot of money to die comfortably.

31 The healthy stomach is nothing if not conservative. Few radicals have good digestions.
ch.VI

32 How thankful we ought to feel that Wordsworth was only a poet and not a musician. Fancy a symphony by Wordsworth! Fancy having to sit it out! And fancy what it would have been if he had written fugues!
ch.VIII

33 The history of art is the history of revivals.

34 Genius...has been defined as a supreme capacity for taking trouble...It might be more fitly described as a supreme capacity for getting its possessors into pains of all kinds, and keeping them therein so long as the genius remains.
ch.XI

35 Talking it over, we agreed that Blake was no good

because he learnt Italian at over 60 to study Dante, and we knew Dante was no good because he was so fond of Virgil, and Virgil was no good because Tennyson ran him, and as for Tennyson—well, Tennyson goes without saying.
ch. XII

1 An Apology for the Devil: It must be remembered that we have only heard one side of the case. God has written all the books.
ch.XIV

2 God is Love, I dare say. But what a mischievous devil Love is.

3 To live is like to love—all reason is against it, and all healthy instinct for it.

4 The public buys its opinions as it buys its meat, or takes in its milk, on the principle that it is cheaper to do this than to keep a cow. So it is, but the milk is more likely to be watered.
ch.XVII

5 I do not mind lying but I hate inaccuracy.
ch.XIX

6 The world will, in the end, follow only those who have despised as well as served it.
ch.XXIV

7 An honest God's the noblest work of man.
Further extracts from the Note Books, selected and edited by A. Bartholomew (1934), p.26. See 270:17, 379:24

8 'Man wants but little here below' but likes that little good—and not too long in coming.
p.61. See 231:7, 588:8

9 Dulce et decorum est desipere in loco.
p.92. See 260:17, 261:20

10 Jesus! with all thy faults I love thee still.
p.117

11 My Lord, I do not believe. Help thou mine unbelief.
Note Books, selected and edited by G. Keynes and B. Hill (1951), p.284

12 Taking numbers into account, I should think more mental suffering had been undergone in the streets leading from St George's, Hanover Square, than in the condemned cells of Newgate.
The Way of All Flesh, ch.13

13 They would have been equally horrified at hearing the Christian religion doubted, and at seeing it practised.
ch.15

14 The advantage of doing one's praising for oneself is that one can lay it on so thick and exactly in the right places.
ch.34

15 There's many a good tune played on an old fiddle.
ch.61

16 'Tis better to have loved and lost, than never to have lost at all.
ch.77. See 536:16

17 Yet meet we shall, and part, and meet again, Where dead men meet on lips of living men.
Life after Death

18 I would not be—not quite—so pure as you.
A Prayer

19 O God! Oh Montreal!
Psalm of Montreal

20 Preferrest thou the gospel of Montreal to the gospel of

Hellas,
The gospel of thy connexion with Mr Spurgeon's haberdasher to the gospel of the Discobolus?
Yet none the less blasphemed he beauty saying, 'The Discobolus hath no gospel,
But my brother-in-law is haberdasher to Mr Spurgeon.'

21 Not on sad Stygian shore, nor in clear sheen Of far Elysian plain, shall we meet those Among the dead whose pupils we have been, Nor those great shades whom we have held as foes.
Seven Sonnets (1904), I

22 It was very good of God to let Carlyle and Mrs Carlyle marry one another and so make only two people miserable instead of four, besides being very amusing.
Letter to Miss Savage, 21 Nov. 1884

WILLIAM BUTLER 1535–1618

23 Doubtless God could have made a better berry [strawberry], but doubtless God never did.
Walton, *Compleat Angler,* pt.i, ch.5

JOHN BYROM 1692–1763

24 Some say, that Signor Bononcini, Compar'd to Handel's a mere ninny; Others aver, to him, that Handel Is scarcely fit to hold a candle. Strange! that such high dispute shou'd be 'Twixt Tweedledum and Tweedledee.
Epigram on the Feuds between Handel and Bononcini

25 God bless the King, I mean the Faith's Defender; God bless—no harm in blessing—the Pretender; But who Pretender is, or who is King, God bless us all—that's quite another thing.
To an Officer in the Army

LORD BYRON 1788–1824

26 For what were all these country patriots born? To hunt, and vote, and raise the price of corn?
The Age of Bronze, xiv

27 Year after year they voted cent per cent, Blood, sweat, and tear-wrung millions—why? for rent!

28 And wilt thou weep when I am low?
And Wilt Thou Weep?

29 Just like a coffin clapt in a canoe. [A gondola.]
Beppo, st.19

30 In short, he was a perfect cavaliero, And to his very valet seem'd a hero.
st.33. See 162:24

31 His heart was one of those which most enamour us, Wax to receive, and marble to retain.
st.34

32 'Tis true, your budding Miss is very charming, But shy and awkward at first coming out, So much alarm'd, that she is quite alarming, All Giggle, Blush; half Pertness and half Pout; And glancing at Mamma, for fear there's harm in What you, she, it, or they, may be about, The nursery still leaps out in all they utter— Besides, they always smell of bread and butter.
st.39

1 Know ye the land where the cypress and myrtle
   Are emblems of deeds that are done in their clime?
Where the rage of the vulture, the love of the turtle,
   Now melt into sorrow, now madden to crime!
The Bride of Abydos, c.I.st.1

2 Where the virgins are soft as the roses they twine,
And all, save the spirit of man, is divine?

3 The blind old man of Scio's rocky isle.
c.II.st.2

4 Mark! where his carnage and his conquests cease!
He makes a solitude, and calls it—peace!
st.20. See 531:7

5 Adieu, adieu! my native shore
   Fades o'er the waters blue.
Childe Harold's Pilgrimage, c.I.st.13

6 My native land—Good Night!

7 Here all were noble, save Nobility.
st.85

8 War, war is still the cry, 'War even to the knife!'
st.86. See 368:8

9 A schoolboy's tale, the wonder of an hour!
c.II.st.2

10 Well didst thou speak, Athena's wisest son!
'All that we know is, nothing can be known.'
st.7

11 Ah! happy years! once more who would not be a boy?
st.23

12 None are so desolate but something dear,
   Dearer than self, possesses or possess'd
A thought, and claims the homage of a tear.
st.24

13 Fair Greece! sad relic of departed worth!
Immortal, though no more; though fallen, great!
st.73

14 Hereditary bondsmen! know ye not
Who would be free themselves must strike the blow?
st.76

15 Where'er we tread 'tis haunted, holy ground.
st.88

16 What is the worst of woes that wait on age?
   What stamps the wrinkle deeper on the brow?
To view each loved one blotted from life's page,
   And be alone on earth, as I am now.
st.98

17 Ada! sole daughter of my house and heart.
c.III.st.1

18 Once more upon the waters! yet once more!
And the waves bound beneath me as a steed
That knows his rider.
st.2

19   Years steal
Fire from the mind as vigour from the limb;
And life's enchanted cup but sparkles near the brim.
st.8

20 There was a sound of revelry by night,
   And Belgium's capital had gather'd then
Her beauty and her chivalry, and bright
   The lamps shone o'er fair women and brave men;
A thousand hearts beat happily; and when
   Music arose with its voluptuous swell,
Soft eyes look'd love to eyes which spake again,
   And all went merry as a marriage bell;

But hush! hark! a deep sound strikes like a rising
  knell!
st.11

21 Did ye not hear it?—No; 'twas but the wind,
   Or the car rattling o'er the stony street;
On with the dance! let joy be unconfined;
   No sleep till morn, when Youth and Pleasure meet
To chase the glowing Hours with flying feet.
st.12

22 Arm! Arm! it is—it is—the cannon's opening roar!

23 Within a window'd niche of that high hall
Sate Brunswick's fated chieftain.
st.23

24 He rush'd into the field, and, foremost fighting, fell.

25 Or whispering, with white lips—'The foe! they come!
  they come!'
st.25

26 Grieving, if aught inanimate e'er grieves,
Over the unreturning brave,—alas!
st.27

27   The earth is cover'd thick with other clay,
    Which her own clay shall cover, heap'd and pent,
Rider and horse,—friend, foe,—in one red burial
  blent!
st.28

28   Life will suit
Itself to Sorrow's most detested fruit,
Like to the apples on the Dead Sea's shore,
All ashes to the taste.
st. 34

29 There sunk the greatest, nor the worst of men,
Whose spirit, antithetically mixt,
One moment of the mightiest, and again
On little objects with like firmness fixt. [Napoleon.]
st.36

30 Quiet to quick bosoms is a hell.
st.42

31 The castled crag of Drachenfels
Frowns o'er the wide and winding Rhine.
st.55

32 But these are deeds which should not pass away,
And names that must not wither.
st.67

33 Lake Leman woos me with its crystal face.
st.68

34 To fly from, need not be to hate, mankind.
st.69

35 I live not in myself, but I become
Portion of that around me; and to me
High mountains are a feeling, but the hum
Of human cities torture.
st.72

36 The self-torturing sophist, wild Rousseau.
st.77

37 Sapping a solemn creed with solemn sneer. [Gibbon.]
st.107

38 I have not loved the world, nor the world me;
   I have not flatter'd its rank breath, nor bow'd
To its idolatries a patient knee.
st.113

39   I stood
Among them, but not of them; in a shroud

Of thoughts which were not their thoughts.

1 I stood in Venice, on the Bridge of Sighs:
  A palace and a prison on each hand.
  c.IV.st.1

2 Where Venice sate in state, throned on her hundred
  isles!

3 The spouseless Adriatic mourns her lord.
  st.11

4 The moon is up, and yet it is not night;
  Sunset divides the sky with her; a sea
  Of glory streams along the Alpine height
  Of blue Friuli's mountains; Heaven is free
  From clouds, but of all colours seems to be,—
  Melted to one vast Iris of the West,—
  Where the day joins the past Eternity.
  st.27

5 The Ariosto of the North. [Scott.]
  st.40

6 Italia! oh Italia! thou who hast
  The fatal gift of beauty.
  st.42

7 Love watching Madness with unalterable mien.
  st.72

8 Then farewell, Horace; whom I hated so,
  Not for thy faults, but mine.
  st.77

9 Oh Rome! my country! city of the soul!
  st.78

10 The Niobe of nations! there she stands,
   Childless and crownless, in her voiceless woe.
   st.79

11 Yet, Freedom! yet thy banner, torn, but flying,
   Streams like the thunder-storm *against* the wind.
   st.98

12 Alas! our young affections run to waste,
   Or water but the desert.
   st.120

13 Of its own beauty is the mind diseased.
   st.122

14 Time, the avenger!
   st.130

15 The arena swims around him— he is gone,
   Ere ceased the inhuman shout which hail'd the wretch
       who won.
   st.140

16 He heard it, but he heeded not—his eyes
   Were with his heart, and that was far away;
   He reck'd not of the life he lost nor prize,
   But where his rude hut by the Danube lay,
   There were his young barbarians all at play,
   There was their Dacian mother— he, their sire,
   Butcher'd to make a Roman holiday.
   st.141

17 A ruin—yet what ruin! from its mass
   Walls, palaces, half-cities, have been rear'd.
   st.143

18 While stands the Coliseum, Rome shall stand;
   When falls the Coliseum, Rome shall fall;
   And when Rome falls—the World.
   st.145

19 The Lord of the unerring bow,

The God of life, and poesy, and light.
st.161

20   So young, so fair,
   Good without effort, great without a foe.
   st.172

21 Oh! that the desert were my dwelling-place,
   With one fair spirit for my minister,
   That I might all forget the human race,
   And, hating no one, love but only her!
   st.177

22 There is a pleasure in the pathless woods,
   There is a rapture on the lonely shore,
   There is society, where none intrudes,
   By the deep sea and music in its roar:
   I love not man the less, but Nature more,
   From these our interviews, in which I steal
   From all I may be, or have been before,
   To mingle with the Universe, and feel
   What I can ne'er express, yet cannot all conceal.
   st.178

23 Roll on, thou deep and dark blue Ocean—roll!
   Ten thousand fleets sweep over thee in vain;
   Man marks the earth with ruin—his control
   Stops with the shore.
   st.179

24 He sinks into thy depths with bubbling groan,
   Without a grave, unknell'd, uncoffin'd, and unknown.

25 Time writes no wrinkle on thine azure brow:
   Such as creation's dawn beheld, thou rollest now.
   st.182

26 Dark-heaving—boundless, endless, and sublime,
   The image of eternity.
   st.183

27 And I have loved thee, Ocean! and my joy
   Of youthful sports was on thy breast to be
   Borne, like thy bubbles, onward: from a boy
   I wanton'd with thy breakers.
   st.184

28 The glory and the nothing of a name.
   Churchill's Grave

29 The fatal facility of the octo-syllabic verse.
   The Corsair, preface

30 Such hath it been—shall be—beneath the sun
   The many still must labour for the one.
   c.I.st.8

31 There was a laughing devil in his sneer.
   st.9

32 Much hath been done, but more remains to do—
   Their galleys blaze—why not their city too?
   c.II.st.4

33 The weak alone repent.
   st.10

34 Oh! too convincing—dangerously dear—
   In woman's eye the unanswerable tear!
   st.15

35   She for him had given
   Her all on earth, and more than all in heaven!
   c.III.st.17

36 He left a Corsair's name to other times,
   Link'd with one virtue, and a thousand crimes.
   st.24

37 Slow sinks, more lovely ere his race be run,

Along Morea's hills the setting sun;
Not, as in northern climes, obscurely bright,
But one unclouded blaze of living light.
Curse of Minerva, I.1, and **The Corsair**, III.1

1 The Assyrian came down like the wolf on the fold,
And his cohorts were gleaming in purple and gold;
And the sheen of their spears was like stars on the sea,
When the blue wave rolls nightly on deep Galilee.
Destruction of Sennacherib

2 For the Angel of Death spread his wings on the blast,
And breathed in the face of the foe as he pass'd.

3 I wish he would explain his explanation.
Don Juan, c.I, dedication st.2

4 The intellectual eunuch Castlereagh.
st.11

5 My way is to begin with the beginning.
st.7

6 In virtues nothing earthly could surpass her,
Save thine 'incomparable oil', Macassar!
st.17

7 But—Oh! ye lords of ladies intellectual,
Inform us truly, have they not hen-peck'd you all?
st.22

8   She,
Was married, charming, chaste, and twenty-three.
st.59

9 What men call gallantry, and gods adultery,
Is much more common where the climate's sultry.
st.63

10 Christians have burnt each other, quite persuaded
That all the Apostles would have done as they did.
st.83

11 A little still she strove, and much repented,
And whispering 'I will ne'er consent'—consented.
st.117

12 Sweet is revenge—especially to women.
st.124

13 Pleasure's a sin, and sometimes sin's a pleasure.
st.133

14 Man's love is of man's life a thing apart,
'Tis woman's whole existence.
st.194

15 So for a good old-gentlemanly vice,
I think I must take up with avarice.
st.216

16 There's nought, no doubt, so much the spirit calms
As rum and true religion.
c.II.st.34

17 'Twas twilight, and the sunless day went down
Over the waste of waters.
st.49

18 A solitary shriek, the bubbling cry
Of some strong swimmer in his agony.
st.53

19   If this be true, indeed,
Some Christians have a comfortable creed.
st.86

20 He could, perhaps, have pass'd the Hellespont,
As once (a feat on which ourselves we prided)
Leander, Mr Ekenhead, and I did.
st.105

21 Let us have wine and women, mirth and laughter,

Sermons and soda-water the day after.
st.178

22 Man, being reasonable, must get drunk;
The best of life is but intoxication.
st.179

23   A group that's quite antique,
Half naked, loving, natural, and Greek.
st.194

24 Alas! the love of women! it is known
To be a lovely and a fearful thing!
st.199

25 In her first passion woman loves her lover,
In all the others all she loves is love.
c.III.st.3

26 'Tis melancholy, and a fearful sign
Of human frailty, folly, also crime,
That love and marriage rarely can combine,
Although they both are born in the same clime;
Marriage from love, like vinegar from wine—
A sad, sour, sober beverage—by time
Is sharpen'd from its high celestial flavour,
Down to a very homely household savour.
st.5

27 Romances paint at full length people's wooings,
But only give a bust of marriages:
For no one cares for matrimonial cooings,
There's nothing wrong in a connubial kiss:
Think you, if Laura had been Petrarch's wife,
He would have written sonnets all his life?
st.8

28 All tragedies are finish'd by a death,
All comedies are ended by a marriage.
st.9

29 Dreading that climax of all human ills,
The inflammation of his weekly bills.
st.35

30 He was the mildest manner'd man
That ever scuttled ship or cut a throat,
With such true breeding of a gentleman,
You never could divine his real thought.
st.41

31 But Shakspeare also says, 'tis very silly
'To gild refined gold, or paint the lily.'
st.76. See 452:25

32 The isles of Greece, the isles of Greece!
Where burning Sappho loved and sung,
Where grew the arts of war and peace,
Where Delos rose, and Phoebus sprung!
Eternal summer gilds them yet,
But all, except their sun, is set.
st.86, 1

33 The mountains look on Marathon—
And Marathon looks on the sea;
And musing there an hour alone,
I dream'd that Greece might still be free.
3

34 A king sate on the rocky brow
Which looks o'er sea-born Salamis;
And ships, by thousands, lay below,
And men in nations;—all were his!
He counted them at break of day—
And when the sun set where were they?
4

1 For what is left the poet here?
For Greeks a blush—for Greece a tear.
6

2 Earth! render back from out thy breast
A remnant of our Spartan dead!
Of the three hundred grant but three,
To make a new Thermopylae!
7

3 Fill high the cup with Samian wine!
9

4 Place me on Sunium's marbled steep,
    Where nothing, save the waves and I,
May hear our mutual murmurs sweep;
    There, swan-like, let me sing and die:
A land of slaves shall ne'er be mine—
Dash down yon cup of Samian wine!
16

5 Milton's the prince of poets—so we say;
    A little heavy, but no less divine.
st.91

6 A drowsy frowzy poem, call'd the 'Excursion',
Writ in a manner which is my aversion.
st.94

7 We learn from Horace, 'Homer sometimes sleeps';
We feel without him, Wordsworth sometimes wakes.
st.98

8 Ave Maria! 'tis the hour of prayer!
Ave Maria! 'tis the hour of love!
st.103

9 Imagination droops her pinion.
c.IV.st.3

10 And if I laugh at any mortal thing,
'Tis that I may not weep.
st.4

11 'Whom the gods love die young' was said of yore.
st.12. See 336:25

12 'Arcades ambo', *id est*—blackguards both.
st.93. See 560:3

13 I've stood upon Achilles' tomb,
And heard Troy doubted; time will doubt of Rome.
st.101

14 When amatory poets sing their loves
    In liquid lines mellifluously bland,
And pair their rhymes as Venus yokes her doves.
c.V.st.1

15 I have a passion for the name of 'Mary',
    For once it was a magic sound to me:
And still it half calls up the realms of fairy
    Where I beheld what never was to be.
st.4

16 And put himself upon his good behaviour.
st.47

17 That all-softening, overpowering knell,
The tocsin of the soul—the dinner-bell.
st.49

18 Not to admire is all the art I know.
st.101. See 258:17, 380:10

19 Why don't they knead two virtuous souls for life
Into that moral centaur, man and wife?
st.158

20 There is a tide in the affairs of women,
    Which, taken at the flood, leads—God knows where.
c.VI.st.2. See 451:27

21 A lady of a 'certain age', which means
Certainly aged.
st.69

22 A 'strange coincidence', to use a phrase
By which such things are settled now-a-days.
st.78

23 'Let there be light' said God, 'and there was light!'
'Let there be blood!' says man, and there's a sea!
c.VII.st.41

24 Oh, Wellington! (or 'Villainton')—for Fame
Sounds the heroic syllables both ways.
c.IX.st.1

25 Call'd 'Saviour of the Nations'—not yet saved,
And 'Europe's Liberator'—still enslaved.
[Wellington.]
st.5

26 Never had mortal man such opportunity,
Except Napoleon, or abused it more.
st.9

27 That water-land of Dutchmen and of ditches.
c.X.st.63

28 When Bishop Berkeley said 'there was no matter',
    And proved it—'twas no matter what he said.
c.XI.st.1

29 But Tom's no more—and so no more of Tom.
st.22

30 And, after all, what is a lie? 'Tis but
    The truth in masquerade.
st.37

31   I—albeit I'm sure I did not know it,
Nor sought of foolscap subjects to be king.—
Was reckon'd, a considerable time,
The grand Napoleon of the realms of rhyme.
st.55

32 John Keats, who was kill'd off by one critique,
Just as he really promised something great,
If not intelligible, without Greek
Contrived to talk about the Gods of late,
Much as they might have been supposed to speak.
Poor fellow! His was an untoward fate;
'Tis strange the mind, that very fiery particle,
Should let itself be snuff'd out by an article.
st.60

33 Nought's permanent among the human race,
Except the Whigs *not* getting into place.
st.82

34 For talk six times with the same single lady,
And you may get the wedding dresses ready.
c.XII.st.59

35   Merely innocent flirtation,
Not quite adultery, but adulteration.
st.63

36 A Prince...
With fascination in his very bow.
st.84

37 A finish'd gentleman from top to toe.

38 Now hatred is by far the longest pleasure;
Men love in haste, but they detest at leisure.
c.XIII.st.4

1 Cervantes smiled Spain's chivalry away.
st.11

2 I hate to hunt down a tired metaphor.
st.36

3 The English winter—ending in July,
   To recommence in August.
st.42

4 Society is now one polish'd horde,
Form'd of two mighty tribes, the *Bores* and *Bored.*
st.95

5 I for one venerate a petticoat.
c.XIV.st.26

6 Of all the horrid, hideous notes of woe,
   Sadder than owl-songs or the midnight blast,
Is that portentous phrase, 'I told you so.'
st.50

7 'Tis strange—but true; for truth is always strange;
Stranger than fiction.
st.101

8 A lovely being, scarcely form'd or moulded,
A rose with all its sweetest leaves yet folded.
c.XV.st.43

9 Between two worlds life hovers like a star,
   'Twixt night and morn, upon the horizon's verge.
How little do we know that which we are!
   How less what we may be!
st.99

10 The antique Persians taught three useful things,
To draw the bow, to ride, and speak the truth.
c.XVI.st.1

11 The loudest wit I e'er was deafen'd with.
st.81

12 And both were young, and one was beautiful.
The Dream, st.2

13 A change came o'er the spirit of my dream.
st.5

14 Still must I hear?—shall hoarse Fitzgerald bawl
His creaking couplets in a tavern hall.
English Bards and Scotch Reviewers, l.1

15   I'll publish, right or wrong:
Fools are my theme, let satire be my song.
l.5

16 'Tis pleasant, sure, to see one's name in print;
A book's a book, although there's nothing in 't.
l.51

17 A man must serve his time to every trade
Save censure—critics all are ready made.
Take hackney'd jokes from Miller, got by rote,
With just enough of learning to misquote.
l.63

18   As soon
Seek roses in December—ice in June;
Hope constancy in wind, or corn in chaff;
Believe a woman or an epitaph,
Or any other thing that's false, before
You trust in critics, who themselves are sore.
l.75

19 Better to err with Pope, than shine with Pye.
l.102

20 Sense and wit with poesy allied.
l.105

21 Who both by precept and example, shows

That prose is verse, and verse is merely prose.
   [Wordsworth.]
l.241

22 Be warm, but pure: be amorous, but be chaste.
l.306

23 Perverts the Prophets, and purloins the Psalms.
l.326

24 Oh, Amos Cottle!—Phoebus! what a name
To fill the speaking trump of future fame!
l.399

25 The petrifactions of a plodding brain.
l.416

26 To sanction Vice, and hunt Decorum down.
l.621

27 Lords too are bards, such things at times befall,
And 'tis some praise in peers to write at all.
l.719

28 Forsook the labours of a servile state.
Stemm'd the rude storm, and triumph'd over fate.
l.779

29 Let simple Wordsworth chime his childish verse,
And brother Coleridge lull the babe at nurse.
l.917

30 Glory, like the phoenix 'midst her fires,
Exhales her odours, blazes, and expires.
l.959

31 I too can hunt a poetaster down.
l.1064

32 The world is a bundle of hay,
   Mankind are the asses who pull;
Each tugs it a different way,
   And the greatest of all is John Bull.
Epigram

33 Fare thee well! and if for ever,
   Still for ever, fare thee well.
Fare Thee Well!

34 I only know we loved in vain—
I only feel—Farewell!!—Farewell!
Farewell! if ever Fondest Prayer

35 Dark tree, still sad when others' grief is fled,
The only constant mourner o'er the dead! [A cypress.]
The Giaour, l.286

36 Or lend fresh interest to a twice-told tale.
Hints from Horace, l.184

37 Friendship is Love without his wings!
Hours of Idleness. L'Amitié

38 I have tasted the sweets and the bitters of love.
To Rev. J.T. Becher

39 Though women are angels, yet wedlock's the devil.
To Eliza

40 But the poor dog, in life the firmest friend,
The first to welcome, foremost to defend.
Inscription on a Newfoundland Dog

41 Then receive him as best such an advent becomes,
With a legion of cooks, and an army of slaves!
The Irish Avatar

42 More happy, if less wise.
The Island, c.II.st.11

43 Jack was embarrassed—never hero more,
And as he knew not what to say, he swore.
c.IV.st.5

1 Who killed John Keats?
   'I,' says the Quarterly,
   So savage and Tartarly;
   ''Twas one of my feats.'
   John Keats

2 His madness was not of the head, but heart.
   Lara, c.I.st.18

3 Maid of Athens, ere we part,
   Give, oh give me back my heart!
   Or, since that has left my breast,
   Keep it now, and take the rest!
   Maid of Athens

4 By thy cold breast and serpent smile,
   By thy unfathom'd gulfs of guile,
   By that most seeming virtuous eye,
   By thy shut soul's hypocrisy;
   By the perfection of thine art
   Which pass'd for human thine own heart;
   By thy delight in others' pain,
   And by thy brotherhood of Cain,
   I call upon thee! and compel
   Thyself to be thy proper Hell!
   Manfred, I.i.242

5 Old man! 'tis not so difficult to die.
   III.iv.151

6   You have deeply ventured;
   But all must do so who would greatly win.
   Marino Faliero, I.ii

7 'Tis done—but yesterday a King!
   And arm'd with Kings to strive—
   And now thou art a nameless thing:
   So abject—yet alive!
   Ode to Napoleon Bonaparte

8 The Arbiter of others' fate
   A Suppliant for his own!

9 The Cincinnatus of the West. [Washington.]

10 It is not in the storm nor in the strife
   We feel benumb'd, and wish to be no more,
   But in the after-silence on the shore,
   When all is lost, except a little life.
   On Hearing Lady Byron was Ill

11 My days are in the yellow leaf;
   The flowers and fruits of love are gone;
   The worm, the canker, and the grief
   Are mine alone!
   On This Day I Complete my Thirty-Sixth Year

12 Seek out—less often sought than found—
   A soldier's grave, for thee the best;
   Then look around, and choose thy ground,
   And take thy rest.

13 Yet in my lineaments they trace
   Some features of my father's face.
   Parisina

14 Eternal spirit of the chainless mind!
   Brightest in dungeons, Liberty! thou art.
   Sonnet on Chillon

15 Chillon! thy prison is a holy place,
   And thy sad floor an altar—for 'twas trod,
   Until his very steps have left a trace
   Worn, as if thy cold pavement were a sod,
   By Bonnivard! May none those marks efface!
   For they appeal from tyranny to God.

16 My hair is grey, but not with years,
   Nor grew it white
   In a single night,
   As men's have grown from sudden fears.
   The Prisoner of Chillon, st.1

17 Regain'd my freedom with a sigh.
   st.14

18 Thy Godlike crime was to be kind,
   To render with thy precepts less
   The sum of human wretchedness.
   Prometheus

19 Man in portions can foresee
   His own funereal destiny.

20 I am the very slave of circumstance
   And impulse—borne away with every breath!
   Sardanapalus, IV.i

21 She walks in beauty, like the night
   Of cloudless climes and starry skies;
   And all that's best of dark and bright
   Meet in her aspect and her eyes:
   Thus mellow'd to that tender light
   Which heaven to gaudy day denies.
   She Walks in Beauty

22 And on that cheek, and o'er that brow,
   So soft, so calm, yet eloquent,
   The smiles that win, the tints that glow
   But tell of days in goodness spent,
   A mind at peace with all below,
   A heart whose love is innocent!

23 We were a gallant company,
   Riding o'er land, and sailing o'er sea.
   Oh! but we went merrily!
   Siege of Corinth, prologue

24 Born in the garret, in the kitchen bred,
   Promoted thence to deck her mistress' head.
   A Sketch

25 So, we'll go no more a roving
   So late into the night,
   Though the heart be still as loving,
   And the moon be still as bright.
   So, We'll Go No More a Roving

26 Though the night was made for loving,
   And the day returns too soon,
   Yet we'll go no more a-roving
   By the light of the moon.

27 There be none of Beauty's daughters
   With a magic like thee.
   Stanzas for Music. There be none of Beauty's daughters

28 There's not a joy the world can give like that it takes
   away.
   There's not a joy the world can give

29 Oh, talk not to me of a name great in story;
   The days of our youth are the days of our glory;
   And the myrtle and ivy of sweet two-and-twenty
   Are worth all your laurels, though ever so plenty.
   Stanzas Written on the Road between Florence and Pisa

30 I knew it was love, and I felt it was glory.

31 I am ashes where once I was fire.
   To the Countess of Blessington

32 My boat is on the shore,
   And my bark is on the sea;
   But, before I go, Tom Moore,

Here's a double health to thee!
To Thomas Moore

1 Here's a sigh to those who love me,
    And a smile to those who hate;
And, whatever sky's above me,
    Here's a heart for every fate.

2 My Murray.
To Mr. Murray

3 The fault was Nature's fault not thine,
    Which made thee fickle as thou art.
To a Youthful Friend

4 And when we think we lead, we are most led.
The Two Foscari, II.i.361

5 The angels all were singing out of tune,
And hoarse with having little else to do,
Excepting to wind up the sun and moon,
Or curb a runaway young star or two.
The Vision of Judgement, st.2

6 In whom his qualities are reigning still,
Except that household virtue, most uncommon,
Of constancy to a bad, ugly woman.
st.12

7 As he drew near, he gazed upon the gate
Ne'er to be entered more by him or Sin,
With such a glance of supernatural hate
As made Saint Peter wish himself within;
He patter'd with his keys at a great rate,
And sweated through his apostolic skin:
Of course his perspiration was but ichor,
Or some such other spiritual liquor.
st.25

8 Yet still between his Darkness and his Brightness
There pass'd a mutual glance of great politeness.
st.35

9   Satan met his ancient friend
With more hauteur, as might an old Castilian
Poor noble meet a mushroom rich civilian.
st.36

10 And when the tumult dwindled to a calm,
I left him practising the hundredth psalm.
st.106

11 Seductive Waltz!
The Waltz

12 Voluptuous Waltz!

13 When we two parted
    In silence and tears,
Half broken-hearted
    To sever for years,
Pale grew thy cheek and cold,
    Colder thy kiss.
When We Two Parted

14 If I should meet thee
    After long years,
How should I greet thee?—
    With silence and tears.

15 Through life's road, so dim and dirty,
I have dragg'd to three-and-thirty.
What have these years left to me?
Nothing—except thirty-three.
Diary, 21 Jan. 1821. In Moore, *Life of Byron*

16 You should have a softer pillow than my heart.
To his wife. E.C. Mayne, ed., *The Life and Letters of Anne Isabella, Lady Noel Byron*, ch.11

17 Wordsworth—stupendous genius! damned fool.
Letter to James Hogg, 1816

18 Love in this part of the world is no sinecure.
Letter to John Murray from Venice, 27 Dec. 1816

19 No *Manual*, no letters, no tooth-powder, no *extract*
from Moore's *Italy* concerning Marino Falieri, no
nothing—as a man hallooed out at one of Burdett's
elections, after a long ululatus of No Bastille! No
Governor Aris! No '—God knows what';—but his *ne
plus ultra* was, 'no nothing!'
Letter to Murray, 4 June 1817

20 I am sure my bones would not rest in an English
grave, or my clay mix with the earth of that country. I
believe the thought would drive me mad on my
deathbed, could I suppose that any of my friends
would be base enough to convey my carcass back to
your soil.
7 June 1819

21 The Princess of Parallelograms.
(Of Annabella Milbanke, to Lady Melbourne)

22 I awoke one morning and found myself famous.
(Referring to the instantaneous success of *Childe Harold*). Moore,
Life of Byron, I, 347

H.J. BYRON 1834–1884

23 Life's too short for chess.
Our Boys, Act I

JAMES BRANCH CABELL 1879–1958

24 A man possesses nothing certainly save a brief loan of
his own body: and yet the body of man is capable of
much curious pleasure.
Jurgen, ch.20

25 The optimist proclaims that we live in the best of all
possible worlds; and the pessimist fears this is true.
The Silver Stallion, bk.iv, ch.26

AUGUSTUS CAESAR
see AUGUSTUS

JULIUS CAESAR 102?–44 B.C.

26 *Gallia est omnis divisa in partes tres.*
Gaul as a whole is divided into three parts.
De Bello Gallico, I.i

27 *Fere libenter homines id quod volunt credunt.*
Men willingly believe what they wish.
iii.18

28 *Et tu, Brute?*
You too Brutus?
Oral trad. See 450:1 and Philemon Holland, trans., Suetonius,
Historie of Twelve Caesars (1606), 'Some have written that as M.
Brutus came running upon him, he said "καὶ σύ, τέκνον",
"And you, my son."'

29 *Veni, vidi, vici.*
I came, I saw, I conquered.
Suetonius, *Divus Julius*, xxxvii.2. (Inscription displayed in
Caesar's Pontic triumph, or, according to Plutarch, I.2, written in
a letter by Caesar, announcing the victory of Zela which concluded
the Pontic campaign)

30 The die is cast.
xxxii. At the crossing of the Rubicon. Often quoted in Latin,
'*Iacta alea est,*' but originally spoken in Greek: Plutarch,
Pompey, 60.2

1 Caesar's wife must be above suspicion.
Oral trad. See Plutarch, *Lives*, Julius Caesar, x.6

2 Thou hast Caesar and his fortune with thee.
xxxviii.3. Tr. North

3 Caesar, when he first went into Gaul, made no scruple
to profess 'That he had rather be first in a village than
second at Rome'.
Bacon, *Advancement of Learning*, II, xxiii, 36

PEDRO CALDERÓN DE LA BARCA 1600–1681

4   *Aún en sueños*
no se pierde el hacer bien.
Even in dreams good works are not wasted.
La Vida es Sueño (1636), II

5 *Qué es la vida? Un frenesí.*
Qué es la vida? Una ilusión,
una sombra, una ficción,
y el mayor bien es pequeño;
que toda la vida es sueño,
y los sueños, sueños son.
What is life? a frenzy. What is life? An illusion, a
shadow, a fiction. And the greatest good is of slight
worth, as all life is a dream, and dreams are dreams.
See 355:5

CALIGULA A.D. 12–41

6 *Utinam populus Romanus unam cervicem haberet!*
Would that the Roman people had but one neck!
Suetonius, *Life of Caligula*, 30

CALLIMACHUS c.305–c.240 B.C.

7

I abhor, too, the roaming lover, nor do I drink from
every well; I loathe all things held in common.
Epigrams, ed. R. Pfeiffer (1949-53), 28. *Anth. Pal.*, 12.43

8 μέγα βιβλίον ἴσον τῷ μεγάλῳ κακῷ.
A great book is like great evil.
Fragments, ed. R. Pfeiffer, 465. Proverbially reduced to
μέγα βιβλίον μέγα κακόν. 'Great book, great evil'

CHARLES ALEXANDRE DE CALONNE 1734–1802

9 *Madame, si c'est possible, c'est fait; impossible? cela*
se fera.
Madam, if a thing is possible, consider it done; the
impossible? that will be done.
J. Michelet, *Histoire de la Révolution Française* (1847), vol.I,
pt.ii, sect 8. Better known as the U.S. Armed Forces slogan, 'The
difficult we do immediately; the impossible takes a little longer.'

C.S. CALVERLEY 1831–1884

10 The farmer's daughter hath soft brown hair;
      (Butter and eggs and a pound of cheese)
And I met with a ballad, I can't say where,
      Which wholly consisted of lines like these.
Ballad

11 And this song is consider'd a perfect gem,
And as to the meaning, it's what you please.

12 O Beer! O Hodgson, Guinness, Allsopp, Bass!
Names that should be on every infant's tongue!
Beer

13 I cannot sing the old songs now!
      It is not that I deem them low;
'Tis that I can't remember how
      They go.
Changed. See 152:23

14 Aspect anything but bland.
Charades, vi

15 You see this pebble-stone? It's a thing I bought
Of a bit of a chit of a boy i' the mid o' the day—
I like to dock the smaller parts-o'-speech,
As we curtail the already curtail'd cur
(You catch the paronomasia, play 'po' words?).
The Cock and the Bull

16 Donn'd galligaskins, antigropeloes,
And so forth; and, complete with hat and gloves,
One on and one a'dangle in my hand,
And ombrifuge (Lord love you!), case o' rain.

17 A bare-legg'd beggarly son of a gun.

18 Fiddlepin's end! Get out, you blazing ass!
Gabble o' the goose. Don't bugaboo-baby *me!*

19 Life is with such all beer and skittles;
They are not difficult to please
About their victuals.
Contentment

20 For king-like rolls the Rhine,
And the scenery's divine,
And the victuals and the wine
                                          Rather good.
Dover to Munich

21 Forever! 'Tis a single word!
      Our rude forefathers deemed it two:
Can you imagine so absurd
                                          A view?
Forever

22 For I've read in many a novel that, unless they've
      souls that grovel,
Folks *prefer* in fact a hovel to your dreary marble
      halls.
In the Gloaming

23 Grinder, who serenely grindest
At my door the Hundredth Psalm.
Lines on Hearing the Organ

24 Meaning, however, is no great matter.
Lovers, and a Reflection

25 Thro' the rare red heather we dance together,
      (O love my Willie!) and smelt for flowers:
I must mention again it was gorgeous weather,
      Rhymes are so scarce in this world of ours.

26 Study first propriety.
Of Propriety

27 How Eugene Aram, though a thief, a liar, and a
      murderer,
Yet, being intellectual, was amongst the noblest of
      mankind.
Of Reading

28 Thou, who when fears attack,
Bidst them avaunt, and Black
Care, at the horseman's back
      Perching, unseatest;
Sweet, when the morn is grey;
Sweet, when they've cleared away
Lunch; and at close of day

Possibly sweetest.
Ode to Tobacco

1 I have a liking old
   For thee, though manifold
   Stories, I know, are told
       Not to thy credit.

GENERAL CAMBRONNE 1770–1842

2 *La Garde meurt, mais ne se rend pas.*
   The Guards die but do not surrender.
   Attr. to Cambronne when called upon to surrender at Waterloo.
   Cambronne denied the saying at a banquet at Nantes, 19 Sept. 1830

3 *Merde!*
   Said to be Cambronne's actual reply to the call to surrender:
   euphemistically known as '*Le mot de Cambronne*'.

CHARLES PRATT, LORD CAMDEN 1714–1794

4 [The British parliament has no right to tax the
   Americans.] Taxation and representation are
   inseparable...whatever is a man's own, is absolutely
   his own; no man hath a right to take it from him
   without his consent either expressed by himself or
   representative; whoever attempts to do it, attempts an
   injury; whoever does it, commits a robbery; he throws
   down and destroys the distinction between liberty and
   slavery.
   House of Lords, 7 Mar. 1766. See 365:25

WILLIAM CAMDEN 1551–1623

5 My friend, judge not me,
   Thou seest I judge not thee.
   Betwixt the stirrup and the ground
   Mercy I asked, mercy I found.
   Remains. Epitaph for a Man Killed by Falling from His Horse

BARON CAMPBELL 1779–1861

6 So essential did I consider an Index to be to every
   book, that I proposed to bring a Bill into parliament to
   deprive an author who publishes a book without an
   Index of the privilege of copyright; and, moreover, to
   subject him, for his offence, to a pecuniary penalty.
   Lives of the Chief Justices, preface to vol.iii, which included an
   index to the previously published vols.

MRS. PATRICK CAMPBELL 1865–1940

7 Some day you'll eat a pork chop, Joey, and then God
   help all women.
   To George Bernard Shaw, a vegetarian. Alexander Woollcott,
   While Rome Burns, Some Neighbours, 3

8 I don't mind where people make love, so long as they
   don't do it in the street and frighten the horses.
   Oral tradition

9 Marriage is the result of the longing for the deep, deep
   peace of the double bed after the hurly-burly of the
   chaise-longue.
   Oral tradition

ROY CAMPBELL 1901–1957

10   Giraffes! —a People
   Who live between the earth and skies,
   Each in his lone religious steeple,

Keeping a light-house with his eyes.
Dreaming Spires

11 Write with your spade, and garden with your pen,
    Shovel your couplets to their long repose.
    And type your turnips down the field in rows.
    The Georgiad (1931), pt.ii

12 You praise the firm restraint with which they write—
    I'm with you there, of course:
    They use the snaffle and the curb all right,
    But where's the bloody horse?
    On Some South African Novelists

13 South Africa, renowned both far and wide
    For politics and little else beside.
    The Wayzgoose (1928)

THOMAS CAMPBELL 1777–1844

14 Of Nelson and the North
    Sing the glorious day's renown,
    When to battle fierce came forth
    All the might of Denmark's crown,
    And her arms along the deep proudly shone,—
    By each gun the lighted brand
    In a bold determined hand;
    And the Prince of all the land
    Led them on.
    Battle of the Baltic

15 There was silence deep as death,
    And the boldest held his breath
    For a time.

16 Let us think of them that sleep,
    Full many a fathom deep,
    By thy wild and stormy steep,
    Elsinore!

17 O leave this barren spot to me!
    Spare, woodman, spare the beechen tree.
    The Beech-Tree's Petition

18 To-morrow let us do or die!
    Gertrude of Wyoming, pt.iii, 37

19 To live in hearts we leave behind
       Is not to die.
    Hallowed Ground

20 On the green banks of Shannon, when Sheelah was
       nigh,
    No blithe Irish lad was so happy as I;
    No harp like my own could so cheerily play,
    And wherever I went was my poor dog Tray.
    The Harper

21 On Linden, when the sun was low,
    All bloodless lay the untrodden snow,
    And dark as winter was the flow
    Of Iser, rolling rapidly.
    Hohenlinden

22 The combat deepens. On, ye brave,
    Who rush to glory, or the grave!
    Wave, Munich! all thy banners wave,
    And charge with all thy chivalry!

23 Better be courted and jilted
    Than never be courted at all.
    The Jilted Nymph

24 'Tis the sunset of life gives me mystical lore,
    And coming events cast their shadows before.
    Lochiel's Warning

1 A chieftain to the Highlands bound
   Cries, 'Boatman, do not tarry!
   And I'll give thee a silver pound
   To row us o'er the ferry.'
   Lord Ullin's Daughter

2 O, I'm the chief of Ulva's isle,
   And this Lord Ullin's daughter.

3 I'll meet the raging of the skies,
   But not an angry father.

4 One lovely hand she stretched for aid,
   And one was round her lover.

5 The waters wild went o'er his child,
   And he was left lamenting.

6 'Tis distance lends enchantment to the view,
   And robes the mountain in its azure hue.
   Pleasures of Hope, pt.i, l.7

7 Hope, for a season, bade the world farewell,
   And Freedom shrieked—as Kosciusko fell!
   l.381

8 What millions died—that Caesar might be great!
   pt.ii, l.174

9 Truth, ever lovely,—since the world began
   The foe of tyrants, and the friend of man.
   l.347

10 What though my winged hours of bliss have been,
   Like angel-visits, few and far between?
   l.375

11 It was not strange; for in the human breast
   Two master-passions cannot co-exist.
   Theodric, l.488

12 Ye Mariners of England
   That guard our native seas,
   Whose flag has braved, a thousand years,
   The battle and the breeze—
   Your glorious standard launch again
   To match another foe!
   And sweep through the deep,
   While the stormy winds do blow,—
   While the battle rages loud and long,
   And the stormy winds do blow.
   Ye Mariners of England

13 With thunders from her native oak
   She quells the floods below.

14 An original something, fair maid, you would win me
   To write—but how shall I begin?
   For I fear I have nothing original in me—
   Excepting Original Sin.
   **To a Young Lady, Who Asked Me to Write Something
   Original for Her Album**

15 Now Barabbas was a publisher.
   Often attributed to Byron

THOMAS CAMPION d. 1620

16 Rose-cheeked Laura, come;
   Sing thou smoothly with thy beauty's
   Silent music, either other
      Sweetly gracing.
   Observations in the Art of English Poesie. Laura

17 When to her lute Corinna sings,
   Her voice revives the leaden strings,
   And both in highest notes appear,
   As any challeng'd echo clear.

But when she doth of mourning speak,
Ev'n with her sighs the strings do break.
A Book of Airs, vi

18 Follow your Saint, follow with accents sweet;
   Haste you, sad notes, fall at her flying feet.
   x

19 Good thoughts his only friends,
      His wealth a well-spent age,
   The earth his sober inn
      And quiet pilgrimage.
   xviii

20 Never weather-beaten sail more willing bent to shore,
   Never tired pilgrim's limbs affected slumber more.
   Two Books of Airs. Divine and Moral Songs, xi

21   Kind are her answers,
   But her performance keeps no day;
      Breaks time, as dancers
   From their own Music when they stray.
   Third Book of Airs, vii

22 There is a garden in her face,
   Where roses and white lilies grow;
   A heav'nly paradise is that place,
   Wherein all pleasant fruits do flow.
   There cherries grow, which none may buy
   Till 'Cherry ripe' themselves do cry.
   Fourth Book of Airs, vii. See 3:18, 248:21

23 Those cherries fairly do enclose
   Of orient pearl a double row;
   Which when her lovely laughter shows,
   They look like rosebuds fill'd with snow.

ALBERT CAMUS 1913–1960

24 *La lutte elle-même vers les sommets suffit à remplir un
   coeur d'homme. Il faut imaginer Sisyphe heureux.*
   The struggle to the top alone will make a human heart
   swell. Sisyphus must be regarded as happy.
   Le Mythe de Sisyphe (1942), last words

GEORGE CANNING 1770–1827

25 In matters of commerce the fault of the Dutch
   Is offering too little and asking too much.
   The French are with equal advantage content,
   So we clap on Dutch bottoms just twenty per cent.
   **Dispatch, in Cipher, To Sir Charles Bagot, English
   Ambassador at the Hague,** 31 Jan. 1826

26 Needy Knife-grinder! whither are you going?
   Rough is the road, your wheel is out of order—
   Bleak blows the blast;—your hat has got a hole in't.
      So have your breeches.
   The Friend of Humanity and the Knife-Grinder

27 *I* give thee sixpence! I will see thee damn'd first—
   Wretch! whom no sense of wrongs can rouse to
      vengeance;
   Sordid, unfeeling, reprobate, degraded,
         Spiritless outcast!

28 A steady patriot of the world alone,
   The friend of every country but his own. [The
      Jacobin.]
   New Morality, l.113. See 185:14, 366:6

29 And finds, with keen discriminating sight,
   Black's not so black;—nor white so very white.
   l.199

1 Give me the avowed, erect and manly foe;
Firm I can meet, perhaps return the blow;
But of all plagues, good Heaven, thy wrath can send,
Save me, oh, save me, from the candid friend.
1.207

2 Pitt is to Addington
As London is to Paddington.
The Oracle, c.1803-4

3 Man, only—rash, refined, presumptuous man,
Starts from his rank, and mars creation's plan.
Progress of Man, 1.55

4 A sudden thought strikes me, let us swear an eternal
friendship.
The Rovers, I.i

5 Whene'er with haggard eyes I view
This Dungeon, that I'm rotting in,
I think of those Companions true
Who studied with me at the U-
    -NIVERSITY OF GOTTINGEN,-
    -NIVERSITY OF GOTTINGEN.
Song

6 Sun, moon, and thou vain world, adieu.

7 Away with the cant of 'Measures not men'!—the idle
supposition that it is the harness and not the horses
that draw the chariot along. If the comparison must be
made, if the distinction must be taken, men are
everything, measures comparatively nothing.
House of Commons, 1801

8 I called the New World into existence, to redress the
balance of the Old.
Speech, 12 Dec. 1826

KING CANUTE 994?-1035

9 Merrily sang the monks in Ely
When Cnut, King, rowed thereby;
Row, my knights, near the land,
And hear we these monks' song.
Attr. **Song of the Monks of Ely,** *Historia Eliensis* (1066). Green,
Conquest of England, ix

MARQUIS DOMENICO CARACCIOLO
1715-1789

10 *Il y a en Angleterre soixante sectes religieuses
différentes, et une seule sauce.*
In England there are sixty different religions, and only
one sauce.
Attr. N. & Q., Dec. 1968

RICHARD CAREW 1555-1620

11 Take the miracle of our age, Sir Philip Sidney.
An Epistle on the Excellency of the English Tongue

THOMAS CAREW 1595?-1639?

12 He that loves a rosy cheek,
    Or a coral lip admires,
Or, from star-like eyes, doth seek
    Fuel to maintain his fires;
As old Time makes these decay,
So his flames must waste away.
Disdain Returned

13 Know, Celia (since thou art so proud,)
'Twas I that gave thee thy renown.

Thou had'st in the forgotten crowd
Of common beauties liv'd unknown,
Had not my verse extoll'd thy name,
And with it imped the wings of fame.
Ingrateful Beauty Threatened

14 Good to the poor, to kindred dear,
To servants kind, to friendship clear,
To nothing but herself severe.
Inscription on Tomb of Lady Mary Wentworth

15 So though a virgin, yet a bride
To every Grace, she justified
A chaste polygamy, and died.

16 Give me more love or more disdain;
The torrid or the frozen zone:
Bring equal ease unto my pain;
The temperate affords me none.
Mediocrity in Love Rejected

17 The purest soul that e'er was sent
Into a clayey tenement.
On the Lady Mary Villiers

18 Ask me no more where Jove bestows,
When June is past, the fading rose;
For in your beauty's orient deep
These flowers, as in their causes, sleep.
A Song

19 Ask me no more whither doth haste
The nightingale when May is past;
For in your sweet dividing throat
She winters and keeps warm her note.

20 Ask me no more if east or west
The Phoenix builds her spicy nest;
For unto you at last she flies,
And in your fragrant bosom dies.

HENRY CAREY 1693?-1743

21 Aldiborontiphoscophornio!
Where left you Chrononhotonthologos?
Chrononhotonthologos, I.i

22 His cogitative faculties immers'd
In cogibundity of cogitation.

23 To thee, and gentle Rigdum-Funnidos,
Our gratulations flow in streams unbounded.
iii

24 God save our gracious king!
Long live our noble king!
    God save the king!
God Save the King. (But see 252:24)

25 Confound their politics,
Frustrate their knavish tricks.

26 Of all the girls that are so smart
    There's none like pretty Sally,
She is the darling of my heart,
    And she lives in our alley.
Sally in our Alley

27 Of all the days that's in the week
    I dearly love but one day—
And that's the day that comes betwixt
    A Saturday and Monday.

WILLIAM CARLETON 1794-1869

28 Things at home are crossways, and Betsey and I are

out.
Farm Ballads. **Betsey and I Are Out**

JANE WELSH CARLYLE 1801–1866

1 I am not at all the sort of person you and I took me for.
Letter to Thomas Carlyle, 7 May 1822

THOMAS CARLYLE 1795–1881

2 A well-written Life is almost as rare as a well-spent one.
Critical and Miscellaneous Essays, vol.i. **Richter**

3 The three great elements of modern civilization, Gunpowder, Printing, and the Protestant Religion.
State of German Literature. See 28:9

4 The 'golden-calf of Self-love.'
Burns

5 It is the Age of Machinery, in every outward and inward sense of that word.
vol.ii. **Signs of the Times**

6 The Bible-Society...is found, on inquiry, to be...a machine for converting the Heathen.

7 Thought, he [Dr. Cabanis] is inclined to hold, is still secreted by the brain; but then Poetry and Religion (and it is really worth knowing) are 'a product of the smaller intestines'!

8 What is all knowledge too but recorded experience, and a product of history; of which, therefore, reasoning and belief, no less than action and passion, are essential materials?
On History

9 History is the essence of innumerable biographies.
See 131:31

10 The foul sluggard's comfort: 'It will last my time.'
vol.iii. **Count Cagliostro. Flight Last**

11 This Mirabeau's work, then, is done. He sleeps with the primeval giants. He has gone over to the majority: *Abiit ad plures.*
Mirabeau. See 373:1

12 There is no life of a man, faithfully recorded, but is a heroic poem of its sort, rhymed or unrhymed.
vol.iv. **Sir Walter Scott**

13 Under all speech that is good for anything there lies a silence that is better. Silence is deep as Eternity; speech is shallow as Time.

14 It can be said of him [Scott], When he departed, he took a man's life along with him. No sounder piece of British manhood was put together in that eighteenth century of Time.

15 A witty statesman said, you might prove anything by figures.
Chartism, ch.2

16 Surely of all 'rights of man', this right of the ignorant man to be guided by the wiser, to be, gently or forcibly, held in the true course by him, is the indisputablest.
ch.6

17 In epochs when cash payment has become the sole nexus of man to man.

18 'Genius' (which means transcendent capacity of taking

trouble, first of all).
Frederick the Great, bk.iv, ch.3. See 106:21

19 If they could forget, for a moment, the correggiosity of Correggio, and the learned babble of the saleroom and varnishing auctioneer.
ch.6. See 519:29

20 Happy the people whose annals are blank in history-books!
bk.xvi, ch.1

21 France was long a despotism tempered by epigrams.
History of the French Revolution, pt.I, bk.i, ch.1

22 A whiff of grapeshot.
bk.v, ch.3

23 History a distillation of rumour.
bk.vii, ch.5

24 The gospel according to Jean Jacques.
pt.II, bk.i, ch.6

25 The difference between Orthodoxy or My-doxy and Heterodoxy or Thy-doxy.
bk.iv, ch.2

26 The seagreen Incorruptible. [Robespierre.]
ch.4

27 Aristocracy of the Moneybag.
bk.vii, ch.7

28 It is well said, in every sense, that a man's religion is the chief fact with regard to him.
Heroes and Hero-Worship, i. **The Hero as Divinity**

29 Worship is transcendent wonder.

30 No sadder proof can be given by a man of his own littleness than disbelief in great men.

31 No great man lives in vain. The history of the world is but the biography of great men.
See 131:9

32 The greatest of faults, I should say, is to be conscious of none.
ii. **The Hero as Prophet**

33 The Hero can be Poet, Prophet, King, Priest or what you will, according to the kind of world he finds himself born into.
iii. **The Hero as Poet**

34 In books lies the *soul* of the whole Past Time; the articulate audible voice of the Past, when the body and material substance of it has altogether vanished like a dream.
v. **The Hero as Man of Letters**

35 The true University of these days is a collection of books.

36 Adversity is sometimes hard upon a man; but for one man who can stand prosperity, there are a hundred that will stand adversity.

37 I hope we English will long maintain our *grand talent pour le silence.*
vi. **The Hero as King**

38 Maid-servants, I hear people complaining, are getting instructed in the 'ologies'.
Inaugural Address at Edinburgh, 1866

39 Speech is human, silence is divine, yet also brutish and dead: therefore we must learn both arts.
Journal

40 Respectable Professors of the Dismal Science.

[Political Economy.]
Latter-Day Pamphlets, No.1. **The Present Time**

1 Little other than a redtape Talking-machine, and unhappy Bag of Parliamentary Eloquence.

2 A healthy hatred of scoundrels.
No.2. **Model Prisons**

3 Nature admits no lie.
No.5. **Stump Orator**

4 A Parliament speaking through reporters to Buncombe and the twenty-seven millions mostly fools.
No.6. **Parliaments**

5 'May the Devil fly away with the fine arts!' exclaimed…in my hearing, one of our most distinguished public men.
No.8

6 The unspeakable Turk should be immediately struck out of the question.
Letter to G. Howard, 24 Nov. 1876

7 Transcendental moonshine.
Life of John Sterling, pt.i, ch.15

8 The progress of human society consists…in…the better and better apportioning of wages to work.
Past and Present, bk.i, ch.3

9 Brothers, I am sorry I have got no Morrison's Pill for curing the maladies of Society.
ch.4

10 Blessed is he who has found his work; let him ask no other blessedness.
bk.iii, ch.11

11 Captains of industry.
bk.iv, ch.4

12 He who first shortened the labour of copyists by device of *Movable Types* was disbanding hired armies, and cashiering most Kings and Senates, and creating a whole new democratic world: he had invented the art of printing.
Sartor Resartus, bk.i, ch.5

13 Man is a tool-using animal…Without tools he is nothing, with tools he is all.

14 Whoso has sixpence is sovereign (to the length of sixpence) over all men; commands cooks to feed him, philosophers to teach him, kings to mount guard over him,—to the length of sixpence.

15 Language is called the garment of thought: however, it should rather be, language is the flesh-garment, the body, of thought.
ch.11

16 The end of man is an action and not a thought, though it were the noblest.
bk.ii, ch.6

17 The everlasting No.
ch.7, title

18 The folly of that impossible precept, 'Know thyself'; till it be translated into this partially possible one, 'Know what thou canst work at'.
See 9:21

19 Man's unhappiness, as I construe, comes of his greatness; it is because there is an Infinite in him, which with all his cunning he cannot quite bury under the Finite.
ch.9

20 Close thy Byron; open thy Goethe.

21 'Do the duty which lies nearest thee', which thou knowest to be a duty! Thy second duty will already have become clearer.

22 Be no longer a chaos, but a world, or even worldkin. Produce! Produce! Were it but the pitifullest infinitesimal fraction of a product, produce it in God's name! 'Tis the utmost thou hast in thee: out with it, then.

23 As the Swiss Inscription says: *Sprechen ist silbern, Schweigen ist golden* (Speech is silvern, Silence is golden); or as I might rather express it: Speech is of Time, Silence is of Eternity.
bk.iii, ch.3

24 A *big*, fierce, weeping, hungry man, not a strong one.
(Of Thackeray.) Letter to R.W. Emerson, 9 Sept. 1853

25 I don't pretend to understand the Universe—it's a great deal bigger than I am…People ought to be modester.
To Wm. Allingham. D.A. Wilson and D. Wilson MacArthur, *Carlyle in Old Age*

26 If Jesus Christ were to come to-day, people would not even crucify him. They would ask him to dinner, and hear what he had to say, and make fun of it.
D.A. Wilson, *Carlyle at his Zenith*

27 It were better to perish than to continue schoolmastering.
D.A. Wilson, *Carlyle Till Marriage*

28 Macaulay is well for a while, but one wouldn't *live* under Niagara.
R.M. Milnes, *Notebook*, 1838

29 A good book is the purest essence of a human soul.
Speech in support of the London Library, 1840. F. Harrison, *Carlyle and the London Library*

30 *Margaret Fuller.* I accept the universe.
Carlyle: Gad! she'd better!
Attr.

ANDREW CARNEGIE 1835–1919

31 Of every thousand dollars spent in so-called charity today, it is probable that nine hundred and fifty dollars is unwisely spent.
North American Review, June 1889, **'The Gospel of Wealth'**, pt.I

32 The man who dies…rich dies disgraced.

JULIA A. CARNEY 1823–1908

33 Little drops of water,
  Little grains of sand,
Make the mighty ocean
  And the beauteous land.

And the little moments,
  Humble though they be,
Make the mighty ages
  Of eternity.
Little Things (1845). Reprinted in *Juvenile Missionary Magazine*, 10, Apr. 1853

JOSEPH EDWARDS CARPENTER 1813–1885

34 What are the wild waves saying
  Sister, the whole day long,

That ever amid our playing,
   I hear but their low lone song?
What are the Wild Waves Saying?

LEWIS CARROLL 1832–1898

1 What I tell you three times is true.
The Hunting of the Snark, Fit 1. **The Landing**

2 He had forty-two boxes, all carefully packed,
   With his name painted clearly on each;
But, since he omitted to mention the fact,
   They were all left behind on the beach.

3 He would answer to 'Hi!' or to any loud cry,
   Such as 'Fry me!' or 'Fritter-my-wig!'

4 His intimate friends called him 'Candle-ends',
   And his enemies, 'Toasted-cheese'.

5 Then the bowsprit got mixed with the rudder
   sometimes.

6 But the principal failing occurred in the sailing,
   And the Bellman, perplexed and distressed,
Said he *had* hoped, at least, when the wind blew due
   East,
That the ship would *not* travel due West!
Fit 2. **The Bellman's Speech**

7 But oh, beamish nephew, beware of the day,
   If your Snark be a Boojum! For then
You will softly and suddenly vanish away,
   And never be met with again!
Fit 3. **The Baker's Tale**

8 They sought it with thimbles, they sought it with care;
   They pursued it with forks and hope;
They threatened its life with a railway-share;
   They charmed it with smiles and soap.
Fit 5. **The Beaver's Lesson**

9 For the Snark *was* a Boojum, you see.
Fit 8. **The Vanishing**

10 He thought he saw an Elephant,
   That practised on a fife:
He looked again, and found it was
   A letter from his wife.
'At length I realize,' he said,
   'The bitterness of life!'
Sylvie and Bruno, ch.5

11 He thought he saw a Buffalo
   Upon the chimney-piece:
He looked again, and found it was
   His sister's husband's niece.
'Unless you leave this house,' he said,
   'I'll send for the Police!'
ch.6

12 He thought he saw a Rattlesnake
   That questioned him in Greek,
He looked again and found it was
   The Middle of Next Week.
'The one thing I regret,' he said,
   'Is that it cannot speak!'

13 He thought he saw a Banker's Clerk
   Descending from the bus:
He looked again, and found it was
   A Hippopotamus:
'If this should stay to dine,' he said,
   'There won't be much for us.'
ch.7

14 'What is the use of a book', thought Alice, 'without
pictures or conversations?'
Alice's Adventures in Wonderland, ch.1

15 Do cats eat bats?...Do bats eat cats?

16 'Curiouser and curiouser!' cried Alice.
ch.2

17 How doth the little crocodile
   Improve his shining tail,
And pour the waters of the Nile
   On every golden scale!
See 565:21

18 How cheerfully he seems to grin,
   How neatly spreads his claws,
And welcomes little fishes in
   With gently smiling jaws!

19 'I'll be judge, I'll be jury,' said cunning old Fury;
   'I'll try the whole cause, and condemn you to death.'
ch.3

20 The Duchess! The Duchess! Oh my dear paws! Oh my
fur and whiskers!
ch.4

21 'I can't explain *myself,* I'm afraid, sir,' said Alice,
'because I'm not myself, you see.' 'I don't see,' said
the Caterpillar.
ch.5

22 'You are old, Father William,' the young man said,
   'And your hair has become very white;
And yet you incessantly stand on your head—
   Do you think, at your age, it is right?'

'In my youth,' Father William replied to his son,
   'I feared it might injure the brain;
But now that I'm perfectly sure I have none,
   Why, I do it again and again.'
See 514:7

23 'I have answered three questions, and that is enough,'
   Said his father; 'don't give yourself airs!
Do you think I can listen all day to such stuff?
   Be off, or I'll kick you downstairs!'
See 83:27

24 'I shall sit here,' he said, 'on and off, for days and
days.'
ch.6

25 'If everybody minded their own business,' said the
Duchess in a hoarse growl, 'the world would go round
a deal faster than it does.'

26 Speak roughly to your little boy,
   And beat him when he sneezes;
He only does it to annoy,
   Because he knows it teases.

27 This time it vanished quite slowly, beginning with the
end of the tail, and ending with the grin, which
remained some time after the rest of it had gone. [The
Cheshire Cat.]

28 'Have some wine,' the March Hare said in an
encouraging tone. Alice looked all round the table, but
there was nothing on it but tea. 'I don't see any wine,'
she remarked. 'There isn't any,' said the March Hare.
ch.7

29 'Then you should say what you mean,' the March
Hare went on. 'I do,' Alice hastily replied; 'at
least—at least I mean what I say—that's the same
thing, you know.'

'Not the same thing a bit!' said the Hatter. 'Why, you might just as well say that "I see what I eat" is the same thing as "I eat what I see!"'

1 'It was the *best* butter,' the March Hare meekly replied.

2 Twinkle, twinkle, little bat!
How I wonder what you're at!
Up above the world you fly!
Like a teatray in the sky.
See 532:1

3 'Take some more tea,' the March Hare said to Alice, very earnestly.
'I've had nothing yet,' Alice replied in an offended tone, 'so I can't take more.'
'You mean you can't take *less*,' said the Hatter: 'it's very easy to take *more* than nothing.'

4 Let's all move one place on.

5 The Queen was in a furious passion, and went stamping about, and shouting, 'Off with his head!' or 'Off with her head!' about once in a minute.
ch.8

6 Everything's got a moral, if you can only find it.
ch.9

7 Take care of the sense, and the sounds will take care of themselves.

8 'That's nothing to what I could say if I chose,' the Duchess replied.

9 'Just about as much right,' said the Duchess, 'as pigs have to fly.'

10 I only took the regular course...the different branches of Arithmetic—Ambition, Distraction, Uglification and Derision.

11 The Drawling-master was an old conger-eel, that used to come once a week: *he* taught us Drawling, Stretching, and Fainting in Coils.

12 'That's the reason they're called lessons,' the Gryphon remarked: 'because they lessen from day to day.'

13 'Will you walk a little faster?' said a whiting to a snail,
'There's a porpoise close behind us, and he's treading on my tail.'
ch.10

14 Will you, won't you, will you, won't you, will you join the dance?

15 The further off from England the nearer is to France—
Then turn not pale, beloved snail, but come and join the dance.

16 'Tis the voice of the lobster; I heard him declare,
'You have baked me too brown, I must sugar my hair.'
See 565:25

17 Soup of the evening, beautiful Soup!

18 'Write that down,' the King said to the jury, and the jury eagerly wrote down all three dates on their slates, and then added them up, and reduced the answer to shillings and pence.
ch.11

19 'Where shall I begin, please your Majesty?' he asked.
'Begin at the beginning,' the King said, gravely, 'and go on till you come to the end: then stop.'

20 '*Un*important, of course, I meant,' the King hastily said, and went on to himself in an undertone, 'important—unimportant—unimportant—important—' as if he were trying which word sounded best.
ch.12

21 'That's not a regular rule: you invented it just now.'
'It's the oldest rule in the book,' said the King.
'Then it ought to be Number One,' said Alice.

22 They told me you had been to her,
And mentioned me to him:
She gave me a good character,
But said I could not swim.

23 No! No! Sentence first—verdict afterwards.

24 I never loved a dear Gazelle—
Nor anything that cost me much:
High prices profit those who sell,
But why should I *be fond of such?*
Phantasmagoria (1911 ed.), **Tema con Variazioni.** See 356:25

25 Yet what are all such gaieties to me
Whose thoughts are full of indices and surds?
$$x^2 + 7x + 53$$
$$= \tfrac{11}{3}$$
from **Four Riddles,** I

26 'The horror of that moment,' the King went on, 'I shall never, *never* forget!' 'You will, though,' the Queen said, 'if you don't make a memorandum of it.'
Through the Looking-Glass, ch.1

27 'My precious Lily! My imperial kitten!'—
'Imperial fiddlestick!'

28 'Twas brillig, and the slithy toves
Did gyre and gimble in the wabe;
All mimsy were the borogoves,
And the mome raths outgrabe.

'Beware the Jabberwock, my son!
The jaws that bite, the claws that catch!'

29 And as in uffish thought he stood,
The Jabberwock, with eyes of flame,
Came whiffling through the tulgey wood,
And burbled as it came!

One, two! One, two! And through and through
The vorpal blade went snicker-snack!
He left it dead, and with its head
He went galumphing back.

'And hast thou slain the Jabberwock?
Come to my arms, my beamish boy!
O frabjous day! Callooh! Callay!'
He chortled in his joy.

30 Curtsey while you're thinking what to say. It saves time.
ch.2

31 Speak in French when you can't think of the English for a thing.

32 Now, *here,* you see, it takes all the running *you* can do, to keep in the same place. If you want to get somewhere else, you must run at least twice as fast as that!

33 Tweedledum and Tweedledee
Agreed to have a battle;
For Tweedledum said Tweedledee
Had spoilt his nice new rattle.

Just then flew down a monstrous crow,
   As black as a tar-barrel;
Which frightened both the heroes so,
   They quite forgot their quarrel.
ch.4

1 If you think we're wax-works, you ought to pay, you know. Wax-works weren't made to be looked at for nothing. Nohow!

2 'Contrariwise,' continued Tweedledee, 'if it was so, it might be; and if it were so, it would be: but as it isn't, it ain't. That's logic.'

3 The sun was shining on the sea,
   Shining with all his might:
He did his very best to make
   The billows smooth and bright—
And this was odd, because it was
   The middle of the night.

4 'It's very rude of him,' she said
   'To come and spoil the fun!'

5 The Walrus and the Carpenter
   Were walking close at hand;
They wept like anything to see
   Such quantities of sand:
'If this were only cleared away,'
   They said, 'it would be grand!'

'If seven maids with seven mops
   Swept it for half a year,
Do you suppose,' the Walrus said,
   'That they could get it clear?'
'I doubt it,' said the Carpenter,
   And shed a bitter tear.

6 But four young Oysters hurried up,
   All eager for the treat:
Their coats were brushed, their faces washed,
   Their shoes were clean and neat—
And this was odd, because, you know,
   They hadn't any feet.

7 'The time has come,' the Walrus said,
   'To talk of many things:
Of shoes—and ships—and sealing wax—
   Of cabbages—and kings—
And why the sea is boiling hot—
   And whether pigs have wings.'

8 'A loaf of bread,' the Walrus said,
   'Is what we chiefly need:
Pepper and vinegar besides
   Are very good indeed—
Now if you're ready, Oysters dear,
   We can begin to feed.'

9 The Carpenter said nothing but
   'The butter's spread too thick!'

10 'I weep for you,' the Walrus said:
   'I deeply sympathize.'
With sobs and tears he sorted out
   Those of the largest size,
Holding his pocket-handkerchief
   Before his streaming eyes.

11   But answer came there none—
And this was scarcely odd because
   They'd eaten every one.
See 415:21

12 'Let's fight till six, and then have dinner,' said Tweedledum.

13 'You know,' he said very gravely, 'it's one of the most serious things that can possibly happen to one in a battle—to get one's head cut off.'

14 'I'm very brave generally,' he went on in a low voice: 'only to-day I happen to have a headache.'

15 The rule is, jam to-morrow and jam yesterday—but never jam to-day.
ch.5

16 'It's a poor sort of memory that only works backwards,' the Queen remarked.

17 Consider anything, only don't cry!

18 Why, sometimes I've believed as many as six impossible things before breakfast.

19 With a name like yours, you might be any shape, almost.
ch.6

20 They gave it me,—for an un-birthday present.

21 'There's glory for you!' 'I don't know what you mean by "glory",' Alice said. 'I meant, "there's a nice knock-down argument for you!"' 'But "glory" doesn't mean "a nice knock-down argument",' Alice objected. 'When *I* use a word,' Humpty Dumpty said in a rather scornful tone, 'it means just what I choose it to mean—neither more nor less.'

22 'The question is,' said Humpty Dumpty, 'which is to be master—that's all.'

23 I can explain all the poems that ever were invented—and a good many that haven't been invented just yet.

24 '*I* can repeat poetry as well as other folk if it comes to that—' 'Oh, it needn't come to that!' Alice hastily said.

25 The little fishes of the sea,
They sent an answer back to me.

The little fishes' answer was
'We cannot do it, Sir, because—'

26 I took a kettle large and new,
Fit for the deed I had to do.

27 I said it very loud and clear;
I went and shouted in his ear.

But he was very stiff and proud;
He said 'You needn't shout so loud!'

And he was very proud and stiff;
He said 'I'd go and wake them, if—'

28 You see it's like a portmanteau—there are two meanings packed up into one word.

29 He's an Anglo-Saxon Messenger—and those are Anglo-Saxon attitudes.
ch.7

30 The other Messenger's called Hatta. I must have *two* you know—to come and go. One to come, and one to go.

31 'There's nothing like eating hay when you're faint.'...'I didn't say there was nothing *better*,' the King replied, 'I said there was nothing *like* it.'

32 'I'm sure nobody walks much faster than I do!'

'He can't do that,' said the King, 'or else he'd have been here first.'

1 It's as large as life, and twice as natural!

2 If you'll believe in me, I'll believe in you.

3 The [White] Knight said...'It's my own invention.'
ch.8

4 But you've no idea what a difference it makes, mixing it with other things—such as gunpowder and sealing-wax.

5 I'll tell thee everything I can:
    There's little to relate.
I saw an aged, aged man,
    A-sitting on a gate.

6 He said, 'I look for butterflies
    That sleep among the wheat:
I make them into mutton-pies,
    And sell them in the street.'

7 Or madly squeeze a right-hand foot
    Into a left-hand shoe.

8 'Speak when you're spoken to!' the Red Queen sharply interrupted her.
ch.9

9 No admittance till the week after next!

10 It isn't etiquette to cut any one you've been introduced to. Remove the joint.

11 Un-dish-cover the fish, or dishcover the riddle.

12 I am fond of children (except boys).
Letter to Kathleen Eschwege. S.D. Collingwood, The Life and Letters of Lewis Carroll (1898), p.416

JOHN CARTWRIGHT 1740–1824

13 One man shall have one vote.
People's Barrier Against Undue Influence (1780), p.5

PHOEBE CARY 1824–1871

14 And though hard be the task,
'Keep a stiff upper lip'.
Keep a Stiff Upper Lip

REVD. EDWARD CASWALL 1814–1878

15 Jesu, the very thought of Thee
With sweetness fills the breast.
Jesu, The Very Thought of Thee (tr. from Latin)

16 My God, I love Thee; not because
I hope for heaven thereby.
My God, I Love Thee (tr. from Latin)

EMPRESS CATHERINE THE GREAT 1729–1796

17 *Moi, je serai autocrate: c'est mon métier. Et le bon Dieu me pardonnera: c'est son métier.*
I shall be an autocrat: that's my trade. And the good Lord will forgive me: that's his.
Attr. See also 244:13

THE ELDER CATO, THE CENSOR 234–149 B.C

18 *Delenda est Carthago.*

Carthage must be destroyed.
Pliny the Elder, *Naturalis Historia*, xv.18.74

CATULLUS 87–54? B.C.

19 *Cui dono lepidum novum libellum*
Arido modo pumice expolitum?
Here's my small book out, nice and new,
Fresh-bound—whom shall I give it to?
Carmina, i, tr. Sir William Marris

20   *Namque tu solebas*
Meas esse aliquid putare nugas.
For you used to think my trifles were worth something.

21 *Plus uno maneat perenne saeclo.*
May it live and last for more than a century.

22 *Lugete, O Veneres Cupidinesque,*
Et quantum est hominum venustiorum.
Passer mortuus est meae puellae,
Passer, deliciae meae puellae.
Mourn, you powers of Charm and Desire, and all you who are endowed with charm. My lady's sparrow is dead, the sparrow which was my lady's darling.
iii

23 *Qui nunc it per iter tenebricosum*
Illuc, unde negant redire quemquam.
Now he goes along the darksome road, thither whence they say no one returns.

24 *Sed haec prius fuere.*
All this is over now.
iv

25 *Vivamus, mea Lesbia, atque amemus,*
Rumoresque senum severiorum
Omnes unius aestimemus assis.
Soles occidere et redire possunt:
Nobis cum semel occidit brevis lux
Nox est perpetua una dormienda.
My sweetest Lesbia let us live and love,
And though the sager sort our deeds reprove,
Let us not weigh them: Heav'n's great lamps do dive
Into their west, and straight again revive,
But soon as once set is our little light,
Then must we sleep one ever-during night.
v. Tr. Campion, *A Book of Airs*, i

26 *Da mi basia mille, deinde centum,*
Dein mille altera, dein secunda centum,
Deinde usque altera mille, deinde centum.
Give me a thousand kisses, then a hundred, then another thousand, then a second hundred, then yet another thousand, then a hundred.

27 *Miser Catulle, desinas ineptire,*
Et quod vides perisse perditum ducas.
Poor Catullus, drop your silly fancies, and what you see is lost let it be lost.
viii

28 *Paene insularum, Sirmio, insularumque*
Ocelle...
O quid solutis est beatius curis?
Cum mens onus reponit, ac peregrino
Labore fessi venimus larem ad nostrum,
Desideratoque acquiescimus lecto.
Hoc est quod unum est pro laboribus tantis.
Salve O venusta Sirmio atque hero gaude;
Gaudete vosque O Lydiae lacus undae;

Ridete quidquid est domi cachinnorum.
Sirmio, bright eye of peninsulas and islands...Ah,
    what is more blessed than to put cares away, when
    the mind lays by its burden, and tired with labour of
    far travel we have come to our own home and rest
    on the couch we have longed for? This it is which
    alone is worth all these toils. Hail, sweet Sirmio,
    and make cheer for your master. Rejoice ye too,
    waters of the Lydian lake, and laugh out aloud all
    the laughter you have at your command.
xxxi

1 *Nam risu inepto res ineptior nulla est.*
For there is nothing sillier than a silly laugh.
xxxix

2 *Iam ver egelidos refert tepores.*
Now Spring restores balmy warmth.
xlvi

3 *Gratias tibi maximas Catullus*
Agit pessimus omnium poeta,
Tanto pessimus omnium poeta,
Quanto tu optimus omnium's patronum.
Catullus gives you warmest thanks,
And he the worst of poets ranks;
As much the worst of bards confessed,
As you of advocates the best.
xlix, tr. Sir William Marris

4 *Ille mi par esse deo videtur,*
Ille, si fas est, superare divos,
Qui sedens adversus identidem te
        Spectat et audit
Dulce ridentem, misero quod omnis
Eripit sensus mihi.
Like to a god he seems to me,
Above the gods, if so may be,
Who sitting often close to thee
        May see and hear
Thy lovely laugh: ah, luckless man!
li, tr. Sir William Marris. Itself a translation of 414:6

5 *Caeli, Lesbia nostra, Lesbia illa,*
Illa Lesbia, quam Catullus unam
Plus quam se atque suos amavit omnes,
Nunc in quadriviis et angiportis
Glubit magnanimos Remi nepotes.
O Caelius, our Lesbia, that Lesbia whom Catullus
    once loved uniquely, more than himself and more
    than all his own, now at the crossroads and in the
    alleyways has it off with the high-minded
    descendants of Remus.
lviii

6 *Ut flos in saeptis secretus nascitur hortis,*
Ignotus pecori, nullo contusus aratro,
Quem mulcent aurae, firmat sol, educat imber;
Multi illum pueri, multae optavere puellae.
As a flower grows concealed in an enclosed garden,
    unknown to the cattle, bruised by no plough, which
    the breezes caress, the sun makes strong, and the
    rain brings out; many boys and many girls long for
    it.
lxii.39

7   *Sed mulier cupido quod dicit amanti,*
In vento et rapida scribere oportet aqua.
But what a woman says to her lusting lover it is best to
    write in wind and swift-flowing water.
lxx

8 *Desine de quoquam quicquam bene velle mereri,*
    Aut aliquem fieri posse putare pium.
Give up wanting to deserve any thanks from anyone,
    or thinking that anybody can be grateful.
lxxiii

9 *Siqua recordanti benefacta priora voluptas*
Est homini.
If a man can take any pleasure in recalling the thought
    of kindnesses done.
lxxvi

10 *Difficile est longum subito deponere amorem.*
It is difficult suddenly to lay aside a long-cherished
    love.

11 *Si vitam puriter egi.*
If I have led a pure life.

12 *O di, reddite mi hoc pro pietate mea.*
O gods, grant me this in return for my piety.

13 *Chommoda dicebat, si quando commoda vellet*
Dicere.
'Hamenities' he used to say, meaning 'amenities'. (Of
    Arrius.)
lxxxiv

14 *Odi et amo: quare id faciam, fortasse requiris.*
    Nescio, sed fieri sentio et excrucior.
I hate and I love: why I do so you may well ask. I do
    not know, but I feel it happen and am in agony.
lxxxv

15 *Multas per gentes et multa per aequora vectus*
    Advenio has miseras, frater, ad inferias,
Ut te postremo donarem munere mortis
    Et mutam nequiquam alloquerer cinerem.
Quandoquidem fortuna mihi tete abstulit ipsum,
    Heu miser indigne frater adempte mihi,
Nunc tamen interea haec prisco quae more parentum
    Tradita sunt tristi munere ad inferias,
Accipe fraterno multum manantia fletu,
    Atque in perpetuum, frater, ave atque vale.
By many lands and over many a wave
I come, my brother, to your piteous grave,
To bring you the last offering in death
And o'er dumb dust expend an idle breath;
For fate has torn your living self from me,
And snatched you, brother, O, how cruelly!
Yet take these gifts, brought as our fathers bade
For sorrow's tribute to the passing shade;
A brother's tears have wet them o'er and o'er;
And so, my brother, hail, and farewell evermore!
ci, tr. Sir William Marris

16 *At non effugies meos iambos.*
You shan't evade
These rhymes I've made.
Fragments, tr. Sir William Marris

CONSTANTINE CAVAFY 1863–1933

17 What shall become of us without any barbarians?
Those people were a kind of solution.
Expecting the Barbarians

EDITH CAVELL 1865–1915

18 Standing, as I do, in the view of God and eternity I
realize that patriotism is not enough. I must have no

hatred or bitterness towards anyone.
Spoken to the chaplain who attended her before her execution by firing squad, 12 Oct. 1915. *The Times*, 23 Oct. 1915

COUNT CAVOUR 1810–1861

1 *Noi siamo pronti a proclamare nell' Italia questo gran principio: Libera Chiesa in libero Stato.*
We are ready to proclaim throughout Italy this great principle: a free church in a free state.
Speech, 27 Mar. 1861. William de la Rive, *Remin. of Life and Character of Count Cavour* (1862), ch.13, p.276

WILLIAM CAXTON c.1421–1491

2 The worshipful father and first founder and embellisher of ornate eloquence in our English, I mean Master Geoffrey Chaucer.
Epilogue to Caxton's edition (?1478) of Chaucer's translation of Boethius, *The Consolacion of Philosophie*, 93 verso

3 It is notoriously known through the universal world that there be nine worthy and the best that ever were. That is to wit three paynims, three Jews, and three Christian men. As for the paynims they were...the first Hector of Troy,...the second Alexander the Great; and the third Julius Caesar....As for the three Jews...the first was Duke Joshua...; the second David, King of Jerusalem; and the third Judas Maccabaeus.... And sith the said Incarnation...was first the noble Arthur.... The second was Charlemagne or Charles the Great...; and the third and last was Godfrey of Bouillon.
Malory, *Le Morte D'Arthur*, Original Preface

4 I, according to my copy, have done set it in imprint, to the intent that noble men may see and learn the noble acts of chivalry, the gentle and virtuous deeds that some knights used in those days.
*

ROBERT CECIL
see SALISBURY

THOMAS OF CELANO c.1190–1260

5 *Dies irae, dies illa,*
Solvet saeclum in favilla,
Teste David cum Sibylla.
That day, the day of wrath, will turn the universe to ashes, as David foretells (and the Sibyl too).
Dies irae, 1. Attr. Printed in Missal, Mass for the Dead

6 *Tuba mirum sparget sonum*
Per sepulchra regionum,
Coget omnes ante thronum.

Mors stupebit et natura,
Cum resurget creatura
Iudicanti responsura.

Liber scriptus proferetur,
In quo totum continetur
Unde mundus iudicetur.
The trumpet will fling out a wonderful sound through the tombs of all regions, it will drive everyone before the throne. Death will be aghast and so will nature, when creation rises again to make answer to the judge. The written book will be brought forth, in which everything is included whereby the world

will be judged.
7

7 *Rex tremendae maiestatis,*
Qui salvandos salvas gratis,
Salva me, fons pietatis!
O King of tremendous majesty, who freely saves those who should be saved, save me, O source of pity!
22

8 *Inter oves locum praesta*
Et ab haedis me sequestra
Statuens in parte dextra.
Among the sheep set me a place and separate me from the goats, standing me on the right-hand side.
43

MRS. CENTLIVRE 1667?–1723

9 The real Simon Pure.
A Bold Stroke for a Wife, V.i

10 And lash the vice and follies of the age.
The Man's Bewitched, prologue. See 159:20

11 He is as melancholy as an unbrac'd drum.
Wonder, II.i

MIGUEL DE CERVANTES 1547–1616

12 *El Caballero de la Triste Figura.*
The Knight of the Doleful Countenance.
Don Quixote, pt.i, ch.19

13 *La mejor salsa del mundo es el hambre.*
Hunger is the best sauce in the world.
pt.ii, ch.5

14 *El pan comido y la compañía deshecha.*
With the bread eaten up, up breaks the company.
ch.7

15 [Sancho asks whether, to get to heaven, we ought not all to become monks.]
No todos podemos ser frailes y muchos son los caminos por donde lleva Dios a los suyos al cielo. Religión es la caballeria.
We cannot all be friars, and many are the ways by which God leads his own to eternal life. Religion *is* knight-errantry.
ch.8

16 *Es un entreverado loco, lleno de lúcidos intervalos.*
He's a muddle-headed fool, with frequent lucid intervals.
(Sancho Panza, of Don Quixote.) ch.18

17 *Dos linages sólos hay en el mundo, como decía una abuela mía, que son el tenir y el no tenir.*
There are only two families in the world, as a grandmother of mine used to say: the haves and the have-nots.
ch.20

18 *Digo, paciencia y barajar.*
What I say is, patience, and shuffle the cards.
ch.23

19 *La diligencia es madre de la buena ventura y la pereza, su contrario, jamás llegó al término que pide un buen deseo.*
Diligence is the mother of good fortune, and idleness, its opposite, never led to good intention's goal.

20 *Bien haya el que inventó el sueño, capa que cubre todos los humanos pensamientos, manjar que quita la*

*hambre, agua que ahuyenta la sed, fuego que calienta
el frío, frío que templa el ardor, y, finalmente, moneda
general con que todas las cosas se compran, balanza y
peso que iguala al pastor con el rey y al simple con el
discreto.*

Blessings on him who invented sleep, the mantle that
covers all human thoughts, the food that satisfies
hunger, the drink that slakes thirst, the fire that warms
cold, the cold that moderates heat, and, lastly, the
common currency that buys all things, the balance and
weight that equalises the shepherd and the king, the
simpleton and the sage.
ch.68

1 *Los buenos pintores imitan la naturaleza, pero los
malos la vomitan.*
Good painters imitate nature, bad ones spew it up.
El Licenciado Vidriera

2 *Puesto ya el pie en el estribo.*
With one foot already in the stirrup.
Preface to **Persiles y Sigismunda** (four days before his death)

PATRICK REGINALD CHALMERS 1872–1942

3 What's lost upon the roundabouts we pulls up on the
   swings!
Green Days and Blue Days: Roundabouts and Swings

JOSEPH CHAMBERLAIN 1836–1914

4 Provided that the City of London remains as it is at
   present, the clearing-house of the world.
   Guildhall, London, 19 Jan. 1904

5 Learn to think Imperially.

6 The day of small nations has long passed away. The
   day of Empires has come.
   Birmingham, 12 May 1904

7 We are not downhearted. The only trouble is, we
   cannot understand what is happening to our
   neighbours.
   Smethwick, 18 Jan. 1906

NEVILLE CHAMBERLAIN 1869–1940

8 In war, whichever side may call itself the victor, there
   are no winners, but all are losers.
   Kettering, 3 July 1938

9 How horrible, fantastic, incredible, it is that we should
   be digging trenches and trying on gas-masks here
   because of a quarrel in a far-away country between
   people of whom we know nothing.
   (Of Germany's annexation of the Sudetenland.) Radio broadcast,
   27 Sept. 1938. K.Feiling, *Life of Neville Chamberlain*, bk.iv,
   ch.28

10 I believe it is peace for our time…peace with honour.
    After Munich Agreement. 30 Sept. 1938. See 185:15

11 Hitler has missed the bus.
    Central Hall, Westminster, 4 April 1940

HADDON CHAMBERS 1860–1921

12 The long arm of coincidence.
    Captain Swift (1888), Act II

NICOLAS-SÉBASTIEN CHAMFORT 1741–1794

13 *Vivre est une maladie dont le sommeil nous soulage*

*toutes les 16 heures. C'est un palliatif. La mort est le
remède.*
Living is an illness to which sleep provides relief every
sixteen hours. It's a palliative. The remedy is death.
Maximes et Pensées (1796), ch.2

14 *Des qualités trop supérieures rendent souvent un
homme moins propre à la société. On ne va pas au
marché avec des lingots; on y va avec de l'argent ou
de la petite monnaie.*
Qualities too elevated often unfit a man for society.
We don't take ingots with us to market; we take silver
or small change.
ch.3

15 *L'amour, tel qu'il existe dans la société, n'est que
l'échange de deux fantaisies et le contact de deux
épidermes.*
Love, in the form in which it exists in society, is
nothing but the exchange of two fantasies and the
superficial contact of two bodies.
ch.6

16 *Je dirais volontiers des métaphysiciens ce que
Scalinger disait des Basques, on dit qu'ils
s'entendent, mais je n'en crois rien.*
I am tempted to say of metaphysicians what Scalinger
used to say of the Basques: they are said to understand
one another, but I don't believe a word of it.
ch.7

17 *Les pauvres sont les nègres de l'Europe.*
The poor are Europe's blacks.
ch.8

18 *Sois mon frère, ou je te tue.*
Be my brother, or I kill you.
Oeuvres, I, 'Notice sur la vie de Chamfort'. Interpretation of
'Fraternité ou la mort'. See 9:13

JOHN CHANDLER 1806–1876

19 Conquering kings their titles take
From the foes they captive make:
Jesu, by a nobler deed,
From the thousands He hath freed.
Hymns Ancient and Modern. (Tr. from Latin)

RAYMOND CHANDLER 1888–1959

20 It was about eleven o'clock in the morning,
mid-October, with the sun not shining and a look of
hard wet rain in the clearness of the foothills. I was
wearing my powder-blue suit, with dark blue shirt, tie
and display handkerchief, black brogues, black wool
socks with dark blue clocks on them. I was neat,
clean, shaved and sober, and I didn't care who knew
it.
The Big Sleep, ch.1

21 The demand was for constant action; if you stopped to
think you were lost. When in doubt have a man come
through a door with a gun in his hand. This could get
to be pretty silly but somehow it didn't seem to matter.
The Simple Art of Murder (1950), preface, referring to the policy
of light crime fiction magazines

22 Down these mean streets a man must go who is not
himself mean; who is neither tarnished nor afraid.
The Simple Art of Murder

CHARLES CHAPLIN 1889–1977

1 *Priest:* May the Lord have mercy on your soul.
Verdoux: Why not? After all, it belongs to Him.
Monsieur Verdoux (1947)

ARTHUR CHAPMAN 1873–1935

2 Out where the handclasp's a little stronger,
Out where the smile dwells a little longer,
That's where the West begins.
Out where the West Begins

GEORGE CHAPMAN 1559?–1634?

3   I know an Englishman,
Being flatter'd, is a lamb; threaten'd, a lion.
Alphonsus, Emperor of Germany, I.ii

4 Berenice's ever-burning hair.
Blind Beggar of Alexandria

5 Speed his plough.
Bussy D'Ambois, I.i

6 Who to himself is law, no law doth need,
Offends no law, and is a king indeed.
II.i

7 Terror of darkness! O, thou king of flames!
V.i

8 There is no danger to a man, that knows
What life and death is; there's not any law,
Exceeds his knowledge; neither is it lawful
That he should stoop to any other law.
He goes before them, and commands them all,
That to himself is a law rational.
Byron's Conspiracy, III.i

9 O incredulity! the wit of fools,
That slovenly will spit on all things fair,
The coward's castle, and the sluggard's cradle.
De Guiana, l.82

10 We have watered our horses in Helicon.
May-Day, III.iii

11 For one heat, all know, doth drive out another,
One passion doth expel another still.
Monsieur D'Olive, V.i

12 I am ashamed the law is such an ass.
Revenge for Honour, III.ii

13 They're only truly great who are truly good.
V.ii

14 A poem, whose subject is not truth, but things like
truth.
Revenge of Bussy D'Ambois, dedication

15 Danger, the spur of all great minds.
V.i

16 And let a scholar all Earth's volumes carry,
He will be but a walking dictionary.
Tears of Peace, l.266

KING CHARLES I 1600–1649

17 Never make a defence or apology before you be
accused.
Letter to Lord Wentworth, 3 Sept. 1636

18 I see all the birds are flown.
Said in the House of Commons, 4 Jan. 1642, after attempting to
arrest the Five Members. *Parliamentary History,* vol.II (1807),
col.1010

19 As to the King, the Laws of the Land will clearly
instruct you for that…For the People; and truly I desire
their Liberty and Freedom, as much as any Body: but
I must tell you, that their Liberty and Freedom consists
in having the Government of those Laws, by which
their Life and their Goods may be most their own; 'tis
not for having share in Government [Sirs] that is
nothing pertaining to 'em. A Subject and a Sovereign
are clean different things…If I would have given way
to an arbitrary way, for to have all Laws chang'd
according to the Power of the Sword, I needed not to
have come here; and therefore I tell you (and I pray
God it be not laid to your Charge) that I am the Martyr
of the People.
Speech on the scaffold, 30 Jan. 1649. Rushworth, *Historical
Collections* (1703-8), vol.vi

20 I die a Christian, according to the Profession of the
Church of England, as I found it left me by my Father.

KING CHARLES II 1630–1685

21 It is upon the navy under the Providence of God that
the safety, honour, and welfare of this realm do chiefly
attend.
Articles of War (1652), Preamble

22 Better than a play.
(On the Debates in the House of Lords on Lord Ross's Divorce
Bill, 1670.) A. Bryant, *King Charles II*

23 This is very true: for my words are my own, and my
actions are my ministers'.
Reply to Lord Rochester's Epitaph on him. See 406:18

24 He [Charles II] said once to myself, he was no atheist,
but he could not think God would make a man
miserable only for taking a little pleasure out of the
way.
Burnet, *History of My Own Time,* vol.I, bk.ii, ch.1

25 He [Lauderdale] told me, the king spoke to him to let
that [Presbytery] go, for it was not a religion for
gentlemen.
ch.2

26 His nonsense suits their nonsense.
ch.11. Of Woolly, afterward Bishop of Clonfert, ('a very honest
man, but a very great blockhead') who had gone from house to
house trying to persuade Nonconformists to go to church.

27 King Charles gave him [Godolphin] a short character
when he was page, which he maintained to his life's
end, of being never *in* the way, nor *out* of the way.
vol.II, bk.iii, ch.11, n. (The Earl of Dartmouth)

28 Let not poor Nelly starve.
ch.17

29 I am sure no man in England will take away my life to
make you King. [To his brother James.]
W. King, *Political & Lit. Anecdotes*

30 He had been, he said, an unconscionable time dying;
but he hoped that they would excuse it.
Macaulay, *Hist. England,* 1849, vol.i, ch.4, p.437

EMPEROR CHARLES V 1500–1558

31 *Je parle espagnol à Dieu, italien aux femmes, français
aux hommes et allemand à mon cheval.*
To God I speak Spanish, to women Italian, to men
French, and to my horse—German.
Attr.

PIERRE CHARRON 1541–1603

1 *La vraye science et le vray étude de l'homme, c'est l'homme.*
The true science and study of man is man.
De la Sagesse (1601), bk.I, ch.i

SALMON PORTLAND CHASE 1808–1873

2 No more slave States: no slave Territories.
Platform of the Free Soil National Convention, 1848

3 The Constitution, in all its provisions, looks to an indestructible Union composed of indestructible States.
Decision in Texas v. White, 7 Wallace, 725

4 The way to resumption is to resume.
Letter to Horace Greeley, 17 May 1866

EARL OF CHATHAM
see WILLIAM PITT

FRANÇOIS-RENÉ DE CHATEAUBRIAND 1768–1848

5 *L'écrivain original n'est pas celui qui n'imite personne, mais celui que personne ne peut imiter.*
The original writer is not he who refrains from imitating others, but he who can be imitated by none.
Génie du Christianisme

GEOFFREY CHAUCER 1340?–1400
All line references are to the various fragments as collected in *The Works of Geoffrey Chaucer*, ed. F.N. Robinson, 2nd edition (1957)

6 Ful craftier to pley she was
Than Athalus, that made the game
First of the ches, so was his name.
The Book of the Duchess, l.662

7 Whan that Aprill with his shoures soote
The droghte of March hath perced to the roote.
The Canterbury Tales, General Prologue, l.1

8 And smale foweles maken melodye,
That slepen al the nyght with open ye
(So priketh hem nature in hir corages);
Thanne longen folk to goon on pilgrimages.
l.9

9　　　　He loved chivalrie,
Trouthe and honour, freedom and curteisie.
l.45

10 He was a verray, parfit gentil knyght.
l.72

11 He was as fressh as is the month of May.
l.92

12 He koude songes make and wel endite.
l.95

13 Curteis he was, lowely, and servysable,
And carf biforn his fader at the table.
l.99

14 Hire gretteste ooth was but by Seinte Loy.
l.120

15 Ful weel she soong the service dyvyne,
Entuned in hir nose ful semely,
And Frenssh she spak ful faire and fetisly,
After the scole of Stratford atte Bowe,

For Frenssh of Parys was to hire unknowe.
l.122

16 She wolde wepe, if that she saugh a mous
Kaught in a trappe, if it were deed or bledde.
Of smale houndes hadde she that she fedde
With rosted flessh, or milk and wastel-breed.
But soore wepte she if oon of hem were deed.
l.144

17 Of smal coral aboute hire arm she bar
A peire of bedes, gauded al with grene,
And theron heng a brooch of gold ful sheene,
On which ther was first write a crowned A,
And after *Amor vincit omnia.*
l.158

18 He yaf nat of that text a pulled hen,
That seith that hunters ben nat hooly men.
l.177

19 A Frere there was, a wantowne and a merye.
l.208

20 He knew the tavernes well in every toun.
l.240

21 He was the beste beggere in his hous.
l.252

22 Somwhat he lipsed, for his wantownesse,
To make his Englissh sweete upon his tonge.
l.264

23 A Clerk ther was of Oxenford also,
That unto logyk hadde longe ygo.
As leene was his hors as is a rake,
And he nas nat right fat, I undertake,
But looked holwe, and therto sobrely.
l.285

24 For hym was levere have at his beddes heed
Twenty bookes, clad in blak or reed
Of Aristotle and his philosophie,
Than robes riche, or fithele, or gay sautrie.
But al be that he was a philosophre,
Yet hadde he but litel gold in cofre.
l.293

25 And gladly wolde he lerne and gladly teche.
l.308

26 Nowher so bisy a man as he ther nas,
And yet he semed bisier than he was.
l.321

27 For he was Epicurus owene sone.
l.336

28 It snewed in his hous of mete and drynke.
l.345

29 A Shipman was ther, wonynge fer by weste;
For aught I woot, he was of Dertemouthe.
l.388

30 His studie was but litel on the Bible.
l.438

31 She was a worthy womman al hir lyve:
Housbondes at chirche dore she hadde fyve,
Withouten oother compaignye in youthe,—
But thereof nedeth nat to speke as nowthe.
And thries hadde she been at Jerusalem;
She hadde passed many a straunge strem;
At Rome she hadde been, and at Boloigne,
In Galice at Seint-Jame, and at Coloigne.
l.459

32 A good man was ther of religioun,

And was a povre Persoun of a Toun.
1.477

1 This noble ensample to his sheep he yaf,
That first he wroghte, and afterward he taughte.
1.496

2 If gold ruste, what shall iren do?
1.500

3 But Cristes loore and his apostles twelve
He taughte, but first he folwed it hymselve.
1.527

4 A Somonour was ther with us in that place,
That hadde a fyr-reed cherubynnes face,
For saucefleem he was, with eyen narwe.
As hoot he was and lecherous as a sparwe.
1.623

5 Wel loved he garleek, oynons, and eek lekes,
And for to drynken strong wyn, reed as blood.
1.634

6 His walet lay biforn hym in his lappe,
Bretful of pardoun, comen from Rome al hoot.
1.686

7 He hadde a croys of latoun ful of stones,
And in a glas he hadde pigges bones.
But with thise relikes, whan that he fond
A povre person dwellynge upon lond,
Upon a day he gat hym moore moneye
Than that the person gat in monthes tweye;
And thus, with feyned flaterye and japes,
He made the person and the peple his apes.
1.699

8 'O stormy peple! unsad and evere untrewe!'
The Clerk's Tale, 1.995

9 Grisilde is deed, and eek hire pacience,
And bothe atones buryed in Ytaille;
For which I crie in open audience,
No wedded man so hardy be t'assaille
His wyves pacience in trust to fynde
Grisildis, for in certein he shal faille.
The Clerk's Tale: Lenvoy de Chaucer, 1.1177

10 Ye archewyves, stondeth at defense,
Syn ye be strong as is a greet camaille;
Ne suffreth nat that men yow doon offense.
And sklendre wyves, fieble as in bataille,
Beth egre as a tygre yond in Ynde;
Ay clappeth as a mille, I yow consaille.
1.1195

11 Be ay of chiere as light as leef on lynde,
And lat hym care, and wepe, and wrynge, and waille!
1.1211

12 For o thyng, sires, saufly dar I seye,
That freendes everych oother moot obeye,
If they wol longe holden compaignye.
Love wol nat been constreyned by maistrye.
Whan maistrie comth, the God of Love anon
Beteth his wynges, and farewel, he is gon!
Love is a thyng as any spirit free.
Wommen, of kynde, desiren libertee,
And nat to been constreyned as a thral;
And so doon men, if I sooth seyen shal.
The Franklin's Tale, 1.761

13 Til that the brighte sonne loste his hewe;
For th'orisonte hath reft the sonne his lyght;

This is as muche to seye as it was nyght!
1.1016

14 Trouthe is the hyest thing that man may kepe.
1.1479

15 The carl spak oo thing, but he thoghte another.
The Friar's Tale, 1.1568

16 And therefore, at the kynges court, my brother,
Ech man for hymself, ther is noon oother.
The Knight's Tale, 1.1181

17 And whan a beest is deed he hath no peyne;
But man after his deeth moot wepe and pleyne.
1.1319

18 The bisy larke, messager of day.
1.1491

19 For pitee renneth soone in gentil herte.
1.1761

20 The smylere with the knyf under the cloke.
1.1999

21 Up roos the sonne, and up roos Emelye.
1.2273

22 What is this world? what asketh men to have?
Now with his love, now in his colde grave.
1.2777

23 She is mirour of alle curteisye.
The Man of Law's Tale, 1.166

24 Have ye nat seyn somtyme a pale face,
Among a prees, of hym that hath be lad
Toward his deeth, wher as hym gat no grace,
And swich a colour in his face hath had,
Men myghte knowe his face that was bistad,
Amonges alle the faces in that route?
1.645

25 Lat take a cat, and forstre hym wel with milk
And tendre flessh, and make his couche of silk,
And lay hym seen a mous go by the wal,
Anon he weyveth milk and flessh and al,
And every deyntee that is in that hous,
Swich appetit hath he to ete a mous.
The Manciple's Tale, 1.175

26 Kepe wel they tonge, and thenk upon the crowe.
1.362

27 And what is bettre than wisedoom? Womman. And
what is bettre than a good womman? Nothyng.
The Tale of Melibee, 1.1107

28 'Tehee!' quod she, and clapte the wyndow to.
The Miller's Tale, 1.3740

29 For certein, whan that Fortune list to flee,
Ther may no man the cours of hire withholde.
The Monk's Tale, 1.1995

30 Ful wys is he that kan hymselven knowe!
1.2139

31 Redeth the grete poete of Ytaille
That highte Dant, for he kan al devyse
Fro point to point, nat o word wol he faille.
1.2460

32 His coomb was redder than the fyn coral,
And batailled as it were a castle wal;
His byle was blak, and as the jeet it shoon;
Lyk asure were his legges and his toon;
His nayles whitter than the lylye flour,
And lyk the burned gold was his colour.
This gentil cok hadde in his governaunce

Sevene hennes for to doon al his plesaunce,
Whiche were his sustres and his paramours,
And wonder lyk to hym, as of colours;
Of whiche the faireste hewed on hir throte
Was cleped fair damoysele Pertelote.
The Nun's Priest's Tale, 1.2859

1 Whan that the month in which the world bigan,
That highte March, whan God first maked man.
1.3187

2 And daun Russell the fox stirte up atones.
1.3334

3 And on a Friday fil al this meschaunce.
1.3341

4 Mordre wol out, that se we day by day.
1.4241

5 Thanne peyne I me to strecche forth the nekke,
And est and west upon the peple I bekke.
The Pardoner's Prologue, 1.395

6 O wombe! O bely! O stynkyng cod
Fulfilled of dong and of corrupcioun!
The Pardoner's Tale, 1.534

7 'What, carl, with sory grace!'
1.717

8 And lightly as it comth, so wol we spende.
1.781

9 He kan nat stynte of syngyng by the weye.
The Prioress's Tale, 1.557

10 Yet in oure asshen olde is fyr yreke.
The Reeve's Prologue, 1.3882

11 'The gretteste clerkes been noght wisest men.'
The Reeve's Tale, 1.4054

12 So was hir joly whistle wel ywet.
1.4155

13 Thou lookest as thou woldest fynde an hare,
For evere upon the ground I se thee stare.
Prologue to Sir Thopas, 1.696

14 He hadde a semely nose.
Sir Thopas, 1.729

15 'By God,' quod he, 'for pleynly, at a word,
Thy drasty rymyng is nat worth a toord!'
1.929

16 Experience though noon auctoritee
Were in this world, is right ynogh for me
To speke of wo that is in mariage.
The Wife of Bath's Prologue, 1.1

17 Yblessed be god that I have wedded fyve!
Welcome the sixte, whan that evere he shal.
For sothe, I wol nat kepe me chaast in al.
Whan myn housbonde is fro the world ygon,
Som Cristen man shall wedde me anon.
1.44

18 The bacon was nat fet for hem, I trowe,
That som men han in Essex at Dunmowe.
1.217

19 But, Lord Crist! whan that it remembreth me
Upon my yowthe, and on my jolitee,
It tikleth me aboute myn herte roote.
Unto this day it dooth myn herte boote
That I have had my world as in my tyme.
1.469

20 And for to se, and eek for to be seye

Of lusty folk.
1.552

21 But yet I hadde alwey a coltes tooth.
Gat-tothed I was, and that bicam me weel.
1.602

22 This is a long preamble of a tale!
1.831

23 Of which mayde anon, maugree hir heed,
By verray force, he rafte hire maydenhed.
The Wife of Bath's Tale, 1.887

24 'My lige lady, generally,' quod he,
'Wommen desiren to have sovereynetee
As wel over hir housbond as hir love.'
1.1037

25 That he is gentil that dooth gentil dedis.
1.1170

26   Venus clerk, Ovide,
That hath ysowen wonder wide
The grete god of Loves name.
The House of Fame, 1.1487

27 And she was fayr as is the rose in May.
The Legend of Cleopatra, 1.613

28 A thousand tymes have I herd men telle
That ther ys joy in hevene and peyne in helle,
And I acorde wel that it ys so;
But, natheless, yet wot I wel also
That ther nis noon dwellyng in this contree,
That eyther hath in hevene or helle ybe,
Ne may of hit noon other weyes witen,
But as he hath herd seyd, or founde it writen;
For by assay ther may no man it preve.
But God forbede but men shulde leve
Wel more thing then men han seen with ye!
Men shal not wenen every thing a lye
But yf himself yt seeth, or elles dooth;
For, God wot, thing is never the lasse sooth,
Thogh every wight ne may it nat ysee.
Bernard the monk ne saugh nat all, pardee!
The Legend of Good Women, The Prologue, 1.1

29 And as for me, though that I konne but lyte,
On bokes for to rede I me delyte,
And to hem yive I feyth and ful credence,
And in myn herte have hem in reverence
So hertely, that ther is game noon
That fro by bokes maketh me to goon,
But yt be seldom on the holyday,
Save, certeynly, whan that the month of May
Is comen, and that I here the foules synge,
And that the floures gynnen for to sprynge,
Farewel my bok, and my devocioun!
1.29

30   Of al the floures in the mede,
Thanne love I most thise floures white and rede,
Swiche as men callen daysyes in our toun.
1.41

31 That wel by reson men it calle may
The 'dayesye,' or elles the 'ye of day,'
The emperice and flour of floures alle.
I pray to God that faire mote she falle,
And alle that lovel floures, for hire sake!
1.183

32 That lyf so short, the craft so long to lerne,

Th' assay so hard, so sharp the conquerynge.
The Parliament of Fowls, 1.1. See 251:8

1 Thou shalt make castels thanne in Spayne,
And dreme of joye, all but in vayne.
The Romaunt of the Rose, 1.2573

2 For it is seyd, 'man maketh ofte a yerde
With which the maker is hymself ybeten.'
Troilus and Criseyde, i, 1.740

3 But love a womman that she woot it nought,
And she wol quyte it that thow shalt nat fele;
Unknowe, unkist, and lost, that is unsought.
1.807

4 O wynd, o wynd, the weder gynneth clere.
ii, 1.2

5 So longe mote ye lyve, and alle proude,
Til crowes feet be growen under youre yë.
1.402

6 And we shall speek of the somwhat, I trow,
Whan thow art gon, to don thyn eris glow!
1.1021

7 It is nought good a slepyng hound to wake.
iii, 1.764

8 For I have seyn, of a ful misty morwe
Folowen ful ofte a myrie someris day.
1.1060

9 Right as an aspes leef she gan to quake.
1.1200

10 And as the newe abaysed nyghtyngale,
That stynteth first whan she bygynneth to synge.
1.1233

11 For of fortunes sharpe adversitee
The worst kynde of infortune is this,
A man to han ben in prosperitee,
And it remembren, whan it passed is.
1.1625. See 89:6, 171:8

12 Oon ere it herde, at tothir out it wente.
iv, 1.434

13 But manly sette the world on six and sevene;
And if thow deye a martyr, go to hevene!
1.622

14 For tyme ylost may nought recovered be.
1.1283

15 Ye, fare wel al the snow of ferne yere!
v, 1.1176

16 Ek gret effect men write in place lite;
Th' entente is al, and nat the letrres space.
1.1629

17 Go, litel bok, go, litel myn tragedye,
Ther God thi makere yet, er that he dye,
So sende myght to make in som comedye!
But litel bok, no makyng thow n'envie,
But subgit be to alle poesye;
And kis the steppes, where as thow seest pace
Virgile, Ovide, Omer, Lucan, and Stace.

And for ther is so gret diversite
In Englissh and in writyng of oure tonge,
So prey I God that non myswrite the,
Ne the mysmetre for defaute of tonge.
And red wherso thow be, or elles songe,
That thow be understonde, God I biseche!
1.1786

18 And whan that he was slayn in this manere,

His lighte goost ful blisfully is went
Up to the holughnesse of the eighthe spere,
In convers letyng everich element;
And ther he saugh, with ful avysement,
The erratik sterres, herkenyng armonye
With sownes ful of hevenyssh melodie.

And down from thennes faste he gan avyse
This litel spot of erthe, that with the se
Embraced is, and fully gan despise
This wrecched world, and held al vanite
To respect of the pleyn felicite
That is in hevene above.
1.1807

19 O yonge, fresshe folkes, he or she,
In which that love up groweth with youre age,
Repeyreth hom fro worldly vanyte,
And of youre herte up casteth the visage
To thilke God that after his ymage
Yow made, and thynketh al nys but a faire
This world, that passeth soone as floures faire.

And loveth hym, the which that right for love
Upon a crois, our soules for to beye,
First start, and roos, and sit in hevene above;
For he nyl falsen no wight, dar I seye,
That wol his herte al holly on hym leye.
And syn he best to love is, and most meke,
What nedeth feynede loves for to seke?

Lo here, of payens corsed olde rites,
Lo here, what alle hire goddes may availle;
Lo here, thise wrecched worldes appetites;
Lo here, the fyn and guerdoun for travaille
Of Jove, Appollo, of Mars, of swich rascaille!
1.1835

20 O moral Gower, this book I directe
To the.
1.1856

21 Flee fro the prees, and dwelle with sothfastnesse.
Truth: Balade de Bon Conseyle, 1.1

22 Forth, pilgrim, forth! Forth, beste, out of they stal!
Know thy contree, look up, thank God of al;
Hold the heye wey, and lat thy gost thee lede;
And trowth thee shal delivere, it is no drede.
1.18

ANTON CHEKHOV 1860–1904

23 When a lot of remedies are suggested for a disease,
that means it can't be cured.
The Cherry Orchard (1903-4), II.i

24 Great God in Heaven, the Cherry Orchard is now
mine...I've bought the estate where my father and
grandfather were slaves, where they weren't even
allowed inside the kitchen. I must be dreaming, I must
be imagining it all.
III

25 *Medvedenko:* Why do you wear black all the time?
Masha: I'm in mourning for my life, I'm unhappy.
The Seagull (1896), I

26 *Nina:* Your play's hard to act, there are no living
people in it.
Treplev: Living people! We should show life neither
as it is nor as it ought to be, but as we see it in our
dreams.

1 Women can't forgive failure.
II

2 *Nina:* I'm a seagull. No, that's wrong. Remember you
shot a seagull? A man happened to come along, saw it
and killed it, just to pass the time. A plot for a short
story.
IV

3 People don't notice whether it's winter or summer
when they're happy. If I lived in Moscow I don't think
I'd care what the weather was like.
Three Sisters (1900-1), II

4 Man has been endowed with reason, with the power to
create, so that he can add to what he's been given. But
up to now he hasn't been a creator, only a destroyer.
Forests keep disappearing, rivers dry up, wild life's
become extinct, the climate's ruined and the land
grows poorer and uglier every day.
Uncle Vanya, I

5 A woman can become a man's friend only in the
following stages—first an acquaintance, next a
mistress, and only then a friend.
II

6 *Sonya:* I'm not beautiful.
Helen: You have lovely hair.
Sonya: No, when a woman isn't beautiful, people
always say, 'You have lovely eyes, you have lovely
hair.'
III

EARL OF CHESTERFIELD 1694–1773

7 Unlike my subject will I frame my song,
It shall be witty and it sha'n't be long.
Epigram on 'Long' Sir Thomas Robinson. D.N.B.

8 The picture plac'd the busts between,
    Adds to the thought much strength;
Wisdom and Wit are little seen,
    But Folly's at full length.
**Wit and Wisdom of Lord Chesterfield. Epigrams. On the
Picture of Richard Nash...between the Busts of...Newton
and...Pope...at Bath.** (Attr. also to Mrs. Jane Brereton)

9 In scandal, as in robbery, the receiver is always
thought as bad as the thief.
Advice to his Son. Rules for Conversation, Scandal

10 In my mind, there is nothing so illiberal and so
ill-bred, as audible laughter.
Graces, Laughter. See 137:1, 159:22

11 In my opinion, parsons are very like other men, and
neither the better nor the worse for wearing a black
gown.
Letter to his son, 5 Apr. 1746

12 The knowledge of the world is only to be acquired in
the world, and not in a closet.
4 Oct. 1746

13 An injury is much sooner forgotten than an insult.
9 Oct. 1746

14 Courts and camps are the only places to learn the
world in.
2 Oct. 1747

15 There is a Spanish proverb, which says very justly,
Tell me whom you live with, and I will tell you who
you are.
9 Oct. 1747

16 Take the tone of the company that you are in.

17 Do as you would be done by is the surest method that
I know of pleasing.
16 Oct. 1747

18 I recommend you to take care of the minutes: for
hours will take care of themselves.
6 Nov. 1747

19 Advice is seldom welcome; and those who want it the
most always like it the least.
29 Jan. 1748

20 Speak of the moderns without contempt, and of the
ancients without idolatry.
22 Feb. 1748

21 Wear your learning, like your watch in a private
pocket: and do not merely pull it out and strike it;
merely to show that you have one.

22 If you happen to have an Elzevir classic in your
pocket, neither show it nor mention it.

23 I am neither of a melancholy nor a cynical disposition,
and am as willing and as apt to be pleased as anybody;
but I am sure that, since I have had the full use of my
reason, nobody has ever heard me laugh.
9 Mar. 1748

24 If Shakespeare's genius had been cultivated, those
beauties, which we so justly admire in him, would
have ben undisgraced by those extravagancies, and
that nonsense, with which they are so frequently
accompanied.
1 Apr. 1748

25 Women, then, are only children of a larger growth:
they have an entertaining tattle, and sometimes wit;
but for solid, reasoning good-sense, I never knew in
my life one that had it, or who reasoned or acted
consequentially for four and twenty hours together.
5 Sept. 1748. See 195:15

26 A man of sense only trifles with them [women], plays
with them, humours and flatters them, as he does with
a sprightly and forward child; but he neither consults
them about, nor trusts them with, serious matters.

27 It must be owned, that the Graces do not seem to be
natives of Great Britain; and I doubt, the best of us
here have more of rough than polished diamond.
18 Nov. 1748

28 Idleness is only the refuge of weak minds.
20 July 1749

29 Women are much more like each other than men: they
have, in truth, but two passions, vanity and love; these
are their universal characteristics.
19 Dec. 1749

30 Putting moral virtues at the highest, and religion at the
lowest, religion must still be allowed to be a collateral
security, at least, to virtue; and every prudent man
will sooner trust to two securities than to one.
8 Jan. 1750

31 Knowledge may give weight, but accomplishments
give lustre, and many more people see than weigh.
8 May 1750

32 Is it possible to love such a man? No. The utmost I
can do for him is to consider him as a respectable
Hottentot. [Lord Lyttelton.]
28 Feb. 1751

33 It is commonly said, and more particularly by Lord

Shaftesbury, that ridicule is the best test of truth.
6 Feb. 1752

1 Every woman is infallibly to be gained by every sort of flattery, and every man by one sort or other.
16 Mar. 1752

2 A chapter of accidents.
16 Feb. 1753

3 In matters of religion and matrimony I never give any advice; because I will not have anybody's torments in this world or the next laid to my charge.
Letter to A.C. Stanhope, 12 Oct. 1765

4 Religion is by no means a proper subject of conversation in a mixed company.
Undated Letter to his Godson, No.112

5 Cunning is the dark sanctuary of incapacity.
Letters from a Celebrated Nobleman to his Heir (1783), **Letter to his godson and heir, to be delivered after his own death**

6 I...could not help reflecting in my way upon the singular ill-luck of this my dear country, which, as long as ever I remember it, and as far back as I have read, has always been governed by the only two or three people, out of two or three millions, totally incapable of governing, and unfit to be trusted.
Works, ed. M. Maty (1777-9), vol.II. **Miscellaneous Pieces**, xlv. First published in *The World,* 7 Oct. 1756.

7 Tyrawley and I have been dead these two years; but we don't choose to have it known.
Boswell's *Johnson,* 3 Apr. 1773

8 He once exclaimed to Anstis, Garter King at Arms, 'You foolish man, you do not even know your own foolish business.'
Jesse, *Memoirs of the Court of England from 1688 to Geo. II,* vol.ii

9 Give Dayrolles a chair.
Last words. W.H. Craig, *Life of Chesterfield*

G.K. CHESTERTON 1874–1936

10 Are they clinging to their crosses,
              F.E. Smith?
Antichrist, or the Reunion of Christendom

11 Talk about the pews and steeples
        And the cash that goes therewith!
But the souls of Christian peoples...
              Chuck it, Smith!

12 They spoke of progress spiring round,
        Of Light and Mrs Humphry Ward—
It is not true to say I frowned,
        Or ran about the room and roared;
I might have simply sat and snored—
        I rose politely in the club
And said, 'I feel a little bored;
        Will some one take me to a pub?'
A Ballade of an Anti-Puritan

13 Prince, Prince-Elective on the modern plan,
        Fulfilling such a lot of people's Wills,
You take the Chiltern Hundreds while you can—
        A storm is coming on the Chiltern Hills.
A Ballade of the First Rain

14 The strangest whim has seized me...After all
I think I will not hang myself to-day.
A Ballade of Suicide

15 Before the gods that made the gods
        Had seen their sunrise pass,

The White Horse of the White Horse Vale
        Was cut out of the grass.
Ballad of the White Horse, bk.i

16 I tell you naught for your comfort,
        Yea, naught for your desire,
Save that the sky grows darker yet
        And the sea rises higher.

17 For the great Gaels of Ireland
        Are the men that God made mad,
For all their wars are merry,
        And all their songs are sad.
bk.ii

18 The thing on the blind side of the heart,
        On the wrong side of the door,
The green plant groweth, menacing
        Almighty lovers in the spring;
There is always a forgotten thing,
        And love is not secure.
bk.iii

19   Because it is only Christian men
Guard even heathen things.

20 'The high tide!' King Alfred cried.
        'The high tide and the turn!'
bk.vii

21 Nelson turned his blindest eye
        On Naples and on liberty.
Blessed are the Peacemakers

22 When fishes flew and forests walked
        And figs grew upon thorn,
Some moment when the moon was blood
        Then surely I was born.

With monstrous head and sickening cry
        And ears like errant wings,
The devil's walking parody
        On all four-footed things.
The Donkey

23 Fools! For I also had my hour;
        One far fierce hour and sweet:
There was a shout about my ears,
        And palms before my feet.

24 The men that worked for England
        They have their graves at home...
And they that rule in England,
        In stately conclave met,
Alas, alas for England
        They have no graves as yet.
Elegy in a Country Churchyard

25 They died to save their country and they only saved the world.
The English Graves

26 But since he stood for England
        And knew what England means,
Unless you give him bacon
        You must not give him beans.
The Englishman

27 When Man is the Turk, and the Atheist,
        Essene, Erastian Whig,
And the Thug and the Druse and the Catholic
        And the crew of the Captain's gig.
The Higher Unity. See 225:16

28 White founts falling in the courts of the sun,

And the Soldan of Byzantium is smiling as they run.
Lepanto

1 The cold queen of England is looking in the glass;
The shadow of the Valois is yawning at the Mass.

2 Strong gongs groaning as the guns boom far,
Don John of Austria is going to the war.

3 Then the tuckets, then the trumpets, then the cannon,
and he comes.
Don John laughing in the brave beard curled,
Spurning of his stirrups like the thrones of all the
world,
Holding his head up for a flag of all the free.
Love-light of Spain—hurrah!
Death-light of Africa!
Don John of Austria
Is riding to the sea.

4 It is he that saith not 'Kismet'; it is he that knows not
Fate;
It is Richard, it is Raymond, it is Godfrey in the gate!

5 The walls are hung with velvet that is black and soft as
sin,
And little dwarfs creep out of it and little dwarfs creep
in.

6 Cervantes on his galley sets the sword back in the
sheath
(*Don John of Austria rides homeward with a wreath.*)

7 And they think we're burning witches when we're only
burning weeds.
Me Heart

8 The legend of an epic hour
A child I dreamed, and dream it still,
Under the great grey water-tower
That strikes the stars on Campden Hill.
The Napoleon of Notting Hill, dedication

9 John Grubby, who was short and stout
And troubled with religious doubt,
Refused about the age of three
To sit upon the curate's knee.
The New Freethinker

10 Before the Roman came to Rye or out to Severn
strode,
The rolling English drunkard made the rolling English
road.
The Rolling English Road

11 The night we went to Birmingham by way of Beachy
Head.

12 My friends, we will not go again or ape an ancient
rage,
Or stretch the folly of our youth to be the shame of
age,
But walk with clearer eyes and ears this path that
wandereth,
And see undrugged in evening light the decent hall of
death;
For there is good news yet to hear and fine things to be
seen,
Before we go to Paradise by way of Kensal Green.

13 And a few men talked of freedom, while England
talked of ale.
The Secret People

14 We only know the last sad squires ride slowly towards
the sea,

And a new people takes the land: and still it is not we.

15 Smile at us, pay us, pass us; but do not quite forget.
For we are the people of England, that never have
spoken yet.

16 Lord Lilac thought it rather rotten
That Shakespeare should be quite forgotten,
And therefore got on a Committee
With several chaps out of the City.
The Shakespeare Memorial

17 The souls most fed with Shakespeare's flame
Still sat unconquered in a ring,
Remembering him like anything.

18 God made the wicked Grocer
For a mystery and a sign.
That men might shun the awful shops
And go to inns to dine.
Song Against Grocers

19 He keeps a lady in a cage
Most cruelly all day,
And makes her count and calls her 'Miss'
Until she fades away.

20 He crams with cans of poisoned meat
The subjects of the King
And when they die by thousands
Why, he laughs like anything.

21 The righteous minds of innkeepers
Induce them now and then
To crack a bottle with a friend
Or treat unmoneyed men.

22 And I dream of the days when work was scrappy,
And rare in our pockets the mark of the mint,
And we were angry and poor and happy,
And proud of seeing our names in print.
A Song of Defeat

23 They haven't got no noses,
The fallen sons of Eve.
The Song of Quoodle

24 And goodness only knowses
The Noselessness of Man.

25 But I, I cannot read it
(Although I run and run)
Of them that do not have the faith,
And will not have the fun.
The Song of the Strange Ascetic

26 Where his aunts, who are not married,
Demand to be divorced.

27 Tea, although an Oriental,
Is a gentleman at least;
Cocoa is a cad and coward,
Cocoa is a vulgar beast.
The Song of Right and Wrong

28 And Noah he often said to his wife when he sat down
to dine,
'I don't care where the water goes if it doesn't get into
the wine.'
Wine and Water

29 All slang is metaphor, and all metaphor is poetry.
The Defendant. A Defence of Slang

30 One sees great things from the valley; only small
things from the peak.
The Hammer of God

1 The artistic temperament is a disease that afflicts
amateurs.
Heretics (1905), ch.17

2 The human race, to which so many of my readers
belong.
The Napoleon of Notting Hill, ch.1

3 Mr Blatchford is not only an early Christian, he is the
only early Christian who ought really to have been
eaten by lions.
Orthodoxy (1909), 3. **Suicide of Thought**

4 Mr Shaw is (I suspect) the only man on earth who has
never written any poetry.

5 Tradition means giving votes to the most obscure of
all classes, our ancestors. It is the democracy of the
dead. Tradition refuses to submit to the small and
arrogant oligarchy of those who merely happen to be
walking about. All democrats object to men being
disqualified by the accident of birth; tradition objects
to their being disqualified by the accident of death.
4. **The Ethics of Elfland**

6 There is nothing the matter with Americans except
their ideals. The real American is all right; it is the
ideal American who is all wrong.
New York Times, 1 Feb. 1931. Reprinted in *Sidelights*

7 Hardy went down to botanize in the swamp, while
Meredith climbed towards the sun. Meredith became,
at his best, a sort of daintily dressed Walt Whitman:
Hardy became a sort of village atheist brooding and
blaspheming over the village idiot.
The Victorian Age in Literature, ch.2

8 He [Tennyson] could not think up to the height of his
own towering style.
ch.3

9 The Christian ideal has not been tried and found
wanting. It has been found difficult; and left untried.
What's Wrong with the World (1910), i.5. **The Unfinished
Temple**

10 If a thing is worth doing, it is worth doing badly.
iv.14. **Folly and Female Education**

11 Chesterton taught me this: the only way to be sure of
catching a train is to miss the one before it.
P. Daninos, *Vacances à tous prix* (1958), 'Le supplice de l'heure'

WILLIAM CHILLINGWORTH 1602–1644

12 The Bible and the Bible only is the religion of
Protestants.
The Religion of Protestants (1637)

13 I once knew a man out of courtesy help a lame dog
over a stile, and he for requital bit his fingers.

RUFUS CHOATE 1799–1859

14 Its constitution the glittering and sounding generalities
of natural right which make up the Declaration of
Independence.
Letter to the Maine Whig State Central Committee, 9 Aug. 1856.
See 208:14

PROFESSOR NOAM CHOMSKY 1928–

15 Colourless green ideas sleep furiously.
An example of a sentence which, though grammatically
acceptable, is without meaning. *Syntactic Structures* (1957), 2.3

16 As soon as questions of will or decision or reason or

choice of action arise, human science is at a loss.
Television interview, 30 Mar. 1978. See *The Listener,* 6 Apr.
1978

CHUANG TSE 4th–3rd cent. B.C.

17 I do not know whether I was then a man dreaming I
was a butterfly, or whether I am now a butterfly
dreaming I am a man.
H.A. Giles, *Chuang Tse,* ch.2

CHARLES CHURCHILL 1731–1764

18 Greatly his foes he dreads, but more his friends;
He hurts me most who lavishly commends.
The Apology, l.19

19 Though by whim, envy, or resentment led,
They damn those authors whom they never read.
The Candidate, l.57

20 The only difference, after all their rout,
Is, that the one is in, the other out.
The Conference, l.165

21 The danger chiefly lies in acting well;
No crime's so great as daring to excel.
An Epistle to William Hogarth, l.51

22 Candour, who, with the charity of Paul,
Still thinks the best, whene'er she thinks at all,
With the sweet milk of human kindness bless'd,
The furious ardour of my zeal repress'd.
l.55

23 By different methods different men excel;
But where is he who can do all things well?
l.573

24   Be England what she will,
With all her faults, she is my country still.
The Farewell, l.27. See 166:33

25 It can't be Nature, for it is not sense.
l.200

26 England—a happy land we know,
Where follies naturally grow.
The Ghost, bk.i, l.111

27 And adepts in the speaking trade
Keep a cough by them ready made.
bk.ii, l.545

28 Who wit with jealous eye surveys,
And sickens at another's praise.
l.663

29 Just to the windward of the law.
bk.iii, l.56

30 [Johnson:] He for subscribers baits his hook,
And takes your cash; but where's the book?
No matter where; wise fear, you know,
Forbids the robbing of a foe;
But what, to serve our private ends,
Forbids the cheating of our friends?
l.801

31 A joke's a very serious thing.
bk.iv, l.1386

32 Old-age, a second child, by Nature curs'd
With more and greater evils than the first,
Weak, sickly, full of pains; in ev'ry breath
Railing at life, and yet afraid of death.
Gotham, i, l.212

33 Keep up appearances; there lies the test;

The world will give thee credit for the rest.
Outward be fair, however foul within;
Sin if thou wilt, but then in secret sin.
Night, 1.311

1 As one with watching and with study faint,
   Reel in a drunkard, and reel out a saint.
   1.323

2 Who often, but without success, have pray'd
   For apt Alliteration's artful aid.
   The Prophecy of Famine, 1.85

3 And Nature gave thee, open to distress,
   A heart to pity, and a hand to bless.
   1.177

4 He sicken'd at all triumphs but his own.
   The Rosciad, 1.64

5 To mischief trained, e'en from his mother's womb,
   Grown old in fraud, tho' yet in manhood's bloom.
   Adopting arts, by which gay villains rise,
   And reach the heights, which honest men despise;
   Mute at the bar, and in the senate loud,
   Dull 'mongst the dullest, proudest of the proud;
   A pert, prim Prater of the *northern* race,
   Guilt in his heart, and famine in his face.
   1.69. [Alexander Wedderburn, later Lord Loughborough.]

6 Ne'er blush'd unless, in spreading Vice's snares,
   She blunder'd on some virtue unawares.
   1.137

7 Genius is of no country.
   1.207

8 He mouths a sentence, as curs mouth a bone.
   1.322

9 Fashion—a word which knaves and fools may use,
   Their knavery and folly to excuse.
   1.455

10 So much they talk'd, so very little said.
   1.550

11 Learn'd without sense, and venerably dull.
   1.592

12 Not without Art, but yet to Nature true,
   She charms the town with humour just, yet new.
   1.699

13 But, spite of all the criticizing elves,
   Those who would make us feel, must feel themselves.
   1.961

14 The two extremes appear like man and wife,
   Coupled together for the sake of strife.
   1.1005

15 Where he falls short, 'tis Nature's fault alone;
   Where he succeeds, the merit's all his own.
   1.1025

16 The best things carried to excess are wrong.
   1.1039

17 With the persuasive language of a tear.
   The Times, 1.308

LORD RANDOLPH CHURCHILL 1849–1894

18 Ulster will fight; Ulster will be right.
   Letter, 7 May 1886

19 The old gang. [Members of the Conservative
   Government.]
   House of Commons, 7 Mar. 1878

20 For the purposes of recreation he [Mr. Gladstone] has

selected the felling of trees, and we may usefully
remark that his amusements, like his politics, are
essentially destructive...The forest laments in order
that Mr Gladstone may perspire.
Speech on Financial Reform, Blackpool, 24 Jan. 1884.

21 He [Gladstone] told them that he would give them and
   all other subjects of the Queen much legislation, great
   prosperity, and universal peace, and he has given them
   nothing but chips. Chips to the faithful allies in
   Afghanistan, chips to the trusting native races of South
   Africa, chips to the Egyptian fellah, chips to the
   British farmer, chips to the manufacturer and the
   artisan, chips to the agricultural labourer, chips to the
   House of Commons itself.

22 An old man in a hurry. [Gladstone.]
   To the Electors of South Paddington, June 1886

23 All great men make mistakes. Napoleon forgot
   Blücher, I forgot Goschen.
   Leaves from the Notebooks of Lady Dorothy Nevill, p.21

24 I never could make out what those damned dots
   meant. (Decimal points.)
   W.S.Churchill, *Lord Randolph Churchill,* vol.ii, p.184

WINSTON CHURCHILL 1874–1965

25 A labour contract into which men enter voluntarily for
   a limited and for a brief period, under which they are
   paid wages which they consider adequate, under which
   they are not bought or sold and from which they can
   obtain relief...on payment of £17.10s., the cost of
   their passage, may not be a desirable contract, may
   not be a healthy or proper contract, but it cannot in the
   opinion of His Majesty's Government be classified as
   slavery in the extreme acceptance of the word without
   some risk of terminological inexactitude.
   House of Commons, 22 Feb. 1906. See R.S. Churchill, *Winston
   S. Churchill* (1967), II.167: 'This celebrated example of
   polysyllabic humour was always to be misunderstood and to be
   regarded as a nice substitute for "lie" which it plainly was not
   intended to be.'

26 The maxim of the British people is 'Business as
   usual'.
   Guildhall, 9 Nov. 1914

27 I remember, when I was a child, being taken to the
   celebrated Barnum's circus, which contained an
   exhibition of freaks and monstrosities, but the
   exhibit...which I most desired to see was the one
   described as 'The Boneless Wonder'. My parents
   judged that that spectacle would be too revolting and
   demoralising for my youthful eyes, and I have waited
   50 years to see the boneless wonder sitting on the
   Treasury Bench.
   House of Commons, 28 Jan. 1931

28 I cannot forecast to you the action of Russia. It is a
   riddle wrapped in a mystery inside an enigma.
   Broadcast talk, 1 Oct. 1939

29 I would say to the House, as I said to those who have
   joined this Government, 'I have nothing to offer but
   blood, toil, tears and sweat'.
   House of Commons, 13 May 1940

30 Victory at all costs, victory in spite of all terror,
   victory however long and hard the road may be; for
   without victory there is no survival.

31 We shall go on to the end, we shall fight in France, we
   shall fight on the seas and oceans, we shall fight with

growing confidence and growing strength in the air, we shall defend our island, whatever the cost may be, we shall fight on the beaches, we shall fight on the landing grounds, we shall fight in the fields and in the streets, we shall fight in the hills; we shall never surrender.
4 June 1940

1 Let us therefore brace ourselves to our duties and so bear ourselves that if the British Empire and its Commonwealth last for a thousand years men will still say, 'This was their finest hour'.
18 June 1940

2 Never in the field of human conflict was so much owed by so many to so few.
20 Aug. 1940

3 The British Empire and the United States will have to be somewhat mixed up together in some of their affairs for mutual and general advantage. For my own part, looking out for the future, I do not view the process with any misgivings. I could not stop it if I wished; no one can stop it. Like the Mississippi, it just keeps rolling along. Let it roll. Let it roll on full flood, inexorable, irresistible, benignant, to broader lands and better days.

4 We are waiting for the long-promised invasion. So are the fishes.
Radio Broadcast to the French people, 21 Oct. 1940

5 I do not resent criticism, even when, for the sake of emphasis, it parts for the time with reality.
House of Commons, 22 Jan. 1941

6 Give us the tools, and we will finish the job.
Radio Broadcast, 9 Feb. 1941. (Addressing President Roosevelt.)

7 This whipped jackal [Mussolini], who, to save his own skin, has made of Italy a vassal state of Hitler's Empire, is frisking up by the side of the German tiger with yelps not only of appetite—that could be understood—but even of triumph.
House of Commons, Apr. 1941

8 Do not let us speak of darker days; let us rather speak of sterner days. These are not dark days: these are great days—the greatest days our country has ever lived; and we must all thank God that we have been allowed, each of us according to our stations, to play a part in making these days memorable in the history of our race.
Harrow School, 29 Oct. 1941

9 What kind of people do they [the Japanese] think we are?
To U.S. Congress, 24 Dec. 1941

10 When I warned them [the French Government] that Britain would fight on alone whatever they did, their Generals told their Prime Minister and his divided Cabinet: 'In three weeks England will have her neck wrung like a chicken.'
Some chicken! Some neck!
To the Canadian Parliament, 30 Dec. 1941

11 This is not the end. It is not even the beginning of the end. But it is, perhaps, the end of the beginning.
Mansion House, 10 Nov. 1942. (Of the Battle of Egypt.)

12 I have not become the King's First Minister in order to preside over the liquidation of the British Empire.

13 The soft under-belly of the Axis.
Report on the War Situation, House of Commons, 11 Nov. 1942

14 Not a seat but a springboard. (North Africa.)
Radio Broadcast, 29 Nov. 1942

15 There is no finer investment for any community than putting milk into babies.
21 Mar. 1943

16 You may take the most gallant sailor, the most intrepid airman, or the most audacious soldier, put them at a table together—what do you get? *The sum of their fears.*
On the Chiefs of Staffs system, 16 Nov. 1943. H. Macmillan, *The Blast of War*, ch.16

17 There are few virtues that the Poles do not possess—and there are few mistakes they have ever avoided.
House of Commons, 16 Aug. 1945

18 An iron curtain has descended across the Continent.
Address at Westminster College, Fulton, U.S.A., 5 Mar. 1946. The expression 'iron curtain' had been previously applied by others to the Soviet Union or its sphere of influence, e.g., Ethel Snowden, *Through Bolshevik Russia* (1920); Dr. Goebbels, *Das Reich* (25 Feb. 1945); and by Churchill himself in a cable to President Truman (4 June 1945).

19 Many forms of government have been tried, and will be tried in this world of sin and woe. No one pretends that democracy is perfect or all-wise. Indeed, it has been said that democracy is the worst form of Government except all those other forms that have been tried from time to time.
House of Commons, 11 Nov. 1947

20 To jaw-jaw is better than to war-war.
Washington, 26 June 1954

21 It was the nation and the race dwelling all round the globe that had the lion's heart. I had the luck to be called upon to give the roar.
Speech at Palace of Westminster on his 80th birthday, 30 Nov. 1954

22 Headmasters have powers at their disposal with which Prime Ministers have never yet been invested.
My Early Life (1930), ch.2

23 By being so long in the lowest form [at Harrow] I gained an immense advantage over the cleverer boys...I got into my bones the essential structure of the normal British sentence—which is a noble thing. Naturally I am biased in favour of boys learning English; and then I would let the clever ones learn Latin as an honour, and Greek as a treat.

24 It is a good thing for an uneducated man to read books of quotations.
ch.9

25 In war, resolution; in defeat, defiance; in victory, magnanimity; in peace, goodwill.
Epigram after the Great War, 1914–18. Sir Edward Marsh, *A Number of People* (1939), p.152. Later used as the 'Moral of the Work' in each volume of *The Second World War.*

26 On the night of the tenth of May [1940], at the outset of this mighty battle, I acquired the chief power in the State, which henceforth I wielded in ever-growing measure for five years and three months of world war, at the end of which time, all our enemies having surrendered unconditionally or being about to do so, I was immediately dismissed by the British electorate from all further conduct of their affairs.
vol.i, *The Gathering Storm* (1948), p.526

27 The loyalties which centre upon number one are enormous. If he trips he must be sustained. If he

makes mistakes they must be covered. If he sleeps he must not be wantonly disturbed. If he is no good he must be pole-axed.
vol.ii, *Their Finest Hour* (1949), p.15

1 No one can guarantee success in war, but only deserve it.
p.484

2 When you have to kill a man it costs nothing to be polite.
(On the ceremonial form of the declaration of war against Japan, 8 Dec. 1941.) vol.iii, *The Grand Alliance* (1950), p.543

3 Dictators ride to and fro upon tigers which they dare not dismount. And the tigers are getting hungry.
While England Slept (1936)

4 I have watched this famous island descending incontinently, fecklessly, the stairway which leads to a dark gulf. It is a fine broad stairway at the beginning, but after a bit the carpet ends. A little farther on there are only flagstones, and a little farther on still these break beneath your feet.

5 In defeat, unbeatable; in victory, unbearable.
(Of Viscount Montgomery.) Edward Marsh, *Ambrosia and Small Beer*, ch.5

6 This is the sort of English up with which I will not put.
Attr. comment against clumsy avoidance of a preposition at the end of a sentence. E. Gowers, *Plain Words*, ch.9, 'Troubles with Prepositions', i

7 Don't talk to me about naval tradition. It's nothing but rum, sodomy and the lash.
Sir Peter Gretton, *Former Naval Person*, ch.1. Sometimes quoted as 'Rum, buggery and the lash'; compare 'Rum, bum, and bacca' and 'Ashore it's wine women and song, aboard it's rum, bum and concertina', naval catch-phrases dating from the nineteenth century.

COLLEY CIBBER 1671–1757

8 Whilst thus I sing, I am a King,
   Altho' a poor blind boy.
The Blind Boy

9 Oh! how many torments lie in the small circle of a wedding-ring!
The Double Gallant, I.ii

10 One had as good be out of the world, as out of the fashion.
Love's Last Shift, Act II

11 What! now your fire's gone, you would knock me down with the butt-end, would you?
The Refusal, Act I

12 Off with his head—so much for Buckingham.
Richard III, (adapted from Shakespeare) IV.iii

13 Conscience avaunt, *Richard's* himself again:
Hark! the shrill trumpet sounds, to horse, away,
My soul's in arms, and eager for the fray.
V.iii

14 Perish the thought!
v

15 Stolen sweets are best.
The Rival Fools, Act I

CICERO 106–43 B.C.

16 *Dicit enim tamquam in Platonis* πολιτείᾳ, *non tamquam in Romuli faece sententiam.*

For he delivers his opinions as though he were living in Plato's Republic rather than among the dregs of Romulus. (Of M. Porcius Cato, the Younger.)
Ad Atticum, II.i.8

17 There is nothing so absurd but some philosopher has said it.
De Divinatione, ii.58

18 *Vulgo enim dicitur: Iucundi acti labores.*
For it is commonly said: completed labours are pleasant.
De Finibus, ii.105

19 *Salus populi suprema est lex.*
The good of the people is the chief law.
De Legibus, III.iii.8

20 *'Ipse dixit.' 'Ipse' autem erat Pythagoras.*
'He himself said it', and this 'himself' was Pythagoras.
De Natura Deorum, I.v.10

21 *Summum bonum.*
The highest good.
De Officiis, I.ii.5

22 *Cedant arma togae, concedant laurea laudi.*
Let war yield to peace, laurels to paeans.
xxii.82

23 *Numquam se minus otiosum esse quam cum otiosus, nec minus solum quam cum solus esset.*
Never less idle than when wholly idle, nor less alone than when wholly alone.
III.i.1

24 *Mens cuiusque is est quisque.*
The spirit is the true self.
De Republica, vi.26

25 *Quousque tandem abutere, Catilina, patientia nostra?*
How long will you abuse our patience, Catiline?
In Catilinam, I.i.1

26 *O tempora, O mores!*
Oh, the times! Oh, the manners!

27 *Abiit, excessit, evasit, erupit.*
He departed, he withdrew, he strode off, he broke forth.
II.i.1

28 *Civis Romanus sum.*
I am a Roman citizen.
In Verrem, V.lvii.147

29 *Quod di omen avertant.*
May the gods avert this omen.
Philippic, III.xiv.35

30 *Nervos belli, pecuniam infinitam.*
The sinews of war, unlimited money.
V.ii.5

31 *Silent enim leges inter arma.*
Laws are inoperative in war.
Pro Milone, IV.xi

32 *Cui bono?*
To whose profit?
XII.xxxii (Quoting L. Cassius Longinus)

33 *Id quod est praestantissimum maximeque optabile omnibus sanis et bonis et beatis, cum dignitate otium.*
The thing which is the most outstanding and chiefly to be desired by all healthy and good and well-off persons, is leisure with honour.
Pro Sestio, xlv.98

1 I would rather be wrong, by God, with Plato than be correct with those men. (The Pythagoreans.)
Tusculanae disputationes, I.xvii.39

2 *O fortunatam natam me consule Romam!*
O happy Rome, born when I was consul!
Juvenal, x.122

JOHN CLARE 1793–1864

3 When badgers fight then everyone's a foe.
Badger

4 He could not die when the trees were green,
    For he loved the time too well.
The Dying Child

5   My life hath been one chain of contradictions,
Madhouses, prisons, whore-shops.
The Exile

6 They took me from my wife, and to save trouble
I wed again, and made the error double.

7   Here let the Muse oblivion's curtain draw,
    And let man think—for God hath often saw
Things here too dirty for the light of day;
    For in a madhouse there exists no law.
Now stagnant grows my too refinèd clay;
I envy birds their wings to fly away.

8 Pale death, the grand physician, cures all pain;
The dead rest well who lived for joys in vain.

9   Hopeless hope hopes on and meets no end,
Wastes without springs and homes without a friend.

10 When words refuse before the crowd
    My Mary's name to give,
The muse in silence sings aloud:
    And there my love will live.
First Love

11 A quiet, pilfering, unprotected race.
Gypsies

12 I am—yet what I am, none cares or knows;
    My friends forsake me like a memory lost:
I am the self-consumer of my woes.
I Am

13 Untroubling and untroubled where I lie
The grass below, above, the vaulted sky.

14 When fishes leap in silver stream…
And forest bees are humming near,
And cowslips in boys' hats appear…
We then may say that May is come.
May. See N. Ault, *A Treasury of Unfamiliar Lyrics* (1938),
p.473

15 The present is the funeral of the past,
And man the living sepulchre of life.
The Past

16 Summers pleasures they are gone like to visions every
    one
And the cloudy days of autumn and of winter cometh
    on
I tried to call them back but unbidden they are gone
Far away from heart and eye and for ever far away.
Remembrances

17 Dear Sir,—I am in a Madhouse and quite forget your
name or who you are.
Letter, 1860

EARL OF CLARENDON 1609–1674

18 Without question, when he [Hampden] first drew the
sword, he threw away the scabbard.
History of the Rebellion, ed. Macray (1888), III.vii.84

19 He [Hampden] had a head to contrive, a tongue to
persuade, and a hand to execute any mischief.

20 He [Falkland]…would, with a shrill and sad accent,
ingeminate the word *Peace, Peace.*
233

21 So enamoured on peace that he would have been glad
the King should have bought it at any price.

22 He [Cromwell] will be looked upon by posterity as a
brave bad man.
xv, last line

CLARIBEL (MRS. C.A. BARNARD) 1840–1869

23 I cannot sing the old songs
I sang long years ago,
For heart and voice would fail me,
And foolish tears would flow.
Fireside Thoughts

JOHN CLARKE fl. 1639

24 He that would thrive
Must rise at five;
He that hath thriven
May lie till seven.
Paraemiologia Anglo-Latina (1639)

25 Home is home, though it be never so homely.

APPIUS CLAUDIUS CAECUS fl. 312–279 B.C.

26 *Faber est suae quisque fortunae.*
Each man is the smith of his own fortune.
'Sallust', *Epistulae ad Caesarem senem*, I.i.2

KARL VON CLAUSEWITZ 1780–1831

27 *Der Krieg ist nichts als eine Fortsetzung der
politschen Verkehrs mit Einmischung anderer Mittel.*
War is nothing but the continuation of politics with the
admixture of other means.
Vom Kriege, (memorial ed. 1952) p.888, commonly rendered in
the form 'War is the continuation of politics by other means'.

HENRY CLAY 1777–1852

28 I had rather be right than be President.
To Senator Preston of South Carolina, 1839

29 The gentleman [Josiah Quincy] can not have forgotten
his own sentiments, uttered even on the floor of this
House, 'peaceably if we can, forcibly if we must'.
Speech, 8 Jan. 1813. See 403:24

GEORGES CLEMENCEAU 1841–1929

30 *Quatorze? Le bon Dieu n'a que dix.*
Fourteen? The good Lord has only ten.
Attr. comment on hearing of Woodrow Wilson's Fourteen Points
(1918)

31 War is much too serious a thing to be left to the
military.
Attr. Also attr. Talleyrand and Briand. See, e.g., John Bailey,
Letters and Diaries (1935), p.176

POPE CLEMENT XIII 1693–1769

1 *Sint ut sunt aut non sint.*
Let them be as they are or not be at all.
Reply to request for changes in the constitutions of the Society of
Jesus, 27 Jan. 1762. See J.A.M. Crétineau-Joly, *Clément XIV et
les Jésuites* (1847), p.370n.

GROVER CLEVELAND 1837–1908

2 I have considered the pension list of the republic a roll
of honour.
Veto of Dependent Pension Bill, 5 July 1888

JOHN CLEVELAND 1613–1658

3 Here lies wise and valiant dust,
Huddled up, 'twixt fit and just:
Strafford, who was hurried hence
'Twixt treason and convenience.
He spent his time here in a mist,
A *Papist*, yet a *Calvinist*.
His Prince's nearest joy and grief;
He had, yet wanted, all relief:
The Prop and Ruin of the State,
The people's violent love and hate:
One in extremes lov'd and abhor'd.
Riddles lie here, or in a word,
Here lies blood; and let it lie
Speechless still, and never cry.
Epitaph on the Earl of Strafford

4 Had Cain been Scot, God would have changed his
doom,
Nor forced him wander, but confined him home.
The Rebel Scot

LORD CLIVE 1725–1774

5 By God, Mr Chairman, at this moment I stand
astonished at my own moderation!
Reply during Parliamentary cross-examination, 1773

6 I feel that I am reserved for some end or other.
Words when his pistol failed to go off twice, in his attempt to
commit suicide. G.R. Gleig, *Life*, ch.1

ARTHUR HUGH CLOUGH 1819–1861

7 Rome, believe me, my friend, is like its own Monte
Testaceo,
Merely a marvellous mass of broken and castaway
wine-pots.
Amours de Voyage, c.I.ii

8 The horrible pleasure of pleasing inferior people.
xi

9 Am I prepared to lay down my life for the British
female?
Really, who knows?...
Ah, for a child in the street I could strike; for the
full-blown lady—
Somehow, Eustace, alas! I have not felt the vocation.
c.II.iv

10 But for his funeral train which the bridegroom sees in
the distance,
Would he so joyfully, think you, fall in with the
marriage-procession?
c.III.vi

11 Allah is great, no doubt, and Juxtaposition his

prophet.

12 Mild monastic faces in quiet collegiate cloisters.
ix

13 Whither depart the souls of the brave that die in the
battle,
Die in the lost, lost fight, for the cause that perishes
with them?
c.V.vi

14 The grave man, nicknamed Adam.
The Bothie of Tober-na-Vuolich, i

15 Petticoats up to the knees, or even, it might be, above
them,
Matching their lily-white legs with the clothes that they
trod in the wash-tub!
ii

16 Good, too, Logic, of course; in itself, but not in fine
weather.

17 Sesquipedalian blackguard.

18 Grace is given of God, but knowledge is bought in the
market.
iv

19 They are married, and gone to New Zealand.
ix

20   Delicious. Ah!
What else is like the gondola?
Dipsychus, sc.v

21 They may talk as they please about what they call
pelf,
And how one ought never to think of one's self,
And how pleasures of thought surpass eating and
drinking—
My pleasure of thought is the pleasure of thinking
How pleasant it is to have money, heigh ho!
How pleasant it is to have money.

22 'There is no God,' the wicked saith,
'And truly it's a blessing,
For what he might have done with us
It's better only guessing.'
vi

23 But country folks who live beneath
The shadow of the steeple;
The parson and the parson's wife,
And mostly married people;

Youths green and happy in first love,
So thankful for illusion;
And men caught out in what the world
Calls guilt, in first confusion;

And almost every one when age,
Disease, or sorrows strike him,
Inclines to think there is a God,
Or something very like Him.

24 Home, Rose, and home, Provence and La Palie.
Les Vaches

25 Thou shalt have one God only; who
Would be at the expense of two?
The Latest Decalogue

26 Thou shalt not kill; but need'st not strive
Officiously to keep alive.

27 Do not adultery commit;
Advantage rarely comes of it.

28 Thou shalt not steal; an empty feat,

When it's so lucrative to cheat.

1 Thou shalt not covet; but tradition
Approves all forms of competition.

2 What voice did on my spirit fall,
Peschiera, when thy bridge I crost?
''Tis better to have fought and lost,
Than never to have fought at all.'
Peschiera. See 536:16

3 As ships, becalmed at eve, that lay
    With canvas drooping, side by side,
Two towers of sail at dawn of day
    Are scarce long leagues apart descried.
Qua Cursum Ventus

4 Say not the struggle naught availeth,
    The labour and the wounds are vain,
The enemy faints not, nor faileth,
    And as things have been, things remain.

If hopes were dupes, fears may be liars;
    It may be, in yon smoke concealed,
Your comrades chase e'en now the fliers,
    And, but for you, possess the field.

For while the tired waves, vainly breaking,
    Seem here no painful inch to gain,
Far back through creeks and inlets making
    Comes silent, flooding in, the main.

And not by eastern windows only,
    When daylight comes, comes in the light,
In front the sun climbs slow, how slowly,
    But westward, look, the land is bright.
Say Not the Struggle Naught Availeth

5 That out of sight is out of mind
Is true of most we leave behind.
Songs in Absence, That Out of Sight

6 What shall we do without you? Think where we are.
Carlyle has led us all out into the desert, and he has
left us there.
Parting words to Emerson, 15 July 1848. See E.E. Hale, *James
Russell Lowell and his Friends* (1889), ch.19

WILLIAM COBBETT 1762–1835

7 The slavery of the tea and coffee and other slop-kettle.
Advice to Young Men, letter i, 31

8 Nouns of number, or multitude, such as *Mob*,
Parliament, Rabble, House of Commons, Regiment,
Court of King's Bench, Den of Thieves, and the like.
English Grammar, letter xvii, **Syntax as Relating to Pronouns**

9 From a very early age, I had imbibed the opinion, that
it was every man's duty to do all that lay in his power
to leave his country as good as he had found it.
Political Register, 22 Dec. 1832

10 But what is to be the fate of the great wen [London] of
all? The monster, called…'the metropolis of the
empire'?
Rural Rides

RICHARD COBDEN 1804–1865

11 I believe it has been said that one copy of *The Times*
contains more useful information than the whole of the
historical works of Thucydides.
Speech, Manchester, 27 Dec. 1850

JEAN COCTEAU 1889–1963

12 *Vivre est une chute horizontale.*
Life is falling sideways.
Opium, 1930 ed., p.37

13 *Victor Hugo…un fou qui se croyait Victor Hugo.*
Victor Hugo…A madman who thought he was Victor
Hugo.
See **Opium,** 1930 ed., p.77

SIR ASTON COKAYNE 1608–1684

14 Sydney, whom we yet admire
Lighting our little torches at his fire.
Funeral Elegy on Mr. Michael Drayton

DESMOND COKE 1879–1931

15 His blade struck the water a full second before any
other…until…as the boats began to near the
winning-post, his own was dipping into the water *twice*
as fast as any other.
Sandford of Merton (1903), ch.xii. Often quoted as 'All rowed
fast but none so fast as stroke', and attr. to Ouida.

SIR EDWARD COKE 1552–1634

16 Magna Charta is such a fellow, that he will have no
sovereign.
On the Lords' Amendment to the Petition of Right, 17 May 1628.
Rushworth, *Hist. Coll.*, 1659, i

17 How long soever it hath continued, if it be against
reason, it is of no force in law.
Institutes: Commentary upon Littleton. First Institute, 62a

18 Reason is the life of the law, nay the common law
itself is nothing else but reason…The law, which is the
perfection of reason.
97b

19 The gladsome light of Jurisprudence.
epilogus

20 Syllables govern the world.

21 For a man's house is his castle, *et domus sua cuique
est tutissimum refugium.*
Third Institute, cap.73

22 Six hours in sleep, in law's grave study six,
Four spend in prayer, the rest on Nature fix.
Pandects, lib.II, tit.iv, **De in Jus vocando.** See 283:13

23 The house of every one is to him as his castle and
fortress.
Semayne's Case, 5 Rep.91b

24 They [corporations] cannot commit treason, nor be
outlawed, nor excommunicate, for they have no souls.
Sutton's Hospital Case, 10 Rep.32b

HARTLEY COLERIDGE 1796–1849

25 But what is Freedom? Rightly understood,
A universal licence to be good.
Liberty

26 She is not fair to outward view
    As many maidens be;
Her loveliness I never knew
    Until she smiled on me;
Oh! then I saw her eye was bright,
A well of love, a spring of light.
Song. She is not Fair

1 Her very frowns are fairer far,
Than smiles of other maidens are.

LORD COLERIDGE 1820–1894

2 I speak not of this college or of that, but of the
University as a whole; and, gentlemen, what a *whole*
Oxford is!
G.W.E. Russell, *Collections and Recollections*, ch.29

MARY COLERIDGE 1861–1907

3 Egypt's might is tumbled down
   Down a-down the deeps of thought;
Greece is fallen and Troy town,
Glorious Rome hath lost her crown,
   Venice' pride is nought.

But the dreams their children dreamed
   Fleeting, unsubstantial, vain.
Shadowy as the shadows seemed
Airy nothing, as they deemed,
   These remain.
Poems (1908), cxxi

4 Some hang above the tombs,
Some weep in empty rooms,
I, when the iris blooms,
   Remember.
cxlvi

SAMUEL TAYLOR COLERIDGE 1772–1834

5 It is an ancient Mariner,
And he stoppeth one of three.
'By thy long grey beard and glittering eye,
Now wherefore stopp'st thou me?'
The Ancient Mariner, pt.i

6 He holds him with his skinny hand,
'There was a ship,' quoth he.
'Hold off! unhand me, grey-beard loon!'
Eftsoons his hand dropt he.

He holds him with his glittering eye...
He cannot choose but hear;
And thus spake on that ancient man,
The bright-eyed Mariner.

7 The Sun came up upon the left.
Out of the sea came he!
And he shone bright, and on the right
Went down into the sea.

8 The Wedding-Guest here beat his breast,
For he heard the loud bassoon.

9 And ice, mast-high, came floating by,
As green as emerald.

10 'God save thee, ancient Mariner!
From the fiends that plague thee thus!—
Why look'st thou so?'—With my cross-bow
I shot the Albatross.

11 Nor dim nor red, like God's own head,
The glorious Sun uprist.
pt.ii

12 We were the first that ever burst
Into that silent sea.

13 As idle as a painted ship
Upon a painted ocean.

14 Water, water, every where,
And all the boards did shrink;
Water, water, every where.
Nor any drop to drink.

The very deep did rot: O Christ!
That ever this should be!
Yea, slimy things did crawl with legs
Upon the slimy sea.

15 *Her* lips were red, *her* looks were free,
Her locks were yellow as gold:
Her skin was white as leprosy,
The Night-mare LIFE-IN-DEATH was she,
Who thicks man's blood with cold.

16 The Sun's rim dips; the stars rush out:
At one stride comes the dark.

17 We listened and looked sideways up!

18 The hornèd Moon, with one bright star
Within the nether tip.

19 'I fear thee, ancient Mariner!
I fear thy skinny hand!
And thou art long, and lank, and brown,
As is the ribbed sea-sand.'
pt.iv

20 Alone, alone, all, all alone,
Alone on a wide wide sea!
And never a saint took pity on
My soul in agony.

21 And a thousand thousand slimy things
Lived on; and so did I.

22 A spring of love gushed from my heart,
And I blessed them unaware.

23 Oh Sleep! it is a gentle thing,
Beloved from pole to pole,
To Mary Queen the praise be given!
She sent the gentle sleep from Heaven,
That slid into my soul.
pt.v

24 Sure I had drunken in my dreams,
And still my body drank.

25 We were a ghastly crew.

26 It ceased; yet still the sails made on
A pleasant noise till noon,
A noise like of a hidden brook
In the leafy month of June,
That to the sleeping woods all night
Singeth a quiet tune.

27 Like one, that on a lonesome road
Doth walk in fear and dread,
And having once turned round walks on,
And turns no more his head;
Because he knows, a frightful fiend
Doth close behind him tread.
pt.vi

28 No voice; but oh! the silence sank
Like music on my heart.

29 I pass, like night, from land to land;
I have strange power of speech.
pt.vii

30 He prayeth well, who loveth well
Both man and bird and beast.

He prayeth best, who loveth best
All things both great and small;
For the dear God who loveth us,
He made and loveth all.

1 He went like one that hath been stunned,
And is of sense forlorn:
A sadder and a wiser man,
He rose the morrow morn.

2 And the Spring comes slowly up this way.
Christabel, pt.i

3 A sight to dream of, not to tell!

4 Alas! they had been friends in youth;
But whispering tongues can poison truth;
And constancy lives in realms above;
And life is thorny; and youth is vain;
And to be wroth with one we love
Doth work like madness in the brain.
pt.ii

5 In Köhln, a town of monks and bones,
And pavements fang'd with murderous stones
And rags, and hags, and hideous wenches;
I counted two and seventy stenches,
All well defined, and several stinks!
Ye Nymphs that reign o'er sewers and sinks,
The river Rhine, it is well known,
Doth wash your city of Cologne;
But tell me, Nymphs, what power divine
Shall henceforth wash the river Rhine?
Cologne

6 Well! If the Bard was weatherwise, who made
The grand old ballad of Sir Patrick Spence.
Dejection: an Ode

7 I see them all so excellently fair,
I see, not feel, how beautiful they are!

8 I may not hope from outward forms to win
The passion and the life, whose fountains are within.

9 O Lady! we receive but what we give,
And in our life alone does Nature live.

10 From his brimstone bed at break of day
A walking the Devil is gone,
To visit his snug little farm the earth,
And see how his stock goes on.
The Devil's Thoughts. (Written jointly with Southey.)

11 His jacket was red and his breeches were blue,
And there was a hole where the tail came through.

12 He saw a Lawyer killing a viper
On a dunghill hard by his own stable;
And the Devil smiled, for it put him in mind
Of Cain and his brother, Abel.

13 He saw a cottage with a double coach-house,
A cottage of gentility;
And the Devil did grin, for his darling sin
Is pride that apes humility.

14 As he went through Cold-Bath Fields he saw
A solitary cell;
And the Devil was pleased, for it gave him a hint
For improving his prisons in Hell.

15 What is an Epigram? a dwarfish whole,
Its body brevity, and wit its soul.
Epigram

16 Swans sing before they die—'twere no bad thing,

Did certain persons die before they sing.
Epigram on a Volunteer Singer

17 That he who many a year with toil of breath
Found death in life, may here find life in death.
Epitaph for Himself

18 Ere sin could blight or sorrow fade,
Death came with friendly care:
The opening bud to Heaven convey'd
And bade it blossom *there.*
Epitaph on an Infant

19 Forth from his dark and lonely hiding-place
(Portentous sight!) the owlet Atheism,
Sailing on obscene wings athwart the noon,
Drops his blue-fringèd lids, and holds them close,
And hooting at the glorious sun in Heaven,
Cries out, 'Where is it?'
Fears in Solitude

20 With what deep worship I have still adored
The spirit of divinest Liberty.
France

21 The frost performs its secret ministry,
Unhelped by any wind.
Frost at Midnight

22 Only that film, which fluttered on the grate,
Still flutters there, the sole unquiet thing.

23 Therefore all seasons shall be sweet to thee,
Whether the summer clothe the general earth
With greenness, or the redbreast sit and sing
Betwixt the tufts of snow on the bare branch
Of mossy apple-tree, while the nigh thatch
Smokes in the sun-thaw; whether the eave-drops fall
Heard only in the trances of the blast,
Or if the secret ministry of frost
Shall hang them up in silent icicles,
Quietly shining to the quiet moon.

24 And visited all night by troops of stars.
Hymn before Sun rise, in the Vale of Chamouni

25 On awaking he...instantly and eagerly wrote down the
lines that are here preserved. At this moment he was
unfortunately called out by a person on business from
Porlock.
Kubla Khan, Preliminary note

26 In Xanadu did Kubla Khan
A stately pleasure-dome decree:
Where Alph, the sacred river, ran
Through caverns measureless to man
Down to a sunless sea.
So twice five miles of fertile ground
With walls and towers were girdled round.

27 But oh! that deep romantic chasm which slanted
Down the green hill athwart a cedarn cover!
A savage place! as holy and enchanted
As e'er beneath a waning moon was haunted
By woman wailing for her demon-lover!
And from this chasm, with ceaseless turmoil seething,
As if this earth in fast thick pants were breathing,
A mighty fountain momently was forced.

28 Five miles meandering with a mazy motion
Through wood and dale the sacred river ran.

29 And 'mid this tumult Kubla heard from far
Ancestral voices prophesying war!

30 A damsel with a dulcimer

In a vision once I saw:
It was an Abyssinian maid,
And on her dulcimer she played,
Singing of Mount Abora.

1 Weave a circle round him thrice,
And close your eyes with holy dread,
For he on honey-dew hath fed,
And drunk the milk of Paradise.

2 All thoughts, all passions, all delights,
    Whatever stirs this mortal frame,
All are but ministers of Love,
    And feed his sacred flame.
Love

3 Trochee trips from long to short.
Metrical Feet

4 Iambics march from short to long;—
With a leap and a bound the swift Anapaests throng.

5 Choose thou whatever suits the line;
Call me Sappho, call me Chloris,
Call me Lalage or Doris,
    Only, only call me thine.
Names (from Lessing's *Die Namen*.)

6 With Donne, whose muse on dromedary trots,
Wreathe iron pokers into true-love knots.
On Donne's Poetry

7 In the hexameter rises the fountain's silvery column;
    In the pentameter aye falling in melody back.
Ovidian Elegiac Metre

8 But still the heart doth need a language, still
Doth the old instinct bring back the old names.
Piccolomini, II.iv (from Schiller.)

9 So for the mother's sake the child was dear,
And dearer was the mother for the child.
*Sonnet to a Friend Who Asked How I Felt When the Nurse
First Presented My Infant to Me*

10 Well, they are gone, and here must I remain,
This lime-tree bower my prison!
This Lime-Tree Bower my Prison, l.1

11   When the last rook
Beat its straight path along the dusky air.
l.68

12   A charm
For thee, my gentle-hearted Charles, to whom
No sound is dissonant which tells of Life.
l.74

13 We ne'er can be
Made happy by compulsion.
The Three Graves, pt.IV.xii

14 All Nature seems at work. Slugs leave their lair—
    The bees are stirring—birds are on the wing—
And Winter slumbering in the open air,
    Wears on his smiling face a dream of Spring!
And I the while, the sole unbusy thing,
Nor honey make, nor pair, nor build, nor sing.
Work Without Hope

15 Work without hope draws nectar in a sieve,
And hope without an object cannot live.

16 Poor little Foal of an oppressed race!
I love the languid patience of thy face.
To a Young Ass

17 Like some poor nigh-related guest,
That may not rudely be dismist;

Yet hath outstay'd his welcome while,
And tells the jest without the smile.
Youth and Age

18 He who begins by loving Christianity better than Truth
will proceed by loving his own sect or church better
than Christianity, and end by loving himself better than
all.
Aids to Reflection: Moral and Religious Aphorisms, XXV

19 The most happy marriage I can picture or imagine to
myself would be the union of a deaf man to a blind
woman.
Allsop, *Recollections* (1836)

20 If men could learn from history, what lessons it might
teach us! But passion and party blind our eyes, and the
light which experience gives is a lantern on the stern,
which shines only on the waves behind us!
(18 Dec. 1831)

21 Until you understand a writer's ignorance, presume
yourself ignorant of his understanding.
Biographia Literaria, ch.12

22 That willing suspension of disbelief for the moment,
which constitutes poetic faith.
ch.14

23 Our *myriad-minded* Shakespeare. *Note*
'Ανὴρ μυριόνους, a phrase which I have borrowed
from a Greek monk, who applies it to a Patriarch of
Constantinople.
ch.15

24 No man was ever yet a great poet, without being at the
same time a profound philosopher.

25 The dwarf sees farther than the giant, when he has the
giant's shoulder to mount on.
The Friend, i, Essay 8. See 41:25

26 Reviewers are usually people who would have been
poets, historians, biographers, &c., if they could; they
have tried their talents at one or at the other, and have
failed; therefore they turn critics.
Lectures on Shakespeare and Milton, i

27 Summer has set in with its usual severity.
Quoted in Lamb's letter to V. Novello, 9 May 1826

28 The last speech, [Iago's soliloquoy] the
motive-hunting of motiveless malignity—how awful!
Notes on the Tragedies of Shakespeare, Othello

29 From whatever place I write you will expect that part
of my 'Travels' will consist of excursions in my own
mind.
Satyrane's Letters, ii. [*The Friend*, 7 Dec. 1809 No. 16.
Biographia Literaria]

30 You abuse snuff! Perhaps it is the final cause of the
human nose.
Table Talk, 4 Jan. 1823

31 To see him [Kean] act, is like reading Shakespeare by
flashes of lightning.
27 Apr. 1823

32 I wish our clever young poets would remember my
homely definitions of prose and poetry; that is prose ;
words in their best order;—poetry ; the *best* words in
the best order.
12 July 1827

33 The man's desire is for the woman; but the woman's
desire is rarely other than for the desire of the man.
23 July 1827

34 My mind is in a state of philosophical doubt as to

animal magnetism.
30 Apr. 1830

1 Poetry is certainly something more than good sense, but it must be good sense at all events; just as a palace is more than a house, but it must be a house, at least.
9 May 1830

2 Swift was *anima Rabelaisii habitans in sicco*—the soul of Rabelais dwelling in a dry place.
15 June 1830

3 In politics, what begins in fear usually ends in folly.
5 Oct. 1830

4 The misfortune is, that he [Tennyson] has begun to write verses without very well understanding what metre is.
24 Apr. 1833

5 I am glad you came in to punctuate my discourse, which I fear has gone on for an hour without any stop at all.
29 June 1833

6 When I was a boy, I was fondest of Aeschylus; in youth and middle-age I preferred Euripides; now in my declining years I prefer Sophocles. I can now at length see that Sophocles is the most perfect. Yet he never rises to the sublime simplicity of Aeschylus—a simplicity of design, I mean—nor diffuses himself in the passionate outpourings of Euripides.
1 July 1833

7 That passage is what I call the sublime dashed to pieces by cutting too close with the fiery four-in-hand round the corner of nonsense.
20 Jan. 1834

8 I believe Shakespeare was not a whit more intelligible in his own day than he is now to an educated man, except for a few local allusions of no consequence. He is of no age—nor of any religion, or party or profession. The body and substance of his works came out of the unfathomable depths of his own oceanic mind: his observation and reading, which was considerable, supplied him with the drapery of his figures.
15 Mar. 1834

9 Poor Lamb, if he wants any *knowledge,* he may apply to me.
Ascribed by Lamb in a letter to Southey, 28 July 1798

WILLIAM COLLINGBOURNE d 1484

10 The Cat, the Rat, and Lovell our dog
Rule all England under a hog.
R. Holinshed, *Chronicles* (1586), iii.746. Of Sir William Catesby (d.1485), Sir Richard Ratcliffe (d.1485), Lord Lovell (1454–?1487) (whose crest was a dog), and King Richard III (whose emblem was a wild boar). Collingbourne was executed on Tower Hill.

JESSE COLLINGS 1831–1920

11 Three acres and a cow.
Phrase used in his land-reform propaganda of 1885. See 339:16

ADMIRAL COLLINGWOOD 1750–1810

12 Now, gentlemen, let us do something today which the world may talk of hereafter.
Said before the Battle of Trafalgar, 21 Oct. 1805. G.L. Newnham Collingwood, ed., *Correspondence and Memoir of Lord Collingwood*

R.G. COLLINGWOOD 1889–1943

13 Perfect freedom is reserved for the man who lives by his own work, and in that work does what he wants to do.
Speculum Mentis, Prologue

CHURTON COLLINS 1848–1908

14 To ask advice is in nine cases out of ten to tout for flattery.
Maxims and Reflections, No.59

MORTIMER COLLINS 1827–1876

15 A man is as old as he's feeling,
A woman as old as she looks.
The Unknown Quantity

WILLIAM COLLINS 1721–1759

16 To fair Fidele's grassy tomb
Soft maids and village hinds shall bring
Each opening sweet of earliest bloom,
And rifle all the breathing spring.
Dirge in Cymbeline

17 If aught of oaten stop, or pastoral song,
May hope, O pensive Eve, to soothe thine ear.
Ode to Evening

18 Now air is hush'd, save where the weak-ey'd bat,
With short shrill shriek flits by on leathern wing,
Or where the beetle winds
His small but sullen horn,
As oft he rises 'midst the twilight path,
Against the pilgrim borne in heedless hum.

19 How sleep the brave, who sink to rest,
By all their country's wishes blest!
Ode Written in the Year 1746

20 By fairy hands their knell is rung,
By forms unseen their dirge is sung.

21 With eyes up-rais'd, as one inspir'd,
Pale Melancholy sate retir'd,
And from her wild sequester'd seat,
In notes by distance made more sweet,
Pour'd thro' the mellow horn her pensive soul.
The Passions, an Ode for Music

22 In hollow murmurs died away.

23 Too nicely Jonson knew the critic's part,
Nature in him was almost lost in Art.
Verses to Sir Thomas Hanmer

GEORGE COLMAN 1732–1794

24 Love and a cottage! Eh, Fanny! Ah, give me indifference and a coach and six!
The Clandestine Marriage, I.ii

GEORGE COLMAN THE YOUNGER 1762–1836

25 Oh, London is a fine town,
A very famous city,
Where all the streets are paved with gold,
And all the maidens pretty.
The Heir at Law (1797), I.ii

1 Not to be sneezed at.
II.i

2 Says he, 'I am a handsome man, but I'm a gay deceiver.'
Love Laughs at Locksmiths (1808), Act II

3 Johnson's style was grand and Gibbon's elegant; the stateliness of the former was sometimes pedantic, and the polish of the latter was occasionally finical. Johnson marched to kettle-drums and trumpets; Gibbon moved to flutes and hautboys: Johnson hewed passages through the Alps, while Gibbon levelled walks through parks and gardens.
Random Records (1830), i.121

4 My father was an eminent button maker—but I had a soul above buttons—I panted for a liberal profession.
Sylvester Daggerwood (1795), I.x

5 His heart runs away with his head.
Who Wants a Guinea? (1805), I.i

6 Impaling worms to torture fish.
Lady of the Wreck, c.II.l.18

7 When taken, To be well shaken.
My Nightgown and Slippers (1797), **Newcastle Apothecary**

CHARLES CALEB COLTON 1780?-1832

8 When you have nothing to say, say nothing.
Lacon (1820), vol.i, No.183

9 Examinations are formidable even to the best prepared, for the greatest fool may ask more than the wisest man can answer.
No.322

10 If you would be known, and not know, vegetate in a village; if you would know, and not be known, live in a city.
No.334

11 Man is an embodied paradox, a bundle of contradictions.
No.408

IVY COMPTON-BURNETT 1892–1969

12 'Time has too much credit,' said Bridget. 'I never agree with the compliments paid to it. It is not a great healer. It is an indifferent and perfunctory one. Sometimes it does not heal at all. And sometimes when it seems to, no healing has been necessary.'
Darkness and Day (1951), ch.7

13 'We may as well imagine the scene.'
'No, my mind baulks at it.'
'Mine does worse. It constructs it.'
A Family and a Fortune (1939), ch.9

14 'She still seems to me in her own way a person born to command,' said Luce…
'I wonder if anyone is born to obey,' said Isabel.
'That may be why people command rather badly, that they have no suitable material to work on.'
Parents and Children (1941), ch.3

AUGUSTE COMTE 1798–1857

15 M. Comte used to reproach his early English admirers with maintaining the 'conspiracy of silence' concerning his later performances.
J.S. Mill, **Auguste Comte and Positivism** (1865), p.199

PRINCE DE CONDÉ 1621–1686

16 *Silence! Voilà l'ennemi!*
Hush! Here comes the enemy!
As Bourdaloue mounted the pulpit at St. Sulpice

WILLIAM CONGREVE 1670–1729

17 Is there in the world a climate more uncertain than our own? And, which is a natural consequence, is there any where a people more unsteady, more apt to discontent, more *saturnine, dark,* and *melancholic* than our selves? Are we not of all people the most unfit to be alone, and most unsafe to be trusted with our selves?
Amendments of Mr. Collier's False and Imperfect Citations

18 Careless she is with artful care,
Affecting to seem unaffected.
Amoret

19 She likes her self, yet others hates
For that which in herself she prizes;
And while she laughs at them, forgets
She is the thing that she despises.

20 It is the business of a comic poet to paint the vices and follies of human kind.
The Double Dealer (1694), **Epistle Dedicatory. See 138:10**

21 Retired to their tea and scandal, according to their ancient custom.
I.i

22 There is nothing more unbecoming a man of quality than to laugh; Jesu, 'tis such a vulgar expression of the passion!
iv. See 137:1

23 Tho' marriage makes man and wife one flesh, it leaves 'em still two fools.
II.iii

24 She lays it on with a trowel.
III.x

25 When people walk hand in hand there's neither overtaking nor meeting.
IV.ii

26 See how love and murder will out.
vi

27 No mask like open truth to cover lies,
As to go naked is the best disguise.
V.vi

28 I cannot help it, if I am naturally more delighted with any thing that is amiable, than with any thing that is wonderful.
Preface to Dryden

29 What he [Dryden] has done in any one species, or distinct kind, would have been sufficient to have acquired him a great name. If he had written nothing but his Prefaces, or nothing but his Songs, or his Prologues, each of them would have intituled him to the preference and distinction of excelling in his kind.

30 The good receiv'd, the giver is forgot.
Epistle to Lord Halifax, l.40

31 Music alone with sudden charms can bind
The wand'ring sense, and calm the troubled mind.
Hymn to Harmony

32 Ah! Madam,…you know every thing in the world but your perfections, and you only know not those,

because 'tis the top of perfection not to know them.
Incognita (1692)

1 I am always of the opinion with the learned, if they
speak first.

2 But soon as e'er the beauteous idiot spoke,
Forth from her coral lips such folly broke,
Like balm the trickling nonsense heal'd my wound,
And what her eyes enthral'd, her tongue unbound.
Lesbia

3 I confess freely to you, I could never look long upon a
monkey, without very mortifying reflections.
Letter to Dennis, concerning Humour in Comedy, 1695

4 Has he not a rogue's face?...a hanging-look to
me...has a damn'd Tyburn-face, without the benefit o'
the Clergy...
Love for Love (1695), II.vii

5 I came upstairs into the world; for I was born in a
cellar.

6 What, wouldst thou have me turn pelican, and feed
thee out of my own vitals?

7 I know that's a secret, for it's whispered every where.
III.iii

8 He that first cries out stop thief, is often he that has
stoln the treasure.
xiv

9 Women are like tricks by slight of hand,
Which, to admire, we should not understand.
IV.xxi

10 A branch of one of your antediluvian families, fellows
that the flood could not wash away.
V.ii

11 To find a young fellow that is neither a wit in his own
eye, nor a fool in the eye of the world, is a very hard
task.

12 Aye, 'tis well enough for a servant to be bred at an
University. But the education is a little too pedantic
for a gentleman.
iii

13 Nay, for my part I always despised Mr *Tattle* of all
things; nothing but his being my husband could have
made me like him less.
xi

14 Music has charms to sooth a savage breast.
The Mourning Bride (1697), I.i

15 Heav'n has no rage, like love to hatred turn'd,
Nor Hell a fury, like a woman scorn'd.
III.viii

16   Is he then dead?
What, dead at last, quite, quite for ever dead!
V.xi

17 In my conscience I believe the baggage loves me, for
she never speaks well of me her self, nor suffers any
body else to rail at me.
The Old Bachelor (1693), I.i

18 One of love's April-fools.

19 The Devil watches all opportunities.
vi

20 Man was by Nature Woman's cully made:
We never are, but by ourselves, betrayed.
III.i

21 Bilbo's the word, and slaughter will ensue.
vii

22 Ask all the tyrants of thy sex, if their fools are not
known by this party-coloured livery—I am melancholy
when thou art absent; look like an ass when thou art
present; wake for thee, when I should sleep, and even
dream of thee, when I am awake; sigh much, drink
little, eat less, court solitude, am grown very
entertaining to my self, and (as I am informed) very
troublesome to everybody else. If this be not love, it is
madness, and then it is pardonable—Nay yet a more
certain sign than all this; I give thee my money.
x

23 Eternity was in that moment.
IV.vii

24 You were about to tell me something, child—but you
left off before you began.
viii

25 Now am I slap-dash down in the mouth.
ix

26 Well, Sir Joseph, you have such a winning way with
you.
V.vii

27 *Sharper:* Thus grief still treads upon the heels of
pleasure:
Marry'd in haste, we may repent at leisure.
Setter: Some by experience find those words
mis-plac'd:
At leisure marry'd, they repent in haste.
viii and ix

28 I could find it in my heart to marry thee, purely to be
rid of thee.
x

29 Courtship to marriage, as a very witty prologue to a
very dull Play.

30 Wou'd I were free from this restraint,
Or else had hopes to win her;
Wou'd she cou'd make of me a saint,
Or I of her a sinner.
Song: Pious Selinda Goes to Prayers

31 For 'tis some virtue, virtue to commend.
To Sir Godfrey Kneller

32 They come together like the Coroner's Inquest, to sit
upon the murdered reputations of the week.
The Way of the World (1700), I.i

33 Ay, ay, I have experience: I have a wife, and so forth.
iii

34 I always take blushing either for a sign of guilt, or of
ill breeding.
ix

35 Say what you will, 'tis better to be left than never to
have been loved.
II.i

36 Here she comes i' faith full sail, with her fan spread
and streamers out, and a shoal of fools for tenders.
iv

37 *Millamant:* O ay, letters—I had letters—I am
persecuted with letters—I hate letters—no body knows
how to write letters; and yet one has 'em, one does not
know why—They serve one to pin up one's hair.
Witwoud: ...Pray, Madam, do you pin up your hair
with all your letters: I find I must keep copies.
Millamant: Only with those in verse, Mr Witwoud. I

never pin up my hair with prose.

1 Beauty is the lover's gift.

2 A little disdain is not amiss; a little scorn is alluring.
III.v

3 Love's but a frailty of the mind
When 'tis not with ambition join'd.
xii

4 O, nothing is more alluring than a levee from a couch
in some confusion.
IV.i

5 I nauseate walking; 'tis a country diversion, I loathe
the country.
iv

6 My dear liberty, shall I leave thee? My faithful
solitude, my darling contemplation, must I bid you
then adieu? Ay-h adieu—My morning thoughts,
agreeable wakings, indolent slumbers, all ye *douceurs,*
ye *sommeils du matin,* adieu—I can't do't, 'tis more
than impossible.
v

7 Don't let us be familiar or fond, nor kiss before folks,
like my Lady Fadler and Sir Francis: Nor go to
Hyde-Park together the first Sunday in a new chariot,
to provoke eyes and whispers, and then never be seen
there together again; as if we were proud of one
another the first week, and asham'd of one another
ever after...Let us be very strange and well-bred: Let
us be as strange as if we had been married a great
while, and as well-bred as if we were not married at
all.

8 These articles subscrib'd, if I continue to endure you a
little longer, I may by degrees dwindle into a wife.

9 I hope you do not think me prone to any iteration of
nuptials.
xii

JAMES M. CONNELL 1852–1929

10 The people's flag is deepest red;
It shrouded oft our martyred dead,
And ere their limbs grew stiff and cold,
Their heart's blood dyed its every fold.
    Then raise the scarlet standard high!
    Within its shade we'll live or die.
    Tho' cowards flinch and traitors sneer,
    We'll keep the red flag flying here.
The Red Flag (1889), in H.E. Piggot, *Songs that made History,*
ch.6

CYRIL CONNOLLY 1903–1974

11 The Mandarin style...is beloved by literary pundits, by
those who would make the written word as unlike as
possible to the spoken one. It is the title of those
writers whose tendency is to make their language
convey more than they mean or more than they feel.
Enemies of Promise (1938), pt.I. **Predicament,** ch.ii

12 She [the artist's wife] will know that there is no more
sombre enemy of good art than the pram in the hall.
pt.II. **The Charlock's Shade,** ch.xiv

13 There is no fury like an ex-wife searching for a new
lover.
The Unquiet Grave (1944), Part I. **Ecce Gubernator**

14 Arrival-Angst is closely connected with guilt, with the
dread of something terrible having happened during
our absence. Death of parents. Entry of bailiffs. Flight
of loved one. Sensations worse at arriving in the
evening than in the morning, and much worse at
Victoria and Waterloo, than at Paddington.

15 Imprisoned in every fat man a thin one is wildly
signalling to be let out.
Part II. **Te Palinure Petens.** See 365:11

16 It is closing time in the gardens of the West and from
now on an artist will be judged only by the resonance
of his solitude or the quality of his despair.
'Comment', *Horizon,* Nos. 120-121, Dec. 1949–Jan. 1950. (Final
Issue)

JOSEPH CONRAD 1857–1924

17 The conquest of the earth, which mostly means the
taking it away from those who have a different
complexion or slightly flatter noses than ourselves, is
not a pretty thing when you look into it too much.
The Heart of Darkness (1902), ch.1

18 Mistah Kurtz—he dead.
ch.3

19 In the destructive element immerse...that was the
way.
Lord Jim (1900), ch.20

20 The terrorist and the policeman both come from the
same basket.
The Secret Agent (1907), ch.4

21 He walked frail, insignificant, shabby, miserable—and
terrible in the simplicity of his idea calling madness
and despair to the regeneration of the world. Nobody
looked at him. He passed on unsuspected and deadly,
like a pest in the street full of men.
closing words

22 The scrupulous and the just, the noble, humane, and
devoted natures; the unselfish and the intelligent may
begin a movement—but it passes away from them.
They are not the leaders of a revolution. They are its
victims.
Under Western Eyes (1911), Part II, ch.3

23 There was a completeness in it, something solid like a
principle, and masterful like an instinct—a disclosure
of something secret—of that hidden something, that
gift of good and evil that makes racial difference, that
shapes the fate of nations.
Youth (1898)

24 I remember my youth and the feeling that will never
come back any more—the feeling that I could last for
ever, outlast the sea, the earth, and all men; the
deceitful feeling that lures us on to perils, to love, to
vain effort—to death; the triumphant conviction of
strength, the heat of life in the handful of dust, that
glow in the heart that with every year grows dim,
grows cold, grows small, and expires—and expires,
too soon, too soon—before life itself.

HENRY CONSTABLE 1562–1613

25 Diaphenia, like the daffadowndilly,
    White as the sun, fair as the lily,
Heigh ho, how I do love thee!
    I do love thee as my lambs
    Are beloved of their dams;

How blest were I if thou wouldst prove me!
Diaphenia

JOHN CONSTABLE 1776–1837

1 The sound of water escaping from mill-dams, etc,
willows, old rotten planks, slimy posts, and
brickwork, I love such things....those scenes made me
a painter and I am grateful.
Leslie, *Life of John Constable* (1843), ch.5. Letter to John Fisher,
23 Oct. 1821

2 There is nothing ugly; *I never saw an ugly thing in my
life:* for let the form of an object be what it
may,—light, shade, and perspective will always make
it beautiful.
ch.17

3 The amiable but eccentric Blake...said of a beautiful
drawing of an avenue of fir trees...'Why, this is not
drawing, but *inspiration.*'...[Constable] replied, 'I
never knew it before; I meant it for drawing'.

4 In Claude's landscape all is lovely—all amiable—all is
amenity and repose;—the calm sunshine of the heart.
ch.18. A Course of Lectures to the Royal Institution. Lecture II, 2
June 1836.

BENJAMIN CONSTANT 1767–1834

5 *Dîner avec Robinson, écolier de Schelling. Son
travail sur l'esthétique du Kant. Idées très
ingénieuses. L'art pour l'art et sans but; tout but
dénature l'art. Mais l'art atteint au but qu'il n'a pas.*
Dinner with [Crabb] Robinson, a pupil of Schelling.
His work on Kant's aesthetics. Very clever notions.
Art for art's sake and with no purpose; any purpose
perverts art. But art achieves a purpose which is not its
own.
Journal intime, 11 février 1804

EMPEROR CONSTANTINE 288?–337

6 *In hoc signo vinces.*
In this sign shalt thou conquer.
Traditional form of words of Constantine's vision (312). Reported
in Greek, τούτῳ νίκα, 'By this, conquer', Eusebius, *Life of
Constantine,* i.28

ELIZA COOK 1818–1889

7 I love it, I love it; and who shall dare
To chide me for loving that old arm-chair?
The Old Arm-chair

8 Better build schoolrooms for 'the boy',
Than cells and gibbets for 'the man'.
A Song for the Ragged Schools

CALVIN COOLIDGE 1872–1933

9 I do not choose to run for President in 1928.
Announcement in 1927

10 He said he was against it.
On being asked what had been said by a clergyman who preached
on sin.

11 The business of America is business.
Speech before Society of American Newspaper Editors, 17 Jan.
1925

12 They hired the money, didn't they?
With reference to the war debts incurred by England and others
(1925)

BISHOP RICHARD CORBET 1582–1635

13 Farewell, rewards and Fairies,
Good housewives now may say,
For now foul sluts in dairies
Do fare as well as they.
The Fairies' Farewell

14 Who of late for cleanliness,
Finds sixpence in her shoe?

15 By which we note the Fairies
Were of the old profession;
Their songs were Ave Marys,
Their dances were procession.

PIERRE CORNEILLE 1606–1684

16 *A vaincre sans péril, on triomphe sans gloire.*
When there is no peril in the fight, there is no glory in
the triumph.
Le Cid (1637), II.ii

17 *Faites votre devoir et laissez faire aux dieux.*
Do your duty, and leave the issue to the Gods.
Horace (1640), II.viii

18 *Un premier mouvement ne fut jamais un crime.*
A first impulse was never a crime.
V.iii. See 355:11

FRANCES CORNFORD 1886–1960

19 Whoso maintains that I am humbled now
(Who wait the Awful Day) is still a liar;
I hope to meet my Maker brow to brow
And find my own the higher.
Epitaph for a Reviewer

20 How long ago Hector took off his plume,
Not wanting that his little son should cry,
Then kissed his sad Andromache goodbye—
And now we three in Euston waiting-room.
Parting in Wartime

21 A young Apollo, golden-haired,
Stands dreaming on the verge of strife,
Magnificently unprepared
For the long littleness of life.
Rupert Brooke

22 O fat white woman whom nobody loves,
Why do you walk through the fields in gloves...
Missing so much and so much?
To a Fat Lady Seen from a Train

F.M. CORNFORD 1874–1943

23 Every public action which is not customary, either is
wrong or, if it is right, is a dangerous precedent. It
follows that nothing should ever be done for the first
time.
Microcosmographia Academica, vii

MME CORNUEL 1605–1694

24 *Il n'y a point de héros pour son valet de chambre.*
No man is a hero to his valet.
Lettres de Mlle Aïssé, xii, 13 août, 1728

CORONATION SERVICE

25 We present you with this Book, the most valuable
thing that this world affords. Here is wisdom; this is

the royal Law; these are the lively Oracles of God.
The Presenting of the Holy Bible. See L.G. Wickham Legge, *English Coronation Records* (1901), p.334

CORREGGIO c.1489–1534

1 *Anch' io sono pittore!*
I, too, am a painter.
On seeing Raphael's 'St. Cecilia' at Bologna, c.1525

WILLIAM CORY 1823–1892

2 Jolly boating weather,
And a hay harvest breeze,
Blade on the feather,
Shade off the trees
Swing, swing together
With your body between your knees.
Eton Boating Song, see E. Parker, *Floreat* (1923), p.109. First
published in *Eton Scrap Book,* 1865

3   Nothing in life shall sever
The chain that is round us now.

4 They told me, Heraclitus, they told me you were
     dead,
They brought me bitter news to hear and bitter tears to
     shed.
I wept as I remembered how often you and I
Had tired the sun with talking and sent him down the
     sky.
Heraclitus. Translation of Callimachus, *Epigrams,* 2

5 You promise heavens free from strife,
     Pure truth, and perfect change of will;
But sweet, sweet is this human life,
     So sweet, I fain would breathe it still;
Your chilly stars I can forgo,
This warm kind world is all I know.
Mimnermus in Church

6 All beauteous things for which we live
     By laws of space and time decay.
But Oh, the very reason why
I clasp them, is because they die.

CHARLES COTTON 1630–1687

7 The shadows now so long do grow,
That brambles like tall cedars show,
Molehills seem mountains, and the ant
Appears a monstrous elephant.
Evening Quatrains, iii

ÉMILE COUÉ 1857–1926

8 *Tous les jours, à tous points de vue, je vais de mieux
en mieux.*
Every day, in every way, I am getting better and
better.
Formula in his clinic at Nancy

VICTOR COUSIN 1792–1867

9 *Il faut de la religion pour la religion, de la morale
pour la morale, comme de l'art pour l'art...le beau ne
peut être la voie ni de l'utile, ni du bien, ni du saint; il
ne conduit qu'à lui-même.*
We must have religion for religion's sake, morality for
morality's sake, as with art for art's sake...the
beautiful cannot be the way to what is useful, or to

what is good, or to what is holy; it leads only to itself.
Du vrai, du beau, et du bien (Sorbonne lecture, 1818). See 162:5

THOMAS COVENTRY, BARON COVENTRY 1578–1640

10 The dominion of the sea, as it is an ancient and
undoubted right of the crown of England, so it is the
best security of the land. The wooden walls are the
best walls of this kingdom.
Speech to the Judges, 17 June 1635. See Rushworth, *Hist. Coll.*
(1680), vol.ii, p.297

NOËL COWARD 1899–1973

11 Very flat, Norfolk.
Private Lives, I

12 Extraordinary how potent cheap music is.

13 It didn't look like a biscuit box did it? I've always felt
that it might. [Of the Taj Mahal.]

14 Certain women should be struck regularly, like gongs.
III

15 Don't let's be beastly to the Germans
When our Victory is ultimately won.
Don't Let's Be Beastly to the Germans (1943)

16 They had him thrown out of a club in Bombay
For, apart from his Mess-bills exceeding his pay,
He took to pig-sticking in *quite* the wrong way.
I wonder what happened to him!
I Wonder what Happened to Him from *Sigh No More* (1945)

17 I believe that since my life began
The most I've had is just a talent to amuse.
Heigh-o,
If love were all.
If Love were all from *Bitter Sweet* (1929)

18 Mad about the boy,
It's pretty funny but I'm mad about the boy.
He has a gay appeal
That makes me feel
There may be something sad about the boy.
Mad about the Boy from *Words and Music* (1932)

19 Mad dogs and Englishmen go out in the mid-day sun;
The Japanese don't care to, the Chinese wouldn't dare
     to;
Hindus and Argentines sleep firmly from twelve to
     one,
But Englishmen detest a
Siesta.
Mad Dogs and Englishmen

20 In the mangrove swamps where the python romps
There is peace from twelve till two.
Even caribous lie around and snooze,
For there's nothing else to do.
In Bengal, to move at all
Is seldom, if ever done.

21 Don't put your daughter on the stage, Missis
     Worthington
Don't put your daughter on the stage.
Mrs. Worthington

22 She refused to begin the 'Beguine'
Tho' they besought her to
And with language profane and obscene
She curs'd the man who taught her to

She curs'd Cole Porter too!
Nina from *Sigh No More* (1945)

1 Poor little rich girl
You're a bewitched girl,
Better beware!
Poor Little Rich Girl from *Charlot's Revue* of 1926

2 We have been able to dispose of
Rows and rows and rows of
Gainsboroughs and Lawrences
Some sporting prints of Aunt Florence's
Some of which were rather rude.
The Stately Homes of England from *Operette* (1938)

3 The Stately Homes of England
How beautiful they stand,
To prove the upper classes
Have still the upper hand.
See 244:21

4 Tho' the pipes that supply the bathroom burst
And the lavat'ry makes you fear the worst
It was used by Charles the First
Quite informally
And later by George the Fourth
On a journey North.

5 The Stately Homes of England,
Tho' rather in the lurch,
Provide a lot of chances
For Psychical Research—
There's the ghost of a crazy younger son
Who murder'd in Thirteen Fifty-One,
An extremely rowdy Nun
Who resented it,
And people who come to call
Meet her in the hall.

ABRAHAM COWLEY 1618–1667

6 Love in her sunny eyes does basking play;
Love walks the pleasant mazes of her hair;
Love does on both her lips for ever stray;
And sows and reaps a thousand kisses there.
In all her outward parts Love's always seen;
    But, oh, he never went within.
The Change

7 The thirsty earth soaks up the rain,
And drinks, and gapes for drink again.
The plants suck in the earth, and are
With constant drinking fresh and fair.
Drinking

8 Fill all the glasses there, for why
Should every creature drink but I,
Why, man of morals, tell me why?

9 God the first garden made, and the first city Cain.
The Garden

10 The world's a scene of changes, and to be
Constant, in Nature were inconstancy.
Inconstancy

11 Well then; I now do plainly see
This busy world and I shall ne'er agree;
The very honey of all earthly joy
Does of all meats the soonest cloy,
    And they (methinks) deserve my pity,
Who for it can endure the stings,
The crowd, and buz, and murmurings

Of this great hive, the city.
The Mistress, or Love Verses

12 Nothing so soon the drooping spirits can raise
As praises from the men, whom all men praise.
Ode upon a Copy of Verses of My Lord Broghill's

13 This only grant me, that my means may lie
Too low for envy, for contempt too high.
Of Myself

14 Acquaintance I would have, but when't depends
Not on the number, but the choice of friends.

15 Poet and Saint! to thee alone are given
The two most sacred names of earth and Heaven.
On the Death of Mr. Crashaw

16 Hail, Bard triumphant! and some care bestow
On us, the Poets Militant below!

17 Ye fields of Cambridge, our dear Cambridge, say,
Have ye not seen us walking every day?
Was there a tree about which did not know
    The love betwixt us two?
On William Harvey

18 Lukewarmness I account a sin
As great in love as in religion.
The Request

19 Life is an incurable disease.
To Dr. Scarborough, vi

20 Hence, ye profane; I hate ye all;
Both the great vulgar, and the small.
Trans. of Horace, bk.iii, ode 1. See 260:13

MRS. HANNAH COWLEY 1743–1809

21 Five minutes! Zounds! I have been five minutes too
late all my life-time!
The Belle's Stratagem (1780), I.i

22 Vanity, like murder, will out.
iv

23 But what is woman?—only one of Nature's agreeable
blunders.
Who's the Dupe?, II

WILLIAM COWPER 1731–1800

24 Regions Caesar never knew
    Thy posterity shall sway,
Where his eagles never flew,
    None invincible as they.
Boadicea

25 Grief is itself a med'cine.
Charity, l.159

26 He found it inconvenient to be poor.
l.189

27 India's spicy shores.
l.442

28 No learned disputants would take the field,
Sure not to conquer, and sure not to yield;
Both sides deceiv'd, if rightly understood,
Pelting each other for the public good.
l.620

29 Spare the poet for his subject's sake.
l.636

30 Though syllogisms hang not on my tongue,
I am not surely always in the wrong!
'Tis hard if all is false that I advance—

A fool must now and then be right, by chance.
Conversation, l.93

1 A noisy man is always in the right.
l.114

2 A tale should be judicious, clear, succinct;
The language plain, and incidents well link'd;
Tell not as new what ev'ry body knows;
And, new or old, still hasten to a close.
l.235

3 The pipe, with solemn interposing puff,
Makes half a sentence at a time enough;
The dozing sages drop the drowsy strain,
Then pause, and puff—and speak, and pause again.
l.245

4 Pernicious weed! whose scent the fair annoys,
Unfriendly to society's chief joys,
Thy worst effect is banishing for hours
The sex whose presence civilizes ours.
l.251

5 His wit invites you by his looks to come,
But when you knock it never is at home.
l.303

6 Whose only fit companion is his horse.
l.412

7 War lays a burden on the reeling state,
And peace does nothing to relieve the weight.
Expostulation, l.306

8 And hast thou sworn, on ev'ry slight pretence,
Till perjuries are common as bad pence,
While thousands, careless of the damning sin,
Kiss the book's outside who ne'er look within.
l.386

9 The man that hails you Tom or Jack,
And proves by thumps upon your back
    How he esteems your merit,
Is such a friend, that one had need
Be very much his friend indeed
    To pardon or to bear it.
Friendship

10 Pleasure is labour too, and tires as much.
Hope, l.20

11 Men deal with life as children with their play,
Who first misuse, then cast their toys away.
l.127

12   The multitudes beguil'd
In vain opinion's waste and dang'rous wild.
Ten thousand rove the brakes and thorns among,
Some eastward, and some westward, and all wrong.
l.278

13 Could he with reason murmur at his case,
Himself sole author of his own disgrace?
l.316

14 And diff'ring judgements serve but to declare
That truth lies somewhere, if we knew but where.
l.423

15 John Gilpin was a citizen
    Of credit and renown,
A train-band captain eke was he
    Of famous London town.
John Gilpin

16 My sister and my sister's child,
    Myself and children three,
Will fill the chaise; so you must ride

On horseback after we.

17 O'erjoy'd was he to find
That, though on pleasure she was bent,
She had a frugal mind.

18 So down he came; for loss of time,
    Although it griev'd him sore,
Yet loss of pence, full well he knew,
    Would trouble him much more.

19 Nor stopp'd till where he had got up
    He did again get down.

20 Beware of desp'rate steps. The darkest day
(Live till tomorrow) will have pass'd away.
The Needless Alarm, l.132

21 Hence jarring sectaries may learn
Their real int'rest to discern;
That brother should not war with brother,
And worry and devour each other.
The Nightingale and Glow-Worm

22 No dancing bear was so genteel,
Or half so dégagé.
Of Himself

23 Oh! for a closer walk with God,
    A calm and heav'nly frame;
A light to shine upon the road
    That leads me to the Lamb!
Olney Hymns, 1

24 There is a fountain fill'd with blood
    Drawn from Emmanuel's veins,
And sinners, plunged beneath that flood,
    Lose all their guilty stains.
15

25 Hark, my soul! it is the Lord;
'Tis thy Saviour, hear his word;
Jesus speaks, and speaks to thee;
'Say, poor sinner, lov'st thou me?'
18

26 God moves in a mysterious way
    His wonders to perform;
He plants his footsteps in the sea,
    And rides upon the storm.
35

27 Ye fearful saints fresh courage take,
The clouds ye so much dread
Are big with mercy, and shall break
In blessings on your head.

28 Behind a frowning providence
He hides a smiling face.

29 Blind unbelief is sure to err,
    And scan his work in vain;
God is his own interpreter,
    And he will make it plain.

30 Toll for the brave—
    The brave! that are no more:
All sunk beneath the wave,
    Fast by their native shore.
On the Loss of the Royal George

31 His sword was in the sheath,
    His fingers held the pen,
When Kempenfelt went down
    With twice four hundred men.

32 Oh, fond attempt to give a deathless lot

To names ignoble, born to be forgot!
On Observing Some Names of Little Note Recorded in the Biographia Britannica

1 There goes the parson, oh! illustrious spark,
   And there, scarce less illustrious, goes the clerk!

2 Oh that those lips had language! Life has pass'd
   With me but roughly since I heard thee last.
   Those lips are thine—thy own sweet smiles I see,
   The same that oft in childhood solac'd me.
   On the Receipt of My Mother's Picture, l.1

3 Thy morning bounties ere I left my home,
   The biscuit, or confectionary plum.
   l.60

4 Perhaps a frail memorial, but sincere,
   Not scorn'd in heav'n, though little notic'd here.
   l.72

5 I shall not ask Jean Jacques Rousseau,
   If birds confabulate or no.
   Pairing Time Anticipated

6 Unmiss'd but by his dogs and by his groom.
   The Progress of Error, l.95

7 Oh, laugh or mourn with me the rueful jest,
   A cassock'd huntsman and a fiddling priest!
   l.110

8 Himself a wand'rer from the narrow way,
   His silly sheep, what wonder if they stray?
   l.118

9 Remorse, the fatal egg by pleasure laid.
   l.239

10 As creeping ivy clings to wood or stone,
    And hides the ruin that it feeds upon.
    l.285

11 How much a dunce that has been sent to roam
    Excels a dunce that has been kept at home.
    l.415

12   Judgment drunk, and brib'd to lose his way,
    Winks hard, and talks of darkness at noon-day.
    l.450

13 Thou god of our idolatry, the press...
    Thou fountain, at which drink the good and wise;
    Thou ever-bubbling spring of endless lies;
    Like Eden's dread probationary tree,
    Knowledge of good and evil is from thee.
    l.461

14 Laugh at all you trembled at before.
    l.592

15 Then, shifting his side, (as a lawyer knows how).
    Report of a Adjudged Case

16 The disencumber'd Atlas of the state.
    Retirement, l.394

17 He likes the country, but in truth must own,
    Most likes it, when he studies it in town.
    l.573

18   Philologists who chase
    A panting syllable through time and space,
    Start it at home, and hunt it in the dark,
    To Gaul, to Greece, and into Noah's ark.
    l.619

19 Absence of occupation is not rest,
    A mind quite vacant is a mind distress'd.
    l.623

20 Beggars invention and makes fancy lame.
    l.709

21 I praise the Frenchman, his remark was shrewd—
    How sweet, how passing sweet, is solitude!
    But grant me still a friend in my retreat,
    Whom I may whisper—solitude is sweet.
    l.739

22 The lie that flatters I abhor the most.
    Table Talk, l.88

23 Admirals, extoll'd for standing still,
    Or doing nothing with a deal of skill.
    l.192

24 The Frenchman, easy, debonair, and brisk,
    Give him his lass, his fiddle, and his frisk,
    Is always happy, reign whoever may,
    And laughs the sense of mis'ry far away.
    l.236

25 Freedom has a thousand charms to show,
    That slaves, howe'er contented, never know.
    l.260

26 Stamps God's own name upon a lie just made,
    To turn a penny in the way of trade.
    l.420

27 But he (his musical finesse was such,
    So nice his ear, so delicate his touch)
    Made poetry a mere mechanic art;
    And ev'ry warbler has his tune by heart. [Pope.]
    l.654

28 Thus first necessity invented stools,
    Convenience next suggested elbow-chairs,
    And luxury the accomplish'd Sofa last.
    The Task, bk.i, *The Sofa,* l.86

29 The nurse sleeps sweetly, hir'd to watch the sick,
    Whom, snoring, she disturbs.
    l.89

30 He, not unlike the great ones of mankind,
    Disfigures earth; and, plotting in the dark,
    Toils much to earn a monumental pile,
    That may record the mischiefs he has done. [The
        mole.]
    l.274

31 God made the country, and man made the town.
    l.749

32 Slaves cannot breathe in England, if their lungs
    Receive our air, that moment they are free;
    They touch our country, and their shackles fall.
    bk.ii, *The Timepiece,* l.40. See 7:7

33 England, with all thy faults, I love thee still—
    My country!
    l.206. See 148:24

34 I would not yet exchange thy sullen skies,
    And fields without a flow'r, for warmer France
    With all her vines.
    l.212

35 There is a pleasure in poetic pains
    Which only poets know.
    l.285

36 Variety's the very spice of life,
    That gives it all its flavour.
    l.606

37   Let her pass, and, chariotted along

In guilty splendour, shake the public ways.
bk.iii, **The Garden,** l.69

1 I was a stricken deer, that left the herd
Long since.
l.108. See 434:16

2   Charge
His mind with meanings that he never had.
l.148

3 Great contest follows, and much learned dust
Involves the combatants.
l.161

4 From reveries so airy, from the toil
Of dropping buckets into empty wells,
And growing old in drawing nothing up!
l.188

5   Newton, childlike sage!
Sagacious reader of the works of God.
l.252

6   Detested sport,
That owes its pleasures to another's pain.
l.326

7 How various his employments, whom the world
Calls idle.
l.352

8 Studious of laborious ease.
l.361

9 Who loves a garden loves a greenhouse too.
l.566

10 To combat may be glorious, and success
Perhaps may crown us; but to fly is safe.
l.686

11 Now stir the fire, and close the shutters fast,
Let fall the curtains, wheel the sofa round,
And, while the bubbling and loud-hissing urn
Throws up a steamy column, and the cups,
That cheer but not inebriate, wait on each,
So let us welcome peaceful ev'ning in.
bk.iv, **The Winter Evening,** l.34. See 41:21

12 'Tis pleasant through the loopholes of retreat
To peep at such a world; to see the stir
Of the great Babel, and not feel the crowd.
l.88

13 I crown thee king of intimate delights,
Fire-side enjoyments, home-born happiness.
l.139

14   A Roman meal;...
          a radish and an egg.
ll.168-73

15 The slope of faces, from the floor to th' roof,
(As if one master-spring controll'd them all),
Relax'd into a universal grin.
l.202

16 With spots quadrangular of di'mond form,
Ensanguin'd hearts, clubs typical of strife,
And spades, the emblem of untimely graves.
l.217

17 I never fram'd a wish, or form'd a plan,
That flatter'd me with hopes of earthly bliss,
But there I laid the scene.
l.695

18 Shaggy, and lean, and shrewd, with pointed ears

And tail cropp'd short, half lurcher and half cur.
bk.v, **The Winter Morning Walk,** l.45

19 Great princes have great playthings.
l.175

20 But war's a game, which, were their subjects wise,
Kings would not play at.
l.187

21 And the first smith was the first murd'rer's son.
l.219

22 He is the freeman whom the truth makes free.
l.733

23   Knowledge dwells
In heads replete with thoughts of other men;
Wisdom in minds attentive to their own.
bk.vi, **The Winter Walk at Noon,** l.89

24 Knowledge is proud that he has learn'd so much;
Wisdom is humble that he knows no more.
l.96

25 Books are not seldom talismans and spells.
l.98

26 Nature is but a name for an effect,
Whose cause is God.
l.223

27 A cheap but wholesome salad from the brook.
l.304

28 I would not enter on my list of friends
(Tho' grac'd with polish'd manners and fine sense,
Yet wanting sensibility) the man
Who needlessly sets foot upon a worm.
l.560

29   Stillest streams
Oft water fairest meadows, and the bird
That flutters least is longest on the wing.
l.929

30 Public schools 'tis public folly feeds.
Tirocinium, l.250

31 The parson knows enough who knows a duke.
l.403

32   As a priest,
A piece of mere church furniture at best.
l.425

33   Tenants of life's middle state,
Securely plac'd between the small and great.
l.807

34 Greece, sound thy Homer's, Rome thy Virgil's name,
But England's Milton equals both in fame.
To John Milton

35 Humility may clothe an English dean.
Truth, l.118

36 He has no hope who never had a fear.
l.298

37 His mind his kingdom, and his will his law.
l.406

38 I am monarch of all I survey,
     My right there is none to dispute;
From the centre all round to the sea
     I am lord of the fowl and the brute.
Oh, solitude! where are the charms
     That sages have seen in thy face?
Better dwell in the midst of alarms,
     Than reign in this horrible place.
Verses Supposed to be Written by Alexander Selkirk

1 [On Johnson's inadequate treatment of *Paradise Lost*]
Oh! I could thresh his old jacket till I made his pension
jingle in his pockets.
Letters. To the Revd. W. Unwin, 31 Oct. 1779

2 Our severest winter, commonly called the spring.
8 June 1783

3 He kissed likewise the maid in the kitchen, and
seemed upon the whole a most loving, kissing,
kind-hearted gentleman.
To the Revd. J. Newton, 29 Mar. 1784

GEORGE CRABBE 1754–1832

4 What is a church?—Our honest sexton tells,
'Tis a tall building, with a tower and bells.
The Borough, letter ii, **The Church,** l.11

5 Virtues neglected then, adored become,
And graces slighted, blossom on the tomb.
l.133

6 Intrigues half-gather'd, conversation-scraps,
Kitchen-cabals, and nursery-mishaps.
letter iii, **The Vicar,** l.71

7 Habit with him was all the test of truth,
'It must be right: I've done it from my youth.'
l.138

8 Lo! the poor toper whose untutor'd sense,
Sees bliss in ale, and can with wine dispense;
Whose head proud fancy never taught to steer,
Beyond the muddy ecstasies of beer.
Inebriety, l.120. Imitation of Pope: see 379:5

9 This, books can do—nor this alone: they give
New views to life, and teach us how to live;
They soothe the grieved, the stubborn they chastise;
Fools they admonish, and confirm the wise.
Their aid they yield to all: they never shun
The man of sorrow, nor the wretch undone;
Unlike the hard, the selfish, and the proud,
They fly not sullen from the suppliant crowd;
Nor tell to various people various things,
But show to subjects, what they show to kings.
The Library, l.41

10 With awe around these silent walks I tread:
These are the lasting mansions of the dead.
l.105

11 And mighty folios first, a lordly band,
Then quartos, their well-order'd ranks maintain,
And light octavos fill a spacious plain;
See yonder, ranged in more frequented rows,
A humbler band of duodecimos.
l.128

12 Fashion, though Folly's child, and guide of fools,
Rules e'en the wisest, and in learning rules.
l.167

13 Coldly profane, and impiously gay.
l.265

14 The murmuring poor, who will not fast in peace:
The Newspaper, l.158

15 A master-passion is the love of news.
l.279

16 Our farmers round, well pleased with constant gain,
Like other farmers, flourish and complain.
The Parish Register, pt.i, **Baptisms,** l.273

17 Who often reads, will sometimes wish to write.
Tales, xi, **Edward Shore,** l.109

18 The wife was pretty, trifling, childish, weak;
She could not think, but would not cease to speak.
xiv, **Struggles of Conscience,** l.343

19 But 'twas a maxim he had often tried,
That right was right, and there he would abide.
xv, **The Squire and the Priest,** l.365

20 That all was wrong because not all was right.
xix, **The Convert,** l.313

21 He tried the luxury of doing good.
Tales of the Hall, iii, **Boys at School,** l.139

22 Secrets with girls, like loaded guns with boys,
Are never valued till they make a noise.
xi, **The Maid's Story,** l.84

23 'The game', he said, 'is never lost till won.'
xv, **Gretna Green,** l.334

24 The face the index of a feeling mind.
xvi, **Lady Barbara,** l.124

25 Love warps the mind a little from the right.
xxi, **Smugglers and Poachers,** l.216

26 Lo! where the heath, with withering brake grown o'er,
Lends the light turf that warms the neighbouring poor;
From thence a length of burning sand appears,
Where the thin harvest waves its wither'd ears;
Rank weeds, that every art and care defy,
Reign o'er the land, and rob the blighted rye:
There thistles stretch their prickly arms afar,
And to the ragged infant threaten war;
There poppies, nodding, mock the hope of toil;
There the blue bugloss paints the sterile soil;
Hardy and high, above the slender sheaf,
The slimy mallow waves her silky leaf;
O'er the young shoot the charlock throws a shade,
And clasping tares cling round the sickly blade.
The Village, bk.i, l.63

27 And the cold charities of man to man.
l.245

28 A potent quack, long versed in human ills,
Who first insults the victim whom he kills;
Whose murd'rous hand a drowsy Bench protect,
And whose most tender mercy is neglect.
l.282

HART CRANE 1899–1932

29 O Sleepless as the river under thee,
Vaulting the sea, the prairies' dreaming sod,
Unto us lowliest sometime sweep, descend
And of the curveship lend a myth to God.
The Bridge

30 You who desired so much—in vain to ask—
Yet fed your hunger like an endless task,
Dared dignify the labor, bless the quest—
Achieved that stillness ultimately best,

Being, of all, least sought for: Emily, Hear!
To Emily Dickinson

31 And yet this great wink of eternity,
Of rimless floods, unfettered leewardings,
Samite sheeted and processioned where
Her undinal vast belly moonward bends,
Laughing the wrapt inflections of our love;

Take this Sea, whose diapason knells
On scrolls of silver snowy sentences,
The sceptered terror of whose session rends
As her demeanors motion well or ill,

All but the pieties of lovers' hands.
Voyages, II

ARCHBISHOP CRANMER 1489–1556

1 This was the hand that wrote it, therefore it shall
suffer first punishment.
At the stake, 21 March 1556. Green, *Short History of the English
People*, p.367

RICHARD CRASHAW 1612?–1649

2 *Nympha pudica Deum vidit, et erubuit.*
The conscious water saw its God, and blushed.
Epigrammata Sacra. Aquae in Vinum Versae (His own
translation.)

3 Love's passives are his activ'st part.
The wounded is the wounding heart.
The Flaming Heart upon the Book of Saint Teresa, 1.73

4 By all the eagle in thee, all the dove.
1.95

5 Love, thou art absolute sole Lord
Of life and death.
Hymn to the Name & Honour of the Admirable Saint Teresa,
1.1

6 Gloomy night embrac'd the place
Where the noble Infant lay.
The Babe look't up and shew'd his face;
In spite of darkness, it was day.
It was Thy day, sweet! and did rise
Not from the East, but from thine eyes.
Hymn of the Nativity, 1.17

7 Poor World (said I) what wilt thou do
To entertain this starry stranger?
Is this the best thou canst bestow?
A cold, and not too cleanly, manger?
Contend, ye powers of heav'n and earth
To fit a bed for this huge birth.
1.37

8 Welcome, all wonders in one sight!
Eternity shut in a span.
1.79

9 I would be married, but I'd have no wife,
I would be married to a single life.
On Marriage

10 Lo here a little volume, but large book.
Prayer...prefixed to a little Prayer-book

11 It is love's great artillery
Which here contracts itself and comes to lie
Close couch'd in your white bosom.

12 Two walking baths; two weeping motions;
Portable, and compendious oceans.
Saint Mary Magdalene, or The Weeper, xix

13 All is Caesar's; and what odds
So long as Caesar's self is God's?
Steps to the Temple, Mark 12

14 And when life's sweet fable ends,
Soul and body part like friends;
No quarrels, murmurs, no delay;
A kiss, a sigh, and so away.
Temperance

15 Whoe'er she be,
That not impossible she
That shall command my heart and me;

Where'er she lie,
Lock'd up from mortal eye,
In shady leaves of destiny.
Wishes to His Supposed Mistress

JULIA CRAWFORD fl. 1835

16 Kathleen Mavourneen! the grey dawn is breaking,
The horn of the hunter is heard on the hill;
The lark from her light wing the bright dew is shaking;
Kathleen Mavourneen! what, slumbering still?
Oh! hast thou forgotten how soon we must sever?
Oh! hast thou forgotten this day we must part?
It may be for years, and it may be for ever,
Oh! why art thou silent, thou voice of my heart?
Kathleen Mavourneen. Metropolitan Magazine, London, 1835

BISHOP MANDELL CREIGHTON 1843–1901

17 No people do so much harm as those who go about
doing good.
Life (1904), vol.ii, p.503

SIR RANULPHE CREWE 1558–1646

18 And yet time hath his revolution; there must be a
period and an end to all temporal things, *finis rerum,*
an end of names and dignities and whatsoever is
terrene; and why not of De Vere? Where is Bohun,
where's Mowbray, where's Mortimer? Nay, which is
more and most of all, where is Plantagenet? They are
entombed in the urns and sepulchres of mortality. And
yet let the name and dignity of De Vere stand so long
as it pleaseth God.
Oxford Peerage Case, 1625. See *D.N.B.*

OLIVER CROMWELL 1599–1658

19 A few honest men are better than numbers.
Letter to Sir W. Spring, Sept. 1643

20 Such men as had the fear of God before them and as
made some conscience of what they did...the plain
russet-coated captain that knows what he fights for and
loves what he knows.
Letter of Sept. 1643. Carlyle, *Letters and Speeches of Oliver
Cromwell*

21 I beseech you, in the bowels of Christ, think it
possible you may be mistaken.
Letter to the General Assembly of the Church of Scotland, 3 Aug.
1650

22 The dimensions of this mercy are above my thoughts.
It is, for aught I know, a crowning mercy.
Letter for the Honourable William Lenthall, 4 Sept. 1651

23 Not what they want but what is good for them.
Attr.

24 Mr Lely, I desire you would use all your skill to paint
my picture truly like me, and not flatter me at all; but
remark all these roughnesses, pimples, warts, and
everything as you see me, otherwise I will never pay a
farthing for it.
Walpole, *Anecdotes of Painting*, ch.12

25 Take away that fool's bauble, the mace.
At the dismissal of the Rump Parliament, 20 Apr. 1653. Bulstrode
Whitelock, *Memorials* (1682), p.554. Often quoted as 'Take away
these baubles'.

26 You have sat too long here for any good you have
been doing. Depart, I say, and let us have done with

you. In the name of God, go!
Addressing the Rump Parliament, 20 Apr. 1653. See Bulstrode
Whitelock, *Memorials* (1682), p.554. Quoted by L.S. Amery from
the back benches of Neville Chamberlain's Government, House of
Commons, 7 May 1940.

1 It's a maxim not to be despised, 'Though peace be
made, yet it's interest that keeps peace.'
Speech to Parliament, 4 Sept. 1654

2 Necessity hath no law. Feigned necessities, imaginary
necessities,…are the greatest cozenage that men can
put upon the Providence of God, and make pretences
to break known rules by.
12 Sept. 1654

3 Your poor army, those poor contemptible men, came
up hither.
21 Apr. 1657

4 You have accounted yourselves happy on being
environed with a great ditch from all the world
besides.
25 Jan. 1658

5 My design is to make what haste I can to be gone.
Last words. Morley, *Life*, v, ch.10

RICHARD ASSHETON, VISCOUNT CROSS
1823–1914

6 [When the House of Lords laughed at his speech in
favour of Spiritual Peers]
I hear a smile.
G.W.E. Russell, *Collections and Recollections*, ch.29

BISHOP RICHARD CUMBERLAND 1631–1718

7 It is better to wear out than to rust out.
G. Horne, *The Duty of Contending for the Faith*

E.E. CUMMINGS 1894–1962

8 who knows if the moon's
a balloon, coming out of a keen city
in the sky—filled with pretty people?
& [AND] (1925), N&:VII

9 the Cambridge ladies who live in furnished souls.
the Cambridge ladies

10 'next to of course god america i
love you land of the pilgrims' and so forth oh
say can you see by the dawn's early my
country 'tis of centuries come and go
and are no more what of it we should worry
in every language even deafanddumb
thy sons acclaim your glorious name by gorry
by jingo by gee by gosh by gum
why talk of beauty what could be more beautiful than these heroic happy dead
who rushed like lions to the roaring slaughter
they did not stop to think they died instead
then shall the voice of liberty be mute?'

He spoke. And drank rapidly a glass of water.
next to of course god

11 pity this busy monster, manunkind,

not. Progress is a comfortable disease.
pity this busy monster, manunkind

12   listen: there's a hell
of a good universe next door; let's go.

ALLAN CUNNINGHAM 1784–1842

13 A wet sheet and a flowing sea,
A wind that follows fast
And fills the white and rustling sail
And bends the gallant mast.
A Wet Sheet and a Flowing Sea

14 It's hame and it's hame, hame fain wad I be,
O, hame, hame, hame to my ain countree!
It's hame and It's hame. Hogg includes this poem among his
Jacobite Relics, i.135. In his notes, i.294, he says he took it from
Cromek's *Galloway and Nithsdale Relics*, and supposes that it
owed much to Allan Cunningham

WILL CUPPY 1884–1949

15 The Dodo never had a chance. He seems to have been
invented for the sole purpose of becoming extinct and
that was all he was good for.
How to Become Extinct

JOHN PHILPOT CURRAN 1750–1817

16 The condition upon which God hath given liberty to
man is eternal vigilance; which condition if he break,
servitude is at once the consequence of his crime, and
the punishment of his guilt.
Speech on the Right of Election of Lord Mayor of Dublin, 10 July
1790

LORD CURZON OF KEDLESTON 1859–1925

17 I hesitate to say what the functions of the modern
journalist may be; but I imagine that they do not
exclude the intelligent anticipation of facts even before
they occur.
House of Commons, 29 Mar. 1898

18 No gentleman has soup at luncheon.
Attr. by Evelyn Waugh in *Noblesse oblige* by A.S.C. Ross and
others (1956), p.73

ST. CYPRIAN d. 258

19 *Habere non potest Deum patrem qui ecclesiam non
habet matrem.*
He cannot have God for his father who has not the
church for his mother.
De Cath. Eccl. Unitate, vi. See 21:19

SAMUEL DANIEL 1562–1619

20   Princes in this case
Do hate the traitor, though they love the treason.
Tragedy of Cleopatra, IV.i

21   Unless above himself he can
Erect himself, how poor a thing is man!
To the Lady Margaret, Countess of Cumberland, xii

22 Custom that is before all law, Nature that is above all
art.
A Defence of Rhyme

23 And who, in time, knows whither we may vent
The treasure of our tongue, to what strange shores
This gain of our best glory shall be sent,
T'enrich unknowing nations with our stores?
What worlds in th'yet unformed Occident
May come refin'd with th'accents that are ours?
Musophilus, l.957

24   But years hath done this wrong,

To make me write too much, and live too long.
Philotas, [Ded.] **To the Prince**, l.108

1 Care-charmer Sleep, son of the sable Night,
Brother to Death, in silent darkness born:
Relieve my languish, and restore the light,
With dark forgetting of my care return,
And let the day be time enough to mourn
The shipwreck of my ill adventured youth:
Let waking eyes suffice to wail their scorn,
Without the torment of the night's untruth.
Sonnets to Delia, liv

DANTE 1265–1321

2 *Nel mezzo del cammin di nostra vita.*
In the middle of the road of our life.
Divina Commedia (ed. Sinclair, 1971). **Inferno**, i.1

3 *PER ME SI VA NELLA CITTÀ DOLENTE,*
PER ME SI VA NELL' ETERNO DOLORE,
PER ME SI VA TRA LA PERDUTA GENTE...
LASCIATE OGNI SPERANZA VOI CH'ENTRATE!
This way for the sorrowful city. This way for eternal
   suffering. This way to join the lost
   people...Abandon all hope, you who enter!
iii.1. Inscription at the entrance to Hell

4 *Non ragioniam di lor, ma guarda, e passa.*
Let us not speak of them, but look, and pass on.
51

5 *Il gran rifiuto.*
The great refusal.
60

6 *Onorate l'altissimo poeta.*
Honour to the greatest poet.
iv.80

7 *Il maestro di color che sanno.*
The master of them that know. [Aristotle.]
131

8 *Nessun maggior dolore,*
Che ricordarsi del tempo felice
Nella miseria.
There is no greater sorrow than to recall a time of
   happiness in misery.
v.121. See 89:6

9 *Noi leggiavamo un giorno per diletto*
Di Lancialotto, come amor lo strinse:
Soli eravamo, e sanza alcun sospetto.
We were reading one day for recreation of Lancelot,
   how love constrained him: we were alone and
   completely unsuspecting.
127

10 *Galeotto fu il libro e chi lo scrisse:*
Quel giorno più non vi leggemmo avante.
A Galeotto [a pander] was the book and writer too:
   that day therein we read no more.
137

11 *Siete voi qui, ser Brunetto?*
Are *you* here, Advocate Brunetto?
xv.30. Brunetto Latini, old and respected friend of Dante,
encountered in hell with other 'Sodomites'.

12 *La cara e buona imagine paterna.*
The dear and kindly paternal image.
83

13 *Considerate la vostra semenza:*
Fatti non foste a viver come bruti,

Ma per seguir virtute e canoscenza.
Consider your origins: you were not made that you
   might live as brutes, but so as to follow virtue and
   knowledge.
xxvi.118

14 *E quindi uscimmo a riveder le stelle.*
Thence we came forth to see the stars again.
xxxiv.139

15 *Puro e disposto a salire alle stelle.*
Pure and ready to mount to the stars.
Purgatorio, xxxiii.145

16 *E'n la sua volontade è nostra pace.*
In His will is our peace.
Paradiso, iii.85

17 *Tu proverai sì come sa di sale*
Lo pane altrui, e com'è duro calle
Lo scendere e'l salir per l'altrui scale.
You shall find out how salt is the taste of another
   man's bread, and how hard is the way up and down
   another man's stairs.
xvii.58

18 *L'amor che muove il sole e l'altre stelle.*
The love that moves the sun and the other stars.
xxxiii.145

DANTON 1759–1794

19 *De l'audace, et encore de l'audace, et toujours de*
l'audace!
Boldness, and again boldness, and always boldness!
Speech to the Legislative Committee of General Defence, 2 Sept.
1792. *Le Moniteur*, 4 Sept. 1792

20 Thou wilt show my head to the people: it is worth
showing.
5 Apr. 1794. Carlyle, *French Revolution*, bk.VI, ch.2

GEORGE DARLEY 1795–1846

21   O blest unfabled Incense Tree,
That burns in glorious Araby.
Nepenthe, l.147

CHARLES DARWIN 1809–1882

22 I have tried lately to read Shakespeare, and found it so
intolerably dull that it nauseated me.
Autobiography (ed. G. de Beer, 1974), p.83

23 A hairy quadruped, furnished with a tail and pointed
ears, probably arboreal in its habits.
Descent of Man (1871), ch.21

24 We must, however, acknowledge, as it seems to me,
that man with all his noble qualities,...still bears in his
bodily frame the indelible stamp of his lowly origin.
final words

25 I have called this principle, by which each slight
variation, if useful, is preserved, by the term of
Natural Selection.
The Origin of Species (1859), ch.3

26 We will now discuss in a little more detail the struggle
for existence.

27 The expression often used by Mr Herbert Spencer of
the Survival of the Fittest is more accurate, and is
sometimes equally convenient.
See 514:30

28 It is interesting to contemplate an entangled bank,

clothed with many plants of many kinds, with birds singing on the bushes, with various insects flitting about, and with worms crawling through the damp earth, and to reflect that these elaborately constructed forms, so different from each other, and dependent upon each other in so complex a manner, have all been produced by laws acting around us...Growth with Reproduction; Inheritance...Variability...a Ratio of Increase so high as to lead to a Struggle for Life, and as a consequence to Natural Selection, entailing Divergence of Character and the Extinction of less-improved forms.
ch.15

1 What a book a devil's chaplain might write on the clumsy, wasteful, blundering, low, and horribly cruel works of nature!
Letter to J.D. Hooker, 13 July 1856

ERASMUS DARWIN 1731–1802

2 A fool...is a man who never tried an experiment in his life.
Letter from Maria Edgeworth to Sophy Ruxton, 9 Mar. 1792

3 No, Sir, because I have time to think before I speak, and don't ask impertinent questions. [When asked if he found his stammering very inconvenient.]
Sir Francis Darwin, *Reminiscences of My Father's Everyday Life,* appendix to his edition of Charles Darwin, *Autobiography* (1877)

CHARLES DAVENANT 1656–1714

4 Custom, that unwritten law,
By which the people keep even kings in awe.
Circe, II.iii

SIR WILLIAM DAVENANT 1606–1668

5 Had laws not been, we never had been blam'd;
For not to know we sinn'd is innocence.
Dryden Miscellany, vi.i.226

6 In ev'ry grave make room, make room!
The world's at an end, and we come, we come.
The Law against Lovers, III.i

7 For I must go where lazy Peace
Will hide her drowsy head;
And, for the sport of kings, increase
The number of the dead.
The Soldier Going to the Field

JOHN DAVIDSON 1857–1909

8 A runnable stag, a kingly crop.
A Runnable Stag

SIR JOHN DAVIES 1569–1626

9 Wedlock, indeed, hath oft compared been
To public feasts where meet a public rout,
Where they that are without would fain go in
And they that are within would fain go out.
A Contention Betwixt a Wife, a Widow, and a Maid for Precedence, l.193

10 Skill comes so slow, and life so fast doth fly,
We learn so little and forget so much.
Nosce Teipsum, xix

11 I know my life's a pain and but a span,
I know my sense is mock'd in every thing;

And to conclude, I know myself a man,
Which is a proud and yet a wretched thing.
xlv

12 Wit to persuade, and beauty to delight.
Orchestra, v

SCROPE DAVIES c.1783–1852

13 Babylon in all its desolation is a sight not so awful as that of the human mind in ruins.
Letter to Thomas Raikes, May 1835. See T. Raikes, *Journal, 1831 to 1847* (1856), vol.ii

W.H. DAVIES 1870–1940

14 The simple bird that thinks two notes a song.
April's Charms

15 A rainbow and a cuckoo's song
May never come together again;
May never come
This side the tomb.
A Great Time

16 It was the Rainbow gave thee birth,
And left thee all her lovely hues.
The Kingfisher

17 What is this life if, full of care,
We have no time to stand and stare?
Leisure

BETTE DAVIS 1908–

18 Fasten your seatbelts. It's going to be a bumpy night.
All About Eve (1950), script by Joseph Mankiewicz

JEFFERSON DAVIS 1808–1889

19 All we ask is to be let alone.
Attr., Inaugural Address as President of the Confederate States of America, 18 Feb. 1861

THOMAS DAVIS 1814–1845

20 Come in the evening, or come in the morning,
Come when you're looked for, or come without warning.
The Welcome

CECIL DAY-LEWIS 1904–1972

21   Hurry! We burn
For Rome so near us, for the phoenix moment
When we have thrown off this traveller's trance
And mother-naked and ageless-ancient
Wake in her warm nest of renaissance.
Flight to Italy

22 Tempt me no more; for I
Have known the lightning's hour,
The poet's inward pride,
The certainty of power.
The Magnetic Mountain (1933), pt.III

23 It is the logic of our times,
No subject for immortal verse—
That we who lived by honest dreams
Defend the bad against the worse.
Where are the War Poets?

STEPHEN DECATUR 1779–1820

1 Our country! In her intercourse with foreign nations, may she always be in the right; but our country, right or wrong.
Decatur's Toast (1816), see A.S. Mackenzie, *Life of Decatur*, ch.xiv

DANIEL DEFOE 1661?–1731

2 The best of men cannot suspend their fate:
The good die early, and the bad die late.
Character of the late Dr. S. Annesley

3 We lov'd the doctrine for the teacher's sake.

4 Nature has left this tincture in the blood,
That all men would be tyrants if they could.
The Kentish Petition, addenda, l.11

5 I was born in the year 1632, in the city of York, of a good family, though not of that county, my father being a foreigner of Bremen, who settled first at Hull.
The Life and Adventures of Robinson Crusoe, pt.i

6 Robin, Robin, Robin Crusoe, poor Robin Crusoe! Where are you, Robin Crusoe? Where are you? Where have you been? [The parrot.]

7 It happened one day, about noon, going towards my boat, I was exceedingly surprised with the print of a man's naked foot on the shore, which was very plain to be seen in the sand. I stood like one thunderstruck, or as if I had seen an apparition.

8 I takes my man Friday with me.

9 In trouble to be troubl'd
Is to have your trouble doubl'd.
Robinson Crusoe, The Farther Adventures

10 Necessity makes an honest man a knave.
Serious Reflections of Robinson Crusoe, ch.2

11 Wherever God erects a house of prayer,
The Devil always builds a chapel there;
And 'twill be found, upon examination,
The latter has the largest congregation.
The True-Born Englishman, pt.i, l.1. See 32:14

12 From this amphibious ill-born mob began
That vain, ill-natur'd thing, an Englishman.
l.132

13 Your Roman-Saxon-Danish-Norman English.
l.139

14 Great families of yesterday we show,
And lords whose parents were the Lord knows who.
l.374

15 And of all plagues with which mankind are curst,
Ecclesiastic tyranny's the worst.
pt.ii, l.299

16 When kings the sword of justice first lay down,
They are no kings, though they possess the crown.
Titles are shadows, crowns are empty things,
The good of subjects is the end of kings.
l.313

CHARLES DE GAULLE 1890–1970

17 *On ne peut rassembler les français que sous le coup de la peur. On ne peut pas rassembler à froid un pays qui compte 265 spécialités de fromages.*
The French will only be united under the threat of danger. Nobody can simply bring together a country that has 265 kinds of cheese.
Speech after the *recul* of the R.P.P. at the elections of 1951

THOMAS DEKKER 1570?–1641?

18 That great fishpond (the sea).
The Honest Whore, pt.i.I.ii

19   The best of men
That e'er wore earth about him, was a sufferer,
A soft, meek, patient, humble, tranquil spirit,
The first true gentleman that ever breath'd.

20 Art thou poor, yet hast thou golden slumbers?
      Oh sweet content!
Art thou rich, yet is thy mind perplexed?
      Oh, punishment!
Dost thou laugh to see how fools are vexed
To add to golden numbers, golden numbers?
O, sweet content, O, sweet, O, sweet content!
      Work apace, apace, apace, apace;
      Honest labour bears a lovely face;
Then hey nonny, nonny; hey nonny, nonny.
Patient Grissil, Act I

21 Canst drink the waters of the crisped spring?
      O sweet content!
Swim'st thou in wealth, yet sink'st in thine own tears?
      O punishment!

22 Golden slumbers kiss your eyes,
Smiles awake you when you rise:
Sleep, pretty wantons, do not cry,
And I will sing a lullaby:
Rock them, rock them, lullaby.
IV.ii

WALTER DE LA MARE 1873–1956

23 Ann, Ann!
      Come! quick as you can!
There's a fish that *talks*
      In the frying-pan.
Alas, Alack

24 Oh, no man knows
Through what wild centuries
Roves back the rose.
All That's Past

25 Very old are we men;
Our dreams are tales
Told in dim Eden
By Eve's nightingales;
We wake and whisper awhile,
But, the day gone by,
Silence and sleep like fields
Of amaranth lie.

26 He is crazed with the spell of far Arabia,
They have stolen his wits away.
Arabia

27 Here lies a most beautiful lady,
      Light of step and heart was she;
I think she was the most beautiful lady
      That ever was in the West Country.
But beauty vanishes; beauty passes;
      However rare—rare it be;
And when I crumble, who will remember
      This lady of the West Country?
Epitaph

1 When I lie where shades of darkness
   Shall no more assail mine eyes.
   Fare Well, i

2 Memory fades, must the remembered
   Perishing be?

3 Look thy last on all things lovely,
   Every hour—let no night
   Seal thy sense in deathly slumber
   Till to delight
   Thou have paid thy utmost blessing;
   Since that all things thou wouldst praise
   Beauty took from those who loved them
   In other days.
   iii

4 In Hans' old Mill his three black cats
   Watch the bins for the thieving rats.
   Whisker and claw, they crouch in the night,
   Their five eyes smouldering green and bright:...
   Jekkel, and Jessup, and one-eyed Jill.
   Five Eyes

5 Nought but vast sorrow was there—
   The sweet cheat gone.
   The Ghost

6 Three jolly gentlemen,
   In coats of red,
   Rode their horses
   Up to bed.
   The Huntsmen

7 'Is there anybody there?' said the traveller,
   Knocking on the moonlit door.
   The Listeners

8 'Tell them I came, and no one answered,
   That I kept my word,' he said.

9 Never the least stir made the listeners.

10 Ay, they heard his foot upon the stirrup,
    And the sound of iron on stone,
    And how the silence surged softly backward,
    When the plunging hoofs were gone.

11 It's a very odd thing—
    As odd as can be—
    That whatever Miss T eats
    Turns into Miss T.
    Miss T

12 What is the world, O soldiers?
        It is I:
    I, this incessant snow,
        This northern sky;
    Soldiers, this solitude
        Through which we go
        Is I.
    Napoleon

13 And there, in the moonlight, dark with dew,
        Asking not wherefore nor why,
    Would brood like a ghost, and as still as a post,
        Old Nicholas Nye.
    Nicholas Nye

14 Three jolly Farmers
    Once bet a pound
    Each dance the others would
    Off the ground.
    Off the Ground

15 And still would remain

My wit to try—
My worn reeds broken,
    The dark tarn dry,
All words forgotten—
    Thou, Lord, and I.
The Scribe

16 Slowly, silently, now the moon
    Walks the night in her silver shoon.
    Silver

17 Of all the trees in England,
        Oak, Elder, Elm, and Thorn,
    The Yew alone burns lamps of peace
        For them that lie forlorn.
    Trees

18 Of all the trees in England,
        Her sweet three corners in,
    Only the Ash, the bonnie Ash
        Burns fierce while it is green.

DEMETRIUS THE CYNIC 1st cent. A.D.

19 *...si sociale animal et in commune genitus mundum ut
    unam omnium domum spectat...*
    ...if [man], being a social animal and created for a
    communal existence, regards the world as the one and
    only home for everyone...
    One of the prerequisites for a balanced stoical philosophy. Seneca,
    De Beneficiis, VII.i.7

SIR JOHN DENHAM 1615–1669

20 Youth, what man's age is like to be doth show;
    We may our ends by our beginnings know.
    Of Prudence, 1.225

21 Such is our pride, our folly, or our fate,
    That few, but such as cannot write, translate.
    To Richard Fanshaw (c. 1643, first printed 1648)

LORD DENMAN 1779–1854

22 Trial by jury itself, instead of being a security to
    persons who are accused, will be a delusion, a
    mockery, and a snare.
    Judgement in O'Connell v. the Queen, 4 Sept. 1844

C.J. DENNIS 1876–1938

23 Me name is Mud.
    The Sentimental Bloke: A Spring Song, st.2 (1916)

JOHN DENNIS 1657–1734

24 A man who could make so vile a pun would not
    scruple to pick a pocket.
    The Gentleman's Magazine (1781), p.324 (Edit. note)

25 Damn them! They will not let my play run, but they
    steal my thunder!
    W.S. Walsh, *Handy-book of Literary Curiosities*

THOMAS DE QUINCEY 1785–1859

26 The burden of the incommunicable.
    Confessions of an English Opium Eater, pt.i

27 So, then, Oxford Street, stony-hearted stepmother,
    thou that listenest to the sighs of orphans, and drinkest
    the tears of children, at length I was dismissed from
    thee.

1 It was a Sunday afternoon, wet and cheerless: and a duller spectacle this earth of ours has not to show than a rainy Sunday in London.
pt.ii, **The Pleasures of Opium**

2 Thou hast the keys of Paradise, oh just, subtle, and mighty opium!

3 Everlasting farewells! and again, and yet again reverberated—everlasting farewells!
pt.iii, **The Pains of Opium**

4 Murder Considered as One of the Fine Arts.
Essay

5 If once a man indulges himself in murder, very soon he comes to think little of robbing; and from robbing he comes next to drinking and sabbath-breaking, and from that to incivility and procrastination.
Supplementary Papers

6 There is first the literature of *knowledge*, and secondly, the literature of *power*.
Essays on the Poets; Pope

7 Books, we are told, propose to *instruct* or to *amuse*. Indeed!…The true antithesis to knowledge, in this case, is not *pleasure*, but *power*. All that is literature seeks to communicate power; all that is not literature, to communicate knowledge.
Letters to a Young Man, letter iii. De Quincey adds that he is indebted for this distinction to 'many years' conversation with Mr. Wordsworth'.

EDWARD STANLEY, EARL OF DERBY
1799–1869

8 When I first came into Parliament, Mr Tierney, a great Whig authority, used always to say that the duty of an Opposition was very simple—it was, to oppose everything, and propose nothing.
House of Commons, 4 June 1841

9 The foreign policy of the noble Earl [Russell]…may be summed up in two short homely but expressive words:—'meddle and muddle'.
Speech on the Address, House of Lords, 4 Feb. 1864

DESCARTES 1596–1650

10 *Cogito, ergo sum.*
I think, therefore I am.
Le Discours de la Méthode

11 *Le bon sens est la chose du monde la mieux partagée, car chacun pense en être bien pourvu.*
Common sense is the best distributed commodity in the world, for every man is convinced that he is well supplied with it.

12 *Repugnare ut detur vacuum sive in quo nulla plane sit res.*
[That] it is contrary to reason to say that there is a vacuum or space in which there is absolutely nothing.
Principia Philosophica, pt.II, xvi, tr. E.S. Haldane and G.R.T. Ross

CAMILLE DESMOULINS 1760–1794

13 My age is that of the *bon Sansculotte Jésus*, an age fatal to Revolutionists.
Answer at his trial. Carlyle, *French Revolution*, bk.vi, ch.2

PHILIPPE NÉRICAULT called DESTOUCHES
1680–1754

14 *Les absents ont toujours tort.*
The absent are always in the wrong.
L'Obstacle imprévu, I.vi

EDWARD DE VERE, EARL OF OXFORD
see OXFORD

ROBERT DEVEREUX, EARL OF ESSEX
see ESSEX

SERGE DIAGHILEV 1872–1929

15 *Étonne-moi.*
Said to Jean Cocteau who was questioning his lack of praise and encouragement in 1912. Cocteau continues, 'In 1917, the evening of the première of *Parade,* I surprised him'.
The Journals of Jean Cocteau, 1

CHARLES DIBDIN 1745–1814

16 Did you ever hear of Captain Wattle?
He was all for love and a little for the bottle.
Captain Wattle and Miss Roe

17 For a soldier I listed, to grow great in fame,
And be shot at for sixpence a-day.
Charity

18 In every mess I finds a friend,
In every port a wife.
Jack in his Element

19 What argufies sniv'ling and piping your eye?
Poor Jack

20 But the standing toast that pleased the most
Was—The wind that blows, the ship that goes,
And the lass that loves a sailor!
The Round Robin

21 Here, a sheer hulk, lies poor Tom Bowling,
The darling of our crew.
Tom Bowling

22 Faithful, below, he did his duty;
But now he's gone aloft.

THOMAS DIBDIN 1771–1841

23 Oh! what a snug little Island,
A right little, tight little Island!
The Snug Little Island

CHARLES DICKENS 1812–1870

BARNABY RUDGE

24 Rather a tough customer in argeyment, Joe, if anybody was to try and tackle him. [Parkes.]
ch.1

25 Something will come of this. I hope it mayn't be human gore. [Simon Tappertit.]
ch.4

26 Polly put the kettle on, we'll all have tea. [Grip.]
ch.17

27 'There are strings,' said Mr Tappertit, '…in the human

heart that had better not be wibrated.'
ch.22

1 Oh gracious, why wasn't I born old and ugly? [Miss Miggs.]
ch.70

BLEAK HOUSE

2 Jarndyce and Jarndyce still drags its dreary length before the Court, perennially hopeless.
ch.1

3 This is a London particular...A fog, miss.
ch.3

4 Educating the natives of Borrioboola-Gha, on the left bank of the Niger. [Mrs. Jellyby.]
ch.4

5 The wind's in the east...I am always conscious of an uncomfortable sensation now and then when the wind is blowing in the east. [Mr. Jarndyce.]
ch.6

6 I only ask to be free. The butterflies are free. Mankind will surely not deny to Harold Skimpole what it concedes to the butterflies!

7 'Not to put too fine a point upon it'—a favourite apology for plain-speaking with Mr Snagsby.
ch.11

8 He wos wery good to me, he wos! [Jo.]

9 He [Mr. Turveydrop] is celebrated, almost everywhere, for his Deportment. [Caddy.]
ch.14

10 'It was a maxim of Captain Swosser's', said Mrs Badger, 'speaking in his figurative naval manner, that when you make pitch hot, you cannot make it too hot; and that if you only have to swab a plank, you should swab it as if Davy Jones were after you.'
ch.17

11 The Professor made the same remark, Miss Summerson, in his last illness; when (his mind wandering) he insisted on keeping his little hammer under the pillow, and chipping at the countenances of the attendants. The ruling passion! [Mrs. Badger.]
See 377:13

12 What is peace? Is it war? No. Is it strife? No. [Mr. Chadband.]
ch.19

13 The Chadband style of oratory is widely received and much admired.

14 You are a human boy, my young friend. A human boy. O glorious to be a human boy!...
    O running stream of sparkling joy
    To be a soaring human boy! [Mr. Chadband.]

15 Jobling, there *are* chords in the human mind. [Guppy.]
ch.20

16 'It is,' says Chadband, 'the ray of rays, the sun of suns, the moon of moons, the star of stars. It is the light of Terewth.'
ch.25

17 Lo, the city is barren, I have seen but an eel.

18 It's my old girl that advises. She has the head. But I never own to it before her. Discipline must be maintained. [Mr. Bagnet.]
ch.27

19 It is a melancholy truth that even great men have their poor relations.
ch.28

20 Never have a mission, my dear child. [Mr. Jellyby.]
ch.30

21 England has been in a dreadful state for some weeks. Lord Coodle would go out, and Sir Thomas Doodle wouldn't come in, and there being nobody in Great Britain (to speak of) except Coodle and Doodle, there has been no Government.
ch.40

22 She's Colour-Sergeant of the Nonpareil battalion. [Mr. Bagnet.]
ch.52

THE CHIMES

23 O let us love our occupations,
Bless the squire and his relations,
Live upon our daily rations,
And always know our proper stations.
2nd Quarter

A CHRISTMAS CAROL

24 'God bless us every one!' said Tiny Tim, the last of all.
stave 3

25 It *was* a turkey! He could never have stood upon his legs, that bird. He would have snapped 'em off short in a minute, like sticks of sealing-wax.
stave 5

DAVID COPPERFIELD

26 'Somebody's sharp.' 'Who is?' asked the gentleman, laughing. I looked up quickly; being curious to know. 'Only Brooks of Sheffield,' said Mr Murdstone. I was relieved to find that it was only Brooks of Sheffield; for, at first, I really thought it was I.
ch.2

27 'I am a lone lorn creetur',' were Mrs Gummidge's words,...'and everythink goes contrairy with me.'
ch.3

28 'I feel it more than other people,' said Mrs Gummidge.

29 I'd better go into the house, and die and be a riddance! [Mrs. Gummidge.]

30 She's been thinking of the old 'un! [Mr. Peggotty, of Mrs. Gummidge.]

31 Barkis is willin'.
ch.5

32 'There was a gentleman here yesterday,' he said—'a stout gentleman, by the name of Topsawyer...he came in here,...ordered a glass of this ale—*would* order it—I told him not—drank it, and fell dead. It was too old for him. It oughtn't to be drawn; that's the fact.' [The Waiter.]

33 I live on broken wittles—and I sleep on the coals. [The Waiter.]

34 'When a man says he's willin',' said Mr Barkis,... 'it's

as much as to say, that a man's waitin' for a answer.'
ch.8

1 Experientia does it—as papa used to say. [Mrs. Micawber.]
ch.11

2 I have known him [Micawber] come home to supper with a flood of tears, and a declaration that nothing was now left but a jail; and go to bed making a calculation of the expense of putting bow-windows to the house, 'in case anything turned up,' which was his favourite expression.

3 I never will desert Mr Micawber. [Mrs. Micawber.]
ch.12

4 Annual income twenty pounds, annual expenditure nineteen nineteen six, result happiness. Annual income twenty pounds, annual expenditure twenty pounds ought and six, result misery. [Mr. Micawber]

5 Mr Dick had been for upwards of ten years endeavouring to keep King Charles the First out of the Memorial; but he had been constantly getting into it, and was there now.
ch.14

6 I am well aware that I am the 'umblest person going....My mother is likewise a very 'umble person. We live in a numble abode. [Uriah Heep.]
ch.16

7 The mistake was made of putting some of the trouble out of King Charles's head into my head.
ch.17

8 We are so very 'umble. [Uriah Heep].

9 'Orses and dorgs is some men's fancy. They're wittles and drink to me—lodging, wife, and children—reading, writing and 'rithmetic—snuff, tobacker, and sleep.
ch.19

10 I only ask for information. [Miss Rosa Dartle.]
ch.20

11 'It was as true', said Mr Barkis, '...as taxes is. And nothing's truer than them.'
ch.21. See 218:18

12 What a world of gammon and spinnage it is, though, ain't it! [Miss Mowcher.]
ch.22

13 Other things are all very well in their way, but give me Blood! [Mr. Waterbrook.]
ch.25

14 I assure you she's the dearest girl. [Traddles.]
ch.27

15 Accidents will occur in the best-regulated families; and in families not regulated by that pervading influence which sanctifies while it enhances the—a—I would say, in short, by the influence of Woman, in the lofty character of Wife, they may be expected with confidence, and must be borne with philosophy. [Mr. Micawber.]
ch.28

16 He told me, only the other day, that it was provided for. That was Mr Micawber's expression, 'Provided for.' [Traddles.]

17 'People can't die, along the coast,' said Mr Peggotty, 'except when the tide's pretty nigh out. They can't be born, unless it's pretty nigh in—not properly born, till

flood. He's a going out with the tide.'
ch.30

18 Mrs Crupp had indignantly assured him that there wasn't room to swing a cat there; but, as Mr Dick justly observed to me, sitting down on the foot of the bed, nursing his leg, 'You know, Trotwood, I don't want to swing a cat. I never do swing a cat. Therefore, what does that signify to *me*!'
ch.35

19 It's only my child-wife. [Dora.]
ch.44

20 Circumstances beyond my individual control. [Mr. Micawber.]
ch.49

21 I'm Gormed—and I can't say no fairer than that! [Mr. Peggotty.]
ch.63

DOMBEY AND SON

22 He's tough, ma'am, tough is J.B. Tough, and devilish sly! [Major Bagstock.]
ch.7

23 There was no light nonsense about Miss Blimber...She was dry and sandy with working in the graves of deceased languages. None of your live languages for Miss Blimber. They must be dead—stone dead—and then Miss Blimber dug them up like a Ghoul.
ch.11

24 As to Mr Feeder, B.A., Doctor Blimber's assistant, he was a kind of human barrel-organ, with a little list of tunes at which he was continually working, over and over again, without any variation.

25 If I could have known Cicero, and been his friend, and talked with him in his retirement at Tusculum (beautiful Tusculum), I could have died contented. [Mrs. Blimber.]

26 'Wal'r, my boy,' replied the Captain, 'in the Proverbs of Solomon you will find the following words, "May we never want a friend in need, nor a bottle to give him!" When found, make a note of.' [Captain Cuttle.]
ch.15

27 Train up a fig-tree in the way it should go, and when you are old sit under the shade of it. [Captain Cuttle.]
ch.19

28 Cows are my passion. [Mrs. Skewton.]
ch.21

29 Mr Toots devoted himself to the cultivation of those gentle arts which refine and humanize existence, his chief instructor in which was an interesting character called the Game Chicken, who was always to be heard of at the bar of the Black Badger, wore a shaggy white great-coat in the warmest weather, and knocked Mr Toots about the head three times a week.
ch.22

30 It's of no consequence. [Mr. Toots.]

31 The bearings of this observation lays in the application of it. [Bunsby.]
ch.23

32 Say, like those wicked Turks, there is no What's-his-name but Thingummy, and

What-you-may-call-it is his prophet! [Mrs. Skewton.]
ch.27

1 I positively adore Miss Dombey;—I—I am perfectly
sore with loving her. [Mr. Toots.]
ch.30

2 If you could see my legs when I take my boots off,
you'd form some idea of what unrequited affection is.
[Mr. Toots.]
ch.48

EDWIN DROOD

3 Stranger, pause and ask thyself the question, Canst
thou do likewise? If not, with a blush retire.
ch.4

4 'Dear me,' said Mr Grewgious, peeping in, 'it's like
looking down the throat of Old Time.'
ch.9

5 'Umps', said Mr Grewgious.
ch.11

GREAT EXPECTATIONS

6 Much of my unassisted self...I struggled through the
alphabet as if it had been a bramble-bush; getting
considerably worried and scratched by every letter.
After that, I fell among those thieves, the nine figures,
who seemed every evening to do something new to
disguise themselves and baffle recognition.
ch.7

7 Your sister is given to government. [Joe Gargery.]

8 'He calls the knaves, Jacks, this boy,' said Estella with
disdain, before our first game was out.
ch.8

9 I had cherished a profound conviction that her bringing
me up by hand, gave her no right to bring me up by
jerks.

10 On the Rampage, Pip, and off the Rampage, Pip; such
is Life! [Joe Gargery.]
ch.15

11 Get hold of portable property. [Wemmick.]
ch.24

12 You don't object to an aged parent, I hope?
[Wemmick.]
ch.25

13 'Have you seen anything of London, yet?' [Herbert.]
'Why, yes: Sir—but we didn't find that it come up to
its likeness in the red bills—it is there drawd too
architectooralooral.' [Joe Gargery.]
ch.27

14 'Halloa! Here's a church!...Let's go in!...Here's Miss
Skiffins! Let's have a wedding.' [Wemmick.]
ch.55

HARD TIMES

15 Now, what I want is, Facts...Facts alone are wanted in
life. [Mr. Gradgrind.]
bk.i, ch.1

LITTLE DORRIT

16 Whatever was required to be done, the Circumlocution
Office was beforehand with all the public departments

in the art of perceiving—HOW NOT TO DO IT.
bk.i, ch.10

17 Look here. Upon my soul you mustn't come into the
place saying you want to know, you know. [Barnacle
Junior.]

18 One remark...I wish to make, one explanation I wish
to offer, when your Mama came and made a scene of
it with my Papa and when I was called down into the
little breakfast-room where they were looking at one
another with your Mama's parasol between them
seated on two chairs like mad bulls what was I to do?
[Flora Finching.]
ch.13

19 The Great Fire of London was not the fire in which
your Uncle George's workshops was burned down.
[Mr. F.'s Aunt]

20 I hate a fool! [Mr. F.'s Aunt.]

21 Take a little time—count five-and-twenty,
Tattycoram. [Mr. Meagles.]
ch.16

22 There's milestones on the Dover Road! [Mr. F.'s
Aunt.]
ch.23

23 You can't make a head and brains out of a brass knob
with nothing in it. You couldn't when your Uncle
George was living; much less when he's dead. [Mr.
F.'s Aunt.]

24 He [Mr. Finching] proposed seven times once in a
hackney-coach once in a boat once in an pew once on
a donkey at Tunbridge Wells and the rest on his knees.
[Flora Finching.]
ch.24

25 I revere the memory of Mr F. as an estimable man and
most indulgent husband, only necessary to mention
Asparagus and it appeared or to hint at any little
delicate thing to drink and it came like magic in a pint
bottle it was not ecstasy but it was comfort. [Flora
Finching.]

26 Father is rather vulgar, my dear. The word Papa,
besides, gives a pretty form to the lips. Papa, potatoes,
poultry, prunes, and prism, are all very good words
for the lips: especially prunes and prism. [Mrs.
General.]
bk.ii, ch.5

27 Dante—known to that gentleman [Mr. Sparkler] as an
eccentric man in the nature of an Old File, who used to
put leaves round his head, and sit upon a stool for
some unaccountable purpose, outside the cathedral at
Florence.
ch.6

28 Once a gentleman, and always a gentleman. [Rigaud.]
ch.28

MARTIN CHUZZLEWIT

29 The Lord No Zoo. [Toby Chuzzlewit.]
ch.1

30 'The name of those fabulous animals (pagan, I regret
to say) who used to sing in the water, has quite
escaped me.' Mr George Chuzzlewit suggested
'Swans.' 'No,' said Mr Pecksniff. 'Not swans. Very
like swans, too. Thank you.' The
nephew...propounded 'Oysters.' 'No,' said Mr

Pecksniff,...'nor oysters. But by no means unlike oysters; a very excellent idea; thank you, my dear sir, very much. Wait. Sirens! Dear me! sirens, of course.' ch.4

1 Any man may be in good spirits and good temper when he's well dressed. There an't much credit in that. [Mark Tapley.] ch.5

2 Some credit in being jolly. [Mark Tapley.]

3 A highly geological home-made cake.

4 'Let us be merry.' Here he took a captain's biscuit. [Mr. Pecksniff.]

5 With affection beaming in one eye, and calculation shining out of the other. [Mrs. Todgers.] ch.8

6 Charity and Mercy. Not unholy names, I hope? [Mr. Pecksniff.] ch.9

7 'Do not repine, my friends,' said Mr Pecksniff, tenderly. 'Do not weep for me. It is chronic.'

8 Let us be moral. Let us contemplate existence. [Mr. Pecksniff.]

9 Here's the rule for bargains: 'Do other men, for they would do you.' That's the true business precept. [Jonas Chuzzlewit.] ch.11

10 'Mrs Harris,' I says, 'leave the bottle on the chimley-piece, and don't ask me to take none, but let me put my lips to it when I am so dispoged.' [Mrs. Gamp.] ch.19

11 Some people...may be Rooshans, and others may be Prooshans; they are born so, and will please themselves. Them which is of other naturs thinks different. [Mrs. Gamp.]

12 Therefore I *do* require it, which I makes confession, to be brought reg'lar and draw'd mild. [Mrs. Gamp.] ch.25

13 'She's the sort of woman now,' said Mould,...'one would almost feel disposed to bury for nothing: and do it neatly, too!'

14 He'd make a lovely corpse. [Mrs. Gamp.]

15 All the wickedness of the world is print to him. [Mrs. Gamp.] ch.26

16 'Sairey,' says Mrs Harris, 'sech is life. Vich likeways is the hend of all things!' [Mrs. Gamp.] ch.29

17 We never knows wot's hidden in each other's hearts; and if we had glass winders there, we'd need keep the shutters up, some on us, I do assure you! [Mrs Gamp.]

18 Our backs is easy ris. We must be cracked-up, or they rises, and we snarls...You'd better crack up, you had! [Chollop.] ch.33

19 Our fellow-countryman is a model of a man, quite fresh from Natur's mould!...Rough he may be. So air our Barrs. Wild he may be. So air our Buffalers. [Pogram.] ch.34

20 A lane was made; and Mrs Hominy, with the aristocratic stalk, the pocket handkerchief, the clasped hands, and the classical cap, came slowly up it, in a procession of one.

21 'To be presented to a Pogram,' said Miss Codger, 'by a Hominy, indeed, a thrilling moment is it in its impressiveness on what we call our feelings.'

22 'Mind and matter,' said the lady in the wig, 'glide swift into the vortex of immensity. Howls the sublime, and softly sleeps the calm Ideal, in the whispering chambers of Imagination.'

23 'The Ankworks package,'...'I wish it was in Jonadge's belly, I do,' cried Mrs Gamp; appearing to confound the prophet with the whale in this miraculous aspiration. ch.40

24 Oh Sairey, Sairey, little do we know wot lays afore us! [Mrs. Gamp.]

25 I know'd she wouldn't have a cowcumber! [Betsey Prig.] ch.49

26 'Who deniges of it?' Mrs Gamp enquired.

27 Ever since afore her First, which Mr Harris who was dreadful timid went and stopped his ears in a empty dog-kennel, and never took his hands away or come out once till he was showed the baby, wen bein' took with fits, the doctor collared him and laid him on his back upon the airy stones, and she was told to ease her mind, his owls was organs. [Mrs. Gamp.]

28 No, Betsey! Drink fair, wotever you do! [Mrs. Gamp.]

29 'Bother Mrs Harris!' said Betsey Prig....'I don't believe there's no sich a person!'

30 The words she spoke of Mrs Harris, lambs could not forgive...nor worms forget. [Mrs. Gamp.]

31 Which fiddle-strings is weakness to expredge my nerves this night! [Mrs. Gamp.] ch.51

32 Farewell! Be the proud bride of a ducal coronet, and forget me!... Unalterably, never yours, Augustus. [Augustus Moddle.] ch.54

NICHOLAS NICKLEBY

33 United Metropolitan Improved Hot Muffin and Crumpet Baking and Punctual Delivery Company. ch.2

34 EDUCATION.—At Mr Wackford Squeers's Academy, Dotheboys Hall, at the delightful village of Dotheboys, near Greta Bridge in Yorkshire, Youth are boarded, clothed, booked, furnished with pocket-money, provided with all necessaries, instructed in all languages living and dead, mathematics, orthography, geometry, astronomy, trigonometry, the use of the globes, algebra, single stick (if required), writing, arithmetic, fortification, and every other branch of classical literature. Terms, twenty guineas per annum. No extras, no vacations, and diet unparalleled. ch.3

35 He had but one eye, and the popular prejudice runs in

favour of two. [Mr. Squeers.]
ch.4

1 Serve it right for being so dear. [Mr. Squeers.]
ch.5

2 Subdue your appetites my dears, and you've conquered human natur. [Mr. Squeers.]

3 Here's richness! [Mr. Squeers.]

4 C-l-e-a-n, clean, verb active, to make bright, to scour. W-i-n, win, d-e-r, der, winder, a casement. When the boy knows this out of the book, he goes and does it. [Mr. Squeers.]
ch.8

5 As she frequently remarked when she made any such mistake, it would be all the same a hundred years hence. [Mrs. Squeers.]
ch.9

6 There are only two styles of portrait painting; the serious and the smirk. [Miss La Creevy.]
ch.10

7 Oh! they're too beautiful to live, much too beautiful! [Mrs. Kenwigs.]
ch.14

8 Sir, My pa requests me to write to you, the doctors considering it doubtful whether he will ever recuvver the use of his legs which prevents his holding a pen. [Fanny Squeers.]
ch.15

9 I am screaming out loud all the time I write and so is my brother which takes off my attention rather and I hope will excuse mistakes. [Fanny Squeers.]

10 I pity his ignorance and despise him. [Fanny Squeers.]

11 This is all very well, Mr Nickleby, and very proper, so far as it goes—so far as it goes, but it doesn't go far enough. [Mr. Gregsbury.]
ch.16

12 We've got a private master comes to teach us at home, but we ain't proud, because ma says it's sinful. [Mrs. Kenwigs.]

13 'What's the water in French, sir?' 'L'eau,' replied Nicholas. 'Ah!' said Mr Lillywick, shaking his head mournfully. 'I thought as much. Lo, eh? I don't think anything of that language—nothing at all.'

14 'It's very easy to talk,' said Mrs Mantalini. 'Not so easy when one is eating a demnition egg,' replied Mr Mantalini; 'for the yolk runs down the waistcoat, and yolk of egg does not match any waistcoat but a yellow waistcoat, demmit.'
ch.17

15 What's the demd total? [Mr Mantalini.]
ch.21

16 Language was not powerful enough to describe the infant phenomenon.
ch.23

17 'The unities, sir,...are a completeness—a kind of a universal dovetailedness with regard to place and time.' [Mr. Curdle.]
ch.24

18 She's the only sylph I ever saw, who could stand upon one leg, and play the tambourine on her other knee, like a sylph. [Mr. Crummles.]
ch.25

19 I am a demd villain! I will fill my pockets with change for a sovereign in half-pence and drown myself in the Thames...I will become a demd, damp, moist, unpleasant body! [Mr. Mantalini.]
ch.34

20 Bring in the bottled lightning, a clean tumbler, and a corkscrew. [The Gentleman in the Small-clothes.]
ch.49

21 All is gas and gaiters. [The Gentleman in the Small-clothes.]

22 My life is one demd horrid grind! [Mr. Mantalini.]
ch.64

23 He has gone to the demnition bow-wows. [Mr. Mantalini.]

THE OLD CURIOSITY SHOP

24 Is the old min agreeable? [Dick Swiveller.]
ch.2

25 What is the odds so long as the fire of soul is kindled at the taper of conwiviality, and the wing of friendship never moults a feather! [Dick Swiveller.]

26 Fan the sinking flame of hilarity with the wing of friendship; and pass the rosy wine. [Dick Swiveller.]
ch.7

27 Codlin's the friend, not Short. [Codlin.]
ch.19

28 If I know'd a donkey wot wouldn't go
To see Mrs Jarley's waxwork show,
Do you think I'd acknowledge him,
                              Oh no no!
ch.27

29 I never nursed a dear Gazelle, to glad me with its soft black eye, but when it came to know me well, and love me, it was sure to marry a market-gardener. [Dick Swiveller.]
ch.56. See 356:25

30 'Did you ever taste beer?' 'I had a sip of it once,' said the small servant. 'Here's a state of things!' cried Mr Swiveller....'She never tasted it—it can't be tasted in a sip!'
ch.57

31 It was a maxim with Foxey—our revered father, gentlemen—'Always suspect everybody.' [Sampson Brass.]
ch.66

OLIVER TWIST

32 Oliver Twist has asked for more! [Bumble.]
ch.2

33 Known by the sobriquet of 'The artful Dodger.'
ch.8

34 'Hard,' replied the Dodger. 'As nails,' added Charley Bates.
ch.9

35 There is a passion for hunting something deeply implanted in the human breast.
ch.10

36 I'll eat my head. [Mr. Grimwig.]
ch.14

37 I only know two sorts of boys. Mealy boys, and beef-faced boys. [Mr. Grimwig.]

1 Oh, Mrs Corney, what a prospect this opens! What a opportunity for a jining of hearts and house-keepings! [Bumble.]
ch.27

2 'If the law supposes that,' said Mr Bumble…'the law is a ass—a idiot.'
ch.51. See 140:12

OUR MUTUAL FRIEND

3 A literary man—*with* a wooden leg. [Mr. Boffin on Silas Wegg.]
bk.1, ch.5

4 Professionally he declines and falls, and as a friend he drops into poetry. [Mr. Boffin on Silas Wegg.]

5 Why then we should drop into poetry. [Boffin.]

6 Decline-and-Fall-Off-The-Rooshan-Empire. [Mr. Boffin.]

7 'Mrs Boffin, Wegg,' said Boffin, 'is a highflyer at Fashion.'

8 Meaty jelly, too, especially when a little salt, which is the case when there's ham, is mellering to the organ. [Silas Wegg.]

9 'It is Rooshan; ain't it, Wegg?'
'No, sir. Roman. Roman.'
'What's the difference, Wegg?'
'The difference, sir?—There you place me in a difficulty, Mr Boffin. Suffice it to observe, that the difference is best postponed to some other occasion when Mrs Boffin does not honour us with her company.'

10 Mr Podsnap settled that whatever he put behind him he put out of existence….Mr Podsnap had even acquired a peculiar flourish of his right arm in often clearing the world of its most difficult problems, by sweeping them behind him.
ch.11

11 The question [with Mr. Podsnap] about everything was, would it bring a blush into the cheek of the young person?

12 'This Island was Blest, Sir, to the Direct Exclusion of such Other Countries as—as there may happen to be. And if we were all Englishmen present, I would say,' added Mr Podsnap…'that there is in the Englishman a combination of qualities, a modesty, an independence, a responsibility, a repose, combined with an absence of everything calculated to call a blush into the cheek of a young person, which one would seek in vain among the Nations of the Earth.'

13 I think…that it is the best club in London. [Mr. Twemlow, on the House of Commons.]
bk.ii, ch.3

14 I don't care whether I am a Minx, or a Sphinx. [Lavvy.]
ch.8

15 A slap-up gal in a bang-up chariot.

16 O Mrs Higden, Mrs Higden, you was a woman and a mother, and a mangler in a million million. [Sloppy.]
bk.iii, ch.9

17 He'd be sharper than a serpent's tooth, if he wasn't as dull as ditch water. [Fanny Cleaver.]
ch.10

18 T'other governor. [Mr Riderhood.]
bk.iv, ch.1

19 I want to be something so much worthier than the doll in the doll's house. [Bella.]
ch.5

20 The dodgerest of the dodgers. [Mr. Fledgeby.]
ch.8

21 The Golden Dustman.
ch.11

PICKWICK PAPERS

22 He had used the word in its Pickwickian sense…He had merely considered him a humbug in a Pickwickian point of view. [Mr Blotton.]
ch.1

23 Heads, heads…!…five children—mother—tall lady, eating sandwiches—forgot the arch—crash—knock—children look round—mother's head off—sandwich in her hand—no mouth to put it in—head of a family off—shocking, shocking! [Jingle.]
ch.2

24 'I am ruminating,' said Mr Pickwick, 'on the strange mutability of human affairs.'
'Ah, I see—in at the palace door one day, out at the window the next. Philosopher, sir?'
'An observer of human nature, sir,' said Mr Pickwick.

25 Half-a-crown in the bill, if you look at the waiter.—Charge you more if you dine at a friend's than they would if you dined in the coffee-room. [Jingle.]

26 Not presume to dictate, but broiled fowl and mushrooms—capital thing! [Jingle.]

27 Kent, sir—everybody knows Kent—apples, cherries, hops, and women. [Jingle.]

28 'It wasn't the wine,' murmured Mr Snodgrass, in a broken voice, 'It was the salmon.'
ch.8

29 I wants to make your flesh creep. [The Fat Boy.]

30 'It's always best on these occasions to do what the mob do.' 'But suppose there are two mobs?' suggested Mr Snodgrass. 'Shout with the largest,' replied Mr Pickwick.
ch.13

31 'Can I unmoved see thee dying
      On a log,
         Expiring frog!' [Mrs. Leo Hunter.]
ch.15

32 'Sir,' said Mr Tupman, 'you're a fellow.' 'Sir,' said Mr Pickwick, 'you're another!'

33 Tongue; well that's a wery good thing when it an't a woman's. [Mr Weller.]
ch.19

34 Battledore and shuttlecock's a wery good game, vhen you an't the shuttlecock and two lawyers the battledores, in which case it gets too excitin' to be pleasant.
ch.20

35 Mr Weller's knowledge of London was extensive and peculiar.

36 Be wery careful o' vidders all your life. [Mr. Weller.]

1 The wictim o' connubiality, as Blue Beard's domestic chaplain said, with a tear of pity, ven he buried him. [Mr. Weller.]

2 'It's a wery remarkable circumstance, sir,' said Sam, 'that poverty and oysters always seem to go together.' ch.22

3 It's over, and can't be helped, and that's one consolation, as they always says in Turkey, ven they cuts the wrong man's head off. [Sam Weller.] ch.23

4 Dumb as a drum vith a hole in it, sir. [Sam Weller.] ch.25

5 Wery glad to see you, indeed, and hope our acquaintance may be a long 'un, as the gen'l'm'n said to the fi'pun' note. [Sam Weller.]

6 Our noble society for providing the infant negroes in the West Indies with flannel waistcoats and moral pocket handkerchiefs. ch.27

7 Wen you're a married man, Samivel, you'll understand a good many things as you don't understand now; but vether it's worth while goin' through so much to learn so little, as the charity-boy said ven he got to the end of the alphabet, is a matter o' taste. [Mr. Weller.]

8 'Eccentricities of genius, Sam,' said Mr Pickwick. ch.30

9 Keep yourself *to* yourself. [Mr. Raddle.] ch.32

10 Pursuit of knowledge under difficulties, Sammy? [Mr. Weller.] ch.33

11 A double glass o' the inwariable, [Mr. Weller.]

12 Poetry's unnat'ral; no man ever talked poetry 'cept a beadle on boxin' day, or Warren's blackin' or Rowland's oil, or some o' them low fellows. [Mr. Weller.]

13 Wot's the good o' callin' a young 'ooman a Wenus or a angel, Sammy? [Mr. Weller.]

14 'That's rather a sudden pull up, ain't it, Sammy?' inquired Mr Weller. 'Not a bit on it,' said Sam; 'she'll vish there wos more, and that's the great art o' letter writin'.'

15 If your governor don't prove a alleybi, he'll be what the Italians call reg'larly flummoxed. [Mr. Weller.]

16 She's a swellin' wisibly before my wery eyes. [Mr. Weller.]

17 It's my opinion, sir, that this meeting is drunk, sir! [Mr. Stiggins.]

18 A Being, erect upon two legs, and bearing all the outward semblance of a man, and not of a monster. [Buzfuz.] ch.34

19 Chops and Tomata sauce. Yours, Pickwick.

20 'Do you spell it with a "V" or a "W"?' inquired the judge. 'That depends upon the taste and fancy of the speller, my Lord,' replied Sam.

21 Put it down a we, my Lord, put it down a we. [Mr. Weller.]

22 'Little to do, and plenty to get, I suppose?' said Sergeant Buzfuz, with jocularity. 'Oh, quite enough to get, sir, as the soldier said ven they ordered him three hundred and fifty lashes,' replied Sam. 'You must not tell us what the soldier, or any other man, said, sir,' interposed the judge; 'it's not evidence.'

23 'Yes, I have a pair of eyes,' replied Sam, 'and that's just it. If they wos a pair o' patent double million magnifyin' gas microscopes of hextra power, p'raps I might be able to see through a flight o' stairs and a deal door; but bein' only eyes, you see my wision's limited.'

24 Oh Sammy, Sammy, vy worn't there a alleybi! [Mr. Weller.]

25 Miss Bolo rose from the table considerably agitated, and went straight home, in a flood of tears and a Sedan chair. ch.35

26 A friendly swarry, consisting of a boiled leg of mutton with the usual trimmings. ch.37

27 'That 'ere young lady,' replied Sam. 'She knows wot's wot, she does.'

28 *We* know, Mr Weller—we, who are men of the world—that a good uniform must work its way with the women, sooner or later. [The Gentleman in Blue.]

29 You're a amiably-disposed young man, sir, I don't think. [Sam Weller.] ch.38

30 'And a bird-cage, sir,' says Sam. 'Veels vithin veels, a prison in a prison.' ch.40

31 'It would make anyone go to sleep, that bedstead would, whether they wanted to or not.' [Mr. Roker.] 'I should think,' said Sam,...'poppies was nothing to it.' ch.41

32 *They* don't mind it; it's a regular holiday to them—all porter and skittles. [Sam Weller.]

33 The have-his-carcase, next to the perpetual motion, is vun of the blessedest things as wos ever made. [Sam Weller.] ch.43

34 Anythin' for a quiet life, as the man said wen he took the sitivation at the lighthouse. [Sam Weller.]

35 Wich puts me in mind o' the man as killed hisself on principle, wich o' course you've heerd on, sir. [Sam Weller.] ch.44

36 Which is your partickler wanity? Vich wanity do you like the flavour on best, sir? [Sam Weller.] ch.45

37 You've got the key of the street, my friend. [Lowten.] ch.47

38 'Never...see...a dead postboy, did you?' inquired Sam...'No,' rejoined Bob, 'I never did.' 'No!' rejoined Sam triumphantly. 'Nor never vill; and there's another thing that no man never see, and that's

a dead donkey.'
ch.51

1 'Vell, gov'ner, ve must all come to it, one day or another.'
'So we must, Sammy,' said Mr Weller the elder.
'There's a Providence in it all,' said Sam.
'O' course there is,' replied his father with a nod of grave approval. 'Wot 'ud become of the undertakers vithout it, Sammy?'
ch.52

2 ''Cos a coachman's a privileged indiwidual,' replied Mr Weller, looking fixedly at his son. ''Cos a coachman may do vithout suspicion wot other men may not; 'cos a coachman may be on the wery amicablest terms with eighty mile o' females, and yet nobody think that he ever means to marry any vun among them.'

SKETCHES BY BOZ

3 A smattering of everything, and a knowledge of nothing. [Minerva House.]
Tales, ch.3. **Sentiment**

4 Grief never mended no broken bones, and as good people's wery scarce, what I says is, make the most on 'em.
Scenes, ch.22. **Gin-Shops**

A TALE OF TWO CITIES

5 It was the best of times, it was the worst of times, it was the age of wisdom, it was the age of foolishness, it was the epoch of belief, it was the epoch of incredulity, it was the season of Light, it was the season of Darkness, it was the spring of hope, it was the winter of despair, we had everything before us, we had nothing before us, we were all going direct to Heaven, we were all going direct the other way.
bk.i, ch.1

6 I pass my whole life, miss, in turning an immense pecuniary Mangle. [Mr. Lorry.]
ch.4

7 A likely thing...If it was ever intended that I should go across salt water, do you suppose Providence would have cast my lot in an island? [Miss Pross.]

8 If you must go flopping yourself down, flop in favour of your husband and child, and not in opposition to 'em. [Jerry Cruncher.]
bk.ii, ch.1

9 'I tell thee,' said madame—'that although it is a long time on the road, it is on the road and coming. I tell thee it never retreats, and never stops.' [Mme Defarge.]
ch.16

10 'It is possible—that it may not come, during our lives...We shall not see the triumph.' [Defarge.]
'We shall have helped it,' returned madame.

11 There might be medical doctors...a cocking their medical eyes. [Jerry Cruncher.]
bk.iii, ch.9

12 It is a far, far better thing that I do, than I have ever done; it is a far, far better rest that I go to, than I have ever known. [Sydney Carton's thoughts on the scaffold.]
ch.15

EMILY DICKINSON 1830–1886

13 After great pain, a formal feeling comes—
The Nerves sit ceremonious, like Tombs—
The stiff Heart questions was it He, that bore,
And Yesterday, or Centuries before?
After great pain, a formal feeling comes

14 This is the Hour of Lead—
Remembered, if outlived,
As Freezing persons, recollect the Snow—
First—Chill—then Stupor—then the letting go.

15 Because I could not stop for Death—
He kindly stopped for me—
The Carriage held but just Ourselves—
And Immortality.
Because I could not stop for Death

16 Since then—'tis Centuries—and yet
Feels shorter than the Day
I first surmised the Horses Heads
Were toward Eternity.

17 The Bustle in a House
The Morning after Death
Is solemnest of industries
Enacted upon Earth—

The Sweeping up the Heart
And putting love away
We shall not want to use again
Until Eternity.
The Bustle in a House

18 What fortitude the Soul contains,
That it can so endure
The accent of a coming Foot—
The opening of a Door.
Elysium is as far as to

19 I heard a Fly buzz—when I died...
With Blue—uncertain stumbling Buzz—
Between the light—and me—
And then the Windows failed—and then
I could not see to see.
I heard a Fly buzz—when I died

20 My life closed twice before its close;
It yet remains to see
If Immortality unveil
A third event to me,

So huge, so hopeless to conceive
As these that twice befel.
Parting is all we know of heaven
And all we need of hell.
My life closed twice before its close

21 The Soul selects her own Society—
Then—shuts the Door—
To her divine Majority—
Present no more.
The Soul selects her own Society

22 I've known her—from an ample nation—
Choose One—
Then—close the Valves of her attention—
Like Stone.

23 Success is counted sweetest
By those who ne'er succeed.
To comprehend a nectar
Requires sorest need.
Success is counted sweetest

1 There's a certain Slant of light,
Winter Afternoons—
That oppresses like the Heft
Of Cathedral Tunes—

Heavenly Hurt, it gives us—
We can find no scar,
But internal difference,
Where the Meanings, are.
There's a certain Slant of light

2 This quiet Dust was Gentlemen and Ladies
      And Lads and Girls—
Was laughter and ability and Sighing,
      And Frocks and Curls.
This quiet Dust was Gentlemen and Ladies

3 What Soft—Cherubic Creatures—
These Gentlewomen are—
One would as soon assault a Plush—
Or violate a Star—

Such Dimity Convictions—
A Horror so refined
Of freckled Human Nature—
Of Deity—ashamed.
What Soft—Cherubic Creatures

JOHN DICKINSON 1732–1808

4 Our cause is just. Our union is perfect.
Declaration on Taking Up Arms in 1775

5 Then join hand in hand, brave Americans all,—
By uniting we stand, by dividing we fall.
The Liberty Song (1768). *Memoirs of the Historical Soc. of Pennsylvania,* vol.xiv

DENIS DIDEROT 1713–1784

6 *L'esprit de l'escalier.*
Staircase wit.
An untranslatable phrase, the meaning of which is that one only thinks on one's way downstairs of the smart retort one might have made in the drawing-room. ***Paradoxe sur le Comédien***

7 *Voyez-vous cet oeuf. C'est avec cela qu'on renverse toutes les écoles de théologie, et tous les temples de la terre.*
See this egg. It is with this that all the schools of theology and all the temples of the earth are to be overturned.
Le Rêve de d'Alembert, pt.i

WENTWORTH DILLON, EARL OF ROSCOMMON
see ROSCOMMON

DIOGENES c.400–c.325 B.C.

8 *"μικρόν", εἶπεν, "ἀπὸ τοῦ ἡλίου μετάστηθι."*
Alexander...asked him if he lacked anything. 'Yea,' said he, 'that I do: that you stand out of my sun a little.'
Plutarch, *Life of Alexander,* 14 (North's translation)

DIONYSIUS OF HALICARNASSUS fl. 30–7 B.C.

9 History is philosophy from examples.
Ars Rhetorica, xi.2

BENJAMIN DISRAELI 1804–1881

10 Though I sit down now, the time will come when you will hear me.
Maiden speech, 7 Dec. 1837. Meynell, *Disraeli,* i.43

11 The Continent will not suffer England to be the workshop of the world.
House of Commons, 15 Mar. 1838

12 Thus you have a starving population, an absentee aristocracy, and an alien Church, and in addition the weakest executive in the world. That is the Irish Question.
16 Feb. 1844

13 The noble Lord [Lord Stanley] is the Rupert of Parliamentary discussion.
24 Apr. 1844. See 107:2

14 The right hon Gentleman [Sir Robert Peel] caught the Whigs bathing, and walked away with their clothes.
28 Feb. 1845

15 Protection is not a principle, but an expedient.
17 Mar. 1845

16 A Conservative Government is an organized hypocrisy.

17 He traces the steam-engine always back to the tea-kettle.
11 Apr. 1845

18 Justice is truth in action.
11 Feb. 1851

19 I read this morning an awful, though monotonous, manifesto in the great organ of public opinion, which always makes me tremble: Olympian bolts; and yet I could not help fancying amid their rumbling terrors I heard the plaintive treble of the Treasury Bench.
13 Feb. 1851

20 He [Sir C. Wood] has to learn that petulance is not sarcasm, and that insolence is not invective.
16 Dec. 1852

21 England does not love coalitions.

22 Finality is not the language of politics.
28 Feb. 1859

23 This shows how much easier it is to be critical than to be correct.
24 Jan. 1860

24 To put an end to these bloated armaments.
8 May 1862

25 He seems to think that posterity is a pack-horse, always ready to be loaded.
3 June 1862

26 Colonies do not cease to be colonies because they are independent.
5 Feb. 1863

27 You are not going, I hope, to leave the destinies of the British Empire to prigs and pedants.

28 Never take anything for granted.
Salthill, 5 Oct. 1864

29 I hold that the characteristic of the present age is craving credulity.
Meeting of Society for Increasing Endowments of Small Livings in the Diocese of Oxford, 25 Nov. 1864

30 Man, my Lord [Bishop Wilberforce], is a being born to believe.

1 Party is organized opinion.

2 Is man an ape or an angel? Now I am on the side of the angels.

3 Assassination has never changed the history of the world.
House of Commons, 1 May 1865

4 Change is inevitable. In a progressive country change is constant.
Edinburgh, 29 Oct. 1867

5 I had to prepare the mind of the country, and...to educate our party.

6 We have legalized confiscation, consecrated sacrilege, and condoned high treason.
House of Commons, 27 Feb. 1871

7 I believe that without party Parliamentary government is impossible.
Manchester, 3 Apr. 1872

8 You behold a range of exhausted volcanoes. (Of the Treasury Bench.)

9 Increased means and increased leisure are the two civilizers of man.

10 A University should be a place of light, of liberty, and of learning.
House of Commons, 11 Mar. 1873

11 An author who speaks about his own books is almost as bad as a mother who talks about her own children.
At Banquet given by Glasgow to Lord Rector, 19 Nov. 1873

12 Upon the education of the people of this country the fate of this country depends.
House of Commons, 15 June 1874

13 He is a great master of gibes and flouts and jeers. (The Marquis of Salisbury.)
5 Aug. 1874

14 Cosmopolitan critics, men who are the friends of every country save their own.
Guildhall, 9 Nov. 1877. See 129:28, 366:6

15 Lord Salisbury and myself have brought you back peace—but a peace I hope with honour.
House of Commons, 16 July 1878. See 412:19

16 A series of congratulatory regrets. (Lord Harrington's Resolution on the Berlin Treaty.)
At Banquet in Riding School, Knightsbridge, 27 July 1878

17 A sophistical rhetorician, inebriated with the exuberance of his own verbosity. (Gladstone.)

18 The hare-brained chatter of irresponsible frivolity.
Guildhall, London, 9 Nov. 1878

19 One of the greatest of Romans, when asked what were his politics, replied, *Imperium et Libertas.* That would not make a bad programme for a British Ministry.
Mansion House, London, 10 Nov. 1879

20 The key of India is London.
House of Lords, 5 Mar. 1881

21 Damn your principles! Stick to your party.
Attr. (To Bulwer Lytton.) Latham, *Famous Sayings*

22 Protection is not only dead, but damned. (c. 1850)
Monypenny and Buckle, *Life of Disraeli*, iii.241

23 Pray remember, Mr Dean, no dogma, no Dean.
iv.368

24 We authors, Ma'am. (To Queen Victoria.)
v.49

25 I am dead: dead, but in the Elysian fields. (Said to a peer on his elevation to the House of Lords.)
522

26 When I want to read a novel I write one.
vi.636

27 She is an excellent creature, but she never can remember which came first, the Greeks or the Romans. [Of his wife.]
G.W.E. Russell, *Collections and Recollections*, ch.1

28 Everyone likes flattery; and when you come to Royalty you should lay it on with a trowel.
(To Matthew Arnold.) ch.23

29 Your Majesty is the head of the literary profession. (To Queen Victoria.)

30 Never complain and never explain.
J. Morley, *Life of Gladstone*, i.122

31 Between ourselves, I could floor them all. This *entre nous*: I was never more confident of anything than that I could carry everything before me in that House. The time will come.
Letters, 7 Feb. 1833

32 In the 'Town' yesterday, I am told 'some one asked Disraeli, in offering himself for Marylebone, on what he intended *to stand.* "On my head," was the reply.'
8 Apr. 1833

33 There can be no economy where there is no efficiency.
To Constituents, 3 Oct. 1868

34 Tadpole and Taper were great friends. Neither of them ever despaired of the Commonwealth.
Coningsby (1844), bk.i, ch.1

35 No Government can be long secure without a formidable Opposition.
bk.ii, ch.1

36 The Arch-Mediocrity who presided, rather than ruled, over this Cabinet of Mediocrities.

37 Conservatism discards Prescription, shrinks from Principle, disavows Progress; having rejected all respect for antiquity, it offers no redress for the present, and makes no preparation for the future.
ch.5

38 'A sound Conservative government,' said Taper, musingly. 'I understand: Tory men and Whig measures.'
ch.6

39 Almost everything that is great has been done by youth.
bk.iii, ch.1

40 Youth is a blunder; Manhood a struggle; Old Age a regret.

41 It seems to me a barren thing this Conservatism—an unhappy cross-breed, the mule of politics that engenders nothing.
ch.5

42 I have been ever of opinion that revolutions are not to be evaded.
bk.iv, ch.11

43 The depositary of power is always unpopular.

1 Where can we find faith in a nation of sectaries?
ch.13

2 Man is only truly great when he acts from the
passions.

3 I grew intoxicated with my own eloquence.
Contarini Fleming (1832), pt.i, ch.7

4 Read no history: nothing but biography, for that is life
without theory.
ch.23

5 The practice of politics in the East may be defined by
one word—dissimulation.
pt.v, ch.10

6 His Christianity was muscular.
Endymion (1880), ch.14

7 The Athanasian Creed is the most splendid
ecclesiastical lyric ever poured forth by the genius of
man.
ch.54

8 The sweet simplicity of the three per cents.
ch.91. See 524:2

9 I believe they went out, like all good things, with the
Stuarts.
ch.99

10 What we anticipate seldom occurs; what we least
expected generally happens.
Henrietta Temple (1837), bk.ii, ch.4

11 Time is the great physician.
bk.vi, ch.9

12 They [the Furies] mean well; their feelings are strong,
but their hearts are in the right place.
The Infernal Marriage (1834), pt.i, 1

13 The blue ribbon of the turf. [The Derby.]
Life of Lord George Bentinck (1854), ch.26

14 Every day when he looked into the glass, and gave the
last touch to his consummate toilette, he offered his
grateful thanks to Providence that his family was not
unworthy of him.
Lothair (1870), ch.1

15 'I could have brought you some primroses, but I do
not like to mix violets with anything.'
'They say primroses make a capital salad,' said Lord
St Jerome.
ch.13

16 A Protestant, if he wants aid or advice on any matter,
can only go to his solicitor.
ch.27

17 London; a nation, not a city.

18 The gondola of London. [A hansom.]

19 When a man fell into his anecdotage it was a sign for
him to retire from the world.
ch.28

20 He was not an intellectual Croesus, but his pockets
were full of sixpences.

21 The greatest misfortune that ever befell man was the
invention of printing. Printing has destroyed
education...The essence of education is the education
of the body...What I admire in the order to which you
belong is that they do live in the air; that they excel in
athletic sports; that they can only speak one language;
and that they never read. This is not a complete
education, but it is the highest education since the

Greek.
ch.29

22 Every woman should marry—and no man.
ch.30

23 You know who the critics are? The men who have
failed in literature and art.
ch.35. See 157:26

24 'My idea of an agreeable person,' said Hugo Bohun,
'is a person who agrees with me.'
ch.41

25 St Aldegonde had a taste for marriages and public
executions.
ch.88

26 'I rather like bad wine,' said Mr Mountchesney; 'one
gets so bored with good wine.'
Sybil (1845), bk.i, ch.1

27 The Egremonts had never said anything that was
remembered, or done anything that could be recalled.
ch.3

28 To do nothing and get something, formed a boy's
ideal of a manly career.
ch.5

29 'Two nations; between whom there is no intercourse
and no sympathy; who are as ignorant of each other's
habits, thoughts, and feelings, as if they were dwellers
in different zones, or inhabitants of different planets;
who are formed by a different breeding, are fed by a
different food, are ordered by different manners, and
are not governed by the same laws.'
'You speak of—' said Egremont, hesitatingly.
'THE RICH AND THE POOR.'
bk.ii, ch.5

30 Little things affect little minds.
bk.iii, ch.2

31 Mr Kremlin himself was distinguished for ignorance,
for he had only one idea,—and that was wrong.
bk.iv, ch.5. See 275:34

32 I was told that the Privileged and the People formed
Two Nations.
ch.8

33 The Youth of a Nation are the trustees of Posterity.
bk.vi, ch.13

34 That fatal drollery called a representative government.
Tancred (1847), bk.ii, ch.13

35 A majority is always the best repartee.
ch.14

36 All is race; there is no other truth.

37 The East is a career.

38 London is a modern Babylon.
bk.v, ch.5

39 The microcosm of a public school.
Vivian Grey (1826), bk.i, ch.2

40 I hate definitions.
bk.ii, ch.6

41 Experience is the child of Thought, and Thought is the
child of Action. We cannot learn men from books.
bk.v, ch.1

42 There is moderation even in excess.
bk.vi, ch.1

43 I repeat...that all power is a trust—that we are
accountable for its exercise—that, from the people,

and for the people, all springs, and all must exist.
ch.7

1 All Paradise opens! Let me die eating ortolans to the sound of soft music!
The Young Duke (1831), bk.i, ch.10

2 A *dark* horse, which had never been thought of, and which the careless St James had never even observed in the list, rushed past the grand stand in sweeping triumph.
bk.ii, ch.5

3 'The age of chivalry is past,' said May Dacre. 'Bores have succeeded to dragons.'

4 A man may speak very well in the House of Commons, and fail very completely in the House of Lords. There are two distinct styles requisite: I intend, in the course of my career, if I have time, to give a specimen of both.
bk.v, ch.6

5 I never deny; I never contradict; I sometimes forget.
Said to Lord Esher of his relations with Queen Victoria. Elizabeth Longford, *Victoria R.I*, ch.27

6 I will not go down to posterity talking bad grammar.
Said while correcting proofs of his last Parliamentary speech, 31 March 1881. Blake, *Disraeli, ch.32*

7 There are three kinds of lies: lies, damned lies and statistics.
Attr. Mark Twain, *Autobiography*, I.246

ISAAC D'ISRAELI 1766–1848

8 He wreathed the rod of criticism with roses. [Bayle.]
Curiosities of Literature, 1834, vol.i, p.20

9 There is an art of reading, as well as an art of thinking, and an art of writing.
Literary Character, ch.11

AUSTIN DOBSON 1840–1921

10 And where are the galleons of Spain?
Ballad to Queen Elizabeth

11 Fame is a food that dead men eat,—
I have no stomach for such meat.
Fame is a Food that Dead Men Eat

12 The ladies of St James's!
   They're painted to the eyes,
Their white it stays for ever,
   Their red it never dies:
But Phyllida, my Phyllida!
   Her colour comes and goes;
It trembles to a lily,—
   It wavers to a rose.
The Ladies of St. James's

13 Time goes, you say? Ah no!
Alas, Time stays, *we* go.
The Paradox of Time

14 I intended an Ode,
   And it turned to a Sonnet.
It began *à la mode*,
I intended an Ode;
But Rose crossed the road
   In her latest new bonnet;
I intended an Ode;

And it turned to a Sonnet.
Rose-Leaves

PHILIP DODDRIDGE 1702–1751

15 O God of Bethel, by whose hand
   Thy people still are fed,
Who through this weary pilgrimage
   Hast all our fathers led.
Hymns (1755). **O God of Bethel**

MARY ABIGAIL DODGE
see GAIL HAMILTON

BUBB DODINGTON 1691–1762

16 Love thy country, wish it well,
   Not with too intense a care,
'Tis enough, that when it fell,
   Thou its ruin didst not share.
Spence, *Anecdotes*

AELIUS DONATUS fl. 4th cent. A.D.

17 *Pereant, inquit, qui ante nos nostra dixerunt.*
Confound those who have said our remarks before us.
St. Jerome, *Commentary on Ecclesiastes*, 1. Migne, *Patrologiae Lat. Cursus*, 23.390. See 544:16

JOHN DONNE 1571?–1631

18 Twice or thrice had I loved thee,
Before I knew thy face or name.
So in a voice, so in a shapeless flame,
Angels affect us oft, and worshipped be.
Air and Angels

19 And new philosophy calls all in doubt,
The element of fire is quite put out;
The sun is lost, and th'earth, and no man's wit
Can well direct him where to look for it.
And freely men confess that this world's spent,
When in the planets and the firmament
They seek so many new; they see that this
Is crumbled out again to his atomies.
'Tis all in pieces, all coherence gone;
All just supply and all relation.
An Anatomy of the World, First Anniversary, 1.205

20 She, she is dead; she's dead; when thou know'st this,
Thou know'st how dry a cinder this world is.
1.427

21 Cloth'd in her virgin white integrity.
Funeral Elegy, 1.75

22   Just such disparity
As is 'twixt air and Angels' purity,
'Twixt women's love, and men's will ever be.

23 All other things, to their destruction draw,
   Only our love hath no decay;
This, no to-morrow hath, nor yesterday,
Running it never runs from us away,
But truly keeps his first, last, everlasting day.
The Anniversary

24 Come live with me, and be my love,
And we will some new pleasures prove
Of golden sands, and crystal brooks,
With silken lines, and silver hooks.
The Bait. See 329:23, 404:9, 495:16

1 A naked thinking heart, that makes no show,
Is to a woman, but a kind of ghost.
The Blossom, 1.27

2   Meet me at London, then,
    Twenty days hence, and thou shalt see
Me fresher, and more fat, by being with men,
Than if I had stayed still with her and thee.
1.33

3 The day breaks not, it is my heart.
Break of Day (Attr. also to John Dowland)

4 For God's sake hold your tongue, and let me love.
The Canonization

5 Dear love, for nothing less than thee
Would I have broke this happy dream,
    It was a theme
For reason, much too strong for fantasy,
Therefore thou wak'd'st me wisely; yet
My dream thou brok'st not, but continued'st it.
The Dream

6 Love built on beauty, soon as beauty, dies.
Elegies, No.2. **The Anagram**

7 No Spring, nor Summer beauty hath such grace,
As I have seen in one Autumnal face.
No.9. **The Autumnal**

8 So, if I dream I have you, I have you.
For, all our joys are but fantastical.
No.10. **The Dream**

9 I will not look upon the quick'ning sun,
But straight her beauty to my sense shall run;
The air shall note her soft, the fire most pure;
Water suggest her clear, and the earth sure;
Time shall not lose our passages; the spring
How fresh our love was in the beginning;
The summer how it ripened in the ear;
And autumn, what our golden harvests were.
The winter I'll not think on to spite thee,
But count it a lost season, so shall she.
No. 12. **His Parting from Her**

10 By our first strange and fatal interview
By all desires which thereof did ensue.
No.16. **On His Mistress**

11   All will spy in thy face
A blushing womanly discovering grace.

12 Nurse, O! my love is slain; I saw him go
O'er the white Alps alone.

13 Whoever loves, if he do not propose
The right true end of love, he's one that goes
To sea for nothing but to make him sick.
No.18. **Love's Progress**

14   The straight Hellespont between
The Sestos and Abydos of her breasts.

15   We easily know
By this these angels from an evil sprite,
Those set our hairs, but these our flesh upright.
No.19. **Going to Bed**

16 Licence my roving hands, and let them go,
Before, behind, between, above, below.
O my America! my new-found-land,
My kingdom, safliest when with one man mann'd.

17 O strong and long-liv'd death, how cam'st thou in?
Epicedes and Obsequies. Elegy on Mrs. Boulstred, 1.21

18 Hail, Bishop Valentine, whose day this is,

All the air is thy Diocese.
Epithalamions. 1, **On the Lady Elizabeth and Count Palatine being Married on St. Valentine's Day**

19 The household bird, with the red stomacher.

20 So, so, break off this last lamenting kiss,
Which sucks two souls, and vapours both away,
Turn thou ghost that way, and let me turn this,
And let our selves benight our happiest day.
The Expiration

21 Where, like a pillow on a bed,
A pregnant bank swelled up, to rest
The violet's reclining head,
Sat we two, one another's best.
The Extasy

22 So to'entergraft our hands, as yet
Was all the means to make us one,
And pictures in our eyes to get
Was all our propagation.

23 And whilst our souls negotiate there,
We like sepulchral statues lay;
All day, the same our postures were,
And we said nothing, all the day.

24 But O alas, so long, so far
Our bodies why do we forbear?
They're ours, though they're not we, we are
The intelligencies, they the sphere.

25 So must pure lovers' souls descend
T'affections, and to faculties,
Which sense may reach and apprehend,
Else a great Prince in prison lies.

26 O wrangling schools, that search what fire
Shall burn this world, had none the wit
Unto this knowledge to aspire,
That this her fever might be it?
A Fever

27 Who ever comes to shroud me, do not harm
Nor question much
That subtle wreath of hair, which crowns my arm;
The mystery, the sign you must not touch,
    For 'tis my outward soul,
Viceroy to that, which then to heaven being gone,
    Will leave this to control,
And keep these limbs, her Province, from dissolution.
The Funeral

28 What ere she meant by it, bury it with me,
    For since I am
Love's martyr, it might breed idolatry,
If into other's hands these relics came;
    As 'twas humility
To afford to it all that a soul can do,
    So, 'tis some bravery,
That since you would save none of me, I bury some of you.

29 I wonder by my troth, what thou, and I
Did, till we lov'd? were we not wean'd till then?
But suck'd on country pleasures, childishly?
Or snorted we in the Seven Sleepers den?
The Good-Morrow

30 And now good morrow to our waking souls,
Which watch not one another out of fear.

31 Without sharp North, without declining West.

32 That All, which always is All everywhere,

Which cannot sin, and yet all sins must bear,
Which cannot die, yet cannot choose but die.
Holy Sonnets (1). **Annunciation**

1 Immensity cloistered in thy dear womb,
Now leaves his well belov'd imprisonment.
Nativity

2 I am a little world made cunningly
Of elements, and an angelic sprite.
Holy Sonnets (2), v

3 At the round earth's imagined corners, blow
Your trumpets, Angels, and arise, arise
From death, you numberless infinities
Of souls, and to your scattered bodies go.
vii

4 All whom war, dearth, age, agues, tyrannies,
Despair, law, chance, hath slain.

5 Death be not proud, though some have called thee
Mighty and dreadful, for thou art not so,
For those whom thou think'st thou dost overthrow,
Die not, poor death, nor yet canst thou kill me.
From rest and sleep, which but thy pictures be,
Much pleasure, then from thee much more must flow,
And soonest our best men with thee do go,
Rest of their bones and soul's delivery.
x

6 One short sleep past, we wake eternally,
And death shall be no more; death, thou shalt die.

7 What if this present were the world's last night?
xiii

8 Batter my heart, three person'd God; for, you
As yet but knock, breathe, shine, and seek to mend.
xiv

9 Take me to you, imprison me, for I
Except you enthrall me, never shall be free,
Nor ever chaste, except you ravish me.

10   As thou
Art jealous, Lord, so I am jealous now,
Thou lov'st not, till from loving more, thou free
My soul: whoever gives, takes liberty:
      O, if thou car'st not whom I love
Alas, thou lov'st not me.
Hymn to Christ, at the author's last going into Germany

11 Seal then this bill of my Divorce to all.

12 To see God only, I go out of sight:
      And to scape stormy days, I choose
      An everlasting night.

13 Wilt thou forgive that sin, where I begun,
Which is my sin, though it were done before?
Wilt thou forgive those sins through which I run
And do them still, though still I do deplore?
When thou hast done, thou hast not done,
      For I have more.

Wilt thou forgive that sin, by which I'have won
Others to sin, and made my sin their door?
Wilt thou forgive that sin which I did shun
A year or two, but wallowed in a score?
When thou hast done, thou hast not done,
      For I have more.
Hymn to God the Father

14 Since I am coming to that holy room,
Where, with thy quire of Saints for evermore,
I shall be made thy Music; as I come

I tune the instrument here at the door,
And what I must do then, think here before.
Hymn to God my God in My Sickness

15 Will no other vice content you?
The Indifferent

16 Rob me, but bind me not, and let me go.

17 And by Love's sweetest part, Variety, she swore.

18 And said, alas, some two or three
Poor heretics in love there be,
Which think to stablish dangerous constancy.

19 Stand still, and I will read to thee
A lecture, Love, in love's philosophy.
A Lecture in the Shadow

20 Love is a growing or full constant light;
And his first minute, after noon, is night.

21 When I died last, and, Dear, I die
As often as from thee I go,
Though it be but an hour ago,
And lovers' hours be full eternity.
The Legacy

22 Sir, more than kisses, letters mingle souls.
Letters to Severall Personages, To Sir Henry Wotton

23 And seeing the snail, which everywhere doth roam,
Carrying his own house still, still is at home,
Follow (for he is easy paced) this snail,
Be thine own palace, or the world's thy gaol.

24 If yet I have not all thy love,
Dear, I shall never have it all.
Lovers' Infiniteness

25 I long to talk with some old lover's ghost,
Who died before the god of love was born.
Love's Deity

26 Rebel and Atheist too, why murmur I,
As though I felt the worst that love could do?

27 'Tis the year's midnight, and it is the day's.
Nocturnal upon St. Lucy's Day

28   The world's whole sap is sunk:
The general balm th'hydroptic earth hath drunk.

29 As till God's great *Venite* change the song.
Of the Progress of the Soul, Second Anniversary, 1.44

30 Think then, my soul, that death is but a groom,
Which brings a taper to the outward room.
1.85

31   Her pure and eloquent blood
Spoke in her cheeks, and so distinctly wrought,
That one might almost say, her body thought.
1.244

32 Whose twilights were more clear, than our mid-day.
1.463

33 Thou art the proclamation; and I am
The trumpet, at whose voice the people came.
1.527

34 I sing the progress of a deathless soul.
Progress of the Soul, i

35 Great Destiny the Commissary of God.
iv

36 To my six lustres almost now outwore.
v

37 This soul to whom Luther, and Mahomet were

Prisons of flesh.
vii

1 So, of a lone unhaunted place possesst,
Did this soul's second inn, built by the guest,
   This living buried man, this quiet mandrake, rest.
xvi

2 Is any kind subject to rape like fish?
xxix

3 Nature's great masterpiece, an Elephant,
The only harmless great thing...
Still sleeping stood; vexed not his fantasy
Black dreams; like an unbent bow, carelessly,
   His sinewy proboscis did remissly lie.
xxxix

4   She knew treachery,
Rapine, deceit, and lust, and ills enow
To be a woman.
li

5 When my grave is broke up again
Some second guest to entertain,
(For graves have learnt that woman-head
To be to more than one a bed)
   And he that digs it spies
A bracelet of bright hair about the bone,
   Will he not let us alone?
The Relic

6   On a huge hill,
Cragged, and steep, Truth stands, and he that will
Reach her, about must, and about must go.
Satyre III, l.79

7 Sweetest love, I do not go,
For weariness of thee,
Nor in hope the world can show
A fitter Love for me;
   But since that I
Must die at last, 'tis best,
To use my self in jest
Thus by feigned deaths to die.
Song

8 Go, and catch a falling star,
Get with child a mandrake root,
Tell me, where all past years are,
Or who cleft the Devil's foot.
Song, Go and Catch a Falling Star

9   And swear
          No where
Lives a woman true and fair.

10 Though she were true, when you met her,
And last, till you write your letter,
          Yet she
          Will be
False, ere I come, to two, or three.

11   Busy old fool, unruly Sun,
          Why dost thou thus,
Through windows, and through curtains call on us?
Must to thy motions lovers' seasons run?
The Sun Rising

12 Love, all alike, no season knows, nor clime,
Nor hours, days, months, which are the rags of time.

13 This bed thy centre is, these walls thy sphere.

14 Send me not this, nor that, t'increase my store,

But swear thou think'st I love thee, and no more.
The Token

15 I am two fools, I know,
For loving, and for saying so
In whining Poetry.
The Triple Fool

16 I have done one braver thing
Than all the Worthies did,
And yet a braver thence doth spring,
Which is, to keep that hid.
The Undertaking

17 So let us melt, and make no noise,
No tear-floods, nor sigh-tempests move,
'Twere profanation of our joys
To tell the laity our love.
A Valediction Forbidding Mourning

18 Thy firmness makes my circle just,
And makes me end, where I begun.

19 But I do nothing upon my self, and yet I am mine own
Executioner.
Devotions upon Emergent Occasions. Meditation XII

20 No man is an *Island*, entire of it self; every man is a
piece of the *Continent*, a part of the *main*; if a *clod* be
washed away by the *sea*, *Europe* is the less, as well as
if a *promontory* were, as well as if a *manor* of thy
friends or of *thine own* were; any man's *death*
diminishes *me*, because I am involved in *Mankind*;
And therefore never send to know for whom the *bell*
tolls; It tolls for *thee.*
Meditation XVII

21 John Donne, Anne Donne, Un-done.
Letter to his Wife

22 Man is but earth; 'Tis true; but earth is the centre.
That man who dwells upon himself, who is always
conversant in himself, rests in his true centre.
LXXX Sermons (1640), v, Christmas Day, 1627

23 It [Death] comes equally to us all, and makes us all
equal when it comes. The ashes of an Oak in the
Chimney, are no epitaph of that Oak, to tell me how
high or how large that was; It tells me not what flocks
it sheltered while it stood, nor what men it hurt when
it fell. The dust of great persons' graves is speechless
too, it says nothing, it distinguishes nothing: As soon
the dust of a wretch whom thou wouldest not, as of a
Prince whom thou couldest not look upon, will trouble
thine eyes, if the wind blow it thither; and when a
whirlwind hath blown the dust of the Churchyard into
the Church, and the man sweeps out the dust of the
Church into the Churchyard, who will undertake to sift
those dusts again, and to pronounce, This is the
Patrician, this is the noble flower, and this the
yeomanly, this the Plebeian bran.
xv, 8 March 1621/2

24 There is nothing that God hath established in a
constant course of nature, and which therefore is done
every day, but would seem a Miracle, and exercise our
admiration, if it were done but once.
xxii, Easter Day, 25 March 1627

25 Poor intricated soul! Riddling, perplexed,
labyrinthical soul!
xlviii, 25 Jan. 1628/9

26 A day that hath no *pridie*, nor *postridie*, yesterday
doth not usher it in, nor tomorrow shall not drive it

out. *Methusalem*, with all his hundreds of years, was but a mushroom of a night's growth, to this day, And all the four Monarchies, with all their thousands of years, and all the powerful Kings and all the beautiful Queens of this world, were but as a bed of flowers, some gathered at six, some at seven, some at eight, All in one Morning, in respect of this Day.
lxxiii, 30 Apr. 1626. **Eternity**

1 I throw myself down in my Chamber, and I call in, and invite God, and his Angels thither, and when they are there, I neglect God and his Angels, for the noise of a fly, for the rattling of a coach, for the whining of a door.
lxxx, 12 Dec. 1626. **At the Funeral of Sir William Cokayne**

2 A memory of yesterday's pleasures, a fear of tomorrow's dangers, a straw under my knee, a noise in mine ear, a light in mine eye, an anything, a nothing, a fancy, a Chimera in my brain, troubles me in my prayer. So certainly is there nothing, nothing in spiritual things, perfect in this world.

3 They shall awake as *Jacob* did, and say as *Jacob* said, *Surely the Lord is in this place,* and *this is no other but the house of God, and the gate of heaven,* And into that gate they shall enter, and in that house they shall dwell, where there shall be no Cloud nor Sun, no darkness nor dazzling, but one equal light, no noise nor silence, but one equal music, no fears nor hopes, but one equal possession, no foes nor friends, but one equal communion and Identity, no ends nor beginnings, but one equal eternity.
XXVI Sermons (1660), x, 29 Feb 1627/8

LORD ALFRED DOUGLAS 1870–1945

4 I am the Love that dare not speak its name.
Two Loves

BISHOP GAVIN DOUGLAS 1474?–1522

5 And all small fowlys singis on the spray: Welcum the lord of lycht and lamp of day.
Eneados, bk.xii, prol.l.251

JAMES DOUGLAS, EARL OF MORTON d. 1581

6 Here lies he who neither feared nor flattered any flesh.
Of John Knox, said as he was buried, 26 Nov. 1572. G.R. Preedy, *Life of John Knox,* VII

KEITH DOUGLAS 1920–1944

7 If at times my eyes are lenses through which the brain explores constellations of feeling my ears yielding like swinging doors admit princes to the corridors into the mind, do not envy me. I have a beast on my back.
Fragment from *Bête Noire,* England, 1944

8 And all my endeavours are unlucky explorers come back, abandoning the expedition; the specimens, the lilies of ambition still spring in their climate, still unpicked: but time, time is all I lacked to find them, as the great collectors before me.
On a Return from Egypt, England, 1944

9 Remember me when I am dead and simplify me when I'm dead.
Simplify me when I'm dead, ?May 1941

10 But she would weep to see today how on his skin the swart flies move; the dust upon the paper eye and the burst stomach like a cave.

For here the lover and killer are mingled who had one body and one heart. And death who had the soldier singled has done the lover mortal hurt.
Vergissmeinnicht, Tunisia, 1943

LORENZO DOW 1777–1834

11 Observing the doctrine of Particular Election...and those who preached it up to make the Bible clash and contradict itself, by preaching somewhat like this: You can and you can't—You shall and you shan't—You will and you won't—And you will be damned if you do— And you will be damned if you don't.
Reflections on the Love of God, vi (1836), 30

ERNEST DOWSON 1867–1900

12 I have forgot much, Cynara! gone with the wind, Flung roses, roses, riotously, with the throng, Dancing, to put thy pale, lost lilies out of mind; But I was desolate and sick of an old passion,
    Yea, all the time, because the dance was long: I have been faithful to thee, Cynara! in my fashion.
Non Sum Qualis Eram

13 They are not long, the weeping and the laughter,
    Love and desire and hate:
I think they have no portion in us after
    We pass the gate.

They are not long, the days of wine and roses:
    Out of a misty dream
Our path emerges for a while, then closes
    Within a dream.
Vitae Summa Brevis

SIR ARTHUR CONAN DOYLE 1859–1930

14 What of the bow? The bow was made in England: Of true wood, of yew-wood, The wood of English bows.
Song of the Bow

15 Singularity is almost invariably a clue. The more featureless and commonplace a crime is, the more difficult is it to bring it home.
The Adventures of Sherlock Holmes. **The Boscombe Valley Mystery**

16 A little monograph on the ashes of one hundred and forty different varieties of pipe, cigar, and cigarette tobacco.

17 The husband was a teetotaller, there was no other woman, and the conduct complained of was that he had drifted into the habit of winding up every meal by taking out his false teeth and hurling them at his wife.
A Case of Identity

18 It has long been an axiom of mine that the little things are infinitely the most important.

1 It is my belief, Watson, founded upon my experience, that the lowest and vilest alleys of London do not present a more dreadful record of sin than does the smiling and beautiful countryside.
Copper Beeches

2 A man should keep his little brain attic stocked with all the furniture that he is likely to use, and the rest he can put away in the lumber room of his library, where he can get it if he wants it.
Five Orange Pips

3 It is quite a three-pipe problem.
The Red-Headed League

4 I have nothing to do to-day. My practice is never very absorbing.

5 To Sherlock Holmes she [Irene Adler] is always *the* woman.
Scandal in Bohemia

6 You see, but you do not observe.

7 It is a capital mistake to theorize before one has data.

8 You know my methods, Watson.
The Memoirs of Sherlock Holmes. The Crooked Man

9 'Excellent!' I [Dr. Watson] cried. 'Elementary,' said he [Holmes].

10 'It is my duty to warn you that it will be used against you,' cried the Inspector, with the magnificent fair play of the British criminal law.
Dancing Men

11 He [Professor Moriarty] is the Napoleon of crime.
The Final Problem

12 'The practice is quiet,' said I [Dr. Watson], 'and I have an accommodating neighbour.'

13 My practice could get along very well for a day or two.
The Naval Treaty

14 You mentioned your name as if I should recognize it, but beyond the obvious facts that you are a bachelor, a solicitor, a Freemason, and an asthmatic, I know nothing whatever about you.
The Norwood Builder

15 A long shot, Watson; a very long shot!
Silver Blaze

16 'Is there any other point to which you would wish to draw my attention?'
'To the curious incident of the dog in the night-time.'
'The dog did nothing in the night-time.'
'That was the curious incident,' remarked Sherlock Holmes.

17 We have not yet met our Waterloo, Watson, but this is our Marengo.
The Return of Sherlock Holmes. Abbey Grange

18 You will ruin no more lives as you ruined mine. You will wring no more hearts as you wrung mine. I will free the world of a poisonous thing. Take that, you hound, and that!—and that!—and that!—and that!
Charles Augustus Milverton

19 Now, Watson, the fair sex is your department.
The Second Stain

20 There is a spirituality about the face, however...which the typewriter does not generate. The lady is a musician.
The Solitary Cyclist

21 All other men are specialists, but his specialism is omniscience.
His Last Bow. Bruce-Partington Plans

22 'I [Sherlock Holmes] followed you—' 'I saw no one.' 'That is what you may expect to see when I follow you.'
The Devil's Foot

23 Good old Watson! You are the one fixed point in a changing age.
His Last Bow

24 But here, unless I am mistaken, is our client.
Wisteria Lodge

25 There is but one step from the grotesque to the horrible.

26 The giant rat of Sumatra, a story for which the world is not yet prepared.
The Case Book. Sussex Vampire

27 They were the footprints of a gigantic hound!
The Hound of the Baskervilles, ch.2

28 Detection is, or ought to be, an exact science, and should be treated in the same cold and unemotional manner. You have attempted to tinge it with romanticism, which produces much the same effect as if you worked a love-story or an elopement into the fifth proposition of Euclid.
The Sign of Four

29 An experience of women which extends over many nations and three separate continents.

30 How often have I said to you that when you have eliminated the impossible, whatever remains, *however improbable*, must be the truth?

31 You know my methods. Apply them.

32 The Baker Street irregulars.

33 London, that great cesspool into which all the loungers of the Empire are irresistibly drained.
A Study in Scarlet

34 'Wonderful!' I [Dr. Watson] ejaculated. 'Commonplace,' said Holmes.

35 'I should have more faith,' he said; 'I ought to know by this time that when a fact appears opposed to a long train of deductions it invariably proves to be capable of bearing some other interpretation.'

36 'I am inclined to think—' said I [Dr Watson]. 'I should do so,' Sherlock Holmes remarked, impatiently.
The Valley of Fear

37 The vocabulary of 'Bradshaw' is nervous and terse, but limited.

38 Mediocrity knows nothing higher than itself, but talent instantly recognizes genius.

SIR FRANCIS DOYLE 1810–1888

39 Last night, among his fellow roughs, He jested, quaff'd, and swore.
The Private of the Buffs

40 His creed no parson ever knew, For this was still his 'simple plan,' To have with clergymen to do

As little as a Christian can.
The Unobtrusive Christian

SIR FRANCIS DRAKE 1540?–1596

1 There must be a beginning of any great matter, but the continuing unto the end until it be thoroughly finished yields the true glory.
Dispatch to Sir Francis Walsingham, 17 May 1587. Navy Records Society, vol. XI (1898), p.134

2 There is plenty of time to win this game, and to thrash the Spaniards too.
Attr. D.N.B.

3 I remember Drake, in the vaunting style of a soldier, would call the Enterprise the singeing of the King of Spain's Beard. (Of the expedition to Cadiz, 1587.)
Bacon, *Considerations touching a War with Spain* (*Harleian Misc.* 1745, vol.v, p.85, col.1)

4 I must have the gentleman to haul and draw with the mariner, and the mariner with the gentleman…I would know him, that would refuse to set his hand to a rope, but I know there is not any such here.
Corbett, *Drake and the Tudor Navy*, i.249

JOSEPH RODMAN DRAKE 1795–1820

5 Forever float that standard sheet!
Where breathes the foe but falls before us,
With Freedom's soil beneath our feet,
And Freedom's banner streaming o'er us?
The American Flag, New York Evening Post, 29 May 1819.
Attr. also to Fitz-Greene Halleck

MICHAEL DRAYTON 1562–1631

6 Ill news hath wings, and with the wind doth go,
Comfort's a cripple and comes ever slow.
The Barrons' Wars, bk.II, xxviii

7 He of a temper was so absolute,
As that it seem'd when Nature him began,
She meant to shew all, that might be in man.
bk.III, xl

8 The mind is free, whate'er afflict the man,
A King's a King, do Fortune what she can.
bk.V, xxxvi

9 Thus when we fondly flatter our desires,
Our best conceits do prove the greatest liars.
bk.VI, xciv

10 Fair stood the wind for France
When we our sails advance,
Nor now to prove our chance
     Longer will tarry.
To the Cambro-Britons. **Agincourt**

11 O when shall English men
With such acts fill a pen?
Or England breed again
     Such a King Harry?

12 When Time shall turn those amber locks to grey,
My verse again shall gild and make them gay.
England's Heroic Epistles. **Henry Howard, Earl of Surrey, to the Lady Geraldine**, l.123

13 Had in him those brave translunary things,
That the first poets had. [Marlowe.]
To Henry Reynolds, of Poets and Poesy, l.106

14 For that fine madness still he did retain

Which rightly should possess a poet's brain.
l.109

15 Next these, learn'd Jonson, in this list I bring,
Who had drunk deep of the Pierian spring.
l.129

16 I pray thee leave, love me no more,
     Call home the heart you gave me,
I but in vain the saint adore,
     That can, but will not, save me.
To His Coy Love

17 These poor half-kisses kill me quite.

18 That shire which we the heart of England well may call. [Warwickshire.]
Poly-olbion, song xiii, l.2

19 Crave the tuneful nightingale to help you with her lay,
The ousel and the throstlecock, chief music of our May.
Shepherd's Garland, eclogue iii, 17–18

20 Queens hereafter shall be glad to live
Upon the alms of thy superfluous praise.
Sonnets. Idea, vi

21 Since there's no help, come let us kiss and part,
Nay, I have done: you get no more of me,
And I am glad, yea glad with all my heart,
That thus so cleanly, I myself can free,
Shake hands for ever, cancel all our vows,
And when we meet at any time again,
Be it not seen in either of our brows,
That we one jot of former love retain;
Now at the last gasp of Love's latest breath,
When his pulse failing, Passion speechless lies,
When Faith is kneeling by his bed of death,
And Innocence is closing up his eyes,
Now if thou wouldst, when all have given him over,
From death to life, thou might'st him yet recover.
lxi

WILLIAM DRENNAN 1754–1820

22 The men of the Emerald Isle.
Erin

JOHN DRINKWATER 1882–1937

23 Moon-washed apples of wonder.
Moonlit Apples

THOMAS DRUMMOND 1797–1840

24 Property has its duties as well as its rights.
Letter to the Earl of Donoughmore, 22 May 1838

WILLIAM DRUMMOND 1585–1649

25 Only the echoes which he made relent,
Ring from their marble caves repent, repent.
For the Baptist

26 Phoebus, arise,
And paint the sable skies,
With azure, white, and red.
Song (ii)

27 I long to kiss the image of my death.
Sonnet ix, **Sleep, Silence Child**

28   A morn
Of bright carnations did o'erspread her face.
xlvi

JOHN DRYDEN 1631–1700

1 In pious times, ere priestcraft did begin,
Before polygamy was made a sin.
Absalom and Achitophel, pt.i, l.1

2 Then Israel's monarch, after Heaven's own heart,
His vigorous warmth did, variously, impart
To wives and slaves: and, wide as his command,
Scatter'd his Maker's image through the land.
l.7

3 Whate'er he did was done with so much ease,
In him alone, 'twas natural to please.
l.27

4 The Jews, a headstrong, moody, murmuring race
As ever tried the extent and stretch of grace,
God's pampered people, whom, debauched with ease,
No king could govern nor no God could please.
l.45

5 Plots, true or false, are necessary things,
To raise up commonwealths and ruin kings.
l.83

6 Of these the false Achitophel was first,
A name to all succeeding ages curst.
For close designs and crooked counsels fit,
Sagacious, bold, and turbulent of wit,
Restless, unfixed in principles and place,
In power unpleas'd, impatient of disgrace;
A fiery soul, which working out its way,
Fretted the pigmy body to decay:
And o'er informed the tenement of clay.
A daring pilot in extremity;
Pleased with the danger, when the waves went high
He sought the storms; but for a calm unfit,
Would steer too nigh the sands to boast his wit.
Great wits are sure to madness near alli'd,
And thin partitions do their bounds divide.
l.150

7 Why should he, with wealth and honour blest,
Refuse his age the needful hours of rest?
Punish a body which he could not please;
Bankrupt of life, yet prodigal of ease?
And all to leave what with his toil he won
To that unfeather'd two-legged thing, a son.
l.165

8 In friendship false, implacable in hate:
Resolv'd to ruin or to rule the state.
l.173

9 The people's prayer, the glad diviner's theme,
The young men's vision and the old men's dream!
l.238

10 All empire is no more than power in trust.
l.411

11 Better one suffer, than a nation grieve.
l.416

12 But far more numerous was the herd of such
Who think too little and who talk too much.
l.533

13 A man so various that he seem'd to be
Not one, but all mankind's epitome.
Stiff in opinions, always in the wrong;
Was everything by starts, and nothing long:
But, in the course of one revolving moon,
Was chemist, fiddler, statesman, and buffoon.
l.545

14 Railing and praising were his usual themes;
And both (to show his judgement) in extremes:
So over violent, or over civil,
That every man, with him, was God or Devil.
l.555

15 In squandering wealth was his peculiar art:
Nothing went unrewarded, but desert.
Beggar'd by fools, whom still he found too late:
He had his jest, and they had his estate.
l.559

16 During his office treason was no crime,
The sons of Belial had a glorious time.
l.597

17 Youth, beauty, graceful action seldom fail:
But common interest always will prevail:
And pity never ceases to be shown
To him, who makes the people's wrongs his own.
l.723

18 For who can be secure of private right,
If sovereign sway may be dissolv'd by might?
Nor is the people's judgement always true:
The most may err as grossly as the few.
l.779

19 Never was patriot yet, but was a fool.
l.968

20 Beware the fury of a patient man.
l.1005

21 Doeg, though without knowing how or why,
Made still a blund'ring kind of melody;
Spurr'd boldly on, and dash'd through thick and thin,
Through sense and nonsense, never out nor in;
Free from all meaning, whether good or bad,
And in one word, heroically mad.
pt.ii, l.412

22 Rhyme is the rock on which thou art to wreck.
l.486

23   The god-like hero sate
    On his imperial throne;
    His valiant peers were plac'd around;
Their brows with roses and with myrtles bound.
    (So should desert in arms be crowned:)
The lovely Thais by his side,
Sate like a blooming Eastern bride
In flow'r of youth and beauty's pride.
    Happy, happy, happy, pair!
        None but the brave,
        None but the brave,
None but the brave deserves the fair.
Alexander's Feast, l.4

24   With ravish'd ears
    The monarch hears,
    Assumes the god,
    Affects to nod,
And seems to shake the spheres.
l.42

25 Bacchus ever fair, and ever young.
l.48

26 Sound the trumpets; beat the drums;
    Flush'd with a purple grace:
    He shows his honest face:
Now give the hautboys breath; he comes, he comes.
l.50

1 Drinking is the soldier's pleasure;
   Rich the treasure;
   Sweet the pleasure;
Sweet is pleasure after pain.
1.57

2 And thrice he routed all his foes, and thrice he slew
   the slain.
1.68

3 Fallen from his high estate,
   And welt'ring in his blood:
Deserted at his utmost need
By those his former bounty fed;
On the bare earth expos'd he lies,
With not a friend to close his eyes.
1.78

4 Revolving in his alter'd soul
   The various turns of chance below.
1.85

5 Softly sweet, in Lydian measures,
Soon he sooth'd his soul to pleasures.
War, he sung, is toil and trouble;
Honour but an empty bubble.
   Never ending, still beginning,
Fighting still, and still destroying,
   If the world be worth thy winning,
Think, oh think, it worth enjoying.
   Lovely Thais sits beside thee,
   Take the good the gods provide thee.
1.97

6 Sigh'd and look'd, and sigh'd again.
1.120

7 And, like another Helen, fir'd another Troy.
1.154

8 Could swell the soul to rage, or kindle soft desire.
1.160

9 Let old Timotheus yield the prize,
   Or both divide the crown;
He rais'd a mortal to the skies;
   She drew an angel down.
1.177

10 Errors, like straws, upon the surface flow;
He who would search for pearls must dive below.
All for Love, Prologue

11 My love's a noble madness.
II.i

12 Fool that I was, upon my eagle's wings
I bore this wren, till I was tired with soaring,
And now he mounts above me.

13   Give, you gods,
Give to your boy, your Caesar,
The rattle of a globe to play withal,
This gewgaw world, and put him cheaply off:
I'll not be pleased with less than Cleopatra.

14 The wretched have no friends.
III.i

15 Men are but children of a larger growth;
Our appetites as apt to change as theirs,
And full as craving too, and full as vain.
IV.i

16 Your Cleopatra; Dolabella's Cleopatra; every man's
Cleopatra.

17 Welcome, thou kind deceiver!
Thou best of thieves; who, with an easy key,
Dost open life, and, unperceived by us,
Even steal us from ourselves.
V.i

18 I am devilishly afraid, that's certain; but...I'll sing,
that I may seem valiant.
Amphitryon, II.i

19 Whistling to keep myself from being afraid.
III.i

20 I never saw any good that came of telling truth.

21 As one that neither seeks, nor shuns his foe.
Annus Mirabilis, xli

22 By viewing nature, nature's handmaid art,
   Makes mighty things from small beginnings grow:
Thus fishes first to shipping did impart,
   Their tail the rudder, and their head the prow.
clv

23 And on the lunar world securely pry.
clxiv

24 An horrid stillness first invades the ear,
And in that silence we the tempest fear.
Astraea Redux, l.7

25 He made all countries where he came his own.
1.76

26 Death, in itself, is nothing; but we fear,
To be we know not what, we know not where.
Aureng-Zebe, IV.i

27   None would live past years again,
Yet all hope pleasure in what yet remain;
And, from the dregs of life, think to receive,
What the first sprightly running could not give.

28 And made almost a sin of abstinence.
Character of a Good Parson, l.11

29 I am as free as nature first made man,
Ere the base laws of servitude began,
When wild in woods the noble savage ran.
The Conquest of Granada, pt.i, I.i

30 Forgiveness to the injured does belong;
But they ne'er pardon, who have done the wrong.
pt.ii, I.ii

31 Thou strong seducer, opportunity!
IV.iii

32 Old as I am, for ladies' love unfit,
The power of beauty I remember yet.
Cymon and Iphigenia, l.1

33 When beauty fires the blood, how love exalts the
   mind.
1.41

34 He trudg'd along unknowing what he sought,
And whistled as he went, for want of thought.
1.84

35 She hugg'd th' offender, and forgave th' offence.
1.367. See 22:1

36 Ill fortune seldom comes alone.
1.392

37 Of seeming arms to make a short essay,
Then hasten to be drunk, the business of the day.
1.407

38 Bold knaves thrive without one grain of sense,

But good men starve for want of impudence.
Epilogue to Constantine the Great

1 Theirs was the giant race before the flood.
Epistles, To Mr. Congreve, l.5

2 Heav'n, that but once was prodigal before,
To Shakespeare gave as much; she could not give him
   more.
1.62

3 How blessed is he, who leads a country life,
Unvex'd with anxious cares, and void of strife!
Who studying peace, and shunning civil rage,
Enjoy'd his youth, and now enjoys his age:
All who deserve his love, he makes his own;
And, to be lov'd himself, needs only to be known.
To John Driden of Chesterton, l.1

4 Lord of yourself, uncumber'd with a wife.
l.18

5 Better to hunt in fields, for health unbought,
Than fee the doctor for a nauseous draught.
The wise, for cure, on exercise depend;
God never made his work, for man to mend.
1.92

6 Ev'n victors are by victories undone.
1.164

7 His colours laid so thick on every place,
As only showed the paint, but hid the face.
To Sir R. Howard, l.75

8 Here lies my wife: here let her lie!
Now she's at rest, and so am I.
Epitaph Intended for Dryden's Wife

9 For he was great, ere fortune made him so.
Heroic Stanzas (On the Death of Oliver Cromwell), vi

10 She fear'd no danger, for she knew no sin.
The Hind and the Panther, pt.i, l.4

11 And doom'd to death, though fated not to die.
l.8

12 For truth has such a face and such a mien
As to be lov'd needs only to be seen.
1.33

13 My thoughtless youth was winged with vain desires,
My manhood, long misled by wandering fires,
Followed false lights; and when their glimpse was
   gone
My pride struck out new sparkles of her own.
Such was I, such by nature still I am;
Be Thine the glory, and be mine the shame!
Good life be now my task: my doubts are done;
(What more could fright my faith than Three in One?)
l.72

14 Reason to rule, but mercy to forgive:
The first is law, the last prerogative.
1.261

15 For all have not the gift of martyrdom.
pt.ii, 1.59

16 Either be wholly slaves or wholly free.
1.285

17 Much malice mingled with a little wit
Perhaps may censure this mysterious writ.
pt.iii, l.1

18 For present joys are more to flesh and blood
Than a dull prospect of a distant good.
1.364

19 By education most have been misled;
So they believe, because they so were bred.
The priest continues what the nurse began,
And thus the child imposes on the man.
1.389

20 The wind was fair, but blew a mack'rel gale.
1.456

21 T'abhor the makers, and their laws approve,
Is to hate traitors and the treason love.
1.706

22 For those whom God to ruin has design'd,
He fits for fate, and first destroys their mind.
1.1093. See 10:1, 199:15

23 And love's the noblest frailty of the mind.
The Indian Emperor, II.ii. See 420:20

24 Repentance is the virtue of weak minds.
III.i

25 For all the happiness mankind can gain
Is not in pleasure, but in rest from pain.
IV.i

26 That fairy kind of writing which depends only upon
the force of imagination.
King Arthur, Dedication

27 All heiresses are beautiful.
I.i

28 War is the trade of kings.
II.ii

29 Fairest Isle, all isles excelling,
Seat of pleasures, and of loves;
Venus here will choose her dwelling,
And forsake her Cyprian groves.
V. **Song of Venus**

30 Three poets, in three distant ages born,
Greece, Italy and England did adorn.
The first in loftiness of thought surpass'd;
The next in majesty, in both the last:
The force of nature could no farther go;
To make a third she join'd the former two.
Lines on Milton

31 Ovid, the soft philosopher of love.
Love Triumphant, II.i

32 Thou tyrant, tyrant Jealousy,
Thou tyrant of the mind!
Song of Jealousy

33 All human things are subject to decay,
And, when fate summons, monarchs must obey.
Mac Flecknoe, l.1

34 The rest to some faint meaning make pretence,
But Shadwell never deviates into sense.
Some beams of wit on other souls may fall,
Strike through and make a lucid interval;
But Shadwell's genuine night admits no ray,
His rising fogs prevail upon the day.
1.19

35 Thy genius calls thee not to purchase fame
In keen iambics, but mild anagram:
Leave writing plays, and choose for thy command
Some peaceful province in Acrostic Land.
There thou mayest wings display and altars raise,
And torture one poor word ten thousand ways.
1.203

36 I am resolved to grow fat and look young till forty,
and then slip out of the world with the first wrinkle and

the reputation of five-and-twenty.
The Maiden Queen, III.i

1 I am to be married within these three days; married
past redemption.
Marriage à la Mode, I.i

2 We loathe our manna, and we long for quails.
The Medal, l.131

3 But treason is not own'd when 'tis descried;
Successful crimes alone are justified.
l.207

4 Whatever is, is in its causes just.
Oedipus (1679), III.i

5 We know not what you can desire or hope,
To please you more, but burning of a *Pope*.
Epilogue

6 But love's a malady without a cure.
Palamon and Arcite, bk.ii, l.110

7 Fool, not to know that love endures no tie,
And Jove but laughs at lovers' perjury.
l.148. See 366:11

8 And Antony, who lost the world for love.
l.607

9 Repentance is but want of power to sin.
bk.iii, l.813

10 Since ev'ry man who lives is born to die,
And none can boast sincere felicity,
With equal mind, what happens, let us bear,
Nor joy nor grieve too much for things beyond our
care.
Like pilgrims to th' appointed place we tend;
The world's an inn, and death the journey's end.
l.883

11 A virgin-widow and a *Mourning Bride*.
l.927

12 But 'tis the talent of our English nation,
Still to be plotting some new reformation.
Prologue at Oxford, 1680

13 So poetry, which is in Oxford made
An art, in London only is a trade.
Prologue to the University of Oxon, 1684

14 Oxford to him a dearer name shall be,
Than his own mother University.
Thebes did his green unknowing youth engage,
He chooses Athens in his riper age.
Prologue to the University of Oxford

15 And this unpolished rugged verse I chose
As fittest for discourse and nearest prose.
Religio Laici, ad fin.

16 I strongly wish for what I faintly hope:
Like the day-dreams of melancholy men,
I think and think on things impossible,
Yet love to wander in that golden maze.
Rival Ladies, III.i

17 A very merry, dancing, drinking,
Laughing, quaffing, and unthinking time.
Secular Masque, l.39

18 Joy rul'd the day, and Love the night.
l.81

19 *Momus:* All, all of a piece throughout;
Thy chase had a beast in view; [pointing to Diana]
Thy wars brought nothing about; [to Mars]
Thy lovers were all untrue. [to Venus]

Janus: 'Tis well an old age is out,
Chronos: And time to begin a new.
l.86

20 For secrets are edged tools,
And must be kept from children and from fools.
Sir Martin Mar-All, II.ii

21 From harmony, from heavenly harmony
This universal frame began:
From harmony to harmony
Through all the compass of the notes it ran,
The diapason closing full in Man.
A Song for St. Cecilia's Day, i

22 What passion cannot Music raise and quell?
ii

23 The trumpet's loud clangour
Excites us to arms.
iii

24 The soft complaining flute.
iv

25 The trumpet shall be heard on high,
The dead shall live, the living die,
And Music shall untune the sky.
Grand Chorus

26 There is a pleasure sure,
In being mad, which none but madmen know!
The Spanish Friar, I.i

27 And, dying, bless the hand that gave the blow.
II.ii

28 They say everything in the world is good for
something.
III.ii

29 Mute and magnificent, without a tear.
Threnodia Augustalis, ii

30 Men met each other with erected look,
The steps were higher that they took;
Friends to congratulate their friends made haste;
And long inveterate foes saluted as they passed.
iv

31 Freedom which in no other land will thrive,
Freedom an English subject's sole prerogative.
x

32 Thou youngest virgin-daughter of the skies,
Made in the last promotion of the blest.
To the Memory of Mrs. Killigrew, l.1

33 Wit will shine
Through the harsh cadence of a rugged line.
To the Memory of Mr. Oldham

34 And he, who servilely creeps after sense,
Is safe, but ne'er will reach an excellence.
Tyrannic Love, Prologue

35 All delays are dangerous in war.
I.i

36 Pains of love be sweeter far
Than all other pleasures are.
IV.i

37 We must beat the iron while it is hot, but we may
polish it at leisure.
Aeneis, Dedication

38 I trade both the living and the dead, for the
enrichment of our native language.

39 Every age has a kind of universal genius, which

inclines those that live in it to some particular studies.
Essay of Dramatic Poesy (1688)

1 A thing well said will be wit in all languages.

2 He was the man who of all modern, and perhaps
ancient poets, had the largest and most comprehensive
soul...He was naturally learn'd; he needed not the
spectacles of books to read Nature: he looked inwards,
and found her there...He is many times flat, insipid;
his comic wit degenerating into clenches, his serious
swelling into bombast. But he is always great.
[Shakespeare.]

3 He invades authors like a monarch; and what would be
theft in other poets, is only victory in him. [Ben
Jonson.]

4 If by the people you understand the multitude, the *hoi
polloi*, 'tis no matter what they think; they are
sometimes in the right, sometimes in the wrong: their
judgement is a mere lottery.

5 He [Shakespeare] is the very Janus of poets; he wears
almost everywhere two faces; and you have scarce
begun to admire the one, ere you despise the other.
Essay on the Dramatic Poetry of the Last Age

6 One of the greatest, most noble, and most sublime
poems which either this age or nation has produced.
[Paradise Lost.]
Essays, **Apology for Heroic Poetry**

7 What judgment I had increases rather than diminishes;
and thoughts, such as they are, come crowding in so
fast upon me, that my only difficulty is to choose or
reject; to run them into verse or to give them the other
harmony of prose.
Fables, **Preface**

8 'Tis sufficient to say [of Chaucer], according to the
proverb, that here is God's plenty.

9 He [Chaucer] is a perpetual fountain of good sense.

10 One of our late great poets is sunk in his reputation,
because he could never forgive any conceit which
came in his way; but swept like a drag-net, great and
small. There was plenty enough, but the dishes were
ill-sorted; whole pyramids of sweetmeats, for boys and
women; but little of solid meat for men.

11 How easy it is to call rogue and villain, and that
wittily! But how hard to make a man appear a fool, a
blockhead, or a knave, without using any of those
opprobrious terms! To spare the grossness of the
names, and to do the thing yet more severely, is to
draw a full face, and to make the nose and cheeks
stand out, and yet not to employ any depth of
shadowing.
Of Satire

12 Sure the poet...spewed up a good lump of clotted
nonsense at once.
On Settle

13 A man may be capable, as Jack Ketch's wife said of
his servant, of a plain piece of work, a bare hanging;
but to make a malefactor die sweetly was only
belonging to her husband.

14 There are many who understand Greek and Latin, and
yet are ignorant of their Mother Tongue.
Sylvae (Poetical Miscellanies, pt.II. 1685), preface

15 Happy the man, and happy he alone,

He, who can call to-day his own:
He who, secure within, can say,
To-morrow do thy worst, for I have lived to-day.
Trans. of Horace, III, xxix

16 Not Heav'n itself upon the past has pow'r;
But what has been, has been, and I have had my hour.

17 I can enjoy her while she's kind;
But when she dances in the wind,
And shakes the wings, and will not stay,
I puff the prostitute away. [Fortune.]

18 Look round the habitable world! how few
Know their own good; or knowing it, pursue.
Trans. of Juvenal, X

19 To see and be seen, in heaps they run;
Some to undo, and some to be undone.
Trans. of Ovid, *Art of Love*, I.109

20 Who, for false quantities, was whipt at school.
Trans. of Persius, *Satires*, I.135

21 She knows her man, and when you rant and swear,
Can draw you to her *with a single hair.*
V.246

22 Arms, and the man I sing, who, forced by fate,
And haughty Juno's unrelenting hate...
Trans. of Virgil, *Aeneid,* I.i

23 Cousin Swift, you will never be a poet.
Johnson, *Lives of the Poets:* Swift

ALEXANDER DUBCEK 1921–

24 Communism with a human face.
Attr. A resolution by the party group in the Ministry of Foreign
Affairs, in 1968, referred to Czechoslovak foreign policy acquiring
'its own defined face'. *Rudé právo*, 14 Mar. 1968

JOACHIM DU BELLAY 1522–1560

25 *France, mère des arts, des armes et des lois.*
France, mother of arts, of warfare, and of laws.
Sonnets

26 *Heureux qui comme Ulysse a fait un beau voyage
Ou comme cestuy là qui conquit la toison,
Et puis est retourné, plein d'usage et raison,
Vivre entre ses parents le reste de son aage!*
Happy he who like Ulysses has made a great journey,
or like that man who won the Fleece and then came
home, full of experience and good sense, to live the
rest of his time among his family!

27 *Plus que le marbre dur me plaist l'ardoise fine,*
*Plus mon Loyre Gaulois, que le Tybre Latin,
Plus mon petit Lyré, que le mont Palatin,
Et plus que l'air marin la doulceur Angevin.*
I love thin slate more than hard marble, my Gallic
Loire more than the Latin Tiber, my little Liré more
than the Palatine Hill, and more than the sea air the
sweetness of Anjou.

MME DU DEFFAND 1697–1780

28 *La distance n'y fait rien; il n'y a que le premier pas
qui coûte.*
The distance is nothing; it is only the first step that is
difficult.
Commenting on the legend that St. Denis, carrying his head in his
hands, walked two leagues. Letter to d'Alembert, 7 July 1763

GEORGE DUFFIELD 1818–1888

1 Stand up!—stand up for Jesus!
The Psalmist, **Stand Up, Stand Up for Jesus**

ALEXANDRE DUMAS 1802–1870

2 *Cherchons la femme.*
Let us look for the woman.
Les Mohicans de Paris, passim (*Cherchez la femme.* Attributed to Joseph Fouche.)

3 *Tous pour un, un pour tous.*
All for one, one for all.
Les Trois Mousquetiers, passim

GEORGE DU MAURIER 1834–1894

4 Life ain't all beer and skittles, and more's the pity;
but what's the odds, so long as you're happy?
Trilby, pt.1

5 The salad, for which, like everybody else I ever met,
he had a special receipt of his own.

6 A little work, a little play
To keep us going—and so, good-day!

A little warmth, a little light
Of love's bestowing—and so, good-night!

A little fun, to match the sorrow
Of each day's growing—and so, good-morrow!

A little trust that when we die
We reap our sowing! and so—good-bye!

GENERAL DUMOURIEZ 1739–1823

7 *Les courtisans qui l'entourent n'ont rien oublié et n'ont rien appris.*
The courtiers who surround him have forgotten nothing and learnt nothing.
Of Louis XVIII, at the time of the Declaration of Verona, Sept. 1795. *Examen.* Later used by Napoleon in his Declaration to the French on his return from Elba. See 531:17

WILLIAM DUNBAR 1465?–1530?

8 I that in heill wes and gladnes
Am trublit now with gret seiknes
And feblit with infirmitie:
  Timor mortis conturbat me.
Lament for the Makaris

9 London, thou art of townes *A per se.*
London, 1.1

10 London, thou art the flower of cities all!
Gemme of all joy, jasper of jocunditie.
1.16

11 Fair be their wives, right lovesom, white and small.
1.46

12 Thy famous Maire, by pryncely governaunce,
With sword of justice thee ruleth prudently.
No Lord of Parys, Venyce, or Floraunce
In dignitye or honour goeth to hym nigh.
1.49

13 All love is lost but upon God alone.
The Merle and the Nightingale, ii

JOHN DUNNING, BARON ASHBURTON 1731–1783

14 The influence of the Crown has increased, is increasing, and ought to be diminished.
Motion passed in the House of Commons, 1780

JAMES DUPORT 1606–1679

15 *Quem Jupiter vult perdere, dementat prius.*
Whom God would destroy He first sends mad.
Homeri Gnomologia (1660), p.282. See 10:1

RICHARD DUPPA 1770–1831

16 In language, the ignorant have prescribed laws to the learned.
Maxims (1830), 252

SIR EDWARD DYER c.1540–1607

17 My mind to me a kingdom is,
  Such present joys therein I find,
That it excels all other bliss
  That earth affords or grows by kind.
Though much I want which most would have,
Yet still my mind forbids to crave.
My Mind to Me a Kingdom Is

JOHN DYER 1700?–1758

18 A little rule, a little sway,
A sunbeam in a winter's day,
Is all the proud and mighty have
Between the cradle and the grave.
Grongar Hill, 1.89

JOHN DYER fl. 1714

19 And he that will this health deny,
Down among the dead men let him lie.
Toast: Here's a Health to the King

MARIA EDGEWORTH 1767–1849

20 Well! some people talk of morality, and some of religion, but give me a little snug property.
The Absentee, ch.2

21 And all the young ladies…said…that to be sure a love match was the only thing for happiness, where the parties could any way afford it.
Castle Rackrent **(Continuation of Memoirs)**

22 I've a great fancy to see my own funeral afore I die.

23 Come when you're called;
And do as you're bid;
Shut the door after you;
And you'll never be chid.
The Contrast, ch.1

24 Business was his aversion; pleasure was his business.
ch.2

THOMAS ALVA EDISON 1847–1931

25 Genius is one per cent inspiration and ninety-nine per cent perspiration.
Life (1932), ch.24

JAMES EDMESTON 1791–1867

26 Lead us, Heavenly Father, lead us
  O'er the world's tempestuous sea;

Guard us, guide us, keep us, feed us,
 For we have no help but Thee.
Sacred Lyrics, Set 2. **Lead Us, Heavenly Father**

KING EDWARD III 1312–1377

1 Also say to them, that they suffre hym this day to
wynne his spurres, for if god be pleased, I woll this
journey be his, and the honoure therof.
(Of the Black Prince at Crécy, 1345. Commonly quoted as 'Let
the boy win his spurs.') Berners, *Froissart's Chronicle,* 1812, I,
cxxx, 158

KING EDWARD VII 1841–1910

2 I thought everyone must know that a *short* jacket is
always worn with a silk hat at a private view in the
morning.
Sir P. Magnus, *Edward VII,* ch.19

KING EDWARD VIII 1894–1972

3 These works [derelict steel-works] brought all these
people here. Something must be done to find them
work.
Speaking in S. Wales during the Depression. F. Donaldson,
Edward VIII (1974), ch.19

4 I have found it impossible to carry the heavy burden
of responsibility and to discharge my duties as King as
I would wish to do without the help and support of the
woman I love.
Broadcast, 11 Dec. 1936

RICHARD EDWARDES 1523?–1566

5 In going to my naked bed, as one that would have
   slept,
 I heard a wife sing to her child, that long before had
   wept.
 She sighed sore, and sang full sweet, to bring the babe
   to rest,
 That would not cease, but cried still in sucking at her
   breast.
 She was full weary of her watch and grieved with her
   child,
 She rocked it, and rated it, till that on her it smiled.
 Then did she say, 'Now have I found this proverb true
   to prove:
 The falling out of faithful friends, renewing is of
   love.'
Amantium Irae, ed. 1580

JONATHAN EDWARDS 1629–1712

6 The bodies of those that made such a noise and tumult
when alive, when dead, lie as quietly among the
graves of their neighbours as any others.
Procrastination

JONATHAN EDWARDS 1703–1758

7 Of all Insects no one is more wonderfull than the
spider especially with Respect to their sagacity and
admirable way of working...I...once saw a very large
spider to my surprise swimming in the air...and Others
have assured me that they Often have seen spiders fly,
the appearance is truly very Pretty and Pleasing.
Of Insects, written in his early youth, see *Andover Review* XIII,
pp.5-13 (1890)

OLIVER EDWARDS 1711–1791

8 I have tried too in my time to be a philosopher; but, I
don't know how, cheerfulness was always breaking in.
Boswell's *Johnson,* 17 Apr. 1778

9 For my part now, I consider supper as a turnpike
through which one must pass, in order to get to bed.
[Boswell's note: I am not absolutely sure but this was
my own suggestion, though it is truly in the character
of Edwards.]

ALBERT EINSTEIN 1879–1955

10 *Gott würfelt nicht.*
 God does not play dice. [Einstein's habitually
 expressed reaction to the quantum theory.]
 B. Hoffman, *Albert Einstein, Creator and Rebel,* ch.10

GEORGE ELIOT 1819–1880

11 It was a pity he couldna be hatched o'er again, an'
hatched different.
Adam Bede (1859), ch.18

12 Our deeds determine us, as much as we determine our
deeds.
ch.29

13 Mrs Poyser 'has her say out'.
ch.32

14 It's them as take advantage that get advantage i' this
world.

15 A maggot must be born i' the rotten cheese to like it.

16 He was like a cock who thought the sun had risen to
hear him crow.
ch.33

17 We hand folks over to God's mercy, and show none
ourselves.
ch.42

18 I'm not one o' those as can see the cat i' the dairy, an'
wonder what she's come after.
ch.52

19 I'm not denyin' the women are foolish: God Almighty
made 'em to match the men.
ch.53

20 Gossip is a sort of smoke that comes from the dirty
tobacco-pipes of those who diffuse it: it proves nothing
but the bad taste of the smoker.
Daniel Deronda (1874–6), bk.ii, ch.13

21 A difference of taste in jokes is a great strain on the
affections.
ch.15

22 There is a great deal of unmapped country within us
which would have to be taken into account in an
explanation of our gusts and storms.
bk.iii, ch.24

23 Friendships begin with liking or gratitude—roots that
can be pulled up.
bk.iv, ch.32

24 Half the sorrows of women would be averted if they
could repress the speech they know to be useless; nay,
the speech they have resolved not to make.
Felix Holt (1866), ch.2

25 An election is coming. Universal peace is declared,
and the foxes have a sincere interest in prolonging the

lives of the poultry.
ch.5

1 A little daily embroidery had been a constant element in Mrs Transome's life; that soothing occupation of taking stitches to produce what neither she nor any one else wanted, was then the resource of many a well-born and unhappy woman.
ch.7

2 Speech is often barren; but silence also does not necessarily brood over a full nest. Your still fowl, blinking at you without remark, may all the while be sitting on one addled egg; and when it takes to cackling will have nothing to announce but that addled delusion.
ch.15

3 A woman can hardly ever choose...she is dependent on what happens to her. She must take meaner things, because only meaner things are within her reach.
ch.27

4 There's many a one who would be idle if hunger didn't pinch him; but the stomach sets us to work.
ch.30

5 'Abroad', that large home of ruined reputations.
epilogue

6 A woman dictates before marriage in order that she may have an appetite for submission afterwards.
Middlemarch (1871–2), ch.9

7 He said he should prefer not to know the sources of the Nile, and that there should be some unknown regions preserved as hunting-grounds for the poetic imagination.

8 Among all forms of mistake, prophecy is the most gratuitous.
ch.10

9 A woman, let her be as good as she may, has got to put up with the life her husband makes for her.
ch.25

10 A man is seldom ashamed of feeling that he cannot love a woman so well when he sees a certain greatness in her: nature having intended greatness for men.
ch.39

11 Though, as we know, she was not fond of pets that must be held in the hands or trodden on, she was always attentive to the feelings of dogs, and very polite if she had to decline their advances.

12 Poor Dagley read a few verses [of the Bible] sometimes on a Sunday evening, and the world was at least not darker to him than it had been before.

13 It was a room where you had no reason for sitting in one place rather than in another.
ch.54

14 Our deeds still travel with us from afar,
And what we have been makes us what we are.
heading to ch.70

15 This is a puzzling world, and Old Harry's got a finger in it.
The Mill on the Floss (1860), bk.iii, ch.9

16 It was written down by a hand that waited for the heart's prompting: it is the chronicle of a solitary hidden anguish, struggle, trust and triumph. [*The Imitation of Christ*.]
bk.iv, ch.3

17 I've never any pity for conceited people, because I think they carry their comfort about with them.
bk.v, ch.4

18 The happiest women, like the happiest nations, have no history.
bk.vi, ch.3

19 If you please to take the privilege o' sitting down.
ch.4

20 I should like to know what is the proper function of women, if it is not to make reasons for husbands to stay at home, and still stronger reasons for bachelors to go out.
ch.6

21 'Character', says Novalis, in one of his questionable aphorisms—'character is destiny.'
See 364:9

22 In every parting there is an image of death.
Scenes of Clerical Life (1857), **Amos Barton**, ch.10

23 Errors look so very ugly in persons of small means—one feels they are taking quite a liberty in going astray; whereas people of fortune may naturally indulge in a few delinquencies.
Janet's Repentance, ch.25

24 Animals are such agreeable friends—they ask no questions, they pass no criticisms.
Mr. Gilfil's Love-Story, ch.7

25 Nothing is so good as it seems beforehand.
Silas Marner (1861), ch.18

26 Debasing the moral currency.
Essay in *Theophrastus Such* (1879)

27 Oh may I join the choir invisible
Of those immortal dead who live again
In minds made better by their presence.
*Poems: **Oh May I Join the Choir Invisible***

28   'Tis God gives skill,
But not without men's hands: He could not make
Antonio Stradivari's violins
Without Antonio.
Stradivarius, l.140

29 By the time you receive this letter I shall...have been married to Mr J.W. Cross...who now that I am alone sees his happiness in the dedication of his life to me.
Letter to Barbara Bodichon, 5 May 1880

30 She, stirred somewhat beyond her wont, and taking as her text the three words which have been used so often as the inspiring trumpet-calls of men—the words *God, Immortality, Duty*—pronounced, with terrible earnestness, how inconceivable was the *first*, how unbelievable the *second*, and yet how peremptory and absolute the third. Never, perhaps, have sterner accents affirmed the sovereignty of impersonal and unrecompensing Law.
F.W.H. Myers, 'George Eliot', *Century Magazine*, Nov. 1881

31 I am not an optimist but a meliorist.
Laurence Housman, *A.E.H.* (1937), p.72

T.S. ELIOT 1888–1965

32 Because I do not hope to turn again
Because I do not hope
Because I do not hope to turn.
Ash Wednesday, 1

33 Because I do not hope to know again

The infirm glory of the positive hour.

1 Because these wings are no longer wings to fly
But merely vans to beat the air
The air which is now thoroughly small and dry
Smaller and dryer than the will
Teach us to care and not to care
Teach us to sit still.

2   Turning
Wearily, as one would turn to nod good-bye to
    Rochefoucauld,
If the street were time and he at the end of the street.
The Boston Evening Transcript

3 Where is the Life we have lost in living?
Where is the wisdom we have lost in knowledge?
Where is the knowledge we have lost in information?
Choruses from 'The Rock', I

4 I shall not want Capital in Heaven,
    For I shall meet Sir Alfred Mond.
We two shall lie together, lapt
    In a five per cent Exchequer Bond.
A Cooking Egg

5 Where are the eagles and the trumpets?

    Buried beneath some snow-deep Alps.
Over buttered scones and crumpets
    Weeping, weeping multitudes
Droop in a hundred A.B.C.'s.

6 Stone, bronze, stone, steel, stone, oakleaves, horses'
    heels
Over the paving.
Coriolan, I. Triumphal March

7 (And Easter Day, we didn't get to the country,
    So we took young Cyril to church. And they rang a
    bell
And he said right out loud, *crumpets.)*

8   Don't throw away that sausage,
It'll come in handy. He's artful. Please, will you
Give us a light?
Light
Light
Et les soldats faisaient la haie? ILS LA FAISAIENT.

9 The clock has stopped in the dark.
The Family Reunion, II.iii

10 Round and round the circle
Completing the charm
So the knot be unknotted
The crossed be uncrossed
The crooked be made straight
And the curse be ended.

11 Sometimes these cogitations still amaze
The troubled midnight and the noon's repose.
La Figlia Che Piange

12 Time present and time past
Are both perhaps present in time future,
And time future contained in time past.
Four Quartets. Burnt Norton, 1

13 Footfalls echo in the memory
Down the passage which we did not take
Towards the door we never opened
Into the rose-garden. My words echo
Thus, in your mind.

14   Human kind

Cannot bear very much reality.

15 At the still point of the turning world. Neither flesh
    nor fleshless;
Neither from nor towards; at the still point, there the
    dance is,
But neither arrest nor movement.
2

16   Time past and time future
Allow but a little consciousness.
To be conscious is not to be in time
But only in time can the moment in the rose-garden,
The moment in the arbour where the rain beat,
The moment in the draughty church at smokefall
Be remembered; involved with past and future.
Only through time time is conquered.

17   Words strain,
Crack and sometimes break, under the burden,
Under the tension, slip, slide, perish,
Decay with imprecision, will not stay in place,
Will not stay still.
5

18 In my beginning is my end.
East Coker, 1

19   A way of putting it—not very satisfactory:
A periphrastic study in a worn-out poetical fashion,
Leaving one still with the intolerable wrestle
With words and meanings.
2

20   We are only undeceived
Of that which, deceiving, could no longer harm.

21 The wounded surgeon plies the steel
That questions the distempered part;
Beneath the bleeding hands we feel
The sharp compassion of the healer's art
Resolving the enigma of the fever chart.
4

22 The whole earth is our hospital
Endowed by the ruined millionaire,
Wherein, if we do well, we shall
Die of the absolute paternal care
That will not leave us, but prevents us everwhere.

23   Each venture
Is a new beginning, a raid on the inarticulate
With shabby equipment always deteriorating
In the general mess of imprecision of feeling.
5

24 There is only the fight to recover what has been lost
And found and lost again and again: and now, under
    conditions
That seem unpropitious. But perhaps neither gain nor
    loss.
For us, there is only the trying. The rest is not our
    business.

25 Our concern was speech, and speech impelled us
To purify the dialect of the tribe
And urge the mind to aftersight and foresight.
Little Gidding, 2

26 From wrong to wrong the exasperated spirit
    Proceeds, unless restored by the refining fire
    Where you must move in measure, like a dancer.

27 We cannot revive old factions
We cannot restore old policies

Or follow an antique drum.

3

1 What we call the beginning is often the end
And to make an end is to make a beginning.
The end is where we start from.
5

2 We shall not cease from exploration
And the end of all our exploring
Will be to arrive where we started
And know the place for the first time.

3 An old man in a dry month.
Gerontion

4 Signs are taken for wonders. 'We would see a sign!'
The word within a word, unable to speak a word,
Swaddled with darkness. In the juvescence of the
year
Came Christ the tiger.

In depraved May, dogwood and chestnut, flowering
judas,
To be eaten, to be divided, to be drunk
Among whispers.

5 After such knowledge, what forgiveness?

6   Unnatural vices
Are fathered by our heroism.

7 And he'll say, as he scratches himself with his claws,
'Well, the Theatre's certainly not what it was.
These modern productions are all very well,
But there's nothing to equal, from what I hear tell,
    That moment of mystery
    When I made history
As Firefrorefiddle, the Fiend of the Fell.'
Gus: The Theatre Cat

8 We are the hollow men
We are the stuffed men
Leaning together
Headpiece filled with straw. Alas!
The Hollow Men, 1

9 *Here we go round the prickly pear*
Prickly pear prickly pear.
5

10 Between the idea
And the reality
Between the motion
And the act
Falls the Shadow.

11 This is the way the world ends
Not with a bang but a whimper.

12 A cold coming we had of it,
Just the worst time of the year
For a journey, and such a long journey:
The ways deep and the weather sharp,
The very dead of winter.
Journey of the Magi. See 4:7

13 And the cities hostile and the towns unfriendly
And the villages dirty and charging high prices.

14 And an old white horse galloped away in the meadow.

15   But set down
This set down
This: were we led all that way for
Birth or Death? There was a Birth, certainly,
We had evidence and no doubt. I had seen birth and
death,
But had thought they were different; this Birth was
Hard and bitter agony for us, like Death, our death.
We returned to our places, these Kingdoms,
But no longer at ease here, in the old dispensation,
With an alien people clutching their gods.
I should be glad of another death.

16 Cling, swing,
Spring, sing,
Swing up into the apple-tree.
Landscapes. I. **New Hampshire**

17   Let us go then, you and I,
When the evening is spread out against the sky
Like a patient etherized upon a table.
The Love Song of J. Alfred Prufrock

18 In the room the women come and go
Talking of Michelangelo.

    The yellow fog that rubs its back upon the
        window-panes,
The yellow smoke that rubs its muzzle on the
        window-panes,
Licked its tongue into the corners of the evening.

19 There will be time, there will be time
To prepare a face to meet the faces that you meet;
There will be a time to murder and create,
And time for all the works and days of hands
That lift and drop a question on your plate.

20 I have measured out my life with coffee spoons.

21 I should have been a pair of ragged claws
Scuttling across the floors of silent seas.

22 Should I, after tea and cakes and ices,
Have the strength to force the moment to its crisis?

23 I have seen the moment of my greatness flicker,
And I have seen the eternal Footman hold my coat, and
    snicker,
And in short, I was afraid.

24 No! I am not Prince Hamlet, nor was meant to be;
Am an attendant lord, one that will do
To swell a progress, start a scene or two.

25   I grow old...I grow old...
I shall wear the bottoms of my trousers rolled.

    Shall I part my hair behind? Do I dare to eat a
        peach?
I shall wear white flannel trousers, and walk upon the
    beach.
I have heard the mermaids singing, each to each;

I do not think that they will sing to me.

26 Macavity, Macavity, there's no one like Macavity,
There never was a Cat of such deceitfulness and
    suavity.
He always has an alibi, and one or two to spare:
At whatever time the deed took place—MACAVITY
    WASN'T THERE!
Macavity: The Mystery Cat

27 I am aware of the damp souls of housemaids
Sprouting despondently at area gates.
Morning at the Window

28 When Mr Apollinax visited the United States
His laughter tinkled among the teacups.
I thought of Fragilion, that shy figure among the
    birch-trees,

And of Priapus in the shrubbery
Gaping at the lady in the swing.
Mr. Apollinax

1 Polyphiloprogenitive
The sapient sutlers of the Lord
Drift across the window-panes
In the beginning was the Word.
Mr. Eliot's Sunday Morning Service

2 Yet we have gone on living,
Living and partly living.
Murder in the Cathedral, pt.I

3 Friendship should be more than biting Time can sever.

4 The last temptation is the greatest treason:
To do the right deed for the wrong reason.

5 The Naming of Cats is a difficult matter,
It isn't just one of your holiday games;
At first you may think I'm as mad as a hatter
When I tell you a cat must have THREE DIFFERENT
NAMES.
The Naming of Cats

6 When you notice a cat in profound meditation,
The reason, I tell you, is always the same:
His mind is engaged in a rapt contemplation
Of the thought, of the thought, of the thought of his
name:
His ineffable effable
Effanineffable
Deep and inscrutable singular Name.

7 The winter evening settles down
With smell of steaks in passageways.
Six o'clock.
The burnt-out ends of smoky days.
Preludes, I

8 The worlds revolve like ancient women
Gathering fuel in vacant lots.

9 Every street lamp that I pass
Beats like a fatalistic drum,
And through the spaces of the dark
Midnight shakes the memory
As a madman shakes a dead geranium.

Half-past one,
The street-lamp sputtered,
The street-lamp muttered,
The street-lamp said, 'Regard that woman
Who hesitates toward you in the light of the door
Which opens on her like a grin.'
Rhapsody on a Windy Night

10 Regard the moon,
La lune ne garde aucune rancune.

11 Paint me the bold anfractuous rocks
Faced by the snarled and yelping seas.
Sweeney Erect

12 You'd be bored.
Birth, and copulation, and death.
That's all the facts when you come to brass tacks:
Birth, and copulation and death.
I've been born, and once is enough.
Sweeney Agonistes, Fragment of an Agon

13 *Where the breadfruit fall*
And the penguin call
And the sound is the sound of the sea
Under the bam

Under the boo
Under the bamboo tree.

14 Apeneck Sweeney spreads his knees
Letting his arms hang down to laugh,
The zebra stripes along his jaw
Swelling to maculate giraffe.
Sweeney Among the Nightingales

15 Gloomy Orion and the Dog
Are veiled; and hushed the shrunken seas;
The person in the Spanish cape
Tries to sit on Sweeney's knees.

16 The host with someone indistinct
Converses at the door apart,
The nightingales are singing near
The convent of the Sacred Heart,

And sang within the bloody wood
When Agamemnon cried aloud
And let their liquid siftings fall
To stain the stiff dishonoured shroud.

17 April is the cruellest month, breeding
Lilacs out of the dead land, mixing
Memory and desire, stirring
Dull roots with spring rain.
Winter kept us warm, covering
Earth in forgetful snow, feeding
A little life with dried tubers.
The Waste Land. 1. **The Burial of the Dead**

18 I read, much of the night, and go south in the winter.

19 And I will show you something different from either
Your shadow at morning striding behind you,
Or your shadow at evening rising to meet you
I will show you fear in a handful of dust.

20 Unreal City,
Under the brown fog of a winter dawn,
A crowd flowed over London Bridge, so many,
I had not thought death had undone so many.

21 Flowed up the hill and down King William Street,
To where Saint Mary Woolnoth kept the hours
With a dead sound on the final stroke of nine.

22 'O keep the Dog far hence, that's friend to men,
'Or with his nails he'll dig it up again!
'You! hypocrite lecteur!—mon semblable,—mon
frère!'
See 35:5, 567:9

23 The Chair she sat in, like a burnished throne,
Glowed on the marble.
2. **A Game of Chess.** See 422:2

24 And still she cried, and still the world pursues,
'Jug Jug' to dirty ears.

25 O O O O that Shakespeherian Rag—
It's so elegant
So intelligent.

26 A rat crept softly through the vegetation
Dragging its slimy belly on the bank
While I was fishing in the dull canal
On a winter evening round behind the gashouse
Musing upon the king my brother's wreck
And on the king my father's death before him.
3. **The Fire Sermon**

27 But at my back from time to time I hear
The sound of horns and motors, which shall bring

Sweeney to Mrs Porter in the spring.
O the moon shone bright on Mrs Porter
And on her daughter
They wash their feet in soda water.
See 332:19

1 I Tiresias, old man with wrinkled dugs
Perceived the scene, and foretold the rest—
I too awaited the expected guest.
He, the young man carbuncular, arrives,
A small house agent's clerk, with one bold stare,
One of the low on whom assurance sits
As a silk hat on a Bradford millionaire.

2 And I Tiresias have foresuffered all
Enacted on this same divan or bed.

3 When lovely woman stoops to folly and
Paces about her room again, alone,
She smoothes her hair with automatic hand,
And puts a record on the gramophone.
See 231:31

4 O City city, I can sometimes hear
Beside a public bar in Lower Thames Street,
The pleasant whining of a mandoline
And a clatter and a chatter from within
Where fishermen lounge at noon: where the walls
Of Magnus Martyr hold
Inexplicable splendour of Ionian white and gold.

5 'Trams and dusty trees.
Highbury bore me. Richmond and Kew
Undid me. By Richmond I raised my knees
Supine on the floor of a narrow canoe.'

6 Phlebas the Phoenician, a fortnight dead,
Forgot the cry of gulls, and the deep sea swell
And the profit and loss.
4. **Death by Water**

7 Consider Phlebas, who was once handsome and tall as
you.

8 Who is the third who walks always beside you?
When I count, there are only you and I together
But when I look ahead up the white road
There is always another one walking beside you.
5. **What the Thunder Said**

9 A woman drew her long black hair out tight
And fiddled whisper music on those strings.

10 In this-decayed hole among the mountains
In the faint moonlight, the grass is singing
Over the tumbled graves, about the chapel
There is the empty chapel, only the wind's home.

11 The awful daring of a moment's surrender.

12 These fragments have I shored against my ruins.

13 Webster was much possessed by death
And saw the skull beneath the skin;
And breastless creatures under ground
Leaned backward with a lipless grin.
Whispers of Immortality

14 Grishkin is nice: her Russian eye
Is underlined for emphasis;
Uncorseted, her friendly bust
Gives promise of pneumatic bliss.

15 The critic, one would suppose, if he is to justify his
existence, should endeavour to discipline his personal
prejudices and cranks—tares to which we are all

subject—and compose his differences with as many of
his fellows as possible, in the common pursuit of true
judgement.
The Function of Criticism (1923), i

16 The only way of expressing emotion in the form of art
is by finding an 'objective correlative'; in other words,
a set of objects, a situation, a chain of events which
shall be the formula of that *particular* emotion; such
that when the external facts, which must terminate in
sensory experience, are given, the emotion is
immediately evoked.
Hamlet (1919)

17 In the seventeenth century a dissociation of sensibility
set in from which we have never recovered.
The Metaphysical Poets

18 Poetry is not a turning loose of emotion, but an escape
from emotion; it is not the expression of personality,
but an escape from personality.
Tradition and the Individual Talent, II

QUEEN ELIZABETH I 1533–1603

19 'Twas God the word that spake it,
He took the Bread and brake it;
And what the word did make it;
That I believe, and take it.
Answer on being asked her opinion of Christ's presence in the
Sacrament. S. Clarke, *Marrow of Ecclesiastical History*, pt.ii,
Life of Queen Elizabeth, ed. 1675

20 The queen of Scots is this day leichter of a fair son,
and I am but a barren stock.
Memoirs of Sir James Melville (1549–93)

21 Anger makes dull men witty, but it keeps them poor.
Bacon, *Apophthegms*, 5

22 Like strawberry wives, that laid two or three great
strawberries at the mouth of their pot, and all the rest
were little ones.
54

23 Good-morning, gentlemen both. [To a delegation of
eighteen tailors.]
Chamberlin, *Sayings of Queen Elizabeth*, p.28

24 To your text, Mr Dean! to your text!
p.137

25 I am your anointed Queen. I will never be by violence
constrained to do anything. I thank God that I am
endued with such qualities that if I were turned out of
the Realm in my petticoat I were able to live in any
place in Christome.
p.142

26 I will make you shorter by the head.
p.224

27 The daughter of debate, that eke discord doth sow.
[Mary Queen of Scots.]
p.301

28 Madam I may not call you; mistress I am ashamed to
call you; and so I know not what to call you; but
howsoever, I thank you. [To the wife of the
Archbishop of Canterbury. The Queen did not approve
of married clergy.]
Harington, *Brief View of the State of the Church*, 1607

29 God may pardon, you, but I never can. [To the
Countess of Nottingham.]
See Hume, *History of England under the House of Tudor*, vol.ii,
ch.7

1 If thy heart fails thee, climb not at all.
Lines written on a window after 404:14. Fuller, *Worthies of England*, vol.i, p.419

2 *Semper eadem.* (Ever the same.)
Motto

3 As for me, I see no such great cause why I should either be fond to live or fear to die. I have had good experience of this world, and I know what it is to be a subject and what to be a sovereign. Good neighbours I have had, and I have met with bad: and in trust I have found treason.
Speech to Parliament, 1586. Camden's *Annals*, p.98

4 I know I have the body of a weak and feeble woman, but I have the heart and stomach of a king, and of a king of England too; and think foul scorn that Parma or Spain, or any prince of Europe, should dare to invade the borders of my realm.
Speech to the Troops at Tilbury on the Approach of the Armada, 1588

5 Though God hath raised me high, yet this I count the glory of my crown: that I have reigned with your loves.
The Golden Speech, 1601. D'Ewes's *Journal*, p.659

6 Must! Is *must* a word to be addressed to princes? Little man, little man! thy father, if he had been alive, durst not have used that word.
To Robert Cecil, on her death-bed. J.R. Green, *A Short History of the English People*, ch.vii

JOHN ELLERTON 1826–1893

7 The day Thou gavest, Lord, is ended,
The darkness falls at Thy behest.
A Liturgy for Missionary Meetings

JANE ELLIOT 1727–1805

8 I've heard them lilting, at the ewe milking.
  Lasses a' lilting, before dawn of day;
But now they are moaning, on ilka green loaning;
  The flowers of the forest are a' wede away.
The Flowers of the Forest (1756) (Popular version of the traditional lament for Flodden.)

CHARLOTTE ELLIOTT 1789–1871

9 'Christian! seek not yet repose,'
Hear thy guardian angel say;
Thou art in the midst of foes—
  'Watch and pray.'
Morning and Evening Hymns

10 Just as I am, without one plea
But that Thy blood was shed for me,
And that Thou bidd'st me come to Thee,
  O Lamb of God, I come!
Invalid's Hymn Book (1834)

EBENEZER ELLIOTT 1781–1849

11 What is a communist? One who hath yearnings
For equal division of unequal earnings.
Epigram

12 When wilt thou save the people?
  Oh, God of Mercy! when?
The people, Lord, the people!

Not thrones and crowns, but men!
The People's Anthem

GEORGE ELLIS 1753–1815

13 Snowy, Flowy, Blowy,
Showery, Flowery, Bowery,
Hoppy, Croppy, Droppy,
Breezy, Sneezy, Freezy.
The Twelve Months

HAVELOCK ELLIS 1859–1939

14 Every artist writes his own autobiography.
The New Spirit. Tolstoi II

ELSTOW

15 Elstow ['One Elstow, a friar of the order of Observant Friars'] smiling said...'With thanks to God we know the way to heaven, to be as ready by water as by land, and therefore we care not which way we go.'
When threatened with drowning by Henry VIII. Stow, *Annales*, 1615, p.543

PAUL ELUARD 1895–1952

16 *Adieu tristesse*
Bonjour tristesse
Tu es inscrite dans les lignes du plafond.
Farewell sadness
Good day sadness
You are inscribed in the lines of the ceiling.
A peine défigurée

RALPH WALDO EMERSON 1803–1882

17 If the red slayer think he slays,
  Or if the slain think he is slain,
They know not well the subtle ways
  I keep, and pass, and turn again.
Brahma

18 I am the doubter and the doubt,
  And I the hymn the Brahmin sings.

19 By the rude bridge that arched the flood,
  Their flag to April's breeze unfurl'd,
Here once the embattled farmers stood,
  And fired the shot heard round the world.
Hymn Sung at the Completion of the Concord Monument

20 Good-bye, proud world! I'm going home:
Thou art not my friend, and I'm not thine.
Good-bye

21 Things are in the saddle,
  And ride mankind.
Ode, Inscribed to W.H. Channing

22 I like a church; I like a cowl;
I love a prophet of the soul;
And on my heart monastic aisles
Fall like sweet strains, or pensive smiles;
Yet not for all his faith can see,
Would I that cowlèd churchman be.
The Problem

23 He builded better than he knew;—
The conscious stone to beauty grew.

24 The frolic architecture of the snow.
The Snowstorm

1 Wilt thou seal up the avenues of ill?
Pay every debt, as if God wrote the bill.
Solution

2 So nigh is grandeur to our dust,
    So near is God to man,
When Duty whispers low, *Thou must*,
    The youth replies, *I can*.
Voluntaries, iii

3 Make yourself necessary to someone.
Conduct of Life. Considerations by the way

4 All sensible people are selfish, and nature is tugging at every contract to make the terms of it fair.

5 A person seldom falls sick, but the bystanders are animated with a faint hope that he will die.

6 Art is a jealous mistress.
Wealth

7 We say the cows laid out Boston. Well, there are worse surveyors.

8 The louder he talked of his honour, the faster we counted our spoons.
Worship. See 275:1

9 London is the epitome of our times, and the Rome of to-day.
English Traits, xviii. **Result**

10 This aged England...pressed upon by transitions of trade and...competing populations,—I see her not dispirited, not weak, but well remembering that she has seen dark days before;—indeed, with a kind of instinct that she sees a little better in a cloudy day, and that, in storm of battle and calamity, she has a secret vigour and a pulse like a cannon.
xix. **Speech at Manchester** (1847)

11 Nothing astonishes men so much as common-sense and plain dealing.
Essays, xii. **Art**

12 Though we travel the world over to find the beautiful we must carry it with us or we find it not.

13 Beware when the great God lets loose a thinker on this planet.
x. **Circles**

14 Conversation is a game of circles. In conversation we pluck up the *termini* which bound the common of silence on every side.

15 People wish to be settled: only as far as they are unsettled is there any hope for them.

16 Nothing great was ever achieved without enthusiasm.

17 To fill the hour—that is happiness.
xiv. **Experience**

18 The wise through excess of wisdom is made a fool.

19 The years teach much which the days never know.

20 A friend may well be reckoned the masterpiece of Nature.
vi. **Friendship**

21 The only reward of virtue is virtue; the only way to have a friend is to be one.

22 Tart, cathartic virtue.
viii. **Heroism**

23 It was a high counsel that I once heard given to a young person, 'Always do what you are afraid to do.'

24 There is properly no history; only biography.
i. **History**

25 Men are conservatives when they are least vigorous, or when they are most luxurious. They are conservatives after dinner.
New England Reformers

26 The reward of a thing well done, is to have done it.

27 We are wiser than we know.
ix. **The Over-Soul**

28 Words are also actions, and actions are a kind of words.
xiii. **The Poet**

29 It is not metres, but a metre-making argument, that makes a poem.

30 We are symbols, and inhabit symbols.

31 Language is fossil poetry.

32 Good men must not obey the laws too well.
xix. **Politics**

33 In skating over thin ice, our safety is in our speed.
vii. **Prudence**

34 To believe your own thought, to believe that what is true for you in your private heart is true for all men,—that is genius.
ii. **Self-Reliance**

35 To-morrow a stranger will say with masterly good sense precisely what we have thought and felt all the time, and we shall be forced to take with shame our own opinion from another.

36 Society everywhere is in conspiracy against the manhood of every one of its members.

37 Whoso would be a man must be a nonconformist.

38 A foolish consistency is the hobgoblin of little minds, adored by little statesmen and philosophers and divines. With consistency a great soul has simply nothing to do.

39 Is it so bad, then, to be misunderstood? Pythagoras was misunderstood, and Socrates, and Jesus, and Luther, and Copernicus, and Galileo, and Newton, and every pure and wise spirit that ever took flesh. To be great is to be misunderstood.

40 I like the silent church before the service begins, better than any preaching.

41 If you would not be known to do anything, never do it.
iv. **Spiritual Laws**

42 What is a weed? A plant whose virtues have not been discovered.
Fortune of the Republic

43 We are always getting ready to live, but never living.
Journals, 13 Apr. 1834

44 I hate quotations.
May 1849

45 Old age brings along with its uglinesses the comfort that you will soon be out of it,—which ought to be a substantial relief to such discontented pendulums as we are. To be out of the war, out of debt, out of the drouth, out of the blues, out of the dentist's hands, out of the second thoughts, mortifications, and remorses that inflict such twinges and shooting pains,—out of the next winter, and the high prices, and company

below your ambition,—surely these are soothing hints.
1864

1 By necessity, by proclivity,—and by delight, we all quote.
Letters and Social Aims. **Quotation and Originality**

2 Next to the originator of a good sentence is the first quoter of it.

3 When Nature has work to be done, she creates a genius to do it.
Method of Nature

4 Every hero becomes a bore at last.
Representative Men. **Uses of Great Men**

5 Talent alone cannot make a writer. There must be a man behind the book.
Goethe

6 Is not marriage an open question, when it is alleged, from the beginning of the world, that such as are in the institution wish to get out; and such as are out wish to get in.
Montaigne

7 Never read any book that is not a year old.
Society and Solitude. **Books**

8 Hitch your wagon to a star.
Civilization

9 We boil at different degrees.
Eloquence

10 One of our statesmen said, 'The curse of this country is eloquent men.'

11 America is a country of young men.
Old Age

12 'Tis the good reader that makes the good book.
Success

13 Invention breeds invention.
Works and Days

14 Glittering generalities! They are blazing ubiquities.
Attr. remark on 148:14

15 If a man write a better book, preach a better sermon, or make a better mouse-trap than his neighbour, tho' he build his house in the woods, the world will make a beaten path to his door.
Mrs. Sarah S.B. Yule (1856–1916) credits the quotation to Emerson in her *Borrowings* (1889), stating in *The Docket*, Feb. 1912, that she copied this in her handbook from a lecture delivered by Emerson. The quotation was the occasion of a long controversy, owing to Elbert Hubbard's claim to its authorship.

WILLIAM EMPSON 1906–

16 Waiting for the end, boys, waiting for the end.
What is there to be or do?
What's become of me or you?
Are we kind or are we true?
Sitting two and two, boys, waiting for the end.
Just a Smack at Auden

17 Slowly the poison the whole blood stream fills.
It is not the effort nor the failure tires.
The waste remains, the waste remains and kills.
Missing Dates

FRIEDRICH ENGELS 1820–1895

18 *Der Staat wird nicht 'abgeschaft', er stirbt ab.*

The State is not 'abolished', *it withers away.*
Anti-Dühring, III.ii

THOMAS DUNN ENGLISH 1819–1902

19 Oh! don't you remember sweet Alice, Ben Bolt,
 Sweet Alice, whose hair was so brown,
Who wept with delight when you gave her a smile,
 And trembled with fear at your frown?
Ben Bolt

ENNIUS 239–169 B.C.

20 *O Tite tute Tati tibi tanta tyranne tulisti!*
O tyrant Titus Tatius, what a lot you brought upon yourself!
Annals 1. Priscianus (*Grammatici Latini*, ed. H. Keil *et al.*, Leipzig, 1857-80, II, 591, 5)

21 *At tuba terribili sonitu taratantara dixit.*
And the trumpet in terrible tones went taratantara.
Annals 2. Priscianus (*Grammatici Latini*, ed. H. Keil *et al.*, Leipzig, 1857-80, II, 450, 2)

22 *Unus homo nobis cunctando restituit rem.*
One man by delaying put the state to rights for us.
Annals 12. Cicero, *De Off.*, I, 24, 84

23 *Moribus antiquis res stat Romana virisque.*
The Roman state survives by its ancient customs and its manhood.
Annals. St. Augustine, *De Civ. Dei*, 2, 21

ROBERT DEVEREUX, EARL OF ESSEX 1566–1601

24 Reasons are not like garments, the worse for wearing.
To Lord Willoughby, 4 Jan. 1598-9. See N. & Q., Ser.X, vol.ii, p.23

HENRI ESTIENNE 1531–1598

25 *Si jeunesse savoit; si vieillesse pouvoit.*
If youth knew; if age could.
Les Prémices, Épigramme cxci

SIR GEORGE ETHEREGE 1635?–1691

26 I must confess I am a fop in my heart; ill customs influence my very senses, and I have been so used to affectation that without the help of the air of the court what is natural cannot touch me.
Letter to Mr. Poley, 2/12 Jan. 1687/8

27 Few of our plays can boast of more wit than I have heard him speak at a supper. [Sir Charles Sedley.]
Letter to Mr. Will. Richards, undated

28 I walk within the purlieus of the Law.
Love in a Tub, I.iii

29 When love grows diseas'd, the best thing we can do is put it to a violent death; I cannot endure the torture of a lingring and consumptive passion.
The Man of Mode, II.ii

30 Writing, Madam, 's a mechanic part of wit! A gentleman should never go beyond a song or a billet.
IV.i

31 What e'er you say, I know all beyond High-Park's a desart to you.
V.ii

EUCLID fl. c.300 B.C.

1 *Quod erat demonstrandum.* (trans. from the Greek).
Which was to be proved.

2 A line is length without breadth.

3 There is no 'royal road' to geometry.
Said to Ptolemy I. Proclus, *Comment on Euclid,* Prol. G.20

EURIPIDES 480–406 B.C.

4 ἡ γλῶσσ' ὀμώμοχ', ἡ δὲ φρὴν ἀνώμοτος.
My tongue swore, but my mind's unsworn.
Hippolytus, 612

ABEL EVANS 1679–1737

5 Under this stone, Reader, survey
Dead Sir John Vanbrugh's house of clay.
Lie heavy on him, Earth! for he
Laid many heavy loads on thee!
Epitaph on Sir John Vanbrugh, Architect of Blenheim Palace

JOHN EVELYN 1620–1706

6 This knight was indeed a valiant gentleman; but not a
little given to romance, when he spake of himself.
Diary, 6 Sept. 1651

7 Mulberry Garden, now the only place of refreshment
about the town for persons of the best quality to be
exceedingly cheated at.
10 May 1654

8 That miracle of a youth, Mr Christopher Wren.
11 July 1654

9 I saw Hamlet Prince of Denmark played, but now the
old plays began to disgust this refined age.
26 Nov. 1661

DAVID EVERETT 1769–1813

10 You'd scarce expect one of my age
To speak in public on the stage;
And if I chance to fall below
Demosthenes or Cicero,
Don't view me with a critic's eye,
But pass my imperfections by.
Large streams from little fountains flow,
Tall oaks from little acorns grow.
Lines Written for a School Declamation

VISCOUNT EVERSLEY
see CHARLES SHAW-LEFEVRE

GAVIN EWART 1916–

11 Miss Twye was soaping her breasts in the bath
When she heard behind her a meaning laugh
And to her amazement she discovered
A wicked man in the bathroom cupboard.
Miss Twye

WILLIAM NORMAN EWER 1885–1976

12 I gave my life for freedom—This I know:
For those who bade me fight had told me so.
Five Souls, 1917

13 How odd
Of God

To choose
The Jews.
How Odd. See 95:13

F.W. FABER 1814–1863

14 The music of the Gospel leads us home.
Oratory Hymns. **The Pilgrims of the Night**

ROBERT FABYAN d. 1513

15 Finally he paid the debt of nature.
New Chronicles, pt.i, xli

16 King Henry [I] being in Normandy, after some
writers, fell from or with his horse, whereof he caught
his death; but Ranulphe says he took a surfeit by eating
of a lamprey, and thereof died.
ccxxix. Ranulphus Higden's account, *Polychronicon* VII.xvii,
does not attribute Henry's death to any direct cause. Fabyan may
have derived the notion of 'surfeit' from an anonymous and rather
fanciful translation of Higden's *nocuerat* as 'chargede his
stomake'. See Harleian ms 2261, f.354.b.

17 The Duke of Clarence...then being a prisoner in the
Tower, was secretly put to death and drowned in a
barrel of Malmesey wine within the said Tower.
vol.II, **1477.** Early editions have the spelling 'malvesye'.

CLIFTON FADIMAN

18 I encountered the mama of dada again. [Gertrude
Stein.]
Appreciations, Gertrude Stein

LUCIUS CARY, VISCOUNT FALKLAND
1610?–1643

19 When it is not necessary to change, it is necessary not
to change.
A Speech concerning Episcopacy [delivered 1641]. *A Discourse
of Infallibility,* 1660

MICHAEL FARADAY 1791–1867

20 Tyndall, I must remain plain Michael Faraday to the
last; and let me now tell you, that if I accepted the
honour which the Royal Society desires to confer upon
me, I would not answer for the integrity of my
intellect for a single year.
On being offered the Presidency of the Royal Society. J. Tyndall,
Faraday as a Discoverer (1868), 'Illustrations of Character'

EDWARD FARMER 1809?–1876

21 I have no pain, dear mother, now;
But oh! I am so dry:
Just moisten poor Jim's lips once more;
And, mother, do not cry!
The Collier's Dying Child. See 6:1

GEORGE FARQUHAR 1678–1707

22 Sir, you shall taste my *Anno Domini.*
The Beaux' Stratagem, I.i

23 I have fed purely upon ale; I have eat my ale, drank
my ale, and I always sleep upon ale.

24 My Lady Bountiful.

25 Says little, thinks less, and does—nothing at all, faith.

26 'Tis still my maxim, that there is no scandal like rags,

nor any crime so shameful as poverty.

1 There's some diversion in a talking blockhead; and since a woman must wear chains, I would have the pleasure of hearing 'em rattle a little.
II.ii

2 No woman can be a beauty without a fortune.

3 I believe they talked of me, for they laughed consumedly.
III.i

4 'Twas for the good of my country that I should be abroad.—Anything for the good of one's country—I'm a Roman for that.
ii

5 Captain is a good travelling name, and so I take it.

6 *Aimwell:* Then you understand Latin, Mr Bonniface?
Bonniface: Not I, Sir, as the saying is, but he talks it so very fast that I'm sure it must be good.

7 There are secrets in all families.
iii

8 How a little love and good company improves a woman!
IV.i

9 It is a maxim that man and wife should never have it in their power to hang one another.
ii

10 Spare all I have, and take my life.
V.ii

11 I hate all that don't love me, and slight all that do.
The Constant Couple, I.ii

12 Grant me some wild expressions, Heavens, or I shall burst—...Words, words or I shall burst.
V.iii

13 Charming women can true converts make,
We love the precepts for the teacher's sake.
See 173:3

14 Crimes, like virtues, are their own rewards.
The Inconstant, IV.ii

15 'Tis an old saying, Like master, like man; why not as well, Like mistress, like maid?
Love and a Bottle, I.i

16 Money is the sinews of love, as of war.
II.i. See 151:30

17 Poetry's a mere drug, Sir.
III.ii

18 He answered the description the page gave to a T, Sir.
IV.iii

19 Hanging and marriage, you know, go by Destiny.
The Recruiting Officer, III.ii

20 I cou'd be mighty foolish, and fancy my self mighty witty; Reason still keeps its throne, but it nods a little, that's all.

21 A lady, if undrest at Church, looks silly,
One cannot be devout in dishabilly.
The Stage Coach, prologue

22 I'm privileg'd to be very impertinent, being an Oxonian.
Sir Harry Wildair, II.i

23 The King of Spain is dead.
ii

DAVID GLASGOW FARRAGUT 1801–1870

24 Damn the torpedoes! Full speed ahead.
At the battle of Mobile Bay, 5 Aug. 1864. 'Torpedoes' were mines. But see Capt. A.T. Mahan, *Admiral Farragut* (1892), ch.10

DEAN FARRAR 1831–1903

25 Russell...acted invariably from the highest principles.
Eric, or Little by Little, pt.i, ch.3

26 Russell, let me always call you Edwin, and call me Eric.
ch.4

27 'What a surly devil that is,' said Eric,...
'A surly—? Oh, Eric, that's the first time I ever heard you swear.
ch.8

28 'By heavens, this is *too* bad!' he exclaimed, stamping his foot with anger. 'What have I ever done to you young blackguards, that you should treat me thus?'
pt.ii, ch.1

29 They all drank his health with the usual honours:—
'...For he's a jolly good fe-el-low, which nobody can deny.'
Julian Home, ch.21

WILLIAM FAULKNER 1897–1962

30 He [the writer] must teach himself that the basest of all things is to be afraid; and, teaching himself that, forget it forever leaving no room in his workshop for anything but the old verities and truths of the heart, the old universal truths lacking which any story is ephemeral and doomed—love and honor and pity and pride and compassion and sacrifice.
Nobel Prize Speech, Stockholm, 10 Dec. 1950

GUY FAWKES 1570–1606

31 A desperate disease requires a dangerous remedy.
6 Nov. 1605. See D.N.B.

GEOFFREY FEARON

32 The 'angry young men' of England (who refuse to write grammatically and syntactically in order to flaunt their proletarian artistry).
Times Literary Supplement, 4 Oct. 1957 but see also R. West, *Black Lamb and Grey Falcon* (1941), 'Dalmatia'

EMPEROR FERDINAND I 1503–1564

33 *Fiat justitia et pereat mundus.*
Let justice be done, though the world perish.
Motto. Johannes Manlius, *Locorum Communium Collectanea* (Basle, 1563), II, 290. See 565:8

WILLIAM PITT FESSENDEN 1806–1869

34 Repudiate the repudiators.
Presidential Campaign Slogan, 1868

LUDWIG FEUERBACH 1804–1872

35 *Der Mensch ist, was er isst.*
Man is what he eats.
Advertisement to Moleschott, *Lehre der Nahrungsmittel: Für das Volk* (1850). See 93:9

EUGENE FIELD 1850–1895

1 But I, when I undress me
    Each night, upon my knees,
Will ask the Lord to bless me,
    With apple pie and cheese.
Apple Pie and Cheese

2 Wynken, Blynken, and Nod one night
    Sailed off in a wooden shoe—
Sailed on a river of crystal light,
    Into a sea of dew.
Wynken, Blynken, and Nod

3 He played the King as though under momentary
apprehension that someone else was about to play the
ace.
Of Creston Clarke as King Lear. Attr. to a review in the *Denver
Tribune*, c.1880

HENRY FIELDING 1707–1754

4 '*Tace*, madam,' answered Murphy, 'is Latin for a
candle.'
Amelia, bk.i, ch.10

5 It hath been often said, that it is not death, but dying,
which is terrible.
bk.iii, ch.4

6 When widows exclaim loudly against second
marriages, I would always lay a wager, that the man,
if not the wedding-day, is absolutely fixed on.
bk.vi, ch.8

7 One fool at least in every married couple.
bk.ix, ch.4

8 There is not in the universe a more ridiculous, nor a
more contemptible animal, than a proud clergyman.
ch.10

9 One of my illustrious predecessors.
Covent-Garden Journal, No.3, 11 Jan. 1752

10 Oh! The roast beef of England,
And old England's roast beef.
The Grub Street Opera, III.iii

11 He in a few minutes ravished this fair creature, or at
least would have ravished her, if she had not, by a
timely compliance, prevented him.
Jonathan Wild, bk.iii, ch.7

12 But pray, Mr Wild, why bitch?
ch.8

13 To whom nothing is given, of him can nothing be
required.
Joseph Andrews, bk.ii, ch.8

14 I describe not men, but manners; not an individual,
but a species.
bk.iii, ch.1

15 They are the affectation of affectation.
ch.3

16 Public schools are the nurseries of all vice and
immorality.
ch.5

17 Some folks rail against other folks, because other folks
have what some folks would be glad of.
bk.iv, ch.6

18 Love and scandal are the best sweeteners of tea.
Love in Several Masques, IV.xi

19 Yes, I had two strings to my bow; both golden ones,
agad! and both cracked.
V.xiii

20 I have lived long enough in the world to see that
necessity is a bad recommendation to favours...which
as seldom fall to those who really want them, as to
those who really deserve them.
The Modern Husband (first performed 1731), II.v

21 Map me no maps, sir, my head is a map, a map of the
whole world.
Rape upon Rape, II.v

22 Every physician almost hath his favourite disease.
Tom Jones, bk.ii, ch.9

23 When I mention religion, I mean the Christian
religion; and not only the Christian religion, but the
Protestant religion; and not only the Protestant religion
but the Church of England.
bk.iii, ch.3

24 Thwackum was for doing justice, and leaving mercy to
heaven.
ch.10

25 What is commonly called love, namely the desire of
satisfying a voracious appetite with a certain quantity
of delicate white human flesh.
bk.vi, ch.1

26 O! more than Gothic ignorance.
bk.vii, ch.3

27 'I did not mean to abuse the cloth; I only said your
conclusion was a *non sequitur*.'—
'You are another,' cries the sergeant, 'an you come to
that, no more a *sequitur* than yourself.'
bk.ix, ch.6

28 An amiable weakness.
bk.x, ch.8

29 His designs were strictly honourable, as the phrase is;
that is, to rob a lady of her fortune by way of
marriage.
bk.xi, ch.4

30 Composed that monstrous animal a husband and wife.
bk.xv, ch.9

31 Nay, you may call me coward if you will; but if that
little man there upon the stage is not frightened, I
never saw any man frightened in my life.
bk.xvi, ch.5

32 'He the best player!' cries Partridge, with a
contemptuous sneer. 'Why, I could act as well as he
myself. I am sure, if I had seen a ghost, I should have
looked in the very same manner, and done just as he
did...The king for my money! He speaks all his words
distinctly, half as loud again as the other. Anybody
may see he is an actor.'

33 All Nature wears one universal grin.
Tom Thumb the Great, I.i

34 To sun my self in Huncamunca's eyes.
iii

35 When I'm not thank'd at all, I'm thank'd enough,
I've done my duty, and I've done no more.

36 The dusky night rides down the sky,
    And ushers in the morn;
The hounds all join in glorious cry,
    The huntsman winds his horn:

And a-hunting we will go.
A-Hunting We Will Go

RONALD FIRBANK 1886–1926

1 There was a pause—just long enough for an angel to
pass, flying slowly.
Vainglory, 6

L'ABBÉ EDGEWORTH DE FIRMONT
1745–1807

2 *Fils de Saint Louis, montez au ciel.*
Son of Saint Louis, ascend to heaven.
Attr. words to Louis XVI as he mounted the steps of the guillotine
at his execution, 1793. No documentary proof at all.

LORD FISHER 1841–1920

3 Sack the lot!
The Times, 2 Sept. 1919

CHARLES FITZGEFFREY 1575?–1638

4 And bold and hard adventures t' undertake,
Leaving his country for his country's sake.
Sir Francis Drake (1596), st.213

EDWARD FITZGERALD 1809–1883

5 Awake! for Morning in the Bowl of Night
Has flung the Stone that puts the Stars to Flight:
    And Lo! the Hunter of the East has caught
The Sultan's Turret in a Noose of Light.
The Rubáiyát of Omar Khayyám (1859), 1

6 Dreaming when Dawn's Left Hand was in the Sky
I heard a Voice within the Tavern cry,
    'Awake, my Little ones, and fill the Cup
Before Life's Liquor in its Cup be dry.'
2

7   In divine
High piping Pehlevi, with 'Wine! Wine! Wine!
    Red Wine!'—the Nightingale cries to the Rose
That yellow Cheek of hers to incarnadine.
6
That sallow cheek of hers to incarnadine. (ed.4 1879)

8 And look—a thousand Blossoms with the Day
Woke—and a thousand scatter'd into Clay.
8

9 But come with old Khayyám and leave the Lot
Of Kaikobad and Kaikhosru forgot:
    Let Rustum lay about him as he will,
Or Hatim Tai cry Supper—heed them not.
9

10 Each Morn a thousand Roses brings, you say;
Yes, but where leaves the Rose of Yesterday?
    And this first Summer month that brings the Rose,
Shall take Jamshyd and Kaikobad away.
9 (ed.4)

11 Here with a Loaf of Bread beneath the bough,
A Flask of Wine, a Book of Verse—and Thou
    Beside me singing in the Wilderness—
And Wilderness is Paradise enow.
11
A Book of Verses underneath the Bough,
A Jug of Wine, a Loaf of Bread—and Thou
    Beside me singing in the Wilderness—
Oh, Wilderness were Paradise enow! 12 (ed.4)

12 Ah, take the Cash in hand and waive the Rest;
Oh, the brave Music of a *distant* Drum!
12
Ah, take the Cash, and let the Credit go,
Nor heed the rumble of a distant Drum! 13 (ed.4)

13 Think, in this batter'd Caravanserai
Whose Doorways are alternate Night and Day,
    How Sultan after Sultan with his Pomp
Abode his Hour or two, and went his way.
15
Think, in this batter'd Caravanserai
Whose Portals are alternate Night and Day,
    How Sultan after Sultan with his Pomp
Abode his destin'd Hour, and went his way. 17 (ed.4)

14 They say the Lion and the Lizard keep
The Courts where Jamshyd gloried and drank deep:
    And Bahram, that great Hunter—the Wild Ass
Stamps o'er his Head, and he lies fast asleep.
17
…but cannot break his Sleep. 18 (ed.4)

15 I sometimes think that never blows so red
The Rose as where some buried Caesar bled;
    That every Hyacinth the Garden wears
Dropt in her Lap from some once lovely Head.
18

16 Ah, my Belovéd, fill the Cup that clears
TO-DAY of past Regrets and Future Fears:
    To-morrow!—Why, To-morrow I may be
Myself with Yesterday's Sev'n thousand Years.
20

17 Lo! some we loved, the loveliest and best
That Time and Fate of all their Vintage prest,
    Have drunk their Cup a Round or two before,
And one by one crept silently to Rest.
21
For some we loved, the loveliest and best
That from his Vintage rolling Time hath prest. 22 (ed.4)

18 Ah, make the most of what we yet may spend,
Before we too into the Dust descend;
    Dust into Dust, and under Dust, to lie,
Sans Wine, sans Song, sans Singer, and—sans End!
23

19 Oh, come with old Khayyám, and leave the Wise
To talk; one thing is certain, that Life flies;
    One thing is certain, and the Rest is Lies;
The Flower that once hath blown for ever dies.
26
Oh threats of Hell and Hopes of Paradise!
One thing at least is certain—*This* Life flies;
One thing is certain and the rest is Lies;
The Flower that once has blown for ever dies. 63 (ed.4)

20 Myself when young did eagerly frequent
Doctor and Saint, and heard great argument
    About it and about: but evermore
Came out by the same Door as I went.
27
Came out by the same Door wherein I went. (ed.4)

21 With them the Seed of Wisdom did I sow,
And with mine own hand wrought to make it grow;
    And this was all the Harvest that I reap'd—
'I came like Water, and like Wind I go'.
28

22 Ah, fill the Cup:—what boots it to repeat
How Time is slipping underneath our Feet:
    Unborn TO-MORROW, and dead YESTERDAY,

Why fret about them if TO-DAY be sweet!
37

1 You know, my Friends, with what a brave Carouse
I made a Second Marriage in my house;
    Divorced old barren Reason from my Bed,
And took the Daughter of the Vine to Spouse.
55 (ed.4)

2 The Grape that can with Logic absolute
The Two-and-Seventy jarring Sects confute.
43

3 For in and out, above, about, below,
'Tis nothing but a Magic Shadow-show,
    Played in a Box whose Candle is the Sun,
Round which we Phantom Figures come and go.
46

4 Strange, is it not? that of the myriads who
Before us pass'd the door of Darkness through,
    Not one returns to tell us of the Road,
Which to discover we must travel too.
64 (ed.4)

5 'Tis all a Chequer-board of Nights and Days
Where Destiny with Men for Pieces plays:
    Hither and thither moves, and mates, and slays,
And one by one back in the Closet lays.
49
But helpless Pieces of the Game He plays
Upon this Chequer-board of Nights and Days;
    Hither and thither moves, and checks, and slays,
And one by one back in the Closet lays. 69 (ed.4)

6 The Ball no question makes of Ayes and Noes,
But Here or There as strikes the Player goes;
    And He that toss'd you down into the Field,
He knows about it all—HE knows—HE knows!
70 (ed.4)

7 The Moving Finger writes; and, having writ,
Moves on: nor all thy Piety nor Wit
    Shall lure it back to cancel half a Line,
Nor all thy Tears wash out a Word of it.
51 ...your Tears... 71 (ed.4)

8 And that inverted Bowl we call The Sky,
Whereunder crawling coop't we live and die,
    Lift not thy hands to *It* for help—for It
Rolls impotently on as Thou or I.
52
...they call the Sky...
As impotently moves as you or I. 72 (ed.4)

9 Drink! for you know not whence you came, nor why:
Drink! for you know not why you go, nor where.
74 (ed.4)

10 After a momentary silence spake
Some Vessel of a more ungainly Make;
    'They sneer at me for leaning all awry;
What! did the Hand then of the Potter shake?'
86 (ed.4)

11 'Who *is* the Potter, pray, and who the Pot?'
60

12 Then said another—'Surely not in vain
My Substance from the common Earth was ta'en,
    That He who subtly wrought me into Shape,
Should stamp me back to common Earth again'.
61

13 Indeed the Idols I have loved so long
Have done my credit in this World much wrong:
    Have drown'd my Glory in a Shallow Cup

And sold my Reputation for a Song.
93 (ed.4)

14 And much as Wine has play'd the Infidel,
And robb'd me of my Robe of Honour—Well,
    I often wonder what the Vintners buy
One half so precious as the Goods they sell.
71 ...the stuff they sell. 95 (ed.4)

15 Alas, that Spring should vanish with the Rose!
That Youth's sweet-scented Manuscript should close!
    The Nightingale that in the Branches sang,
Ah, whence, and whither flown again, who knows!
72

16 Ah Love! could thou and I with Fate conspire
To grasp this sorry Scheme of Things entire,
    Would not we shatter it to bits—and then
Re-mould it nearer to the Heart's Desire!
73
Ah Love! could you and I with Him conspire. 94 (ed.4)

17 Ah, Moon of my Delight who know'st no wane,
The Moon of Heav'n is rising once again:
    How oft hereafter rising shall she look
Through this same Garden after me—in vain!
74
Yon rising Moon that looks for us again.
How oft hereafter will she wax and wane;
    How oft hereafter rising look for us
Through this same Garden—and for *one* in vain! 100 (ed.4)

18 And when Thyself with shining Foot shall pass
Among the Guests Star-scattered on the Grass,
    And in thy joyous Errand reach the Spot
Where I made one—turn down an empty Glass!
75
And when like her, O Saki, you shall pass...
And in your joyous errand reach the spot. 101 (ed.4)

19 Mrs Browning's death is rather a relief to me, I must
say: no more Aurora Leighs, thank God! A woman of
real genius, I know; but what is the upshot of it all?
She and her sex had better mind the kitchen and their
children; and perhaps the poor: except in such things
as little novels, they only devote themselves to what
men do much better, leaving that which men do worse
or not at all.
Letter to W.H. Thompson, 15 July 1861. For Browning's
rejoinder see 106:1

20 Taste is the feminine of genius.
To J.R. Lowell, Oct. 1877

21 A Mr Wilkinson, a clergyman.
Hallam Tennyson, *Tennyson*, ii.276. An imitation of
Wordsworth's worst style.

F. SCOTT FITZGERALD 1896–1940

22 In the real dark night of the soul it is always three
o'clock in the morning.
The Crack-Up, ed. E. Wilson (1945), John Peale Bishop, *The
Hours*. The phrase 'dark night of the soul' was used as the Spanish
title of a work by St. John of the Cross known in English as *The
Ascent of Mount Carmel* (1578-80)

23 Her voice is full of money.
The Great Gatsby, ch.7

24 Let me tell you about the very rich. They are different
from you and me.
The Rich Boy. 'Notebooks E' in *The Crack-Up* records Ernest
Hemingway's rejoinder: 'Yes, they have more money.'

ROBERT FITZSIMMONS 1862–1917

1 The bigger they come, the harder they fall.
Said before his fight with Jefferies in San Francisco, 9 June 1899

GUSTAVE FLAUBERT 1821–1880

2 *Nous ferons tout ce qui nous plaira! nous laisserons pousser notre barbe!*
We'll do just as we like! We'll grow beards!
Bouvard et Pécuchet, ch.1

3 *Les livres ne se font pas comme les enfants, mais comme les pyramides…et ça ne sert à rien! et ça reste dans le désert!…Les chacals pissent au bas et les bourgeois montent dessus.*
Books are made not like children but like pyramides…and they're just as useless! and they stay in the desert!…Jackals piss at their foot and the bourgeois climb up on them.
Letter to Ernest Feydeau (1821-73), Nov./Dec. 1857

JAMES ELROY FLECKER 1884–1915

4 For pines are gossip pines the wide world through.
Brumana

5 Half to forget the wandering and the pain,
Half to remember days that have gone by,
And dream and dream that I am home again!

6 Noon strikes on England, noon on Oxford town,
Beauty she was statue cold—there's blood upon her gown:
Noon of my dreams, O noon!
Proud and godly kings had built her, long ago,
With her towers and tombs and statues all arow,
With her fair and floral air and the love that lingers there,
And the streets where the great men go.
The Dying Patriot

7 West of these out to seas colder than the Hebrides I must go
Where the fleet of stars is anchored and the young star-captains glow.

8 The dragon-green, the luminous, the dark, the serpent-haunted sea.
The Gates of Damascus. West Gate

9 We who with songs beguile your pilgrimage
And swear that Beauty lives though lilies die,
We Poets of the proud old lineage
Who sing to find your hearts, we know not why,—
What shall we tell you? Tales, marvellous tales
Of ships and stars and isles where good men rest.
The Golden Journey to Samarkand (1913), Prologue

10 When the great markets by the sea shut fast
All that calm Sunday that goes on and on:
When even lovers find their peace at last,
And Earth is but a star, that once had shone.

11 How splendid in the morning glows the lily; with what grace he throws
His supplication to the rose.
Hassan (1922), I.i

12 And some to Meccah turn to pray, and I toward thy bed, Yasmin.

13   For one night or the other night
Will come the Gardener in white, and gathered flowers are dead, Yasmin.

14 For lust of knowing what should not be known,
We take the Golden Road to Samarkand.
V.ii

15 And once I touched a broken girl
And knew that marble bled.
Oak and Olive

16 I have seen old ships sail like swans asleep
Beyond that village which men still call Tyre,
With leaden age o'ercargoed, dipping deep
For Famagusta and the hidden sun
That rings black Cyprus with a lake of fire.
The Old Ships (1915)

17 But now through friendly seas they softly run,
Painted the mid-sea blue or the shore-sea green,
Still patterned with the vine and grapes in gold.

18 And with great lies about his wooden horse
Set the crew laughing, and forgot his course.

19 It was so old a ship—who knows, who knows?
And yet so beautiful, I watched in vain
To see the mast burst open with a rose,
And the whole deck put on its leaves again.

20 And walk with you, and talk with you, like any other boy.
Riouopéroux

21 A ship, an isle, a sickle moon—
With few but with how splendid stars
The mirrors of the sea are strewn
Between their silver bars.
A Ship, an Isle, and a Sickle Moon

22 And old Maeonides the blind
Said it three thousand years ago.
To a Poet a Thousand Years Hence

23 O friend unseen, unborn, unknown,
Student of our sweet English tongue,
Read out my words at night, alone:
I was a poet, I was young.

RICHARD FLECKNOE d. 1678?

24 Still-born Silence! thou that art
Floodgate of the deeper heart.
Miscellania (1653)

MARJORY FLEMING 1803–1811

25 A direful death indeed they had
That would put any parent mad
But she was more than usual calm
She did not give a singel dam.
Journal, p.29

26 The most devilish thing is 8 times 8 and 7 times 7 it is what nature itselfe cant endure.
p.47

27 To-day I pronounced a word which should never come out of a lady's lips it was that I called John a Impudent Bitch.
p.51

28 I am going to turn over a new life and am going to be a very good girl and be obedient to Isa Keith, here there is plenty of gooseberries which makes my teeth watter.
p.76

29 I hope I will be religious again but as for regaining my

character I despare.
p.80

1 An annibabtist is a thing I am not a member of.
p.99

2 Sentiment is what I am not acquainted with.

3 My dear Isa,
    I now sit down on my botom to answer all your kind
    and beloved letters which you was so good as to
    write to me.
Letters. I, To Isabella

4 O lovely O most charming pug
    Thy graceful air and heavenly mug...
    His noses cast is of the roman
    He is a very pretty weoman
    I could not get a rhyme for roman
    And was obligded to call it weoman.
Poems

PAUL FLEMING 1609–1640

5 *Des grossen Vaters Helm ist viel zu weit dem Sohne.*
The mighty father's helm is far too big for his son.
Die jetzigen Deutschen

ANDREW FLETCHER OF SALTOUN 1655–1716

6 I knew a very wise man so much of Sir Chr—'s
sentiment, that he believed if a man were permitted to
make all the ballads, he need not care who should
make the laws of a nation.
Political Works. **Letter to the Marquis of Montrose, and
Others** (1703)

JOHN FLETCHER 1579–1625
See also under BEAUMONT

7 Best while you have it use your breath,
    There is no drinking after death.
The Bloody Brother (with Jonson and others), II.ii, song

8 And he that will go to bed sober,
    Falls with the leaf still in October.

9 Three merry boys, and three merry boys,
    And three merry boys are we,
    As ever did sing in a hempen string
    Under the Gallows-Tree.
III.ii

10 Come, we are stark naught all, bad's the best of us.
IV.ii

11 Death hath so many doors to let out life.
The Custom of the Country (with Massinger), II.ii. See
336:1, 420:11, 566:26

12 But what is past my help, is past my care.
The Double Marriage (with Massinger), I.i

13 Our acts our angels are, or good or ill,
    Our fatal shadows that walk by us still.
An Honest Man's Fortune, Epilogue

14 *Leon:* I have heard you are poetical.
    Mallfort: Something given that way.
The Lover's Progress (rev. Massinger), I.i

15 Deeds, not words shall speak me.
III.vi

16 I find the medicine worse than the malady.
III.ii

17 Nothing's so dainty sweet, as lovely melancholy.
The Nice Valour (with Middleton), III.iii, song

18 'Tis virtue, and not birth that makes us noble:
    Great actions speak great minds, and such should
      govern.
The Prophetess (with Massinger), II.iii

19 Are you at ease now? Is your heart at rest?
    Now you have got a shadow, an umbrella
    To keep the scorching world's opinion
    From your fair credit.
Rule a Wife and Have a Wife, III.i

20 I'll have a fling.
v

21 Daisies smell-less, yet most quaint,
                    And sweet thyme true,
    Primrose first born child of Ver,
    Merry Springtime's Harbinger.
Two Noble Kinsmen (with Shakespeare), I.i

22 Care-charming Sleep, thou easer of all woes,
    Brother to Death.
Valentinian, V.ii, song

23 Come sing now, sing; for I know ye sing well,
    I see ye have a singing face.
The Wild-Goose Chase, II.ii

24 Whistle and she'll come to you.
Wit Without Money, IV.iv

25 Charity and beating begins at home.
V.ii

26 Have you not maggots in your brains?
Women Pleased, III.iv

PHINEAS FLETCHER 1582–1650

27 Poorly (poor man) he liv'd; poorly (poor man) he
    di'd.
The Purple Island (1633), I.xix

28 His little son into his bosom creeps,
    The lively picture of his father's face.
XII.vi

29 Drop, drop, slow tears,
      And bathe those beauteous feet,
    Which brought from Heav'n
      The news and Prince of Peace.
An Hymn

30 In your deep floods
      Drown all my faults and fears;
    Not let His eye
      See sin, but through my tears.

31 Love is like linen often chang'd, the sweeter.
Sicelides (1614), III.v

32 The coward's weapon, poison.
V.iii

33 Love's tongue is in the eyes.
Piscatory Eclogues (1633), eclog. V, xiii

JEAN-PIERRE CLARIS DE FLORIAN 1755–1794

34 *Plaisir d'amour ne dure qu'un moment,
    Chagrin d'amour dure toute la vie.*
Love's pleasure lasts but a moment; love's sorrow
    lasts all through life.
Celestine. See 327:19

JOHN FLORIO 1553?–1625

1 England is the paradise of women, the purgatory of
men, and the hell of horses.
Second Frutes (1591)

DR F.J. FOAKES JACKSON 1855–1941

2 It's no use trying to be *clever*—we are all clever here;
just try to be *kind*—a little kind.
Said to a recently elected young don at Jesus College, Cambridge.
Oral tradition. Noted in A.C. Benson's Commonplace Book

MARSHAL FOCH 1851–1929

3 *Mon centre cède, ma droite recule, situation
excellente. J'attaque!*
My centre is giving way, my right is in retreat;
situation excellent. I shall attack.
Aston, *Biography of Foch* (1929), ch.13

JOSÉ DA FONSECA
and PEDRO CAROLINO fl. 1855

4 The walls have hearsay.
O Novo Guia da Conversação em Portuguez e Inglez (1855),
Idiotisms and Proverbs. Selections from this book were first
published in England by James Millington in 1883 under the title
English as she is spoke: or a Jest in sober earnest.

5 *Por dinheiro baila o perro.* Nothing some money
nothing of Swiss.
A literal translation of the Portuguese proverb would be *The dog
dances for money.* It is suspected that the *Novo Guia* was prepared
with the help of a French-English dictionary. See 404:5

SAMUEL FOOTE 1720–1777

6 Born in a cellar,...and living in a garret.
The Author (1757), II

7 So she went into the garden to cut a cabbage-leaf, to
make an apple-pie; and at the same time a great
she-bear, coming up the street, pops its head into the
shop. 'What! no soap?' So he died, and she very
imprudently married the barber; and there were
present the Picninnies, and the Joblillies, and the
Garyalies, and the grand Panjandrum himself, with the
little round button at top, and they all fell to playing
the game of catch as catch can, till the gun powder ran
out at the heels of their boots.
Farrago composed by Foote to test the vaunted memory of the
actor Charles Macklin. See *Quarterly Review* (1854), 95.516

8   For as the old saying is,
When house and land are gone and spent
Then learning is most excellent.
Taste (1752), I.i

9 He is not only dull in himself, but the cause of
dullness in others.
Boswell, *Life of Johnson*, ed. Powell, IV, p.178. Parody of
441:3

MISS C.F. FORBES 1817–1911

10 The sense of being well-dressed gives a feeling of
inward tranquillity which religion is powerless to
bestow.
Emerson, *Social Aims*

HENRY FORD 1863–1947

11 History is more or less bunk.
Chicago Tribune, 25 May 1916

JOHN FORD c.1586–1639

12 Tempt not the stars, young man, thou canst not play
With the severity of fate.
The Broken Heart (1633), I.iii

13 I am...a mushroom
On whom the dew of heaven drops now and then.

14 The joys of marriage are the heaven on earth,
Life's paradise, great princess, the soul's quiet,
Sinews of concord, earthly immortality,
Eternity of pleasures; no restoratives
Like to a constant woman.
II.ii

15   There's not a hair
Sticks on my head but, like a leaden plummet,
It sinks me to the grave: I must creep thither;
The journey is not long.
IV.ii

16 He hath shook hands with time.
V.ii

17 We can drink till all look blue.
The Lady's Trial (1638), IV.ii

18   Tell us, pray, what devil
This melancholy is, which can transform
Men into monsters.
III.i

19 Parthenophil is lost, and I would see him;
For he is like to something I remember,
A great while since, a long, long time ago.
The Lover's Melancholy (1629)

20   Why, I hold fate
Clasp'd in my fist, and could command the course
Of time's eternal motion, hadst thou been
One thought more steady than an ebbing sea.
'Tis Pity She's a Whore (1633), V.iv

HOWELL FORGY 1908–

21 Praise the Lord, and pass the ammunition.
Attr. when a Naval Lt., at Pearl Harbor, 7 Dec. 1941

E.M. FORSTER 1879–1970

22 They go forth into it [the world] with well-developed
bodies, fairly developed minds, and undeveloped
hearts. [Public schoolboys.]
Abinger Harvest (1936), pt.I, **Notes on the English Character,**
first published 1920

23 Everything must be like something, so what is this
like?
Our Diversions, 3 'The Doll Souse', first published 1924

24 Yes—oh dear yes—the novel tells a story.
Aspects of the Novel, ch.2

25 I felt for a moment that the whole Wilcox family was
a fraud, just a wall of newspapers and motor-cars and
golf-clubs, and that if it fell I should find nothing
behind it but panic and emptiness.
Howards End, ch.4

26 All men are equal—all men, that is to say, who

possess umbrellas.
ch.6

1 Personal relations are the important thing for ever and ever, and not this outer life of telegrams and anger.
ch.19

2 Only connect! That was the whole of her sermon. Only connect the prose and the passion, and both will be exalted, and human love will be seen at its highest.
ch.22

3 Death destroys a man; the idea of Death saves him.
ch.27

4 The good societies say, 'I tell you to do this because I am Cambridge'. The bad ones say, 'I tell you to do that because I am the great world'—not 'because I am Peckham', or 'Billingsgate', or 'Park Lane', but 'because I am the great world'. They lie.
The Longest Journey, ch.7

5 The very wood seems to be made of mud, the inhabitants of mud moving.
A Passage to India, ch.1

6 'I don't think I understand people very well. I only know whether I like or dislike them.' 'Then you are an Oriental.'
ch.2

7 The so-called white races are really pinko-gray.
ch.7

8 The echo in a Marabar cave…is entirely devoid of distinction…Hope, politeness, the blowing of a nose, the squeak of a bat, all produce 'boum'
ch.14

9 God si Love. Is this the final message of India?
ch.33

10 I do not believe in Belief…Lord I disbelieve—help thou my unbelief.
Two Cheers for Democracy, pt.2. **What I Believe.** See 119:11

11 My law-givers are Erasmus and Montaigne, not Moses and St Paul.

12 I hate the idea of causes, and if I had to choose between betraying my country and betraying my friend, I hope I should have the guts to betray my country.

13 So Two cheers for Democracy: one because it admits variety and two because it permits criticism. Two cheers are quite enough: there is no occasion to give three. Only Love the Beloved Republic deserves that.

14 Works of art, in my opinion, are the only objects in the material universe to possess internal order, and that is why, though I don't believe that only art matters, I do believe in Art for Art's sake.
Art for Art's Sake. See 162:5, 163:9

15 Creative writers are always greater than the causes that they represent.
Gide and George

CHARLES FOSTER 1828–1904

16 Isn't this a billion dollar country?
At the 51st Congress; retorting to a Democratic gibe about a 'million dollar Congress'. Also attr. Thomas B. Reed.

SIR GEORGE FOSTER 1847–1931

17 In these somewhat troublesome days when the great

Mother Empire stands splendidly isolated in Europe.
Canadian House of Commons, 16 Jan. 1896

CHARLES FOURIER 1772–1837

18 *L'extension des privilèges des femmes est le principe général de tous progrès sociaux.*
The extension of women's rights is the basic principle of all social progress.
Théorie des Quatre Mouvements (1808), II.iv

CHARLES JAMES FOX 1749–1806

19 How much the greatest event it is that ever happened in the world! and how much the best!
On the Fall of the Bastille. Letter to Fitzpatrick, 30 July 1789. Russell, *Life and Times of C.J. Fox,* vol.ii, p.361

20 He was uniformly of an opinion which, though not a popular one, he was ready to aver, that the right of governing was not property but a trust.
On Pitt's scheme of Parliamentary Reform. J.L. Hammond, *C.J. Fox* (1903), p.75

21 No man could be so wise as Thurlow looked.
Campbell, *Lives of the Lord Chancellors* (1846), vol.v, p.661

22 I die happy.
Last Words, Russell, *op.cit.,* vol.iii, ch.69

GEORGE FOX 1624–1691

23 I told them I lived in the virtue of that life and power that took away the occasion of all wars.
Fox had been offered a captaincy in the army of the Commonwealth, against the forces of the King, in 1651. **Journal,** ed. N. Penney (1911), vol.I, p.11

HENRY FOX
see 1ST LORD HOLLAND

HENRY RICHARD VASSALL FOX
see 3RD LORD HOLLAND

HENRY STEPHEN FOX 1791–1846

24 I am so changed that my oldest creditors would hardly know me.
After an illness. Quoted by Byron in a letter to John Murray, 8 May 1817

ANATOLE FRANCE 1844–1924

25 *Désarmer les forts et armer les faibles ce serait changer l'ordre social que j'ai mission de conserver. La justice est la sanction des injustices établies.*
To disarm the strong and arm the weak would be to change the social order which it's my job to preserve. Justice is the means by which established injustices are sanctioned.
Crainquebille, iv

26 *La majestueuse égalité des lois, qui interdit au riche comme au pauvre de coucher sous les ponts, de mendier dans les rues et de voler du pain.*
The majestic egalitarianism of the law, which forbids rich and poor alike to sleep under bridges, to beg in the streets, and to steal bread.
Le Lys Rouge (1894), ch.7

27 *Il fut des temps barbares et gothiques où les mots avaient un sens; alors les écrivains exprimaient des*

pensées.
It was in the barbarous, gothic times when words had a meaning; in those days, writers expressed thoughts.
La Vie Littéraire (1888-92), vol.II. **M. Charles Morice**

FRANCIS I 1494–1547

1 *De toutes choses ne m'est demeuré que l'honneur et la vie qui est saulve.*
Of all I had, only honour and life have been spared.
Letter to his mother after his defeat at Pavia, 1525. *Collection des Documents Inédits sur l'Histoire de France* (1847), I, 129. Usually cited as *'Tout est perdu fors l'honneur'* (All is lost save honour).

ST. FRANCIS DE SALES 1567–1622

2 *Ce sont les grans feux qui s'enflamment au vent, mays les petitz s'esteignent si on ne les y porte a couvert.*
Big fires flare up in a wind, but little ones are blown out unless they are carried in under cover.
Introduction à la vie dévote (1609), pt.III, ch.34

BENJAMIN FRANKLIN 1706–1790

3 Remember, that time is money.
Advice to Young Tradesman (1748)

4 No nation was ever ruined by trade.
Essays. Thoughts on Commercial Subjects

5 The having made a young girl miserable may give you frequent bitter reflection; none of which can attend the making of an old woman happy.
On the Choice of a Mistress (i.e. wife)

6 A little neglect may breed mischief,…for want of a nail, the shoe was lost; for want of a shoe the horse was lost; and for want of a horse the rider was lost.
Maxims…Prefixed to *Poor Richard's Almanack* (1758)

7 Some are weather-wise, some are otherwise.
Poor Richard's Almanack, Feb. 1735

8 Necessity never made a good bargain.
Apr. 1735

9 Three may keep a secret, if two of them are dead.
July 1735

10 At twenty years of age, the will reigns; at thirty, the wit; and at forty, the judgement.
June 1741

11 Dost thou love life? Then do not squander time, for that's the stuff life is made of.
June 1746

12 Many have been ruined by buying good pennyworths.
Sept. 1747

13 He that lives upon hope will die fasting.
1758, preface

14 We must indeed all hang together, or, most assuredly, we shall all hang separately.
Remark to John Hancock, at the Signing of the Declaration of Independence, 4 July 1776

15 Man is a tool-making animal.
Boswell, *Life of Johnson,* 7 Apr. 1778

16 Here Skugg
Lies snug
As a bug
In a rug.
Letter to Georgiana Shipley on the death of her squirrel, 26 Sept. 1772. 'Skug' was a dialect word meaning 'squirrel'.

17 There never was a good war, or a bad peace.
Letter to Quincy, 11 Sept. 1783

18 But in this world nothing can be said to be certain, except death and taxes.
Letter to Jean Baptiste Le Roy, 13 Nov. 1789

19 What is the use of a new-born child?
When asked what was the use of a new invention. J. Parton, *Life and Times of Benjamin Franklin* (1864), pt.IV, ch.17

20　　　　　The body of
Benjamin Franklin, printer,
(Like the cover of an old book,
Its contents worn out,
And stript of its lettering and gilding)
Lies here, food for worms!
Yet the work itself shall not be lost,
For it will, as he believed, appear once more
In a new
And more beautiful edition,
Corrected and amended
By its Author!
Epitaph for himself. See 553:22

21 *Ça ira.*
That will go its way.
Oral trad. Remark made in Paris, 1776-7, on the American War of Independence. Taken up in the French Revolution and used as the refrain of the song to the tune *'Carillon national'* by 1790. Ladré later claimed to have written the words.

FREDERICK THE GREAT 1712–1786

22 My people and I have come to an agreement which satisfies us both. They are to say what they please, and I am to do what I please.
Ascribed

23 *Ihr Racker, wollt ihr ewig leben?*
Rascals, would you live for ever?
When the Guards hesitated, at Kolin, 18 June 1757

E.A. FREEMAN 1823–1892

24 A saying which fell from myself in one of the debates in Congregation on the Modern Language Statute has been quoted in several places…'chatter about Shelley'…I mentioned that I had lately read a review of a book about Shelley in which the critic…praised or blamed the author…for his 'treatment of the Harriet problem'.
Contemporary Review, Oct. 1887: 'Literature and Language'. The two phrases are often telescoped as 'chatter about Harriet'.

JOHN HOOKHAM FRERE 1769–1846

25 The feather'd race with pinions skim the air—
Not so the mackerel, and still less the bear!
Progress of Man, l.34

26 Ah! who has seen the mailed lobster rise,
Clap her broad wings, and soaring claim the skies?
l.44

ROBERT FROST 1874–1963

27 I have been one acquainted with the night.
I have walked out in rain—and back in rain.
I have outwalked the furthest city light.

I have looked down the saddest city lane.
I have passed by the watchman on his beat

And dropped my eyes, unwilling to explain.
Acquainted with the Night

1 I'd like to get away from earth awhile
And then come back to it and begin over.
May no fate willfully misunderstand me
And half grant what I wish and snatch me away
Not to return. Earth's the right place for love:
I don't know where it's likely to get better.
I'd like to go by climbing a birch tree,
And climb black branches up a snow-white trunk
Toward heaven, till the tree could bear no more,
But dipped its top and set me down again.
That would be good both going and coming back.
One could do worse than be a swinger of birches.
Birches

2 'Home is the place where, when you have to go there,
They have to take you in'.

'I should have called it
Something you somehow haven't to deserve.'
The Death of the Hired Man

3 They cannot scare me with their empty spaces
Between stars—on stars where no human race is.
I have it in me so much nearer home
To scare myself with my own desert places.
Desert Places

4 Spades take up leaves
No better than spoons,
And bags full of leaves
Are light as balloons.
Gathering Leaves

5 The land was ours before we were the land's.
The Gift Outright

6 Such as we were we gave ourselves outright
(The deed of gift was many deeds of war)
To the land vaguely realizing westward,
But still unstoried, artless, unenhanced,
Such as she was, such as she would become.

7 Forgive, O Lord, my little jokes on Thee
And I'll forgive Thy great big one on me.
In the clearing, **Cluster of Faith**

8 Something there is that doesn't love a wall.
North of Boston (1914). **Mending Wall**

9 My apple trees will never get across
And eat the cones under his pines, I tell him.
He only says, 'Good fences make good neighbours.'

10 Two roads diverged in a wood, and I—
I took the one less traveled by,
And that has made all the difference.
The Road Not Taken

11 Whoever it is that leaves him out so late,
When other creatures have gone to stall and bin,
Ought to be told to come and take him in.
The Runaway

12 The woods are lovely, dark, and deep,
But I have promises to keep,
And miles to go before I sleep,
And miles to go before I sleep.
Stopping by Woods on a Snowy Evening

13 To err is human, not to, animal.
The White-tailed Hornet

14 The ruling passion in man is not as Viennese as is
claimed. It is rather a gregarious instinct to keep

together by minding each other's business. Grex rather
than sex.
The Constant Symbol

15 Writing free verse is like playing tennis with the net
down.
Address at Milton Academy, Milton, Mass., 17 May 1935

16 Poetry is what gets lost in translation.
Attr.

J.A. FROUDE 1818–1894

17 Wild animals never kill for sport. Man is the only one
to whom the torture and death of his fellow-creatures
is amusing in itself.
Oceana (1886), ch.5

18 Men are made by nature unequal. It is vain, therefore,
to treat them as if they were equal.
Short Studies on Great Subjects. 3rd Ser (1877). **Party Politics**

19 Experience teaches slowly, and at the cost of
mistakes.

20 Fear is the parent of cruelty.

CHRISTOPHER FRY 1907–

21 This is the morning to take the air.
The Boy with a Cart (1938)

22 You can't be beaten by a piece of timber; it isn't
princely in a man to be beaten by a piece of timber.

23 There's a dreariness in dedicated spirits
That makes the promised land seem older than the
fish.
The Dark is Light Enough (1954), Act I

24   I sometimes think
His critical judgement is so exquisite
It leaves us nothing to admire except his opinion.
Act II

25   In our plain defects
We already know the brotherhood of man.

26 Out there, in the sparkling air, the sun and the rain
Clash together like the cymbals clashing
When David did his dance. I've an April blindness.
You're hidden in a cloud of crimson catherine-wheels.
The Lady's Not For Burning (1948), Act I

27   What, after all,
Is a halo? It's only one more thing to keep clean.

28   You bubble-mouthing, fog-blathering,
Chin-chuntering, chap-flapping, liturgical,
Turgidical, base old man!

29   Am I invisible?
Am I inaudible? Do I merely festoon
The room with my presence?

30   Using words
That are only fit for the Bible.
Act II

31 We should be like stars now that it's dark;
Use ourselves up to the last bright dregs
And vanish in the morning.

32   The moon is nothing
But a circumambulating aphrodisiac
Divinely subsidized to provoke the world
Into a rising birth-rate.
Act III

1   I hear
A gay modulating anguish, rather like music.

2 The Great Bear is looking so geometrical
One would think that something or other could be
   proved.

3 *Margaret:* She must be lost.
Nicholas: Who isn't? The best
Thing we can do is to make wherever we're lost in
Look as much like home as we can.

4 It's all this smell of cooped-up angels
Worries me.
A Sleep of Prisoners (1951)

5 Run on, keep your head down, cross at the double
The bursts of open day between the nights.

6   I hope
I've done nothing so monosyllabic as to cheat.
A spade is never so merely a spade as the word
Spade would imply.
Venus Observed (1950), II.i

7 Over all the world
Men move unhoming, and eternally
Concerned: a swarm of bees who have lost their
   queen.

8   What a minefield
Life is! One minute you're taking a stroll in the sun,
The next your legs and arms are all over the hedge.
There's no dignity in it.
A Yard of Sun (1970), Act II

9 There may always be another reality
To make fiction of the truth we think we've arrived at.

RICHARD BUCKMINSTER FULLER 1895–

10   God, to me, it seems,
is a verb
not a noun,
proper or improper.
No More Secondhand God. See 267:9

THOMAS FULLER 1608–1661

11 A proverb is much matter decocted into few words.
The History of the Worthies of England (1662), ch.2

12 Worldly wealth he cared not for, desiring only to make
both ends meet. [Of Edmund Grindall.]
Worthies of Cumberland

13 Know most of the rooms of thy native country before
thou goest over the threshold thereof.
The Holy State and the Profane State (1642), bk.ii, ch.4. **Of
Travelling**

14 A little skill in antiquity inclines a man to Popery; but
depth in that study brings him about again to our
religion.
ch.6. **The True Church Antiquary**

15 But our captain counts the Image of God nevertheless
his image, cut in ebony as if done in ivory.
ch.20. **The Good Sea-Captain**

16 Light (God's eldest daughter) is a principal beauty in
building.
bk.iii, ch.7. **Of Building**

17 Anger is one of the sinews of the soul.
ch.8. **Of Anger**

18 Learning hath gained most by those books by which

the printers have lost.
ch.18. **Of Books**

19 He was one of a lean body and visage, as if his eager
soul, biting for anger at the clog of his body, desired to
fret a passage through it.
bk.v, ch.19. **Life of the Duke of Alva**

THOMAS FULLER 1654–1734

20 It is a silly game where nobody wins.
Gnomologia (1732), No. 2880

21 We are all Adam's children but silk makes the
difference.
No.5425

HENRY FUSELI 1741–1825

22 Blake is damned good to steal from!
Gilchrist, *Life of Blake* (1863), ch.vii

ROSE FYLEMAN 1877–1957

23 There are fairies at the bottom of our garden.
Fairies and Chimneys

THOMAS GAINSBOROUGH 1727–1788

24 We are all going to Heaven, and Vandyke is of the
company.
Attr. last words. Boulton, *Thomas Gainsborough*, ch.9

REVD. THOMAS GAISFORD 1779–1855

25 Nor can I do better, in conclusion, than impress upon
you the study of Greek literature, which not only
elevates above the vulgar herd, but leads not
infrequently to positions of considerable emolument.
Christmas Day Sermon in the Cathedral, Oxford. Revd. W.
Tuckwell, *Reminiscences of Oxford* (2nd ed., 1907), p.124

HUGH GAITSKELL 1906–1963

26 There are some of us who will fight and fight and
fight again to save the party we love.
Speech, Labour Party Conference, Scarborough, 5 Oct. 1960

GAIUS 2nd cent. A.D.

27 *Damnosa hereditas.*
Ruinous inheritance.
Institutes, ii.163

J.K. GALBRAITH 1908–

28 In the affluent society no useful distinction can be
made between luxuries and necessaries.
The Affluent Society, ch.21.iv

GALILEO GALILEI 1564–1642

29 *Eppur si muove.*
But it does move.
Attr. to Galileo after his recantation in 1632. The earliest
apppearance of the phrase is perhaps in Baretti, *Italian Library*
(1757), p.52

JOHN GALSWORTHY 1867–1933

30 He [Jolyon] was afflicted by the thought that where
Beauty was, nothing ever ran quite straight, which, no

doubt, was why so many people looked on it as immoral.
In Chancery (1920), ch.13

1 Nobody tells me anything. [James Forsyte.]
The Man of Property (1906), pt.I, ch.i

JOHN GALT 1779–1839

2 From the lone shieling of the misty island
Mountains divide us, and the waste of seas—
Yet still the blood is strong, the heart is Highland,
And we in dreams behold the Hebrides!
Fair these broad meads, these hoary woods are grand;
But we are exiles from our fathers' land.
Attr. *Canadian Boat Song ('The Lone Shieling')*. 'Noctes
Ambrosianae', XLVI, Blackwoods Magazine, Sept. 1829

GRETA GARBO 1905–

3 I want to be alone.
Grand Hotel (1932), script by William A. Drake.
The phrase had frequently been attributed to Garbo before being
used in the film; she seems in fact to have said on various
occasions (off screen) 'I want to be left alone' and 'Why don't
they leave me alone.'

FEDERICO GARCÍA LORCA 1899–1936

4 *Verte desnuda es recordar la Tierra.*
To see you naked is to recall the Earth.
Casida de la mujer tendida

5 *A las cinco de la tarde.*
A las cinco en punto de la tarde.
At five in the afternoon. At exactly five in the afternoon.
Llanto por Ignacio Sánchez Mejías, 1

6 *Que no quiero verla!*
I don't want to see it!
2

7 *Verde que te quiero verde,*
Verde viento. Verde ramas.
Green I love you green. Green wind. Green branches.
Romance sonámbulo

RICHARD GARDINER b. c.1533

8 Sowe Carrets in your Gardens, and humbly praise God for them, as for a singular and great blessing.
Profitable Instructions for the Manuring, Sowing and Planting of Kitchen Gardens (1599)

JAMES A. GARFIELD 1831–1881

9 Fellow-citizens: God reigns, and the Government at Washington lives!
Speech on Assassination of Lincoln, 1865

GIUSEPPE GARIBALDI 1807–1882

10 *Soldati, io esco da Roma. Chi vuole continuare la guerra contro lo straniero venga con me. Non posso offrirgli nè onori nè stipendi; gli offro fame, sete, marcie forzate, battaglie e morte. Chi ama la patria mi segua.*
Men, I'm getting out of Rome. Anyone who wants to carry on the war against the outsiders, come with me. I can't offer you either honours or wages; I offer you hunger, thirst, forced marches, battles and death.

Anyone who loves his country, follow me.
Guerzoni, *Garibaldi* (1882), I. p.331. (The speech was not recorded verbatim.)

DAVID GARRICK 1717–1779

11 Prologues precede the piece—in mournful verse;
As undertakers—walk before the hearse.
Apprentice, prologue

12 Are these the choice dishes the Doctor has sent us?
Is this the great poet whose works so content us?
This Goldsmith's fine feast, who has written fine books?
Heaven sends us good meat, but the Devil sends cooks.
On Doctor Goldsmith's Characteristical Cookery

13 Here lies Nolly Goldsmith, for shortness call'd Noll,
Who wrote like an angel, but talk'd like poor Poll.
Impromptu Epitaph. See 231:16, 278:19

14 I've that within—for which there are no plaisters.
Prologue to Goldsmith's *She Stoops to Conquer*

15 A fellow-feeling makes one wond'rous kind.
An Occasional Prologue on Quitting the Theatre, 10 June 1776

16 Kitty, a fair, but frozen maid,
    Kindled a flame I still deplore;
The hood-wink'd boy I call'd in aid,
Much of his near approach afraid.
    So fatal to my suit before.
A Riddle. *Lady's Magazine,* June 1762

WILLIAM LLOYD GARRISON 1805–1879

17 I am in earnest—I will not equivocate—I will not excuse—I will not retreat a single inch—and I will be heard!
Salutatory Address of *The Liberator,* 1 Jan. 1831

18 Our country is the world—our countrymen are all mankind.
Prospectus of *The Liberator,* 15 Dec. 1837

19 The compact which exists between the North and the South is 'a covenant with death and an agreement with hell'.
Resolution adopted by the Massachusetts Anti-Slavery Society, 27 Jan. 1843. See 58:22

SIR SAMUEL GARTH 1661–1719

20 Hard was their lodging, homely was their food;
For all their luxury was doing good.
Claremont (1715), 1.148

21 A barren superfluity of words.
The Dispensary (1699), c.2, 1.95

MRS. GASKELL 1810–1865

22 A man...is *so* in the way in the house!
Cranford (1851-3), ch.1

23 [The Cranford ladies'] dress is very independent of fashion; as they observe, 'What does it signify how we dress here at Cranford, where everybody knows us?' And if they go from home, their reason is equally cogent: 'What does it signify how we dress here, where nobody knows us?'

24 Get her a flannel waistcoat and flannel drawers, ma'am, if you wish to keep her alive. But my advice is, kill the poor creature at once. [Capt. Brown on

Miss Betsey Barker's cow.]

1 We were none of us musical, though Miss Jenkyns
beat time, out of time, by way of appearing to be so.

2 'It is very pleasant dining with a bachelor,' said Miss
Matty, softly, as we settled ourselves in the
counting-house. 'I only hope it is not improper; so
many pleasant things are!'
ch.4

3 Bombazine would have shown a deeper sense of her
loss. [Miss Jenkyns.]
ch.7

4 That kind of patriotism which consists in hating all
other nations.
Sylvia's Lovers (1863), ch.1

GAVARNI 1804–1866

5 *Les enfants terribles.*
The embarrassing young.
Title of a series of prints

JOHN GAY 1685–1732

6   I rage, I melt, I burn,
The feeble God has stabb'd me to the heart.
Acis and Galatea (c.1720), ii

7 Bring me an hundred reeds of decent growth,
To make a pipe for my capacious mouth.

8 O ruddier than the cherry,
O sweeter than the berry.

9 Wou'd you gain the tender creature?
Softly, gently, kindly treat her,
   Suff'ring is the lover's part.
Beauty by constraint, possessing,
You enjoy but half the blessing,
   Lifeless charms, without the heart.

10 Love sounds the alarm, and Fear is a flying.

11 How, like a moth, the simple maid
   Still plays about the flame!
The Beggar's Opera (1728), Act I, sc.iv, air iv

12 Our Polly is a sad slut! nor heeds what we have taught
her.
I wonder any man alive will ever rear a daughter!
sc.viii, air vii

13 Do you think your mother and I should have liv'd
comfortably so long together, if ever we had been
married?

14 Can Love be controll'd by advice?
air viii

15 Well, Polly; as far as one woman can forgive another,
I forgive thee.
air ix

16 *Polly:* Then all my sorrows are at an end.
Mrs Peachum: A mighty likely speech, in troth, for a
wench who is just married!

17 Money, wife, is the true fuller's earth for reputations,
there is not a spot or a stain but what it can take out.
sc.ix

18 The comfortable estate of widowhood, is the only
hope that keeps up a wife's spirits.
sc.x

19 Away, hussy. Hang your husband and be dutiful.

20 Even butchers weep!
sc.xii

21 Pretty Polly, say,
When I was away,
Did your fancy never stray
   To some newer lover?
sc.xiii, air xiv

22 If with me you'd fondly stray.
Over the hills and far away.
air xvi

23 O what pain it is to part!
air xvii

24 We retrench the superfluities of mankind.
Act II, sc.i

25 Fill ev'ry glass, for wine inspires us,
   And fires us
With courage, love and joy.
Women and wine should life employ.
Is there ought else on earth desirous?
air xix

26 If the heart of a man is deprest with cares,
The mist is dispell'd when a woman appears.
sc.iii, air xxi

27 I must have women. There is nothing unbends the
mind like them.

28 Youth's the season made for joys,
   Love is then our duty.
sc.iv, air xxii

29 To cheat a man is nothing; but the woman must have
fine parts indeed who cheats a woman!

30 Man may escape from rope and gun;
   Nay, some have outliv'd the doctor's pill:
Who takes a woman must be undone,
   That basilisk is sure to kill.
The fly that sips treacle is lost in the sweets,
So he that tastes woman, woman, woman,
   He that tastes woman, ruin meets.
sc.viii, air xxvi

31 *Macheath:* Have you no bowels, no tenderness, my
dear Lucy, to see a husband in these circumstances?
Lucy: A husband!
Macheath: In ev'ry respect but the form.
sc.ix

32 I am ready, my dear Lucy, to give you satisfaction—if
you think there is any in marriage?

33 In one respect indeed, our employment may be
reckoned dishonest, because, like great Statesmen, we
encourage those who betray their friends.
sc.x

34 I think you must ev'n do as other widows—buy
yourself weeds, and be cheerful.
sc.xi

35 How happy could I be with either,
   Were t'other dear charmer away!
But while ye thus tease me together,
   To neither a word will I say.
sc.xiii, air xxxv

36 One wife is too much for one husband to hear,
But two at a time there's no mortal can bear.
This way, and that way, and which way I will,
What would comfort the one, t'other wife would take

ill.
Act III, sc.xi, air liii

1 The charge is prepar'd; the lawyers are met;
The Judges all rang'd (a terrible show!).
air lvii

2 She who has never lov'd, has never liv'd.
The Captives (1724), II.i

3 If e'er your heart has felt the tender passion
You will forgive this just, this pious fraud.
IV.x

4 She who trifles with all
Is less likely to fall
Than she who but trifles with one.
The Coquet Mother and the Coquet Daughter

5 Then nature rul'd, and love, devoid of art,
Spoke the consenting language of the heart.
Dione, prologue

6 Behold the victim of Parthenia's pride!
He saw, he sigh'd, he lov'd, was scorn'd and died.
I.i

7 He best can pity who has felt the woe.
II.ii

8   Woman's mind
Oft' shifts her passions, like th'inconstant wind;
Sudden she rages, like the troubled main,
Now sinks the storm, and all is calm again.
v

9 A woman's friendship ever ends in love.
IV.vi

10 Whence is thy learning? Hath thy toil
O'er books consum'd the midnight oil?
Fables (1727), introduction, l.15. See 403:10

11 Where yet was ever found a mother,
Who'd give her booby for another?
iii. **The Mother, the Nurse, and the Fairy**, l.33

12 Envy's a sharper spur than pay,
No author ever spar'd a brother,
Wits are gamecocks to one another.
x. **The Elephant and the Bookseller**, l.74

13 An open foe may prove a curse,
But a pretended friend is worse.
xvii. **The Shepherd's Dog and the Wolf**, l.33

14 Those who in quarrels interpose,
Must often wipe a bloody nose.
xxxiv. **The Mastiff**, l.1

15 Fools may our scorn, not envy raise,
For envy is a kind of praise.
xliv. **The Hound and the Huntsman**, l.29

16 And when a lady's in the case,
You know, all other things give place.
l. **The Hare and Many Friends**, l.41

17 Give me, kind heaven, a private station,
A mind serene for contemplation.
(1738), ii. **The Vulture, the Sparrow, and Other Birds**, l.69

18 Studious of elegance and ease,
Myself alone I seek to please.
viii. **The Man, the Cat, the Dog, and the Fly**, l.127

19 Behold the bright original appear.
A Letter to a Lady, l.85

20 Praising all alike, is praising none.
l.114

21 One always zealous for his country's good.
l.118

22 Life is a jest; and all things show it.
I thought so once; but now I know it.
My Own Epitaph

23 Variety's the source of joy below,
From whence still fresh revolving pleasures flow.
In books and love, the mind one end pursues,
And only change th'expiring flame renews.
On a Miscellany of Poems

24 Whether we can afford it or no, we must have
superfluities.
Polly (1729), I.i

25 No, sir, tho' I was born and bred in England, I can
dare to be poor, which is the only thing now-a-days
men are asham'd of.
xi

26 An inconstant woman, tho' she has no chance to be
very happy, can never be very unhappy.
xiv

27   No retreat.
        No retreat.
They must conquer or die who've no retreat.
II.x

28 All in the Downs the fleet was moor'd,
The streamers waving in the wind,
When black-ey'd Susan came aboard.
Sweet William's Farewell to Black-Eyed Susan

29 They'll tell thee, sailors, when away,
In ev'ry port a mistress find.

30 Adieu, she cries! and wav'd her lily hand.

31 A miss for pleasure, and a wife for breed.
The Toilette

SIR ERIC GEDDES 1875–1937

32 The Germans, if this Government is returned, are
going to pay every penny; they are going to be
squeezed, as a lemon is squeezed—until the pips
squeak. My only doubt is not whether we can squeeze
hard enough, but whether there is enough juice.
Speech, Cambridge, 10 Dec. 1918. *Cambridge Daily News*, 3/2

LLOYD GEORGE 1863–1945

33 What is our task? To make Britain a fit country for
heroes to live in.
Speech, Wolverhampton, 24 Nov. 1918

KING GEORGE I 1660–1727

34 I hate all Boets and Bainters.
Campbell, *Lives of the Chief Justices*, ch.30, Lord Mansfield

KING GEORGE II 1683–1760

35 *Non, j'aurai des maîtresses.*
No, I shall have mistresses.
Reply to Queen Caroline when, as she lay dying, she urged him to
marry again. Her reply to this was '*Ah! mon dieu! cela n'empêche
pas*'. Hervey, *Memoirs of George the Second* (1848), vol.ii

36 Mad, is he? Then I hope he will *bite* some of my other
generals.
Reply to the Duke of Newcastle who complained that General
Wolfe was a madman. Willson, *The life and letters of James
Wolfe*, ch.17

KING GEORGE III 1738–1820

1 Born and educated in this country I glory in the name of Briton.
Speech from the Throne, 1760

2 'Was there ever,' cried he, 'such stuff as great part of Shakespeare? Only one must not say so! But what think you?—what?—Is there not sad stuff? what?—what?'
To Fanny Burney (in her *Diary*, 19 Dec. 1785)

KING GEORGE IV 1762–1830

3 Harris, I am not well; pray get me a glass of brandy.
On first seeing Caroline of Brunswick. Earl of Malmesbury, *Diaries*, 5 Apr. 1795

KING GEORGE V 1865–1936

4 I have many times asked myself whether there can be more potent advocates of peace upon earth through the years to come than this massed multitude of silent witnesses to the desolation of war.
On the battlefield cemeteries in Flanders, 1922. Gavin Stamp (ed.), *Silent Cities* (1977), p.19

5 How is the Empire?
Last words. *The Times*, 21 Jan. 1936

EDWARD GIBBON 1737–1794

6 My early and invincible love of reading, which I would not exchange for the treasures of India.
Autobiography (World's Classics ed.), p.27

7 To the University of Oxford I acknowledge no obligation; and she will as cheerfully renounce me for a son, as I am willing to disclaim her for a mother. I spent fourteen months at Magdalen College: they proved the fourteen months the most idle and unprofitable of my whole life.
p.36

8 If I inquire into the manufactures of the monks of Magdalen, if I extend the inquiry to the other colleges of Oxford and Cambridge, a silent blush, or a scornful frown, will be the only reply. The fellows or monks of my time were decent easy men, who supinely enjoyed the gifts of the founder.

9 Their dull and deep potations excused the brisk intemperance of youth.

10 Dr — well remembered that he had a salary to receive, and only forgot that he had a duty to perform.
p.44

11 It was here that I suspended my religious inquiries (aged 17).
p.63

12 I saw and loved.
p.83

13 I sighed as a lover, I obeyed as a son.

14 Crowds without company, and dissipation without pleasure. [Of London.]
p.90

15 The captain of the Hampshire grenadiers...has not been useless to the historian of the Roman empire.
p.106. (Referring to his own army service.)

16 It was at Rome, on the 15th of October, 1764, as I sat musing amidst the ruins of the Capitol, while the barefoot friars were singing vespers in the Temple of Jupiter, that the idea of writing the decline and fall of the city first started to my mind.
p.160

17 The first of earthly blessings, independence.
p.176

18 I will not dissemble the first emotions of joy on the recovery of my freedom, and, perhaps, the establishment of my fame. But my pride was soon humbled, and a sober melancholy was spread over my mind, by the idea that I had taken an everlasting leave of an old and agreeable companion, and that whatsoever might be the future date of my History, the life of the historian must be short and precarious.
p.205

19 My English text is chaste, and all licentious passages are left in the decent obscurity of a learned language.
p.212

20 I must reluctantly observe that two causes, the abbreviation of time, and the failure of hope, will always tinge with a browner shade the evening of life.
p.221

21 The various modes of worship, which prevailed in the Roman world, were all considered by the people as equally true; by the philosopher, as equally false; and by the magistrate, as equally useful. And thus toleration produced not only mutual indulgence, but even religious concord.
The Decline and Fall of the Roman Empire (1776–88), ch.2

22 The principles of a free constitution are irrecoverably lost, when the legislative power is nominated by the executive.
ch.3

23 His reign is marked by the rare advantage of furnishing very few materials for history; which is, indeed, little more than the register of the crimes, follies, and misfortunes of mankind.
(Of Antoninus Pius, Roman Emperor, 137–161 A.D.) See 561:10

24 If a man were called to fix the period in the history of the world during which the condition of the human race was most happy and prosperous, he would, without hesitation, name that which elapsed from the death of Domitian to the accession of Commodus.

25 Twenty-two acknowledged concubines, and a library of sixty-two thousand volumes attested the variety of his inclinations; and from the productions which he left behind him, it appears that both the one and the other were designed for use rather than for ostentation.
[Emperor Gordian the Younger.]
ch.7

26 All taxes must, at last, fall upon agriculture.
ch.8

27 Corruption, the most infallible symptom of constitutional liberty.
ch.21

28 In every deed of mischief he [Comenus] had a heart to resolve, a head to contrive, and a hand to execute.
ch.48. See 152:19

29 All that is human must retrograde if it does not advance.
ch.71

ORLANDO GIBBONS 1583–1625

1 The silver swan, who, living had no note,
When death approached unlocked her silent throat.
from *The First Set of Madrigals and Motets of Five Parts* (1612)

STELLA GIBBONS 1902–

2 Something nasty in the woodshed.
Cold Comfort Farm (1932), *passim*

3 Every year, in the fulness o'summer, when the
sukebind hangs heavy from the wains...'tes the same.
And when the spring comes her hour is upon her
again. 'Tes the hand of Nature, and we women cannot
escape it.
ch.5

4 [Mr. Mybug] said that, by god, D.H. Lawrence was
right when he had said there must be a dumb, dark,
dull, bitter belly-tension between a man and a woman,
and how else could this be achieved save in the long
monotony of marriage?
ch.20

WILFRED GIBSON 1878–1962

5 The heart-break in the heart of things.
Lament (1926). See 557:17

ANDRÉ GIDE 1869–1951

6 *Hugo—hélas!*
When asked to name the greatest poet of the nineteenth century.
André Gide-Paul Valéry Correspondance 1890–1942, p.494

SIR HUMPHREY GILBERT 1539?–1583

7 We are as near to heaven by sea as by land!
Richard Hakluyt, *Voyages* (1600), iii, p.159. See 206:15

W.S. GILBERT 1836–1911

8 Down went the owners—greedy men whom hope of
gain allured:
Oh, dry the starting tear, for they were heavily
insured.
The 'Bab' Ballads (1866–71), **Etiquette**

9 He had often eaten oysters, but had never had enough.

10 There were captains by the hundred, there were
baronets by dozens.
Ferdinando and Elvira

11 Only find out who it is that writes those lovely cracker
mottoes!

12 The padre said, 'Whatever have you been and gone
and done?'
Gentle Alice Brown

13 From a highly impossible tree
In a highly impossible scene.
Only a Dancing Girl

14 Which is pretty, but I don't know what it means.
Story of Prince Agib

15 Then they began to sing
That extremely lovely thing,
'*Scherzando! ma non troppo ppp.*'

16 Oh, I am a cook and a captain bold,
And the mate of the *Nancy* brig,

And a bo'sun tight, and a midshipmite,
And the crew of the captain's gig.
The Yarn of the 'Nancy Bell'

17 He led his regiment from behind—
He found it less exciting.
The Gondoliers (1899), I

18 That celebrated,
Cultivated,
Underrated
Nobleman,
The Duke of Plaza Toro!

19 Of that there is no manner of doubt—
No probable, possible shadow of doubt—
No possible doubt whatever.

20 His terrible taste for tippling.

21 A taste for drink, combined with gout,
Had doubled him up for ever.

22 Oh, 'tis a glorious thing, I ween,
To be a regular Royal Queen!
No half-and-half affair, I mean,
But a right-down regular Royal Queen!

23 All shall equal be.
The Earl, the Marquis, and the Dook,
The Groom, the Butler, and the Cook,
The Aristocrat who banks with Coutts,
The Aristocrat who cleans the boots.

24 But the privilege and pleasure
That we treasure beyond measure
Is to run on little errands for the Ministers of State.
II

25 With the gratifying feeling that our duty has been
done!

26 Take a pair of sparkling eyes,
Hidden, ever and anon,
In a merciful eclipse.

27 Take my counsel, happy man;
Act upon it, if you can!

28 He wished all men as rich as he
(And he was rich as rich could be),
So to the top of every tree
Promoted everybody.

29 Ambassadors cropped up like hay,
Prime Ministers and such as they
Grew like asparagus in May,
And dukes were three a penny.

30 When every blessed thing you hold
Is made of silver, or of gold,
You long for simple pewter.
When you have nothing else to wear
But cloth of gold and satins rare,
For cloth of gold you cease to care—
Up goes the price of shoddy.

31 When every one is somebodee,
Then no one's anybody.

32 I see no objection to stoutness, in moderation.
Iolanthe (1882), I

33 For I'm to be married to-day—to-day—
Yes, I'm to be married to-day!

34 Thou the singer; I the song!

35 Bow, bow, ye lower middle classes!

Bow, bow, ye tradesmen, bow, ye masses.

1 The Law is the true embodiment
Of everything that's excellent.
It has no kind of fault or flaw,
And I, my Lords, embody the Law.

2 The constitutional guardian I
Of pretty young wards in Chancery,
All very agreeable girls—and none
Are over the age of twenty-one.
    A pleasant occupation for
    A rather susceptible Chancellor!

3 For I'm not so old, and not so plain,
And I'm quite prepared to marry again.

4 Spurn not the nobly born
        With love affected,
Nor treat with virtuous scorn
        The well-connected.

5 Hearts just as pure and fair
May beat in Belgrave Square
As in the lowly air
                Of Seven Dials.

6 When I went to the Bar as a very young man,
    (Said I to myself—said I),
I'll work on a new and original plan,
    (Said I to myself—said I).

7 My son in tears—and on his wedding day!

8 When all night long a chap remains
On sentry-go, to chase monotony
He exercises of his brains,
That is, assuming that he's got any.
Though never nurtured in the lap
Of luxury, yet I admonish you,
I am an intellectual chap,
And think of things that would astonish you.
I often think it's comical
    How Nature always does contrive
That every boy and every gal,
    That's born into the world alive,
Is either a little Liberal,
    Or else a little Conservative!
    II

9 When in that House MPs divide,
If they've a brain and cerebellum too,
They have to leave that brain outside,
And vote just as their leaders tell 'em to.

10   The prospect of a lot
Of dull MPs in close proximity,
All thinking for themselves is what
No man can face with equanimity.

11 The House of Peers, throughout the war,
Did nothing in particular,
    And did it very well:
Yet Britain set the world ablaze
In good King George's glorious days!

12 When you're lying awake with a dismal headache, and
    repose is taboo'd by anxiety,
I conceive you may use any language you choose to
    indulge in, without impropriety.

13 For you dream you are crossing the Channel, and
    tossing about in a steamer from Harwich—
Which is something between a large bathing machine

and a very small second class carriage.

14 And you're giving a treat (penny ice and cold meat) to
    a party of friends and relations—
They're a ravenous horde—and they all came on board
    at Sloane Square and South Kensington Stations.
And bound on that journey you find your attorney
    (who started that morning from Devon);
He's a bit undersized, and you don't feel surprised
    when he tells you he's only eleven.

15 In your shirt and your socks (the black silk with gold
    clocks), crossing Salisbury Plain on a bicycle.

16 The shares are a penny, and ever so many are taken by
    Rothschild and Baring,
And just as a few are allotted to you, you awake with a
    shudder despairing.

17   The darkness is gone
    Ditto ditto my song.

18 A wandering minstrel I—
A thing of shreds and patches,
Of ballads, songs and snatches,
And dreamy lullaby!
The Mikado (1885), I

19   And I am right,
        And you are right,
And all is right as right can be!

20 I can trace my ancestry back to a protoplasmal
primordial atomic globule. Consequently, my family
pride is something in-conceivable. I can't help it. I
was born sneering.

21 It revolts me, but I do it!

22 I accept refreshment at any hands, however lowly.

23 I am happy to think that there will be no difficulty in
finding plenty of people whose loss will be a distinct
gain to society at large.

24 As some day it may happen that a victim must be
    found,
    I've got a little list—I've got a little list
Of society offenders who might well be under ground
    And who never would be missed—who never would
    be missed!

25 The idiot who praises, with enthusiastic tone,
All centuries but this, and every country but his own.
See 129:28, 185:14, 366:6

26 They wouldn't be sufficiently degraded in their own
estimation unless they were insulted by a very
considerable bribe.

27 Three little maids from school are we,
Pert as a schoolgirl well can be,
Filled to the brim with girlish glee.

28 Life is a joke that's just begun.

29 Three little maids who, all unwary,
Come from a ladies' seminary.

30 Modified rapture!

31 Awaiting the sensation of a short, sharp shock,
From a cheap and chippy chopper on a big black
block.

32 Ah, pray make no mistake,
    We are not shy;
We're very wide awake,

The moon and I!
II

1   Sing a merry madrigal.

2   Here's a how-de-doo!

3   Matrimonial devotion
    Doesn't seem to suit her notion.

4   Ha! ha! Family Pride, how do you like *that*, my buck?

5   My object all sublime
        I shall achieve in time—
    To let the punishment fit the crime—
            The punishment fit the crime;
        And make each prisoner pent
        Unwillingly represent
        A source of innocent merriment!
        Of innocent merriment.

6   The music-hall singer attends a series
    Of masses and fugues and 'ops'
        By Bach, interwoven
        With Spohr and Beethoven,
    At classical Monday Pops.

7   The billiard sharp whom any one catches,
        His doom's extremely hard—
            He's made to dwell—
            In a dungeon cell
        On a spot that's always barred.
    And there he plays extravagant matches
        In fitless finger-stalls
            On a cloth untrue
            With a twisted cue
        And elliptical billiard balls.

8   I drew my snickersnee!

9   Though trunkless, yet
        It couldn't forget
    The deference due to me!

10 I have a left shoulder-blade that is a miracle of
    loveliness. People come miles to see it. My right elbow
    has a fascination that few can resist.

11 Something lingering, with boiling oil in it, I fancy.

12 Merely corroborative detail, intended to give artistic
    verisimilitude to an otherwise bald and unconvincing
    narrative.

13 The flowers that bloom in the spring,
            Tra la,
    Have nothing to do with the case.

14 I've got to take under my wing,
            Tra la,
    A most unattractive old thing,
            Tra la,
    With a caricature of a face.
    And that's what I mean when I say, or I sing,
    'Oh bother the flowers that bloom in the spring.'

15 On a tree by a river a little tom-tit
    Sang 'Willow, titwillow, titwillow!'
    And I said to him, 'Dicky-bird, why do you sit
    Singing Willow, titwillow, titwillow?'

16 'Is it weakness of intellect, birdie?' I cried,
    'Or a rather tough worm in your little inside?'
    With a shake of his poor little head he replied,
    'Oh, willow, titwillow, titwillow!'

17 He sobbed and he sighed, and a gurgle he gave,

Then he plunged himself into the billowy wave,
And an echo arose from the suicide's grave—
    'Oh willow, titwillow, titwillow!'

18   There's a fascination frantic
        In a ruin that's romantic;
    Do you think you are sufficiently decayed?

19 Twenty love-sick maidens we,
    Love-sick all against our will.
    Patience (1881), I

20 If you're anxious for to shine in the high aesthetic line
        as a man of culture rare.

21 You must lie upon the daisies and discourse in novel
        phrases of your complicated state of mind,
    The meaning doesn't matter if it's only idle chatter of
        a transcendental kind.
            And everyone will say,
            As you walk your mystic way,
    'If this young man expresses himself in terms too deep
        for *me*,
    Why, what a very singularly deep young man this deep
        young man must be!'

22 For Art stopped short in the cultivated court of the
        Empress Josephine.

23 Then a sentimental passion of a vegetable fashion
        must excite your languid spleen,
    An attachment à la Plato for a bashful young potato, or
        a not too French French bean!
    Though the Philistines may jostle, you will rank as an
        apostle in the high aesthetic band,
    If you walk down Piccadilly with a poppy or a lily in
        your medieval hand.
            And everyone will say,
            As you walk your flowery way,
    'If he's content with a vegetable love which would
        certainly not suit *me*,
    Why, what a most particularly pure young man this
        pure young man must be!'

24 While this magnetic,
        Peripatetic
    Lover, he lived to learn,
        By no endeavour
        Can magnet ever
    Attract a Silver Churn!
    II

25 'High diddle diddle'
    Will rank as an idyll,
    If I pronounce it chaste!

26 Francesca di Rimini, miminy, piminy,
    Je-ne-sais-quoi young man!

27 A greenery-yallery, Grosvenor Galley,
    Foot-in-the-grave young man!

28 A Sewell & Cross young man,
    A Howell & James young man,
    A pushing young particle—'What's the next article?'
    Waterloo House young man!

29 I'm called Little Buttercup—dear Little Buttercup,
    Though I could never tell why.
    H.M.S. Pinafore (1878), I

30 I am the Captain of the *Pinafore*;
    And a right good captain too!

31 And I'm never, never sick at sea!

What, never?
No, never!
What, *never*?
Hardly ever!
He's hardly ever sick at sea!
Then give three cheers, and one cheer more,
For the hardy Captain of the *Pinafore*!

1 You're exceedingly polite,
And I think it only right
To return the compliment.

2 Though 'Bother it' I may
Occasionally say,
I never use a big, big D—

3 And so do his sisters, and his cousins and his aunts!
His sisters and his cousins,
Whom he reckons up by dozens,
And his aunts!

4 When I was a lad I served a term
As office boy to an Attorney's firm.
I cleaned the windows and I swept the floor,
And I polished up the handle of the big front door.
I polished up that handle so carefullee
That now I am the Ruler of the Queen's Navee!

5 And I copied all the letters in a big round hand.

6 I always voted at my party's call,
And I never thought of thinking for myself at all.

7 Stick close to your desks and never go to sea,
And you all may be Rulers of the Queen's Navee!

8 Things are seldom what they seem,
Skim milk masquerades as cream.
II

9 He is an Englishman!
For he himself has said it,
And it's greatly to his credit,
That he is an Englishman!

10 For he might have been a Roosian,
A French, or Turk, or Proosian,
Or perhaps Ital-ian!
But in spite of all temptations
To belong to other nations,
He remains an Englishman!

11 The other, upper crust,
A regular patrician.

12 It is, it is a glorious thing
To be a Pirate King.
The Pirates of Penzance (1879), I

13 The question is, had he not been
A thing of beauty,
Would she be swayed by quite as keen
A sense of duty?

14 Poor wandering one!
Though thou hast surely strayed,
Take heart of grace,
Thy steps retrace,
Poor wandering one!

15 Take heart, fair days will shine;
Take any heart, take mine!

16 I'm very good at integral and differential calculus,
I know the scientific names of beings animalculous;
In short, in matters vegetable, animal, and mineral,

I am the very model of a modern Major-General.

17 About binomial theorems I'm teeming with a lot of news,
With many cheerful facts about the square on the hypoteneuse.

18 When the foeman bares his steel,
Tarantara, tarantara!
We uncomfortable feel,
Tarantara.
II

19 When constabulary duty's to be done,
A policeman's lot is not a happy one.

20 When the enterprising burglar's not a-burgling.

21 When the coster's finished jumping on his mother—
He loves to lie a-basking in the sun.

22 They are no members of the common throng;
They are all noblemen who have gone wrong!

23 No Englishman unmoved that statement hears,
Because, with all our faults, we love our House of Peers.

24 With all our faults, we love our Queen.

25 Politics we bar,
They are not our bent:
On the whole we are
Not intelligent.
Princess Ida (1884), I

26 Yet everybody says I'm such a disagreeable man!
And I can't think why!

27 To everybody's prejudice I know a thing or two;
I can tell a woman's age in half a minute—and I do!

28 Man is Nature's sole mistake!
II

29 Oh, don't the days seem lank and long
When all goes right and nothing goes wrong,
And isn't your life extremely flat
With nothing whatever to grumble at!
III

30 All baronets are bad.
Ruddigore (1887), I

31 I'll wager in their joy they kissed each other's cheek
(Which is what them furriners do).

32 You must stir it and stump it,
And blow your own trumpet,
Or trust me, you haven't a chance.

33 He combines the manners of a Marquis with the morals of a Methodist.

34 When he's excited he uses language that would make your hair curl.

35 If a man can't forge his own will, whose will can he forge?
II

36 Some word that teems with hidden meaning—like Basingstoke.

37 This particularly rapid, unintelligible patter
Isn't generally heard, and if it is it doesn't matter.

38 Time was when Love and I were well acquainted.
The Sorcerer (1877), I

39 Forsaking even military men.

1 I was a pale young curate then.

2   Oh! My name is John Wellington Wells,
I'm a dealer in magic and spells.

3 So I fell in love with a rich attorney's
  Elderly ugly daughter.
Trial by Jury (1875)

4 She may very well pass for forty-three
  In the dusk with a light behind her!

5 For now I am a Judge,
  And a good Judge too.

6 And a good job too!

7 Is life a boon?
  If so, it must befall
    That Death, whene'er he call,
Must call too soon.
The Yeoman of the Guard (1888), I

8 I have a song to sing O!
Sing me your song, O!

9 It's a song of a merryman, moping mum,
Whose soul was sad, and whose glance was glum,
Who sipped no sup, and who craved no crumb,
  As he sighed for the love of a ladye.

10 'Tis ever thus with simple folk—an accepted wit has
but to say 'Pass the mustard', and they roar their ribs
out!
II

ERIC GILL 1882–1940

11 That state is a state of Slavery in which a man does
what he likes to do in his spare time and in his working
time that which is required of him.
Slavery and Freedom (1918)

W.E. GLADSTONE 1809–1898

12 You cannot fight against the future. Time is on our
side.
Speech on the Reform Bill, 1866

13 [The Turks] one and all, bag and baggage, shall, I
hope, clear out from the province they have desolated
and profaned.
House of Commons, 7 May 1877

14 The resources of civilization are not yet exhausted.
Leeds, Speech at Banquet, 7 Oct. 1881

15 It is perfectly true that these gentlemen [the Irish Land
League] wish to march through rapine to disintegration
and dismemberment of the Empire, and, I am sorry to
say, even to the placing of different parts of the
Empire in direct hostility one with the other.
Knowsley, 27 Oct. 1881

16 I would tell them of my own intention to keep my own
counsel...and I will venture to recommend them, as an
old Parliamentary hand, to do the same.
House of Commons, 21 Jan. 1886

17 All the world over, I will back the masses against the
classes.
Liverpool, 28 June 1886

18 We are part of the community of Europe, and we must
do our duty as such.
Carnarvon, 10 Apr. 1888

19 This is the negation of God erected into a system of
Government.
*First Letter to the Earl of Aberdeen on the State persecutions of
the Neapolitan Government,* 8, 1851, p.9n

20 It is not a Life at all. It is a Reticence, in three
volumes.
On J.W. Cross's *Life of George Eliot.* E.F. Benson, *As We Were*
(1930), ch.6

MRS. HANNAH GLASSE fl. 1747

21 Take your hare when it is cased...
The Art of Cookery Made Plain and Easy (1747), ch.1. Cased ;
skinned. The proverbial 'First catch your hare', recorded since
c. 1300, has frequently been misattributed to Mrs. Glasse.

DUKE OF GLOUCESTER 1743–1805

22 Another damned, thick, square book! Always
scribble, scribble, scribble! Eh! Mr Gibbon?
Best's *Literary Memorials.* (Boswell's *Johnson,* vol.ii, p.2n)

WILLIAM FREDERICK, 2nd DUKE OF
GLOUCESTER 1776–1834

23 Who's Silly Billy now?
Lending his own nick-name to William IV, his nephew. G. Smith,
Lectures and Essays (1881), 'A Wirepuller of Kings'

A.D. GODLEY 1856–1925

24 What is this that roareth thus?
Can it be a Motor Bus?
Yes, the smell and hideous hum
Indicat Motorem Bum...
How shall wretches live like us
Cincti Bis Motoribus?
Domine, defende nos
Contra hos Motores Bos!
The Motor Bus. Letter to C.R.L.F., 10 Jan. 1914

HERMANN GOERING 1893–1946

25 Guns will make us powerful; butter will only make us
fat.
Radio Broadcast, summer of 1936, often misquoted as 'Guns
before butter'.

JOHANN WOLFGANG VON GOETHE
1749–1832

26 Lord Byron is only great as a poet; as soon as he
reflects, he is a child.
Conversations with Eckermann, 18 Jan. 1825

27 *Im übrigen ist es zuletzt die grösste Kunst, sich zu
beschränken und zu isolieren.*
For the rest of it, the last and greatest art is to limit and
isolate oneself.
20 Apr. 1825

28 *Ich kenne mich auch nicht und Gott soll mich auch
davor behüten.*
I do not know myself, and God forbid that I should.
10 Apr. 1829. See 9:21

29 *Es irrt der Mensch, so lang er strebt.*
Man is in error throughout his strife.
Faust, pt.i (1808). **Prolog im Himmel**

30 *Zwei Seelen wohnen, ach! in meiner Brust.*
Two souls dwell, alas! in my breast.
Vor dem Thor

1 *Ich bin der Geist der stets verneint.*
I am the spirit that always denies.
Studierzimmer

2 *Entbehren sollst Du! sollst entbehren!*
Das ist der ewige Gesang.
Deny yourself! You must deny yourself!
That is the song that never ends.

3 *Grau, teurer Freund, ist alle Theorie*
Und grün des Lebens goldner Baum.
All theory, dear friend, is grey, but the golden tree of
  actual life springs ever green.

4 *Meine Ruh' ist hin,*
Mein Herz ist schwer.
My peace is gone,
My heart is heavy.
Gretchen am Spinnrad

5 *Die Tat ist alles, nichts der Ruhm.*
The deed is all, and not the glory.
pt. ii (1832). **Hochgebirg**

6 *Das Ewig-Weibliche zieht uns hinan.*
Eternal Woman draws us upward.
last line

7 *Du musst herrschen und gewinnen,*
Oder dienen und verlieren,
Leiden oder triumphieren
Amboss oder Hammer sein.
You must be master and win, or serve and lose, grieve
  or triumph, be the anvil or the hammer.
Der Gross-Cophta (1791), Act ii

8 *Wenn es eine Freude ist das Gute zu geniessen, so ist*
es eine grössere das Bessere zu empfinden, und in der
Kunst ist das Beste gut genug.
Since it is a joy to have the benefit of what is good, it
  is a greater one to experience what is better, and in art
  the best is good enough.
Italienische Reise (1816–17), 3 Mar. 1787

9 *Der Aberglaube ist die Poesie des Lebens.*
Superstition is the poetry of life.
Sprüche in Prosa (1819), iii

10 *Es bildet ein Talent sich in der Stille,*
Sich ein Charakter in dem Strom der Welt.
Talent develops in quiet places, character in the full
  current of human life.
Torquato Tasso (1790), i.2

11 *Über allen Gipfeln*
Ist Ruh'.
Over all the mountain tops is peace.
Wanderers Nachtlied

12 *Wer nie sein Brot mit Tränen ass,*
Wer nie die kummervollen Nächte
Auf seinem Bette weinend sass,
Der kennt euch nicht, ihr himmlischen Mächte.
Who never ate his bread in sorrow,
Who never spent the darksome hours
Weeping and watching for the morrow
He knows ye not, ye heavenly powers.
Wilhelm Meisters Lehrjahre (1795–6), II.13. Tr. Carlyle

13 *Kennst du das Land, wo die Zitronen blühn?*
Im dunkeln Laub die Gold-Orangen glühn,
Ein sanfter Wind vom blauen Himmel weht,
Die Myrte still und hoch der Lorbeer steht—
Kennst du es wohl?
    Dahin! Dahin!

Möcht ich mit dir, o mein Geliebter, ziehn!
Know you the land where the lemon-trees bloom? In
  the dark foliage the gold oranges glow; a soft wind
  hovers from the sky, the myrtle is still and the laurel
  stands tall—do you know it well? There, there, I
  would go, O my beloved, with thee!
III.i

14 *Mehr Licht!*
More light!
Attr. dying words. (Actually: *'Macht doch den zweiten*
Fensterladen auch auf, damit mehr Licht hereinkomme': 'Open
the second shutter, so that more light can come in.')

15 *Ohne Hast, aber ohne Rast.*
Without haste, but without rest.
Motto

OLIVER GOLDSMITH 1730–1774

16 Sweet Auburn, loveliest village of the plain,
Where health and plenty cheered the labouring swain,
Where smiling spring its earliest visit paid,
And parting summer's lingering blooms delayed.
The Deserted Village (1770), l.1

17 The bashful virgin's side-long looks of love,
The matron's glance that would those looks reprove.
l.29

18 Ill fares the land, to hast'ning ills a prey,
Where wealth accumulates, and men decay;
Princes and lords may flourish, or may fade;
A breath can make them, as a breath has made;
But a bold peasantry, their country's pride,
When once destroy'd, can never be supplied.
A time there was, ere England's griefs began,
When every rood of ground maintain'd its man;
For him light labour spread her wholesome store,
Just gave what life requir'd, but gave no more;
His best companions, innocence and health;
And his best riches, ignorance of wealth.
l.51

19 How happy he who crowns in shades like these,
A youth of labour with an age of ease.
l.99

20 Bends to the grave with unperceiv'd decay,
While resignation gently slopes the way;
And, all his prospects bright'ning to the last,
His heaven commences ere the world be pass'd.
l.109

21 The watchdog's voice that bay'd the whisp'ring wind,
And the loud laugh that spoke the vacant mind.
l.121. See 137:1

22 A man he was to all the country dear,
And passing rich with forty pounds a year;
Remote from towns he ran his godly race,
Nor e'er had chang'd nor wished to change his place;
Unpractis'd he to fawn, or seek for power,
By doctrines fashion'd to the varying hour;
Far other aims his heart had learned to prize,
More skill'd to raise the wretched than to rise.
l.141

23 He chid their wand'rings, but reliev'd their pain.
l.150

24 At church, with meek and unaffected grace,
His looks adorn'd the venerable place;
Truth from his lips prevail'd with double sway,

And fools, who came to scoff, remain'd to pray.
l.177

1 Even children follow'd with endearing wile,
And pluck'd his gown, to share the good man's smile.
l.183

2 A man severe he was, and stern to view;
I knew him well, and every truant knew;
Well had the boding tremblers learn'd to trace
The day's disasters in his morning face;
Full well they laugh'd with counterfeited glee,
At all his jokes, for many a joke had he;
Full well the busy whisper, circling round,
Convey'd the dismal tidings when he frown'd;
Yet he was kind; or if severe in aught,
The love he bore to learning was in fault.
l.197

3 In arguing too, the parson own'd his skill,
For e'en though vanquish'd, he could argue still;
While words of learned length, and thund'ring sound
Amazed the gazing rustics rang'd around,
And still they gaz'd, and still the wonder grew,
That one small head could carry all he knew.
l.211

4 The white-wash'd wall, the nicely sanded floor,
The varnish'd clock that click'd behind the door;
The chest contriv'd a double debt to pay,
A bed at night, a chest of drawers by day.
l.227

5   How wide the limits stand
Between a splendid and a happy land.
l.267

6 In all the silent manliness of grief.
l.384

7 Man wants but little here below,
   Nor wants that little long.
Edwin and Angelina, or the Hermit (1766). See 588:8

8 The doctor found, when she was dead,—
   Her last disorder mortal.
Elegy on Mrs. Mary Blaize

9 Good people all, of every sort,
   Give ear unto my song;
And if you find it wond'rous short,
   It cannot hold you long.
Elegy on the Death of a Mad Dog

10 That still a godly race he ran,
   Whene'er he went to pray.

11 The naked every day he clad,
   When he put on his clothes.

12 And in that town a dog was found,
   As many dogs there be,
Both mongrel, puppy, whelp, and hound,
   And curs of low degree.

13 The dog, to gain some private ends,
   Went mad and bit the man.

14 The man recover'd of the bite,
   The dog it was that died.

15 Brutes never meet in bloody fray,
   Nor cut each other's throats, for pay.
Logicians Refuted, l.39

16 Our Garrick's a salad; for in him we see
Oil, vinegar, sugar, and saltness agree.
Retaliation (1774), l.11. See 221:13

17 Who, too deep for his hearers, still went on refining,
And thought of convincing, while they thought of dining;
Though equal to all things, for all things unfit,
Too nice for a statesman, too proud for a wit. [Edmund Burke].
l.35

18 Here lies David Garrick, describe me, who can,
An abridgement of all that was pleasant in man.
l.93

19 As a wit, if not first, in the very first line. [Garrick.]
l.96

20 On the stage he was natural, simple, affecting;
'Twas only that when he was off he was acting.
   [Garrick.]
l.101

21 When they talk'd of their Raphaels, Correggios, and stuff,
He shifted his trumpet, and only took snuff.
   [Reynolds.]
l.145

22 Let schoolmasters puzzle their brain,
   With grammar, and nonsense, and learning,
Good liquor, I stoutly maintain,
   Gives genius a better discerning.
She Stoops to Conquer, I.i, song

23 Remote, unfriended, melancholy, slow,
Or by the lazy Scheldt, or wandering Po.
The Traveller (1764), l.1

24 Where'er I roam, whatever realms to see,
My heart untravell'd fondly turns to thee;
Still to my brother turns with ceaseless pain,
And drags at each remove a lengthening chain.
l.7

25 Such is the patriot's boast, where'er we roam,
His first, best country ever is, at home.
l.73

26 At night returning, every labour sped,
He sits him down the monarch of a shed;
Smiles by his cheerful fire, and round surveys
His children's looks, that brighten at the blaze;
While his lov'd partner, boastful of her hoard,
Displays her cleanly platter on the board.
l.191

27 To men of other minds my fancy flies,
Embosom'd in the deep where Holland lies.
Methinks her patient sons before me stand,
Where the broad ocean leans against the land.
l.282

28 Pride in their port, defiance in their eye,
I see the lords of human kind pass by.
l.327

29 Laws grind the poor, and rich men rule the law.
l.386

30 In every government, though terrors reign,
Though tyrant kings, or tyrant laws restrain,
How small, of all that human hearts endure,
That part which laws or kings can cause or cure!
l.427

31 When lovely woman stoops to folly
   And finds too late that men betray,
What charm can soothe her melancholy,
   What art can wash her guilt away?

The only art her guilt to cover,
    To hide her shame from every eye,
To give repentance to her lover
    And wring his bosom—is to die.
Song from *The Vicar of Wakefield*, ch.29

1 As writers become more numerous, it is natural for readers to become more indolent.
The Bee (1759), No. 175. **Upon Unfortunate Merit**

2 He writes indexes to perfection.
The Citizen of the World (1762), letter 29

3 To a philosopher no circumstance, however trifling, is too minute.
letter 30

4 'Did I say so?' replied he coolly; 'to be sure, if I said so, it was so.'
letter 54

5 The true use of speech is not so much to express our wants as to conceal them.
Essays, v. **The Use of Language**

6 I hate the French because they are all slaves, and wear wooden shoes.
xxiv. **Distresses of a Common Soldier**

7 This same philosophy is a good horse in the stable, but an arrant jade on a journey.
The Good-Natured Man (1768), I

8 We must touch his weaknesses with a delicate hand. There are some faults so nearly allied to excellence, that we can scarce weed out the fault without eradicating the virtue.

9 All his faults are such that one loves him still the better for them.

10 I'm now no more than a mere lodger in my own house.

11 Friendship is a disinterested commerce between equals; love, an abject intercourse between tyrants and slaves.

12 Don't let us make imaginary evils, when you know we have so many real ones to encounter.

13 *Leontine:* An only son, sir, might expect more indulgence.
Croaker: An only father, Sir, might expect more obedience.

14 I am told he makes a very handsome corpse, and becomes his coffin prodigiously.

15 Silence is become his mother tongue.
II

16 All men have their faults; too much modesty is his.

17 You, that are going to be married, think things can never be done too fast; but we, that are old, and know what we are about, must elope methodically, madam.

18 In my time, the follies of the town crept slowly among us, but now they travel faster than a stagecoach.
She Stoops to Conquer (1773), I

19 I love every thing that's old; old friends, old times, old manners, old books, old wines.

20 As for disappointing them I should not so much mind; but I can't abide to disappoint myself.

21 Is it one of my well-looking days, child? Am I in face to-day?

22 The very pink of perfection.

23 In a concatenation accordingly.

24 I'll be with you in the squeezing of a lemon.

25 It's a damned long, dark, boggy, dirty, dangerous way.

26 This is Liberty-Hall, gentlemen.
II

27 The first blow is half the battle.

28 Was there ever such a cross-grained brute?
III

29 Women and music should never be dated.

30 As for murmurs, mother, we grumble a little now and then, to be sure. But there's no love lost between us.
IV

31 A book may be amusing with numerous errors, or it may be very dull without a single absurdity.
The Vicar of Wakefield (1761–2, published 1766) advertisement

32 I was ever of opinion, that the honest man who married and brought up a large family, did more service than he who continued single and only talked of population.
ch.1

33 I chose my wife, as she did her wedding gown, not for a fine glossy surface, but such qualities as would wear well.

34 All our adventures were by the fire-side, and all our migrations from the blue bed to the brown.

35 The virtue which requires to be ever guarded is scarcely worth the sentinel.
ch.5

36 With other fashionable topics, such as pictures, taste, Shakespeare, and the musical glasses.

37 Mr Burchell...at the conclusion of every sentence would cry out '*Fudge!*'—an expression which displeased us all.
ch.11

38 Conscience is a coward, and those faults it has not strength enough to prevent it seldom has justice enough to accuse.
ch.13

39 It seemed to me pretty plain, that they had more of love than matrimony in them.
ch.16

40 There is no arguing with Johnson; for when his pistol misses fire, he knocks you down with the butt end of it.
Boswell, *Life of Johnson*, 26 Oct. 1769. See 151:11

41 As I take my shoes from the shoemaker, and my coat from the tailor, so I take my religion from the priest.
9 Apr. 1773

SAMUEL GOLDWYN 1882–1974

42 In two words: im possible.
Alva Johnson, *The Great Goldwyn*

43 You can include me out.
See Zierold, *The Hollywood Tycoons* (1969), ch.3

44 For years I have been known for saying 'Include me out'; but today I am giving it up for ever.
Address at Balliol College, Oxford, 1 Mar. 1945

ADAM LINDSAY GORDON 1833–1870

1 Life is mostly froth and bubble,
    Two things stand like stone,
Kindness in another's trouble,
    Courage in your own.
Ye Wearie Wayfarer, Fytte 8

1ST LORD GOSCHEN 1831–1907

2 I have the courage of my opinions, but I have not the temerity to give a political blank cheque to Lord Salisbury.
House of Commons, 19 Feb. 1884

3 We have stood alone in that which is called isolation—our splendid isolation, as one of our colonial friends was good enough to call it.
Lewes, 26 Feb. 1896. See 217:17

EDMUND GOSSE 1849–1928

4 A sheep in sheep's clothing.
Of T. Sturge Moore, c.1906. Ferris Greenslet, *Under the Bridge*, ch.12. Also attr. Winston Churchill of Clement Attlee.

DEAN GOULBURN 1818–1897

5 Let the scintillations of your wit be like the coruscations of summer lightning, lambent but innocuous.
Sermon at Rugby. Revd. W. Tuckwell, *Reminiscences of Oxford* (2nd ed., 1907), p.272

JOHN GOWER 1330?–1408

6 It hath and schal ben evermor
That love is maister wher he wile.
Confessio Amantis (1386–90), prologue, 1.34

SIR ERNEST GOWERS 1880–1966

7 It is not easy nowadays to remember anything so contrary to all appearances as that officials are the servants of the public; and the official must try not to foster the illusion that it is the other way round.
Plain Words, ch. 3, The Elements

CLEMENTINA STIRLING GRAHAM 1782–1877

8 The best way to get the better of temptation is just to yield to it.
Mystifications (1859), Soirée at Mrs Russel's

HARRY GRAHAM 1874–1936

9 Weep not for little Léonie
Abducted by a French *Marquis*!
Though loss of honour was a wrench
Just think how it's improved her French.
More Ruthless Rhymes for Heartless Homes. Compensation

10 O'er the rugged mountain's brow
    Clara threw the twins she nursed,
And remarked, 'I wonder now
    Which will reach the bottom first?'
Ruthless Rhymes for Heartless Homes. Calculating Clara

11 Aunt Jane observed, the second time
    She tumbled off a bus,
The step is short from the Sublime
    To the Ridiculous.
Equanimity

12 'There's been an accident!' they said,
'Your servant's cut in half; he's dead!'
'Indeed!' said Mr Jones, 'and please
Send me the half that's got my keys.'
Mr. Jones

13 Billy, in one of his nice new sashes,
Fell in the fire and was burnt to ashes;
Now, although the room grows chilly,
I haven't the heart to poke poor Billy.
Tender-Heartedness

JAMES GRAHAM, MARQUIS OF MONTROSE 1612–1650

14 He either fears his fate too much,
    Or his deserts are small,
That puts it not unto the touch
    To win or lose it all.
My Dear and Only Love

15 But if thou wilt be constant then,
    And faithful of thy word,
I'll make thee glorious by my pen,
    And famous by my sword.

16 Let them bestow on every airth a limb;
Then open all my veins, that I may swim
To thee, my Maker! in that crimson lake;
Then place my parboiled head upon a stake—
Scatter my ashes—strew them in the air;—
Lord! since thou know'st where all these atoms are,
I'm hopeful thou'lt recover once my dust,
And confident thou'lt raise me with the just.
Lines written on the Window of his Jail the Night before his Execution

KENNETH GRAHAME 1859–1932

17 Aunt Maria flung herself on him [the curate]. 'O Mr Hodgitts!' I heard her cry, 'you are brave! for my sake do not be rash!' He was not rash.
The Golden Age (1895). The Burglars

18 Believe me, my young friend, there is *nothing*—absolutely nothing—half so much worth doing as simply messing about in boats.
The Wind in the Willows (1908), ch.1

19 The clever men at Oxford
    Know all that there is to be knowed.
But they none of them know one half as much
    As intelligent Mr Toad.
ch.10

JAMES GRAINGER 1721?–1766

20 What is fame? an empty bubble;
Gold? a transient, shining trouble.
Solitude, 1.96

ULYSSES S. GRANT 1822–1885

21 I purpose to fight it out on this line, if it takes all summer.
Dispatch to Washington, from head-quarters in the field, 11 May 1864

22 I know no method to secure the repeal of bad or obnoxious laws so effective as their stringent

execution.
Inaugural Address, 4 Mar. 1869

1 No terms except unconditional and immediate
surrender can be accepted. I propose to move
immediately upon your works.
*To Simon Bolivar Buckner, whom he was besieging in Fort
Donelson, 16 Feb. 1862*

2 Let us have peace.
Letter of acceptance of nomination, 29 May 1868

3 Let no guilty man escape, if it can be avoided...No
personal considerations should stand in the way of
performing a public duty.
Indorsement of a letter relating to the Whiskey Ring, 29 July 1875

GEORGE GRANVILLE, BARON LANSDOWNE
1666–1735

4 I'll be this abject thing no more;
 Love, give me back my heart again.
Adieu l'Amour

5 Of all the plagues with which the world is curst,
Of every ill, a woman is the worst.
The British Enchanters (1706), II.i

6 Bright as the day, and like the morning, fair,
Such Cloe is...and common as the air.
Cloe

7 O Love! thou bane of the most generous souls!
Thou doubtful pleasure, and thou certain pain.
Heroic Love (1698), II.i

8 'Tis the talk, and not the intrigue, that's the crime.
The She Gallants (1696), III.i

9 Cowards in scarlet pass for men of war.
V

LORD GRANVILLE 1819–1907

10 Spheres of action.
*Letter to Count Münster, 29 April 1885. Sir Edward Hertslet, Map
of Africa by Treaty (1894), vol.ii, p.596. See 7:17*

ROBERT GRAVES 1895–

11 His eyes are quickened so with grief,
He can watch a grass or leaf
Every instant grow.
Lost Love

12 'Complaints is many and various
And my feet are cold,' says Aquarius,
'There's Venus objects to Dolphin-scales,
And Mars to Crab-spawn found in my pails,
 And the pump has frozen to-night,
 And the pump has frozen to-night.'
Star-talk

PATRICK, 6TH LORD GRAY d.1612

13 A dead woman bites not.
*Oral tradition. Gray advocated the execution of Mary, Queen of
Scots, 1587. See J.B. Black, The Reign of Elizabeth
(1558–1603), 2nd edn. (1959), ch.10: The Master of Gray
whispered...'Mortui non mordent'.*

THOMAS GRAY 1716–1771

14 Ruin seize thee, ruthless King!
 Confusion on thy banners wait,
Tho' fann'd by Conquest's crimson wing

They mock the air with idle state.
The Bard (1757), I.i

15 Weave the warp, and weave the woof,
 The winding-sheet of Edward's race.
Give ample room, and verge enough
 The characters of hell to trace.
II.i

16 Fair laughs the morn, and soft the zephyr blows,
 While proudly riding o'er the azure realm
In gallant trim the gilded vessel goes,
 Youth on the prow, and Pleasure at the helm;
Regardless of the sweeping whirlwind's sway,
That, hush'd in grim repose, expects his evening prey.
ii

17 Ye towers of Julius, London's lasting shame,
With many a foul and midnight murther fed.
iii

18 The curfew tolls the knell of parting day,
 The lowing herd wind slowly o'er the lea,
The ploughman homeward plods his weary way,
 And leaves the world to darkness and to me.

Now fades the glimmering landscape on the sight,
 And all the air a solemn stillness holds,
Save where the beetle wheels his droning flight,
 And drowsy tinklings lull the distant folds.
Elegy in a Country Churchyard (1742–50), 1

19 Save that from yonder ivy-mantled tow'r,
 The moping owl does to the moon complain.
3

20 Beneath those rugged elms, that yew-tree's shade,
 Where heaves the turf in many a mouldering heap,
Each in his narrow cell for ever laid,
 The rude forefathers of the hamlet sleep.

The breezy call of incense-breathing Morn,
 The swallow twitt'ring from the straw-built shed,
The cock's shrill clarion, or the echoing horn,
 No more shall rouse them from their lowly bed.
4

21 Let not ambition mock their useful toil,
 Their homely joys, and destiny obscure;
Nor grandeur hear with a disdainful smile,
 The short and simple annals of the poor.

The boast of heraldry, the pomp of pow'r,
 And all that beauty, all that wealth e'er gave,
Awaits alike th' inevitable hour,
 The paths of glory lead but to the grave.
8

22 Can storied urn or animated bust
 Back to its mansion call the fleeting breath?
Can honour's voice provoke the silent dust,
 Or flatt'ry soothe the dull cold ear of death?
11

23 Full many a gem of purest ray serene,
 The dark unfathom'd caves of ocean bear:
Full many a flower is born to blush unseen,
 And waste its sweetness on the desert air.

Some village-Hampden, that with dauntless breast
 The little tyrant of his fields withstood;
Some mute inglorious Milton here may rest,
 Some Cromwell guiltless of his country's blood.
14

24   Nor circumscrib'd alone

    Their growing virtues, but their crimes confin'd;
    Forbad to wade through slaughter to a throne,
      And shut the gates of mercy on mankind.
    17

1 Far from the madding crowd's ignoble strife,
      Their sober wishes never learn'd to stray;
    Along the cool sequester'd vale of life
      They kept the noiseless tenor of their way.
    19

2 For who to dumb Forgetfulness a prey,
      This pleasing anxious being e'er resign'd,
    Left the warm precincts of the cheerful day,
      Nor cast one longing ling'ring look behind?
    22

3 Mindful of th' unhonour'd dead.
    24

4 Here rests his head upon the lap of Earth
      A youth to fortune and to fame unknown.
    Fair Science frown'd not on his humble birth,
      And Melancholy mark'd him for her own.
    30

5 He gave to Mis'ry all he had, a tear,
      He gain'd from Heav'n ('twas all he wish'd) a
          friend.
    31

6 What female heart can gold despise?
      What cat's averse to fish?
    Ode on the Death of a Favourite Cat (1747)

7 A fav'rite has no friend!

8 Not all that tempts your wand'ring eyes
    And heedless hearts, is lawful prize;
    Nor all, that glisters, gold.

9 Ye distant spires, ye antique towers,
      That crown the wat'ry glade.
    Ode on a Distant Prospect of Eton College (1742, published
    1747), 1.1

10 Urge the flying ball.
    1.30

11 Still as they run they look behind,
    They hear a voice in every wind,
      And snatch a fearful joy.
    1.38

12 Alas, regardless of their doom,
      The little victims play!
    No sense have they of ills to come,
      Nor care beyond to-day.
    1.51

13 To each his suff'rings, all are men,
      Condemn'd alike to groan;
    The tender for another's pain,
      Th' unfeeling for his own.

    Yet ah! why should they know their fate?
    Since sorrow never comes too late,
      And happiness too swiftly flies.
    Thought would destroy their paradise.
    No more; where ignorance is bliss,
      'Tis folly to be wise.
    1.91

14 Servitude that hugs her chain.
    Ode for Music, 1.6

15 The meanest flowret of the vale,
    The simplest note that swells the gale,

    The common sun, the air, and skies,
    To him are opening paradise.
    Ode on the Pleasure Arising from Vicissitude, 1.49

16 The Attic warbler pours her throat,
    Responsive to the cuckoo's note.
    Ode on the Spring, 1.5

17 The bloom of young desire and purple light of love.
    The Progess of Poesy (1754, published 1757), i.3

18   Far from the sun and summer-gale,
    In thy green lap was Nature's darling laid,
    What time, where lucid Avon stray'd,
    To him the mighty Mother did unveil
    Her aweful face: the dauntless child
    Stretch'd forth his little arms, and smiled.
    iii.1 (Shakespeare.)

19 Nor second he, that rode sublime
      Upon the seraph-wings of ecstasy,
      The secrets of th' abyss to spy.
    He pass'd the flaming bounds of place and time:
    The living throne, the sapphire-blaze,
    Where angels tremble, while they gaze,
    He saw; but blasted with excess of light,
    Closed his eyes in endless night.
    2 (Milton.)

20 Beyond the limits of a vulgar fate,
    Beneath the good how far—but far above the great.
    3

21 Too poor for a bribe, and too proud to importune,
    He had not the method of making a fortune.
    Sketch of his own Character

22 The language of the age is never the language of
    poetry, except among the French, whose verse, where
    the thought or image does not support it, differs in
    nothing from prose.
    Letters. 103, To West [8] Apr., [1742]

23 It has been usual to catch a mouse or two (for form's
    sake) in public once a year.
    [On refusing the Laureateship.] 259, To Mason, 19 Dec. 1757

24 Any fool may write a most valuable book by chance,
    if he will only tell us what he heard and saw with
    veracity.
    475, To Walpole, 25 Feb. 1768

25 I shall be but a shrimp of an author.

HORACE GREELY 1811–1872

26 Go West, young man, and grow up with the country.
    Hints toward Reform. See 513:11

MATTHEW GREEN 1696–1737

27 They politics like ours profess,
    The greater prey upon the less.
    The Grotto (1732), 1.69

28 To cure the mind's wrong biass, spleen,
    Some recommend the bowling green,
    Some, hilly walks; all, exercise;
    Fling but a stone, the giant dies.
    Laugh and be well.
    The Spleen (1737), 1.89

29 Or to some coffee-house I stray,
    For news, the manna of a day,
    And from the hipp'd discourses gather

That politics go by the weather.
l.168

1 Who their ill-tasted, home-brewed prayer
To the State's mellow forms prefer.
l.336

2 By happy alchemy of mind
They turn to pleasure all they find.
l.610

GRAHAM GREENE 1904–

3 Against the beautiful and the clever and the
successful, one can wage a pitiless war, but not
against the unattractive.
The Heart of the Matter (1948), bk.1, pt.1, ch.2

4 They had been corrupted by money, and he had been
corrupted by sentiment. Sentiment was the more
dangerous, because you couldn't name its price. A
man open to bribes was to be relied upon below a
certain figure, but sentiment might uncoil in the heart
at a name, a photograph, even a smell remembered.

5 Any victim demands allegiance.
bk.3, pt.1, ch.1

6 His hilarity was like a scream from a crevasse.

7 Perhaps if I wanted to be understood or to understand
I would bamboozle myself into belief, but I am a
reporter; God exists only for leader-writers.
The Quiet American (1955), pt.I, ch.iv.2

ROBERT GREENE 1560?–1592

8 Cupid abroad was lated in the night,
His wings were wet with ranging in the rain.
Sonnet: Cupid Abroad was Lated

9 Hangs in the uncertain balance of proud time.
Friar Bacon and Friar Bungay (1594), 111.i

10 Ah! were she pitiful as she is fair,
Or but as mild as she is seeming so.
Pandosto, or Dorastus and Fawnia (1588)

11 Ah! what is love! It is a pretty thing,
As sweet unto a shepherd as a king,
  And sweeter too;
For kings have cares that wait upon a crown,
And cares can make the sweetest love to frown.
  Ah then, ah then,
If country loves such sweet desires do gain,
What lady would not love a shepherd swain?
The Shepherd's Wife's Song

12 For there is an upstart crow, beautified with our
feathers, that with his tiger's heart wrapped in a
player's hide, supposes he is as well able to bumbast
out a blank verse as the best of you; and being an
absolute *Iohannes fac totum,* is in his own conceit the
only Shake-scene in a country.
Groatsworth of Wit Bought with a Million of Repentance
(1592)

POPE GREGORY THE GREAT c.540–604

13 *Non Angli sed Angeli.*
Not Angles but Angels.
Bede, *Historia Ecclesiastica,* II.i, recorded: *Responsum est, quod
Angli vocarentur. At ille: 'Bene,' inquit; 'nam et angelicam
habent faciem, et tales angelorum in caelis decet esse coheredes.'*
They answered that they were called Angles. 'It is well,' he said,
'for they have the faces of angels, and such should be the co-heirs
of the angels of heaven.'

STEPHEN GRELLET 1773–1855

14 I expect to pass through this world but once; any good
thing therefore that I can do, or any kindness that I can
show to any fellow-creature, let me do it now; let me
not defer or neglect it, for I shall not pass this way
again.
Attr. See John o' London's *Treasure Trove* (1925). Many other
claimants to authorship

JULIAN GRENFELL 1888–1915

15 The naked earth is warm with Spring,
  And with green grass and bursting trees
Leans to the sun's kiss glorying,
  And quivers in the sunny breeze;

And life is colour and warmth and light
  And a striving evermore for these;
And he is dead, who will not fight;
  And who dies fighting has increase.

The fighting man shall from the sun
Take warmth, and life from the glowing earth.
Into Battle, published in *The Times,* 27 May 1915

SIR FULKE GREVILLE 1554–1628

16 Oh wearisome condition of humanity!
Born under one law, to another bound.
Mustapha (1609), V.iv

17 Silence augmenteth grief, writing increaseth rage,
Stal'd are my thoughts, which loved and lost, the
    wonder of our age,
Yet quick'ned now with fire, though dead with frost
    ere now,
Enraged I write, I know not what: dead, quick, I know
    not how.
Elegy on the Death of Sir Philip Sidney

18 Fulke Greville, Servant to Queen Elizabeth,
Councillor to King James, and Friend to Sir Philip
Sidney.
Epitaph written for himself, on his Monument in Warwick

LORD GREY OF FALLODON 1862–1933

19 The lamps are going out all over Europe; we shall not
see them lit again in our lifetime.
3 Aug. 1914. *Twenty-Five Years, 1892–1916* (1925), vol.ii,
ch.18

NICHOLAS GRIMALD 1519–1562

20 Of all the heavenly gifts that mortal men commend,
What trusty treasure in the world can countervail a
    friend?
Of Friendship

GEORGE GROSSMITH 1847–1912
and WEEDON GROSSMITH 1854–1919

21 What's the good of a home if you are never in it?
The Diary of a Nobody (1894), ch.1

22 I...recognized her as a woman who used to work years
ago for my old aunt at Clapham. It only shows how
small the world is.
ch.2

1 He [Gowing] suggested we should play 'Cutlets', a game we never heard of. He sat on a chair, and asked Carrie to sit on his lap, an invitation which dear Carrie rightly declined.
ch.7

2 I left the room with silent dignity, but caught my foot in the mat.
ch.12

3 I am a poor man, but I would gladly give ten shillings to find out who sent me the insulting Christmas card I received this morning.
ch.13

PHILIP GUEDALLA 1889–1944

4 The little ships, the unforgotten Homeric catalogue of *Mary Jane* and *Peggy IV*, of *Folkestone Belle, Boy Billy*, and *Ethel Maud*, of *Lady Haig* and *Skylark*...the little ships of England brought the Army home.
Mr. Churchill (1941). (Evacuation of Dunkirk.)

5 The work of Henry James has always seemed divisible by a simple dynastic arrangement into three reigns: James I, James II, and the Old Pretender.
Collected Essays, vol.iv. **Men of Letters: Mr. Henry James**

TEXAS GUINAN 1884–1933

6 Fifty million Frenchmen can't be wrong.
Attr. *New York World-Telegram*, 21 Mar. 1931

MRS. DOROTHY FRANCES GURNEY 1858–1932

7 The kiss of the sun for pardon,
    The song of the birds for mirth,
One is nearer God's Heart in a garden
    Than anywhere else on earth.
God's Garden

NELL GWYN 1650–1687

8 Pray, good people, be civil. I am the Protestant whore.
In Oxford, during the Popish Terror, 1681. Bevan, *Nell Gwyn*, ch.xiii

EMPEROR HADRIAN A.D. 76–138

9 *Animula vagula blandula,*
Hospes comesque corporis,
Quae nunc abibis in loca
Pallidula rigida nudula,
Nec ut soles dabis iocos!
Ah! gentle, fleeting, wav'ring sprite,
Friend and associate of this clay!
    To what unknown region borne,
Wilt thou now wing thy distant flight?
No more with wonted humour gay,
    But pallid, cheerless, and forlorn.
J.W. Duff (ed.), *Minor Latin Poets* (1934), 445. Trans. Byron, *Adrian's Address to His Soul When Dying*

C.F.S. HAHNEMANN 1755–1843

10 *Similia similibus curantur.*
Like cures like.
Motto of homoeopathic medicine. Hahnemann seems to have used this formula, but with *curentur:* Let similars be treated by similars. Paracelsus (1493–1541), not acknowledged as an influence by Hahnemann, wrote *Simile similis cura: non contrarium (Fragmenta Medica).*

EARL HAIG 1861–1928

11 Every position must be held to the last man: there must be no retirement. With our backs to the wall, and believing in the justice of our cause, each one of us must fight on to the end.
Order to the British Troops, 12 Apr. 1918

EDWARD EVERETT HALE 1822–1909

12 'Do you pray for the senators, Dr Hale?' 'No, I look at the senators and I pray for the country.'
Van Wyck Brooks, *New England Indian Summer* (1940), p.418n.

SIR MATTHEW HALE 1609–1676

13 Christianity is part of the Common Law of England.
Historia Placitorum Coronae, ed. Sollom Emlyn (1736). Also in W. Blackstone *Commentaries on the Laws of England*, iv, 1765

NATHAN HALE 1755–1776

14 I only regret that I have but one life to lose for my country.
Speech before being executed as a spy by the British, 22 Sept. 1776. See 1:22

MRS. SARAH JOSEPHA HALE 1788–1879

15 Mary had a little lamb,
    Its fleece was white as snow,
And everywhere that Mary went
    The lamb was sure to go.
Poems for Our Children (1830). **Mary's Little Lamb**

T.C. HALIBURTON 1796–1865

16 I want you to see Peel, Stanley, Graham, Shiel, Russell, Macaulay, Old Joe, and so on. These men are all upper crust here.
The Attaché, or Sam Slick in England (1843-4), ch.24

GEORGE SAVILE, MARQUIS OF HALIFAX 1633–1695

17 Love is a passion that hath friends in the garrison.
Advice to a Daughter (1688). **Behaviour and Conversation**

18 This innocent word 'Trimmer' signifies no more than this, that if men are together in a boat, and one part of the company would weigh it down on one side, another would make it lean as much to the contrary.
Character of a Trimmer (1685, printed 1688), preface

19 There is...no fundamental, but that *every supreme power must be arbitrary.*
Political, Moral, and Miscellaneous Thoughts and Reflections (1750). **Of Fundamentals**

20 When the People contend for their Liberty, they seldom get anything by their Victory but new masters.
Of Prerogative, Power and Liberty

21 Power is so apt to be insolent and Liberty to be saucy, that they are very seldom upon good Terms.

22 Men are not hanged for stealing horses, but that horses may not be stolen.
Of Punishment

23 Most men make little other use of their speech than to

give evidence against their own understanding.
Of Folly and Fools

1 Anger is never without an argument, but seldom with
a good one.
Of Anger

2 Malice is of a low stature, but it hath very long arms.
Of Malice and Envy

3 The best way to suppose what may come, is to
remember what is past.
Miscellaneous, 'Experience'

4 To the question, What shall we do to be saved in this
World? there is no other answer but this, Look to your
Moat.
A Rough Draft of a New Model at Sea

5 He [Halifax] had said he had known many kicked
down stairs, but he never knew any kicked up stairs
before.
Burnet, *Original Memoirs* (c.1697)

BISHOP JOSEPH HALL 1574–1656

6 I first adventure, follow me who list
And be the second English satirist.
Virgidemiae (1597), Prologue

7 Perfection is the child of Time.
Works (1625), p.670

FITZ-GREENE HALLECK 1790–1867

8 They love their land because it is their own,
    And scorn to give aught other reason why;
Would shake hands with a king upon his throne,
    And think it kindness to his Majesty.
Connecticut

9 Green be the turf above thee,
Friend of my better days!
None knew thee but to love thee,
Nor named thee but to praise.
On the Death of J.R. Drake

FRIEDRICH HALM 1806–1871

10 *Mein Herz ich will dich fragen:*
Was ist denn Liebe? Sag'!—
'Zwei Seelen und ein Gedanke,
Zwei Herzen und ein Schlag!'
What love is, if thou wouldst be taught,
    Thy heart must teach alone—
Two souls with but a single thought,
    Two hearts that beat as one.
Der Sohn der Wildnis (1842), Act II *ad fin.* Trans. by Maria
Lovell in *Ingomar the Barbarian*

ADMIRAL W.F. ('BULL') HALSEY 1882-1959

11 Our ships have been salvaged and are retiring at high
speed toward the Japanese fleet.
Radio Message, Oct. 1944 after Japanese claims that most of the
American Third Fleet had been sunk or were retiring

P.G. HAMERTON 1834–1894

12 The art of reading is to skip judiciously.
The Intellectual Life (1873), pt.iv, letter iv

ALEXANDER HAMILTON 1755?–1804

13 A national debt, if it is not excessive, will be to us a
national blessing.
Letter to Robert Morris, 30 Apr. 1781

GAIL HAMILTON (MARY A. DODGE) 1833–1896

14 The total depravity of inanimate things.
Epigram

SIR WILLIAM HAMILTON 1788–1856

15 Truth, like a torch, the more it's shook it shines.
Discussions on Philosophy (1852), title page

16 On earth there is nothing great but man; in man there
is nothing great but mind.
Lectures on Metaphysics (1859-60)

CHRISTOPHER HAMPTON 1946–

17 If I had to give a definition of capitalism I would say:
the process whereby American girls turn into American
women.
Savages (1973), 16

JOHN HANCOCK 1737–1793

18 There, I guess King George will be able to read that.
Remark on signing the Declaration of Independence, 4 July 1776

MINNY MAUD HANFF 1880–1942

19 Since then they called him Sunny Jim.
Advertisement for Force, a breakfast food, c.1902

EDMOND HARAUCOURT 1856–1941

20 *Partir c'est mourir un peu,*
C'est mourir à ce qu'on aime:
On laisse un peu de soi-même
En toute heure et dans tout lieu.
To go away is to die a little, it is to die to that which
    one loves: everywhere and always, one leaves
    behind a part of oneself.
Seul (1891), **Rondel de l'Adieu**

KEIR HARDIE 1856–1915

21 From his childhood onward this boy [the future
Edward VIII] will be surrounded by sycophants and
flatterers by the score—[*Cries of* 'Oh, oh!']—and will
be taught to believe himself as of a superior creation.
[*Cries of* 'Oh, oh!'] A line will be drawn between him
and the people whom he is to be called upon some day
to reign over. In due course, following the precedent
which has already been set, he will be sent on a tour
round the world, and probably rumours of a
morganatic alliance will follow—[*Loud cries of* 'Oh,
oh!' *and* 'Order!']—and the end of it all will be that
the country will be called upon to pay the bill. [*Cries
of* Divide!]
House of Commons, 28 June 1894

THOMAS HARDY 1840–1928

22   Come again, with the feet
That were light on the green as a thistledown ball,

And those mute ministrations to one and to all
    Beyond a man's saying sweet.
After the Visit

1 When the Present has latched its postern behind my
    tremulous stay,
    And the May month flaps its glad green leaves like
      wings,
    Delicate-filmed as new-spun silk, will the neighbours
    say,
    'He was a man who used to notice such things'?
Afterwards

2 Some nocturnal blackness, mothy and warm,
When the hedgehog travels furtively over the lawn.

3 'Peace upon earth!' was said. We sing it,
And pay a million priests to bring it.
After two thousand years of mass
We've got as far as poison-gas.
Christmas: 1924

4   In a solitude of the sea
        Deep from human vanity,
And the Pride of Life that planned her, stilly couches
she.

        Steel chambers, late the pyres
        Of her salamandrine fires,
Cold currents thrid, and turn to rhythmic tidal lyres.

        Over the mirrors meant
        To glass the opulent
The sea-worm crawls—grotesque, slimed, dumb,
    indifferent.
The Convergence of the Twain. Lines on the Loss of the *Titanic*,
I

5   Dim moon-eyed fishes near
        Gaze at the gilded gear
And query: 'What does this vaingloriousness down
    here?'
V

6   And as the smart ship grew
        In stature, grace, and hue,
In shadowy silent distance grew the Iceberg too.

        Alien they seemed to be:
        No mortal eye could see
The intimate welding of their later history,

        Or sign that they were bent
        By paths coincident
On being twin halves of one august event,

        Till the Spinner of the Years
        Said 'Now!' And each one hears,
And consummation comes, and jars two hemispheres.
VIII

7 At once a voice arose among
    The bleak twigs overhead
In a full-hearted evensong
    Of joy illimited;
An aged thrush, frail, gaunt, and small,
    In blast-beruffled plume,
Had chosen thus to fling his soul
    Upon the growing gloom.

So little cause for carollings
    Of such ecstatic sound
Was written on terrestrial things
    Afar or nigh around,
That I could think there trembled through

His happy good-night air
Some blessed Hope, whereof he knew
    And I was unaware.
The Darkling Thrush

8 Young Hodge the Drummer never knew—
    Fresh from his Wessex home—
The meaning of the broad Karoo,
    The Bush, the dusty loam.
Drummer Hodge

9 Yet portion of that unknown plain
    Will Hodge for ever be;
His homely Northern breast and brain
    Grow to some Southern tree,
And strange-eyed constellations reign
    His stars eternally.

10   Ah, no; the years, the years;
Down their carved names the rain-drop ploughs.
During Wind and Rain

11 What of the Immanent Will and its designs?—
- It works unconsciously as heretofore,
Eternal artistries in Circumstance.
The Dynasts (1903-08), pt.i. Fore-Scene

12   Like a knitter drowsed,
Whose fingers play in skilled unmindfulness,
The Will has woven with an absent heed
Since life first was; and ever so will weave.

13 The nether sky opens, and Europe is disclosed as a
prone and emaciated figure, the Alps shaping like a
backbone, and the branching mountain-chains like
ribs, the peninsular plateau of Spain forming a head.
Stage Direction

14 A local cult called Christianity.
I.vi

15 My argument is that War makes rattling good history;
but Peace is poor reading.
II.v

16 But O, the intolerable antilogy
Of making figments feel!
IV.vi

17 William Dewy, Tranter Reuben, Farmer Ledlow late
    at plough,
        Robert's kin, and John's, and Ned's,
And the Squire, and Lady Susan, lie in Mellstock
    churchyard now!
Friends Beyond

18   Yet at mothy curfew-tide,
And at midnight when the noon-heat breathes it back
    from walls and leads,

They've a way of whispering to me—fellow-wight
    who yet abide—
        In the muted, measured note
Of a ripple under archways, or a lone cave's stillicide.

19 Ye mid burn the old bass-viol that I set such value by.

20 If ye break my best blue china, children, I shan't care
or ho.

21 Well, World, you have kept faith with me,
    Kept faith with me;
Upon the whole you have proved to be
    Much as you said you were.
He Never Expected Much [or] **A Consideration.** On his 86th
birthday

22   'I do not promise overmuch,

Child; overmuch;
Just neutral-tinted haps and such,'
You said to minds like mine.

1 I am the family face;
Flesh perishes, I live on.
Heredity

2 But Time, to make me grieve,
Part steals, lets part abide;
And shakes this fragile frame at eve
With throbbings of noontide.
I Look Into My Glass

3 Let him in whose ears the low-voiced Best is killed by
the clash of the First,
Who holds that if way to the Better there be, it exacts
a full look at the worst,
Who feels that delight is a delicate growth cramped by
crookedness, custom, and fear,
Get him up and be gone as one shaped awry; he
disturbs the order here.
In Tenebris

4 I'm a labouring man, and know but little,
Or nothing at all;
But I can't help thinking that stone once echoed
The voice of Paul.
In the British Museum

5 Only a man harrowing clods
In a slow silent walk
With an old horse that stumbles and nods
Half asleep as they stalk.

Only thin smoke without flame
From the heaps of couch grass;
Yet this will go onward the same
Though Dynasties pass.

Yonder a maid and her wight
Come whispering by:
War's annals will cloud into night
Ere their story die.
In Time of 'The Breaking of Nations'

6 Let me enjoy the earth no less
Because the all-enacting Might
That fashioned forth its loveliness
Had other aims than my delight.
Let Me Enjoy the Earth

7 Here's not a modest maiden elf
But dreads the final Trumpet,
Lest half of her should rise herself,
And half some sturdy strumpet!
The Levelled Churchyard

8 What of the faith and fire within us
Men who march away
Ere the barn-cocks say
Night is growing gray?
Men Who March Away

9 In the third-class seat sat the journeying boy
And the roof-lamp's oily flame
Played on his listless form and face,
Bewrapt past knowing to what he was going,
Or whence he came.
Midnight on the Great Western

10 Your face, and the God-curst sun, and a tree,
And a pond edged with grayish leaves.
Neutral Tones

11 A car comes up, with lamps full-glare,

That flash upon a tree:
It has nothing to do with me,
And whangs along in a world of its own,
Leaving a blacker air.
Nobody Comes

12 That long drip of human tears.
On an Invitation to the United States

13 Christmas Eve, and twelve of the clock.
'Now they are all on their knees,'
An elder said as we sat in a flock
By the embers in hearthside ease.
The Oxen

14 So fair a fancy few would weave
In these years! Yet, I feel,
If someone said on Christmas Eve,
'Come; see the oxen kneel,

'In the lonely barton by yonder coomb
Our childhood used to know',
I should go with him in the gloom,
Hoping it might be so.

15 Queer are the ways of a man I know:
He comes and stands
In a careworn craze,
And looks at the sands
And the seaward haze
With moveless hands
And face and gaze,
Then turns to go...
And what does he see when he gazes so?
The Phantom Horsewoman

16 We shall see her no more
On the balcony
Smiling, while hurt, at the roar
As of a surging sea
From the stormy sturdy band
Who have doomed her lord's cause,
Though she waves her little hand
As it were applause.
The Rejected Member's Wife (Jan. 1906)

17 Read that moderate man Voltaire.
The Respectable Burgher

18 Love is lame at fifty years.
The Revisitation

19 —'You left us in tatters, without shoes or socks,
Tired of digging potatoes, and spudding up docks;
And now you've gay bracelets and bright feathers
three!'—
'Yes: that's how we dress when we're ruined,' said
she.
The Ruined Maid

20 A little ball of feather and bone.
Shelley's Skylark

21   Every branch big with it,
Bent every twig with it;
Every fork like a white web-foot;
Every street and pavement mute:
Some flakes have lost their way, and grope back
upward, when
Meeting those meandering down they turn and descend
again.
Snow in the Suburbs

22 A baby watched a ford, whereto
A wagtail came for drinking;

A blaring bull went wading through,
   The wagtail showed no shrinking.
Wagtail and Baby

1 A perfect gentleman then neared;
   The wagtail, in a winking,
With terror rose and disappeared;
   The baby fell a-thinking.

2 This is the weather the cuckoo likes,
   And so do I;
When showers betumble the chestnut spikes,
   And nestlings fly:
And the little brown nightingale bills his best,
And they sit outside at 'The Travellers' Rest'.
Weathers

3 This is the weather the shepherd shuns,
   And so do I.

4 And drops on gate-bars hang in a row,
And rooks in families homeward go,
   And so do I.

5 When I set out for Lyonnesse,
   A hundred miles away,
   The rime was on the spray,
And starlight lit my lonesomeness
When I set out for Lyonnesse
   A hundred miles away.
When I Set Out for Lyonnesse

6 When I came back from Lyonnesse
   With magic in my eyes,
All marked with mute surmise
My radiance rare and fathomless,
When I came back from Lyonnesse
   With magic in my eyes!

7 Goodbye is not worth while.
Without Ceremony

8 It says that Life would signify
   A thwarted purposing:
      That we come to live, and are called to die.
      Yes, that's the thing
      In fall, in spring,
      That Yell'ham says:—
   'Life offers—to deny!'
Yell'ham-Wood's Story

9 The kingly brilliance of Sirius pierced the eye with a steely glitter, the star called Capella was yellow, Aldebaran and Betelgueux shone with a fiery red. To persons standing alone on a hill during a clear midnight such as this, the roll of the world eastward is almost a palpable movement.
Far From the Madding Crowd (1874), ch.2

10 A nice unparticular man.
ch.8

11 We ought to feel deep cheerfulness that a happy Providence kept it from being any worse.

12 Ah! stirring times we live in—stirring times.
ch.15

13 Five decades hardly modified the cut of a gaiter, the embroidery of a smock-frock, by the breadth of a hair. Ten generations failed to alter the turn of a single phrase. In these Wessex nooks the busy outsider's ancient times are only old; his old times are still new; his present is futurity.
ch.22

14 Ethelberta breathed a sort of exclamation, not right out, but stealthily, like a parson's damn.
The Hand of Ethelberta (1875), ch.26

15 Done because we are too menny.
Jude the Obscure (1895), pt.vi, ch.2

16 'Well, poor soul; she's helpless to hinder that or anything now,' answered Mother Cuxsom. 'And all her shining keys will be took from her, and her cupboards opened, and things a' didn't wish seen, anybody will see; and her little wishes and ways will all be as nothing.'
The Mayor of Casterbridge (1894), ch.18

17 Dialect words—those terrible marks of the beast to the truly genteel.
ch.20

18   Michael Henchard's Will.
That Elizabeth-Jane Farfrae be not told of my death,
   or made to grieve on account of me.
   & that I be not buried in consecrated ground.
   & that no sexton be asked to toll the bell.
   & that nobody is wished to see my dead body.
   & that no murners walk behind me at my funeral.
   & that no flours be planted on my grave.
   & that no man remember me.
To this I put my name.
ch.45

19 The heaven being spread with this pallid screen and the earth with the darkest vegetation, their meeting-line at the horizon was clearly marked. In such contrast the heath wore the appearance of an instalment of night which had taken up its place before its astronomical hour was come: darkness had to a great extent arrived hereon, while day stood distinct in the sky.
The Return of the Native (1878), ch.1

20 In fact, precisely at this transitional point of its nightly roll into darkness the great and particular glory of the Egdon waste began, and nobody could be said to understand the heath who had not been there at such a time.

21 The great inviolate place had an ancient permanence which the sea cannot claim. Who can say of a particular sea that it is old? Distilled by the sun, kneaded by the moon, it is renewed in a year, in a day, or in an hour. The sea changed, the fields changed, the rivers, the villages, and the people changed, yet Egdon remained.

22 A little one-eyed, blinking sort o' place.
Tess of the D'Urbervilles (1891), ch.1

23 Always washing, and never getting finished.
ch.4

24 The New Testament was less a Christiad than a Pauliad to his intelligence.
ch.25

25 'Justice' was done, and the President of the Immortals (in Aeschylean phrase) had ended his sport with Tess.
ch.59

26 Good, but not religious-good.
Under the Greenwood Tree (1872), ch.2

27 That man's silence is wonderful to listen to.
ch.14

1 You was a good man, and did good things.
The Woodlanders (1887), ch.48

JULIUS HARE 1795–1855
and AUGUSTUS HARE 1792–1834

2 Truth, when witty, is the wittiest of all things.
Guesses at Truth (1827), Series 1

3 The ancients dreaded death: the Christian can only fear dying.

4 Half the failures in life arise from pulling in one's horse as he is leaping.

5 Purity is the feminine, Truth the masculine, of Honour.

6 Every Irishman, the saying goes, has a potato in his head.

MAURICE EVAN HARE 1886–1967

7 Alfred de Musset
Used to call his cat Pusset.
His accent was affected.
That was only to be expected.
Byway in Biography

8 There once was a man who said, 'Damn!
It is borne in upon me I am
      An engine that moves
      In predestinate grooves,
I'm not even a bus, I'm a tram.'
Written, as above, at St. John's College, Oxford, in 1905

SIR JOHN HARINGTON 1561–1612

9   When I make a feast,
I would my guests should praise it, not the cooks.
Epigrams (1618), bk.i, No.5. **Against Writers that Carp at Other Men's Books**

10 Treason doth never prosper, what's the reason?
For if it prosper, none dare call it treason.
bk.iv, No.5. **Of Treason**

KING HAROLD OF ENGLAND 1022–1066

11 He will give him seven feet of English ground, or as much more as he may be taller than other men.
His offer to Harald Sigurdson, invading England. Snorri Sturluson, *Heimskringla*, X. xci

JOEL CHANDLER HARRIS 1848–1908

12 'Law, Brer Tarrypin!' sez Brer Fox, sezee, 'you ain't see no trouble yit. Ef you wanter see sho' nuff trouble, you des oughter go 'longer me; I'm de man w'at kin show you trouble,' sezee.
Nights with Uncle Remus (1883), ch.17

13 W'en folks git ole en strucken wid de palsy, dey mus speck ter be laff'd at.
ch.23

14 Hit look lak sparrer-grass, hit feel like sparrer-grass, hit tas'e lak sparrer-grass, en I bless ef 'taint sparrer-grass.
ch.27

15 All by my own-alone self.
ch.36

16 We er sorter po'ly, Sis Tempy, I'm 'blige ter you.

You know w'at de jay-bird say ter der squinch-owl!
'I'm sickly but sassy.'
ch.50

17 Oh, whar shill we go w'en de great day comes,
Wid de blowin' er de trumpits en de bangin' er de drums?
How many po' sinners'll be kotched out late
En find no latch ter de golden gate?
Uncle Remus: His Songs and Sayings (1880), i

18 How duz yo' sym'tums seem ter segashuate?
Uncle Remus. Legends of the Old Plantation (1881), ch.2. **Tar-Baby Story**

19 Tar-baby ain't sayin' nuthin', en Brer Fox, he lay low.

20 Bred en bawn in a brier-patch!
ch.4

21 Lounjun 'roun' en suffer'n'.
ch.12

22 Ole man Know-All died las' year.
ch.34, **Plantation Proverbs**

23 Licker talks mighty loud w'en it git loose fum de jug.

24 Hongry rooster don't cackle w'en he fine a wum.

25 Youk'n hide de fier, but w'at you gwine do wid de smoke?

BRET HARTE 1836–1902

26 And on that grave where English oak and holly
      And laurel wreaths entwine
Deem it not all a too presumptuous folly,—
      This spray of Western pine!
Dickens in Camp

27 Thar ain't no sense
In gittin' riled!
Jim

28 If, of all words of tongue and pen,
The saddest are, 'It might have been,'
More sad are these we daily see:
'It is, but hadn't ought to be!'
Mrs. Judge Jenkins. See 571:19

29 Which I wish to remark,
And my language is plain,
That for ways that are dark
And for tricks that are vain,
The heathen Chinee is peculiar,
Which the same I would rise to explain.
Plain Language from Truthful James (1870)

30 We are ruined by Chinese cheap labour.

31 He wore, I think, a chasuble, the day when first we met.
The Ritualist

32 I reside at Table Mountain, and my name is Truthful James;
I am not up to small deceit, or any sinful games.
The Society upon the Stanislaus

33 And he smiled a kind of sickly smile, and curled up on the floor,
And the subsequent proceedings interested him no more.

L.P. HARTLEY 1895–1972

34 The past is a foreign country: they do things

differently there.
The Go-Between, Prologue

M. LOUISE HASKINS 1875–1957

1 And I said to the man who stood at the gate of the year: 'Give me a light that I may tread safely into the unknown'. And he replied: 'Go out into the darkness and put your hand into the hand of God. That shall be to you better than light and safer than a known way.'
The Desert (c.1908), Introduction. Quoted by King George VI in a Christmas Broadcast, 25 Dec. 1939

STEPHEN HAWES d. 1523?

2 When the lytle byrdes swetely dyd syng
Laudes to their maker early in the mornyng.
Passetyme of Pleasure (1506, printed 1509), cap.33, xxxiii

3 For though the day be never so longe,
At last the belles ringeth to evensonge.
cap.42

REVD. R.S. HAWKER 1803–1875

4 And have they fixed the where and when?
   And shall Trelawny die?
Here's twenty thousand Cornish men
   Will know the reason why!
Song of the Western Men. The last three lines have existed since the imprisonment by James II, 1688, of the seven Bishops, including Trelawny, Bishop of Bristol.

NATHANIEL HAWTHORNE 1804–1864

5 Dr Johnson's morality was as English an article as a beefsteak.
Our Old Home (1863), **Lichfield and Uttoxeter**

IAN HAY 1876–1952

6 What do you mean, funny? Funny-peculiar or funny-ha-ha?
The Housemaster (1936), Act III

J. MILTON HAYES fl. 1911

7 There's a one-eyed yellow idol to the north of Khatmandu,
There's a little marble cross below the town;
There's a broken-hearted woman tends the grave of Mad Carew
And the Yellow God forever gazes down.
The Green Eye of the Yellow God (1911)

WILLIAM HAZLITT 1778–1830

8 His sayings are generally like women's letters; all the pith is in the postscript. [Charles Lamb.]
Conversations of Northcote. (Boswell Redivivus, 1826-7)

9 The only specimen of Burke is, *all that he wrote.*
English Literature, ch.ix. **Character of Mr. Burke**

10 He writes as fast as they can read, and he does not write himself down.
ch.xiv. **Sir Walter Scott**

11 His worst is better than any other person's best.

12 His works (taken together) are almost like a new edition of human nature. This is indeed to be an author!

13 The round-faced man in black entered, and dissipated all doubts on the subject, by beginning to talk. He did not cease while he stayed; nor has he since, that I know of. [Coleridge.]
ch.xvii. **My First Acquaintance with Poets**

14 'For those two hours,' he [Coleridge] afterwards was pleased to say, 'he was conversing with W.H.'s forehead!'

15 So have I loitered my life away, reading books, looking at pictures, going to plays, hearing, thinking, writing on what pleased me best. I have wanted only one thing to make me happy, but wanting that have wanted everything.

16 You will hear more good things on the outside of a stagecoach from London to Oxford than if you were to pass a twelvemonth with the undergraduates, or heads of colleges, of that famous university.
The Ignorance of the Learned

17 He [Coleridge] talked on for ever; and you wished him to talk on for ever.
Lectures on the English Poets. Lecture viii, **On the Living Poets**

18 The dupe of friendship, and the fool of love; have I not reason to hate and to despise myself? Indeed I do; and chiefly for not having hated and despised the world enough.
The Plain Speaker (1826). **On the Pleasure of Hating**

19 The love of liberty is the love of others; the love of power is the love of ourselves.
Political Essays (1819). **'The Times' Newspaper**

20 Those who make their dress a principal part of themselves, will, in general, become of no more value than their dress.
On the Clerical Character

21 There is nothing good to be had in the country, or if there is, they will not let you have it.
1817. **Observations on Mr. Wordsworth's *Excursion***

22 The art of pleasing consists in being pleased.
Round Table, vol.i. **On Manner**

23 The greatest offence against virtue is to speak ill of it.
Sketches and Essays (1839). **On Cant and Hypocrisy**

24 The most fluent talkers or most plausible reasoners are not always the justest thinkers.
On Prejudice

25 We never do anything well till we cease to think about the manner of doing it.

26 There is an unseemly exposure of the mind, as well as of the body.
On Disagreeable People

27 A nickname is the heaviest stone that the devil can throw at a man.
Nicknames

28 Rules and models destroy genius and art.
On Taste

29 But of all footmen the lowest class is *literary footmen.*
Footmen

30 One of the pleasantest things in the world is going on a journey; but I like to go by myself.
Table Talk, xix. **On Going a Journey**

31 When I am in the country I wish to vegetate like the country.

32 Give me the clear blue sky over my head, and the

green turf beneath my feet, a winding road before me, and a three hours' march to dinner—and then to thinking! It is hard if I cannot start some game on these lone heaths.

1 The English (it must be owned) are rather a foul-mouthed nation.
xxii. **On Criticism**

2 We can scarcely hate any one that we know.

3 No young man believes he shall ever die.
Uncollected Essays, xviii. **On the Feeling of Immortality in Youth**

4 Well, I've had a happy life.
Last words. W.C. Hazlitt, *Memoirs of William Hazlitt,* 1867

EDWARD HEATH 1916–

5 It is the unpleasant and unacceptable face of capitalism but one should not suggest that the whole of British industry consists of practices of this kind.
House of Commons, 15 May 1973

BISHOP REGINALD HEBER 1783–1826

6 What though the spicy breezes
Blow soft o'er Ceylon's isle;
Though every prospect pleases,
And only man is vile:

In vain with lavish kindness
The gifts of God are strown;
The heathen in his blindness
Bows down to wood and stone.
From Greenland's Icy Mountains. This is the most familiar version. Bishop Heber originally wrote 'The savage in his blindness'. He altered this, and also altered 'Ceylon's' to 'Java's'.

7 They climb'd the steep ascent of Heav'n
Through peril, toil and pain;
O God, to us may grace be given
To follow in their train.
The Son of God Goes Forth

G.W.F. HEGEL 1770–1831

8 What experience and history teach is this—that people and governments never have learned anything from history, or acted on principles deduced from it.
Philosophy of History. Introduction

HEINRICH HEINE 1797–1856

9 *Ich weiss nicht, was soll es bedeuten,*
Dass ich so traurig bin;
Ein Märchen aus alten Zeiten,
Das kommt mir nicht aus dem Sinn.
I know not why I am so sad; I cannot get out of my head a fairy-tale of olden times.
Die Loreley

10 *Sie hatten sich beide so herzlich lieb,*
Spitzbübin war sie, er war ein Dieb.
They loved each other beyond belief—
She was a strumpet, he was a thief.
Neue Gedichte (1844), **Romanzen,** I. 'Ein Weib'. Trans. Louis Untermeyer (1938)

11 *Hört ihr das Glöckchen klingeln? Kniet nieder—Man bringt die Sakramente einem sterbenden Gotte.*
Do you hear the little bell tinkle? Kneel down. They

are bringing the sacraments to a dying god.
Zur Geschichte der Religion und Philosophie in Deutschland (1834), bk.2

12 *Dieses merkt Euch, Ihr stolzen Männer det Tat. Ihr seid nichts als unbewusste Handlanger der Gedankenmänner. . .Maximilan Robespierre war nichts als die Hand von Jean Jacques Rousseau, die blutige Hand, die aus dem Schosse der Zeit den Leib hervorzog, dessen Seele Rousseau geschaffen.*
Note this, you proud men of action. You are nothing but the unconscious hodmen of the men of ideas. . .Maximilian Robespierre was nothing but the hand of Jean Jacques Rousseau, the bloody hand that drew from the womb of time the body whose soul Rousseau had created.
bk. 3

13 *Dieu me pardonnera. C'est son métier.*
God will pardon me. It is His trade.
On his deathbed. Edmond and Charles Goncourt, *Journal,* 23 Feb. 1863

14   *Dort, wo man Bücher*
Verbrennt, verbrennt man auch am Ende Menschen.
Whenever books are burned men also, in the end, are burned.
Almansor (1820–1), l. 245

LILLIAN HELLMAN 1905–

15 I cannot and will not cut my conscience to fit this year's fashions.
Letter to the Honourable John S. Wood, Chairman of the House Committee on un-American Activities, 19 May 1952

SIR ARTHUR HELPS 1813–1875

16 Reading is sometimes an ingenious device for avoiding thought.
Friends in Council (1847, 1853), bk.ii, ch.1

17 What a blessing this smoking is! perhaps the greatest that we owe to the discovery of America.
series II, 1859, vol.i, ch.1, **Worry**

18 There is one statesman of the present day, of whom I always say that he would have escaped making the blunders that he has made if he had only ridden more in omnibuses.
vol.ii, ch.9, **On Government**

C.-A. HELVÉTIUS 1715–1771

19 *L'éducation nous faisait ce que nous sommes.*
Education makes us what we are.
Discours XXX, ch.30

MRS. HEMANS 1793–1835

20 The boy stood on the burning deck
Whence all but he had fled;
The flame that lit the battle's wreck
Shone round him o'er the dead.
Casabianca

21 The stately homes of England,
How beautiful they stand!
Amidst their tall ancestral trees,
O'er all the pleasant land.
The Homes of England

JOHN HEMING d.1630
and HENRY CONDELL d.1627

1 Well! it is now public, and you will stand for your privileges we know: to read, and censure. Do so, but buy it first. That doth best commend a book, the stationer says.
Preface to the First Folio Shakespeare, 1623

2 Who, as he was a happy imitator of Nature, was a most gentle expresser of it. His mind and hand went together: And what he thought, he uttered with that easiness, that we have scarce received from him a blot.

ERNEST HEMINGWAY 1898–1961

3 But did thee feel the earth move?
For Whom the Bell Tolls (1940), ch.13

W.E. HENLEY 1849–1903

4 Out of the night that covers me,
Black as the Pit from pole to pole,
I thank whatever gods may be
For my unconquerable soul.

In the fell clutch of circumstance,
I have not winced nor cried aloud:
Under the bludgeonings of chance
My head is bloody, but unbowed.
Echoes (1888), iv. **Invictus. In Mem. R.T.H.B.**

5 It matters not how strait the gate,
How charged with punishments the scroll,
I am the master of my fate:
I am the captain of my soul.

6 Madam Life's a piece in bloom
Death goes dogging everywhere;
She's the tenant of the room,
He's the ruffian on the stair.
ix. **To W.R.**

7 A late lark twitters from the quiet skies.
xxxv. **Margaritae Sororis**

8 Night with her train of stars.
And her great gift of sleep.

9 So be my passing!
My task accomplished and the long day done,
My wages taken, and in my heart
Some late lark singing,
Let me be gathered to the quiet west,
The sundown splendid and serene,
Death.

10 Or ever the Knightly years were gone
With the old world to the grave,
I was a King in Babylon
And you were a Christian Slave.
xxxvii. **To W.A.**

11 What have I done for you,
    England, my England?
What is there I would not do,
    England, my own?
For England's Sake (1900), iii. **Pro Rege Nostro**

12 Valiant in velvet, light in ragged luck,
Most vain, most generous, sternly critical,
Buffoon and poet, lover and sensualist:
A deal of Ariel, just a streak of Puck,

Much Antony, of Hamlet most of all,
And something of the Shorter-Catechist. [Stevenson.]
In Hospital, xxv. **Apparition**

HENRI IV 1553–1610

13 *Je veux qu'il n'y ait si pauvre paysan en mon royaume qu'il n'ait tous les dimanches sa poule au pot.*
I want there to be no peasant in my kingdom so poor that he is unable to have a chicken in his pot every Sunday.
Hardouin de Péréfixe, *Hist. de Henry le Grand*, 1681

14 *Pends-toi, brave Crillon; nous avons combattu à Arques et tu n'y étais pas.*
Hang yourself, brave Crillon; we fought at Arques and you were not there.
Traditional form given by Voltaire to a letter of Henri to Crillon. *Lettres missives de Henri IV, Collection des documents inédits de l'histoire de France*, vol.iv, 1847, p.848. Henri's actual words, in a letter to Crillon of 20 Sept. 1597, were *Brave Crillon, pendez-vous de n'avoir été ici près de moi lundi dernier à la plus belle occasion qui se soit jamais vue et qui peut-être se verra jamais.*

15 *Paris vaut bien une messe.*
Paris is well worth a mass.
Attr. either to Henri IV or to his minister Sully, in conversation with Henri. *Caquets de l'Accouchée*, 1622

16 The wisest fool in Christendom.
Of James I of England. Remark attr. to Henri IV and Sully. The French is not known

MATTHEW HENRY 1662–1714

17 The better day, the worse deed.
Exposition of the Old and New Testaments (1708-10), Genesis III.vi

18 To their own second and sober thoughts.
Job VI.xxix

19 He rolls it under his tongue as a sweet morsel.
Ps. XXXVI.ii

20 They that die by famine die by inches.
Ps. LIX.xv

21 Men of polite learning and a liberal education.
Acts X.i

22 All this and heaven too.
Attr.

O. HENRY 1862–1910

23 Life is made up of sobs, sniffles, and smiles, with sniffles predominating.
The Gift of the Magi

24 Turn up the lights, I don't want to go home in the dark.
Last words, quoting popular song. C.A. Smith, *O. Henry*, ch.9

PATRICK HENRY 1736–1799

25 Caesar had his Brutus—Charles the First, his Cromwell—and George the Third—('Treason,' cried the Speaker)...*may profit by their example.* If *this* be treason, make the most of it.
Speech in the Virginia Convention, May 1765. Wirt, *Patrick Henry* (1818), p.65

26 I am not a Virginian, but an American.
Speech in the Virginia Convention, Sept. 1774

27 I know not what course others may take; but as for

me, give me liberty, or give me death!
20 Mar. 1775. Wirt, *Patrick Henry* (1818), p.123

KING HENRY II 1133–1189

1 Will no one revenge me of the injuries I have sustained
from one turbulent priest?
Of St. Thomas Becket (Dec. 1170). Oral trad. See G. Lyttelton,
History of the Life of King Henry the Second (1769), IV, p.353;
also Herbert of Bosham, *Vita S. Thomae* in *Materials for the
History of Archbishop Thomas Becket* (Rolls Series), III (1887),
p.487

KING HENRY VIII 1491–1547

2 The King found her so different from her
picture...that...he swore they had brought him a
Flanders mare. [Anne of Cleves.]
Smollett, *Hist. of England* (ed.3, 1759), vi.68

3 This man hath the right sow by the ear. [Of Cranmer.]
Attr.

BISHOP JOSEPH HENSHAW 1603–1679

4 One doth but breakfast here, another dines, he that
liveth longest doth but sup; we must all go to bed in
another world.
Horae Succisivae (1631), pt.I

HERACLITUS fl. 513 B.C.

5 πάντα χωρεῖ, οὐδὲν μένει.
Everything flows and nothing stays.
Plato, *Cratylus*, 402a

6 δὶς ἐς τὸν αὐτὸν ποταμὸν οὐκ ἂν ἐμβαίης.
You can't step twice into the same river.

A.P. HERBERT 1890–1971

7 Don't let's go to the dogs to-night,
For mother will be there.
Don't Let's Go to the Dogs

8 Don't tell my mother I'm living in sin,
Don't let the old folks know:
Don't tell my twin that I breakfast on gin,
He'd never survive the blow.
Don't Tell My Mother

9 Let's find out what everyone is doing,
And then stop everyone from doing it.
Let's Stop Somebody

10 As my poor father used to say
In 1863,
Once people start on all this Art
Good-bye, moralitee!
And what my father used to say
Is good enough for me.
Lines for a Worthy Person

11 Well, fancy giving money to the Government!
Might as well have put it down the drain.
Fancy giving money to the Government!
Nobody will see the stuff again.
Well, they've no idea what money's for—
Ten to one they'll start another war.
I've heard a lot of silly things, but, Lor'!
Fancy giving money to the Government!
Too Much!

12 He didn't ought to come to bed in boots.
Riverside Nights

13 The Common Law of England has been laboriously
built about a mythical figure—the figure of 'The
Reasonable Man'.
Uncommon Law (1935), p.1

14 People must not do things for fun. We are not here for
fun. There is no reference to fun in any Act of
Parliament.
p.28

15 If elderly bishops were seen leaving the Athenaeum
with jugs of stout in their hands the casual observer
would form an impression of the character of that
institution which would be largely unjust.
p.33

16 The critical period in matrimony is breakfast-time.
p.98

17 The Englishman never enjoys himself except for a
noble purpose.
p.198

18 For any ceremonial purposes the otherwise excellent
liquid, water, is unsuitable in colour and other
respects.
p.272

19 An Act of God was defined as *something which no
reasonable man could have expected.*
p.316

LORD HERBERT OF CHERBURY 1583–1648

20 Now that the April of your youth adorns
The garden of your face.
Ditty: Now That the April

GEORGE HERBERT 1593–1633

21 He that makes a good war makes a good peace.
Outlandish Proverbs, 420

22 He that lives in hope danceth without musick.
1006

23 I read, and sigh, and wish I were a tree—
For sure then I should grow
To fruit or shade; at least some bird would trust
Her household to me, and I should be just.
The Temple (1633). Affliction

24 Ah, my dear God, though I am clean forgot,
Let me not love Thee, if I love Thee not.

25 How well her name an 'Army' doth present.
In whom the 'Lord of Hosts' did pitch His tent!
Anagram, Mary

26 Let all the world in ev'ry corner sing
My God and King.
The heav'ns are not too high,
His praise may thither fly;
The earth is not too low,
His praises there may grow.
Let all the world in ev'ry corner sing
My God and King.
The Church with psalms must shout,
No door can keep them out:
But above all, the heart
Must bear the longest part.
Antiphon

27 Hearken unto a Verser, who may chance

Rhyme thee to good, and make a bait of pleasure:
A verse may find him who a sermon flies,
And turn delight into a sacrifice.
The Church Porch, i

1   Drink not the third glass—which thou
canst not tame
When once it is within thee.
v

2   Dare to be true: nothing can need a lie;
A fault, which needs it most, grows two thereby.
xiii

3   O England, full of sin, but most of sloth;
Spit out thy phlegm, and fill thy breast with glory.
xvi

4   Wit's an unruly engine, wildly striking
Sometimes a friend, sometimes the engineer.
xli

5   But love is lost, the way of friendship's gone,
Though David had his Jonathan, Christ his John.
xlvi

6   Be calm in arguing; for fierceness makes
Error a fault and truth discourtesy.
lii

7   Calmness is great advantage; he that lets
Another chafe, may warm him at his fire.
liii

8   Who aimeth at the sky
Shoots higher much than he that means a tree.
lvi

9   Man is God's image; but a poor man is
Christ's stamp to boot.
lxiv

10 Kneeling ne'er spoil'd silk stocking; quit thy state;
All equal are within the Church's gate.
lxviii

11   O, be drest;
Stay not for th' other pin! Why, thou hast lost
A joy for it worth worlds.
lxix

12 Judge not the preacher, for he is thy Judge;
If thou mislike him, thou conceiv'st him not:
God calleth preaching folly: do not grudge
To pick out treasures from an earthen pot:
The worst speaks something good; if all want sense,
God takes a text, and preacheth patience.
lxxii

13 Look not on pleasures as they come, but go.
lxxvii

14 I struck the board, and cried, 'No more;
I will abroad.'
What, shall I ever sigh and pine?
My lines and life are free; free as the road,
Loose as the wind, as large as store.
Shall I be still in suit?
Have I no harvest but a thorn
To let me blood, and not restore
What I have lost with cordial fruit?
Sure there was wine
Before my sighs did dry it; there was corn
Before my tears did drown it;
Is the year only lost to me?
Have I no bays to crown it?
The Collar

15   Away! take heed;
I will abroad.
Call in thy death's-head there, tie up thy fears;
He that forbears
To suit and serve his need
Deserves his load.
But as I rav'd and grew more fierce and wild
At every word,
Methought I heard one calling, 'Child';
And I replied, 'My Lord.'

16 Love is swift of foot;
Love's a man of war,
And can shoot,
And can hit from far.
Discipline

17 I got me flowers to strew Thy way,
I got me boughs off many a tree;
But Thou wast up by break of day,
And brought'st Thy sweets along with Thee.
Easter Song

18 Teach me, my God and King,
In all things Thee to see,
And what I do in any thing
To do it as for Thee.

A man that looks on glass,
On it may stay his eye;
Or if he pleaseth, through it pass,
And then the heaven espy.
The Elixir

19 A servant with this clause
Makes drudgery divine;
Who sweeps a room as for Thy laws
Makes that and th' action fine.

20 Oh that I were an orange-tree,
That busy plant!
Then I should ever laden be,
And never want
Some fruit for Him that dressed me.
Employment

21 Who would have thought my shrivel'd heart
Could have recovered greenness?
The Flower

22 And now in age I bud again,
After so many deaths I live and write;
I once more smell the dew and rain,
And relish versing: O, my only Light,
It cannot be
That I am he
On whom Thy tempests fell all night.

23 Death is still working like a mole,
And digs my grave at each remove.
Grace

24 I made a posy while the day ran by;
Here will I smell my remnant out, and tie
My life within this band;
But Time did beckon to the flow'rs, and they
By noon most cunningly did steal away,
And wither'd in my hand.
Life

25 Love bade me welcome; yet my soul drew back,
Guilty of dust and sin.
But quick-ey'd Love, observing me grow slack
From my first entrance in,

Drew nearer to me, sweetly questioning
          If I lack'd any thing.
Love

1 'You must sit down,' says Love, 'and taste My meat.'
        So I did sit and eat.

2   For us the winds do blow,
The earth resteth, heav'n moveth, fountains flow;
   Nothing we see but means our good,
    As our delight or as our treasure;
The whole is either our cupboard of food
    Or cabinet of pleasure.
Man

3 Oh mighty love! Man is one world, and hath
   Another to attend him.

4   When boyes go first to bed,
They step into their voluntarie graves.
Mortification

5 Prayer the Church's banquet...
Exalted manna, gladness of the best,
Heaven in ordinary, man well drest,
The Milkie Way, the bird of Paradise...
The land of spices; something understood.
Prayer

6 When God at first made man,
Having a glass of blessings standing by;
Let us (said he) pour on him all we can:
Let the world's riches, which dispersed lie,
Contract into a span.
The Pulley

7 He would adore my gifts instead of Me,
And rest in Nature, not the God of Nature:
   So both should losers be.

8   Yet let him keep the rest,
But keep them with repining restlessness;
Let him be rich and weary, that at least,
If goodness lead him not, yet weariness
   May toss him to My breast.

9 But who does hawk at eagles with a dove?
The Sacrifice, xxiii

10 Lord, with what care Thou hast begirt us round!
Parents first season us; then schoolmasters
Deliver us to laws; they send us, bound
To rules of reason, holy messengers,

Pulpits and Sundays, sorrow dogging sin,
Afflictions sorted, anguish of all sizes,
Fine nets and stratagems to catch us in,
Bibles laid open, millions of surprises.
Sin

11 Yet all these fences and their whole array
One cunning bosom sin blows quite away.

12 Grasp not at much, for fear thou losest all.
The Size

13 The God of love my Shepherd is,
And He that doth me feed,
While He is mine, and I am His,
What can I want or need?
23rd Psalm

14 Lord, make me coy and tender to offend:
In friendship, first I think if that agree
       Which I intend
Unto my friend's intent and end;

I would not use a friend as I use Thee.
Unkindness

15 My friend may spit upon my curious floor;
Would he have gold? I lend it instantly;
       But let the poor,
And Thou within them, starve at door:
I cannot use a friend as I use Thee.

16 Sweet day, so cool, so calm, so bright,
The bridal of the earth and sky,
The dew shall weep thy fall to-night;
       For thou must die.

Sweet rose, whose hue angry and brave
Bids the rash gazer wipe his eye,
Thy root is ever in its grave,
       And thou must die.

Sweet spring, full of sweet days and roses,
A box where sweets compacted lie.
Virtue

17 Only a sweet and virtuous soul,
Like season'd timber, never gives;
But though the whole world turn to coal,
       Then chiefly lives.

ROBERT HERRICK 1591–1674

18 I sing of brooks, of blossoms, birds, and bowers:
Of April, May, of June, and July-flowers.
I sing of May-poles, Hock-carts, wassails, wakes,
Of bride-grooms, brides, and of their bridal-cakes.
Hesperides (1648). **Argument of his Book**

19 And once more yet (ere I am laid out dead)
Knock at a star with my exalted head.
The Bad Season Makes the Poet Sad

20 Fair pledges of a fruitful tree,
   Why do ye fall so fast?
   Your date is not so past;
But you may stay yet here a while,
   To blush and gently smile;
   And go at last.
Blossoms

21 Cherry-ripe, ripe, ripe, I cry,
Full and fair ones; come and buy:
If so be, you ask me where
They do grow? I answer, there,
Where my Julia's lips do smile;
There's the land, or cherry-isle.
Cherry-Ripe. See 3:18, 129:22

22 Get up, get up for shame, the blooming morn
Upon her wings presents the god unshorn.
Corinna's Going a-Maying

23 Get up, sweet Slug-a-bed, and see
The dew bespangling herb and tree.

24   'Tis sin,
Nay, profanation to keep in.

25 Come, let us go, while we are in our prime;
And take the harmless folly of the time.

26 So when or you or I are made
A fable, song, or fleeting shade;
All love, all liking, all delight
Lies drown'd with us in endless night.
Then while time serves, and we are but decaying;
Come, my Corinna, come, let's go a-Maying.

1 With thousand such enchanting dreams, that meet
To make sleep not so sound, as sweet.
A Country Life: to his Brother, M. Tho. Herrick

2 A sweet disorder in the dress
Kindles in clothes a wantonness:
A lawn about the shoulders thrown
Into a fine distraction…
A careless shoe-string, in whose tie
I see a wild civility:
Do more bewitch me, than when Art
Is too precise in every part.
Delight in Disorder

3 More discontents I never had
Since I was born, than here;
Where I have been, and still am sad,
    In this dull Devonshire.
Discontents in Devon

4 It is the end that crowns us, not the fight.
The End

5 Only a little more
I have to write,
Then I'll give o'er,
And bid the world Good-night.
His Poetry his Pillar

6 When I a verse shall make,
Know I have prayed thee
For old religion's sake,
Saint Ben, to aid me.
His Prayer to Ben Jonson

7 Roses at first were white,
    Till they co'd not agree,
Whether my Sappho's breast,
    Or they more white sho'd be.
How Roses Came Red

8 'Twixt kings and tyrants there's this difference
    known;
Kings seek their subjects' good: tyrants their own.
Kings and Tyrants

9 Love is a circle that doth restless move
In the same sweet eternity of love.
Love What It Is

10 Good morrow to the day so fair;
Good morning, Sir, to you:
Good morrow to mine own torn hair
    Bedabbled with the dew.
The Mad Maid's Song

11 Her eyes the glow-worm lend thee,
The shooting-stars attend thee;
    And the elves also,
    Whose little eyes glow,
Like the sparks of fire, befriend thee.
The Night-Piece, to Julia

12 Night makes no difference 'twixt the Priest and Clerk;
Joan as my Lady is as good i' th' dark.
No Difference i' th' Dark

13 Made us nobly wild, not mad.
Ode for Ben Jonson

14 Out-did the meat, out-did the frolic wine.

15 Fain would I kiss my Julia's dainty leg,
Which is as white and hairless as an egg.
On Julia's Legs

16 Men are suspicious; prone to discontent:

Subjects still loathe the present Government.
Present Government Grievous

17 Praise they that will times past, I joy to see
My self now live: this age best pleaseth me.
The Present Time Best Pleaseth

18 Some ask'd how pearls did grow, and where?
Then spoke I to my girl,
To part her lips, and shew'd them there
The quarelets of pearl.
The Rock of Rubies, and the Quarry of Pearls

19 Attempt the end, and never stand to doubt;
Nothing's so hard, but search will find it out.
Seek and Find

20 A little saint best fits a little shrine,
A little prop best fits a little vine,
As my small cruse best fits my little wine.
A Ternary of Littles, upon a Pipkin of Jelly sent to a Lady

21 A little stream best fits a little boat;
A little lead best fits a little float;
As my small pipe best fits my little note.

A little meat best fits a little belly,
As sweetly, Lady, give me leave to tell ye,
This little pipkin fits this little jelly.

22 Give me a kiss, add to that kiss a score;
Then to that twenty, add a hundred more:
A thousand to that hundred: so kiss on,
To make that thousand up a million.
Treble that million, and when that is done,
Let's kiss afresh, as when we first begun.
To Anthea: Ah, My Anthea! See 136:26

23 Now is the time, when all the lights wax dim;
And thou (Anthea) must withdraw from him
Who was thy servant.
To Anthea: Now is the Time

24 For my Embalming (Sweetest) there will be
No Spices wanting, when I'm laid by thee.

25 Bid me to live, and I will live
Thy Protestant to be:
Or bid me love, and I will give
A loving heart to thee.
To Anthea, Who May Command Him Anything

26 Bid me to weep, and I will weep,
While I have eyes to see.

27 Bid me despair, and I'll despair,
Under that cypress tree:
Or bid me die, and I will dare
E'en Death, to die for thee.

Thou art my life, my love, my heart,
The very eyes of me:
And hast command of every part,
To live and die for thee.

28 Fair daffodils, we weep to see
You haste away so soon:
As yet the early-rising sun
Has not attain'd his noon.
    Stay, stay,
Until the hasting day
    Has run
But to the even-song;
And, having pray'd together, we
Will go with you along.

We have short time to stay, as you,

We have as short a Spring;
As quick a growth to meet decay,
As you or any thing.
To Daffodils

1 Sweet, be not proud of those two eyes,
Which star-like sparkle in their skies.
To Dianeme

2 That ruby which you wear
Sunk from the tip of your soft ear
Will last to be a precious stone
When all your world of beauty's gone.

3 I dare not ask a kiss;
I dare not beg a smile;
Lest having that, or this,
I might grow proud the while.

No, no, the utmost share
Of my desire, shall be
Only to kiss that air,
That lately kissed thee.
To Electra

4 He loves his bonds, who when the first are broke,
Submits his neck unto a second yoke.
To Love

5 Gather ye rosebuds while ye may,
Old Time is still a-flying:
And this same flower that smiles to-day,
To-morrow will be dying.
To the Virgins, to Make Much of Time

6 Then be not coy, but use your time;
And while ye may, go marry:
For having lost but once your prime,
You may for ever tarry.

7 Her pretty feet
Like snails did creep
A little out, and then,
As if they started at bo-peep,
Did soon draw in agen.
Upon her Feet

8 Whenas in silks my Julia goes,
Then, then (methinks) how sweetly flows
That liquefaction of her clothes.

Next, when I cast mine eyes and see
That brave vibration each way free;
O how that glittering taketh me!
Upon Julia's Clothes

9 So smooth, so sweet, so silv'ry is thy voice,
As, could they hear, the damn'd would make no noise,
But listen to thee (walking in thy chamber)
Melting melodious words, to lutes of amber.
Upon Julia's Voice

10 Here a little child I stand,
Heaving up my either hand;
Cold as paddocks though they be,
Here I lift them up to Thee,
For a benison to fall
On our meat, and on us all. Amen.
Noble Numbers. Another Grace for a Child

11 In prayer the lips ne'er act the winning part,
Without the sweet concurrence of the heart.
The Heart

12 When the artless doctor sees
No one hope, but of his fees,

And his skill runs on the lees;
Sweet Spirit, comfort me!

When his potion and his pill,
Has, or none, or little skill,
Meet for nothing, but to kill;
Sweet Spirit, comfort me!
His Litany to the Holy Spirit

13 But, for Man's fault, then was the thorn,
Without the fragrant rose-bud, born;
But ne'er the rose without the thorn.
The Rose

14 Lord, Thou hast given me a cell
Wherein to dwell,
A little house, whose humble roof
Is weather-proof;
Under the spars of which I lie
Both soft, and dry.
A Thanksgiving to God for his House

15 If any thing delight me for to print
My book, 'tis this; that Thou, my God, art in't.
To God

16 To work a wonder, God would have her shown,
At once, a bud, and yet a rose full-blown.
The Virgin Mary

JAMES HERVEY 1714–1758

17 E'en crosses from his sov'reign hand
Are blessings in disguise.
Reflections on a Flower-Garden

LORD HERVEY 1696–1743

18 Whoever would lie usefully should lie seldom.
Memoirs of the Reign of George II, vol.I, ch.19

HESIOD c.700 B.C.

19 πλέον ἥμισυ παντός.
The half is greater than the whole.
Works and Days, 40

LORD HEWART 1870–1943

20 It is not merely of some importance but is of
fundamental importance that justice should not only be
done, but should manifestly and undoubtedly be seen
to be done.
Rex v. Sussex Justices, 9 Nov. 1923 (King's Bench Reports,
1924, vol.i, p.259)

JOHN HEYWOOD 1497?–1580?

21 All a green willow, willow;
All a green willow is my garland.
The Green Willow

THOMAS HEYWOOD 1574?–1641

22 Seven cities warr'd for Homer, being dead,
Who, living, had no roof to shroud his head.
The Hierarchy of the Blessed Angels (1635). See 7:14

SIR SEYMOUR HICKS 1871–1949

23 You will recognize, my boy, the first sign of old age:
it is when you go out into the streets of London and
realize for the first time how young the policemen

look.
Attr. C. Pulling, *They Were Singing*, 7

W.E. HICKSON 1803–1870

1 'Tis a lesson you should heed,
   Try, try again.
   If at first you don't succeed,
   Try, try again.
   Try and Try Again

AARON HILL 1685–1750

2 Tender-handed stroke a nettle,
      And it stings you for your pains;
   Grasp it like a man of mettle,
      And it soft as silk remains.
   Verses Written on Window

JOE HILL 1879–1914

3 You will eat (You will eat)
      Bye and bye (Bye and bye)
   In that glorious land above the sky (Way up high)
      Work and pray (Work and pray)
   Live on hay (Live on hay)
      You'll get pie in the sky when you die (That's a
      lie.)
   The Preacher and the Slave

REVD. ROWLAND HILL 1744–1833

4 He did not see any reason why the devil should have
   all the good tunes.
   E.W.Broome, *Rev. Rowland Hill*, vii

HILLEL 'THE ELDER' ?70 B.C.–A.D. 10?

5 A name made great is a name destroyed.
   Pirque Aboth. See *Sayings of the Jewish Fathers*, ed. C. Taylor
   (1877), i.14

6 If I am not for myself who is for me; and being for my
   own self what am I? If not now when?
   15

HIPPOCLEIDES 6th cent. B.C.

7 οὐ φροντὶς Ἱπποκλείδῃ.
   Hippocleides doesn't care.
   Herodotus, *Histories*, vi.129.4

HIPPOCRATES 5th cent. B.C.

8 ὁ βίος βραχύς, ἡ δὲ τέχνη μακρή.
   The life so short, the craft so long to learn.
   Aphorisms, I.i. Trans. by Chaucer. See 143:32.
   Often quoted in Latin as *Ars longa, vita brevis*. See Seneca, *De
   Brevitate Vitae*, 1

ADOLF HITLER 1889–1945

9 *Die breite Masse eines Volkes...einer grossen Lüge
   leichter zum Opfer fällt als einer kleinen.*
   The broad mass of a nation...will more easily fall
   victim to a big lie than to a small one.
   Mein Kampf, I.x

10 I go the way that Providence dictates with the

assurance of a sleepwalker.
Speech in Munich, 15 Mar. 1936, after the successful
re-occupation of the Rhineland, against the experts' advice. See
Alan Bullock, *Hitler, A Study in Tyranny* (1952), ch.7, pt.i

11 My patience is now at an end.
   Speech, 26 Sept. 1938

12 It is the last territorial claim which I have to make in
   Europe. [The Sudetenland.]

THOMAS HOBBES 1588–1679

13 True and False are attributes of speech, not of things.
   And where speech is not, there is neither Truth nor
   Falsehood.
   Leviathan (1651), pt.i, ch.4

14 Geometry (which is the only science that it hath
   pleased God hitherto to bestow on mankind).

15 Words are wise men's counters, they do but reckon by
   them: but they are the money of fools, that value them
   by the authority of an Aristotle, a Cicero, or a
   Thomas, or any other doctor whatsoever, if but a man.

16 They that approve a private opinion, call it opinion;
   but they that mislike it, heresy: and yet heresy
   signifies no more than private opinion.
   ch.11

17 During the time men live without a common power to
   keep them all in awe, they are in that condition which
   is called war; and such a war as is of every man
   against every man...the nature of war consisteth not in
   actual fighting, but in the known disposition thereto
   during all the time there is no assurance to the
   contrary.
   ch.13

18 No arts; no letters; no society; and which is worst of
   all, continual fear and danger of violent death; and the
   life of man, solitary, poor, nasty, brutish, and short.

19 Force, and fraud, are in war the two cardinal virtues.

20 They that are discontented under *monarchy,* call it
   tyranny; and they that are displeased with *aristocracy,*
   call it *oligarchy:* so also, they which find themselves
   grieved under a *democracy,* call it *anarchy,* which
   signifies the want of government; and yet I think no
   man believes, that want of government, is any new
   kind of government.
   pt.ii, ch.19

21 The Papacy is not other than the Ghost of the deceased
   Roman Empire, sitting crowned upon the grave
   thereof.
   pt.iv, ch.47

22 Laughter is nothing else but sudden glory arising from
   some sudden conception of some eminency in
   ourselves, by comparison with the infirmity of others,
   or with our own formerly.
   Human Nature (1640, published 1650), ix

23 He was wont to say that if he had read as much as
   other men, he should have known no more than other
   men.
   Aubrey, *Life of Hobbes*

24 I am about to take my last voyage, a great leap in the
   dark.
   Last words. Watkins, *Anecdotes of Men of Learning*

JOHN CAM HOBHOUSE, BARON BROUGHTON 1786–1869

1 When I invented the phrase 'His Majesty's Opposition' [Canning] paid me a compliment on the fortunate hit.
Recollections of a Long Life (1865), ii, ch.12

RALPH HODGSON 1871–1962

2 'Twould ring the bells of Heaven
The wildest peal for years,
If Parson lost his senses
And people came to theirs,
And he and they together
Knelt down with angry prayers
For tamed and shabby tigers
And dancing dogs and bears,
And wretched, blind, pit ponies,
And little hunted hares.
The Bells of Heaven

3 See an old unhappy bull,
Sick in soul and body both.
The Bull

4 Eve, with her basket, was
Deep in the bells and grass,
Wading in bells and grass
Up to her knees,
Plucking a dish of sweet
Berries and plums to eat,
Down in the bells and grass
Under the trees.
Eve

5 Reason has moons, but moons not hers,
　Lie mirror'd on her sea,
Confounding her astronomers,
　But, O! delighting me.
Reason Has Moons

6 I climbed a hill as light fell short,
And rooks came home in scramble sort,
And filled the trees and flapped and fought
And sang themselves to sleep.
The Song of Honour

7 When stately ships are twirled and spun
Like whipping tops and help there's none
And mighty ships ten thousand ton
Go down like lumps of lead.

8 I stood upon that silent hill
And stared into the sky until
My eyes were blind with stars and still
I stared into the sky.

9 Time, you old gypsy man,
　Will you not stay,
Put up your caravan
　Just for one day?
Time, You Old Gypsy Man

10 Last week in Babylon,
　Last night in Rome,
Morning, and in the crush
　Under Paul's dome.

HEINRICH HOFFMANN 1809-1894

11 Augustus was a chubby lad;
Fat ruddy cheeks Augustus had:
And everybody saw with joy
The plump and hearty, healthy boy.
He ate and drank as he was told,
And never let his soup get cold.
But one day, one cold winter's day,
He screamed out, 'Take the soup away!
O take the nasty soup away!
I won't have any soup today.'
Struwwelpeter (1845, translated 1848). **Augustus**

12 Here is cruel Frederick, see!
A horrid wicked boy was he.
Cruel Frederick

13 At this, good Tray grew very red,
And growled, and bit him till he bled.

14 Let me see if Philip can
Be a little gentleman;
Let me see, if he is able
To sit still for once at table.
Fidgety Philip

15 But fidgety Phil,
He won't sit still;
He wriggles
And giggles,
And then, I declare,
Swings backwards and forwards,
And tilts up his chair,
Just like any rocking-horse—
'Philip! I am getting cross!'

16 Look at little Johnny there,
Little Johnny Head-In-Air!
Johnny Head-In-Air

17 Silly little Johnny, look,
You have lost your writing-book!

18 The door flew open, in he ran,
The great, long, red-legged scissor-man.
The Little Suck-a-Thumb

19 'Ah!' said Mamma, 'I knew he'd come
To naughty little Suck-a-Thumb.'

20 He finds it hard, without a pair
Of spectacles, to shoot the hare.
The hare sits snug in leaves and grass,
And laughs to see the green man pass.
The Man Who Went Out Shooting

21 And now she's trying all she can,
To shoot the sleepy, green-coat man.

22 Anything to me is sweeter
Than to see Shock-headed Peter.
Shock-Headed Peter

JAMES HOGG 1770–1835

23 Where the pools are bright and deep
Where the gray trout lies asleep,
Up the river and o'er the lea
That's the way for Billy and me.
A Boy's Song

24 God bless our Lord the King!
God save our lord the king!
　God save the king!
Make him victorious,
Happy, and glorious,
Long to reign over us:

God save the king!
Jacobite Relics of Scotland (1819-20), ii.50. **God Save The King.** See 130:24

1 We'll o'er the water, we'll o'er the sea,
We'll o'er the water to Charlie;
Come weel, come wo, we'll gather and go,
And live or die wi' Charlie.
76. **O'er the Water to Charlie**

2 Cock up your beaver, and cock it fu' sprush;
We'll over the Border and gi'e them a brush;
There's somebody there we'll teach better behaviour.
Hey, Johnnie lad, cock up your beaver!
127. **Cock Up Your Beaver**

1ST LORD HOLLAND 1705-1774

3 If Mr Selwyn calls again, shew him up: if I am alive I shall be delighted to see him; and if I am dead he would like to see me.
During his last illness. J.H. Jesse, *George Selwyn and his Contemporaries*, 1844, vol.iii, p.50

3RD LORD HOLLAND 1733-1840

4 Nephew of Fox, and friend of Grey,—
Enough my meed of fame
If those who deign'd to observe me say
I injur'd neither name.
Lady Holland, *Memoir of Rev. Sydney Smith* (1855), i.334

REVD. JOHN H. HOLMES 1879-1964

5 The universe is not hostile, nor yet is it friendly. It is simply indifferent.
A Sensible Man's View of Religion (1933)

OLIVER WENDELL HOLMES 1809-1894

6 Sweet is the scene where genial friendship plays
The pleasing game of interchanging praise.
An After-Dinner Poem

7 Fate tried to conceal him by naming him Smith.
[Samuel Francis Smith.] **The Boys**

8 Have you heard of the wonderful one-hoss shay,
That was built in such a logical way
It ran a hundred years to a day?
The Deacon's Masterpiece

9 A general flavor of mild decay.

10 Lean, hungry, savage anti-everythings.
A Modest Request

11 Wisdom has taught us to be calm and meek,
To take one blow, and turn the other cheek;
It is not written what a man shall do
If the rude caitiff smite the other too!
Non-Resistance

12 And, when you stick on conversation's burrs,
Don't strew your pathway with those dreadful *urs*.
A Rhymed Lesson

13 Man wants but little drink below,
But wants that little strong.
A Song of other Days. See 231:7, 588:8

14 To be seventy years young is sometimes far more cheerful and hopeful than to be forty years old.
On the Seventieth Birthday of Julia Ward Howe

15 Man has his will,—but woman has her way.
The Autocrat of the Breakfast-Table (1858), ch.1

16 The axis of the earth sticks out visibly through the centre of each and every town or city.
ch.6

17 The world's great men have not commonly been great scholars, nor its great scholars great men.

18 His humid front the cive, anheling, wipes.
And dreams of erring on ventiferous ripes.
ch.11. **Aestivation**

19 Depart,—be off,—excede,—evade,—erump!
See 151:27

20 It is the province of knowledge to speak and it is the privilege of wisdom to listen.
The Poet at the Breakfast Table (1872), ch.10

21 A moment's insight is sometimes worth a life's experience.
The Professor at the Breakfast Table (1860), ch.10

JOHN HOME 1722-1808

22 My name is Norval; on the Grampian hills
My father feeds his flocks; a frugal swain,
Whose constant cares were to increase his store.
Douglas (1756), II.1

23   He seldom errs
Who thinks the worst he can of womankind.
III.iii

24 Like Douglas conquer, or like Douglas die.
v

25 Bold and erect the Caledonian stood,
Old was his mutton and his claret good;
Let him drink port, the English Statesman cried—
He drank the poison and his spirit died.
Lockhart, *Life of Scott*, IV, ch.v

HOMER 8th cent. B.C.

26 μῆνιν ἄειδε, θεά, Πηληϊάδεω Ἀχιλῆος
οὐλομένην, ἣ μυρί' Ἀχαιοῖς ἄλγε' ἔθηκε.
Achilles' cursed anger sing, O goddess, that son of Peleus, which started a myriad sufferings for the Achaeans.
Achilles' wrath, to Greece the direful spring
Of woes unnumbered, heavenly goddess, sing.
(Alexander Pope's translation.)
Iliad, i.1

27 ἔπεα πτερόεντα.
Winged words.
201

28 οὐ νέμεσις Τρῶας καὶ ἐϋκνήμιδας Ἀχαιοὺς
τοιῆδ' ἀμφὶ γυναικὶ πολὺν χρόνον ἄλγεα πάσχειν.
αἰνῶς ἀθανάτῃσι θεῇς εἰς ὦπα ἔοικεν.
It is no cause for anger that the Trojans and the well-greaved Achaeans have suffered for so long over *such* a woman: she is wondrously like the immortal goddesses to look upon.
iii.156. Of Helen

29 οἵη περ φύλλων γενεή, τοίη δὲ καὶ ἀνδρῶν.
Like that of leaves is a generation of men.
vi.146

30 αἰὲν ἀριστεύειν καὶ ὑπείροχον ἔμμεναι ἄλλων.

Always to be best, and to be distinguished above the rest.
208

1 δακρυόεν γελάσασα.
Smiling through her tears.
484

2 εἷς οἰωνὸς ἄριστος, ἀμύνεσθαι περὶ πάτρης.
This is the one best omen, to fight in defence of one's country.
xii.243

3 κεῖτο μέγας μεγαλωστί, λελασμένος ἱπποσυνάων.
He lay great and greatly fallen, forgetful of his chivalry.
xvi.776

4 ἄνδρα μοι ἔννεπε, Μοῦσα, πολύτροπον, ὃς μάλα πολλὰ
πλάγχθη, ἐπεὶ Τροίης ἱερὸν πτολίεθρον ἔπερσε,
πολλῶν δ' ἀνθρώπων ἴδεν ἄστεα καὶ νόον ἔγνω.
Tell me, Muse, of the man of many tricks, who wandered far and wide after he had sacked Troy's sacred city, and saw the towns of many men and knew their mind.
Odyssey, i.1. Of Odysseus

5 ῥοδοδάκτυλος Ἠώς.
Rosy-fingered dawn.
ii.1, and elsewhere

6 βουλοίμην κ' ἐπάρουρος ἐὼν θητευέμεν ἄλλω
ἀνδρὶ παρ' ἀκλήρω, ᾧ μὴ βίοτος πολὺς εἴη,
ἢ πᾶσιν νεκύεσσι καταφθιμένοισιν ἀνάσσειν.
I would rather be tied to the soil as another man's serf, even a poor man's, who hadn't much to live on himself, than be King of all these the dead and destroyed.
xi.489

WILLIAM HONE 1780–1842

7 John Jones may be described as 'one of the *has beens*.'
Every-Day Book (1826-7), vol.ii, 820

THOMAS HOOD 1799–1845

8 It was not in the winter
    Our loving lot was cast!
It was the time of roses,
    We plucked them as we passed!
Ballad: It Was Not in the Winter

9 Take her up tenderly,
Lift her with care;
Fashion'd so slenderly,
'Young, and so fair!
The Bridge of Sighs

10 Mad from life's history,
Glad to death's mystery,
Swift to be hurl'd—
Anywhere, anywhere,
Out of the world!

11 Much study had made him very lean,
    And pale, and leaden-ey'd.
The Dream of Eugene Aram

12 Two stern-faced men set out from Lynn,
    Through the cold and heavy mist;
And Eugene Aram walked between,
    With gyves upon his wrist.

13 Ben Battle was a soldier bold,
    And used to war's alarms:
But a cannon-ball took off his legs,
    So he laid down his arms!
Faithless Nelly Gray

14 For here I leave my second leg,
    And the Forty-second Foot!

15 The love that loves a scarlet coat
    Should be more uniform.

16 His death, which happen'd in his berth,
    At forty-odd befell:
They went and told the sexton, and
    The sexton toll'd the bell.
Faithless Sally Brown

17 I remember, I remember,
The house where I was born,
The little window where the sun
Came peeping in at morn;
He never came a wink too soon,
Nor brought too long a day,
But now, I often wish the night
Had borne my breath away!
I Remember

18 I remember, I remember,
The fir trees dark and high;
I used to think their slender tops
Were close against the sky:
It was a childish ignorance,
But now 'tis little joy
To know I'm farther off from heav'n
Than when I was a boy.

19 He never spoils the child and spares the rod,
But spoils the rod and never spares the child.
The Irish Schoolmaster, xii

20 But evil is wrought by want of thought,
    As well as want of heart!
The Lady's Dream

21 For that old enemy the gout
    Had taken him in toe!
Lieutenant Luff

22 Alas! my everlasting peace
    Is broken into pieces.
Mary's Ghost

23 And then, in the fulness of joy and hope,
Seem'd washing his hands with invisible soap,
    In imperceptible water.
Miss Kilmansegg (1841-3). **Her Christening**

24 There's Bardus, a six-foot column of fop,
A lighthouse without any light atop.
Her First Step

25 For one of the pleasures of having a rout,
Is the pleasure of having it over.
Her Dream

26 Home-made dishes that drive one from home.
Her Misery

27 No sun—no moon!
No morn—no noon
No dawn—no dusk—no proper time of day.
No!

28 No warmth, no cheerfulness, no healthful ease,
No comfortable feel in any member—
No shade, no shine, no butterflies, no bees,

No fruits, no flowers, no leaves, no birds,—
November!

1 I saw old Autumn in the misty morn
Stand shadowless like Silence, listening
To silence.
Ode: Autumn

2   The bird forlorn,
That singeth with her breast against a thorn.
The Plea of the Midsummer Fairies (1827), xxx

3 When Eve upon the first of Men
   The apple press'd with specious cant,
Oh! what a thousand pities then
   That Adam was not Adamant!
A Reflection

4 She stood breast high amid the corn,
Clasp'd by the golden light of morn,
Like the sweetheart of the sun,
Who many a glowing kiss had won.
Ruth

5 Sure, I said, heav'n did not mean,
Where I reap thou shouldst but glean,
Lay thy sheaf adown and come,
Share my harvest and my home.

6 With fingers weary and worn,
With eyelids heavy and red,
A woman sat, in unwomanly rags,
Plying her needle and thread—
Stitch! stitch! stitch!
In poverty, hunger, and dirt.
The Song of the Shirt (1843)

7 O! men with sisters dear,
   O! men with mothers and wives!
It is not linen you're wearing out,
   But human creatures' lives!

8 Oh! God! that bread should be so dear,
   And flesh and blood so cheap!

9 No blessed leisure for love or hope,
   But only time for grief!

10 My tears must stop, for every drop
   Hinders needle and thread!

11 There is a silence where hath been no sound,
There is a silence where no sound may be,
In the cold grave—under the deep deep sea,
Or in the wide desert where no life is found.
Sonnet. Silence

12 A wife who preaches in her gown,
And lectures in her night-dress!
The Surplice Question

13 Our hands have met, but not our hearts;
Our hands will never meet again.
To a False Friend

14 What is a modern poet's fate?
To write his thoughts upon a slate;
The critic spits on what is done,
Gives it a wipe—and all is gone.
See Hallam Tennyson, *Alfred Lord Tennyson, A Memoir* (1897),
vol.ii, ch.3. Not found in Hood's *Complete Works*.

15 There are three things which the public will always
clamour for, sooner or later: namely, Novelty,
novelty, novelty.
Announcement of *Comic Annual* for 1836

16 The sedate, sober, silent, serious, sad-coloured sect.
[Quakers.]
The Doves and the Crows

17 'Extremes meet', as the whiting said with its tail in its
mouth.

18 Holland...lies so low they're only saved by being
dammed.
Up the Rhine. To Rebecca Page (1839)

RICHARD HOOKER 1554?–1600

19 He that goeth about to persuade a multitude, that they
are not so well governed as they ought to be, shall
never want attentive and favourable hearers.
Of the Laws of Ecclesiastical Polity (1594,1597), bk.I.i

20 Of Law there can be no less acknowledged, than that
her seat is the bosom of God, her voice the harmony
of the world: all things in heaven and earth do her
homage, the very least as feeling her care, and the
greatest as not exempted from her power.
xvi

21 Change is not made without inconvenience, even from
worse to better.
Quoted by Johnson, as from Hooker, in the Preface to the *English
Dictionary*

ELLEN STURGIS HOOPER 1816–1841

22 I slept, and dreamed that life was Beauty;
I woke, and found that life was Duty.
Beauty and Duty (1840)

PRESIDENT HERBERT HOOVER 1874–1964

23 The American system of rugged individualism.
Campaign speech, New York, 22 Oct. 1928

24 Our country has deliberately undertaken a great social
and economic experiment, noble in motive and
far-reaching in purpose. [The Eighteenth Amendment,
enacting Prohibition.]
Letter to Senator W.H. Borah, 28 Feb. 1928

25 Older men declare war. But it is youth that must fight
and die.
Speech to Republican National Convention, Chicago, 27 June
1944

ANTHONY HOPE 1863–1933

26 Economy is going without something you do want in
case you should, some day, want something you
probably won't want.
The Dolly Dialogues (1894), No.12

27 'You oughtn't to yield to temptation.'
'Well, somebody must, or the thing becomes absurd.'
No. 14

28 'Boys will be boys—'
'And even that...wouldn't matter if we could only
prevent girls from being girls.'
No. 16

29 '*Bourgeois,*' I observed, 'is an epithet which the
riff-raff apply to what is respectable, and the
aristocracy to what is decent.'
No. 17

30 I wish you would read a little poetry sometimes. Your
ignorance cramps my conversation.
No. 22

1 Good families are generally worse than any others.
The Prisoner of Zenda (1894), ch.1

2 His foe was folly and his weapon wit.
Inscription on the tablet to W.S. Gilbert, Victoria Embankment,
London (1915)

LAURENCE HOPE (MRS. M.H. NICOLSON)
1865–1904

3 Pale hands I loved beside the Shalimar,
Where are you now? Who lies beneath your spell?
The Garden of Kama and other Love Lyrics from India
(1901). **Pale Hands I Loved**

4 Pale hands, pink-tipped, like lotus-buds that float
On those cool waters where we used to dwell,
I would have rather felt you round my throat
Crushing out life than waving me farewell.

5 Less than the dust beneath thy chariot wheel,
Less than the weed that grows beside thy door,
Less than the rust that never stained thy sword,
Less than the need thou hast in life of me,
    Even less am I.
Less than the Dust

GERARD MANLEY HOPKINS 1844–1889

6 Wild air, world-mothering air,
Nestling me everywhere.
The Blessed Virgin Compared to the Air We Breathe

7 Not, I'll not, carrion comfort, Despair, not feast on
    thee;
Not untwist—slack they may be—these last strands of
    man
In me or, most weary, cry *I can no more.* I can;
Can something, hope, wish day come, not choose not
    to be.
Carrion Comfort

8   That night, that year
Of now done darkness I wretch lay wrestling with (my
    God!) my God.

9 Towery city and branchy between towers.
Duns Scotus' Oxford

10 Cuckoo-echoing, bell-swarmèd, lark-charmèd,
rook-racked, river-rounded.

11 Didst fettle for the great grey drayhorse his bright and
    battering sandal!
Felix Randal

12 The world is charged with the grandeur of God.
    It will flame out like shining from shook foil;...
Generations have trod, have trod, have trod;
    And all is seared with trade; bleared, smeared with
        toil;
    And wears man's smudge and shares man's smell:
        the soil
Is bare now, nor can foot feel, being shod.
God's Grandeur

13   Because the Holy Ghost over the bent
World broods with warm breast and with ah! bright
    wings.

14 Elected Silence, sing to me
And beat upon my whorlèd ear,
Pipe me to pastures still and be
The music that I care to hear.
The Habit of Perfection

15 Palate, the hutch of tasty lust,
Desire not to be rinsed with wine:
The can must be so sweet, the crust
So fresh that come in fasts divine!

16 And you unhouse and house the Lord.

17   I have desired to go
        Where springs not fail,
To fields where flies no sharp and sided hail
    And a few lilies blow.

    And I have asked to be
        Where no storms come,
Where the green swell is in the havens dumb,
    And out of the swing of the sea.
Heaven-Haven

18 What would the world be, once bereft
Of wet and wildness? Let them be left,
O let them be left, wildness and wet;
Long live the weeds and the wilderness yet.
Inversnaid

19 No worst, there is none. Pitched past pitch of grief,
More pangs will, schooled at forepangs, wilder wring.
Comforter, where, where is your comforting?
No Worst, there is None

20 O the mind, mind has mountains; cliffs of fall
Frightful, sheer, no-man-fathomed. Hold them cheap
May who ne'er hung there.

21   Here! creep,
Wretch, under a comfort serves in a whirlwind: all
Life death does end and each day dies with sleep.

22 Glory be to God for dappled things.
Pied Beauty

23 All things counter, original, spare, strange;
    Whatever is fickle, freckled (who knows how?)
        With swift, slow; sweet, sour; adazzle, dim;
He fathers-forth whose beauty is past change:
        Praise him.

24   The glassy peartree leaves and blooms, they brush
        The descending blue; that blue is all in a rush
With richness.
Spring

25 Margaret, are you grieving
Over Goldengrove unleaving?
Spring and Fall. To a young child

26 Ah! as the heart grows older
It will come to such sights colder
By and by, not spare a sigh
Though worlds of wanwood leafmeal lie,
And yet you *will* weep and know why.

27 It is the blight man was born for,
It is Margaret you mourn for.

28 Look at the stars! look, look up at the skies!
O look at all the fire-folk sitting in the air!
The bright boroughs, the circle-citadels there!
The Starlight Night

29 Ah well! it is all a purchase, all is a prize.
Buy then! bid then!—What?— Prayer, patience, alms,
    vows.
Look, look: a May-mess, like on orchard boughs!
Look! March-bloom, like on mealed-with-yellow
    sallows!
These are indeed the barn; withindoors house

The shocks. This piece-bright paling shuts the spouse
Christ home, Christ and his mother and all his
    hallows.

1 I am all at once what Christ is, since he was what I
    am, and
This Jack, joke, poor potsherd, patch, matchwood,
    immortal diamond,
        Is immortal diamond.
That Nature is a Heraclitean Fire

2 Thou art indeed just, Lord, if I contend
With thee; but, sir, so what I plead is just.
Why do sinners' ways prosper? and why must
Disappointment all I endeavour end?
Thou Art Indeed Just, Lord

3   Birds build—but not I build; no, but strain,
Time's eunuch, and not breed one work that wakes.
Mine, O thou lord of life, send my roots rain.

4 I caught this morning morning's minion, kingdom of
    daylight's dauphin, dapple-dawn-drawn Falcon.
The Windhover

5   My heart in hiding
Stirred for a bird,—the achieve of, the mastery of the
    thing!

6   I did say yes
O at lightning and lashed rod;
Thou heardst me truer than tongue confess
    Thy terror, O Christ, O God.
The Wreck of the Deutschland, I.2

7   How a lush-kept plush-capped sloe
    Will, mouthed to flesh-burst,
Gush!—flush the man, the being with it, sour or
    sweet,
Brim, in a flash, full!
8

JOSEPH HOPKINSON 1770–1842

8 Hail, Columbia! happy land!
Hail, ye heroes! heaven-born band!
Hail, Columbia! Porcupine's Gazette, 20 Apr. 1798

HORACE 65–8 B.C.

9   *Ut turpiter atrum*
Desinat in piscem mulier formosa superne.
So that what is a beautiful woman on top ends in a
    black and ugly fish.
Ars Poetica, 3

10   *'Pictoribus atque poetis*
Quidlibet audendi semper fuit aequa potestas.'
Scimus, et hanc veniam petimusque damusque
    vicissim.
'Painters and poets alike have always had licence to
    dare anything.' We know that, and we both claim
    and allow to others in their turn this indulgence.
9

11 *Inceptis gravibus plerumque et magna professis*
Purpureus, late qui splendeat, unus et alter
Adsuitur pannus.
Frequently with serious works and ones of great
    import, some purple patch or other is stitched on, to
    show up far and wide.
14

12   *Brevis esse laboro,*

Obscurus fio.
I strive to be brief, and I become obscure.
25

13 *Dixeris egregie notum si callida verbum*
Reddiderit iunctura novum.
You will have written exceptionally well if, by skilful
    arrangement of your words, you have made an
    ordinary one seem original.
47

14 *Multa renascentur quae iam cecidere, cadentque*
Quae nunc sunt in honore vocabula, si volet usus,
Quem penes arbitrium est et ius et norma loquendi.
Many terms which have now dropped out of favour,
    will be revived, and those that are at present
    respectable will drop out, if usage so choose, with
    whom resides the decision and the judgement and
    the code of speech.
70

15 *Grammatici certant et adhuc sub iudice lis est.*
Scholars dispute, and the case is still before the courts.
78

16 *Proicit ampullas et sesquipedalia verba.*
Throws aside his paint-pots and his words a foot and a
    half long.
97

17 *Difficile est proprie communia dicere.*
It is hard to utter common notions in an individual
    way.
128

18 *Parturient montes, nascetur ridiculus mus.*
Mountains will heave in childbirth, and a silly little
    mouse will be born.
139

19 *Non fumum ex fulgore, sed ex fumo dare lucem*
Cogitat.
His thinking does not result in smoke after the flashing
    fire, but in light emerging from the smoke.
143

20 *Semper ad eventum festinat et in medias res*
Non secus ac notas auditorem rapit.
He always hurries to the main event and whisks his
    audience into the middle of things as though they
    knew already.
148

21 *Difficilis, querulus, laudator temporis acti*
Se puero, castigator censorque minorum.
Multa ferunt anni venientes commoda secum,
Multa recedentes adimunt.
Tiresome, complaining, a praiser of the times that
    were when he was a boy, a castigator and censor of
    the young generation. The years as they come bring
    a lot of advantages with them, but as they go by they
    take a lot away too.
173

22   *Vos exemplaria Graeca*
Nocturna versate manu, versate diurna.
For your own good, turn the pages of your Greek
    exemplars by night and by day.
268

23 *Grais ingenium, Grais dedit ore rotundo*
Musa loqui.
To the Greeks the Muse gave native wit, to the Greeks

the gift of graceful eloquence.
323

1 *Omne tulit punctum qui miscuit utile dulci,*
Lectorem delectando pariterque monendo.
He has gained every point who has mixed practicality
with pleasure, by delighting the reader at the same
time as instructing him.
343

2 *Indignor quandoque bonus dormitat Homerus.*
I'm aggrieved when sometimes even excellent Homer
nods.
359

3 *Ut pictura poesis.*
The making of a poem is like that of a painting.
361

4 *Mediocribus esse poetis*
Non homines, non di, non concessere columnae.
Not gods, nor men, nor even booksellers have put up
with poets' being second-rate.
372

5 *Tu nihil invita dices faciesve Minerva.*
You will get nothing written or created unless Minerva
helps.
385

6 *Nonumque prematur in annum,*
Membranis intus positis: delere licebit
Quod non edideris; nescit vox missa reverti.
Let it be kept till the ninth year, the manuscript put
away at home: you may destroy whatever you
haven't published; once out, what you've said can't
be stopped.
388. See 258:22

7 *Nullius addictus iurare in verba magistri,*
Quo me cumque rapit tempestas, deferor hospes.
Not bound to swear allegiance to any master, wherever
the wind takes me I travel as a visitor.
Epistles, I.i.14. *Nullius in verba* is the motto of the Royal
Society.

8 *Condicio dulcis sine pulvere palmae.*
The happy state of getting the victor's palm without
the dust of racing.
51

9 *Hic murus aeneus esto,*
Nil conscire sibi, nulla pallescere culpa.
Let this be your wall of brass, to have nothing on your
conscience, no guilt to make you turn pale.
60

10 *Si possis recte, si non, quocumque modo rem.*
If possible honestly, if not, somehow, make money.
66

11 *Olim quod vulpes aegroto cauta leoni*
Respondit referam: 'quia me vestigia terrent,
Omnia te adversum spectantia, nulla retrorsum.'
Let me remind you what the wary fox said once upon a
time to the sick lion: 'Because those footprints scare
me, all directed your way, none coming back.'
73

12 *Quidquid delirant reges plectuntur Achivi.*
For any madness of their kings, it is the Greeks who
take the beating.
ii.14

13 *Nos numerus sumus et fruges consumere nati.*

We are just statistics, born to consume resources.
27

14 *Dimidium facti qui coepit habet: sapere aude.*
To have begun is half the job: be bold and be sensible.
40

15 *Ira furor brevis est.*
Anger is a short madness.
62

16 *Omnem crede diem tibi diluxisse supremum.*
Grata superveniet quae non sperabitur hora.
Me pinguem et nitidum bene curata cute vises
Cum ridere voles Epicuri de grege porcum.
Believe each day that has dawned is your last. Some
hour to which you have not been looking forward
will prove lovely. As for me, if you want a good
laugh, you will come and find me fat and sleek, in
excellent condition, one of Epicurus' herd of pigs.
iv.13

17 *Nil admirari prope res est una, Numici,*
Solaque quae possit facere et servare beatum.
To marvel at nothing is just about the one and only
thing, Numicius, that can make a man happy and
keep him that way.
vi.1

18 *Naturam expellas furca, tamen usque recurret.*
You may drive out nature with a pitchfork, yet she'll
be constantly running back.
x.24

19 *Caelum non animum mutant qui trans mare currunt.*
Strenua nos exercet inertia: navibus atque
Quadrigis petimus bene vivere. Quod petis hic est,
Est Ulubris, animus si te non deficit aequus.
They change their clime, not their frame of mind, who
rush across the sea. We work hard at doing nothing:
we look for happiness in boats and carriage rides.
What you are looking for is here, is at Ulubrae, if
only peace of mind doesn't desert you.
xi.27

20 *Concordia discors.*
Harmony in discord.
xii.19

21 *Principibus placuisse viris non ultima laus est.*
Non cuivis homini contingit adire Corinthum.
It is not the least praise to have pleased leading men.
Not everyone is lucky enough to get to Corinth.
xvii.35

22 *Et semel emissum volat irrevocabile verbum.*
And once sent out a word takes wing irrevocably.
xviii.71. See 258:6

23 *Nam tua res agitur, paries cum proximus ardet.*
For it is your business, when the wall next door
catches fire.
84

24 *Fallentis semita vitae.*
The pathway of a life unnoticed.
103

25 *Prisco si credis, Maecenas docte, Cratino,*
Nulla placere diu nec vivere carmina possunt
Quae scribuntur aquae potoribus.
If you believe Cratinus from days of old, Maecenas,
(as you must know) no verse can give pleasure for
long, nor last, that is written by drinkers of water.
xix.1

1 *O imitatores, servum pecus.*
O imitators, you slavish herd.
19

2 *Graecia capta ferum victorem cepit et artes*
Intulit agresti Latio.
Greece, once overcome, overcame her wild conqueror,
and brought the arts into rustic Latium.
II.i.156

3 *Si foret in terris, rideret Democritus.*
If he were on earth, Democritus would laugh at the
sight.
194

4 *Atque inter silvas Academi quaerere verum.*
And seek for truth in the groves of Academe.
ii.45

5 *Multa fero, ut placem genus irritabile vatum.*
I have to put up with a lot, to please the sensitive race
of poets.
102

6 *Quid te exempta iuvat spinis de pluribus una?*
Vivere si recte nescis, decede peritis.
Lusisti satis, edisti satis atque bibisti:
Tempus abire tibi est.
What pleasure does it give to be rid of one thorn out of
many? If you don't know how to live right, give
way to those who are expert at it. You have had
enough fun, eaten and drunk enough: time you were
off.
212

7 *Beatus ille, qui procul negotiis,*
Ut prisca gens mortalium,
Paterna rura bubus exercet suis,
Solutus omni faenore.
He's happy who, far away from business, like the race
of men of old, tills his ancestral fields with his own
oxen, unbound by any interest to pay.
Epodes, ii.1

8 *Maecenas atavis edite regibus,*
O et praesidium et dulce decus meum.
Maecenas, descended from royal forebears, oh and my
stronghold and my pride and joy!
Odes, I.i.1

9 *Indocilis pauperiem pati.*
Hard to train to accept being poor.
18

10 *Quodsi me lyricis vatibus inseres,*
Sublimi feriam sidera vertice.
And if you include me among the lyric poets, I'll hold
my head so high it'll strike the stars.
35

11 *Animae dimidium meae.*
The half of my own life.
iii.8. Of Virgil.

12 *Illi robur et aes triplex*
Circa pectus erat, qui fragilem truci
Commisit pelago ratem
Primus.
His breast must have been protected all round with oak
and three-ply bronze, who first launched his frail
boat on the rough sea.
9

13 *Pallida Mors aequo pulsat pede pauperum tabernas*
Regumque turris.

Pale Death kicks his way equally into the cottages of
the poor and the castles of kings.
iv.13

14 *Vitae summa brevis spem nos vetat incohare longam.*
Life's short span forbids us to enter on far-reaching
hopes.
15

15 *Quis multa gracilis te puer in rosa*
Perfusus liquidis urget odoribus
Grato, Pyrrha, sub antro?
Cui flavam religas comam,
Simplex munditiis?
Who's the slim boy now, dripping with scent, who's
pressing you down, Pyrrha, on a pile of rose-petals,
in the pleasant shade of some rock? For whom are
you dressing your golden hair, simply but with such
style?
v.1

16 *Nil desperandum Teucro duce et auspice.*
Teucer shall lead and his star shall preside.
No cause for despair, then.
vii.27. Tr. James Michie

17 *Cras ingens iterabimus aequor.*
Tomorrow we'll be back on the vast ocean.
32

18 *Quid sit futurum cras fuge quaerere et*
Quem Fors dierum cumque dabit lucro
Appone.
Drop the question what tomorrow may bring, and
count as profit every day that Fate allows you.
ix.13

19 *Tu ne quaesieris, scire nefas, quem mihi, quem tibi*
Finem di dederint.
Do not try to find out—we're forbidden to
know—what end the gods have in store for me, or
for you.
xi.1

20   *Dum loquimur, fugerit invida*
Aetas: carpe diem, quam minimum credula postero.
While we're talking, time will have meanly run on:
pick today's fruits, not relying on the future in the
slightest.
7

21   *Felices ter et amplius*
Quos irrupta tenet copula nec malis
Divulsus querimoniis
Suprema citius solvet amor die.
Thrice blest (and more) are the couple whose ties are
unbroken and whose love, never strained by nasty
quarrels, will not slip until their dying day.
xiii.17

22 *O matre pulchra filia pulchrior.*
What a beautiful mother, and yet more beautiful
daughter!
xvi.1

23 *Integer vitae scelerisque purus.*
Of unblemished life and spotless record.
xxii.1

24 *Dulce ridentem Lalagen amabo,*
Dulce loquentem.
I will go on loving Lalage, who laughs so sweetly and
talks so sweetly.
23

1 *Multis ille bonis flebilis occidit,*
Nulli flebilior quam tibi.
Many good men should weep for his death, but you
most of all.
xxiv.9

2 *Parcus deorum cultor et infrequens.*
Not a devoted or regular worshipper of the gods.
xxxiv.1

3 *Nunc est bibendum, nunc pede libero*
Pulsanda tellus.
Now for drinks, now for some dancing with a good
beat.
xxxvii.1

4 *Persicos odi, puer, apparatus.*
I hate all that Persian gear, boy.
xxxviii.1

5 *Mitte sectari, rosa quo locorum*
Sera moretur.
Stop looking for the place where a late rose may yet
linger.
3

6 *Aequam memento rebus in arduis*
Servare mentem.
When things are steep, remember to stay level-headed.
II.iii.1

7 *Omnes eodem cogimur, omnium*
Versatur urna serius ocius
Sors exitura et nos in aeternum
Exsilium impositura cumbae.
Sheep driven deathward. Sooner or later Fate's
Urn shakes, the lot comes leaping for each of us
And books a one-way berth in Charon's
Boat on the journey to endless exile.
25. Tr. James Michie

8 *Ille terrarum mihi praeter omnis*
Angulus ridet.
That corner of the world smiles for me more than
anywhere else.
vi.13

9 *Auream quisquis mediocritatem*
Diligit.
Someone who loves the golden mean.
x.5

10 *Eheu fugaces, Postume, Postume,*
Labuntur anni.
Ah me, Postumus, Postumus, the fleeting years are
slipping by.
xiv.1

11 *Nihil est ab omni*
Parte beatum.
Nothing is an unmixed blessing.
xvi.27

12 *Credite posteri.*
Believe me, you who come after me!
xix.2

13 *Odi profanum vulgus et arceo;*
Favete linguis; carmina non prius
Audita Musarum sacerdos
Virginibus puerisque canto.
I hate the unholy masses and I keep away from them.
Hush your tongues; as a priest of the Muses, I sing
songs never heard before to virgin girls and boys.
III.i.1

14 *Omne capax movet urna nomen.*
The enormous tombola shakes up everyone's name.
16

15 *Post equitem sedet atra Cura.*
At the rider's back sits dark Anxiety.
40

16 *Cur valle permutem Sabina*
Divitias operosiores?
Why should I exchange my Sabine valley for riches
which just make more trouble?
47

17 *Dulce et decorum est pro patria mori.*
Lovely and honourable it is to die for one's country.
ii.13

18 *Iustum et tenacem propositi virum*
Non civium ardor prava iubentium,
Non vultus instantis tyranni
Mente quatit solida.
For a just man and one with a firm grasp of his
intentions, neither the heated passions of his
fellow-citizens ordaining something awful, nor the
face of a tyrant before his very eyes, will shake him
in his firm-based mind.
iii.1

19 *Si fractus illabatur orbis,*
Impavidum ferient ruinae.
If the world should break and fall on him, its ruins
would strike him unafraid.
7

20 *Aurum irrepertum et sic melius situm.*
Gold undiscovered (and all the better for being so).
49

21 *Non sine dis animosus infans.*
An adventurous child, thanks to the gods.
iv.20

22 *Fratresque tendentes opaco*
Pelion imposuisse Olympo.
And the brothers attempting to get Pelion perched on
top of shady Olympus.
51. Of two gigantic heroes trying to reach heaven.

23 *Vis consili expers mole ruit sua.*
Force, if unassisted by judgement, collapses through
its own mass.
65

24 *O magna Carthago, probrosis*
Altior Italiae ruinis!
O mighty Carthage, all the loftier for the shocking
collapse of Italy!
v.39

25 *Delicta maiorum immeritus lues.*
Undeservedly you will atone for the sins of your
fathers.
vi.1

26 *Damnosa quid non imminuit dies?*
Aetas parentum peior avis tulit
Nos nequiores, mox daturos
Progeniem vitiosiorem.
What do the ravages of time not injure? Our parents'
age (worse than our grandparents') has produced us,
more worthless still, who will soon give rise to a yet
more vicious generation.
45

27 *Donec gratus eram tibi.*

In the days when I was dear to you.
ix.1

1 *Tecum vivere amem, tecum obeam libens.*
With you I should love to live, with you be ready to
  die.
24

2 *Splendide mendax et in omne virgo*
  Nobilis aevum.
Gloriously deceitful and a virgin renowned for ever.
xi.35. Of the Danaid Hypermestra.

3 *O fons Bandusiae splendidior vitro.*
O spring of Bandusia, glinting more than glass.
xiii.1

4 *Non ego hoc ferrem calidus iuventa*
  Consule Planco.
I shouldn't have put up with this when I was a
  hot-blooded youth (and Plancus was consul).
xiv.27

5 *O nata mecum consule Manlio*
  …pia testa.
O trusty wine-jar, born the same year as I (when
  Manlius was consul).
xxi.1

6 *Vixi puellis nuper idoneus*
Et militavi non sine gloria;
  Nunc arma defunctumque bello
  Barbiton hic paries habebit.
My life with girls has ended, though till lately I was up
  to it and soldiered on not ingloriously; now on this
  wall will hang my weapons and my lyre, discharged
  from the war.
xxvi.1

7 *Fumum et opes strepitumque Romae.*
The smoke and wealth and din of Rome.
xxix.12

8 *Exegi monumentum aere perennius.*
I have executed a memorial longer lasting than bronze.
xxx.1

9 *Non omnis moriar.*
I shall not altogether die.
6

10 *Non sum qualis eram bonae*
Sub regno Cinarae. Desine, dulcium
  Mater saeva Cupidinum.
I am not as I was when dear Cinara was my queen.
  Don't force me, cruel mother of the lovely Cupids.
IV.i.3

11 *Quod spiro et placeo, si placeo, tuum est.*
That I make poetry and give pleasure (if I give
  pleasure) are because of you.
iii.24

12 *Merses profundo: pulchrior evenit.*
Plunge it in deep water: it comes up more beautiful.
iv.65

13   *Occidit, occidit*
Spes omnis et fortuna nostri
  Nominis Hasdrubale interempto.
All our hope is fallen, fallen, and the luck of our name
  lost with Hasdrubal.
70

14 *Diffugere nives, redeunt iam gramina campis*
  Arboribusque comae.
The snows have dispersed, now grass returns to the

fields and leaves to the trees.
vii.1

15 *Immortalia ne speres, monet annus et almum*
  Quae rapit hora diem.
Not to hope for things to last for ever, is what the year
  teaches and even the hour which snatches a nice day
  away.
7

16 *Damna tamen celeres reparant caelestia lunae:*
  Nos ubi decidimus
Quo pater Aeneas, quo Tullus dives et Ancus,
  Pulvis et umbra sumus.
Yet moons swiftly wax again after they have waned.
  We, when we have gone down to join our father
  Aeneas, and Tullus who was so rich, and Ancus, we
  are but dust and a shadow.
13

17 *Dignum laude virum Musa vetat mori.*
The man worthy of praise the Muse forbids to die.
viii.28

18 *Vixere fortes ante Agamemnona*
Multi; sed omnes illacrimabiles
  Urgentur ignotique longa
  Nocte, carent quia vate sacro.
Many brave men lived before Agamemnon's time; but
  they are all, unmourned and unknown, covered by
  the long night, because they lack their sacred poet.
ix.25

19 *Non possidentem multa vocaveris*
Recte beatum: rectius occupat
  Nomen beati, qui deorum
  Muneribus sapienter uti
Duramque callet pauperiem pati
Peiusque leto flagitium timet.
Not the owner of many possessions will you be right to
  call happy: he more rightly deserves the name of
  happy who knows how to use the gods' gifts wisely
  and to put up with rough poverty, and who fears
  dishonour more than death.
45

20 *Misce stultitiam consiliis brevem:*
  Dulce est desipere in loco.
Mix a little foolishness with your serious plans: it's
  lovely to be silly at the right moment.
xii.27

21 *Qui fit, Maecenas, ut nemo, quam sibi sortem*
Seu ratio dederit seu fors obiecerit, illa
Contentus vivat, laudet diversa sequentis?
How is it, Maecenas, that no one lives contented with
  his lot, whether he has planned it for himself or fate
  has flung him into it, but yet he praises those who
  follow different paths?
Satires, I.i.1

22   *Mutato nomine de te*
Fabula narratur.
Change the name and it's about you, that story.
69

23 *Est modus in rebus, sunt certi denique fines,*
Quos ultra citraque nequit consistere rectum.
Things have their due measure; there are ultimately
  fixed limits, beyond which, or short of which,
  something must be wrong.
106

24 *Hoc genus omne.*

All that tribe.
ii.2

1   *Ab ovo*
Usque ad mala.
From the egg right through to the apples.
iii.6. Meaning, from the start to the finish (of a meal).

2 *Etiam disiecti membra poetae.*
Even though broken up, the limbs of a poet.
iv.62. Of Ennius.

3 *Hic niger est, hunc tu, Romane, caveto.*
That man's a blackguard; Roman, watch out for that
man.
85

4   *Ad unguem*
Factus homo.
An accomplished man to his finger-tips.
v.32

5   *Credat Iudaeus Apella,*
Non ego.
Let Apella the Jew believe it; I shan't.
100

6 *Sic me servavit Apollo.*
Thus did Apollo rescue me.
ix.78

7 *Solventur risu tabulae, tu missus abibis.*
The case will be dismissed with a laugh. You will get
off scot-free.
II.i.86. Tr. H.R. Fairclough

8 *Par nobile fratrum.*
A noble pair of brothers.
iii.243

9 *Hoc erat in votis: modus agri non ita magnus,*
Hortus ubi et tecto vicinus iugis aquae fons
Et paulum silvae super his foret.
This was one of my prayers: for a parcel of land not so
very large, which should have a garden and a spring
of ever-flowing water near the house, and a bit of
woodland as well as these.
vi.1

10 *Responsare cupidinibus, contemnere honores*
Fortis, et in se ipso totus, teres, atque rotundus.
Strong enough to answer back to desires, to despise
distinctions, and a whole man in himself, polished
and well-rounded.
vii.85

BISHOP SAMUEL HORSLEY 1733–1806

11 In *this* country, my Lords,...the individual
subject...'has nothing to do with the laws but to obey
them.'
House of Lords, 13 Nov. 1795. Bishop Horsley was defending a
maxim which he had earlier used in committee.

A.E. HOUSMAN 1859–1936

12 From Clee to heaven the beacon burns,
    The shires have seen it plain,
From north and south the sign returns
And beacons burn again.
A Shropshire Lad (1896), 1. **1887**

13 The saviours come not home tonight:
    Themselves they could not save.

It dawns in Asia, tombstones show

And Shropshire names are read;
And the Nile spills his overflow
    Beside the Severn's dead.

14 Loveliest of trees, the cherry now
Is hung with bloom along the bough,
And stands about the woodland ride
Wearing white for Eastertide.

Now of my threescore years and ten,
Twenty will not come again,
And take from seventy springs a score,
It only leaves me fifty more.

And since to look at things in bloom
Fifty springs are little room,
About the woodlands I will go
To see the cherry hung with snow.
2

15 Up, lad: thews that lie and cumber
    Sunlit pallets never thrive;
Morns abed and daylight slumber
    Were not meant for man alive.

Clay lies still, but blood's a rover;
    Breath's a ware that will not keep.
Up, lad: when the journey's over
    There'll be time enough to sleep.
4. **Reveillé**

16 They hang us now in Shrewsbury jail:
    The whistles blow forlorn,
And trains all night groan on the rail
    To men that die at morn.
9

17 And naked to the hangman's noose
    The morning clocks will ring
A neck God made for other use
    Than strangling in a string.

18 So here I'll watch the night and wait
    To see the morning shine,
When he will hear the stroke of eight
    And not the stroke of nine.

19 Afield for palms the girls repair,
    And sure enough the palms are there,
And each will find by hedge or pond
    Her waving silver-tufted wand.
10. **March**

20 When I was one-and-twenty
    I heard a wise man say,
'Give crowns and pounds and guineas
    But not your heart away;
Give pearls away and rubies,
    But keep your fancy free.'
But I was one-and-twenty,
    No use to talk to me.
13

21 Look not in my eyes, for fear
    They mirror true the sight I see,
And there you find your face too clear
    And love it and be lost like me.
One the long night through must lie
    Spent in star-defeated sighs,
But why should you as well as I
    Perish? gaze not in my eyes.
15

22 Twice a week the winter thorough

Here stood I to keep the goal:
Football then was fighting sorrow
  For the young man's soul.

Now in Maytime to the wicket
Out I march with bat and pad:
See the son of grief at cricket
  Trying to be glad.
17

1 Oh, when I was in love with you,
   Then I was clean and brave,
  And miles around the wonder grew
   How well did I behave.

  And now the fancy passes by,
   And nothing will remain,
  And miles around they'll say that I
   Am quite myself again.
18

2 Eyes the shady night has shut
  Cannot see the record cut,
  And silence sounds no worse than cheers
  After earth has stopped the ears.
   19. To an Athlete Dying Young

3 And round that early-laurelled head
  Will flock to gaze the strengthless dead,
  And find unwithered on its curls
  The garland briefer than a girl's.

4 In summertime on Bredon
   The bells they sound so clear;
  Round both the shires they ring them
   In steeples far and near,
   A happy noise to hear.

  Here of a Sunday morning
   My love and I would lie,
  And see the coloured counties,
   And hear the larks so high
   About us in the sky.
   21. Bredon Hill

5 'Come all to church, good people,'—
   Oh, noisy bells, be dumb;
  I hear you, I will come.

6 The lads in their hundreds to Ludlow come in for the
   fair,
  There's men from the barn and the forge and the
   mill and the fold,
  The lads for the girls and the lads for the liquor are
   there,
  And there with the rest are the lads that will never
   be old.
23

7 I wish one could know them, I wish there were tokens
   to tell
  The fortunate fellows that now you can never
   discern.

8 They carry back bright to the coiner the mintage of
   man,
  The lads that will die in their glory and never be
   old.

9 'Is my team ploughing,
   That I was used to drive
  And hear the harness jingle
   When I was man alive?'
27

10 The goal stands up, the keeper
   Stands up to keep the goal.

11 Yes, lad, I lie easy,
   I lie as lads would choose;
  I cheer a dead man's sweetheart,
   Never ask me whose.

12 High the vanes of Shrewsbury gleam
  Islanded in Severn stream.
  28. The Welsh Marches

13 Others, I am not the first,
  Have willed more mischief than they durst.
30

14 On Wenlock Edge the wood's in trouble;
   His forest fleece the Wrekin heaves;
  The gale, it plies the saplings double,
   And thick on Severn snow the leaves.
31

15 There, like the wind through woods in riot,
   Through him the gale of life blew high;
  The tree of man was never quiet:
   Then 'twas the Roman, now 'tis I.

  The gale, it plies the saplings double,
   It blows so hard, 'twill soon be gone:
  Today the Roman and his trouble
   Are ashes under Uricon.

16 From far, from eve and morning
   And yon twelve-winded sky,
  The stuff of life to knit me
   Blew hither: here am I.
32

17 Speak now, and I will answer;
   How shall I help you, say;
  Ere to the wind's twelve quarters
   I take my endless way.

18 On the idle hill of summer,
   Sleepy with the flow of streams,
  Far I hear the steady drummer
   Drumming like a noise in dreams.
35

19 East and west on fields forgotten
   Bleach the bones of comrades slain,
  Lovely lads and dead and rotten;
   None that go return again.

20 White in the moon the long road lies,
   The moon stands blank above;
  White in the moon the long road lies
   That leads me from my love.
36

21 You and I must keep from shame
  In London streets the Shropshire name;
  On banks of Thames they must not say
  Severn breeds worse men than they.
37

22 Into my heart an air that kills
   From yon far country blows:
  What are those blue remembered hills,
   What spires, what farms are those?

  That is the land of lost content,
   I see it shining plain,
  The happy highways where I went
   And cannot come again.
40

1 And bound for the same bourn as I,
   On every road I wandered by,
   Trod beside me, close and dear,
   The beautiful and death-struck year.
   41

2 Shot? so quick, so clean an ending?
   Oh that was right, lad, that was brave.
   44

3 Be still, my soul, be still; the arms you bear are
        brittle,
   Earth and high heaven are fixt of old and founded
        strong.
   48

4 Men loved unkindness then, but lightless in the quarry
   I slept and saw not; tears fell down, I did not
        mourn;
   Sweat ran and blood sprang out and I was never sorry:
   Then it was well with me, in days ere I was born.

5 Be still, be still, my soul; it is but for a season:
   Let us endure an hour and see injustice done.

6 Think no more; 'tis only thinking
   Lays lads underground.
   49

7 *Clunton and Clunbury,*
   Clungunford and Clun,
   Are the quietest places
   Under the sun.
   50. Version of a traditional rhyme.

8 'Tis a long way further than Knighton,
   A quieter place than Clun,
   Where doomsday may thunder and lighten
   And little 'twill matter to one.

9 For when the knife has slit
   The throat across from ear to ear
   'Twill bleed because of it.
   53

10 With rue my heart is laden
   For golden friends I had,
   For many a rose-lipt maiden
   And many a lightfoot lad.

   By brooks too broad for leaping
   The lightfoot lads are laid;
   The rose-lipt girls are sleeping
   In fields where roses fade.
   54

11 'Terence, this is stupid stuff:
   You eat your victuals fast enough;
   There can't be much amiss, 'tis clear,
   To see the rate you drink your beer.
   But oh, good Lord, the verse you make,
   It gives a chap the belly-ache.'
   62

12 Say, for what were hop-yards meant,
   Or why was Burton built on Trent?
   Oh many a peer of England brews
   Livelier liquor than the Muse,
   And malt does more than Milton can
   To justify God's ways to man.

13 Oh I have been to Ludlow fair
   And left my necktie God knows where,
   And carried half way home, or near,
   Pints and quarts of Ludlow beer:

Then the world seemed none so bad,
And I myself a sterling lad;
And down in lovely muck I've lain,
Happy till I woke again.

14 Therefore, since the world has still
   Much good, but much less good than ill,
   And while the sun and moon endure
   Luck's a chance, but trouble's sure,
   I'd face it as a wise man would,
   And train for ill and not for good.

15 They put arsenic in his meat
   And stared aghast to watch him eat;
   They poured strychnine in his cup
   And shook to see him drink it up.

16 —I tell the tale that I heard told.
   Mithridates, he died old.

17 I hoed and trenched and weeded,
      And took the flowers to fair:
   I brought them home unheeded;
      The hue was not the wear.

18 Comrade, look not on the west:
   'Twill have the heart out of your breast.
   Last Poems (1922), 1. **The West**

19 I 'listed at home for a lancer,
   Oh who would not sleep with the brave?
   6. **Lancer**

20 The chestnut casts his flambeaux, and the flowers
      Stream from the hawthorn on the wind away,
   The doors clap to, the pane is blind with showers.
      Pass me the can, lad; there's an end of May.
   9

21 We for a certainty are not the first
      Have sat in taverns while the tempest hurled
   Their hopeful plans to emptiness, and cursed
      Whatever brute and blackguard made the world.

22 The troubles of our proud and angry dust
      Are from eternity, and shall not fail.
   Bear them we can, and if we can we must.
      Shoulder the sky, my lad, and drink your ale.

23 But men at whiles are sober
      And think by fits and starts,
   And if they think, they fasten
      Their hands upon their hearts.
   10

24 The laws of God, the laws of man,
   He may keep that will and can.
   12

25 I, a stranger and afraid
   In a world I never made.

26 And since, my soul, we cannot fly
   To Saturn nor to Mercury,
   Keep we must, if keep we can,
   These foreign laws of God and man.

27 Oh let not man remember
      The soul that God forgot,
   But fetch the county kerchief
      And noose me in the knot
   And I will rot.
   14

28 He stood, and heard the steeple
      Sprinkle the quarters on the morning town.

One, two, three, four, to market-place and people
   It tossed them down.

Strapped, noosed, nighing his hour,
   He stood and counted them and cursed his luck;
And then the clock collected in the tower
   Its strength, and struck.
15. Eight O'Clock

1 The night is freezing fast,
   Tomorrow comes December;
     And winterfalls of old
Are with me from the past;
   And chiefly I remember
     How Dick would hate the cold.

Fall, winter, fall; for he,
   Prompt hand and headpiece clever,
     Has woven a winter robe,
And made of earth and sea
   His overcoat for ever,
     And wears the turning globe.
20

2 The candles burn their sockets,
   The blinds let through the day,
The young man feels his pockets
   And wonders what's to pay.
21

3 *The King with half the East at heel is marched from*
     lands of morning;
   Their fighters drink the rivers up, their shafts
     benight the air.
And he that stands will die for nought, and home
   there's no returning.
   The Spartans on the sea-wet rock sat down and
     combed their hair.
25. The Oracles

4 Many things I thought of then,
Battle, and the loves of men,
Cities entered, oceans crossed,
Knowledge gained and virtue lost,
Careless folly done and said,
And the lovely way that led
To the slimepit and the mire
And the everlasting fire.
31. Hell Gate

5 And the portress foul to see
Lifted up her eyes on me
Smiling, and I made reply:
'Met again, my lass,' said I.
Then the sentry turned his head,
Looked, and knew me, and was Ned.

6 I sought them far and found them,
   The sure, the straight, the brave,
The hearts I lost my own to,
   The souls I could not save.
They braced their belts about them,
   They crossed in ships the sea,
They sought and found six feet of ground,
   And there they died for me.
32

7 These, in the day when heaven was falling,
   The hour when earth's foundations fled,
Followed their mercenary calling
   And took their wages and are dead.

Their shoulders held the sky suspended;

They stood, and earth's foundations stay;
   What God abandoned, these defended,
And saved the sum of things for pay.
37. Epitaph on an Army of Mercenaries

8 Tell me not here, it needs not saying,
   What tune the enchantress plays
In aftermaths of soft September
   Or under blanching mays,
For she and I were long acquainted
   And I knew all her ways.
40

9 The cuckoo shouts all day at nothing
   In leafy dells alone;
And traveller's joy beguiles in autumn
   Hearts that have lost their own.

10 For nature, heartless, witless nature,
   Will neither care nor know
What stranger's feet may find the meadow
   And trespass there and go,
Nor ask amid the dews of morning
   If they are mine or no.

11 Wenlock Edge was umbered
   And bright was Abdon Burf,
And warm between them slumbered
   The smooth green miles of turf.
41. Fancy's Knell

12 Tomorrow, more's the pity,
   Away we both must hie,
To air the ditty,
   And to earth I.

13 They say my verse is sad: no wonder;
   Its narrow measure spans
Tears of eternity, and sorrow,
   Not mine, but man's.

This is for all ill-treated fellows
   Unborn and unbegot,
For them to read when they're in trouble
   And I am not.
More Poems (1936), epigraph

14 I to my perils
   Of cheat and charmer
   Came clad in armour
     By stars benign.
6

15 When green buds hang in the elm like dust
   And sprinkle the lime like rain,
Forth I wander, forth I must,
   And drink of life again.
9

16 The weeping Pleiads wester,
   And the moon is under seas.
10

17 The rainy Pleiads wester,
   Orion plunges prone,
The stroke of midnight ceases,
   And I lie down alone.
11

18 Crossing alone the nighted ferry
   With the one coin for fee,
Whom, on the wharf of Lethe waiting,
   Count you to find? Not me.

The brisk fond lackey to fetch and carry,

The true, sick-hearted slave,
Expect him not in the just city
And free land of the grave.
23

1 Because I liked you better
   Than suits a man to say,
   It irked you, and I promised
   To throw the thought away.
   31

2 Halt by the headstone naming
   The heart no longer stirred,
   And say the lad that loved you
   Was one that kept his word.

3 Here dead lie we because we did not choose
   To live and shame the land from which we sprung.
   Life, to be sure, is nothing much to lose;
   But young men think it is, and we were young.
   36

4 I did not lose my heart in summer's even,
   When roses to the moonrise burst apart:
   When plumes were under heel and lead was flying,
   In blood and smoke and flame I lost my heart.

   I lost it to a soldier and a foeman,
   A chap that did not kill me, but he tried;
   That took the sabre straight and took it striking
   And laughed and kissed his hand to me and died.
   37

5 Good-night; ensured release,
   Imperishable peace,
   Have these for yours.
   48. **Parta Quies**

6 When the bells justle in the tower
   The hollow night amid,
   Then on my tongue the taste is sour
   Of all I ever did.
   Collected Poems (1939), **Additional Poems,** 9

7 The stars have not dealt me the worst they could do:
   My pleasures are plenty, my troubles are two.
   But oh, my two troubles they reave me of rest,
   The brains in my head and the heart in my breast.
   17

8 Oh who is that young sinner with the handcuffs on his
   wrists?
   And what has he been after that they groan and shake
   their fists?
   And wherefore is he wearing such a
   conscience-stricken air?
   Oh they're taking him to prison for the colour of his
   hair.

   'Tis a shame to human nature, such a head of hair as
   his;
   In the good old time 'twas hanging for the colour that
   it is;
   Though hanging isn't bad enough and flaying would be
   fair
   For the nameless and abominable colour of his hair.
   18

9 O suitably attired in leather boots
   Head of a traveller, wherefore seeking whom
   Whence by what way how purposed art thou come
   To this well-nightingaled vicinity?
   My object in enquiring is to know.
   But if you happen to be deaf and dumb

And do not understand a word I say,
Nod with your hand to signify as much.
Fragment of a Greek Tragedy, Trinity Magazine, Feb. 1921;
first published in *The Bromsgrovian,* 1883

10 Mud's sister, not himself, adorns my shoes.

11 Reader, behold! this monster wild
   Has gobbled up the infant child.
   The infant child is not aware
   It has been eaten by the bear.
   Infant Innocence. Laurence Housman, *A.E.H.* (1937), p.256

12 Three minutes' thought would suffice to find this out,
   but thought is irksome and three minutes is a long
   time.
   Juvenalis Saturae (ed.) (1905), Preface

13 The arsenals of divine vengeance, if I may so describe
   the Bodleian library.

14 Gentlemen who use MSS as drunkards use
   lamp-posts—not to light them on their way but to
   dissimulate their instability.
   M. Manilii Astronomicon Liber Primus (ed.) (1903),
   introduction, I

15 If a man will comprehend the richness and variety of
   the universe, and inspire his mind with a due measure
   of wonder and of awe, he must contemplate the human
   intellect not only on its heights of genius but in its
   abysses of ineptitude; and it might be fruitlessly
   debated to the end of time whether Richard Bentley or
   Elias Stoeber was the more marvellous work of the
   Creator: Elias Stoeber, whose reprint of Bentley's
   text, with a commentary intended to confute it, saw the
   light in 1767 at Strasbourg, a city still famous for its
   geese.
   II. Of earlier editors of Manilius

16 *Ueberlieferungsgeschichte...*is a longer and nobler
   name than fudge.
   Preface to his (1927) edition of Lucan, *De Bello Civili*

17 Experience has taught me, when I am shaving of a
   morning, to keep watch over my thoughts, because, if
   a line of poetry strays into my memory, my skin
   bristles so that the razor ceases to act.
   The Name and Nature of Poetry (1933)

18 The University which once saw Wordsworth drunk and
   once saw Porson sober will see a better scholar than
   Wordsworth, and a better poet than Porson, betwixt
   and between.
   Speech at farewell dinner, University College, London, before
   going to Cambridge as Kennedy Professor of Latin, 1911.
   Laurence Housman, *A.E.H.* (1937), p.101

JULIA WARD HOWE 1819–1910

19 Mine eyes have seen the glory of the coming of the
   Lord:
   He is trampling out the vintage where the grapes of
   wrath are stored.
   Battle Hymn of the American Republic (Dec. 1861)

JAMES HOWELL 1594?–1666

20 Some hold translations not unlike to be
   The wrong side of a Turkey tapestry.
   Familiar Letters (1645–55), bk.i, let.6

21 One hair of a woman can draw more than a hundred
   pair of oxen.
   bk.ii, let.4

1 This life at best is but an inn,
And we the passengers.
let.73

MARY HOWITT 1799–1888

2 Buttercups and daisies,
Oh, the pretty flowers;
Coming ere the Springtime,
To tell of sunny hours.
Buttercups and Daisies

3 'Will you walk into my parlour?' said a spider to a
fly:
''Tis the prettiest little parlour that ever you did spy.'
The Spider and the Fly

EDMOND HOYLE 1672–1769

4 When in doubt, win the trick.
Hoyle's Games (c. 1756). **Whist, Twenty-four Short Rules for
Learners**

FRIEDRICH VON HÜGEL 1852–1926

5 The golden rule is, to help those we love to escape
from us; and never try to begin to help people, or
influence them till they ask, but wait for them. (To his
niece, in conversation.)
Letters...to a Niece (1928), introduction

THOMAS HUGHES 1822–1896

6 Tom and his younger brothers as they grew up, went
on playing with the village boys without the idea of
equality or inequality (except in wrestling, running,
and climbing) ever entering their heads, as it doesn't
till it's put there by Jack Nastys or fine ladies' maids.
Tom Brown's Schooldays, pt.i, ch.3

7 He never wants anything but what's right and fair;
only when you come to settle what's right and fair, it's
everything that he wants and nothing that you want.
And that's his idea of a compromise. Give me the
Brown compromise when I'm on his side.
pt.ii, ch.2

8 It's more than a game. It's an institution. [Cricket.]
ch.7

VICTOR HUGO 1802–1885

9 *Le mot, c'est le Verbe, et le Verbe, c'est Dieu.*
The word is the Verb, and the Verb is God.
Contemplations (1856), I.viii

10 *Souffrons, mais souffrons sur les cimes.*
If suffer we must, let's suffer on the heights.
Les Malheureux

11 *On résiste à l'invasion des armées; on ne résiste pas à
l'invasion des idées.*
A stand can be made against invasion by an army; no
stand can be made against invasion by an idea.
Histoire d'un Crime, La Chute, X

12 *La symétrie, c'est l'ennui, et l'ennui est le fond même
du deuil. Le désespoir baîlle.*
Symmetry is tedious, and tedium is the very basis of
mourning. Despair yawns.
Les Misérables, vol.II, bk.iv, ch.1

13 *Jésus a pleuré, Voltaire a souri; c'est de cette larme
divine et de ce sourire humain qu'est faite la douceur*

de la civilisation actuelle. (Applaudissements
prolongés.)
Jesus wept; Voltaire smiled. Of that divine tear and of
that human smile the sweetness of present civilisation
is composed. (*Hearty applause.*)
Transcript of centenary oration on Voltaire, 30 May 1878

DAVID HUME 1711–1776

14 Custom, then, is the great guide of human life.
An Enquiry Concerning Human Understanding (1748), sec.5,
pt.1

15 If we take in our hand any volume; of divinity or
school metaphysics, for instance; let us ask, *Does it
contain any abstract reasoning concerning quantity or
number?* No. *Does it contain any experimental
reasoning, concerning matter of fact and existence?*
No. Commit it then to the flames: for it can contain
nothing but sophistry and illusion.
sec.12, pt.III

16 Avarice, the spur of industry, is so obstinate a
passion, and works its way through so many real
dangers and difficulties, that it is not likely to be
scared by an imaginary danger, which is so small that
it scarcely admits of calculation.
Essays (1741–2). **Of Civil Liberty**

17 Beauty in things exists in the mind which
contemplates them.
Of Tragedy

18 There is not to be found, in all history, any miracle
attested by a sufficient number of men, of such
unquestioned good sense, education, and learning, as
to secure us against all delusion in themselves; of such
undoubted integrity, as to place them beyond all
suspicion of any design to deceive others; of such
credit and reputation in the eyes of mankind, as to
have a great deal to lose in case of their being detected
in any falsehood; and at the same time attesting facts,
performed in such a public manner, and in so
celebrated a part of the world, as to render the
detection unavoidable.
Of Miracles, Pt.2

19 Their credulity increases his impudence: and his
impudence overpowers their credulity.

20 We soon learn that there is nothing mysterious or
supernatural in the case, but that all proceeds from the
usual propensity of mankind towards the marvellous,
and that, though this inclination may at intervals
receive a check from sense and learning, it can never
be thoroughly extirpated from human nature.

21 The Christian religion not only was at first attended
with miracles, but even at this day cannot be believed
by any reasonable person without one. Mere reason is
insufficient to convince us of its veracity: and whoever
is moved by faith to assent to it, is conscious of a
continued miracle in his own person, which subverts
all the principles of his understanding, and gives him a
determination to believe what is most contrary to
custom and experience.

22 It cannot reasonably be doubted, but a little miss,
dressed in a new gown for a dancing-school ball,
receives as complete enjoyment as the greatest orator,
who triumphs in the splendour of his eloquence, while
he governs the passions and resolutions of a numerous

assembly.
The Sceptic

1 Never literary attempt was more unfortunate than my Treatise of Human Nature. It fell *dead-born from the Press*.
My Own Life (1777), ch.1

2 Opposing one species of superstition to another, set them a quarrelling; while we ourselves, during their fury and contention, happily make our escape into the calm, though obscure, regions of philosophy.
The Natural History of Religion (1757), xv

G.W. HUNT 1829?–1904

3 We don't want to fight, but, by jingo if we do,
We've got the ships, we've got the men, we've got the money too.
We've fought the Bear before, and while Britons shall be true,
The Russians shall not have Constantinople.
We Don't Want to Fight. Music hall song, 1878

LEIGH HUNT 1784–1859

4 Abou Ben Adhem (may his tribe increase!)
Awoke one night from a deep dream of peace,
And saw, within the moonlight in his room,
Making it rich, and like a lily in bloom,
An angel writing in a book of gold:—
Exceeding peace had made Ben Adhem bold,
And to the presence in the room he said,
'What writest thou?'—The vision raised its head,
And with a look made of all sweet accord,
Answered, 'The names of those who love the Lord.'
Abou Ben Adhem and the Angel

5   'I pray thee then,
Write me as one that loves his fellow-men.'

6 And lo! Ben Adhem's name led all the rest.

7 You strange, astonished-looking, angle-faced,
Dreary-mouthed, gaping wretches of the sea.
The Fish, the Man, and the Spirit

8 'By God!' said Francis, 'rightly done!' and he rose from where he sat:
'No love,' quoth he, 'but vanity, sets love a task like that.'
The Glove and the Lions

9 The laughing queen that caught the world's great hands.
The Nile

10 Jenny kissed me when we met,
Jumping from the chair she sat in;
Time, you thief, who love to get
Sweets into your list, put that in:
Say I'm weary, say I'm sad,
Say that health and wealth have missed me,
Say I'm growing old, but add,
Jenny kissed me.
Rondeau

11 Stolen sweets are always sweeter,
Stolen kisses much completer,
Stolen looks are nice in chapels,
Stolen, stolen, be your apples.
Song of Fairies Robbing an Orchard

12 Where the light woods go seaward from the town.
The Story of Rimini, i, l.18

13 The two divinest things this world has got,
A lovely woman in a rural spot!
iii, l.257

14 A pleasure so exquisite as almost to amount to pain.
Letter to Alexander Ireland, 2 June 1848

ANNE HUNTER 1742–1821

15 My mother bids me bind my hair
    With bands of rosy hue,
Tie up my sleeves with ribbons rare,
    And lace my bodice blue.
My Mother Bids Me Bind My Hair

WILLIAM HUNTER 1718–1783

16 Some physiologists will have it that the stomach is a mill;—others, that it is a fermenting vat;—others again that it is a stew-pan;—but in my view of the matter, it is neither a mill, a fermenting vat, nor a stew-pan—but a *stomach*, gentlemen, a *stomach*.
MS. note from his lectures. Epigraph to J.A. Paris, *A Treatise on Diet* (1824)

SIR GERALD HURST 1877–1957

17 One of the mysteries of human conduct is why adult men and women all over England are ready to sign documents which they do not read, at the behest of canvassers whom they do not know, binding them to pay for articles which they do not want, with money which they have not got.
Closed Chapters (1942), p.141

JOHN HUSS c.1372–1415

18 *O sancta simplicitas!*
O holy simplicity!
At the stake, seeing an old peasant bringing a faggot to throw on the pile. Zincgreff-Weidner, *Apophthegmata*, (Amsterdam, 1653), pt.iii, p.383. See 272:20

FRANCIS HUTCHESON 1694–1746

19 Wisdom denotes the pursuing of the best ends by the best means.
Inquiry into the Original of our Ideas of Beauty and Virtue (1725). Treatise I, sec.v, 18

20 That action is best, which procures the greatest happiness for the greatest numbers.
Treatise II. **Concerning Moral Good and Evil**, sec.3, 8

ALDOUS HUXLEY 1894–1963

21 A million million spermatozoa,
    All of them alive:
Out of their cataclysm but one poor Noah
    Dare hope to survive.
Fifth Philosopher's Song

22   But when the wearied Band
Swoons to a waltz, I take her hand,
And there we sit in peaceful calm,
Quietly sweating palm to palm.
Frascati's

23 Your maiden modesty would float face down,

And men would weep upon your hinder parts.
Leda

1 Beauty for some provides escape,
Who gain a happiness in eyeing
The gorgeous buttocks of the ape
Or Autumn sunsets exquisitely dying.
Ninth Philosopher's Song

2 Then brim the bowl with atrabilious liquor!
We'll pledge our Empire vast across the flood:
For Blood, as all men know, than water's thicker,
But water's wider, thank the Lord, than Blood.

T.H. HUXLEY 1825–1895

3 Science is nothing but trained and organized common
sense, differing from the latter only as a veteran may
differ from a raw recruit: and its methods differ from
those of common sense only as far as the guardsman's
cut and thrust differ from the manner in which a
savage wields his club.
Collected Essays, iv. **The Method of Zadig**

4 Every variety of philosophical and theological opinion
was represented there [the Metaphysical Society], and
expressed itself with entire openness; most of my
colleagues were *-ists* of one sort or another; and,
however kind and friendly they might be, I, the man
without a rag of a label to cover himself with, could
not fail to have some of the uneasy feelings which
must have beset the historical fox when, after leaving
the trap in which his tail remained, he presented
himself to his normally elongated companions. So I
took thought, and invented what I conceived to be the
appropriate title of 'agnostic'.
v. **Agnosticism**

5 The great tragedy of Science—the slaying of a
beautiful hypothesis by an ugly fact.
viii. **Biogenesis and Abiogenesis**

6 The chess-board is the world; the pieces are the
phenomena of the universe; the rules of the game are
what we call the laws of Nature. The player on the
other side is hidden from us. We know that his play is
always fair, just, and patient. But also we know, to
our cost, that he never overlooks a mistake, or makes
the smallest allowance for ignorance.
Lay Sermons, &c., iii. **A Liberal Education**

7 Some experience of popular lecturing had convinced
me that the necessity of making things plain to
uninstructed people was one of the very best means of
clearing up the obscure corners in one's own mind.
Man's Place in Nature, Preface to 1894 edition

8 If some great Power would agree to make me always
think what is true and do what is right, on condition of
being turned into a sort of clock and wound up every
morning before I got out of bed, I should instantly
close with the offer.
On Descartes' Discourse on Method. **Method & Results,** iv

9 If a little knowledge is dangerous, where is the man
who has so much as to be out of danger?
On Elementary Instruction in Physiology (1877)

10 Logical consequences are the scarecrows of fools and
the beacons of wise men.
Science and Culture, ix. **On the Hypothesis that Animals are
Automata**

11 Irrationally held truths may be more harmful than
reasoned errors.
xii. **The Coming of Age of the Origin of Species**

12 It is the customary fate of new truths to begin as
heresies and to end as superstitions.

13 I asserted—and I repeat—that a man has no reason to
be ashamed of having an ape for his grandfather. If
there were an ancestor whom I should feel shame in
recalling it would rather be a *man*—a man of restless
and versatile intellect—who, not content with an
equivocal success in his own sphere of activity,
plunges into scientific questions with which he has no
real acquaintance, only to obscure them by an aimless
rhetoric, and distract the attention of his hearers from
the real point at issue by eloquent digressions and
skilled appeals to religious prejudice.
Replying to Bishop Samuel Wilberforce in the debate on Darwin's
theory of evolution during the meeting of the British Association
at Oxford, 30 June 1860. See *Life and Letters of Thomas Henry
Huxley* (1900), vol.i, p.185, letter from J.R. Green to Professor
Boyd Dawkins. Huxley, in a letter to Francis Darwin agreed that
this account was fair if not wholly accurate: there is no reliable
verbatim transcript.

14 I am too much of a sceptic to deny the possibility of
anything.
Letter to Herbert Spencer, 22 March 1886

EDWARD HYDE
see EARL OF CLARENDON

DOLORES IBÁRRURI 'LA PASIONARIA'
1895–

15 *No pasarán!*
They shall not pass.
H. Thomas, *The Spanish Civil War* (1961), ch.16. See 363:17

16 It is better to die on your feet than to live on your
knees.
Speech in Paris, 3 Sept. 1936

HENRIK IBSEN 1828–1906

17 The worst enemy of truth and freedom in our society
is the compact majority. Yes, the damned, compact,
liberal majority.
An Enemy of the People (1882), Act 4

18 The majority has the might—more's the pity—but it
hasn't right…The minority is always right.

19 You should never have your best trousers on when you
turn out to fight for freedom and truth.
Act 5

20 The strongest man in the world is the man who stands
alone.

21 It's not just what we inherit from our mothers and
fathers that haunts us. It's all kinds of old defunct
theories, all sorts of old defunct beliefs, and things like
that. It's not that they actually *live* on in us; they are
simply lodged there, and we cannot get rid of them.
I've only to pick up a newspaper and I seem to see
ghosts gliding between the lines.
Ghosts (1881), Act 2

22 Mother, give me the sun.
Act 3

23 Ten o'clock…and back he'll come. I can just see him.
With vine leaves in his hair. Flushed and confident.
Hedda Gabler (1890), Act 2

1 People don't do such things!
Act 4

2 Youth will come here and beat on my door, and force
its way in.
The Master Builder (1892), Act 1

3 Castles in the air—they're so easy to take refuge in. So
easy to build, too.
Act 3

4 Take the life-lie away from the average man and
straight away you take away his happiness.
The Wild Duck (1884), Act 5

IVAN ILLICH 1926–

5 In a consumer society there are inevitably two kinds of
slaves: the prisoners of addiction and the prisoners of
envy.
Tools for Conviviality (1973)

DEAN INGE 1860–1954

6 To become a popular religion, it is only necessary for
a superstition to enslave a philosophy.
Outspoken Essays, Second Series (1922), ch.III. **The Idea of
Progress.** First published as the Romanes Lecture, 1920

7 Democracy is only an experiment in government, and
it has the obvious disadvantage of merely counting
votes instead of weighing them.
Possible Recovery?

8 Literature flourishes best when it is half a trade and
half an art.
The Victorian Age (1922), p.49

9 A man may build himself a throne of bayonets, but he
cannot sit on it.
Marchant (ed.), *Wit and Wisdom of Dean Inge,* No. 108

10 The nations which have put mankind and posterity
most in their debt have been small states—Israel,
Athens, Florence, Elizabethan England.
No.181

11 *Nisi monumentum requiris, circumspice.* (Of the
traffic outside St. Paul's.)
Attr.

JEAN INGELOW 1820–1897

12 Play uppe, play uppe, O Boston bells!
Play all your changes, all your swells.
The High Tide on the Coast of Lincolnshire, 1571

13 Play uppe 'The Brides of Enderby'.

14 'Cusha! Cusha! Cusha!' calling
E'er the early dews were falling,
Farre away I heard her song.

15 Come uppe, Whitefoot, come uppe Lightfoot,
Come uppe Jetty, rise and follow,
Jetty, to the milking shed.

16 But each will mourn her own (she saith)
And sweeter woman ne'er drew breath
Than my sonne's wife, Elizabeth.

ROBERT G. INGERSOLL 1833–1899

17 An honest God is the noblest work of man.
Gods, pt.1, p.2. See 119:7, 379:24

18 In nature there are neither rewards nor

punishments—there are consequences.
Lectures & Essays, 3rd Series. **Some Reasons Why,** viii

J.A.D. INGRES 1780–1867

19 *Le dessin est la probité de l'art.*
Drawing is the true test of art.
Pensées d'Ingres, 1922, p.70

WASHINGTON IRVING 1783–1859

20 A woman's whole life is a history of the affections.
The Sketch Book (1819–20). **The Broken Heart**

21 A tart temper never mellows with age, and a sharp
tongue is the only edged tool that grows keener with
constant use.
Rip Van Winkle

22 They who drink beer will think beer.
Stratford-on-Avon

23 Free-livers on a small scale; who are prodigal within
the compass of a guinea.
The Stout Gentleman

24 I am always at a loss to know how much to believe of
my own stories.
Tales of a Traveller (1824), To the Reader

25 There is a certain relief in change, even though it be
from bad to worse; as I have found in travelling in a
stage-coach, that it is often a comfort to shift one's
position and be bruised in a new place.

26 The almighty dollar, that great object of universal
devotion throughout our land, seems to have no
genuine devotees in these peculiar villages.
Wolfert's Roost (1855). **The Creole Village**

CHRISTOPHER ISHERWOOD 1904–

27 The common cormorant or shag
Lays eggs inside a paper bag
The reason you will see no doubt
It is to keep the lightning out.
But what these unobservant birds
Have never noticed is that herds
Of wandering bears may come with buns
And steal the bags to hold the crumbs.
The Common Cormorant

28 I am a camera with its shutter open, quite passive,
recording, not thinking.
Goodbye to Berlin, **A Berlin Diary,** Autumn 1930

PRESIDENT ANDREW JACKSON 1767–1845

29 You are uneasy; you never sailed with *me* before, I
see.
J. Parton, *Life of Jackson,* vol.iii, ch.35

30 Our Federal Union: it must be preserved.
Toast given on the Jefferson Birthday Celebration, 13 Apr. 1830.
Benton, *Thirty Years' View,* vol.1

JACOPONE DA TODI c.1230–1306

31 *Stabat Mater dolorosa,*
Iuxta crucem lacrimosa
Dum pendebat Filius.
There was standing the sorrowing Mother, beside the
cross weeping while her Son hung upon it.
Stabat Mater dolorosa. Hymn also ascribed to Pope Innocent III
and St. Bonaventure

REVD. RICHARD JAGO 1715–1781

1 With leaden foot time creeps along
  While Delia is away.
Absence

KING JAMES I OF ENGLAND AND VI OF SCOTLAND 1566–1625

2 A branch of the sin of drunkenness, which is the root of all sins.
A Counterblast to Tobacco (1604)

3 A custom loathsome to the eye, hateful to the nose, harmful to the brain, dangerous to the lungs, and in the black, stinking fume thereof, nearest resembling the horrible Stygian smoke of the pit that is bottomless.

4 Herein is not only a great vanity, but a great contempt of God's good gifts, that the sweetness of man's breath, being a good gift of God, should be wilfully corrupted by this stinking smoke.

5 I will govern according to the common weal, but not according to the common will.
December, 1621. J.R. Green, *History of the English People*, Vol.III, bk.vii, ch.4

6 Dr Donne's verses are like the peace of God; they pass all understanding.
Saying recorded by Archdeacon Plume (1630–1704)

KING JAMES V OF SCOTLAND 1512–1542

7 It cam' wi' a lass, it will gang wi' a lass.
Said on his deathbed of the crown of Scotland; David Hume, *History of England*, vol.iv, ch.33 records 'It came with a woman…and it will go with one.' It is unlikely that James V spoke with a strong Scottish accent.

HENRY JAMES 1843–1916

8 It takes a great deal of history to produce a little literature.
Life of Nathaniel Hawthorne (1879)

9 [Thoreau] was worse than provincial—he was parochial.
ch.4

10 The only obligation to which in advance we may hold a novel, without incurring the accusation of being arbitrary, is that it be interesting.
Partial Portraits. **The Art of Fiction**

11 Experience is never limited, and it is never complete; it is an immense sensibility, a kind of huge spider-web of the finest silken threads suspended in the chamber of consciousness, and catching every air-borne particle in its tissue.

12 What is character but the determination of incident? what is incident but the illustration of character?

13 We must grant the artist his subject, his idea, his *donné*: our criticism is applied only to what he makes of it.

14 Dramatise, dramatise!
Prefaces (1909). **The Altar of the Dead** (1909), and elsewhere

15 The note I wanted; that of the strange and sinister embroidered on the very type of the normal and easy.

16 The terrible *fluidity* of self-revelation.
The Ambassadors (1903)

17 The deep well of unconscious cerebration.
The American (1877)

18 The historian, essentially, wants more documents than he can really use; the dramatist only wants more liberties than he can really take.
The Aspern Papers, &c (1888)

19 The fatal futility of Fact.
The Spoils of Poynton, &c (1897)

20 Live all you can; it's a mistake not to. It doesn't so much matter what you do in particular, so long as you have your life. If you haven't had that what *have* you had?
The Ambassadors (1903), bk.5, ch.2

21 She was a woman who, between courses, could be graceful with her elbows on the table.
bk.7, ch.16

22 Vereker's secret, my dear man—the general intention of his books: the string the pearls were strung on, the buried treasure, the figure in the carpet.
The Figure in the Carpet (1897), ch.11

23 The black and merciless things that are behind the great possessions.
The Ivory Tower (1917), Notes, p.287

24 Cats and monkeys, monkeys and cats—all human life is there.
The Madonna of the Future (1879)

25 Tennyson was not Tennysonian.
Terminations (1895). **The Middle Years**

26 Print it as it stands—beautifully.
The Death of the Lion, x

27 To kill a human being is, after all, the least injury you can do him.
My Friend Bingham (1867)

28 The superiority of one man's opinion over another's is never so great as when the opinion is about a woman.
The Tragic Muse (1890), ch.9

29 The perfect presence of mind, unconfused, unhurried by emotion, that any artistic performance requires and that all, whatever the instrument, require in exactly the same degree.
ch.19

30 Summer afternoon—summer afternoon; to me those have always been the two most beautiful words in the English language.
Edith Wharton, *A Backward Glance*, ch.10

31 So here it is at last, the distinguished thing. [Of his own death.]
ch.14

32 I remember once saying to Henry James, in reference to a novel of the type that used euphemistically to be called 'unpleasant': 'You know, I was rather disappointed; that book wasn't nearly as bad as I expected'; to which he replied, with his incomparable twinkle: 'Ah, my dear, the abysses are all so shallow.'
Edith Wharton, *The House of Mirth*. Introduction to the World's Classics edition (1936), ii

33 I can stand a great deal of gold. [On seeing a particularly grand drawing room.]
Attr. by D. McCarthy, *The Legend of the Master* (compiled by S. Nowell-Smith, 1947) 'Social Occasions'.

34 Some beflagged jam pots, I understand, my dear Fred, let into the soil at long but varying distances. A swoop, a swing, a flourish of steel, a dormy. [On

golf.]
Attr. by E.F. Benson, 'Lamb House'.

1 Poor Gissing...struck me as quite particularly marked
out for what is called in his and my profession an
unhappy ending.
Letter to Sir Sidney Colvin, 1903

2 It is art that *makes* life, makes interest, makes
importance, for our consideration and application of
these things, and I know of no substitute whatever for
the force and beauty of its process.
Letter to H.G. Wells, 10 July 1915

WILLIAM JAMES 1842–1910

3 The moral flabbiness born of the bitch-goddess
SUCCESS. That—with the squalid cash interpretation
put on the word success—is our national disease.
Letter to H.G. Wells, 11 Sept. 1906

JEAN PAUL (J.P.F. RICHTER) 1763–1825

4 Providence has given to the French the empire of the
land, to the English that of the sea, and to the Germans
that of the air.
Quoted by Thomas Carlyle, in the *Edinburgh Review*, 1827

PRESIDENT THOMAS JEFFERSON 1743–1826

5 When in the course of human events, it becomes
necessary for one people to dissolve the political bonds
which have connected them with another, and to
assume among the powers of the earth the separate and
equal station to which the laws of nature and of
Nature's God entitle them, a decent respect to the
opinions of mankind requires that they should declare
the causes which impel them to the separation.
Declaration of Independence, 4 July 1776: Preamble

6 We hold these truths to be sacred and undeniable; that
all men are created equal and independent, that from
that equal creation they derive rights inherent and
inalienable, among which are the preservation of life,
and liberty, and the pursuit of happiness.
Original draft for the Declaration of Independence. See 8:14

7 In the full tide of successful experiment.
First Inaugural Address, 4 March 1801

8 Peace, commerce, and honest friendship with all
nations—entangling alliances with none.

9 A little rebellion now and then is a good thing.
Letter to James Madison, 30 Jan. 1787

10 The tree of liberty must be refreshed from time to time
with the blood of patriots and tyrants. It is its natural
manure.
To W.S. Smith, 13 Nov. 1787

11 Whenever a man has cast a longing eye on them
[offices], a rottenness begins in his conduct.
To Tench Coxe, 1799

12 If the principle were to prevail of a common law [i.e a
single government] being in force in the United
States...it would become the most corrupt government
on the earth.
To Gideon Granger, 13 Aug. 1800

13 To seek out the best through the whole Union we must
resort to other information, which, from the best of
men, acting disinterestedly and with the purest

motives, is sometimes incorrect.
Letter to Elias Shipman and others of New Haven, 12 July 1801

14 To attain all this [universal republicanism], however,
rivers of blood must yet flow, and years of desolation
pass over; yet the object is worth rivers of blood, and
years of desolation.
To John Adams, 4 Sept. 1823

15 If a due participation of office is a matter of right, how
are vacancies to be obtained? Those by death are few;
by resignation none.
Usually quoted, 'Few die and none resign'.

16 Indeed I tremble for my country when I reflect that
God is just.
Notes on Virginia (1784), Query xviii. **Manners**

17 When a man assumes a public trust, he should
consider himself as public property.
Remark to Baron von Humboldt, 1807. Rayner, *Life of Jefferson*
(1834), p.356

18 No duty the Executive had to perform was so trying as
to put the right man in the right place.
J.B. MacMaster, *History of the People of the U.S.*, vol.ii, ch.13,
p.586

FRANCIS, LORD JEFFREY 1773–1850

19 This will never do.
On Wordsworth's 'Excursion'. *Edinburgh Review*, Nov. 1814, p.1

ST. JEROME c.342–420

20 *Venerationi mihi semper fuit non verbosa rusticitas,
sed sancta simplicitas.*
I have revered always not crude verbosity, but holy
simplicity.
Letters, 57, xii (*Patrologia Latina* xxii, 579)

21 Hooly writ is the scripture of puplis, for it is maad,
that alle puplis schulden knowe it.
Attr. See J. Forshall and F. Madden (eds.), *The Holy Bible...in
the Earliest English Versions...* Oxford (1850), Prologue
(probably by John Purvey, c.1353–c.1428), ch.xv

JEROME K. JEROME 1859–1927

22 It is impossible to enjoy idling thoroughly unless one
has plenty of work to do.
The Idle Thoughts of an Idle Fellow (1889). **On Being Idle**

23 Love is like the measles; we all have to go through it.
On Being in Love

24 George goes to sleep at a bank from ten to four each
day, except Saturdays, when they wake him up and
put him outside at two.
Three Men in a Boat (1889), ch.2

25 But there, everything has its drawbacks, as the man
said when his mother-in-law died, and they came down
on him for the funeral expenses.
ch.3

26 I like work: it fascinates me. I can sit and look at it for
hours. I love to keep it by me: the idea of getting rid
of it nearly breaks my heart.
ch.15

DOUGLAS JERROLD 1803–1857

27 Honest bread is very well—it's the butter that makes
the temptation.
The Catspaw (1850), Act III

1 Religion's in the heart, not in the knees.
The Devil's Ducat (1830), I.ii

2 He is one of those wise philanthropists who, in a time of famine, would vote for nothing but a supply of toothpicks.
Wit and Opinions of Douglas Jerrold (1859), **A Philanthropist**

3 Love's like the measles—all the worse when it comes late in life.

4 The best thing I know between France and England is—the sea.
The Anglo-French Alliance

5 That fellow would vulgarize the day of judgment.
A Comic Author

6 The ugliest of trades have their moments of pleasure. Now, if I were a grave-digger, or even a hangman, there are some people I could work for with a great deal of enjoyment.
Ugly Trades

7 Earth is here [Australia] so kind, that just tickle her with a hoe and she laughs with a harvest.
A Land of Plenty

8 Some people are so fond of ill-luck that they run half-way to meet it.
Meeting Troubles Half-way

9 He was so good he would pour rose-water over a toad.
A Charitable Man

10 Talk to him of Jacob's ladder, and he would ask the number of the steps.
A Matter-of-fact Man

11 We love peace, as we abhor pusillanimity; but not peace at any price. There is a peace more destructive of the manhood of living man than war is destructive of his material body. Chains are worse than bayonets.
Peace

12 If an earthquake were to engulf England to-morrow, the English would manage to meet and dine somewhere among the rubbish, just to celebrate the event.
Blanchard Jerrold, *Life of D. Jerrold*, ch.14

13 The only athletic sport I ever mastered was backgammon.
W. Jerrold, *Douglas Jerrold* (1914), vol.i, ch.1, p.22

BISHOP JOHN JEWEL 1522–1571

14 In old time we had treen [wooden] chalices and golden priests, but now we have treen priests and golden chalices.
Certain Sermons Preached Before the Queen's Majesty (1609), p.176

ST. JOHN OF THE CROSS 1542–1591

15 *Muero porque no muero.*
I die because I do not die.
Coplas del alma que pena por ver a dios

16 *Con un no saber sabiendo.*
With a knowing ignorance.
Coplas hechas sobre un éxtasis de alta contemplación

JOHN OF SALISBURY c.1115–1180

17 *Siquidem uita breuis, sensus hebes, neglegentiae torpor, inutilis occupatio, nos paucula scire*

permittunt, et eadem iugiter excutit et auellit ab animo fraudatrix scientiae, inimica et infida semper memoriae nouerca, obliuio.
The brevity of our life, the dullness of our senses, the torpor of our indifference, the futility of our occupation, suffer us to know but little: and that little is soon shaken and then torn from the mind by that traitor to learning, that hostile and faithless stepmother to memory, oblivion.
Prologue to the Policraticus (C.C.J. Webb's edition, vol.i, p.12, ll.13-16) Tr. Helen Waddell

HIRAM JOHNSON 1866–1945

18 The first casualty when war comes is truth.
Speech, U.S. Senate, 1917

LIONEL JOHNSON 1867–1902

19 There Shelley dream'd his white Platonic dreams.
Oxford

20 　　　　In her ears the chime
Of full, sad bells brings back her old springtide.

21 I know you: solitary griefs,
Desolate passions, aching hours.
The Precept of Silence

22 The saddest of all Kings
Crown'd, and again discrown'd.
By the Statue of King Charles I at Charing Cross

23 Alone he rides, alone,
The fair and fatal king.

PHILANDER CHASE JOHNSON 1866–1939

24 Cheer up, the worst is yet to come.
Shooting Stars. See *Everybody's Magazine*, May 1920

SAMUEL JOHNSON 1709–1784

25 The rod produces an effect which terminates in itself. A child is afraid of being whipped, and gets his task, and there's an end on't; whereas, by exciting emulation and comparisons of superiority, you lay the foundation of lasting mischief; you make brothers and sisters hate each other.
Boswell, *Life of Johnson* (L.F. Powell's revision of G.B. Hill's edition), vol.i, p.46

26 In my early years I read very hard. It is a sad reflection, but a true one, that I knew almost as much at eighteen as I do now.
p.56. 20 July 1763

27 *Johnson:* I had no notion that I was wrong or irreverent to my tutor.
Boswell: That, Sir, was great fortitude of mind.
Johnson: No, Sir; stark insensibility.
p.60. 5 Nov. 1728

28 Sir, we are a nest of singing birds.
Of Pembroke College, Oxford. p.75. 1730

29 It is incident to physicians, I am afraid, beyond all other men, to mistake subsequence for consequence.
Review of Dr. Lucas's *Essay on Waters.* p.91n. 25 Nov. 1734

30 He was a vicious man, but very kind to me. If you call a dog *Hervey*, I shall love him.
p.106. 1737

31 My old friend, Mrs Carter, could make a pudding as

well as translate Epictetus.
p.123n. 1738

1 Tom Birch is as brisk as a bee in conversation; but no sooner does he take a pen in his hand, than it becomes a torpedo to him, and benumbs all his faculties.
p.159. 1743

2 I'll come no more behind your scenes, David; for the silk stockings and white bosoms of your actresses excite my amorous propensities.
p.201. 1750

3 A man may write at any time, if he will set himself doggedly to it.
p.203. Mar. 1750

4 Thy body is all vice, and thy mind all virtue.
To Beauclerk. p.250. 1752

5 I had done all I could; and no man is well pleased to have his all neglected, be it ever so little.
p.261. Letter to Lord Chesterfield, 7 Feb. 1755

6 The shepherd in Virgil grew at last acquainted with Love, and found him a native of the rocks.

7 Is not a Patron, my Lord, one who looks with unconcern on a man struggling for life in the water, and, when he has reached ground, encumbers him with help? The notice which you have been pleased to take of my labours, had it been early, had been kind; but it has been delayed till I am indifferent, and cannot enjoy it; till I am solitary, and cannot impart it; till I am known, and do not want it.

8 A fly, Sir, may sting a stately horse and make him wince; but one is but an insect, and the other is a horse still.
p.263, n.3

9 This man I thought had been a Lord among wits; but, I find, he is only a wit among Lords.
Of Lord Chesterfield. p.266. 1754

10 They teach the morals of a whore, and the manners of a dancing master.
Of Lord Chesterfield's *Letters*. p.266. 1754

11 There are two things which I am confident I can do very well: one is an introduction to any literary work, stating what it is to contain, and how it should be executed in the most perfect manner; the other is a conclusion, shewing from various causes why the execution has not been equal to what the author promised to himself and to the public.
p.292. 1755

12 Ignorance, madam, pure ignorance.
When asked by a lady why he defined 'pastern' as the 'knee' of a horse, in his Dictionary. p.293. 1755

13 Lexicographer: a writer of dictionaries, a harmless drudge.
p.296. 1755

14 I have protracted my work till most of those whom I wished to please have sunk into the grave; and success and miscarriage are empty sounds.
p.297. 1755

15 If a man does not make new acquaintance as he advances through life, he will soon find himself left alone. A man, Sir, should keep his friendship in constant repair.
p.300. 1755

16 The booksellers are generous liberal-minded men.
p.304. 1756

17 The worst of Warburton is, that he has a rage for saying something, when there's nothing to be said.
p.329. 1758

18 No man will be a sailor who has contrivance enough to get himself into a jail; for being in a ship is being in a jail, with the chance of being drowned...A man in a jail has more room, better food, and commonly better company.
p.348. 16 Mar. 1759

19 'Are you a botanist, Dr Johnson?'
'No, Sir, I am not a botanist; and (alluding, no doubt, to his near sightedness) should I wish to become a botanist, I must first turn myself into a reptile.'
p.377. 20 July 1762

20 *Boswell*: I do indeed come from Scotland, but I cannot help it...
Johnson: That, Sir, I find, is what a very great many of your countrymen cannot help.
p.392. 16 May 1763

21 The notion of liberty amuses the people of England, and helps to keep off the *taedium vitae*. When a butcher tells you that *his heart bleeds for his country* he has, in fact, no uneasy feeling.
p.394. 16 May 1763

22 Yes, Sir, many men, many women, and many children.
On Dr. Blair's asking whether any man of a modern age could have written *Ossian*. p.396. 24 May 1763

23 It was like leading one to talk of a book when the author is concealed behind the door.

24 He insisted on people praying with him; and I'd as lief pray with Kit Smart as any one else.
p.397. 24 May 1763

25 He did not love clean linen; and I have no passion for it.
Of Kit Smart

26 You *may* abuse a tragedy, though you cannot write one. You may scold a carpenter who has made you a bad table, though you cannot make a table. It is not your trade to make tables.
Of literary criticism. p.409. 25 June 1763

27 I am afraid he has not been in the inside of a church for many years; but he never passes a church without pulling off his hat. This shews that he has good principles.
Of Dr. John Campbell. p.418. 1 July 1763

28 He is the richest author that ever grazed the common of literature.
Of Dr. John Campbell

29 Great abilities are not requisite for an Historian...Imagination is not required in any high degree.
p.424. 6 July 1763

30 Norway, too, has noble wild prospects; and Lapland is remarkable for prodigious noble wild prospects. But, Sir, let me tell you, the noblest prospect which a Scotchman ever sees, is the high road that leads him to England!
p.425. 6 July 1763

31 A man ought to read just as inclination leads him; for

what he reads as a task will do him little good.
p.428. 14 July 1763

1 But if he does really think that there is no distinction between virtue and vice, why, Sir, when he leaves our houses let us count our spoons.
p.432. 14 July 1763

2 You never find people labouring to convince you that you may live very happily upon a plentiful fortune.
p.441. 20 July 1763

3 Truth, Sir, is a cow, which will yield such people [sceptics] no more milk, and so they are gone to milk the bull.
p.444. 21 July 1763

4 Young men have more virtue than old men; they have more generous sentiments in every respect.
p.445. 22 July 1763

5 Your levellers wish to level *down* as far as themselves; but they cannot bear levelling *up* to themselves.
p.448. 21 July 1763

6 It is no matter what you teach them [children] first, any more than what leg you shall put into your breeches first.
p.452. 26 July 1763

7 Why, Sir, Sherry [Thomas Sheridan] is dull, naturally dull; but it must have taken him a great deal of pains to become what we now see him. Such an excess of stupidity, Sir, is not in Nature.
p.453. 28 July 1763

8 It is burning a farthing candle at Dover, to shew light at Calais.
Of Thomas Sheridan's influence on the English language. p.454. 28 July 1763

9 [To a woman of the town, accosting him]
No, no, my girl...it won't do.
p.457. 28 July 1763

10 A woman's preaching is like a dog's walking on his hinder legs. It is not done well; but you are surprised to find it done at all.
p.463. 31 July 1763

11 I look upon it, that he who does not mind his belly will hardly mind anything else.
p.467. 5 Aug. 1763

12 This was a good dinner enough, to be sure; but it was not a dinner to *ask* a man to.
p.470. 5 Aug. 1763

13 We could not have had a better dinner had there been a *Synod of Cooks*.

14 Don't, Sir, accustom yourself to use big words for little matters. It would *not* be *terrible,* though I *were* to be detained some time here.
p.471. 6 Aug. 1763

15 [Of Bishop Berkeley's theory of the non-existence of matter, Boswell observed that though they were satisfied it was not true, they were unable to refute it. Johnson struck his foot against a large stone, till he rebounded from it, saying]
I refute it *thus.*

16 A very unclubable man.
Sir John Hawkins. p.480n. 1764

17 That all who are happy, are equally happy, is not true. A peasant and a philosopher may be equally *satisfied,*

but not equally *happy.* Happiness consists in the multiplicity of agreeable consciousness.
vol.ii, p.9. Feb. 1766

18 It is our first duty to serve society, and, after we have done that, we may attend wholly to the salvation of our own souls. A youthful passion for abstracted devotion should not be encouraged.
p.10. Feb. 1766

19 Our tastes greatly alter. The lad does not care for the child's rattle, and the old man does not care for the young man's whore.
p.14. Spring, 1766

20 It was not for me to bandy civilities with my Sovereign.
p.35. Feb. 1767

21 I love Robertson, and I won't talk of his book.
p.53. 1768

22 Sir, if a man has a mind to *prance,* he must study at Christ-Church and All-Souls.
p.68n. Autumn, 1769

23 Let me smile with the wise, and feed with the rich.
p.79. 6 Oct. 1769

24 We *know* our will is free, and *there's* an end on't.
p.82. 16 Oct. 1769

25 Inspissated gloom.
p.90

26 I do not know, Sir, that the fellow is an infidel; but if he be an infidel, he is an infidel as a dog is an infidel; that is to say, he has never thought upon the subject.
p.95. 19 Oct. 1769

27 Shakespeare never had six lines together without a fault. Perhaps you may find seven, but this does not refute my general assertion.
p.96. 19 Oct. 1769

28 I would not *coddle* the child.
p.101. 26 Oct. 1769

29 Why, Sir, most schemes of political improvement are very laughable things.
p.102. 26 Oct. 1769

30 There is no idolatry in the Mass. They believe God to be there, and they adore him.
p.105. 26 Oct. 1769

31 It matters not how a man dies, but how he lives. The act of dying is not of importance, it lasts so short a time.
p.106. 26 Oct. 1769

32 Burton's *Anatomy of Melancholy,* he said, was the only book that ever took him out of bed two hours sooner than he wished to rise.
p.121. 1770

33 Want of tenderness is want of parts, and is no less a proof of stupidity than depravity.
p.122. 1770

34 That fellow seems to me to possess but one idea, and that is a wrong one.
p.126. 1770

35 Johnson observed, that 'he did not care to speak ill of any man behind his back, but he believed the gentleman was an *attorney.*'

36 The triumph of hope over experience.
Of a man who remarried immediately after the death of a wife with whom he had been very unhappy. p.128. 1770

1 Every man has a lurking wish to appear considerable in his native place.
p.141. Letter to Sir Joshua Reynolds, 17 July 1771

2 It is so far from being natural for a man and woman to live in a state of marriage that we find all the motives which they have for remaining in that connection, and the restraints which civilized society imposes to prevent separation, are hardly sufficient to keep them together.
p.165. 31 Mar. 1772

3 Nobody can write the life of a man, but those who have eat and drunk and lived in social intercourse with him.
p.166. 31 Mar. 1772

4 I would not give half a guinea to live under one form of government rather than another. It is of no moment to the happiness of an individual.
p.170. 31 Mar. 1772

5 Sir, I perceive you are a vile Whig.
To Sir Adam Fergusson

6 There is a remedy in human nature against tyranny, that will keep us safe under every form of government.

7 A man who is good enough to go to heaven, is good enough to be a clergyman.
p.171. 5 Apr. 1772

8 There is more knowledge of the heart in one letter of Richardson's, than in all *Tom Jones.*
p.174. 6 Apr. 1772

9 Why, Sir, if you were to read Richardson for the story, your impatience would be so much fretted that you would hang yourself.
p.175. 6 Apr. 1772

10 Much may be made of a Scotchman, if he be *caught* young.
On Lord Mansfield, who was educated in England. p.194. Spring 1772

11 He has, indeed, done it very well; but it is a foolish thing well done.
On Goldsmith's apology in the *London Chronicle* for beating Evans the bookseller. p.210. 3 Apr. 1773

12 All intellectual improvement arises from leisure.
p.219. 13 Apr. 1773

13 *Elphinston:* What, have you not read it through?... *Johnson:* No, Sir, do *you* read books *through*?
p.226. 19 Apr. 1773

14 Read over your compositions, and where ever you meet with a passage which you think is particularly fine, strike it out.
Quoting a college tutor. p.237. 30 Apr. 1773

15 The woman's a whore, and there's an end on't.
Of Lady Diana Beauclerk. p.247. 7 May 1773

16 I hope I shall never be deterred from detecting what I think a cheat, by the menaces of a ruffian.
p.298. Letter to James Macpherson, 20 Jan. 1775

17 The Irish are a fair people;—they never speak well of one another.
p.307. 1775

18 There are few ways in which a man can be more innocently employed than in getting money.
p.323. 27 Mar. 1775

19 He [Thomas Gray] was dull in a new way, and that made many people think him *great.*
p.327. 28 Mar. 1775

20 I never think I have hit hard, unless it rebounds.
p.335. 2 Apr. 1775

21 I think the full tide of human existence is at Charing-Cross.
p.337. 2 Apr. 1775

22 George the First knew nothing, and desired to know nothing; did nothing, and desired to do nothing; and the only good thing that is told of him is, that he wished to restore the crown to its hereditary successor.
p.342. 6 Apr. 1775

23 It is wonderful, when a calculation is made, how little the mind is actually employed in the discharge of any profession.
p.344. 6 Apr. 1775

24 A man will turn over half a library to make one book.

25 Patriotism is the last refuge of a scoundrel.
p.348. 7 Apr. 1775

26 That is the happiest conversation where there is no competition, no vanity, but a calm quiet interchange of sentiments.
p.359. 14 Apr. 1775

27 Their learning is like bread in a besieged town: every man gets a little, but no man gets a full meal.
On the Scots. p.363. 18 Apr. 1775

28 Knowledge is of two kinds. We know a subject ourselves, or we know where we can find information upon it.
p.365. 18 Apr. 1775

29 Politics are now nothing more than a means of rising in the world.
p.369. 1775

30 Players, Sir! I look upon them as no better than creatures set upon tables and joint stools to make faces and produce laughter, like dancing dogs.
p.404. 1775

31 In lapidary inscriptions a man is not upon oath.
p.407. 1775

32 There is now less flogging in our great schools than formerly, but then less is learned there; so that what the boys get at one end they lose at the other.

33 When men come to like a sea-life, they are not fit to live on land.
p.438. 18 Mar. 1776

34 Nothing odd will do long. *Tristram Shandy* did not last.
p.449. 20 Mar. 1776

35 There is nothing which has yet been contrived by man, by which so much happiness is produced as by a good tavern or inn.
p.452. 21 Mar. 1776

36 Marriages would in general be as happy, and often more so, if they were all made by the Lord Chancellor.
p.461. 22 Mar. 1776

37 Questioning is not the mode of conversation among gentlemen.
p.472. Mar. 1776

38 Fine clothes are good only as they supply the want of other means of procuring respect.
p.475. 27 Mar. 1776

1 If a madman were to come into this room with a stick in his hand, no doubt we should pity the state of his mind; but our primary consideration would be to take care of ourselves. We should knock him down first, and pity him afterwards.
vol.iii, p.11. 3 Apr. 1776

2 Consider, Sir, how should you like, though conscious of your innocence, to be tried before a jury for a capital crime, once a week.

3 We would all be idle if we could.
p.13. 3 Apr. 1776

4 No man but a blockhead ever wrote, except for money.
p.19. 5 Apr. 1776

5 It is better that some should be unhappy than that none should be happy, which would be the case in a general state of equality.
p.26. 7 Apr. 1776

6 A man who has not been in Italy, is always conscious of an inferiority, from his not having seen what it is expected a man should see. The grand object of travelling is to see the shores of the Mediterranean.
p.36. 11 Apr. 1776

7 'Sir, what is poetry?'
'Why Sir, it is much easier to say what it is not. We all *know* what light is; but it is not easy to *tell* what it is.'
p.38 10 Apr. 1776

8 Nay, Madam, when you are declaiming, declaim; and when you are calculating, calculate.
To Mrs. Thrale, who had interrupted him and Boswell by a lively extravagant sally on the expense of clothing children. p.49. 26 Apr. 1776

9 Every man of any education would rather be called a rascal, than accused of deficiency in *the graces*.
p.54. May 1776

10 Sir, you have but two topics, yourself and me. I am sick of both.
p.57. May 1776

11 Dine with Jack Wilkes, Sir! I'd as soon dine with Jack Ketch.
p.66. 'This has been circulated as if actually said by Johnson; when the truth is, it was only *supposed* by me.' (Boswell's note.)

12 Sir, it is not so much to be lamented that Old England is lost, as that the Scotch have found it.
p.78. 15 May 1776

13 *Olivarii Goldsmith, Poetae, Physici, Historici, Qui nullum fere scribendi genus non tetigit, Nullum quod tetigit non ornavit.*
To Oliver Goldsmith, A Poet, Naturalist, and Historian, who left scarcely any style of writing untouched, and touched none that he did not adorn.
p.82. 22 June 1776. Epitaph on Goldsmith

14 Hermit hoar, in solemn cell,
   Wearing out life's evening gray;
Smite thy bosom, sage, and tell,
   What is bliss, and which the way?
Thus I spoke; and speaking sigh'd;
   —Scarce repressed the starting tear;—
When the smiling sage reply'd—
   —Come, my lad, and drink some beer.
p.159. 18 Sept. 1777

15 If I had no duties, and no reference to futurity, I would spend my life in driving briskly in a post-chaise with a pretty woman.
p.162. 19 Sept. 1777

16 Depend upon it, Sir, when a man knows he is to be hanged in a fortnight, it concentrates his mind wonderfully.
p.167. 19 Sept. 1777

17 When a man is tired of London, he is tired of life; for there is in London all that life can afford.
p.178. 20 Sept. 1777

18 He who praises everybody praises nobody.
p.225n.

19 Round numbers are always false.
p.226, n.4. 30 Mar. 1778

20 Accustom your children constantly to this; if a thing happened at one window and they, when relating it, say that it happened at another, do not let it pass, but instantly check them; you do not know where deviation from truth will end.
p.228. 31 Mar. 1778

21 All argument is against it; but all belief is for it.
Of the appearance of the spirit of a person after death. p.230. 31 Mar. 1778

22 John Wesley's conversation is good, but he is never at leisure. He is always obliged to go at a certain hour. This is very disagreeable to a man who loves to fold his legs and have out his talk, as I do.

23 Though we cannot out-vote them we will out-argue them.
p.234. 3 Apr. 1778

24 Seeing Scotland, Madam, is only seeing a worse England.
p.248. 7 Apr. 1778

25 Goldsmith, however, was a man, who, whatever he wrote, did it better than any other man could do.
p.253. 9 Apr. 1778

26 Every man thinks meanly of himself for not having been a soldier, or not having been at sea.
p.265. 10 Apr. 1778

27 A mere antiquarian is a rugged being.
p.278. Letter to Boswell, 23 Apr. 1778

28 Johnson had said that he could repeat a complete chapter of 'The Natural History of Iceland', from the Danish of Horrebow, the whole of which was exactly thus:—'CHAP. LXXII. *Concerning snakes*. There are no snakes to be met with throughout the whole island.'
p.279. 13 Apr. 1778

29 A country governed by a despot is an inverted cone.
p.283. 14 Apr. 1778

30 I am willing to love all mankind, *except an American*.
p.290. 15 Apr. 1778

31 As the Spanish proverb says, 'He, who would bring home the wealth of the Indies, must carry the wealth of the Indies with him.' So it is in travelling; a man must carry knowledge with him, if he would bring home knowledge.
p.302. 17 Apr. 1778

32 Sir, the insolence of wealth will creep out.
p.316. 18 Apr. 1778

33 All censure of a man's self is oblique praise. It is in order to shew how much he can spare.
p.323. 25 Apr. 1778

1 Sir, there are rascals in all countries.
On Boswell's expressing surprise at finding a Staffordshire Whig. p.326. 28 Apr. 1778

2 I have always said, the first Whig was the Devil.

3 It is thus that mutual cowardice keeps us in peace. Were one half of mankind brave and one half cowards, the brave would be always beating the cowards. Were all brave, they would lead a very uneasy life; all would be continually fighting; but being all cowards, we go on very well.

4 Were it not for imagination, Sir, a man would be as happy in the arms of a chambermaid as of a Duchess.
p.341. 9 May 1778

5 There are innumerable questions to which the inquisitive mind can in this state receive no answer: Why do you and I exist? Why was this world created? Since it was to be created, why was it not created sooner?

6 Dr Mead lived more in the broad sunshine of life than almost any man.
p.355. 16 May 1778

7 Claret is the liquor for boys; port for men; but he who aspires to be a hero must drink brandy.
p.381. 7 Apr. 1779

8 A man who exposes himself when he is intoxicated, has not the art of getting drunk.
p.389. 24 Apr. 1779

9 Remember that all tricks are either knavish or childish.
p.396. Letter to Boswell, 9 Sept. 1779

10 Worth seeing? yes; but not worth going to see.
Of the Giant's Causeway. p.410. 12 Oct. 1779

11 If you are idle, be not solitary; if you are solitary, be not idle.
p.415. Letter to Boswell, 27 Oct. 1779. See 117:3

12 When Charles Fox said something to me once about Catiline's Conspiracy, I withdrew my attention and thought about Tom Thumb.
p.512. Letter from Mrs. Piozzi to W.A. Conway, 21 Aug. 1819

13 Among the anfractuosities of the human mind, I know not if it may not be one, that there is a superstitious reluctance to sit for a picture.
vol.iv, p.4. 1780

14 Clive, sir, is a good thing to sit by; she always understands what you say.
Of Kitty Clive. p.7. 1780

15 I have got no further than this: Every man has a right to utter what he thinks truth, and every other man has a right to knock him down for it. Martyrdom is the test.
p.12. 1780

16 They are forced plants, raised in a hot-bed; and they are poor plants; they are but cucumbers after all.
Of Gray's *Odes*. p.13. 1780

17 A Frenchman must be always talking, whether he knows anything of the matter or not; an Englishman is content to say nothing, when he has nothing to say.
p.15. 1780

18 Sir, your wife, under pretence of keeping a bawdy-house, is a receiver of stolen goods.
During an exchange of coarse raillery customary among people travelling upon the Thames. p 26. 1780

19 No man was more foolish when he had not a pen in his hand, or more wise when he had.
Of Goldsmith. See 221:13

20 Depend upon it that if a man talks of his misfortunes there is something in them that is not disagreeable to him; for where there is nothing but pure misery there never is any recourse to the mention of it.
p.31. 1780

21 Supposing...a wife to be of a studious or argumentative turn, it would be very troublesome: for instance,—if a woman should continually dwell upon the subject of the Arian heresy.
p.32. 1780

22 No man speaks concerning another, even suppose it be in his praise, if he thinks he does not hear him, exactly as he would, if he thought he was within hearing.

23 I believe that is true. The dogs don't know how to write trifles with dignity.
Reply to Fowke who had observed that in writing biography, Johnson infinitely exceeded his contemporaries. p.34, n.5

24 Mrs Montagu has dropt me. Now, Sir, there are people whom one should like very well to drop, but would not wish to be dropped by.
p.73. Mar. 1781

25 This merriment of parsons is mighty offensive.
p.76. Mar. 1781

26 He fills a chair.
Of Mr. Dudley Long. p.81. 1 Apr. 1781

27 We are not here to sell a parcel of boilers and vats, but the potentiality of growing rich, beyond the dreams of avarice.
At the sale of Thrale's brewery. p.87. 6 Apr. 1781. See 355:14

28 'The woman had a bottom of good sense.' The word '*bottom*' thus introduced, was so ludicrous,...that most of us could not forbear tittering... 'Where's the merriment?...I say the *woman* was *fundamentally* sensible.'
p.99. 20 Apr. 1781

29 Classical quotation is the *parole* of literary men all over the world.
p.102. 8 May 1781

30 Why, that is, because, dearest, you're a dunce.
To Miss Monckton, afterwards Lady Corke, who said that Sterne's writings affected her. p.109. May 1781

31 I have two very cogent reasons for not printing any list of subscribers;—one, that I have lost all the names,—the other, that I have spent all the money.
p.111. May 1781

32 My friend [Johnson] was of opinion, that when a man of rank appeared in that character [as an author], he deserved to have his merit handsomely allowed.
p.114. May 1781

33 Always, Sir, set a high value on spontaneous kindness. He whose inclination prompts him to cultivate your friendship of his own accord, will love you more than one whom you have been at pains to attach to you.
p.115. May 1781

34 A wise Tory and a wise Whig, I believe, will agree. Their principles are the same, though their modes of thinking are different.
p.117. Written statement given to Boswell, May 1781

35 Officious, innocent, sincere,

Of every friendless name the friend.

Yet still he fills affection's eye,
Obscurely wise, and coarsely kind.
p.127. 20 Jan. 1782. On the death of Mr. Levett

1 Then, with no throbs of fiery pain,
No cold gradations of decay,
Death broke at once the vital chain,
And freed his soul the nearest way.

2 Resolve not to be poor: whatever you have, spend
less. Poverty is a great enemy to human happiness; it
certainly destroys liberty, and it makes some virtues
impracticable and others extremely difficult.
p.157. 7 Dec. 1782

3 I hate a fellow whom pride, or cowardice, or laziness
drives into a corner, and who does nothing when he is
there but sit and *growl*; let him come out as I do, and
bark.
p.161, n.3. 14 Nov. 1782

4 I never have sought the world; the world was not to
seek me.
p.172. 23 Mar. 1783

5 How few of his friends' houses would a man choose to
be at when he is sick.
p.181. 1783

6 There is a wicked inclination in most people to
suppose an old man decayed in his intellects. If a
young or middle-aged man, when leaving a company,
does not recollect where he laid his hat, it is nothing;
but if the same inattention is discovered in an old man,
people will shrug up their shoulders, and say, 'His
memory is going.'

7 A man might write such stuff for ever, if he would
abandon his mind to it.
Of Ossian. p.183. 1783

8 Sir, there is no settling the point of precedency
between a louse and a flea.
To Maurice Morgann who asked him whether he reckoned Derrick
or Smart the better poet. p.192. 1783

9 When I observed he was a fine cat, saying, 'why yes,
Sir, but I have had cats whom I liked better than this';
and then as if perceiving Hodge to be out of
countenance, adding, 'but he is a very fine cat, a very
fine cat indeed.'
p.197. 1783

10 Sir, I have never slept an hour less, nor eat an ounce
less meat. I would have knocked the factious dogs [the
Whigs] on the head, to be sure; but I was not *vexed*.
p.220. 15 May 1783

11 My dear friend, clear your *mind* of cant...You may
talk in this manner; it is a mode of talking in Society:
but don't *think* foolishly.
p.221. 15 May 1783

12 As I know more of mankind I expect less of them, and
am ready now to call a man *a good man*, upon easier
terms than I was formerly.
p.239. Sept. 1783

13 Boswell is a very clubable man.
p.254n. 1783

14 I should as soon think of contradicting a Bishop.
Of George Psalmanazar, whom he reverenced for his piety. p.274.
15 May 1784

15 If a man were to go by chance at the same time with
[Edmund] Burke under a shed, to shun a shower, he

would say—'this is an extraordinary man.'
p.275

16 It is as bad as bad can be: it is ill-fed, ill-killed,
ill-kept, and ill-drest.
The roast mutton he had for dinner at an inn. p.284. 3 June 1784

17 *Johnson*: As I cannot be sure that I have fulfilled the
conditions on which salvation is granted, I am afraid I
may be one of those who shall be damned (looking
dismally).
Dr. Adams: What do you mean by damned?
Johnson (passionately and loudly): Sent to Hell, Sir,
and punished everlastingly.
p.299. 1784

18 Milton, Madam, was a genius that could cut a
Colossus from a rock; but could not carve heads upon
cherry-stones.
To Miss Hannah More, who had expressed a wonder that the poet
who had written *Paradise Lost* should write such poor Sonnets.
p.305. 13 June 1784

19 Don't cant in defence of savages.
p.308. 15 June 1784

20 It might as well be 'Who drives fat oxen should
himself be fat.'
p.313. June 1784. Parody of 94:4

21 Sir, I have found you an argument; but I am not
obliged to find you an understanding.

22 No man is a hypocrite in his pleasures.
p.316. June 1784

23 Dublin, though a place much worse than London, is
not so bad as Iceland.
Letter to Mrs. Christopher Smart. p.359n. 1791

24 Who can run the race with Death?
p.360. Letter to Dr. Burney, 2 Aug. 1784

25 Sir, I look upon every day to be lost, in which I do
not make a new acquaintance.
p.374. Nov. 1784

26 I will be conquered; I will not capitulate.
Talking of his illness

27 Are you sick or are you sullen?
p.380. Letter to Boswell, 3 Nov. 1784

28 Long-expected one-and-twenty,
Ling'ring year, at length is flown;
Pride and pleasure, pomp and plenty
Great [Sir John], are now your own.
p.413. Dec. 1784

29 An odd thought strikes me:—we shall receive no
letters in the grave.

30 A lawyer has no business with the justice or injustice
of the cause which he undertakes, unless his client
asks his opinion, and then he is bound to give it
honestly. The justice or injustice of the cause is to be
decided by the judge.
Boswell, *Tour to the Hebrides (Life*, vol.v), 15 Aug. 1773, p.175

31 Let him go abroad to a distant country; let him go to
some place where he is *not* known. Don't let him go to
the devil where he is known!
18 Aug., p.194

32 I have, all my life long, been lying till noon; yet I tell
all young men, and tell them with great sincerity, that
nobody who does not rise early will ever do any good.
14 Sept., p.299

33 I inherited a vile melancholy from my father, which

has made me mad all my life, at least not sober.
16 Sept., p.302

1 I am always sorry when any language is lost, because languages are the pedigree of nations.
18 Sept., p.310

2 No, Sir; there were people who died of dropsies, which they contracted in trying to get drunk.
Johnson, railing against Scotland, had said that the wine the Scots had before the Union would not make them drunk. Boswell assured Johnson there was much drunkenness. 23 Sept., p.326

3 A cucumber should be well sliced, and dressed with pepper and vinegar, and then thrown out, as good for nothing.
5 Oct., p.354

4 Come, let me know what it is that makes a Scotchman happy!
Calling for a gill of whisky. 23 Oct., p.393

5 Sir, are you so grossly ignorant of human nature, as not to know that a man may be very sincere in good principles, without having good practice?
25 Oct., p.403

6 I am sorry I have not learned to play at cards. It is very useful in life: it generates kindness and consolidates society.
21 Nov., p.433

7 This world where much is to be done and little to be known.
Johnsonian Miscellanies ed. G.B. Hill (1897), vol.i. Prayers and Meditations. Against inquisitive and perplexing Thoughts, p.118

8 Corneille is to Shakespeare...as a clipped hedge is to a forest.
Anecdotes of Johnson by Mrs. Piozzi, p.187

9 Wheresoe'er I turn my view,
All is strange, yet nothing new;
Endless labour all along,
Endless labour to be wrong;
Phrase that time hath flung away,
Uncouth words in disarray.
Trick'd in antique ruff and bonnet,
Ode, and elegy, and sonnet.
p.190

10 If the man who turnips cries,
Cry not when his father dies,
'Tis a proof that he had rather
Have a turnip than his father.
Burlesque of Lope de Vega's lines, 'Si a quien los leones vence,' &c. p.193

11 Dear Bathurst (said he to me one day) was a man to my very heart's content: he hated a fool, and he hated a rogue, and he hated a whig; he was a very good hater.
p.204

12 He will not, whither he is now gone, find much difference, I believe, either in the climate or the company.
Of a Jamaica gentleman, then lately dead. p.211

13 One day at Streatham...a young gentleman called to him suddenly, and I suppose he thought disrespectfully, in these words: 'Mr Johnson, would you advise me to marry?' 'I would advise no man to marry, Sir,' returns for answer in a very angry tone Dr Johnson, 'who is not likely to propagate understanding.'
p.213

14 *Goldsmith*: Here's such a stir about a fellow that has written one book [Beattie's *Essay on Truth*], and I have written many.
Johnson: Ah, Doctor, there go two-and-forty sixpences you know to one guinea.
p.269

15 It is very strange, and very melancholy, that the paucity of human pleasures should persuade us ever to call hunting one of them.
p.288

16 Was there ever yet anything written by mere man that was wished longer by its readers, excepting *Don Quixote, Robinson Crusoe,* and the *Pilgrim's Progress*?
p.332

17 Books that you may carry to the fire, and hold readily in your hand, are the most useful after all.
vol.ii. Apophthegms from Hawkins's edition of Johnson's works, p.2

18 A man is in general better pleased when he has a good dinner upon his table, than when his wife talks Greek.
p.11

19 I would rather see the portrait of a dog that I know, than all the allegorical paintings they can shew me in the world.
p.15

20 I have heard him assert, that a tavern chair was the throne of human felicity.
Extracts from Hawkins's *Life of Johnson*, p.91

21 I dogmatise and am contradicted, and in this conflict of opinions and sentiments I find delight.
p.92

22 Abstinence is as easy to me, as temperance would be difficult.
Anecdotes by Hannah More, p.197

23 Of music Dr Johnson used to say that it was the only sensual pleasure without vice.
Anecdotes by William Seward, p.301

24 Difficult do you call it, Sir? I wish it were impossible.
Of the performance of a celebrated violinist. p.308

25 What is written without effort is in general read without pleasure.
p.309

26 As with my hat upon my head
I walk'd along the Strand,
I there did meet another man
With his hat in his hand.
Anecdotes by George Steevens, p.315

27 Love is the wisdom of the fool and the folly of the wise.
From William Cooke's *'Life of Samuel Foote'*, p.393

28 Fly fishing may be a very pleasant amusement; but angling or float fishing I can only compare to a stick and a string, with a worm at one end and a fool at the other.
Attrib. Johnson by Hawker in *Instructions to Young Sportsmen* (1859), p.197. Not found in his works. See N. & Q., 11 Dec. 1915

29 Madam, before you flatter a man so grossly to his face, you should consider whether or not your flattery is worth his having.
Remark to Hannah More. Mme D'Arblay, *Diary and Letters* (1891 edn.), vol.i, ch.ii, p.55 (Aug. 1778)

1 A general anarchy prevails in my kitchen.
ch.iii, p.63 (Sept. 1778)

2 Every man has, some time in his life, an ambition to
be a wag.
vol.iii, ch.xlvi, p.413 (1 June 1792)

3 I know not, madam, that you have a right, upon moral
principles, to make your readers suffer so much.
To Mrs. Sheridan, after publication of her novel *Memoirs of Miss
Sydney Biddulph* (1763)

4 In all pointed sentences, some degree of accuracy
must be sacrificed to conciseness.
On the Bravery of the English Common Soldier. Works
(1787), vol.x, p.286

5 It is the fate of those who toil at the lower
employments of life...to be exposed to censure,
without hope of praise; to be disgraced by miscarriage,
or punished for neglect...Among these unhappy
mortals is the writer of dictionaries...Every other
author may aspire to praise; the lexicographer can only
hope to escape reproach.
Dictionary of the English Language (1775), Preface

6 I am not yet so lost in lexicography, as to forget that
words are the daughters of earth, and that things are
the sons of heaven. Language is only the instrument of
science, and words are but the signs of ideas: I wish,
however, that the instrument might be less apt to
decay, and that signs might be permanent, like the
things which they denote.
See 326:19

7 Every quotation contributes something to the stability
or enlargement of the language.
Of citations of usage in a dictionary

8 But these were the dreams of a poet doomed at last to
wake a lexicographer.

9 If the changes that we fear be thus irresistible, what
remains but to acquiesce with silence, as in the other
insurmountable distresses of humanity? It remains that
we retard what we cannot repel, that we palliate what
we cannot cure.

10 The chief glory of every people arises from its
authors.

11 *Dull.* 8. To make dictionaries is dull work.

12 *Excise.* A hateful tax levied upon commodities.

13 *Net.* Anything reticulated or decussated at equal
distances, with interstices between the intersections.

14 *Oats.* A grain, which in England is generally given to
horses, but in Scotland supports the people.

15 *Patron.* Commonly a wretch who supports with
insolence, and is paid with flattery.

16 *Whig.* The name of a faction.

17 Every man is, or hopes to be, an idler.
The Idler (1758-60), No.1

18 When two Englishmen meet, their first talk is of the
weather.
No.11

19 Promise, large promise, is the soul of an
advertisement.
No.41

20 He is no wise man who will quit a certainty for an
uncertainty.
No.57

21 Nothing is more hopeless than a scheme of merriment.
No.58

22 A Scotchman must be a very sturdy moralist who does
not love Scotland better than truth.
Journey to the Western Islands of Scotland (1775). **Col**

23 At seventy-seven it is time to be in earnest.

24 Whatever withdraws us from the power of our senses;
whatever makes the past, the distant, or the future,
predominate over the present, advances us in the
dignity of thinking beings.
Inch Kenneth

25 I do not much wish well to discoveries, for I am
always afraid they will end in conquest and robbery.
Letter to W.S. Johnson, 4 Mar. 1773

26 Grief is a species of idleness.
To Mrs. Thrale, 17 Mar. 1773

27 There is no wisdom in useless and hopeless sorrow.
To Mrs. Thrale, 12 Apr. 1781

28 A hardened and shameless tea-drinker, who has for
twenty years diluted his meals with only the infusion
of this fascinating plant; whose kettle has scarcely time
to cool; who with tea amuses the evening, with tea
solaces the midnight, and with tea welcomes the
morning.
Review in the *Literary Magazine*, vol.ii, No.xiii. 1757

29 The reciprocal civility of authors is one of the most
risible scenes in the farce of life.
Life of Sir Thomas Browne, first published as preface to his 1756
edition of *Christian Morals*·

30 The true genius is a mind of large general powers,
accidentally determined to some particular direction.
Lives of the English Poets (1779-81). **Cowley**

31 Language is the dress of thought.
See 568:25

32 We are perpetually moralists, but we are
geometricians only be chance. Our intercourse with
intellectual nature is necessary; our speculations upon
matter are voluntary, and at leisure.
Milton

33 An acrimonious and surly republican.

34 The great source of pleasure is variety.
Butler

35 The father of English criticism.
Dryden

36 I am disappointed by that stroke of death, which has
eclipsed the gaiety of nations and impoverished the
public stock of harmless pleasure. [Garrick's death.]
Edmund Smith

37 About things on which the public thinks long it
commonly attains to think right.
Addison

38 Whoever wishes to attain an English style, familiar
but not coarse, and elegant but not ostentatious, must
give his days and nights to the volumes of Addison.

39 In the character of his Elegy I rejoice to concur with
the common reader; for by the common sense of
readers uncorrupted with literary prejudices...must be
finally decided all claim to poetical honours.
Gray

40 A man, doubtful of his dinner, or trembling at a
creditor, is not much disposed to abstracted

meditation, or remote enquiries.
Collins

1 This play [*The Beggar's Opera*]...was first offered to Cibber and his brethren at Drury-Lane, and rejected; it being then carried to Rich, had the effect, as was ludicrously said, of making Gay *rich* and Rich *gay*.
John Gay

2 He washed himself with oriental scrupulosity.
Swift

3 Friendship is not always the sequel of obligation.
James Thomson

4 There are minds so impatient of inferiority that their gratitude is a species of revenge, and they return benefits, not because recompense is a pleasure, but because obligation is a pain.
The Rambler, 15 Jan. 1751

5 I have laboured to refine our language to grammatical purity, and to clear it from colloquial barbarisms, licentious idioms, and irregular combinations.
14 Mar. 1752

6 The business of a poet, said Imlac, is to examine, not the individual, but the species;...he does not number the streaks of the tulip, or describe the different shades in the verdure of the forest.
Rasselas (1759), ch.10

7 He [the poet] must write as the interpreter of nature, and the legislator of mankind, and consider himself as presiding over the thoughts and manners of future generations; as a being superior to time and place.

8 Human life is everwhere a state in which much is to be endured, and little to be enjoyed.
ch.11

9 Marriage has many pains, but celibacy has no pleasures.
ch.26

10 Example is always more efficacious than precept.
ch.29

11 Integrity without knowledge is weak and useless, and knowledge without integrity is dangerous and dreadful.
ch.41

12 The endearing elegance of female friendship.
ch.45

13 The power of punishment is to silence, not to confute.
Sermons (1788), No.xxiii

14 Notes are often necessary, but they are necessary evils.
Plays of William Shakespeare, with Notes (1765), preface

15 A quibble is to Shakespeare what luminous vapours are to the traveller: he follows it at all adventures; it is sure to lead him out of his way and sure to engulf him in the mire.

16 It must be at last confessed that, as we owe everything to him [Shakespeare], he owes something to us; that, if much of our praise is paid by perception and judgement, much is likewise given by custom and veneration. We fix our eyes upon his graces and turn them from his deformities, and endure in him what we should in another loathe or despise.

17 I have always suspected that the reading is right which requires many words to prove it wrong, and the emendation wrong that cannot without so much labour

appear to be right.

18 How is it that we hear the loudest yelps for liberty among the drivers of negroes?
Taxation No Tyranny (1775)

19 A generous and elevated mind is distinguished by nothing more certainly than an eminent degree of curiosity.
Dedication of his English trans. of Fr. J. Lobo's *Voyage to Abyssinia* (1735), signed 'the editor' but attr. to Johnson in Boswell's *Life*, i.89

20 Unmov'd tho' witlings sneer and rivals rail;
Studious to please, yet not asham'd to fail.
Irene (1736-7, produced 1749), prologue

21 How small, of all that human hearts endure,
That part which laws or kings can cause or cure!
Still to ourselves in every place consigned,
Our own felicity we make or find:
With secret course, which no loud storms annoy,
Glides the smooth current of domestic joy.
Lines added to Goldsmith's 'Traveller' (1764). See 231:30

22 Here falling houses thunder on your head,
And here a female atheist talks you dead.
London (1738), l.17

23 Of all the griefs that harrass the distress'd,
Sure the most bitter is a scornful jest;
Fate never wounds more deep the gen'rous heart,
Than when a blockhead's insult points the dart.
l.166

24 This mournful truth is ev'rywhere confess'd,
Slow rises worth by poverty depress'd.
l.176

25 When learning's triumph o'er her barb'rous foes
First rear'd the Stage, immortal Shakespeare rose;
Each change of many-colour'd life he drew,
Exhausted worlds, and then imagin'd new:
Existence saw him spurn her bounded reign,
And panting Time toil'd after him in vain.
Prologue at the Opening of the Theatre in Drury Lane, 1747

26 Hard is his lot, that here by fortune plac'd,
Must watch the wild vicissitudes of taste;
With ev'ry meteor of caprice must play,
And chase the new-blown bubbles of the day.

27 The stage but echoes back the public voice.
The drama's laws the drama's patrons give,
For we that live to please, must please to live.

28 Let observation with extensive view,
Survey mankind, from China to Peru;
Remark each anxious toil, each eager strife,
And watch the busy scenes of crowded life.
The Vanity of Human Wishes (1749), l.1

29 Deign on the passing world to turn thine eyes,
And pause awhile from letters to be wise;
There mark what ills the scholar's life assail,
Toil, envy, want, the patron, and the jail.
See nations slowly wise, and meanly just,
To buried merit raise the tardy bust.
l.157

30 A frame of adamant, a soul of fire,
No dangers fright him and no labours tire.
l.193

31 His fall was destined to a barren strand,
A petty fortress, and a dubious hand;
He left the name, at which the world grew pale,

To point a moral, or adorn a tale. [Charles XII of Sweden.]
1.219

1 'Enlarge my life with multitude of days!'
In health, in sickness, thus the suppliant prays:
Hides from himself its state, and shuns to know,
That life protracted is protracted woe.
Time hovers o'er, impatient to destroy,
And shuts up all the passages of joy.
1.225

2 Superfluous lags the vet'ran on the stage.
1.308

3 In life's last scene what prodigies surprise,
Fears of the brave, and follies of the wise!
From Marlb'rough's eyes the streams of dotage flow,
And Swift expires a driv'ler and a show.
1.315

4 What ills from beauty spring.
1.321

5 Still raise for good the supplicating voice,
But leave to Heaven the measure and the choice.
1.351

6 With these celestial Wisdom calms the mind,
And makes the happiness she does not find.
1.367

JOHN BENN JOHNSTONE 1803–1891

7 I want you to assist me in forcing her on board the lugger; once there, I'll frighten her into marriage.
Since quoted as: Once aboard the lugger and the maid is mine.
The Gipsy Farmer

HANNS JOHST 1890–

8 *Wenn ich Kultur höre...entsichere ich meinen Browning!*
Whenever I hear the word 'culture'...I release the safety-catch on my pistol.
Schlageter (1934), I.i. Often attrib. Goering

AL JOLSON 1886–1950

9 You ain't heard nothin' yet, folks.
In the first talking film, *The Jazz Singer*, July 1927

HENRY ARTHUR JONES 1851–1929
and HENRY HERMAN 1832–1894

10 O God! Put back Thy universe and give me yesterday.
The Silver King

JOHN PAUL JONES 1747–1792

11 I have not yet begun to fight.
On being hailed to know whether he had struck his flag, as his ship was sinking, 23 Sept. 1779. De Koven, *Life and Letters of J.P. Jones*, vol.i

SIR WILLIAM JONES 1746–1794

12 My opinion is, that power should always be distrusted, in whatever hands it is placed.
Lord Teignmouth, *Life of Sir W. Jones* (1835), vol.i. Letter to Lord Althorpe, 5 Oct. 1782

13 Seven hours to law, to soothing slumber seven,

Ten to the world allot, and *all* to Heaven.
vol.ii. Lines in substitution for Sir E. Coke's lines: Six hours in sleep, [&c.]. See 154:22

BEN JONSON 1573?–1637

14 Fortune, that favours fools.
The Alchemist (1610), prologue

15 Thou look'st like Antichrist in that lewd hat.
IV.vii

16 I will eat exceedingly, and prophesy.
Bartholomew Fair (1614), I.vi

17 Neither do thou lust after that tawney weed tobacco.
II.vi

18 When I mock poorness, then heaven make me poor.
The Case is Altered (1598-9), III.i

19 *People:* The Voice of Cato is the voice of Rome.
Cato: The voice of Rome is the consent of heaven!
Catiline his Conspiracy (1611), III.i

20 Where it concerns himself,
Who's angry at a slander makes it true.

21 Slow, slow, fresh fount, keep time with my salt tears:
Yet, slower, yet; O faintly, gentle springs:
List to the heavy part the music bears,
Woe weeps out her division, when she sings.
Cynthia's Revels (1600), I.i

22 So they be ill men,
If they spake worse, 'twere better: for of such
To be dispraised, is the most perfect praise.
III.ii

23 True happiness
Consists not in the multitude of friends,
But in the worth and choice.

24 Queen and huntress, chaste and fair,
Now the sun is laid to sleep,
Seated in thy silver chair,
State in wonted manner keep:
Hesperus entreats thy light,
Goddess, excellently bright.
v.iii

25 If he were
To be made honest by an act of parliament,
I should not alter in my faith of him.
The Devil is an Ass (1616), IV.i

26 Alas, all the castles I have, are built with air, thou know'st.
Eastward Ho (1604), II.ii.226

27 Still to be neat, still to be drest,
As you were going to a feast;
Still to be powder'd, still perfum'd,
Lady, it is to be presumed,
Though art's hid causes are not found,
All is not sweet, all is not sound.

Give me a look, give me a face,
That makes simplicity a grace;
Robes loosely flowing, hair as free:
Such sweet neglect more taketh me,
Than all the adulteries of art;
They strike mine eyes, but not my heart.
Epicoene (1609), I.i

28 Rest in soft peace, and, ask'd say here doth lye
Ben Jonson his best piece of poetrie.
Epigrams (1672), xlv. **On My First Son**

1 But that which most doth take my Muse and me,
Is a pure cup of rich Canary wine,
Which is the Mermaid's now, but shall be mine.
ci. **Inviting a Friend to Supper**

2 Weep with me, all you that read
This little story:
And know for whom a tear you shed
Death's self is sorry.
'Twas a child that so did thrive
In grace and feature,
As Heaven and Nature seem'd to strive
Which own'd the creature.
Years he number'd scarce thirteen
When Fates turn'd cruel,
Yet three fill'd Zodiacs had he been
The stage's jewel;
And did act, what now we moan,
Old men so duly,
As sooth the Parcae thought him one,
He play'd so truly.
So, by error, to his fate
They all consented;
But viewing him since, alas, too late!
They have repented;
And have sought (to give new birth)
In baths to steep him;
But being so much too good for earth,
Heaven vows to keep him.
cxx. **An Epitaph on Salomon Pavy, a Child of Queen Elizabeth's Chapel**

3 Underneath this stone doth lie
As much beauty as could die;
Which in life did harbour give
To more virtue than doth live.
cxxiv. **Epitaph on Elizabeth L.H.**

4 Helter skelter, hang sorrow, care'll kill a cat, up-tails all, and a louse for the hangman.
Every Man in His Humour (1598), I.iii

5 Ods me, I marvel what pleasure or felicity they have in taking their roguish tobacco. It is good for nothing but to choke a man, and fill him full of smoke and embers.
III.v

6 I do honour the very flea of his dog.
IV.ii

7 I have it here in black and white.

8 It must be done like lightning.
v

9 There shall be no love lost.
Every Man out of His Humour (1599), II.i

10 Blind Fortune still
Bestows her gifts on such as cannot use them.
ii

11 Follow a shadow, it still flies you,
Seem to fly it, it will pursue:
So court a mistress, she denies you;
Let her alone, she will court you.
Say, are not women truly, then,
Styl'd but the shadows of us men?
The Forest (1616), vii. **Song: That Women are but Men's Shadows**

12 Drink to me only with thine eyes,
And I will pledge with mine;
Or leave a kiss but in the cup,

And I'll not look for wine.
The thirst that from the soul doth rise
Doth ask a drink divine;
But might I of Jove's nectar sup,
I would not change for thine.

I sent thee late a rosy wreath,
Not so much honouring thee,
As giving it a hope that there
It could not wither'd be.
ix. **To Celia**

13 Ramp up my genius, be not retrograde;
But boldly nominate a spade a spade.
The Poetaster (1601), v.i

14 Detraction is but baseness' varlet;
And apes are apes, though clothed in scarlet.

15 This is Mab, the Mistress-Fairy
That doth nightly rob the dairy.
The Satyr (1603)

16 Tell proud Jove,
Between his power and thine there is no odds:
'Twas only fear first in the world made gods.
Sejanus (1603), II.ii

17 This figure that thou here seest put,
It was for gentle Shakespeare cut,
Wherein the graver had a strife
With Nature, to out-do the life:
O could he but have drawn his wit
As well in brass, as he has hit
His face; the print would then surpass
All that was ever writ in brass:
But since he cannot, reader, look
Not on his picture, but his book.
On the Portrait of Shakespeare, To the Reader

18 While I confess thy writings to be such,
As neither man, nor muse, can praise too much.
To the Memory of My Beloved, the Author, Mr. William Shakespeare

19 Soul of the Age!
The applause! delight! the wonder of our stage!
My Shakespeare, rise; I will not lodge thee by
Chaucer, or Spenser, or bid Beaumont lie
A little further, to make thee a room:
Thou art a monument, without a tomb,
And art alive still, while thy book doth live,
And we have wits to read, and praise to give.

20 Marlowe's mighty line.

21 And though thou hadst small Latin, and less Greek.

22 To hear thy buskin tread,
And shake a stage: or, when thy socks were on,
Leave thee alone, for the comparison
Of all that insolent Greece or haughty Rome
Sent forth, or since did from their ashes come.

23 He was not of an age, but for all time!

24 For a good poet's made, as well as born.

25 Sweet Swan of Avon! what a sight it were
To see thee in our waters yet appear,
And make those flights upon the banks of Thames,
That so did take Eliza, and our James!

26 Well, they talk we shall have no more Parliaments,
God bless us!
The Staple of News (1625), III.i

1 I remember the players have often mentioned it as an honour to Shakespeare that in his writing (whatsoever he penned) he never blotted out a line. My answer hath been 'Would he had blotted a thousand'. Which they thought a malevolent speech. I had not told posterity this, but for their ignorance, who chose that circumstance to commend their friend by wherein he most faulted; and to justify mine own candour: for I loved the man, and do honour his memory, on this side idolatry, as much as any. He was (indeed) honest, and of an open and free nature; had an excellent phantasy, brave notions, and gentle expressions; wherein he flowed with that facility, that sometimes it was necessary he should be stopped: *sufflaminandus erat*, as Augustus said of Haterius. His wit was in his own power, would the rule of it had been so too...But he redeemed his vices with his virtues. There was ever more in him to be praised than to be pardoned.
Timber, or Discoveries made upon Men and Matter (1641). De Shakespeare Nostrati. Augustus in Haterium. See 245:2

2 The fear of every man that heard him was, lest he should make an end. [Bacon.]
Dominus Verulamius

3 Talking and eloquence are not the same: to speak, and to speak well, are two things.
Praecept. Element

4 Have you seen but a bright lily grow,
    Before rude hands have touch'd it?
Have you mark'd but the fall o' the snow
    Before the soil hath smutch'd it?...
O so white! O so soft! O so sweet is she!
The Underwood (1640). Celebration of Charis, iv. **Her Triumph**

5 She is Venus when she smiles;
But she's Juno when she walks,
And Minerva when she talks.
v. **His Discourse with Cupid**

6 Greek was free from rhyme's infection,
Happy Greek, by this protection,
    Was not spoiled:
Whilst the Latin, queen of tongues,
Is not yet free from rhyme's wrongs,
    But rests foiled.
29. **A Fit of Rhyme against Rhyme**

7 England's high Chancellor: the destin'd heir,
In his soft cradle, to his father's chair.
51. **On Lord Bacon's [Sixtieth] Birthday**

8 It is not growing like a tree
In bulk, doth make men better be;
Or standing long an oak, three hundred year,
To fall a log at last, dry, bald, and sere:
    A lily of a day,
    Is fairer far in May,
Although it fall and die that night;
It was the plant and flower of light.
In small proportions we just beauties see;
And in short measures, life may perfect be.
70. **To the Immortal Memory...of...Sir Lucius Carey and Sir H. Morison**

9 What gentle ghost, besprent with April dew,
Hails me so solemnly to yonder yew?
83. **Elegy on the Lady Jane Pawlet**

10 The voice so sweet, the words so fair,
As some soft chime had stroked the air;

And though the sound were parted thence,
Still left an echo in the sense.
84. **Eupheme**

11 Calumnies are answered best with silence.
Volpone (1605), II.ii

12 Come, my Celia, let us prove,
While we can, the sports of love.
III.v. See 136:25

13 Suns, that set, may rise again;
But if once we lose this light,
'Tis with us perpetual night.

14 Our drink shall be prepared gold and amber;
Which we will take, until my roof whirl around
With the *vertigo*: and my dwarf shall dance.

15 You have a gift, sir, (thank your education,)
Will never let you want, while there are men,
And malice, to breed causes. [To a lawyer.]
V.i

16   Mischiefs feed
Like beasts, till they be fat, and then they bleed.
viii

17 His censure of the English poets was this...
That Donne...deserved hanging.
That Shakespeare wanted Art.
Conversations with William Drummond of Hawthornden (1619), III

THOMAS JORDAN 1612?–1685

18 They pluck't communion tables down
    And broke our painted glasses;
They threw our altars to the ground
    And tumbled down the crosses.
They set up Cromwell and his heir—
    The Lord and Lady Claypole—
Because they hated Common Prayer,
    The organ and the maypole.
How the War began (1664)

JOHN JORTIN 1698–1770

19 *Palmam qui meruit, ferat.*
Let him who has won it bear the palm.
Lusus Poetici (1722): **Ad Ventos.** Adopted as motto by Lord Nelson.

BENJAMIN JOWETT 1817–1893

20 One man is as good as another until he has written a book.
Abbott and Campbell, *Letters of B. Jowett* (1899), i.248

21 At Oxford, as you know, we follow the Cambridge lead, sometimes with uncertain steps.
Letter to Professor Marshall, 5 Jan. 1886

22 I hope our young men will not grow into such *dodgers* as these old men are. I believe everything a *young* man says to me. (Attr.)
'Notes and Sayings'

23 Nowhere probably is there more true feeling, and nowhere worse taste, than in a churchyard—both as regards the monuments and the inscriptions. Scarcely a word of true poetry anywhere.

24 Young men make great mistakes in life; for one thing, they idealize love too much.

1 My dear child, you must believe in God in spite of what the clergy tell you.
Private conversation with Margot Asquith, shortly after the near-fatal illness a year before his death. Asquith, *Autobiography*, ch.8

JAMES JOYCE 1882–1941

2 Riverrun, past Eve and Adam's, from swerve of shore to bend of bay, brings us by a commodius vicus of recirculation back to Howth Castle and Environs.
Finnegans Wake (1939), standard edition. Opening words.

3 That ideal reader suffering from an ideal insomnia.
p.120

4 When is a man not a man?...when he is a—yours till the rending of the rocks—Sham.
p.170

5 The flushpots of Euston and the hanging garments of Marylebone.
p.192

6   O
        tell me all about
    Anna Livia! I want to hear all
about Anna Livia. Well, you know Anna Livia?
Yes, of course, we all know Anna Livia. Tell me all.
  Tell me now.
p.196

7 If you don't like my story get out of the punt.
p.206

8 Can't hear with the waters of. The chittering waters of. Flittering bats, fieldmice bawk talk. Ho! Are you not gone ahome?...Dark hawks hear us. Night! Night! My ho head halls. I feel as heavy as yonder stone...Beside the rivering waters of, hitherandthithering waters of. Night!
p.215

9 Quiet takes back her folded fields.
p.244

10 Loud, heap miseries upon us yet entwine our arts with laughters low!
p.259

11 All moanday, tearsday, wailsday, thumpsday, frightday, shatterday.
p.301

12 Three quarks for Muster Mark!
p.383

13 The Gracehoper was always jigging ajog, hoppy on akkant of his joyicity.
p.414

14 Soft morning, city!
p.619

15 Poor Parnell! he cried loudly. My dead King!
A Portrait of the Artist as a Young Man (1916), ch.1

16 Ireland is the old sow that eats her farrow.
ch.5

17 Pity is the feeling which arrests the mind in the presence of whatsoever is grave and constant in human sufferings and unites it with the human sufferer. Terror is the feeling which arrests the mind in the presence of whatsoever is grave and constant in human sufferings and unites it with the secret cause.

18 The mystery of esthetic like that of material creation is accomplished. The artist, like the God of the creation, remains within or behind or beyond or above his handiwork, invisible, refined out of existence, indifferent, paring his fingernails.

19 April 26...Welcome, O life! I go to encounter for the millionth time the reality of experience and to forge in the smithy of my soul the uncreated conscience of my race.
April 27. Old father, old artificer, stand me now and ever in good stead.
closing words

20 The snotgreen sea. The scrotumtightening sea.
Ulysses (1922). **Telemachus**

21 It is a symbol of Irish art. The cracked lookingglass of a servant.

22 I fear those big words, Stephen said, which make us so unhappy.
Nestor

23 History is a nightmare from which I am trying to awake.

24 Lawn Tennyson, gentleman poet.
Proteus

25 The statue of the onehandled adulterer. [Nelson.]
Aeolus

26 A base barreltone voice.
Lestrygonians

27 A man of genius makes no mistakes. His errors are volitional and are the portals of discovery.
Scylla and Charybdis

28 Greater love than this, he said, no man hath that a man lay down his wife for a friend. Go thou and do likewise. Thus, or words to that effect, saith Zarathustra, sometime regius professor of French letters to the University of Oxtail.
Oxen of the Sun

29 The heaventree of stars hung with humid nightblue fruit.
Ithaca

30 And I thought well as well him as another and then I asked him with my eyes to ask again yes and then he asked me would I yes to say yes my mountain flower and first I put my arms around him yes and drew him down to me so he could feel my breasts all perfume yes and his heart was going like mad and yes I said yes I will Yes.
Penelope, closing words

EMPEROR JULIAN THE APOSTATE c.332–363

31 *Vicisti, Galilaee.*
You have won, Galilean.
Supposed dying words; but a late embellishment of Theodoret, *Hist. Eccles.*, iii.25

DAME JULIAN OF NORWICH 1343–1443

32 Sin is behovely, but all shall be well and all shall be well and all manner of thing shall be well.
Revelations of Divine Love, ch.27

33 Wouldest thou wit thy Lord's meaning in this thing? Wit it well: Love was his meaning. Who shewed it thee? Love. What shewed He thee? Love. Wherefore shewed it He? for Love...Thus was I learned that Love

is our Lord's meaning.
ch.86

'JUNIUS' fl. 1770

1 The liberty of the press is the *Palladium* of all the civil, political, and religious rights of an Englishman.
Letters, *Public Advertiser* (1769–71), dedication

2 The right of election is the very essence of the constitution.
Letter 11, 24 Apr. 1769

3 Is this the wisdom of a great minister? or is it the ominous vibration of a pendulum?
Letter 12, 30 May 1769

4 There is a holy mistaken zeal in politics as well as in religion. By persuading others, we convince ourselves.
Letter 35, 19 Dec. 1769

5 Whether it be the heart to conceive, the understanding to direct, or the hand to execute.
Letter 37, 19 Mar. 1770. See 152:19

6 The injustice done to an individual is sometimes of service to the public.
Letter 41, 14 Nov. 1770

7 As for Mr Wedderburne, there is something about him, which even treachery cannot trust.
Letter 49, 22 June 1771

EMPEROR JUSTINIAN c.482–565

8 Justice is the constant and perpetual wish to render to every one his due.
Institutes, I.i.1

JUVENAL A.D. c.60–c.130

9 *Difficile est saturam non scribere.*
It's hard not to write satire.
Satires, i.30

10 *Probitas laudatur et alget.*
Honesty is praised and left to shiver.
i.74. Tr. G.G. Ramsay

11 *Si natura negat, facit indignatio versum.*
Even if nature says no, indignation makes me write verse.
79

12 *Quidquid agunt homines, votum timor ira voluptas Gaudia discursus nostri farrago libelli est.*
Everything mankind does, their hope, fear, rage, pleasure, joys, business, are the hotch-potch of my little book.
85

13 *Quis tulerit Gracchos de seditione querentes?*
Who would put up with the Gracchi complaining about subversion?
ii.24

14 *Nemo repente fuit turpissimus.*
No one ever suddenly became depraved.
83

15 *Iam pridem Syrus in Tiberim defluxit Orontes Et linguam et mores.*
The Syrian Orontes has now for long been pouring into the Tiber, with its own language and ways of behaving.

16 *Grammaticus, rhetor, geometres, pictor, aliptes,*

Augur, schoenobates, medicus, magus, omnia novit Graeculus esuriens: in caelum iusseris ibit.
Scholar, public speaker, geometrician, painter, physical training instructor, diviner of the future, rope-dancer, doctor, magician, the hungry little Greek can do everything: send him to—Heaven (and he'll go there).
iii.76

17 *Nil habet infelix paupertas durius in se Quam quod ridiculos homines facit.*
The misfortunes of poverty carry with them nothing harder to bear than that it exposes men to ridicule.
152

18 *Haud facile emergunt quorum virtutibus obstat Res angusta domi.*
It's not easy for people to rise out of obscurity when they have to face straitened circumstances at home.
164

19   *Omnia Romae Cum pretio.*
Everything in Rome is expensive.
183

20 *Rara avis in terris nigroque simillima cycno.*
A rare bird on this earth, like nothing so much as a black swan.
vi.165

21 *Hoc volo, sic iubeo, sit pro ratione voluntas.*
I will have this done, so I order it done; let my will replace reasoned judgement.
223

22 *'Pone seram, cohibe.' Sed quis custodiet ipsos Custodes? Cauta est et ab illis incipit uxor.*
'Bolt her in, keep her indoors.' But who is to guard the guards themselves? Your wife arranges accordingly and begins with them.
347

23   *Tenet insanabile multos Scribendi cacoethes et aegro in corde senescit.*
Many suffer from the incurable disease of writing, and it becomes chronic in their sick minds.
vii.51

24 *Occidit miseros crambe repetita magistros.*
That cabbage hashed up again and again proves the death of the wretched teachers.
154

25 *Summum crede nefas animam praeferre pudori Et propter vitam vivendi perdere causas.*
Count it the greatest sin to prefer mere existence to honour, and for the sake of life to lose the reasons for living.
viii.83

26 *Cantabit vacuus coram latrone viator.*
Travel light and you can sing in the robber's face.
x.22

27   *Verbosa et grandis epistula venit A Capreis.*
A huge wordy letter came from Capri.
71. The Emperor Tiberius's letter to the Senate that caused the downfall of Sejanus, A.D. 31.

28   *Duas tantum res anxius optat, Panem et circenses.*
Only two things does he worry about or long

for—bread and the big match.
80. Of the citizen these days.

1   *Expende Hannibalem: quot libras in duce summo*
    Invenies?
    Weigh Hannibal: how many pounds will you find in
    that great general?
    147

2   *I, demens, et saevas curre per Alpes*
    Ut pueris placeas et declamatio fias.
    Off you go, madman, and hurry across the horrible
    Alps, duly to delight schoolboys and become a
    subject for practising speech-making.
    166

3   *Mors sola fatetur*
    Quantula sint hominum corpuscula.
    Death alone reveals how small are men's poor bodies.
    172

4   *Orandum est ut sit mens sana in corpore sano.*
    You should pray to have a sound mind in a sound
    body.
    356

5   *Prima est haec ultio, quod se*
    Iudice nemo nocens absolvitur.
    This is the first of punishments, that no guilty man is
    acquitted if judged by himself.
    xiii.2

6   *Quippe minuti*
    Semper et infirmi est animi exiguique voluptas
    Ultio. Continuo sic collige, quod vindicta
    Nemo magis gaudet quam femina.
    Indeed, it's always a paltry, feeble, tiny mind that
    takes pleasure in revenge. You can deduce it
    without further evidence than this, that no one
    delights more in vengeance than a woman.
    189

7   *Maxima debetur puero reverentia, siquid*
    Turpe paras, nec tu pueri contempseris annos.
    A child deserves the maximum respect; if you ever
    have something disgraceful in mind, don't ignore
    your son's tender years.
    xiv.47

IMMANUEL KANT 1724–1804

8   Two things fill the mind with ever new and increasing
    wonder and awe, the more often and the more
    seriously reflection concentrates upon them: the starry
    heaven above me and the moral law within me.
    Critique of Practical Reason, conclusion

9   *Ich soll niemals anders verfahren, als so, dass ich*
    auch wollen könne, meine Maxime solle ein
    allgemeines Gesetz werden.
    I am never to act otherwise than so *that I could also*
    will that my maxim should become a universal law.
    Grundlegung zur Metaphysik der Sitten, trans. T.K. Abbott,
    Section I

10 *Endlich gibt es einen Imperativ, der, ohne irgend eine*
    andere durch ein gewisses Verhalten zu erreichende
    Absicht als Bedingung zum Grunde zu legen, dieses
    Verhalten unmittelbar gebietet. Dieser Imperativ ist
    kategorisch...Dieser Imperativ mag der der
    Sittlichkeit heissen.
    Finally, there is an imperative which commands a
    certain conduct immediately, without having as its
    condition any other purpose to be attained by it. This

imperative is Categorical...This imperative may be
called that of Morality.
Section II

11 *Wer den Zweck will, will (so fern die Vernunft auf*
    seine Handlungen entscheidenden Einfluss hat) auch
    das dazu unentbehrlich notwendige Mittel, das in
    seiner Gewalt ist.
    Whoever wills the end, wills also (so far as reason
    decides his conduct) the means in his power which are
    indispensably necessary thereto.

12 *...weil Glückseligkeit nicht ein Ideal der Vernunft,*
    sondern der Einbildung ist.
    ...because happiness is not an ideal of reason but of
    imagination.

13 *Handle so, dass du die Menschheit, sowohl in deiner*
    Person, als in der Person eines jeden andern, jederzeit
    zugleich als Zweck, niemals bloss als Mittel brauchest.
    So act as to treat humanity, whether in thine own
    person or in that of any other, in every case as an end
    withal, never as means only.

14 *Aus so krummem Holze, als woraus der Mensch*
    gemacht ist, kann nichts ganz gerades gezimmert
    werden.
    Out of the crooked timber of humanity no straight
    thing can ever be made.
    Idee zu einer allgemeinen Geschichte in weltbürgerlicher
    Absicht

ALPHONSE KARR 1808–1890

15 *Plus ça change, plus c'est la même chose.*
    The more things change, the more they are the same.
    Les Guêpes, Jan. 1849. vi

16 *Si l'on veut abolir la peine de mort en ce cas, que MM*
    les assassins commencent.
    If we are to abolish the death penalty, I should like to
    see the first step taken by our friends the murderers.

CHRISTOPH KAUFMANN 1753–1795

17 *Sturm und Drang.*
    Storm and stress.
    Phrase suggested to F.M. Klinger (1752–1831) as a better title for
    his play originally called *Der Wirrwarr,* the suggestion was
    adopted, the play produced in 1777, and a literary period was thus
    named.

DENIS KEARNEY 1847–1907

18 Horny-handed sons of toil.
    Speech, San Francisco, c.1878. See 319:9

JOHN KEATS 1795–1821

19 The imagination of a boy is healthy, and the mature
    imagination of a man is healthy; but there is a space of
    life between, in which the soul is in a ferment, the
    character undecided, the way of life uncertain, the
    ambition thick-sighted: thence proceeds mawkishness.
    Endymion (1818), preface

20 A thing of beauty is a joy for ever:
    Its loveliness increases; it will never
    Pass into nothingness; but still will keep
    A bower quiet for us, and a sleep
    Full of sweet dreams, and health, and quiet breathing.
    bk.i, l.1

1   The grandeur of the dooms
We have imagined for the mighty dead.
l.20

2 They must be always with us, or we die.
l.33

3   Who, of men, can tell
That flowers would bloom, or that green fruit would
  swell
To melting pulp, that fish would have bright mail,
The earth its dower of river, wood, and vale,
The meadows runnels, runnels pebble-stones,
The seed its harvest, or the lute its tones,
Tones ravishment, or ravishment its sweet
If human souls did never kiss and greet?
l.835

4   Here is wine,
Alive with sparkles—never, I aver,
Since Ariadne was a vintager,
So cool a purple.
bk.ii, l.442

5   To Sorrow,
   I bade good-morrow,
And thought to leave her far away behind;
   But cheerly, cheerly,
   She loves me dearly;
She is so constant to me, and so kind.
bk.iv, l.173

6   Their smiles,
Wan as primroses gather'd at midnight
By chilly finger'd spring.
l.969

7 Sweet are the pleasures that to verse belong,
And doubly sweet a brotherhood in song.
Epistle to G.F. Mathew

8   It is a flaw
In happiness, to see beyond our bourn,—
It forces us in summer skies to mourn,
It spoils the singing of the nightingale.
Epistle to J.H. Reynolds, l.82

9 St Agnes' Eve—Ah, bitter chill it was!
The owl, for all his feathers, was a-cold;
The hare limp'd trembling through the frozen grass,
And silent was the flock in woolly fold.
The Eve of Saint Agnes, 1

10 The sculptur'd dead on each side seem to freeze,
Emprison'd in black, purgatorial rails.
2

11 The silver, snarling trumpets 'gan to chide.
4

12 Soft adorings from their loves receive
Upon the honey'd middle of the night.
6

13 The music, yearning like a God in pain.
7

14 A poor, weak, palsy-stricken, churchyard thing.
18

15 Out went the taper as she hurried in;
Its little smoke, in pallid moonshine, died.
23

16 A casement high and triple-arch'd there was,
All garlanded with carven imag'ries
Of fruits, and flowers, and bunches of knot-grass,
And diamonded with panes of quaint device,

Innumerable of stains and splendid dyes,
As are the tiger-moth's deep-damask'd wings.
24

17   By degrees
Her rich attire creeps rustling to her knees.
26

18 Her soft and chilly nest.
27

19 As though a rose should shut, and be a bud again.

20 And still she slept an azure-lidded sleep,
In blanched linen, smooth, and lavender'd,
While he from forth the closet brought a heap
Of candied apple, quince, and plum, and gourd,
With jellies soother than the creamy curd,
And lucent syrops, tinct with cinnamon;
Manna and dates, in argosy transferr'd
From Fez; and spiced dainties, every one,
From silken Samarcand to cedar'd Lebanon.
30

21 He play'd an ancient ditty, long since mute,
In Provence call'd, 'La belle dame sans mercy'.
33

22 And the long carpets rose along the gusty floor.
40

23 And they are gone: aye, ages long ago
These lovers fled away into the storm.
42

24 The Beadsman, after thousand aves told,
For aye unsought-for slept among his ashes cold.

25 Dry your eyes—O dry your eyes,
For I was taught in Paradise
To ease my breast of melodies.
Fairy's Song

26 Fanatics have their dreams, wherewith they weave
A paradise for a sect.
The Fall of Hyperion, l.1

27 'None can usurp this height', return'd that shade,
'But those to whom the miseries of the world
Are misery, and will not let them rest.'
l.147

28 The poet and the dreamer are distinct,
Diverse, sheer opposite, antipodes.
The one pours out a balm upon the world,
The other vexes it.
l.199

29 Ever let the fancy roam,
Pleasure never is at home.
Fancy, l.1

30 O sweet Fancy! let her loose;
Summer's joys are spoilt by use.
l.9

31 Where's the cheek that doth not fade,
Too much gaz'd at? Where's the maid
Whose lip mature is ever new?
l.69

32   Where's the face
One would meet in every place?
l.73

33 Deep in the shady sadness of a vale
Far sunken from the healthy breath of morn,
Far from the fiery noon, and eve's one star,

Sat gray-hair'd Saturn, quiet as a stone.
Hyperion, bk.i, l.1

1   No stir of air was there,
Not so much life as on a summer's day
Robs not one light seed from the feather'd grass,
But where the dead leaf fell, there did it rest.
l.7

2   The Naiad 'mid her reeds
Press'd her cold finger closer to her lips.
l.13

3 That large utterance of the early Gods.
l.51

4 O aching time! O moments big as years!
l.64

5 As when, upon a trancèd summer-night,
Those green-rob'd senators of mighty woods,
Tall oaks, branch-charmèd by the earnest stars,
Dream, and so dream all night without a stir.
l.72

6   Sometimes eagle's wings,
Unseen before by Gods or wondering men,
Darken'd the place.
l.182

7 And still they were the same bright, patient stars.
l.353

8 Knowledge enormous makes a God of me.
bk.iii, l.113

9 Why were they proud? again we ask aloud,
Why in the name of Glory were they proud?
Isabella, 16

10 So the two brothers and their murder'd man
        Rode past fair Florence.
27

11 And she forgot the stars, the moon, the sun,
        And she forgot the blue above the trees,
        And she forgot the dells where waters run,
        And she forgot the chilly autumn breeze;
She had no knowledge when the day was done,
        And the new morn she saw not: but in peace
Hung over her sweet Basil evermore.
53

12   'For cruel 'tis,' said she,
'To steal my Basil-pot away from me.'
62

13   And then there crept
A little noiseless noise among the leaves,
Born of the very sigh that silence heaves.
I Stood Tip-toe upon a Little Hill

14 Here are sweet peas, on tiptoe for a flight.

15 Oh, what can ail thee, Knight at arms
        Alone and palely loitering;
The sedge is wither'd from the lake,
        And no birds sing.
La Belle Dame Sans Merci

16 I see a lily on thy brow,
        With anguish moist and fever dew;
And on thy cheek a fading rose
        Fast withereth too.

I met a lady in the meads
        Full beautiful, a faery's child;
Her hair was long, her foot was light,
        And her eyes were wild.

17 I set her on my pacing steed,
        And nothing else saw all day long;
For sideways would she lean, and sing
        A faery's song.

18 She look'd at me as she did love,
        And made sweet moan.

19 And sure in language strange she said,
        'I love thee true!'

20 And there I shut her wild, wild eyes
        With kisses four.

21   'La belle Dame sans Merci
        Hath thee in thrall!'

I saw their starv'd lips in the gloam
        With horrid warning gapèd wide,
And I awoke, and found me here
        On the cold hill side.

22 She was a gordian shape of dazzling hue,
Vermilion-spotted, golden, green, and blue;
Striped like a zebra, freckled like a pard,
Eyed like a peacock, and all crimson barr'd.
Lamia, pt.i, l.47

23 Real are the dreams of Gods, and smoothly pass
Their pleasures in a long immortal dream.
l.127

24 Love—in a hut, with water and a crust,
Is—Love, forgive us!—cinders, ashes, dust;
Love in a palace is perhaps at last
More grievous torment than a hermit's fast.
pt.ii, l.1

25 That purple-lined palace of sweet sin.
l.31

26 In pale contented sort of discontent.
l.135

27   Do not all charms fly
At the mere touch of cold philosophy?
There was an awful rainbow once in heaven:
We know her woof, her texture; she is given
In the dull catalogue of common things.
Philosophy will clip an Angel's wings.
l.229

28 Souls of poets dead and gone,
What Elysium have ye known,
Happy field or mossy cavern,
Choicer than the Mermaid Tavern?
Have ye tippled drink more fine
Than mine host's Canary wine?
Lines on the Mermaid Tavern

29 Pledging with contented smack
The Mermaid in the Zodiac.

30 This living hand, now warm and capable
Of earnest grasping, would, if it were cold
And in the icy silence of the tomb,
So haunt thy days and chill thy dreaming nights
That thou wouldst wish thine own heart dry of blood
So in my veins red life might stream again,
And thus be conscience-calm'd—see here it is—
I hold it towards you.
Lines Supposed to have been Addressed to Fanny Brawne

31 Bards of Passion and of Mirth,
Ye have left your souls on earth!

Have ye souls in heaven too?
Ode. Written on the blank page before Beaumont and Fletcher's
Fair Maid of the Inn.

1 Where the nightingale doth sing
  Not a senseless, tranced thing,
  But divine melodious truth.

2 Thou still unravish'd bride of quietness,
    Thou foster-child of silence and slow time.
Ode on a Grecian Urn

3   What men or gods are these? What maidens loth?
  What mad pursuit? What struggle to escape?
    What pipes and timbrels? What wild ecstasy?

4 Heard melodies are sweet, but those unheard
    Are sweeter; therefore, ye soft pipes, play on;
  Not to the sensual ear, but, more endear'd,
    Pipe to the spirit ditties of no tone.

5 For ever wilt thou love, and she be fair!

6 For ever piping songs for ever new.

7   For ever warm and still to be enjoy'd,
    For ever panting and for ever young;
  All breathing human passion far above,
    That leaves a heart high-sorrowful and cloy'd,
      A burning forehead, and a parching tongue.

8 Who are these coming to the sacrifice?
    To what green altar, O mysterious priest,
  Lead'st thou that heifer lowing at the skies,
    And all her silken flanks with garlands drest?
  What little town by river or sea shore,
    Or mountain-built with peaceful citadel,
      Is emptied of this folk, this pious morn?

9   O Attic shape! Fair attitude!

10   Thou, silent form, dost tease us out of thought
  As doth eternity: Cold Pastoral!

11 'Beauty is truth, truth beauty,'—that is all
    Ye know on earth, and all ye need to know.

12 Rich in the simple worship of a day.
Ode to May

13 No, no, go not to Lethe, neither twist
    Wolf's-bane, tight-rooted, for its poisonous wine.
Ode on Melancholy

14 Nor let the beetle, nor the death-moth be
    Your mournful Psyche.

15 But when the melancholy fit shall fall
    Sudden from heaven like a weeping cloud,
  That fosters the droop-headed flowers all,
    And hides the green hill in an April shroud;
  Then glut thy sorrow on a morning rose,
    Or on the rainbow of the salt sand-wave,
      Or on the wealth of globèd peonies;
  Or if thy mistress some rich anger shows,
    Emprison her soft hand and let her rave,
      And feed deep, deep upon her peerless eyes.

She dwells with Beauty—Beauty that must die;
    And Joy, whose hand is ever at his lips
Bidding adieu; and aching Pleasure nigh,
    Turning to Poison while the bee-mouth sips:
Ay, in the very temple of delight
    Veil'd Melancholy has her sovran shrine.
      Though seen of none save him whose strenuous
        tongue
Can burst Joy's grape against his palate fine;

His soul shall taste the sadness of her might,
    And be among her cloudy trophies hung.

16 My heart aches, and a drowsy numbness pains
    My sense, as though of hemlock I had drunk.
Ode to a Nightingale

17 'Tis not through envy of thy happy lot,
    But being too happy in thine happiness,—
      That thou, light-winged Dryad of the trees,
        In some melodious plot
  Of beechen green, and shadows numberless,
    Singest of summer in full-throated ease.

18 O, for a draught of vintage! that hath been
    Cool'd a long age in the deep-delved earth,
Tasting of Flora and the country green,
    Dance, and Provençal song, and sunburnt mirth!
O for a beaker full of the warm South,
    Full of the true, the blushful Hippocrene,
      With beaded bubbles winking at the brim,
        And purple-stained mouth;
That I might drink, and leave the world unseen,
    And with thee fade away into the forest dim.

Fade far away, dissolve, and quite forget
    What thou among the leaves hast never known,
The weariness, the fever, and the fret,
  Here, where men sit and hear each other groan.

19   Where youth grows pale, and spectre-thin, and dies.
    Where but to think is to be full of sorrow
      And leaden-eyed despairs.

20 Away! away! for I will fly to thee,
    Not charioted by Bacchus and his pards,
But on the viewless wings of Poesy,
    Though the dull brain perplexes and retards:
Already with thee! tender is the night,
    And haply the Queen-Moon is on her throne,
      Clustered around by all her starry Fays;
        But here there is no light,
Save what from heaven is with the breezes blown
    Through verdurous glooms and winding mossy
      ways.

I cannot see what flowers are at my feet,
    Nor what soft incense hangs upon the boughs.

21   Fast fading violets cover'd up in leaves;
      And mid-May's eldest child,
  The coming musk-rose, full of dewy wine,
    The murmurous haunt of flies on summer eves.

22 Darkling I listen; and, for many a time
    I have been half in love with easeful Death,
Call'd him soft names in many a mused rhyme,
    To take into the air my quiet breath;
Now more than ever seems it rich to die,
    To cease upon the midnight with no pain,
      While thou art pouring forth thy soul abroad
        In such an ecstasy!
Still wouldst thou sing, and I have ears in vain—
    To thy high requiem become a sod.

23 Thou wast not born for death, immortal Bird!
    No hungry generations tread thee down;
The voice I hear this passing night was heard
    In ancient days by emperor and clown:
Perhaps the self-same song that found a path
    Through the sad heart of Ruth, when sick for home,
    She stood in tears amid the alien corn;

The same that oft-times hath
Charm'd magic casements, opening on the foam
Of perilous seas, in faery lands forlorn.

Forlorn! the very word is like a bell
To toll me back from thee to my sole self!
Adieu! the fancy cannot cheat so well
As she is fam'd to do, deceiving elf.
Adieu! adieu! thy plaintive anthem fades
Past the near meadows, over the still stream,
Up the hill-side; and now 'tis buried deep
In the next valley-glades:
Was it a vision, or a waking dream?
Fled is that music:—Do I wake or sleep?

1 'Mid hush'd, cool-rooted flowers, fragrant-eyed,
Blue, silver-white, and budded Tyrian.
Ode to Psyche

2 Nor virgin-choir to make delicious moan
Upon the midnight hour.

3 Yes, I will be thy priest, and build a fane
In some untrodden region of my mind,
Where branched thoughts, new grown with pleasant pain,
Instead of pines shall murmur in the wind.

4 A bright torch, and a casement ope at night,
To let the warm Love in!

5 O fret not after knowledge—I have none,
And yet my song comes native with the warmth.
O fret not after knowledge—I have none,
And yet the Evening listens.
O Thou Whose Face

6 Stop and consider! life is but a day;
A fragile dew-drop on its perilous way
From a tree's summit; a poor Indian's sleep
While his boat hastens to the monstrous steep
Of Montmorenci.
Sleep and Poetry, l.85

7 O for ten years, that I may overwhelm
Myself in poesy; so I may do the deed
That my own soul has to itself decreed.
l.96

8 They sway'd about upon a rocking horse,
And thought it Pegasus.
l.186

9 They shall be accounted poet kings
Who simply tell the most heart-easing things.
l.267

10 I had a dove and the sweet dove died;
And I have thought it died of grieving:
O, what could it grieve for? Its feet were tied,
With a silken thread of my own hand's weaving.
Song

11 Bright star, would I were steadfast as thou art—
Not in lone splendour hung aloft the night
And watching, with eternal lids apart,
Like nature's patient, sleepless Eremite,
The moving waters at their priestlike task
Of pure ablution round earth's human shores.
Sonnets. Bright Star

12 Still, still to hear her tender-taken breath,
And so live ever—or else swoon to death.

13 The day is gone, and all its sweets are gone!
Sweet voice, sweet lips, soft hand, and softer
breast.
The Day Is Gone

14 Four seasons fill the measure of the year;
There are four seasons in the mind of men.
Four Seasons

15 Happy is England! I could be content
To see no other verdure than its own;
To feel no other breezes than are blown
Through its tall woods with high romances blent.
Happy is England!

16 Happy is England, sweet her artless daughters;
Enough their simple loveliness for me.

17 Much have I travell'd in the realms of gold,
And many goodly states and kingdoms seen.
On First Looking into Chapman's Homer

18 Then felt I like some watcher of the skies
When a new planet swims into his ken;
Or like stout Cortez when with eagle eyes
He star'd at the Pacific—and all his men
Look'd at each other with a wild surmise—
Silent, upon a peak in Darien.

19 Mortality
Weighs heavily on me like unwilling sleep.
On Seeing the Elgin Marbles

20 Yet the sweet converse of an innocent mind,
Whose words are images of thought refin'd,
Is my soul's pleasure; and it sure must be
Almost the highest bliss of human-kind,
When to thy haunts two kindred spirits flee.
O Solitude!

21 The poetry of earth is never dead:
When all the birds are faint with the hot sun,
And hide in cooling trees, a voice will run
From hedge to hedge about the new-mown mead.
On the Grasshopper and Cricket

22 It keeps eternal whisperings around
Desolate shores, and with its mighty swell
Gluts twice ten thousand Caverns.
On the Sea

23 O Chatterton! how very sad thy fate!
To Chatterton

24 Other spirits there are standing apart
Upon the forehead of the age to come.
To Haydon, ii

25 Aye on the shores of darkness there is light,
And precipices show untrodden green,
There is a budding morrow in midnight,
There is a triple sight in blindness keen.
To Homer

26 Glory and loveliness have pass'd away.
To Leigh Hunt. Dedication of *Poems*, 1817

27 To one who has been long in city pent;
'Tis very sweet to look into the fair
And open face of heaven.
To One Who Has Been Long

28 O soft embalmer of the still midnight,
Shutting, with careful fingers and benign,
Our gloom-pleas'd eyes.
To Sleep

29 Turn the key deftly in the oiled wards,
And seal the hushed Casket of my Soul.

30 When I have fears that I may cease to be

Before my pen has glean'd my teeming brain.
When I Have Fears

1 When I behold upon the night's starr'd face,
Huge cloudy symbols of a high romance.

2   Then on the shore
Of the wide world I stand alone, and think
Till love and fame to nothingness do sink.

3 In a drear-nighted December,
    Too happy, happy tree,
Thy branches ne'er remember
    Their green felicity.
Stanzas

4 But were there ever any
    Writh'd not at passing joy?
To know the change and feel it,
When there is none to heal it,
    Nor numbed sense to steel it,
    Was never said in rhyme.

5 Season of mists and mellow fruitfulness,
    Close bosom-friend of the maturing sun;
Conspiring with him how to load and bless
    With fruit the vines that round the thatch-eaves run.
To Autumn

6 Who hath not seen thee oft amid thy store?
    Sometimes whoever seeks abroad may find
Thee sitting careless on a granary floor,
    Thy hair soft-lifted by the winnowing wind;
Or on a half-reap'd furrow sound asleep,
    Drows'd with the fume of poppies, while thy hook
    Spares the next swath and all its twined flowers.

7 Where are the songs of Spring? Ay, where are they?
    Think not of them, thou hast thy music too.

8 Then in a wailful choir the small gnats mourn
    Among the river sallows, borne aloft
    Or sinking as the light wind lives or dies.

9 The red-breast whistles from a garden-croft;
    And gathering swallows twitter in the skies.

10 Woman! when I behold thee flippant, vain,
    Inconstant, childish, proud, and full of fancies.
Woman! When I Behold Thee

11 I remember your saying that you had notions of a good
Genius presiding over you. I have of late had the same
thought—for things which [I] do half at random are
afterwards confirmed by my judgment in a dozen
features of propriety. Is it too daring to fancy
Shakespeare this Presider?
Letters. To B.R. Haydon, 10/11 May 1817

12 I am quite disgusted with literary men.
To Benjamin Bailey, 8 Oct. 1817

13 A long poem is a test of invention which I take to be
the Polar star of poetry, as fancy is the sails, and
imagination the rudder.

14 A man should have the fine point of his soul taken off
to become fit for this world.
To J.H. Reynolds, 22 Nov. 1817

15 I am certain of nothing but the holiness of the heart's
affections and the truth of imagination—what the
imagination seizes as beauty must be truth—whether it
existed before or not.
To Benjamin Bailey, 22 Nov. 1817

16 I have never yet been able to perceive how anything

can be known for truth by consecutive reasoning—and
yet it must be.

17 O for a life of sensations rather than of thoughts!

18 The excellency of every art is its intensity, capable of
making all disagreeables evaporate, from their being in
close relationship with beauty and truth.
To G. and T. Keats, 21 Dec. 1817

19 Negative Capability, that is, when a man is capable of
being in uncertainties, mysteries, doubts, without any
irritable reaching after fact and reason—Coleridge, for
instance, would let go by a fine isolated verisimilitude
caught from the Penetralium of mystery, from being
incapable of remaining content with half-knowledge.

20 There is nothing stable in the world; uproar's your
only music.
To G. and T. Keats, 13 Jan. 1818

21 So I do believe...that works of genius are the first
things in this world.

22 For the sake of a few fine imaginative or domestic
passages, are we to be bullied into a certain philosophy
engendered in the whims of an egotist.
To J.H. Reynolds, 3 Feb. 1818

23 We hate poetry that has a palpable design upon
us—and if we do not agree, seems to put its hand in its
breeches pocket. Poetry should be great and
unobtrusive, a thing which enters into one's soul, and
does not startle or amaze it with itself, but with its
subject.

24 Poetry should surprise by a fine excess, and not by
singularity; it should strike the reader as a wording of
his own highest thoughts, and appear almost a
remembrance. Its touches of beauty should never be
half-way, thereby making the reader breathless, instead
of content. The rise, the progress, the setting of
imagery should, like the sun, come natural to him.
To John Taylor, 27 Feb. 1818

25 If poetry comes not as naturally as leaves to a tree it
had better not come at all.

26 I have good reason to be content, for thank God I can
read and perhaps understand Shakespeare to his
depths.

27 Scenery is fine—but human nature is finer.
To Benjamin Bailey, 13 Mar. 1818

28 It is impossible to live in a country which is
continually under hatches...Rain! Rain! Rain!
To J.H. Reynolds, 10 Apr. 1818 (from Devon)

29 I have been hovering for some time between the
exquisite sense of the luxurious and a love for
philosophy—were I calculated for the former I should
be glad—but as I am not I shall turn all my soul to the
latter.
To John Taylor, 24 Apr. 1818

30 Axioms in philosophy are not axioms until they are
proved upon our pulses: we read fine things but never
feel them to the full until we have gone the same steps
as the author.
To J.H. Reynolds, 3 May 1818

31 I am in that temper that if I were under water I would
scarcely kick to come to the top.
To Benjamin Bailey, 21 May 1818

32 Were it in my choice I would reject a petrarchal

coronation—on account of my dying day, and because women have cancers.
To Benjamin Bailey, 10 June 1818

1 I do think better of womankind than to suppose they care whether Mister John Keats five feet high likes them or not.
To Benjamin Bailey, 18 July 1818

2 I wish I could say Tom was any better. His identity presses upon me so all day that I am obliged to go out.
Of his youngest brother. To C.W. Dilke, 21 Sept. 1818

3 I never was in love—yet the voice and the shape of a woman has haunted me these two days.
To J.H. Reynolds, 22 Sept. 1818

4 There is an awful warmth about my heart like a load of immortality.

5 In Endymion, I leaped headlong into the sea, and thereby have become better acquainted with the soundings, the quicksands, and the rocks, than if I had stayed upon the green shore, and piped a silly pipe, and took tea and comfortable advice.
To James Hessey, 9 Oct. 1818

6 I would sooner fail than not be among the greatest.

7 As to the poetical character itself (I mean that sort of which, if I am anything, I am a member; that sort distinguished from the Wordsworthian or egotistical sublime; which is a thing *per se* and stands alone) it is not itself—it has no self...It has as much delight in conceiving an Iago as an Imogen.
To Richard Woodhouse, 27 Oct. 1818

8 A poet is the most unpoetical of anything in existence, because he has no identity; he is continually informing [?] and filling some other body.

9 I think I shall be among the English Poets after my death.
To George and Georgiana Keats, 14 Oct. 1818

10 The roaring of the wind is my wife and the stars through the window pane are my children. The mighty abstract idea I have of beauty in all things stifles the more divided and minute domestic happiness...The opinion I have of the generality of women—who appear to me as children to whom I would rather give a sugar plum than my time, forms a barrier against matrimony which I rejoice in.

11 I never can feel certain of any truth but from a clear perception of its beauty.
To George and Georgiana Keats, 16 Dec. 1818–4 Jan. 1819

12 A man's life of any worth is a continual allegory.
To George and Georgiana Keats, 18 Feb. 1819

13 Shakespeare led a life of allegory: his works are the comments on it.

14 I have come to this resolution—never to write for the sake of writing or making a poem, but from running over with any little knowledge or experience which many years of reflection may perhaps give me; otherwise I shall be dumb.
To B.R. Haydon, 8 Mar. 1819

15 It is true that in the height of enthusiasm I have been cheated into some fine passages: but that is not the thing.

16 I should like the window to open onto the Lake of Geneva—and there I'd sit and read all day like the

picture of somebody reading.
To Fanny Keats, 13 Mar. 1819

17 I go among the fields and catch a glimpse of a stoat or a fieldmouse peeping out of the withered grass—The creature hath a purpose and its eyes are bright with it—I go amongst the buildings of a city and I see a man hurrying along—to what? The Creature has a purpose and his eyes are bright with it.
To George and Georgiana Keats, 19 Mar. 1819

18 Nothing ever becomes real till it is experienced—even a proverb is no proverb to you till your life has illustrated it.

19 Call the world if you please 'The vale of Soul-making'.

20 I have met with women whom I really think would like to be married to a poem, and to be given away by a novel.
To Fanny Brawne, 8 July 1819

21 I have two luxuries to brood over in my walks, your loveliness and the hour of my death. O that I could have possession of them both in the same minute.
To Fanny Brawne, 25 July 1819

22 My friends should drink a dozen of Claret on my Tomb.
To Benjamin Bailey, 14 Aug. 1819

23 I am convinced more and more day by day that fine writing is next to fine doing, the top thing in the world.
To. J.H. Reynolds, 24 Aug. 1819

24 Give me books, fruit, french wine and fine weather and a little music out of doors, played by somebody I do not know.
To Fanny Keats, 29 Aug. 1819

25 All clean and comfortable I sit down to write.
To George and Georgiana Keats, 17 Sept. 1819

26 The only means of strengthening one's intellect is to make up one's mind about nothing—to let the mind be a thoroughfare for all thoughts. Not a select party.

27 You have ravished me away by a power I cannot resist; and yet I could resist till I saw you; and even since I have seen you I have endeavoured often 'to reason against the reason of my Love'.
To Fanny Brawne, 13 Oct. 1819

28 'If I should die', said I to myself, 'I have left no immortal work behind me—nothing to make my friends proud of my memory—but I have loved the principle of beauty in all things, and if I had had time I would have made myself remembered.'
To Fanny Brawne, Feb. 1820?

29 I long to believe in immortality...If I am destined to be happy with you here—how short is the longest life. I wish to believe in immortality—I wish to live with you for ever.
To Fanny Brawne, July 1820

30 I wish you could invent some means to make me at all happy without you. Every hour I am more and more concentrated in you; every thing else tastes like chaff in my mouth.
To Fanny Brawne, Aug. 1820

31 You, I am sure, will forgive me for sincerely remarking that you might curb your magnanimity, and be more of an artist, and load every rift of your subject

with ore.
To Shelley, Aug. 1820

1 He already seemed to feel the flowers growing over
him.
Words reported by Severn. W. Sharp, *Life and Letters of Severn,*
ch.4

2 I shall soon be laid in the quiet grave—thank God for
the quiet grave—O! I can feel the cold earth upon
me—the daisies growing over me—O for this
quiet—it will be my first.
Joseph Severn, letter to John Taylor, 6 Mar. 1821

3 Here lies one whose name was writ in water.
Epitaph. Lord Houghton, *Life of Keats,* ii.91

JOHN KEBLE 1792–1866

4 The trivial round, the common task,
Would furnish all we ought to ask;
Room to deny ourselves; a road
To bring us, daily, nearer God.
The Christian Year (1827). **Morning**

5 There is a book, who runs may read,
    Which heavenly truth imparts,
And all the lore its scholars need,
    Pure eyes and Christian hearts.
Septuagesima

6 The voice that breathed o'er Eden.
Holy Matrimony

GEORGE KEITH, 5th EARL MARISCHAL
1553–1623

7 They haif said: Quhat say they? Lat thame say.
Motto of the Earls Marischal of Scotland, inscribed at Marischal
College, founded by the fifth Earl at Aberdeen in 1593. A
similarly defiant motto in Greek has been found engraved in
remains from classical antiquity.

FRANK B. KELLOGG 1856–1937

8 The high contracting parties solemnly declare in the
names of their respective peoples that they condemn
recourse to war for the solution of international
controversies, and renounce it as an instrument of
national policy in their relations with one another. The
high contracting parties agree that the settlement or
solution of all disputes or conflicts of whatever nature
or of whatever origin they may be, which may rise
among them, shall never be sought except by pacific
means.
Peace Pact, signed at Paris, 27 Aug. 1928

THOMAS À KEMPIS
See THOMAS

BISHOP THOMAS KEN 1637–1711

9 Teach me to live, that I may dread
The grave as little as my bed.
Evening Hymn. Glory to Thee My God This Night

JOHN FITZGERALD KENNEDY 1917–1963

10 And so, my fellow Americans: ask not what your
country can do for you—ask what you can do for your
country. My fellow citizens of the world: ask not what
America will do for you, but what together we can do

for the freedom of man.
Inaugural address, 20 Jan. 1961. Not the first use of this form of
words: a similiar exhortation may be found in the funeral oration
for John Greenleaf Whittier.

11 All free men, wherever they may live, are citizens of
Berlin. And therefore, as a free man, I take pride in
the words *Ich bin ein Berliner.*
Speech at City Hall, West Berlin, 26 June 1963

LADY CAROLINE KEPPEL 1735–?

12 What's this dull town to me?
    Robin's not near.
He whom I wished to see,
    Wished for to hear;
Where's all the joy and mirth
Made life a heaven on earth?
O! they're all fled with thee,
    Robin Adair.
Robin Adair

RALPH KETTELL 1563–1643

13 Here is Hey for Garsington! and Hey for Cuddesdon!
and Hey Hockley! but here's nobody cries, Hey for
God Almighty!
Sermon at Garsington Revel. Aubrey, *Brief Lives*

FRANCIS SCOTT KEY 1779–1843

14 'Tis the star-spangled banner; O long may it wave
O'er the land of the free, and the home of the brave!
The Star-Spangled Banner (1814)

J.M. KEYNES 1883–1946

15 I do not know which makes a man more
conservative—to know nothing but the present, or
nothing but the past.
The End of Laisser-Faire (1926), I

16 Marxian Socialism must always remain a portent to the
historians of Opinion—how a doctrine so illogical and
so dull can have exercised so powerful and enduring an
influence over the minds of men, and, through them,
the events of history.
III

17 The important thing for Government is not to do
things which individuals are doing already, and to do
them a little better or a little worse; but to do those
things which at present are not done at all.
IV. See 365:22, 549:31

18 I think that Capitalism, wisely managed, can probably
be made more efficient for attaining economic ends
than any alternative system yet in sight, but that in
itself it is in many ways extremely objectionable.
V

19 This goat-footed bard, this half-human visitor to our
age from the hag-ridden magic and enchanted woods
of Celtic antiquity. [Lloyd George.]
Essays and Sketches in Biography (1933)

20 Practical men, who believe themselves to be quite
exempt from any intellectual influences, are usually
the slaves of some defunct economist. Madmen in
authority, who hear voices in the air, are distilling
their frenzy from some academic scribbler of a few

years back.
The General Theory of Employment Interest and Money
(1936), ch.24.v

1 There are the *Trade-Unionists*, once the oppressed,
now the tyrants, whose selfish and sectional
pretensions need to be bravely opposed.
Liberalism and Labour (1926)

2 For him [Keynes] the short run was much more
significant than the long run—that long run in which,
as he used to say, 'we are all dead'.
A.C. Pigou, *Proceedings of the British Academy*, v.32, p.13

[ALFRED] JOYCE KILMER 1886–1918

3 I think that I shall never see
A poem lovely as a tree.
Trees (1914)

4 Poems are made by fools like me,
But only God can make a tree.

REVD. FRANCIS KILVERT 1840–1879

5 Of all noxious animals, too, the most noxious is a
tourist. And of all tourists the most vulgar, ill-bred,
offensive and loathsome is the British tourist.
Diary, 5 Apr. 1870

6 The Vicar of St Ives says the smell of fish there is
sometimes so terrific as to stop the church clock.
21 July 1870

7 An angel satyr walks these hills.
20 June 1871

8 It is a fine thing to be out on the hills alone. A man
can hardly be a beast or a fool alone on a great
mountain.
On the Black Mountain in Wales. 29 May 1871

BENJAMIN FRANKLIN KING 1857–1894

9 Nothing to do but work,
Nothing to eat but food,
Nothing to wear but clothes
To keep one from going nude.
The Pessimist

10 Nothing to breathe but air,
Quick as a flash 'tis gone;
Nowhere to fall but off,
Nowhere to stand but on!

BISHOP HENRY KING 1592–1669

11 Sleep on, my Love, in thy cold bed,
Never to be disquieted!
My last good night! Thou wilt not wake
Till I thy fate shall overtake:
Till age, or grief, or sickness must
Marry my body to that dust
It so much loves; and fill the room
My heart keeps empty in thy tomb.
The Exequy

12 But hark! My pulse like a soft drum
Beats my approach, tells thee I come.

13 We that did nothing study but the way
To love each other, with which thoughts the day
Rose with delight to us, and with them set,

Must learn the hateful art, how to forget.
The Surrender

REVD. MARTIN LUTHER KING 1929–1968

14 A riot is at bottom the language of the unheard.
Chaos or Community (1967), ch.4

15 I have a dream that one day this nation will rise up,
live out the true meaning of its creed: we hold these
truths to be self-evident, that all men are created
equal.
Washington, 27 Aug. 1963. The phrase 'I have a dream' was used
by him in other speeches during the summer of that year.

CHARLES KINGSLEY 1819–1875

16 Airly Beacon, Airly Beacon;
Oh the pleasant sight to see
Shires and towns from Airly Beacon,
While my love climb'd up to me!
Airly Beacon

17 Airly Beacon, Airly Beacon;
Oh the weary haunt for me,
All alone on Airly Beacon,
With his baby on my knee!

18 The merry brown hares came leaping
Over the crest of the hill,
Where the clover and corn lay sleeping
Under the moonlight still.
The Bad Squire

19 Be good, sweet maid, and let who can be clever;
Do lovely things, not dream them, all day long;
And so make Life, and Death, and that For Ever,
One grand sweet song.
A Farewell. To C.E.G.

20 Leave to Robert Browning
Beggars, fleas, and vines;
Leave to squeamish Ruskin
Popish Apennines,
Dirty stones of Venice
And his gas-lamps seven;
We've the stones of Snowdon
And the lamps of heaven.
Letter to Thomas Hughes

21 What we can we will be,
Honest Englishmen.
Do the work that's nearest,
Though it's dull at whiles,
Helping, when we meet them,
Lame dogs over stiles.

22 Welcome, wild North-easter!
Shame it is to see
Odes to every zephyr;
Ne'er a verse to thee.
Ode to the North-East Wind

23 'Tis the hard grey weather
Breeds hard English men.

24 Come; and strong within us
Stir the Vikings' blood;
Bracing brain and sinew;
Blow, thou wind of God!

25 'O Mary, go and call the cattle home,
And call the cattle home,
And call the cattle home,

Across the sands of Dee.'
The western wind was wild and dank with foam,
And all alone went she.
The Sands of Dee

1 The western tide crept up along the sand,
And o'er and o'er the sand,
And round and round the sand,
As far as eye could see.
The rolling mist came down and hid the land:
And never home came she.

2 Three fishers went sailing away to the west,
Away to the west as the sun went down;
Each thought on the woman who loved him the best,
And the children stood watching them out of the town.
The Three Fishers

3 For men must work, and women must weep,
And there's little to earn, and many to keep,
Though the harbour bar be moaning.

4 I once had a sweet little doll, dears
The prettiest doll in the world;
Her cheeks were so red and so white, dears,
And her hair was so charmingly curled.
Songs from *The Water Babies* (1863). **My Little Doll**

5 When all the world is young, lad,
And all the trees are green;
And every goose a swan, lad,
And every lass a queen;
Then hey for boot and horse, lad,
And round the world away:
Young blood must have its course, lad,
And every dog his day.
Young and Old

6 To be discontented with the divine discontent, and to
be ashamed with the noble shame, is the very germ and
first upgrowth of all virtue.
Health and Education (1874), p.20

7 We have used the Bible as if it was a constable's
handbook—an opium-dose for keeping beasts of
burden patient while they are being overloaded.
Letters to the Chartists, no.2. See 333:6

8 He did not know that a keeper is only a poacher turned
outside in, and a poacher a keeper turned inside out.
The Water Babies (1863), ch.1

9 As thorough an Englishman as ever coveted his
neighbour's goods.
ch.4

10 And still the lobster held on.
ch.5

11 Mrs Bedonebyasyoudid is coming.

12 The loveliest fairy in the world; and her name is Mrs
Doasyouwouldbedoneby.

13 All the butterflies and cockyolybirds would fly past
me.
ch.8

14 Till the coming of the Cocqcigrues.

15 More ways of killing a cat than choking her with
cream.
Westward Ho! (1855), ch.20

16 Eustace is a man no longer; he is become a thing, a
tool, a Jesuit.
ch.23

17 Truth, for its own sake, had never been a virtue with

the Roman clergy.
Review of Froude's *History of England*, in *Macmillan's
Magazine*, Jan. 1864

18 Some say that the age of chivalry is past, that the
spirit of romance is dead. The age of chivalry is never
past, so long as there is a wrong left unredressed on
earth.
Mrs C. Kingsley, *Life* (1879), vol.ii, ch.28

HUGH KINGSMILL 1889–1949

19 What, still alive at twenty-two,
A clean upstanding chap like you?
Sure, if your throat 'tis hard to slit,
Slit your girl's, and swing for it.
Two Poems after A.E. Housman, 1

20 But bacon's not the only thing
That's cured by hanging from a string.

21 'Tis Summer Time on Bredon,
And now the farmers swear;
The cattle rise and listen
In valleys far and near,
And blush at what they hear.

But when the mists in autumn
On Bredon top are thick,
The happy hymns of farmers
Go up from fold and rick,
The cattle then are sick.
2

RUDYARD KIPLING 1865–1936

22 When you've shouted 'Rule Britannia', when you've
sung 'God save the Queen',
When you've finished killing Kruger with your mouth.
The Absent-Minded Beggar

23 He's an absent-minded beggar, and his weaknesses are
great—
But we and Paul must take him as we find him—
He's out on active service, wiping something off a
slate—
And he's left a lot of little things behind him!

24 Duke's son—cook's son—son of a hundred Kings—
(Fifty thousand horse and foot going to Table Bay!)

25 Pass the hat for your credit's sake, and
pay—pay—pay!

26 England's on the anvil—hear the hammers ring—
Clanging from the Severn to the Tyne!
Never was a blacksmith like our Norman King—
England's being hammered, hammered, hammered
into line!
The Anvil

27 Oh, East is East, and West is West, and never the
twain shall meet,
Till Earth and Sky stand presently at God's great
Judgment Seat;
But there is neither East nor West, Border, nor Breed,
nor Birth,
When two strong men stand face to face, though they
come from the ends of earth!
The Ballad of East and West

28 And the talk slid north, and the talk slid south,
With the sliding puffs from the hookah-mouth.
Four things greater than all things are,—

Women and Horses and Power and War.
Ballad of the King's Jest

1 It was not part of their blood,
   It came to them very late
   With long arrears to make good,
   When the English began to hate.
The Beginnings

2 Ah! What avails the classic bent
   And what the cultured word,
   Against the undoctored incident
   That actually occurred?
The Benefactors. See 308:26

3 And a woman is only a woman, but a good cigar is a
   Smoke.
The Betrothed

4 'Oh, where are you going to, all you Big Steamers,
   With England's own coal, up and down the salt seas?'
   'We are going to fetch you your bread and your butter,
   Your beef, pork, and mutton, eggs, apples, and
   cheese.'
Big Steamers

5 'For the bread that you eat and the biscuits you nibble,
   The sweets that you suck and the joints that you carve,
   They are brought to you daily by all us Big Steamers—
   And if any one hinders our coming you'll starve!'

6 We're foot—slog—slog—slog—sloggin' over Africa—
   Foot—foot—foot—foot—sloggin' over Africa—
   (Boots—boots—boots—boots—movin' up an' down
   again!)
   There's no discharge in the war!
Boots. See 55:25

7 I've a head like a concertina, I've a tongue like a
   button-stick,
   I've a mouth like an old potato, and I'm more than a
   little sick,
   But I've had my fun o' the Corp'ral's Guard; I've
   made the cinders fly,
   And I'm here in the Clink for a thundering drink and
   blacking the Corporal's eye.
Cells

8 Take of English earth as much
   As either hand may rightly clutch.
   In the taking of it breathe
   Prayer for all who lie beneath...
   Lay that earth upon thy heart,
   And thy sickness shall depart!
A Charm

9 These were our children who died for our lands...
   But who shall return us the children?
The Children

10 Land of our birth, we pledge to thee
   Our love and toil in the years to be;
   When we are grown and take our place,
   As men and women with our race.
The Children's Song

11 That we, with Thee, may walk uncowed
   By fear or favour of the crowd.

12 Teach us delight in simple things,
   And mirth that has no bitter springs;
   Forgiveness free of evil done,
   And love to all men 'neath the sun!

13 High noon behind the tamarisks—the sun is hot above
   us—

As at Home the Christmas Day is breaking wan.
   They will drink our healths at dinner—those who tell
   us how they love us,
   And forget us till another year be gone!
Christmas in India

14 We must go back with Policeman Day—
   Back from the City of Sleep!
The City of Sleep

15 Gold is for the mistress—silver for the maid—
   Copper for the craftsman cunning at his trade.
   'Good!' said the Baron, sitting in his hall,
   'But Iron—Cold Iron—is master of them all.'
Cold Iron

16 We know that the tail must wag the dog, for the horse
   is drawn by the cart;
   But the Devil whoops, as he whooped of old: 'It's
   clever, but is it Art?'
The Conundrum of the Workshops

17 By the favour of God we might know as much—as
   our father Adam knew!

18 It is always a temptation to a rich and lazy nation,
   To puff and look important and to say:-
   'Though we know we should defeat you, we have not
   the time to meet you.
   We will therefore pay you cash to go away.'

   And that is called paying the Dane-geld;
   But we've proved it again and again,
   That if once you have paid him the Dane-geld
   You never get rid of the Dane.
Dane-Geld

19 'What are the bugles blowin' for?' said
   Files-on-Parade.
   'To turn you out, to turn you out,' the
   Colour-Sergeant said.
Danny Deever

20 'For they're hangin' Danny Deever, you can hear the
   Dead March play,
   The Regiment's in 'ollow square—they're hangin' 'im
   to-day;
   They've taken of 'is buttons off an' cut 'is stripes
   away,
   An' they're hangin' Danny Deever in the mornin'.'

21 The 'eathen in 'is blindness bows down to wood an'
   stone;
   'E don't obey no orders unless they is 'is own;
   'E keeps 'is side-arms awful: 'e leaves 'em all about,
   An' then comes up the Regiment an' pokes the 'eathen
   out.
The 'Eathen. See 244:6

22 The 'eathen in 'is blindness must end where 'e began,
   But the backbone of the Army is the
   Non-commissioned man!

23 Who are neither children nor Gods, but men in a world
   of men!
England's Answer

24 Winds of the World, give answer! They are
   whimpering to and fro—
   And what should they know of England who only
   England know?
The English Flag

25 I could not look on Death, which being known,

Men led me to him, blindfold and alone.
Epitaphs of the War. The Coward

1 But it never really mattered till the English grew
   polite.
   Et Dona Ferentes

2 'Something hidden. Go and find it. Go and look
   behind the Ranges—
   Something lost behind the Ranges. Lost and waiting
   for you. Go.'
   The Explorer

3 Yes, your 'Never-never country'—yes, your 'edge of
   cultivation'
   And 'No sense in going further'—till I crossed the
   range to see.
   God forgive me! No *I* didn't. It's God's present to our
   nation.
   Anybody might have found it, but—His whisper
   came to Me!

4 When the Himalayan peasant meets the he-bear in his
   pride,
   He shouts to scare the monster, who will often turn
   aside.
   But the she-bear thus accosted rends the peasant tooth
   and nail
   For the female of the species is more deadly than the
   male.
   The Female of the Species

5 Man propounds negotiations, Man accepts the
   compromise.
   Very rarely will he squarely push the logic of a fact
   To its ultimate conclusion in unmitigated act.

6 For all we have and are,
   For all our children's fate,
   Stand up and take the war.
   The Hun is at the gate!
   For All We Have and Are

7 There is but one task for all—
   One life for each to give.
   What stands if Freedom fall?
   Who dies if England live?

8 So 'ere's to you, Fuzzy-Wuzzy, at your 'ome in the
   Soudan;
   You're a pore benighted 'eathen but a first-class
   fightin' man;
   An' 'ere's to you, Fuzzy-Wuzzy, with your 'ayrick
   'ead of 'air—
   You big black boundin' beggar—for you broke a
   British square!
   Fuzzy-Wuzzy

9 'E's all 'ot sand an' ginger when alive,
   An' 'e's generally shammin' when 'e's dead.

10 We're poor little lambs who've lost our way,
       Baa! Baa! Baa!
    We're little black sheep who've gone astray,
       Baa-aa-aa!
    Gentleman-rankers out on the spree,
    Damned from here to Eternity,
    God ha' mercy on such as we,
       Baa! Yah! Bah!
    Gentleman-Rankers

11 We have done with Hope and Honour, we are lost to
    Love and Truth,
    We are dropping down the ladder rung by rung;

And the measure of our torment is the measure of our
   youth.
God help us, for we knew the worst too young!
See 113:7

12 Our England is a garden that is full of stately views,
   Of borders, beds and shrubberies and lawns and
      avenues,
   With statues on the terraces and peacocks strutting by;
   But the Glory of the Garden lies in more than meets
      the eye.
   The Glory of the Garden

13 The Glory of the Garden it abideth not in words.

14 Our England is a garden, and such gardens are not
      made
   By singing:—'Oh, how beautiful!' and sitting in the
      shade,
   While better men than we go out and start their
      working lives
   At grubbing weeds from gravel paths with broken
      dinner-knives.

15 Oh, Adam was a gardener, and God who made him
      sees
   That half a proper gardener's work is done upon his
      knees,
   So when your work is finished, you can wash your
      hands and pray
   For the Glory of the Garden, that it may not pass
      away!
   And the Glory of the Garden it shall never pass away!

16 In the Carboniferous Epoch we were promised
      abundance for all,
   By robbing selected Peter to pay for collective Paul;
   But though we had plenty of money, there was nothing
      our money could buy,
   And the Gods of the Copybook Headings said: *'If you
   don't work, you die'.*
   The Gods of the Copybook Headings

17 The uniform 'e wore
   Was nothin' much before,
   An' rather less than 'arf o' that be'ind.
   Gunga Din

18 An' for all 'is dirty 'ide
   'E was white, clear white, inside
   When 'e went to tend the wounded under fire!

19 So I'll meet 'im later on
   At the place where 'e is gone—
   Where it's always double drills and no canteen.
   'E'll be squattin' on the coals
   Givin' drink to poor damned souls,
   An' I'll get a swig in Hell from Gunga Din.

20 Though I've belted you an' flayed you,
   By the livin' Gawd that made you,
   You're a better man than I am, Gunga Din!

21 What is a woman that you forsake her,
   And the hearth-fire and the home-acre,
   To go with the old grey Widow-maker?
   Harp Song of the Dane Women

22 If you can keep your head when all about you
      Are losing theirs and blaming it on you,
   If you can trust yourself when all men doubt you,
      But make allowance for their doubting too;
   If you can wait and not be tired by waiting,
      Or being lied about, don't deal in lies,

Or being hated, don't give way to hating,
   And yet don't look too good, nor talk too wise:

If you can dream—and not make dreams your master;
   If you can think—and not make thoughts your aim;
If you can meet with Triumph and Disaster
   And treat those two impostors just the same.
If—

1 If you can make one heap of all your winnings
      And risk it on one turn of pitch-and-toss,
   And lose, and start again at your beginnings
      And never breathe a word about your loss.

2 If you can talk with crowds and keep your virtue,
      Or walk with Kings—nor lose the common touch,
   If neither foes nor loving friends can hurt you,
      If all men count with you, but none too much;
   If you can fill the unforgiving minute
      With sixty seconds' worth of distance run,
   Yours is the Earth and everything that's in it,
      And—which is more—you'll be a Man, my son!

3 There are nine and sixty ways of constructing tribal
      lays,
   And—every—single—one—of—them—is—right!
   In the Neolithic Age

4 Then ye returned to your trinkets; then ye contented
      your souls
   With the flannelled fools at the wicket or the muddied
      oafs at the goals.
   The Islanders

5 He wrote that monarchs were divine,
      And left a son who—proved they weren't!
   James I

6 For agony and spoil
      Of nations beat to dust,
   For poisoned air and tortured soil
      And cold, commanded lust,
   And every secret woe
      The shuddering waters saw—
   Willed and fulfilled by high and low—
      Let them relearn the Law.
   Justice. October, 1918

7 Yes, weekly from Southampton,
      Great steamers, white and gold,
   Go rolling down to Rio
      (Roll down—roll down to Rio!).
   And I'd like to roll to Rio
      Some day before I'm old!
   Just-So Stories (1902). **Beginning of the Armadilloes**

8 I've never seen a Jaguar,
      Nor yet an Armadill-
   o dilloing in his armour,
      And I s'pose I never will.

9 The Camel's hump is an ugly lump
      Which well you may see at the Zoo;
   But uglier yet is the Hump we get
      From having too little to do.
   How the Camel Got His Hump

10 We get the Hump—
      Cameelious Hump—
   The Hump that is black and blue!

11 The cure for this ill is not to sit still,
      Or frowst with a book by the fire;
   But to take a large hoe and a shovel also,
      And dig till you gently perspire.

12 I keep six honest serving-men
      (They taught me all I knew);
   Their names are What and Why and When
      And How and Where and Who.
   I keep six honest serving-men

13 Old Man Kangaroo first, Yellow-Dog Dingo behind.
   Sing-Song of Old Man Kangaroo

14 For Allah created the English mad—the maddest of all
      mankind!
   Kitchener's School

15 But the things you will learn from the Yellow an'
      Brown,
   They'll 'elp you a lot with the White!
   The Ladies

16 An' I learned about women from 'er!

17 I've taken my fun where I've found it,
      An' now I must pay for my fun,
   For the more you 'ave known o' the others
      The less will you settle to one;
   An' the end of it's sittin' and thinkin',
      An' dreamin' Hell-fires to see.
   So be warned by my lot (which I know you will not),
      An' learn about women from me!

18 For the Colonel's Lady an' Judy O'Grady
      Are sisters under their skins!

19 And Ye take mine honour from me if Ye take away
      the sea!
   The Last Chantey

20 Now this is the Law of the Jungle—as old and as true
      as the sky;
   And the Wolf that shall keep it may prosper, but the
      Wolf that shall break it must die.
   The Law of the Jungle

21 It was our fault, and our very great fault—and now we
      must turn it to use.
   We have forty million reasons for failure, but not a
      single excuse.
   So the more we work and the less we talk the better
      results we shall get.
   We have had an Imperial lesson; it may make us an
      Empire yet!
   The Lesson

22 And that's how it all began, my dears,
      And that's how it all began!
   The Light that Failed (1890), chapter heading

23 There's a whisper down the field where the year has
      shot her yield,
      And the ricks stand grey to the sun,
   Singing:—'Over then, come over, for the bee has quit
      the clover,
      And your English summer's done.'

   You have heard the beat of the off-shore wind,
      And the thresh of the deep-sea rain;
   You have heard the song—how long? how long?
      Pull out on the trail again!
   Ha' done with the Tents of Shem, dear lass,
      We've seen the seasons through,
   And it's time to turn on the old trail, our own trail, the
      out trail,
   Pull out, pull out, on the Long Trail—the trail that is
      always new!
   The Long Trail

24 It's North you may run to the rime-ringed sun,

Or South to the blind Horn's hate;
Or East all the way into Mississippi Bay,
Or West to the Golden Gate.

1 There be triple ways to take, of the eagle or the snake,
Or the way of a man with a maid;
But the sweetest way to me is a ship's upon the sea
In the heel of the North-East Trade.
See 55:1

2 Lord, Thou hast made this world below the shadow of
a dream,
An', taught by time, I tak' it so—exceptin' always
Steam.
From coupler-flange to spindle-guide I see Thy Hand,
O God—
Predestination in the stride o' yon connectin'-rod.
McAndrew's Hymn

3 Yon's strain, hard strain, o' head an' hand, for though
Thy Power brings
All skill to naught, Ye'll understand a man must think
o' things.

4 Mister McAndrew, don't you think steam spoils
romance at sea?

5 By the old Moulmein Pagoda, lookin' eastward to the
sea,
There's a Burma girl a-settin', and I know she thinks
o' me;
For the wind is in the palm-trees, an' the temple-bells
they say:
'Come you back, you British soldier; come you back
to Mandalay!'
Come you back to Mandalay,
Where the old Flotilla lay:
Can't you 'ear their paddles chunkin' from Rangoon to
Mandalay?
On the road to Mandalay,
Where the flyin'-fishes play,
An' the dawn comes up like thunder outer China 'crost
the Bay!
Mandalay

6 An' I seed her first a-smokin' of a whackin' white
cheroot,
An' a-wastin' Christian kisses on an 'eathen idol's
foot.

7 I am sick o' wastin' leather on these gritty
pavin'-stones,
An' the blasted English drizzle wakes the fever in my
bones;
Tho' I walks with fifty 'ousemaids outer Chelsea to the
Strand,
An' they talks a lot o' lovin', but wot do they
understand?
Beefy face an' grubby 'and—
Law! Wot do they understand?
I've a neater, sweeter maiden in a cleaner, greener
land!

8 Ship me somewheres east of Suez, where the best is
like the worst,
Where there aren't no Ten Commandments, an' a man
can raise a thirst;
For the temple-bells are callin', an' it's there that I
would be—
By the old Moulmein Pagoda, looking lazy at the sea.

9 For a man he must go with a woman, which women
don't understand—
Or the sort that say they can see it, they aren't the
marrying brand.
The 'Mary Gloster'

10 I'm sick of the hired women. I'll kiss my girl on her
lips!

11 Nice while it lasted, an' now it is over—
Tear out your 'eart an' good-bye to your lover!
What's the use o' grievin', when the mother that bore
you
(Mary, pity women!) knew it all before you?
Mary, Pity Women

12 Mines reported in the fairway,
Warn all traffic and detain.
'Sent up *Unity, Claribel, Assyrian, Stormcock,* and
Golden Gain.
Mine Sweepers

13 Good rest to all
That keep the Jungle Law.
Morning Song in the Jungle

14 If I were hanged on the highest hill,
Mother o' mine, O mother o' mine!
I know whose love would follow me still,
Mother o' mine, O mother o' mine!
Mother O' Mine

15 'Have you news of my boy Jack?'
   Not this tide.
'When d'you think that he'll come back?'
   Not with this wind blowing, and this tide.
My Boy Jack

16 The depth and dream of my desire,
The bitter paths wherein I stray—
Thou knowest Who hast made the Fire,
Thou knowest Who hast made the Clay.
My New-cut Ashlar

17 One stone the more swings into place
In that dread Temple of Thy worth.
It is enough that, through Thy Grace,
I saw nought common on Thy Earth.

18 Now it is not good for the Christian's health to hustle
the Aryan brown,
For the Christian riles, and the Aryan smiles, and it
weareth the Christian down;
And the end of the fight is a tombstone white with the
name of the late deceased,
And the epitaph drear: 'A Fool lies here who tried to
hustle the East.'
The Naulahka (1892), heading of ch.5

19 The Saxon is not like us Normans. His manners are
not so polite.
But he never means anything serious till he talks about
justice and right,
When he stands like an ox in the furrow with his sullen
set eyes on your own,
And grumbles, 'This isn't fair dealing,' my son, leave
the Saxon alone.
Norman and Saxon

20 A Nation spoke to a Nation,
A Throne sent word to a Throne:
'Daughter am I in my mother's house,
But mistress in my own.
The gates are mine to open,
As the gates are mine to close,

And I abide by my Mother's House.'
Said our Lady of the Snows.
Our Lady of the Snows

1 The toad beneath the harrow knows
Exactly where each tooth-point goes;
The butterfly upon the road
Preaches contentment to that toad.
Pagett M.P.

2 The Three in One, the One in Three? Not so!
To my own Gods I go.
It may be they shall give me greater ease
Than your cold Christ and tangled Trinities.
Plain Tales from the Hills (1888). Chapter heading to **Lispeth**

3 There is sorrow enough in the natural way
From men and women to fill our day;
But when we are certain of sorrow in store,
Why do we always arrange for more?
Brothers and Sisters, I bid you beware
Of giving your heart to a dog to tear.
The Power of the Dog

4 The Celt in all his variants from Builth to Ballyhoo,
His mental processes are plain—one knows what he
will do,
And can logically predicate his finish by his start.
The Puzzler

5 For undemocratic reasons and for motives not of
State,
They arrive at their conclusions—largely inarticulate.
Being void of self-expression they confide their views
to none;
But sometimes in a smoking room, one learns why
things were done.
Of the English

6 Valour and Innocence
Have latterly gone hence
To certain death by certain shame attended.
The Queen's Men

7 God of our fathers, known of old,
Lord of our far-flung battle-line,
Beneath whose awful Hand we hold
Dominion over palm and pine—
Lord God of Hosts, be with us yet,
Lest we forget—lest we forget!

The tumult and the shouting dies;
The Captains and the Kings depart:
Still stands Thine ancient sacrifice,
An humble and a contrite heart.
Lord God of Hosts, be with us yet,
Lest we forget—lest we forget!
Recessional (1897)

8 Lo, all our pomp of yesterday
Is one with Nineveh and Tyre!

9 If, drunk with sight of power, we loose
Wild tongues that have not Thee in awe,
Such boastings as the Gentiles use,
Or lesser breeds without the Law.

10 For heathen heart that puts her trust
In reeking tube and iron shard,
All valiant dust that builds on dust,
And, guarding, calls not Thee to guard,
For frantic boast and foolish word—
Thy mercy on Thy People, Lord!

11 If England was what England seems,

An' not the England of our dreams,
But only putty, brass, an' paint,
'Ow quick we'd drop 'er! But she ain't!
The Return

12 English they be and Japanee that hang on the Brown
Bear's flank,
And some be Scot, but the worst of the lot, and the
boldest thieves, be Yank!
The Rhyme of the Three Sealers

13 And I've lost Britain, and I've lost Gaul,
And I've lost Rome and, worst of all,
I've lost Lalage!
Rimini

14 Brother, thy tail hangs down behind!
Road Song of the Bandar-Log

15 No one thinks of winter when the grass is green!
A St. Helena Lullaby

16 You can go where you please, you can skid up the
trees, but you don't get away from the guns!
Screw-guns

17 But remember, please, the Law by which we live,
We are not built to comprehend a lie,
We can neither love nor pity nor forgive,
If you make a slip in handling us you die!
The Secret of the Machines

18 Cheer for the Sergeant's weddin'—
Give 'em one cheer more!
Grey gun-'orses in the lando,
An' a rogue is married to a whore.
The Sergeant's Weddin'

19 Shillin' a day,
Bloomin' good pay—
Lucky to touch it, a shillin' a day!
Shillin' a Day

20 Give 'im a letter—
Can't do no better,
Late Troop-Sergeant-Major an'—runs with a letter!
Think what 'e's been,
Think what 'e's seen.
Think of 'is pension an'—
GAWD SAVE THE QUEEN!

21 There was two-an'-thirty Sergeants,
There was Corp'rals forty-one,
There was just nine 'undred rank an' file
To swear to a touch o' sun.
The Shut-Eye Sentry

22 If you wake at midnight, and hear a horse's feet,
Don't go drawing back the blind, or looking in the
street,
Them that asks no questions isn't told a lie.
Watch the wall, my darling, while the Gentlemen go
by!
Five and twenty ponies,
Trotting through the dark—
Brandy for the Parson,
'Baccy for the Clerk;
Laces for a lady, letters for a spy,
Watch the wall, my darling, while the Gentlemen go
by!
A Smuggler's Song

23 'E's a kind of a giddy harumfrodite—soldier an' sailor
too!
Soldier an' Sailor too!

1 I'm the Prophet of the Utterly Absurd,
   Of the Patently Impossible and Vain.
   The Song of the Banjo

2 I am all that ever went with evening dress!

3 There's never a wave of all her waves
   But marks our English dead.
   The Song of the Dead, ii

4 If blood be the price of admiralty,
   Lord God, we ha' paid in full!

5 For the Lord our God Most High
   He hath made the deep as dry,
   He hath smote for us a pathway to the ends of all the
   earth!
   A Song of the English

6 Keep ye the law—be swift in all obedience—
   Clear the land of evil, drive the road and bridge the
   ford.
   Make ye sure to each his own
   That he reap where he hath sown;
   By the peace among our peoples let men know we
   serve the Lord!

7 Ere Mor the Peacock flutters, ere the Monkey People
   cry,
   Ere Chil the Kite swoops down a furlong sheer,
   Through the Jungle very softly flits a shadow and a
   sigh—
   He is Fear, O Little Hunter, he is Fear!
   The Song of the Little Hunter

8 But thy throat is shut and dried, and thy heart against
   thy side
   Hammers: 'Fear, O Little Hunter—this is Fear!'

9 Mithras, God of the Morning, our trumpets waken the
   Wall!
   'Rome is above the Nations, but Thou art over all!'
   A Song to Mithras

10 They sit at the Feet—they hear the Word—they see
   how truly the Promise runs.
   They have cast their burden upon the Lord, and—the
   Lord He lays it on Martha's Sons!
   The Sons of Martha

11 An' it all goes into the laundry,
   But it never comes out in the wash,
   'Ow we're sugared about by the old men
   ('Eavy-sterned amateur old men!)
   That 'amper an' 'inder an' scold men
   For fear o' Stellenbosch!
   Stellenbosch

12 The barrow and the camp abide,
   The sunlight and the sward.
   Sussex

13 And here the sea-fogs lap and cling
   And here, each warning each,
   The sheep-bells and the ship-bells ring
   Along the hidden beach.

14 Little, lost, Down churches praise
   The Lord who made the hills.

15 Huge oaks and old, the which we hold
   No more than Sussex weed.

16 God gives all men all earth to love,
   But, since man's heart is small,
   Ordains for each one spot shall prove
   Belovèd over all.

Each to his choice, and I rejoice
   The lot has fallen to me
In a fair ground—in a fair ground—
   Yea, Sussex by the sea!
See 390:6

17 One man in a thousand, Solomon says,
   Will stick more close than a brother.
   The Thousandth Man

18 But the Thousandth Man will stand by you side
   To the gallows-foot—and after!

19 Though we called your friend from his bed this night,
   he could not speak to you,
   For the race is run by one and one and never by two
   and two.
   Tomlinson

20 For the sin ye do by two and two ye must pay for one
   by one!

21 And—the God that you took from a printed book be
   with you, Tomlinson!

22 Oh, it's Tommy this, an' Tommy that, an' 'Tommy,
   go away';
   But it's 'Thank you, Mister Atkins,' when the band
   begins to play.
   Tommy

23 It's Tommy this, an' Tommy that, an' 'Chuck him
   out, the brute!'
   But it's 'Saviour of 'is country' when the guns begin to
   shoot.

24 Then it's Tommy this, an' Tommy that, an' 'Tommy
   'ow's yer soul?'
   But it's 'Thin red line of 'eroes' when the drums begin
   to roll.

25 Of all the trees that grow so fair,
   Old England to adorn,
   Greater are none beneath the Sun,
   Than Oak, and Ash, and Thorn.
   A Tree Song. The association of these trees is traditional

26 Ellum she hateth mankind and waiteth
   Till every gust be laid
   To drop a limb on the head of him
   That anyway trusts her shade.

27 England shall bide till Judgement Tide,
   By Oak, and Ash, and Thorn!

28 I tell this tale, which is strictly true,
   Just by way of convincing you
   How very little, since things were made,
   Things have altered in the building trade.
   A Truthful Song

29 A fool there was and he made his prayer
   (Even as you and I!)
   To a rag and a bone and a hank of hair
   (We called her the woman who did not care)
   But the fool he called her his lady fair—
   (Even as you and I!)
   The Vampire

30 Oh, was there ever sailor free to choose,
   That didn't settle somewhere near the sea?
   The Virginity

31 They shut the road through the woods
   Seventy years ago.
   Weather and rain have undone it again,
   And now you would never know

There was once a road through the woods.
The Way Through the Woods

1 You will hear the beat of a horse's feet,
  And the swish of a skirt in the dew,
  Steadily cantering through
  The misty solitudes,
  As though they perfectly knew
  The old lost road through the woods—
  But there is no road through the woods!

2 Father, Mother, and Me,
  Sister and Auntie say
  All the people like us are We,
  And every one else is They.
  We and They

3 And only The Master shall praise us, and only The
    Master shall blame;
  And no one shall work for money, and no one shall
    work for fame,
  But each for the joy of the working, and each, in his
    separate star,
  Shall draw the Thing as he sees It for the God of
    Things as They are!
  When Earth's Last Picture

4 When 'Omer smote 'is bloomin' lyre,
    'E'd 'eard men sing by land an' sea;
  An' what 'e thought 'e might require,
    'E went an' took—the same as me!
  When 'Omer Smote. (Barrack-Room Ballads (1892):
  Introduction)

5 They knew 'e stole; 'e knew they knowed.
    They didn't tell, nor make a fuss,
  But winked at 'Omer down the road,
    An' 'e winked back—the same as us!

6 Take up the White Man's burden—
    Send forth the best ye breed—
  Go, bind your sons to exile
    To serve your captives' need;
  To wait in heavy harness
    On fluttered folk and wild—
  Your new-caught, sullen peoples,
    Half-devil and half-child.
  The White Man's Burden

7 By all ye cry or whisper,
    By all ye leave or do,
  The silent, sullen peoples
    Shall weigh your Gods and you.

8 Take up the White Man's burden—
    And reap his old reward:
  The blame of those ye better,
    The hate of those ye guard.

9 'Ave you 'eard o' the Widow at Windsor
    With a hairy gold crown on 'er 'ead?
  She 'as ships on the foam—she 'as millions at 'ome,
    An' she pays us poor beggars in red.
  The Widow at Windsor

10 Take 'old o' the Wings o' the Mornin',
     An' flop round the earth till you're dead;
   But you won't get away from the tune that they play
     To the bloomin' old rag over 'ead.

11 Down to Gehenna or up to the Throne,
     He travels the fastest who travels alone.
   The Winners

12 Good hunting!
   The Jungle Book (1894). Kaa's Hunting

13 We be of one blood, thou and I.

14 'Nice,' said the small 'stute Fish. 'Nice but nubbly.'
   Just So Stories (1902). How the Whale Got His Throat

15 You must *not* forget the Suspenders, Best Beloved.

16 He had his Mummy's leave to paddle, or else he
   would never have done it, because he was a man of
   infinite-resource-and-sagacity.

17 Most 'scruciating idle.
   How the Camel Got His Hump

18 'Humph yourself!'
     And the Camel humphed himself.

19 There lived a Parsee from whose hat the rays of the
   sun were reflected in more-than-oriental-splendour.
   How the Rhinoceros Got His Skin

20 An Elephant's Child—who was full of 'satiable
   curtiosity.
   The Elephant's Child

21 The great grey-green, greasy Limpopo River, all set
   about with fever-trees.

22 Led go! You are hurtig be!

23 He walked by himself, and all places were alike to
   him.
   The Cat That Walked by Himself

24 He went back through the Wet Wild Woods, waving
   his wild tail, and walking by his wild lone. But he
   never told anybody.

25 The mad all are in God's keeping.
   Kim (1901), ch.2

26 What's the good of argifying?
   Life's Handicap (1891). On Greenhow Hill

27 Asia is not going to be civilized after the methods of
   the West. There is too much Asia and she is too old.
   The Man Who Was

28 Let it be clearly understood that the Russian is a
   delightful person till he tucks in his shirt.

29 Man that is born of woman is small potatoes and few
   in the hill.
   The Head of the District

30 Some were married, which was bad, and some did
   other things which were worse.
   The Mark of the Beast

31 You haf too much Ego in your Cosmos.
   Bertran and Bimi

32 She was as immutable as the Hills. But not quite so
   green.
   Plain Tales from the Hills (1888). Venus Annodomini

33 Every one is more or less mad on one point.
   On the Strength of a Likeness

34 Open and obvious devotion from any sort of man is
   always pleasant to any sort of woman.

35 Take my word for it, the silliest woman can manage a
   clever man; but it needs a very clever woman to
   manage a fool.
   Three and—an Extra

36 Lalun is a member of the most ancient profession in
   the world.
   Soldiers Three (1888). On the City Wall

37 Being kissed by a man who didn't wax his moustache

was—like eating an egg without salt.
The Gadsbys. Poor Dear Mamma

1 Steady the Buffs.

2 Been trotting out the Gorgonzola!

3 Almost inevitable Consequences.
Fatima

4 I gloat! Hear me gloat!
Stalky & Co. (1899). **The Ambush**

5 It's boy; only boy.
An Unsavoury Interlude

6 We ain't goin' to have any beastly Erickin'.
The Moral Reformers

7 'This man,' said M'Turk, with conviction, 'is *the*
Gadarene Swine.'
The Flag of Their Country

8 A Jelly-bellied Flag-flapper.

9 'Tisn't beauty, so to speak, nor good talk necessarily.
It's just IT. Some women'll stay in a man's memory if
they once walked down a street.
Traffics and Discoveries (1904). **Mrs. Bathurst**

10 Once upon a time there was a Man and his Wife and a
Tertium Quid.
Wee Willie Winkie (1888). **At the Pit's Mouth**

11 Gawd knows, an' 'E won't split on a pal.
Drums of the Fore and Aft

12 A Soldier of the Great War Known unto God.
Inscription on gravestones above unidentified bodies, chosen by
Kipling as literary adviser for the Imperial War Graves
Commission, 1919. Gavin Stamp (ed.), *Silent Cities* (1977), p.13

13 Power without responsibility—the prerogative of the
harlot throughout the ages.
In conversation with Max Aitken (Lord Beaverbrook); later used
by Stanley Baldwin. See Lord Baldwin, *Address to the Kipling
Society*, Oct. 1971

LORD KITCHENER 1850–1916

14 You are ordered abroad as a soldier of the King to help
our French comrades against the invasion of a common
enemy. You have to perform a task which will need
your courage, your energy, your patience. Remember
that the honour of the British Army depends on your
individual conduct. It will be your duty not only to set
an example of discipline and perfect steadiness under
fire but also to maintain the most friendly relations
with those whom you are helping in this struggle. In
this new experience you may find temptations both in
wine and women. You must entirely resist both
temptations, and, while treating all women with
perfect courtesy, you should avoid any intimacy. Do
your duty bravely. Fear God. Honour the King.
A message to the soldiers of the British Expeditionary Force,
1914, to be kept by each soldier in his Active Service Pay-Book.
Sir G. Arthur, *Life of Kitchener*, vol.iii, p.27. See 80:25

PAUL KLEE 1879–1940

15 An *active* line on a walk moving freely, without goal.
A walk for a walk's sake.
Pedagogical Sketchbook (1925), 1.1

FRIEDRICH KLOPSTOCK 1724–1803

16 God and I both knew what it meant once; now God

alone knows.
C. Lombroso, *The Man of Genius* (1891), pt.I, ch.2. Also attr. to
Browning in the form 'When [*Sordello*] was written, God and
Robert Browning knew what it meant; now only God knows.'

MARY KNOWLES 1733–1807

17 He [Dr. Johnson] gets at the substance of a book
directly; he tears out the heart of it.
Boswell's *Johnson* (ed. 1934), vol.iii, p.284. 15 Apr. 1778

JOHN KNOX 1505–1572

18 *Un homme avec Dieu est toujours dans la majorité.*
A man with God is always in the majority.
Inscription on the Reformation Monument, Geneva, Switzerland

19 The First Blast of the Trumpet Against the Monstrous
Regiment of Women.
Title of Pamphlet, 1558

MGR. RONALD KNOX 1888–1957

20 When suave politeness, tempering bigot zeal,
Corrected *I believe* to *One does feel.*
Absolute and Abitofhell (1913)

21 O God, for as much as without Thee
We are not enabled to doubt Thee,
    Help us all by Thy grace
    To convince the whole race
It knows nothing whatever about Thee.
Attr. Langford Reed, *The Limerick Book*

22 There once was a man who said 'God
Must think it exceedingly odd
    If he find that this tree
    Continues to be
When there's no one about in the Quad.'
For the answer see 4:29

23 Evangelical vicar, in want of a portable, second-hand
font, would dispose, for the same, of a portrait, in frame,
of the Bishop, elect, of Vermont.
Advertisement placed in a newspaper. See W.S. Baring-Gould,
The Lure of the Limerick, pt. I. ch. 1. n. 5

VICESIMUS KNOX 1752–1821

24 That learning belongs not to the female character, and
that the female mind is not capable of a degree of
improvement equal to that of the other sex, are narrow
and unphilosophical prejudices.
Essays, vol.3, 142. (*The British Essayists* (1823), vol.37)

25 All sensible people agree in thinking that large
seminaries of young ladies, though managed with all
the vigilance and caution which human abilities can
exert, are in danger of great corruption.
Liberal Education, vol.I. sect.27, **On the literary education of
women**

26 Can anything be more absurd than keeping women in
a state of ignorance, and yet so vehemently to insist on
their resisting temptation?
See Mary Wollstonecraft, *A Vindication of the Rights of Woman*
(1792)

ALEXANDER KORDA 1893–1956

27 It's not enough to be Hungarian, you must have talent
too.
c.1935. See K. Kulik, *Alexander Korda* (1975), p.142

PAUL KRUGER 1825–1904

1 A bill of indemnity…for raid by Dr Jameson and the British South Africa Company's troops. The amount falls under two heads—first material damage, total of claim, £577,938 3s.3d.; second, moral or intellectual damage, total of claim, £1,000,000.
Communicated to House of Commons by Joseph Chamberlain, 18 Feb. 1897

THOMAS KYD 1558?–1594?

2 What outcries pluck me from my naked bed?
The Spanish Tragedy (1592), II.v.1

3 Oh eyes, no eyes, but fountains fraught with tears;
Oh life, no life, but lively form of death;
Oh world, no world, but mass of public wrongs.
III.ii.1

4 Thus must we toil in other men's extremes,
That know not how to remedy our own.
vi.1

5 I am never better than when I am mad. Then methinks
I am a brave fellow; then I do wonders. But reason
abuseth me, and there's the torment, there's the hell.
vii a.169 (1602 edn.)

6 My son—and what's a son? A thing begot
Within a pair of minutes, thereabout,
A lump bred up in darkness.
xi. Additions, 1.5

7   Duly twice a morning
Would I be sprinkling it with fountain water.
At last it grew, and grew, and bore, and bore,
Till at the length
It grew a gallows and did bear our son,
It bore thy fruit and mine: O wicked, wicked plant.
xii. Additions, 1.66

8 Why then I'll fit you.
IV.i.69

9 For what's a play without a woman in it?
96

HENRY LABOUCHERE 1831–1912

10 He [Labouchere] did not object, he once said, to Gladstone's always having the ace of trumps up his sleeve, but only to his pretence that God had put it there.
D.N.B. See also Thorold, *Life of Henry Labouchere*, ch.15:
'[Gladstone] cannot refrain from perpetually bringing an ace down his sleeve, even when he has only to play fair to win the trick.'

JEAN DE LA BRUYÈRE 1645–1696

11 *Tout est dit et l'on vient trop tard depuis plus de sept mille ans qu'il y a des hommes et qui pensent.*
Everything has been said, and we are more than seven thousand years of human thought too late.
Les Caractères (1688). **Des Ouvrages de l'Esprit**

12 *C'est un métier que de faire un livre, comme de faire une pendule: il faut plus que de l'esprit pour être auteur.*
Making a book is a craft, as is making a clock; it takes more than wit to become an author.

13 *Le commencement et le déclin de l'amour se font sentir par l'embarras où l'on est de se trouver seuls.*
The onset and the waning of love make themselves felt in the uneasiness experienced at being alone together.
Du Coeur

14 *Le peuple n'a guère d'esprit et les grands n'ont point d'âme…faut-il opter, je ne balance pas, je veux être peuple.*
The people have little intelligence, the great no heart…if I had to choose I should have no hesitation: I would be of the people.
Des Grands

15 *Entre le bon sens et le bon goût il y a la différence de la cause et son effet.*
Between good sense and good taste there is the same difference as between cause and effect.
Des Jugements

NIVELLE DE LA CHAUSSÉE 1692–1754

16 *Quand tout le monde a tort, tout le monde a raison.*
When everyone is wrong, everyone is right.
La Gouvernante (1747), I.iii

JEAN DE LA FONTAINE 1621–1695

17 *Aide-toi, le ciel t'aidera.*
Help yourself, and heaven will help you.
Fables (1668), vi.18. **Le Chartier Embourbé**

18 *Je plie et ne romps pas.*
I bend and I break not.
i.22. **Le Chêne et le Roseau**

19 *C'est double plaisir de tromper le trompeur.*
It is doubly pleasing to trick the trickster.
ii.15. **Le Coq et le Renard**

20 *Il connaît l'univers et ne se connaît pas.*
He knows the world and does not know himself.
(1678–9), viii.26. **Démocrite et les Abdéritains**

21 *La raison du plus fort est toujours la meilleure.*
The reason of the strongest is always the best.
i.10. **Le Loup et l'Agneau**

22 *La mort ne surprend point le sage,*
Il est toujours prêt à partir.
Death never takes the wise man by surprise; he is always ready to go.
viii.1. **La Mort et le Mourant.** See 354:13

JULES LAFORGUE 1860–1887

23 *Ah! que la vie est quotidienne.*
Oh, what a day-to-day business life is.
Complainte sur certains ennuis (1885)

ALPHONSE DE LAMARTINE 1790–1869

24 *Un seul être vous manque, et tout est dépeuplé.*
Only one being is wanting, and your whole world is bereft of people.
Premières Méditations poétiques (1820), **L'Isolement**

LADY CAROLINE LAMB 1785–1828

25 Mad, bad, and dangerous to know.
Of Byron, in her journal after their first meeting at a ball in March 1812. See Jenkins, *Lady Caroline Lamb* (1932), ch.6

CHARLES LAMB 1775–1834

1 I have no ear.
Essays of Elia (1820–23). **A Chapter on Ears**

2 I even think that sentimentally I am disposed to harmony. But organically I am incapable of a tune.

3 'Presents', I often say, 'endear Absents.'
A Dissertation upon Roast Pig

4 It argues an insensibility.

5 Why have we none [i.e. no grace] for books, those spiritual repasts—a grace before Milton—a grace before Shakspeare—a devotional exercise proper to be said before reading the Faerie Queene?
Grace Before Meat

6 Coleridge holds that a man cannot have a pure mind who refuses apple-dumplings. I am not certain but he is right.

7 I am, in plainer words, a bundle of prejudices—made up of likings and dislikings.
Imperfect Sympathies

8 I have been trying all my life to like Scotchmen, and am obliged to desist from the experiment in despair.

9 She unbent her mind afterwards—over a book.
Mrs. Battle's Opinions on Whist

10 In everything that relates to science, I am a whole Encyclopaedia behind the rest of the world.
The Old and the New Schoolmaster

11 A votary of the desk—a notched and cropt scrivener—one that sucks his substance, as certain sick people are said to do, through a quill.
Oxford in the Vacation

12 The human species, according to the best theory I can form of it, is composed of two distinct races, *the men who borrow,* and *the men who lend.*
The Two Races of Men

13 What a liberal confounding of those pedantic distinctions of *meum* and *tuum!*

14 I mean your *borrowers of books*—those mutilators of collections, spoilers of the symmetry of shelves, and creators of odd volumes.

15 To lose a volume to C[oleridge] carries some sense and meaning in it. You are sure that he will make one hearty meal on your viands, if he can give no account of the platter after it.

16 I love to lose myself in other men's minds. When I am not walking, I am reading; I cannot sit and think. Books think for me.
Last Essays of Elia (1833). **Detached Thoughts on Books and Reading**

17 I can read any thing which I call a book. There are things in that shape which I cannot allow for such. In this catalogue of books which are no books—biblia a-biblia—I reckon Court Calendars, Directories…the works of Hume, Gibbon, Robertson, Beattie, Soame Jenyns, and, generally, all those volumes which 'no gentleman's library should be without'.

18 Things in books' clothing.

19 Milton almost requires a solemn service of music to be played before you enter upon him.

20 A poor relation—is the most irrelevant thing in nature.
Poor Relations

21 Cultivate simplicity, Coleridge.
Letter to Coleridge, 8 Nov. 1796

22 Separate from the pleasure of your company, I don't much care if I never see another mountain in my life.
Letter to William Wordsworth, 30 Jan. 1801

23 The man must have a rare recipe for melancholy, who can be dull in Fleet Street.
The Londoner, in letter to Thomas Manning, 15 Feb. 1802

24 Nursed amid her noise, her crowds, her beloved smoke—what have I been doing all my life, if I have not lent out my heart with usury to such scenes?

25 I have made a little scale, supposing myself to receive the following various accessions of dignity from the king, who is the fountain of honour—As at first, 1, Mr C. Lamb;…10th, Emperor Lamb; 11th, Pope Innocent, higher than which is nothing but the Lamb of God.
Letter to Thomas Manning, 2 Jan. 1810

26 Nothing puzzles me more than time and space; and yet nothing troubles me less, as I never think about them.

27 I was at Hazlitt's marriage, and had like to have been turned out several times during the ceremony. Anything awful makes me laugh. I misbehaved once at a funeral.
Letter to Southey, 9 Aug. 1815

28 This very night I am going to leave off tobacco! Surely there must be some other world in which this unconquerable purpose shall be realized. The soul hath not her generous aspirings implanted in her in vain.
Letter to Thomas Manning, 26 Dec. 1815

29 His face when he repeats his verses hath its ancient glory, an Archangel a little damaged. [Coleridge.]
Letter to Wordsworth, 26 Apr. 1816

30 The rogue gives you Love Powders, and then a strong horse drench to bring 'em off your stomach that they mayn't hurt you. [Coleridge.]
23 Sept. 1816

31 Fanny Kelly's divine plain face.
Letter to Mrs. Wordsworth, 18 Feb. 1818

32 How I like to be liked, and what I do to be liked!
Letter to D. Wordsworth, 8 Jan. 1821

33 Who first invented Work—and tied the free
And holy-day rejoicing spirit down
To the ever-haunting importunity
Of business, in the green fields, and the town—
To plough—loom—anvil—spade—and, oh, most sad,
To this dry drudgery of the desk's dead wood?
Letter to Barton, Sept. 1822

34 Those fellows hate us. [Booksellers and authors.]
9 Jan. 1823

35 We should be modest for a modest man—as he is for himself.
Letter to Mrs. Montagu, Summer 1827

36 You are knee deep in clover.
Letter to C.C. Clarke, Dec. 1828

37 When my sonnet was rejected, I exclaimed, 'Damn the age; I will write for Antiquity!'
Letter to B.W. Procter, 22 Jan. 1829

38 Books of the true sort, not those things in boards that moderns mistake for books—what they club for at

book clubs.
Letter to J. Gillman, 30 Nov. 1829

1 Half as sober as a judge.
Letter to Mr. and Mrs. Moxon, Aug. 1833

2 The greatest pleasure I know, is to do a good action by
stealth, and to have it found out by accident.
Table Talk by the late Elia. *The Athenaeum,* 4 Jan. 1834

3 What a lass that were to go a-gipseying through the
world with.
The Jovial Crew. *The Examiner,* July 1819

4 The uncommunicating muteness of fishes.
A Quakers' Meeting

5 For thy sake, Tobacco, I
Would do any thing but die.
A Farewell to Tobacco, l.122

6 I have had playmates, I have had companions,
In my days of childhood, in my joyful school-days,—
All, all are gone, the old familiar faces.
The Old Familiar Faces

7 If ever I marry a wife,
I'll marry a landlord's daughter,
For then I may sit in the bar,
And drink cold brandy and water.
Written in a copy of *Coelebs in Search of a Wife*

8 At Godwin's...they [Lamb, Holcroft, and Coleridge]
were disputing fiercely which was the best—Man as he
was, or man as he is to be. 'Give me,' says Lamb,
'man as he is *not* to be.'
Hazlitt, *English Literature,* ch.xvii. My First Acquaintance with
Poets

9 Martin, if dirt were trumps, what hands you would
hold!
Leigh Hunt, *Lord Byron and his Contemporaries* (1828), p.299

10 I do not [know the lady]; but damn her at a venture.
E.V. Lucas, *Charles Lamb* (1905), vol.i, p.320, note

11 I noted one odd saying of Lamb's that 'the last breath
he drew in he wished might be through a pipe and
exhaled in a pun'.
Macready, *Journal,* 9 Jan. 1834

12 Dr Parr...asked him, how he had acquired his power
of smoking at such a rate? Lamb replied, 'I toiled after
it, sir, as some men toil after virtue.'
Talfourd, *Memoirs of Charles Lamb* (1892), p.262

MARY LAMB 1764–1847

13 He [Henry Crabb Robinson] says he never saw a man
so happy in *three wives* as Mr Wordsworth is.
Letter to Sarah Hutchinson, Nov. 1816

14 A child's a plaything for an hour.
Parental Recollections

JOHN GEORGE LAMBTON, FIRST EARL OF DURHAM 1792–1840

15 £40,000 a year a moderate income—such a one as
a man *might jog on with.*
The Creevey Papers (13 Sept. 1821), ii.32

LETITIA ELIZABETH LANDON 1802–1838

16 Few, save the poor, feel for the poor.
The Poor

WALTER SAVAGE LANDOR 1775–1864

17 Around the child bent all the three
Sweet Graces: Faith, Hope, Charity.
Around the man bend other faces:
Pride, Envy, Malice, are his Graces.
Around the Child

18 Hail, ye indomitable heroes, hail!
Despite of all your generals ye prevail.
The Crimean Heroes

19 Death stands above me, whispering low
I know not what into my ear;
Of his strange language all I know
Is, there is not a word of fear.
Epigrams, c. **Death**

20 I strove with none; for none was worth my strife;
Nature I loved, and, next to Nature, Art;
I warmed both hands before the fire of life;
It sinks, and I am ready to depart.
Finis

21 He says, *my reign is peace,* so slays
A thousand in the dead of night.
Are you all happy now? he says,
And those he leaves behind cry *quite*.
He swears he will have no contention,
And sets all nations by the ears;
He shouts aloud, *No intervention*!
Invades, and drowns them all in tears.
A Foreign Ruler (1863)

22 Past ruin'd Ilion Helen lives,
Alcestis rises from the shades;
Verse calls them forth; 'tis verse that gives
Immortal youth to mortal maids.
Ianthe

23 Ireland never was contented...
Say you so? You are demented.
Ireland was contented when
All could use the sword and pen,
And when Tara rose so high
That her turrets split the sky,
And about her courts were seen
Liveried Angels robed in green,
Wearing, by St Patrick's bounty,
Emeralds big as half a county.
The Last Fruit Off an Old Tree (1853), **Epigrams** LXXXIV

24 I loved him not; and yet now he is gone
I feel I am alone.
I check'd him while he spoke; yet, could he speak,
Alas! I would not check.
The Maid's Lament

25 Proud word you never spoke, but you will speak
Four not exempt from pride some future day.
Resting on one white hand a warm wet cheek
Over my open volume you will say,
'This man loved *me*!' then rise and trip away.
Proud Word You Never Spoke

26 Ah, what avails the sceptred race!
Ah, what the form divine!
What every virtue, every grace!
Rose Aylmer, all were thine.

Rose Aylmer, whom these wakeful eyes
May weep, but never see,
A night of memories and of sighs

I consecrate to thee.
Rose Aylmer

1 There is delight in singing, tho' none hear
Beside the singer.
To Robert Browning

2 Thee gentle Spenser fondly led;
But me he mostly sent to bed.
To Wordsworth: Those Who Have Laid the Harp Aside

3 How many verses have I thrown
Into the fire because the one
Peculiar word, the wanted most,
Was irrecoverably lost.
Verses Why Burnt

4 Well I remember how you smiled
To see me write your name upon
The soft sea-sand—'O! what a child!
You think you're writing upon stone!'

I have since written what no tide
Shall ever wash away, what men
Unborn shall read o'er ocean wide
And find Ianthe's name again.
Well I Remember How You Smiled

5 I know not whether I am proud,
But this I know, I hate the crowd.
With an Album. See 260:13

6 George the First was always reckoned
Vile, but viler George the Second;
And what mortal ever heard
Any good of George the Third?
When from earth the Fourth descended
God be praised the Georges ended!
Epigram in *The Atlas*, 28 Apr. 1855. See N. & Q., 3 May 1902, pp.318, 354

7 Laodameia died; Helen died; Leda, the beloved of Jupiter, went before.
Imaginary Conversations (1824–29). **Aesop and Rhodope,** i

8 There are no fields of amaranth on this side of the grave: there are no voices, O Rhodope! that are not soon mute, however tuneful: there is no name, with whatever emphasis of passionate love repeated, of which the echo is not faint at last.

9 He who first praises a good book becomingly, is next in merit to the author.
Alfieri and Salomon the Florentine Jew

10 Prose on certain occasions can bear a great deal of poetry: on the other hand, poetry sinks and swoons under a moderate weight of prose.
Archdeacon Hare and Walter Landor

11 I hate false words, and seek with care, difficulty, and moroseness, those that fit the thing.
Bishop Burnet and Humphrey Hardcastle

12 Goodness does not more certainly make men happy than happiness makes them good.
Lord Brooke and Sir Philip Sidney

13 States, like men, have their growth, their manhood, their decrepitude, their decay.
Pollio and Calvus

14 Clear writers, like clear fountains, do not seem so deep as they are; the turbid look the most profound.
Southey and Porson (1823).

15 Fleas know not whether they are upon the body of a giant or upon one of ordinary size.

SIR EDWIN LANDSEER 1802–1873

16 If people only knew as much about painting as I do, they would never buy my pictures.
Said to W.P. Frith. Campbell Lennie, *Landseer the Victorian Paragon*, ch.12

ANDREW LANG 1844–1912

17 St Andrews by the Northern Sea,
That is a haunted town to me!
Almae Matres

18 And through the music of the languid hours
They hear like Ocean on a western beach
The surge and thunder of the Odyssey.
As One That for a Weary Space has Lain

19 If the wild bowler thinks he bowls,
Or if the batsman thinks he's bowled,
They know not, poor misguided souls,
They too shall perish unconsoled.
I am the batsman and the bat,
I am the bowler and the ball,
The umpire, the pavilion cat,
The roller, pitch, and stumps, and all.
Brahma. See 206:17

JULIA S. LANG 1921–

20 Are you sitting comfortably? Then I'll begin.
Preamble to children's story in *Listen With Mother*, B.B.C. radio programme, from 1950

FREDERICK LANGBRIDGE 1849–1923

21 Two men look out through the same bars:
One sees the mud, and one the stars.
A Cluster of Quiet Thoughts (1896) (Religious Tract Society Publication)

WILLIAM LANGLAND 1330?–1400?

22 In a somer seson whan soft was the sonne.
The Vision of William concerning Piers the Plowman (ed. Skeat), B Text, Prologue, l.1

23 A faire felde ful of folke fonde I there bytwene
Of alle manner of men, the mene and riche,
Worchyng and wandryng as the worlde asketh.
l.17

24 A glotoun of wordes.
l.139

25 Ac on a May morwenyng on Maluerne hulles
Me byfel for to slepe for weyrynesse of wandryng.
C Text, Passus 1, l.6

26 Bakers and brewers, bouchers and cokes—
For thees men doth most harme to the mene puple.
Passus 4, l.80

27 Grammere, that grounde is of alle.
Passus 18, l.107

28 'After sharpest shoures,' quath Pees [Peace] 'most sheene is the sonne;
Ys no weder warmer than after watery cloudes.'
Passus 21, l.456

ARCHBISHOP STEPHEN LANGTON d. 1228

29 *Veni, Sancte Spiritus,*
Et emitte coelitus
Lucis tuae radium.

Come, Holy Spirit, and send out from heaven the beam
of your light.
The 'Golden Sequence' for Whitsunday. Attr.

1 *Lava quod est sordidum,*
Riga quod est aridum,
Sana quod est saucium,
Flecte quod est rigidum,
Fove quod est frigidum,
Rege quod est devium.
Wash what is dirty, water what is dry, heal what is
wounded. Bend what is stiff, warm what is cold,
guide what goes off the road.

LÂO TSE ?6th cent. B.C.

2 Heaven and Earth are not ruthful;
To them the Ten Thousand Things are but as straw
dogs.
Tao-te-ching, 5. Tr. Arthur Waley. (The Ten Thousand Things:
all life forms. Straw dogs: sacrificial tokens.)

PHILIP LARKIN 1922–

3 What are days for?
Days are where we live
They come they wake us
Time and time over.
They are to be happy in;
Where can we live but days?
Days

4 Nothing, like something, happens anywhere.
I Remember, I Remember

5 Perhaps being old is having lighted rooms
Inside your head, and people in them, acting.
People you know, yet can't quite name.
The Old Fools

6 Why should I let the toad *work*
  Squat on my life?
Can't I use my wit as a pitchfork
  And drive the brute off?
Toads

7 Give me your arm, old toad;
Help me down Cemetery Road.
Toads Revisited

DUC DE LA ROCHEFOUCAULD 1613–1680

8 *Dans l'adversité de nos meilleurs amis, nous trouvons*
toujours quelque chose qui ne nous déplaît pas.
In the misfortune of our best friends, we always find
something which is not displeasing to us.
Réflexions ou Maximes Morales (1665), 99

9 *Nous avons tous assez de force pour supporter les*
maux d'autrui.
We are all strong enough to bear the misfortunes of
others.
Réflexions ou Sentences et Maximes Morales (1678), 19

10 *Il est plus honteux de se défier de ses amis que d'en*
être trompé.
It is more shameful to spurn one's friends than to be
duped by them.
84

11 *Il y a de bons mariages, mais il n'y en a point de*
délicieux.

There are good marriages, but no delightful ones.
113

12 *L'hypocrisie est un hommage que le vice rend à la*
vertu.
Hypocrisy is a tribute which vice pays to virtue.
218

13 *C'est une grande habileté que de savoir cacher son*
habileté.
The height of cleverness is to be able to conceal it.
245

14 *Il n'y a guère d'homme assez habile pour connaître*
tout le mal qu'il fait.
There is scarcely a single man sufficiently aware to
know all the evil he does.
269

15 *L'absence diminue les médiocres passions, et*
augmente les grandes, comme le vent éteint les
bougies, et allume le feu.
Absence diminishes commonplace passions and
increases great ones, as the wind extinguishes candles
and kindles fire.
276. See 117:6, 218:2

16 *La reconnaissance de la plupart des hommes n'est*
qu'une secrète envie de recevoir de plus grands
bienfaits.
In most of mankind gratitude is merely a secret hope
for greater favours.
298

17 *L'accent du pays où l'on est né demeure dans l'esprit*
et dans le coeur comme dans le langage.
The accent of one's birthplace lingers in the mind and
in the heart as it does in one's speech.
342

18 *On n'est jamais si malheureux qu'on croit, ni si*
heureux qu'on espère.
One is never as unhappy as one thinks, nor as happy as
one hopes.
Sentences et Maximes de Morale, Dutch edition (1664), 128

DUC DE LA ROCHEFOUCAULD-LIANCOURT
1747–1827

19 Louis XVI: *C'est une grande révolte.*
La Rochefoucauld-Liancourt: *Non, Sire, c'est une*
grande révolution.
('It is a big revolt.' 'No, Sir, a big revolution.')
When the Fall of the Bastille was reported at Versailles, 1789. F.
Dreyfus, *La Rochefoucauld-Liancourt* (1903), ch.II, sect iii

BISHOP HUGH LATIMER c.1485–1555

20 *Gutta cavat lapidem, non vi sed saepe cadendo.*
The drop of rain maketh a hole in the stone, not by
violence, but by oft falling.
7th Sermon preached before Edward VI (1549). See 366:27

21 Be of good comfort Master Ridley, and play the man.
We shall this day light such a candle by God's grace in
England, as (I trust) shall never be put out.
16 Oct. 1555. Foxe, *Actes and Monuments* (1562–3), 1570 edn.,
p.1937

BONAR LAW 1858–1923

22 If, therefore, war should ever come between these two
countries [Great Britain and Germany], which Heaven
forbid! it will not, I think, be due to irresistible natural

laws, it will be due to the want of human wisdom.
House of Commons, 27 Nov. 1911

1 I said [in 1911] that if ever war arose between Great
Britain and Germany it would not be due to inevitable
causes, for I did not believe in inevitable war. I said it
would be due to human folly.
6 Aug. 1914

D.H. LAWRENCE 1885–1930

2 To the Puritan all things are impure, as somebody
says.
Etruscan Places (1932). **Cerveteri**

3 She is dear to me in the middle of my being. But the
gold and flowing serpent is coiling up again, to sleep
at the root of my tree.
The Man Who Died (1931), pt.ii

4 Be a good animal, true to your animal instincts.
The White Peacock (1911), pt.ii, ch.2. See 514:25

5 Along the avenue of cypresses,
All in their scarlet cloaks and surplices
Of linen, go the chanting choristers,
The priests in gold and black, the villagers.
Giorno dei Morti

6 How beastly the bourgeois is
especially the male of the species.
How beastly the bourgeois is

7 So now it is vain for the singer to burst into clamour
With the great black piano appassionato. The glamour
Of childish days is upon me, my manhood is cast
Down in the flood of remembrance, I weep like a child
    for the past.
Piano

8 Now it is autumn and the falling fruit
and the long journey towards oblivion…
Have you built your ship of death, O have you?
O build your ship of death, for you will need it.
The Ship of Death

9 Not I, not I, but the wind that blows through me!
Song of a man who has come through

10 Never trust the artist. Trust the tale. The proper
function of a critic is to save the tale from the artist
who created it.
Studies in Classic American Literature (1924), ch.1

11 It is lurid and melodramatic, but it is true.
ch.6

T.E. LAWRENCE 1888–1935

12 I loved you, so I drew these tides of men into my
    hands
    and wrote my will across the sky in stars
To earn you Freedom, the seven pillared worthy
    house,
    that your eyes might be shining for me
        When we came.
Epigraph to *The Seven Pillars of Wisdom*. 'To S.A.'

EMMA LAZARUS 1849–1887

13   Give me your tired, your poor,
Your huddled masses yearning to breathe free.
The New Colossus

STEPHEN LEACOCK 1869–1944

14 Lord Ronald…flung himself upon his horse and rode
madly off in all directions.
Nonsense Novels (1911). **Gertrude the Governess**

EDWARD LEAR 1812–1888

15 There was an Old Man with a beard,
Who said, 'It is just as I feared!—
    Two Owls and a Hen,
    Four Larks and a Wren,
Have all built their nests in my beard!'
Book of Nonsense (1846)

16 There was an Old Man in a tree,
Who was horribly bored by a bee;
    When they said, 'Does it buzz?'
    He replied, 'Yes, it does!
It's a regular brute of a bee!'

17 There was an old Lady of Chertsey,
Who made a remarkable curtsey:
    She whirled round and round,
    Till she sunk underground,
Which distressed all the people of Chertsey.

18 There was an old man who said, 'Hush!
I perceive a young bird in this bush!'
    When they said, 'Is it small?'
    He replied, 'Not at all!
It is four times as big as the bush!'

19 Nasticreechia Krorluppia.
Nonsense Botany (1870)

20 'How pleasant to know Mr Lear!'
    Who has written such volumes of stuff!
Some think him ill-tempered and queer,
    But a few think him pleasant enough.
Nonsense Songs (1871), preface

21 He has ears, and two eyes, and ten fingers,
    Leastways if you reckon two thumbs;
Long ago he was one of the singers,
    But now he is one of the dumbs.

22 He drinks a good deal of Marsala
But never gets tipsy at all.

23 He has many friends, laymen and clerical.
Old Foss is the name of his cat:
    His body is perfectly spherical,
    He weareth a runcible hat.

24 He reads but he cannot speak Spanish,
    He cannot abide ginger-beer:
Ere the days of his pilgrimage vanish,
    How pleasant to know Mr Lear!

25 On the coast of Coromandel
Where the early pumpkins blow,
    In the middle of the woods,
    Lived the Yonghy-Bonghy-Bò.
Two old chairs, and half a candle;—
One old jug without a handle,—
    These were all his worldly goods.
The Courtship of the Yonghy-Bonghy-Bó

26   'Gaze upon the rolling deep
    (Fish is plentiful and cheap)
As the sea my love is deep!'
Said the Yonghy-Bonghy-Bó.
    Lady Jingly answered sadly,

And her tears began to flow—
    'Your proposal comes too late.'

1 I can merely be your friend.

2 When awful darkness and silence reign
Over the great Gromboolian plain,
    Through the long, long wintry nights.
When the angry breakers roar
As they beat on the rocky shore;—
When Storm-clouds brood on the towering heights
    Of the Hills of the Chankly Bore.
The Dong with the Luminous Nose

3 And those who watch at that midnight hour
From Hall or Terrace or lofty Tower,
Cry as the wild light passes along,—
'The Dong!—the Dong!
The wandering Dong through the forest goes!
The Dong!—the Dong!
The Dong with Luminous Nose!'

4 And who so happy,—O who,
As the Duck and the Kangaroo?
The Duck and the Kangaroo

5 O My agéd Uncle Arly!
Sitting on a heap of Barley
    Thro' the silent hours of night,—
Close beside a leafy thicket:—
On his nose there was a Cricket,—
In his hat a Railway-Ticket;—
(But his shoes were far too tight.)
Incidents in the Life of my Uncle Arly

6 Far and few, far and few,
    Are the lands where the Jumblies live;
Their heads are green, and their hands are blue,
    And they went to sea in a Sieve.
The Jumblies

7   In spite of all their friends could say,
On a winter's morn, on a stormy day,
    In a Sieve they went to sea!

8 They called aloud 'Our Sieve ain't big,
But we don't care a button! We don't care a fig!'

9 And they brought an Owl, and a useful Cart,
And a pound of Rice, and a Cranberry Tart,
    And a hive of silvery Bees.
And they brought a Pig, and some green Jack-daws,
And a lovely Monkey with lollipop paws,
And forty bottles of Ring-Bo-Ree,
    And no end of Stilton Cheese.

10   Till Mrs Discobbolos said
    'Oh! W! X! Y! Z!
    It has just come into my head—
Suppose we should happen to fall!!!!
                Darling Mr Discobbolos?'
Mr. and Mrs. Discobbolos

11 The Owl and the Pussy-Cat went to sea
    In a beautiful pea-green boat.
They took some honey, and plenty of money,
    Wrapped up in a five-pound note.
The Owl looked up to the Stars above
    And sang to a small guitar,
'Oh lovely Pussy! O Pussy, my love,
    What a beautiful Pussy you are.'
The Owl and the Pussy-Cat

12 Pussy said to the Owl, 'You elegant fowl!

How charmingly sweet you sing!
O let us be married! too long we have tarried:
    But what shall we do for a ring?'
They sailed away for a year and a day,
    To the land where the Bong-tree grows,
And there in a wood a Piggy-wig stood
    With a ring at the end of his nose.

13 'Dear Pig, are you willing to sell for one shilling
    Your ring?' Said the Piggy, 'I will.'

14 They dined on mince, and slices of quince,
    Which they ate with a runcible spoon;
And hand in hand, on the edge of the sand,
    They danced by the light of the moon.

15 Ploffskin, Pluffskin, Pelican jee!
We think no birds so happy as we!
Plumpskin, Plashkin, Pelican jill!
We think so then, and we thought so still!
The Pelican Chorus

16 We live on the Nile. The Nile we love.
By night we sleep on the cliffs above.
By day we fish, and at eve we stand
On long bare islets of yellow sand.

17 The Pobble who has no toes
Had once as many as we;
When they said, 'Some day you may lose them all';—
He replied,—'Fish fiddle de-dee!'

His Aunt Jobiska made him drink
Lavender water tinged with pink,
For she said, 'The world in general knows
There's nothing so good for a Pobble's toes!'
The Pobble Who Has No Toes

18 For his Aunt Jobiska said, 'No harm
Can come to his toes if his nose is warm,
And it's perfectly known that a Pobble's toes
Are safe, provided he minds his nose.'

19   When boats or ships came near him
He tinkledy-binkledy-winkled a bell.

20 He has gone to fish, for his Aunt Jobiska's
Runcible Cat with crimson whiskers!

21 And she made him a feast at his earnest wish
Of eggs and buttercups fried with fish;—
And she said, 'It's a fact the whole world knows,
That Pobbles are happier without their toes.'

22 'But the longer I live on this Crumpetty Tree
The plainer than ever it seems to me
That very few people come this way
And that life on the whole is far from gay!'
    Said the Quangle-Wangle Quee.
The Quangle-Wangle's Hat

23 Two old Bachelors were living in one house;
One caught a Muffin, the other caught a Mouse.
The Two Old Bachelors

24 And what can we expect if we haven't any dinner,
But to lose our teeth and eyelashes and keep on
    growing thinner?

25 Who, or why, or which, or what,
Is the Akond of Swat?
1888 edn. **The Akond of Swat**

26 There was an old person of Slough,
Who danced at the end of a bough;
    But they said, 'If you sneeze,

You might damage the trees,
You imprudent old person of Slough.'
One Hundred Nonsense Pictures and Rhymes

1 There was an old person of Ware,
Who rode on the back of a bear:
When they asked,—'Does it trot?'—
He said, 'Certainly not!
He's a Moppsikon Floppsikon bear.'

2 There was an old person of Dean,
Who dined on one pea and one bean;
For he said, 'More than that,
Would make me too fat,'
That cautious old person of Dean.

3 There was an old man of Thermopylae,
Who never did anything properly;
But they said, 'If you choose
To boil eggs in your shoes,
You shall never remain in Thermopylae.'

MARY ELIZABETH LEASE 1853–1933

4 Kansas had better stop raising corn and begin raising hell.
Attr.

LE CORBUSIER 1887–1965

5 *La maison est une machine à habiter.*
A house is a living-machine.
Vers une architecture (1923), p.ix

ALEXANDRE AUGUSTE LEDRU-ROLLIN 1807–1874

6 *Eh! je suis leur chef, il fallait bien les suivre.*
Ah well! I am their leader, I really ought to follow them!
E. de Mirecourt, *Histoire Contemporaine* no.79, 'Ledru-Rollin' (1857)

HENRY LEE 1756–1818

7 A citizen, first in war, first in peace, and first in the hearts of his countrymen.
Resolutions Adopted by the Congress on the Death of Washington, 19 Dec. 1799; moved by John Marshall and misquoted in his *Life of Washington* as '…first in the hearts of his fellow citizens.'

NATHANIEL LEE 1653?–1692

8 When the sun sets, shadows, that showed at noon
But small, appear most long and terrible.
Oedipus (1679), IV.i

9 He speaks the kindest words, and looks such things,
Vows with so much passion, swears with so much grace.
That 'tis a kind of Heaven to be deluded by him.
The Rival Queens (1677), I

10 'Tis beauty calls and glory leads the way.

11 Then he will talk, Good Gods,
How he will talk.
III

12 When Greeks joined Greeks, then was the tug of war!
IV.ii

13 Philip fought men, but Alexander women.

14 Man, false man, smiling, destructive man.
Theodosius (1680), III.ii

HENRY SAMBROOKE LEIGH 1837–1883

15 The rapturous, wild, and ineffable pleasure
Of drinking at somebody else's expense.
Carols of Cockayne (1869). Stanzas to an Intoxicated Fly

CHARLES G. LELAND 1824–1903

16 Hans Breitmann gife a barty—
Vhere ish dat barty now?
Hans Breitmann's Barty (1857)

17 All goned afay mit de lager-beer—
Afay in de ewigkeit!

18 They saw a Dream of Loveliness descending from the train.
Brand New Ballads. The Masher

LENIN (VLADIMIR ILYICH ULYANOV) 1870–1924

19 The methods of the liberals were aptly and graphically hit off by the Trudovik Sedelnikov at a meeting on May 9 in the Panina Palace. When a liberal is abused, he says: Thank God they didn't beat me. When he is beaten, he thanks God they didn't kill him. When he is killed, he will thank God that his immortal soul has been delivered from its mortal clay.
The Government's Falsification of the Duma and the Tasks of the Social-Democrats. Proletary, no.10, Dec. 1906. Tr. in *Collected Works*, Moscow (1962), ed. C. Dutt, Vol.11

20 We shall now proceed to construct the socialist order.
Opening words of congress after the capture of the Winter Palace, 26 Oct. 1917, Trotsky, *History of the Russian Revolution*, ch.10

21 The substitution of the proletarian for the bourgeois state is impossible without a violent revolution.
State and Revolution, (1917), ch.1.4

22 Communism is Soviet power plus the electrification of the whole country.
Report at the eighth All-Russia Congress of Soviets on the work of the Council of People's Commissars, 22 Dec. 1920

SPEAKER WILLIAM LENTHALL 1591–1662

23 I have neither eye to see, nor tongue to speak here, but as the House is pleased to direct me.
4 Jan. 1642. Said to Charles I, who had asked if he saw any of the five M.P.s whom the King had ordered to be arrested. Rushworth, *Historical Collections* (1703–08), iv.238

LEONARDO DA VINCI 1452–1519

24 The poet ranks far below the painter in the representation of visible things, and far below the musician in that of invisible things.
Selections from the Notebooks, World's Classics edn., p.198

25 Every man at three years old is half his height.
MS. in Library of Institute of France, H. 31 recto

G.E. LESSING 1729–1781

26 *Gestern liebt' ich,*
Heute leid' ich,
Morgen sterb' ich:
Dennoch denk' ich
Heut und morgen
Gern an gestern.

Yesterday I loved, today I suffer, tomorrow I die: but I still think fondly, today and tomorrow, of yesterday.
Lied aus dem Spanischen

1 *Ein einziger dankbarer Gedanke gen Himmel ist das vollkommenste Gebet.*
One single grateful thought raised to heaven is the most perfect prayer.
Minna von Barnhelm (1767), ii.7

2 *Wenn Gott in seiner Rechten alle Wahrheit und in seiner Linken den einzigen, immer regen Trieb nach Wahrheit, obgleich mit dem Zusatz, mich immer und ewig zu irren, verschlossen hielte und spräche zu mir: Wähle! ich fiele ihm mit Demut in seine Linke und sagte: Vater, gieb! Die reine Wahrheit ist ja doch nur für Dich allein.*
If God were to hold out enclosed in His right hand all Truth, and in His left hand just the active search for Truth, though with the condition that I should ever err therein, and should say to me: Choose! I should humbly take His left hand and say: Father! Give me this one; absolute Truth belongs to Thee alone.
Wolfenbüttler Fragmente

ADA LEVERSON 1865–1936

3 The last gentleman in Europe.
Of Oscar Wilde. Wilde, *Letters to the Sphinx*. 'Reminiscences', 2

DUC DE LÉVIS 1764–1830

4 *Noblesse oblige.*
Nobility has its obligations.
Maximes et Réflexions, 1812 ed., **Morale**, 'Maximes et Préceptes', lxxiii

5 *Gouverner, c'est choisir.*
To govern is to make choices.
Politique, 'Maximes de Politique', xix

G.H. LEWES 1817–1878

6 Murder, like talent, seems occasionally to run in families.
The Physiology of Common Life (1859), ch.12

7 We must never assume that which is incapable of proof.
ch.13

C.S. LEWIS 1898–1963

8 A sensible human once said…'She's the sort of woman who lives for others—you can tell the others by their hunted expression.'
The Screwtape Letters (1942), XXVI

9 Term, holidays, term, holidays, till we leave school, and then work, work, work till we die.
Surprised by Joy, ch.4

SIR GEORGE CORNEWALL LEWIS 1806–1863

10 Life would be tolerable but for its amusements.
D.N.B.

WLAZIU VALENTINO ('LEE') LIBERACE 1920–

11 I cried all the way to the bank.
Liberace: An Autobiography, ch.2. After hostile criticism

CHARLES-JOSEPH, PRINCE DE LIGNE 1735–1814

12 *Le congrès ne marche pas, il danse.*
The Congress makes no progress; it dances.
La Garde-Chambonas, *Souvenirs du Congrès de Vienne, 1814–1815,* c.I

ABRAHAM LINCOLN 1809–1865

13 The ballot is stronger than the bullet.
Speech, 19 May 1856

14 'A house divided against itself cannot stand.' I believe this government cannot endure permanently, half slave and half free.
Speech, 16 June 1858. See 68:27

15 You can fool all the people some of the time, and some of the people all the time, but you can not fool all the people all of the time.
Attr. words in a speech at Clinton, 8 Sept. 1858. N.W. Stephenson, *Autobiography of A. Lincoln* (1927). Attr. also to Phineas Barnum

16 What is conservatism? Is it not adherence to the old and tried, against the new and untried?
Speech, 27 Feb. 1860

17 Let us have faith that right makes might; and in that faith let us to the end, dare to do our duty as we understand it.

18 I take the official oath to-day with no mental reservations, and with no purpose to construe the Constitution or laws by any hypercritical rules.
First Inaugural Address, 4 Mar. 1861

19 This country, with its institutions, belongs to the people who inhabit it. Whenever they shall grow weary of the existing government, they can exercise their constitutional right of amending it, or their revolutionary right to dismember or overthrow it.

20 I think the necessity of being *ready* increases.—Look to it.
The whole of a letter to Governor Andrew Curtin of Pennsylvania, 8 Apr. 1861

21 My paramount object in this struggle is to save the Union…If I could save the Union without freeing any slave, I would do it; and if I could save it by freeing all the slaves, I would do it; and if I could save it by freeing some and leaving others alone, I would also do that…I have here stated my purpose according to my views of official duty and I intend no modification of my oft-expressed personal wish that all men everywhere could be free.
Letter to Horace Greeley, 22 Aug. 1862

22 In giving freedom to the slave, we assure freedom to the free,—honourable alike in what we give and what we preserve.
Annual Message to Congress, 1 Dec. 1862

23 Fourscore and seven years ago our fathers brought forth upon this continent a new nation, conceived in liberty, and dedicated to the proposition that all men are created equal…In a larger sense we cannot dedicate, we cannot consecrate, we cannot hallow this ground. The brave men, living and dead, who struggled here, have consecrated it far above our power to add or detract. The world will little note, nor long remember, what we say here, but it can never forget what they did here. It is for us, the living, rather

to be dedicated here to the unfinished work which they who fought here have thus far so nobly advanced. It is rather for us to be here dedicated to the great task remaining before us, that from these honoured dead we take increased devotion to that cause for which they gave the last full measure of devotion; that we here highly resolve that the dead shall not have died in vain, that this nation, under God, shall have a new birth of freedom; and that government of the people, by the people, and for the people, shall not perish from the earth.
Address at Dedication of National Cemetery at Gettysburg, 19 Nov. 1863. See 368:26

1 I claim not to have controlled events, but confess plainly that events have controlled me.
Letter to A.G. Hodges, 4 Apr. 1864

2 It is not best to swap horses while crossing the river.
Reply to National Union League, 9 June 1864. J.G. Nicolay and J. Hay, *Abraham Lincoln*, bk.ix

3 With malice toward none; with charity for all; with firmness in the right, as God gives us to see the right, let us strive on to finish the work we are in: to bind up the nation's wounds; to care for him who shall have borne the battle, and for his widow and his orphan, to do all which may achieve and cherish a just and lasting peace among ourselves, and with all nations.
Second Inaugural Address, 4 Mar. 1865

4 People who like this sort of thing will find this the sort of thing they like.
Judgement on a book. G.W.E. Russell, *Collections and Recollections*, ch.30

5 The Lord prefers common-looking people. That is why he makes so many of them.
James Morgan, *Our President*, ch.6

6 So you're the little woman who wrote the book that made this great war!
On meeting Harriet Beecher Stowe. Carl Sandburg, *Abraham Lincoln: The War Years*, vol.II, ch.39

7 As President, I have no eyes but constitutional eyes; I cannot see you.
Attr. reply to the South Carolina Commissioners

GEORGE LINLEY 1798–1865

8 Among our ancient mountains,
And from our lovely vales,
Oh, let the prayer re-echo:
'God bless the Prince of Wales!'
God Bless the Prince of Wales

WALTER LIPPMANN 1889–

9 I doubt whether the student can do a greater work for his nation in this grave moment of its history than to detach himself from its preoccupations, refusing to let himself be absorbed by distractions about which, as a scholar, he can do almost nothing.
The Scholar in a Troubled World, (1932)

MAXIM LITVINOFF 1876–1951

10 Peace is indivisible.
First used publicly 25 Feb. 1920. A.U. Pope, *Maxim Litvinoff*, p.234. Also used in a speech to the 16th Plenum of the League of Nations on 1 July 1936. See *Against Aggression* (1939), p.45

LIVY 59 B.C.–A.D. 17 or 64 B.C.–A.D. 12

11 *Vae victis.*
Down with the defeated.
Ab Urbe Condita, 5.48.9. Shouted by Brennus, the Gallic King, who had captured Rome (390 B.C.), but a proverbial cry.

12 *Pugna magna victi sumus.*
In a battle, a big one, the defeated were us!
22.7.8. The announcement of the Roman disaster in Hannibal's ambush at Lake Trasimene (217 B.C.)

JOHN LOCKE 1632–1704

13 New opinions are always suspected, and usually opposed, without any other reason but because they are not already common.
An Essay concerning Human Understanding (1690), dedicatory epistle

14 Nature never makes excellent things for mean or no uses.
bk.ii, ch.1, sec.15

15 No man's knowledge here can go beyond his experience.
sec.19

16 It is one thing to show a man that he is in an error, and another to put him in possession of truth.
bk.iv, ch.7, sec.11

17 All men are liable to error; and most men are, in many points, by passion or interest, under temptation to it.
ch.20, sec.17

FREDERICK LOCKER-LAMPSON 1821–1895

18 If you lift a guinea-pig up by the tail
His eyes drop out!
A Garden Lyric

19 The world's as ugly, ay, as sin,
And almost as delightful.
The Jester's Plea

20 And many are afraid of God—
And more of Mrs Grundy.

21 Some men are good for righting wrongs,—
And some for writing verses.

JOHN GIBSON LOCKHART 1794–1854

22 It is a better and a wiser thing to be a starved apothecary than a starved poet; so back to the shop Mr John, back to 'plasters, pills, and ointment boxes.'
Review of Keats's *Endymion* in *Blackwood's Magazine*, 1818; authorship attr. to Lockhart.

23 Here, early to bed, lies kind William Maginn,
Who with genius, wit, learning, life's trophies to win,
Had neither great Lord nor rich cit of his kin,
Nor discretion to set himself up as to tin...
But at last he was beat, and sought help of the bin
(All the same to the Doctor, from claret to gin),
Which led swiftly to gaol, with consumption therein;
It was much, when the bones rattled loose in his skin,
He got leave to die here, out of Babylon's din.
Barring drink and the girls, I ne'er heard of a sin:
Many worse, better few, than bright, broken Maginn.
Epitaph for William Maginn (1794–1842), in William Maginn, *Miscellanies* (1885), vol.I, p.xviii

315

1 Here lies that peerless peer Lord Peter,
  Who broke the laws of God and man and metre.
  Epitaph for Patrick ('Peter'), Lord Robertson. Sir Walter Scott,
  Journal, vol.i, p.259, n.2

FRANCIS LOCKIER 1667–1740

2 In all my travels I never met with any one Scotchman
  but what was a man of sense. I believe everybody of
  that country that has any, leaves it as fast as they can.
  Joseph Spence, *Anecdotes* (1858), p.55

THOMAS LODGE 1558?–1625

3 Love, in my bosom, like a bee,
  Doth suck his sweet.
  Love, In My Bosom

4 Heigh ho, would she were mine!
  Rosalind's Description

FRIEDRICH VON LOGAU 1604–1655

5 *Gottesmühlen mahlen langsam, mahlen aber trefflich
  klein;
  Ob aus Langmut Er sich säumet, bringt mit Schärf' Er
  alles ein.*
  Though the mills of God grind slowly, yet they grind
  exceeding small;
  Though with patience He stands waiting, with
  exactness grinds He all.
  Sinngedichte (1653), III.ii.24 (tr. H.W. Longfellow)

HENRY WADSWORTH LONGFELLOW
1807–1882

6 I shot an arrow into the air,
  It fell to earth, I knew not where.
  The Arrow and the Song

7 Thou, too, sail on, O Ship of State!
  Sail on, O Union, strong and great!
  Humanity with all its fears,
  With all the hopes of future years,
  Is hanging breathless on thy fate!
  The Building of the Ship

8 Ye are better than all the ballads
  That ever were sung or said;
  For ye are living poems,
  And all the rest are dead.
  Children

9 Between the dark and the daylight,
  When the night is beginning to lower,
  Comes a pause in the day's occupations,
  That is known as the Children's Hour.
  The Children's Hour

10 The cares that infest the day
  Shall fold their tents, like the Arabs,
  And as silently steal away.
  The Day is Done

11 If you would hit the mark, you must aim a little above
  it;
  Every arrow that flies feels the attraction of earth.
  Elegiac Verse

12 This is the forest primeval.
  Evangeline (1847), introduction, l.1

13 Sorrow and silence are strong, and patient endurance
  is godlike.
  pt.II, l.60

14 The shades of night were falling fast,
  As through an Alpine village passed
  A youth, who bore, 'mid snow and ice,
  A banner with the strange device,
      Excelsior!
  Excelsior

15 'Try not the Pass!' the old man said;
  'Dark lowers the tempest overhead.'

16 A traveller, by the faithful hound,
  Half-buried in the snow was found.

17 Giotto's tower,
  The lily of Florence blossoming in stone.
  Giotto's Tower

18 I like that ancient Saxon phrase, which calls
  The burial-ground God's-Acre!
  God's-Acre

19 The heights by great men reached and kept
  Were not attained by sudden flight,
  But they, while their companions slept,
  Were toiling upward in the night.
  The Ladder of Saint Augustine

20 Standing, with reluctant feet,
  Where the brook and river meet,
  Womanhood and childhood fleet!
  Maidenhood

21 The men that women marry,
  And why they marry them, will always be
  A marvel and a mystery to the world.
  Michael Angelo, pt.I, vi

22 I remember the black wharves and the slips,
  And the sea-tides tossing free;
  And Spanish sailors with bearded lips,
  And the beauty and mystery of the ships,
  And the magic of the sea.
  And the voice of that wayward song
  Is singing and saying still:
  'A boy's will is the wind's will
  And the thoughts of youth are long, long thoughts.'
  My Lost Youth

23 A solid man of Boston.
  A comfortable man, with dividends,
  And the first salmon and the first green peas.
  New England Tragedies (1868), John Endicott, IV.i

24 *Emigravit* is the inscription on the tombstone where he
  lies;
  Dead he is not, but departed,—for the artist never
  dies. [Of Albrecht Dürer.]
  Nuremberg, xiii

25 Listen, my children, and you shall hear
  Of the midnight ride of Paul Revere,
  On the eighteenth of April in Seventy-five.
  Paul Revere's Ride (1861)

26 A hurry of hoofs in a village street,
  A shape in the moonlight, a bulk in the dark,
  And beneath, from the pebbles, in passing, a spark
  Struck out from a steed flying fearless and fleet:
  That was all! And yet, through the gloom and the
  light,
  The fate of a nation was riding that night.

27 Not in the clamour of the crowded street,
  Not in the shouts and plaudits of the throng,

But in ourselves, are triumph and defeat.
The Poets

1 Tell me not, in mournful numbers,
    Life is but an empty dream!
For the soul is dead that slumbers,
    And things are not what they seem.

Life is real! Life is earnest!
    And the grave is not its goal;
Dust thou art, to dust returnest,
    Was not spoken of the soul.
A Psalm of Life

2 Art is long, and Time is fleeting,
    And our hearts, though stout and brave,
Still, like muffled drums, are beating
    Funeral marches to the grave.
See 251:8

3 Trust no Future, howe'er pleasant!
    Let the dead Past bury its dead!
Act,—act in the living Present!
    Heart within, and God o'erhead!

4 Lives of great men all remind us
    We can make our lives sublime,
And, departing, leave behind us
    Footprints on the sands of time.

5 Let us, then, be up and doing,
    With a heart for any fate;
Still achieving, still pursuing,
    Learn to labour and to wait.

6 There is no flock, however watched and tended,
    But one dead lamb is there!
There is no fireside, howsoe'er defended,
    But has one vacant chair!
Resignation

7 A Lady with a Lamp shall stand
In the great history of the land,
    A noble type of good,
    Heroic womanhood.
Santa Filomena

8 The forests, with their myriad tongues,
    Shouted of liberty;
And the Blast of the Desert cried aloud,
    With a voice so wild and free,
That he started in his sleep and smiled
    At their tempestuous glee.
The Slave's Dream

9 Gitche Manito, the mighty.
The Song of Hiawatha (1855), i. **The Peace-Pipe**

10 By the shore of Gitche Gumee,
By the shining Big-Sea-Water,
Stood the wigwam of Nokomis,
Daughter of the Moon, Nokomis.
Dark behind it rose the forest,
Rose the black and gloomy pine-trees,
Rose the firs with cones upon them;
Bright before it beat the water,
Beat the clear and sunny water,
Beat the shining Big-Sea-Water.
iii. **Hiawatha's Childhood**

11 From the waterfall he named her,
Minnehaha, Laughing Water.
iv. **Hiawatha and Mudjekeewis**

12 As unto the bow the cord is,
So unto the man is woman;

Though she bends him, she obeys him,
Though she draws him, yet she follows;
Useless each without the other!
x. **Hiawatha's Wooing**

13 Onaway! Awake, beloved!
xi. **Hiawatha's Wedding-feast**

14 He is dead, the sweet musician!
He the sweetest of all singers!
He has gone from us for ever,
He has moved a little nearer
To the Master of all music,
To the Master of all singing!
O my brother, Chibiabos!
xv. **Hiawatha's Lamentation**

15 The secret anniversaries of the heart.
Sonnets. Holidays

16 He seemed the incarnate 'Well, I told you so!'
Tales of a Wayside Inn, pt.I (1863), **The Poet's Tale. The Birds of Killingworth**

17 Ships that pass in the night, and speak each other in
    passing;
Only a signal shown and a distant voice in the
    darkness;
So on the ocean of life we pass and speak one another,
Only a look and a voice; then darkness again and a
    silence.
pt.III (1874), **The Theologian's Tale. Elizabeth**, iv

18 Under the spreading chestnut tree
    The village smithy stands;
The smith, a mighty man is he,
    With large and sinewy hands;
And the muscles of his brawny arms
    Are strong as iron bands.
The Village Blacksmith

19 Each morning sees some task begin,
    Each evening sees it close;
Something attempted, something done,
    Has earned a night's repose.

20 It was the schooner Hesperus,
    That sailed the wintry sea;
And the skipper had taken his little daughter,
    To bear him company.
The Wreck of the Hesperus

21 But the father answered never a word,
    A frozen corpse was he.

22 There was a little girl
Who had a little curl
Right in the middle of her forehead,
When she was good
She was very, very good,
But when she was bad she was horrid.
B.R.T. Machetta, *Home Life of Longfellow*

23 The square root of half a number of bees, and also
eight-ninths of the whole, alighted on the jasmines,
and a female buzzed responsive to the hum of the male
inclosed at night in a water-lily. O, beautiful damsel,
tell me the number of bees.
Kavanagh, ch.4

FREDERICK LONSDALE 1881–1934

24 Don't keep finishing your sentences. I am not a bloody

fool.
Frances Donaldson, *Child of the Twenties* (1959), p.11

ANITA LOOS 1893–

1 A girl like I.
Gentlemen Prefer Blondes (1925), *passim*

2 Fate keeps on happening.
ch.2 (heading)

3 Kissing your hand may make you feel very very good but a diamond and safire bracelet lasts forever.
ch.4

4 You have got to be a Queen to get away with a hat like that.

5 Fun is fun but no girl wants to laugh all of the time.

6 So then Dr Froyd said that all I needed was to cultivate a few inhibitions and get some sleep.
ch.5

FEDERICO GARCÍA LORCA
see GARCÍA LORCA

LOUIS XIV 1638–1715

7 *Il n'y a plus de Pyrénées.*
The Pyrenees have ceased to exist.
At the accession of his grandson to the throne of Spain, 1700. Attr. Voltaire, *Siècle de Louis XIV*, ch.28

8 *L'État c'est moi.*
I am the State.
Attr. remark before the Parlement de Paris, 13 Apr. 1655. Dulaure, *Histoire de Paris* (1834), vol.6, p.298. Probably apocryphal.

9 *Toutes les fois que je donne une place vacante, je fais cent mécontents et un ingrat.*
Every time I make an appointment, I make one ungrateful person and a hundred with a grievance.
Voltaire, *Siècle de Louis XIV*, ch.26

10 *J'ai failli attendre.*
I almost had to wait.
Attrib. expression of impatience. Attribution doubted by e.g. E. Fournier, *L'Esprit dans l'Histoire* (4th edition, 1884), ch.xlviii

LOUIS XVIII 1755–1824

11 *L'exactitude est la politesse des rois.*
Punctuality is the politeness of kings.
Attr. *Souvenirs de J. Lafitte* (1844), bk.1, ch.3

RICHARD LOVELACE 1618–1658

12   Am not I shot
With the self-same artillery?
Amyntor from Beyond the Sea to Alexis

13 Lucasta that bright northern star.

14 Forbear, thou great good husband, little ant.
The Ant

15 When Love with unconfined wings
    Hovers within my gates;
And my divine Althea brings
    To whisper at the grates:
When I lie tangled in her hair,
    And fettered to her eye;
The Gods, that wanton in the air,

Know no such liberty.
To Althea, From Prison

16 When flowing cups run swiftly round
With no allaying Thames.

17 When thirsty grief in wine we steep,
    When healths and draughts go free,
Fishes, that tipple in the deep,
    Know no such liberty.

18 Stone walls do not a prison make
    Nor iron bars a cage;
Minds innocent and quiet take
    That for an hermitage;
If I have freedom in my love,
    And in my soul am free;
Angels alone, that soar above,
    Enjoy such liberty.

19 If to be absent were to be
    Away from thee;
Or that when I am gone,
    You or I were alone;
Then my Lucasta might I crave
Pity from blust'ring wind, or swallowing wave.
To Lucasta, Going Beyond the Seas

20 Tell me not (Sweet) I am unkind,
    That from the nunnery
Of thy chaste breast, and quiet mind,
    To war and arms I fly.

True; a new mistress now I chase,
    The first foe in the field;
And with a stronger faith embrace
    A sword, a horse, a shield.

Yet this inconstancy is such,
    As you too shall adore;
I could not love thee (Dear) so much,
    Lov'd I not honour more.
To Lucasta, Going to the Wars

SAMUEL LOVER 1797–1868

21 When once the itch of literature comes over a man, nothing can cure it but the scratching of a pen.
Handy Andy (1842), ch.36

22 'Now women are mostly troublesome cattle to deal with mostly', said Goggins.

ROBERT LOWE, VISCOUNT SHERBROOKE 1811–1892

23 I believe it will be absolutely necessary that you should prevail on our future masters to learn their letters.
House of Commons, 15 July 1867, on the passing of the Reform Bill. Popularized as 'We must educate our masters.'

24 The Chancellor of the Exchequer is a man whose duties make him more or less of a taxing machine. He is intrusted with a certain amount of misery which it is his duty to distribute as fairly as he can.
House of Commons, 11 Apr. 1870

AMY LOWELL 1856–1943

25 And the softness of my body will be guarded from embrace
By each button, hook, and lace.

For the man who should loose me is dead,
Fighting with the Duke in Flanders,
In a pattern called a war.
Christ! What are patterns for?
Patterns

JAMES RUSSELL LOWELL 1819–1891

1 An' you've gut to git up airly
  Ef you want to take in God.
  The Biglow Papers, First Series (1848), No.1

2 You've a darned long row to hoe.

3 I du believe in Freedom's cause,
  Ez fur away ez Payris is;
  I love to see. her stick her claws
  In them infarnal Phayrisees;
  It's wal enough agin a king
  To dror resolves an' triggers,—
  But libbaty's a kind o' thing
  Thet don't agree with niggers.
  No.6. **The Pious Editor's Creed**

4 I *don't* believe in princerple,
  But O, I *du* in interest.

5 It ain't by princerples nor men
  My preudunt course is steadied,—
  I scent wich pays the best, an' then
  Go into it baldheaded.

6 She thought no v'ice hed sech a swing
  Ez hisn in the choir;
  My! when he made Ole Hundred ring,
  She *knowed* the Lord was nigher.
  Introduction to the Second Series (1867), **The Courtin'**

7 We've a war, an' a debt, an' a flag; an' ef this
  Ain't to be inderpendunt, why, wut on airth is?
  Second Series, No.4

8 There comes Poe with his raven like Barnaby Rudge,
  Three-fifths of him genius, and two-fifths sheer fudge.
  A Fable for Critics (1848), l.1215

9 No man is born into the world, whose work
  Is not born with him; there is always work,
  And tools to work withal, for those who will:
  And blessèd are the horny hands of toil!
  A Glance Behind the Curtain, l.201

10 These pearls of thought in Persian gulfs were bred,
  Each softly lucent as a rounded moon;
  The diver Omar plucked them from their bed,
  Fitzgerald strung them on an English thread.
  In a Copy of Omar Khayyám

11 Before Man made us citizens, great Nature made us
  men.
  On the Capture of Fugitive Slaves

12 Once to every man and nation comes the moment to
  decide,
  In the strife of Truth with Falsehood, for the good or
  evil side.
  The Present Crisis

13 Truth forever on the scaffold, Wrong forever on the
  throne,—
  Yet that scaffold sways the future, and, behind the dim
  unknown,
  Standeth God within the shadow, keeping watch above
  his own.

14 New occasions teach new duties: Time makes ancient
  good uncouth;
  They must upward still, and onward, who would keep
  abreast of Truth.

15 May is a pious fraud of the almanac.
  Under the Willows, l.21

16 A wise scepticism is the first attribute of a good critic.
  Among My Books. Shakespeare Once More

17 Let us be of good cheer, however, remembering that
  the misfortunes hardest to bear are those which never
  come.
  Democracy and Addresses. Democracy

18 There is no good in arguing with the inevitable. The
  only argument available with an east wind is to put on
  your overcoat.

ROBERT LOWELL 1917–1977

19 I saw the spiders marching through the air,
  Swimming from tree to tree that mildewed day
    In latter August when the hay
    Came creaking to the barn...

    Let there pass
  A minute, ten, ten trillion; but the blaze
  Is infinite, eternal, this is death,
  To die and know it. This is the Black Widow, death.
  Mr. Edwards and the Spider. See 200:7

20 These are the tranquillized *Fifties,*
  and I am forty. Ought I to regret my seedtime?
  I was a fire-breathing Catholic C.O.,
  and made my manic statement,
  telling off the state and president, and then
  sat waiting sentence in the bull pen
  beside a negro boy with curlicues
  of marijuana in his hair.
  Memories of West Street and Lepke

WILLIAM LOWNDES 1652–1724

21 Take care of the pence, and the pounds will take care
  of themselves.
  Lord Chesterfield, letter to his son, 5 Feb. 1750. In an earlier
  letter (6 Nov. 1747) the formula is given as '...for the pounds...'

LUCAN A.D. 39–65

22   *Quis iustis induit arma*
  Scire nefas, magno se iudice quisque tuetur:
  Victrix causa deis placuit, sed victa Catoni.
  It is not granted to know which man took up arms with
  more right on his side. Each pleads his cause before
  a great judge: the winning cause pleased the gods,
  but the losing one pleased Cato.
  Bellum Civile, I.126

23 *Stat magni nominis umbra.*
  There stands the ghost of a great name.
  Works, I.135

24 *Nil actum credens, dum quid superesset agendum.*
  Thinking nothing done while anything remained to be
  done.
  II.657

25   *Coniunx*
  Est mihi, sunt nati: dedimus tot pignora fatis.
  I have a wife, I have sons: all of them hostages given
  to fate.
  VII.661

1 *Jupiter est quodcumque vides, quocumque moveris.*
Jupiter is whatever you see, whichever way you move.
IX.580

LUCILIUS d.102/1 B.C.

2 *Maior erat natu; non omnia possumus omnes.*
He was older; there are some things we cannot all do.
See Macrobius, *Saturnalia*, VI.i.35

LUCRETIUS 94?–55 B.C.

3 *Ergo vivida vis animi pervicit, et extra*
Processit longe flammantia moenia mundi
Atque omne immensum peragravit, mente animoque.
So the vital strength of his spirit won through, and he
made his way far outside the flaming walls of the
world and ranged over the measureless whole, both
in mind and spirit.
De Rerum Natura, i.72. Of Epicurus.

4 *Tantum religio potuit suadere malorum.*
So much wrong could religion induce.
101

5   *Nil posse creari*
De nilo.
Nothing can be created out of nothing.
155

6 *Suave, mari magno turbantibus aequora ventis,*
E terra magnum alterius spectare laborem;
Non quia vexari quemquamst iucunda voluptas,
Sed quibus ipse malis careas quia cernere suave est.
Suave etiam belli certamina magna tueri
Per campos instructa tua sine parte pericli.
Sed nil dulcius est, bene quam munita tenere
Edita doctrina sapientum templa serena,
Despicere unde queas alios passimque videre
Errare atque viam palantis quaerere vitae,
Certare ingenio, contendere nobilitate,
Noctes atque dies niti praestante labore
Ad summas emergere opes rerumque potiri.
Lovely it is, when the winds are churning up the
waves on the great sea, to gaze out from the land on
the great efforts of someone else; not because it's an
enjoyable pleasure that somebody is in difficulties,
but because it's lovely to realize what troubles you
are yourself spared. Lovely also to witness great
battle-plans of war, carried out across the plains,
without your having any share in the danger. But
nothing is sweeter than to occupy the quiet precincts
that are well protected by the teachings of the wise,
from where you can look down on others and see
them wandering all over the place, getting lost and
seeking the way in life, striving by their wits, pitting
their noble birth, by night and by day struggling by
superior efforts to rise to power at the top and make
all theirs.
ii.1

7 *Augescunt aliae gentes, aliae minuuntur,*
Inque brevi spatio mutantur saecla animantum
Et quasi cursores vitai lampada tradunt.
Some races increase, others are reduced, and in a short
while the generations of living creatures are changed
and like runners relay the torch of life.
7

8 *Nil igitur mors est ad nos neque pertinet hilum,*

Quandoquidem natura animi mortalis habetur.
Death therefore is nothing to us nor does it concern us
a scrap, seeing that the nature of the spirit we
possess is something mortal.
iii.830

9 *Scire licet nobis nil esse in morte timendum*
Nec miserum fieri qui non est posse neque hilum
Differre an nullo fuerit iam tempore natus,
Mortalem vitam mors cum immortalis ademit.
We can know there is nothing to be feared in death,
that one who is not cannot be made unhappy, and
that it matters not a scrap whether one might ever
have been born at all, when death that is immortal
has taken over one's mortal life.
866

10 *Vitaque mancipio, nulli datur, omnibus usu.*
And life is given to none freehold, but it is leasehold
for all.
971

11   *Medio de fonte leporum*
Surgit amari aliquid quod in ipsis floribus angat.
From the midst of the fountain of delights rises
something bitter that chokes them all amongst the
flowers.
iv.1133

FRAY LUIS DE LEÓN c.1527–1591

12   *Que descansada vida*
la del que huye el mundanal ruido,
y sigue la escondida
senda, por donde han ido
los pocos sabios que en el mundo han sido!
What a relaxed life is that which flees the worldly
clamour, and follows the hidden path down which
have gone the few wise men there have been in the
world!
Vida Retirada

13 *Dicebamus hesterno die.*
We were saying yesterday.
On resuming a lecture at Salamanca University (1577) after five
years' imprisonment. Attr. in, e.g., A.F.G. Bell, *Luis de León*,
ch.8

MARTIN LUTHER 1483–1546

14 *Darum gibt unser Herr Gott gemeiniglich Reichtum*
den grossen Eseln, denen er sonst nichts gönnt.
So our Lord God commonly gives riches to those gross
asses to whom He vouchsafes nothing else.
Colloquia (collected 1566, J. Aurifaber), ch.XX

15 *Esto peccator et pecca fortiter, sed fortius fide et*
gaude in Christo.
Be a sinner and sin strongly, but more strongly have
faith and rejoice in Christ.
Letter to Melanchthon. **Epistolae**, Jena (1556), i.345

16 *Hier stehe ich. Ich kann nicht anders. Gott helfe mir.*
Amen.
Here stand I. I can do no other. God help me. Amen.
Speech at the Diet of Worms, 18 Apr. 1521

17 The confidence and faith of the heart alone make both
God and an idol.
Large Catechism, pt.I. 'The First Commandment', 1

18 Whatever your heart clings to and confides in that is
really your God.

1 *Wer nicht liebt Wein, Weib und Gesang,*
  Der bleibt ein Narr sein Leben lang.
  Who loves not woman, wine, and song
  Remains a fool his whole life long.
  Attr. Written in the Luther room in the Wartburg, but no proof
  exists of its authorship

2 *Ein' feste Burg ist unser Gott,*
  Ein' gute Wehr und Waffen.
  A safe stronghold our God is still,
  A trusty shield and weapon.
  Klug'sche Gesangbuch (1529). Tr. Carlyle

3 *Wenn ich gewusst hätte, dass so viel Teufel auf mich*
  gezielet hätten, als Ziegel auf den Dächern waren zu
  Worms, wäre ich dennoch eingeritten.
  If I had heard that as many devils would set on me in
  Worms as there are tiles on the roofs, I should none
  the less have ridden there.
  Luthers Sämmtliche Schriften (1745), xvi.14

JOHN LYDGATE 1370?–1451?

4 Woord is but wynd; leff woord and tak the dede.
  Secrees of Old Philisoffres, l.1224

5 Sithe off oure language he [Chaucer] was the
  lodesterre.
  Falls of Princes (1430-38), prol. l.252

6 Sithe he off Inglissh in makyng was the beste,
  Preie onto God to yiue his soule good reste.
  l.356

7 Comparisouns doon offte gret greuaunce.
  bk.iii, l.2188

8 Love is mor than gold or gret richesse.
  The Story of Thebes (c.1420), pt.III, l.2716

JOHN LYLY 1554?–1606

9 *Campaspe:* Were women never so fair, men would be
  false.
  Apelles: Were women never so false, men would be
  fond.
  Campaspe (1584), III.iii

10 Cupid and my Campaspe play'd
  At cards for kisses, Cupid paid.
  III.v

11 At last he set her both his eyes;
  She won, and Cupid blind did rise.
  O Love! has she done this to thee?
  What shall, alas! become of me?

12 What bird so sings, yet so does wail?
  O 'tis the ravish'd nightingale.
  Jug, jug, jug, jug, tereu, she cries,
  And still her woes at midnight rise.
  V.i

13 How at heaven's gates she claps her wings,
  The morn not waking till she sings. [The lark.]

14 Be valiant, but not too venturous. Let thy attire be
  comely, but not costly.
  Euphues: the Anatomy of Wit (1578, Arber), p.39

15 Night hath a thousand eyes.
  Maides Metamorphose (1600), III.i

16 If all the earth were paper white
  And all the sea were ink
  'Twere not enough for me to write

As my poor heart doth think.
  Works, ed. Bond (1902), vol.iii, p.452

BARON LYNDHURST 1772–1863

17 Campbell has added another terror to death.
  On being assured that he had not yet been included in Lord
  Campbell's *Lives of the Lord Chancellors;* attr. by Sir H. Poland.
  See E. Bowen-Rowlands, *Seventy-Two Years At the Bar,* ch.10.
  See 569:6

LYSANDER d. 395 B.C.

18 Deceive boys with toys, but men with oaths.
  Plutarch, *Lives, Lysander,* 8

H.F. LYTE 1793–1847

19 Abide with me; fast falls the eventide;
  The darkness deepens; Lord, with me abide;
  When other helpers fail, and comforts flee,
  Help of the helpless, O, abide with me.

  Swift to its close ebbs out life's little day;
  Earth's joys grow dim, its glories pass away;
  Change and decay in all around I see;
  O Thou, who changest not, abide with me.
  Abide with Me

GEORGE, LORD LYTTELTON 1709–1773

20 What is your sex's earliest, latest care,
  Your heart's supreme ambition?—To be fair.
  Advice to a Lady (1733), l.17

21 Seek to be good, but aim not to be great;
  A woman's noblest station is retreat.
  l.51

22 Where none admire, 'tis useless to excel;
  Where none are beaux, 'tis vain to be a belle.
  Soliloquy of a Beauty in the Country

E.R. BULWER, 1ST EARL OF LYTTON
see OWEN MEREDITH

WARD McALLISTER 1827–1895

23 There are only about four hundred people in New York
  society.
  Interview with Charles H. Crandall in the *New York Tribune,*
  1888. D. Amer. B.

GENERAL DOUGLAS MACARTHUR 1880–1964

24 I shall return.
  Message on leaving Corregidor for Australia. 11 Mar. 1942

LORD MACAULAY 1800–1859

25 Attend, all ye who list to hear our noble England's
  praise;
  I tell of the thrice famous deeds she wrought in ancient
  days.
  The Armada (1842)

26 Night sank upon the dusky beach, and on the purple
  sea,
  Such night in England ne'er had been, nor e'er again
  shall be.

27 The rugged miners poured to war from Mendip's
  sunless caves.

1 The sentinel on Whitehall gate looked forth into the
night.

2 At once on all her stately gates arose the answering
fires;
At once the wild alarum clashed from all her reeling
spires.

3 And broader still became the blaze, and louder still the
din,
As fast from every village round the horse came
spurring in;
And eastward straight from wild Blackheath the
warlike errand went,
And roused in many an ancient hall the gallant squires
of Kent.

4 Till Belvoir's lordly terraces the sign to Lincoln sent,
And Lincoln sped the message on o'er the wide vale of
Trent;
Till Skiddaw saw the fire that burned on Gaunt's
embattled pile,
And the red glare on Skiddaw roused the burghers of
Carlisle.

5 Obadiah Bind-their-kings-in-chains-and-their-
nobles-with-links-of-iron.
The Battle of Naseby. (Name of the supposed author. See
399:24.)

6 Oh, wherefore come ye forth in triumph from the
north,
With your hands, and your feet, and your raiment all
red?
And wherefore doth your rout send forth a joyous
shout?
And whence be the grapes of the wine-press which ye
tread?

7 And the Man of Blood was there, with his long
essenced hair,
And Astley, and Sir Marmaduke, and Rupert of the
Rhine.

8 To my true king I offer'd free from stain
Courage and faith; vain faith, and courage vain.
A Jacobite's Epitaph

9 For him I languished in a foreign clime,
Grey-haired with sorrow in my manhood's prime;
Heard on Lavernia Scargill's whispering trees,
And pined by Arno for my lovelier Tees.

10 By those white cliffs I never more must see,
By that dear language which I spake like thee,
Forget all feuds, and shed one English tear
O'er English dust. A broken heart lies here.

11 Lars Porsena of Clusium
By the nine gods he swore
That the great house of Tarquin
Should suffer wrong no more.
By the Nine Gods he swore it,
And named a trysting day,
And bade his messengers ride forth,
East and west and south and north,
To summon his array.
Lays of Ancient Rome (1842). Horatius, 1

12 The harvests of Arretium,
This year, old men shall reap.
This year, young boys in Umbro
Shall plunge the struggling sheep;

And in the vats of Luna,
This year, the must shall foam
Round the white feet of laughing girls
Whose sires have marched to Rome.
8

13 And with a mighty following
To join the muster came
The Tusculan Mamilius,
Prince of the Latian name.
12

14 But the Consul's brow was sad,
And the Consul's speech was low,
And darkly looked he at the wall,
And darkly at the foe.
26

15 Then out spake brave Horatius,
The Captain of the Gate:
'To every man upon this earth
Death cometh soon or late.
And how can man die better
Than facing fearful odds,
For the ashes of his fathers,
And the temples of his Gods?'
27

16 To save them from false Sextus
That wrought the deed of shame.
28

17 'Now who will stand on either hand,
And keep th_ bridge with me?'
29

18 Then none was for a party;
Then all were for the state;
Then the great man helped the poor,
And the poor man loved the great:
Then lands were fairly portioned;
Then spoils were fairly sold:
The Romans were like brothers
In the brave days of old.
31

19 Was none who would be foremost
To lead such dire attack;
But those behind cried 'Forward!'
And those before cried 'Back!'
50

20 'Come back, come back, Horatius!'
Loud cried the Fathers all.
'Back, Lartius! back, Herminius!
Back, ere the ruin fall!'
53

21 'Oh, Tiber! father Tiber
To whom the Romans pray,
A Roman's life, a Roman's arms,
Take thou in charge this day!'
59

22 And even the ranks of Tuscany
Could scarce forbear to cheer.
60

23 When the oldest cask is opened,
And the largest lamp is lit;...
With weeping and with laughter
Still is the story told,
How well Horatius kept the bridge

In the brave days of old.
69-70

1 Those trees in whose dim shadow
  The ghastly priest doth reign,
The priest who slew the slayer,
  And shall himself be slain.
The Battle of Lake Regillus, 10

2 Let no man stop to plunder,
  But slay, and slay, and slay;
The Gods who live for ever
  Are on our side to-day.
35

3 Knowledge advances by steps, and not by leaps.
Essays and Biographies. History (*Edinburgh Review*, May 1828)

4 The English Bible, a book which, if everything else in our language should perish, would alone suffice to show the whole extent of its beauty and power.
John Dryden (Jan. 1828)

5 His imagination resembled the wings of an ostrich. It enabled him to run, though not to soar.

6 The business of everybody is the business of nobody.
Historical Essays Contributed to the 'Edinburgh Review'. Hallam's 'Constitutional History' (Sept. 1828)

7 The gallery in which the reporters sit has become a fourth estate of the realm.

8 He knew that the essence of war is violence, and that moderation in war is imbecility. [John Hampden.]
Lord Nugent's 'Memorials of Hampden' (Dec. 1831)

9 The reluctant obedience of distant provinces generally costs more than it [the territory] is worth.
War of the Succession in Spain (Jan. 1833)

10 Biographers, translators, editors, all, in short, who employ themselves in illustrating the lives or writings of others, are peculiarly exposed to the *Lues Boswelliana*, or disease of admiration.
William Pitt, Earl of Chatham (Jan. 1834)

11 The highest intellects, like the tops of mountains, are the first to catch and to reflect the dawn.
Sir James Mackintosh (July 1835)

12 The history of England is emphatically the history of progress.

13 The rising hope of those stern and unbending Tories who follow, reluctantly and mutinously, a leader whose experience and eloquence are indispensable to them, but whose cautious temper and moderate opinions they abhor. [Sir Robert Peel.]
Gladstone on Church and State (Apr. 1839)

14 Every schoolboy knows who imprisoned Montezuma, and who strangled Atahualpa.
Lord Clive (Jan. 1840)

15 They [the Nabobs] raised the price of everything in their neighbourhood, from fresh eggs to rotten boroughs.

16 She [the Roman Catholic Church] may still exist in undiminished vigour when some traveller from New Zealand shall, in the midst of a vast solitude, take his stand on a broken arch of London Bridge to sketch the ruins of St Paul's.
Von Ranke (Oct. 1840). See 563:9

17 She [the Church of Rome] thoroughly understands what no other church has ever understood, how to deal with enthusiasts.

18 The Chief Justice was rich, quiet, and infamous.
Warren Hastings (Oct. 1841)

19 The great Proconsul.

20 That temple of silence and reconciliation where the enmities of twenty generations lie buried.
[Westminster Abbey.]

21 In order that he might rob a neighbour whom he had promised to defend, black men fought on the coast of Coromandel, and red men scalped each other by the Great Lakes of North America.
Frederic the Great (Apr. 1842)

22 As civilization advances, poetry almost necessarily declines.
Literary Essays Contributed to the 'Edinburgh Review'. Milton (Aug. 1825)

23 Perhaps no person can be a poet, or can even enjoy poetry, without a certain unsoundness of mind.

24 There is only one cure for the evils which newly acquired freedom produces; and that is freedom.

25 Many politicians of our time are in the habit of laying it down as a self-evident proposition, that no people ought to be free till they are fit to use their freedom. The maxim is worthy of the fool in the old story, who resolved not to go into the water till he had learnt to swim. If men are to wait for liberty till they become wise and good in slavery, they may indeed wait for ever.

26 On the rich and the eloquent, on nobles and priests, they looked down with contempt: for they esteemed themselves rich in a more precious treasure, and eloquent in a more sublime language, nobles by the right of an earlier creation, and priests by the imposition of a mightier hand. [The Puritans.]

27 Out of his surname they have coined an epithet for a knave, and out of his Christian name a synonym for the Devil.
Machiavelli (Mar. 1827)

28 Nothing is so useless as a general maxim.

29 We have heard it said that five per cent is the natural interest of money.
Southey's 'Colloquies on Society' (Jan. 1830)

30 His writing bears the same relation to poetry which a Turkey carpet bears to a picture. There are colours in the Turkey carpet out of which a picture might be made. There are words in Mr Montgomery's writing which, when disposed in certain orders and combinations, have made, and will make again, good poetry. But, as they now stand, they seem to be put together on principle in such a manner as to give no image of anything 'in the heavens above, or in the earth beneath, or in the waters under the earth.'
Mr. Robert Montgomery's Poems (Apr. 1830). See 47:24

31 The use of a mirror, we submit, is not to be painted upon.

32 His theory is therefore this, that God made the thunder, but that the lightning made itself.

33 He had a head which statuaries loved to copy, and a foot the deformity of which the beggars in the street mimicked.
Moore's 'Life of Lord Byron' (June 1830)

1 We know no spectacle so ridiculous as the British public in one of its periodical fits of morality.

2 We prefer a gipsy by Reynolds to his Majesty's head on a sign-post.

3 From the poetry of Lord Byron they drew a system of ethics, compounded of misanthropy and voluptuousness, a system in which the two great commandments were, to hate your neighbour, and to love your neighbour's wife.

4 It is not easy to make a simile go on all fours.
John Bunyan (Dec. 1830)

5 The Life of Johnson is assuredly a great, a very great work. Homer is not more decidedly the first of heroic poets, Shakespeare is not more decidedly the first of dramatists, Demosthenes is not more decidedly the first of orators, than Boswell is the first of biographers.
Samuel Johnson (Sept. 1831)

6 They knew luxury; they knew beggary; but they never knew comfort.

7 In the foreground is that strange figure which is as familiar to us as the figures of those among whom we have been brought up, the gigantic body, the huge massy face, seamed with the scars of disease, the brown coat, the black worsted stockings, the grey wig with the scorched foretop, the dirty hands, the nails bitten and pared to the quick.

8 The conformation of his mind was such that whatever was little seemed to him great, and whatever was great seemed to him little.
Horace Walpole (Oct. 1833)

9 With the dead there is no rivalry. In the dead there is no change. Plato is never sullen. Cervantes is never petulant. Demosthenes never comes unseasonably. Dante never stays too long. No difference of political opinion can alienate Cicero. No heresy can excite the horror of Bossuet.
Lord Bacon (July 1837)

10 An acre in Middlesex is better than a principality in Utopia.

11 We now turn away from the checkered spectacle of so much glory and so much shame.

12 What schoolboy of fourteen is ignorant of this remarkable circumstance?
Sir William Temple (Oct. 1838)

13 He was a rake among scholars, and a scholar among rakes. [Richard Steele.]
The Life and Writings of Addison (July 1843)

14 The old philosopher is still among us in the brown coat with the metal buttons and the shirt which ought to be at wash, blinking, puffing, rolling his head, drumming with his fingers, tearing his meat like a tiger, and swallowing his tea in oceans.
Life of Johnson, (ad fin.)

15 I shall cheerfully bear the reproach of having descended below the dignity of history.
History of England, vol.i (1849), ch.1

16 Thus our democracy was, from an early period, the most aristocratic, and our aristocracy the most democratic in the world.

17 Persecution produced its natural effect on them. It found them a sect; it made them a faction.

18 It was a crime in a child to read by the bedside of a sick parent one of those beautiful collects which had soothed the griefs of forty generations of Christians.
ch.2

19 The Puritan hated bear-baiting, not because it gave pain to the bear, but because it gave pleasure to the spectators.

20 The object of oratory alone is not truth, but persuasion.
Works (1898), vol.xi. **Essay on Athenian Orators**

21 History, abounding with kings thirty feet high, and reigns thirty thousand years long—and geography made up of seas of treacle and seas of butter.
Minute, as Member of Supreme Council of India, 2 Feb. 1835

22 Dark and terrible beyond any season within my remembrance of political affairs was the day of their flight. Far darker and far more terrible will be the day of their return. [The Tory Government, defeated in Nov. 1830.]
Speech, 20 Sept. 1831

23 A broken head in Cold Bath Fields produces a greater sensation among us than three pitched battles in India.
10 July 1833

24 Thank you, madam, the agony is abated. [Reply, aged four.]
Trevelyan, *Life and Letters of Macaulay*, ch.1

25 I shall not be satisfied unless I produce something which shall for a few days supersede the last fashionable novel on the tables of young ladies.
ch.9

26 We were regaled by a dogfight...How odd that people of sense should find any pleasure in being accompanied by a beast who is always spoiling conversation.
ch.14

ROSE MACAULAY 1889–1958

27 'Take my camel, dear,' said my aunt Dot as she climbed down from this animal on her return from High Mass.
The Towers of Trebizond (1956), p.1

GENERAL McAULIFFE 1898–1975

28 Nuts!
Reply to German demand for surrender of 101st Airborne Division men trapped at Bastogne, Belgium, 23 Dec. 1944

GENERAL GEORGE B. McCLELLAN 1826–1885

29 All quiet along the Potomac.
Attr. in the American Civil War. See 38:8

DR. JOHN McCRAE 1872–1918

30 In Flanders fields the poppies blow
Between the crosses, row on row,
   That mark our place.
In Flanders Fields. Ypres Salient, 3 May 1915

31   If ye break faith with us who die
We shall not sleep, though poppies grow
   In Flanders fields.

C.B. MACDONALD 1855–1939

1 When ye come to play golf ye maun hae a heid!
Scotland's Gift—Golf (1928)
(A caddy at St. Andrews named Lang Willie was teaching one of
the professors of the university the noble game. The professor was
not a promising pupil.—Willie fairly got out of patience and said
to him: 'Ye see, Professor, as long as ye are learning thae lads at
the College Latin and Greek it is easy work, but when ye come to
play golf ye maun hae a heid!')

GEORGE MACDONALD 1824–1905

2 Where did you come from, baby dear?
Out of the everywhere into here.
At the Back of the North Wind (1871), xxxiii, Song

3 Here lie I, Martin Elginbrodde:
Hae mercy o' my soul, Lord God;
As I wad do, were I Lord God,
And ye were Martin Elginbrodde.
David Elginbrod (1863), bk.i, ch.13

4 They all were looking for a king
To slay their foes, and lift them high;
Thou cam'st, a little baby thing,
That made a woman cry.
That Holy Thing

WILLIAM McGONAGALL 1825–1902

5 Alas! Lord and Lady Dalhousie are dead, and buried
  at last,
Which causes many people to feel a little downcast.
The Death of Lord and Lady Dalhousie

6 Beautiful Railway Bridge of the Silv'ry Tay!
Alas, I am very sorry to say
That ninety lives have been taken away
On the last Sabbath day of 1879,
Which will be remember'd for a very long time.
The Tay Bridge Disaster

ANTONIO MACHADO 1875–1939

7 *Yo vivo en paz con los hombres*
y en guerra con mis entrañas.
I am living at peace with men and at war with my
  innards.
Campos de Castilla (1917), **Proverbios y Cantares**, xxii

NICCOLÒ MACHIAVELLI 1469–1527

8 As a prince must be able to act just like a beast, he
should learn from the fox and the lion; because the lion
does not defend himself against traps, and the fox does
not defend himself against wolves. So one has to be a
fox in order to recognize traps, and a lion to frighten
off wolves.
The Prince, XVIII

CHARLES MACKAY 1814–1889

9 There's a good time coming, boys,
  A good time coming.
The Good Time Coming

SIR COMPTON MACKENZIE 1883–1972

10 You are offered a piece of bread and butter that feels
like a damp handkerchief and sometimes, when

cucumber is added to it, like a wet one. [An English
tea party.]
Vestal Fire (1927), ch.3

SIR JAMES MACKINTOSH 1765–1832

11 Men are never so good or so bad as their opinions.
Ethical Philosophy (1830), 6. Bentham

12 The Commons, faithful to their system, remained in a
wise and masterly inactivity.
Vindiciae Gallicae (1791), 1

ARCHIBALD MACLEISH 1892–

13 A Poem should be palpable and mute
As a globed fruit,

Dumb
As old medallions to the thumb,

Silent as the sleeve-worn stone
Of casement ledges where the moss has grown—

A poem should be wordless
As the flight of birds.
Ars poetica

14 A poem should not mean
But be.

MURDOCH McLENNAN fl. 1715

15 There's some say that we wan, some say that they
  wan,
  Some say that nane wan at a', man;
But one thing I'm sure, that at Sheriffmuir
  A battle there was which I saw, man:
And we ran, and they ran, and they ran, and we ran,
  And we ran; and they ran awa', man!
Sheriffmuir. Roxburghe Ballads (1889), vol.vi. In Hogg's
Jacobite Relics, 1821, vol.ii, the last line is: 'But Florence ran
fastest of a', man.' (Florence was the Marquis of Huntley's horse)

MARSHALL McLUHAN 1911–

16 In a culture like ours, long accustomed to splitting and
dividing all things as a means of control, it is
sometimes a bit of a shock to be reminded that, in
operational and practical fact, the medium is the
message.
Understanding Media (1964), pt.i, ch.1

MARSHAL MACMAHON 1808–1893

17 *J'y suis, j'y reste.*
Here I am, and here I stay.
At the taking of the Malakoff, 8 Sept. 1855. MacMahon later cast
doubt on the attribution: *'Je ne crois pas...avoir donné à ma
pensée cette forme lapidaire.'* See Hanoteaux, *Histoire de la
France Contemporaine,* vol.II, ch.1, sect.i

HAROLD MACMILLAN 1894–

18 Let's be frank about it; most of our people have never
had it so good.
Speech at Bedford, 20 July 1957. 'You Never Had It So Good'
was the Democratic Party slogan in the U.S. election campaign of
1952.

19 On 7 January [1958]...I made a short and carefully
prepared statement...I referred to 'some recent
difficulties' in our affairs at home which had 'caused
me a little anxiety'. However, 'I thought the best thing

to do was to settle up these little local difficulties and then to turn to the wider vision of the Commonwealth.'
Referring to the sterling crisis and to Thorneycroft's resignation. *Riding The Storm, 1956–1959* (1971), ch.11, **Money and Men**

1 The most striking of all the impressions I have formed since I left London a month ago is of the strength of this African national consciousness...The wind of change is blowing through this continent.
Speech to the South African Houses of Parliament, Cape Town, 3 Feb. 1960. The speech was drafted by Sir David Hunt as described by him in *On the Spot: An Ambassador Remembers* (1975)

LEONARD MACNALLY 1752–1820

2 This lass so neat, with smiles so sweet,
Has won my right good-will,
I'd crowns resign to call thee mine,
Sweet lass of Richmond Hill.
The Lass of Richmond Hill. E. Duncan, *Minstrelsy of England* (1905), i.254. Attr. also to W. Upton in *Oxford Song Book*, and to W. Hudson in Baring-Gould, *English Minstrelsie* (1895), iii.54

LOUIS MACNEICE 1907–1963

3 All of London littered with remembered kisses.
Autumn Journal, iv

4 Better authentic mammon than a bogus god.
xii

5 Good-bye now, Plato and Hegel,
The shop is closing down;
They don't want any philosopher-kings in England,
There ain't no universals in this man's town.
xiii

6 There will be time to audit
The accounts later, there will be sunlight later
And the equation will come out at last.
xxiv

7 It's no go the merrygoround, it's no go the rickshaw,
All we want is a limousine and a ticket for the peepshow.
Bagpipe Music

8 It's no go the picture palace, it's no go the stadium,
It's no go the country cot with a pot of pink geraniums,
It's no go the Government grants, it's no go the elections,
Sit on your arse for fifty years and hang your hat on a pension.

It's no go my honey love, it's no go my poppet;
Work your hands from day to day, the winds will blow the profit.
The glass is falling hour by hour, the glass will fall for ever,
But if you break the bloody glass, you won't hold up the weather.

9 Why, then, do I loiter round these chartered sanctuaries,
Holding the basin to gowned and spectacled Pilates
While they suffer those ghosts [classical authors] to be martyred over and over.
A Classical Education

10 A poet like a pale candle guttering
On a worn window-sill in the wind.

11 Time was away and somewhere else,

There were two glasses and two chairs
And two people with the one pulse
(Somebody stopped the moving stairs):
Time was away and somewhere else.
Meeting Point

12 So they were married—to be the more together—
And found they were never again so much together.
Novelettes, II. **Les Sylphides**

13 I am not yet born; O fill me
With strength against those who would freeze my humanity, would dragoon me into a lethal automaton, would make me a cog in a machine, a thing with one face, a thing, and against all those who would dissipate my entirety, would blow me like thistledown hither and thither or hither and thither like water held in the hands would spill me.

let them not make me a stone and let them not spill me
Otherwise kill me.
Prayer before Birth

14 World is crazier and more of it than we think,
Incorrigibly plural.
Snow

15 The sunlight on the garden
Hardens and grows cold,
We cannot cage the minute
Within its nets of gold,
When all is told
We cannot beg for pardon.
The Sunlight on the Garden

16 Our freedom as free lances
Advances towards its end;
The earth compels, upon it
Sonnets and birds descend;
And soon, my friend,
We shall have no time for dances.

GEOFFREY MADAN 1895–1947

17 The devil finds some mischief still for hands that have not learnt how to be idle.
L.S.N., *Twelve Reflections* (privately printed, 1934)

18 The dust of exploded beliefs may make a fine sunset.

SAMUEL MADDEN 1686–1765

19 Words are men's daughters, but God's sons are things.
Boulter's Monument (1745), 1.377

MAURICE MAETERLINCK 1862–1949

20 *Il n'y a pas de morts.*
There are no dead.
L'Oiseau bleu (1909), IV.ii

ARCHBISHOP MAGEE 1821–1891

21 It would be better that England should be free than that England should be compulsorily sober.
Speech on the Intoxicating Liquor Bill, House of Lords, 2 May 1872

MAGNA CARTA 1215

1 *Quod Anglicana ecclesia libera sit.*
That the English Church shall be free.
1

2 *Nullus liber homo capiatur, vel imprisonetur, aut dissaisiatur, aut utlagetur, aut exuletur, aut aliquo modo destruator, nec super eum ibimus, nec super eum mittemus, nisi per legale judicium parium suorum vel per legem terrae.*
No free man shall be taken or imprisoned or dispossessed, or outlawed or exiled, or in any way destroyed, nor will we go upon him, nor will we send against him except by the lawful judgement of his peers or by the law of the land.
39

3 *Nulli vendemus, nulli negabimus aut differemus, rectum aut justitiam.*
To no man will we sell, or deny, or delay, right or justice.
40

SIR JOHN PENTLAND MAHAFFY 1839–1919

4 [On distinguishing the Irish bull from similar freaks of language.] The Irish bull is always pregnant.
Oral trad.

ALFRED T. MAHAN 1840–1914

5 Those far distant, storm-beaten ships, upon which the Grand Army never looked, stood between it and the dominion of the world.
The Influence of Sea Power upon the French Revolution and Empire, 1793–1812 (1892), ii.118

GUSTAV MAHLER 1860–1911

6 *Endlich fortissimo!*
At last, *fortissimo!*
On visiting Niagara. K. Blankopf, *Mahler*, ch.8

SIR HENRY MAINE 1822–1888

7 Except the blind forces of Nature, nothing moves in this world which is not Greek in its origin.
Village Communities (1871)

JOSEPH DE MAISTRE 1753–1821

8 *Toute nation a le gouvernement qu'elle mérite.*
Every country has the government it deserves.
Lettres et Opuscules Inédits, i. p.215, 15 Aug. 1811

STÉPHANE MALLARMÉ 1842–1898

9 *La chair est triste, hélas! et j'ai lu tous les livres.*
The flesh, alas, is wearied; and I have read all the books there are.
Brise Marin

10 *Le vierge, le vivace et le bel aujourd'hui.*
That virgin, vital, fine day: today.
Plusieurs Sonnets

11 *Un coup de dés jamais n'abolira le hasard.*
A throw of the dice will never eliminate chance.
Cosmopolis, May 1897

DAVID MALLET 1705?–1765

12 O grant me, Heaven, a middle state,
Neither too humble nor too great;
More than enough, for nature's ends,
With something left to treat my friends.
Imitation of Horace. See 262:9

GEORGE LEIGH MALLORY 1886–1924

13 Because it is there.
Answer to the question repeatedly asked him on his American lecture tour of 1923, 'Why do you want to climb Mt. Everest?' D. Robertson, *George Mallory* (1969), p.215

SIR THOMAS MALORY d. 1471

14 Whoso pulleth out this sword of this stone and anvil is rightwise King born of all England.
Le Morte D'Arthur (finished 1469–70, printed 1485), bk.i, ch.4

15 This beast went to the well and drank, and the noise was in the beast's belly like unto the questing of thirty couple hounds, but all the while the beast drank there was no noise in the beast's belly.
ch.19

16 Me repenteth, said Merlin; because of the death of that lady thou shalt strike a stroke most dolorous that ever man struck, except the stroke of our Lord, for thou shalt hurt the truest knight and the man of most worship that now liveth, and through that stroke three kingdoms shall be in great poverty, misery and wretchedness twelve years, and the knight shall not be whole of that wound for many years.
bk.ii, ch.8

17 Ah, my little son, thou hast murdered thy mother! And therefore I suppose thou that art a murderer so young, thou art full likely to be a manly man in thine age...when he is christened let call him Tristram, that is as much to say as a sorrowful birth.
bk.viii, ch.1

18 Meanwhile came Sir Palomides, the good knight, following the questing beast that had in shape like a serpent's head and a body like a leopard, buttocked like a lion and footed like a hart. And in his body there was such a noise as it had been twenty couple of hounds questing [yelping], and such noise that beast made wheresomever he went.
bk.ix, ch.12

19 God defend me, said Dinadan, for the joy of love is too short, and the sorrow thereof, and what cometh thereof, dureth over long.
bk.x, ch.56

20 Now I thank God, said Sir Launcelot, for His great mercy of that I have seen, for it sufficeth me. For, as I suppose, no man in this world hath lived better than I have done, to achieve that I have done.
bk.xvii, ch.16

21 Fair lord, salute me to my lord, Sir Launcelot, my father, and as soon as ye see him, bid him remember of this unstable world.
ch.22

22 Thus endeth the story of the Sangreal, that was briefly drawn out of French into English, the which is a story chronicled for one of the truest and the holiest that is in this world.
ch.23, end

1 The month of May was come, when every lusty heart beginneth to blossom, and to bring forth fruit; for like as herbs and trees bring forth fruit and flourish in May, in likewise every lusty heart that is in any manner a lover, springeth and flourisheth in lusty deeds.
bk.xviii, ch.25

2 Therefore all ye that be lovers call unto your remembrance the month of May, like as did Queen Guenevere, for whom I make here a little mention, that while she lived she was a true lover, and therefore she had a good end.

3 Through this man and me hath all this war been wrought, and the death of the most noblest knights of the world; for through our love that we have loved together is my most noble lord slain.
bk.xxi, ch.9

4 Wherefore, madam, I pray you kiss me and never no more. Nay, said the queen, that shall I never do, but abstain you from such works: and they departed. But there was never so hard an hearted man but he would have wept to see the dolour that they made.
ch.10

5 And Sir Launcelot awoke, and went and took his horse, and rode all that day and all night in a forest, weeping.

6 Then Sir Launcelot never after ate but little meat, ne drank, till he was dead.
ch.12

7 I saw the angels heave up Sir Launcelot unto heaven, and the gates of heaven opened against him.

8 Said Sir Ector...Sir Launcelot...thou wert never matched of earthly knight's hand; and thou wert the courteoust knight that ever bare shield; and thou wert the truest friend to thy lover that ever bestrad horse; and thou wert the truest lover of a sinful man that ever loved woman; and thou wert the kindest man that ever struck with sword; and thou wert the goodliest person that ever came among press of knights; and thou wert the meekest man and the gentlest that ever ate in hall among ladies; and thou wert the sternest knight to thy mortal foe that ever put spear in the rest.
ch.13

THOMAS ROBERT MALTHUS 1766–1834

9 Population, when unchecked, increases in a geometrical ratio. Subsistence only increases in an arithmetical ratio.
The Principle of Population (1798), 1

W.R. MANDALE nineteenth century

10 Up and down the City Road,
In and out the Eagle,
That's the way the money goes—
Pop goes the weasel!
Pop Goes the Weasel

MANILIUS 1st cent. A.D.

11 *Eripuitque Jovi fulmen viresque tonandi.*
And snatched from Jove the lightning shaft and power

to thunder.
Astronomica, i.104. Of human intelligence

MRS. MANLEY 1663–1724

12 No time like the present.
The Lost Lover (1696), IV.i

HORACE MANN 1796–1859

13 The object of punishment is, prevention from evil; it never can be made impulsive to good.
Lectures and Reports on Education (1845), 1867 edn., lecture vii

14 Lost, yesterday, somewhere between Sunrise and Sunset, two golden hours, each set with sixty diamond minutes. No reward is offered, for they are gone forever.
Lost, Two Golden Hours

LORD JOHN MANNERS, DUKE OF RUTLAND 1818–1906

15 Let wealth and commerce, laws and learning die,
But leave us still our old nobility!
England's Trust (1841), pt.III, l.227

LORD MANSFIELD 1705–1793

16 The constitution does not allow reasons of state to influence our judgments: God forbid it should! We must not regard political consequences; however formidable soever they might be: if rebellion was the certain consequence, we are bound to say '*fiat justitia, ruat caelum*'.
Rex v. Wilkes, 8 June 1768

17 Consider what you think justice requires, and decide accordingly. But never give your reasons; for your judgement will probably be right, but your reasons will certainly be wrong.
Advice to a newly appointed colonial governor ignorant in the law. Campbell, *Lives of the Chief Justices*, ch.40

MAO TSE-TUNG 1893–1976

18 Letting a hundred flowers blossom and a hundred schools of thought contend is the policy.
Speech, 2 May 1956. Roderick MacFarquhar, *Origins of the Cultural Revolution* (1974), vol. 1, p. 51

19 Every Communist must grasp the truth, 'Political power grows out of the barrel of a gun.'
Selected Works (Peking, 1961), vol.II. **Problems of War and Strategy,** ii, 6 Nov. 1938

20 The atomic bomb is a paper tiger which the US reactionaries use to scare people. It looks terrible, but in fact it isn't. . .All reactionaries are paper tigers.
vol. IV. **Talk with Anna Louise Strong,** Aug. 1946

WILLIAM LEARNED MARCY 1786–1857

21 To the victor belong the spoils of the enemy.
Parton, *Life of Jackson* (1860), vol.iii, p.378

QUEEN MARIE-ANTOINETTE 1755–1793

22 *Qu'ils mangent de la brioche.*
Let them eat cake.
On being told that her people had no bread. Attributed to Marie-Antoinette, but much older. Rousseau refers in his

Confessions, 1740, to a similar remark, as a well known saying. Louis XVIII in his *Relation d'un Voyage à Bruxelles et à Coblentz en 1791* (1823, p.59) attributes to Marie-Thérèse (1638–83), wife of Louis XIV, *'Que ne mangent-ils de la croûte de pâté?'* ('Why don't they eat pastry?')

SARAH, 1ST DUCHESS OF MARLBOROUGH
1660–1744

1 The Duke returned from the wars today and did pleasure me in his top-boots.
Oral trad. Attr. in various forms

2 For painters, poets and builders have very high flights, but they must be kept down.
Letter to the Duchess of Bedford, 21 June 1734. Gladys Scott Thomson, *The Russells in Bloomsbury (1669–1771)* (1940), ch.9

CHRISTOPHER MARLOWE 1564–1593

3 Sweet Analytics, 'tis thou hast ravished me.
Doctor Faustus (1588?, published 1604), I.i.6

4 I'll have them fly to India for gold,
Ransack the ocean for orient pearl.
80

5 I'll have them wall all Germany with brass,
And make swift Rhine circle fair Wertenberg.
I'll have them fill the public schools with silk,
Wherewith the students shall be bravely clad.
86

6 *Faustus:* And what are you that live with Lucifer?
Mephistopheles: Unhappy spirits that fell with Lucifer,
Conspired against our God with Lucifer,
And are for ever damned with Lucifer.
iii.69

7 Why this is hell, nor am I out of it:
Thinkst thou that I who saw the face of God,
And tasted the eternal joys of heaven,
Am not tormented with ten thousand hells
In being deprived of everlasting bliss!
76

8 Hell hath no limits nor is circumscrib'd
In one self place, where we are is Hell,
And where Hell is, there must we ever be.
And to be short, when all the world dissolves,
And every creature shall be purified,
All places shall be hell that are not heaven.
II.i.120

9 Have not I made blind Homer sing to me?
ii.26

10 Was this the face that launch'd a thousand ships,
And burnt the topless towers of Ilium?
Sweet Helen, make me immortal with a kiss!
Her lips suck forth my soul: see, where it flies!
Come Helen, come give me my soul again.
Here will I dwell, for heaven be in these lips,
And all is dross that is not Helena.
V.i.97

11 Now hast thou but one bare hour to live,
And then thou must be damned perpetually;
Stand still you ever-moving spheres of heaven,
That time may cease, and midnight never come.
Fair nature's eye, rise, rise again and make
Perpetual day, or let this hour be but
A year, a month, a week, a natural day,
That Faustus may repent and save his soul.
O lente, lente currite noctis equi:

The stars move still, time runs, the clock will strike,
The devil will come, and Faustus must be damn'd.
O I'll leap up to my God: who pulls me down?
See see where Christ's blood streams in the firmament.
One drop would save my soul, half a drop, ah my Christ.
ii.127

12 Mountains and hills, come, come and fall on me,
And hide me from the heavy wrath of God.
146

13 You stars that reigned at my nativity,
Whose influence hath allotted death and hell,
Now draw up Faustus like a foggy mist,
Into the entrails of yon labouring cloud,
That when you vomit forth into the air,
My limbs may issue from your smoky mouths,
So that my soul may but ascend to heaven.
151

14 Ah, Pythagoras' metempsychosis, were that true,
This soul should fly from me, and I be chang'd
Unto some brutish beast.
168

15 O soul, be changed into little water drops,
And fall into the ocean, ne'er be found:
My God, my God, look not so fierce on me.
179

16 Cut is the branch that might have grown full straight,
And burnèd is Apollo's laurel bough,
That sometime grew within this learned man.
epilogue

17 My men, like satyrs grazing on the lawns,
Shall with their goat feet dance an antic hay.
Edward II (1593), I.i.59

18 It lies not in our power to love, or hate,
For will in us is over-rul'd by fate.
When two are stripped, long ere the course begin,
We wish that one should lose, the other win;
And one especially do we affect
Of two gold ingots, like in each respect.
The reason no man knows; let it suffice,
What we behold is censured by our eyes.
Where both deliberate, the love is slight;/
Who ever loved that loved not at first sight?
Hero and Leander (published 1598). First Sestiad, l.167. See 426:19

19 I count religion but a childish toy,
And hold there is no sin but ignorance.
The Jew of Malta (c. 1592), prologue

20 Thus methinks should men of judgement frame
Their means of traffic from the vulgar trade,
And, as their wealth increaseth, so enclose
Infinite riches in a little room.
I.i.34

21 As for myself, I walk abroad o' nights
And kill sick people groaning under walls:
Sometimes I go about and poison wells.
II.iii.172

22 *Barnadine:* Thou hast committed—
Barabas: Fornication? But that was in another country: and besides, the wench is dead.
IV.i.40

23 Come live with me, and be my love,
And we will all the pleasures prove,

That valleys, groves, hills and fields,
Woods or steepy mountain yields.
The Passionate Shepherd to his Love. See
187:24, 404:9, 495:16

1 By shallow rivers, to whose falls,
Melodious birds sing madrigals.

2 From jigging veins of rhyming mother-wits,
And such conceits as clownage keeps in pay,
We'll lead you to the stately tents of war.
Tamburlaine the Great (1587 or earlier, published 1590),
prologue

3 Zenocrate, lovelier than the Love of Jove,
Brighter than is the silver Rhodope,
Fairer than whitest snow on Scythian hills.
pt.I, 1.283

4 Our swords shall play the orators for us.
1.328

5 With Nature's pride, and richest furniture,
His looks do menace heaven and dare the Gods.
1.351

6 Accurst be he that first invented war.
1.664

7 Is it not passing brave to be a King,
And ride in triumph through Persepolis?
1.758

8 Nature that fram'd us of four elements,
Warring within our breasts for regiment,
Doth teach us all to have aspiring minds:
Our souls, whose faculties can comprehend
The wondrous Architecture of the world:
And measure every wand'ring planet's course,
Still climbing after knowledge infinite,
And always moving as the restless Spheres,
Will us to wear ourselves and never rest,
Until we reach the ripest fruit of all,
That perfect bliss and sole felicity,
The sweet fruition of an earthly crown.
1.869

9 Virtue is the fount whence honour springs.
1.1769

10 Ah fair Zenocrate, divine Zenocrate,
Fair is too foul an epithet for thee.
1.1916

11 What is beauty saith my sufferings, then?
If all the pens that ever poets held
Had fed the feeling of their masters' thoughts,
And every sweetness that inspir'd their hearts,
Their minds, and muses on admired themes:
If all the heavenly quintessence they still
From their immortal flowers of Poesy,
Wherein as in a mirror we perceive
The highest reaches of a human wit;
If these had made one poem's period,
And all combin'd in beauty's worthiness,
Yet should there hover in their restless heads
One thought, one grace, one wonder at the least,
Which into words no virtue can digest.
But how unseemly is it for my sex,
My discipline of arms and chivalry,
My nature, and the terror of my name,
To harbour thoughts effeminate and faint!
Save only that in Beauty's just applause,
With whose instinct the soul of man is touched,
And every warrior that is rapt with love

Of fame, of valour, and of victory,
Must needs have beauty beat on his conceits:
I thus conceiving and subduing both,
That which hath stopp'd the tempest of the Gods,
Even from the fiery-spangled veil of heaven,
To feel the lovely warmth of shepherds' flames,
And march in cottages of strowed reeds,
Shall give the world to note, for all my birth,
That Virtue solely is the sum of glory,
And fashions men with true nobility.
1.1941

12 Now walk the angels on the walls of heaven,
As sentinels to warn th' immortal souls,
To entertain divine Zenocrate.
pt.II, 1.2983

13 Yet let me kiss my Lord before I die,
And let me die with kissing of my Lord.
1.3037

14 Helen, whose beauty summoned Greece to arms,
And drew a thousand ships to Tenedos.
1.3055

15 More childish valourous than manly wise.
1.3690

16 Holla, ye pampered Jades of Asia:
What, can ye draw but twenty miles a day?
1.3980. See 441:25

17 Tamburlaine, the Scourge of God, must die.
1.4641

SHACKERLEY MARMION 1603–1639

18 Familiarity begets boldness.
The Antiquary (1636 or earlier, published 1641), Act I

19 Great joys, like griefs, are silent.
Holland's Leaguer (1632), V.i

DON MARQUIS 1878–1937

20 girls we was all of us ladies
we was o what the hell
and once a lady always game
by crikey blood will tell.
archy and mehitabel, xxxv. **mehitabel dances with boreas**

21 but wotthehell archy wotthehell
jamais triste archy jamais triste
that is my motto.
xlvi. **mehitabel sees paris**

22 toujours gai, archy, toujours gai.
archys life of mehitabel, i. **the life of mehitabel the cat**

23   the great open spaces
where cats are cats.
xiv. **mehitabel has an adventure**

24 honesty is a good
thing but
it is not profitable to
its possessor
unless it is
kept under control.
xl. **archygrams**

25 as I was crawling
through the holes in
a swiss cheese
the other
day it occurred to

me to wonder
what a swiss cheese
would think if
a swiss cheese
could think and after
cogitating for some
time I said to myself
if a swiss cheese
could think
it would think that
a swiss cheese
was the most important
thing in the world
just as everything that
can think at all
does think about itself.

1 did you ever
notice that when
a politician
does get an idea
he usually
gets it all wrong.

2 now and then
there is a person born
who is so unlucky
that he runs into accidents
which started out to happen
to somebody else.
xli. *archy says*

CAPTAIN MARRYAT 1792–1848

3 There's no getting blood out of a turnip.
Japhet in Search of a Father (1836), ch.4

4 As savage as a bear with a sore head.
The King's Own (1830), ch.26

5 If you please, ma'am, it was a very little one. [The
nurse excusing her illegitimate baby.]
Mr. Midshipman Easy (1836), ch.3

6 All zeal...all zeal, Mr Easy.
ch.9

7 I never knows the children. It's just six of one and
half-a-dozen of the other.
The Pirate (1836), ch.4

MARTIAL b. A.D. 43

8 *Non est, crede mihi, sapientis dicere 'Vivam':*
Sera nimis vita est crastina: vive hodie.
Believe me, wise men don't say 'I shall live to do
that', tomorrow's life's too late; live today.
Epigrammata, I.xv

9 *Non amo te, Sabidi, nec possum dicere quare:*
Hoc tantum possum dicere, non amo te.
I don't love you, Sabidius, and I can't tell you why;
all I can tell you is this, that I don't love you.
xxxii

10 *Laudant illa sed ista legunt.*
They praise those works, but they're not the ones they
read.
IV.xlix

11   *Bonosque*
Soles effugere atque abire sentit,
Qui nobis pereunt et imputantur.

Each of us feels the good days speed and depart, and
they're lost to us and counted against us.
V.xx

12 *Non est vivere, sed valere vita est.*
Life's not just being alive, but being well.
VI.lxx

13 *Difficilis facilis, iucundus acerbus es idem:*
Nec tecum possum vivere nec sine te.
Difficult or easy, pleasant or bitter, you are the same
you: I cannot live with you—nor without you.
XII.xlvi (xlvii)

14 *Rus in urbe.*
Country in the town.
lvii

ANDREW MARVELL 1621–1678

15 Where the remote Bermudas ride
In th' ocean's bosom unespied.
Bermudas

16 He hangs in shades the orange bright,
Like golden lamps in a green night. . .
And makes the hollow seas, that roar,
Proclaim the ambergris on shore.
He cast (of which we rather boast)
The Gospel's pearls upon our coast.

17 O let our voice his praise exalt,
Till it arrive at Heaven's vault:
Which thence (perhaps) rebounding, may
Echo beyond the Mexique Bay.

18 My love is of a birth as rare
As 'tis for object strange and high:
It was begotten by despair
Upon impossibility.

Magnanimous Despair alone
Could show me so divine a thing,
Where feeble Hope could ne'er have flown
But vainly flapt its tinsel wing.
The Definition of Love

19 As lines so loves oblique may well
Themselves in every angle greet
But ours so truly parallel,
Though infinite can never meet.

Therefore the love which us doth bind,
But Fate so enviously debars,
Is the conjunction of the mind,
And opposition of the stars.

20 Choosing each stone, and poising every weight,
Trying the measures of the breadth and height;
Here pulling down, and there erecting new,
Founding a firm state by proportions true.
The First Anniversary of the Government under Oliver
Cromwell, l.245

21 How vainly men themselves amaze
To win the palm, the oak, or bays;
And their uncessant labours see
Crown'd from some single herb or tree,
Whose short and narrow vergèd shade
Does prudently their toils upbraid;
While all flowers and all trees do close
To weave the garlands of repose.
The Garden, 1

22 Fair quiet, have I found thee here,

331

And Innocence thy Sister dear!

2

1 Society is all but rude,
To this delicious solitude.

2 The Gods, that mortal beauty chase,
Still in a tree did end their race.
Apollo hunted Daphne so,
Only that she might laurel grow.
And Pan did after Syrinx speed,
Not as a nymph, but for a reed.

4

3 What wond'rous life is this I lead!
Ripe apples drop about my head;
The luscious clusters of the vine
Upon my mouth do crush their wine;
The nectarine and curious peach,
Into my hands themselves do reach;
Stumbling on melons, as I pass,
Insnar'd with flow'rs, I fall on grass.

5

4 Meanwhile the mind, from pleasure less,
Withdraws into its happiness.

6

5 Annihilating all that's made
To a green thought in a green shade.

6 Here at the fountain's sliding foot,
Or at some fruit-tree's mossy root,
Casting the body's vest aside,
My soul into the boughs does glide.

7

7 Such was that happy garden-state,
While man there walk'd without a mate.

8

8 But 'twas beyond a mortal's share
To wander solitary there:
Two Paradises 'twere in one
To live in Paradise alone.

9 He nothing common did or mean
Upon that memorable scene:
    But with his keener eye
    The axe's edge did try. [Charles I.]
An Horatian Ode upon Cromwell's Return from Ireland
(1650), l.57

10 But bowed his comely head,
Down as upon a bed.
l.63

11 And now the Irish are ashamed
To see themselves in one year tamed:
    So much one man can do
    That does both act and know.
l.75

12 Ye living lamps, by whose dear light
The nightingale does sit so late,
And studying all the summer night,
Her matchless songs does meditate.

Ye country comets, that portend
No war, nor prince's funeral,
Shining unto no higher end
Then to presage the grasses' fall.
The Mower to the Glow-worms

13 It is a wond'rous thing, how fleet
'Twas on those little silver feet.
With what a pretty skipping grace,

It oft would challenge me the race:
And when 't had left me far away,
'Twould stay, and run again, and stay.
For it was nimbler much than hinds;
And trod, as on the four winds.
The Nymph Complaining for the Death of her Fawn

14 I have a garden of my own,
But so with roses overgrown,
And lilies, that you would it guess
To be a little wilderness.

15 Had it liv'd long, it would have been
Lilies without, roses within.

16 For though the whole world cannot shew such
    another,
Yet we'd better by far have him than his brother. [Of
    Charles II.]
The Statue in Stocks-Market

17 He is Translation's thief that addeth more,
As much as he that taketh from the store
Of the first author.
To...Dr. Witty

18 Had we but world enough, and time,
This coyness, Lady, were no crime.
We would sit down, and think which way
To walk, and pass our long love's day.
Thou by the Indian Ganges' side
Shouldst rubies find: I by the tide
Of Humber would complain. I would
Love you ten years before the Flood:
And you should if you please refuse
Till the conversion of the Jews.
My vegetable love should grow
Vaster than empires, and more slow.
To His Coy Mistress

19 But at my back I always hear
Time's wingèd chariot hurrying near.
And yonder all before us lie
Deserts of vast eternity.
Thy beauty shall no more be found;
Nor, in thy marble vault, shall sound
My echoing song: then worms shall try
That long preserved virginity:
And your quaint honour turn to dust;
And into ashes all my lust.
The grave's a fine and private place,
But none I think do there embrace.

20 Let us roll all our strength and all
Our sweetness up into one ball,
And tear our pleasures with rough strife
Thorough the iron gates of life:
Thus, though we cannot make our sun
Stand still, yet we will make him run.

21 What need of all this marble crust
T' impark the wanton mote of dust?
Upon Appleton House, to my Lord Fairfax, iii

22 Thrice happy he who, not mistook,
Hath read in Nature's mystic book.
lxxiii

23 But now the salmon-fishers moist
Their leathern boats begin to hoist;
And, like Antipodes in shoes,
Have shod their heads in their canoes.
How tortoise-like, but not so slow,

These rational amphibii go!
lxxxxvii

GROUCHO MARX 1895–1977

1 Either he's dead or my watch has stopped.
A Day at the Races (1937), script by Robert Pirosh, George
Seaton, George Oppenheim

KARL MARX 1818–1883

2 A spectre is haunting Europe—The spectre of
Communism.
The Communist Manifesto (1848), opening words

3 The history of all hitherto existing society is the
history of class struggle.

4 The workers have nothing to lose in this [revolution]
but their chains. They have a world to gain. Workers
of the world, unite!
closing words

5 From each according to his abilities, to each according
to his needs.
Criticism of the Gotha Programme (1875). See 29:25

6 Religion…is the opium of the people.
Critique of Hegel's Philosophy of Right (1843–4), Introduction.
See 297:7

7 Mankind always sets itself only such problems as it
can solve; since, looking at the matter more closely, it
will always be found that the task itself arises only
when the material conditions for its solution already
exist or are at least in the process of formation.
A Critique of Political Economy (1859), preface, tr. D. McLellan

8 And even when a society has got upon the right track
for the discovery of the natural laws of its
movement—and it is the ultimate aim of this work, to
lay bare the economic law of motion of modern
society—it can neither clear by bold leaps, nor remove
by legal enactments, the obstacles offered by the
successive phases of its normal development. But it
can shorten and lessen the birth-pangs.
Das Kapital, Preface (25 July 1865) to the 1st German edn.
(1867)

9 Hegel says somewhere that all great events and
personalities in world history reappear in one fashion
or another. He forgot to add: the first time as tragedy,
the second as farce.
The Eighteenth Brumaire of Louis Napoleon (1852), 1

10 The philosophers have only interpreted the world in
various ways; the point is to change it.
Theses on Feuerbach (1888), xi

11 What I did that was new was to prove…that the class
struggle necessarily leads to the dictatorship of the
proletariat.
Letter to Weydemeyer 5 Mar. 1852. The phrase 'dictatorship of
the proletariat' had earlier been used in the Constitution of the
World Society of Revolutionary Communists (1850), signed by
Marx, Engels, Adam and J. Vidil, G. Julian Harney, and August
Willich. Marx claimed that the phrase had been coined by Auguste
Blanqui (1805–1881), but it has not been found in this form in
Blanqui's work. See Marx, *Political Writings* (ed. Fernbach,
1973), vol.1, p.24.

12 All I know is that I am not a Marxist.
Attr. in Engels, letter to C. Schmidt, 5 Aug. 1890

MARY TUDOR 1516–1558

13 When I am dead and opened, you shall find 'Calais'

lying in my heart.
Holinshed, *Chronicles*, iii.1160

QUEEN MARY 1867–1953

14 Well, Mr Baldwin! *this* is a pretty kettle of fish!
(The abdication crisis, 1936.) James Pope-Hennessy, *Life of
Queen Mary* (1959), ch.7.i

15 Really! this might be Roumania!
ii

16 So *that's* what hay looks like.
ch.8.i

JOHN MASEFIELD 1878–1967

17 I have seen dawn and sunset on moors and windy hills
Coming in solemn beauty like slow old tunes of Spain.
Beauty

18 Quinquireme of Nineveh from distant Ophir
Rowing home to haven in sunny Palestine,
With a cargo of ivory,
And apes and peacocks,
Sandalwood, cedarwood, and sweet white wine.
Cargoes. See 50:34

19 Dirty British coaster with a salt-caked smoke stack,
Butting through the Channel in the mad March days,
With a cargo of Tyne coal,
Road-rail, pig-lead,
Firewood, iron-ware, and cheap tin trays.

20 Oh some are fond of Spanish wine, and some are fond
   of French,
And some'll swallow tay and stuff fit only for a
   wench.
Captain Stratton's Fancy

21 Oh some are fond of fiddles, and a song well sung,
And some are all for music for to lilt upon the tongue;
But mouths were made for tankards, and for sucking
   at the bung,
Says the old bold mate of Henry Morgan.

22 In the dark womb where I began
My mother's life made me a man.
Through all the months of human birth
Her beauty fed my common earth.
I cannot see, nor breathe, nor stir,
But through the death of some of her.
C.L.M.

23 I have seen flowers come in stony places
And kind things done by men with ugly faces,
And the gold cup won by the worst horse at the races,
So I trust, too.
An Epilogue

24 To get the whole world out of bed
And washed, and dressed, and warmed, and fed,
To work, and back to bed again,
Believe me, Saul, costs worlds of pain.
The Everlasting Mercy (1911)

25 And he who gives a child a treat
Makes joy-bells ring in Heaven's street,
And he who gives a child a home
Builds palaces in Kingdom come,
And she who gives a baby birth
Brings Saviour Christ again to Earth.

26 The corn that makes the holy bread
By which the soul of man is fed,

The holy bread, the food unpriced,
Thy everlasting mercy, Christ.

1 Death opens unknown doors. It is most grand to die.
Pompey the Great (1910). i. **The Chief Centurions. 'Man is a sacred city'**

2 One road leads to London,
  One road runs to Wales,
My road leads me seawards
  To the white dipping sails.
Roadways

3 Most roads lead men homewards,
  My road leads me forth.

4 I must down to the seas again, to the lonely sea and
    the sky,
And all I ask is a tall ship and a star to steer her by,
And the wheel's kick and the wind's song and the
    white sail's shaking,
And a grey mist on the sea's face and a grey dawn
    breaking.
Sea Fever

5 I must down to the seas again, for the call of the
    running tide
Is a wild call and a clear call that may not be denied.

6 I must down to the seas again, to the vagrant gypsy
    life,
To the gull's way and the whale's way where the
    wind's like a whetted knife;
And all I ask is a merry yarn from a laughing
    fellow-rover,
And quiet sleep and a sweet dream when the long
    trick's over.

7 Friends and loves we have none, nor wealth, nor
    blessed abode,
But the hope of the City of God at the other end of the
    road.
The Seekers

8 It is good to be out on the road, and going one knows
    not where,
Going through meadow and village, one knows not
    whither nor why.
Tewkesbury Road

9 It's a warm wind, the west wind, full of birds' cries;
I never hear the west wind but tears are in my eyes.
For it comes from the west lands, the old brown hills,
And April's in the west wind, and daffodils.
The West Wind

THE MASS IN LATIN

10 *Asperges me, Domine, hyssopo, et mundabor.*
Sprinkle me with hyssop, O Lord, and I shall be
cleansed.
Anthem at Sprinkling the Holy Water. See 393:5

11 *Dominus vobiscum.*
  Et cum spiritu tuo.
The Lord be with you.
  And with thy spirit.

12 *In Nomine Patris, et Filii, et Spiritus Sancti.*
In the Name of the Father, and of the Son, and of the
Holy Ghost.
The Ordinary of the Mass

13 *Introibo ad altare Dei.*

I will go unto the altar of God.
See 392:11

14 *Gloria Patri, et Filio, et Spiritui Sancto.*
    Sicut erat in principio, et nunc, et semper, et in
    saecula saeculorum.
Glory be to the Father, and to the Son, and to the Holy
Ghost.
    As it was in the beginning, is now, and ever shall
    be, world without end.
See 384:15

15 *Confiteor Deo omnipotenti, beatae Mariae semper*
    Virgini, beato Michaeli Archangelo, beato Joanni
    Baptistae, sanctis Apostolis Petro et Paulo, omnibus
    sanctis, et tibi, Pater, quia peccavi nimis cogitatione,
    verbo, et opere, mea culpa, mea culpa, mea maxima
    culpa.
I confess to almighty God, to blessed Mary ever
Virgin, to blessed Michael the Archangel, to blessed
John the Baptist, to the holy Apostles Peter and Paul,
to all the saints, and to you, Father, that I have sinned
exceedingly in thought, word, and deed, through my
fault, through my fault, through my most grievous
fault.

16 *Kyrie eleison, Kyrie eleison, Kyrie eleison.*
    Christe eleison, Christe eleison, Christe eleison.
Lord, have mercy upon us.
    Christ, have mercy upon us.

17 *Requiem aeternam dona eis, Domine: et lux perpetua*
    luceat eis.
Grant them eternal rest, O Lord; and let perpetual light
shine on them.
[To be said only at Masses for the dead.]

18 *Gloria in excelsis Deo, et in terra pax hominibus*
    bonae voluntatis. Laudamus te, benedicimus te,
    adoramus te, glorificamus te.
Glory be to God on high, and on earth peace to men of
good will. We praise thee, we bless thee, we adore
thee, we glorify thee.

19 *Deo gratias.*
Thanks be to God.

20 *Credo in unum Deum, Patrem omnipotentem, factorem*
    coeli et terrae, visibilium omnium et invisibilium.
    Et in unum Dominum Jesum Christum Filium Dei
    unigenitum, et ex Patre natum ante omnia saecula:
    Deum de Deo, lumen de lumine, Deum verum de Deo
    vero; genitum non factum, consubstantialem Patri, per
    quem omnia facta sunt. Qui propter nos homines, et
    propter nostram salutem, descendit de coelis; et
    incarnatus est de Spiritu Sancto, ex Maria Virgine; ET
    HOMO FACTUS EST. Crucifixus etiam pro nobis,
    sub Pontio Pilato passus, et sepultus est. Et resurrexit
    tertia die, secundum Scripturas; et ascendit in coelum;
    sedet ad dexteram Patris; et iterum venturus est cum
    gloria, judicare vivos et mortuos; cuius regni non erit
    finis.
    Et in Spiritum Sanctum, Dominum vivificantem, qui ex
    Patre Filioque procedit; qui cum Patre et Filio simul
    adoratur, et conglorificatur; qui locutus est per
    Prophetas. Et unam sanctam Catholicam et
    Apostolicam Ecclesiam. Confiteor unum Baptisma in
    remissionem peccatorum. Et expecto resurrectionem
    mortuorum, et vitam venturi saeculi.
I believe in one God, the Father almighty, maker of
heaven and earth, and of all things visible and

invisible.

And in one Lord Jesus Christ, the only begotten Son of God, and born of the Father before all ages; God of God, light of light; true God of true God; begotten, not made; consubstantial to the Father, by whom all things were made. Who for us men, and for our salvation, came down from heaven; and became incarnate by the Holy Ghost, of the Virgin Mary; AND WAS MADE MAN. He was crucified also for us, suffered under Pontius Pilate, and was buried. And the third day he rose again according to the Scriptures; and ascended into heaven, sitteth at the right hand of the Father; and he is to come again with glory, to judge both the living and the dead; of whose kingdom there shall be no end.

And in the Holy Ghost, the Lord and giver of life, who proceedeth from the Father and the Son; who together with the Father and the Son, is adored and glorified; who spoke by the Prophets. And one holy Catholic and Apostolic Church. I confess one Baptism for the remission of sins. And I expect the resurrection of the dead, and the life of the world to come.
See 384:26, 387:10

1 *Oremus.*
Let us pray.

2 *Sursum corda.*
Lift up your hearts.
See 387:21

3 *Dignum et justum est.*
It is right and fitting.
See 387:23

4 *Sanctus, sanctus, sanctus, Dominus Deus Sabaoth. Pleni sunt coeli et terra gloria tua. Hosanna in excelsis. Benedictus qui venit in nomine Domini.*
Holy, holy, holy, Lord God of Hosts. Heaven and earth are full of thy glory. Hosanna in the highest. Blessed is he that cometh in the name of the Lord.
See 81:24, 387:23

5 *Pater noster, qui es in coelis, sanctificetur nomen tuum; adveniat regnum tuum; fiat voluntas tua sicut in coelo, et in terra; panem nostrum quotidianum da nobis hodie; et dimitte nobis debita nostra, sicut et nos dimittimus debitoribus nostris; et ne nos inducas in tentationem.*
     Sed libera nos a malo.
Our Father, who art in heaven, hallowed be thy name; thy kingdom come; thy will be done on earth, as it is in heaven; give us this day our daily bread; and forgive us our trespasses, as we forgive them that trespass against us; and lead us not into temptation.
     But deliver us from evil.
See 64:24

6 *Pax Domini sit semper vobiscum.*
The peace of the Lord be always with you.

7 *Agnus Dei, qui tollis peccata mundi, miserere nobis. Agnus Dei, qui tollis peccata mundi, dona nobis pacem.*
Lamb of God, who takest away the sins of the world, have mercy on us.
Lamb of God, who takest away the sins of the world, give us peace.

8 *Domine, non sum dignus ut intres sub tectum meum; sed tantum dic verbo, et sanabitur anima mea.*
Lord, I am not worthy that thou shouldst enter under

my roof; but say only the word, and my soul shall be healed.
See 65:14

9 *Ite missa est.*
Go, you are dismissed.

10 *Requiescant in pace.*
May they rest in peace.
[In Masses for the dead.]

11 *In principio erat Verbum, et Verbum erat apud Deum, et Deus erat Verbum.*
In the beginning was the Word, and the Word was with God, and the Word was God.
See 71:21

12 VERBUM CARO FACTUM EST.
THE WORD WAS MADE FLESH.
See 71:27

PHILIP MASSINGER 1583–1640

13 Ambition, in a private man a vice,
Is, in a prince, the virtue.
The Bashful Lover (licensed 1636, published 1655), I.ii

14 He that would govern others, first should be
The master of himself.
The Bondman (licensed 1623, printed 1624), I.iii

15 Pray enter
You are learned Europeans and we worse
Than ignorant Americans.
The City Madam (1658), III.iii

16 Soar not too high to fall; but stoop to rise.
The Duke of Milan (1623), I.ii

17   Greatness, with private men
Esteem'd a blessing, is to me a curse;
And we, whom, for our high births, they conclude
The only freemen, are the only slaves.
Happy the golden mean!
The Great Duke of Florence (1627, printed 1635), I.i. See 260:9

18   I am driven
Into a desperate strait and cannot steer
A middle course.
III.i

19   Verity, you brach!
The devil turned precisian?
A New Way to Pay Old Debts (c.1625, printed 1632), I.i

20 Patience, the beggar's virtue.
V.i

21 Some undone widow sits upon my arm,
And takes away the use of 't; and my sword,
Glued to my scabbard with wrong'd orphans' tears,
Will not be drawn.

22   View yourselves
In the deceiving mirror of self-love.
The Parliament of Love (licensed 1624), I.v

23 What pity 'tis, one that can speak so well,
Should in his actions be so ill!
III.iii

24   All words,
And no performance!
IV.ii

25   Serves and fears
The fury of the many-headed monster,

The giddy multitude.
The Unnatural Combat (c.1619, printed 1639), III.ii

1 Death has a thousand doors to let out life:
I shall find one.
A Very Woman, V.iv. See 215:11, 420:11, 566:26

LORD JUSTICE SIR JAMES MATHEW 1830–1908

2 In England, Justice is open to all, like the Ritz hotel.
R.E. Megarry, *Miscellany-at-Law* (1955), p.254. See 4:13

SOMERSET MAUGHAM 1874–1965

3 People ask you for criticism, but they only want praise.
Of Human Bondage (1915), ch.50

4 Dying is a very dull, dreary affair. And my advice to you is to have nothing whatever to do with it.
Robin Maugham, *Escape from the Shadows*, 5

BILL MAULDIN 1921–

5 I feel like a fugitive from th' law of averages.
Up Front (1946), p.39

JONATHAN MAYHEW 1720–1766

6 Rulers have no authority from God to do mischief.
A Discourse Concerning Unlimited Submission and Non-Resistance to the Higher Powers, 30 Jan. 1750

HUGHES MEARNS 1875–1965

7 As I was going up the stair
I met a man who wasn't there.
He wasn't there again to-day.
I wish, I wish he'd stay away.
The Psychoed

COSIMO DE MEDICI 1389–1464

8 We read that we ought to forgive our enemies; but we do not read that we ought to forgive our friends.
Bacon, *Apophthegms*, 206

LORENZO DE' MEDICI 1449–1492

9 *Quant' è bella giovinezza*
   Che si fugge tuttavia!
   Chi vuol esser lieto, sia:
   Di doman non c'è certezza.
How beautiful is youth, that is always slipping away! Whoever wants to be happy, let him be so: about tomorrow there's no knowing.
Trionfo di Bacco ed Arianna

LORD MELBOURNE 1779–1848

10 I wish I was as cocksure of anything as Tom Macaulay is of everything.
Earl Cowper, *Preface to Lord Melbourne's Papers* (1889), p.xii

11 What all the wise men promised has not happened, and what all the d—d fools said would happen has come to pass.
Of Catholic Emancipation. H. Dunckley, *Lord Melbourne* (1890)

12 I like the Garter; there is no damned merit in it.
On the Order of the Garter

13 Things have come to a pretty pass when religion is allowed to invade the sphere of private life.
Remark on hearing an evangelical sermon. G.W.E. Russell, *Collections and Recollections*, ch.6

14 Now, is it to lower the price of corn, or isn't it? It is not much matter which we say, but mind, we must all say *the same*.
(At a Cabinet meeting.) Attr. See Bagehot, *The English Constitution*, ch.1

15 Nobody ever did anything very foolish except from some strong principle.
Lord David Cecil, *The Young Melbourne*, ch.9

16 God help the Minister that meddles with art!
Lord David Cecil, *Lord M*, ch.3

17 What I want is men who will support me when I am in the wrong.
ch.4. 'Reply to a politician' who said 'I will support you as long as you are in the right.'

18 I have always thought complaints of ill-usage contemptible, whether from a seduced disappointed girl or a turned out Prime Minister.
After his dismissal by William IV. See letter from Emily Eden to Mrs. Lister, 23 Nov. 1834, in *Miss Eden's Letters*, ed. V. Dickinson (1919)

19 Damn it all, another Bishop dead,—I verily believe they die to vex me.
Attr.

20 The worst of the present day [1835] is that men hate one another so damnably. For my part I love them all.
Attr.

21 I don't know, Ma'am, why they make all this fuss about education; none of the Pagets can read or write, and they get on well enough. [To the Queen.]
Attr.

22 While I cannot be regarded as a pillar, I must be regarded as a buttress of the church, because I support it from the outside.
Attr.

HERMAN MELVILLE 1819–1891

23 Call me Ishmael.
Moby Dick, ch.1, opening words

GILLES MÉNAGE 1613–1692

24 *Comme nous nous entretenions de ce qui pouvait rendre heureux, je lui dis;* Sanitas sanitatum, et omnia sanitas.
While we were discussing what could make one happy, I said to him: *Sanitas sanitatum et omnia sanitas.*
Ménagiana (1693), p.166. Part of a conversation with Jean-Louis Guez de Balzac (1594–1654). See 83:14

MENANDER 342/1–293/89 B.C.

25 ὃν οἱ θεοὶ φιλοῦσιν ἀποθνῄσκει νέος.
Whom the gods love dies young.
Dis Exapaton, fr.4

GEORGE MEREDITH 1828–1909

26 Overhead, overhead
Rushes life in a race,
As the clouds the clouds chase;
   And we go,

And we drop like the fruits of the tree,
    Even we,
    Even so.
Dirge in Woods

1 Under yonder beech-tree single on the greensward,
    Couched with her arms behind her golden head,
    Knees and tresses folded to slip and ripple idly,
    Lies my young love sleeping in the shade.
Love in the Valley, i

2 She whom I love is hard to catch and conquer,
    Hard, but O the glory of the winning were she won!
ii

3 Lovely are the curves of the white owl sweeping
    Wavy in the dusk lit by one large star.
Lone on the fir-branch, his rattle-note unvaried,
    Brooding o'er tne gloom, spins the brown eve-jar.
Darker grows the valley, more and more forgetting:
    So were it with me if forgetting could be willed.
Tell the grassy hollow that holds the bubbling
    well-spring,
    Tell it to forget the source that keeps it filled.
v

4 Love that so desires would fain keep her changeless;
    Fain would fling the net, and fain have her free.
vi

5 On a starred night Prince Lucifer uprose.
Tired of his dark dominion swung the fiend…
He reached a middle height, and at the stars,
Which are the brain of heaven, he looked, and sank.
Around the ancient track marched, rank on rank,
The army of unalterable law.
Lucifer in Starlight

6 He fainted on his vengefulness, and strove
To ape the magnanimity of love.
Modern Love (1862), ii

7 Not till the fire is dying in the grate,
Look we for any kinship with the stars.
iv

8 And if I drink oblivion of a day,
So shorten I the stature of my soul.
xii

9 'I play for Seasons; not Eternities!'
Says Nature.
xiii

10 A kiss is but a kiss now! and no wave
Of a great flood that whirls me to the sea.
But, as you will! we'll sit contentedly,
And eat our pot of honey on the grave.
xxix

11   That rarest gift
To Beauty, Common Sense.
xxxii

12 O have a care of natures that are mute!
xxxv

13 God, what a dancing spectre seems the moon.
xxxix

14   In tragic life, God wot,
No villain need be! Passions spin the plot:
We are betrayed by what is false within.
xliii

15 Love, that had robbed us of immortal things,
This little moment mercifully gave,
Where I have seen across the twilight wave

The swan sail with her young beneath her wings.
xlvii

16 Their sense is with their senses all mixed in,
Destroyed by subtleties these women are!
xlviii

17 Thus piteously Love closed what he begat:
The union of this ever diverse pair!
These two were rapid falcons in a snare,
Condemned to do the flitting of a bat.
l

18 Ah, what a dusty answer gets the soul
When hot for certainties in this our life!

19 Narrows the world to my neighbour's gate.
Seed Time

20 We spend our lives in learning pilotage,
And grow good steersmen when the vessel's crank!
The Wisdom of Eld

21 Enter these enchanted woods,
        You who dare.
The Woods of Westermain

22 Thoughts of heroes were as good as warming-pans.
Beauchamp's Career (1874-5), ch.4

23 They that make of his creed a strait jacket for
humanity.
ch.29

24 'Tis Ireland gives England her soldiers, her generals
too.
Diana of the Crossways (1885), ch.2

25 She did not seduce, she ravished.
ch.7

26 She was a lady of incisive features bound in stale
parchment.
ch.14

27 Between the ascetic rocks and the sensual whirlpools.
ch.37

28 There is nothing the body suffers the soul may not
profit by.
ch.43

29 A Phoebus Apollo turned fasting friar.
The Egoist (1879), ch.2

30 A dainty rogue in porcelain.
ch.5

31 Cynicism is intellectual dandyism.
ch.7

32 In…the book of Egoism, it is written, Possession
without obligation to the object possessed approaches
felicity.
ch.14

33 None of your dam punctilio.
One of Our Conquerors (1890-91), ch.1

34 I expect that Woman will be the last thing civilized by
Man.
The Ordeal of Richard Feverel (1859), ch.1

35 In action Wisdom goes by majorities.

36 Who rises from prayer a better man, his prayer is
answered.
ch.12

37 Away with Systems! Away with a corrupt world! Let
us breathe the air of the Enchanted island.
Golden lie the meadows; golden run the streams; red
gold is on the pine-stems. The sun is coming down to

earth, and walks the fields and the waters.
The sun is coming down to earth, and the fields and
the waters shout to him golden shouts.
ch.19

1 Kissing don't last: cookery do!
ch.28

2 Speech is the small change of silence.
ch.34

3 Italia, Italia shall be free.
Vittoria (1866), ch.21

4 Much benevolence of the passive order may be traced
to a disinclination to inflict pain upon oneself.
ch.42

OWEN MEREDITH (E.R.B. LYTTON, EARL OF LYTTON) 1831–1891

5 Genius does what it must, and Talent does what it
can.
Last Words of a Sensitive Second-Rate Poet

6 We may live without poetry, music and art;
We may live without conscience, and live without
heart;
We may live without friends; we may live without
books;
But civilized man cannot live without cooks.
Lucile (1860), pt.1, c.2.xix

7 He may live without books,—what is knowledge but
grieving?
He may live without hope,—what is hope but
deceiving?
He may live without love,—what is passion but
pining?
But where is the man that can live without dining?
xxiv

DIXON LANIER MERRITT 1879–1954

8 A wonderful bird is the pelican,
His bill will hold more than his belican.
He can take in his beak
Food enough for a week,
But I'm damned if I see how the helican.
The Pelican

LE CURÉ MESLIER 1664?–1733

9 *Il me souvient à ce sujet d'un souhait que faisait
autrefois un homme, qui n'avait ni science ni
étude...Il souhaitait, disait-il...que tous les grands de
la terre et que tous les nobles fussent pendus et
étranglés avec les boyaux des prêtres. Pour ce qui est
de moi...je souhaitais d'avoir les bras et la force
d'Hercule pour purger le monde de tout vice et de
toute iniquité, et pour avoir le plaisir d'assommer tous
ces monstres d'erreurs et d'iniquité qui font gémir si
pitoyablement tous les peuples de la terre.*
I remember, on this matter, the wish made once by an
ignorant, uneducated man...He said he wished...that
all the great men in the world and all the nobility could
be hanged, and strangled in the guts of priests. For
myself...I wish I could have the strength of Hercules to
purge the world of all vice and sin, and the pleasure of
destroying all those monsters of error and sin [priests]
who make all the peoples of the world groan so

pitiably.
Testament (ed. R. Charles, 1864), I.ch.2. Often quoted as *'Je
voudrais... que le dernier des rois fût étranglé avec les boyaux du
dernier prêtre'* or in Diderot's version:
*Et des boyaux du dernier prêtre
Serrons le cou du dernier roi.*

PRINCE METTERNICH 1773–1859

10 *L'erreur n'a jamais approché de mon esprit.*
Error has never approached my spirit.
(Spoken to Guizot in 1848.) Guizot, *Mémoires* (1858–1867),
vol.IV, p.21

11 *Italien ist ein geographischer Begriff.*
Italy is a geographical expression.
Letter, 19 Nov. 1849

CHARLOTTE MEW 1869–1928

12   She sleeps up in the attic there
                       Alone, poor maid. 'Tis but a stair
Betwixt us. Oh! my God! the down,
The soft young down of her, the brown,
The brown of her—her eyes, her hair, her hair!
The Farmer's Bride

ALICE MEYNELL 1847–1922

13 I must not think of thee; and, tired yet strong,
I shun the thought that lurks in all delight—
The thought of thee—and in the blue heaven's height,
And in the sweetest passage of a song.
Renouncement

14 With the first dream that comes with the first sleep
I run, I run, I am gathered to thy heart.

15 She walks—the lady of my delight—
    A shepherdess of sheep.
The Shepherdess

HUGO MEYNELL 1727–1808

16 The chief advantage of London is, that a man is
always so near his burrow.
Boswell, *Johnson* (ed. 1934), vol.iii, p.379. 1 Apr. 1779

17 For anything I see, foreigners are fools.
vol.iv, p.15. 1780

THOMAS MIDDLETON 1570?–1627

18   I never heard
Of any true affection, but 'twas nipt
With care.
Blurt, Master-Constable (published 1602), III.i.39

19 By many a happy accident.
No Wit, No Help, Like a Woman's (1613?, published 1657),
IV.i.66

20 There's no hate lost between us.
The Witch (before 1627, printed 1778), IV.iii.10

JOHN STUART MILL 1806–1873

21 Ask yourself whether you are happy, and you cease to
be so.
Autobiography (1873), ch.5

22 No great improvements in the lot of mankind are
possible, until a great change takes place in the

fundamental constitution of their modes of thought.
ch.7

1 As often as a study is cultivated by narrow minds, they will draw from it narrow conclusions.
Auguste Comte and Positivism (1865), p.82

2 The Conservatives...being by the law of their existence the stupidest party.
Considerations on Representative Government (1861), ch.vii, footnote

3 When society requires to be rebuilt, there is no use in attempting to rebuild it on the old plan.
Dissertations and Discussions, vol.i (1859), **Essay on Coleridge**, p.423

4 Unearned increment.
vol.iv (1876), p.299

5 I will call no being good, who is not what I mean when I apply that epithet to my fellow-creatures; and if such a being can sentence me to hell for not so calling him, to hell I will go.
Examination of Sir William Hamilton's Philosophy (1865), ch.7

6 The sole end for which mankind are warranted, individually or collectively, in interfering with the liberty of action of any of their number, is self-protection.
On Liberty (1859), ch.1

7 The only purpose for which power can be rightfully exercised over any member of a civilized community, against his will, is to prevent harm to others. His own good, either physical or moral, is not a sufficient warrant.

8 If all mankind minus one, were of one opinion, and only one person were of the contrary opinion, mankind would be no more justified in silencing that one person, than he, if he had the power, would be justified in silencing mankind.
ch.2

9 We can never be sure that the opinion we are endeavouring to stifle is a false opinion; and if we were sure, stifling it would be an evil still.

10 A party of order or stability, and a party of progress or reform, are both necessary elements of a healthy state of political life.

11 The liberty of the individual must be thus far limited; he must not make himself a nuisance to other people.
ch.3

12 All good things which exist are the fruits of originality.

13 Liberty consists in doing what one desires.
ch.5

14 The worth of a State, in the long run, is the worth of the individuals composing it.

15 A State which dwarfs its men, in order that they may be more docile instruments in its hands even for beneficial purposes—will find that with small men no great thing can really be accomplished.

16 When the land is cultivated entirely by the spade and no horses are kept, a cow is kept for every three acres of land.
Principles of Political Economy (1848). **A Treatise on Flemish Husbandry**

17 The great majority of those who speak of perfectibility as a dream, do so because they feel that it is one which

would afford them no pleasure if it were realized.
Speech on Perfectibility (1828)

18 The principle which regulates the existing social relations between the two sexes—the legal subordination of one sex to the other—is wrong in itself, and now one of the chief hindrances to human improvement; and...it ought to be replaced by a principle of perfect equality, admitting no power or privilege on the one side, nor disability on the other.
The Subjection of Women (1869), ch.1

19 The moral regeneration of mankind will only really commence, when the most fundamental of the social relations [marriage] is placed under the rule of equal justice, and when human beings learn to cultivate their strongest sympathy with an equal in rights and cultivation.
ch.4

20 If we may be excused the antithesis, we should say that eloquence is *heard*, poetry is *overheard*.
Thoughts on Poetry and its varieties (1859)

21 The most important thing women have to do is to stir up the zeal of women themselves.
Letter to Alexander Bain, 14 July 1869

22 Were there but a few hearts and intellects like hers this earth would already become the hoped-for heaven.
Epitaph (1858-9) for his wife Harriet, cemetery of St. Véran, near Avignon. See M. St.J. Packe, *Life of John Stuart Mill* (1954), bk.VII, ch. iii

EDNA ST. VINCENT MILLAY 1892–1950

23 Gently they go, the beautiful, the tender, the kind;
Quietly they go, the intelligent, the witty, the brave.
I know. But I do not approve. And I am not resigned.
The Buck in the Snow, III, **Dirge without Music**

24 Childhood is not from birth to a certain age and at a
    certain age
The child is grown, and puts away childish things,

Childhood is the kingdom where nobody dies.

Nobody that matters, that is.
Childhood is the Kingdom where Nobody dies

25 Man has never been the same since God died.

He has taken it very hard. Why, you'd think it was
    only yesterday,
The way he takes it.
Not that he says much, but he laughs much louder than
    he used to,
And he can't bear to be left alone even for a minute,
    and he can't
Sit still.
Conversation at Midnight, IV

26 My candle burns at both ends;
    It will not last the night;
But ah, my foes, and oh my friends—
    It gives a lovely light!
A Few Figs from Thistles (1920). **First Fig**

27 Was it for this I uttered prayers,
And sobbed and cursed and kicked the stairs,
That now, domestic as a plate,
I should retire at half-past eight?
Grown-up

28 Euclid alone has looked on Beauty bare.
The Harp-Weaver (1923), 4, sonnet 22

29 Death devours all lovely things:

Lesbia with her sparrow
Shares the darkness,—presently
Every bed is narrow.
Passer Mortuus Est. See 136:22

1 After all, my erstwhile dear,
My no longer cherished,
Need we say it was not love,
Just because it perished?

ALICE DUER MILLER 1874–1942

2 I am American bred,
I have seen much to hate here—much to forgive,
But in a world where England is finished and dead,
I do not wish to live.
The White Cliffs (1940)

WILLIAM MILLER 1810–1872

3 Wee Willie Winkie rins through the town,
Up stairs and down stairs in his nicht-gown,
Tirling at the window, crying at the lock,
Are the weans in their bed, for it's now ten o'clock?
Willie Winkie (1841)

A.A. MILNE 1882–1956

4 They're changing guard at Buckingham Palace—
Christopher Robin went down with Alice.
Alice is marrying one of the guard.
'A soldier's life is terrible hard,'
Says Alice.
When We Were Very Young (1924). **Buckingham Palace**

5 James James
Morrison Morrison
Weatherby George Dupree
Took great
Care of his Mother
Though he was only three.
Disobedience

6 You must never go down to the end of the town if you
don't go down with me.

7 The King asked
The Queen, and
The Queen asked
The Dairymaid:
'Could we have some butter for
The Royal slice of bread?'
The King's Breakfast

8 I do like a little bit of butter to my bread!

9 The King said
'Butter, eh?'
And bounced out of bed.

10 *What* is the matter with Mary Jane?
She's perfectly well and she hasn't a pain,
And it's lovely rice pudding for dinner again,—
What *is* the matter with Mary Jane?
Rice Pudding

11 Little Boy kneels at the foot of the bed,
Droops on the little hands, little gold head;
Hush! Hush! Whisper who dares!
Christopher Robin is saying his prayers.
Vespers

12 Isn't it funny

How a bear likes honey?
Buzz! Buzz! Buzz!
I wonder why he does?
Winnie-the-Pooh (1926), ch.1

13 I am a Bear of Very Little Brain, and long words
Bother me.
ch.4

14 'Pathetic', he said. 'That's what it is. Pathetic'.
ch.6

15 Time for a little something.

16 On Monday, when the sun is hot,
I wonder to myself a lot:
'Now is it true, or is it not,
'That what is which and which is what?'
ch.7

17 When I was young, we *always* had mornings like this.
Toad of Toad Hall (1929), II.3. Milne's dramatization of Kenneth
Grahame's *The Wind in the Willows*.

LORD MILNER 1854–1925

18 If we believe a thing to be bad, and if we have a right
to prevent it, it is our duty to try to prevent it and to
damn the consequences. [The Peers and the Budget.]
Speech at Glasgow, 26 Nov. 1909

JOHN MILTON 1608–1674

19 Such sweet compulsion doth in music lie.
Arcades (?1633), 1.68

20 Blest pair of Sirens, pledges of Heaven's joy,
Sphere-born harmonious sisters, Voice and Verse.
At a Solemn Music

21 Where the bright Seraphim in burning row
Their loud up-lifted Angel trumpets blow.

22 Before the starry threshold of Jove's Court
My mansion is.
Comus (1634), 1.1

23 Above the smoke and stir of this dim spot,
Which men call Earth.
1.5

24 Yet some there be that by due steps aspire
To lay their just hands on that golden key
That opes the palace of Eternity.
1.12

25 Rich and various gems inlay
The unadornèd bosom of the deep.
1.22

26 An old, and haughty nation proud in arms.
1.33

27 And the gilded car of day,
His glowing axle doth allay
In the steep Atlantic stream.
1.95

28 What hath night to do with sleep?
1.122

29 Come, knit hands, and beat the ground,
In a light fantastic round.
1.143

30   When the grey-hooded Even
Like a sad votarist in palmer's weed,
Rose from the hindmost wheels of Phoebus' wain.
1.188

1   O thievish Night,
Why shouldst thou, but for some felonious end,
In thy dark lantern thus close up the stars
That nature hung in heaven, and filled their lamps
With everlasting oil, to give due light
To the misled and lonely traveller?
l.195

2 Was I deceived, or did a sable cloud
Turn forth her silver lining on the night?
l.221

3 Sweet Echo, sweetest nymph, that liv'st unseen
    Within thy airy shell
By slow Meander's margent green,
    And in the violet-embroidered vale.
l.230

4 Can any mortal mixture of earth's mould
Breathe such divine enchanting ravishment?
l.244

5 Such sober certainty of waking bliss
I never heard till now.
l.263

6   Shepherd, I take thy word,
And trust thy honest offer'd courtesy,
Which oft is sooner found in lowly sheds
With smoky rafters, than in tap'stry halls
And courts of princes.
l.321

7 With thy long levell'd rule of streaming light.
l.340

8 Virtue could see to do what virtue would
By her own radiant light, though sun and moon
Were in the flat sea sunk. And Wisdom's self
Oft seeks to sweet retired solitude,
Where with her best nurse Contemplation
She plumes her feathers, and lets grow her wings
That in the various bustle of resort
Were all to-ruffled, and sometimes impair'd.
He that has light within his own clear breast
May sit i' th' centre and enjoy bright day;
But he that hides a dark soul and foul thoughts
Benighted walks under the midday sun.
l.373

9 Where an equal poise of hope and fear
Does arbitrate th' event, my nature is
That I incline to hope rather than fear,
And gladly banish squint suspicion.
l.410

10 'Tis Chastity, my brother, Chastity:
She that has that, is clad in complete steel.
l.420

11 How charming is divine philosophy!
Not harsh, and crabbed as dull fools suppose,
But musical as is Apollo's lute,
And a perpetual feast of nectared sweets,
Where no crude surfeit reigns.
l.476

12 What the sage poets taught by th' heavenly Muse,
Storied of old in high immortal verse
Of dire chimeras and enchanted isles
And rifted rocks whose entrance leads to Hell,—
For such there be, but unbelief is blind.
l.515

13 And fill'd the air with barbarous dissonance.
l.550

14   I was all ear,
And took in strains that might create a soul
Under the ribs of Death.
l.560

15   Against the threats
Of malice or of sorcery, or that power
Which erring man call chance, this I hold firm:
Virtue may be assailed, but never hurt,
Surprised by unjust force, but not enthralled.
l.586

16 O foolishness of men! that lend their ears
To those budge doctors of the Stoic fur,
And fetch their precepts from the Cynic tub,
Praising the lean and sallow Abstinence.
l.706

17 Beauty is Nature's coin, must not be hoarded,
But must be current, and the good thereof
Consists in mutual and partaken bliss.
l.739

18 Beauty is Nature's brag, and must be shown
In courts, at feasts, and high solemnities,
Where most may wonder at the workmanship;
It is for homely features to keep home,
They had their name thence; coarse complexions
And cheeks of sorry grain will serve to ply
The sampler, and to tease the huswife's wool.
What need a vermeil-tinctur'd lip for that,
Love-darting eyes, or tresses like the morn?
l.745

19 Obtruding false rules pranked in reason's garb.
l.759

20 Sabrina fair,
    Listen where thou art sitting
Under the glassy, cool, translucent wave,
    In twisted braids of lilies knitting
The loose train of thy amber-dropping hair.
l.859

21 Thus I set my printless feet
O'er the cowslip's velvet head,
That bends not as I tread.
l.897

22 Love virtue, she alone is free,
She can teach ye how to climb
Higher than the sphery chime;
Or, if virtue feeble were,
Heaven itself would stoop to her.
l.1019

23 Hence, vain deluding joys,
The brood of Folly without father bred.
Il Penseroso (1632), l.1

24 As thick and numberless
    As the gay motes that people the sunbeams.
l.7

25 Hail divinest Melancholy.
l.12

26 Come, pensive Nun, devout and pure,
Sober, steadfast, and demure.
l.31

27 And join with thee calm Peace, and Quiet,
Spare Fast, that oft with gods doth diet.
l.45

1 And add to these retired Leisure,
That in trim gardens takes his pleasure.
1.49

2 Sweet bird, that shunn'st the noise of folly,
Most musical, most melancholy!
1.61

3   I walk unseen
On the dry smooth-shaven green,
To behold the wandering moon,
Riding near her highest noon,
Like one that had been led astray
Through the heav'n's wide pathless way;
And oft, as if her head she bow'd,
Stooping through a fleecy cloud.
1.65

4 Oft, on a plat of rising ground,
I hear the far-off curfew sound
Over some wide-watered shore,
Swinging slow with sullen roar.
1.73

5 Where glowing embers through the room
Teach light to counterfeit a gloom,
Far from all resort of mirth,
Save the cricket on the hearth.
1.79

6 Or bid the soul of Orpheus sing
Such notes as, warbled to the string,
Drew iron tears down Pluto's cheek.
1.105

7 Where more is meant than meets the ear.
1.120

8 While the bee with honied thigh,
That at her flowery work doth sing,
And the waters murmuring
And such consort as they keep,
Entice the dewy-feather'd sleep.
1.142

9 But let my due feet never fail
To walk the studious cloister's pale.
1.155

10 With antique pillars massy proof,
And storied windows richly dight,
Casting a dim religious light.
There let the pealing organ blow,
To the full-voiced quire below,
In service high, and anthems clear
As may, with sweetness, through mine ear,
Dissolve me into ecstasies,
And bring all Heaven before mine eyes.
1.158

11 Till old experience do attain
To something like prophetic strain.
1.173

12 Hence, loathed Melancholy,
Of Cerberus, and blackest Midnight born,
In Stygian cave forlorn,
'Mongst horrid shapes, and shrieks, and sights
unholy.
L'Allegro (1632), l.1

13 So buxom, blithe, and debonair.
1.24

14 Haste thee Nymph, and bring with thee
Jest and youthful jollity,

Quips and cranks, and wanton wiles,
Nods, and becks, and wreathed smiles.
1.25

15 Sport that wrinkled Care derides,
And Laughter holding both his sides.
Come, and trip it as ye go
On the light fantastic toe,
And in thy right hand lead with thee
The mountain nymph, sweet Liberty.
1.31

16 Mirth, admit me of thy crew,
To live with her, and live with thee,
In unreproved pleasures free.
1.38

17 While the cock with lively din
Scatters the rear of darkness thin,
And to the stack, or the barn door,
Stoutly struts his dames before.
1.49

18 Right against the eastern gate,
Where the great Sun begins his state.
1.59

19   The ploughman near at hand,
Whistles o'er the furrowed land,
And the milkmaid singeth blithe,
And the mower whets his scythe,
And every shepherd tells his tale
Under the hawthorn in the dale.
1.63

20 Meadows trim with daisies pied,
Shallow brooks and rivers wide.
Towers, and battlements it sees
Bosom'd high in tufted trees,
Where perhaps some beauty lies,
The cynosure of neighbouring eyes.
1.75

21 Of herbs, and other country messes,
Which the neat-handed Phyllis dresses.
1.85

22 To many a youth, and many a maid,
Dancing in the chequered shade.
And young and old come forth to play
On a sunshine holiday.
1.95

23 Then to the spicy nut-brown ale.
1.100

24 Towered cities please us then,
And the busy hum of men.
1.117

25 Store of ladies, whose bright eyes
Rain influence, and judge the prize
Of wit or arms.
1.121

26 And pomp, and feast, and revelry,
With mask, and antique pageantry,
Such sights as youthful poets dream,
On summer eves by haunted stream.
Then to the well-trod stage anon,
If Jonson's learnèd sock be on,
Or sweetest Shakespeare, Fancy's child,
Warble his native wood-notes wild,
And ever against eating cares,
Lap me in soft Lydian airs,

Married to immortal verse
Such as the meeting soul may pierce
In notes, with many a winding bout
Of linked sweetness long drawn out.
l.127

1 Such strains as would have won the ear
Of Pluto, to have quite set free
His half regain'd Eurydice.
l.148

2 Yet once more, O ye laurels, and once more
Ye myrtles brown, with ivy never sere,
I come to pluck your berries harsh and crude,
And with forc'd fingers rude,
Shatter your leaves before the mellowing year.
Bitter constraint and sad occasion dear
Compels me to disturb your season due,
For Lycidas is dead, dead ere his prime,
Young Lycidas and hath not left his peer.
Who would not sing for Lycidas? he knew
Himself to sing and build the lofty rhyme.
He must not float upon his watery bier
Unwept, and welter to the parching wind
Without the meed of some melodious tear.
Lycidas (1637), l.1

3 Hence with denial vain, and coy excuse.
l.18

4 For we were nursed upon the self-same hill.
l.23

5 But, O the heavy change, now thou art gone,
Now thou art gone, and never must return!
l.37

6   The woods and desert caves,
With wild thyme and the gadding vine o'ergrown.
l.39

7 Where were ye, Nymphs, when the remorseless deep
Closed o'er the head of your loved Lycidas?
l.50

8 Alas! what boots it with uncessant care
To tend the homely, slighted, shepherd's trade,
And strictly meditate the thankless Muse?
Were it not better done, as others use,
To sport with Amaryllis in the shade,
Or with the tangles of Neaera's hair.
Fame is the spur that the clear spirit doth raise
(That last infirmity of noble mind)
To scorn delights, and live laborious days;
But the fair guerdon when we hope to find,
And think to burst out into sudden blaze,
Comes the blind Fury with th' abhorred shears
And slits the thin-spun life.
l.64

9 Fame is no plant that grows on mortal soil.
l.78

10 It was that fatal and perfidious bark
Built in th' eclipse, and rigged with curses dark,
That sunk so low that sacred head of thine.
l.100

11 Last came, and last did go,
The Pilot of the Galilean lake,
Two massy keys he bore of metals twain,
The golden opes, the iron shuts amain.
l.108

12   Such as for their bellies' sake,

Creep and intrude, and climb into the fold.
Of other care they little reckoning make,
Than how to scramble at the shearers' feast,
And shove away the worthy bidden guest.
Blind mouths! that scarce themselves know how to
    hold
A sheep-hook, or have learn'd aught else the least
That to the faithful herdman's art belongs!
l.114

13   Their lean and flashy songs
Grate on their scrannel pipes of wretched straw,
The hungry sheep look up, and are not fed,
But, swoln with wind and the rank mist they draw,
Rot inwardly and foul contagion spread;
Besides what the grim wolf with privy paw
Daily devours apace, and nothing said.
But that two-handed engine at the door
Stands ready to smite once, and smite no more.
l.123

14 Return, Alpheus, the dread voice is past
That shrunk thy streams; return Sicilian Muse.
l.132

15 Bring the rathe primrose that forsaken dies,
The tufted crow-toe, and pale jessamine,
The white pink, and the pansy freakt with jet,
The glowing violet,
The musk-rose, and the well-attir'd woodbine,
With cowslips wan that hang the pensive head,
And every flower that sad embroidery wears.
Bid amaranthus all his beauty shed,
And daffadillies fill their cups with tears,
To strew the laureate hearse where Lycid lies.
l.142

16 Whether beyond the stormy Hebrides,
Where thou perhaps under the whelming tide
Visit'st the bottom of the monstrous world;
Or whether thou, to our moist vows denied,
Sleepst by the fable of Bellerus old,
Where the great Vision of the guarded mount
Looks toward Namancos and Bayona's hold.
Look homeward, Angel, now, and melt with ruth.
l.156

17 For Lycidas your sorrow is not dead,
Sunk though he be beneath the watery floor;
So sinks the day-star in the ocean bed,
And yet anon repairs his drooping head,
And tricks his beams, and with new spangled ore,
Flames in the forehead of the morning sky:
So Lycidas sunk low, but mounted high,
Through the dear might of Him that walked the waves.
l.166

18 There entertain him all the saints above,
In solemn troops and sweet societies
That sing, and singing in their glory move,
And wipe the tears for ever from his eyes.
l.178

19 Thus sang the uncouth swain to th' oaks and rills,
While the still morn went out with sandals gray;
He touch'd the tender stops of various quills,
With eager thought warbling his Doric lay.
l.186

20 At last he rose, and twitch'd his mantle blue;
To-morrow to fresh woods, and pastures new.
l.192

1 What needs my Shakespeare for his honour'd bones,
The labour of an age in piled stones,
Or that his hallow'd relics should be hid
Under a star-y-pointing pyramid?
On Shakespeare (1630)

2 O fairest flower, no sooner blown but blasted,
Soft silken primrose fading timelessly.
On the Death of a Fair Infant, Dying of a Cough (1628), l.1

3 This is the month, and this the happy morn,
Wherein the Son of Heaven's eternal King,
Of wedded maid, and virgin mother born,
Our great redemption from above did bring;
For so the holy sages once did sing,
That He our deadly forfeit should release,
And with His Father work us a perpetual peace.
On the Morning of Christ's Nativity (1629), l.1

4 The star-led wizards haste with odours sweet!
l.23

5 It was the winter wild
While the Heav'n-born child
All meanly wrapt in the rude manger lies,
Nature in awe to him
Had doff't her gawdy trim
With her great Master so to sympathize.
l.29

6 Nor war, nor battle's sound
Was heard the world around,
The idle spear and shield were high uphung.
l.53

7 The stars with deep amaze
Stand fixt in stedfast gaze
Bending one way their precious influence
And will not take their flight
For all the morning light,
Or Lucifer that often warned them thence,
But in their glimmering orbs did glow
Until their Lord himself bespake and bid them go.
l.69

8 Perhaps their loves, or else their sheep,
Was all that did their silly thoughts so busy keep.
l.91

9 The helmed Cherubim
And sworded Seraphim,
Are seen in glittering ranks with wings display'd.
l.112

10 Ring out ye crystal spheres,
Once bless our human ears
(If ye have power to touch our senses so)
And let your silver chime
Move in melodious time;
And let the base of heav'n's deep organ blow,
And with your ninefold harmony
Make up full consort to th' angelic symphony.
l.125

11 For if such holy song
Enwrap our fancy long,
Time will run back, and fetch the age of gold
And speckled Vanity
Will sicken soon and die.
l.133

12 Swinges the scaly horror of his folded tail.
l.172

13 The oracles are dumb,

No voice or hideous hum
Runs through the arched roof in words deceiving.
Apollo from his shrine
Can no more divine,
With hollow shriek the steep of Delphos leaving.
l.173

14 So when the sun in bed,
Curtain'd with cloudy red,
Pillows his chin upon an orient wave.
l.229

15 But see the Virgin blest,
Hath laid her Babe to rest,
Time is our tedious song should here have ending.
l.237

16 Showed him his room where he must lodge that night,
Pulled off his boots, and took away the light.
If any ask for him, it shall be said,
'Hobson has supped, and's newly gone to bed.'
On the University Carrier

17 Fly, envious Time, till thou run out thy race:
Call on the lazy leaden-stepping hours.
On Time, l.1

18 Rhyme being no necessary adjunct or true ornament of
poem or good verse, in longer works especially, but
the invention of a barbarous age, to set off wretched
matter and lame metre.
The Verse. Preface to *Paradise Lost* (1667), 1668 ed.

19 The troublesome and modern bondage of Rhyming.

20 Of Man's first disobedience, and the fruit
Of that forbidden tree, whose mortal taste
Brought death into the world, and all our woe,
With loss of Eden.
bk.i, l.1

21 Things unattempted yet in prose or rhyme.
l.16

22   What in me is dark
Illumine, what is low raise and support;
That to the highth of this great argument
I may assert eternal Providence,
And justify the ways of God to Men.
l.22

23 The infernal serpent; he it was, whose guile,
Stirr'd up with envy and revenge, deceived
The mother of mankind.
l.34

24   Him the Almighty Power
Hurled headlong flaming from th' ethereal sky
With hideous ruin and combustion down
To bottomless perdition, there to dwell
In adamantine chains and penal fire
Who durst defy th' Omnipotent to arms.
l.44

25 A dungeon horrible, on all sides round
As one great furnace flam'd; yet from those flames
No light, but rather darkness visible
Serv'd only to discover sights of woe,
Regions of sorrow, doleful shades, where peace
And rest can never dwell, hope never comes
That comes to all.
l.60

26   But O how fall'n! how changed
From him who, in the happy realms of light,
Clothed with transcendent brightness didst outshine

Myriads though bright.
1.84

1 United thoughts and counsels, equal hope,
And hazard in the glorious enterprise.
1.88

2   Yet not for those
Nor what the potent victor in his rage
Can else inflict do I repent or change,
Though changed in outward lustre; that fixed mind
And high disdain, from sense of injured merit.
1.94

3   What though the field be lost?
All is not lost; th' unconquerable will,
And study of revenge, immortal hate,
And courage never to submit or yield:
And what is else not to be overcome?
1.105

4 Vaunting aloud, but racked with deep despair.
1.126

5 Fall'n Cherub, to be weak is miserable
Doing or suffering; but of this be sure,
To do ought good never will be our task,
But ever to do ill our sole delight.
1.157

6 And out of good still to find means of evil.
1.165

7 What reinforcement we may gain from hope,
If not, what resolution from despair.
1.190

8   The will
And high permission of all-ruling Heaven
Left him at large to his own dark designs,
That with reiterated crimes he might
Heap on himself damnation.
1.211

9 Is this the region, this the soil, the clime,
Said then the lost Archangel, this the seat
That we must change for Heav'n, this mournful gloom
For that celestial light?
1.242

10   Farewell happy fields
Where joy for ever dwells: Hail horrors, hail
Infernal world, and thou profoundest Hell
Receive thy new possessor: one who brings
A mind not to be changed by place or time.
The mind is its own place, and in it self
Can make a Heav'n of Hell, a Hell of Heav'n.
1.249

11 Here we may reign secure, and in my choice
To reign is worth ambition though in hell:
Better to reign in hell, than serve in heav'n.
1.261

12 His spear, to equal which the tallest pine
Hewn on Norwegian hills, to be the mast
Of some great ammiral, were but a wand,
He walk'd with to support uneasy steps
Over the burning marle.
1.292

13 Thick as autumnal leaves that strow the brooks
In Vallombrosa, where th' Etrurian shades
High over-arch'd embower.
1.302

14 First Moloch, horrid king, besmear'd with blood

Of human sacrifice, and parents' tears.
1.392

15   For spirits when they please
Can either sex assume, or both; so soft
And uncompounded is their essence pure...
          in what shape they choose,
Dilated or condensed, bright or obscure,
Can execute their aery purposes.
1.423

16 Astarte, Queen of Heav'n, with crescent horns.
1.439

17   Thammuz came next behind,
Whose annual wound in Lebanon allur'd
The Syrian damsels to lament his fate
In amorous ditties all a summer's day,
While smooth Adonis from his native rock
Ran purple to the sea.
1.446

18   And when night
Darkens the streets, then wander forth the sons
Of Belial, flown with insolence and wine.
1.500

19 Th' imperial ensign, which full high advanced
Shone like a meteor streaming to the wind.
1.536

20 Sonorous metal blowing martial sounds:
At which the universal host upsent
A shout that tore hell's concave, and beyond
Frighted the reign of Chaos and old Night.
1.540

21   Anon they move
In perfect phalanx to the Dorian mood
Of flutes and soft recorders.
1.549

22   That small infantry
Warred on by cranes. [Pygmies.]
1.575

23   What resounds
In fable or romance of Uther's son
Begirt with British and Armoric knights;
And all who since, baptized or infidel
Jousted in Aspramont or Montalban,
Damasco, or Marocco, or Trebisond,
Or whom Biserta sent from Afric shore
When Charlemain with all his peerage fell
By Fontarabbia.
1.579

24   The sun...
In dim eclipse disastrous twilight sheds
On half the nations, and with fear of change
Perplexes monarchs.
1.594

25   Who overcomes
By force, hath overcome but half his foe.
1.648

26   Mammon led them on,
Mammon, the least erected Spirit that fell
From heav'n, for ev'n in heav'n his looks and thoughts
Were always downward bent, admiring more
The riches of heaven's pavement, trodden gold,
Than aught divine or holy else enjoy'd
In vision beatific.
1.678

1   Let none admire
That riches grow in hell; that soil may best
Deserve the precious bane.
1.690

2   Anon out of the earth a fabric huge
Rose like an exhalation.
1.710

3   From morn
To noon he fell, from noon to dewy eve,
A summer's day; and with the setting sun
Dropt from the zenith like a falling star.
1.742

4   Nor aught availed him now
To have built in heav'n high tow'rs nor did he scape
By all his engines, but was headlong sent
With his industrious crew to build in hell.
1.748

5   Pandoemonium, the high capitol
Of Satan and his peers.
1.756

6   High on a throne of royal state, which far
Outshone the wealth of Ormus and of Ind,
Or where the gorgeous East with richest hand
Showers on her kings barbaric pearl and gold,
Satan exalted sat, by merit raised
To that bad eminence; and from despair
Thus high uplifted beyond hope.
bk.ii, l.1

7   The strongest and the fiercest Spirit
That fought in Heav'n; now fiercer by despair.
His trust was with th' Eternal to be deemed
Equal in strength, and rather than be less
Cared not to be at all.
1.44

8   My sentence is for open war: of wiles
More unexpert, I boast not.
1.51

9   Belial, in act more graceful and humane;
A fairer person lost not Heav'n; he seemed
For dignity compos'd and high exploit:
But all was false and hollow; though his tongue
Dropt manna, and could make the worse appear
The better reason.
1.109

10   For who would lose,
Though full of pain, this intellectual being,
Those thoughts that wander through eternity,
To perish rather, swallowed up and lost
In the wide womb of uncreated night,
Devoid of sense and motion?
1.146

11   There to converse, with everlasting groans,
Unrespited, unpitied, unreprieved,
Ages of hopeless end.
1.184

12   Thus Belial with words clothed in reason's garb
Counselled ignoble ease, and peaceful sloth,
Not peace.
1.226

13   Our torments also may in length of time
Become our elements.
1.274

14   With grave

Aspect he rose, and in his rising seem'd
A pillar of state; deep on his front engraven
Deliberation sat and public care;
And princely counsel in his face yet shone,
Majestic though in ruin.
1.300

15   To sit in darkness here
Hatching vain empires.
1.377

16   Who shall tempt with wand'ring feet
The dark unbottom'd infinite abyss
And through the palpable obscure find out
His uncouth way.
1.404

17   Long is the way
And hard, that out of hell leads up to light.
1.432

18   O shame to men! devil with devil damn'd
Firm concord holds, men only disagree
Of creatures rational.
1.496

19   In discourse more sweet
(For eloquence the soul, song charms the sense,)
Others apart sat on a hill retir'd,
In thoughts more elevate, and reason'd high
Of providence, foreknowledge, will, and fate,
Fix'd fate, free will, foreknowledge absolute,
And found no end, in wand'ring mazes lost.
1.555

20   Of good and evil much they argued then,
Of happiness and final misery,
Passion and apathy, and glory and shame,
Vain wisdom all, and false philosophy.
1.562

21   The parching air
Burns frore, and cold performs th' effect of fire.
1.594

22   Feel by turns the bitter change
Of fierce extremes, extremes by change more fierce.
1.598

23   O'er many a frozen, many a fiery Alp,
Rocks, caves, lakes, fens, bogs, dens, and shades of
   death,
A universe of death, which God by curse
Created evil, for evil only good,
Where all life dies, death lives, and Nature breeds,
Perverse, all monstrous, all prodigious things,
Abominable, unutterable, and worse
Than fables yet have feigned, or fear conceived,
Gorgons and Hydras, and Chimaeras dire.
1.620

24   The other shape,
If shape it might be call'd that shape had none
Distinguishable in member, joint, or limb,
Or substance might be call'd that shadow seem'd,
For each seem'd either; black it stood as night,
Fierce as ten furies, terrible as hell,
And shook a dreadful dart; what seem'd his head
The likeness of a kingly crown had on.
1.666

25   Whence and what art thou, execrable shape?
1.681

26   Incens'd with indignation Satan stood

Unterrifi'd, and like a comet burn'd
That fires the length of Ophiucus huge
In th' arctic sky, and from his horrid hair
Shakes pestilence and war.
l.707

1   Their fatal hands
No second stroke intend.
l.712

2   I fled, and cry'd out, *Death*;
Hell trembled at the hideous name, and sigh'd
From all her caves, and back resounded, *Death*.
l.787

3   On a sudden open fly
With impetuous recoil and jarring sound
Th' infernal doors, and on their hinges grate
Harsh thunder.
l.879

4   Chaos umpire sits,
And by decision more embroils the fray
By which he reigns: next him high arbiter
Chance governs all.
l.907

5 Sable-vested Night, eldest of things.
l.962

6 With ruin upon ruin, rout on rout,
Confusion worse confounded.
l.995

7 So he with difficulty and labour hard
Moved on, with difficulty and labour he.
l.1021

8 Then feed on thoughts, that voluntary move
Harmonious numbers; as the wakeful bird
Sings darkling, and in shadiest covert hid,
Tunes her nocturnal note. Thus with the year
Seasons return, but not to me returns
Day, or the sweet approach of ev'n or morn,
Or sight of vernal bloom, or summer's rose,
Or flocks, or herds, or human face divine;
But cloud instead, and ever-during dark
Surrounds me, from the cheerful ways of men
Cut off, and for the book of knowledge fair
Presented with a universal blank
Of Nature's works to me expung'd and raz'd,
And wisdom at one entrance quite shut out.
bk.iii, l.37

9 Dark with excessive bright.
l.380

10 So on this windy sea of land, the Fiend
Walked up and down alone bent on his prey.
l.440

11 Into a Limbo large and broad, since called
The Paradise of Fools, to few unknown.
l.495

12 For neither man nor angel can discern
Hypocrisy, the only evil that walks
Invisible, except to God alone.
l.682

13   At whose sight all the stars
Hide their diminished heads.
bk.iv, l.34

14 Warring in Heav'n against Heav'n's matchless King.
l.41

15 Me miserable! which way shall I fly

Infinite wrath, and infinite despair?
Which way I fly is Hell; myself am Hell;
And in the lowest deep a lower deep
Still threatening to devour me opens wide,
To which the Hell I suffer seems a Heaven.
l.73

16 So farewell hope, and with hope farewell fear,
Farewell remorse: all good to me is lost;
Evil be thou my Good.
l.108

17   When to them who sail
Beyond the Cape of Hope, and now are past
Mozambic, off at sea north-east winds blow
Sabean odours from the spicy shore
Of Araby the Blest, with such delay
Well pleased they slack their course, and many a
    league
Cheered with the grateful smell old Ocean smiles.
l.159

18 So clomb this first grand thief into God's fold:
So since into his church lewd hirelings climb.
Thence up he flew, and on the tree of life,
The middle tree and highest there that grew,
Sat like a cormorant.
l.192

19 Groves whose rich trees wept odorous gums and balm,
Others whose fruit burnished with golden rind
Hung amiable, Hesperian fables true,
If true, here only.
l.248

20 Flowers of all hue, and without thorn the rose.
l.256

21   Not that fair field
Of Enna, where Proserpin gathering flowers
Herself a fairer flower by gloomy Dis
Was gathered, which cost Ceres all that pain.
l.268

22 For contemplation he and valour formed;
For softness she and sweet attractive grace,
He for God only, she for God in him:
His fair large front and eye sublime declared
Absolute rule.
l.297

23   Which implied
Subjection, but required with gentle sway
And by her yielded, by him best received;
Yielded with coy submission, modest pride,
And sweet reluctant amorous delay.
l.307

24 Adam, the goodliest man of men since born
His sons; the fairest of her daughters Eve.
l.323

25 The savoury pulp they chew, and in the rind
Still as they thirsted scooped the brimming stream.
l.335

26 Sporting the lion ramped, and in his paw,
Dandled the kid; bears, tigers, ounces, pards
Gamboll'd before them, th' unwieldy elephant
To make them mirth us'd all his might, and wreathed
His lithe proboscis.
l.343

27 So spake the Fiend, and with necessity,

The tyrant's plea, excus'd his devilish deeds.
1.393

1   These two
Imparadised in one another's arms,
The happier Eden, shall enjoy their fill
Of bliss on bliss.
1.505

2 Now came still evening on, and twilight gray
Had in her sober livery all things clad;
Silence accompanied, for beast and bird,
They to their grassy couch, these to their nests,
Were slunk, all but the wakeful nightingale;
She all night long her amorous descant sung;
Silence was pleas'd: now glow'd the firmament
With living sapphires: Hesperus that led
The starry host, rode brightest, till the moon,
Rising in clouded majesty, at length
Apparent queen unveil'd her peerless light,
And o'er the dark her silver mantle threw.
1.598

3 God is thy law, thou mine: to know no more
Is woman's happiest knowledge and her praise.
With thee conversing I forget all time.
1.637

4 Sweet is the breath of morn, her rising sweet,
With charm of earliest birds.
1.641

5   Sweet the coming on
Of grateful evening mild, then silent night
With this her solemn bird and this fair moon,
And these the gems of Heav'n, her starry train.
1.646

6 Millions of spiritual creatures walk the earth
Unseen, both when we wake, and when we sleep.
1.677

7   Into their inmost bower
Handed they went; and eas'd the putting off
These troublesome disguises which we wear,
Strait side by side were laid, nor turned I ween
Adam from his fair spouse, nor Eve the rites
Mysterious of connubial love refus'd:
Whatever hypocrites austerely talk
Of purity and place and innocence,
Defaming as impure what God declares
Pure, and commands to some, leaves free to all.
1.738

8 Hail wedded love, mysterious law, true source
Of human offspring, sole propriety,
In Paradise of all things common else.
1.750

9   Sleep on,
Blest pair; and O yet happiest if ye seek
No happier state, and know to know no more.
1.773

10   Him there they found
Squat like a toad, close at the ear of Eve.
1.799

11 But wherefore thou alone? Wherefore with thee
Came not all hell broke loose?
1.917

12 Then when I am thy captive talk of chains,
Proud limitary Cherub.
1.970

13   His sleep
Was aery light, from pure digestion bred.
bk.v, l.3

14 My fairest, my espoused, my latest found,
Heaven's last best gift, my ever new delight.
1.18

15 Best image of myself and dearer half.
1.95

16 On earth join all ye creatures to extol
Him first, him last, him midst, and without end.
1.164

17 A wilderness of sweets.
1.294

18 So saying, with despatchful looks in haste
She turns, on hospitable thoughts intent.
1.331

19   Nor jealousy
Was understood, the injured lover's hell.
1.449

20   Freely we serve,
Because we freely love, as in our will
To love or not; in this we stand or fall.
1.538

21   What if earth
Be but the shadow of Heaven, and things therein
Each to other like, more than on earth is thought?
1.574

22 Hear all ye Angels, progeny of light,
Thrones, Dominations, Princedoms, Virtues, Powers.
1.600

23 All seemed well pleased, all seemed but were not all.
1.617

24   Yonder starry sphere
Of planets and of fixed in all her wheels
       ...mazes intricate,
Eccentric, intervolved, yet regular
Then most, when most irregular they seem;
And in their motions harmony divine
So smoothes her charming tones that God's own ear
Listens delighted.
1.620

25 Satan, so call him now, his former name
Is heard no more in heaven.
1.655

26 Servant of God, well done, well hast thou fought
The better fight, who singly hast maintained
Against revolted multitudes the cause
Of truth, in word mightier than they in arms.
bk.vi, l.29

27   Headlong themselves they threw
Down from the verge of Heaven, eternal wrath
Burnt after them to the bottomless pit.
1.864

28 Standing on earth, not rapt above the Pole,
More safe I sing with mortal voice, unchang'd
To hoarse or mute, though fall'n on evil days,
On evil days though fall'n, and evil tongues.
bk.vii, l.23

29   Drive far off the barb'rous dissonance
Of Bacchus and his revellers.
1.32

30   Necessity and chance

Approach not me, and what I will is fate.
1.172

1   There Leviathan
Hugest of living creatures, on the deep
Stretch'd like a promontory sleeps or swims,
And seems a moving land, and at his gills
Draws in, and at his trunk spouts out a sea.
1.412

2 The Planets in their stations list'ning stood,
While the bright Pomp ascended jubilant.
Open, ye everlasting gates, they sung,
Open, ye heavens, your living doors; let in
The great Creator from his work return'd
Magnificent, his six days' work, a world.
1.563

3   He his fabric of the Heavens
Hath left to their disputes, perhaps to move
His laughter at their quaint opinions wide
Hereafter, when they come to model Heaven
And calculate the stars, how they will wield
The mighty frame, how build, unbuild, contrive
To save appearances, how gird the sphere
With centric and eccentric scribbled o'er,
Cycle and epicycle, orb in orb.
bk.viii, 1.76

4   Heaven is for thee too high
To know what passes there; be lowly wise:
Think only what concerns thee and thy being.
1.172

5 Tell me, how may I know him, how adore,
From whom I have that thus I move and live,
And feel that I am happier than I know?
1.280

6   In solitude
What happiness? Who can enjoy alone,
Or all enjoying, what contentment find?
1.364

7   So absolute she seems
And in herself complete, so well to know
Her own, that what she wills to do or say
Seems wisest, virtuousest, discreetest, best.
1.547

8   Oft-times nothing profits more
Than self-esteem, grounded on just and right
Well manag'd.
1.571

9 My celestial Patroness, who deigns
Her nightly visitation unimplor'd,
And dictates to me slumb'ring, or inspires
Easy my unpremeditated verse:
Since first this subject for heroic song
Pleas'd me long choosing, and beginning late.
bk.ix, 1.21

10   Unless an age too late, or cold
Climate, or years damp my intended wing.
1.44

11 The serpent subtlest beast of all the field.
1.86

12 For solitude sometimes is best society,
And short retirement urges sweet return.
1.249

13 As one who long in populous city pent,
Where houses thick and sewers annoy the air,

Forth issuing on a summer's morn to breathe
Among the pleasant villages and farms
Adjoin'd, from each thing met conceives delight.
1.445

14 She fair, divinely fair, fit love for Gods.
1.489

15 God so commanded, and left that command
Sole daughter of his voice; the rest, we live
Law to ourselves, our reason is our law.
1.652

16   Her rash hand in evil hour
Forth reaching to the fruit, she pluck'd, she eat:
Earth felt the wound, and Nature from her seat
Sighing through all her works gave signs of woe
That all was lost.
1.780

17 O fairest of creation! last and best
Of all God's works! creature in whom excell'd
Whatever can to sight or thought be form'd,
Holy, divine, good, amiable, or sweet!
1.896

18   For with thee
Certain my resolution is to die;
How can I live without thee, how forgo
Thy sweet converse and love so dearly joined,
To live again in these wild woods forlorn?
1.906

19   Flesh of flesh,
Bone of my bone thou art, and from thy state
Mine never shall be parted, weal or woe.
1.915

20   What thou art is mine;
Our state cannot be sever'd, we are one,
One flesh; to lose thee were to lose myself.
1.957

21   Yet I shall temper so
Justice with mercy.
bk.x, 1.77

22   He hears
On all sides, from innumerable tongues,
A dismal universal hiss, the sound
Of public scorn.
1.506

23   Oh! why did God,
Creator wise, that peopled highest Heaven
With Spirits masculine, create at last
This novelty on Earth, this fair defect
Of Nature?
1.888

24 Demoniac frenzy, moping melancholy,
And moon-struck madness.
bk.xi, 1.485

25 Nor love thy life, nor hate; but what thou liv'st
Live well, how long or short permit to Heaven.
1.553

26   The evening star,
Love's harbinger.
1.588

27   For now I see
Peace to corrupt no less than war to waste.
1.779

28 In me is no delay; with thee to go,
Is to stay here; without thee here to stay,

Is to go hence unwilling; thou to me
Art all things under Heaven, all places thou,
Who for my wilful crime art banished hence.
bk.xii, l.615

1 They looking back, all th' eastern side beheld
Of Paradise, so late their happy seat,
Wav'd over by that flaming brand, the Gate
With dreadful faces throng'd and fiery arms.
Some natural tears they dropped, but wiped them
    soon;
The world was all before them, where to choose
Their place of rest, and Providence their guide:
They hand in hand with wandering steps and slow
Through Eden took their solitary way.
l.641

2 Skill'd to retire, and in retiring draw
Hearts after them tangled in amorous nets.
Paradise Regained (1671), bk.ii, l.161

3 Ladies of th' Hesperides, that seemed
Fairer than feign'd of old, or fabled since
Of faery damsels met in forest wide
By knights of Logres, or of Lyones,
Lancelot or Pelleas, or Pellenore.
l.357

4 Of whom to be dispraised were no small praise.
bk.iii, l.56

5 But on Occasion's forelock watchful wait.
l.173

6 As he who, seeking asses, found a kingdom. [Saul.]
l.242

7   The childhood shows the man,
As morning shows the day. Be famous then
By wisdom; as thy empire must extend,
So let extend thy mind o'er all the world.
bk.iv, l.220

8 Athens, the eye of Greece, mother of arts
And eloquence, native to famous wits
Or hospitable, in her sweet recess,
City or suburban, studious walks and shades;
See there the olive grove of Academe,
Plato's retirement, where the Attic bird
Trills her thick-warbled notes the summer long.
l.240

9 The first and wisest of them all professed
To know this only, that he nothing knew.
l.293

10   Who reads
Incessantly, and to his reading brings not
A spirit and judgment equal or superior
(And what he brings, what needs he elsewhere seek?)
Uncertain and unsettled still remains,
Deep versed in books and shallow in himself.
l.322

11 In them is plainest taught, and easiest learnt,
What makes a nation happy, and keeps it so.
l.361

12 But headlong joy is ever on the wing.
The Passion, l.5

13 A little onward lend thy guiding hand
To these dark steps, a little further on.
Samson Agonistes (1671), l.1

14 Ask for this great deliverer now, and find him

Eyeless in Gaza, at the mill with slaves.
l.40

15 O dark, dark, dark, amid the blaze of noon,
Irrecoverably dark, total eclipse
Without all hope of day!
l.80

16 The sun to me is dark
And silent as the moon,
When she deserts the night
Hid in her vacant interlunar cave.
l.86

17 To live a life half dead, a living death.
l.100

18 Ran on embattled armies clad in iron,
And, weaponless himself,
Made arms ridiculous.
l.129

19   Wisest men
Have erred, and by bad women been deceived;
And shall again, pretend they ne'er so wise.
l.210

20 Just are the ways of God,
And justifiable to men;
Unless there be who think not God at all.
l.293

21   Of such doctrine never was there school,
But the heart of the fool,
And no man therein doctor but himself.
l.297

22 But what availed this temperance, not complete
Against another object more enticing?
What boots it at one gate to make defence,
And at another to let in the foe?
l.558

23 My race of glory run, and race of shame,
And I shall shortly be with them that rest.
l.597

24   That grounded maxim
So rife and celebrated in the mouths
Of wisest men; that to the public good
Private respects must yield.
l.865

25 Yet beauty, though injurious, hath strange power,
After offence returning, to regain
Love once possess'd.
l.1003

26 Love-quarrels oft in pleasing concord end.
l.1008

27 Lords are lordliest in their wine.
l.1418

28 For evil news rides post, while good news baits.
l.1538

29 And as an ev'ning dragon came,
Assailant on the perched roosts
And nests in order rang'd
Of tame villatic fowl.
l.1692

30 Like that self-begotten bird
In the Arabian woods embost,
That no second knows nor third,
And lay erewhile a holocaust.
l.1699

31 And though her body die, her fame survives,

A secular bird, ages of lives.
l.1706

1   Samson hath quit himself
Like Samson, and heroically hath finish'd
A life heroic.
l.1709

2 Nothing is here for tears, nothing to wail
Or knock the breast; no weakness, no contempt,
Dispraise or blame; nothing but well and fair,
And what may quiet us in a death so noble.
l.1721

3 All is best, though we oft doubt,
What th' unsearchable dispose
Of highest wisdom brings about,
And ever best found in the close.
l.1745

4 His servants he with new acquist
Of true experience from this great event
With peace and consolation hath dismiss'd,
And calm of mind all passion spent.
l.1752

5 O nightingale, that on yon bloomy spray
Warbl'st at eve, when all the woods are still.
Sonnet i. **To the Nightingale**

6 How soon hath Time, the subtle thief of youth
Stoln on its wing my three and twentieth year.
ii. **On his having arrived at the age of twenty-three**

7 I did but prompt the age to quit their clogs,
By the known rules of ancient liberty,
When straight a barbarous noise environs me
Of owls and cuckoos, asses, apes, and dogs.
xii. **On the Same [Detraction, etc.]**

8 Licence they mean when they cry Liberty;
For who loves that, must first be wise and good.

9 Avenge, O Lord, thy slaughtered saints, whose bones
Lie scattered on the Alpine mountains cold;
Ev'n them who kept thy truth so pure of old,
When all our fathers worshipped stocks and stones,
Forget not.
xv. **On the late Massacre in Piedmont**

10 When I consider how my light is spent,
E're half my days, in this dark world and wide,
And that one Talent which is death to hide,
Lodg'd with me useless, though my Soul more bent
To serve therewith my Maker, and present
My true account, lest He returning chide;
'Doth God exact day-labour, light deny'd?'
I fondly ask; But Patience, to prevent
That murmur, soon replies, 'God doth not need
Either man's work or his own gifts. Who best
Bear his mild yoke, they serve him best, his State
Is Kingly. Thousands at his bidding speed
And post o'er Land and Ocean without rest:
They also serve who only stand and wait.
xvi. **On His Blindness**

11 In mirth, that after no repenting draws.
xviii. **To Cyriac Skinner**

12 Methought I saw my late espousèd Saint
Brought to me like Alcestis from the grave.
xix. **On His Deceased Wife**

13 Love, sweetness, goodness, in her person shined.

14 But O as to embrace me she inclined,
I waked, she fled, and day brought back my night.

15 New Presbyter is but old Priest writ large.
On the New Forcers of Conscience under the Long Parliament

16 For what can war but endless war still breed?
On the Lord General Fairfax

17   Peace hath her victories
No less renowned than war.
To the Lord General Cromwell, May 1652

18 He who would not be frustrate of his hope to write
well hereafter in laudable things ought himself to be a
true poem.
An Apology against a Pamphlet…against Smectymnuus (1642),
introd. to 1

19 His words…like so many nimble and airy servitors trip
about him at command.
12

20 For this is not the liberty which we can hope, that no
grievance ever should arise in the Commonwealth,
that let no man in this world expect; but when
complaints are freely heard, deeply considered, and
speedily reformed, then is the utmost bound of civil
liberty attained that wise men look for.
Areopagitica (1644)

21 Books are not absolutely dead things, but do contain a
potency of life in them to be as active as that soul was
whose progeny they are; nay they do preserve as in a
vial the purest efficacy and extraction of that living
intellect that bred them.

22 As good almost kill a man as kill a good book: who
kills a man kills a reasonable creature, God's image;
but he who destroys a good book, kills reason itself,
kills the image of God, as it were in the eye.

23 A good book is the precious life-blood of a master
spirit, embalmed and treasured up on purpose to a life
beyond life.

24 He that can apprehend and consider vice with all her
baits and seeming pleasures, and yet abstain, and yet
distinguish, and yet prefer that which is truly better, he
is the true wayfaring Christian. I cannot praise a
fugitive and cloistered virtue, unexercised and
unbreathed, that never sallies out and sees her
adversary, but slinks out of the race, where that
immortal garland is to be run for, not without dust and
heat. Assuredly we bring not innocence into the world,
we bring impurity much rather: that which purifies us
is trial, and trial is by what is contrary.

25 If we think to regulate printing thereby to rectify
manners, we must regulate all recreations and
pastimes, all that is delightful to man…It will ask more
than the work of twenty licensers to examine all the
lutes, the violins, and the guitars in every house…and
who shall silence all the airs and madrigals, that
whisper softness in chambers?

26 To be still searching what we know not by what we
know, still closing up truth to truth as we find it (for
all her body is homogeneal and proportional), this is
the golden rule in theology as well as in arithmetic,
and makes up the best harmony in a church.

27 God is decreeing to begin some new and great period
in His Church, even to the reforming of Reformation
itself. What does He then but reveal Himself to His
servants, and as His manner is, first to His
Englishmen?

1 Behold now this vast city [London]; a city of refuge, the mansion-house of liberty, encompassed and surrounded with His protection.

2 Where there is much desire to learn, there of necessity will be much arguing, much writing, many opinions; for opinion in good men is but knowledge in the making.

3 Methinks I see in my mind a noble and puissant nation rousing herself like a strong man after sleep, and shaking her invincible locks. Methinks I see her as an eagle mewing her mighty youth, and kindling her undazzled eyes at the full midday beam.

4 Give me the liberty to know, to utter, and to argue freely according to conscience, above all liberties.

5 Though all the winds of doctrine were let loose to play upon the earth, so Truth be in the field, we do injuriously by licensing and prohibiting to misdoubt her strength. Let her and Falsehood grapple; who ever knew Truth put to the worse, in a free and open encounter?

6 Let not England forget her precedence of teaching nations how to live.
The Doctrine and Discipline of Divorce (1643)

7 I owe no light or leading received from any man in the discovery of this truth.
The Judgement of Martin Bucer Concerning Divorce

8 I call therefore a complete and generous education that which fits a man to perform justly, skilfully and magnanimously all the offices both private and public of peace and war.
Of Education (1644)

9 Ornate rhetorick taught out of the rule of Plato,...To which poetry would be made subsequent, or indeed rather precedent, as being less subtle and fine, but more simple, sensuous and passionate.

10 In those vernal seasons of the year, when the air is calm and pleasant, it were an injury and sullenness against Nature not to go out, and see her riches, and partake in her rejoicing with Heaven and Earth.

11 What I have spoken, is the language of that which is not called amiss *The good old Cause.*
The Ready and Easy Way to Establish a Free Commonwealth (1660)

12 But because about the manner and order of this government, whether it ought to be Presbyterial, or Prelatical, such endless question, or rather uproar is arisen in this land, as may be justly termed, what the fever is to the physicians, the eternal reproach of the divines.
The Reason of Church Government Urged Against Prelaty (1641), preface

13 This manner of writing [i.e. prose] wherein knowing myself inferior to myself...I have the use, as I may account it, but of my left hand.
bk.ii, introd. to ch.1

14 By labour and intent study (which I take to be my portion in this life) joined with the strong propensity of nature, I might perhaps leave something so written to after-times, as they should not willingly let it die.

15 The land had once enfranchised herself from this impertinent yoke of prelaty, under whose inquisitorious and tyrannical duncery no free and

splendid wit can flourish.

16 Beholding the bright countenance of truth in the quiet and still air of delightful studies.

17 None can love freedom heartily, but good men; the rest love not freedom, but licence.
The Tenure of Kings and Magistrates (1648-9)

18 No man who knows aught, can be so stupid to deny that all men naturally were born free.

COMTE DE MIRABEAU 1749–1791

19 *La guerre est l'industrie nationale de la Prusse.*
War is the national industry of Prussia.
Attr. to Mirabeau by Albert Sorel, based on his Introduction to his *Monarchie Prussienne*

MISSAL

20 *O felix culpa, quae talem ac tantum meruit habere Redemptorem.*
O happy fault, which has deserved to have such and so mighty a Redeemer.
'Exsultet' on Holy Saturday

MARGARET MITCHELL 1900–1949

21 After all, tomorrow is another day.
Gone with the Wind (1936), closing words.

MARY RUSSELL MITFORD 1787–1855

22 I have discovered that our great favourite, Miss Austen, is my country-woman...with whom mamma before her marriage was acquainted. Mamma says that she was then the prettiest, silliest, most affected, husband-hunting butterfly she ever remembers.
Letter to Sir William Elford, 3 Apr. 1815

NANCY MITFORD 1904–1973

23 'Always be civil to the girls, you never know who they may marry' is an aphorism which has saved many an English spinster from being treated like an Indian widow.
Love in a Cold Climate, pt.1, ch.2. See 3:5

24 'Twenty-three and a quarter minutes past', Uncle Matthew was saying furiously, 'in precisely six and three-quarter minutes the damned fella will be late.'
ch.13

25 When the loo paper gets thicker and the writing paper thinner it's always a bad sign, at home.
pt.2, ch.2

26 Like all the very young we took it for granted that making love is child's play.
The Pursuit of Love, ch.3

27 I loathe abroad, nothing would induce me to live there...and, as for foreigners, they are all the same, and they all make me sick.
ch.10

28 Abroad is unutterably bloody and foreigners are fiends.
ch.15

EMILIO MOLA d. 1937

29 *La quinta columna.*

The fifth column.
A reference to Mola's expectation of help from civilians in Madrid, reported in *Mundo Obrero* in the first week of Oct. 1936; but the phrase may not have been coined with direct reference to the Madrid offensive, since there is doubt over the number of columns deployed in his march on the city. See, e.g., G. Hills, *The Battle for Madrid* (1976), p.85n, and *Madrid: Servicio Histórico Militar*, La Marcha sobre Madrid (1968), p.88 n.70

MOLIÈRE (J.-B. POQUELIN) 1622–1673

1 *Présentez toujours le devant au monde.*
Always show your front to the world.
L'Avare (1668), III.ii

2 *Il faut manger pour vivre et non pas vivre pour manger.*
One should eat to live, and not live to eat.
v

3 M. Jourdain: *Quoi? quand je dis: 'Nicole, apportez-moi mes pantoufles, et me donnez mon bonnet de nuit', c'est de la prose?*
Maître de Philosophie: *Oui, Monsieur.*
M. Jourdain: *Par ma foi! il y a plus de quarante ans que je dis de la prose sans que j'en susse rien.*
M. Jourdain: What? when I say: 'Nicole, bring me my slippers, and give me my night-cap,' is that prose?
Philosophy Teacher: Yes, Sir.
M. Jourdain: Good heavens! For more than forty years I have been speaking prose without knowing it.
Le Bourgeois Gentilhomme (1670), II.iv

4 *Tout ce qui n'est point prose est vers; et tout ce qui n'est point vers est prose.*
All that is not prose is verse; and all that is not verse is prose.

5 *Ah, la belle chose que de savoir quelque chose.*
Ah, it's a lovely thing, to know a thing or two.
vi

6 *Je voudrais bien savoir si la grande règle de toutes les règles n'est pas de plaire.*
I shouldn't be surprised if the greatest rule of all weren't to give pleasure.
Critique de L'École des Femmes (1663), vii

7 *C'est une étrange entreprise que celle de faire rire les honnêtes gens.*
It's an odd job, making decent people laugh.

8 *On ne meurt qu'une fois, et c'est pour si longtemps!*
One dies only once, and it's for such a long time!
Le Dépit Amoureux (1656), V.iii

9 *Qui vit sans tabac n'est pas digne de vivre.*
He who lives without tobacco is not worthy to live.
Dom Juan (1665), I.i

10 *Je vis de bonne soupe et non de beau langage.*
It's good food and not fine words that keeps me alive.
Les Femmes Savantes (1672), II.vii

11 *Guenille, si l'on veut: ma guenille m'est chère.*
Rags and tatters, if you like: I am fond of my rags and tatters.

12 *Un sot savant est sot plus qu'un sot ignorant.*
A knowledgeable fool is a greater fool than an ignorant fool.
IV.iii

13 *Les livres cadrent mal avec le mariage.*
Reading goes ill with the married state.
V.iii

14 *Que diable allait-il faire dans cette galère?*
What the devil would he be doing in this gang?
Les Fourberies de Scapin (1671), II.vii

15 *Vous l'avez voulu, Georges Dandin, vous l'avez voulu.*
You asked for it, George Dandin, you asked for it.
Georges Dandin (1668), I.ix

16 *L'on a le temps d'avoir les dents longues, lorsqu'on attend pour vivre le trépas de quelqu'un.*
You've time to get hungry, while you're waiting for someone's death to get a living.
Le Médecin malgré lui (1666), II.ii

17 Géronte: *Il me semble que vous les placez autrement qu'ils ne sont: que le coeur est du côté gauche, et le foie du côté droit.*
Sganarelle: *Oui, cela était autrefois ainsi, mais nous avons changé tout cela, et nous faisons maintenant la médecine d'une méthode toute nouvelle.*
Géronte: It seems to me you are locating them wrongly: the heart is on the left and the liver is on the right.
Sganarelle: Yes, in the old days that was so, but we have changed all that, and we now practise medicine by a completely new method.
iv

18 *Il faut, parmi le monde, une vertu traitable.*
Virtue, in the great world, should be amenable.
Le Misanthrope (1666), I.i

19 *C'est une folie à nulle autre seconde,*
De vouloir se mêler à corriger le monde.
Of all human follies there's none could be greater
Than trying to render our fellow-men better.

20 *On doit se regarder soi-même un fort long temps,*
Avant que de songer à condamner les gens.
We should look long and carefully at ourselves before we pass judgement on others.
III.vii

21 *C'est un homme expéditif, qui aime à dépêcher ses malades; et quand on a à mourir, cela se fait avec lui le plus vite du monde.*
He's an expeditious man, who likes to hurry his patients along; and when you have to die, he sees to that quickest in all the world.
Monsieur de Pourceaugnac (1669), I.vii

22 *Ils commencent ici par faire pendre un homme et puis ils lui font son procès.*
Here [in Paris] they hang a man first, and try him afterwards.
III.ii

23 *Les gens de qualité savent tout sans avoir jamais rien appris.*
People of quality know everything without ever having been taught anything.
Les Précieuses Ridicules (1659), X

24 *Assassiner c'est le plus court chemin.*
Assassination is the quickest way.
Le Sicilien (1668), XIII

25 *Ah, pour être dévot, je n'en suis pas moins homme.*
I am not the less human for being devout.
Le Tartuffe (1664), III.iii

26 *Le ciel défend, de vrai, certains contentements*
Mais on trouve avec lui des accommodements.
God, it is true, does some delights condemn,

But 'tis not hard to come to terms with Him.
IV.v

1 *Le scandale du monde est ce qui fait l'offense,*
Et ce n'est pas pécher que pécher en silence.
It is public scandal that constitutes offence, and to sin in secret is not to sin at all.

2 *L'homme est, je vous l'avoue, un méchant animal.*
Man, I can assure you, is a nasty creature.
V.vi

3 *Il m'est permis de reprendre mon bien où je le trouve.*
It is permitted me to take good fortune where I find it.
Grimarest, *Vie de Molière* (1704), p.14

HELMUTH VON MOLTKE 1800–1891

4 *Der ewige Friede ist ein Traum, und nicht einmal ein schöner und der Krieg ein Glied in Gottes Weltordnung…Ohne den Krieg wurde die Welt in Materialismus versumpfen.*
Everlasting peace is a dream, and not even a pleasant one; and war is a necessary part of God's arrangement of the world…Without war, the world would slide dissolutely into materialism.
Letter to Dr. J.K. Bluntschli, 11 Dec. 1880

DUKE OF MONMOUTH 1649–1685

5 Do not hack me as you did my Lord Russell.
Words to his Executioner. Macaulay, *History of England*, vol.i, ch.5

LADY MARY WORTLEY MONTAGU 1689–1762

6 This world consists of men, women, and Herveys.
Letters, vol.i, p.67

7 But the fruit that can fall without shaking,
   Indeed is too mellow for me.
Letters and Works. Answered, for Lord William Hamilton

8 And we meet, with champagne and a chicken, at last.
The Lover

9 General notions are generally wrong.
Letter to Mr. Wortley Montagu, 28 Mar. 1710

10 Civility costs nothing and buys everything.
Letter to the Countess of Bute, 30 May 1756

11 People wish their enemies dead—but I do not; I say give them the gout, give them the stone!
Letter from Horace Walpole to the Earl of Harcourt, 17 Sept. 1778

MONTAIGNE 1533–1592

12 *Pour juger des choses grandes et hautes, il faut une âme de même, autrement nous leur attribuons le vice qui est le nôtre.*
To make judgements about great and high things, a soul of the same stature is needed; otherwise we ascribe to them that vice which is our own.
Essais, I.xiv. [References are to M. Rat's edition of the *Essais* (1958) which, in accordance with the Strowski and Gebelin text (1906–1933), conflates the 1580 edition of books I and II, the revised and enlarged 1588 edition of all three books, and later manuscript additions published posthumously.]

13 *Il faut être toujours botté et prêt à partir.*
One should always have one's boots on, and be ready to leave.
xx

14 *Je veux…que la mort me trouve plantant mes choux,*
mais nonchalant d'elle, et encore plus de mon jardin imparfait.
I want death to find me planting my cabbages, but caring little for it, and much more for my imperfect garden.

15 *'Le continuel ouvrage de votre vie, c'est bâtir la mort.'*
The ceaseless labour of your life is to build the house of death.

16 *'L'utilité du vivre n'est pas en l'espace, elle est en l'usage; tel a vécu longtemps qui a peu vécu…Il gît en votre volonté, non au nombre des ans, que vous ayez assez vécu.'*
The value of life lies not in the length of days but in the use you make of them; he has lived for a long time who has little lived. Whether you have lived enough depends not on the number of your years but on your will.

17 *Il faut noter, que les jeux d'enfants ne sont pas jeux: et les faut juger en eux, comme leurs plus sérieuses actions.*
It should be noted that children at play are not playing about; their games should be seen as their most serious-minded activity.
xxiii

18 *Si on me presse de dire pourquoi je l'aimais, je sens que cela ne se peut s'exprimer, qu'en répondant: 'Parce que c'était lui; parce que c'était moi.'*
If I am pressed to say why I loved him, I feel it can only be explained by replying: 'Because it was he; because it was me.'
[Of his friend Étienne de la Boétie.] xxviii

19 *Il n'y a guère moins de tourment au gouvernement d'une famille que d'un état entier…et, pour être les occupations domestiques moins importantes, elles n'en sont pas moins importunes.*
There is scarcely any less bother in the running of a family than in that of an entire state. And domestic business is no less importunate for being less important.
xxxix

20 *Il se faut réserver une arrière boutique toute notre, toute franche, en laquelle nous établissons notre vraie liberté et principale retraite et solitude.*
A man should keep for himself a little back shop, all his own, quite unadulterated, in which he establishes his true freedom and chief place of seclusion and solitude.

21 *La plus grande chose du monde, c'est de savoir être à soi.*
The greatest thing in the world is to know how to be one's own.

22 *La gloire et le repos sont choses qui ne peuvent loger en même gîte.*
Fame and tranquillity can never be bedfellows.

23 *Mon métier et mon art c'est vivre.*
Living is my job and my art.
II.vi

24 *La vertue refuse la facilité pour compagne…elle demande un chemin âpre et épineux.*
Virtue shuns ease as a companion. It demands a rough and thorny path.
xi

1 *Notre religion est faite pour extirper les vices; elle les couvre, les nourrit, les incite.*
Our religion is made so as to wipe out vices; it covers them up, nourishes them, incites them.
xii

2 *Quand je me joue à ma chatte, qui sait si elle passe son temps de moi plus que je ne fais d'elle?*
When I play with my cat, who knows whether she isn't amusing herself with me more than I am with her?

3 *'Que sais-je?'*
What do I know?

4 *L'homme est bien insensé. Il ne saurait forger un ciron, et forge des Dieux à douzaines.*
Man is quite insane. He wouldn't know how to create a maggot, and he creates Gods by the dozen.

5 *Ceux qui ont apparié notre vie à un songe, ont eu de la raison, à l'aventure plus qu'ils ne pensaient...Nous veillons dormants, et veillants dormons.*
Those who have likened our life to a dream were more right, by chance, than they realised. We are awake while sleeping, and waking sleep.

6 *Quelqu'un pourrait dire de moi que j'ai seulement fait ici un amas de fleurs étrangères, m'y ayant fourni du mien que le filet à les lier.*
It could be said of me that in this book I have only made up a bunch of other men's flowers, providing of my own only the string that ties them together.
III.xii

BARON DE MONTESQUIEU 1689–1755

7 *Les grands seigneurs ont des plaisirs, le peuple a de la joie.*
Great lords have their pleasures, but the people have fun.
Pensées Diverses

8 *Les Anglais sont occupés; ils n'ont pas le temps d'être polis.*
The English are busy; they don't have time to be polite.

FIELD-MARSHAL MONTGOMERY 1887–1976

9 The U.S. has broken the second rule of war. That is, don't go fighting with your land army on the mainland of Asia. Rule One is don't march on Moscow. I developed these two rules myself.
Of American policy in Vietnam. Chalfont, *Montgomery of Alamein* (1976), p.318

ROBERT MONTGOMERY 1807–1855

10 The solitary monk who shook the world.
Luther, Man's Need and God's Supply (1842), l.68

CASIMIR, COMTE DE MONTROND 1768–1843

11 *Défiez-vous des premiers mouvements parce qu'ils sont bons.*
Have no truck with first impulses as they are always generous ones.
Attr., Comte J. d'Estournel, *Derniers Souvenirs*. Also attr. Talleyrand. See 162:18

MARQUIS OF MONTROSE
see JAMES GRAHAM

PROFESSOR CLEMENT C. MOORE 1779–1863

12 'Twas the night before Christmas, when all through the house
Not a creature was stirring, not even a mouse;
The stockings were hung by the chimney with care,
In hopes that St Nicholas soon would be there.
A Visit from St. Nicholas. *Troy Sentinel,* 23 Dec. 1823

EDWARD MOORE 1712–1757

13 This is adding insult to injuries.
The Foundling (1747–8), V.ii

14 I am rich beyond the dreams of avarice.
The Gamester (1753), II.ii

GEORGE MOORE 1852–1933

15 All reformers are bachelors.
The Bending of the Bough (1900), Act I

16 Art must be parochial in the beginning to become cosmopolitan in the end.
Hail and Farewell! (1911–14), 1925 edn., vol.i, p.5

17 Acting is therefore the lowest of the arts, if it is an art at all.
Mummer-Worship

MARIANNE MOORE 1887–1972

18   O to be a dragon
a symbol of the power of Heaven.
O to Be a Dragon

19 I, too, dislike it: there are things that are important beyond all this fiddle.
  Reading it, however, with a perfect contempt for it, one discovers in
it after all, a place for the genuine.
Poetry

20 Nor till the poets among us can be
  'literalists of
    the imagination'—above
      insolence and triviality and can present

for inspection, 'imaginary gardens with real toads in them,' shall we have
  it. [Poetry.]

21 My father used to say
  'Superior people never make long visits.'
Silence

22 Self-reliant like the cat—
  that takes its prey to privacy,
the mouse's limp tail hanging like a shoelace from its mouth.

STURGE MOORE 1870–1944

23 Then, cleaving the grass, gazelles appear
(The gentler dolphins of kindlier waves)
With sensitive heads alert of ear;
Frail crowds that a delicate hearing saves.
The Gazelles

THOMAS MOORE 1779–1852

1 For you know, dear—I may, without vanity, hint—
 Though an angel should write, still 'tis *devils* must
 print.
 The Fudges in England (1835), letter iii, l.64

2 Yet, who can help loving the land that has taught us
 Six hundred and eighty-five ways to dress eggs?
 The Fudge Family in Paris (1818), letter viii, l.64

3 A Persian's Heaven is easily made;
 'Tis but black eyes and lemonade.
 Intercepted Letters, vi

4 Believe me, if all those endearing young charms,
  Which I gaze on so fondly today,
 Were to change by tomorrow, and fleet in my arms,
  Like fairy gifts fading away!
 Thou wouldst still be ador'd as this moment thou art,
  Let thy loveliness fade as it will,
 And, around the dear ruin, each wish of my heart
  Would entwine itself verdantly still.
 Irish Melodies (1807). **Believe Me, if all those Endearing
 Young Charms**

5 No, the heart that has truly lov'd never forgets,
  But as truly loves on to the close,
 As the sun-flower turns on her god, when he sets,
  The same look which she turn'd when he rose.

6 Eyes of most unholy blue!
 By that Lake

7 You may break, you may shatter the vase, if you will,
 But the scent of the roses will hang round it still.
 Farewell! But Whenever

8 Go where glory waits thee,
 But, while fame elates thee,
  Oh! still remember me.
 Go Where Glory

9 The harp that once through Tara's halls
  The soul of music shed,
 Now hangs as mute on Tara's walls
  As if that soul were fled.—
 So sleeps the pride of former days,
  So glory's thrill is o'er;
 And hearts, that once beat high for praise,
  Now feel that pulse no more.
 The Harp that Once

10 Thus freedom now so seldom wakes,
  The only throb she gives,
 Is when some heart indignant breaks,
  To show that still she lives.

11 Lesbia hath a beaming eye,
  But no one knows for whom it beameth.
 Lesbia Hath

12 No, there's nothing half so sweet in life
  As love's young dream.
 Love's Young Dream

13 The Minstrel Boy to the war is gone,
  In the ranks of death you'll find him;
 His father's sword he has girded on,
  And his wild harp slung behind him.
 The Minstrel Boy

14 Oh! blame not the bard.
 Oh! Blame Not

15 Oh! breathe not his name, let it sleep in the shade,

Where cold and unhonour'd his relics are laid.
 Oh! Breathe not his Name

16 Rich and rare were the gems she wore,
 And a bright gold ring on her wand she bore.
 Rich and Rare

1·7 She is far from the land where her young hero sleeps,
  And lovers are round her, sighing:
 But coldly she turns from their gaze, and weeps,
  For her heart in his grave is lying.
 She is Far

18 My only books
  Were woman's looks,
 And folly's all they've taught me.
 The Time I've Lost

19 'Tis sweet to think, that, where'er we rove,
 We are sure to find something blissful and dear,
 And that, when we're far from the lips we love,
 We've but to make love to the lips we are near.
 'Tis Sweet to Think

20 'Tis the last rose of summer
  Left blooming alone;
 All her lovely companions
  Are faded and gone.
 'Tis the Last Rose

21 Then awake! the heavens look bright, my dear;
 'Tis never too late for delight, my dear;
  And the best of all ways
  To lengthen our days
 Is to steal a few hours from the night, my dear!
 The Young May Moon

22 Where I love I must not marry;
 Where I marry, cannot love.
 Juvenile Poems. **Love and Marriage**

23 'Twere more than woman to be wise;
 'Twere more than man to wish thee so!
 The Ring (ed. 1882)

24 To love you was pleasant enough,
 And, oh! 'tis delicious to hate you!
 To—When I Lov'd You

25 Oh! ever thus, from childhood's hour,
  I've seen my fondest hopes decay;
 I never lov'd a tree or flow'r,
  But 'twas the first to fade away.
 I never nurs'd a dear gazelle,
  To glad me with its soft black eye,
 But when it came to know me well,
  And love me, it was sure to die!
 Lalla Rookh (1817). **The Fire-Worshippers**, i. l.279

26 Like Dead Sea fruits, that tempt the eye,
  But turn to ashes on the lips!
 l.484

27 One Morn a Peri at the gate
 Of Eden stood, disconsolate.
 Paradise and the Peri, l.1

28 But Faith, fanatic Faith, once wedded fast
 To some dear falsehood, hugs it to the last.
 The Veiled Prophet, iii. l.356

29 'Come, come', said Tom's father, 'at your time of
  life,
  'There's no longer excuse for thus playing the rake—
 'It is time you should think, boy, of taking a wife'—
  'Why, so it is, father—whose wife shall I take?'
 Miscellaneous Poems. **A Joke Versified**

1 Disguise our bondage as we will,
'Tis woman, woman, rules us still.
Sovereign Woman

2 Oft, in the stilly night,
　　Ere Slumber's chain has bound me,
Fond Memory brings the light
　　Of other days around me.
National Airs (1815). **Oft in the Stilly Night**

3 There was a little Man, and he had a little Soul,
And he said, 'Little Soul, let us try, try, try'.
Satirical and Humorous Poems. **Little Man and Little Soul**

4 Your priests, whate'er their gentle shamming,
Have always had a taste for damning.
The Twopenny Post-Bag (1813), letter iv

5 Good at a fight, but better at a play,
Godlike in giving, but—the devil to pay!
On a Cast of Sheridan's Hand. Memoirs of the Life of R.B. Sheridan (1825), p.712

THOMAS OSBERT MORDAUNT 1730–1809

6 Sound, sound the clarion, fill the fife,
　　Throughout the sensual world proclaim,
One crowded hour of glorious life
　　Is worth an age without a name.
Verses Written During the War, 1756–1763. The Bee, 12 Oct. 1791

HANNAH MORE 1745–1833

7 For you'll ne'er mend your fortunes, nor help the just cause,
By breaking of windows, or breaking of laws.
Address to the Meeting in Spa Fields (1817). H. Thompson, *Life* (1838), p.398

8 Small habits, well pursued betimes,
May reach the dignity of crimes.
Florio, l.77

9 He lik'd those literary cooks
Who skim the cream of others' books;
And ruin half an author's graces
By plucking bon-mots from their places.
l.123

10 　　　　Did not God
Sometimes withhold in mercy what we ask,
We should be ruined at our own request.
Moses in the Bulrushes (1782), pt.i, l.34

11 The sober comfort, all the peace which springs
From the large aggregate of little things;
On these small cares of daughter, wife, or friend,
The almost sacred joys of home depend.
Sensibility, l.315

SIR THOMAS MORE 1478–1535

12 'In good faith, I rejoiced, son,' quoth he, 'that I had given the devil a foul fall, and that with those Lords I had gone so far, as without great shame I could never go back again.'
Roper, *Life of Sir Thomas More* (1935), p.69

13 'By god body, master More, *Indignatio principis mors est.*'
'Is that all, my Lord?' quoth he. 'Then in good faith is there no more difference between your grace and me, but that I shall die to-day, and you to-morrow.'
p.71

14 Son Roper, I thank our Lord the field is won.
p.73

15 Is not this house [the Tower of London] as nigh heaven as my own?
p.83

16 I pray you, master Lieutenant, see me safe up, and my coming down let me shift for my self. [On mounting the scaffold.]
p.103

17 Pluck up thy spirits, man, and be not afraid to do thine office; my neck is very short; take heed therefore thou strike not awry, for saving of thine honesty. [To the Executioner.]

18 This hath not offended the king. [As he drew his beard aside on placing his head on the block.]
Bacon, *Apophthegms,* 22

19 Your sheep, that were wont to be so meek and tame, and so small eaters, now, as I hear say, be become so great devourers, and so wild, that they eat up and swallow down the very men themselves.
Utopia (1516), bk.I

20 I cumber you goode Margaret muche, but I woulde be sorye, if it shoulde be any lenger than to morrowe, for it is S. Thomas evin and the vtas of Sainte Peter and therefore to morowe longe I to goe to God, it were a daye very meete and conveniente for me. I neuer liked your maner towarde me better then when you kissed me laste for I loue when doughterly loue and deere charitie hathe no laisor to looke to worldely curtesye. Fare well my deere childe and praye for me, and I shall for you and all your freindes that we maie merily meete in heaven.
Last letter to Margaret Roper, his daughter, 5 July 1535 (ed. E.F. Rogers, 1947). More was beheaded the following morning.

THOMAS MORELL 1703–1784

21 See, the conquering hero comes!
Sound the trumpets, beat the drums!
Joshua (1748), pt.iii (Libretto for Handel's oratorio)

CHRISTIAN MORGENSTERN 1871–1914

22 *Es war einmal ein Lattenzaun,*
mit Zwischenraum, hindurchzuschaun.

Ein Architekt, der dieses sah,
stand eines Abends plötzlich da—

und nahm den Zwischenraum heraus
und baute draus ein grosses Haus.

One time there was a picket fence
with space to gaze from hence to thence.

An architect who saw this sight
approached it suddenly one night,

removed the spaces from the fence
and built of them a residence.
Galgenlieder (1905), **Der Lattenzaun;** tr. Max Knight, 1963

LORD MORLEY (VISCOUNT MORLEY OF BLACKBURN) 1838–1923

23 That most delightful way of wasting time. [Letter-writing.]
Critical Miscellanies (1886), ii. **Life of Geo. Eliot,** p.96

24 The whole of the golden Gospel of Silence is now

effectively compressed in thirty-five volumes.
Carlyle, p.195

LORD MORLEY (3rd EARL OF MORLEY) 1843–1905

1 I am always very glad when Lord Salisbury makes a great speech,…It is sure to contain at least one blazing indiscretion which it is a delight to remember.
Speech, Hull, 25 Nov. 1887

'COUNTESS MORPHY' (MARCELLE AZRA FORBES) fl. 1930–50

2 The tragedy of English cooking is that 'plain' cooking cannot be entrusted to 'plain' cooks.
English Recipes (1935), p.17

CHARLES MORRIS 1745–1838

3 If one must have a villa in summer to dwell,
Oh, give me the sweet shady side of Pall Mall!
The Contrast

4 A house is much more to my taste than a tree,
And for groves, oh! a good grove of chimneys for me.

DESMOND MORRIS 1928–

5 There are one hundred and ninety-three living species of monkeys and apes. One hundred and ninety-two of them are covered with hair. The exception is a naked ape self-named *Homo sapiens*.
The Naked Ape (1967), Introduction

GENERAL GEORGE POPE MORRIS 1802–1864

6 Woodman, spare that tree!
  Touch not a single bough!
In youth it sheltered me,
  And I'll protect it now.
Woodman, Spare That Tree (1830)

WILLIAM MORRIS 1834–1896

7 What is this, the sound and rumour? What is this that all men hear,
Like the wind in hollow valleys when the storm is drawing near,
Like the rolling on of ocean in the eventide of fear?
'Tis the people marching on.
Chants for Socialists (1885), The March of the Workers

8 Nor for my words shall ye forget your tears,
Or hope again for aught that I can say,
The idle singer of an empty day.
The Earthly Paradise (1868–70). An Apology

9 Dreamer of dreams, born out of my due time,
Why should I strive to set the crooked straight?
Let it suffice me that my murmuring rhyme
Beats with light wing against the ivory gate,
Telling a tale not too importunate
To those who in the sleepy region stay,
Lulled by the singer of an empty day.
See 48:23

10 Forget six counties overhung with smoke,
Forget the snorting steam and piston stroke,
Forget the spreading of the hideous town;
Think rather of the pack-horse on the down,

And dream of London, small and white and clean,
The clear Thames bordered by its gardens green.
Prologue. **The Wanderers**, 1.1

11 Had she come all the way for this,
To part at last without a kiss?
Yea, had she borne the dirt and rain
That her own eyes might see him slain
Beside the haystack in the floods?
The Haystack in the Floods

12 But lo, the old inn, and the lights, and the fire,
And the fiddler's old tune and the shuffling of feet;
Soon for us shall be quiet and rest and desire,
And to-morrow's uprising to deeds shall be sweet.
The Message of the March Winds

13 And ever she sung from noon to noon,
'Two red roses across the moon.'
Two Red Roses Across the Moon

14 Have nothing in your houses that you do not know to be useful, or believe to be beautiful.
Hopes and Fears for Art (1882), p.108

J.B. MORTON ('BEACHCOMBER') 1893–1979

15 Hush, hush,
Nobody cares!
Christopher Robin
Has
  Fallen
    Down-
      Stairs.
By the Way (1931), 18 Dec. **Now We are Sick. See 340:11**

THOMAS MORTON 1764?–1838

16 Approbation from Sir Hubert Stanley is praise indeed.
A Cure for the Heartache (1797), V.ii

17 I eat well, and I drink well, and I sleep well—but that's all.
A Roland for an Oliver (1819), I.ii

18 Always ding, dinging Dame Grundy into my ears—what will Mrs Grundy zay? What will Mrs Grundy think?
Speed the Plough (1798), I.i

SIR OSWALD MOSLEY 1896–

19 I am not, and never have been, a man of the right. My position was on the left and is now in the centre of politics.
Letter to *The Times*, 26 Apr. 1968

JOHN LOTHROP MOTLEY 1814–1877

20 As long as he lived, he was the guiding-star of a whole brave nation, and when he died the little children cried in the streets. [William of Orange.]
Rise of the Dutch Republic (1856), pt.vi, ch.vii

21 Give us the luxuries of life, and we will dispense with its necessities.
O.W. Holmes, *Autocrat of the Breakfast-Table*, ch.6

PETER ANTHONY MOTTEUX 1660–1718

22 The devil was sick, the devil a monk wou'd be;
The devil was well, and the devil a monk he'd be.
Translation of Rabelais, *Gargantua and Pantagruel* (1693), bk.iv (1708 edn.) ch.24. Version of a medieval Latin proverb.

WILHELM MÜLLER 1794–1827

1 *Vom Abendrot zum Morgenlicht*
Ward mancher Kopf zum Greise.
Wer glaubt's? Und meiner ward es nicht
Auf dieser ganzen Reise.
Between dusk and dawn many a head has turned
white. Who can believe it? And mine has not
changed on all this long journey.
Die Winterreise, 14. Der greise Kopf

ALFRED DE MUSSET 1810–1857

2 *Mon verre n'est pas grand mais je bois dans mon*
verre.
The glass I drink from is not large, but at least it is my
own.
La Coupe et les Lèvres

3 *Le seul bien qui me rest au monde*
Est d'avoir quelquefois pleuré.
The only good thing left to me is that I have
sometimes wept.
Poèmes

4 *Malgré moi l'infini me tourmente.*
I can't help it, the idea of the infinite torments me.
Premières Poésies. L'Espoir en Dieu

VLADIMIR NABOKOV 1891–1977

5 Lolita, light of my life, fire of my loins.
Lolita, ch.1

IAN NAIRN 1930–

6 If what is called development is allowed to multiply at
the present rate, then by the end of the century Great
Britain will consist of isolated oases of preserved
monuments in a desert of wire, concrete roads, cosy
plots and bungalows...Upon this new Britain the
REVIEW bestows a name in the hope that it will
stick—SUBTOPIA. [Making an ideal of suburbia.]
Architectural Review, June 1955, p.365

SIR WILLIAM NAPIER 1785–1860

7 Then was seen with what a strength and majesty the
British soldier fights.
History of the War in the Peninsula (1828–40), bk.xii, ch.6,
Albuera

NAPOLEON I 1769–1821

8 *Soldats, songez que, du haut de ces pyramides,*
quarante siècles vous contemplent.
Think of it, soldiers; from the summit of these
pyramids, forty centuries look down upon you.
Speech to the Army of Egypt on 21 July 1798, before the Battle of
the Pyramids. Gourgaud, *Mémoires, Guerre d'Orient*, i, p.160

9 *Tout soldat français porte dans sa giberne le bâton de*
maréchal de France.
Every French soldier carries in his cartridge-pouch the
baton of a marshal of France.
E. Blaze, *La Vie Militaire sous l'Empire*, I.v

10 *A la guerre, les trois quarts sont des affaires morales,*
la balance des forces réelles n'est que pour un autre
quart.
In war, three-quarters turns on personal character and
relations; the balance of manpower and materials

counts only for the remaining quarter.
Correspondance de Napoléon Ier, xvii, no.14276 (Observations
sur les affaires d'Espagne, Saint-Cloud, 27 août 1808)

11 *Du sublime au ridicule il n'y a qu'un pas.*
There is only one step from the sublime to the
ridiculous.
To De Pradt, Polish ambassador, after the retreat from Moscow in
1812. De Pradt, *Histoire de l'Ambassade dans le grand-duché de
Varsovie en 1812*, ed.1815, p.215. See 367:21

12 *Quant au courage moral, il avait trouvé fort rare,*
disait-il, celui de deux heures après minuit;
c'est-à-dire le courage de l'improviste.
As to moral courage, I have very rarely met with two
o'clock in the morning courage: I mean instantaneous
courage.
Las Cases, Mémorial de Ste-Hélène, Dec. 4-5, 1815

13 *Les savants conçurent une autre idée tout-à-fait*
étrangère au bienfait de l'unité de poids et de
mesures; ils y adaptèrent la numération décimale, en
prenant le mètre pour unité; ils supprimèrent tous les
nombres complexes. Rien n'est plus contraire à
l'organisation de l'esprit, de la mémoire et de
l'imagination...Le nouveau système de poids et
mesures sera un sujet d'embarras et de difficultés pour
plusieurs générations...C'est tourmenter le peuple par
des vétilles!!!
The scientists had another idea which was totally at
odds with the benefits to be derived from the
standardization of weights and measures; they adapted
to them the decimal system, on the basis of the metre
as a unit; they suppressed all complicated numbers.
Nothing is more contrary to the organization of the
mind, of the memory, and of the imagination...The
new system of weights and measures will be a
stumbling block and the source of difficulties for
several generations...It's just tormenting the people
with trivia!!!
Of the introduction of the metric system. *Mémoires...écrits à
Ste-Hélène...*(Paris 1823–25), vol.IV. ch.xvi.4

14 *La carrière ouverte aux talents.*
The career open to talents.
O'Meara, *Napoleon in Exile* (1822), vol.i, p.103

15 *L'Angleterre est une nation de boutiquiers.*
England is a nation of shopkeepers.
Attr. by B.E. O'Meara, *Napoleon at St. Helena*, vol. ii. See
1:9, 509:12

16 Has he luck?
Attr. Habitually asked, to assess a man's probable practical value.
See A.J.P. Taylor, *Politics in Wartime* (1964), ch.16

17 An army marches on its stomach.
Attr. See, e.g., *Windsor Magazine*, 1904, p.268. Probably
condensed from a long passage in Las Cases, *Mémorial de
Ste-Hélène* (Nov. 1816). Also attr. to Frederick the Great.

OGDEN NASH 1902–1971

18 One would be in less danger
From the wiles of a stranger
If one's own kin and kith
Were more fun to be with.
Family Court

19 Candy
   Is dandy
   But liquor
   Is quicker.
Reflections on Ice-Breaking

1 When I consider how my life is spent,
I hardly ever repent.
Reminiscent Reflection. See 351:10

2 I think that I shall never see
A billboard lovely as a tree
Indeed, unless the billboards fall
I'll never see a tree at all.
Song of the Open Road. See 296:3

3 Mr Lionel Fortague said he would settle down on
Innisfree, the home of iridescent chitchat,
He said he would a small cabin build there, of clay and
wattles made.
Everyone said did he mean he would build a small
cabin there, made of clay and wattles?
Mr Lionel Fortague said yes, but his way of putting it
was more poetic.
Everyone said maybe, but they were all out of wattles...
He a fierce-looking dog at an annual clearance sale
bought, and it the people of Innisfree one by one to
bite he instructed.
My, he was disappointed.
He had forgotten that a bargain dog never bites.
The Strange Case of Mr. Fortague's Disappointment

4 The turtle lives 'twixt plated decks
Which practically conceal its sex.
I think it clever of the turtle
In such a fix to be so fertile.
The Turtle

5 Sure, deck your lower limbs in pants;
Yours are the limbs, my sweeting.
You look divine as you advance—
Have you seen yourself retreating?
What's the Use?

THOMAS NASHE 1567–1601

6 O, tis a precious apothegmaticall Pedant, who will
finde matter inough to dilate a whole day of the first
invention of *Fy, fa, fum,* I smell the bloud of an
English-man.
Have with you to Saffron-walden (1596), fol.iii

7 Brightness falls from the air;
Queens have died young and fair;
Dust hath closed Helen's eye.
I am sick, I must die.
    Lord have mercy on us.
In Time of Pestilence

8 From winter, plague and pestilence, good lord, deliver
us!
Songs from ***Summer's Last Will and Testament*** (1592?,
published 1600)

9 Spring, the sweet spring, is the year's pleasant king;
Then blooms each thing, then maids dance in a ring,
Cold doth not sting, the pretty birds do sing:
    Cuckoo, jug-jug, pu-we, to-witta-woo

JAMES BALL NAYLOR 1860–1945

10 King David and King Solomon
    Led merry, merry lives,
With many, many lady friends
    And many, many wives;
But when old age crept over them,
    With many, many qualms,
King Solomon wrote the Proverbs
And King David wrote the Psalms.
David and Solomon

HORATIO, LORD NELSON 1758–1805

11 It is my turn now; and if I come back, it is yours.
Exercising his privilege, as second lieutenant, to board a prize ship
before the Master. Southey, *Life of Nelson,* ch.1, Nelson's
Memoir of His Services.

12 You must consider every man your enemy who speaks
ill of your king: and...you must hate a Frenchman as
you hate the devil.
ch.3

13 Westminster Abbey or victory!
At the battle of Cape St. Vincent, ch.4

14 Before this time to-morrow I shall have gained a
peerage, or Westminster Abbey.
Battle of the Nile, ch.5

15 Victory is not a name strong enough for such a scene.
At the battle of the Nile

16 It is warm work; and this day may be the last to any of
us at a moment. But mark you! I would not be
elsewhere for thousands.
At the battle of Copenhagen, ch.7

17 I have only one eye,—I have a right to be blind
sometimes:...I really do not see the signal!
At the battle of Copenhagen

18 In honour I gained them, and in honour I will die with
them.
When asked to cover the stars on his uniform, ch.9

19 I believe my arrival was most welcome, not only to
the Commander of the Fleet but almost to every
individual in it; and when I came to explain to them
the *'Nelson touch',* it was like an electric shock. Some
shed tears, all approved—'It was new—it was
singular—it was simple!'...Some may be Judas's; but
the majority are much pleased with my commanding
them.
Letter to Lady Hamilton, 1 Oct. 1805

20 England expects that every man will do his duty.
At the battle of Trafalgar

21 This is too warm work, Hardy, to last long.

22 Thank God, I have done my duty.

23 Kiss me, Hardy.

EMPEROR NERO A.D. 37–68

24 *Qualis artifex pereo!*
What an artist dies with me!
Suetonius, *Life of Nero,* xlix.1

GÉRARD DE NERVAL 1808–1855

25 *Dieu est mort! le ciel est vide—*
Pleurez! enfants, vous n'avez plus de père.
God is dead! Heaven is empty—Weep, children, you
no longer have a father.
Epigraph to **Le Christ aux Oliviers, Les Chimères** (1854).
Nerval's summary of a passage in Jean Paul, **Blumen- Frucht- und
Dornstücke** (1796-7), in which God's children are referred to as
'orphans'

26 *Je suis le ténébreux,—le veuf,—l'inconsolé,*
Le prince d'Aquitaine à la tour abolie:
Ma seule étoile est morte, et mon luth constellé
Porte le soleil noir de la mélancholie.

I am the darkly shaded, the bereaved, the inconsolate,
the prince of Aquitaine, with the blasted tower. My
only *star* is dead, and my star-strewn lute carries on
it the black *sun* of *melancholy*.
El Desdichado

1 *En quoi un homard est-il plus ridicule qu'un
chien...ou [que] toute autre bête dont on se fait suivre?
J'ai le goût des homards, qui sont tranquilles, sérieux,
savent les secrets de la mer, n'aboient pas et n'avalent
pas la monade des gens comme les chiens, si
antipathiques à Goethe, lequel pourtant n'était pas
fou.*
Why should a lobster be any more ridiculous than a
dog...or any other animal that one chooses to take for
a walk? I have a liking for lobsters. They are peaceful,
serious creatures. They know the secrets of the sea,
they don't bark, and they don't gnaw upon one's
monadic privacy like dogs do. And Goethe had an
aversion to dogs, and he wasn't mad.
In justification of his walking a lobster, on a lead, in the gardens
of the Palais Royal. T. Gautier, *Portraits et Souvenirs Littéraires*
(1875). Tr. Richard Holmes, in Gautier, *My Phantoms* (1976),
p.149

PROFESSOR ALLAN NEVINS 1890–1971

2 The former allies had blundered in the past by offering
Germany too little, and offering even that too late,
until finally Nazi Germany had become a menace to
all mankind.
Article in *Current History*, May 1935

SIR HENRY NEWBOLT 1862–1938

3 Admirals all, for England's sake,
   Honour be yours, and fame!
And honour, as long as waves shall break,
   To Nelson's peerless name!
Admirals All, i

4 He clapped the glass to his sightless eye,
   And 'I'm damned if I see it', he said.
See 360:17

5 'Qui procul hinc', the legend's writ,—
   The frontier-grave is far away—
'Qui ante diem periit:
   Sed miles, sed pro patria.'
The Island Race. Clifton Chapel

6 'Take my drum to England, hang et by the shore,
   Strike et when your powder's runnin' low;
If the Dons sight Devon, I'll quit the port o' Heaven,
   An' drum them up the Channel as we drummed them
      long ago.'
Drake's Drum (1896)

7 Drake he's in his hammock till the great Armadas
      come.
   (Capten, art tha sleepin' there below?)
Slung atween the round shot, listenin' for the drum,
   An' dreamin' arl the time o' Plymouth Hoe.
Call him on the deep sea, call him up the Sound,
   Call him when ye sail to meet the foe;
Where the old trade's plyin' an' the old flag flyin'
   They shall find him ware an' wakin', as they found
      him long ago!

8 There's a breathless hush in the Close to-night—
   Ten to make and the match to win—
A bumping pitch and a blinding light,

An hour to play and the last man in.
And it's not for the sake of a ribboned coat,
   Or the selfish hope of a season's fame,
But his Captain's hand on his shoulder smote—
   'Play up! play up! and play the game!'
Vitaï Lampada

9 The voice of the schoolboy rallies the ranks:
   'Play up! play up! and play the game!'

10 Now the sunset breezes shiver,
   And she's fading down the river,
But in England's song for ever
   She's the Fighting Téméraire.
The Fighting Téméraire

11 'Ye have robb'd,' said he, 'ye have slaughter'd and
      made an end,
Take your ill-got plunder, and bury the dead.'
He Fell Among Thieves

12 But cared greatly to serve God and the King,
   And keep the Nelson touch.
Minora Sidera. See 360:19

CARDINAL NEWMAN 1801–1890

13 It is very difficult to get up resentment towards
persons whom one has never seen.
Apologia pro Vita Sua (1864). Mr. Kingsley's Method of
Disputation

14 There is such a thing as legitimate warfare: war has its
laws; there are things which may fairly be done, and
things which may not be done...He has attempted (as I
may call it) to *poison the wells*.

15 I will vanquish, not my Accuser, but my judges.
True Mode of meeting Mr. Kingsley

16 I used to wish the Arabian Tales were true.
History of My Religious Opinions to the Year 1833

17 Two and two only supreme and luminously
self-evident beings, myself and my Creator.

18 For years I used almost as proverbs what I considered
to be the scope and issue of his [Thomas Scott's]
doctrine, 'Holiness rather than peace', and 'Growth the
only evidence of life'.

19 It would be a gain to the country were it vastly more
superstitious, more bigoted, more gloomy, more fierce
in its religion than at present it shows itself to be.
History of My Religious Opinions from 1833 to 1839

20 From the age of fifteen, dogma has been the
fundamental principle of my religion: I know no other
religion; I cannot enter into the idea of any other sort
of religion; religion, as a mere sentiment, is to me a
dream and a mockery.

21 This is what the Church is said to want, not party
men, but sensible, temperate, sober, well-judging
persons, to guide it through the channel of
no-meaning, between the Scylla and Charybdis of Aye
and No.
History of My Religious Opinions from 1839 to 1841

22 I recollect an acquaintance saying to me that 'the Oriel
Common Room stank of Logic'.
History of My Religious Opinions from 1841 to 1845

23 Trinity had never been unkind to me. There used to be
much snap-dragon growing on the walls opposite my
freshman's rooms there, and I had for years taken it as
the emblem of my own perpetual residence even unto

death in my University.

On the morning of the 23rd I left the Observatory. I have never seen Oxford since, excepting its spires, as they are seen from the railway.

1 Ten thousand difficulties do not make one doubt.
Position of my Mind since 1845

2 What must be the face-to-face antagonist, by which to withstand and baffle the fierce energy of passion and the all-corroding, all-dissolving scepticism of the intellect in religious enquiries.

3 It is almost a definition of a gentleman to say that he is one who never inflicts pain.
The Idea of a University (1852). **Knowledge and Religious Duty**

4 She [the Catholic Church] holds that it were better for sun and moon to drop from heaven, for the earth to fail, and for all the many millions who are upon it to die of starvation in extremest agony, as far as temporal affliction goes, than that one soul, I will not say, should be lost, but should commit one single venial sin, should tell one wilful untruth,...or steal one poor farthing without excuse.
Lectures on Anglican Difficulties (1852). Lecture VIII

5 And this is all that is known, and more than all—yet nothing to what the angels know— of the life of a servant of God, who sinned and repented, and did penance and washed out his sins, and became a Saint, and reigns with Christ in heaven.
Lives of the English Saints: Hermit Saints. 'The Legend of Saint Bettelin'. This passage attr. to Newman; the phrase 'and more than all' may have been added by J.A. Froude.

6 *Ex umbris et imaginibus in veritatem.*
From shadows and types to the reality.
Motto

7 *Cor ad cor loquitur.*
Heart speaks to heart.
Motto adopted for his coat-of-arms as cardinal. 1879

8 It is as absurd to argue men, as to torture them, into believing.
Sermon at Oxford, 11 Dec. 1831

9 May He support us all the day long, till the shades lengthen, and the evening comes, and the busy world is hushed, and the fever of life is over, and our work is done! Then in His mercy may He give us a safe lodging, and a holy rest, and peace at the last.
Sermon, 1834. 'Wisdom and Innocence'

10 When men understand what each other mean, they see, for the most part, that controversy is either superfluous or hopeless.
Sermon at Oxford, Epiphany, 1839

11 Firmly I believe and truly
   God is Three, and God is One;
And I next acknowledge duly
   Manhood taken by the Son.
The Dream of Gerontius (1865)

12 Praise to the Holiest in the height,
   And in the depth be praise;
In all his words most wonderful,
   Most sure in all His ways.

13 O wisest love! that flesh and blood
   Which did in Adam fail,
Should strive afresh against their foe,
   Should strive and should prevail.

14 Lead, kindly Light, amid the encircling gloom,

Lead thou me on;
The night is dark, and I am far from home,
   Lead thou me on.
Keep Thou my feet; I do not ask to see
The distant scene; one step enough for me.
The Pillar of Cloud. Lead Kindly Light (1833)

15 And with the morn those Angel faces smile,
Which I have loved long since, and lost awhile.

16 *We can believe what we choose.* We are answerable for what we choose to believe.
Letter to Mrs. William Froude, 27 June 1848

17 Though you can believe what you choose, you must believe what you ought.
3 July 1848

SIR ISAAC NEWTON 1642–1727

18 Nature is very consonant and conformable with herself.
Opticks (1730 ed.), bk.III, pt.i, qu.30

19 If I have seen further it is by standing on the shoulders of giants.
Letter to Robert Hooke, 5 Feb. 1675/6. See 41:25

20 I do not know what I may appear to the world, but to myself I seem to have been only like a boy playing on the sea-shore, and diverting myself in now and then finding a smoother pebble or a prettier shell than ordinary, whilst the great ocean of truth lay all undiscovered before me.
L.T. More, *Isaac Newton* (1934), p.664

21 O Diamond! Diamond! thou little knowest the mischief done!
Remark to a dog who knocked down a candle and so set fire to some papers and 'destroyed the almost finished labours of some years'. Thomas Maude, *Wensley-Dale...a Poem* (1780), p.28, note

EMPEROR NICHOLAS I OF RUSSIA 1796–1855

22 *Nous avons sur les bras un homme malade—un homme gravement malade.*
We have on our hands a sick man—a very sick man. [The sick man of Europe, the Turk.]
Parliamentary Papers. Accounts and Papers, vol.lxxi, pt.5. Eastern Papers, p.2. Sir G.H. Seymour to Lord John Russell, 11 Jan. 1853

23 Russia has two generals in whom she can confide—Generals Janvier and Février.
Attr. See *Punch*, 10 Mar. 1853

ROBERT NICHOLS 1893–1944

24 Was there love once? I have forgotten her. Was there grief once? grief yet is mine.
Fulfilment

NICIAS c.470–413 B.C.

25 ἄνδρες γὰρ πόλις, καὶ οὐ τείχη οὐδὲ νῆες ἀνδρῶν κεναί.
For a city consists in its men, and not in its walls nor ships empty of men.
Speech to the defeated Athenian army at Syracuse, 413 B.C. Thucydides, vii.77

REINHOLD NIEBUHR 1892–1971

26 Man's capacity for justice makes democracy possible, but man's inclination to injustice makes democracy

necessary.
The Children of Light and the Children of Darkness (1944),
foreword

FRIEDRICH NIETZSCHE 1844–1900

1 *Ich lehre euch den Übermenschen. Der Mensch ist
Etwas, das überwunden werden soll.*
I teach you the superman. Man is something to be
surpassed.
Also Sprach Zarathustra. Prologue (1883)

2 *Auf Andere warte ich. . .auf Höhere, Stärkere,
Sieghaftere, Wohlgemutere, Solche, die rechtwinklig
gebaut sind an Leib und Seele: lachende Löwen
müssen kommen.*
For others do I wait. . .for higher ones, stronger ones,
more triumphant ones, merrier ones, for such as are
built squarely in body and soul: laughing lions must
come
IV, **Die Begrüssung**

3 *Das Erbarmen Gottes mit der einzigen Not, die alle
Paradiese an sich haben, kennt keine Grenzen: er
schuf alsbald noch andere Tiere. Erster Fehlgriff
Gottes: der Mensch fand die Tiere nicht
unterhaltend,—er herrschte über sie, er wollte nicht
einmal 'Tier' sein.*
[Man found a solitary existence tedious.] There are no
limits to God's compassion with Paradises over their
one universally felt want: he immediately created
other animals besides. God's first blunder: Man didn't
find the animals amusing,—he dominated them, and
didn't even want to be an 'animal'.
Der Antichrist, 48

4 *Das Weib war der zweite Fehlgriff Gottes.*
Woman was God's second blunder.

5 *Wie ich den Philosophen verstehe, als einen
furchtbaren Explosionsstoff, vor dem Alles in Gefahr
ist.*
What I understand by 'philosopher': a terrible
explosive in the presence of which everything is in
danger.
Ecce Homo, **Die Unzeitgemässen**

6 *Gott ist tot: aber so wie die Art der Menschen ist,
wird es vielleicht noch jahrtausendlang Höhlen geben,
in denen man seinen Schatten zeigt.*
God is dead: but considering the state the species Man
is in, there will perhaps be caves, for ages yet, in
which his shadow will be shown.
Die Fröhliche Wissenschaft, III, 108

7 *Moralität ist Herden-Instinkt im Einzelnen.*
Morality is the herd-instinct in the individual.
116

8 *Der christliche Entschluss, die Welt hässlich und
schlecht zu finden, hat die Welt hässlich und schlecht
gemacht.*
The Christian resolution to find the world ugly and bad
has made the world ugly and bad.
130

9 *Glaubt es mir!—das Geheimniss, um die grösste
Fruchtbarkeit und den grössten Genuss vom Dasein
einzuernten, heisst:* gefährlich leben!
Believe me! The secret of reaping the greatest
fruitfulness and the greatest enjoyment from life is to

live dangerously!
IV, 283

10 *Wer mit Ungeheuern kämpft, mag zusehn, dass er
nicht dabei zum Ungeheuer wird. Und wenn du lange
in einen Abgrund blickst, blickt der Abgrund auch in
dich hinein.*
He who fights with monsters might take care lest he
thereby become a monster. And if you gaze for long
into an abyss, the abyss gazes also into you.
Jenseits von Gut und Böse, IV, 146

11 *Der Gedanke an den Selbstmord ist ein starkes
Trostmittel: mit ihm kommt man gut über manche böse
Nacht hinweg.*
The thought of suicide is a great source of comfort:
with it a calm passage is to be made across many a bad
night.
157

12 *Herren-Moral und Sklaven-Moral.*
Master-morality and slave-morality.
IX.260

13 *Der Witz ist das Epigramm auf den Tod eines
Gefühls.*
Wit is the epitaph of an emotion.
Menschliches, Allzumenschliches, II.i, 202

14 *Auf dem Grunde aller dieser vornehmen Rassen ist
das Raubtier, die prachtvolle nach Beute und Sieg
lüstern schweifende blonde Bestie nicht zu verkennen.*
At the base of all these aristocratic races the predator is
not to be mistaken, the splendorous blond beast, avidly
rampant for plunder and victory.
Zur Genealogie der Moral, I, 11

FLORENCE NIGHTINGALE 1820–1910

15 Sir Douglas Dowson, after a short speech, stepped
forward and handed the insignia of the Order [of
Merit] to Miss Nightingale. Propped up by pillows she
dimly recognized that some kind of compliment was
being paid her. 'Too kind—too kind,' she murmured;
and she was not ironical.
Lytton Strachey, *Eminent Victorians*, 'Florence Nightingale'

16 To understand God's thoughts we must study
statistics, for these are the measure of his purpose.
Attr. See K. Pearson, *Life...of Francis Galton*, vol.II, ch.xiii,
sect.i

GENERAL R.-G. NIVELLE 1856–1924

17 *Ils ne passeront pas.*
They shall not pass.
Used as a slogan throughout the defence of Verdun and often
attributed to Marshal Pétain. Nivelle's Order of the Day in late
June 1916 read '*Vous ne les laisserez pas passer.*' Taken up by
the Republicans in the Spanish Civil War as '*No pasarán!*'

ALBERT J. NOCK 1873–1945

18 It is an economic axiom as old as the hills that goods
and services can be paid for only with goods and
services.
Memoirs of a Superfluous Man, III, ch.3

THOMAS NOEL 1799–1861

19 Rattle his bones over the stones;

He's only a pauper, whom nobody owns!
Rhymes and Roundelays (1841), **The Pauper's Drive**

CHARLES HOWARD, DUKE OF NORFOLK
1746–1815

1 I cannot be a good Catholic; I cannot go to heaven; and if a man is to go to the devil, he may as well go thither from the House of Lords as from any other place on earth.
Henry Best, *Personal and Literary Memorials* (1829), ch.18

CHRISTOPHER NORTH (PROFESSOR JOHN WILSON) 1785–1854

2 Minds like ours, my dear James, must always be above national prejudices, and in all companies it gives me true pleasure to declare, that, as a people, the English are very little indeed inferior to the Scotch.
Noctes Ambrosianae, No.28 (Oct. 1826)

3 Laws were made to be broken.
No.24 (May 1830)

4 Insultin the sun, and quarrellin wi' the equawtor. [Ettrick Shepherd.]

5 Animosities are mortal, but the Humanities live for ever.
No.35 (Aug. 1834)

6 I cannot sit still, James, and hear you abuse the shopocracy.
No.39 (Feb. 1835)

SIR STAFFORD NORTHCOTE, 1ST EARL OF IDDESLEIGH 1818–1887

7 Argue as you please, you are nowhere, that grand old man, the Prime Minister, insists on the other thing.
Of Gladstone. Speech at Liverpool, 12 Apr. 1882

MRS. CAROLINE NORTON 1808–1877

8 For death and life, in ceaseless strife,
   Beat wild on this world's shore,
And all our calm is in that balm—
   Not lost but gone before.
Not Lost but Gone Before

NOVALIS (FRIEDRICH VON HARDENBERG) 1772–1801

9 *Oft fühl ich jetzt...[und] je tiefer ich einsehe, dass Schicksal und Gemüt Namen eines Begriffes sind.*
I often feel, and ever more deeply I realize, that fate and character are the same conception.
Heinrich von Ofterdingen (1802), bk.II. Often quoted as 'Character is destiny' or 'Character is fate'. See, e.g., 201:21

10 *Ein Gott-betrunkener Mensch.*
A God-intoxicated man.
Attr. remark about Spinoza

ALFRED NOYES 1880–1958

11 Go down to Kew in lilac-time, in lilac-time, in lilac-time;
   Go down to Kew in lilac-time (it isn't far from London!)
Barrel Organ

12 The wind was a torrent of darkness among the gusty trees,
The moon was a ghostly galleon tossed upon cloudy seas,
The road was a ribbon of moonlight over the purple moor,
And the highwayman came riding—
      Riding—riding—
The highwayman came riding, up to the old inn-door.
The Highwayman

13 The landlord's black-eyed daughter,
      Bess, the landlord's daughter,
Plaiting a dark red love-knot into her long black hair.

14 Look for me by moonlight;
      Watch for me by moonlight;
I'll come to thee by moonlight, though hell should bar the way!

SEAN O'CASEY 1884–1964

15 I ofen looked up at the sky an' assed meself the question—what is the stars, what is the stars? [Boyle.]
Juno and the Paycock (1924), I

16 The whole counthry's in a state of chassis. [Boyle.]
II. Meaning 'a state of chaos'. In Act I and Act III (last line) used of the whole world.

17 Sacred Heart of the Crucified Jesus, take away our hearts o' stone...an' give us hearts o' flesh!...Take away this murdherin' hate...an' give us Thine own eternal love! [Mrs. Tancred.]

18 The Polis as Polis, in this city, is Null an' Void! [Mrs Madigan.]
III. Of the Police

WILLIAM OCCAM c.1280–1349

19 *Entia non sunt multiplicanda praeter necessitatem.*
No more things should be presumed to exist than are absolutely necessary.
'Occams's Razor'. Ancient philosophical principle, often attributed to Occam, but used by many earlier thinkers. Not found in this form in his writings, though he frequently used similar expressions, e.g. *Pluralitas non est ponenda sine necessitate* (*Quodlibeta*, c.1324, V, Q.i).

ADOLPH S. OCHS 1858–1935

20 All the news that's fit to print.
Motto of the *New York Times*

JAMES OGILVY, FIRST EARL OF SEAFIELD 1664–1730

21 Now there's ane end of ane old song.
As he signed the engrossed exemplification of the Act of Union, 1706. *Lockhart Papers* (1817), i.223

DANIEL O'CONNELL 1775–1847

22 [Sir Robert] Peel's smile: like the silver plate on a coffin.
Hansard, 26 Feb. 1835, quoting J.P. Curran (1750—1817), Irish politician and lawyer

JOHN O'KEEFFE 1747–1833

23 Amo, amas, I love a lass,
   As a cedar tall and slender;
Sweet cowslip's grace

Is her nom'native case,
And she's of the feminine gender.
The Agreeable Surprise (1781), II.ii

1 Fat, fair and forty were all the toasts of the young men.
Irish Mimic (1795), ii

2 You should always except the present company.
London Hermit (1793), I.ii

DENNIS O'KELLY 1720?–1787

3 Eclipse first, the rest nowhere.
Epsom, 3 May 1769. *Annals of Sporting,* vol.ii, p.271. D.N.B. gives the occasion as the Queen's Plate at Winchester, 1769.

WILLIAM OLDYS 1696–1761

4 Busy, curious, thirsty fly,
Gently drink, and drink as I;
Freely welcome to my cup.
The Fly (1732)

FRANK WARD O'MALLEY 1875–1932

5 Life is just one damned thing after another.
Attr. See *Literary Digest,* 5 Nov. 1932. Also attr. Elbert Hubbard

JOHN OPIE 1761–1807

6 [When asked with what he mixed his colours.]
I mix them with my brains, sir.
Samuel Smiles, *Self-Help,* ch.4

BARONESS ORCZY 1865–1947

7 We seek him here, we seek him there,
Those Frenchies seek him everywhere.
Is he in heaven?—Is he in hell?
That demmed, elusive Pimpernel?
The Scarlet Pimpernel (1905), ch.12

GEORGE ORWELL 1903–1950

8 Four legs good, two legs bad.
Animal Farm (1945), ch.3

9 All animals are equal but some animals are more equal than others.
ch.10

10 Whatever is funny is subversive, every joke is ultimately a custard pie... A dirty joke is...a sort of mental revolution.
The Art of Donald McGill (1945)

11 I'm fat, but I'm thin inside. Has it ever struck you that there's a thin man inside every fat man, just as they say there's a statue inside every block of stone?
Coming Up For Air (1939), Part I, ch.3. See 161:15

12 Big Brother is watching you.
1984 (1949), p.1

13 *Doublethink* means the power of holding two contradictory beliefs in one's mind simultaneously, and accepting both of them.
pt.II, ch.9

14 If you want a picture of the future, imagine a boot stamping on a human face—for ever.
pt.III, ch.3

15 Good prose is like a window pane.
Collected Essays (1968), vol.I. **Why I Write**

16 Nine times out of ten a revolutionary is merely a climber with a bomb in his pocket.
Review of F.C. Green, *Stendhal*

17 To see what is in front of one's nose needs a constant struggle.
vol.IV. **In Front of Your Nose**

18 At 50, everyone has the face he deserves.
Closing words, MS Notebook, 17 Apr. 1949

DOROTHY OSBORNE (LADY TEMPLE) 1627–1695

19 All letters, methinks, should be as free and easy as one's discourse, not studied as an oration, nor made up of hard words like a charm.
Letter to Sir Wm. Temple, Oct. 1653

ARTHUR O'SHAUGHNESSY 1844–1881

20 We are the music makers,
    We are the dreamers of dreams,
Wandering by lone sea-breakers,
    And sitting by desolate streams;—
World-losers and world-forsakers,
    On whom the pale moon gleams:
We are the movers and shakers
    Of the world for ever, it seems.
Ode

21 For each age is a dream that is dying,
    Or one that is coming to birth.

JOHN L. O'SULLIVAN 1813–1895

22 Understood as a central consolidated power, managing and directing the various general interests of the society, all government is evil, and the parent of evil...The best government is that which governs least.
Introduction to *The United States Magazine and Democratic Review* (1837)

23 Our manifest destiny to overspread the continent allotted by Providence for the free development of our yearly multiplying millions.
vol.xvii, July-Aug. 1845, p.5

24 A torchlight procession marching down your throat.
Description of some whisky. G.W.E. Russell, *Collections and Recollections,* ch.19

JAMES OTIS 1725–1783

25 Taxation without representation is tyranny.
Watchword (coined 1761?) of the American Revolution. See Samuel Eliot Morison, 'James Otis', *Dict. Am. Biog.*, xiv.102

THOMAS OTWAY 1652–1685

26 These are rogues that pretend to be of a religion now! Well, all I say is, honest atheism for my money.
The Atheist, Act III, l.31

27 Ere man's corruptions made him wretched, he
Was born most noble that was born most free;
Each of himself was lord; and unconfin'd
Obey'd the dictates of his godlike mind.
Don Carlos (1676), Act II, l.3

1 Destructive, damnable, deceitful woman!
The Orphan (1680), Act III, l.586

2 And for an apple damn'd mankind.
l.594

3 You wags that judge by rote, and damn by rule.
Titus and Berenice (1677), prologue, l.3

4 Oh woman! lovely woman! Nature made thee
To temper man: we had been brutes without you;
Angels are painted fair, to look like you;
There's in you all that we belive of heav'n,
Amazing brightness, purity, and truth,
Eternal joy, and everlasting love.
Venice Preserv'd (1681/2), Act I, l.337

5 No praying, it spoils business.
Act II, l.87

SIR THOMAS OVERBURY 1581–1613

6 He disdains all things above his reach, and preferreth
all countries before his own.
Miscellaneous Works. An Affectate Traveller

7 You cannot name any example in any heathen author
but I will better it in Scripture.
Crumms Fal'n From King James's Table, 10

OVID 43 B.C–A.D. 17

8 *Procul omen abesto!*
Far be that fate from us!
Amores, I.xiv.41

9 *Procul hinc, procul este, severae!*
Far hence, keep far from me, you grim women!
II.i.3

10 *Spectatum veniunt, veniunt spectentur ut ipsae.*
The women come to see the show, they come to make
a show themselves.
Ars Amatoria, i.99

11 *Iuppiter ex alto periuria ridet amantum.*
Jupiter from on high laughs at lovers' perjuries.
633

12 *Forsitan et nostrum nomen miscebitur istis.*
Perhaps my name too will be linked with theirs.
iii.339

13 *Chaos, rudis indigestaque moles.*
Chaos, a rough and unordered mass.
Metamorphoses, i.7

14 *Medio tutissimus ibis.*
A middle course is the safest for you to take.
ii.137

15 *Inopem me copia fecit.*
Plenty has made me poor.
iii.466

16 *Ipse docet quid agam; fas est et ab hoste doceri.*
He himself teaches what I should do; it is right to be
taught by the enemy.
iv.428

17 *Video meliora, proboque;*
Deteriora sequor.
I see the better way, and approve it; I follow the
worse.
vii.20

18 *Tempus edax rerum.*

Time the devourer of everything.
xv.234

19 *Iamque opus exegi, quod nec Iovis ira, nec ignis,*
Nec poterit ferrum, nec edax abolere vetustas.
And now I have finished the work, which neither the
wrath of Jove, nor fire, nor the sword, nor
devouring age shall be able to destroy.
871

20 *Principiis obsta; sero medicina paratur*
Cum mala per longas convaluere moras.
Stop it at the start, it's late for medicine to be prepared
when disease has grown strong through long delays.
Remedia Amoris, 91

21 *Qui finem quaeris amoris,*
Cedet amor rebus; res age, tutus eris.
You who seek an end of love, love will yield to
business: be busy, and you will be safe.
143

22 *Teque, rebellatrix, tandem, Germania, magni*
Triste caput pedibus supposuisse ducis!
How you, rebellious Germany, laid your wretched
head beneath the feet of the great general.
Tristia, III.xii.47

23 *Sponte sua carmen numeros veniebat ad aptos,*
Et quod temptabam dicere versus erat.
Of its own accord my song would come in the right
rhythms, and what I was trying to say was poetry.
IV.x.25

24 *Vergilium vidi tantum.*
I just saw Virgil.
51

25 *Adde quod ingenuas didicisse fideliter artes*
Emollit mores nec sinit esse feros.
Add the fact that to have conscientiously studied the
liberal arts refines behaviour and does not allow it to
be savage.
Epistulae Ex Ponto, II.ix.47

26 *Ut desint vires, tamen est laudanda voluntas.*
Though the strength is lacking, yet the willingness is to
be praised.
III.iv.79

27 *Gutta cavat lapidem, consumitur anulus usu.*
Dripping water hollows out a stone, a ring is worn
away by use.
IV.x.5

JOHN OWEN 1560?–1622

28 God and the doctor we alike adore
But only when in danger, not before;
The danger o'er, both are alike requited,
God is forgotten, and the Doctor slighted.
Epigrams

ROBERT OWEN 1771–1858

29 All the world is queer save thee and me, and even thou
art a little queer.
To his partner, W. Allen on severing business relations at New
Lanark 1828. Attr.

WILFRED OWEN 1893–1918

30 Above all, this book is not concerned with Poetry.
The subject of it is War, and the Pity of War.
The Poetry is in the pity.
Poems (1920), Preface

1 All the poet can do today is to warn.
That is why the true Poets must be truthful.

2 What passing-bells for these who die as cattle?
   Only the monstrous anger of the guns.
   Only the stuttering rifles' rapid rattle
Can patter out their hasty orisons.
Anthem for Doomed Youth

3   The pallor of girls' brows shall be their pall;
Their flowers the tenderness of patient minds,
And each slow dusk a drawing-down of blinds.

4 Move him into the sun...
If anything might rouse him now
The kind old sun will know.
Futility

5 Was it for this the clay grew tall?
—O what made fatuous sunbeams toil
   To break earth's sleep at all?

6 Red lips are not so red
As the stained stones kissed by the English dead.
Greater Love

7 So secretly, like wrongs hushed-up, they went:
They were not ours.
We never heard to which front these were sent.

Nor, there, if they yet mock what women meant
Who gave them flowers.
The Send-Off

8 Hour after hour they ponder the warm field,—
And the far valley behind, where the buttercup
Had blessed with gold their slow boots coming up.
Spring Offensive

9 It seemed that out of battle I escaped
Down some profound dull tunnel, long since scooped
Through granites which titanic wars had groined.
Strange Meeting

10 'Strange friend,' I said, 'here is no cause to mourn.'
'None,' said the other, 'save the undone years,
The hopelessness. Whatever hope is yours
Was my life also; I went hunting wild
After the wildest beauty in the world.'

11 For by my glee might many men have laughed,
And of my weeping something have been left,
Which must die now. I mean the truth untold,
The pity of war, the pity war distilled.
Now men will go content with what we spoiled,
Or, discontent, boil bloody, and be spilled.
They will be swift with swiftness of the tigress,
None will break ranks, though nations trek from
   progress.

12 I am the enemy you killed, my friend.

COUNT OXENSTIERNA 1583–1654

13 Dost thou not know, my son, with how little wisdom
the world is governed?
Letter to his son, 1648

EDWARD DE VERE, EARL OF OXFORD
1550–1604

14 If women could be fair and yet not fond.
Women's Changeableness

BARRY PAIN 1864–1928

15 The cosy fire is bright and gay,
The merry kettle boils away
   And hums a cheerful song.
I sing the saucer and the cup;
Pray, Mary, fill the teapot up,
   And do not make it strong.
The Poets at Tea. **Cowper**

16 Pour, varlet, pour the water,
The water steaming hot!
A spoonful for each man of us,
Another for the pot!
Macaulay

17 As the sin that was sweet in the sinning
Is foul in the ending thereof,
As the heat of the summer's beginning
Is past in the winter of love:
O purity, painful and pleading!
O coldness, ineffably gray!
O hear us, our handmaid unheeding,
And take it away!
Swinburne

18 I think that I am drawing to an end:
For on a sudden came a gasp for breath,
And stretching of the hands, and blinded eyes,
And a great darkness falling on my soul.
O Hallelujah!...Kindly pass the milk.
Tennyson

19 'Come, little cottage girl, you seem
To want my cup of tea;
And will you take a little cream?
Now tell the truth to me.'

She had a rustic, woodland grin
Her cheek was soft as silk,
And she replied, 'Sir, please put in
A little drop of milk.'
Wordsworth

TOM PAINE 1737–1809

20 It is necessary to the happiness of man that he be
mentally faithful to himself. Infidelity does not consist
in believing, or in disbelieving, it consists in
professing to believe what one does not believe.
The Age of Reason (1794), pt.i

21 The sublime and the ridiculous are often so nearly
related, that it is difficult to class them separately. One
step above the sublime, makes the ridiculous; and one
step above the ridiculous, makes the sublime again.
pt.ii (1795), p.20

22 Government, even in its best state, is but a necessary
evil; in its worst state, an intolerable one.
Government, like dress, is the badge of lost
innocence; the palaces of kings are built upon the ruins
of the bowers of paradise.
Common Sense (1776), ch.1

23 As to religion, I hold it to be the indispensable duty of
government to protect all conscientious professors
thereof, and I know of no other business which
government hath to do therewith.
ch.4

1 These are the times that try men's souls. The summer soldier and the sunshine patriot will, in this crisis, shrink from the service of their country; but he that stands it *now*, deserves the love and thanks of men and women.
The Crisis, Intro. (Dec. 1776)

2 The final event to himself [Mr Burke] has been, that as he rose like a rocket, he fell like the stick.
Letter to the Addressers on the late Proclamation (1792), p.4

3 [Burke] is not affected by the reality of distress touching his heart, but by the showy resemblance of it striking his imagination. He pities the plumage, but forgets the dying bird. [Of Burke's *Reflections on the Revolution in France*.]
The Rights of Man (1791), p.26

4 Lay then the axe to the root, and teach governments humanity. It is their sanguinary punishments which corrupt mankind.
p.33

5 My country is the world, and my religion is to do good.
pt.ii (1792), ch.5

6 A share in two revolutions is living to some purpose.
See Eric Foner, *Tom Paine and Revolutionary America* (1976), ch.7

7 The religion of humanity.
Attr. by Edmund Gosse

JOSÉ DE PALAFOX 1780–1847

8 War to the knife.
On 4 Aug. 1808, at the siege of Saragossa, the French general Verdier sent a one-word suggestion: 'Capitulation'. Palafox replied '*Guerra y cuchillo*' (War and the knife), later reported as '*Guerra a cuchillo*' and commonly rendered as above. The correctness of the former is confirmed by its appearance, at the behest of Palafox himself, on survivors' medals. Gómez de Arteche, *Guerra de la Independencia* (1868–1903), II, iv

REVD. WILLIAM PALEY 1743–1805

9 Who can refute a sneer?
Principles of Moral and Political Philosophy (1785), bk.v, ch.9

LORD PALMERSTON 1784–1865

10 I therefore fearlessly challenge the verdict which this House...is to give...whether, as the Roman, in days of old, held himself free from indignity, when he could say *Civis Romanus sum;* so also a British subject, in whatever land he may be, shall feel confident that the watchful eye and the strong arm of England will protect him against injustice and wrong.
House of Commons, 25 June 1850, in the Don Pacifico debate

11 You may call it coalition, you may call it the accidental and fortuitous concurrence of atoms.
Of a projected Palmerston-Disraeli coalition. House of Commons, 5 Mar. 1857

12 What is merit? The opinion one man entertains of another.
Carlyle, *Critical and Miscellaneous Essays*, viii, 'Shooting Niagara'

13 Die, my dear Doctor, that's the last thing I shall do!
Attr. last words

DOROTHY PARKER 1893–1967

14 Oh, life is a glorious cycle of song,
A medley of extemporanea;
And love is a thing that can never go wrong,
And I am Marie of Roumania.
Comment

15 Four be the things I'd been better without:
Love, curiosity, freckles, and doubt.
Inventory

16 Men seldom make passes
At girls who wear glasses.
News Item

17 Why is it no one ever sent me yet
One perfect limousine, do you suppose?
Ah no, it's always just my luck to get
One perfect rose.
One Perfect Rose

18 Razors pain you;
Rivers are damp;
Acids stain you;
And drugs cause cramp.
Guns aren't lawful;
Nooses give;
Gas smells awful;
You might as well live.
Résumé

19 By the time you swear you're his,
Shivering and sighing,
And he vows his passion is
Infinite, undying—
Lady, make a note of this:
One of you is lying.
Unfortunate Coincidence

20 And I'll stay off Verlaine too; he was always chasing Rimbauds.
The Little Hours (The Penguin Dorothy Parker, 1977)

21 She ran the whole gamut of the emotions from A to B.
Of Katharine Hepburn in a Broadway play

22 Dear Mary, We all knew you had it in you.
Telegram sent after a much-publicised pregnancy

23 How could they tell?
[On being told of the death of President Coolidge.]
John Keats, *You might as well live* (1971), Foreword

24 If all the girls attending it [the Yale Prom] were laid end to end, I wouldn't be at all surprised.
A. Woollcott, *While Rome Burns*, 'Some Neighbours', IV: Our Mrs. Parker

MARTIN PARKER d. 1656?

25 You gentlemen of England
Who live at home at ease,
How little do you think
On the dangers of the seas.
The Valiant Sailors. See *Early Naval Ballads* (Percy Society, 1841), p.34

THEODORE PARKER 1810–1860

26 There is what I call the American idea...This idea demands...a democracy, that is, a government of all the people, by all the people, for all the people; of course, a government after the principles of eternal justice, the unchanging law of God; for shortness'

sake, I will call it the idea of freedom.
Speech at N.E. Anti-Slavery Convention, Boston, 29 May 1850.
Discourses of Slavery (1863), i

C. NORTHCOTE PARKINSON 1909–

1 Work expands so as to fill the time available for its
completion.
Parkinson's Law (1958), I, opening words

CHARLES STEWART PARNELL 1846–1891

2 No man has a right to fix the boundary of the march of
a nation; no man has a right to say to his
country—thus far shalt thou go and no further.
Speech at Cork, 21 Jan. 1885

BLAISE PASCAL 1623–1662

3 *La dernière chose qu'on trouve en faisant un ouvrage,
est de savoir celle qu'il faut mettre la première.*
The last thing one knows in constructing a work is
what to put first.
Pensées, ed. L. Brunschvicg (5th edn. 1909), i.19

4 *Quand on voit le style naturel, on est tout étonné et
ravi, car on s'attendait de voir un auteur, et on trouve
un homme.*
When we see a natural style, we are quite surprised
and delighted, for we expected to see an author and we
find a man.
29

5 *Tout le malheur des hommes vient d'une seule chose,
qui est de ne savoir pas demeurer en repos dans une
chambre.*
All the misfortunes of men derive from one single
thing, which is their inability to be at ease in a room
[at home].
ii.139

6 *Le nez de Cléopâtre: s'il eût été plus court, toute la
face de la terre aurait changé.*
Had Cleopatra's nose been shorter, the whole face of
the world would have changed.
162

7 *Le silence éternel de ces espaces infinis m'effraie.*
The eternal silence of these infinite spaces [the
heavens] terrifies me.
iii.206

8 *Le dernier acte est sanglant, quelque belle que soit la
comédie en tout le reste.*
The last act is bloody, however charming the rest of
the play may be.
210

9 *On mourra seul.*
We shall die alone.
211

10 *Le coeur a ses raisons que la raison ne connaît point.*
The heart has its reasons which reason knows nothing
of.
iv.277

11 *L'homme n'est qu'un roseau, le plus faible de la
nature; mais c'est un roseau pensant.*
Man is only a reed, the weakest thing in nature; but he
is a thinking reed.
vi.347

12 *Le moi est haïssable.*

'I' is hateful.
vii.455

13 *Tu ne me chercherais pas si tu ne me possédais.
Ne t'inquiete donc pas.*
You would not be looking for Me if you did not
possess Me. So do not be uneasy.
555

14 *Je n'ai fait celle-ci plus longue que parce que je n'ai
pas eu le loisir de la faire plus courte.*
I have made this letter longer than usual, only because
I have not had the time to make it shorter.
Lettres Provinciales (1657), xvi

15 *FEU. Dieu d'Abraham, Dieu d'Isaac, Dieu de Jacob,
non des philosophes et savants. Certitude. Certitude.
Sentiment. Joie. Paix.*
FIRE. God of Abraham, God of Isaac, God of Jacob,
not of the philosophers and scholars. Certainty.
Certainty. Feeling. Joy. Peace.
On a paper dated 23 Nov. 1654, stitched into the lining of his coat
and found after his death.

LOUIS PASTEUR 1822–1895

16 *Dans les champs de l'observation le hasard ne
favorise que les esprits préparés.*
Where observation is concerned, chance favours only
the prepared mind.
Address given on the inauguration of the Faculty of Science,
University of Lille, 7 Dec. 1854.
*De nos jours, le hasard ne favorise l'invention que pour des
esprits préparés aux découvertes par de patientes études et de
persévérants efforts. 'Pourquoi la France n'a pas trouvé
d'hommes supérieurs au moment du péril,' La Salut public,*
Lyons, Mar. 1871

17 *Il n'existe pas de sciences appliquées, mais seulement
des applications de la science.*
There are no such things as applied sciences, only
applications of science.
Address, 11 Sept. 1872, *Comptes rendus des travaux du Congrès
viticole et séricicole de Lyon, 9–14 septembre 1872,* p.49

WALTER PATER 1839–1894

18 Hers is the head upon which all 'the ends of the world
are come', and the eyelids are a little weary. [Mona
Lisa.]
Studies in the History of the Renaissance (1873) **Leonardo da
Vinci** (1869)

19 She is older than the rocks among which she sits; like
the vampire, she has been dead many times, and
learned the secrets of the grave; and has been a diver in
deep seas, and keeps their fallen day about her; and
trafficked for strange webs with Eastern merchants:
and, as Leda, was the mother of Helen of Troy, and as
Saint Anne, the mother of Mary; and all this has been
to her but as the sound of lyres and flutes, and lives
only in the delicacy with which it has moulded the
changing lineaments, and tinged the eyelids and the
hands.

20 All art constantly aspires towards the condition of
music.
The School of Giorgione

21 To burn always with this hard, gemlike flame, to
maintain this ecstasy, is success in life.
Conclusion

22 Not to discriminate every moment some passionate

attitude in those about us, and in the brilliance of their gifts some tragic dividing of forces on their ways is, on this short day of frost and sun, to sleep before evening.

COVENTRY PATMORE 1823–1896

1 Kind souls, you wonder why, love you,
    When you, you wonder why, love none.
We love, Fool, for the good we do,
    Not that which unto us is done!
The Angel in the House (1854–62), 1904 edn., bk.I, c.vi, Prelude 4, **A Riddle Solved**

2 I drew my bride, beneath the moon,
    Across my threshold; happy hour!
But, ah, the walk that afternoon
    We saw the water-flags in flower!
c.viii, Prelude 3, **The Spirit's Epochs**, l.9

3 'I saw you take his kiss!' ''Tis true.'
    'O modesty!' ''Twas strictly kept:
He thought me asleep; at least, I knew
    He thought I thought he thought I slept.'
bk.II, c.viii, Prelude 3, **The Kiss**

4 Some dish more sharply spiced than this
Milk-soup men call domestic bliss.
Olympus, l.15

5 So, till to-morrow eve, my Own, adieu!
Parting's well-paid with soon again to meet,
Soon in your arms to feel so small and sweet,
Sweet to myself that am so sweet to you!
The Unknown Eros (1877), bk.I, vii, **The Azalea**, l.22

6 With all my will, but much against my heart,
We two now part.
My Very Dear,
Our solace is, the sad road lies so clear.
It needs no art,
With faint, averted feet
And many a tear,
In our opposed paths to persevere.
xvi, **A Farewell**, l.1

7 He that but once too nearly hears
The music of forfended spheres
Is thenceforth lonely, and for all
His days as one who treads the Wall
Of China, and, on this hand, sees
Cities and their civilities
And, on the other, lions.
The Victories of Love, bk.I.ii. **From Mrs. Graham**, l.15

MARK PATTISON 1813–1884

8 In research the horizon recedes as we advance, and is no nearer at sixty than it was at twenty. As the power of endurance weakens with age, the urgency of the pursuit grows more intense...And research is always incomplete.
Isaac Casaubon (1875), ch.10

JAMES PAYN 1830–1898

9 I had never had a piece of toast
Particularly long and wide,
But fell upon the sanded floor,

And always on the buttered side.
Chambers's Journal, 2 Feb. 1884. See 356:25

J.H. PAYNE 1791–1852

10 Mid pleasures and palaces though we may roam,
Be it ever so humble, there's no place like home;
A charm from the skies seems to hallow us there,
Which, seek through the world, is ne'er met with
    elsewhere.
Home, home, sweet, sweet home!
There's no place like home! there's no place like
    home!
Clari, the Maid of Milan (1823), **Home, Sweet Home**

THOMAS LOVE PEACOCK 1785–1866

11 Ancient sculpture is the true school of modesty. But where the Greeks had modesty, we have cant; where they had poetry, we have cant; where they had patriotism, we have cant; where they had anything that exalts, delights, or adorns humanity, we have nothing but cant, cant, cant.
Crotchet Castle (1831) ch.7

12 A book that furnishes no quotations is, *me judice*, no book—it is a plaything.
ch.9

13 The march of mind has marched in through my back parlour shutters, and out again with my silver spoons, in the dead of night. The policeman, who was sent down to examine, says my house has been broken open on the most scientific principles.
ch.17

14 A Sympathizer would seem to imply a certain degree of benevolent feeling. Nothing of the kind. It signifies a ready-made accomplice in any species of political villainy.
Gryll Grange (1861), ch.1

15 Nothing can be more obvious than that all animals were created solely and exclusively for the use of man.
Headlong Hall (1816), ch.2

16 'Indeed, the loaves and fishes are typical of a mixed diet; and the practice of the Church in all ages shows—'
'That it never loses sight of the loaves and the fishes.'

17 'I distinguish the picturesque and the beautiful, and I add to them, in the laying out of grounds, a third and distinct character, which I call *unexpectedness*.'
'Pray, sir,' said Mr Milestone, 'by what name do you distinguish this character, when a person walks round the grounds for the second time?'
ch.4

18 Sir, I have quarrelled with my wife; and a man who has quarrelled with his wife is absolved from all duty to his country.
Nightmare Abbey (1818), ch.11

19 He remembered too late on his thorny green bed,
Much that well may be thought cannot wisely be said.
Crotchet Castle (1831): **The Priest and the Mulberry Tree**, st.5

20 Long night succeeds thy little day
    Oh blighted blossom! can it be,
That this gray stone and grassy clay
    Have closed our anxious care of thee?
Epitaph on his Daughter. *Works of Peacock*, ed. Henry Cole (1875), Biographical Notice by E. Nicolls

1 Frail as thy love, the flowers were dead
      Ere yet the evening sun was set:
   But years shall see the cypress spread,
      Immutable as my regret.
   The Grave of Love

2 The mountain sheep are sweeter,
      But the valley sheep are fatter;
   We therefore deemed it meeter
      To carry off the latter.
   The Misfortunes of Elphin (1823), ch.11. **The War-Song of Dinas Vawr**

3 In a bowl to sea went wise men three,
      On a brilliant night in June:
   They carried a net, and their hearts were set
      On fishing up the moon.
   The Wise Men of Gotham

PEDRO I, EMPEROR OF BRAZIL (PEDRO IV OF PORTUGAL) 1798–1834

4 *Como é para o bem de todos e a felicidade geral da nação, estou pronto. Diga ao povo que fico.*
   As it is for the good of all and the general happiness of the nation, I am ready and willing. Tell the people I'm staying.
   In response to a popular delegation, and in defiance of a decree from Lisbon requiring his return, 9 Sept. 1822. Commonly rendered *Fico* (I'm staying).

SIR ROBERT PEEL 1788–1850

5 I may be a Tory. I may be an illiberal—but...Tory as I am, I have the further satisfaction of knowing that there is not a single law connected with my name which has not had as its object some mitigation of the criminal law; some prevention of abuse in the exercise of it; or some security for its impartial administration.
   House of Commons, 1 May 1827

GEORGE PEELE 1558?–1597?

6 Fair and fair, and twice so fair,
      As fair as any may be;
   The fairest shepherd on our green,
      A love for any lady.
   Works, ed. A.H. Bullen, vol.i. **The Arraignment of Paris** (c.1581), I.ii.55 **Song of Oenone and Paris**

7 What thing is love for (well I wot) love is a thing.
   It is a prick, it is a sting,
   It is a pretty, pretty thing;
   It is a fire, it is a coal
   Whose flame creeps in at every hole.
   vol.ii. **Miscellaneous Poems. The Hunting of Cupid**, l.1

8 His golden locks time hath to silver turn'd;
      O time too swift, O swiftness never ceasing!
   His youth 'gainst time and age hath ever spurn'd
      But spurn'd in vain; youth waneth by increasing:
   Beauty, strength, youth, are flowers but fading seen;
   Duty, faith, love, are roots, and ever green.

   His helmet now shall make a hive for bees,
      And, lovers' sonnets turn'd to holy psalms,
   A man-at-arms must now serve on his knees,
      And feed on prayers, which are age his alms:
   But though from court to cottage he depart,
   His saint is sure of his unspotted heart...

   Goddess, allow this aged man his right,

To be your beadsman now that was your knight.
Polyhymnia (1590), **Sonnet ad finem. A Farewell to Arms**

9 When as the rye reach to the chin,
   And chopcherry, chopcherry ripe within,
   Strawberries swimming in the cream,
   And schoolboys playing in the stream,
   Then O, then O, then O, my true love said,
   Till that time come again,
   She could not live a maid.
   The Old Wives' Tale, l.81

1ST EARL OF PEMBROKE 1501?–1570

10 Out ye whores, to work, to work, ye whores, go spin.
    Aubrey, *Brief Lives*. Commonly quoted as 'Go spin, you jades, go spin.' See Sir W. Scott, *Journal*, 9 Feb. 1826

2ND EARL OF PEMBROKE c.1534–1601

11 A parliament can do any thing but make a man a woman, and a woman a man.
    Quoted in Speech made by his son, the 4th Earl on 11 Apr. 1648, proving himself Chancellor of Oxford. *Harleian Miscellany* (1810), Vol.5, p.113

10th EARL OF PEMBROKE 1734–1794

12 Dr Johnson's sayings would not appear so extraordinary, were it not for his *bow-wow way.*
    Boswell, *Life of Johnson*, 27 Mar. 1775, note

VLADIMIR PENIAKOFF 1897–1951

13 A message came on the wireless for me. It said 'SPREAD ALARM and DESPONDENCY'...The date was, I think, May 18th, 1942.
    Private Army, II, v.128. See also Army Act 42 & 43 Vict.33 sect.5 (1879): 'Every person subject to military law who...spreads reports calculated to create unnecessary alarm or despondency...shall...be liable to suffer penal servitude.'

WILLIAM PENN 1644–1718

14 It is a reproach to religion and government to suffer so much poverty and excess.
    Some Fruits of Solitude, in Reflections and Maxims relating to the conduct of Humane Life (1693), pt.i, No.52

15 Men are generally more careful of the breed of their horses and dogs than of their children.
    No.85

16 The taking of a Bribe or Gratuity, should be punished with as severe Penalties as the defrauding of the State.
    No.384

SAMUEL PEPYS 1633–1703

17 Strange the difference of men's talk!
    Diary, 4 Jan. 1659–60

18 I stayed up till the bell-man came by with his bell just under my window as I was writing of this very line, and cried, 'Past one of the clock, and a cold, frosty, windy morning.'
    16 Jan. 1659–60

19 And so to bed.
    20 Apr. 1660

20 A silk suit, which cost me much money, and I pray God to make me able to pay for it.
    1 July 1660

1 I went out to Charing Cross, to see Major-general Harrison hanged, drawn, and quartered; which was done there, he looking as cheerful as any man could do in that condition.
13 Oct. 1660

2 Very merry, and the best fritters that ever I eat in my life.
26 Feb: 1660–1 (Shrove Tues.)

3 A good honest and painful sermon.
17 Mar. 1661

4 If ever I was foxed it was now.
23 Apr. 1661

5 But methought it lessened my esteem of a king, that he should not be able to command the rain.
19 July 1662

6 I see it is impossible for the King to have things done as cheap as other men.
21 July 1662

7 But Lord! to see the absurd nature of Englishmen, that cannot forbear laughing and jeering at everything that looks strange.
27 Nov. 1662

8 My wife, who, poor wretch, is troubled with her lonely life.
19 Dec. 1662

9 Went to hear Mrs Turner's daughter…play on the harpsichon; but, Lord! it was enough to make any man sick to hear her; yet was I forced to commend her highly.
1 May 1663

10 A woman sober, and no high flyer, as he calls it.
27 May 1663

11 Most of their discourse was about hunting, in a dialect I understand very little.
22 Nov. 1663

12 While we were talking came by several poor creatures carried by, by constables, for being at a conventicle…I would to God they would either conform, or be more wise, and not be catched!
7 Aug. 1664

13 Pretty witty Nell. [Nell Gwynne.]
3 Apr. 1665

14 Strange to see how a good dinner and feasting reconciles everybody.
9 Nov. 1665

15 Strange to say what delight we married people have to see these poor fools decoyed into our condition.
25 Dec. 1665

16 Music and women I cannot but give way to, whatever my business is.
9 Mar. 1665–6

17 And mighty proud I am (and ought to be thankful to God Almighty) that I am able to have a spare bed for my friends.
8 Aug. 1666

18 I bless God I do find that I am worth more than ever I yet was, which is £6,200, for which the Holy Name of God be praised!
31 Oct. 1666

19 But it is pretty to see what money will do.
21 Mar. 1667–8

20 This day my wife made it appear to me that my late entertainment this week cost me above £12, an expense which I am almost ashamed of, though it is but once in a great while, and is the end for which, in the most part, we live, to have such a merry day once or twice in a man's life.
6 Mar. 1669

21 And so I betake myself to that course, which is almost as much as to see myself go into my grave—for which, and all the discomforts that will accompany my being blind, the good God prepare me!
Closing words, 31 May 1669

PERICLES c.495–429 B.C.

22 φιλοκαλοῦμέν τε γὰρ μετ' εὐτελείας καὶ φιλοσοφοῦμεν ἄνευ μαλακίας.
Our love of what is beautiful does not lead to extravagance; our love of the things of the mind does not make us soft.
Funeral Oration, Athens, 430 B.C., as reported by Thucydides, *Histories* ii.40, 1. Trans. Rex Warner

23 ἀνδρῶν γὰρ ἐπιφανῶν πᾶσα γῆ τάφος.
For famous men have the whole earth as their memorial.
43, 3. Trans. Rex Warner

24 τῆς τε γὰρ ὑπαρχούσης φύσεως μὴ χείροσι γενέσθαι ὑμῖν μεγάλη ἡ δόξα καὶ ἧς ἂν ἐπ' ἐλάχιστον ἀρετῆς πέρι ἢ ψόγου ἐν τοῖς ἄρσεσι κλέος ᾖ.
Your great glory is not to be inferior to what God has made you, and the greatest glory of a woman is to be least talked about by men, whether they are praising you or criticizing you.
45, 2. Trans. Rex Warner

CHARLES PERRAULT 1628–1703

25 *'Anne, ma soeur Anne, ne vois-tu rien venir?' Et la soeur Anne lui répondit, 'Je ne vois rien que le soleil qui poudroye, et l'herbe qui verdoye.'*
'Anne, sister Anne, do you see nothing coming?' And her sister Anne replied, 'I see nothing but the sun making a dust, and the grass looking green.'
Histoires et Contes du Temps Passé (1697)

PERSIUS A.D. 34–62

26 *Nec te quaesiveris extra.*
And don't consult anyone's opinions but your own.
Satires, i.7

27 *Virtutem videant intabescantque relicta.*
Let them recognize virtue and rot for having lost it.
iii.38

28 *Venienti occurrite morbo.*
Confront disease at its onset.
64. See 366:20

29 *Tecum habita: noris quam sit tibi curta supellex.*
Live with yourself: get to know how poorly furnished you are.
iv.52

PETRONIUS A.D. 1st cent.

30 *Canis ingens, catena vinctus, in pariete erat pictus superque quadrata littera scriptum 'Cave canem.'*
A huge dog, tied by a chain, was painted on the wall and over it was written in capital letters 'Beware of the

dog.'
Satyricon: Cena Trimalchionis, 29.1

1 *Abiit ad plures.*
He's gone to join the majority.
42.5. Meaning the dead.

2 *Nam Sibyllam quidem Cumis ego ipse oculis meis vidi in ampulla pendere, et cum illi pueri dicerent:*
Σίβυλλα, τί θελεις; *respondebat illa:* ἀποθανεῖν θέλω
'I saw the Sibyl at Cumae'
(One said) 'with mine own eye.
She hung in a cage, and read her rune
    To all the passers-by.
Said the boys, "What wouldst thou, Sibyl?"
    She answered, "I would die."'
48.8. Tr. D.G. Rossetti, *Fragments. The Sibyl*

3 *Horatii curiosa felicitas.*
Horace's precisely lucky strikes.
Satyricon, 118

4 *Habes confitentem reum.*
Your prisoner admits the crimes.
130

5 *Foeda est in coitu et brevis voluptas*
Et taedet Veneris statim peractae.
Delight of lust is gross and brief
And weariness treads on desire.
A. Baehrens, *Poetae Latinae Minores*, vol.IV, no.101. Tr. Helen Waddell.

PHEIDIPPIDES or PHILIPPIDES d. 490 B.C.

6 χαίρετε, νικῶμεν.
Greetings, we win.
Lucian, III.64, *Pro Lapsu inter salutandum*, para.iii. Before dying, having run to Athens with news of the Battle of Marathon.

EDWARD JOHN PHELPS 1822–1900

7 The man who makes no mistakes does not usually make anything.
Speech at Mansion House, 24 Jan. 1899

REAR ADMIRAL 'JACK' PHILIP 1840–1900

8 Don't cheer, men; those poor devils are dying.
At the Battle of Santiago, 4 July 1898. Allan Westcott, John Woodward Philip, *Dict. Am. Biog.*

AMBROSE PHILIPS 1675?–1749

9 The flowers anew, returning seasons bring!
But beauty faded has no second spring.
The First Pastoral (1709), Lobbin, 1.55

STEPHEN PHILLIPS 1864–1915

10 A man not old, but mellow, like good wine.
Ulysses (1902), III.ii

WENDELL PHILLIPS 1811–1884

11 Every man meets his Waterloo at last.
Speeches (1880), Lecture at Brooklyn, N.Y., 1 Nov. 1859

12 We live under a government of men and morning newspapers.
Address: The Press

PINDAR 518–438 B.C.

13 ἄριστον μὲν ὕδωρ.
Water is excellent.
Olympian Odes, I.1

14 φωνᾶντα συνετοῖσιν. ἐς δὲ τὸ πᾶν ἑρμηνέων χατίζει.
(Weapons) that speak to the wise; but in general they need interpreters.
II.85

15 μή, φίλα ψυχά, βίον ἀθάνατον
σπεῦδε, τὰν δ' ἔμπρακτον ἄντλει μαχανάν.
My soul, do not seek immortal life, but exhaust the realm of the possible.
Pythian Odes, III.109

SIR ARTHUR WING PINERO 1855–1934

16 Put me into something loose.
The Gay Lord Quex (1899), III

17 What beautiful fruit! I love fruit when it's expensive.
The Second Mrs. Tanqueray (1893), Act I

HAROLD PINTER 1930–

18 I can't drink Guinness from a thick mug. I only like it out of a thin glass.
The Caretaker (1959), Act I

19 If only I could get down to Sidcup. I've been waiting for the weather to break.

WILLIAM PITT, EARL OF CHATHAM 1708–1778

20 The atrocious crime of being a young man...I shall neither attempt to palliate nor deny.
House of Commons, 27 Jan. 1741

21 I rejoice that America has resisted. Three millions of people, so dead to all the feelings of liberty, as voluntarily to submit to be slaves, would have been fit instruments to make slaves of the rest.
14 Jan. 1766

22 I cannot give them my confidence; pardon me, gentlemen, confidence is a plant of slow growth in an aged bosom: youth is the season of credulity.

23 Unlimited power is apt to corrupt the minds of those who possess it.
House of Lords, 9 Jan. 1770. See 1:5

24 There is something behind the throne greater than the King himself.
2 Mar. 1770

25 We have a Calvinistic creed, a Popish liturgy, and an Arminian clergy.
19 May 1772

26 If I were an American, as I am an Englishman, while a foreign troop was landed in my country, I never would lay down my arms,—never—never—never!
18 Nov. 1777

27 You cannot conquer America.

28 I invoke the genius of the Constitution!

29 The poorest man may in his cottage bid defiance to all the forces of the Crown. It may be frail—its roof may shake—the wind may blow through it—the storm may enter—the rain may enter—but the King of England

cannot enter!—all his force dares not cross the threshold of the ruined tenement!
Date unknown. Lord Brougham, *Statesmen in the Time of George III* (1839), vol.I

1 Our watchword is security.
Attr.

2 The lungs of London. [The parks.]
William Windham, in a Speech in House of Commons, 30 June 1808

WILLIAM PITT 1759–1806

3 Necessity is the plea for every infringement of human freedom. It is the argument of tyrants; it is the creed of slaves.
House of Commons, 18 Nov. 1783

4 We must recollect...what it is we have at stake, what it is we have to contend for. It is for our property, it is for our liberty, it is for our independence, nay, for our existence as a nation; it is for our character, it is for our very name as Englishmen, it is for everything dear and valuable to man on this side of the grave.
22 July 1803

5 England has saved herself by her exertions, and will, as I trust, save Europe by her example.
Guildhall, 1805

6 Roll up that map; it will not be wanted these ten years.
On a map of Europe, after hearing the news of the Battle of Austerlitz Dec. 1805. Lord Stanhope, *Life of the Rt. Hon. William Pitt* (1862), vol.iv, p.369

7 Oh, my country! how I leave my country!
Last words. Stanhope (1879), iii. p.397; in the 1st edn. (1862), iv, p.369, the words were given as 'How I love my country' and in G. Rose, *Diaries and Correspondence*, 23 Jan. 1806, as simply 'My country! oh, my country!' Oral tradition reports the alternative, 'I think I could eat one of Bellamy's veal pies.'

PLATO c.429–347 B.C.

8 Σωκράτη φησὶν ἀδικεῖν τούς τε νέους διαφθείροντα καὶ θεοὺς οὓς ἡ πόλις νομίζει οὐ νομίζοντα, ἕτερα δὲ δαιμόνια καινά.
It is said that Socrates commits a crime by corrupting the young men and not recognizing the gods that the city recognizes, but some other new religion.
Apologia, 24b

9 Socrates, I shall not accuse you as I accuse others, of getting angry and cursing me when I tell them to drink the poison imposed by the authorities. I know you on the contrary in your time here to be the noblest and gentlest and best man of all who ever came here; and now I am sure you are not angry with me, for you know who are responsible, but with them.
Phaedo, 116c. Spoken by Socrates' jailor

10 This was the end, Echechrates, of our friend; a man of whom we may say that of all whom we met at that time he was the wisest and justest and best.
118. Of Socrates' death

11 οὐ γὰρ περὶ τοῦ ἐπιτυχόντος ὁ λόγος, ἀλλὰ περὶ τοῦ ὅντινα τρόπον χρὴ ζῆν.
For our discussion is on no trifling matter, but on the right way to conduct our lives.
Republic, VIII, 352d

12 οὐ μὲν οὖν τῇ ἀληθείᾳ, φάναι, ὦ φιλούμενε Ἀγάθων, δύνασαι ἀντιλέγειν, ἐπεὶ Σωκράτει γε οὐδὲν χαλεπόν.

But, my dearest Agathon, it is truth which you cannot contradict; you can without any difficulty contradict Socrates.
Symposium, 201

PLAUTUS d. c.184 B.C.

13 *Lupus est homo homini, non homo, quom qualis sit non novit.*
A man is a wolf rather than a man to another man, when he hasn't yet found out what he's like.
Asinaria, 495. Often cited simply as *Homo homini lupus* (A man is a wolf to another man.)

14 *Dictum sapienti sat est.*
What's been said is enough for anyone with sense.
Persa, 729. Proverbially later, *Verbum sapienti sat est*, A word is enough for the wise.

15 Labrax: *Una littera plus sum quam medicus.*
Gripus: *Tum tu Mendicus es?*
Labrax: *Tetigisti acu.*
Labrax: One letter more than a medical man, that's what I am.
Gripus: Then you're a mendicant?
Labrax: You've hit the point.
Rudens, 1305

PLINY A.D. 23/24–79

16 *Brutum fulmen.*
A harmless thunderbolt.
Historia Naturalis, II.xliii

17 *Sal Atticum.*
Attic wit.
xxxi.87

WILLIAM PLOMER 1903–1973

18 A rose-red sissy half as old as time.
The Playboy of the Demi-World (1938). See 108:4

19 Fissures appeared in football fields
And houses in the night collapsed.
The Thames flowed backward to its source,
The last trickle seemed to disappear
Swiftly, like an adder to its hole,
And here and there along the river-bed
The stranded fish gaped among empty tins;
Face downward lay the huddled suicides
Like litter that a riot leaves.
The Silent Sunday

PLUTARCH A.D.c.50–c. 120

20 He who cheats with an oath acknowledges that he is afraid of his enemy, but that he thinks little of God.
Lives: Lysander, 8. See 321:18

EDGAR ALLAN POE 1809–1849

21 This maiden she lived with no other thought
Than to love and be loved by me.
Annabel Lee (1849)

22 I was a child and she was a child,
In this kingdom by the sea;
But we loved with a love which was more than love—
I and my Annabel Lee.

23 And so, all the night-tide, I lie down by the side
Of my darling, my darling, my life and my bride

In her sepulchre there by the sea,
In her tomb by the side of the sea.

1 Keeping time, time, time,
   In a sort of Runic rhyme,
To the tintinnabulation that so musically wells
   From the bells, bells, bells, bells.
   The Bells (1849), l.9

2 All that we see or seem
   Is but a dream within a dream.
   A Dream within a Dream, l.10

3 The fever call'd 'Living'
   Is conquer'd at last.
   For Annie

4 Once upon a midnight dreary, while I pondered, weak
      and weary,
   Over many a quaint and curious volume of forgotten
      lore,
   While I nodded, nearly napping, suddenly there came
      a tapping,
   As of some one gently rapping, rapping at my
      chamber door.
   The Raven (1845), i

5 Eagerly I wished the morrow,—vainly had I sought to
      borrow
   From my books surcease of sorrow—sorrow for the
      lost Lenore—
   For the rare and radiant maiden whom the angels name
      Lenore—
         Nameless here for evermore.
   ii

6 Take thy beak from out my heart, and take thy form
      from off my door!
         Quoth the Raven, 'Nevermore'.
   xvii

7 Helen, thy beauty is to me
      Like those Nicean barks of yore,
   That gently, o'er a perfumed sea,
      The weary, wayworn wanderer bore
      To his own native shore.

   On desperate seas long wont to roam,
      Thy hyacinth hair, thy classic face,
   Thy Naiad airs have brought me home,
      To the glory that was Greece
      And the grandeur that was Rome.
   To Helen, l.1

JOHN POMFRET 1667–1702

8 We live and learn, but not the wiser grow.
   Reason (1700), l.112

MADAME DE POMPADOUR 1721–1764

9 *Après nous le déluge.*
   After us the deluge.
   Madame de Hausset, *Mémoires,* p.19

JOHN POOLE 1786?–1872

10 I hope I don't intrude?
   Paul Pry (1825), I.ii

ALEXANDER POPE 1688–1744

11 To wake the soul by tender strokes of art,

To raise the genius, and to mend the heart;
To make mankind, in conscious virtue bold,
Live o'er each scene, and be what they behold:
For this the Tragic Muse first trod the stage.
Prologue to Addison's *Cato* (1713), l.1

12 A brave man struggling in the storms of fate,
   And greatly falling with a falling state.
   While Cato gives his little senate laws,
   What bosom beats not in his country's cause?
   l.21

13 Poetic Justice, with her lifted scale;
   Where, in nice balance, truth with gold she weighs,
   And solid pudding against empty praise.
   The Dunciad (1728), bk.i, l.52

14 Now night descending, the proud scene was o'er,
   But liv'd, in Settle's numbers, one day more.
   l.89

15 While pensive poets painful vigils keep,
   Sleepless themselves, to give their readers sleep.
   l.93

16 Or where the pictures for the page atone,
   And Quarles is sav'd by beauties not his own.
   l.139

17 And gentle dullness ever loves a joke.
   bk.ii, l.34

18 A brain of feathers, and a heart of lead.
   l.44

19 All crowd, who foremost shall be damn'd to fame.
   bk.iii, l.158

20 Flow Welsted, flow! like thine inspirer, beer,
   Tho' stale, not ripe; tho' thin, yet never clear;
   So sweetly mawkish, and so smoothly dull;
   Heady, not strong; o'erflowing tho' not full.
   l.169

21 Proceed, great days! 'till learning fly the shore,
   'Till Birch shall blush with noble blood no more,
   'Till Thames see Eaton's sons for ever play,
   'Till Westminster's whole year be holiday,
   'Till Isis' elders reel, their pupils sport,
   And Alma Mater lie dissolv'd in port!
   l.333

22 A wit with dunces, and a dunce with wits.
   bk.iv (1742), l.90

23 May you, may Cam, and Isis, preach it long,
   The Right Divine of Kings to govern wrong.
   l.187

24 With the same cement, ever sure to bind,
   We bring to one dead level ev'ry mind.
   Then take him to develop, if you can,
   And hew the block off, and get out the man.
   l.267

25   She mark'd thee there,
   Stretch'd on the rack of a too easy chair,
   And heard thy everlasting yawn confess
   The pains and penalties of idleness.
   l.341

26 See skulking Truth to her old cavern fled,
   Mountains of casuistry heap'd o'er her head!
   Philosophy, that lean'd on Heav'n before,
   Shrinks to her second cause, and is no more.
   Physic of Metaphysic begs defence,
   And Metaphysic calls for aid on Sense!
   l.641

1 Religion blushing veils her sacred fires,
And unawares Morality expires.
1.649

2 Lo! thy dread empire, Chaos! is restor'd;
Light dies before thy uncreating word;
Thy hand, great Anarch! lets the curtain fall,
And universal darkness buries all.
1.653

3 Vital spark of heav'nly flame!
Quit, oh quit this mortal frame:
Trembling, hoping, ling'ring, flying,
Oh the pain, the bliss of dying!
The Dying Christian to his Soul (1713). See 237:9

4 Tell me, my soul, can this be death?

5 What beck'ning ghost, along the moonlight shade
Invites my step, and points to yonder glade?
Elegy to the Memory of an Unfortunate Lady (1717), 1.1

6 Is it, in heav'n, a crime to love too well?
1.6

7 Is there no bright reversion in the sky,
For those who greatly think, or bravely die?
1.9

8 Ambition first sprung from your blest abodes;
The glorious fault of angels and of gods.
1.13

9 On all the line a sudden vengeance waits,
And frequent hearses shall besiege your gates.
1.37

10 By foreign hands thy dying eyes were clos'd,
By foreign hands thy decent limbs compos'd,
By foreign hands thy humble grave adorn'd,
By strangers honour'd, and by strangers mourn'd!
1.51

11 No, make me mistress to the man I love;
If there be yet another name more free,
More fond than mistress, make me that to thee!
Eloisa to Abelard (1717), 1.88

12 Of all affliction taught a lover yet,
'Tis sure the hardest science to forget!
How shall I lose the sin, yet keep the sense,
And love the offender, yet detest th'offence?
How the dear object from the crime remove,
Or how distinguish penitence from love?
1.189. See 22:1

13 How happy is the blameless Vestal's lot?
The world forgetting, by the world forgot.
1.207

14 See my lips tremble, and my eye-balls roll,
Suck my last breath, and catch my flying soul!
1.323

15 You beat your pate, and fancy wit will come;
Knock as you please, there's nobody at home.
Epigram

16 I am his Highness' dog at Kew;
Pray, tell me sir, whose dog are you?
Epigram Engraved on the Collar of a Dog which I gave to his Royal Highness

17 Sir, I admit your gen'ral rule
That every poet is a fool;
But you yourself may serve to show it,
That every fool is not a poet.
Epigram from the French

18 Shut, shut the door, good John! fatigu'd I said,

Tie up the knocker; say I'm sick, I'm dead.
The Dog-star rages!
Epistle to Dr. Arbuthnot (1735), 1.1 (Imitation of Horace)

19 Is there a parson, much bemus'd in beer,
A maudlin poetess, a rhyming peer,
A clerk, foredoom'd his father's soul to cross,
Who pens a stanza, when he should engross?
1.15

20 Fir'd that the house reject him, ''Sdeath I'll print it,
And shame the fools.'
1.61

21 You think this cruel? take it for a rule,
No creature smarts so little as a fool.
Let peals of laughter, Codrus! round thee break,
Thou unconcern'd canst hear the mighty crack:
Pit, box, and gall'ry in convulsions hurl'd,
Thou stand'st unshook amidst a bursting world.
1.83. See 2:30, 260:18

22 Destroy his fib or sophistry—in vain!
The creature's at his dirty work again.
1.91

23 As yet a child, nor yet a fool to fame,
I lisp'd in numbers, for the numbers came.
I left no calling for this idle trade,
'No duty broke, no father disobey'd.
The Muse but serv'd to ease some friend, not wife,
To help me thro' this long disease, my life.
1.127. See 366:23

24 Pretty! in amber to observe the forms
Of hairs, or straws, or dirt, or grubs, or worms!
The things, we know, are neither rich nor rare,
But wonder how the Devil they got there.
1.169

25 And he, whose fustian's so sublimely bad,
It is not poetry, but prose run mad.
1.187

26   Were there one whose fires
True genius kindles, and fair fame inspires;
Blest with each talent, and each art to please,
And born to write, converse, and live with ease:
Should such a man, too fond to rule alone,
Bear, like the Turk, no brother near the throne,
View him with scornful, yet with jealous eyes,
And hate for arts that caus'd himself to rise;
Damn with faint praise, assent with civil leer,
And, without sneering, teach the rest to sneer;
Willing to wound, and yet afraid to strike,
Just hint a fault, and hesitate dislike. [Addison.]
1.193. See 584:2

27 Alike reserv'd to blame, or to commend,
A tim'rous foe, and a suspicious friend;
Dreading ev'n fools, by flatterers besieged,
And so obliging, that he ne'er oblig'd;
Like Cato, give his little senate laws,
And sit attentive to his own applause. [Addison.]
1.207

28 Who but must laugh, if such a man there be?
Who would not weep, if Atticus were he! [Addison.]
1.215

29 But still the great have kindness in reserve,
He help'd to bury whom he help'd to starve.
1.247

30 Let Sporus tremble—'What? that thing of silk,

Sporus, that mere white curd of ass's milk?
Satire or sense, alas! can Sporus feel?
Who breaks a butterfly upon a wheel?' [Lord Hervey.]
l.305

1 Yet let me flap this bug with gilded wings,
This painted child of dirt, that stinks and stings. [Lord Hervey.]
l.309

2 Eternal smiles his emptiness betray,
As shallow streams run dimpling all the way. [Lord Hervey.]
l.315

3 And he himself one vile antithesis.
l.325

4 A cherub's face, a reptile all the rest. [Lord Hervey.]
l.331

5 Unlearn'd, he knew no schoolman's subtle art,
No language, but the language of the heart.
By nature honest, by experience wise,
Healthy by temp'rance, and by exercise.
l.398

6 Such were the notes, thy once-loved Poet sung,
Till Death untimely stopp'd his tuneful tongue.
Epistle to the Earl of Oxford and Earl Mortimer (1721), l.1

7 She went, to plain-work, and to purling brooks,
Old-fashion'd halls, dull aunts, and croaking rooks:
She went from op'ra, park, assembly, play,
To morning-walks, and pray'rs three hours a day;
To part her time 'twixt reading and Bohea,
To muse, and spill her solitary tea,
Or o'er cold coffee trifle with the spoon,
Court the slow clock, and dine exact at noon;
Divert her eyes with pictures in the fire,
Hum half a tune, tell stories to the squire.
Epistle to Miss Blount, on her leaving the Town after the Coronation, l.11

8 To observations which ourselves we make,
We grow more partial for th' observer's sake.
Epistles to Several Persons Ep.i. **To Lord Cobham** (1734), l.11

9 Like following life thro' creatures you dissect,
You lose it in the moment you detect.
l.29

10 Alas! in truth the man but chang'd his mind,
Perhaps was sick, in love, or had not din'd.
l.127

11 'Tis from high life high characters are drawn;
A saint in crape is twice a saint in lawn.
l.135

12 'Tis Education forms the common mind,
Just as the twig is bent, the tree's inclin'd.
l.149

13 Search then the Ruling Passion: There, alone,
The wild are constant and the cunning known;
The fool consistent, and the false sincere;
Priests, princes, women, no dissemblers here.
This clue once found, unravels all the rest.
l.174

14 Old politicians chew on wisdom past,
And totter on in bus'ness to the last.
l.228

15 'Odious! in woollen! 'twould a saint provoke!'
l.246

16 'One would not, sure, be frightful when one's dead:

And—Betty—give this cheek a little red.'
l.250

17 Most women have no characters at all.
Ep.ii. **To a Lady** (1735), l.2

18 Choose a firm cloud, before it fall, and in it
Catch, ere she change, the Cynthia of this minute.
l.19

19 A very heathen in the carnal part,
Yet still a sad, good Christian at her heart.
l.67

20 Chaste to her husband, frank to all beside,
A teeming mistress, but a barren bride.
l.71

21 Wise wretch! with pleasures too refin'd to please,
With too much spirit to be e'er at ease,
With too much quickness ever to be taught;
With too much thinking to have common thought:
You purchase pain with all that joy can give,
And die of nothing but a rage to live.
l.95

22 'With ev'ry pleasing, ev'ry prudent part,
Say, what can Cloe want?'—She wants a heart.
l.159

23 Virtue she finds too painful an endeavour,
Content to dwell in decencies for ever.
l.163

24 In men, we various ruling passions find,
In women, two almost divide the kind;
Those, only fix'd, they first or last obey,
The love of pleasure, and the love of sway.
l.207

25 Men, some to bus'ness, some to pleasure take;
But ev'ry woman is at heart a rake:
Men, some to quiet, some to public strife;
But ev'ry lady would be Queen for life.
l.215

26 Still round and round the ghosts of beauty glide,
And haunt the places where their honour died.
See how the world its veterans rewards!
A youth of frolics, an old age of cards.
l.241

27 She who ne'er answers till a husband cools,
Or, if she rules him, never shows she rules;
Charms by accepting, by submitting sways,
Yet has her humour most, when she obeys.
l.261

28 And mistress of herself, though China fall.
l.268

29 Woman's at best a contradiction still.
l.270

30 Who shall decide, when doctors disagree,
And soundest casuists doubt, like you and me?
Ep.iii. **To Lord Bathurst** (1733), l.1

31 But thousands die, without or this or that,
Die, and endow a college, or a cat.
l.95

32 The ruling passion, be it what it will,
The ruling passion conquers reason still.
l.153

33 In the worst inn's worst room, with mat half-hung,
The floors of plaister, and the walls of dung,
On once a flock-bed, but repaired with straw,
With tape-tied curtains, never meant to draw,

The George and Garter dangling from that bed
Where tawdry yellow strove with dirty red,
Great Villiers lies.
l.299

1 Gallant and gay, in Cliveden's proud alcove,
The bow'r of wanton Shrewsbury and love.
l.307

2 Where London's column, pointing at the skies,
Like a tall bully, lifts the head, and lies.
l.339

3 Consult the genius of the place in all.
Ep.iv. **To Lord Burlington** (1731), l.57

4 To rest, the cushion and soft Dean invite,
Who never mentions Hell to ears polite.
l.149

5 Another age shall see the golden ear
Imbrown the slope, and nod on the parterre,
Deep harvests bury all his pride has plann'd,
And laughing Ceres re-assume the land.
l.173

6 Statesman, yet friend to truth! of soul sincere,
In action faithful, and in honour clear;
Who broke no promise, serv'd no private end,
Who gain'd no title, and who lost no friend.
Ep.v. **To Mr. Addison** (1721), l.67

7 Nature, and Nature's laws lay hid in night:
God said, *Let Newton be!* and all was light.
Epitaphs. Intended for Sir Isaac Newton. See 517:14

8 Of manners gentle, of affections mild;
In wit, a man; simplicity, a child:
With native humour temp'ring virtuous rage,
Form'd to delight at once and lash the age.
On Mr. Gay

9 Here rests a woman, good without pretence,
Blest with plain reason, and with sober sense.
On Mrs. Corbet

10 Let such teach others who themselves excel,
And censure freely who have written well.
An Essay on Criticism (1711), l.15

11 Some are bewilder'd in the maze of schools,
And some made coxcombs nature meant but fools.
l.26

12 Some have at first for wits, then poets pass'd,
Turn'd critics next, and prov'd plain fools at last.
l.36

13 A little learning is a dang'rous thing;
Drink deep, or taste not the Pierian spring:
There shallow draughts intoxicate the brain,
And drinking largely sobers us again.
l.215. See 193:15

14 Hills peep o'er hills, and Alps on Alps arise!
l.232

15 Whoever thinks a faultless piece to see
Thinks what ne'er was, nor is, nor e'er shall be.
l.253

16 Poets, like painters, thus unskill'd to trace
The naked nature and the living grace,
With gold and jewels cover ev'ry part,
And hide with ornaments their want of art.
l.293

17 True wit is nature to advantage dress'd,

What oft was thought, but ne'er so well express'd.
l.297

18 Such labour'd nothings, in so strange a style,
Amaze th' unlearn'd, and make the learned smile.
l.326

19 Be not the first by whom the new are tried,
Nor yet the last to lay the old aside.
l.335

20   As some to church repair,
Not for the doctrine, but the music there,
These equal syllables alone require,
Tho' oft the ear the open vowels tire;
While expletives their feeble aid do join;
And ten low words oft creep in one dull line.
l.342

21 Where'er you find 'the cooling western breeze',
In the next line, it 'whispers through the trees':
If crystal streams 'with pleasing murmurs creep',
The reader's threaten'd, not in vain, with 'sleep':
Then, at the last and only couplet fraught
With some unmeaning thing they call a thought,
A needless Alexandrine ends the song,
That, like a wounded snake, drags its slow length
   along.
l.350

22 True ease in writing comes from art, not chance,
As those move easiest who have learn'd to dance.
'Tis not enough no harshness gives offence,
The sound must seem an echo to the sense.
l.362

23 But when loud surges lash the sounding shore,
The hoarse, rough verse should like the torrent roar:
When Ajax strives, some rock's vast weight to throw,
The line too labours, and the words move slow.
l.368

24 Yet let not each gay turn thy rapture move;
For fools admire, but men of sense approve.
l.390

25 What woeful stuff this madrigal would be,
In some starv'd hackney sonneteer, or me?
But let a lord once own the happy lines,
How the wit brightens! how the style refines!
l.418

26 Some praise at morning what they blame at night;
But always think the last opinion right.
l.430

27 To err is human, to forgive, divine.
l.525

28 All seems infected that th'infected spy,
As all looks yellow to the jaundic'd eye.
l.558

29 Men must be taught as if you taught them not,
And things unknown propos'd as things forgot.
l.574

30 The bookful blockhead, ignorantly read,
With loads of learned lumber in his head.
l.612

31 For fools rush in where angels fear to tread.
l.625

32 But where's the man, who counsel can bestow,
Still pleas'd to teach, and yet not proud to know?
Unbiass'd, or by favour, or by spite:
Not dully prepossess'd, nor blindly right;

Tho' learn'd, well-bred; and tho' well-bred, sincere;
Modestly bold, and humanly severe:
Who to a friend his faults can freely show,
And gladly praise the merit of a foe?
l.631

1 Awake, my St John! leave all meaner things
To low ambition, and the pride of kings.
Let us (since Life can little more supply
Than just to look about us and to die)
Expatiate free o'er all this scene of man;
A mighty maze! but not without a plan.
An Essay on Man. Epistle i (1733), l.1

2 Eye Nature's walks, shoot folly as it flies,
And catch the manners living as they rise.
Laugh where we must, be candid where we can;
But vindicate the ways of God to man.
Say first, of God above or man below,
What can we reason, but from what we know.
l.13

3 Observe how system into system runs,
What other planets circle other suns.
l.25

4 Who sees with equal eye, as God of all,
A hero perish, or a sparrow fall,
Atoms or systems into ruin hurl'd,
And now a bubble burst, and now a world.
l.87

5 Hope springs eternal in the human breast;
Man never Is, but always To be blest.
The soul, uneasy, and confin'd from home,
Rests and expatiates in a life to come.
Lo, the poor Indian! whose untutor'd mind
Sees God in clouds, or hears him in the wind;
His soul proud Science never taught to stray
Far as the solar walk or milky way;
Yet simple Nature to his hope has giv'n,
Behind the cloud-topp'd hill, an humbler heav'n.
l.95

6 But thinks, admitted to that equal sky,
His faithful dog shall bear him company.
l.111

7 Pride still is aiming at the bless'd abodes,
Men would be angels, angels would be gods.
Aspiring to be gods if angels fell,
Aspiring to be angels men rebel.
l.125

8 Why has not man a microscopic eye?
For this plain reason, man is not a fly.
l.193

9 The spider's touch, how exquisitely fine!
Feels at each thread, and lives along the line.
l.217

10 All are but parts of one stupendous whole,
Whose body Nature is, and God the soul.
l.267

11 All nature is but art unknown to thee;
All chance, direction which thou canst not see;
All discord, harmony not understood;
All partial evil, universal good;
And, spite of pride, in erring reason's spite,
One truth is clear, 'Whatever IS, is RIGHT.'
l.289

12 Know then thyself, presume not God to scan,

The proper study of mankind is man.
Plac'd on this isthmus of a middle state,
A being darkly wise, and rudely great:
With too much knowledge for the sceptic side,
With too much weakness for the stoic's pride,
He hangs between; in doubt to act or rest,
In doubt to deem himself a god, or beast;
In doubt his mind or body to prefer;
Born but to die, and reas'ning but to err;
Alike in ignorance, his reason such,
Whether he thinks too little or too much.
Ep.ii (1733), l.1. See 141:1

13 Created half to rise, and half to fall;
Great lord of all things, yet a prey to all;
Sole judge of truth, in endless error hurl'd;
The glory, jest, and riddle of the world!
l.15

14 Go, teach eternal wisdom how to rule—
Then drop into thyself, and be a fool!
l.29

15 Fix'd like a plant on his peculiar spot,
To draw nutrition, propagate, and rot.
l.63

16 Vice is a monster of so frightful mien,
As, to be hated, needs but to be seen;
Yet seen too oft, familiar with her face,
We first endure, then pity, then embrace.
But where th' extreme of vice, was ne'er agreed:
Ask where's the North? at York, 'tis on the Tweed;
In Scotland, at the Orcades; and there,
At Greenland, Zembla, or the Lord knows where.
l.217

17 The learn'd is happy nature to explore,
The fool is happy that he knows no more.
l.263

18 Behold the child, by nature's kindly law
Pleas'd with a rattle, tickled with a straw.
l.275

19 Scarfs, garters, gold, amuse his riper stage,
And beads and pray'r-books are the toys of age:
Pleas'd with this bauble still, as that before;
Till tir'd, he sleeps, and life's poor play is o'er.
l.279

20 For forms of government let fools contest;
Whate'er is best administer'd is best:
For modes of faith, let graceless zealots fight;
His can't be wrong whose life is in the right:
In faith and hope the world will disagree,
But all mankind's concern is charity.
Ep.iii (1733), l.303

21 O Happiness! our being's end and aim!
Good, pleasure, ease, content! whate'er thy name:
That something still which prompts th' eternal sigh,
For which we bear to live, or dare to die.
Ep.iv (1734), l.1

22 Worth makes the man, and want of it, the fellow;
The rest is all but leather or prunella.
l.203

23 What can ennoble sots, or slaves, or cowards?
Alas! not all the blood of all the Howards.
l.215

24 A wit's a feather, and a chief a rod;

An honest man's the noblest work of God.
l.247

1 If parts allure thee, think how Bacon shin'd,
The wisest, brightest, meanest of mankind:
Or ravish'd with the whistling of a name,
See Cromwell, damn'd to everlasting fame!
l.281

2 Slave to no sect, who takes no private road,
But looks through Nature, up to Nature's God.
l.331

3 Form'd by thy converse, happily to steer
From grave to gay, from lively to severe.
l.379

4 Shall then this verse to future age pretend
Thou wert my guide, philosopher, and friend?
That urg'd by thee, I turn'd the tuneful art
From sounds to things, from fancy to the heart;
For wit's false mirror held up nature's light;
Shew'd erring pride, whatever is, is right;
That reason, passion, answer one great aim;
That true self-love and social are the same;
That virtue only makes our bliss below;
And all our knowledge is, ourselves to know.
l.389

5 There St John mingles with my friendly bowl
The feast of reason and the flow of soul.
Imitations of Horace. Hor.II, Sat.1 (1733). **To Mr. Fortescue,**
l.127

6 For I, who hold sage Homer's rule the best,
Welcome the coming, speed the going guest.
Hor.II, Sat.2 (1734). **To Mr. Bethel,** l.159. See 380:25

7 Our Gen'rals now, retir'd to their estates,
Hang their old trophies o'er the garden gates,
In life's cool ev'ning satiate of applause.
Hor.I, Ep.1 (1738). **To Lord Bolingbroke,** l.7

8 Not to go back, is somewhat to advance,
And men must walk at least before they dance.
l.53

9 Get place and wealth, if possible, with grace;
If not, by any means get wealth and place.
l.103

10 Not to admire, is all the art I know,
To make men happy, and to keep them so.
Hor.I, Ep.6 (1738). **To Mr. Murray,** l.1. See 258:17

11 The worst of madmen is a saint run mad.
l.27

12 Shakespeare (whom you and ev'ry play-house bill
Style the divine, the matchless, what you will)
For gain, not glory, wing'd his roving flight,
And grew immortal in his own despite.
Hor.II, Ep.1 (1737). **To Augustus,** l.69

13 Who now reads Cowley? if he pleases yet,
His moral pleases, not his pointed wit.
l.75

14 The people's voice is odd,
It is, and it is not, the voice of God.
l.89. See 3:9

15 Waller was smooth; but Dryden taught to join
The varying verse, the full-resounding line,
The long majestic march, and energy divine.
l.267

16 Ev'n copious Dryden wanted, or forgot,

The last and greatest art, the art to blot.
l.280

17 There still remains, to mortify a wit,
The many-headed monster of the pit.
l.304

18 Let humble Allen, with an awkward shame,
Do good by stealth, and blush to find it fame.
Epilogue (1738), Dial.i, l.135

19 Ask you what provocation I have had?
The strong antipathy of good to bad.
Dial.ii, l.197

20 Yes, I am proud; I must be proud to see
Men not afraid of God, afraid of me.
l.208

21 Vain was the chief's and sage's pride.
They had no poet and they died!
Hor.IV, Ode 9, l.12

22 Ye gods! annihilate but space and time,
And make two lovers happy.
Martinus Scriblerus...or The Art of Sinking in Poetry, ch.11
(Miscellanies, 1727)

23 Happy the man, whose wish and care
A few paternal acres bound,
Content to breathe his native air,
In his own ground.
Ode on Solitude (1717)

24 Thus let me live, unseen, unknown,
Thus unlamented let me die;
Steal from the world, and not a stone
Tell where I lie.

25 Welcome the coming, speed the parting guest.
Odyssey (1725–6), xv.83

26 'Has she no faults then (Envy says) Sir?'
Yes, she has one, I must aver:
When all the world conspires to praise her,
The woman's deaf, and does not hear.
On a Certain Lady at Court (1727–8)

27 Where'er you walk, cool gales shall fan the
glade,
Trees, where you sit, shall crowd into a shade:
Where'er you tread, the blushing flow'rs shall rise,
And all things flourish where you turn your eyes.
Pastorals (1709), **Summer,** l.73

28 What dire offence from am'rous causes springs,
What mighty contests rise from trivial things.
The Rape of the Lock (1714), c.i, l.1

29 Now lap-dogs give themselves the rousing shake,
And sleepless lovers, just at twelve, awake:
Thrice rung the bell, the slipper knock'd the ground,
And the press'd watch return'd a silver sound.
l.15

30 They shift the moving Toyshop of their heart.
l.100

31 Here files of pins extend their shining rows,
Puffs, powders, patches, bibles, billet-doux.
l.137

32 Bright as the sun, her eyes the gazers strike,
And, like the sun, they shine on all alike.
c.ii, l.13

33 If to her share some female errors fall,
Look on her face, and you'll forget 'em all.
l.17

1 Fair tresses man's imperial race insnare,
And beauty draws us with a single hair.
l.27

2 Here thou, great Anna! whom three realms obey,
Dost sometimes counsel take—and sometimes tea.
c.iii, l.7

3 At ev'ry word a reputation dies.
l.16

4 The hungry judges soon the sentence sign,
And wretches hang that jury-men may dine.
l.21

5 Let Spades be trumps! she said, and trumps they were.
l.46

6 For lo! the board with cups and spoons is crown'd,
The berries crackle, and the mill turns round;
On shining altars of Japan they raise
The silver lamp; the fiery spirits blaze:
From silver spouts the grateful liquors glide,
While China's earth receives the smoking tide:
At once they gratify their scent and taste,
And frequent cups prolong the rich repast.
l.105

7 Coffee, (which makes the politician wise,
And see through all things with his half-shut eyes)
Sent up in vapours to the Baron's brain
New stratagems, the radiant lock to gain.
l.117

8 Not louder shrieks to pitying heav'n are cast,
When husbands, or when lapdogs breathe their last.
l.157

9 Here in a grotto, shelter'd close from air,
And screen'd in shades from day's detested glare,
She sighs for ever on her pensive bed,
Pain at her side, and Megrim at her head.
c.iv, l.21

10 Sir Plume, of amber snuff-box justly vain,
And the nice conduct of a clouded cane.
l.123

11 Beauties in vain their pretty eyes may roll;
Charms strike the sight, but merit wins the soul.
c.v, l.33

12 Thou Great First Cause, least understood!
  Who all my sense confin'd
To know but this, that Thou art good,
  And that myself am blind.
The Universal Prayer

13 Teach me to feel another's woe,
  To hide the fault I see;
That mercy I to others show,
  That mercy show to me.

14 See! from the brake the whirring pheasant springs,
And mounts exulting on triumphant wings:
Short is his joy; he feels the fiery wound,
Flutters in blood, and panting beats the ground.
Ah! what avail his glossy, varying dyes,
His purple crest, and scarlet-circled eyes,
The vivid green his shining plumes unfold,
His painted wings and breast that flames with gold?
Windsor Forest, l.111

15 This is the Jew
That Shakespeare drew.
Of Macklin's performance of Shylock, 14 Feb. 1741. Baker, Reed
& Jones, *Biographia Dramatica* (1812), vol.I, pt.ii, p.469

16 Party-spirit, which at best is but the madness of many
for the gain of a few.
Letters. To E. Blount, 27 Aug. 1714

17 How often are we to die before we go quite off this
stage? In every friend we lose a part of ourselves, and
the best part.
To Swift, 5 Dec. 1732

18 To endeavour to work upon the vulgar with fine sense,
is like attempting to hew blocks with a razor.
Thoughts on Various Subjects (1706)

19 A man should never be ashamed to own he has been in
the wrong, which is but saying, in other words, that he
is wiser to-day than he was yesterday.

20 It is with narrow-souled people as with narrow-necked
bottles: the less they have in them, the more noise they
make in pouring it out.

21 When men grow virtuous in their old age, they only
make a sacrifice to God of the devil's leavings.

22 The most positive men are the most credulous.

23 Here am I, dying of a hundred good symptoms.
15 May 1744. Joseph Spence, *Anecdotes by and about Alexander
Pope,* p.637

SIR KARL POPPER 1902–

24 The open society and its enemies.
Book title (1945)

25 Piecemeal social engineering resembles physical
engineering in regarding the *ends* as beyond the
province of technology.
The Poverty of Historicism, III, 21

RICHARD PORSON 1759–1808

26 When Dido found Aeneas would not come,
She mourn'd in silence, and was Di-do-dum.
Epigram: On Latin Gerunds. J.S. Watson, *Life of Porson*
(1861), p.418

27 The Germans in Greek
Are sadly to seek:
Not five in five score,
But ninety-five more:
All, save only Herman,
And Herman's a German.
M.L. Clarke, *Life of Porson,* ch.vii

28 Madoc will be read,—when Homer and Virgil are
forgotten. [To Southey.]
Samuel Rogers, *Table Talk,* p.330

29 I went to Frankfort, and got drunk
With that most learn'd professor, Brunck;
I went to Worts, and got more drunken
With that more learn'd professor, Ruhnken.
Facetiae Cantabrigienses (1825)

30 Life is too short to learn German.
T.L. Peacock, *Gryll Grange,* ch.3

BEILBY PORTEUS 1731–1808

31   One murder made a villain,
Millions a hero.
Death (1759), l.155

32 War its thousands slays, Peace its ten thousands.
l.179

33   Teach him how to live,

And, oh! still harder lesson! how to die.
1.319

BEATRIX POTTER 1866–1943

1 Don't go into Mr McGregor's garden: your Father had
an accident there; he was put in a pie by Mrs
McGregor.
The Tale of Peter Rabbit (1902)

BISHOP HENRY CODMAN POTTER 1835–1908

2 We have exchanged the Washingtonian dignity for the
Jeffersonian simplicity, which in due time came to be
only another name for the Jacksonian vulgarity.
Address, Washington Centennial, 30 Apr. 1889

EUGÈNE POTTIER 1816–1887

3 *Debout! les damnés de la terre!*
    Debout! les forçats de la faim!
La raison tonne en son cratère,
    C'est l'éruption de la fin.
Du passé faisons table rase,
    Foule esclave, debout, debout,
Le monde va changer de base,
    Nous ne sommes rien, soyons tout!
        C'est la lutte finale
            Groupons-nous, et, demain,
            L'Internationale
            Sera le genre humain.
On your feet, you damned souls of the earth! On your
feet, inmates of hunger's prison! Reason is rumbling
in its crater, and its final eruption is on its way. Let
us wipe clean the slate of the past—on your feet,
you enslaved multitude, on your feet—the world is
to undergo a fundamental change: we are nothing,
let us be everything! This is the final conflict: let us
form up and, tomorrow, the International will
encompass the human race.
L'Internationale, in H.E. Piggot, *Songs that made History*
(1937), ch.6

EZRA POUND 1885–1972

4 Winter is icummen in,
Lhude sing Goddamm,
Raineth drop and staineth slop,
And how the wind doth ramm!
        Sing: Goddamm.
Ancient Music. See 7:18

5 Blue, blue is the grass about the river
And the willows have overfilled the close garden.
And within, the mistress, in the midmost of her youth,
White, white of face, hesitates, passing the door.
Slender, she puts forth a slender hand;

And she was a courtezan in the old days,
And she has married a sot,
Who now goes drunkenly out
And leaves her too much alone.
The Beautiful Toilet, By Mei Sheng B.C. 140

6 Hang it all, Robert Browning,
        there can but be the one 'Sordello'.
Cantos, 2

7 Palace in smoky light,

Troy but a heap of smouldering boundary stones.
4

8 *With Usura*

With usura hath no man a house of good stone
each block cut smooth and well fitting
that design might cover their face.
45

9 WITH USURA
wool comes not to market
sheep bringeth no gain with usura
Usura is a murrain, usura
blunteth the needle in the maid's hand
and stoppeth the spinner's cunning.

10 Usura rusteth the chisel
It rusteth the craft and the craftsman.

11 Azure hath a canker by usura; cramoisi is unbroidered
Emerald findeth no Memling
Usura slayeth the child in the womb
It stayeth the young man's courting
It hath brought palsey to bed, lyeth
between the young bride and her bridegroom
        CONTRA NATURA
They have brought whores for Eleusis
Corpses are set to banquet
at behest of usura.

12 What thou lovest well remains,
        the rest is dross
What thou lov'st well shall not be reft from thee
What thou lov'st well is thy true heritage.
81

13 The ant's a centaur in his dragon world.
Pull down thy vanity, it is not man
Made courage, or made order, or made grace.
        Pull down thy vanity, I say pull down.
Learn of the green world what can be thy place
In scaled invention or true artistry,
Pull down thy vanity,
                Paquin pull down!
The green casque has outdone your elegance.

14 But to have done instead of not doing
        this is not vanity
To have, with decency, knocked
That a Blunt should open
        To have gathered from the air a live tradition
or from a fine old eye the unconquered flame
This is not vanity.
        Here error is all in the not done,
all in the diffidence that faltered.

15 Yet you ask on what account I write so many
        love-lyrics
And whence this soft book comes into my mouth.
Neither Calliope nor Apollo sung these things into my
        ear,
        My genius is no more than a girl.
If she with ivory fingers drive a tune through the lyre,
        We look at the process.
How easy the moving fingers; if hair is mussed on her
        forehead,
If she goes in a gleam of Cos, in a slither of dyed
        stuff,
There is a volume in the matter.
Homage to Sextus Propertius (1917), V, 2

1 For three years, out of key with his time,
He strove to resuscitate the dead art
Of poetry; to maintain the 'sublime'
In the old sense.
Hugh Selwyn Mauberley, I

2 Bent resolutely on wringing lilies from the acorns;
Capaneus; trout for factitious bait.

3 His true Penelope was Flaubert,
He fished by obstinate isles;
Observed the elegance of Circe's hair
Rather than the mottoes on sun-dials.

4 Better mendacities
Than the classics in paraphrase!
II

5 The tea-rose tea-gown, etc.
Supplants the *mousseline* of Cos,
The pianola 'replaces'
Sappho's barbitos.
III

6 Christ follows Dionysus,
Phallic and ambrosial
Made way for macerations;
Caliban casts out Ariel.

7 All things are a flowing,
Sage Heracleitus says;
But a tawdry cheapness
Shall outlast our days.
See 246:5

8 Even the Christian beauty
Defects—after Samothrace;
We see τὸ καλόν
Decreed in the market place.

9 O bright Apollo,
τίν' ἄνδρα, τίν' ἥρωα, τινα θεόν,
What god, man, or hero
Shall I place a tin wreath upon!

10 There died a myriad,
And of the best, among them,
For an old bitch gone in the teeth,
For a botched civilization.
V

11 The apparition of these faces in the crowd;
Petals, on a wet, black bough.
Lustra (1915), **In a Station of the Metro**

12 I make a pact with you, Walt Whitman—
I have detested you long enough...
It was you that broke the new wood,
Now is a time for carving.
We have one sap and one root—
Let there be commerce between us.
A Pact

13 Even in my dreams you have denièd yourself to me
And sent me only your handmaids.
τὸ καλόν [Good]

14 Suddenly discovering in the eyes of the very beautiful
Normande cocotte
The eyes of the very learned British Museum assistant.
Pagani's, November 8

15 O woe, woe,
People are born and die,
We also shall be dead pretty soon

Therefore let us act as if we were dead already.
Mr. Housman's Message

16 At fourteen I married My Lord you.
I never laughed, being bashful.
Lowering my head, I looked at the wall.
Called to, a thousand times, I never looked back.

At fifteen I stopped scowling,
I desired my dust to be mingled with yours
Forever and forever and forever.
Why should I climb the look out?

At sixteen you departed,
You went into far Ku-to-yen, by the river of swirling
eddies,
And you have been gone five months.
The monkeys make sorrowful noise overhead.
The River Merchant's Wife: A Letter, By Rihaku

17 The leaves fall early this autumn, in wind.
The paired butterflies are already yellow with August
Over the grass in the West garden;
They hurt me. I grow older.
If you are coming down through the narrows of the
river Kiang,
Please let me know beforehand,
And I will come out to meet you
                    As far as Cho-fu-sa.

18 He hath not heart for harping, nor in ring-having
Nor winsomeness to wife, nor world's delight
Nor any whit else save the wave's slash,
Yet longing comes upon him to fare forth on the
water.
Bosque taketh blossom, cometh beauty of berries,
Fields to fairness, land fares brisker,
All this admonisheth man eager of mood,
The heart turns to travel so that he then thinks
On flood-ways to be far departing.
Cuckoo calleth with gloomy crying,
He singeth summerward, bodeth sorrow,
The bitter heart's blood.
The Seafarer. From the Anglo-Saxon

19 There come now no Kings nor Caesars
Nor gold-giving lords like those gone.
Howe'er in mirth most magnified,
Whoe'er lived in life most lordliest,
Drear all this excellence, delights undurable!
Waneth the watch, but the world holdeth.
Tomb hideth trouble. The blade is layed low.
Earthly glory ageth and seareth.

20 I had over-prepared the event,
        that much was ominous.
With middle-ageing care
        I had laid out just the right books.
I had almost turned down the pages.
Villanelle: the psychological hour

21 Music begins to atrophy when it departs too far from
the dance;...poetry begins to atrophy when it gets too
far from music.
ABC of Reading (1934), Warning

22 One of the pleasures of middle age is to *find out* that
one WAS right, and that one was much righter than
one knew at say 17 or 23.
ch.1, 2

23 Literature is news that STAYS news.
ch.2

1 Great literature is simply language charged with meaning to the utmost possible degree.
How to Read (1931), Pt.II

SIR JOHN POWELL 1645–1713

2 Let us consider the reason of the case. For nothing is law that is not reason.
Coggs v. Bernard, 2 Lord Raymond, 911

JOHN O'CONNOR POWER

3 The mules of politics: without pride of ancestry, or hope of posterity.
Quoted in H.H. Asquith, *Memories and Reflections*, i.123. See 185:41

WINTHROP MACKWORTH PRAED 1802–1839

4 My own Araminta, say 'No!'
A Letter of Advice

5 Of science and logic he chatters
  As fine and as fast as he can;
Though I am no judge of such matters,
  I'm sure he's a talented man.
The Talented Man

6 For all who understood admired,
  And some who did not understand them.
The Vicar

PRAYER BOOK 1662

7 It hath been the wisdom of the Church of England, ever since the first compiling of her Publick Liturgy, to keep the mean between the two extremes, of too much stiffness in refusing, and of too much easiness in admitting any variation from it.
The Preface

8 There was never any thing by the wit of man so well devised, or so sure established, which in continuance of time hath not been corrupted.
Concerning the Service of the Church

9 Dearly beloved brethren, the Scripture moveth us in sundry places to acknowledge and confess our manifold sins and wickedness; and that we should not dissemble nor cloke them before the face of Almighty God our heavenly Father; but confess them with an humble, lowly, penitent, and obedient heart.
Morning Prayer. After the beginning Sentences

10 I pray and beseech you, as many as are here present, to accompany me with a pure heart, and humble voice, unto the throne of the heavenly grace.

11 We have erred, and strayed from thy ways like lost sheep. We have followed too much the devices and desires of our own hearts.
General Confession

12 We have left undone those things which we ought to have done; And we have done those things which we ought not to have done; And there is no health in us.

13 Restore thou them that are penitent; According to thy promises declared unto mankind in Christ Jesu our Lord. And grant, O most merciful Father, for his sake; That we may hereafter live a godly, righteous, and sober life.

14 And forgive us our trespasses, As we forgive them that trespass against us.
The Lord's Prayer. See 64:24

15 Glory be to the Father, and to the Son: and to the Holy Ghost; As it was in the beginning, is now, and ever shall be: world without end. Amen.
Gloria. See 334:14

16 We praise thee, O God: we acknowledge thee to be the Lord.
All the earth doth worship thee: the Father everlasting.
To thee all Angels cry aloud: the Heavens, and all the Powers therein.
To thee Cherubin, and Seraphin: continually do cry,
Holy, Holy, Holy: Lord God of Sabaoth;
Heaven and earth are full of the Majesty: of thy Glory.
The glorious company of the Apostles: praise thee.
The goodly fellowship of the Prophets: praise thee.
The noble army of Martyrs: praise thee.
Te Deum. See 11:3

17 When thou hadst overcome the sharpness of death: thou didst open the Kingdom of Heaven to all believers.

18 Day by day: we magnify thee;
And we worship thy Name: ever world without end.
Vouchsafe, O Lord: to keep us this day without sin.
O Lord, have mercy upon us: have mercy upon us.
O Lord, let thy mercy lighten upon us: as our trust is in thee.
O Lord, in thee have I trusted: let me never be confounded.
See 11:4

19 O all ye Works of the Lord, bless ye the Lord.
Benedicite. See 83:16

20 O ye Waters that be above the Firmament, bless ye the Lord.

21 O ye Showers, and Dew, bless ye the Lord: praise him, and magnify him for ever.
O ye Winds of God, bless ye the Lord: praise him, and magnify him for ever.

22 O ye Dews, and Frosts, bless ye the Lord: praise him, and magnify him for ever.
O ye Frost and Cold, bless ye the Lord: praise him and magnify him for ever.
O ye Ice and Snow, bless ye the Lord: praise him and magnify him for ever.
O ye Nights, and Days, bless ye the Lord: praise him, and magnify him for ever.

23 O let the Earth bless the Lord: yea, let it praise him, and magnify him for ever.

24 O all ye Green Things upon the Earth, bless ye the Lord: praise him, and magnify him for ever.

25 O ye Whales, and all that move in the Waters, bless ye the Lord: praise him, and magnify him for ever.

26 I believe in God the Father Almighty, Maker of heaven and earth: And in Jesus Christ his only Son our Lord, Who was conceived by the Holy Ghost, Born of the Virgin Mary, Suffered under Pontius Pilate, Was crucified, dead, and buried, He descended into hell; The third day he rose again from the dead, He ascended into heaven, And sitteth on the right hand of God the Father Almighty; From thence he shall come to judge the quick and the dead.
I believe in the Holy Ghost; The holy Catholick Church; The Communion of Saints; The Forgiveness

of sins; The Resurrection of the body, And the life everlasting. Amen.
The Apostles' Creed. See 334:20, 387:10

1 Give peace in our time, O Lord.
Versicle

2 O God, who art the author of peace and lover of concord, in knowledge of whom standeth our eternal life, whose service is perfect freedom; Defend us thy humble servants in all assaults of our enemies.
Second Collect, for Peace

3 Grant that this day we fall into no sin, neither run into any kind of danger.
Third Collect, for Grace

4 In Quires and Places where they sing, here followeth the Anthem.
Rubric after Third Collect

5 Endue her plenteously with heavenly gifts; grant her in health and wealth long to live.
Prayer for the Queen's Majesty

6 Almighty God, the fountain of all goodness.
Prayer for the Royal Family

7 Almighty and everlasting God, who alone workest great marvels; Send down upon our Bishops, and Curates, and all Congregations committed to their charge, the healthful Spirit of thy grace; and that they may truly please thee, pour upon them the continual dew of thy blessing.
Prayer for the Clergy and People

8 Almighty God, who hast given us grace at this time with one accord to make our common supplications unto thee; and dost promise, that when two or three are gathered together in thy Name thou wilt grant their requests: Fulfil now, O Lord, the desires and petitions of thy servants, as may be most expedient for them.
Prayer of St. Chrysostom

9 O God, from whom all holy desires, all good counsels, and all just works do proceed; Give unto thy servants that peace which the world cannot give.
Evening Prayer. Second Collect

10 Lighten our darkness, we beseech thee, O Lord; and by thy great mercy defend us from all perils and dangers of this night.
Third Collect

11 Whosoever will be saved: before all things it is necessary that he hold the Catholick Faith.
At Morning Prayer. Athanasian Creed. *Quicunque vult*

12 And the Catholick Faith is this: That we worship one God in Trinity, and Trinity in Unity;
Neither confounding the Persons: nor dividing the Substance.

13 There are not three incomprehensibles, nor three uncreated: but one uncreated, and one incomprehensible.

14 Perfect God, and perfect Man: of a reasonable soul and human flesh subsisting; Equal to the Father, as touching his Godhead: and inferior to the Father, as touching his Manhood.

15 Have mercy upon us miserable sinners.
The Litany

16 From all evil and mischief; from sin, from the crafts and assaults of the devil; from thy wrath, and from everlasting damnation,

Good Lord, deliver us.
From all blindness of heart; from pride, vain-glory, and hypocrisy; from envy, hatred, and malice, and from all uncharitableness,
Good Lord, deliver us.
From fornication, and all other deadly sin; and from all the deceits of the world, the flesh, and the devil,
Good Lord, deliver us.
From lightning and tempest; from plague, pestilence, and famine; from battle and murder, and from sudden death,
Good Lord, deliver us.

17 By thine Agony and bloody Sweat; by thy Cross and Passion; by thy precious Death and Burial; by thy glorious Resurrection and Ascension; and by the coming of the Holy Ghost,
Good Lord, deliver us.
In all time of our tribulation; in all time of our wealth; in the hour of death, and in the day of judgement,
Good Lord, deliver us.

18 That it may please thee to illuminate all Bishops, Priests, and Deacons, with true knowledge and understanding of thy Word; and that both by their preaching and living they may set it forth, and show it accordingly;
We beseech thee to hear us, good Lord.

19 That it may please thee to strengthen such as do stand; and to comfort and help the weak-hearted; and to raise up them that fall; and finally to beat down Satan under our feet;
We beseech thee to hear us, good Lord.

20 That it may please thee to preserve all that travel by land or by water, all women labouring of child, all sick persons, and young children; and to shew thy pity upon all prisoners and captives;
We beseech thee to hear us, good Lord.
That it may please thee to defend, and provide for, the fatherless children, and widows, and all that are desolate and oppressed;
We beseech thee to hear us, good Lord.

21 That it may please thee to give and preserve to our use the kindly fruits of the earth, so as in due time we may enjoy them;
We beseech thee to hear us, good Lord.

22 O God, merciful Father, that despisest not the sighing of a contrite heart, nor the desire of such as be sorrowful; Mercifully assist our prayers that we make before thee in all our troubles and adversities, whensoever they oppress us.

23 O God, whose nature and property is ever to have mercy and to forgive, receive our humble petitions; and though we be tied and bound by the chain of our sins, yet let the pitifulness of thy great mercy loose us; for the honour of Jesus Christ, our Mediator and Advocate.
Prayers and Thanksgivings, upon Several Occasions

24 O God, the Creator and Preserver of all mankind, we humbly beseech thee for all sorts and conditions of men.
Collect or Prayer for all Conditions of Men

25 We pray for the good estate of the Catholick Church; that it may be so guided and governed by thy good Spirit, that all who profess and call themselves

Christians may be led into the way of truth.

1 We commend to thy fatherly goodness all those, who are any ways afflicted, or distressed, in mind, body, or estate; that it may please thee to comfort and relieve them, according to their several necessities, giving them patience under their sufferings, and a happy issue out of all their afflictions.

2 We bless thee for our creation, preservation, and all the blessings of this life; but above all, for thine inestimable love in the redemption of the world by our Lord Jesus Christ; for the means of grace, and for the hope of glory.
General Thanksgiving

3 O God our heavenly Father, who by thy gracious providence dost cause the former and the latter rain to descend upon the earth, that it may bring forth fruit for the use of man; We give thee humble thanks that it hath pleased thee, in our great necessity, to send us at the last a joyful rain upon thine inheritance, and to refresh it when it was dry.
Thanksgiving for Rain

4 Almighty God, give us grace that we may cast away the works of darkness, and put upon us the armour of light, now in the time of this mortal life, in which thy Son Jesus Christ came to visit us in great humility.
Collects. 1st Sunday in Advent

5 Blessed Lord, who hast caused all holy Scriptures to be written for our learning; Grant that we may in such wise hear them read, mark, learn, and inwardly digest them, that by patience, and comfort of thy holy Word, we may embrace, and ever hold fast the blessed hope of everlasting life.
2nd Sunday in Advent

6 That whereas, through our sins and wickedness, we are sore let and hindered in running the race that is set before us, thy bountiful grace and mercy may speedily help and deliver us.
4th Sunday in Advent

7 O Lord, we beseech thee mercifully to receive the prayers of thy people which call upon thee; and grant that they may both perceive and know what things they ought to do, and also may have grace and power faithfully to fulfil the same.
1st Sunday after Epiphany

8 O God, who knowest us to be set in the midst of so many and great dangers, that by reason of the frailty of our nature we cannot always stand upright; Grant to us such strength and protection, as may support us in all dangers, and carry us through all temptations.
4th Sunday after Epiphany

9 Almighty God, who seest that we have no power of ourselves to help ourselves; Keep us both outwardly in our bodies, and inwardly in our souls; that we may be defended from all adversities which may happen to the body, and from all evil thoughts which may assault and hurt the soul.
2nd Sunday in Lent

10 We humbly beseech thee, that, as by thy special grace preventing us thou dost put into our minds good desires, so by thy continued help we may bring the same to good effect.
Easter Day

11 Grant us so to put away the leaven of malice and wickedness, that we may alway serve thee in pureness of living and truth.
1st Sunday after Easter

12 O Almighty God, who alone canst order the unruly wills and affections of sinful men; Grant unto thy people, that they may love the thing which thou commandest, and desire that which thou dost promise; that so, among the sundry and manifold changes of the world, our hearts may surely there be fixed, where true joys are to be found.
4th Sunday after Easter

13 We beseech thee, leave us not comfortless; but send to us thine Holy Ghost to comfort us, and exalt us unto the same place whither our Saviour Christ is gone before.
Sunday after Ascension Day

14 God, who as at this time, didst teach the hearts of thy faithful people, by the sending to them the light of thy Holy Spirit; Grant us by the same Spirit to have a right judgement in all things.
Whit-Sunday

15 Because through the weakness of our mortal nature we can do no good thing without thee, grant us the help of thy grace, that in keeping of thy commandments we may please thee, both in will and deed.
1st Sunday after Trinity

16 O God, the protector of all that trust in thee, without whom nothing is strong, nothing is holy; Increase and multiply upon us thy mercy; that, thou being our ruler and guide, we may so pass through things temporal, that we finally lose not the things eternal.
4th Sunday after Trinity

17 Grant, O Lord, we beseech thee, that the course of this world may be so peaceably ordered by thy governance, that thy Church may joyfully serve thee in all godly quietness.
5th Sunday after Trinity

18 O God, who hast prepared for them that love thee such good things as pass man's understanding; Pour into our hearts such love toward thee, that we, loving thee above all things, may obtain thy promises, which exceed all that we can desire.
6th Sunday after Trinity

19 Lord of all power and might, who art the author and giver of all good things; Graft in our hearts the love of thy Name, increase in us true religion, nourish us with all goodness, and of thy great mercy keep us in the same.
7th Sunday after Trinity

20 Pour down upon us the abundance of thy mercy; forgiving us those things whereof our conscience is afraid.
12th Sunday after Trinity

21 O God, forasmuch as without thee we are not able to please thee; Mercifully grant, that thy Holy Spirit may in all things direct and rule our hearts.
19th Sunday after Trinity

22 Grant, we beseech thee, merciful Lord, to thy faithful people pardon and peace, that they may be cleansed from all their sins, and serve thee with a quiet mind.
21st Sunday after Trinity

23 Lord, we beseech thee to keep thy household the

Church in continual godliness.
22nd Sunday after Trinity

1 Grant that those things which we ask faithfully we may obtain effectually.
23rd Sunday after Trinity

2 Stir up, we beseech thee, O Lord, the wills of thy faithful people; that they, plenteously bringing forth the fruit of good works, may of thee be plenteously rewarded.
25th Sunday after Trinity

3 Give us grace, that, being not like children carried away with every blast of vain doctrine, we may be established in the truth of thy holy Gospel.
St. Mark's Day. 25 April

4 O Almighty God, who hast knit together thine elect in one communion and fellowship, in the mystical body of thy Son Christ our Lord; Grant us grace so to follow thy blessed Saints in all virtuous and godly living, that we may come to those unspeakable joys, which thou hast prepared for them that unfeignedly love thee.
All Saints' Day. 1 November

5 So many as intend to be partakers of the holy Communion shall signify their names to the Curate, at least some time the day before.
And if any of those be an open and notorious evil liver, or have done any wrong to his neighbours by word or deed, so that the Congregation be thereby offended; the Curate, having knowledge thereof, shall call him and advertise him, that in any wise he presume not to come to the Lord's Table, until he have openly declared himself to have truly repented and amended his former naughty life.
Holy Communion. Introductory rubric

6 The Table, at the Communion-time having a fair white linen cloth upon it, shall stand in the Body of the Church, or in the Chancel.

7 Almighty God, unto whom all hearts be open, all desires known, and from whom no secrets are hid; Cleanse the thoughts of our hearts by the inspiration of thy Holy Spirit, that we may perfectly love thee, and worthily magnify thy holy Name.
Collect

8 Incline our hearts to keep this law.
Response to Commandments

9 Thou shalt do no murder.
6th Commandment. See 47:24

10 I believe in one God the Father Almighty, Maker of heaven and earth, And of all things visible and invisible:
And in one Lord Jesus Christ, the only-begotten Son of God, Begotten of his Father before all worlds, God of God, Light of Light, Very God of very God, Begotten, not made, Being of one substance with the Father, By whom all things were made.
Nicene Creed. See 334:20, 384:26

11 And I believe in the Holy Ghost, the Lord and giver of life, Who proceedeth from the Father and the Son, Who with the Father and the Son together is worshipped and glorified, Who spake by the Prophets. And I believe one Catholick and Apostolick Church.

12 Let us pray for the whole state of Christ's Church militant here in earth.
Prayer for the Church Militant

13 We humbly beseech thee most mercifully to accept our alms and oblations, and to receive these our prayers, which we offer unto thy Divine Majesty; beseeching thee to inspire continually the universal Church with the spirit of truth, unity, and concord: And grant, that all they that do confess thy holy Name may agree in the truth of thy holy Word, and live in unity, and godly love.

14 Grant unto her whole Council, and to all that are put in authority under her, that they may truly and indifferently minister justice.
(Of the Queen's government.)

15 Give grace, O heavenly Father, to all Bishops and Curates, that they may both by their life and doctrine set forth thy true and lively Word.

16 We most humbly beseech thee of thy goodness, O Lord, to comfort and succour all them, who in this transitory life are in trouble, sorrow, need, sickness, or any other adversity. And we also bless thy holy Name for all thy servants departed this life in thy faith and fear.

17 Because it is requisite, that no man should come to the holy Communion, but with a full trust in God's mercy, and with a quiet conscience; therefore if there be any of you, who by this means cannot quiet his own conscience herein, but requireth further comfort or counsel, let him come to me, or to some other discreet and learned Minister of God's Word, and open his grief.
First Exhortation

18 Ye that do truly and earnestly repent you of your sins, and are in love and charity with your neighbours, and intend to lead a new life, following the commandments of God, and walking from henceforth in his holy ways; Draw near with faith, and take this holy Sacrament to your comfort; and make your humble confession to Almighty God, meekly kneeling upon your knees.
The Invitation

19 We do earnestly repent, And are heartily sorry for these our misdoings; The remembrance of them is grievous unto us; The burden of them is intolerable.
General Confession

20 Hear what comfortable words our Saviour Christ saith unto all that truly turn to him.
The Comfortable Words

21 Lift up your hearts.
Versicles and Responses. See 335:2

22 It is meet and right so to do.

23 It is very meet, right, and our bounden duty, that we should at all times, and in all places, give thanks unto thee, O Lord, Holy Father, Almighty, Everlasting God.
Therefore with Angels and Archangels, and with all the company of heaven, we laud and magnify thy glorious Name; evermore praising thee, and saying, Holy, holy, holy, Lord God of hosts, heaven and earth are full of thy glory: Glory be to thee, O Lord most High.
Hymn of Praise. See 81:24, 335:3

24 Almighty God, our heavenly Father, who of thy

tender mercy didst give thine only Son Jesus Christ to suffer death upon the cross for our redemption; who made there (by his one oblation of himself once offered) a full, perfect, and sufficient sacrifice, oblation, and satisfaction, for the sins of the whole world.
Prayer of Consecration

1 Who, in the same night that he was betrayed, took Bread; and, when he had given thanks, he brake it, and gave it to his disciples, saying, Take, eat, this is my Body which is given for you: Do this in remembrance of me. Likewise after supper he took the Cup; and, when he had given thanks, he gave it to them, saying, Drink ye all of this; for this is my Blood of the New Testament, which is shed for you and for many for the remission of sins: Do this, as oft as ye shall drink it, in remembrance of me.

2 Although we be unworthy, through our manifold sins, to offer unto thee any sacrifice, yet we beseech thee to accept this our bounden duty and service; not weighing our merits, but pardoning our offences.
1st Prayer of Oblation

3 We are very members incorporate in the mystical body of thy Son, which is the blessed company of all faithful people; and are also heirs through hope of thy everlasting kingdom.
2nd (alternative) Prayer of Oblation

4 The blessing of God Almighty, the Father, the Son, and the Holy Ghost, be amongst you and remain with you always.
The Blessing

5 Assist us mercifully, O Lord, in these our supplications and prayers, and dispose the way of thy servants towards the attainment of everlasting salvation; that, among all the changes and chances of this mortal life, they may ever be defended by thy most gracious and ready help.
Collects after the Offertory, 1

6 Prevent us, O Lord, in all our doings with thy most gracious favour, and further us with thy continual help; that in all our works, begun, continued, and ended in thee, we may glorify thy holy Name.
4

7 Those things, which for our unworthiness we dare not, and for our blindness we cannot ask, vouchsafe to give us, for the worthiness of thy Son Jesus Christ our Lord.
5

8 It is expedient that Baptism be administered in the vulgar tongue.
Publick Baptism of Infants. Introductory rubric

9 O merciful God, grant that the old Adam in this Child may be so buried, that the new man may be raised up in him.
Invocation of blessing on the child

10 Humbly we beseech thee to grant, that he, being dead unto sin, and living unto righteousness, and being buried with Christ in his death, may crucify the old man, and utterly abolish the whole body of sin.
Thanksgiving

11 And as for you, who have now by Baptism put on Christ, it is your part and duty also, being made the children of God and of the light, by faith in Jesus

Christ, to walk answerably to your Christian calling, and as becometh the children of light.
Publick Baptism of Such as are of Riper Years. Priest's final address

12 Question. What is your Name?
Answer. N or M.
Question. Who gave you this Name?
Answer. My Godfathers and Godmothers in my Baptism; wherein I was made a member of Christ, the child of God, and an inheritor of the kingdom of heaven.
Catechism

13 I should renounce the devil and all his works, the pomps and vanity of this wicked world, and all the sinful lusts of the flesh.

14 Question. What dost thou chiefly learn by these Commandments?
Answer. I learn two things: my duty towards God, and my duty to my Neighbour.

15 My duty towards my Neighbour, is to love him as myself, and to do to all men, as I would they should do unto me.

16 To submit myself to all my governors, teachers, spiritual pastors and masters.

17 To keep my hands from picking and stealing, and my tongue from evil-speaking, lying, and slandering.

18 Not to covet nor desire other men's goods; but to learn and labour truly to get mine own living, and to do my duty in that state of life, unto which it shall please God to call me.

19 Question. How many Sacraments hath Christ ordained in his Church?
Answer. Two only, as generally necessary to salvation, that is to say, Baptism, and the Supper of the Lord.
Question. What meanest thou by this word Sacrament?
Answer. I mean an outward and visible sign of an inward and spiritual grace.

20 Our help is in the name of the Lord;
Who hath made heaven and earth.
Order of Confirmation. See 398:9

21 Lord, hear our prayers.
And let our cry come unto thee.

22 Defend, O Lord, this thy Child [or this thy Servant] with thy heavenly grace, that he may continue thine for ever; and daily increase in thy holy Spirit more and more, until he come unto thy everlasting kingdom.

23 If any of you know cause, or just impediment, why these two persons should not be joined together in holy Matrimony, ye are to declare it. This is the first [second, or third] time of asking.
Solemnization of Matrimony. The Banns

24 Dearly beloved, we are gathered together here in the sight of God, and in the face of this congregation, to join together this Man and this Woman in holy Matrimony.
Exhortation

25 Which holy estate Christ adorned and beautified with his presence, and first miracle that he wrought, in Cana of Galilee; and is commended of Saint Paul to be honourable among all men: and therefore not by any to be enterprised, nor taken in hand, unadvisedly, lightly,

or wantonly, to satisfy men's carnal lusts and appetites, like brute beasts that have no understanding.

1 First, It was ordained for the procreation of children, to be brought up in the fear and nurture of the Lord, and to the praise of his holy Name.

2 If any man can shew any just cause, why they may not lawfully be joined together, let him now speak, or else hereafter for ever hold his peace.

3 Wilt thou have this Woman to thy wedded wife, to live together after God's ordinance in the holy estate of Matrimony? Wilt thou love her, comfort her, honour, and keep her in sickness and in health; and, forsaking all other, keep thee only unto her, so long as ye both shall live?
Betrothal

4 I *N* take thee *N* to my wedded husband, to have and to hold from this day forward, for better for worse, for richer for poorer, in sickness and in health, to love, cherish, and to obey, till death us do part, according to God's holy ordinance; and thereto I give thee my troth.
The Man will have used the words 'I plight thee my troth' and not 'to obey'.

5 With this Ring I thee wed, with my body I thee worship, and with all my worldly goods I thee endow.
Wedding

6 Those whom God hath joined together let no man put asunder.

7 Forasmuch as *N* and *N* have consented together in holy wedlock, and have witnessed the same before God and this company, and thereto have given and pledged their troth either to other, and have declared the same by giving and receiving of a Ring, and by joining of hands; I pronounce that they be Man and Wife together.
Minister's declaration

8 Peace be to this house, and to all that dwell in it.
Visitation of the Sick

9 Unto God's gracious mercy and protection we commit thee.

10 The Office ensuing is not to be used for any that die unbaptized, or excommunicate, or have laid violent hands upon themselves.
Burial of the Dead. Introductory rubric

11 Man that is born of a woman hath but a short time to live, and is full of misery.
First anthem. See 52:26

12 In the midst of life we are in death.

13 Forasmuch as it hath pleased Almighty God of his great mercy to take unto himself the soul of our dear brother here departed, we therefore commit his body to the ground; earth to earth, ashes to ashes, dust to dust; in sure and certain hope of the Resurrection to eternal life, through our Lord Jesus Christ; who shall change our vile body, that it may be like unto his glorious body, according to the mighty working, whereby he is able to subdue all things to himself.
Interment

14 Blessed is the man that hath not walked in the counsel of the ungodly, nor stood in the way of sinners: and hath not sat in the seat of the scornful.
Psalms 1:1

15 Why do the heathen so furiously rage together: and why do the people imagine a vain thing?
2:1

16 Let us break their bonds asunder: and cast away their cords from us.
3

17 The Lord shall have them in derision.
4

18 Thou shalt bruise them with a rod of iron: and break them in pieces like a potter's vessel.
9

19 Kiss the Son, lest he be angry, and so ye perish from the right way: if his wrath be kindled, (yea, but a little,) blessed are all they that put their trust in him.
12

20 Stand in awe, and sin not: commune with your own heart, and in your chamber, and be still.
4:4

21 Lord, lift thou up: the light of thy countenance upon us.
7

22 I will lay me down in peace, and take my rest.
9

23 The Lord will abhor both the bloodthirsty and deceitful man.
5:6

24 Make thy way plain before my face.
8

25 Let them perish through their own imaginations.
11

26 I am weary of my groaning; every night wash I my bed: and water my couch with my tears.
6:6

27 Away from me, all ye that work vanity.
8

28 Out of the mouth of very babes and sucklings hast thou ordained strength, because of thine enemies: that thou mightest still the enemy, and the avenger.
For I will consider thy heavens, even the works of thy fingers: the moon and the stars, which thou hast ordained.
What is man, that thou art mindful of him: and the son of man, that thou visitest him?
Thou madest him lower than the angels: to crown him with glory and worship.
8:2

29 Up, Lord, and let not man have the upper hand.
9:19

30 He that said in his heart, Tush, I shall never be cast down: there shall no harm happen unto me.
10:6

31 Upon the ungodly he shall rain snares, fire and brimstone, storm and tempest: this shall be their portion to drink.
11:7

32 Help me, Lord, for there is not one godly man left: for the faithful are minished from among the children of men.
They talk of vanity every one with his neighbour: they do but flatter with their lips, and dissemble in their double heart.
12:1

1 How long wilt thou forget me, O Lord, for ever: how long wilt thou hide thy face from me?
13:1

2 The fool hath said in his heart: There is no God. They are corrupt, and become abominable in their doings: there is none that doeth good, no not one.
14:1

3 They are all gone out of the way, they are altogether become abominable.
4

4 Lord, who shall dwell in thy tabernacle: or who shall rest upon thy holy hill?
Even he, that leadeth an uncorrupt life: and doeth the thing which is right, and speaketh the truth from his heart.
He that hath used no deceit in his tongue, nor done evil to his neighbour: and hath not slandered his neighbour.
15:1

5 He that sweareth unto his neighbour, and disappointeth him not: though it were to his own hindrance.
He that hath not given his money upon usury: nor taken reward against the innocent.
Whoso doeth these things: shall never fall.
5

6 The lot is fallen unto me in a fair ground: yea, I have a goodly heritage.
16:7. The Authorized Version of the Bible (Psalms 16:6) has 'The lines are fallen unto me in pleasant places'.

7 Thou shalt not leave my soul in hell: neither shalt thou suffer thy Holy One to see corruption.
11

8 He rode upon the cherubims, and did fly: he came flying upon the wings of the wind.
18:10

9 At the brightness of his presence his clouds removed: hailstones, and coals of fire.
12

10 With the help of my God I shall leap over the wall.
29

11 The heavens declare the glory of God: and the firmament sheweth his handy-work.
One day telleth another: and one night certifieth another.
There is neither speech nor language: but their voices are heard among them.
Their sound is gone out into all lands: and their words into the ends of the world.
In them hath he set a tabernacle for the sun: which cometh forth as a bridegroom out of his chamber, and rejoiceth as a giant to run his course.
19:1

12 The law of the Lord is an undefiled law, converting the soul: the testimony of the Lord is sure, and giveth wisdom unto the simple.
The statutes of the Lord are right, and rejoice the heart: the commandment of the Lord is pure, and giveth light unto the eyes.
The fear of the Lord is clean, and endureth for ever: the judgements of the Lord are true, and righteous altogether.
More to be desired are they than gold, yea, than much fine gold: sweeter also than honey, and the honey-comb.
7

13 Who can tell how oft he offendeth: O cleanse thou me from my secret faults.
Keep thy servant also from presumptuous sins, lest they get the dominion over me: so shall I be undefiled, and innocent from the great offence.
Let the words of my mouth, and the meditation of my heart: be alway acceptable in thy sight,
O Lord: my strength, and my redeemer.
12

14 Some put their trust in chariots, and some in horses: but we will remember the Name of the Lord our God.
20:7

15 They intended mischief against thee: and imagined such a device as they are not able to perform.
21:11

16 My God, my God, look upon me; why hast thou forsaken me: and art so far from my health, and from the words of my complaint?
O my God, I cry in the day-time, but thou hearest not: and in the night-season also I take no rest.
22:1. See 68:24

17 But as for me, I am a worm, and no man: a very scorn of men, and the out-cast of the people.
All they that see me laugh me to scorn: they shoot out their lips, and shake their heads, saying,
He trusted in God, that he would deliver him: let him deliver him, if he will have him.
6

18 Many oxen are come about me: fat bulls of Basan close me in on every side.
12

19 I am poured out like water, and all my bones are out of joint: my heart also in the midst of my body is even like melting wax.
14

20 They pierced my hands and my feet; I may tell all my bones: they stand staring and looking upon me.
They part my garments among them: and cast lots upon my vesture.
17

21 The Lord is my shepherd: therefore can I lack nothing.
He shall feed me in a green pasture: and lead me forth beside the waters of comfort.
23:1

22 Yea, though I walk through the valley of the shadow of death, I will fear no evil: for thou art with me; thy rod and thy staff comfort me.
Thou shalt prepare a table before me against them that trouble me: thou hast anointed my head with oil, and my cup shall be full.
But thy loving-kindness and mercy shall follow me all the days of my life: and I will dwell in the house of the Lord for ever.
4

23 The earth is the Lord's, and all that therein is: the compass of the world, and they that dwell therein.
24:1

24 Lift up your heads, O ye gates, and be ye lift up, ye everlasting doors: and the King of glory shall come in.
Who is the King of glory: it is the Lord strong and

mighty, even the Lord mighty in battle.
7

1 Even the Lord of hosts, he is the King of glory.
10

2 O remember not the sins and offences of my youth.
25:6

3 Deliver Israel, O God: out of all his troubles.
21

4 Examine me, O Lord, and prove me: try out my reins and my heart.
26:2

5 I will wash my hands in innocency, O Lord: and so will I go to thine altar;
That I may shew the voice of thanksgiving: and tell of all thy wondrous works.
6

6 My foot standeth right: I will praise the Lord in the congregation.
12

7 The Lord is my light, and my salvation; whom then shall I fear: the Lord is the strength of my life; of whom then shall I be afraid?
27:1. See 83:5

8 Teach me thy way, O Lord: and lead me in the right way, because of mine enemies.
13

9 I should utterly have fainted: but that I believe verily to see the goodness of the Lord in the land of the living.
15

10 The voice of the Lord breaketh the cedar-trees: yea, the Lord breaketh the cedars of Libanus.
He maketh them also to skip like a calf: Libanus also, and Sirion, like a young unicorn.
29:5

11 The voice of the Lord maketh the hinds to bring forth young, and discovereth the thick bushes.
8

12 The Lord shall give strength unto his people: the Lord shall give his people the blessing of peace.
10

13 Sing praises unto the Lord, O ye saints of his: and give thanks unto him for a remembrance of his holiness.
For his wrath endureth but the twinkling of an eye, and in his pleasure is life: heaviness may endure for a night, but joy cometh in the morning.
30:4

14 Then cried I unto thee, O Lord: and gat me to my Lord right humbly.
8

15 Into thy hands I commend my spirit.
31:6. See 71:14

16 Blessed is the man unto whom the Lord imputeth no sin: and in whose spirit there is no guile.
For while I held my tongue: my bones consumed away through my daily complaining.
32:2

17 For this shall every one that is godly make his prayer unto thee, in a time when thou mayest be found: but in the great water-floods they shall not come nigh him.
7

18 I will inform thee, and teach thee in the way wherein thou shalt go: and I will guide thee with mine eye.
Be ye not like to horse and mule, which have no understanding: whose mouths must be held with bit and bridle, lest they fall upon thee.
Great plagues remain for the ungodly: but whoso putteth his trust in the Lord, mercy embraceth him on every side.
9

19 Sing unto the Lord a new song: sing praises lustily unto him with a good courage.
33:3

20 A horse is counted but a vain thing to save a man: neither shall he deliver any man by his great strength.
16

21 O taste and see, how gracious the Lord is: blessed is the man that trusteth in him.
34:8

22 The lions do lack, and suffer hunger: but they who seek the Lord shall want no manner of thing that is good.
10

23 What man is he that lusteth to live: and would fain see good days?
Keep thy tongue from evil: and thy lips, that they speak no guile.
Eschew evil, and do good: seek peace, and ensue it.
12

24 They rewarded me evil for good: to the great discomfort of my soul.
35:12

25 O deliver my soul from the calamities which they bring on me, and my darling from the lions.
17

26 Fret not thyself because of the ungodly.
37:1

27 The meek-spirited shall possess the earth: and shall be refreshed in the multitude of peace.
11

28 I have been young, and now am old: and yet saw I never the righteous forsaken, nor his seed begging their bread.
25

29 I myself have seen the ungodly in great power: and flourishing like a green bay-tree.
I went by, and lo, he was gone: I sought him, but his place could no where be found.
Keep innocency, and take heed unto the thing that is right: for that shall bring a man peace at the last.
36

30 I held my tongue, and spake nothing: I kept silence, yea, even from good words; but it was pain and grief to me.
My heart was hot within me, and while I was thus musing the fire kindled: and at the last I spake with my tongue;
Lord, let me know mine end, and the number of my days: that I may be certified how long I have to live.
39:3

31 For man walketh in a vain shadow, and disquieteth himself in vain: he heapeth up riches, and cannot tell who shall gather them.
7

1 I waited patiently for the Lord: and he inclined unto me, and heard my calling.
He brought me also out of the horrible pit, out of the mire and clay: and set my feet upon the rock, and ordered my goings.
40:1

2 Sacrifice, and meat-offering, thou wouldest not: but mine ears hast thou opened.
Burnt-offerings, and sacrifice for sin, hast thou not required: then said I, Lo, I come.
In the volume of the book it is written of me, that I should fulfil thy will, O my God.
8

3 Thou art my helper and redeemer: make no long tarrying, O my God.
21

4 Blessed is he that considereth the poor and needy: the Lord shall deliver him in the time of trouble.
41:1

5 Yea, even mine own familiar friend, whom I trusted: who did also eat of my bread, hath laid great wait for me.
9. The Authorized Version of the Bible has '...hath lifted up his heel against me'.

6 Like as the hart desireth the water-brooks: so longeth my soul after thee, O God.
42:1

7 Why art thou so full of heaviness, O my soul: and why art thou so disquieted within me?
6

8 My God, my soul is vexed within me: therefore will I remember thee concerning the land of Jordan, and the little hill of Hermon.
One deep calleth another, because of the noise of the water-pipes: all thy waves and storms are gone over me.
8

9 I will say unto the God of my strength, Why hast thou forgotten me: why go I thus heavily, while the enemy oppresseth me?
My bones are smitten asunder as with a sword: while mine enemies that trouble me cast me in the teeth;
Namely, while they say daily unto me: Where is now thy God?
11. See 234:13

10 Give sentence with me, O God, and defend my cause against the ungodly people: O deliver me from the deceitful and wicked man.
43:1

11 O send out thy light and thy truth, that they may lead me: and bring me unto thy holy hill, and to thy dwelling.
And that I may go unto the altar of God, even unto the God of my joy and gladness: and upon the harp will I give thanks unto thee, O God, my God.
3

12 O put thy trust in God: for I will yet give him thanks, which is the help of my countenance, and my God.
6

13 We have heard with our ears, O God, our fathers have told us: what thou hast done in their time of old.
44:1

14 My heart is inditing of a good matter: I speak of the

things which I have made unto the King.
My tongue is the pen: of a ready writer.
45:1

15 Thou hast loved righteousness, and hated iniquity: wherefore God, even thy God, hath anointed thee with the oil of gladness above thy fellows.
8

16 Kings' daughters were among thy honourable women: upon thy right hand did stand the queen in a vesture of gold, wrought about with divers colours.
10

17 The King's daughter is all glorious within: her clothing is of wrought gold.
She shall be brought unto the King in raiment of needlework: the virgins that be her fellows shall bear her company, and shall be brought unto thee.
14

18 Instead of thy fathers thou shalt have children: whom thou mayest make princes in all lands.
17

19 God is our hope and strength: a very present help in trouble.
Therefore will we not fear, though the earth be moved: and though the hills be carried into the midst of the sea.
46:1

20 God is in the midst of her, therefore shall she not be removed: God shall help her, and that right early.
The heathen make much ado, and the kingdoms are moved: but God hath shewed his voice, and the earth shall melt away.
The Lord of hosts is with us: the God of Jacob is our refuge.
5

21 He maketh wars to cease in all the world: he breaketh the bow, and knappeth the spear in sunder, and burneth the chariots in the fire.
Be still then, and know that I am God: I will be exalted among the heathen, and I will be exalted in the earth.
9

22 O clap your hands together, all ye people: O sing unto God with the voice of melody.
47:1

23 He shall subdue the people under us: and the nations under our feet.
3

24 God is gone up with a merry noise: and the Lord with the sound of the trump.
5

25 For lo, the kings of the earth: are gathered, and gone by together.
They marvelled to see such things: they were astonished, and suddenly cast down.
48:3

26 Thou shalt break the ships of the sea: through the east-wind.
6

27 Walk about Sion, and go round about her: and tell the towers thereof.
Mark well her bulwarks, set up her houses: that ye may tell them that come after.
11

28 Wise men also die, and perish together: as well as the

ignorant and foolish, and leave their riches for other.
And yet they think that their houses shall continue for
ever: and that their dwelling-places shall endure from
one generation to another; and call the lands after their
own names.
Nevertheless, man will not abide in honour: seeing he
may be compared unto the beasts that perish; this is the
way of them.
49:10

1 They lie in the hell like sheep, death gnaweth upon
them, and the righteous shall have domination over
them in the morning: their beauty shall consume in the
sepulchre out of their dwelling.
14

2 All the beasts of the forest are mine: and so are the
cattle upon a thousand hills.
50:10

3 Thinkest thou that I will eat bulls' flesh: and drink the
blood of goats?
13

4 Wash me throughly from my wickedness: and cleanse
me from my sin.
For I acknowledge my faults: and my sin is ever before
me.
Against thee only have I sinned, and done this evil in
thy sight.
51:2

5 Behold, I was shapen in wickedness: and in sin hath
my mother conceived me.
But lo, thou requirest truth in the inward parts: and
shalt make me to understand wisdom secretly.
Thou shalt purge me with hyssop, and I shall be clean:
thou shalt wash me, and I shall be whiter than snow.
Thou shalt make me hear of joy and gladness: that the
bones which thou hast broken may rejoice.
5. See 334:10

6 Make me a clean heart, O God: and renew a right
spirit within me.
Cast me not away from thy presence: and take not thy
holy Spirit from me.
O give me the comfort of thy help again: and stablish
me with thy free Spirit.
10

7 Deliver me from blood-guiltiness, O God.
14

8 Thou shalt open my lips, O Lord: and my mouth shall
shew thy praise.
For thou desirest no sacrifice, else would I give it
thee: but thou delightest not in burnt-offerings.
The sacrifice of God is a troubled spirit: a broken and
contrite heart, O God, shalt thou not despise.
O be favourable and gracious unto Sion: build thou the
walls of Jerusalem.
15

9 Then shall they offer young bullocks upon thine altar.
19

10 O that I had wings like a dove: for then would I flee
away, and be at rest.
55:6

11 It was even thou, my companion: my guide, and mine
own familiar friend.
We took sweet counsel together: and walked in the
house of God as friends.
14

12 The words of his mouth were softer than butter, having
war in his heart: his words were smoother than oil, and
yet they be very swords.
22

13 Thou tellest my flittings; put my tears into thy bottle:
are not these things noted in thy book?
56:8

14 Under the shadow of thy wings shall be my refuge,
until this tyranny be over-past.
57:1

15 God shall send forth his mercy and truth: my soul is
among lions.
And I lie even among the children of men, that are set
on fire: whose teeth are spears and arrows, and their
tongue a sharp sword.
Set up thyself, O God, above the heavens: and thy
glory above all the earth.
They have laid a net for my feet, and pressed down my
soul: they have digged a pit before me, and are fallen
into the midst of it themselves.
4

16 Awake up, my glory; awake, lute and harp: I myself
will awake right early.
9

17 They are as venomous as the poison of a serpent: even
like the deaf adder that stoppeth her ears;
Which refuseth to hear the voice of the charmer: charm
he never so wisely.
58:4

18 Gilead is mine, and Manasses is mine: Ephraim also is
the strength of my head; Judah is my law-giver;
Moab is my wash-pot; over Edom will I cast out my
shoe: Philistia, be thou glad of me.
60:7

19 Their delight is in lies; they give good words with
their mouth, but curse with their heart.
62:4

20 As for the children of men, they are but vanity: the
children of men are deceitful upon the weights, they
are altogether lighter than vanity itself.
O trust not in wrong and robbery, give not yourselves
unto vanity: if riches increase, set not your heart upon
them.
God spake once, and twice I have also heard the same:
that power belongeth unto God;
And that thou, Lord, art merciful: for thou rewardest
every man according to his work.
9

21 My soul thirsteth for thee, my flesh also longeth after
thee: in a barren and dry land where no water is.
63:2

22 These also that seek the hurt of my soul: they shall go
under the earth.
Let them fall upon the edge of the sword: that they
may be a portion for foxes.
10

23 Thou, O God, art praised in Sion: and unto thee shall
the vow be performed in Jerusalem.
Thou that hearest the prayer: unto thee shall all flesh
come.
65:1

1 Thou that art the hope of all the ends of the earth, and of them that remain in the broad sea.
Who in his strength setteth fast the mountains: and is girded about with power.
Who stilleth the raging of the sea: and the noise of his waves, and the madness of the people.
5

2 Thou visitest the earth, and blessest it: thou makest it very plenteous.
9

3 Thou waterest her furrows, thou sendest rain into the little valleys thereof: thou makest it soft with the drops of rain, and blessest the increase of it.
Thou crownest the year with thy goodness: and thy clouds drop fatness.
They shall drop upon the dwellings of the wilderness: and the little hills shall rejoice on every side.
The folds shall be full of sheep: the valleys also shall stand so thick with corn, that they shall laugh and sing.
11

4 God be merciful unto us, and bless us: and shew us the light of his countenance, and be merciful unto us;
That thy way may be known upon earth: thy saving health among all nations.
Let the people praise thee, O God: yea, let all the people praise thee.
67:1

5 Then shall the earth bring forth her increase: and God, even our own God, shall give us his blessing.
6

6 Let God arise, and let his enemies be scattered: let them also that hate him flee before him.
68:1

7 O sing unto God, and sing praises unto his name: magnify him that rideth upon the heavens, as it were upon an horse; praise him in his name JAH, and rejoice before him.
He is a Father of the fatherless, and defendeth the cause of the widows: even God in his holy habitation.
He is the God that maketh men to be of one mind in an house, and bringeth the prisoners out of captivity: but letteth the runagates continue in scarceness.
O God, when thou wentest forth before the people: when thou wentest through the wilderness,
the earth shook, and the heavens dropped at the presence of God.
4

8 The Lord gave the word: great was the company of the preachers.
Kings with their armies did flee, and were discomfited: and they of the household divided the spoil.
Though ye have lien among the pots, yet shall ye be as the wings of a dove: that is covered with silver wings, and her feathers like gold.
11

9 Why hop ye so, ye high hills? this is God's hill, in which it pleaseth him to dwell.
16

10 Thou art gone up on high, thou hast led captivity captive, and received gifts for men.
18

11 The zeal of thine house hath even eaten me.
69:9

12 Thy rebuke hath broken my heart; I am full of heaviness: I looked for some to have pity on me, but there was no man, neither found I any to comfort me.
They gave me gall to eat: and when I was thirsty they gave me vinegar to drink.
21

13 Let their habitation be void: and no man to dwell in their tents.
26

14 Let them be wiped out of the book of the living: and not be written among the righteous.
29

15 Let them be ashamed and confounded that seek after my soul: let them be turned backward and put to confusion that wish me evil.
Let them for their reward be soon brought to shame: that cry over me, There, there.
70:2

16 I am become as it were a monster unto many: but my sure trust is in thee.
71:6

17 Cast me not away in the time of age: forsake me not when my strength faileth me.
8

18 Give the King thy judgements, O God: and thy righteousness unto the King's son.
72:1

19 The mountains also shall bring peace: and the little hills righteousness unto the people.
3

20 His dominion shall be also from the one sea to the other: and from the flood unto the world's end.
They that dwell in the wilderness shall kneel before him: his enemies shall lick the dust.
The Kings of Tharsis and of the isles shall give presents: the kings of Arabia and Saba shall bring gifts.
All kings shall fall down before him: all nations shall do him service.
8

21 He shall live, and unto him shall be given of the gold of Arabia.
15

22 Therefore fall the people unto them: and thereout suck they no small advantage.
Tush, say they, how should God perceive it: is there knowledge in the most High?
73:10

23 Then thought I to understand this: but it was too hard for me.
Until I went into the sanctuary of God: then understood I the end of these men.
15

24 O deliver not the soul of thy turtle-dove unto the multitude of the enemies: and forget not the congregation of the poor for ever.
74:20

25 The earth is weak, and all the inhabiters thereof: I bear up the pillars of it.
75:4

26 For promotion cometh neither from the east, nor from

the west: nor yet from the south.
And why? God is the Judge: he putteth down one, and setteth up another.
7

1 In Jewry is God known: his Name is great in Israel.
At Salem is his tabernacle: and his dwelling in Sion.
76:1

2 I have considered the days of old: and the years that are past.
77:5

3 Hear my law, O my people: incline your ears unto the words of my mouth.
I will open my mouth in a parable: I will declare hard sentences of old;
Which we have heard and known: and such as our fathers have told us.
78:1

4 Not to be as their forefathers, a faithless and stubborn generation: a generation that set not their heart aright, and whose spirit cleaveth not stedfastly unto God.
9

5 He divided the sea, and let them go through: he made the waters to stand on an heap.
14

6 He rained down manna also upon them for to eat: and gave them food from heaven.
So man did eat angels' food: for he sent them meat enough.
25

7 So the Lord awaked as one out of sleep: and like a giant refreshed with wine.
66

8 Turn us again, O God: shew the light of thy countenance, and we shall be whole.
80:3

9 Sing we merrily unto God our strength: make a cheerful noise unto the God of Jacob.
Take the psalm, bring hither the tabret: the merry harp with the lute.
Blow up the trumpet in the new-moon: even in the time appointed, and upon our solemn feast-day.
81:1

10 I have said, Ye are gods: and ye are all children of the most Highest.
But ye shall die like men: and fall like one of the princes.
82:6

11 O how amiable are thy dwellings: thou Lord of hosts!
My soul hath a desire and longing to enter into the courts of the Lord: my heart and my flesh rejoice in the living God.
Yea, the sparrow hath found her an house, and the swallow a nest where she may lay her young: even thy altars, O Lord of hosts, my King and my God.
84:1

12 Blessed is the man whose strength is in thee: in whose heart are thy ways.
Who going through the vale of misery use it for a well: and the pools are filled with water.
They will go from strength to strength: and unto the God of gods appeareth every one of them in Sion.
5

13 For one day in thy courts: is better than a thousand.

I had rather be a door-keeper in the house of my God: than to dwell in the tents of ungodliness.
10

14 Wilt thou not turn again, and quicken us: that thy people may rejoice in thee?
85:6

15 Mercy and truth are met together: righteousness and peace have kissed each other.
Truth shall flourish out of the earth: and righteousness hath looked down from heaven.
10

16 Very excellent things are spoken of thee: thou city of God.
87:2

17 Lord, thou hast been our refuge: from one generation to another.
Before the mountains were brought forth, or ever the earth and the world were made: thou art God from everlasting, and world without end.
90:1

18 For a thousand years in thy sight are but as yesterday: seeing that is past as a watch in the night.
As soon as thou scatterest them they are even as a sleep: and fade away suddenly like the grass.
In the morning it is green, and groweth up: but in the evening it is cut down, dried up, and withered.
4

19 The days of our age are threescore years and ten; and though men be so strong that they come to fourscore years: yet is their strength then but labour and sorrow; so soon passeth it away, and we are gone.
10

20 So teach us to number our days: that we may apply our hearts unto wisdom.
12

21 For he shall deliver thee from the snare of the hunter: and from the noisome pestilence.
He shall defend thee under his wings, and thou shalt be safe under his feathers: his faithfulness and truth shall be thy shield and buckler.
Thou shalt not be afraid for any terror by night: nor for the arrow that flieth by day;
For the pestilence that walketh in darkness: nor for the sickness that destroyeth in the noon-day.
A thousand shall fall beside thee, and ten thousand at thy right hand: but it shall not come nigh thee.
91:3

22 For thou, Lord, art my hope: thou hast set thine house of defence very high.
There shall no evil happen unto thee: neither shall any plague come nigh thy dwelling.
For he shall give his angels charge over thee: to keep thee in all thy ways.
They shall bear thee in their hands: that thou hurt not thy foot against a stone.
Thou shalt go upon the lion and adder: the young lion and the dragon shalt thou tread under thy feet.
9

23 With long life will I satisfy him: and shew him my salvation.
16

24 The Lord is King, and hath put on glorious apparel: the Lord hath put on his apparel, and girded himself with strength.

He hath made the round world so sure: that it cannot be moved.
93:1

1 The floods are risen, O Lord, the floods have lift up their voice: the floods lift up their waves.
The waves of the sea are mighty, and rage horribly: but yet the Lord, who dwelleth on high, is mightier.
Thy testimonies, O Lord, are very sure: holiness becometh thine house for ever.
4

2 He that planted the ear, shall he not hear: or he that made the eye, shall he not see?
94:9

3 O come, let us sing unto the Lord: let us heartily rejoice in the strength of our salvation.
Let us come before his presence with thanksgiving: and shew ourselves glad in him with psalms.
95:1. See 83:7

4 In his hand are all the corners of the earth: and the strength of the hills is his also.
The sea is his, and he made it: and his hands prepared the dry land.
O come, let us worship and fall down: and kneel before the Lord our Maker.
For he is the Lord our God: and we are the people of his pasture, and the sheep of his hand.
To-day if ye will hear his voice, harden not your hearts: as in the provocation, and as in the day of temptation in the wilderness;
When your fathers tempted me: proved me, and saw my works.
Forty years long was I grieved with this generation, and said: It is a people that do err in their hearts, for they have not known my ways;
Unto whom I sware in my wrath: that they should not enter into my rest.
4

5 Ascribe unto the Lord the honour due unto his Name: bring presents, and come into his courts.
O worship the Lord in the beauty of holiness: let the whole earth stand in awe of him.
96:8

6 The Lord is King, the earth may be glad thereof: yea, the multitude of the isles may be glad thereof.
97:1

7 O sing unto the Lord a new song: for he hath done marvellous things.
With his own right hand, and with his holy arm: hath he gotten himself the victory.
98:1

8 Praise the Lord upon the harp: sing to the harp with a psalm of thanksgiving.
With trumpets also, and shawms: O shew yourselves joyful before the Lord the King.
6

9 With righteousness shall he judge the world: and the people with equity.
10

10 The Lord is King, be the people never so impatient: he sitteth between the cherubims, be the earth never so unquiet.
99:1

11 O be joyful in the Lord, all ye lands: serve the Lord with gladness, and come before his presence with a song.
Be ye sure that the Lord he is God: it is he that hath made us, and not we ourselves; we are his people, and the sheep of his pasture.
100:1. See 83:8

12 I am become like a pelican in the wilderness: and like an owl that is in the desert.
I have watched, and am even as it were a sparrow: that sitteth alone upon the house-top.
102:6

13 Thou, Lord, in the beginning hast laid the foundation of the earth: and the heavens are the work of thy hands.
They shall perish, but thou shalt endure: they all shall wax old as doth a garment;
And as a vesture shalt thou change them, and they shall be changed: but thou art the same, and thy years shall not fail.
25

14 Praise the Lord, O my soul: and forget not all his benefits.
103:2

15 Who satisfieth thy mouth with good things: making thee young and lusty as an eagle.
5

16 The Lord is full of compassion and mercy: long-suffering, and of great goodness.
He will not alway be chiding: neither keepeth he his anger for ever.
8

17 For look how high the heaven is in comparison of the earth: so great is his mercy also toward them that fear him.
Look how wide also the east is from the west: so far hath he set our sins from us.
Yea, like as a father pitieth his own children: even so is the Lord merciful unto them that fear him.
For he knoweth whereof we are made: he remembereth that we are but dust.
The days of man are but as grass: for he flourisheth as a flower of a field.
For as soon as the wind goeth over it, it is gone: and the place thereof shall know it no more.
11

18 Who layeth the beams of his chambers in the waters: and maketh the clouds his chariot, and walketh upon the wings of the wind.
He maketh his angels spirits: and his ministers a flaming fire.
He laid the foundations of the earth: that it never should move at any time.
Thou coveredst it with the deep like as with a garment: the waters stand in the hills.
104:3

19 Thou hast set them their bounds which they shall not pass: neither turn again to cover the earth.
He sendeth the springs into the rivers: which run among the hills.
All beasts of the field drink thereof: and the wild asses quench their thirst.
Beside them shall the fowls of the air have their habitation: and sing among the branches.
9

20 He bringeth forth grass for the cattle: and green herb

for the service of men;

That he may bring food out of the earth, and wine that maketh glad the heart of man: and oil to make him a cheerful countenance, and bread to strengthen man's heart.

The trees of the Lord also are full of sap: even the cedars of Libanus which he hath planted.
14

1 The high hills are a refuge for the wild goats: and so are the stony rocks for the conies.

He appointed the moon for certain seasons: and the sun knoweth his going down.

Thou makest darkness that it may be night: wherein all the beasts of the forest do move.

The lions roaring after their prey: do seek their meat from God.

The sun ariseth, and they get them away together: and lay them down in their dens.

Man goeth forth to his work, and to his labour: until the evening.

O Lord, how manifold are thy works, in wisdom hast thou made them all; the earth is full of thy riches.

So is the great and wide sea also: wherein are creeping things innumerable, both small and great beasts.

There go the ships, and there is that Leviathan: whom thou hast made to take his pastime therein.

These wait all upon thee: that thou mayest give them meat in due season.
18

2 The earth shall tremble at the look of him: if he do but touch the hills, they shall smoke.
32

3 He had sent a man before them: even Joseph, who was sold to be a bond-servant;

Whose feet they hurt in the stocks: the iron entered into his soul.
105:17

4 The king sent, and delivered him: the prince of the people let him go free.

He made him lord also of his house: and ruler of all his substance;

That he might inform his princes after his will: and teach his senators wisdom.
20

5 Yea, they thought scorn of that pleasant land: and gave no credence to his word;

But murmured in their tents: and hearkened not unto the voice of the Lord.
106:24

6 Thus were they stained with their own works: and went a whoring with their own inventions.
38

7 O that men would therefore praise the Lord for his goodness: and declare the wonders that he doeth for the children of men!

For he satisfieth the empty soul: and filleth the hungry soul with goodness.

Such as sit in darkness, and in the shadow of death: being fast bound in misery and iron;

Because they rebelled against the words of the Lord: and lightly regarded the counsel of the most Highest.
107:8

8 Their soul abhorred all manner of meat: and they were

even hard at death's door.
18

9 They that go down to the sea in ships: and occupy their business in great waters;

These men see the works of the Lord: and his wonders in the deep.
23

10 They reel to and fro, and stagger like a drunken man: and are at their wit's end.

So when they cry unto the Lord in their trouble: he delivereth them out of their distress.

For he maketh the storm to cease: so that the waves thereof are still.

Then are they glad, because they are at rest: and so he bringeth them unto the heaven where they would be.
27

11 The Lord said unto my Lord: Sit thou on my right hand, until I make thine enemies thy footstool.
110:1

12 Thou art a Priest for ever after the order of Melchisedech.
4

13 The fear of the Lord is the beginning of wisdom: a good understanding have all they that do thereafter; the praise of it endureth for ever.
111:10

14 A good man is merciful, and lendeth: and will guide his words with discretion.

For he shall never be moved: and the righteous shall be had in everlasting remembrance.
112:5

15 He maketh the barren woman to keep house: and to be a joyful mother of children.
113:8

16 When Israel came out of Egypt: and the house of Jacob from among the strange people,

Judah was his sanctuary: and Israel his dominion.

The sea saw that, and fled: Jordan was driven back.

The mountains skipped like rams: and the little hills like young sheep.
114:1

17 Not unto us, O Lord, not unto us, but unto thy Name give the praise.
115:1. See 83:10

18 They have mouths, and speak not: eyes have they, and see not.

They have ears, and hear not: noses have they, and smell not.

They have hands, and handle not: feet have they, and walk not: neither speak they through their throat.
5

19 The snares of death compassed me round about: and the pains of hell gat hold upon me.
116:3

20 And why? thou hast delivered my soul from death: mine eyes from tears, and my feet from falling.
8

21 I said in my haste, All men are liars.
10

22 I will pay my vows now in the presence of all his people: right dear in the sight of the Lord is the death of his saints.
13

1 The right hand of the Lord hath the pre-eminence: the right hand of the Lord bringeth mighty things to pass.
118:16

2 The same stone which the builders refused: is become the head-stone in the corner.
This is the Lord's doing: and it is marvellous in our eyes.
This is the day which the Lord hath made: we will rejoice and be glad in it.
22

3 Blessed be he that cometh in the Name of the Lord: we have wished you good luck, ye that are of the house of the Lord.
26

4 Wherewithal shall a young man cleanse his way: even by ruling himself after thy word.
119:9

5 The law of thy mouth is dearer unto me: than thousands of gold and silver.
72

6 Thy word is a lantern unto my feet: and a light unto my paths.
105

7 Woe is me that I am constrained to dwell with Mesech: and to have my habitation among the tents of Kedar.
120:4

8 I labour for peace, but when I speak unto them therof: they make them ready to battle.
6

9 I will lift up mine eyes unto the hills: from whence cometh my help.
My help cometh even from the Lord: who hath made heaven and earth.
He will not suffer thy foot to be moved: and he that keepeth thee will not sleep.
Behold, he that keepeth Israel: shall neither slumber not sleep.
The Lord himself is thy keeper: the Lord is thy defence upon thy right hand;
So that the sun shall not burn thee by day: neither the moon by night.
121:1

10 The Lord shall preserve thy going out, and thy coming in: from this time forth for evermore.
8

11 I was glad when they said unto me: We will go into the house of the Lord.
Our feet shall stand in thy gates: O Jerusalem.
Jerusalem is built as a city: that is at unity in itself.
For thither the tribes go up, even the tribes of the Lord.
122:1

12 O pray for the peace of Jerusalem: they shall prosper that love thee.
Peace be within thy walls: and plenteousness with thy palaces.
For my brethren and companions' sakes: I will wish thee prosperity.
6

13 If the Lord himself had not been on our side, now may Israel say: if the Lord himself had not been on our side, when men rose up against us;

They had swallowed us up quick: when they were so wrathfully displeased at us.
124:1

14 Our soul is escaped even as a bird out of the snare of the fowler: the snare is broken, and we are delivered.
Our help standeth in the Name of the Lord: who hath made heaven and earth.
6

15 The hills stand about Jerusalem: even so standeth the Lord round about his people, from this time forth for evermore.
125:2

16 When the Lord turned again the captivity of Sion: then were we like unto them that dream.
Then was our mouth filled with laughter: and our tongue with joy.
126:1

17 Turn our captivity, O Lord: as the rivers in the south.
They that sow in tears: shall reap in joy.
He that now goeth on his way weeping, and beareth forth good seed: shall doubtless come again with joy, and bring his sheaves with him.
5

18 Except the Lord build the house: their labour is but lost that build it.
Except the Lord keep the city: the watchman waketh but in vain.
127:1. See 83:12

19 Like as the arrows in the hand of the giant: even so are the young children.
Happy is the man that hath his quiver full of them: they shall not be ashamed when they speak with their enemies in the gate.
5

20 Thy wife shall be as the fruitful vine: upon the walls of thine house.
Thy children like the olive-branches: round about thy table.
128:3

21 Many a time have they fought against me from my youth up: may Israel now say.
129:1

22 But they have not prevailed against me.
The plowers plowed upon my back: and made long furrows.
2

23 Out of the deep have I called unto thee, O Lord: Lord, hear my voice.
O let thine ears consider well: the voice of my complaint.
If thou, Lord, wilt be extreme to mark what is done amiss: O Lord, who may abide it?
130:1. See 83:13

24 My soul fleeth unto the Lord: before the morning watch, I say, before the morning watch.
6

25 Lord, I am not high-minded: I have no proud looks.
I do not exercise myself in great matters: which are too high for me.
131:1

26 Behold, how good and joyful a thing it is: brethren, to dwell together in unity!
133:1

1 He smote divers nations: and slew mighty kings;
Sehon king of the Amorites, and Og the king of
Basan: and all the kingdoms of Canaan;
And gave their land to be an heritage: even an heritage
unto Israel his people.
135:10

2 O give thanks unto the Lord, for he is gracious: and
his mercy endureth for ever.
136:1

3 By the waters of Babylon we sat down and wept: when
we remembered thee, O Sion.
As for our harps, we hanged them up: upon the trees
that are therein.
For they that led us away captive required of us then a
song, and melody, in our heaviness: Sing us one of the
songs of Sion.
How shall we sing the Lord's song: in a strange land?
If I forget thee, O Jerusalem: let my right hand forget
her cunning.
If I do not remember thee, let my tongue cleave to the
roof of my mouth: yea, if I prefer not Jerusalem in my
mirth.
137:1

4 O Lord, thou hast searched me out, and known me:
thou knowest my down-sitting, and mine up-rising;
thou understandest my thoughts long before.
139:1

5 Such knowledge is too wonderful and excellent for
me: I cannot attain unto it.
Whither shall I go then from thy Spirit: or whither
shall I go then from thy presence?
If I climb up into the heaven, thou art there: if I go
down to hell, thou art there also.
If I take the wings of the morning: and remain in the
uttermost parts of the sea;
Even there also shall thy hand lead me: and thy right
hand shall hold me.
If I say, Peradventure the darkness shall cover me:
then shall my night be turned to day.
Yea, the darkness is no darkness with thee, but the
night is as clear as the day: the darkness and light to
thee are both alike.
5

6 I will give thanks unto thee, for I am fearfully and
wonderfully made.
13

7 Thine eyes did see my substance, yet being imperfect:
and in thy book were all my members written;
Which day by day were fashioned: when as yet there
were none of them.
15

8 Try me, O God, and seek the ground of my heart:
prove me, and examine my thoughts.
23

9 Let the lifting up of my hands be an evening sacrifice.
Set a watch, O Lord, before my mouth: and keep the
door of my lips.
141:2

10 Let the ungodly fall into their own nets together: and
let me ever escape them.
11

11 Enter not into judgement with thy servant: for in thy
sight shall no man living be justified.
143:2

12 Save me, and deliver me from the hand of strange
children: whose mouth talketh of vanity, and their
right hand is a right hand of iniquity.
That our sons may grow up as the young plants: and
that our daughters may be as the polished corners of
the temple.
144:11

13 That our sheep may bring forth thousands and ten
thousands in our streets.
That our oxen may be strong to labour, that there be no
decay: no leading into captivity, and no complaining in
our streets.
13

14 The Lord upholdeth all such as fall: and lifteth up all
those that are down.
145:14

15 Thou givest them their meat in due season.
Thou openest thine hand: and fillest all things living
with plenteousness.
15

16 O put not your trust in princes, nor in any child of
man: for there is no help in them.
146:2

17 The Lord looseth men out of prison: the Lord giveth
sight to the blind.
7

18 The Lord careth for the strangers; he defendeth the
fatherless and widow: as for the way of the ungodly,
he turneth it upside down.
9

19 A joyful and pleasant thing it is to be thankful.
The Lord doth build up Jerusalem: and gather together
the out-casts of Israel.
He healeth those that are broken in heart: and giveth .
medicine to heal their sickness.
He telleth the number of the stars: and calleth them all
by their names.
147:1

20 He hath no pleasure in the strength of an horse:
neither delighteth he in any man's legs.
10

21 He giveth snow like wool: and scattereth the
hoar-frost like ashes.
He casteth forth his ice like morsels: who is able to
abide his frost?
16

22 Praise the Lord upon earth: ye dragons, and all deeps;
Fire and hail, snow and vapours: wind and storm,
fulfilling his word.
148:7

23 Young men and maidens, old men and children, praise
the Name of the Lord: for his Name only is excellent,
and his praise above heaven and earth.
12

24 Let the saints be joyful with glory: let them rejoice in
their beds.
Let the praises of God be in their mouth: and a
two-edged sword in their hands;
To be avenged of the heathen: and to rebuke the
people;
To bind their kings in chains: and their nobles with
links of iron.
149:5

1 Praise him upon the well-tuned cymbals: praise him
upon the loud cymbals.
Let every thing that hath breath: praise the Lord.
150:5

2 Be pleased to receive into thy Almighty and most
gracious protection the persons of us thy servants, and
the Fleet in which we serve.
Forms of Prayer to be Used at Sea. 1st prayer

3 That we may be...a security for such as pass on the
seas upon their lawful occasions.

4 We therefore commit his body to the deep, to be
turned into corruption, looking for the resurrection of
the body (when the Sea shall give up her dead).
At the Burial of their Dead at Sea

5 Come, Holy Ghost, our souls inspire,
And lighten with celestial fire.
Thou the anointing Spirit art,
Who dost thy seven-fold gifts impart.

Thy blessed Unction from above,
Is comfort, life, and fire of love.
Enable with perpetual light
The dulness of our blinded sight.

Anoint and cheer our soiled face
With the abundance of thy grace.
Keep far our foes, give peace at home:
Where thou art guide, no ill can come.
Ordering of Priests. Veni, Creator Spiritus

6 Holy Scripture containeth all things necessary to
salvation.
Articles of Religion (1562). 6

7 Man is very far gone from original righteousness.
9

8 It is a thing plainly repugnant to the Word of God, and
the custom of the Primitive Church, to have publick
Prayer in the Church, or to minister the Sacraments in
a tongue not understood of the people.
24

9 The sacrifices of Masses, in the which it was
commonly said, that the Priest did offer Christ for the
quick and the dead, to have remission of pain or guilt,
were blasphemous fables, and dangerous deceits.
31

10 The Bishop of Rome hath no jurisdiction in this Realm
of England.
37

11 It is lawful for Christian men, at the commandment of
the Magistrate, to wear weapons, and serve in the
wars.

12 The Riches and Goods of Christians are not common,
as touching the right, title, and possession of the same,
as certain Anabaptists do falsely boast.
38

13 A Man may not marry his Mother.
Table of Kindred and Affinity

KEITH PRESTON 1884–1927

14 Of all the literary scenes
Saddest this sight to me:
The graves of little magazines
Who died to make verse free.
The Liberators

JACQUES PRÉVERT 1900–1977

15   *Notre Père qui êtes aux cieux*
        Restez-y
   Et nous nous resterons sur la terre.
Our Father which art in heaven, stay there; and as for
us, we shall stay on the earth.
Paroles (1946), Pater Noster

16 *Je suis comme je suis*
Je suis faite comme ça.
I am the way I am. That's the way I'm made.
Je suis comme je suis

17 *Il a mis le café*
Dans la tasse
Il a mis le lait
Dans la tasse de café
Il a mis le sucre
Dans le café au lait
Avec la petite cuiller
Il a tourné
Il a bu le café au lait
Et il a reposé la tasse
Sans me parler.
He put the coffee in the cup. He put the milk in the cup
of coffee. He put the sugar in the white coffee, with
the tea-spoon, he stirred. He drank the white coffee
and he put the cup down. Without speaking to me.
Déjeuner du Matin

MATTHEW PRIOR 1664–1721

18 He's half absolv'd who has confess'd.
Alma, c.ii, 1.22

19 Dear Cloe, how blubber'd is that pretty face!
A Better Answer [to Cloe Jealous]

20 Odds life! must one swear to the truth of a song?

21 I court others in verse: but I love thee in prose:
And they have my whimsies, but thou hast my heart.

22 The song too daring, and the theme too great!
Carmen Seculare, 1.308

23 Be to her virtues very kind;
Be to her faults a little blind;
Let all her ways be unconfin'd;
And clap your padlock—on her mind.
An English Padlock, 1.79

24 To John I ow'd great obligation;
   But John, unhappily, thought fit
To publish it to all the nation:
   Sure John and I are more than quit.
Epigram

25 Nobles and heralds, by your leave,
   Here lies what once was Matthew Prior;
The son of Adam and of Eve,
   Can Bourbon or Nassau go higher?
Epitaph

26 And oft the pangs of absence to remove
By letters, soft interpreters of love.
Henry and Emma, 1.147

27 For the idiom of words very little she heeded,
Provided the matter she drove at succeeded,
She took and gave languages just as she needed.
Jinny the Just

28 Venus, take my votive glass;
   Since I am not what I was,

What from this day I shall be,
   Venus, let me never see.
The Lady who Offers her Looking-Glass to Venus

1 The merchant, to secure his treasure,
   Conveys it in a borrowed name:
  Euphelia serves to grace my measure;
   But Chloe is my real flame.
An Ode

2 He rang'd his tropes, and preach'd up patience;
  Back'd his opinion with quotations.
Paulo Purganti and his Wife, l.138

3 Entire and sure the monarch's rule must prove,
  Who founds her greatness on her subjects' love.
Prologue Spoken...on Her Majesty's Birthday, 1704, l.17

4 Cur'd yesterday of my disease,
  I died last night of my physician.
The Remedy Worse than the Disease

5 Abra was ready ere I call'd her name;
  And, though I call'd another, Abra came.
Solomon (1718), bk.ii, l.362

6 What is a King?—a man condemn'd to bear
  The public burden of the nation's care.
bk.iii, l.275

7 For as our diff'rent ages move,
   'Tis so ordained, would Fate but mend it,
  That I shall be past making love,
   When she begins to comprehend it.
To a Child of Quality of Five Years Old

8 From ignorance our comfort flows,
  The only wretched are the wise.
To the Hon. Charles Montague, l.35

9 No, no; for my virginity,
  When I lose that, says Rose, I'll die:
  Behind the elms last night, cried Dick,
  Rose, were you not extremely sick?
A True Mind

10 I never strove to rule the roast,
   She ne'er refus'd to pledge my toast.
The Turtle and the Sparrow, l.334

11 They never taste who always drink;
   They always talk, who never think.
Upon this Passage in Scaligerana

ALEXANDRE PRIVAT D'ANGLEMONT 1820?–1859

12 *Je les ai épatés, les bourgeois.*
  I flabbergasted them, the *bourgeois*.
Attr. Also attr. to Baudelaire, in the form *Il faut épater le bourgeois*.

ADELAIDE ANN PROCTER 1825–1864

13 Seated one day at the organ,
   I was weary and ill at ease,
  And my fingers wandered idly
   Over the noisy keys.
Legends and Lyrics (1858). A Lost Chord

14 But I struck one chord of music,
   Like the sound of a great Amen.

PROPERTIUS b. c.51 B.C.

15 *Navita de ventis, de tauris narrat arator,*
   Enumerat miles vulnera, pastor oves.

The seaman tells stories of winds, the ploughman of
   bulls; the soldier details his wounds, the shepherd
   his sheep.
Elegies, II.i.43

16 *Quod si deficiant vires, audacia certe*
   Laus erit: in magnis et voluisse sat est.
Even if strength fail, boldness at least will deserve
   praise: in great endeavours even to have had the
   will is enough.
x.5

17 *Cedite Romani scriptores, cedite Grai!*
   Nescioquid maius nascitur Iliade.
Make way, you Roman writers, make way, Greeks!
   Something greater than the Iliad is born.
xxxiv.65. Of Virgil's *Aeneid*

PROTAGORAS c.481–411 B.C.

18 Man is the measure of all things.
Plato, *Theaetetus*, 160d

PIERRE-JOSEPH PROUDHON 1809–1865

19 *La propriété c'est le vol.*
Property is theft.
Qu'est-ce que la Propriété? (1840), ch.1

MARCEL PROUST 1871–1922

20 *Longtemps je me suis couché de bonne heure.*
For a long time I used to go to bed early.
A la Recherche du Temps Perdu, tr. C.K. Scott-Moncrieff and
S. Hudson (1922–1931), *Du côté de chez Swann*, opening
sentence

21 *Et il ne fut plus question de Swann chez les Verdurin.*
After which there was no more talk of Swann at the
Verdurins'.
pt.II

22 Une dame prétentieuse: *Que pensez-vous de l'amour?*
Mme Leroi: *L'amour? Je le fais souvent, mais je n'en
parle jamais.*
A pushing lady: What are your views on love?
Mme Leroi: Love? I make it constantly but I never talk
about it.
Le Côté de Guermantes, vol.I, ch.3. G.D. Painter, in *Marcel
Proust*, vol.I, ch.7, traces this exchange to a conversation between
Mme Lydie Aubernon and Mme Laure Baignères, at a *soirée* held
by the former.

23 *On l'enterra, mais toute la nuit funèbre, aux vitrines
éclairées, ses livres disposés trois par trois veillaient
commes des anges aux ailes éployées et semblaient,
pour celui qui n'était plus, le symbole de sa
résurrection.*
They buried him, but all through the night of
mourning, in the lighted windows, his books arranged
three by three kept watch like angels with outspread
wings and seemed, for him who was no more, the
symbol of his resurrection.
La Prisonnière, vol. I, ch. 1

24 *Ces dépèches dont M. de Guermantes avait
spirituellement fixé le modèle: 'Impossible venir,
mensonge suit.'*
One of those telegrams of which M. de Guermantes
had wittily fixed the formula: 'Cannot come, lie
follows'.
Le Temps Retrouvé, vol.I, ch.1. See 41:17

1 *Les vrais paradis sont les paradis qu'on a perdus.*
The true paradises are paradises we have lost.
.vol.II, ch.3

WILLIAM JEFFREY PROWSE 1836–1870

2 Though the latitude's rather uncertain,
And the longitude also is vague,
The persons I pity who know not the city,
The beautiful city of Prague.
The City of Prague

PUBLILIUS SYRUS 1st cent. B.C.

3 *Inopi beneficium bis dat qui dat celeriter.*
He gives the poor man twice as much good who gives
quickly.
Sententiae, 274. J.W. and A.M. Duff, *Minor Latin Poets*, Loeb edn.
(1934). Proverbially *Bis dat qui cito dat* (He gives twice who gives soon.)

4 *Formosa facies muta commendatio est.*
A beautiful face is a mute recommendation.
199. Tr. Bacon, *Apophthegms*, 12

5 *Iudex damnatur ubi nocens absolvitur.*
The judge is condemned when the guilty party is
acquitted.
296

6 *Necessitas dat legem non ipsa accipit.*
Necessity gives the law without itself acknowledging
one.
444. Proverbially *Necessitas non habet legem* (Necessity has no
law.)

JOHN PUDNEY 1909–1977

7 Do not despair
For Johnny head-in-air;
He sleeps as sound
As Johnny underground.
For Johnny

8 Better by far
For Johnny-the-bright-star,
To keep your head
And see his children fed.

WILLIAM PULTENEY, EARL OF BATH
1684–1764

9 Since twelve honest men have decided the cause,
And were judges of fact, tho' not judges of laws.
The Honest Jury, iii. In *The Craftsman*, 1731, vol.5, 337. Refers
to Sir Philip Yorke's unsuccessful prosecution of *The Craftsman*
(1729)

PUNCH

10 Advice to persons about to marry.—'Don't.'
vol.viii, p.1. 1845

11 The Half-Way House to Rome, Oxford.
vol.xvi, p.36. 1849

12 What is better than presence of mind in a railway
accident? Absence of body.
p.231. 1849

13 Never do to-day what you can put off till to-morrow.
vol.xvii, p.241. 1849

14 Who's 'im, Bill?
A stranger!

'Eave 'arf a brick at 'im.
vol.xxvi, p.82. 1854

15 What is Matter?—Never mind.
What is Mind?—No matter.
vol.xxix, p.19. 1855

16 '*Peccavi*—I've Scinde' wrote Lord Ellen so proud.
More briefly Dalhousie wrote—'*Vovi*—I've Oude'.
vol.xxx, p.118. 1856. See 575:8

17 It ain't the 'unting as 'urts 'im, it's the 'ammer,
'ammer, 'ammer along the 'ard 'igh road.
p.218. 1856

18 Mun, a had na' been the-erre abune two hours
when—*bang*—went saxpence!!!
vol.liv, p.235. 1868

19 Cats is 'dogs' and rabbits is 'dogs' and so's Parrats,
but this 'ere 'Tortis' is a insect, and there ain't no
charge for it.
vol.lvi, p.96. 1869

20 Nothink for nothink 'ere, and precious little for
sixpence.
vol.lvii, p.152. 1869

21 Sure, the next train has gone ten minutes ago.
vol.lx, p.206. 1871

22 It appears the Americans have taken umbrage.
The deuce they have! Whereabouts is that?
vol.lxiii, p.189. 1872

23 Go directly—see what she's doing, and tell her she
mustn't.
p.202. 1872

24 There was one poor tiger that hadn't *got* a Christian.
vol.lxviii, p.143. 1875

25 There was an old owl liv'd in an oak
The more he heard, the less he spoke;
The less he spoke, the more he heard
O, if men were all like that wise bird!
p.155. 1875

26 It's worse than wicked, my dear, it's vulgar.
Almanac. 1876

27 What did you take out of the bag, Mamma? *I* only got
sixpence.
vol.lxx, p.139. 1876

28 I never read books—I *write* them.
vol.lxxiv, p.210. 1878

29 I am not hungry; but thank goodness, I am greedy.
vol.lxxv, p.290. 1878

30 *Bishop:*
Who is it that sees and hears all we do, and before
whom even I am but as a crushed worm?
Page:
The Missus my Lord.
vol.lxxix, p.63. 1880

31 Ah whiles hae ma doobts aboot the meenister.
p.275. 1880

32 What sort of a doctor is he?
Oh, well, I don't know very much about his ability;
but he's got a very good bedside manner!
vol.lxxxvi, p.121. 1884

33 I used your soap two years ago; since then I have used
no other.
p.197. 1884

34 Don't look at me, Sir, with—ah—in that tone of

voice.
vol.lxxxvii, p.38. 1884

1 Oh yes! I'm sure he's not so fond of me as at first.
He's away so much, neglects me dreadfully, and he's
so cross when he comes home. What *shall* I do?
Feed the brute!
vol.lxxxix, p.206. 1885

2 Nearly all our best men are dead! Carlyle, Tennyson,
Browning, George Eliot!—I'm not feeling very well
myself.
vol.civ, p.210. 1893

3 Botticelli isn't a wine, you Juggins! Botticelli's a
cheese!
vol.cvi, p.270. 1894

4 I'm afraid you've got a bad egg, Mr Jones.
Oh no, my Lord, I assure you! Parts of it are
excellent!
vol.cix, p.222. 1895

5 Look here, Steward, if this is coffee, I want tea; but if
this is tea, then I wish for coffee.
vol.cxxiii, p.44. 1902

ISRAEL PUTNAM 1718–1790

6 Men, you are all marksmen—don't one of you fire
until you see the whites of their eyes.
Bunker Hill, 1775. Frothingham, *History of the Siege of Boston*
(1873), ch.5, note. Also attributed to William Prescott (1726-95)

PYRRHUS 319–272 B.C

7 One more such victory and we are lost.
Plutarch, *Pyrrhus*. After defeating the Romans at Asculum, 279
B.C.

FRANCIS QUARLES 1592–1644

8 I wish thee as much pleasure in the reading, as I had in
the writing.
Emblems (1643). To the Reader

9 The heart is a small thing, but desireth great matters.
It is not sufficient for a kite's dinner, yet the whole
world is not sufficient for it.
bk.i, No.12. Hugo de Anima

10 We spend our midday sweat, our midnight oil;
We tire the night in thought, the day in toil.
bk.ii, No.2, l.33

11 Be wisely worldly, be not worldly wise.
l.46

12 Man is Heaven's masterpiece.
No.6, Epig.6

13 Thou art my way; I wander, if thou fly;
Thou art my light; if hid, how blind am I!
Thou art my life; if thou withdraw, I die.
bk.iii, No.7

14 Our God and soldiers we alike adore
Ev'n at the brink of danger; not before:
After deliverance, both alike requited,
Our God's forgotten, and our soldiers slighted.
Epigram

15 My soul, sit thou a patient looker-on;
Judge not the play before the play is done:
Her plot hath many changes; every day
Speaks a new scene; the last act crowns the play.
Epigram. Respice Finem

16 No man is born unto himself alone;
Who lives unto himself, he lives to none.
Esther, Sect.1, Medit.1

17 He teaches to deny that faintly prays.
A Feast for Worms (1620), Sect.7, Medit.7, l.2

18 Man is man's A.B.C. There is none that can
Read God aright, unless he first spell Man.
Hieroglyphics of the Life of Man (1638), i, l.1

19 He that begins to live, begins to die.
Epig.1

20 Physicians of all men are most happy; what good
success soever they have, the world proclaimeth, and
what faults they commit, the earth covereth.
iv. **Nicocles**

21 We'll cry both arts and learning down,
And hey! then up go we!
The Shepherd's Oracles (1646). Eclogue xi. **Song of Anarchus,**
iv

FRANÇOIS QUESNAY 1694–1774

22 *Vous ne connaissez qu'une seule règle du commerce;
c'est (pour me servir de vos propres termes) de laisser
passer et de laisser faire tous les acheteurs et tous les
vendeurs quelconques.*
You recognize but one rule of commerce; that is (to
avail myself of your own terms) to allow free passage
and freedom of action to all buyers and sellers
whoever they may be.
Letter from M. Alpha: see Salleron, *François Quesnay et la
Physiocratie* (1958), II.940. Also attr. Marquis d'Argenson,
Mémoires (1736). See 9:10, 11:25

SIR ARTHUR QUILLER-COUCH 1863–1944

23 The best is the best, though a hundred judges have
declared it so.
Oxford Book of English Verse (1900), Preface

JOSIAH QUINCY 1772–1864

24 As it will be the right of all, so it will be the duty of
some, definitely to prepare for a separation, amicably
if they can, violently if they must.
Abridgement of Debates of Congress, 14 Jan. 1811, vol.iv, p.327

QUINTILIAN A.D.c.35–c.100

25 *Satura quidem tota nostra est.*
Verse satire indeed is entirely our own.
Institutio Oratoria, 10.1.93. Meaning Roman as opposed to
Greek.

FRANÇOIS RABELAIS 1494?–c.1553

26 *L'appétit vient en mangeant.*
The appetite grows by eating.
Gargantua (1534), I.v

27 *Natura vacuum abhorret.*
Nature abhors a vacuum.
Quoting, in Latin, article of ancient wisdom. Compare Plutarch,
Moralia, 'De placitis philosophorum', I. xviii

28 *Fay ce que vouldras.*
Do what you like.
lvii

29 *Quaestio subtilissima, utrum chimera in vacuo
bombinans possit comedere secundas intentiones.*

A most subtle question: whether a chimera
bombinating in a vacuum can devour second
intentions.
Pantagruel, II.vii

1 *Il aurait répondu à un page...'Je vais quérir un grand
peut-être...' Puis il avait expiré en disant 'Tirez le
rideau, la farce est jouée'.*
He answered a page...'I am going to seek a great
perhaps...' Then he died, saying 'Bring down the
curtain, the farce is played out.'
Attr. last words. See Jean Fleury, *Rabelais et ses oeuvres* (1877),
vol.I, ch.3, pt.15, p.130. Fleury adds, *'Rien, dans les
contemporains, m'autorise ces récits...Tout cela fait partie de la
légende rabelaisienne.'*

JEAN RACINE 1639–1699

2 *C'était pendant l'horreur d'une profonde nuit.*
It was during the horror of a deep night.
Athalie (1691), ii.5

3 *Elle flotte, elle hésite; en un mot, elle est femme.*
She floats, she hesitates; in a word, she's a woman.
iii.3

4 *Ce n'est plus une ardeur dans mes veines cachée:
C'est Vénus tout entière à sa proie attachée.*
It's no longer a warmth hidden in my veins: it's Venus
     entire and whole fastening on her prey.
Phèdre (1677), I.iii

5 *Point d'argent, point de Suisse, et ma porte était
close.*
No money, no service, and my door stayed shut.
Les Plaideurs (1668), I.i

6 *Sans argent l'honneur n'est qu'une maladie.*
Honour, without money, is just a disease.

VICE-ADMIRAL THOMAS RAINBOROWE
d. 1648

7 The poorest he that is in England hath a life to live as
the greatest he.
In the Army debates at Putney, 29 Oct. 1647. Peacock, *Life of
Rainborowe*.

SIR WALTER RALEGH 1552?–1618

8 Now what is love? I pray thee, tell.
It is that fountain and that well,
Where pleasure and repentance dwell.
It is perhaps that saucing bell,
That tolls all in to heaven or hell:
And this is love, as I hear tell.
A Description of Love

9 If all the world and love were young,
  And truth in every shepherd's tongue,
These pretty pleasures might me move
To live with thee, and be thy love.
Answer to Marlow. See 187:24, 329:23, 495:16

10 Go, Soul, the body's guest,
   Upon a thankless arrant:
Fear not to touch the best;
   The truth shall be thy warrant:
     Go, since I needs must die,
     And give the world the lie.
The Lie, i

11 Only we die in earnest, that's no jest.
On the Life of Man

12 Give me my scallop-shell of quiet,
My staff of faith to walk upon,
My scrip of joy, immortal diet,
My bottle of salvation,
My gown of glory, hope's true gage,
And thus I'll take my pilgrimage.
The Passionate Man's Pilgrimage

13 'As you came from the holy land
   Of Walsinghame,
Met you not with my true love
   By the way as you came?'

'How shall I know your true love,
   That have met many one
As I went to the holy land,
   That have come, that have gone?'
Walsinghame

14 Fain would I climb, yet fear I to fall.
Line written on a Window-Pane. Fuller, *Worthies of England*,
vol.i, p.419. See 206:1

15 Even such is Time, which takes in trust
Our youth, our joys, and all we have,
And pays us but with age and dust;
Who in the dark and silent grave,
When we have wandered all our ways,
Shuts up the story of our days:
And from which earth, and grave, and dust,
The Lord shall raise me up, I trust.
Written the night before his death. Found in his Bible in the
Gate-house at Westminster

16 O eloquent, just, and mighty Death!...thou hast drawn
together all the farstretched greatness, all the pride,
cruelty, and ambition of man, and covered it all over
with these two narrow words, *Hic jacet.*
A History of the World (1614), bk.v, ch.vi, 12

17 [Feeling the edge of the axe before his execution:]
'Tis a sharp remedy, but a sure one for all ills.
David Hume, *History of Great Britain* (1754), vol.i, ch.iv, p.72

18 [When asked which way he preferred to lay his head
on the block:]
So the heart be right, it is no matter which way the
head lies.
W. Stebbing, *Sir Walter Raleigh*, ch.xxx

19 I have a long journey to take, and must bid the
company farewell.
Edward Thompson, *Sir Walter Raleigh*, ch.26

SIR WALTER RALEIGH 1861–1922

20 I wish I loved the Human Race;
I wish I loved its silly face;
I wish I liked the way it walks;
I wish I liked the way it talks;
And when I'm introduced to one
I wish I thought *What Jolly Fun!*
Laughter from a Cloud (1923), p.228. **Wishes of an Elderly
Man**

JULIAN RALPH 1853–1903

21 News value.
Lecture to Brander Matthews's English Class, Columbia, 1892.
Thomas Beer, *Mauve Decade*

SRINIVASA RAMANUJAN 1887–1920

22 No, it is a very interesting number; it is the smallest

number expressible as a sum of two cubes in two different ways.
Hardy had referred to a cab's number—1729—as 'dull'. The cube roots for the two sums are 1 and 12, and 9 and 10. *Collected Papers of Srinivasa Ramanujan* (1927), Notice by G.H. Hardy, iv

TERENCE RATTIGAN 1911–1977

1 A nice respectable, middle-class, middle-aged maiden lady, with time on her hands and the money to help her pass it...Let us call her Aunt Edna...Aunt Edna is universal, and to those who feel that all the problems of the modern theatre might be saved by her liquidation, let me add that...She is also immortal.
Collected Plays (1953), Vol.II, Preface

2 *Brian:* Elle a des idées au-dessus de sa gare.
Kenneth: You can't do it like that. You can't say au-dessus de sa gare. It isn't that sort of station.
French Without Tears (1937), Act I

CHARLES READE 1814–1884

3 *Courage, mon ami, le diable est mort!*
The Cloister and the Hearth (1861), ch.24, and *passim*

4 Sow an act, and you reap a habit. Sow a habit, and you reap a character. Sow a character, and you reap a destiny.
Attr. See N. & Q., 9th series, vol.12, p.377

HENRY REED 1914–

5 To-day we have naming of parts. Yesterday
We had daily cleaning. And tomorrow morning,
We shall have what to do after firing. But to-day,
To-day we have naming of parts.
Naming of Parts (1946)

6 And this you can see is the bolt. The purpose of this
Is to open the breech, as you see. We can slide it
Rapidly backwards and forwards: we call this
Easing the spring. And rapidly backwards and
    forwards
The early bees are assaulting and fumbling the
    flowers:
They call it easing the Spring.

7 And the various holds and rolls and throws and
    breakfalls
Somehow or other I always seemed to put
In the wrong place. And as for war, my wars
    Were global from the start.
Unarmed Combat

JOHN REED 1887–1920

8 Ten Days that Shook the World.
Book title, 1919

GENERAL JOSEPH REED 1741–1785

9 I am not worth purchasing, but such as I am, the King of Great Britain is not rich enough to do it.
U.S. Congress, 11 Aug. 1878. Reed understood himself to have been offered a bribe on behalf of the British Crown.

JULES RENARD 1864–1910

10 *Les bourgeois, ce sont les autres.*

The bourgeois are other people.
Journal, 28 Jan. 1890

DR. MONTAGUE JOHN RENDALL 1862–1950

11 Nation shall speak peace unto nation.
Written as the motto of the BBC in 1927 by Dr. Rendall, one of the first Governors of the Corporation

JEAN RENOIR 1894–1979

12 Is it possible to succeed without any act of betrayal?
My Life and My Films (1974), 'Nana', p.86

PIERRE RENOIR 1841–1919

13 *C'étaient des fous, mais ils avaient cette petite flamme qui ne s'éteint pas.*
They were madmen; but they had in them that little flame which is not to be snuffed out. [The men of the French Commune.]
Jean Renoir, *Renoir*, pt.II, 1962 edn., p.136

FREDERIC REYNOLDS 1764–1841

14 How goes the enemy? [Said by Mr. Ennui, 'the timekiller'.]
The Dramatist (1789), I.i

15 Now do take my advice, and write a play—if any incident happens, remember, it is better to have written a damned play, than no play at all—it snatches a man from obscurity.

SIR JOSHUA REYNOLDS 1723–1792

16 If you have great talents, industry will improve them: if you have but moderate abilities, industry will supply their deficiency.
Discourse to Students of the Royal Academy, 11 Dec. 1769

17 A mere copier of nature can never produce anything great.
14 Dec. 1770

18 He who resolves never to ransack any mind but his own, will be soon reduced, from mere barrenness, to the poorest of all imitations; he will be obliged to imitate himself, and to repeat what he has before often repeated.
10 Dec. 1774

19 I should desire that the last words which I should pronounce in this Academy, and from this place, might be the name of—Michael Angelo.
10 Dec. 1790

20 He [Dr. Johnson] has no formal preparation, no flourishing with his sword; he is through your body in an instant.
Boswell's *Johnson* (ed. 1934), vol.ii, p.365, 18 Apr. 1775

21 He [Johnson] qualified my mind to think justly.
vol.iii, p.369, n.3; and Northcote, *Reynolds*, vol.ii, p.282

22 Taste does not come by chance: it is a long and laborious task to acquire it.
James Northcote, *Life of Sir Joshua Reynolds* (1818), 2nd edn. (revised and augmented) of *Memoirs of Sir Joshua Reynolds* (1813-15), vol.i, p.264

GRANTLAND RICE 1880–1954

23 For when the One Great Scorer comes

To write against your name,
He marks—not that you won or lost—
But how you played the game.
Alumnus Football

SIR STEPHEN RICE 1637–1715

1   I will drive a coach and six horses through the Act of
Settlement.
W. King, *State of the Protestants of Ireland* (1672), ch.3, sect.8,
p.6

MANDY RICE-DAVIES 1944–

2   He would, wouldn't he?
When told that Lord Astor had denied her allegations. Trial of
Stephen Ward, 29 June, 1963

BISHOP GEORGE RIDDING 1828–1904

3   I feel a feeling which I feel you all feel.
Sermon in the London Mission of 1885. G.W.E. Russell,
Collections and Recollections, ch.29

RAINER MARIA RILKE 1875–1926

4   *So leben wir und nehmen immer Abschied.*
Thus we live, forever taking leave.
Duineser Elegien, VIII

5   One day (for this there are now already, especially in
northern lands, reliable signs, eloquent and
illuminating), one day there will be the girl, and the
woman, whose character will no longer provide a mere
contrast for masculinity, but something self-justifying,
something in connection with which one thinks not of
a complement and a limitation, but of life and
existence: the womanly person…[This will provide a
basis for a new kind of love.] The love which consists
in this, that two solitudes protect and limit and greet
each other.
Briefe an einem jungen Dichter (1929), 14 May 1904

MARTIN RINKART 1586–1649

6   *Nun danket alle Gott.*
Now thank you all your God.
Das Danklied (1636). Sung as a hymn to the tune by Johann
Crüger (1598–1662) composed in 1649

ARTHUR RIMBAUD 1854–1891

7   *Je m'en allais, les poings dans mes poches crevées;*
Mon paletot aussi devenait idéal.
I was walking along, hands in holey pockets; my
overcoat also was entering the realms of the ideal.
Ma Bohème

8   *Ô saisons, ô châteaux!*
Quelle âme est sans défauts?
O seasons, O castles! What soul is without fault?
Ô saisons, ô châteaux

9   *A noir, E blanc, I rouge, U vert, O bleu: voyelles,*
Je dirais quelque jour vos naissances latentes…
I, pourpres, sang craché, rire des lèvres belles
Dans la colère ou les ivresses pénitentes.
A black, E white, I red, U green, O blue: vowels,
some day I will tell of the births that may be yours.
I, purples, coughed-up blood, laughter of beautiful

lips in anger or penitent drunkennesses.
Voyelles

ANTOINE DE RIVAROL 1753–1801

10   *Ce qui n'est pas clair n'est pas français.*
What is not clear is not French.
Discours sur l'Universalité de la Langue Française (1784)

MAXIMILIEN ROBESPIERRE 1758–1794

11   *Toute loi qui viole les droits imprescriptibles de*
l'homme, est essentiellement injuste et tyrannique; elle
n'est point une loi.
Any law which violates the indefeasible rights of man
is essentially unjust and tyrannical; it is not a law at
all.
Déclaration des Droits de l'homme, 24 Apr. 1793, XVIII. This
article, in slightly different form, is recorded as having figured in
Robespierre's *Projet* of 21 Apr. 1793.

12   *Toute institution qui ne suppose pas le peuple bon, et*
le magistrat corruptible, est vicieuse.
Any institution which does not suppose the people
good, and the magistrate corruptible, is evil.
XIX

SIR BOYLE ROCHE 1743–1807

13   He regretted that he was not a bird, and could not be in
two places at once.
Attr.

14   Mr Speaker, I smell a rat; I see him forming in the air
and darkening the sky; but I'll nip him in the bud.
Attr.

JOHN WILMOT, EARL OF ROCHESTER
1647–1680

15   Since 'tis Nature's law to change,
Constancy alone is strange.
A Dialogue between Strephon and Daphne, 1.31

16   What vain, unnecessary things are men!
How well we do without 'em!
Fragment

17   'Is there then no more?'
She cries. 'All this to love and rapture's due;
Must we not pay a debt to pleasure too?'
The Imperfect Enjoyment

18   Here lies a great and mighty king
Whose promise none relies on;
He never said a foolish thing,
Nor ever did a wise one.
The King's Epitaph. An alternative version of the first line is:
'Here lies our sovereign lord the King.' For Charles II's answer
see 140:23

19   Love…
That cordial drop heaven in our cup has thrown
To make the nauseous draught of life go down.
A Letter from Artemisia in the Town to Chloe in the Country

20   An age in her embraces past,
Would seem a winter's day.
The Mistress

21   Reason, an *ignis fatuus* of the mind,
Which leaves the light of nature, sense, behind.
A Satire Against Mankind, 1.11

22   Then Old Age, and Experience, hand in hand,

Lead him to Death, and make him understand,
After a search so painful, and so long
That all his life he has been in the wrong.
Huddled in dirt the reasoning engine lies,
Who was so proud, so witty and so wise.
l.25

1 For all men would be cowards if they durst.
l.158

2 A merry monarch, scandalous and poor.
A Satire on King Charles II for which he was banished from the Court, l.19

3 Ancient person, for whom I
All the flattering youth defy,
Long be it ere thou grow old,
Aching, shaking, crazy, cold;
      But still continue as thou art,
      Ancient person of my heart.
A Song of a Young Lady to her Ancient Lover

4 The best good man, with the worst-natur'd muse.
To Lord Buckhurst

5 French truth, Dutch prowess, British policy,
Hibernian learning, Scotch civility,
Spaniards' Dispatch, Danes' Wit, are mainly seen in
   thee.
Upon Nothing

THEODORE ROETHKE 1908–1963

6 I wake to sleep, and take my waking slow.
I feel my fate in what I cannot fear.
I learn by going where I have to go.
The Waking

SAMUEL ROGERS 1763–1855

7 Think nothing done while aught remains to do.
Human Life (1819), l.49. See 319:24

8 But there are moments which he calls his own,
Then, never less alone than when alone,
Those whom he loved so long and sees no more,
Loved and still loves—not dead—but gone before,
He gathers round him.
l.755

9 By many a temple half as old as Time.
Italy. A Farewell (1828), ii.5

10 Go—you may call it madness, folly;
      You shall not chase my gloom away.
There's such a charm in melancholy,
      I would not, if I could, be gay.
To—, 1814

11 It doesn't much signify whom one marries, for one is
sure to find next morning that it was someone else.
Table Talk (ed. Alexander Dyce, 1860)

12 When a new book is published, read an old one.
Attr.

THOROLD ROGERS 1823–1890

13 Sir, to be facetious it is not necessary to be indecent.
In imitation of Samuel Johnson. Also attributed to Birkbeck Hill.
John Bailey, *Dr. Johnson and his Circle*

14 While ladling butter from alternate tubs
Stubbs butters Freeman, Freeman butters Stubbs.
Attr. in W.H. Hutton, *Letters of Bishop Stubbs*

MME ROLAND 1754–1793

15 *O liberté! O liberté! que de crimes on commet en ton nom!*
O liberty! O liberty! what crimes are committed in thy name!
Lamartine, *Histoire des Girondins* (1847), livre li, ch.8

16 The more I see of men, the better I like dogs.
Attr.

FR. ROLFE, BARON CORVO 1860–1913

17 Pray for the repose of His soul. He was so tired.
Hadrian VII (1904), last words

PIERRE DE RONSARD 1524–1585

18 *Quand vous serez bien vieille, au soir, à la chandelle,*
Assise auprès du feu, dévidant et filant,
Direz, chantant mes vers, en vous émerveillant,
Ronsard me célébrait du temps que j'étais belle.
When you are very old, and sit in the candle-light at
   evening spinning by the fire, you will say, as you
   murmur my verses, a wonder in your eyes, 'Ronsard
   sang of me in the days when I was fair.'
Sonnets pour Hélène (1578), ii.43

PRESIDENT FRANKLIN D. ROOSEVELT 1882–1945

19 I pledge you—I pledge myself—to a new deal for the
American people.
Chicago Convention, 2 July 1932. (See also N. & Q., cxciv, p.529.)

20 Let me assert my firm belief that the only thing we
have to fear is fear itself.
First Inaugural Address, 4 Mar. 1933

21 In the field of world policy; I would dedicate this
nation to the policy of the good neighbour.

22 I see one-third of a nation ill-housed, ill-clad,
ill-nourished.
Second Inaugural Address, 20 Jan. 1937

23 When peace has been broken anywhere, the peace of
all countries everywhere is in danger.
Fireside Chat, 3 Sept. 1939

24 A radical is a man with both feet firmly planted in the
air.
Broadcast address to Forum on Current Problems, 26 Oct. 1939

25 We must be the great arsenal of democracy.
29 Dec. 1940

26 In the future days, which we seek to make secure, we
look forward to a world founded upon four essential
human freedoms.
The first is freedom of speech and
expression—everywhere in the world.
The second is freedom of every person to worship God
in his own way—everywhere in the world.
The third is freedom from want…
The fourth is freedom from fear.
Address to Congress, 6 Jan. 1941

PRESIDENT THEODORE ROOSEVELT 1858–1919

27 I wish to preach, not the doctrine of ignoble ease, but

the doctrine of the strenuous life.
Hamilton Club, Chicago, 10 Apr. 1899

1 There is a homely adage which runs 'Speak softly and carry a big stick; you will go far.'
Minnesota State Fair, 2 Sept. 1901

2 The first requisite of a good citizen in this Republic of ours is that he shall be able and willing to pull his weight.
New York, 11 Nov. 1902

3 A man who is good enough to shed his blood for the country is good enough to be given a square deal afterwards. More than that no man is entitled to, and less than that no man shall have.
At the Lincoln Monument, Springfield (Illinois), 4 June 1903

4 The men with the muck-rakes are often indispensable to the well-being of society; but only if they know when to stop raking the muck.
At the laying of the corner-stone of the Office Building of House of Representatives, 14 Apr. 1906

5 Every reform movement has a lunatic fringe.
Speaking of the Progressive Party, in 1913

6 There can be no fifty-fifty Americanism in this country. There is room here for only 100 per cent Americanism, only for those who are Americans and nothing else.
Republican Convention, Saratoga

7 We demand that big business give the people a square deal; in return we must insist that when any one engaged in big business honestly endeavors to do right he shall himself be given a square deal.
Autobiography (1913), p.615

8 Hyphenated Americans.
Metropolitan Magazine, Oct. 1915, p.7

WENTWORTH DILLON, EARL OF ROSCOMMON 1633?–1685

9 But words once spoke can never be recall'd.
Art of Poetry (1680), l.438. See 258:22

10 Choose an author as you choose a friend.
Essay on Translated Verse (1684), l.96

11 Immodest words admit of no defence,
For want of decency is want of sense.
l.113

12 The multitude is always in the wrong.
l.183

LORD ROSEBERY 1847–1929

13 Before Irish Home Rule is conceded by the Imperial Parliament, England as the predominant member of the three kingdoms will have to be convinced of its justice and equity.
House of Lords, 11 Mar. 1894

14 Imperialism, sane Imperialism, as distinguished from what I may call wild-cat Imperialism, is nothing but this—a larger patriotism.
Speech at a City Liberal Club dinner, 5 May 1899

15 It is beginning to be hinted that we are a nation of amateurs.
Rectorial Address, Glasgow, 16 Nov. 1900

16 I must plough my furrow alone.
City of London Liberal Club, 19 July 1901

17 The fly-blown phylacteries of the Liberal Party.
Chesterfield, 16 Dec. 1901

PILOT OFFICER V.A. ROSEWARNE 1916–1940

18 The universe is so vast and so ageless that the life of one man can only be justified by the measure of his sacrifice.
Last letter to his mother, published in *The Times* 18 June 1940, and inscribed on the portrait of the 'Young Airman' by Frank Salisbury in the R.A.F. Museum, Hendon

ALAN C. ROSS 1907–

19 'U' and 'Non-U'.
Upper Class English Usage, Bulletin de la Société Neo-Philologique de Helsinki 1954. Reprinted in *Noblesse Oblige* (1956), ed. Nancy Mitford

SIR RONALD ROSS 1857–1932

20 This day relenting God
  Hath placed within my hand
A wondrous thing; and God
  Be praised. At His command,

Seeking His secret deeds
  With tears and toiling breath,
I find thy cunning seeds,
  O million-murdering Death.

I know this little thing
  A myriad men may save.
O Death, where is thy sting?
  Thy victory, O Grave?
In Exile, VI. **Reply**, i. See 77:1. Of his part in the discovery of the life-cycle of the malaria parasite.

CHRISTINA ROSSETTI 1830–1894

21 Oh where are you going with your love-locks flowing?
Amor Mundi, i

22 This downhill path is easy, but there's no turning back.
v

23 My heart is like a singing bird
Whose nest is in a watered shoot;
My heart is like an apple-tree
Whose boughs are bent with thickset fruit;
My heart is like a rainbow shell
That paddles in a halcyon sea;
My heart is gladder than all these
Because my love is come to me.
A Birthday

24 Because the birthday of my life
Is come, my love is come to me.

25 'Come cheer up, my lads, 'tis to glory we steer'—
As the soldier remarked whose post lay in the rear.
Couplet

26 Come to me in the silence of the night;
  Come in the speaking silence of a dream;
Come with soft rounded cheeks and eyes as bright
  As sunlight on a stream;
    Come back in tears,
O memory, hope, love of finished years.
Echo

27 For there is no friend like a sister
In calm or stormy weather;

To cheer one on the tedious way,
To fetch one if one goes astray,
To lift one if one totters down,
To strengthen whilst one stands.
Goblin Market (1862)

1 In the bleak mid-winter
  Frosty wind made moan,
Earth stood hard as iron,
  Water like a stone;
Snow had fallen, snow on snow,
  Snow on snow,
In the bleak mid-winter,
  Long ago.
Mid-Winter

2 The hope I dreamed of was a dream,
  Was but a dream; and now I wake,
Exceeding comfortless, and worn, and old,
  For a dream's sake.
Mirage

3 Remember me when I am gone away,
  Gone far away into the silent land.
Remember

4 Better by far you should forget and smile
Than that you should remember and be sad.

5 O Earth, lie heavily upon her eyes;
Seal her sweet eyes weary of watching, Earth.
Rest

6 Silence more musical than any song.

7 Oh roses for the flush of youth,
  And laurel for the perfect prime;
But pluck an ivy branch for me
  Grown old before my time.
Song: 'Oh Roses for the Flush'

8 When I am dead, my dearest,
  Sing no sad songs for me;
Plant thou no roses at my head,
  Nor shady cypress tree:
Be the green grass above me
  With showers and dewdrops wet;
And if thou wilt, remember,
  And if thou wilt, forget.
Song: 'When I am Dead'

9 And dreaming through the twilight
  That doth not rise nor set,
Haply I may remember,
  And haply may forget.

10 Gone were but the Winter,
  Come were but the Spring,
I would go to a covert
  Where the birds sing.
Spring Quiet

11 Does the road wind up-hill all the way?
  Yes, to the very end.
Will the day's journey take the whole long day?
  From morn to night, my friend.
Up-Hill

12 Will there be beds for me and all who seek?
  Yea, beds for all who come.

DANTE GABRIEL ROSSETTI 1828–1882

13 Like the sweet apple which reddens upon the topmost
bough,

A-top on the topmost twig,—which the pluckers
  forgot, somehow,—
Forgot it not, nay, but got it not, for none could get it
till now.
Beauty: A Combination from Sappho. See 414:7

14 The blessed damozel leaned out
  From the gold bar of Heaven;
Her eyes were deeper than the depth
  Of waters stilled at even;
She had three lilies in her hand,
  And the stars in her hair were seven.
The Blessed Damozel (1850), i

15 Her hair that lay along her back
  Was yellow like ripe corn.
ii

16 So high, that looking downward thence,
  She scarce could see the sun.
v

17   As low as where this earth
Spins like a fretful midge.
vi

18 And the souls mounting up to God
  Went by her like thin flames.
vii

19 'We two,' she said, 'will seek the groves
  Where the lady Mary is,
With her five handmaidens, whose names
  Are five sweet symphonies,
Cecily, Gertrude, Magdalen,
  Margaret and Rosalys.'
xviii

20 Was it a friend or foe that spread these lies?
Nay, who but infants question in such wise?
'Twas one of my most intimate enemies.
Fragment

21 A sonnet is a moment's monument,—
Memorial from the Soul's eternity
To one dead deathless hour.
The House of Life (1881), pt.I. Introd.

22 I was a child beneath her touch,—a man
When breast to breast we clung, even I and she,—
A spirit when her spirit looked through me,—
A god when all our life-breath met to fan
Our life-blood, till love's emulous ardours ran,
Fire within fire, desire in deity.
vi. **The Kiss**

23 'Tis visible silence, still as the hour-glass.
xix. **Silent Noon**

24 Deep in the sun-searched growths the dragon-fly
Hangs like a blue thread loosened from the sky:—
So this wing'd hour is dropt to us from above.
Oh! clasp we to our hearts, for deathless dower,
This close-companioned inarticulate hour
When twofold silence was the song of love.

25 They die not,—for their life was death,—but cease;
And round their narrow lips the mould falls close.
pt.II. lxxi. **The Choice**, i

26 Nay, come up hither. From this wave-washed mound
Unto the furthest flood-brim look with me;
Then reach on with thy thought till it be drown'd.
Miles and miles distant though the last line be,
And though thy soul sail leagues and leagues beyond,—

Still, leagues beyond those leagues, there is more sea.
iii

1 Give honour unto Luke Evangelist;
For he it was (the aged legends say)
Who first taught Art to fold her hands and pray.
lxxiv. **Old and New Art,** i

2 Lo! as that youth's eyes burned at thine, so went
Thy spell through him, and left his straight neck bent
And round his heart one strangling golden hair.
lxxviii. **Body's Beauty**

3 I do not see them here; but after death
God knows I know the faces I shall see,
Each one a murdered self, with low last breath.
'I am thyself,—what hast thou done to me?'
'And I—and I—thyself', (lo! each one saith,)
'And thou thyself to all eternity!'
lxxxvi. **Lost Days**

4 Look in my face; my name is Might-have-been;
I am also called No-more, Too-late, Farewell.
xcvii. **A Superscription**

5 Sleepless with cold commemorative eyes.

6 When vain desire at last and vain regret
Go hand in hand to death, and all is vain,
What shall assuage the unforgotten pain
And teach the unforgetful to forget?
ci. **The One Hope**

7 Unto the man of yearning thought
And aspiration, to do nought
Is in itself almost an act.
Soothsay, x

8 I have been here before,
    But when or how I cannot tell:
I know the grass beyond the door,
    The sweet keen smell,
The sighing sound, the lights around the shore.
Sudden Light, i

9 From perfect grief there need not be
Wisdom or even memory:
One thing then learnt remains to me,—
The woodspurge has a cup of three.
The Woodspurge

10 Conception, my boy, *fundamental brainwork,* is what
makes the difference in all art.
Letter to Hall Caine, in Caine's *Recollections of Rossetti* (1882)

GIOACCHINO ROSSINI 1792–1868

11 *Monsieur Wagner a de beaux moments, mais de
mauvais quart d'heures.*
Wagner has lovely moments but awful quarters of an
hour.
Said to Emile Naumann, April 1867. Naumann, *Italienische
Tondichter* (1883), IV, 541

EDMOND ROSTAND 1868–1918

12 Cyrano: *Il y a malgré vous quelque chose
Que j'emporte, et ce soir, quand j'entrerai chez Dieu,
Mon salut balaiera largement le seuil bleu,
Quelque chose que sans un pli, sans une tache,
J'emporte malgré vous…et c'est…*
Roxane: *C'est?…*
Cyrano: *Mon panache!*
Cyrano: There is, in spite of you, something which I
    shall take with me. And tonight, when I go into

God's house, my bow will make a wide sweep
across the blue threshold. Something which, with
not a crease, not a mark, I'm taking away in spite of
you…and it's…
Roxane: It's…
Cyrano: My panache!
Cyrano de Bergerac, V.iv

13 *Le seul rêve intéresse,
Vivre sans rêve, qu'est-ce?
Et j'aime la Princesse
    Lointaine.*
The dream, alone, is of interest. What is life, without
a dream? And I love the Distant Princess.
La Princesse Lointaine, I.iv

LEO C. ROSTEN 1908–

14 Any man who hates dogs and babies can't be all bad.
Of W.C. Fields, and often attributed to him. Speech at Masquers'
Club dinner, 16 Feb. 1939. See letter, *T.L.S.* 24 Jan. 1975

NORMAN ROSTEN

15 And there's the outhouse poet, anonymous:
        Soldiers who wish to be a hero
            Are practically zero
        But those who wish to be civilians
            Jesus they run into millions.
The Big Road (1946), pt.V

CLAUDE-JOSEPH ROUGET DE LISLE
1760–1836

16 *Allons, enfants de la patrie,
Le jour de gloire est arrivé.*
Come, children of our country, the day of glory has
arrived.
La Marseillaise (25 Apr. 1792)

JEAN-JACQUES ROUSSEAU 1712–1778

17 *L'homme est né libre, et partout il est dans les fers.*
Man was born free, and everywhere he is in chains.
Du Contrat Social, ch.1

DR. ROUTH 1755–1854

18 You will find it a very good practice always to verify
your references, sir!
Burgon, *Quarterly Review,* July 1878, vol.cxlvi, p.30, and *Lives
of Twelve Good Men* (1888 edn.), vol I, p.73

NICHOLAS ROWE 1674–1718

19 That false Lothario!
The Fair Penitent (1703), II.i

20 The evening of my age.
IV.i

21 I feel the pangs of disappointed love.

22 Is this that haughty, gallant, gay Lothario?
V.i

23 Like Helen, in the night when Troy was sack'd,
Spectatress of the mischief which she made.

24 Death is the privilege of human nature,
And life without it were not worth our taking.

25 Think on the sacred dictates of thy faith,
And let that arm thy virtue, to perform

What Cato's daughter durst not,—live Aspasia,
And dare to be unhappy.
Tamerlane (1702), IV.i

WILLIAM ROWLEY 1585?–1642?

1 Art thou gone in haste?
   I'll not forsake thee;
Run'st thou ne'er so fast,
   I'll o'ertake thee:
O'er the dales, o'er the downs,
Through the green meadows,
From the fields through the towns,
To the dim shadows.
The Thracian Wonder (1661), ascribed to Rowley and, improbably, John Webster, I.i

MATTHEW ROYDON fl. 1580–1622

2 A sweet attractive kind of grace,
   A full assurance given by looks,
Continual comfort in a face,
   The lineaments of Gospel books;
I trow that countenance cannot lie,
Whose thoughts are legible in the eye.
An Elegy, or Friend's Passion, for his Astrophill (i.e. Sir Philip Sidney) (1593), xviii

3 Was never eye, did see that face,
   Was never ear, did hear that tongue,
Was never mind, did mind his grace,
   That ever thought the travel long—
      But eyes, and ears, and ev'ry thought,
      Were with his sweet perfections caught.
xix

DAMON RUNYON 1884–1946

4 More than somewhat.
P. rase used frequently in Runyon's work, and adopted as book-title in 1937.

JOHN RUSKIN 1819–1900

5 You know there are a great many odd styles of architecture about; you don't want to do anything ridiculous; you hear of me, among others, as a respectable architectural man-milliner; and you send for me, that I may tell you the leading fashion.
The Crown of Wild Olive (1866), 53, lecture ii. **Traffic**

6 Thackeray settled like a meat-fly on whatever one had got for dinner, and made one sick of it.
Fors Clavigera (1871–84), letter xxxi

7 I have seen, and heard, much of Cockney impudence before now; but never expected to hear a coxcomb ask two hundred guineas for flinging a pot of paint in the public's face.
[On Whistler's 'Nocturne in Black and Gold'] letter lxxix, 18 June 1877. See 569:23

8 No person who is not a great sculptor or painter can be an architect. If he is not a sculptor or painter, he can only be a *builder*.
Lectures on Architecture and Painting (1853), 61, Addenda

9 Life without industry is guilt, and industry without art is brutality.
Lectures on Art, 3. **The Relation of Art to Morals**, 23 Feb. 1870

10 What is poetry? The suggestion, by the imagination, of noble grounds for the noble emotions.
Modern Painters (1888), vol.iii

11 All violent feelings…produce in us a falseness in all our impressions of external things, which I would generally characterize as the 'Pathetic Fallacy'.

12 Mountains are the beginning and the end of all natural scenery.
vol.iv, pt.v, ch.20, 1

13 There was a rocky valley between Buxton and Bakewell,…divine as the vale of Tempe; you might have seen the gods there morning and evening,—Apollo and the sweet Muses of the Light…You enterprised a railroad,…you blasted its rocks away…And now, every fool in Buxton can be at Bakewell in half-an-hour, and every fool in Bakewell at Buxton.
Praeterita (1885-9), III.iv. **Joanna's Cave**, 84, note

14 All books are divisible into two classes: the books of the hour, and the books of all time.
Sesame and Lilies (1865), Lecture i. **Of Kings' Treasuries**, 8

15 But whether thus submissively or not, at least be sure that you go to the author to get at his meaning, not to find yours.
13

16 Which of us…is to do the hard and dirty work for the rest—and for what pay? Who is to do the pleasant and clean work, and for what pay?
30, note

17 What do we, as a nation, care about books? How much do you think we spend altogether on our libraries, public or private, as compared with what we spend on our horses?
32

18 How long most people would look at the best book before they would give the price of a large turbot for it!

19 We call ourselves a rich nation, and we are filthy and foolish enough to thumb each other's books out of circulating libraries!

20 I believe the right question to ask, respecting all ornament, is simply this: Was it done with enjoyment—was the carver happy while he was about it?
The Seven Lamps of Architecture (1849), ch.5. **The Lamp of Life**

21 Better the rudest work that tells a story or records a fact, than the richest without meaning. There should not be a single ornament put upon great civic buildings, without some intellectual intention.
ch.6. **The Lamp of Memory**, 7

22 When we build, let us think that we build for ever.
10

23 Remember that the most beautiful things in the world are the most useless; peacocks and lilies for instance.
The Stones of Venice (1851-3), vol.i, ch.2, 17

24 The purest and most thoughtful minds are those which love colour the most.
vol.ii, ch.5, 30

25 Fine art is that in which the hand, the head, and the heart of man go together.
The Two Paths (1859), Lecture ii

26 Not only is there but one way of *doing* things rightly,

but there is only one way of *seeing* them, and that is, seeing the whole of them.

1 Nobody cares much at heart about Titian; only there is a strange undercurrent of everlasting murmur about his name, which means the deep consent of all great men that he is greater than they.

2 No human being, however great, or powerful, was ever so free as a fish.
Lecture v

3 Labour without joy is base. Labour without sorrow is base. Sorrow without labour is base. Joy without labour is base.
Time and Tide (1867), letter v

4 Your honesty is *not* to be based either on religion or policy. Both your religion and policy must be based on *it*. Your honesty must be based, as the sun is, in vacant heaven; poised, as the lights in the firmament, which have rule over the day and over the night.
letter viii

5 To make your children *capable of honesty* is the beginning of education.

6 I hold it for indisputable, that the first duty of a State is to see that every child born therein shall be well housed, clothed, fed and educated, till it attain years of discretion. But in order to the effecting this the Government must have an authority over the people of which we now do not so much as dream.
letter xiii

7 It ought to be quite as natural and straightforward a matter for a labourer to take his pension from his parish, because he has deserved well of his parish, as for a man in higher rank to take his pension from his country, because he has deserved well of his country.
Unto this Last (1862), preface, 6 (4)

8 The force of the guinea you have in your pocket depends wholly on the default of a guinea in your neighbour's pocket. If he did not want it, it would be of no use to you.
Essay ii, 27

9 Soldiers of the ploughshare as well as soldiers of the sword.
Essay iii, 54

10 Government and co-operation are in all things the laws of life; anarchy and competition the laws of death.

11 Whereas it has long been known and declared that the poor have no right to the property of the rich, I wish it also to be known and declared that the rich have no right to the property of the poor.

12 There is no wealth but life.
Essay iv, 77

13 Each book that a young girl touches should be bound in white vellum.
Said to Jane E. Harrison. *Reminiscences of a Student's Life*, ch.2

14 There is really no such thing as bad weather, only different kinds of good weather.
Quoted by Lord Avebury

BERTRAND RUSSELL 1872–1970

15 Mathematics, rightly viewed, possesses not only truth, but supreme beauty—a beauty cold and austere, like that of sculpture.
Mysticism and Logic (1918), ch.4

16 This method is, to define as the number of a class the class of all classes similar to the given class.
Principles of Mathematics, pt.II, ch.11, sect.iii (1903)

17 It is undesirable to believe a proposition when there is no ground whatever for supposing it true.
Sceptical Essays (1928), p.1

LORD JOHN RUSSELL 1792–1878

18 It is impossible that the whisper of a faction should prevail against the voice of a nation.
Letter to T. Attwood, Oct. 1831, after the rejection in the House of Lords of the Reform Bill (7 Oct. 1831)

19 If peace cannot be maintained with honour, it is no longer peace.
Greenock, 19 Sept. 1853

20 Among the defects of the Bill, which were numerous, one provision was conspicuous by its presence and another by its absence.
Speech to the electors of the City of London, Apr. 1859

21 A proverb is one man's wit and all men's wisdom.
Ascribed

JOHN RUSSELL 1919–

22 Certain phrases stick in the throat, even if they offer nothing that is analytically improbable. 'A dashing Swiss officer' is one such.
Paris (1960), ch.11

SIR WILLIAM HOWARD RUSSELL 1820–1907

23 They dashed on towards that *thin red line tipped with steel*.
The British Expedition to the Crimea (1877), p.156. Of the Russians charging the British. Russell's original dispatch to *The Times*, 25 Oct. 1854, read 'This thin red streak tipped with a line of steel', *The War* (1855)

LORD RUTHERFORD 1871–1937

24 We haven't the money, so we've got to think.
Attr. in Prof. R.V. Jones, 1962 Brunel Lecture, 14 Feb. 1962

GILBERT RYLE 1900–1976

25 The dogma of the Ghost in the machine.
The Concept of Mind (1949), passim

VICTORIA SACKVILLE-WEST 1892–1962

26 The greater cats with golden eyes
Stare out between the bars.
King's Daughter, II.i

WARHAM ST. LEGER 1850–c.1915

27 There is a fine stuffed chavender,
A chavender, or chub,
That decks the rural pavender,
The pavender, or pub,
Wherein I eat my gravender,
My gravender, or grub.
The Chavender, or Chub, st.1

CHARLES-AUGUSTIN SAINTE-BEUVE
1804–1869

1   *Et Vigny plus secret,*
Comme en sa tour d'ivoire, avant midi rentrait.
    And Vigny more reserved,
Returned ere noon, within his ivory tower.
Les Pensées d'Août, à M. Villemain, p.152

'SAKI' (H.H. MUNRO) 1870–1916

2 'The man is a common murderer.'
'A common murderer, possibly, but a very uncommon cook.'
Beasts and Super-Beasts (1914). **The Blind Spot**

3 When she inveighed eloquently against the evils of capitalism at drawing-room meetings and Fabian conferences she was conscious of a comfortable feeling that the system, with all its inequalities and iniquities, would probably last her time. It is one of the consolations of middle-aged reformers that the good they inculcate must live after them if it is to live at all.
The Byzantine Omelette

4 Waldo is one of those people who would be enormously improved by death.
The Feast of Nemesis

5 Romance at short notice was her speciality.
The Open Window

6 He's simply got the instinct for being unhappy highly developed.
The Chronicles of Clovis (1911). **The Match-Maker**

7 Oysters are more beautiful than any religion…There's nothing in Christianity or Buddhism that quite matches the sympathetic unselfishness of an oyster.

8 There are so many things to complain of in this household that it would never have occurred to me to complain of rheumatism.
The Quest

9 Never be a pioneer. It's the Early Christian that gets the fattest lion.
Reginald (1904), **Reginald's Choir Treat**

10 The cook was a good cook, as cooks go; and as cooks go she went.
Reginald on Besetting Sins

11 Women and elephants never forget an injury.

12 Addresses are given to us to conceal our whereabouts.
Reginald in Russia (1910). **Cross Currents**

13 The Western custom of one wife and hardly any mistresses.
A Young Turkish Catastrophe

14 But, good gracious, you've got to educate him first. You can't expect a boy to be vicious till he's been to a good school.
The Baker's Dozen

15 In baiting a mouse-trap with cheese, always leave room for the mouse.
The Square Egg (1924). **The Infernal Parliament**

16 Children with Hyacinth's temperament don't know better as they grow older; they merely know more.
The Toys of Peace (1919). **Hyacinth**

GEORGE AUGUSTUS SALA 1828–1896

17 And now, Sir, we will take a walk down Fleet Street.

Motto of the *Temple Bar* magazine (1860). Ascribed to Dr. Johnson.

LORD SALISBURY 1830–1903

18 No lesson seems to be so deeply inculcated by the experience of life as that you never should trust experts. If you believe the doctors, nothing is wholesome: if you believe the theologians, nothing is innocent: if you believe the soldiers, nothing is safe. They all require to have their strong wine diluted by a very large admixture of insipid common sense.
Letter to Lord Lytton, 15 June 1877. Lady Gwendolen Cecil, *Life of Robert, Marquis of Salisbury*, vol.II, ch.4

19 We are part of the community of Europe and we must do our duty as such.
Speech at Caernarvon, 11 Apr. 1888. Lady Gwendolen Cecil, *Life of Robert, Marquis of Salisbury*, vol.IV, ch.4

20 I cannot help thinking that in discussions of this kind, a great deal of misapprehension arises from the popular use of maps on a small scale. As with such maps you are able to put a thumb on India and a finger on Russia, some persons at once think that the political situation is alarming and that India must be looked to. If the noble Lord would use a larger map—say one on the scale of the Ordnance Map of England—he would find that the distance between Russia and British India is not to be measured by the finger and thumb, but by a rule.
House of Commons, 11 June 1877

21 By office boys for office boys.
Of the Daily Mail. See H. Hamilton Fyfe, *Northcliffe, an Intimate Biography*, ch.4

SALLUST c.86–c.35 B.C.

22 *Alieni appetens, sui profusus.*
Greedy for the property of others, extravagant with his own.
Catiline, 5

23 *Quieta movere magna merces videbatur.*
Just to stir things up seemed a great reward in itself.
21

24 *Esse quam videri bonus malebat.*
He preferred to be rather than to seem good.
54. Of Cato

25 *Punica fide.*
With Carthaginian trustworthiness.
Jugurtha, 108, 3. Meaning treachery.

CARL SANDBURG 1878–1967

26 The fog comes
on little cat feet.

It sits looking
over harbor and city
on silent haunches
and then moves on.
Fog

27 Pile the bodies high at Austerlitz and Waterloo.
Shovel them under and let me work—
        I am the grass; I cover all.
  Grass

GEORGE SANTAYANA 1863–1952

1 Progress, far from consisting in change, depends on retentiveness...Those who cannot remember the past are condemned to fulfil it.
Life of Reason (1905-6), vol.I, ch.xii. **Flux and Constancy in Human Nature**

2 Reason is not come to repeat the universe but to fulfil it.
vol.V, ch.ii. **History**

3 Music is essentially useless, as life is: but both lend utility to their conditions.
Little Essays (1920), pt.iii, no.54

4 Never since the heroic days of Greece has the world had such a sweet, just, boyish master. It will be a black day for the human race when scientific blackguards, conspirators, churls, and fanatics manage to supplant him.
Soliloquies in England (1922), 9. **The British Character**

5 For an idea ever to be fashionable is ominous, since it must afterwards be always old-fashioned.
Winds of Doctrine (1913). **Modernism and Christianity**

SAPPHO b. c.612 B.C.

6 φαίνεταί μοι κῆνος ἴσος θέοισιν
ἔμμεν' ὤνηρ, ὄττις ἐνάντιός τοι
ἰσδάνει καὶ πλάσιον ἀδυ φωνεί-
  σας ὑπακούει

καὶ γελαίσας ἰμέροεν, τό μ' ἦ μὰν
καρδίαν ἐν στήθεσιν ἐπτόαισεν,
ὡς γὰρ ἔς σ' ἴδω βρόχε', ὤς με φώναι-
  σ' οὐδ' ἒν ἔτ' εἴκει,

ἀλλ' ἄκαν μεν γλῶσσα πεπαγε, λέπτον
δ' αὔτικα χρῶι πῦρ ὑπαδεδρόμηκεν,
ὀππάτεσσι δ' οὐδ' ἒν ὄρημμ', ἐπιρρόμ-
  βεισι δ' ἄκουαι,

κὰδ δέ μ' ἴδρως κακχέεται, τρόμος δὲ
παῖσαν ἄγρει, χλωροτέρα δὲ ποίας
ἔμμι, τεθνάκην δ' ὀλίγω 'πιδεύης
  φαίνομ' ἔμ' αὔται.

That man seems to me on a par with the gods who sits in your company and listens to you so close to him speaking sweetly and laughing sexily, such a thing makes my heart flutter in my breast, for when I see you even for a moment, then power to speak another word fails me, instead my tongue freezes into silence, and at once a gentle fire has caught throughout my flesh, and I see nothing with my eyes, and there's a drumming in my ears, and sweat pours down me, and trembling seizes all of me, and I become paler than grass, and I seem to fail almost to the point of death in my very self.
D.L. Page, *Lyrica Selecta Graeca* (1968)

7 οἷον τὸ γλυκύμαλον ἐρεύθεται ἄκρω ἐπ' ὕσδω,
ἄκρον ἐπ' ἀκροτάτω, λελάθοντο δὲ μαλοδρόπηες,
οὐ μὰν ἐκλελάθοντ', ἀλλ' οὐκ ἐδύναντ' ἐπίκεσθαι.
Just as the sweet-apple reddens on the high branch, high on the highest, and the apple-pickers missed it, or rather did not miss it out, but dared not reach it.
105(a). Of a girl before her marriage

JEAN-PAUL SARTRE 1905–

8 *Alors, c'est ça l'Enfer. Je n'aurais jamais cru...Vous vous rappelez: le soufre, le bûcher, le gril...Ah! quelle plaisanterie. Pas besoin de gril, l'Enfer, c'est les Autres.*
So that's what Hell is. I'd never have believed it...Do you remember, brimstone, the stake, the gridiron?...What a joke! No need of a gridiron, [when it come to] Hell, it's other people.
Huis Clos, sc.v

9 *Trois heures, c'est toujours trop tard ou trop tôt pour tout ce qu'on veut faire.*
Three o'clock is always too late or too early for anything you want to do.
La Nausée, **Vendredi**

SIEGFRIED SASSOON 1886–1967

10 If I were fierce and bald and short of breath,
  I'd live with scarlet Majors at the Base,
And speed glum heroes up the line to death.
Base Details

11 And when the war is done and youth stone dead
I'd toddle safely home and die—in bed.

12 I'd like to see a Tank come down the stalls,
Lurching to rag-time tunes, or 'Home, sweet Home,'—
And there'd be no more jokes in Music-halls
To mock the riddled corpses round Bapaume.
'Blighters'

13 Does it matter?—losing your legs?...
For people will always be kind,
And you need not show that you mind
When others come in after hunting
To gobble their muffins and eggs.

Does it matter?—losing your sight?...
There's such splendid work for the blind;
And people will always be kind,
As you sit on the terrace remembering
And turning your face to the light.
Does it Matter?

14 Why do you lie with your legs ungainly huddled,
And one arm bent across your sullen, cold
Exhausted face?
The Dug-Out

15 You are too young to fall asleep for ever;
And when you sleep you remind me of the dead.

16 Everyone suddenly burst out singing.
Everyone Sang

17   The song was wordless;
The singing will never be done.

18 'Good morning; good morning!' the general said
When we met him last week on our way to the line.
Now the soldiers he smiled at are most of 'em dead,
And we're cursing his staff for incompetent swine.
'He's a cheery old card,' grunted Harry to Jack
As they slogged up to Arras with rifle and pack...
But he did for them both with his plan of attack.
The General

19 They have spoken lightly of my deathless friends,
(Lamps for my gloom, hands guiding where I
  stumble,)
Quoting, for shallow conversational ends,
What Shelley shrilled, what Blake once wildly

muttered...
How can they use such names and not be humble?
I have sat silent; angry at what they uttered.
The Grandeur of Ghosts

1 In me the tiger sniffs the rose.
The Heart's Journey, VIII

2 *Alone...*the word is life endured and known.
XII

3 Here sleeps the Silurist; the loved physician;
The face that left no portraiture behind;
The skull that housed white angels and had vision
Of daybreak through the gateways of the mind.
XXIII. **At the Grave of Henry Vaughan**

4 A sallow waiter brings me beans and pork...
Outside there's fury in the firmament.
Ice-cream, of course, will follow; and I'm content.
O Babylon! O Carthage! O New York!
Storm on Fifth Avenue

RICHARD SAVAGE d. 1743

5 Perhaps been poorly rich, and meanly great,
The slave of pomp, a cipher in the state.
The Bastard (1728), l.39

GEORGE SAVILE, MARQUIS OF HALIFAX
see HALIFAX

DOROTHY L. SAYERS 1893–1957

6 I admit it is more fun to punt than to be punted, and
that a desire to have all the fun is nine-tenths of the law
of chivalry.
Gaudy Night, ch.14

7 As I grow older and older,
And totter towards the tomb,
I find that I care less and less
Who goes to bed with whom.
That's why I never read modern novels

FRIEDRICH VON SCHELLING 1775–1854

8 Architecture in general is frozen music.
Philosophie der Kunst (1809)

FRIEDRICH VON SCHILLER 1759–1805

9 *Freude, schöner Götterfunken,*
Tochter aus Elysium,
Wir betreten feuertrunken,
Himmlische, dein Heiligtum.
Deine Zauber binden wieder,
Was die Mode streng geteilt,
Alle Menschen werden Brüder
Wo dein sanfter Flügel weilt.
Joy, beautiful radiance of the gods, daughter of
Elysium, we set foot in your heavenly shrine dazzled
by your brilliance. Your charms re-unite what
common use has harshly divided: all men become
brothers under your tender wing.
An die Freude (1786)

10 *Mit der Dummheit kämpfen Götter selbst vergebens.*
With stupidity the gods themselves struggle in vain.
Die Jungfrau von Orleans (1801), III.vi

11 *Die Weltgeschichte ist das Weltgericht.*
The world's history is the world's judgement.
First lecture as Prof. of History, Jena. 26 May 1789

PROFESSOR E.F. SCHUMACHER 1911–1977

12 Small is beautiful.
Title of book (1973)

CARL SCHURZ 1829–1906

13 Our country, right or wrong! When right, to be kept
right; when wrong, to be put right!
Speech, U.S. Senate, 1872. See 173:1

ALEXANDER SCOTT 1525?–1584?

14 Love is ane fervent fire,
Kindled without desire,
Short pleasure, long displeasure;
Repentance is the hire;
And pure treasure without measure.
Love is ane fervent fire.
Lo, What it is to Love (c. 1568)

C.P. SCOTT 1846–1932

15 The newspaper is of necessity something of a
monopoly, and its first duty is to shun the temptations
of monopoly. Its primary office is the gathering of
news. At the peril of its soul it must see that the supply
is not tainted. Neither in what it gives, nor in what it
does not give, nor in the mode of presentation, must
the unclouded face of truth suffer wrong. Comment is
free but facts are sacred.
Manchester Guardian, 6 May 1926

16 Television? The word is half Latin and half Greek. No
good can come of it.
Attr.

CAPTAIN ROBERT FALCON SCOTT 1868–1912

17 Great God! this is an awful place. [The South Pole.]
Journal, 17 Jan. 1912

18 For God's sake look after our people.
25 Mar. 1912

19 Had we lived, I should have had a tale to tell of the
hardihood, endurance, and courage of my companions
which would have stirred the heart of every
Englishman. These rough notes and our dead bodies
must tell the tale.
Message to the Public

SIR WALTER SCOTT 1771–1832

20 To the Lords of Convention 'twas Claver'se who
spoke,
'Ere the King's crown shall fall there are crowns to be
broke;
So let each cavalier who loves honour and me,
Come follow the bonnet of Bonny Dundee.
Come fill up my cup, come fill up my can,
Come saddle your horses, and call up your men;
Come open the West Port, and let me gang free,
And it's room for the bonnets of Bonny Dundee!'
Bonny Dundee. (*The Doom of Devorgoil,* 1830, Act II, sc.ii).
See 418:30

21 The valiant Knight of Triermain

Rung forth his challenge-blast again,
But answer came there none.
The Bridal of Triermain (1813), c.III.x

1 The stag at eve had drunk his fill,
Where danced the moon on Monan's rill,
And deep his midnight lair had made
In lone Glenartney's hazel shade.
The Lady of the Lake (1810), c.I.i

2 His ready speech flow'd fair and free,
In phrase of gentlest courtesy;
Yet seem'd that tone, and gesture bland,
Less used to sue than to command.
xxi

3 Huntsman, rest! thy chase is done.
xxxii

4 Hail to the Chief who in triumph advances!
c.II.xix

5 He is gone on the mountain,
He is lost to the forest,
Like a summer-dried fountain,
When our need was the sorest.
c.III.xvi

6 Respect was mingled with surprise,
And the stern joy which warriors feel
In foemen worthy of their steel.
c.V.x

7 Where, where was Roderick then?
One blast upon his bugle-horn
Were worth a thousand men!
c.VI.xviii

8 The way was long, the wind was cold,
The Minstrel was infirm and old;
His wither'd cheek and tresses grey,
Seem'd to have known a better day.
The Lay of the Last Minstrel (1805), introd. l.1

9 The last of all the Bards was he,
Who sung of Border chivalry;
For, welladay! their date was fled,
His tuneful brethren all were dead;
And he, neglected and oppress'd,
Wish'd to be with them, and at rest.
l.7

10 The unpremeditated lay.
l.18

11 Vengeance, deep-brooding o'er the slain,
Had lock'd the source of softer woe;
And burning pride and high disdain
Forbade the rising tear to flow.
c.I.ix

12 What shall be the maiden's fate?
Who shall be the maiden's mate?
xvi

13 If thou would'st view fair Melrose aright,
Go visit it by the pale moonlight;
For the gay beams of lightsome day
Gild, but to flout, the ruins grey.
c.II.i

14 Strange sounds along the chancel pass'd,
The banner wav'd without a blast.
xvi

15 Yet somewhat was he chill'd with dread,
And his hair did bristle upon his head.

16 I cannot tell how the truth may be;

I say the tale as 'twas said to me.
xxii

17 In peace, Love tunes the shepherd's reed;
In war, he mounts the warrior's steed;
In halls, in gay attire is seen;
In hamlets, dances on the green.
Love rules the court, the camp, the grove,
And men below, and saints above;
For love is heaven, and heaven is love.
c.III.ii

18 For ne'er
Was flattery lost on poet's ear:
A simple race! they waste their toil
For the vain tribute of a smile.
c.IV, conclusion

19 Call it not vain; they do not err,
Who say, that when the Poet dies,
Mute Nature mourns her worshipper,
And celebrates his obsequies.
c.V.i

20 It is the secret sympathy,
The silver link, the silken tie,
Which heart to heart, and mind to mind,
In body and in soul can bind.
xiii

21 Breathes there the man, with soul so dead,
Who never to himself hath said,
This is my own, my native land!
Whose heart hath ne'er within him burn'd,
As home his footsteps he hath turn'd
From wandering on a foreign strand!
c.VI.i

22 Despite those titles, power, and pelf,
The wretch, concentred all in self,
Living, shall forfeit fair renown,
And, doubly dying, shall go down
To the vile dust, from whence he sprung,
Unwept, unhonour'd, and unsung.

O Caledonia! stern and wild,
Meet nurse for a poetic child!
Land of brown heath and shaggy wood,
Land of the mountain and the flood,
Land of my sires! what mortal hand
Can e'er untie the filial band
That knits me to thy rugged strand!

23 O! many a shaft, at random sent,
Finds mark the archer little meant!
And many a word, at random spoken,
May soothe or wound a heart that's broken.
The Lord of the Isles (1813), c.V.xviii

24 O hush thee, my babie, thy sire was a knight,
Thy mother a lady, both lovely and bright.
Lullaby of an Infant Chief

25 Then hush thee, my darling, take rest while you may,
For strife comes with manhood, and waking with day.

26 O lovers' eyes are sharp to see,
And lovers' ears in hearing.
The Maid of Neidpath

27 November's sky is chill and drear,
November's leaf is red and sear.
Marmion (1808), c.I, introd. i

28 To him, as to the burning levin,

Short, bright, resistless course was given.
vi

1 Had'st thou but liv'd, though stripp'd of power,
A watchman on the lonely tower. [On Pitt.]
viii

2 Now is the stately column broke,
The beacon-light is quench'd in smoke,
The trumpet's silver sound is still,
The warder silent on the hill! [On Pitt.]

3 Drop upon Fox's grave the tear,
'Twill trickle to his rival's bier;
O'er Pitt's the mournful requiem sound,
And Fox's shall the notes rebound.
xi

4 But search the land of living men,
Where wilt thou find their like agen?

5 His square-turn'd joints, and strength of limb,
Show'd him no carpet knight so trim,
But in close fight a champion grim,
    In camps a leader sage.
c.I.v

6 And come he slow, or come he fast,
It is but Death who comes at last.
c.II.xxx

7 Still is thy name in high account,
    And still thy verse has charms,
Sir David Lindesay of the Mount,
    Lord Lion King-at-arms!
c.IV.vii

8 O, young Lochinvar is come out of the west,
Through all the wide Border his steed was the best.
c.V.xii

9 So faithful in love, and so dauntless in war,
There never was knight like the young Lochinvar.

10 For a laggard in love, and a dastard in war,
Was to wed the fair Ellen of brave Lochinvar.

11 'O come ye in peace here, or come ye in war,
Or to dance at our bridal, young Lord Lochinvar?'

12 'To lead but one measure, drink one cup of wine.'

13 She look'd down to blush, and she look'd up to sigh,
With a smile on her lips and a tear in her eye,
He took her soft hand, ere her mother could bar,—
'Now tread we a measure!' said young Lochinvar.

14 'She is won! we are gone, over bank, bush, and scaur;
They'll have fleet steeds that follow' quoth young
    Lochinvar.

15 Heap on more wood!—the wind is chill;
But let it whistle as it will,
We'll keep our Christmas merry still.
c.VI, introd. i

16 England was merry England, when
Old Christmas brought his sports again.
'Twas Christmas broach'd the mightiest ale;
'Twas Christmas told the merriest tale;
A Christmas gambol oft could cheer
The poor man's heart through half the year.
iii

17 My castles are my King's alone,
From turret to foundation-stone—
The hand of Douglas is his own.
xiii

18   'And dar'st thou then
To beard the lion in his den,
The Douglas in his hall?
And hop'st thou thence unscathed to go?
No, by Saint Bride of Bothwell, no!
Up drawbridge, grooms—what, warder, ho!
Let the portcullis fall.'
xiv

19 O what a tangled web we weave,
When first we practise to deceive!
xvii

20 And such a yell was there,
Of sudden and portentous birth,
As if men fought upon the earth,
And fiends in upper air.
xxv

21 O Woman! in our hours of ease,
Uncertain, coy, and hard to please,
And variable as the shade
By the light quivering aspen made;
When pain and anguish wring the brow,
A ministering angel thou!
xxx

22 'Charge, Chester, charge! On, Stanley, on!'
Were the last words of Marmion.
xxxii

23 O, for a blast of that dread horn,
On Fontarabian echoes borne!
xxxiii

24 The stubborn spear-men still made good
Their dark impenetrable wood,
Each stepping where his comrade stood,
    The instant that he fell.
xxxiv

25 Still from the sire the son shall hear
Of the stern strife, and carnage drear,
    Of Flodden's fatal field,
Where shiver'd was fair Scotland's spear,
    And broken was her shield!

26 To all, to each, a fair good-night,
And pleasing dreams, and slumbers light!
L'envoy

27 Pibroch of Donuil Dhu,
    Pibroch of Donuil,
Wake thy wild voice anew,
    Summon Clan-Conuil.
Come away, come away,
    Hark to the summons!
Come in your war array,
    Gentles and commons.
Pibroch of Donuil Dhu

28 Leave untended the herd,
    The flock without shelter;
Leave the corpse uninterr'd,
    The bride at the altar.

29 See yon pale stripling! when a boy,
A mother's pride, a father's joy!
Rokeby (1813), c.III.xv

30 O, Brignal banks are wild and fair,
    And Greta woods are green,
And you may gather garlands there
    Would grace a summer queen.
xvi

1 You...whirl'd them to the back o' beyont.
The Antiquary (1816), ch.2

2 It's no fish ye're buying—it's men's lives.
ch.11

3 Widow'd wife, and married maid,
Betrothed, betrayer, and betray'd!
The Betrothed (1825), ch.15

4 Woman's faith, and woman's trust—
Write the characters in dust.
ch.20

5 Look not thou on beauty's charming,—
Sit thou still when kings are arming,—
Taste not when the wine-cup glistens,—
Speak not when the people listens,—
Stop thine ear against the singer,—
From the red gold keep thy finger;—
Vacant heart and hand, and eye,—
Easy live and quiet die.
The Bride of Lammermoor (1819), ch.3

6 I live by twa trades, sir,...fiddle, sir, and spade; filling
the world, and emptying of it.
ch.24

7 Her winding-sheet is up as high as her throat already.
ch.34

8 An ower true tale.

9 Touch not the cat but a glove.
The Fair Maid of Perth (1828), ch.34. but ; without.

10 But no one shall find me rowing against the stream. I
care not who knows it—I write for the general
amusement.
The Fortunes of Nigel (1822), introductory epistle

11 It's ill taking the breeks aff a wild Highlandman.
ch.5

12 For a con-si-de-ra-tion.
ch.22

13 O Geordie, Jingling Geordie, it was grand to hear
Baby Charles laying down the guilt of dissimulation,
and Steenie lecturing on the turpitude of incontinence.
ch.31

14 *Mrs. Bertram:* That sounds like nonsense, my dear.
Mr. Bertram: May be so, my dear; but it may be very
good law for all that.
Guy Mannering (1815), ch.9

15 Sophia, as you well know, followed me to India. She
was as innocent as gay; but, unfortunately for us both,
as gay as innocent.
ch.12. See 588:7

16 Gin by pailfuls, wine in rivers,
Dash the window-glass to shivers!
For three wild lads were we, brave boys,
And three wild lads were we;
Thou on the land, and I on the sand,
And Jack on the gallows-tree!
ch.34

17 The ancient and now forgotten pastime of high jinks.
ch.36

18 The hour is come, but not the man.
The Heart of Midlothian (1818), ch.4, heading

19 The passive resistance of the Tolbooth-gate.
ch.6

20 Jock, when ye hae naething else to do, ye may be ay
sticking in a tree; it will be growing, Jock, when ye're
sleeping.
ch.8

21 Proud Maisie is in the wood,
Walking so early,
Sweet Robin sits in the bush,
Singing so rarely.
ch.40

22 'Pax vobiscum' will answer all queries.
Ivanhoe (1819), ch.26

23 His morning walk was beneath the elms in the
churchyard; 'for death,' he said, 'had been his
next-door neighbour for so many years, that he had no
apology for dropping the acquaintance.'
A Legend of Montrose (1819), introd.

24 March, march, Ettrick and Teviotdale,
Why the deil dinna ye march forward in order?
March, march, Eskdale and Liddesdale,
All the Blue Bonnets are bound for the Border.
The Monastery (1820), ch.25

25 Ah! County Guy, the hour is nigh,
The sun has left the lea,
The orange flower perfumes the bower,
The breeze is on the sea.
Quentin Durward (1823), ch.4

26 And it's ill speaking between a fou man and a fasting.
Redgauntlet (1824), Letter 11, **Wandering Willie's Tale**

27 Better a finger off, as ay wagging.
ch.2

28 The ae half of the warld thinks the tither daft.
ch.7

29 But with the morning cool repentance came.
Rob Roy (1817), ch.12

30 Come fill up my cup, come fill up my cann,
Come saddle my horses, and call up my man;
Come open your gates, and let me gae free,
I daurna stay langer in bonny Dundee.
ch.23. See 415:20

31 There's a gude time coming.
ch.32

32 Speak out, sir, and do not Maister or Campbell
me— my foot is on my native heath, and my name is
MacGregor!
ch.34

33 Fair, fat, and forty.
St. Ronan's Well (1823), ch.7

34 The play-bill, which is said to have announced the
tragedy of Hamlet, the character of the Prince of
Denmark being left out.
The Talisman (1825), introd. For an earlier report of this anecdote
see *T.L.S.* 3 June 1939

35 Rouse the lion from his lair.
ch.6

36 But I must say to the Muse of fiction, as the Earl of
Pembroke said to the ejected nun of Wilton, 'Go spin,
you jade, go spin!'
Journal, 9 Feb. 1826. See 371:10

37 The Big Bow-Wow strain I can do myself like any now
going; but the exquisite touch, which renders ordinary
commonplace things and characters interesting, from
the truth of the description and the sentiment, is denied
to me. [On Jane Austen.]
14 Mar. 1826. See 371:12

38 I would like to be there, were it but to see how the cat

jumps.
7 Oct. 1826

1 The blockheads talk of my being like
Shakespeare—not fit to tie his brogues.
11 Dec. 1826

2 I never saw a richer country or to speak my mind a
finer people. The worst of them is the bitter and
envenomed dislike which they have to each other their
factions have been so long envenomed and having so
little ground to fight their battle in that they are like
people fighting with daggers in a hogshead.
Letter to Joanna Baillie, 12 Oct. 1825

3 All men who have turned out worth anything have had
the chief hand in their own education.
Letter to J.G. Lockhart, c.16 June 1830

4 We shall never learn to feel and respect our real calling
and destiny, unless we have taught ourselves to
consider every thing as moonshine, compared with the
education of the heart.
To J.G. Lockhart (Aug. 1825), quoted in Lockhart's *Life of Sir
Walter Scott*, vol. 6 (1837), ch.2

SCOTTISH METRICAL PSALMS 1650

5 The Lord's my shepherd, I'll not want.
    He makes me down to lie
In pastures green: he leadeth me
    the quiet waters by.
My soul he doth restore again;
    and me to walk doth make
Within the paths of righteousness,
    ev'n for his own name's sake.

Yea, though I walk in death's dark vale,
    yet will I fear none ill:
For thou art with me; and thy rod
    and staff me comfort still.
My table thou hast furnished
    in presence of my foes;
My head thou dost with oil anoint,
    and my cup overflows.
Psalm xxiii.1. See 390:22

6 I to the hills will lift mine eyes
    from whence doth come mine aid.
Psalm cxxi.1. See 398:9

7 The race that long in darkness pin'd
    have seen a glorious light.
Paraphrase 19. Isaiah ix.2

SIR CHARLES SEDLEY 1639?–1701

8 Ah, Chloris! that I now could sit
    As unconcerned as when
Your infant beauty could beget
    No pleasure, nor no pain!
Child and Maiden

9 Love still has something of the sea
    From whence his mother rose.
Love still has Something

10 Phyllis is my only joy,
    Faithless as the winds or seas;
Sometimes coming, sometimes coy,
    Yet she never fails to please.
Song

11   She deceiving,
      I believing;
What need lovers wish for more?

12 Phyllis, without frown or smile,
Sat and knotted all the while.
Song [Phyllis Knotting]

13 Not, Celia, that I juster am
    Or better than the rest,
For I would change each hour like them,
    Were not my heart at rest.
Song [To Celia]

14 Why then should I seek farther store,
    And still make love anew;
When change itself can give no more,
    'Tis easy to be true.

ALAN SEEGER 1888–1916

15 I have a rendezvous with Death
At some disputed barricade.
I Have a Rendezvous with Death (*North American Review*, Oct.
1916)

SIR JOHN SEELEY 1834–1895

16 We [the English] seem, as it were, to have conquered
and peopled half the world in a fit of absence of mind.
The Expansion of England (1883), Lecture I

17 History is past politics, and politics present history.
The Growth of British Policy (1895)

JOHN SELDEN 1584–1654

18 *Scrutamini scripturas.* These two words have undone
the world.
Table Talk (1689), 1892 edn. p.10. **Bible Scripture.** See 72:3

19 Old friends are best. King James used to call for his
old shoes; they were easiest for his feet.
p.71. **Friends**

20 'Tis not the drinking that is to be blamed, but the
excess.
p.78. **Humility**

21 Ignorance of the law excuses no man; not that all men
know the law, but because 'tis an excuse every man
will plead, and no man can tell how to confute him.
p.99. **Law**

22 Take a straw and throw it up into the air, you shall see
by that which way the wind is.
p.105. **Libels**

23 Marriage is nothing but a civil contract.
p.109. **Marriage**

24 There never was a merry world since the fairies left
off dancing, and the Parson left conjuring.
p.130. **Parson**

25 There is not anything in the world so much abused as
this sentence, *Salus populi suprema lex esto.*
p.131. **People.** See 151:19

26 Pleasure is nothing else but the intermission of pain,
the enjoying of something I am in great trouble for till
I have it.
p.132. **Pleasure**

1 Preachers say, Do as I say, not as I do.
p.147. **Preaching**

W.C. SELLAR 1898–1951
and **R.J. YEATMAN** 1898?–1968

2 The Roman Conquest was, however, a *Good Thing*.
1066, And All That (1930), ch.1

3 The memorable epitaph: *'Honi soie qui mal y pense'*
('Honey, your silk stocking's hanging down').
ch.25

4 The Cavaliers (Wrong but Wromantic) and the
Roundheads (Right but Repulsive).
ch.35

5 Charles II was always very merry and was therefore
not so much a king as a Monarch.
ch.36

6 The National Debt is a very Good Thing and it would
be dangerous to pay it off for fear of Political
Economy.
ch.38

7 Napoleon's armies always used to march on their
stomachs, shouting: 'Vive l'Intérieur!'
ch.48

8 A Bad Thing, America was thus clearly top nation,
and History came to a .
ch. 62

SENECA 4 B.C./A.D. 1–65

9 Eternal law has arranged nothing better than this, that
it has given us one way in to life, but many ways out.
Epistulae Morales, 70.14

10 *Homines dum docent discunt.*
Even while they teach, men learn.
Letters, 7.8

11 Anyone can stop a man's life, but no one his death; a
thousand doors open on to it.
Phoenissae, 152

ROBERT W. SERVICE 1874–1958

12 Ah! the clock is always slow;
It is later than you think.
Ballads of a Bohemian. **Spring,** ii

13 This is the Law of the Yukon, that only the Strong
shall thrive;
That surely the Weak shall perish, and only the Fit
survive.
Dissolute, damned, and despairful, crippled and
palsied and slain,
This is the Will of the Yukon,—Lo! how she makes it
plain!
Songs of a Sourdough (1907). **The Law of the Yukon**

14 Back of the bar, in a solo game, sat Dangerous Dan
McGrew,
And watching his luck was his light-o'-love, the lady
that's known as Lou.
The Shooting of Dan McGrew

WILLIAM SEWARD 1801–1872

15 The Constitution devotes the domain to union, to
justice, to defence, to welfare, and to liberty. But there

is a higher law than the Constitution.
U.S. Senate, 11 Mar. 1850

16 I know, and all the world knows, that revolutions
never go backward.
At Rochester on the Irrepressible Conflict, Oct. 1858

EDWARD SEXBY d. 1658

17 Killing no Murder Briefly Discourst in Three
Questions.
Title of Pamphlet, 1657

ANNE SEXTON 1928–1974

18 In a dream you are never eighty.
Old

THOMAS SHADWELL 1642?–1692

19 Words may be false and full of art,
Sighs are the natural language of the heart.
Psyche (1674), Act III

20 And wit's the noblest frailty of the mind.
A True Widow (1678-9), II.i. See 196:23

21 The haste of a fool is the slowest thing in the world.
III.i

22 Every man loves what he is good at.
V.i

23 Instantly, in the twinkling of a bed-staff.
Virtuoso (1676), I.i

**ANTHONY ASHLEY COOPER, 1ST EARL OF
SHAFTESBURY** 1621–1683

24 'People differ in their discourse and profession about
these matters, but men of sense are really but of one
religion.'...'Pray, my lord, what religion is that which
men of sense agree in?' 'Madam,' says the earl
immediately, 'men of sense never tell it.'
Bishop Burnet, *History of My Own Time*, vol.I, bk.ii, ch.1, note
by Onslow

WILLIAM SHAKESPEARE 1564–1616

The line number is given without brackets where the scene is all
verse up to the quotation and the line number is certain, and in
square brackets where prose makes it variable. All references are
to the Oxford Standard Authors Shakespeare in one volume.

ALL'S WELL THAT ENDS WELL

25   It were all one
That I should love a bright particular star
And think to wed it, he is so above me.
I.i.[97]

26 The hind that would be mated with the lion
Must die of love.
[103]

27 Your virginity, your old virginity, is like one of our
French withered pears; it looks ill, it eats drily.
[176]

28 Our remedies oft in ourselves do lie
Which we ascribe to heaven.
[235]

29 It is like a barber's chair that fits all buttocks.
II.ii.[18]

1 A young man married is a man that's marred.
iii.[315]

2 I know a man that had this trick of melancholy sold a
goodly manor for a song.
III.ii.[8]

3 The web of our life is of a mingled yarn, good and ill
together: our virtues would be proud if our faults
whipped them not; and our crimes would despair if
they were not cherished by our own virtues.
IV.iii.[83]

4 The flowery way that leads to the broad gate and the
great fire.
v.[58]. See 460:17

5   Praising what is lost
Makes the remembrance dear.
V.iii.19

ANTONY AND CLEOPATRA

6 The triple pillar of the world transform'd
Into a strumpet's fool.
I.i.12

7 *Cleopatra:* If it be love indeed, tell me how much.
Antony: There's beggary in the love that can be
reckoned.
Cleopatra: I'll set a bourn how far to be belov'd.
Antony: Then must thou needs find out new heaven,
new earth.
14

8 Kingdoms are clay; our dungy earth alike
Feeds beast as man; the nobleness of life
Is to do thus; when such a mutual pair
And such a twain can do't.
35

9 In Nature's infinite book of secrecy
A little I can read.
ii.[11]

10 You shall be yet far fairer than you are.
[18]

11 You shall be more beloving than belov'd.
[24]

12 O excellent! I love long life better than figs.
[34]

13 Mine, and most of our fortunes, to-night, shall
be,—drunk to bed.
[47]

14 But a worky-day fortune.
[57]

15   On the sudden
A Roman thought hath struck him.
[90]

16 The nature of bad news infects the teller.
[103]

17 These strong Egyptian fetters I must break,
Or lose myself in dotage.
[125]

18 There's a great spirit gone!
[131]

19 I must from this enchanting queen break off;
Ten thousand harms, more than the ills I know,
My idleness doth hatch.
[137]

20 I have seen her die twenty times upon far poorer

moment. I do think there is mettle in death which
commits some loving act upon her, she hath such a
celerity in dying.
[150]

21 O sir! you had then left unseen a wonderful piece of
work which not to have been blessed withal would
have discredited your travel.
[164]

22 Indeed the tears live in an onion that should water this
sorrow.
[181]

23   If you find him sad,
Say I am dancing; if in mirth, report
That I am sudden sick.
iii.3

24 *Charmian:* In each thing give him way, cross him in
nothing.
Cleopatra: Thou teachest like a fool; the way to lose
him.
9

25 In time we hate that which we often fear.
12

26 Eternity was in our lips and eyes,
Bliss in our brows bent.
35

27 Though age from folly could not give me freedom,
It does from childishness.
57

28   Courteous lord, one word.
Sir, you and I must part, but that's not it:
Sir, you and I have lov'd, but there's not it;
That you know well: something it is I would,—
O! my oblivion is a very Antony,
And I am all forgotten.
86

29   On the Alps
It is reported thou didst eat strange flesh,
Which some did die to look on.
iv.66

30 Give me to drink mandragora...
That I might sleep out this great gap of time
My Antony is away.
v.4

31 O happy horse, to bear the weight of Antony!
Do bravely, horse, for wot'st thou whom thou mov'st?
The demi-Atlas of this earth, the arm
And burgonet of men. He's speaking now,
Or murmuring 'Where's my serpent of old Nile?'
21

32   Think on me,
That am with Phoebus' amorous pinches black,
And wrinkled deep in time? Broad-fronted Caesar,
When thou wast here above the ground I was
A morsel for a monarch, and great Pompey
Would stand and make his eyes grow in my brow;
There would he anchor his aspect and die
With looking on his life.
27

33   My salad days,
When I was green in judgment, cold in blood,
To say as I said then!
73

34 I do not much dislike the matter, but

The manner of his speech.
II.ii.117

1   Take Antony
Octavia to his wife; whose beauty claims
No worse a husband than the best of men.
133

2 The barge she sat in, like a burnish'd throne,
Burn'd on the water; the poop was beaten gold,
Purple the sails, and so perfumed, that
The winds were love-sick with them, the oars were
    silver,
Which to the tune of flutes kept stroke, and made
The water which they beat to follow faster,
As amorous of their strokes. For her own person,
It beggar'd all description; she did lie
In her pavilion,—cloth-of-gold of tissue,—
O'er-picturing that Venus where we see
The fancy outwork nature; on each side her
Stood pretty-dimpled boys, like smiling Cupids,
With divers-colour'd fans, whose wind did seem
To glow the delicate cheeks which they did cool,
And what they undid did.
[199]

3 Her gentlewomen, like the Nereides,
So many mermaids, tended her i' the eyes,
And made their bends adornings; at the helm
A seeming mermaid steers; the silken tackle
Swell with the touches of those flower-soft hands,
That yarely frame the office. From the barge
A strange invisible perfume hits the sense
Of the adjacent wharfs. The city cast
Her people out upon her, and Antony,
Enthron'd i' the market-place, did sit alone,
Whistling to the air; which, but for vacancy,
Had gone to gaze on Cleopatra too
And made a gap in nature.
[214]

4   I saw her once
Hop forty paces through the public street;
And having lost her breath, she spoke, and panted
That she did make defect perfection,
And, breathless, power breathe forth.
[236]

5 Age cannot wither her, nor custom stale
Her infinite variety; other women cloy
The appetites they feed, but she makes hungry
Where most she satisfies; for vilest things
Become themselves in her, that the holy priests
Bless her when she is riggish.
[243]

6 I have not kept the square, but that to come
Shall all be done by the rule.
iii.6

7 I' the east my pleasure lies.
40

8 Attendants: The music, ho!
Cleopatra: Let it alone; let's to billiards: come,
    Charmian.
v.2

9 Give me mine angle; we'll to the river: there—
My music playing far off—I will betray
Tawny-finn'd fishes; my bended hook shall pierce
Their slimy jaws; and, as I draw them up,
I'll think them every one an Antony,

And say, 'Ah, ha!' you're caught.
10

10 I laugh'd him out of patience; and that night
I laugh'd him into patience: and next morn,
Ere the ninth hour, I drunk him to his bed.
19

11   There is gold, and here
My bluest veins to kiss; a hand that kings
Have lipp'd, and trembled kissing.
28

12 Though it be honest, it is never good
To bring bad news; give to a gracious message
A host of tongues, but let ill tidings tell
Themselves when they be felt.
85

13 I will praise any man that will praise me.
vi.[88]

14 Lepidus: What manner o' thing is your crocodile?
Antony: It is shaped, sir, like itself, and it is as broad
as it hath breadth; it is just so high as it is, and moves
with its own organs; it lives by that which nourisheth
it; and the elements once out of it, it transmigrates.
Lepidus: What colour is it of?
Antony: Of its own colour too.
Lepidus: 'Tis a strange serpent.
Antony: 'Tis so; and the tears of it are wet.
vii.[47]

15 He sends so poor a pinion of his wing,
Which had superfluous kings for messengers
Not many moons gone by.
III.x.4

16   He wears the rose
Of youth upon him.
xi.20

17 Against the blown rose may they stop their nose,
That kneel'd unto the buds.
39

18   Yet he that can endure
To follow with allegiance a fall'n lord,
Does conquer him that did his master conquer,
And earns a place i' the story.
43

19   Your Caesar's father oft,
When he hath mus'd of taking kingdoms in,
Bestow'd his lips on that unworthy place,
As it rain'd kisses.
82

20 I found you as a morsel, cold upon
Dead Caesar's trencher.
116

21 To let a fellow that will take rewards
And say 'God quit you!' be familiar with
My playfellow, your hand; this kingly seal
And plighter of high hearts.
123

22 Let's have one other gaudy night: call to me
All my sad captains; fill our bowls once more;
Let's mock the midnight bell.
182

23   Since my lord
Is Antony again, I will be Cleopatra.
185

24 To business that we love we rise betime,

And go to 't with delight.
IV.iv.20

1   O! my fortunes have
Corrupted honest men.
v.16

2   I am alone the villain of the earth,
And feel I am so most.
vi.30

3   *Cleopatra:* Lord of lords!
O infinite virtue! com'st thou smiling from
The world's great snare uncaught?
Antony: My nightingale,
We have beat them to their beds.
viii.16

4   O sovereign mistress of true melancholy,
The poisonous damp of night disponge upon me,
That life, a very rebel to my will,
May hang no longer on me.
ix.12

5   The hearts
That spaniel'd me at heels, to whom I gave
Their wishes, do discandy, melt their sweets
On blossoming Caesar.
x.33

6   The soul and body rive not more in parting
Than greatness going off.
xi.5

7   Sometimes we see a cloud that's dragonish;
A vapour sometime like a bear or lion,
A tower'd citadel, a pendant rock,
A forked mountain, or blue promontory
With trees upon 't, that nod unto the world
And mock our eyes with air: thou hast seen these
    signs;
They are black vesper's pageants.
xii.2

8   That which is now a horse, even with a thought
The rack dislimns, and makes it indistinct,
As water is in water.
9

9   Unarm, Eros; the long day's task is done,
And we must sleep.
35

10   Lie down, and stray no further. Now all labour
Mars what it does; yea, very force entangles
Itself with strength...
        Stay for me:
Where souls do couch on flowers, we'll hand in hand,
And with our sprightly port make the ghosts gaze;
Dido and her Aeneas shall want troops,
And all the haunt be ours.
47

11   I will be
A bridegroom in my death, and run into 't
As to a lover's bed.
99

12   All strange and terrible events are welcome,
But comforts we despise.
xiii.3

13   *Antony:* Not Caesar's valour hath o'erthrown Antony
But Antony's hath triumphed on itself.
Cleopatra: So it should be, that none but Antony

Should conquer Antony.
14

14   I am dying, Egypt, dying; only
I here importune death awhile, until
Of many thousand kisses the poor last
I lay upon thy lips.
18

15   The miserable change now at my end
Lament nor sorrow at; but please your thoughts
In feeding them with those my former fortunes
Wherein I liv'd, the greatest prince o' the world,
The noblest; and do now not basely die,
Not cowardly put off my helmet to
My countryman; a Roman by a Roman
Valiantly vanquished.
51

16   Hast thou no care of me? shall I abide
In this dull world, which in thy absence is
No better than a sty? O! see my women,
The crown o' the earth doth melt. My lord!
O! wither'd is the garland of the war,
The soldier's pole is fall'n; young boys and girls
Are level now with men; the odds is gone,
And there is nothing left remarkable
Beneath the visiting moon.
60

17   No more, but e'en a woman and commanded
By such poor passion as the maid that milks
And does the meanest chares.
73

18   What's brave, what's noble,
Let's do it after the high Roman fashion,
And make death proud to take us.
86

19   A rarer spirit never
Did steer humanity; but you, gods, will give us
Some faults to make us men.
V.i.31

20   My desolation does begin to make
A better life. 'Tis paltry to be Caesar;
Not being Fortune, he's but Fortune's knave,
A minister of her will; and it is great
To do that thing that ends all other deeds,
Which shackles accidents, and bolts up change,
Which sleeps, and never palates more the dug,
The beggar's nurse and Caesar's.
ii.1

21   Nor once be chastis'd with the sober eye
Of dull Octavia. Shall they hoist me up
And show me to the shouting varletry
Of censuring Rome? Rather a ditch in Egypt
Be gentle grave unto me! rather on Nilus' mud
Lay me stark naked, and let the water-flies
Blow me into abhorring!
54

22   His legs bestrid the ocean; his rear'd arm
Crested the world; his voice was propertied
As all the tuned spheres, and that to friends;
But when he meant to quail and shake the orb,
He was as rattling thunder. For his bounty,
There was no winter in 't; an autumn was
That grew the more by reaping; his delights
Were dolphin-like, they show'd his back above
The element they liv'd in; in his livery

Walk'd crowns and crownets, realms and islands were
As plates dropp'd from his pocket.
82

1 He words me, girls, he words me, that I should not
Be noble to myself.
190

2 Finish, good lady; the bright day is done,
And we are for the dark.
192

3   Antony
Shall be brought drunken forth, and I shall see
Some squeaking Cleopatra boy my greatness
I' the posture of a whore.
217

4 My resolution's plac'd, and I have nothing
Of woman in me; now from head to foot
I am marble-constant, now the fleeting moon
No planet is of mine.
237

5 His biting is immortal; those that do die of it do seldom
or never recover.
[246]

6 A very honest woman, but something given to lie.
[251]

7 I wish you all joy of the worm.
[260]

8 Indeed there is no goodness in the worm.
[267]

9 I know that a woman is a dish for the gods, if the
devil dress her not.
[274]

10 Give me my robe, put on my crown; I have
Immortal longings in me.
[282]

11   Husband, I come:
Now to that name my courage prove my title!
I am fire and air; my other elements
I give to baser life.
[289]

12 If thou and nature can so gently part,
The stroke of death is as a lover's pinch,
Which hurts, and is desir'd.
[296]

13 If thus thou vanishest, thou tell'st the world
It is not worth leave-taking.
[299]

14 *Cleopatra:* If she first meet the curled Antony,
He'll make demand of her, and spend that kiss
Which is my heaven to have. Come, thou mortal
   wretch,
With thy sharp teeth this knot intrinsicate
Of life at once untie; poor venomous fool,
Be angry, and dispatch. O! couldst thou speak,
That I might hear thee call great Caesar ass
Unpolicied.
Charmian: O eastern star!
Cleopatra: Peace! peace!
Dost thou not see my baby at my breast,
That sucks the nurse asleep?
[303]

15 Now boast thee, death, in thy possession lies
A lass unparallel'd.
[317]

16 It is well done, and fitting for a princess
Descended of so many royal kings.
[328]

17   She looks like sleep,
As she would catch a second Antony
In her strong toil of grace.
[347]

18 She hath pursu'd conclusions infinite
Of easy ways to die.
[356]

19 She shall be buried by her Antony:
No grave upon the earth shall clip in it
A pair so famous.
[359]

AS YOU LIKE IT

20 Fleet the time carelessly, as they did in the golden
world.
I.i.[126]

21 Let us sit and mock the good housewife Fortune from
her wheel, that her gifts may henceforth be bestowed
equally.
ii.[35]

22 How now, wit! whither wander you?
[60]

23 Thus men may grow wiser every day: it is the first
time that I ever heard breaking of ribs was sport for
ladies.
[146]

24 Only in the world I fill up a place, which may be
better supplied when I have made it empty.
[206]

25 Wear this for me, one out of suits with fortune,
That could give more, but that her hand lacks means.
[263]

26 Sir, you have wrestled well, and overthrown
More than your enemies.
[271]

27 Hereafter, in a better world than this,
I shall desire more love and knowledge of you.
[301]

28 Thus must I from the smoke into the smother;
From tyrant duke unto a tyrant brother.
[304]

29 O, how full of briers is this working-day world!
iii.[12]

30 We'll have a swashing and a martial outside,
As many other mannish cowards have
That do outface it with their semblances.
[123]

31 Hath not old custom made this life more sweet
Than that of painted pomp? Are not these woods
More free from peril than the envious court?
Here feel we but the penalty of Adam,
The seasons' difference; as, the icy fang
And churlish chiding of the winter's wind,
Which, when it bites and blows upon my body,
Even till I shrink with cold, I smile and say,
'This is no flattery.'
II.i.2

32 Sweet are the uses of adversity,
Which like the toad, ugly and venomous,

Wears yet a precious jewel in his head;
And this our life, exempt from public haunt,
Finds tongues in trees, books in the running brooks,
Sermons in stones, and good in everything.
12

1   The big round tears
Cours'd one another down his innocent nose,
In piteous chase.
38

2 Sweep on, you fat and greasy citizens!
55

3 I love to cope him in these sullen fits,
For then he's full of matter.
67

4 Unregarded age in corners thrown.
iii.42

5   Though I look old, yet I am strong and lusty;
For in my youth I never did apply
Hot and rebellious liquors in my blood.
47

6 Therefore my age is as a lusty winter,
Frosty, but kindly.
52

7 O good old man! how well in thee appears
The constant service of the antique world,
When service sweat for duty, not for meed!
Thou art not for the fashion of these times,
Where none will sweat but for promotion,
And having that, do choke their service up
Even with the having.
56

8 Ay, now am I in Arden; the more fool I. When I was
at home I was in a better place; but travellers must be
content.
iv.[16]

9 In thy youth thou wast as true a lover
As ever sigh'd upon a midnight pillow.
[26]

10 If thou remember'st not the slightest folly
That ever love did make thee run into,
Thou hast not lov'd.
[34]

11 We that are true lovers run into strange capers.
[53]

12 Thou speakest wiser than thou art ware of.
[57]

13 I shall ne'er be ware of mine own wit till I break my
shins against it.
[59]

14 Under the greenwood tree
Who loves to lie with me,
And turn his merry note
Unto the sweet bird's throat,
Come hither, come hither, come hither:
    Here shall he see
      No enemy
But winter and rough weather.
v.1

15 I can suck melancholy out of a song as a weasel sucks
eggs.
[12]

16 Who doth ambition shun
And loves to live i' the sun,

Seeking the food he eats,
And pleas'd with what he gets.
[38]

17 I'll go to sleep if I can; if I cannot, I'll rail against all
the first-born of Egypt.
[60]

18 A fool, a fool! I met a fool i' the forest,
A motley fool; a miserable world!
As I do live by food, I met a fool;
Who laid him down and bask'd him in the sun,
And rail'd on Lady Fortune in good terms,
In good set terms, and yet a motley fool.
'Good morrow, fool,' quoth I. 'No, sir,' quoth he,
'Call me not fool till heaven hath sent me fortune.'
vii.12

19 And so, from hour to hour, we ripe and ripe,
And then from hour to hour, we rot and rot:
And thereby hangs a tale.
26

20 My lungs began to crow like chanticleer,
That fools should be so deep-contemplative,
And I did laugh sans intermission
An hour by his dial. O noble fool!
A worthy fool! Motley's the only wear.
30

21 O worthy fool! One that hath been a courtier,
And says, if ladies be but young and fair,
They have the gift to know it: and in his brain,—
Which is as dry as the remainder biscuit
After a voyage,—he hath strange places cramm'd
With observation, the which he vents
In mangled forms.
36

22   I must have liberty
Withal, as large a charter as the wind,
To blow on whom I please.
47

23 If ever you have look'd on better days,
If ever been where bells have knoll'd to church,
If ever sat at any good man's feast,
If ever from your eyelids wip'd a tear,
And know what 'tis to pity, and be pitied,
Let gentleness my strong enforcement be.
113

24   All the world's a stage,
And all the men and women merely players:
They have their exits and their entrances;
And one man in his time plays many parts,
His acts being seven ages. At first the infant,
Mewling and puking in the nurse's arms.
And then the whining schoolboy, with his satchel,
And shining morning face, creeping like snail
Unwillingly to school. And then the lover,
Sighing like furnace, with a woful ballad
Made to his mistress' eyebrow. Then a soldier,
Full of strange oaths, and bearded like the pard,
Jealous in honour, sudden and quick in quarrel,
Seeking the bubble reputation
Even in the cannon's mouth. And then the justice,
In fair round belly with good capon lin'd,
With eyes severe, and beard of formal cut,
Full of wise saws and modern instances;
And so he plays his part. The sixth age shifts
Into the lean and slipper'd pantaloon,

With spectacles on nose and pouch on side,
His youthful hose well sav'd a world too wide
For his shrunk shank; and his big manly voice,
Turning again towards childish treble, pipes
And whistles in his sound. Last scene of all,
That ends this strange eventful history,
Is second childishness, and mere oblivion,
Sans teeth, sans eyes, sans taste, sans everything.
139

1 Blow, blow, thou winter wind,
Thou art not so unkind
        As man's ingratitude:
Thy tooth is not so keen,
Because thou art not seen,
        Although thy breath be rude.
Heigh-ho! sing, heigh-ho! unto the green holly:
Most friendship is feigning, most loving mere folly.
        Then heigh-ho! the holly!
            This life is most jolly.

Freeze, freeze, thou bitter sky,
That dost not bite so nigh
        As benefits forgot:
Though thou the waters warp,
Thy sting is not so sharp
        As friend remember'd not.
174

2 Run, run, Orlando: carve on every tree
The fair, the chaste, and unexpressive she.
III.ii.9

3 He that wants money, means, and content is without
three good friends.
[25]

4 I earn that I eat, get that I wear, owe no man hate,
envy no man's happiness, glad of other men's good,
content with my harm.
[78]

5 From the east to western Ind,
No jewel is like Rosalind.
[94]

6 Let us make an honourable retreat; though not with
bag and baggage, yet with scrip and scrippage.
[170]

7 O wonderful, wonderful, and most wonderful
wonderful! and yet again wonderful, and after that,
out of all whooping!
[202]

8 It is as easy to count atomies as to resolve the
propositions of a lover.
[246]

9 Do you not know I am a woman? when I think, I must
speak.
[265]

10 I do desire we may be better strangers.
[276]

11 You have a nimble wit; I think 'twas made of
Atalanta's heels.
[294]

12 Jaques: I do not like her name.
Orlando: There was no thought of pleasing you when
she was christened.
[283]

13 Jaques: Time travels in divers paces with divers
persons...

Orlando: Who stays it still withal?
Jaques: With lawyers in the vacation; for they sleep
between term and term.
[328]

14 There were none principal; they were all like one
another as half-pence are; every one fault seeming
monstrous till his fellow fault came to match it.
[376]. Of women's offences.

15 Truly, I would the gods had made thee poetical.
iii.[16]

16 I am not a slut, though I thank the gods I am foul.
[40]

17   Down on your knees,
And thank heaven, fasting, for a good man's love.
v.57

18 I pray you, do not fall in love with me,
For I am falser than vows made in wine.
[72]

19 Dead shepherd, now I find thy saw of might:
'Who ever lov'd that lov'd not at first sight?'
[81]. See 329:18

20 Jaques: Nay then, God be wi' you, an you talk in
blank verse. (Exit)
Rosalind: Farewell, Monsieur Traveller: look you lisp
and wear strange suits, disable all the benefits of your
own country, be out of love with your nativity, and
almost chide God for making you the countenance you
are, or I will scarce think you have swam in a
gondola.
IV.i.[33]

21 Come, woo me, woo me; for now I am in a holiday
humour, and like enough to consent.
[70]

22 You were better speak first, and when you were
gravelled for lack of matter, you might take occasion
to kiss.
[75]

23 Men are April when they woo, December when they
wed: maids are May when they are maids, but the sky
changes when they are wives.
[153]

24 O coz, coz, coz, my pretty little coz, that thou didst
know how many fathom deep I am in love!
[217]

25 The horn, the horn, the lusty horn
Is not a thing to laugh to scorn.
IV.ii.[17]

26 Chewing the food of sweet and bitter fancy.
iii.[103]

27 Your brother and my sister no sooner met, but they
looked; no sooner looked but they loved; no sooner
loved but they sighed; no sooner sighed but they asked
one another the reason; no sooner knew the reason but
they sought the remedy: and in these degrees have they
made a pair of stairs to marriage which they will climb
incontinent, or else be incontinent before marriage.
V.ii.[36]

28 Oh! how bitter a thing it is to look into happiness
through another man's eyes.
[48]

29 Phebe: Good shepherd, tell this youth what 'tis to
love.
Silvius: It is to be all made of sighs and tears...

It is to be all made of faith and service...
It is to be all made of fantasy,
All made of passion, and all made of wishes;
All adoration, duty, and observance;
All humbleness, all patience, and impatience;
All purity, all trial, all obeisance.
[90]

1 'Tis like the howling of Irish wolves against the
moon.
[120]

2 It was a lover and his lass,
   With a hey, and a ho, and a hey nonino,
That o'er the green cornfield did pass,
   In the spring time, the only pretty ring time,
When birds do sing, hey ding a ding, ding;
Sweet lovers love the spring.

Between the acres of the rye,
   With a hey, and a ho, and a hey nonino,
These pretty country folks would lie,
   In the spring time, &c.

This carol they began that hour,
   With a hey, and a ho, and a hey nonino,
How that a life was but a flower,
   In the spring time, &c.

And therefore take the present time,
   With a hey, and a ho, and a hey nonino;
For love is crowned with the prime
   In the spring time, &c.
iii.[18]

3 Here comes a pair of very strange beasts, which in all
tongues are called fools.
iv.[36]

4 A poor virgin, sir, an ill-favoured thing, sir, but mine
own: a poor humour of mine, sir, to take that that no
man else will. Rich honesty dwells like a miser, sir, in
a poor house, as your pearl in your foul oyster.
[60]

5 The retort courteous...the quip modest...the reply
churlish...the reproof valiant...the countercheck
quarrelsome...the lie circumstantial...the lie direct.
[96]. Of the degrees of the lie.

6 Your 'if' is the only peace-maker; much virtue in 'if'
[108]

7 He uses his folly like a stalking-horse, and under the
presentation of that he shoots his wit.
[112]

8 If it be true that 'good wine needs no bush', 'tis true
that a good play needs no epilogue.
Epilogue [3]

THE COMEDY OF ERRORS

9 They brought one Pinch, a hungry, lean-fac'd villain,
A mere anatomy, a mountebank,
A threadbare juggler, and a fortune-teller,
A needy, hollow-ey'd, sharp-looking wretch,
A living-dead man.
V.i.238

CORIOLANUS

10 He's a very dog to the commonalty.
I.i.[29]

11 The kingly crowned head, the vigilant eye,
The counsellor heart, the arm our soldier,

Our steed the leg, the tongue our trumpeter.
[121]

12 What's the matter, you dissentious rogues,
That, rubbing the poor itch of your opinion,
Make yourselves scabs?
[170]

13   They threw their caps
As they would hang them on the horns o' the moon,
Shouting their emulation.
[218]

14 I am known to be...one that loves a cup of hot wine
with not a drop of allaying Tiber in't.
II.i.[52]

15   Bid them wash their faces,
And keep their teeth clean.
[65]

16 My gracious silence, hail!
[194]

17   Custom calls me to 't:
What custom wills, in all things should we do't,
The dust on antique time would lie unswept,
And mountainous error be too highly heap'd
For truth to o'erpeer.
II.iii.[124]

18 I thank you for your voices, thank you,
Your most sweet voices.
[179]

19 How youngly he began to serve his country,
How long continu'd.
[244]

20 For the mutable, rank-scented many, let them
Regard me as I do not flatter, and
Therein behold themselves.
III.i.65

21 Hear you this Triton of the minnows? mark you
His absolute 'shall'?
88

22 On both sides more respect.
180

23 You common cry of curs! whose breath I hate
As reek o' the rotten fens, whose loves I prize
As the dead carcases of unburied men
That do corrupt my air,—I banish you.
iii.118

24   Despising,
For you, the city, thus I turn my back:
There is a world elsewhere.
131

25   The beast
With many heads butts me away.
IV.i.1

26 Thou hast a grim appearance, and thy face
Bears a command in't; though thy tackle's torn,
Thou show'st a noble vessel. What's thy name?
v.[66]

27 Let me have war, say I; it exceeds peace as far as day
does night; it's spritely, waking, audible, and full of
vent. Peace is a very apoplexy, lethargy: mulled, deaf,
sleepy, insensible; a getter of more bastard children
than war's a destroyer of men.
[237]

28   I'll never
Be such a gosling to obey instinct, but stand

As if a man were author of himself
And knew no other kin.
V.iii.34

1   Like a dull actor now,
I have forgot my part, and I am out,
Even to a full disgrace.
40

2   O! a kiss
Long as my exile, sweet as my revenge!
Now, by the jealous queen of heaven, that kiss
I carried from thee, dear, and my true lip
Hath virgin'd it e'er since.
44

3   Chaste as the icicle
That's curdied by the frost from purest snow,
And hangs on Dian's temple.
65

4   The god of soldiers,
With the consent of supreme Jove, inform
Thy thoughts with nobleness; that thou mayst prove
To shame unvulnerable, and stick i' the wars
Like a great sea-mark, standing every flaw,
And saving those that eye thee!
70

5   Thou hast never in thy life
Show'd thy dear mother any courtesy;
When she—poor hen! fond of no second brood—
Has cluck'd thee to the wars, and safely home,
Loaden with honour.
160

6 If you have writ your annals true, 'tis there,
That, like an eagle in a dove-cote, I
Flutter'd your Volscians in Corioli:
Alone I did it.
v.114

CYMBELINE

7 If she be furnish'd with a mind so rare,
She is alone the Arabian bird, and I
Have lost the wager. Boldness be my friend!
Arm me, audacity.
I.vi.16

8   Cytherea,
How bravely thou becom'st thy bed! fresh lily,
And whiter than the sheets! That I might touch!
But kiss: one kiss! Rubies unparagon'd,
How dearly they do't! 'Tis her breathing that
Perfumes the chamber thus; the flame of the taper
Bows toward her, and would under-peep her lids
To see the enclosed lights, now canopied
Under these windows, white and azure lac'd
With blue of heaven's own tinct.
II.ii.14

9   On her left breast
A mole cinque-spotted, like the crimson drops
I' the bottom of a cowslip.
37

10 Hark! hark! the lark at heaven's gate sings,
      And Phoebus 'gins arise,
His steeds to water at those springs
      On chalic'd flowers that lies;
And winking Mary-buds begin

To ope their golden eyes:
With everything that pretty is,
      My lady sweet, arise!
iii.[22]

11 Is there no way for men to be, but women
Must be half-workers?
v.1

12   I thought her
As chaste as unsunn'd snow.
12

13 The natural bravery of your isle, which stands
As Neptune's park, ribbed and paled in
With rocks unscalable, and roaring waters.
III.i.18

14 O, for a horse with wings!
ii.[49]

15   What should we speak of
When we are old as you? when we shall hear
The rain and wind beat dark December, how,
In this our pinching cave, shall we discourse
The freezing hours away? We have seen nothing.
iii.35

16   Some jay of Italy,
Whose mother was her painting, hath betray'd him:
Poor I am stale, a garment out of fashion.
iv.[51]

17 Hath Britain all the sun that shines?
[139]

18   Weariness
Can snore upon the flint when resty sloth
Finds the down pillow hard.
vi.33

19 Great griefs, I see, medicine the less.
IV.ii.243

20   Though mean and mighty rotting
Together, have one dust, yet reverence—
That angel of the world—doth make distinction
Of place 'tween high and low.
246

21 Thersites' body is as good as Ajax'
When neither are alive.
252

22 Fear no more the heat o' the sun,
      Nor the furious winter's rages;
Thou thy worldly task hast done,
      Home art gone and ta'en thy wages:
Golden lads and girls all must,
As chimney-sweepers, come to dust.

Fear no more the frown o' the great,
      Thou art past the tyrant's stroke:
Care no more to clothe and eat;
      To thee the reed is as the oak:
The sceptre, learning, physic, must
All follow this, and come to dust.

Fear no more the lightning flash,
      Nor the all-dreaded thunder-stone;
Fear not slander, censure rash;
      Thou hast finish'd joy and moan:
All lovers young, all lovers must
Consign to thee, and come to dust.

No exorciser harm thee!
      Nor no witchcraft charm thee!

Ghost unlaid forbear thee!
   Nothing ill come near thee!
Quiet consummation have:
And renowned be thy grave!
258

1 Every good servant does not all commands.
  V.i.6

2 He that sleeps feels not the toothache.
  iv.[176]

3 He spake of her as Dian had hot dreams,
  And she alone were cold.
  v.181

HAMLET

4 You come most carefully upon your hour.
  I.i.6

5 For this relief much thanks; 'tis bitter cold
  And I am sick at heart.
  8

6 Not a mouse stirring.
  10

7 *Bernardo:* What! is Horatio there?
  Horatio: A piece of him.
  19

8 What! has this thing appear'd again to-night?
  21

9 Look, where it comes again!
  40

10 But in the gross and scope of my opinion,
  This bodes some strange eruption to our state.
  68

11   This sweaty haste
  Doth make the night joint-labourer with the day.
  77

12 In the most high and palmy state of Rome,
  A little ere the mightiest Julius fell,
  The graves stood tenantless and the sheeted dead
  Did squeak and gibber in the Roman streets.
  113

13   The moist star
  Upon whose influence Neptune's empire stands
  Was sick almost to doomsday with eclipse.
  118

14 I'll cross it, though it blast me.
  127

15 We do it wrong, being so majestical,
  To offer it the show of violence;
  For it is, as the air, invulnerable,
  And our vain blows malicious mockery.
  143

16 And then it started like a guilty thing
  Upon a fearful summons.
  148

17 It faded on the crowing of the cock.
  Some say that ever 'gainst that season comes
  Wherein our Saviour's birth is celebrated,
  The bird of dawning singeth all night long;
  And then, they say, no spirit can walk abroad;
  The nights are wholesome; then no planets strike,
  No fairy takes, nor witch hath power to charm,
  So hallow'd and so gracious is the time.
  157

18 But, look, the morn, in russet mantle clad,
  Walks o'er the dew of yon high eastern hill.
  166

19 Though yet of Hamlet our dear brother's death
  The memory be green...
  Therefore our sometime sister, now our queen,...
  Have we, as 'twere with a defeated joy,
  With one auspicious and one dropping eye,
  With mirth in funeral and with dirge in marriage,
  In equal scale weighing delight and dole,
  Taken to wife.
  ii.1

20 The head is not more native to the heart,
  The hand more instrumental to the brain,
  Than is the throne of Denmark to thy father.
  47

21 A little more than kin, and less than kind.
  65

22 Not so, my lord; I am too much i' the sun.
  67

23 Good Hamlet, cast thy nighted colour off,
  And let thine eye look like a friend on Denmark.
  68

24 *Queen:* Thou know'st 'tis common; all that live must
    die,
  Passing through nature to eternity.
  Hamlet: Ay, madam, it is common.
  72

25 Seems, madam! Nay, it is; I know not 'seems'.
  'Tis not alone my inky cloak, good mother,
  Nor customary suits of solemn black,
  Nor windy suspiration of forc'd breath,
  No, nor the fruitful river in the eye,
  Nor the dejected 'haviour of the visage,
  Together with all forms, modes, shows of grief,
  That can denote me truly; these indeed seem,
  For they are actions that a man might play:
  But I have that within which passeth show;
  These but the trappings and the suits of woe.
  76

26   But to persever
  In obstinate condolement is a course
  Of impious stubbornness; 'tis unmanly grief;
  It shows a will most incorrect to heaven,
  A heart unfortified, a mind impatient.
  92

27 *Hamlet:* I shall in all my best obey you, madam.
  King: Why, 'tis a loving and a fair reply.
  120

28 O! that this too too solid flesh would melt,
  Thaw, and resolve itself into a dew;
  Or that the Everlasting had not fix'd
  His canon 'gainst self-slaughter! O God! O God!
  How weary, stale, flat, and unprofitable
  Seem to me all the uses of this world.
  Fie on't! O fie! 'tis an unweeded garden,
  That grows to seed; things rank and gross in nature
  Possess it merely. That it should come to this!
  But two months dead: nay, not so much, not two:
  So excellent a king; that was, to this,
  Hyperion to a satyr: so loving to my mother,
  That he might not beteem the winds of heaven
  Visit her face too roughly. Heaven and earth!
  Must I remember? Why, she would hang on him,

As if increase of appetite had grown
By what it fed on; and yet, within a month,
Let me not think on't: Frailty, thy name is woman!
A little month; or ere those shoes were old
With which she follow'd my poor father's body,
Like Niobe, all tears; why she, even she,—
O God! a beast, that wants discourse of reason,
Would have mourn'd longer,—married with mine
   uncle,
My father's brother, but no more like my father
Than I to Hercules.
129

1 It is not, nor it cannot come to good;
But break, my heart, for I must hold my tongue!
158

2 A truant disposition, good my lord.
169

3 We'll teach you to drink deep ere you depart.
175

4 Thrift, thrift, Horatio! the funeral bak'd meats
Did coldly furnish forth the marriage tables.
Would I had met my dearest foe in heaven
Ere I had ever seen that day, Horatio!
180

5 He was a man, take him for all in all,
I shall not look upon his like again.
187

6 In the dead vast and middle of the night.
198

7 Armed at points exactly, cap-a-pe.
200

8   Distill'd
Almost to jelly with the act of fear.
204

9 These hands are not more like.
212

10 But answer made it none.
215

11 A countenance more in sorrow than in anger.
231

12 While one with moderate haste might tell a hundred.
237

13 *Hamlet:* His beard was grizzled, no?
Horatio: It was, as I have seen it in his life,
A sable silver'd.
239

14 Give it an understanding, but no tongue.
249

15   All is not well;
I doubt some foul play.
254

16   Foul deeds will rise,
Though all the earth o'erwhelm them, to men's eyes.
256

17 And keep you in the rear of your affection,
Out of the shot and danger of desire.
The chariest maid is prodigal enough
If she unmask her beauty to the moon.
iii.34

18 Do not, as some ungracious pastors do,
Show me the steep and thorny way to heaven,
Whiles, like a puff'd and reckless libertine,

Himself the primrose path of dalliance treads,
And recks not his own rede.
47

19 And these few precepts in thy memory
Look thou character. Give thy thoughts no tongue,
Nor any unproportion'd thought his act.
Be thou familiar, but by no means vulgar;
The friends thou hast, and their adoption tried,
Grapple them to thy soul with hoops of steel;
But do not dull thy palm with entertainment
Of each new-hatch'd, unfledg'd comrade. Beware
Of entrance to a quarrel; but, being in,
Bear't that th' opposed may beware of thee.
Give every man thine ear, but few thy voice;
Take each man's censure, but reserve thy judgment.
Costly thy habit as thy purse can buy,
But not express'd in fancy; rich, not gaudy;
For the apparel oft proclaims the man,
And they in France of the best rank and station
Are most select and generous, chief in that.
Neither a borrower, nor a lender be;
For loan oft loses both itself and friend,
And borrowing dulls the edge of husbandry,
This above all: to thine own self be true,
And it must follow, as the night the day,
Thou canst not then be false to any man.
58

20   You speak like a green girl,
Unsifted in such perilous circumstance.
101

21 Ay, springes to catch woodcocks. I do know,
When the blood burns, how prodigal the soul
Lends the tongue vows: these blazes, daughter,
Giving more light than heat, extinct in both,
Even in their promise, as it is a-making,
You must not take for fire.
115

22 *Hamlet:* The air bites shrewdly; it is very cold.
Horatio: It is a nipping and an eager air.
iv.1

23 But to my mind,—though I am native here,
And to the manner born,—it is a custom
More honour'd in the breach than the observance.
14

24 Angels and ministers of grace defend us!
Be thou a spirit of health or goblin damn'd,
Bring with thee airs from heaven or blasts from hell,
Be thy intents wicked or charitable,
Thou com'st in such a questionable shape
That I will speak to thee: I'll call thee Hamlet,
King, father; royal Dane, O! answer me:
Let me not burst in ignorance; but tell
Why thy canoniz'd bones hearsed in death,
Have burst their cerements; why the sepulchre,
Wherein we saw thee quietly inurn'd,
Hath op'd his ponderous and marble jaws,
To cast thee up again. What may this mean,
That thou, dead corse again in complete steel
Revisit'st thus the glimpses of the moon,
Making night hideous; and we fools of nature
So horridly to shake our disposition
With thoughts beyond the reaches of our souls?
39

25 I do not set my life at a pin's fee;

And for my soul, what can it do to that,
Being a thing immortal as itself?
65

1   Unhand me, gentlemen,
By heaven! I'll make a ghost of him that lets me.
84

2 Something is rotten in the state of Denmark.
90

3 Alas! poor ghost.
v.4

4 I am thy father's spirit;
Doom'd for a certain term to walk the night.
9

5   But that I am forbid
To tell the secrets of my prison-house,
I could a tale unfold whose lightest word
Would harrow up thy soul, freeze thy young blood,
Make thy two eyes, like stars, start from their spheres,
Thy knotted and combined locks to part,
And each particular hair to stand an end,
Like quills upon the fretful porpentine:
But this eternal blazon must not be
To ears of flesh and blood. List, list, O, list!
13

6 Revenge his foul and most unnatural murder.
25

7 Murder most foul, as in the best it is;
But this most foul, strange, and unnatural.
27

8 And duller shouldst thou be than the fat weed
That rots itself in ease on Lethe wharf,
Wouldst thou not stir in this.
32

9   O my prophetic soul!
My uncle!
40

10 But, soft! methinks I scent the morning air.
58

11 In the porches of mine ears.
63

12 Thus was I, sleeping, by a brother's hand,
Of life, of crown, of queen, at once dispatch'd;
Cut off even in the blossoms of my sin,
Unhousel'd, disappointed, unanel'd,
No reckoning made, but sent to my account
With all my imperfections on my head:
O, horrible! O, horrible! most horrible!
If thou hast nature in thee, bear it not.
74

13   Leave her to heaven,
And to those thorns that in her bosom lodge,
To prick and sting her.
86

14 The glow-worm shows the matin to be near,
And 'gins to pale his uneffectual fire.
89

15   Remember thee!
Ay, thou poor ghost, while memory holds a seat
In this distracted globe. Remember thee!
Yea, from the table of my memory
I'll wipe away all trivial fond records,
All saws of books, all forms, all pressures past,

That youth and observation copied there.
95

16 O most pernicious woman!
O villain, villain, smiling, damned villain!
My tables,—meet it is I set it down,
That one may smile, and smile, and be a villain;
At least I'm sure it may be so in Denmark.
105

17 *Hamlet:* There's ne'er a villain dwelling in all
     Denmark,
But he's an arrant knave.
Horatio: There needs no ghost, my lord, come from
     the grave,
To tell us this.
123

18 These are but wild and whirling words, my lord.
133

19 It is an honest ghost, that let me tell you.
138

20 *Hic et ubique?* then we'll shift our ground.
156

21 Well said, old mole! canst work i' the earth so fast?
162

22 O day and night, but this is wondrous strange!
164

23 There are more things in heaven and earth, Horatio,
Than are dreamt of in your philosophy.
166

24 To put an antic disposition on.
172

25 Rest, rest, perturbed spirit.
182

26 The time is out of joint; O cursed spite,
That ever I was born to set it right!
188

27 By indirections find directions out.
II.i.66

28 Lord Hamlet, with his doublet all unbrac'd;
No hat upon his head; his stockings foul'd,
Ungarter'd, and down-gyved to his ancle.
78

29 This is the very ecstasy of love.
101

30 Brevity is the soul of wit.
ii.90

31   To define true madness,
What is't but to be nothing else but mad?
93

32 More matter with less art.
95

33 That he is mad, 'tis true; 'tis true 'tis pity;
And pity 'tis 'tis true: a foolish figure;
But farewell it, for I will use no art.
97

34 That's an ill phrase, a vile phrase; 'beautified' is a vile
phrase.
[110]

35 Doubt thou the stars are fire;
    Doubt that the sun doth move;
Doubt truth to be a liar;
    But never doubt I love.
[115]

1 Lord Hamlet is a prince, out of thy star.
[141]

2 And he, repulsed,—a short tale to make,—
Fell into a sadness, then into a fast,
Thence to a watch, thence into a weakness,
Thence to a lightness; and by this declension
Into the madness wherein now he raves,
And all we wail for.
[146]

3 Let me be no assistant for a state,
But keep a farm, and carters.
[166]

4 *Polonius:* Do you know me, my lord?
Hamlet: Excellent well; you are a fishmonger.
[173]

5 Ay, sir; to be honest, as this world goes, is to be one
man picked out of ten thousand.
[179]

6 Still harping on my daughter.
[190]

7 *Polonius:* What do you read, my lord?
Hamlet: Words, words, words.
[195]

8 The satirical rogue says here that old men have grey
beards, that their faces are wrinkled, their eyes purging
thick amber and plum-tree gum, and that they have a
plentiful lack of wit, together with most weak hams:
all of which, sir, though I most potently and
powerfully believe, yet I hold it not honesty to have it
thus set down.
[201]

9 Though this be madness, yet there is method in't.
[211]

10 *Polonius:* My honourable lord, I will most humbly
take my leave of you.
Hamlet: You cannot, sir, take from me any thing that I
will more willingly part withal; except my life, except
my life, except my life.
[221]

11 *Guildenstern:* On Fortune's cap we are not the very
button.
Hamlet: Nor the soles of her shoe?
Rosencrantz: Neither, my lord.
Hamlet: Then you live about her waist, or in the
middle of her favours?
Guildenstern: Faith, her privates, we.
Hamlet: In the secret parts of Fortune? O! most true;
she is a strumpet. What news?
Rosencrantz: None, my lord, but that the world's
grown honest.
Hamlet: Then is doomsday near.
[237]

12 There is nothing either good or bad, but thinking
makes it so.
[259]

13 O God! I could be bounded in a nut-shell, and count
myself a king of infinite space, were it not that I have
bad dreams.
[263]

14 Beggar that I am, I am poor even in thanks.
[286]

15 It goes so heavily with my disposition that this goodly
frame, the earth, seems to me a sterile promontory;
this most excellent canopy, the air, look you, this
brave o'erhanging firmament, this majestical roof
fretted with golden fire, why, it appears no other thing
to me but a foul and pestilent congregation of vapours.
What a piece of work is a man! How noble in reason!
how infinite in faculty! in form, in moving, how
express and admirable! in action how like an angel! in
apprehension how like a god! the beauty of the world!
the paragon of animals! And yet, to me, what is this
quintessence of dust? man delights not me; no, nor
woman neither, though, by your smiling, you seem to
say so.
[316]

16 He that plays the king shall be welcome; his majesty
shall have tribute of me.
[341]

17 There is something in this more than natural, if
philosophy could find it out.
[392]

18 I am but mad north-north-west; when the wind is
southerly, I know a hawk from a handsaw.
[405]

19 The great baby you see there is not yet out of his
swaddling-clouts.
[410]

20 The best actors in the world, either for tragedy,
comedy, history, pastoral, pastoral-comical,
historical-pastoral, tragical-historical,
tragical-comical-historical-pastoral, scene individable,
or poem unlimited. Seneca cannot be too heavy, nor
Plautus too light.
[424]

21 One fair daughter and no more,
The which he loved passing well.
[435]

22 Come, give us a taste of your quality.
[460]

23 The play, I remember, pleased not the million; 'twas
caviare to the general.
[465]

24 But who, O! who had seen the mobled queen.
[533]

25 Good my lord, will you see the players well bestowed?
Do you hear, let them be well used; for they are the
abstracts and brief chronicles of the time: after your
death you were better have a bad epitaph than their ill
report while you live.
[553]

26 Use every man after his desert, and who should 'scape
whipping?
[561]

27 O, what a rogue and peasant slave am I:
Is it not monstrous that this player here,
But in a fiction, in a dream of passion,
Could force his soul so to his own conceit
That from her working all his visage wann'd,
Tears in his eyes, distraction in 's aspect,
A broken voice, and his whole function suiting
With forms to his conceit? and all for nothing!
For Hecuba!
What's Hecuba to him or he to Hecuba
That he should weep for her?
[584]

1   He would drown the stage with tears,
And cleave the general ear with horrid speech,
Make mad the guilty, and appal the free,
Confound the ignorant, and amaze, indeed,
The very faculties of eyes and ears.
[596]

2   I,
A dull and muddy-mettled rascal, peak,
Like John-a-dreams, unpregnant of my cause,
And can say nothing.
[601]

3   Am I a coward?
Who calls me villain? breaks my pate across?
Plucks off my beard and blows it in my face?
Tweaks me by the nose? gives me the lie i' the throat,
As deep as to the lungs?
[606]

4 But I am pigeon-liver'd, and lack gall
To make oppression bitter, or ere this
I should have fatted all the region kites
With this slave's offal. Bloody, bawdy villain!
Remorseless, treacherous, lecherous, kindless villain!
[613]

5   I have heard,
That guilty creatures sitting at a play
Have by the very cunning of the scene
Been struck so to the soul that presently
They have proclaim'd their malefactions;
For murder, though it have no tongue, will speak
With most miraculous organ.
[625]

6   The play's the thing
Wherein I'll catch the conscience of the king.
[641]

7 'Tis too much prov'd—that with devotion's visage
And pious action, we do sugar o'er
The devil himself.
III.i.47

8 To be, or not to be: that is the question:
Whether 'tis nobler in the mind to suffer
The slings and arrows of outrageous fortune,
Or to take arms against a sea of troubles,
And by opposing end them? To die: to sleep;
No more; and, by a sleep to say we end
The heart-ache and the thousand natural shocks
That flesh is heir to, 'tis a consummation
Devoutly to be wish'd. To die, to sleep;
To sleep: perchance to dream: ay, there's the rub;
For in that sleep of death what dreams may come
When we have shuffled off this mortal coil,
Must give us pause. There's the respect
That makes calamity of so long life;
For who would bear the whips and scorns of time,
The oppressor's wrong, the proud man's contumely,
The pangs of dispriz'd love, the law's delay,
The insolence of office, and the spurns
That patient merit of the unworthy takes,
When he himself might his quietus make
With a bare bodkin? Who would fardels bear,
To grunt and sweat under a weary life,
But that the dread of something after death,
The undiscover'd country from whose bourn
No traveller returns, puzzles the will,
And makes us rather bear those ills we have,

Than fly to others that we know not of?
Thus conscience doth make cowards of us all;
And thus the native hue of resolution
Is sicklied o'er with the pale cast of thought,
And enterprises of great pith and moment
With this regard their currents turn awry,
And lose the name of action.
56

9   Nymph, in thy orisons
Be all my sins remember'd.
89

10   For, to the noble mind,
Rich gifts wax poor when givers prove unkind.
100

11 Get thee to a nunnery: why wouldst thou be a breeder
of sinners? I am myself indifferent honest; but yet I
could accuse me of such things that it were better my
mother had not borne me. I am very proud,
revengeful, ambitious; with more offences at my beck
than I have thoughts to put them in, imagination to
give them shape, or time to act them in. What should
such fellows as I do crawling between heaven and
earth? We are arrant knaves, all; believe none of us.
[124]

12 Be thou as chaste as ice, as pure as snow, thou shalt
not escape calumny. Get thee to a nunnery, go;
farewell.
[142]

13 I have heard of your paintings too, well enough. God
hath given you one face and you make yourselves
another.
[150]

14 I say, we will have no more marriages.
[156]

15 O! what a noble mind is here o'erthrown:
The courtier's, soldier's, scholar's, eye, tongue,
   sword;
The expectancy and rose of the fair state,
The glass of fashion, and the mould of form,
The observed of all observers, quite, quite, down!
And I, of ladies most deject and wretched,
That suck'd the honey of his music vows,
Now see that noble and most sovereign reason,
Like sweet bells jangled, out of tune and harsh;
That unmatch'd form and figure of blown youth,
Blasted with ecstasy: O! woe is me,
To have seen what I have seen, see what I see!
[159]

16 Speak the speech, I pray you, as I pronounced it to
you, trippingly on the tongue; but if you mouth it, as
many of your players do, I had as lief the town-crier
spoke my lines. Nor do not saw the air too much with
your hand, thus; but use all gently: for in the very
torrent, tempest, and—as I may say—whirlwind of
passion, you must acquire and beget a temperance,
that may give it smoothness. O! it offends me to the
soul to hear a robustious periwig-pated fellow tear a
passion to tatters, to very rags, to split the ears of the
groundlings, who for the most part are capable of
nothing but inexplicable dumb-shows and noise: I
would have such a fellow whipped for o'erdoing
Termagant; it out-herods Herod: pray you, avoid it.
ii.1

17 Be not too tame neither, but let your own discretion be

your tutor: suit the action to the word, the word to the action; with this special observance, that you o'erstep not the modesty of nature; for anything so overdone is from the purpose of playing, whose end, both at the first and now, was and is, to hold, as 'twere, the mirror up to nature; to show virtue her own feature, scorn her own image, and the very age and body of the time his form and pressure. Now, this overdone, or come tardy off, though it make the unskilful laugh, cannot but make the judicious grieve; the censure of which one must in your allowance o'erweigh a whole theatre of others. O! there be players that I have seen play, and heard others praise, and that highly, not to speak it profanely, that, neither having the accent of Christians nor the gait of Christian, pagan, nor man, have so strutted and bellowed that I have thought some of nature's journeymen had made men and not made them well, they imitated humanity so abominably.
[19]

1 Since my dear soul was mistress of her choice
And could of men distinguish, her election
Hath seal'd thee for herself.
[68]

2   Give me that man
That is not passion's slave, and I will wear him
In my heart's core, ay, in my heart of heart,
As I do thee.
[76]

3 It is a damned ghost we have seen,
And my imaginations are as foul
As Vulcan's stithy.
[87]

4 The chameleon's dish: I eat the air,
promise-crammed; you cannot feed capons so.
[98]

5 Here's metal more attractive.
[117]

6 That's a fair thought to lie between maids' legs.
[126]

7 Die two months ago, and not forgotten yet? Then there's hope a great man's memory may outlive his life half a year; but, by'r lady, he must build churches then.
[140]

8 For, O! for, O! the hobby-horse is forgot.
[145]

9 Marry, this is miching mallecho; it means mischief.
[148]

10 *Ophelia:* 'Tis brief, my lord.
Hamlet: As woman's love.
[165]

11 The lady doth protest too much, methinks.
[242]

12 *Hamlet:* No, no, they do but jest, poison in jest; no offence i' the world.
King: What do you call the play?
Hamlet: The Mouse-trap.
[247]

13 We that have free souls, it touches us not: let the galled jade wince, our withers are unwrung.
[255]

14 The story is extant, and writ in very choice Italian.
[277]

15 What! frighted with false fire?
[282]

16 Why, let the stricken deer go weep,
   The hart ungalled play;
For some must watch, while some must sleep:
   So runs the world away.
[287]

17 O wonderful son, that can so astonish a mother!
[347]

18 The proverb is something musty.
[366]

19 It will discourse most eloquent music.
[381]

20 You would play upon me; you would seem to know my stops; you would pluck out the heart of my mystery; you would sound me from my lowest note to the top of my compass.
[387]

21 Do you think I am easier to be played on than a pipe? Call me what instrument you will, though you can fret me, you cannot play upon me.
[393]

22 *Hamlet:* Do you see yonder cloud that's almost in shape of a camel?
Polonius: By the mass, and 'tis like a camel, indeed.
Hamlet: Methinks it is like a weasel.
Polonius: It is backed like a weasel.
Hamlet: Or like a whale?
Polonius: Very like a whale.
[400]

23 They fool me to the top of my bent.
[408]

24 By and by is easily said.
[411]

25 'Tis now the very witching time of night,
When churchyards yawn and hell itself breathes out
Contagion to this world: now could I drink hot blood,
And do such bitter business as the day
Would quake to look on.
[413]

26 Let me be cruel, not unnatural;
I will speak daggers to her, but use none.
[420]

27 O! my offence is rank, it smells to heaven.
iii.36

28 O wretched state! O bosom black as death!
O limed soul, that struggling to be free
Art more engaged!
67

29 Now might I do it pat, now he is praying.
73

30 He took my father grossly, full of bread,
With all his crimes broad blown, as flush as May;
And how his audit stands who knows save heaven?
80

31 My words fly up, my thoughts remain below:
Words without thoughts never to heaven go.
97

32 Tell him his pranks have been too broad to bear with.
iv.2

33 You go not, till I set you up a glass

Where you may see the inmost part of you.
19

1 How now! a rat? Dead, for a ducat, dead!
23

2 A bloody deed! almost as bad, good mother,
As kill a king, and marry with his brother.
28

3 Thou wretched, rash, intruding fool, farewell!
I took thee for thy better.
31

4   Such an act
       ... makes marriage vows
As false as dicers' oaths; O! such a deed
As from the body of contraction plucks
The very soul, and sweet religion makes
A rhapsody of words.
40

5   Ay me! what act,
That roars so loud, and thunders in the index?
51

6 Look here, upon this picture, and on this.
53

7 Could you on this fair mountain leave to feed,
And batten on this moor?
66

8 You cannot call it love, for at your age
The hey-day in the blood is tame, it's humble,
And waits upon the judgment.
68

9   Speak no more;
Thou turn'st mine eyes into my very soul.
88

10   Nay, but to live
In the rank sweat of an enseamed bed,
Stew'd in corruption, honeying and making love
Over the nasty sty.
91

11 A cut-purse of the empire and the rule,
That from a shelf the precious diadem stole,
And put it in his pocket!
99

12 A king of shreds and patches.
102

13 Conceit in weakest bodies strongest works.
113

14   Mother, for love of grace,
Lay not that flattering unction to your soul.
142

15   Confess yourself to heaven;
Repent what's past; avoid what is to come.
149

16 For in the fatness of these pursy times,
Virtue itself of vice must pardon beg.
153

17 *Queen:* O Hamlet! thou hast cleft my heart in twain.
Hamlet: O! throw away the worser part of it,
And live the purer with the other half.
156

18 Assume a virtue, if you have it not.
That monster, custom, who all sense doth eat,
Of habits devil, is angel yet in this.
160

19 And when you are desirous to be bless'd,
I'll blessing beg of you.
171

20 I must be cruel only to be kind.
178

21 For 'tis the sport to have the enginer
Hoist with his own petar: and it shall go hard
But I will delve one yard below their mines,
And blow them at the moon.
206

22 I'll lug the guts into the neighbour room.
212

23   Indeed this counsellor
Is now most still, most secret, and most grave,
Who was in life a foolish prating knave.
213

24 He keeps them, like an ape doth nuts, in the corner of
his jaw; first mouthed, to be last swallowed.
IV.ii.[19]

25   Diseases desperate grown,
By desperate appliances are reliev'd,
Or not at all.
iii.9

26 A certain convocation of politic worms are e'en at
him. Your worm is your only emperor for diet.
[21]

27 A man may fish with the worm that hath eat of a king,
and eat of the fish that hath fed of that worm.
[29]

28 We go to gain a little patch of ground,
That hath in it no profit but the name.
iv.18

29 How all occasions do inform against me,
And spur my dull revenge! What is a man,
If his chief good and market of his time
Be but to sleep and feed? a beast, no more.
Sure he that made us with such large discourse,
Looking before and after, gave us not
That capability and god-like reason
To fust in us unus'd.
32

30   Some craven scruple
Of thinking too precisely on the event.
40

31   Rightly to be great
Is not to stir without great argument,
But greatly to find quarrel in a straw
When honour's at the stake.
53

32 How should I your true love know
    From another one?
By his cockle hat and staff,
    And his sandal shoon.
v.[23]

33 He is dead and gone, lady,
    He is dead and gone,
At his head a grass-green turf;
    At his heels a stone.
[29]

34 White his shroud as the mountain snow...
    Larded with sweet flowers;
Which bewept to the grave did go

With true-love showers.
[36]

1 Lord! we know what we are, but know not what we
may be.
[43]

2 Then up he rose, and donn'd his clothes.
[53]

3 Come, my coach! Good-night, ladies; good-night,
sweet ladies; good night, good-night.
[72]

4 When sorrows come, they come not single spies,
But in battalions.
[78]

5   We have done but greenly
In hugger-mugger to inter him.
[83]

6 There's such divinity doth hedge a king,
That treason can but peep to what it would.
[123]

7 To hell, allegiance! vows, to the blackest devil!
Conscience and grace, to the profoundest pit!
I dare damnation.
[130]

8 Nature is fine in love, and where 'tis fine
It sends some precious instance of itself
After the thing it loves.
[160]

9 They bore him barefac'd on the bier;
Hey non nonny, nonny, hey nonny;
And in his grave rain'd many a tear.
[163]

10 There's rosemary, that's for remembrance; pray, love,
remember: and there is pansies, that's for thoughts.
[174]

11 There's fennel for you, and columbines; there's rue
for you; and here's some for me; we may call it herb
of grace o' Sundays. O! you must wear your rue with a
difference. There's a daisy; I would give you some
violets, but they withered all when my father died.
They say he made a good end,—
For bonny sweet Robin is all my joy.
[179]

12 No, no, he is dead;
Go to thy death-bed,
He never will come again.
[191]

13 He is gone, he is gone,
And we cast away moan;
God ha' mercy on his soul!
[196]

14 His means of death, his obscure burial,
No trophy, sword, nor hatchment o'er his bones,
No noble rite nor formal ostentation.
[213]

15 And where the offence is let the great axe fall.
[218]

16 It warms the very sickness in my heart,
That I shall live and tell him to his teeth,
'Thus diddest thou.'
vii.55

17 A very riband in the cap of youth,
Yet needful too; for youth no less becomes
The light and careless livery that it wears

Than settled age his sables and his weeds,
Importing health and graveness.
77

18 No place, indeed should murder sanctuarize.
127

19 There is a willow grows aslant a brook,
That shows his hoar leaves in the glassy stream;
There with fantastic garlands did she come,
Of crow-flowers, nettles, daisies, and long purples,
That liberal shepherds give a grosser name,
But our cold maids do dead men's fingers call them:
There, on the pendent boughs her coronet weeds
Clambering to hang, an envious sliver broke,
When down her weedy trophies and herself
Fell in the weeping brook. Her clothes spread wide,
And, mermaid-like, awhile they bore her up;
Which time she chanted snatches of old tunes,
As one incapable of her own distress.
167

20 Too much of water hast thou, poor Ophelia,
And therefore I forbid my tears; but yet
It is our trick, nature her custom holds,
Let shame say what it will.
186

21 Is she to be buried in Christian burial that wilfully
seeks her own salvation?
V.i.1

22 There is no ancient gentlemen but gardeners, ditchers
and grave-makers; they hold up Adam's profession.
[32]

23 *First Clown:* What is he that builds stronger than
either the mason, the shipwright, or the carpenter?
Second Clown: The gallows-maker; for that frame
outlives a thousand tenants.
[44]

24 Cudgel thy brains no more about it, for your dull ass
will not mend his pace with beating.
[61]

25 The houses that he makes last till doomsday.
[64]

26 Has this fellow no feeling of his business?
[71]

27 This might be the pate of a politician...one that would
circumvent God, might it not?
[84]

28 How absolute the knave is! we must speak by the
card, or equivocation will undo us.
[147]

29 The age is grown so picked that the toe of the peasant
comes so near the heel of the courtier, he galls his
kibe.
[150]

30 *First Clown:* He that is mad, and sent into England.
Hamlet: Ay, marry; why was he sent into England?
First Clown: Why, because he was mad; he shall
recover his wits there; or, if he do not, 'tis no great
matter there.
Hamlet: Why?
First Clown: 'Twill not be seen in him there; there the
men are as mad as he.
[160]

31 Alas, poor Yorick. I knew him, Horatio; a fellow of
infinite jest, of most excellent fancy; he hath borne me

on his back a thousand times; and now, how abhorred in my imagination it is! my gorge rises at it. Here hung those lips that I have kissed I know not how oft. Where be your gibes now? your gambols? your songs? your flashes of merriment, that were wont to set the table on a roar? Not one now, to mock your own grinning? quite chap-fallen? Now get you to my lady's chamber, and tell her, let her paint an inch thick, to this favour she must come; make her laugh at that. [201]

1 To what base uses we may return, Horatio!
[222]

2 Imperious Caesar, dead, and turn'd to clay,
Might stop a hole to keep the wind away.
[235]

3 We should profane the service of the dead,
To sing a requiem, and such rest to her
As to peace-parted souls.
[258]

4   Lay her i' the earth;
And from her fair and unpolluted flesh
May violets spring! I tell thee, churlish priest,
A ministering angel shall my sister be,
When thou liest howling.
[260]

5 Sweets to the sweet: farewell!
[265]

6 I thought thy bride-bed to have deck'd, sweet maid,
And not have strewed thy grave.
[267]

7 For, though I am not splenetive and rash
Yet have I in me something dangerous.
[283]

8 I lov'd Ophelia: forty thousand brothers
Could not, with all their quantity of love,
Make up my sum.
[291]

9 And thus a while the fit will work on him;
Anon, as patient as the female dove,
When that her golden couplets are disclos'd,
His silence will sit drooping.
[307]

10 This grave shall have a living monument.
[319]

11 There's a divinity that shapes our ends,
Rough-hew them how we will.
ii.10

12 I once did hold it, as our statists do,
A baseness to write fair, and labour'd much
How to forget that learning; but, sir, now
It did me yeoman's service.
33

13 But, sure, the bravery of his grief did put me
Into a towering passion.
79

14 But thou wouldst not think how ill all's here about my heart.
[222]

15 Not a whit, we defy augury; there's a special providence in the fall of a sparrow. If it be now, 'tis not to come; if it be not to come, it will be now; if it be not now, yet it will come: the readiness is all.
[232]

16 I have shot mine arrow o'er the house,
And hurt my brother.
[257]

17 Now the king drinks to Hamlet!
[292]

18 A hit, a very palpable hit.
[295]

19 Why, as a woodcock to mine own springe, Osric;
I am justly kill'd with my own treachery.
[320]

20 O villany! Ho! let the door be lock'd:
Treachery! seek it out.
[325]

21 The point envenom'd too!—
Then, venom, to thy work.
[335]

22   This fell sergeant, death,
Is swift in his arrest.
[350]

23   Report me and my cause aright
To the unsatisfied.
[353]

24 I am more an antique Roman than a Dane.
[355]

25 If thou didst ever hold me in thy heart,
Absent thee from felicity awhile,
And in this harsh world draw thy breath in pain,
To tell my story.
[360]

26 The potent poison quite o'ercrows my spirit.
[367]

27 The rest is silence.
[372]

28 Now cracks a noble heart. Good-night, sweet prince,
And flights of angels sing thee to thy rest!
[373]

29 The ears are senseless that should give us hearing,
To tell him his commandment is fulfill'd,
That Rosencrantz and Guildenstern are dead.
[383]

30   Let four captains
Bear Hamlet, like a soldier, to the stage;
For he was likely, had he been put on,
To have prov'd most royally.
[409]

31 Go, bid the soldiers shoot.
[417]

HENRY IV, Part 1

32 So shaken as we are, so wan with care.
I.i.1

33   In those holy fields
Over whose acres walk'd those blessed feet,
Which fourteen hundred years ago were nail'd
For our advantage, on the bitter cross.
24

34 Unless hours were cups of sack, and minutes capons, and clocks the tongues of bawds, and dials the signs of leaping-houses, and the blessed sun himself a fair hot wench in flame-colour'd taffeta, I see no reason why thou shouldst be so superfluous to demand the time of

day.
ii.[7]

1 Let us be Diana's foresters, gentlemen of the shade, minions of the moon.
[28]

2 *Falstaff:* And is not my hostess of the tavern a most sweet wench?
Prince: As the honey of Hybla, my old lad of the castle.
[44]

3 What, in thy quips and thy quiddities?
[50]

4 Shall there be gallows standing in England when thou art king, and resolution thus fobbed as it is with the rusty curb of old father antick, the law?
[66]

5 Thou hast the most unsavoury similes.
[89]

6 I would to God thou and I knew where a commodity of good names were to be bought.
[92]

7 O! thou hast damnable iteration, and art, indeed, able to corrupt a saint.
[101]

8 Now am I, if a man should speak truly, little better than one of the wicked.
[105]

9 I'll be damned for never a king's son in Christendom.
[108]

10 Why, Hal, 'tis my vocation, Hal; 'tis no sin for a man to labour in his vocation.
[116]. Of stealing.

11 How agrees the devil and thee about thy soul, that thou soldest him on Good Friday last for a cup of Madeira and a cold capon's leg?
[126]

12 If he fight longer than he sees reason, I'll forswear arms.
[206]

13 If all the year were playing holidays,
To sport would be as tedious as to work;
But when they seldom come, they wish'd for come.
[226]

14 And as the soldiers bore dead bodies by,
He call'd them untaught knaves, unmannerly,
To bring a slovenly, unhandsome corpse
Betwixt the wind and his nobility.
With many holiday and lady terms
He question'd me.
iii.42

15 So pester'd with a popinjay.
50

16   It was great pity, so it was,
This villainous saltpetre should be digg'd
Out of the bowels of the harmless earth,
Which many a good tall fellow had destroy'd
So cowardly; and but for these vile guns,
He would himself have been a soldier.
59

17 To put down Richard, that sweet lovely rose,
And plant this thorn, this canker, Bolingbroke.
175

18   O! the blood more stirs
To rouse a lion than to start a hare.
197

19 By heaven methinks it were an easy leap
To pluck bright honour from the pale-fac'd moon,
Or dive into the bottom of the deep,
Where fathom-line could never touch the ground,
And pluck up drowned honour by the locks.
201

20 Why, what a candy deal of courtesy
This fawning greyhound then did proffer me!
251

21 I know a trick worth two of that.
II.i.[40]

22 At hand, quoth pick-purse.
[53]

23 We have the receipt of fern-seed, we walk invisible.
[95]

24 I am bewitched with the rogue's company. If the rascal have not given me medicines to make me love him, I'll be hanged.
ii.[19]

25 Go hang thyself in thine own heir-apparent garters!
[49]

26 On, bacons, on!
[99]

27 It would be argument for a week, laughter for a month, and a good jest for ever.
[104]

28   Falstaff sweats to death
And lards the lean earth as he walks along.
[119]

29 Out of this nettle, danger, we pluck this flower, safety.
iii.[11]

30 A good plot, good friends, and full of expectation; an excellent plot, very good friends.
[21]

31 Away, you trifler! Love! I love thee not,
I care not for thee, Kate: this is no world
To play with mammets and to tilt with lips:
We must have bloody noses and crack'd crowns.
[95]

32   Constant you are,
But yet a woman: and for secrecy,
No lady closer; for I well believe
Thou wilt not utter what thou dost not know.
[113]

33 I am not yet of Percy's mind, the Hotspur of the North; he that kills me some six or seven dozen of Scots at a breakfast, washes his hands, and says to his wife, 'Fie upon this quiet life! I want work.'
iv.[116]

34 There live not three good men unhanged in England, and one of them is fat and grows old.
[146]

35 Call you that backing of your friends? A plague upon such backing! give me them that will face me.
[168]

36 A plague of all cowards, still say I.
[175]

1 I am a Jew else; an Ebrew Jew.
[201]

2 Nay that's past praying for: I have peppered two of them: two I am sure I have paid, two rogues in buckram suits. I tell thee what, Hal, if I tell thee a lie, spit in my face, call me horse. Thou knowest my old ward; here I lay, and thus I bore my point. Four rogues in buckram let drive at me,—
[214]

3 O monstrous! eleven buckram men grown out of two.
[247]

4 These lies are like the father that begets them; gross as a mountain, open, palpable.
[253]

5 Give you a reason on compulsion! if reasons were as plentiful as blackberries I would give no man a reason upon compulsion, I.
[267]

6 Mark now, how a plain tale shall put you down.
[285]

7 What a slave art thou, to hack thy sword as thou hast done, and then say it was in fight!
[292]

8 Instinct is a great matter, I was a coward on instinct.
[304]

9 Ah! no more of that, Hal, an thou lovest me.
[316]

10 What doth gravity out of his bed at midnight?
[328]

11 A plague of sighing and grief! it blows a man up like a bladder.
[370]

12 I will do it in King Cambyses' vein.
[430]

13 Peace, good pint-pot!
[443]

14 Shall the blessed sun of heaven prove a micher and eat blackberries? a question not to be asked.
[454]

15 There is a devil haunts thee in the likeness of a fat old man; a tun of man is thy companion.
[498]

16 That roasted Manningtree ox with the pudding in his belly, that reverend vice, that grey iniquity, that father ruffian, that vanity in years.
[504]

17 If sack and sugar be a fault, God help the wicked!
[524]

18 No, my good lord; banish Peto, banish Bardolph, banish Poins; but for sweet Jack Falstaff, kind Jack Falstaff, true Jack Falstaff, valiant Jack Falstaff, and therefore more valiant, being, as he is, old Jack Falstaff, banish not him thy Harry's company: banish not him thy Harry's company: banish plump Jack and banish all the world.
[528]

19 Play out the play.
[539]

20 O monstrous! but one half-pennyworth of bread to this intolerable deal of sack!
[598]

21 *Glendower:* At my nativity

The front of heaven was full of fiery shapes,
Of burning cressets; and at my birth
The frame and huge foundation of the earth
Shak'd like a coward.
Hotspur: Why, so it would have done at the same
season, if your mother's cat had but kittened.
III.i.13

22 And all the courses of my life do show
I am not in the roll of common men.
[42]

23 *Glendower:* I can call spirits from the vasty deep.
Hotspur: Why, so can I, or so can any man;
But will they come when you do call for them?
[53]

24 I'll have the current in this place damm'd up,
And here the smug and silver Trent shall run
In a new channel, fair and evenly.
[102]

25 I had rather be a kitten and cry mew
Than one of these same metre ballad-mongers.
[128]

26 That would set my teeth nothing on edge,
Nothing so much as mincing poetry:
'Tis like the forc'd gait of a shuffling nag.
[132]

27 And such a deal of skimble-skamble stuff
As puts me from my faith.
[153]

28   O! he's as tedious
As a tired horse, a railing wife;
Worse than a smoky house. I had rather live
With cheese and garlic in a windmill, far,
Than feed on cates and have him talk to me
In any summer-house in Christendom.
[158]

29 I understand thy kisses, and thou mine,
And that's a feeling disputation.
[204]

30   Thy tongue
Makes Welsh as sweet as ditties highly penn'd,
Sung by a fair queen in a summer's bower,
With ravishing division, to her lute.
[207]

31 Now I perceive the devil understands Welsh.
[233]

32 You swear like a comfit-maker's wife.
[252]

33 Swear me, Kate, like a lady as thou art,
A good mouth-filling oath.
[257]

34 The skipping king, he ambled up and down
With shallow jesters and rash bavin wits.
ii.60

35   Being daily swallow'd by men's eyes,
They surfeited with honey and began
To loathe the taste of sweetness, whereof a little
More than a little is by much too much.
So, when he had occasion to be seen,
He was but as the cuckoo is in June,
Heard, not regarded.
70

36 My near'st and dearest enemy.
123

1 Well, I'll repent, and that suddenly, while I am in some liking; I shall be out of heart shortly, and then I shall have no strength to repent.
iii.[5]

2 Company, villanous company, hath been the spoil of me.
[10]

3 Come, sing me a bawdy song; make me merry.
[15]

4 Shall I not take mine ease in mine inn but I shall have my pocket picked?
[91]

5 Thou knowest in the state of innocency Adam fell; and what should poor Jack Falstaff do in the days of villany. Thou seest I have more flesh than another man, and therefore more frailty.
[184]

6   Where is his son,
That nimble-footed madcap Prince of Wales,
And his comrades, that daff'd the world aside,
And bid it pass?
IV.i.94

7 I saw young Harry, with his beaver on,
His cushes on his thighs, gallantly arm'd,
Rise from the ground like feather'd Mercury,
And vaulted with such ease into his seat,
As if an angel dropp'd down from the clouds,
To turn and wind a fiery Pegasus,
And witch the world with noble horsemanship.
104

8 Doomsday is near; die all, die merrily.
134

9 I have misus'd the king's press damnably.
ii.[13]

10 The cankers of a calm world and a long peace.
[32]

11 I am as vigilant as a cat to steal cream.
[64]

12 Tut, tut; good enough to toss; food for powder, food for powder; they'll fill a pit as well as better: tush, man, mortal men, mortal men.
[72]

13 Greatness knows itself.
iii.74

14 For mine own part, I could be well content
To entertain the lag-end of my life
With quiet hours.
V.i.23

15 Rebellion lay in his way, and he found it.
28

16 I do not think a braver gentleman,
More active-valiant or more valiant-young,
More daring or more bold, is now alive
To grace this latter age with noble deeds.
For my part, I may speak it to my shame,
I have a truant been to chivalry.
89

17 *Falstaff:* I would it were bed-time, Hal, and all well.
Prince: Why, thou owest God a death.
[125]. See 442:7

18 Honour pricks me on. Yea, but how if honour prick me off when I come on? how then? Can honour set-to a leg? No. Or an arm? No. Or take away the grief of a wound? No. Honour hath no skill in surgery, then? No. What is honour? A word. What is that word, honour? Air. A trim reckoning! Who hath it? He that died o' Wednesday. Doth he feel it? No. Doth he hear it? No. It is insensible then? Yea, to the dead. But will it not live with the living? No. Why? Detraction will not suffer it. Therefore I'll none of it: honour is a mere scutcheon: and so ends my catechism.
[131]

19 O gentlemen! the time of life is short;
To spend that shortness basely were too long.
ii.81

20 Now, *Esperance!* Percy! and set on.
96

21 I like not such grinning honour as Sir Walter hath: give me life; which if I can save, so; if not, honour comes unlooked for, and there's an end.
iii.[61]

22 Two stars keep not their motion in one sphere.
iv.65

23 But thought's the slave of life, and life time's fool;
And time, that takes survey of all the world,
Must have a stop.
[81]

24   Fare thee well, great heart!
Ill-weav'd ambition, how much art thou shrunk!
When that this body did contain a spirit,
A kingdom for it was too small a bound;
But now two paces of the vilest earth
Is room enough: this earth, that bears thee dead,
Bears not alive so stout a gentleman.
[87]

25 Thy ignominy sleep with thee in the grave,
But not remember'd in thy epitaph!
What! old acquaintance! could not all this flesh
Keep in a little life? Poor Jack, farewell!
I could have better spar'd a better man.
[100]

26   Full bravely hast thou flesh'd
Thy maiden sword.
[132]

27 Lord, Lord, how this world is given to lying! I grant you I was down and out of breath; and so was he; but we rose both at an instant, and fought a long hour by Shrewsbury clock.
[148]

28 For my part, if a lie may do thee grace,
I'll gild it with the happiest terms I have.
[161]

29 I'll purge, and leave sack, and live cleanly, as a nobleman should do.
[168]

HENRY IV, Part 2

30 I speak of peace, while covert enmity
Under the smile of safety wounds the world.
Induction, 9

31   Rumour is a pipe
Blown by surmises, jealousies, conjectures,
And of so easy and so plain a stop
That the blunt monster with uncounted heads,
The still-discordant wavering multitude,

Can play upon it.
15

1 Even such a man, so faint, so spiritless,
So dull, so dead in look, so woe-begone,
Drew Priam's curtain in the dead of night,
And would have told him, half his Troy was burn'd.
I.i.70

2 Yet the first bringer of unwelcome news
Hath but a losing office, and his tongue
Sounds ever after as a sullen bell,
Remember'd knolling a departed friend.
100

3 The brain of this foolish-compounded clay, man, is
not able to invent anything that tends to laughter, more
than I invent or is invented on me: I am not only witty
in myself, but the cause that wit is in other men. I do
here walk before thee like a sow that hath
overwhelmed all her litter but one.
ii.[7]

4 A rascally yea-forsooth knave.
[40]

5 Your lordship, though not clean past your youth, hath
yet some smack of age in you, some relish of the
saltness of time.
[111]

6 This apoplexy is, as I take it, a kind of lethargy, an't
please your lordship; a kind of sleeping in the blood, a
whoreson tingling.
[127]

7 It is the disease of not listening, the malady of not
marking, that I am troubled withal.
[139]

8 I am as poor as Job, my lord, but not so patient.
[145]

9 Well, I am loath to gall a new-healed wound.
[169]

10 Have you not a moist eye, a dry hand, a yellow cheek,
a white beard, a decreasing leg, an increasing belly? Is
not your voice broken, your wind short, your chin
double, your wit single, and every part about you
blasted with antiquity, and will you yet call yourself
young? Fie, fie, fie, Sir John!
[206]

11 My lord, I was born about three of the clock in the
afternoon, with a white head, and something of a
round belly. For my voice, I have lost it with hollaing,
and singing of anthems.
[213]

12 *Chief Justice:* God send the prince a better companion!
Falstaff: God send the companion a better prince! I
cannot rid my hands of him.
[227]

13 All you that kiss our lady Peace at home.
[236]

14 It was always yet the trick of our English nation, if
they have a good thing, to make it too common.
[244]

15 I would to God my name were not so terrible to the
enemy as it is: I were better to be eaten to death with
rust than to be scoured to nothing with perpetual
motion.
[247]

16 I can get no remedy against this consumption of the

purse: borrowing only lingers and lingers it out, but
the disease is incurable.
[268]

17   When we mean to build,
We first survey the plot, then draw the model;
And when we see the figure of the house,
Then we must rate the cost of the erection;
Which if we find outweighs ability,
What do we then but draw anew the model
In fewer offices, or at last desist
To build at all?
iii.[41]

18 A hundred mark is a long one for a poor lone woman
to bear; and I have borne, and borne, and borne; and
have been fubbed off, and fubbed off, and fubbed off,
from this day to that day, that it is a shame to be
thought on.
II.i.[36]

19 Away, you scullion! you rampallion! you fustilarian!
I'll tickle your catastrophe.
[67]

20 Thou didst swear to me upon a parcel-gilt goblet,
sitting in my Dolphin-chamber, at the round table, by
a sea-coal fire, upon Wednesday in Wheeson week.
[97]

21 Doth it not show vilely in me to desire small beer?
ii.[7]

22 I do now remember the poor creature, small beer.
[12]

23 Let the end try the man.
[52]

24   He was indeed the glass
Wherein the noble youth did dress themselves.
iii.21

25   Shall pack-horses,
And hollow pamper'd jades of Asia,
Which cannot go but thirty miles a day,
Compare with Caesars, and with Cannibals,
And Trojan Greeks? nay, rather damn them with
King Cerberus; and let the welkin roar.
iv. [176]. See 330:16

26 By my troth, captain, these are very bitter words.
[183]

27 Thou whoreson little tidy Bartholomew boar-pig, when
wilt thou leave fighting o' days, and foining o' nights,
and begin to patch up thine old body for heaven?
[249]

28 Is it not strange that desire should so many years
outlive performance?
[283]

29   O sleep! O gentle sleep!
Nature's soft nurse, how have I frighted thee,
That thou no more wilt weigh mine eyelids down
And steep my senses in forgetfulness?
Why rather, sleep, liest thou in smoky cribs,
Upon uneasy pallets stretching thee,
And hush'd with buzzing night-flies to thy slumber,
Than in the perfum'd chambers of the great,
Under the canopies of costly state,
And lull'd with sound of sweetest melody?
III.i.5

30   Then, happy low, lie down!

Uneasy lies the head that wears a crown.
30

1   O God! that one might read the book of fate,
And see the revolution of the times
Make mountains level, and the continent,—
Weary of solid firmness,—melt itself
Into the sea!
45

2   O! if this were seen,
The happiest youth, viewing his progress through,
What perils past, what crosses to ensue,
Would shut the book, and sit him down and die.
54

3   There is a history in all men's lives,
Figuring the nature of the times deceas'd,
The which observ'd, a man may prophesy,
With a near aim, of the main chance of things
As yet not come to life, which in their seeds
And weak beginnings lie intreasured.
80

4   A soldier is better accommodated than with a wife.
ii.[73]

5   Most forcible Feeble.
[181]

6   We have heard the chimes at midnight.
[231]

7   I care not; a man can die but once; we owe God a
death.
[253]. See 440:17

8   He that dies this year is quit for the next.
[257]

9   Lord, Lord! how subject we old men are to this vice
of lying.
[329]

10 When a' was naked, he was, for all the world, like a
forked radish, with a head fantastically carved upon it
with a knife.
[335]

11 Talks as familiarly of John a Gaunt as if he had been
sworn brother to him.
[348]

12 Against ill chances men are ever merry,
But heaviness foreruns the good event.
IV.ii.81

13 That I may justly say with the hook-nosed fellow of
Rome, 'I came, saw, and overcame.'
iii.[44]

14 A man cannot make him laugh; but that's no marvel;
he drinks no wine.
[95]

15 A good sherris-sack hath a two-fold operation in it. It
ascends me into the brain; dries me there all the foolish
and dull and crudy vapours which environ it; makes it
apprehensive, quick, forgetive, full of nimble fiery and
delectable shapes; which, deliver'd o'er to the voice,
the tongue, which is the birth, becomes excellent wit.
The second property of your excellent sherris is, the
warming of the blood; which, before cold and settled,
left the liver white and pale, which is the badge of
pusillanimity and cowardice: but the sherris warms it
and makes it course from the inwards to the parts
extreme. It illumineth the face, which, as a beacon,
gives warning to all the rest of this little kingdom,

man, to arm; and then the vital commoners and inland
petty spirits muster me all to their captain, the heart,
who, great and puffed up with this retinue, doth any
deed of courage; and this valour comes of sherris. So
that skill in the weapon is nothing without sack, for
that sets it a-work; and learning, a mere hoard of gold
kept by a devil till sack commences it and sets it in act
and use.
[103]

16 If I had a thousand sons, the first human principle I
would teach them should be, to forswear thin
potations.
[133]

17 O polish'd perturbation! golden care!
That keep'st the ports of slumber open wide
To many a watchful night! Sleep with it now!
Yet not so sound, and half so deeply sweet
As he whose brow with homely biggin bound
Snores out the watch of night.
v.22

18 This sleep is sound indeed; this is a sleep
That from this golden rigol hath divorc'd
So many English kings.
34

19 Thy wish was father, Harry, to that thought.
91

20   Commit
The oldest sins the newest kind of ways.
124

21 It hath been prophesied to me many years
I should not die but in Jerusalem,
Which vainly I suppos'd the Holy Land.
But bear me to that chamber; there I'll lie:
In that Jerusalem shall Harry die.
235

22 Any pretty little tiny kickshaws, tell William cook.
V.i.[29]

23 This is the English, not the Turkish court;
Not Amurath an Amurath succeeds,
But Harry, Harry.
ii.47

24 Sorrow so royally in you appears,
That I will deeply put the fashion on.
51

25 My father is gone wild into his grave.
123

26 'Tis merry in hall when beards wag all.
iii.[35]

27 A foutra for the world, and worldlings base!
I speak of Africa and golden joys.
[100]

28 Under which king, Bezonian? speak, or die!
[116]

29 Let us take any man's horses; the laws of England are
at my commandment.
[139]

30 I know thee not, old man: fall to thy prayers;
How ill white hairs become a fool and jester!
I have long dream'd of such a kind of man,
So surfeit-swell'd, so old, and so profane,
v.[52]

31 Make less thy body hence, and more thy grace;
Leave gormandising; know the grave doth gape

For thee thrice wider than for other men.
[57]

1 Presume not that I am the thing I was.
[61]

2 Where, for anything I know, Falstaff shall die of a sweat, unless already a' be killed with your hard opinions; for Oldcastle died a martyr, and this is not the man.
Epilogue, [32]

HENRY V

3 O! for a Muse of fire, that would ascend
The brightest heaven of invention;
A kingdom for a stage, princes to act
And monarchs to behold the swelling scene.
Chorus, 1

4　　　　Can this cockpit hold
The vasty fields of France? or may we cram
Within this wooden O the very casques
That did affright the air at Agincourt?
11

5 Consideration like an angel came,
And whipp'd the offending Adam out of him.
I.i.28

6　　　　When he speaks,
The air, a charter'd libertine, is still.
47

7 O noble English! that could entertain
With half their forces the full pride of France,
And let another half stand laughing by,
All out of work, and cold for action.
ii.111

8 And make your chronicle as rich with praise
As is the owse and bottom of the sea
With sunken wrack and sumless treasuries.
163

9　　　　For so work the honey-bees,
Creatures that by a rule in nature teach
The act of order to a peopled kingdom.
They have a king and officers of sorts;
Where some, like magistrates, correct at home,
Others, like merchants, venture trade abroad,
Others, like soldiers, armed in their stings,
Make boot upon the summer's velvet buds;
Which pillage they with merry march bring home
To the tent-royal of their emperor:
Who, busied in his majesty, surveys
The singing masons building roofs of gold,
The civil citizens kneading up the honey,
The poor mechanic porters crowding in
Their heavy burdens at his narrow gate,
The sad-ey'd justice, with his surly hum,
Delivering o'er to executors pale
The lazy yawning drone.
187

10 *King Henry:* What treasure, uncle?
Exeter: Tennis-balls, my liege.
258

11 His present and your pains we thank you for:
When we have match'd our rackets to these balls,
We will in France, by God's grace, play a set
Shall strike his father's crown into the hazard.
260

12 Now all the youth of England are on fire,
And silken dalliance in the wardrobe lies;
Now thrive the armourers, and honour's thought
Reigns solely in the breast of every man:
They sell the pasture now to buy the horse,
Following the mirror of all Christian kings,
With winged heels, as English Mercuries.
For now sits Expectation in the air
And hides a sword from hilts unto the point
With crowns imperial, crowns and coronets,
Promis'd to Harry and his followers.
II. Chorus, 1

13 O England! model to thy inward greatness,
Like little body with a mighty heart,
What might'st thou do, that honour would thee do,
Were all thy children kind and natural!
But see thy fault!
16

14 I dare not fight; but I will wink and hold out mine iron.
i.[7]

15 For, lambkins, we will live.
[134]

16 Would I were with him, wheresome'er he is, either in heaven or in hell.
iii.[7]

17 He's in Arthur's bosom, if ever man went to Arthur's bosom. A' made a finer end, and went away an it had been any christom child; a' parted even just between twelve and one, even at the turning o' the tide: for after I saw him fumble with the sheets and play with flowers and smile upon his fingers' ends, I knew there was but one way; for his nose was as sharp as a pen, and a' babbled of green fields.
[9]

18 So a' cried out 'God, God, God!' three or four times: now I, to comfort him, bid him a' should not think of God, I hoped there was no need to trouble himself with any such thoughts yet. So a' bade me lay more clothes on his feet: I put my hand into the bed and felt them, and they were as cold as any stone; then I felt to his knees, and so upward, and upward, and all was as cold as any stone.
[19]

19 *Boy:* Yes, that a' did; and said they were devils incarnate.
Hostess: A' never could abide carnation; 'twas a colour he never liked.
Boy: A' said once, the devil would have him about women.
[33]

20　　　　Trust none;
For oaths are straws, men's faiths are wafer-cakes,
And hold-fast is the only dog, my duck.
[53]

21 Once more unto the breach, dear friends, once more;
Or close the wall up with our English dead!
In peace there's nothing so becomes a man
As modest stillness and humility:
But when the blast of war blows in our ears,
Then imitate the action of the tiger;
Stiffen the sinews, summon up the blood,
Disguise fair nature with hard-favour'd rage;

Then lend the eye a terrible aspect.
III.i.1

1   On, on you noblest English!
Whose blood is fet from fathers of war-proof;
Fathers that, like so many Alexanders,
Have in these parts from morn till even fought,
And sheath'd their swords for lack of argument.
17

2   And you, good yeomen,
Whose limbs were made in England, show us here
The mettle of your pasture.
25

3 I see you stand like greyhounds in the slips,
Straining upon the start. The game's afoot:
Follow your spirit; and, upon this charge
Cry 'God for Harry! England and Saint George!'
31

4 Would I were in an alehouse in London! I would give
all my fame for a pot of ale, and safety.
ii.[13]

5 Men of few words are the best men.
[40]

6 A' never broke any man's head but his own, and that
was against a post when he was drunk.
[43]

7 One Bardolph, if your majesty know the man: his face
is all bubukles, and whelks, and knobs, and flames o'
fire.
vi.[110]

8 Give them great meals of beef and iron and steel, they
will eat like wolves and fight like devils.
vii.[166]

9 Now entertain conjecture of a time
When creeping murmur and the poring dark
Fills the wide vessel of the universe.
From camp to camp, through the foul womb of night,
The hum of either army stilly sounds,
That the fix'd sentinels almost receive
The secret whispers of each other's watch.
Fire answers fire, and through their paly flames
Each battle sees the other's umber'd face:
Steed threatens steed, in high and boastful neighs
Piercing the night's dull ear; and from the tents
The armourers, accomplishing the knights,
With busy hammers closing rivets up,
Give dreadful note of preparation.
IV. Chorus, 1

10 The royal captain of this ruin'd band.
29

11 A largess universal, like the sun
His liberal eye doth give to every one,
Thawing cold fear.
43

12 A little touch of Harry in the night.
47

13   Yet sit and see;
Minding true things by what their mockeries be.
52

14 Gloucester, 'tis true that we are in great danger;
The greater therefore should our courage be.
i.1

15 Thus may we gather honey from the weed,

And make a moral of the devil himself.
11

16 Discuss unto me; art thou officer?
Or art thou base, common and popular?
37

17 The king's a bawcock, and a heart of gold,
A lad of life, an imp of fame,
Of parents good, of fist most valiant:
I kiss his dirty shoe, and from my heart-string
I love the lovely bully.
44

18 If you would take the pains but to examine the wars of
Pompey the Great, you shall find, I warrant you, that
there is no tiddle-taddle nor pibble-pabble in Pompey's
camp.
[69]

19 Though it appear a little out of fashion,
There is much care and valour in this Welshman.
[86]

20 I think the king is but a man, as I am: the violet smells
to him as it doth to me.
[106]

21 I am afeard there are few die well that die in a battle;
for how can they charitably dispose of any thing when
blood is their argument?
[149]

22 Every subject's duty is the king's; but every subject's
soul is his own.
[189]

23 Upon the king! let us our lives, our souls,
Our debts, our careful wives,
Our children, and our sins lay on the king!
We must bear all. O hard condition!
[250]

24   What infinite heart's ease
Must kings neglect, that private men enjoy!
And what have kings that privates have not too,
Save ceremony, save general ceremony?
[256]

25 'Tis not the balm, the sceptre and the ball,
The sword, the mace, the crown imperial,
The intertissued robe of gold and pearl,
The farced title running 'fore the king,
The throne he sits on, nor the tide of pomp
That beats upon the high shore of this world,
No, not all these, thrice-gorgeous ceremony,
Not all these, laid in bed majestical,
Can sleep so soundly as the wretched slave,
Who with a body fill'd and vacant mind
Gets him to rest, cramm'd with distressful bread;
Never sees horrid night, the child of hell,
But, like a lackey, from the rise to set
Sweats in the eye of Phoebus, and all night
Sleeps in Elysium.
[280]

26 O God of battles! steel my soldiers' hearts;
Possess them not with fear; take from them now
The sense of reckoning, if the opposed numbers
Pluck their hearts from them.
[309]

27   O! that we now had here
But one ten thousand of those men in England

That do no work to-day.
iii.16

1 If we are mark'd to die, we are enow
To do our country loss; and if to live,
The fewer men, the greater share of honour.
20

2 If it be a sin to covet honour
I am the most offending soul alive.
31

3 He which hath no stomach to this fight,
Let him depart; his passport shall be made,
And crowns for convoy put into his purse:
We would not die in that man's company
That fears his fellowship to die with us.
This day is called the feast of Crispian:
He that outlives this day and comes safe home,
Will stand a tip-toe when this day is nam'd,
And rouse him at the name of Crispian.
He that shall live this day, and see old age,
Will yearly on the vigil feast his neighbours,
And say, 'To-morrow is Saint Crispian:'
Then will he strip his sleeve and show his scars,
And say, 'These wounds I had on Crispin's day.'
Old men forget: yet all shall be forgot,
But he'll remember with advantages
What feats he did that day. Then shall our names,
Familiar in his mouth as household words,
Harry the King, Bedford and Exeter,
Warwick and Talbot, Salisbury and Gloucester,
Be in their flowing cups freshly remember'd.
This story shall the good man teach his son;
And Crispin Crispian shall ne'er go by,
From this day to the ending of the world,
But we in it shall be remembered;
We few, we happy few, we band of brothers;
For he to-day that sheds his blood with me
Shall be my brother; be he ne'er so vile
This day shall gentle his condition:
And gentlemen in England, now a-bed
Shall think themselves accurs'd they were not here,
And hold their manhoods cheap whiles any speaks
That fought with us upon Saint Crispin's day.
35

4 Thou damned and luxurious mountain goat.
iv.[20]

5 There is a river in Macedon, and there is also
moreover a river at Monmouth: it is called Wye at
Monmouth; but it is out of my prains what is the name
of the other river; but 'tis all one, 'tis alike as my
fingers is to my fingers, and there is salmons in both.
vii.[28]

6   But now behold,
In the quick forge and working-house of thought,
How London doth pour out her citizens.
V. Chorus, 22

7 Were now the general of our gracious empress,—
As in good time he may,—from Ireland coming,
Bringing rebellion broached on his sword.
30

8 There is occasions and causes why and wherefore in
all things.
i.[3]

9 Not for Cadwallader and all his goats.
[29]

10 By this leek, I will most horribly revenge.
[49]

11   Let it not disgrace me
If I demand before this royal view,
What rub or what impediment there is,
Why that the naked, poor, and mangled Peace,
Dear nurse of arts, plenties, and joyful births,
Should not in this best garden of the world,
Our fertile France, put up her lovely visage?
ii.31

12   Her fallow leas
The darnel, hemlock and rank fumitory
Doth root upon, while that the coulter rusts
That should deracinate such savagery;
The even mead, that erst brought sweetly forth
The freckled cowslip, burnet, and green clover,
Wanting the scythe, all uncorrected, rank,
Conceives by idleness, and nothing teems
But hateful docks, rough thistles, kecksies, burs,
Losing both beauty and utility.
44

13 For these fellows of infinite tongue, that can rhyme
themselves into ladies' favours, they do always reason
themselves out again.
[162]

14 Shall not thou and I, between Saint Denis and Saint
George, compound a boy, half-French, half-English,
that shall go to Constantinople and take the Turk by
the beard?
[218]

15 It is not a fashion for the maids in France to kiss
before they are married.
[287]

16 God, the best maker of all marriages,
Combine your hearts in one.
[387]

HENRY VI, Part 1

17 Hung be the heavens with black, yield day to night!
I.i.1

18 Expect Saint Martin's summer, halcyon days.
ii.131

19   Unbidden guests
Are often welcomest when they are gone.
II.ii.55

20 But in these nice sharp quillets of the law,
Good faith, I am no wiser than a daw.
iv.17

21 *Plantagenet:* Let him that is a true-born gentleman,
And stands upon the honour of his birth,
If he suppose that I have pleaded truth,
From off this brier pluck a white rose with me.
Somerset: Let him that is no coward nor no flatterer,
But dare maintain the party of the truth,
Pluck a red rose from off this thorn with me.
27

22 Delays have dangerous ends.
III.ii.33

23 I owe him little duty and less love.
IV.iv.34

24 So doth the swan her downy cygnets save,

Keeping them prisoners underneath her wings.
V.iii.56

1 She's beautiful and therefore to be woo'd;
She is a woman, therefore to be won.
78. See 486:15

HENRY VI, Part 2

2 Put forth thy hand, reach at the glorious gold.
I.ii.11

3 Is this the fashion of the court of England?
Is this the government of Britain's isle,
And this the royalty of Albion's king?
iii.[46]

4 She bears a duke's revenues on her back,
And in her heart she scorns our poverty.
[83]

5 Could I come near your beauty with my nails
I'd set my ten commandments in your face.
[144]

6 What stronger breastplate than a heart untainted!
Thrice is he arm'd that hath his quarrel just,
And he but naked, though lock'd up in steel,
Whose conscience with injustice is corrupted.
III.ii.232

7 Forbear to judge, for we are sinners all.
Close up his eyes, and draw the curtain close;
And let us all to meditation.
iii.31

8 The gaudy, blabbing, and remorseful day
Is crept into the bosom of the sea.
IV.i.1

9 True nobility is exempt from fear:
More can I bear than you dare execute.
129

10 I say it was never merry world in England since
gentlemen came up.
ii.[10]

11 *Cade:* There shall be in England seven halfpenny
loaves sold for a penny; the three-hooped pot shall
have ten hoops; and I will make it felony to drink
small beer. All the realm shall be in common, and in
Cheapside shall my palfrey go to grass. And when I am
king,—as king I will be,—...there shall be no money;
all shall eat and drink on my score; and I will apparel
them all in one livery, that they may agree like
brothers, and worship me their lord.
Dick: The first thing we do, let's kill all the lawyers.
[73]

12 Is not this a lamentable thing, that of the skin of an
innocent lamb should be made parchment? that
parchment, being scribbled o'er, should undo a man?
[88]

13 And Adam was a gardener.
[146]

14 Thou hast most traitorously corrupted the youth of the
realm in erecting a grammar school: and whereas,
before, our forefathers had no other books but the
score and the tally, thou hast caused printing to be
used; and, contrary to the king, his crown and dignity,
thou hast built a paper-mill.
vii.[35]

15 Away with him! away with him! he speaks Latin.
[62]

HENRY VI, Part 3

16 O tiger's heart wrapp'd in a woman's hide!
I.iv.137

17 This battle fares like to the morning's war,
When dying clouds contend with growing light,
What time the shepherd, blowing of his nails,
Can neither call it perfect day nor night.
II.v.1

18 O God! methinks it were a happy life,
To be no better than a homely swain;
To sit upon a hill, as I do now,
To carve out dials, quaintly, point by point,
Thereby to see the minutes how they run,
How many make the hour full complete;
How many hours bring about the day;
How many days will finish up the year;
How many years a mortal man may live.
21

19 Gives not the hawthorn bush a sweeter shade
To shepherds, looking on their silly sheep,
Than doth a rich embroider'd canopy
To kings that fear their subjects' treachery?
42

20 Peace! impudent and shameless Warwick, peace;
Proud setter up and puller down of kings.
III.iii.156

21 A little fire is quickly trodden out,
Which, being suffer'd, rivers cannot quench.
IV.viii.7

22 Lo! now my glory smear'd in dust and blood;
My parks, my walks, my manors that I had,
Even now forsake me; and, of all my lands
Is nothing left me but my body's length.
Why, what is pomp, rule, reign, but earth and dust?
And, live we how we can, yet die we must.
V.ii.23

23 Suspicion always haunts the guilty mind;
The thief doth fear each bush an officer.
vi.11

24 Down, down to hell; and say I sent thee thither.
67

HENRY VIII

25 Heat not a furnace for your foe so hot
That it do singe yourself.
I.i.140

26 If I chance to talk a little wild, forgive me;
I had it from my father.
iv.26

27 Go with me, like good angels, to my end;
And, as the long divorce of steel falls on me,
Make of your prayers one sweet sacrifice,
And lift my soul to heaven.
II.i.75

28 *Chamberlain:* It seems the marriage with his brother's
wife
Has crept too near his conscience.
Suffolk: No; his conscience

Has crept too near another lady.
ii.[17]

1　　　Heaven will one day open
The king's eyes, that so long have slept upon
This bold bad man.
[42]. See 516:1

2　　　I would not be a queen
For all the world.
45

3 Orpheus with his lute made trees,
And the mountain-tops that freeze,
　　Bow themselves when he did sing:
To his music plants and flowers
Ever sprung; as sun and showers
　　There had made a lasting spring.

Everything that heard him play,
Even the billows of the sea,
　　Hung their heads, and then lay by.
In sweet music is such art,
Killing care and grief of heart
　　Fall asleep, or hearing die.
III.i.3

4 Heaven is above all yet; there sits a judge,
That no king can corrupt.
99

5 A spleeny Lutheran.
ii.100

6　　　Then to breakfast with
What appetite you have.
203

7　　　I shall fall
Like a bright exhalation in the evening,
And no man see me more.
226

8　　　In all you writ to Rome, or else
To foreign princes, *Ego et Rex meus*
Was still inscrib'd; in which you brought the king
To be your servant.
313

9 Farewell! a long farewell, to all my greatness!
This is the state of man: to-day he puts forth
The tender leaves of hope; to-morrow blossoms,
And bears his blushing honours thick upon him;
The third day comes a frost, a killing frost;
And, when he thinks, good easy man, full surely
His greatness is a-ripening, nips his root,
And then he falls, as I do. I have ventur'd,
Like little wanton boys that swim on bladders,
This many summers in a sea of glory,
But far beyond my depth: my high-blown pride
At length broke under me, and now has left me
Weary and old with service, to the mercy
Of a rude stream that must for ever hide me.
Vain pomp and glory of this world, I hate ye:
I feel my heart new open'd. O how wretched
Is that poor man that hangs on princes' favours!
There is, betwixt that smile we would aspire to,
That sweet aspect of princes, and their ruin,
More pangs and fears than wars or women have;
And when he falls, he falls like Lucifer,
Never to hope again.
352

10 A peace above all earthly dignities,

A still and quiet conscience.
380

11 A load would sink a navy.
384

12 Cromwell, I charge thee, fling away ambition:
By that sin fell the angels; how can man then,
The image of his Maker, hope to win by't?
Love thyself last: cherish those hearts that hate thee;
Corruption wins not more than honesty.
Still in thy right hand carry gentle peace,
To silence envious tongues: be just, and fear not.
Let all the ends thou aim'st at be thy country's,
Thy God's, and truth's: then if thou fall'st, O
　　Cromwell!
Thou fall'st a blessed martyr.
441

13 Had I but serv'd my God with half the zeal
I serv'd my king, he would not in mine age
Have left me naked to mine enemies.
456

14 She had all the royal makings of a queen.
IV.i.87

15 An old man, broken with the storms of state
Is come to lay his weary bones among ye;
Give him a little earth for charity.
ii.21

16 He gave his honours to the world again,
His blessed part to Heaven, and slept in peace.
29

17 So may he rest; his faults lie gently on him!
31

18　　　He was a man
Of an unbounded stomach.
33

19 His promises were, as he then was, mighty;
But his performance, as he is now, nothing.
41

20 Men's evil manners live in brass; their virtues
We write in water.
45

21 He was a scholar, and a ripe and good one;
Exceeding wise, fair-spoken, and persuading:
Lofty and sour to them that lov'd him not;
But, to those men that sought him, sweet as summer.
51

22 Those twins of learning that he rais'd in you,
Ipswich and Oxford!
58

23 After my death I wish no other herald,
No other speaker of my living actions,
To keep mine honour from corruption,
Than such an honest chronicler as Griffith.
69

24　　　I had thought
They had parted so much honesty among 'em,—
At least, good manners,—as not thus to suffer
A man of his place, and so near our favour,
To dance attendance on their lordships' pleasures,
And at the door too, like a post with packets.
V.ii.26

25　　　'Tis a cruelty
To load a falling man.
76

1 In her days every man shall eat in safety
   Under his own vine what he plants; and sing
   The merry songs of peace to all his neighbours.
   v.34

2   Those about her
   From her shall read the perfect ways of honour.
   37

3 Nor shall this peace sleep with her; but as when
   The bird of wonder dies, the maiden phoenix,
   Her ashes new-create another heir
   As great in admiration as herself.
   40

4   Some come to take their ease
   And sleep an act or two.
   Epilogue, 2

JULIUS CAESAR

5 Hence! home, you idle creatures, get you home:
   Is this a holiday?
   I.i.1

6 You blocks, you stones, you worse than senseless
           things!
   O you hard hearts, you cruel men of Rome,
   Knew you not Pompey?
   [39]

7 *Caesar:* Who is it in the press that calls on me?
   I hear a tongue, shriller than all the music,
   Cry 'Caesar'. Speak; Caesar is turn'd to hear.
   Soothsayer: Beware the ides of March.
   ii.15

8 He is a dreamer; let us leave him: pass.
   24

9 I am not gamesome: I do lack some part
   Of that quick spirit that is in Antony.
   28

10 Brutus, I do observe you now of late:
   I have not from your eyes that gentleness
   And show of love as I was wont to have:
   You bear too stubborn and too strange a hand
   Over your friend that loves you.
   32

11   Poor Brutus, with himself at war,
   Forgets the shows of love to other men.
   46

12 Set honour in one eye and death i' the other,
   And I will look on both indifferently.
   86

13 Well, honour is the subject of my story.
   I cannot tell what you and other men
   Think of this life: but, for my single self,
   I had as lief not be as live to be
   In awe of such a thing as I myself.
   92

14 I was born free as Caesar; so were you:
   We both have fed as well, and we can both
   Endure the winter's cold as well as he:
   For once, upon a raw and gusty day,
   The troubl'd Tiber chafing with her shores,
   Caesar said to me, 'Dar'st thou, Cassius, now,
   Leap in with me into this angry flood,
   And swim to yonder point?' Upon the word,
   Accoutred as I was, I plunged in,
   And bade him follow...

But ere we could arrive the point propos'd,
Caesar cried, 'Help me, Cassius, or I sink!'
I, as Aeneas, our great ancestor,
Did from the flames of Troy upon his shoulder
The old Anchises bear, so from the waves of Tiber
Did I the tired Caesar. And this man
Is now become a god.
97

15 He had a fever when he was in Spain,
   And when the fit was on him, I did mark
   How he did shake; 'tis true, this god did shake;
   His coward lips did from their colour fly,
   And that same eye whose bend doth awe the world
   Did lose his lustre.
   119

16   Ye gods, it doth amaze me,
   A man of such a feeble temper should
   So get the start of the majestic world,
   And bear the palm alone.
   128

17 Why, man, he doth bestride the narrow world
   Like a Colossus; and we petty men
   Walk under his huge legs, and peep about
   To find ourselves dishonourable graves.
   Men at some time are masters of their fates:
   The fault, dear Brutus, is not in our stars,
   But in ourselves, that we are underlings.
   134

18 'Brutus' will start a spirit as soon as 'Caesar'.
   Now in the names of all the gods at once,
   Upon what meat doth this our Caesar feed,
   That he is grown so great?
   146

19 When could they say, till now, that talk'd of Rome,
   That her wide walls encompass'd but one man?
   Now is it Rome indeed and room enough,
   When there is in it but one only man.
   153

20 Let me have men about me that are fat;
   Sleek-headed men and such as sleep o' nights;
   Yond' Cassius has a lean and hungry look;
   He thinks too much: such men are dangerous.
   191

21 Would he were fatter! but I fear him not:
   Yet if my name were liable to fear,
   I do not know the man I should avoid
   So soon as that spare Cassius. He reads much;
   He is a great observer, and he looks
   Quite through the deeds of men; he loves no plays,
   As thou dost, Antony; he hears no music;
   Seldom he smiles, and smiles in such a sort
   As if he mock'd himself, and scorn'd his spirit,
   That could be mov'd to smile at anything.
   Such men as he be never at heart's ease,
   Whiles they behold a greater than themselves,
   And therefore are they very dangerous.
   I rather tell thee what is to be fear'd
   Than what I fear, for always I am Caesar.
   197

22 'Tis very like: he hath the falling sickness.
   [255]

23 *Cassius:* Did Cicero say any thing?
   Casca: Ay, he spoke Greek.
   Cassius: To what effect?

Casca: Nay, an I tell you that, I'll ne'er look you i' the face again; but those that understood him smiled at one another and shook their heads; but, for mine own part, it was Greek to me.
[282]

1   Yesterday the bird of night did sit,
Even at noon-day, upon the market-place,
Hooting and shrieking.
iii.26

2   Cassius from bondage will deliver Cassius.
90

3   Nor stony tower, nor walls of beaten brass,
Nor airless dungeon, nor strong links of iron,
Can be retentive to the strength of spirit;
But life, being weary of these worldly bars,
Never lacks power to dismiss itself.
93

4   It is the bright day that brings forth the adder;
And that craves wary walking.
II.i.14

5   'Tis a common proof,
That lowliness is young ambition's ladder,
Whereto the climber-upward turns his face;
But when he once attains the upmost round,
He then unto the ladder turns his back,
Looks in the clouds, scorning the base degrees
By which he did ascend.
21

6   Between the acting of a dreadful thing
And the first motion, all the interim is
Like a phantasma, or a hideous dream:
The genius and the mortal instruments
Are then in council; and the state of man,
Like to a little kingdom, suffers then
The nature of an insurrection.
63

7   O conspiracy!
Sham'st thou to show thy dangerous brow by night,
When evils are most free?
77

8   Let us be sacrificers, but not butchers, Caius.
166

9   Let's carve him as a dish fit for the gods,
Not hew him as a carcass fit for hounds.
173

10 For he is superstitious grown of late,
Quite from the main opinion he held once
Of fantasy, of dreams, and ceremonies.
195

11 But when I tell him he hates flatterers,
He says he does, being then most flattered.
207

12 Enjoy the honey-heavy dew of slumber.
230

13   What! is Brutus sick,
And will he steal out of his wholesome bed
To dare the vile contagion of the night?
263

14   That great vow
Which did incorporate and make us one.
272

15 *Portia:* Dwell I but in the suburbs
Of your good pleasure? If it be no more,

Portia is Brutus' harlot, not his wife.
Brutus: You are my true and honourable wife,
As dear to me as are the ruddy drops
That visit my sad heart.
285

16 I grant I am a woman, but, withal,
A woman that Lord Brutus took to wife;
I grant I am a woman, but, withal,
A woman well-reputed, Cato's daughter.
Think you I am no stronger than my sex,
Being so fathered and so husbanded?
292

17 Nor heaven nor earth have been at peace to-night.
ii.1

18 *Calphurnia:* When beggars die, there are no comets seen;
The heavens themselves blaze forth the death of princes.
Caesar: Cowards die many times before their deaths;
The valiant never taste of death but once.
Of all the wonders that I yet have heard,
It seems to me most strange that men should fear;
Seeing that death, a necessary end,
Will come when it will come.
30

19   Danger knows full well
That Caesar is more dangerous than he:
We are two lions litter'd in one day,
And I the elder and more terrible:
And Caesar shall go forth.
44

20 The cause is in my will: I will not come.
71

21 See! Antony, that revels long o' nights,
Is notwithstanding up.
116

22 O constancy! be strong upon my side;
Set a huge mountain 'tween my heart and tongue;
I have a man's mind, but a woman's might.
How hard it is for women to keep counsel!
iv.6

23 *Caesar:* The ides of March are come.
Soothsayer: Ay, Caesar; but not gone.
III.i.1

24   Be not fond,
To think that Caesar bears such rebel blood
That will be thaw'd from the true quality
With that which melted fools; I mean sweet words,
Low-crooked curtsies, and base spaniel fawning.
Thy brother by decree is banished:
If thou dost bend and pray and fawn for him,
I spurn thee like a cur out of my way.
39

25 If I could pray to move, prayers would move me;
But I am constant as the northern star,
Of whose true-fix'd and resting quality
There is no fellow in the firmament.
The skies are painted with unnumber'd sparks,
They are all fire and every one doth shine,
But there's but one in all doth hold his place:
So, in the world; 'tis furnish'd well with men,
And men are flesh and blood, and apprehensive;
Yet in the number I do know but one
That unassailable holds on his rank,

Unshak'd of motion: and that I am he,
Let me a little show it, even in this,
That I was constant Cimber should be banish'd,
And constant do remain to keep him so.
59

1 *Et tu, Brute?* Then fall, Caesar!
77. See 126:28

2 Ambition's debt is paid.
83

3 That we shall die, we know; 'tis but the time
And drawing days out, that men stand upon.
99

4 He that cuts off twenty years of life
Cuts off so many years of fearing death.
101

5 *Cassius:* How many ages hence
Shall this our lofty scene be acted o'er,
In states unborn, and accents yet unknown!
Brutus: How many times shall Caesar bleed in sport.
111

6 O mighty Caesar! dost thou lie so low?
Are all thy conquests, glories, triumphs, spoils,
Shrunk to this little measure?
148

7   Your swords, made rich
With the most noble blood of all this world.
155

8   Live a thousand years,
I shall not find myself so apt to die:
No place will please me so, no mean of death,
As here by Caesar, and by you cut off,
The choice and master spirits of this age.
159

9 Had I as many eyes as thou hast wounds,
Weeping as fast as they stream forth thy blood,
It would become me better than to close
In terms of friendship with thine enemies.
200

10 The enemies of Caesar shall say this;
Then, in a friend, it is cold modesty.
212

11 O! pardon me, thou bleeding piece of earth,
That I am meek and gentle with these butchers;
Thou art the ruins of the noblest man
That ever lived in the tide of times.
254

12   Caesar's spirit, ranging for revenge,
With Ate by his side, come hot from hell,
Shall in these confines, with a monarch's voice
Cry, 'Havoc!' and let slip the dogs of war;
That this foul deed shall smell above the earth
With carrion men, groaning for burial.
270

13 Passion, I see, is catching.
283

14 Not that I loved Caesar less, but that I loved Rome
more.
ii.[22]

15 As he was valiant, I honour him: but, as he was
ambitious, I slew him.
[27]

16 Who is here so base that would be a bondman? If any,
speak; for him have I offended. Who is here so rude

that would not be a Roman? If any, speak; for him
have I offended. Who is here so vile that will not love
his country? If any, speak; for him have I offended. I
pause for a reply.
[31]

17 Friends, Romans, countrymen, lend me your ears;
I come to bury Caesar, not to praise him.
The evil that men do lives after them,
The good is oft interred with their bones;
So let it be with Caesar. The noble Brutus
Hath told you Caesar was ambitious;
If it were so, it was a grievous fault;
And grievously hath Caesar answer'd it.
Here, under leave of Brutus and the rest,—
For Brutus is an honourable man;
So are they all, all honourable men,—
Come I to speak in Caesar's funeral.
[79]

18 He was my friend, faithful and just to me:
But Brutus says he was ambitious;
And Brutus is an honourable man.
[91]

19 When that the poor have cried, Caesar hath wept;
Ambition should be made of sterner stuff.
[97]

20   On the Lupercal
I thrice presented him a kingly crown
Which he did thrice refuse: was this ambition?
[101]

21 You all did love him once, not without cause.
[108]

22 O judgment! thou art fled to brutish beasts,
And men have lost their reason.
[110]

23 But yesterday the word of Caesar might
Have stood against the world; now lies he there,
And none so poor to do him reverence.
[124]

24 The will, the will! we will hear Caesar's will.
[145]

25 You are not wood, you are not stones, but men;
And, being men, hearing the will of Caesar,
It will inflame you, it will make you mad.
[148]

26 If you have tears, prepare to shed them now.
You all do know this mantle: I remember
The first time ever Caesar put it on;
'Twas on a summer's evening, in his tent,
That day he overcame the Nervii.
[174]

27 See what a rent the envious Casca made.
[180]

28 This was the most unkindest cut of all;
For when the noble Caesar saw him stab,
Ingratitude, more strong than traitors' arms,
Quite vanquish'd him: then burst his mighty heart;
And, in his mantle muffling up his face,
Even at the base of Pompey's statua,
Which all the while ran blood, great Caesar fell.
O! what a fall was there, my countrymen;
Then I, and you, and all of us fell down,
Whilst bloody treason flourish'd over us.
O! now you weep, and I perceive you feel

The dint of pity; these are gracious drops.
[188]

1 I come not, friends, to steal away your hearts:
I am no orator, as Brutus is;
But, as you know me all, a plain, blunt man,
That love my friend.
[220]

2 For I have neither wit, nor words, nor worth,
Action, nor utterance, nor power of speech,
To stir men's blood; I only speak right on;
I tell you that which you yourselves do know.
[225]

3   But were I Brutus,
And Brutus Antony, there were an Antony
Would ruffle up your spirits, and put a tongue
In every wound of Caesar, that should move
The stones of Rome to rise and mutiny.
[230]

4   He hath left you all his walks,
His private arbours, and new-planted orchards,
On this side Tiber; he hath left them you,
And to your heirs for ever; common pleasures,
To walk abroad, and recreate yourselves.
[252]

5 Here was a Caesar! when comes such another?
[257]

6 Now let it work; mischief, thou art afoot,
Take thou what course thou wilt!
[265]

7   Fortune is merry,
And in this mood will give us anything.
[271]

8 Tear him for his bad verses, tear him for his bad
verses.
iii.[34]

9 He shall not live; look, with a spot I damn him.
IV.i.6

10 This is a slight unmeritable man,
Meet to be sent on errands.
12

11 When love begins to sicken and decay,
It useth an enforced ceremony.
There are no tricks in plain and simple faith.
ii.20

12 Let me tell you, Cassius, you yourself
Are much condemn'd to have an itching palm.
iii.7

13   Shall we now
Contaminate our fingers with base bribes?
23

14 I had rather be a dog, and bay the moon,
Than such a Roman.
27

15 Away, slight man!
37

16 I'll use you for my mirth, yea, for my laughter,
When you are waspish.
49

17   For mine own part,
I shall be glad to learn of noble men.
53

18 You wrong me every way; you wrong me, Brutus;

19 I said an elder soldier, not a better:
Did I say 'better'?
55

19 Do not presume too much upon my love;
I may do that I shall be sorry for.
63

20 There is no terror, Cassius, in your threats;
For I am arm'd so strong in honesty
That they pass by me as the idle wind,
Which I respect not.
66

21 By heaven, I had rather coin my heart,
And drop my blood for drachmas, than to wring
From the hard hands of peasants their vile trash
By any indirection.
72

22 A friend should bear his friend's infirmities,
But Brutus makes mine greater than they are.
85

23 Cassius is aweary of the world;
Hated by one he loves; brav'd by his brother;
Check'd like a bondman; all his faults observ'd,
Set in a note-book, learn'd, and conn'd by rote,
To cast into my teeth.
94

24 O Cassius! you are yoked with a lamb
That carries anger as the flint bears fire;
Who, much enforced, shows a hasty spark,
And straight is cold again.
109

25 O Cassius! I am sick of many griefs.
143

26 Good reasons must, of force, give place to better.
202

27 The enemy increaseth every day;
We, at the height, are ready to decline.
There is a tide in the affairs of men,
Which, taken at the flood, leads on to fortune;
Omitted, all the voyage of their life
Is bound in shallows and in miseries.
On such a full sea are we now afloat,
And we must take the current when it serves,
Or lose our ventures.
215

28 The deep of night is crept upon our talk,
And nature must obey necessity.
225

29 This was an ill beginning of the night:
Never come such division 'tween our souls!
233

30 *Brutus:* Then I shall see thee again?
Ghost: Ay, at Philippi.
Brutus: Why, I will see thee at Philippi, then.
283

31 But for your words, they rob the Hybla bees,
And leave them honeyless.
V.i.34

32 If we do meet again, why, we shall smile!
If not, why then, this parting was well made.
118

33   O! that a man might know
The end of this day's business, ere it come;
But it sufficeth that the day will end,

And then the end is known.
123

1 This day I breathed first: time is come round,
And where I did begin, there shall I end;
My life is run his compass.
iii.23

2 O hateful error, melancholy's child!
Why dost thou show, to the apt thoughts of men,
The things that are not?
67

3 O Julius Caesar! thou art mighty yet!
Thy spirit walks abroad, and turns our swords
In our own proper entrails.
94

4   I had rather have
Such men my friends than enemies.
iv.28

5 Thou seest the world, Volumnius, how it goes;
Our enemies have beat us to the pit:
It is more worthy to leap in ourselves,
Than tarry till they push us.
v.22

6 Thou art a fellow of a good respect;
Thy life hath had some smatch of honour in it.
Hold then my sword, and turn away thy face,
While I do run upon it.
45

7 This was the noblest Roman of them all;
All the conspirators save only he
Did that they did in envy of great Caesar;
He, only, in a general honest thought
And common good to all, made one of them.
His life was gentle, and the elements
So mix'd in him that Nature might stand up
And say to all the world, 'This was a man!'
68

KING JOHN

8   Hadst thou rather be a Faulconbridge
And like thy brother, to enjoy thy land,
Or the reputed son of Coeur-de-Lion,
Lord of thy presence and no land beside.
I.i.134

9 And if his name be George, I'll call him Peter;
For new-made honour doth forget men's names.
186

10 Sweet, sweet, sweet poison for the age's tooth.
213

11 Courage mounteth with occasion.
II.i.82

12 Saint George, that swinged the dragon and e'er since
Sits on his horse back at mine hostess' door.
288

13 Mad world! mad kings! mad composition!
561

14 That smooth-fac'd gentleman, tickling Commodity,
Commodity, the bias of the world.
573

15 Well, whiles I am a beggar, I will rail,
And say there is no sin, but to be rich;
And, being rich, my virtue then shall be,

To say there is no vice, but beggary.
593

16 Thou wear a lion's hide! doff it for shame,
And hang a calf's-skin on those recreant limbs!
III.i.128

17   No Italian priest
Shall tithe or toll in our dominions.
153

18 Old Time the clock-setter, that bald sexton, Time.
324

19 Bell, book, and candle shall not drive me back,
When gold and silver becks me to come on.
iii.12

20 Grief fills the room up of my absent child,
Lies in his bed, walks up and down with me,
Puts on his pretty looks, repeats his words,
Remembers me of all his gracious parts,
Stuffs out his vacant garments with his form:
Then have I reason to be fond of grief.
iv.93

21 Life is as tedious as a twice-told tale,
Vexing the dull ear of a drowsy man.
108

22 Heat me these irons hot.
IV.i.1

23 Methinks nobody should be sad but I:
Yet I remember, when I was in France,
Young gentlemen would be as sad as night,
Only for wantonness.
13

24   Will you put out mine eyes?
These eyes that never did nor never shall
So much as frown on you?
56

25   To be possess'd with double pomp,
To guard a title that was rich before,
To gild refined gold, to paint the lily,
To throw a perfume on the violet,
To smooth the ice, or add another hue
Unto the rainbow, or with taper light
To seek the beauteous eye of heaven to garnish,
Is wasteful and ridiculous excess.
ii.9

26 The spirit of the time shall teach me speed.
176

27 Another lean unwash'd artificer
Cuts off his tale and talks of Arthur's death.
201

28 How oft the sight of means to do ill deeds
Makes ill deeds done!
219

29 Heaven take my soul, and England keep my bones!
iii.10

30 Whate'er you think, good words, I think, were best.
28

31   None of you will bid the winter come
To thrust his icy fingers in my maw;
Nor let my kingdom's rivers take their course
Through my burn'd bosom; nor entreat the north
To make his bleak winds kiss my parched lips
And comfort me with cold. I do not ask you much:
I beg cold comfort; and you are so strait

And so ingrateful you deny me that.
V.vii.36

1 This England never did, nor never shall,
Lie at the proud foot of a conqueror,
But when it first did help to wound itself.
Now these her princes are come home again,
Come the three corners of the world in arms,
And we shall shock them: nought shall make us rue,
If England to itself do rest but true.
112

KING LEAR

2 Nothing will come of nothing: speak again.
I.i.[92]

3 *Lear:* So young, and so untender?
Cordelia: So young, my lord, and true.
Lear: Let it be so; thy truth then be thy dower:
For, by the sacred radiance of the sun,
The mysteries of Hecate and the night,
By all the operation of the orbs
From whom we do exist and cease to be,
Here I disclaim all my paternal care,
Propinquity and property of blood,
And as a stranger to my heart and me
Hold thee from this for ever.
[108]

4 Come not between the dragon and his wrath.
[124]

5   I want that glib and oily art
To speak and purpose not; since what I well intend,
I'll do't before I speak.
[227]

6 It is no vicious blot nor other foulness,
No unchaste action, or dishonour'd step,
That hath depriv'd me of your grace and favour,
But even for want of that for which I am richer,
A still-soliciting eye, and such a tongue
That I am glad I have not, though not to have it
Hath lost me in your liking.
[230]

7   Love is not love
When it is mingled with regards that stand
Aloof from the entire point.
[241]

8 Fairest Cordelia, that art most rich, being poor;
Most choice, forsaken; and most lov'd, despis'd!
[253]

9   Why bastard? wherefore base?
When my dimensions are as well compact,
My mind as generous, and my shape as true,
As honest madam's issue? Why brand they us
With base? with baseness? bastardy? base, base?
Who in the lusty stealth of nature take
More composition and fierce quality
Than doth, within a dull, stale, tired bed,
Go to creating a whole tribe of fops,
Got 'tween asleep and wake?
ii.6

10   I grow, I prosper;
Now, gods, stand up for bastards!
21

11 This is the excellent foppery of the world, that, when
we are sick in fortune,—often the surfeit of our own
behaviour,— we make guilty of our own disasters the
sun, the moon, and the stars; as if we were villains by
necessity, fools by heavenly compulsion, knaves,
thieves, and treachers by spherical predominance,
drunkards, liars, and adulterers by an enforced
obedience of planetary influence; and all that we are
evil in, by a divine thrusting on: an admirable evasion
of whoremaster man, to lay his goatish disposition to
the charge of a star! My father compounded with my
mother under the dragon's tail, and my nativity was
under *ursa major,* so that it follows I am rough and
lecherous. 'Sfoot! I should have been that I am had the
maidenliest star in the firmament twinkled on my
bastardizing.
[132]

12 Pat he comes, like the catastrophe of the old comedy;
my cue is villanous melancholy, with a sigh like Tom
o' Bedlam.
[150]

13 *Lear:* Dost thou know me, fellow?
Kent: No, sir; but you have that in your countenance
which I would fain call master.
Lear: What's that?
Kent: Authority.
iv.[28]

14 Not so young, sir, to love a woman for singing, nor so
old to dote on her for any thing.
[40]

15 Have more than thou showest,
Speak less than thou knowest,
Lend less than thou owest.
[132]

16 *Lear:* Dost thou call me fool, boy?
Fool: All thy other titles thou hast given away; that
thou wast born with.
[163]

17 Ingratitude, thou marble-hearted fiend,
More hideous, when thou show'st thee in a child,
Than the sea-monster.
[283]

18 Into her womb convey sterility!
Dry up in her the organs of increase.
[302]

19 How sharper than a serpent's tooth it is
To have a thankless child!
[312]

20 O! let me not be mad, not mad, sweet heaven;
Keep me in temper; I would not be mad!
v.[51]

21 Thou whoreson zed! thou unnecessary letter!
II.ii.[68]

22 Goose, if I had you upon Sarum plain,
I'd drive ye cackling home to Camelot.
[88]

23 Sir, 'tis my occupation to be plain:
I have seen better faces in my time
Than stands on any shoulder that I see
Before me at this instant.
[98]

24   Down, thou climbing sorrow!
Thy element's below.
iv.[57]

25   O, sir! you are old;

Nature in you stands on the very verge
Of her confine.
[148]

1   You see me here, you gods, a poor old man,
As full of grief as age; wretched in both!
[275]

2   Touch me with noble anger,
And let not women's weapons, water-drops,
Stain my man's cheeks! No, you unnatural hags,
I will have such revenges on you both
That all the world shall—I will do such things,—
What they are yet I know not,—but they shall be
The terrors of the earth. You think I'll weep;
No, I'll not weep:
I have full cause of weeping, but this heart
Shall break into a hundred thousand flaws
Or ere I'll weep. O fool! I shall go mad.
[279]

3   Contending with the fretful elements;
Bids the wind blow the earth into the sea,
Or swell the curled waters 'bove the main,
That things might change or cease.
III.i.4

4   Blow, winds, and crack your cheeks! rage! blow!
You cataracts and hurricanoes, spout
Till you have drench'd our steeples, drown'd the
    cocks!
You sulphurous and thought-executing fires,
Vaunt-couriers to oak-cleaving thunderbolts,
Singe my white head! And thou, all-shaking thunder,
Strike flat the thick rotundity o' the world!
Crack nature's moulds, all germens spill at once
That make ingrateful man!
ii.1

5   Rumble thy bellyful! Spit, fire! Spout, rain!
Nor rain, wind, thunder, fire, are my daughters:
I tax not you, you elements, with unkindness;
I never gave you kingdom, call'd you children,
You owe me no subscription: then, let fall
Your horrible pleasure; here I stand, your slave,
A poor, infirm, weak, and despis'd old man.
14

6   There was never yet fair woman but she made mouths
in a glass.
[35]

7   No, I will be the pattern of all patience; I will say
nothing.
[37]

8   Marry, here's grace and a cod-piece; that's a wise man
and a fool.
[40]

9   Things that love night
Love not such nights as these.
[42]

10   Close pent-up guilts,
Rive your concealing continents, and cry
These dreadful summoners grace. I am a man
More sinned against than sinning.
[57]

11 The art of our necessities is strange,
That can make vile things precious.
[70]

12 He that has a little tiny wit,

With hey, ho, the wind and the rain,
Must make content with his fortunes fit,
Though the rain it raineth every day.
[74]

13   When the mind's free,
The body's delicate.
iv.11

14 O! that way madness lies; let me shun that.
21

15 Poor naked wretches, wheresoe'er you are,
That bide the pelting of this pitiless storm,
How shall your houseless heads and unfed sides,
Your looped and window'd raggedness, defend you
From seasons such as these?
28

16   Take physic, pomp;
Expose thyself to feel what wretches feel.
33

17 Pillicock sat on Pillicock-hill:
Halloo, halloo, loo, loo!
[75]

18 A serving-man, proud in heart and mind: that curled
my hair, wore gloves in my cap, served the lust of my
mistress's heart, and did the act of darkness with her;
swore as many oaths as I spake words, and broke them
in the sweet face of heaven; one that slept in the
contriving of lust, and waked to do it. Wine loved I
deeply, dice dearly, and in woman out-paramoured the
Turk.
[84]

19 Keep thy foot out of brothels, thy hand out of
plackets, thy pen from lenders' books, and defy the
foul fiend.
[96]

20 Thou art the thing itself; unaccommodated man is no
more but such a poor, bare, forked animal as thou art.
Off, off, you lendings! Come; unbutton here.
[109]

21 'Tis a naughty night to swim in.
[113]

22 This is the foul fiend Flibbertigibbet: he begins at
curfew, and walks till the first cock; he gives the web
and the pin, squints the eye, and makes the harelip;
mildews the white wheat, and hurts the poor creatures
of earth.
[118]

23 The green mantle of the standing pool.
[136]

24 The prince of darkness is a gentleman.
[148]

25 Poor Tom's a-cold.
[151]

26 I will keep still with my philosopher.
[180]

27 Child Roland to the dark tower came,
His word was still, Fie, foh, and fum,
I smell the blood of a British man.
[185]. See 360:6

28 He's mad that trusts in the tameness of a wolf, a
horse's health, a boy's love, or a whore's oath.
vi.[20]

29   The little dogs and all,

Tray, Blanch, and Sweet-heart, see, they bark at me.
[65]

1 Mastiff, greyhound, mongrel grim,
Hound or spaniel, brach or lym;
Or bobtail tike, or trundle-tail;
Tom will make them weep and wail.
[71]

2 By the kind gods, 'tis most ignobly done
To pluck me by the beard.
vii.[35]

3 I am tied to the stake, and I must stand the course.
[54]

4 *Cornwall:* Out, vile jelly!
Where is thy lustre now?
Gloucester: All dark and comfortless.
[83]

5 Yet better thus, and known to be contemn'd,
Than still contemn'd and flatter'd. To be worst,
The lowest and most dejected thing of fortune,
Stands still in esperance, lives not in fear:
The lamentable change is from the best;
The worst returns to laughter.
IV.i.1

6 I have no way, and therefore want no eyes;
I stumbled when I saw.
18

7 Might I but live to see thee in my touch,
I'd say I had eyes again.
23

8   The worst is not,
So long as we can say, 'This is the worst.'
27

9 As flies to wanton boys, are we to the gods;
They kill us for their sport.
36

10 You are not worth the dust which the rude wind
Blows in your face.
ii.30

11 Wisdom and goodness to the vile seem vile;
Filths savour but themselves.
38

12   It is the stars,
The stars above us, govern our conditions.
iii.[34]

13   He was met even now
As mad as the vex'd sea; singing aloud;
Crown'd with rank fumitor and furrow weeds,
With burdocks, hemlock, nettles, cuckoo-flowers,
Darnel, and all the idle weeds that grow
In our sustaining corn.
iv.1

14 How fearful
And dizzy 'tis to cast one's eyes so low!
The crows and choughs that wing the midway air
Show scarce so gross as beetles; half-way down
Hangs one that gathers samphire, dreadful trade!
Methinks he seems no bigger than his head.
The fishermen that walk upon the beach
Appear like mice, and yond tall anchoring bark
Diminish'd to her cock, her cock a buoy
Almost too small for sight. The murmuring surge,
That on the unnumber'd idle pebbles chafes,

Cannot be heard so high.
vi.12

15 They told me I was every thing; 'tis a lie, I am not
ague-proof.
[107]

16 *Gloucester:* Is't not the king?
Lear: Ay, every inch a king:
When I do stare, see how the subject quakes.
I pardon that man's life. What was thy cause?
Adultery?
Thou shalt not die: die for adultery! No:
The wren goes to't, and the small gilded fly
Does lecher in my sight.
Let copulation thrive.
[110]

17 *Lear:* The fitchew nor the soiled horse goes to't
With a more riotous appetite.
Down from the waist they are Centaurs,
Though women all above:
But to the girdle do the Gods inherit,
Beneath is all the fiends':
There's hell, there's darkness, there is the sulphurous
     pit,
Burning, scalding, stench, consumption; fie, fie, fie!
     pah, pah! Give me an ounce of civet, good
     apothecary, to sweeten my imagination; there's
     money for thee.
Gloucester: O! let me kiss that hand!
Lear: Let me wipe it first; it smells of mortality.
Gloucester: O ruin'd piece of nature! This great world
Should so wear out to nought.
[125]

18 A man may see how this world goes with no eyes.
Look with thine ears: see how yond justice rails upon
yond simple thief. Hark, in thine ear: change places;
and, handy-dandy, which is the justice, which is the
thief?
[154]

19 Thou rascal beadle, hold thy bloody hand!
Why dost thou lash that whore? Strip thine own back;
Thou hotly lust'st to use her in that kind
For which thou whipp'st her.
[165]

20   Plate sin with gold,
And the strong lance of justice hurtless breaks;
Arm it in rags, a pigmy's straw doth pierce it.
[170]

21   Get thee glass eyes;
And, like a scurvy politician, seem
To see the things thou dost not.
[175]

22 I know thee well enough; thy name is Gloucester:
Thou must be patient; we came crying hither:
Thou know'st the first time that we smell the air
We waul and cry.
[182]

23 When we are born we cry that we are come
To this great stage of fools.
[187]

24   Mine enemy's dog,
Though he had bit me, should have stood that night
Against my fire.
vii.36

25 Thou art a soul in bliss; but I am bound

Upon a wheel of fire, that mine own tears
Do scald like molten lead.
46

1 I am a very foolish, fond old man,
Fourscore and upward, not an hour more or less;
And, to deal plainly,
I fear I am not in my perfect mind.
60

2   Men must endure
Their going hence, even as their coming hither:
Ripeness is all.
V.ii.9

3   Come, let's away to prison;
We two alone will sing like birds i' the cage:
When thou dost ask me blessing, I'll kneel down,
And ask of thee forgiveness: and we'll live,
And pray, and sing, and tell old tales, and laugh
At gilded butterflies, and hear poor rogues
Talk of court news; and we'll talk with them too,
Who loses, and who wins; who's in, who's out;
And take upon 's the mystery of things,
As if we were God's spies; and we'll wear out,
In a wall'd prison, packs and sets of great ones
That ebb and flow by the moon.
iii.8

4 Upon such sacrifices, my Cordelia,
The gods themselves throw incense.
20

5 The gods are just, and of our pleasant vices
Make instruments to plague us.
[172]

6 The wheel is come full circle.
[176]

7   His flaw'd heart,—
Alack! too weak the conflict to support;
'Twixt two extremes of passion, joy and grief,
Burst smilingly.
[198]

8 Howl, howl, howl, howl! O! you are men of stones:
Had I your tongue and eyes, I'd use them so
That heaven's vaults should crack. She's gone for
ever!
[259]

9 *Kent:* Is this the promis'd end?
Edgar: Or image of that horror?
Albion: Fall and cease?
[265]

10   Her voice was ever soft,
Gentle and low, an excellent thing in woman.
[274]

11 And my poor fool is hang'd! No, no, no life!
Why should a dog, a horse, a rat, have life,
And thou no breath at all? Thou'lt come no more,
Never, never, never, never, never!
Pray you, undo this button.
[307]

12 Vex not his ghost: O! let him pass; he hates him
That would upon the rack of this tough world
Stretch him out longer.
[314]

13 The weight of this sad time we must obey,
Speak what we feel; not what we ought to say.
The oldest hath borne most: we that are young,

Shall never see so much, nor live so long.
[325]

LOVE'S LABOUR'S LOST

14 Let fame, that all hunt after in their lives,
Live register'd upon our brazen tombs,
And then grace us in the disgrace of death;
When, spite of cormorant devouring Time,
The endeavour of this present breath may buy
That honour which shall bate his scythe's keen edge,
And make us heirs of all eternity.
I.i.1

15 Study is like the heaven's glorious sun,
    That will not be deep-search'd with saucy looks;
Small have continual plodders ever won,
    Save base authority from others' books.
These earthly godfathers of Heaven's lights
    That give a name to every fixed star,
Have no more profit of their shining nights
    Than those that walk and wot not what they are.
84

16   At Christmas I no more desire a rose
Than wish a snow in May's new-fangled mirth;
    But like of each thing that in season grows.
·105

17 If I break faith, this word shall speak for me,—
I am forsworn 'on mere necessity'.
[152]

18 The world was very guilty of such a ballad some three
ages since; but, I think, now 'tis not to be found.
ii.[117]

19 Assist me some extemporal god of rime, for I am sure
I shall turn sonneter. Devise, wit; write, pen; for I am
for whole volumes in folio.
[192]

20 Beauty is bought by judgment of the eye,
Not utter'd by base sale of chapmen's tongues.
II.i.15

21   A merrier man,
Within the limit of becoming mirth,
I never spent an hour's talk withal.
66

22 Did not I dance with you in Brabant once?
[114]

23 Your wit's too hot, it speeds too fast, 'twill tire.
[119]

24 Thy own wish wish I thee in every place!
[178]

25 Warble, child; make passionate my sense of hearing.
III.i.1

26 This wimpled, whining, purblind, wayward boy,
This senior-junior, giant-dwarf, Dan Cupid;
Regent of love rhymes, lord of folded arms,
The anointed sovereign of sighs and groans,
Liege of all loiterers and malecontents,
Dread prince of plackets, king of codpieces,
Sole imperator and great general
Of trotting 'paritors: O my little heart!
[189]

27 A wightly wanton with a velvet brow,
With two pitch balls stuck in her face for eyes;
Ay, and, by heaven, one that will do the deed
Though Argus were her eunuch and her guard:

And I to sigh for her! to watch for her!
To pray for her!
[206]

1 He hath not fed of the dainties that are bred in a book;
he hath not eat paper, as it were; he hath not drunk
ink.
IV.ii.[25]

2 Old Mantuan! old Mantuan! Who understandeth thee
not, loves thee not.
[102]

3 Here are only numbers ratified; but, for the elegancy,
facility, and golden cadence of poesy, *caret*. Ovidius
Naso was the man: and why, indeed, Naso, but for
smelling out the odoriferous flowers of fancy, the jerks
of invention?
[126]

4 Did not the heavenly rhetoric of thine eye,
   'Gainst whom the world cannot hold argument,
Persuade my heart to this false perjury?
   Vows for thee broke deserve not punishment.
iii.[60]

5 Thou for whom e'en Jove would swear
Juno but an Ethiop were;
And deny himself for Jove,
Turning mortal for thy love.
[117]

6 From women's eyes this doctrine I derive:
They are the ground, the books, the academes,
From whence doth spring the true Promethean fire.
[302]

7 For where is any author in the world
Teaches such beauty as a woman's eye?
[312]

8 But love, first learned in a lady's eyes,
Lives not alone immured in the brain,
But, with the motion of all elements,
Courses as swift as thought in every power,
And gives to every power a double power,
Above their functions and their offices.
It adds a precious seeing to the eye;
A lover's eyes will gaze an eagle blind;
A lover's ears will hear the lowest sound,
When the suspicious head of theft is stopp'd:
Love's feeling is more soft and sensible
Than are the tender horns of cockled snails:
Love's tongue proves dainty Bacchus gross in taste.
For valour, is not love a Hercules,
Still climbing trees in the Hesperides?
Subtle as Sphinx; as sweet and musical
As bright Apollo's lute, strung with his hair;
And when Love speaks, the voice of all the gods
Makes heaven drowsy with the harmony.
Never durst poet touch a pen to write
Until his ink were temper'd with Love's sighs.
[327]

9 From women's eyes this doctrine I derive:
They sparkle still the right Promethean fire;
They are the books, the arts, the academes,
That show, contain, and nourish all the world.
[350]

10 He draweth out the thread of his verbosity finer than
the staple of his argument.
V.i.[18]

11 *Bone? bone,* for *bene:* Priscian a little scratched;

'twill serve.
[31]

12 *Moth:* They have been at a great feast of languages,
and stolen the scraps.
Costard: O! they have lived long on the alms-basket of
words. I marvel thy master hath not eaten thee for a
word; for thou art not so long by the head as
honorificabilitudinitatibus: thou art easier swallowed
than a flap-dragon.
[39]

13 The posteriors of this day; which the rude multitude
call the afternoon.
[96]

14   Had she been light, like you,
Of such a merry, nimble, stirring spirit,
She might ha' been a grandam ere she died;
And so may you; for a light heart lives long.
ii.15

15 Taffeta phrases, silken terms precise,
   Three-pil'd hyperboles, spruce affectation,
Figures pedantical; these summer flies
   Have blown me full of maggot ostentation:
I do forswear them.
407

16 Henceforth my wooing mind shall be express'd
   In russet yeas and honest kersey noes:
And, to begin, wench,—so God help me, la!—
My love to thee is sound, sans crack or flaw.
413

17 A jest's prosperity lies in the ear
Of him that hears it, never in the tongue
Of him that makes it.
[869]

18 When daisies pied and violets blue
      And lady-smocks all silver-white
   And cuckoo-buds of yellow hue
      Do paint the meadows with delight,
   The cuckoo then, on every tree,
Mocks married men; for thus sings he,
            Cuckoo;
Cuckoo, cuckoo; O, word of fear,
Unpleasing to a married ear!
[902]

19 When icicles hang by the wall,
      And Dick the shepherd, blows his nail,
   And Tom bears logs into the hall,
      And milk comes frozen home in pail,
   When blood is nipp'd and ways be foul,
Then nightly sings the staring owl,
            Tu-who;
Tu-whit, tu-who—a merry note,
While greasy Joan doth keel the pot.

When all aloud the wind doth blow,
And coughing drowns the parson's saw;
And birds sit brooding in the snow,
And Marion's nose looks red and raw,
When roasted crabs hiss in the bowl.
[920]

20 The words of Mercury are harsh after the songs of
Apollo. You, that way: we, this way.
[938]

MACBETH

1 *First Witch:* When shall we three meet again
In thunder, lightning, or in rain?
Second Witch: When the hurly-burly's done,
When the battle's lost and won.
Third Witch: That will be ere the set of sun.
First Witch: Where the place?
Second Witch: Upon the heath.
Third Witch: There to meet with Macbeth.
First Witch: I come, Graymalkin!
Second Witch: Paddock calls.
Third Witch: Anon!
All: Fair is foul, and foul is fair:
Hover through the fog and filthy air.
I.i.1

2 What bloody man is that?
ii.1

3 Brave Macbeth,— well he deserves that name,—
Disdaining fortune, with his brandish'd steel,
Which smok'd with bloody execution,
Like valour's minion carv'd out his passage
Till he fac'd the slave;
Which ne'er shook hands, nor bade farewell to him,
Till he unseam'd him from the nave to the chaps,
And fix'd his head upon our battlements.
16

4 They
Doubly redoubled strokes upon the foe:
Except they meant to bathe in reeking wounds,
Or memorize another Golgotha,
I cannot tell.
38

5 Bellona's bridegroom, lapp'd in proof,
Confronted him with self-comparisons,
Point against point, rebellious arm 'gainst arm,
Curbing his lavish spirit.
55

6 A sailor's wife had chestnuts in her lap,
And munch'd, and munch'd, and munch'd: 'Give
me,' quoth I:
'Aroint thee, witch!' the rump-fed ronyon cries.
Her husband's to Aleppo gone, master o' the Tiger:
But in a sieve I'll thither sail,
And, like a rat without a tail,
I'll do, I'll do, and I'll do.
iii.4

7 Sleep shall neither night nor day
Hang upon his pent-house lid.
He shall live a man forbid.
Weary se'nnights nine times nine
Shall he dwindle, peak, and pine:
Though his bark cannot be lost,
Yet it shall be tempest-tost.
19

8 *Third Witch:* A drum! a drum!
Macbeth doth come.
All: The weird sisters, hand in hand,
Posters of the sea and land,
Thus do go about, about.
30

9 So foul and fair a day I have not seen.
38

10 What are these,
So withered, and so wild in their attire,

That look not like th' inhabitants o' the earth,
And yet are on 't? Live you? or are you aught
That man may question? You seem to understand me,
By each at once her choppy finger laying
Upon her skinny lips: you should be women,
And yet your beards forbid me to interpret
That you are so.
39

11 If you can look into the seeds of time,
And say which grain will grow and which will not,
Speak then to me, who neither beg nor fear
Your favours nor your hate.
58

12 Stay, you imperfect speakers, tell me more.
70

13 Say, from whence
You owe this strange intelligence? or why
Upon this blasted heath you stop our way
With such prophetic greeting?
72

14 The earth hath bubbles, as the water has,
And these are of them.
79

15 Were such things here as we do speak about?
Or have we eaten on the insane root
That takes the reason prisoner?
83

16 What! can the devil speak true?
107

17 The Thane of Cawdor lives: why do you dress me
In borrow'd robes?
108

18 Oftentimes, to win us to our harm,
The instruments of darkness tell us truths;
Win us with honest trifles, to betray's
In deepest consequence.
123

19 Two truths are told,
As happy prologues to the swelling act
Of the imperial theme.
127

20 This supernatural soliciting
Cannot be ill, cannot be good; if ill,
Why hath it given me earnest of success,
Commencing in a truth? I am Thane of Cawdor:
If good, why do I yield to that suggestion
Whose horrid image doth unfix my hair
And make my seated heart knock at my ribs,
Against the use of nature? Present fears
Are less than horrible imaginings;
My thought, whose murder yet is but fantastical,
Shakes so my single state of man that function
Is smother'd in surmise, and nothing is
But what is not.
130

21 Come what come may,
Time and the hour runs through the roughest day.
146

22 *Malcolm:* Nothing in his life
Became him like the leaving it: he died
As one that had been studied in his death
To throw away the dearest thing he owed
As 'twere a careless trifle.

Duncan: There's no art
To find the mind's construction in the face;
He was a gentleman on whom I built
An absolute trust.
iv.7

1 Glamis thou art, and Cawdor; and shalt be
What thou art promis'd. Yet I do fear thy nature;
It is too full o' the milk of human kindness
To catch the nearest way; thou wouldst be great,
Art not without ambition; but without
The illness should attend it; what thou wouldst highly,
That thou wouldst holily; wouldst not play false,
And yet wouldst wrongly win; thou'dst have, great
    Glamis,
That which cries, 'Thus thou must do, if thou have it';
And that which rather thou dost fear to do
Than wishest should be undone. Hie thee hither
That I may pour my spirits in thine ear,
And chastise with the valour of my tongue
All that impedes thee from the golden round,
Which fate and metaphysical aid doth seem
To have thee crown'd withal.
v.[16]

2   The raven himself is hoarse
That croaks the fatal entrance of Duncan
Under my battlements. Come, you spirits
That tend on mortal thoughts! unsex me here,
And fill me from the crown to the toe top full
Of direst cruelty; make thick my blood,
Stop up the access and passage to remorse,
That no compunctious visitings of nature
Shake my fell purpose, nor keep peace between
The effect and it! Come to my woman's breasts,
And take my milk for gall, you murdering ministers,
Wherever in your sightless substances
You wait on nature's mischief! Come, thick night,
And pall thee in the dunnest smoke of hell,
That my keen knife see not the wound it makes,
Nor heaven peep through the blanket of the dark,
To cry 'Hold, hold!'
[38]

3 Your face, my thane, is as a book where men
May read strange matters. To beguile the time,
Look like the time; bear welcome in your eye,
Your hand, your tongue: look like the innocent flower,
But be the serpent under't.
[63]

4 *Duncan:* This castle hath a pleasant seat; the air
Nimbly and sweetly recommends itself
Unto our gentle senses.
Banquo: This guest of summer,
The temple-haunting martlet, does approve
By his lov'd mansionry that the heaven's breath
Smells wooingly here: no jutty, frieze,
Buttress, nor coign of vantage, but this bird
Hath made his pendent bed and procreant cradle:
Where they most breed and haunt, I have observ'd,
The air is delicate.
vi.1

5 If it were done when 'tis done, then 'twere well
It were done quickly: if the assassination
Could trammel up the consequence, and catch
With his surcease success; that but this blow
Might be the be-all and the end-all here,
But here, upon this bank and shoal of time,

We'd jump the life to come. But in these cases
We still have judgment here; that we but teach
Bloody instructions, which, being taught, return,
To plague the inventor; this even-handed justice
Commends the ingredients of our poison'd chalice
To our own lips.
vii.1

6   Besides, this Duncan
Hath borne his faculties so meek, hath been
So clear in his great office, that his virtues
Will plead like angels trumpet-tongu'd, against
The deep damnation of his taking-off;
And pity, like a naked new-born babe,
Striding the blast, or heaven's cherubim, hors'd
Upon the sightless couriers of the air,
Shall blow the horrid deed in every eye,
That tears shall drown the wind. I have no spur
To prick the sides of my intent, but only
Vaulting ambition, which o'erleaps itself,
And falls on the other.
16

7 We will proceed no further in this business:
He hath honour'd me of late; and I have bought
Golden opinions from all sorts of people.
31

8   Was the hope drunk,
Wherein you dress'd yourself? hath it slept since,
And wakes it now, to look so green and pale
At what it did so freely? From this time
Such I account thy love. Art thou afeard
To be the same in thine own act and valour
As thou art in desire? Wouldst thou have that
Which thou esteem'st the ornament of life,
And live a coward in thine own esteem,
Letting 'I dare not' wait upon 'I would,'
Like the poor cat i' the adage?
35

9 I dare do all that may become a man;
Who dares do more is none.
46

10 *Lady Macbeth:* I have given suck, and know
How tender 'tis to love the babe that milks me:
I would, while it was smiling in my face,
Have plucked my nipple from his boneless gums,
And dash'd the brains out, had I so sworn as you
Have done to this.
Macbeth: If we should fail,—
Lady Macbeth: We fail!
But screw your courage to the sticking-place,
And we'll not fail.
54

11   Bring forth men-children only;
For thy undaunted mettle should compose
Nothing but males.
72

12 False face must hide what the false heart doth know.
82

13   There's husbandry in heaven;
Their candles are all out.
II.i.4

14 A heavy summons lies like lead upon me,
And yet I would not sleep.
6

15 Is this a dagger which I see before me,

The handle toward my hand? Come, let me clutch
   thee:
I have thee not, and yet I see thee still.
Art thou not, fatal vision, sensible
To feeling as to sight? or art thou but
A dagger of the mind, a false creation,
Proceeding·from the heat-oppressed brain?
33

1   Now o'er the one half-world
Nature seems dead, and wicked dreams abuse
The curtain'd sleep; witchcraft celebrates
Pale Hecate's offerings; and wither'd murder,
Alarum'd by his sentinel, the wolf,
Whose howl's his watch, thus with his stealthy pace,
With Tarquin's ravishing strides, toward his design
Moves like a ghost. Thou sure and firm-set earth,
Hear not my steps, which way they walk, for fear
The very stones prate of my whereabout,
And take the present horror from the time,
Which now suits with it. Whiles I threat he lives:
Words to the heat of deeds too cold breath gives.
I go, and it is done; the bell invites me.
Hear it not, Duncan; for it is a knell
That summons thee to heaven or to hell.
49

2 That which hath made them drunk hath made me bold,
What hath quench'd them hath given me fire.
ii.1

3 It was the owl that shriek'd, the fatal bellman,
Which gives the stern'st good-night.
4

4   The attempt and not the deed,
Confounds us.
12

5   Had he not resembled
My father as he slept I had done't.
14

6 I have done the deed. Didst thou not hear a noise?
16

7   Wherefore could not I pronounce 'Amen'?
I had most need of blessing, and 'Amen'
Stuck in my throat.
32

8 Methought I heard a voice cry, 'Sleep no more!
Macbeth does murder sleep,' the innocent sleep,
Sleep that knits up the ravell'd sleave of care,
The death of each day's life, sore labour's bath,
Balm of hurt minds, great nature's second course,
Chief nourisher in life's feast.
36

9 Glamis hath murder'd sleep, and therefore Cawdor
Shall sleep no more, Macbeth shall sleep no more!
43

10 You do unbend your noble strength to think
So brainsickly of things.
46

11 *Macbeth:* I am afraid to think what I have done;
Look on't again I dare not.
Lady Macbeth: Infirm of purpose!
Give me the daggers. The sleeping and the dead
Are but as pictures; 'tis the eye of childhood
That fears a painted devil. If he do bleed
I'll gild the faces of the grooms withal;

For it must seem their guilt.
52

12   Whence is that knocking?
How is't with me, when every noise appals me?
58

13 Will all great Neptune's ocean wash this blood
Clean from my hand? No, this my hand will rather
The multitudinous seas incarnadine,
Making the green one red.
61

14 A little water clears us of this deed.
68

15 Here's a knocking, indeed! If a man were porter of
hell-gate he should have old turning the key. Knock,
knock, knock! Who's there i' the name of Beelzebub?
Here's a farmer that hanged himself on the expectation
of plenty.
iii.1

16 Who's there i' the other devil's name! Faith, here's an
equivocator, that could swear in both the scales
against either scale; who committed treason enough
for God's sake, yet could not equivocate to heaven: O!
come in, equivocator.
[9]

17 This place is too cold for hell. I'll devil-porter it no
further: I had thought to have let in some of all
professions, that go the primrose way to the everlasting
bonfire.
[19]. See 421:4

18 *Porter:* Drink, sir, is a great provoker of three things.
Macduff: What three things does drink especially
provoke?
Porter: Marry, sir, nose-painting, sleep, and urine.
Lechery, sir, it provokes, and unprovokes; it provokes
the desire, but it takes away the performance.
[28]

19 The labour we delight in physics pain.
[56]

20 The night has been unruly: where we lay
Our chimneys were blown down; and, as they say,
Lamentings heard i' the air; strange screams of death,
And prophesying with accents terrible
Of dire combustion and confus'd events
New-hatch'd to the woeful time. The obscure bird
Clamour'd the live-long night: some say the earth
Was feverous and did shake.
[60]

21 O horror! horror! horror! Tongue nor heart
Cannot conceive nor name thee!
[70]

22 Confusion now hath made his masterpiece!
Most sacrilegious murder hath broke ope
The Lord's anointed temple, and stole thence
The life o' the building!
[72]

23 Shake off this downy sleep, death's counterfeit,
And look on death itself! up, up, and see
The great doom's image!
[83]

24 *Macduff:* Our royal master's murder'd!
Lady Macbeth: Woe, alas!
What! in our house?
[95]

1 Had I but died an hour before this chance,
I had liv'd a blessed time; for, from this instant,
There's nothing serious in mortality:
All is but toys; renown and grace is dead,
The wine of life is drawn, and the mere lees
Is left this vault to brag of.
[98]

2 Who can be wise, amazed, temperate, and furious,
Loyal and neutral, in a moment? No man.
[115]

3 *Lady Macbeth:* Help me hence, ho!
Macduff: Look to the lady.
[125]

4   Where we are,
There's daggers in men's smiles: the near in blood,
The nearer bloody.
[146]

5 A falcon, towering in her pride of place,
Was by a mousing owl hawk'd at and kill'd.
iv.12

6 Thou hast it now: King, Cawdor, Glamis, all,
As the weird women promis'd; and, I fear,
Thou play'dst most foully for't.
III.i.1

7 *Banquo:* Go not my horse the better,
I must become a borrower of the night
For a dark hour or twain.
Macbeth: Fail not our feast.
26

8   To be thus is nothing;
But to be safely thus.
48

9 *First Murderer:* We are men, my liege.
Macbeth: Ay, in the catalogue ye go for men.
91

10 *Second Murderer:* I am one, my liege,
Whom the vile blows and buffets of the world
Have so incens'd, that I am reckless what
I do to spite the world.
First Murderer: I another,
So weary with disasters, tugg'd with fortune,
That I would set my life on any chance,
To mend it or be rid on't.
108

11 Leave no rubs nor botches in the work.
134

12 *Lady Macbeth:* Things without all remedy
Should be without regard: what's done is done.
Macbeth: We have scotch'd the snake, not killed it:
She'll close and be herself, whilst our poor malice
Remains in danger of her former tooth.
But let the frame of things disjoint, both the worlds
suffer,
Ere we will eat our meal in fear, and sleep
In the affliction of these terrible dreams
That shake us nightly. Better be with the dead,
Whom we, to gain our peace, have sent to peace,
Than on the torture of the mind to lie
In restless ecstasy. Duncan is in his grave;
After life's fitful fever he sleeps well;
Treason has done his worst: nor steel, nor poison,
Malice domestic, foreign levy, nothing,

Can touch him further.
ii.11

13   Ere the bat hath flown
His cloister'd flight, ere, to black Hecate's summons
The shard-borne beetle with his drowsy hums
Hath rung night's yawning peal, there shall be done
A deed of dreadful note.
40

14 Be innocent of the knowledge, dearest chuck,
Till thou applaud the deed. Come, seeling night,
Scarf up the tender eye of pitiful day,
And with thy bloody and invisible hand,
Cancel and tear to pieces that great bond
Which keeps me pale! Light thickens, and the crow
Makes wing to the rooky wood;
Good things of day begin to droop and drowse,
Whiles night's black agents to their preys do rouse.
45

15 The west yet glimmers with some streaks of day:
Now spurs the lated traveller apace
To gain the timely inn.
iii.5

16 Ourself will mingle with society
And play the humble host.
iv.3

17   Now I am cabin'd, cribb'd, confin'd, bound in
To saucy doubts and fears.
24

18 Now good digestion wait on appetite,
And health on both!
38

19 Which of you have done this?
49

20 Thou canst not say I did it: never shake
Thy gory locks at me.
50

21 What man dare, I dare;
Approach thou like the rugged Russian bear,
The arm'd rhinoceros or the Hyrcan tiger,
Take any shape but that, and my firm nerves
Shall never tremble.
99

22   Hence, horrible shadow!
Unreal mockery, hence!
106

23 Stand not upon the order of your going,
But go at once.
119

24 *Macbeth:* It will have blood, they say; blood will have
blood:
Stones have been known to move and trees to speak;
Augurs and understood relations augur
By maggot-pies and choughs and rooks brought forth
The secret'st man of blood. What is the night?
Lady Macbeth: Almost at odds with morning, which is
which.
122

25   I am in blood
Stepp'd in so far that, should I wade no more,
Returning were as tedious as go o'er.
136

26 You lack the season of all natures, sleep.
141

1   Security
Is mortals' chiefest enemy.
v.32

2 Round about the cauldron go;
In the poison'd entrails throw.
Toad, that under cold stone
Days and nights hast thirty-one
Swelter'd venom sleeping got,
Boil thou first i' the charmed pot.
Double, double toil and trouble;
Fire burn and cauldron bubble.
IV.i.4

3 Eye of newt, and toe of frog,
Wool of bat, and tongue of dog,
Adder's fork, and blind-worm's sting,
Lizard's leg, and howlet's wing,
For a charm of powerful trouble,
Like a hell-broth boil and bubble.
14

4 Liver of blaspheming Jew,
Gall of goat, and slips of yew
Sliver'd in the moon's eclipse,
Nose of Turk, and Tartar's lips,
Finger of birth-strangled babe
Ditch-deliver'd by a drab,
Make the gruel thick and slab.
26

5 *Second Witch:* By the pricking of my thumbs,
Something wicked this way comes.
                    Open, locks,
                        Whoever knocks.
Macbeth: How now, you secret, black, and midnight
   hags!
What is't you do?
Witches: A deed without a name.
44

6 Be bloody, bold, and resolute; laugh to scorn
The power of man, for none of woman born
Shall harm Macbeth.
79

7 But yet, I'll make assurance double sure,
And take a bond of fate.
83

8 Macbeth shall never vanquish'd be until
Great Birnam wood to high Dunsinane hill
Shall come against him.
92

9 Show his eyes, and grieve his heart;
Come like shadows, so depart!
110

10 What! will the line stretch out to the crack of doom?
117

11 His flight was madness: when our actions do not,
Our fears do make us traitors.
ii.3

12   He loves us not;
He wants the natural touch; for the poor wren,
The most diminutive of birds, will fight—
Her young ones in her nest—against the owl.
8

13 *Son:* And must they all be hanged that swear and lie?
Lady Macduff: Every one.
Son: Who must hang them?

Lady Macduff: Why, the honest men.
Son: Then the liars and swearers are fools, for there
are liars and swearers enow to beat the honest men and
hang up them.
[51]

14 Angels are bright still, though the brightest fell.
iii.22

15 Stands Scotland where it did?
164

16 What! man; ne'er pull your hat upon your brows;
Give sorrow words: the grief that does not speak
Whispers the o'er-fraught heart, and bids it break.
208

17 *Malcolm:* Let's make us medicine of our great
      revenge,
To cure this deadly grief.
Macduff: He has no children. All my pretty ones?
Did you say all? O hell-kite! All?
What! all my pretty chickens and their dam,
At one fell swoop?
216

18 *Malcolm:* Dispute it like a man.
Macduff: I shall do so;
But I must also feel it as a man.
219

19 *Doctor:* You see her eyes are open.
Gentlewoman: Ay, but their sense is shut.
V.i.[27]

20 Out, damned spot! out, I say! One; two: why then, 'tis
time to do't. Hell is murky! Fie, my lord, fie! a
soldier, and afeard? What need we fear who knows it,
when none can call our power to account? Yet who
would have thought the old man to have had so much
blood in him?
[38]

21 The Thane of Fife had a wife: where is she now?
What! will these hands ne'er be clean? No more o'
that, my lord, no more o' that: you mar all with this
starting.
[46]

22 Here's the smell of the blood still: all the perfumes of
Arabia will not sweeten this little hand. Oh! oh! oh!
[55]

23 I would not have such a heart in my bosom for the
dignity of the whole body.
[60]

24 Wash your hands, put on your night-gown; look not so
pale.
[67]

25 What's done cannot be undone. To bed, to bed, to
bed.
[74]

26 Foul whisperings are abroad. Unnatural deeds
Do breed unnatural troubles; infected minds
To their deaf pillows will discharge their secrets;
More needs she the divine than the physician.
[78]

27 Those he commands move only in command,
Nothing in love; now does he feel his title
Hang loose about him, like a giant's robe
Upon a dwarfish thief.
ii.19

28 Bring me no more reports; let them fly all:

Till Birnam wood remove to Dunsinane
I cannot taint with fear.
iii.1

1 The devil damn thee black, thou cream-faced loon!
Where gott'st thou that goose look?
11

2 I have lived long enough: my way of life
Is fall'n into the sear, the yellow leaf;
And that which should accompany old age,
As honour, love, obedience, troops of friends,
I must not look to have; but, in their stead,
Curses, not loud but deep, mouth-honour, breath,
Which the poor heart would fain deny, and dare not.
22

3 *Macbeth:* Canst thou not minister to a mind diseas'd,
Pluck from the memory a rooted sorrow,
Raze out the written troubles of the brain,
And with some sweet oblivious antidote
Cleanse the stuff'd bosom of that perilous stuff
Which weighs upon the heart?
Doctor: Therein the patient
Must minister to himself.
Macbeth: Throw physic to the dogs; I'll none of it.
37

4 Hang out our banners on the outward walls;
The cry is still, 'They come'; our castle's strength
Will laugh a siege to scorn.
v.1

5 I have almost forgot the taste of fears.
The time has been my senses would have cool'd
To hear a night-shriek, and my fell of hair
Would at a dismal treatise rouse and stir
As life were in't. I have supp'd full with horrors;
Direness, familiar to my slaughterous thoughts,
Cannot once start me.
9

6 She should have died hereafter;
There would have been a time for such a word,
To-morrow, and to-morrow, and to-morrow,
Creeps in this petty pace from day to day,
To the last syllable of recorded time;
And all our yesterdays have lighted fools
The way to dusty death. Out, out, brief candle!
Life's but a walking shadow, a poor player,
That struts and frets his hour upon the stage,
And then is heard no more; it is a tale
Told by an idiot, full of sound and fury,
Signifying nothing.
16

7 If that which he avouches does appear,
There is nor flying hence, nor tarrying here.
I 'gin to be aweary of the sun,
And wish the estate o' the world were now undone.
Ring the alarum-bell! Blow, wind! come, wrack!
At least we'll die with harness on our back.
47

8 *Macbeth:* I bear a charmed life, which must not yield
To one of woman born.
Macduff: Despair thy charm;
And let the angel who thou still hast serv'd
Tell thee, Macduff was from his mother's womb
Untimely ripp'd.
vii.41

9   Lay on, Macduff;

And damn'd be him that first cries, 'Hold, enough!'
62

10 *Siward:* Had he his hurts before?
Ross: Ay, on the front.
Siward: Why, then, God's soldier be he!
Had I as many sons as I have hairs,
I would not wish them to a fairer death.
75

MEASURE FOR MEASURE

11   Now, as fond fathers,
Having bound up the threat'ning twigs of birch,
Only to stick it in their children's sight
For terror, not to use, in time the rod
Becomes more mock'd than fear'd; so our decrees,
Dead to infliction, to themselves are dead,
And liberty plucks justice by the nose;
The baby beats the nurse, and quite athwart
Goes all decorum.
I.iii.23

12 I hold you as a thing ensky'd and sainted;
By your renouncement an immortal spirit,
And to be talk'd with in sincerity,
As with a saint.
iv.34

13 Your brother and his lover have embrac'd:
As those that feed grow full, as blossoming time
That from the seedness the bare fallow brings
To teeming foison, even so her plenteous womb
Expresseth his full tilth and husbandry.
40

14   A man whose blood
Is very snow-broth; one who never feels
The wanton stings and motions of the sense,
But doth rebate and blunt his natural edge
With profits of the mind, study and fast.
57

15 We must not make a scarecrow of the law,
Setting it up to fear the birds of prey,
And let it keep one shape, till custom make it
Their perch and not their terror.
II.i.1

16 'Tis one thing to be tempted, Escalus,
Another thing to fall. I not deny,
The jury, passing on the prisoner's life,
May in the sworn twelve have a thief or two
Guiltier than him they try.
17

17 This will last out a night in Russia,
When nights are longest there.
[144]

18 There is a vice that most I do abhor,
And most desire should meet the blow of justice,
For which I would not plead, but that I must;
For which I must not plead, but that I am
At war 'twixt will and will not.
ii.29

19 Condemn the fault and not the actor of it?
37

20 No ceremony that to great ones 'longs,
Not the king's crown, nor the deputed sword,
The marshal's truncheon, nor the judge's robe,
Become them with one half so good a grace

As mercy does.
59

1   O! it is excellent
To have a giant's strength, but it is tyrannous
To use it like a giant.
107

2   Man, proud man,
Drest in a little brief authority,
Most ignorant of what he's most assur'd,
His glassy essence, like an angry ape,
Plays such fantastic tricks before high heaven,
As make the angels weep.
117

3 Great men may jest with saints; 'tis wit in them,
But, in the less foul profanation.
127

4 That in the captain's but a choleric word,
Which in the soldier is flat blasphemy.
130

5   Is this her fault or mine?
The tempter or the tempted, who sins most?
162

6 O cunning enemy, that, to catch a saint,
With saints dost bait thy hook! Most dangerous
Is that temptation that doth goad us on
To sin in loving virtue; never could the strumpet,
With all her double vigour, art and nature,
Once stir my temper; but this virtuous maid
Subdues me quite. Ever till now
When men were fond, I smil'd and wonder'd how.
180

7 Might there not be a charity in sin
To save this brother's life?
iv.64

8 *Claudio:* The miserable have no other medicine
But only hope:
I have hope to live, and am prepar'd to die.
Duke: Be absolute for death; either death or life
Shall thereby be the sweeter. Reason thus with life:
If I do lose thee, I do lose a thing
That none but fools would keep: a breath thou art
Servile to all the skyey influences,
That dost this habitation, where thou keep'st,
Hourly afflict. Merely, thou art death's fool;
For him thou labour'st by thy flight to shun,
And yet run'st toward him still.
III.i.2

9   If thou art rich, thou'rt poor;
For, like an ass whose back with ingots bows,
Thou bear'st thy heavy riches but a journey,
And death unloads thee.
25

10   Thou hast nor youth nor age;
But, as it were, an after-dinner's sleep,
Dreaming on both; for all thy blessed youth
Becomes as aged, and doth beg the alms
Of palsied eld.
32

11   Dar'st thou die?
The sense of death is most in apprehension,
And the poor beetle, that we tread upon,
In corporal sufferance finds a pang as great

As when a giant dies.
75

12   If I must die,
I will encounter darkness as a bride,
And hug it in mine arms.
81

13   Sure, it is no sin;
Or of the deadly seven it is the least.
108

14 *Claudio:* Death is a fearful thing.
Isabella: And shamed life a hateful.
Claudio: Ay, but to die, and go we know not where;
To lie in cold obstruction and to rot;
This sensible warm motion to become
A kneaded clod; and the delighted spirit
To bathe in fiery floods, or to reside
In thrilling region of thick-ribbed ice;
To be imprisoned in the viewless winds,
And blown with restless violence round about
The pendant world; or to be worse than worst
Of those that lawless and incertain thoughts
Imagine howling: 'tis too horrible!
The weariest and most loathed worldly life
That age, ache, penury, and imprisonment
Can lay on nature, is a paradise
To what we fear of death.
114

15   O, fie, fie, fie!
Thy sin's not accidental, but a trade.
146

16 The hand that hath made you fair hath made you
good.
[182]

17 Virtue is bold, and goodness never fearful.
[214]

18 There, at the moated grange, resides this dejected
Mariana.
[279]

19 Some report a sea-maid spawn'd him; some that he
was begot between two stock-fishes. But it is certain
that when he makes water his urine is congealed ice.
ii.[117]

20 A very superficial, ignorant, unweighing fellow.
[151]

21 Take, O take those lips away,
    That so sweetly were forsworn;
And those eyes, the break of day,
    Lights that do mislead the morn:
But my kisses bring again, bring again;
Seals of love, but seal'd in vain, seal'd in vain.
IV.i.1

22   Though music oft hath such a charm
To make bad good, and good provoke to harm.
16

23 He will discredit our mystery.
ii.[29]

24 Every true man's apparel fits your thief.
[46]

25 A man that apprehends death no more dreadfully but
as a drunken sleep; careless, reckless, and fearless of
what's past, present, or to come; insensible of
mortality, and desperately mortal.
[148]

1 O! death's a great disguiser.
[185]

2 I am a kind of burr; I shall stick.
iii.[193]

3 O! your desert speaks loud; and I should wrong it,
To lock it in the wards of covert bosom,
When it deserves, with characters of brass,
A forted residence 'gainst the tooth of time,
And razure of oblivion.
V.i.12

4   Let the devil
Be sometime honour'd for his burning throne.
[289]

5 Haste still pays haste, and leisure answers leisure;
Like doth quit like, and Measure still for Measure.
[411]

6 They say best men are moulded out of faults,
And, for the most, become much more the better
For being a little bad: so may my husband.
[440]

THE MERCHANT OF VENICE

7 *Antonio:* In sooth I know not why I am so sad:
It wearies me; you say it wearies you;
But how I caught it, found it, or came by it,
What stuff 'tis made of, whereof it is born,
I am to learn;
And such a want-wit sadness makes of me,
That I have much ado to know myself.
Salarino: Your mind is tossing on the ocean;
There, where your argosies with portly sail,—
Like signiors and rich burghers on the flood,
Or, as it were, the pageants of the sea,—
Do overpeer the petty traffickers,
That curtsy to them, do them reverence,
As they fly by them with their woven wings.
I.i.1

8   Now, by two-headed Janus,
Nature hath fram'd strange fellows in her time.
50

9 You have too much respect upon the world:
They lose it that do buy it with much care.
74

10 I hold the world but as the world, Gratiano;
A stage where every man must play a part,
And mine a sad one.
77

11 Why should a man, whose blood is warm within,
Sit like his grandsire cut in alabaster?
83

12 There are a sort of men whose visages
Do cream and mantle like a standing pond,
And do a wilful stillness entertain,
With purpose to be dress'd in an opinion
Of wisdom, gravity, profound conceit;
As who should say, 'I am Sir Oracle,
And when I ope my lips let no dog bark!'
O, my Antonio, I do know of these,
That therefore only are reputed wise,
For saying nothing.
88

13   Fish not, with this melancholy bait,
For this fool gudgeon, this opinion.
101

14   Silence is only commendable
In a neat's tongue dried and a maid not vendible.
111

15 Gratiano speaks an infinite deal of nothing, more than any man in all Venice. His reasons are as two grains of wheat, hid in two bushels of chaff: you shall seek all day ere you find them; and, when you have them, they are not worth the search.
114

16 My purse, my person, my extremest means
Lie all unlock'd to your occasions.
[139]

17 In Belmont is a lady richly left,
And she is fair, and fairer than the word,
Of wondrous virtues; sometimes from her eyes
I did receive fair speechless messages.
[162]

18 By my troth, Nerissa, my little body is aweary of this great world.
ii.1

19 They are as sick that surfeit with too much, as they that starve with nothing. It is no mean happiness, therefore, to be seated in the mean: superfluity comes sooner by white hairs, but competency lives longer.
[5]

20 If to do were as easy as to know what were good to do, chapels had been churches, and poor men's cottages princes' palaces. It is a good divine that follows his own instructions; I can easier teach twenty what were good to be done, than be one of *the* twenty to follow mine own teaching.
[13]

21 He doth nothing but talk of his horse.
[43]

22 God made him, and therefore let him pass for a man.
[59]

23 If I should marry him, I should marry twenty husbands.
[66]

24 I think he bought his doublet in Italy, his round hose in France, his bonnet in Germany, and his behaviour everywhere.
[78]

25 I will do anything, Nerissa, ere I will be married to a sponge.
[105]

26 There is not one among them but I dote on his very absence.
[117]

27 Ships are but boards, sailors but men; there be land-rats and water-rats, land-thieves and water-thieves.
iii.[22]

28 I will buy with you, sell with you, talk with you, walk with you, and so following; but I will not eat with you, drink with you, nor pray with you. What news on the Rialto?
[36]

29 How like a fawning publican he looks!
I hate him for he is a Christian;
But more for that in low simplicity

He lends out money gratis, and brings down
The rate of usance here with us in Venice.
If I can catch him once upon the hip,
I will feed fat the ancient grudge I bear him.
He hates our sacred nation, and he rails,
Even there where merchants most do congregate,
On me, my bargains, and my well-won thrift,
Which he calls interest.
[42]

1 The devil can cite Scripture for his purpose.
An evil soul, producing holy witness,
Is like a villain with a smiling cheek,
A goodly apple rotten at the heart.
O, what a goodly outside falsehood hath!
[99]

2 Signior Antonio, many a time and oft
In the Rialto you have rated me
About my moneys and my usances:
Still have I borne it with a patient shrug,
For sufferance is the badge of all our tribe.
You call me misbeliever, cut-throat dog,
And spet upon my Jewish gabardine,
And all for use of that which is mine own.
[107]

3 You that did void your rheum upon my beard,
And foot me as you spurn a stranger cur
Over your threshold: moneys is your suit.
What should I say to you? Should I not say,
'Hath a dog money? Is it possible
A cur can lend three thousand ducats?' or
Shall I bend low, and in a bondman's key,
With bated breath, and whispering humbleness,
Say this:—
'Fair sir, you spat on me Wednesday last;
You spurn'd me such a day; another time
You call'd me dog; and for these courtesies
I'll lend you thus much moneys?'
[118]

4 O father Abram! what these Christians are,
Whose own hard dealing teaches them suspect
The thoughts of others!
[161]

5 *Antonio:* This Hebrew will turn Christian, he grows
   kind.
   Bassanio: I like not fair terms and a villain's mind.
[179]

6 Mislike me not for my complexion,
The shadow'd livery of the burnish'd sun,
To whom I am a neighbour and near bred.
II.i.1

7 My conscience, hanging about the neck of my heart,
says very wisely to me, 'my honest friend Launcelot,
being an honest man's son,'—or rather an honest
woman's son;—for, indeed, my father did something
smack, something grow to, he had a kind of
taste;—well, my conscience says, 'Launcelot, budge
not.' 'Budge.' says the fiend. 'Budge not,' says my
conscience. 'Conscience,' say I, 'you counsel well;'
'fiend,' say I, 'you counsel well.'
ii.[13]

8 The boy was the very staff of my age, my very prop.
[71]

9 It is a wise father that knows his own child.
[83]

10 Truth will come to light; murder cannot be hid long.
[86]

11 There is some ill a-brewing towards my rest.
For I did dream of money-bags to-night.
v.17

12 Then it was not for nothing that my nose fell
a-bleeding on Black-Monday.
[24]

13 Lock up my doors; and when you hear the drum,
And the vile squealing of the wry-neck'd fife,
Clamber not you up to the casements then,
Nor thrust your head into the public street
To gaze on Christian fools with varnish'd faces,
But stop my house's ears, I mean my casements;
Let not the sound of shallow foppery enter
My sober house.
[29]

14 Love is blind, and lovers cannot see
The pretty follies that themselves commit.
vi.36

15 What! must I hold a candle to my shames?
41

16   Men that hazard all
Do it in hope of fair advantages:
A golden mind stoops not to shows of dross.
vii.18

17 Had you been as wise as bold,
Young in limbs, in judgment old,
Your answer had not been inscroll'd.
70

18 My daughter! O my ducats! O my daughter!
Fled with a Christian! O my Christian ducats!
Justice! the law! my ducats, and my daughter!
viii.15

19 What many men desire! that 'many' may be meant
By the fool multitude, that choose by show,
Not learning more than the fond eye doth teach;
Which pries not to the interior; but, like the martlet,
Builds in the weather on the outward wall,
Even in the force and road of casualty.
I will not choose what many men desire,
Because I will not jump with common spirits
And rank me with the barbarous multitude.
ix.25

20   Let none presume
To wear an undeserved dignity.
O! that estates, degrees, and offices
Were not deriv'd corruptly, and that clear honour
Were purchased by the merit of the wearer.
How many then should cover that stand bare;
How many be commanded that command;
How much low peasantry would then be glean'd
From the true seed of honour; and how much honour
Pick'd from the chaff and ruin of the times
To be new varnish'd!
39

21 The portrait of a blinking idiot.
54

22 The fire seven times tried this:
Seven times tried that judgment is
That did never choose amiss.
Some there be that shadows kiss;

Such have but a shadow's bliss.
63

1 Thus hath the candle sing'd the moth.
O, these deliberate fools!
79

2 The Goodwins, I think they call the place; a very
dangerous flat, and fatal, where the carcasses of many
a tall ship lie buried, as they say, if my gossip Report
be an honest woman of her word.
III.i.[4]

3 Let him look to his bond.
[51, 52, 54]

4 Hath not a Jew eyes? hath not a Jew hands, organs,
dimensions, senses, affections, passions? fed with the
same food, hurt with the same weapons, subject to the
same diseases, healed by the same means, warmed and
cooled by the same winter and summer, as a Christian
is? If you prick us, do we not bleed? if you tickle us,
do we not laugh? if you poison us, do we not die? and
if you wrong us, shall we not revenge? If we are like
you in the rest, we will resemble you in that.
63

5 The villany you teach me I will execute, and it shall go
hard but I will better the instruction.
[76]

6 Thou stick'st a dagger in me.
[118]

7 *Tubal:* One of them showed me a ring that he had of
your daughter for a monkey.
Shylock: Out upon her! Thou torturest me, Tubal: it
was my turquoise; I had it of Leah when I was a
bachelor: I would not have given it for a wilderness of
monkeys.
[126]

8   He makes a swan-like end
Fading in music.
ii.44

9 Tell me where is fancy bred.
   Or in the heart or in the head?
How begot, how nourished?
   Reply, reply.

It is engender'd in the eyes,
With gazing fed; and fancy dies
In the cradle where it lies.
   Let us all ring fancy's knell:
   I'll begin it,—Ding, dong, bell.
63

10 So may the outward shows be least themselves:
The world is still deceived with ornament.
In law, what plea so tainted and corrupt
But, being season'd with a gracious voice,
Obscures the show of evil? In religion,
What damned error, but some sober brow
Will bless it and approve it with a text,
Hiding the grossness with fair ornament?
There is no vice so simple but assumes
Some mark of virtue on his outward parts.
73

11   Ornament is but the guiled shore
To a most dangerous sea; the beauteous scarf
Veiling an Indian beauty; in a word,
The seeming truth which cunning times put on

To entrap the wisest.
97

12 How all the other passions fleet to air,
As doubtful thoughts, and rash-embrac'd despair,
And shuddering fear, and green-ey'd jealousy.
108

13 You see me, Lord Bassanio, where I stand,
Such as I am: though for myself alone
I would not be ambitious in my wish,
To wish myself much better; yet, for you
I would be trebled twenty times myself;
A thousand times more fair, ten thousand times
More rich;
That only to stand high in your account,
I might in virtues, beauties, livings, friends,
Exceed account: but the full sum of me
Is sum of nothing; which, to term in gross,
Is an unlesson'd girl, unschool'd, unpractis'd;
Happy in this, she is not yet so old
But she may learn; happier than this,
She is not bred so dull but she can learn.
149

14 I wish you all the joy that you can wish.
191

15 Here are a few of the unpleasant'st words
That ever blotted paper!
252

16 I will have my bond.
iii.17

17 This comes too near the praising of myself.
iv.22

18 How every fool can play upon the word!
v.[48]

19 Wilt thou show the whole wealth of thy wit in an
instant? I pray thee, understand a plain man in his
plain meaning.
[62]

20 You'll ask me, why I rather choose to have
A weight of carrion flesh than to receive
Three thousand ducats: I'll not answer that:
But say it is my humour: is it answer'd?
IV.i.40

21 Some men there are love not a gaping pig;
Some, that are mad if they behold a cat;
And others, when the bagpipe sings i' the nose,
Cannot contain their urine.
47

22 There is no firm reason to be render'd,
Why he cannot abide a gaping pig;
Why he, a harmless necessary cat;
Why he, a wauling bagpipe.
53

23 I am not bound to please thee with my answer.
65

24 What judgment shall I dread, doing no wrong?
89

25 I am a tainted wether of the flock,
Meetest for death: the weakest kind of fruit
Drops earliest to the ground.
114

26 I never knew so young a body with so old a head.
[163]

27 *Portia:* Then must the Jew be merciful.

Shylock: On what compulsion must I? tell me that.
Portia: The quality of mercy is not strain'd,
It droppeth as the gentle rain from heaven
Upon the place beneath: it is twice bless'd;
It blesseth him that gives and him that takes:
'Tis mightiest in the mightiest: it becomes
The throned monarch better than his crown;
His sceptre shows the force of temporal power,
The attribute to awe and majesty,
Wherein doth sit the dread and fear of kings;
But mercy is above this sceptred sway,
It is enthroned in the hearts of kings,
It is an attribute to God himself,
And earthly power doth then show likest God's
When mercy seasons justice. Therefore, Jew,
Though justice be thy plea, consider this,
That in the course of justice none of us
Should see salvation: we do pray for mercy,
And that same prayer doth teach us all to render
The deeds of mercy.
[182]

1 My deeds upon my head! I crave the law.
[206]

2 Wrest once the law to your authority:
To do a great right, do a little wrong.
[215]

3 *Portia:* There is no power in Venice
Can alter a decree established:
'Twill be recorded for a precedent,
And many an error by the same example
Will rush into the state.
Shylock: A Daniel come to judgment! yea, a Daniel!
O wise young judge, how I do honour thee!
[218]

4 An oath, an oath, I have an oath in heaven:
Shall I lay perjury upon my soul?
No, not for Venice.
[228]

5   I charge you by the law,
Whereof you are a well-deserving pillar,
Proceed to judgment.
[238]

6 The court awards it, and the law doth give it.
[301]

7   Thyself shalt see the act;
For, as thou urgest justice, be assur'd
Thou shalt have justice, more than thou desir'st.
[315]

8 A second Daniel, a Daniel, Jew!
Now, infidel, I have thee on the hip.
[334]

9 I thank thee, Jew, for teaching me that word.
[342]

10 Nay, take my life and all; pardon not that:
You take my house when you do take the prop
That doth sustain my house; you take my life
When you do take the means whereby I live.
[375]

11 He is well paid that is well satisfied.
[416]

12 I see, sir, you are liberal in offers:
You taught me first to beg, and now methinks

You teach me how a beggar should be answer'd.
[439]

13 The moon shines bright: in such a night as this,
When the sweet wind did gently kiss the trees
And they did make no noise, in such a night
Troilus methinks mounted the Troyan walls,
And sigh'd his soul toward the Grecian tents,
Where Cressid lay that night.
V.i.1

14   In such a night
Stood Dido with a willow in her hand
Upon the wild sea-banks, and waft her love
To come again to Carthage.
9

15 How sweet the moonlight sleeps upon this bank!
Here will we sit, and let the sounds of music
Creep in our ears; soft stillness and the night
Become the touches of sweet harmony.
Sit, Jessica: look, how the floor of heaven
Is thick inlaid with patines of bright gold:
There's not the smallest orb which thou behold'st
But in this motion like an angel sings
Still quiring to the young-eyed cherubins;
Such harmony is in immortal souls;
But, whilst this muddy vesture of decay
Doth grossly close it in, we cannot hear it.
54

16 I am never merry when I hear sweet music.
69

17 The man that hath no music in himself,
Nor is not mov'd with concord of sweet sounds,
Is fit for treasons, stratagems, and spoils;
The motions of his spirit are dull as night,
And his affections dark as Erebus:
Let no such man be trusted.
79

18 *Portia:* How far that little candle throws his beams!
So shines a good deed in a naughty world.
Nerissa: When the moon shone, we did not see the
candle.
Portia: So doth the greater glory dim the less:
A substitute shines brightly as a king
Until a king be by, and then his state
Empties itself, as doth an inland brook
Into the main of waters.
90

19 The crow doth sing as sweetly as the lark
When neither is attended, and I think
The nightingale, if she should sing by day,
When every goose is cackling, would be thought
No better a musician than the wren.
How many things by season season'd are
To their right praise and true perfection!
Peace, ho! the moon sleeps with Endymion,
And would not be awak'd!
102

20 This night methinks is but the daylight sick.
124

21 Let me give light, but let me not be light:
For a light wife doth make a heavy husband.
129

22 These blessed candles of the night.
220

THE MERRY WIVES OF WINDSOR

1 I will make a Star-Chamber matter of it.
I.i.1

2 She has brown hair, and speaks small like a woman.
[48]

3 I had rather than forty shillings I had my Book of
Songs and Sonnets here.
[205]

4 'Convey,' the wise it call. 'Steal!' foh! a fico for the
phrase!
iii.[30]

5 Here will be an old abusing of God's patience, and the
king's English.
iv.[5]

6 We burn daylight.
II.i.[54]

7 Faith, thou hast some crotchets in thy head now.
[158]

8 Why, then the world's mine oyster,
Which I with sword will open.
ii.2

9 *Falstaff:* Of what quality was your love, then?
Ford: Like a fair house built upon another man's
ground; so that I have lost my edifice by mistaking the
place where I erected it.
[228]

10 He capers, he dances, he has eyes of youth, he writes
verses, he speaks holiday, he smells April and May.
III.ii.[71]

11 O, what a world of vile ill-favour'd faults
Looks handsome in three hundred pounds a year!
iv.[32]

12 If I be served such another trick, I'll have my brains
ta'en out, and buttered, and give them to a dog for a
new year's gift.
v.[7]

13 You may know by my size that I have a kind of
alacrity in sinking.
[12]

14 He so takes on yonder with my husband; so rails
against all married mankind; so curses all Eve's
daughters, of what complexion soever; and so buffets
himself on the forehead, crying, 'Peer out, peer out!'
that any madness I ever yet beheld seemed but
tameness, civility and patience, to this his distemper he
is in now.
IV.ii.[22]

15 This is the third time; I hope good luck lies in odd
numbers...There is divinity in odd numbers, either in
nativity, chance or death.
V.i.2

16 Fairies, black, grey, green, and white,
You moonshine revellers, and shades of night,
You orphan heirs of fixed destiny,
Attend your office and your quality.
v.43

A MIDSUMMER NIGHT'S DREAM

17   Question your desires;
Know of your youth, examine well your blood,
Whether, if you yield not to your father's choice,
You can endure the livery of a nun,

For aye to be in shady cloister mew'd,
To live a barren sister all your life,
Chanting faint hymns to the cold fruitless moon.
Thrice blessed they that master so their blood,
To undergo such maiden pilgrimage;
But earthlier happy is the rose distill'd,
Than that which withering on the virgin thorn
Grows, lives, and dies, in single blessedness.
I.i.67

18 Ay me! for aught that ever I could read,
Could ever hear by tale or history,
The course of true love never did run smooth.
132

19 O hell! to choose love by another's eye.
140

20   If there were a sympathy in choice,
War, death, or sickness did lay siege to it,
Making it momentany as a sound,
Swift as a shadow, short as any dream,
Brief as the lightning in the collied night,
That, in a spleen, unfolds both heaven and earth,
And ere a man hath power to say, 'Behold!'
The jaws of darkness do devour it up:
So quick bright things come to confusion.
141

21 Your eyes are lodestars! and your tongue's sweet air
More tuneable than lark to shepherd's ear,
When wheat is green, when hawthorn buds appear.
183

22 How happy some o'er other some can be!
Through Athens I am thought as fair as she;
But what of that? Demetrius thinks not so;
He will not know what all but he do know;
And as he errs, doting on Helen's eyes,
So I, admiring of his qualities.
Things base and vile, holding no quantity,
Love can transpose to form and dignity.
Love looks not with the eyes, but with the mind,
And therefore is wing'd Cupid painted blind.
226

23 The most lamentable comedy, and most cruel death of
Pyramus and Thisby.
ii.[11]

24 Masters, spread yourselves.
[16]

25 If I do it, let the audience look to their eyes.
[28]

26 I could play Ercles rarely, or a part to tear a cat in, to
make all split.
[31]

27 This is Ercles' vein, a tyrant's vein.
[43]

28 Nay, faith, let me not play a woman; I have a beard
coming.
[50]

29 I will roar, that I will do any man's heart good to hear
me; I will roar, that I will make the duke say, 'Let him
roar again, let him roar again.'
[73]

30 I will roar you as gently as any sucking dove; I will
roar you as 'twere any nightingale.
[85]

31 Pyramus is a sweet-faced man; a proper man, as one

shall see in a summer's day.
[89]

1 Hold, or cut bow-strings.
[115]

2 *Puck:* How now, spirit! whither wander you?
Fairy: Over hill, over dale,
    Thorough bush, thorough brier,
Over park, over pale,
    Thorough flood, thorough fire,
I do wander everywhere,
Swifter than the moone's sphere;
And I serve the fairy queen,
To dew her orbs upon the green:
The cowslips tall her pensioners be;
In their gold coats spots you see;
Those be rubies, fairy favours,
In those freckles live their savours:
I must go seek some dew-drops here,
And hang a pearl in every cowslip's ear.
II.i.1

3 The wisest aunt, telling the saddest tale,
Sometime for three-foot stool mistaketh me;
Then slip I from her bum, down topples she,
And 'tailor' cries, and falls into a cough;
And then the whole quire hold their hips and loff.
51

4 Ill met by moonlight, proud Titania.
60

5 The fold stands empty in the drowned field,
And crows are fatted with the murrion flock;
The nine men's morris is filled up with mud.
96

6 Therefore the moon, the governess of floods,
Pale in her anger, washes all the air,
That rheumatic diseases do abound:
And thorough this distemperature we see
The seasons alter: hoary-headed frosts
Fall in the fresh lap of the crimson rose.
103

7 Since once I sat upon a promontory,
And heard a mermaid on a dolphin's back
Uttering such dulcet and harmonious breath,
That the rude sea grew civil at her song,
And certain stars shot madly from their spheres,
To hear the sea-maid's music.
149

8 But I might see young Cupid's fiery shaft
Quench'd in the chaste beams of the wat'ry moon,
And the imperial votaress passed on,
In maiden meditation, fancy-free.
Yet mark'd I where the bolt of Cupid fell:
It fell upon a little western flower,
Before milk-white, now purple with love's wound,
And maidens call it, Love-in-idleness.
161

9 I'll put a girdle round about the earth
In forty minutes.
175

10 I know a bank whereon the wild thyme blows,
Where oxlips and the nodding violet grows
Quite over-canopied with luscious woodbine,
With sweet musk-roses, and with eglantine:
There sleeps Titania some time of the night,
Lull'd in these flowers with dances and delight;

And there the snake throws her enamell'd skin,
Weed wide enough to wrap a fairy in.
249

11 You spotted snakes with double tongue,
Thorny hedge-hogs, be not seen;
Newts, and blind-worms, do no wrong;
Come not near our fairy queen.
ii.9

12 Weaving spiders come not here;
Hence you long-legg'd spinners, hence!
Beetles black, approach not near;
Worm nor snail, do no offence.
20

13 Night and silence! who is here?
Weeds of Athens he doth wear.
70

14 God shield us!—a lion among ladies, is a most
dreadful thing; for there is not a more fearful
wild-fowl than your lion living.
III.i.[32]

15 Look in the almanack; find out moonshine, find out
moonshine.
[55]

16 What hempen home-spuns have we swaggering here,
So near the cradle of the fairy queen?
[82]

17 Bless thee, Bottom! bless thee! thou art translated.
[124]

18 *Bottom:* The ousel-cock, so black of hue,
    With orange-tawny bill,
The throstle with his note so true,
    The wren with little quill.
Titania: What angel wakes me from my flowery bed?
[131]

19 Out of this wood do not desire to go.
[159]

20 As wild geese that the creeping fowler eye,
Or russet-pated choughs, many in sort,
Rising and cawing at the gun's report,
Sever themselves, and madly sweep the sky;
So, at his sight, away his fellows fly.
ii.20

21 Lord, what fools these mortals be!
115

22   So we grew together,
Like to a double cherry, seeming parted,
But yet an union in partition;
Two lovely berries moulded on one stem;
So, with two seeming bodies, but one heart.
208

23 Ay, do, persever, counterfeit sad looks,
Make mouths upon me when I turn my back.
237

24 O! when she's angry she is keen and shrewd.
She was a vixen when she went to school:
And though she be but little, she is fierce.
323

25   Night's swift dragons cut the clouds full fast,
And yonder shines Aurora's harbinger;
At whose approach, ghosts, wandering here and there,
Troop home to churchyards.
379

26 Cupid is a knavish lad,

Thus to make poor females mad.
440

1   Jack shall have Jill;
        Nought shall go ill;
The man shall have his mare again,
And all shall be well.
461

2 I must to the barber's, mounsieur, for methinks I am
marvellous hairy about the face.
IV.i.[25]

3 I have a reasonable good ear in music: let us have the
tongs and the bones.
[32]

4 Methinks I have a great desire to a bottle of hay: good
hay, sweet hay, hath no fellow.
[37]

5 I pray you, let none of your people stir me: I have an
exposition of sleep come upon me.
[43]

6 My Oberon! what visions have I seen!
Methought I was enamour'd of an ass.
[82]

7 I was with Hercules and Cadmus once,
When in a wood of Crete they bay'd the bear
With hounds of Sparta: never did I hear...
So musical a discord, such sweet thunder.
[118]

8   Saint Valentine is past:
Begin these wood-birds but to couple now?
[145]

9 I have had a dream, past the wit of man to say what
dream it was.
[211]

10 The eye of man hath not heard, the ear of man hath
not seen, man's hand is not able to taste, his tongue to
conceive, nor his heart to report, what my dream was.
[218]

11 The lunatic, the lover, and the poet,
Are of imagination all compact:
One sees more devils than vast hell can hold,
That is, the madman; the lover, all as frantic,
Sees Helen's beauty in a brow of Egypt:
The poet's eye, in a fine frenzy rolling,
Doth glance from heaven to earth, from earth to
    heaven;
And, as imagination bodies forth
The forms of things unknown, the poet's pen
Turns them to shapes, and gives to airy nothing
A local habitation and a name.
Such tricks hath strong imagination,
That, if it would but apprehend some joy,
It comprehends some bringer of that joy;
Or in the night, imagining some fear,
How easy is a bush suppos'd a bear!
V.i.7

12 What revels are in hand? Is there no play,
To ease the anguish of a torturing hour?
36

13 *A tedious brief scene of young Pyramus*
And his love Thisbe: very tragical mirth.
Merry and tragical! tedious and brief!
That is, hot ice and wondrous strange snow.
56

14 For never anything can be amiss,
When simpleness and duty tender it.
82

15 Out of this silence yet I pick'd a welcome;
And in the modesty of fearful duty
I read as much as from the rattling tongue
Of saucy and audacious eloquence.
100

16 If we offend, it is with our good will.
    That you should think, we come not to offend,
But with good will. To show our simple skill,
    That is the true beginning of our end.
Consider then we come but in despite.
    We do not come as minding to content you,
Our true intent is. All for your delight,
    We are not here.
[108]

17 Whereat, with blade, with bloody blameful blade,
He bravely broach'd his boiling bloody breast.
[148]

18 I see a voice: now will I to the chink,
To spy an I can hear my Thisby's face.
[195]

19 The best in this kind are but shadows, and the worst
are no worse, if imagination amend them.
[215]

20 The iron tongue of midnight hath told twelve;
Lovers, to bed; 'tis almost fairy time.
[372]

21 Now the hungry lion roars,
    And the wolf behowls the moon;
Whilst the heavy ploughman snores,
    All with weary task fordone.
ii.1

22   Not a mouse
Shall disturb this hallow'd house:
I am sent with broom before,
To sweep the dust behind the door.
17

23 If we shadows have offended,
Think but this, and all is mended,
That you have but slumber'd here
While these visions did appear.
54

MUCH ADO ABOUT NOTHING

24 A victory is twice itself when the achiever brings
home full numbers.
I.i.[8]

25 He hath indeed better bettered expectation than you
must expect of me to tell you how.
[15]

26 He is a very valiant trencher-man.
[52]

27 I see, lady, the gentleman is not in your books.
[79]

28 *Beatrice:* I wonder that you will still be talking,
Signior Benedick: nobody marks you.
Benedick: What! my dear Lady Disdain, are you yet
living?
[121]

1 Shall I never see a bachelor of three-score again?
[209]

2 In time the savage bull doth bear the yoke.
[271]

3 Lord! I could not endure a husband with a beard on his face: I had rather lie in the woollen.
II.i.[31]

4 Would it not grieve a woman to be over-mastered with a piece of valiant dust? to make an account of her life to a clod of wayward marl?
[64]

5 I have a good eye, uncle: I can see a church by daylight.
[86]

6 Speak low, if you speak love.
[104]

7 Friendship is constant in all other things
Save in the office and affairs of love.
[184]

8 She speaks poniards, and every word stabs: if her breath were as terrible as her terminations, there were no living near her; she would infect to the north star.
[257]

9 I will go on the slightest errand now to the Antipodes that you can devise to send me on; I will fetch you a toothpicker now from the furthest inch of Asia; bring you the length of Prester John's foot; fetch you a hair off the Great Cham's beard; do you any embassage to the Pigmies, rather than hold three words' conference with this harpy.
[274]

10 Silence is the perfectest herald of joy: I were but little happy, if I could say how much.
[319]

11 Speak, cousin, or, if you cannot, stop his mouth with a kiss.
[322]

12 *Don Pedro:* Out of question, you were born in a merry hour.
Beatrice: No, sure, my lord, my mother cried; but then there was a star danced, and under that was I born.
[348]

13 She is never sad but when she sleeps; and not ever sad then, for I have heard my daughter say, she hath often dreamed of unhappiness and waked herself with laughing.
[360]

14 I have known, when he would have walked ten miles afoot to see a good armour; and now will he lie ten nights awake, carving the fashion of a new doublet.
iii.[16]

15 Is it not strange, that sheeps' guts should hale souls out of men's bodies?
[62]

16 Sigh no more, ladies, sigh no more,
    Men were deceivers ever;
One foot in sea, and one on shore,
To one thing constant never.
        Then sigh not so,
        But let them go,
    And be you blithe and bonny,
Converting all your sounds of woe

Into Hey nonny, nonny.
[65]

17 Sits the wind in that corner?
[108]

18 Doth not the appetite alter? A man loves the meat in his youth that he cannot endure in his age.
[258]

19 The world must be peopled. When I said I would die a bachelor, I did not think I should live till I were married.
[262]

20   Now begin;
For look where Beatrice, like a lapwing, runs
Close by the ground, to hear our counsel.
III.1.23

21 Disdain and scorn ride sparkling in her eyes.
51

22 Contempt, farewell! and maiden pride, adieu!
    No glory lives behind the back of such.
And, Benedick, love on; I will requite thee,
    Taming my wild heart to thy loving hand.
109

23 He hath a heart as sound as a bell, and his tongue is the clapper; for what his heart thinks his tongue speaks.
ii.[12]

24 Well, every one can master a grief but he that has it.
[28]

25 A' brushes his hat a mornings; what should that bode?
[41]

26 The barber's man hath been seen with him; and the old ornament of his cheek hath already stuffed tennis-balls.
[45]

27 To be a well-favoured man is the gift of fortune; but to write and read comes by nature
iii.[14]

28 Well, for your favour, sir, why, give God thanks, and make no boast of it; and for your writing and reading, let that appear when there is no need of such vanity. You are thought here to be the most senseless and fit man for the constable of the watch.
[19]

29 You shall comprehend all vagrom men.
[25]

30 For the watch to babble and to talk is most tolerable and not to be endured.
[36]

31 The most peaceable way for you, if you do take a thief, is, to let him show himself what he is and steal out of your company.
[61]

32 I thank God, I am as honest as any man living, that is an old man and no honester than I.
v.[15]

33 Comparisons are odorous.
[18]

34 A good old man, sir; he will be talking: as they say, 'when the age is in, the wit is out.'
[36]

35 Well, God's a good man.
[39]

1 O! what men dare do! what men may do! what men
daily do, not knowing what they do!
IV.i.[19]

2 I do love nothing in the world so well as you: is not
that strange?
[271]

3 O God, that I were a man! I would eat his heart in the
market-place.
[311]

4 Flat burglary as ever was committed.
ii.[54]

5 O that he were here to write me down an ass! but,
masters, remember that I am an ass; though it be not
written down, yet forget not that I am an ass.
[80]

6 Patch grief with proverbs.
V.i.17

7   There was never yet philosopher
That could endure the toothache patiently.
35

8 In a false quarrel there is no true valour.
[121]

9 What though care killed a cat, thou hast mettle enough
in thee to kill care.
[135]

10 No, I was not born under a riming planet.
ii.[40]

11 Good morrow, masters: put your torches out,
The wolves have prey'd; and look, the gentle day,
Before the wheels of Phoebus, round about
Dapples the drowsy east with spots of grey.
iii.24

OTHELLO

12   'Tis the curse of the service,
Preferment goes by letter and affection,
Not by the old gradation, where each second
Stood heir to the first.
I.i.35

13   You shall mark
Many a duteous and knee-crooking knave,
That, doting on his own obsequious bondage,
Wears out his time, much like his master's ass,
For nought but provender.
44

14 In following him, I follow but myself.
58

15 But I will wear my heart upon my sleeve
For daws to peck at: I am not what I am.
64

16 Even now, now, very now, an old black ram
Is tupping your white ewe.
88

17 'Zounds! sir, you are one of those that will not serve
God if the devil bid you.
108

18 Your daughter and the Moor are now making the beast
with two backs.
[117]

19 Though I do hate him as I do hell-pains,
Yet, for necessity of present life,
I must show out a flag and sign of love,

Which is indeed but sign.
[155]

20 Though in the trade of war I have slain men,
Yet do I hold it very stuff o' the conscience
To do no contriv'd murder: I lack iniquity
Sometimes to do me service.
ii.1

21 Keep up your bright swords, for the dew will rust
them.
59

22 I'll refer me to all things of sense,
Whether a maid so tender, fair, and happy,
So opposite to marriage that she shunn'd
The wealthy curled darlings of our nation,
Would ever have, to incur a general mock,
Run from her guardage to the sooty bosom
Of such a thing as thou.
64

23   My particular grief
Is of so flood-gate and o'bearing nature
That it engluts and swallows other sorrows
And it is still itself.
iii.55

24 *Othello:* Most potent, grave, and reverend signiors,
My very noble and approv'd good masters,
That I have ta'en away this old man's daughter,
It is most true; true, I have married her:
The very head and front of my offending
Hath this extent, no more. Rude am I in my speech,
And little bless'd with the soft phrase of peace;
For since these arms of mine had seven years' pith,
Till now some nine moons wasted, they have us'd
Their dearest action in the tented field;
And little of this great world can I speak,
More than pertains to feats of broil and battle;
And therefore little shall I grace my cause
In speaking for myself. Yet, by your gracious
patience,
I will a round unvarnish'd tale deliver
Of my whole course of love; what drugs, what
charms,
What conjuration, and what mighty magic,
For such proceeding I am charg'd withal,
I won his daughter.
Brabantio: A maiden never bold;
Of spirit so still and quiet, that her motion
Blush'd at herself.
76

25 Her father lov'd me; oft invited me;
Still question'd me the story of my life
From year to year, the battles, sieges, fortunes
That I have pass'd.
I ran it through, even from my boyish days
To the very moment that he bade me tell it;
Wherein I spake of most disastrous chances,
Of moving accidents by flood and field,
Of hair-breadth 'scapes i' the imminent deadly breach,
Of being taken by the insolent foe
And sold to slavery, of my redemption thence
And portance in my travel's history;
Wherein of antres vast and desarts idle,
Rough quarries, rocks and hills whose heads touch
heaven,
It was my hint to speak, such was the process;

And of the Cannibals that each other eat,
The Anthropophagi, and men whose heads
Do grow beneath their shoulders. This to hear
Would Desdemona seriously incline.
128

1 And often did beguile her of her tears,
When I did speak of some distressful stroke
That my youth suffer'd. My story being done,
She gave me for my pains a world of sighs:
She swore, in faith, 'twas strange, 'twas passing
strange;
'Twas pitiful, 'twas wondrous pitiful:
She wish'd she had not heard it, yet she wish'd
That heaven had made her such a man; she thank'd
me,
And bade me, if I had a friend that lov'd her,
I should but teach him how to tell my story,
And that would woo her. Upon this hint I spake:
She lov'd me for the dangers I had pass'd,
And I lov'd her that she did pity them.
This only is the witchcraft I have us'd.
156

2 I do perceive here a divided duty.
181

3 The robb'd that smiles steals something from the thief.
208

4 But words are words; I never yet did hear
That the bruis'd heart was pierced through the ear.
218

5 The tyrant custom, most grave senators,
Hath made the flinty and steel couch of war
My thrice-driven bed of down.
[230]

6   If I be left behind,
A moth of peace, and he go to the war,
The rites for which I love him are bereft me,
And I a heavy interim shall support
By his dear absence. Let me go with him.
[257]

7 Roderigo: I will incontinently drown myself.
Iago: Well, if thou dost, I shall never love thee after.
Why, thou silly gentleman!
Roderigo: It is silliness to live when to live is torment;
and then have we a prescription to die when death is
our physician.
[307]

8 Virtue! a fig! 'tis in ourselves that we are thus, or
thus. Our bodies are our gardens, to the which our
wills are gardeners.
[323]

9 Put money in thy purse.
[345]

10 These Moors are changeable in their wills;—fill thy
purse with money:—the food that to him now is as
luscious as locusts, shall be to him shortly as bitter as
coloquintida.
[352]

11 There are many events in the womb of time which
will be delivered.
[377]

12 He hath a person and a smooth dispose
Fram'd to make women false.
The Moor is of a free and open nature,

That thinks men honest that but seem to be so.
[403]

13 I have't; it is engender'd; hell and night
Must bring this monstrous birth to the world's light.
[409]

14 Our great captain's captain.
II.i.74

15   You are pictures out of doors,
Bells in your parlours, wild cats in your kitchens,
Saints in your injuries, devils being offended,
Players in your housewifery, and housewives in your
beds.
109

16   Do not put me to't,
For I am nothing if not critical.
118

17 I am not merry, but I do beguile
The thing I am by seeming otherwise.
122

18 Iago: She that was ever fair and never proud,
Had tongue at will and yet was never loud,
Never lack'd gold and yet went never gay,
Fled from her wish and yet said 'Now I may,'
She that being anger'd, her revenge being nigh,
Bade her wrong stay and her displeasure fly,
She that in wisdom never was so frail
To change the cod's head for the salmon's tail,
She that could think and ne'er disclose her mind,
See suitors following and not look behind,
She was a wight, if ever such wight were,—
Desdemona: To do what?
Iago: To suckle fools and chronicle small beer.
Desdemona: O most lame and impotent conclusion!
148

19 With as little a web as this will I ensnare as great a fly
as Cassio.
[169]

20 Othello: If it were now to die,
'Twere now to be most happy, for I fear
My soul hath her content so absolute
That not another comfort like to this
Succeeds in unknown fate.
Desdemona: The heavens forbid
But that our loves and comforts should increase
Even as our days do grow!
[192]

21 A slipper and subtle knave, a finder-out of occasions,
that has an eye can stamp and counterfeit advantages,
though true advantage never present itself; a devilish
knave! Besides, the knave is handsome, young, and
hath all those requisites in him that folly and green
minds look after; a pestilent complete knave! and the
woman hath found him already.
[247]

22 Make the Moor thank me, love me, and reward me
For making him egregiously an ass
And practising upon his peace and quiet
Even to madness.
[320]

23 I have very poor and unhappy brains for drinking: I
could well wish courtesy would invent some other
custom of entertainment.
iii.[34]

1 My boat sails freely, both with wind and stream.
[66]

2 *Cassio:* 'Fore God, an excellent song.
Iago: I learned it in England, where indeed they are
most potent in potting; your Dane, your German, and
your swag-bellied Hollander,—drink, ho!—are nothing
to your English.
[78]

3 'Tis pride that pulls the country down.
[99]

4 Silence that dreadful bell! it frights the isle
From her propriety.
[177]

5 But men are men; the best sometimes forget.
[243]

6 Thy honesty and love doth mince this matter.
[249]

7 Reputation, reputation, reputation! O! I have lost my
reputation. I have lost the immortal part of myself, and
what remains is bestial. My reputation, Iago, my
reputation!
[264]

8 O thou invisible spirit of wine! if thou hast no name to
be known by, let us call thee devil!
[285]

9 O God! that men should put an enemy in their mouths
to steal away their brains; that we should, with joy,
pleasance, revel, and applause, transform ourselves
into beasts.
[293]

10 Come, come; good wine is a good familiar creature if
it be well used; exclaim no more against it.
[315]

11 How poor are they that have not patience!
What wound did ever heal but by degrees?
[379]

12 O! thereby hangs a tail.
III.i.[8]

13   My lord shall never rest;
I'll watch him tame, and talk him out of patience;
His bed shall seem a school, his board a shrift;
I'll intermingle every thing he does
With Cassio's suit.
iii.22

14 Excellent wretch! Perdition catch my soul
But I do love thee! and when I love thee not,
Chaos is come again.
90

15 By heaven, he echoes me,
As if there were some monster in his thought
Too hideous to be shown.
106

16 Good name in man and woman, dear my lord,
Is the immediate jewel of their souls;
Who steals my purse steals trash; 'tis something,
          nothing;
'Twas mine, 'tis his, and has been slave to thousands;
But he that filches from me my good name
Robs me of that which not enriches him,
And makes me poor indeed.
155

17   O! beware, my lord, of jealousy;
It is the green-ey'd monster which doth mock

The meat it feeds on.
165

18 In Venice they do let heaven see the pranks
They dare not show their husbands; their best
          conscience
Is not to leave't undone, but keep't unknown.
202

19 I humbly do beseech you of your pardon
For too much loving you.
212

20 Not to affect many proposed matches
Of her own clime, complexion, and degree,
Whereto, we see, in all things nature tends;
Foh! one may smell in such, a will most rank,
Foul disposition, thoughts unnatural.
229

21   If I do prove her haggard,
Though that her jesses were my dear heart-strings,
I'd whistle her off and let her down the wind,
To prey at fortune. Haply, for I am black,
And have not those soft parts of conversation
That chamberers have, or, for I am declin'd
Into the vale of years—yet that's not much—
She's gone, I am abus'd; and my relief
Must be to loathe her. O curse of marriage!
That we can call these delicate creatures ours,
And not their appetites. I had rather be a toad,
And live upon the vapour of a dungeon,
Than keep a corner in the thing I love
For others' uses.
260

22 If she be false, O! then heaven mocks itself.
I'll not believe it.
278

23   Trifles light as air
Are to the jealous confirmations strong
As proofs of holy writ.
323

24   Not poppy, nor mandragora,
Nor all the drowsy syrups of the world,
Shall ever medicine thee to that sweet sleep
Which thou ow'dst yesterday.
331

25 I had been happy, if the general camp,
Pioners and all, had tasted her sweet body,
So I had nothing known. O! now, for ever
Farewell the tranquil mind; farewell content!
Farewell the plumed troop and the big wars
That make ambition virtue! O, farewell!
Farewell the neighing steed and the shrill trump,
The spirit-stirring drum, the ear-piercing fife,
The royal banner, and all quality,
Pride, pomp, and circumstance of glorious war!
And, O you mortal engines, whose rude throats
The immortal Jove's dread clamours counterfeit,
Farewell! Othello's occupation's gone!
346

26   O wretched fool!
That liv'st to make thine honesty a vice.
O monstrous world! Take note, take note, O world!
To be direct and honest is not safe.
376

27 This denoted a foregone conclusion.
429

1   Like to the Pontick sea,
Whose icy current and compulsive course
Ne'er feels retiring ebb, but keeps due on
To the Propontic and the Hellespont,
Even so my bloody thoughts, with violent pace,
Shall ne'er look back, ne'er ebb to humble love,
Till that a capable and wide revenge
Swallow them up.
454

2 For here's a young and sweating devil here,
That commonly rebels. 'Tis a good hand,
A frank one.
iv.43

3 That handkerchief
Did an Egyptian to my mother give.
56

4 'Tis true; there's magic in the web of it;
A sibyl, that had number'd in the world
The sun to course two hundred compasses,
In her prophetic fury sew'd the work;
The worms were hallow'd that did breed the silk,
And it was dy'd in mummy which the skilful
Conserv'd of maidens' hearts.
70

5   Jealous souls will not be answer'd so;
They are not ever jealous for the cause,
But jealous for they are jealous.
158

6 What! keep a week away? seven days and nights?
Eight score eight hours? and lovers' absent hours,
More tedious than the dial eight score times?
O, weary reckoning!
172

7   O! it comes o'er my memory,
As doth the raven o'er the infected house,
Boding to all.
IV.i.20

8 Work on,
My medicine, work! Thus credulous fools are caught.
45

9   'Tis the strumpet's plague
To beguile many and be beguil'd by one.
97

10 I would have him nine years a-killing.
[186]

11 My heart is turned to stone; I strike it, and it hurts my
hand. O! the world hath not a sweeter creature; she
might lie by an emperor's side and command him
tasks.
[190]

12 An admirable musician! O, she will sing the
savageness out of a bear.
[197]

13 But yet the pity of it, Iago! O! Iago, the pity of it,
Iago!
[205]

14 O well-painted passion!
[268]

15 Goats and monkeys!
[274]

16   Is this the noble nature
Whom passion could not shake? whose solid virtue
The shot of accident nor dart of chance

Could neither graze nor pierce?
[277]

17 Your mystery, your mystery; nay, dispatch.
ii.29

18   Had it pleas'd heaven
To try me with affliction, had he rain'd
All kinds of sores, and shames, on my bare head,
Steep'd me in poverty to the very lips,
Given to captivity me and my utmost hopes,
I should have found in some part of my soul
A drop of patience; but, alas! to make me
The fixed figure for the time of scorn
To point his slow and moving finger at;
Yet could I bear that too; well, very well.
But there, where I have garner'd up my heart,
Where either I must live or bear no life,
The fountain from the which my current runs
Or else dries up; to be discarded thence!
Or keep it as a cistern for foul toads
To knot and gender in! Turn thy complexion there,
Patience, thou young and rose-lipp'd cherubin;
Ay, there, look grim as hell!
46

19   O thou weed!
Who art so lovely fair and smell'st so sweet
That the sense aches at thee, would thou hadst ne'er
       been born!
66

20 Heaven stops the nose at it and the moon winks.
76

21   I cry you mercy, then;
I took you for that cunning whore of Venice
That married with Othello. You, mistress,
That have the office opposite to Saint Peter,
And keep the gate of hell!
87

22 Those that do teach young babes
Do it with gentle means and easy tasks;
He might have chid me so; for, in good faith,
I am a child to chiding.
111

23 I will be hang'd, if some eternal villain,
Some busy and insinuating rogue,
Some cogging cozening slave, to get some office,
Have not devis'd this slander.
130

24   Unkindness may do much;
And his unkindness may defeat my life,
But never taint my love.
159

25 *Emilia:* I would you had never seen him.
Desdemona: So would not I; my love doth so approve
       him,
That even his stubbornness, his checks and frowns...
Have grace and favour in them.
iii.18

26 My mother had a maid call'd Barbara;
She was in love, and he she lov'd proved mad
And did forsake her; she had a song of 'willow;'
An old thing 'twas, but it express'd her fortune,
And she died singing it; that song to-night
Will not go from my mind.
26

27 The poor soul sat sighing by a sycamore tree,

Sing all a green willow;
Her hand on her bosom, her head on her knee,
Sing willow, willow, willow:
The fresh streams ran by her, and murmur'd her
    moans;
Sing willow, willow, willow:
Her salt tears fell from her, and soften'd the stones;—
Sing willow, willow, willow:
Sing all a green willow must be my garland.
[41]. See 250:21

1 *Desdemona:* Mine eyes do itch;
Doth that bode weeping?
Emilia: 'Tis neither here nor there.
[59]

2 Who would not make her husband a cuckold to make
him a monarch?
[76]

3 He hath a daily beauty in his life.
That makes me ugly.
V.i.19

4   This is the night
That either makes me or fordoes me quite.
128

5 It is the cause, it is the cause, my soul;
Let me not name it to you, you chaste stars!
It is the cause. Yet I'll not shed her blood,
Nor scar that whiter skin of hers than snow,
And smooth as monumental alabaster.
Yet she must die, else she'll betray more men.
Put out the light, and then put out the light:
If I quench thee, thou flaming minister,
I can again thy former light restore,
Should I repent me; but once put out thy light,
Thou cunning'st pattern of excelling nature,
I know not where is that Promethean heat
That can thy light relume. When I have pluck'd the
    rose,
I cannot give it vital growth again,
It needs must wither: I'll smell it on the tree.
O balmy breath, that dost almost persuade
Justice to break her sword! One more, one more.
Be thus when thou art dead, and I will kill thee,
And love thee after. One more, and this the last:
So sweet was ne'er so fatal. I must weep,
But they are cruel tears; this sorrow's heavenly,
It strikes where it doth love.
ii.1

6 Alas! why gnaw you so your nether lip?
Some bloody passion shakes your very frame;
These are portents, but yet, I hope, I hope
They do not point on me.
43

7 Kill me to-morrow; let me live to-night!
80

8 It is the very error of the moon;
She comes more near the earth than she was wont,
And makes men mad.
107

9   Murder's out of tune,
And sweet revenge grows harsh.
113

10 *Emilia:* O! who hath done this deed?
Desdemona: Nobody; I myself; farewell.
121

11 *Othello:* She's like a liar gone to burning hell;
'Twas I that kill'd her.
Emilia: O! the more angel she,
And you the blacker devil.
127

12   Nay, had she been true,
If heaven would make me such another world
Of one entire and perfect chrysolite,
I'd not have sold her for it.
141

13   May his pernicious soul
Rot half a grain a day! he lies to the heart:
She was too fond of her most filthy bargain.
153

14 Thou hast not half the power to do me harm
As I have to be hurt.
160

15 You told a lie, an odious damned lie;
Upon my soul, a lie, a wicked lie.
178

16   Are there no stones in heaven
But what serve for the thunder?
232

17 Every puny whipster gets my sword.
242

18   I will play the swan,
And die in music.
245

19 Who can control his fate?
264

20 Be not afraid, though you do see me weapon'd;
Here is my journey's end, here is my butt,
And very sea-mark of my utmost sail.
265

21   O ill-starr'd wench!
Pale as thy smock! when we shall meet at compt,
This look of thine will hurl my soul from heaven,
And fiends will snatch at it. Cold, cold, my girl!
Even like thy chastity.
O! cursed, cursed slave. Whip me, ye devils,
From the possession of this heavenly sight!
Blow me about in winds! roast me in sulphur!
Wash me in steep-down gulfs of liquid fire!
O Desdemona! Desdemona! dead!
271

22 An honourable murderer, if you will;
For nought did I in hate, but all in honour.
293

23 I have done the state some service, and they know 't;
No more of that. I pray you, in your letters,
When you shall these unlucky deeds relate,
Speak of me as I am; nothing extenuate,
Nor set down aught in malice: then, must you speak
Of one that lov'd not wisely but too well;
Of one not easily jealous, but, being wrought,
Perplex'd in the extreme; of one whose hand,
Like the base Indian, threw a pearl away
Richer than all his tribe; of one whose subdu'd eyes
Albeit unused to the melting mood,
Drop tears as fast as the Arabian trees
Their med'cinable gum. Set you down this;
And say besides, that in Aleppo once,
Where a malignant and a turban'd Turk

Beat a Venetian and traduc'd the state,
I took by the throat the circumcised dog,
And smote him thus.
338

1 *Gratiano:* All that's spoke is marred.
Othello: I kiss'd thee ere I kill'd thee, no way but this,
Killing myself to die upon a kiss.
356

PERICLES, PRINCE OF TYRE

2 See where she comes apparell'd like the spring.
I.i.12

3 Few love to hear the sins they love to act.
92

4 *Third Fisherman:* Master, I marvel how the fishes live
in the sea.
First Fisherman: Why, as men do a-land: the great
ones eat up the little ones.
II.i.[29]

5   O you gods!
Why do you make us love your goodly gifts,
And snatch them straight away?
III.i.22

RICHARD II

6 Old John of Gaunt, time-honour'd Lancaster.
I.i.1

7 Let's purge this choler without letting blood.
153

8 The purest treasure mortal times afford
Is spotless reputation; that away,
Men are but gilded loam or painted clay.
A jewel in a ten-times-barr'd-up chest
Is a bold spirit in a loyal breast.
Mine honour is my life; both grow in one;
Take honour from me, and my life is done.
177

9 We were not born to sue, but to command.
196

10 The language I have learn'd these forty years,
My native English, now I must forego;
And now my tongue's use is to me no more
Than an unstringed viol or a harp.
iii.159

11 I am too old to fawn upon a nurse,
Too far in years to be a pupil now.
170

12 But what thou art, God, thou, and I do know;
And all too soon, I fear, the king shall rue.
204

13 How long a time lies in one little word!
Four lagging winters and four wanton springs
End in a word; such is the breath of kings.
213

14 Things sweet to taste prove in digestion sour.
236

15 Must I not serve a long apprenticehood
To foreign passages, and in the end,
Having my freedom, boast of nothing else
But that I was a journeyman to grief?
271

16 All places that the eye of heaven visits

Are to a wise man ports and happy havens.
Teach thy necessity to reason thus;
There is no virtue like necessity.
275

17 O! who can hold a fire in his hand
By thinking on the frosty Caucasus?
Or cloy the hungry edge of appetite,
By bare imagination of a feast?
Or wallow naked in December snow
By thinking on fantastic summer's heat?
O, no! the apprehension of the good
Gives but the greater feeling to the worse.
294

18 More are men's ends mark'd than their lives before:
The setting sun, and music at the close,
As the last taste of sweets, is sweetest last,
Writ in remembrance more than things long past.
II.i.11

19 Methinks I am a prophet new inspir'd,
And thus expiring do foretell of him:
His rash fierce blaze of riot cannot last,
For violent fires soon burn out themselves;
Small showers last long, but sudden storms are short;
He tires betimes that spurs too fast betimes.
31

20 This royal throne of kings, this scepter'd isle,
This earth of majesty, this seat of Mars,
This other Eden, demi-paradise,
This fortress built by Nature for herself
Against infection and the hand of war,
This happy breed of men, this little world,
This precious stone set in the silver sea,
Which serves it in the office of a wall,
Or as a moat defensive to a house,
Against the envy of less happier lands,
This blessed plot, this earth, this realm, this England,
This nurse, this teeming womb of royal kings,
Fear'd by their breed and famous by their birth,
Renowned for their deeds as far from home,—
For Christian service and true chivalry,—
As is the sepulchre in stubborn Jewry
Of the world's ransom, blessed Mary's Son:
This land of such dear souls, this dear, dear land,
Dear for her reputation through the world,
Is now leas'd out,—I die pronouncing it,—
Like to a tenement or pelting farm:
England, bound in with the triumphant sea,
Whose rocky shore beats back the envious siege
Of watery Neptune, is now bound in with shame,
With inky blots, and rotten parchment bonds:
That England, that was wont to conquer others,
Hath made a shameful conquest of itself.
40

21 These words hereafter thy tormentors be!
136

22   Lay aside life-harming heaviness,
And entertain a cheerful disposition.
ii.3

23 I am a stranger here in Gloucestershire:
These high wild hills and rough uneven ways
Draw out our miles and make them wearisome.
iii.2

24 I count myself in nothing else so happy

As in a soul remembering my good friends.
46

1 Grace me no grace, nor uncle me no uncle.
87

2 The caterpillars of the commonwealth.
166

3 Things past redress are now with me past care.
171

4 Eating the bitter bread of banishment.
III.i.21

5 Not all the water in the rough rude sea
Can wash the balm from an anointed king;
The breath of worldly men cannot depose
The deputy elected by the Lord.
For every man that Bolingbroke hath press'd
To lift shrewd steel against our golden crown,
God for his Richard hath in heavenly pay
A glorious angel; then, if angels fight,
Weak men must fall, for heaven still guards the right.
ii.54

6 O! call back yesterday, bid time return.
69

7 Is not the king's name twenty thousand names?
Arm, arm, my name! A puny subject strikes
At thy great glory.
85

8 The worst is death, and death will have his day.
103

9 O villains, vipers, damn'd without redemption!
Dogs, easily won to fawn on any man!
Snakes, in my heart-blood warm'd, that sting my
heart!
Three Judases, each one thrice worse than Judas!
Would they make peace? terrible hell make war
Upon their spotted souls for this offence!
129

10 Of comfort no man speak:
Let's talk of graves, of worms, and epitaphs;
Make dust our paper, and with rainy eyes
Write sorrow on the bosom of the earth.
Let's choose executors, and talk of wills.
144

11 For God's sake, let us sit upon the ground
And tell sad stories of the death of kings:
How some have been depos'd, some slain in war,
Some haunted by the ghosts they have depos'd,
Some poison'd by their wives, some sleeping kill'd;
All murder'd: for within the hollow crown
That rounds the mortal temples of a king
Keeps Death his court, and there the antick sits,
Scoffing his state and grinning at his pomp;
Allowing him a breath, a little scene,
To monarchize, be fear'd, and kill with looks,
Infusing him with self and vain conceit
As if this flesh which walls about our life
Were brass impregnable; and humour'd thus
Comes at the last, and with a little pin
Bores through his castle wall, and farewell king!
155

12 See, see, King Richard doth himself appear,
As doth the blushing discontented sun
From out the fiery portal of the east.
iii.62

13 The purple testament of bleeding war.
94

14 O! that I were as great
As is my grief, or lesser than my name,
Or that I could forget what I have been,
Or not remember what I must be now.
136

15 What must the king do now? Must he submit?
The king shall do it: must he be depos'd?
The king shall be contented: must he lose
The name of king? o' God's name, let it go.
I'll give my jewels for a set of beads,
My gorgeous palace for a hermitage,
My gay apparel for an almsman's gown,
My figur'd goblets for a dish of wood,
My sceptre for a palmer's walking staff,
My subjects for a pair of carved saints,
And my large kingdom for a little grave,
A little little grave, an obscure grave;
Or I'll be buried in the king's highway,
Some way of common trade, where subjects' feet
May hourly trample on their sovereign's head;
For on my heart they tread now whilst I live;
And buried once, why not upon my head?
143

16 Shall we play the wantons with our woes,
And make some pretty match with shedding tears?
164

17 Go, bind thou up yon dangling apricocks,
Which, like unruly children, make their sire
Stoop with oppression of their prodigal weight.
iv.29

18 Old Adam's likeness, set to dress this garden.
73

19 Here did she fall a tear; here, in this place,
I'll set a bank of rue, sour herb of grace;
Rue, even for ruth, here shortly shall be seen,
In the remembrance of a weeping queen.
104

20 Peace shall go sleep with Turks and infidels,
And in this seat of peace tumultuous wars
Shall kin with kin and kind with kind confound;
Disorder, horror, fear and mutiny
Shall here inhabit, and this land be call'd
The field of Golgotha and dead men's skulls.
IV.i.139

21 God save the king! Will no man say, amen?
Am I both priest and clerk? Well then, amen.
172

22 Give me the crown. Here, cousin, seize the crown;
Here cousin,
On this side my hand and on that side thine.
Now is this golden crown like a deep well
That owes two buckets filling one another;
The emptier ever dancing in the air,
The other down, unseen, and full of water:
That bucket down and full of tears am I,
Drinking my griefs, whilst you mount up on high.
181

23 You may my glories and my state depose,
But not my griefs; still am I king of those.
192

1 Now mark me how I will undo myself.
203

2 With mine own tears I wash away my balm,
With mine own hands I give away my crown.
207

3 God pardon all oaths that are broke to me!
God keep all vows unbroke are made to thee!
214

4 Mine eyes are full of tears, I cannot see:
And yet salt water blinds them not so much
But they can see a sort of traitors here.
Nay, if I turn my eyes upon myself,
I find myself a traitor with the rest.
244

5 A brittle glory shineth in this face:
As brittle as the glory is the face.
287

6   This is the way
To Julius Caesar's ill-erected tower.
V.i.1

7   I am sworn brother, sweet,
To grim Necessity, and he and I
Will keep a league till death.
20

8 In winter's tedious nights sit by the fire
With good old folks, and let them tell thee tales
Of woeful ages, long ago betid;
And ere thou bid good night, to quit their grief,
Tell thou the lamentable tale of me,
And send the hearers weeping to their beds.
40

9 That were some love but little policy.
84

10 As in a theatre, the eyes of men,
After a well-grac'd actor leaves the stage,
Are idly bent on him that enters next,
Thinking his prattle to be tedious;
Even so, or with much more contempt, men's eyes
Did scowl on Richard.
ii.23

11   Who are the violets now
That strew the green lap of the new come spring?
46

12 He prays but faintly and would be denied.
iii.103

13 I have been studying how I may compare
This prison where I live unto the world.
v.1

14   How sour sweet music is,
When time is broke, and no proportion kept!
So is it in the music of men's lives.
42

15 I wasted time, and now doth time waste me.
49

16 Mount, mount, my soul! thy seat is up on high,
Whilst my gross flesh sinks downwards here to die.
112

RICHARD III

17 Now is the winter of our discontent
Made glorious summer by this sun of York.
I.i.1

18 Grim-visag'd war hath smooth'd his wrinkl'd front;
And now, instead of mounting barbed steeds,
To fright the souls of fearful adversaries,—
He capers nimbly in a lady's chamber
To the lascivious pleasing of a lute.
But I, that am not shap'd for sportive tricks,
Nor made to court an amorous looking-glass;
I, that am rudely stamp'd, and want love's majesty
To strut before a wanton ambling nymph;
I, that am curtail'd of this fair proportion,
Cheated of feature by dissembling nature,
Deform'd, unfinish'd, sent before my time
Into this breathing world, scarce half made up,
And that so lamely and unfashionable
That dogs bark at me, as I halt by them;
Why, I, in this weak piping time of peace,
Have no delight to pass away the time.
9

19 And therefore, since I cannot prove a lover,
To entertain these fair well-spoken days,
I am determined to prove a villain,
And hate the idle pleasures of these days.
28

20 No beast so fierce but knows some touch of pity.
ii.71

21 Teach not thy lip such scorn, for it was made
For kissing, lady, not for such contempt.
172

22 Was ever woman in this humour woo'd?
Was ever woman in this humour won?
229

23 Cannot a plain man live and think no harm,
But that his simple truth must be abus'd
By silken, sly, insinuating Jacks?
iii.51

24 Since every Jack became a gentleman
There's many a gentle person made a Jack.
72

25 And thus I clothe my naked villany
With odd old ends stol'n forth of holy writ,
And seem a saint when most I play the devil.
336

26 O, I have pass'd a miserable night,
So full of ugly sights, of ghastly dreams,
That, as I am a Christian faithful man,
I would not spend another such a night,
Though 'twere to buy a world of happy days,
So full of dismal terror was the time!
iv.2

27 Lord, Lord! methought what pain it was to drown:
What dreadful noise of water in mine ears!
What sights of ugly death within mine eyes!
Methought I saw a thousand fearful wracks;
A thousand men that fishes gnaw'd upon;
Wedges of gold, great anchors, heaps of pearl,
Inestimable stones, unvalu'd jewels,
All scatter'd in the bottom of the sea.
Some lay in dead men's skulls; and in those holes
Where eyes did once inhabit, there were crept
As 'twere in scorn of eyes, reflecting gems,
That woo'd the slimy bottom of the deep,
And mock'd the dead bones that lay scatter'd by.
21

1 Clarence is come,—false, fleeting, perjur'd Clarence.
55

2 Woe to the land that's govern'd by a child!
II.iii.11. See 56:3

3 So wise so young, they say, do never live long.
III.i.79

4 My Lord of Ely, when I was last in Holborn,
I saw good strawberries in your garden there.
iv.31

5 Talk'st thou to me of 'ifs'? Thou art a traitor:
Off with his head!
74

6 I am not in the giving vein to-day.
IV.ii.115

7 The sons of Edward sleep in Abraham's bosom.
iii.38

8 Thou cam'st on earth to make the earth my hell.
A grievous burden was thy birth to me;
Tetchy and wayward was thy infancy;
Thy school-days frightful, desperate, wild and furious;
Thy prime of manhood daring, bold, and venturous;
Thy age confirm'd, proud, subtle, sly, and bloody,
More mild, but yet more harmful, kind in hatred;
What comfortable hour canst thou name
That ever grac'd me in thy company?
iv.167

9 An honest tale speeds best being plainly told.
359

10 Harp not on that string.
365

11 True hope is swift, and flies with swallow's wings;
Kings it makes gods, and meaner creatures kings.
V.ii.23

12 The king's name is a tower of strength.
iii.12

13 Give me another horse! bind up my wounds!
Have mercy, Jesu! Soft! I did but dream.
O coward conscience, how dost thou afflict me!
178

14 My conscience hath a thousand several tongues,
And every tongue brings in a several tale,
And every tale condemns me for a villain.
194

15 I shall despair. There is no creature loves me;
And if I die, no soul will pity me:
Nay, wherefore should they, since that I myself
Find in myself no pity to myself?
201

16 By the apostle Paul, shadows to-night
Have struck more terror to the soul of Richard
Than can the substance of ten thousand soldiers.
217

17 Conscience is but a word that cowards use,
Devis'd at first to keep the strong in awe.
310

18 A horse! a horse! my kingdom for a horse!
iv.7

19 Slave! I have set my life upon a cast,
And I will stand the hazard of the die.
9

ROMEO AND JULIET

20 From forth the fatal loins of these two foes
A pair of star-cross'd lovers take their life.
Prologue

21 The fearful passage of their death-mark'd love,
And the continuance of their parents' rage,
Which, but their children's end, nought could remove,
Is now the two hours' traffick of our stage.

22 Do you bite your thumb at us, sir?
I.i.[50]

23 I do not bite my thumb at you, sir; but I bite my
thumb, sir.
[56]

24 She will not stay the siege of loving terms,
Nor bide the encounter of assailing eyes,
Nor ope her lap to saint-seducing gold.
[218]

25   'Tis not hard, I think,
For men so old as we to keep the peace.
ii.2

26 *Paris:* Younger than she are happy mothers made.
Capulet: And too soon marr'd are those so early made.
12

27 And then my husband—God be with his soul!
A' was a merry man—took up the child:
'Yea,' quoth he, 'dost thou fall upon thy face?
Thou wilt fall backward when thou hast more wit;
Wilt thou not, Jule?' and, by my halidom,
The pretty wretch left crying, and said 'Ay'...
Pretty fool, it stinted and said 'Ay.'
iii.39

28 O! then, I see, Queen Mab hath been with you...
She is the fairies' midwife, and she comes
In shape no bigger than an agate-stone
On the forefinger of an alderman,
Drawn with a team of little atomies
Athwart men's noses as they lie asleep:
Her waggon-spokes made of long spinners' legs;
The cover, of the wings of grasshoppers;
The traces, of the smallest spider's web;
The collars, of the moonshine's watery beams;
Her whip, of cricket's bone; the lash, of film;
Her waggoner, a small grey-coated gnat,
Not half so big as a round little worm
Prick'd from the lazy finger of a maid;
Her chariot is an empty hazel-nut,
Made by the joiner squirrel or old grub,
Time out o' mind the fairies' coach-makers.
And in this state she gallops night by night
Through lovers' brains, and then they dream of love;
O'er courtiers' knees, that dream on curtsies straight;
O'er lawyers' fingers, who straight dream on fees;
O'er ladies' lips, who straight on kisses dream;
Which oft the angry Mab with blisters plagues,
Because their breaths with sweetmeats tainted are.
Sometimes she gallops o'er a courtier's nose,
And then dreams he of smelling out a suit;
And sometimes comes she with a tithe-pig's tail,
Tickling a parson's nose as a' lies asleep,
Then dreams he of another benefice;
Sometimes she driveth o'er a soldier's neck,
And then dreams he of cutting foreign throats,
Of breaches, ambuscadoes, Spanish blades,
Of healths five fathom deep; and then anon

Drums in his ear, at which he starts and wakes;
And, being thus frighted, swears a prayer or two,
And sleeps again. This is that very Mab
That plats the manes of horses in the night;
And bakes the elf-locks in foul sluttish hairs,
Which once untangled much misfortune bodes;
This is the hag, when maids lie on their backs,
That presses them and learns them first to bear,
Making them women of good carriage.
iv.53

1   You and I are past our dancing days.
v.[35]

2   O! she doth teach the torches to burn bright.
It seems she hangs upon the cheek of night
Like a rich jewel in an Ethiop's ear;
Beauty too rich for use, for earth too dear.
[48]

3   Gentlemen, prepare not to be gone;
We have a trifling foolish banquet towards.
[125]

4   My only love sprung from my only hate!
Too early seen unknown, and known too late!
[142]

5   He jests at scars, that never felt a wound.
But, soft! what light through yonder window breaks?
It is the east, and Juliet is the sun.
II.ii.1

6   It is my lady; O! it is my love:
O! that she knew she were.
10

7   See! how she leans her cheek upon her hand:
O! that I were a glove upon that hand,
That I might touch that cheek.
23

8   O Romeo, Romeo! wherefore art thou Romeo?
Deny thy father, and refuse thy name;
Or, if thou wilt not, be but sworn my love,
And I'll no longer be a Capulet.
33

9   What's in a name? that which we call a rose
By any other name would smell as sweet.
43

10 With love's light wings did I o'er-perch these walls;
For stony limits cannot hold love out,
And what love can do that dares love attempt.
66

11 Thou know'st the mask of night is on my face,
Else would a maiden blush bepaint my cheek
For that which thou hast heard me speak tonight.
85

12 Fain would I dwell on form, fain, fain deny
What I have spoke: but farewell compliment!
88

13   At lovers' perjuries,
They say, Jove laughs. O gentle Romeo!
If thou dost love, pronounce it faithfully:
Or if thou think'st I am too quickly won,
I'll frown and be perverse and say thee nay,
So thou wilt woo; but else, not for the world.
In truth, fair Montague, I am too fond.
92. See 366:11

14   I'll prove more true

Than those that have more cunning to be strange.
100

15 *Romeo:* Lady, by yonder blessed moon I swear
That tips with silver all these fruit-tree tops,—
Juliet: O! swear not by the moon, the inconstant
moon,
That monthly changes in her circled orb,
Lest that thy love prove likewise variable.
Romeo: What shall I swear by?
Juliet: Do not swear at all;
Or, if thou wilt, swear by thy gracious self,
Which is the god of my idolatry.
107

16 It is too rash, too unadvis'd, too sudden;
Too like the lightning, which doth cease to be
Ere one can say it lightens. Sweet, good-night!
This bud of love, by summer's ripening breath,
May prove a beauteous flower when next we meet.
118

17 My bounty is as boundless as the sea,
My love as deep; the more I give to thee,
The more I have, for both are infinite.
133

18 Love goes toward love, as schoolboys from their
books;
But love from love, toward school with heavy looks.
156

19 *Juliet:* O! for a falconer's voice,
To lure this tassel-gentle back again.
Bondage is hoarse, and may not speak aloud,
Else would I tear the cave where Echo lies,
And make her airy tongue more hoarse than mine,
With repetition of my Romeo's name.
Romeo: It is my soul that calls upon my name:
How silver-sweet sound lovers' tongues by night,
Like softest music to attending ears!
158

20 *Juliet:* 'Tis almost morning; I would have thee gone;
And yet no further than a wanton's bird,
Who lets it hop a little from her hand,
Like a poor prisoner in his twisted gyves,
And with a silk thread plucks it back again,
So loving-jealous of his liberty.
Romeo: I would I were thy bird.
Juliet: Sweet, so would I:
Yet I should kill thee with much cherishing.
Good-night, good-night! parting is such sweet sorrow
That I shall say good-night till it be morrow.
Romeo: Sleep dwell upon thine eyes, peace in thy
breast!
Would I were sleep and peace, so sweet to rest!
176

21 One, two, and the third in your bosom.
iv.[24]

22 O flesh, flesh, how art thou fishified!
[41]

23 I am the very pink of courtesy.
[63]

24 A gentleman, nurse, that loves to hear himself talk,
and will speak more in a minute than he will stand to
in a month.
[156]

25   O! so light a foot

Will ne'er wear out the everlasting flint.
vi.16

1 Thy head is as full of quarrels as an egg is full of
meat.
III.i.[23]

2 Men's eyes were made to look, and let them gaze;
I will not budge for no man's pleasure, I.
[59]

3 No, 'tis not so deep as a well, nor so wide as a church
door; but 'tis enough, 'twill serve.
[100]

4   A plague o' both your houses!
They have made worms' meat of me.
[112]

5 O! I am Fortune's fool.
[142]

6 Gallop apace, you fiery-footed steeds,
Towards Phoebus' lodging; such a waggoner
As Phaethon would whip you to the west,
And bring in cloudy night immediately.
Spread thy close curtain, love-performing night!
That runaway's eyes may wink, and Romeo
Leap to these arms, untalk'd of and unseen!
Lovers can see to do their amorous rites
By their own beauties; or, if love be blind,
It best agrees with night. Come, civil night,
Thou sober-suited matron, all in black.
ii.1

7 Come, night! come, Romeo! come, thou day in night!
For thou wilt lie upon the wings of night,
Whiter than new snow on a raven's back.
Come, gentle night; come, loving, black-brow'd
night,
Give me my Romeo: and, when he shall die,
Take him and cut him out in little stars,
And he will make the face of heaven so fine
That all the world will be in love with night,
And pay no worship to the garish sun.
17

8   He was not born to shame:
Upon his brow shame is ashamed to sit.
91

9 Romeo, come forth; come forth, thou fearful man:
Affliction is enamour'd of thy parts,
And thou art wedded to calamity.
iii.1

10 Thou cutt'st my head off with a golden axe,
And smil'st upon the stroke that murders me.
22

11 Adversity's sweet milk, philosophy.
54

12   Hang up philosophy!
Unless philosophy can make a Juliet.
56

13 Wilt thou be gone? it is not yet near day:
It was the nightingale, and not the lark,
That pierc'd the fearful hollow of thine ear;
Nightly she sings on yon pomegranate tree:
Believe me, love, it was the nightingale.
v.1

14 Night's candles are burnt out, and jocund day
Stands tiptoe on the misty mountain tops.
9

15 I have more care to stay than will to go.
23

16 Villain and he be many miles asunder.
82

17 Thank me no thankings, nor proud me no prouds.
153

18 Is there no pity sitting in the clouds,
That sees into the bottom of my grief?
198

19 Romeo's a dishclout to him.
221

20 Sirrah, go hire me twenty cunning cooks.
IV.ii.2

21 Farewell! God knows when we shall meet again.
I have a faint cold fear thrills through my veins,
That almost freezes up the heat of life.
iii.14

22   Out, alas! she's cold;
Her blood is settled, and her joints are stiff;
Life and these lips have long been separated:
Death lies on her like an untimely frost
Upon the sweetest flower of all the field.
v.25

23 My bosom's lord sits lightly on his throne;
And all this day an unaccustom'd spirit
Lifts me above the ground with cheerful thoughts.
V.i.3

24 Is it even so? then I defy you, stars.
24

25 Being holiday, the beggar's shop is shut.
56

26 *Romeo:* The world is not thy friend nor the world's
law:
The world affords no law to make thee rich;
Then be not poor, but break it, and take this.
Apothecary: My poverty, but not my will, consents.
Romeo: I pay thy poverty, and not thy will.
72

27 Tempt not a desperate man.
iii.59

28 One writ with me in sour misfortune's book.
82

29 How oft when men are at the point of death
Have they been merry! which their keepers call
A lightning before death.
88

30   Beauty's ensign yet
Is crimson in thy lips and in thy cheeks,
And death's pale flag is not advanced there.
94

31   Shall I believe
That unsubstantial Death is amorous,
And that the lean abhorred monster keeps
Thee here in dark to be his paramour?
For fear of that I still will stay with thee,
And never from this palace of dim night
Depart again: here, here will I remain
With worms that are thy chambermaids; O! here
Will I set up my everlasting rest,
And shake the yoke of inauspicious stars
From this world-wearied flesh. Eyes, look your last!
Arms, take your last embrace! and, lips, O you
The doors of breath, seal with a righteous kiss

A dateless bargain to engrossing death!
102

1 Seal up the mouth of outrage for a while,
Till we can clear these ambiguities.
216

THE TAMING OF THE SHREW

2 Look in the chronicles; we came in with Richard
Conqueror.
Induction i.[4]

3 As Stephen Sly, and old John Naps of Greece,
And Peter Turf, and Henry Pimpernell,
And twenty more such names and men as these,
Which never were nor no man ever saw.
ii.[95]

4 No profit grows where is no pleasure ta'en;
In brief, sir, study what you most affect.
I.i.39

5 Nothing comes amiss, so money comes withal.
ii.[82]

6 O! this learning, what a thing it is.
[163]

7 She is your treasure, she must have a husband;
I must dance bare-foot on her wedding day,
And, for your love to her, lead apes in hell.
II.i.32

8 Say that she rail; why then I'll tell her plain
She sings as sweetly as a nightingale:
Say that she frown; I'll say she looks as clear
As morning roses newly wash'd with dew:
Say she be mute and will not speak a word;
Then I'll commend her volubility,
And say she uttereth piercing eloquence.
171

9   You are call'd plain Kate,
And bonny Kate, and sometimes Kate the curst;
But, Kate, the prettiest Kate in Christendom;
Kate of Kate-Hall, my super-dainty Kate,
For dainties are all cates: and therefore, Kate,
Take this of me, Kate of my consolation.
186

10 Kiss me Kate, we will be married o' Sunday.
318

11   She shall watch all night:
And if she chance to nod I'll rail and brawl,
And with the clamour keep her still awake.
This is the way to kill a wife with kindness.
IV.i.[208]

12 What say you to a piece of beef and mustard?
iii.[23]

13 *Petruchio:* It shall be what o'clock I say it is.
Hortensio: Why, so this gallant will command the sun.
[197]

14   O vile,
Intolerable, not to be endur'd!
V.ii.93

15 Fie, fie! unknit that threatening unkind brow,
And dart not scornful glances from those eyes,
To wound thy lord, thy king, thy governor.
137

16 A woman mov'd is like a fountain troubled,

Muddy, ill-seeming, thick, bereft of beauty.
143

17 Thy husband is thy lord, thy life, thy keeper,
Thy head, thy sovereign; one that cares for thee,
And for thy maintenance commits his body
To painful labour both by sea and land.
147

18 Such duty as the subject owes the prince,
Even such a woman oweth to her husband.
156

19 I am asham'd that women are so simple
To offer war where they should kneel for peace.
162

THE TEMPEST

20 What cares these roarers for the name of king?
I.i.[18]

21 He hath no drowning mark upon him; his complexion
is perfect gallows.
[33]

22 Now would I give a thousand furlongs of sea for an
acre of barren ground; long heath, brown furze, any
thing. The wills above be done! but I would fain die a
dry death.
[70]

23   O! I have suffer'd
With those that I saw suffer: a brave vessel,
Who had, no doubt, some noble creatures in her,
Dash'd all to pieces. O! the cry did knock
Against my very heart. Poor souls, they perish'd.
ii.5

24   What seest thou else
In the dark backward and abysm of time?
49

25 Your tale, sir, would cure deafness.
106

26   My library
Was dukedom large enough.
109

27 The still-vexed Bermoothes.
229

28 For this, be sure, tonight thou shalt have cramps.
325

29 You taught me language; and my profit on't
Is, I know how to curse: the red plague rid you,
For learning me your language!
363

30 Come unto these yellow sands,
     And then take hands:
Curtsied when you have, and kiss'd,—
     The wild waves whist,—
Foot it featly here and there;
And, sweet sprites, the burden bear.
375

31 This music crept by me upon the waters,
Allaying both their fury, and my passion,
With its sweet air.
389

32 Full fathom five thy father lies;
     Of his bones are coral made:
Those are pearls that were his eyes:
     Nothing of him that doth fade,

But doth suffer a sea-change
Into something rich and strange.
Sea-nymphs hourly ring his knell:
              Ding-dong.
Hark! now I hear them,—ding-dong, bell.
394

1 The fringed curtains of thine eye advance,
And say what thou seest yond.
405

2   At the first sight
They have changed eyes.
437

3 He receives comfort like cold porridge.
II.1.10

4 Look, he's winding up the watch of his wit, by and by
it will strike.
[12]

5 What's past is prologue.
[261]

6 They'll take suggestion as a cat laps milk.
[296]

7 A very ancient and fish-like smell.
ii.[27]

8 When they will not give a doit to relieve a lame
beggar, they will lay out ten to see a dead Indian.
[33]

9 Misery acquaints a man with strange bedfellows.
[42]

10 Well, here's my comfort. [*Drinks.*]
The master, the swabber, the boatswain and I,
    The gunner and his mate,
Lov'd Mall, Meg, and Marian and Margery,
    But none of us car'd for Kate;
    For she had a tongue with a tang,
    Would cry to a sailor, 'Go hang!'
[48]

11 'Ban, 'Ban, Ca-Caliban,
Has a new master—Get a new man.
[197]

12 *Ferdinand:* Wherefore weep you?
Miranda: At mine unworthiness, that dare not offer
What I desire to give; and much less take
What I shall die to want.
III.i.76

13 *Miranda:* I am your wife, if you will marry me;
If not, I'll die your maid: to be your fellow
You may deny me; but I'll be your servant
Whether you will or no.
Ferdinand: My mistress, dearest;
And thus I humble ever.
Miranda: My husband then?
Ferdinand: Ay, with a heart as willing
As bondage e'er of freedom: here's my hand.
Miranda: And mine, with my heart in't.
83

14 Thou deboshed fish thou.
ii.[30]

15 Flout 'em, and scout 'em; and scout 'em, and flout
'em;
Thought is free.
[133]

16 He that dies pays all debts.
[143]

17 Be not afeard: the isle is full of noises,
Sounds and sweet airs, that give delight, and hurt not.
[147]

18   In dreaming,
The clouds methought would open and show riches
Ready to drop upon me; that, when I wak'd
I cried to dream again.
[152]

19 Thy banks with pioned and twilled brims,
Which spongy April at thy hest betrims,
To make cold nymphs chaste crowns.
IV.i.64

20 Our revels now are ended. These our actors,
As I foretold you, were all spirits and
Are melted into air, into thin air:
And, like the baseless fabric of this vision,
The cloud-capp'd towers, the gorgeous palaces,
The solemn temples, the great globe itself,
Yea, all which it inherit, shall dissolve
And, like this insubstantial pageant faded,
Leave not a rack behind. We are such stuff
As dreams are made on, and our little life
Is rounded with a sleep.
148

21 I do begin to have bloody thoughts.
[221]

22   We shall lose our time,
And all be turn'd to barnacles, or to apes
With foreheads villanous low.
[250]

23 Ye elves of hills, brooks, standing lakes, and groves;
And ye, that on the sands with printless foot
Do chase the ebbing Neptune and do fly him
When he comes back; you demi-puppets, that
By moonshine do the green sour ringlets make
Whereof the ewe not bites.
V.i.33

24   This rough magic
I here abjure...
         I'll break my staff,
Bury it certain fathoms in the earth,
And, deeper than did ever plummet sound,
I'll drown my book.
50

25 Where the bee sucks, there suck I
In a cowslip's bell I lie;
There I couch when owls do cry.
On the bat's back I do fly
After summer merrily:
Merrily, merrily shall I live now
Under the blossom that hangs on the bough.
88

26 How may goodly creatures are there here!
How beauteous mankind is! O brave new world,
That has such people in't.
182

TIMON OF ATHENS

27 'Tis not enough to help the feeble up,
But to support him after.
I.i.108

28 He that loves to be flattered is worthy o' the flatterer.
[233]

1   The strain of man's bred out
Into baboon and monkey.
[260]

2 I wonder men dare trust themselves with men.
ii.[45]

3 Immortal gods, I crave no pelf;
I pray for no man but myself.
[64]

4 Like madness is the glory of this life.
[141]

5 Men shut their doors against a setting sun.
[152]

6 Nothing emboldens sin so much as mercy.
III.v.3

7 Uncover, dogs, and lap.
vi.[96]

8 You fools of fortune, trencher-friends, time's flies.
[107]

9 We have seen better days.
IV.ii.27

10 O! the fierce wretchedness that glory brings us.
30

11 He has almost charmed me from my profession, by
persuading me to it.
iii.[457]

12   My long sickness
Of health and living now begins to mend,
And nothing brings me all things.
V.i.[191]

13   Tell them, that, to ease them of their griefs,
Their fears of hostile strokes, their aches, losses,
Their pangs of love, with other incident throes
That nature's fragile vessel doth sustain
In life's uncertain voyage, I will some kindness do
     them.
[203]

14 Timon hath made his everlasting mansion
Upon the beached verge of the salt flood;
Who once a day with his embossed froth
The turbulent surge shall cover.
[220]

TITUS ANDRONICUS

15 She is a woman, therefore may be woo'd;
She is a woman, therefore may be won;
She is Lavinia, therefore must be lov'd.
What, man! more water glideth by the mill
Than wots the miller of; and easy it is
Of a cut loaf to steal a shive, we know.
II.i.82. See 446:1

16 Come, and take choice of all my library,
And so beguile thy sorrow.
IV.i.34

17 The eagle suffers little birds to sing,
And is not careful what they mean thereby.
iv.[82]

18 If one good deed in all my life I did,
I do repent it from my very soul.
V.iii.[189]

TROILUS AND CRESSIDA

19   O! that her hand,

In whose comparison all whites are ink,
Writing their own reproach; to whose soft seizure
The cygnet's down is harsh, and spirit of sense
Hard as the palm of ploughman.
I.i.[57]

20 I have had my labour for my travail.
[73]

21   Women are angels, wooing:
Things won are done; joy's soul lies in the doing;
That she belov'd knows nought that knows not this:
Men prize the thing ungain'd more than it is.
ii.[310]

22 The heavens themselves, the planets, and this centre
Observe degree, priority, and place,
Insisture, course, proportion, season, form,
Office, and custom, in all line of order.
iii.85

23   O! when degree is shak'd,
Which is the ladder to all high designs,
The enterprise is sick.
101

24 Take but degree away, untune that string,
And, hark! what discord follows; each thing meets
In mere oppugnancy.
109

25   The general's disdain'd
By him one step below, he by the next,
That next by him beneath; so every step,
Exampled by the first pace that is sick
Of his superior, grows to an envious fever
Of pale and bloodless emulation.
129

26   We are soldiers;
And may that soldier a mere recreant prove,
That means not, hath not, or is not in love!
286

27 And in such indexes, although small pricks
To their subsequent volumes, there is seen
The baby figure of the giant mass
Of things to come at large.
343

28 The plague of Greece upon thee, thou mongrel
beef-witted lord!
II.i.[13]

29 Achilles...who wears his wit in his belly, and his guts
in his head, I'll tell you what I say of him.
[78]

30   You have both said well;
And on the cause and question now in hand
Have gloz'd but superficially; not much
Unlike young men, whom Aristotle thought
Unfit to hear moral philosophy.
ii.163

31   Thus to persist
In doing wrong extenuates not wrong,
But makes it much more heavy.
186

32 I am giddy, expectation whirls me round.
The imaginary relish is so sweet
That it enchants my sense.
III.ii.[17]

33 This is the monstruosity in love, lady, that the will is
infinite, and the execution confined; that the desire is

boundless, and the act a slave to limit.
[85]

1   To be wise, and love,
Exceeds man's might.
[163]

2 I am as true as truth's simplicity,
And simpler than the infancy of truth.
[176]

3 Time hath, my lord, a wallet at his back,
Wherein he puts alms for oblivion,
A great-siz'd monster of ingratitudes:
Those scraps are good deeds past; which are devour'd
As fast as they are made, forgot as soon
As done.
iii.145

4   Perseverance, dear my lord,
Keeps honour bright: to have done, is to hang
Quite out of fashion, like a rusty mail
In monumental mockery.
150

5   Time is like a fashionable host
That slightly shakes his parting guest by the hand,
And with his arms outstretch'd, as he would fly,
Grasps in the comer: welcome ever smiles,
And farewell goes out sighing.
165

6   Beauty, wit,
High birth, vigour of bone, desert in service,
Love, friendship, charity, are subjects all
To envious and calumniating time.
One touch of nature makes the whole world kin,
That all with one consent praise new-born gawds,
Though they are made and moulded of things past,
And give to dust that is a little gilt
More laud than gilt o'er-dusted.
171

7 A plague of opinion! a man may wear it on both sides,
like a leather jerkin.
[267]

8 How my achievements mock me!
IV.ii.[72]

9 You smile, and mock me, as if I meant naughtily.
iii.38

10 My love admits no qualifying dross.
iv.9

11 What a pair of spectacles is here!
[Pandarus, of the lovers] [13]

12 We two, that with so many thousand sighs
Did buy each other, must poorly sell ourselves
With the rude brevity and discharge of one.
Injurious time now with a robber's haste
Crams his rich thievery up, he knows not how:
As many farewells as be stars in heaven,
With distinct breath and consign'd kisses to them,
He fumbles up into a loose adieu,
And scants us with a single famish'd kiss,
Distasted with the salt of broken tears.
[39]

13   Fie, fie upon her!
There's language in her eye, her cheek, her lip,
Nay, her foot speaks; her wanton spirits look out
At every joint and motive of her body.
v.54

14 What's past, and what's to come is strew'd with husks
And formless ruin of oblivion.
165

15   The end crowns all,
And that old common arbitrator, Time,
Will one day end it.
223

16 Lechery, lechery; still, wars and lechery: nothing else
holds fashion.
V.ii.192

17 Words, words, mere words, no matter from the heart.
iii.[109]

18 Hector is dead; there is no more to say.
x.22

19 O world! world! world! thus is the poor agent
despised. O traitors and bawds, how earnestly are you
set a-work, and how ill requited! why should our
endeavour be so loved, and the performance so
loathed?
[36]

TWELFTH NIGHT

20 If music be the food of love, play on;
Give me excess of it, that, surfeiting,
The appetite may sicken, and so die.
That strain again! it had a dying fall:
O! it came o'er my ear like the sweet sound
That breathes upon a bank of violets,
Stealing and giving odour! Enough! no more:
'Tis not so sweet now as it was before.
O spirit of love! how quick and fresh art thou,
That notwithstanding thy capacity
Receiveth as the sea, nought enters there,
Of what validity and pitch soe'er,
But falls into abatement and low price,
Even in a minute: so full of shapes is fancy,
That it alone is high fantastical.
I.i.1

21 O! when mine eyes did see Olivia first,
Methought she purg'd the air of pestilence.
That instant was I turn'd into a hart,
And my desires, like fell and cruel hounds,
E'er since pursue me.
19

22 And what should I do in Illyria?
My brother he is in Elysium.
ii.2

23 He's as tall a man as any's in Illyria.
iii.[21]

24 He plays o' the viol-de-gamboys, and speaks three or
four languages word for word without book, and hath
all the good gifts of nature.
[27]

25 Methinks sometimes I have no more wit than a
Christian or an ordinary man has; but I am a great
eater of beef, and I believe that does harm to my wit.
[90]

26 *Sir Andrew:* I would I had bestowed that time in the
tongues that I have in fencing, dancing, and
bear-baiting. O! had I but followed the arts!
Sir Toby: Then hadst thou had an excellent head of
hair.
[99]

1 Wherefore are these things hid? wherefore have these
gifts a curtain before 'em? are they like to take dust,
like Mistress Mall's picture? why dost thou not go to
church in a galliard, and come home in a coranto? My
very walk should be a jig.
[135]

2 Is it a world to hide virtues in?
[142]

3   They shall yet belie thy happy years
That say thou art a man: Diana's lip
Is not more smooth and rubious; thy small pipe
Is as the maiden's organ, shrill and sound;
And all is semblative a woman's part.
iv.30

4 Many a good hanging prevents a bad marriage.
v.[20]

5 What says Quinapalus? 'Better a witty fool than a
foolish wit.'
[37]

6 Virtue that transgresses is but patched with sin; and sin
that amends is but patched with virtue.
[52]

7 Good my mouse of virtue, answer me.
[68]

8 A plague o' these pickle herring!
[127]

9 Not yet old enough for a man, nor young enough for a
boy; as a squash is before 'tis a peascod, or a codling
when 'tis almost an apple: 'tis with him in standing
water, between boy and man. He is very
well-favoured, and he speaks very shrewishly: one
would think his mother's milk were scarce out of him.
[166]

10 I would be loath to cast away my speech, for besides
that it is excellently well penned, I have taken great
pains to con it.
[184]

11 I can say little more than I have studied, and that
question's out of my part.
[191]

12 *Olivia:* 'Tis in grain, sir; 'twill endure wind and
  weather.
Viola: 'Tis beauty truly blent, whose red and white
Nature's own sweet and cunning hand laid on:
Lady, you are the cruell'st she alive
If you will lead these graces to the grave
And leave the world no copy.
Olivia: O! sir I will not be so hard-hearted; I will give
  out divers schedules of my beauty: it shall be
  inventoried, and every particle and utensil labelled
  to my will: as *Item*, Two lips, indifferent red; *Item*,
  Two grey eyes with lids to them; *Item*, One neck,
  one chin, and so forth.
[257]

13 Make me a willow cabin at your gate,
And call upon my soul within the house;
Write loyal cantons of contemned love,
And sing them loud even in the dead of night;
Halloo your name to the reverberate hills,
And make the babbling gossip of the air
Cry out, 'Olivia!' O! you should not rest
Between the elements of air and earth,

But you should pity me!
[289]

14   'What is your parentage?'
'Above my fortune, yet my state is well:
I am a gentleman.'
[310]

15 She is drowned already, sir, with salt water, though I
seem to drown her remembrance again with more.
II.i.[31]

16 Not to be a-bed after midnight is to be up betimes.
iii.1

17 O mistress mine! where are you roaming?
O! stay and hear; your true love's coming,
  That can sing both high and low.
Trip no further, pretty sweeting;
Journeys end in lovers meeting,
  Every wise man's son doth know...

What is love? 'tis not hereafter;
Present mirth hath present laughter;
  What's to come is still unsure:
In delay there lies no plenty;
Then come kiss me, sweet and twenty,
  Youth's a stuff will not endure.
[42]

18 Am not I consanguineous? am I not of her blood?
Tillyvally, lady.
[85]

19 He does it with a better grace, but I do it more natural.
[91]

20 Is there no respect of place, persons, nor time, in you?
[100]

21 Dost thou think, because thou art virtuous, there shall
be no more cakes and ale?
[124]

22 *Maria:* Marry, sir, sometimes he is a kind of puritan.
Sir Andrew: O, if I thought that, I'd beat him like a
dog!
[153]

23 I will drop in his way some obscure epistles of love;
wherein by the colour of his beard, the shape of his
leg, the manner of his gait, the expressure of his eye,
forehead, and complexion, he shall find himself most
feelingly personated.
[171]

24 I was adored once too.
[200]

25 My purpose is, indeed, a horse of that colour.
[184]

26 Now, good Cesario, but that piece of song,
That old and antique song we heard last night;
Methought it did relieve my passion much,
More than light airs and recollected terms
Of these most brisk and giddy-paced times:
Come, but one verse.
iv.2

27 *Duke:* If ever thou shalt love,
In the sweet pangs of it remember me;
For such as I am all true lovers are:
Unstaid and skittish in all motions else,
Save in the constant image of the creature
That is belov'd. How dost thou like this tune?
Viola: It gives a very echo to the seat

Where love is enthron'd.
15

1   Let still the woman take
An elder than herself, so wears she to him,
So sways she level in her husband's heart:
For, boy, however we do praise ourselves,
Our fancies are more giddy and unfirm,
More longing, wavering, sooner lost and worn,
Than women's are.
29

2 Then let thy love be younger than thyself,
Or thy affection cannot hold the bent.
36

3 Mark it, Cesario; it is old and plain.
The spinsters and the knitters in the sun
And the free maids that weave their thread with bones
Do use to chant it: it is silly sooth,
And dallies with the innocence of love,
Like the old age.
43

4 Come away, come away, death,
    And in sad cypress let me be laid;
Fly away, fly away, breath:
    I am slain by a fair cruel maid.
My shroud of white, stuck all with yew,
    O! prepare it.
My part of death no one so true
    Did share it.
51

5 Now, the melancholy god protect thee, and the tailor
make thy doublet of changeable taffeta, for thy mind is
a very opal.
[74]

6   There is no woman's sides
Can bide the beating of so strong a passion
As love doth give my heart; no woman's heart
So big, to hold so much; they lack retention.
Alas! their love may be call'd appetite,
No motion of the liver, but the palate,
That suffer surfeit, cloyment, and revolt;
But mine is all as hungry as the sea,
And can digest so much.
[95]

7 *Viola:* My father had a daughter lov'd a man,
As it might be, perhaps, were I a woman,
I should your lordship.
Duke: And what's her history?
Viola: A blank, my lord. She never told her love,
But let concealment, like a worm i' the bud,
Feed on her damask cheek: she pin'd in thought;
And with a green and yellow melancholy,
She sat like patience on a monument,
Smiling at grief. Was not this love indeed?
We men may say more, swear more; but, indeed,
Our shows are more than will; for still we prove
Much in our vows, but little in our love.
[108]

8 I am all the daughters of my father's house,
And all the brothers too.
[122]

9 How now, my metal of India!
v.[17]

10 Here comes the trout that must be caught with

tickling.
[25]

11 Contemplation makes a rare turkey-cock of him: how
he jets under his advanced plumes!
[35]

12 Now is the woodcock near the gin.
[93]

13 I may command where I adore.
[117]

14 But be not afraid of greatness: some men are born
great, some achieve greatness, and some have
greatness thrust upon them.
[158]

15 Let thy tongue tang arguments of state; put thyself into
the trick of singularity. She thus advises thee that sighs
for thee. Remember who commended thy yellow
stockings, and wished to see thee ever cross-gartered.
[165]

16 Jove and my stars be praised! Here is yet a postscript.
[190]

17 He will come to her in yellow stockings, and 'tis a
colour she abhors; and cross-gartered, a fashion she
detests.
[220]

18 Now Jove, in his next commodity of hair, send thee a
beard.
III.i.[51]

19 This fellow's wise enough to play the fool,
And to do that well craves a kind of wit.
[68]

20 Taste your legs, sir; put them to motion.
[88]

21 Most excellent accomplished lady, the heavens rain
odours on you!
[96]

22   'Twas never merry world
Since lowly feigning was called compliment.
[110]

23 O world! how apt the poor are to be proud.
[141]

24 O! what a deal of scorn looks beautiful
In the contempt and anger of his lip.
[159]

25 Love sought is good, but giv'n unsought is better.
[170]

26 They have been grand-jurymen since before Noah was
a sailor.
ii.[18]

27 You should then have accosted her, and with some
excellent jests, fire-new from the mint, you should
have banged the youth into dumbness.
[23]

28 You are now sailed into the north of my lady's
opinion; where you will hang like an icicle on a
Dutchman's beard.
[29]

29 I had as lief be a Brownist as a politician.
[35]

30 As many lies as will lie in thy sheet of paper, although
the sheet were big enough for the bed of Ware in
England, set 'em down.
[51]

1 If he were opened, and you find so much blood in his liver as will clog the foot of a flea, I'll eat the rest of the anatomy.
[68]

2 Look, where the youngest wren of nine comes.
[73]

3 He does smile his face into more lines than are in the new map with the augmentation of the Indies.
[85]

4 In the south suburbs, at the Elephant,
Is best to lodge.
iii.39

5 I think we do know the sweet Roman hand.
iv.[31]

6 Why, this is very midsummer madness.
[62]

7 What, man! defy the devil: consider, he's an enemy to mankind.
[109]

8 Go, hang yourselves all! you are idle shallow things: I am not of your element.
[138]

9 If this were played upon a stage now, I could condemn it as an improbable fiction.
[142]

10 More matter for a May morning.
[158]

11 Still you keep o' the windy side of the law.
[183]

12 Fare thee well; and God have mercy upon one of our souls! He may have mercy upon mine, but my hope is better; and so look to thyself.
[185]

13 Nay, let me alone for swearing.
[204]

14 He is knight dubbed with unhatched rapier, and on carpet consideration.
[260]

15 I am one that had rather go with sir priest than sir knight; I care not who knows so much of my mettle.
[300]

16 Out of my lean and low ability
I'll lend you something.
[380]

17 I hate ingratitude more in a man
Than lying, vainness, babbling drunkenness,
Or any taint of vice whose strong corruption
Inhabits our frail blood.
[390]

18 In nature there's no blemish but the mind;
None can be call'd deform'd but the unkind.
[403]

19 Out, hyperbolical fiend!
IV.ii.[29]

20 For I am one of those gentle ones that will use the devil himself with courtesy.
[37]

21 *Clown:* What is the opinion of Pythagoras concerning wild fowl?
Malvolio: That the soul of our grandam might haply inhabit a bird.
Clown: What thinkest thou of his opinion?

Malvolio: I think nobly of the soul, and no way approve his opinion.
[55]

22 Leave thy vain bibble-babble.
[106]

23 We took him for a coward, but he's the very devil incardinate.
V.i.[185]

24 Why have you suffer'd me to be imprison'd,
Kept in a dark house, visited by the priest,
And made the most notorious geck and gull
That e'er invention played on? Tell me why.
[353]

25 Thus the whirligig of time brings in his revenges.
[388]

26 I'll be revenged on the whole pack of you.
[390]

27 When that I was and a little tiny boy,
   With hey, ho, the wind and the rain;
A foolish thing was but a toy,
   For the rain it raineth every day.

But when I came to man's estate,
   With hey, ho, the wind and the rain;
'Gainst knaves and thieves men shut their gates,
   For the rain it raineth every day.

But when I came, alas! to wive,
   With hey, ho, the wind and the rain;
By swaggering could I never thrive,
   For the rain it raineth every day.

But when I came unto my beds,
   With hey, ho, the wind and the rain;
With toss-pots still had drunken heads,
   For the rain it raineth every day.

A great while ago the world begun,
   With hey, ho, the wind and the rain;
But that's all one, our play is done,
   And we'll strive to please you every day.
[401]

THE TWO GENTLEMEN OF VERONA

28 Home-keeping youth have ever homely wits.
I.i.2

29 He was more than over shoes in love.
24

30 I have no other but a woman's reason:
I think him so, because I think him so.
ii.23

31 Fie, fie! how wayward is this foolish love
That, like a testy babe, will scratch the nurse
And presently all humbled kiss the rod!
55

32 Poor wounded name! my bosom, as a bed
Shall lodge thee till thy wound be throughly heal'd.
111

33 O! how this spring of love resembleth
   The uncertain glory of an April day,
Which now shows all the beauty of the sun,
   And by and by a cloud takes all away!
iii.84

34 Or as one nail by strength drives out another,
So the remembrance of my former love

Is by a newer object quite forgotten.
II.iv.194

1 Except I be by Silvia in the night,
There is no music in the nightingale;
Unless I look on Silvia in the day,
There is no day for me to look upon.
III.i.178

2 Much is the force of heaven-bred poesy.
ii.71

3 A man I am cross'd with adversity.
IV.i.12

4 Who is Sylvia? what is she,
    That all our swains commend her?
Holy, fair, and wise is she;
    The heaven such grace did lend her,
That she might admired be.

Is she kind as she is fair?
    For beauty lives with kindness:
Love doth to her eyes repair,
    To help him of his blindness;
And, being help'd, inhabits there.

Then to Silvia let us sing,
    That Silvia is excelling;
She excels each mortal thing
    Upon the dull earth dwelling;
To her let us garlands bring.
ii.40

5 How use doth breed a habit in man!
V.iv.1

6   O heaven! were man
But constant, he were perfect.
110

THE WINTER'S TALE

7   We were, fair queen,
Two lads that thought there was no more behind
But such a day to-morrow as to-day,
And to be boy eternal.
I.ii.62

8 We were as twinn'd lambs that did frisk i' the sun,
And bleat the one at the other: what we chang'd
Was innocence for innocence; we knew not
The doctrine of ill-doing, no, nor dream'd
That any did.
67

9 But to be paddling palms and pinching fingers,
As now they are, and making practis'd smiles,
As in a looking-glass.
116

10 How like, methought, I then was to this kernel,
This squash, this gentleman.
160

11 Make that thy question, and go rot!
324

12   A sad tale's best for winter.
I have one of sprites and goblins.
II.i.24

13 It is a heretic that makes the fire,
Not she which burns in 't.
iii.114

14 I am a feather for each wind that blows.
153

15   What's gone and what's past help
Should be past grief.
III.ii.[223]

16 *Exit, pursued by a bear*. iii. Stage Direction.

17 When daffodils begin to peer,
    With heigh! the doxy, over the dale,
Why, then comes in the sweet o' the year;
    For the red blood reigns in the winter's pale.

The white sheet bleaching on the hedge,
    With heigh! the sweet birds, O, how they sing!
Doth set my pugging tooth on edge;
    For a quart of ale is a dish for a king.

The lark, that tirra-lirra chants,
    With, heigh! with, heigh! the thrush and the jay,
Are summer songs for me and my aunts,
    While we lie tumbling in the hay.
IV.ii.1

18 My father named me Autolycus; who being, as I am,
littered under Mercury, was likewise a snapper-up of
unconsidered trifles.
[24]

19 For the life to come, I sleep out the thought of it.
[30]

20 Prig, for my life, prig; he haunts wakes, fairs, and
bear-baitings.
[109]

21 Jog on, jog on the foot-path way,
    And merrily hent the stile-a:
A merry heart goes all the day,
    Your sad tires in a mile-a.
[133]

22 For you there's rosemary and rue; these keep
Seeming and savour all the winter long.
iii.74

23   The fairest flowers o' the season
Are our carnations and streak'd gillyvors,
Which some call nature's bastards.
81

24   I'll not put
The dibble in earth to set one slip of them.
99

25   Here's flowers for you;
Hot lavender, mints, savory, marjoram;
The marigold, that goes to bed wi' the sun,
And with him rises weeping.
103

26   O Proserpina!
For the flowers now that frighted thou let'st fall
From Dis's waggon! daffodils,
That come before the swallow dares, and take
The winds of March with beauty; violets dim,
But sweeter than the lids of Juno's eyes
Or Cytherea's breath; pale prime-roses,
That die unmarried, ere they can behold
Bright Phoebus in his strength,—a malady
Most incident to maids; bold oxlips and
The crown imperial; lilies of all kinds,
The flower-de-luce being one.
116

27 *Perdita:* Sure this robe of mine
Doth change my disposition.
Florizel: What you do
Still betters what is done. When you speak, sweet,

I'd have you do it ever: when you sing,
I'd have you buy and sell so; so give alms;
Pray so; and, for the ordering your affairs,
To sing them too: when you do dance, I wish you
A wave o' the sea, that you might ever do
Nothing but that; move still, still so,
And own no other function: each your doing,
So singular in each particular,
Crowns what you are doing in the present deed,
That all your acts are queens.
134

1   Good sooth, she is
The queen of curds and cream.
160

2 Lawn as white as driven snow.
[220]

3 I love a ballad in print, a-life, for then we are sure they
are true.
[262]

4 The self-same sun that shines upon his court
Hides not his visage from our cottage, but
Looks on alike.
[457]

5 Being now awake, I'll queen it no inch further,
But milk my ewes and weep.
[462]

6 Prosperity's the very bond of love,
Whose fresh complexion and whose heart together
Affliction alters.
[586]

7 Ha, ha! what a fool Honesty is! and Trust his sworn
brother, a very simple gentleman!
[608]

8 Though I am not naturally honest, I am so sometimes
by chance.
[734]

9 I will but look upon the hedge and follow you.
[862]

10   Stars, stars!
And all eyes else dead coals.
V.i.67

11   Still, methinks,
There is an air comes from her: what fine chisel
Could ever yet cut breath?
iii.77

12   O! she's warm.
If this be magic, let it be an art
Lawful as eating.
109

THE PASSIONATE PILGRIM

13 Crabbed age and youth cannot live together:
Youth is full of pleasance, age is full of care.
xii

14 Age, I do abhor thee, youth, I do adore thee.

THE PHOENIX AND THE TURTLE

15 Let the bird of loudest lay,
On the sole Arabian tree,
Herald sad and trumpet be,

To whose sound chaste wings obey.
1.1.

THE RAPE OF LUCRECE

16 What I have done is yours; what I have to do is yours;
being part in all I have, devoted yours.
Dedication

17 Beauty itself doth of itself persuade
The eyes of men without an orator.
1.29

18 Who buys a minute's mirth to wail a week?
Or sells eternity to get a toy?
For one sweet grape who will the vine destroy?
1.213

19 Time's glory is to calm contending kings,
To unmask falsehood, and bring truth to light.
1.939

20 And now this pale swan in her watery nest
Begins the sad dirge of her certain ending.
1.1611

SONNETS

21 To the onlie begetter of these insuing sonnets, Mr.
W.H.
Dedication (also attr. Thomas Thorpe)

22 From fairest creatures we desire increase,
That thereby beauty's rose might never die.
1

23 When forty winters shall besiege thy brow,
And dig deep trenches in thy beauty's field.
2

24 Thou art thy mother's glass, and she in thee
Calls back the lovely April of her prime.
3

25 Music to hear, why hear'st thou music sadly?
Sweets with sweets war not, joy delights in joy:
Why lov'st thou that which thou receiv'st not gladly,
Or else receiv'st with pleasure thine annoy?
If the true concord of well-tuned sounds,
By unions married, do offend thine ear,
They do but sweetly chide thee.
8

26 When lofty trees I see barren of leaves,
Which erst from heat did canopy the herd,
And summer's green all girded up in sheaves,
Borne on the bier with white and bristly beard.
12

27 If I could write the beauty of your eyes
And in fresh numbers number all your graces,
The age to come would say, 'This poet lies;
Such heavenly touches ne'er touch'd earthly faces.'
So should my papers, yellow'd with their age,
Be scorn'd, like old men of less truth than tongue,
And your true rights be term'd a poet's rage
And stretched metre of an antique song.
17

28 Shall I compare thee to a summer's day?
Thou art more lovely and more temperate:
Rough winds do shake the darling buds of May,
And summer's lease hath all too short a date:
Sometimes too hot the eye of heaven shines,
And often is his gold complexion dimm'd;

And every fair from fair sometime declines,
By chance, or nature's changing course untrimm'd;
But thy eternal summer shall not fade,
Nor lose possession of that fair thou ow'st,
Nor shall death brag thou wander'st in his shade,
When in eternal lines to time thou grow'st;
    So long as men can breathe, or eyes can see,
    So long lives this, and this gives life to thee.
  18

1 My glass shall not persuade me I am old,
So long as youth and thou are of one date;
But when in thee time's furrows I behold,
Then look I death my days should expiate.
  22

2 As an unperfect actor on the stage,
Who with his fear is put beside his part,
Or some fierce thing replete with too much rage,
Whose strength's abundance weakens his own heart;
So I, for fear of trust, forget to say
The perfect ceremony of love's rite.
  23

3 O! let my books be then the eloquence
And dumb presagers of my speaking breast.

4 The painful warrior famoused for fight,
After a thousand victories once foil'd,
Is from the book of honour razed quite,
And all the rest forgot for which he toil'd.
  25

5 Weary with toil, I haste me to my bed,
The dear repose for limbs with travel tired;
But then begins a journey in my head
To work my mind, when body's work's expired.
  27

6 When in disgrace with fortune and men's eyes
I all alone beweep my outcast state,
And trouble deaf heaven with my bootless cries,
And look upon myself and curse my fate,
Wishing me like to one more rich in hope,
Featur'd like him, like him with friends possess'd,
Desiring this man's art, and that man's scope,
With what I most enjoy contented least;
Yet in these thoughts myself almost despising,
Haply I think on thee,—and then my state,
Like to the lark at break of day arising
From sullen earth, sings hymns at heaven's gate;
    For thy sweet love remember'd such wealth brings
    That then I scorn to change my state with kings.
  29

7 When to the sessions of sweet silent thought
I summon up remembrance of things past,
I sigh the lack of many a thing I sought,
And with old woes new wail my dear times' waste:
Then can I drown an eye, unus'd to flow,
For precious friends hid in death's dateless night,
And weep afresh love's long since cancell'd woe,
And moan the expense of many a vanish'd sight:
Then can I grieve at grievances foregone,
And heavily from woe to woe tell o'er
The sad account of fore-bemoaned moan,
Which I new pay as if not paid before.
    But if the while I think on thee, dear friend,
    All losses are restor'd and sorrows end.
  30

8   Since he died, and poets better prove,

Theirs for their style I'll read, his for his love.
  32

9 Full many a glorious morning have I seen
Flatter the mountain-tops with sovereign eye,
Kissing with golden face the meadows green,
Gilding pale streams with heavenly alchemy.
  33

10 But, out! alack! he was but one hour mine,
The region cloud hath mask'd him from me now.
    Yet him for this my love no whit disdaineth;
    Suns of the world may stain when heaven's sun
      staineth.

11 Why didst thou promise such a beauteous day,
And make me travel forth without my cloak
To let base clouds o'ertake me in my way,
Hiding thy bravery in their rotten smoke?
  34

12 Roses have thorns, and silver fountains mud;
Clouds and eclipses stain both moon and sun,
And loathsome canker lives in sweetest bud.
All men make faults.
  35

13 As a decrepit father takes delight
To see his active child do deeds of youth,
So I, made lame by fortune's dearest spite,
Take all my comfort of thy worth and truth.
  37

14 Against that time when thou shalt strangely pass,
And scarely greet me with that sun, thine eye,
When love, converted from the thing it was,
Shall reasons find of settled gravity.
  49

15 What is your substance, whereof are you made,
That millions of strange shadows on you tend?
  53

16 O! how much more doth beauty beauteous seem
By that sweet ornament which truth doth give!
  54

17 Not marble, nor the gilded monuments
Of princes, shall outlive this powerful rime;
But you shall shine more bright in these contents
Than unswept stone, besmear'd with sluttish time.
  55

18 Being your slave, what should I do but tend
Upon the hours and times of your desire?
I have no precious time at all to spend,
Nor services to do, till you require.
Nor dare I chide the world-without-end hour
Whilst I, my sovereign, watch the clock for you,
Nor think the bitterness of absence sour
When you have bid your servant once adieu;
Nor dare I question with my jealous thought
Where you may be, or your affairs suppose,
But like a sad slave, stay and think of nought
Save, where you are, how happy you make those.
    So true a fool is love that in your will,
    Though you do anything, he thinks no ill.
  57

19 Like as the waves make towards the pebbled shore,
So do our minutes hasten to their end.
  60

20 Time doth transfix the flourish set on youth
And delves the parallels in beauty's brow.

1 Sin of self-love possesseth all mine eye.
62

2 When I have seen by Time's fell hand defac'd
The rich-proud cost of outworn buried age.
64

3 When I have seen the hungry ocean gain
Advantage on the kingdom of the shore.

4 Since brass, nor stone, nor earth, nor boundless sea,
But sad mortality o'ersways their power,
How with this rage shall beauty hold a plea,
Whose action is no stronger than a flower?
65

5 Tir'd with all these, for restful death I cry,
As to behold desert a beggar born,
And needy nothing trimm'd in jollity,
And purest faith unhappily forsworn,
And gilded honour shamefully misplac'd,
And maiden virtue rudely strumpeted,
And right perfection wrongfully disgrac'd,
And strength by limping sway disabled,
And art made tongue-tied by authority,
And folly—doctor-like—controlling skill,
And simple truth miscall'd simplicity,
And captive good attending captain ill:
　　Tir'd with all these, from these I would be gone,
　　Save that, to die, I leave my love alone.
66

6 No longer mourn for me when I am dead
Than you shall hear the surly sullen bell
Give warning to the world that I am fled
From this vile world, with vilest worms to dwell.
71

7 That time of year thou mayst in me behold
When yellow leaves, or none, or few, do hang
Upon those boughs which shake against the cold,
Bare ruin'd choirs, where late the sweet birds sang.
In me thou see'st the twilight of such day
As after sunset fadeth in the west;
Which by and by black night doth take away,
Death's second self, that seals up all in rest.
73

8 This thou perceiv'st, which makes thy love more
　　strong,
To love that well which thou must leave ere long.

9 O! know, sweet love, I always write of you,
And you and love are still my argument;
So all my best is dressing old words new,
Spending again what is already spent.
76

10 Time's thievish progress to eternity.
77

11 Was it the proud full sail of his great verse,
Bound for the prize of all too precious you,
That did my ripe thoughts in my brain inhearse,
Making their tomb the womb wherein they grew?
86

12 　　　　　　　That affable familiar ghost
Which nightly gulls him with intelligence.

13 Farewell! thou art too dear for my possessing,
And like enough thou know'st thy estimate:
The charter of thy worth gives thee releasing;
My bonds in thee are all determinate.
For how do I hold thee but by thy granting?

And for that riches where is my deserving?
The cause of this fair gift in me is wanting,
And so my patent back again is swerving.
Thyself thou gav'st, thy own worth then not knowing,
Or me, to whom thou gav'st it, else mistaking;
So thy great gift, upon misprision growing,
Comes home again, on better judgment making.
　　Thus have I had thee, as a dream doth flatter,
　　In sleep a king, but, waking, no such matter.
87

14 Ah, do not, when my heart hath 'scap'd this sorrow,
Come in the rearward of a conquer'd woe;
Give not a windy night a rainy morrow,
To linger out a purpos'd overthrow.
90

15 They that have power to hurt and will do none,
That do not do the thing they most do show,
Who, moving others, are themselves as stone,
Unmoved, cold, and to temptation slow;
They rightly do inherit heaven's graces,
And husband nature's riches from expense;
They are the lords and owners of their faces,
Others but stewards of their excellence.
The summer's flower is to the summer sweet,
Though to itself it only live and die,
But if that flower with base infection meet,
The basest weed outbraves his dignity:
　　For sweetest things turn sourest by their deeds;
　　Lilies that fester smell far worse than weeds.
94

16 How like a winter hath my absence been
From thee, the pleasure of the fleeting year!
What freezings have I felt, what dark days seen!
What old December's bareness every where!
97

17 From you have I been absent in the spring,
When proud-pied April, dress'd in all his trim,
Hath put a spirit of youth in everything.
98

18 To me, fair friend, you never can be old,
For as you were when first your eye I ey'd,
Such seems your beauty still. Three winters cold
Have from the forests shook three summers' pride,
Three beauteous springs to yellow autumn turn'd
In process of the seasons have I seen,
Three April perfumes in three hot Junes burn'd,
Since first I saw you fresh, which yet are green.
Ah! yet doth beauty, like a dial-hand,
Steal from his figure, and no pace perceiv'd;
So your sweet hue, which methinks still doth stand,
Hath motion, and mine eye may be deceiv'd:
　　For fear of which, hear this, thou age unbred:
　　Ere you were born was beauty's summer dead.
104

19 When in the chronicle of wasted time
I see descriptions of the fairest wights,
And beauty making beautiful old rime,
In praise of ladies dead and lovely knights.
106

20 For we, which now behold these present days,
Have eyes to wonder, but lack tongues to praise.

21 Not mine own fears, nor the prophetic soul
Of the wide world dreaming on things to come,
Can yet the lease of my true love control,

Suppos'd as forfeit to a confin'd doom.
The mortal moon hath her eclipse endur'd,
And the sad augurs mock their own presage.
107

1 And thou in this shalt find thy monument,
When tyrants' crests and tombs of brass are spent.

2 O! never say that I was false of heart,
Though absence seem'd my flame to qualify.
109

3 Alas! 'tis true I have gone here and there,
And made myself a motley to the view,
Gor'd mine own thoughts, sold cheap what is most
     dear,
Made old offences of affections new;
Most true it is that I have look'd on truth
Askance and strangely; but, by all above,
These blenches gave my heart another youth,
And worse essays prov'd thee my best of love.
110

4   My nature is subdu'd
To what it works in, like the dyer's hand;
Pity me, then, and wish I were renew'd.
111

5 Let me not to the marriage of true minds
Admit impediments. Love is not love
Which alters when it alteration finds,
Or bends with the remover to remove:
O, no! it is an ever-fixed mark,
That looks on tempests and is never shaken;
It is the star to every wandering bark,
Whose worth's unknown, although his height be
     taken.
Love's not Time's fool, though rosy lips and cheeks
Within his bending sickle's compass come;
Love alters not with his brief hours and weeks,
But bears it out even to the edge of doom.
     If this be error, and upon me prov'd,
     I never writ, nor no man ever lov'd.
116

6 What potions have I drunk of Siren tears,
Distill'd from limbecks foul as hell within,
Applying fears to hopes, and hopes to fears,
Still losing when I saw myself to win!
119

7 The expense of spirit in a waste of shame
Is lust in action; and till action, lust
Is perjur'd, murderous, bloody, full of blame,
Savage, extreme, rude, cruel, not to trust;
Enjoyed no sooner but despised straight;
Past reason hunted; and no sooner had,
Past reason hated, as a swallow'd bait,
On purpose laid to make the taker mad:
Mad in pursuit, and in possession so;
Had, having, and in quest to have, extreme;
A bliss in proof,—and prov'd, a very woe;
Before, a joy propos'd; behind, a dream.
     All this the world well knows; yet none knows well:
     To shun the heaven that leads men to this hell.
129

8 My mistress' eyes are nothing like the sun;
Coral is far more red than her lips' red:
If snow be white, why then her breasts are dun;
If hairs be wires, black wires grow on her head.
130

9 And yet, by heaven, I think my love as rare
As any she belied with false compare.

10 Whoever hath her wish, thou hast thy *Will*,
And *Will* to boot, and *Will* in over-plus.
135

11 When my love swears that she is made of truth,
I do believe her, though I know she lies.
138

12 Two loves I have of comfort and despair,
Which like two spirits do suggest me still:
The better angel is a man right fair,
The worser spirit a woman colour'd ill.
144

13 Poor soul, the centre of my sinful earth,
[Fool'd by] these rebel powers that thee array,
Why dost thou pine within and suffer dearth,
Painting thy outward walls so costly gay?
Why so large cost, having so short a lease,
Dost thou upon thy fading mansion spend?
146

14 So shalt thou feed on Death, that feeds on men,
And Death once dead, there's no more dying then.

15 Past cure I am, now Reason is past care,
And frantic-mad with evermore unrest;
My thoughts and my discourse as madmen's are,
At random from the truth vainly express'd;
     For I have sworn thee fair, and thought thee bright,
     Who art as black as hell, as dark as night.
147

SONNETS TO SUNDRY NOTES OF MUSIC

16 Live with me and be my love,
And we will all the pleasures prove.
That hills and valleys, dales and fields,
And all the craggy mountains yields.
v. See 187:24, 329:23, 404:9

VENUS AND ADONIS

17 If the first heir of my invention prove deformed, I
shall be sorry it had so noble a godfather.
Dedication

18 Hunting he lov'd, but love he laugh'd to scorn.
l.4

19 Bid me discourse, I will enchant thine ear,
Or like a fairy trip upon the green,
Or, like a nymph, with long dishevell'd hair,
Dance on the sands, and yet no footing seen:
     Love is a spirit all compact of fire,
     Not gross to sink, but light, and will aspire.
l.145

20 Round-hoof'd, short-jointed, fetlocks shag and long,
Broad breast, full eye, small head and nostril wide,
High crest, short ears, straight legs and passing strong,
Thin mane, thick tail, broad buttock, tender hide:
     Look, what a horse should have he did not lack,
     Save a proud rider on so proud a back.
l.295

21 By this, poor Wat, far off upon a hill,
Stands on his hinder legs with listening ear,
To hearken if his foes pursue him still.
l.697

22 Good friend, for Jesu's sake forbear

To dig the dust enclosed here.
Blest be the man that spares these stones,
And curst be he that moves my bones.
Epitaph on his tomb at Stratford-on-Avon, supposed to have been chosen by himself.

1 Item, I give unto my wife my second best bed, with the furniture.
Will, 1616

GEORGE BERNARD SHAW 1856–1950

2 All great truths begin as blasphemies.
Annajanska (1917), p.262

3 One man that has a mind and knows it, can always beat ten men who havnt and dont.
The Apple Cart (1929), Act I

4 What Englishman will give his mind to politics as long as he can afford to keep a motor car?

5 I never resist temptation, because I have found that things that are bad for me do not tempt me.
Act II

6 You can always tell an old soldier by the inside of his holsters and cartridge boxes. The young ones carry pistols and cartridges: the old ones, grub.
Arms and the Man (1898), Act I

7 I never apologise.
Act III

8 You're not a man, you're a machine.

9 He is a barbarian, and thinks that the customs of his tribe and island are the laws of nature.
Caesar and Cleopatra (1898), Act II

10 When a stupid man is doing something he is ashamed of, he always declares that it is his duty.
Act III

11 He who has never hoped can never despair.
Act IV

12 A man of great common sense and good taste,—meaning thereby a man without originality or moral courage.
Notes. Julius Caesar

13 We have no more right to consume happiness without producing it than to comsume wealth without producing it.
Candida (1898), Act I

14 Do you think that the things people make fools of themselves about are any less real and true than the things they behave sensibly about?

15 It is easy—terribly easy—to shake a man's faith in himself. To take advantage of that to break a man's spirit is devil's work.

16 I'm only a beer teetotaller, not a champagne teetotaller.
Act III

17 The worst sin towards our fellow creatures is not to hate them, but to be indifferent to them: that's the essence of inhumanity.
The Devil's Disciple, (1897), Act II

18 I never expect a soldier to think.
Act III

19 The British soldier can stand up to anything except the British War Office.

20 Stimulate the phagocytes.
The Doctor's Dilemma (1906), Act I

21 All professions are conspiracies against the laity.

22 I believe in Michael Angelo, Velasquez, and Rembrandt; in the might of design, the mystery of color, the redemption of all things by Beauty everlasting, and the message of Art that has made these hands blessed.

23 With the single exception of Homer, there is no eminent writer, not even Sir Walter Scott, whom I can despise so entirely as I despise Shakespeare when I measure my mind against his…It would positively be a relief to me to dig him up and throw stones at him.
Dramatic Opinions and Essays (1907), vol.II, p.52

24 Parentage is a very important profession; but no test of fitness for it is ever imposed in the interest of children.
Everybody's Political What's What (1944),ch.ix, p.74

25 It's all that the young can do for the old, to shock them and keep them up to date.
Fanny's First Play (1911), Induction

26 You don't expect me to know what to say about a play when I don't know who the author is, do you?…If it's by a good author, it's a good play, naturally. That stands to reason.
Epilogue

27 The one point on which all women are in furious secret rebellion against the existing law is the saddling of the right to a child with the obligation to become the servant of a man.
Getting Married (1908), Preface

28 What God hath joined together no man ever shall put asunder: God will take care of that.
p.216

29 When you loved me I gave you the whole sun and stars to play with. I gave you eternity in a single moment, strength of the mountains in one clasp of your arms, and the volume of all the seas in one impulse of your soul.
p.278

30 We possessed all the universe together; and you ask me to give you my scanty wages as well. I have given you the greatest of all things; and you ask me to give you little things. I gave you your own soul: you ask me for my body as a plaything. Was it not enough? Was it not enough?

31 I am a woman of the world, Hector; and I can assure you that if you will only take the trouble always to do the perfectly correct thing, and to say the perfectly correct thing, you can do just what you like.
Heartbreak House (1917), Act I

32 Go anywhere in England, where there are natural, wholesome, contented, and really nice English people; and what do you always find? That the stables are the real centre of the household.
Act III

33 The captain is in his bunk, drinking bottled ditchwater; and the crew is gambling in the forecastle. She will strike and sink and split. Do you think the laws of God will be suspended in favour of England because you were born in it?

34 Money is indeed the most important thing in the world; and all sound and successful personal and

national morality should have this fact for its basis.
The Irrational Knot (1905), Preface, p.xiv

1 Though the Life Force supplies us with its own purpose, it has no other brains to work with than those it has painfully and imperfectly evolved in our heads.
p.xxv

2 Reminiscences make one feel so deliciously aged and sad.
ch.14

3 A man who has no office to go to—I don't care who he is—is a trial of which you can have no conception.
ch.18

4 What really flatters a man is that you think him worth flattering.
John Bull's Other Island (1907), Act IV

5 There are only two qualities in the world: efficiency and inefficiency; and only two sorts of people: the efficient and the inefficient.

6 The greatest of evils and the worst of crimes is poverty.
Major Barbara (1907), Preface

7 The universal regard for money is the one hopeful fact in our civilization, the one sound spot in our social conscience. Money is the most important thing in the world. It represents health, strength, honour, generosity, and beauty as conspicuously as the want of it represents illness, weakness, disgrace, meanness, and ugliness.

8 Cusins is a very nice fellow, certainly: nobody would ever guess that he was born in Australia.
Act I

9 Nobody can say a word against Greek: it stamps a man at once as an educated gentleman.

10 Wot prawce Selvytion nah?
Act II

11 I am a Millionaire. That is my religion.

12 I am a sort of collector of religions: and the curious thing is that I find I can believe in them all.

13 I cant talk religion to a man with bodily hunger in his eyes.

14 You darent handle high explosives; but youre all ready to handle honesty and truth and justice and the whole duty of man, and kill one another at that game. What a country! What a world!
Act III

15 Nothing is ever done in this world until men are prepared to kill one another if it is not done.

16 Our political experiment of democracy, the last refuge of cheap misgovernment.
Man and Superman (1903), Epistle Dedicatory, p.xxi

17 A lifetime of happiness! No man alive could bear it: it would be hell on earth.
Act I

18 We are ashamed of everything that is real about us; ashamed of ourselves, of our relatives, of our incomes, of our accents, of our opinions, of our experience, just as we are ashamed of our naked skins.

19 The more things a man is ashamed of, the more respectable he is.

20 Vitality in a woman is a blind fury of creation.

21 The true artist will let his wife starve, his children go barefoot, his mother drudge for his living at seventy, sooner than work at anything but his art.

22 Is the devil to have all the passions as well as all the good tunes?
See 251:4

23 Very nice sort of place, Oxford, I should think, for people that like that sort of place.
Act II

24 You think that you are Ann's suitor; that you are the pursuer and she the pursued; that it is your part to woo, to persuade, to prevail, to overcome. Fool: it is you who are the pursued, the marked down quarry, the destined prey.

25 It is a woman's business to get married as soon as possible, and a man's to keep unmarried as long as he can.

26 You can be as romantic as you please about love, Hector; but you mustnt be romantic about money.

27 Hell is full of musical amateurs: music is the brandy of the damned.
Act III

28 An Englishman thinks he is moral when he is only uncomfortable.

29 As an old soldier I admit the cowardice: it's as universal as seasickness, and matters just as little.

30 When the military man approaches, the world locks up its spoons and packs off its womankind.

31 What is virtue but the Trade Unionism of the married?

32 Those who talk most about the blessings of marriage and the constancy of its vows are the very people who delare that if the chain were broken and the prisoners left free to choose, the whole social fabric would fly asunder. You cannot have the argument both ways. If the prisoner is happy, why lock him in? If he is not, why pretend that he is?

33 There are two tragedies in life. One is not to get your heart's desire. The other is to get it.
Act IV. See 555:2

34 Do not do unto others as you would they should do unto you. Their tastes may not be the same.
Maxims for Revolutionists (by 'John Tanner'): **'The Golden Rule'.**

35 The Golden Rule is that there are no golden rules.

36 Democracy substitutes election by the incompetent many for appointment by the corrupt few.
'Democracy'

37 Liberty means responsibility. That is why most men dread it.
'Liberty'

38 He who can, does. He who cannot teaches.
'Education'

39 Marriage is popular because it combines the maximum of temptation with the maximum of opportunity.
'Marriage'

40 When domestic servants are treated as human beings it is not worth while to keep them.
'Servants'

41 If you strike a child, take care that you strike it in anger, even at the risk of maiming it for life. A blow in

cold blood neither can nor should be forgiven.
'How to Beat Children'

1 The reasonable man adapts himself to the world: the unreasonable one persists in trying to adapt the world to himself. Therefore all progress depends on the unreasonable man.
'Reason'

2 The man who listens to Reason is lost: Reason enslaves all whose minds are not strong enough to master her.

3 Home is the girl's prison and the woman's workhouse.
'Women in the Home'

4 Every man over forty is a scoundrel.
'Stray Sayings'

5 Youth, which is forgiven everything, forgives itself nothing: age, which forgives itself anything, is forgiven nothing.

6 There is nothing so bad or so good that you will not find Englishmen doing it; but you will never find an Englishman in the wrong. He does everything on principle. He fights you on patriotic principles; he robs you on business principles; he enslaves you on imperial principles.
The Man of Destiny (1897)

7 An English army led by an Irish general: that might be a match for a French army led by an Italian general.

8 A great devotee of the Gospel of Getting On.
Mrs. Warren's Profession (1893), Act IV

9 The fickleness of the women I love is only equalled by the infernal constancy of the women who love me.
The Philanderer (1893), Act II

10 It is clear that a novel cannot be too bad to be worth publishing...It certainly is possible for a novel to be too good to be worth publishing.
Plays Pleasant and Unpleasant (1898), vol.1, Preface, p.vi

11 There is only one religion, though there are a hundred versions of it.
vol.2, Preface, p.vii

12 The English have no respect for their language, and will not teach their children to speak it...It is impossible for an Englishman to open his mouth, without making some other Englishman despise him.
Pygmalion (1912), Preface

13 *Pickering:* Have you no morals, man?
Doolittle: Can't afford them, Governor.
Act II

14 I'm one of the undeserving poor: that's what I am. Think of what that means to a man. It means that he's up agen middle class morality all the time...What is middle class morality? Just an excuse for never giving me anything.

15 Gin was mother's milk to her.
Act III

16 Walk! Not bloody likely. I am going in a taxi.

17 Assassination is the extreme form of censorship.
The Rejected Statement, Pt.I

18 If ever I utter an oath again may my soul be blasted to eternal damnation!
St. Joan (1923), Sc.ii

19 How can what an Englishman believes be heresy? It is

a contradiction in terms.
Sc.iv

20 Must then a Christ perish in torment in every age to save those that have no imagination?
Epilogue

21 Well, sir, you never can tell. That's a principle in life with me, sir, if you'll excuse my having such a thing.
You Never Can Tell (1897), Act II

22 If you are going to have doctors you had better have doctors well off; just as if you are going to have a landlord you had better have a rich landlord. Taking all the round of professions and occupations, you will find that every man is the worse for being poor; and the doctor is a specially dangerous man when poor.
The Socialist Criticism of the Medical Profession. Paper read to the Medico-Legal Society, 16 Feb. 1909

23 England is still governed from Langar Rectory, from Shrewsbury School, from Cambridge, with their annexes of the Stock Exchange and the solicitors' offices; and even if the human products of these institutions were all geniuses, they would finally wreck any modern civilized country after maintaining themselves according to their own notions at the cost of the squalor and slavery of four-fifths of its inhabitants.
Introductory essay to S. Butler's *The Way of All Flesh*, World's Classics edn. (1936)

THOMAS SHAW 1694–1751

24 I hate a *cui bono* man.
Attr. Boswell's *Life of Johnson*, IV, 112. May 1781

LORD SHAWCROSS 1902–

25 'The question is,' said Humpty Dumpty, 'which is to be master—that's all.'
We are the masters at the moment, and not only at the moment, but for a very long time to come.
House of Commons, 2 Apr. 1946. Often misquoted as 'We are the masters now.' See 135:22

CHARLES SHAW-LEFEVRE, VISCOUNT EVERSLEY 1794–1888

26 What is that fat gentleman in such a passion about?
Remark as a child on hearing Mr. Fox speak in Parliament.
G.W.E. Russell, *Collections and Recollections*, ch.11

PATRICK SHAW STEWART 1888–1917

27 I saw a man this morning
    Who did not wish to die;
I ask, and cannot answer
    If otherwise wish I.
Written during the Gallipoli expedition, 1915. N. Mosley, *Julian Grenfell* (1976), ch.31

28 I will go back this morning
    From Imbros over the sea;
Stand in the trench, Achilles,
    Flame-capped, and shout for me.

RICHARD SHEALE sixteenth century

29 For Witherington needs must I wail,
    As one in doleful dumps;
For when his legs were smitten off,

He fought upon his stumps.
Ballad of Chevy Chase, Pt. II, x

JOHN SHEFFIELD, DUKE OF BUCKINGHAM
see BUCKINGHAM

MARY WOLLSTONECRAFT SHELLEY
1797–1851

1 Mrs Shelley was choosing a school for her son, and asked the advice of this lady, who gave for advice—to use her own words to me—'Just the sort of banality, you know, one does come out with: "Oh, send him somewhere where they will teach him to think for himself!"'...Mrs Shelley answered: 'Teach him to think for himself? Oh, my God, teach him rather to think like other people!'
Matthew Arnold, *Essays in Criticism, Second Series; Shelley*

PERCY BYSSHE SHELLEY 1792–1822

2 The cemetery is an open space among the ruins, covered in winter with violets and daisies. It might make one in love with death, to think that one should be buried in so sweet a place.
Adonais (1821). Preface

3 I weep for Adonais—he is dead!
O, weep for Adonais! though our tears
Thaw not the frost which binds so dear a head!
I

4 Most musical of mourners, weep again!
Lament anew, Urania!—He died,
Who was the Sire of an immortal strain,
Blind, old and lonely.
IV

5   He went, unterrified,
Into the gulf of death; but his clear Sprite
Yet reigns o'er earth; the third among the sons of
     light.
V

6 To that high Capital, where kingly Death
Keeps his pale court in beauty and decay,
He came.
VII

7   The quick Dreams,
The passion-winged Ministers of thought.
IX

8 Lost Angel of a ruin'd Paradise!
She knew not 'twas her own; as with no stain
She faded, like a cloud which had outwept its rain.
X

9   Desires and Adorations,
Wingèd Persuasions and veiled Destinies,
Splendours, and Glooms, and glimmering Incarnations
Of hopes and fears, and twilight·Phantasies;
And Sorrow, with her family of Sighs,
And Pleasure, blind with tears, led by the gleam
Of her own dying smile instead of eyes,
Came in slow pomp.
XIII

10 Ah, woe is me! Winter is come and gone,
But grief returns with the revolving year.
XVIII

11 The great morning of the world when first

God dawned on Chaos.
XIX

12 Alas! that all we loved of him should be,
But for our grief, as if it had not been,
And grief itself be mortal!
XXI

13 Whence are we, and why are we? Of what scene
The actors or spectators?

14 As long as skies are blue, and fields are green,
Evening must usher night, night urge the morrow,
Month follow month with woe, and year wake year to
     sorrow.

15 Why didst thou leave the trodden paths of men
Too soon, and with weak hands though mighty heart
Dare the unpastured dragon in his den?
XXVII

16 The herded wolves, bold only to pursue;
The obscene ravens, clamorous o'er the dead.
XXVIII

17 A pard-like Spirit, beautiful and swift—
A Love in desolation masked;—a Power
Girt round with weakness;—it can scarce uplift
The weight of the superincumbent hour;
It is a dying lamp, a falling shower,
A breaking billow;—even whilst we speak
Is it not broken?
XXXII

18 Our Adonais has drunk poison—oh!
What deaf and viperous murderer could crown
Life's early cup with such a draught of woe?
XXXVI

19 He wakes or sleeps with the enduring dead;
Thou canst not soar where he is sitting now—
Dust to the dust! but the pure spirit shall flow
Back to the burning fountain whence it came,
A portion of the Eternal.
XXXVIII

20 He hath awakened from the dream of life—
'Tis we, who lost in stormy visions, keep
With phantoms an unprofitable strife,
And in mad trance, strike with our spirit's knife
Invulnerable nothings.
XXXIX

21 He has out-soared the shadow of our night;
Envy and calumny and hate and pain,
And that unrest which men miscall delight,
Can touch him not and torture not again;
From the contagion of the world's slow stain
He is secure, and now can never mourn
A heart grown cold, a head grown grey in vain.
XL

22 He lives, he wakes,—'tis Death is dead, not he.
XLI

23 He is made one with Nature: there is heard
His voice in all her music, from the moan
Of thunder, to the song of night's sweet bird.
XLII

24 He is a portion of the loveliness
Which once he made more lovely.
XLIII

25 What Adonais is, why fear we to become?
LI

26 The One remains, the many change and pass;

Heaven's light forever shines, Earth's shadows fly;
Life, like a dome of many-coloured glass,
Stains the white radiance of Eternity,
Until Death tramples it to fragments.
LII

1 The soul of Adonais, like a star,
Beacons from the abode where the Eternal are.
LV

2   Arethusa arose
        From her couch of snows
In the Acroceraunian mountains,—
        From cloud and from crag,
        With many a jag,
Shepherding her bright fountains.
Arethusa

3 A widow bird sate mourning for her love
        Upon a wintry bough;
The frozen wind crept on above,
        The freezing stream below.

There was no leaf upon the forest bare,
        No flower upon the ground,
And little motion in the air
        Except the mill-wheel's sound.
Charles the First (1822), sc.v, l.10

4 I wield the flail of the lashing hail,
        And whiten the green plains under,
And then again I dissolve it in rain,
        And laugh as I pass in thunder.
The Cloud (1819)

5 And I all the while bask in Heaven's blue smile,
        Whilst he is dissolving in rains.

6 That orbèd maiden, with white fire laden,
        Whom mortals call the Moon,
Glides glimmering o'er my fleece-like floor,
        By the midnight breezes strewn;
And wherever the beat of her unseen feet,
        Which only the angels hear,
May have broken the woof of my tent's thin roof,
        The stars peep behind her and peer;
And I laugh to see them whirl and flee
        Like a swarm of golden bees,
When I widen the rent in my wind-built tent,
        Till the calm rivers, lakes, and seas,
Like strips of the sky fallen through me on high,
        Are each paved with the moon and these.

7 I am the daughter of Earth and Water,
        And the nursling of the Sky;
I pass through the pores of the ocean and shores;
        I change, but I cannot die,
For after the rain when with never a stain
        The pavilion of Heaven is bare,
And the winds and sunbeams with their convex gleams
        Build up the blue dome of air,
I silently laugh at my own cenotaph,
        And out of the caverns of rain,
Like a child from the womb, like a ghost from the
        tomb,
        I arise and unbuild it again.

8   How wonderful is Death,
        Death and his brother Sleep!
One pale as the yonder wan and horned moon,
        With lips of lurid blue,
The other glowing like the vital morn,

When throned on ocean's wave
    It breathes over the world:
Yet both so passing strange and wonderful!
The Daemon of the World, Part I, 1,1. See also *Queen Mab*,
opening lines.

9 I never was attached to that great sect,
Whose doctrine is that each one should select
Out of the crowd a mistress or a friend,
And all the rest, though fair and wise, commend
To cold oblivion.
Epipsychidion (1821), l.149

10   The beaten road
Which those poor slaves with weary footsteps tread,
Who travel to their home among the dead
By the broad highway of the world, and so
With one chained friend, perhaps a jealous foe,
The dreariest and the longest journey go.
l.154

11 True Love in this differs from gold and clay,
That to divide is not to take away.
l.160

12   An isle under Ionian skies,
Beautiful as a wreck of Paradise.
l.422

13 I pant, I sink, I tremble, I expire!
l.591

14 Chameleons feed on light and air:
Poets' food is love and fame.
An Exhortation

15   Time's printless torrent grew
A scroll of crystal, blazoning the name
Of Adonais!
Fragment on Keats

16 My spirit like a charmed bark doth swim
    Upon the liquid waves of thy sweet singing.
Fragment: To One Singing. See 503:11

17 Good-night? ah! no; the hour is ill
    Which severs those it should unite;
Let us remain together still,
    Then it will be *good* night.
Good Night

18 Life may change, but it may fly not;
Hope may vanish, but can die not;
Truth be veiled, but still it burneth;
Love repulsed,—but it returneth!
Hellas (1822), l.34

19 Let there be light! said Liberty,
And like sunrise from the sea,
Athens arose!
l.682

20 The world's great age begins anew,
The golden years return,
The earth doth like a snake renew
Her winter weeds outworn;
Heaven smiles, and faiths and empires gleam,
Like wrecks of a dissolving dream.
l.1060

21 A loftier Argo cleaves the main,
Fraught with a later prize;
Another Orpheus sings again,
And loves, and weeps, and dies.
A new Ulysses leaves once more

Calypso for his native shore.
1.1072

1 Although a subtler Sphinx renew
Riddles of death Thebes never knew.
1.1082

2 Another Athens shall arise,
And to remoter time
Bequeath, like sunset to the skies,
The splendour of its prime;
And leave, if nought so bright may live,
All earth can take or Heaven can give.
1.1090

3 O cease! must hate and death return?
Cease! must men kill and die?
Cease! drain not to its dregs the urn
Of bitter prophecy.
The world is weary of the past,
Oh, might it die or rest at last!
1.1102

4 I pursued a maiden and clasped a reed.
Gods and men, we are all deluded thus!
It breaks in our bosom and then we bleed.
Hymn of Pan

5 The awful shadow of some unseen Power
Floats though unseen among us,—visiting
This various world with as inconstant wing
As summer winds that creep from flower to flower.
Hymn to Intellectual Beauty (1816)

6 While yet a boy I sought for ghosts, and sped
Through many a listening chamber, cave and ruin,
And starlight wood, with fearful steps pursuing
Hopes of high talk with the departed dead.

7 The day becomes more solemn and serene
When noon is past—there is a harmony
In autumn, and a lustre in its sky,
Which through the summer is not heard or seen,
As if it could not be, as if it had not been!

8 I arise from dreams of thee
In the first sweet sleep of night.
When the winds are breathing low,
And the stars are shining bright.
The Indian Serenade

9 Oh lift me from the grass!
I die! I faint! I fail!
Let thy love in kisses rain
On my lips and eyelids pale.

10   I love all waste
And solitary places; where we taste
The pleasure of believing what we see
Is boundless, as we wish our souls to be.
Julian and Maddalo (1818), 1.14

11 Thou Paradise of exiles, Italy!
1.57

12 Me—who am as a nerve o'er which do creep
The else unfelt oppressions of this earth.
1.449

13   Most wretched men
Are cradled into poetry by wrong:
They learn in suffering what they teach in song.
1.543

14 O world! O life! O time!
On whose last steps I climb,
Trembling at that where I had stood before;

When will return the glory of your prime?
No more—Oh, never more!
A Lament

15 Fresh spring, and summer, and winter hoar,
Move my faint heart with grief, but with delight
No more—Oh, never more!

16 We watched the ocean and the sky together,
Under the roof of blue Italian weather.
Letter to Maria Gisborne (1820), 1.146

17   London, that great sea, whose ebb and flow
At once is deaf and loud, and on the shore
Vomits its wrecks, and still howls on for more.
1.193

18 You will see Coleridge—he who sits obscure
In the exceeding lustre and the pure
Intense irradiation of a mind,
Which, through its own internal lightning blind,
Flags wearily through darkness and despair—
A cloud-encircled meteor of the air,
A hooded eagle among blinking owls.
You will see Hunt—one of those happy souls
Which are the salt of the earth, and without whom
This world would smell like what it is—a tomb.
1.202

19   Have you not heard
When a man marries, dies, or turns Hindoo,
His best friends hear no more of him?
1.235

20   His fine wit
Makes such a wound, the knife is lost in it. [T.L.
Peacock]
1.240

21 When the lamp is shattered
The light in the dust lies dead—
When the cloud is scattered
The rainbow's glory is shed.
When the lute is broken,
Sweet tones are remembered not;
When the lips have spoken,
Loved accents are soon forgot.
Lines: When the Lamp

22 When hearts have once mingled
Love first leaves the well-built nest;
The weak one is singled
To endure what it once possessed.
O Love! who bewailest
The frailty of things here,
Why choose you the frailest
For your cradle, your home, and your bier?

23 Beneath is spread like a green sea
The waveless plain of Lombardy,
Bounded by the vaporous air,
Islanded by cities fair;
Underneath Day's azure eyes
Ocean's nursling, Venice lies,
A peopled labyrinth of walls,
Amphitrite's destined halls.
Lines written amongst the Euganean Hills (1818), 1.90

24 Sun-girt city, thou hast been
Ocean's child, and then his queen;
Now is come a darker day,
And thou soon must be his prey.
1.115

1 The fountains mingle with the river,
    And the rivers with the ocean;
The winds of heaven mix for ever
    With a sweet emotion;
Nothing in the world is single;
    All things, by a law divine,
In one another's being mingle.
    Why not I with thine?
Love's Philosophy

2 I met Murder in the way—
He had a mask like Castlereagh.
The Mask of Anarchy (1819), II

3 His big tears, for he wept full well,
Turned to mill-stones as they fell.

And the little children, who
Round his feet played to and fro,
Thinking every tear a gem,
Had their brains knocked out by them.
IV. Of 'Fraud' (Lord Eldon)

4 Rise like Lions after slumber
In unvanquishable number—
Shake your chains to earth like dew
Which in sleep had fallen on you—
Ye are many—they are few.
XXXVIII and XCI

5 Its horror and its beauty are divine.
The 'Medusa' of Leonardo da Vinci

6 Nought may endure but Mutability.
Mutability

7 I stood within the City disinterred;
And heard the autumnal leaves like light footfalls
Of spirits passing through the streets; and heard
The Mountain's slumbrous voice at intervals
Thrill through those roofless halls.
Ode to Naples (1820), l.1

8 O wild West Wind, thou breath of Autumn's being,
Thou, from whose unseen presence the leaves dead
Are driven, like ghosts from an enchanter fleeing,

Yellow, and black, and pale, and hectic red,
Pestilence-stricken multitudes: O thou,
Who chariotest to their dark wintry bed

The winged seeds, where they lie cold and low,
Each like a corpse within its grave, until
Thine azure sister of the spring shall blow

Her clarion o'er the dreaming earth, and fill
(Driving sweet buds like flocks to feed in air)
With living hues and odours plain and hill:

Wild Spirit, which art moving everywhere;
Destroyer and preserver; hear, oh, hear!
Ode to the West Wind (1819), l.1

9   There are spread
On the blue suface of thine aëry surge,
Like the bright hair uplifted from the head

Of some fierce Maenad, even from the dim verge
Of the horizon to the zenith's height,
The locks of the approaching storm.
l.18

10 Thou who didst waken from his summer dreams
The blue Mediterranean, where he lay,
Lulled by the coil of his crystalline streams

Beside a pumice isle in Baiae's bay,

And saw in sleep old palaces and towers
Quivering within the wave's intenser day,

All overgrown with azure moss and flowers
    So sweet, the sense faints picturing them.
l.29

11   Far below
The sea-blooms and the oozy woods which wear
The sapless foliage of the ocean, know

Thy voice, and suddenly grow gray with fear,
And tremble and despoil themselves.
l.38

12 If I were a dead leaf thou mightest bear;
If I were a swift cloud to fly with thee;
A wave to pant beneath thy power, and share

The impulse of thy strength, only less free
Than thou, O uncontrollable!
l.43

13 Oh, lift me as a wave, a leaf, a cloud!
I fall upon the thorns of life! I bleed!

A heavy weight of hours has chained and bowed
One too like thee: tameless, and swift, and proud.

Make me thy lyre, even as the forest is:
What if my leaves are falling like its own?
The tumult of thy mighty harmonies

Will take from both a deep, autumnal tone,
Sweet though in sadness.
l.53

14 And, by the incantation of this verse,

Scatter, as from an unextinguished hearth
Ashes and sparks, my words among mankind!
Be through my lips to unawakened earth

The trumpet of a prophecy! O, Wind,
If Winter comes, can Spring be far behind?
l.65

15 I met a traveller from an antique land
Who said: Two vast and trunkless legs of stone
Stand in the desert.
Ozymandias

16 'My name is Ozymandias, king of kings:
Look on my works, ye Mighty, and despair!'
Nothing beside remains. Round the decay
Of that colossal wreck, boundless and bare
The lone and level sands stretch far away.

17 Hell is a city much like London—
A populous and smoky city.
Peter Bell the Third (1819), pt.3. **Hell,** i

18 But from the first 'twas Peter's drift
    To be a kind of moral eunuch,
He touched the hem of Nature's shift,
    Felt faint—and never dared uplift
    The closest, all-concealing tunic.
pt.4. **Sin,** xi

19   Ere Babylon was dust,
The Magus Zoroaster, my dead child,
Met his own image walking in the garden,
That apparition, sole of men, he saw.
Prometheus Unbound (1819), I.191

20 Cruel he looks, but calm and strong,
Like one who does, not suffers wrong.
238

21 It doth repent me: words are quick and vain;

Grief for awhile is blind, and so was mine.
I wish no living thing to suffer pain.
303

1 Kingly conclaves stern and cold
Where blood with guilt is bought and sold.
530

2 The good want power, but to weep barren tears.
The powerful goodness want: worse need for them.
The wise want love; and those who love want wisdom.
625

3   Peace is in the grave.
The grave hides all things beautiful and good:
I am a God and cannot find it there.
638

4 The dust of creeds outworn.
697

5 On a poet's lips I slept
Dreaming like a love-adept
In the sound his breathing kept.
737

6 He will watch from dawn to gloom
The lake-reflected sun illume
The yellow bees in the ivy-bloom,
Nor heed, nor see, what things they be;
But from these create he can
Forms more real than living man,
Nurslings of immortality!
743

7   To be
Omnipotent but friendless is to reign.
II.iv.47

8 He gave man speech, and speech created thought,
Which is the measure of the universe.
73

9 All spirits are enslaved which serve things evil.
110

10 Fate, Time, Occasion, Chance, and Change? To these
All things are subject but eternal Love.
119

11   My soul is an enchanted boat,
         Which, like a sleeping swan, doth float
Upon the silver waves of thy sweet singing.
v.72. See 500:16

12 The loathsome mask has fallen, the man remains
Sceptreless, free, uncircumscribed, but man
Equal, unclassed, tribeless, and nationless,
Exempt from awe, worship, degree, the king
Over himself; just, gentle, wise: but man
Passionless?—no, yet free from guilt or pain,
Which were, for his will made or suffered them,
Nor yet exempt, though ruling them like slaves,
From chance, and death, and mutability,
The clogs of that which else might oversoar
The loftiest star of unascended heaven,
Pinnacled dim in the intense inane.
III.iii.193

13 Familiar acts are beautiful through love.
IV.403

14 A traveller from the cradle to the grave
Through the dim night of this immortal day.
551

15 To suffer woes which Hope thinks infinite;
To forgive wrongs darker than death or night;

To defy Power, which seems omnipotent;
To love, and bear; to hope till Hope creates
From its own wreck the thing it contemplates;
   Neither to change, nor falter, nor repent;
This, like thy glory, Titan, is to be
Good, great and joyous, beautiful and free;
This is alone Life, Joy, Empire and Victory.
570

16 That sweet bondage which is freedom's self.
Queen Mab (1813), c.9, l.76

17 I dreamed that, as I wandered by the way,
   Bare Winter suddenly was changed to Spring,
And gentle odours led my steps astray,
   Mixed with a sound of water's murmuring
Along a shelving bank of turf, which lay
   Under a copse, and hardly dared to fling
Its green arms round the bosom of the stream,
   But kissed it and then fled, as thou mightst in
      dream.
The Question

18 There grew pied wind-flowers and violets,
   Daisies, those pearled Arcturi of the earth,
The constellated flower that never sets.

19 And in the warm hedge grew lush eglantine,
   Green cowbind and the moonlight-coloured may,
And cherry-blossoms, and white cups, whose wine
   Was the bright dew, yet drained not by the day;
And wild roses, and ivy serpentine,
   With its dark buds and leaves, wandering astray;
And flowers azure, black, and streaked with gold,
   Fairer than any wakened eyes behold.

20 And nearer to the river's trembling edge
   There grew broad flag-flowers, purple, pranked with
      white,
And starry river buds among the sedge,
   And floating water-lilies, broad and bright.

21 With hue like that when some great painter dips
   His pencil in the gloom of earthquake and eclipse.
The Revolt of Islam (1818), c.5. xxiii

22 A Sensitive Plant in a garden grew.
The Sensitive Plant (1820), pt.I, l.1

23 And the rose like a nymph to the bath addressed,
Which unveiled the depth of her glowing breast,
Till, fold after fold, to the fainting air
The soul of her beauty and love lay bare.
l.29

24 And the jessamine faint, and the sweet tuberose,
The sweetest flower for scent that blows.
l.37

25 Rarely, rarely, comest thou,
Spirit of Delight!
Song

26 I love all that thou lovest,
   Spirit of Delight:
The fresh Earth in new leaves dressed,
   And the starry night;
Autumn evening, and the morn
When the golden mists are born.

27 I love snow, and all the forms
Of the radiant frost.

28   Everything almost
Which is Nature's, and may be

Untainted by man's misery.

1 I love tranquil solitude,
    And such society
As is quiet, wise, and good;
    Between thee and me
What difference? but thou dost possess
The things I seek, not love them less.

2 Men of England, wherefore plough
For the lords who lay you low?
Song to the Men of England

3 The seed ye sow, another reaps;
The wealth ye find, another keeps;
The robes ye weave, another wears;
The arms ye forge, another bears.

Sow seed—but let no tyrant reap;
Find wealth—let no impostor heap;
Weave robes—let not the idle wear;
Forge arms, in your defence to bear.

4 Lift not the painted veil which those who live
Call Life.
Sonnet

5   He sought,
For his lost heart was tender, things to love,
But found them not, alas! nor was there aught
The world contains, the which he could approve.
Through the unheeding many he did move,
A splendour among shadows, a bright blot
Upon this gloomy scene, a Spirit that strove
For truth, and like the Preacher found it not.

6 An old, mad, blind, despised, and dying king.
Sonnet: England in 1819

7 Away! the moor is dark beneath the moon,
Rapid clouds have drank the last pale beam of even:
Away! the gathering winds will call the darkness soon,
And profoundest midnight shroud the serene lights of
    heaven.
Stanzas.—April 1814

8 The City's voice itself is soft like Solitude's.
Stanzas Written in Dejection, near Naples (1818)

9 I see the waves upon the shore,
Like light dissolved in star-showers, thrown.

10 Alas! I have nor hope nor health,
    Nor peace within nor calm around,
Nor that content surpassing wealth
    The sage in meditation found,
    And walked with inward glory crowned.

11 I could lie down like a tired child,
    And weep away the life of care
Which I have borne and yet must bear,
    Till death like sleep might steal on me.

12 Music, when soft voices die,
Vibrates in the memory—
Odours, when sweet violets sicken,
Live within the sense they quicken.

Rose leaves, when the rose is dead,
Are heaped for the beloved's bed;
And so thy thoughts, when thou art gone,
Love itself shall slumber on.
To—

13 One word is too often profaned
    For me to profane it,

One feeling too falsely disdained
    For thee to disdain it.
To—

14 The desire of the moth for the star,
    Of the night for the morrow,
The devotion to something afar
    From the sphere of our sorrow.

15 Hail to thee, blithe Spirit!
    Bird thou never wert,
That from Heaven, or near it,
    Pourest thy full heart
In profuse strains of unpremeditated art.
To a Skylark (1819)

16 And singing still dost soar, and soaring ever singest.

17 Like an unbodied joy whose race is just begun.

18 Thou art unseen, but yet I hear thy shrill delight.

19 Like a Poet hidden
    In the light of thought,
Singing hymns unbidden,
    Till the world is wrought
To sympathy with hopes and fears it heeded not.

20 Chorus Hymeneal,
    Or triumphal chant,
Matched with thine would be all
    But an empty vaunt,
A thing wherein we feel there is some hidden want.

21 What objects are the fountains
    Of thy happy strain?
What fields, or waves, or mountains?
    What shapes of sky or plain?
What love of thine own kind? what ignorance of pain?

22 With thy clear keen joyance
    Languor cannot be:
Shadow of annoyance
    Never came near thee:
Thou lovest—but ne'er knew love's sad satiety.

23 We look before and after;
    We pine for what is not;
Our sincerest laughter
    With some pain is fraught;
Our sweetest songs are those that tell of saddest
    thought.

24 Better than all measures
    Of delightful sound,
Better than all treasures
    That in books are found,
Thy skill to poet were, thou scorner of the ground!

Teach me half the gladness
    That thy brain must know,
Such harmonious madness
    From my lips would flow
The world should listen then—as I am listening now.

25 I am gone into the fields
To take what this sweet hour yields;—
Reflection, you may come to-morrow,
Sit by the fireside with Sorrow.—
You with the unpaid bill, Despair,
You, tiresome verse-reciter, Care,—
I will pay you in the grave,—
Death will listen to your stave.
To Jane: The Invitation

1 Less oft is peace in Shelley's mind,
Than calm in waters, seen.
To Jane: The Recollection

2 Swiftly walk over the western wave,
Spirit of Night!
Out of the misty eastern cave,
Where, all the long and lone daylight,
Thou wovest dreams of joy and fear,
Which make thee terrible and dear,—
Swift be thy flight!
To Night

3 Blind with thine hair the eyes of Day;
Kiss her until she be wearied out,
Then wander o'er city, and sea, and land,
Touching all with thine opiate wand—
Come, long-sought!

4 Death will come when thou art dead,
Soon, too soon—
Sleep will come when thou art fled;
Of neither would I ask the boon
I ask of thee, beloved Night—
Swift be thine approaching flight,
Come soon, soon!

5 Art thou pale for weariness
Of climbing heaven, and gazing on the earth,
Wandering companionless
Among the stars that have a different birth,—
And ever changing, like a joyless eye
That finds no object worth its constancy?
To the Moon

6 In honoured poverty thy voice did weave
Songs consecrate to truth and liberty,—
Deserting these, thou leavest me to grieve,
Thus having been, that thou shouldst cease to be.
To Wordsworth

7 And like a dying lady, lean and pale,
Who totters forth, wrapped in a gauzy veil.
The Waning Moon

8 A lovely lady, garmented in light
From her own beauty.
The Witch of Atlas (1820, pub.1824), v

9 For she was beautiful—her beauty made
The bright world dim, and everything beside
Seemed like the fleeting image of a shade.
xii

10 A single word even may be a spark of inextinguishable thought.
A Defence of Poetry (1821)

11 The rich have become richer, and the poor have
become poorer; and the vessel of the state is driven
between the Scylla and Charybdis of anarchy and
despotism.

12 Poetry is the record of the best and happiest moments
of the happiest and best minds.

13 Poets are...the trumpets which sing to battle and feel
not what they inspire...Poets are the unacknowledged
legislators of the world.
See 282:7

14 When it was a matter of wonder how Keats, who was
ignorant of Greek, could have written his 'Hyperion',
Shelley, whom envy never touched, gave as a reason,

'Because he *was* a Greek'.
W.S. Landor, *Imaginary Conversations. Southey and Landor*, ii

WILLIAM SHENSTONE 1714–1763

15 Whoe'er has travell'd life's dull round,
Where'er his stages may have been,
May sigh to think he still has found
The warmest welcome, at an inn.
At an Inn at Henley

16 Laws are generally found to be nets of such a texture,
as the little creep through, the great break through, and
the middle-sized are alone entangled in.
Essays on Men, Manners, and Things (vol.ii of *Works*,
1764-9), **On Politics**. See 512:23

17 A Fool and his words are soon parted; a man of genius
and his money.
On Reserve

PHILIP HENRY SHERIDAN 1831–1888

18 The only good Indian is a dead Indian.
Attr., at Fort Cobb, Jan. 1869

RICHARD BRINSLEY SHERIDAN 1751–1816

19 Not a translation—only *taken from the French*.
The Critic (1779), I.i

20 The newspapers! Sir, they are the most
villainous—licentious—abominable—infernal—Not
that I ever read them—no—I make it a rule never to
look into a newspaper.

21 If it is abuse—why one is always sure to hear of it from
one damned good-natured friend or other!

22 Egad, I think the interpreter is the hardest to be
understood of the two!
ii

23 Yes, sir, puffing is of various sorts; the principal are,
the puff direct, the puff preliminary, the puff
collateral, the puff collusive, and the puff oblique, or
puff by implication.

24 No scandal about Queen Elizabeth, I hope?
II.i

25 I open with a clock striking, to beget an awful
attention in the audience: it also marks the time, which
is four o'clock in the morning, and saves a description
of the rising sun, and a great deal about gilding the
eastern hemisphere.
ii

26 Inconsolable to the minuet in Ariadne!

27 The Spanish fleet thou *canst* not see because—
It is not yet in sight!

28 All that can be said is, that two people happened to hit
on the same thought—and Shakespeare made use of it
first, that's all.
III.i

29 *Burleigh comes forward, shakes his head, and exit.*
Sneer: He is very perfect indeed. Now pray, what did
he mean by that?
Puff: Why, by that shake of the head, he gave you to
understand that even though they had more justice in
their cause and wisdom in their measures, yet, if there
was not a greater spirit shown on the part of the
people, the country would at last fall a sacrifice to the

hostile ambition of the Spanish monarchy.
Sneer: The devil!—did he mean all that by shaking his head?
Puff: Every word of it. If he shook his head as I taught him.

1 *Whiskerandos:* And Whiskerandos quits this bustling scene
For all eter—
Beefeater: —nity—he would have added, but stern death
Cut short his being, and the noun at once!

2 I wish sir, you would practise this without me. I can't stay dying here all night.

3 O Lord, sir, when a heroine goes mad she always goes into white satin.

4 An oyster may be crossed in love.

5 I was struck all of a heap.
The Duenna (1775), II.ii

6 Conscience has no more to do with gallantry than it has with politics.
iv

7 The throne *we* honour is the *people's choice.*
Pizarro (1799), II.i

8 Illiterate him, I say, quite from your memory.
The Rivals (1775), I.ii

9 'Tis safest in matrimony to begin with a little aversion.

10 Madam, a circulating library in a town is as an evergreen tree of diabolical knowledge! It blossoms through the year! And depend on it, Mrs Malaprop, that they who are so fond of handling the leaves, will long for the fruit at last.

11 You gentlemen's gentlemen are so hasty.
II.ii

12 He is the very pine-apple of politeness!
III.iii

13 An aspersion upon my parts of speech!

14 If I reprehend any thing in this world, it is the use of my oracular tongue, and a nice derangement of epitaphs!

15 She's as headstrong as an allegory on the banks of the Nile.

16 Too civil by half.
iv

17 Our ancestors are very good kind of folks; but they are the last people I should choose to have a visiting acquaintance with.
IV.i

18 No caparisons, miss, if you please. Caparisons don't become a young woman.
ii

19 You are not like Cerberus, three gentlemen at once, are you?

20 The quarrel is a very pretty quarrel as it stands; we should only spoil it by trying to explain it.
iii

21 There's nothing like being used to a thing.
V.iii

22 My valour is certainly going!—it is sneaking off! I feel it oozing out as it were at the palms of my hands!

23 I own the soft impeachment.

24 Thro' all the drama—whether damned or not—
Love gilds the scene, and women guide the plot.
Epilogue

25 Tale-bearers are as bad as the tale-makers.
The School for Scandal (1777), I.i

26 You shall see them on a beautiful quarto page, where a neat rivulet of text shall meander through a meadow of margin.

27 You had no taste when you married me.
ii

28 *Mrs. Candour:* I'll swear her colour is natural: I have seen it come and go.
Lady Teazle: I dare swear you have ma'am; it goes off at night, and comes again in the morning.
II.ii

29 Here is the whole set! a character dead at every word.

30 I'm called away by particular business. But I leave my character behind me.

31 Here's to the maiden of bashful fifteen;
Here's to the widow of fifty;
Here's to the flaunting, extravagant quean;
And here's to the housewife that's thrifty.
Let the toast pass,—
Drink to the lass,
I'll warrant she'll prove an excuse for the glass.
III.iii. Song

32 Here's to the charmer whose dimples we prize;
Now to the maid who has none, sir;
Here's to the girl with a pair of blue eyes,
And here's to the nymph with but one, sir.

33 An unforgiving eye, and a damned disinheriting countenance.
IV.i

34 *Rowley:* I believe there is no sentiment he has such faith in as that 'charity begins at home'.
Sir Oliver Surface: And his, I presume, is of that domestic sort which never stirs abroad at all.
V.i

35 There is no trusting appearances.
ii

36 The Right Honourable gentleman is indebted to his memory for his jests, and to his imagination for his facts.
Speech in Reply to Mr. Dundas. T. Moore, *Life of Sheridan* (1825), II.471

37 You write with ease, to show your breeding,
But easy writing's vile hard reading.
Clio's Protest. See T. Moore, *Life of Sheridan*, I.55

38 A man may surely be allowed to take a glass of wine by his own fireside.
On being encountered drinking a glass of wine in the street, while watching his theatre, the Drury Lane, burn down. II.20

39 Won't you come into the garden? I would like my roses to see you.
To a young lady. Attr. in *The Perfect Hostess*

GENERAL SHERMAN 1820–1891

40 There is many a boy here to-day who looks on war as all glory, but, boys, it is all hell.
Speech, Columbus, Ohio, 11 Aug. 1880. Lewis, *Sherman, Fighting Prophet*

1 I will not accept if nominated, and will not serve if elected.
Telegram to General Henderson on being urged to stand as Republican candidate in the U.S. Presidential election of 1884. *Memoirs*, 4th edition (to which his children had added a new chapter, XXVII, in which this text appears as the memory of Sherman's son who was present at its drafting).

JAMES SHIRLEY 1596–1666

2 The glories of our blood and state
Are shadows, not substantial things;
There is no armour against fate;
    Death lays his icy hand on kings:
        Sceptre and crown
        Must tumble down,
And in the dust be equal made
With the poor crooked scythe and spade.
The Contention of Ajax and Ulysses (1659), I.iii

3 The garlands wither on your brow;
    Then boast no more your mighty deeds!

4 Only the actions of the just
Smell sweet, and blossom in their dust.

5 I presume you're mortal, and may err.
The Lady of Pleasure (1635), II.ii

6   How little room
Do we take up in death, that, living know
No bounds?
The Wedding, (1626), IV.iv

THE SHORTER CATECHISM

7 'What is the chief end of man?'
'To glorify God and to enjoy him for ever'

J.H. SHORTHOUSE 1834–1903

8 'The Church of England,' I said, seeing that Mr Inglesant paused, 'is no doubt a compromise.'
John Inglesant (1880), ch.40

9 In all probability 'Wordsworth's standard of intoxication was miserably low'
Remark to some Wordsworthians who were deploring W.'s confession that he got drunk at Cambridge. G.W.E. Russell, *Collections and Recollections*, ch.8

HENRY SIDGWICK 1838–1900

10 We think so because other people all think so,
Or because—or because—after all we do think so,
Or because we were told so, and think we must think so,
Or because we once thought so, and think we still think so,
Or because having thought so, we think we *will* think so.
Arthur Sidgwick and Mrs. E.M. Sidgwick, *Henry Sidgwick* (1906), end of ch.11

ALGERNON SIDNEY 1622–1683

11 Liars ought to have good memories.
Discourses concerning Government (1698), ch.II, xv

12 Men lived like fishes; the great ones devour'd the small.
xviii

13 'Tis not necessary to light a candle to the sun.
xxiii

SIR PHILIP SIDNEY 1554–1586

14 Shallow brooks murmur most, deep silent slide away.
The Arcadia (1590), bk.i, **First Eclogues, Lalus and Dorus**, st.ii

15 Who shoots at the mid-day sun, though he be sure he shall never hit the mark; yet as sure he is he shall shoot higher than who aims but at a bush.
bk.ii

16 My true love hath my heart and I have his,
By just exchange one for the other giv'n;
I hold his dear, and mine he cannot miss,
There never was a better bargain driv'n.
bk.iii

17 Biting my truant pen, beating myself for spite,
'Fool,' said my Muse to me, 'look in thy heart and write'.
Astrophel and Stella (1591), Sonnet 1

18 With how sad steps, O Moon, thou climb'st the skies!
How silently, and with how wan a face!
What! may it be that even in heavenly place
That busy archer his sharp arrows tries?
Sonnet 31

19 Do they call virtue there ungratefulness?

20 Come, Sleep! O Sleep, the certain knot of peace,
    The baiting-place of wit, the balm of woe,
The poor man's wealth, the prisoner's release,
    Th' indifferent judge between the high and low.
Sonnet 39

21 Take thou of me smooth pillows, sweetest bed;
    A chamber deaf to noise and blind to light,
A rosy garland and a weary head.

22 That sweet enemy, France.
Sonnet 41

23 They love indeed who quake to say they love.
Sonnet 54

24 Doubt you to whom my Muse these notes intendeth,
    Which now my breast o'ercharged to music lendeth?
To you, to you, all song of praise is due;
    Only in you my song begins and endeth.
First song

25 Oh heav'nly fool, thy most kiss-worthy face
Anger invests with such a lovely grace,
That Anger's self I needs must kiss again.
Sonnet 73

26 I never drank of Aganippe well,
    Nor ever did in shade of Tempe sit,
And Muses scorn with vulgar brains to dwell;
    Poor layman I, for sacred rites unfit...
I am no pick-purse of another's wit.
Sonnet 74

27 Highway, since you my chief Parnassus be,
    And that my Muse, to some ears not unsweet,
Tempers her words to trampling horses' feet
    More oft than to a chamber melody,
Now blessed you, bear onward blessed me
    To her, where I my heart, safe-left, shall meet.
Sonnet 84

28 Leave me, O Love, which reacheth but to dust;
    And thou, my mind, aspire to higher things;

Grow rich in that which never taketh rust;
   Whatever fades, but fading pleasure brings.
Certain Sonnets

1 O fair! O sweet! When I do look on thee,
   In whom all joys so well agree,
Heart and soul do sing in me,
   Just accord all music makes.
To the Tune of a Spanish Song

2 With a tale forsooth he cometh unto you, with a tale
which holdeth children from play, and old men from
the chimney corner. [The poet.]
Defence of Poesie (1579-80, pub. 1595)

3 Certainly I must confess mine own barbarousness, I
never heard the old song of Percy and Douglas, that I
found not my heart moved more than with a trumpet.

4 Philip of Macedon reckoned a horse-race won at
Olympus among his three fearful felicities.

5 I will not wish unto you the ass's ears of Midas, nor to
be driven by a poet's verses, as Bubonax was, to hang
himself, nor to be rhymed to death, as is said to be
done in Ireland.

6 Thy necessity is yet greater than mine.
On giving his water-bottle to a dying soldier on the battle-field of
Zutphen, 1586. Sir Fulke Greville, *Life* (1652). The word
'necessity' is more often quoted as 'need'

ABBÉ EMMANUEL JOSEPH SIEYÈS 1748–1836

7 *La mort, sans phrases.*
Death, without rhetoric.
Attr. to Sieyès on voting in the French Convention for the death of
Louis XVI, 19 Jan. 1793. Afterwards repudiated by him

8 *J'ai vécu.*
I survived.
When asked what he had done during the French Revolution. V.
Mignet, 'Notice Historique sur la Vie et les Travaux de M. le
Comte de Sieyès'. *Recueil des Lectures...28 Déc. 1836.* He
afterwards stated he could not recall having said it.

SIMONIDES c.556–468 B.C.

9 ὦ ξεῖν', ἀγγέλλειν Λακεδαιμονίοις ὅτι τῇδε
   κείμεθα τοῖς κείνων ῥήμασι πειθόμενοι.

Go, tell the Spartans, thou who passest by,
   That here obedient to their laws we lie.
Herodotus, *Histories*, vii, 228.

GEORGE R. SIMS 1847–1922

10 It is Christmas Day in the Workhouse.
The Dagonet and Other Poems (1903)

EDITH SITWELL 1887–1964

11 Jane Jane
   Tall as a crane
   The morning light creaks down again.
Aubade

12 Daisy and Lily
Lazy and silly
Walk by the shore of the wan grassy sea
Talking once more 'neath a swan-bosomed tree.
Façade. Waltz

13 Still falls the Rain—
Dark as the world of man, black as our loss—

Blind as the nineteen hundred and forty nails
Upon the Cross.
The Raids 1940. Still falls the Rain

SIR OSBERT SITWELL 1892–1969

14 The British Bourgeoisie
Is not born,
And does not die,
But, if it is ill,
It has a frightened look in its eyes.
At the House of Mrs. Kinfoot

15 *Educ:* during the holidays from Eton.
Who's Who

JOHN SKELTON 1460?–1529

16 Far may be sought
Erst ye can find
So courteous, so kind,
As Merry Margaret, the midsummer flower,
Gentle as falcon or hawk of the tower.
To Mistress Margaret Hussey

17 With solace and gladness,
Much mirth and no madness,
All good and no badness;
So joyously,
So maidenly,
So womanly,
Her demeaning.

18 She is the violet,
The daisy delectable,
The columbine commendable,
The jelofer amiable;
For this most goodly flower,
This blossom of fresh colour,
So Jupiter me succour,
She flourisheth new and new
In beauty and virtue.
The Commendations of Mistress Jane Scrope

19 For the soul of Philip Sparrow,
That was late slain at Carrow
Among the Nunnes Black,
For that sweet soul's sake
And for all sparrows' souls
Set in our bead-rolls,
Pater noster qui
With an *Ave Mari.*
The Sparrow's Dirge

B.F. SKINNER 1904–

20 Education is what survives when what has been learnt
has been forgotten.
Education in 1984. *New Scientist*, 21 May 1964, p.484

CHRISTOPHER SMART 1722–1771

21 For I will consider my Cat Jeoffry.
For he is the servant of the Living God, duly and daily
   serving Him.
Jubilate Agno, XIX.51

22 For he counteracts the powers of darkness by his
   electrical skin and glaring eyes,
For he counteracts the Devil, who is death, by brisking

about the Life.
XX.15

1 He sung of God—the mighty source
Of all things—the stupendous force
    On which all strength depends;
From whose right arm, beneath whose eyes,
All period, pow'r, and enterprize
    Commences, reigns, and ends.
Song to David (1763), st.18

2 For Adoration all the ranks
Of angels yield eternal thanks,
    And David in the midst.
st.51

3 Strong is the horse upon his speed;
Strong in pursuit the rapid glede,
    Which makes at once his game:
Strong the tall ostrich on the ground;
Strong thro' the turbulent profound
    Shoots xiphias to his aim.

Strong is the lion—like a coal
His eye-ball—like a bastion's mole
    His chest against his foes:
Strong, the gier-eagle on his sail,
Strong against tide, th' enormous whale
    Emerges as he goes.

Where ask is have, where seek is find,
    Where knock is open wide.
st.75

4 Glorious the sun in mid-career;
Glorious th' assembled fires appear;
    Glorious the comet's train:
Glorious the trumpet and alarm;
Glorious th' almighty stretch'd-out arm;
    Glorious th' enraptur'd main.

Glorious the northern lights astream;
Glorious the song, when God's the theme;
    Glorious the thunder's roar:
Glorious hosanna from the den;
Glorious the catholic amen;
    Glorious the martyr's gore.

Glorious—more glorious is the crown
Of Him that brought salvation down
    By meekness, call'd thy Son;
Thou that stupendous truth believ'd,
And now the matchless deed's achiev'd,
    Determined, dared, and done.
st.84

SAMUEL SMILES 1812–1904

5 His [Dr. Priestley's] appointment [to act as astronomer
to Captain Cook's expedition to the southern seas] had
been cancelled, as the Board of Longitude objected to
his theology.
Men of Invention and Industry (1904), ch.3

6 Cecil's despatch of business was extraordinary, his
maxim being, 'The shortest way to do many things is
to do only one thing at once.'
Self-Help (1859), ch.9

7 A place for everything, and everything in its place.
Thrift (1875), ch.5

ADAM SMITH 1723–1790

8 And thus, *Place*, that great object which divides the
wives of aldermen, is the end of half the labours of
human life; and is the cause of all the tumult and
bustle, all the rapine and injustice, which avarice and
ambition have introduced into this world.
The Theory of Moral Sentiments, I.iii.2.8

9 The rich only select from the heap what is most
precious and agreeable. They consume little more than
the poor, and in spite of their natural selfishness and
rapacity...they divide with the poor the produce of all
their improvements. They are led by an invisible hand
to make nearly the same distribution of the necessaries
of life which would have been made, had the earth
been divided into equal portions among all its
inhabitants.
IV.i.10

10 People of the same trade seldom meet together, even
for merriment and diversion, but the conversation ends
in a conspiracy against the public, or in some
contrivance to raise prices.
Wealth of Nations (ed. Todd, 1976), I.x.c.27

11 With the greater part of rich people, the chief
enjoyment of riches consists in the parade of riches,
which in their eyes is never so complete as when they
appear to possess those decisive marks of opulence
which nobody can possess but themselves.
xi.c.31

12 To found a great empire for the sole purpose of raising
up a people of customers, may at first sight appear a
project fit only for a nation of shopkeepers. It is,
however, a project altogether unfit for a nation of
shopkeepers; but extremely fit for a nation whose
government is influenced by shopkeepers.
IV.vii.c.63. See 1:9, 359:15

13 It is the interest of every man to live as much at his
ease as he can; and if his emoluments are to be
precisely the same, whether he does, or does not
perform some very laborious duty, it is certainly his
interest, at least as interest is vulgarly understood,
either to neglect it altogether, or, if he is subject to
some authority which will not suffer him to do this, to
perform it in as careless and slovenly a manner as that
authority will permit.
V.i.f.7

14 The discipline of colleges and universities is in
general contrived, not for the benefit of the students,
but for the interest, or more properly speaking, for the
ease of the masters.
15

15 There is no art which one government sooner learns of
another than that of draining money from the pockets
of the people.
ii. h. 12

16 Without a union with Great Britain, the inhabitants of
Ireland are not likely for many ages to consider
themselves as one people.
iii.89

17 If any of the provinces of the British empire cannot be
made to contribute towards the support of the whole
empire, it is surely time that Great Britain should free
herself from the expense of defending those provinces
in time of war, and of supporting any part of their civil
or military establishments in time of peace, and

endeavour to accommodate her future views and designs to the real mediocrity of her circumstances.
92

1 Be assured, my young friend, that there is a great deal of *ruin* in a nation.
Correspondence of Sir John Sinclair (1831), i.390-91

ALEXANDER SMITH 1830–1867

2 Like a pale martyr in his shirt of fire.
A Life Drama (1853), ii

ALFRED EMANUEL SMITH 1873–1944

3 No matter how thin you slice it, it's still baloney.
Speech, 1936

4 The kiss of death.
Speech, 1926, referring to William Randolph Hearst's support of Ogden Mills

F.E. SMITH
see BIRKENHEAD

JAMES SMITH 1775–1839
and 'HORACE' [HORATIO] SMITH 1779–1849

5 In Craven-street, Strand, ten attorneys find place,
And ten dark coal-barges are moor'd at its base.
Fly, honesty, fly! seek some safer retreat;
For there's craft in the river, and craft in the street.
Craven Street, Strand

6 Hail, glorious edifice, stupendous work!
God bless the Regent and the Duke of York!
Rejected Addresses (1812). No.1. **Loyal Effusion**, l.1

7 Who makes the quartern loaf and Luddites rise?
Who fills the butcher's shops with large blue flies?
l.48

8 What stately vision mocks my waking sense?
Hence, dear delusion, sweet enchantment, hence!
No.3. **An Address Without a Phoenix**

9 In the name of the Prophet—figs!
No.10. **Johnson's Ghost**

LANGDON SMITH 1858–1918

10 When you were a tadpole, and I was a fish,
In the Palaeozoic time,
And side by side in the ebbing tide
We sprawled through the ooze and slime.
A Toast to a Lady. (*The Scrap-Book*, April 1906)

LOGAN PEARSALL SMITH 1865–1946

11 There are two things to aim at in life: first, to get what you want; and after that, to enjoy it. Only the wisest of mankind achieve the second.
Afterthoughts (1931), ch.1. **Life and Human Nature**

12 There are few sorrows, however poignant, in which a good income is of no avail.

13 There is more felicity on the far side of baldness than young men can possibly imagine.
ch.2. **Age and Death**

14 Most people sell their souls, and live with a good conscience on the proceeds.
ch.3. **Other People**

15 When people come and talk to you of their

aspirations, before they leave you had better count your spoons.
See 207:8, 275:1

16 Married women are kept women, and they are beginning to find it out.

17 It is the wretchedness of being rich that you have to live with rich people.
ch.4. **In the World**

18 Eat with the rich, but go to the play with the poor, who are capable of joy.
See 355:7

19 To suppose, as we all suppose, that we could be rich and not behave as the rich behave, is like supposing that we could drink all day and keep absolutely sober.

20 A best-seller is the gilded tomb of a mediocre talent.
ch.5. **Art and Letters**

21 People say that life is the thing, but I prefer reading.
ch.6. **Myself**

22 The old know what they want; the young are sad and bewildered.
Last Words (1933)

23 Thank heavens, the sun has gone in, and I don't have to go out and enjoy it.

SAMUEL FRANCIS SMITH 1808–1895

24 My country, 'tis of thee,
Sweet land of liberty,
     Of thee I sing:
Land where my fathers died,
Land of the pilgrims' pride,
From every mountain-side
     Let freedom ring.
America (1831)

STEVIE SMITH 1902–1971

25 Oh I am a cat that likes to
Gallop about doing good.
The Galloping Cat

26 Nobody heard him, the dead man,
But still he lay moaning:
I was much further out than you thought
And not waving but drowning.
Not Waving But Drowning

27 This Englishwoman is so refined
She has no bosom and no behind.
This Englishwoman

REVD. SYDNEY SMITH 1771–1845

28 It requires a surgical operation to get a joke well into a Scotch understanding. Their only idea of wit…is laughing immoderately at stated intervals.
Lady Holland, *Memoir* (1st ed. 1855), vol.I, ch.2, p.15

29 I heard him [Jeffrey] speak disrespectfully of the Equator!
p.17

30 That knuckle-end of England—that land of Calvin, oat-cakes, and sulphur.

31 Take short views, hope for the best, and trust in God.
ch.6, p.48

1 Looked as if she had walked straight out of the Ark.
ch.7, p.157

2 No furniture so charming as books.
ch.9, p.240

3 Madam, I have been looking for a person who disliked gravy all my life; let us swear eternal friendship.
p.257

4 How can a bishop marry? How can he flirt? The most he can say is, 'I will see you in the vestry after service.'
p.258

5 Not body enough to cover his mind decently with; his intellect is improperly exposed.

6 I have, alas, only one illusion left, and that is the Archbishop of Canterbury.
p.259

7 You find people ready enough to do the Samaritan, without the oil and twopence.
p.261

8 As the French say, there are three sexes—men, women, and clergymen.
p.262

9 Praise is the best diet for us, after all.
p.265

10 Daniel Webster struck me much like a steam-engine in trousers.
p.267

11 My definition of marriage:…it resembles a pair of shears, so joined that they cannot be separated; often moving in opposite directions, yet always punishing anyone who comes between them.
ch.11, p.363

12 He [Macaulay] is like a book in breeches.

13 He [Macaulay] has occasional flashes of silence, that make his conversation perfectly delightful.

14 Let onion atoms lurk within the bowl,
And, scarce-suspected, animate the whole.
Recipe for Salad, p.373

15 Serenely full, the epicure would say,
Fate cannot harm me, I have dined to-day.

16 Deserves to be preached to death by wild curates.
p.384

17 I never read a book before reviewing it; it prejudices a man so.
H. Pearson, *The Smith of Smiths* (1934), ch.iii, p.54

18 It is a place with only one post a day…In the country I always fear that creation will expire before tea-time.
ch.5, p.92

19 Minorities…are almost always in the right.
ch.9, p.220

20 —'s idea of heaven is, eating *pâtés de foie gras* to the sound of trumpets.
ch.10, p.236

21 What a pity it is that we have no amusements in England but vice and religion!

22 Let the Dean and Canons lay their heads together and the thing will be done. (It being proposed to surround St Paul's with a wooden pavement.)
p.237

23 Death must be distinguished from dying, with which it is often confused.
ch.11, p.271

24 The only way to deal with such a man as O'Connell is to hang him up and erect a statue to him under the gallows.
p.272

25 What two ideas are more inseparable than Beer and Britannia?

26 I am just going to pray for you at St Paul's, but with no very lively hope of success.
ch.13, p.308

27 Poverty is no disgrace to a man, but it is confoundedly inconvenient.
His Wit and Wisdom (1900), p.89

28 One of the greatest pleasures of life is conversation.
Essays (1877). Female Education, p.103

29 This great spectacle of human happiness.
Waterton's Wanderings, p.465

30 The moment the very name of Ireland is mentioned, the English seem to bid adieu to common feeling, common prudence, and common sense, and to act with the barbarity of tyrants, and the fatuity of idiots.
Peter Plymley's Letters (1929), p.9

31 A Curate—there is something which excites compassion in the very name of a Curate!!!
p.127. Persecuting Bishops

32 Dame Partington…was seen…with mop and pattens…vigorously pushing away the Atlantic Ocean. The Atlantic Ocean beat Mrs Partington.
p.228

33 Bishop Berkeley destroyed this world in one volume octavo; and nothing remained, after his time, but mind; which experienced a similar fate from the hand of Mr Hume in 1739.
Sketches of Moral Philosophy. Introd.

34 We shall generally find that the triangular person has got into the square hole, the oblong into the triangular, and a square person has squeezed himself into the round hole. The officer and the office, the doer and the thing done, seldom fit so exactly that we can say they were almost made for each other.
Lect.ix

35 I never could find any man who could think for two minutes together.
Lect.xix

36 The motto I proposed for the [*Edinburgh*] *Review* was: *Tenui musam meditamur avena*—'We cultivate literature upon a little oatmeal.'
Works (1859), vol.i, Preface, p.v

37 We can inform Jonathan what are the inevitable consequences of being too fond of glory;—Taxes upon every article which enters into the mouth, or covers the back, or is placed under the foot…taxes on everything on earth, and the waters under the earth.
vol.i. Review of Seybert's *Statistical Annals of the United States*, p.291

38 The schoolboy whips his taxed top—the beardless youth manages his taxed horse, with a taxed bridle, on a taxed road;—and the dying Englishman, pouring his medicine, which has paid seven per cent, into a spoon that has paid fifteen per cent—flings himself back upon his chintz bed, which has paid twenty-two per cent—and expires in the arms of an apothecary who

has paid a licence of a hundred pounds for the privilege of putting him to death.

1 What bishops like best in their clergy is a dropping-down-deadness of manner.
vol.ii, **First Letter to Archdeacon Singleton**, p.271. Note

2 There is not a better man in England than Lord John Russell; but his worst failure is, that he is utterly ignorant of all moral fear; there is nothing he would not undertake. I believe he would perform the operation for the stone—build St Peter's—or assume (with or without ten minutes' notice) the command of the Channel Fleet; and no one would discover by his manner that the patient had died—the church tumbled down—and the Channel Fleet been knocked to atoms.
Second letter to Archdeacon Singleton, 1838, p.275

3 I like, my dear Lord, the road you are travelling, but I don't like the pace you are driving; too similar to that of the son of Nimshi. I always feel myself inclined to cry out, Gently, John, gently down hill. Put on the drag.
Letter to Lord John Russell, p.300

4 Where etiquette prevents me from doing things disagreeable to myself, I am a perfect martinet.
Letters. To Lady Holland, 6 Nov. 1842

5 I look upon Switzerland as an inferior sort of Scotland.
To Lord Holland, 1815

6 Tory and Whig in turns shall be my host,
I taste no politics in boil'd and roast.
To John Murray. Nov. 1834

7 What would life be without arithmetic, but a scene of horrors?
To Miss —, 22 July 1835

8 I am convinced digestion is the great secret of life.
To Arthur Kinglake, 30 Sept. 1837

9 I have no relish for the country; it is a kind of healthy grave.
To Miss G. Harcourt, 1838

10 I have seen nobody since I saw you, but persons in orders. My only varieties are vicars, rectors, curates, and every now and then (by way of turbot) an archdeacon.
To Miss Berry, 28 Jan. 1843

11 Science is his forte, and omniscience his foible.
[William Whewell.]
Isaac Todhunter, *William Whewell* (1876), i.410

TOBIAS SMOLLETT 1721–1771

12 I think for my part one half of the nation is mad—and the other not very sound.
The Adventures of Sir Launcelot Greaves (1760–2), ch.6

13 He was formed for the ruin of our sex.
Roderick Random (1748), ch.22

14 That great Cham of literature, Samuel Johnson.
Letter to John Wilkes, 16 Mar. 1759. Boswell's *Johnson* (1934), vol.i, p.348

C.P. SNOW 1905–

15 The official world, the corridors of power, the dilemmas of conscience and egotism—she disliked them all.
Homecomings (1956), ch.22. See also ch.14 'those powerful anonymous *couloirs*'. Snow used the phrase as the title of a subsequent novel: *Corridors of Power* (1964).

16 A good many times I have been present at gatherings of people who, by the standards of the traditional culture, are thought highly educated and who have with considerable gusto been expressing their incredulity at the illiteracy of scientists. Once or twice I have been provoked and have asked the company how many of them could describe the Second Law of Thermodynamics. The response was cold: it was also negative.
The Two Cultures, Rede Lecture, 1959, ch.1

SOCRATES 469–399 B.C.

17 ὁ δὲ ἀνεξέταστος βίος οὐ βιωτὸς ἀνθρώπῳ.
The unexamined life is not worth living.
Plato, *Apology*, 38a

18 But already it is time to depart, for me to die, for you to go on living; which of us takes the better course, is concealed from anyone except God.
42a

19 A man should feel confident concerning his soul, who has renounced those pleasures and fineries that go with the body, as being alien to him, and considering them to result more in harm than in good, but has pursued the pleasures that go with learning and made the soul fine with no alien but rather its own proper refinements, moderation and justice and courage and freedom and truth; thus it is ready for the journey to the world below.
Plato, *Phaedo*, 114d

20 'What do you say about pouring a libation to some god from this cup? Is it allowed or not?'
'We only prepare just the right amount to drink, Socrates,' he said [the jailor.]
'I understand,' he went on; 'but it is allowed and necessary to pray to the gods, that my moving from hence to there may be blessed; thus I pray, and so be it.'
117b

21 ὦ Κρίτων, τῷ Ἀσκληπιῷ ὀφείλομεν ἀλεκτρυόνα. ἀλλὰ ἀπόδοτε καὶ μὴ ἀμελήσητε.
Crito, we owe a cock to Aesculapius; please pay it and don't let it pass.
118. Last words

22 πόσων ἐγὼ χρείαν οὐκ ἔχω.
How many things I can do without!
On looking at a multitude of wares exposed for sale. Diogenes Laertius, *Lives of the Eminent Philosophers*, II.25

SOLON c.630–c.555 B.C.

23 Laws are like spider's webs: if some poor weak creature come up against them, it is caught; but a bigger one can break through and get away.
Diogenes Laertius, *Lives of the Eminent Philosophers*, I.58

24 γηράσκω δ' αἰεὶ πολλὰ διδασκόμενος.
I grow old ever learning many things.
Poetae Lyrici Graeci (ed. Bergk), Solon, 18

25 πρὶν δ' ἂν τελευτήσῃ, ἐπισχεῖν μηδὲ καλέειν κω ὄλβιον, ἀλλ' εὐτυχέα.
Call no man happy till he dies, he is at best but

fortunate.
Herodotus, *Histories*, i.32

ALEXANDER SOLZHENITSYN 1918–

1 The salvation of mankind lies only in making everything the concern of all.
Nobel Lecture, 1970

WILLIAM SOMERVILLE 1675–1742

2   My hoarse-sounding horn
Invites thee to the chase, the sport of kings;
Image of war, without its guilt.
The Chace (1735), bk.i, l.13. See 172:7

3 Hail, happy Britain! highly favoured isle,
And Heaven's peculiar care!
l.84

SOPHOCLES 496–406 B.C.

4 ὦ παῖ, γένοιο πατρὸς εὐτυχέστερος.
My son, may you be happier than your father.
Ajax, 550

5 ἐχθρῶν ἄδωρα δῶρα κοὐκ ὀνήσιμα.
Enemies' gifts are no gifts and do no good.
665

6 θεοῖς τέθνηκεν οὗτος, οὐ κείνοισιν, οὔ.
His death concerns the gods, not those men, no!
970. Of Ajax's enemies, the Greek leaders

7 πολλὰ τὰ δεινὰ κοὐδὲν ἀν-
θρώπου δεινότερον πέλει.
There are many wonderful things, and nothing is more wonderful than man.
Antigone, 332

8 μὴ φῦναι τὸν ἅπαντα νι-
κᾷ λόγον.
Not to be born is, past all prizing, best.
Oedipus Coloneus, 1224. Tr. R.W. Jebb

9 "πῶς," ἔφη, "ὦ Σοφόκλεις, ἔχεις πρὸς τἀφροδίσια;
ἔτι οἷός τε εἶ γυναικὶ συγγίγνεσθαι;" καὶ ὅς,
"εὐφήμει," ἔφη, "ὦ ἄνθρωπε. ἀσμενέστατα μέντοι
αὐτὸ ἀπέφυγον, ὥσπερ λυττῶντα τινα καὶ ἄγριον
δεσπότην ἀποδράς."
Someone asked Sophocles, 'How do you feel now about sex? Are you still able to have a woman?' He replied, 'Hush, man; most gladly indeed am I rid of it all, as though I had escaped from a mad and savage master.'
Plato, *Republic*, I, 329b

CHARLES HAMILTON SORLEY 1895–1915

10 We swing ungirded hips,
And lightened are our eyes,
The rain is on our lips,
We do not run for prize.
The Song of the Ungirt Runners

JOHN L.B. SOULE 1815–1891

11 Go West, young man, go West!
Editorial, *Terre Haute* (Indiana) *Express* (1851). See 235:26

REVD. ROBERT SOUTH 1634–1716

12 An Aristotle was but the rubbish of an Adam, and Athens but the rudiments of Paradise.
Sermons, vol.I.ii

THOMAS SOUTHERNE 1660–1746

13   And when we're worn,
Hack'd hewn with constant service, thrown aside
To rust in peace, or rot in hospitals.
The Loyal Brother (1682), Act I

ROBERT SOUTHEY 1774–1843
See also under Coleridge

14 It was a summer evening,
    Old Kaspar's work was done,
And he before his cottage door
    Was sitting in the sun,
And by him sported on the green
His little grandchild Wilhelmine.
The Battle of Blenheim

15 He came to ask what he had found,
That was so large, and smooth, and round.

16 Now tell us all about the war,
And what they fought each other for.

17 But what they fought each other for,
    I could not well make out.

18 But things like that, you know, must be
    At every famous victory.

19 Great praise the Duke of Marlbro' won,
    And our good Prince Eugene.

20 'And everybody praised the Duke,
    Who this great fight did win.'
'But what good came of it at last?'
    Quoth little Peterkin.
'Why that I cannot tell,' said he,
'But 'twas a famous victory.'

21 My name is Death: the last best friend am I.
Carmen Nuptiale. The Lay of the Laureate. The Dream, lxxxvii

22 And this way the water comes down at Lodore.
The Cataract of Lodore

23 Curses are like young chickens, they always come home to roost.
The Curse of Kehama (1810). Motto

24 And Sleep shall obey me,
    And visit thee never,
And the Curse shall be on thee
    For ever and ever.
II.14

25 Hark! at the Golden Palaces
The Brahmin strikes the hour.
V.1

26 They sin who tell us love can die.
With life all other passions fly,
    All others are but vanity.
X.10

27 Thou hast been call'd, O Sleep! the friend of Woe,
But 'tis the happy who have called thee so.
XV.12

28 No stir in the air, no stir in the sea,

The ship was still as she could be.
The Inchcape Rock

1 And then they knew the perilous rock,
And blest the Abbot of Aberbrothok.

2 O Christ! It is the Inchcape Rock!

3 Sir Ralph the Rover tore his hair;
He curst himself in his despair.

4 Blue, darkly, deeply, beautifully blue.
Madoc (1805). Pt.I, **Madoc in Wales.** V, Lincoya, l.102

5 We wage no war with women nor with priests.
XV, **The Excommunication**, l.65

6 What will not woman, gentle woman dare,
When strong affection stirs her spirit up?
Pt.II, **Madoc in Aztlan.** II, **The Tidings**, l.125

7 You are old, Father William, the young man cried,
The few locks which are left you are grey;
You are hale, Father William, a hearty old man,
Now tell me the reason, I pray.
The Old Man's Comforts, and how he Gained them

8 You are old, Father William, the young man cried
And pleasures with youth pass away,
And yet you lament not the days that are gone,
Now tell me the reason, I pray.

9 In the days of my youth I remembered my God!
And He hath not forgotten my age.

10 The Monk my son, and my daughter the Nun.
The Old Woman of Berkeley

11 A vague, a dizzy, a tumultuous joy.
Thalaba the Destroyer (1801), bk.III.xix

12 The arts babblative and scribblative.
Colloquies on the Progress and Prospects of Society (1829).
Coll.x. Pt.ii

13 The march of intellect.
Coll.xiv

14 Your true lover of literature is never fastidious.
The Doctor (1812), ch.17

15 Show me a man who cares no more for one place than
another, and I will show you in that same person one
who loves nothing but himself. Beware of those who
are homeless by choice.
ch.34

16 Live as long as you may, the first twenty years are the
longest half of your life.
ch.130

17 The death of Nelson was felt in England as something
more than a public calamity; men started at the
intelligence, and turned pale, as if they had heard of
the loss of a dear friend.
The Life of Nelson (1813), ch.9

18 She has made me half in love with a cold climate.
Letter to his brother Thomas, 28 Apr. 1797

ROBERT SOUTHWELL 1561?–1595

19 As I in hoary winter's night stood shivering in the
snow,
Surprised I was with sudden heat which made my
heart to glow;
And lifting up a fearful eye to view what fire was
near,
A pretty Babe all burning bright did in the air appear.
The Burning Babe (1595)

20 Times go by turns, and chances change by course,
From foul to fair, from better hap to worse.
Times go by Turns. See 11:5

21 Before my face the picture hangs,
That daily should put me in mind
Of those cold qualms, and bitter pangs,
That shortly I am like to find:
But yet alas full little I
Do think hereon that I must die.
Upon the Image of Death

JOHN SPARROW 1906–

22 Chill on the brow and in the breast
The frost of years is spread—
Soon we shall take our endless rest
With the unfeeling dead.

Insensibly, ere we depart,
We grow more cold, more kind:
Age makes a winter in the heart,
An autumn in the mind.
Grave Epigrams (1974), viii

23 That indefatigable and unsavoury engine of pollution,
the dog.
Letter to *The Times*, 30 Sept. 1975

HERBERT SPENCER 1820–1903

24 Science is organized knowledge.
Education (1861), ch.2

25 People are beginning to see that the first requisite to
success in life is to be a good animal.

26 Absolute morality is the regulation of conduct in such
a way that pain shall not be inflicted.
Essays (1891), vol.iii, p.152. **Prison Ethics**

27 The ultimate result of shielding men from the effects
of folly, is to fill the world with fools.
p.354. **State Tamperings with Money and Banks**

28 The Republican form of Government is the highest
form of government; but because of this it requires the
highest type of human nature—a type nowhere at
present existing.
p.478. **The Americans**

29 Evolution…is—a change from an indefinite,
incoherent homogeneity, to a definite coherent
heterogeneity.
First Principles (1862), ch.16, 138

30 It cannot but happen…that those will survive whose
functions happen to be most nearly in equilibrium with
the modified aggregate of external forces…This
survival of the fittest implies multiplication of the
fittest.
Principles of Biology (1865), pt.iii, ch.12, **Indirect
Equilibration**, 164

31 How often misused words generate misleading
thoughts.
Principles of Ethics, bk.I, pt.ii, ch.8, 152

32 Progress, therefore, is not an accident, but a
necessity…It is a part of nature.
Social Statics (1850), pt.i, ch.2, 4

33 A clever theft was praiseworthy amongst the Spartans;
and it is equally so amongst Christians, provided it be
on a sufficiently large scale.
pt.ii, ch.16, 3

1 Education has for its object the formation of character.
ch.17, 4

2 Opinion is ultimately determined by the feelings, and not by the intellect.
pt.iv, ch.30, 8

3 No one can be perfectly free till all are free; no one can be perfectly moral till all are moral; no one can be perfectly happy till all are happy.
16

4 It was remarked to me by the late Mr Charles Roupell...that to play billards well was a sign of an ill-spent youth.
Duncan, *Life and Letters of Spencer* (1908), ch.20, p.298

5 French art, if not sanguinary, is usually obscene.
'Two', *Home Life with Herbert Spencer* (1906), ch.IV, p.115

STEPHEN SPENDER 1909–

6 As she will live who, candle-lit
Floats upon her final breath
The ceiling of the frosty night
And her white room beneath
Wearing not like destruction, but
Like a white dress, her death.
Elegy for Margaret, vi

7 I think continually of those who were truly great—
The names of those who in their lives fought for life,
Who wore at their hearts the fire's centre.
I Think Continually of Those

8 Born of the sun they travelled a short while towards the sun,
And left the vivid air signed with their honour.

9   Their collected
Hearts wound up with love, like little watch springs.
The Living Values

10 Never being, but always at the edge of Being.
Preludes, 10. (*Collected Poems*, 1955)

11 My parents kept me from children who were rough
Who threw words like stones and who wore torn clothes.
11

12 What I had not foreseen
Was the gradual day
Weakening the will
Leaking the brightness away.
12

13 After the first powerful, plain manifesto
The black statement of pistons, without more fuss
But gliding like a queen, she leaves the station.
29. **The Express**

14 Eye, gazelle, delicate wanderer,
Drinker of horizon's fluid line.
35

15 The word bites like a fish.
Shall I throw it back free
Arrowing to that sea
Where thoughts lash tail and fin?
Or shall I pull it in
To rhyme upon a dish?
Word

EDMUND SPENSER 1552?–1599

16 The merry cuckoo, messenger of Spring,

His trumpet shrill hath thrice already sounded.
Amoretti (1595). Sonnet xix

17 Most glorious Lord of life, that on this day
Didst make thy triumph over death and sin:
And, having harrow'd hell, didst bring away
Captivity thence captive, us to win.
lxviii

18 So let us love, dear Love, like as we ought,
—Love is the lesson which the Lord us taught.

19 Fresh spring the herald of love's mighty king,
In whose coat armour richly are display'd
All sorts of flowers the which on earth do spring
In goodly colours gloriously array'd.
lxx

20 One day I wrote her name upon the strand,
But came the waves and washed it away:
Again I wrote it with a second hand,
But came the tide, and made my pains his prey.
Vain man, said she, that dost in vain assay,
A mortal thing so to immortalize,
For I myself shall like to this decay,
And eke my name be wiped out likewise.
Not so, quoth I, let baser things devise
To die in dust, but you shall live by fame:
My verse your virtues rare shall eternize,
And in the heavens write your glorious name,
Where when as death shall all the world subdue,
Our love shall live, and later life renew.
lxxv

21 Triton blowing loud his wreathed horn.
Colin Clout's Come Home Again (1595), l.245

22 So love is Lord of all the world by right.
l.883

23 What more felicity can fall to creature,
Than to enjoy delight with liberty.
Complaints (1591). **Muiopotmos**, l.209

24 Of such deep learning little had he need,
Ne yet of Latin, ne of Greek that breed
Doubts 'mongst Divines, and difference of texts,
From whence arise diversity of sects,
and hateful heresies.
Prosopopoia or Mother Hubbard's Tale, l.385

25 Open the temple gates unto my love,
Open them wide that she may enter in.
Epithalamion (1595), l.204

26 Ah! when will this long weary day have end,
And lend me leave to come unto my love?
l.278

27 Song made in lieu of many ornaments,
With which my love should duly have been deck'd.
l.427

28 The generall end therefore of all the book is to fashion a gentleman or noble person in vertuous and gentle discipline.
The Faerie Queen (1596), preface

29 Fierce wars and faithful loves shall moralize my song.
bk.I, introd. i.1

30 A gentle knight was pricking on the plain.
c.I.i

31 But on his breast a bloody cross he bore,
The dear remembrance of his dying Lord.
ii

32 But of his cheer did seem too solemn sad;

Yet nothing did he dread, but ever was ydrad.

1 A bold bad man, that dar'd to call by name
Great Gorgon, Prince of darkness and dead night.
xxxvii. See 447:1

2   Her angel's face
As the great eye of heaven shined bright,
And made a sunshine in the shady place;
Did never mortal eye behold such heavenly grace.
c.III.vi

3 And all the hinder parts, that few could spy,
Were ruinous and old, but painted cunningly.
c.IV.v

4 The Noble heart, that harbours virtuous thought,
And is with child of glorious great intent,
Can never rest, until it forth have brought
Th' eternal brood of glory excellent.
c.V.i

5   A cruel crafty Crocodile,
Which in false grief hiding his harmful guile,
Doth weep full sore, and sheddeth tender tears.
xviii

6 Still as he fled, his eye was backward cast,
As if his fear still followed him behind.
c.IX.xxi

7 That darksome cave they enter, where they find
That cursed man, low sitting on the ground,
Musing full sadly in his sullen mind.
xxxv

8 Sleep after toil, port after stormy seas,
Ease after war, death after life does greatly please.
xl

9 Death is the end of woes: die soon, O fairy's son.
xlvii

10 So double was his pains, so double be his praise.
bk.II, c.II.xxv

11 Upon her eyelids many Graces sate,
Under the shadow of her even brows.
c.III.xxv

12 And all for love, and nothing for reward.
c.VIII.ii

13 So passeth, in the passing of a day,
Of mortal life the leaf, the bud, the flower,
No more doth flourish after first decay,
That erst was sought to deck both bed and bower,
Of many a Lady, and many a Paramour:
Gather therefore the Rose, whilst yet is prime,
For soon comes age, that will her pride deflower:
Gather the Rose of love, whilst yet is time,
Whilst loving thou mayst loved be with equal crime.
c.XII.lxxv

14   The dunghill kind
Delights in filth and foul incontinence:
Let Grill be Grill, and have his hoggish mind.
lxxxvii

15 Whether it divine tobacco were,
Or Panachaea, or Polygony,
She found, and brought it to her patient dear.
bk.III, c.V.xxxii

16 Hard is to teach an old horse amble true.
c.VIII.xxvi

17 And painful pleasure turns to pleasing pain.
c.X.lx

18 And as she look'd about, she did behold,
How over that same door was likewise writ,
Be bold, be bold, and everywhere Be bold...
At last she spied at that room's upper end
Another iron door, on which was writ
Be not too bold.
c.XI.liv

19 Dan Chaucer, well of English undefiled,
On Fame's eternal beadroll worthy to be filed.
bk.IV, c.II.xxxii

20 For all that nature by her mother wit
Could frame in earth.
c.X.xxi

21 O sacred hunger of ambitious minds.
bk.V, c.XII.i

22 A monster, which the Blatant beast men call,
A dreadful fiend of gods and men ydrad.
xxxvii

23 The gentle mind by gentle deeds is known.
For a man by nothing is so well bewray'd,
As by his manners.
bk.VI, c.III.i

24 What man that sees the ever-whirling wheel
Of Change, the which all mortal things doth sway,
But that thereby doth find, and plainly feel,
How Mutability in them doth play
Her cruel sports, to many men's decay?
bk.VII, c.VI.i

25 For all that moveth doth in Change delight:
But thenceforth all shall rest eternally
With Him that is the God of Sabbaoth hight:
O that great Sabbaoth God, grant me that Sabbaoth's
sight.
c.VIII.ii

26 So you great Lord, that with your counsel sway
The burden of this kingdom mightily,
With like delights sometimes may eke delay,
The rugged brow of careful Policy.
[Dedicatory Sonnets] **To Sir Christopher Hatton**

27 That beauty is not, as fond men misdeem,
An outward show of things, that only seem.
An Hymn in Honour of Beauty (1596), l.90

28 For of the soul the body form doth take;
For soul is form, and doth the body make.
l.132

29 I was promis'd on a time,
To have reason for my rhyme;
From that time unto this season,
I received nor rhyme nor reason.
Lines on his Pension. Attr.

30 Calm was the day, and through the trembling air,
Sweet breathing Zephyrus did softly play.
Prothalamion (1596), l.1

31 With that, I saw two Swans of goodly hue,
Come softly swimming down along the Lee;
Two fairer Birds I yet did never see:
The Snow which doth the top of Pindus strew,
Did never whiter show,
Nor Jove himself when he a Swan would be
For love of Leda, whiter did appear.
l.37

32 So purely white they were,
That even the gentle stream, the which them bare,

Seem'd foul to them, and bade his billows spare
To wet their silken feathers, lest they might
Soil their fair plumes with water not so fair
And mar their beauties bright,
That shone as Heaven's light,
Against their Bridal day, which was not long:
Sweet Thames, run softly, till I end my Song.
l.46

1 At length they all to merry London came,
To merry London, my most kindly nurse,
That to me gave this life's first native source.
l.127

2 To be wise and eke to love,
Is granted scarce to God above.
The Shepherd's Calendar (1579), **March. Willy's Emblem**

3 Bring hither the Pink and purple Columbine,
     With Gillyflowers:
Bring Coronation, and Sops in wine,
     Worn of paramours.
Strew the ground with Daffadowndillies,
And Cowslips, and Kingcups, and loved Lilies:
     The pretty Pawnce,
     And the Chevisaunce,
Shall match with the fair flower Delice.
April, l.136

4 And he that strives to touch the stars,
     Oft stumbles at a straw.
July, l.99

5 Uncouth unkist, said the old famous Poet Chaucer.
The Shepherd's Calendar. **Letter to Gabriel Harvey**

6 So now they have made our English tongue a
gallimaufry or hodgepodge of all other speeches.

BARUCH SPINOZA 1632–1677

7 *Sedula curavi, humanas actiones non ridere, non
lugere, neque detestare, sed intelligere.*
I have striven not to laugh at human actions, not to
weep at them, nor to hate them, but to understand
them.
Tractatus Politicus 1, iv

REVD. WILLIAM ARCHIBALD SPOONER
1844–1930

8 You will find as you grow older that the weight of
rages will press harder and harder on the employer.
Sir W. Hayter, *Spooner* (1977), ch.6. Many other Spoonerisms,
such as those given in the previous editions of O.D.Q., are now
known to be apocryphal.

9 Poor soul, very sad; her late husband, you know, a
very sad death—eaten by missionaries—poor soul!

SIR CECIL ARTHUR SPRING-RICE 1858–1918

10 I vow to thee, my country—all earthly things above—
Entire and whole and perfect, the service of my love.
Last Poem

11 I am the Dean of Christ Church, Sir:
There's my wife; look well at her.
She's the Broad and I'm the High;
We are the University.
The Masque of Balliol, composed by and current among members
of Balliol College, Oxford, in the late 1870s. This first couplet
(identified as by C.A. Spring-Rice) was unofficially altered to:

12 I am the Dean, and this is Mrs Liddell;

She is the first and I the second fiddle.
See also 7:1. 37:8

J.C. (SIR JOHN) SQUIRE 1884–1958

13 God heard the embattled nations sing and shout
'Gott strafe England!' and 'God save the King!'
God this, God that, and God the other thing—
'Good God', said God, 'I've got my work cut out.'
Epigrams, no.1, **'The Dilemma'**

14 It did not last: the Devil howling 'Ho!
Let Einstein be!' restored the status quo.
Answer to 378:7

MME DE STAEL 1766–1817

15 *Tout comprendre rend très indulgent.*
To be totally understanding makes one very indulgent.
Corinne (1807), lib.iv, ch.2

JOSEPH STALIN 1879–1953

16 The Pope! How many divisions has *he* got?
When asked by Laval to encourage Catholicism in Russia to
conciliate the Pope, 13 May 1935. Churchill, *The Second World
War,* vol.i, 'The Gathering Storm', ch.8

SIR HENRY MORTON STANLEY 1841–1904

17 Dr Livingstone, I presume?
How I found Livingstone (1872), ch.11

COLONEL C.E. STANTON 1859–1933

18 Lafayette, we are here!
Address delivered at the grave of Lafayette, Paris, 4 July 1917.
Often attr. to General John J. Pershing, but disclaimed by him

EDWIN McMASTERS STANTON 1814–1869

19 Now he belongs to the ages.
Of Abraham Lincoln, after his assassination, 15 Apr. 1865. I.M.
Tarbell, *Life of Abraham Lincoln* (1900), vol.II, p.244

JOHN STARK 1728–1822

20 We beat them to-day or Molly Stark's a widow.
Before Battle of Bennington, 16 Aug. 1777. Appleton,
Cyclopaedia of American Biography, vol.v

ENID STARKIE d. 1970

21 Unhurt people are not much good in the world.
Joanna Richardson, *Enid Starkie,* ch.18

SIR RICHARD STEELE 1672–1729

22 I have often thought that a story-teller is born, as well
as a poet.
The Guardian, No.24

23 Gained universal applause by explaining a passage in
the game-act.
The Spectator, No.2

24 I have heard Will Honeycomb say, A Woman seldom
Writes her Mind but in her Postscript.
No.79

25 We were in some little time fixed in our seats, and sat
with that dislike which people not too good-natured

usually conceive of each other at first sight.
No.132

1 The noblest motive is the public good.
No.200. Motto in Ed. 1744

2 There are so few who can grow old with a good grace.
No.263

3 Will Honeycomb calls these over-offended ladies the outrageously virtuous.
No.266

4 Fashion, the arbiter, and rule of right.
No.478. Motto in Ed.1744

5 It is to be noted that when any part of this paper appears dull there is a design in it.
The Tatler, No.38

6 Though her mien carries much more invitation than command, to behold her is an immediate check to loose behaviour; to love her is a liberal education.
No.49

7 Every man is the maker of his own fortune.
No.52

8 The insupportable labour of doing nothing.
No.54

9 Reading is to the mind what exercise is to the body.
No.147

10 The truth of it is, the first rudiments of education are given very indiscreetly by most parents.
No.173

11 Let your precept be, Be easy.
No.196

12 It was very prettily said, that we may learn the little value of fortune by the persons on whom heaven is pleased to bestow it.
No.203. See 320:14

13 These ladies of irresistible modesty are those who make virtue unamiable.
No.217

14 I fared like a distressed Prince who calls in a powerful Neighbour to his Aid; I was undone by my Auxiliary; when I had once called him in, I could not subsist without Dependance on him.
Preface of vol.iv (1711). On his co-editorship, with Addison, of *The Spectator*

LINCOLN STEFFENS 1866–1936

15 I have seen the future, and it works.
After visiting Moscow in 1919, Steffens said to Bernard Baruch 'I have been over into the future, and it works.' He later improved the expression, and used it frequently in the shorter form. William C. Bullitt, the U.S. diplomat with whom Steffens was travelling, claimed he was rehearsing this formula long before seeing Lenin's Russia. J. Kaplan, *Lincoln Steffens* (1975), ch.13, ii

GERTRUDE STEIN 1874–1946

16 Pigeons on the grass alas.
Four Saints in 3 Acts, III.ii

17 Rose is a rose is a rose is a rose.
Sacred Emily

18 You're all a lost generation.
Quoting (in translation), in a particular reference to 'all of you young people who served in the war', a mechanic's rebuke (in French) to his apprentice, who had made a shoddy repair to her car. E. Hemingway, *A Moveable Feast,* ch.3. Used as the epigraph to Hemingway's *The Sun Also Rises* (1926).

19 What *is* the answer?...In that case, what is the question?
Last words. Donald Sutherland, *Gertrude Stein, A Biography of her Work* (1951), ch.6

SIR JAMES FITZJAMES STEPHEN 1829–1894

20 The way in which the man of genius rules is by persuading an efficient minority to coerce an indifferent and self-indulgent majority.
Liberty, Equality and Fraternity (1873), ch.II

21 Progress has its drawbacks and they are great and serious.

J.K. STEPHEN 1859–1892

22 Two voices are there: one is of the deep;
It learns the storm-cloud's thunderous melody,
Now roars, now murmurs with the changing sea,
Now bird-like pipes, now closes soft in sleep:
And one is of an old half-witted sheep
Which bleats articulate monotony,
And indicates that two and one are three,
That grass is green, lakes damp, and mountains steep
And, Wordsworth, both are thine.
Lapsus Calami (1896). A Sonnet. See 582:18

23   Good Lord! I'd rather be
Quite unacquainted with the A.B.C.
Than write such hopeless rubbish as thy worst.

24 Will there never come a season
Which shall rid us from the curse
Of a prose which knows no reason
And an unmelodious verse...
When there stands a muzzled stripling,
Mute, beside a muzzled bore:
When the Rudyards cease from kipling
And the Haggards Ride no more.
To R.K.

25 Ah! Matt.: old age has brought to me
Thy wisdom, less thy certainty:
The world's a jest, and joy's a trinket:
I knew that once: but now—I think it.
Senex to Matt. Prior

JAMES STEPHENS 1882–1950

26 I heard a sudden cry of pain!
There is a rabbit in a snare.
The Snare

27 Little One! Oh, Little One!
I am searching everywhere!

LAURENCE STERNE 1713–1768

28 They order, said I, this matter better in France.
A Sentimental Journey (1768), 1.1

29 I had had an affair with the moon, in which there was neither sin nor shame.
The Monk. Calais

30 The Sentimental Traveller (meaning thereby myself) who have travell'd, and of which I am now sitting down to give an account—as much out of necessity, and the *besoin de voyager,* as any one in the class.
Preface. In the Desobligeant

31 As an English man does not travel to see English men,

I retired to my room.

1 —You need not tell me what the proposal was, said she, laying her hand upon both mine, as she interrupted me.—A man, my good Sir, has seldom an offer of kindness to make to a woman, but she has a presentment of it some moments before.
The Remise. Calais

2 I pity the man who can travel from Dan to Beersheba, and cry, 'tis all barren.
In the Street. Calais

3 Having been in love with one princess or another, almost all my life, and I hope I shall go on so, till I die, being firmly persuaded, that if I ever do a mean action, it must be in some interval betwixt one passion and another.
Montriul

4 Vive l'amour! et vive la bagatelle!
The letter

5 Hail ye small sweet courtesies of life.
The Pulse. Paris

6 There are worse occupations in this world than feeling a woman's pulse.

7 'I can't get out,—I can't get out,' said the starling.
The Passport. The Hotel at Paris

8 He gave a deep sigh—I saw the iron enter into his soul!
The Captive. Paris

9 I think there is a fatality in it—I seldom go to the place I set out for.
The Address. Versailles

10 They [the French] are a loyal, a gallant, a generous, an ingenious, and good-temper'd people as is under heaven—if they have a fault, they are too *serious.*
The Character. Versailles

11 God tempers the wind, said Maria, to the shorn lamb.
Maria. From a French proverb, but familiar in Sterne's form of words

12 Dear sensibility! source inexhausted of all that's precious in our joys, or costly in our sorrows!
The Bourbonnois

13 If the supper was to my taste—the grace which followed it was much more so.
The Supper

14 But the fille de chambre hearing there were words between us, and fearing that hostilities would ensue in due course, had crept silently out of her closet, and it being totally dark, had stolen so close to our beds, that she had got herself into the narrow passage which separated them, and had advanced so far up as to be in a line betwixt her mistress and me—
So that when I stretched out my hand, I caught hold of the fille de chambre's
The Case of Delicacy

15 I live in a constant endeavour to fence against the infirmities of ill health, and other evils of life, by mirth; being firmly persuaded that every time a man smiles,—but much more so, when he laughs, that it adds something to this Fragment of Life.
Tristram Shandy (1760–67). Dedication

16 I wish either my father or my mother, or indeed both of them, as they were in duty both equally bound to it, had minded what they were about when they begot

me.
bk.I, ch.1, opening words

17 'Pray, my dear,' quoth my mother, 'have you not forgot to wind up the clock?'—'Good G—!' cried my father, making an exclamation, but taking care to moderate his voice at the same time,—'Did ever woman, since the creation of the world, interrupt a man with such a silly question?'

18 As we jog on, either laugh with me, or at me, or in short do anything,—only keep your temper.
ch.6

19 'Tis known by the name of perseverance in a good cause,—and of obstinacy in a bad one.
ch.17

20 What is the character of a family to an hypothesis? my father would reply.
ch.21

21 My uncle Toby would never offer to answer this by any other kind of argument, than that of whistling half a dozen bars of Lillabullero.

22 Digressions, incontestably, are the sunshine;—they are the life, the soul of reading;—take them out of this book for instance,—you might as well take the book along with them.
ch.22

23 I should have no objection to this method, but that I think it must smell too strong of the lamp.
ch.23

24 'I'll not hurt thee,' says my uncle Toby, rising from his chair, and going across the room, with the fly in his hand,—'I'll not hurt a hair of thy head:—Go,' says he, lifting up the sash, and opening his hand as he spoke, to let it escape;—'go, poor devil, get thee gone, why should I hurt thee?—This world surely is wide enough to hold both thee and me.'
bk.ii, ch.12

25 Whenever a man talks loudly against religion,—always suspect that it is not his reason, but his passions which have got the better of his creed.
ch.17

26 'Sir,' replied Dr Slop, 'it would astonish you to know what improvements we have made of late years in all branches of obstetrical knowledge, but particularly in that one single point of the safe and expeditious extraction of the foetus,—which has received such lights, that, for my part (holding up his hands) I declare I wonder how the world has—.'
'I wish,' quoth my uncle Toby, 'you had seen what prodigious armies we had in Flanders.'
ch.18

27 It is the nature of an hypothesis, when once a man has conceived it, that it assimilates every thing to itself, as proper nourishment; and, from the first moment of your begetting it, it generally grows the stronger by every thing you see, hear, read, or understand. This is of great use.
bk.ii, ch.19

28 'Our armies swore terribly in Flanders,' cried my uncle Toby,—'but nothing to this.'
bk.iii, ch.11

29 The corregiescity of Corregio.
ch.12. See 131:19

30 Of all the cants which are canted in this canting

world,—though the cant of hypocrites may be the worst,—the cant of criticism is the most tormenting!

1 Is this a fit time, said my father to himself, to talk of Pensions and Grenadiers?
bk.iv, ch.5 (complete)

2 There is a North-west passage to the intellectual World.
ch.42

3 'There is no terror, brother Toby, in its looks, but what it borrows from groans and convulsions—and the blowing of noses, and the wiping away of tears with the bottoms of curtains, in a dying man's room—Strip it of these, what is it?'—''Tis better in battle than in bed', said my uncle Toby.
bk.v, ch.3. Of death

4 Prejudice of education, he would say, is the devil,—and the multitudes of them which we suck in with our mother's milk—are the devil and all.—We are haunted with them, brother Toby, in all our lucubrations and researches; and was a man fool enough to submit tamely to what they obtruded upon him,—what would his book be?...nothing but a farrago of the clack of nurses, and of the nonsense of the old women (of both sexes) throughout the kingdom.
ch.16

5 'The poor soul will die:—'
'He shall not die, by G—', cried my uncle Toby.—The Accusing Spirit, which flew up to heaven's chancery with the oath, blush'd as he gave it in;—and the Recording Angel, as he wrote it down, dropp'd a tear upon the word, and blotted it out for ever.
bk.vi, ch.8

6 To say a man is fallen in love,—or that he is deeply in love,—or up to the ears in love,—and sometimes even over head and ears in it,—carries an idiomatical kind of implication, that love is a thing below a man:—this is recurring again to Plato's opinion, which, with all his divinityship,—I hold to be damnable and heretical:—and so much for that.
Let love therefore be what it will,—my uncle Toby fell into it.
ch.37

7 My brother Toby, quoth she, is going to be married to Mrs Wadman.
Then he will never, quoth my father, lie diagonally in his bed again as long as he lives.
ch.39

8 'A soldier,' cried my Uncle Toby, interrupting the corporal, 'is no more exempt from saying a foolish thing, Trim, than a man of letters.'—'But not so often, an' please your honour,' replied the corporal.
bk.viii, ch.19

9 An eye full of gentle salutations—and soft responses—...whispering soft—like the last low accents of an expiring saint...It did my uncle Toby's business.
ch.25

10 'I am half distracted, Captain Shandy,' said Mrs Wadman,...'a mote—or sand—or something—I know not what, has got into this eye of mine—do look into it.'...In saying which, Mrs Wadman edged herself close in beside my uncle Toby,...'Do look into

it'—said she....
If thou lookest, uncle Toby,...thou art undone.

11 Every time I kiss thy hand to bid adieu, and every absence which follows it, are preludes to that eternal separation which we are shortly to make.
bk.ix, ch.8

12 Said my mother, 'what is all this story about?'—'A Cock and a Bull,' said Yorick.
ch.33

13 This sad vicissitude of things.
Sermon xv

WALLACE STEVENS 1879–1955

14 The only emperor is the emperor of ice-cream.
The Emperor of Ice-Cream

15 Poetry is the supreme fiction, madame.
A High-Toned old Christian Woman

16 Just as my fingers on these keys
Make music, so the selfsame sounds
On my spirit make a music, too.

Music is feeling, then, not sound.
Peter Quince at the Clavier, I

17 Beauty is momentary in the mind—
The fitful tracing of a portal;
But in the flesh it is immortal.
The body dies; the body's beauty lives.
IV

18 Complacencies of the peignoir, and late
Coffee and oranges in a sunny chair.
And the green freedom of a cockatoo
Upon a rug mingle to dissipate
The holy hush of ancient sacrifice.
Sunday Morning, I

ADLAI STEVENSON 1900–1965

19 Someone asked me...how I felt, and I was reminded of a story that a fellow-townsman of ours used to tell—Abraham Lincoln...He [a boy in Mr. Lincoln's story] said that he was too old to cry, but it hurt too much to laugh.
Speech, after electoral defeat, 5 Nov. 1942

20 As the girl said, 'A kiss on the wrist feels good, but, a diamond bracelet lasts forever.'
Address given to Chicago Council on Foreign Relations, 22 Mar. 1946. See 318:3

21 Making peace is harder than making war.

22 He [Mr. Stevenson], derided the Secretary [of State] for boasting of his brinkmanship—the art of bringing up to the edge of the nuclear abyss.
New York Times, 26 Feb. 1956

ROBERT LOUIS STEVENSON 1850–1894

23 The harmless art of knucklebones has seen the fall of the Roman empire and the rise of the United States.
Across the Plains (1892). VII. The Lantern-Bearers, i

24 The bright face of danger.
iv

25 Every one lives by selling something.
IX. Beggars, iii

26 Our frailties are invincible, our virtues barren; the battle goes sore against us to the going down of the

sun.
XI. Pulvis et Umbra, i

1 Surely we should find it both touching and inspiriting, that in a field from which success is banished, our race should not cease to labour.
ii

2 Still obscurely fighting the lost fight of virtue, still clinging, in the brothel or on the scaffold, to some rag of honour, the poor jewel of their souls!

3 A mortified appetite is never a wise companion.
XII. A Christmas Sermon, i

4 To be honest, to be kind—to earn a little and to spend a little less, to make upon the whole a family happier for his presence, to renounce when that shall be necessary and not be embittered, to keep a few friends, but these without capitulation—above all, on the same grim condition, to keep friends with himself—here is a task for all that a man has of fortitude and delicacy.

5 Here lies one who meant well, tried a little, failed much:—surely that may be his epitaph, of which he need not be ashamed.
iv

6 Politics is perhaps the only profession for which no preparation is thought necessary.
Familiar Studies of Men and Books (1882). **'Yoshida-Torajiro'**

7 Am I no a bonny fighter? [Alan Breck.]
Kidnapped (1886), ch.10

8 I've a grand memory for forgetting, David. [Alan Breck.]
ch.18

9 I have thus played the sedulous ape to Hazlitt, to Lamb, to Wordsworth, to Sir Thomas Browne, to Defoe, to Hawthorne, to Montaigne, to Baudelaire and to Obermann.
Memories and Portraits (1887), ch.4

10 Each has his own tree of ancestors, but at the top of all sits Probably Arboreal.
ch.6, **Pastoral.** See 171:23

11 Lamplough was genteel, Eno was omnipresent; Lamplough was trite, Eno original and abominably vulgar...Am I, then, to sink with Lamplough, or to soar with Eno?
More New Arabian Nights: The Dynamiter (1885). **The Superfluous Mansion**

12 He who was prepared to help the escaping murderer or to embrace the impenitent thief, found, to the overthrow of all his logic, that he objected to the use of dynamite.

13 'Or Opulent Rotunda Strike the Sky,' said the shopman to himself, in the tone of one considering a verse. 'I suppose it would be too much to say "orotunda", and yet how noble it were! "Or Opulent Orotunda Strike the Sky." But that is the bitterness of arts; you see a good effect, and some nonsense about sense continually intervenes.'
Epilogue of the Cigar Divan

14 These are my politics: to change what we can; to better what we can; but still to bear in mind that man is but a devil weakly fettered by some generous beliefs and impositions; and for no word however sounding, and no cause however just and pious, to relax the stricture of these bonds.

15 The devil, depend upon it, can sometimes do a very gentlemanly thing.
The New Arabian Nights (1882). **The Suicide Club. Story of the Young Man with the Cream Tarts**

16 Is there anything in life so disenchanting as attainment?
The Adventure of the Hansom Cab

17 I regard you with an indifference closely bordering on aversion.
The Rajah's Diamond. Story of the Bandbox

18 For my part, I travel not to go anywhere, but to go. I travel for travel's sake. The great affair is to move.
Travels with a Donkey (1879). **Cheylard and Luc**

19 I own I like definite form in what my eyes are to rest upon; and if landscapes were sold, like the sheets of characters of my boyhood, one penny plain and twopence coloured, I should go the length of twopence every day of my life.
Father Apollinaris

20 A faddling hedonist.
The Boarders

21 Fifteen men on the dead man's chest
Yo-ho-ho, and a bottle of rum!
Drink and the devil had done for the rest—
Yo-ho-ho, and a bottle of rum!
Treasure Island (1883), ch.1

22 Tip me the black spot.
ch.3

23 Many's the long night I've dreamed of cheese—toasted, mostly. [Ben Gunn.]
ch.15

24 In marriage, a man becomes slack and selfish, and undergoes a fatty degeneration of his moral being.
Virginibus Puerisque (1881), I.i

25 Acidulous vestals.

26 They have never been in love, or in hate.

27 Even if we take matrimony at its lowest, even if we regard it as no more than a sort of friendship recognised by the police.

28 A little amateur painting in water-colours shows the innocent and quiet mind.

29 Lastly (and this is, perhaps, the golden rule), no woman should marry a teetotaller, or a man who does not smoke.

30 Marriage is a step so grave and decisive that it attracts light-headed, variable men by its very awfulness.

31 Marriage is like life in this—that it is a field of battle, and not a bed of roses.

32 Times are changed with him who marries; there are no more by-path meadows, where you may innocently linger, but the road lies long and straight and dusty to the grave.
ii

33 To marry is to domesticate the Recording Angel. Once you are married, there is nothing left for you, not even suicide, but to be good.

34 Man is a creature who lives not upon bread alone, but principally by catchwords.

35 The cruellest lies are often told in silence.
iv. **Truth of Intercourse**

1 Old and young, we are all on our last cruise.
Crabbed Age and Youth

2 Youth is the time to go flashing from one end of the world to the other both in mind and body; to try the manners of different nations; to hear the chimes at midnight; to see sunrise in town and country; to be converted at a revival; to circumnavigate the metaphysics, write halting verses, run a mile to see a fire, and wait all day long in the theatre to applaud 'Hernani'
See 442:6

3 It is better to be a fool than to be dead.

4 There is no duty we so much underrate as the duty of being happy.
III. **An Apology for Idlers**

5 He sows hurry and reaps indigestion.

6 By the time a man gets well into the seventies his continued existence is a mere miracle.
V. **Aes Triplex**

7 Philosophy, in its more rigid sense, has been at the same work for ages; and...has the honour of laying before us...her contribution towards the subject: that life is a Permanent Possibility of Sensation.

8 Even if the doctor does not give you a year, even if he hesitates about a month, make one brave push and see what can be accomplished in a week.

9 To travel hopefully is a better thing than to arrive, and the true success is to labour.
VI. **El Dorado**

10 Though we are mighty fine fellows nowadays, we cannot write like Hazlitt.
X. **Walking Tours**

11 What hangs people...is the unfortunate circumstance of guilt.
The Wrong Box (with Lloyd Osbourne, 1889), ch.7

12 Nothing like a little judicious levity.

13 Between the possibility of being hanged in all innocence, and the certainty of a public and merited disgrace, no gentleman of spirit could long hesitate.
ch.10

14 'The "Athaeneum", that was the name! Golly, what a paper!' '"Athenaeum", you mean,' said Morris.
ch.15

15 I believe in an ultimate decency of things.
Letter, 23 Aug. 1893

16 In winter I get up at night
And dress by yellow candle-light.
In summer, quite the other way,—
I have to go to bed by day.

I have to go to bed and see
The birds still hopping on the tree,
Or hear the grown-up people's feet
Still going past me in the street.
A Child's Garden of Verses (1885). I. **Bed in Summmer**

17 A child should always say what's true,
And speak when he is spoken to,
And behave mannerly at table:
At least as far as he is able.
V. **Whole Duty of Children**

18 Whenever the moon and stars are set,
Whenever the wind is high,

All night long in the dark and wet,
A man goes riding by.
Late in the night when the fires are out,
Why does he gallop and gallop about?
IX. **Windy Nights**

19 When I am grown to man's estate
I shall be very proud and great,
And tell the other girls and boys
Not to meddle with my toys.
XII. **Looking Forward**

20 When I was sick and lay a-bed,
I had two pillows at my head,
And all my toys beside me lay
To keep me happy all the day...

I was the giant great and still
That sits upon the pillow-hill,
And sees before him, dale and plain,
The pleasant land of counterpane.
XVI. **The Land of Counterpane**

21 The child that is not clean and neat,
With lots of toys and things to eat,
He is a naughty child, I'm sure—
Or else his dear papa is poor.
XIX. **System**

22 The world is so full of a number of things,
I'm sure we should all be as happy as kings.
XXIV. **Happy Thought**

23 If you would grow great and stately,
You must try to walk sedately.
XXVII. **Good and Bad Children**

24 A birdie with a yellow bill
Hopped upon the window-sill,
Cocked his shining eye and said:
'Ain't you 'shamed, you sleepy-head?'
XXXIV. **Time to Rise**

25 Must we to bed indeed? Well then,
Let us arise and go like men,
And face with an undaunted tread
The long black passage up to bed.
XLI. **North-West Passage. I. Good-Night**

26 But all that I could think of, in the darkness and the cold,
Was that I was leaving home and my folks were growing old.
Christmas at Sea

27 Give to me the life I love,
Let the lave go by me,
Give the jolly heaven above
And the byway nigh me.
Bed in the bush with stars to see,
Bread I dip in the river—
There's the life for a man like me,
There's the life for ever.
Songs of Travel (1896). I. **The Vagabond**

28 Let the blow fall soon or late,
Let what will be o'er me;
Give the face of earth around
And the road before me.
Wealth I seek not, hope nor love,
Nor a friend to know me;
All I seek, the heaven above
And the road below me.

29 I will make you brooches and toys for your delight

Of bird-song at morning and star-shine at night.
I will make a palace fit for you and me
Of green days in forests and blue days at sea.
I will make my kitchen, and you shall keep your room,
Where white flows the river and bright blows the broom,
And you shall wash your linen and keep your body white
In rainfall at morning and dewfall at night.
XI

1 Bright is the ring of words
    When the right man rings them,
Fair the fall of songs
    When the singer sings them.
Still they are carolled and said—
    On wings they are carried—
After the singer is dead
    And the maker buried.
XIV

2 In the highlands, in the country places,
Where the old plain men have rosy faces,
And the young fair maidens
        Quiet eyes.
XV

3 Trusty, dusky, vivid, true,
With eyes of gold and bramble-dew,
Steel-true and blade-straight,
The great artificer
Made my mate.
XXV. **My Wife**

4 Sing me a song of a lad that is gone,
    Say, could that lad be I?
Merry of soul he sailed on a day
    Over the sea to Skye.
XLII

5 Be it granted to me to behold you again in dying,
    Hills of home! and to hear again the call;
Hear about the graves of the martyrs the peewees crying,
    And hear no more at all.
XLV. **To S.R. Crockett**

6 Of all my versè, like not a single line;
But like my title, for it is not mine.
That title from a better man I stole;
Ah, how much better, had I stol'n the whole!
Underwoods (1887). Foreword. See 285:4

7 Go, little book, and wish to all
Flowers in the garden, meat in the hall,
A bin of wine, a spice of wit,
A house with lawns enclosing it,
A living river by the door,
A nightingale in the sycamore!
bk.I.i. Envoy. See 144:17

8 The gauger walked with willing foot,
And aye the gauger played the flute;
And what should Master Gauger play
But 'Over the hills and far away'?
ii. **A Song of the Road**

9 There's nothing under Heav'n so blue
That's fairly worth the travelling to.
iv

10 Under the wide and starry sky
Dig the grave and let me lie.

Glad did I live and gladly die,
    And I laid me down with a will.
This be the verse you grave for me:
'Here he lies where he longed to be;
Home is the sailor, home from sea,
    And the hunter home from the hill.'
xxi. **Requiem**

11 If I have faltered more or less
In my great task of happiness;
If I have moved among my race
And shown no glorious morning face;
If beams from happy human eyes
Have moved me not; if morning skies,
Books, and my food, and summer rain
Knocked on my sullen heart in vain:—
Lord, thy most pointed pleasure take
And stab my spirit broad awake;
Or, Lord, if too obdurate I,
Choose thou, before that spirit die,
A piercing pain, a killing sin,
And to my dead heart run them in!
xxii. **The Celestial Surgeon**

12 Unfrowning caryatides.
xxiii. **Our Lady of the Snows**

13 I am a kind of farthing dip,
    Unfriendly to the nose and eyes;
A blue-behinded ape, I skip
    Upon the trees of Paradise.
xxx. **A Portrait**

EDWARD STILLINGFLEET 1635–1699

14 'My Lord,' a certain nobleman is said to have observed, after sitting next to [Richard] Bentley at dinner, 'that chaplain of yours is a very extraordinary man.' Stillingfleet agreed, adding, 'Had he but the gift of humility, he would be the most extraordinary man in Europe.'
R.J. White, *Dr. Bentley* (1965), ch.4

TOM STOPPARD 1937–

15 *Guildenstern:* ...Maidens aspiring to godheads—
Rosenkrantz: And vice versa.
Rosenkrantz and Guildenstern Are Dead (1967), Act I

16 I can do you blood and love without the rhetoric, and I can do you blood and rhetoric without the love and I can do you all three concurrent or consecutive but I can't do you love and rhetoric without the blood. Blood is compulsory—they're all blood you see.

17 To sum up: your father, whom you love, dies, you are his heir, you come back to find that hardly was the corpse cold before his younger brother popped on to his throne and into his sheets, thereby offending both legal and natural practice. Now why exactly are you behaving in this extraordinary manner.

18 The bad end unhappily, the good unluckily. That is what tragedy means.
Act II. See 573:3

HARRIET BEECHER STOWE 1811–1896

19 'Who was your mother?' 'Never had none!' said the child, with another grin. 'Never had any mother? What do you mean? Where were you born?' 'Never

was born!' persisted Topsy.
Uncle Tom's Cabin (1852), ch.20

1 'Do you know who made you?' 'Nobody, as I knows
on,' said the child, with a short laugh...'I 'spect I
grow'd.'

LORD STOWELL 1745–1836

2 The elegant simplicity of the three per cents.
Lord Campbell, *Lives of the Lord Chancellors* (1857), vol.x,
ch.212, p.218

3 A precedent embalms a principle.
An Opinion, while Advocate-General, 1788. Attr.

LYTTON STRACHEY 1880–1932

4 The time was out of joint, and he was only too
delighted to have been born to set it right.
Of Hurrell Froude. **Eminent Victorians**, I. **Cardinal Manning**,
ii. See 431:26

BISHOP WILLIAM STUBBS 1825–1901

5 Froude informs the Scottish youth
That parsons do not care for truth.
The Reverend Canon Kingsley cries
History is a pack of lies.
What cause for judgments so malign?
A brief reflection solves the mystery—
Froude believes Kingsley a divine,
And Kingsley goes to Froude for history.
Letter to J.R. Green, 17 Dec. 1871. **Letters of Stubbs** (1904),
p.162

SIR JOHN SUCKLING 1609–1642

6 Why so pale and wan, fond lover?
Prithee, why so pale?
Will, when looking well can't move her,
Looking ill prevail?
Prithee, why so pale?
Aglaura (1637), IV.i. Song

7 Quit, quit, for shame, this will not move:
This cannot take her.
If of herself she will not love,
Nothing can make her:
The devil take her!

8 Her feet beneath her petticoat,
Like little mice, stole in and out,
As if they fear'd the light.
A Ballad upon a Wedding (1646), viii

9 For streaks of red were mingled there,
Such as are on a Catherine pear
(The side that's next the sun).

10 Her lips were red, and one was thin,
Compar'd to that was next her chin
(Some bee had stung it newly).
xi

11 At length the candle's out, and now
All that they had not done they do:
What that is, who can tell?
But I believe it was no more
Than thou and I have done before
With Bridget, and with Nell.

12 I prithee send me back my heart,
Since I cannot have thine:

For if from yours you will not part,
Why then shouldst thou have mine?
Song. I Prithee Send me Back

13 But love is such a mystery,
I cannot find it out:
For when I think I'm best resolv'd,
I then am in most doubt.

14 Out upon it, I have loved
Three whole days together;
And am like to love three more,
If it prove fair weather.

Time shall moult away his wings,
Ere he shall discover
In the whole wide world again
Such a constant lover.
A Poem with the Answer

15 Had it any been but she,
And that very face,
There had been at least ere this
A dozen dozen in her place.

SUETONIUS C.A.D. 69–c. 130

16 *Festina lente.* [σπεῦδε βραδέως.]
Make haste slowly.
Augustus, 25

17 *Ita feri ut se mori sentiat.*
Strike him so that he can feel that he is dying.
Caligula, 30

MAXIMILIEN DE BETHUNE, DUC DE SULLY 1559–1641

18 *Les anglais s'amusent tristement selon l'usage de leur pays.*
The English take their pleasures sadly after the fashion
of their country.
Memoirs, c.1630

SU TUNG-P'O 1036–1101

19 Families, when a child is born
Want it to be intelligent.
I, through intelligence,
Having wrecked my whole life,
Only hope the baby will prove
Ignorant and stupid.
Then he will crown a tranquil life
By becoming a Cabinet Minister.
On the Birth of his Son, tr. Arthur Waley, *170 Chinese Poems*
(1918), p.98

HENRY HOWARD, EARL OF SURREY 1517?–1547

20 Martial, the things for to attain
The happy life be these, I find:
The riches left, not got with pain;
The fruitful ground, the quiet mind;

The equal friend; no grudge nor strife;
No charge or rule nor governance;
Without disease the healthful life;
The household of continuance.
The Happy Life

21 The chaste wife wise, without debate;

Such sleeps as may beguile the night;
Content thyself with thine estate;
Neither wish death, nor fear his might.

R.S. SURTEES 1803–1864

1 More people are flattered into virtue than bullied out of vice.
The Analysis of the Hunting Field (1846), ch.1

2 The only infallible rule we know is, that the man who is always talking about being a gentleman never is one.
Ask Mamma (1858), ch.1

3 Major Yammerton was rather a peculiar man, inasmuch as he was an ass, without being a fool.
ch.25

4 'Unting is all that's worth living for—all time is lost wot is not spent in 'unting—it is like the hair we breathe—if we have it not we die—it's the sport of kings, the image of war without its guilt, and only five-and-twenty per cent of its danger.
Handley Cross (1843), ch.7. See 172:7

5 'Unting fills my thoughts by day, and many a good run I have in my sleep. Many a dig in the ribs I gives Mrs J when I think they're running into the warmint (renewed cheers). No man is fit to be called a sportsman wot doesn't kick his wife out of bed on a haverage once in three weeks!
ch.11

6 Tell me a man's a fox-hunter, and I loves him at once.

7 He will bring his nightcap with him, for where the M.F.H. dines he sleeps, and where the M.F.H. sleeps he breakfasts.
ch.15

8 I'll fill hup the chinks wi' cheese.

9 Well did that great man, I think it was Sir Walter Scott, but if it warn't, 'twas little Bartley, the bootmaker, say, that there was no young man wot would not rather have a himputation on his morality than on his 'ossmanship.
ch.16

10 It ar'n't that I loves the fox less, but that I loves the 'ound more.

11 I can stand a wast of praise.
ch.24

12 Unless a man has a good many servants, he had better have them cleanin' his 'oss than cleanin' his breeches.
ch.27

13 Paid for catching my 'oss, 6d.
ch.29

14 Con-found all presents wot eat!
ch.37

15 Hellish dark, and smells of cheese!
ch.50

16 'Hurrah! blister my kidneys!' exclaimed he in delight, 'it is a frost!—the dahlias are dead!'
ch.59

17 Three things I never lends—my 'oss, my wife, and my name.
Hillingdon Hall (1845), ch.33

18 Every man shouting in proportion to the amount of his subscription.
Jorrocks's Jaunts and Jollities (1838). No.1. **Swell and the Surrey**

19 Jorrocks, who is not afraid of 'the pace' so long as there is no leaping.

20 Champagne certainly gives one werry gentlemanly ideas, but for a continuance, I don't know but I should prefer mild hale.
No.9. **Mr. Jorrocks in Paris**

21 No one knows how ungentlemanly he can look, until he has seen himself in a shocking bad hat.
Mr. Facey Romford's Hounds (1865), ch.9

22 Better be killed than frightened to death.
ch.32

23 Thinking that life would be very pleasant if it were not for its enjoyments.
See 314:10

24 These sort of boobies think that people come to balls to do nothing but dance; whereas everyone knows that the real business of a ball is either to look out for a wife, to look after a wife, or to look after somebody else's wife.
ch.56

25 The young ladies entered the drawing-room in the full fervour of sisterly animosity.
Mr. Sponge's Sporting Tour (1853), ch.17

26 Women never look so well as when one comes in wet and dirty from hunting.
ch.21

27 He was a gentleman who was generally spoken of as having nothing a-year, paid quarterly.
ch.24

28 There is no secret so close as that between a rider and his horse.
ch.31

29 When at length they rose to go to bed, it struck each man as he followed his neighbour upstairs that the one before him walked very crookedly.
ch.35

HANNEN SWAFFER 1879–1962

30 Freedom of the press in Britain is freedom to print such of the proprietor's prejudices as the advertisers don't object to.
In conversation with Tom Driberg, c.1928

JONATHAN SWIFT 1667–1745

31 I conceive some scattered notions about a superior power to be of singular use for the common people, as furnishing excellent materials to keep children quiet when they grow peevish, and providing topics of amusement in a tedious winter-night.
An Argument Against Abolishing Christianity (1708)

32 Satire is a sort of glass, wherein beholders do generally discover everybody's face but their own.
The Battle of the Books (1704), preface

33 Instead of dirt and poison we have rather chosen to fill our hives with honey and wax; thus furnishing mankind with the two noblest of things, which are sweetness and light.

34 I have heard of a man who had a mind to sell his house, and therefore carried a piece of brick in his

pocket, which he shewed as a pattern to encourage purchasers.
The Drapier's Letters, No. 2 (4 Aug. 1724)

1 He [the emperor] is taller by almost the breadth of my nail than any of his court, which alone is enough to strike an awe into the beholders.
Gulliver's Travels (1726). **Voyage to Lilliput,** ch.2

2 The colonel and his officers were in much pain, especially when they saw me take out my penknife.

3 He put this engine [a watch] to our ears, which made an incessant noise like that of a water-mill; and we conjecture it is either some unknown animal, or the god that he worships; but we are more inclined to the latter opinion.

4 It is alleged indeed, that the high heels are most agreeable to our ancient constitution: but however this be, his Majesty hath determined to make use of only low heels in the administration of the government.
ch.4

5 I cannot but conclude the bulk of your natives to be the most pernicious race of little odious vermin that nature ever suffered to crawl upon the surface of the earth.
Voyage to Brobdingnag, ch.6

6 And he gave it for his opinion, that whoever could make two ears of corn or two blades of grass to grow upon a spot of ground where only one grew before, would deserve better of mankind, and do more essential service to his country than the whole race of politicians put together.
ch.7

7 He had been eight years upon a project for extracting sun-beams out of cucumbers, which were to be put into vials hermetically sealed, and let out to warm the air in raw inclement summers.
Voyage to Laputa, etc., ch.5

8 These unhappy people were proposing schemes for persuading monarchs to choose favourites upon the score of their wisdom, capacity and virtue; of teaching ministers to consult the public good; of rewarding merit, great abilities and eminent services; of instructing princes to know their true interest by placing it on the same foundation with that of their people: of choosing for employment persons qualified to exercise them; with many other wild impossible chimeras, that never entered before into the heart of man to conceive, and confirmed in me the old observation, that there is nothing so extravagant and irrational which some philosophers have not maintained for truth.
ch.6

9 I said the thing which was not.
A Voyage to the Houyhnhnms, ch.3

10 I told him...that we ate when we were not hungry, and drank without the provocation of thirst.
ch.6

11 Plaguy twelvepenny weather.
Journal to Stella, 26 Oct. 1710

12 'Tis very warm weather when one's in bed.
8 Nov. 1710

13 We are so fond of one another, because our ailments are the same.
1 Feb. 1711

14 Will she pass in a crowd? Will she make a figure in a country church?
9 Feb. 1711

15 I love good creditable acquaintance; I love to be the worst of the company.
17 May 1711

16 He was a fiddler, and consequently a rogue.
25 July 1711

17 He showed me his bill of fare to tempt me to dine with him; poh, said I, I value not your bill of fare, give me your bill of company.
2 Sept. 1711

18 We were to do more business after dinner; but after dinner is after dinner—an old saying and a true, 'much drinking, little thinking'.
26 Feb. 1712

19 Monday is parson's holiday.
3 Mar. 1712

20 Proper words in proper places, make the true definition of a style.
Letter to a Young Clergyman, 9 Jan. 1720

21 If Heaven had looked upon riches to be a valuable thing, it would not have given them to such a scoundrel.
Letter to Miss Vanhomrigh, 12-13 Aug. 1720

22 You have but a very few years to be young and handsome in the eyes of the world; and as few months to be so in the eyes of a husband, who is not a fool.
Letter to a Young Lady on her Marriage (1723)

23 I have ever hated all nations, professions and communities, and all my love is towards individuals...But principally I hate and detest that animal called man; although I heartily love John, Peter, Thomas, and so forth.
Letter to Pope, 29 Sept. 1725

24 Not die here in a rage, like a poisoned rat in a hole.
Letter to Bolingbroke, 21 Mar. 1729

25 Surely man is a broomstick!
A Meditation upon a Broomstick (1710)

26 I have been assured by a very knowing American of my acquaintance in London, that a young healthy child well nursed is at a year old a most delicious, nourishing, and wholesome food, whether stewed, roasted, baked, or boiled, and I make no doubt that it will equally serve in a fricassee, or a ragout.
A Modest Proposal for Preventing the Children of Ireland from being a Burden to their Parents or Country (1729)

27 I mean, you lie—under a mistake.
Polite Conversation (1738). Dialogue 1

28 Why every one as they like; as the good woman said when she kissed her cow.

29 She wears her clothes, as if they were thrown on her with a pitchfork.

30 Faith, that's as well said, as if I had said it myself.
Dialogue 2

31 Lord, I wonder what fool it was that first invented kissing!

32 I'll give you leave to call me anything, if you don't call me spade.

33 I always love to begin a journey on Sundays, because I shall have the prayers of the church, to preserve all that travel by land, or by water.

1 It is a maxim, that those to whom everybody allows the second place, have an undoubted title to the first.
   A Tale of a Tub, (1704), Dedication

2 Books, like men their authors, have no more than one way of coming into the world, but there are ten thousand to go out of it, and return no more.

3 Satire, being levelled at all, is never resented for an offence by any.
   Preface

4 What though his head be empty, provided his commonplace book be full.
   Digression in Praise of Digression

5 Last week I saw a woman flayed, and you will hardly believe, how much it altered her person for the worse.
   ch.IX

6 I never saw, heard, nor read, that the clergy were beloved in any nation where Christianity was the religion of the country. Nothing can render them popular, but some degree of persecution.
   Thoughts on Religion (1768)

7 We have just enough religion to make us hate, but not enough to make us love one another.
   Thoughts on Various Subjects (1706)

8 When a true genius appears in the world, you may know him by this sign, that the dunces are all in confederacy against him.

9 What they do in heaven we are ignorant of; what they do *not* we are told expressly, that they neither marry, nor are given in marriage.
   See 67:21

10 The reasons why so few marriages are happy, is, because young ladies spend their time in making nets, not in making cages.

11 Few are qualified to shine in company; but it is in most men's power to be agreeable.

12 Every man desires to live long; but no man would be old.

13 A nice man is a man of nasty ideas.

14 Old men and comets have been reverenced for the same reason; their long beards, and pretences to foretell events.

15 I never wonder to see men wicked, but I often wonder to see them not ashamed.

16 Laws are like cobwebs, which may catch small flies, but let wasps and hornets break through.
   A Tritical Essay upon the Faculties of the Mind (1709). See 512:23

17 There is nothing in this world constant, but inconstancy.

18 Good God! what a genius I had when I wrote that book. *[The Tale of a Tub.]*
   Sir Walter Scott, *Life of Swift. Works of Swift* (1824), vol.i, p.89

19 I shall be like that tree, I shall die at the top.
   Sir Walter Scott, *Memoirs of Swift*

20 How haughtily he cocks his nose,
   To tell what every schoolboy knows.
   The Country Life, l.81

21 Only take this rule along,
   Always to advise her wrong;
   And reprove her when she's right;

   She may then grow wise for spite.
   Daphne (1730), l.35

22 In all distresses of our friends,
   We first consult our private ends;
   While nature, kindly bent to ease us,
   Points out some circumstance to please us.
   Verses on the Death of Dr. Swift (1731), l.7

23 Poor Pope will grieve a month, and Gay
   A week, and Arbuthnot a day.
   St John himself will scarce forbear
   To bite his pen, and drop a tear.
   The rest will give a shrug, and cry,
   'I'm sorry—but we all must die!'
   l.207

24 Yet malice never was his aim;
   He lash'd the vice, but spared the name;
   No individual could resent,
   Where thousands equally were meant.
   l.512

25 He gave the little wealth he had
   To build a house for fools and mad;
   And show'd, by one satiric touch,
   No nation wanted it so much.
   l.538

26 A coming shower your shooting corns presage.
   A Description of a City Shower (1710), l.9

27 They never would hear,
   But turn the deaf ear,
   As a matter they had no concern in.
   Dingley and Brent (1724), ii

28 I often wish'd that I had clear,
   For life, six hundred pounds a-year,
   A handsome house to lodge a friend,
   A river at my garden's end,
   A terrace walk, and half a rood
   Of land, set out to plant a wood.
   Imitation of Horace (1714), bk.II, sat.vi, l.1. See 262:9

29 Nor do they trust their tongue alone,
   But speak a language of their own;
   Can read a nod, a shrug, a look,
   Far better than a printed book;
   Convey a libel in a frown,
   And wink a reputation down.
   The Journal of a Modern Lady (1729), l.188

30 Hail, fellow, well met,
   All dirty and wet:
   Find out, if you can,
   Who's master, who's man.
   My Lady's Lamentation (1728), l.171

31 Th' artillery of words.
   Ode to...Sancroft (1692), i

32 Philosophy! the lumber of the schools.
   Ode to Sir W. Temple (1692), ii

33 Say, Britain, could you ever boast,—
   Three poets in an age at most?
   Our chilling climate hardly bears
   A sprig of bays in fifty years.
   On Poetry (1733), l.5

34 Then, rising with Aurora's light,
   The Muse invoked, sit down to write;
   Blot out, correct, insert, refine,
   Enlarge, diminish, interline.
   l.85

1 As learned commentators view
In Homer more than Homer knew.
1.103

2 So geographers, in Afric-maps,
With savage-pictures fill their gaps;
And o'er unhabitable downs
Place elephants for want of towns.
1.177

3 He gives directions to the town,
To cry it up, or run it down.
1.269

4 Hobbes clearly proves, that every creature
Lives in a state of war by nature.
1.319

5 So, naturalists observe, a flea
Hath smaller fleas that on him prey;
And these have smaller fleas to bite 'em,
And so proceed *ad infinitum*.
Thus every poet, in his kind,
Is bit by him that comes behind.
1.337

6 Walls have tongues, and hedges ears.
*A Pastoral Dialogue between Richmond Lodge and Marble
Hill* (1727), 1.8

7 Humour is odd, grotesque, and wild,
Only by affectation spoil'd;
'Tis never by invention got,
Men have it when they know it not.
To Mr. Delany (1718), 1.25

8 Hated by fools, and fools to hate,
Be that my motto and my fate.
1.171

9 In Church your grandsire cut his throat;
To do the job too long he tarry'd,
He should have had my hearty vote,
To cut his throat before he marry'd.
Verses on the Upright Judge

10 'Libertas et natale solum':
Fine words! I wonder where you stole 'em.
Whitshed's Motto on his Coach (1724)

11 A beggarly people!
A church and no steeple! [Of St Ann's Church,
Dublin.]
Attr. to Swift by Malone. See Prior, *Life of Malone* (1860), p.381

12 *Ubi saeva indignatio ulterius cor lacerare nequit.*
Where fierce indignation can no longer tear his heart.
Swift's Epitaph

ALGERNON CHARLES SWINBURNE 1837–1909

13 Superflux of pain.
Anactoria, 1.27

14 Maiden, and mistress of the months and stars
Now folded in the flowerless fields of heaven.
Atalanta in Calydon (1865). *Collected Poetical Works* (1924),
vol.ii, p.247, 1.1

15 When the hounds of spring are on winter's traces,
The mother of months in meadow or plain
Fills the shadows and windy places
With lisp of leaves and ripple of rain;
And the brown bright nightingale amorous
Is half assuaged for Itylus,
For the Thracian ships and the foreign faces,
The tongueless vigil and all the pain.
Chorus, p.249

16 Bind on thy sandals, O thou most fleet,
Over the splendour and speed of thy feet;
For the faint east quickens, the wan west shivers,
Round the feet of the day and the feet of the night.

Where shall we find her, how shall we sing to her,
Fold our hands round her knees, and cling?
O that man's heart were as fire and could spring to
her,
Fire, or the strength of the streams that spring!

17 For winter's rains and ruins are over,
And all the season of snows and sins;
The days dividing lover and lover,
The light that loses, the night that wins;
And time remembered is grief forgotten,
And frosts are slain and flowers begotten,
And in green underwood and cover
Blossom by blossom the spring begins.

18 And Pan by noon and Bacchus by night,
Fleeter of foot than the fleet-foot kid,
Follows with dancing and fills with delight
The Maenad and the Bassarid;
And soft as lips that laugh and hide
The laughing leaves of the tree divide,
And screen from seeing and leave in sight
The god pursuing, the maiden hid.
p.250

19 The wolf that follows, the fawn that flies.

20 Before the beginning of years
There came to the making of man
Time with a gift of tears,
Grief with a glass that ran.
p.258

21 Strength without hands to smite,
Love that endures for a breath;
Night, the shadow of light,
And Life, the shadow of death.

22 We have seen thee, O love, thou art fair; thou art
goodly, O Love.
p.273

23 For words divide and rend;
But silence is most noble till the end.
p.299

24 For a day and a night Love sang to us, played with us,
Folded us round from the dark and the light;
And our hearts were fulfilled with the music he made
with us,
Made with our hands and our lips while he stayed with
us,
Stayed in mid passage his pinions from flight
For a day and a night.
At Parting

25 Shall I strew on thee rose or rue or laurel,
Brother, on this that was the veil of thee?
Or quiet sea-flower moulded by the sea,
Or simplest growth of meadow-sweet or sorrel?
Ave atque Vale, i

26 Now all strange hours and all strange loves are over,
Dreams and desires and sombre songs and sweet,
Hast thou found place at the great knees and feet
Of some pale Titan-woman like a lover
Such as thy vision here solicited,

Under the shadow of her fair vast head,
The deep division of prodigious breasts,
 The solemn slope of mighty limbs asleep?
vi

1 Sleep; and if life was bitter to thee, pardon,
 If sweet, give thanks; thou hast no more to live;
 And to give thanks is good, and to forgive.
xvii

2 Villon, our sad bad glad mad brother's name.
Ballad of François Villon

3 O slain and spent and sacrificed
People, the grey-grown speechless Christ.
Before a Crucifix. Poetical Works (1924), vol.i, p.744

4 We shift and bedeck and bedrape us,
 Thou art noble and nude and antique.
Dolores (1866), vii

5 Change in a trice
The lilies and languors of virtue
 For the raptures and roses of vice.
ix

6 O splendid and sterile Dolores,
 Our Lady of Pain.

7 Ah beautiful passionate body
That never has ached with a heart!
xi

8 But sweet as the rind was the core is;
 We are fain of thee still, we are fain,
O sanguine and subtle Dolores,
 Our Lady of Pain.
xiii

9 The delight that consumes the desire,
 The desire that outruns the delight.
xiv

10 For the crown of our life as it closes
 Is darkness, the fruit thereof dust;
No thorns go as deep as a rose's,
 And love is more cruel than lust.
Time turns the old days to derision,
 Our loves into corpses or wives;
And marriage and death and division
 Make barren our lives.
xx

11 What ailed us, O gods, to desert you
 For creeds that refuse and restrain?
Come down and redeem us from virtue,
 Our Lady of Pain.
xxxv

12 I shall remember while the light lives yet
And in the night time I shall not forget.
Erotion

13 There was a poor poet named Clough,
Whom his friends all united to puff,
 But the public, though dull,
 Had not such a skull
As belonged to believers in Clough.
Essays and Studies (1875), **Matthew Arnold** (printed as prose)

14 Bright with names that men remember, loud with
 names that men forget.
Eton: An Ode

15 What adders came to shed their coats?
 What coiled obscene
Small serpents with soft stretching throats

Caressed Faustine?
Faustine (1862)

16 Those eyes the greenest of things blue,
 The bluest of things grey.
Félise

17 In a coign of the cliff between lowland and highland,
At the sea-down's edge between windward and lee,
Walled round with rocks as an inland island,
 The ghost of a garden fronts the sea.
A Forsaken Garden

18 The fields fall southward, abrupt and broken,
To the low last edge of the long lone land.
If a step should sound or a word be spoken,
 Would a ghost not rise at the strange guest's hand?
So long have the grey bare walls lain guestless,
Through branches and briars if a man make way,
He shall find no life but the sea-wind's, restless
 Night and day.

19 'For the foam-flowers endure when the rose-blossoms
 wither
 And men that love lightly may die—but we?'
And the same wind sang and the same waves
 whitened,
And or ever the garden's last petals were shed,
In the lips that had whispered, the eyes that had
 lightened,
 Love was dead.

20 Stretched out on the spoils that his own hand spread.
As a god self-slain on his own strange altar,
 Death lies dead.

21 Here, where the world is quiet;
Here, where all trouble seems
Dead winds' and spent waves' riot
In doubtful dreams of dreams.
The Garden of Proserpine

22 Pale, beyond porch and portal,
 Crowned with calm leaves, she stands
Who gathers all things mortal
 With cold immortal hands.

23 Dead dreams of days forsaken,
Blind buds that snows have shaken,
Wild leaves that winds have taken,
 Red strays of ruined springs.

24 We are not sure of sorrow,
 And joy was never sure.

25 From too much love of living,
 From hope and fear set free,
We thank with brief thanksgiving
 Whatever gods may be
That no man lives forever,
That dead men rise up never;
That even the weariest river
 Winds somewhere safe to sea.

26 Calling a crowned man royal
That was no more than a king.
The Halt before Rome

27 Fiddle, we know, is diddle: and diddle, we take it, is
 dee.
The Heptalogia. The Higher Pantheism in a Nutshell. See
533:29

28 Green leaves of thy labour, white flowers of thy

thought, and red fruit of thy death.
Hertha

1 But God, if a God there be, is the substance of men
    which is man.
Hymn of Man

2 Glory to Man in the highest! for Man is the master of
    things.

3 Yea, is not even Apollo, with hair and harpstring of
    gold,
    A bitter God to follow, a beautiful God to behold?
    I am sick of singing: the bays burn deep and chafe: I
        am fain
    To rest a little from praise and grievous pleasure and
        pain.
Hymn to Proserpine

4 Wilt thou yet take all, Galilean? but these thou shalt
    not take,
    The laurel, the palms and the paean, the breasts of the
        nymphs in the brake;
    Breasts more soft than a dove's, that tremble with
        tenderer breath;
    And all the wings of the Loves, and all the joy before
        death.

5 Thou hast conquered, O pale Galilean; the world has
    grown grey from Thy breath;
    We have drunken of things Lethean, and fed on the
        fullness of death.
    Laurel is green for a season, and love is sweet for a
        day;
    But love grows bitter with treason, and laurel outlives
        not May.
    See 286:31

6 For the old faiths loosen and fall, the new years ruin
    and rend.

7 Though the feet of thine high priests tread where thy
    lords and our forefathers trod,
    Though these that were Gods are dead, and thou being
        dead art a God,
    Though before thee the throned Cytherean be fallen,
        and hidden her head,
    Yet thy kingdom shall pass, Galilean, thy dead shall go
        down to thee dead.

8 As the deep dim soul of a star.

9 A little soul for a little bears up this corpse which is
    man.

10 I remember the way we parted,
    The day and the way we met;
    You hoped we were both broken-hearted,
    And knew we should both forget.
An Interlude

11 And the best and the worst of this is
    That neither is most to blame,
    If you have forgotten my kisses
    And I have forgotten your name.

12 Swallow, my sister, O sister swallow,
    How can thine heart be full of the spring?
    A thousand summers are over and dead.
    What hast thou found in the spring to follow?
    What hast thou found in thine heart to sing?
    What wilt thou do when the summer is shed?
Itylus (1864)

13 Sister, my sister, O fleet sweet swallow,

Thy way is long to the sun and the south;
But I, fulfilled of my heart's desire,
    Shedding my song upon height, upon hollow,
From tawny body and sweet small mouth
    Feed the heart of the night with fire.

I the nightingale all spring through,
    O swallow, sister, O changing swallow,
All spring through till the spring be done,
    Clothed with the light of the night on the dew,
Sing, while the hours and the wild birds follow,
    Take flight and follow and find the sun.

14 Till life forget and death remember,
    Till thou remember and I forget.

15 The small slain body, the flower-like face,
    Can I remember if thou forget?

16 Thou hast forgotten, O summer swallow,
    But the world shall end when I forget.

17 Apples of gold for the king's daughter.
The King's Daughter

18 Ah, yet would God this flesh of mine might be
    Where air might wash and long leaves cover me;
    Where tides of grass break into foam of flowers,
    Or where the wind's feet shine along the sea.
Laus Veneris (1866)

19 Until God loosen over sea and land
    The thunder of the trumpets of the night.

20 But you would have felt my soul in a kiss,
    And known that once if I loved you well;
    And I would have given my soul for this
    To burn for ever in burning hell.
Les Noyades

21 If love were what the rose is,
    And I were like the leaf,
    Our lives would grow together
    In sad or singing weather,
    Blown fields or flowerful closes,
    Green pleasure or grey grief.
A Match

22 Ask nothing more of me, sweet;
    All I can give you I give.
    Heart of my heart, were it more,
    More would be laid at your feet:
    Love that should help you to live,
    Song that should spur you to soar.
The Oblation

23 They have tied the world in a tether,
    They have bought over God with a fee.
A Song in Time of Order (1852)

24 The strong sea-daisies feast on the sun.
The Triumph of Time

25 A broken blossom, a ruined rhyme.

26   Content you;
    The gate is strait; I shall not be there.

27 I will go back to the great sweet mother,
    Mother and lover of men, the sea.
    I will go down to her, I and no other,
    Close with her, kiss her and mix her with me.

28 I shall sleep, and move with the moving ships,
    Change as the winds change, veer in the tide.

29 There lived a singer in France of old
    By the tideless dolorous midland sea.

In a land of sand and ruin and gold
There shone one woman, and none but she.

1 Sweet red splendid kissing mouth.
Translations from Villon. **Complaint of the fair Armouress**

2 There's no good girl's lip out of Paris.
Ballad of the Women of Paris

JOHN ADDINGTON SYMONDS 1840–1893

3 These things shall be! A loftier race
Than e'er the world hath known shall rise,
With flame of freedom in their souls,
And light of knowledge in their eyes.
Hymn

JOHN MILLINGTON SYNGE 1871–1909

4 A man who is not afraid of the sea will soon be
drownded for he will be going out on a day he
shouldn't. But we do be afraid of the sea, and we do
only be drownded now and again.
The Aran Islands, Pt.II

5 I've lost the only playboy of the western world.
The Playboy of the Western World, III, closing words

TACITUS A.D. 55 or 56–c.120

6 *Nunc terminus Britanniae patet, atque omne ignotum
pro magnifico est.*
Now the boundary of Britain is revealed, and
everything unknown is held to be glorious.
Agricola, 30. Allegedly reporting a British leader, 'Calgacus'.

7 *Solitudinem faciunt pacem appellant.*
They make a wilderness and call it peace.

8 *Proprium humani ingenii est odisse quem laeseris.*
It is part of human nature to hate the man you have
hurt.
42

9 *Tu vero felix, Agricola, non vitae tantum claritate, sed
etiam opportunitate mortis.*
You were indeed fortunate, Agricola, not only in the
distinction of your life, but also in the lucky timing of
your death.
45

10 *Sine ira et studio.*
Without either anger or zealousness.
Annals, i.1

11 *Elegantiae arbiter.*
The authority on taste.
xvi.18. Of Petronius

12 *Rara temporum felicitate ubi sentire quae velis et quae
sentias dicere licet.*
These times having the rare good fortune that you may
think what you like and say what you think.
Histories, i.1

13 *Maior privato visus dum privatus fuit, et omnium
consensu capax imperii nisi imperasset.*
He seemed much greater than a private citizen while he
still was a private citizen, and had he never become
emperor everyone would have agreed that he had the
capacity to reign.
49. Of the Emperor Galba

14 *Etiam sapientibus cupido gloriae novissima exuitur.*
Love of fame is the last thing even learned men can

bear to be parted from.
iv.6

CHARLES-MAURICE DE TALLEYRAND 1754–1838

15 *Surtout, Messieurs, point de zèle.*
Above all, gentlemen, not the slightest zeal.
P. Chasles, *Voyages d'un critique à travers la vie et les livres*
(1868), vol.2, p.407

16 *Qui n'a pas vécu dans les années voisines de 1789 ne
sait pas ce que c'est que le plaisir de vivre.*
He who has not lived during the years around 1789 can
not know what is meant by the pleasure of life.
M. Guizot, *Mémoires pour servir à l'histoire de mon temps*
(1858), I, 6

17 *Ils n'ont rien appris, ni rien oublié.*
They have learnt nothing, and forgotten nothing.
Attributed to Talleyrand by the Chevalier de Panat in a letter to
Mallet du Pan, Jan. 1796, 'Personne n'est corrigé, personne n'a su
ni rien oublier ni rien apprendre.' *Mémoires et correspondance de
Mallet du Pan* (1851), II.196. See 199:7

18 *Quelle triste vieillesse vous vous préparez.*
What a sad old-age you are preparing for yourself.
J.J.M.C. Amédée Pichot, *Souvenirs Intimes sur M. de
Talleyrand*, 'Le Pour et le Contre.' A young diplomat had prided
himself, in front of Talleyrand, on his ignorance of whist.

19 *Voilà le commencement de la fin.*
This is the beginning of the end.
Attr. On the announcement of Napoleon's defeat at Borodino,
1812. Sainte-Beuve, *M. de Talleyrand* (1870), ch.3

NAHUM TATE 1652–1715
and NICHOLAS BRADY 1659–1726

20 As pants the hart for cooling streams
When heated in the chase.
New Version of the Psalms (1696). **As Pants the Hart**

21 Through all the changing scenes of life.
Through all the Changing

22 While shepherds watch'd their flocks by night,
All seated on the ground,
The Angel of the Lord came down,
And glory shone around.
Supplement to the New Version of the Psalms (1700). **While
Shepherds Watched**

ANN TAYLOR 1782–1866
and JANE TAYLOR 1783–1824

23 I thank the goodness and the grace
Which on my birth have smiled,
And made me, in these Christian days,
A happy English child.
Hymns for Infant Minds, I. **A Child's Hymn of Praise**

24 'Tis a *credit* to any good girl to be neat,
But quite a *disgrace* to be fine.
Hymns for Sunday Schools. **The Folly of Finery**

25 Who ran to help me when I fell,
And would some pretty story tell,
Or kiss the place to make it well?
    My Mother.
Original Poems. **My Mother**. (By Ann Taylor)

26 How pleasant it is, at the end of the day,
No follies to have to repent;
But reflect on the past, and be able to say,

That my time has been properly spent.
Rhymes for the Nursery. The Way to be Happy. (By Jane Taylor)

1 Twinkle, twinkle, little star,
How I wonder what you are!
Up above the world so high,
Like a diamond in the sky!
The Star. (By Jane Taylor)

BAYARD TAYLOR 1825–1878

2 Till the sun grows cold,
And the stars are old,
And the leaves of the Judgment Book unfold.
Bedouin Song. Refrain

BISHOP JEREMY TAYLOR 1613–1667

3 As our life is very short, so it is very miserable, and therefore it is well it is short.
The Rule and Exercise of Holy Dying (1651), ch.i, sect.4

4 Too quick a sense of a constant infelicity.
5

5 Every school-boy knows it.
On the Real Presence, V, par.I

6 The union of hands and hearts.
Sermons. The Marriage Ring, pt.i

TOM TAYLOR 1817–1880

7 Hawkshaw, the detective.
The Ticket-of-leave Man, IV.i. Commonly remembered, and delivered, in the form 'I am Hawkshaw, the detective'.

ARCHBISHOP FREDERICK TEMPLE 1821–1902

8 'My aunt was suddenly prevented from going a voyage in a ship what went down—would you call that a case of Providential interference?'
'Can't tell: didn't know your aunt.'
Sandford, *Memoirs of Archbishop Temple,* (1906), vol. II, p. 705

9 There is a certain class of clergyman whose mendicity is only equalled by their mendacity.
Remark at a meeting of the Ecclesiastical Commissioners quoted by Sir George Leveson Gower, *Years of Endeavour* (1942)

SIR WILLIAM TEMPLE 1628–1699

10 When all is done, human life is, at the greatest and the best, but like a froward child, that must be play'd with and humoured a little to keep it quiet till it falls asleep, and then the care is over.
Essay on Poetry, ad fin.

ARCHBISHOP WILLIAM TEMPLE 1881–1944

11 In place of the conception of the Power-State we are led to that of the Welfare-State.
Citizen and Churchman (1941), ch.II

12 Christianity is the most materialistic of all great religions.
Reading in St John's Gospel, vol.I (1939), Introduction

13 'Are you not,' a Rugby master had asked him in discussing one of his [schoolboy] essays, 'a little out of your depth here?' 'Perhaps, Sir,' was the confident reply, 'but I can swim.'
F.A. Iremonger, *William Temple*

SIR JOHN TENNIEL 1820–1914

14 Dropping the pilot.
Caption of a cartoon and title of a poem in *Punch,* 29 March 1890, referring to the departure from office of Bismark

ALFRED, LORD TENNYSON 1809–1892

15 For nothing worthy proving can be proven,
Nor yet disproven: wherefore thou be wise,
Cleave ever to the sunnier side of doubt.
The Ancient Sage (1885), l.66

16 Her arms across her breast she laid;
She was more fair than words can say:
Bare-footed came the beggar maid
Before the king Cophetua.
In robe and crown the king stept down,
To meet and greet her on her way;
'It is no wonder,' said the lords,
'She is more beautiful than day.'

As shines the moon in clouded skies,
She in her poor attire was seen:
One praised her ankles, one her eyes,
One her dark hair and lovesome mien.
So sweet a face, such angel grace,
In all that land had never been:
Cophetua sware a royal oath:
'This beggar maid shall be my queen!'
The Beggar Maid (1842)

17 Break, break, break,
On thy cold gray stones, O Sea!
And I would that my tongue could utter
The thoughts that arise in me.
Break, Break, Break (1842)

18 And the stately ships go on
To their haven under the hill;
But O for the touch of a vanish'd hand,
And the sound of a voice that is still!

19 A happy bridesmaid makes a happy bride.
The Bridesmaid (1830), l.4

20 I come from haunts of coot and hern,
I make a sudden sally
And sparkle out among the fern,
To bicker down a valley.
The Brook (1864), l.23

21 For men may come and men may go,
But I go on for ever.
l.33

22 The Lord let the house of a brute to the soul of a man,
And the man said, 'Am I your debtor?'
And the Lord—'Not yet: but make it as clean as you can,
And then I will let you a better.'
By an Evolutionist (1889)

23 Half a league, half a league,
Half a league onward,
All in the valley of Death
Rode the six hundred.
The Charge of the Light Brigade (1854)

24 'Forward the Light Brigade!'
Was there a man dismay'd?

Not tho' the soldier knew
  Some one had blunder'd:
Their's not to make reply,
Their's not to reason why,
Their's but to do and die:
Into the valley of Death
  Rode the six hundred.

Cannon to right of them
Cannon to left of them,
Cannon in front of them
  Volley'd and thunder'd.

1 Into the jaws of Death,
   Into the mouth of Hell.

2 Come not, when I am dead,
     To drop thy foolish tears upon my grave,
   To trample round my fallen head,
     And vex the unhappy dust thou wouldst not save.
   Come Not, When I Am Dead (1842), i

3 Sunset and evening star,
     And one clear call for me!
   And may there be no moaning of the bar
     When I put out to sea.
   Crossing the Bar (1889)

4 Twilight and evening bell,
     And after that the dark!
   And may there be no sadness of farewell,
     When I embark;

   For tho' from out our bourne of Time and Place
     The flood may bear me far,
   I hope to see my Pilot face to face
     When I have crost the bar.

5 O Love what hours were thine and mine,
   In lands of palm and southern pine;
     In lands of palm, of orange-blossom,
   Of olive, aloe, and maize and vine.
   The Daisy (1847), i

6 A daughter of the gods, divinely tall
     And most divinely fair. [Iphigenia.]
   A Dream of Fair Women (1833), l.87

7 He clasps the crag with crooked hands;
   Close to the sun in lonely lands,
   Ring'd with the azure world, he stands.
   The wrinkled sea beneath him crawls;
   He watches from his mountain walls,
   And like a thunderbolt he falls.
   The Eagle (1842)

8 The curate; he was fatter than his cure.
   Edwin Morris (1842), l.15

9 God made the woman for the man,
   And for the good and increase of the world.
   l.50

10   Slight Sir Robert with his watery smile
     And educated whisker.
     l.128

11 And when they buried him the little port
    Had seldom seen a costlier funeral.
    Enoch Arden (1864)

12 O mighty-mouth'd inventor of harmonies,
    O skill'd to sing of Time or Eternity,
      God-gifted organ-voice of England,
      Milton, a name to resound for ages.
    Experiments. Milton: Alcaics

13   All that bowery loneliness,
     The brooks of Eden mazily murmuring.

14 O you chorus of indolent reviewers.
    Milton: Hendecasyllabics

15 The mellow lin-lan-lone of evening bells.
    Far-Far-Away (1889)

16 O Love, O fire! once he drew
    With one long kiss my whole soul thro'
    My lips, as sunlight drinketh dew.
    Fatima (1833), iii

17 Row us out from Desenzano, to your Sirmione row!
    Frater Ave atque Vale

18 Tenderest of Roman poets nineteen-hundred years
      ago,
    'Frater Ave atque Vale'—as we wander'd to and fro
    Gazing at the Lydian laughter of the Garda lake below
    Sweet Catullus' all-but-island, olive-silvery Sirmio!
    See 136:28

19 More black than ashbuds in the front of March.
    The Gardener's Daughter (1842), l.28

20 A sight to make an old man young.
    l.140

21 Then she rode forth, clothed on with chastity.
    Godiva (1842), l.53

22 With twelve great shocks of sound, the shameless
      noon
    Was clash'd and hammer'd from a hundred towers.
    l.74

23   Ah! when shall all men's good
     Be each man's rule, and universal Peace
     Lie like a shaft of light across the land?
     The Golden Year (1842), l.47

24 Thro' all the circle of the golden year.
    l.51

25 That a lie which is all a lie may be met and fought
      with outright,
    But a lie which is part a truth is a harder matter to
      fight.
    The Grandmother (1847), viii

26 That man's the true Conservative
    Who lops the moulder'd branch away.
    Hands All Round (1885), i

27 Pray God our greatness may not fail
    Thro' craven fears of being great.
    iii

28 Gigantic daughter of the West,
    We drink to thee across the flood…
    For art thou not of British blood?
    iv. In original version, published in *The Examiner*, 7 Feb. 1852

29 Speak to Him thou for He hears, and Spirit with Spirit
      can meet—
    Closer is He than breathing, and nearer than hands and
      feet.
    The Higher Pantheism (1847), vi

30 Wearing the white flower of a blameless life,
    Before a thousand peering littlenesses,
    In that fierce light which beats upon a throne,
    And blackens every blot.
    The Idylls of the King (1842–1885), Dedication, l.24

31 Man's word is God in man.
    The Coming of Arthur, l.132

1 Clothed in white samite, mystic, wonderful.
1.284, and **The Passing of Arthur**, 1.199

2 Rain, rain, and sun! a rainbow in the sky!
A young man will be wiser by and by;
An old man's wit may wander ere he die.
1.402

3 From the great deep to the great deep he goes.
1.410

4 Blow trumpet, for the world is white with May.
1.481

5 Live pure, speak true, right wrong, follow the King—
Else, wherefore born?
Gareth and Lynette, 1.117

6   The city is built
To music, therefore never built at all,
And therefore built for ever.
1.272

7 Lightly was her slender nose
Tip-tilted like the petal of a flower.
1.576

8 Too late, too late! ye cannot enter now.
Guinevere, 1.168

9 For manners are not idle, but the fruit
Of loyal nature, and of noble mind.
1.333

10 The children born of thee are sword and fire,
Red ruin, and the breaking up of laws.
1.422

11 To reverence the King, as if he were
Their conscience, and their conscience as their King,
To break the heathen and uphold the Christ,
To ride abroad redressing human wrongs,
To speak no slander, no, nor listen to it,
To honour his own word as if his God's.
1.465

12 To love one maiden only, cleave to her,
And worship her by years of noble deeds,
Until they won her; for indeed I knew
Of no more subtle master under heaven
Than is the maiden passion for a maid,
Not only to keep down the base in man,
But teach high thought, and amiable words
And courtliness, and the desire of fame,
And love of truth, and all that makes a man.
1.472

13   He never mocks,
For mockery is the fume of little hearts.
1.627

14 I thought I could not breathe in that fine air
That pure severity of perfect light—
I yearn'd for warmth and colour which I found
In Lancelot.
1.640

15 It was my duty to have loved the highest:
It surely was my profit had I known:
It would have been my pleasure had I seen.
We needs must love the highest when we see it,
Not Lancelot, nor another.
1.652

16 To where beyond these voices there is peace.
1.692

17 For good ye are and bad, and like to coins,
Some true, some light, but every one of you

Stamp'd with the image of the King.
The Holy Grail, 1.25

18 The cup, the cup itself, from which our Lord
Drank at the last sad supper with his own.
1.46

19 God make thee good as thou art beautiful.
1.136

20 For when was Lancelot wanderingly lewd?
1.148

21 I, maiden, round thee, maiden, bind my belt.
1.159

22   Ye follow wandering fires
Lost in the quagmire!
1.319

23 I will be deafer than the blue-eyed cat,
And thrice as blind as any noon-tide owl,
To holy virgins in their ecstasies,
Henceforward.
1.865

24 So spake the King: I knew not all he meant.
1.919

25 Elaine the fair, Elaine the loveable,
Elaine, the lily maid of Astolat.
Lancelot and Elaine, 1.1

26   To me
He is all fault who hath no fault at all:
For who loves me must have a touch of earth.
1.131

27   In me there dwells
No greatness, save it be some far-off touch
Of greatness to know well I am not great.
1.447

28 I know not if I know what true love is,
But if I know, then, if I love not him,
I know there is none other I can love.
1.672

29 The shackles of an old love straiten'd him,
His honour rooted in dishonour stood,
And faith unfaithful kept him falsely true.
1.870

30 Sweet is true love tho' given in vain, in vain;
And sweet is death who puts an end to pain.
1.1000

31   Never yet
Was noble man but made ignoble talk.
He makes no friend who never made a foe.
1.1080

32 Our bond is not the bond of man and wife.
1.1199

33 'Forgive me; mine was jealousy in love.'
He answer'd with his eyes upon the ground,
'That is love's curse; pass on, my Queen, forgiven.'
1.1340

34 Free love—free field—we love but while we may.
The Last Tournament, 1.281

35 The dirty nurse, Experience, in her kind
Hath foul'd me.
1.317

36 The greater man, the greater courtesy.
1.628

37 The ptarmigan that whitens ere his hour

Woos his own end.
l.692

1 Our hoard is little, but our hearts are great.
The Marriage of Geraint, l.352

2 For man is man and master of his fate.
l.355

3 Hark, by the bird's song ye may learn the nest.
l.359

4 They take the rustic murmur of their bourg
For the great wave that echoes round the world.
l.419

5 Brave hearts and clean! and yet—God guide
them—young.
Merlin and Vivien, l.29

6 Unfaith in aught is want of faith in all.
l.387

7 It is the little rift within the lute,
That by and by will make the music mute,
And ever widening slowly silence all.
l.388

8 And trust me not at all or all in all.
l.396

9 Man dreams of fame while woman wakes to love.
l.458

10 With this for motto, 'Rather use than fame'.
l.478

11   Where blind and naked Ignorance
Delivers brawling judgments, unashamed,
On all things all day long.
l.662

12 But every page having an ample marge,
And every marge enclosing in the midst
A square of text that looks a little blot.
l.667

13 And none can read the text, not even I;
And none can read the comment but myself.
l.679

14 O selfless man and stainless gentleman!
l.790

15 Defaming and defacing, till she left
Not even Lancelot brave, nor Galahad clean.
l.802

16 For men at most differ as Heaven and Earth,
But women, worst and best, as Heaven and Hell.
l.812

17 Face-flatterer and backbiter are the same.
l.822

18 O great and sane and simple race of brutes
That own no lust because they have no law!
Pelleas and Ettarre, l.471

19 I found Him in the shining of the stars,
I mark'd Him in the flowering of His fields,
But in His ways with men I find Him not.
The Passing of Arthur, l.9

20 So all day long the noise of battle roll'd
Among the mountains by the winter sea.
l.170

21 On one side lay the Ocean, and on one
Lay a great water, and the moon was full.
l.179

22 Authority forgets a dying king.
l.289

23 Clothed with his breath, and looking, as he walk'd,
Larger than human on the frozen hills.
He heard the deep behind him, and a cry
Before.
l.350

24 The days darken round me, and the years,
Among new men, strange faces, other minds.
l.405

25 And slowly answer'd Arthur from the barge:
'The old order changeth, yielding place to new,
And God fulfils himself in many ways,
Lest one good custom should corrupt the world.'
l.407

26 If thou shouldst never see my face again,
Pray for my soul. More things are wrought by prayer
Than this world dreams of. Wherefore, let thy voice
Rise like a fountain for me night and day.
For what are men better than sheep or goats
That nourish a blind life within the brain,
If, knowing God, they lift not hands of prayer
Both for themselves and those who call them friend?
For so the whole round earth is every way
Bound by gold chains about the feet of God.
l.414

27   I am going a long way
With these thou seest—if indeed I go
(For all my mind is clouded with a doubt)—
To the island-valley of Avilion;
Where falls not hail, or rain, or any snow,
Nor ever wind blows loudly; but it lies
Deep-meadow'd, happy, fair with orchard lawns
And bowery hollows crown'd with summer sea,
Where I will heal me of my grievous wound.
l.424

28   Like some full-breasted swan
That, fluting a wild carol ere her death,
Ruffles her pure cold plume, and takes the flood
With swarthy webs.
l.434

29 Believing where we cannot prove.
In Memoriam A.H.H. (1850), prologue. (The numbering of the
Cantos includes the additional Canto No. xxxix, first published in
1869)

30 Thou madest man, he knows not why,
He thinks he was not made to die;
And thou hast made him: thou art just.

31 Our little systems have their day;
They have their day and cease to be:
They are but broken lights of thee,
And thou, O Lord, art more than they.

32 Let knowledge grow from more to more,
But more of reverence in us dwell;
That mind and soul, according well,
May make one music as before.

33 I held it truth, with him who sings
To one clear harp in divers tones,
That men may rise on stepping-stones
Of their dead selves to higher things.
i

34   For words, like Nature, half reveal

And half conceal the Soul within.
v

1 But, for the unquiet heart and brain,
    A use in measured language lies;
    The sad mechanic exercise,
Like dull narcotics, numbing pain.

2   And common is the commonplace,
And vacant chaff well meant for grain.
vi

3   Never morning wore
To evening, but some heart did break.

4   His heavy-shotted hammock-shroud
Drops in his vast and wandering grave.

5 Dark house, by which once more I stand
    Here in the long unlovely street,
    Doors, where my heart was used to beat
So quickly, waiting for a hand.
vii

6 And ghastly thro' the drizzling rain
On the bald street breaks the blank day.

7   Or where the kneeling hamlet drains
The chalice of the grapes of God.
x

8   The last red leaf is whirl'd away,
The rooks are blown about the skies.
xv

9 Thou comest, much wept for: such a breeze
    Compell'd thy canvas.
xvii

10   And from his ashes may be made
The violet of his native land.
xviii

11 There twice a day the Severn fills;
    The salt sea-water passes by,
    And hushes half the babbling Wye,
And makes a silence in the hills.
xix

12 I do but sing because I must,
And pipe but as the linnets sing.
xxi

13 The Shadow cloak'd from head to foot,
Who keeps the keys of all the creeds.
xxiii

14   And Thought leapt out to wed with Thought
Ere Thought could wed itself with Speech.

15 I envy not in any moods
    The captive void of noble rage,
    The linnet born within the cage,
That never knew the summer woods.
xxvii

16 'Tis better to have loved and lost
Than never to have loved at all.

17 The time draws near the birth of Christ.
xxviii

18 From every house the neighbours met,
    The streets were fill'd with joyful sound,
    A solemn gladness even crown'd
The purple brows of Olivet.

Behold a man raised up by Christ!
    The rest remaineth unreveal'd;
    He told it not; or something seal'd

The lips of that Evangelist.
xxxi

19 Her eyes are homes of silent prayer.
xxxii

20 Short swallow-flights of song, that dip
    Their wings in tears, and skim away.
xlviii

21 Be near me when my light is low,
    When the blood creeps, and the nerves prick
    And tingle; and the heart is sick,
And all the wheels of Being slow.

Be near me when the sensuous frame
    Is rack'd with pains that conquer trust;
    And Time, a maniac scattering dust,
And Life, a Fury slinging flame.
l

22 How many a father have I seen,
    A sober man, among his boys,
    Whose youth was full of foolish noise.
liii

23 Hold thou the good: define it well:
    For fear divine Philosophy
    Should push beyond her mark, and be
Procuress to the Lords of Hell.

24 Oh yet we trust that somehow good
    Will be the final goal of ill.
liv

25 That nothing walks with aimless feet;
    That not one life shall be destroy'd,
    Or cast as rubbish to the void,
When God hath made the pile complete.

26 Behold, we know not anything;
    I can but trust that good shall fall
    At last—far off—at last, to all,
And every winter change to spring.

So runs my dream: but what am I?
    An infant crying in the night:
    An infant crying for the light:
And with no language but a cry.

27   So careful of the type she seems,
So careless of the single life.
lv

28   The great world's altar-stairs
That slope thro' darkness up to God.

29 Man...
Who trusted God was love indeed
    And love Creation's final law—
    Tho' Nature, red in tooth and claw
With ravine, shriek'd against his creed.
lvi

30   Dragons of the prime,
    That tare each other in their slime,
Were mellow music match'd with him.

31 Peace; come away: the song of woe
    Is after all an earthly song:
    Peace; come away: we do him wrong
To sing so wildly: let us go.
lvii

32   The passing of the sweetest soul
That ever look'd with human eyes.

33 O Sorrow, wilt thou live with me

No casual mistress, but a wife.
lix

1   As some divinely gifted man,
    Whose life in low estate began
And on a simple village green;

Who breaks his birth's invidious bar,
    And grasps the skirts of happy chance,
    And breasts the blows of circumstance,
And grapples with his evil star.
lxiv

2   So many worlds, so much to do,
    So little done, such things to be.
lxxiii

3   Death has made
His darkness beautiful with thee.
lxxiv

4   And round thee with the breeze of song
To stir a little dust of praise.
lxxv

5   O last regret, regret can die!
lxxviii

6   Laburnums, dropping-wells of fire.
lxxxiii

7   God's finger touch'd him, and he slept.
lxxxv

8   He brought an eye for all he saw;
    He mixt in all our simple sports;
    They pleased him, fresh from brawling courts
And dusty purlieus of the law.
lxxxix. See 208:28

9   When rosy plumelets tuft the larch,
    And rarely pipes the mounted thrush:
    Or underneath the barren bush
Flits by the sea-blue bird of March.
xci

10 You tell me, doubt is Devil-born.
xcvi

11 There lives more faith in honest doubt,
Believe me, than in half the creeds.

12 Their meetings made December June,
Their every parting was to die.
xcvii

13 He seems so near and yet so far.

14 Ring out, wild bells, to the wild sky,
    The flying cloud, the frosty light:
    The year is dying in the night;
Ring out, wild bells, and let him die.

Ring out the old, ring in the new,
    Ring, happy bells, across the snow:
    The year is going, let him go;
Ring out the false, ring in the true.
cvi

15 Ring out a slowly dying cause,
    And ancient forms of party strife;
    Ring in the nobler modes of life,
With sweeter manners, purer laws.

Ring out the want, the care, the sin,
    The faithless coldness of the times;
    Ring out, ring out my mournful rhymes,
But ring the fuller minstrel in.

Ring out false pride in place and blood,

The civic slander and the spite;
    Ring in the love of truth and right,
Ring in the common love of good.

Ring out old shapes of foul disease;
    Ring out the narrowing lust of gold;
    Ring out the thousand wars of old,
Ring in the thousand years of peace.

Ring in the valiant man and free,
    The larger heart, the kindlier hand;
    Ring out the darkness of the land;
Ring in the Christ that is to be.

16   Not the schoolboy heat,
The blind hysterics of the Celt.
cix

17 And thus he bore without abuse
    The grand old name of gentleman,
    Defamed by every charlatan,
And soil'd with all ignoble use.
cxi

18 Now fades the last long streak of snow
    Now burgeons every maze of quick
    About the flowering squares and thick
By ashen roots the violets blow.
cxv

19   And drown'd in yonder living blue
The lark becomes a sightless song.

20   There, where the long street roars, hath been
The stillness of the central sea.
cxxiii

21 And thou art worthy; full of power;
    As gentle; liberal-minded, great,
    Consistent; wearing all that weight
Of learning lightly like a flower.
cxxxi, st.13

22   One God, one law, one element,
        And one far-off divine event,
To which the whole creation moves.
st.37

23 The voice of the dead was a living voice to me.
    In the Valley of Cauteretz (1847)

24 Below the thunders of the upper deep;
    Far, far beneath in the abysmal sea,
    His ancient, dreamless, uninvaded sleep
The Kraken sleepeth.
    The Kraken

25 There hath he lain for ages and will lie
    Battening upon huge seaworms in his sleep,
    Until the latter fire shall heat the deep.

26 At me you smiled, but unbeguiled
    I saw the snare, and I retired:
    The daughter of a hundred Earls,
    You are not one to be desired.
    Lady Clara Vere de Vere (1833), i

27 A simple maiden in her flower
    Is worth a hundred coats-of-arms.
    ii

28 Her manners had not that repose
    Which stamps the caste of Vere-de-Vere.
    v

29   From yon blue heavens above us bent
    The gardener Adam and his wife
        Smile at the claims of long descent.

Howe'er it be, it seems to me,
  'Tis only noble to be good.
Kind hearts are more than coronets,
  And simple faith than Norman blood.
vi

1 Oh! teach the orphan-boy to read,
  Or teach the orphan-girl to sew.

2 On either side the river lie
Long fields of barley and of rye,
That clothe the wold and meet the sky;
And thro' the field the road runs by
  To many-tower'd Camelot.
The Lady of Shalott (1833), pt.i

3 Willows whiten, aspens quiver,
Little breezes dusk and shiver.

4 But who hath seen her wave her hand?
Or at the casement seen her stand?
Or is she known in all the land,
  The Lady of Shalott?

5 Only reapers, reaping early
In among the bearded barley,
Hear a song that echoes cheerly
From the river winding clearly
  Down to tower'd Camelot.

6 She hath no loyal knight and true,
  The Lady of Shalott.
pt.ii

7 Or when the moon was overhead,
Came two young lovers lately wed;
'I am half sick of shadows,' said
  The Lady of Shalott.

8 A bow-shot from her bower-eaves,
He rode between the barley-sheaves,
The sun came dazzling thro' the leaves
And flamed upon the brazen greaves
  Of bold Sir Lancelot.
A red-cross knight for ever kneel'd
To a lady in his shield,
That sparkled on the yellow field,
  Beside remote Shalott.
pt.iii

9 All in the blue unclouded weather
Thick-jewell'd shone the saddle-leather,
The helmet and the helmet-feather
Burn'd like one burning flame together,
  As he rode down to Camelot.

10 'Tirra lirra,' by the river
  Sang Sir Lancelot.

11 She left the web, she left the loom,
She made three paces thro' the room
She saw the water-lily bloom,
She saw the helmet and the plume,
  She look'd down to Camelot.
Out flew the web and floated wide;
The mirror crack'd from side to side;
'The curse is come upon me,' cried
  The Lady of Shalott.

12 Who is this? and what is here?
And in the lighted palace near
Died the sound of royal cheer;
And they cross'd themselves for fear,
  All the knights at Camelot:

But Lancelot mused a little space;
He said, 'She has a lovely face;
God in his mercy lend her grace,
  The Lady of Shalott.'
pt.iv

13 Slander, meanest spawn of Hell.
The Letters (1842)

14 Airy, fairy Lilian.
Lilian (1830)

15 Comrades, leave me here a little, while as yet 'tis early morn:
Leave me here, and when you want me, sound upon the bugle-horn.
Locksley Hall (1842), l.1

16 Here about the beach I wander'd, nourishing a youth sublime
With the fairy tales of science, and the long result of Time.
l.11

17 In the Spring a livelier iris changes on the burnish'd dove;
In the Spring a young man's fancy lightly turns to thoughts of love.
l.19

18 And our spirits rush'd together at the touching of the lips.
l.38

19 As the husband is, the wife is: thou art mated with a clown,
And the grossness of his nature will have weight to drag thee down.

He will hold thee, when his passion shall have spent its novel force,
Something better than his dog, a little dearer than his horse.
l.47

20   This is truth the poet sings,
That a sorrow's crown of sorrow is remembering happier things.
l.75. See 89:6, 171:8

21 Like a dog, he hunts in dreams.
l.79

22 O, I see thee old and formal, fitted to thy petty part,
With a little hoard of maxims preaching down a daughter's heart.
l.93

23 But the jingling of the guinea helps the hurt that Honour feels.
l.105

24 Men, my brothers, men the workers, ever reaping something new:
That which they have done but earnest of the things that they shall do:

For I dipt into the future, far as human eye could see,
Saw the Vision of the world, and all the wonder that would be;

Saw the heavens fill with commerce, argosies of magic sails,
Pilots of the purple twilight, dropping down with costly bales;

Heard the heavens fill with shouting, and there rain'd a ghastly dew

From the nations' airy navies grappling in the central
 blue;

Far along the world-wide whisper of the south-wind
 rushing warm,
With the standards of the peoples plunging thro' the
 thunder-storm;

Till the war-drum throbb'd no longer, and the
 battle-flags were furl'd
In the Parliament of man, the Federation of the world.
l.117

1 Science moves, but slowly slowly, creeping on from
 point to point.
l.134

2 Yet I doubt not thro' the ages one increasing purpose
 runs,
And the thoughts of men are widen'd with the process
 of the suns.
l.137

3 Knowledge comes, but wisdom lingers.
l.143

4 I am shamed thro' all my nature to have loved so
 slight a thing.
l.148

5 Woman is the lesser man, and all thy passions match'd
 with mine,
Are as moonlight unto sunlight, and as water unto
 wine.
l.151

6 I will take some savage woman, she shall rear my
 dusky race.
l.168

7 I the heir of all the ages, in the foremost files of time.
l.178

8   Forward, forward let us range,
Let the great world spin for ever down the ringing
 grooves of change.
l.181

9 Better fifty years of Europe than a cycle of Cathay.
l.184

10 He is but a landscape-painter,
 And a village maiden she.
The Lord of Burleigh (1842), l.7

11 Weeping, weeping late and early,
 Walking up and pacing down,
Deeply mourn'd the Lord of Burleigh,
 Burleigh-house by Stamford-town.
l.89

12 'Courage!' he said, and pointed toward the land,
'This mounting wave will roll us shoreward soon.'
In the afternoon they came unto a land
In which it seemed always afternoon.
The Lotos-Eaters (1833)

13 Music that gentlier on the spirit lies,
Than tir'd eyelids upon tir'd eyes.
Choric Song, i

14 There is no joy but calm!
ii

15 Death is the end of life; ah, why
Should life all labour be?
iv

16   Live and lie reclined
On the hills like Gods together, careless of mankind.

For they lie beside their nectar, and the bolts are hurl'd
Far below them in the valleys, and the clouds are
 lightly curl'd
Round their golden houses, girdled with the gleaming
 world.

17 Surely, surely, slumber is more sweet than toil, the
 shore
Than labour in the deep mid-ocean, wind and wave
 and oar;
Oh rest ye, brother mariners, we will not wander
 more.

18 The long mechanic pacings to and fro,
The set gray life, and apathetic end.
Love and Duty (1842), l.17

19   Earn well the thrifty months, nor wed
Raw Haste, half-sister to Delay.
Love thou thy Land (1833), xxiv

20   I saw the flaring atom-streams
And torrents of her myriad universe,
Ruining along the illimitable inane.
Lucretius (1868), l.38

21   Nor at all can tell
Whether I mean this day to end myself,
Or lend an ear to Plato where he says,
That men like soldiers may not quit the post
Allotted by the Gods.
l.145

22 Passionless bride, divine Tranquillity,
Yearn'd after by the wisest of the wise,
Who fail to find thee, being as thou art
Without one pleasure and without one pain.
l.265

23   Weeded and worn the ancient thatch
Upon the lonely moated grange.

She only said, 'My life is dreary,
 He cometh not,' she said;
She said, 'I am aweary, aweary.
 I would that I were dead!'

Her tears fell with the dews at even;
 Her tears fell ere the dews were dried.
Mariana (1830). See 464:18

24 She wept, 'I am aweary, aweary,
 O God, that I were dead!'

25 I hate that dreadful hollow behind the little wood.
Maud (1855), Pt.I.i.1

26 For I trust if an enemy's fleet came yonder round by
 the hill,
And the rushing battle-bolt sang from the three-decker
 out of the foam,
That the smooth-faced snubnosed rogue would leap
 from his counter and till,
And strike, if he could, were it but with his cheating
 yardwand, home.
13

27 Faultily faultless, icily regular, splendidly null,
Dead perfection, no more.
ii

28 The passionate heart of the poet is whirl'd into folly
 and vice.
iv.7

29 And most of all would I flee from the cruel madness
 of love—

The honey of poison-flowers and all the measureless
   ill.
  10

1 That jewell'd mass of millinery,
    That oil'd and curl'd Assyrian Bull.
    vi.6

2 She came to the village church,
    And sat by a pillar alone;
    An angel watching an urn
    Wept over her, carved in stone.
    viii

3   I heard no longer
    The snowy-banded, dilettante,
    Delicate-handed priest intone.

4 Ah God, for a man with heart, head, hand,
    Like some of the simple great ones gone
    For ever and ever by,
    One still strong man in a blatant land,
    Whatever they call him, what care I,
    Aristocrat, democrat, autocrat—one
    Who can rule and dare not lie.

    And ah for a man to arise in me,
    That the man I am may cease to be!
    x.5

5 Birds in the high Hall-garden
    When twilight was falling,
    Maud, Maud, Maud, Maud,
    They were crying and calling.
    xii.1

6 I kiss'd her slender hand,
    She took the kiss sedately;
    Maud is not seventeen,
    But she is tall and stately.
    4

7 Gorgonised me from head to foot
    With a stony British stare.
    xiii.2

8 A livelier emerald twinkles in the grass,
    A purer sapphire melts into the sea.
    xviii.6

9 Come into the garden, Maud,
    For the black bat, night, has flown
    Come into the garden, Maud,
    I am here at the gate alone;
    And the woodbine spices are wafted abroad,
    And the musk of the rose is blown.

    For a breeze of morning moves,
    And the planet of Love is on high,
    Beginning to faint in the light that she loves
    On a bed of daffodil sky.
    xxii.1

10 All night has the casement jessamine stirr'd
    To the dancers dancing in tune;
    Till a silence fell with the waking bird,
    And a hush with the setting moon.
    3

11 Queen rose of the rosebud garden of girls.
    9

12 There has fallen a splendid tear
    From the passion-flower at the gate.
    She is coming, my dove, my dear;
    She is coming, my life, my fate;
    The red rose cries, 'She is near, she is near;'

And the white rose weeps, 'She is late;'
The larkspur listens, 'I hear, I hear;'
  And the lily whispers, 'I wait.'

She is coming, my own, my sweet;
  Were it ever so airy a tread,
My heart would hear her and beat,
  Were it earth in an earthy bed;
My dust would hear her and beat,
  Had I lain for a century dead;
Would start and tremble under her feet,
  And blossom in purple and red.
10

13 O that 'twere possible
    After long grief and pain
    To find the arms of my true love
    Round me once again!
    Pt.II.iv.1

14 But the churchmen fain would kill their church,
    As the churches have kill'd their Christ.
    v.2

15 O me, why have they not buried me deep enough?
    Is it kind to have made me a grave so rough,
    Me, that was never a quiet sleeper?
    11

16 My life has crept so long on a broken wing
    Thro' cells of madness, haunts of horror and fear,
    That I come to be grateful at last for a little thing.
    Pt.III.vi.1

17 When the face of night is fair on the dewy downs,
    And the shining daffodil dies.

18 The blood-red blossom of war with a heart of fire.
    4

19 It is better to fight for the good, than to rail at the ill;
    I have felt with my native land, I am one with my
      kind,
    I embrace the purpose of God, and the doom assign'd.
    5

20 You must wake and call me early, call me early,
      mother dear;
    To-morrow 'ill be the happiest time of all the glad
      New-year;
    Of all the glad New-year, mother, the maddest
      merriest day;
    For I'm to be Queen o' the May, mother, I'm to be
      Queen o' the May.
    The May Queen (1833)

21 Launch your vessel,
    And crowd your canvas,
    And, ere it vanishes
    Over the margin,
    After it, follow it,
    Follow The Gleam.
    Merlin and The Gleam (1886)

22   What, it's you,
    The padded man—that wears the stays.
    The New Timon and the Poets (1846)

23 What profits now to understand
    The merits of a spotless shirt—
    A dapper boot—a little hand—
    If half the little soul is dirt?

24 Dosn't thou 'ear my 'erse's legs, as they canters
      awaäy?
    Proputty, proputty, proputty—that's what I 'ears 'em

saäy.
Northern Farmer. New Style (1847)

1 But I knaw'd a Quaäker feller as often 'as towd me
   this:
   'Doänt thou marry for munny, but goä wheer munny
   is!'

2 Taäke my word for it, Sammy, the poor in a loomp is
   bad.

3 An' I thowt a said whot a owt to 'a said an' I coom'd
   awaäy.
   Northern Farmer. Old Style (1847)

4 Do godamoighty knaw what a's doing a-taäkin' o'
   meä?

5 Bury the Great Duke
   With an empire's lamentation,
   Let us bury the Great Duke
   To the noise of the mourning of a mighty nation.
   Ode on the Death of the Duke of Wellington (1854), i

6 The last great Englishman is low.
   iii

7 Foremost captain of his time,
   Rich in saving common-sense,
   And, as the greatest only are,
   In his simplicity sublime.
   O good grey head which all men knew!
   iv

8 O fall'n at length that tower of strength
   Which stood four-square to all the winds that blew!

9 For this is England's greatest son,
   He that gain'd a hundred fights,
   Nor ever lost an English gun.
   vi

10 In that world-earthquake, Waterloo!

11 That sober freedom out of which there springs
   Our loyal passion for our temperate kings.
   vii

12 Who never sold the truth to serve the hour,
   Nor palter'd with Eternal God for power.

13 Truth-teller was our England's Alfred named.

14 Not once or twice in our rough island-story,
   The path of duty was the way to glory.
   viii

15 Speak no more of his renown,
   Lay your earthly fancies down,
   And in the vast cathedral leave him,
   God accept him, Christ receive him.
   ix

16 There lies a vale in Ida, lovelier
   Than all the valleys of Ionian hills.
   Oenone (1833), l.1

17 O mother Ida, many-fountain'd Ida.
   l.22

18   Then to the bower they came,
   Naked they came to that smooth-swarded bower,
   And at their feet the crocus brake like fire,
   Violet, amaracus, and asphodel,
   Lotos and lilies.
   l.92

19   Because right is right, to follow right
   Were wisdom in the scorn of consequence.
   l.147

20 I built my soul a lordly pleasure-house,
   Wherein at ease for aye to dwell.
   The Palace of Art (1833), i

21 Still as, while Saturn whirls, his stedfast shade
   Sleeps on his luminous ring.
   iv

22   An English home—gray twilight pour'd
   On dewy pasture, dewy trees,
   Softer than sleep—all things in order stored,
   A haunt of ancient Peace.
   xxii

23   Two godlike faces gazed below;
   Plato the wise, and large-brow'd Verulam,
   The first of those who know.
   xli

24 Vex not thou the poet's mind
   With thy shallow wit;
   Vex not thou the poet's mind;
   For thou canst not fathom it.
   The Poet's Mind (1830)

25 Dark-brow'd sophist, come not anear:
   All the place is holy ground.

26 For some cry 'Quick' and some cry 'Slow ,
   But, while the hills remain,
   Up hill 'Too-slow' will need the whip,
   Down hill 'Too-quick', the chain.
   Politics (1889)

27 With prudes for proctors, dowagers for deans,
   And sweet girl-graduates in their golden hair.
   The Princess (1847), prologue, l.141

28 As thro' the land at eve we went,
   And pluck'd the ripen'd ears,
   We fell out, my wife and I,
   O we fell out I know not why,
   And kiss'd again with tears.
   And blessings on the falling out
   That all the more endears,
   When we fall out with those we love
   And kiss again with tears!
   ii. Song

29 O hard, when love and duty clash!
   ii, l.273

30   Follow'd then
   A classic lecture, rich in sentiment,
   With scraps of thundrous Epic lilted out
   By violet-hooded Doctors, elegies
   And quoted odes, and jewels five-words long,
   That on the stretch'd forefinger of all Time
   Sparkle for ever.
   l.351

31 Sweet and low, sweet and low,
   Wind of the western sea,
   Low, low, breathe and blow,
   Wind of the western sea!
   Over the rolling waters go,
   Come from the dying moon, and blow,
   Blow him again to me;
   While my little one, while my pretty one, sleeps.
   iii. Song

32 The splendour falls on castle walls
   And snowy summits old in story:
   The long light shakes across the lakes,
   And the wild cataract leaps in glory.

Blow, bugle, blow, set the wild echoes flying,
Blow, bugle; answer, echoes, dying, dying, dying.

O hark, O hear! how thin and clear,
   And thinner, clearer, farther going!
O sweet and far from cliff and scar
   The horns of Elfland faintly blowing!
iv. Song (1)

1 O love, they die in yon rich sky,
   They faint on hill or field or river:
Our echoes roll from soul to soul,
   And grow for ever and for ever.

2 Tears, idle tears, I know not what they mean,
Tears from the depth of some divine despair
Rise in the heart, and gather to the eyes,
In looking on the happy Autumn-fields,
And thinking of the days that are no more.
Song (2)

3 So sad, so fresh, the days that are no more.

4 Ah, sad and strange as in dark summer dawns
The earliest pipe of half-awaken'd birds
To dying ears, when unto dying eyes
The casement slowly grows a glimmering square;
So sad, so strange, the days that are no more.

Dear as remembered kisses after death,
And sweet as those by hopeless fancy feign'd
On lips that are for others: deep as love,
Deep as first love, and wild with all regret;
O Death in Life, the days that are no more.

5 O Swallow, Swallow, flying, flying South,
Fly to her, and fall upon her gilded eaves,
And tell her, tell her, what I tell to thee.

O tell her, Swallow, thou that knowest each,
That bright and fierce and fickle is the South,
And dark and true and tender is the North.
Song (3)

6 O tell her, Swallow, that thy brood is flown:
Say to her, I do but wanton in the South,
But in the North long since my nest is made.

7 Thy voice is heard thro' rolling drums,
   That beat to battle where he stands;
Thy face across his fancy comes,
   And gives the battle to his hands:
A moment, while the trumpets blow,
   He sees his brood about thy knee;
The next, like fire he meets the foe,
   And strikes him dead for thine and thee.
Song (4)

8 Man is the hunter; woman is his game:
The sleek and shining creatures of the chase,
We hunt them for the beauty of their skins;
They love us for it, and we ride them down.
v, 1.147

9 Man for the field and woman for the hearth:
Man for the sword and for the needle she:
Man with the head and woman with the heart:
Man to command and woman to obey;
All else confusion.
1.427

10 Home they brought her warrior dead.
She nor swoon'd, nor utter'd cry:
All her maidens, watching said,

'She must weep or she will die.'
vi. Song

11 Rose a nurse of ninety years,
Set his child upon her knee—
Like summer tempest came her tears—
'Sweet my child, I live for thee.'

12   The woman is so hard
Upon the woman.
1.205

13 Ask me no more: what answer should I give?
I love not hollow cheek or faded eye:
Yet, O my friend, I will not have thee die!
Ask me no more, lest I should bid thee live;
               Ask me no more.
vii. Song (1)

14 Now sleeps the crimson petal, now the white;
Nor waves the cypress in the palace walk;
Nor winks the gold fin in the porphyry font:
The fire-fly wakens: waken thou with me.

Now droops the milk-white peacock like a ghost,
And like a ghost she glimmers on to me.

Now lies the Earth all Danaë to the stars,
And all thy heart lies open unto me.

Now slides the silent meteor on, and leaves
A shining furrow, as thy thoughts in me.

Now folds the lily all her sweetness up,
And slips into the bosom of the lake:
So fold thyself, my dearest, thou, and slip
Into my bosom and be lost in me.
Song (2)

15 Come down, O maid, from yonder mountain height:
What pleasure lives in height?
Song (3)

16 For Love is of the valley, come thou down
And find him; by the happy threshold, he,
Or hand in hand with Plenty in the maize,
Or red with spirted purple of the vats,
Or foxlike in the vine; nor cares to walk
With Death and Morning on the silver horns.

17   Sweet is every sound,
Sweeter thy voice, but every sound is sweet;
Myriads of rivulets hurrying thro' the lawn,
The moan of doves in immemorial elms,
And murmuring of innumerable bees.

18 The woman's cause is man's: they rise or sink
Together.
1.243

19   Happy he
With such a mother! faith in womankind
Beats with his blood, and trust in all things high
Comes easy to him, and tho' he trip and fall
He shall not blind his soul with clay.
1.308

20 No little lily-handed Baronet he,
A great broad-shoulder'd genial Englishman,
A lord of fat prize-oxen and of sheep,
A raiser of huge melons and of pine,
A patron of some thirty charities,
A pamphleteer on guano and on grain.
Conclusion, 1.84

21 At Flores in the Azores Sir Richard Grenville lay,
And a pinnace, like a fluttered bird, came flying from

far away:
'Spanish ships of war at sea! we have sighted
  fifty-three!'
Then sware Lord Thomas Howard: ''Fore God I am no
  coward;
But I cannot meet them here, for my ships are out of
  gear,
And the half my men are sick. I must fly, but follow
  quick.
We are six ships of the line; can we fight with
  fifty-three?'

Then spake Sir Richard Grenville: 'I know you are no
  coward;
You fly them for a moment to fight with them again.
But I've ninety men and more that are lying sick
  ashore.
I should count myself the coward if I left them, my
  Lord Howard,
To these Inquisition dogs and the devildoms of Spain.'

So Lord Howard past away with five ships of war that
  day,
Till he melted like a cloud in the silent summer
  heaven.
The Revenge (1880), i

1 And Sir Richard said again: 'We be all good English
    men.
   Let us bang these dogs of Seville, the children of the
    devil,
   For I never turn'd my back upon Don or devil yet.'
   iv

2 And the sun went down, and the stars came out far
    over the summer sea,
   But never a moment ceased the fight of the one and the
    fifty-three.
   ix

3 'Sink me the ship, Master Gunner—sink her, split her
    in twain!
   Fall into the hands of God, not into the hands of
    Spain!'

   And the gunner said 'Ay, ay', but the seamen made
    reply:
   'We have children, we have wives,
   And the Lord hath spared our lives.'
   xi

4 And they praised him to his face with their courtly
    foreign grace;
   But he rose upon their decks, and he cried:
   'I have fought for Queen and Faith like a valiant man
    and true;
   I have only done my duty as a man is bound to do:
   With a joyful spirit I Sir Richard Grenville die!'
   And he fell upon their decks, and he died.
   xiii

5 And the little Revenge herself went down by the island
    crags
   To be lost evermore in the main.
   xiv

6 Form, Form, Riflemen Form!
   Riflemen Form! (1892)

7 What does little birdie say
   In her nest at peep of day?
   Sea Dreams (1864), l.281

8 My strength is as the strength of ten,

Because my heart is pure.
Sir Galahad (1842)

9 A man had given all other bliss,
   And all his worldly worth for this,
   To waste his whole heart in one kiss
     Upon her perfect lips.
   Sir Launcelot and Queen Guinevere (1842)

10 Alone and warming his five wits,
   The white owl in the belfry sits.
   Song. The Owl (1830)

11 The woods decay, the woods decay and fall,
   The vapours weep their burthen to the ground,
   Man comes and tills the field and lies beneath,
   And after many a summer dies the swan.
   Me only cruel immortality
   Consumes: I wither slowly in thine arms,
   Here at the quiet limit of the world.
   Tithonus (c.1833, pub.1860), l.1

12 Why wilt thou ever scare me with thy tears,
   And make me tremble lest a saying learnt,
   In days far-off, on that dark earth, be true?
   'The gods themselves cannot recall their gifts.'
   l.46

13 Of happy men that have the power to die,
   And grassy barrows of the happier dead.
   l.70

14 God gives us love. Something to love
     He lends us; but, when love is grown
   To ripeness, that on which it throve
     Falls off, and love is left alone.
   To J.S., iv

15 Her court was pure; her life serene;
     God gave her peace; her land reposed;
     A thousand claims to reverence closed
   In her as Mother, Wife, and Queen.
   To the Queen (1851)

16 You'll have no scandal while you dine,
   But honest talk and wholesome wine.
   To the Revd. F.D. Maurice, v

17 All the charm of all the Muses often flowering in a
     lonely word.
   To Virgil (1889), iii

18   I salute thee, Mantovano,
   I that loved thee since my day began,
   Wielder of the stateliest measure ever moulded by the
     lips of man.
   x

19 This truth within thy mind rehearse,
   That in a boundless universe
   Is boundless better, boundless worse.
   The Two Voices (1833), ix

20 No life that breathes with human breath
   Has ever truly long'd for death.
   cxxxii

21 It little profits that an idle king,
   By this still hearth, among these barren crags,
   Match'd with an aged wife, I mete and dole
   Unequal laws unto a savage race.
   Ulysses (1842), l.1

22   I will drink
   Life to the lees: all times I have enjoy'd
   Greatly, have suffer'd greatly, both with those
   That loved me, and alone; on shore, and when

Thro' scudding drifts the rainy Hyades
Vext the dim sea: I am become a name;
For always roaming with a hungry heart
Much have I seen and known; cities of men
And manners, climates, councils, governments,
Myself not least, but honour'd of them all;
And drunk delight of battle with my peers,
Far on the ringing plains of windy Troy.
I am a part of all that I have met;
Yet all experience is an arch wherethro'
Gleams that untravell'd world, whose margin fades
For ever and for ever when I move.
How dull it is to pause, to make an end,
To rust unburnish'd, not to shine in use!
As tho' to breathe were life.
1.6

1   This gray spirit yearning in desire
To follow knowledge like a sinking star,
Beyond the utmost bound of human thought.
1.30

2 This is my son, mine own Telemachus.
1.33

3 There lies the port; the vessel puffs her sail:
There gloom the dark broad seas. My mariners
Souls that have toil'd, and wrought, and thought with
     me—
That ever with a frolic welcome took
The thunder and the sunshine, and opposed
Free hearts, free foreheads—you and I are old;
Old age hath yet his honour and his toil;
Death closes all: but something ere the end,
Some work of noble note, may yet be done,
Not unbecoming men that strove with gods.
The lights begin to twinkle from the rocks:
The long day wanes: the slow moon climbs: the deep
Moans round with many voices. Come, my friends,
'Tis not too late to seek a newer world.
Push off, and sitting well in order smite
The sounding furrows; for my purpose holds
To sail beyond the sunset, and the baths
Of all the western stars, until I die.
It may be that the gulfs will wash us down:
It may be we shall touch the Happy Isles,
And see the great Achilles, whom we knew.
Tho' much is taken, much abides; and tho'
We are not now that strength which in old days
Moved earth and heaven; that which we are, we are;
One equal temper of heroic hearts,
Made weak by time and fate, but strong in will
To strive, to seek, to find, and not to yield.
1.44

4 What is it all but a trouble of ants in the gleam of a
     million million of suns?
Vastness (1889)

5 Fur hoffens we talkt o' my darter es died o' the fever
     at fall:
An' I thowt 'twur the will o' the Lord, but Miss Annie
     she said it wur draäins.
The Village Wife (1880), ii

6 Bitter barmaid, waning fast!
The Vision of Sin (1842), IV.ii

7 Let us have a quiet hour,
     Let us hob-and-nob with Death.
iii

8 Every moment dies a man,
     Every moment one is born.
ix

9 O plump head-waiter at the Cock,
     To which I must resort,
How goes the time? 'Tis five o'clock.
     Go fetch a pint of port.
Will Waterproof's Lyrical Monologue (1842), i

10 I grow in worth, and wit, and sense,
     Unboding critic-pen,
Or that eternal want of pence,
     Which vexes public men.
vi

11 A land of settled government,
     A land of just and old renown,
     Where Freedom slowly broadens down
From precedent to precedent.
'You ask me, why' (1833), iii

12 While I live, the owls!
When I die, the GHOULS!!!
Written in 1869 in Hallam Tennyson's commonplace book by the
side of an epigram on a poet's fate by Thomas Hood. H.
Tennyson, *Alfred, Lord Tennyson* (1898), ii, ch.3. See 255:14

13 A louse in the locks of literature.
Said of Churton Collins to Edmund Gosse. Evan Charteris, *Life
and Letters of Sir Edmund Gosse* (1931), ch.xiv

TERENCE c.190–159 B.C.

14 *Hinc illae lacrimae.*
Hence all those tears shed.
Andria, 126

15 *Amantium irae amoris integratio est.*
Lovers' rows make love whole again.
555

16 *Nullumst iam dictum quod non dictum sit prius.*
Nothing has yet been said that's not been said before.
Eunuchus. Prolog. 41

17 *Homo sum; humani nil a me alienum puto.*
I am a man, I count nothing human foreign to me.
Heauton Timorumenos, 77

18 *Fortis fortuna adiuvat.*
Fortune aids the brave.
Phormio, 203

19 *Quot homines tot sententiae: suo' quoique mos.*
There are as many opinions as there are people: each
has his own correct way.
454

ST. TERESA OF ÁVILA 1512–1582

20 *Oh, válame Dios, Señor cómo apretáis a vestros
amadores!*
Alas, O Lord, to what a state dost Thou bring those
who love Thee!
Interior Castles (Mansions), trans. by the Benedictines of
Stanbrook, 1921, VI, xi, 6

TERTULLIAN A.D. c.160–c.225

21 *O testimonium animae naturaliter Christianae.*
O evidence of a naturally Christian soul!
Apologeticus, 17

22 *Plures efficimus quoties metimur a vobis, semen est
sanguis Christianorum.*
As often as we are mown down by you, the more we

grow in numbers; the blood of Christians is the seed.
50,13. Traditionally cited as, The blood of the martyrs is the seed
of the Church.

1 *Certum est quia impossibile est.*
It is certain because it is impossible.
De Carne Christi, 5. Often quoted as, *Credo quia impossibile.*

EDWARD TESCHEMACHER nineteenth century

2 Where my caravan has rested,
Flowers I leave you on the grass.
Where My Caravan Has Rested

A.S.J. TESSIMOND 1902–1962

3 Cats, no less liquid than their shadows,
   Offer no angles to the wind.
They slip, diminished, neat, through loopholes
   Less than themselves.
Cats, II

WILLIAM MAKEPEACE THACKERAY
1811–1863

4 He who meanly admires mean things is a Snob.
The Book of Snobs (1848), ch.2

5 It is impossible, in our condition of Society, not to be
sometimes a Snob.
ch.3

6 'Tis not the dying for a faith that's so hard, Master
Harry—every man of every nation has done that—'tis
the living up to it that is difficult.
The History of Henry Esmond (1852), bk.i, ch.6

7 'Tis strange what a man may do, and a woman yet
think him an angel.
ch.7

8 We love being in love, that's the truth on't.
bk.ii, ch.15

9 Why do they always put mud into coffee on board
steamers? Why does the tea generally taste of boiled
boots?
The Kickleburys on the Rhine (1850)

10 Kind, cheerful, merry Dr Brighton.
The Newcomes (1853-5), bk.i, ch.9

11 What money is better bestowed than that of a
school-boy's tip?
ch.16

12 As the last bell struck, a peculiar sweet smile shone
over his face, and he lifted up his head a little, and
quickly said, 'Adsum!' and fell back. It was the word
we used at school, when names were called; and lo,
he, whose heart was as that of a little child, had
answered to his name, and stood in the presence of
The Master.
ch.80

13 Yes, I am a fatal man, Madame Fribsbi. To inspire
hopeless passion is my destiny. [Mirobolant.]
Pendennis (1848-50), ch.23

14 Remember, it is as easy to marry a rich woman as a
poor woman.
ch.28

15 For a slashing article, sir, there's nobody like the
Capting.
ch.32

16 The *Pall Mall Gazette* is written by gentlemen for

gentlemen.

17 Business first; pleasure afterwards. [Queen of
Paflagonia.]
The Rose and the Ring (1855), ch.1

18 Runs not a river by my palace wall? Have I not sacks
to sew up wives withal? [Valoroso.]
ch.9

19 'No business before breakfast, Glum!' says the King.
'Breakfast first, business next.' [Valoroso.]
ch.11

20 My bold, my beautiful, my Bulbo! [Angelica.]

21 This I set down as a positive truth. A woman with fair
opportunities and without a positive hump, may marry
whom she likes.
Vanity Fair (1847-8), ch.4

22 [Miss Crawley] had been in France—and loved, ever
after, French novels, French cookery, and French
wines.
ch.10

23 Whenever he met a great man he grovelled before
him, and my-lorded him as only a free-born Briton can
do.
ch.13

24 If a man's character is to be abused, say what you
will, there's nobody like a relation to do the business.
ch.19

25 Them's my sentiments! [Fred Bullock.]
ch.21

26 Darkness came down on the field and city: and Amelia
was praying for George, who was lying on his face,
dead, with a bullet through his heart.
ch.32

27 Nothing like blood, sir, in hosses, dawgs, and men.
[James Crawley.]
ch.35

28 How to live well on nothing a year.
Title of ch.36

29 Ah! *Vanitas Vanitatum!* Which of us is happy in this
world? Which of us has his desire? or, having it, is
satisfied?—Come, children, let us shut up the box and
the puppets, for our play is played out.
ch.67

30 There's no sweeter tobacco comes from Virginia, and
no better brand than the Three Castles.
The Virginians (1857-59), ch.1

31 Ho, pretty page, with the dimpled chin
That never has known the barber's shear,
All your wish is woman to win,
This is the way that boys begin.
   Wait till you come to Forty Year.
The Age of Wisdom

32 There were three sailors of Bristol City
Who took a boat and went to sea.
But first with beef and captain's biscuits
And pickled pork they loaded she.
There was gorging Jack and guzzling Jimmy,
And the youngest he was little Billee.
Now when they got as far as the Equator
They'd nothing left but one split pea.
Little Billee

33 Says gorging Jim to guzzling Jacky,
We have no wittles, so we must eat *we*.

1 There's little Bill as is young and tender,
We're old and tough—so let's eat *he*.

2 He scarce had said his Cathechism,
When up he jumps: 'There's land I see!
There's Jerusalem and Madagascar,
And North and South Amerikey.
There's the British Fleet a-riding at anchor,
With Admiral Napier, K.C.B.'

3 Werther had a love for Charlotte
    Such as words could never utter;
Would you know how first he met her?
    She was cutting bread and butter.

Charlotte was a married lady,
    And a moral man was Werther,
And for all the wealth of Indies,
    Would do nothing for to hurt her.

So he sighed and pined and ogled,
    And his passion boiled and bubbled,
Till he blew his silly brains out
    And no more was by it troubled.

Charlotte, having seen his body
    Borne before her on a shutter,
Like a well-conducted person,
    Went on cutting bread and butter.
Sorrows of Werther

4 Oh, Vanity of vanities!
    How wayward the decrees of Fate are;
How very weak the very wise,
    How very small the very great are!
Vanitas Vanitatum

LOUIS ADOLPHE THIERS 1797–1877

5 *[Le roi] règne et le peuple se gouverne.*
The king reigns, and the people govern themselves.
Le National, 20 Jan. 1830. The article in which this appears was unsigned. In *Le National*, 4 Feb. 1830, a signed article by Thiers states *'Le roi n'administre pas, ne gouverne pas, il règne.'*

THOMAS À KEMPIS c.1380–1471

6 I would far rather feel remorse than know how to define it.
Of the Imitation of Christ, I.i.3

7 *O quam cito transit gloria mundi.*
Oh how quickly the world's glory passes away!
iii.6. See 11:1

8 Seek not to know who said this or that, but take note of what has been said.
v.1

9 It is much safer to be in a subordinate position than in one of authority.
ix.1

10 *Nam homo proponit, sed Deus disponit.*
For man plans, but God arranges.
xix.2

11 *Numquam sis ex toto otiosus, sed aut legens, aut scribens, aut orans, aut meditans, aut aliquid utilitatis pro communi laborans.*
Never to be completely idle, but either reading, or writing, or praying, or meditating, or working at something useful for all in common.
4

12 Would that we had spent one whole day well in this world!
xxiii.2

13 We are sometimes stirred by emotion and take it for zeal.
II.v.i

14 *Si libenter crucem portas portabit te.*
If you bear the cross gladly, it will bear you.
xii.5

15 *De duobus malis minus est semper eligendum.*
Of the two evils the lesser is always to be chosen.
III.xii.2

ST. THOMAS AQUINAS c.1225–1274

16 *Pange, lingua, gloriosi*
    Corporis mysterium,
Sanguinisque pretiosi,
    Quem in mundi pretium
Fructus ventris generosi
    Rex effudit gentium.
Sing, my tongue, of the mystery of the glorious Body,
    and of the precious Blood shed to redeem the world
    by the King of all peoples, the fruit of a noble womb.
Pange Lingua Gloriosi. Corpus Christi hymn

17 *Tantum ergo sacramentum*
    Veneremur cernui;
Et antiquum documentum
    Novo cedat ritui.
Therefore we, before him bending,
    This great Sacrament revere;
Types and shadows have their ending,
    For the newer rite is here.
Tr. J.M. Neale, E. Caswall, and others. *English Hymnal*, 326

BRANDON THOMAS 1856–1914

18 I'm Charley's aunt from Brazil—where the nuts come from.
Charley's Aunt (1892), Act 1

DYLAN THOMAS 1914–1953

19 Though they go mad they shall be sane,
Though they sink through the sea they shall rise again;
Though lovers be lost love shall not;
And death shall have no dominion.
And death shall have no dominion. See 75:2

20 I can never remember whether it snowed for six days and six nights when I was twelve or whether it snowed for twelve days and twelve nights when I was six.
A Child's Christmas in Wales (1954)

21 The gong was bombilating, and Mrs Prothero was announcing ruin like a town crier in Pompeii.

22 Years and years and years ago, when I was a boy, when there were wolves in Wales, and birds the colour of red-flannel petticoats whisked past the harp-shaped hills...when we rode the daft and happy hills bareback, it snowed and it snowed.

23 Do not go gentle into that good night,
Old age should burn and rave at close of day;
Rage, rage against the dying of the light.
Do not go gentle into that good night

24 And you, my father, there on that sad height,
Curse, bless, me now with your fierce tears I pray.

1 Now as I was young and easy under the apple boughs
  About the lilting house and happy as the grass was
    green.
  Fern Hill

2 Oh as I was young and easy in the mercy of his
    means,
      Time held me green and dying
      Though I sang in my chains like the sea.

3 The force that through the green fuse drives the flower
  Drives my green age; that blasts the roots of trees
  Is my destroyer.
  And I am dumb to tell the crooked rose
  My youth is bent by the same wintry fever.
  The force that through the green fuse drives the flower

4 The hand that signed the paper felled a city;
  Five sovereign fingers taxed the breath,
  Doubled the globe of death and halved a country;
  These five kings did a king to death.
  The hand that signed the paper

5 The hand that signed the treaty bred a fever,
  And famine grew, and locusts came;
  Great is the hand that holds dominion over
  Man by a scribbled name.

6   It was my thirtieth year to heaven
  Woke to my hearing from harbour and neighbour wood
      And the mussel pooled and the heron
        Priested shore.
  Poem in October

7   Pale rain over the dwindling harbour
  And over the sea wet church the size of a snail
      With its horns through mist and the castle
        Brown as owls
        But all the gardens
  Of spring and summer were blooming in the tall tales
  Beyond the border and under the lark full cloud.
      There could I marvel
        My birthday
  Away but the weather turned around.
  A refusal to mourn the death, by fire, of a child in London

8 After the first death, there is no other.
  A refusal to mourn the death, by fire, of a child in London

9 It is spring, moonless night in the small town, starless
  and bible-black, the cobblestreets silent and the
  hunched, courters'-and-rabbits' wood limping invisible
  down to the sloeblack, slow, black, crowblack,
  fishingboat-bobbing sea.
  Under Milk Wood (1954)

10 *Mr Pritchard:* I must dust the blinds and then I must
  raise them.
  Mrs Ogmore-Pritchard: And before you let the sun in,
  mind it wipes its shoes.

11 Gomer Owen who kissed her once by the pig-sty when
  she wasn't looking and never kissed her again although
  she was looking all the time.

12 Nothing grows in our garden, only washing. And
  babies.

13 Oh, what can I do? I'll *never* be refined if I twitch.

14 You just wait. I'll sin till I blow up!

15 Dylan talked copiously, then stopped.
  'Somebody's boring me,' he said, 'I think it's me.'
  Rayner Heppenstall, *Four Absentees* (1960), xvi

EDWARD THOMAS 1878–1917

16 Yes. I remember Adlestrop—
  The name, because one afternoon
  Of heat the express train drew up there
  Unwontedly. It was late June.
  Adlestrop

17 The past is the only dead thing that smells sweet.
  Early One Morning

18 If I should ever by chance grow rich
  I'll buy Codham, Cockridden, and Childerditch,
  Roses, Pyrgo, and Lapwater,
  And let them all to my elder daughter.
  If I should ever by chance

19 I have come to the borders of sleep,
  The unfathomable deep
  Forest where all must lose
  Their way, however straight,
  Or winding, soon or late;
  They cannot choose.
  Lights Out

20 Out in the dark over the snow
  The fallow fawns invisible go
  With the fallow doe;
  And the winds blow
  Fast as the stars are slow.
  Out in the Dark

21 As well as any bloom upon a flower
  I like the dust on the nettles, never lost
  Except to prove the sweetness of a shower.
  Tall Nettles

FRANCIS THOMPSON 1859–1907

22 Pontifical Death, that doth the crevasse bridge
  To the steep and trifid God.
  Anthem of Earth

23 And thou—what needest with thy tribe's black tents
  Who hast the red pavilion of my heart?
  Arab Love Song

24 It is little I repair to the matches of the Southron folk,
  Though my own red roses there may blow;
  It is little I repair to the matches of the Southron folk,
    Though the red roses crest the caps I know.
  For the field is full of shades as I near the shadowy
    coast,
  And a ghostly batsman plays to the bowling of a
    ghost,
  And I look through my tears on a soundless-clapping
    host
    As the run-stealers flicker to and fro,
      To and fro:—
    O my Hornby and my Barlow long ago!
  At Lord's

25 The fairest things have fleetest end,
    Their scent survives their close:
  But the rose's scent is bitterness
    To him that loved the rose.
  Daisy

26 She went her unremembering way,
    She went and left in me
  The pang of all the partings gone,
    And partings yet to be.

  She left me marvelling why my soul
    Was sad that she was glad;

At all the sadness in the sweet,
The sweetness in the sad.

1 Nothing begins and nothing ends
That is not paid with moan;
For we are born in other's pain,
And perish in our own.

2 Ah, for a heart less native to high Heaven,
A hooded eye, for jesses and restraint,
Or for a will accipitrine to pursue!
The Dread of Height

3 Go, songs, for ended is our brief sweet play;
Go, children of swift joy and tardy sorrow:
And some are sung, and that was yesterday,
And some unsung, and that may be to-morrow.
Envoy

4 Spring is come home with her world-wandering feet.
And all things are made young with young desires.
The Night of Forebeing. Ode to Easter

5 Let even the slug-abed snail upon the thorn
Put forth a conscious horn!

6 Look for me in the nurseries of Heaven.
To My Godchild

7 And all man's Babylons strive but to impart
The grandeurs of his Babylonian heart.
The Heart, ii

8 I fled Him, down the nights and down the days;
I fled Him, down the arches of the years;
I fled Him, down the labyrinthine ways
Of my own mind; and in the mist of tears
I hid from Him, and under running laughter.
The Hound of Heaven

9 But with unhurrying chase,
And unperturbèd pace,
Deliberate speed, majestic instancy,
They beat—and a Voice beat
More instant than the Feet—
'All things betray thee, who betrayest Me.'

10 (For, though I knew His love Who followed,
Yet was I sore adread
Lest, having Him, I must have naught beside.)

11 Fear wist not to evade, as Love wist to pursue.

12 I said to Dawn: Be sudden—to Eve: Be soon.

13 To all swift things for swiftness did I sue;
Clung to the whistling mane of every wind.

14 Came on the following Feet,
And a Voice above their beat—
'Naught shelters thee, who wilt not shelter Me.'

15 I was heavy with the even
When she lit her glimmering tapers
Round the day's dead sanctities.

16 My harness piece by piece Thou hast hewn from me
And smitten me to my knee.

17 Yea, faileth now even dream
The dreamer, and the lute the lutanist;
Even the linked fantasies, in whose blossomy twist
I swung the earth a trinket at my wrist.

18 Ah! must—
Designer infinite!—
Ah! must Thou char the wood ere Thou canst limn
with it?

19 Such is; what is to be?
The pulp so bitter, how shall taste the rind?

20 Yet ever and anon a trumpet sounds
From the hid battlements of Eternity;
Those shaken mists a space unsettle, then
Round the half-glimpsèd turrets slowly wash again.

21 Now of that long pursuit
Comes on at hand the bruit;
That Voice is round me like a bursting sea:
'And is thy earth so marred,
Shattered in shard on shard?
Lo, all things fly thee, for thou fliest Me!'

22 All which I took from thee I did but take,
Not for thy harms,
But just that thou might'st seek it in My arms.

23 Halts by me that footfall:
Is my gloom, after all,
Shade of His hand, outstretched caressingly?
'Ah, fondest, blindest, weakest,
I am He whom thou seekest!
Thou dravest love from thee, who dravest Me.'

24 O world invisible, we view thee,
O world intangible, we touch thee,
O world unknowable, we know thee,
Inapprehensible, we clutch thee!
In No Strange Land

25 'Tis ye, 'tis your estrangèd faces,
That miss the many-splendoured thing.

But (when so sad thou canst not sadder)
Cry;—and upon thy so sore loss
Shall shine the traffic of Jacob's ladder
Pitched betwixt Heaven and Charing Cross.

Yea, in the night, my Soul, my daughter,
Cry,—clinging Heaven by the hems;
And lo, Christ walking on the water
Not of Gennesareth, but Thames!

26 There is no expeditious road
To pack and label men for God,
And save them by the barrel-load.
A Judgment in Heaven, epilogue

27 Summer set lip to earth's bosom bare,
And left the flushed print in a poppy there.
The Poppy

28 The sleep-flower sways in the wheat its head,
Heavy with dreams, as that with bread:
The goodly grain and the sun-flushed sleeper
The reaper reaps, and Time the reaper.

I hang 'mid men my needless head,
And my fruit is dreams, as theirs is bread:
The goodly men and the sun-hazed sleeper
Time shall reap, but after the reaper
The world shall glean of me, me the sleeper.

29 What heart could have thought you?—
Past our devisal
(O filigree petal!)
Fashioned so purely,
Fragilely, surely,
From what Paradisal
Imagineless metal,
Too costly for cost?
To a Snowflake

1   His hammer of wind,
And His graver of frost.

2   Wake! for the Ruddy Ball has taken flight
That scatters the slow Wicket of the Night;
    And the swift Batsman of the Dawn has driven
Against the Star-spiked Rails a fiery Smite.
Wake! for the Ruddy Ball has Taken Flight. J.C. Squire, *Apes
and Parrots.* See 212:5

3   And, while she feels the heavens lie bare,
She only talks about her hair.
The Way of a Maid

WILLIAM HEPWORTH THOMPSON 1810–1886

4   I never could have supposed that we should have had
so soon to regret the departure of our dear friend the
late Professor.
On Seeley's inaugural lecture as Professor of History at
Cambridge, following Charles Kingsley. A.J. Balfour, *Chapters
of Autobiography* (1930), ch.4

5   We are none of us infallible—not even the youngest of
us.
Remark referring to G.W. Balfour, then Junior Fellow of Trinity.
G.W.E. Russell, *Collections and Recollections*, ch.18

6   What time he can spare from the adornment of his
person he devotes to the neglect of his duties.
Of Sir Richard Jebb, afterwards Professor of Greek at Cambridge.
M.R. Bobbit, *With Dearest Love to All*, ch.7

JAMES THOMSON 1700–1748

7   When Britain first, at heaven's command,
Arose from out the azure main,
This was the charter of the land,
And guardian angels sung this strain:
    'Rule, Britannia, rule the waves;
    Britons never will be slaves.'
Alfred: a Masque (1740), Act II, Scene the last

8   A pleasing land of drowsyhead it was.
The Castle of Indolence (1748), c.I.vi

9   A bard here dwelt, more fat than bard beseems
Who, void of envy, guile, and lust of gain,
On virtue still, and nature's pleasing themes,
Poured forth his unpremeditating strain.
lxviii

10 Delightful task! to rear the tender thought,
To teach the young idea how to shoot.
The Seasons (1728), **Spring**, l.1152

11 An elegant sufficiency, content,
Retirement, rural quiet, friendship, books.
l.1161

12 The sober-suited songstress. [The nightingale.]
Summer, l.746

13 Ships, dim-discovered, dropping from the clouds.
l.946

14 Or sighed and looked unutterable things.
l.1188

15 Autumn nodding o'er the yellow plain
Comes jovial on.
Autumn, l.2

16 While listening senates hang upon thy tongue.
l.15

17   For loveliness
Needs not the foreign aid of ornament,
But is when unadorned adorned the most.
l.204

18 Poor is the triumph o'er the timid hare!
l.401

19   He stands at bay,
And puts his last weak refuge in despair.
The big round tears run down his dappled face;
He groans in anguish; while the growling pack,
Blood-happy, hang at his fair jutting chest,
And mark his beauteous chequered sides with gore.
l.452. Of a stag. See 425:1

20 Find other lands beneath another sun.
l.1286

21 See, Winter comes to rule the varied year,
Sullen and sad.
Winter, l.1

22   Welcome, kindred glooms!
Congenial horrors, hail!
l.5

23 The redbreast, sacred to the household gods,
Wisely regardful of the embroiling sky,
In joyless fields and thorny thickets leaves
His shivering mates, and pays to trusted man
His annual visit.
l.246

24   Studious let me sit,
And hold high converse with the mighty dead.
l.431

25 Oh! Sophonisba! Sophonisba! oh!
Sophonisba (1730), III.ii

26 How the heart listened while he pleading spoke!
While on the enlightened mind, with winning art,
His gentle reason so persuasive stole
That the charmed hearer thought it was his own.
To the Memory of the Lord Talbot (1737), l.103

JAMES THOMSON 1834–1882

27 The City is of Night; perchance of Death,
But certainly of Night.
The City of Dreadful Night

28 As we rush, as we rush in the train,
The trees and the houses go wheeling back,
But the starry heavens above that plain
Come flying on our track.
Sunday at Hampstead, x

29 Give a man a horse he can ride,
Give a man a boat he can sail.
Sunday up the River, xv

LORD THOMSON OF FLEET 1894–1977

30 It's just like having a licence to print your own
money.
(After the opening of Scottish commercial television.) Braddon,
Roy Thomson of Fleet Street, p.240

HENRY DAVID THOREAU 1817–1862

31 I heartily accept the motto, 'That government is best
which governs least'; and I should like to see it acted
up to more rapidly and systematically. Carried out, it
finally amounts to this, which I also believe,— 'That
government is best which governs not at all.'
Civil Disobedience (1849). See 365:22

1 Under a government which imprisons any unjustly, the true place for a just man is also a prison.

2 I have travelled a good deal in Concord.
Walden (1854). **Economy**

3 As if you could kill time without injuring eternity.

4 The mass of men lead lives of quiet desperation.

5 It is a characteristic of wisdom not to do desperate things.

6 I have lived some thirty years on this planet, and I have yet to hear the first syllable of valuable or even earnest advice from my seniors.

7 There are now-a-days professors of philosophy but not philosophers.

8 I long ago lost a hound, a bay horse, and a turtle-dove, and am still on their trail.

9 In any weather, at any hour of the day or night, I have been anxious to improve the nick of time, and notch it on my stick too; to stand on the meeting of two eternities, the past and the future, which is precisely the present moment; to toe that line.

10 It is true, I never assisted the sun materially in his rising, but, doubt not, it was of the last importance only to be present at it.

11 Tall arrowy white pines.

12 The owner of the axe, as he released his hold on it, said that it was the apple of his eye; but I returned it sharper than I received it.

13 For more than five years I maintained myself thus solely by the labor of my hands, and I found, that by working about six weeks in a year, I could meet all the expenses of living.

14 As for Doing-good, that is one of the professions which are full. Moreover, I have tried it fairly, and, strange as it may seem, am satisfied that it does not agree with my constitution.

15 The government of the world I live in was not framed, like that of Britain, in after-dinner conversations over the wine.
conclusion

16 I wanted to live deep and suck out all the marrow of life...to drive life into a corner, and reduce it to its lowest terms, and, if it proved to be mean, why then to get the whole and genuine meanness of it, and publish its meanness to the world; or if it were sublime, to know it by experience, and be able to give a true account of it in my next excursion.
Where I lived, and what I lived for

17 Our life is frittered away by detail...Simplify, simplify.

18 The three-o'-clock in the morning courage, which Bonaparte thought was the rarest.
Sounds. See 359:12

19 Wherever a man goes, men will pursue him and paw him with their dirty institutions, and, if they can, constrain him to belong to their desperate oddfellow society.
The Village

20 I frequently tramped eight or ten miles through the deepest snow to keep an appointment with a beech-tree, or a yellow birch, or an old acquaintance among the pines.
Winter Visitors

21 I once had a sparrow alight upon my shoulder for a moment while I was hoeing in a village garden, and I felt that I was more distinguished by that circumstance than I should have been by any epaulet I could have worn.

22 It has been proposed that the town should adopt for its coat of arms a field verdant, with the Concord circling nine times round.
A Week on the Concord and Merrimack Rivers (1849). **Concord River**

23 It takes two to speak the truth,—one to speak, and another to hear.
Wednesday

24 Some circumstantial evidence is very strong, as when you find a trout in the milk.
Journal, 11 Nov. 1850 (pub. 1903)

25 I do not perceive the poetic and dramatic capabilities of an anecdote or story which is told me, its significance, till some time afterwards...We do not enjoy poetry unless we know it to be poetry.
1 Oct. 1856

26 Not that the story need be long, but it will take a long while to make it short.
Letter to Mr. B., 16 Nov. 1857. See 369:14

27 *Emerson:* Why are you here?
Thoreau: Why are you not here?
Thoreau was in prison for failure to pay taxes. Oral tradition in Emerson family, discounted for lack of documentary evidence. Harding, *A Thoreau Handbook* (1959), p.8

28 It were treason to our love
And a sin to God above
One iota to abate
Of a pure impartial hate.
Indeed, Indeed I Cannot Tell (1852)

JAMES THURBER 1894–1961

29 It's a Naïve Domestic Burgundy, Without Any Breeding, But I Think You'll be Amused by its Presumption.
Men, Women and Dogs. Cartoon caption

30 Well, if I Called the Wrong Number, Why Did You Answer the Phone?

31 All Right, Have It Your Way—You Heard a Seal Bark.
The Seal in the Bedroom. Cartoon caption

EDWARD, FIRST BARON THURLOW 1731–1806

32 Corporations have neither bodies to be punished, nor souls to be condemned, they therefore do as they like.
Poynder, *Literary Extracts* (1844), vol.I. Usually quoted as 'Did you ever expect a corporation to have a conscience, when it has no soul to be damned, and no body to be kicked?'

EDWARD, SECOND BARON THURLOW 1781–1829

33 Nature is always wise in every part.
To a Bird, that haunted the Waters of Lacken, in the Winter

TIBULLUS c.50–19 B.C.

34 *Te spectem, suprema mihi cum venerit hora,*

Et teneam moriens deficiente manu.
May I be looking at you when my last hour has come,
  and dying may I hold you with my weakening hand.
I.i.59

1 *Te propter nullos tellus tua postulat imbres,*
  Arida nec pluvio supplicat herba Iovi,
Because of you your land never pleads for showers,
  nor does its parched grass pray to Jupiter the
  Rain-giver.
vii.25. Of the Nile in Egypt

CHIDIOCK TICHBORNE 1558?–1586

2 My prime of youth is but a frost of cares;
My feast of joy is but a dish of pain;
My crop of corn is but a field of tares;
And all my good is but vain hope of gain.
The day is past, and yet I saw no sun;
And now I live, and now my life is done.
Elegy. (Written in the Tower before his execution)

THOMAS TICKELL 1686–1740

3 There taught us how to live; and (oh! too high
The price for knowledge) taught us how to die.
Epitaph. On the Death of Mr. Addison, l.81. In Tickell's
edition of Addison's *Works* (1721), preface, p.xx

PAUL TILLICH 1886–1965

4 He who knows about depth knows about God.
The Shaking of the Foundations (1962 ed.), p.64

MATTHEW TINDAL 1657–1733

5 Matters of fact, which as Mr Budgell somewhere
observes, are very stubborn things.
Will of Matthew Tindal (1733), p.23

EMPEROR TITUS A.D. 39–81

6 *Recordatus quondam super cenam, quod nihil cuiquam*
toto die praestitisset, memorabilem illam meritoque
laudatam vocem edidit: 'Amici, diem perdidi.'
On reflecting at dinner that he had done nothing to help
anybody all day, he uttered those memorable and
praiseworthy words: 'Friends, I have lost a day.'
Suetonius, *Titus*, 8, i

JOHN TOBIN 1770–1804

7 The man that lays his hand upon a woman,
Save in the way of kindness, is a wretch
Whom 't were gross flattery to name a coward.
The Honeymoon, II.i

ALEXIS DE TOCQUEVILLE 1805–1859

8 *L'esprit français est de ne pas vouloir de* supérieur.
L'esprit anglais de vouloir des inférieurs. *Le Français*
lève les yeux sans cesse au-dessus de lui avec
inquiétude. L'Anglais les baisse au-dessous de lui
avec complaisance. C'est de part et d'autre de
l'orgueil, mais entendu de manière différente.
The French want no-one to be their *superior.* The
English want *inferiors.* The Frenchman constantly
raises his eyes above him with anxiety. The
Englishman lowers his beneath him with satisfaction.

On either side it is pride, but understood in a different
way.
Voyage en Angleterre et en Irlande de 1835, 18 May

9 *C'est au milieu de ce cloaque infect que la plus grande*
fleuve de l'industrie humaine prend sa source et va
féconder l'univers. De cet égout immonde, l'or pur
s'écoule. C'est là que l'esprit humain se perfectionne
et s'abrutit; que la civilisation produit ses merveilles
et que l'homme civilisée redevient presque sauvage.
It is from the midst of this putrid sewer that the
greatest river of human industry springs up and carries
fertility to the whole world. From this foul drain pure
gold flows forth. Here it is that humanity achieves for
itself both perfection and brutalization, that civilization
produces its wonders, and that civilized man becomes
again almost a savage.
Of Manchester. 2 July

LEO TOLSTOY 1828–1910

10 All happy families resemble one another, but each
unhappy family is unhappy in its own way.
Anna Karenina (1875-7), pt.i, ch.1. Tr. Maude

11 It is amazing how complete is the delusion that beauty
is goodness.
The Kreutzer Sonata, 5. Tr. Maude

12 Our body is a machine for living. It is organized for
that, it is its nature. Let life go on in it unhindered and
let it defend itself, it will do more than if you paralyse
it by encumbering it with remedies.
War and Peace (1868-9), bk.X, ch.29. Tr. A. and L. Maude

13 Pure and complete sorrow is as impossible as pure and
complete joy.
bk.XV, ch.1

14 Art is not a handicraft, it is the transmission of feeling
the artist has experienced.
What is Art? (1898), ch.19. Tr. Maude

15 I sit on a man's back, choking him and making him
carry me, and yet assure myself and others that I am
very sorry for him and wish to ease his lot by all
possible means—except by getting off his back.
What Then Must We Do? (1886), ch.16. Tr. Maude

CYRIL TOURNEUR c.1575–1626

16 Does the silk-worm expend her yellow labours
For thee? for thee does she undo herself?
The Revenger's Tragedy (1607), III.v.71

THOMAS TRAHERNE 1637?–1674

17 You never enjoy the world aright, till the sea itself
floweth in your veins, till you are clothed with the
heavens, and crowned with the stars: and perceive
yourself to be the sole heir of the whole world, and
more than so, because men are in it who are every one
sole heirs as well as you. Till you can sing and rejoice
and delight in God, as misers do in gold, and kings in
sceptres, you never enjoy the world.
Centuries of Meditations. Cent.i, 29

18 The corn was orient and immortal wheat, which never
should be reaped, nor was ever sown. I thought it had
stood from everlasting to everlasting.
Cent.iii, 3

19 The Men! O what venerable and reverend creatures did

the aged seem! Immortal Cherubims! And young men glittering and sparkling Angels, and maids strange seraphic pieces of life and beauty! Boys and girls tumbling in the street, and playing, were moving jewels. I knew not that they were born or should die; but all things abided eternally as they were in their proper places.

1 The hands are a sort of feet, which serve us in our passage towards Heaven, curiously distinguished into joints and fingers, and fit to be applied to any thing which reason can imagine or desire.
Meditations on the Six Days of Creation (1717), vi, p.78

2 Contentment is a sleepy thing
   If it in death alone must die;
A quiet mind is worse than poverty,
   Unless it from enjoyment spring!
That's blessedness alone that makes a King!
Of Contentment

3   I within did flow
With seas of life, like wine.
Wonder, iii

HENRY DUFF TRAILL 1842–1900

4 Look in my face. My name is Used-to-was;
   I am also called Played-out and Done-to-death,
And It-will-wash-no-more.
After Dilettante Concetti [i.e. Dante Gabriel Rossetti], viii. See 410:4

JOSEPH TRAPP 1679–1747

5 The King, observing with judicious eyes
The state of both his universities,
To Oxford sent a troop of horse, and why?
That learned body wanted loyalty;
To Cambridge books, as very well discerning
How much that loyal body wanted learning.
On George I's Donation of the Bishop of Ely's Library to Cambridge University. Nichols, *Literary Anecdotes,* vol.iii, p.330. For the reply see 97:26

BEN TRAVERS 1886–

6 One night Mr and Mrs Reginald Bingham went to Ciro's. They had been married only about six months. Mr Bingham had never been to Ciro's before in his life. His surprise, therefore, upon seeing his wife there, was considerable.
Mischief (1926), ch.1

HERBERT TRENCH 1865–1923

7 Come, let us make love deathless, thou and I.
To Arolilia, No.2

RICHARD TRENCH, ARCHBISHOP OF DUBLIN 1807–1886

8 England, we love thee better than we know.
Gibraltar

G.M. TREVELYAN 1876–1962

9 Disinterested intellectual curiosity is the life blood of real civilisation.
English Social History (1942), preface, viii

10 Education...has produced a vast population able to read but unable to distinguish what is worth reading.
ch.18

ANTHONY TROLLOPE 1815–1882

11 He must have known me had he seen me as he was wont to see me, for he was in the habit of flogging me constantly. Perhaps he did not recognize me by my face.
Autobiography (1883), ch.1

12 Take away from English authors their copyrights, and you would very soon take away from England her authors.
ch.6

13 Three hours a day will produce as much as a man ought to write.
ch.15

14 Of all the needs a book has the chief need is that it be readable.
ch.19

15 I think that Plantagenet Palliser, Duke of Omnium, is a perfect gentleman. If he be not, then I am unable to describe a gentleman.
ch.20

16 She [Mrs. Stanhope] was rich in apparel, but not bedizened with finery...she well knew the great architectural secret of decorating her constructions, and never descended to construct a decoration.
Barchester Towers (1857), ch.9

17 'Unhand it, sir!' said Mrs Proudie. From what scrap of dramatic poetry she had extracted the word cannot be said; but it must have rested on her memory, and now seemed opportunely dignified for the occasion.
ch.11

18 No man thinks there is much ado about nothing when the ado is about himself.
The Bertrams (1859), ch.27

19 Those who have courage to love should have courage to suffer.

20 How I did respect you when you dared to speak the truth to me! Men don't know women, or they would be harder to them.
The Claverings (1867), ch.15

21 The comic almanacs give us dreadful pictures of January and February; but, in truth, the months which should be made to look gloomy in England are March and April. Let no man boast himself that he has got through the perils of winter till at least the seventh of May.
Doctor Thorne (1858), ch.47

22 For the most of us, if we do not talk of ourselves, or at any rate of the individual circles of which we are the centres, we can talk of nothing. I cannot hold with those who wish to put down the insignificant chatter of the world.
Framley Parsonage (1860), ch.10

23 It's dogged as does it. It ain't thinking about it.
The Last Chronicle of Barset (1867), ch.61

24 With many women I doubt whether there be any more effectual way of touching their hearts than ill-using them and then confessing it. If you wish to get the sweetest fragrance from the herb at your feet, tread on

it and bruise it.
Miss Mackenzie (1865), ch.10

1 We cannot bring ourselves to believe it possible that a foreigner should in any respect be wiser than ourselves. If any such point out to us our follies, we at once claim those follies as the special evidences of our wisdom.
Orley Farm (1862), ch.18

2 It is because we put up with bad things that hotel-keepers continue to give them to us.

3 As for conceit, what man will do any good who is not conceited? Nobody holds a good opinion of a man who has a low opinion of himself.
ch.22

4 A fainéant government is not the worst government that England can have. It has been the great fault of our politicians that they have all wanted to do something.
Phineas Finn (1869), ch.13

5 Mr Turnbull had predicted evil consequences...and was now doing the best in his power to bring about the verification of his own prophecies.
ch.25

6 Perhaps there is no position more perilous to a man's honesty than that...of knowing himself to be quite loved by a girl whom he almost loves himself.
ch.50

7 Men are so seldom really good. They are so little sympathetic. What man thinks of changing himself so as to suit his wife? And yet men expect that women shall put on altogether new characters when they are married, and girls think that they can do so.
Phineas Redux (1874), ch.3

8 It is the necessary nature of a political party in this country to avoid, as long as it can be avoided, the consideration of any question which involves a great change...The best carriage horses are those which can most steadily hold back against the coach as it trundles down the hill.
ch.4

9 To think of one's absent love is very sweet; but it becomes monotonous after a mile or two of a towing-path, and the mind will turn away to Aunt Sally, the Cremorne Gardens, and financial questions. I doubt whether any girl would be satisfied with her lover's mind if she knew the whole of it.
The Small House at Allington (1864), ch.4

10 Why is it that girls so constantly do this,—so frequently ask men who have loved them to be present at their marriages with other men? There is no triumph in it. It is done in sheer kindness and affection. They intend to offer something which shall soften and not aggravate the sorrow that they have caused...I fully appreciate the intention, but in honest truth, I doubt the eligibility of the proffered entertainment.
ch.9

11 It may almost be a question whether such wisdom as many of us have in our mature years has not come from the dying out of the power of temptation, rather than as the results of thought and resolution.
ch.14

12 And, above all things, never think that you're not good enough yourself. A man should never think that. My belief is that in life people will take you very much at your own reckoning.
ch.32

13 The tenth Muse, who now governs the periodical press.
The Warden (1855), ch.14

14 Is it not singular how some men continue to obtain the reputation of popular authorship without adding a word to the literature of their country worthy of note?...To puff and to get one's self puffed have become different branches of a new profession.
The Way We Live Now (1875), ch.1

15 Love is like any other luxury. You have no right to it unless you can afford it.
ch.84

LEV TROTSKY 1879–1940

16 Old age is the most unexpected of all the things that happen to a man.
Diary in Exile, 8 May 1935

17 In a serious struggle there is no worse cruelty than to be magnanimous at an inopportune time.
The History of the Russian Revolution, tr. M. Eastman (1933), vol.IV, ch.7

18 Where force is necessary, one should make use of it boldly, resolutely, and right to the end. But it is as well to know the limitations of force; to know where to blend force with manoeuvre, assault with conciliation.
Was nun? (1932), p.106

HARRY S. TRUMAN 1884–1972

19 The buck stops here.
Hand-lettered sign on President Truman's desk. Phillips, *The Truman Presidency,* ch.12

20 If you can't stand the heat, get out of the kitchen.
Mr. Citizen, ch.15. Perhaps proverbial in origin, possibly echoing the expression 'kitchen cabinet'.

MARTIN TUPPER 1810–1889

21 A good book is the best of friends, the same to-day and for ever.
Proverbial Philosophy, Series I (1838). **Of Reading**

A.-R.-J. TURGOT 1727–1781

22 *Eripuit coelo fulmen, sceptrumque tyrannis.*
He snatched the lightning shaft from heaven, and the sceptre from tyrants.
A.N. de Condorcet, *Vie de Turgot* (1786), *Oeuvres Complètes* (Paris, 1804), 5, p.230. Inscription composed for a bust of Benjamin Franklin, inventor of the lightning conductor. See 328:11

WALTER JAMES REDFERN TURNER 1889–1946

23 Chimborazo, Cotopaxi,
They had stolen my soul away!
Romance, vii

MARK TWAIN 1835–1910

24 There was things which he stretched, but mainly he told the truth.
The Adventures of Huckleberry Finn (1884), ch.1

1 There was some books...One was *Pilgrim's Progress,*
about a man that left his family, it didn't say why. I
read considerable in it now and then. The statements
was interesting, but tough. Another was *Friendship's
Offering,* full of beautiful stuff and poetry; but I didn't
read the poetry.
ch.17

2 All kings is mostly rapscallions.
ch.23

3 Hain't we got all the fools in town on our side? and
ain't that a big enough majority in any town?
ch.26

4 If there was two birds sitting on a fence, he would bet
you which one would fly first.
The Celebrated Jumping Frog (1865), p.17

5 I don't see no p'ints about that frog that's any better'n
any other frog.
p.20

6 Soap and education are not as sudden as a massacre,
but they are more deadly in the long run.
*The Facts concerning the Recent Resignation. Sketches New &
Old* (1900), p.350

7 It is by the goodness of God that in our country we
have those three unspeakably precious things: freedom
of speech, freedom of conscience, and the prudence
never to practise either of them.
Following the Equator (1897), heading of ch.20

8 Man is the only animal that blushes. Or needs to.
heading of ch.27

9 They spell it Vinci and pronounce it Vinchy;
foreigners always spell better than they pronounce.
The Innocents Abroad (1869), ch.19

10 I do not want Michael Angelo for breakfast...for
luncheon—for dinner—for tea—for supper—for
between meals.
ch.27

11 Lump the whole thing! say that the Creator made Italy
from designs by Michael Angelo!

12 Guides cannot master the subtleties of the American
joke.

13 If you've got a nice *fresh* corpse, fetch him out!

14 At bottom he was probably fond of them, but he was
always able to conceal it. [On Thomas Carlyle and
Americans.]
My First Lie

15 An experienced, industrious, ambitious, and often
quite picturesque liar.
Private History of a Campaign that Failed

16 When angry, count a hundred; when very angry,
swear.
Pudd'nhead Wilson's Calendar, March

17 There's plenty of boys that will come hankering and
gruvvelling around when you've got an apple, and beg
the core off you; but when *they've* got one, and you
beg for the core and remind them how you give them a
core one time, they make a mouth at you and say thank
you 'most to death, but there ain't-a-going to be no
core.
Tom Sawyer Abroad (1894), ch.1

18 There ain't no way to find out why a snorer can't hear
himself snore.
ch.10

19 Adam was but human—this explains it all. He did not
want the apple for the apple's sake, he wanted it only
because it was forbidden.
The Tragedy of Pudd'nhead Wilson (1894), heading of ch.2

20 Whoever has lived long enough to find out what life
is, knows how deep a debt of gratitude we owe to
Adam, the first great benefactor of our race. He
brought death into the world.
heading of ch.3. See 344:20

21 The cross of the Legion of Honour has been conferred
upon me. However, few escape that distinction.
A Tramp Abroad (1880), ch.8

22 The report of my death was an exaggeration.
Cable from Europe to the Associated Press

23 There is a sumptuous variety about the New England
weather that compels the stranger's admiration—and
regret. The weather is always doing something there;
always attending strictly to business; always getting up
new designs and trying them on the people to see how
they will go. But it gets through more business in
spring than in any other season. In the spring I have
counted one hundred and thirty-six different kinds of
weather inside of four-and-twenty hours.
The Weather. Speech at dinner of New England Society, New
York, 22 Dec. 1876. *Speeches* (1910), p.59

24 A verb has a hard time enough of it in this world when
its all together. It's downright inhuman to split it up.
But that's just what those Germans do. They take part
of a verb and put it down here, like a stake, and they
take the other part of it and put it away over yonder
like another stake, and between these two limits they
just shovel in German.
Address at dinner of the Nineteenth Century Club, New York, 20
Nov. 1900, to the toast, 'The Disappearance of Literature'

25 Something that everybody wants to have read and
nobody wants to read. [A classic.]

DOMITIUS ULPIAN d. 228

26 *Nulla iniuria est, quae in volentem fiat.*
No injustice is done to someone who wants that thing
done.
Corpus Iuris Civilis, Digests 47, X.i.5. Usually cited in the form
Volenti non fit iniuria, To someone who wants it no injustice
occurs.

MIGUEL DE UNAMUNO 1864–1937

27 *Fe que no duda es fe muerta.*
Faith which does not doubt is dead faith.
La Agonía del Cristianismo, p.34

28 Cure yourself of the condition of bothering about how
you look to other people. Be concerned only...with the
idea God has of you.
Vida de D. Quijote y Sancho, p.27

ARCHBISHOP JAMES USSHER 1581–1656

29 Which beginning of time [the Creation] according to
our Chronologie, fell upon the entrance of the night
preceding the twenty third day of *Octob.* in the year of
the Julian Calendar, 710 [i.e. B.C. 4004].
The Annals of the World (1658), p.1

PAUL VALÉRY 1871–1945

1 *Il faut n'appeler* Science: *que* l'ensemble des recettes qui réussissent toujours.—*Tout le reste est* littérature.
The term *Science* should not be given to anything but *the aggregate of the recipes that are always successful.* All the rest is *literature.*
Moralités (1932), p.41. See 556:9

SIR JOHN VANBRUGH 1664–1726

2 The want of a thing is perplexing enough, but the possession of it is intolerable.
The Confederacy (1705), I.ii

3 Much of a muchness.
The Provok'd Husband (1728), I.i

4 *Belinda:* Ay, but you know we must return good for evil.
Lady Brute: That may be a mistake in the translation.
The Provok'd Wife (1697), I.i

5 Thinking is to me the greatest fatigue in the world.
The Relapse (1696), II.i

6 No man worth having is true to his wife, or can be true to his wife, or ever was, or ever will be so.
III.ii

WILLIAM HENRY VANDERBILT 1821–1885

7 The public be damned!
Reply to a question whether the public should be consulted about luxury trains. A.W. Cole, Letter, *New York Times,* 25 Aug. 1918

BARTOLOMEO VANZETTI 1888–1927

8 Sacco's name will live in the hearts of the people and in their gratitude when Katzmann's and yours bones will be dispersed by time, when your name, your laws, institutions, and your false god are but a deem remomoring of a cursed past in which man was wolf to the man.
Statement disallowed by Judge Thayer in the Dedham, Massachusetts, court which convicted Sacco and Vanzetti of murder and robbery. Both were sentenced to death on 9 Apr. 1927, the eulogy was written down by Vanzetti on the following day, and both men were executed on 23 August. Katzmann was the prosecuting attorney. F. Russell, *Tragedy in Dedham* (1963), ch.17. See 374:13

CHARLES JOHN VAUGHAN 1816–1897

9 Must you go? Can't you stay?
Remark with which he broke up awkward breakfast parties of schoolboys who were too shy to go. Story retold with the words transposed, 'Can't you go? Must you stay?' G.W.E. Russell, *Collections and Recollections,* ch.24

HENRY VAUGHAN 1622–1695

10 Man is the shuttle, to whose winding quest
And passage through these looms
God order'd motion, but ordain'd no rest.
Silex Scintillans (1650-55), **Man**

11 Wise Nicodemus saw such light
As made him know his God by night.

Most blest believer he!
Who in that land of darkness and blind eyes
Thy long expected healing wings could see
When Thou didst rise!
And, what can never more be done,

Did at midnight speak with the Sun!
The Night, l.5

12 Dear Night! this world's defeat;
The stop to busy fools; care's check and curb;
The day of spirits; my soul's calm retreat
Which none disturb!
l.25

13 My soul, there is a country
Far beyond the stars,
Where stands a wingèd sentry
All skilful in the wars;
There, above noise and danger,
Sweet Peace is crown'd with smiles,
And One born in a manger
Commands the beauteous files.
Peace

14 Happy those early days, when I
Shin'd in my angel-infancy.
Before I understood this place
Appointed for my second race,
Or taught my soul to fancy aught
But a white, celestial thought;
When yet I had not walked above
A mile or two from my first love,
And looking back—at that short space—
Could see a glimpse of His bright face.
The Retreat, l.1

15 And in those weaker glories spy
Some shadows of eternity.
l.13

16 But felt through all this fleshly dress
Bright shoots of everlastingness.
l.19

17 Some men a forward motion love,
But I by backward steps would move,
And when this dust falls to the urn,
In that state I came, return.
l.29

18 They are all gone into the world of light,
And I alone sit lingering here;
Their very memory is fair and bright,
And my sad thoughts doth clear.
They Are All Gone

19 I see them walking in an air of glory,
Whose light doth trample on my days:
My days, which are at best but dull and hoary,
Mere glimmering and decays.

20 Dear, beauteous death! the jewel of the just,
Shining nowhere but in the dark;
What mysteries do lie beyond thy dust,
Could man outlook that mark!

21 And yet, as angels in some brighter dreams
Call to the soul when man doth sleep,
So some strange thoughts transcend our wonted themes,
And into glory peep.

22 I saw Eternity the other night,
Like a great ring of pure and endless light,
All calm, as it was bright;
And round beneath it, Time in hours, days, years,
Driv'n by the spheres
Like a vast shadow mov'd; in which the world

And all her train were hurl'd.
The World

THORSTEIN VEBLEN 1857–1929

1 Conspicuous consumption of valuable goods is a
means of reputability to the gentleman of leisure.
The Theory of the Leisure Class (1899), ch.iv

2 From the foregoing survey of the growth of
conspicuous leisure and consumption, it appears that
the utility of both alike for the purposes of reputability
lies in the element of waste that is common to both. In
the one case it is a waste of time and effort, in the
other it is a waste of goods.

VEGETIUS 4th–5th cent. A.D.

3 *Qui desiderat pacem, praeparet bellum.*
Let him who desires peace, prepare for war.
De Re Mil. 3, prol. Usually cited in the form *Si vis pacem, para
bellum* (If you want peace, prepare for war.)

VENANTIUS FORTUNATUS c.530–c.610

4 *Pange, lingua, gloriosi
Proelium certaminis.*
Sing, my tongue, of the battle in the glorious struggle.
Pange lingua gloriosi. Passiontide hymn, see J.P. Migne,
Patrologia Latina, 88

5 *Vexilla regis prodeunt,
Fulget crucis mysterium;
Qua vita mortem pertulit,
Et morte vitam protulit.*
The banners of the king advance, the mystery of the
cross shines bright; where his life went through with
death, and from death brought forth life.
Vexilla Regis. Analecta Hymnica, 50, No.67, p.74

6 *Regnavit a ligno Deus.*
God reigned from the wood.

PIERRE VERGNIAUD 1753–1793

7 *Il a été permis de craindre que la Révolution, comme
Saturne, dévorât successivement tous ses enfants.*
There was reason to fear that the Revolution, like
Saturn, might devour in turn each one of her children.
Lamartine, *Histoire des Girondins* (1847), bk.xxxviii, ch.20

PAUL VERLAINE 1844–1896

8 *Les sanglots longs
Des violons
De l'automne
Blessent mon coeur
D'une langueur
Monotone.*
The drawn-out sobs of the violins of autumn wound
my heart with a monotonous languor.
Chanson de l'automne

9 *Et tout le reste est littérature.*
All the rest is mere fine writing.
Jadis et Naguère (1885). *L'art poétique*

10 *Et, Ô ces voix d'enfants chantants dans la coupole!*
And oh those children's voices, singing beneath the

dome!
Parsifal, A Jules Tellier

EMPEROR VESPASIAN A.D. 9–79

11 *Pecunia non olet.*
Money has no smell.
Traditional summary of Suetonius, *Vespasian,* 23,3. Vespasian
was answering Titus's objection to his tax on public lavatories;
holding a coin to Titus's nose and being told it didn't smell, he
replied:
Atqui e lotio est.
Yet that's made from urine.

12 *Vae, puto deus fio.*
Woe is me, I think I am becoming a god.
Suetonius, *Vespasian,* 23,4. Said when fatally ill

QUEEN VICTORIA 1819–1901

13 I will be good.
To Baroness Lehzen, 11 Mar. 1830. Martin, *The Prince Consort*
(1875), vol.i, p.13

14 The Queen is most anxious to enlist every one who can
speak or write to join in checking this mad, wicked
folly of 'Woman's Rights', with all its attendant
horrors, on which her poor feeble sex is bent,
forgetting every sense of womanly feeling and
propriety. Lady— ought to get a *good whipping.*
It is a subject which makes the Queen so furious that
she cannot contain herself. God created men and
women different—then let them remain each in their
own position.
Letter to Sir Theodore Martin, 29 May 1870

15 The danger to the country, to Europe, to her vast
Empire, which is involved in having all these great
interests entrusted to the shaking hand of an old, wild,
and incomprehensible man of $82\frac{1}{2}$, is very great!
On Gladstone's last appointment as Prime Minister. Letter to Lord
Lansdowne, 12 Aug. 1892

16 Move Queen Anne? Most certainly not! Why it might
some day be suggested that *my* statue should be
moved, which I should much dislike.
When it was suggested that the statue of Queen Anne outside St.
Paul's should be moved, on the occasion of the Diamond Jubilee
in 1887. Duke of Portland, *Men, Women and Things,* ch.5

17 We are not amused.
Attr. *Notebooks of a Spinster Lady,* 2 Jan. 1900

18 We are not interested in the possibilities of defeat; they
do not exist.
To A.J. Balfour, in 'Black Week', Dec. 1899

19 He [Mr Gladstone] speaks to Me as if I was a public
meeting.
G.W.E. Russell, *Collections and Recollections,* ch.14

GORE VIDAL 1925–

20 It is not enough to succeed. Others must fail.
Revd. G. Irvine, *Antipanegyric for Tom Driberg,* 8 Dec. 1976

JOSÉ ANTONIO VIERA GALLO 1943–

21 *El socialismo puede llegar solo en bicicleta.*
Socialism can only arrive by bicycle.
Ivan Illich, *Energy & Equity* (1974), quoting the Under Secretary
of Justice in the Chilean Government of Salvador Allende

ALFRED DE VIGNY 1797–1863

1 *J'aime la majesté des souffrances humaines.*
I love the majesty of human suffering.
La Maison du Berger (1844)

2 *Seul le silence est grand; tout le reste est faiblesse…*
Fais énergiquement ta longue et lourde tâche…
Puis, après, comme moi, souffre et meurs sans parler.
Silence alone is great; all else is feebleness…
Perform with all your heart your long and heavy task…
Then as do I, say naught, but suffer and die.
La Mort du Loup (1838)

PHILIPPE-AUGUSTE VILLIERS DE L'ISLE-ADAM 1838–1889

3 *Vivre? les serviteurs feront cela pour nous.*
Living? The servants will do that for us.
Axël (1890), IV, sect 2

FRANÇOIS VILLON b. 1431

4 *Frères humains qui après nous vivez,*
N'ayez les cuers contre nous endurcis,
Car, se pitié de nous povres avez,
Dieu en aura plus tost de vous mercis…
Mais priez Dieu que tous nous veuille absoudre!
Brothers in humanity who live after us, let not your
hearts be hardened against us, for, if you take pity
on us poor ones, God will be more likely to have
mercy on you. But pray God that he may be willing
to absolve us all.
Ballade des pendus

5 *Mais où sont les neiges d'antan?*
But where are the snows of yesteryear?
Le Grand Testament (1461). **Ballade des Dames du Temps
Jadis.** Tr. D.G. Rossetti

6 *En ceste foy je veuil vivre et mourir.*
In this faith I wish to live and to die.
Ballade pour prier Nostre Dame

ST. VINCENT OF LERINS d. c.450

7 *Quod semper, quod ubique, quod ab omnibus creditum
est.*
What is always, what is everywhere, what is by all
people believed.
Commonitorium, ii

VIRGIL 70–19 B.C.

8 *Arma virumque cano, Troiae qui primus ab oris*
Italiam fato profugus Laviniaque venit
Litora, multum ille et terris iactatus et alto
Vi superum, saevae memorem Iunonis ob iram.
I sing of arms and the man who first from the shores
of Troy came destined an exile to Italy and the
Lavinian beaches, much buffeted he on land and on
the deep by force of the gods because of fierce
Juno's never-forgetting anger.
Aeneid, i.1

9 *Tantaene animis caelestibus irae?*
Why such great anger in those heavenly minds?
11

10 *Tantae molis erat Romanam condere gentem.*
So massive was the effort to found the Roman nation.
33

11 *Apparent rari nantes in gurgite vasto.*
Odd figures swimming were glimpsed in the waste of
waters.
118

12 *Constitit hic arcumque manu celerisque sagittas*
Corripuit fidus quae tela gerebat Achates.
Hereupon he stopped and took up in his hand a bow
and swift arrows, the weapons that trusty Achates
carried.
187

13 *O passi graviora, dabit deus his quoque finem.*
O you who have borne even heavier things, God will
grant an end to these too.
199

14 *Forsan et haec olim meminisse iuvabit.*
Maybe one day we shall be glad to remember even
these things.
203

15 *Dux femina facti.*
The leader of the enterprise a woman.
364

16 *Dixit et avertens rosea cervice refulsit,*
Ambrosiaeque comae divinum vertice odorem
Spiravere; pedes vestis defluxit ad imos,
Et vera incessu patuit dea.
She said no more and as she turned away there was a
bright glimpse of the rosy glow of her neck, and
from her ambrosial head of hair a heavenly
fragrance wafted; her dress flowed down right to her
feet, and in her walk it showed, she was in truth a
goddess.
402

17 *'En Priamus. Sunt hic etiam sua praemia laudi,*
Sunt lacrimae rerum et mentem mortalia tangunt.
Solve metus; feret haec aliquam tibi fama salutem.'
Sic ait atque animum pictura pascit inani.
'Look, there's Priam! Even here prowess has its due
rewards, there are tears shed for things even here
and mortality touches the heart. Abandon your
fears; I tell you, this fame will stand us somehow in
good stead.' So he spoke, and fed his thoughts on
the unreal painting.
461

18 *Di tibi, si qua pios respectant numina, si quid*
Usquam iustitiae est et mens sibi conscia recti,
Praemia digna ferant.
Surely as the divine powers take note of the dutiful,
surely as there is any justice anywhere and a mind
recognizing in itself what is right, may the gods
bring you your earned rewards.
603

19 *Non ignara mali miseris succurrere disco.*
No stranger to trouble myself I am learning to care for
the unhappy.
630

20 *Infandum, regina, iubes renovare dolorem.*
A grief too much to be told, O queen, you bid me
renew.
ii.3

21   *Quaeque ipse miserrima vidi*
Et quorum pars magna fui.
And the most miserable things which I myself saw and
of which I was a major part.
5

1   *Equo ne credite, Teucri.*
Quidquid id est, timeo Danaos et dona ferentis.
Do not trust the horse, Trojans. Whatever it is, I fear
   the Greeks even when they bring gifts.
48

2   *Crimine ab uno*
Disce omnis.
From the one crime recognize them all as culprits.
65

3 *Tacitae per amica silentia lunae.*
Through the friendly silence of the soundless
   moonlight.
255

4 *Tempus erat quo prima quies mortalibus aegris*
Incipit et dono divum gratissima serpit.
It was the time when first sleep begins for weary
   mortals and by the gift of the gods creeps over them
   most welcomely.
268

5   *Quantum mutatus ab illo*
Hectore qui redit exuvias indutus Achilli.
How greatly changed from that Hector who comes
   home wearing the armour stripped from Achilles!
274

6   *Fuimus Troes, fuit Ilium et ingens*
Gloria Teucrorum.
We Trojans are at an end, Ilium has ended and the
   vast glory of the Teucrians.
325

7   *Moriamur et in media arma ruamus.*
Una salus victis nullam sperare salutem.
Let us die even as we rush into the midst of the battle.
   The only safe course for the defeated is to expect no
   safety.
353

8 *Dis aliter visum.*
The gods thought otherwise.
428

9 *Non tali auxilio nec defensoribus istis*
Tempus eget.
Now is not the hour that requires such help, nor those
   defenders.
521

10   *Quid non mortalia pectora cogis,*
Auri sacra fames!
What do you not drive human hearts into, cursed
   craving for gold!
iii.56

11 *Monstrum horrendum, informe, ingens, cui lumen*
ademptum.
A monster horrendous, hideous and vast, deprived of
   sight.
658

12 *Quis fallere possit amantem?*
Who could deceive a lover?
iv.296

13   *Nec me meminisse pigebit Elissae*
Dum memor ipse mei, dum spiritus hos regit artus.
Nor will it ever upset me to remember Elissa so long
   as I can remember who I am, so long as the breath
   of life controls these limbs.
335. Aeneas, of Dido

14   *Varium et mutabile semper*

Femina.
Fickle and changeable always is woman.
569. Richard Stanyhurst's translation (1582):
    A windfane changabil huf puffe
Always is a woomman.

15 *Exoriare aliquis nostris ex ossibus ultor.*
Arise, you avenger someone, from my bones.
625

16 *Hos successus alit: possunt, quia posse videntur.*
These success encourages: they can because they think
   they can.
v.231

17   *Bella, horrida bella,*
Et Thybrim multo spumantem sanguine cerno.
I see wars, horrible wars, and the Tiber foaming with
   much blood.
vi.86

18   *Facilis descensus Averno:*
Noctes atque dies patet atri ianua Ditis;
Sed revocare gradum superasque evadere ad auras,
Hoc opus, hic labor est.
Easy is the way down to the Underworld: by night and
   by day dark Dis's door stands open; but to withdraw
   one's steps and to make a way out to the upper air,
   that's the task, that is the labour.
126

19 *Procul, o procul este, profani.*
Far off, Oh keep far off, you uninitiated ones.
258

20 *Ibant obscuri sola sub nocte per umbram*
Perque domos Ditis vacuas et inania regna.
Darkling they went under the lonely night through the
   shadow and through the empty dwellings and
   unsubstantial realms of Dis.
268

21 *Vestibulum ante ipsum primisque in faucibus Orci*
Luctus et ultrices posuere cubilia Curae,
Pallentesque habitant Morbi tristisque Senectus,
Et Metus et malesuada Fames ac turpis Egestas,
Terribiles visu formae, Letumque Labosque.
Before the very forecourt and in the opening of the
   jaws of hell Grief and avenging Cares have placed
   their beds, and wan Diseases and sad Old Age live
   there, and Fear and Hunger that urges to
   wrongdoing, and shaming Destitution, figures
   terrible to see, and Death and Toil.
273

22 *Stabant orantes primi transmittere cursum*
Tendebantque manus ripae ulterioris amore.
They stood begging to be the first to make the voyage
   over and they reached out their hands in longing for
   the further shore.
313

23 *Inventas aut qui vitam excoluere per artis*
Quique sui memores aliquos fecere merendo:
Omnibus his nivea cinguntur tempora vitta.
Or those who have improved life by the knowledge
   they have found out, and those who have made
   themselves remembered by some for their services:
   round the brows of all these is worn a snow-white
   band.
663

24 *Spiritus intus alit, totamque infusa per artus*
Mens agitat molem et magno se corpore miscet.

The spirit within nourishes, and mind instilled
   throughout the living parts activates the whole mass
   and mingles with the vast frame.
726

1 *Excudent alii spirantia mollius aera*
  (Credo equidem), vivos ducent de marmore vultus,
  Orabunt causas melius, caelique meatus
  Describent radio et surgentia sidera dicent:
  Tu regere imperio populos, Romane, memento
  (Hae tibi erunt artes), pacique imponere morem,
  Parcere subiectis et debellare superbos.
  Others shall shape bronzes more smoothly so that they
   seem alive (yes, I believe it), shall mould from
   marble living faces, shall better plead their cases in
   court, and shall demonstrate with a pointer the
   motions of the heavenly bodies and tell the stars as
   they rise: you, Roman, make your task to rule
   nations by your government (these shall be your
   skills), to impose ordered ways upon a state of
   peace, to spare those who have submitted and to
   subdue the arrogant.
847

2 *Heu, miserande puer, si qua fata aspera rumpas,*
  Tu Marcellus eris. Manibus date lilia plenis.
  Alas, pitiable boy—if only you might break your cruel
   fate!—you are to be Marcellus. Give me lilies in
   armfuls.
882

3 *Sunt geminae Somni portae, quarum altera fertur*
  Cornea, qua veris facilis datur exitus umbris,
  Altera candenti perfecta nitens elephanto,
  Sed falsa ad caelum mittunt insomnia Manes.
  There are two gates of Sleep, one of which it is held is
   made of horn and by it real ghosts have easy egress;
   the other shining fashioned of gleaming white ivory,
   but deceptive are the visions the Underworld sends
   that way to the light.
893

4   *Geniumque loci primamque deorum*
  Tellurem Nymphasque et adhuc ignota precatur
  Flumina.
  He prays to the spirit of the place and to Earth the first
   of the gods and to the Nymphs and as yet unknown
   rivers.
vii.136

5 *Flectere si nequeo superos, Acheronta movebo.*
  If I am unable to make the gods above relent, I shall
   move Hell.
312

6 *O mihi praeteritos referat si Iuppiter annos.*
  Oh if only Jupiter would give me back my past years.
  viii. 560

7 *Quadripedante putrem sonitu quatit ungula campum.*
  Hooves with a galloping sound are shaking the
   powdery plain.
596

8 *Macte nova virtute, puer, sic itur ad astra.*
  Blessings on your young courage, boy; that's the way
   to the stars.
ix.641

9 *Audentis Fortuna iuvat.*
  Fortune assists the bold.
  x.284

10 *Experto credite.*

Trust one who has gone through it.
xi.283

11 *Tityre, tu patulae recubans sub tegmine fagi*
  Silvestrem tenui Musam meditaris avena.
  Tityrus, you who lie under cover of the spreading
   beech-tree, you are practising your pastoral music on
   a thin stalk.
  Eclogue, i.1

12 *O Meliboee, deus nobis haec otia fecit.*
  O Meliboeus, it is a god that has made this peaceful
   life for us.
6

13 *At nos hinc alii sitientis ibimus Afros,*
  Pars Scythiam et rapidum cretae veniemus Oaxen
  Et penitus toto divisos orbe Britannos.
  But we from here are to go some to arid Africa,
   another group to Scythia and others of us shall come
   to the Oaxes swirling with clay, and amongst the
   Britons who are kept far away from the whole
   world.
64

14 *Formosum pastor Corydon ardebat Alexin,*
  Delicias domini, nec quid speraret habebat.
  The shepherd Corydon was in hot love with handsome
   Alexis, his master's favourite, but he was not getting
   anything he hoped for.
ii.1

15 *O formose puer, nimium ne crede colori.*
  O handsome lad, don't trust too much in your
   complexion.
17

16 *Quem fugis, a! demens? Habitarunt di quoque silvas.*
  Ah, madman! Whom are you running away from?
   Gods too have lived in the woods.
60

17 *Trahit sua quemque voluptas.*
  Everyone is dragged on by their favourite pleasure.
65

18 *Malo me Galatea petit, lasciva puella,*
  Et fugit ad salices et se cupit ante videri.
  Galatea throws an apple at me, sexy girl, and runs
   away into the willows and wants to have been
   spotted.
iii.64

19 *Latet anguis in herba.*
  There's a snake hidden in the grass.
93

20 *Non nostrum inter vos tantas componere lites.*
  It's not in my power to decide such a great dispute
   between you.
108

21 *Claudite iam rivos, pueri; sat prata biberunt.*
  Close the sluices now, lads; the fields have drunk
   enough.
111

22 *Sicelides Musae, paulo maiora canamus!*
  Non omnis arbusta iuvant humilesque myricae;
  Si canimus silvas, silvae sint consule dignae.
   Ultima Cumaei venit iam carminis aetas;
  Magnus ab integro saeclorum nascitur ordo.
  Iam redit et virgo, redeunt Saturnia regna,
  Iam nova progenies caelo demittitur alto.
  Sicilian Muses, let us sing of rather greater things. Not

everyone likes bushes and low tamarisks; if we sing
of the woods, let them be woods of consular
dignity.

Now has come the last age according to the oracle at
Cumae; the great series of lifetimes starts anew. Now
too the virgin goddess returns, the golden days of
Saturn's reign return, now a new race descends from
high heaven.
iv.1

1 *Incipe, parve puer, risu cognoscere matrem.*
Begin, baby boy, to recognize your mother with a
smile.
60

2 *Incipe, parve puer: qui non risere parenti,*
Nec deus hunc mensa, dea nec dignata cubili est.
Begin, baby boy: if you haven't had a smile for your
parent, then neither will a god think you worth
inviting to dinner, nor a goddess to bed.
62

3 *Ambo florentes aetatibus, Arcades ambo,*
Et cantare pares et respondere parati.
Both in the flower of their youth, Arcadians both, and
matched and ready alike to start a song and to
respond.
vii.4

4 *Saepibus in nostris parvam te roscida mala*
(Dux ego vester eram) vidi cum matre legentem.
Alter ab undecimo tum me iam acceperat annus,
Iam fragilis poteram a terra contingere ramos:
Ut vidi, ut perii, ut me malus abstulit error!
In our orchard I saw you picking dewy apples with
your mother (I was showing you the way). I had
just turned twelve years old, I could reach the brittle
branches even from the ground: how I saw you! how
I fell in love! how an awful madness swept me
away!
viii.37

5 *Nunc scio quid sit Amor.*
Now I know what Love is.
43

6 *Non omnia possumus omnes.*
We can't all do everything.
63. Attributed to Lucilius, Macrobius, *Saturnalia*, vi.1.35

7   *Et me fecere poetam*
Pierides, sunt et mihi carmina, me quoque dicunt
Vatem pastores; sed non ego credulus illis.
Nam neque adhuc Vario videor nec dicere Cinna
Digna, sed argutos inter strepere anser olores.
Me too the Muses made write verse. I have songs of
my own, the shepherds call me also a poet; but I'm
not inclined to trust them. For I don't seem yet to
write things as good either as Varius or as Cinna,
but to be a goose honking amongst tuneful swans.
ix.32

8 *Omnia vincit Amor: et nos cedamus Amori.*
Love conquers all things: let us too give in to Love.
x.69

9 *Ite domum saturae, venit Hesperus, ite capellae.*
Go on home, you have fed full, the evening star is
coming, go on, my she-goats.
77

10 *Ultima Thule.*
Farthest Thule.
Georgics, i.30

11 *Nosque ubi primus equis Oriens adflavit anhelis*
Illic sera rubens accendit lumina Vesper.
And when the rising sun has first breathed on us with
his panting horses, over there the red evening-star is
lighting his late lamps.
250

12 *Ter sunt conati imponere Pelio Ossam*
Scilicet atque Ossae frondosum involvere Olympum;
Ter pater exstructos disiecit fulmine montis.
Three times they endeavoured to pile Ossa on Pelion,
no less, and to roll leafy Olympus on top of Ossa;
three times our Father scattered the heaped-up
mountains with a thunderbolt.
281

13 *O fortunatos nimium, sua si bona norint,*
Agricolas!
O farmers excessively fortunate if only they recognized
their blessings!
ii.458

14 *Felix qui potuit rerum cognoscere causas.*
Lucky is he who has been able to understand the
causes of things.
490

15 *Fortunatus et ille deos qui novit agrestis.*
Fortunate too is the man who has come to know the
gods of the countryside.
493

16 *Optima quaeque dies miseris mortalibus aevi*
Prima fugit; subeunt morbi tristisque senectus
Et labor, et durae rapit inclementia mortis.
All the best days of life slip away from us poor mortals
first; illnesses and dreary old age and pain sneak up,
and the fierceness of harsh death snatches away.
iii.66

17 *Sed fugit interea, fugit inreparabile tempus.*
But meanwhile it is flying, irretrievable time is flying.
284

18 *Hi motus animorum atque haec certamina tanta*
Pulveris exigui iactu compressa quiescent.
All these spirited movements and such great contests
as these will be contained and quieten down by the
throwing of a little dust.
iv.86. Of the battle of the bees

19 *Non aliter, si parva licet componere magnis,*
Cecropias innatus apes amor urget habendi
Munere quamque suo.
Just so, if one may compare small things with great, an
innate love of getting drives these Attic bees each
with his own function.
176

20 *Sic vos non vobis mellificatis apes.*
Sic vos non vobis nidificatis aves.
Sic vos non vobis vellera fertis oves.
Thus you bees make honey not for yourselves. Thus
you birds build nests not for yourselves. Thus you
sheep bear fleeces not for yourselves.
Attr. On Bathyllus' claiming the authorship of certain lines by
Virgil

VOLTAIRE 1694–1778

21 *Si nous ne trouvons pas des choses agréables, nous*
trouverons du moins des choses nouvelles.
If we do not find anything pleasant, at least we shall

find something new.
Candide (1759), ch.17

1 *Dans ce pays-ci il est bon de tuer de temps en temps un amiral pour encourager les autres.*
In this country [England] it is thought well to kill an admiral from time to time to encourage the others.
ch.23

2 *Tout est pour le mieux dans le meilleur des mondes possibles.*
All is for the best in the best of possible worlds.
ch.30

3 *Cela est bien dit, répondit Candide, mais il faut cultiver notre jardin.*
'That is well said,' replied Candide, 'but we must cultivate our garden.' (We must attend to our own affairs.)

4 *Ils ne se servent de la pensée que pour autoriser leurs injustices, et n'emploient les paroles que pour déguiser leurs pensées.*
[Men] use thought only to justify their injustices, and speech only to conceal their thoughts.
Dialogue xiv. Le Chapon et la Poularde

5 *Le mieux est l'ennemi du bien.*
The best is the enemy of the good.
Dict. Philosophique (1764). **Art Dramatique**

6 *La superstition met le monde entier en flammes; la philosophie les éteint.*
Superstition sets the whole world in flames; philosophy quenches them.
Superstition

7 *Tous les genres sont bons hors le genre ennuyeux.*
All styles are good save the tiresome kind.
L'Enfant Prodigue (1736), preface

8 *Si Dieu n'existait pas, il faudrait l'inventer.*
If God did not exist, it would be necessary to invent him.
Épîtres, xcvi. **A l'Auteur du Livre des Trois Imposteurs**

9 *Ce corps qui s'appelait et qui s'appelle encore le saint empire romain n'était en aucune manière ni saint, ni romain, ni empire.*
This agglomeration which was called and which still calls itself the Holy Roman Empire was neither holy, nor Roman, nor an empire.
Essai sur les Moeurs et l'Esprit des Nations (1769), lxx

10 *En effet, l'histoire n'est que le tableau des crimes et des malheurs.*
Indeed, history is nothing more than a tableau of crimes and misfortunes.
L'Ingénu (1767), ch.10

11 *Quoi que vous fassiez, écrasez l'infâme, et aimez qui vous aime.*
Whatever you do, stamp out abuses, and love those who love you.
Letter to M. d'Alembert, 28 Nov. 1762

12 *Il est plaisant qu'on fait une vertu du vice de chasteté; et voilà encore une drôle de chasteté que celle qui mène tout droit les hommes au péché d'Onan, et les filles aux pâles couleurs!*
It is amusing that a virtue is made of the vice of chastity; and it's a pretty odd sort of chastity at that, which leads men straight into the sin of Onan, and girls to the waning of their colour.
Letter to M. Mariott, 28 Mar. 1766

13 *Je ne suis pas comme une dame de la cour de Versailles, qui disait: c'est bien dommage que l'aventure de la tour de Babel ait produit la confusion des langues; sans cela tout le monde aurait toujours parlé français.*
I am not like a lady at the court of Versailles, who said: 'What a dreadful pity that the bother at the tower of Babel should have got language all mixed up; but for that, everyone would always have spoken French.'
Letter to Catherine the Great, 26 May 1767

14 *Le superflu, chose très nécessaire.*
The superfluous is very necessary.
Le Mondain (1736), v.22

15 *C'est une des superstitions de l'esprit humain d'avoir imaginé que la virginité pouvait être une vertu.*
It is one of the superstitions of the human mind to have imagined that virginity could be a virtue.
Notebooks, ed. T. Besterman, 2nd edn. (1968), vol.II, **The Leningrad Notebooks** (c.1735–c.1750), p.455

16 *Il faut qu'il y ait des moments tranquilles dans les grands ouvrages, comme dans la vie après les instants de passions, mais non pas des moments de dégoût.*
There ought to be moments of tranquillity in great works, as in life after the experience of passions, but not moments of disgust.
The Piccini Notebooks, p.500

17 *Il faut, dans le gouvernement, des bergers et des bouchers.*
Governments need to have both shepherds and butchers.
p.517

18 *Dieu n'est pas pour les gros bataillons, mais pour ceux qui tirent le mieux.*
God is on the side not of the heavy batallions, but of the best shots.
p.547. See 117:7

19 *On doit des égards aux vivants; on ne doit aux morts que la vérité.*
We owe respect to the living; to the dead we owe only truth.
Oeuvres (1785), vol.I, p.15n. (**Première Lettre sur Oedipe**)

20 *La foi consiste à croire ce que la raison ne croit pas...Il ne suffit pas qu'une chose soit possible pour la croire.*
Faith consists in believing when it is beyond the power of reason to believe. It is not enough that a thing be possible for it to be believed.
Questions sur l'Encyclopédie

21 *Le secret d'ennuyer est...de tout dire.*
The way to be a bore is to say everything.
Sept Discours en vers sur l'Homme, VI. **Sur la Nature de l'Homme**. v.174-5

22 When Voltaire was asked why no woman has ever written a tolerable tragedy, 'Ah (said the Patriarch) the composition of a tragedy requires *testicles.*'
Letter from Byron to John Murray, 2 Apr. 1817

23 *Habacuc était capable de tout.*
Habakkuk was capable of anything.
Attr. See N. & Q., clxxxi.46

24 I disapprove of what you say, but I will defend to the death your right to say it.
Attr. in S.G. Tallentyre, *The Friends of Voltaire* (1907), p.199

RICHARD WAGNER 1813–1883

1 *Frisch weht der Wind*
der Heimat zu:—
mein irisch Kind,
wo weilest du?
Freshly blows the wind to the homeland: my Irish
child, where are you staying?
Tristan und Isolde, I.i

ARTHUR WALEY 1889–1966

2 What is hard today is to censor one's own thoughts—
To sit by and see the blind man
On the sightless horse, riding into the bottomless
abyss.
Censorship

HENRY WALLACE 1888–1965

3 The century on which we are entering—the century
which will come out of this war—can be and must be
the century of the common man.
Address: **The Price of Free World Victory,** 8 May 1942

WILLIAM ROSS WALLACE d. 1881

4 The hand that rocks the cradle
Is the hand that rules the world.
John o'London's Treasure Trove

GRAHAM WALLAS 1858–1932

5 The little girl had the making of a poet in her who,
being told to be sure of her meaning before she spoke,
said: 'How can I know what I think till I see what I
say?'
The Art of Thought

EDMUND WALLER 1606–1687

6 So was the huntsman by the bear oppress'd,
Whose hide he sold—before he caught the beast!
Battle of the Summer Islands, ii, 1.111

7 Poets that lasting marble seek
Must carve in Latin or in Greek.
Of English Verse

8 Others may use the ocean as their road,
Only the English make it their abode.
Of a War with Spain, 1.25

9 The soul's dark cottage, batter'd and decay'd
Lets in new light through chinks that time has made;
Stronger by weakness, wiser men become,
As they draw near to their eternal home.
Leaving the old, both worlds at once they view,
That stand upon the threshold of the new.
On the Foregoing Divine Poems, 1.18

10 That which her slender waist confin'd
Shall now my joyful temples bind;
No monarch but would give his crown
His arms might do what this has done.
On a Girdle

11 Rome, though her eagle through the world had flown,
Could never make this island all her own.
Panegyric to My Lord Protector, xvii

12 Illustrious acts high raptures do infuse,
And every conqueror creates a Muse.
xlvi

13 Go, lovely Rose!
Tell her, that wastes her time and me,
That now she knows,
When I resemble her to thee,
How sweet and fair she seems to be.
Song: 'Go Lovely Rose!'

14 Small is the worth
Of beauty from the light retir'd;
Bid her come forth,
Suffer herself to be desir'd,
And not blush so to be admir'd.

15 Why came I so untimely forth
Into a world which, wanting thee,
Could entertain us with no worth,
Or shadow of felicity?
To My Young Lady Lucy Sidney

16 So all we know
Of what they do above,
Is that they happy are, and that they love.
Upon the Death of My Lady Rich, 1.75

17 Under the tropic is our language spoke,
And part of Flanders hath receiv'd our yoke.
Upon the Death of the Lord Protector, 1.21

HORACE WALPOLE, FOURTH EARL OF ORFORD 1717–1797

18 Alexander at the head of the world never tasted the
true pleasure that boys of his own age have enjoyed at
the head of a school.
Letters. To Montagu, 6 May 1736

19 Our supreme governors, the mob.
To Mann, 7 Sept. 1743

20 [Lovat] was beheaded yesterday, and died extremely
well, without passion, affectation, buffoonery or
timidity: his behaviour was natural and intrepid.
To Mann, 10 Apr. 1747

21 [Strawberry Hill] is a little plaything-house that I got
out of Mrs Chenevix's shop, and is the prettiest bauble
you ever saw. It is set in enamelled meadows, with
filigree hedges.
To Conway, 8 June 1747

22 But, thank God! the Thames is between me and the
Duchess of Queensberry.

23 Every drop of ink in my pen ran cold.
To Montagu, 3 July 1752

24 It has the true rust of the Barons' Wars.
To Bentley, Sept. 1753

25 At present, nothing is talked of, nothing admired, but
what I cannot help calling a very insipid and tedious
performance: it is a kind of novel, called *The Life and
Opinions of Tristram Shandy;* the great humour of
which consists in the whole narration always going
backwards.
To Dalrymple, 4 Apr. 1760

26 One of the greatest geniuses that ever existed,
Shakespeare, undoubtedly wanted taste.
To Wren, 9 Aug. 1764

27 The works of Richardson...which are pictures of high
life as conceived by a bookseller, and romances as they

would be spiritualized by a Methodist preacher.
To Mann, 20 Dec. 1764

1 At Madame du Deffand's, an old blind *débauchée* of wit.
To Conway, 6 Oct. 1765

2 What has one to do, when one grows tired of the world, as we both do, but to draw nearer and nearer, and gently waste the remains of life with friends with whom one began it?
To Montagu, 21 Nov. 1765

3 It is charming to totter into vogue.
To Selwyn, 2 Dec. 1765

4 Yes, like Queen Eleanor in the ballad, I sunk at Charing Cross, and have risen in the Faubourg St Germain.
To Gray, 25 Jan. 1766

5 The best sun we have is made of Newcastle coal.
To Montagu, 15 June 1768

6 Everybody talks of the constitution, but all sides forget that the constitution is extremely well, and would do very well, if they would but let it alone.
To Mann, 18-19 Jan. 1770

7 It was easier to conquer it [the East] than to know what to do with it.
To Mann, 27 Mar. 1772

8 The way to ensure summer in England is to have it framed and glazed in a comfortable room.
To Cole, 28 May 1774

9 The next Augustan age will dawn on the other side of the Atlantic. There will, perhaps, be a Thucydides at Boston, a Xenophon at New York, and, in time, a Virgil at Mexico, and a Newton at Peru. At last, some curious traveller from Lima will visit England and give a description of the ruins of St Paul's, like the editions of Balbec and Palmyra.
To Mann, 24 Nov. 1774

10 By the waters of Babylon we sit down and weep, when we think of thee, O America!
To Mason, 12 June 1775

11 This world is a comedy to those that think, a tragedy to those that feel.
To the Countess of Upper Ossory, 16 Aug. 1776

12 Tell me, ye divines, which is the most virtuous man, he who begets twenty bastards, or he who sacrifices an hundred thousand lives?
To Mann, 7 July 1778

13 When will the world know that peace and propagation are the two most delightful things in it?

14 The life of any man written under the direction of his family, did nobody honour.
To Cole, 1 Sept. 1778

15 When men write for profit, they are not very delicate.

16 Easy I am so far, that the ill success of the American war has saved us from slavery—in truth, I am content that liberty will exist anywhere, and amongst Englishmen, even cross the Atlantic.
To Mann, 25 Feb. 1779

17 When people will not weed their own minds, they are apt to be overrun with nettles.
To Lady Ailesbury, 10 July 1779

18 Prognostics do not always prove prophecies,—at least

the wisest prophets make sure of the event first.
To Thos. Walpole, 19 Feb. 1785

19 It is the story of a mountebank and his zany.
Of Boswell's *Tour to the Hebrides*. To Conway, 6 Oct. 1785

20 All his [Sir Joshua Reynolds's] own geese are swans, as the swans of others are geese.
To the Countess of Upper Ossory, 1 Dec. 1786

21 I do not dislike the French from the vulgar antipathy between neighbouring nations, but for their insolent and unfounded airs of superiority.
To Hannah More, 14 Oct. 1787

22 Virtue knows to a farthing what it has lost by not having been vice.
L. Kronenberger, *The extraordinary Mr. Wilkes* (1974), Part 3, ch.2, 'The Ruling Class'

SIR HUGH WALPOLE 1884–1941

23 'Tisn't life that matters! 'Tis the courage you bring to it.
Fortitude (1913), opening sentence

SIR ROBERT WALPOLE, FIRST EARL OF ORFORD 1676–1745

24 They now *ring* the bells, but they will soon *wring* their hands.
On the declaration of war with Spain, 1739. W. Coxe, *Memoirs of Sir Robert Walpole* (1798), vol.i, p.618

25 Madam, there are fifty thousand men slain this year in Europe, and not one Englishman.
To Queen Caroline, 1734. Hervey, *Memoirs* (1848), vol.i, p.398

26 My Lord Bath, you and I are now two as insignificant men as any in England.
To Pulteney, Earl of Bath, on their promotion to the House of Lords. W. King, *Political & Literary Anecdotes* (1819), p.43

27 The balance of power.
House of Commons, 13 Feb. 1741

WILLIAM WALSH 1663–1708

28 And sadly reflecting,
That a lover forsaken
    A new love may get,
But a neck when once broken
    Can never be set.
The Despairing Lover, l.17

29 By partners, in each other kind,
Afflictions easier grow;
In love alone we hate to find
Companions of our woe.
Song, Of All the Torments

30 I can endure my own despair,
But not another's hope.

IZAAK WALTON 1593–1683

31 Angling may be said to be so like the mathematics, that it can never be fully learnt.
The Compleat Angler (1653), Epistle to the Reader

32 And for winter fly-fishing it is as useful as an almanac out of date.

33 As no man is born an artist, so no man is born an angler.

34 I shall stay him no longer than to wish him a rainy

evening to read this following discourse; and that if he. be an honest angler, the east wind may never blow when he goes a-fishing.

1 I am, Sir, a Brother of the Angle.
pt.i, ch.1

2 Angling is somewhat like poetry, men are to be born so.

3 Sir Henry Wotton…was also a most dear lover, and a frequent practiser of the art of angling; of which he would say, 'it was an employment for his idle time, which was then not idly spent…a rest to his mind, a cheerer of his spirits, a diverter of sadness, a calmer of unquiet thoughts, a moderator of passions, a procurer of contentedness; and that it begat habits of peace and patience in those that professed and practised it.'

4 Good company and good discourse are the very sinews of virtue.
ch.2

5 An excellent angler, and now with God.
ch.4

6 I love such mirth as does not make friends ashamed to look upon one another next morning.
ch.5

7 A good, honest, wholesome, hungry breakfast.

8 No man can lose what he never had.

9 In so doing, use him as though you loved him.
ch.8. Instructions for baiting a hook with a live frog.

10 This dish of meat is too good for any but anglers, or very honest men.

11 I love any discourse of rivers, and fish and fishing.
ch.18

12 Look to your health; and if you have it, praise God, and value it next to a good conscience; for health is the second blessing that we mortals are capable of; a blessing that money cannot buy.
ch.21

13 Let the blessing of St Peter's Master be…upon all that are lovers of virtue; and dare trust in His providence; and be quiet; and go a-Angling.

14 But God, who is able to prevail, wrestled with him, as the Angel did with Jacob, and marked him; marked him for his own.
Life of Donne

15 The great Secretary of Nature and all learning, Sir Francis Bacon.
Life of Herbert

16 Of this blest man, let his just praise be given, Heaven was in him, before he was in heaven.
Written in Dr. Richard Sibbes's *Returning Backslider,* now preserved in Salisbury Cathedral Library

BISHOP WILLIAM WARBURTON 1698–1779

17 Orthodoxy is my doxy; heterodoxy is another man's doxy.
To Lord Sandwich. Priestley, *Memoirs* (1807), vol.i, p.372

ARTEMUS WARD (CHARLES FARRAR BROWNE) 1834–1867

18 I now bid you a welcome adoo.
Artemus Ward His Book. **The Shakers**

19 'Mister Ward, don't yur blud bile at the thawt that three million and a half of your culled brethren air a clanking their chains in the South?' Sez I, 'not a bile! Let 'em clank!'
Oberlin

20 If you mean gettin hitched, I'M IN!
The Showman's Courtship

21 My pollerticks, like my religion, bein of a exceedin accommodatin character.
The Crisis

22 Shall we sell our birthrite for a mess of potash?

23 N.B. This is rote Sarcasticul.
A Visit to Brigham Young

24 I girdid up my Lions & fled the Seen.

25 Did you ever hav the measels, and if so how many?
The Census

26 The female woman is one of the greatest institooshuns of which this land can boste.
Woman's Rights

27 By a sudden and adroit movement I placed my left eye agin the Secesher's fist.
Thrilling Scenes in Dixie

28 The ground flew up and hit me in the hed.

29 I presunted myself at Betty's bedside late at nite, with considerbul licker koncealed about my persun.
Betsy-Jain Re-orgunised

30 The happy marrid man dies in good stile at home, surrounded by his weeping wife and children. The old batchelor don't die at all—he sort of rots away, like a polly-wog's tail.
Draft in Baldinsville

31 It is a pity that Chawcer, who had geneyus, was so unedicated. He's the wuss speller I know of.
Artemus Ward in London, ch.4. **At the Tomb of Shakespeare**

32 He [Brigham Young] is dreadfully married. He's the most married man I ever saw in my life.
Artemus Ward's Lecture

33 Why is this thus? What is the reason of this thusness?

34 I am happiest when I am idle. I could live for months without performing any kind of labour, and at the expiration of that time I should feel fresh and vigorous enough to go right on in the same way for numerous more months.
Pyrotechny. III. **Pettingill**

35 Why care for grammar as long as we are good?
V

36 Let us all be happy, and live within our means, even if we have to borrer the money to do it with.
Science and Natural History

MRS. HUMPHRY WARD 1851–1920

37 'Propinquity does it'—as Mrs Thornburgh is always reminding us.
Robert Elsmere (1888), bk.i, ch.2

REVD. NATHANIEL WARD 1578–1652

38 The world is full of care, much like unto a bubble; Woman and care, and care and women, and women and care and trouble.
Epigram. Attr. by Ward to a lady at the Court of the Queen of Bohemia. *Simple Cobler's Boy* (1648), p.25

GEORGE WASHINGTON 1732–1799

1 Father, I cannot tell a lie, I did it with my little
hatchet.
Attr. Mark Twain, *Mark Twain as George Washington.* Another
version is: I can't tell a lie, Pa; you know I can't tell a lie. I did
cut it with my hatchet. Weems, *Washington,* (Fifth edition, 1806)

2 It is our true policy to steer clear of permanent alliance
with any portion of the foreign world.
Farewell Address to the People of the United States, 17 Sept. 1796

3 Labour to keep alive in your breast that little spark of
celestial fire, called conscience.
Rules of Civility and Decent Behaviour. Sparks, *Life of
Washington* (1839), vol.ii, p.109

4 We must consult Brother Jonathan.
Said to have been a frequent remark of his during the American
Revolution, referring to Jonathan Trumbull, 1710-85, Governor of
Connecticut. *Publications of the Colonial Society of
Massachusetts* (1905), vol.vii, p.94

5 Put none but Americans on guard to-night.
Attr. based on his circular letter to regimental commanders, 30
Apr. 1777

ROWLAND WATKYNS fl. 1662

6 I love him not, but shew no reason can
Wherefore, but this, *I do not love* the man.
Flamma sine fumo. Antipathy. See 331:9

7 For every marriage then is best in tune,
When that the wife is May, the husband June.
**To the most Courteous and Fair Gentlewoman, Mrs. Elinor
Williams**

WILLIAM WATSON 1559?–1603

8 *Fiat justitia et ruant coeli.*
Let justice be done though the heavens fall.
*A Decacordon of Ten Quodlibeticall Questions Concerning
Religion and State* (1602). First citation in an English work of a
famous maxim. See 210:33

SIR WILLIAM WATSON 1858–1936

9 April, April,
Laugh thy girlish laughter;
Then, the moment after,
Weep thy girlish tears!
April

10 O be less beautiful, or be less brief.
Autumn

11 How all her care was but to be fair,
And all her task to be sweet.
The Heart of the Rose

12 Who never negligently yet
Fashioned an April violet,
Nor would forgive, did June disclose
Unceremoniously the rose.
Nature's Way

13 The staid, conservative,
Came-over-with-the-Conqueror type of mind.
A Study in Contrasts, i, I.42

ISAAC WATTS 1674–1748

14 Lord, I ascribe it to Thy grace,
And not to chance, as others do,
That I was born of Christian race,

And not a Heathen, or a Jew.
Divine Songs for Children, vi. **Praise for the Gospel**

15 There's no repentance in the grave.
x. **Solemn Thoughts of God and Death**

16 There is a dreadful Hell,
And everlasting pains;
There sinners must with devils dwell
In darkness, fire, and chains.
xi. **Heaven and Hell**

17 Let dogs delight to bark and bite,
For God hath made them so;
Let bears and lions growl and fight,
For 'tis their nature too.
xvi. **Against Quarrelling**

18 But, children, you should never let
Such angry passions rise;
Your little hands were never made
To tear each other's eyes.

19 Whatever brawls disturb the street,
There should be peace at home.
xvii. **Love between Brothers and Sisters**

20 Birds in their little nests agree
And 'tis a shameful sight,
When children of one family
Fall out, and chide, and fight.

21 How doth the little busy bee
Improve each shining hour,
And gather honey all the day
From every opening flower!
xx. **Against Idleness and Mischief**

22 In works of labour, or of skill,
I would be busy too;
For Satan finds some mischief still
For idle hands to do.

23 One sickly sheep infects the flock,
And poisons all the rest.
xxi. **Against Evil Company**

24 Let me be dress'd fine as I will,
Flies, worms, and flowers, exceed me still.
xxii. **Against Pride in Clothes**

25 'Tis the voice of the sluggard; I heard him complain,
'You have wak'd me too soon, I must slumber again'.
As the door on its hinges, so he on his bed,
Turns his sides and his shoulders and his heavy head.
Moral Songs, i. **The Sluggard**

26 How rude are the boys that throw pebbles and mire.
ii. **Innocent Play**

27 I'll not willingly offend,
Nor be easily offended;
What's amiss I'll strive to mend,
And endure what can't be mended.
vi. **Good Resolution**

28 Hark! from the tombs a doleful sound.
Hymns and Spiritual Songs, bk.ii, No.63. **Hark! from the
Tombs**

EVELYN WAUGH 1903–1966

29 The sound of the English county families baying for
broken glass.
Decline and Fall (1928), Prelude

30 'We class schools, you see, into four grades: Leading
School, First-rate School, Good School, and School.

Frankly', said Mr Levy, 'School is pretty bad.'
Pt.I. ch.1

1 You can't get into the soup in Ireland, do what you like.
ch.3

2 For generations the British bourgeoisie have spoken of themselves as gentlemen, and by that they have meant, among other things, a self-respecting scorn of irregular perquisites. It is the quality that distinguishes the gentleman from both the artist and the aristocrat.
ch.6

3 Feather-footed through the plashy fen passes the questing vole.
Scoop (1938), bk.I, ch.1

4 Up to a point, Lord Copper.
Meaning 'No'. *passim*

5 Lady Peabury was in the morning room reading a novel; early training gave a guilty spice to this recreation, for she had been brought up to believe that to read a novel before luncheon was one of the gravest sins it was possible for a gentlewoman to commit.
Work Suspended (1942), **An Englishman's Home** [1939]

BEATRICE WEBB 1848–1943

6 If I ever felt inclined to be timid as I was going into a room full of people, I would say to myself, 'You're the cleverest member of one of the cleverest families in the cleverest class of the cleverest nation in the world, why should you be frightened?'
Bertrand Russell, *Portraits from Memory* (1956), VIII. Sidney and Beatrice Webb

SIDNEY WEBB 1859–1947

7 The inevitability of gradualness.
Presidential address to the annual conference of the Labour Party, 1920

8 Marriage is the waste-paper basket of the emotions.
Attr. by Beatrice Webb. Bertrand Russell, *Portraits from Memory* (1956), VIII. Sidney and Beatrice Webb

DANIEL WEBSTER 1782–1852

9 There is always room at the top.
When advised not to become a lawyer as the profession was overcrowded

10 The people's government, made for the people, made by the people, and answerable to the people.
Second Speech in the Senate on Foot's Resolution, 26 Jan. 1830

11 Liberty and Union, now and forever, one and inseparable!

12 On this question of principle, while actual suffering was yet afar off, they [the Colonies] raised their flag against a power, to which, for purposes of foreign conquest and subjugation, Rome, in the height of her glory, is not to be compared; a power which has dotted over the surface of the whole globe with her possessions and military posts, whose morning drum-beat, following the sun, and keeping company with the hours, circles the earth with one continuous and unbroken strain of the martial airs of England.
Speech in the Senate on the President's Protest, 7 May 1834

13 Thank God, I—I also—am an American!
Speech on the Completion of Bunker Hill Monument, 17 June 1843

14 The Law: It has honoured us, may we honour it.

15 I was born an American; I will live an American; I shall die an American.
Speech in the Senate on 'The Compromise Bill', 17 July 1850

16 Fearful concatenation of circumstances.
Argument on the Murder of Captain Joseph White

JOHN WEBSTER 1580?–1625?

17 Vain the ambition of kings
Who seek by trophies and dead things,
To leave a living name behind,
And weave but nets to catch the wind.
The Devil's Law-Case, V.iv

18 *Ferdinand:* And women like that part which, like the lamprey,
Hath never a bone in't.
Duchess: Fie, sir!
Ferdinand: Nay,
I mean the tongue; variety of courtship:
What cannot a neat knave with a smooth tale
Make a woman believe?
The Duchess of Malfi (1623), ed. C.B. Wheeler (1915), I.ii.43

19 Unequal nature, to place women's hearts
So far upon the left side.
II.v.33

20   Why should only I...
Be cas'd up, like a holy relic? I have youth
And a little beauty.
III.ii.135

21 Raised by that curious engine, your white hand.
297

22   O, that it were possible,
We might but hold some two days' conference
With the dead!
IV.ii.18

23 I have made a soap-boiler costive.
117

24 I am Duchess of Malfi still.
146

25 Glories, like glow-worms, afar off shine bright,
But looked to near, have neither heat nor light.
148

26 I know death hath ten thousand several doors
For men to take their exits.
222. See 215:11, 336:1, 420:11

27 *Ferdinand:* Cover her face; mine eyes dazzle: she died young.
Bosola: I think not so; her infelicity
Seem'd to have years too many.
267

28 Physicians are like kings,—they brook no contradiction.
V.ii.72

29 We are merely the stars' tennis-balls, struck and bandied
Which way please them.
iv.53

30 Is not old wine wholesomest, old pippins toothsomest, old wood burn brightest, old linen wash whitest? Old

soldiers, sweethearts, are surest, and old lovers are soundest.
Westward Hoe (1607), II.ii

1   Fortune's a right whore:
If she give aught, she deals it in small parcels,
That she may take away all at one swoop.
The White Devil (1612), I.i.4

2 'Tis just like a summer birdcage in a garden; the birds that are without despair to get in, and the birds that are within despair, and are in a consumption, for fear they shall never get out.
ii.47

3 A mere tale of a tub, my words are idle.
II.i.92

4 Only the deep sense of some deathless shame.
ii.67

5 Cowardly dogs bark loudest.
III.i.163

6 A rape! a rape!...
Yes, you have ravish'd justice;
Forced her to do your pleasure.
271

7 There's nothing sooner dry than women's tears.
V.iii.192

8 Call for the robin-red-breast and the wren,
Since o'er shady groves they hover,
And with leaves and flowers do cover
The friendless bodies of unburied men.
iv.100

9 But keep the wolf far thence that's foe to men,
For with his nails he'll dig them up again.
108

10 We think caged birds sing, when indeed they cry.
128

11 And of all axioms this shall win the prize,—
'Tis better to be fortunate than wise.
vi.183

12 There's nothing of so infinite vexation
As man's own thoughts.
206

13 My soul, like to a ship in a black storm,
Is driven, I know not whither.
248

14 Prosperity doth bewitch men, seeming clear;
But seas do laugh, show white, when rocks are near.
250

15   I have caught
An everlasting cold; I have lost my voice
Most irrecoverably.
270

JOSIAH WEDGWOOD 1730–1795

16 Am I not a man and a brother.
Legend on Wedgwood cameo depicting a kneeling negro slave in chains, reproduced in facsimile in E. Darwin, *The Botanic Garden* pt.1 (1791), facing p.87

THOMAS EARLE WELBY 1881–1933

17 'Turbot, Sir,' said the waiter, placing before me two fishbones, two eyeballs, and a bit of black

mackintosh.
The Dinner Knell

DUKE OF WELLINGTON 1769–1852

18 Not upon a man from the colonel to the private in a regiment—both inclusive. We may pick up a marshal or two perhaps; but not worth a damn.
On being asked whether he calculated upon any desertion in Buonaparte's army. *Creevey Papers*, ch.x, p.228

19 It has been a damned serious business—Blücher and I have lost 30,000 men. It has been a damned nice thing—the nearest run thing you ever saw in your life...By God! I don't think it would have done if I had not been there.
p.236

20 All the business of war, and indeed all the business of life, is to endeavour to find out what you don't know by what you do; that's what I called 'guessing what was at the other side of the hill'.
Croker Papers (1885), vol.iii, p.276

21 I believe I forgot to tell you I was made a Duke.
Postscript to a letter to his nephew Henry Wellesley, 22 May 1814

22 I never saw so many shocking bad hats in my life.
On seeing the first Reformed Parliament. Sir William Fraser, *Words on Wellington* (1889), p.12

23 You must build your House of Parliament upon the river: so...that the populace cannot exact their demands by sitting down round you.
p.163

24 The battle of Waterloo was won on the playing fields of Eton.
See Montalembert, *De l'Avenir Politique de l'Angleterre* (1856). The attribution was refuted by the 7th Duke.

25 The next greatest misfortune to losing a battle is to gain such a victory as this.
S. Rogers, *Recollections* (1859), p.215

26 'What a glorious thing must be a victory, Sir.' 'The greatest tragedy in the world, Madam, except a defeat.'
footnote

27 I always say that, next to a battle lost, the greatest misery is a battle gained.
Frances, Lady Shelley, *Diary*, p.102

28 So he is a fool, and a d—d fool; but he can take Rangoon.
G.W.E. Russell, *Collections and Recollections*, ch.2. On its being objected that he had always spoken of Lord Combermere as a fool, and yet had proposed him as commander of an expedition to take Rangoon. The story is probably apocryphal: Wellington thought highly of Combermere, who, moreover, was never involved in the Rangoon campaign.

29 In my situation as Chancellor of the University of Oxford, I have been much exposed to authors.

30 Not half so surprised as I am now, Mum!
On being asked by Mrs. Arbuthnot if he had not been surprised at Waterloo

31 I have no small talk and Peel has no manners.
ch.14

32 Hard pounding this, gentlemen; let's see who will pound longest.
At Waterloo. Sir W. Scott, *Paul's Letters* (1815)

33 I used to say of him [Napoleon] that his presence on

the field made the difference of forty thousand men.
Stanhope, *Notes of Conversations with the Duke of Wellington*, 2 Nov. 1831

1 Ours [our army] is composed of the scum of the earth—the mere scum of the earth.
4 Nov. 1831

2 My rule always was to do the business of the day in the day.
2 Nov. 1835

3 What is the best to be done for the country? How can the Government be carried on?
18 May 1839

4 Beginning reform is beginning revolution.
Mrs. Arbuthnot's Journal, 7 Nov. 1830

5 I hate the whole race...There is no believing a word they say—your professional poets, I mean—there never existed a more worthless set than Byron and his friends for example.
Noted in Lady Salisbury's diary, 26 Oct. 1833. C. Oman, *The Gascoyne Heiress* (1968), III

6 When I reflect upon the characters and attainments of some of the general officers of this army, and consider that these are the persons on whom I am to rely to lead columns against the French, I tremble; and as Lord Chesterfield said of the generals of his day, 'I only hope that when the enemy reads the list of their names, he trembles as I do.'
Dispatch to Torrens, 29 Aug. 1810. Usually quoted as 'I don't know what effect these men will have upon the enemy, but, by God, they frighten me.' Also attributed to George III.

7 [To a gentleman who accosted him in the street saying, 'Mr. Jones, I believe?']
If you believe that you will believe anything.
Attr.

8 There is no mistake; there has been no mistake; and there shall be no mistake.
Wellingtoniana (1852), p.78

9 Up Guards and at them again!
Letter from Captain Batty 22 June 1815. Booth, *Battle of Waterloo*. See also Croker, *Correspondence and Diaries* (1884), III, 280

10 Publish and be damned.
Attr. According to legend, Wellington wrote these words across a blackmailing letter from Stockdale, publisher of Harriette Wilson's *Memoirs*, and posted it back to him. See Elizabeth Pakenham, *Wellington: The Years of the Sword* (1969), ch.10

H.G. WELLS 1866–1946

11 The thing his novel is *about* is always there. It is like a church lit but without a congregation to distract you, with every light and line focused on the high altar. And on the altar, very reverently placed, intensely there, is a dead kitten, an egg-shell, a bit of string. [Of Henry James.]
Boon, ch.4, sect.3

12 In the Country of the Blind the One-eyed Man is King.
The Country of the Blind

13 'I'm a Norfan, both sides,' he would explain, with the air of one who had seen trouble.
Kipps, bk.i, ch.6, I

14 'I expect,' he said, 'I was thinking jest what a Rum Go everything is. I expect it was something like that.'
bk.iii, ch.3, 8

15 The Social Contract is nothing more or less than a vast conspiracy of human beings to lie to and humbug themselves and one another for the general Good. Lies are the mortar that bind the savage individual man into the social masonry.
Love and Mr. Lewisham, ch.23

16 Human history becomes more and more a race between education and catastrophe.
The Outline of History, ch.40 of the 1951 edn.

CHARLES WESLEY 1707–1788

17 Gentle Jesus, meek and mild,
    Look upon a little child;
Pity my simplicity,
    Suffer me to come to thee.
Hymns and Sacred Poems (1742), **Gentle Jesus, Meek and Mild**

JOHN WESLEY 1703–1791

18 I look upon all the world as my parish.
Journal, 11 June 1739

19 Once in seven years I burn all my sermons; for it is a shame if I cannot write better sermons now than I did seven years ago.
1 Sept. 1778

20 Though I am always in haste, I am never in a hurry.
Select Letters (1837). Letter to a member of the Society. 10 Dec. 1777

21 Do all the good you can,
By all the means you can,
In all the ways you can,
In all the places you can,
At all the times you can,
To all the people you can,
As long as ever you can.
Letters (1915). **Rule of Conduct**

22 Let it be observed, that slovenliness is no part of religion; that neither this, nor any text of Scripture, condemns neatness of apparel. Certainly this is a duty, not a sin. 'Cleanliness is, indeed, next to godliness.'
Sermons, No. xciii. **On Dress**

23 Beware you be not swallowed up in books! An ounce of love is worth a pound of knowledge.
R. Southey, *Life of Wesley* (1820), ch.16

24 We should constantly use the most common, little, easy words (so they are pure and proper) which our language affords.
Of preaching to 'plain people'

REVD. SAMUEL WESLEY 1662–1735

25 Style is the dress of thought; a modest dress,
Neat, but not gaudy, will true critics please.
An Epistle to a Friend concerning Poetry (1700)

MAE WEST 1892?–

26 'Goodness, what beautiful diamonds.'
'Goodness had nothing to do with it, dearie.'
Night After Night (1932), script by Vincent Lawrence

27 Why don't you come up sometime, see me?
She Done Him Wrong (1933). Commonly misquoted as 'Come up and see me sometime'.

DAME REBECCA WEST 1892–

1 A life of immorality which involves posing as a page-boy in an Italian hotel must have been something so rich and strange that few of us could forebear to pause and inquire.
The Strange Necessity (1928). **The Tosh Horse**

2 God forbid that any book should be banned. The practice is as indefensible as infanticide.

RICHARD BETHELL, LORD WESTBURY 1800–1873

3 Then, sir, you will turn it over once more in what you are pleased to call your mind.
Related by Jowett and denied, not very convincingly, by Westbury. T.A. Nash, *Life of Lord Westbury* (1888), bk.2, ch.12

EDWARD NOYES WESTCOTT 1846–1898

4 They say a reasonable amount o' fleas is good fer a dog—keeps him from broodin' over bein' a dog, mebbe.
David Harum, ch.32

JOHN FANE, LORD WESTMORLAND 1759–1841

5 *Merit,* indeed!…We are come to a pretty pass if they talk of *merit* for a bishopric.
Noted in Lady Salisbury's diary, 9 Dec. 1835. C. Oman, *The Gascoyne Heiress* (1968), V

SIR CHARLES WETHERELL 1770–1846

6 Then there is my noble and biographical friend who has added a new terror to death.
Of Lord Campbell. Lord St. Leonards, *Misrepresentations in Campbell's Lives of Lyndhurst and Brougham* (1869), p.3. See 321:17

ROBERT WEVER fl. 1550

7 In a harbour grene aslepe whereas I lay,
The byrdes sang swete in the middes of the day,
I dreamèd fast of mirth and play:
    In youth is pleasure, in youth is pleasure.
Lusty Juventus

EDITH WHARTON 1862–1937

8 Mrs Ballinger is one of the ladies who pursue Culture in bands, as though it were dangerous to meet it alone.
Xingu (1916), ch.1

9 Another unsettling element in modern art is that common symptom of immaturity, the dread of doing what has been done before.
The Writing of Fiction, ch.1, pt.iii

THOMAS, 1st MARQUIS OF WHARTON 1648–1715

10 Ho, Brother *Teague,* dost hear de Decree?
    Lilli Burlero Bullena-la.
Dat we shall have a new Debity,
    Lilli Burlero Bullena-la.
A New Song. Written 1687; published on a single sheet 1688; first collected, in the above form, as 'Song' in *Poems on Affairs of State* (1704), vol.III, p.231

RICHARD WHATELY, ARCHBISHOP OF DUBLIN 1787–1863

11 Preach not because you have to say something, but because you have something to say.
Apophthegms

12 Happiness is no laughing matter.
p.218

13 It is a folly to expect men to do all that they may reasonably be expected to do.
p.219

14 Honesty is the best policy; but he who is governed by that maxim is not an honest man.

15 'Never forget, gentlemen,' he said, to his astonished hearers, as he held up a copy of the 'Authorized Version' of the Bible, 'never forget that this is *not* the Bible,' then, after a moment's pause, he continued, 'This, gentlemen, is only a *translation* of the Bible.'
To a meeting of his diocesan clergy. H. Solly, *These Eighty Years* (1893), vol.II. ch.ii, p.81

WILLIAM WHEWELL 1794–1866

16 Hence no force however great can stretch a cord however fine into an horizontal line which is accurately straight: there will always be a bending downwards.
Elementary Treatise on Mechanics, (1819), ch.IV, prob.ii. Often cited as an example of accidental metre and rhyme, and changed in later editions.

JAMES McNEILL WHISTLER 1834–1903

17 I am not arguing with you—I am telling you.
The Gentle Art of Making Enemies (1890)

18 Art is upon the Town!
'Ten O'Clock' (1885)

19 Listen! There never was an artistic period. There never was an Art-loving nation.

20 Nature is usually wrong.

21 'I only know of two painters in the world,' said a newly introduced feminine enthusiast to Whistler, 'yourself and Velasquez.' 'Why,' answered Whistler in dulcet tones, 'why drag in Velasquez?'
D.C. Seitz, *Whistler Stories* (1913), p.27

22 [In answer to a lady who said that a landscape reminded her of his work]
Yes madam, Nature is creeping up.
p.9

23 [In answer to the question 'For two days' labour, you ask two hundred guineas?']
No, I ask it for the knowledge of a lifetime.
p.40

24 You shouldn't say it is not good. You should say you do not like it; and then, you know, you're perfectly safe.
p.35

25 [Answering Oscar Wilde's 'I wish I had said that']
You will, Oscar, you will.
L.C. Ingleby, *Oscar Wilde*, p.67

WILLIAM WHITING 1825–1878

26 O hear us when we cry to Thee

For those in peril on the sea.
Eternal Father Strong to Save

WALT WHITMAN 1819–1892

1 Silent and amazed even when a little boy,
   I remember I heard the preacher every Sunday put God
      in his statements,
   As contending against some being or influence.
   A Child's Amaze

2 Full of life now, compact, visible,
   I, forty year old the eighty-third year of the States,
   To one a century hence or any number of centuries
      hence,
   To you yet unborn these, seeking you.
   Full of life now

3 Give me the splendid silent sun with all his beams
      full-dazzling!
   Give Me the Splendid Silent Sun

4 I dream'd in a dream I saw a city invincible to the
      attacks of the whole of the rest of the earth,
   I dream'd that was the new city of Friends.
   I Dream'd in a Dream

5 The institution of the dear love of comrades.
   I Hear it was Charged against Me

6 Me imperturbe, standing at ease in Nature.
   Me Imperturbe

7 O Captain! my Captain! our fearful trip is done,
   The ship has weather'd every rack, the prize we
      sought is won,
   The port is near, the bells I hear, the people all
      exulting.
   O Captain! My Captain! (1865-6), i

8 The ship is anchor'd safe and sound, its voyage closed
      and done.
   From fearful trip the victor ship comes in with object
      won;
   Exult O shores, and ring O bells! But I with mournful
      tread
   Walk the deck my Captain lies, Fallen cold and dead.
   iii

9 Out of the cradle endlessly rocking,
   Out of the mocking-bird's throat, the musical shuttle…
   A reminiscence sing.
   Out of the Cradle endlessly Rocking (1860)

10 Come my tan-faced children,
    Follow well in order, get your weapons ready,
    Have you your pistols? have you your sharp-edged
       axes?
         Pioneers! O pioneers!
    Pioneers! O Pioneers! (1865)

11 Beautiful that war and all its deeds of carnage must in
       time be utterly lost,
    That the hands of the sisters Death and Night
       incessantly softly wash again, and ever again, this
       soil'd world;
    For my enemy is dead, a man as divine as myself is
       dead,
    I look where he lies white-faced and still in the
       coffin—I draw near,
    Bend down and touch lightly with my lips the white
       face in the coffin.
    Reconciliation

12 What do you see Walt Whitman?

Who are they you salute, and that one after another
   salute you?
Salut au monde

13 Camerado, this is no book,
    Who touches this touches a man,
    (Is it night? Are we here together alone?)
    It is I you hold and who holds you.
    I spring from the pages into your arms—decease calls
       me forth.
    So Long!

14 Where the populace rise at once against the
       never-ending audacity of elected persons.
    Song of the Broad Axe (1856), 5, 1.12

15 Where women walk in public processions in the streets
       the same as the men,
    Where they enter the public assembly and take places
       the same as the men;
    Where the city of the faithfullest friends stands,
    Where the city of the cleanliness of the sexes stands,
    Where the city of the healthiest fathers stands,
    Where the city of the best-bodied mothers stands,
    There the great city stands.
    1.20

16 I celebrate myself, and sing myself.
    Song of Myself (1855), 1

17 Urge and urge and urge,
    Always the procreant urge of the world.
    3

18 A child said *What is the grass?* fetching it to one with
       full hands
    How could I answer the child? I do not know what it is
       any more than he.

    I guess it must be the flag of my disposition, out of the
       hopeful green stuff woven.

    Or I guess it is the handkerchief of the Lord,
    A scented gift and remembrancer designedly dropt,
    Bearing the owner's name someway in the corners,
       that we may see and remark, and say *Whose?*…
    And now it seems to me the beautiful uncut hair of
       graves.
    6

19 Has any one supposed it lucky to be born?
    I hasten to inform him or her, it is just as lucky to die
       and I know it.
    7

20 I also say it is good to fall, battles are lost in the same
       spirit in which they are won.
    18

21 I believe a leaf of grass is no less than the
       journey-work of the stars,
    And the pismire is equally perfect, and a grain of
       sand, and the egg of the wren,
    And the tree toad is a chef-d'oeuvre for the highest,
    And the running blackberry would adorn the parlors of
       heaven.
    31

22 I think I could turn and live with animals, they are so
       placid and self-contain'd,
    I stand and look at them long and long.
    They do not sweat and whine about their condition,
    They do not lie awake in the dark and weep for their
       sins,
    They do not make me sick discussing their duty to

God,
Not one is dissatisfied, not one is demented with the
   mania of owning things,
Not one kneels to another, nor to his kind that lived
   thousands of years ago,
Not one is respectable or unhappy over the whole
   earth.
32

1   Behold, I do not give lectures or a little charity,
    When I give I give myself.
    39

2   My rendezvous is appointed, it is certain,
    The Lord will be there and wait till I come on perfect
       terms,
    The great Camerado, the lover true for whom I pine
       will be there.
    44

3   I have said that the soul is not more than the body,
    And I have said that the body is not more than the
       soul,
    And nothing, not God, is greater to one than one's self
       is.
    47

4   In the faces of men and women I see God, and in my
       own face in the glass,
    I find letters from God dropt in the street, and every
       one is sign'd by God's name,
    And I leave them where they are, for I know that
       wheresoe'er I go,
    Others will punctually come for ever and ever.

5   Do I contradict myself?
    Very well then I contradict myself,
    (I am large, I contain multitudes.)
    50

6   I sound my barbaric yawp over the roofs of the world.
    51

7   Afoot and light-hearted I take to the open road,
    Healthy, free, the world before me,
    The long brown path before me leading wherever I
       choose.
    Song of the Open Road, I, l.1

8   The earth, that is sufficient,
    I do not want the constellations any nearer,
    I know they are very well where they are,
    I know they suffice for those who belong to them.
    l.8

9   I will put in my poems that with you is heroism upon
       land and sea,
    And I will report all heroism from an American point
       of view.
    Starting from Paumanok (1860), 6

10 This dust was once the man,
    Gentle, plain, just and resolute, under whose cautious
       hand,
    Against the foulest crime in history known in any land
       or age,
    Was saved the Union of these States.
    This Dust was Once a Man

11 The earth does not argue,
    Is not pathetic, has no arrangements,
    Does not scream, haste, persuade, threaten, promise,
    Makes no discriminations, has no conceivable failures,

Closes nothing, refuses nothing, shuts none out.
To the sayers of words, 2

12 When lilacs last in the dooryard bloom'd,
    And the great star early droop'd in the western sky in
       the night,
    I mourn'd, and yet shall mourn with ever-returning
       spring.
    When Lilacs Last in the Dooryard Bloom'd (1865-6), 1

13 Come lovely and soothing death,
    Undulate round the world, serenely arriving, arriving,
    In the day, in the night, to all, to each,
    Sooner or later, delicate death.
    Prais'd be the fathomless universe,
    For life and joy, and for objects and knowledge
       curious,
    And for love, sweet love—but praise! praise! praise!
    For the sure-enwinding arms of cool-enfolding death.
    14

14 These United States.
    A Backward Glance O'er Travell'd Roads (1888), 'These
    States' is *passim* in Whitman's verse

JOHN GREENLEAF WHITTIER 1807–1892

15 Up from the meadows rich with corn,
    Clear in the cool September morn,

    The clustered spires of Frederick stand
    Green-walled by the hills of Maryland.
    Barbara Frietchie, l.1

16 Up the street came the rebel tread,
    Stonewall Jackson riding ahead.
    l.23

17 'Shoot, if you must, this old gray head,
    But spare your country's flag,' she said.

    A shade of sadness, a blush of shame,
    Over the face of the leader came.
    l.35

18 'Who touches a hair of yon gray head
    Dies like a dog! March on!' he said.
    l.41

19 For all sad words of tongue or pen,
    The saddest are these: 'It might have been!'
    Maud Muller, l.105

20 The Indian Summer of the heart!
    Memories, ix

21 O brother man! fold to thy heart thy brother.
    Worship, l.49

ROBERT WHITTINGTON fl.1520

22 As time requireth, a man of marvellous mirth and
    pastimes, and sometime of as sad gravity, as who say:
    a man for all seasons.
    [Of Sir Thomas More.] *Vulgaria* (1521). pt.II, **De constructione
    nominum.** Erasmus famously applied the idea to More, writing in
    his prefatory letter to *In Praise of Folly* (1509), in Latin, that he
    played *'omnium horarum hominem.'*

BENJAMIN WHORF 1897–1941

23 We dissect nature along lines laid down by our native
    language...Language is not simply a reporting device
    for experience but a defining framework for it.
    Thinking in Primitive Communities, in Hoyer (ed.), *New
    Directions in the Study of Language*, 1964

CORNELIUS WHURR c.1845

1 What lasting joys the man attend
Who has a polished female friend.
The Accomplished Female Friend

GEORGE JOHN WHYTE-MELVILLE 1821–1878

2 Then drink, puppy, drink, and let ev'ry puppy drink,
That is old enough tó lap and to swallow;
For he'll grow into a hound, so we'll pass the bottle
   round,
And merrily we'll whoop and we'll holloa.
Drink, Puppy, Drink, chorus

BISHOP SAMUEL WILBERFORCE 1805–1873

3 If I were a cassowary
On the plains of Timbuctoo,
I would eat a missionary,
Cassock, band, and hymn-book too.
Impromptu verse, ascribed also to W.M. Thackeray

RICHARD WILBUR 1921–

4 We milk the cow of the world, and as we do
We whisper in her ear, 'You are not true.'
Epistemology, ii

ELLA WHEELER WILCOX 1855–1919

5 Laugh and the world laughs with you;
   Weep, and you weep alone;
For the sad old earth must borrow its mirth,
   But has trouble enough of its own.
Solitude

6 So many gods, so many creeds,
   So many paths that wind and wind,
While just the art of being kind
   Is all the sad world needs.
The World's Need

OSCAR WILDE 1854–1900

7 He did not wear his scarlet coat,
   For blood and wine are red,
And blood and wine were on his hands
   When they found him with the dead.
The Ballad of Reading Gaol (1898), pt.I.i

8 I never saw a man who looked
   With such a wistful eye
Upon that little tent of blue
   Which prisoners call the sky.
iii

9 When a voice behind me whispered low,
   'That fellow's got to swing.'
iv

10 Yet each man kills the thing he loves,
   By each let this be heard,
Some do it with a bitter look,
   Some with a flattering word.
The coward does it with a kiss,
   The brave man with a sword!
vii

11 Like two doomed ships that pass in storm
   We had crossed each other's way:
But we made no sign, we said no word,

We had no word to say.
II.xii

12 The Governor was strong upon
   The Regulations Act:
The Doctor said that Death was but
   A scientific fact:
And twice a day the Chaplain called,
   And left a little tract.
III.iii

13 Something was dead in each of us,
   And what was dead was Hope.
xxxi

14 And the wild regrets, and the bloody sweats,
   None knew so well as I:
For he who lives more lives than one
   More deaths than one must die.
xxxvii

15 I know not whether Laws be right,
   Or whether Laws be wrong;
All that we know who lie in gaol
   Is that the wall is strong;
And that each day is like a year,
   A year whose days are long.
V.i

16 How else but through a broken heart
   May Lord Christ enter in?
xiv

17   And yet, and yet,
These Christs that die upon the barricades,
God knows it I am with them, in some things.
Sonnet to Liberty: Not that I Love Thy Children

18 All her bright golden hair
   Tarnished with rust,
She that was young and fair
   Fallen to dust.
Requiescat

19 O Singer of Persephone!
In the dim meadows desolate
Dost thou remember Sicily?
Theocritus

20 A little sincerity is a dangerous thing, and a great deal
of it is absolutely fatal.
The Critic as Artist, Part 2

21 Ah! don't say that you agree with me. When people
agree with me I always feel that I must be wrong.

22 As long as war is regarded as wicked, it will always
have its fascination. When it is looked upon as vulgar,
it will cease to be popular.

23 There is no sin except stupidity.

24 Art never expresses anything but itself.
The Decay of Lying (1891), p.43

25 Really, if the lower orders don't set us a good
example, what on earth is the use of them?
The Importance of Being Earnest (1895), Act I

26 It is very vulgar to talk like a dentist when one isn't a
dentist. It produces a false impression.

27 The truth is rarely pure, and never simple.

28 In married life three is company and two none.

29 I have invented an invaluable permanent invalid called
Bunbury, in order that I may be able to go down into
the country whenever I choose.

1 To lose one parent, Mr Worthing, may be regarded as a misfortune; to lose both looks like carelessness.

2 All women become like their mothers. That is their tragedy. No man does. That's his.

3 The good ended happily, and the bad unhappily. That is what Fiction means. [Miss Prism on her novel.]
Act II

4 The chapter on the Fall of the Rupee you may omit. It is somewhat too sensational.

5 I hope you have not been leading a double life, pretending to be wicked and being really good all the time. That would be hypocrisy.

6 Charity, dear Miss Prism, charity! None of us are perfect. I myself am peculiarly susceptible to draughts.

7 On an occasion of this kind it becomes more than a moral duty to speak one's mind. It becomes a pleasure.

8 I couldn't help it. I can resist everything except temptation.
Lady Windermere's Fan (1891), Act I

9 Many a woman has a past, but I am told that she has a least a dozen, and that they all fit.

10 Do you know, Mr Hopper, dear Agatha and I are so much interested in Australia. It must be so pretty with all the dear little kangaroos flying about. [Duchess of Berwick.]
Act II

11 We are all in the gutter, but some of us are looking at the stars.
Act III

12 There is nothing in the whole world so unbecoming to a woman as a Nonconformist conscience.

13 A man who knows the price of everything and the value of nothing.
Definition of a cynic

14 *Dumby:* Experience is the name every one gives to their mistakes.
Cecil Graham: One shouldn't commit any.
Dumby: Life would be very dull without them.

15 There is no such thing as a moral or an immoral book. Books are well written, or badly written.
The Picture of Dorian Gray (1891), preface

16 The nineteenth century dislike of Realism is the rage of Caliban seeing his own face in the glass.

17 The moral life of man forms part of the subject matter of the artist, but the morality of art consists in the perfect use of an imperfect medium.

18 There is only one thing in the world worse than being talked about, and that is not being talked about.
ch.1

19 A man cannot be too careful in the choice of his enemies.

20 A cigarette is the perfect type of a perfect pleasure. It is exquisite, and it leaves one unsatisfied. What more can one want?
ch.6

21 It is better to be beautiful than to be good. But...it is better to be good than to be ugly.
ch.17

22 Anybody can be good in the country.
ch.19

23 As for the virtuous poor, one can pity them, of course, but one cannot possibly admire them.
The Soul of Man under Socialism

24 Democracy means simply the bludgeoning of the people by the people for the people.

25 *Mrs Allonby:* They say, Lady Hunstanton, that when good Americans die they go to Paris.
Lady Hunstanton: Indeed? And when bad Americans die, where do they go to?
Lord Illingworth: Oh, they go to America.
A Woman of No Importance (1893), Act I. See 11:13

26 The youth of America is their oldest tradition. It has been going on now for three hundred years.

27 The English country gentleman galloping after a fox—the unspeakable in full pursuit of the uneatable.

28 One should never trust a woman who tells one her real age. A woman who would tell one that, would tell one anything.

29 *Lord Illingworth:* The Book of Life begins with a man and a woman in a garden.
Mrs Allonby: It ends with Revelations.

30 Children begin by loving their parents; after a time they judge them; rarely, if ever, do they forgive them.

31 To be in it [society] is merely a bore. But to be out of it simply a tragedy.
Act III

32 You should study the Peerage, Gerald...It is the best thing in fiction the English have ever done.

33 No publisher should ever express an opinion of the value of what he publishes. That is a matter entirely for the literary critic to decide...A publisher is simply a useful middle-man. It is not for him to anticipate the verdict of criticism.
Letter in *St. James's Gazette*, 28 June 1890

34 A thing is not necessarily true because a man dies for it.
Sebastian Melmoth (1904), p.12. *Oscariana* (1910), p.8

35 *Voulez-vous savoir le grand drame de ma vie? C'est que j'ai mis mon génie dans ma vie; je n'ai mis que mon talent dans mes ouvres.*
Do you want to know the great drama of my life? It's that I have put my genius into my life; all I've put into my works is my talent.
Spoken to André Gide. Gide, *Oscar Wilde: In Memoriam*

36 [At the New York Custom House]
I have nothing to declare except my genius.
F. Harris, *Oscar Wilde* (1918), p.75

37 'Will you very kindly tell me, Mr Wilde, in your own words, your viewpoint of George Meredith?'
'George Meredith is a prose Browning, and so is Browning.'
'Thank you. His style?'
'Chaos, illumined by flashes of lightning.'
Ada Leverson, *Letters to the Sphinx* (1930), 'Reminiscences', 1

38 There seems to be some curious connection between piety and poor rhymes.
E.V. Lucas (ed.), *A Critic in Pall Mall* (1919), 'Sententiae'

39 Work is the curse of the drinking classes.
H. Pearson, *Life of Oscar Wilde* (1946), ch.12

1 He has fought a good fight and has had to face every difficulty except popularity.
Unpublished character sketch of W.E. Henley written for Rothenstein's *English Portraits.* See W. Rothenstein, *Men and Memories,* vol. I, ch.25

2 He [Bernard Shaw] hasn't an enemy in the world, and none of his friends like him.
Shaw, *Sixteen Self Sketches,* ch.17

3 [A huge fee for an operation was mentioned]
'Ah, well, then, I suppose that I shall have to die beyond my means.'
R.H. Sherard, *Life of Oscar Wilde* (1906), p.421

KAISER WILHELM II 1859–1941

4 It is my Royal and Imperial Command that you concentrate your energies, for the immediate present, upon one single purpose, and that is that you address all your skill and all the valour of my soldiers to exterminate first the treacherous English, and to walk over General French's contemptible little Army.
Of the British Expeditionary Force. Order dated Headquarters, Aix-la-Chapelle, 19 Aug. 1914, as reported in *The Times,* 1 Oct. 1914

JOHN WILKES 1727–1797

5 The chapter of accidents is the longest chapter in the book.
Attr. by Southey in *The Doctor* (1837), vol.iv, p.166

6 'Wilkes,' said Lord Sandwich, 'you will die either on the gallows, or of the pox.'
'That,' replied Wilkes blandly, 'must depend on whether I embrace your lordship's principles or your mistress.'
Charles Chenevix-Trench, *Portrait of a Patriot* (1962)., ch 3. But see H. Brougham, *Statesmen of George III,* third series (1843), p. 189. Also attr. Samuel Foote.

EMMA HART WILLARD 1787–1870

7 Rocked in the cradle of the deep.
Song

KING WILLIAM III 1650–1702

8 'Do you not see your country is lost?' asked the Duke of Buckingham. 'There is one way never to see it lost' replied William, 'and that is to die in the last ditch.'
Burnet, *History of his own Times* (1715), i.457

9 Every bullet has its billet.
John Wesley, *Journal,* 6 June 1765

WILLIAM CARLOS WILLIAMS 1883–1963

10 so much depends
upon

a red wheel
barrow

glazed with rain
water

beside the white
chickens.
The Red Wheelbarrow

11 Is it any better in Heaven, my friend Ford,
Than you found it in Provence?
To Ford Madox Ford in Heaven

12 I will teach you my townspeople how to perform a funeral
for you have it over a troop of artists—
unless one should scour the world—
you have the ground sense necessary.
Tract

NATHANIEL PARKER WILLIS 1806–1867

13 At present there is no distinction among the upper ten thousand of the city.
Necessity for a Promenade Drive

WENDELL WILLKIE 1892–1944

14 The Constitution does not provide for first and second class citizens.
New York Herald Tribune, 13 June 1944

CHARLES ERWIN WILSON 1890–1961

15 For many years I thought what was good for our country was good for General Motors, and vice versa.
Testimony before the Senate Armed Services Committee, Jan. 1953

SIR HAROLD WILSON 1916–

16 That doesn't mean, of course, that the pound here in Britain—in your pocket or purse or in your bank—has been devalued.
Ministerial Broadcast, 19 Nov. 1967

17 The Britain that is going to be forged in the white heat of this revolution.
Speech at the Labour Party conference, Scarborough, 1 Oct. 1963. Usually quoted as 'the white heat of the technological revolution.'

18 A week is a long time in politics.
Phrase used a number of times in 1965-6

HARRIETTE WILSON 1789–1846

19 I shall not say why and how I became, at the age of fifteen, the mistress of the Earl of Craven.
Memoirs, First sentence

JOHN WILSON
see CHRISTOPHER NORTH

PRESIDENT WOODROW WILSON 1856–1924

20 There is such a thing as a man being too proud to fight.
Address at Philadelphia, 10 May 1915

21 We have stood apart, studiously neutral.
Message to Congress, 7 Dec. 1915

22 Armed neutrality.
26 Feb. 1917

23 A little group of wilful men reflecting no opinion but their own have rendered the great Government of the United States helpless and contemptible.
Statement made on 4 Mar. 1917 after a successful filibuster against his bill to arm American merchant ships against German submarine attacks

24 The world must be made safe for democracy.
Address to Congress, 2 Apr. 1917

1 Open covenants of peace openly arrived at.
Address to Congress, 8 Jan. 1918. First of *Fourteen Points.*

2 It is indispensable that the governments associated against Germany should know beyond a peradventure with whom they are dealing.
Note to Germany, 14 Oct. 1918

3 Sometimes people call me an idealist. Well, that is the way I know I am an American. America is the only idealistic nation in the world.
Address at Sioux Falls, 8 Sept. 1919

ANNE FINCH, LADY WINCHILSEA 1661–1720

4 For see! where on the Bier before ye lies
The pale, the fall'n, th' untimely Sacrifice
To your mistaken Shrine, to your false Idol Honour.
All is Vanity, iii

5 Nor will in fading silks compose
Faintly the inimitable rose.
The Spleen

6 Now the Jonquille o'ercomes the feeble brain;
We faint beneath the aromatic pain.

WILLIAM WINDHAM 1750–1810

7 Those entrusted with arms...should be persons of some substance and stake in the country.
House of Commons, 22 July 1807

CATHERINE WINKWORTH 1827–1878

8 *Peccavi*—I have Sindh.
Of Sir Charles Napier's conquest of Sind (1843). Pun sent to *Punch*, 13 May 1844, and printed as 'the most laconic despatch ever issued', supposedly sent by Napier to Lord Ellenborough, *Punch*, vi, p.209, 18 May 1844. See N.M. Billimoria, *Proceedings of the Sind Historical Society*, II (1938) and N. & Q., cxcix (1954), p.219.

ROBERT CHARLES WINTHROP 1809–1894

9 A Star for every State, and a State for every Star.
Speech on Boston Common, 27 Aug. 1862

CARDINAL WISEMAN 1802–1865

10 Dr Wiseman was particularly pleased by the conversion of a Mr Morris, who, as he said, was 'the author of the essay...on the best method of prooving Christianity to the Hindoos.'
Lytton Strachey, *Eminent Victorians*, I.iii

OWEN WISTER 1860–1938

11 When you call me that, *smile.*
The Virginian (1902), ch.2

GEORGE WITHER 1588–1667

12 Shall I, wasting in despair,
   Die because a woman's fair?
Or make pale my cheeks with care,
   'Cause another's rosy are?
Be she fairer than the day,
Or the flow'ry meads in May;
   If she think not well of me,
   What care I how fair she be?
Sonnet

13 I loved a lass, a fair one,
   As fair as e'er was seen;
She was indeed a rare one,
   Another Sheba queen.
I Loved a Lass, a Fair One

LUDWIG WITTGENSTEIN 1889–1951

14 *Die Welt ist alles, was der Fall ist.*
The world is everything that is the case.
Tractatus Logico-Philosophicus (1922), 1

15 *Die Logik muss für sich selber sorgen.*
Logic must take care of itself.
5.473

16 *Die Welt des Glücklichen ist eine andere als die des Unglücklichen.*
The world of the happy is quite another than the world of the unhappy.
6.43

17 *Wovon man nicht sprechen kann, darüber muss man schweigen.*
Whereof one cannot speak, thereon one must remain silent.
7

P.G. WODEHOUSE 1881–1975

18 There was another ring at the front door. Jeeves shimmered out and came back with a telegram.
Carry on Jeeves (1925). **Jeeves Takes Charge**

19 He spoke with a certain what-is-it in his voice, and I could see that, if not actually disgruntled, he was far from being gruntled.
The Code of the Woosters (1938)

20 Slice him where you like, a hellhound is always a hellhound.

21 To my daughter Leonora without whose never-failing sympathy and encouragement this book would have been finished in half the time.
The Heart of a Goof (1926), dedication

22 Her hair was a deep chestnut, her eyes blue, her nose small and laid back with about as much loft as a light iron.
Chester Forgets Himself

23 The lunches of fifty-seven years had caused his chest to slip down to the mezzanine floor.

24 While they were content to peck cautiously at the ball, he never spared himself in his efforts to do it a violent injury.

25 She fitted into my biggest arm-chair as if it had been built round her by someone who knew they were wearing arm-chairs tight about the hips that season.
My Man Jeeves (1919). **Jeeves and the Unbidden Guest**

26 What with excellent browsing and sluicing and cheery conversation and what-not the afternoon passed quite happily.

27 Ice formed on the butler's upper slopes.
Pigs Have Wings (1952), ch.5. pt.i

28 The Right Hon was a tubby little chap who looked as if he had been poured into his clothes and had forgotten to say 'When!'
Very Good Jeeves (1930). **Jeeves and the Impending Doom**

1 …the unpleasant, acrid smell of burned poetry…
Young Men in Spats (1936). **The Fiery Wooing of Mordred**

CHARLES WOLFE 1791–1823

2 Not a drum was heard, not a funeral note,
As his corse to the rampart we hurried.
The Burial of Sir John Moore at Corunna, i

3 We buried him darkly at dead of night,
The sods with our bayonets turning.
ii

4 But he lay like a warrior taking his rest,
With his martial cloak around him.
iii

5 We carved not a line, and we raised not a stone—
But we left him alone with his glory.
viii

HUMBERT WOLFE 1886–1940

6 You cannot hope
to bribe or twist,
thank God! the
British journalist.

But, seeing what
the man will do
unbribed, there's
no occasion to.
The Uncelestial City, Bk.I. ii.2. **Over the Fire**

JAMES WOLFE 1727–1759

7 The General…repeated nearly the whole of Gray's
Elegy…adding, as he concluded, that he would prefer
being the author of that poem to the glory of beating
the French to-morrow.
J. Playfair, *Biogr. Acc. of J. Robinson* in *Transactions R. Soc.
Edinb.* (1814), vii. 499

8 Now God be praised, I will die in peace.
Dying words. J. Knox, *Historical Journal of Campaigns,
1757-60* (1769), ed. 1914, vol.ii, p.114

MARY WOLLSTONECRAFT 1759–1797

9 The *divine right* of husbands, like the divine right of
kings, may, it is hoped, in this enlightened age, be
contested without danger.
A Vindication of the Rights of Woman (1792), ch.3

10 A king is always a king—and a woman always a
woman: his authority and her sex ever stand between
them and rational converse.
ch.4

11 I do not wish them [women] to have power over men;
but over themselves.

12 When a man seduces a woman, it should, I think, be
termed a *left-handed* marriage.

CARDINAL WOLSEY 1475?–1530

13 Father Abbot, I am come to lay my bones amongst
you.
Cavendish, *Negotiations of Thomas Woolsey* (1641), p.108

14 Had I but served God as diligently as I have served the
King, he would not have given me over in my gray
hairs.
p.113

MRS. HENRY WOOD 1814–1887

15 Dead! and…never called me mother.
East Lynne (dramatized version by T.A. Palmer, 1874). These
words do not occur in the novel

LIEUT.-COMMANDER THOMAS WOODROOFE 1899–1978

16 The Fleet is all lit up.
First live outside broadcast, Coronation Spithead review, May
1937. See A. Briggs, *A History of Broadcasting in the United
Kingdom*, vol.II (1965), pt.ii, 2

VIRGINIA WOOLF 1882–1941

17 It is vain and foolish to talk of knowing Greek.
The Common Reader (1925), **On Not Knowing Greek**

18 She bore about with her, she could not help knowing
it, the torch of her beauty; she carried it erect into any
room that she entered; and after all, veil it as she
might, and shrink from the monotony of bearing that it
imposed on her, her beauty was apparent. She had
been admired. She had been loved.
To the Lighthouse (1927), I.8

19 So that is marriage, Lily thought, a man and a woman
looking at a girl throwing a ball.
13

20 I have lost friends, some by death…others through
sheer inability to cross the street.
The Waves (1931), p.202

DOROTHY WORDSWORTH 1771–1855

21 When we were in the woods beyond Gowbarrow park
we saw a few daffodils close to the waterside…But as
we went along there were more and yet more and at
last under the boughs of the trees, we saw that there
was a long belt of them along the shore, about the
breadth of a country turnpike road. I never saw
daffodils so beautiful they grew among the mossy
stones about and about them, some rested their heads
upon these stones as on pillow for weariness and the
rest tossed and reeled and danced and seemed as if they
verily laughed with the wind that blew upon them over
the lake.
The Grasmere Journals, 15 Apr. 1802

ELIZABETH WORDSWORTH 1840–1932

22 If all the good people were clever,
And all clever people were good,
The world would be nicer than ever
We thought that it possibly could.

But somehow, 'tis seldom or never
The two hit it off as they should;
The good are so harsh to the clever,
The clever so rude to the good!
St. Christopher and Other Poems: **Good and Clever**

WILLIAM WORDSWORTH 1770–1850

23 My apprehensions come in crowds;
I dread the rustling of the grass;
The very shadows of the clouds

Have power to shake me as they pass.
The Affliction of Margaret — (1807)

1 And three times to the child I said,
'Why, Edward, tell me why?'
Anecdote for Fathers (1798)

2 Action is transitory,—a step, a blow,
The motion of a muscle, this way or that—
'Tis done, and in the after-vacancy
We wonder at ourselves like men betrayed:
Suffering is permanent, obscure and dark,
And shares the nature of infinity.
The Borderers (1842), III.1539

3 Who is the happy Warrior? Who is he
That every man in arms should wish to be?
It is the generous spirit, who, when brought
Among the tasks of real life, hath wrought
Upon the plan that pleased his childish thought:
Whose high endeavours are an inward light
That makes the path before him always bright:
Who, with a natural instinct to discern
What knowledge can perform, is diligent to learn.
Character of the Happy Warrior (1807)

4 Ah! then, if mine had been the Painter's hand,
To express what then I saw; and add the gleam,
The light that never was, on sea or land,
The consecration, and the Poet's dream.
Elegiac Stanzas (on a picture of Peele Castle in a storm, 1807)

5 Not in the lucid intervals of life
That come but as a curse to party strife...
Is Nature felt, or can be.
Evening Voluntaries (1835), iv

6   By grace divine,
Not otherwise, O Nature, we are thine.

7 On Man, on Nature, and on Human Life,
Musing in solitude.
The Excursion (1814), preface, 1.1

8   The Mind of Man—
My haunt, and the main region of my song.
1.40

9 Oh! many are the Poets that are sown
By Nature; men endowed with highest gifts,
The vision and the faculty divine;
Yet wanting the accomplishment of verse.
bk.i, 1.77

10 What soul was his, when from the naked top
Of some bold headland, he beheld the sun
Rise up, and bathe the world in light!
1.198

11   The good die first,
And they whose hearts are dry as summer dust
Burn to the socket.
1.500

12 This dull product of a scoffer's pen.
bk.ii, 1.484. Of *Candide*

13 The intellectual power, through words and things,
Went sounding on, a dim and perilous way!
bk.iii, 1.700

14 Society became my glittering bride,
And airy hopes my children.
1.735

15 'Tis a thing impossible, to frame
Conceptions equal to the soul's desires;
And the most difficult of tasks to *keep*

Heights which the soul is competent to gain.
bk.iv, 1.136

16   I have seen
A curious child, who dwelt upon a tract
Of inland ground applying to his ear
The convolutions of a smooth-lipped shell;
To which, in silence hushed, his very soul
Listened intensely; and his countenance soon
Brightened with joy; for from within were heard
Murmurings, whereby the monitor expressed
Mysterious union with its native sea.
1.1132

17 'To every Form of being is assigned',
Thus calmly spoke the venerable Sage,
'An *active* Principle.'
bk.ix, 1.1

18 The rapt one, of the godlike forehead,
The heaven-eyed creature sleeps in earth:
And Lamb, the frolic and the gentle,
Has vanished from his lonely hearth.
Extempore Effusion upon the Death of James Hogg (1835)

19 How fast has brother followed brother,
From sunshine to the sunless land!

20   The wiser mind
Mourns less for what age takes away
Than what it leaves behind.
The Fountain (1800)

21 Bliss was it in that dawn to be alive,
But to be young was very heaven!
French Revolution, as it Appeared to Enthusiasts (1809), and
The Prelude, bk.xi, 1.108

22 The moving accident is not my trade;
To freeze the blood I have no ready arts:
'Tis my delight, alone in summer shade,
To pipe a simple song for thinking hearts.
Hart-leap Well (1800), pt.2, 1.1

23 'Tis he whom you so long have lost,
He whom you love, your Idiot Boy.
The Idiot Boy (1798), 1.370

24   As her mind grew worse and worse,
Her body—it grew better.
1.415

25   All shod with steel
We hissed along the polished ice, in games
Confederate.
Influence of Natural Objects (1809) and *The Prelude*, bk.i, 1.414

26   Leaving the tumultuous throng
To cut across the reflex of a star;
Image, that flying still before me, gleamed
Upon the glassy plain.

27   Yet still the solitary cliffs
Wheeled by me—even as if the earth had rolled
With visible motion her diurnal round!
(also *The Prelude*, bk.i, 1.458)

28 I travelled among unknown men
In lands beyond the sea;
Nor, England! did I know till then
What love I bore to thee.
I Travelled among Unknown Men (1807)

29 I wandered lonely as a cloud
That floats on high o'er vales and hills,
When all at once I saw a crowd,
A host, of golden daffodils;

Beside the lake, beneath the trees,
Fluttering and dancing in the breeze.
I Wandered Lonely as a Cloud (1807)

1 A poet could not but be gay,
In such a jocund company:
I gazed—and gazed—but little thought
What wealth to me the show had brought:

For oft, when on my couch I lie
In vacant or in pensive mood,
They flash upon that inward eye
Which is the bliss of solitude;
And then my heart with pleasure fills,
And dances with the daffodils.

2   The gods approve
The depth, and not the tumult, of the soul.
Laodamia (1815), l.74

3 Of all that is most beauteous—imaged there
In happier beauty; more pellucid streams,
An ampler ether, a diviner air,
And fields invested with purpureal gleams.
l.103

4   I have owed to them,
In hours of weariness, sensations sweet,
Felt in the blood, and felt along the heart;
And passing even into my purer mind,
With tranquil restoration:—feelings too
Of unremembered pleasure: such, perhaps,
As have no slight or trivial influence
On that best portion of a good man's life,
His little, nameless, unremembered, acts
Of kindness and of love.
Lines composed a few miles above Tintern Abbey (1798), l.26

5   That blessed mood,
In which the burthen of the mystery,
In which the heavy and the weary weight
Of all this unintelligible world,
Is lightened.
l.37

6   For nature then
(The coarser pleasures of my boyish days,
And their glad animal movements all gone by)
To me was all in all.—I cannot paint
What then I was. The sounding cataract
Haunted me like a passion: the tall rock,
The mountain, and the deep and gloomy wood,
Their colours and their forms, were then to me
An appetite; a feeling and a love,
That had no need of a remoter charm,
By thought supplied, nor any interest
Unborrowed from the eye.
l.72

7   I have learned
To look on nature, not as in the hour
Of thoughtless youth; but hearing often-times
The still, sad music of humanity,
Nor harsh nor grating, though of ample power
To chasten and subdue. And I have felt
A presence that disturbs me with the joy
Of elevated thoughts; a sense sublime
Of something far more deeply interfused,
Whose dwelling is the light of setting suns,
And the round ocean and the living air,
And the blue sky, and in the mind of man.
l.88

8 A power is passing from the earth
To breathless Nature's dark abyss;
But when the great and good depart,
What is it more than this—

That Man who is from God sent forth,
Doth yet again to God return?—
Such ebb and flow must ever be,
Then wherefore should we mourn?
Lines on the Expected Dissolution of Mr. Fox (1807)

9 And much it grieved my heart to think
What man has made of man.
Lines Written in Early Spring (1798)

10 I chanced to see at break of day
The solitary child.
Lucy Gray (1800)

11 Sweet Highland Girl, a very shower
Of beauty is thy earthly dower.
Memorials of a Tour in Scotland, 1803. vi. **To a Highland Girl**

12 What, you are stepping westward?
viii. **Stepping Westward**

13 Behold her, single in the field,
    Yon solitary Highland lass!
ix. **The Solitary Reaper**

14 Will no one tell me what she sings?—
Perhaps the plaintive numbers flow
For old, unhappy, far-off things,
And battles long ago.

15 Some natural sorrow, loss, or pain
That has been, and may be again.

16 The music in my heart I bore,
Long after it was heard no more.

17   The good old rule
Sufficeth them, the simple plan,
That they should take, who have the power,
    And they should keep who can.
xi. **Rob Roy's Grave**

18 Degenerate Douglas! Oh, the unworthy lord!
xii. **Sonnet**

19 My heart leaps up when I behold
    A rainbow in the sky:
So was it when my life began;
So is it now I am a man;
So be it when I shall grow old,
    Or let me die!
The Child is father of the Man;
And I could wish my days to be
Bound each to each by natural piety.
My Heart Leaps Up (1807)

20   Move along these shades
In gentleness of heart; with gentle hand
Touch—for there is a spirit in the woods.
Nutting (1800)

21 But Thy most dreaded instrument
In working out a pure intent,
Is man,—arrayed for mutual slaughter,
Yea, Carnage is Thy daughter.
Ode, 1815 (Imagination—ne'er before content, 1816)

22 There was a time when meadow, grove, and stream,
The earth, and every common sight,
    To me did seem
    Apparelled in celestial light,
The glory and the freshness of a dream.

It is not now as it hath been of yore;—
  Turn wheresoe'er I may,
  By night or day,
The things which I have seen I now can see no more.

  The rainbow comes and goes,
  And lovely is the rose,
  The moon doth with delight
Look round her when the heavens are bare,
  Waters on a starry night
  Are beautiful and fair;
  The sunshine is a glorious birth:
  But yet I know, where'er I go,
That there hath passed away a glory from the earth.
Ode. Intimations of Immortality (1807), i

1 A timely utterance gave that thought relief,
And I again am strong.
iii

2 The winds come to me from the fields of sleep.

3 Shout round me, let me hear thy shouts, thou happy
  Shepherd-boy.

4   The sun shines warm,
And the Babe leaps up on his Mother's arm.
iv

5 —But there's a tree of many, one,
A single field which I have looked upon,
Both of them speak of something that is gone:
  The pansy at my feet
  Doth the same tale repeat:
Whither is fled the visionary gleam?
Where is it now, the glory and the dream?

Our birth is but a sleep and a forgetting:
  The Soul that rises with us, our life's Star,
Hath had elsewhere its setting,
  And cometh from afar;
Not in entire forgetfulness,
And not in utter nakedness,
But trailing clouds of glory do we come
  From God, who is our home:
Heaven lies about us in our infancy!
Shades of the prison-house begin to close
  Upon the growing boy,
But he beholds the light, and whence it flows,
  He sees it in his joy;
The youth, who daily farther from the east
  Must travel, still is Nature's priest,
  And by the vision splendid
  Is on his way attended;
At length the man perceives it die away,
And fade into the light of common day.

6 As if his whole vocation
Were endless imitation.
vii

7   Thou Eye among the blind,
That, deaf and silent, read'st the eternal deep
Haunted for ever by the eternal mind.
viii

8 Why with such earnest pains dost thou provoke
The years to bring the inevitable yoke,
Thus blindly with thy blessedness at strife?
Full soon thy Soul shall have her earthly freight,
And custom lie upon thee with a weight,
Heavy as frost, and deep almost as life!

9 O joy! that in our embers

Is something that doth live,
That nature yet remembers
What was so fugitive!
The thought of our past years in me doth breed
Perpetual benediction.
ix

10 Not for these I raise
The song of thanks and praise;
  But for those obstinate questionings
  Of sense and outward things,
  Fallings from us, vanishings;
  Blank misgivings of a creature
Moving about in worlds not realised,
High instincts before which our mortal nature
Did tremble like a guilty thing suprised.

11 Our noisy years seem moments in the being
Of the eternal Silence: truths that wake,
  To perish never.

12 Hence in a season of calm weather
  Though inland far we be,
Our souls have sight of that immortal sea
  Which brought us hither,
  Can in a moment travel thither,
And see the children sport upon the shore,
And hear the mighty waters rolling evermore.

13 Though nothing can bring back the hour
Of splendour in the grass, of glory in the flower;
We will grieve not, rather find
Strength in what remains behind...
In the faith that looks through death,
In years that bring the philosophic mind.

And O, ye fountains, meadows, hills and groves,
Forbode not any severing of our loves!
Yet in my heart of hearts I feel your might;
I only have relinquished one delight
To live beneath your more habitual sway.

14 Another race hath been, and other palms are won.
Thanks to the human heart by which we live,
Thanks to its tenderness, its joys and fears,
To me the meanest flower that blows can give
Thoughts that do often lie too deep for tears.

15 Stern daughter of the voice of God!
O Duty! if that name thou love
Who art a light to guide, a rod
To check the erring and reprove.
Ode to Duty (1807)

16 Thou dost preserve the stars from wrong;
And the most ancient heavens, through Thee, are fresh
  and strong.

17   Sweetest melodies
Are those by distance made more sweet.
Personal Talk (1807), ii. See 158:21

18 There's something in a flying horse,
There's something in a huge balloon;
But through the clouds I'll never float
Until I have a little Boat,
Shaped like the crescent moon.
Peter Bell (1819), prologue, l.1

19 A primrose by a river's brim
A yellow primrose was to him,
And it was nothing more.
pt.i, l.249

1 He gave a groan, and then another,
Of that which went before the brother,
And then he gave a third.
l.443

2 Is it a party in a parlour?
Cramm'd just as they on earth were cramm'd—
Some sipping punch, some sipping tea,
But, as you by their faces see,
All silent and all damn'd!
(pt.i, st.66 in MS of 1819, later omitted)

3 Physician art thou?—one, all eyes,
Philosopher!—a fingering slave,
One that would peep and botanize
Upon his mother's grave?
A Poet's Epitaph (1800)

4 A reasoning, self-sufficing thing,
An intellectual All-in-all!

5 In common things that round us lie
Some random truths he can impart,—
The harvest of a quiet eye,
That broods and sleeps on his own heart.

But he is weak; both Man and Boy,
Hath been an idler in the land;
Contented if he might enjoy
The things which others understand.

—Come hither in thy hour of strength;
Come, weak as is a breaking wave.

6 I recoil and droop, and seek repose
In listlessness from vain perplexity,
Unprofitably travelling toward the grave.
The Prelude (1850), bk.i, l.265

7 Made one long bathing of a summer's day.
l.290

8 Fair seed-time had my soul, and I grew up
Fostered alike by beauty and by fear.
l.301

9   When the deed was done
I heard among the solitary hills
Low breathings coming after me, and sounds
Of undistinguishable motion, steps
Almost as silent as the turf they trod.
l.321

10   Though mean
Our object and inglorious, yet the end
Was not ignoble.
l.328

11 Dust as we are, the immortal spirit grows
Like harmony in music; there is a dark
Inscrutable workmanship that reconciles
Discordant elements, makes them cling together
In one society.
l.340

12   The grim shape
Towered up between me and the stars, and still,
For so it seemed, with purpose of its own
And measured motion like a living thing,
Strode after me.
l.382

13   For many days, my brain
Worked with a dim and undetermined sense
Of unknown modes of being.
l.391

14   Huge and mighty forms that do not live
Like living men, moved slowly through the mind
By day, and were a trouble to my dreams.
l.398

15   I was taught to feel, perhaps too much,
The self-sufficing power of Solitude.
bk.ii, l.76

16   To thee
Science appears but, what in truth she is,
Not as our glory and our absolute boast,
But as a succedaneum, and a prop
To our infirmity.
l.211

17   Where the statue stood
Of Newton, with his prism and silent face,
The marble index of a mind for ever
Voyaging through strange seas of Thought, alone.
bk.iii, l.61

18   Spirits overwrought
Were making night do penance for a day
Spent in a round of strenuous idleness.
bk.iv, l.376

19 Even forms and substances are circumfused
By that transparent veil with light divine,
And, through the turnings intricate of verse,
Present themselves as objects recognised,
In flashes, and with glory not their own.
bk.v, l.601

20   We were brothers all
In honour, as in one community,
Scholars and gentlemen.
bk.ix, l.227

21   All things have second birth;
The earthquake is not satisfied at once.
bk.x, l.83

22   In the People was my trust,
And in the virtues which mine eyes had seen.
bk.xi, l.11

23 Not in Utopia—subterranean fields,—
Or some secreted island, Heaven knows where!
But in the very world, which is the world
Of all of us,—the place where, in the end
We find our happiness, or not at all!
l.140

24   There is
One great society alone on earth:
The noble Living and the noble Dead.
l.393

25   I shook the habit off
Entirely and for ever, and again
In Nature's presence stood, as now I stand,
A sensitive being, a *creative* soul.
bk.xii, l.204

26   Imagination, which, in truth,
Is but another name for absolute power
And clearest insight, amplitude of mind,
And Reason in her most exalted mood.
bk.xiv, l.190

27 There was a roaring in the wind all night;
The rain came heavily and fell in floods;
But now the sun is rising, calm and bright.
Resolution and Independence (1807), i

28 I thought of Chatterton, the marvellous boy,

The sleepless soul, that perished in his pride;
Of him who walked in glory and in joy,
Following his plough, along the mountain side:
By our own spirits are we deified:
We poets in our youth begin in gladness;
But thereof comes in the end despondency and
    madness.
vii

1 His words came feebly, from a feeble chest,
But each in solemn order followed each,
With something of a lofty utterance drest—
Choice words, and measured phrase, above the reach
Of ordinary men; a stately speech;
Such as grave Livers do in Scotland use.
xiv

2   The fear that kills;
And hope that is unwilling to be fed;
Cold, pain, and labour, and all fleshly ills;
And mighty Poets in their misery dead.
—Perplexed, and longing to be comforted,
My question eagerly I did renew.
'How is it that you live, and what is it you do?'
xvii

3 At the corner of Wood Street, when daylight appears,
Hangs a Thrush that sings loud, it has sung for three
    years:
Poor Susan has passed by the spot, and has heard
In the silence of morning the song of the Bird.

'Tis a note of enchantment; what ails her? She sees
A mountain ascending, a vision of trees;
Bright volumes of vapour through Lothbury glide,
And a river flows on through the vale of Cheapside.
The Reverie of Poor Susan

4 I thought of Thee, my partner and my guide,
As being past away—Vain sympathies!
For, backward, Duddon! as I cast my eyes,
I see what was, and is, and will abide;
Still glides the Stream, and shall for ever glide;
The Form remains, the Function never dies.
The River Duddon (1820), xxxiv. **After-Thought**

5 Enough, if something from our hands have power
To live, and act, and serve the future hour;
And if, as toward the silent tomb we go,
Through love, through hope, and faith's transcendent
    dower,
We feel that we are greater than we know.

6 She dwelt among the untrodden ways
    Beside the springs of Dove,
A maid whom there were none to praise
    And very few to love:

A violet by a mossy stone
    Half hidden from the eye!
Fair as a star, when only one
    Is shining in the sky.

She lived unknown, and few could know
    When Lucy ceased to be;
But she is in her grave, and, oh,
    The difference to me!
She Dwelt Among the Untrodden Ways (1800)

7 She was a phantom of delight
When first she gleamed upon my sight.
She was a Phantom of Delight (1807)

8 I saw her upon nearer view,

A spirit, yet a woman too!
Her household motions light and free,
And steps of virgin liberty;
A countenance in which did meet
Sweet records, promises as sweet;
A creature not too bright or good
For human nature's daily food;
For transient sorrows, simple wiles,
Praise, blame, love, kisses, tears, and smiles.

And now I see with eye serene,
The very pulse of the machine;
A being breathing thoughtful breath,
A traveller betwixt life and death;
The reason firm, the temperate will,
Endurance, foresight, strength, and skill;
A perfect woman, nobly planned,
To warn, to comfort, and command;
And yet a spirit still, and bright
With something of angelic light.

9 For still, the more he works, the more
Do his weak ankles swell.
Simon Lee (1798)

10 A slumber did my spirit seal;
    I had no human fears:
She seemed a thing that could not feel
    The touch of earthly years.

No motion has she now, no force;
    She neither hears nor sees;
Rolled round in earth's diurnal course,
    With rocks, and stones, and trees.
A Slumber did My Spirit Seal (1800)

11 Love had he found in huts where poor men lie;
His daily teachers had been woods and rills,
The silence that is in the starry sky,
The sleep that is among the lonely hills.
Song at the Feast of Brougham Castle (1807)

12 O Man, that from thy fair and shining youth
Age might but take the things Youth needed not!
The Small Celandine (There is a flower, 1807)

13 Another year!—another deadly blow!
Another mighty Empire overthrown!
And we are left, or shall be left, alone.
Sonnets. Another year! (1807)

14 Earth has not anything to show more fair;
Dull would he be of soul who could pass by
A sight so touching in its majesty:
This City now doth, like a garment, wear
The beauty of the morning; silent, bare,
Ships, towers, domes, theatres, and temples lie
Open unto the fields, and to the sky;
All bright and glittering in the smokeless air.
Composed upon Westminster Bridge (1807)

15 Dear God! the very houses seem asleep;
And all that mighty heart is lying still!

16 A genial hearth, a hospitable board,
And a refined rusticity.
A genial hearth (1822)

17   Not choice
But habit rules the unreflecting herd.
Grant that by this (1822)

18 It is a beauteous evening, calm and free,
The holy time is quiet as a nun,

Breathless with adoration.
It is a beauteous evening (1807)

1 Dear Child! dear Girl! that walkest with me here
If thou appear untouched by solemn thought,
Thy nature is not therefore less divine.
Thou liest in Abraham's bosom all the year;
And worshipp'st at the temple's inner shrine,
God being with thee when we know it not.

2 It is not to be thought of that the Flood
Of British freedom, which, to the open sea
Of the world's praise, from dark antiquity
Hath flowed, 'with pomp of waters, unwithstood'...
Should perish.
It is not to be thought of (1807)

3   In our halls is hung
Armoury of the invincible Knights of old:
We must be free or die, who speak the tongue
That Shakespeare spake; the faith and morals hold
Which Milton held.—In everything we are sprung
Of Earth's first blood, have titles manifold.

4 Jones! as from Calais southward you and I
Went pacing side by side, this public Way
Streamed with the pomp of a too-credulous day.
Jones! as from Calais (1807). Referring to 14 July 1790.

5 Milton! thou shouldst be living at this hour:
England hath need of thee; she is a fen
Of stagnant waters: altar, sword, and pen,
Fireside, the heroic wealth of hall and bower,
Have forfeited their ancient English dower
Of inward happiness.
Milton! thou shouldst (1807)

6   Some happy tone
Of meditation, slipping in between
The beauty coming and the beauty gone.
Most sweet it is (1835)

7 Nuns fret not at their convent's narrow room;
And hermits are contented with their cells.
Nuns fret not (1807)

8 In sundry moods, 'twas pastime to be bound
Within the Sonnet's scanty plot of ground;
Pleased if some souls (for such there needs must be)
Who have felt the weight of too much liberty,
Should find some solace there, as I have found.

9 Plain living and high thinking are no more:
The homely beauty of the good old cause
Is gone; our peace, our fearful innocence,
And pure religion breathing household laws.
O friend! I know not (1807)

10 Once did she hold the gorgeous East in fee,
And was the safeguard of the West.
Once did she hold

11 Venice, the eldest Child of Liberty.
She was a maiden City, bright and free.

12 Isis and Cam, to patient Science dear!
Open your gates (1822)

13 A Poet!—He hath put his heart to school,
Nor dares to move unpropped upon the staff
Which Art hath lodged within his hand—must laugh
By precept only, and shed tears by rule.
A Poet! He hath put his heart (1842)

14 Scorn not the Sonnet; Critic, you have frowned,
Mindless of its just honours; with this key

Shakespeare unlocked his heart.
Scorn not the Sonnet (1827)

15 Surprised by joy—impatient as the Wind
I turned to share the transport—Oh! with whom
But Thee, deep buried in the silent tomb.
Surprised by joy (1815)

16 Tax not the royal Saint with vain expense,
With ill-matched aims the Architect who planned—
Albeit labouring for a scanty band
Of white-robed Scholars only—this immense
And glorious work of fine intelligence!
Give all thou canst; high Heaven rejects the lore
Of nicely-calculated less or more.
Tax not the royal Saint (1822). Of King's College Chapel, Cambridge.

17 Though fallen thyself, never to rise again,
Live, and take comfort. Thou hast left behind
Powers that will work for thee; air, earth, and skies;
There's not a breathing of the common wind
That will forget thee; thou hast great allies;
Thy friends are exultations, agonies,
And love, and man's unconquerable mind.
Toussaint, the most unhappy man (1803)

18 Two Voices are there; one is of the sea,
One of the mountains; each a mighty Voice,
In both from age to age thou didst rejoice,
They were thy chosen music, Liberty!
Two Voices are there (1807)

19 The world is too much with us; late and soon,
Getting and spending, we lay waste our powers:
Little we see in Nature that is ours.
The world is too much with us (1807)

20   Great God! I'd rather be
A Pagan suckled in a creed outworn,
So might I, standing on this pleasant lea,
Have glimpses that would make me less forlorn;
Have sight of Proteus rising from the sea,
Or hear old Triton blow his wreathed horn.
See 515:21

21 What fond and wayward thoughts will slide
Into a Lover's head!
'O mercy!' to myself I cried,
'If Lucy should be dead!'
Strange Fits of Passion (1800)

22 Up! up! my friend, and quit your books;
  Or surely you'll grow double.
The Tables Turned (1798)

23   Our meddling intellect
Misshapes the beauteous forms of things:—
  We murder to dissect.

Enough of science and of art;
  Close up these barren leaves.
Come forth, and bring with you a heart
  That watches and receives.

24 I've measured it from side to side:
'Tis three feet long and two feet wide.
The Thorn (1798), iii [early reading]

25 O blithe new-comer! I have heard,
I hear thee and rejoice.
O Cuckoo! Shall I call thee bird,
Or but a wandering voice?
To the Cuckoo (O blithe new-comer!, 1807)

26 Oft on the dappled turf at ease

I sit, and play with similes,
Loose types of things through all degrees.
To the Same Flower [Daisy] (With little here to do, 1807)

1 Type of the wise who soar, but never roam;
True to the kindred points of heaven and home!
To a Skylark (Ethereal minstrel!, 1827)

2 There's a flower that shall be mine,
'Tis the little celandine.
To the Small Celandine (Pansies, lilies, 1807)

3 Spade! with which Wilkinson hath tilled his lands,
And shaped these pleasant walks by Emont's side,
Thou art a tool of honour in my hands;
I press thee, through the yielding soil, with pride.
To the Spade of a Friend (1807)

4 But an old age, serene and bright,
And lovely as a Lapland night,
Shall lead thee to thy grave.
To a Young Lady (1802)

5 A simple child, dear brother Jim
That lightly draws its breath,
And feels its life in every limb,
What should it know of death?
We are Seven (1798). The words 'dear brother Jim' were omitted
in the 1815 edition of his poems.

6 I take my little porringer
And eat my supper there.

7 'But they are dead; those two are dead!
Their spirits are in Heaven!'
'Twas throwing words away; for still
The little Maid would have her will,
And said, 'Nay, we are seven!'

8 The Poet writes under one restriction only, namely,
that of the necessity of giving pleasure to a human
Being possessed of that information which may be
expected from him, not as a lawyer, a physician, a
mariner, an astronomer or a natural philosopher, but as
a Man.
Lyrical Ballads, preface to 2nd edn. (1802)

9 Poetry is the breath and finer spirit of all knowledge;
it is the impassioned expression which is in the
countenance of all science.

10 Poetry is the spontaneous overflow of powerful
feelings: it takes its origin from emotion recollected in
tranquillity.

11 Never forget what I believe was observed to you by
Coleridge, that every great and original writer, in
proportion as he is great and original, must himself
create the taste by which he is to be relished.
Letter to Lady Beaumont, 21 May 1807

SIR HENRY WOTTON 1568–1639

12 How happy is he born and taught
That serveth not another's will;
Whose armour is his honest thought,
And simple truth his utmost skill!
The Character of a Happy Life, i

13 Who God doth late and early pray
More of his grace than gifts to lend;
And entertains the harmless day
With a religious book, or friend.

This man is freed from servile bands,
Of hope to rise, or fear to fall:—

Lord of himself, though not of lands,
And having nothing, yet hath all.
v

14 He first deceas'd; she for a little tri'd
To live without him: lik'd it not, and di'd.
Death of Sir Albertus Moreton's Wife

15 You meaner beauties of the night,
That poorly satisfy our eyes,
More by your number, than your light;
You common people of the skies,
What are you when the moon shall rise?
On His Mistress, the Queen of Bohemia

16 In *Architecture* as in all other *Operative* Arts, the *end*
must direct the *Operation.* The *end* is to build well.
Well building hath three Conditions. *Commodity,
Firmness,* and *Delight.*
Elements of Architecture (1624), pt.I

17 Take heed of thinking, *The farther you go from the
church of Rome, the nearer you are to God.*
Izaak Walton, *Sir Henry Wotton,* in Christopher Wordsworth,
Ecclesiastical Biography (1810), vol.V, p.44; first published in
Walton's first edition of *Reliquiae Wottonianae* (1651)

18 An ambassador is an honest man sent to lie abroad for
the good of his country.
Written in the Album of Christopher Fleckmore (1604). Izaak
Walton, *Life*

SIR THOMAS WYATT 1503?–1542

19 And wilt thou leave me thus?
Say nay, say nay, for shame.
An Appeal

20 What should I say,
Since faith is dead,
And Truth away
From you is fled?
Farewell

21 They flee from me, that sometime did me seek
With naked foot, stalking in my chamber.
I have seen them gentle, tame, and meek,
That now are wild, and do not remember
That sometime they put themselves in danger
To take bread at my hand.
Remembrance

22 When her loose gown from her shoulders did fall,
And she me caught in her arms long and small,
Therewith all sweetly did me kiss
And softly said, 'Dear heart how like you this?'

23 My lute, awake! perform the last
Labour that thou and I shall waste,
An end that I have now begun;
For when this song is sung and past,
My lute, be still, for I have done.
To his Lute

WILLIAM WYCHERLEY 1640?–1716

24 A mistress should be like a little country retreat near
the town, not to dwell in constantly, but only for a
night and away.
The Country Wife (1672-3), Act I.i

25 Go to your business, I say, pleasure, whilst I go to my
pleasure, business.
Act II

26 Nay, you had both felt his desperate deadly daunting

dagger:—there are your d's for you!
The Gentleman Dancing-Master (1671-2), Act V

1 Fy! madam, do you think me so ill bred as to love a
husband?
Love in a Wood (1671), III.iv

2 You [drama critics] who scribble, yet hate all who
write...
And with faint praises one another damn.
The Plain Dealer (1677), prologue

GEORGE WYNDHAM 1863–1913

3 Over the construction of Dreadnoughts...What the
people said was, 'We want eight, and we won't wait.'
Wigan, 27 Mar. 1909

ANDREW OF WYNTOUN 1350?–1420?

4 Quhen Alysander oure kyng wes dede,
    That Scotland led in luve and le,
Away wes sons of ale and brede,
    Of wyne and wax, of gamyn and gle;
Oure gold wes changyd into lede,
    Cryst, borne into virgynyte,
Succour Scotland, and remede,
    That stad is in perplexyte.
The Orygynale Cronykil, vol.i, p.401, edn. 1795

XENOPHON c.428/7–c.354 B.C.

5 θάλαττα θάλαττα.
The sea! the sea!
Anabasis, IV.vii.24

AUGUSTIN, MARQUIS DE XIMÉNÈZ 1726–1817

6 *Attaquons dans ses eaux*
La perfide Albion!
Let us attack in her own waters perfidious Albion!
L'Ère des Français (Oct. 1793). *Poésies Révolutionnaires et*
contre-révolutionnaires (Paris, 1821), I, p.160. See 90:14

THOMAS RUSSELL YBARRA b. 1880

7 A Christian is a man who feels
Repentance on a Sunday
For what he did on Saturday
And is going to do on Monday.
The Christian (1909)

W.F. YEAMES R.A. 1835–1918

8 And when did you last see your father?
Title of painting (1878) now in the Walker Art Gallery, Liverpool

W.B. YEATS 1865–1939

9 A line will take us hours maybe;
Yet if it does not seem a moment's thought,
Our stitching and unstitching has been naught.
Adam's Curse

10 When I was young,
I had not given a penny for a song
Did not the poet sing it with such airs
That one believed he had a sword upstairs.
All Things can Tempt me

11 O body swayed to music, O brightening glance,

How can we know the dancer from the dance?
Among School Children, VIII

12 A starlit or a moonlit dome disdains
All that man is,
All mere complexities,
The fury and the mire of human veins.
Byzantium

13 That dolphin-torn, that gong-tormented sea.

14 The intellect of man is forced to choose
Perfection of the life, or of the work.
The Choice

15 Now that my ladder's gone,
I must lie down where all the ladders start,
In the foul rag-and-bone shop of the heart.
The Circus Animals' Desertion, III

16 I made my song a coat
Covered with embroideries
Out of old mythologies
From heel to throat;
But the fools caught it,
Wore it in the world's eyes
As though they'd wrought it.
Song, let them take it,
For there's more enterprise
In walking naked.
A Coat

17 The years like great black oxen tread the world,
And God the herdsman goads them on behind,
And I am broken by their passing feet.
The Countess Cathleen, Act IV

18 The Light of Lights
Looks always on the motive, not the deed,
The Shadow of Shadows on the deed alone.

19 A woman can be proud and stiff
When on love intent;
But Love has pitched his mansion in
The place of excrement;
For nothing can be sole or whole
That has not been rent.
Crazy Jane talks to the Bishop

20 Nor dread nor hope attend
A dying animal;
A man awaits his end
Dreading and hoping all.
Death

21 He knows death to the bone—
Man has created death.

22 Down by the salley gardens my love and I did meet;
She passed the salley gardens with little snow-white
    feet.
She bid me take love easy, as the leaves grow on the
    tree;
But I, being young and foolish, with her would not
    agree.

In a field by the river my love and I did stand,
And on my leaning shoulder she laid her snow-white
    hand.
She bid me take life easy, as the grass grows on the
    weirs;
But I was young and foolish, and now am full of tears.
Down by the Salley Gardens

23 She was more beautiful than thy first love,

This lady by the trees.
A Dream of Death, early version

1   I have met them at close of day
Coming with vivid faces
From counter or desk among grey
Eighteenth-century houses.
I have passed with a nod of the head
Or polite meaningless words,
And thought before I had done
Of a mocking tale or a gibe
To please a companion
Around the fire at the club,
Being certain that they and I
But lived where motley is worn:
All changed, changed utterly:
A terrible beauty is born.
Easter 1916

2   Too long a sacrifice
Can make a stone of the heart.

3   I see a schoolboy when I think of him,
With face and nose pressed to a sweet-shop window,
For certainly he sank into his grave
His senses and his heart unsatisfied,
And made—being poor, ailing and ignorant,
Shut out from all the luxury of the world,
The coarse-bred son of a livery-stable keeper—
Luxuriant song.
Ego Dominus Tuus. Of Keats.

4   Those great honey-coloured
Ramparts at your ear.
For Anne Gregory

5   Only God, my dear,
Could love you for yourself alone
And not your yellow hair.

6   Never to have lived is best, ancient writers say;
Never to have drawn the breath of life, never to have
     looked into the eye of day;
The second best's a gay goodnight and quickly turn
     away.
From 'Oedipus at Colonus'

7   The ghost of Roger Casement
Is beating on the door.
The Ghost of Roger Casement

8   But weigh this song with the great and their pride;
I made it out of a mouthful of air,
Their children's children shall say they have lied.
He thinks of those who have Spoken Evil of his Beloved

9   Had I the heavens' embroidered cloths,
Enwrought with golden and silver light,
The blue and the dim and the dark cloths
Of night and light and the half-light,
I would spread the cloths under your feet:
But I, being poor, have only my dreams;
I have spread my dreams under your feet;
Tread softly because you tread on my dreams.
He wishes for the Cloths of Heaven

10   I mourn for that most lonely thing; and yet God's will
     be done:
I knew a phoenix in my youth, so let them have their
     day.
His Phoenix

11   The light of evening, Lissadell,
Great windows open to the south

Two girls in silk kimonos, both
Beautiful, one a gazelle.
In Memory of Eva Gore-Booth and Con Markiewicz

12   The innocent and the beautiful
Have no enemy but time.

13   I am accustomed to their lack of breath,
But not that my dear friend's dear son,
Our Sidney and our perfect man,
Could share in that discourtesy of death.
In Memory of Major Robert Gregory, VI

14   Out-worn heart, in a time out-worn,
Come clear of the nets of wrong and right;
Laugh, heart, again in the grey twilight,
Sigh, heart, again in the dew of the morn.
Into the Twilight

15   Nor law, nor duty bade me fight,
Nor public men, nor cheering crowds,
A lonely impulse of delight
Drove to this tumult in the clouds;
I balanced all, brought all to mind,
The years to come seemed waste of breath,
A waste of breath the years behind
In balance with this life, this death.
An Irish Airman Forsees his Death

16   None other knows what pleasures man
     At table or in bed.
What shall I do for pretty girls
     Now my old bawd is dead?
John Kinsella's Lament for Mrs. Mary Moore

17   I will arise and go now, and go to Innisfree,
And a small cabin build there, of clay and wattles
     made:
Nine bean-rows will I have there, a hive for the
     honey-bee,
And live alone in the bee-loud glade.

And I shall have some peace there, for peace comes
     dropping slow,
Dropping from the veils of the morning to where the
     cricket sings;
There midnight's all a-glimmer, and noon a purple
     glow,
And evening full of the linnet's wings.

I will arise and go now, for always night and day
I hear lake water lapping with low sounds by the
     shore;
While I stand on the roadway, or on the pavements
     gray,
I hear it in the deep heart's core.
The Lake Isle of Innisfree

18   Of a land where even the old are fair,
And even the wise are merry of tongue.
The Land of Heart's Desire

19   Land of Heart's Desire,
Where beauty has no ebb, decay no flood,
But joy is wisdom, Time an endless song.

20   What lively lad most pleasured me
Of all that with me lay?
I answer that I gave my soul
And loved in misery,
But had great pleasure with a lad
That I loved bodily.

Flinging from his arms I laughed
To think his passion such

He fancied that I gave a soul
Did but our bodies touch,
And laughed upon his breast to think
Beast gave beast as much.
A Last Confession

1 A sudden blow: the great wings beating still
Above the staggering girl, her thighs caressed
By the dark webs, her nape caught in his bill,
He holds her hapless breast upon his breast.

How can those terrified vague fingers push
The feathered glory from her loosening thighs?
Leda and the Swan

2 A shudder in the loins engenders there
The broken wall, the burning roof and tower
And Agamemnon dead.

3 Our master Caesar is in the tent,
Where the maps are spread,
His eyes fixed upon nothing,
A hand under his head.
Like a long-legged fly upon the stream
His mind moves upon silence.
Long-legged Fly

4 What were all the world's alarms
To mighty Paris when he found
Sleep upon a golden bed
That first dawn in Helen's arms?
Lullaby

5 In the Junes that were warmer than these are, the
     waves were more gay,
When I was a boy with never a crack in my heart.
The Meditation of the Old Fisherman

6 Think where man's glory most begins and ends,
And say my glory was I had such friends.
The Municipal Gallery Revisited, VII

7 Why, what could she have done, being what she is?
Was there another Troy for her to burn?
No Second Troy

8 Where, where but here have Pride and Truth,
That long to give themselves for wage,
To shake their wicked sides at youth
Restraining reckless middle age?
On hearing that the Students of our New University have joined
the Agitation against Immoral Literature

9 A pity beyond all telling
Is hid in the heart of love.
The Pity of Love

10 Rose of all Roses, Rose of all the World!
The Rose of Battle

11 That is no country for old men. The young
In one another's arms, birds in the trees
—Those dying generations—at their song,
The salmon-falls, the mackerel-crowded seas,
Fish, flesh, or fowl, commend all summer long
Whatever is begotten, born, and dies.
Sailing to Byzantium, I

12 An aged man is but a paltry thing,
A tattered coat upon a stick, unless
Soul clap its hands and sing, and louder sing
For every tatter in its mortal dress.
II

13 And therefore I have sailed the seas and come
To the holy city of Byzantium.

14 Bald heads, forgetful of their sins,

Old, learned, respectable bald heads
Edit and annotate the lines
That young men tossing on their beds,
Rhymed out in love's despair
To flatter beauty's ignorant ear.

All shuffle there; all cough in ink;
All wear the carpet with their shoes;
All think what other people think;
All know the man their neighbour knows.
Lord, what would they say
Did their Catullus walk that way?
The Scholars

15 Turning and turning in the widening gyre
The falcon cannot hear the falconer;
Things fall apart; the centre cannot hold;
Mere anarchy is loosed upon the world,
The blood-dimmed tide is loosed, and everywhere
The ceremony of innocence is drowned;
The best lack all conviction, while the worst
Are full of passionate intensity.
The Second Coming

16 And what rough beast, its hour come round at last,
Slouches towards Bethlehem to be born?

17 A woman of so shining loveliness
That men threshed corn at midnight by a tress.
The Secret Rose

18 When shall the stars be blown about the sky,
Like the sparks blown out of a smithy, and die?
Surely thine hour has come, thy great wind blows,
Far-off, most secret, and inviolate Rose?

19 Was it for this the wild geese spread
The grey wing upon every tide;
For this that all that blood was shed,
For this Edward Fitzgerald died,
And Robert Emmet and Wolfe Tone,
All that delirium of the brave?
Romantic Ireland's dead and gone,
It's with O'Leary in the grave.
September 1913

20 I thought no more was needed
Youth to prolong
Than dumb-bell and foil
To keep the body young.
O who could have foretold
That the heart grows old?
A Song

21 And pluck till time and times are done
The silver apples of the moon
The golden apples of the sun.
The Song of Wandering Aengus

22 A girl arose that had red mournful lips
And seemed the greatness of the world in tears,
Doomed like Odysseus and the labouring ships
And proud as Priam murdered with his peers;

Arose, and on the instant clamorous eaves,
A climbing moon upon an empty sky,
And all that lamentation of the leaves,
Could but compose man's image and his cry.
The Sorrow of Love

23 You think it horrible that lust and rage
Should dance attention upon my old age;
They were not such a plague when I was young;

What else have I to spur me into song?
The Spur

1 Pythagoras planned it. Why did the people stare?
His numbers, though they moved or seemed to move
In marble or in bronze, lacked character.
But boys and girls, pale from the imagined love
Of solitary beds, knew what they were,
That passion could bring character enough,
And pressed at midnight in some public place
Live lips upon a plummet-measured face.

No! Greater than Pythagoras, for the men
That with a mallet or a chisel modelled these
Calculations that look but casual flesh, put down
All Asiatic vague immensities,
And not the banks of oars that swam upon
The many-headed foam at Salamis.
Europe put off that foam when Phidias
Gave women dreams and dreams their looking-glass.
The Statues

2 When Pearse summoned Cuchulain to his side,
What stalked through the Post Office? What intellect,
What calculation, number, measurement, replied?
We Irish, born into that ancient sect
But thrown upon this filthy modern tide
And by its formless spawning fury wrecked,
Climb to our proper dark, that we may trace
The lineaments of a plummet-measured face.

3 Swift has sailed into his rest;
Savage indignation there
Cannot lacerate his breast.
Imitate him if you dare,
World-besotted traveller; he
Served human liberty.
Swift's Epitaph. See 528:12

4 But was there ever dog that praised his fleas?
*To a Poet, who would have me Praise certain Bad Poets,
Imitators of His and Mine*

5 I know what wages beauty gives,
How hard a life her servant lives,
Yet praise the winters gone:
There is not a fool can call me friend,
And I may dine at journey's end
With Landor and with Donne.
To a Young Beauty

6 Red Rose, proud Rose, sad Rose of all my days!
To the Rose upon the Rood of Time

7 Measurement began our might.
Under Ben Bulben, IV

8 Irish poets, learn your trade,
Sing whatever is well made,
Scorn the sort now growing up
All out of shape from toe to top,
Their unremembering hearts and heads
Base-born products of base beds.
Sing the peasantry, and then
Hard-riding country gentlemen,
The holiness of monks, and after
Porter-drinkers' randy laughter.
V

9 Cast your mind on other days
That we in coming days may be
Still the indomitable Irishry.

10 Under bare Ben Bulben's head

In Drumcliff churchyard Yeats is laid...
On limestone quarried near the spot
By his command these words are cut:

> *Cast a cold eye*
> *On life, on death.*
> *Horseman, pass by!*

VI

11 While on the shop and street I gazed
My body of a sudden blazed;
And twenty minutes more or less
It seemed, so great my happiness,
That I was blessèd and could bless.
Vacillation

12 When you are old and gray and full of sleep,
And nodding by the fire, take down this book,
And slowly read, and dream of the soft look
Your eyes had once, and of their shadows deep;

How many loved your moments of glad grace,
And loved your beauty with love false or true,
But one man loved the pilgrim soul in you,
And loved the sorrows of your changing face;

And bending down beside the glowing bars,
Murmur, a little sadly, how Love fled
And paced upon the mountains overhead
And hid his face amid a crowd of stars.
When you are Old

13 My son is now between nine and ten and should begin
Greek at once...Do not teach him one word of Latin.
The Roman people were the classical decadence, their
literature form without matter. They destroyed Milton,
the French seventeenth and our eighteenth century, and
our schoolmasters even today read Greek with Latin
eyes.
Explorations, sel. Mrs. W.B. Yeats (1962), II.iv. **A Letter to
Michael's schoolmaster**

14 Greece, could we but approach it with eyes as young
as its own, might renew our youth.

EDWARD YOUNG 1683–1765

15   Be wise with speed;
A fool at forty is a fool indeed.
Love of Fame: The Universal Passion (1725-8), Sat.ii, l.281

16 For who does nothing with a better grace?
Sat.iv, l.86

17 With skill she vibrates her eternal tongue,
For ever most divinely in the wrong.
Sat.vi, l.106

18 For her own breakfast she'll project a scheme,
Nor take her tea without a stratagem.
l.187

19 One to destroy, is murder by the law;
And gibbets keep the lifted hand in awe;
To murder thousands, takes a specious name,
War's glorious art, and gives immortal fame.
Sat.vii, l.55

20 How commentators each dark passage shun,
And hold their farthing candle to the sun.
l.97

21 Tir'd Nature's sweet restorer, balmy sleep!
He, like the world, his ready visit pays
Where fortune smiles; the wretched he forsakes.
The Complaint: Night Thoughts (1742-5), Night i, l.1

1 Night, sable goddess! from her ebon throne
In rayless majesty, now stretches forth
Her leaden sceptre o'er a slumb'ring world.
l.18

2   We take no note of Time
But from its Loss.
l.55

3 Be wise to-day; 'tis madness to defer.
l.390

4 Procrastination is the thief of time.
l.393

5 At thirty a man suspects himself a fool;
Knows it at forty, and reforms his plan;
At fifty chides his infamous delay,
Pushes his prudent purpose to resolve;
In all the magnanimity of thought
Resolves; and re-resolves; then dies the same.
l.417

6 All men think all men mortal, but themselves.
l.424

7   Beautiful as sweet!
And young as beautiful! and soft as young!
And gay as soft! and innocent as gay.
Night iii, l.81

8 Shall our pale, wither'd hands be still stretch'd out,
Trembling, at once, with Eagerness and Age?
With Avarice, and Convulsions grasping hand?
Grasping at Air! for what has Earth beside?
Man wants but little; nor that little, long.
Night iv, l.118

9 A God all mercy is a God unjust.
l.233

10 By night an atheist half believes a God.
Night v, l.176

11 To know the world, not love her, is thy point,
She gives but little, nor that little, long.
Night viii, l.1276

12 Devotion! daughter of astronomy!
An undevout astronomer is mad.
Night ix, l.769

13 Life is the desert, life the solitude;
Death joins us to the great majority.
The Revenge (1721), Act IV

14 You are so witty, profligate, and thin,
At once we think thee Milton, Death, and Sin.
Epigram on Voltaire

GEORGE W. YOUNG 1846–1919

15 Your lips, on my own, when they printed 'Farewell',
Had never been soiled by the 'beverage of hell';
But they come to me now with the bacchanal sign,
And the lips that touch liquor must never touch mine.
The Lips That Touch Liquor Must Never Touch Mine; also
attr., in a different form, to Harriet A. Glazebrook

ISRAEL ZANGWILL 1864–1926

16 Scratch the Christian and you find the pagan—spoiled.
Children of the Ghetto (1892), bk.ii, ch.6

17 America is God's Crucible, the great Melting-Pot
where all the races of Europe are melting and
re-forming!
The Melting Pot (1908), Act I

EMILIANO ZAPATA 1879?–1919

18 *Muchos de ellos, por complacer a tiranos, por un
puñado de monedas, o por cohecho o soborno, están
derramando la sangre de sus hermanos.*
Many of them, so as to curry favour with tyrants, for a
fistful of coins, or through bribery or corruption, are
making the blood of their brothers spurt forth.
Of the *maderistas* who, in Zapata's view, had betrayed the
revolutionary cause. *Plan de Ayala,* 28 Nov. 1911, para.10

ÉMILE ZOLA 1840–1902

19 *Ne me regardez plus comme ça, parce que vous allez
vous user les yeux.*
Don't go on looking at me like that, because you'll
wear your eyes out.
La Bête Humaine (1889–90), ch.5

20 *J'accuse.*
I accuse.
Title of an open letter to the President of the French Republic, in
connection with the Dreyfus case, published in *L'Aurore,* 13 Jan.
1898

INDEX

NOTE. The order of the index both in the keywords and in the entries following each keyword is strictly alphabetical. Singular and plural nouns (including their possessive forms) are grouped separately: for 'with some old lover's ghost' see 'lover'; for 'at lovers' perjuries' see 'lovers'. All spellings and word forms appear in the index precisely as they do in the main text.

Foreign words are included in the general alphabetical scheme. A separate Greek index follows the main index.

The references show the author's name, usually in an abbreviated form, followed by the page and item numbers: 163:15 = quotation 15 on page 163.

To save space, the definite and indefinite articles, and the words Oh, O, but, and, for, as, have been dropped from the beginning of most entries, and the alphabetical order is thus decided by more significant words: 'And is it true' is shown as 'is it true'.

Les a. ont toujours tort   DEST 175:14
Absolute: A. across the hall   BELL 39:28
a. power corrupts   ACTON 1:5
A. rule   MILT 347:22
Be a. for death   SHAK 464:8
foreknowledge a.   MILT 346:19
hath her content so a.   SHAK 474:20
So a. she seems   MILT 349:7
yet how peremptory and a.   ELIOT 201:30
absolutism: a. moderated by assassination
                                         ANON 5:5
absolv'd: half a. who has confess'd
                                         PRIOR 400:18
absolve: be willing to a. us all   VILL 557:4
absolved: a. from all duty to his   PEAC 370:18
absolvitur: damnatur ubi nocens a.
                                         PUBL 402:5
absouldre: que tous nous veuille a.
                                         VILL 557:4
Abstain: A. from fleshly lusts   BIBLE 80:24
Abstinence: A. is as easy to me   JOHN 280:22
A. sows sand all over   BLAKE 86:20
lean and sallow A.   MILT 341:16
made almost a sin of a.   DRYD 195:28
total a. is easier than   AUG 21:22
abstinent: Multi quidem facilius se a.
                                         AUG 21:22
Abstract: A. liberty   BURKE 109:21
abstracted: disposed to a. meditation
                                         JOHN 281:40
abstracts: a. and brief chronicles
                                         SHAK 432:25
abstulit: ut me malus a. error   VIRG 560:4
absurd: a. but some philosopher   CIC 151:17
It is as a. to argue men   NEWM 362:8
Proving a. all written   BROW 100:5
rather a. about the past   BEER 37:12
scientific faith's a.   BROW 100:21
thing becomes a.   HOPE 255:27
absurdity: dull without a single a.
                                         GOLD 232:31
abundance: a. of the heart the mouth
                                         BIBLE 66:9
he shall have a.   BIBLE 68:4
sound of a. of rain   BIBLE 51:10
upon us the a. of thy mercy   PRAY 386:20
were promised a. for all   KIPL 299:16
Whose strength's a. weakens   SHAK 493:2
abuse: a. in public and to read   BORR 89:26
If it is a.   SHER 505:21
more dangerous the a.   BURKE 109:1
will you a. our patience   CIC 151:25
abused: a. it more   BYRON 123:26
man's character is to be a.   THAC 545:24
much a. as this sentence   SELD 419:25
abuses: attended with considerable a.
                                         BURKE 109:3
stamp out a.   VOLT 561:11
abusing: old a. of God's patience   SHAK 469:5
Abydos: Sestos and A. of her breasts
                                         DONNE 188:14
abysm: backward and a. of time   SHAK 484:24
abyss: a. gazes also into you   NIET 363:10
breathless Nature's dark a.   WORD 578:8
edge of the nuclear a.   STEV 520:22
into the bottomless a.   WALEY 562:2
secrets of th' a. to spy   GRAY 235:19
abysses: a. are all so shallow   JAMES 271:32
in its a. of ineptitude   HOUS 266:15
Abyssinian: It was an A. maid   COL 156:30
Academe: there the olive grove of A.
                                         MILT 350:8
truth in the groves of A.   HOR 259:4
academes: ground, the books, the a.
                                         SHAK 457:6
academy: groves of *their* a.   BURKE 111:12
Mr Wackford Squeers's A.   DICK 179:34
accent: a. of a coming Foot   DICK 183:18
L'a. du pays où l'on est   LA R 310:17
with a shrill and sad a.   CLAR 152:20

accents: a. of an expiring saint   STER 520:9
A. uncertain   BROW 100:35
a. yet unknown   SHAK 450:5
caught his clear a.   BROW 102:5
come refin'd with th'a.   DAN 170:23
follow with a. sweet   CAMP 129:18
Loved a. are soon forgot   SHEL 501:21
acceptable: a. unto God   BIBLE 75:15
a. year of the Lord   BIBLE 60:8
be alway a. in thy sight   PRAY 390:13
this is a. with God   BIBLE 80:26
accepted: a. wit has but to say 'Pass
                                         GILB 229:10
accepteth: God now a. thy works   BIBLE 55:28
accepting: Charms by a.   POPE 377:27
accepts: Man a. the compromise   KIPL 299:5
accident: By many a happy a.   MIDD 338:19
disqualified by the a. of death   CHES 148:5
have it found out by a.   LAMB 308:2
of a. nor dart of chance   SHAK 476:16
Accidents: A. will occur in the
best-regulated   DICK 177:15
chapter of a.   CHES 146:2
chapter of a. is the longest   WILK 574:5
Of moving a. by flood   SHAK 473:25
that he runs into a.   MARQ 331:2
Which shackles a.   SHAK 423:20
accipitrine: will a. to pursue   THOM 548:2
accommodatin: exceedin a. character
                                         WARD 564:21
*accommodements: trouve avec lui des
a.*   MOL 353:26
accompany: a. me with a pure heart
                                         PRAY 384:10
accomplice: signifies a ready-made a.
                                         PEAC 370:14
accomplished: a. man to his finger-tips
                                         HOR 262:4
desire a. is sweet   BIBLE 53:37
material creation is a.   JOYCE 286:18
what can be a. in a week   STEV 522:8
accomplishments: a. give lustre   CHES 145:31
accord: a. to make our common
supplications   PRAY 385:8
Should of his own a.   ANON 8:24
according: each a. to his abilities MARX 333:5
accosted: should then have a. her
                                         SHAK 489:27
account: a. wife and children   BACON 26:32
accurate and exhaustive a.   BEER 37:13
sent to my a.   SHAK 431:12
Such I a. thy love   SHAK 459:8
they shall give a. thereof   BIBLE 66:10
accuracy: of a. must be sacrificed   JOHN 281:4
accurate: a. and exhaustive account
                                         BEER 37:13
accurs'd: themselves a. they were not
here   SHAK 445:3
accursed: a. power which stands   BELL 39:21
Accurst: A. be he that first invented
                                         MARL 330:6
accuse: J'a.   ZOLA 588:20
yet I could a. me of such   SHAK 433:11
accused: apology before you be a.
                                         CHAR 140:17
security to persons who are a.   DENM 174:22
than a. of deficiency   JOHN 277:9
Accuser: not my A., but my judges
                                         NEWM 361:15
accustomed: a. to their lack of breath
                                         YEATS 585:13
ace: a. of trumps up his sleeve   LAB 306:10
was about to play the a.   FIELD 211:3
aces: hands that hold the a.   BETJ 42:13
Achaeans: A. have suffered for so
                                         HOMER 253:28
myriad sufferings for the A.   HOMER 253:26
Achates: fidus quae tela gerebat A.
                                         VIRG 557:12
ache: has made my heart to a.   BLAKE 87:7

ached: never has a. with a heart   SWIN 529:7
Acheronta: A. movebo   VIRG 559:5
aches: That the sense a. at thee   SHAK 476:19
achieve: a. of, the mastery of   HOPK 257:5
I shall a. in time   GILB 227:5
Our patience will a. more   BURKE 111:24
to a. that I have done   MAL 327:20
achieved: It is a.   BIBLE 83:23
achievements: How my a. mock me
                                         SHAK 487:8
achieving: Still a., still pursuing LONG 317:5
Achilles: A.' cursed anger sing   HOMER 253:26
A. wears his wit in his   SHAK 486:29
armour stripped from A.   VIRG 558:5
I've stood upon A.' tomb   BYRON 123:13
name A. assumed   BROW 97:14
see the great A.   TENN 544:3
Stand in the trench, A.   SHAW 498:28
to work out A. his armour   BROW 95:18
Aching: A., shaking   ROCH 407:3
Achitophel: these the false A. was first
                                         DRYD 194:6
Achivi: reges plectuntur A.   HOR 258:12
Acids: A. stain you   PARK 368:18
Acidulous: A. vestals   STEV 521:25
Ackney Marshes: You could see to 'A.
                                         BAT 35:3
acknowledge: a. thee to be the Lord
                                         PRAY 384:16
I a. my faults   PRAY 393:4
acorns: Tall oaks from little a.   EVER 209:10
wringing lilies from the a.   POUND 383:2
Acquaintance: A. I would have   COWL 164:14
first an a., next a mistress   CHEK 145:5
have a visiting a. with   SHER 506:17
hope our a. may be a long   DICK 182:5
I do not make a new a.   JOHN 279:25
love good creditable a.   SWIFT 526:15
man does not make new a.   JOHN 274:15
Should auld a. be forgot   BURNS 112:30
acquainted: a. with grief   BIBLE 59:21
been one a. with the night   FROST 218:27
Love and I were well a.   GILB 228:38
Sentiment is what I am not a.   FLEM 215:2
she and I were long a.   HOUS 265:8
acquent: When we were first a.
                                         BURNS 114:12
acquiesce: remains but to a. with silence
                                         JOHN 281:9
acquitted: guilty party is a.   PUBL 402:5
acre: furlongs of sea for an a.   SHAK 484:24
acres: few paternal a. bound   POPE 380:23
lass that has a. o' charms   BURNS 114:6
Three a. and a cow   COLL 158:11
acrimonious: a. and surly republican
                                         JOHN 281:33
Acroceraunian: In the A. mountains
                                         SHEL 500:2
Acrostic: peaceful province in A. Land
                                         DRYD 196:35
act: a. in the living Present   LONG 317:3
a. of darkness with her   SHAK 454:18
a. of dying is not of importance   JOHN 275:31
A. of God was defined   HERB 246:19
A. upon it   GILB 225:27
I could a. as well as he   FIEL 211:32
in any A. of Parliament   HERB 246:14
in itself almost an a.   ROSS 410:7
it is the foolishest a.   BROW 96:33
made honest by an a.   JONS 283:25
motion And the a.   ELIOT 203:10
nobility is the a. of time   BACON 26:39
princes to a.   SHAK 443:3
prologues to the swelling a.   SHAK 458:19
Regulations A.   WILDE 572:12
same in thine own a.   SHAK 459:8
sins they love to a.   SHAK 478:3
sleep an a. or two   SHAK 448:4
To see him a.   COL 157:31
what a., That roars so   SHAK 435:5

within the meaning of the A.   ANON 4:21
Your play's hard to a.   CHEK 144:26
acte: dernier a. est sanglant   PASC 369:8
acted: reasoned or a. consequentially
                                    CHES 145:25
this our lofty scene be a.   SHAK 450:5
acti: Iucundi a. labores   CIC 151:18
laudator temporis a.   HOR 257:21
Acting: A. is therefore the lowest
                                    MOORE 355:17
a. of a dreadful thing   SHAK 449:6
danger chiefly lies in a.   CHUR 148:21
when he was off he was a.   GOLD 231:20
Action: A. is transitory   WORD 577:2
cold for a.   SHAK 443:7
end of man is an a.   CARL 132:16
imitate the a. of the tiger   SHAK 443:21
In a. faithful   POPE 378:6
Is lust in a.   SHAK 495:7
Let a single completed a.   BOIL 89:11
lose the name of a.   SHAK 433:8
suit the a. to the word   SHAK 433:17
Thought is the child of A.   DISR 186:41
to you the a. of Russia   CHUR 149:28
with the liberty of a.   MILL 339:6
actions: a. that a man might play
                                    SHAK 429:25
best of all our a. tend   BUTL 118:16
Great a. are not always   BUTL 117:28
Great a. speak great minds   FLET 215:18
laugh at human a.   SPIN 517:7
leurs plus sérieuses a.   MONT 354:17
my a. are my ministers'   CHAR 140:23
Only the a. of the just   SHIR 507:4
person doing interesting a.   BAG 28:30
poor centre of a man's a.   BACON 27:36
Should in his a. be so ill   MASS 335:23
Words are also a.   EMER 207:28
active: *a.* line on a walk moving KLEE 305:15
a. Principle   WORD 577:17
active-valiant: More a. or more
valiant-young   SHAK 440:16
actor: Anybody may see he is an a.
                                    FIEL 211:32
Like a dull a. now   SHAK 428:1
unperfect a. on the stage   SHAK 493:2
well-grac'd a. leaves the stage   SHAK 480:10
actors: a. or spectators   SHEL 499:13
best a. in the world   SHAK 432:20
actresses: a. excite my amorous JOHN 274:2
acts: a. being seven ages   SHAK 425:24
first four a. already past   BERK 41:20
He who desires but a. not   BLAKE 88:15
Illustrious a. high raptures   WALL 562:12
nameless, unremembered, a.   WORD 578:4
Our a. our angels are   FLET 215:13
person a. his own creations   BROW 103:4
That all your a. are queens   SHAK 491:27
actum: Nil a. credens   LUCAN 319:24
acu: Tetigisti a.   PLAU 374:15
Acus: Pulveris Tormentarii, et A.
                                    BACON 28:9
Ada: A.! sole daughter of my   BYRON 120:17
adage: poor cat i' the a.   SHAK 459:8
Adam: A. from his fair spouse   MILT 348:7
A. Had 'em   ANON 4:12
A., the goodliest man   MILT 347:24
A. was a gardener   KIPL 299:15
A. was a gardener   SHAK 446:13
A. was but human   TWAIN 554:17
A. was not deceived   BIBLE 79:10
deep sleep to fall upon A.   BIBLE 45:11
gardener A. and his wife   TENN 537:29
hold up A.'s profession   SHAK 436:22
in A. all die   BIBLE 76:22
nicknamed A.   CLOU 153:14
old A. in this Child   PRAY 388:9
Old A.'s likeness   SHAK 479:18
Old A. the carrion crow   BEDD 36:26
our father A. knew   KIPL 298:17

past Eve and A.'s   JOYCE 286:2
penalty of A.   SHAK 424:31
rubbish of an A.   SOUTH 513:12
son of A. and of Eve   PRIOR 400:25
That A. was not Adamant   HOOD 255:3
Which did in A. fail   NEWM 362:13
Whilst A. slept   ANON 8:21
whipp'd the offending A.   SHAK 443:5
adamant: frame of a.   JOHN 282:30
That Adam was not A.   HOOD 255:3
adapts: reasonable man a. himself
                                    SHAW 498:1
adazzle: sweet, sour; a., dim   HOPK 256:23
added: then a. them up   CARR 134:18
things shall be a. unto you   BIBLE 64:31
Adder: A.'s fork   SHAK 462:3
a. that stoppeth her ears   PRAY 393:17
go upon the lion and a.   PRAY 395:22
like an a. to its hole   PLOM 374:19
stingeth like an a.   BIBLE 54:24
that brings forth the a.   SHAK 449:4
adders: What a. came to shed their
                                    SWIN 529:15
addeth: Translation's thief that a.
                                    MARV 332:17
addicted: Salteena was not very a. ASHF 17:9
addiction: prisoners of a.   ILL 270:5
Addison: A. approved   BUDG 106:19
nights to the volumes of A.   JOHN 281:38
addled: announce but that a. delusion
                                    ELIOT 201:2
Addresses: A. are given to us to conceal
                                    SAKI 413:12
adepts: a. in the speaking trade CHUR 148:27
Adeste: A., fideles   ANON 10:4
Adieu: A., she cries   GAY 223:30
fumbles up into a loose a.   SHAK 487:12
thou vain world, a.   CANN 130:6
ad infinitum: so proceed a.   SWIFT 528:5
adire: homini contingit a. Corinthum
                                    HOR 258:21
Adlestrop: I remember A.   THOM 547:16
administer'd: Whate'er is best a. is
                                    POPE 379:20
administration: a. of the government
                                    SWIFT 526:4
made a criticism of a.   BAG 28:23
security for its impartial a.   PEEL 371:5
admiral: kill an a. from time   VOLT 561:1
Admirals: A. all   NEWB 361:3
A., extoll'd for standing   COWP 166:23
admiralty: blood be the price of a. KIPL 303:4
admirari: Nil a. prope res est una
                                    HOR 258:17
admiration: disease of a.   MAC 323:10
great in a. as herself   SHAK 448:3
admir'd: not blush so to be a.   WALL 562:14
admire: cannot possibly a. them
                                    WILDE 573:23
happiness is to a. without desiring
                                    BRAD 91:11
Not to a. is all the art   BYRON 123:18
Not to a., is all the art   POPE 380:10
scarce begun to a. the one   DRYD 198:5
th' a. his sleight of hand   BUTL 118:6
to a. except his opinion   FRY 219:24
to a., we should not understand   CONG 160:9
Where none a.   LYTT 321:22
admired: all who understood a.   PRAED 384:6
That she might a. be   SHAK 491:4
admirers: he became his a.   AUDEN 19:3
admires: a. mean things is a Snob
                                    THAC 545:4
admiring: cure for a. the House of Lords
                                    BAG 29:6
admit: never to a. them in your AUST 23:19
admits: genuine night a. no ray DRYD 196:34
admittance: No a. till the week after
                                    CARR 136:9
admonish: Fools they a.   COWP 168:9

yet I a. you   GILB 226:8
ado: a. is about himself   TROL 552:18
heathen make much a.   PRAY 392:20
Adonais: blazoning the name Of A.
                                    SHEL 500:15
I weep for A.   SHEL 499:3
What A. is   ~ SHEL 499:25
Adonis: While smooth A. from his
                                    MILT 345:17
adopted: By roads 'not a.'   BETJ 44:8
adoption: received the Spirit of a. BIBLE 75:8
adorable: strongly a. tennis-girl's hand
                                    BETJ 44:8
Adoration: A. all the ranks   SMART 509:2
a., duty, and observance   SHAK 426:29
Breathless with a.   WORD 581:18
Adorations: Desires and A.   SHEL 499:9
adore: a. him, Christ the Lord   ANON 10:5
may command where I a.   SHAK 489:13
positively a. Miss Dombey   DICK 178:1
soldiers we alike a.   QUAR 403:14
would a. my gifts instead   HERB 248:7
adored: I was a. once too   SHAK 488:24
adoremus: Venite a. Dominum   ANON 10:5
adorings: Soft a. from their loves
                                    KEATS 289:12
adorn: none that he did not a.   JOHN 277:13
adorned: Christ a. and beautified
                                    PRAY 388:25
when unadorned a. the most   THOM 549:17
adornings: made their bends a.   SHAK 422:3
adornment: a. of his person he devotes
                                    THOM 549:6
adorns: a. my shoes   HOUS 266:10
adread: Yet was I sore a.   THOM 548:10
Adriatic: spouseless A. mourns her
                                    BYRON 121:3
Adsuitur: A. pannus   HOR 257:11
Adsum: 'A!' and fell back   THAC 545:12
adulation: betrayed him by their a.
                                    BURKE 109:5
Adult: Dreaming of A. Education BETJ 44:11
adulteration: quite adultery, but a.
                                    BYRON 123:35
adulterer: statue of the onehandled a.
                                    JOYCE 286:25
adulteries: Than all the a. of art JONS 283:27
adulterous: evil and a. generation
                                    BIBLE 66:11
adultery: die for a.   SHAK 455:16
Do not a. commit   CLOU 153:27
gods a.   BYRON 122:9
Not quite a.   BYRON 123:35
Thou shalt not commit a.   BIBLE 47:24
woman taken in a.   BIBLE 72:9
Adultress: very good eye at an A. AUST 23:30
advance: is somewhat to a.   POPE 380:8
retrograde if it does not a.   GIBB 224:29
advances: had to decline their a. ELIOT 201:11
advantage: a. of the preacher than
                                    BURKE 108:14
A. rarely comes of it   CLOU 153:27
French are with equal a.   CANN 129:25
It's them as take a.   ELIOT 200:14
thereout suck they no small a.   PRAY 394:22
undertaking of Great A.   ANON 4:11
advantages: bring a lot of a. with them
                                    HOR 257:21
Do it in hope of fair a.   SHAK 466:16
stamp and counterfeit a.   SHAK 474:21
adventure: a. brave and new   BROW 104:5
will be an awfully big a.   BARR 34:15
adventures: a. were by the fire-side
                                    GOLD 232:34
hard a. t' undertake   FITZ 212:4
adventurous: a. child   HOR 260:21
adversary: a. had written a book BIBLE 52:38
Agree with thine a. quickly   BIBLE 64:13
because your a. the devil   BIBLE 80:33

adversitate: *Nam in omni a. fortunae*
  BOET 89:6
adversité: *Dans l'a. de nos meilleurs*
  LA R 310:8
adversities: all our troubles and a.
  PRAY 385:22
adversity: a. doth best discover virtue
  BACON 25:21
a. is the blessing BACON 25:18
a. is not without comforts BACON 25:20
A. is sometimes hard upon CARL 131:36
A.'s sweet milk SHAK 483:11
any other a. PRAY 387:16
bread of a. BIBLE 58:28
brother is born for a. BIBLE 54:11
in the day of a. consider BIBLE 55:21
Like old companions in a. BRY 106:9
man I am cross'd with a. SHAK 491:3
men contending with a. BURT 116:24
Sweet are the uses of a. SHAK 424:32
advertise: shall call him and a. him
  PRAY 387:5
advertisement: is the soul of an a.
  JOHN 281:19
advertisers: a. don't object SWAF 525:30
Advice: A. is seldom welcome CHES 145:19
earnest a. from my seniors THOR 550:6
Love be controll'd by a. GAY 222:14
matrimony I never give any a. CHES 146:3
tea and comfortable a. KEATS 294:5
To ask a. is in nine cases COLL 158:14
woman seldom asks a. before ADD 2:23
advise: would a. no man to marry
  JOHN 280:13
advises: It's my old girl that a. DICK 176:18
thus a. thee that sighs SHAK 489:15
advocate: intellect of an a. BAG 29:17
our Mediator and A. PRAY 385:23
advocates: a. of peace upon earth GEOR 224:4
you of a. the best CAT 137:3
aedificaverit: *Nisi Dominus a. domum*
  BIBLE 83:12
Aeneas: as A., our great ancestor
  SHAK 448:14
Dido and her A. shall want SHAK 423:10
down to join our father A. HOR 261:16
Quo pater A. HOR 261:16
aeneus: *Hic murus a. esto* HOR 258:9
Aequam: *A. memento rebus in arduis*
  HOR 260:6
aequo: *Pallida Mors a.* HOR 259:13
aequor: *Cras ingens iterabimus a.*
  HOR 259:17
aequus: *animus si te non deficit a.* HOR 258:19
aere: *monumentum a. perennius* HOR 261:8
aery: execute their a. purposes MILT 345:15
aes: *robur et a. triplex* HOR 259:12
Aeschylus: I was fondest of A. COL 158:6
Aesculapius: we owe a cock to A.
  SOCR 512:21
aesthetic: high a. line GILB 227:22
high a. band GILB 227:23
aestimemus: *Omnes unius a. assis* CAT 136:25
Aetas: *A. parentum peior avis* HOR 260:26
fugerit invida A. HOR 259:20
Aetolian: Through Europe to the A. shore
  ARN 13:9
afar: peace to you which were a. BIBLE 77:22
afeard: Be not a. SHAK 485:17
soldier, and a. SHAK 462:20
affair: had an a. with the moon STER 518:29
affaire: then *quelle a.* BLUC 89:1
affairs: tide in the a. of women
  BYRON 123:20
tide in the a. of men SHAK 451:27
affectation: have been so used to a.
  ETH 208:26
spruce a. SHAK 457:15
They are the a. of affectation FIEL 211:15
wits to sophistry and a. BACON 28:12

affected: His accent was a. HARE 242:7
Really I believe I'm so a. BEAR 35:11
Affecting: A. to seem unaffected
  CONG 159:18
affection: heard Of any true a. MIDD 338:18
in the rear of your a. SHAK 430:17
still he fills a.'s eye JOHN 278:35
thy a. cannot hold SHAK 489:2
When strong a. stirs her SOUT 514:6
With a. beaming in one DICK 179:5
your a. on things above BIBLE 78:25
affections: his a. dark as Erebus SHAK 468:17
holiness of the heart's a. and the truth
  KEATS 293:15
is a history of the a. IRV 270:20
offences of a. new SHAK 495:3
our young a. run to waste BYRON 121:12
souls descend T'a. DONNE 188:25
unruly wills and a. PRAY 386:12
Affects: A. to nod DRYD 194:24
afflicted: he was a. BIBLE 59:22
afflicting: most a. to a parent's mind
  AUST 23:18
Affliction: A. alters SHAK 492:6
A. is enamour'd of thy SHAK 483:9
all a. taught a lover yet POPE 376:12
bread of a. and with water BIBLE 51:20
Remembering mine a. and my misery
  BIBLE 60:29
saveth in time of a. BIBLE 62:21
thee in the furnace of a. BIBLE 59:14
To try me with a. SHAK 476:18
waters of a. BIBLE 58:28
Afflictions: A. sorted HERB 248:10
A. easier grow WALSH 563:29
describing the a. of Job BACON 25:19
affluent: a. society no useful distinction
  GALB 220:28
afford: can a. to keep a motor car
  SHAW 496:4
Can't a. them SHAW 498:13
parties could any way a. it EDG 199:21
unless you can a. it TROL 553:15
Whether we can a. it or no GAY 223:24
Afield: A. for palms the girls HOUS 262:19
afire: bush a. with God BROW 97:33
afloat: full sea are we now a. SHAK 451:27
afraid: a. of me POPE 380:20
a. of the sea will soon SYNGE 531:4
a. to look upon God BIBLE 47:5
a. to speak evil of dignities BIBLE 81:1
do what you are a. to do EMER 207:23
I am a. to think what SHAK 460:11
I am devilishly a. DRYD 195:18
in short, I was a. ELIOT 203:23
keep myself from being a. DRYD 195:19
many are a. of God LOCK 315:20
not so much a. of death BROW 96:20
of his near approach a. GARR 221:16
see all, nor be a. BROW 104:2
stranger and a. HOUS 264:25
that he is a. of his enemy PLUT 374:20
they were sore a. BIBLE 69:9
we do be a. of the sea SYNGE 531:4
whereof our conscience is a. PRAY 386:20
whom then shall I be a. PRAY 391:7
yet a. of death CHUR 148:32
yet a. to strike POPE 376:26
Afric: geographers, in A.-maps SWIFT 528:2
Africa: all A. and her prodigies BROW 96:12
are to go some to arid A. VIRG 559:13
silent over A. BROW 101:9
speak of A. and golden joys SHAK 442:27
Till China and A. meet AUDEN 18:9
African: strength of this A. national
  MACM 326:1
after: a. many a summer dies TENN 543:11
'A. sharpest shoures LANG 309:28
A. such knowledge ELIOT 203:5
A. the first death THOM 547:8

tell them that come a. PRAY 392:27
you who come a. me HOR 260:12
aftermaths: In a. of soft September
  HOUS 265:8
afternoon: rude multitude the call the a.
  SHAK 457:13
Summer a. JAMES 271:30
which it seemed always a. TENN 539:12
aftersight: mind to a. and foresight
  ELIOT 202:25
after-silence: in the a. on the shore
  BYRON 125:10
after-times: something so written to a.
  MILT 352:14
after-tram-ride: a. quiet BETJ 43:19
Afton: sweet A. BURNS 113:27
Agag: A. came unto him delicately
  BIBLE 50:5
again: Come a., with the feet HARDY 238:22
comfort of thy help a. PRAY 393:6
hang the man over a. BARH 33:9
I do it again and a. CARR 133:22
Against: A. my fire SHAK 455:24
A. thee only have I sinned PRAY 393:4
hand will be a. every man BIBLE 46:5
He said he was a. it COOL 162:10
I have somewhat a. thee BIBLE 81:16
is not with me is a. me BIBLE 66:6
Shall come a. him SHAK 462:8
who can be a. us BIBLE 75:12
Agamemnon: A. dead YEATS 586:2
When A. cried aloud ELIOT 204:16
Agamemnona: *Vixere fortes ante A.*
  HOR 261:18
Aganippe: I never drank of A. well
  SIDN 507:26
agate-stone: shape no bigger than an
  SHAK 481:28
age: a. are threescore years PRAY 395:19
A. cannot wither her SHAK 422:5
a. fatal to Revolutionists DESM 175:13
a. from folly could not SHAK 421:27
A., I do abhor thee SHAK 492:14
a. in her embraces past ROCH 406:20
a. is a dream that is dying OSH 365:21
a. is as a lusty winter SHAK 425:6
A. is deformed BAST 35:2
A. makes a winter SPAR 514:22
A. might but take the things WORD 581:12
a. of chivalry is gone BURKE 111:9
a. of chivalry is never KING 297:18
a. shall be able to destroy OVID 366:19
A. shall not weary them BINY 84:10
a., which forgives itself SHAW 498:5
A. will not be defied BACON 27:6
all the faults of the a. BALF 30:5
arrogance of a. must submit BURKE 110:23
Athens in his riper a. DRYD 197:14
away in the time of a. PRAY 394:17
buried in a good old a. BIBLE 46:4
companions for middle a. BACON 26:34
Crabbed a. and youth SHAK 492:13
Diseases and sad Old A. VIRG 558:21
evening of my a. ROWE 410:20
Every a. has a kind DRYD 197:9
fetch the a. of gold MILT 344:11
flower of their a. BIBLE 49:33
full of grief as a. SHAK 454:1
governed their rude a. BAG 28:28
hath yet some smack of a. SHAK 441:5
He died in a good old a. BIBLE 51:40
He is of a. BIBLE 72:15
He is of no a. COL 158:8
He was not of an a. JONS 284:23
if a. could EST 208:25
invention of a barbarous a. MILT 344:18
Is common at your a. BELL 38:25
labour with an a. of ease GOLD 230:19
less for what a. takes away WORD 577:20
Let a. approve of youth BROW 104:13

now enjoys his a.	DRYD 196:3
Now has come the last a.	VIRG 559:22
now in a. I bud again	HERB 247:22
Old A. a regret	DISR 185:40
Old a. brings along with	EMER 207:45
Old a. is the most unexpected	TROT 553:16
old a. of cards	POPE 377:26
pays us but with a.	RAL 404:15
poison for the a.'s tooth	SHAK 452:10
soon comes a.	SPEN 516:13
tell a woman's a.	GILB 228:27
Than settled a. his sables	SHAK 436:17
That men call a.	BROO 94:7
this a. best pleaseth me	HERR 249:17
thou a. unbred	SHAK 494:18
Thou hast nor youth nor a.	SHAK 464:10
tiresomeness of old a.	ANON 10:13
To complain of the a. we	BURKE 108:17
Towards the a. of twenty-six	BELL 39:5
To youth and a. in common	ARN 15:13
very staff of my a.	SHAK 466:8
vice and follies of the a.	CENT 138:10
wealth a well-spent a.	CAMP 129:19
well stricken in a.	BIBLE 46:6
'when the a. is	SHAK 472:34
who tells one her real a.	WILDE 573:28
with Eagerness and A.	YOUNG 588:8
With leaden a. o'ercargoed	FLEC 214:16
worth an a. without a name	MORD 357:6
aged: a. man is but a paltry	YEATS 586:1
don't object to an a. parent	DICK 178:12
I saw an a., aged man	CARR 136:5
reverend creatures did the a.	TRAH 551:19
ageless-ancient: mother-naked and a.	
	DAY-L 172:21
agendum: dum quid superesset a.	
	LUCAN 319:24
agent: is the poor a. despised	SHAK 487:19
agents: night's black a.	SHAK 461:14
ages: acts being seven a.	SHAK 425:24
A. of hopeless end	MILT 346:11
a. of imagination this	BLAKE 88:26
heir of all the a.	TENN 539:7
next a.	BACON 28:14
Now he belongs to the a.	STAN 517:19
our diff'rent a. move	PRIOR 401:7
ageth: Earthly glory a. and seareth	
	POUND 383:19
aggravating: She was an a. child	BELL 39:12
aggregate: From the large a. of little	
	MORE 357:11
aghast: stared a. to watch him eat	
	HOUS 264:15
Agincourt: affright the air at A.	SHAK 443:4
a-gley: Gang aft a.	BURNS 115:22
a-glimmer: There midnight's all a.	
	YEATS 585:17
Agnes: St A.' Eve	KEATS 289:7
agnostic: appropriate title of 'a.'	HUXL 269:4
Agnus: A. Dei	MASS 335:7
agonies: exultations, a., And love	
	WORD 582:17
Agony: A. and bloody Sweat	PRAY 385:17
a. and spoil	KIPL 300:6
a. is abated	MAC 324:24
Hard and bitter a. for us	ELIOT 203:15
intense the a.	BRON 93:21
it happen and am in a.	CAT 137:14
strong swimmer in his a.	BYRON 122:18
agree: a. in the truth of thy	PRAY 387:13
a. the kettle and the earthen	BIBLE 63:3
A. with thine adversary	BIBLE 64:13
colours will a. in the dark	BACON 27:32
does not a. with my constitution	THOR 550:14
in their little nests a.	BELL 40:6
Music and sweet Poetry a.	BARN 34:2
they may a. like brothers	SHAK 446:11
When people a. with me	WILDE 572:21
whom all joys so well a.	SIDN 508:1
world and I shall ne'er a.	COWL 164:11

agreeable: himself a most a. fellow	
	AUST 22:10
Is the old min a.	DICK 180:24
most men's power to be a.	SWIFT 527:11
'My idea of an a. person	DISR 186:24
agreement: death and an a. with hell'	
	GARR 221:19
with hell are we at a.	BIBLE 58:22
agrestis: ille deos qui novit a.	VIRG 560:15
agri: modus a. non ita magnus	HOR 262:9
agriculture: fall upon a.	GIBB 224:26
agua: a. que ahuyenta la sed	CERV 138:20
ague-proof: I am not a.	SHAK 455:15
Ahab: ran before A.	BIBLE 51:12
a-hunting: a. we will go	FIEL 211:36
We daren't go a.	ALL 3:20
Aid: Summoned the Immediate A.	COWP 168:9
Their a. they yield	BELL 39:8
Aide-toi: A., le ciel t'aidera	LA F 306:17
aik: lean'd my back unto an a.	BALL 32:10
ail: what can a. thee	KEATS 290:15
ailes: a. de géant l'empêchent	BAUD 35:6
ailing: poor, a. and ignorant	YEATS 585:3
ailments: because our a. are the same	
	SWIFT 526:13
aim: at which all things a.	ARIS 12:6
you must a. a little above	LONG 316:11
aimai: plus j'a. ma patrie	BELL 40:17
aime: C'est mourir à ce qu'on a.	HAR 238:20
Et j'a. la Princesse	ROST 410:13
aimeth: Who a. at the sky	HERB 247:8
aimez: et a. qui vous aime	VOLT 561:11
aiming: a. at a million	BROW 100:38
aimless: nothing walks with a. feet	
	TENN 536:25
obscure them by an a. rhetoric	HUXL 269:13
aims: a. his heart had learned	GOLD 230:22
other a. than my delight	HARDY 240:6
aim'st: Let all the ends thou a.	SHAK 447:12
ain't: she a.	KIPL 302:11
You a. heard nothin' yet	JOLS 283:9
air: a., a charter'd libertine	SHAK 443:6
a. a live tradition	POUND 382:14
a. a solemn stillness holds	GRAY 234:18
a. broke into a mist with	BROW 103:11
a. is delicate	SHAK 459:4
a. might wash and long	SWIN 530:18
a. Nimbly and sweetly	SHAK 459:4
a. shall note her soft	DONNE 188:9
a. signed with their honour	SPEN 515:8
are built with a.	JONS 283:26
Behold the fowls of the a.	BIBLE 64:28
breathing English a.	BROO 94:30
burning fills the startled a.	BELL 40:7
diviner a.	WORD 578:3
excellent canopy, the a.	SHAK 432:15
fair and floral a.	FLEC 214:6
firmly planted in the a.	ROOS 407:24
I am fire and a.	SHAK 424:11
into thin a.	SHAK 485:20
Leaving a blacker a.	HARDY 240:11
let out to warm the a.	SWIFT 526:7
merely vans to beat the a.	ELIOT 202:1
morning to take the a.	FRY 219:21
my heart an a. that kills	HOUS 263:22
nipping and an eager a.	SHAK 430:22
ocean and the living a.	WORD 578:7
one that beateth the a.	BIBLE 76:9
Only to kiss that a.	HERR 250:3
other painters fleet to a.	SHAK 467:12
out of a mouthful of a.	YEATS 585:8
Out of the a. a voice	AUDEN 20:10
over the fowl of the a.	BIBLE 45:4
parching a. Burns frore	MILT 346:21
There is an a. comes from	SHAK 492:11
through the trembling a.	SPEN 516:30
To a. the ditty	HOUS 265:12
'twixt a. and Angels' purity	DONNE 187:22
with pinions skim the a.	FRERE 218:25
world-mothering a.	HOPK 256:6

airly: you've gut to git up a.	LOW 319:1
Airly Beacon: Shires and towns from	
A.	KING 296:16
airman: most intrepid a.	CHUR 150:16
airports: a. almost deserted	AUDEN 19:2
airs: a. from heaven or blasts	SHAK 430:24
'don't give yourself a.	CARR 133:23
poet sing it with such a.	YEATS 584:10
Sounds and sweet a.	SHAK 485:17
Airy: A., fairy Lilian	TENN 538:14
a. subtleties in religion	BROW 96:8
Ajalon: in the valley of A.	BIBLE 49:4
Ajax: Thersites' body is as good as A.	
	SHAK 428:21
a-killing: have him nine years a.	SHAK 476:10
Akond: Is the A. of Swat	LEAR 312:25
al: nat kepe me chaast in a.	CHAU 143:17
alabaster: a. box of very precious	BIBLE 68:8
his grandsire cut in a.	SHAK 465:11
smooth as monumental a.	SHAK 477:5
alacrity: kind of a. in sinking	SHAK 469:13
ALARM: A. and DESPONDENCY	
	PEN 371:13
Glorious the trumpet and a.	SMART 509:4
alarms: Swept with confused a. of struggle	
	ARN 12:23
were all the world's a.	YEATS 586:4
alarum: At once the wild a. clashed	
	MAC 322:2
Alas: A. but cannot help nor	AUDEN 20:17
Albatross: I shot the A.	COL 155:10
Albion: La perfide A.	XIM 584:6
Alcestis: me like A. from the grave	
	MILT 351:12
alchemy: By happy a. of mind	GREEN 236:2
aldermen: divides the wives of a.	
	SMITH 509:8
Aldershot: Furnish'd and burnish'd by	
A.	BETJ 44:6
ale: a. is a dish for a king	SHAK 491:17
be no more cakes and a.	SHAK 488:21
broach'd the mightiest a.	SCOTT 417:16
drink your a.	HOUS 264:22
Good a.	BORR 90:8
have fed purely upon a.	FARQ 209:23
my fame for a pot of a.	SHAK 444:4
Of jolly good a. and old	ANON 5:21
...ordered a glass of this a.	DICK 176:32
spicy nut-brown a.	MILT 342:23
wes sons of a. and brede	WYNT 584:13
while England talked of a.	CHES 147:13
alehouse: were in an a. in London	
	SHAK 444:4
Aleppo: Her husband's to A. gone	
	SHAK 458:6
Alexander: A. at the head of the world	
	WALP 562:18
A. women	LEE 313:13
If I were not A.	ALEX 3:12
Alexandrine: needless A. ends the song	
	POPE 378:21
Alexin: pastor Corydon ardebat A.	
	VIRG 559:14
Alfred: high tide!' King A.	CHES 146:20
Truth-teller was our England's A.	
	TENN 541:18
alget: Probitas laudatur et a.	JUV 287:10
alibi: He always has an a.	ELIOT 203:26
Alice: A., where art thou	BUNN 107:8
don't you remember sweet A.	ENGL 208:19
Alien: A. they seemed to be	HARDY 239:6
tears amid the a. corn	KEATS 291:23
With an a. people clutching	ELIOT 203:15
Alieni: A. appetens	SALL 413:22
alienum: humani nil a me a. puto	TER 544:17
alights: Daintily a. Elaine	BETJ 43:13
alike: light to thee are both a.	PRAY 399:5
Looks on a.	SHAK 492:4
there should be none a.	BROW 96:31

aliquid: *Meas esse a. putare nugas*
                                               CAT 136:20
aliquo: *aut a. modo destruator* MAGN 327:2
aliter: *Dis a. visum*   VIRG 558:8
Alive: A. like patterns a murmuration
                                               AUDEN 20:6
a. so stout a gentleman   SHAK 440:24
A. with sparkles   KEATS 289:4
Christ shall all be made a.   BIBLE 76:22
I am a. for evermore   BIBLE 81:15
if I am a. I shall be delighted   HOLL 253:3
is a. again   BIBLE 70:21
it in that dawn to be a.   WORD 577:21
Life's not just being a.   MART 331:12
living which are yet a.   BIBLE 55:14
Looking as if she were a.   BROW 102:21
noise and tumult when a.   EDW 200:6
Officiously to keep a.   CLOU 153:26
show that one's a.   BURN 112:22
still a. at twenty-two   KING 297:19
that he is no longer a.   BENT 41:5
When I was man a.   HOUS 263:9
all: a. for love   SPEN 516:12
A. for one   DUMAS 199:3
A. for your delight   SHAK 471:16
a. goes right and nothing   GILB 228:29
a. hell broke loose   MILT 348:11
A. is for the best   VOLT 561:2
A. men make faults   SHAK 493:12
a. our yesterdays have   SHAK 463:6
A.'s right with the world   BROW 103:21
A. that a man hath will   BIBLE 52:8
a. that's best of dark   BYRON 125:21
a. the rest forgot   SHAK 493:4
a. the silent manliness   GOLD 231:6
A. things are lawful   BIBLE 76:10
A. things bright and beautiful   ALEX 3:13
a. things to all men'   ANON 6:11
A. things to all men   BIBLE 76:7
A. things were made   BIBLE 71:22
A. this and heaven too   HENRY 245:22
a. to Heaven   JONES 283:13
a. we have and are   KIPL 299:6
A. we have willed or hoped   BROW 98:19
always is A. everywhere   DONNE 188:32
are a. gone out of the way   PRAY 390:3
because not a. was right   COWP 168:20
everything the concern of a.   SOLZ 513:1
Her a. on earth   BYRON 121:35
man for a. seasons   WHIT 571:22
not at all or all in a.   TENN 535:8
nothing brings me a. things   SHAK 486:12
Then a. were for the state   MAC 322:18
this is a. that is known   NEWM 362:5
to have his a. neglected   JOHN 274:5
upholdeth a. such as fall   PRAY 399:14
When a. night long a chap   GILB 226:8
When A. the world is young   KING 297:5
Allah: A. created the English   KIPL 300:14
A. is great   CLOU 153:11
Allaying: A. both their fury   SHAK 484:31
drop of a. Tiber   SHAK 427:14
allegiance: Any victim demands a.
                                               GREE 236:5
religious a.   BAG 28:21
To hell, a.   SHAK 436:7
to swear a. to any master   HOR 258:7
allegorical: a. paintings they can shew
                                               JOHN 280:19
allegory: headstrong as an a.   SHER 506:15
Shakespeare led a life of a.   KEATS 294:13
Which things are an a.   BIBLE 77:16
worth is a continual a.   KEATS 294:12
allemand: hommes et a. à mon cheval
                                               CHAR 140:31
alles: Die Welt ist a.   WITT 575:14
alleviate: a. so severe a misfortune
                                               AUST 23:18
alley: she lives in our a.   CAREY 130:26

alleybi: governor don't prove a a.
                                               DICK 182:15
vy won't there a a.   DICK 182:24
alleys: a. of London do not present
                                               DOYLE 192:1
alleyways: crossroads and in the a. CAT 137:5
allgemeines: Maxime solle ein a. Gesetz
                                               KANT 288:9
alliance: clear of permanent a.   WASH 565:2
rumours of a morganatic a.   HARD 238:21
alliances: entangling a. with none JEFF 272:8
allied: nearly a. to excellence   GOLD 232:8
allies: thou hast great a.   WORD 582:17
All-in-all: intellectual A.   WORD 580:4
Alliteration: apt A.'s artful aid   CHUR 149:2
allotted: a. death and hell   MARL 329:13
allow: a. their names to be mentioned
                                               AUST 23:19
all-round: he was a wonderful a. man
                                               BEER 38:6
Allsopp: Guinness, A., Bass   CALV 127:12
All-Souls: at Christ-Church and A.
                                               JOHN 275:22
alluring: little scorn is a.   CONG 161:2
more a. than a levee from   CONG 161:4
Almack: to A.'s too   ANST 11:8
Alma Mater: A. lie dissolv'd in port
                                               POPE 375:21
almanac: useful as an a. out of date
                                               WALT 563:32
Almighty: A.'s orders to perform ADD 1:14
arrow from the A.'s bow   BLAKE 86:6
almond: a. tree shall flourish   BIBLE 56:11
alms: accept our a. and oblations PRAY 387:13
a. Of palsied eld   SHAK 464:10
a. of thy superfluous praise   DRAY 193:20
he puts a. for oblivion   SHAK 487:3
When thou doest a.   BIBLE 64:22
alms-basket: long on the a. of words
                                               SHAK 457:12
aloe: olive, a.   TENN 533:5
aloft: now he's gone a.   DIBD 175:22
alone: all a. went she   KING 296:25
A. he rides   JOHN 273:23
A. I did it   SHAK 428:6
a. on a hill during a clear   HARDY 241:9
A. on a wide wide sea   COL 155:20
A., poor maid   MEW 338:12
alone than when wholly a.   CIC 151:23
A. word is   SASS 415:2
Are we here together a.   WHIT 570:13
be a. on earth   BYRON 120:16
bear the palm a.   SHAK 448:16
down a. bent on his prey   MILT 347:10
experienced at being a. together LA B 306:13
I feel I am a.   LAND 308:24
I lie down a.   HOUS 265:17
Ill fortune seldom comes a.   DRYD 195:36
In leafy dells a.   HOUS 265:9
is the man who stands a.   IBSEN 269:20
it a. is high fantastical   SHAK 487:20
I want to be a.   GARBO 221:3
leaves her too much a.   POUND 382:5
left him a. with his glory   WOLFE 576:5
let me a. for swearing   SHAK 490:13
Let me a.   BIBLE 52:20
Lives not a.   BLAKE 85:20
love is left a.   TENN 543:14
mortal millions live a.   ARN 13:12
most unfit to be a.   CONG 159:17
never less a. than when   ROG 407:8
One is one and all a.   ANON 6:5
shall be left, a.   WORD 581:13
shalt be, art, a.   ARN 13:11
sparrow: that sitteth a.   PRAY 396:12
that the man should be a.   BIBLE 45:10
they would but let it a.   WALP 563:6
things were a. with theirs   BETJ 42:9
To live in Paradise a.   MARV 332:8
trodden the winepress a.   BIBLE 60:11

we ask is to be let a.   DAVIS 172:19
we were a. and completely   DANTE 171:9
Will he not let us a.   DONNE 190:5
Aloof: A. from the entire point   SHAK 453:7
aloud: thee all Angels cry a.   PRAY 384:16
Alpes: et saevas curre per A.   JUV 288:2
Alph: A., the sacred river   COL 156:26
Alpha: 'I am A. and Omega   AUDEN 21:7
I am A. and Omega   BIBLE 81:10
alphabet: got to the end of the a. DICK 182:7
struggled through the a.   DICK 178:6
Alpheus: A., the dread voice is   MILT 343:14
Alpine: on the A. mountains cold MILT 351:9
Alps: A. on Alps arise   POPE 378:14
A. shaping like a backbone   HARDY 239:13
beneath some snow-deep A.   ELIOT 202:5
fading a. and archipelagoes   ALDR 3:11
O'er the white A. alone   DONNE 188:12
also: hell, thou art there a.   PRAY 399:5
altar: a. with this inscription   BIBLE 74:12
self-slain on his own strange a. SWIN 529:20
so will I go to thine a.   PRAY 391:5
that I may go unto the a.   PRAY 392:11
To what green a.   KEATS 291:8
altars: even thy a., O Lord   PRAY 395:11
shining a. of Japan they raise   POPE 381:6
threw our a. to the ground   JORD 285:18
altar-stairs: great world's a.   TENN 536:28
alter: the past, historians can   BUTL 118:21
not a. in my faith of him   JONS 283:25
Will it a. my life altogether   AUDEN 21:2
alteram: Audi partem a.   AUG 21:20
alteration: alters when it a. finds SHAK 495:1
altered: how much it a. her person
                                               SWIFT 527:5
alternative: unhappy a. is before you
                                               AUST 23:15
alternatives: more a., the more difficult
                                               ALL 3:19
Althea: my divine A. brings   LOV 318:15
Altior: A. Italiae ruinis   HOR 260:24
altissimo: Onorate l'a. poeta   DANTE 171:6
Altogether: A. elsewhere   AUDEN 18:16
I shall not a. die   HOR 261:9
righteous a.   PRAY 390:12
altrui: Lo pane a.   DANTE 171:17
alway: He will not a. be chiding   PRAY 396:16
I am with you a.   BIBLE 68:25
always: a. with us, or we die   KEATS 289:2
It wasn't a. like this   AUDEN 19:15
man with God is a.   KNOX 305:18
research is a. incomplete   PATT 370:8
third who walks a. beside   ELIOT 205:8
Alysander: Quhen A. oure kyng wes
                                               WYNT 584:4
am: grace of God I am what I a.   BIBLE 76:19
Here I a., and here I stay   MACM 325:17
I AM THAT I A.   BIBLE 47:7
I am the way I a.   PREV 400:16
therefore I a.   DESC 175:20
what I a., none cares   CLARE 152:12
amabam: Nondum a.   AUG 21:12
amantem: Quis fallere possit a.   VIRG 558:12
amanti: mulier cupido quod dicit a.
                                               CAT 137:7
Amantium: A. irae amoris integratio
                                               TER 544:15
amantum: alto periuria ridet a.   OVID 366:11
amaracus: Violet, a., and asphodel
                                               TENN 541:18
amaranth: Of a. lie   DE L 173:25
amaranthus: Bid a. all his beauty shed
                                               MILT 343:15
amare: amans a.   AUG 21:12
amari: Surgit a. aliquid quod   LUCR 320:11
Amaryllis: To sport with A.   MILT 343:8
amateur: a. painting in water-colours
                                               STEV 521:28
Eavy-sterned a. old men   KIPL 303:11
amateurs: disease that afflicts a.   CHES 148:1

that we are a nation of a.	ROS 408:15
amavi: *Sero te a.*	AUG 21:16
amavit: *Cras amet qui nunquam a.*	ANON 10:11
amaz'd: a., and curious	BURNS 115:10
Amaze: A. th' unlearn'd	POPE 378:18
these cogitations still a.	ELIOT 202:11
vainly men themselves a.	MARV 331:21
amazed: a., temperate, and furious	
	SHAK 461:2
Silent and a. even when	WHIT 570:1
ambassador: a. is an honest man sent	
	WOTT 583:18
Ambassadors: A. cropped up like hay	
	GILB 225:29
amber: be prepared gold and a.	JONS 285:14
ceiling of a.	ARN 13:7
in a. to observe the forms	POPE 376:24
to lutes of a.	HERR 250:9
ambergris: Proclaim the a. on shore	
	MARV 331:16
ambiguities: Till we can clear these a.	
	SHAK 484:1
Ambition: A., Distraction	CARR 134:10
A. first sprung from your	POPE 376:8
A., in a private man	MASS 335:13
a. mock their useful toil	GRAY 234:21
A.'s debt is paid	SHAK 450:2
A. should be made of sterner	SHAK 450:19
a. to be a wag	JOHN 281:2
Art not without a.	SHAK 459:1
Cromwell was a man in whom a.	
	BURKE 111:29
fling away a.	SHAK 447:12
Ill-weav'd a.	SHAK 440:24
lowliness is young a.'s ladder	SHAK 449:5
specimens, the lilies of a.	DOUG 191:8
that a. can creep as well	BURKE 112:9
That make a. virtue	SHAK 475:25
'tis not with a. join'd	CONG 161:3
To low a.	POPE 379:1
Vaulting a.	SHAK 459:6
was this a.	SHAK 450:20
Who doth a. shun	SHAK 425:16
Your heart's supreme a.	LYTT 321:20
ambitious: Brutus says he was a.	
	SHAK 450:18
he was a.	SHAK 450:15
hunger of a. minds	SPEN 516:21
told you Caesar was a.	SHAK 450:17
would not be a. in my wish	SHAK 467:13
ambo: *Arcades a.*	VIRG 560:3
Amboss: *A. oder Hammer sein*	GOET 230:7
âme: *grands n'ont point d'â.*	LA B 306:14
Quelle â. est sans défauts	RIMB 406:8
Amelia: A. was praying for George	
	THAC 545:24
amemus: *atque a.*	CAT 136:25
Amen: A.' Stuck in my throat	SHAK 460:7
Glorious the catholic a.	SMART 509:4
sound of a great A.	PROC 401:14
Will no man say, a.	SHAK 479:21
amenable: should be a.	MOL 353:18
amenities: meaning 'a.'	CAT 137:13
America: America! A.	BATES 35:4
A. is a country of young	EMER 208:11
A. is God's Crucible	ZANG 588:17
A. is just ourselves	ARN 15:14
A. is the only idealistic	WILS 575:3
A., thou half-brother	BAIL 29:22
A. was thus clearly top	SELL 420:8
ask not what A. will do	KENN 295:10
business of A. is business	COOL 162:11
'next to of course god a.	CUMM 170:10
O my A.	DONNE 188:16
than *whole* A.	BURKE 109:20
there is A.	BURKE 109:19
think of thee, O A.	WALP 563:10
to the discovery of A.	HELPS 244:17
You cannot conquer A.	PITT 373:27

youth of A. is their oldest	WILDE 573:26
American: A. girls turn into American	
	HAMP 238:17
A. system of rugged individualism	
	HOOV 255:23
except an A.	JOHN 277:30
fallen in love with A. names	BENET 40:19
I also—am an A.	WEBS 566:13
I am A. bred	MILL 340:2
I shall die an A.	WEBS 566:15
new deal for the A.	ROOS 407:19
real A. is all right	CHES 148:6
subtleties of the A. joke	TWAIN 554:12
Virginian, but an A.	HENRY 245:26
what I call the A. idea	PARK 368:26
Americanism: can be no fifty-fifty A.	
	ROOS 408:6
Americans: A. on guard to-night	WASH 565:5
are A. and nothing else	ROOS 408:6
Good A.	APPL 11:13
Hyphenated A.	ROOS 408:8
when bad A. die	WILDE 573:25
worse Than ignorant A.	MASS 335:15
Amerikey: North and South A.	THAC 546:2
amet: *Cras a. qui nunquam amavit*	
	ANON 10:11
amethyst: last an a.	BROW 97:34
amiability: found to have gained in a.	
	BUTL 118:28
amiable: a. weakness	FIEL 211:28
a. words	TENN 534:12
how a. are thy dwellings	PRAY 395:11
with any thing that is a.	CONG 159:28
amiably-disposed: You're a a. young	
man	DICK 182:29
amicably: a. if they can	QUIN 403:24
Amicus: *A. Plato*	ARIS 12:12
amiral: *A. pour encourager les*	VOLT 561:1
amis: *de se défier de ses a.*	LA R 310:10
Nos a., les ennemis	BER 41:15
amiss: All is a.	BARN 34:4
Nothing comes a.	SHAK 484:5
Nothing shall come a.	BUCK 106:18
to mark what is done a.	PRAY 398:23
amitié: *L'a. de la connaissance*	BUSS 117:5
l'a. ferme les yeux	ANON 9:11
ammer: 'a. along the 'ard 'igh	PUNCH 402:17
ammiral: mast Of some great A.	MILT 345:12
ammunition: pass the a.	FORGY 216:21
Amo: A., amas	OKEE 364:23
Non a. te, Sabidi	MART 331:9
Odi et a.	CAT 137:14
among: a. the English Poets after	
	KEATS 294:9
how a. so many millions	BROW 96:31
What are they a. so many	BIBLE 72:4
amongst: a. you and remain with	PRAY 388:4
Amor: *A. vincit omnia*	CHAU 141:17
Cedet a. rebus	OVID 366:21
come a. lo strinse	DANTE 171:9
L'a. che muove il sole	DANTE 171:18
Nunc scio quid sit A.	VIRG 560:5
Omnia vincit a.	VIRG 560:8
Suprema citius solvet a.	HOR 259:21
amorem: *longum subito deponere a.*	
	CAT 137:10
Amorites: Sehon king of the A.	PRAY 399:1
amorous: a. ditties all a summer's	
	MILT 345:17
a. of their strokes	SHAK 422:2
be a., but be chaste	BYRON 124:22
court an a. looking-glass	SHAK 480:18
excite my a. propensities	JOHN 274:2
sweet reluctant a. delay	MILT 347:23
unsubstantial Death is a.	SHAK 483:31
Amour: beginning of an A.	BEHN 38:10
commencement et le déclin de l'a.	
	LA B 306:13
faire l'a. en tout temps	BEAU 35:17
L'a. est aveugle	ANON 9:11

L'a.? Je le fais souvent	PROU 401:22
L'a., tel qu'il existe	CHAM 139:15
L'a. vient de l'aveuglement	BUSS 117:5
quitter L'a. de ma mie	ANON 9:17
Vive l'a.	STER 519:4
amphibii: These rational a. go	MARV 332:23
amphibious: this a. ill-born mob began	
	DEFOE 173:12
Amphitrite: A.'s destined halls	SHEL 501:23
ample: cabin'd a. Spirit	ARN 14:6
from an a. nation	DICK 183:22
ampulla: *meis vidi in a. pendere*	PETR 373:2
ampullas: *a. et sesquipedalia verba*	
	HOR 257:16
Amurath: Not A. an Amurath succeeds	
	SHAK 442:23
amuse: is just a talent to a.	COW 163:17
Amused: be A. by its Presumption	
	THUR 550:29
We are not a.	VICT 556:17
amusement: not cough my own a.	
	AUST 23:12
providing topics of a.	SWIFT 525:31
write for the general a.	SCOTT 418:10
amusements: his a., like his politics	
	CHUR 149:20
tolerable but for its a.	LEWIS 314:10
amusent: *anglais s'a. tristement*	
	SULLY 524:18
amusing: a. herself with me more	
	MONT 355:2
book may be a. with numerous	GOLD 232:31
Anabaptists: A. do falsely boast	PRAY 400:12
anagram: mild a.	DRYD 196:35
Anak: sons of A.	BIBLE 48:11
Analytics: Sweet A.	MARL 329:3
anapaestic: rolling a.	BROW 98:16
Anapaests: bound the swift A. throng	
	COL 157:4
anarchy: a. and competition	RUSK 412:10
and despotism	SHEL 505:11
a. prevails in my kitchen	JOHN 281:1
Mere a. is loosed upon	YEATS 586:15
servitude is the cure of a.	BURKE 109:30
Anathema: Let him be A. Maran-atha	
	BIBLE 77:3
anatomy: eat the rest of the a.	SHAK 490:1
mere a.	SHAK 427:9
ancestors: from the wisdom of our a.	
	BURKE 108:21
has his own tree of a.	STEV 521:10
look backward to their a.	BURKE 111:7
Our a. are very good kind	SHER 506:17
ancestral: a. fields with his own	HOR 259:7
ancestry: I can trace my a. back	GILB 226:20
without pride of a.	POWER 384:3
Anchises: old A. bear	SHAK 448:14
anchor: a. his aspect and die	SHAK 421:32
anchor'd: ship is a. safe and sound	
	WHIT 570:8
anchored: stars is a. and the young	
	FLEC 214:7
ancient: a. grudge I bear him	SHAK 465:29
a. nobility is the act	BACON 26:39
A. of days did sit	BIBLE 61:8
a. permanence which	HARDY 241:21
A. person of my heart	ROCH 407:3
A. times were the youth	BACON 25:10
ape an a. rage	CHES 147:12
both so a. and so fresh	AUG 21:16
From a. melody have ceas'd...	BLAKE 88:10
intruders on his a. home	ARN 14:21
It is an a. Mariner	COL 155:5
Time makes a. good uncouth	LOW 319:14
very a. and fish-like smell	SHAK 485:7
With the a. is wisdom	BIBLE 52:24
worlds revolve like a.	ELIOT 204:8
ancients: a. dreaded death	HARE 242:3
a. without idolatry	CHES 145:20
anders: *Ich kann nicht a.*	LUTH 320:16

Anderson: John A. my jo BURNS 114:12
Andrea del Sarto: A. apears for a moment BEER 37:25
anecdotage: man fell into his a. it DISR 186:19
anfractuosities: Among the a. of the human JOHN 278:13
anfractuous: Paint me the bold a. ELIOT 204:11
angat: quod in ipsis floribus a. LUCR 320:11
Angel: A. did with Jacob WALT 564:14
A. of a ruin'd Paradise SHEL 499:8
a. of the Lord came upon BIBLE 69:9
A. of the Lord came down TATE 531:22
a. satyr walks these hills KILV 296:7
a. took up a stone like BIBLE 82:24
a. to pass, flying slowly FIRB 212:1
a. watching an urn TENN 540:2
a. writing in a book HUNT 268:4
beautiful and ineffectual a. ARN 16:10
better a. is a man right fair SHAK 495:12
domesticate the Recording A. STEV 521:33
drive an a. from your door BLAKE 88:4
Her a.'s face SPEN 516:2
in action how like an a. SHAK 432:15
Is man an ape or an a. DISR 185:2
ministering a. thou SCOTT 417:21
ministering a. shall my SHAK 437:4
more a. she SHAK 477:11
'ooman a Wenus or a a. DICK 182:13
prepared to paint an a. BROW 102:30
Recording A., as he wrote STER 520:5
reverence— That a. SHAK 428:20
She drew an a. down DRYD 195:9
sigh is the sword of an A. BLAKE 86:6
Though an a. should write MOORE 356:1
What a. wakes me from my SHAK 470:18
White as an a. is the English BLAKE 88:2
Who wrote like an a. GARR 221:13
woman yet think him an a. THAC 545:7
Angeli: Non Angli sed A. GREG 236:13
angelic: With something of a. light WORD 581:8
angel-infancy: Shin'd in my a. VAUG 555:14
angel of death: a. has been abroad throughout BRIG 93:1
A. spread his wings BYRON 122:2
Angelorum: A. chori ANON 10:14
angels: all the a. stood round BIBLE 81:32
A. affect us oft DONNE 187:18
a. all were singing out BYRON 126:5
A. alone, that soar above LOV 318:18
A. and ministers of grace SHAK 430:24
A. are bright still SHAK 462:14
A. are painted fair OTWAY 366:4
A. came and ministered BIBLE 64:4
a. heave up Sir Launcelot MAL 328:7
a. in some brighter dreams VAUG 555:21
a. of God ascending BIBLE 46:18
a. with outspread wings PROU 401:23
a. would be gods POPE 379:7
By that sin fell the a. SHAK 447:12
entertained a. unawares BIBLE 80:3
flights of a. sing thee SHAK 437:28
fools rush in where a. POPE 378:31
Four a. to my bed ANON 6:15
glittering and sparkling A. TRAH 551:19
God and a. to be lookers on BACON 24:24
Hear all ye A. MILT 348:22
He maketh his a. spirits PRAY 396:18
his a. charge over thee PRAY 395:22
if a. fight SHAK 479:5
little lower than the a. BETJ 43:4
madest him lower than the a. PRAY 389:28
make the a. weep SHAK 464:2
Michael and his a. fought BIBLE 82:11
neglect God and his A. DONNE 191:1
nor life, nor a. BIBLE 75:13
nothing to what the a. know NEWM 362:5
Now walk the a. MARL 330:12

Our acts our a. are FLET 215:13
So man did eat a.' food PRAY 395:6
Therefore with A. and Archangels PRAY 387:23
this smell of cooped-up a. FRY 220:4
tongues of men and of a. BIBLE 76:14
To thee all A. cry aloud PRAY 384:16
'-triumph and sorrow for a. BROW 102:7
'twixt air and A.' purity DONNE 187:22
Where a. tremble GRAY 235:19
angel-visits: Like a. CAMP 129:10
anger: Achilles' cursed a. sing HOMER 253:26
a. as the flint bears fire SHAK 451:24
a. in those heavenly minds VIRG 557:9
A. invests with such SIDN 507:25
A. is a short madness HOR 258:15
A. is never without HAL 238:1
A. is one of the sinews FULL 220:17
A. makes dull men witty ELIZ 205:21
either a. or zealousness TAC 531:10
He that is slow to a. is BIBLE 54:9
his a. is not turned away BIBLE 57:27
In the contempt and a. SHAK 489:24
Juno's never-forgetting a. VIRG 557:8
keepeth he his a. for ever PRAY 396:16
life of telegrams and a. FORS 217:1
more in sorrow than in a. SHAK 430:11
that you strike it in a. SHAW 497:41
thy mistress some rich a. KEATS 291:15
Touch me with noble a. SHAK 454:2
anges: a. aux ailes éployées PROU 401:23
Angevin: l'air marin la douleur A. DU B 198:27
angiportis: Nunc in quadriviis et a. CAT 137:5
anglais: a. s'amusent tristement SULLY 524:18
L'A. les baisse au-dessous TOCQ 551:8
Les A. sont occupés MONT 355:8
Angle: Brother of the A. WALT 564:1
Give me mine a. SHAK 422:9
Themselves in every a. greet MARV 331:19
angler: excellent a., and now with God WALT 564:5
so no man is born an a. WALT 563:33
that if he be an honest a. WALT 563:34
anglers: too good for any but a. WALT 564:10
Angles: Not A. but Angels GREG 236:13
Offer no a. to the wind TESS 545:3
Angleterre: L'A. est une nation de boutiquiers NAP 359:15
la perfide A. BOSS 90:14
Anglicana: A. ecclesia libera MAGN 327:1
Angling: A. is somewhat like poetry WALT 564:2
A. may be said to be so WALT 563:31
a. or float fishing I can JOHN 280:28
be quiet; and go a-A. WALT 564:13
practiser of the art of a. WALT 564:3
Anglo-Saxon: natural idol of the A. BAG 29:4
those are A. attitudes CARR 135:29
vigour of our old A. breed ARN 15:27
angry: a. and poor and happy CHES 147:22
a. at a slander makes it JONS 283:20
a. with a man for loving BACON 27:8
'a. young men' of England FEAR 210:32
be a. with his judgment BROW 96:4
Be ye a. and sin not BIBLE 78:1
I was a. with my friend BLAKE 87:21
not an a. father CAMP 129:3
proud and a. dust HOUS 264:22
that's a. with me BROW 96:7
When he was a. BECK 36:19
when she's a. she is keen SHAK 470:24
when very a., swear TWAIN 554:8
anguis: Latet a. in herba VIRG 559:19
anguish: a. of all sizes HERB 248:10
gay modulating a. FRY 220:1
of a solitary hidden a. ELIOT 201:16
To ease the a. of a torturing SHAK 471:12
With a. moist and fever KEATS 290:16

Angulus: A. ridet HOR 260:8
angusta: Res a. domi JUV 287:18
anheling: cive, a., wipes HOLM 253:18
anhelis: equis Oriens adflavit a. VIRG 560:11
Animae: A. dimidium meae HOR 259:11
a. naturaliter Christianae TERT 544:21
animal: a., and mineral GILB 228:16
Be a good a. LAWR 311:4
being a social a. and created DEM 174:19
by nature a political a. ARIS 12:7
Cet a. est très méchant ANON 9:4
coitum omne a. triste ANON 10:17
constitution a religious a. BURKE 111:18
doubt as to a. magnetism COL 157:34
either some unknown a. SWIFT 526:3
err is human, not to, a. FROST 219:13
life is to be a good a. SPEN 514:20
Man is a noble a. BROW 97:23
only a. that blushes TWAIN 554:8
their glad a. movements WORD 578:6
This a. is very bad ANON 9:4
animalculous: scientific names of beings a. GILB 228:16
Animals: A. are such agreeable friends ELIOT 201:24
a. were created solely PEAC 370:15
a. will not look AUDEN 20:17
could turn and live with a. WHIT 570:26
Man didn't find the a. NIET 363:3
animam: Liberavi a. meam BERN 41:24
animate: scarce-suspected, a. the whole SMITH 511:14
Animosities: A. are mortal NORTH 364:5
dissensions and a. of mankind BURKE 111:3
animosity: fervour of sisterly a. SURT 525:25
animosus: Non sine dis a. infans HOR 260:21
Animula: A. vagula blandula HADR 237:9
animum: Caelum non a. mutant HOR 258:19
anise: mint and a. and cummin BIBLE 67:24
Anjou: air the sweetness of A. DU B 198:27
ankles: Do his weak a. swell WORD 581:9
One praised her a. TENN 532:16
Ann: A., Ann DE L 173:23
Anna: we all know A. Livia JOYCE 286:6
Annabel Lee: I and my A. POE 374:22
annals: a. are blank in history-books CARL 131:20
simple a. of the poor GRAY 234:21
Anne: ma soeur A. PERR 372:25
Move Queen A. VICT 556:16
annibabtist: a. is a thing I am not FLEM 215:1
annihilate: a. but space and time POPE 380:22
Annihilating: A. all that's made MARV 332:5
Annihilation: Oblivion is a kind of A. BROW 95:14
anniversaries: secret a. of the heart LONG 317:15
Anno Domini: you shall taste my A. FARQ 209:22
annotate: Edit and a. the lines YEATS 586:14
announcing: a. ruin like a town crier THOM 546:21
annoy: He only does it to a. CARR 133:26
annoyance: Shadow of a. SHEL 504:22
annuity: a. is a very serious business AUST 23:24
annus: monet a. et almum HOR 261:15
anointed: a. Solomon BIBLE 50:30
hast a. my head with oil PRAY 390:22
wash the balm from an a. SHAK 479:5
anointing: Thou the a. Spirit art PRAY 400:5
another: a. shall gird thee BIBLE 73:17
a. Troy for her to burn YEATS 586:7
censure or condemn a. BROW 96:32
fair house built upon a. SHAK 469:9
happiness through a. man's eyes SHAK 426:28
love one a. or die AUDEN 20:9
members one of a. BIBLE 77:29
not spend a. such a night SHAK 480:26
setteth up a. PRAY 394:26

taste of a. man's bread DANTE 171:17
to choose love by a.'s SHAK 469:19
when comes such a. SHAK 451:5
woman can forgive a. GAY 222:15
anser: argutos inter strepere a. olores
VIRG 560:7
Answer: A. a fool according BIBLE 54:31
a. came there none CARR 135:11
a. came there none SCOTT 415:21
a. made it none SHAK 430:10
A. not a fool according BIBLE 54:31
He would a. to 'Hi CARR 133:3
I will a. HOUS 263:17
man's waitin' for a a. DICK 176:34
please thee with my a. SHAK 467:23
silver a. rang...'Not Death BROW 98:9
soft a. turneth away wrath BIBLE 54:4
than the wisest man can a. COLT 159:9
They sent an a. back to me CARR 135:25
what a dusty a. gets MER 337:18
what a. should I give TENN 542:13
What *is* the a. STEIN 518:19
Why Did You A. the Phone THUR 550:30
answerably: a. to your Christian calling
PRAY 388:11
answer'd: grievously hath Caesar a. it
SHAK 450:17
answered: a. some AUDEN 21:9
He a. the description FARQ 210:18
his prayer is a. MER 337:36
no one a. DE L 174:8
answers: Kind are her a. CAMP 129:21
ant: a.'s a centaur in his POUND 382:13
good husband, little a. LOV 318:14
Go to the a. thou sluggard BIBLE 53:21
antagonist: a. over the edge of a precipice
BRAM 91:21
Our a. is our helper BURKE 111:23
antan: où sont les neiges d'a. VILL 557:5
antediluvian: one of your a. families
CONG 160:10
anthem: thy plaintive a. fades KEATS 291:23
anthems: a. clear MILT 342:10
Anthropophagi: A., and men whose
heads SHAK 473:25
anti: savage a.-everythings HOLM 253:10
antic: dance an a. hay MARL 329:17
To put an a. disposition SHAK 431:24
Antichrist: like A. in that lewd hat
JONS 283:15
anticipate: What we a. seldom occurs
DISR 186:10
anticipation: intelligent a. of facts
CURZ 170:17
antidote: sharp a. against disgrace
BURKE 111:9
some sweet oblivious a. SHAK 463:3
antigropeloes: Donn'd galligaskins, a.
CALV 127:16
antilogy: intolerable a. HARDY 239:16
antipathies: myself those common a.
BROW 96:28
antipathy: I have no a. BROW 96:27
strong a. of good to bad POPE 380:19
Antipodes: like A. in shoes MARV 332:23
sheer opposite, a. KEATS 289:28
slightest errand now to the A. SHAK 472:9
antiquarian: mere a. is a rugged being
JOHN 277:27
antiquates: which a. antiquities BROW 97:12
antique: follow an a. drum ELIOT 202:27
group that's quite a. BYRON 122:23
hat of a. shape ARN 14:13
noble and nude and a. SWIN 529:4
traveller from an a. land SHEL 502:15
Antiquitas: A. saeculi juventus mundi
BACON 25:10
Antiquities: A. are history defaced
BACON 24:18
which antiquates a. BROW 97:12

antiquity: about you blasted with a.
SHAK 441:10
I will write for A. LAMB 307:37
little skill in a. inclines FULL 220:14
rejected all respect for a. DISR 185:37
antithesis: he himself one vile a. POPE 377:3
Antony: A., Enthron'd i' the market-place
SHAK 422:3
Antony Should conquer A. SHAK 423:13
first meet the curled A. SHAK 424:14
Much A. HENL 245:12
my oblivion is a very A. SHAK 421:28
quick spirit that is in A. SHAK 448:9
shall be buried by her A. SHAK 424:19
Since my lord Is A. again SHAK 422:23
there were an A. SHAK 451:3
think them every one an A. SHAK 422:9
would catch a second A. SHAK 424:17
ants: trouble of a. TENN 544:4
anulus: consumitur a. usu OVID 366:27
anvil: be the a. or the hammer GOET 230:7
England's on the a. KIPL 297:26
My sledge and a. lie declined ANON 6:19
sword of this stone and a. MAL 327:14
anxiety: 'caused me a little a.' MACM 325:19
repose is taboo'd by a. GILB 226:12
rider's back sits dark A. HOR 260:15
anxious: closed our a. care of thee
PEAC 370:20
Unvex'd with a. cares DRYD 196:3
you're a. for to shine GILB 227:20
any: If a. of you know cause PRAY 388:23
anybody: 'Is there a. there DE L 174:7
Then no one's a. GILB 225:31
anything: Nobody tells me a. GALS 221:1
old to dote on her for a. SHAK 453:14
Ready to be a. BROW 97:24
anywhere: peace has been broken a.
ROOS 407:23
apart: of man's life a thing a. BYRON 122:14
Things fall a. YEATS 586:15
We have stood a. WILS 574:21
apathetic: gray life, and a. end TENN 539:18
ape: a. an ancient rage CHES 147:12
a. for his grandfather HUXL 269:13
a. the magnanimity of love MER 337:6
blue-behinded a. STEV 523:3
exception is a naked a. MORR 358:5
Is man an a. or an angel DISR 185:2
like an a. doth nuts SHAK 435:24
played the sedulous a. STEV 521:9
their manners from the A. BELL 38:26
Apeneck: A. Sweeney spreads his
ELIOT 204:14
apes: a., and peacocks BIBLE 50:34
a. and peacocks MAS 333:18
a. are apes JONS 284:14
barnacles, or to a. SHAK 485:22
lead a. in hell SHAK 484:7
Now for dogs and a. BROW 100:37
person and the peple his a. CHAU 142:7
pride that a. humility COL 156:13
aphorism: corroboration of this a. BIRK 84:12
aphrodisiac: circumambulating a. FRY 219:32
Aphrodite: Blonde A. rose up excited
AUDEN 18:3
Apollo: A. from his shrine MILT 344:13
A. hunted Daphne so MARV 332:2
bright A. POUND 383:9
bright A.'s lute SHAK 457:8
burn'd in A.'s laurel MARL 329:16
harsh after the songs of A. SHAK 457:20
is not even A. SWIN 530:3
Neither Calliope nor A. POUND 382:15
Phoebus A. turned fasting MER 337:20
Sic me servavit A. HOR 262:6
'Tis A. comes leading ARN 13:8
young A. CORN 162:21
Apollos: A. watered BIBLE 75:31
Apollyon: his name is A. BUNY 107:14

apologise: I never a. SHAW 496:7
A pology: A. for the Devil BUTL 119:1
Never make a defence or a. CHAR 140:17
apoplexy: Peace is a very a. SHAK 427:27
This a. is SHAK 441:6
apostle: great a. of the Philistines ARN 16:6
meet to be called an a. BIBLE 76:19
rank as an a. in the high GILB 227:23
apostles: am the least of the a. BIBLE 76:19
A. would have done as they BYRON 122:10
Cristes loore and his a. CHAU 142:3
glorious company of the A. PRAY 384:16
He gave some, a. BIBLE 77:28
true a. of equality ARN 15:16
Twelve for the twelve a. ANON 6:5
Apostolick: Catholick and A. Church
PRAY 387:11
apothecary: ointment of the a. to send
BIBLE 56:1
starved a. than a starved poet LOCK 315:22
apothegmaticall: precious a. Pedant
NASHE 360:6
appalling: Drifts the a. snow AUDEN 18:10
apparel: a. oft proclaims the man
SHAK 430:19
hath put on glorious a. PRAY 395:24
She was rich in a. TROL 552:16
apparition: a. of these faces POUND 383:11
a., sole of men SHEL 502:19
was an a. AUBR 18:2
appassionato: black piano a. LAWR 311:7
Appeal: A. from Philip drunk ANON 4:22
a. to the understanding BAG 28:30
I a. unto Caesar BIBLE 74:23
they a. from tyranny to God BYRON 125:15
appeals: a. to diffused feeling BAG 28:30
appear: a. considerable in his JOHN 276:1
let that a. when there SHAK 472:28
appearance: a. of Your Majesty BIBLE 44:21
looketh on the outward a. BIBLE 50:6
Thou hast a grim a. SHAK 427:26
appearances: contrive To save a. MILT 349:3
Keep up a. CHUR 148:33
There is no trusting a. SHER 506:35
appeareth: that a. for a little time
BIBLE 80:16
appetit: a. hath he to ete a mous CHAU 142:25
L'a. vient en mangeant RAB 403:26
appetite: a. may sicken SHAK 487:20
Doth not the a. alter SHAK 472:18
good digestion wait on a. SHAK 461:18
increase of a. had grown SHAK 429:28
mortified a. is never STEV 521:3
satisfying a voracious a. FIEL 211:25
their love may be call'd a. SHAK 489:6
What a. you have SHAK 447:6
With a more riotous a. SHAK 455:17
appetites: men's carnal lusts and a.
PRAY 388:25
not their a. SHAK 475:21
Our a. as apt to change DRYD 195:15
Subdue your a. my dears DICK 180:2
thise wrecched worldes a. CHAU 144:19
Applaud: A. us when we run BURKE 110:19
Till thou a. the deed SHAK 461:14
applause: attentive to his own a. POPE 376:27
Gained universal a. STEE 517:23
it were a. HARDY 240:16
sunshine and with a. BUNY 107:19
that in Beauty's just a. MARL 330:11
apple: a. damn'd mankind OTWAY 366:7
a. for the apple's sake TWAIN 554:19
a. press'd with specious HOOD 255:3
a. trees will never get FROST 219:9
Galatea throws an a. at me VIRG 559:18
goodly a. rotten SHAK 466:1
him as the a. of his eye BIBLE 48:30
it was the a. of his eye THOR 550:12
Just as the sweet-a. reddens SAPP 414:7
Like the sweet a. which ROSS 409:13

Of candied a. KEATS 289:20
there vor me the a. tree BARN 33:28
trees of small green a. BETJ 43:7
when 'tis almost an a. SHAK 488:9
With a. pie and cheese FIELD 211:1
young and easy under the a. THOM 547:1
apple-dumplings: pure mind who refuses
a. LAMB 307:6
apple-pie: to make an a. FOOTE 216:7
was an a. ANON 4:25
apples: a., cherries DICK 181:27
A. of gold for the king's SWIN 530:17
comfort me with a. BIBLE 56:21
Like to the a. on the Dead BYRON 120:28
Moon-washed a. of wonder DRIN 193:23
Ripe a. drop about my head MARV 332:3
saw you picking dewy a. VIRG 560:4
silver a. of the moon YEATS 586:21
spoken is like a. of gold BIBLE 54:26
stolen, be your a. HUNT 268:11
apple-tree: My heart is like an a. ROSS 408:23
Swing up into the a. ELIOT 203:16
applications: a. for situations AUDEN 20:2
seulement des a. de la science PAST 369:17
applied: such things as a. sciences
PAST 369:17
apply: a. new remedies must expect
BACON 26:28
a. our hearts unto wisdom PRAY 395:20
appointed: even in the time a. PRAY 395:9
house a. for all living BIBLE 52:36
appointment: a. by the corrupt few
SHAW 497:36
a. with a beech-tree THOR 550:20
Every time I make an a. LOUI 318:9
apprehend: it would but a. some joy
SHAK 471:11
apprehension: a. of the good SHAK 478:17
of death is most in a. SHAK 464:11
apprehensions: My a. come in crowds
WORD 576:23
apprentice: a. for to bind BALL 30:8
appris: Ils n'ont rien a. TALL 531:17
oublié et n'ont rien a. DUM 199:7
sans avoir jamais rien a. MOL 353:23
approach: Much of his near a. afraid
GARR 221:16
snuff the a. of tyranny BURKE 109:23
Approbation: A. from Sir Hubert Stanley
MORT 358:16
approve: I do not a. MILL 339:23
it and a. it with a text SHAK 467:10
men of sense a. POPE 378:24
my love doth so a. him SHAK 476:25
which he could a. SHEL 504:5
apricocks: thou up yon dangling a.
SHAK 479:17
April: A., April WATS 565:9
A. is the cruellest month ELIOT 204:17
A. of your youth adorns HERB 246:20
A.'s in the west wind MAS 334:9
blossoming boughs of A. BRID 92:8
Calls back the lovely A. SHAK 492:24
England are March and A. TROL 552:21
green hill in an A. shroud KEATS 291:15
I've an A. blindness FRY 219:26
Men are A. when they woo SHAK 426:23
Now that A.'s there BROW 101:5
sweet love seemed that A. BRID 92:20
Three A. perfumes in three SHAK 494:18
uncertain glory of an A. day SHAK 490:33
When proud-pied A. SHAK 494:17
Which spongy A. at thy SHAK 485:19
April-fools: One of love's A. CONG 160:18
Aprill: Whan that A. with his shoures
CHAU 141:7
aprons: made themselves a. BIBLE 45:16
apt: find myself so a. to die SHAK 450:8
aptitude: grande a. à la patience BUFF 106:21
greater a. for patience BUFF 106:21

aquae: scribuntur a. potoribus HOR 258:25
Aquitaine: prince d'A. à la tour NERV 360:26
Arabia: all the perfumes of A. SHAK 462:22
A. and Saba shall bring PRAY 394:20
given of the gold of A. PRAY 394:21
with the spell of far A. DE L 173:26
Arabian: On the sole A. tree SHAK 492:15
She is alone the A. bird SHAK 428:7
wish the A. Tales were true NEWM 361:16
Arabians: Cretes and A. BIBLE 73:23
Arabs: like the A. LONG 316:10
Araby: Of A. the Blest MILT 347:17
That burns in glorious A. DARL 171:21
Aral Sea: shine upon the A. ARN 15:1
Aram: Eugene A. walked between
HOOD 254:12
Araminta: A., say 'No PRAED 384:4
aratro: nullo contusus a. CAT 137:6
Arbiter: A. of others' fate BYRON 125:8
Elegantiae. TAC 531:11
high a. Chance governs MILT 347:4
arbitrary: supreme power must be a.
HAL 237:19
arbitrate: Does a. th' event MILT 341:9
who shall a. BROW 104:7
arbitrator: that old common a. SHAK 487:15
Arboreal: of all sits Probably A. STEV 521:10
probably a. in its habits DARW 171:23
arbour: a. where the rain beat ELIOT 202:16
arbours: His private a. SHAK 451:4
arbusta: Non omnis a. iuvant humilesque
VIRG 559:22
Arcades: A. ambo VIRG 560:3
'A. ambo.' *id est* BYRON 123:12
Arcadia: *Et in A. ego* ANON 10:12
Arcadians: A. both VIRG 560:3
arceo: Odi profanum vulgus et a. HOR 260:13
Archangel: A. a little damaged LAMB 307:29
Archangels: Therefore with Angels and
A. PRAY 387:23
Archbishop: is the A. of Canterbury
SMITH 511:6
Lord A. of Rheims BARH 33:11
archdeacon: (by way of turbot) an a.
SMITH 512:10
archer: a. his sharp arrows tries SIDN 507:18
mark the a. little meant SCOTT 416:23
arches: down the a. of the years THOM 548:8
archewyves: a., stondeth at defense
CHAU 142:10
arch-flatterer: well said that 'the a.
BACON 26:30
archipelagoes: fading alps and a. ALDR 3:11
Architect: aims the A. who planned
WORD 582:16
a., one of the greatest BARH 33:7
painter can be an a. RUSK 411:8
architectooraloorol: it is there drawd
too a. DICK 178:13
architectural: respectable a. man-milliner
RUSK 411:5
well knew the great a. TROL 552:16
Architecture: A. in general is frozen
SCH 415:8
frolic a. of the snow EMER 206:24
many odd styles of a. about RUSK 411:5
New styles of a. AUDEN 20:7
wondrous A. of the world MARL 330:8
archways: Of a ripple under a. HARDY 239:18
archy: jamais triste a. MARQ 330:21
arcs: earth the broken a. BROW 98:18
Arcturi: pearled A. of the earth SHEL 503:18
Arden: now am I in A. SHAK 425:8
ardet: paries cum proximus a. HOR 258:23
ardeur: a. dans mes veines cachée RAC 404:4
ardor: frío que templa el a. CERV 138:20
ardour: a. of my zeal repress'd CHUR 148:22
ardua: Per a. ad astra ANON 10:16
arduis: Aequam memento rebus in a.
HOR 260:6

are: actions a. what they are BUTL 117:10
a. strangers before thee BIBLE 51:39
know that which we a. BYRON 124:9
Let them be as they a. CLEM 153:1
so very indubitably a. BEER 37:23
we know what we a. SHAK 436:1
will tell you what you a. BRIL 93:9
arena: a. swims around him BYRON 121:15
Arethusa: A. arose SHEL 500:2
argent: l'a. ou de la petite monnaie
CHAM 139:14
Sans a. l'honneur n'est RAC 404:6
argifying: What's the good of a. KIPL 304:26
Argo: loftier A. cleaves SHEL 500:21
argosies: a. of magic sails TENN 538:24
your a. with portly sail SHAK 465:7
argue: earth does not a. WHIT 571:11
he could a. still GOLD 231:3
It is as absurd to a. men NEWM 362:8
argues: heart a., not the mind ARN 13:20
It a. an insensibility LAMB 307:4
argufies: a. sniv'ling and piping DIBD 175:19
arguing: Be calm in a. HERB 247:6
I am not a. with you WHIS 569:17
in a. with the inevitable LOW 319:18
necessity will be much a. MILT 352:2
There is no a. with Johnson GOLD 232:40
argument: All a. is against it JOHN 277:21
A.'s hot to the close BROW 102:11
heard great a. FITZ 212:20
highth of this great a. MILT 344:22
I have found you an a. JOHN 279:21
is never without an a. HAL 238:1
It is the a. of tyrants PITT 374:3
It would be a. for a week SHAK 438:27
love are still my a. SHAK 494:9
nice knock-down a. for you CARR 135:1
than the staple of his a. SHAK 457:10
their swords for lack of a. SHAK 444:1
This is a rotten a. ANON 8:8
Tories own no a. but force BROW 97:26
to stir without great a. SHAK 435:31
Whigs admit no force but a. BROW 97:26
argumentative: be of a studious or a.
JOHN 278:21
arguments: No a. shall be wanting
AUST 23:18
tongue tang a. of state SHAK 489:15
Argus: Though A. were her eunuch
SHAK 456:27
argutos: a. inter strepere anser VIRG 560:7
Ariadne: Inconsolable to the minuet in
A. SHER 505:26
Since A. was a vintager KEATS 289:4
Arian: three sips the A. frustrate BROW 105:6
Ariel: Caliban casts out A. POUND 383:6
deal of A. HENL 245:12
aright: sought the Lord a. BURNS 113:6
Ariosto: A. of the North BYRON 121:5
arise: ah for a man to a. in me TENN 540:4
a. and unbuild it again SHEL 500:7
A. from their graves BLAKE 87:22
A., shine BIBLE 60:7
I will a. and go now YEATS 585:11
Let God a. PRAY 394:6
My lady sweet, a. SHAK 428:10
ariseth: sun a. PRAY 397:1
Aristocracy: A. of the Moneybag
CARL 131:27
a. to what is decent HOPE 255:29
a. the most democratic MAC 324:16
Aristocrat: A. who banks with Coutts
GILB 225:23
aristocratic: a. class from the Philistines
ARN 15:19
Aristotle: A. was but the rubbish
SOUTH 513:12
follow this counsel of A. ASCH 17:4
Of A. and his philosophie CHAU 141:24
whom A. thought SHAK 486:30

Arithmetic: different branches of A.
CARR 134:10
would life be without a. SMITH 512:7
arithmetical: increases in an a. ratio
MALT 328:9
ark: him an a. of bulrushes BIBLE 46:41
Noe entered into the a. BIBLE 67:32
straight out of the A. SMITH 511:1
two unto Noah into the A. BIBLE 45:34
arm: almighty stretch'd-out a. SMART 509:4
a. Crested the world SHAK 423:22
A. it in rags SHAK 455:20
a. of the Lord revealed BIBLE 59:20
a. our soldier SHAK 427:11
by a stretched out a. BIBLE 48:19
eye and the strong a. of England
PALM 368:10
gather the lambs with his a. BIBLE 59:7
Human on my faithless a. AUDEN 19:17
lang's my a. BURNS 115:16
one a. bent across your SASS 414:14
rebellious arm 'gainst a. SHAK 458:5
seal upon thine a. BIBLE 57:11
shewed strength with his a. BIBLE 69:6
smal coral aboute hire a. CHAU 141:17
undone widow sits upon my a. MASS 335:21
with his holy a. PRAY 396:7
Arma: *A. virumque cano* VIRG 557:8
Cedant a. togae CIC 151:22
Moriamur et in media a. ruamus VIRG 558:7
Nunc a. defunctumque bello HOR 261:6
Quis iustis induit a. LUCAN 319:22
Silent enim leges inter a. CIC 151:31
Armadas: hammock till the great A.
NEWB 361:7
Armadill: Nor yet an A.- KIPL 300:8
Armageddon: in the Hebrew tongue A.
BIBLE 82:21
armaments: end to these bloated a.
DISR 184:24
arm-chair: loving that old a. ELIZ 162:7
of the Fortieth spare A. BROW 100:19
arm-chairs: wearing a. tight WOD 575:25
arm'd: a. so strong in honesty SHAK 451:20
I'm a. with more than complete ANON 6:4
Armed: A. at points exactly SHAK 430:7
A. neutrality WILS 574:22
goeth on to meet the a. BIBLE 53:6
want as an a. man BIBLE 53:22
armies: a. swore terribly in Flanders
STER 519:28
embattled a. clad in iron MILT 350:18
ignorant a. clash by night ARN 12:23
interested in a. and fleets AUDEN 18:15
Kings with their a. did flee PRAY 394:8
prodigious a. we had in Flanders STER 519:26
Arminian: A. clergy PITT 373:25
armonye: herkenyng a. CHAU 144:18
armor: a. of a righteous cause BRYAN 106:7
Armoric: Begirt with British and A.
MILT 345:23
armour: a. stripped from Achilles VIRG 558:5
a. wherein he trusted BIBLE 69:36
Came clad in a. HOUS 265:14
dilloing in his a. KIPL 300:8
In whose coat a. richly SPEN 515:19
Put on the whole a. of God BIBLE 78:9
put upon us the a. of light PRAY 386:4
There is no a. against fate SHIR 507:2
us put on the a. of light BIBLE 75:24
Whose a. is his honest WOTT 583:12
work out Achilles his a. BROW 95:18
you the whole a. of God BIBLE 78:10
armourers: a., accomplishing SHAK 444:9
Now thrive the a. SHAK 443:12
Armoury: A. of the invincible Knights
WORD 582:3
arms: are the everlasting a. BIBLE 48:33
a. against a sea of troubles SHAK 433:8
a. along the deep proudly CAMP 128:14

A., and the man DRYD 198:22
a. and the man who first VIRG 557:8
a. burd Helen dropt BALL 31:4
a. long and small WYATT 583:22
A., take your last embrace SHAK 483:31
a. with more right on his LUCAN 319:22
a. ye forge, another bears SHEL 504:3
a. you bear are brittle HOUS 264:3
beauty summoned Greece to a. MARL 330:14
corners of the world in a. SHAK 453:1
defy th' Omnipotent to a. MILT 344:24
find the a. of my true love TENN 540:13
first dawn in Helen's a. YEATS 586:4
Flinging from her a. YEATS 585:20
His a. might do what this WALL 562:10
if my love were in my a. ANON 8:16
I'll forswear a. SHAK 438:12
Imparadised in one another's a. MILT 348:1
in my a. till break AUDEN 19:17
it hath very long a. HAL 238:2
Its green a. round SHEL 503:17
Leap to these a. SHAK 483:6
lord of folded a. SHAK 456:26
mightier than they in a. MILT 348:26
might'st seek it in My a. THOM 548:22
My soul's in a. CIBB 151:13
nation proud in a. MILT 340:26
of a state a. do flourish BACON 27:34
So he laid down his a. HOOD 254:13
sure-enwinding a. WHIT 571:13
Those entrusted with a. WIND 575:7
To war and a. I fly LOV 318:20
Army: A. is the Non-commissioned
KIPL 298:22
a. marches on its stomach ANON 9:3
a. marches on its stomach NAP 359:17
a. of unalterable law MER 337:5
a. would be a base rabble BURKE 110:5
contemptible little A. WILH 574:4
England brought the A. home GUED 237:4
English a. led by an Irish SHAW 498:7
fighting with your land a. MONT 355:9
Grand A. never looked MAHAN 327:5
hum of either a. SHAK 444:9
my great a. which I sent BIBLE 61:14
name an 'A.' doth present HERB 246:25
noble a. of Martyrs PRAY 384:16
terrible as an a. with banners BIBLE 57:5
Your poor a. CROM 170:3
Aroint: A. thee, witch SHAK 458:6
aromatic: faint beneath the a. pain
WINC 575:6
arose: he a. and followed him BIBLE 65:21
Arques: we fought at A. and you
HENR 245:14
arrange: do we always a. for more KIPL 302:3
arrangement: a. of your words HOR 257:13
arrangements: has no a. WHIT 571:11
arrayed: all his glory was not a. BIBLE 64:30
arrears: pay glad life's a. BROW 104:1
With long a. to make good KIPL 298:1
arrest: Is swift in his a. SHAK 437:22
neither a. nor movement ELIOT 202:15
arrests: a. the mind in the presence
JOYCE 286:17
Arrival-Angst: A. is closely connected
CONN 161:14
arrive: been at to a. where I am BUNY 107:38
be to a. where we started ELIOT 203:2
better thing than to a. STEV 522:9
arriving: a. in the evening than CONN 161:14
arrogance: a. of age must submit
BURKE 110:23
arrogant: submitted and to subdue the
a. VIRG 559:1
arrow: a. from the Almighty's BLAKE 86:6
a. that flieth by day PRAY 395:21
Every a. that flies feels LONG 316:4
I have shot mine a. o'er SHAK 437:16
I shot an a. into the air LONG 316:6

arrows: a. in the hand of the giant
PRAY 398:19
Bring me my a. of desire BLAKE 86:16
busy archer his sharp a. SIDN 507:18
slings and a. of outrageous SHAK 433:8
spend mine a. upon them BIBLE 48:32
teeth are spears and a. PRAY 393:15
arse: Sit on your a. for fifty MACN 326:8
arsenal: great a. of democracy ROOS 407:25
arsenals: a. of divine vengeance HOUS 266:13
arsenic: They put a. in his meat HOUS 264:15
art: all the adulteries of A. JONS 283:27
A. and Science cannot exist BLAKE 86:7
a. can wash her guilt GOLD 231:31
a. constantly aspires towards PATER 369:20
a. for art's sake and with CONS 162:5
a. for art's sake…the beautiful COUS 163:9
a., in London only is DRYD 197:13
A. is a jealous mistress EMER 207:6
A. is long LONG 317:2
A. is not a handicraft TOLS 551:14
a. is the history of revivals BUTL 118:33
A. is the only thing that BOWEN 91:2
a. is to limit and isolate GOET 229:27
A. is upon the Town WHIS 569:18
a. made tongue-tied SHAK 494:5
A. most cherishes BROW 102:26
A. must be parochial MOORE 355:16
A. never expresses anything WILDE 572:24
a. of getting drunk JOHN 278:8
a. of our necessities is SHAK 454:11
A.'s subject is the human AUDEN 19:16
A. stopped short GILB 227:22
believe in A. for Art's sake FORS 217:14
clever, but is it A. KIPL 298:16
Desiring this man's a. SHAK 493:6
despise A. and Science BLAKE 86:9
devoid of a. GAY 223:5
difference in all a. ROSS 410:10
each a. to please POPE 376:26
emotion in the form of a. ELIOT 205:16
ensnaring a. BURNS 113:7
est la probité de l'a. INGR 270:19
every a. is its intensity KEATS 293:18
failed in literature and a. DISR 186:23
faithful herdman's a. belongs MILT 343:12
Fine a. is that in which RUSK 411:25
French a., if not sanguinary SPEN 515:5
glib and oily a. SHAK 453:5
glory and good of A. BROW 104:34
Grotesque A. in English Poetry BAG 29:20
him was almost lost in A. COLL 158:23
in a. the best is good GOET 230:8
in writing comes from a. POPE 378:22
is the a. of the possible BISM 84:20
is the true test of a. INGR 270:19
It is a. that *makes* life JAMES 272:2
I turn'd the tuneful a. POPE 380:4
l'a. beau ne peut être la COUS 163:9
L'a. pour l'art et sans CONS 162:5
last and greatest a. POPE 380:16
Living is my job and my a. MONT 354:23
message of A. SHAW 496:22
Minister that meddles with a. MELB 336:16
models destroy genius and a. HAZL 243:28
morality of A. consists WILDE 573:17
More matter with less a. SHAK 431:32
Must learn the hateful a. KING 296:13
nature is the a. of God BROW 96:13
nature's handmaid is DRYD 195:22
next to Nature, A. LAND 308:20
Not without a. CHUR 149:12
ornaments their want of a. POPE 378:16
people start on all this A. HERB 246:10
resuscitate the dead a. Of poetry
POUND 383:1
staff Which A. hath lodged WORD 582:13
strains of unpremeditated a. SHEL 504:15
symbol of Irish a. JOYCE 286:21
That Shakespeare wanted A. JONS 285:17

Though a.'s hid causes | JONS 283:27
trade and half an a. | INGE 270:8
unsettling element in modern a. | WHAR 569:9
when A. Is too precise | HERR 249:2
Who first taught A. | ROSS 410:1
without a. is brutality | RUSK 411:9
works of a. | ALB 3:7
artes: a. Intulit agresti | HOR 259:2
didicisse fideliter a. | OVID 366:25
(Hae tibi erunt a.) | VIRG 559:1
artful: He's a. | ELIOT 202:8
Arthur: He's in A.'s bosom | SHAK 443:17
talks of A.'s death | SHAK 452:27
article: be snuff'd out by an a. | BYRON 123:32
of being the correct a. | ASHF 17:12
'What's the next a. | GILB 227:28
artifex: Qualis a. pereo | NERO 360:24
artificer: Another lean unwash'd a. | SHAK 452:27
great a. Made my mate | STEV 523:3
Old father, old a. | JOYCE 286:19
artificial: All things are a. | BROW 96:13
artificially: people hang together a. | BUTL 118:29
artillery: Th' a. of words | SWIFT 527:31
With the self-same a. | LOV 318:12
artisan: give employment to the a. | BELL 39:29
artist: a., like the God | JOYCE 286:18
a. never dies | LONG 316:24
a. writes his own autobiography | ELLIS 206:14
grant the a. his subject | JAMES 271:13
Never trust the a. | LAWR 311:10
no man is born an a. | WALT 563:33
true a. will let his wife | SHAW 497:21
West and from now on an a. | CONN 161:16
What an a. dies with me | NERO 360:24
artistic: a. performance requires | JAMES 271:29
a. temperament is a disease | CHES 148:1
give a. verisimilitude | GILB 227:12
artistries: Eternal a. in Circumstance | HARDY 239:11
artistry: scaled invention or true a. | POUND 382:13
Art-loving: There never was an A. nation | WHIS 569:19
arts: a. into rustic Latium | HOR 259:2
cry both a. and learning | QUAR 403:21
Dear nurse of a. | SHAK 445:11
fam'd in all great a. | ARN 15:11
gentle a. which refine | DICK 177:29
had I but followed the a. | SHAK 487:26
hate for a. that caus'd | POPE 376:26
His virtues were his a. | BURKE 112:13
is the bitterness of a. | STEV 521:13
liberal a. refines behaviour | OVID 366:25
mechanical a. and merchandise | BACON 27:34
mother of a. And eloquence | MILT 350:8
No a.; no letters | HOBB 251:18
our a. with laughters low | JOYCE 286:10
therefore the lowest of the a. | MOORE 355:17
Where grew the a. of war | BYRON 122:32
artus: dum spiritus hos regit a. | VIRG 558:13
totamque infusa per a. | VIRG 558:24
Aryan: health to hustle the A. | KIPL 301:18
ascendant: became lord of the a. | BURKE 109:6
ascended: He a. into heaven | PRAY 384:26
ascendeth: smoke of their torment a. | BIBLE 82:17
ascending: angels of God a. and descending | BIBLE 46:18
Ascension: glorious Resurrection and A. | PRAY 385:17
ascetic: a. rocks and the sensual | MER 337:27
ascribe: a. to an opponent motives | BARR 34:9
A. unto the Lord the honour | PRAY 396:5
Ash: Oak, and A., and Thorn | KIPL 303:25
Only the A. | DE L 174:18

ashamed: are a. of our naked skins | SHAW 497:18
a. thereof | BROW 96:20
be a. to own he has been | POPE 381:19
does not make friends a. | WALT 564:6
doing something he is a. | SHAW 496:10
Hope maketh not a. | BIBLE 74:41
Let them be a. and confounded | PRAY 394:15
more things a man is a. | SHAW 497:19
Nor ever once a. | ARN 12:19
to be a. with the noble | KING 297:6
to beg I am a. | BIBLE 70:23
wonder to see them not a. | SWIFT 527:15
ashbuds: More black than a. | TENN 533:19
ashes: All a. to the taste | BYRON 120:28
Are a. under Uricon | HOUS 263:15
a. new-create another heir | SHAK 448:3
a. of an Oak in the Chimney | DONNE 190:23
a. of his fathers | MAC 322:15
a. to ashes | PRAY 389:13
a. where once I was fire | BYRON 125:31
from his a. may be made | TENN 536:10
into a. all my lust | MARV 332:19
little monograph on the a. | DOYLE 191:16
Scatter my a. | GRAH 233:16
sour grapes and a. | ASHF 17:14
turn the universe to a. | CEL 138:5
turn to a. on the lips | MOORE 356:26
unto them beauty for a. | BIBLE 60:9
Asia: army on the mainland of A. | MONT 355:9
churches which are in A. | BIBLE 81:9
churches which are in A. | BIBLE 81:12
It dawns in A. | HOUS 262:13
much A. and she is too old | KIPL 304:27
ye pampered Jades of A. | MARL 330:16
Asiatic: A. vague immensities | YEATS 587:1
aside: turned a. and wept | AYT 24:8
ask: all that we a. or think | BIBLE 77:26
a. amid the dews of morning | HOUS 265:10
A., and it shall be given | BIBLE 65:2
A. me no more where Jove | CAREW 130:18
A. me no more | TENN 542:13
A. the booksellers of London | BURKE 111:17
blindness we cannot a. | PRAY 388:7
greatest fool may a. more | COLT 159:9
things which we a. faithfully | PRAY 387:1
Where a. is have | SMART 509:3
you a. me for my body | SHAW 496:30
asked: I have a. to be | HOPK 256:17
Oliver Twist has a. for more | DICK 180:32
You a. for it | MOL 353:15
Askelon: not in the streets of A. | BIBLE 50:16
asketh: Every one that a. receiveth | BIBLE 65:3
asking: is the first time of a. | PRAY 388:23
offering too little and a. | CANN 129:25
asks: a. no questions isn't told | KIPL 302:22
asleep: are too young to fall a. | SASS 414:15
Fall a., or hearing die | SHAK 447:3
Got 'tween a. and wake | SHAK 453:9
he lies fast a. | FITZ 212:14
men were all a. the snow | BRID 92:12
sucks the nurse a. | SHAK 424:14
those that are a. to speak | BIBLE 57:10
very houses seem a. | WORD 581:15
Where the winds are all a. | ARN 13:6
asp: play on the hole of the a. | BIBLE 58:11
asparagus: Grew like a. in May | GILB 225:29
mention A. and it appeared | DICK 178:25
Aspect: A. anything but bland | CALV 127:14
aspens: a. quiver | TENN 538:3
Asperges: A. me | MASS 334:10
A. me hyssopo | BIBLE 83:6
aspersion: a. upon my parts of speech | SHER 506:13
aspes: a. leef she gan to quake | CHAU 144:9
asphodel: Violet, amaracus, and a. | TENN 541:18

aspiration: yearning thought And a. | ROSS 410:7
aspirations: talk to you of their a. | SMITH 510:15
aspire: be that by due steps a. | MILT 340:24
crouch whom the rest bade a. | BROW 102:6
from their graves and a. | BLAKE 87:22
light, and will a. | SHAK 495:19
aspired: I am he that a. to KNOW | BROW 103:3
aspires: All art constantly a. towards | PATER 369:20
Aspiring: A. to be angels men rebel | POPE 379:7
us all to have a. minds | MARL 330:8
ass: ashamed the law is such an a. | CHAP 140:12
a. his master's crib | BIBLE 57:15
a.'s ears of Midas | SIDN 508:5
a. when thou art present | CONG 160:22
a. will not mend his pace | SHAK 436:24
a., without being a fool | SURT 525:3
Bumble...'the law is a a. | DICK 181:2
Caesar a. Unpolicied | SHAK 424:14
jaw of an a. have I slain | BIBLE 49:24
making him egregiously an a. | SHAK 474:22
nor his a. | BIBLE 47:24
to write me down an a. | SHAK 473:5
was enamour'd of an a. | SHAK 471:6
Wild A. | FITZ 212:14
Assailant: A. on the perched roosts | MILT 350:29
assaille: a. His wyves pacience | CHAU 142:9
assassination: absolutism moderated by a. | ANON 5:5
A. has never changed | DISR 185:3
A. is the quickest way | MOL 353:24
A. is the extreme form | SHAW 498:17
if the a. Could trammel | SHAK 459:5
Assassiner: A. c'est le plus court | MOL 353:24
assassins: que MM les a. commencent | KARR 288:16
assault: thoughts which may a. and hurt | PRAY 386:9
assaults: crafts and a. of the devil | PRAY 385:16
in all a. of our enemies | PRAY 385:2
assay: a. ther may no man it preve | CHAU 143:28
Th' a. so hard | CHAU 143:32
assembled: Once again a. here | BUCK 106:16
assemblies: calling of a. | BIBLE 57:17
assembly: parliament is a *deliberative* a. | BURKE 109:12
assent: a. with civil leer | POPE 376:26
asses: Death hath a.' ears | BEDD 36:27
Mankind are the a. who pull | BYRON 124:32
riches to those gross a. | LUTH 320:14
seeking a. | MILT 350:6
wild a. quench their thirst | PRAY 396:19
asshen: Yet in oure a. olde is | CHAU 143:10
assis: Omnes unius aestimemus a. | CAT 136:25
assistant: learned British Museum a. | POUND 383:14
me be no a. for a state | SHAK 432:3
assisted: never a. the sun | THOR 550:10
assuage: a. the unforgotten pain | ROSS 410:6
Assume: A. a virtue | SHAK 435:18
We must never a. that which | LEWES 314:7
assumed: name Achilles a. | BROW 97:14
Assumes: A. the god | DRYD 194:24
assuming: a. that he's got any | GILB 226:8
assurance: full a. given by looks | ROYD 411:2
I'll make a. double sure | SHAK 462:7
laws is the a. of incorruption | BIBLE 62:19
One of the low on whom a. | ELIOT 205:1
Assyrian: A. came down like the wolf | BYRON 122:1
oil'd and curl'd A. Bull | TENN 540:1

Assyrians: She doted upon the A. her
BIBLE 60:37
Astarte: A., Queen of Heav'n   MILT 345:16
Astolat: lily maid of A.   TENN 534:25
astonish: of things that would a.   GILB 226:8
that can so a. a mother   SHAK 434:17
astonished: a. at my own moderation
CLIVE 153:5
astonishment: Your a.'s odd   ANON 4:29
astra: Per ardua ad a.   ANON 10:16
sic itur ad a.   VIRG 559:8
astray: like sheep have gone a.   BIBLE 59:22
odours led my steps a.   SHEL 503:17
one that had been led a.   MILT 342:3
were as sheep going a.   BIBLE 80:27
astronomer: undevout a. is mad
YOUNG 588:12
astronomers: Confounding her a.
HODG 252:5
astronomy: daughter of a.   YOUNG 588:12
asunder: bones are smitten a.   PRAY 392:9
let not man put a.   BIBLE 67:8
together let no man put a.   PRAY 389:6
asure: Lyk a. were his legges   CHAU 142:32
Atahualpa: who strangled A.   MAC 323:14
Atalanta: 'twas made of A.'s heels
SHAK 426:11
ate: a. a good supper at night   ANST 11:7
a. his bread in sorrow   GOET 230:12
a. when we were not hungry   SWIFT 526:10
never after a. but little   MAL 328:6
With A. by his side   SHAK 450:12
Athalus: Than A.   CHAU 141:6
Athanasian: A. Creed is the most splendid
DISR 186:7
atheism: honest a. for my money
OTWAY 365:26
inclineth man's mind to a.   BACON 25:24
miracle to convince a.   BACON 25:23
owlet A.   COL 156:19
atheist: a. brooding and blaspheming
CHES 148:7
a.-laugh's a poor exchange   BURNS 113:18
By night an a. half believes   YOUNG 588:17
here a female a. talks   JOHN 282:22
he was no a.   CHAR 140:24
is the Turk, and the A.   CHES 146:27
Rebel and A. too   DONNE 189:26
Athenaeum: A. with jugs of stout
HERB 246:15
A.'', you mean   STEV 522:14
Athenians: A. and strangers which
BIBLE 74:11
Athens: Another A. shall arise   SHEL 501:2
A. arose   SHEL 500:19
A. but the rudiments   SOUTH 513:12
A., Florence   INGE 270:10
A., the eye of Greece   MILT 350:8
Truths as refin'd as ever A.   ARMS 12:16
Ye men of A.   BIBLE 74:12
athirst: that is a. of the fountain   BIBLE 82:32
Atkins: Thank you, Mister A.   KIPL 303:22
Atlantic: A. Ocean beat Mrs Partington
SMITH 511:32
In the steep A. stream   MILT 340:27
other side of the A.   WALP 563:9
To where the A. raves   ARN 14:21
Atlas: demi-A. of this earth   SHAK 421:31
disencumber'd A. of the state   COWP 166:16
atomic: a. bomb is a paper tiger   MAO 328:20
primordial a. globule   GILB 226:20
atomies: easy to count a.   SHAK 426:8
Atoms: A. of Democritus   BLAKE 86:24
A. or systems into ruin   POPE 379:4
fortuitous concurrence of a.   PALM 368:11
atom-streams: I saw the flaring a.
TENN 539:20
atrabilious: bowl with a. liquor   HUXL 269:2
attach: Where people wish to a.   AUST 23:5

attachment: a. à la Plato for a bashful
GILB 227:23
attack: dared a. my Chesterton   BELL 39:27
I shall a.   FOCH 216:3
attacked: when a. it defends itself   ANON 9:4
attain: I cannot a. unto it   PRAY 399:5
attained: Were not a. by sudden flight
LONG 316:19
attainment: so disenchanting as a.
STEV 521:16
attaque: Quand on l'a. il se défend   ANON 9:4
attempt: a. and not the deed   SHAK 460:4
A. the end   HERR 249:19
can do that dares love a.   SHAK 482:10
fond a. to give a deathless   COWP 165:32
attempted: Something a., something
done   LONG 317:19
attend: Another to a. him   HERB 248:3
attendance: To dance a. on their lordships'
SHAK 447:24
attendant: Am an a. lord   ELIOT 203:24
attendants: countenances of the a.
DICK 176:11
attended: Is on his way a.   WORD 579:5
attendre: J'ai failli a.   LOUI 318:10
attention: a. of the nation is concentrated
BAG 28:30
awful a. in the audience   SHER 505:25
close the Valves of her a.   DICK 183:22
serious a. than history   ARIS 12:10
attentions: a. proceed from the impulse
AUST 23:13
attentive: a. and favourable hearers
HOOK 255:19
sit a. to his own applause   POPE 376:27
Attic: A. shape   KEATS 291:9
A. warbler pours her throat   GRAY 235:16
A. wit   PLINY 374:17
glory of the A. stage   ARN 15:10
sleeps up in the a. there   MEW 338:12
where the A. bird   MILT 350:8
Atticus: if A. were he   POPE 376:28
attire: bride her a.   BIBLE 60:15
My Love in her a. doth   ANON 6:20
attired: suitably a. in leather   HOUS 266:9
attitudes: those are Anglo-Saxon a.
CARR 135:29
attorney: gentleman was an a.   JOHN 275:35
in love with a rich a.'s   GILB 229:3
office boy to an A.'s   GILB 228:4
attorneys: ten a. find place   SMITH 510:5
Attract: A. a Silver Churn   GILB 227:24
attraction: flies feels the a. of earth
LONG 316:11
attracts: commerce which now a. the
envy   BURKE 109:15
attribute: grandest moral a.   BARR 34:20
is an a. to God himself   SHAK 467:27
attributes: False are a. of speech
HOBB 251:13
Auburn: Sweet A.   GOLD 230:16
auctioneer: saleroom and varnishing
a.   CARL 131:19
auctoritee: Experience though noon a.
CHAU 143:16
audace: et toujours de l'a.   DANT 171:19
audacia: a. certe Laus erit   PROP 401:16
audacious: saucy and a. eloquence
SHAK 471:15
audacity: Arm me, a.   SHAK 428:7
a. of elected persons   WHIT 570:14
aude: sapere a.   HOR 258:14
audendi: Quidlibet a. semper fuit   HOR 257:10
Audi: A. partem alteram   AUG 21:20
audible: a., and full of vent   SHAK 427:27
audience: a. into the middle of thi   HOR 257:20
a. look to their eyes   SHAK 469:25
audit: a. The accounts later   MACN 326:6
how his a. stands who knows   SHAK 434:30

auditorem: secus ac notas a. rapit
HOR 257:20
Augescunt: A. aliae gentes   LUCR 320:7
augmentation: with the a. of the Indies
SHAK 490:3
augur: a. misgovernment   BURKE 109:23
He bored with his a.   BALL 31:3
Augurs: A. and understood relations
SHAK 461:24
a. mock their own presage   SHAK 494:21
augury: we defy a.   SHAK 437:15
August: already yellow with A.
POUND 383:17
A. for the people and their   AUDEN 18:12
To recommence in A.   BYRON 124:3
Augustan: next A. age will dawn   WALP 563:9
Augustus: A. was a chubby lad   HOFF 252:11
aujourd'hui: le vivace et le bel a.
MALL 327:10
auld: 'tis a. it waxeth cauld   BALL 32:10
aunt: didn't know your a.   TEMP 532:8
I had an a. in Yucatan   BELL 40:4
Until Matilda's A. succeeded   BELL 39:9
Aunt Edna: A. is universal   RATT 405:1
aunts: a., who are not married   CHES 147:26
his cousins and his a.   GILB 228:3
Auream: A. quisquis mediocritatem
HOR 260:2
Auri: A. sacra fames   VIRG 558:10
Aurora: yonder shines A.'s harbinger
SHAK 470:25
Aurum: A. irrepertum et sic melius
HOR 260:20
ausrechnen: nicht a., was es kostet
BREC 91:26
Austen: great favourite, Miss A., MITF 352:22
austere: beauty cold and a.   RUSS 412:15
knewest that I was an a. man   BIBLE 71:1
Australia: so much interested in A.
WILDE 573:10
that he was born in A.   SHAW 497:8
Austria: Don John of A. is going   CHES 147:2
Don John of A. Is riding   CHES 147:3
auteur: l'esprit pour être a.   LA B 306:12
s'attendait de voir un a.   PASC 369:4
author: a. and giver of all good   PRAY 386:19
a. is concealed behind   JOHN 274:23
a. of peace and lover   PRAY 385:2
a. to get at his meaning   RUSK 411:15
a. who speaks about his   DISR 185:11
be but a shrimp of an a.   GRAY 235:25
Choose an a. as you choose   ROOS 408:10
four qualities of his a.   ARN 16:11
If it's by a good a.   SHAW 496:26
Jesus the a. and finisher   BIBLE 79:35
man were a. of himself   SHAK 427:28
next in merit to the a.   LAND 309:9
No a. ever spar'd a brother   GAY 223:12
ruin half an a.'s graces   MORE 357:4
sole a. of his own disgrace   COWP 165:13
store Of the first a.   MARV 332:1
than wit to become an a.   LA B 306:12
This is indeed to be an a.   HAZL 243:12
where is any a. in the world   SHAK 457:7
authoress: ever dared to be an a.   AUST 24:2
authorities: poison imposed by the a.
PLATO 374:9
authority: are put in a. under her
PRAY 387:14
A. forgets a dying king   TENN 535:22
base a. from others' books   SHAK 456:15
by the a. of an Aristotle   HOBB 251:15
Drest in a little brief a.   SHAK 464:2
Even reproofs from a. ought   BACON 26:25
Government must have an a.   RUSK 412:6
I am a man under a.   BIBLE 65:15
nor to usurp a. over   BIBLE 79:9
position than in one of a.   THOM 546:9
Rulers have no a. from   MAYH 336:6
taught them as one having a.   BIBLE 65:13

Authorized: 'A. Version' of the Bible
WHAT 569:15
authors: been much exposed to a.
WELL 567:29
English a. their copyrights TROL 552:12
people arises from its a. JOHN 281:10
reciprocal civility of a. JOHN 281:29
So let great a. have their BACON 24:15
They damn those a. whom CHUR 148:19
We a. DISR 185:24
authorship: reputation of popular a.
TROL 553:11
autobiography: artist writes his own
a. ELLIS 206:14
autocrate: je serai a. CATH 136:17
Autolycus: My father named me A.
SHAK 491:18
automne: violons De l'a. VERL 556:8
autres: ce sont les a. REN 405:10
l'Enfer, c'est les A. SART 414:8
pour encourager les a. VOLT 561:1
autumn: a. and of winter cometh
CLARE 152:16
a. and the falling fruit LAWR 311:8
a. evening ARN 14:8
A. evening SHEL 503:26
a. in the mind SPAR 514:22
A. nodding o'er the yellow THOM 549:15
A. sunsets exquisitely HUXL 269:1
a. was That grew the more SHAK 423:22
a., what our golden harvests DONNE 188:9
I saw old A. in the misty HOOD 255:1
leaves fall early this a. POUND 383:17
melancholy A. comes to Wembley
BETJ 42:16
springs to yellow a. turn'd SHAK 494:18
there is a harmony In a. SHEL 501:7
This a. morning BROW 101:20
thou breath of A.'s being SHEL 502:8
traveller's joy beguiles in a. HOUS 265:9
when the mists in a. KING 297:21
autumnal: deep, a. tone SHEL 502:13
have seen in one A. face DONNE 188:7
autumn-evenings: When the long dark
a. come BROW 99:17
Autumn-fields: looking on the happy
A. TENN 542:2
Auxiliary: I was undone by my A.
STEE 518:14
avails: a. the sceptred race LAND 308:26
Avarice: A., the spur of industry
HUME 267:16
beyond the dreams of a. JOHN 278:27
beyond the dreams of a. MOORE 355:14
I must take up with a. BYRON 122:15
low drudgery of a. BURKE 108:7
Avatar: In Vishnu-land what A. BROW 100:8
avaunt: Conscience a. CIBB 151:13
ave: a. atque vale CAT 137:15
A. Caesar ANON 10:7
A. Maria ANON 10:8
A. verum corpus ANON 10:9
With an A. Mari SKEL 508:19
Ave Maria: A.! 'tis the hour of prayer
BYRON 123:8
Avenge: A., O Lord MILT 351:9
avenger: enemy, and the a. PRAY 389:28
you a. someone VIRG 558:15
averages: fugitive from th' law of a.
MAUL 336:5
Averno: Facilis descensus A. VIRG 558:18
aversion: begin with a little a. SHER 506:9
closely bordering on a. STEV 521:17
manner which is my a. BYRON 123:6
avert: May the gods a. this omen CIC 151:29
aveugle: L'amour est a. ANON 9:11
aveuglement: L'amour vient de l'a.
BUSS 117:5
Avilion: island-valley of A. TENN 535:27
avis: Rara a. in terris nigroque JUV 287:20

avoid: a. what is to come SHAK 435:15
avoiding: superstition in a. superstition
BACON 27:22
Avon: Sweet Swan of A. JONS 284:25
where lucid A. stray'd GRAY 235:18
awaäy: 'a said an' I coom'd a. TENN 541:3
awaiting: a. instructions Jellings BEER 38:2
A. the sensation of a short GILB 226:31
Awake: A., beloved LONG 317:13
A., my heart BRID 92:7
A., O north wind BIBLE 56:29
Being now a. SHAK 492:5
clamour keep her still a. SHAK 484:11
England! a. BLAKE 86:11
myself will a. right early PRAY 393:16
They shall a. as Jacob did DONNE 191:3
use its guard staying a. BIBLE 83:12
We're very wide a. GILB 226:32
which I am trying to a. JOYCE 286:23
will he lie ten nights a. SHAK 472:14
awaked: must be a. BIBLE 51:9
So the Lord a. as one out PRAY 395:7
aware: infant child is not a. HOUS 266:11
made a. BROO 94:30
away: a.! for I will fly KEATS 291:20
A. from me PRAY 389:27
a. his fellows fly SHAK 470:20
A. we both must hie HOUS 265:12
black night doth take a. SHAK 494:7
get a. from earth awhile FROST 219:1
keep a week a. SHAK 476:6
kiss, a sigh, and so a. CRAS 169:14
they get them a. together PRAY 397:1
To get the Men to go a. BELL 39:9
awe: a. into the beholders SWIFT 526:1
Exempt from a. SHEL 503:12
eye whose bend doth a. SHAK 448:15
in a., and sin not PRAY 389:20
In a. of such a thing SHAK 448:13
increasing wonder and a. KANT 288:8
pity and mournful a. ARN 13:8
to keep the strong in a. SHAK 481:17
aweary: Cassius is a. of the world
SHAK 451:23
'gin to be a. of the sun SHAK 463:7
'I am a. TENN 539:24
my little body is a. SHAK 465:18
awf'lly: It's a. bad luck on Diana BETJ 42:21
awful: this is an a. place SCOTT 415:17
awkward: a. squad fire over me BURNS 116:9
awry: at me for leaning all a. FITZ 213:10
be gone as one shaped a. HARDY 240:3
axe: a. is laid unto the root BIBLE 63:39
a.'s edge did try MARV 332:9
head off with a golden a. SHAK 483:10
Lizzie Borden took an a. ANON 6:12
offence is let the great a. SHAK 436:5
owner of the a. THOR 550:12
then the a. to the root PAINE 368:4
axes: you your sharp-edged a. WHIT 570:10
Axioms: A. in philosophy are not
KEATS 293:30
axis: a. of the earth sticks HOLM 253:16
soft under-belly of the A. CHUR 150:13
axle: His glowing a. doth allay MILT 340:27
axletree: a. of the chariot-wheel BACON 27:33
Ay: it stinted and said 'A. SHAK 481:27
Aye: Charybdis of A. and No NEWM 361:21
Ayr: Auld A. BURNS 115:4
Azores: At Flores in the A. Sir TENN 542:21
Azure: A. hath a canker by usura
POUND 382:11
a. sister of the spring SHEL 502:8
outdares Stokes in a. feats BROW 103:27
azure-lidded: still she slept an a. sleep
KEATS 289:20
B: B. bit it ANON 4:25
Baa: B.! Baa KIPL 299:10
babblative: arts b. and scribblative
SOUT 514:12

babble: learned b. of the saleroom
CARL 131:19
babbled: a' b. of green fields SHAK 443:17
babbler: What will this b. say BIBLE 74:10
Babe: B. all burning bright did SOUT 514:19
B. leaps up on his Mother's WORD 579:4
Come little b. BRET 92:6
Finger of birth-strangled b. SHAK 462:4
Hath laid her B. to rest MILT 344:15
if my young b. were born BALL 32:11
like a naked new-born b. SHAK 459:6
love the b. that milks SHAK 459:10
to bring the b. to rest EDW 200:5
Babel: bother at the tower of B. VOLT 561:13
babes: mouth of very b. and sucklings
PRAY 389:28
newborn b. BIBLE 80:22
babies: bit the b. in the cradles BROW 103:15
hates dogs and b. ROST 410:14
than putting milk into b. CHUR 150:15
Bab-lock-hithe: stripling Thames at B.
ARN 14:14
baboon: Into b. and monkey SHAK 486:1
baby: b. beats the nurse SHAK 463:11
b. boy VIRG 560:1
b. fell a-thinking HARDY 241:1
b. figure of the giant SHAK 486:27
B. in an ox's stall BETJ 42:8
first b. laughed BARR 34:13
great b. you see there SHAK 432:19
not see my b. at my breast SHAK 424:14
till he was showed the b. DICK 179:27
With his b. on my knee KING 296:17
Babylon: B. in all its desolation DAV 172:13
B. is fallen BIBLE 82:16
B.! O Carthage SASS 415:4
B. THE GREAT BIBLE 82:23
B. we sit down and weep WALP 563:10
Ere B. was dust SHEL 502:19
great city B. be thrown down BIBLE 82:24
I was a King in B. HENL 245:10
waters of B. we sat PRAY 399:3
Babylonian: jargon of their B. pulpits
BURKE 111:6
Babylons: all man's B. strive THOM 548:7
bacchanal: me now with the b. sign
YOUNG 588:15
Bacchus: B. ever fair DRYD 194:25
dainty B. gross in taste SHAK 457:8
Not charioted by B. KEATS 291:20
Of B. and his revellers MILT 348:29
Pan by noon and B. by night SWIN 528:18
Baccy: 'B. for the Clerk KIPL 302:22
Bach: By B. GILB 227:6
bachelor: b. of three-score again SHAK 472:1
facts that you are a b. DOYLE 192:14
I said I would die a b. SHAK 472:19
pleasant dining with a b. GASK 222:2
bachelors: All reformers are b.
MOORE 355:15
reasons for b. to go out ELIOT 201:20
Two old B. were living LEAR 312:23
back: at my b. from time to time
ELIOT 204:27
B. and side go bare ANON 5:21
b. to the shop Mr John LOCK 315:22
bolt is shot b. ARN 12:22
borne me on his b. SHAK 436:31
by thumps upon your b. COWP 165:9
come b., Horatius MAC 322:20
I sit on a man's b. TOLS 551:15
lean'd my b. unto an aik BALL 32:10
looking b. BIBLE 69:25
never turned his b. BROW 98:32
one by one b. in the Closet FITZ 213:5
plowers plowed upon my b. PRAY 398:22
rider on so proud a b. SHAK 495:20
stamp me to the b. to common FITZ 213:12
them to the b. o' beyont SCOTT 418:1
there's no turning b. ROSS 408:22

think that he'll come b. — KIPL 301:15
wife looked b. — BIBLE 46:8
will b. the masses against — GLAD 229:17
backbiter: Face-flatterer and b. are — TENN 535:17
backbone: Alps shaping like a b. — HARDY 239:13
b. of the Army is the Non-commissioned — KIPL 298:22
backgammon: I ever mastered was b. — JERR 273:13
background: landscape but a b. — AUDEN 19:16
backing: always b. into the limelight — BERN 42:1
plague upon such b. — SHAK 438:35
backs: making the beast with two b. — SHAK 473:18
Our b. is easy ris — DICK 179:18
when maids lie on their b. — SHAK 481:28
With our b. to the wall — HAIG 237:11
backward: drew me b. by the hair — BROW 98:9
I by b. steps would move — VAUG 555:17
let them be turned b. — PRAY 394:15
look b. to their ancestors — BURKE 111:7
Thames flowed b. to its — PLOM 374:19
Thou wilt fall b. when — SHAK 481:27
backwards: memory that only works b. — CARR 135:16
bacon: b.'s not the only thing — KING 297:20
b. was nat fet for hem — CHAU 143:18
Unless you give him b. — CHES 146:26
bacons: On, b., on — SHAK 438:26
bad: b., and dangerous to know — LAMB 306:25
b. die late — DEFOE 173:2
b. end unhappily — STOP 523:18
B. laws are the worst sort — BURKE 110:20
b. news infects the teller — SHAK 421:16
b.'s the best of us — FLET 215:10
B. Thing — SELL 420:8
because we put up with b. — TROL 553:2
being a little b. — SHAK 465:6
bold b. man — SHAK 447:1
bold b. man — SPEN 516:1
Defend the b. against — DAY-L 172:23
find the world ugly and b. — NIET 363:8
good ye are and b. — TENN 534:17
her badness when she's b. — BARR 34:17
it's always a b. sign — MITF 352:25
never so good or so b. — MACK 325:11
nothing either good or b. — SHAK 432:12
Persecution is a b. — BROW 96:16
sad and b. and mad — BROW 100:8
sad b. glad — SWIN 529:2
shocking b. hats in my life — WELL 567:22
so much b. in the best — ANON 8:2
such thing as b. weather — RUSK 412:14
This animal is very b. — ANON 9:4
To bring b. news — SHAK 422:12
To make b. good — SHAK 464:22
was not really b. at heart — BELL 39:12
When b. men combine — BURKE 108:22
bade: b. betwixt their shores — ARN 13:13
crouch whom the rest b. aspire — BROW 102:6
badge: b. of pusillanimity — SHAK 442:15
sufferance is the b. — SHAK 466:2
badgers: When b. fight then everyone's — CLARE 152:3
badly: it is worth doing b. — CHES 148:10
badness: To the b. of her badness — BARR 34:17
baffled: b., get up and begin again — BROW 102:1
matter is not easily b. — BAG 28:31
bag: b. and baggage — GLAD 229:13
eggs inside a paper b. — ISH 270:27
not with b. and baggage — SHAK 426:6
wages to put it into a b. — BIBLE 62:2
bagatelle: et vive la b. — STER 519:4
baggage: believe the b. loves me — CONG 160:17

bagpipe: when the b. sings i' — SHAK 467:21
Baiae: Beside a pumice isle in B.'s — SHEL 502:10
bailiff: b.'s daughter of Islington — BALL 30:9
loved the b.'s daughter — BALL 30:7
baîlle: Le désespoir b. — HUGO 267:12
Bainters: hate all Boets and B. — GEOR 223:34
bait: swallow'd b. — SHAK 495:7
trout for factitious b. — POUND 383:2
baits: while good news b. — MILT 350:26
baked: 'You have b. me too brown — CARR 134:16
baker: b. rhymes for his pursuit — BROW 105:4
Bakers: B. and brewers — LANG 309:26
Baker Street: B. irregulars — DOYLE 192:32
Bakewell: valley between Buxton and B. — RUSK 411:13
balaiera: salut b. largement le seuil — ROST 410:12
balance: at the b. let's be mute — BURNS 112:26
b. of power — WALP 563:27
In b. with this life — YEATS 585:15
small dust of the b. — BIBLE 59:8
uncertain b. of proud time — GREE 236:9
weigh thy words in a b. — BIBLE 63:12
balanced: I b. all — YEATS 585:15
balances: Thou art weighed in the b. — BIBLE 61:6
balanza: b. y peso que iguala al — CERV 138:20
Balbec: editions of B. and Palmyra — WALP 563:9
bald: b. and unconvincing narrative — GILB 227:12
bare mountain tops are b. — ARN 16:7
If I were fierce and b. — SASS 414:10
respectable b. heads — YEATS 586:14
thou b. head — BIBLE 51:24
we found him b. too — BROW 100:35
baldheaded: Go into it b. — LOW 319:5
baldness: felicity on the far side of b. — SMITH 510:13
with a b. full of grandeur — ARN 16:7
bales: beach undid his corded b. — ARN 14:21
dropping down with costly b. — TENN 538:24
Balkans: damned silly thing in the B. — BISM 84:26
ball: at a girl throwing a b. — WOOLF 576:19
B. no question makes — FITZ 213:6
Only wind it into a b. — BLAKE 86:8
peck cautiously at the b. — WOD 575:24
real business of a b. — SURT 525:24
Ruddy B. has taken flight — THOM 549:2
Urge the flying b. — GRAY 235:10
ballad: b. of Sir Patrick Spence — COL 156:6
I love a b. in print — SHAK 492:3
I met with a b. — CALV 127:10
very guilty of such a b. — SHAK 456:18
ballad-mongers: of these same metre b. — SHAK 439:25
ballads: b., songs and snatches — GILB 226:18
better than all the b. — LONG 316:8
permitted to make all the b. — FLET 215:8
ballet: b. of bloodless categories — BRAD 91:10
Balliol: B. made me — BELL 40:14
balloon: moon's a b. — CUMM 170:8
something in a huge b. — WORD 579:18
balloons: Are light as b. — FROST 219:4
ballot: b. is stronger than — LINC 314:13
balls: elliptical billiard b. — GILB 227:7
our rackets to these b. — SHAK 443:11
two pitch b. — SHAK 456:27
Ballyhoo: variants from Builth to B. — KIPL 302:4
Balm: B. of hurt minds — SHAK 460:8
b. th'hydroptic earth hath — DONNE 189:28
Can wash the b. from — SHAK 479:5
Is there no b. in Gilead — BIBLE 60:21
our calm is in that b. — NORT 364:8
out a b. upon the world — KEATS 289:28
wept odorous gums and b. — MILT 347:19

baloney: it's still b. — SMITH 510:3
Balzac: All B.'s novels occupy — BROW 99:3
bamboo: Under the b. tree — ELIOT 204:13
bamboozle: to understand I would b. — GREE 236:7
banal: Eldorado b. de tous les vieux — BAUD 35:8
Banbury: To B. came — BRAT 91:24
band: captain of this ruin'd b. — SHAK 444:10
heaven-born b. — HOPK 257:8
high aesthetic b. — GILB 227:23
stormy sturdy b. — HARDY 240:16
we b. of brothers — SHAK 445:3
when the wearied B. — HUXL 268:22
bandaged: death b. my eyes — BROW 103:32
bands: drew them…with b. of love — BIBLE 61:12
loose the b. of Orion — BIBLE 53:5
loose the b. of wickedness — BIBLE 60:4
Bandusiae: fons B. splendidior vitro — HOR 261:3
bandy: b. civilities with my Sovereign — JOHN 275:20
Would not have b. children — BLAKE 87:20
bane: Deserve the precious b. — MILT 346:1
thou b. of the most generous — GRAN 234:7
bang: b. these dogs of Seville — TENN 543:1
b.—went saxpence — PUNCH 402:18
with a b. but a whimper — ELIOT 203:11
banged: b. the youth into dumbness — SHAK 489:27
banish: b. not him thy Harry's — SHAK 439:18
b. plump Jack and banish — SHAK 439:18
Everything did b. moan — BARN 33:32
I b. you — SHAK 427:23
banish'd: constant Cimber should be b. — SHAK 449:25
banished: b. man — BALL 31:10
brother by decree is b. — SHAK 449:24
from which success is b. — STEV 521:1
my wilful crime art b. hence — MILT 349:28
banishing: worst effect is b. for hours — COWP 165:4
banishment: bitter bread of b. — SHAK 479:4
bank: Along a shelving b. of turf — SHEL 503:17
b. and shoal of time — SHAK 459:5
contemplate an entangled b. — DARW 171:28
cried all the way to the b. — LIB 314:11
George goes to sleep at a b. — JER 272:24
moonlight sleeps upon this b. — SHAK 468:15
pregnant b. swelled up — DONNE 188:21
Banker: thought he saw a B.'s Clerk — CARR 133:13
Bankrupt: B. of life — DRYD 194:7
banks: b. and braes o' bonny Doon — BURNS 116:6
letters from b. — AUDEN 20:2
Thy b. with pioned — SHAK 485:19
banned: that any book should be b. — WEST 569:2
banner: b. wav'd without a blast — SCOTT 416:14
b. with the strange device — LONG 316:14
Freedom's b. streaming — DRAKE 193:5
His b. over me was love — BIBLE 56:20
'Tis the star-spangled b. — KEY 295:14
yet thy b. — BYRON 121:11
banners: all thy b. wave — CAMP 128:22
b. of the king advance — VEN 556:5
Hang out our b. — SHAK 463:4
terrible as an army with b. — BIBLE 57:5
banquet: Corpses are set to b. — POUND 382:11
trifling foolish b. towards — SHAK 482:3
banqueting: beggar by b. upon borrowing — BIBLE 63:6
banter: how does fortune b. us — BOL 89:13
Baptism: B., and the Supper — PRAY 388:19
Godmothers in my B. — PRAY 388:12
that B. be administered — PRAY 388:8
baptize: I b. with water — BIBLE 71:29

bar: Back of the b. — SERV 420:14
b. in Lower Thames Street — ELIOT 205:4
b. of the Black Badger — DICK 177:29
be no moaning of the b. — TENN 533:3
door and b. for thy mouth — BIBLE 63:12
Get up and b. the door — BALL 31:1
his birth's invidious b. — TENN 537:1
Mute at the b. — CHUR 149:5
When I have crost the b. — TENN 533:4
When I went to the B. — GILB 226:6
Barabbas: At least we withstand B. — BROW 101:4
Now B. was a robber — BIBLE 72:45
Now B. was a publisher — CAMP 129:15
barajar: paciencia y b. — CERV 138:18
Barbara: mother had a maid call'd B. — SHAK 476:26
Barbara Allen: Her name was B. — SHAK 476:26
barbares: temps b. et gothiques — FRAN 217:27
Barbarian: B., Scythian — BIBLE 78:26
He is a b. — SHAW 496:9
barbarians: become of us without any b. — CAV 137:17
Greeks, and to the B. — BIBLE 74:30
his young b. all at play — BYRON 121:16
in my own mind the B. — ARN 15:19
with the B. quite left — ARN 15:14
barbaric: b. yawp over the roofs — WHIT 571:6
barbarisms: clear it from colloquial b. — JOHN 282:5
barbarity: act with the b. of tyrants — SMITH 511:30
barbarous: air with b. dissonance — MILT 341:13
invention of a b. age — MILT 344:18
me with the b. multitude — SHAK 466:19
This b. philosophy — BURKE 111:11
barbarousness: must confess mine own b. — SIDN 508:3
barbe: laisserons pousser notre b. — FLAU 214:2
barber: b.'s chair that fits all — SHAK 420:29
has known the b.'s shear — THAC 545:31
I must to the b.'s — SHAK 471:2
Barbiton: B. hic paries habebit — HOR 261:5
bard: blame not the B. — MOORE 356:14
Hear the voice of the B. — BLAKE 87:13
he was the wisest b. — BEHN 38:11
If the B. was weatherwise — COL 156:6
more fat than b. beseems — THOM 549:9
Bardolph: banish B. — SHAK 439:18
Bards: B. of Passion and of Mirth — KEATS 290:31
last of all the B. was he — SCOTT 416:9
worst of b. confessed — CAT 137:3
bare: Back and side go b. — ANON 5:21
b. mountain tops are bald — ARN 16:7
B. ruin'd choirs — SHAK 494:7
beauty and love lay b. — SHEL 503:23
they b. children to them — BIBLE 45:33
Though I go b. — ANON 5:21
barefac'd: bore him b. on the bier — SHAK 436:9
barefoot: b. friars were singing — GIBB 224:16
makes shoes go b. himself — BURT 116:16
bareness: old December's b. — SHAK 494:16
bargain: b. dog never bites — NASH 360:3
dateless b. to engrossing death — SHAK 483:31
fond of her most filthy b. — SHAK 477:13
Necessity never made a good b. — FRAN 218:8
never was a better b. driv'n — SIDN 507:16
bargains: b., and my well-won thrift — SHAK 465:29
barge: b. she sat — SHAK 422:2
Baring: taken by Rothschild and B. — GILB 226:16
bark: come out as I do, and b. — JOHN 279:3
fatal and perfidious b. — MILT 343:10
my b. is on the sea — BYRON 125:32
spirit like a charmed b. — SHEL 500:16

star to every wandering b. — SHAK 495:5
That dogs b. at me — SHAK 480:18
they b. at me — SHAK 454:29
they don't b. — NERV 361:1
Though his b. cannot be — SHAK 458:7
yond tall anchoring b. — SHAK 455:14
You Heard a Seal B. — THUR 550:31
Barkis: B. is willin' — DICK 176:31
barley: fields of b. and of rye — TENN 538:2
In among the bearded b. — TENN 538:5
Sitting on a heap of B. — LEAR 312:5
Barleycorn: John B. should die — BURNS 114:13
Barlow: my Hornby and my B. — THOM 547:24
barmaid: Bitter b., waning fast — TENN 544:6
barmie: b. noddle's working prime — BURNS 113:23
barn: from the b. and the forge — HOUS 263:6
barn-cocks: Ere the b. say — HARDY 240:8
barns: nor gather into b. — BIBLE 64:28
Baronetage: up any book but the B. — AUST 23:7
baronets: All b. are bad — GILB 228:30
there were b. by dozens — GILB 225:10
Barons: rust of the B.' Wars — WALP 562:24
barouche-landau: They will have their b. — AUST 22:16
Barrack: B. and bivouac shall be — AUDEN 19:11
barred: spot that's always b. — GILB 227:7
barrel: b. of Malmesey wine within — FABY 209:17
handful of meal in a b. — BIBLE 51:7
barrel-load: save them by the b. — THOM 548:26
barrel-organ: was a kind of human b. — DICK 177:24
barreltone: base b. voice — JOYCE 286:26
barren: b. and dry land where no — PRAY 393:21
b. sister all your life — SHAK 469:17
b. superfluity of words — GARTH 221:21
b. woman to keep house — PRAY 397:15
Close up these b. leaves — WORD 582:23
I am but a b. stock — ELIZ 205:20
Make b. our lives — SWIN 529:10
none is b. among them — BIBLE 56:26
'tis all b. — STER 519:2
underneath the b. bush — TENN 537:9
barricade: At some disputed b. — SEEG 419:15
barricades: Christs that die upon the b. — WILDE 572:17
barrier: b. against matrimony which — KEATS 294:10
barring: b. of the door — BALL 30:21
barrow: b. and the camp abide — KIPL 303:12
red wheel b. — WILL 574:10
barrows: grassy b. of the happier dead — TENN 543:13
bars: Between their silver b. — FLEC 214:21
out through the same b. — LANG 309:21
weary of these worldly b. — SHAK 449:3
barton: lonely b. by yonder coomb — HARDY 240:14
barty: Hans Breitmann gife a b. — LEL 313:16
Basan: fat bulls of B. — PRAY 390:18
Og the king of B. — PRAY 399:1
base: b. and ignoble creature — BACON 25:25
b. barreltone voice — JOYCE 286:26
b., common and popular — SHAK 444:16
b. old man — FRY 219:28
keep down the b. in man — TENN 534:12
Labour without joy is b. — RUSK 412:3
scarlet Majors at the B. — SASS 414:10
scorning the b. degrees — SHAK 449:5
Things b. and vile — SHAK 469:22
To what b. uses we may — SHAK 437:1
wherefore b. — SHAK 453:9

Base-born: B. products of base beds — YEATS 587:8
baseless: b. fabric of this vision — SHAK 485:20
basely: To spend that shortness b. — SHAK 440:19
baseness: child of ignorance and b. — BACON 25:31
baser: I give to b. life — SHAK 424:11
lewd fellows of the b. — BIBLE 74:1
bashful: never laughed, being b. — POUND 383:16
Plato for a b. young potato — GILB 227:23
bashfulness: England a particular b. — ADD 2:21
basia: Da mi b. mille — CAT 136:26
basically: b. I'm viable from ten — BETJ 42:14
Basil: over her sweet B. evermore — KEATS 290:11
basilisk: That b. is sure to kill — GAY 222:30
Basil-pot: 'To steal my B. away from — KEATS 290:12
basin: Holding the b. to gowned — MACN 326:9
stare in the b. — AUDEN 18:10
Basingstoke: hidden meaning—like B. — GILB 228:36
bask: b. in Heaven's blue smile — SHEL 500:5
baskets: that remained twelve b. — BIBLE 66:24
basking: loves to lie a-b. in the sun — GILB 228:21
bason: tip up b. and a hose — ASHF 17:8
Basques: Scalinger used to say of the B. — CHAM 139:16
Bass: Guinness, Allsopp, B. — CALV 127:12
Bassarid: Maenad and the B. — SWIN 528:18
bassoon: he heard the loud b. — COL 155:8
bass-viol: Ye mid burn the old b. — HARDY 239:19
bastard: getter of more b. children — SHAK 427:27
Why b. — SHAK 453:9
bastardizing: firmament twinkled on my b. — SHAK 453:11
bastards: he who begets twenty b. — WALP 563:12
stand up for b. — SHAK 453:10
Which some call nature's b. — SHAK 491:23
bastion: like a b.'s mole — SMART 509:3
bat: b. that flits at close — BLAKE 85:11
black b., night — TENN 540:9
Ere the b. hath flown — SHAK 461:13
I march with b. and pad — HOUS 262:22
On the b.'s back I do — SHAK 485:25
squeak of a b. — FORS 217:8
where the weak-ey'd b. — COLL 158:18
Wool of b. — SHAK 462:3
batailled: b. as it were a castle — CHAU 142:32
bataillons: n'est pas pour les gros b. — VOLT 561:18
batallions: side not of the heavy b. — VOLT 561:18
batchelor: old b. don't die at all — WARD 564:30
bated: With b. breath — SHAK 466:3
bath: b. room has got a tip up — ASHF 17:8
can ever be tired of B. — AUST 23:3
nymph to the b. addressed — SHEL 503:23
soaping her breasts in the b. — EWART 209:11
sore labour's b. — SHAK 460:8
bathe: b. those beauteous feet — FLET 215:29
to b. in reeking wounds — SHAK 458:4
bathing: b. machine and a very small — GILB 226:13
b. of a summer's day — WORD 580:7
Gentleman caught the Whigs b. — DISR 184:14
Bath-rabbim: by the gate of B. — BIBLE 57:9
baths: b. Of all the western stars — TENN 544:3
Having b. in Camden Town — BETJ 42:6
Two walking b. — CRAS 159:1
bâtir: c'est b. la mort — MONT 354:15
baton: b. of a marshal of France — NAP 359:9

bats: are like b. amongst birds   BACON 27:23
...Do b. eat cats   CARR 133:15
Flittering b.   JOYCE 286:8
batsman: b. plays to the bowling   THOM 547:24
if the b. thinks he's bowled   LANG 309:19
swift B. of the Dawn has   THOM 549:2
battaglie: b. e morte   GAR 221:10
batten: b. on this moor   SHAK 435:7
Battening: B. upon huge seaworms   TENN 537:25
Batter: B. my heart   DONNE 189:8
battle: Agreed to have a b.   CARR 134:33
at Sheriffmuir A b. there was   MCL 325:15
b., a big one   LIVY 315:12
B., and the loves of men   HOUS 265:4
b. fares like to the morning's   SHAK 446:17
b. goes sore against us   STEV 520:26
better in b. than in bed   STER 520:3
brave that die in the b.   CLOU 153:13
day long the noise of b.   TENN 535:20
die well that die in a b.   SHAK 444:21
drunk delight of b. with   TENN 543:22
Each b. sees the other's   SHAK 444:9
first blow is half the b.   GOLD 232:27
forefront of the hottest b.   BIBLE 50:19
foremost in b. was Mary Ambree   BALL 31:8
from b. and murder   PRAY 385:16
he smelleth the b. afar   BIBLE 53:7
into the midst of the b.   VIRG 558:7
Lord mighty in b.   PRAY 390:24
misfortune to losing a b.   WELL 567:25
next to a b. lost   WELL 567:27
nor the b. to the strong   BIBLE 55:30
Nor war, nor b.'s sound   MILT 344:6
of the b. in the glorious   VEN 556:4
prepare himself to the b.   BIBLE 76:15
See the front o' b. lour   BURNS 114:34
That beat to b. where he   TENN 542:7
that it is a field of b.   STEV 521:31
they make them ready to b.   PRAY 389:8
to feats of broil and b.   SHAK 473:24
trumpets which sing to b.   SHEL 505:13
When the b.'s lost   SHAK 458:1
battle-bolt: rushing b. sang from TENN 539:26
Battledore: B. and shuttlecock's   DICK 181:34
battle-flags: b. were furl'd   TENN 538:20
battlements: b. it sees   MILT 342:20
came and perched on b.   BEER 38:2
fix'd his head upon our b.   SHAK 458:3
From the hid b. of Eternity   THOM 548:20
battles: b. and death   GAR 221:10
b. are lost in the same   WHIT 570:20
b. long ago   WORD 578:14
b., sieges, fortunes   SHAK 473:25
God of b.   SHAK 444:26
that I have fought his b.   BUNY 107:38
three pitched b. in India   MAC 324:23
bauble: Pleas'd with this b. still   POPE 379:19
Take away that fool's b.   CROM 169:25
Baum: grün des Lebens goldner B.   GOET 230:3
bavin: shallow jesters and rash b.   SHAK 439:34
bawcock: king's a b.   SHAK 444:17
bawd: Now my old b. is dead   YEATS 585:16
bawdy: Bloody, b. villain   SHAK 433:4
bawdy-house: pretence of keeping a b.   JOHN 278:18
bawl: bang and roar and b.   BELL 39:28
bawling: b. what it likes   ARN 15:20
bay: b. the moon   SHAK 451:14
He stands at b.   THOM 549:19
baying: families b. for broken   WAUGH 565:29
bayonets: Chains are worse than b.   JERR 273:11
himself a throne of b.   INGE 270:9
sods with our b. turning   WOLFE 576:3
bays: b. burn deep and chafe   SWIN 530:3
Have I no b. to crown it   HERB 247:14

sprig of b. in fifty years   SWIFT 527:33
bay-tree: flourishing like a green b.   PRAY 391:29
be: b. rather than to seem   SALL 413:24
b. the people never so   PRAY 396:10
b. what they behold   POPE 375:11
is that which shall b.   BIBLE 55:7
Let them b. as they are   CLEM 153:1
To b., or not to be   SHAK 433:8
beach: about the b. I wander'd   TENN 538:16
all left behind on the b.   CARR 133:2
b. undid his corded bales   ARN 14:21
only pebble on the b.   BRAI 91:17
beached: b. verge of the salt flood   SHAK 486:14
Beachy Head: Birmingham by way of B.   CHES 147:11
beacon: face, which, as a b.   SHAK 442:15
From Clee to heaven the b.   HOUS 262:12
beacon-light: b. is quench'd in smoke   SCOTT 417:2
Beacons: B. from the abode where   SHEL 500:1
b. of wise men   HUXL 269:10
beaded: With b. bubbles winking   KEATS 291:18
beadroll: On Fame's eternal b. worthy   SPEN 516:19
bead-rolls: Set in our b.   SKEL 508:19
Beadsman: B., after thousand aves   KEATS 289:24
b. now that was your knight   PEELE 371:8
beak: He can take in his b.   MERR 338:8
thy b. from out my heart   POE 375:6
beaker: b. full of the warm South   KEATS 291:18
Beale: Miss Buss and Miss B.   ANON 6:16
be-all: b. and the end-all here   SHAK 459:5
beam: b. that is in thine own   BIBLE 64:34
b. upon my inward view   ARN 13:4
beameth: one knows for whom it b.   MOORE 356:11
beamish: b. nephew   CARR 133:7
my b. boy   CARR 134:29
beams: b. of his chambers   PRAY 396:18
moonshine's watery b.   SHAK 481:28
tricks his b.   MILT 343:17
bean: dined on one pea and one b.   LEAR 313:2
home of the b. and the cod   BOSS 90:13
not too French French b.   GILB 227:23
bean-flowers: b.' boon   BROW 100:13
bean-rows: Nine b. will I have there   YEATS 585:17
beans: You must not give him b. CHES 146:26
Bear: B. of Very Little Brain   MILNE 340:13
b. onward blessed me   SIDN 507:27
B. them we can   HOUS 264:22
b. the palm alone   SHAK 448:16
b. the yoke in his youth   BIBLE 60:30
b. up the pillars of it   PRAY 394:25
b. with a sore head   MARR 331:4
has been eaten by the b.   HOUS 266:11
How a b. likes honey   MILNE 340:12
huntsman that by the b. oppress'd   WALL 562:6
is a bush suppos'd a b.   SHAK 471:11
like the rugged Russian b.   SHAK 461:21
makes us rather b. those   SHAK 433:8
Moppsikon Floppsikon b.   LEAR 313:1
More can I b. than you   SHAK 446:9
my safe old b.   BETJ 44:9
No dancing b. was so genteel   COWP 165:22
pursued by a b.   SHAK 491:16
rode on the back of a b.   LEAR 313:1
still less the b.   FRERE 218:25
Their habits from the B.   BELL 38:26
there's no mortal can b.   GAY 222:36
They shall b. thee in their   PRAY 395:22
To pardon or to b. it   COWP 165:9
We must b. all   SHAK 444:23

We've fought the B. before   HUNT 268:3
which we b. to live   POPE 379:21
wounded spirit who can b.   BIBLE 54:13
ye cannot b. them now   BIBLE 72:39
bear-baiting: Puritan hated b.   MAC 324:19
bear-baitings: fairs, and b.   SHAK 491:20
beard: b. of formal cut   SHAK 425:24
brave b. curled   CHES 155:5
by the colour of his b.   SHAK 488:23
endure a husband with a b.   SHAK 472:3
grey b. and glittering eye   COL 155:5
His b. was grizzled   SHAK 430:13
icicle on a Dutchman's b.   SHAK 489:28
I have a b. coming   SHAK 469:28
King of Spain's B.   DRAKE 193:3
Plucks off my b. and blows   SHAK 433:3
send thee a b.   SHAK 489:18
To b. the lion in his den   SCOTT 417:18
To pluck me by the b.   SHAK 455:2
void your rheum upon my b.   SHAK 466:3
was an Old Man with a b.   LEAR 311:15
with white and bristly b.   SHAK 492:26
bearded: b. like the pard   SHAK 425:24
beards: their long b.   SWIFT 527:14
'Tis merry in hall when b.   SHAK 442:26
We'll grow b.   FLAU 214:2
your b. forbid me to interpret   SHAK 458:10
Beardsley: belong to the B. period   BEER 37:11
Beareth: B. all things   BIBLE 76:14
that b. up things light   BACON 27:5
bearing: from the monotony of b.   WOOLF 576:18
bearings: b. of this observation   DICK 177:31
bears: dancing dogs and b.   HODG 252:2
Let b. and lions growl   WATTS 565:17
wandering b. may come with buns ISH 270:27
beast: be a b. or a fool alone   KILV 296:8
B. gave beast as much   YEATS 585:20
b. who is always spoiling   MAC 324:26
b. With many heads   SHAK 427:25
count the number of the b.   BIBLE 82:14
doubt the maw-crammed b.   BROW 104:3
evil b. hath devoured him   BIBLE 46:29
Feeds b. as man   SHAK 421:8
following the questing b.   MAL 327:18
I have a b. on my back   DOUG 191:7
just b.   ANON 4:9
making the b. with two backs   SHAK 473:18
name of the b.   BIBLE 82:13
No b. so fierce but knows   SHAK 480:20
noise in the b.'s belly   MAL 327:15
preeminence above a b.   BIBLE 55:13
regardeth the life of his b.   BIBLE 53:34
solitude is either a wild b.   BACON 26:14
splendorous blond b.   NIET 363:14
terrible marks of the b.   HARDY 241:17
what rough b.   YEATS 586:16
Who is like unto the b.   BIBLE 82:12
worship the b. and his image   BIBLE 82:17
beastie: tim'rous b.   BURNS 115:20
beasties: ghosties and long-leggety b.   ANON 5:8
beastly: let's be b. to the Germans   COW 163:15
Beasts: B. did leap and birds did BARN 33:32
b. of the forest are mine   PRAY 393:2
b. of the field drink thereof   PRAY 396:19
b. of the forest do move   PRAY 397:1
b. that have no understanding   PRAY 388:25
be compared unto the b.   PRAY 392:28
charming as the b.   AUDEN 19:12
elders and the four b.   BIBLE 81:32
fought with b. at Ephesus   BIBLE 76:24
four b. and four and twenty   BIBLE 81:27
four b. full of eyes   BIBLE 81:23
man is of kin to the b.   BACON 25:25
manner of four-footed b.   BIBLE 73:37
beat: b. down Satan under our   PRAY 385:19
b. him when he sneezes   CARR 133:26

B. its straight path along COL 157:11
b. of a horse's feet KIPL 304:1
b. of her unseen feet SHEL 500:6
b. of the off-shore wind KIPL 300:23
b. the ground MILT 340:29
b. their swords into plowshares BIBLE 57:19
b. them to their beds SHAK 423:3
b. upon that house BIBLE 65:12
can always b. ten men who SHAW 496:3
could b. three *Frenchmen* ADD 2:19
enemies have b. us to the pit SHAK 452:5
I'd b. him like a dog SHAK 488:22
though Miss Jenkyns b. time GASK 222:1
Voice above their b. THOM 548:14
waves that b. on Heaven's BLAKE 85:15
We b. them to-day or Molly STARK 517:20
when thy heart began to b. BLAKE 87:15
ye b. my people to pieces BIBLE 57:20
beaten: b. by a piece of timber FRY 219:22
Thrice was I b. with rods BIBLE 77:12
beateth: not as one that b. the air BIBLE 76:9
beating: b. in the void his luminous ARN 16:10
b. myself for spite SIDN 507:17
Charity and b. begins at home FLET 215:25
daily the b. of man's heart AUDEN 20:6
glory of the French WOLFE 576:7
Greeks who take the b. HOR 258:12
hear the b. of his wings BRIG 93:1
hearts b. each to each BROW 102:14
Is b. on the door YEATS 585:7
not mend his pace with b. SHAK 436:24
than driven by b. ASCH 17:1
Beatrice: You whisper 'B.' BROW 102:30
Beats: B. all the lies you can BLAKE 85:14
light which b. upon a throne TENN 533:30
beatum: Parte b. HOR 260:11
possit facere et servare b. HOR 258:17
vocaveris Recte b. HOR 261:7
Beatus: B. *ille* HOR 259:7
B. *vir qui timet Dominum* BIBLE 83:9
beau: l'art pour l'art...le b. COUS 163:9
Beaumont: rare B. lie BASSE 35:1
beauté: tout n'est qu'ordre et b. BAUD 35:7
beauteous: b. chequered sides with THOM 549:19
b. flower when next we SHAK 482:16
How b. mankind is SHAK 485:26
love all b. things BRID 92:10
Of all that is most b. WORD 578:3
Beauties: B. in vain their pretty POPE 381:11
By their own b. SHAK 483:6
Of common b. liv'd unknown CAREW 130:13
proportions we just b. see JONS 285:8
sav'd by b. not his own POPE 375:16
unripened b. of the north ADD 1:19
You meaner b. of the night WOTT 583:15
beautified: adorned and b. with his presence PRAY 388:25
'b.' is a vile phrase SHAK 431:34
b. with our feathers GREE 236:12
beautiful: acts are b. through love SHEL 503:13
Against the b. GREE 236:3
All things bright and b. ALEX 3:13
art for art's sake...the b. COUS 163:9
b. and ineffectual angel ARN 16:10
b. and death-struck year HOUS 264:1
b. are thy feet with shoes BIBLE 57:7
B. as a wreck of Paradise SHEL 500:12
B. as sweet YOUNG 588:7
b. face is a mute PUBL 402:4
b. God to behold SWIN 530:3
B. must be the mountains BRID 92:17
B. Railway Bridge MCG 325:6
b., the tender, the kind MILL 339:23
b. things in the world RUSK 411:23
b. than any religion SAKI 413:7
B. that war and all its WHIT 570:11
b. than thy first love YEATS 584:23

b. woman on top HOR 257:9
b. words in the English JAMES 271:30
be less b. WATS 565:10
believe to be b. MORR 358:14
deal of scorn looks b. SHAK 489:24
entirely b. AUDEN 19:17
has made His darkness b. TENN 537:3
Here lies a most b. lady DE L 173:27
How b. upon the mountains BIBLE 59:18
how b. they are COL 156:7
how b. KIPL 299:14
indeed appear b. outward BIBLE 67:25
innocent and the b. YEATS 585:12
it comes up more b. HOR 261:12
one was b. BYRON 124:12
Our love of what is b. PER 372:22
'She is more b. than day TENN 532:16
She's b. and therefore SHAK 446:1
she was b. SHEL 505:9
Small is b. SCH 415:12
thee good as thou art b. TENN 534:19
they're too b. to live DICK 180:7
to be b. than to be good WILDE 573:21
when a woman isn't b. CHEK 145:6
will always make it b. CONS 162:2
world over to find the b. EMER 207:12
yet more b. daughter HOR 259:22
beautifully: Print it as it stands—b. JAMES 271:26
beauty: After the wildest b. OWEN 367:10
alike by b. and by fear WORD 580:8
alone has looked on B. bare MILL 339:28
b. beat on his conceits MARL 330:11
B. by constraint GAY 222:9
b. calls and glory leads LEE 313:10
b. cold and austere RUSS 412:15
b. coming and the beauty WORD 582:6
b. draws us with a single POPE 381:1
b. faded has no second PHIL 373:9
B. for some provides escape HUXL 269:1
b. from the light retir'd WALL 562:14
B. in things exists HUME 267:17
B. is bought by judgment SHAK 456:21
B. is momentary STEV 520:17
B. is Nature's coin MILT 341:17
B. is Nature's brag MILT 341:18
b. is the mind diseased BYRON 121:13
B. is the lover's gift CONG 161:1
'B. is truth KEATS 291:11
B. itself doth of itself SHAK 492:17
b. like slow old tunes MAS 333:17
B. lives though lilies FLEC 214:9
b. lives with kindness SHAK 491:4
b. making beautiful old SHAK 494:19
b. of Israel is slain BIBLE 50:16
b. of the good old cause WORD 582:9
B.'s conquest of your AUDEN 20:21
B.'s ensign yet SHAK 483:30
B. she was statue cold FLEC 214:6
b.'s rose might never SHAK 492:22
b.'s self she is ANON 6:20
b. that hath not some strangeness BACON 25:28
B. that must die KEATS 291:15
b. that we should desire BIBLE 59:21
b., though injurious MILT 350:25
b. to delight DAV 172:12
B. took from those who DE L 174:3
B. too rich for use SHAK 482:2
B. unadorn'd BEHN 38:19
b. vanishes DE L 173:27
B., wit, High birth SHAK 487:6
bereft of b. SHAK 484:16
body's b. lives STEV 520:17
born was b.'s summer dead SHAK 494:18
Christian b. Defects POUND 383:8
clear perception of its b. KEATS 294:11
close relationship with b. KEATS 293:18
deep trenches in thy b.'s SHAK 492:23
delusion that b. is goodness TOLS 551:11

delves the parallels in b.'s SHAK 493:20
dreamed that life was B. HOOP 255:22
fatal gift of b. BYRON 121:6
fathers-forth whose b. HOPK 256:23
force and b. of its process JAMES 272:2
give unto them b. for ashes BIBLE 60:9
He hath a daily b. in his SHAK 477:3
Her b. fed my common earth MAS 333:22
her b. was apparent WOOLF 576:18
home and b. BRAH 91:16
horror and its b. are divine SHEL 502:5
I know what wages b. gives YEATS 587:5
In b. and virtue SKEL 508:18
in your b.'s orient deep CAREW 130:18
is simply order and b. BAUD 35:7
is the best part of b. BACON 25:27
June for b.'s heightening ARN 15:4
Lord in the b. of holiness PRAY 396:5
Losing both b. and utility SHAK 445:1
loved the principle of b. KEATS 294:28
more doth b. beauteous seem SHAK 493:16
much b. as could die JONS 284:3
near your b. with my nails SHAK 446:5
No b. she doth miss ANON 6:20
No woman can be a b. without FARQ 210:2
power of b. I remember DRYD 195:32
principal b. in building FULL 220:16
rarest gift To B. MER 337:1
redemption of all things by B. SHAW 496:22
round the ghosts of b. glide POPE 377:26
seizes as b. must be truth KEATS 293:15
She walks in b. BYRON 125:21
shower Of b. WORD 578:11
simple b. and nought else BROW 100:29
soul of her b. and love SHEL 503:23
straight her b. to my sense DONNE 188:9
such b. as a woman's eye SHAK 457:7
Such seems your b. still SHAK 494:18
terrible b. is born YEATS 585:1
That b. is not SPEN 516:27
their b. shall consume PRAY 393:1
thing of b. GILB 228:13
thing of b. is a joy KEATS 288:20
thou B. both so ancient AUG 21:16
thought that where B. was GALS 220:30
thy b. is to me POE 375:7
Thy b. shall no more be MARV 332:19
'Tis b. truly blent SHAK 488:12
To flatter b.'s ignorant YEATS 586:14
unmask her b. to the moon SHAK 430:17
What ills from b. spring JOHN 283:4
What is b. saith my sufferings MARL 330:1
When b. fires the blood DRYD 195:33
Where b. has no ebb YEATS 585:19
Where perhaps some b. lies MILT 342:20
whose b. claims SHAK 422:1
winds of March with b. SHAK 491:26
with this rage shall b. SHAK 494:4
write the b. of your eyes SHAK 492:27
Your infant b. could beget SEDL 419:8
your world of b.'s gone HERR 250:2
youth And a little b. WEBS 566:20
beaux: Where none are b. LYTT 321:22
beaver: Cock up your b. HOGG 253:2
Harry, with his b. on SHAK 440:7
became: b. his'admirers AUDEN 19:3
because: b. I think him so SHAK 490:30
B. it is there MALL 327:13
'B. it was he MONT 354:18
becks: b., and wreathed smiles MILT 342:14
become: do all that may b. a man SHAK 459:9
becomes: b. his coffin prodigiously GOLD 232:14
peace there's nothing so b. SHAK 443:21
becometh: holiness b. thine house PRAY 396:1
bed: able to have a spare b. PEPYS 372:17
Are the weans in their b. MILL 340:3
b. after the hurly-burly CAMP 128:9
b. and procreant cradle SHAK 459:4

b. at night — GOLD 231:4
B. be blest that I lie — ANON 6:15
B. in the bush with stars — STEV 522:27
b. I sought him whom my — BIBLE 56:25
b. of Ware in England — SHAK 489:30
better in battle than in b. — STER 520:3
bounced out of b. — MILNE 340:9
die—in b. — SASS 414:11
drunk to b. — SHAK 421:13
dull, stale, tired b. — SHAK 453:9
earth in an earthy b. — TENN 540:12
ever on her pensive b. — POPE 381:9
Every b. is narrow — MILL 339:29
every night wash I my b. — PRAY 389:26
go to b. in another world — HENS 246:4
grave as little as my b. — KEN 295:9
have to go to b. by day — STEV 522:16
heaped for the beloved's b. — SHEL 504:12
His b. shall seem a school — SHAK 475:13
I drunk him to his b. — SHAK 422:10
I haste me to my b. — SHAK 493:5
I in my b. again — ANON 8:16
In going to my naked b. — EDW 200:5
in thy cold b. — KING 296:11
I put my hand into the b. — SHAK 443:18
I toward thy b. — FLEC 214:12
I used to go to b. early — PROU 401:20
kick his wife out of b. — SURT 525:5
lawn I lie in b. — AUDEN 20:18
lie *diagonally* in his b. — STER 520:9
Lord Tomnoddy went home to b. — BARH 33:9
make my b. — BALL 30:12
make my b. soon — BALL 31:5
me he mostly sent to b. — LAND 309:2
migrations from the blue b. — GOLD 232:34
Must we to b. indeed — STEV 522:25
newly gone to b. — MILT 344:16
nor a goddess to b. — VIRG 560:2
not a b. of roses — STEV 521:31
ought to come to b. in boots — HERB 246:12
pluck me from my naked b. — KYD 306:2
so to b. — PEPYS 371:19
sweat of an enseamed b. — SHAK 435:10
take up thy b. — BIBLE 72:1
This b. thy centre is — DONNE 190:13
thy b. Of crimson joy — BLAKE 87:12
To b., to bed, to bed — SHAK 462:25
to deck both b. and bower — SPEN 516:13
weather when one's in b. — SWIFT 526:12
When boyes go first to b. — HERB 248:4
Who goes to b. with whom — SAY 415:7
whole world out of b. — MAS 333:24
wife my second best b. — SHAK 496:1
bedes: peire of b. — CHAU 141:17
bedfellows: acquaints a man with strange
   b. — SHAK 485:9
Poverty has strange b. — BULW 107:6
Bedlam: with a sigh like Tom o' B. — SHAK 453:12
Bedonebyasyoudid: Mrs B. is coming — KING 297:11
beds: beat them to their b. — SHAK 423:3
hearers weeping to their b. — SHAK 480:8
them rejoice in their b. — PRAY 399:24
when I came unto my b. — SHAK 490:27
Will there be b. for me — ROSS 409:12
bedside: Betty's b. late at nite — WARD 564:29
got a very good b. manner — PUNCH 402:32
bed-staff: in the twinkling of a b. — SHAD 420:23
bed-time: I would it were b. — SHAK 440:17
bee: b. has quit the clover — KIPL 300:23
b.'s kiss — BROW 101:15
b. with honied thigh — MILT 342:8
brisk as a b. in conversation — JOHN 274:1
doth the little busy b. — WATTS 565:21
horribly bored by a b. — LEAR 311:16
like a b. — LODGE 316:3
(Some b. had stung it newly) — SUCK 524:10
Where the b. sucks — SHAK 485:25

beech: appointment with a b.-tree — THOR 550:20
yonder b.-tree single — MER 337:1
beech-tree: cover of the spreading b. — VIRG 559:11
beef: am a great eater of b. — SHAK 487:25
b. and captain's biscuits — THAC 545:32
piece of b. and mustard — SHAK 484:12
roast b. of England — FIEL 211:10
beefsteak: English an article as a b. — HAWT 243:5
beef-witted: thou mongrel b. lord — SHAK 486:28
beefy: b. ATS — BETJ 42:18
bee-loud: live alone in the b. glade — YEATS 585:17
bee-mouth: to Poison while the b. — KEATS 291:15
been: b. and gone and done — GILB 225:12
if it had not b. — SHEL 499:12
'Thou hast b. — ARN 13:11
Beer: B.! O Hodgson — CALV 127:12
chronicle small b. — SHAK 474:18
'Did you ever taste b. — DICK 180:30
drink beer will think b. — IRV 270:22
drink some b. — JOHN 277:14
felony to drink small b. — SHAK 446:11
I'm only a b. teetotaller — SHAW 496:14
in me to desire small b. — SHAK 441:21
inseparable than B. and Britannia — SMITH 511:25
Life ain't all b. and skittles — DU M 199:4
like thine inspirer, b. — POPE 375:20
muddy ecstasies of b. — COWP 168:3
parson, much bemus'd in b. — POPE 376:19
poor creature, small b. — SHAK 441:22
quarts of Ludlow beer — HOUS 264:13
rate you drink your b. — HOUS 264:11
such all b. and skittles — CALV 127:19
Beer-sheba: From Dan even to B. — BIBLE 49:30
travel from Dan to B. — STER 519:2
bees: b. are stirring — COL 157:14
b. each with his own function — VIRG 560:19
b. make honey not for yourselves — VIRG 560:20
b. who have lost their — FRY 220:7
early b. are assaulting — REED 405:6
forest b. are humming near — CLARE 152:14
hive of silvery B. — LEAR 312:9
Like a swarm of golden b. — SHEL 500:6
murmuring of innumerable b. — TENN 542:17
of half a number of b. — LONG 317:23
rob the Hybla b. — SHAK 451:31
yellow b. in the ivy-bloom — SHEL 503:6
beest: b. is deed he hath no peyne — CHAU 142:17
bees-winged: was it his b. eyes — BETJ 42:4
Beethoven: With Spohr and B. — GILB 227:6
beetle: Nor let the b. — KEATS 291:14
poor b. — SHAK 464:11
Save where the b. wheels — GRAY 234:18
shard-borne b. with his — SHAK 461:13
where the b. winds — COLL 158:18
Beetles: B. black — SHAK 470:12
Show scarce so gross as b. — SHAK 455:14
befall: it must b. — GILB 229:7
beflagged: b. jam pots — JAMES 271:34
before: art not what thou wast b. — AYT 24:4
B., behind — DONNE 188:16
b. the flood they were — BIBLE 67:32
doing what has been done b. — WHAR 569:9
I have been here b. — ROSS 410:8
large a trunk b. — BELL 38:28
said our remarks b. — DON 187:1
Saviour Christ is gone b. — PRAY 386:13
sent b. my time — SHAK 480:18
that's not been said b. — TER 544:16
those b. cried 'Back — MAC 322:19
those things which are b. — BIBLE 78:18

Was nothin' much b. — KIPL 299:17
beforehand: so good as it seems b. — ELIOT 201:25
beg: to b. I am ashamed — BIBLE 70:23
to b. in the streets — FRAN 217:26
We cannot b. for pardon — MACN 326:15
you b. for the core — TWAIN 554:17
You taught me first to b. — SHAK 468:12
began: All things b. in order — BROW 95:20
dark womb where I b. — MAS 333:22
first the human race b. — BURNS 113:21
left off before you b. — CONG 160:24
that's how it all b. — KIPL 300:22
was it when my life b. — WORD 578:19
begetter: To the onlie b. of these — SHAK 492:21
beggar: Bare-footed came the b. maid — TENN 532:16
b. by banqueting upon borrowing — BIBLE 63:6
b. should be answer'd — SHAK 468:12
b.'s nurse and Caesar's — SHAK 423:20
B. that I am — SHAK 432:14
behold desert a b. born — SHAK 494:5
certain b. named Lazarus — BIBLE 70:28
He's an absent-minded b. — KIPL 297:23
whiles I am a b. — SHAK 452:15
beggar'd: It b. all description — SHAK 422:2
beggarly: b. people — SWIFT 528:11
Beggars: B., fleas — KING 296:20
B. invention and makes — COWP 166:20
When b. die — SHAK 449:18
beggary: b. in the love that can — SHAK 421:7
no vice, but b. — SHAK 452:15
they knew b. — MAC 324:6
begged: HOMER b. his Bread — ANON 7:14
beggere: beste b. in his hous — CHAU 141:21
begging: his seed b. their bread — PRAY 391:28
Begin: 'B. at the beginning — CARR 134:19
b. charges which once begun — BACON 26:10
B. these wood-birds — SHAK 471:8
get up and b. again — BROW 102:1
My way is to b. with — BYRON 122:5
Then I'll b. — LANG 309:20
where I did b. — SHAK 452:1
will b. with certainties — BACON 24:16
beginning: been told you from the b. — BIBLE 59:9
Before the b. of years — SWIN 528:20
b. and the ending — BIBLE 81:10
b. God created the heaven — BIBLE 44:22
b. is often the end — ELIOT 203:1
b. of any great matter — DRAKE 193:1
B. reform is beginning — WELL 568:4
Each venture Is a new b. — ELIOT 202:23
end of the b. — CHUR 150:11
In my b. is my end — ELIOT 202:18
In the b. was the Word — BIBLE 71:21
it was in the b. — PRAY 384:15
Lord is the b. of wisdom — PRAY 397:13
That is the true b. — SHAK 471:16
that was the b. of fairies — BARR 34:13
thing is the b. of an Amour — BEHN 38:10
This is the b. of the end — TALL 531:19
Thou, Lord, in the b. — PRAY 396:13
Which b. of time according — USSH 554:29
beginnings: may our ends by our b. — DENH 174:20
mighty things from small b. — DRYD 195:22
begins: He that b. to live — QUAR 403:19
she b. to comprehend it — PRIOR 401:7
world's great age b. anew — SHEL 500:20
begot: b. Within a pair of minutes — KYD 306:2
mother on his father him b. — BLAKE 87:2
some that he was b. between — SHAK 464:19
were about when they b. me — STER 519:16
Begotten: B., not made — PRAY 387:1
hath b. the drops of dew — BIBLE 53:4
only b. of the Father — BIBLE 71:27

Whatever is b.   YEATS 586:11
Begriffes: *Gemüt Namen eines B.*   NOV 364:9
beguile: kiaugh and care b.   BURNS 113:5
So b. thy sorrow   SHAK 486:16
To b. many and be beguil'd   SHAK 476:9
To b. the time   SHAK 459:3
beguiled: serpent b. me   BIBLE 45:19
beguiles: traveller's joy b. in autumn
                                                                            HOUS 265:9
Beguine: refused to begin the 'B.'
                                                                            COW 163:22
begun: have not yet b. to fight   JONES 283:11
To have b. is half   HOR 258:14
works, b., continued   PRAY 388:6
behave: b. as the rich behave   SMITH 510:19
How well did I b.   HOUS 263:1
behaving: b. in this extraordinary
                                                                            STOP 523:17
language and ways of b.   JUV 287:15
behaviour: himself upon his good b.
                                                                            BYRON 123:16
immediate check to loose b.   STEE 518:6
liberal arts refines b.   OVID 366:25
of good b.   BIBLE 79:12
there we'll teach better b.   HOGG 253:2
beheaded: was b. yesterday   WALP 562:20
beheld: Where I b. what never was
                                                                            BYRON 123:15
behemoth: Behold now b.   BIBLE 53:8
behind: At such a little tail b.   BELL 38:28
b., between   DONNE 188:16
B. the cloud-topp'd hill   POPE 379:5
b. the throne greater than   PITT 373:24
B. you swiftly the figure   AUDEN 18:18
Broad before and broad b.   BETJ 44:14
come no more b. your scenes   JOHN 274:2
dusk with a light b.   GILB 229:4
has no bosom and no b.   SMITH 510:27
Scratches its innocent b.   AUDEN 19:19
those b. cried 'Forward   MAC 322:19
those things which are b.   BIBLE 78:18
turn thee b. me   BIBLE 51:32
whatever he put b. him   DICK 181:10
Behold: B. an Israelite indeed   BIBLE 71:32
b. a pale horse   BIBLE 81:29
b. a white horse   BIBLE 82:25
B. my mother and my brethren   BIBLE 66:15
B. the man   BIBLE 83:22
b. us with Thy blessing   BUCK 106:16
b. with prejudice the French   BROW 96:28
be what they b.   POPE 375:11
to b. you again in dying   STEV 523:5
beholden: b. to Machiavel and others
                                                                          BACON 24:25
be'ind: less than 'arf o' that b.   KIPL 299:17
Being: always at the edge of B.   SPEN 515:10
B., erect upon two legs   DICK 182:18
have our b.   BIBLE 74:14
in the middle of my b.   LAWR 311:3
Of unknown modes of b.   WORD 580:13
selfish b. all my life   AUST 23:21
will call no b. good   MILL 339:5
beings: human b. are born free   ANON 4:14
bekke: west upon the peple I b.   CHAU 143:5
Belbroughton: B. Road is bonny   BETJ 43:12
Belgium: lightly drawn until B.   ASQ 17:17
Belgrave Square: May beat in B.   GILB 226:5
Belial: B., in act more graceful   MILT 346:9
thou son of B.   BIBLE 50:24
wander forth the sons Of B.   MILT 345:18
belie: shall yet b. thy happy years   SHAK 488:3
belied: she b. with false compare   SHAK 495:9
belief: all b. is for it   JOHN 277:21
bamboozle myself into b.   GREE 236:7
b. of truth   BACON 27:31
believe in B. I disbelieve   FORS 217:10
loved each other beyond b.   HEINE 244:10
beliefs: dust of exploded b.   MADAN 326:18
generous b. and impositions   STEV 521:14
sorts of old defunct b.   IBSEN 269:21

two contradictory b.   ORW 365:13
believe: b. also in me   BIBLE 72:30
b. and take for granted   BACON 27:18
B. a woman or an epitaph   BYRON 124:18
b. everything a *young* man   JOW 285:22
b. in God in spite of what   JOW 286:1
b. in God the Father   PRAY 384:26
b. what one does not believe   PAINE 367:20
brain that won't b.   BLAKE 85:11
Corrected *I b.* to *One does feel*   KNOX 305:20
Do you b. in fairies   BARR 34:16
Firmly I b. and truly   NEWM 362:11
him a determination to b.   HUME 267:21
I b. in Michael Angelo   SHAW 496:22
I b. it was no more   SUCK 524:11
I do b. her   SHAK 495:11
I do not b.   BUTL 119:11
I don't b. a word of it   CHAM 139:16
If you b. that you will   WELL 568:7
If you'll b. in me   CARR 136:2
is a being born to b.   DISR 184:30
I will not b.   BIBLE 73:10
Let Apella the Jew b. it   HOR 262:5
little ones which b. in me   BIBLE 67:3
Lord, I b.   BIBLE 68:35
potently and powerfully b.   SHAK 432:8
power of reason to b.   VOLT 561:20
preaching to save them that b.   BIBLE 75:29
Though ye b. not me   BIBLE 72:21
to b. of my own stories   IRV 270:24
To b. only possibilities   BROW 96:24
To b. your own thought   EMER 207:34
undesirable to b. a proposition   RUSS 412:17
We can b. what we choose   NEWM 362:16
whom shall my soul b.   BROW 104:7
willingly b. what they wish   CAES 126:27
Will ne'er b.   BLAKE 85:17
ye will not b.   BIBLE 71:43
you must b. what you ought   NEWM 362:17
believed: against hope b. in hope   BIBLE 74:40
all that b. were together   BIBLE 73:24
seen, and yet have b.   BIBLE 73:12
what is by all people b.   VINC 557:7
Who hath b. our report   BIBLE 59:20
believer: Most blest b. he   VAUG 555:11
believers: belonged to b. in Clough
                                                                        SWIN 529:13
Kingdom of Heaven to all b.   PRAY 384:17
believes: that he more readily b.   BACON 28:7
believeth: b. all things   BIBLE 76:14
b. he that it is the sound   BIBLE 53:7
b. in him should not perish   BIBLE 71:38
b. on me hath everlasting   BIBLE 72:7
Believing: B. where we cannot prove
                                                                        TENN 535:29
Be not faithless, but b.   BIBLE 73:11
heads of parties against b.   ARB 11:19
She deceiving, I b.   SEDL 419:11
torture them, into b.   NEWM 362:8
bell: be asked to toll the b.   HARDY 241:18
B., book, and candle   SHAK 452:19
b. invites me   SHAK 460:1
b.-swarmed   HOPK 256:10
ever after as a sullen b.   SHAK 441:2
heart as sound as a b.   SHAK 472:23
hear the surly sullen b.   SHAK 494:6
mock the midnight b.   SHAK 422:22
sexton toll'd the b.   HOOD 254:16
Silence that dreadful b.   SHAK 475:4
they rang a b.   ELIOT 202:7
Thrice rung the b.   POPE 380:29
tinkledy-binkledy-winkled a b.   LEAR 312:19
to know for whom the *b.*   DONNE 190:20
Twilight and evening b.   TENN 533:4
very word is like a b.   KEATS 291:23
Bella: B., *horrida bella*   VIRG 558:17
belle: *Garde bien ta b. folie*   BANV 33:1
'La b. dame sans mercy'   KEATS 289:21
belles: b. ringeth to evensonge   HAWES 243:3
belli: Nervos b.   CIC 151:30

bellies: Such as for their b.' sake   MILT 343:12
Bellman: B., perplexed and distressed
                                                                        CARR 133:6
fatal b.   SHAK 460:3
I stayed up till the b.   PEPYS 371:18
Bellona: B.'s bridegroom   SHAK 458:5
bellows: My b. too have lost their   ANON 6:19
bell-rope: swam to the b. and grasped
                                                                        BEER 37:14
Bells: B. are booming down   BETJ 43:7
b., bells, bells   POE 375:1
b. have knoll'd to church   SHAK 425:23
b. justle in the tower   HOUS 266:6
b. of Hell go ting-a-ling-a-ling   ANON 7:4
b. they sound so clear   HOUS 263:4
broke into a mist with b.   BROW 103:11
Down in the b. and grass   HODG 252:4
I heard the church b. hollowing   BETJ 44:9
Like sweet b. jangled   SHAK 433:15
lin-lan-lone of evening b.   TENN 533:15
noisy b., be dumb   HOUS 263:5
sad b. brings back her   JOHN 273:20
'Twould ring the b. of Heaven   HODG 252:2
bellum: praeparet b.   VEG 556:3
belly: b. God send thee good ale   ANON 5:21
b. is as bright ivory overlaid   BIBLE 57:4
b. is like an heap of wheat   BIBLE 57:8
b. of the fish three days   BIBLE 61:22
b. will hardly mind anything   JOHN 275:11
filled his b. with the husks   BIBLE 70:19
increasing b.   SHAK 441:10
individual b. and orders   AUDEN 20:15
its slimy b. on the bank   ELIOT 204:26
it was in Jonadge's b.   DICK 179:23
meat best fits a little b.   HERR 249:21
my b. was bitter   BIBLE 82:9
noise in the beast's b.   MAL 327:15
something of a round b.   SHAK 441:11
wears his wit in his b.   SHAK 486:29
Whose God is their b.   BIBLE 78:19
belly-ache: It gives a chap the b. HOUS 264:11
bellyful: Rumble thy b.   SHAK 454:5
belly-tension: bitter b. between a man
                                                                        GIBB 225:4
Belmont: B. is a lady richly left   SHAK 465:17
belong: suffice for those who b.   WHIT 571:8
To b. to other nations   GILB 228:10
belongs: it b. to Him   CHAP 140:1
belov'd: be more beloving than b.
                                                                        SHAK 421:11
bourn how far to be b.   SHAK 421:7
Shall never be b. by men   BLAKE 85:12
That she b. knows nought   SHAK 486:21
beloved: b. come into his garden   BIBLE 56:29
b. is white and ruddy   BIBLE 57:3
beloved more than another b.   BIBLE 57:2
Dearly b.   PRAY 388:24
man greatly b.   BIBLE 61:9
My b. is mine   BIBLE 56:24
This is my b.   BIBLE 57:4
This is my b. Son   BIBLE 63:40
voice of my b. that knocketh   BIBLE 57:1
beloving: be more b. than belov'd
                                                                        SHAK 421:11
below: above, b.   DONNE 188:16
By him one step b.   SHAK 486:25
journey to the world b.   SOCR 512:19
love is a thing b. a man   STER 520:6
Thy element's b.   SHAK 453:24
belt: bind my b.   TENN 534:21
belted: Though I've b. you an'   KIPL 299:20
belts: They braced their b. about   HOUS 265:6
Belvoir: Till B.'s lordly terraces   MAC 322:4
bely: O wombe! O b.   CHAU 143:6
Ben: Saint B., to aid me   HERR 249:6
Ben Bolt: remember sweet Alice, B.
                                                                        ENGL 208:19
Bench: hand a drowsy B. protect
                                                                        COWP 168:28
suppose I am on the B.   BIRK 84:16

bend: I b. and I break not　　LA F 306:18
Bends: B. to the grave with unperceiv'd
　　　　　　　　　　　　　GOLD 230:20
made their b. adornings　　SHAK 422:3
That b. not as I tread　　MILT 341:21
Though she b. him　　LONG 317:12
bene: *bone,* for *b.*　　SHAK 457:11
Beneath: B. is all the fiends'　　SHAK 455:17
some springing from b.　　BACON 24:20
that is in the earth b.　　BIBLE 47:24
Benedicite: *B., omnia opera Domini*
　　　　　　　　　　　　　BIBLE 83:16
benediction: Perpetual b.　　WORD 579:9
Benedictus: *B. qui venit in nomine*
　　　　　　　　　　　　　MASS 335:4
benefacta: *Siqua recordanti b. priora*
　　　　　　　　　　　　　CAT 137:9
benefactor: first great b. of our race
　　　　　　　　　　　　　TWAIN 554:20
benefice: dreams he of another b.
　　　　　　　　　　　　　SHAK 481:28
beneficial: hands even for b. purposes
　　　　　　　　　　　　　MILL 339:15
benefit: b. of a people whom he
　　　　　　　　　　　　　BURKE 110:26
b. of the students　　SMITH 509:14
without the b. o' the Clergy　　CONG 160:4
benefits: bite so nigh As b. forgot SHAK 426:1
forget not all his b.　　PRAY 396:14
benevolence: b. of mankind does most
　　　　　　　　　　　　　BAG 29:18
b. of the passive order　　MER 338:4
Bengal: In B., to move at all　　COW 163:20
benight: selves b. our happiest day
　　　　　　　　　　　　　DONNE 188:20
their shafts b. the air　　HOUS 265:3
Benighted: B. walks under the midday
　　　　　　　　　　　　　MILT 341:8
benign: By stars b.　　HOUS 265:14
under that b. sky　　BRON 94:1
benison: b. of hot water　　BROO 94:9
b. to fall On our meat　　HERR 250:10
Benjamin: of the tribe of B.　　BIBLE 78:16
bent: b. to make some port he　　ARN 15:2
Just as the twig is b.　　POPE 377:12
My youth is b. by the same　　THOM 547:3
They are not our b.　　GILB 228:25
Bentley: B. or Elias Stoeber was HOUS 266:15
Bequeath: B., like sunset　　SHEL 501:2
bereav'd: if b. of light　　BLAKE 88:2
bereft: b. Of wet and wildness　　HOPK 256:18
bergers: *des b. et des bouchers* VOLT 561:17
Berkeley: B. destroyed this world
　　　　　　　　　　　　　SMITH 511:33
When Bishop B. said 'there　　BYRON 123:28
Berliner: words *Ich bin ein B.*　　KENN 295:11
Bermoothes: still-vexed B.　　SHAK 484:27
Bermudas: Where the remote B. ride
　　　　　　　　　　　　　MARV 331:15
Bernard: B. the monk ne saugh nat
　　　　　　　　　　　　　CHAU 143:28
berries: cometh beauty of b.　　POUND 383:18
I come to pluck your b.　　MILT 343:2
Two lovely b. moulded　　SHAK 470:22
berry: could have made a better b.
　　　　　　　　　　　　　BUTL 119:23
sweeter than the b.　　GAY 222:8
berth: which happen'd in his b.　　HOOD 254:16
beryl: gold rings set with the b.　　BIBLE 57:4
beschränken: *sich zu b. und zu isolieren*
　　　　　　　　　　　　　GOET 229:27
beseech: I pray and b. you　　PRAY 384:10
We b. thee to hear us　　PRAY 385:18
beside: thou art b. thyself　　BIBLE 74:25
thousand shall fall b.　　PRAY 395:21
besiege: forty winters shall b.　　SHAK 492:23
besoin: *b. de voyager*　　STER 518:30
besought: Tho' they b. her　　COW 163:22
bespake: their Lord himself b.　　MILT 344:7

Bessere: *grössere das B. zu empfinden*
　　　　　　　　　　　　　GOET 230:8
best: ae b. dance e'er cam　　BURNS 113:13
All is b.　　MILT 351:3
All is for the b.　　VOLT 561:2
all our b. men are dead　　PUNCH 403:2
Always to be b.　　HOMER 253:30
bad's the b. of us　　FLET 215:10
b. administer'd is best　　POPE 379:20
b. and happiest moments　　SHEL 505:12
b. and the worst of this　　SWIN 530:11
b. and worst, and parted　　BROO 94:6
b. be still　　ARN 13:14
b. chosen language　　AUST 22:31
b. days of life　　VIRG 560:16
b. government is that which　　OSUL 365:22
b. in this kind are　　SHAK 471:19
b. is like the worst　　KIPL 301:8
b. is the best　　QUIL 403:23
b. is the enemy　　VOLT 561:5
b. is yet to be　　BROW 104:2
b. lack all conviction　　YEATS 586:15
b. of all possible worlds　　CAB 126:25
b. that has been known　　ARN 16:17
B., to forget　　BROW 104:35
b. trousers on when you　　IBSEN 269:19
b. words in the best order　　COL 157:32
ears the low-voiced B.　　HARDY 240:3
Fear not to touch the b.　　RAL 404:10
he made the b. of this　　BURNS 113:26
in art the b. is good　　GOET 230:8
is the b. of all trades　　BELL 40:15
is the b. part of beauty　　BACON 25:27
It was the b. of times　　DICK 183:5
lamentable change is from the b.　　SHAK 455:5
loveliest and the b.　　BELL 39:20
loveliest and b.　　FITZ 212:17
one another's b.　　DONNE 188:21
On that b. portion　　WORD 578:4
past all prizing, b.　　SOPH 513:8
propagate the b. that is known　　ARN 16:1
Send forth the b. ye breed　　KIPL 304:6
strongest is always the b.　　LA F 306:21
than any other person's b.　　HAZL 243:11
To seek out the b. through　　JEFF 272:13
wisest and justest and b.　　PLATO 374:10
beste: b., out of they stal　　CHAU 144:22
in der Kunst ist das B.　　GOET 230:8
Bestie: *lüstern schweifende blonde B.*
　　　　　　　　　　　　　NIET 363:14
bestow: Let them b. on every airth
　　　　　　　　　　　　　GRAH 233:16
Bestows: B. her gifts on such　　JONS 284:10
bestride: doth b. the narrow world
　　　　　　　　　　　　　SHAK 448:17
best-seller: b. is the gilded tomb
　　　　　　　　　　　　　SMITH 510:20
b. was a book which somehow　　BOOR 89:21
bet: he would b. you which one TWAIN 554:4
betake: b. myself to that course PEPYS 372:21
Bethel: God of B.　　DODD 187:15
Bethlehem: come ye to B.　　ANON 10:4
Slouches towards B.　　YEATS 586:19
venite in B.　　ANON 10:4
betimes: that spurs too fast b.　　SHAK 478:19
betray: 'All things b. thee　　THOM 548:9
b.'s In deepest consequence　　SHAK 458:18
B. sweet Jenny's unsuspecting　　BURNS 113:7
b. Tawny-finn'd fishes　　SHAK 422:9
else she'll b. more men　　SHAK 477:5
encourage those who b.　　GAY 222:33
finds too late that men b.　　GOLD 231:31
guts to b. my country　　FORS 217:12
betrayal: succeed without any act of b.
　　　　　　　　　　　　　REN 405:12
betray'd: Betrothed, betrayer, and b.
　　　　　　　　　　　　　SCOTT 418:3
betrayed: at ourselves like men b.
　　　　　　　　　　　　　WORD 577:2
b. by what is false within　　MER 337:14

b. him by their adulation　　BURKE 109:5
by ourselves, b.　　CONG 160:20
same night that he was b.　　PRAY 388:1
betrayer: Betrothed, b., and betray'd
　　　　　　　　　　　　　SCOTT 418:3
betrayeth: which is he that b. thee
　　　　　　　　　　　　　BIBLE 73:18
Betrothed: B., betrayer, and betray'd
　　　　　　　　　　　　　SCOTT 418:3
Betsey: B. and I are out　　CARL 130:28
Bette: *Auf seinem B. weinen sass*
　　　　　　　　　　　　　GOET 230:12
better: am getting better and b.　　COUE 163:8
B. be courted and jilted　　CAMP 128:23
B. by far you should forget　　ROSS 409:4
b. day　　HENRY 245:17
b. for worse　　PRAY 389:4
B. is the end of a thing　　BIBLE 55:19
b. supplied when I have　　SHAK 424:24
b. than all the ballads　　LONG 316:8
B. than all measures　　SHEL 504:24
b. than light and safer　　HASK 243:1
b. to be left than never　　CONG 160:35
b. to have loved and lost　　BUTL 119:16
b. to have loved and lost　　TENN 536:15
b. to marry than to burn　　BIBLE 76:2
blame of those ye b.　　KIPL 304:8
did it b. than any other　　JOHN 277:25
far, far b. thing　　DICK 183:12
from b. hap to worse　　SOUT 514:20
have better spar'd a b.　　SHAK 440:25
He is not b.　　ANON 4:17
holds that if way to the B.　　HARDY 240:3
home I was in a b. place　　SHAK 425:8
in a b. world than this　　SHAK 424:27
is b. than a thousand　　PRAY 395:13
is b. to be a fool than　　STEV 522:3
I see the b. way　　OVID 366:17
It is b. that some should　　JOHN 277:5
it is much b. than likely　　BRON 94:2
I took thee for thy b.　　SHAK 435:3
knows of a b. 'ole　　BAIR 29:23
loves him still the b.　　GOLD 232:9
made b. by their presence　　ELIOT 201:27
make a b. mouse-trap　　EMER 208:15
nae b. than he should be　　BURNS 113:12
never b. than when I am mad　　KYD 306:17
party breaks up the b.　　AUST 22:13
render our fellow-men b.　　MOL 353:19
say there was nothing *b.*　　CARR 135:31
see b. days　　BEHN 38:15
Seem'd to have known a b. day　　SCOTT 416:8
seen b. faces in my time　　SHAK 453:18
she'd b.　　CARL 132:30
Something b. than his dog　　TENN 538:19
talk I'm kent the b.　　BURNS 114:32
that which is truly b.　　MILT 351:24
to b. what we can　　STEV 521:14
We have seen b. days　　SHAK 486:9
which of us takes the b.　　SOCR 512:18
will b. it in Scripture　　OVER 366:7
will b. the instruction　　SHAK 467:5
You are no b. than you　　BEAU 36:2
you have look'd on b. days　　SHAK 425:23
You're a b. man than　　KIPL 299:20
bettered: b. expectation than you
　　　　　　　　　　　　　SHAK 471:25
betters: Still b. what is done　　SHAK 491:27
between: anyone who comes b. them
　　　　　　　　　　　　　SMITH 511:11
b., above　　DONNE 188:16
b. France and England　　JERR 273:4
b. his Darkness and his　　BYRON 126:8
B. the dark and the daylight　　LONG 316:9
B. two worlds life hovers　　BYRON 124:9
something b. compliments　　AUST 22:27
wasn't for the 'ouses in b.　　BAT 35:3
betwixt: b. and between　　HOUS 266:18
that's the day that comes b.　　CAREY 130:27

beverage: soiled by the 'b. of hell'
          YOUNG 588:15
Beware: B. of the scribes   BIBLE 68:37
 B. of the dog   PETR 372:30
 B. the ides of March   SHAK 448:7
beweep: alone b. my outcast state SHAK 493:6
bewept: Which b. to the grave did
         SHAK 435:34
bewildered: young are sad and b.
         SMITH 510:22
bewitch: Do more b. me   HERR 249:2
bewitched: I am b. with the rogue's
         SHAK 438:24
Bewrapt: B. past knowing to what
         HARDY 240:9
bewrayeth: Thy speech b. thee BIBLE 68:19
beye: our soules for to b.   CHAU 144:19
beyond: are not b. all conjecture BROW 97:14
 b. the knowledge of a man
 is there anything b.   BEAU 35:16
         BROO 94:10
 loved each other b. belief HEINE 244:10
 organism to live b. its income BUTL 118:27
beyont: them to the back o' b. SCOTT 418:1
Bezonian: B. speak   SHAK 442:28
bias: b. of the world   SHAK 452:14
bibble-babble: Leave thy vain b.
         SHAK 490:22
bibendum: Nunc est b.   HOR 260:3
bibisti: edisti satis atque b.   HOR 259:6
Bible: are only fit for the B.   FRY 219:30
 B. as if it was a constable's KING 297:7
 B. clash and contradict   DOW 191:11
 B. only is the religion   CHIL 148:12
 big ha'-B.   BURNS 113:9
 English B.   MAC 323:4
 knows even his B.   ARN 15:22
 read the B. day and night BLAKE 85:22
 that book is the B.   ARN 16:13
 to be hanged with the B.   AUBR 17:23
 translation of the B.   WHAT 569:15
 was but litel on the B.   CHAU 141:30
bible-black: starless and b. THOM 547:9
bibles: b., billet-doux   POPE 380:31
 B. laid open   HERB 248:10
Bible-Society: B. found   CARL 131:6
bicicleta: puede llegar solo en b. VIER 556:21
bicker: To b. down a valley TENN 532:20
bicycle: Salisbury Plain on a b. GILB 226:15
 Socialism can only arrive by b. VIER 556:21
bid: b. the soldiers shoot   SHAK 437:31
bide: b. by the buff   BURNS 114:5
Bidst: B. them avaunt   CALV 127:28
bien: mieux est l'ennemi du b. VOLT 561:5
 mon b. où je le trouve   MOL 354:3
bienfaits: recevoir de plus grands b.
         LA R 310:16
bier: float upon his watery b. MILT 343:2
 him barefac'd on the b.   SHAK 436:9
big: b. business give the people ROOS 408:7
 b. enough majority in any TWAIN 554:3
 b. squadrons against   BUSS 117:7
 b. words for little   JOHN 275:14
 die will be an awfully b. adventure
         BARR 34:15
 fear those b. words   JOYCE 286:22
 letters in a b. round hand GILB 228:5
Big Brother: B. is watching you ORW 365:12
bigger: b. they come   FITZ 214:1
 seems no b. than his head SHAK 455:14
biggin: whose brow with homely b.
         SHAK 442:17
Big-Sea-Water: By the shining B.
         LONG 317:10
Bilbo: B.'s the word   CONG 160:21
bill: b. of fare to tempt me SWIFT 526:1
 b. of indemnity...for raid KRUG 306:1
 b. of my Divorce to all DONNE 189:11
 birdie with a yellow b. STEV 522:24
 Half-a-crown in the b.   DICK 181:25
 Take thy b.   BIBLE 70:24

There's little B. as is   THAC 546:1
billards: play b. well   SPEN 515:4
billboard: b. lovely as a tree NASH 360:2
Billee: youngest he was little B. THAC 545:32
billet: Every bullet has its b. WILL 574:9
billiard: b. sharp whom any one catches
         GILB 227:7
 elliptical b. balls   GILB 227:7
billiards: let's to b.   SHAK 422:8
billing: fond, and b.   BUTL 118:7
billion: this a b. dollar country FOST 217:16
billow: breaking b.   SHEL 499:17
billowing: sail in amply b. gown BELL 39:28
billows: b. smooth and bright CARR 135:3
 Even the b. of the sea   SHAK 447:3
billowy: plunged himself into the b.
         GILB 227:17
bills: children but as b. of charges
         BACON 26:32
 inflammation of his weekly b. BYRON 122:29
Billy: heart to poke poor B. GRAH 233:13
 Who's Silly B. now   GLOU 229:23
bin: have gone to stall and b. FROST 219:11
bind: apprentice for to b. BALL 30:8
 b. another to its delight BLAKE 87:19
 b. their kings in chains PRAY 399:24
 b. the sweet influences BIBLE 53:5
 b. up the nation's wounds LINC 315:3
 b. your sons to exile   KIPL 304:6
 body and in soul can b. SCOTT 416:20
 ever sure to b.   POPE 375:24
 Rob me, but b. me not DONNE 189:16
binds: who b. to himself a Joy BLAKE 86:18
Bingham: B. had never been to Ciro's
         TRAV 552:6
Binnorie: bonnie milldams o' B. BALL 30:14
binomial: b. theorems I'm teeming
         GILB 228:17
Biographers: B., translators MAC 323:10
 Boswell is the first of b. MAC 324:5
biographical: b. friend who has added
         WETH 569:6
biographies: essence of innumerable
 b.   CARL 131:9
Biography: B. is about chaps BENT 41:3
 b. of great men   CARL 131:31
 no history; only b.   EMER 207:24
 nothing but b.   DISR 186:4
birch: nor fasting, nor b. BLAKE 87:20
 to go by climbing a b. FROST 219:1
bird: at the voice of the b. BIBLE 56:11
 b. forlorn   HOOD 255:2
 b. of dawning singeth all SHAK 429:17
 b. of night did sit   SHAK 449:1
 b. of wonder dies   SHAK 448:3
 b.'s song ye may learn TENN 535:3
 b. That flutters least COWP 167:29
 b. that thinks two notes DAV 172:14
 B. thou never wert   SHEL 504:15
 b. would trust Her household HERB 246:23
 Dromedary is a cheerful b. BELL 38:27
 fell with the waking b. TENN 540:10
 forgets the dying b.   PAINE 368:3
 further than a wanton's b. SHAK 482:20
 heart is like a singing b. ROSS 408:23
 household b.   DONNE 188:19
 in the sight of any b. BIBLE 53:14
 is escaped even as a b. PRAY 398:14
 I would I were thy b. SHAK 482:20
 Let the b. of loudest lay SHAK 492:15
 Like that self-begotten b. MILT 350:30
 obscure b.   SHAK 460:20
 rare b. on this earth JUV 287:20
 regretted that he was not a b. ROCHE 406:13
 sea-blue b. of March TENN 537:9
 secular b.   MILT 350:31
 Shall I call thee b.   WORD 582:25
 Stirred for a b.   HOPK 257:5
 Sweet b., that shunn'st MILT 342:2
 Unto the sweet b.'s throat SHAK 425:14

wakeful b. Sings darkling MILT 347:8
 were all like that wise b. PUNCH 402:25
 widow b. sate mourning SHEL 500:3
 young b. in this bush LEAR 311:18
birdcage: summer b. in a garden WEBS 567:2
bird-haunted: b. English lawn ARN 14:1
birdie: b. with a yellow bill STEV 522:24
 What does little b. say TENN 543:7
birds: are like bats amongst b. BACON 27:23
 Beasts did leap and b. BARN 33:32
 b. are on the wing   COL 157:14
 B. build   HOPK 257:3
 B. in the high Hall-garden TENN 540:5
 B. in their little nests BELL 40:6
 B. in their little nests WATTS 565:20
 b. of the air have nests BIBLE 65:18
 b. sit brooding   SHAK 457:19
 b. still hopping   STEV 522:16
 b. the colour of red-flannel THOM 546:22
 children casual as b. AUDEN 18:5
 diminutive of b., will fight SHAK 462:12
 happy as b. in the spring BLAKE 87:20
 I envy b. their wings CLARE 152:5
 If b. confabulate or no COWP 166:5
 Melodious b. sing madrigals MARL 330:1
 nest of singing b.   JOHN 273:28
 no b. sing   KEATS 290:15
 pipe of half-awaken'd b. TENN 542:4
 see all the b. are flown CHAR 140:18
 sing like b. i' the cage SHAK 456:3
 song of the b. for mirth GURN 237:7
 so that the b. of the air BIBLE 66:20
 suffers little b. to sing SHAK 486:17
 time of the singing of b. BIBLE 56:22
 Two fairer b. I yet did SPEN 516:31
 very merciful to the b. ANON 8:15
 We think caged b. sing WEBS 567:1
 what these unobservant b. ISH 270:27
 where late the sweet b. sang SHAK 494:7
 With charm of earliest b. MILT 348:4
 you b. build nests not VIRG 560:20
bird-song: b. at morning and star-shine
         STEV 522:29
Birmingham: B. by way of Beachy Head
         CHES 147:11
 no great hopes from B. AUST 22:18
Birnam wood: B. to high Dunsinane
 hill   SHAK 462:8
 Till B. remove to Dunsinane SHAK 462:28
birth: at my b.   SHAK 439:21
 Beauty, wit, High b. SHAK 487:6
 bed for this huge b. CRAS 169:7
 B., and copulation ELIOT 204:12
 bring this monstrous b. SHAK 474:13
 draws near the b. of Christ TENN 536:17
 grievous burden was thy b. SHAK 481:8
 his b.'s invidious bar TENN 537:1
 I had seen b. and death ELIOT 203:15
 laid us as we lay at b. ARN 13:17
 Nobility of b. commonly BACON 27:1
 one that is coming to b. OSH 365:21
 Our b. is but a sleep WORD 579:5
 Saviour's b. is celebrated SHAK 429:17
 she who gives a baby b. MAS 333:25
 sudden and portentous b. SCOTT 417:20
 Terms like grace, new b. ARN 16:18
 that have a different b. SHEL 505:5
 There was a B.   ELIOT 203:15
 to say as a sorrowful b. MAL 327:17
 virtue, and not b.   FLET 215:18
birthday: Because the b. of my life
         ROSS 408:24
 marvel My b. Away THOM 547:7
birth-pangs: shorten and lessen the b.
         MARX 333:8
birth-place: b. of valour BURNS 114:26
birth-rate: Into a rising b. FRY 219:32
birthright: Esau selleth his b. for a mess
         BIBLE 46:12
 sold his b. unto Jacob BIBLE 46:14

birthrite: b. for a mess of potash
WARD 564:22
births: b. of living creatures BACON 26:27
joyful b. SHAK 445:11
which are the b. of time BACON 26:27
birth-strangled: Finger of b. babe
SHAK 462:4
bis: b. dat qui dat celeriter PUBL 402:3
biscuit: b., or confectionary plum
COWP 166:3
dry as the remainder b. SHAK 425:21
he took a captain's b. DICK 179:4
biscuit box: didn't look like a b. did it
COW 163:13
biscuits: eat and the b. you nibble KIPL 298:5
with beef and captain's b. THAC 545:32
Bishop: another B. dead MELB 336:19
B.-Elect of Vermont KNOX 305:23
B. of Rome hath no jurisdiction PRAY 400:10
b. then must be blameless BIBLE 79:12
desire the office of a b. BIBLE 79:11
How can a b. marry SMITH 511:4
Shepherd and B. of your souls BIBLE 80:27
think of contradicting a B. JOHN 279:14
bishopric: talk of *merit* for a b. WEST 569:5
bishops: b. like best in their clergy
SMITH 512:1
If elderly b. were seen HERB 246:15
Send down upon our B. PRAY 385:7
thee to illuminate all B. PRAY 385:18
to all B. and Curates PRAY 387:15
bisier: he semed b. than he was CHAU 141:26
bisy: Nowher so b. a man as he CHAU 141:26
bit: b. by him that comes behind SWIFT 528:5
b. him till he bled HOFF 252:13
b. the babies in the cradles BROW 103:15
held with b. and bridle PRAY 391:18
requital b. his fingers CHIL 148:13
Though he had b. me SHAK 455:24
Went mad and b. the man GOLD 231:13
Bitch: called John a Impudent B.
FLEM 214:27
old b. gone in the teeth POUND 383:10
why b. FIEL 211:12
bitch-goddess: flabbiness born of the
b. SUCCESS JAMES 272:3
bite: b. some of my other generals
GEOR 223:36
b. so nigh As benefits forgot SHAK 426:1
b. the hand that fed BURKE 112:10
forbear To b. his pen SWIFT 527:23
man recover'd of the b. GOLD 231:14
you b. your thumb at us SHAK 481:22
bites: bargain dog never is NASH 360:3
dog b. a man BOG 89:9
biteth: last it b. like a serpent BIBLE 54:24
biting: His b. is immortal SHAK 424:5
more than b. Time can sever ELIOT 204:3
bitter: be not b. against them BIBLE 78:27
b. belly-tension between GIBB 225:4
b. bread of banishment SHAK 479:4
B. God to follow SWIN 530:3
does truth sound b. BROW 102:9
do such b. business SHAK 434:25
end is b. as wormwood BIBLE 53:20
life unto the b. in soul BIBLE 52:14
love grows b. with treason SWIN 530:5
make misfortunes more b. BACON 27:3
mirth that has no b. springs KIPL 298:12
my belly was b. BIBLE 82:9
pulp so b. THOM 548:19
shortly as b. as coloquintida SHAK 474:10
Some do it with a b. look WILDE 572:10
something b. that chokes LUCR 320:11
sweet water and b. BIBLE 80:15
these are very b. words SHAK 441:26
bitterness: of death is past BIBLE 50:5
must have no hatred or b. CAV 137:18
rose's scent is b. THOM 547:25
scorn in the b. of his soul BIBLE 62:26

think the b. of absence sour SHAK 493:18
years in the b. of my soul BIBLE 59:3
bivouac: Barrack and b. shall be
AUDEN 19:11
blabbing: b., and remorseful day SHAK 446:8
black: be a b. man or a fair man ADD 2:7
be the heavens with b. SHAK 445:17
b. and merciless things JAMES 271:23
B. as the Pit from pole HENL 245:4
b., but comely BIBLE 56:16
b. eyes and lemonade MOORE 356:3
b. it stood as night MILT 346:24
b. men fought on the coast MAC 323:21
b. piano appassionato LAWR 311:7
b. ram Is tupping SHAK 473:16
Black's not so b. CANN 129:29
b. *sun* of *melancholy* NERV 360:26
b. vesper's pageants SHAK 423:7
customary suits of solemn b. SHAK 429:25
devil damn thee b. SHAK 463:1
I am b. SHAK 475:21
I am b. BLAKE 88:2
it here in b. and white JONS 284:7
More b. than ashbuds TENN 533:19
night's b. agents SHAK 461:14
read'st b. where I read white BLAKE 85:22
shall not neutralize the b. BROW 104:31
sloeblack, slow, b., crowblack THOM 547:9
They were as b. as they BALL 32:7
Tip me the b. spot STEV 521:22
velvet that is b. and soft CHES 147:5
vexed not his fantasy B. DONNE 190:3
Who art as b. as hell SHAK 495:15
worse for wearing a b. gown CHES 145:11
you wear b. all the time CHEK 144:25
blackberries: plentiful as b. SHAK 439:5
prove a micher and eat b. SHAK 439:14
sit round it and pluck b. BROW 97:33
blackberry: running b. would adorn
WHIT 570:21
blackbird: b.'s tune BROW 100:13
b., what a boy you are BROWN 95:11
blackbirds: full of b. than of cherries
ADD 2:25
blackens: b. all the water about ADD 2:24
b. every blot TENN 533:30
blacker: Leaving a b. air HARDY 240:11
blackguard: brute and b. made the world
HOUS 264:21
Sesquipedalian b. CLOU 153:17
That man's a b. HOR 262:3
blackguards: b. both BYRON 123:12
ever done to you young b. FARR 210:28
Blackheath: from wild B. MAC 322:3
blacking: drink and b. the Corporal's
KIPL 298:7
blacksmith: Never was a b. like our
KIPL 297:26
Black Widow: This is the B. LOW 319:19
bladder: blows a man up like a b.
SHAK 439:11
bladders: boys that swim on b. SHAK 447:9
blade: b. is layed low POUND 383:19
cling round the sickly b. COWP 168:26
destroy a b. of grass BOTT 90:17
His b. struck the water COKE 154:15
vorpal b. went snicker-snack CARR 134:29
with bloody blameful b. SHAK 471:17
blade-straight: Steel-true and b. STEV 523:3
blains: breaking forth with b. BIBLE 47:14
Blake: B. is damned good to steal FUS 220:22
B. was no good BUTL 118:35
B. went dotty as he sang AUDEN 18:20
what B. once wildly muttered... SASS 414:19
blame: Alike reserv'd to b. POPE 376:27
am not disposed to b. him BURKE 109:5
b. of those ye better KIPL 304:8
only The Master shall b. KIPL 304:3
That neither is most to b. SWIN 530:11

blameless: bishop then must be b.
BIBLE 79:12
white flower of a b. life TENN 533:30
blanch: plain when counsellors b.
BACON 25:39
Tray, B., and Sweet-heart SHAK 454:29
blanching: under b. mays HOUS 265:8
bland: Aspect anything but b. CALV 127:14
composed and b. ARN 14:4
lines mellifluously b. BYRON 123:14
tone, and gesture b. SCOTT 416:2
blandula: Animula vagula b. HADR 237:9
Blank: B. to Zoroaster on his BROW 102:35
political b. cheque GOSC 233:2
Presented with a universal b. MILT 347:8
you talk in b. verse SHAK 426:20
blanket: right side of the b. ASHF 17:12
through the b. of the dark SHAK 459:2
blankets: rough male kiss of b. BROO 94:8
blasphemies: great truths begin as b.
SHAW 496:2
blaspheming: brooding and b. over the
village CHES 148:7
Liver of b. Jew SHAK 462:4
blasphemous: were b. fables PRAY 400:9
blasphemy: b. against the Holy Ghost
BIBLE 66:7
soldier is flat b. SHAK 464:4
blast: banner wav'd without a b.
SCOTT 416:14
B. of the Desert cried LONG 317:8
b. of war blows in our SHAK 443:21
every b. of vain doctrine PRAY 387:3
in the trances of the b. COL 156:23
One b. upon his bugle-horn SCOTT 416:7
though it b. me SHAK 429:14
blasted: about you b. with antiquity
SHAK 441:10
b. heath you stop our way SHAK 458:13
b. with excess of light GRAY 235:19
B. with ecstasy SHAK 433:15
no sooner blown but b. MILT 344:2
you b. its rocks away RUSK 411:13
blasts: airs from heaven or b. SHAK 430:24
Blatant: which the B. beast men SPEN 516:22
blaze: broader still became the b. MAC 322:3
heavens themselves b. forth the death
SHAK 449:18
that brighten at the b. GOLD 231:26
unclouded b. of living light BYRON 121:37
blazed: My body of a sudden b.
YEATS 587:11
blazes: b., and expires BYRON 124:30
blazing: you b. ass CALV 127:18
blazon: this eternal b. must not be
SHAK 431:5
Bleach: B. the bones of comrades
HOUS 263:19
bleaching: white sheet b. on the hedge
SHAK 491:17
bleak: In the b. mid-winter ROSS 409:1
bleat: b. the one at the other SHAK 491:8
bled: bit him till he b. HOFF 252:13
knew that marble b. FLEC 214:15
bleed: Caesar b. in sport SHAK 450:5
do we not b. SHAK 467:4
I b. SHEL 502:13
If he do b. SHAK 460:11
mee downe and b. a while BALL 31:15
our bosom and then we b. SHEL 501:4
'Twill b. because of it HOUS 264:9
bleeding: pageant of his b. heart ARN 13:9
testament of b. war SHAK 479:13
thou b. piece of earth SHAK 450:11
blemish: lamb shall be without b.
BIBLE 47:16
there's no b. but the mind SHAK 490:18
without fear and without b. ANON 9:5
blenches: These b. gave my heart SHAK 495:3
Bless: B. her when she is riggish SHAK 422:5

b. the hand that gave DRYD 197:27
B. the Lord BIBLE 83:16
B. the squire and his relations DICK 176:23
b. ye the Lord PRAY 384:19
Curse, b., me now THOM 546:24
except thou b. me BIBLE 46:24
'God b. us every one DICK 176:24
him how to load and b. KEATS 293:5
was blessèd and could b. YEATS 587:11
Blessed: B. are the poor in spirit BIBLE 64:6
B. are the eyes which see BIBLE 69:29
B. are the dead which die BIBLE 82:18
b. are the horny hands LOW 319:9
B. art thou among women ANON 10:8
b. art thou among women BIBLE 69:4
B. be he that cometh PRAY 398:3
b. be the name of the Lord BIBLE 52:7
b. damozel leaned out ROSS 409:14
B. is he who has found CARL 132:10
B. is the man that endureth BIBLE 80:8
B. is the man that hath PRAY 389:14
B. is the man unto whom PRAY 391:16
b. is the man that trusteth PRAY 391:21
B. is the man whose strength PRAY 395:12
b. mutter of the mass BROW 99:14
b. the latter end of Job BIBLE 53:13
b. they that master so SHAK 469:17
B. to give than to receive BIBLE 74:19
buttercup Had b. with gold OWEN 367:8
call her b. BIBLE 55:4
generations shall call me b. BIBLE 69:5
hence to there may be b. SOCR 512:20
His b. part to Heaven SHAK 447:16
How b. is he DRYD 196:3
I b. them unaware COL 155:22
I was b. and could bless YEATS 587:11
Judge none b. before his BIBLE 63:1
That b. mood WORD 578:5
This b. plot SHAK 478:20
Thou fall'st a b. martyr SHAK 447:12
thou hast altogether b. BIBLE 48:16
what all the b. Evil's BROW 99:8
whom thou blessest is b. BIBLE 48:13
blessedness: b. alone that makes a King TRAH 552:2
blindly with thy b. at strife WORD 579:8
in single b. SHAK 469:17
Blesses: B. his stars ADD 1:17
blessest: visitest the earth, and b. PRAY 394:2
blesseth: It b. him that gives SHAK 467:27
blessing: behold us with Thy b. BUCK 106:16
b. of God Almighty PRAY 388:4
b. of the Old Testament BACON 25:18
b. that money cannot buy WALT 564:12
come as a boon and a b. ANON 8:5
continual dew of thy b. PRAY 385:7
contrariwise b. BIBLE 80:30
daughter would have been a b. AUST 23:18
hath taken away thy b. BIBLE 46:17
I'll b. beg of you SHAK 435:19
in the pursuit of the b. AUST 22:30
shall give us his b. PRAY 394:5
When thou dost ask me b. SHAK 456:3
You enjoy but half the b. GAY 222:9
blessings: Are b. in disguise HERV 250:17
b. on the falling out TENN 541:28
Having a glass of b. standing HERB 248:6
In b. on your head COWP 165:27
they recognized their b. VIRG 560:13
blest: always To be b. POPE 379:5
Bed be b. that I lie ANON 6:15
B. pair of Sirens MILT 340:20
last promotion of the b. DRYD 197:32
their country's wishes b. COLL 158:19
blew: b. his silly brains out THAC 546:3
hotched an' b. wi' might BURNS 115:11
blight: is the b. man was born HOPK 256:27
Blimber: nonsense about Miss B. DICK 177:23
blind: Altho' a poor b. boy CIBB 151:8

b. as any noon-tide owl TENN 534:23
b. his soul with clay TENN 542:19
b. Homer sing MARL 329:9
b. man in a dark room BOWEN 90:23
b. man On the sightless WALEY 562:2
b., now I see BIBLE 72:16
b. old man of Scio's rocky BYRON 120:3
B. to Galileo on his turret BROW 102:35
B. with thine hair SHEL 505:3
Country of the B. the One-eyed WELLS 568:12
Cupid b. did rise LYLY 321:11
eyes were b. with stars HODG 252:8
eyes will gaze an eagle b. SHAK 457:8
giveth sight to the b. PRAY 399:17
go drawing back the b. KIPL 302:22
halt, and the b. BIBLE 70:12
her faults a little b. PRIOR 400:23
if the blind lead the b. BIBLE 66:29
I was eyes to the b. BIBLE 52:35
Love is b. ANON 9:11
man to a b. woman COL 157:19
of darkness and b. eyes VAUG 555:11
old, mad, b. SHEL 504:6
old Maeonides the b. FLEC 214:22
own internal lightning b. SHEL 501:18
passion and party b. COL 157:20
splendid work for the b. SASS 414:13
That myself am b. POPE 381:12
That nourish a b. life TENN 535:26
Thou Eye among the b. WORD 579:7
though she be b. BACON 26:13
though she's painted b. BUTL 118:14
unbelief is b. MILT 341:12
will accompany my being b. PEPYS 372:21
wing'd Cupid painted b. SHAK 469:22
Ye b. guides BIBLE 67:24
blinded: dulness of our b. sight PRAY 400:5
blindfold: b. and alone KIPL 298:25
blindly: nor b. right POPE 378:32
blindness: From all b. of heart PRAY 385:16
is a triple sight in b. KEATS 292:25
I've an April b. FRY 219:26
our b. we cannot ask PRAY 388:7
To help him of his b. SHAK 491:4
blinds: b. let through the day HOUS 265:2
dusk a drawing-down of b. OWEN 367:3
blind-worm: b.'s sting SHAK 462:3
blind-worms: b., do no wrong SHAK 470:11
blinking: b. sort o' place HARDY 241:22
portrait of a b. idiot SHAK 466:21
blisfully: His lighte goost ful b. CHAU 144:18
Bliss: B. in our brows bent SHAK 421:26
b. in proof SHAK 495:7
B. was it in that dawn WORD 577:21
certainty of waking b. MILT 341:5
deprived of everlasting b. MARL 329:7
each to his point of b. BROW 105:20
had given all other b. TENN 543:9
highest b. of human-kind KEATS 292:20
it will be b. BETJ 43:15
Milk-soup men call domestic b. PATM 370:4
mutual and partaken b. MILT 341:17
Of bliss on b. MILT 348:1
promise of pneumatic b. ELIOT 200:21
Thou art a soul in b. SHAK 455:25
where ignorance is b. GRAY 235:13
Which is the b. of solitude WORD 578:1
with hopes of earthly b. COWP 167:17
blister: b. my kidneys SURT 525:16
blithe: be you b. and bonny SHAK 472:16
buxom, b., and debonair MILT 342:13
Hail to thee, b. Spirit SHEL 504:15
No b. Irish lad was so CAMP 128:20
No lark more b. than he BICK 83:28
block: chopper on a big black b. GILB 226:31
each b. cut smooth POUND 382:8
old b. itself BURKE 110:22
blockhead: bookful b. POPE 378:30
if I had not been a b. ADD 2:17

man but a b. ever wrote JOHN 277:4
when a b.'s insult points JOHN 282:23
blocks: You b., you stones SHAK 448:6
Blond: B. comme un soleil d'Italie BANV 33:1
blonde: b. Bestie nicht zu verkennen NIET 363:14
blood: am I not of her b. SHAK 488:18
b. and smoke and flame HOUS 266:4
b. and wine are red WILDE 572:7
B., as all men know HUXL 269:2
b. be the price of admiralty KIPL 303:4
b. in his liver as will SHAK 490:1
B. is compulsory STOP 523:16
b. is fet from fathers SHAK 444:1
B. is very snow-broth SHAK 463:14
b. more stirs SHAK 438:18
b. of all the Howards POPE 379:23
b. Of human sacrifice MILT 345:14
B. of Jesus whispers BICK 84:4
b. of patriots and tyrants JEFF 272:10
B. of the New Testament PRAY 388:1
b. ran down the stairs AUDEN 21:7
b. reigns in the winter's SHAK 491:5
b.'s a rover HOUS 262:15
b. will have blood SHAK 461:24
b. with guilt is bought SHEL 503:1
blow in cold b. SHAW 497:41
by crikey b. will tell MARQ 330:20
choler without letting b. SHAK 478:7
drink the b. of goats PRAY 393:3
drop my b. for drachmas SHAK 451:21
examine well your b. SHAK 469:4
flesh and b. so cheap HOOD 255:8
fountain fill'd with b. COWP 165:24
from kindred b. BURKE 110:2
getting b. out of a turnip MARR 331:3
give me B. DICK 177:13
good enough to shed his b. ROOS 408:3
guiltless of his country's b. GRAY 234:23
have had so much b. in him SHAK 462:20
Her b. is settled SHAK 483:22
Here's the smell of the b. SHAK 462:22
His b. be on us BIBLE 68:22
I am innocent of the b. BIBLE 68:21
in b. Stepp'd in so far SHAK 461:25
Inhabits our frail b. SHAK 490:1
kind of sleeping in the b. SHAK 441:6
'Let there be b. BYRON 123:23
make thick my b. SHAK 459:2
Man of B. was there MAC 322:1
man shall his b. be shed BIBLE 45:39
men are flesh and b. SHAK 449:25
moment when the moon was b. CHES 146:22
most noble b. SHAK 450:7
near in b. SHAK 461:4
Neptune's ocean wash this b. SHAK 460:13
not against flesh and b. BIBLE 78:10
Nothing like b. THAC 545:24
nothing to offer but b. CHUR 149:29
now could I drink hot b. SHAK 434:25
out through b. and iron BISM 84:25
pride in place and b. TENN 537:15
Propinquity and property of b. SHAK 453:3
pure and eloquent b. DONNE 189:31
rivers of b. must yet flow JEFF 272:14
See see where Christ's b. MARL 329:11
shedding of b. is no remission BIBLE 79:29
shed innocent b. BIBLE 60:1
smear'd in dust and b. SHAK 446:22
smell the b. of a British SHAK 454:27
summon up the b. SHAK 443:21
Sweat ran and b. sprang HOUS 264:4
that all that b. was shed YEATS 586:19
that sheds his b. with me SHAK 445:3
there's b. upon her gown FLEC 214:6
they stream forth thy b. SHAK 450:3
thicks man's b. with cold COL 155:15
this tincture in the b. DEFOE 173:4
Tiber foaming with much b. VIRG 558:17
voice of thy brother's b. BIBLE 45:26

warming of the b.   SHAK 442:15
was not part of their b.   KIPL 298:1
We be of one b.   KIPL 304:13
When beauty fires the b.   DRYD 195:33
when b. is their argument   SHAK 444:21
When b. is nipp'd and ways   SHAK 457:19
When the b. creeps   TENN 536:21
Which all the while ran b.   SHAK 450:28
white in the b. of the Lamb   BIBLE 82:2
whose b. is warm within   SHAK 465:11
Young b. must have its   KING 297:5

blood-dimmed: b. tide is loosed
   YEATS 586:15

blood-guiltiness: Deliver me from b.
   PRAY 393:7

Blood-happy: B., hang at his fair jutting
   THOM 549:19

bloodless: ballet of b. categories   BRAD 91:10
b. lay the untrodden snow   CAMP 128:21

blood-red: one glorious b.   BROW 101:8

blood-thirsty: b. clinging to life   ARN 15:24
b. and deceitful man   PRAY 389:23

blood-tinctured: Shows a heart within
b.   BROW 98:3

bloody: Agony and b. Sweat   PRAY 385:17
begin to have b. thoughts   SHAK 485:21
b., bold, and resolute   SHAK 462:6
b. hand that drew from   HEINE 244:12
b. noses and crack'd crowns   SHAK 438:31
breast a b. cross he bore   SPEN 515:31
discontent, boil b.   OWEN 367:11
Even so my b. thoughts   SHAK 476:1
last act is b.   PASC 369:8
My head is b.   HENL 245:4
Not b. likely   SHAW 498:16
sang within the b. wood   ELIOT 204:16
subtle, sly, and b.   SHAK 481:8
teach B. instructions   SHAK 459:5
What b. man is that   SHAK 458:2
wipe a b. nose   GAY 223:14
with b. blameful blade   SHAK 471:17
Woe to the b. city   BIBLE 61:26
wrong with our b. ships   BEAT 35:12

bloom: b. is gone   ARN 15:5
b. of the year in the bag   BROW 98:30
b. of young desire   GRAY 235:17
flowers that b. in the spring   GILB 227:13
Full on thy b.   BURNS 115:19
How can ye b. sae fresh   BURNS 116:6
Madam Life's a piece in b.   HENL 245:6
opening sweet of earliest b.   COLL 158:16
sort of b. on a woman   BARR 34:18
to look at things in b.   HOUS 262:14
with b. along the bough   HOUS 262:14

blooming: Left b. alone   MOORE 356:20
were b. in the tall tales   THOM 547:7

blooms: Then b. each thing   NASHE 360:9

blossom: blood-red b. of war   TENN 540:18
b. as the rose   BIBLE 58:32
B. by blossom the spring   SWIN 528:17
b. in purple and red   TENN 540:12
b. in their dust   SHIR 507:4
b. that hangs on the bough   SHAK 485:25
Bosque taketh b.   POUND 383:18
broken b.   SWIN 530:25
full spring-tide of b.   BETJ 43:12
may not b. into a Duchess   AIL 3:5
rank tongue b. into speech   BROW 99:24
This b. of fresh colour   SKEL 508:18

blossoming: b. boughs of April in laughter
   BRID 92:8

blossoms: even in the b. of my sin
   SHAK 431:12
thousand B. with the Day   FITZ 212:8
to-morrow b.   SHAK 447:9

blot: art to b.   POPE 380:16
blackens every b.   TENN 533:30
B. out   SWIFT 527:34
It is no vicious b. nor   SHAK 453:6
not b. out his name out   BIBLE 81:18

received from him a b.   HEM 245:2
that looks a little b.   TENN 535:12
This world's no b.   BROW 100:31

blotted: b. it out for ever   STER 520:5
one b. from life's page   BYRON 120:16
That ever b. paper   SHAK 467:15
'Would he had b. a thousand'   JONS 285:1

bloud: b. of an English-man   NASHE 360:6

blow: another deadly b.   WORD 581:13
B. him again to me   TENN 541:31
b. in cold blood   SHAW 497:41
b. them at the moon   SHAK 435:21
B., thou wind of God   KING 296:24
b., thou winter wind   SHAK 426:1
b. upon my garden   BIBLE 56:29
B. up the trumpet   PRAY 395:9
B., winds   SHAK 454:4
b. your own trumpet   GILB 228:32
first b. is half the battle   GOLD 232:27
hand that gave the b.   DRYD 197:27
I'll sin till I b. up   THOM 547:14
Let the b. fall soon   STEV 522:28
stocks in fragrant b.   ARN 15:6
sudden b.   YEATS 586:1
To b. on whom I please   SHAK 425:22
when wilt thou b.   ANON 8:16
who gets his b. in fust   BILL 84:6
winds shoreward b.   ARN 13:5

bloweth: wind b. where it listeth BIBLE 71:36

Blown: B. by surmises   SHAK 440:31
no sooner b. but blasted   MILT 344:2
once hath b. for ever dies   FITZ 212:19
rooks are b. about   TENN 536:8
stars be b. about the sky   YEATS 586:18
when a whirlwind hath b.   DONNE 190:23

blows: b. and buffets of the world
   SHAK 461:10
B. out his brains upon   BROW 105:4
It b. so hard   HOUS 263:15
think that never b. so red   FITZ 212:15
vain b. malicious mockery   SHAK 429:15

blubber'd: how b. is that pretty face
   PRIOR 400:19

blud: don't yur b. bile   WARD 564:19

blude: a' the b. that's shed   BALL 32:6
They waded thro' red b.   BALL 32:6

blude-red: Drinking the b. wine   BALL 31:16

bludgeoning: b. of the people   WILDE 573:24

bludgeonings: Under the b. of chance
   HENL 245:4

blue: All's b.   BROW 98:34
beautifully b.   SOUT 514:4
b. and the dim   YEATS 585:9
b. days at sea   STEV 522:29
b. is the grass about   POUND 382:5
b. remembered hills   HOUS 263:22
by the buff and the b.   BURNS 114:5
drink till all look b.   FORD 216:17
drown'd in yonder living b.   TENN 537:19
Eyes of most unholy b.   MOORE 356:6
forgot the b. above the trees   KEATS 290:11
girl with a pair of b. eyes   SHER 506:32
Hobbs hints b.   BROW 103:27
mid-sea b. or the shore-sea   FLEC 214:17
that b. is all in a rush   HOPK 256:24
that little tent of b.   WILDE 572:8
too expressive to be b.   ARN 13:4

Blue Beard: B.'s domestic chaplain
   DICK 182:1

blue-bottle: b. fly on a rather large
   BARH 33:5

bluest: b. of things grey   SWIN 529:16

blunder: At so grotesque a b.   BENT 41:10
it is a b.   BOUL 90:19
Woman was God's second b.   NIET 363:4

blunder'd: b. on some virtue unawares
   CHUR 149:6
Some one had b.   TENN 532:24

blunders: b. that he has made HELPS 244:18
of Nature's agreeable b.   COWL 164:23

blunt: b. his natural edge   SHAK 463:14
plain, b. man   SHAK 451:1
That a B. should open   POUND 382:14

blush: b. at what they hear   KING 297:21
b. to find it fame   POPE 380:18
bring a b. into the cheek   DICK 181:11
flower is born to b. unseen   GRAY 234:23
Greeks a b.   BYRON 123:1
not b. so to be admir'd   WALL 562:14
She look'd down to b.   SCOTT 417:13
'Till Birch shall b. with   POPE 375:21

blush'd: Ne'er b. unless   CHUR 149:6
water saw its God, and b.
   CRAS 169:2

blushes: only animal that b.   TWAIN 554:8

blushful: b. Hippocrene   KEATS 291:18

blushing: b. discontented sun   SHAK 479:12
b. honours thick upon him   SHAK 447:9
I always take b. either   CONG 160:34

Blut: sich nur durch B. und Eisen BISM 84:25

board: his b. a shrift   SHAK 475:13
hospitable b.   WORD 581:16
I struck the b.   HERB 247:14

boarded: Youth are b.   DICK 179:34

boards: all the b. did shrink   COL 155:14
not those things in b.   LAMB 307:38
Ships are but b.   SHAK 465:27

boar-pig: little tidy Bartholomew b.
   SHAK 441:27

boast: Anabaptists do falsely b. PRAY 400:12
B. not thyself of to morrow   BIBLE 54:36
b. of more wit than I have   ETH 208:27
frantic b. and foolish   KIPL 302:10
girdeth on his harness b.   BIBLE 51:16
glory and our absolute b.   WORD 580:16
none can b. sincere felicity   DRYD 197:10
Such is the patriot's b.   GOLD 231:25
Then b. no more your mighty   SHIR 507:3

boasteth: then he b.   BIBLE 54:19

boastful: b. of her hoard   GOLD 231:26

boastings: Such b. as the Gentiles KIPL 302:9

Boasts: B. two soul-sides   BROW 102:36

boat: beautiful pea-green b.   LEAR 312:11
frail b. on the rough sea   HOR 259:12
Give a man a b. he can sail   THOM 549:29
My b. is on the shore   BYRON 125:32
My b. sails freely   SHAK 475:1
soul is an enchanted b.   SHEL 503:11
Until I have a little B.   WORD 579:18
Who took a b. and went   THAC 545:32

boating: Jolly b. weather   CORY 163:2

Boatman: B., do not tarry   CAMP 129:1

boats: b. began to near the winning-post
   COKE 154:15
b. or ships came near him   LEAR 312:19
look for happiness in b.   HOR 258:19

bobtail: Or b. tike, or trundle-tail SHAK 455:1

bodes: b. some strange eruption SHAK 429:10

bodice: lace my b. blue   HUNT 268:15

bodies: b. a living sacrifice   BIBLE 75:15
b. of those that made such   EDW 200:6
both outwardly in our b.   PRAY 386:9
Corporations have neither b.   THUR 550:32
Did but our b. touch   YEATS 585:20
friendless b. of unburied men   WEBS 567:8
of their b. have failed   BACON 27:4
Our b. are our gardens   SHAK 474:8
Our b. why do we forbear   DONNE 188:24
Pile the b. high at Austerlitz   SAND 413:27
rough notes and our dead b.   SCOTT 415:19
small are men's poor b.   JUV 288:3
soldiers bore dead b.   SHAK 438:14
superficial contact of two b. CHAM 139:15
to your scattered b. go   DONNE 189:3
with two seeming b.   SHAK 470:22
with well-developed b.   FORS 216:22

bodily: lad That I loved b.   YEATS 585:20

Boding: B. to all   SHAK 476:7

bodkin: With a bare b.   SHAK 433:8

Bodleian: describe the B. library HOUS 266:13

is like a b. in breeches · SMITH 511:12
is worthy to open the b. · BIBLE 81:26
I won't talk of his b. · JOHN 275:21
Kiss the b.'s outside · COWP 165:8
knows this out of the b. · DICK 180:4
leaves of the Judgment B. · TAYL 532:2
library to make one b. · JOHN 276:24
look at the best b. · RUSK 411:18
Making a b. is a craft · LA B 306:12
moral or an immoral b. · WILDE 573:15
most valuable b. by chance · GRAY 235:24
name out of the b. of life · BIBLE 81:18
note it in a b. · BIBLE 58:25
not throw this b. about · BELL 38:23
of the b. of the living · PRAY 394:14
oldest rule in the b. · CARR 134:21
printed b. be with you · KIPL 303:21
provided his commonplace b. · SWIFT 527:4
publishes a b. without an Index · CAMP 128:6
read a b. before reviewing · SMITH 511:17
reader seldom peruses a b. · ADD 2:7
religious b., or friend · WOTT 583:13
square b. · GLOU 229:22
substance of a b. directly · KNOW 305:17
take down this b. · YEATS 587:12
that makes the good b. · EMER 208:12
There is a b. · KEBLE 295:5
they were printed in a b. · BIBLE 52:30
things noted in thy b. · PRAY 393:13
thing which I call a b. · LAMB 307:17
this b. I directe · CHAU 144:20
this is no b. · WHIT 570:13
this square old yellow B. · BROW 104:14
until he has written a b. · JOW 285:20
was the b. and writer too · DANTE 171:10
was the only b. that ever · JOHN 275:32
'What is the use of a b.' · CARR 133:14
When a new b. is published · ROG 407:12
when I wrote that b. · SWIFT 527:18
where's the b. · CHUR 148:30
while thy b. doth live · JONS 284:19
who destroys a good b. · MILT 351:22
who first praises a b. · LAND 309:9
will find one English b. · ARN 16:13
woman who wrote the b. · LINC 315:6
Would shut the b. · SHAK 442:2
write in a b. · BIBLE 81:12
written b. will be brought · CEL 138:6
book clubs: what they club for at b.
· LAMB 307:38
bookes: Twenty b., clad in blak · CHAU 141:24
bookful: b. blockhead · POPE 378:30
books: authority from others' b. · SHAK 456:15
B., and my food · STEV 523:11
B. are made not like children · FLAU 214:3
B. are not seldom talismans · COWP 167:25
B. are not absolutely dead · MILT 351:21
b. at the British Museum · BUTL 118:22
b. be then the eloquence · SHAK 493:3
b. by which the printers · FULL 220:18
b. can do · COWP 168:9
b. consum'd the midnight · GAY 223:10
b. in the running brooks · SHAK 424:32
B., like men their authors · SWIFT 527:2
B. must follow sciences · BACON 25:6
b. of all time · RUSK 411:14
b. of the hour · RUSK 411:14
B. of the true sort · LAMB 307:38
B. that you may carry · JOHN 280:17
B. think for me · LAMB 307:16
b., those spiritual repasts · LAMB 307:5
B., we are told · DE Q 175:7
b. were opened · BIBLE 61:8
B. will speak plain · BACON 25:39
b. with the fat of others' · BURT 116:13
cannot learn men from b. · DISR 186:41
care about b. · RUSK 411:17
cream of others' b. · MORE 357:9
days is a collection of b. · CARL 131:35
Deep versed in b. and shallow · MILT 350:10

do *you* read b. *through* · JOHN 276:13
equal skill to Cambridge b. · BROW 97:26
From my b. surcease · POE 375:5
furniture so charming as b. · SMITH 511:2
general intention of his b. · JAMES 271:22
gentleman is not in your b. · SHAK 471:27
Give me b. · KEATS 294:24
ground, the b., the academes · SHAK 457:6
has written all the b. · BUTL 119:1
He may live without b. · MER 338:7
his b. arranged three · PROU 401:23
his b. were read · BELL 39:19
In b. and love · GAY 223:23
In b. lies the *soul* · CARL 131:34
I never read b. · PUNCH 402:28
laid out just the right b. · POUND 383:20
many b. there is no end · BIBLE 56:13
mean your *borrowers of b.* · LAMB 307:14
My only b. · MOORE 356:18
not swallowed up in b. · WESL 568:23
of books which are no b. · LAMB 307:14
old b. · GOLD 232:19
quit your b. · WORD 582:22
read all the b. there are · MALL 327:9
Some b. are to be tasted · BACON 27:19
spectacles of b. to read Nature · DRYD 198:2
studied b. than men · BACON 28:13
That in b. are found · SHEL 504:24
Things in b.' clothing · LAMB 307:18
to thumb each other's b. · RUSK 411:19
Wherever b. are burned men also
· HEINE 244:14
written three b. on the soul · BROW 100:5
bookseller: life as conceived by a b.
· WALP 562:27
booksellers: Ask the b. of London
· BURKE 111:17
b. have put up with poets' · HOR 258:4
b. are generous liberal-minded · JOHN 274:16
booming: Bells are b. down the bohreens
· BETJ 43:7
boon: bean-flowers' b. · BROW 100:13
b. and a blessing to men · ANON 8:5
Is life a b. · GILB 229:7
Boot: B., saddle · BROW 99:27
imagine a b. stamping · ORW 365:14
Make b. upon the summer's · SHAK 443:9
boote: day it dooth myn herte b. · CHAU 143:19
boots: Aristocrat who cleans the b.
· GILB 225:23
attired in leather b. · HOUS 266:9
Books from B.' · BETJ 43:6
B.—boots—boots · KIPL 298:6
generally taste of boiled b. · THAC 545:9
legs when I take my b. · DICK 178:2
ought to come to bed in b. · HERB 246:12
pleasure me in his top-b. · MARL 329:1
Pulled off his b. · MILT 344:16
should always have one's b. · MONT 354:13
Their b. are heavy · AUDEN 20:5
bo-peep: if they started at b. · HERR 250:7
Border: B. and gi'e them a brush · HOGG 253:2
b. see Israel set · BROW 101:3
she gaed o'er the b. · BURNS 112:37
bore: awhile they b. her up · SHAK 436:19
be in it is merely a b. · WILDE 573:31
b. me in the southern wild · BLAKE 88:2
b. within their breasts · AYT 24:5
Every hero becomes a b. · EMER 208:4
It b. thy fruit and mine · KYD 306:7
way to be a b. is to say · VOLT 561:21
Bored: *Bores* and B. · BYRON 124:4
He b. with his augur · BALL 31:3
'I feel a little b. · CHES 146:12
'one gets so b. with good · DISR 186:26
was horribly b. by a bee · LEAR 311:16
Bores: B. and *Bored* · BYRON 124:4
'B. have succeeded to dragons · DISR 187:3
Borgias: last night with the B. · BEER 37:18
boring: 'Somebody's b. me · THOM 547:15

born: been b. to set it right · STR 524:4
bondwoman was b. after the flesh
· BIBLE 77:16
B. but to die · POPE 379:12
B. in a cellar · FOOTE 216:6
B. in the garret · BYRON 125:24
b. King of the Jews · BIBLE 63:31
b. most noble that was · OTWAY 365:27
B. of the sun they travelled · SPEN 515:8
B. of the Virgin Mary · PRAY 384:26
B. on our shoulders · BROW 100:34
b. out of my due time · MORR 358:9
b. the same year as I · HOR 261:5
b. to be forgot · COWP 165:32
b. to write · POPE 376:26
b. under a riming planet · SHAK 473:10
b. we cry that we are come · GREV 236:16
b. when I was consul · CIC 152:2
b. with a different face · BLAKE 86:15
ever have been b. at all · LUCR 320:9
Every moment one is b. · TENN 544:8
Godolphin Horne was nobly b. · BELL 38:33
He was not b. to shame · SHAK 483:8
house where I was b. · HOOD 254:17
human beings are b. free · ANON 4:14
I am not yet b. · MACN 326:13
if anyone is b. to obey · COMP 159:14
in days ere I was b. · HOUS 264:4
In the days ere I was b. · BLUNT 89.5
is the blight man was b. · HOPK 256:27
I was b. about trouble · SHAK 441:11
I was b. free as Caesar · SHAK 448:14
I was b. in a cellar · CONG 160:5
I was b. in the year 1632 · DEFOE 173:5
I was b. sneering · GILB 226:20
I was b. to set it right · SHAK 431:26
I was free b. · BIBLE 74:21
man if he had not been b. · BIBLE 68:10
Man is b. unto trouble · BIBLE 52:17
Man that is b. of a woman · BIBLE 52:26
Man that is b. of a woman · PRAY 389:11
Man was b. free · ROUS 410:17
man who lives is b. to die · DRYD 197:10
men naturally were b. free · MILT 352:18
natural to die as to be b. · BACON 26:3
Never was b. · STOWE 523:19
No man is b. unto himself · QUAR 403:16
Not to be b. is the best · AUDEN 18:13
Not to be b. · BACON 28:18
Not to be b. is · SOPH 513:8
of one b. out of due time · BIBLE 76:13
other powerless to be b. · ARN 13:8
perish wherein I was b. · BIBLE 52:11
soon as we were b. · BIBLE 62:17
sucker b. every minute · BARN 34:6
supposed it lucky to be b. · WHIT 570:19
terrible beauty is b. · YEATS 585:1
that a story-teller is b. · STEE 517:22
That's b. into the world · GILB 226:8
that thou wast b. with · SHAK 453:16
Then surely I was b. · CHES 146:22
They can't be b. · DICK 177:11
time to be b. · BIBLE 55:12
'Tis less than to be b. · BEAU 36:10
took the trouble to be b. · BEAU 35:18
To one of woman b. · SHAK 463:8
to the manner b. · SHAK 430:23
unto us a child is b. · BIBLE 58:7
virgin mother b. · MILT 344:3
was b. of Christian race · WATTS 565:14
wasn't I b. old and ugly · DICK 176:1
we are b. in other's pain · THOM 548:1
were b. in a merry hour · SHAK 472:12
We were not b. to sue · SHAK 478:9
when a child is b. · SU T 524:19
wherefore b. · TENN 534:5
Where thou wast b. · BALL 30:9
who are b. of thee · BENS 40:24
world he finds himself b. · CARL 131:33

borne: b. away with every breath
                                      BYRON 125:20
  b. it with a patient shrug   SHAK 466:2
  b. me a man of strife   BIBLE 60:23
  Had b. my breath away   HOOD 254:17
  I have b., and borne   SHAK 441:18
  my mother had not b. me   SHAK 433:11
  who have b. even heavier   VIRG 557:13
borogoves: All mimsy were the b.
                                    CARR 134:28
boroughs: bright b.   HOPK 256:28
  fresh eggs to rotten b.   MAC 323:15
borrer: b. the money to do it with
                                   WARD 564:36
borrow: earth must b. its mirth WILC 572:5
  men who b.   LAMB 307:12
borrow'd: dress me In b. robes SHAK 458:17
borrowed: Conveys it in a b. name
                                   PRIOR 401:1
borrower: become a b. of the night
                                   SHAK 461:7
  b., nor a lender be   SHAK 430:19
borrowers: I mean your *b. of books*
                                  LAMB 307:14
borrowing: beggar by banqueting upon
  b.   BIBLE 63:6
  b. only lingers and lingers   SHAK 441:16
bosom: b. beats not in his country's
                                   POPE 375:12
  b. black as death   SHAK 434:28
  b. of the urgent West   BRID 92:19
  carried into Abraham's b.   BIBLE 70:28
  carry them in his b.   BIBLE 59:7
  Cleanse the stuff'd b.   SHAK 463:3
  guardage to the sooty b.   SHAK 473:22
  has no b. and no behind   SMITH 510:27
  in your fragrant b. dies   CAREW 130:20
  leaning on Jesus' b.   BIBLE 72:28
  little son into his b.   FLET 215:28
  man take fire in his b.   BIBLE 53:23
  my b., as a bed   SHAK 490:32
  My b.'s lord sits lightly   SHAK 483:23
  sleep in Abraham's b.   SHAK 481:7
  third in your b.   SHAK 482:21
  those thorns that in her b. SHAK 431:13
  Through my burn'd b.   SHAK 452:31
  wring his b.   GOLD 231:31
bosoms: b. of your actresses excite
                                    JOHN 274:2
  hang and brush their b.   BROW 105:26
  Quiet to quick b. is a hell BYRON 120:30
Bosque: B. taketh blossom POUND 383:18
Bossuet: excite the horror of B. MAC 324:9
Boston: B. bells   ING 270:4
  B. man is the east wind   APPL 11:12
  B.'s a hole   BROW 102:20
  say the cows laid out B.   EMER 207:7
  solid man of B.   LONG 316:23
  this is good old B.   BOSS 90:13
bo'sun: b. tight   GILB 225:16
Boswell: B. is the first of biographers
                                 MAC 324:5
Boswelliana: exposed to the *Lues B.*
                                MAC 323:10
botanist: I am not a b.   JOHN 274:19
botanize: down to b. in the swamp
                                  CHES 148:7
  that would peep and b.   WORD 580:3
botched: b. civilization POUND 383:10
botches: Leave no rubs nor b. SHAK 461:11
both: a Norfan, b. sides   WELLS 568:13
  b. were faiths   ARN 13:8
  gentlemen b.   ELIZ 205:23
  long as ye b. shall live   PRAY 389:3
  may wear it on b. sides   SHAK 487:7
bother: 'Oh b. the flowers that GILB 227:14
  Though 'B. it' I may   GILB 228:2
botom: I now sit down on my b. FLEM 215:3
botté: toujours b. et prêt à partir
                                MONT 354:13

Botticelli: B.'s a *cheese* PUNCH 403:3
bottle: crack a b. with a friend CHES 147:21
  farthest b. labelled 'Ether' BROW 100:7
  great desire to a b. of hay SHAK 471:4
  'leave the b. on the chimley-piece
                                      DICK 179:10
  little for the b.   DIBD 175:16
  My b. of salvation   RAL 404:12
  nor a b. to give him   DICK 177:26
  put my tears into thy b. PRAY 393:13
  we'll pass the b. round WHYT 572:2
bottles: forty b. of Ring-Bo-Ree LEAR 312:9
  new wine into old b.   BIBLE 65:25
bottom: b. of the monstrous world
                                   MILT 343:16
  scatter'd in the b. of the sea SHAK 480:27
  Which will reach the b. GRAH 233:10
  woman had a b. of good sense JOHN 278:28
bottomless: after them to the b. pit
                                   MILT 348:27
  Law is a b. pit   ARB 11:20
  riding into the b. abyss WALEY 562:2
  smoke of the pit that is b. JAM 271:3
bouchers: des bergers et des b. VOLT 561:17
boue: La nostalgie de la b. AUG 21:11
bough: blossom that hangs on the b.
                                   SHAK 485:25
  of Bread beneath the b. FITZ 212:11
  Touch not a single b.   MORR 358:6
  with bloom along the b. HOUS 262:14
boughs: b. and the brushwood sheaf
                                   BROW 101:5
  b. which shake against SHAK 494:7
  I got me b. off many   HERB 247:17
bought: b. over God with a fee SWIN 530:23
  guilt is b. and sold   SHEL 503:1
  have b. it at any price CLAR 152:21
  knowledge is b. in the market CLOU 153:18
bougies: le vent éteint les b. LA R 310:15
boum: all produce 'b.'   FORS 217:8
bounced: b. out of bed   MILNE 340:9
bound: b. him a thousand years BIBLE 82:27
  b. in the spirit unto Jerusalem BIBLE 74:18
  fast b. in misery   PRAY 397:7
  Fresh-b.   CAT 136:19
  my duty as a man is b.   TENN 543:4
  tied and b. by the chain PRAY 385:23
  to another b.   GREV 236:16
  utmost b. of human thought TENN 544:1
boundary: has a right to fix the b.
                                   PARN 369:2
  of smouldering b. stones POUND 382:7
bounded: could be b. in a nut-shell
                                   SHAK 432:13
bounden: b. duty and service PRAY 388:2
  our b. duty   PRAY 387:23
bounding: heart less b. at emotion ARN 15:9
boundless: believing what we see Is b.
                                   SHEL 501:10
  b. better, boundless worse TENN 543:19
  b., endless   BYRON 121:26
  bounty is as b. as the sea SHAK 482:17
  that the desire is b.   SHAK 486:33
bounds: flaming b. of place and time
                                  GRAY 235:19
  hast set them their b.   PRAY 396:19
bounties: Thy morning b. ere I left
                                  COWP 166:3
bounty: his b., There was no winter
                                  SHAK 423:22
  lust of the goat is the b. BLAKE 88:21
  My b. is as boundless   SHAK 482:17
  those his former b. fed DRYD 195:3
bour: twa sisters sat in a b. BALL 30:14
Bourbon: Can B. or Nassau go higher
                                 PRIOR 400:25
bourg: rustic murmur of their b. TENN 535:4
bourgeois: b. are other people REN 405:10
  'B.,' I observed, 'is an epithet' HOPE 255:29
  How beastly the b. is   LAWR 311:6

pissent au bas et les b. montent FLAU 214:3
  proletarian for the b.   LENIN 313:21
Bourgeoisie: British B. SITW 508:14
  generations the British b. WAUGH 566:2
bourn: bound for the same b. HOUS 264:1
  b. how far to be belov'd SHAK 421:7
  to see beyond our b.   KEATS 289:8
bousing: While we sit b. at the nappy
                                  BURNS 115:3
boutique: arrière b. toute notre MONT 354:20
*boutiquiers: L'Angleterre est une nation
de b.*   NAP 359:15
bow: all griefs which b.   ARN 14:24
  b. my knees unto the Father BIBLE 77:24
  b. myself in the house BIBLE 51:29
  b. of burning gold   BLAKE 86:16
  B. themselves when he did SHAK 447:3
  b., ye tradesmen   GILB 225:35
  certain man drew a b.   BIBLE 51:21
  do set my b. in the cloud BIBLE 45:40
  fascination in his very b. BYRON 123:36
  from the Almighty's b. BLAKE 86:6
  he breaketh the b.   PRAY 392:21
  Jesus every knee should b. BIBLE 78:1
  like an unbent b.   DONNE 190:3
  Lord of the unerring b. BYRON 121:19
  my b. will make a wide ROST 410:12
  reason doth buckle and b. BACON 24:19
  strong men shall b. themselves BIBLE 56:11
  Thou shalt not b. down BIBLE 47:24
  To draw the b.   BYRON 124:10
  two strings to my b.   FIEL 211:19
  unto the b. the cord is LONG 317:15
bow'd: it b. and syne it brake BALL 32:10
  We b. our head and held ARN 13:16
bowed: At her feet he b. BIBLE 49:11
  hours has chained and b. SHEL 502:13
bowels: Have you no b. GAY 222:31
  in the b. of Christ   CROM 169:21
  shutteth up his b. of compassion BIBLE 81:4
bower: b. quiet for us   KEATS 288:20
  lime-tree b. my prison COL 157:10
  queen in a summer's b. SHAK 439:30
  that smooth-swarded b. TENN 541:18
  to deck both bed and b. SPEN 516:3
bower-eaves: bow-shot from her b.
                                   TENN 538:8
bowers: green and pleasant b. BLAKE 86:12
bowery: All that b. loneliness TENN 533:13
  b. hollows crown'd with TENN 535:27
bowl: b. to sea went wise men PEAC 371:3
  golden b. be broken   BIBLE 56:11
  inverted B. we call The Sky FITZ 213:8
  Love in a golden b.   BLAKE 85:19
  Morning in the B. of Night FITZ 212:5
bowler: If the wild b. thinks he LANG 309:19
Bowling: lies poor Tom B. DIBD 175:21
  plays to the b. of a ghost THOM 547:24
  Some recommend the b. green GREEN 235:28
bow'r: b. of wanton Shrewsbury POPE 378:1
Bows: B. toward her   SHAK 428:8
  wood of English b.   DOYLE 191:4
bow-shot: b. from her bower-eaves
                                   TENN 538:8
bowsprit: b. got mixed with the rudder
                                   CARR 133:5
bow-strings: cut b.   SHAK 470:1
bow-windows: putting b. to the house
                                   DICK 177:2
Bow-Wow: Big B. strain I can do
                                  SCOTT 418:37
  were it not for his *b.* way PEMB 371:1
bow-wows: gone to the demnition b.
                                   DICK 180:23
box: b. where sweets compacted HERB 248:16
  having an alabaster b. BIBLE 68:8
  to him and said 'B. about AUBR 17:26
  twelve good men into a b. BROU 95:4
boxes: He had forty-two b. CARR 133:2
  holsters and cartridge b. SHAW 496:6

boy: Alas, pitiable b.   VIRG 559:2
Altho' a poor blind b.   CIBB 151:8
b.'s love   SHAK 454:28
b. stood on the burning   HEM 244:20
b.'s will is the wind's   LONG 316:22
b. to be vicious till he's   SAKI 413:14
b. with never a crack   YEATS 586:5
compound a b.   SHAK 445:14
good-humoured b.   BEER 37:21
hood-wink'd b. I call'd   GARR 221:16
like any other b.   FLEC 214:20
Mad about the b.   COW 163:18
more who would not be a b.   BYRON 120:11
nor young enough for a b.   SHAK 488:9
only b.   KIPL 305:5
purblind, wayward b.   SHAK 456:26
roughly to your little b.   CARR 133:26
saw a little vulgar B.   BARH 33:19
seat sat the journeying b.   HARDY 240:9
Smiling the b. fell dead   BROW 101:16
squeaking Cleopatra b.   SHAK 424:3
Take the thanks of a b.   BEEC 37:9
that were when he was a b.   HOR 257:21
To be a soaring human b.   DICK 176:14
to be b. eternal   SHAK 491:7
Upon the growing b.   WORD 579:5
was and a little tiny b.   SHAK 490:27
what a b. you are   BROWN 95:11
When I was a little b.   ANON 8:19
boyaux: étranglés avec les b.   MESL 338:9
boyes: When b. go first to bed   HERB 248:4
boys: among his b.   TENN 536:22
B. and girls tumbling   TRAH 551:19
b. get at one end they   JOHN 276:32
b. that swim on bladders   SHAK 447:9
'B. will be boys   HOPE 255:28
Christian b. I can scarcely   ARN 16:27
Deceive b. with toys   LYS 321:18
flies to wanton b.   SHAK 455:9
is the way that b. begin   THAC 545:31
men that were b. when   BELL 40:11
of children (except b.   CARR 136:12
office boys for office b.   SAL 413:21
only know two sorts of b.   DICK 180:37
three merry b. are we   FLET 215:9
to virgin girls and b.   HOR 260:13
Bozrah: dyed garments from B.   BIBLE 60:10
Brabant: I dance with you in B.   SHAK 456:22
brace: b. ourselves to our duties   CHUR 150:1
b. their belts about them   HOUS 265:6
bracelet: b. of bright hair about   DONNE 190:5
diamond b. lasts forever   STEV 520:20
bracelets: b. and bright feathers   HARDY 240:19
braces: Damn b.   BLAKE 88:23
brach: b. or lym   SHAK 455:1
Bracing: B. brain and sinew   KING 296:24
bracken: through b. turning brown   BRAD 91:8
Bradford: silk hat on a B. millionaire   ELIOT 205:1
Bradshaw: vocabulary of 'B.' is   DOYLE 192:37
braes: among thy green b.   BURNS 113:27
banks and b. o' bonny Doon   BURNS 116:6
brag: Beauty is Nature's b.   MILT 341:18
Is left this vault to b.   SHAK 461:1
Nor shall death b. thou   SHAK 492:28
Brahmin: B. strikes the hour   SOUT 513:25
I the hymn The B. sings   EMER 206:18
braided: she has b. her yellow hair   BALL 32:1
braids: twisted b. of lilies knitting   MILT 341:20
brain: alone immured in the b.   SHAK 457:8
ascends me into the b.   SHAK 442:15
Bear of Very Little B.   MILNE 340:13
b. attic stocked with all   DOYLE 192:2
b. of feathers   POPE 375:18
b. perplexes and retards   KEATS 291:20
b. that won't believe   BLAKE 85:11

b. to think again   BRON 93:21
b. Worked with a dim   WORD 580:13
Chimera in my b.   DONNE 191:2
draughts intoxicate the b.   POPE 378:13
fibre from the b. does tear   BLAKE 85:10
from the heat-oppressed b.   SHAK 459:15
glean'd my teeming b.   KEATS 292:30
harmful to the b.   JAM 271:3
instrumental to the b.   SHAK 429:20
it might injure the b.   CARR 133:22
let my b. lie also   BROW 102:34
petrifactions of a plodding b.   BYRON 124:25
schoolmasters puzzle their b.   GOLD 231:22
stars, Which are the b.   MER 337:5
tares of mine own b.   BROW 96:18
through which the b. explores   DOUG 191:7
to leave that b. outside   GILB 226:9
What hand and b. went ever   BROW 101:26
brained: large-b. woman   BROW 98:15
brain-pan: weak is their b.   BLAKE 87:1
brains: Blows out his b. upon   BROW 105:4
b. in my head and the heart   HOUS 266:7
b. out of a brass knob   DICK 178:23
b. ta'en out, and buttered   SHAK 469:12
Cudgel thy b. no more about   SHAK 436:24
dash'd the b. out   SHAK 459:10
Had their b. knocked out   SHEL 502:3
He exercises of his b.   GILB 226:8
I mix them with my b.   OPIE 365:6
no other b. to work with   SHAW 497:1
not maggots in your b.   FLET 215:26
Till he blew his silly b.   THAC 546:3
to steal away their b.   SHAK 475:9
brainsickly: So b. of things   SHAK 460:10
brainwork: *fundamental b.*   ROSS 410:10
brake: he b. that gallant ship   BALL 30:19
his neck b.   BIBLE 49:39
it bow'd and syne it b.   BALL 32:10
brakes: rove the b. and thorns   COWP 165:12
bramble-bush: if it had been a b.   DICK 178:6
bramble-dew: With eyes of gold and b.   STEV 523:3
brambles: nettles and b. in the fortresses   BIBLE 58:31
bran: this the Plebeian b.   DONNE 190:23
Branch: B. shall grow out of his   BIBLE 58:9
Cut is the b. that might   MARL 329:16
Every b. big with it   HARDY 240:21
lops the moulder'd b.   TENN 533:26
reddens on the high b.   SAPP 414:7
branches: b. of the frankincense   BIBLE 63:27
lodge in the b. thereof   BIBLE 66:20
sing among the b.   PRAY 396:19
Thy b. ne'er remember   KEATS 293:3
branchy: city and b. between towers   HOPK 256:9
brand: over by that flaming b.   MILT 350:1
brandy: be a hero must drink b.   JOHN 278:7
B. for the Parson   KIPL 302:22
is the b. of the damned   SHAW 497:27
pray get me a glass of b.   GEOR 224:3
There's some are fou o' b.   BURNS 114:9
brass: am become as sounding b.   BIBLE 76:14
b., nor stone   SHAK 494:4
evil manners live in b.   SHAK 447:20
feet like unto fine b.   BIBLE 81:14
that was ever writ in b.   JONS 284:17
this be your wall of b.   HOR 258:9
wall all Germany with b.   MARL 329:5
brav'd: b. by his brother   SHAK 451:23
brave: adventure b. and new   BROW 104:5
b. beard curled   CHES 147:3
B. hearts and clean   TENN 535:5
B. Macbeth   SHAK 458:3
b. man with a sword   WILDE 572:10
b. men lived before Agamemnon's   HOR 261:18
b. Music of a *distant*   FITZ 212:12
b. new world   SHAK 485:26
b. old Scottish Cavalier   AYT 24:11

Fortune aids the b.   TER 544:18
home of the b.   KEY 295:14
How sleep the b.   COLL 158:19
'I'm very b. generally   CARR 135:14
intelligent, the witty, the b.   MILL 339:23
In the b. days of old   MAC 322:18
late to-morrow to be b.   ARMS 12:17
make one b. push   STEV 522:8
None but the b.   DRYD 194:23
Of the b. and innocent   AUDEN 19:7
passing b. to be a King   MARL 330:7
posterity as a b. bad man   CLAR 152:22
souls of the b. that die in the battle   CLOU 153:13
straight, the b.   HOUS 265:6
that delirium in the b.   YEATS 586:19
that was b.   HOUS 264:2
Then I was clean and b.   HOUS 263:1
Toll for the b.   COWP 165:30
What's b., what's noble   SHAK 423:18
with what a b. Carouse   FITZ 213:1
would not sleep with the b.   HOUS 264:19
braver: I have done one b. thing   DONNE 190:16
not think a b. gentleman   SHAK 440:16
bravery: b. of his grief did put   SHAK 437:13
Hiding thy b. in their   SHAK 493:11
natural b. of your isle   SHAK 428:13
braw: He was a b. gallant   BALL 30:16
brawler: not a b., not covetous   BIBLE 79:12
brawling: b. woman in a wide house   BIBLE 54:20
brawls: Whatever b. disturb   WATTS 565:19
Brazil: B.—where the nuts   THOM 546:18
breach: More honour'd in the b.   SHAK 430:23
Once more unto the b.   SHAK 443:21
bread: ate his b. in sorrow   GOET 230:12
bit of butter to my b.   MILNE 340:8
bitter b. of banishment   SHAK 479:4
b. and butter that feels   MACK 325:10
b. and flesh in the morning   BIBLE 51:6
b. and the big match   JUV 287:28
b. eaten in secret is pleasant   BIBLE 53:28
b. enough and to spare   BIBLE 70:19
B. I dip in the river   STEV 522:27
b. of adversity   BIBLE 58:28
b. of affliction and with   BIBLE 51:20
b. to strengthen man's   PRAY 396:20
Cast thy b. upon the waters   BIBLE 56:5
cramm'd with distressful b.   SHAK 444:25
eat thy b. with joy   BIBLE 55:28
face shalt thou eat b.   BIBLE 45:22
'For the b. that you eat   KIPL 298:5
half-pennyworth of b.   SHAK 439:20
Here with a Loaf of B.   FITZ 212:11
HOMER begged his B.   ANON 7:14
Honest b. is very well   JERR 272:27
Jesus took b.   BIBLE 68:11
lives not upon b. alone   STEV 521:34
loaf of b.   CARR 135:8
Man doth not live by b.   BIBLE 48:22
Man shall not live by b.   BIBLE 64:1
Royal slice of b.   MILNE 340:7
smell of b. and butter   BYRON 119:32
taste of another man's b.   DANTE 171:17
that b. should be so dear   HOOD 255:8
that makes the holy b.   MAS 333:26
that which is not b.   BIBLE 59:25
Their learning is like b.   JOHN 276:27
theirs is b.   THOM 548:28
them in breaking of b.   BIBLE 71:19
took B.   PRAY 388:1
took the B. and brake it   ELIZ 205:19
to steal b.   FRAN 217:26
To take b. at my hand   WYATT 583:21
unleavened b.   BIBLE 47:17
unleavened b. of sincerity   BIBLE 75:36
us this day our daily b.   BIBLE 64:24
was cutting b. and butter   THAC 546:3
who did also eat of my b.   PRAY 392:5

whom if his son ask b.   BIBLE 65:4
With the b. eaten up   CERV 138:14
breadfruit: *Where the b. fall*   ELIOT 204:13
breadth: 'Let me have length and b.
    BALL 31:14
whole b. of the way   BUNY 107:15
break: b. a man's spirit is devil's
    SHAW 496:15
B., break, break   TENN 532:17
b. faith with us who die   MCCR 324:31
b., my heart   SHAK 430:1
b. the ice by some whose   BACON 25:41
bruised reed shall he not b.   BIBLE 59:11
chanced to see at b. of day   WORD 578:10
I bend and I b. not   LA F306:18
I'll b. my staff   SHAK 485:24
lark at b. of day   SHAK 493:6
of nature round him b.   ADD 2:30
sighs the strings do b.   CAMP 129:17
that ye b. every yoke   BIBLE 60:4
thyself must b. at last   ARN 13:14
us b. their bonds asunder   PRAY 389:16
ye b. my best blue china   HARDY 239:20
you b. the bloody glass   MACN 326:8
breakers: I wanton'd with thy b.
    BYRON 121:27
breaketh: he b. the bow   PRAY 392:21
Lord b. the cedar-trees   PRAY 391:10
breakfalls: rolls and throws and b.
    REED 405:7
breakfast: All too soon the tiny b.   BETJ 42:7
b. she'll project a scheme   YOUNG 587:18
Hope is a good b.   BACON 25:8
impossible things before b.   CARR 135:18
'No business before b.   THAC 545:19
One doth but b. here   HENS 246:4
period in matrimony is b.-time   HERB 246:16
That b.   BELL 39:2
Then to b. with   SHAK 447:6
twin that I b. on gin   HERB 246:8
want Michael Angelo for b.   TWAIN 554:10
'Where shall we our b. take   BALL 32:7
wholesome, hungry b.   WALT 564:7
breakfasted: b. with you and shall sup
    BRUCE 106:2
breakfasts: sleeps he b.   SURT 525:7
breaking: b. of ribs was sport   SHAK 424:23
b. up of laws   TENN 534:10
b. what it likes   ARN 15:20
By b. of windows   MORE 357:7
England take pleasure in b.   ANON 7:22
known of them in b. of bread   BIBLE 71:19
breaks: b. a butterfly upon a wheel
    POPE 376:30
day b. not   DONNE 188:3
It b. in our bosom   SHEL 501:4
some heart indignant b.   MOORE 356:10
where Helicon b. down   ARN 13:2
breast: back somewhere in our b.   ARN 12:22
b. o'ercharged to music   SIDN 507:24
broach'd his boiling bloody b.   SHAK 471:17
charms to sooth a savage b.   CONG 160:14
depth of her glowing b.   SHEL 503:23
eternal in the human b.   POPE 379:5
God within my b.   BRON 93:19
hapless b. upon his breast   YEATS 586:1
heart out of your b.   HOUS 264:18
in my b.   GOET 229:30
laughed upon his b.   YEATS 585:20
render back from out thy b.   BYRON 123:2
soft hand, and softer b.   KEATS 292:13
stood b. high amid the corn   HOOD 255:4
That singeth with her b.   HOOD 255:2
unwonted calm pervades his b.   ARN 12:22
When breast to b. we clung   ROSS 409:22
World broods with warm b.   HOPK 256:13
breastie: what a panic's in thy b.
    BURNS 115:20
breastless: b. creatures under ground
    ELIOT 205:13

breastplate: b. of judgment the Urim
    BIBLE 48:1
b. of righteousness   BIBLE 78:10
b. of faith and love   BIBLE 79:2
b. than a heart untainted   SHAK 446:6
breasts: all night betwixt my b.   BIBLE 56:18
b. are like two young roes   BIBLE 56:26
b. of the nymphs   SWIN 530:4
b. the blows of circumstance   TENN 537:1
division of prodigious b.   SWIN 528:26
feel my b all perfume   JOYCE 286:30
Sestos and Abydos of her b.   DONNE 188:14
she hath no b.   BIBLE 57:13
soaping her b. in the bath   EWART 209:11
why then her b. are dun   SHAK 495:8
within their b. the grief   AYT 24:5
breath: accustomed to their lack of b.
    YEATS 585:13
All the b. and the bloom   BROW 98:30
Although thy b. be rude   SHAK 426:1
are but the b. of kings   BURNS 113:10
bald and short of b.   SASS 414:10
b. can make them   GOLD 230:1
breathing thoughtful b.   WORD 581:8
b. of worldly men cannot   SHAK 479:5
B.'s a ware that will   HOUS 262:15
b. thou art   SHAK 464:8
Clothed with his b.   TENN 535:23
Could ever yet cut b.   SHAK 492:11
deeds too cold b. gives   SHAK 460:1
down and out of b.   SHAK 440:27
dust expend an idle b.   CAT 137:15
every thing that hath b.   PRAY 400:1
flutter'd and fail'd for b.   ARN 14:6
fly away, b.   SHAK 489:4
from the healthy b. of morn   KEATS 289:33
Had borne my b. away   HOOD 254:17
having lost her b.   SHAK 422:4
hear her tender-taken b.   KEATS 292:12
heaven's b. Smells wooingly   SHAK 459:4
last b. he drew in   LAMB 308:11
mansion call the fleeting b.   GRAY 234:22
our head and held our b.   ARN 13:16
sweeter woman ne'er drew b.   ING 270:16
Sweet is the b. of morn   MILT 348:4
sweetness of man's b.   JAM 271:4
tears and toiling b.   ROSS 408:20
That lightly draws its b.   WORD 583:5
this present b. may buy   SHAK 456:14
thou no b. at all   SHAK 456:11
waste of b. the years behind   YEATS 585:15
world draw thy b. in pain   SHAK 437:25
year with toil of b.   COL 156:17
you have it use your b.   FLET 215:7
breathe: b. not his name   MOORE 356:15
b. the air of the Enchanted   MER 337:37
like the hair we b.   SURT 525:4
So long as men can b.   SHAK 492:28
tho' to b. were life   TENN 543:22
breathed: b. into his nostrils   BIBLE 45:7
This day I b. first   SHAK 452:1
Breathes: B. there the man   SCOTT 416:21
breathing: b. English air   BROO 94:30
B. out threatenings   BIBLE 73:32
Closer is He than b.   TENN 533:29
In the sound his b. kept   SHEL 503:5
quiet b.   KEATS 288:20
rifle all the b. spring   COLL 158:16
breathings: Low b. coming after me
    WORD 580:9
breathless: b. hush in the Close to-night
    NEWB 361:3
B. with adoration   WORD 581:18
breaths: b. with sweetmeats tainted
    SHAK 481:28
bred: strain of man's b.   SHAK 486:1
brede: wes sons of ale and b.   WYNT 584:4
Bredon: In summertime on B.   HOUS 263:4
bree: little abune her b.   BALL 32:1

breeches: He is like a book in b.
    SMITH 511:12
jacket was red and his b.   COL 156:11
'oss than cleanin' his b.   SURT 525:12
So have your b.   CANN 129:26
breed: b. of their horses   PENN 371:15
b. one work that wakes   HOPK 257:3
endless war still b.   MILT 351:10
Fear'd by their b.   SHAK 478:20
This happy b.   SHAK 478:20
Where they most b. and haunt   SHAK 459:4
breeder: thou be a b. of sinners   SHAK 433:11
breedeth: Severity b. fear   BACON 26:25
breeding: such true b. of a gentleman
    BYRON 122:30
though spoiled i' the b.   BROME 93:12
Breeds: B. hard English men   KING 296:23
lesser b. without the Law   KIPL 302:9
breeks: b. aff a wild Highlandman
    SCOTT 418:11
breeze: b. is on the sea   SCOTT 418:25
b. of morning moves   TENN 540:9
such a b.   TENN 536:9
'the cooling western b.'   POPE 378:21
thee with the b. of song   TENN 537:4
volleying rain and tossing b.   ARN 15:5
breezes: Little b. dusk and shiver   TENN 538:3
other b. than are blown   KEATS 292:15
Breezy: B., Sneezy   ELLIS 206:13
breite: b. Masse eines Volkes   HITL 251:9
Brekekekex: B. koax koax   ARIS 12:5
Bremen: being a foreigner of B.   DEFOE 173:5
brent: Your bonny brow was b.
    BURNS 114:12
brethren: Behold my mother and my
  b.   BIBLE 66:15
b. and companions' sakes   PRAY 398:12
Dearly beloved b.   PRAY 384:9
joyful a thing it is: b.   PRAY 398:26
least of these my b.   BIBLE 68:7
thee and me...for we be b.   BIBLE 46:2
tuneful b. all were dead   SCOTT 416:9
breuis: uita b., sensus hebes   JOHN 273:17
Brevis: B. *esse laboro*   HOR 257:12
Vitae summa b. spem   HOR 259:14
Brevity: B. is the soul of wit   SHAK 431:30
Its body b.   COL 156:15
brewer: not a b.'s servant   BLAKE 87:8
brewers: Bakers and b.   LANG 309:26
brewery: take me to a b.   ANON 6:1
brews: many a peer of England b.
    HOUS 264:12
Bribe: taking of a B. or Gratuity   PENN 371:16
to b. or twist   WOLFE 576:6
Too poor for a b.   GRAY 235:21
very considerable b.   GILB 226:26
bribes: man open to b. was to be   GREE 236:4
our fingers with base b.   SHAK 451:13
brick: 'Eave 'arf a b. at 'im   PUNCH 402:14
I inherited it b. and left   AUG 22:5
piece of b. in his pocket   SWIFT 525:34
bricks: carried the b. to Lawley   BETJ 44:2
Bridal: Against their B. day   SPEN 516:32
b. of the earth and sky   HERB 248:16
to dance at our b.   SCOTT 417:11
bride: barren b.   POPE 377:20
became my glittering b.   WORD 577:14
b. adorned for her husband   BIBLE 82:30
b. at the altar   SCOTT 417:20
b. her attire   BIBLE 60:15
bridesmaid makes a happy b.   TENN 532:13
darling, my life and my b.   POE 374:23
encounter darkness as a b.   SHAK 464:12
I drew my b.   PATM 370:2
is ready to be thy b.   BALL 30:9
like a blooming Eastern b.   DRYD 194:23
Passionless b.   TENN 539:22
proud b. of a ducal coronet   DICK 179:4
unravish'd b. of quietness   KEATS 291:2

virgin-widow and a *Mourning B.*
DRYD 197:11
yet a b. CAREW 130:15
young b. and her bridegroom POUND 382:11
bride-bed: thought thy b. to have deck'd
SHAK 437:6
bridegroom: Bellona's b. SHAK 458:5
b. in my death SHAK 423:11
b. out of his chamber PRAY 390:11
funeral train which the b. CLOU 153:10
Like a b. from his room AYT 24:9
young bride and her b. POUND 382:11
bride-grooms: Of b. HERR 248:18
brides: b., and of their bridal-cakes
HERR 248:18
uppe 'The B. of Enderby' ING 270:13
bridesmaid: happy b. makes a happy
bride TENN 532:19
Bridge: Beautiful Railway B. MCG 325:6
keep the b. with me MAC 322:17
well Horatius kept the b. MAC 322:23
when thy b. I crost CLOU 154:2
(Which goes with B. BELL 39:21
Bridge of Sighs: on the B. BYRON 121:1
bridle: be held with bit and b. PRAY 391:18
with a taxed b. SMITH 511:38
bridle-ring: took him by the b. BALL 30:9
bridles: She heard the b. ring BALL 32:2
bridleth: b. not his tongue BIBLE 80:11
brief: be less b. WATS 565:10
B. as the lightning SHAK 469:20
Drest in a little b. authority SHAK 464:2
I strive to be b. HOR 257:12
lust is gross and b. PETR 373:5
tedious and b. SHAK 471:13
'Tis b., my lord SHAK 434:10
briefer: garland b. than a girl's HOUS 263:3
brier: b. shall come up the myrtle
BIBLE 59:28
thorough b. SHAK 470:2
brier-patch: Bred en bawn in a b.
HARR 242:20
briers: b. is this working-day SHAK 424:29
bright: All things b. and beautiful ALEX 3:13
Behold the b. original appear GAY 223:19
b. and fierce and fickle TENN 542:5
B. as the day GRAN 234:6
b. blot SHEL 504:5
b., broken Maginn LOCK 315:23
b. day is done SHAK 424:2
b. face of danger STEV 520:24
b. girdle furl'd ARN 12:23
b. in the fruitful valleys BRID 92:17
B. is the ring of words STEV 523:1
b. things come to confusion SHAK 469:20
b. to the coiner HOUS 263:8
burning b. BLAKE 87:14
creature not too b. or good WORD 581:8
Dark with excessive b. MILT 347:9
garden of b. images BRAM 91:22
It is the b. day that brings SHAK 449:4
Keep up your b. swords SHAK 473:21
obscurely b. BYRON 121:37
on earth your fame is b. BRID 92:18
purpose and his eyes are b. KEATS 294:17
thought thee b. SHAK 495:15
was a young lady named B. BULL 106:22
you shall shine more b. SHAK 493:17
brightness: being the b. of his glory
BIBLE 79:28
b. didst outshine Myriads MILT 344:26
B. falls from the air NASHE 360:7
b. in their failing eyes BLUN 89:2
b. of his presence his PRAY 390:9
b., purity, and truth OTWAY 366:4
his Darkness and his B. BYRON 126:8
Leaking the b. away SPEN 515:12
Brighton: cheerful, merry Dr B. THAC 545:10
Brignal: B. banks are wild and fair
SCOTT 417:30

Brig o' Dread: From B. when thou may'st
BALL 31:7
brilliant: envy of b. men BEER 37:28
less b. pen BEER 37:13
brillig: 'Twas b. CARR 134:28
brim: bubbles winking at the b. KEATS 291:18
sparkles near the b. BYRON 120:19
brimstone: From his b. bed at break
COL 156:10
rain snares, fire and b. PRAY 389:31
bring: b. in cloudy night immediately
SHAK 483:6
B. me my arrows of desire BLAKE 86:16
B. out number BLAKE 88:18
b. up the rear in heaven BROW 96:26
knowest not what a day may b. BIBLE 54:36
would b. home knowledge JOHN 277:31
bringer: first b. of unwelcome news
SHAK 441:2
bringeth: him that b. good tidings
BIBLE 59:18
bringing: that her b. me up by hand DICK 178:9
brinkmanship: boasting of his b.
STEV 520:22
brioche: Qu'ils mangent de la b. MAR 328:22
brisk: b. as a bee in conversation JOHN 274:1
b. fond lackey to fetch HOUS 265:18
spoke a b. little somebody BROW 99:1
brisker: land fares b. POUND 383:18
brisking: by b. about the Life SMART 508:22
bristle: his hair did b. upon his SCOTT 416:15
bristles: memory, my skin b. HOUS 266:17
Bristol: he is not member of B. BURKE 109:12
were three sailors of B. THAC 545:32
Britain: boundary of B. is revealed TAC 531:6
B. all the sun that shines SHAK 428:17
B., could you ever boast SWIFT 527:33
Hail, happy B. SOM 513:3
I've lost B. KIPL 302:13
Yet B. set the world ablaze GILB 226:11
Britannia: B., rule the waves THOM 549:7
inseparable than Beer and B. SMITH 511:25
brither: lo'ed him like a vera b. BURNS 115:5
British: art thou not of B. blood TENN 533:28
B. Bourgeoisie SITW 508:14
B. bourgeoisie have spoken WAUGH 566:2
B. Fleet a-riding at anchor THAC 546:2
B. journalist WOLFE 576:6
B. manhood was put together CARL 131:14
B. policy ROCH 407:5
B. soldier can stand up SHAW 496:19
dismissed by the B. electorate CHUR 150:26
Flood Of B. freedom WORD 582:2
greatness of the *B.* Nation ADD 2:19
majesty the B. soldier fights NAP 359:7
provinces of the B. empire SMITH 509:17
smell the blood of a B. SHAK 454:27
so ridiculous as the B. MAC 324:1
With a stony B. stare TENN 540:7
with B. and Armoric knights MILT 345:23
world less known by the B. BORR 90:3
British Empire: B. and the United States
CHUR 150:3
destinies of the B. DISR 184:27
liquidation of the B. CHUR 150:12
British Islands: than these selfsame B.
BORR 90:3
British Museum: keep my books at the
B. BUTL 118:22
very learned B. assistant POUND 383:14
British Public: B., ye who like me not
BROW 104:16
Briton: glory in the name of B. GEOR 224:1
only a free-born B. can do THAC 545:23
Britons: amongst the B. who are VIRG 559:13
B. never will be slaves THOM 549:7
brittle: arms you bear are b. HOUS 264:3
b. glory shineth in this SHAK 480:5
broached: Bringing rebellion b. SHAK 445:7

Broad: B. and I'm the High SPR 517:11
b. is the way BIBLE 65:6
B. of Church and broad BETJ 44:14
b. on the roots of things BROW 98:17
b. sunshine of life JOHN 278:6
brooks too b. for leaping HOUS 264:10
make b. their phylacteries BIBLE 67:22
broader: b. lands and better days CHUR 150:3
brogues: not fit to tie his b. SCOTT 419:1
broiled: piece of a b. fish BIBLE 71:20
broke: b. any man's head but his SHAK 446:6
he b. forth CIC 151:27
Vows for thee b. deserve SHAK 457:4
Who b. the laws of God LOCK 316:1
you b. a British square KIPL 299:8
you that b. the new wood POUND 383:12
broken: baying for b. glass WAUGH 565:29
bright, b. Maginn LOCK 315:23
b. and castaway wine-pots CLOU 153:7
b. and contrite heart PRAY 393:8
b. head in Cold Bath Fields MAC 324:23
b. open on the most scientific PEAC 370:13
b. the lock and splintered AUDEN 20:5
b. with the storms of state SHAK 447:15
charm they have b. BRID 92:15
cord is not quickly b. BIBLE 55:15
earth the b. arcs BROW 98:18
else but through a b. heart WILDE 572:16
healeth those that are b. PRAY 399:19
I am b. by their passing YEATS 584:17
Is it not b. SHEL 499:17
Laws were made to be b. NORTH 364:3
Naught b. save this body BROO 94:28
neck when once b. WALSH 563:28
Nor a b. thing mend BELL 40:10
pitcher be b. at the fountain BIBLE 56:11
sound of b. glass BELL 40:5
thou hast b. may rejoice PRAY 393:5
touched a b. girl FLEC 214:15
When the lute is b. SHEL 501:21
brokenhearted: To bind up the b. BIBLE 60:8
We had ne'er been b. BURNS 112:29
You hoped we were both b. SWIN 530:10
broker: honest b. BISM 84:23
bronze: gold and lungs of b. BELL 39:28
longer lasting than b. HOR 261:8
with oak and three-ply b. HOR 259:12
bronzes: Others shall shape b. more
VIRG 559:1
broo: eels boil'd in b.' BALL 31:5
brooch: theron heng a b. of gold CHAU 141:17
brooches: b. and toys for your delight
STEV 522:29
brood: eternal b. of glory excellent
SPEN 516:4
fond of no second b. SHAK 428:5
He sees his b. about thy TENN 542:7
that thy b. is flown TENN 542:6
brooding: atheist b. and blaspheming
CHES 148:7
broods: b. and sleeps on his own WORD 580:5
World b. with warm breast HOPK 256:13
brook: b. and river meet LONG 316:20
b. Into the main SHAK 468:18
dwelt by the b. Cherith BIBLE 51:6
Fell in the weeping b. SHAK 436:19
noise like of a hidden b. COL 155:26
brooks: b. are Thames's tributaries ARN 15:8
b. of Eden mazily murmuring TENN 533:13
b. too broad for leaping HOUS 264:10
'Only B. of Sheffield DICK 176:26
Shallow b. murmur most SIDN 507:14
broom: bright blows the b. STEV 522:29
I am sent with b. before SHAK 471:22
broomstick: Surely man is a b. SWIFT 526:25
Brot: sein B. mit Tränen ass GOET 230:12
brothels: b. with bricks of Religion
BLAKE 88:20
Keep thy foot out of b. SHAK 454:19
brother: Am I my b.'s keeper BIBLE 45:25

Am I not a man and a b.   WEDG 567:16
Be my b.   CHAM 139:18
brav'd by his b.   SHAK 451:23
b. and his lover have embrac'd   SHAK 463:13
b. by decree is banished   SHAK 449:24
b. is born for adversity   BIBLE 54:11
b. of death exacteth   BROW 95:24
b. of death exacteth   BROW 96:1
B. of the Angle   WALT 564:1
b. should not war with   COWP 165:21
b.'s tears have wet them   CAT 137:15
dawn is my b.   BELL 39:16
Death and his b. Sleep   SHEL 500:8
Esau my b. is a hairy   BIBLE 46:15
far have him than his b.   MARV 332:16
fold to thy heart thy b.   WHIT 571:21
glad mad b.'s   SWIN 529:2
Had it been his b.   ANON 5:15
hand of every man's b.   BIBLE 45:38
has brother followed b.   WORD 577:19
hateth his b.   BIBLE 81:7
his b. is dead   BIBLE 46:35
hurt my b.   SHAK 437:16
I am a b. to dragons   BIBLE 52:37
king my b.'s wreck   ELIOT 204:26
marriage with his b.'s wife   SHAK 446:28
marry with his b.   SHAK 435:2
My b..he is in Elysium   SHAK 487:22
our dear b. here departed   PRAY 389:13
stick more close than a b.   KIPL 303:17
Still to my b. turns with   GOLD 231:24
Strong B. in God   BELL 40:8
Thy b. came with subtilty   BIBLE 46:17
tyrant duke unto a tyrant b.   SHAK 424:28
voice of thy b.'s blood   BIBLE 45:26
Your b. and my sister   SHAK 426:27
brotherhood: already know the b. of
  man   FRY 219:25
by thy b. of Cain   BYRON 125:4
crown thy good with b.   BATES 35:4
doubly sweet a b. in song   KEATS 289:7
Love the b.   BIBLE 80:25
brotherly: Let b. love continue BIBLE 80:3
brothers: all men become b. under SCH 415:9
all the b. too   SHAK 489:8
b. attempting to get Pelion   HOR 260:22
B. in humanity who live   VILL 557:4
forty thousand b.   SHAK 437:8
noble pair of b.   HOR 262:8
Romans were like b.   MAC 322:18
So the two b. and their   KEATS 290:10
they may agree like b.   SHAK 446:11
we band of b.   SHAK 445:3
We were b. all   WORD 580:20
brow: b. of labour this crown BRYAN 106:8
b. with homely biggin bound   SHAK 442:17
Chill on the b.   SPAR 514:22
Consul's b. was sad   MAC 322:14
his eyes grow in my b.   SHAK 421:32
meet my Maker brow to b.   CORN 162:19
o'er that b.   BYRON 125:22
of a southward-facing b.   ARN 14:21
rugged b. of careful Policy   SPEN 516:26
speech in that victorious b.   ARN 14:24
That great b.   BROW 99:19
that threatening unkind b.   SHAK 484:15
wanton with a velvet b.   SHAK 456:27
Whether on Ida's shady b.   BLAKE 88:10
Your bonny b. was brent   BURNS 114:12
brown: b. Greek manuscripts   BROW 99:13
b. of her—her eyes   MEW 338:12
from the Yellow an' B.   KIPL 300:15
She has b. hair   SHAK 469:2
smile o' the b. old earth   BROW 101:20
browner: always tinge with a b. GIBB 224:20
Browning: *entsichere ich meinen B.*
                                   JOHST 283:8
from B. some 'Pomegranate'   BROW 98:3
Hang it all, Robert B.   POUND 382:6
Leave to Robert B.   KING 296:20

Meredith is a prose B.   WILDE 573:37
Mrs B.'s death is rather   FITZ 213:19
Tennyson and B.   BAG 29:20
Brownist: be a B. as a politician SHAK 489:29
brows: Gathering her b. like gathering
                                   BURNS 115:3
girls' b. shall be their pall   OWEN 367:3
round the b. of all these   VIRG 558:23
shadow of her even b.   SPEN 516:11
browsing: b. and sluicing and cheery
                                   WOD 575:26
bruise: b. them with a rod of iron
                                   PRAY 389:18
It shall b. thy head   BIBLE 45:20
bruised: be b. in a new place IRV 270:25
b. reed shall he not break   BIBLE 59:11
staff of this b. reed   BIBLE 51:38
was b. for our iniquities   BIBLE 59:22
bruisers: sneer at the b. of England
                                   BORR 90:6
bruit: Comes on at hand the b. THOM 548:21
meurt le b. parmi le vent   APOL 11:10
Brunetto: *you* here, Advocate B.
                                   DANTE 171:11
brunt: Bear the b.   BROW 104:1
brush: Border and gi'e them a b. HOGG 253:2
hang and b. their bosoms   BROW 105:26
never b. their hair   BELL 38:26
work with so fine a b.   AUST 24:3
brushes: A' b. his hat a mornings
                                   SHAK 472:25
brushwood: lowest boughs and the b.
                                   BROW 101:5
Brust: in meiner B.   GOET 229:30
brutal: stupid and b. in the history BEEC 37:5
brutality: industry without art is b.
                                   RUSK 411:9
brute: b. beasts that have no PRAY 388:21
b. I might have been   BROW 104:4
cursed Whatever b.   HOUS 264:21
Et tu, B.   CAES 126:28
Et tu, B.   SHAK 450:1
Feed the b.   PUNCH 403:1
house of a b. to the soul   TENN 532:22
It's a regular b. of a bee   LEAR 311:16
such a cross-grained b.   GOLD 232:28
Brutes: B. never meet in bloody GOLD 231:15
had been b. without you   OTWAY 366:4
sane and simple race of b.   TENN 535:18
that you might live as b.   DANTE 171:13
bruti: non foste a viver come b. DANTE 171:13
brutish: nasty, b., and short HOBB 251:18
Unto some b. beast   MARL 329:14
Brutum: B. fulmen   PLINY 374:16
Brutus: B. is an honourable man
                                   SHAK 450:17
B. makes mine greater than   SHAK 451:22
B.' will start a spirit   SHAK 448:18
is B. sick   SHAK 449:13
Portia is B.' harlot   SHAK 449:15
that Lord B. took to wife   SHAK 449:16
You too B.   CAES 126:28
bubble: is mostly froth and b. GORD 233:1
now a b. burst   POPE 379:4
world's a b.   BACON 28:15
bubbles: beaded b. winking at the brim
                                   KEATS 291:18
earth hath b.   SHAK 458:14
new-blown b. of the day   JOHN 282:26
bubukles: his face is all b.   SHAK 444:7
bubus: Paterna rura b.   HOR 259:7
Bücher: wo man B. verbrennt   HEINE 244:14
buck: b. stops here   TRUM 553:19
bucket: nations are as a drop of a b.
                                   BIBLE 59:8
That b. down and full   SHAK 479:22
buckets: dropping b. into empty wells
                                   COWP 167:4
Buckingham: so much for B.   CIBB 151:12

Buckingham Palace: changing guard
  at B.   MILNE 340:4
buckle: reason doth b. and bow BACON 24:19
buckler: carry the b. unto Samson
                                   BROW 96:14
shall be thy shield and b.   PRAY 395:21
bucklers: there hang a thousand b.
                                   BIBLE 56:26
buckram: eleven b. men grown out
                                   SHAK 439:3
Four rogues in b. let drive   SHAK 439:2
bud: be a b. again   KEATS 289:19
b., and yet a rose full-blown   HERR 250:16
leaf, the b., the flower   SPEN 516:13
now in age I b. again   HERB 247:22
opening b. to Heaven convey'd   COL 156:18
This b. of love   SHAK 482:16
budding: b. morrow in midnight
                                   KEATS 292:25
budge: b. doctors of the Stoic MILT 341:16
B..' says the fiend   SHAK 466:7
I will not b. for no man's   SHAK 483:2
buds: Blind b. that snows have SWIN 529:23
b. hang in the elm like   HOUS 265:15
darling b. of May   SHAK 492:28
(Driving sweet b. like   SHEL 502:8
green b. they were swellin'   BALL 30:10
starry river b.   SHEL 503:20
That kneel'd unto the b.   SHAK 422:17
buff: bide by the b. and the blue BURNS 114:5
Buffalo: B. Upon the chimney-piece
                                   CARR 133:11
buffeted: ye be b. for your faults BIBLE 80:26
buffets: Whom the vile blows and b.
                                   SHAK 461:10
Buffoon: B. and poet   HENL 245:12
statesman, and b.   DRYD 194:13
Buffs: Steady the B.   KIPL 305:1
bug: b. with gilded wings   POPE 377:1
bugaboo-baby: Don't b. *me*   CALV 127:18
Bugg: Stiggins, B.   ARN 15:26
bugle: b., blow   TENN 541:32
One blast upon his b.-horn   SCOTT 416:7
bugle-horn: sound upon the b. TENN 538:15
bugles: 'What are the b. blowin' KIPL 298:19
bugloss: There the blue b. paints
                                   COWP 168:26
build: Birds b.   HOPK 257:3
b. the Perfect City time   AUDEN 19:12
b. thou the walls of Jerusalem   PRAY 393:8
B. up the blue dome   SHEL 500:7
b. your House of Parliament   WELL 567:23
end is to b. well   WOTT 583:16
Except the Lord b. the house   PRAY 398:18
intending to b. a tower   BIBLE 70:14
So easy to b.   IBSEN 270:3
think that we b. for ever   RUSK 411:22
to b. the house of death   MONT 354:15
When we mean to b.   SHAK 441:17
builder: he can only be a *b.*   RUSK 411:8
maker and b. is God   BIBLE 79:32
builders: b. have laboured in vain
                                   BIBLE 83:3
painters, poets and b.   MARL 329:2
stone which the b. refused   PRAY 398:2
building: altered in the b. trade KIPL 303:28
castle or b. not in decay   BACON 26:38
principal beauty in b.   FULL 220:16
pursuit for the B. up of Jerusalem
                                   BLAKE 86:10
we have a b. of God   BIBLE 77:6
buildings: put upon great civic b.
                                   RUSK 411:21
builds: What is he that b. stronger
                                   SHAK 436:23
built: b. by the guest   DONNE 190:1
b. his house upon the sand   BIBLE 65:12
B. in th' eclipse   MILT 343:10
b. to comprehend a lie   KIPL 302:17
is almost lost that b. it   BROW 97:19

Lord has b. the house   BIBLE 83:12
Prisons are b. with stones   BLAKE 88:20
therefore b. for ever   TENN 534:6
we have b. do we discern   ARN 13:23
Builth: variants from B. to Ballyhoo
  KIPL 302:4
Bulbo: my beautiful, my B.   THAC 545:20
bull: are gone to milk the b.   JOHN 275:3
blaring b. went wading   HARDY 240:22
Cock and a B.   STER 520:12
curl'd Assyrian B.   TENN 540:1
Irish b. is always pregnant   MAH 327:4
savage b. doth bear the yoke   SHAK 472:2
See an old unhappy b.   HODG 252:3
bullet: Every b. has its billet   WILL 574:9
is stronger than the b.   LINC 314:13
with a b. through his heart   THAC 545:26
bullets: With b. made of platinum   BELL 38:30
bull-fighters: b. of Spain   BORR 90:6
bullied: b. out of vice   SURT 525:1
bullocks: wisdom...whose talk is of b.
  BIBLE 63:20
young b. upon thine altar   PRAY 393:9
bulls: eat b.' flesh   PRAY 393:3
fat b. of Basan   PRAY 390:18
ploughman of b.   PROP 401:15
two chairs like mad b.   DICK 178:18
bully: I love the lovely b.   SHAK 444:17
Like a tall b.   POPE 378:2
mentality, too, is b.   BEER 38:1
bulrushes: took for him an ark of b.
  BIBLE 46:41
bulwark: floating b. of the island   BLAC 85:4
bulwarks: Mark well her b.   PRAY 392:27
bum: Then slip I from her b.   SHAK 470:3
bumbast: to b. out a blank verse   GREE 236:12
bump: that go b. in the night   ANON 5:8
Bunbury: permanent invalid called B.
  WILDE 572:29
bunch: b. of other men's flowers   MONT 355:6
Buncombe: through reporters to B.
  CARL 132:4
bundle: b. of prejudices   LAMB 307:7
buns: bears may come with b.   ISH 270:27
Bunyan: genius in literature—B.   ARN 16:23
buona: b. imagine paterna   DANTE 171:12
burbled: b. as it came   CARR 134:29
burd: arms b. Helen dropt   BALL 31:4
burden: bear the b. and the heat   ARN 13:23
b. and heat of the day   BIBLE 67:15
b. of them is intolerable   PRAY 387:19
b. of the nation's care   PRIOR 401:6
grievous b. was thy birth to me   SHAK 481:8
Is the b. of my song   ANON 6:13
my b. is light   BIBLE 66:5
Take up the White Man's b.   KIPL 304:6
They have cast their b.   KIPL 303:10
burdens: to undo the heavy b.   BIBLE 60:4
Burg: Ein' feste B. ist unser   LUTH 321:2
burghers: Like signiors and rich b.
  SHAK 465:7
roused the b. of Carlisle   MAC 322:4
burglar: When the enterprising b.'s
  GILB 228:20
burglary: Flat b. as ever was committed
  SHAK 473:4
burgonet: arm And b. of men   SHAK 421:31
Burgundy: It's a Naïve Domestic B.
  THUR 550:29
burial: buried in Christian b.   SHAK 436:21
groaning for b.   SHAK 450:12
his obscure b.   SHAK 436:14
in one red b. blent   BYRON 120:27
thy precious Death and B.   PRAY 385:17
burial-ground: b. God's-Acre   LONG 316:18
buried: be b. in a good old age   BIBLE 46:4
be b. in so sweet a place   SHEL 499:2
being b. with Christ   PRAY 388:10
B. beneath some snow-deep   ELIOT 202:5
b., He descended into   PRAY 384:26

Half-b. in the snow was   LONG 316:16
I'll be b. in the king's   SHAK 479:15
rich-proud cost of outworn b.   SHAK 494:2
Rose as where some b. Caesar   FITZ 212:15
shall be b. by her Antony   SHAK 424:19
They b. him   PROU 401:23
they b. him the little port   TENN 533:11
they not b. me deep enough   TENN 540:15
This living b. man   DONNE 190:1
twenty generations lie b.   MAC 323:20
Upon my b. body lay   BEAU 36:8
We b. him darkly at dead   WOLFE 576:3
Burke: only specimen of B. is   HAZL 243:9
time with B. under a shed   JOHN 279:15
Burleigh: mourn'd the Lord of B.
  TENN 539:11
burn: beacons b. again   HOUS 262:12
better to marry than to b.   BIBLE 76:2
b. the old bass-viol that   HARDY 239:19
B. to the socket   WORD 577:11
B. upward each to his point   BROW 105:20
Did not our heart b. within   BIBLE 71:18
I rage, I melt, I b.   GAY 222:6
Old age should b. and rave   THOM 546:23
shall not b. thee by day   PRAY 398:9
To b. always with th   PATER 369:21
To b. for ever in burning   SWIN 530:20
violent fires soon b. out   SHAK 478:19
We b. daylight   SHAK 469:6
years I b. all my sermons   WESL 568:19
Burn'd: B. on the water   SHAK 422:2
Through my b. bosom   SHAK 452:31
burnèd: b. is Apollo's laurel   MARL 329:16
bush b. with fire   BIBLE 47:3
his clothes not be b.   BIBLE 53:23
I give my body to be b.   BIBLE 76:14
smell of b. poetry   WOD 576:1
Wherever books are b. men   HEINE 244:14
burneth: b. the chariots   PRAY 392:21
burning: bow of b. gold   BLAKE 86:16
b. and a shining light   BIBLE 72:2
b. bright   BLAKE 87:14
b. fiery furnace   BIBLE 61:3
B. for burning   BIBLE 47:25
b. of a *Pope*   DRYD 197:5
b. of the leaves   BINY 84:8
b. Sappho loved and sung   BYRON 122:32
b. witches when we're only   CHES 147:7
firebrand plucked out of the b.   BIBLE 61:20
pretty Babe all b. bright   SOUT 514:19
smell of b. fills the startled   BELL 40:7
their eyes are b.   AUDEN 20:5
your lights b.   BIBLE 70:6
burnish'd: Furnish'd and b. by Aldershot
  BETJ 44:6
Burns: B., Shelley, were with us BROW 102:5
Lovely B. has charms   BURNS 114:16
Not she which b. in 't   SHAK 491:13
burnt-offerings: thou delightest not in
b.   PRAY 393:8
burnt-out: b. ends of smoky days
  ELIOT 204:7
burr: I am a kind of b.'s   SHAK 465:2
Burrow: B. awhile and build   BROW 98:17
is always so near his b.   MEYN 338:16
burrows: b. of the Nightmare   AUDEN 18:10
burrs: Do roses stick like b.   BROW 105:27
burst: b. Joy's grape   KEATS 291:15
B. smilingly   SHAK 456:7
first that ever b.   COL 155:12
Let me not b. in ignorance   SHAK 430:24
mast b. open with a rose   FLEC 214:19
moonlit cedar what a b.   ARN 14:2
suddenly b. out singing   SASS 414:16
then b. his mighty heart   SHAK 450:28
words or I shall b.   FARQ 210:12
bursts: b. come crowding through   ARN 14:3
b. of open day between   FRY 220:5
burthen: vapours weep their b.   TENN 543:11
which the b. of the mystery   WORD 578:5

Burton: why was B. built on Trent
  HOUS 264:12
Bury: B. it certain fathoms   SHAK 485:24
B. my heart at Wounded Knee   BENET 40:20
b. whom he help'd to starve   POPE 376:29
disposed to b. for nothing   DICK 179:13
I b. some of you   DONNE 188:28
I come to b. Caesar   SHAK 450:17
Let the dead b. their dead   BIBLE 65:19
Past b. its dead   LONG 317:3
they'll meet to b.   BROO 94:16
bus: Descending from the b.   CARR 133:13
I'm not even a b.   HARE 242:8
She tumbled off a b.   GRAH 233:11
bush: Bed in the b. with stars   STEV 522:27
b. burned with fire   BIBLE 47:3
B., the dusty loam   HARDY 239:8
every common b. afire   BROW 97:33
fear each b. an officer   SHAK 446:23
flame? The B. is bare   BROW 98:29
is a b. suppos'd a bear   SHAK 471:11
Thorough b.   SHAK 470:2
young bird in this b.   LEAR 311:18
bushel: neither under a b.   BIBLE 70:1
bushes: discovereth the thick b.   PRAY 391:11
likes b. and low tamarisks   VIRG 559:22
busied: b. in his majesty   SHAK 443:9
business: annuity is a very serious b.
  AUST 23:24
be about my Father's b.   BIBLE 69:13
B. first   THAC 545:17
b. of America is business   COOL 162:11
b. of everybody is   MAC 323:6
b. of the wealthy man   BELL 39:29
b. of the day   DRYD 195:37
b. of the day in the day   WELL 568:2
b. that we love we rise   SHAK 422:24
B. was his aversion   EDG 199:24
did my uncle Toby's b.   STER 520:9
everybody minded their own b.   CARR 133:25
far away from b.   HOR 259:7
If it's b. of consequence   BARH 33:10
importunity Of b.   LAMB 307:33
In civil b.   BACON 25:31
it is your b.   HOR 258:23
know your own foolish b.   CHES 146:8
lucrative b. of mystery   BURKE 108:12
my b. is to Create   BLAKE 86:2
my pleasure, b.   WYCH 583:25
'No b. before breakfast   THAC 545:19
occupy their b. in great   PRAY 397:9
On a thousand b. women   BETJ 42:6
our b. to lose innocence   BOWEN 91:6
people is 'B. as usual'   CHUR 149:26
person on b. from Porlock   COL 156:25
praying, it spoils b.   OTWAY 366:5
proceed no further in this b.   SHAK 459:7
projects than for settled b.   BACON 27:39
requisite in b. than dispatch   ADD 1:12
rest is not our b.   ELIOT 202:24
robs you on b. principles   SHAW 498:6
servants of b.   BACON 26:21
That's the true b. precept   DICK 179:9
to do your own b.   BIBLE 79:1
Treasury is the spring of b.   BAG 28:22
We demand that big b. give   ROOS 408:7
woman's b. to get married   SHAW 497:25
busk: wherefore should I b. my heid
  BALL 32:10
bus'ness: some to b.   POPE 377:25
Buss: Miss B. and Miss Beale   ANON 6:16
bust: her friendly b.   ELIOT 205:14
merit raise the tardy b.   JOHN 282:29
only give a b. of marriages   BYRON 122:27
storied urn or animated b.   GRAY 234:22
Bustle: B. in a House   DICK 183:17
of all the tumult and b.   SMITH 509:8
busts: picture plac'd the b. between
  CHES 145:8
busy: b., and you will be safe   OVID 366:21

Caledonia: O C.! stern and wild
                              SCOTT 416:22
support C.'s cause   BURNS 114:5
Caledonian: Bold and erect the C. stood
                              HOME 253:25
calf: also to skip like a c.   PRAY 391:10
Bring hither the fatted c.   BIBLE 70:20
c. and the young lion   BIBLE 58:10
When he killed a c. he   AUBR 17:27
calf's-skin: hang a c. on those recreant
                              SHAK 452:16
Caliban: Ban, Ca-C.   SHAK 485:11
C. casts out Ariel   POUND 383:6
rage of C.   WILDE 573:16
call: all who profess and c.   PRAY 385:25
c. a dog *Hervey*   JOHN 273:30
c. back yesterday   SHAK 479:6
c. of the running tide   MAS 334:5
c. you, Shepherd   ARN 14:10
go and c. me cattle home   KING 296:25
I tried to c. them back   CLARE 152:16
leave to c. me anything   SWIFT 526:32
let me always c. you Edwin FARR 210:26
Must c. too soon   GILB 229:7
of thy people which c.   PRAY 386:7
one clear c. for me   TENN 533:3
only c. me thine   COL 157:5
people who come to c.   COW 164:5
shall please God to c. me PRAY 388:18
they come when you do c.   SHAK 439:23
thing which I c. a book   LAMB 307:17
wake and c. me early   TENN 540:20
What shall I c. thee   BLAKE 88:1
When you c. me that   WIST 575:11
who can c. to-day his own DRYD 198:15
will c. no being good   MILL 339:5
call'd: though I c. another   PRIOR 401:5
calle: *e com'è duro c.*   DANTE 171:17
called: c. the chess-board white BROW 99:5
c. them by wrong names   BROW 99:11
C. to, a thousand times   POUND 383:16
I c. not   BIBLE 49:35
many are c.   BIBLE 67:18
Out of the deep have I c. PRAY 398:23
vocation wherewith ye are c. BIBLE 77:27
calleth: c. them all by their names
                              PRAY 399:19
One deep c. another   PRAY 392:8
calling: answerably to your Christian
c.   PRAY 388:11
dignity of this high c.   BURKE 110:7
heard my c.   PRAY 392:1
Calliope: C. nor Apollo sung these
                              POUND 382:15
calls: press that c. on me   SHAK 448:7
calm: all is c. again   GAY 223:8
all our c. is in that balm NORT 364:8
c. of mind all passion   MILT 351:4
C. was the day   SPEN 516:30
cankers of a c. world   SHAK 440:10
famous, c., and dead   BROW 100:34
Hence in a season of c.   WORD 579:12
Nor peace within nor c.   SHEL 504:10
There is no joy but c.   TENN 539:14
Time's glory is to c. contending SHAK 492:19
unwonted c. pervades his breast ARN 12:22
was more than usual c.   FLEM 214:25
calme: *Luxe, c. et volupté*   BAUD 35:7
calmer: c. of unquiet thoughts WALT 564:3
Calmness: C. is great advantage HERB 247:7
Calumnies: C. are answered best with
                              JONS 285:11
calumny: thou shalt not escape c.
                              SHAK 433:12
Calvin: that land of C.   SMITH 510:30
Calvinist: *Papist*, yet a C.   CLEV 153:3
Calvinistic: We have a C. creed PITT 373:25
Calypso: Ulysses leaves once more C.
                              SHEL 500:21
Cam: Isis and C.   WORD 582:12

camaille: strong as is a greet c.   CHAU 142:10
Camberley: Into nine-o'clock C.   BETJ 44:8
Cambridge: C. ladies who live in furnished
                              CUMM 170:9
C. people rarely smile   BROO 94:23
do this because I am C.'   FORS 217:4
from Shrewsbury School, from C.
                              SHAW 498:23
gently back at Oxford or C. BEER 37:22
more attractive than C.   BAED 28:19
skill to C. books he sent BROW 97:26
To C. books   TRAPP 552:5
we follow the C. lead   JOW 285:21
Ye fields of C.   COWL 164:17
Cambyses: do it in King C.' vein
                              SHAK 439:12
Camden Town: Having baths in C. BETJ 42:6
came: angel of the Lord c. upon BIBLE 69:9
By the way as you c.   RAL 404:13
C. Christ the tiger   ELIOT 203:4
c. in with Richard Conqueror SHAK 484:2
c. in with the Conqueror   BROME 93:12
C. out by the same Door   FITZ 212:20
He c. unto his own   BIBLE 71:26
I c., I saw, I conquered   CAES 126:29
'I c.' like Water   FITZ 212:21
I c., saw, and overcame   SHAK 442:13
In that state I c.   VAUG 555:17
camel: almost in shape of a c.   SHAK 434:22
C. humphed himself   KIPL 304:18
C.'s hump is an ugly lump KIPL 300:9
It is easier for a c.   BIBLE 67:11
raiment of c.'s hair   BIBLE 63:37
swallow a c.   BIBLE 67:24
Take my c., dear   MAC 324:27
Camelot: To many-tower'd C. TENN 538:2
ye cackling home to C.   SHAK 453:22
camera: I am a c. with its shutter ISH 270:28
Camerado: C., this is no book WHIT 570:13
great C.   WHIT 571:2
Camilla: respectable family resided C.
                              BURN 112:16
caminos: *fraires y muchos son los c.*
                              CERV 138:15
cammin: *mezzo del c. di nostra vita*
                              DANTE 171:2
camp: From camp to c.   SHAK 444:9
Campden Hill: strikes the stars on C.
                              CHES 147:8
camps: Courts and c. are the only
                              CHES 145:14
can: because they think they c. VIRG 558:16
c. must be so sweet   HOPK 256:15
C. something, hope,   HOPK 256:7
dance while you c.   AUDEN 18:13
He who c., does   SHAW 497:38
I c.   EMER 207:2
if we c. we must   HOUS 264:22
Pass me the c.   HOUS 264:20
You c. and you can't   DOW 191:11
Cana: in C. of Galilee   PRAY 388:25
canal: fishing in the dull c. ELIOT 204:26
swimming along the old c. BETJ 44:2
canard: *Mettez un c. sur un lac* AUG 21:11
Cancel: C. and tear to pieces that
                              SHAK 461:14
it back to c. half a Line FITZ 213:7
cancers: because women have c.
                              KEATS 293:32
candid: be c. where we can   POPE 379:2
from the c. friend   CANN 130:1
candidate: good dog, like a good c.
                              BECK 36:18
candle: Bell, book, and c.   SHAK 452:19
Box whose C. is the Sun   FITZ 213:3
brief c.   SHAK 463:6
burning a farthing c. at Dover JOHN 275:8
friends called him 'C.-ends' CARR 133:4
hath the c. sing'd the moth SHAK 467:1
hold a c. to my shames   SHAK 466:15

'is Latin for a c.   FIEL 211:4
is to set a c. in the sun BURT 116:32
light a c. of understanding BIBLE 62:8
little c. throws his beams SHAK 468:18
My c. burns at both ends   MILL 339:26
poet like a pale c. guttering MACN 326:10
their farthing c. to the sun YOUNG 587:20
this day light such a c.   LAT 310:21
to light a c. to the sun   SIDN 507:13
when he hath lighted a c. BIBLE 70:1
candle-light: c. at evening spinning
                              RONS 407:18
Colours seen by c.   BROW 98:5
dress by yellow c.   STEV 522:16
candle-lighte: Fire and fleet and c. BALL 31:6
candles: blessed c. of the night SHAK 468:22
c. burn their sockets   HOUS 265:2
Night's c. are burnt out   SHAK 483:14
Their c. are all out   SHAK 459:13
wind extinguishes c.   LA R 310:15
candlestick: c. upon the plaister BIBLE 61:5
Candlestick-maker: C. much acquaints
                              BROW 105:4
candlesticks: seven golden c. BIBLE 81:13
Candour: C., who, with the charity
                              CHUR 148:22
Candy: C. Is dandy   NASH 359:19
cane: conduct of a clouded c. POPE 381:10
canem: *littera scriptum 'Cave c.* PETR 372:30
canker: Azure hath a c. by usura
                              POUND 382:11
c., Bolingbroke   SHAK 438:17
loathsome c. lives in sweetest SHAK 493:12
cankers: c. of a calm world SHAK 440:10
cankerworm: c., and the caterpillar
                              BIBLE 61:14
Cannibals: of the C. that each other
                              SHAK 473:25
with Caesars, and with C. SHAK 441:25
cannie: c. wee thing   BURNS 113:1
cannon: c.'s opening roar BYRON 120:22
C. to right of them   TENN 532:24
Even in the c.'s mouth   SHAK 425:24
then the c.   CHES 147:3
cannon-ball: c. took off his legs HOOD 254:13
cannot: her gifts on such as c. JONS 284:10
I c. sing the old songs   CLAR 152:23
some things we c. all do   LUC 320:2
cano: *Arma virumque c.*   VIRG 557:8
canoe: coffin clapt in a c. BYRON 119:29
floor of a narrow c.   ELIOT 205:5
canoes: their heads in their c. MARV 332:23
canonized: many (questionless) c.
                              BROW 96:17
canonizes: death c. and sanctifies
                              BURKE 109:5
canopied: c. Under these windows
                              SHAK 428:8
canopies: Under the c. of costly SHAK 441:29
canopy: doth a rich embroider'd c.
                              SHAK 446:19
Canossa: We will not go to C. BISM 84:21
cant: c. in defence of savages JOHN 279:19
c. of hypocrites may be   STER 519:30
clear your *mind* of c. may JOHN 279:11
Let them c. about decorum BURNS 114:20
press'd with specious c.   HOOD 255:3
stamp is the c. of *Not men* BURKE 108:23
we have nothing but c.   PEAC 370:11
Cantate: *C. Domino canticum novum*
                              BIBLE 83:7
canteen: double drills and no c. KIPL 299:19
Canterbury: is the Archbishop of C.
                              SMITH 511:6
cantering: Steadily c. through KIPL 304:1
canters: they c. awaäy   TENN 540:24
canticle: sweetest c. is *Nunc dimittis*
                              BACON 26:4
canticum: *Cantate Domino c. novum*
                              BIBLE 83:7

cantie: Contented wi' little and c.
BURNS 113:4
canton: establish the robin's plucky c.
AUDEN 20:15
cantons: loyal c. of contemned love
SHAK 488:13
canvas: Compell'd thy c. TENN 536:9
crowd your c. TENN 540:21
canvassers: c. whom they do not know
HURST 268:17
canvasses: good in c. and factions
BACON 25:40
cap: riband in the c. of youth SHAK 436:17
Stuck a *feather* in his c. BANGS 32:16
capa: c. que cubre todos los CERV 138:20
Capability: Negative C. KEATS 293:19
That c. and god-like reason SHAK 435:29
capable: Habacuc était c. de tout
VOLT 561:23
capacious: pipe for my c. mouth GAY 222:7
capacity: described as a supreme c.
BUTL 118:34
that he had the c. to reign TAC 531:13
transcendent c. of taking trouble CARL 131:18
wisdom, c. and virtue SWIFT 526:8
cap-a-pe: Armed at points exactly, c.
SHAK 430:7
caparisons: No c., miss SHER 506:18
capax: c. imperii nisi imperasset TAC 531:13
Cape: Beyond the C. of Hope MILT 347:17
Round the c. of a sudden BROW 103:9
Capella: star called C. was yellow
HARDY 241:9
caper: Till first ae c. BURNS 115:11
capers: c. nimbly in a lady's chamber
SHAK 480:18
He c., he dances SHAK 469:10
lovers run into strange c. SHAK 425:11
capiatur: Nullus liber homo c. MAGN 327:2
capitaine: c. de vingt-quatre soldats
ANON 9:8
Capital: shall not want C. in Heaven
ELIOT 202:4
To that high C. SHEL 499:6
Capitalism: C., wisely managed KEYN 295:18
definition of c. HAMP 238:17
unacceptable face of c. HEATH 244:5
capitulate: I will not c. JOHN 279:26
capon: of Madeira and a cold c.'s
SHAK 438:11
capons: you cannot feed c. so SHAK 434:4
Capri: wordy letter came from C. JUV 287:27
caprice: ev'ry meteor of c. must play
JOHN 282:26
caprices: which has her c. BURKE 110:15
caps: roses crest the c. I know THOM 547:24
They threw their c. SHAK 427:13
capta: Graecia c. ferum victorem HOR 259:2
Captain: C. is a good travelling FARQ 210:5
c. is in his bunk SHAW 496:33
c. of the Hampshire grenadiers...has
GIBB 224:15
c.'s but a choleric word SHAK 464:4
C. Webb from Dawley BETJ 44:2
crew of the c.'s gig GILB 225:16
Foremost c. of his time TENN 541:7
I am a cook and a c. bold GILB 225:16
I am the C. of the *Pinafore* GILB 227:30
I am the c. of my soul HENL 245:5
O Captain! my C. WHIT 570:7
Our great captain's c. SHAK 474:14
plain russet-coated c. CROM 169:20
royal c. of this ruin'd band SHAK 444:10
Saying 'C. BALL 31:3
their c., the heart SHAK 442:15
Walk the deck my C. lies WHIT 570:8
captains: All my sad c. SHAK 422:22
c. and rulers clothed BIBLE 60:37
C. and the Kings depart KIPL 302:7
c. couragious whom death BALL 31:8

C. of industry CARL 132:11
There were c. by the hundred GILB 225:10
thunder of the c. BIBLE 53:7
Capting: there's nobody like the C.
THAC 545:15
captive: Captivity thence c. SPEN 515:17
From the foes they c. make CHAN 139:19
they that led us away c. PRAY 399:3
thou hast led captivity c. PRAY 394:10
when I am thy c. MILT 348:12
captives: proclaim liberty to the c. BIBLE 60:8
To serve your c.' need KIPL 304:6
upon all prisoners and c. PRAY 385:20
captivity: no leading into c. PRAY 399:13
prisoners out of c. PRAY 394:7
turned again the c. of Sion PRAY 398:16
Turn our c. PRAY 398:17
Capulets: than in the tomb of the C.
BURKE 108:6
caput: c. pedibus supposuisse OVID 366:22
car: afford to keep a motor c. SHAW 496:4
gilded c. of day MILT 340:27
Put the c. away AUDEN 19:15
cara: c. e buona imagine DANTE 171:12
caravan: Put up your c. HODG 252:9
Where my c. has rested TESC 545:2
Caravanserai: in this batter'd C. FITZ 212:13
Carboniferous: In the C. Epoch we were
KIPL 299:16
carbuncular: young man c. ELIOT 205:1
carcase: Wheresoever the c. is BIBLE 67:30
carcases: dead c. of unburied men
SHAK 427:23
carcass: him as a c. fit for hounds
SHAK 449:9
card: 'He's a cheery old c. SASS 414:18
we must speak by the c. SHAK 436:28
Cardinal: Jackdaw sat on the C.'s chair
BARH 33:11
cards: be that can pack the c. BACON 25:40
not learned to play at c. JOHN 280:6
play'd At c. for kisses LYLY 321:10
shuffle the c. CERV 138:18
some were playing c. BALL 31:3
care: absolute paternal c. ELIOT 202:22
age is full of c. SHAK 492:13
are now with me past c. SHAK 479:3
beneath Thy special c. BETJ 43:6
c. and valour in this Welshman SHAK 444:19
C., at the horseman's CALV 127:28
c. fifty times more BAG 28:29
Careless she is with artful c. CONG 159:18
c. of all the churches BIBLE 77:12
c.'s check and curb VAUG 555:12
c. to stay than will SHAK 483:15
c. where the water goes CHES 147:28
Deliberation sat and public c. MILT 346:14
disclaim all my paternal c. SHAK 453:3
do buy it with much c. SHAK 465:9
enough in thee to kill c. SHAK 473:9
forgather wi' Sorrow and C. BURNS 113:4
Hast thou no c. of me SHAK 423:16
Have closed our anxious c. PEAC 370:20
Heaven's peculiar c. SOM 513:3
her c. was but to be fair WATS 565:11
Hippocleides doesn't c. HILL 251:7
I c. for nobody BICK 84:1
I c. not two-pence BEAU 36:3
I shan't c. or ho HARDY 239:20
is past my c. FLET 215:12
kiaugh and c. beguile BURNS 113:5
Killing c. and grief of heart SHAK 447:3
learning to c. for the unhappy VIRG 557:19
least as feeling her c. HOOK 255:20
nipt With c. MIDD 338:18
Nor c. beyond to-day GRAY 235:12
now Reason is past c. SHAK 495:15
ravell'd sleave of c. SHAK 460:8
Sport that wrinkled C. MILT 342:15
Take c. of the pence LOWN 319:21

then the c. is over TEMP 532:9
things beyond our c. DRYD 197:10
tiresome verse-reciter, C. SHEL 504:25
to take c. of the minutes CHES 145:18
us to care and not to c. ELIOT 202:1
we don't c. a button LEAR 312:8
weep away the life of c. SHEL 504:11
Will neither c. nor know HOUS 265:10
With middle-ageing c. POUND 383:20
with what c. Thou hast HERB 248:10
women and c. and trouble WARD 564:38
Young ladies should take c. AUST 22:17
Cared: C. not to be at all MILT 346:7
Gallio c. for none of those BIBLE 74:15
career: boy's ideal of a manly c. DISR 186:28
which might damage his c. BARR 34:20
careful: c. of the type she seems TENN 536:21
carefully: come most c. upon your hour
SHAK 429:4
Careless: C. folly done and said HOUS 265:4
C. she is with artful care CONG 159:18
first fine c. rapture BROW 101:6
So c. of the single life TENN 536:27
'twere a c. trifle SHAK 458:22
carelessly: unbent bow, c. DONNE 190:3
carelessness: lose both looks like c.
WILDE 573:1
With carefullest c. BETJ 44:6
carent: c. quia vate sacro HOR 261:18
cares: blessed than to put c. away CAT 136:28
c. that infest the day LONG 316:10
c. were to increase his HOME 253:22
devil has ended his c. BROW 102:13
ever against eating c. MILT 342:26
hell Grief and avenging C. VIRG 558:21
Hush, hush, Nobody c. MORT 358:15
kings have c. that wait GREE 236:11
one c. for none of them AUST 24:1
these small c. of daughter MORE 357:1
youth is but a frost of c. TICH 551:2
caret: golden cadence of poesy, c.
SHAK 457:3
careth: c. not for the sheep BIBLE 72:19
Carew: tends the grave of Mad C.
HAYES 243:7
carf: c. biforn his fader CHAU 141:13
cargo: With a c. of ivory MAS 333:18
caribous: c. lie around and snooze
COW 163:20
caricature: With a c. of a face GILB 227:14
carl: c., with sory grace CHAU 143:7
carl-hemp: Thou stalk o' c. in man
BURNS 115:14
Carlisle: You may go to C.'s ANST 11:8
Carlyle: C. and Mrs Carlyle marry
BUTL 119:22
C. has led us all out into CLOU 154:6
carmina: placere diu nec vivere c.
HOR 258:25
sunt et mihi c. VIRG 560:7
carnage: all its deeds of c. WHIT 570:11
c. and his conquests cease BYRON 120:4
C. is Thy daughter WORD 578:21
carnal: men's c. lusts and appetites
PRAY 388:25
carnally: to be c. minded is death BIBLE 75:7
carnation: A' never could abide c.
SHAK 443:19
carnations: Are our c. and streak'd
SHAK 491:23
Of bright c. did o'erspread DRUM 193:28
Soon will the musk c. break ARN 15:6
CARO: VERBUM C. FACTUM EST
MASS 335:12
carol: This c. they began that SHAK 427:2
wild c. ere her death TENN 535:28
carolled: Still they are c. and said STEV 523:1
Carouse: with what a brave C. FITZ 213:1
carpe: c. diem HOR 259:20
carpenter: Is not this the c.'s son BIBLE 66:22

understood Christ was a c.   BLAKE 87:8
Walrus and the C.   CARR 135:5
You may scold a c. who   JOHN 274:26
carpet: All wear the c. with their
   YEATS 586:14
colours in the Turkey c.   MAC 323:30
figure in the c.   JAMES 271:22
him no c. knight so trim   SCOTT 417:5
on c. consideration   SHAK 490:14
carpets: c. rose along the gusty   KEATS 289:22
Over thick c. with a deadened   BETJ 42:12
carping: obnoxious to each c. tongue
   BRAD 91:13
Carrets: Sowe C. in your Gardens
   GARD 221:8
Carriage: C. held but just Ourselves
   DICK 183:15
very small second class c.   GILB 226:13
women of good c.   SHAK 481:28
carried: being not like children c.   PRAY 387:3
carrion: c. comfort, Despair   HOPK 256:7
With c. men   SHAK 450:12
Carrow: That was late slain at C.
   SKEL 508:19
carry: Books that you may c.   JOHN 280:17
c. a letter to my love   BALL 30:20
c. everything before me   DISR 185:31
c. the buckler unto Samson   BROW 96:14
c. their comfort about   ELIOT 201:17
c. them in his bosom   BIBLE 59:7
c. the moon in my pocket   BROW 102:13
c. within us the wonders   BROW 96:12
certain we can c. nothing out   BIBLE 79:17
choking him and making him c.   TOLS 551:15
man must c. knowledge with   JOHN 277:31
softly and a big stick   ROOS 408:1
cart: horse is drawn by the c.   KIPL 298:16
useful C.   LEAR 312:9
carters: keep a farm, and c.   SHAK 432:3
Carthage: C. must be destroyed   CATO 136:18
O C.! O New York   SASS 415:4
Carthaginian: With C. trustworthiness
   SALL 413:25
Carthago: Delenda est C.   CATO 136:18
magna C.   HOR 260:24
cartridge: holsters and c. boxes   SHAW 496:6
carve: c. heads upon cherry-stones
   JOHN 279:18
c. on every tree   SHAK 426:2
Let's c. him as a dish fit   SHAK 449:9
To c. out dials   SHAK 446:18
ye c. my epitaph aright   BROW 99:13
carved: c. names the rain-drop   HARDY 239:10
head fantastically c.   SHAK 442:10
carving: Now is a time for c.   POUND 383:12
caryatides: Unfrowning c.   STEV 523:12
Casca: what a rent the envious C.
   SHAK 450:27
cas'd: c. up, like a holy relic   WEBS 566:20
case: c. is concluded   AUG 22:2
c. will be dismissed with   HOR 262:7
Clutching a little c.   AUDEN 18:9
corpse in the c. with a sad   BARH 33:16
everything that is the c.   WITT 575:14
nothing to do with the c.   GILB 227:13
this c. is that case   ARAB 11:16
when a lady's in the c.   GAY 223:16
casement: c. high and triple-arch'd
   KEATS 289:16
c. ope at night   KEATS 292:4
c. slowly grows a glimmering   TENN 542:4
ghost of Roger C.   YEATS 585:7
casements: Charm'd magic c.   KEATS 291:23
cash: c. that goes therewith   CHES 146:11
In epochs when c. payment   CARL 131:17
takes your c.   CHUR 148:30
take the C. in hand   FITZ 212:12
with the squalid c. interpretation   JAMES 272:3
Casket: hushed C. of my Soul   KEATS 292:29
casse: tout c.   ANON 9:20

Cassius: C. from bondage will deliver
   SHAK 449:2
C. is aweary of the world   SHAK 451:23
Dar'st thou, C.   SHAK 448:14
cassock'd: c. huntsman and a fiddling
   COWP 166:7
cassowary: If I were a c.   WILB 572:3
Cast: C. a cold eye   YEATS 587:10
c. away the works of darkness   PRAY 386:4
C. me not away from thy   PRAY 393:6
c. off the works of darkness   BIBLE 75:24
C. thy bread upon the waters   BIBLE 56:5
c. ye your pearls before   BIBLE 65:1
first c. a stone at her   BIBLE 72:10
have c. their burden upon   KIPL 303:10
have set my life upon a c.   SHAK 481:19
he c. into the sea   BIBLE 70:30
I will in no wise c. out   BIBLE 72:6
loath to c. away my speech   SHAK 488:10
more he c. away   BUNY 107:34
Nor c. one longing ling'ring   GRAY 235:2
over Edom will I c.   PRAY 393:18
suddenly c. down   PRAY 392:25
trouble me c. me in the teeth   PRAY 392:9
Tush, I shall never be c.   PRAY 389:30
will I c. out of my sight   BIBLE 50:31
castaway: I myself should be a c.   BIBLE 76:9
mighty is vilely c.   BIBLE 50:16
castels: make c. thanne in Spayne
   CHAU 144:1
casteth: He c. out devils through   BIBLE 65:28
Castilian: might an old C.   BYRON 126:9
castitatem: Da mihi c. et continentiam
   AUG 21:14
castle: c., called Doubting-Castle
   BUNY 107:20
c. or building not in decay   BACON 26:38
him as his c. and fortress   COKE 154:23
man's house is his c.   COKE 154:21
my old lad of the c.   SHAK 438:2
rich man in his c.   ALEX 3:14
splendour falls on c. walls   TENN 541:32
This c. hath a pleasant   SHAK 459:4
castled: c. crag of Drachenfels   BYRON 120:31
Castle Downe: Look owre the C.   BALL 30:17
Castlereagh: He had a mask like C.
   SHEL 502:2
intellectual eunuch C.   BYRON 122:4
castles: all the c. I have   JONS 283:26
C. in the air   IBSEN 270:3
My c. are my King's alone   SCOTT 417:17
casual: children c. as birds   AUDEN 18:5
half-believers in our c. creeds   ARN 14:17
casualty: first c. when war   JOHN 273:18
force and road of c.   SHAK 466:19
casuistry: Mountains of c. heap'd
   POPE 375:26
casuists: soundest c. doubt   POPE 377:30
cat: c. in profound meditation   ELIOT 204:6
c.'s mew rise to a scream   AUDEN 20:8
C., the Rat, and Lovell   COLL 158:10
deafer than the blue-eyed c.   TENN 534:23
Foss is the name of his c.   LEAR 311:23
Had Tiberius been a c.   ARN 14:4
Hanging of his c. on Monday   BRAT 91:24
harmless necessary c.   SHAK 467:22
I am a c. that likes   SMITH 510:25
it might have been c.   BARH 33:6
I will consider my C. Jeoffry   SMART 508:21
killing a c. than choking   KING 297:15
Lat seen a c.   CHAU 142:25
mother's c. had but kittened   SHAK 439:21
part to tear a c.   SHAK 469:26
pavilion c.   LANG 309:19
poor c. i' the adage   SHAK 459:8
room to swing a c.   DICK 177:18
Runcible C. with crimson   LEAR 312:20
see the c. i' the dairy   ELIOT 200:18
Self-reliant like the c.   MOORE 355:22
suggestion as a c. laps milk   SHAK 485:6

to see how the c. jumps   SCOTT 418:38
Touch not the c.   SCOTT 418:9
very fine c. indeed   JOHN 279:9
vigilant as a c. to steal cream   SHAK 440:11
What c.'s averse to fish   GRAY 235:6
When I play with my c.   MONT 355:2
catalogue: dull c. of common things
   KEATS 290:27
in the c. ye go for men   SHAK 461:9
cataract: sounding c.   WORD 578:6
wild c. leaps in glory   TENN 541:32
cataracts: You c. and hurricanoes
   SHAK 454:4
catastrophe: between education and c.
   WELLS 568:16
c. of the old comedy   SHAK 453:12
I'll tickle your c.   SHAK 441:19
catch: c. my flying soul   POPE 376:14
game of catch as c. can   FOOTE 216:7
hard to c. and conquer   MER 337:2
Perdition c. my soul   SHAK 475:14
usual to c. a mouse or two   GRAY 235:23
catched: not be c.   PEPYS 372:12
catching: c. a train is to miss   CHES 148:11
Passion, I see, is c.   SHAK 450:13
poverty's c.   BEHN 38:17
catchwords: principally by c.   STEV 521:34
catechism: so ends my c.   SHAK 440:18
Catechist: something of the Shorter-C.
   HENL 245:12
Categorical: This imperative is C.
imperative   KANT 288:10
categories: ballet of bloodless c.   BRAD 91:10
caterpillar: c., and the palmerworm
   BIBLE 61:14
c. on the leaf   BLAKE 85:13
caterpillars: c. of the commonwealth
   SHAK 479:2
cates: Than feed on c. and have   SHAK 439:28
Cathay: Europe than a cycle of C.
   TENN 539:9
Cathechism: scarce had said his C.
   THAC 546:2
Cathedral: Heft Of C. Tunes   DICK 184:1
in the vast c. leave him   TENN 541:15
Catherine: Such as are on a C. pear
   SUCK 524:9
catherine-wheels: in a cloud of crimson
c.   FRY 219:26
Catholic: Druse and the C.   CHES 146:27
I cannot be a good C.   NORF 364:1
Catholick: C. and Apostolick Church
   PRAY 387:11
holy C. Church   PRAY 384:26
that he hold the C. Faith   PRAY 385:11
Catiline: abuse our patience, C.   CIC 151:25
Cato: C.'s daughter durst not   ROWE 410:25
C.'s daughter   SHAK 449:16
Like C.   POPE 376:27
losing one pleased C.   LUCAN 319:22
What C. did   BUDG 106:19
Cats: C. is 'dogs' and rabbits   PUNCH 402:19
C., no less liquid than   TESS 545:3
Do c. eat bats   CARR 133:15
dogs and killed the c.   BROW 103:15
greater c. with golden eyes   SACK 412:26
Mill his three black c.   DE L 174:4
monkeys and c.   JAMES 271:24
Naming of C. is a difficult   ELIOT 204:5
where cats are c.   MARQ 330:23
cattle: are mostly troublesome c.
   LOVER 318:22
c. rise and listen   KING 297:21
c. upon a thousand hills   PRAY 393:2
forth grass for the c.   PRAY 396:20
go and call the c. home   KING 296:25
over the c.   BIBLE 45:4
these who die as c.   OWEN 367:2
unknown to the c.   CAT 137:6

Catullus: C. gives you warmest thanks
CAT 137:3
Did their C. walk that YEATS 586:14
Poor C. CAT 136:27
caught: 'Ah, ha!' you're c. SHAK 422:9
before he c. the beast WALL 562:6
c. at God's skirts BROW 101:18
c. his clear accents BROW 102:5
c. in her arms long WYATT 583:22
his sweet perfections c. ROYD 411:3
if he be c. young JOHN 276:10
must be c. with tickling SHAK 489:10
ram c. in a thicket BIBLE 46:11
cauld: 'tis auld it waxeth c. BALL 32:10
cauldron: Fire burn and c. bubble
SHAK 462:2
Round about the c. go SHAK 462:2
causa: c. finita est AUG 22:2
Victrix c. deis placuit LUCAN 319:22
causas: vitam vivendi perdere c. JUV 287:25
cause: beauty of the good old c. WORD 582:9
between c. and effect LA B 306:15
called amiss *The good old C.* MILT 352:11
c. is in my will SHAK 449:20
c. of dullness in others FOOTE 216:9
c. of Freedom is the cause BOWL 91:7
c., or just impediment PRAY 388:23
c. that perishes with them CLOU 153:13
c. that wit is in other SHAK 441:3
c. this evil is upon us BIBLE 61:21
defendeth the c. of widows PRAY 394:7
defend my c. against PRAY 392:10
final c. of the human nose COL 157:30
Freedom is the c. of God BOWL 91:7
have full c. of weeping SHAK 454:2
increased devotion to that c. LINC 314:23
in the justice of our c. HAIG 237:11
it is the c., my soul SHAK 477:5
judge thou my c. BIBLE 60:32
man can shew any just c. PRAY 389:2
no c. however just STEV 521:14
Our c. is just DICK 184:4
perseverance in a good c. STER 519:19
Report me and my c. aright SHAK 437:23
Ring out a slowly dying c. TENN 537:15
So little c. for carollings HARDY 239:7
support Caledonia's c. BURNS 114:5
Thou Great First C. POPE 381:12
unites it with the secret c. JOYCE 286:17
unpregnant of my c. SHAK 433:2
Causer: C. of this BARN 34:4
causes: c. that they represent FORS 217:15
is in its c. just DRYD 197:4
is the knowledge of c. BACON 28:6
understand the c. of things VIRG 560:14
cautiously: do c. ANON 10:18
Cavalier: brave old Scottish C. AYT 24:11
So let each c. who loves SCOTT 415:20
cavalier: he was a perfect c. BYRON 119:30
Cavaliers: C. (Wrong but Wromantic)
SELL 420:4
cavat: Gutta c. lapidem OVID 366:27
cave: burst stomach like a c. DOUG 191:10
echo in a Marabar c. FORS 217:8
her vacant interlunar c. MILT 350:16
In this our pinching c. SHAK 428:15
littera scriptum 'C. canem PETR 372:30
lone c.'s stillicide HARDY 239:18
tear the c. where Echo SHAK 482:19
That darksome c. they enter SPEN 516:7
Caveant: C. consules ne quid res publica
ANON 10:10
Cave of Adullam: called his political
C. BRIG 93:5
cavern: skulking Truth to her old c.
POPE 375:26
Caverns: Gluts twice ten thousand C.
KEATS 292:14
out of the c. of rain SHEL 500:7
Sand-strewn c. ARN 13:6

caves: unfathom'd c. of ocean bear
GRAY 234:23
woods and desert c. MILT 343:6
caveto: tu, Romane, c. HOR 262:3
caviare: 'twas c. to the general SHAK 432:23
Cawdor: Glamis thou art, and C. SHAK 459:1
Thane of C. lives SHAK 458:17
cawing: Rising and c. at the gun's
SHAK 470:20
Cease: C.! must men kill SHEL 501:3
c. upon the midnight with KEATS 291:22
C., ye prudes BURNS 114:16
Fall and c. SHAK 456:9
have fears that I may c. KEATS 292:30
He did not c. while he HAZL 243:13
He maketh wars to c. PRAY 392:21
maketh the storm to c. PRAY 397:10
night shall not c. BIBLE 45:37
not c. from Mental Fight BLAKE 86:16
that thou shouldst c. to be SHEL 505:6
things might change or c. SHAK 454:3
to see me c. to live ARN 15:12
whom we do exist and c. SHAK 453:3
ceased: it c. to be with Sarah BIBLE 46:6
ceases: Love c. to be a pleasure BEHN 38:12
ceasing: Remembering without c.
BIBLE 78:30
Without c. I make mention BIBLE 74:29
Cecilia: Blessed C. AUDEN 18:4
'It is only C. AUST 22:31
cedar: moonlit c. what a burst ARN 14:2
cedars: brambles like tall c. show COTT 163:7
c. of Libanus which he PRAY 396:20
devour the c. of Lebanon BIBLE 49:19
excellent as the c. BIBLE 57:4
cedar-trees: Lord breaketh the c.
PRAY 391:10
Cedite: C. Romani scriptores PROP 401:17
ceiling: c. of amber ARN 13:7
in the lines of the c. ELUA 206:16
celandine: 'Tis the little c. WORD 583:2
celebrat: semper c. superna curia ABEL 1:1
celebrate: just to c. the event JERR 273:12
celebrated: Saviour's birth is c. SHAK 429:17
celebrates: c. his obsequies SCOTT 416:19
heavenly court for ever c. ABEL 1:1
celebrity: c. is a person who is known
BOOR 89:20
celerity: hath such a c. in dying SHAK 421:20
celestial: Apparelled in c. light WORD 578:22
lighten with c. fire PRAY 400:5
that c. light MILT 345:9
Celia: C. (since thou art so proud
CAREW 130:13
celibacy: c. has no pleasures JOHN 282:9
cell: Each in his narrow c. GRAY 234:20
solitary c. COL 156:14
Thou hast given me a c. HERR 250:14
cellar: Born in a c. FOOTE 216:6
I was born in a c. CONG 160:5
Cellarer: Old Simon the C. keeps BELL 38:22
cells: c. and gibbets for 'the man' ELIZ 162:8
contented with their c. WORD 582:7
Celt: blind hysterics of the C. TENN 537:16
C. in all his variants KIPL 302:4
Celtic: enchanted woods of C. antiquity
KEYN 295:19
cement: With the same c. POPE 375:24
cemetery: c. is an open space among
SHEL 499:2
Help me down C. Road LARK 310:7
cenotaph: laugh at my own c. SHEL 500:7
censor: to c. one's own thoughts
WALEY 562:2
censorship: extreme form of c. SHAW 498:17
censure: All c. of a man's self JOHN 277:33
c. freely who have written POPE 378:10
c. or condemn another BROW 96:32
c. this mysterious writ DRYD 196:17
I do not presume to c. BURKE 109:5

Take each man's c. SHAK 430:19
to read, and c. HEM 245:1
censured: behold is c. by our eyes
MARL 329:18
censuring: varletry Of c. Rome SHAK 423:21
centaur: c. in his dragon world POUND 382:13
c., man and wife BYRON 123:19
Centaurs: from the waist they are C.
SHAK 455:17
centre: c. cannot hold YEATS 586:15
earth is the c. DONNE 190:22
Mon c. cède FOCH 216:3
My c. is giving way FOCH 216:3
now in the c. of politics MOSL 358:19
poor c. of a man's actions BACON 27:36
which the c. is everywhere ANON 7:27
centres: of which we are the c. TROL 552:22
centric: c. and eccentric scribbled MILT 349:3
centum: deinde c. CAT 136:26
centuries: All c. but this GILB 226:25
forty c. look down upon NAP 359:8
I shall lie through c. BROW 99:14
century: c. of the common man WALL 562:3
intellectual life of our c. ARN 15:25
last for more than a c. CAT 136:21
Rafael made a c. of sonnets BROW 102:28
seventeenth c. a dissociation ELIOT 205:17
To one a c. hence or any WHIT 570:2
Cerberus: damn them with King C.
SHAK 441:25
loathed Melancholy, Of C. MILT 342:12
You are not like C. SHER 506:19
cerebration: well of unconscious c.
JAMES 271:17
cerements: Have burst their c. SHAK 430:24
ceremonial: any c. purposes the otherwise
HERB 246:18
ceremonies: of dreams, and c. SHAK 449:16
ceremony: c. of innocence is drowned
YEATS 586:15
It useth an enforced c. SHAK 451:11
No c. that to great ones SHAK 463:20
perfect c. of love's rite SHAK 493:2
save general c. SHAK 444:24
thrice-gorgeous c. SHAK 444:25
Ceres: laughing C. re-assume the land
POPE 378:5
which cost C. all that pain MILT 347:21
certain: c. because it is impossible
TERT 545:1
c. hope of the Resurrection PRAY 389:13
dirge of her c. ending SHAK 492:20
more c. than incertainties BARN 34:3
one thing is c. FITZ 212:19
To c. death by certain KIPL 302:6
certain age: lady of a 'c. BYRON 123:21
Certainly: C. the growth of the fore-brain
AUDEN 19:10
certain place: receive your reward in
a c. BROWN 95:8
certainties: man will begin with c.
BACON 24:16
When hot for c. in this MER 337:18
certainty: c. for an uncertainty JOHN 281:20
sober c. of waking bliss MILT 341:5
certamina: animorum atque haec c. tanta
VIRG 560:14
etiam belli c. magna tueri LUCR 320:6
Certare: C. ingenio LUCR 320:6
certezza: Di doman non c'è c. MED 336:9
certified: c. how long I have to live
PRAY 391:30
certifieth: one night c. another PRAY 390:11
certitude: Nor c. ARN 12:23
Cervantes: C. is never petulant MAC 324:9
C. on his galley sets CHES 147:6
C. smiled Spain's chivalry BYRON 124:1
cervicem: populus Romanus unam c.
CAL 127:6

cesspool: that great c. into which
DOYLE 192:33
Ceylon: Blow soft o'er C.'s isle HEBER 244:6
Cézanne: All C.'s apples I would
AUDEN 19:16
chaast: wol nat kepe me c. in al CHAU 143:17
chacals: c. pissent au bas et les FLAU 214:3
Chadband: C. style of oratory is DICK 176:13
chafe: Champ and c. and toss ARN 13:5
he that lets Another c. HERB 247:7
chaff: c. well meant for grain TENN 536:2
chaffinch: c. sings on the orchard
BROW 101:5
Chagrin: C. d'amour dure toute la
FLOR 215:34
chain: bound by the c. of our sins
PRAY 385:23
broke at once the vital c. JOHN 279:1
c. that is round us now CORY 163:3
flesh to feel the c. BRON 93:21
hill 'Too-quick', the c. TENN 541:26
remove a lengthening c. GOLD 231:24
that Homer's golden c. BURT 116:31
chained: hours has c. and bowed SHEL 502:13
chains: adamantine c. and penal fire
MILT 344:24
am thy captive talk of c. MILT 348:12
bind their kings in c. PRAY 399:24
c. about the feet of God TENN 535:26
C. and slaverie BURNS 114:34
C. are worse than bayonets JERR 273:11
clanking their c. WARD 564:19
everywhere he is in c. ROUS 410:17
sang in my c. like the sea THOM 547:2
Shake your c. to earth SHEL 502:4
since a woman must wear c. FARQ 210:1
Chair: C. she sat ELIOT 204:23
Give Dayrolles a c. CHES 146:9
has one vacant c. LONG 317:6
He fills a c. JOHN 278:26
It is like a barber's c. SHAK 420:29
La c. est triste MALL 327:9
sat on the Cardinal's c. BARH 33:11
Seated in thy silver c. JONS 283:24
to his father's c. JONS 285:7
chairs: next suggested elbow-c. COWP 166:28
two glasses and two c. MACN 326:11
chaise-longue: hurly-burly of the c.
CAMP 128:3
chalcedony: third c. BROW 97:34
chalice: c. of the grapes of God TENN 536:7
chalices: treen priests and golden c.
JEWEL 273:14
Cham: That great C. of literature
SMOL 512:14
chamber: bridegroom out of his c.
PRAY 390:11
cannot find a c. in the inn ANON 9:1
c. deaf to noise SIDN 507:21
heart, and in your c. PRAY 389:20
into the conference c. BEVAN 44:17
stalking in my c. WYATT 583:21
chambermaid: of a c. as of a Duchess
JOHN 278:4
chambermaids: With worms that are
thy c. SHAK 483:31
chambers: in the c. of the East BLAKE 88:10
of his c. in the waters PRAY 396:18
perfum'd c. of the great SHAK 441:29
chambre: demeurer en repos dans une
c. PASC 369:5
chameleon: c.'s dish SHAK 434:4
Chameleons: C. feed on light and air
SHEL 500:14
Champ: C. and chafe and toss ARN 13:5
Champagne: C. certainly gives one
SURT 525:20
not a c. teetotaller SHAW 496:16
with c. and a chicken MONT 354:3
Women and C. BELL 39:21

champion: in close fight a c. grim
SCOTT 417:5
chance: accident nor dart of c. SHAK 476:16
bludgeonings of c. HENL 245:4
C., and Change SHEL 503:10
c., and death, and mutability SHEL 503:12
c. favours only the prepared PAST 369:16
high arbiter C. governs MILT 347:4
it was by c. BRAD 91:13
law, c., hath slain DONNE 189:4
of the main c. of things SHAK 442:3
skirts of happy c. TENN 537:1
various turns of c. below DRYD 195:4
voice to come in as by c. BACON 25:41
Which erring man call c. MILT 341:15
will never eliminate c. MALL 327:11
would set my life on any c. SHAK 461:10
Chancellor: C. of the Exchequer is
LOWE 318:24
C. of the University WELL 567:29
England's high C. JONS 285:7
rather susceptible C. GILB 226:2
Chancery: pretty young wards in C.
GILB 226:2
chances: c. change by course SOUT 514:20
changes and c. of this mortal PRAY 388:5
choose Between the c. AUDEN 21:6
spake of most disastrous c. SHAK 473:25
chang'd: man but c. his mind POPE 377:10
Change: all that moveth doth in C.
SPEN 516:25
bolts up c. SHAK 423:20
certain relief in c. IRV 270:25
Chance, and C. SHEL 503:10
C. and decay in all around LYTE 321:19
C. as the winds change SWIN 530:28
c., but I cannot die SHEL 500:7
C. came o'er the spirit BYRON 124:13
C. is not made without HOOK 255:21
c. of heart AUDEN 20:7
c. our vile body PRAY 389:13
c. best carriage horses TROL 553:8
C. the name and it's about HOR 261:22
c. th'expiring flame renews GAY 223:23
dead there is no c. MAC 324:9
did you c. your stockings AUST 22:17
Doth c. my disposition SHAK 491:27
ever-whirling wheel Of C. SPEN 516:24
extremes by c. more fierce MILT 346:22
fill my pockets with c. DICK 180:19
God cannot c. the past AGAT 3:4
heavy c. MILT 343:5
How will the c. strike BROW 99:20
is necessary not to c. FALK 209:19
I would c. each hour like SEDL 419:13
I would not c. for thine JONS 284:12
lamentable c. is from the best SHAK 455:5
like a c. in the weather AUDEN 21:2
love will c. in growing old BRID 92:20
miserable c. now at my SHAK 423:15
more things c. KARR 288:15
Neither to c. SHEL 503:15
nor wished to c. GOLD 230:22
nous avons c. tout cela MOL 353:17
point is to c. MARX 333:10
progressive country c. DISR 185:4
ringing grooves of c. TENN 539:8
scorn to c. my state SHAK 493:6
take silver or small c. CHAM 139:14
that love could never c. BRID 92:20
That we must c. for Heav'n MILT 345:9
things might c. or cease SHAK 454:3
thou ever c. Kate into Nan BLAKE 86:1
To c. the cod's head SHAK 474:18
to c. what we can STEV 521:14
To know the c. and feel KEATS 293:4
vesture shalt thou c. them PRAY 396:13
we c. with them ANON 11:5
When c. itself can give SEDL 419:14
wind of c. is blowing MACM 326:1

with fear of c. MILT 345:24
without the means of some c. BURKE 111:4
changeable: Moors are c. in their wills
SHAK 474:10
changed: c. from that Hector who VIRG 558:5
c. into little water drops MARL 329:15
c. that my oldest creditors FOX 217:24
c. utterly YEATS 585:1
that it be not c. BIBLE 61:7
they shall be c. PRAY 396:13
Though c. in outward lustre MILT 345:2
we shall all be c. BIBLE 76:29
changefu: seen sae mony c.' years
BURNS 114:15
changeless: would fain keep her c. MER 337:4
changes: c. and chances of this PRAY 388:5
Her plot hath many c. QUAR 403:15
If the c. that we fear JOHN 281:9
Play all your c. ING 270:12
sundry and manifold c. PRAY 386:12
changest: who c. not LYTE 321:19
changing: c. guard at Buckingham Palace
MILNE 340:4
c. scenes of life TATE 531:21
What man thinks of c. TROL 553:7
Chankly Bore: Of the Hills of the C.
LEAR 312:2
Channel: Butting through the C. MAS 333:19
new c., fair and evenly SHAK 439:24
you are crossing the C. GILB 226:13
channels: through the c. of the ear
AUDEN 20:3
chant: triumphal c. SHEL 504:20
chantants: O ces voix d'enfants c.
VERL 556:10
chante: on le c. BEAU 35:14
chanted: c. snatches of old tunes
SHAK 436:19
chanticleer: lungs began to crow like
c. SHAK 425:20
Chanting: C. faint hymns to the cold
SHAK 469:17
Chaos: C. illumined WILDE 573:37
C. is come again SHAK 475:14
C.! is restor'd POPE 376:2
C., rudis indigestaque OVID 366:13
C. umpire sits MILT 347:4
God dawned on C. SHEL 499:11
reign of C. and old Night MILT 345:20
chap: c. that did not kill me HOUS 266:4
second eleven sort of c. BARR 34:8
chapel: decent whitewashed c. BETJ 43:7
There is the empty c. ELIOT 205:10
chapels: Stolen looks are nice in c.
HUNT 268:11
Chaplain: twice a day the C. called
WILDE 572:12
Chapman: Mr C.'s yea was yea BENT 41:4
chapmen: base sale of c.'s tongues
SHAK 456:20
chaps: from the nave to the c. SHAK 458:3
several c. out of the City CHES 147:16
chapter: c. of accidents CHES 146:2
c. of accidents WILK 574:5
c. of 'The Natural History JOHN 277:28
char: c. the wood ere Thou canst
THOM 548:18
character: belongs not to the female c.
KNOX 305:24
c. dead at every word SHER 506:29
c. in the full current GOET 230:10
'c. is destiny ELIOT 201:21
c. of a family to an hypothesis STER 519:20
entailing Divergence of C. DARW 171:28
I leave my c. behind me SHER 506:30
man's c. is to be abused THAC 545:24
object the formation of c. SPEN 515:1
passion could bring c. YEATS 587:1
personal c. and relations NAP 359:10
regaining my c. I despare FLEM 214:29

She gave me a good c. CARR 134:22
short c. when he was page CHAR 140:27
Sow a c. READE 405:4
that fate and c. are NOV 364:9
What is c. but the determination
JAMES 271:12
characteristic: c. of the English Monarchy
BAG 28:28
characters: c. of hell to trace GRAY 234:15
from high life high c. POPE 377:11
Most women have no c. POPE 377:17
Who have c. to lose BURNS 114:20
Charakter: Sich ein C. in dem Strom
GOET 230:10
Charge: 'C., Chester, charge! SCOTT 417:22
c. is prepar'd GAY 223:1
c. or rule nor governance SURR 524:20
c. with all thy chivalry CAMP 128:22
C. you more if you dine DICK 181:25
shall give his angels c. PRAY 395:22
charged: c. the troops of error BROW 96:5
is c. with the grandeur HOPK 256:12
charges: children but as bills of c.
BACON 26:32
ought warily to begin c. BACON 26:10
chariest: c. maid is prodigal enough
SHAK 430:17
Charing-Cross: human existence is at
C. JOHN 276:21
I sunk at C. WALP 563:4
Pitched betwixt Heaven and C. THOM 548:25
chariot: Bring me my c. of fire BLAKE 86:16
c. of Israel BIBLE 51:22
maketh the clouds his c. PRAY 396:18
slap-up gal in a bang-up c. DICK 181:15
charioted: c. by Bacchus and his pards
KEATS 291:20
chariotest: c. to their dark wintry SHEL 502:8
chariots: burneth the c. in the fire
PRAY 392:21
c., and some in horses PRAY 390:14
tarry the wheels of his c. BIBLE 49:12
chariot-wheel: axletree of the c.
BACON 27:33
charitably: how can they c. dispose
SHAK 444:21
charitie: doughterly loue and deere c.
MORE 357:20
charities: cold c. of man to man COWP 168:27
patron of some thirty c. TENN 542:20
charity: Candour, who, with the c.
CHUR 148:22
C. and beating begins FLET 215:25
C. and Mercy DICK 179:6
C., dear Miss Prism WILDE 573:6
c. edifieth BIBLE 76:5
c. envieth not BIBLE 76:14
C. never faileth BIBLE 76:14
C. shall cover the multitude BIBLE 80:32
C. suffereth long BIBLE 76:14
c. vaunteth not itself BIBLE 76:14
c. will hardly water BACON 26:33
c. with your neighbours PRAY 387:18
faith, hope, c. BIBLE 76:14
greatest of these is c. BIBLE 76:14
have not c. BIBLE 76:14
healing voice of Christian c. BURKE 111:2
him a little earth for c. SHAK 447:15
lectures or a little c. WHIT 571:1
living need c. ARN 12:20
Love, friendship, c. SHAK 487:6
mankind's concern is c. POPE 379:20
spent in so-called c. today CARN 132:31
that 'c. begins at home' SHER 506:34
there not be a c. in sin SHAK 464:7
with c. for all LINC 315:3
charlatan: Defamed by every c. TENN 537:17
Charlemain: When C. with all his peerage
MILT 345:23
Charles: my gentle-hearted C. COL 157:12

used by C. the First COW 164:4
Charles II: C. was always very merry
SELL 420:5
Charles the First: King C. out of the
Memorial DICK 177:5
Charlie: We'll o'er the water to C.
HOGG 253:1
charlock: shoot the c. throws a shade
COWP 168:26
Charlotte: C. has been writing a book
BRON 94:2
Werther had a love for C. THAC 546:3
charm: c. can soothe her melancholy
GOLD 231:31
c. he never so wisely PRAY 393:17
c. of all the Muses often TENN 543:17
c. of powerful trouble SHAK 462:3
c. they have broken BRID 92:15
Completing the c. ELIOT 202:10
powers of C. and Desire CAT 136:22
such a c. in melancholy ROG 407:10
charmed: Boil thou first i' the c. SHAK 462:2
c. it with smiles and soap CARR 133:8
c. me from my profession SHAK 486:11
I bear a c. life SHAK 463:8
charmer: hear the voice of the c.
PRAY 393:17
perils Of cheat and c. HOUS 265:14
Were t'other dear c. away GAY 222:35
charming: c. is divine philosophy
MILT 341:11
Every thing that is c. AUST 23:23
innocent and c. as the beasts AUDEN 19:12
So smoothes her c. tones MILT 348:24
charmingly: How c. sweet you sing
LEAR 312:12
Charms: C. strike the sight POPE 381:11
c. the town with humour CHUR 149:12
lass that has acres o' c. BURNS 114:6
Music has to sooth CONG 160:14
those endearing young c. MOORE 356:4
what drugs, what c. SHAK 473:24
Charrington: Outside C.'s we waited
BETJ 43:18
charter: c. of thy worth gives thee
SHAK 494:13
This was the c. of the land THOM 549:7
charts: busied in c. BAG 29:11
Charybdis: Scylla and C. NEWM 361:21
Scylla and C. SHEL 505:11
chase: c. of honours and distinction
BURKE 108:7
c. the glowing Hours with BYRON 120:21
In piteous c. SHAK 425:1
shining creatures of the c. TENN 542:8
Thy c. had a beast in view DRYD 197:19
thy c. is done SCOTT 416:3
When heated in the c. TATE 531:20
Wherein he doth forever c. ARN 12:22
with unhurrying c. THOM 548:9
chasing: he was always c. Rimbauds
PARK 368:20
chasm: romantic c. which slanted COL 156:7
chasse: souvenirs sont cors de c. APOL 11:10
chassis: counthry's in a state of c.
OCAS 364:16
chaste: Be thou as c. as ice SHAK 433:12
C. as the icicle SHAK 428:3
c. as unsunn'd snow SHAK 428:12
c. polygamy CAREW 130:15
C. to her husband POPE 377:20
cold nymphs c. crowns SHAK 485:19
If I pronounce it c. GILB 227:25
married, charming, c. BYRON 122:8
My English text is c. GIBB 224:19
Nor ever c. DONNE 189:9
nunnery Of thy c. breast LOV 318:20
chasten: power To c. and subdue WORD 578:7
chasteneth: Lord loveth he c. BIBLE 80:1
chasteté: une vertu du vice de c. VOLT 561:12

chastis'd: Nor once be c. with SHAK 423:21
chastise: c. with the valour of my SHAK 459:1
chastised: father hath c. you with whips
BIBLE 51:3
having been a little c. BIBLE 62:13
chastisement: c. of our peace was upon
BIBLE 59:22
chastity: clothed on with c. TENN 533:21
Even like thy c. SHAK 477:21
Give me c. and continency AUG 21:14
made of the vice of c. VOLT 561:12
that c. of honour BURKE 111:10
'Tis C., my brother MILT 341:10
chasuble: He wore, I think, a c.
HARTE 242:31
châteaux: Ô saisons, ô c. RIMB 406:8
Chatham: C. with his sabre drawn
ANON 5:10
everyday politics than a C. BAG 28:25
chats: spoiled the women's c. BROW 103:15
chatte: Quand je me joue à ma c. MONT 355:2
chatter: c. about Shelley FREE 218:24
insignificant c. of the world TROL 552:22
matter if it's only idle c. GILB 227:21
chatters: science and logic he c. PRAED 384:5
Chatterton: C.! how very sad thy fate
KEATS 292:23
C., the marvellous boy WORD 580:28
Chaucer: C., well of English undefiled
SPEN 516:19
mean Master Geoffrey C. CAXT 138:2
old famous Poet C. SPEN 517:5
To learned C. BASSE 35:1k
chavender: There is a fine stuffed c.
ST L 412:27
Chawcer: It is a pity that C. WARD 564:31
cheap: c. and chippy chopper GILB 226:31
done as c. as other men PEPYS 372:6
flesh and blood so c. HOOD 255:8
hold their manhoods c. SHAK 445:3
maketh himself c. BACON 25:37
sold c. what is most dear SHAK 495:3
cheaper: principle that it is c. BUTL 119:4
cheaply: put him c. off DRYD 195:13
cheapness: tawdry c. Shall outlast
POUND 383:7
Cheapside: in C. shall my palfrey
SHAK 446:11
through the vale of C. WORD 581:3
cheat: detecting what I think a c. JOHN 276:16
he may c. at cards genteelly BOSW 90:16
it's so lucrative to c. CLOU 153:28
perils Of c. and charmer HOUS 265:14
so monosyllabic as to c. FRY 220:6
sweet c. gone DE L 174:5
To c. a man is nothing GAY 222:29
Cheated: C. of feature by dissembling
SHAK 480:18
enthusiasm I have been c. KEATS 294:15
Of being c. BUTL 118:6
Old men who never c. BETJ 42:12
quality to be exceedingly c. EVEL 209:7
cheating: Forbids the c. of our friends
CHUR 148:30
cheats: c. with an oath acknowledges
PLUT 374:20
check: dreadful is the c. BRON 93:21
immediate c. to loose behaviour STEE 518:6
I would not c. LAND 308:24
To c. the erring and reprove WORD 579:15
Check'd: C. like a bondman SHAK 451:23
cheek: bring a blush into the c. DICK 181:1
C. of hers to incarnadine FITZ 212:7
c. to him that smiteth BIBLE 60:31
Feed on her damask c. SHAK 489:7
give this c. a little red POPE 377:16
hangs upon the c. of night SHAK 482:2
Her c. was soft as silk PAIN 367:19
He that loves a rosy c. CAREW 130:12
iron tears down Pluto's c. MILT 342:6

kissed each other's c.   GILB 228:31
leans her c. upon her hand   SHAK 482:7
old ornament of his c.   SHAK 472:26
on thy c. a fading rose   KEATS 290:16
smite thee on thy right c.   BIBLE 64:17
Where's the c. that doth   KEATS 289:31
yellow c.   SHAK 441:10
cheeks: c. of sorry grain wi   MILT 341:18
crack your c.   SHAK 454:4
Fat ruddy c. Augustus had   HOFF 252:11
Her c. were so red   KING 297:4
Spoke in her c.   DONNE 189:31
cheer: Be of good c..   BIBLE 66:26
be of good c.   BIBLE 72:41
c. us when we recover   BURKE 110:19
Could scarce forbear to c.   MAC 322:22
Died the sound of royal c.   TENN 538:12
Don't c.   PHIL 373:8
Greet the unseen with a c.   BROW 98:33
let thy heart c. thee   BIBLE 56:10
That c. but not inebriate   COWP 167:11
to c. but not inebriate   BERK 41:21
Cheer'd: C. up himself with ends
    BUTL 117:31
cheerer: c. of his spirits   WALT 564:3
cheerful: c. countenance, and bread
    PRAY 396:20
c. noise unto the God   PRAY 395:9
Dromedary is a c. bird   BELL 38:27
entertain a c. disposition   SHAK 478:22
ground with c. thoughts   SHAK 483:23
heart maketh a c. countenance   BIBLE 54:5
he looking as c. as any   PEPYS 372:1
loveth a c. giver   BIBLE 77:9
more c. and hopeful than   HOLM 253:14
cheerfulness: c. was always breaking
    EDW 200:8
cheerioh: 'c.' and 'cheeri-bye'   BETJ 42:18
cheers: sounds no worse than c.   HOUS 263:2
cheese: baiting a mouse-trap with c.
    SAKI 413:15
Botticelli's a c.   PUNCH 403:3
c. and garlic in a windmill   SHAK 439:28
fill hup the chinks wi' c.   SURT 525:8
like some valley c.   AUDEN 20:14
night I've dreamed of c.   STEV 521:23
smells of c.   SURT 525:15
swiss c. would think   MARQ 330:25
that has 265 kinds of c.   DE G 173:17
With apple pie and c.   FIELD 211:1
cheeses: ate the c. out of the vats
    BROW 103:15
chef: *je suis leur c.*   LEDR 313:6
chef-d'oeuvre: tree toad is a c.   WHIT 570:21
chemin: *c'est le plus court c.*   MOL 353:24
chemist: c., fiddler, statesman   DRYD 194:13
cheque: c. and the postal order   AUDEN 20:1
political blank c.   GOSC 233:2
Chequer-board: C. of Nights and Days
    FITZ 213:5
chequered: beauteous c. sides with gore
    THOM 549:19
cherchᵉrais: *c. pas si tu ne me possédais*
    PASC 369:13
cherish: c. those hearts that hate   SHAK 447:12
love, c., and to obey   PRAY 389:4
Then c. pity   BLAKE 88:4
cherishing: kill thee with much c.
    SHAK 482:20
Cherith: dwelt by the brook C.   BIBLE 51:6
cheroot: of a whackin' white c.   KIPL 301:6
cherries: c., hops   DICK 181:27
There c. grow   ALIS 3:18
There c. grow   CAMP 129:22
cherry: c. now   HOUS 262:14
C. Orchard is now mine…I've   CHEK 144:24
C.-ripe   HERR 248:21
Like to a double c.   SHAK 470:22
ruddier than the c.   GAY 222:8
see the c. hung with snow   HOUS 262:14

Till c. ripe themselves   ALIS 3:18
Till 'C. ripe' themselves   CAMP 129:22
cherry-blossoms: c., and white cups
    SHEL 503:19
cherry-isle: There's the land, or c.
    HERR 248:21
cherry-stones: not carve heads upon c.
    JOHN 279:18
Chertsey: There was an old Lady of C.
    LEAR 311:17
cherub: c.'s face   POPE 377:4
Cherubic: C. Creatures— These
    Gentlewomen   DICK 184:3
cherubim: c. does cease to sing   BLAKE 85:10
heaven's c.   SHAK 459:6
helmed C.   MILT 344:9
That the C. may cry   ANON 10:14
cherubims: He rode upon the c.   PRAY 390:8
Immortal C.   TRAH 551:19
sitteth between the c.   PRAY 396:10
Cherubin: To thee C.   PRAY 384:16
cherubins: quiring to the young-eyed
    c.   SHAK 468:15
cherubynnes: fyr-reed c. face   CHAU 142:4
ches: First of the c.   CHAU 141:6
chess: Life's too short for c.   BYRON 126:23
chess-board: called the c. white   BROW 99:5
c. is the world   HUXL 269:6
chest: caused his c. to slip down   WOD 575:23
c. of drawers by day   GOLD 231:4
His c. against his foes   SMART 509:3
men on the dead man's c.   STEV 521:21
Chester: 'Charge, C., charge!   SCOTT 417:22
Chesterton: dared attack my C.   BELL 39:27
chestnut: c. casts his flambeaux   HOUS 264:20
dogwood and c.   ELIOT 203:4
showers betumble the c.   HARDY 241:2
Under the spreading c. tree   LONG 317:18
chestnuts: sailor's wife had c.   SHAK 458:6
cheval: *hommes et allemand à mon c.*
    CHAR 140:31
Chevalier: *C. sans peur et sans reproche*
    ANON 9:5
chew: savoury pulp they c.   MILT 347:25
chewed: few to be c. and digested
    BACON 27:19
cheweth: yet he c. not the cud   BIBLE 48:6
chewing: c. little bits of string   BELL 38:34
Chicken: character called the Game C.
    DICK 177:29
c. in his pot every Sunday   HENR 245:13
Some c.   CHUR 150:10
with champagne and a c.   MONT 354:8
chickens: Curses are like young c.
    SOUT 513:23
gathereth her c. under her wings   BIBLE 67:26
pretty c. and their dam   SHAK 462:17
chid: He c. their wand'rings   GOLD 230:23
chide: c. the world-without-end   SHAK 493:18
They do but sweetly c.   SHAK 492:25
chiding: c. of the winter's wind   SHAK 424:31
He will not alway be c.   PRAY 396:16
I am a child to c.   SHAK 476:22
chief: c. of the ways of God   BIBLE 53:9
Hail to the C. who in triumph   SCOTT 416:4
I'm the c. of Ulva's isle   CAMP 129:2
Sinners; of whom I am c.   BIBLE 79:8
chiefest: c. among ten thousand   BIBLE 57:3
Chief Justice: C. was rich   MAC 323:18
chieftain: c. to the Highlands bound
    CAMP 129:1
Great c. o' the puddin'-race   BURNS 115:16
Sate Brunswick's fated c.   BYRON 120:23
chiels: Facts are c. that winna ding
    BURNS 113:14
chiens: *monade des gens comme les c.*
    NERV 361:1
Chiesa: *Libera C. in libero Stato*   CAV 138:1
child: adventurous c.   HOR 260:21
angel is the English c.   BLAKE 88:2

Around the c. bend all   LAND 308:17
Behold the c.   POPE 379:18
care for the c.'s rattle   JOHN 275:19
c. deserves the maximum   JUV 288:7
C.! do not throw this   BELL 38:23
c. imposes on the man   DRYD 196:19
c. in the street I could   CLOU 153:9
c. is afraid of being whipped   JOHN 273:25
C. is father of the Man   WORD 578:19
c. is known by his doings   BIBLE 54:17
c. may joy to hear   BLAKE 87:25
c. of glorious great intent   SPEN 516:4
c. of God   PRAY 388:12
c.'s a plaything   LAMB 308:14
c. should always say what's   STEV 522:17
c. that is not clean   STEV 522:21
Defend, O Lord, this thy C.   PRAY 388:22
father that knows his own c.   SHAK 466:9
friend or c. I speak   ARN 13:8
had been any christom c.   SHAK 443:17
happy English c.   TAYL 531:23
healthy c. well nursed is   SWIFT 526:26
heard one calling, 'C.'   HERB 247:15
He never spoils the c.   HOOD 254:19
he who gives a c. a treat   MAS 333:25
I am a c. to chiding   SHAK 476:22
If you strike a c.   SHAW 497:41
Is it well with the c.   BIBLE 51:25
is to see that every c.   RUSK 412:6
It was a crime in a c.   MAC 324:18
I was a c. and she was   POE 374:22
leave a c. alone   BROW 104:22
lie down like a tired c.   SHEL 504:11
like a froward c.   TEMP 532:9
little c. shall lead them   BIBLE 58:10
making love is c.'s play   MITF 352:26
mother's sake the c. was dear   COL 157:9
my Irish c.   WAGN 562:1
named the c. I-chabod   BIBLE 49:40
nicest c. I ever knew   BELL 38:32
On a cloud I saw a c.   BLAKE 87:9
receive one such little c.   BIBLE 67:3
room up of my absent c.   SHAK 452:20
saddling of the right to a c.   SHAW 496:27
seen A curious c.   WORD 577:16
Set his c. upon her knee   TENN 542:11
She was an aggravating c.   BELL 39:12
sing to the c. on thy knee   BRID 92:21
slayeth the c. in the womb   POUND 382:11
solitary c.   WORD 578:10
spoil the c.   BUTL 118:2
sucking c. shall play   BIBLE 58:11
that's govern'd by a c.   SHAK 481:2
This painted c. of dirt   POPE 377:1
thou show'st thee in a c.   SHAK 453:17
To have a thankless c.   SHAK 453:19
To see his active c. do   SHAK 493:13
Train up a c. in the way   BIBLE 54:22
'Twas a c. that so did   JONS 284:2
unto us a c. is born   BIBLE 58:7
use of a new-born c.   FRAN 218:19
was a c. beneath her touch   ROSS 409:22
waters wild went o'er his c.   CAMP 129:5
when a c. is born   SU T 524:19
When I was a c.   BIBLE 76:14
when thy king is a c.   BIBLE 56:3
While the c. was yet alive   BIBLE 50:22
woman forget her sucking c.   BIBLE 58:9
would not *coddle* the c.   JOHN 275:28
wretched c. expires   BELL 39:2
yet a c.   POPE 376:23
childbirth: Mountains will heave in c.
    HOR 257:18
Childe Roland: 'C. to the Dark Tower
    came   BROW 99:30
Childhood: C. is the kingdom where
    MILL 339:24
c. shows the man   MILT 350:7
From his c. onward this   HARD 238:21
Our c. used to know'   HARDY 240:14

that oft in c. solac'd me	COWP 166:2	they bare c. to them	BIBLE 45:33	c. and master spirits	SHAK 450:8
'tis the eye of c.	SHAK 460:11	those c.'s voices	VERL 556:10	c. dishes the Doctor has	GARR 221:12
Womanhood and c. fleet	LONG 316:30	thou shalt bring forth c.	BIBLE 45:21	c. of friends	COWL 164:14
childish: again towards c. treble	SHAK 425:24	thou shalt have c.	PRAY 392:18	C. words	WORD 581:1
are either knavish or c.	JOHN 278:9	We are the c. of God	BIBLE 75:9	decision or reason or c.	CHOM 148:16
c. valourous than manly	MARL 330:15	'We have c.	TENN 543:3	Each to his c.	KIPL 303:16
glamour Of c. days	LAWR 311:7	Were all thy c. kind	SHAK 443:13	honour is the *people's c.*	SHER 506:7
I put away c. things	BIBLE 76:14	When c. of one family	WATTS 565:20	in the worth and c.	JONS 283:23
It was a c. ignorance	HOOD 254:18	When the voices of c. are	BLAKE 88:3	money and you takes your c.	ANON 9:2
my c. wave of pity	BETJ 43:19	which holdeth c. from play	SIDN 508:2	more difficult the c.	ALL 3:19
Wordsworth chime his c.	BYRON 124:29	who appear to me as c.	KEATS 294:10	take c. of all my library	SHAK 486:16
childishness: Is second c.	SHAK 425:24	wife and c. hath given hostages	BACON 26:31	there were a sympathy in c.	SHAK 469:20
It does from c.	SHAK 421:27	wife and c. but as bills	BACON 26:32	was mistress of her c.	SHAK 434:1
childless: have proceeded from c. men		wiser than the c. of light	BIBLE 70:25	choir: c. of heaven and furniture	BERK 41:19
	BACON 27:4	Women, then, are only c.	CHES 145:25	c. the small gnats mourn	KEATS 293:8
children: Accustom your c. constantly		Would not have bandy c.	BLAKE 87:20	I join the c. invisible	ELIOT 201:27
	JOHN 277:20	young c.	PRAY 385:20	**choirs:** Bare ruin'd c.	SHAK 494:7
airy hopes my c.	WORD 577:14	**child-wife:** It's only my c.	DICK 177:19	**choisir:** *c'est c.*	LEVIS 314:5
all our c.'s fate	KIPL 299:6	**chill:** bitter c. it was	KEATS 289:9	**choke:** c. the word	BIBLE 66:17
be called the c. of God	BIBLE 64:6	C. on the brow	SPAR 514:22	do c. their service up	SHAK 425:7
become as little c.	BIBLE 67:2	First—C.—then Stupor	DICK 183:14	nothing but to c. a man	JONS 284:5
becometh the c. of light	PRAY 388:11	So haunt thy days and c.	KEATS 290:30	**choked:** thorns sprang up and c. them
call'd you c.	SHAK 454:5	**Chillon:** C.! thy prison is a holy			BIBLE 66:16
c. at play are not playing	MONT 354:17		BYRON 125:15	**chokes:** something bitter that c.	LUCR 320:15
C. begin by loving their	WILDE 573:30	**chilly:** c. stars I can forgo	CORY 163:5	**choking:** cat than c. her with cream
c. born of thee are sword	TENN 534:10	I feel c. and grown old	BROW 105:26		KING 297:15
c. *capable of honesty* is	RUSK 412:5	**Chiltern Hundreds:** take the C. while		c. him and making him carry	TOLS 551:15
c. carried away with every	PRAY 387:3	you can	CHES 146:13	**choleric:** captain's but a c. word	SHAK 464:4
c. *casual as birds*	AUDEN 18:5	**Chimborazo:** C., Cotopaxi	TURN 553:23	**Chommoda:** C. dicebat	CAT 137:13
c. cried in the streets	MOTL 358:20	**chime:** let your silver c.	MILT 344:10	**choose:** *can believe what we c.*	NEWM 362:16
c. died in the streets	AUDEN 18:15	some soft c. had stroked	JONS 285:10	can believe what you c.	NEWM 362:17
c. follow'd with endearing	GOLD 231:1	**Chimera:** C. in my brain	DONNE 191:2	c. A Jewish God	BROW 95:13
c. in England take pleasure	ANON 7:22	*utrum c. in vacuo bombinans*	RAB 403:29	C. an author as you choose	ROOS 408:10
c. in Holland take pleasure	ANON 7:22	**chimeras:** dire c. and enchanted isles		c. life that both thou	BIBLE 48:29
c. *innocent and charming*	AUDEN 19:12		MILT 341:12	c. love by another's eye	SHAK 469:19
c. in whom is no faith	BIBLE 48:31	other wild impossible c.	SWIFT 526:8	c. the good	BIBLE 58:3
c. like the olive-branches	PRAY 398:20	**chimes:** heard the c. at midnight	SHAK 442:6	c. Their place of rest	MILT 350:1
C. of the future age	BLAKE 87:17	hear the c. at midnight	STEV 522:2	c. thou whatever suits	COL 157:5
c., quietly talking alone	BOWEN 91:3	**chimney:** Who smoked like a c.	BARH 33:17	c. time is to save time	BACON 26:7
c.'s teeth are set	BIBLE 60:34	**chimney-piece:** Buffalo Upon the c.		I lie as lads would c.	HOUS 263:11
c. stood watching them	KING 297:2		CARR 133:11	leading wherever I c.	WHIT 571:7
C. sweeten labours	BACON 27:3	**chimneys:** good grove of c. for me		Let's c. executors	SHAK 479:10
C. with Hyacinth's temperament	SAKI 413:16		MORR 358:4	not c. not to be	HOPK 256:7
c., you should never let	WATTS 565:18	Our c. were blown down	SHAK 460:20	that c. by show	SHAK 466:19
Come my tan-faced c.	WHIT 570:10	So your c. I sweep	BLAKE 88:5	They cannot c.	THOM 547:14
committed by c. on children	BOWEN 91:3	**chimney-sweepers:** c., come to dust		To c. The Jews	EWER 209:13
doeth for the c. of men	PRAY 397:7		SHAK 428:22	**Choosing:** C. each stone	MARV 331:20
dogs than of their c.	PENN 371:15	**chin:** rye reach to the c.	PEELE 371:9	just c. so	BROW 99:25
even so are the young c.	PRAY 398:19	**China:** from C. to Peru	JOHN 282:28	**chop:** day you'll eat a pork c.	CAMP 128:7
father pitieth his own c.	PRAY 396:17	infusion of a C. plant	ADD 2:11	**chopcherry:** c. ripe within	PEELE 371:9
fathers, provoke not your c.	BIBLE 78:7	though C. fall	POPE 377:28	**chopper:** cheap and chippy c.	GILB 226:31
fathers upon the c. unto	BIBLE 47:24	Till C. and Africa meet	AUDEN 18:9	**Chops:** C. and Tomata sauce	DICK 182:19
fear death as c.	BACON 26:1	treads the Wall Of C.	PATM 370:7	**chord:** feel for the common c.	BROW 98:22
fond of c. (except boys)	CARR 136:12	ye break my best blue c.	HARDY 239:20	I struck one c. of music	PROC 401:14
He has no c.	SHAK 462:17	**Chinamen:** With C.	BELL 40:6	**chords:** *are* c. in the human mind
Her c. arise up	BIBLE 55:4	**Chinee:** heathen C. is peculiar	HARTE 242:29		DICK 176:15
her c. came from school	BURT 116:34	**Chinese:** ruined by C. cheap labour		**choristers:** go the chanting c.	LAWR 311:5
His c.'s looks	GOLD 231:26		HARTE 242:30	**chortled:** He c. in his joy	CARR 134:29
I have gathered thy c.	BIBLE 67:26	**chinks:** fill hup the c. wi' cheese	SURT 525:8	**Chorus:** C. Hymeneal	SHEL 504:20
imposed in the interest of c.	SHAW 496:24	**chintzy:** c. cheeriness	BETJ 42:10	**chose:** c. him five smooth stones	BIBLE 50:11
I never knows the c.	MARR 331:7	**chip:** Not merely a c.	BURKE 110:22	**chosen:** best c. language	AUST 22:31
keep c. quiet	SWIFT 525:31	**chipping:** c. at the countenances	DICK 176:11	c. thee in the furnace	BIBLE 59:14
kept from c. and from fools	DRYD 197:20	**chippy:** cheap and c. chopper	GILB 226:31	fast that I have c.	BIBLE 60:4
kitchen and their c.	FITZ 213:19	**chips:** given them nothing but c.	CHUR 149:21	few are c.	BIBLE 67:18
known as the C.'s Hour	LONG 316:9	**chirche:** Housbondes at c. dore she		hath c. the weak things	BIBLE 75:30
little c.'s dower	BROW 101:7		CHAU 141:31	Mary hath c. that good part	BIBLE 69:35
many c.	JOHN 274:22	**chisel:** Usura rusteth the c.	POUND 382:10	name is rather to be c.	BIBLE 54:21
me from c. who were rough	SPEN 515:11	**chitchat:** home of iridescent c.	NASH 360:3	opponent of the c. people	ARN 16:3
Men are but c. of a larger	DRYD 195:15	**chivalrie:** He loved c.	CHAU 141:9	ye are a c. generation	BIBLE 80:23
neither c. nor Gods	KIPL 298:23	**chivalry:** age of c. is gone	BURKE 111:9	Ye have not c. me	BIBLE 72:37
Nourish thy c.	BIBLE 62:6	age of c. is never past	KING 297:18	**choughs:** c. and rooks brought forth
of the c. of the light	ARN 16:3	age of c. is past	DISR 187:3		SHAK 461:24
old men and c.	PRAY 399:23	Cervantes smiled Spain's c.	BYRON 124:1	crows and c. that wing	SHAK 455:14
procreation of c.	PRAY 389:1	Christian service and true c.	SHAK 478:20	**choux:** *trouve plantant mes c.*	MONT 354:14
Rachel weeping for her c.	BIBLE 63:34	forgetful of his c.	HOMER 254:3	**Christ:** am all at once what C. is	HOPK 257:1
see his c. fed	PUDN 402:8	have a truant been to c.	SHAK 440:16	Are they ministers of C.	BIBLE 77:11
see the c. sport upon	WORD 579:12	learn the noble acts of c.	CAXT 138:4	Came C. the tiger	ELIOT 203:4
shall return us the c.	KIPL 298:9	nine-tenths of the law of c.	SAY 415:6	C. and his mother and all	HOPK 256:29
Suffer the little c.	BIBLE 68:36	Who sung of Border c.	SCOTT 416:9	C. being raised from	BIBLE 75:2
Their children's c. shall	YEATS 585:8	**choice:** being just the terrible c.	BROW 104:31	C. came and preached peace	BIBLE 77:22

C. cannot find a chamber	ANON 9:1
C. erecteth his Church	BANC 32:14
C. follows Dionysus	POUND 383:6
C. is all	BIBLE 78:26
C. our passover is sacrificed	BIBLE 75:36
C. perish in torment	SHAW 498:20
C. receive him	TENN 541:15
C. shall all be made alive	BIBLE 76:22
C.'s particular love's	BROW 104:22
C.'s stamp to boot	HERB 247:9
C. walking on the water	THOM 548:25
C. which strengtheneth	BIBLE 78:23
churches have kill'd their C.	TENN 540:14
counted loss for C.	BIBLE 78:17
draws near the birth of C.	TENN 536:17
edifying of the body of C.	BIBLE 77:28
estate C. adorned	PRAY 388:25
grey-grown speechless C.	SWIN 529:3
heathen and uphold the C.	TENN 534:11
in the bowels of C.	CROM 169:21
is C. risen from the dead	BIBLE 76:22
joint-heirs with C.	BIBLE 75:9
last kind word to C.	BROW 104:25
love of C.	BIBLE 77:25
May Lord C. enter	WILDE 572:16
me to live is C.	BIBLE 78:11
now by Baptism put on C.	PRAY 388:11
only we have hope in C.	BIBLE 76:21
Priest did offer C.	PRAY 400:9
Ring in the C. that is	TENN 537:15
Saviour C. again to Earth	MAS 333:25
stature of the fulness of C.	BIBLE 77:28
Thy everlasting mercy, C.	MAS 333:26
to be with C.	BIBLE 78:12
understood C. was a carpenter	BLAKE 87:8
unsearchable riches of C.	BIBLE 77:23
Vision of C. that thou	BLAKE 85:21
We withstood C. then	BROW 101:4
where C.'s blood streams	MARL 329:11
Christ-Church: festal light in C.	ARN 14:16
I am the Dean of C.	SPR 517:11
study at C. and All-Souls	JOHN 275:22
Christe: C. eleison	MASS 334:16
C. receive thy saule	BALL 31:6
christened: pleasing you when she was c.	SHAK 426:12
Christiad: C. than a Pauliad to his	HARDY 241:24
Christian: Because it is only C. men	CHES 146:19
buried in C. burial	SHAK 436:21
C. beauty Defects	POUND 383:8
C. boys I can scarcely	ARN 16:27
C. can only fear dying	HARE 242:3
C. hold for me the glass	ANON 10:14
C. ideal has not been tried	CHES 148:9
C. is a man who feels	YBAR 584:7
C. religion doubted	BUTL 119:13
C. religion not only was	HUME 267:21
C. resolution to find	NIET 363:8
C. service and true chivalry	SHAK 478:20
C.'s health to hustle	KIPL 301:18
darkness fell upon C.	BUNY 107:25
evidence of a naturally C. soul	TERT 544:21
good C. at her heart	POPE 377:19
hate him for he is a C.	SHAK 465:29
he is the only early C.	CHES 148:3
honourable style of a C.	BROW 96:2
I die a C.	CHAR 140:20
I mean the C. religion	FIEL 211:23
is the true wayfaring C.	MILT 351:24
It's the Early C. that	SAKI 413:9
Let every C.	BLAKE 86:10
little as a C. can	DOYLE 192:40
of his C. name a synonym	MAC 323:27
peace a C. can die	ADD 2:29
persuadest me to be a C.	BIBLE 74:27
Scratch the C. and you	ZANG 588:16
souls of C. peoples…	CHES 146:11
That I was born of C. race	WATTS 565:14

This Hebrew will turn C.	SHAK 466:5
three C. men	CAXT 138:3
tiger that hadn't *got* a C.	PUNCH 402:24
to forgive them as a c.	AUST 23:19
to form C. men	ARN 16:27
you were a C. Slave	HENL 245:10
Christianity: age come from C. and journalism	BALF 30:5
C. better than Truth will	COL 157:18
C. is part of the Common	HALE 237:13
C. is the most materialistic	TEMP 532:11
His C. was muscular	DISR 186:6
local cult called C.	HARDY 239:14
prooving C. to the Hindoos	WIS 575:10
that C. is not so much	BUTL 117:8
where C. was the religion	SWIFT 527:6
Christian name: superfluous C. lopped off	ARN 15:27
Christians: blood of C. is the seed	TERT 544:22
call themselves C. may	PRAY 385:25
C. all behave so badly	BAYL 35:9
C. have burnt each other	BYRON 122:10
what these C. are	SHAK 466:4
Christ Jesus: glory in the church by C.	BIBLE 77:26
Christmas: C. gambol oft could cheer	SCOTT 417:16
C. I no more desire a rose	SHAK 456:16
C. morning bells say 'Come	BETJ 42:8
insulting C. card	GROS 237:3
keep our C. merry still	SCOTT 417:15
that C. should fall out	ADD 2:16
'Twas the night before C.	MOORE 355:12
Christmas Day: at Home the C. is breaking	KIPL 298:13
It is C. in the Workhouse	SIMS 508:10
Christmas Eve: C., and twelve	HARDY 240:13
Christopher Robin: C. went down with Alice	MILNE 340:4
C. is saying his prayers	MILNE 340:11
Christs: C. that die upon the barricades	WILDE 572:17
chronic: It is c.	DICK 179:7
chronicle: in the c. of wasted time	SHAK 494:19
it is the c. of a solitary	ELIOT 201:16
make your c. as rich with	SHAK 443:8
chronicler: honest c. as Griffith	SHAK 447:23
chronicles: abstracts and brief c.	SHAK 432:25
Look in the c.	SHAK 484:2
Chrononhotonthologos: Where left you C.	CAREY 130:21
chub: chavender, or c.	ST L 412:27
Chuck: C. it, Smith	CHES 146:11
church: because I persecuted the c.	BIBLE 76:19
bells have knoll'd to c.	SHAK 425:23
best harmony in a c.	MILT 351:26
Broad of C. and broad	BETJ 44:14
buttress of the c.	MELB 336:22
came to the village c.	TENN 540:2
Catholick and Apostolick C.	PRAY 387:11
Christ erecteth his C.	BANC 32:14
c. and no steeple	SWIFT 528:11
C. is said to want	NEWM 361:21
c. lit but without a congregation	WELLS 568:1
C. militant here in earth	PRAY 387:12
C.'s Restoration	BETJ 43:2
C. with psalms must shout	HERB 246:26
'Come all to c.	HOUS 263:5
English C. shall be free	MAGN 327:1
equal are within the C.'s	HERB 247:10
estate of the Catholick C.	PRAY 385:25
ever was the c. for peace	BROW 99:12
fain would kill their c.	TENN 540:14
free c. in a free state	CAV 138:1
glory in the c. by Christ Jesus	BIBLE 77:26

he never passes a c. without	JOHN 274:27
Here's a c.	DICK 178:14
I like a c.	EMER 206:22
I like the silent c. before	EMER 207:40
keep thy household the C.	PRAY 386:23
nearer the C. the further	ANDR 4:8
not the c. for his mother	CYPR 170:19
other c. has ever understood	MAC 323:17
parish c. of Kentish Town	BETJ 43:18
publick Prayer in the C.	PRAY 400:8
rock I will build my c.	BIBLE 66:33
salvation outside the c.	AUG 21:19
see a c. by daylight	SHAK 472:5
some to c. repair	POPE 378:20
there must be the C.	AMBR 4:1
took young Cyril to c.	ELIOT 202:7
wet c. the size of a snail	THOM 547:7
What is a c.	COWP 168:4
who is always at c.	BLAKE 87:20
women to speak in the c.	BIBLE 76:17
churches: care of all the c.	BIBLE 77:12
C. built to please	BURNS 114:19
Down c. praise	KIPL 303:14
he must build c. then	SHAK 434:7
keep silence in the c.	BIBLE 76:16
seven c. which are in Asia	BIBLE 81:9
seven c. which are in Asia	BIBLE 81:12
churchmen: c. fain would kill their	TENN 540:14
life doth well with c.	BACON 26:33
Church of England: been the wisdom of the C.	PRAY 384:7
'C.,' I said	SHOR 507:8
Profession of the C.	CHAR 140:20
Protestant religion but the C.	FIEL 211:23
churchyard: beneath the elms in the c.	SCOTT 418:23
blown the dust of the C.	DONNE 190:23
c. thing	KEATS 289:14
devil in the same c. will	BANC 32:14
lie in Mellstock c. now	HARDY 239:17
of a little country c.	BURKE 108:6
worse taste, than in a c.	JOW 285:23
churchyards: Troop home to c.	SHAK 470:25
When c. yawn and hell itself	SHAK 434:25
Churn: Attract a Silver C.	GILB 227:24
chute: Vivre est une c. horizontale	COCT 154:12
Cicero: If I could have known C.	DICK 177:25
opinion can alienate C.	MAC 324:9
ciel: montez au c.	FIRM 212:2
cielo: Que el c. exista	BORG 89:23
cieux: Père qui êtes aux c.	PREV 400:15
cigar: c., and cigarette tobacco	DOYLE 191:16
good c. is a Smoke	KIPL 298:3
sweet post-prandial c.	BUCH 106:11
cigarette: c. is the perfect type	WILDE 573:20
Cilicia: city in C.	BIBLE 74:20
Cimber: constant C. should be banish'd	SHAK 449:25
Cinara: when dear C. was my queen	HOR 261:10
Cinarae: Sub regno C.	HOR 261:10
Cincinnatus: C. of the West	BYRON 125:9
cinco: c. en punto de la tarde	GARC 221:5
cinder: dry a c. this world	DONNE 187:20
cinders: I've made the c. fly	KIPL 298:7
cinerem: nequiquam alloquerer c.	CAT 137:15
cinguntur: his nivea c. tempora vitta	VIRG 558:20
cinnamon: c. and cloves	BEAU 36:5
tinct with c.	KEATS 289:20
cipher: c. in the state	SAV 415:5
Circe: elegance of C.'s hair	POUND 383:3
circenses: Panem et c.	JUV 287:28
circle: God is a c. of which the centre	ANON 7:27
Love is a c. that doth	HERR 249:9
Round and round the c.	ELIOT 202:10
Weave a c. round him thrice	COL 157:1

wheel is come full c.　　　SHAK 456:6
circles: Conversation is a game of c.
　　　　　　　　　　　EMER 207:14
individual c. of which we are　TROL 552:22
circuitous: foil'd c. wanderer　ARN 15:1
Circumcised: C. the eighth day　BIBLE 78:16
circumcision: c. nor uncircumcision
　　　　　　　　　　　BIBLE 78:26
circumference: everywhere and the c.
is nowhere　　　　　　　ANON 7:27
circumfused: forms and substances are
c.　　　　　　　　　　WORD 580:19
Circumlocution: C. Office was beforehand
　　　　　　　　　　　DICK 178:16
circumspectly: that ye walk c.　BIBLE 78:4
Circumspice: C., si Monumentum
　　　　　　　　　　　BARH 33:7
monumentum requiris, c.　ANON 11:2
Nisi monumentum requiris, c.　INGE 270:11
circumstance: am the very slave of c.
　　　　　　　　　　　BYRON 125:20
breasts the blows of c.　　TENN 537:1
Eternal artistries in C.　　HARDY 239:11
ignorant of this remarkable c.　MAC 324:12
In the fell clutch of c.　　HENL 245:4
Of plastic c.　　　　　　BROW 104:11
pomp, and c.　　　　　　SHAK 475:25
To a philosopher no c.　　GOLD 232:3
Circumstances: C. beyond my individual
　　　　　　　　　　　DICK 177:20
Fearful concatenation of c.　WEBS 566:16
see a husband in these c.　GAY 222:31
circumstantial: c. evidence is very strong
　　　　　　　　　　　THOR 550:24
circumvent: politician...one that would
c. God　　　　　　　　SHAK 436:27
Ciro: Bingham had never been to C.'s
　　　　　　　　　　　TRAV 552:6
cirque: always like a c. of mountains
　　　　　　　　　　　AUDEN 19:12
citadel: mountain-built with peaceful
c.　　　　　　　　　　KEATS 291:8
citadels: circle-c. there　HOPK 256:28
Cities: C. and their civilities　PATM 370:7
C. entered　　　　　　　HOUS 265:4
c. hostile and the towns　ELIOT 203:13
hell to c.　　　　　　　AESC 3:1
Of human c. torture　　　BYRON 120:35
citizen: c. of no mean city　BIBLE 74:20
greater than a private c.　TAC 531:13
he is a c. of the world　BACON 26:20
humblest c. of all　　　BRYAN 106:7
requisite of a good c.　　ROOS 408:2
citizens: Before Man made us c.　LOW 319:11
c. kneading up the honey　SHAK 443:9
first and second class c.　WILL 574:14
you fat and greasy c.　　SHAK 425:2
CITTÀ: PER ME SI VA NELLA C.
DOLENTE　　　　　　DANTE 171:3
city: all the c. on an uproar　BIBLE 74:8
Back from the C. of Sleep　KIPL 298:14
Behold now this vast c.　MILT 352:1
briskly to infect a c.　　AUDEN 18:19
citizen of no mean c.　　BIBLE 74:20
c. and I see a man hurrying　KEATS 294:17
c. consists in its men　　NIC 362:25
c., I can sometimes hear　ELIOT 205:4
c. is barren　　　　　　DICK 176:17
c. is built To music　　TENN 534:6
C. is of Night　　　　　THOM 549:27
c. state of the sponge　AUDEN 20:15
C.'s voice itself is soft　SHEL 504:8
c.: that is at unity　　　PRAY 398:11
c. that is set on an hill　BIBLE 64:8
C. with her dreaming spires　ARN 15:4
crowning c.　　　　　　BIBLE 58:16
Despising, For you, the c.　SHAK 427:24
doth the c. sit solitary　BIBLE 60:27
dream'd in a dream I saw a c. invincible
　　　　　　　　　　　WHIT 570:4

each and every town or c.　HOLM 253:16
Except the Lord keep the c.　PRAY 398:18
first c. Cain　　　　　　COWL 164:9
Happy is that c. which　ANON 5:12
have we no continuing c.　BIBLE 80:5
he looked for a c. which　BIBLE 79:32
holy c., new Jerusalem　BIBLE 82:30
in perils of the c.　　　BIBLE 77:12
live in a c.　　　　　　COLT 159:10
long in populous c. pent　MILT 349:13
looking over harbor and c.　SAND 413:26
Lord guards the c.　　　BIBLE 83:12
people went up into the c.　BIBLE 49:2
pity who know not the c.　PROW 402:2
possession of truth as of a c.　BROW 96:6
rose-red c. 'half as old　BURG 108:4
several chaps out of the C.　CHES 147:16
Shall there be evil in a c.　BIBLE 61:19
She was a maiden C.　　WORD 582:11
Soft morning, c.　　　　JOYCE 286:14
street of the c. was pure gold　BIBLE 82:33
streets and lanes of the c.　BIBLE 70:12
Sun-girt c.　　　　　　SHEL 501:24
than he that taketh a c.　BIBLE 54:9
that great c.　　　　　　BIBLE 82:16
This C. now doth　　　WORD 581:14
this great hive, the c.　COWL 164:11
thou c. of God　　　　　PRAY 395:16
to the oppressing c.　　BIBLE 61:27
We build the Perfect C.　AUDEN 19:12
went about the c. found me　BIBLE 57:2
Where the c. of the faithfullest　WHIT 570:15
who has been long in c.　KEATS 292:27
why not their c. too　　BYRON 121:32
within the C. disinterred　SHEL 502:7
Woe to the bloody c.　　BIBLE 61:26
City of London: C. remains as it is
　　　　　　　　　　　CHAM 139:4
city-square: day in the c.　BROW 105:31
cive: c., anheling, wipes　HOLM 253:16
civet: Give me an ounce of c.　SHAK 455:17
civic: ornament put upon great c. buildings
　　　　　　　　　　　RUSK 411:21
Civics: talk on 'Sex and C.　BETJ 43:1
civil: 'Always be c. to the girls　MITF 352:23
c. to folk he ne'er saw　ANST 11:8
effects from c. discord　ADD 1:25
good people, be c.　　　GWYN 237:8
In c. business　　　　　BACON 25:31
That the rude sea grew c.　SHAK 470:7
Too c. by half　　　　　SHER 506:16
civilian: meet a mushroom rich c.
　　　　　　　　　　　BYRON 126:9
civilians: those who wish to be c.
　　　　　　　　　　　ROST 410:15
civilisation: brutal in the history of c.
　　　　　　　　　　　BEEC 37:5
douceur de la c. actuelle　HUGO 267:13
life blood of real c.　　TREV 552:9
civilities: bandy c. with my Sovereign
　　　　　　　　　　　JOHN 275:20
Cities and their c.　　　PATM 370:7
Civility: C. costs nothing and buys
　　　　　　　　　　　MONT 354:10
I see a wild c.　　　　　HERR 249:2
reciprocal c. of authors　JOHN 281:29
to use the c. of my knee　BROW 96:3
civilization: botched c.　POUND 383:10
c. advances　　　　　　MAC 323:22
great elements of modern c.　CARL 131:3
resources of c. are not　GLAD 229:14
civilized: c. man cannot live without
　　　　　　　　　　　MER 338:6
last thing c. by Man　MER 337:34
civilizers: leisure are the two c.　DISR 185:9
civilizes: sex whose presence c. ours
　　　　　　　　　　　COWP 165:4
Civis: C. Romanus sum　CIC 151:28
could say *C. Romanus sum*　PALM 368:10

civium: Non c. ardor prava iubentium
　　　　　　　　　　　HOR 260:18
clad: naked every day he c.　GOLD 231:11
claes: An' some upo' their c.　BURNS 114:7
claim: last territorial c. which　HITL 251:12
clair: pas c. n'est pas français　RIV 406:10
claith: web o' the silken c.　BALL 31:18
clamavi: De profundis c. ad te　BIBLE 83:13
clan: Against the c. M'Tavish　AYT 24:6
Clan-Conuil: Summon C.　SCOTT 417:27
clank: Let 'em c.　　　WARD 564:19
Clap: C. her broad wings　FRERE 218:26
c. your hands　　　　　BARR 34:16
c. your hands together　PRAY 392:22
doors c.　　　　　　　HOUS 264:20
Soul c. its hands and sing　YEATS 586:12
clappeth: Ay c. as a mille　CHAU 142:10
clapping: tears on a soundless-c.
　　　　　　　　　　　THOM 547:24
clapte: c. the wyndow　CHAU 142:28
Clarence: perjur'd C.　SHAK 481:1
claret: c. crowns his cup　BROW 103:27
C. is the liquor for boys　JOHN 278:7
c. that 'it would be port　BENT 41:11
dozen of C. on my Tomb　KEATS 294:22
was his mutton and his c.　HOME 253:25
clarion: Her c. o'er the dreaming　SHEL 502:8
Clash: sun and the rain C.　FRY 219:26
clash'd: Was c. and hammer'd from
　　　　　　　　　　　TENN 533:22
clasp: reason why I c. them　CORY 163:6
clasps: c. the crag with crooked　TENN 533:7
class: c. distinction　　BETJ 43:6
c. struggle necessarily leads　MARX 333:1
c. the class of all classes　RUSS 412:16
Englishman of our upper c.　ARN 15:17
history of c. struggle　MARX 333:3
Like many of the upper c.　BELL 40:5
Philistines proper, or middle c.　ARN 15:19
someone of the middle c.　BELL 39:30
this c. we have a designation　ARN 15:18
classes: divisible into two great c.　BEER 37:17
masses against the c.　GLAD 229:17
ye lower middle c.　　GILB 225:35
classic: happen to have an Elzevir c.
　　　　　　　　　　　CHES 145:22
tread on c. ground　　ADD 2:4
What avails the c. bent　KIPL 298:2
classical: c. Monday Pops　GILB 227:6
C. quotation is the *parole*　JOHN 278:29
classics: Than the c. in paraphrase
　　　　　　　　　　　POUND 383:4
clatter: c. and a chatter from within
　　　　　　　　　　　ELIOT 205:4
Claudel: will pardon Paul C.　AUDEN 19:8
Claudite: C. iam rivos　VIRG 559:21
claw: Nature, red in tooth and c.　TENN 536:29
claws: been a pair of ragged c.　ELIOT 203:21
c. that catch　　　　　CARR 134:28
How neatly spreads his c.　CARR 133:18
to see her stick her c.　LOW 319:3
clay: associate of this c.　HADR 237:9
blind his soul with c.　TENN 542:19
C. lies still　　　　　　HOUS 262:15
c. say to him that fashioneth　BIBLE 59:13
cover'd thick with other c.　BYRON 120:27
knowest Who hast made the C.　KIPL 301:16
Making a woman of c.　AUDEN 21:7
of c. and wattles made　YEATS 585:17
out of the mire and c.　PRAY 392:1
Potter and c. endure　BROW 104:10
potter power over the c.　BIBLE 75:14
this the c. grew tall　OWEN 367:5
thousand scatter'd into C.　FITZ 212:8
clean: All c. and comfortable　KEATS 294:5
Brave hearts and c.　　TENN 535:5
c., verb active　　　　DICK 180:4
fear of the Lord is c.　PRAY 390:12
He did not love c. linen　JOHN 274:5
I shall be c.　　　　　PRAY 393:5

keep their teeth c.   SHAK 427:15
make it as c. as you can   TENN 532:22
Make me a c. heart   PRAY 393:6
nor Galahad c.   TENN 535:15
one more thing to keep c.   FRY 219:27
small and white and c.   MORR 358:10
so c. an ending   HOUS 264:2
that is not c. and neat   STEV 522:21
Then I was c. and brave   HOUS 263:1
these hands ne'er be c.   SHAK 462:21
cleaned: c. the windows and I swept
    GILB 228:4
cleanin: c.' his 'oss than cleanin' SURT 525:12
cleaning: We had daily c.   REED 405:5
Cleanliness: C. is, indeed   WESL 568:22
c. of the sexes stands   WHIT 570:15
Who of late for c.   CORB 162:14
cleanse: c. me from my sin   PRAY 393:4
C. the stuff'd bosom   SHAK 463:3
C. the thoughts of our   PRAY 387:7
c. thou me from my secret   PRAY 390:13
Wherewithal shall a young man c.
    PRAY 398:4
cleansed: doors of perception were c.
    BLAKE 88:28
What God hath c.   BIBLE 74:1
Clear: C. the land of evil   KIPL 303:6
c. your *mind* of cant   JOHN 279:11
is not c. is not French   RIV 406:10
night is as c. as the day   PRAY 399:5
sad road lies so c.   PATM 370:6
So c. in his great office   SHAK 459:6
clearing: very best means of c. up
    HUXL 269:7
clearing-house: c. of the world CHAM 139:4
clears: little water c. us of this SHAK 460:14
cleave: c. the general ear with SHAK 433:1
c. the wood and there am   ANON 7:11
shall c. unto his wife   BIBLE 45:13
tongue c. to the roof   PRAY 399:3
cleaveth: whose spirit c. not stedfastly
    PRAY 395:4
cleaving: c. the grass, gazelles MOORE 355:23
Clee: C. to heaven the beacon HOUS 262:12
clemens: O c., o pia   ANON 10:19
Cleopatra: C.'s nose been shorter PASC 369:6
every man's C.   DRYD 195:16
Had gone to gaze on C. too   SHAK 422:3
I will be C.   SHAK 422:23
pleased with less than C.   DRYD 195:13
squeaking C. boy   SHAK 424:3
clercs: La trahison des c.   BENDA 40:18
clergy: bishops like best in their c.
    SMITH 512:1
of what the c. tell you   JOW 286:1
that the c. were beloved   SWIFT 527:6
without the benefit o' the C.   CONG 160:4
clergyman: c. whose mendicity is only
    TEMP 532:8
good enough to be a c.   JOHN 276:7
Mr Wilkinson, a c.   FITZ 213:21
than a proud c.   FIEL 211:8
clergymen: men, women, and c. SMITH 511:8
To have with to do   DOYLE 192:40
Cleric: C. before   BUTL 117:32
Clerk: C. ther was of Oxenford CHAU 141:23
less illustrious, goes the c.   COWP 166:1
small house agent's c.   ELIOT 205:1
thought he saw a Banker's C.   CARR 133:13
clerkes: c. been noght wisest men
    CHAU 143:11
clever: c., but is it Art   KIPL 298:16
c. theft was praiseworthy   SPEN 514:33
c. to a fault   BROW 99:7
c. woman to manage a fool   KIPL 304:35
good people were c.   WORD 576:22
let who can be c.   KING 296:19
Some parts were c.   ANON 8:12
we are all c. here   FOAK 216:2
cleverest: 'You're the c. member WEBB 566:6

cleverness: c. is to be able to conceal
    LA R 310:13
cliff: In a coign of the c. between SWIN 529:17
In c. to the sea   ARN 13:2
cliffs: of the chalk c. of Dover   BALD 29:28
where down cloudy c.   ARN 14:21
white c. I never more   MAC 322:10
Yet still the solitary c.   WORD 577:27
climate: chilling c. hardly bears SWIFT 527:33
c. more uncertain than   CONG 159:17
C., or years damp my intended   MILT 349:10
in the c. or the company   JOHN 280:12
love with a cold c.   SOUT 514:18
climax: that c. of all human ills
    BYRON 122:29
climb: can teach ye how to c.   MILT 341:22
church lewd hirelings c.   MILT 347:18
c. not at all   ELIZ 206:1
Fain would I c.   RAL 404:14
I c. up into the heaven   PRAY 399:5
should I c. the look out   POUND 383:16
climb'd: While my love c. up to me
    KING 296:16
climbed: Meredith c. towards the sun
    CHES 148:7
climber: c. with a bomb in his pocket
    ORW 365:16
climber-upward: Whereto the c. turns
his   SHAK 449:5
climbing: weariness Of c. heaven SHEL 505:5
clime: after that sweet golden c. BLAKE 87:22
marvel save in Eastern c.   BURG 108:4
They change their c.   HOR 258:19
this the soil, the c.   MILT 345:9
climes: Of cloudless c. and starry
    BYRON 125:21
Cling: C., swing   ELIOT 203:16
clinging: blood-thirsty c. to life   ARN 15:24
clings: heart c. to and confides LUTH 320:18
Clive: What I like about C.   BENT 41:5
Cliveden: in C.'s proud alcove POPE 378:1
cloak: travel forth without my c. SHAK 493:11
With his martial c. around   WOLFE 576:4
cloaque: c. infect que la plus grande
    TOCQ 551:9
clock: c. collected in the tower HOUS 264:28
c. has stopped in the dark   ELIOT 202:9
c. is always slow   SERV 420:12
Court the slow c.   POPE 377:7
forgot to wind up the c.   STER 519:17
is making a c.   LA B 306:12
open with a c. striking   SHER 505:25
to stop the church c.   KILV 296:6
turned into a sort of c.   HUXL 269:8
varnish'd c. that click'd   GOLD 231:4
watch the c. for you   SHAK 493:18
clocks: c. the tongues of bawds SHAK 437:34
morning c. will ring   HOUS 262:17
clock-setter: Old Time the c. SHAK 452:18
clod: to a c. of wayward marl   SHAK 472:4
clogs: age to quit their c.   MILT 351:7
c. of that which else might   SHEL 503:12
cloister: to be in shady c. mew'd
    SHAK 469:17
To walk the studious c.'s   MILT 342:9
cloistered: fugitive and c. virtue MILT 351:24
cloisters: in quiet collegiate c.   CLOU 153:12
cloke: not dissemble nor c. them PRAY 384:9
with the knyf under the c.   CHAU 142:20
close: c. the drama with the day BERK 41:20
c. the wall up with our   SHAK 443:21
C. to the sun in lonely   TENN 533:7
C. with her, kiss her   SWIN 530:27
c. your eyes with holy   COL 157:1
Doth c. behind him tread   COL 155:27
ever best found in the c.   MILT 351:3
I have met them at c.   YEATS 585:1
still hasten to a c.   COWP 165:2
Closed: C. his eyes in endless GRAY 235:19
c. up the flesh instead   BIBLE 45:11

close-lipp'd: c. Patience for our only
    ARN 14:18
Closer: C. is He than breathing TENN 533:29
friend that sticketh c.   BIBLE 54:14
Closes: C. nothing, refuses nothing
    WHIT 571:11
fields or flowerful c.   SWIN 530:21
closet: not in a c.   CHES 145:12
one by one back in the C.   FITZ 213:5
closing time: c. in the gardens CONN 161:16
cloth: fair white linen c.   PRAY 387:6
On a c. untrue   GILB 227:7
clothe: c. my naked villany   SHAK 436:2
clothed: captains and rulers c. BIBLE 60:37
C., and in his right mind   BIBLE 68:31
c., fed and educated   RUSK 412:6
c. on with chastity   TENN 533:21
C. with transcendent brightness MILT 344:26
C. with his breath   TENN 535:23
man c. in soft raiment   BIBLE 66:2
who c. you in scarlet   BIBLE 50:17
woman c. with the sun   BIBLE 82:10
words c. in reason's   MILT 346:12
ye c. me   BIBLE 68:6
clothes: donn'd his c.   SHAK 436:2
Her c. spread wide   SHAK 436:19
his c. and had forgotten   WOD 575:28
his c. not be burned   BIBLE 53:23
Kindles in c. a wantonness   HERR 249:2
lay more c. on his feet   SHAK 443:18
liquefaction of her c.   HERR 250:8
walked away with their c.   DISR 184:14
When he put on his c.   GOLD 231:11
Who touched my c.   BIBLE 68:32
witnesses laid down their c.   BIBLE 73:28
clothing: c. for the soul divine BLAKE 85:14
come to you in sheep's c.   BIBLE 65:8
Gave thee c. of delight   BLAKE 87:26
her c. is of wrought gold   PRAY 392:1
Things in books' c.   LAMB 307:18
which love to go in long c.   BIBLE 68:37
cloth of gold: c. you cease to care
    GILB 225:30
cloths: heavens' embroidered c. YEATS 585:9
cloud: by and by a c. takes all SHAK 490:33
Choose a firm c.   POPE 377:18
c. of crimson catherine-wheels FRY 219:26
day in a pillar of a c.   BIBLE 47:21
did a sable c.   MILT 341:2
do set my bow in the c.   BIBLE 45:40
Do you see yonder c. that's   SHAK 434:22
entrails of yon labouring c.   MARL 329:13
great a c. of witnesses   BIBLE 79:35
like a c. which had outwept   SHEL 499:8
Like a fiend hid in a c.   BLAKE 87:23
little c. out of the sea   BIBLE 51:11
On a c. I saw a child   BLAKE 87:24
region c. hath mask'd him   SHAK 493:10
see a c. that's dragonish   SHAK 423:7
Stooping through a fleecy c.   MILT 342:3
swift c. to fly with thee   SHEL 502:12
Till he melted like a c.   TENN 542:14
wandered lonely as a c.   WORD 577:29
When the c. is scattered   SHEL 501:21
cloud-continents: great c. of sunset-seas
    ALDR 3:11
Cloudcuckooland: How about 'C.' ARIS 12:3
clouded: mind is c. with a doubt)
    TENN 535:27
Clouds: C. and eclipses stain both
    SHAK 493:12
c. and wind without rain   BIBLE 54:27
c. blew off from a high   BRID 92:13
c. drop fatness   PRAY 394:3
c. I'll never float   WORD 579:18
c. methought would open   SHAK 485:18
c. return after the rain   BIBLE 56:11
clouds the c. chase   MER 336:26
c. ye so much dread   COWP 165:27
dropping from the c.   THOM 549:13

he cometh with c.   BIBLE 81:10
Looks in the c.   SHAK 449:5
maketh the c. his chariot   PRAY 396:18
O c., unfold   BLAKE 86:16
of his presence his c.   PRAY 390:9
Rapid c. have drank   SHEL 504:7
regardeth the c. shall not reap   BIBLE 56:7
Sees God in c.   POPE 379:5
To let base c. o'ertake   SHAK 493:11
to this tumult in the c.   YEATS 585:15
trailing c. of glory   WORD 579:5
When dying c. contend with   SHAK 446:17
White c. on the wing   ALL 3:21
Clough: was a poor poet named C.
                                           SWIN 529:13
clouts: stones and c. make martyrs
                                           BROW 97:9
cloven-footed: be c.   BIBLE 48:6
clover: bee has quit the c.   KIPL 300:23
c. and corn lay sleeping   KING 296:18
You are knee deep in c.   LAMB 307:36
cloves: cinnamon and c.   BEAU 36:5
clown: thou art mated with a c.   TENN 538:19
club: is the best c. in London   DICK 181:13
Legion and Social C.   BETJ 42:13
rose politely in the c.   CHES 146:12
savage wields his c.   HUXL 269:3
clubable: Boswell is a very c. man
                                           JOHN 279:13
clubs: c. typical of strife   COWP 167:16
cluck'd: Has c. thee to the wars   SHAK 428:5
clue: almost invariably a c.   DOYLE 191:15
Clun: quieter place than C.   HOUS 264:8
Clunton: *C. and Clunbury*   HOUS 264:7
clutch: either hand may rightly c.   KIPL 298:8
clutching: c. the inviolable shade   ARN 14:20
C Major: C. of this life   BROW 98:22
Cnut: C., King, rowed   CAN 130:9
coach: drive a c. and six horses   RICE 406:1
hold back against the c.   TROL 553:8
rattling of a c.   DONNE 191:1
coach and six: me indifference and a
c.   COLM 158:24
coach-house: cottage with a double c.
                                           COL 156:13
coach-makers: o' mind the fairies' c.
                                           SHAK 481:28
coachman: c.'s a privileged indiwidual
                                           DICK 183:2
coal: having a live c. in his   BIBLE 57:30
is made of Newcastle c.   WALP 563:5
like a c. His eye-ball   SMART 509:3
whole world turn to c.   HERB 248:17
With a cargo of Tyne c.   MAS 333:19
With England's own c.   KIPL 298:4
coal-barges: ten dark c. are moor'd
                                           SMITH 510:5
coalition: You may call it c.   PALM 368:11
coalitions: England does not love c.
                                           DISR 184:21
coals: all eyes else dead c.   SHAK 492:10
c. of fire upon his head   BIBLE 54:29
c. of fire   PRAY 390:9
I sleep on the c.   DICK 176:33
My c. are spent   ANON 6:19
coarse: c. complexions   MILT 341:18
coarse-bred: c. son of a livery-stable
                                           YEATS 585:3
coast: Gospel's pearls upon our c.
                                           MARV 331:16
I near the shadowy c.   THOM 547:24
coaster: c. with a salt-caked smoke
                                           MAS 333:19
merry Grecian c.   ARN 14:21
coat: him a c. of many colours   BIBLE 46:26
hold my c., and snicker   ELIOT 203:23
I made my song a c.   YEATS 584:16
riband to stick in his c.   BROW 102:4
tattered c. upon a stick   YEATS 586:12
that loves a scarlet c.   HOOD 254:15

coats: Their c. were brushed   CARR 135:6
coats-of-arms: Is worth a hundred c.
                                           TENN 537:27
cobweb: that c. of the brain   BUTL 117:33
cobwebs: Laws are like c.   SWIFT 527:16
cock: before the c. crow   BIBLE 68:12
C. and a Bull   STER 520:12
c.'s shrill clarion   GRAY 234:20
Diminysh'd to her c.   SHAK 455:14
He was like a c. who thought   ELIOT 200:16
immediately the c. crew   BIBLE 68:19
on the crowing of the c.   SHAK 429:17
Our c. won't fight   BEAV 36:14
owe a c. to Aesculapius   SOCR 512:21
plump head-waiter at the C.   TENN 544:9
walks till the first c.   SHAK 454:22
While the c. with lively   MILT 342:17
cockatrice: hand on the c.' den   BIBLE 58:11
cockle: By his c. hat and staff   SHAK 435:32
Cockney: C. impudence before now
                                           RUSK 411:7
cockpit: Can this c. hold   SHAK 443:4
cocks: drown'd the c.   SHAK 454:4
cocksure: c. of anything as Tom Macaulay
                                           MELB 336:10
cockyolybirds: butterflies and c. would
                                           KING 297:13
Cocoa: C. is a vulgar beast   CHES 147:27
cocotte: Normande c.   POUND 383:14
Cocqcigrues: Till the coming of the C.
                                           KING 297:14
cod: of the bean and the c.   BOSS 90:13
stynkyng c. Fulfilled   CHAU 143:6
To change the c.'s head   SHAK 474:18
coddle: I would not c. the child   JOHN 275:28
Codlin: C.'s the friend   DICK 180:27
codling: c. when 'tis almost   SHAK 488:9
cod-piece: here's grace and a c.   SHAK 454:8
codpieces: king of c.   SHAK 456:26
coelitus: *Et emitte c.*   LANG 309:29
coepit: *Dimidium facti qui c.*   HOR 258:14
coerce: minority to c. an indifferent
                                           STEP 518:20
coeur: *c. a ses raisons que la*   PASC 369:10
l'esprit et dans le c.   LA R 310:17
que le c. est du côté   MOL 353:17
Coeur-de-Lion: reputed son of C.
                                           SHAK 452:8
co-exist: master-passions cannot c.
                                           CAMP 129:11
coffee: always put mud into c.   THAC 545:9
C. and oranges in a sunny   STEV 520:18
C., (which makes the politician   POPE 381:7
He put the c. in the cup   PREV 400:17
if this is c.   PUNCH 403:5
slavery of the tea and c.   COBB 154:7
coffee-house: to some c. I stray   GREEN 235:29
coffee spoons: measured out my life with
c.   ELIOT 203:20
coffin: becomes his c. prodigiously
                                           GOLD 232:14
like a c. clapt in a canoe   BYRON 119:29
silver plate on a c.   OCON 364:22
white-faced and still in the c.   WHIT 570:11
cofre: he but litel gold in c.   CHAU 141:24
cog: o' gude swats   BURNS 113:4
make me a c. in a machine   MACN 326:13
cogimur: *Omnes eodem c.*   HOR 260:7
cogitation: In cogibundity of c.   CAREY 130:22
cogitations: Sometimes these c. still amaze
                                           ELIOT 202:11
Cogito: *C., ergo sum*   DESC 175:10
cognizance: c. of men and things
                                           BROW 101:11
cognoscere: *potuit rerum c. causas*
                                           VIRG 560:14
coherence: all c. gone   DONNE 187:19
cohorts: c. were gleaming in purple
                                           BYRON 122:1
coign: c. of the cliff between   SWIN 529:17

nor c. of vantage   SHAK 459:4
coil: c. of his crystalline streams   SHEL 502:10
coin: Beauty is Nature's c.   MILT 341:17
I had rather c. my heart   SHAK 451:21
With the one c. for fee   HOUS 265:18
coincidence: long arm of c.   CHAM 139:12
'strange c.'   BYRON 123:22
coincident: bent By paths c.   HARDY 239:6
coiner: bright to the c.   HOUS 263:8
c. of sweet words   ARN 14:25
coins: like to c.   TENN 534:17
coition: trivial and vulgar way of c.
                                           BROW 96:33
coitu: *Foeda est in c. et brevis*   PETR 373:5
coitum: *Post c. omne animal*   ANON 10:17
cok: c. hadde in his governaunce
                                           CHAU 142:32
cold: all was as c. as any stone   SHAK 443:18
blow in c. blood   SHAW 497:41
Cast a c. eye   YEATS 587:10
caught An everlasting c.   WEBS 567:15
c. and heat   BIBLE 45:37
c. Christ and tangled Trinities   KIPL 302:2
c. coming they had of it   ANDR 4:7
c. commemorative eyes   ROSS 410:5
c., frosty, windy morning   PEPYS 371:18
c. grave she was lain   BALL 32:9
c. hearts and muddy   BURKE 111:11
c. in blood   SHAK 421:33
C. in the earth   BRON 93:22
c., my girl   SHAK 477:21
c. nymphs chaste crowns   SHAK 485:19
c. performs th' effect   MILT 346:21
c. that moderates heat   CERV 138:20
comfort like c. porridge   SHAK 485:3
crazy, c.   ROCH 407:3
darkness and the c.   STEV 522:26
Dick would hate the c.   HOUS 265:1
dwelleth i' the c. o' the moon   BROW 99:24
Even till I shrink with c.   SHAK 424:31
grow more c., more kind   SPAR 514:22
I beg c. comfort   SHAK 432:31
in the midst of a c. war   BAR 34:25
love with a c. climate   SOUT 514:18
of ink in my pen ran c.   WALP 562:23
Of those c. qualms   SOUT 514:21
place is too c. for hell   SHAK 460:17
Poor Tom's a-c.   SHAK 454:25
she alone were c.   SHAK 429:3
shelter me from the c.   BELL 40:11
she's c.   SHAK 483:22
straight is c. again   SHAK 451:24
thicks man's blood with c.   COL 155:15
thou art neither c. nor hot   BIBLE 81:20
'tis bitter c.   SHAK 429:5
To lie in c. obstruction   SHAK 464:14
warm what is c.   LANG 310:1
We called a cold a c.   BENN 40:21
ye Frost and C.   PRAY 384:22
colder: proves the pleasanter the c.
                                           BUTL 118:17
seas c. than the Hebrides   FLEC 214:7
Coldly: C., sadly descends   ARN 14:8
coldness: faithless c. of the times
                                           TENN 537:15
Coleridge: brother C. lull the babe
                                           BYRON 124:29
observed to you by C.   WORD 583:11
You will see C.   SHEL 501:18
Coliseum: While stands the C.   BYRON 121:18
Collapse: 'C. of Stout Party'   ANON 8:10
collar: braw brass c.   BURNS 115:25
collarbone: my silly old c.'s bust   BETJ 42:22
collector: sort of c. of religions   SHAW 497:12
collectors: great c. before me   DOUG 191:8
collects: beautiful c. which had soothed
                                           MAC 324:18
college: Than either school or c.   BURNS 114:8
colleges: a' their c. and schools   BURNS 115:27
discipline of c. and universities   SMITH 509:14

inquiry to the other c.	GIBB 224:8	
collegiate: faces in quiet c. cloisters		
	CLOU 153:12	
Cologne: Doth wash your city of C.		
	COL 156:5	
Colonel: C.'s Lady an' Judy O'Grady		
	KIPL 300:18	
Colonies: C. do not cease to be colonies		
	DISR 184:26	
commerce with our c.	BURKE 109:16	
My hold of the c. is	BURKE 110:2	
Colonus: Singer of sweet C.	ARN 15:10	
color: mystery of c.	SHAW 496:22	
colori: nimium ne crede c.	VIRG 559:15	
colors: c. dont quite match your	ASHF 17:7	
Colossus: genius that could cut a C.		
	JOHN 279:18	
Like a C.	SHAK 448:17	
colour: are those which love c.	RUSK 411:24	
cast thy nighted c. off	SHAK 429:23	
c. I think of little moment	BECK 36:18	
c. which I found In Lancelot	TENN 534:14	
giveth his c. in the cup	BIBLE 54:24	
Her c. comes and goes	DOBS 187:12	
life is c. and warmth	GREN 236:15	
prison for the c. of his hair	HOUS 266:8	
swear her c. is natural	SHER 506:28	
'tis a c. she abhors	SHAK 489:17	
'twas a c. he never liked	SHAK 443:19	
coloured: see the c. counties	HOUS 263:4	
Colourless: C. green ideas	CHOM 148:15	
colours: c. in the Turkey carpet	MAC 323:30	
C. seen by candle-light	BROW 98:5	
c. will agree in the dark	BACON 27:32	
His c. laid so thick	DRYD 196:7	
In goodly c. gloriously	SPEN 515:19	
made him a coat of many c.	BIBLE 46:26	
run The c. from my	BROW 98:10	
Their c. and their forms	WORD 578:6	
wrought about with divers c.	PRAY 392:16	
Colour-Sergeant: She's C. of the Nonpareil		
	DICK 176:22	
coltes: I hadde alwey a c. tooth	CHAU 143:21	
Columbia: C.! happy land	HOPK 257:8	
columbine: c. commendable	SKEL 508:18	
Pink and purple C.	SPEN 517:3	
columbines: fennel for you, and c.		
	SHAK 436:11	
column: is the stately c. broke	SCOTT 417:2	
tower like a public c.	AUDEN 19:11	
Where London's c.	POPE 378:2	
columna: La quinta c.	MOLA 352:29	
columnae: non concessere c.	HOR 258:4	
comae: Arboribusque c.	HOR 261:14	
comam: Cui flavam religas c.	HOR 259:15	
combat: c. deepens	CAMP 128:22	
him that can win the c.	BACON 26:2	
To c. may be glorious	COWP 167:10	
combatants: Involves the c.	COWP 167:3	
combattu: nous avons c. à Arques		
	HENR 245:14	
combed: rock sat down and c. their hair		
	HOUS 265:3	
combine: nations c. each cry	AUDEN 20:15	
When bad men c.	BURKE 108:22	
combustion: Of dire c. and confus'd		
	SHAK 460:20	
With hideous ruin and c.	MILT 344:24	
come: beds for all who c.	ROSS 409:12	
Cannot c., lie follows	PROU 401:24	
C. again, with the feet	HARDY 238:22	
'C. all to church	HOUS 263:5	
C., and he cometh	BIBLE 65:15	
C., friendly bombs	BETJ 44:4	
c. he slow	SCOTT 417:6	
C., Holy Spirit	LANG 309:29	
C. in the speaking silence	ROSS 408:26	
C. into the garden	TENN 540:9	
c. is strew'd with husks	SHAK 487:14	
c., let us sing	PRAY 396:3	

C. like shadows	SHAK 462:9	
C. little babe	BRET 92:6	
C., little cottage girl	PAIN 367:19	
C., my Celia	JONS 285:12	
C. not between the dragon	SHAK 453:4	
c. now no Kings nor Caesars	POUND 383:19	
c. out, thou bloody man	BIBLE 50:24	
C. over into Macedonia	BIBLE 74:6	
c. to make a show themselves	OVID 366:10	
C. unto me	BIBLE 66:5	
C. unto these yellow sands	SHAK 484:30	
c. up sometime, see me	WEST 568:27	
C. up to us and we will	BIBLE 50:2	
C. were but the Spring	ROSS 409:10	
C. what come may	SHAK 458:21	
c. when you're called	EDG 199:23	
c. with old Khayyám	FITZ 212:9	
c. with old Khayyám	FITZ 212:19	
c. without warning	DAVIS 172:20	
dreaming on things to c.	SHAK 494:21	
Even so, c., Lord Jesus	BIBLE 83:4	
He never will c. again	SHAK 436:12	
hour your Lord doth c.	BIBLE 68:1	
I c. quickly	BIBLE 83:2	
it needn't c. to that	CARR 135:24	
I will c.	HOUS 263:5	
I will not c.	SHAK 449:20	
jump the life to c.	SHAK 459:5	
King of glory shall c.	PRAY 390:24	
leave to c. unto my love	SPEN 515:26	
Lo, I c.	PRAY 392:2	
men c. for Mary or Kitty	AUST 23:22	
men may c. and men may	TENN 532:21	
mine hour is not yet c.	BIBLE 71:33	
my love is c. to me	ROSS 408:24	
O c., all ye faithful	ANON 10:4	
Of things to c. at large	SHAK 486:27	
One to c., and one to go	CARR 135:30	
Suffer me to c. to thee	WESL 568:17	
tells thee I c.	KING 296:12	
That it should c. to this	SHAK 429:28	
they c. when you do call	SHAK 439:23	
'tis not to c.	SHAK 437:15	
'twill c. to my father anon'	AUBR 17:26	
ve must all c. to it	DICK 183:1	
Very sorry can't c.	BER 41:17	
What's to c. is still unsure	SHAK 488:17	
wheel is c. full circle	SHAK 456:6	
Where did you c. from	MACD 325:2	
wherefore art thou c.	BIBLE 68:17	
which is to c.	BIBLE 81:9	
whistle, and I'll c. to you	BURNS 116:4	
Will come when it will c.	SHAK 449:18	
will it c. without warning	AUDEN 21:2	
comédie: soit la c. en tout le reste	PASC 369:8	
comedies: c. are ended by a marriage		
	BYRON 122:28	
comedy: catastrophe of the old c.		
	SHAK 453:12	
most lamentable c.	SHAK 469:23	
This world is a c. to those	WALP 563:11	
tragedy, c., history	SHAK 432:20	
comedye: myght to make in som c.		
	CHAU 144:17	
comeliness: He hath no form nor c.		
	BIBLE 59:21	
comely: black, but c.	BIBLE 56:16	
c., but not costly	LYLY 321:14	
perpetual hyperbole is c.	BACON 26:29	
thy speech is c.	BIBLE 56:26	
comer: Grasps in the c.	SHAK 487:5	
comes: all c. to the same thing	BROW 98:25	
book c. into my mouth	POUND 382:15	
c. again in the morning	SHER 506:28	
consummation c.	HARDY 239:6	
late c. round by Rome	BROW 104:24	
Look, where it c. again	SHAK 429:9	
comest: thou c. into thy kingdom	BIBLE 71:12	
Thou c., much wept	TENN 536:9	
comet: Glorious the c.'s train	SMART 509:4	

cometh: Blessed be he that c. in the Name		
	PRAY 398:3	
canst not tell whence it c.	BIBLE 71:36	
c. beauty of berries	POUND 383:18	
He c. not	TENN 539:23	
he c. with clouds	BIBLE 81:10	
Him that c. to me I will	BIBLE 72:6	
master of the house c.	BIBLE 69:1	
no man c. unto the Father	BIBLE 72:32	
comets: Old men and c. have been		
	SWIFT 527:14	
there are no c. seen	SHAK 449:18	
Ye country c.	MARV 332:12	
comfit-maker: You swear like a c.'s		
	SHAK 439:32	
comfort: another c. like to this	SHAK 474:20	
a' the c. we're to get	BURNS 115:24	
beside the waters of c.	PRAY 390:21	
carrion c., Despair	HOPK 256:7	
c. and help the weak-hearted	PRAY 385:19	
c. her	PRAY 389:3	
c. like cold porridge	SHAK 485:3	
c. of thy help again	PRAY 393:6	
C.'s a cripple and comes	DRAY 193:6	
c. serves in a whirlwind	HOPK 256:6	
c. ye my people	BIBLE 59:4	
Continual c. in a face	ROYD 411:2	
here's my c.	SHAK 485:10	
holy Sacrament to your c.	PRAY 387:18	
I beg cold c.	SHAK 452:31	
I have of c. and despair	SHAK 495:12	
Man seeketh in society c.	BACON 25:1	
neither found I any to c. me	PRAY 394:12	
not ecstasy but it was c.	DICK 178:25	
Of c. no man speak	SHAK 479:10	
requireth further c. or counsel	PRAY 387:17	
sober c.	MORE 357:11	
staff me c. still	SCOT 419:5	
Take all my c. of thy worth	SHAK 493:13	
that I may take c. a little	BIBLE 52:20	
they never knew c.	MAC 324:6	
think they carry their c.	ELIOT 201:17	
to c. all that mourn	BIBLE 60:8	
What would c. the one	GAY 222:36	
you naught for your c.	CHES 146:16	
comfortable: Christians have a c. creed		
	BYRON 122:19	
c. estate of widowhood	GAY 222:18	
c. man, with dividends	LONG 316:23	
c. words our Saviour Christ	PRAY 387:20	
c. hour canst thou name	SHAK 481:8	
Progress is a c. disease	CUMM 170:11	
comfortably: liv'd c. so long together		
	GAY 222:13	
lot of money to die c.	BUTL 118:30	
Speak ye c. to Jerusalem	BIBLE 59:4	
comforted: longing to be c.	WORD 581:2	
Lord hath c. his people	BIBLE 59:19	
they shall be c.	BIBLE 64:6	
would not be c.	BIBLE 63:34	
Comforter: C. will not come unto you		
	BIBLE 72:38	
comforters: Miserable c. are ye all		
	BIBLE 52:27	
comforting: where is your c.	HOPK 256:19	
comfortless: All dark and c.	SHAK 455:4	
c., and worn, and old	ROSS 409:2	
leave us not c.	PRAY 386:13	
comforts: c. we despise	SHAK 423:12	
loves and c. should increase	SHAK 474:20	
not without c. and hopes	BACON 25:20	
Which c. while it mocks	BROW 104:4	
comical: I often think it's c.	GILB 226:8	
coming: cold c. we had of it	ELIOT 203:12	
c. after me is preferred	BIBLE 71:29	
c. events cast their shadows	CAMP 128:24	
c. of the King of Heaven	ANON 9:1	
c. of the Son of Man	BIBLE 67:32	
c. of the Cocqcigrues	KING 297:14	
do you see nothing c.	PERR 372:25	

even as their c. hither	SHAK 456:2	**Commodity:** *C., Firmness,* and *Delight*
good both going and c.	FROST 219:1	WOTT 583:16
'He is c.	AYT 24:9	c. of good names were	SHAK 438:6
it is on the road and c.	DICK 183:9	distributed c. in the world	DESC 175:11
She is c., my dove	TENN 540:12	tickling C.	SHAK 452:14
There's a gude time c.	SCOTT 418:31	**common:** are no members of the c.
way of c. into the world	SWIFT 527:2	GILB 228:22
command: commands move only in c.		Ay, madam, it is c.	SHAK 429:24
	SHAK 462:27	base, c. and popular	SHAK 444:16
c. what you will	AUG 21:17	be the century of the c.	WALL 562:3
face Bears a c.	SHAK 427:26	Cloe is...and c. as the air	GRAN 234:6
gallant will c. the sun	SHAK 484:13	c. antipathies that I can	BROW 96:28
hast c. of every part	HERR 249:27	c. enemy and oppressor	BURKE 110:33
I may c. where I adore	SHAK 489:13	c. of silence on every	EMER 207:14
Man to c.	TENN 542:9	c. opinion and uncommon	BAG 29:15
more invitation than c.	STEE 518:6	c. pursuit of true judgement	ELIOT 205:15
mortals to c. success	ADD 1:16	c. sense and observation	BROW 96:18
not be able to c. the rain	PEPYS 372:5	c. sense and good taste	SHAW 496:12
That shall c. my heart	CRAS 169:15	c. task	KEBLE 295:4
used to sue than to c.	SCOTT 416:2	concur with the c. reader	JOHN 281:39
why people c. rather badly	COMP 159:14	dull catalogue of c. things	KEATS 290:27
commanded: God so c.	MILT 349:15	feel for the c. chord	BROW 98:22
many be c. that command	SHAK 466:20	grazed the c. of literature	JOHN 274:28
commandest: thing which thou c.		had all things c.	BIBLE 73:24
	PRAY 386:12	He nothing c. did or mean	MARV 332:9
commandment: c. of the Lord is pure		In c. things that round	WORD 580:5
	PRAY 390:12	Is much more c. where	BYRON 122:9
Commandments: chiefly learn by these		jump with c. spirits	SHAK 466:19
C.	PRAY 388:14	loathe all things held in c.	CALL 127:7
Fear God, and keep his c.	BIBLE 56:14	man is a c. murderer	SAKI 413:2
following the c. of God	PRAY 387:18	nor lose the c. touch	KIPL 300:2
hadst hearkened to my c.	BIBLE 59:15	not in the roll of c. men	SHAK 439:22
in keeping of thy c.	PRAY 386:15	of Christians are not c.	PRAY 400:12
keep my c.	BIBLE 47:24	saw nought c. on Thy Earth	KIPL 301:17
set my ten c. in your face	SHAK 446:5	stamp me back to c.	FITZ 213:12
Ten for the ten c.	ANON 6:5	steals a goose from off a c.	ANON 7:24
there aren't no Ten C.	KIPL 301:8	that call not thou c.	BIBLE 74:1
Commands: C. the beauteous files		they are not already c.	LOCKE 315:13
	VAUG 555:13	things they have in c.	BLUN 89:2
servant does not all c.	SHAK 429:1	to make it too c.	SHAK 441:14
commemorative: cold c. eyes	ROSS 410:5	to speak as the c. people	ASCH 17:4
commencement: c. et le déclin de l'amour		You c. people of the skies	WOTT 583:15
	LA B 306:13	**commonalty:** He's a very dog to the c.
Voilà le c. de la fin	TALL 531:19		SHAK 427:10
commend: c., A tim'rous foe	POPE 376:27	**common-looking:** Lord prefers c. people
forced to c. her highly	PEPYS 372:9		LINC 315:5
hands I c. my spirit	BIBLE 71:14	**commonplace:** common is the c.	TENN 536:2
hands I c. my spirit	PRAY 391:15	'C.,' said Holmes	DOYLE 192:34
That doth best c. a book	HEM 245:1	c. things and characters	SCOTT 418:37
Then I'll c. her volubility	SHAK 484:8	provided his c. book be full	SWIFT 527:4
virtue to c.	CONG 160:31	**Common Prayer:** Because they hated
commendable: Silence is only c.		C.	JORD 285:18
	SHAK 465:14	**Commons:** C., faithful to their	MACK 325:12
commendatio: *Formosa facies muta c.*		**common sense:** admixture of insipid c.
	PUBL 402:4		SAL 413:18
commendation: Small matters win great		C. is the best distributed	DESC 175:11
c.	BACON 25:36	c. and plain dealing	EMER 207:11
commendeth: discommendeth others		gift To Beauty, C.	MER 337:11
obliquely c.	BROW 95:15	Rich in saving c.	TENN 541:7
commends: me most who lavishly c.		trained and organized c.	HUXL 269:3
	CHUR 148:18	**commonwealth:** caterpillars of the c.
comment: can read the c. but myself			SHAK 479:2
	TENN 535:13	c. is fixed and stable	BURKE 110:17
C. is free but facts are	SCOTT 415:15	ever despaired of the C.	DISR 185:34
commentators: c. each dark passage		service and conduct of the c.	BURKE 108:24
shun	YOUNG 587:20	**commonwealths:** raise up c. and ruin
comments: his works are the c.	KEATS 294:13	kings	DRYD 194:5
commerce: c., and honest friendship		**commune:** c. with your own heart
	JEFF 272:8		PRAY 389:20
c. the fault of the Dutch	CANN 129:25	**communi:** *utilitatis pro c. laborans*
c. with our colonies	BURKE 109:16		THOM 546:11
disinterested c. between equals	GOLD 232:11	**communia:** *Difficile est proprie c.*
heavens fill with c.	TENN 538:24		HOR 257:17
Let there be c. between us	POUND 383:12	**communicate:** good and to c. forget
that c. which now attracts	BURKE 109:15		BIBLE 80:6
commit: c. A social science	AUDEN 21:5	**communication:** Let your c. be Yea
c. his body to the ground	PRAY 389:13		BIBLE 64:16
c. his body to the deep	PRAY 400:4	**communications:** Evil c. corrupt good
Committee: therefore got on a C.		manners	BIBLE 76:25
	CHES 147:16	**Communion:** C. of Saints	PRAY 384:26

one equal c. and Identity	DONNE 191:3
partakers of the holy C.	PRAY 387:5
should come to the holy C.	PRAY 387:17
They pluck't c. tables down	JORD 285:18
Communion-time: C. having a fair white
	PRAY 387:6
Communism: C. is Soviet power plus
	LENIN 313:22
C. with a human face	DUBC 198:24
spectre of C.	MARX 333:2
Communist: C. must grasp the truth
	MAO 328:19
What is a c.	ELL 206:11
community: c. of Europe and we must
	SAL 413:19
part of the c. of Europe	GLAD 229:18
compact: Are of imagination all c.
	SHAK 471:11
c. which exists between	GARR 221:19
life now, c., visible	WHIT 570:2
compañía: *El pan comido y la c. deshecha*
	CERV 138:14
companion: appetite is never a wise c.
	STEV 521:3
c. to owls	BIBLE 52:37
earth-born c. An' fellow-mortal
	BURNS 115:21
last C.	BELL 40:8
my c.: my guide	PRAY 393:11
only fit c. is his horse	COWP 165:6
prince a better c.	SHAK 441:12
companioned: close-c. inarticulate hour
	ROSS 409:24
companionless: c. Among the stars
	SHEL 505:5
companions: c. for middle age BACON 26:34
C. of our woe	WALSH 563:29
His best c.	GOLD 230:18
I have had c.	LAMB 308:6
Like old c. in adversity	BRY 106:9
my brethren and c.' sakes	PRAY 389:11
company: before God and this c.	PRAY 389:7
be the worst of the c.	SWIFT 526:15
c. and good discourse are	WALT 564:4
c. below your ambition	EMER 207:45
C. for carrying on an undertaking ANON 4:11
c., hath been the spoil	SHAK 440:2
c. of all faithful people	PRAY 388:3
c. of the heavenly host	BLAKE 88:29
c. of the preachers	PRAY 394:8
crowd is not c.	BACON 26:15
except the present c.	OKEE 365:2
fellows shall bear her c.	PRAY 392:1
give me your bill of c.	SWIFT 526:17
in the climate or the c.	JOHN 280:12
is what I call good c.	AUST 23:8
little love and good c.	FARQ 210:8
married life three is c.	WILDE 572:28
Punctual Delivery C.	DICK 179:33
qualified to shine in c.	SWIFT 527:1
steal out of your c.	SHAK 472:31
Take the tone of the c.	CHES 145:16
up breaks the c.	CERV 138:14
very good c.	AUBR 18:1
whose c. I delight myself	BUNY 107:39
with all the c. of heaven	PRAY 387:23
comparable: nothing c. for shortness
all	BORR 90:11
compare: been studying how I may c.
	SHAK 480:13
c. small things with great	VIRG 560:19
c. thee to a summer's day	SHAK 492:18
she belied with false c.	SHAK 495:9
will not Reason and C.	BLAKE 86:2
compared: c. unto the beasts that
	PRAY 392:28
comparison: by c. with the infirmity
	HOBB 251:22
high the heaven is in c.	PRAY 396:17
Comparisons: C. are odorous	SHAK 472:33

Confronted him with self-c.   SHAK 458:5
Comparisouns: C. doon offte gret
greuaunce   LYDG 321:7
compass: c. of the notes it ran DRYD 197:21
c. of the world   PRAY 390:23
My life is run his c.   SHAK 452:1
note to the top of my c.   SHAK 434:20
compassed: snares of death c. PRAY 397:19
compassion: is full of c. and mercy
                                 BIBLE 62:21
is full of c. and mercy   PRAY 396:16
she should not have c.   BIBLE 59:17
shutteth up his bowels of c.   BIBLE 81:4
something which excites c.   SMITH 511:31
compel: c. them to come   BIBLE 70:13
c. us to be equal upstairs   BARR 34:7
shall c. thee to go a mile   BIBLE 64:18
competency: c. lives longer SHAK 465:19
competition: anarchy and c. the laws
                                 RUSK 412:10
Approves all forms of c.   CLOU 154:1
Complacencies: C. of the peignoir
                                 STEV 520:18
complain: farmers, flourish and c.
                                 COWP 168:16
Never c. and never explain   DISR 185:30
raised a dust and then c.   BERK 41:18
To c. of the age we live   BURKE 108:17
to me to c. of rheumatism   SAKI 413:8
complainers: c. for the public to be
                                 BURKE 108:15
complaining: away through my daily
c.   PRAY 391:16
no c. in our streets   PRAY 399:13
complaint: from the words of my c.
                                 PRAY 390:16
voice of my c.   PRAY 398:23
Complaints: 'C. is many and various
                                 GRAV 234:12
c. of ill-usage contemptible   MELB 336:18
when c. are freely heard   MILT 351:20
complete: c. with hat and gloves CALV 127:16
in herself c.   MILT 349:7
completed: c. labours are pleasant CIC 151:18
complexion: clime, c., and degree
                                 SHAK 475:20
Mislike me not for my c.   SHAK 466:3
often is his gold c. dimm'd   SHAK 492:28
their health and their c.   AUST 22:17
trust too much in your c.   VIRG 559:15
compliance: by a timely c.   FIEL 211:11
to join c. with reason   BURKE 111:26
complicated: c. state of mind GILB 227:21
complies: He that c. against his BUTL 118:13
compliment: farewell c.   SHAK 482:12
feigning was called c.   SHAK 489:22
To return the c.   GILB 228:1
compliments: c. and—and love AUST 22:27
componere: inter vos tantas c. lites
                                 VIRG 559:20
parva licet c. magnis   VIRG 560:19
composed: c. and bland   ARN 14:4
conceived and c. in their wits   ARN 16:9
Composer: contemplation of the first
C.   BROW 97:1
Composing: startle C. mortals AUDEN 18:4
composition: mad c.   SHAK 482:12
compound: c. a boy   SHAK 445:14
comprehend: built to c. a lie KIPL 302:17
c. the richness and variety   HOUS 266:15
shall c. all vagrom men   SHAK 472:29
Time we may c.   BROW 96:10
When she begins to c. it   PRIOR 401:7
comprehended: darkness c. it not
                                 BIBLE 71:23
comprehends: It c. some bringer of that
                                 SHAK 471:11
comprendre: Tout c. rend très indulgent
                                 STAEL 517:15

compromise: Give me the Brown c. when
                                 HUGH 267:7
'is no doubt a c.   SHOR 507:8
compulsion: fools by heavenly c.
                                 SHAK 453:11
Give you a reason on c.   SHAK 439:5
Made happy by c.   COL 157:13
On what c. must   SHAK 467:27
sweet c. doth in music lie   MILT 340:19
compulsive: Whose icy current and c.
                                 SHAK 476:1
compunctious: That no c. visitings
                                 SHAK 459:2
compute: What's done we partly may
c.   BURNS 112:26
Comrade: C., look not on the west
                                 HOUS 264:18
comrades: Bleach the bones of c.
                                 HOUS 263:19
C., leave me here a little   TENN 538:15
of the dear love of c.   WHIT 570:5
Your c. chase e'en now   CLOU 154:4
con: taken great pains to c. SHAK 488:10
conati: Ter sunt c. imponere   VIRG 560:12
concatenation: Fearful c. of circumstances
                                 WEBS 566:16
In a c. accordingly   GOLD 232:23
concave: shout that tore hell's c. MILT 345:20
conceal: cleverness is to be able to c.
                                 LA R 310:13
express our wants as to c.   GOLD 232:5
Fate tried to c. him   HOLM 253:7
should c. it as well   AUST 23:5
us to c. our whereabouts   SAKI 413:12
yet cannot all c.   BYRON 121:22
concealed: book when the author is c.
                                 JOHN 274:23
flower grows c. in an enclosed   CAT 137:6
concealing: all-c. tunic   SHEL 502:18
hazard of c.   BURNS 113:17
Rive your c. continents   SHAK 454:10
concealment: c., like a worm SHAK 489:7
Conceit: C. in weakest bodies strongest
                                 SHAK 435:13
c., what man will do any   TROL 553:3
c. which came in his way   DRYD 198:10
he be wise in his own c.   BIBLE 54:31
him with self and vain c.   SHAK 479:11
is wiser in his own c.   BIBLE 54:35
man wise in his own c.   BIBLE 54:33
suiting With forms to his c.   SHAK 432:27
conceited: never any pity for c. people
                                 ELIOT 201:17
conceits: current and accepted for c.
                                 BACON 24:22
have beauty beat on his c.   MARL 330:1
not wise in you own c.   BIBLE 75:17
Our best c. do prove   DRAY 193:9
such c. as clownage keeps   MARL 330:2
conceive: c. you may use any language
                                 GILB 226:12
virgin shall c.   BIBLE 58:3
Whether it be the heart to c.   JUN 287:5
conceived: poetry is c. and composed
                                 ARN 16:9
sin hath my mother c. me   PRAY 393:5
There is a man child c.   BIBLE 52:11
was c. by the Holy Ghost   PRAY 384:26
Conceives: C. by idleness   SHAK 445:12
conceiving: delight in c. an Iago KEATS 294:7
thus c. and subduing both   MARL 330:11
concentrated: more and more c. in you
                                 KEATS 294:30
concentrates: it c. his mind wonderfully
                                 JOHN 277:16
Conceptions: C. equal to the soul's
                                 WORD 577:15
concern: life and its largest c. ARN 16:21
matter they had no c.   SWIFT 527:27
concerns: Think only what c. thee MILT 349:4

concert: persons acting in c. together
                                 ARAB 11:16
concertina: I've a head like a c. KIPL 298:7
concessions: c. of the weak are BURKE 109:14
conciseness: must be sacrificed to c.
                                 JOHN 281:4
conclave: In stately c. met CHES 146:24
conclaves: Kingly c. stern and cold
                                 SHEL 503:1
concluded: case is c.   AUG 22:2
conclusion: most lame and impotent c.
                                 SHAK 474:18
other is a c.   JOHN 274:11
ultimate c. in unmitigated act   KIPL 299:5
conclusions: c.—largely inarticulate
                                 KIPL 302:5
draw from it narrow c.   MILL 339:1
hath pursu'd c. infinite   SHAK 424:18
sufficient c. from insufficient BUTL 118:26
conclusive: verdict of the world is c.
                                 AUG 21:18
concord: c. of well-tuned sounds
                                 SHAK 492:25
Love-quarrels oft in pleasing c. MILT 350:26
of peace and lover of c.   PRAY 385:2
travelled a good deal in C.   THOR 550:2
truth, unity, and c.   PRAY 387:13
with c. of sweet sounds   SHAK 468:17
with the C. circling nine   THOR 550:22
Concordia: C. discors   HOR 258:20
concubines: Twenty-two acknowledged
c.   GIBB 224:25
concupiscite: sine dolo lac c. BIBLE 83:25
concurrence: fortuitous c. of atoms
                                 PALM 368:11
sweet c. of the heart   HERR 250:11
condamner: de songer à c. les gens
                                 MOL 353:20
condemn: censure or c. another BROW 96:32
C. the fault and not   SHAK 463:19
c. you to death   CARR 133:19
does some delights c.   MOL 353:26
Neither do I c. thee   BIBLE 72:11
nor the years c.   BINY 84:10
they c. recourse to war   KELL 295:8
Condemn'd: C. alike to groan GRAY 235:13
c. to have an itching palm   SHAK 451:12
condemned: c. cells of Newgate BUTL 119:12
C. to do the flitting   MER 337:17
condemns: with which Dr Johnson c.
                                 BURN 112:20
condere: Tantae molis erat Romanam
c.   VIRG 557:10
condescend: c. to men of low estate
                                 BIBLE 75:17
condition: devils in life and c. ASCH 17:3
hard c.   SHAK 444:23
man could do in that c.   PEPYS 372:1
primordial c. of liberty   BAK 29:25
conditions: c. for its solution already
                                 MARX 333:7
c. That seem unpropitious   ELIOT 202:24
govern our c.   SHAK 455:12
sorts and c. of men   PRAY 385:24
condolement: obstinate c. is a course
                                 SHAK 429:26
Conduct: C. is three-fourths ARN 16:21
c. of a losing party   BURKE 111:27
C. the prejudice of good   ANON 4:28
gentlemanly c.   ARN 16:26
into the service and c.   BURKE 108:24
nice c. of a clouded cane   POPE 381:10
regulation of c.   SPEN 514:26
right way to c. our lives   PLATO 374:1
rottenness begins in his c.   JEFF 272:11
what is c.   ARN 16:19
cones: eat the c. under his pines FROST 219:9
firs with c. upon them   LONG 317:10
confederacy: dunces are all in c. against
                                 SWIFT 527:8

Confederate: in games C.   WORD 577:25
conference: c. a ready man   BACON 27:20
   c. With the dead   WEBS 566:22
   naked into the c. chamber   BEVAN 44:17
confess: c. them with an humble   PRAY 384:9
   C. yourself to heaven   SHAK 435:15
   I c. to almighty God   MASS 334:15
confess'd: half absolv'd who has c.
     PRIOR 400:18
confessed: c. that they were strangers
     BIBLE 79:33
confessing: ill-using them and then c.
   it   TROL 552:24
confession: humble c. to Almighty God
     PRAY 387:18
confide: c. their views to none   KIPL 302:5
confidence: c. and faith of the heart
     LUTH 320:17
   c. is a plant of slow growth   PITT 373:22
   In quietness and in c.   BIBLE 58:27
confident: c. thou'lt raise me with
     GRAH 233:16
   Flushed and c.   IBSEN 269:23
   Never glad c. morning again   BROW 102:8
confides: heart clings to and c.   LUTH 320:18
confine: verge Of her c.   SHAK 453:25
confined: execution c.   SHAK 486:33
confirm: c. the feeble knees   BIBLE 58:33
confiscate: c. for safety every private
     AUDEN 19:11
confiscation: We have legalized c. DISR 185:6
confitentem: Habes c. reum   PETR 373:4
Confiteor: C. *Deo omnipotenti* MASS 334:15
conflict: in the field of human c.   CHUR 150:2
   in this c. of opinions   JOHN 280:21
conform: God they would either c.
     PEPYS 372:12
conformable: is very consonant and c.
     NEWT 362:18
Con-found: C. all presents wot eat
     SURT 525:14
   C. their politics   CAREY 130:25
   world to c. the wise   BIBLE 75:30
confounded: Confusion worse c.   MILT 347:6
   let me never be c.   PRAY 384:18
confounding: Neither c. the Persons
     PRAY 385:12
confundar: non c. in aeternum   ANON 11:4
confusion: All else c.   TENN 542:9
   bright things come to c.   SHAK 469:20
   C. now hath made his masterpiece
     SHAK 460:22
   C. on thy banners wait   GRAY 234:14
   C. worse confounded   MILT 347:6
   from a couch in some c.   CONG 161:4
confute: man can tell how to c. him
     SELD 419:21
   not to contradict and c.   BACON 27:18
congratulate: Friends to c. their friends
     DRYD 197:30
congregation: church lit but without a
   c.   WELLS 568:11
   c. of the poor for ever   PRAY 394:24
   in the face of this c.   PRAY 388:24
   landlord to the whole c.   ADD 2:12
   latter has the largest c.   DEFOE 173:11
   pestilent c. of vapours   SHAK 432:15
   praise the Lord in the c.   PRAY 391:6
   so that the C. be thereby   PRAY 387:5
Congregations: all C. committed to their
     PRAY 385:7
congrès: Le c. ne marche pas
     LIGNE 314:12
conies: stony rocks for the c.   PRAY 397:1
conjecture: are not beyond all c. BROW 97:14
   Now entertain c. of a time   SHAK 444:9
conjunction: Is the c. of the mind
     MARV 331:19
   without c.   BROW 96:33
conjuration: What c.   SHAK 473:24
conjuring: Parson left c.   SELD 419:24

connaissance: L'amitié de la c.   BUSS 117:5
connaît: l'univers et ne se c. pas LA F 306:20
conn'd: c. by rote   SHAK 451:23
connect: Only c. the prose   FORS 217:2
connectin'-rod: in the stride o' yon c.
     KIPL 301:2
connubial: Mysterious of c. love refus'd
     MILT 348:7
   nothing wrong in a c. kiss   BYRON 122:27
conquer: Antony Should c. Antony
     SHAK 423:13
   c. or die who've no retreat   GAY 223:27
   hard to catch and c.   MER 337:2
   It was easier to c. it   WALP 563:7
   Like Douglas c.   HOME 253:24
   that did his master c.   SHAK 422:18
   that was wont to c. others   SHAK 478:20
   this sign shalt thou c.   CONS 162:6
   we will c.   BEE 37:3
   You cannot c. Time   AUDEN 18:10
conquer'd: hath c. thee   ARN 15:7
conquered: c., O pale Galilean   SWIN 530:5
   have c. and peopled half   SEEL 419:16
   I came, I saw, I c.   CAES 126:29
   is perpetually to be c.   BURKE 109:19
   I will be c.   JOHN 279:26
   through time time is c.   ELIOT 202:16
conquering: c., and to conquer   BIBLE 81:28
   c. hero comes   MOR 357:21
   C. kings their titles take   CHAN 139:19
Conqueror: came in with Richard C.
     SHAK 484:2
   Came-over-with-the-C. type   WATS 565:13
   every c. creates a Muse   WALL 562:12
   overcame her wild c.   HOR 259:2
   proud foot of a c.   SHAK 453:1
   We came in with the C.   BROME 93:12
conquerynge: so sharp the c.   CHAU 143:32
conquest: c. of the earth   CONR 161:17
   fann'd by C.'s crimson wing   GRAY 234:14
   foreign c. and subjugation   WEBS 566:12
   Hath made a shameful c.   SHAK 478:20
   Roman C. was   SELL 420:2
   will end in c. and robbery   JOHN 281:25
conquests: his carnage and his c.
     BYRON 120:4
   only honourable c.   BURKE 110:7
   To spread her c. farther   BURNS 112:37
consanguineous: Am not I c.   SHAK 488:1
conscia: mens sibi c. recti   VIRG 557:18
conscience: catch the c. of the king
     SHAK 433:6
   celestial fire, called c.   WASH 565:3
   C. has no more to do with   SHER 506:6
   C. is a coward   GOLD 232:38
   C. is but a word that cowards   SHAK 481:17
   c. void of offence   BIBLE 74:22
   c. with injustice is corrupted   SHAK 446:6
   coward c.   SHAK 481:13
   cut my c. to fit this year's   HELL 244:15
   freedom of c.   TWAIN 554:7
   freely according to c.   MILT 352:4
   Has crept too near his c.   SHAK 446:28
   have nothing on your c.   HOR 258:9
   my c. says   SHAK 466:7
   My c. hath a thousand several   SHAK 481:14
   Nonconformist C. makes cowards BEER 37:19
   some c. of what they did   CROM 169:20
   still and quiet c.   SHAK 447:10
   their c. as their King   TENN 534:11
   thus be c.-calm'd   KEATS 290:30
   Thus c. doth make cowards   SHAK 433:8
   uncreated c. of my race   JOYCE 286:19
   We may live without c.   MER 338:6
   whereof our c. is afraid   PRAY 386:20
   with a quiet c.   PRAY 387:17
conscience-stricken: he wearing such
   a c. air   HOUS 266:8
conscious: c. stone to beauty grew
     EMER 206:23

   is to be c. of none   CARL 131:32
consciousness: Allow but a little c.
     ELIOT 202:16
   multiplicity of agreeable c.   JOHN 275:17
   suspended in the chamber of c. JAMES 271:11
conscire: Nil c. sibi   HOR 258:9
consecrate: I c. to thee   LAND 308:26
consecrated: George III was a kind of
   'c. obstruction'   BAG 29:1
   not buried in c. ground   HARDY 241:18
consecration: c., and the Poet's dream
     WORD 577:4
consent: c. began to make excuse
     BIBLE 70:10
   his c. either expressed   CAMD 128:4
   like enough to c.   SHAK 426:21
   Rome is the c. of heaven   JONS 283:19
   secretly...Thou shalt not c.   BIBLE 48:24
   whispering 'I will ne'er c.'   BYRON 122:11
consented: c. together in holy wedlock
     PRAY 389:7
   will ne'er consent'—c.   BYRON 122:11
consenting: c. language of the heart
     GAY 223:5
   Saul was c. unto his death   BIBLE 73:29
consequence: c. of cabinet government
     BAG 28:23
   If it's business of c.   BARH 33:10
   It's of no c.   DICK 177:30
   mistake subsequence for c.   JOHN 273:29
   wisdom in the scorn of c.   TENN 541:19
Consequences: Almost inevitable C.
     KIPL 305:3
   prevent it and to damn the c.   MILN 340:18
   there are c.   ING 270:18
consequentially: reasoned or acted c.
     CHES 145:25
conservation: without the means of its
   c.   BURKE 111:4
Conservatism: barren thing this C.
     DISR 185:41
   C. discards Prescription   DISR 185:37
   What is c.   LINC 314:16
Conservative: 'A sound C. government
     DISR 185:38
   C. Government is an organized DISR 184:16
   else a little C.   GILB 226:8
   That man's the true C.   TENN 533:26
   which makes a man more c.   KEYN 295:15
Conservatives: C. by the law of their
     MILL 339:2
   They are c. after dinner   EMER 207:25
conserver: que j'ai mission de c. FRAN 217:25
Consider: C. anything   CARR 135:17
   c. her ways   BIBLE 53:21
   c. how my light is spent   MILT 351:10
   c. how my life is spent   NASH 360:1
   C. the lilies of the field   BIBLE 64:30
   day of adversity c.   BIBLE 55:21
   I will c. thy heavens   PRAY 389:28
   I will c. my Cat Jeoffry   SMART 508:21
   let thine ears c. well   PRAY 398:23
   Stop and c.   KEATS 292:6
   to weigh and c.   BACON 27:18
considerable: appear c. in his native
     JOHN 276:1
Considerate: C. *la vostra semenza*
     DANTE 171:13
Consideration: C. like an angel came
     SHAK 443:5
   on carpet c.   SHAK 490:14
considered: have c. the days of old
     PRAY 395:2
consiliis: Misce stultitiam c.   HOR 261:20
consistency: foolish c. is the hobgoblin
     EMER 207:38
consolation: c. in a distressed one AUST 23:7
   Kate of my c.   SHAK 484:7
consolations: c. of middle-aged reformers
     SAKI 413:3

console: c. us when we fall   BURKE 110:19
consolidates: kindness and c. society
     JOHN 280:6
consonant: Nature is very c. and
   conformable   NEWT 362:18
consort: such c. as they keep   MILT 342:8
Conspicuous: C. consumption of valuable
     VEBL 556:1
was c. by its presence   RUSS 412:20
conspiracies: All professions are c.
     SHAW 496:21
conspiracy: c. against the manhood
     EMER 207:36
c. against the public   SMITH 509:10
'c. of silence' concerning   COMTE 159:15
less than a vast c.   WELLS 568:15
O c.! Sham'st thou   SHAK 449:7
conspirators: All the c.   SHAK 452:7
conspire: thou and I with Fate c.   FITZ 213:16
Conspired: C. against our God with
     MARL 329:6
conspires: world c. to praise her   POPE 380:26
Conspiring: C. with him how to load
     KEATS 293:5
constable: it was a c.'s handbook   KING 297:7
constabulary: When c. duty's to be done
     GILB 228:19
constancy: blessings of marriage and
   the c.   SHAW 497:32
C. alone is strange   ROCH 406:15
c. lives in realms above   COL 156:4
c. of the women who love   SHAW 498:9
is but c. in a good   BROW 96:15
no object worth its c.   SHEL 505:5
O c.! be strong   SHAK 449:22
Of c. to a bad   BYRON 126:6
to stablish dangerous c.   DONNE 189:18
constant: c. as the northern star   SHAK 449:25
c. do remain to keep him   SHAK 449:25
c. image of the creature   SHAK 488:27
C. in nothing but inconstancy   BARN 34:3
C., in Nature were inconstancy   COWL 164:10
c. service of the antique   SHAK 425:7
C. you are   SHAK 438:32
Friendship is c. in all   SHAK 472:7
if thou wilt be c. then   GRAH 233:15
in a c. course of nature   DONNE 190:24
Like to a c. woman   FORD 216:14
nothing in this world c.   SWIFT 527:17
One here will c. be   BUNY 107:36
sense of a c. infelicity   TAYL 532:4
She is so c. to me   KEATS 289:5
Such a c. lover   SUCK 524:14
To one thing c. never   SHAK 472:16
were man But c.   SHAK 491:6
whatsoever is grave and c.   JOYCE 286:17
Constantinople: Russians shall not have
   C.   HUNT 268:3
constellated: c. flower that never sets
     SHEL 503:18
constellations: c. of feeling   DOUG 191:7
not want the c. any nearer   WHIT 571:8
strange-eyed c. reign   HARDY 239:9
Constitution: C., in all its provisions
     CHASE 141:3
country has its own c.   ANON 5:5
Everybody talks of the c.   WALP 563:6
higher law than the C.   SEW 420:15
I am of a c. so general   BROW 96:27
invoke the genius of the C.   PITT 373:28
principle of the English c.   BLAC 85:5
principles of a free c.   GIBB 224:22
proportioned to the human c.   BERK 41:21
purpose to construe the C.   LINC 314:18
very essence of the c.   JUN 287:2
constitutional: c. guardian   GILB 226:2
c. right of amending it   LINC 314:19
no eyes but c. eyes   LINC 315:7
constitutions: c. of later Greece ruled
     BAG 28:28

constrained: c. to dwell with Mesech
     PRAY 398:7
violence c. to do anything   ELIZ 205:25
constreyned: nat been c. by maistrye
     CHAU 142:12
constructed: defences of peace must
   be c.   ANON 7:16
constructing: last thing one knows in
   c.   PASC 369:3
construction: mind's c. in the face
     SHAK 458:22
constructions: secret of decorating her
   c.   TROL 552:16
constructs: worse. It c. it   COMP 159:13
construe: to c. the Constitution   LINC 314:18
consul: born when I was c.   CIC 152:2
consule: *natam me c. Romam*   CIC 152:2
consules: *Caveant c. ne quid res publica*
     ANON 10:10
consuls: c. see to it that no harm   ANON 10:10
consulted: right to be c.   BAG 29:3
consults: he neither c. them about
     CHES 145:26
consume: born to c. resources   HOR 258:13
c. happiness without producing   SHAW 496:13
their beauty shall c.   PRAY 393:1
They c. little more than   SMITH 509:9
consumed: bush was not c.   BIBLE 47:3
my bones c. away through   PRAY 391:16
consumer: In a c. society there are   ILL 270:5
consumere: *numerus sumus et fruges*
   c.   HOR 258:13
Consumes: cruel immortality C.   TENN 543:11
consummation: c. comes   HARDY 239:6
c. Devoutly to be wish'd   SHAK 433:8
Quiet c. have   SHAK 428:22
consummatum: *'c. est*   BEDE 37:2
C. est   BIBLE 83:23
consumption: against this c. of the purse
     SHAK 441:16
Conspicuous c. of valuable   VEBL 556:1
contact: *deux fantaisies et le c.*   CHAM 139:15
contagion: c. of the world's slow   SHEL 499:21
C. to this world   SHAK 434:25
Rot inwardly and foul c.   MILT 343:13
vile c. of the night   SHAK 449:13
Contaminate: C. our fingers with base
     SHAK 451:13
contemn'd: Than still c. and flatter'd
     SHAK 455:5
contemned: it would utterly be c.
     BIBLE 57:12
contemneth: c. small things shall fall
     BIBLE 63:7
contemplates: in the mind which c. them
     HUME 267:17
contemplation: c. of the first Composer
     BROW 97:1
c. he and valour formed   MILT 347:22
C. makes a rare turkey-cock   SHAK 489:11
Has left for c.   BETJ 43:2
is engaged in a rapt c.   ELIOT 204:6
mind serene for c.   GAY 223:1
with her best nurse C.   MILT 341:8
contemplative: fools should be so deep-c.
     SHAK 425:20
contempt: c. and anger of his lip
     SHAK 489:24
C., farewell   SHAK 472:22
c. of God's good gifts   JAM 271:4
c. too high   COWL 164:13
moderns without c.   CHES 145:20
religion when in rags and c.   BUNY 107:19
they looked down with c.   MAC 323:26
was only an Object of C.   AUST 22:25
contemptible: complaints of ill-usage
   c.   MELB 336:18
c. little Army   WILH 574·4
sacrifice in a c. struggle   BURKE 108:·2
those poor c. men   CROM 170:3

contend: Let's c. no more   BROW 105:35
thought c. is the policy   MAO 328:18
contending: c. against some being
     WHIT 570:1
C. with the fretful elements   SHAK 454:3
let fierce c. nations know   ADD 1:25
content: Be c. with your wages   BIBLE 69:15
c. surpassing wealth   SHEL 504:10
C. thyself with thine estate   SURR 524:21
C. to breathe his native   POPE 380:23
c.! whate'er thy name   POPE 379:21
c. with six foot   BROW 97:24
c. with a vegetable love   GILB 227:23
c. with what we spoiled   OWEN 367:11
c. with my harm   SHAK 426:4
c. with his fortunes fit   SHAK 454:12
hath her c. so absolute   SHAK 474:20
land of lost c.   HOUS 263:22
money, means, and c.   SHAK 426:3
Nothing less will c. me   BURKE 109:20
remaining c. with half-knowledge
     KEATS 293:19
sweet C.   BARN 33:27
sweet c.   DEKK 173:20
Contented: C. if he might enjoy   WORD 580:5
C. wi' little and cantie   BURNS 113:4
he was c. there   ARIS 12:4
king shall be c.   SHAK 479:15
no one lives c.   HOR 261:21
With what I most enjoy c.   SHAK 493:6
contentedness: procurer of c.   WALT 564:3
contention: Let the long c. cease   ARN 13:14
strife and a man of c.   BIBLE 60:23
swears he will have no c.   LAND 308:21
contentious: day and a c. woman   BIBLE 54:39
Contentment: C. is a sleepy thing
     TRAH 552:2
Preaches c. to that toad   KIPL 302:1
what c. find   MILT 349:6
contents: Its c. worn out   FRAN 218:20
Contentus: C. vivat   HOR 261:21
contest: Great c. follows   COWP 167:3
contests: such great c. as these   VIRG 560:18
continency: c.—but not yet   AUG 21:14
You impose c. upon us   AUG 21:17
continent: c.,— Weary of solid firmness
     SHAK 442:1
C. will not suffer England   DISR 184:11
destiny to overspread the c.   OSUL 365:23
man is a piece of the C.   DONNE 190:20
continentiam: *Imperas nobis c.*   AUG 21:17
continents: nations and three separate
   c.   DOYLE 192:29
continual: c. dew of thy blessing   PRAY 385:7
continuance: c., I don't know   SURR 525:20
household of c.   SURR 524:20
Patient c. in well doing   BIBLE 74:33
which in c. of time hath   PRAY 384:8
continue: c. thine for ever   PRAY 388:22
runagates c. in scarceness   PRAY 394:7
which once begun will c.   BACON 26:10
continued: works, begun, c.   PRAY 388:6
continueth: Here c. to rot   ARB 11:21
continuing: c. unto the end until it
     DRAKE 193:1
here have we no c. city   BIBLE 80:5
contortions: c. of the Sibyl without
     BURKE 112:14
contract: every c. to make the terms
     EMER 207:4
healthy or proper c.   CHUR 149:25
nothing but a civil c.   SELD 419:23
Social C. is nothing more   WELLS 568:15
contradict: Do I c. myself   WHIT 571:5
I never c.   DISR 187:5
Read not to c. and confute   BACON 27:18
truth which you cannot c.   PLATO 374:12
contradicted: I dogmatise and am c.
     JOHN 280:21

contradicting: soon think of c. a Bishop JOHN 279:14
contradiction: It is a c. in terms SHAW 498:19
they brook no c. WEBS 566:28
Woman's at best a c. still POPE 377:29
contradictions: bundle of c. COLT 159:11
hath been one chain of c. CLARE 152:5
contrairy: everythink goes c. with me DICK 176:27
contrariwise: c. blessing BIBLE 80:30
'C.,' continued Tweedledee CARR 135:2
contrary: c. to custom and experience HUME 267:21
c. to the decrees of Caesar BIBLE 74:9
trial is by what is c. MILT 351:24
contrast: mere c. for masculinity RILKE 406:5
contree: Know thy c. CHAU 144:22
contrite: broken and c. heart PRAY 393:8
sighing of a c. heart PRAY 385:22
contrivance: Government is a c. of human wisdom BURKE 111:8
contrivances: wisdom of human c. BURKE 109:18
contrive: c. To save appearances MILT 349:3
How Nature always does c. GILB 226:8
control: Who can c. his fate SHAK 477:19
controlled: plainly that events have c. LINC 315:1
controversy: c. is either superfluous NEWM 362:10
contumely: proud man's c. SHAK 433:8
convenience: c. of the business BURKE 108:16
C. next suggested elbow-chairs COWP 166:28
convenient: feed me with food c. BIBLE 54:45
convent: c. of the Sacred Heart ELIOT 204:16
high up in the c. wall AUDEN 21:1
Nuns fret not at their c.'s WORD 582:7
Convention: To the Lords of C. 'twas SCOTT 415:20
Conventionality: C. is not morality BRON 93:14
conversant: is always c. in himself DONNE 190:22
conversation: brisk as a bee in c. JOHN 274:1
C. is a game of circles EMER 207:14
c. perfectly delightful SMITH 511:13
have a great deal of c. AUST 23:8
ignorance cramps my c. HOPE 255:30
pleasures of life is c. SMITH 511:28
proper subject of c. CHES 146:4
Questioning is not the mode of c. JOHN 276:37
That is the happiest c. JOHN 276:26
those soft parts of c. SHAK 475:21
who is always spoiling c. MAC 324:26
you stick on c.'s burrs HOLM 253:12
conversations: after-dinner c. over the wine THOR 550:15
'without pictures or c. CARR 133:14
converse: between them and rational c. WOLL 576:10
c. with the mighty dead THOM 549:24
Form'd by thy c. POPE 380:3
sweet c. of an innocent mind KEATS 292:20
Converses: C. at the door apart ELIOT 204:16
conversing: c. with W.H.'s forehead HAZL 243:14
conversion: Till the c. of the Jews MARV 332:18
converted: Except ye be c. BIBLE 67:2
to be c. at a revival STEV 522:2
When love, c. SHAK 493:14
converting: c. the soul PRAY 390:12
Convey: 'C.,' the wise call it SHAK 469:4
conviction: best lack all c. YEATS 586:15
triumphant c. of strength CONR 161:24
Convictions: Such Dimity C. DICK 184:3
convince: people labouring to c. JOHN 275:2
we c. ourselves JUN 287:4

convincing: c. myself that I am right AUST 23:27
not for the sake of c. BLAKE 87:11
thought of c. GOLD 231:17
too c.—dangerously dear BYRON 121:34
convoy: crowns for c. put into SHAK 445:3
convulsions: gall'ry in c. hurl'd POPE 376:21
conwiviality: kindled at the taper of c. DICK 180:25
Coodle: Lord C. would go out DICK 176:21
cook: c. and a captain bold GILB 225:16
C. is a little unnerved BETJ 42:19
tell William c. SHAK 442:22
very uncommon c. SAKI 413:2
Cookery: C. is become an art BURT 116:19
Kissing don't last: c. do MER 338:1
cooking: tragedy of English c. MORP 358:2
cooks: as c. go she went SAKI 413:10
cannot live without c. MER 338:6
c. are gentlemen BURT 116:19
Devil sends c. GARR 221:12
entrusted to 'plain' c. MORP 358:2
hire me twenty cunning c. SHAK 483:20
lik'd those literary c. MORE 357:9
praise it, not the c. HAR 242:9
there been a *Synod of C.* JOHN 275:13
With a legion of c. BYRON 124:41
cool: garden in the c. of the day BIBLE 45:16
So c. a purple KEATS 289:4
Cool'd: C. a long age in the deep-delved KEATS 291:18
cool-hair'd: Lifting the c. creepers ARN 14:21
coolness: of c. plays upon his face ARN 12:22
coomb: His c. was redder than CHAU 142:32
lonely barton by yonder c. HARDY 240:14
co-operation: Government and c. are RUSK 412:10
coot: haunts of c. and hern TENN 532:20
cope: c. him in these sullen SHAK 425:3
Cophetua: Before the king C. TENN 532:16
copia: Inopem me c. fecit OVID 366:15
copied: I c. all the letters GILB 228:5
copier: c. of nature can never REYN 405:17
copies: I find I must keep c. CONG 160:37
Copper: C. for the craftsman cunning KIPL 298:15
copse: Under a c. SHEL 503:17
copula: Quos irrupta tenet c. HOR 259:21
copulation: c. and death ELIOT 204:12
Let c. thrive SHAK 455:16
copy: according to my c. CAXT 138:4
leave the world no c. SHAK 488:12
statuaries loved to c. MAC 323:33
Copybook: Gods of the C. Headings KIPL 299:16
copyrights: English authors their c. TROL 552:12
coquetry: c. of public opinion BURKE 110:15
Cor: C. ad cor loquitur NEWM 362:7
corages: priketh hem nature in hir c.) CHAU 141:8
coral: c. aboute hire arm she CHAU 141:17
C. is far more red than SHAK 495:8
Of his bones are c. made SHAK 484:32
redder than the fyn c. CHAU 142:32
coranto: come home in a c. SHAK 488:1
corbies: I heard twa c. making BALL 32:8
cord: c. however fine into WHEW 569:16
ever the silver c. be loosed BIBLE 56:11
threefold c. is not quickly BIBLE 55:15
triple c. BURKE 112:5
unto the bow the c. is LONG 317:12
corda: Sursum c. MASS 335:2
cords: cast away their c. from us PRAY 389:16
made a scourge of small c. BIBLE 71:35
core: ain't-a-going to be no c. TWAIN 554:17
sweet as the rind was the c. SWIN 529:8
Corinth: lucky enough to get to C. HOR 258:21

Corinthum: homini contingit adire C. HOR 258:21
cork-heel'd: wat their c. shoon BALL 31:19
corking-pin: c. stuck through his tail BARH 33:5
corkscrew: clean tumbler, and a c. DICK 180:20
corkscrews: heart are as crooked as c. AUDEN 18:13
cormorant: common c. or shag ISH 270:27
Sat like a c. MILT 347:16
spite of c. devouring Time SHAK 456:14
corn: better stop raising c. LEASE 313:4
breast high amid the c. HOOD 255:4
c. is but a field of tares TICH 551:2
c. that makes the holy MAS 333:26
c. was orient and immortal TRAH 551:18
he treadeth out the c. BIBLE 48:25
In our sustaining c. SHAK 455:13
meadows rich with c. WHIT 571:15
raise the price of c. BYRON 119:26
stand so thick with c. PRAY 394:3
tears amid the alien c. KEATS 291:23
that there was c. in Egypt BIBLE 46:33
there was c. HERB 247:14
two ears of c. SWIFT 526:6
Was yellow like ripe c. ROSS 409:15
Where the clover and c. KING 296:18
Cornea: C., qua veris facilis VIRG 559:3
Corneille: C. is to Shakespeare JOHN 280:8
corner: c. in the thing I love SHAK 475:21
c. of a foreign field BROO 94:30
c. of the world smiles HOR 260:8
drive like into a c. THOR 550:16
head-stone in the c. PRAY 398:2
Sits the wind in that c. SHAK 472:17
thing was not done in a c. BIBLE 74:26
corners: all the c. of the earth PRAY 396:4
polished c. of the temple PRAY 399:12
round earth's imagined c. DONNE 189:3
sheet knit at the four c. BIBLE 73:37
three c. of the world SHAK 453:1
Unregarded age in c. thrown SHAK 425:4
cornet: hear the sound of the c. BIBLE 61:3
cornfield: o'er the green c. did pass SHAK 427:2
Cornish: Here's twenty thousand C. men HAWK 243:4
corns: shower your shooting c. SWIFT 527:26
Coromandel: On the coast of C. LEAR 311:25
Coronation: Bring C. SPEN 517:3
reject a petrarchal c. KEATS 293:12
coronet: proud bride of a ducal c. DICK 179:32
coronets: hearts are more than c. TENN 537:29
Corporal: drink and blacking the C.'s KIPL 298:7
Corporations: C. have neither bodies THUR 550:32
corpore: mens sana in c. sano JUV 288:4
Corporis: C. mysterium THOM 546:16
corpse: begin and carry up this c. BROW 100:32
c. in the case with a sad BARH 33:16
Each like a c. within its SHEL 502:8
frozen c. was he LONG 317:21
He'd make a lovely c. DICK 179:14
Leave the c. uninterr'd SCOTT 417:28
makes a very handsome c. GOLD 232:14
slovenly, unhandsome c. SHAK 438:14
this c. which is man SWIN 530:9
you've got a nice *fresh* c. TWAIN 554:13
Corpses: C. are set to banquet POUND 382:11
loves into c. or wives SWIN 529:10
To mock the riddled c. SASS 414:12
corpus: Ave verum c. ANON 10:9
corpuscula: Quantula sint hominum c. JUV 288:3
correct: All present and c. ANON 4:15
c., insert, refine SWIFT 527:34

critical than to be c.   DISR 184:23
each has his own c. way   TER 544:19
with Plato than be c. with   CIC 152:1
correcteth: whom the Lord loveth he
c.   BIBLE 53:15
Correggio: correggiosity of C.   CARL 131:19
Correggios: C., and stuff   GOLD 231:21
corregiescity: c. of Corregio   STER 519:29
Corregio: corregiescity of C.   STER 519:29
correlative: finding an 'objective c.
   ELIOT 205:16
corridors: c. into the mind   DOUG 191:7
c. of power   SNOW 512:15
corriger: *se mêler à c. le monde*   MOL 353:19
corroboration: particular c. of this
aphorism   BIRK 84:12
corroborative: Merely c. detail   GILB 227:12
corrupcioun: Fulfilled of dong and of
c.   CHAU 143:6
corrupt: able to c. a saint   SHAK 438:7
Among a people generally c.   BURKE 110:14
appointment by the c. few   SHAW 497:36
Away with a c. world   MER 337:37
be equally wicked and c.   BURKE 108:20
c., and become abominable   PRAY 390:2
c. government on the earth   JEFF 272:12
C. influence   BURKE 110:16
c. the souls of those they   ARN 13:22
moth and rust doth c.   BIBLE 64:25
one good custom should c.   TENN 535:25
Peace to c. no less than   MILT 349:27
sanguinary punishments which c.
   PAINE 368:4
That do c. my air   SHAK 427:23
That no king can c.   SHAK 447:4
Unlimited power is apt to c.   PITT 373:23
corrupted: conscience with injustice
is c.   SHAK 446:6
c. by this stinking smoke   JAM 271:4
c. the youth of the realm   SHAK 446:14
had been c. by sentiment   GREE 236:4
my fortunes have C.   SHAK 423:1
of time hath not been c.   PRAY 384:8
corruptible: c. must put on incorruption
   BIBLE 76:29
it to obtain a c. crown   BIBLE 76:9
corrupting: c. the young men and not
   PLATO 374:8
corruption: are in danger of great c.
   KNOX 305:25
C., the most infallible   GIBB 224:27
C. wins not more than honesty   SHAK 447:12
It is sown in c.   BIBLE 76:27
of vice whose strong c.   SHAK 490:17
Stew'd in c.   SHAK 435:10
thy Holy One to see c.   PRAY 390:7
to be turned into c.   PRAY 400:4
corruptions: man's c. made him wretched
   OTWAY 365:27
corruptly: Were not deriv'd c.   SHAK 466:20
corrupts: absolute power c.   ACTON 1:5
cors: *souvenirs sont c. de chasse*   APOL 11:10
corse: c. again in complete steel   SHAK 430:24
his c. to the rampart we   WOLFE 576:2
Cortez: like stout C. when with   KEATS 292:18
coruscations: c. of summer lightning
   GOUL 233:5
Corydon: *Formosum pastor C. ardebat*
   VIRG 559:14
For Time, not C.   ARN 15:7
Cos: she goes in a gleam of C.   POUND 382:15
Supplants the *mousseline* of C.   POUND 383:5
cosmogeny: blot out c.   BROW 99:9
cosmopolitan: to become c. in the end
   MOORE 355:16
Cosmos: too much Ego in your C.
   KIPL 304:31
cost: c. of the squalor and slavery
   SHAW 498:23
counteth the c.   BIBLE 70:14

not wish to count the c.   BREC 91:26
rate the c. of the erection   SHAK 441:17
Too costly for c.   THOM 548:29
Why so large c.   SHAK 495:13
coster: c.'s finished jumping   GILB 228:21
costive: have made a soap-boiler c.
   WEBS 566:23
costly: comely, but not c.   LYLY 321:14
c. in our sorrows   STER 519:12
C. thy habit as thy purse   SHAK 430:19
cot: c. with a pot of pink geraniums
   MACN 326:8
Cotopaxi: Chimborazo, C.   TURN 553:23
cottage: c. of gentility   COL 156:13
court to c. he depart   PEELE 371:8
his visage from our c.   SHAK 492:4
left as a c. in a vineyard   BIBLE 57:16
Love and a c.   COLM 158:24
soul's dark c.   WALL 562:9
cottages: march in c. of strowed reeds
   MARL 330:11
cottage-smell: Sweet-William with his
homely c.   ARN 15:6
Cottle: Amos C.   BYRON 124:24
couch: all my frowzy c. in sorrow
   BURNS 113:22
flinty and steel c. of war   SHAK 474:5
home and rest on the c.   CAT 136:28
than a levee from a c.   CONG 161:4
There I c. when owls do cry   SHAK 485:25
water my c. with my tears   PRAY 389:26
when on my c. I lie   WORD 578:1
couché: *Longtemps je me suis c.*   PROU 401:20
make his c. of silk   CHAU 142:25
Couched: C. with her arms behind   MER 337:1
coucher: *pauvre de c. sous les ponts*
   FRAN 217:26
couches: stilly c. she   HARDY 239:4
cough: all c. in ink   YEATS 586:14
falls into a c.   SHAK 470:3
Keep a c. by them ready   CHUR 148:27
coughing: c. drowns the parson's
   SHAK 457:19
coughs: c. when you would kiss   AUDEN 18:10
no discretion in her c.   AUST 23:12
could: I c. not look on Death   KIPL 298:25
coulter: while that the c. rusts   SHAK 445:12
Councillor: C. to King James   GREV 236:18
counsel: darkeneth c. by words   BIBLE 52:41
Dost sometimes c. take   POPE 381:2
execution than for c.   BACON 27:39
follow this c. of Aristotle   ASCH 17:4
his c. was not followed   BIBLE 50:25
in the c. of the ungodly   PRAY 389:14
is for women to keep c.   SHAK 449:22
keep my own c. I will venture   GLAD 229:16
lightly regarded the c.   PRAY 397:7
princely c. in his face   MILT 346:14
requireth further comfort or c.   PRAY 387:17
spirit of c. and might   BIBLE 58:9
Take my c.   GILB 225:27
We took sweet c. together   PRAY 393:11
Who cannot give good c.   BURT 116:26
who c. can bestow   POPE 378:32
'you c. well   SHAK 466:7
Counsellor: C., The mighty God   BIBLE 58:7
this c. Is now most still   SHAK 435:23
counsellors: plain when c. blanch
   BACON 25:39
With kings and c.   BIBLE 52:12
counsels: all good c.   PRAY 385:9
designs and crooked c. fit   DRYD 194:6
United thoughts and c.   MILT 345:1
count: c. five-and-twenty   DICK 178:21
c. the number of the beast   BIBLE 82:14
had better c. your spoons   SMITH 510:15
her c. and calls her 'Miss'   CHES 147:19
I c. it not an inn   BROW 97:3
I c. myself in nothing   SHAK 478:24
If all men c. with you   KIPL 300:2

Let me c. the ways   BROW 98:13
let us c. our spoons   JOHN 275:1
We should c. time   BAIL 29:21
counted: are c. as the small dust   BIBLE 59:8
c. loss for Christ   BIBLE 78:17
c. them and cursed his   HOUS 264:28
faster we c. our spoons   EMER 207:8
countenance: c. was as the sun shineth
   BIBLE 81:14
damned disinheriting c.   SHER 506:33
did the C. Divine   BLAKE 86:16
grim grew his c.   BALL 30:18
heart maketh a cheerful c.   BIBLE 54:5
his c. is as Lebanon   BIBLE 57:4
Knight of the Doleful C.   CERV 138:12
lift up his c. upon thee   BIBLE 48:9
light of thy c. upon us   PRAY 389:21
make him a cheerful c.   PRAY 396:20
making you the c. you are   SHAK 426:20
sharpeneth the c. of his friend   BIBLE 54:40
shew the light of thy c.   PRAY 395:8
trow that c. cannot lie   ROYD 411:2
us the light of his c.   PRAY 394:4
which is the help of my c.   PRAY 392:12
withal of a beautiful c.   BIBLE 50:7
counter: All things c., original   HOPK 256:23
From c. or desk among grey   YEATS 585:1
counteracts: he c. the Devil   SMART 508:22
countercheck: c. quarrelsome   SHAK 427:5
Counterfeit: C. values always resemble
   AUDEN 19:20
c. sad looks   SHAK 470:23
light to c. a gloom   MILT 342:5
stamp and c. advantages   SHAK 474:21
counterfeited: well they laugh'd with
c.   GOLD 231:2
counterpane: pleasant land of c.   STEV 522:20
counterpoint: Too much c.   BEEC 37:4
counters: Words are wise men's c.
   HOBB 251:15
countest: c. the steps of the Sun   BLAKE 87:22
counties: Forget six c. overhung   MORR 358:10
see the coloured c.   HOUS 263:4
counting: c. votes instead of weighing
   INGE 270:7
countrey: I will into some far c.   BALL 30:9
countries: c. where he came his own
   DRYD 195:25
preferreth all c. before his own   OVER 366:6
country: airs make unto me one c.
   BROW 96:29
all these c. patriots born   BYRON 119:26
always zealous for his c.'s   GAY 223:21
America is a c. of young   EMER 208:11
Anybody can be good in the c.   WILDE 573:22
benefits of your own c.   SHAK 426:20
best c. ever is   GOLD 231:25
bosom beats not in his c.'s   POPE 375:12
c. and they only saved   CHES 146:25
c. folks who live beneath   CLOU 153:23
country for our c.'s good   BARR 34:23
c. has its own constitution   ANON 5:5
C. in the town   MART 331:14
C. of the Blind the One-eyed   WELLS 568:12
c. retreat near the town   WYCH 583:24
c. that has 265 kinds   DE G 173:17
c. 'tis of centuries come   CUMM 170:10
c. was good for General   WILS 574:15
departed into their own c.   BIBLE 63:33
ever exist in a free c.   BURKE 110:1
every c. but his own   GILB 226:25
fate of this c. depends   DISR 185:12
Father of his C.   ANON 5:7
fight for its King and c.   ANON 7:19
fit c. for heroes to live   GEOR 223:33
friends of every c. save   DISR 185:14
From yon far c. blows   HOUS 263:22
God made the c.   COWP 166:31
good news from a far c.   BIBLE 54:30
good of one's c.   FARQ 210:4

good to be had in the c.	HAZL 243:21
great deal of unmapped c.	ELIOT 200:22
guts to betray my c.	FORS 217:12
have no relish for the c.	SMITH 512:9
heart bleeds for his c.	JOHN 274:21
he began to serve his c.	SHAK 427:19
He likes the c.	COWP 166:17
his journey into a far c.	BIBLE 70:18
his pension from his c.	RUSK 412:7
his power to leave his c.	COBB 154:9
how I leave my c.	PITT 374:7
I loathe the c.	CONG 161:5
Indeed I tremble for my c.	JEFF 272:16
in defence of one's c.	HOMER 254:2
In the c. of the free	BROW 97:36
in the c. places	STEV 523:2
is to die for one's c.	HOR 260:17
I vow to thee, my c.	SPR 517:10
Leaving his c. for his	FITZ 212:4
life to lose for my c.	HALE 237:14
Love thy c.	DOD 187:16
My c. is the world	PAINE 368:5
My c., 'tis of thee	SMITH 510:24
not see your c. is lost	WILL 574:8
of every c. but his own	CANN 129:28
once to serve our c.	ADD 1:22
Our c. is the world	GARR 221:18
our c., right or wrong	DEC 173:1
Our c., right or wrong	SCH 415:13
prepare the mind of the c.	DISR 185:5
pride that pulls the c.	SHAK 475:3
senators and I pray for the c.	HALE 237:12
shed his blood for the c.	ROOS 408:3
she is my c. still	CHUR 148:24
That is no c. for old men	YEATS 586:11
that was in another c.	MARL 329:22
that will not love his c.	SHAK 450:16
their c.'s wishes blest	COLL 158:19
they've undone his c.	ADD 1:21
this a billion dollar c.	FOST 217:16
thou aim'st at be thy c.'s	SHAK 447:12
to vegetate like the c.	HAZL 243:31
What a c.	SHAW 497:14
what your c. can do for you	KENN 295:10
who leads a c. life	DRYD 196:3
whose c. he has turned	BURKE 110:33
countrymen: Friends, Romans, c.	SHAK 450:17
in perils by mine own c.	BIBLE 77:12
our c. are all mankind	GARR 221:18
countryside: know the gods of the c.	VIRG 560:15
smiling and beautiful c.	DOYLE 192:1
county: English c. families	WAUGH 565:29
coupés: les lauriers sont c.	ANON 9:15
couple: c. whose ties are unbroken	HOR 259:21
wood-birds but to c. now	SHAK 471:8
coupler-flange: c. to spindle-guide I see	KIPL 301:2
couplets: creaking c. in a tavern	BYRON 124:14
Shovel your c. to their	CAMP 128:11
courage: Blessings on your young c.	VIRG 559:8
'C!' he said	TENN 539:12
C. in your own	GORD 233:1
C. is the thing	BARR 34:10
C., mon ami	READE 405:3
C. mounteth with occasion	SHAK 452:11
c. never to submit or yield	MILT 345:3
c. the greater	ANON 8:9
fearful saints fresh c. take	COWP 165:27
I mean instantaneous c.	NAP 359:12
originality or moral c.	SHAW 496:12
screw your c. to the sticking-place	SHAK 459:10
should have c. to suffer	TROL 552:19
strong and of a good c.	BIBLE 48:36
therefore should our c. be	SHAK 444:14

three-o'-clock in the morning c.	THOR 550:18
'Tis the c. you bring	WALP 563:23
unto him with a good c.	PRAY 391:19
vain faith, and c. vain	MAC 322:8
which inspired c. whilst	BURKE 111:10
courageous: captains c. whom death	BALL 31:8
couriers: sightless c. of the air	SHAK 459:6
Vaunt-c. to oak-cleaving thunderbolts	SHAK 454:4
cours: c. of hire withholde	CHAU 142:29
course: betake myself to that c.	PEPYS 372:21
c. of true love never did	SHAK 469:18
forgot his c.	FLEC 214:18
giant to run his c.	PRAY 390:11
I have finished my c.	BIBLE 79:26
I must stand the c.	SHAK 455:3
in the c. of human events	JEFF 272:5
regular c. different branches	CARR 134:10
Take thou what c. thou wilt	SHAK 451:6
court: *Assassiner c'est le plus c. chemin*	MOL 353:24
c. an amorous looking-glass	SHAK 480:18
c. awards it	SHAK 468:6
c. for owls	BIBLE 58:31
C. the slow clock	POPE 377:7
c. to cottage he depart	PEELE 371:8
cultivated c. of the Empress	GILB 227:22
heavenly c. for ever celebrates	ABEL 1:1
Her c. was pure	TENN 543:15
I c. others in verse	PRIOR 400:21
peril than the envious c.	SHAK 424:31
plead their cases in c.	VIRG 559:1
she will c. you	JONS 284:11
Talk of c. news	SHAK 456:3
that shines upon his c.	SHAK 492:4
what a c.	ABEL 1:2
courte: *loisir de la faire plus c.*	PASC 369:14
courted: Better be c. and jilted	CAMP 128:23
courteous: gracious and c. to strangers	BACON 26:20
greeting be c. or rough	AUDEN 21:2
courteoust: thou wert the c. knight	MAL 328:8
courtesies: these c.	SHAK 466:3
ye small sweet c. of life	STER 519:5
courtesy: all women with perfect c.	KITC 305:14
am the very pink of c.	SHAK 482:23
devil himself with c.	SHAK 490:20
Grace of God is in C.	BELL 39:14
greater man, the greater c.	TENN 534:36
In phrase of gentlest c.	SCOTT 416:2
thy dear mother any c.	SHAK 428:5
trust thy honest offer'd c.	MILT 341:6
what a candy deal of c.	SHAK 438:20
courtezan: she was a c. in the old	POUND 382:5
courtier: near the heel of the c.	SHAK 436:29
courting: stayeth the young man's c.	POUND 382:11
courtly: with their c. foreign grace	TENN 543:4
Courts: C. and camps are the only	CHES 145:14
C. for cowards were erected	BURNS 114:19
founts falling in the c.	CHES 146:28
fresh from brawling c.	TENN 537:8
is still before the c.	HOR 257:15
longing to enter into the c.	PRAY 395:11
one day in thy c.	PRAY 395:13
Courtship: C. to marriage	CONG 160:29
cousins: His sisters and his c.	GILB 228:3
Coutts: Aristocrat who banks with C.	GILB 225:23
couvre: *les c., les nourrit, les incite*	MONT 355:1
cove: c. with pushing prow	BROW 102:14
covenant: be for a token of a c.	BIBLE 45:40
c. with death and an agreement	GARR 221:19
have made a c. with death	BIBLE 58:22

covenanted: c. with him for thirty	BIBLE 68:9
covenants: Open c. of peace openly	WILS 575:1
Cover: C. her face	WEBS 566:27
jewels c. ev'ry part	POPE 378:16
leaves and flowers do c.	WEBS 567:8
(Like the c. of an old book	FRAN 218:20
neither turn again to c.	PRAY 396:19
should c. that stand bare	SHAK 466:20
covered: twain he c. his face	BIBLE 57:28
covert: c. from the tempest	BIBLE 58:30
I would go to a c.	ROSS 409:10
covet: c. thy neighbour's house	BIBLE 47:24
sin to c. honour	SHAK 445:2
Thou shalt not c.	CLOU 154:1
coveted: Englishman as ever c. his	KING 297:9
covetous: not a brawler, not c.	BIBLE 79:12
covetousness: all uncleanness, or c.	BIBLE 78:2
cow: c. is kept for every three	MILL 339:16
I never saw a Purple C.	BURG 108:2
isn't grass to graze a c.	BETJ 44:3
Kiss till the c. comes home	BEAU 36:11
milk the c. of the world	WILB 572:4
Three acres and a c.	COLL 158:11
to keep a c.	BUTL 119:4
Truth, Sir, is a c.	JOHN 275:3
when she kissed her c.	SWIFT 526:28
coward: Am I a c.	SHAK 433:3
c. does it with a kiss	WILDE 572:10
c. lips did from their	SHAK 448:15
c.'s castle	CHAP 140:9
c. shame distain his name	BURNS 114:21
c.'s weapon	FLET 215:32
''Fore God I am no c.	TENN 542:1
gross flattery to name a c.	TOBIN 551:7
I was a c. on instinct	SHAK 439:8
live a c. in thine own	SHAK 459:8
may call me c. if you will	FIEL 211:31
No c. soul is mine	BRON 93:18
Shak'd like a c.	SHAK 439:21
We took him for a c.	SHAK 490:23
cowardice: mutual c. keeps us in peace	JOHN 278:3
of pusillanimity and c.	SHAK 442:15
soldier I admit the c.	SHAW 497:29
cowardly: Not c. put off my helmet	SHAK 423:15
cowards: being all c.	JOHN 278:3
conscience doth make c.	SHAK 433:8
Conscience is but a word that c.	SHAK 481:17
Courts for c. were erected	BURNS 114:19
C. die many times before	SHAK 449:18
c. flinch and traitors	CONN 161:10
C. in scarlet pass	GRAN 234:9
many other mannish c. have	SHAK 424:30
Nonconformist Conscience makes c.	BEER 37:19
plague of all c.	SHAK 438:36
would be c. if they durst	ROCH 407:1
cowbind: Green c. and the moonlight-coloured	SHEL 503:19
cowcumber: she wouldn't have a c.	DICK 179:25
cowl: I like a c.	EMER 206:25
Cows: C. are my passion	DICK 177:28
say the c. laid out Boston	EMER 207:7
cowslip: In a c.'s bell I lie	SHAK 485:25
I' the bottom of a c.	SHAK 428:8
O'er the c.'s velvet head	MILT 341:21
Cowslips: C., and Kingcups	SPEN 517:3
c. in boys' hats appear...	CLARE 152:14
c. tall her pensioners	SHAK 470:2
c. wan that hang the pensive	MILT 343:15
coxcombs: c. nature meant but fools	POPE 378:16
coy: c. and tender to offend	HERB 248:14
Then be not c.	HERR 250:6

coyness: c., Lady, were no crime MARV 332:18
coz: my pretty little c. SHAK 426:24
Crabbed: C. age and youth SHAK 492:13
crabs: When roasted c. hiss SHAK 457:19
Crab-spawn: Mars to C. found in my GRAV 234:12
crab-tree: grievous c. cudgel BUNY 107:22
crack: canst hear the mighty c. POPE 376:21
c. in the tea-cup opens AUDEN 18:10
C. nature's moulds SHAK 454:4
heaven's vaults should c. SHAK 456:8
sans c. or flaw SHAK 457:16
snarls...You'd better c. up DICK 179:18
with never a c. in my heart YEATS 586:5
would hear the mighty c. ADD 2:30
crack'd: have bloody noses and c. SHAK 438:31
cracked: c. lookingglass of a servant JOYCE 286:21
cracker: those lovely c. mottoes GILB 225:11
crackling: c. of thorns under a pot BIBLE 55:18
cracks: Now c. a noble heart SHAK 437:28
cradle: bed and procreant c. SHAK 459:4
Between the c. DYER 199:18
frailest For your c. SHEL 501:22
from the c. to the grave SHEL 503:14
In his soft c. JONS 285:7
mountain c. in Pamere ARN 15:1
Out of the c. endlessly WHIT 570:9
Rocked in the c. of the deep WILL 574:7
rocking a grown man in the c. BURKE 110:13
craft: Between c. and credulity BURKE 110:10
c. so long to lerne CHAU 143:32
c. so long to learn HIPP 251:8
there's c. in the river SMITH 510:5
craftier: Ful c. to pley she was CHAU 141:6
crafts: from the c. and assaults PRAY 385:16
craftsman: Copper for the c. cunning KIPL 298:15
rusteth the craft and the c. POUND 382:10
crag: He clasps the c. with crooked TENN 533:7
crags: among these barren c. TENN 543:21
crambe: miseros c. repetita magistros JUV 287:24
cramm'd: they on earth were c. WORD 580:2
cramoisi: c. is unbroidered POUND 382:11
cramped: delicate growth c. by crookedness HARDY 240:3
cramps: tonight thou shalt have c. SHAK 484:28
crams: c. with cans of poisoned CHES 147:20
Cranberry: C. Tart LEAR 312:9
crane: Jane Jane Tall as a c. SITW 508:11
cranes: Warred on by c. MILT 345:22
crank: steersmen when the vessel's c. MER 337:20
cranks: personal prejudices and c. ELIOT 205:15
Quips and c. MILT 342:14
crape: saint in c. is twice POPE 377:11
Cras: C. amet qui nunquam amavit ANON 10:11
C. ingens iterabimus aequor HOR 259:17
crastina: Sera nimis vita est c. MART 331:8
cratère: raison tonne en son c. POTT 382:3
Cratinus: If you believe C. from HOR 258:25
craved: who c. no crumb GILB 229:9
craven: c. fears of being great TENN 533:27
Craven-street: In C. SMITH 510:5
craving: full as c. too DRYD 195:15
crawl: slimy things did c. with COL 155:14
crawling: such fellows as I do c. SHAK 433:11
craze: stands In a careworn c. HARDY 240:15
crazed: He is c. with the spell DE L 173:26
crazier: World is c. and more MACN 326:14
crazy: c., cold ROCH 407:3

creaking: c. couplets in a tavern BYRON 124:14
cream: c. and mantle like a standing SHAK 465:12
milk masquerades as c. GILB 228:8
queen of curds and c. SHAK 492:1
than choking her with c. KING 297:15
vigilant as a cat to steal c. SHAK 440:11
will you take a little c. PAIN 367:19
cream-faced: thou c. loon SHAK 463:1
crease: with not a c. ROST 410:12
create: ashes new-c. another heir SHAK 448:3
c. new heavens and a new BIBLE 60:14
from these c. he can SHEL 503:6
I must C. a System BLAKE 86:2
must himself c. the taste WORD 583:11
strains that might c. a soul MILT 341:14
time to murder and c. ELIOT 203:19
well to c. good precedents BACON 26:24
created: beginning God c. the heaven BIBLE 44:22
c. equal...In a larger sense LINC 314:23
C. half to rise POPE 379:13
he immediately c. other NIET 363:3
image of him that c. him BIBLE 78:26
Male and female c. BIBLE 45:5
Man has c. death YEATS 584:21
men are c. equal JEFF 272:6
that all men are c. equal ANON 8:14
Thou hast c. all things BIBLE 81:25
why was it not c. sooner JOHN 278:5
written or c. unless Minerva HOR 258:5
creating: c. a whole tribe of fops SHAK 453:9
Creation: been present at the C. ALF 3:16
c. groaneth and travaileth BIBLE 75:10
c. will expire before tea-time SMITH 511:18
like the God of the c. JOYCE 286:18
love C.'s final law TENN 536:29
mars c.'s plan CANN 130:3
Such as c.'s dawn beheld BYRON 121:25
We bless thee for our c. PRAY 386:2
when c. rises again CEL 138:6
which the whole c. moves TENN 537:22
woman is a blind fury of c. SHAW 497:20
creations: person acts his own c. BROW 103:4
creative: c. soul WORD 580:25
destruction is also a c. BAK 29:24
Creator: C. and Preserver of all PRAY 385:24
creature more than the C. BIBLE 74:32
depends on his C. BURT 116:31
glory of the C. and the relief BACON 24:17
great C. from his work MILT 349:2
marvellous work of the C. HOUS 266:15
now he hasn't been a c. CHEK 145:4
Remember now thy C. BIBLE 56:11
creatura: Cum resurget c. CEL 138:6
creature: base and ignoble c. BACON 25:25
c. hath a purpose and its KEATS 294:17
c.'s at his dirty work POPE 376:22
God's first C. BACON 28:5
kill the poor c. at once GASK 221:24
Let the living c. lie AUDEN 19:17
served the c. more than the Creator BIBLE 74:32
creatures: births of living c. BACON 26:27
c. great and small ALEX 3:13
generations of living c. LUCR 320:7
goodly c. are there here SHAK 485:26
Hugest of living c. MILT 349:1
meanest of the c. BROW 102:36
other c. have gone to stall FROST 219:11
perverse c. in the world ADD 2:18
take unto other living c. BACON 26:19
than c. set upon tables JOHN 276:30
Credat: C. Iudaeus Apella HOR 262:5
credence: gave no c. to his word PRAY 397:5
yive I feyth and ful c. CHAU 143:29
credit: c. in this World much wrong FITZ 213:13
it's greatly to his c. GILB 228:9

Not to thy c. CALV 128:1
There an't much c. in that DICK 179:1
'Tis a c. to any good girl TAYL 531:24
creditable: love good c. acquaintance SWIFT 526:15
credite: Experto c. VIRG 559:10
creditor: trembling at a c. JOHN 281:40
creditors: c. would hardly know me FOX 217:24
Credo: C. in unum Deum MASS 334:20
credulity: Between craft and c. BURKE 110:10
c. below the milkiness BURKE 108:20
c. increases his impudence HUME 267:19
present age is craving c. DISR 184:29
credulous: positive men are the most c. POPE 381:22
with the pomp of a too-c. WORD 582:4
credulus: sed non ego c. illis VIRG 560:7
credunt: homines id quod volunt c. CAES 126:27
creed: Christians have a comfortable c. BYRON 122:19
c. of a second-rate man BAG 29:16
got the better of his c. STER 519:25
His c. no parson ever knew DOYLE 192:40
it is the c. of slaves PITT 374:3
Pagan suckled in a c. outworn WORD 582:20
shrieked against his c. TENN 536:29
solemn c. with solemn sneer BYRON 120:37
creeds: c. that refuse and restrain SWIN 529:11
dust of c. outworn SHEL 503:4
half-believers in our casual c. ARN 14:17
keys of all the c. TENN 536:13
so many c. WILC 572:6
Vain are the thousand c. BRON 93:20
creep: ambition can c. as well as soar BURKE 112:9
bade me c. past BROW 103:32
C. in our ears SHAK 468:15
C. into thy narrow bed ARN 13:14
it and little dwarfs do CHES 147:5
'with pleasing murmurs c.' POPE 378:21
creepers: Lifting the cool-hair'd c. ARN 14:21
creeping: are c. things innumerable PRAY 397:1
c. thing that creepeth BIBLE 45:4
c. things, and fowls BIBLE 73:37
Creeps: C. in this petty pace SHAK 463:6
c. rustling to her knees KEATS 289:17
creetur: 'I am a lone lorn c. DICK 176:27
Cremorne: C. Gardens TROL 553:9
crept: c. too near his conscience SHAK 446:28
one c. silently to Rest FITZ 212:17
Cretes: C. and Arabians BIBLE 73:23
crevasse: like a scream from a c. GREE 236:6
that doth the c. bridge THOM 547:22
crew: admit me of thy c. MILT 342:16
c. is gambling in the forecastle SHAW 496:33
c. of the Captain's gig CHES 146:21
c. of the captain's gig GILB 225:16
darling of our c. DIBD 175:21
immediately the cock c. BIBLE 68:19
Set the c. laughing FLEC 214:18
We were a ghastly c. COL 155:25
With his industrious c. MILT 346:4
crib: ass his master's c. BIBLE 57:15
cribs: liest thou in smoky c. SHAK 441:29
Cricket: his nose there was a C. LEAR 312:5
Save the c. on the hearth MILT 342:5
son of grief at c. HOUS 262:22
Cricklewood: bound for C. BETJ 43:17
cried: c. all the way to the bank LIB 314:11
c. the little children AUDEN 18:15
from the depths I have c. BIBLE 83:13
I c. to dream again SHAK 485:18
little children c. MOTL 358:20
still she c. ELIOT 204:24
When that the poor have c. SHAK 450:19
Crier: when the C. cried BARH 33:22
cries: heaven with my bootless c. SHAK 493:6

Night and day on me she c.   BALL 31:4
'tailor' c.   SHAK 470:3
crieth: that c. in the wilderness   BIBLE 59:5
crikey: always game by c. blood will tell
    MARQ 330:20
Crillon: brave C.   HENR 245:14
crime: C'est pire qu'un c.   BOUL 90:19
commonplace a c. is   DOYLE 191:15
c. in a child to read   MAC 324:18
c. of being a young man...I   PITT 373:20
c. so shameful as poverty   FARQ 209:26
c. to love too well   POPE 376:6
foulest c. in history   WHIT 571:10
Godlike c. was to be kind   BYRON 125:18
He is the Napoleon of c.   DOYLE 192:11
It is worse than a c.   BOUL 90:19
jury for a capital c.   JOHN 277:2
loved be with equal c.   SPEN 516:13
love, was thought a c.   BLAKE 87:17
No c.'s so great as daring   CHUR 148:21
that's the c.   GRAN 234:8
Who for my wilful c.   MILT 349:28
Crimes: C., like virtues   FARQ 210:14
our c. would despair   SHAK 421:3
reach the dignity of c.   MORE 357:8
register of the c.   GIBB 224:23
Successful c. alone are   DRYD 197:3
tableau des c. et des malheurs   VOLT 561:10
their c. confin'd   GRAY 234:24
thousand c.   BYRON 121:36
what c. are committed   ROL 407:15
With all his c. broad blown   SHAK 434:30
with reiterated c. he might   MILT 345:8
worst of c. is poverty   SHAW 497:6
Crimine: C. ab uno   VIRG 558:2
crimson: in that c. lake   GRAH 233:16
Is c. in thy lips   SHAK 483:30
crisis: force the moment to its c.   ELIOT 203:22
in this c.   PAINE 368:1
Crispian: called the feast of C.   SHAK 445:3
Crispin: C. Crispian shall ne'er   SHAK 445:3
Crist: C.! whan that it remembreth
    CHAU 143:19
Cristen: C. man shall wedde   CHAU 143:17
Cristes: C. loore and his apostles CHAU 142:3
criterion: infallible c. of wisdom
    BURKE 111:27
critic: attribute of a good c.   LOW 319:16
C. and whippersnapper   BROW 99:1
c., one would suppose   ELIOT 205:15
c. spits on what is done   HOOD 255:14
c. to decide...A publisher   WILDE 573:33
nicely Jonson knew the c.'s   COLL 158:23
critical: be c. than to be correct   DISR 184:23
c. judgement is so exquisite   FRY 219:24
c. period in matrimony   HERB 246:16
I am nothing if not c.   SHAK 474:16
criticism: anticipate the verdict of c.
    WILDE 573:33
c. is the most tormenting   STER 519:30
c. of administration   BAG 28:23
father of English c.   JOHN 281:35
I do not resent c.   CHUR 150:5
my own definition of c.   ARN 16:1
our c. is applied only   JAMES 271:13
People ask you for c.   MAUG 336:3
two because it permits c.   FORS 217:13
wreathed the rod of c.   DISR 187:8
criticizing: spite of all the c. elves
    CHUR 149:13
critic-pen: Unboding c.   TENN 544:10
critics: Cosmopolitan c.   DISR 185:14
c. all are ready made   BYRON 124:17
therefore they turn c.   COL 157:26
Turn'd c. next   POPE 378:12
You know who the c. are   DISR 186:23
You trust in c.   BYRON 124:18
croaks: That c. the fatal entrance SHAK 459:2
Crocodile: cruel crafty C.   SPEN 516:5
How doth the little c.   CARR 133:17

manner o' thing is your c.   SHAK 422:14
To these c.'s tears   BURT 116:35
crocodiles: is the wisdom of the c.
    BACON 27:38
crocus: feet the c. brake like fire TENN 541:18
Croesus: not an intellectual C.   DISR 186:20
crois: for love Upon a c.   CHAU 144:19
mais je n'en c. rien   CHAM 139:16
croit: *ce que la raison ne c.*   VOLT 561:20
Cromwell: C. guiltless of his country's
    GRAY 234:23
C.; the Philistine   ARN 16:23
C. was a man in whom ambition
    BURKE 111:29
They set up C. and his heir   JORD 285:18
crony: drouthy c.   BURNS 115:5
crook: such a thumping c.   BETJ 43:4
crooked: c. shall be made straight BIBLE 59:5
c. timber of humanity   KANT 288:14
dumb to tell the c. rose   THOM 547:3
heart are as c. as corkscrews AUDEN 18:13
With your c. heart   AUDEN 18:11
crookedly: before him walked very c.
    SURT 525:29
crookedness: delicate growth cramped
by c.   HARDY 240:3
crop-full: Irks care the c. bird   BROW 104:3
crop-headed: c. Parliament swing
    BROW 99:26
Croppy: C., Droppy   ELLIS 206:13
croquet: c. matches in summer   AUDEN 21:1
cross: before him endured the c. BIBLE 79:35
beside the c. weeping while   JAC 270:31
by thy C. and Passion   PRAY 385:17
c. him in nothing   SHAK 421:24
his breast a bloody c.   SPEN 515:31
I am getting c.   HOFF 252:15
If you bear the c. gladly   THOM 546:14
I'll c. it   SHAK 429:14
mankind upon a c. of gold   BRYAN 106:8
mystery of the c. shines   VEN 556:5
suffer death upon the c.   PRAY 387:24
cross-bow: With my c.   COL 155:10
cross'd: they c. themselves for fear
    TENN 538:12
crossed: c. be uncrossed   ELIOT 202:10
oyster may be c. in love   SHER 506:4
We had c. each other's   WILDE 572:11
crosses: c., row on row   MCCR 324:30
E'en c. from his sov'reign   HERV 250:17
they clinging to their c.   CHES 146:10
tumbled down the c.   JORD 285:18
what c. to ensue   SHAK 442:2
cross-gartered: wished to see thee ever
c.   SHAK 489:15
cross-grained: there ever such a c. brute
    GOLD 232:28
Crossing: C. alone the nighted ferry
    HOUS 265:18
C. the stripling Thames   ARN 14:14
crossroads: c. and in the alleyways CAT 137:5
crossways: Things at home are c.
    CARL 130:28
crotchets: some c. in thy head now
    SHAK 469:7
crouch: c. whom the rest bade aspire
    BROW 102:6
crow: before the cock c.   BIBLE 68:12
c. doth sing as sweetly   SHAK 468:19
c. Makes wing   SHAK 461:14
flew down a monstrous c.   CARR 134:33
had risen to hear him c.   ELIOT 200:16
Old Adam, the carrion c.   BEDD 36:26
there is an upstart c.   GREE 236:12
crowd: c. flowed over London Bridge
    ELIOT 204:20
c. is not company   BACON 26:15
fear or favour of the c.   KIPL 298:11
I hate the c.   LAND 309:5
madding c.'s ignoble strife   GRAY 235:1

not feel the c.   COWP 167:12
of these faces in the c.   POUND 383:11
riotousness of the c. is   ALC 3:9
crowding: come c. in so fast upon
    DRYD 198:7
thick the bursts come c.   ARN 14:3
Crowds: C. without company   GIBB 224:14
Frail c. that a delicate   MOORE 355:23
If you can talk with c.   KIPL 300:2
crowe: thenk upon the c.   CHAU 142:26
crowes feet: Til c. be growen under
    CHAU 144:5
crown: both divide the c.   DRYD 195:9
Caesar's laurel c.   BLAKE 85:16
c. him with glory and worship PRAY 389:28
C. is according   BAG 28:22
c. of our life as it closes   SWIN 529:10
c. o' the earth doth melt   SHAK 423:16
c. ourselves with rosebuds   BIBLE 62:11
c. thy good with brotherhood BATES 35:4
'Ere the King's c. shall   SCOTT 415:20
fruition of an earthly c.   MARL 330:8
Give me the c.   SHAK 479:13
hairy gold c. on 'er 'ead   KIPL 304:9
head a c. of twelve stars   BIBLE 82:10
head that wears a c.   SHAK 441:30
influence of the C. has   DUNN 199:14
labour this c. of thorns   BRYAN 106:8
likeness of a kingly c.   MILT 346:24
mace, the c. imperial   SHAK 444:25
monarch but would give his c.   WALL 562:10
more glorious is the c.   SMART 509:4
Not the king's c.   SHAK 463:20
obtain a corruptible c.   BIBLE 76:9
Of life, of c., of queen   SHAK 431:12
power of the c.   BURKE 108:19
presented him a kingly c.   SHAK 450:20
put on my c.   SHAK 424:10
shall receive the c. of life   BIBLE 80:8
strike his father's c.   SHAK 443:11
That c. the wat'ry glade   GRAY 235:9
thought of hath worn the c.   BIBLE 62:31
will give thee a c. of life   BIBLE 81:17
wished to restore the c.   JOHN 276:22
within the hollow c.   SHAK 479:11
Crown'd: C., and again discrown'd
    JOHN 273:22
C. with rank fumitor   SHAK 455:13
crowned: Calling a c. man royal SWIN 529:26
Crowner: Medical C.'s a queer   BARH 33:14
crownest: c. the year with thy goodness
    PRAY 394:3
crown imperial: oxlips and The c.
    SHAK 491:26
crowning: c. mercy   CROM 169:22
crowns: cold nymphs chaste c.   SHAK 485:19
c. are empty things   DEFOE 173:16
c. for convoy put into   SHAK 445:3
'Give c. and pounds   HOUS 262:20
happy he who c. in shades   GOLD 230:19
I'd c. resign to call thee   MACN 326:2
It is the end that c. us   HERR 249:4
last act c. the play   QUAR 403:15
With c. imperial   SHAK 443:12
crows: c. and choughs that wing SHAK 455:14
crow-toe: tufted c.   MILT 343:15
croyait: c. Victor Hugo   COCT 154:13
croys: c. of latoun ful of stones   CHAU 142:7
crucem: *libenter c. portas portabit te*
    THOM 546:14
Crucible: America is God's C.   ZANG 588:17
crucified: Was c.   PRAY 384:26
Crucifixus: *C. etiam pro nobis*   MASS 334:20
crucify: c. mankind upon a cross
    BRYAN 106:8
c. the old man   PRAY 388:10
people would not even c. him   CARL 132:26
Cruel: C., but composed and bland ARN 14:4
C. he looks   SHEL 502:4
c., not unnatural   SHAK 434:26

Here is c. Frederick HOFF 252:12
horribly c. works of nature DARW 172:1
jealousy is c. as the grave BIBLE 57:11
mercies of the wicked are c. BIBLE 53:34
must be c. only to be kind SHAK 435:20
you c. men of Rome SHAK 448:6
cruellest: April is the c. month ELIOT 204:17
cruell'st: you are the c. she alive
SHAK 488:12
cruelly: I am c. used AUST 23:16
Cruelty: C. has a human heart BLAKE 88:9
c. To load a falling man SHAK 447:25
Fear is the parent of c. FROU 219:20
full Of direst c. SHAK 459:2
cruise: are all on our last c. STEV 522:1
crumble: itself c. to the dust beneath
BROW 98:8
crumbs: bags to hold the c. ISH 270:27
c. which fell from BIBLE 70:28
dogs eat of the c. which BIBLE 66:30
picker-up of learning's c. BROW 100:24
Crumpet: Improved Hot Muffin and
C. DICK 179:33
crumpets: buttered scones and c. ELIOT 202:5
said right out loud, c. ELIOT 202:7
Crumpetty: longer I live on this C. Tree
LEAR 312:22
cruse: little oil in a c. BIBLE 51:7
crush: c. Under Paul's dome HODG 252:10
crush'd: c. beneath the furrow's
BURNS 115:19
crushed: once c. ARN 15:9
Crushing: C. out life than waving HOPE 256:4
Crusoe: poor Robin C. DEFOE 173:6
crust: the c. So fresh HOPK 256:15
These men are all upper c. HAL 237:16
upper c. GILB 228:11
cry: bubbling c. BYRON 122:18
continually do c. PRAY 384:16
C.;—and upon thy so sore THOM 548:25
c. both arts and learning QUAR 403:21
c. did knock SHAK 484:23
c. over me, There, there PRAY 394:15
cuckoo's parting c. ARN 15:5
harlot's c. from street BLAKE 85:17
I c. in the day-time PRAY 390:16
let our c. come unto thee PRAY 388:21
man's image and his c. YEATS 586:22
monstrous head and sickening c. CHES 146:22
nations combine each c. AUDEN 20:15
only don't c. CARR 135:17
righteousness, but behold a c. BIBLE 57:23
stones would immediately c. BIBLE 71:2
that dismal c. rose slowly BROW 98:2
that he was too old to c. STEV 520:19
That the Cherubim may c. ANON 10:14
that we still should c. BACON 28:18
To c. it up SWIFT 528:3
Truth is the c. of all BERK 41:22
utter'd a dreadful c. ARN 14:26
was a great c. in Egypt BIBLE 47:19
We waul and c. SHAK 455:22
What shall I c. BIBLE 59:6
when indeed they c. WEBS 567:10
When we are born we c. SHAK 455:23
crying: infant c. for the light TENN 536:26
one c. in the wilderness BIBLE 63:36
we came c. hither SHAK 455:22
Cryst: C., borne into virgynyte WYNT 584:4
crystal: clear as c. BIBLE 82:35
sea of glass like unto c. BIBLE 81:23
cubes: expressible as a sum of two c.
RAM 404:22
cubili: *dea nec dignata c. est* VIRG 560:2
cubit: one c. unto his stature BIBLE 64:29
cubits: gallows fifty c. high BIBLE 52:4
cuccu: Lhude sing c. ANON 7:18
Cuchulain: Pearse summoned C.
YEATS 587:2

cuckold: not make her husband a c.
SHAK 477:2
Cuckoo: C. calleth with gloomy
POUND 383:18
C.-echoing HOPK 256:10
c. is in June SHAK 439:35
C., jug-jug NASHE 360:9
C.! Shall I call thee WORD 582:25
c. shouts all day at nothing HOUS 265:9
c. then, on every tree SHAK 457:18
heard the c.'s parting cry ARN 15:5
merry c. SPEN 515:16
rainbow and a c.'s song DAV 172:15
Responsive to the c.'s HARDY 241:2
This is the weather the c. HARDY 241:2
cuckoo-buds: c. of yellow hue SHAK 457:18
cucumber: c. should be well sliced
JOHN 280:3
when c. is added to it MACK 325:10
cucumbers: extracting sun-beams out
of c. SWIFT 526:7
lodge in a garden of c. BIBLE 57:16
they are but c. after all JOHN 278:16
cud: yet he cheweth not the c. BIBLE 48:6
Cuddesdon: Hey for C. KEIT 295:13
cudgel: grievous crab-tree c. BUNY 107:22
cue: With a twisted c. GILB 227:7
cuers: *c. contre nous endurcis* VILL 557:4
Cui: *C. bono* CIC 151:32
cui bono: I hate a *c.* man SHAW 498:24
cully: was by Nature Woman's c.
CONG 160:20
culpa: *felix c.* MISS 352:20
mea c. MASS 334:15
nulla pallescere c. HOR 258:9
culprits: recognize them all as c. VIRG 558:2
cultivate: 'but we must c. our garden
VOLT 561:3
c. literature upon a little SMITH 511:36
C. simplicity LAMB 307:21
c. your friendship of his JOHN 278:33
to c. a few inhibitions LOOS 318:6
cultivated: c. court of the Empress
GILB 227:22
Shakespeare's genius had been c.
CHES 145:24
cultivation: equal in rights and c. MILL 339:19
cultiver: *il faut c. notre jardin* VOLT 561:3
culture: c. are the true apostles ARN 15:16
C., the acquainting ourselves ARN 16:17
elaborate defence of c. ARN 15:22
hear the word 'c.' JOHST 283:8
ladies who pursue C. WHAR 569:8
man of c. rare GILB 227:20
cultured: what the c. word KIPL 298:2
Cumae: Sibyl at C. PETR 373:2
Cumaei: *Ultima C. venit iam carminis*
VIRG 559:22
cumber: c. Sunlit pallets HOUS 262:15
I c. you goode Margaret MORE 357:20
cumbered: Martha was c. about much
BIBLE 69:34
cummin: mint and anise and c. BIBLE 67:24
cunctando: *homo nobis c. restituit rem*
ENN 208:22
Cunning: C. is the dark sanctuary CHES 146:5
c. men pass for wise BACON 25:43
have more c. to be strange SHAK 482:14
I find thy c. seeds ROSS 408:20
right hand forget her c. PRAY 399:3
that c. whore of Venice SHAK 476:21
Cup: after supper he took the C. PRAY 388:1
c. itself TENN 534:18
c. of hot wine with not SHAK 427:14
c. won by the worst horse MAS 333:23
enchanted c. but sparkles near BYRON 120:19
Fill high the c. with Samian BYRON 123:3
fill the C. FITZ 212:6
fill the C. that clears FITZ 212:16
fill the C. FITZ 212:22

Freely welcome to my c. OLDYS 365:4
giveth his colour in the c. BIBLE 54:24
Have drunk their C. a Round FITZ 212:17
let this c. pass from me BIBLE 68:14
Life's Liquor in its C. FITZ 212:6
my c. overflows SCOT 419:5
my c. shall be full PRAY 390:22
my Glory in a Shallow C. FITZ 213:13
Perfect the c. as planned BROW 104:13
poured strychnine in his c. HOUS 264:15
sing the saucer and the c. PAIN 367:15
tak a c. o' kindness yet BURNS 112:32
There's Death in the c. BURNS 113:30
To uses of c. BROW 104:12
woodspurge has a c. of three ROSS 410:9
cupboard: glacier knocks in the c.
AUDEN 18:10
is either our c. of food HERB 248:2
man in the bathroom c. EWART 209:11
cupboards: her c. opened HARDY 241:16
Cupid: C. abroad was lated GREE 236:8
C. blind did rise LYLY 321:11
C. is a knavish lad SHAK 470:26
C.'s darts do not feel ANON 6:16
giant-dwarf, Dan C. SHAK 456:26
wing'd C. painted blind SHAK 469:22
Cupidinesque: *Veneres C.* CAT 136:22
cupidinibus: *Responsare c.* HOR 262:10
Cupidinum: *Mater saeva C.* HOR 261:10
cupido: *c. gloriae novissima exuitur*
TAC 531:14
Cupids: mother of the lovely C. HOR 261:10
cups: frequent c. prolong POPE 381:6
When flowing c. run swiftly LOV 318:16
white c. SHEL 503:19
cur: half lurcher and half c. COWP 167:18
I spurn thee like a c. SHAK 449:24
you spurn a stranger c. SHAK 466:3
Cura: *Post equitem sedet atra C.* HOR 260:15
curantur: *Similia similibus c.* HAHN 237:10
curate: c.; he was fatter than TENN 533:5
in the very name of a C. SMITH 511:31
I was a pale young c. then GILB 229:1
sit upon the c.'s knee CHES 147:9
curates: abundant shower of c. has
BRON 93:16
C., and all Congregations PRAY 385:7
preached to death by wild c. SMITH 511:16
to all Bishops and C. PRAY 387:15
curb: c. a runaway young star BYRON 126:1
c. of old father antick SHAK 438:4
might c. your magnanimity KEATS 294:31
use the snaffle and the c. CAMP 128:12
Curbing: C. his lavish spirit SHAK 458:5
Cur'd: C. yesterday of my disease
PRIOR 401:4
curds: queen of c. and cream SHAK 492:1
cure: c. for admiring the House of Lords
BAG 29:6
c. for the evils which MAC 323:24
c. for this ill is not KIPL 300:11
c. the disease and kill BACON 26:17
ill he cannot c. a name ARN 15:12
is no c. for this disease BELL 39:1
is the c. of all diseases BROW 97:2
labour against our own c. BROW 97:2
love's a malady without a c. DRYD 197:6
palliate what we cannot c. JOHN 281:9
servitude is the c. of anarchy BURKE 109:30
To c. this deadly grief SHAK 462:17
was fatter than his c. TENN 533:8
wilt thou c. thine heart BEDD 36:24
cured: c. by hanging from a string
KING 297:20
that means it can't be c. CHEK 144:23
cures: Like c. like HAHN 237:10
curfew: c. tolls the knell of parting
GRAY 234:18
hear the far-off c. sound MILT 342:4
he begins at c. SHAK 454:22

Yet at mothy c.-tide HARDY 239:18
curia: quae c. ABEL 1:2
semper celebrat superna c. ABEL 1:1
curing: Morrison's Pill for c. CARL 132:9
curiosa: Horatii c. felicitas PETR 373:3
curiosities: c. would be quite forgot AUBR 17:22
curiosity: c., freckles PARK 368:15
Disinterested intellectual c. TREV 552:9
eminent degree of c. JOHN 282:19
curious: amaz'd, and c. BURNS 115:10
Be not c. in unnecessary BIBLE 62:23
c. engine, your white hand WEBS 566:21
objects and knowledge c. WHIT 571:13
Curiouser: 'C. and curiouser CARR 133:16
curiously: others to be read but not c. BACON 27:19
curis: solutis est beatius c. CAT 136:28
curl: Who had a little c. LONG 317:22
would make your hair c. GILB 228:34
Curl'd: C. minion ARN 14:25
curled: brave beard c. CHES 147:3
C. like vapour over shrines BROW 98:16
that c. my hair SHAK 454:18
wealthy c. darlings SHAK 473:22
curls: find unwithered on its c. HOUS 263:3
Frocks and C. DICK 184:2
currency: common c. that buys all CERV 138:20
Debasing the moral c. ELIOT 201:26
current: c. and compulsive course SHAK 476:1
c. in this place damm'd SHAK 439:24
smooth c. of domestic joy JOHN 282:21
take the c. when it serves SHAK 451:27
works have been most c. BACON 25:17
currents: regard their c. turn awry SHAK 433:8
curs: c. mouth a bone CHUR 149:8
c. of low degree GOLD 231:12
You common cry of c. SHAK 427:23
curs'd: by Nature c. CHUR 148:32
She c. Cole Porter too COW 163:2
curse: began he to c. and to swear BIBLE 68:19
c. be ended ELIOT 202:10
C., bless, me now THOM 546:24
C. God BIBLE 52:10
c. of this country is eloquent EMER 208:10
C. on his virtues ADD 1:21
C. shall be on thee SOUT 513:24
c. to party strife WORD 577:5
c. with their heart PRAY 393:19
heard such a terrible c. BARH 33:14
I know how to c. SHAK 484:29
is to me a c. MASS 335:17
look upon myself and c. SHAK 493:6
open foe may prove a c. GAY 223:13
'That is love's c. TENN 534:33
'The c. is come upon me TENN 538:11
thee to c. mine enemies BIBLE 48:16
'Tis the c. of the service SHAK 473:12
Work is the c. of the drinking WILDE 573:39
cursed: counted them and c. his HOUS 264:28
c. Whatever brute HOUS 264:21
He c. him in sleeping BARH 33:13
That c. man SPEN 516:7
whom thou cursest is c. BIBLE 48:13
Curses: C. are like young chickens SOUT 513:23
C., not loud but deep SHAK 463:2
so c. all Eve's daughters SHAK 469:14
with c. from pole to pole BLAKE 85:24
curst: all succeeding ages c. DRYD 194:6
c. be he that moves my SHAK 495:22
curtail: we c. the already curtail'd CALV 127:15
curtain: draw the c. close SHAK 446:7
Drew Priam's c. SHAK 441:1
iron c. has descended across CHUR 150:18

saying 'Bring down the c. RAB 404:1
these gifts a c. before 'em SHAK 488:1
'Up with the c. BROW 100:35
when she drew the c. BALL 30:11
Curtain'd: C. with cloudy red MILT 344:14
curtains: c. of Solomon BIBLE 56:16
fringed c. of thine eye SHAK 485:1
Curteis: C. he was CHAU 141:13
curteisie: freedom and c. CHAU 141:9
curteisye: She is mirour of alle c. CHAU 142:23
curtiosity: was full of 'satiable c. KIPL 304:20
Curtsey: C. while you're thinking CARR 134:30
Who made a remarkable c. LEAR 311:17
curtsies: Low-crooked c. SHAK 449:24
that dream on c. straight SHAK 481:28
curveship: c. lend a myth to God CRANE 168:29
Curzon: is George Nathaniel C. ANON 7:1
Cusha: C.!' calling ING 270:14
cushes: His c. on his thighs SHAK 440:7
cushion: c. and soft Dean invite POPE 378:4
custard pie: joke is ultimately a c. ORW 365:10
Custodes: custodiet ipsos C. JUV 287:22
custodierit: Nisi Dominus c. civitatem BIBLE 83:12
custodiet: c. ipsos Custodes JUV 287:22
custom: contrary to c. and experience HUME 267:21
c., and fear HARDY 240:3
C. calls me to 't SHAK 427:17
c. lie upon thee with WORD 579:8
c. loathsome to the eye JAM 271:3
C. reconciles us to everything BURKE 108:10
c. should corrupt the world TENN 535:25
C. that is before all law DAN 170:22
C., that unwritten law DAV 172:4
C., then HUME 267:14
custom to whom c. BIBLE 75:22
Hath not old c. made this SHAK 424:31
nor c. stale SHAK 422:5
sitting at the receipt of c. BIBLE 65:21
That monster, c. SHAK 435:18
customer: tough c. in argeyment DICK 175:24
customers: raising up a people of c. SMITH 509:12
customs: ancient c. and its manhood ENN 208:23
c. of his tribe and island SHAW 496:9
cut: an' c. 'is stripes away KIPL 298:20
Cannot see the record c. HOUS 263:2
cheerful ways of men C. off MILT 347:8
c. his throat before he SWIFT 528:9
C. is the branch that might MARL 329:16
c. my conscience to fit HELL 244:15
c. off out of the land BIBLE 59:23
C. short his being SHER 506:1
guardsman's c. and thrust HUXL 269:3
in the evening it is c. PRAY 395:18
Nor c. each other's throats GOLD 231:15
scuttled ship or c. a throat BYRON 122:30
unkindest c. of all SHAK 450:28
will I c. off Israel out BIBLE 50:31
you can c. that right out AUDEN 19:14
cute: nitidum bene curata c. vises HOR 258:16
Cutlets: suggested we should play 'C.' GROS 237:1
cut-purse: c. of the empire SHAK 435:11
Cuts: C. off so many years SHAK 450:4
cutting: c. all the pictures out BELL 38:23
he of c. foreign throats SHAK 481:28
Went on c. bread and butter THAC 546:3
Cutty-sark: Weel done, C. BURNS 115:11
cygnes: *un lac au milieu des c.* AUG 21:11
cygnet: c.'s down is harsh SHAK 486:19
cygnets: doth the swan her downy c. SHAK 445:24
cymbal: talk but a tinkling c. BACON 26:15

tinkling c. BIBLE 76:14
cymbals: upon the well-tuned c. PRAY 400:1
Cynara: faithful to thee, C. DOWS 191:12
Cynic: precepts from the C. tub MILT 341:16
cynical: of a melancholy nor a c. CHES 145:23
Cynicism: C. is intellectual dandyism MER 337:31
cynosure: c. of neighbouring eyes MILT 342:20
Cynthia: C. of this minute POPE 377:18
cypress: in sad c. let me be laid SHAK 489:4
Nor waves the c. TENN 542:14
shall see the c. spread PEAC 371:1
cypresses: Along the avenue of c. LAWR 311:5
Cyprus: That rings black C. with FLEC 214:16
Cyrano: C.: *Mon panache* ROST 410:12
Cyrene: parts of Libya about C. BIBLE 73:23
Cyril: took young C. to church ELIOT 202:7
Cythera: It's C. BAUD 35:8
Cytherean: throned C. be fallen SWIN 530:7
D: big D. GILB 228:2
there are your d.'s for you WYCH 583:26
Da: D. mi basia mille CAT 136:26
D. mihi castitatem et continentiam AUG 21:14
D. quod iubes et iube quod AUG 21:17
Dad: To meet their D. BURNS 113:5
dada: mama of d. FAD 209:18
daffadillies: d. fill their cups with MILT 343:15
Daffadowndillies: Strew me the ground with D. SPEN 517:3
daff'd: that d. the world aside SHAK 440:6
daffodil: On a bed of d. sky TENN 540:9
shining d. dies TENN 540:17
daffodils: d., That come before SHAK 491:26
dances with the d. WORD 578:1
Fair d. HERR 249:28
host, of golden d. WORD 577:29
I never saw d. so beautiful WORD 576:31
in the west wind, and d. MAS 334:9
When d. begin to peer SHAK 491:17
daft: d. and happy hills THOM 546:22
warld thinks the tither d. SCOTT 418:28
dagger: d. of the mind SHAK 459:15
desperate deadly daunting d. WYCH 583:26
Is this a d. which I see SHAK 459:15
Thou stick'st a d. in me SHAK 467:6
daggers: fighting with d. in a hogshead SCOTT 419:2
Give me the d. SHAK 460:11
I will speak d. to her SHAK 434:26
There's d. in men's smiles SHAK 461:4
Dahin: D.! Dahin GOET 230:13
dahlias: d. are dead SURT 525:16
daily: consumed away through my d. complaining PRAY 391:16
d. beauty in his life SHAK 477:3
d. increase in thy holy PRAY 388:22
Give us this day our d. bread BIBLE 64:24
which cometh upon me d. BIBLE 77:12
Daily Telegraph: young lions of the D. ARN 15:23
dainties: d. are all cates SHAK 484:9
hath not fed of the d. SHAK 457:1
spiced d. KEATS 289:20
daintily: must have things d. served BETJ 42:19
dairies: now foul sluts in d. CORB 162:13
dairy: doth nightly rob the d. JONS 284:1
daisies: Buttercups and d. HOW 267:2
d. growing over me KEATS 295:2
d. pied and violets blue SHAK 457:18
D. smell-less FLET 215:21
D., those pearled Arcturi SHEL 503:18
lie upon the d. and discourse GILB 227:21
Meadows trim with d. pied MILT 342:20
sea-d. feast on the sun SWIN 530:24
Daisy: D. and Lily SITW 508:12
d. delectable SKEL 508:18

thou who mourn'st the D.'s BURNS 115:19
Dalhousie: Lady D. are dead MCG 325:5
dalliance: d. in the wardrobe lies SHAK 443:12
primrose path of d. treads SHAK 430:18
dallies: d. with the innocence SHAK 489:3
dam: did not give a singel d. FLEM 214:25
pretty chickens and their d. SHAK 462:17
damage: moral or intellectual d. KRUG 306:1
which might d. his career BARR 34:20
You might d. the trees LEAR 312:26
damaged: Archangel a little d. LAMB 307:29
damages: He first d. his mind ANON 10:1
Damascus: rivers of D. BIBLE 51:28
dame: 'La belle d. sans mercy' KEATS 289:21
'La belle D. sans Merci KEATS 290:21
sits our sulky sullen d. BURNS 115:3
Dame Lurch: modest D. BLAKE 87:20
dames: Stoutly struts his d. before MILT 342:17
damm'd: current in this place d. SHAK 439:24
dammed: only saved by being d. HOOD 255:18
damn: d. by rule OTWAY 366:3
d. her at a venture LAMB 308:10
'D. the age LAMB 307:37
D. the torpedoes FARR 210:24
d. those authors whom they CHUR 148:19
D. with faint praise POPE 376:26
D. you, Jack BONE 89:1
He doesn't give a d. ANON 7:13
like a parson's d. HARDY 241:14
not worth a d. WELL 567:18
praises one another d. WYCH 584:2
to d. the consequences MILN 340:18
with a spot d. him SHAK 451:9
Damna: D. tamen celeres reparant HOR 261:16
damnation: be blasted to eternal d. SHAW 498:18
deep d. of his taking-off SHAK 459:6
from everlasting d. PRAY 385:16
Heap on himself d. MILT 345:8
I dare d. SHAK 436:7
damnations: Twenty-nine distinct d. BROW 105:7
damn'd: All silent and all d. WORD 580:2
d. to everlasting fame POPE 380:1
foremost shall be d. to fame POPE 375:19
health or goblin d. SHAK 430:24
damned: d. and luxurious mountain SHAK 445:4
D. from here to Eternity KIPL 299:10
d. lies and statistics DISR 187:7
ever d. with Lucifer MARL 329:6
has been a d. nice thing WELL 567:19
I'll be d. for never SHAK 438:9
is the brandy of the d. SHAW 497:27
one d. thing OMAL 365:5
public be d. VAND 555:7
Publish and be d. WELL 568:10
those who shall be d. JOHN 279:17
thou must be d. perpetually MARL 329:11
to have written a d. play REYN 405:15
Water your d. flower-pots BROW 105:5
what those d. dots meant CHUR 149:24
will be d. if you don't DOW 191:11
damnés: les d. de la terre POTT 382:3
damning: always had a taste for d. MOORE 357:4
By d. those they have no BUTL 117:23
careless of the d. sin COWP 165:8
Damnosa: D. hereditas GAIUS 220:27
D. quid non imminuit dies HOR 260:26
damoysele: cleped fair d. Pertelote CHAU 142:32
damozel: blessed d. leaned out ROSS 409:14
damp: d. souls of housemaids ELIOT 203:27
poisonous d. of night disponge SHAK 423:4
damsel: d. with a dulcimer COL 156:30

to every man a d. or two BIBLE 49:13
Dan: Dangerous D. McGrew SERV 420:14
From D. even to Beer-sheba BIBLE 49:30
travel from D. to Beersheba STER 519:2
Danaë: Now lies the Earth all D. TENN 542:14
Danaos: timeo D. et dona VIRG 558:1
dance: ae best d. e'er cam BURNS 113:13
at least before they d. POPE 380:8
d. an antic hay MARL 329:17
d. attendance on their SHAK 447:24
d. is a measured pace BACON 24:23
D. on the sands SHAK 495:19
dancer from the d. YEATS 584:11
d. while you can AUDEN 18:13
d. with you in Brabant SHAK 456:22
departs too far from the d. POUND 383:21
fixed thee mid this d. BROW 104:11
On with the d. BYRON 120:21
there the d. is ELIOT 202:15
time to d. BIBLE 55:12
to d. at our bridal SCOTT 417:11
when you do d. SHAK 491:27
who have learn'd to d. POPE 378:22
will you join the d. CARR 134:14
danced: David d. before the Lord BIBLE 50:18
They d. by the light LEAR 312:14
ye have not d. BIBLE 66:3
dancer: d., coiner of sweet words ARN 14:25
in measure, like a d. ELIOT 202:26
know the d. from the dance YEATS 584:11
dancers: To the d. dancing in tune TENN 540:10
dances: breaks the threaded d. AUDEN 18:10
He capers, he d. SHAK 469:10
In hamlets, d. on the green SCOTT 416:17
makes no progress; it d. LIGNE 314:12
shall have no time for d. MACN 326:16
Their d. were procession CORB 162:15
danceth: in hope d. without musick HERB 246:22
Dan Chaucer: D., mighty Shakespeare BRID 92:9
Dancing: D. in the chequered shade MILT 342:22
Fluttering and d. WORD 577:29
Follows with d. and fills SWIN 528:18
manners of a d. master JOHN 274:10
now for some d. with HOR 260:3
Say I am d. SHAK 421:23
You and I are past our d. SHAK 482:1
dandelions: Sheaves of drooping d. BETJ 43:19
dandyism: Cynicism is intellectual d. MER 337:31
Dane: antique Roman than a D. SHAK 437:24
never get rid of the D. KIPL 298:15
Dane-geld: is called paying the D. KIPL 298:15
Danes: D.' Wit ROCH 407:5
danger: bright face of d. STEV 520:24
d. chiefly lies in acting CHUR 148:21
D. knows full well SHAK 449:19
d. o'er OWEN 366:28
d. of hell fire BIBLE 64:12
D., the spur of all great CHAP 140:15
d. to the country VICT 556:15
everything is in d. NIET 363:5
having any share in the d. LUCR 320:6
in d. of her former tooth SHAK 461:12
in d. of Popery so long ADD 2:19
much as to be out of d. HUXL 269:9
One should be in less d. NASH 359:18
Out of this nettle, d. SHAK 438:29
run into any kind of d. PRAY 385:3
that we are in great d. SHAK 444:14
There is no d. to a man CHAP 140:8
they put themselves in d. WYATT 583:21
dangerous: Beware, I am d. BAG 28:20
D. Dan McGrew SERV 420:14

d. to sit to Sargent ANON 6:8
d. to know LAMB 306:25
fables, and d. deceits PRAY 400:9
have I in me something d. SHAK 437:7
Into the d. world I leapt BLAKE 87:23
is a d. precedent CORN 162:23
little knowledge is d. HUXL 269:9
such men are d. SHAK 448:20
though it were d. to meet WHAR 569:8
To a most d. sea SHAK 467:11
dangerously: from life is to live d. NIET 363:9
Dangers: D. by being despised grow BURKE 111:33
d. fright him and no labours JOHN 282:30
d. I had pass'd SHAK 474:1
fear of tomorrow's d. DONNE 191:2
of so many and great d. PRAY 386:8
perils and d. of this night PRAY 385:10
What d. thou canst make BURNS 115:9
dangling: thou up yon d. apricocks SHAK 479:17
Daniel: D. come to judgment SHAK 468:3
second D. SHAK 468:8
danket: Nun d. alle Gott RINK 406:6
Danny Deever: 'For they're hangin' D. KIPL 298:20
danse: marche pas, il d. LIGNE 314:12
Dant: That highte D. CHAU 142:31
Dante: D.—known to that gentleman DICK 178:27
D. never stays too long MAC 324:9
D. of the dread Inferno BROW 103:1
D. once prepared to paint BROW 102:30
D., who loved well because BROW 102:31
we knew D. was no good BUTL 118:35
Daphne: Apollo hunted D. so MARV 332:2
dapper: d. boot TENN 540:23
dappled: Glory be to God for d. HOPK 256:22
round tears run down his d. THOM 549:19
dapple-dawn-drawn: d. Falcon HOPK 257:4
Dapples: D. the drowsy east SHAK 473:11
dare: always had licence to d. HOR 257:10
d. not trust it without BROW 97:5
D. the unpastured dragon SHEL 499:15
D. to be true HERB 247:2
d. to be unhappy ROWE 410:25
d. to die POPE 379:21
d. to do our duty as we LINC 314:17
do menace heaven and d. MARL 330:5
gentle woman d. SOUT 514:6
I can d. to be poor GAY 223:25
I d. damnation SHAK 436:7
Letting 'I d. not' wait SHAK 459:8
none d. call it treason HAR 242:10
our unworthiness we d. PRAY 388:7
What man dare, I d. SHAK 461:21
what men d. do SHAK 473:1
You who d. MER 337:21
dared: d. attack my Chesterton BELL 39:27
Determined, d., and done SMART 509:4
dares: do that d. love attempt SHAK 482:10
Who d. do more is none SHAK 459:9
Darien: upon a peak in D. KEATS 292:18
daring: d. of a moment's surrender ELIOT 205:11
song too d. PRIOR 400:22
dark: All d. and comfortless SHAK 455:4
Between the d. LONG 316:9
blind man in a d. room BOWEN 90:23
children fear to go in the d. BACON 26:1
Climb to our proper d. YEATS 587:2
clock has stopped in the d. ELIOT 202:9
colours will agree in the d. BACON 27:32
d., amid the blaze MILT 350:15
D. and terrible beyond MAC 324:22
d. and true and tender TENN 542:5
d. as night SHAK 495:15
d. backward and abysm SHAK 484:24
d., boggy GOLD 232:25
d. horse DISR 187:2

'D. lowers the tempest overhead

    LONG 316:15

d. night of the soul   FITZ 213:22
d. sanctuary of incapacity   CHES 146:5
d. Satanic mills   BLAKE 86:16
D. with excessive bright   MILT 347:9
d. womb where I began   MAS 333:22
d. world of sin   BICK 84:4
dim and the d. cloths   YEATS 585:9
ever-during d.   MILT 347:8
great leap in the d.   HOBB 251:24
Hellish d.   SURT 525:15
hides a d. soul   MILT 341:8
Kept in a d. house   SHAK 490:24
Lady is as good i' th' d.   HERR 249:12
made a leap into the d.   BROWN 95:9
murmur and the poring d.   SHAK 444:9
one stride comes the d.   COL 155:16
Out in the d. over   THOM 547:20
saturnine, d., and melancholic   CONG 159:17
That for ways that are d.   HARTE 242:29
through the blanket of the d.   SHAK 459:2
through the spaces of the d.   ELIOT 204:9
us i' the d. to rise   BROW 104:27
want to go home in the d.   HENRY 245:24
we are for the d.   SHAK 424:2
darken: days d. round me   TENN 535:24
darkeneth: d. counsel by words   BIBLE 52:41
darkening: sky is d. like a stain   AUDEN 21:10
darker: let us speak of d. days   CHUR 150:8
Save that the sky grows d.   CHES 146:16
world was at least not d.   ELIOT 201:12
darkling: are here as on a d. plain   ARN 12:23
D. I listen   KEATS 291:22
darkly: d. looked he at the wall   MAC 322:14
through a glass, d.   BIBLE 76:14
darkness: Aye on the shores of d.

    KEATS 292:25

cast away the works of d.   PRAY 386:4
cast off the works of d.   BIBLE 75:24
cast out into outer d.   BIBLE 65:17
d., and in the shadow   PRAY 397:7
D. came down on the field   THAC 545:26
d. comprehended it not   BIBLE 71:23
d. had to a great extent   HARDY 241:19
darkness is no d. with thee   PRAY 399:5
d. over the land of Egypt   BIBLE 47:15
d. that it may be night   PRAY 397:1
d. was upon the face   BIBLE 44:22
Death has made His d.   TENN 537:3
did the act of d. with   SHAK 454:18
encounter d. as a bride   SHAK 464:12
far as light excelleth d.   BIBLE 55:10
great d. falling on my   PAIN 367:18
Great Gorgon, Prince of d.   SPEN 516:1
great horror and d. fell   BUNY 107:25
horror of great d. fell   BIBLE 46:3
instruments of d. tell us truths   SHAK 458:18
in the d. and the cold   STEV 522:26
jaws of d. do devour it   SHAK 469:20
land of d. and the shadow   BIBLE 52:20
land...where the light is as d.   BIBLE 52:21
leaves the world to d.   GRAY 234:18
lie where shades of d.   DE L 174:1
Lighten our d.   PRAY 385:10
lump bred up in d.   KYD 306:6
Men loved d. rather than   BIBLE 71:39
pass'd the door of D.   FITZ 213:4
people that walked in d.   BIBLE 58:6
Peradventure the d. shall   PRAY 399:5
pestilence that walketh in d.   PRAY 395:21
prince of d. is a gentleman   SHAK 454:24
race that long in d. pin'd   SCOT 419:7
rather d. visible   MILT 344:25
Ring out the d. of the land   TENN 537:15
Scatters the rear of d.   MILT 342:17
slope thro' d. up to God   TENN 536:28
Swaddled with d.   ELIOT 203:4
talks of d. at noon-day   COWP 166:12
Terror of d.   CHAP 140:7

To sit in d. here   MILT 346:15
to them that sit in d.   BIBLE 69:7
universal d. buries all   POPE 376:2
When awful d. and silence   LEAR 312:2
winds will call the d.   SHEL 504:7
Yet still between his D.   BYRON 126:8
darksome: he goes along the d. road

    CAT 136:23

spent the d. hours   GOET 230:12
Dark Tower: '*Childe Roland to the D.*

    BROW 99:30

darling: d. buds of May   SHAK 492:28
D. Mr Discobbolos   LEAR 312:10
d., my life and my bride   POE 374:23
my d. from the lions   PRAY 391:25
She is the d. of my heart   CAREY 130:26
which was my lady's d.   CAT 136:22
darlings: wealthy curled d.   SHAK 473:22
Dar'st: D. thou, Cassius   SHAK 448:14
dart: Time shall throw a d.   BROW 97:25
darter: d. es died o' the fever   TENN 544:5
darts: fiery d. of the wicked   BIBLE 78:10
Dasein: grössten Genuss vom D.   NIET 363:9
Dash: D. down yon cup of Samian

    BYRON 123:4

dashing: d. Swiss officer'   RUSS 412:22
dastard: d. in war   SCOTT 417:10
dastards: commands, and d. me   BROW 96:7
dat: *Inopi beneficium bis d.*   PUBL 402:3
data: theorize before one has d.   DOYLE 192:7
date: keep them up to d.   SHAW 496:25
dated: music should never be d.   GOLD 232:29
dateless: d. bargain to engrossing

    SHAK 483:31

dates: Manna and d.   KEATS 289:20
three d. on their slates   CARR 134:18
very few D. in this History   AUST 22:19
daubed: d. it with slime   BIBLE 46:41
daughter: alive will ever rear a d.   GAY 222:12
all to my elder d.   THOM 547:18
bailiff's d. of Islington   BALL 30:9
Carnage is Thy d.   WORD 578:21
Cato's d.   SHAK 449:16
'D. am I in my mother's   KIPL 301:20
d. of a hundred Earls   TENN 537:26
d. of debate   ELIZ 205:27
D. of the Vine to Spouse   FITZ 213:1
d. of the gods   TENN 533:6
d. of Zion is left   BIBLE 57:16
d. went through the river   BUNY 107:37
death of your d. would   AUST 23:18
Duke-and-a-Duchess's d.   BARH 33:26
Elderly ugly d.   GILB 229:3
farmer's d. hath soft brown   CALV 127:1
Gigantic d. of the West   TENN 533:28
gold for the king's d.   SWIN 530:17
had taken his little d.   LONG 317:20
I am the d. of Earth   SHEL 500:7
King's d. is all glorious   PRAY 392:17
landlord's d.   NOYES 364:13
loved the bailiff's d.   BALL 30:7
maxims preaching down a d.'s   TENN 538:22
my ducats! O my d.   SHAK 466:18
My father had a d. lov'd   SHAK 489:7
One fair d. and no more   SHAK 432:21
put your d. on the stage   COW 163:21
so is her d.   BIBLE 60:33
sole of my house   BYRON 120:17
Stern d. of the voice of God   WORD 579:15
Still harping on my d.   SHAK 432:6
this Lord Ullin's d.   CAMP 129:2
Translated D.   AUDEN 18:4
What Cato's d. durst not   ROWE 410:25
Who married Noah's d.   AYT 24:7
yet more beautiful d.   HOR 259:22
youngest virgin-d. of the skies   DRYD 197:32
daughters: be none of Beauty's d.

    BYRON 125:27

came in unto the d. of men   BIBLE 45:33
d. may be as the polished   PRAY 399:12

d. of musick shall be brought   BIBLE 56:11
I am all the d. of my father's   SHAK 489:8
Kings' d. were among thy   PRAY 392:16
so curses all Eve's d.   SHAK 469:14
sweet her artless d.   KEATS 292:16
Words are men's d.   MADD 326:19
words are the d. of earth   JOHN 281:6
ye d. of Jerusalem   BIBLE 56:16
your d. shall prophesy   BIBLE 61:15
Daumier: one small Goya or a D.

    AUDEN 19:16

daunte: whom death could not d.   BALL 31:8
dauntless: d. child   GRAY 235:18
D. the slug-horn to my   BROW 99:30
so d. in war   SCOTT 417:9
dauphin: kingdom of daylight's d.

    HOPK 257:4

David: D. his ten thousands   BIBLE 50:13
D. in the midst   SMART 509:2
D. wrote the Psalms   NAYL 360:10
Teste D. cum Sibylla   CEL 138:5
Though D. had his Jonathan   HERB 247:5
Davy: D. Abominated gravy   BENT 41:6
Davy Jones: if D. were after you   DICK 176:10
daw: I am no wiser than a d.   SHAK 445:20
dawn: catch and to reflect the d.   MAC 323:11
d. comes up like thunder   KIPL 301:5
D. shall over Lethe break   BELL 39:22
Dreaming when D.'s Left   FITZ 212:6
dusk and d. many a head   MULL 359:1
face and a grey d. breaking   MAS 334:4
I said to D.: Be sudden   THOM 548:12
moon on my left and the d.   BELL 39:16
music of its trees at d.   ARN 14:1
Rosy-fingered d.   HOMER 254:5
through night hooting at d.   BEER 38:2
We'd see truth d. together   BROW 99:2
Will sing at d.   BROW 97:27
dawns: It d. in Asia   HOUS 262:13
strange as in dark summer d.   TENN 542:4
day: all in one d.   BOIL 89:11
alternate Night and D.   FITZ 212:13
arrow that flieth by d.   PRAY 395:21
at least in this thy d.   BIBLE 71:3
Believe each d. that has   HOR 258:16
benight our happiest d.   DONNE 188:20
blinds let through the d.   HOUS 265:2
breaks the blank d.   TENN 536:6
bright d. is done   SHAK 424:2
burden and heat of the d.   BIBLE 67:15
bursts of open d. between   FRY 220:5
business of the day in the d.   WELL 568:2
close the drama with the d.   BERK 41:20
compare thee to a summer's d.   SHAK 492:28
d. and a night Love sang   SWIN 528:24
d. and night shall not   BIBLE 45:37
d. becomes more solemn   SHEL 501:7
d. be never so longe   HAWES 243:3
d. brought back my night   MILT 351:14
D. by day   PRAY 384:18
d. in a pillar of a cloud   BIBLE 47:21
d. in which he was taken   BIBLE 73:20
d. is at hand   BIBLE 75:24
d. is gone   KEATS 292:13
d. joins the past Eternity   BYRON 121:4
d. of his wrath is come   BIBLE 81:30
d. of small nations has   CHAM 139:6
d. of the Lord is near   BIBLE 61:17
d. of vengeance of our   BIBLE 60:8
d. perish wherein I was   BIBLE 52:11
d. returns too soon   BYRON 125:26
d. Rose with delight   KING 296:13
d.'s at the morn   BROW 103:21
d.'s dead sanctities   THOM 548:15
d.'s disasters in his   GOLD 231:2
d. star arise in your hearts   BIBLE 80:34
d. that comes betwixt   CAREY 130:27
d. Thou gavest   ELL 206:7
d. which the Lord hath   PRAY 398:21
death of each d.'s life   SHAK 460:8

death was a dark cold d.   AUDEN 19:2
each d. dies with sleep   HOPK 256:21
encounter such a d. as this   AUST 22:10
end of this d.'s business   SHAK 451:33
everlasting d.   DONNE 187:23
Farewell night, welcome d.   BUNY 107:37
foul and fair a d.   SHAK 458:9
from d.'s detested glare   POPE 381:9
garden in the cool of the d.   BIBLE 45:16
Good things of d. begin   SHAK 461:14
go w'en de great d. comes   HARR 242:17
greater light to rule the d.   BIBLE 45:3
guest that tarrieth but a d.   BIBLE 62:18
hair the eyes of D.   SHEL 505:3
have known a better d.   SCOTT 416:8
I have lost a d.   TITUS 551:6
it is not yet near d.   SHAK 483:13
It was Thy d.   CRAS 169:6
joint-labourer with the d.   SHAK 429:11
Joy rul'd the d.   DRYD 197:18
lark at break of d.   SHAK 493:6
left alone with our d.   AUDEN 19:7
long d. wanes   TENN 544:3
more unto the perfect d.   BIBLE 53:19
morning were the first d.   BIBLE 45:1
mouth of the dying d.   AUDEN 19:2
murmur of a summer's d.   ARN 14:11
my arms till break of d.   AUDEN 19:17
night be turned to d.   PRAY 399:5
night do penance for a d.   WORD 580:18
night of this immortal d.   SHEL 503:14
no proper time of d.   HOOD 254:27
Now's the d.   BURNS 114:34
ofte a myrie someris d.   CHAU 144:8
one d. in thy courts   PRAY 395:13
One d. telleth another   PRAY 390:11
'Our d. is our loss   AUDEN 20:15
perfect d. nor night   SHAK 446:17
posteriors of this d.   SHAK 457:13
profit every d. that Fate   HOR 259:18
rainy d. and a contentious   BIBLE 54:39
Round the feet of the d.   SWIN 528:16
shall not burn thee by d.   PRAY 398:9
singer of an empty d.   MORR 358:9
snatches a nice d. away   HOR 261:15
Spirit on the Lord's d.   BIBLE 81:11
stand at the latter d.   BIBLE 52:31
succeeds thy little d.   PEAC 370:20
Sufficient unto the d.   BIBLE 64:32
take the whole long d.   ROSS 409:11
that each d. is like a year   WILDE 572:15
There is no d. for me   SHAK 491:1
There's night and d.   BORR 90:4
this long weary d. have end   SPEN 515:26
thou d. in night   SHAK 483:7
thousand Blossoms with the D.   FITZ 212:8
Underneath D.'s azure   SHEL 501:23
Until the d. break   BIBLE 56:24
what a d. may bring forth   BIBLE 54:36
while d. stood distinct   HARDY 241:19
who dwell in realms of D.   BLAKE 85:18
Without all hope of d.   MILT 350:15
with some streaks of d.   SHAK 461:15
withstand in the evil d.   BIBLE 78:10
Would seem a winter's d.   ROCH 406:20
daybreak: vision Of d.   SASS 415:3
white tremendous d.   BROO 94:29
day-dreams: Like the d. of melancholy
  DRYD 197:16
daye: d. very meete and conveniente
  MORE 357:20
dayeseye: it calle may the 'd.'   CHAU 143:31
day-labour: 'Doth God exact d.   MILT 351:10
daylight: abed and d. slumber   HOUS 262:15
all the long and lone d.   SHEL 505:2
Between the dark and the d.   LONG 316:9
kingdom of d.'s dauphin   HOPK 257:4
methinks is but the d. sick   SHAK 468:20
see a church by d.   SHAK 472:5
We burn d.   SHAK 469:6

Dayrolles: Give D. a chair   CHES 146:9
days: all the d. of my life   PRAY 390:22
all the works and d.   ELIOT 203:19
because the d. are evil   BIBLE 78:4
behold these present d.   SHAK 494:20
best d. of life   VIRG 560:16
broader lands and better d.   CHUR 150:3
burnt-out ends of smoky d.   ELIOT 204:7
cause that the former d.   BIBLE 55:20
Chequer-board of Nights and D.   FITZ 213:5
d. are in the yellow leaf   BYRON 125:11
d. are swifter than a weaver's   BIBLE 52:18
d. dividing lover and lover   SWIN 528:17
d. of golden dreams   BRON 93:24
d. of his pilgrimage vanish   LEAR 311:24
d. of Methuselah were nine   BIBLE 45:31
d. of our youth are   BYRON 125:29
d. of wine and roses   DOWS 191:13
d. seem lank and long   GILB 228:29
d. that are no more   TENN 542:2
d. will finish up the year   SHAK 446:18
drawing d. out   SHAK 450:3
dream of the d. when work   CHES 147:22
end my d. in a tavern   ANON 10:14
fair d. will shine   GILB 228:15
fall'n on evil d.   MILT 348:28
from the d. that have been   BULW 107:1
good d. speed and depart   MART 331:11
I am but two d. old   BLAKE 88:1
In the d. ere I was born   BLUNT 89:5
in the midst of his d.   BIBLE 60:25
length of d. understanding   BIBLE 52:24
Length of d. is in her   BIBLE 53:16
life with multitude of d.   JOHN 283:1
man in his hasty d.   BRID 92:10
number of my d.   PRAY 391:30
of a woman is of few d.   BIBLE 52:26
of d. in goodness spent   BYRON 125:22
our d. on the earth are   BIBLE 51:39
O ye Nights, and D.   PRAY 384:22
see better d.   BEHN 38:15
see good d.   PRAY 391:23
seemed unto him but a few d.   BIBLE 46:21
Six d. shalt thou labour   BIBLE 47:24
teach us to number our d.   PRAY 395:20
that thy d. may be long   BIBLE 47:24
These are not dark d.   CHUR 150:8
these fair well-spoken d.   SHAK 480:19
up the story of our d.   RAL 404:15
We have seen better d.   SHAK 486:9
What are d.   LARK 310:3
day-star: So sinks the d.   MILT 343:17
daysyes: men callen d. in our toun
  CHAU 143:30
day-time: I cry in the d.   PRAY 390:16
dazzled: flowed in it d. their eyes   BALL 31:3
shrine d. by your brilliance   SCH 415:9
De: doctrine of the enclitic D.   BROW 101:1
Deacons: D., with true knowledge
  PRAY 385:18
dead: act as if we were d.   POUND 383:15
After the singer is d.   STEV 523:1
all our best men are d.   PUNCH 403:2
all the rest are d.   LONG 316:8
another Bishop d.   MELB 336:19
any man fears to be d.   BACON 27:41
barrows of the happier d.   TENN 543:13
be a fool than to be d.   STEV 522:3
being d. unto sin   PRAY 388:10
Beside the Severn's d.   HOUS 262:13
Better be with the d.   SHAK 461:12
Blessed are the d. which   BIBLE 82:18
character d. at every word   SHER 506:29
charity more than the d.   ARN 12:20
cheer a d. man's sweetheart   HOUS 263:11
Christ risen from the d.   BIBLE 76:22
clamorous o'er the d.   SHEL 499:16
Come not, when I am d.   TENN 533:2
conference With the d.   WEBS 566:22
converse with the mighty d.   THOM 549:24

d., and buried   PRAY 384:26
d. Are but as pictures   SHAK 460:11
dead bury their d.   BIBLE 65:19
d., but in the Elysian   DISR 185:25
d. Did squeak and gibber   SHAK 429:12
D. flies cause the ointment   BIBLE 56:1
D., for a ducat   SHAK 435:1
D. from the waist down   BROW 101:1
d. hour of the night   BALL 32:2
d. leaf thou mightest bear   SHEL 502:12
d. or my watch has stopped   MARX 333:1
d. shall be raised incorruptible   BIBLE 76:29
d. shall live   DRYD 197:25
d. there is no rivalry   MAC 324:9
d., the sweet musician   LONG 317:14
d. thing that smells sweet   THOM 547:17
d. we owe only truth   VOLT 561:19
d. which he slew at his   BIBLE 49:28
d. whose pupils we have   BUTL 119:21
d., who will not fight   GREN 236:15
d. woman bites not   GRAY 234:13
democracy of the d.   CHES 148:5
dew on the face of the d.   BEERS 38:8
England mourns for her d.   BINY 84:9
Evelyn Hope is d.   BROW 100:25
Faith without works is d.   BIBLE 80:12
famous, calm, and d.   BROW 100:34
fell at his feet as d.   BIBLE 81:14
fortnight d.   ELIOT 205:6
frightful when one's d.   POPE 377:16
gaze the strengthless d.   HOUS 263:3
generally shammin' when 'e's d.   KIPL 299:9
God is d.   NIET 363:6
God is d.   NERV 360:25
Harrow the house of the d.   AUDEN 20:7
Hector is d.   SHAK 487:18
He is d. and gone   SHAK 435:33
Here is d. lie we because   HOUS 266:3
himself must be d.   AUST 23:29
his brother is d.   BIBLE 46:35
if I am d. he would like   HOLL 253:3
'If Lucy should be d.   WORD 582:21
if the d. rise not   BIBLE 76:24
I lain for a century d.   TENN 540:12
imagined for the mighty d.   KEATS 289:1
immortal d. who live again   ELIOT 201:27
I should be d. of joy   BROW 101:21
It struck him d.   BELL 39:29
I would that I were d.   TENN 539:23
judge the quick and the d.   PRAY 384:26
King of all these the d.   HOMER 254:6
King of Spain is d.   FARQ 210:23
kissed by the English d.   OWEN 367:6
ladies d. and lovely knights   SHAK 494:19
Lady Dalhousie are d.   MCG 325:5
lane to the land of the d.   AUDEN 18:10
lasting mansions of the d.   COWP 168:10
living among the d.   BIBLE 71:16
Living and the noble D.   WORD 580:24
Lovely lads and d. and rotten   HOUS 263:9
Lycidas is d.   MILT 343:2
maid is not d., but sleepeth   BIBLE 65:27
Mistah Kurtz—he d.   CONR 161:18
much less when he's d.   DICK 178:23
my enemy is d.   WHIT 570:11
My lady's sparrow is d.   CAT 136:22
mysel' were d. and gane   BALL 32:11
Nobody heard him, the d. man   SMITH 510:26
not d.—but gone before   ROG 407:8
once d. by fate   BEAU 36:1
out ten to see a d. Indian   SHAK 485:8
over the rich D.   BROO 94:7
Past bury its d.   LONG 317:3
profane the service of the d.   SHAK 437:3
quite for ever d.   CONG 160:16
Rejoice ye d.   BRID 92:18
resurrection of the d.   BIBLE 76:22
resurrection of the d.   BIBLE 76:27
resuscitate the d. art Of poetry   POUND 383:1
sculptur'd d. on each side   KEATS 289:10

sea gave up the d. which BIBLE 82:29
Sea shall give up her d. PRAY 400:4
she has been d. many times PATER 369:19
she's d. DONNE 187:20
simplify me when I'm d. DOUG 191:9
Since faith is d. WYATT 583:20
sleeps with the enduring d. SHEL 499:19
Smiling the boy fell d. BROW 101:16
stepping-stones Of their d. selves
   TENN 535:33
strikes him d. for thine TENN 542:7
talk with the departed d. SHEL 501:6
'thanked God my wife was d. BROW 106:1
that are d. to sin BIBLE 74:43
That d. men rise up never SWIN 529:25
that's a d. donkey DICK 182:38
their home among the d. SHEL 500:10
their wages and are d. HOUS 265:7
There are no d. MAET 326:20
they found him with the d. WILDE 572:7
they told me you were d. CORY 163:4
This my son was d. BIBLE 70:21
thou being d. art a God SWIN 530:7
though d. with frost ere now GREV 236:17
'tis Death is d. SHEL 499:22
to my d. heart run them STEV 523:11
Towns contend for HOMER D. ANON 7:14
tuneful brethren all were d. SCOTT 416:9
two months d. SHAK 429:28
Tyrawley and I have been d. CHES 146:7
up with our English d. SHAK 443:21
very d. of Winter ANDR 4:7
voice of the d. was a living TENN 537:23
was beauty's summer d. SHAK 494:18
'we are all d.' KEYN 296:2
wench is d. MARL 329:2
what was d. was Hope WILDE 572:13
when she was d. GOLD 231:8
Where d. men meet on lips BUTL 119:17
Wherefore I praised the d. BIBLE 55:14
where there was not one d. BIBLE 47:19
Who was alive and is d. ANON 5:15
wished to see my d. body HARDY 241:18
within full of d. men's bones BIBLE 67:25
your remind me of the d. SASS 414:15
youth stone d. SASS 414:11
deadly: all other d. sin PRAY 385:16
species is more d. than KIPL 299:4
Dead March: you can hear the D. play
   KIPL 298:20
Deadwood: Tucson and D. and Lost
   BENET 40:19
deaf: chamber d. to noise SIDN 507:21
happen to be d. and dumb HOUS 266:9
He is as d. as a door BRET 92:4
To their d. pillows SHAK 462:26
turn the d. ear SWIFT 527:27
union of a d. man COL 157:19
woman's d. POPE 380:26
deafen'd: loudest wit I e'er was d.
   BYRON 124:11
deafer: d. than the blue-eyed cat TENN 534:23
deafness: mother's d. is very trifling
   AUST 22:12
tale, sir, would cure d. SHAK 484:25
deal: d. by speech than by letter BACON 26:37
d. with life as children COWP 165:11
don't d. in lies KIPL 299:22
great d. of gold JAMES 271:33
himself be given a square d. ROOS 408:7
is a great d. to be said BENT 41:5
new d. for the American ROOS 407:19
to be given a square d. ROOS 408:3
dealbabor: *et super nivem d.* BIBLE 83:6
dealer: d. in magic and spells GILB 229:2
dealing: common-sense and plain d.
   EMER 207:11
peradventure with whom they are d.
   WILS 575:2
Whose own hard d. teaches SHAK 466:4

Dean: cushion and soft D. invite POPE 378:4
D. of Christ Church SPR 517:11
may clothe an English d. COWP 167:35
no dogma, no D. DISR 185:23
not do as the d. pleases AUDEN 21:4
was an old person of D. LEAR 313:2
deans: dowagers for d. TENN 541:27
dear: days when I was d. to you HOR 260:27
d. and kindly paternal DANTE 171:12
d. Brutus SHAK 448:17
d., deluding Woman BURNS 113:25
D. heart how like you WYATT 583:22
d. to me as are the rud SHAK 449:15
d. to me in the middle LAWR 311:3
make thee terrible and d. SHEL 505:2
Plato is d. to me ARIS 12:12
right d. in the sight PRAY 397:22
sold cheap what is most d. SHAK 495:3
that bread should be so d. HOOD 255:8
this dear, d. land SHAK 478:20
too convincing—dangerously d.
   BYRON 121:34
too d. for my possessing SHAK 494:13
was to all the country d. GOLD 230:22
dearer: d. still is truth ARIS 12:12
D. than self BYRON 120:12
d. was the mother COL 157:9
law of thy mouth is d. PRAY 398:5
little d. than his horse TENN 538:19
dearest: assure you she's the d. girl
   DICK 177:14
d., you're a dunce JOHN 278:30
near'st and d. enemy SHAK 439:36
To throw away the d. thing SHAK 458:22
dearie: thinking on my d. BURNS 112:36
Dearly: D. beloved brethren PRAY 384:9
D. beloved PRAY 388:24
dearth: measure in a year of d. BLAKE 88:18
pine within and suffer d. SHAK 495:13
death: added a new terror to d. WETH 569:6
added another terror to d. LYND 321:17
After the first d. THOM 547:8
All in the valley of D. TENN 532:23
allotted d. and hell MARL 329:13
ancients dreaded d. HARE 242:3
any man's d. diminishes DONNE 190:20
apprehends d. no more dreadfully
   SHAK 464:25
are at the point of d. SHAK 483:29
arms of cool-enfolding d. WHIT 571:13
back resounded, D. MILT 347:2
bargain to engrossing d. SHAK 483:31
battles and d. GAR 221:10
Be absolute for d. SHAK 464:8
beauteous d. VAUG 555:20
be carnally minded is d. BIBLE 75:7
been studied in his d. SHAK 458:22
Be thou faithful unto d. BIBLE 81:17
bitterness of d. is past BIBLE 50:5
blaze forth the d. of princes SHAK 449:18
bosom black as d. SHAK 434:28
bridegroom in my d. SHAK 423:11
brother of d. exacteth BROW 95:24
brother of d. exacteth BROW 96:1
Brother to D. FLET 215:22
Brought d. into the world MILT 344:20
build your ship of d. LAWR 311:8
canoniz'd bones hearsed in d. SHAK 430:24
can this be d. POPE 376:4
chance, and d., and mutability SHEL 503:12
come away, d. SHAK 489:4
competition the laws of d. RUSK 412:10
consenting unto his d. BIBLE 73:29
copulation and d. ELIOT 204:12
couragious whom d. could not daunte
   BALL 31:8
cry'd out, D. MILT 347:2
darkness and the shadow of d. BIBLE 52:20
days shall men seek d. BIBLE 82:7
d. after life does greatly SPEN 516:8

D. alone reveals how small JUV 288:3
D. and his brother Sleep SHEL 500:8
D. and Morning on the silver TENN 542:16
D. and Night incessantly WHIT 570:11
D. and Toil VIRG 558:21
d., a necessary end SHAK 449:18
d.; a thousand doors SEN 420:11
d. bandaged my eyes BROW 103:32
d. be not proud DONNE 189:5
d. brag thou wander'st SHAK 492:28
D. broke at once the vital JOHN 279:1
d. came with friendly care COL 156:18
d. canonizes and sanctifies BURKE 109:5
D. closes all TENN 544:3
d. complete the same BROW 104:13
D. devours all lovely things MILL 339:29
D.! ere thou hast slain BROW 97:25
d. gnaweth upon them PRAY 393:1
D. goes dogging everywhere HENL 245:6
D. has a thousand doors MASS 336:1
D. has made His darkness TENN 537:3
D. hath asses' ears BEDD 36:27
d. hath no more dominion BIBLE 75:2
D. hath so many doors FLET 215:11
D. hath this also BACON 26:4
d.,' he said SCOTT 418:23
D., I do conceive myself BROW 96:15
D., in itself DRYD 195:26
D. is a fearful thing SHAK 464:14
d. is as a lover's pinch SHAK 424:12
d. is most in apprehension SHAK 464:11
D. is still working like HERB 247:23
d. is the cure of all diseases BROW 97:2
D. is the end of life TENN 539:15
D. is the privilege ROWE 410:24
d. joins us to the great YOUNG 588:13
D. kicks his way equally HOR 259:13
D. lays his icy hand SHIR 507:2
D. lies dead SWIN 529:20
D. lies on her like SHAK 483:15
D. must be distinguished SMITH 511:23
d. my days should expiate SHAK 493:1
D. never takes the wise LA F 306:22
d. no one so true Did share SHAK 489:4
d. of a political economist BAG 29:12
d. of each day's life SHAK 460:8
d. of your daughter would AUST 23:18
D. opens unknown doors MAS 334:1
D. put down his book AUDEN 20:19
d.'s a great disguiser SHAK 465:1
d.'s counterfeit SHAK 460:23
d. shall have no dominion THOM 546:19
d.'s pale flag is not SHAK 483:30
D.'s second self SHAK 494:7
D.'s self is sorry JONS 284:2
D.'s shadow at the door BLUN 89:2
D. stands above me LAND 308:19
d. that is immortal has LUCR 320:9
d. the journey's end DRYD 197:10
D., the poor man's dearest BURNS 114:24
D. therefore is nothing LUCR 320:8
d. they were not divided BIBLE 50:17
d., thou shalt die DONNE 189:4
D. tramples it to fragments SHEL 499:26
d. unloads thee SHAK 464:9
D. was but A scientific WILDE 572:12
d., whene'er he call GILB 229:7
D., where is thy sting-a-ling-a-ling ANON 7:4
d., where is thy sting BIBLE 77:1
D., where is thy sting ROSS 408:20
d. who had the soldier DOUG 191:10
D. will be aghast and so CEL 138:6
D. will come when thou SHEL 505:4
d. will have his day SHAK 479:8
d. will listen to your SHEL 504:25
D., without rhetoric SIEY 508:7
decent hall of d. CHES 147:12
direful d. indeed they FLEM 214:25
disqualified by the accident of d. CHES 148:5
Doubled the globe of d. THOM 547:4

dread of something after d.   SHAK 433:8
dull cold ear of d.   GRAY 234:22
eaten to d. with rust   SHAK 441:15
eloquent, just, and mighty D.   RAL 404:16
enormously improved by d.   SAKI 413:4
envy of the devil came d.   BIBLE 62:12
even hard at d.'s door   PRAY 397:8
ever truly long'd for d.   TENN 543:20
except d. and taxes   FRAN 218:18
faith that looks through d.   WORD 579:13
fear d. as children   BACON 26:1
Fear d.?—to feel the fog   BROW 103:31
fed on the fullness of d.   SWIN 530:5
first day of our Jubilee is d.   BROW 96:21
friend and enemy is but D.   BROO 94:28
from sudden d.   PRAY 385:16
from the body of this d.   BIBLE 75:6
give me d.   HENRY 245:27
Glad to d.'s mystery   HOOD 254:10
have a rendezvous with D.   SEEG 419:15
have often thought upon d.   BACON 27:40
He brought d. into   TWAIN 554:20
Her feet go down to d.   BIBLE 53:20
heroes when the line to d.   SASS 414:10
His d. concerns the gods   SOPH 513:6
his d. was a dark cold day   AUDEN 19:2
His means of d.   SHAK 436:14
honour in one eye and d.   SHAK 448:12
I could not look on D.   KIPL 298:25
I could not stop for D.   DICK 183:15
idea of D. saves   FORS 217:3
I know d. hath ten thousand   WEBS 566:26
in love with easeful D.   KEATS 291:22
in that sleep of d.   SHAK 433:8
in the hour of d.   PRAY 385:17
in the shadow of d.   BIBLE 69:7
in the shadow of d.   PRAY 397:7
Into the gulf of d.   SHEL 499:5
Into the jaws of D.   TENN 533:1
is 'a covenant with d.   GARR 221:19
is but the shadow of d.   BROW 95:17
is death and the sole d.   BROW 100:10
is no drinking after d.   FLET 215:7
is the Black Widow, d.   LOW 319:19
is the d. of his saints   PRAY 397:22
It is but D. who comes   SCOTT 417:6
I will dare E'en D.   HERR 249:27
keys of hell and of d.   BIBLE 81:15
killed than frightened to d.   SURT 525:22
kiss of d.   SMITH 510:4
kiss the image of my d.   DRUM 193:27
land of the shadow of d.   BIBLE 58:6
last offering in d.   CAT 137:15
Life d. does end and each   HOPK 256:21
Life, the shadow of d.   SWIN 528:21
life went through with d.   VEN 556:5
lively form of d.   KYD 306:3
living d.   MILT 350:17
love is strong as d.   BIBLE 57:11
loveliness and the hour of my d.
  KEATS 294:21
lovely and soothing d.   WHIT 571:13
love thee better after d.   BROW 98:14
lucky timing of your d.   TAC 531:9
made a covenant with d.   BIBLE 58:22
make d. proud to take us   SHAK 423:18
make one in love with death   SHEL 499:2
Man has created d.   YEATS 584:21
many years of fearing d.   SHAK 450:4
marriage and d. and division   SWIN 529:10
may here find life in d.   COL 156:17
midst of life we are in d.   PRAY 389:12
million-murdering D.   ROSS 408:20
Milton, D., and Sin   YOUNG 588:14
must hate and d. return   SHEL 501:3
my father's d. before him   ELIOT 204:26
My name is D.   SOUT 513:21
Neither wish d.   SURR 524:21
no mean of d.   SHAK 450:8
none blessed before his d.   BIBLE 63:1

nor to be rhymed to d.   SIDN 508:5
not so much afraid of d.   BROW 96:20
Now boast thee, d.   SHAK 424:15
of harsh d. snatches away   VIRG 560:16
of no calamity while d.   BROW 96:22
one life and one d.   BROW 101:13
only the stroke of d.   BACON 27:41
overcome the sharpness of d.   PRAY 384:17
owe God a d.   SHAK 442:7
Pale d., the grand physician   CLARE 152:8
perchance of D.   THOM 549:27
Pontifical D.   THOM 547:22
preached to d. by wild curates   SMITH 511:16
precious friends hid in d.'s   SHAK 493:7
quiet us in a d. so noble   MILT 351:2
red fruit of thy d.   SWIN 529:28
remedy is d.   CHAM 139:13
remembered kisses after d.   TENN 542:4
report of my d.   TWAIN 554:22
restful d. I cry   SHAK 494:5
Revenge triumphs over d.   BACON 26:2
Riddles of d. Thebes   SHEL 501:1
room Do we take up in d.   SHIR 507:6
run the race with D.   JOHN 279:24
shall be destroyed is d.   BIBLE 76:23
should be glad of another d.   ELIOT 203:11
should weep for his d.   HOR 260:1
silver answer rang…'Not D.   BROW 98:9
since by man came d.   BIBLE 76:22
Sin, D., and Hell   BUNY 107:33
Sleep is a d.   BROW 97:6
snares of d. compassed   PRAY 397:19
so like d.   BROW 97:5
some one's d.   BROW 99:4
someone's d. to get a living   MOL 353:16
So shalt thou feed on D.   SHAK 495:14
stories of the d. of kings   SHAK 479:11
strange screams of d.   SHAK 460:20
strong and long-liv'd d.   DONNE 188:17
swallow up d. in victory   BIBLE 58:19
Swarm over, D.   BETJ 44:4
sweet is d. who puts   TENN 534:30
sword he sung a song of d.   BLAKE 86:19
talks of Arthur's d.   SHAK 452:27
that d. is but a groom   DONNE 189:30
that discourtesy of d.   YEATS 585:13
that sat on him was D.   BIBLE 81:29
their life was d.   ROSS 409:25
therefore d. is no such   BACON 26:2
There is a d. in the pot   BIBLE 51:26
There's D. in the cup   BURNS 113:30
there shall be no more d.   BIBLE 82:31
think there is mettle in d.   SHAK 421:20
This fell sergeant, d.   SHAK 437:22
thou art d.'s fool   SHAK 464:8
thought d. had undone so many   ELIOT 204:20
thou owest God a d.   SHAK 440:17
thou sleep the sleep of d.   BLAKE 86:11
Thou wast not born for d.   KEATS 291:21
thou wilt bring me to d.   BIBLE 52:36
through the d. of some   MAS 333:22
Till life sleep might   SHEL 504:11
Till D. untimely stopp'd   POPE 377:6
till d. us do part   PRAY 389:4
Till D. forget and d.   SWIN 530:14
'tis D. is dead   SHEL 499:22
to build the house of d.   MONT 354:15
tragedies are finish'd by a d.   BYRON 122:28
traveller betwixt life and d.   WORD 581:8
triumph over d. and sin   SPEN 515:17
ugly d. within mine eyes   SHAK 480:27
Under the ribs of D.   MILT 341:14
universe of d.   MILT 346:23
unsubstantial D. is amorous   SHAK 483:31
us hob-and-nob with D.   TENN 544:7
us in the disgrace of d.   SHAK 456:14
valley of the shadow of d.   PRAY 390:22
vasty hall of d.   ARN 14:6
wages of sin is d.   BIBLE 75:3
walk in d.'s dark vale   SCOT 419:5

was much possessed by d.   ELIOT 205:13
way to dusty d.   SHAK 463:6
we are to abolish the d.   KARR 288:16
What life and d. is   CHAP 140:8
What's d.? You'll love   BROW 103:24
What should it know of d.   WORD 583:5
When d. approached unlocked   GIBB 225:1
when d. is our physician   SHAK 474:7
When D. to either shall   BRID 92:21
where kingly D.   SHEL 499:6
whereof he caught his d.   FABY 209:16
which he slew at his d.   BIBLE 49:28
white dress, her d.   SPEN 515:6
wild carol ere her d.   TENN 535:28
Will keep a league till d.   SHAK 480:7
would fain die a dry d.   SHAK 484:22
yet afraid of d.   CHUR 148:32
deathbed: drive me mad on my d.
  BYRON 126:20
Young Jemmy Grove on his d.   BALL 30:10
deathless: let us make love d.   TREN 552:7
lightly of my d. friends   SASS 414:19
sense of some d. shame   WEBS 567:4
Death-light: D. of Africa   CHES 147:3
death-moth: nor the d. be   KEATS 291:14
deaths: many d. I live and write   HERB 247:22
More d. than one must die   WILDE 572:14
death's-head: Call in thy d. there
  HERB 247:15
death-struck: beautiful and d. year
  HOUS 264:1
deathward: Sheep driven d.   HOR 260:7
debars: Fate so enviously d.   MARV 331:19
Debasing: D. the moral currency
  ELIOT 201:26
debate: daughter of d.   ELIZ 205:27
Rupert of D.   BULW 107:2
debauch: considered as a d. of youth
  BURKE 108:16
débauchée: old blind d. of wit   WALP 563:1
debellare: subiectis et d. superbos   VIRG 559:1
debita: dimitte nobis d. nostra   MASS 335:5
Debity: we shall have a new D.   WHAR 569:10
debonair: buxom, blithe, and d.   MILT 342:13
deboshed: Thou d. fish thou   SHAK 485:14
debout: Foule esclave, d.   POTT 382:3
debt: Ambition's d. is paid   SHAK 452:2
chest contriv'd a double d.   GOLD 231:4
d., an' a flag   LOW 319:7
He'd run in d. by disputation   BUTL 117:14
he paid the d. of nature   FABY 209:15
in d., and in drink   BROME 93:10
national d.   HAM 238:13
National D. is a very Good   SELL 420:6
pay a d. to pleasure   ROCH 406:17
posterity most in their d.   INGE 270:10
debtor: am d. both to the Greeks   BIBLE 74:30
'Am I your d.   TENN 532:22
man a d. to his profession   BACON 25:16
debts: forgive us our d.   BIBLE 64:24
He that dies pays all d.   SHAK 485:16
decades: Five d. hardly modified
  HARDY 241:13
decay: begins to sicken and d.   SHAK 451:11
castle or building not in d.   BACON 26:38
Change and d. in all around   LYTE 321:19
d. no flood   YEATS 585:19
d. Of that colossal wreck   SHEL 502:16
energies of our system will d.   BALF 30:3
flourish after first d.   SPEN 516:13
general flavor of mild d.   HOLM 253:9
laws of space and time d.   CORY 163:6
muddy vesture of d.   SHAK 468:15
myself had like to this d.   SPEN 515:20
quick a growth to meet d.   HERR 249:28
seen my fondest hopes d.   MOORE 356:25
that there be no d.   PRAY 399:13
their decrepitude, their d.   LAND 309:13
things are subject to d.   DRYD 196:33
to many men's d.   SPEN 516:24

decayed: d. hole among the mountains
ELIOT 205:10
you are sufficiently d.   GILB 227:18
decaying: we are but d.   HERR 248:26
decays: Mere glimmering and d. VAUG 555:19
decease: d. calls me forth   WHIT 570:13
decede: d. peritis   HOR 259:6
deceit: d., and lust   DONNE 190:4
I am not up to small d.   HARTE 242:32
used no d. in his tongue   PRAY 390:4
deceitful: bloodthirsty and d. man
PRAY 389:23
children of men are d.   PRAY 393:20
d. and a virgin renowned   HOR 261:2
from the d. and wicked man   PRAY 392:10
heart is d. above all things   BIBLE 60:24
deceitfulness: Cat of such d. and suavity
ELIOT 203:26
deceits: all the d. of the world   PRAY 385:16
fables, and dangerous d.   PRAY 400:9
prophesy.   BIBLE 58:26
Deceive: D. boys with toys   LYS 321:18
d. you with vain words   BIBLE 78:3
don't d. me   ANON 5:3
first we practise to d.   SCOTT 417:19
let not Time d. you   AUDEN 18:10
they lie in wait to d.   BIBLE 77:28
we d. ourselves   BIBLE 81:3
Who could d. a lover   VIRG 558:12
deceived: Adam was not d.   BIBLE 79:10
d. The mother of mankind   MILT 344:23
is still d. with ornament   SHAK 467:10
should we desire to be d.   BUTL 117:10
woman being d. was   BIBLE 79:10
deceiver: I'm a gay d.   COLM 159:2
thou kind d.   DRYD 195:17
deceivers: Men were d. ever   SHAK 472:16
deceiveth: d. his own heart   BIBLE 80:11
deceiving: arched round in words d.
MILT 344:13
d., could no longer harm   ELIOT 202:20
d..mirror of self-love   MASS 335:22
d. your own selves   BIBLE 80:10
She d., I believing   SEDL 419:11
December: D. when they wed   SHAK 426:23
In a drear-nighted D.   KEATS 293:3
old D.'s bareness   SHAK 494:16
rain and wind beat dark D.   SHAK 428:15
Their meetings made D. June   TENN 537:12
Tomorrow comes D.   HOUS 265:1
Decembers: fifteen wild D.   BRON 93:22
decencies: to dwell in d. for ever POPE 377:23
decency: believe in an ultimate d.
STEV 522:15
want of d. is want of sense   ROOS 408:11
decent: aristocracy to what is d.   HOPE 255:29
d. hall of death   CHES 147:12
d. obscurity of a learned   GIBB 224:19
decently: be done d. and in order BIBLE 61:7
deceptive: d. are the visions   VIRG 559:3
decerated: d. dark red as I have somber
ASHF 17:8
decide: comes the moment to d.   LOW 319:12
d. such a great dispute   VIRG 559:20
decidimus: Nos ubi d.   HOR 261:10
decimal: adapted to them the d. system
NAP 359:13
decision: multitudes in the valley of d.
BIBLE 61:17
will or d. or reason   CHOM 148:16
deck: d. put on its leaves again FLEC 214:19
stood on the burning d.   HEM 244:20
to d. her mistress' head   BYRON 125:24
Walk the d. my Captain lies   WHIT 570:8
deck'd: should duly have been d. SPEN 515:27
thy bride-bed to have d.   SHAK 437:6
decks: he fell upon their d.   TENN 543:4
declaim: d.; and when you are calculating
JOHN 277:8
declamatio: Ut pueris placeas et d. JUV 288:2

declare: d., if thou hast understanding
BIBLE 53:2
d. the wonders that he   PRAY 397:7
heavens d. the glory   PRAY 390:11
nothing to d.   WILDE 573:36
ye are to d. it   PRAY 388:23
declension: by this d.   SHAK 432:2
déclin: d. de l'amour se font sentir
LA B 306:13
decline: are ready to d.   SHAK 451:27
D.-and-Fall-Off   DICK 181:6
Morn in weary Night's d.   GIBB 224:16
declined: dear Carrie rightly d.   BLAKE 86:1
decoration: descended to construct a
d.   TROL 552:16
decorum: athwart Goes all d.   SHAK 463:11
Dulce et d. est pro patria   HOR 260:17
hunt D. down   BYRON 124:26
Let them cant about d.   BURNS 114:20
decree: Can alter a d. established SHAK 468:3
d. from Caesar Augustus   BIBLE 69:8
dost hear de D.   WHAR 569:10
establish the d.   BIBLE 61:7
Decreed: D. in the market place POUND 383:8
own soul has to itself d.   KEATS 292:7
decrees: contrary to the d. of Caesar
BIBLE 74:9
decrepitude: their d., their decay
LAND 309:13
decus: praesidium et dulce d.   HOR 259:8
dede: leff woord and tak the d. LYDG 321:4
dedicate: larger sense we cannot d.
LINC 314:23
dedicated: dreariness in d. spirits FRY 219:23
dedication: d. of his life to me ELIOT 201:29
dedis: gentil that dooth gentil d. CHAU 143:25
deductions: long train of d.   DOYLE 192:35
Dee: Across the sands of D.   KING 296:25
Lived on the river D.   BICK 83:28
deed: attempt and not the d.   SHAK 460:4
beest is d. he hath no peyne   CHAU 142:17
bloody d.   SHAK 435:2
blow the horrid d.   SHAK 459:6
both in will and d.   PRAY 386:15
d. is all   GOET 230:5
d. of dreadful note   SHAK 461:13
d. without a name   SHAK 462:5
Fit for the d. I had to do   CARR 135:26
good d. in a naughty   SHAK 468:18
Grisilde in d.   CHAU 142:9
If one good d. in all my   SHAK 486:18
I have done the d.   SHAK 460:6
Shadow of Shadows on the d. YEATS 584:18
she if oon of hem were d.   CHAU 141:16
To do the right d.   ELIOT 204:4
whatever time the d. took place ELIOT 203:26
When the d. was done   WORD 580:9
worse d.   HENRY 245:17
deeds: because their d. were evil BIBLE 71:39
D., not words shall speak   FLET 215:15
d. that some knights used   CAXT 138:4
d. which should not pass   BYRON 120:32
Foul d. will rise   SHAK 430:16
My d. upon my head   SHAK 468:1
nameless in worthy d.   BROW 97:17
Our d. determine us   ELIOT 200:12
Our d. still travel with   ELIOT 201:14
sager sort our d. reprove   CAT 136:25
Seeking His secret d.   ROSS 408:20
deem: In doubt to d. himself   POPE 379:12
deep: commit his body to the d.   PRAY 400:4
day have I been in the d.   BIBLE 77:12
d. almost as life   WORD 579:8
D. as first love   TENN 542:4
D. in the shady sadness   KEATS 289:33
d. like as with a garment   PRAY 396:18
d. sense of some deathless   WEBS 567:4
d. upon her peerless eyes   KEATS 291:15
D. versed in books   MILT 350:10

d. where Holland lies   GOLD 231:27
great deep to the great d.   TENN 534:3
hath made the d. as dry   KIPL 303:5
have they not buried me d.   TENN 540:15
heard the d. behind him   TENN 535:23
her arms along the d. proudly   CAMP 128:14
himself in terms too d.   GILB 227:21
his wonders in the d.   PRAY 397:9
house with d. thatch   BELL 40:11
in the cradle of the d.   WILL 574:7
lowest d. a lower deep   MILT 347:15
Not d. the Poet sees   ARN 14:7
often lie too d. for tears   WORD 579:14
One d. calleth another   PRAY 392:8
one is of the d.   STEP 518:22
Out of the d. have I called   PRAY 398:23
sea my love is d.   LEAR 311:26
singularly d. young man   GILB 227:21
'tis not so d. as a well   SHAK 483:3
too d. for his hearers   GOLD 231:17
unadornèd bosom of the d.   MILT 340:25
upon the face of the d.   BIBLE 44:22
when the remorseless d.   MILT 343:7
deeper: d. than did ever plummet
SHAK 485:24
Her eyes were d. than   ROSS 409:14
shown a d. sense of her loss   GASK 222:3
Deep-hearted: D. man   BROW 98:8
Deep-meadow'd: D., happy   TENN 535:27
deer: Around the dying d.   AYT 24:10
hunting the beautiful d.   AUDEN 18:8
I was a stricken d.   COWP 167:1
let the stricken d. go   SHAK 434:16
deeth: be lad Toward his d.   CHAU 142:24
man after his d. moot wepe   CHAU 142:17
defaced: Antiquities are history d.
BACON 24:18
defacing: Defaming and d.   TENN 535:15
Defamed: D. by every charlatan TENN 537:17
Defaming: D. and defacing   TENN 535:15
défauts: Quelle âme est sans d. RIMB 406:8
defeat: are triumph and d.   LONG 316:21
in d., defiance   CHUR 150:25
possibilities of d.   VICT 556:18
this world's d.   VAUG 555:12
defeated: d. were us   LIVY 315:12
Down with the d.   LIVY 315:11
safe course for the d.   VIRG 558:7
defect: chief d. of Henry King   BELL 38:34
this fair d. Of Nature   MILT 349:21
Defects: Christian beauty D.   POUND 383:8
In our plain d.   FRY 219:25
defence: at one gate to make d.   MILT 350:22
cant in d. of savages   JOHN 279:19
D., not defiance   ANON 5:1
d. of England you no longer   BALD 29:28
d. or apology before you   CHAR 140:17
fight in d. of one's country   HOMER 254:2
house of d. very high   PRAY 395:21
Lord is thy d. upon thy   PRAY 398:9
ready in d.   BURKE 109:23
defences: d. of peace must be constructed
ANON 7:16
defend: d. my cause against   PRAY 392:10
D., O Lord, this thy Child   PRAY 388:22
D. the bad against   DAY-L 172:23
d. to the death your right   VOLT 561:24
D. us thy humble servants   PRAY 385:2
foremost to d.   BYRON 124:40
Le ciel d.   MOL 353:26
mercy d. us from all perils   PRAY 385:10
Quand on l'attaque il se d.   ANON 9:4
we shall d. our island   CHUR 149:31
whom he had promised to d.   MAC 323:21
defended: these d.   HOUS 265:7
defending: sake of d. those who do
BLAKE 87:11
defends: when attacked it d. itself ANON 9:4
defensoribus: Non tali auxilio nec d.
VIRG 558:9

defer: 'tis madness to d. — YOUNG 588:3
deference: d. due to me — GILB 227:9
deferred: Hope d. maketh the heart — BIBLE 53:35
defiance: Defence, not d. — ANON 5:1
  d. in their eye — GOLD 231:28
deficiant: Quod si d. vires — PROP 401:16
deficiente: Et teneam moriens d. manu — TIB 550:34
defied: Age will not be d. — BACON 27:6
défier: honteux de se d. de ses amis — LA R 310:10
defiled: toucheth pitch shall be d. — BIBLE 63:2
defileth: into the mouth d. a man — BIBLE 66:28
define: know how to d. it — THOM 546:6
  To d. true madness — SHAK 431:31
definition: by my own d. of criticism — ARN 16:1
  d. of a gentleman to say — NEWM 362:3
definitions: I hate d. — DISR 186:40
deflower: that will her pride d. — SPEN 516:13
deform'd: None can be call'd d. — SHAK 490:18
deformed: of my invention prove d. — SHAK 495:17
deformity: foot the d. of which — MAC 323:33
defrauding: Penalties as the d. of the State — PENN 371:16
defy: d. the devil — SHAK 490:7
  d. the foul fiend — SHAK 454:19
  d. th' Omnipotent to arms — MILT 344:24
  then I d. you — SHAK 483:24
dégagé: half so d. — COWP 165:22
Degenerate: D. Douglas — WORD 578:18
degeneration: fatty d. of his moral being — STEV 521:24
dégoût: non pas des moments de d. — VOLT 561:16
degraded: wouldn't be sufficiently d. — GILB 226:26
degree: d., priority, and place — SHAK 486:22
  exalted them of low d. — BIBLE 69:6
  when d. is shak'd — SHAK 486:23
Dei: Ad majorem D. gloriam — ANON 10:6
  vox D. — ALC 3:9
deid: y'er a lang time d. — ANON 4:27
deified: our own spirits are we d. — WORD 580:28
de'il: d.'s awa wi' th'Exciseman — BURNS 113:13
Deity: D. offended — BURNS 113:18
  desire in d. — ROSS 409:22
deject: ladies most d. and wretched — SHAK 433:15
dejected: lowest and most d. thing — SHAK 455:5
  Nor the d. 'haviour — SHAK 429:25
delay: chides his infamous d. — YOUNG 588:5
  d. there lies no plenty — SHAK 488:17
  half-taster to D. — TENN 539:19
  sell, or deny, or d. — MAGN 327:3
delayed: d. till I am indifferent — JOHN 274:7
delaying: d. put the state to rights — ENN 208:22
delays: d. are dangerous in war — DRYD 197:35
  D. have dangerous ends — SHAK 445:22
  strong through long d. — OVID 366:20
Delectable: came to the D. Mountains — BUNY 107:23
delectando: Lectorem d. pariterque monendo — HOR 258:1
Delenda: D. est Carthago — CATO 136:18
Delia: While D. is away — JAGO 271:1
deliberate: these d. fools — SHAK 467:1
  Where both d. — MARL 329:18
deliberates: woman that d. is lost — ADD 1:20
Deliberation: D. sat and public care — MILT 346:14
delicacy: has of fortitude and d. — STEV 521:4
delicate: body's d. — SHAK 454:13
  d. death — WHIT 571:13
  delight is a d. growth cramped — HARDY 240:3

these d. creatures ours — SHAK 475:21
they are not very d. — WALP 563:15
Young ladies are d. plants — AUST 22:17
Delice: with the fair flower D. — SPEN 517:3
deliciae: d. meae puellae — CAT 136:22
Delicias: D. domini — VIRG 559:14
délicieux: il n'y en a point de d. — LA R 310:11
delicious: d. story is ripe to tell — AUDEN 20:22
  'tis d. to hate you — MOORE 356:24
deliciously: Reminiscences make one feel so d. — SHAW 497:2
Delicta: D. maiorum immeritus lues — HOR 260:25
delight: All for your d. — SHAK 471:16
  bind another to its d. — BLAKE 87:19
  By thy d. in others' pain — BYRON 125:4
  Commodity, Firmness, and D. — WOTT 583:16
  day Rose with d. — KING 296:13
  d. in conceiving an Iago — KEATS 294:7
  d. is a delicate growth — HARDY 240:3
  d. is in proper young — BURNS 114:17
  d. of battle with my peers — TENN 543:22
  D. of lust is gross — PETR 373:5
  desire that outruns the d. — SWIN 529:9
  Energy is Eternal D. — BLAKE 88:11
  go to 't with d. — SHAK 422:24
  Had other aims than my d. — HARDY 240:6
  have relinquished one d. — WORD 579:13
  Him in whose company I d. — BUNY 107:39
  in the very temple of d. — KEATS 291:15
  labour we d. in physics — SHAK 460:19
  Let dogs d. to bark — WATTS 565:17
  lonely impulse of d. — YEATS 585:15
  Moon of my D. who know'st — FITZ 213:17
  My d. and thy delight — BRID 92:16
  my ever new d. — MILT 348:14
  our d. or as our treasure — HERB 248:2
  rejoice and d. in God — TRAH 551:17
  sentiments I find d. — JOHN 280:21
  She was a phantom of d. — WORD 581:7
  source of little visible d. — BRON 93:25
  Spirit of D. — SHEL 503:25
  Studies serve for d. — BACON 27:15
  sweetest d. of gardens — BROW 95:21
  Teach us d. in simple things — KIPL 298:12
  that give d. — SHAK 485:17
  Their d. is in lies — PRAY 393:19
  There is d. in singing — LAND 309:1
  thing met conceives d. — MILT 349:13
  thought that lurks in all d. — MEYN 338:13
  'Tis never too late for d. — MOORE 356:17
  to d. at once and lash — POPE 378:8
  to do ill our sole d. — MILT 345:5
  to enjoy d. with liberty — SPEN 515:23
  turn d. into a sacrifice — HERB 246:27
  unrest which men miscall d. — SHEL 499:21
  we have a degree of d. — BURKE 108:8
  with d. No more — SHEL 501:15
  yet I hear thy shrill d. — SHEL 504:18
delighted: d. in solitude is either — BACON 26:14
  d. with any thing that — CONG 159:28
  You have d. us long enough — AUST 23:14
delightest: d. not in burnt-offerings — PRAY 393:8
delighteth: d. he in any man's legs — PRAY 399:20
  king d. to honour — BIBLE 52:3
delightful: all that is d. to man — MILT 351:25
  almost as d. — LOCK 315:19
  two most d. things — WALP 563:13
delighting: d. the reader at the same — HOR 258:1
Delights: D. in filth and foul incontinence — SPEN 516:18
  does some d. condemn — MOL 353:26
  his d. Were dolphin-like — SHAK 423:22
  midst of the fountain of d. — LUCR 320:11
  thee king of intimate d. — COWP 167:13

delineation: happiest d. of its varieties — AUST 22:31
delinquencies: naturally indulge in a few d. — ELIOT 201:23
delinquent: condemns a less d. for't — BUTL 118:19
delirant: d. reges plectuntur — HOR 258:12
delirium: All that d. of the brave — YEATS 586:19
delitabill: Storys to rede ar d. — BARB 33:3
Deliver: D. Israel — PRAY 391:3
  d. me from the deceitful — PRAY 392:10
  d. my soul from the calamities — PRAY 391:25
  d. us — PRAY 385:16
  d. us from evil — BIBLE 64:24
  I will d. him unto you — BIBLE 68:9
  let him d. him — PRAY 390:17
  neither shall he d. any — PRAY 391:20
  shall d. me from the body — BIBLE 75:6
delivered: God hath d. him into mine — BIBLE 50:14
  hast d. my soul from death — PRAY 397:20
delivereth: d. them out of their distress — PRAY 397:10
dells: In leafy d. alone — HOUS 265:9
Delphos: hollow shriek the steep of D. — MILT 344:13
deluded: kind of Heaven to be d. — LEE 313:9
  we are all d. thus — SHEL 501:4
déluge: Après nous le d. — POMP 375:9
delusion: announce but that addled d. — ELIOT 201:2
  d., a mockery, and a snare — DENM 174:22
  d. that beauty is goodness — TOLS 551:11
  Hence, dear d. — SMITH 510:8
delusive: d. seduction of martial — BURN 112:21
demand: He'll make d. of her — SHAK 424:14
  superfluous to d. the time of day — SHAK 437:34
Demas: D., greet you — BIBLE 78:29
demd: What's the d. total — DICK 180:15
demens: d.? Habitarunt di quoque — VIRG 559:16
dementat: d. prius — DUP 199:15
demented: d. with the mania of owning — WHIT 570:22
demerit: preacher's merit or d. — BROW 100:4
demeure: Les jours s'en vont je d. — APOL 11:11
demeurer: d. en repos dans une chambre — PASC 369:5
demi-paradise: other Eden, d. — SHAK 478:20
demi-puppets: you d. — SHAK 485:23
democracy: capacity for justice makes d. — NIEB 362:26
  D. and proper drains — BETJ 43:6
  D. is only an experiment — INGE 270:7
  D. means simply the bludgeoning — WILDE 573:24
  d. or absolute oligarchy — ARIS 12:8
  D. resumed her reign — BELL 39:21
  D. substitutes election — SHAW 497:36
  great arsenal of d. — ROOS 407:25
  idea demands…a d. — PARK 368:26
  It is the d. of the dead — CHES 148:5
  must be made safe for d. — WILS 574:24
  perfect d. is therefore — BURKE 111:19
  political experiment of d. — SHAW 497:16
  So Two cheers for D. — FORS 217:13
  thanks to wine-lees and d. — BROW 98:28
  that d. is the worst form — CHUR 150:19
  that of our Author's D. — BENT 40:26
  themselves grieved under a d. — HOBB 251:20
democratic: aristocracy the most d. — MAC 324:16
Democritus: rideret D. — HOR 259:3
demon-lover: woman wailing for her d. — COL 156:27
demonstrandum: Quod erat d. — EUCL 209:1

Demosthenes: D. never comes
unseasonably　　　　　　　MAC 324:9
den: hand on the cockatrice' d.　BIBLE 58:11
made it a d. of thieves　　　BIBLE 67:17
denial: d. vain, and coy excuse　MILT 343:3
denied: faintly and would be d.　SHAK 480:12
if it be but half d.　　　　　BUTL 118:11
in my dreams you have d.　　POUND 383:13
to our moist vows d.　　　　MILT 343:16
denies: spirit that always d.　GOET 230:1
deniges: 'Who d. of it　　　DICK 179:26
denk: d.' ich Heut und morgen　LESS 313:26
Denmark: All the might of D.'s CAMP 128:14
Prince of D. being left out　SCOTT 418:34
rotten in the state of D.　　SHAK 431:2
sure it may be so in D.　　　SHAK 431:16
Than is the throne of D.　　SHAK 429:20
dens: d. and in the rocks　BIBLE 81:30
lay them down in their d.　PRAY 397:1
dentist: vulgar to talk like a d.　WILDE 572:26
dents longues: le temps d'avoir les d.
　　　　　　　　　　　　MOL 353:16
deny: d. a God destroy　　BACON 25:25
I never d.　　　　　　　　DISR 187:5
Life offers—to d.　　　　HARDY 241:8
Room to d. ourselves　　KEBLE 298:14
sell, or d., or delay　　　MAGN 327:3
so ingrateful you d. me　SHAK 452:31
thou shalt d. me thrice　　BIBLE 68:12
yet will I not d. thee　　　BIBLE 68:13
You must d. yourself　　　GOET 230:2
Deo: D. gratias　　　　MASS 334:19
Ille mi par esse d. videtur　CAT 137:4
deorum: Parcus d. cultor et infrequens
　　　　　　　　　　　　HOR 260:2
depart: already it is time to d.　SOCR 512:18
court to cottage he d.　　PEELE 371:8
D.,—be off　　　　　　HOLM 253:19
d. the souls of the brave　CLOU 153:13
Having a desire to d.　　BIBLE 78:12
he will not d. from it　　BIBLE 54:22
I am ready to d.　　　　LAND 308:20
servant d. in peace　　BIBLE 69:12
when the great and good d.　WORD 578:8
departed: Dead he is not, but d. LONG 316:24
d. into their own country　BIBLE 63:33
D. never to return　　　BURNS 116:7
d. this life in thy faith　PRAY 387:16
glory is d. from Israel　BIBLE 49:40
He d., he withdrew　　CIC 151:27
knolling a d. friend　　SHAK 441:2
Lord was d. from him　BIBLE 49:26
our dear brother here d.　PRAY 389:13
departing: flood-ways to be far d.
　　　　　　　　　　　　POUND 383:18
departure: *so soon* to regret the d.
　　　　　　　　　　　　THOM 549:4
their d. is taken for misery　BIBLE 62:13
depend: joys of home d.　MORE 357:11
Dependance: not subsist without D.
　　　　　　　　　　　　STEE 518:14
depends: so much d.　WILL 574:10
dépeuplé: et tout est d.　LAM 306:24
déplaît: chose qui ne nous d. pas LA R 310:8
deponere: Difficile est longum subito
d. amorem　　　　　　CAT 137:10
depopulating: d. his dominions and making
　　　　　　　　　　　　BECK 36:19
Deportment: his D.　　DICK 176:9
depose: glories and my state d.　SHAK 479:23
depositary: d. of power is always
unpopular　　　　　　DISR 185:43
depraved: ever suddenly became d.
　　　　　　　　　　　　JUV 287:14
In d. May　　　　　　ELIOT 203:4
depravity: proof of stupidity than d.
　　　　　　　　　　　　JOHN 275:33
total d. of inanimate things　HAM 238:14
deprest: heart of a man is d.　GAY 222:26
deprived: d. of everlasting bliss　MARL 329:7

depth: d., and not the tumult　WORD 578:2
d. in philosophy bringeth　BACON 25:24
d. in that study brings　FULL 220:14
far beyond my d.　　　SHAK 447:9
He who knows about d. knows　TILL 551:4
little out of your d. here　TEMP 532:12
depths: d. I have cried to thee　BIBLE 83:13
his d. and his shallows　BURNS 115:2
of the unfathomable d.　COL 158:8
deputy: also may be read by d.　BACON 27:19
d. elected by the Lord　SHAK 479:5
deracinate: That should d. such savagery
　　　　　　　　　　　　SHAK 445:12
derangement: nice d. of epitaphs
　　　　　　　　　　　　SHER 506:14
derision: Lord shall have them in d.
　　　　　　　　　　　　PRAY 389:17
turns the old days to d.　SWIN 529:10
Uglification and D.　　CARR 134:10
dernière: La d. chose qu'on trouve
　　　　　　　　　　　　PASC 369:3
Dertemouthe: he was of D.　CHAU 141:29
dés: Un coup de d. jamais n'abolira
　　　　　　　　　　　　MALL 327:1
desart: beyond High-Park's a d.　ETH 208:31
descend: Intervene. O d. as a dove
　　　　　　　　　　　　AUDEN 20:15
into the Dust d.　　　FITZ 212:18
Descended: D. of so many royal kings
　　　　　　　　　　　　SHAK 424:16
descending: island d. incontinently
　　　　　　　　　　　　CHUR 151:4
of God ascending and d.　BIBLE 46:18
descensus: Facilis d. Averno　VIRG 558:18
descent: at the claims of long d.　TENN 537:29
described: d. as a supreme capacity
　　　　　　　　　　　　BUTL 118:34
describing: d. the afflictions of Job
　　　　　　　　　　　　BACON 25:19
Descried: D. at sunrise an emerging
　　　　　　　　　　　　ARN 14:21
description: He answered the d.　FARQ 210:18
descriptions: d. of the fairest wights
　　　　　　　　　　　　SHAK 494:19
deseo: término que pide un buen d.
　　　　　　　　　　　　CERV 138:19
Desert: Blast of the D. cried aloud
　　　　　　　　　　　　LONG 317:8
d. shall rejoice　　　BIBLE 58:32
d. sighs in the bed　AUDEN 18:10
d. were a paradise　BURNS 114:31
every man after his d.　SHAK 432:26
Life is the d.　　　YOUNG 588:13
never will d. Mr Micawber　DICK 177:3
owl that is in the d.　PRAY 396:12
pain'd d. lion　　　ARN 14:26
scare myself with my own d.　FROST 219:3
Stand in the d.　　SHEL 502:15
straight in the d. a highway　BIBLE 59:5
streams in the d.　BIBLE 58:34
that the d. were my dwelling-place
　　　　　　　　　　　　BYRON 121:21
us all out into the d.　CLOU 154:6
water but the d.　　BYRON 121:12
your d. speaks loud　SHAK 465:3
Deserted: D. at his utmost need　DRYD 195:3
Deserts: D. of vast eternity　MARV 332:19
his d. are small　　GRAH 233:14
In the d. of the heart　AUDEN 19:9
When she d. the night　MILT 350:16
deserve: d. any thanks from anyone
　　　　　　　　　　　　CAT 137:8
those who really d. them　FIEL 211:20
we'll d. it　　　　ADD 1:16
wicked to d. such pain　BROW 99:29
would d. better of mankind　SWIFT 526:6
you somehow haven't to d.　FROST 219:2
deserves: everyone has the face he d.
　　　　　　　　　　　　ORW 365:18
has the government it d.　MAIS 327:8

deserving: that riches where is my d.
　　　　　　　　　　　　SHAK 494:13
désespoir: Le d. baîlle　HUGO 267:12
design: appears dull there is a d.　STEE 518:5
in the might of d.　SHAW 496:22
that d. might cover their　POUND 382:8
Designer: D. infinite　THOM 548:18
designing: Say I am d. St Paul's　BENT 41:9
designs: His d. were strictly honourable
　　　　　　　　　　　　FIEL 211:29
Immanent Will and its d.　HARDY 239:11
ladder to all high d.　SHAK 486:23
large to his own dark d.　MILT 345:8
Lofty d. must close　BROW 101:2
Desinat: D. in piscem mulier　HOR 257:9
Desine: D. de quoquam quicquam CAT 137:8
desint: Ut d. vires　OVID 366:26
desipere: Dulce est d. in loco　HOR 261:20
Dulce et decorum est d.　BUTL 119:9
desirable: all of them d. young men
　　　　　　　　　　　　BIBLE 60:37
desir'd: hurts, and is d.　SHAK 424:12
Suffer herself to be d.　WALL 562:14
desire: beauty that we should d.　BIBLE 59:21
bloom of young d. and purple　GRAY 235:17
Bring me my arrows of d.　BLAKE 86:16
depth and dream of my d.　KIPL 301:16
d. accomplished is sweet　BIBLE 53:37
d. and longing to enter　PRAY 395:11
d. at last and vain regret　ROSS 410:6
D. gratified　　　BLAKE 86:20
d. in deity　　　ROSS 409:22
d. of the moth　SHEL 504:14
d. on the part of every　BUTL 118:27
d. other men's goods　PRAY 388:18
d. should so many years　SHAK 441:28
d. that outruns the delight　SWIN 529:9
d. the office of a bishop　BIBLE 79:11
exceed all that we can d.　PRAY 386:21
few things to d. and many　BACON 26:8
fulfilled of my heart's d.　SWIN 530:13
hours and times of your d.　SHAK 493:18
it provokes the d.　SHAK 460:18
kindle soft d.　　DRYD 195:8
Land of Heart's D.　YEATS 585:19
lineaments of gratified d.　BLAKE 86:17
man's d. is for the woman　COL 157:33
mixing Memory and d.　ELIOT 204:1
naught for your d.　CHES 146:16
nearer to the Heart's D.　FITZ 213:16
powers of Charm and D.　CAT 136:22
shall d. to die　　BIBLE 82:7
shot and danger of d.　SHAK 430:17
that the d. is boundless　SHAK 486:33
this fond d.　　　ADD 1:24
thou art in d.　　SHAK 459:8
to get your heart's d.　SHAW 497:33
tongue has its d.　AUDEN 20:22
weariness treads on d.　PETR 373:5
What many men d.　SHAK 466:22
what you can d. or hope　DRYD 197:5
when the d. cometh　BIBLE 53:35
Which of us has his d.　THAC 545:29
wonder and a wild d.　BROW 104:19
Youth pined away with d.　BLAKE 87:22
desired: d. by all healthy and good CIC 151:33
d. to know nothing　JOHN 276:25
I have d. to go　　HOPK 256:17
kings have d. to see　BIBLE 69:29
More to be d. are they　PRAY 390:12
You are not one to be d.　TENN 537:26
desiren: 'Wommen d. to have sovereynetee
　　　　　　　　　　　　CHAU 143:24
desires: all d. known　PRAY 387:7
By all d. which thereof　DONNE 188:10
consists in doing what one d.　MILL 339:13
D. and Adorations　SHEL 499:9
d. and other hopes beset　BRON 93:23
d., like fell and cruel　SHAK 487:21
d. of the heart are　AUDEN 18:13

Dreams and d. and sombre SWIN 528:26
enough to answer back to d. HOR 262:10
from whom all holy d. PRAY 385:9
Fulfil now, O Lord, the d. PRAY 385:8
He who d. but acts not BLAKE 88:15
into our minds good d. PRAY 386:10
much the devices and d. PRAY 384:11
nurse unacted d. BLAKE 88:24
Question your d. SHAK 469:17
shows of things to the d. BACON 24:19
was winged with vain d. DRYD 196:13
we fondly flatter our d. DRAY 193:9
whilst his d. were as warm BURKE 110:21
desirest: thou d. no sacrifice PRAY 393:8
desireth: hart d. the water-brooks PRAY 392:6
Desiring: D. this man's art SHAK 493:6
is to admire without d. BRAD 91:11
desist: d. To build at all SHAK 441:17
desk: dry drudgery of the d.'s LAMB 307:33
From counter or d. among YEATS 585:1
Is but a d. to write upon BUTL 118:1
votary of the d. LAMB 307:11
desks: Stick close to your d. and never
GILB 228:7
desnuda: Verte d. es recordar GARC 221:4
desolate: d. places for themselves
BIBLE 52:12
making his palace d. BECK 36:19
that are d. and oppressed PRAY 385:20
desolated: they have d. and profaned
GLAD 229:13
desolation: Love in d. masked SHEL 499:17
My d. does begin to make SHAK 423:20
see the abomination of d. BIBLE 67:29
years of d. pass over JEFF 272:14
despair: begotten by d. Upon impossibility
MARV 331:18
Bid me d. HERR 249:27
carrion comfort, D. HOPK 256:7
curst himself in his d. SOUT 514:3
depth of some divine d. TENN 542:2
d. to the regeneration CONR 161:21
D. was powerless to destroy BRON 93:24
D. yawns HUGO 267:12
Do not d. PUDN 402:7
from d. Thus high uplifted MILT 346:6
have of comfort and d. SHAK 495:12
Heaven in Hell's d. BLAKE 87:18
I can endure my own d. WALSH 563:30
I shall d. SHAK 481:15
last weak refuge in d. THOM 549:19
near neighbour to D. ARN 14:18
never hoped can never d. SHAW 496:11
No cause for d. HOR 259:16
now fiercer by d. MILT 346:7
owner whereof was Giant D. BUNY 107:20
quality of his d. CONN 161:16
racked with deep d. MILT 345:4
rash-embrac'd d. SHAK 467:12
unpaid bill, D. SHEL 504:25
what resolution from d. MILT 345:7
despaired: ever d. of the Commonwealth
DISR 185:34
despairer: Too quick d. ARN 15:6
despairs: leaden-eyed d. KEATS 291:19
despare: regaining my character I d.
FLEM 214:29
despatchful: with d. looks in haste
MILT 348:18
*desperandum: Nil d. Teucro duce et
auspice* HOR 259:16
desperate: characteristic of wisdom not
to do d. THOR 550:5
d. strait and cannot steer MASS 335:18
Diseases d. grown SHAK 435:25
Tempt not a d. man SHAK 483:27
desperately: d. mortal SHAK 464:25
desperation: lives of quiet d. THOR 550:4
Despicere: D. unde queas alios passimque
LUCR 320:6

despis'd: d. old man SHAK 454:5
despise: d. Shakespeare when I measure
SHAW 496:23
d. them most BURNS 114:29
d. the skylark's song BRON 93:13
ere you d. the other DRYD 198:5
other Englishman d. him SHAW 498:12
pretend to d. Art BLAKE 86:9
reason to hate and to d. HAZL 243:18
shalt thou not d. PRAY 393:8
despised: Dangers by being d. grow
BURKE 111:33
d. and rejected of men BIBLE 59:21
d., and dying king SHEL 504:6
d. as well as served it BUTL 119:6
Enjoyed no sooner but d. SHAK 495:7
my part I always d. Mr CONG 160:13
despises: is the thing that she d. CONG 159:19
despising: d. all manner of *éclat* BAG 29:11
d. the shame BIBLE 79:35
thoughts myself almost d. SHAK 493:6
despite: builds a Hell in Heaven's d.
BLAKE 87:19
D. of all your generals LAND 308:18
despoil: tremble and d. themselves
SHEL 502:11
Despond: name of the slough was D.
BUNY 107:11
despondency: in the end d. and madness
WORD 580:28
last words of Mr D. BUNY 107:37
said 'SPREAD ALARM and D. PEN 371:13
despot: country governed by a d. JOHN 277:29
despotism: anarchy and d. SHEL 505:11
d. tempered by epigrams CARL 131:21
d. will come from either ARIS 12:8
desp'rate: Beware of d. steps COWP 165:20
dessin: Le d. est la probité de INGR 270:19
destinies: d. of the British Empire
DISR 184:27
Persuasions and veiled D. SHEL 499:9
destiny: 'character is d. ELIOT 201:21
D. the Commissary of God DONNE 189:35
D. with Men for Pieces FITZ 213:5
His own funereal d. BYRON 125:19
In shady leaves of d. CRAS 169:15
orphan heirs of fixed d. SHAK 469:16
Our manifest d. to overspread OSUL 365:23
you reap a d. READE 405:4
destitute: worst solitude is to be d.
BACON 25:14
Destitution: shaming D. VIRG 558:21
destroy: after my skin worms d. BIBLE 52:31
age shall be able to d. OVID 366:19
Despair was powerless to d. BRON 93:24
d. a blade of grass BOTT 90:17
D. his fib or sophistry POPE 376:22
Doth the winged life d. BLAKE 86:18
God d. man's nobility BACON 25:25
impatient to d. JOHN 283:1
not to d., but to fulfil BIBLE 64:10
sin will d. a sinner BUNY 107:29
They shall not hurt nor d. BIBLE 58:11
Whom God would d. He first DUP 199:15
destroy'd: d. by Time's devouring
BRAM 91:23
not one life shall be d. TENN 536:25
destroyed: Berkeley d. this world
SMITH 511:33
D. by subtleties these MER 337:16
made great is a name d. HILL 251:5
that shall be d. is death BIBLE 76:23
Destroyer: D. and preserver SHEL 502:8
only a d. CHEK 145:4
destroyeth: sickness that d. PRAY 395:21
destroys: Death d. a man FORS 217:3
first d. their mind DRYD 196:22
he who d. a good book MILT 351:22
destruator: aut aliquo modo d. MAGN 327:2

destruction: d. of the poor is their
BIBLE 53:30
from us to be utter d. BIBLE 62:13
Pride goeth before d. BIBLE 54:8
startles at d. ADD 1:24
that leadeth to d. BIBLE 65:6
to their d. draw DONNE 187:23
urge for d. is also a creative BAK 29:24
destructive: d. forest laments in order
CHUR 149:20
d. of the manhood JERR 273:11
d. man LEE 313:14
In the d. element immerse CONR 161:19
desuper: d., et nubes pluant Justum
BIBLE 83:15
detail: frittered away by d.Simplify
THOR 550:17
Merely corroborative d. GILB 227:12
occupied in trivial d. BAG 29:11
detect: in the moment you d. POPE 377:9
Detection: D. is, or ought to be
DOYLE 192:28
detective: Hawkshaw, the d. TAYL 532:7
Deteriora: D. sequor OVID 366:17
determination: d. to believe what is most
HUME 267:21
determine: Let us d. to die here BEE 37:3
Our deeds d. us ELIOT 200:12
determined: am d. to prove a villain
SHAK 480:19
D., dared, and done SMART 509:4
determining: d. a point of law BURKE 109:28
detest: hate and d. that animal SWIFT 526:23
they d. at leisure BYRON 123:38
yet d. th'offence POPE 376:12
detestare: non lugere, neque d. SPIN 517:7
detested: I have d. you long enough...
POUND 383:12
Detraction: D. is but baseness' varlet
JONS 284:14
D. will not suffer it SHAK 440:18
detrimenti: ne quid res publica d.
ANON 10:10
Deum: D. de Deo MASS 334:20
D. patrem qui ecclesiam* CYPR 170:19
deus: d. nobis haec otia fecit VIRG 559:12
Nec d. hunc mensa VIRG 560:2
puto d. fio VESP 556:12
'Sit D. propitius ANON 10:14
devant: Présentez toujours le d. MOL 353:1
development: contributions to human
d. ARN 15:21
De Vere: why not of D. CREWE 169:18
deviates: Shadwell never d. into sense
DRYD 196:34
deviation: where d. from truth will end
JOHN 277:20
device: imagined such a d. as they
PRAY 390:15
reporting d. for experience WHORF 571:23
devices: d. and desires of our own
PRAY 384:21
Devil: Apology for the D. BUTL 119:1
are of your father the d. BIBLE 72:13
assaults of the d. PRAY 385:16
because your adversary the d. BIBLE 80:33
can the d. speak true SHAK 458:16
children of the d. TENN 543:1
defy the d. SHAK 490:7
D. always builds a chapel DEFOE 173:11
d. a monk wou'd be MOTT 358:22
d. Be sometime honour'd SHAK 465:4
d. can cite Scripture SHAK 466:1
d. damn thee black SHAK 463:1
d., depend upon it STEV 521:15
d. finds some mischief MADAN 326:17
D. fly away with the fine arts CARL 132:5
d. haunts thee in the likeness SHAK 439:15
D., having nothing else BELL 39:24
d. himself with courtesy SHAK 490:20

D. howling 'Ho | SQUI 517:14
d. in the same churchyard | BANC 32:14
d.-porter it no further | SHAK 460:17
D. sends cooks | GARR 221:12
d. should have all | HILL 251:4
d.'s most devilish when | BROW 97:32
d.'s walking parody | CHES 146:22
d. take her | SUCK 524:7
d. taketh him up into | BIBLE 64:3
d., taking him up into | BIBLE 69:16
d. to have all the passions | SHAW 497:22
d. to pay | MOORE 357:5
d. turned precisian | MASS 335:19
d. understands Welsh | SHAK 439:31
D. watches all opportunities | CONG 160:19
D. whoops | KIPL 298:16
Don't let him go to the d. | JOHN 279:31
Drink and the d. had done | STEV 521:21
envy of the d. came death | BIBLE 62:12
first Whig was the D. | JOHN 278:2
flesh, and the d. | PRAY 385:16
given the d. a foul fall | MORE 357:12
he counteracts the D. | SMART 508:22
hoard of gold kept by a d. | SHAK 442:15
How agrees the d. and thee | SHAK 438:11
I dream'd of the d. | ANST 11:7
if the d. dress her not | SHAK 424:9
laughing d. in his sneer | BYRON 121:31
let us call thee d. | SHAK 475:8
make a moral of the d. | SHAK 444:15
man is to go to the d. | NORF 364:1
mischievous d. Love | BUTL 119:2
name a synonym for the D. | MAC 323:27
not serve God if the d. | SHAK 473:17
of the D.'s party without | BLAKE 88:12
problem must puzzle the d. | BURNS 115:2
sacrifice to God of the d.'s | POPE 381:21
should dream of the d. | BARH 33:13
should renounce the d. | PRAY 388:13
sugar o'er The d. himself | SHAK 433:7
That fears a painted d. | SHAK 460:11
To the D. that prompts | BROW 99:26
very d. incardinate | SHAK 490:23
walking the D. is gone | COL 156:10
was God or D. | DRYD 194:14
What a book a d.'s chaplain | DARW 172:1
'What a surly d. that is | FARR 210:27
when most I play the d. | SHAK 480:25
which is the D. | BIBLE 82:27
who cleft the D.'s foot | DONNE 190:8
wonder how the D. they | POPE 376:24
young and sweating d. here | SHAK 476:2
you the blacker d. | SHAK 477:11
devildoms: Inquisition dogs and the d.
| TENN 542:21
devilish: most d. thing is 8 times FLEM 214:26
devils: d. being offended | SHAK 474:15
d. in life and condition | ASCH 17:3
d.'-triumph and sorrow | BROW 102:7
doctrines of d. | BIBLE 79:13
fight like d. | SHAK 444:8
had heard that as many d. | LUTH 321:3
He casteth out d. through | BIBLE 65:28
said they were d. incarnate | SHAK 443:19
still 'tis d. must print | MOORE 356:1
devisal: Past our d. | THOM 548:29
devised: wit of man so well d. | PRAY 384:8
devocioun: Farewell my bok, and my
d. | CHAU 143:29
Devoid: D. of sense and motion MILT 346:10
devoir: d. et laissez faire aux | CORN 162:17
Devon: started that morning from D.
| GILB 226:14
Devonshire: In this dull D. | HERR 249:3
dévot: pour être d. | MOL 353:25
devote: they only d. themselves | FITZ 213:19
devotees: d. in these peculiar villages
| IRV 270:26
Devotion: D.! daughter of astronomy
| YOUNG 588:12

d. to something afar | SHEL 504:14
d. to that cause for which | LINC 314:23
Matrimonial d. | GILB 227:3
Open and obvious d. from | KIPL 304:34
passion for abstracted d. | JOHN 275:18
universal d. throughout our land | IRV 270:26
devour: d. widows' houses | BIBLE 68:37
might d. in turn each one | VERG 556:7
seeking whom he may d. | BIBLE 80:33
tears when they would d. | BACON 27:38
devoured: d. the seven good ears BIBLE 46:32
d. thy living with harlots | BIBLE 70:22
Some evil beast hath d. | BIBLE 46:29
devourer: Time the d. of everything
| OVID 366:18
devourers: be become so great d.
| MORE 357:19
devout: cannot be d. in dishabilly
| FARQ 210:21
less human for being d. | MOL 353:25
dew: Bedabbled with the d. | HERR 249:10
begotten the drops of d. | BIBLE 53:4
besprent with April d. | JONS 285:9
continual d. of thy blessing | PRAY 385:7
dark with d. | DE L 174:13
d. bespangling herb | HERR 248:23
D., bless ye the Lord | PRAY 384:21
d. shall weep thy fall | HERB 248:16
d. will rust them | SHAK 473:21
Drop down d. | BIBLE 83:15
fades awa' like morning d. | BALL 32:10
let there be no d. | BIBLE 50:16
more smell the d. and rain | HERB 247:22
mushroom On whom the d. | FORD 216:13
of the night on the d. | SWIN 530:13
resolve itself into a d. | SHAK 429:28
there rain'd a ghastly d. | TENN 538:24
to meet the morning d. | ARN 15:9
Walks o'er the d. of yon | SHAK 429:18
wine Was the bright d. | SHEL 503:19
dew-drop: fragile d. on its perilous
| KEATS 292:6
dew-drops: must go seek some d. here
| SHAK 470:2
dewfall: rainfall at morning and d.
| STEV 522:29
dews: early d. were falling | ING 270:14
fell ere the d. were dried | TENN 539:23
Nor ask amid the d. | HOUS 265:10
dextra: Statuens in parte d. | CEL 138:8
deyntee: every d. that is in that | CHAU 142:25
diable: le d. est mort | READE 405:3
diabolical: tree of d. knowledge SHER 506:10
diagonally: lie d. in his bed | STER 520:7
Dialect: D. words | HARDY 241:17
in a d. I understand very | PEPYS 372:11
purify the d. of the tribe | ELIOT 202:25
dials: d. the signs of leaping-houses
| SHAK 437:34
To carve out d. | SHAK 446:18
diamond: d. and safire bracelet | LOOS 318:3
d. bracelet lasts forever | STEV 520:20
immortal d. | HOPK 257:1
Like a d. in the sky | TAYL 532:1
rough than polished d. | CHES 145:27
diamonded: d. with panes of quaint
| KEATS 289:16
diamonds: what beautiful d. | WEST 568:26
Dian: hangs on D.'s temple | SHAK 428:3
her as D. had hot dreams | SHAK 429:3
Diana: Great is D. of the Ephesians
| BIBLE 74:17
Let us be D.'s foresters | SHAK 438:1
diapason: d. closing full in Man DRYD 197:21
Diaphenia: D., like the daffadowndilly
| CONS 161:25
diavolo: è un d. incarnato | ASCH 17:3
dibble: d. in earth to set one | SHAK 491:24
dic: sed tantum d. verbo | MASS 335:8
dice: d. dearly | SHAK 454:18

God does not play d. | EINS 200:10
some were playing d. | BALL 31:3
throw of the d. will never | MALL 327:11
Dicebamus: D. hesterno die | LUIS 320:13
dicere: quae sentias d. | TAC 531:12
dicers: vows As false as d.' oaths SHAK 435:4
dices: invita d. faciesve | HOR 258:5
Dick: D. the shepherd | SHAK 457:19
How D. would hate the cold | HOUS 265:1
Dicky-bird: D. why do you sit | GILB 227:15
dictate: Not presume to d. | DICK 181:26
dictates: d. of his godlike mind
| OTWAY 365:27
d. to me slumb'ring | MILT 349:9
sacred d. of thy faith | ROWE 410:25
woman d. before marriage | ELIOT 201:6
Dictators: D. ride to and fro upon
| CHUR 151:3
dictatorship: d. of the proletariat
| MARX 333:11
dictionaries: mortals is the writer of d.
| JOHN 281:5
To make d. is dull work | JOHN 281:11
writer of d. | JOHN 274:3
dictionary: will be but a walking d.
| CHAP 140:16
dictum: quod non d. sit prius | TER 544:16
Did: D. nothing in particular | GILB 226:11
D., till we lov'd | DONNE 188:29
he d. for them both with | SASS 414:18
Of all I ever d. | HOUS 266:6
diddest: 'Thus d. thou | SHAK 436:16
diddle: Fiddle, we know, is d. | SWIN 529:27
'High d. diddle' | GILB 227:25
Dido: D. and her Aeneas shall | SHAK 423:10
D. with a willow in her | SHAK 468:14
Di-do-dum: was D. | PORS 381:26
die: always with us, or we d. | KEATS 289:2
am prepar'd to d. | SHAK 464:7
are about to d. salute you | ANON 10:7
are called to d. | HARDY 241:8
Ay, but to d. | SHAK 464:1
begins to d. | QUAR 403:19
believes he shall ever d. | HAZL 244:3
better to d. on your feet | IBAR 269:16
bid me d. | HERR 249:27
bravely d. | POPE 376:7
break faith with us who d. | MCCR 324:31
by feigned deaths to d. | DONNE 190:7
change, but I cannot d. | SHEL 500:7
Cowards d. many times before | SHAK 449:18
Curse God, and d. | BIBLE 52:10
Dar'st thou d. | SHAK 464:11
dear, d. | BEDD 36:24
did I live and gladly d. | STEV 523:10
d. all, die merrily | SHAK 440:8
D., and endow a college | POPE 377:31
D. because a woman's fair | WITH 575:12
die because I do not d. | JOHN 273:15
d. but once to serve our | ADD 1:22
d. by feigning die by inches | HENRY 245:20
d. for adultery | SHAK 455:16
d. in music | SHAK 477:10
d. in that man's company | SHAK 445:3
d. in the flower of their | BIBLE 49:33
d. in their glory and never | HOUS 263:6
d. is cast | CAES 126:30
D., my dear Doctor | PALM 368:13
d. of starvation | NEWM 362:4
D. of the absolute paternal | ELIOT 202:22
d. soon, O fairy's son | SPEN 516:9
D. to save charges | BURT 116:20
d. when the trees were | CLARE 152:4
d. will be an awfully big | BARR 34:15
d. with harness on our | SHAK 463:7
do now not basely d. | SHAK 423:15
do we not d. | SHAK 467:4
ever seems it rich to d. | KEATS 291:2
every parting was to d. | TENN 537:12
faint hope that he will d. | EMER 207:5

Fall asleep, or hearing d. SHAK 447:3
few d. well SHAK 444:21
find myself so apt to d. SHAK 450:8
forgets that he can d. BROW 96:22
go away is to d. a little HAR 238:20
have to d. beyond my means WILDE 574:3
how can man d. better MAC 322:15
How often are we to d. POPE 381:17
how to d. PORT 381:33
I d. a Christian CHAR 140:20
I d. happy FOX 217:22
I d. pronouncing it SHAK 478:20
If I should d. BROO 94:30
If it were now to d. SHAK 474:20
If we are mark'd to d. SHAK 445:1
I have seen her d. twenty SHAK 421:20
I'll d. for him to-morrow BALL 30:12
I must d. BIBLE 50:3
in Adam all d. BIBLE 76:22
I shall d. at the top SWIFT 527:19
Is not to d. CAMP 128:19
It is most grand to d. MAS 334:1
it was sure to d. MOORE 356:25
I will d. in peace WOLFE 576:8
I will not have thee d. TENN 542:13
"I would d. PETR 373:2
Jerusalem shall Harry d. SHAK 442:21
kiss my Lord before I d. MARL 330:13
Let me d. eating ortolans DISR 187:1
Let us determine to d. BEE 37:3
Let us d. even as we rush VIRG 558:7
live or d. wi' Charlie HOGG 253:1
look about us and to d. POPE 379:1
love one another or d. AUDEN 20:9
lucky to d. and I know it WHIT 570:19
man can d. but once SHAK 442:7
may be smitten, and d. BIBLE 50:19
might it d. or rest at last SHEL 501:3
money to d. comfortably BUTL 118:30
much beauty as could d. JONS 284:3
Muse forbids to d. HOR 261:17
Must d. of love SHAK 420:26
must weep or she will d. TENN 542:10
myself to d. upon a kiss SHAK 478:1
natural to d. as to be born BACON 26:3
night to d. upon the sand ARN 14:26
Not d. here in a rage SWIFT 526:24
not so difficult to d. BYRON 125:5
not to live, but to d. BROW 97:3
not willingly let it d. MILT 352:14
'Now that I come to d. BROW 100:6
Of easy ways to d. SHAK 424:18
of king should ever d. BROW 103:23
Only we d. in earnest RAL 404:11
peace a Christian can d. ADD 2:29
'People can't d. DICK 177:17
persons to d. before they sing COL 156:16
shall break it must d. KIPL 300:20
shall desire to d. BIBLE 82:7
shall not altogether d. HOR 261:19
shall Trelawny d. HAWK 243:4
should d. before I wake ANON 7:3
should d. for the people BIBLE 72:24
since I needs must d. RAL 404:10
Sir Richard Grenville d. TENN 543:4
sit him down and d. SHAK 442:2
stand the hazard of the d. SHAK 481:19
suffer and d. VIGNY 557:2
taught us how to d. TICK 551:3
that have the power to d. TENN 543:13
that I shall d. to-day MORE 357:13
that love lightly may d. SWIN 529:19
that must fight and d. HOOV 255:25
That we shall d., we know SHAK 450:3
Their's but to do and d. TENN 532:24
thereof thou shalt surely d. BIBLE 45:9
These Christs that d. upon WILDE 572:17
these who d. as cattle OWEN 367:2
they d. in yon rich sky TENN 542:1
They must conquer or d. GAY 223:27

think hereon that I must d. SOUT 514:21
thinks he was not made to d. TENN 535:30
Though I should d. with thee BIBLE 68:13
time to d. BIBLE 55:12
to d. for one's country HOR 260:17
to d. in the last dyke BURKE 110:31
to d. in the last ditch WILL 574:8
to d. is gain BIBLE 78:11
To live and d. for thee HERR 249:27
to make a malefactor d. DRYD 198:13
To men that d. at morn HOUS 262:16
To-morrow let us do or d. CAMP 128:18
to morrow we d. BIBLE 76:24
to morrow we shall d. BIBLE 58:15
unwise they seemed to d. BIBLE 62:13
we all must d. SWIFT 527:23
we needs must d. BIBLE 50:23
We shall d. alone PASC 369:9
What I shall d. to want SHAK 485:12
What 'tis to d. BEAU 36:10
When beggars d. SHAK 449:18
When I d., the GHOULS TENN 544:12
when they d. APPL 11:13
when they d. by thousands CHES 147:20
when you have to d. MOL 353:21
Which some did d. to look SHAK 421:29
Who did not wish to d. SHAW 498:27
who lives is born to d. DRYD 197:10
who would wish to d. BORR 90:4
wisdom shall d. with you BIBLE 52:23
Wise men also d. PRAY 392:28
wish to live and to d. VILL 557:6
with you be ready to d. HOR 261:1
work till we d. LEWIS 314:9
Would do any thing but d. LAMB 308:5
wretch that dares not d. BURNS 114:21
ye shall d. like men PRAY 395:10
yet cannot choose but d. DONNE 188:32
yet d. we must SHAK 446:22
yet I love her till I d. ANON 8:1
Yet she must d. SHAK 477:5
you don't work, you d. KIPL 299:16
Dieb: er war ein D. HEINE 244:10
died: been a grandam ere she d. SHAK 457:14
been the same since God d. MILL 339:25
beggar d. BIBLE 70:28
children d. in the streets AUDEN 18:15
children who d. for our lands KIPL 298:9
could have d. contented DICK 177:25
darter es d. o' the fever TENN 544:5
d. by the hand of the Lord BIBLE 47:23
d. extremely well WALP 562:20
d. last night of my physician PRIOR 401:4
d. like a Duke-and-a-Duchess's BARH 33:26
d. to save their country CHES 146:25
d. to succour me BALL 31:4
dog it was that d. GOLD 231:14
Had I but d. an hour before SHAK 461:1
He d. in a good old age BIBLE 51:40
he d. unto sin once BIBLE 75:2
Helen d. LAND 309:7
He that d. o' Wednesday SHAK 440:18
should have d. hereafter SHAK 463:6
There d. a myriad POUND 383:10
there they d. for me HOUS 265:6
These all d. in faith BIBLE 79:33
thought it d. of grieving KEATS 292:10
When I d. last DONNE 189:21
would God I had d. for thee BIBLE 50:26
diem: carpe d. HOR 259:20
d. perdidi TITUS 551:6
d. tibi diluxisse supremum HOR 258:16
dienen: Oder d. und verlieren GOET 230:7
dies: artist never d. LONG 316:24
d. fighting has increase GREN 236:15
D. irae CEL 138:5
D. like a dog WHIT 571:18
d., or turns Hindoo SHEL 501:19
Every moment d. a man BABB 24:13
Every moment d. a man TENN 544:8

gods love d. young MEN 336:25
hath blown for ever d. FITZ 212:19
He that d. pays all debts SHAK 485:16
kingdom where nobody d. MILL 339:24
king never d. BLAC 85:3
marrid man d. in good stile WARD 564:30
matters not how a man d. JOHN 275:31
necessarily true because a man d. WILDE 573:34
One d. only once MOL 353:8
Optima quaeque d. miseris VIRG 560:16
primrose that forsaken d. MILT 343:15
summer d. the swan TENN 543:11
that d. this year is quit SHAK 442:8
Where all life d. MILT 346:23
Who d. if England live KIPL 299:7
who d. rich dies disgraced CARN 132:32
worm that never d. BROO 94:14
diest: Where thou d. BIBLE 49:32
diet: d., humour, air BROW 96:27
d. unparalleled DICK 179:34
Praise is the best d. SMITH 511:9
that oft with gods doth d. MILT 341:27
Dieu: D. en aura plus tost de VILL 557:4
D. est d'ordinaire pour BUSS 117:7
D. est mort NERV 360:25
D. n'est pas pour les gros VOLT 561:18
Je parle espagnol à D. CHAR 140:31
Le bon D. n'a que dix CLEM 152:31
le Verbe, c'est D. HUGO 267:9
Si D. n'existait pas VOLT 561:8
differemus: nulli negabimus aut d. MAGN 327:3
difference: d. between genuine poetry ARN 16:9
d. of taste in jokes ELIOT 200:21
d. of texts SPEN 515:24
d. to me WORD 581:6
evil that makes racial d. CONR 161:23
find much d. JOHN 280:12
Strange the d. of men's PEPYS 371:17
that has made all the d. FROST 219:10
that the d. is best postponed DICK 181:9
upon the d. of an opinion BROW 96:4
different: d. methods different men CHUR 148:23
from those who have a d. CONR 161:17
How d. from us ANON 6:16
other naturs thinks d. DICK 179:11
They are d. from you FITZ 213:24
very d. from the home life ANON 5:20
We boil at d. degrees EMER 208:9
who follow d. paths HOR 261:21
will show you something d. ELIOT 204:19
differential: integral and d. calculus GILB 228:16
differently: they do things d. there HART 242:34
differeth: One star d. from another BIBLE 76:26
Difficile: D. est longum subito deponere CAT 137:10
D. est saturam non JUV 287:9
Difficult: D. do you call it JOHN 280:24
It has been found d. CHES 146:34
more alternatives, the more d. ALL 3:19
'tis not so d. to die BYRON 125:5
which it is d. to speak BURKE 110:30
difficulties: d. do not make one doubt NEWM 362:1
little local d. MACM 325:19
that somebody is in d. LUCR 320:6
difficulty: great d. I am got hither BUNY 107:38
has had to face every d. WILDE 574:1
with d. and labour he MILT 347:7
Diffidence: her name was D. BUNY 107:21
in the d. that faltered POUND 382:14
Diffugere: D. nives HOR 261:14
diffused: appeals to d. feeling BAG 28:30

dig: d. him up and throw stones   SHAW 496:23
d. in the ribs I gives   SURT 525:5
D. the grave and let me   STEV 523:10
d. till you gently perspire   KIPL 300:11
I cannot d.   BIBLE 70:23
nails he'll d. it up again   ELIOT 204:22
with his nails he'll d.   WEBS 567:9
digest: can d. so much   SHAK 489:6
inwardly d. them   PRAY 386:5
digested: few to be chewed and d.
  BACON 27:19
digestion: d. is the great secret   SMITH 512:8
from pure d. bred   MILT 348:13
good d. wait on appetite   SHAK 461:18
sweet to taste prove in d.   SHAK 478:14
digestions: Few radicals have good d.
  BUTL 118:31
diggeth: d. a pit shall fall   BIBLE 56:2
digne: *tabac n'est pas d. de vivre*   MOL 353:9
dignitate: *cum d. otium*   CIC 151:33
dignities: afraid to speak evil of d. BIBLE 81:1
indignities men come to d.   BACON 26:23
dignity: accessions of d. from the king
  LAMB 307:25
below the d. of history   MAC 324:15
d. compos'd and high exploit   MILT 346:9
d. of this high calling   BURKE 110:7
d. of thinking beings   JOHN 281:24
d. of the whole body   SHAK 462:23
equal in d. and rights   ANON 4:14
maintained the d. of history   BOL 89:18
May reach the d. of crimes   MORE 357:8
room with silent d.   GROS 237:2
There's no d. in it   FRY 220:8
To wear an undeserved d.   SHAK 466:20
write trifles with d.   JOHN 278:23
Dignum: *D. et justum est*   MASS 335:3
D. laude virum Musa vetat   HOR 261:17
dignus: *Domine, non sum d.*   MASS 335:8
digression: there began a lang d.
  BURNS 115:26
Digressions: D., incontestably   STER 519:22
digs: d. my grave at each remove
  HERB 247:23
dilectione: *d. hominum et odio vitiorum*
  AUG 22:1
dilettante: snowy-banded, d.   TENN 540:3
Dilige: *D. et quod vis fac*   AUG 21:21
Diligence: D. is the mother of good
  CERV 138:19
diligencia: *La d. es madre de la buena*
  CERV 138:19
dim: d. and perilous way   WORD 577:13
d. and the dark cloths   YEATS 585:9
doth the greater glory d.   SHAK 468:18
Not when the sense is d.   BEEC 37:9
with every year grows d.   CONR 161:24
dimanches: *tous les d. sa poule au pot*
  HENR 245:13
dimensions: d. of this mercy are above
  CROM 169:22
my d. are as well compact   SHAK 453:9
dimidium: *Animae d. meae*   HOR 259:11
D. facti qui coepit   HOR 258:14
diminish: Enlarge, d., interline SWIFT 527:34
Diminish'd: D. to her cock   SHAK 455:14
diminished: ought to be d.   DUNN 199:14
dimittimus: *sicut et nos d. debitoribus*
  MASS 335:5
dimittis: *Nunc d. servum tuum*   BIBLE 83:19
Dimity: Such D. Convictions   DICK 184:3
dimmed: glory of the sun will be d.
  BALF 30:3
di'mond: quadrangular of d. form
  COWP 167:16
dimpled: Stood pretty-d. boys   SHAK 422:2
dimples: charmer whose d. we prize
  SHER 506:32
dimpling: shallow streams run d. POPE 377:2
din: wealth and d. of Rome   HOR 261:7

din'd: had not d.   POPE 377:10
dine: d. somewhere among   JERR 273:12
go to inns to d.   CHES 147:18
hang that jury-men may d.   POPE 381:4
I'd as soon d. with Jack   JOHN 277:11
I d. at Blenheim once   ANON 7:2
I may d. at journey's end   YEATS 587:5
no scandal while you d.   TENN 543:16
this should stay to d.   CARR 133:13
'Where sall we gang and d.   BALL 32:8
dined: 'I d. last night with   BEER 37:18
I have d. to-day   SMITH 511:15
diner-out: philosophic d.   BROW 102:18
dines: d. he sleeps   SURT 525:7
ding: are chiels that winna d.   BURNS 113:14
Dingo: Yellow-Dog D. behind   KIPL 300:13
dining: d. late with peers   BETJ 44:12
that can live without d.   MER 338:7
while they thought of d.   GOLD 231:17
dinner: d. and feasting reconciles
  PEPYS 372:14
d. of herbs where love   BIBLE 54:6
doubtful of his d.   JOHN 281:40
expect if we haven't any d.   LEAR 312:24
good d. upon his table   JOHN 280:18
if you'd watch a d. out   BROW 99:2
more business after d.   SWIFT 526:18
not have had a better d.   JOHN 275:13
They would ask him to d.   CARL 132:26
three hours' march to d.   HAZL 243:32
was not a d. to *ask* a man   JOHN 275:12
'What gat ye to your d.   BALL 31:5
you worth inviting to d.   VIRG 560:2
dinner-bell: tocsin of the soul—the d.
  BYRON 123:17
dinner-knives: gravel paths with broken
d.   KIPL 299:14
Dinted: D. with the silver-pointed
  BROW 102:28
Diocese: All the air is thy D.   DONNE 188:18
Diogenes: I would be D.   ALEX 3:12
Dionysus: Christ follows D.   POUND 383:6
dip: am a kind of farthing d.   STEV 523:13
Diplomacy: Dollar D.   ANON 5:2
dire: d. offence from am'rous   POPE 380:28
direct: d. and honest is not safe SHAK 475:26
House is pleased to d.   LENT 313:23
puff d.   SHER 505:23
things d. and rule our hearts   PRAY 386:21
were all going d. to Heaven   DICK 183:5
directe: this book I d.   CHAU 144:20
directed: all d. your way   HOR 258:11
direction: d. which thou canst not
  POPE 379:11
directions: By indirections find d.
  SHAK 431:27
He gives d. to the town   SWIFT 528:3
rode madly off in all d.   LEAC 311:14
direful: d. death indeed they had FLEM 214:25
something d. in the sound   AUST 22:18
dirge: d. of her certain ending   SHAK 492:20
unseen their d. is sung   COLL 158:20
with d. in marriage   SHAK 429:19
dirt: d. the reasoning engine   ROCH 406:22
half the little soul is d.   TENN 540:23
if d. were trumps   LAMB 308:9
poverty, hunger, and d.   HOOD 255:6
dirty: An' for all 'is d. 'ide   KIPL 299:18
creature's at his d. work   POPE 376:22
d., dangerous way   GOLD 232:25
d. nurse, Experience   TENN 534:35
d. work for the rest   RUSK 411:16
their d. songs and dreary   BROO 94:27
Wash what is d.   LANG 310:1
Dis: by gloomy D. Was gathered MILT 347:21
dark D.'s door stands open   VIRG 558:9
D. aliter visum   VIRG 558:8
unsubstantial realms of D.   VIRG 558:20
disagree: men only d.   MILT 346:18

disagreeable: doing things d. to myself
  SMITH 512:4
enough to tell him d. truths   BULW 107:7
everybody says I'm such a d.   GILB 228:26
disagreeables: making all d. evaporate
  KEATS 293:18
disappeared: He d. in the dead of winter
  AUDEN 19:2
disappears: that nothing really d.
  BACON 25:15
disappoint: can't abide to d. myself
  GOLD 232:20
disappointed: feel the pangs of d. love
  ROWE 410:21
I am d. by that stroke   JOHN 281:36
disappointeth: d. him not   PRAY 390:5
Disappointment: D. all I endeavour end
  HOPK 257:2
disapprove: I d. of what you say VOLT 561:24
disapproves: condemns whatever he d.
  BURN 112:20
Disaster: meet with Triumph and D.
  KIPL 299:22
disasters: day's d. in his morning GOLD 231:2
make guilty of our own d.   SHAK 453:11
So weary with d.   SHAK 461:10
disbelief: d. in great men   CARL 131:30
willing suspension of d.   COL 157:22
discandy: d., melt their sweets   SHAK 423:5
Disce: *D. omnis*   VIRG 558:2
discept: Two must d.   BROW 102:12
discern: that now you can never d.
  HOUS 263:7
we have built do we d.   ARN 13:23
discharge: responsibility and to d. EDW 200:4
there is no d. in that war   BIBLE 55:25
There's no d. in the war   KIPL 298:6
discharged: d. from the war   HOR 261:6
disciple: d. is not above his master
  BIBLE 65:34
d. whom Jesus loved   BIBLE 73:18
only in the name of a d.   BIBLE 65:41
other d. did outrun Peter   BIBLE 73:6
disciples: d., whom Jesus loved BIBLE 72:28
discipline: d. and perfect steadiness
  KITC 305:14
D. must be maintained   DICK 176:18
d. of colleges and universities SMITH 509:14
order and military d.   ANON 4:28
disclaim: d. all my paternal care SHAK 453:3
willing to d. her for a mother   GIBB 224:7
disclose: more and more to d. truth
  BACON 25:5
disco: *mali miseris succurrere d.* VIRG 557:19
Discobbolos: Till Mrs D. said   LEAR 312:10
Discobolus: to the gospel of the D.
  BUTL 119:20
discomfort: great d. of my soul PRAY 391:24
discommendeth: d. others obliquely
commendeth   BROW 95:15
disconsolate: gate Of Eden stood, d.
  MOORE 356:27
discontent: d., boil bloody   OWEN 361:1
is the winter of our d.   SHAK 480:17
pale contented sort of d.   KEATS 290:26
prone to d.   HERR 249:16
youth and age in common—d.   ARN 15:13
discontented: blushing d. sun   SHAK 479:12
that are d. under *monarchy*   HOBB 251:20
To be d. with the divine   KING 297:6
discontents: More d. I never had HERR 249:3
discord: effects from civil d.   ADD 1:25
Harmony in d.   HOR 258:20
that eke d. doth sow   ELIZ 205:27
what d. follows   SHAK 486:24
Discordant: reconciles D. elements
  WORD 580:11
still-d. wavering multitude   SHAK 440:31
Discords: D. make the sweetest airs
  BUTL 118:9

discors: *Concordia d.* HOR 258:20
discountenance: Religious, d. every
BLAKE 86:9
discouragement: There's no d. BUNY 107:36
discourse: came in to punctuate my d.
COL 158:5
d. and nearest prose DRYD 197:15
d. The freezing hours SHAK 428:15
Good company and good d. WALT 564:4
I love any d. of rivers WALT 564:11
nor to find talk and d. BACON 27:18
not the d. of the elders BIBLE 62:27
upon the daisies and d. GILB 227:21
discourtesy: fault and truth d. HERB 247:6
share in that d. of death YEATS 585:13
discover: further to d. truth BACON 24:15
discoverers: They are ill d. that think
BACON 24:21
discovereth: d. the thick bushes PRAY 391:11
discoveries: not much wish well to d.
JOHN 281:25
virtue and consequence of d. BACON 28:9
discovering: d. in the eyes of the very
POUND 383:14
discovery: are the portals of d. JOYCE 286:27
discredit: He will d. our mystery
SHAK 464:23
discredited: would have d. your travel
SHAK 421:21
discreet: d. and learned Minister PRAY 387:17
discretion: guide his words with d.
PRAY 397:14
has no d. in her coughs AUST 23:12
till it attain years of d. RUSK 412:6
woman which is without d. BIBLE 53:32
your own d. be your tutor SHAK 433:17
discreto: *rey y al simple con el d.*
CERV 138:20
discriminate: Not to d. every moment
PATER 369:22
discriminations: Makes no d. WHIT 571:11
discunt: *Homines dum docent d.*
SEN 420:10
disdain: burning pride and high d.
SCOTT 416:11
D. and scorn ride sparkling SHAK 472:21
fixed mind And high d. MILT 345:2
little d. is not amiss CONG 161:2
me more love or more d. CAREW 130:16
my dear Lady D. SHAK 471:28
disdain'd: general's d. SHAK 486:25
disdained: feeling too falsely d. SHEL 504:13
If now I be d. ANON 7:15
disdaineth: this my love no whit d.
SHAK 493:10
disdains: He d. all things above OVER 366:6
diseas'd: minister to a mind d. SHAK 463:3
disease: almost hath his favourite d.
FIEL 211:22
are suggested for a d. CHEK 144:23
Confront d. at its onset PERS 372:28
Cur'd yesterday of my d. PRIOR 401:4
cure the d. and kill BACON 26:17
desperate d. requires FAWK 210:31
d. has grown strong through OVID 366:20
d. is incurable SHAK 441:16
d. of admiration MAC 323:10
d. of modern life ARN 14:19
d. of not listening SHAK 441:7
d. that afflicts amateurs CHES 148:1
is just a d. RAC 404:6
is no cure for this d. BELL 39:1
long d., my life POPE 376:23
out old shapes of foul d. TENN 537:15
Progress is a comfortable d. CUMM 170:11
remedy is worse than the d. BACON 27:13
Without d. the healthful life SURR 524:20
your skin is a shocking d. AUDEN 18:18
diseased: beauty is the mind d. BYRON 121:13
diseases: death is the cure of all d.
BROW 97:2

D. and sad Old Age live VIRG 558:21
D. desperate grown SHAK 435:25
subject to the same d. SHAK 467:4
disenchanting: life so d. as attainment
STEV 521:16
disencumber'd: d. Atlas of the state
COWP 166:16
disentangle: cannot d. ANON 7:15
disfigure: that in a moment can so d.
BROW 96:20
disfigured: snow d. the public statues
AUDEN 19:2
Disfigures: D. earth COWP 166:30
disgrace: d. and ignominy of our BROW 96:20
d. with fortune and men's SHAK 493:6
Even to a full d. SHAK 428:1
grace us in the d. of death SHAK 456:14
public and merited d. STEV 522:13
quite a *d.* to be fine TAYL 531:24
sharp antidote against d. BURKE 111:9
sole author of his own d. COWP 165:13
disgraced: who dies…rich dies d.
CARN 132:32
disgraceful: something d. JUV 288:7
disguise: Are blessings in d. HERV 250:17
D. fair nature with hard-favour'd
SHAK 443:21
go naked is the best d. CONG 159:27
disguiser: death's a great d. SHAK 465:1
disguises: troublesome d. which we wear
MILT 348:7
disgust: began to d. this refined age
EVEL 209:9
not moments of d. VOLT 561:16
disgusted: quite d. with literary men
KEATS 293:1
dish: forth butter in a lordly d. BIBLE 49:10
Let's carve him as a d. SHAK 449:9
woman is a d. for the gods SHAK 424:9
dishabilly: cannot be devout in d.
FARQ 210:21
dishclout: Romeo's a d. to him SHAK 483:19
dishcover: d. the riddle CARR 136:11
dishes: Are these the choice d. GARR 221:12
d. were ill-sorted DRYD 198:10
Home-made d. that drive HOOD 254:26
there's no washing of d. ANON 5:13
were the d. wherein to me AUG 21:13
dishonour: another unto d. BIBLE 75:14
who fears d. HOR 261:19
dishonourable: find ourselves d. graves
SHAK 448:17
dishonour'd: d. step SHAK 453:6
dislecti: *d. membra poetae* HOR 262:2
disinclination: d. to inflict pain upon
MER 338:4
disinheriting: damned d. countenance
SHER 506:33
disintegration: rapine to d. and
dismemberment GLAD 229:15
disinterested: d. endeavour to learn ARN 16:1
d. commerce between equals GOLD 232:11
dislike: do not much d. the matter
SHAK 421:34
sat with that d. which STEE 517:25
dislikings: made up of likings and d.
LAMB 307:7
dismal: d. headache, and repose GILB 226:12
d. tidings when he frown'd GOLD 231:2
of d. terror was the time SHAK 480:26
Professors of the D. Science CARL 131:40
that d. cry rose slowly BROW 98:2
dismay'd: Was there a man d. TENN 532:24
dismemberment: disintegration and d.
of the Empire GLAD 229:15
dismiss: d. us with Thy blessing BUCK 106:17
lacks power to d. itself SHAK 449:3
dismissed: d. by the British electorate
CHUR 150:26
will be d. with a laugh HOR 262:7

disobedience: Of Man's first d. MILT 344:20
upon the children of d. BIBLE 78:3
Disorder: D., horror SHAK 479:20
sweet d. in the dress HERR 249:2
disparity: Just such d. DONNE 187:22
dispatch: requisite in business than d.
ADD 1:12
dispensation: in the old d. ELIOT 203:15
display: does a Human Form d. BLAKE 85:18
displeased: were so wrathfully d. at us
PRAY 398:13
displeasing: something which is not d.
to us LA R 310:8
displeasure: her wrong stay and her d.
SHAK 474:18
dispoged: lips to it when I am so d.
DICK 179:10
disponit: *sed Deus d.* THOM 546:10
dispose: d. the way of thy servants
PRAY 388:5
disposition: Doth change my d. SHAK 491:27
entertain a cheerful d. SHAK 478:22
free have d. to be truthful AUDEN 19:13
horridly to shake our d. SHAK 430:24
must be the flag of my d. WHIT 570:18
of a mild or choleric d. ADD 2:7
to lay his goatish d. SHAK 453:11
To put an antic d. SHAK 431:24
dispraised: d. were no small praise
MILT 350:4
To be d. JONS 283:22
disputants: Our d. put me in mind ADD 2:24
disputation: that's a feeling d. SHAK 439:29
disputations: Doubtful d. BIBLE 75:26
dispute: decide such a great d. VIRG 559:20
D. it like a man SHAK 462:18
right there is none to d. COWP 167:38
disputes: Hath left to their d. MILT 349:3
disquieted: art thou so d. within me
PRAY 392:7
Never to be d. KING 296:11
disquieteth: d. himself in vain PRAY 391:31
disrespectfully: speak d. of the Equator
SMITH 510:29
Diss: with you by train to D. BETJ 43:15
dissaisiatur: *imprisonetur, aut d.* MAGN 327:2
dissatisfied: Not one is d. WHIT 570:22
dissect: thro' creatures you d. POPE 377:9
We d. nature along lines WHORF 571:23
We murder to d. WORD 582:23
dissemble: d. in their double heart
PRAY 389:32
d. sometimes your knowledge BACON 26:5
not d. nor cloke them PRAY 384:9
right to d. your love BICK 83:27
dissembling: Cheated of feature by d.
SHAK 480:18
dissensions: d. and animosities of mankind
BURKE 111:3
dissent: is the dissidence of d. BURKE 109:22
dissentious: you d. rogues SHAK 427:12
dissertates: One d. BROW 102:12
dissidence: it is the d. of dissent
BURKE 109:22
dissimulate: to d. their instability
HOUS 266:14
dissimulation: defined by one word—d.
DISR 186:5
laying down the guilt of d. SCOTT 418:13
dissipation: d. without pleasure GIBB 224:14
dissociation: century a d. of sensibility
ELIOT 205:17
Dissolute: D., damned, and despairful
SERV 420:13
dissolve: d., and quite forget KEATS 291:18
D. me into ecstasies MILT 342:10
dissolved: tabernacle of this house were
d. BIBLE 77:6
dissonance: air with barbarous d. MILT 341:13
far off the barb'rous d. MILT 348:29

dissonant: No sound is d. which tells COL 157:12

distain: coward shame d. his name BURNS 114:21

distance: by d. made more sweet WORD 579:17
d. is nothing DU D 198:28
La d. n'y fait rien DU D 198:28
notes by d. made more sweet COLL 158:21
sixty seconds' worth of d. KIPL 300:2
'Tis d. lends enchantment CAMP 129:6

distant: All places are d. from BURT 116:28
dull prospect of a d. good DRYD 196:18
Music of a d. Drum FITZ 212:12
Ye d. spires GRAY 235:9

Distasted: D. with the salt of broken SHAK 487:12

distastes: without many fears and d. BACON 25:20

distemperature: thorough this d. we see SHAK 470:6

distempered: That questions the d. part ELIOT 202:21

Distilled: D. by the sun HARDY 241:21

distinction: chase of honours and d. BURKE 108:7
d. between virtue and vice JOHN 275:1
few escape that d. TWAIN 554:21
no d. among WILL 574:13
preference and d. of excelling CONG 159:29

distinctions: d. of meum and tuum LAMB 307:13
to despise d. HOR 262:10

distinctive: man's d. mark alone BROW 100:11

distinguish: could of men d. SHAK 434:1

distinguished: at last, the d. thing JAMES 271:31
discept,—has d. BROW 102:12
d. by that circumstance THOR 550:21
d. into joints and fingers TRAH 552:1
man is d. from all other ADD 2:26
to be d. above the rest HOMER 253:30

distinguishes: it d. nothing DONNE 190:23

Distorts: D. the Heavens from pole BLAKE 85:23

distracted: I shall go d. AUST 23:23

Distraction: D., Uglification and Derision CARR 134:10
d. in 's aspect SHAK 432:27

distress: All pray in their d. BLAKE 88:6
could foretell this sore d. BRID 92:22
delivereth them out of their d. PRAY 397:10
incapable of her own d. SHAK 436:19
open to d. CHUR 149:3

distress'd: quite vacant is a mind d. COWP 166:19

distressed: afflicted, or d. PRAY 386:1

distresses: In all d. of our friends SWIFT 527:22

distressful: speak of some d. stroke SHAK 474:1

distribution: same d. of the necessaries SMITH 509:9

disturb: me to d. your season due MILT 343:2
Which none d. VAUG 555:12

disturbed: moment d. its solitude BALF 30:3

disturbs: he d. the order here HARDY 240:3

dìt: d. et l'on vient trop tard LA B 306:11
la peine d'être d. BEAU 35:14

ditch: environed with a great d. CROM 170:4
is to die in the last d. WILL 574:8
Rather a d. in Egypt SHAK 423:21
shall fall into the d. BIBLE 66:29

Ditch-deliver'd: D. by a drab SHAK 462:4

ditchers: d. and grave-makers SHAK 436:22

ditches: water-land of Dutchmen and of d. BYRON 123:27

ditchwater: drinking bottled d. SHAW 496:33

ditties: In amorous d. all a summer's MILT 345:17
Pipe to the spirit d. KEATS 291:4

Ditto: D. ditto my song GILB 226:17

ditty: He play'd an ancient d. KEATS 289:21
To air the d. HOUS 265:12

diurnal: With visible motion her d. WORD 577:27

Diuturnity: D. is a dream and a folly BROW 97:21

divan: Enacted on this same d. ELIOT 205:2

dive: Heav'n's great lamps do d. CAT 136:25
search for pearls must d. DRYD 195:10

diver: d.'s brilliant bow AUDEN 18:10
has been a d. in deep seas PATER 369:19

Divergence: entailing D. of Character DARW 171:28

divers: led away with d. lusts BIBLE 79:24

diversa: laudet d. sequentis HOR 261:21

diversion: 'tis a country d. CONG 161:5

diversite: ther is so gret d. CHAU 144:17

diversities: Now there are d. of gifts BIBLE 76:13

diversity: whence arise d. of sects SPEN 515:24

Divert: D. her eyes with pictures POPE 377:7

dives: quo Tullus d. et Ancus HOR 261:16

divide: d. is not to take away SHEL 500:11
d. with the poor the produce SMITH 509:9
rejoice when they d. the spoil BIBLE 58:6
though he d. the hoof BIBLE 48:6

divided: common use has harshly d. SCH 415:9
death they were not d. BIBLE 50:17
Have they not d. the prey BIBLE 49:13
He d. the sea PRAY 395:5
household he d. the spoil PRAY 394:8
If a house be d. against BIBLE 68:27
perceive here a d. duty SHAK 474:2
Thy kingdom is d. BIBLE 61:6
whole is d. into three parts CAES 126:26

dividends: comfortable man, with d. LONG 316:23

divideth: d. his spoils BIBLE 69:36

dividing: by d. we fall DICK 184:5
days d. lover and lover SWIN 528:17
their gifts some tragic d. PATER 369:22

divine: all are d. ARN 13:3
arsenals of d. vengeance HOUS 266:13
believes Kingsley a d. STUB 524:5
by a d. thrusting SHAK 453:11
by a law d. SHEL 502:1
could d. his real thought BYRON 122:30
depth of some d. despair TENN 542:2
did the Countenance D. BLAKE 86:16
d. enchanting ravishment MILT 341:4
D. of Kings to govern wrong POPE 375:23
d. right of husbands WOLL 576:9
d. than the physician SHAK 462:26
Door— To her d. Majority DICK 183:21
energy d. POPE 380:15
Fanny Kelly's d. plain face LAMB 307:31
heavy, but no less d. BYRON 123:5
horror and its beauty are d. SHEL 502:2
human form d. BLAKE 88:7
inspired by d. revelation BACON 24:20
is not therefore less d. WORD 582:1
It is a good d. that follows SHAK 465:20
one far-off d. event TENN 537:22
some are fou o' love d. BURNS 114:9
Terror the human form d. BLAKE 88:9
their motions harmony d. MILT 348:24
to forgive, d. POPE 378:27
vision and the faculty d. WORD 577:9
what the form d. LAND 308:26
Whether it d. tobacco were SPEN 516:15
worshipp'd by the names d. BLAKE 86:1
wrote that monarchs were d. KIPL 300:5
You look d. as you advance NASH 360:5

divinely: ever most d. in the wrong YOUNG 587:17
most d. fair TENN 533:6

divineness: people hath some d. BACON 25:11
some participation of d. BACON 24:19

divines: eternal reproach of the d. MILT 352:12

divinest: two d. things this world HUNT 268:13

divinity: d. doth hedge a king SHAK 436:6
d. in odd numbers SHAK 469:15
d. or school metaphysics HUME 267:15
d. that shapes our ends SHAK 437:11
doctors of law or d. BURKE 108:12
is something in it of d. BROW 97:1
is surely a piece of d. BROW 97:4
'Tis the d. that stirs ADD 1:24
wingy mysteries in d. BROW 96:8

divisible: Mankind is d. into two BEER 37:17

Division: D. is as bad ANON 6:18
such d. 'tween our souls SHAK 451:29

divisions: Pope! How many d. STAL 517:16

divisos: Et penitus toto d. orbe VIRG 559:13

Divitias: D. operosiores HOR 260:16

divorc'd: d. So many English kings SHAK 442:18

divorce: long d. of steel SHAK 446:27
then this bill of my D. DONNE 189:11

divorced: Demand to be d. CHES 147:26
D. old barren Reason from FITZ 213:1

Dixeris: D. egregie notum si callida HOR 257:13

dixerunt: qui ante nos nostra d. DON 187:17

dixit: 'Ipse d. CIC 151:20

dizzy: d., a tumultuous joy SOUT 514:11
d. 'tis to cast one's eyes SHAK 455:14

do: can't all d. everything VIRG 560:6
d. any man's heart good SHAK 469:29
d. anything well till we HAZL 243:25
D. as I say SELD 420:1
d. as much for my true-love BALL 32:9
D. as you would be done CHES 145:17
d. for pretty girls YEATS 585:16
d. it yourself BARH 33:10
D. lovely things KING 296:19
D. not do unto others SHAW 497:34
d. nothing and get something DISR 186:28
d. only one thing SMIL 509:6
'D. other men DICK 179:9
d. something today which COLL 158:12
d. were as easy as to know SHAK 465:20
D. what you like RAB 403:28
d. ye even so to them BIBLE 65:5
having too little to d. KIPL 300:9
How many things I can d. SOCR 512:22
HOW NOT TO D. IT DICK 178:16
I am to d. what I please FRED 218:22
I can d. no other LUTH 320:16
I'll do, and I'll d. SHAK 458:6
I'll d.'t before I speak SHAK 453:1
'I should d. so DOYLE 192:36
It revolts me, but I d. it GILB 226:17
I will d. such things SHAK 454:2
I would they should d. PRAY 388:15
Let us d. or die BURNS 115:1
Love and d. what you will AUG 21:21
my girl…it won't d. JOHN 275:9
not knowing what they d. SHAK 473:1
one that will d. the deed SHAK 456:27
out what you cannot d. BLAKE 87:6
People don't d. such things IBSEN 270:6
Their's but to d. and die TENN 532:24
they know not what they d. BIBLE 71:11
things we cannot all d. LUC 320:2
This will never d. JEFF 272:19
to d. those things which KEYN 295:17
To-morrow let us d. or die CAMP 128:18
trouble always to d. SHAW 496:31
true and d. what is right HUXL 269:8
'We cannot d. it CARR 135:25

What are we going to d. AUDEN 19:14
Whatever you d. ANON 10:18
what I d. in any thing HERB 247:18
what is it you d. WORD 581:2
What must I d. to be saved BIBLE 74:7
what you are afraid to d. EMER 207:23
who can d. all things well CHUR 148:23
Doasyouwouldbedoneby: her name is
Mrs D. KING 297:12
docent: Homines dum d. discunt SEN 420:10
doceri: fas est et ab hoste d. OVID 366:16
docile: that they may be more d. MILL 339:15
docks: hateful d. SHAK 445:12
spudding up d. HARDY 240:19
doctor: d. found GOLD 231:8
d. full of phrase and fame ARN 15:12
d. is a specially dangerous SHAW 498:22
d.'s thesis On education AUDEN 21:4
God and the d. we alike OWEN 366:28
man therein d. but himself MILT 350:21
outliv'd the d.'s pill GAY 222:30
Than fee the d. for a nauseous DRYD 196:5
When the artless d. sees HERR 250:12
doctors: better have d. well off SHAW 498:22
budge d. of the Stoic MILT 341:16
d. cocking their medical DICK 183:11
d. of law or divinity BURKE 108:12
If you believe the d. SAL 413:18
when d. disagree POPE 377:30
doctrine: about with every wind of d.
BIBLE 77:28
d. of the enclitic *De* BROW 101:1
d. of the strenuous life ROOS 407:27
d. set forth thy true PRAY 387:15
d. so illogical and so KEYN 295:16
every blast of vain d. PRAY 387:3
Not for the d. POPE 378:20
doctrines: By d. fashion'd GOLD 230:22
d. of devils BIBLE 79:13
makes all d. plain and clear BUTL 118:10
documents: England are ready to sign
d. HURST 268:17
wants more d. than he can JAMES 271:18
Dodger: *sobriquet* of 'The artful D.
DICK 180:33
dodgers: dodgerest of the d. DICK 181:20
d. as these old men are JOW 285:22
Dodo: D. never had a chance CUPPY 170:15
doers: be ye d. of the word BIBLE 80:10
does: d.—nothing at all FARQ 209:25
d., not suffers wrong SHEL 502:20
doest: That thou d., do quickly BIBLE 72:29
doeth: Whoso d. these things PRAY 390:5
doff't: Had d. her gawdy trim MILT 344:5
dog: Am I a d. BIBLE 50:12
bargain d. never bites NASH 360:3
Beware of the d. PETR 372:30
call a d. *Hervey* JOHN 273:30
courtesy help a lame d. CHIL 148:13
cut-throat d. SHAK 466:2
Dies like a d. WHIT 571:18
d. bites a man BOG 89:9
d. is turned to his own BIBLE 81:2
d. it was that died GOLD 231:14
d. returneth to his vomit BIBLE 54:32
d. starv'd at his master's BLAKE 85:10
d. that praised his fleas YEATS 587:4
d., to gain some private GOLD 231:13
erigine of pollution, the d. SPAR 514:23
every d. his day KING 297:5
fleas is good fer a d. WEST 569:4
giving your heart to a d. KIPL 302:3
good d., like a good candidate BECK 36:18
'Hath a d. money SHAK 466:3
His faithful d. shall bear POPE 379:6
I'd beat him like a d. SHAK 488:22
I had rather be a d. SHAK 451:14
infidel as a d. is an infidel JOHN 275:26
Is thy servant a d. BIBLE 51:31
Like a d. TENN 538:21

living d. is better than BIBLE 55:27
Lovell our d. COLL 158:10
Mine enemy's d. SHAK 455:24
my poor d. Tray CAMP 128:20
'O keep the D. far hence ELIOT 204:22
ope my lips let no d. SHAK 465:12
Orion and the D. Are veiled ELIOT 204:15
poor d. BYRON 124:40
preaching is like a d.'s JOHN 275:10
see the portrait of a d. JOHN 280:19
Something better than his d. TENN 538:19
tail must wag the d. KIPL 298:16
that town a d. was found GOLD 231:12
'The d. did nothing DOYLE 192:16
tongue of a d. SHAK 462:3
very d. to the commonalty SHAK 427:10
very flea of his d. JONS 284:6
whose d. are you POPE 376:16
You call'd me d. SHAK 466:3
young man's d. with them BIBLE 62:9
dogfight: We were regaled by a d.
MAC 324:26
dogged: It's d. as does it TROL 552:23
doggy: on with their d. life AUDEN 19:19
dog-kennel: his ears in a empty d.
DICK 179:27
dogma: d. has been the fundamental
NEWM 361:20
d. of the Ghost RYLE 412:25
no d., no Dean DISR 185:23
dogmatise: I d. and am contradicted
JOHN 280:21
dogs: attentive to the feelings of d.
ELIOT 201:11
bang these d. of Seville TENN 543:1
barking d. by Highgate Pond BETJ 43:19
better I like d. ROL 407:16
Cowardly d. bark loudest WEBS 567:5
dancing d. and bears HODG 252:2
D., easily won to fawn SHAK 479:9
d. eat of the crumbs which BIBLE 66:30
d. licked his sores BIBLE 70:28
Goethe had an aversion to d. NERV 361:1
hates d. and babies ROST 410:14
Lame d. over stiles KING 296:21
Let d. delight to bark WATTS 565:17
let's go to the d. to-night HERB 246:7
let slip the d. of war SHAK 450:12
like dancing d. JOHN 276:30
little d. and all SHAK 454:29
Mad d. and Englishmen COW 163:19
Now for d. and apes BROW 100:37
of their horses and d. PENN 371:15
That d. bark at me SHAK 480:18
They fought the d. BROW 103:15
they were na men but d. BURNS 116:1
Things are but as straw d. LAO 310:2
Throw physic to the d. SHAK 463:3
Uncover, d., and lap SHAK 486:7
Unmiss'd but by his d. COWP 166:6
without are d. BIBLE 83:3
Dog-star: D. rages POPE 376:18
dogwood: d. and chestnut ELIOT 203:4
doileys: I'm soiling the d. BETJ 42:20
doing: be up and d. LONG 317:5
continuance in well d. BIBLE 74:33
done instead of not d. POUND 382:14
dread of d. what has been done WHAR 569:9
heaven-born privilege of d. ARN 15:20
joy's soul lies in the d. SHAK 486:21
labour of d. nothing STEE 518:8
not be weary in well d. BIBLE 77:20
see what she's d. PUNCH 402:23
still be d. BUTL 117:22
This is the Lord's d. PRAY 398:2
way of d. things rightly RUSK 411:26
what everyone is d. HERB 246:9
What was he d. BROW 98:6
Doing-good: D., that is one THOR 550:14
doings: child is known by his d. BIBLE 54:17

Doleful: Knight of the D. Countenance
CERV 138:12
dolefull'st: there sung the d. ditty BARN 33:32
DOLENTE: ME SI VA NELLA CITTÀ
D. DANTE 171:3
doll: doll in the d.'s house DICK 181:19
once had a sweet little d. KING 297:4
dollar: almighty d. is the only ANON 7:21
almighty d. IRV 270:26
D. Diplomacy ANON 5:2
DOLORE: ME SI VA NELL' ETERNO
D. DANTE 171:3
Nessun maggior d. DANTE 171:8
dolorem: iubes renovare d. VIRG 557:20
Dolores: sanguine and subtle D. SWIN 529:8
splendid and sterile D. SWIN 529:6
dolour: have wept to see the d. MAL 328:4
dolphin: heard a mermaid on a d.'s
SHAK 470:7
his delights Were d.-like SHAK 423:22
That d.-torn YEATS 584:13
Dolphin-chamber: sitting in my D.
SHAK 441:20
dolphins: d. of kindlier waves MOORE 355:23
Dolphin-scales: 'There's Venus objects
to D. GRAV 234:12
dome: Build up the blue d. SHEL 500:7
starlit or a moonlit d. YEATS 584:12
domestic: d. as a plate MILL 339:27
d. business is no less MONT 354:19
d. servants are treated SHAW 497:40
Milk-soup men call d. bliss PATM 370:4
minute d. happiness KEATS 294:19
smooth current of d. joy JOHN 282:21
domesticate: d. the Recording Angel
STEV 521:33
domi: Res angusta d. JUV 287:18
dominant: d.'s persistence till BROW 105:24
domination: d. over them in the morning
PRAY 393:1
military d. of Prussia ASQ 17:17
dominion: death hath no more d. over
BIBLE 75:2
death shall have no d. THOM 546:19
d. of the sea COV 163:10
d. of the world MAHAN 327:5
D. over palm and pine KIPL 302:7
His d. shall be also from PRAY 394:20
I'm truly sorry Man's d. BURNS 115:21
inglorious period of our d. BURKE 110:24
them have d. over the fish BIBLE 45:4
they get the d. over me PRAY 390:13
dominions: of depopulating his d. BECK 36:19
tithe or toll in our d. SHAK 452:17
Dominus: D. custodierit civitatem
BIBLE 83:12
D. illuminatio mea BIBLE 83:5
D. vobiscum MASS 334:11
domum: Ite d. saturae VIRG 557:20
Don: D. different from those BELL 39:28
Remote and ineffectual D. BELL 39:27
turn'd my back upon D. TENN 543:1
dona: d. nobis pacem MASS 335:7
Requiem aeternam d. eis MASS 334:17
timeo Danaos et d. VIRG 558:1
done: anything remained to be d.
LUCAN 319:24
Apostles would have d. BYRON 122:10
been and gone and d. GILB 225:12
consider it d. CAL 127:9
Determined, dared, and d. SMART 509:4
doing what has been d. before WHAR 569:9
d. anything that could DISR 186:27
D. because we are too menny HARDY 241:15
d. instead of not doing POUND 382:14
d. the state some service SHAK 477:23
d. to you young blackguards FARR 210:28
d. with Hope and Honour KIPL 299:11
he has d. it all himself BARR 34:22
he might have d. with us CLOU 153:22

If it were d. when 'tis	SHAK 459:5
I have d. the deed	SHAK 460:6
let us have d. with you	CROM 169:26
much is to be d. and little	JOHN 280:7
part shall be d. away	BIBLE 76:14
petty d.	BROW 101:25
present are not d. at all	KEYN 295:17
reward of a thing well d.	EMER 207:26
Something attempted, something d.	
	LONG 317:19
Something must be d.	EDW 200:3
Still betters what is d.	SHAK 491:27
surprised to find it d. at all	JOHN 275:10
that which shall be d.	BIBLE 55:7
therefore is d. every day	DONNE 190:24
they had not d. they do	SUCK 524:11
Things won are d.	SHAK 486:21
thing was not d. in a corner	BIBLE 74:26
this that thou hast d.	BIBLE 45:18
thou and I have d. before	SUCK 524:11
thou hast not d.	DONNE 189:13
traveller's journey is d.	BLAKE 87:22
we have d. those things	PRAY 394:11
what could she have d.	YEATS 586:7
what hast thou d. to me	ROSS 410:3
What have I d. for you	HENL 245:11
What's d. cannot be undone	SHAK 462:25
what's d. is done	SHAK 461:12
Which of you have d. this	SHAK 461:19
ye have d. it unto me	BIBLE 68:7

Done-to-death: called Played-out and
    D.   TRAI 552:4

dong: cod Fulfilled of d. and of corrupcioun
    CHAU 143:6
D. with Luminous Nose   LEAR 312:3

Don John: D. of Austria is going   CHES 147:2
D. of Austria Is riding   CHES 147:3

donkey: If I know'd a d. wot wouldn't
    DICK 180:28
that's a dead d.   DICK 182:38

Donne: D., whose muse on dromedary
    COL 157:6
Dr D.'s verses are like   JAM 271:6
shorter Poems of D.   AUDEN 21:3
Si le Roi m'avait d.   ANON 9:17
That D. hanging   JONS 285:17
With Landor and with D.   YEATS 587:5

Don Quixote: excepting *D.*   JOHN 280:16

Dons: If the D. sight Devon   NEWB 361:6

Don't: persons about to marry.—'D.
    PUNCH 402:10

Donuil Dhu: Pibroch of D.   SCOTT 417:27

doobts: ma d. aboot the meenister
    PUNCH 402:31

doom: even to the edge of d.   SHAK 495:5
forfeit to a confin'd d.   SHAK 494:21
great d.'s image   SHAK 460:23
His d.'s extremely hard   GILB 227:7
regardless of their d.   GRAY 235:12
scaffold and the d.   AYT 24:9
would have changed his d.   CLEV 153:4

Doom'd: D. for a certain term   SHAK 431:4
d. to death   DRYD 196:11

dooms: grandeur of the d.   KEATS 289:3

Doomsday: D. is near   SHAK 440:8
Then is d. near   SHAK 432:11
Where d. may thunder   HOUS 264:8

Doon: banks and braes o' bonny D.
    BURNS 116:6

door: at the d. too   SHAK 447:24
back at mine hostess' d.   SHAK 452:12
barring of the d.   BALL 30:21
Came out by the same D.   FITZ 212:20
Converses at the d. apart   ELIOT 204:16
d. and bar for thy mouth   BIBLE 63:12
D.— To her divine Majority   DICK 183:21
d. with a gun in his hand   CHAN 139:21
drive an angel from your d.   BLAKE 88:4
even hard at death's d.   PRAY 397:8
gusts shake the d.   ARN 13:7

handle of the big front d.	GILB 228:4
He is as deaf as a d.	BRET 92:4
here and beat on my d.	IBSEN 270:2
I am the d.	BIBLE 72:17
I stand at the d.	BIBLE 81:21
knocking at Preferment's d.	ARN 14:12
lock and splintered the d.	AUDEN 20:5
my d. stayed shut	RAC 404:5
opening of a D.	DICK 183:18
pass'd the d. of Darkness	FITZ 213:4
rapping at my chamber d.	POE 375:4
Shut the d., Wales	BRUM 106:6
Shut the d. after you	EDG 199:23
so wide as a church d.	SHAK 483:3
Towards the d. we never opened	
	ELIOT 202:13
whining of d.	DONNE 191:1
Will it knock on my d.	AUDEN 21:2
wrong side of the d.	CHES 146:18

door-keeper: d. in the house of my God
    PRAY 395:13

doors: death; a thousand d.   SEN 420:11
d. clap   HOUS 264:20
d. of perception were cleansed   BLAKE 88:28
d. shall be shut   BIBLE 56:11
D., where my heart was   TENN 536:5
has been opening the d.   AUST 22:14
many d. to let out life   FLET 215:11
shut their d. against a setting   SHAK 486:5
ten thousand several d.   WEBS 566:26
Th' infernal d.   MILT 347:3
thousand d. to let out life   MASS 336:1
ye everlasting d.   PRAY 390:24
yielding like swinging d.   DOUG 191:7

Doorways: D. are alternate Night   FITZ 212:13

dooryard: When lilacs last in the d.
    WHIT 571:12

Dorchester: Safe in the D. Hotel   BETJ 42:8

Dorian: perfect phalanx to the D.   MILT 345:21

dormienda: *Nox est perpetua una d.*
    CAT 136:25

dormons: *et veillants d.*   MONT 355:5

dormy: flourish of steel, a d.   JAMES 271:34

dotage: eyes the streams of d.   JOHN 283:3
lose myself in d.   SHAK 421:17

dote: d. on her for any thing   SHAK 453:14
I d. on his very absence   SHAK 465:26

doted: d. upon the Assyrians her   BIBLE 60:37

Dotheboys: D. Hall   DICK 179:34

dots: out what those damned d.   CHUR 149:24

Dotting: D. the shoreless watery   ARN 13:12

dotty: Blake went d. as he sang   AUDEN 18:20

double: contriv'd a d. debt to pay   GOLD 231:4
dissemble in their d. heart   PRAY 389:32
d. the Cape of Good Hope   BACON 28:3
d. the vision my eyes do   BLAKE 86:14
d. toil and trouble   SHAK 462:2
lips prevail'd with d. sway   GOLD 230:24
so d. be his praise   SPEN 516:10
surely you'll grow d.   WORD 582:22

doubled: Had d. him up for ever   GILB 225:21

doublet: he bought his d. in Italy
    SHAK 465:24
tailor make thy d. of changeable   SHAK 489:5
with his d. all unbrac'd   SHAK 431:28

Doublethink: *D.* means the power
    ORW 365:13

Doubly: D. redoubled strokes upon
    SHAK 458:4

doubt: are not enabled to d. Thee
    KNOX 305:21
difficulties do not make one d.   NEWM 362:1
d. is Devil-born   TENN 537:10
freckles, and d.   PARK 368:15
in d. to act or rest   POPE 379:12
Is a rift of d. diversified   BROW 99:5
I then am in most d.   SUCK 524:13
mind is clouded with a d.   TENN 535:27
more faith in honest d.   TENN 537:11
never d.   BELL 40:3

never d. I love	SHAK 431:35
never stand to d.	HERR 249:19
No possible d. whatever	GILB 225:19
One may not d. that	BROO 94:11
philosophical d. as to animal	COL 157:34
philosophy calls all in d.	DONNE 187:19
soundest casuists d.	POPE 377:30
Sun and Moon should d.	BLAKE 85:17
sunnier side of d.	TENN 532:15
time will d. of Rome	BYRON 123:13
troubled with religious d.	CHES 147:9
wherefore didst thou d.	BIBLE 66:27
yourself when all men d. you	KIPL 299:22

doubted: Christian religion d.   BUTL 119:13
never d.   BETJ 42:12

doubter: I am the d. and the doubt
    EMER 206:18

Doubtful: D. disputations   BIBLE 75:26

Doubting-Castle: castle, called D.
    BUNY 107:20

Doubtless: D. God could have made
    BUTL 119:23
shall d. come again with   PRAY 398:17

Doubts: breed D. 'mongst Divines
    SPEN 515:24
dissipated all d. on the subject   HAZL 243:13
he shall end in d.   BACON 24:16
He who d. from what he   BLAKE 85:17
my d. are done   DRYD 196:13
To saucy d. and fears   SHAK 461:17

doughterly: d. loue and deere charitie
    MORE 357:20

Douglas: Degenerate D.   WORD 578:11
D. in his hall   SCOTT 417:18
hand of D. is his own   SCOTT 417:17
Like D. conquer   HOME 253:24
old song of Percy and D.   SIDN 508:3

doulceur: *l'air marin la d. Angevin*
    DU B 198:27

douzaines: *et forge des Dieux à d.*
    MONT 355:2

dove: all the d.   CRAS 169:4
be as the wings of a d.   PRAY 394:8
Beside the springs of D.   WORD 581:6
Breasts more soft than a d.'s   SWIN 530:4
changes on the burnish'd d.   TENN 538:17
d. found no rest   BIBLE 45:35
hawk at eagles with a d.   HERB 248:9
I had a d. and the sweet   KEATS 292:10
Intervene. O descend as a d.   AUDEN 20:15
patient as the female d.   SHAK 437:9
that I had wings like a d.   PRAY 393:10

dove-cote: like an eagle in a d.   SHAK 428:6

Dover: chalk cliffs of D.   BALD 29:28
farthing candle at D.   JOHN 275:8

Dover Road: There's milestones on the
    D.   DICK 178:22

doves: d.' eyes within thy locks   BIBLE 56:26
d. opposed the air strike   BART 34:24
harmless as d.   BIBLE 65:33
of d. in immemorial elms   TENN 542:17

dovetailedness: kind of a universal d.
    DICK 180:17

dowagers: d. for deans   TENN 541:27

dower: beauty is thy earthly d.   WORD 578:11
earth its d. of river   KEATS 289:3
faith's transcendent d.   WORD 581:5
little children's d.   BROW 101:7
their ancient English d.   WORD 582:5
thy truth then be thy d.   SHAK 453:3

down: Dead from the waist d.   BROW 101:1
D. among the dead men let   DYER 199:19
d. and out of breath   SHAK 440:27
D. by the salley gardens   YEATS 584:22
D. these mean streets   CHAN 139:22
D., thou climbing sorrow   SHAK 453:24
D. went the owners   GILB 225:9
D. with the defeated   LIVY 315:11
go d. to the sea in ships   PRAY 397:9
he putteth d. one   PRAY 394:26

levellers wish to level *d.*　JOHN 275:5
quite, quite, d.　SHAK 433:15
sloth Finds the d. pillow　SHAK 428:18
soft young d. of her　MEW 338:12
they must be kept d.　MARL 329:2
way d. to the Underworld　VIRG 558:18
you don't go d. with me　MILNE 340:6
downcast: people to feel a little d.　MCG 325:5
downfall: regress is either a d.　BACON 26:23
down-gyved: d. to his ancle　SHAK 431:28
downhearted: Are we d.　ANON 4:23
We are not d.　CHAM 139:7
downhill: This d. path is easy　ROSS 408:22
Downs: D. the fleet was moor'd　GAY 223:28
is fair on the D.　TENN 540:17
that looks on Ilsley d.　ARN 15:3
down-sitting: d., and mine up-rising
　　PRAY 399:4
downstairs: why did you kick me d.
　　BICK 83:27
downward: Were always d. bent MILT 345:26
downwards: could look no way but d.
　　BUNY 107:28
my gross flesh sinks d.　SHAK 480:16
dozen: d. dozen in her place　SUCK 524:15
dozens: Whom he reckons up by d.
　　GILB 228:3
draäins: Annie she said it wur d.　TENN 544:5
drab: Ditch-deliver'd by a d.　SHAK 462:4
Drachenfels: castled crag of D.
　　BYRON 120:31
drachmas: drop my blood for d. SHAK 451:21
drag: have weight to d. thee down
　　TENN 538:19
Put on the d.　SMITH 512:3
dragg'd: have d. to three-and-thirty
　　BYRON 126:15
dragon: angels fought against the d.
　　BIBLE 82:11
between the d. and his wrath　SHAK 453:4
centaur in his d. world　POUND 382:13
Dare the unpastured d.　SHEL 499:15
d.-green　FLEC 214:8
d. shalt thou tread under　PRAY 395:22
ev'ning d. came　MILT 350:29
he laid hold on the d.　BIBLE 82:27
my mother under the d.'s　SHAK 453:11
swinged the d. and e'er since　SHAK 452:12
to be a d.　MOORE 355:18
dragon-fly: sun-searched growths the
　　d.　ROSS 409:24
dragons: be an habitation of d.　BIBLE 58:31
D. in their pleasant palaces　BIBLE 58:12
D. of the prime　TENN 536:30
I am a brother to d.　BIBLE 52:37
ye d., and all deeps　PRAY 399:22
drags: d. at each remove a lengthening
　　GOLD 231:24
d. its slow length along　POPE 378:21
draiglet: She d. a' her petticoatie
　　BURNS 113:2
drain: d. pure gold flows forth　TOCQ 551:9
have put it down the d.　HERB 246:11
drained: yet d. not by the day　SHEL 503:19
drains: Democracy and proper d.　BETJ 43:6
Drake: D. he's in his hammock　NEWB 361:7
drama: close the d. with the day　BERK 41:20
d.'s laws the drama's　JOHN 282:27
Dramatise: D., dramatise　JAMES 271:14
dramatist: d. only wants more liberties
　　JAMES 271:18
drame: savoir le grand d. de ma vie
　　WILDE 573:35
Drang: Sturm und D.　KAUF 288:17
drank: d. my ale　FARQ 209:23
d. Prussic acid without　BARH 33:26
d. without the provocation　SWIFT 526:10
he d. of the brook　BIBLE 51:6
Jamshyd gloried and d.　FITZ 212:14
They all d. his health　FARR 210:29

went to the well and d.　MAL 327:15
drapery: with the d. of his figures　COL 158:8
Drastic: D. measures is Latin　ANST 11:9
draught: cup with such a d. of woe
　　SHEL 499:18
does not think of the d.　AUST 22:14
draughts: peculiarly susceptible to d.
　　WILDE 573:6
draughty: d. church at smokefall
　　ELIOT 202:16
dravest: Thou d. love from thee THOM 548:23
draw: began to d. to our end　BIBLE 62:17
cable can so forcibly d.　BURT 116:33
Can d. you to her *with*　DRYD 198:21
d. Hearts after them　MILT 350:2
D. near with faith　PRAY 387:18
d. the Thing as he sees　KIPL 304:3
is to d. a full face　DRYD 198:11
only used to d. Madonnas　BROW 102:28
thou d. out leviathan with　BIBLE 53:11
drawbacks: everything has its d.　JER 272:25
drawers: waistcoat and flannel d.
　　GASK 221:24
wood and d. of water　BIBLE 49:3
drawing: d. days out　SHAK 450:3
D. is the true test　INGR 270:19
I meant it for d.'　CONS 162:3
no d. back　BRON 94:3
think that I am d. to an end　PAIN 367:18
Drawling: *he* taught us D.　CARR 134:11
drawn: It oughtn't to be d.　DICK 176:32
drayhorse: fettle for the great grey d.
　　HOPK 256:11
Dr Busby: D., a great man　ADD 2:17
dread: d. and fear of kings　SHAK 467:27
d. of doing what has been　WHAR 569:9
let him be your d.　BIBLE 58:4
Nor d. nor hope attend　YEATS 584:20
was he chill'd with d.　SCOTT 416:15
What d. hand　BLAKE 87:15
whence this secret d.　ADD 1:24
Yet nothing did he d.　SPEN 515:32
your eyes with holy d.　COL 157:1
dreaded: Thy most d. instrument
　　WORD 578:21
dreadful: Between the acting of a d.
　　SHAK 449:6
deed of d. note　SHAK 461:13
d. fiend of gods and men　SPEN 516:22
d. is the check　BRON 93:21
Give d. note of preparation　SHAK 444:9
silences Of d. things　AUDEN 18:5
Dreading: D. and hoping all　YEATS 584:20
dreads: Greatly his foes he d.　CHUR 148:18
dream: altogether vanished like a d.
　　CARL 131:34
awakened from the d. of life　SHEL 499:20
behold it was a d.　BUNY 107:27
Diuturnity is a d. and a folly　BROW 97:21
d. doth flatter　SHAK 494:13
D. of Loveliness descending　LEL 313:18
d. of money-bags to-night　SHAK 466:11
d. of the days when work　CHES 147:22
d. of the soft look　YEATS 587:12
d.'s sake　ROSS 409:2
d. that I am home again　FLEC 214:5
each age is a d. that is　OSH 365:21
empty words of a d.　BRID 92:10
faileth now even d.　THOM 548:17
freshness of a d.　WORD 578:22
from a deep d. of peace　HUNT 268:4
glory and the d.　WORD 579:5
He should d. of the devil　BARH 33:13
hope I dreamed of was a d.　ROSS 409:2
I cried to d. again　SHAK 485:18
I did but d.　SHAK 481:13
if I d. I have you　DONNE 188:3
If you can d.　KIPL 299:22
I have a d.　KING 296:15
In a d. you are never　SEXT 420:18

Is but a d. within a dream　POE 375:2
Life is but an empty d.　LONG 317:1
life, that insane d.　BROW 100:22
life, without a d.　ROST 410:13
likened our life to a d.　MONT 355:5
like unto them that d.　PRAY 398:16
lost traveller's d.　BLAKE 86:1
love's young d.　MOORE 356:12
My d. thou brok'st not　DONNE 188:5
not d. them　KING 296:19
o'er the spirit of my d.　BYRON 124:13
perceived they had dreamed a d.
　　BROW 105:19
perchance to d.　SHAK 433:8
perfectibility as a d.　MILL 339:17
phantasma, or a hideous d.　SHAK 449:6
pleasures in a long immortal d. KEATS 290:23
quiet sleep and a sweet d.　MAS 334:6
short as any d.　SHAK 469:20
sights as youthful poets d.　MILT 342:26
sight to d.　COL 156:3
smiling face a d. of Spring　COL 157:14
so d. all night without　KEATS 290:5
So runs my d.　TENN 536:26
That children d. not　BROW 95:23
then they d. of love　SHAK 481:28
thou mightst in d.　SHEL 503:17
vision and the old men's d.　DRYD 194:9
waking d.　KEATS 291:23
With the first d. that　MEYN 338:14
wit of man to say what d.　SHAK 471:9
wrecks of a dissolving d.　SHEL 500:20
you d. you are crossing　GILB 226:13
dream'd: d. in a dream I saw a city
　　WHIT 570:4
d. that Greece might still　BYRON 122:33
I d. of the devil　ANST 11:7
dreamed: child I d.　CHES 147:8
d. that life was Beauty　HOOP 255:22
he d., and behold a ladder　BIBLE 46:18
I d. fast of mirth　WEVER 569:7
night I've d. of cheese　STEV 521:23
perceived they had d. a dream　BROW 105:19
dreamer: d. of dreams...Thou shalt
　　BIBLE 48:23
D. of dreams　MORR 358:9
He is a d.　SHAK 448:8
poet and the d. are distinct　KEATS 289:28
this d. cometh　BIBLE 46:28
dreamers: We are the d. of dreams
　　OSH 365:20
dreaming: City with her d. spires　ARN 15:4
d. through the twilight　ROSS 409:9
I am now a butterfly d.　CHUA 148:17
dreams: affliction of these terrible d.
　　SHAK 461:12
angels in some brighter d.　VAUG 555:21
because you tread on my d.　YEATS 585:9
before us like a land of d.　ARN 12:23
beyond the d. of avarice　JOHN 278:27
days of golden d.　BRON 93:24
Dead of d. days forsaken　SWIN 529:20
dream'd his white Platonic d.　JOHN 273:19
D. and desires and sombre　SWIN 528:26
d. are dreams　CALD 127:5
d. happy as her day　BROO 94:30
d. their children dreamed　COL 155:3
d. you have denied yourself　POUND 383:13
dreamt of in d.　BARH 33:11
Drumming like a noise in d.　HOUS 263:18
Even in d. good works are　CALD 127:4
fantasy Black d.　DONNE 190:3
Heavy with d.　THOM 548:28
he hunts in d.　TENN 538:21
her as Dian had hot d.　SHAK 429:3
I arise from d. of thee　SHEL 501:8
If there were d. to sell　BEDD 36:28
In doubtful d. of dreams　SWIN 529:21
not make d. your master　KIPL 299:22
not that I have bad d.　SHAK 432:13

of d., and ceremonies SHAK 449:10
old men shall dream d. BIBLE 61:15
Our d. are tales DE L 173:25
Phidias Gave women d. YEATS 587:1
pleasing d. SCOTT 417:26
quick D. SHEL 499:7
Real are the d. of Gods KEATS 290:23
rich beyond the d. of avarice MOORE 355:14
sick men's d. BROW 95:23
stuff As d. are made on SHAK 485:20
Than this world d. TENN 535:26
thousand such enchanting d. HERR 249:1
Thou wovest d. of joy SHEL 505:2
were a trouble to my d. WORD 580:14
we see it in our d. CHEK 144:26
who lived by honest d. DAY-L 172:23
wicked d. abuse SHAK 460:1
dreamt: d. of in your philosophy
SHAK 431:23
Drear: D. all this excellence POUND 383:19
vast edges d. ARN 12:23
dreariness: d. in dedicated spirits FRY 219:23
dregs: among the d. of Romulus CIC 151:16
from the d. of life DRYD 195:27
dreme: d. of joye CHAU 144:1
drench: then a strong horse d. LAMB 307:30
drench'd: you have d. our steeples
SHAK 454:4
Drene: Delicately drowns in D. BETJ 43:14
dress: does it signify how we d. GASK 221:23
d. by yellow candle-light STEV 522:16
more value than their d. HAZL 243:20
noble youth did d. themselves SHAK 441:24
Peace, the human d. BLAKE 88:7
sweet disorder in the d. HERR 249:2
through all this fleshly d. VAUG 555:16
we d. when we're ruined HARDY 240:19
dress'd: Let me be d. fine WATTS 565:24
dressed: temper when he's well d. DICK 179:1
dresses: neat-handed Phyllis d. MILT 342:21
dressing: d. old words SHAK 494:9
dressings: every season she hath d.
ANON 6:20
Drest: D. in a little brief authority
SHAK 464:2
drew: I d. my snickersnee GILB 227:8
man d. a bow at a venture BIBLE 51:21
Dr Fell: I do not love you, D. BROWN 95:10
Dr Froyd: So then D. said that all LOOS 318:6
dried: d. up, and withered PRAY 395:18
Drift: D. across the window-panes
ELIOT 204:1
drifting: I am d. with the tide BALL 31:3
drifts: with its dank yellow d. ARN 14:8
drills: double d. and no canteen KIPL 299:19
drink: Aunt Jobiska made him d.
LEAR 312:17
Barring d. and the girls LOCK 315:23
beasts of the field d. PRAY 396:19
be their portion to d. PRAY 389:31
can d. till all look blue FORD 216:17
Doth ask a d. divine JONS 284:12
d., and be merry BIBLE 70:4
d. and blacking the Corporal's KIPL 298:7
d., and forget his poverty BIBLE 55:2
D. and the devil had done STEV 521:21
d. cold brandy and water LAMB 308:7
D. fair DICK 179:28
D.! for you know not whence FITZ 213:9
D. no longer water BIBLE 79:16
D. not the third glass HERB 247:1
d. shall be prepared gold JONS 285:14
D., sir, is a great provoker SHAK 460:18
d. some beer JOHN 277:14
d. that slakes thirst CERV 138:20
d. the blood of goats PRAY 393:3
d. thy wine with a merry BIBLE 55:28
D. to me only with thine JONS 284:12
d. unto one of these little BIBLE 65:41
d. with you SHAK 465:28

D. ye all of this PRAY 388:1
d. your ale HOUS 264:22
eat, and to d. BIBLE 55:26
felony to d. small beer SHAK 446:11
five reasons we should d. ALDR 3:10
Givin' d. to poor damned KIPL 299:19
I d. well MORT 358:17
in debt, and in d. BROME 93:10
Leeze me on d. BURNS 114:8
Let us eat and d. BIBLE 58:15
let us eat and d. BIBLE 76:24
man may d. and no be drunk BURNS 115:13
Man wants but little d. HOLM 253:13
meaning is my meat and d. BROW 100:31
never taste who always d. PRIOR 401:11
Nor any drop to d. COL 155:14
now could I d. hot blood SHAK 434:25
proper d. of Englishmen BORR 90:8
sat down to eat and to d. BIBLE 48:3
Shall sit and d. with me BELL 40:11
shook to see him d. it up HOUS 264:15
Should every creature d. COWL 164:8
strong d. is raging BIBLE 54:15
taste for d. GILB 225:21
that I can d. ANON 5:21
Then d., puppy WHYT 572:2
they may follow strong d. BIBLE 57:25
They will d. our healths KIPL 298:13
thirsty and ye gave me d. BIBLE 68:6
thou gavest meat or d. BALL 31:7
We'll teach you to d. deep SHAK 430:3
drinkers: is written by d. of water
HOR 258:25
drinketh: he d. up a river BIBLE 53:10
sunlight d. dew TENN 533:16
drinking: constant d. fresh and fair
COWL 164:7
dancing, d. DRYD 197:17
days in a tavern d. ANON 10:14
d. at somebody else's expense LEIGH 313:15
d. bottled ditchwater SHAW 496:33
D. is the soldier's pleasure DRYD 195:1
d. largely sobers us again POPE 378:13
D. my griefs SHAK 479:22
D. the blude-red wine BALL 31:16
d. too much of Mr Weston's AUST 22:11
D. watered orange-pulp BROW 105:6
D. when we are not thirsty BEAU 35:17
is the curse of the d. WILDE 573:39
much d., little thinking SWIFT 526:18
There is no d. after death FLET 215:7
they were eating and d. BIBLE 67:32
thought surpass eating and d. CLOU 153:21
'Tis not the d. that is SELD 419:20
unhappy brains for d. SHAK 474:23
drinks: king d. to Hamlet SHAK 437:17
Now for d. HOR 260:3
drip: That long d. of human tears
HARDY 240:12
Dripping: D. along BETJ 44:3
drive: difficult to d. BROU 95:6
d. a coach and six horses RICE 406:1
d. an angel from your door BLAKE 88:4
d. me mad on my deathbed BYRON 126:20
driven: towns all Inns have been d.
BELL 40:16
drives: d. fat oxen should himself
JOHN 279:20
D. my green age THOM 547:3
one nail by strength d. SHAK 490:34
driving: d. briskly in a post-chaise
JOHN 277:15
driving is like the d. of Jehu BIBLE 51:33
drizzle: blasted English d. wakes KIPL 301:7
Dr Johnson: D. condemns whatever he
BURN 112:20
D.'s morality was as English HAWT 243:5
droghte: d. of March hath perced CHAU 141:7
droits: Toute loi qui viole les d. ROB 406:11
drollery: That fatal d. called DISR 186:34

dromedary: Donne, whose muse on d.
COL 157:6
D. is a cheerful bird BELL 38:27
drone: lazy yawning d. SHAK 443:9
droon: I d. twa' ANON 7:12
Droop: D. in a hundred A.B.C.'s
ELIOT 202:5
Droops: D. on the little hands MILNE 340:11
drop: are as a d. of a bucket BIBLE 59:8
clouds d. fatness PRAY 394:3
dance till you d. AUDEN 18:13
d. of allaying Tiber SHAK 427:14
d. of rain maketh a hole LAT 310:20
d., slow tears FLET 215:29
One d. would save my soul MARL 329:11
should like very well to d. JOHN 278:24
Then d. into thyself POPE 379:14
To d. a limb on the head KIPL 303:26
we d. like the fruits MER 336:26
dropped: glory d. from their youth
BROW 105:19
heavens d. at the presence PRAY 394:7
would not wish to be d. JOHN 278:24
dropping: d. down the ladder rung
KIPL 299:11
d. in a very rainy day BIBLE 54:39
D. the pilot TENN 532:14
peace comes d. slow YEATS 585:17
dropping-down-deadness: d. of manner
SMITH 512:1
drops: changed into little water d.
MARL 329:15
D. earliest to the ground SHAK 467:25
d. on gate-bars hang HARDY 241:4
d. That visit my sad heart SHAK 449:15
soft with the d. of rain PRAY 394:3
these are gracious d. SHAK 450:28
dropsies: were people who died of d.
JOHN 280:2
dropt: arms burd Helen d. BALL 31:4
D. from the ruin'd sides BEAU 36:1
D. from the zenith like MILT 346:3
dross: admits no qualifying d. SHAK 487:1
is d. that is not Helena MARL 329:10
stoops not to shows of d. SHAK 466:16
drove: he d. them all out BIBLE 71:35
Drown: D. all my faults and fears
FLET 215:30
d. myself in the Thames...I DICK 180:19
I'll d. my book SHAK 485:24
I will incontinently d. SHAK 474:7
tears shall d. the wind SHAK 459:6
what pain it was to d. SHAK 480:27
drown'd: d. in yonder living blue
TENN 537:19
d. my Glory in a Shallow FITZ 213:13
d. the cocks SHAK 454:4
thy thought till it be d. ROSS 409:26
drownded: d. now and again SYNGE 531:4
drowned: he were d. in the depth BIBLE 67:3
She is d. already SHAK 488:15
drowning: By d. their speaking BROW 103:15
hath no d. mark upon him SHAK 484:21
not waving but d. SMITH 510:26
drowns: Delicately d. in Drene BETJ 43:14
d. things weighty and solid BACON 27:5
drowsy: Dapples the d. east SHAK 473:1
d. numbness pains KEATS 291:16
Nor all the d. syrups SHAK 475:24
these d. approaches of sleep BROW 95:22
Vexing the dull ear of a d. SHAK 452:21
drowsyhead: pleasing land of d. it was
THOM 549:8
drudge: harmless d. JOHN 274:13
drudgery: d. of the desk's dead wood
LAMB 307:33
in the low d. of avarice BURKE 108:7
Makes d. divine HERB 247:19
drug: literature is a d. BORR 90:7
drugs: d. cause cramp PARK 368:18

drum: An' d. them up the Channel
NEWB 361:6
Bang-whang-whang goes the d. BROW 105:31
Beats like a fatalistic d. ELIOT 204:9
d.! a drum SHAK 458:8
Dumb as a d. vith a hole DICK 182:4
follow an antique d. ELIOT 202:27
melancholy as an unbrac'd d. CENT 138:11
Music of a *distant* D. FITZ 212:12
My pulse like a soft d. KING 296:12
Not a d. was heard WOLFE 576:2
spirit-stirring d. SHAK 475:25
when you hear the d. SHAK 466:13
drum-beat: whose morning d. WEBS 566:12
drummer: Far I hear the steady d.
HOUS 263:18
Hodge the D. never knew HARDY 239:8
drumming: Down in the valley d.
AUDEN 20:4
drums: beat the d. DRYD 194:26
beat the d. MOR 357:21
en de bangin' er de d. HARR 242:17
heard thro' rolling d. TENN 542:7
like muffled d. LONG 317:2
when the d. begin to roll KIPL 303:24
drunk: against a post when he was d.
SHAK 444:6
Be not d. with wine BIBLE 78:5
contracted in trying to get d. JOHN 280:2
d. deep of the Pierian DRAY 193:15
d. old wine straightway BIBLE 69:19
d. to bed SHAK 421:13
d. with sight of power KIPL 302:9
eaten and d. enough HOR 259:6
fields have d. enough VIRG 559:21
genteel when he gets d. BOSW 90:16
got d. PORS 381:29
Have d. their Cup a Round FITZ 212:17
he hath not d. ink SHAK 457:1
I d. him to his bed SHAK 422:10
if it be d. moderately BIBLE 63:15
may drink and no be d. BURNS 115:13
must get d. BYRON 122:22
not the art of getting d. JOHN 278:8
once saw Wordsworth d. HOUS 266:18
partly she was d. BURNS 114:18
Philip d. to Philip sober ANON 4:22
that this meeting is d. DICK 182:17
Then hasten to be d. DRYD 195:37
th'hydroptic earth hath d. DONNE 189:28
Was the hope d. SHAK 459:8
when men have well d. BIBLE 71:34
which hath made them d. SHAK 460:2
drunkard: English d. made the rolling
CHES 147:10
Reel in a d. CHUR 149:1
drunkards: MSS as d. use lamp-posts
HOUS 266:14
drunken: dreadfully but as a d. sleep
SHAK 464:25
got more d. PORS 381:29
Shall be brought d. forth SHAK 424:3
stagger like a d. man PRAY 397:10
Sure I had d. in my dreams COL 155:24
They are d. BIBLE 58:23
drunkenly: Who now goes d. out
POUND 382:5
drunkenness: branch of the sin of d.
JAM 271:2
drunkennesses: in anger or penitent d.
RIMB 406:9
Druse: D. and the Catholic CHES 146:27
dry: being d. ALDR 3:10
d. a cinder this world DONNE 187:20
d. as the remainder biscuit SHAK 425:21
d. one's eyes BROW 102:1
d. place, as the shadow BIBLE 58:30
d. the starting tear GILB 225:8
d. your eyes KEATS 289:25
I am so d. ANON 6:1

in a barren and d. land PRAY 393:21
nothing sooner d. WEBS 567:7
old man in a d. month ELIOT 203:3
Rabelais dwelling in a d. place COL 158:2
refresh it when it was d. PRAY 386:3
shall be done in the d. BIBLE 71:10
they whose hearts are d. WORD 577:11
thoroughly small and d. ELIOT 202:1
tones as d. and level AUDEN 20:10
water what is d. LANG 310:1
would fain die a d. death SHAK 484:22
ye d. bones BIBLE 61:2
Dryad: light-winged D. of the trees
KEATS 291:17
Dryden: D. fails to render him ARN 16:12
poetry and the poetry of D. ARN 16:9
drynke: his hous of mete and d. CHAU 141:28
Dublin: D., though a place much JOHN 279:23
ducats: my d.! O my daughter SHAK 466:18
duce: quot libras in d. summo JUV 288:1
Duchess: chambermaid as of a D. JOHN 278:4
D. of Malfi still WEBS 566:24
D. painted on the wall BROW 102:21
D.! The Duchess CARR 133:20
may not blossom into a D. AIL 3:5
Duck: D. and the Kangaroo LEAR 312:4
Put a d. on a lake AUG 21:11
ducks: country stealing d. ARAB 11:18
Four d. on a pond ALL 3:21
duda: Fe que no d. es fe muerta UNAM 554:27
Duddon: backward, D. WORD 581:4
due: d. season we shall reap BIBLE 77:20
d. time we may enjoy them PRAY 385:21
render to every one his d. JUST 287:8
dues: simple d. of fellowship BROW 97:30
therefore to all their d. BIBLE 75:22
dug: never palates more the d. SHAK 423:20
dugs: old man with wrinkled d. ELIOT 205:1
Duke: D. of Plaza Toro GILB 225:18
d.'s revenues on her back SHAK 446:4
everybody praised the D. SOUT 513:20
From tyrant d. unto a tyrant SHAK 424:28
knows enough who knows a d. COWP 167:31
Let us bury the Great D. TENN 541:5
tell you I was made a D. WELL 567:21
dukedom: library Was d. SHAK 484:26
dukes: were three a penny GILB 225:29
Dulce: D. est desipere in loco HOR 261:20
D. et decorum est desipere BUTL 119:9
D. et decorum est pro patria HOR 260:17
D. ridentem CAT 137:4
D. ridentem Lalagen amabo HOR 259:24
dulcet: d. and harmonious breath SHAK 470:7
dulci: miscuit utile d. HOR 258:1
dulcimer: damsel with a d. COL 156:30
d., and all kinds of musick BIBLE 61:3
dulcis: d. virgo Maria ANON 10:19
dull: at best but d. and hoary VAUG 555:19
be very d. without them WILDE 573:14
can be d. in Fleet Street LAMB 307:23
d. and deep potations excused GIBB 224:9
d. and muddy-mettled rascal SHAK 433:2
d. cold ear of death GRAY 234:22
d. product of a scoffer's WORD 577:12
d. without a single absurdity GOLD 232:31
D. would he be of soul WORD 581:14
He was d. in a new way JOHN 276:19
How d. it is to pause TENN 543:22
is not only d. in himself FOOTE 216:9
make dictionaries is d. JOHN 281:11
Of his d. life BEAU 35:19
of this paper appears d. STEE 518:5
Sherry is d. JOHN 275:7
so d. but she can learn SHAK 467:13
so illogical and so d. KEYN 295:16
so smoothly d. POPE 375:20
Though it's d. at whiles KING 296:1
venerably d. CHUR 149:11
wasn't as d. as ditch water DICK 181:17
What's this d. town to me KEPP 295:12

words oft creep in one d. line POPE 378:20
young Woman her name was D. BUNY 107:30
dullard: d.'s envy of brilliant BEER 37:28
duller: d. shouldst thou be than SHAK 431:8
d. spectacle this earth DE Q 175:1
dullness: cause of d. in others FOOTE 216:9
d. of our senses JOHN 273:17
dully: just walking d. along AUDEN 19:18
dulness: d. of our blinded sight PRAY 400:5
dumb: before her shearers is d. BIBLE 59:22
D. as a drum vith a hole DICK 182:4
D., inscrutable and grand ARN 14:4
d. presagers of my speaking SHAK 493:3
D. to Homer BROW 102:35
happen to be deaf and d. HOUS 266:9
noisy bells, be d. HOUS 263:5
otherwise I shall be d. KEATS 294:14
swell is in the havens d. HOPK 256:17
tongue of the d. sing BIBLE 58:34
dumb-bell: Than d. and foil YEATS 586:20
dumbness: banged the youth into d.
SHAK 489:27
dumbs: now he is one of the d. LEAR 311:21
dumb-shows: inexplicable d. and noise
SHAK 433:16
Dummheit: Mit der D. kämpfen Götter
SCH 415:10
dun: then her breasts are d. SHAK 495:8
Duncan: fatal entrance of D. SHAK 459:2
dunce: dearest, you're a d. JOHN 278:30
d. with wits POPE 375:22
Excels a d. that has been COWP 166:11
thou art but a d. BLAKE 86:1
duncery: inquisitorious and tyrannical
d. MILT 352:15
dunces: d. are all in confederacy SWIFT 527:8
Dundee: bonnet of Bonny D. SCOTT 415:20
stay langer in bonny D. SCOTT 418:30
Dunfermline: king sits in D. town
BALL 31:16
dungeon: d. horrible MILT 344:25
D., that I'm rotting in CANN 130:5
In a d. cell GILB 227:7
dungeons: Brightest in d., Liberty
BYRON 125:14
dunghill: d. kind SPEN 516:14
Dunmowe: men han in Essex at D.
CHAU 143:18
dunnest: in the d. smoke of hell SHAK 459:2
Dunsinane: Birnam wood remove to
D. SHAK 462:28
Birnam wood to high D. SHAK 462:8
duodecimos: humbler band of d.
COWP 168:11
dupe: d. of friendship HAZL 243:18
durance: d. vile here must I wake
BURNS 113:22
duration: is a fallacy in d. BROW 97:15
durst: more mischief than they d.
HOUS 263:13
dusk: d. and dawn many a head MULL 359:1
d. with a light behind GILB 229:4
dusky: she shall rear my d. race TENN 539:6
straight path along the d. COL 157:11
dust: All valiant d. that builds KIPL 302:10
are they like to take d. SHAK 488:1
chimney-sweepers, come to d. SHAK 428:22
d. and a shadow HOR 261:16
D. as we are WORD 580:11
d. expend an idle breath CAT 137:15
d, of exploded beliefs MADAN 326:18
d. of great persons' graves DONNE 190:23
d. on antique time would SHAK 427:17
d. return to the earth BIBLE 56:11
d. that is a little gilt SHAK 487:6
d. thou art BIBLE 45:23
D. thou art LONG 317:1
d. to be mingled with yours POUND 383:16
d. to dust PRAY 389:13
D. was Gentlemen and Ladies DICK 184:2

enemies shall lick the d.	PRAY 394:20	I've done my d.	FIEL 211:35
Fallen to d.	WILDE 572:18	little d. and less love	SHAK 445:23
fear in a handful of d.	ELIOT 204:19	Love is then our d.	GAY 222:28
forbear To dig the d.	SHAK 495:22	my d. as a man is bound	TENN 543:4
impark the wanton mote of d.	MARV 332:21	my d. towards God	PRAY 388:14
in the d. be equal made	SHIR 507:2	Nor law, nor d.	YEATS 585:15
in the D. my Vice is laid	ANON 6:19	O D.! if that name	WORD 579:15
into the D. descend	FITZ 212:18	perceive here a divided d.	SHAK 474:2
itself crumble to the d.	BROW 98:8	picket's off d. forever	BEERS 38:8
Less than the d. beneath	HOPE 256:5	sense of d.	GILB 228:13
lies wise and valiant d.	CLEV 153:3	some very laborious d.	SMITH 509:13
life in the handful of d.	CONR 161:24	subject's d. is the king's	SHAK 444:22
like the d. on the nettles	THOM 547:21	Such d. as the subject	SHAK 484:18
man of the d. of the ground	BIBLE 45:7	that he had a d. to perform	GIBB 224:10
much learned d.	COWP 167:3	this is the whole d. of man	BIBLE 56:14
My d. would hear her	TENN 540:12	When D. whispers low	EMER 207:2
not without d. and heat	MILT 351:24	when love and d. clash	TENN 541:29
off the d. of your feet	BIBLE 65:32	When service sweat for d.	SHAK 425:7
proud and angry d.	HOUS 264:22	When simpleness and d.	SHAK 471:14
quaint honour turn to d.	MARV 332:19	*Dux:* D. femina facti	VIRG 557:15
raised a d. and then complain	BERK 41:18	dwarf: d. sees farther than	COL 157:25
remembereth that we are but d.	PRAY 396:17	my d. shall dance	JONS 285:14
rich earth a richer d.	BROO 94:30	dwarfish: d. whole	COL 156:15
small d. of the balance	BIBLE 59:8	dwarfs: like d. on the shoulders	BERN 41:25
smear'd in d. and blood	SHAK 446:22	little d. creep out	CHES 147:5
stir a little d. of praise	TENN 537:4	State which d. its men	MILL 339:15
This d. was once the man	WHIT 571:10	dwell: alone d. for ever	ARN 13:7
this quintessence of d.	SHAK 432:15	Better d. in the midst	COWP 167:38
thou'lt recover once my d.	GRAH 233:16	constrained to d. with Mesech	PRAY 398:7
throwing of a little d.	VIRG 560:18	d. in a corner of the housetop	BIBLE 54:20
To sweep the d. behind	SHAK 471:22	d. in the land of the shadow	BIBLE 58:6
vex the unhappy d. thou	TENN 533:2	Fain would I d. on form	SHAK 482:12
victor's palm without the d.	HOR 258:8	He's made to d.	GILB 227:7
what a d. do I raise	BACON 27:33	I will d. in the house	PRAY 390:22
when this d. falls	VAUG 555:17	man to d. in their tents	PRAY 394:13
with a piece of valiant d.	SHAK 472:4	shall d. in thy tabernacle	PRAY 390:4
writes in d.	BACON 28:16	to all that d. in it	PRAY 389:8
Write the characters in d.	SCOTT 418:4	which it pleaseth him to d.	PRAY 394:9
You are not worth the d.	SHAK 455:10	who d. in realms of Day	BLAKE 85:18
dust-heap: great d. called 'history'		dwelle: d. with sothfastnesse	CHAU 144:21
	BIRR 84:17	dwelleth: d. not in temples made	BIBLE 74:13
Dustman: Golden D.	DICK 181:21	dwelling: holy hill, and to thy d.	PRAY 392:11
dusts: undertake to sift those d.		Whose d. is the light	WORD 578:7
	DONNE 190:23	dwellings: how amiable are thy d.	
dusty: d. answer gets the soul	MER 337:18		PRAY 395:11
Dutch: commerce the fault of the D.		dwells: man who d. upon himself	
	CANN 129:25		DONNE 190:22
D. prowess	ROCH 407:5	She d. with Beauty	KEATS 291:15
Dutchman: icicle on a D.'s beard		dwelt: d. among us	BIBLE 71:27
	SHAK 489:28	d. by the brook Cherith	BIBLE 51:6
Dutchmen: water-land of D. and of ditches		d. in marble halls	BUNN 107:9
	BYRON 123:27	d. in the land of Nod	BIBLE 45:29
duteous: d. and knee-crooking knave		dwindle: by degrees d. into a wife	
	SHAK 473:13		CONG 161:8
duties: brace ourselves to our d.	CHUR 150:1	dyed: d. garments from Bozrah	BIBLE 60:10
to the neglect of his d.	THOM 549:6	in a slither of d. stuff	POUND 382:15
dutiful: powers take note of the d.		dyer: like the d.'s hand	SHAK 495:4
	VIRG 557:18	dyes: stains and splendid d.	KEATS 289:16
duty: adoration, d., and observance		dyin: I think you're d.'	BALL 30:11
	SHAK 426:29	dying: against the d. of the light	THOM 546:23
bounden d. and service	PRAY 388:2	Around the d. deer	AYT 24:10
dare to do our d. as we	LINC 314:17	Authority forgets a d. king	TENN 535:22
declares that it is his d.	SHAW 496:10	be distinguished from d.	SMITH 511:23
'Do the d. which lies nearest	CARL 132:21	behold you again in d.	STEV 523:5
Do your d.	CORN 162:17	bliss of d.	POPE 376:3
d. of an Opposition was	DERBY 175:8	can feel that he is d.	SUET 524:17
d. of being happy	STEV 522:4	Christian can only fear d.	HARE 242:3
d. of government to protect	PAINE 367:23	doubly d.	SCOTT 416:22
d. to speak one's mind	WILDE 573:7	d., bless the hand that	DRYD 197:27
d. was the way to glory	TENN 541:14	d. for a faith that's so	THAC 545:6
Europe and we must do our d.	SAL 413:19	D. is a very dull	MAUG 336:4
every man will do his d.	NELS 360:20	d. may I hold you	TIB 550:34
first d. of a State	RUSK 412:6	d. of a hundred good symptoms	POPE 381:23
first d. to serve society	JOHN 275:18	d. out of the power	TROL 552:11
found that life was D.	HOOP 255:22	D., we live	BROW 104:35
God, Immortality, D.	ELIOT 201:30	d., which is terrible	FIEL 211:5
gratifying feeling that our d.	GILB 225:25	hath such a celerity in d.	SHAK 421:20
I have done my d.	NELS 360:22	I am d., Egypt	SHAK 423:14
I owe a d.	BEHN 38:14	I can't stay d. here all	SHER 506:2
is absolved from all d.	PEAC 370:18	I'm d. now and done	BETJ 44:13

in a d. man's room	STER 520:3		
like a d. lady	SHEL 505:7		
lips of d. men	ARN 14:27		
living indisposeth us for d.	BROW 97:13		
mouth of the d. day	AUDEN 19:2		
sacraments to a d. god	HEINE 244:11		
slip until their d. day	HOR 259:21		
there's no more d. then	SHAK 495:14		
Those d. generations	YEATS 586:11		
those poor devils are d.	PHIL 373:8		
unconscionable time d.	CHAR 140:30		
year is d. in the night	TENN 537:14		
dyke: behind yon auld fail d.	BALL 32:8		
die in the last d. of prevarication			
	BURKE 110:31		
dynamite: objected to the use of d.			
	STEV 521:12		
dyvyne: soong the service d.	CHAU 141:15		
E: A noir, E. blanc, I rouge	RIMB 406:9		
Each: E. in his narrow cell	GRAY 234:20		
hearts beating each to e.	BROW 102:14		
eager: e. for the fray	CIBB 151:15		
eagle: By all the e. in thee	CRAS 169:4		
Does the E. know what is	BLAKE 85:19		
e.-feather	BROW 102:16		
e. mewing her mighty youth	MILT 352:3		
e. suffers little birds	SHAK 486:17		
eyes will gaze an e. blind	SHAK 457:8		
Fate is not an e.	BOWEN 91:5		
gier-e. on his sail	SMART 509:3		
hooded e. among blinking owls	SHEL 501:16		
like an e. in a dove-cote	SHAK 428:6		
of the e. or the snake	KIPL 301:1		
Sometimes e.'s wings	KEATS 290:6		
though her e. through	WALL 562:11		
upon my e.'s wings	DRYD 195:12		
way of an e. in the air	BIBLE 55:1		
young and lusty as an e.	PRAY 396:15		
eagles: e. and the trumpets	ELIOT 202:5		
hawk at e. with a dove	HERB 248:9		
mount up with wings as e.	BIBLE 59:10		
there will the e. be gathered	BIBLE 67:30		
they were swifter than e.	BIBLE 50:17		
ear: beat upon my whorlèd e.	HOPK 256:14		
by the hearing of the e.	BIBLE 53:12		
channels of the e.	AUDEN 20:3		
cleave the general e. with	SHAK 433:1		
close at the e. of Eve	MILT 348:10		
dull cold e. of death	GRAY 234:24		
dull e. of a drowsy man	SHAK 452:21		
e. filled with hearing	BIBLE 55:7		
e. of jealousy heareth	BIBLE 62:10		
e. of man hath not seen	SHAK 471:10		
Give every man thine e.	SHAK 430:19		
hearing e.	BIBLE 54:18		
He that planted the e.	PRAY 396:2		
I have no e.	LAMB 307:1		
meant than meets the e.	MILT 342:7		
Not to the sensual e.	KEATS 291:4		
pierced through the e.	SHAK 474:4		
right sow by the e.	HENR 246:3		
shall see the golden e.	POPE 378:5		
these things into my e.	POUND 382:15		
to soothe thine e.	COLL 158:17		
Unpleasing to a married e.	SHAK 457:18		
Was never e.	ROYD 411:3		
We whisper in her e.	WILB 572:4		
When the e. begins to hear	BRON 93:21		
Earls: daughter of a hundred E.	TENN 537:26		
early: always too late or too e.	SART 414:9		
e. Christian who ought	CHES 148:3		
E. one morning	ANON 5:3		
had it been e.	JOHN 274:7		
marr'd are those so e. made	SHAK 481:26		
myself will awake right e.	PRAY 393:16		
that right e.	PRAY 392:20		
Up in the morning e.	BURNS 116:2		
wake and call me e.	TENN 540:20		
early-laurelled: round that e. head			
	HOUS 263:3		

earn: I e. that I eat	SHAK 426:4	
there's little to e.	KING 297:3	
to e. a monumental pile	COWP 166:30	
Earned: E. a precarious living	ANON 5:4	
Has e. a night's repose	LONG 317:19	
earnest: e. of the things that they	TENN 538:24	
I am in e.	GARR 221:17	
it is time to be in e.	JOHN 281:23	
steadily e. in the pursuit	AUST 22:30	
earnestly: e. repent you of your sins	PRAY 387:18	
earns: e. a place i' the story	SHAK 422:18	
ears: adder that stoppeth her e.	PRAY 393:17	
ass's e. of Midas	SIDN 508:5	
Creep in our e.	SHAK 468:15	
Death hath asses' e.	BEDD 36:27	
devoured the seven good e.	BIBLE 46:32	
e., and hear not	PRAY 397:18	
e. are senseless that should	SHAK 437:29	
e. in an empty dog-kennel	DICK 179:27	
e. like errant wings	CHES 146:22	
e. of every one that heareth	BIBLE 49:37	
earth has stopped the e.	HOUS 263:2	
Enemy e. are listening	ANON 9:18	
have heard with our e.	PRAY 392:13	
hedges e.	SWIFT 528:6	
He that hath e. to hear	BIBLE 68:28	
is he buzzing in my e.	BROW 100:6	
lend me your e.	SHAK 450:17	
let thine e. consider well	PRAY 398:23	
Look with thine e.	SHAK 455:18	
lovers' e. in hearing	SCOTT 416:26	
lover's e. will hear	SHAK 457:8	
my e. yielding like swinging	DOUG 191:7	
Once bless our human e.	MILT 344:10	
pluck'd the ripen'd e.	TENN 541:28	
porches of mine e.	SHAK 431:11	
sets all nations by the e.	LAND 308:21	
stop my house's e.	SHAK 466:13	
there's a drumming in my e.	SAPP 414:6	
to split the e.	SHAK 433:12	
was a shout about my e.	CHES 146:23	
With ravish'd e.	DRYD 194:24	
earth: all the corners of the e.	PRAY 396:4	
all the ends of the e.	PRAY 394:1	
'And is thy e. so marred	THOM 548:21	
are the daughters of e.	JOHN 281:6	
are the salt of the e.	BIBLE 64:7	
blow the e. into the sea	SHAK 454:3	
bowels of the harmless e.	SHAK 438:16	
bring food out of the e.	PRAY 396:20	
canst work i' the e. so	SHAK 431:21	
Cold in the e.	BRON 93:22	
composed of the scum of the e.	WELL 568:1	
Could frame in e.	SPEN 516:20	
created the heaven and the e.	BIBLE 44:22	
differ as Heaven and E.	TENN 535:16	
dust return to the e.	BIBLE 56:11	
E. all Danaë to the stars	TENN 542:14	
E. and high heaven are	HOUS 264:3	
e. a richer dust concealed	BROO 94:30	
e. a trinket at my wrist	THOM 548:24	
e. Be but the shadow	MILT 348:21	
e. breaks up and heaven	BROW 99:20	
e. can take or Heaven can	SHEL 501:2	
e. covereth	QUAR 403:20	
e. does not argue	WHIT 571:11	
e. doth like a snake renew	SHEL 500:20	
e. exhales	BETJ 44:5	
E. felt the wound	MILT 349:16	
E. has not anything	WORD 581:14	
e. has stopped the ears	HOUS 263:2	
e. his sober inn	CAMP 129:19	
e. in an earthy bed	TENN 540:12	
e. is all the home I have	AYT 24:12	
E. is but a star	FLEC 214:10	
e. is cover'd thick with	BYRON 120:27	
e. is not too low	HERB 246:26	
e. is the Lord's	BIBLE 76:11	
e. is the Lord's	PRAY 390:23	
e. is weak	PRAY 394:25	
e. I wait forlorn	ARN 13:8	
E., receive an honoured	AUDEN 19:7	
E.'s crammed with heaven	BROW 97:33	
e.'s foundations stay	HOUS 265:7	
e. shall be full	BIBLE 58:11	
e. shall melt away	PRAY 392:20	
e. shall wail because	BIBLE 81:10	
e. shook	PRAY 394:7	
E.'s shadows fly	SHEL 499:26	
E.'s the right place	FROST 219:1	
E. stood hard as iron	ROSS 409:1	
e. sure	DONNE 188:9	
e. that is not filled with	BIBLE 54:46	
e., that is sufficient	WHIT 571:8	
e. the broken arcs	BROW 98:18	
E. the first of the gods	VIRG 559:4	
e., tideless and inert	BALF 30:3	
earth to make the e. my hell	SHAK 481:8	
e. Was feverous	SHAK 460:20	
e. were paper white	LYLY 321:16	
E. will hold us	ANON 10:13	
even as if the e. had rolled	WORD 577:27	
feels the attraction of e.	LONG 316:11	
feel the e. move	HEM 245:3	
flowery lap of e.	ARN 13:17	
foundation of the e.	PRAY 396:13	
foundations of the e.	BIBLE 53:2	
fresh E. in new leaves	SHEL 503:26	
from which e.	RAL 404:15	
girdle round about the e.	SHAK 470:9	
gives all men all e. to love	KIPL 303:16	
going the way of all the e.	BIBLE 49:5	
going to and fro in the e.	BIBLE 52:5	
hath made heaven and e.	PRAY 398:14	
heaven and e. is named	BIBLE 77:24	
Heaven and E. are not ruthful	LAO 310:2	
Her all on e.	BYRON 121:35	
heroic for e. too hard	BROW 98:20	
huge foundation of the e.	SHAK 439:21	
I find e. not grey	BROW 98:34	
It fell to e.	LONG 316:6	
I will move the e.	ARCH 11:24	
Lay her i' the e.	SHAK 437:4	
Lay that e. upon thy heart	KIPL 298:3	
let the E. bless the Lord	PRAY 384:23	
Lie heavy on him, E.	EVANS 209:5	
life from the glowing e.	GREN 236:15	
life of men on e.	BEDE 37:1	
Lightly gently e.	BEAU 36:8	
like to get away from e.	FROST 219:1	
little e. for charity	SHAK 447:15	
low as where this e.	ROSS 409:17	
made heaven and e.	PRAY 388:20	
Man is but e.	DONNE 190:22	
Man marks the e. with ruin	BYRON 121:23	
meek-spirited shall possess the e.	PRAY 391:27	
must have a touch of e.	TENN 534:26	
naked is warm with Spring	GREN 236:15	
new heaven and a new e.	BIBLE 82:30	
new heaven, new e.	SHAK 421:7	
new heaven and a new e.	BIBLE 60:14	
Nor heaven nor e. have	SHAK 449:17	
nought common on Thy E.	KIPL 301:17	
O E., lie heavily	ROSS 409:5	
Of E.'s first blood	WORD 582:3	
on e. peace	BIBLE 69:11	
our days on the e. are	BIBLE 51:39	
our dungy e. alike	SHAK 421:8	
pilgrims on the e.	BIBLE 79:33	
poetry of e. is never dead	KEATS 292:21	
pure ablution round e.'s	KEATS 292:11	
replenish the e.	BIBLE 45:6	
Rolled round in e.'s diurnal	WORD 581:10	
round e.'s shore	ARN 12:23	
round e.'s imagined corners	DONNE 189:3	
sleepers in that quiet e.	BRON 94:1	
smile o' the brown old e.	BROW 101:20	
so much too good for e.	JONS 284:2	
Standing on e.	MILT 348:28	
Substance from the common E.	FITZ 213:12	
Take of English e. as much	KIPL 298:8	
that creepeth upon the e.	BIBLE 45:4	
there is our e. here	BROW 105:23	
There were giants in the e.	BIBLE 45:33	
they shall inherit the e.	BIBLE 64:6	
th'hydroptic e. hath drunk	DONNE 189:28	
th' inhabitants o' the e.	SHAK 458:10	
This e. of majesty	SHAK 478:20	
this e., this realm	SHAK 478:20	
this goodly frame, the e.	SHAK 432:15	
thou bleeding piece of e.	SHAK 450:11	
though the e. be moved	PRAY 392:19	
to e. I	HOUS 265:12	
tread on E. unguess'd	ARN 14:24	
vilest e. Is room enough	SHAK 440:24	
visitest the e., and blessest	PRAY 394:2	
water under the e.	BIBLE 47:24	
Which men call E.	MILT 340:23	
While the e. remaineth	BIBLE 45:37	
whole e. as their memorial	PER 372:23	
whole e. is our hospital	ELIOT 202:22	
whole round e. is every way	TENN 535:26	
Yours is the E. and everything	KIPL 300:2	
earth-born: e. companion An' fellow-mortal	BURNS 115:21	
earthly: any e. thing	BALL 32:2	
e. godfathers of Heaven's	SHAK 456:15	
earthquake: e. is not satisfied	WORD 580:21	
gloom of e. and eclipse	SHEL 503:21	
If an e. were to engulf	JERR 273:12	
Lord was not in the e.	BIBLE 51:14	
very good against an e.	ADD 2:28	
earthy: man is of the earth, e.	BIBLE 76:28	
ease: another gives its e.	BLAKE 87:18	
be never at heart's e.	SHAK 448:21	
Bring equal e. unto my pain	CAREW 130:16	
doctrine of ignoble e.	ROOS 407:27	
E. after war	SPEN 516:8	
e. in mine inn but I shall	SHAK 440:4	
e. in writing comes from	POPE 378:22	
e. my breast of melodies	KEATS 289:25	
e. of the masters	SMITH 509:14	
e. the anguish of a torturing	SHAK 471:12	
e. them of their griefs	SHAK 486:15	
embers in hearthside e.	HARDY 240:13	
in another's loss of e.	BLAKE 87:19	
labour with an age of e.	GOLD 230:19	
much at his e. as he can	SMITH 509:13	
nature, kindly bent to e.	SWIFT 527:22	
Some come to take their e.	SHAK 448:4	
standing at e. in Nature	WHIT 570:6	
Studious of elegance and e.	GAY 223:18	
Studious of laborious e.	COWP 167:8	
take thine e.	BIBLE 70:4	
thou wilt e. thine heart	BEDD 36:23	
To e. my weary limb	BALL 30:9	
Virtue shuns e. as a companion	MONT 354:24	
Wherein at e. for aye	TENN 541:20	
Who live at home at e.	PARK 368:23	
easer: thou e. of all woes	FLET 215:22	
easier: e. for a camel to go through	BIBLE 67:11	
easing: They call it e. the Spring	REED 405:6	
East: chambers of the E.	BLAKE 88:10	
Dapples the drowsy e.	SHAK 473:1	
E. all the way into Mississippi Bay	KIPL 300:24	
E. and west on fields forgotten	HOUS 263:19	
E. at heel is marched from	HOUS 265:3	
E. is a career	DISR 186:37	
E. is East	KIPL 297:27	
e. my pleasure lies	SHAK 422:7	
e., nor from the west	PRAY 394:26	
e. wind made flesh	APPL 11:12	
e. wind may never blow	WALT 563:34	
faint e. quickens	SWIN 528:16	

fiery portal of the e. SHAK 479:12
from the e. to Jerusalem BIBLE 63:31
gorgeous E. with richest hand MILT 346:6
hold the gorgeous E. in fee WORD 582:10
It is the e. SHAK 482:5
Look how wide also the e. PRAY 396:17
me somewheres e. of Suez KIPL 301:8
on the e. of Eden BIBLE 45:29
practice of politics in the E. DISR 186:5
three kings into the e. BURNS 114:13
wind's in the e. DICK 176:5
eastern: gilding the e. hemisphere
SHER 505:25
marvel save in E. clime BURG 108:4
Out of the misty e. cave SHEL 505:2
Right against the e. gate MILT 342:18
Eastertide: Wearing white for E.
HOUS 262:14
eastward: garden e. in Eden BIBLE 45:7
east-wind: through the e. PRAY 392:26
easy: e. as one's discourse OSB 365:19
E. is the way down VIRG 558:18
E. live and quiet die SCOTT 418:5
e. writing's vile hard SHER 506:37
How e. it is to call rogue DRYD 198:11
If to do were as e. SHAK 465:20
I lie e. HOUS 263:11
Now as I was young and e. THOM 547:1
Of e. ways to die SHAK 424:18
on the rack of a too e. POPE 375:25
precept be, Be e. STEE 518:11
She bid me take love e. YEATS 584:22
type of the normal and e. JAMES 271:15
eat: aghast to watch him e. HOUS 264:15
Butter and honey shall he e. BIBLE 58:3
can not e. but little meat ANON 5:21
Con-found all presents wot e. SURT 525:14
did also e. of my bread PRAY 392:5
down to e. and to drink BIBLE 48:3
e., and to drink BIBLE 55:26
e. bulls' flesh PRAY 393:3
e. but ye have not enough BIBLE 62:2
e., drink BIBLE 70:4
e. his heart in the market-place SHAK 473:3
e. like wolves SHAK 444:8
E. not of it raw BIBLE 47:17
e. our pot of honey MER 337:10
e. the fat of the land BIBLE 46:36
e. the rest of the anatomy SHAK 490:1
e. your victuals fast enough HOUS 264:11
every man shall e. in safety SHAK 448:1
face shalt thou e. bread BIBLE 45:22
great ones e. up the little SHAK 478:4
have meat and cannot e. BURNS 114:14
he hath not e. paper SHAK 457:1
I did e. BIBLE 45:17
I e. well MORT 358:17
I have e. my ale FARQ 209:23
I'll e. my head DICK 180:36
I will e. exceedingly JONS 283:16
I will not e. with you SHAK 465:28
I would e. a missionary WILB 572:3
Let us e. and drink BIBLE 58:15
let us e. and drink BIBLE 76:24
neither should he e. BIBLE 79:5
of toys and things to e. STEV 522:21
One should e. to live MOL 353:2
so we must e. we THAC 545:33
Take, e., this is my Body PRAY 388:1
Tell me what you e. BRIL 93:9
that "I see what I e." CARR 133:29
thou didst e. strange flesh SHAK 421:29
thou shalt not e. of it BIBLE 45:9
thy princes e. in the morning BIBLE 56:3
will e. our meal in fear SHAK 461:12
ye shall e. it in haste BIBLE 47:18
eaten: e. and drunk enough HOR 259:6
e. by missionaries SPOO 517:9
e. on the insane root SHAK 458:15
e. to death with rust SHAK 441:15

He was e. of worms BIBLE 74:3
see God made and e. BROW 99:14
They'd e. every one CARR 135:11
to have been e. by lions CHES 148:3
eater: I am a great e. of beef SHAK 487:25
of the e. came forth meat BIBLE 49:21
eaters: so small e. MORE 357:19
eateth: e. grass as an ox BIBLE 53:8
e. not of the fruit thereof BIBLE 76:6
e. your Master with publicans BIBLE 65:22
eathen: 'e. in 'is blindness bows KIPL 298:21
You're a pore benighted 'e. KIPL 299:8
eating: appetite grows by e. RAB 403:26
e. or opening a window AUDEN 19:18
e. *pâtés de foie gras* SMITH 511:20
they were e. and drinking BIBLE 67:32
thought surpass e. and drinking CLOU 153:21
eats: Man is what he e. FEUE 210:35
That whatever Miss T e. DE L 174:11
Eave: E. 'arf a brick at 'im PUNCH 402:14
eaves: fall upon her gilded e. TENN 542:5
instant clamorous e. YEATS 586:22
ebb: e. and flow must ever be WORD 578:8
ne'er e. to humble love SHAK 476:1
ebbing: steady than an e. sea FORD 216:20
ebony: in e. as if done in ivory FULL 220:15
Ecce: E. homo BIBLE 83:22
Eccentric: intricate, E., intervolved
MILT 348:24
With centric and e. scribbled MILT 349:3
ecclesia: Anglicana e. libera MAGN 327:1
ibi ergo e. AMBR 4:1
ecclesiam: patrem qui e. non habet matrem
CYPR 170:19
Salus extra e. non est AUG 21:19
Ecclesiastes: dixit E. BIBLE 83:14
Ecclesiastic: E. tyranny's the worst
DEFOE 173:15
ecclesiastical: e. lyric ever poured forth
DISR 186:7
ecclesiologist: keen e. BETJ 44:14
echo: e. arose from the suicide's GILB 227:17
E. beyond the Mexique Bay MARV 331:17
e. in a Marabar cave FORS 217:8
e. is not faint at last LAND 309:8
gives a very e. to the seat SHAK 488:27
left an e. in the sense JONS 285:10
My words e. Thus ELIOT 202:13
seem an e. to the sense POPE 378:22
Sweet E., sweetest nymph MILT 341:3
tear the cave where E. SHAK 482:19
echoes: e., dying TENN 541:32
great wave that e. round TENN 535:4
he e. me SHAK 475:15
Only the e. which he made DRUM 193:25
Our e. roll from soul TENN 542:1
stage but e. back the public JOHN 282:27
echoing: e. straits between us thrown
ARN 13:12
éclat: manner of *é.* and eloquence BAG 29:11
eclipse: almost to doomsday with e.
SHAK 429:13
at least an e. BACON 26:23
E. first OKEL 365:3
gloom of earthquake and e. SHEL 503:21
In a merciful e. GILB 225:26
mortal moon hath her e. SHAK 494:21
Sliver'd in the moon's e. SHAK 462:4
sun... In dim e. MILT 345:24
total e. MILT 350:15
eclipsed: e. the gaiety of nations JOHN 281:36
eclipses: Clouds and e. stain both
SHAK 493:12
écoles: toutes les é. de théologie DID 184:7
economic: attaining e. ends KEYN 295:18
e. law of motion of modern MARX 333:8
social and e. experiment HOOV 255:24
economist: death of a political e. BAG 29:12
slaves of some defunct e. KEYN 295:20

Economy: E. is going without something
HOPE 255:26
e. where there is no efficiency DISR 185:33
fear of Political E. SELL 420:6
'Principles of Political E.' BENT 41:8
écrivain: L'é. original n'est pas celui
CHAT 141:5
ecstasies: Dissolve me into e. MILT 342:10
holy virgins in their e. TENN 534:23
ecstasy: Blasted with e. SHAK 433:15
e., is success in life PATER 369:21
In restless e. SHAK 461:12
In such an e. KEATS 291:22
in the e. of being ever BROW 97:24
seraph-wings of e. GRAY 235:19
think thereof without an e. BROW 96:10
This is the very e. of love SHAK 431:29
What will e. KEATS 291:3
edax: Tempus e. rerum OVID 366:18
Eden: attempt a picnic in E. BOWEN 91:6
E.'s dread probationary COWP 166:13
E. took their solitary MILT 350:1
garden eastward in E. BIBLE 45:7
happier E. MILT 348:1
on the east of E. BIBLE 45:29
This other E. SHAK 478:20
voice that breathed o'er E. KEBLE 295:6
edge: always at the e. of Being SPEN 515:10
blunt his natural e. SHAK 463:14
children's teeth are set on e. BIBLE 60:34
my teeth nothing on e. SHAK 439:26
your 'e. of cultivation' KIPL 299:3
edges: vast e. drear ARN 12:23
edideris: Quod non e. HOR 258:6
edification: than the e. of the hearers
BURKE 108:14
edifice: Hail, glorious e. SMITH 510:6
edifieth: charity e. BIBLE 76:5
edifying: e. of the body of Christ BIBLE 77:28
edisti: e. satis atque bibisti HOR 259:6
Edit: E. and annotate the lines YEATS 586:14
edition: more beautiful e. FRAN 218:20
new e. fifty volumes long BROW 99:3
new e. of human nature HAZL 243:12
Edom: over E. will I cast PRAY 393:18
this that cometh from E. BIBLE 60:10
Educ: E.: during the holidays SITW 508:15
educated: e. man's BROW 104:32
e. whisker TENN 533:10
fed and e. RUSK 412:6
once as an e. gentleman SHAW 497:9
than he is now to an e. man COL 158:8
Educating: E. the natives of
Borrioboola-Gha DICK 176:4
education: all this fuss about e. MELB 336:21
between e. and catastrophe WELLS 568:16
chief hand in their own e. SCOTT 419:3
complete and generous e. MILT 352:8
doctor's thesis On e. AUDEN 21:4
E. has for its object SPEN 515:1
E. produced a vast population TREV 552:10
E. is what survives when SKIN 508:20
E. makes a people easy BROU 95:6
E. makes us what we are HELV 244:19
e. most have been misled DRYD 196:19
e. of the body...What I admire DISR 186:21
first rudiments of e. are STEE 518:10
highest e. since the Greek DISR 186:21
is a part of e. BACON 27:27
is the beginning of e. RUSK 412:5
learning and a liberal e. HENRY 245:21
love her is a liberal e. STEE 518:6
Prejudice of e. STER 520:4
Printing has destroyed e. DISR 186:21
Soap and e. are not TWAIN 554:4
(thank your e. JONS 285:15
'Tis E. forms the common POPE 377:12
Upon the e. of the people DISR 185:12
with the e. of the heart SCOTT 419:4
eel: I have seen but an e. DICK 176:17

eels: e. boil'd in broo'   BALL 31:5
efface: May none those marks e.
    BYRON 125:15
effacerai: j'en e. trois   BOIL 89:12
Effanineffable: ineffable effable E.
    ELIOT 204:6
effect: between cause and e.   LA B 306:15
bring the same to good e.   PRAY 386:10
rod produces an e. which   JOHN 273:25
effecting: e. of all things possible
    BACON 28:6
effects: e. from civil discord   ADD 1:25
effectually: faithfully we may obtain
e.   PRAY 387:1
effeminate: harbour thoughts e. and faint
    MARL 330:11
efficiency: economy where there is no
e.   DISR 185:33
e. and inefficiency   SHAW 497:5
efficient: e. and the inefficient   SHAW 497:5
e. minority to coerce   STEP 518:20
effort: e. very nearly killed her   BELL 39:7
if that e. be too great   ANON 6:17
What is written without e.   JOHN 280:25
effraie: ces espaces infinis m'e.   PASC 369:7
effugere: Soles e. atque abire sentit
    MART 331:11
effugies: At non e. meos iambos   CAT 137:16
effusions: e. of wit and humour   AUST 22:31
these were not common e.   BRON 93:17
égalité: majestueuse é. des lois   FRAN 217:26
égards: doit des é. aux vivants   VOLT 561:19
Egdon: glory of the E. waste began
    HARDY 241:20
yet E. remained   HARDY 241:21
Egestas: malesuada Fames ac turpis E.
    VIRG 558:21
egg: afraid you've got a bad e.   PUNCH 403:4
e. boiled very soft is   AUST 22:7
e. of the wren   WHIT 570:21
fatal e. by pleasure laid   COWP 166:9
full of quarrels as an e.   SHAK 483:1
is eating a demnition e.   DICK 180:14
radish and an e.   COWP 167:14
See this e.   DID 184:7
sitting on one addled e.   ELIOT 201:2
that a hen is only an e.'s   BUTL 118:24
white and hairless as an e.   HERR 249:15
eggs: e. and buttercups fried   LEAR 312:21
eighty-five ways to dress e.   MOORE 356:2
fresh e. to rotten boroughs   MAC 323:15
Lays e. inside a paper bag   ISH 270:27
partridge sitteth on e.   BIBLE 60:25
weasel sucks e.   SHAK 425:15
were but to roast their e.   BACON 27:37
egg-shell: dead kitten, an e.   WELLS 568:11
eglantine: warm hedge grew lush e.
    SHEL 503:19
with e.   SHAK 470:10
Ego: E. et Rex meus   SHAK 447:8
Et in Arcadia e.   ANON 10:12
too much E. in your Cosmos   KIPL 304:31
egotist: engendered in the whims of an
e.   KEATS 293:22
egotistical: Wordsworthian or e. sublime
    KEATS 294:7
égout: De cet é. immonde   TOCQ 551:9
egregiously: making him e. an ass
    SHAK 474:22
Egypt: all the first-born of E.   SHAK 425:17
arose up a new king over E.   BIBLE 46:40
darkness over the land of E.   BIBLE 47:15
E.'s might is tumbled   COL 155:3
firstborn in the land of E.   BIBLE 47:18
servant in the land of E.   BIBLE 48:19
that there was corn in E.   BIBLE 46:33
thee out of the land of E.   BIBLE 47:24
there was a great cry in E.   BIBLE 47:19
When Israel came out of E.   PRAY 397:16
wonders in the land of E.   BIBLE 47:11

Egyptian: E. fetters I must break
    SHAK 421:17
handkerchief Did an E.   SHAK 476:3
Egyptians: they spoiled the E.   BIBLE 47:20
Eheu: E. fugaces   HOR 260:10
Ehrlicher: E. Makler   BISM 84:23
eight: 'We want e.   WYND 584:3
will hear the stroke of e.   HOUS 262:18
eighthe: holughnesse of the e. spere
    CHAU 144:18
eighty: dream you are never e.   SEXT 420:18
Einbildung: sondern der E. ist   KANT 288:12
Einstein: Let E. be   SQUI 517:14
Eisen: sich nur durch Blut und E.   BISM 84:25
either: e. reading   THOM 546:11
happy could I be with e.   GAY 222:35
their troth e. to other   PRAY 389:7
Elaine: Daintily alights E.   BETJ 43:13
E., the lily maid of Astolat   TENN 534:25
elbow: e. has a fascination that   GILB 227:10
elbows: with her e. on the table   JAMES 271:21
eld: alms Of palsied e.   SHAK 464:10
elder: e. and more terrible   SHAK 449:19
e. man not at all   BACON 26:35
five days e. than ourselves   BROW 96:10
I said an e. soldier   SHAK 451:18
scent of e. bushes   AUDEN 21:1
woman take An e.   SHAK 489:1
elderly: Mr Salteena was an e. man
    ASHF 17:5
elders: discourse of the e.   BIBLE 62:27
e. and the four beasts   BIBLE 81:32
four and twenty e. fell   BIBLE 81:27
eldest: e. of things   MILT 347:5
eldest son: Earl of Fitzdotterel's e. BROU 95:3
Eldorado: E. banal de tous les vieux
    BAUD 35:8
Eleanor: like Queen E. in the ballad
    WALP 563:4
elect: knit together thine e.   PRAY 387:4
elected: audacity of e. persons   WHIT 570:14
will not serve if e.   SHER 507:1
election: e. by the incompetent many
    SHAW 497:36
e. is coming   ELIOT 200:25
right of e. is the very   JUN 287:2
elections: it's no go the e.   MACN 326:8
electorate: dismissed by the British e.
    CHUR 150:26
Electric: mend the E. Light   BELL 39:29
Runs the red e. train   BETJ 43:13
electrical: e. skin and glaring eyes
    SMART 508:22
Electrician: E. is no longer there   BELL 40:7
electrification: e. of the whole country
    LENIN 313:22
elegance: casque has outdone your e.
    POUND 382:13
e. of female friendship   JOHN 282:12
Studious of e. and ease   GAY 223:18
elegant: e. but not ostentatious   JOHN 281:38
It's so e.   ELIOT 204:25
elegies: e. And quoted odes   TENN 541:30
elegy: e., and sonnet   JOHN 280:9
eleison: Kyrie e.   MASS 334:16
element: e. of fire is quite put DONNE 187:19
I am not of your e.   SHAK 490:8
Thy e.'s below   SHAK 453:24
Elementary: 'E.,' said he   DOYLE 192:9
elements: Become our e.   MILT 346:13
Contending with the fretful e.   SHAK 454:3
e. of modern civilization   CARL 131:3
e. once out of it   SHAK 422:14
e. So mix'd in him   SHAK 452:7
with the motion of all e.   SHAK 457:8
world made cunningly Of e.   DONNE 189:2
elephant: Appears a monstrous e. COTT 163:7
E., Is best to lodge   SHAK 490:4
E., The only harmless   DONNE 190:3
He thought he saw an E.   CARR 133:10

th' unwieldy e.   MILT 347:26
elephanto: candenti perfecta nitens e.
    VIRG 559:3
elephants: Place e. for want of towns
    SWIFT 528:2
Women and e. never forget   SAKI 413:11
Eleusis: have brought whores for E.
    POUND 382:11
elevated: generous and e. mind JOHN 282:19
joy Of e. thoughts   WORD 578:7
elevates: e. above the vulgar herd GAIS 220:25
elevating: wild, melancholy, and e.
    BRON 93:17
elevation: emotion that e. and that fall
    BURKE 111:9
eleven: e. buckram men grown out
    SHAK 439:3
second e. sort of chap   BARR 34:8
tells you he's only e.   GILB 226:14
elf: deceiving e.   KEATS 291:23
not a modest maiden e.   HARDY 240:7
too often a negligent e.   BARH 33:10
Elfland: horns of E. faintly blowing
    TENN 541:32
Elginbrodde: Here lie I, Martin E.
    MACD 325:3
Eli: E., lama sabachthani   BIBLE 68:24
eligendum: malis minus est semper e.
    THOM 546:15
Elijah: E. passed by him   BIBLE 51:15
E. went up by a whirlwind   BIBLE 51:22
spirit of E. doth rest   BIBLE 51:23
Elisha: Elijah doth rest on E.   BIBLE 51:23
E. saw it   BIBLE 51:22
Elizabeth: Than my sonne's wife, E.
    ING 270:16
Ellen: fair E. of brave Lochinvar
    SCOTT 417:10
ELLIOT: E. OF KELLYNCH-HALL
    AUST 23:7
elliptical: e. billiard balls   GILB 227:7
Ellum: E. she hateth mankind   KIPL 303:26
elm: green buds hang in the e. HOUS 265:15
elms: Behind the e. last night   PRIOR 401:9
Beneath those rugged e.   GRAY 234:20
doves in immemorial e.   TENN 542:17
e., Fade into dimness   ARN 14:8
elm-tree: Round the e. bole are   BROW 101:5
elope: must e. methodically   GOLD 232:17
Eloquence: Bag of Parliamentary E.
    CARL 132:1
embellisher of ornate e.   CAXT 138:2
gift of graceful e.   HOR 257:23
his superior e.   BURKE 109:5
intoxicated with my own e.   DISR 186:3
manner of *éclat* and e.   BAG 29:11
mother of arts And e.   MILT 350:8
my books be then the e.   SHAK 493:3
saucy and audacious e.   SHAK 471:15
should say that e. is *heard*   MILL 339:20
eloquent: curse of this country is e.
    EMER 208:10
e. in a more sublime language MAC 323:26
e., just, and mighty Death   RAL 404:16
pure and e. blood   DONNE 189:31
soft, so calm, yet e.   BYRON 125:22
else: e. would I give it thee   PRAY 393:8
elsewhere: Altogether e.   AUDEN 18:16
elsewhere live as they live e.   AMBR 4:2
not be e. for thousands   NELS 360:16
ELUCESCEBAT: E. quoth our friend
    BROW 99:15
elusive: flying and e. shadow   ARN 12:22
elves: all the criticizing e.   CHUR 149:13
e. also   HERR 249:11
Ye e. of hills   SHAK 485:23
Ely: Merrily sang the monks in E. CAN 130:9
Elysian: in the E. fields   DISR 185:25
Elysium: daughter of E.   SCH 415:9
My brother he is in E.   SHAK 487:22

Sleeps in E. — SHAK 444:25
What E. have ye known — KEATS 290:28
Elzevir: E. classic in your pocket — CHES 145:22
emaciated: prone and e. figure HARDY 239:13
embalmer: e. of the still midnight — KEATS 292:28
Embalming: my E. (Sweetest) there — HERR 249:24
embark: When I e. — TENN 533:4
embarras: L'e. des richesses — ALL 3:19
se font sentir par l'e. — LA B 306:13
embarrassed: Jack was e. — BYRON 124:43
embattled: e. nations sing and shout — SQUI 517:13
embellisher: founder and e. of ornate — CAXT 138:2
embers: O joy! that in our e. — WORD 579:9
Where glowing e. through — MILT 342:5
emblem: e. of my own perpetual — NEWM 361:12
e. of untimely graves — COWP 167:16
embody: e. the Law — GILB 226:1
embrace: escaping murderer or to e. — STEV 521:12
his right hand doth e. me — BIBLE 56:21
none I think do there e. — MARV 332:19
pity, then e. — POPE 379:16
to e. me she inclined — MILT 351:14
embraces: age in her e. past — ROCH 406:20
embraceth: mercy e. him on every side — PRAY 391:18
embroideries: Covered with e. YEATS 584:16
embroidery: little daily e. had been — ELIOT 201:1
Emelye: up roos E. — CHAU 142:21
emendation: e. wrong that cannot without — JOHN 282:17
Emerald: E. findeth no Memling — POUND 382:11
e. twinkles in the grass — TENN 540:8
in sight like unto an e. — BIBLE 81:22
Emerald Isle: men of the E. — DREN 193:22
Emeralds: E. big as half a county — LAND 308:23
Emerge: E., and shine upon — ARN 15:1
I shall e. one day — BROW 103:8
emerging: Descried at sunrise an e. prow — ARN 14:21
emigration: e. Has proved most useful — BARR 34:23
Emigravit: E. is the inscription — LONG 316:24
Emily: E., Hear — CRANE 168:30
eminence: raised To that bad e. — MILT 346:6
eminency: of some e. in ourselves — HOBB 251:22
Emmet: Robert E. and Wolfe Tone — YEATS 586:19
Emollit: E. mores nec sinit esse — OVID 366:25
emolument: positions of considerable e. — GAIS 220:25
emoluments: if his e. are to be precisely — SMITH 509:13
emotion: e. and take it for zeal — THOM 546:13
e. in the form of art is — ELIOT 205:16
e. recollected in tranquillity — WORD 583:10
escape from e. — ELIOT 205:18
heart less bounding at e. — ARN 15:9
is the epitaph of an e. — NIET 363:13
morality touched by e. — ARN 16:20
unhurried by e. — JAMES 271:29
emotions: grounds for the noble e. — RUSK 411:10
waste-paper basket of the e. — WEBB 566:8
emperice: e. and flour of floures CHAU 143:31
emperor: ancient days by e. and clown — KEATS 291:23
E. has nothing on at all — AND 4:5
emperor is the e. of ice-cream — STEV 520:14
had he never become e. — TAC 531:13

looking for the sacred E. — BRAM 91:18
emphasis: sake of e. — CHUR 150:5
Empire: Another mighty E. overthrown — WORD 581:13
Britain has lost an E. — ACH 1:4
called...'the metropolis of the e. COBB 154:10
dismemberment of the E. — GLAD 229:15
e. is no more than power — DRYD 194:10
E. stands splendidly isolated — FOST 217:17
great e. and little minds — BURKE 110:6
How is the E. — GEOR 224:5
it may make us an E. yet — KIPL 300:21
Joy, E. and Victory — SHEL 503:15
ni romain, ni e. — VOLT 561:9
preserve the unity of the e. — BURKE 110:4
Rooshan-E. — DICK 181:6
We'll pledge our E. vast — HUXL 269:2
Westward the course of e. — BERK 41:20
wilderness into a glorious e. — BURKE 110:7
Empires: day of E. has come — CHAM 139:6
Hatching vain e. — MILT 346:15
employed: more innocently e. — JOHN 276:18
employment: e. for his idle time WALT 564:3
our e. may be reckoned — GAY 222:33
pleasantness of an e. does — AUST 23:25
To give e. to the artisan — BELL 39:29
employments: How various his e. — COWP 167:7
emporte: quelque chose Que j'e. ROST 410:12
Empress: cultivated court of the E. — GILB 227:22
Emprison: E. her soft hand and let — KEATS 291:15
Emprison'd: E. in black — KEATS 289:10
emptiness: behind it but panic and e. — FORS 216:25
Eternal smiles his e. betray — POPE 377:2
little e. of love — BROO 94:27
empty: e. words of a dream — BRID 92:11
fold stands e. in the drowned SHAK 470:5
heart keeps e. in thy tomb — KING 296:11
he findeth it e. — BIBLE 66:13
he satisfieth the e. soul — PRAY 397:7
idle singer of an e. day — MORR 358:8
men had ever very e. heads — BACON 25:7
rich he hath sent e. away — BIBLE 69:6
There is the e. chapel — ELIOT 205:10
turn down an e. Glass — FITZ 213:18
when I have made it e. — SHAK 424:24
emulation: by exciting e. and comparisons — JOHN 273:25
Of pale and bloodless e. — SHAK 486:25
Shouting their e. — SHAK 427:13
En: 'E. Priamus — VIRG 557:17
Enable: E. with perpetual light — PRAY 400:5
Enacted: E. on this same divan — ELIOT 205:2
enamoured: e. on peace that he would — CLAR 152:21
enchant: I will e. thine ear — SHAK 495:19
Enchanted: breathe the air of the E. — MER 337:37
Of dire chimeras and e. — MILT 341:12
enchanter: like ghosts from an e. — SHEL 502:8
enchantment: distance lends e. to the view — CAMP 129:6
sweet e., hence — SMITH 510:8
'Tis a note of e. — WORD 581:3
enchantments: e. of the Middle Age...Home — ARN 15:25
enchantress: tune the e. plays — HOUS 265:8
enchants: That it e. my sense — SHAK 486:32
enclitic: doctrine of the e. *De* — BROW 101:1
encompass'd: e. but one man — SHAK 448:19
encounter: e. darkness as a bride — SHAK 464:12
encourage: e. those who betray their — GAY 222:33
right to e. — BAG 29:3
to e. the others — VOLT 561:1

encouragement: expression of no-e. — BRAM 91:19
encourager: amiral pour e. les autres — VOLT 561:1
Encyclopaedia: I am a whole E. behind — LAMB 307:10
end: Ages of hopeless e. — MILT 346:11
A' made a finer e. — SHAK 443:17
am reserved for some e. — CLIVE 153:6
as an e. withal, never as means KANT 288:13
began to draw to our e. — BIBLE 62:17
beginning of the e. — TALL 531:19
Better is the e. of a thing — BIBLE 55:19
boys get at one e. they — JOHN 276:32
come to pass but the e. — BIBLE 67:27
e. crowns all — SHAK 487:15
e. in sight was a vice — BROW 105:21
e. is bitter as wormwood — BIBLE 53:20
e. is where we start from — ELIOT 203:1
e. justifies the means — BUS 117:4
e. my days in a tavern — ANON 10:14
e. of all things is — BIBLE 80:31
e. of Job more than his — BIBLE 53:13
e. of man is an action — CARL 132:16
e. of the beginning — CHUR 150:1
e. of this day's business — SHAK 451:33
e. that I have now begun — WYATT 583:23
e. to be without honour — BIBLE 62:16
e. try the man — SHAK 441:23
flood unto the world's e. — PRAY 394:20
God be at my e. — ANON 5:9
God will grant an e. — VIRG 557:13
he shall e. in doubts — BACON 24:16
is the e. that crowns us — HERR 249:4
Is this the promis'd e. — SHAK 456:9
laid e. to end — PARK 368:24
lest he should make an e. — JONS 285:2
let me know mine e. — PRAY 391:30
long weary day have e. — SPEN 515:26
look to the e. — ANON 10:18
make an e. the sooner — BACON 26:6
man awaits his e. — YEATS 584:20
mean this day to e. myself — TENN 539:21
same thing at the e. — BROW 98:25
sans E. — FITZ 212:18
something ere the e. — TENN 544:3
so there's an e. on't — ANON 8:20
therefore then had a good e. — MAL 328:2
there's an e., I think, of kissing BROOK 95:1
there's ane e. of ane old song OGIL 364:21
there's an e. on't — JOHN 275:24
there shall I e. — SHAK 452:1
They say he made a good e. — SHAK 436:11
things have fleetest e. — THOM 547:25
This was the e. — PLATO 374:1
till you come to the e. — CARR 134:19
understood from all of these men PRAY 394:23
We shall go on to the e. — CHUR 149:31
what e. the gods have — HOR 259:19
'What is the chief e. of man — SHOR 507:7
Whoever wills the e. — KANT 288:17
wish it all at an e. — BURN 112:18
world may e. to-night — BROW 101:23
world shall e. when I forget — SWIN 530:16
world without e. — BIBLE 77:26
world without e. — PRAY 384:15
end-all: be the be-all and the e. — SHAK 459:5
endearing: all those e. young charms — MOORE 356:4
children follow'd with e. wile GOLD 231:1
endears: That all the more e. — TENN 541:28
endeavour: By no e. — GILB 227:24
disinterested e. to learn — ARN 16:1
should our e. be so loved — SHAK 487:19
endeavours: e. are unlucky explorers — DOUG 191:8
high e. are an inward light — WORD 577:3
ended: e. in thee — PRAY 388:6
has e. and the vast glory — VIRG 558:6
praised the Georges e. — LAND 309:6

Enderby: uppe 'The Brides of E.   ING 270:13
ending: beginning and the e.   BIBLE 81:10
dirge of her certain e.   SHAK 492:20
profession an unhappy e.   JAMES 272:1
so clean an e.   HOUS 264:2
endless: I take my e. way   HOUS 263:17
Endlich: E. fortissimo   MAHL 327:6
endow: e. a college   POPE 377:31
worldly goods I thee e.   PRAY 389:5
Endowed: E. by the ruined millionaire   ELIOT 202:22
ends: all the e. of the earth   PRAY 394:1
best e. by the best means   HUTC 268:19
divinity that shapes our e.   SHAK 437:11
E. all our month-long love   BRID 92:11
e. by our beginnings know   DENH 174:20
e. thou aim'st at be thy   SHAK 447:12
into the e. of the world   PRAY 390:11
make both e. meet   FULL 220:12
More are men's e. mark'd   SHAK 478:18
To do that thing that e.   SHAK 423:20
worthy e. and expectations   BACON 26:4
Endue: E. her plenteously with   PRAY 385:5
endurance: patient e. is godlike   LONG 316:13
endurcis: les cuers contre nous e.   VILL 557:4
endure: all that human hearts e.   GOLD 231:30
all that human hearts e.   JOHN 282:21
days wear on but I e.   APOL 11:11
e. an hour and see injustice   HOUS 264:5
e. Their going hence   SHAK 456:3
e. the toothache patiently   SHAK 473:7
E. the winter's cold   SHAK 448:14
e. what can't be mended   WATTS 565:27
e. what it once possessed   SHEL 501:22
heaviness may e. for a night   PRAY 391:13
I can e. my own despair   WALSH 563:30
if I continue to e. you   CONG 161:8
immortal spirit must e.   ARN 14:24
nature itselfe cant e.   FLEM 214:26
Potter and clay e.   BROW 104:10
thou shalt e.   PRAY 396:13
We first e.   POPE 379:16
Youth's a stuff will not e.   SHAK 488:17
endured: life e. and known   SASS 415:2
tolerable and not to be e.   SHAK 472:30
which much is to be e.   JOHN 282:8
endureth: e. all things   BIBLE 76:14
mercy e. for ever   PRAY 399:2
the praise of it e.   PRAY 397:13
enemies: all assaults of our e.   PRAY 385:2
called thee to curse mine e.   BIBLE 48:16
E.' gifts are no gifts   SOPH 513:5
e. having surrendered unconditionally   CHUR 150:26
e. of Caesar shall say   SHAK 450:10
e. shall lick the dust   PRAY 394:20
friendship with thine e.   SHAK 450:9
in the choice of his e.   WILDE 573:19
left me naked to mine e.   SHAK 447:13
let his e. be scattered   PRAY 394:6
Love your e.   BIBLE 69:21
make thine e. thy footstool   PRAY 397:11
men my friends than e.   SHAK 452:4
of my most intimate e.   ROSS 409:20
open society and its e.   POPP 381:24
Our e. have beat us   SHAK 452:5
overthrown More than your e.   SHAK 424:26
People wish their e. dead   MONT 354:11
To forgive e. H   BLAKE 87:5
trophies unto the e. of truth   BROW 96:5
with their e. in the gate   PRAY 398:19
enemy: common e. and oppressor   BURKE 110:33
Do be my e.   BLAKE 87:7
e., and the avenger   PRAY 389:28
e. came and sowed tares   BIBLE 66:18
E. ears are listening   ANON 9:18
e. hath done this   BIBLE 66:19
e. increaseth every day   SHAK 451:27
e. in their mouths to steal   SHAK 475:9

e. of truth and freedom   IBSEN 269:17
e. who speaks ill of your   NELS 360:12
friend and e. is but Death   BROO 94:28
hasn't an e. in the world   WILDE 574:2
Have no e. but time   YEATS 585:12
he is afraid of his e.   PLUT 374:20
Here comes the e.   CONDE 159:16
he's an e. to mankind   SHAK 490:7
How goes the e.   REYN 405:14
I am the e. you killed   OWEN 367:12
If thine e. be hungry   BIBLE 54:29
Is mortals' chiefest e.   SHAK 462:1
is no such terrible e.   BACON 26:2
last e. that shall be destroyed   BIBLE 76:23
mine e.   BIBLE 51:18
Mine e.'s dog   SHAK 455:24
my e. is dead   WHIT 570:11
my vision's greatest e.   BLAKE 85:21
near'st and dearest e.   SHAK 439:36
No e. But winter   SHAK 425:14
Our friends, the e.   BER 41:15
that great e. of reason   BROW 96:30
that old e. the gout   HOOD 254:21
That sweet e.   SIDN 507:22
to be taught by the e.   OVID 366:16
while the e. oppresseth me   PRAY 392:9
energies: e. of our system will decay   BALF 30:3
energy: e. divine   POPE 380:15
E. is Eternal Delight   BLAKE 88:11
enfants: e. de la patrie   ROUG 410:16
Les e. terribles   GAV 222:5
que les jeux d'e. ne sont   MONT 354:17
se font pas comme les e.   FLAU 214:3
Enfer: l'E., c'est les Autres   SART 414:8
Enfin: E. Malherbe vint   BOIL 89:10
enflamment: feux qui s'e. au vent FRAN 218:2
enforced: It useth an e. ceremony   SHAK 451:11
engage: e. himself openly and publicly   BLAKE 86:10
engagement: from every honourable e.   BURKE 108:23
engine: curious e., your white hand   WEBS 566:21
e. that moves   HARE 242:8
put this e. to our ears   SWIFT 526:3
that two-handed e.   MILT 343:13
Wit's an unruly e.   HERB 247:4
engineer: furious papa or a mild e.   AUDEN 20:15
engineering: Piecemeal social e. POPP 381:25
engineer: sport to have the e.   SHAK 435:21
engines: e. to play a little   BURKE 111:1
scape By all his e.   MILT 346:4
England: about the defence of E. BALD 29:28
away from E. her authors   TROL 552:12
Be E. what she will   CHUR 148:24
between France and E.   JERR 273:4
children in E. take pleasure   ANON 7:22
cold queen of E. is looking   CHES 147:1
Common Law of E. has been   HERB 246:13
Elizabethan E.   INGE 270:10
E.—a happy land we know   CHUR 148:26
E. and Saint George   SHAK 444:3
E. a particular bashfulness   ADD 2:21
E.! awake   BLAKE 86:11
E. breed again   DRAY 193:11
E. expects that every man   NELS 360:20
E., full of sin   HERB 247:3
E. hath need of thee   WORD 582:5
E., home and beauty   BRAH 91:16
E. invented the phrase   BAG 28:23
E. is a garden that is   KIPL 299:12
E. is a nation of shopkeepers   NAP 359:15
E. is finished and dead   MILL 340:2
E. is still governed from   SHAW 498:23
E. is the paradise of women   FLOR 216:1
E. keep my bones   SHAK 452:29
E. mourns for her dead   BINY 84:9

E., my England   HENL 245:11
E.'s green and pleasant   BLAKE 86:12
E.'s green & pleasant   BLAKE 86:16
E. shall bide till Judgement   KIPL 303:27
E. should be free than   MAGEE 326:21
E.'s on the anvil   KIPL 297:26
E.'s winding sheet   BLAKE 85:17
E. was merry England   SCOTT 417:16
E. was too pure an Air   ANON 7:7
England was what E. seems   KIPL 302:11
E., we love thee better   TREN 552:8
E., with all thy faults   COWP 166:33
ere E.'s griefs began   GOLD 230:18
faithless E.   BOSS 90:14
fashion of the court of E.   SHAK 446:3
get me to E. once again   BROO 94:22
gloomy in E. are March   TROL 552:21
Happy is E.   KEATS 292:15
hear our noble E.'s praise   MAC 321:25
heart of E. well may call   DRAY 193:18
here did E. help me   BROW 101:9
history of E. is emphatically   MAC 323:12
in E.'s song for ever   NEWB 361:10
influenced manners in E.   BURKE 111:15
Ireland gives E. her soldiers   MER 337:24
jurisdiction in this Realm of E.   PRAY 400:10
lamented that Old E. is lost   JOHN 277:12
Let not E. forget her precedence   MILT 352:6
lost the last of E.   BELL 40:16
mad, and sent into E.   SHAK 436:30
martial airs of E.   WEBS 566:12
men that worked for E.   CHES 146:24
Noon strikes on E.   FLEC 214:6
Nor, E.! did I know   WORD 577:28
O E.! model to thy inward   SHAK 443:13
of a king of E. too   ELIZ 206:4
Old E. to adorn   KIPL 303:25
only seeing a worse E.   JOHN 277:24
poison E. at her roots   BOTT 90:17
road that leads him to E.   JOHN 274:30
royal navy of E. hath ever   BLAC 85:4
should they know of E.   KIPL 298:24
Slaves cannot breathe in E.   COWP 166:32
sneer at the bruisers of E.   BORR 90:6
Stately Homes of E.   COW 164:3
stately homes of E.   HEM 244:21
strong arm of E. will protect   PALM 368:10
suffer E. to be the workshop   DISR 184:11
suspended in favour of E.   SHAW 496:33
That is for ever E.   BROO 94:30
The further off from E.   CARR 134:15
This aged E. upon by transitions   EMER 207:10
This E. never did   SHAK 453:1
this E.   SHAK 478:20
this is E.'s greatest   TENN 541:9
to be in E.   BROW 101:5
to ensure summer in E.   WALP 563:8
to the landscape of E.   AUST 22:22
Walk upon E.'s mountains   BLAKE 86:16
we are the people of E.   CHES 147:15
while E. talked of ale   CHES 147:13
Who dies if E. live   KIPL 299:7
With E.'s own coal   KIPL 298:4
worst government that E.   TROL 553:4
youth of E. are on fire   SHAK 443:12
English: Allah created the E. mad   KIPL 300:14
angel is the E. child   BLAKE 88:2
are nothing to your E.   SHAK 475:2
be the second E. satirist   HALL 238:6
bird-haunted E. lawn   ARN 14:1
Breeds hard E. men   KING 296:23
characteristic of the E. Monarchy   BAG 28:28
Dr Johnson's morality was as E.   HAWT 243:5
E. are busy   MONT 355:8
E. are perhaps the least   BAG 29:2
E. are very little indeed   NORTH 364:2
E. army led by an Irish   SHAW 498:7
E. Bible   MAC 323:4

E. Church shall be free — MAGN 327:1
E. county families — WAUGH 565:29
E. drunkard made the rolling — CHES 147:10
E. home — TENN 541:22
E. (it must be owned) a — HAZL 244:1
E. make it their abode — WALL 562:8
E. man does not travel — STER 518:31
E., not the Turkish court — SHAK 442:23
E., now I must forego — SHAK 478:10
E. subject's sole prerogative — DRYD 197:31
E. take their pleasures — SULLY 524:18
E. tongue a gallimaufry — SPEN 517:6
E. would manage to meet — JERR 273:12
favour of boys learning E. — CHUR 150:23
feet of E. ground — HAR 242:11
fine old E. gentleman — ANON 6:10
forfeited their ancient E. dower — WORD 582:5
half-French, half-E. — SHAK 445:14
happy E. child — TAYL 531:23
if he went among the E. — BARR 34:19
I hope we E. will long — CARL 131:37
In an E. lane — BROW 100:12
I shall be among the E. — KEATS 294:9
king's E. — SHAK 469:5
kissed by the E. dead — OWEN 367:6
marks our E. dead — KIPL 303:3
noble E. — SHAK 443:7
not the expression in E. — ARN 16:4
one E. book and one only — ARN 16:13
on that grave where E. — HARTE 242:26
on you noblest E. — SHAK 444:1
principle of the E. constitution — BLAC 85:5
really nice E. people — SHAW 496:32
Roman-Saxon-Danish-Norman E. — DEFOE 173:13
sagacity of E. enterprise — BURKE 109:17
sort of E. up with which — CHUR 151:6
Take of E. earth as much — KIPL 298:8
'tis the talent of our E. — DRYD 197:12
to the E. that of the sea — JEAN 272:4
trick of our E. nation — SHAK 441:14
under an E. heaven — BROO 94:30
When the E. began to hate — KIPL 298:1
wishes to attain an E. style — JOHN 281:38
your E. summer's done — KIPL 300:23
Englishman: broad-shoulder'd genial E. — TENN 542:20
Either for E. or Jew — BLAKE 85:25
E. a combination of qualities — DICK 181:12
E., Being flatter'd — CHAP 140:3
E. believes be heresy — SHAW 498:19
E. could beat three Frenchmen — ADD 2:19
E. is content to say nothing — JOHN 278:17
E. never enjoys himself — HERB 246:17
E. of our upper class — ARN 15:17
E.'s heaven-born privilege — ARN 15:20
E. thinks he is moral when — SHAW 497:28
E. to open his mouth — SHAW 498:12
E. unmoved that statement — GILB 228:23
E. whose heart is — BAG 28:31
find an E. in the wrong — SHAW 498:6
heart of a true *E.* — ADD 2:19
He is an E. — GILB 228:9
He remains an E. — GILB 228:10
ill-natur'd thing, an E. — DEFOE 173:12
last great E. is low — TENN 541:6
not one E. — WALP 563:25
religious rights of an E. — JUN 287:1
smell the bloud of an E. — NASHE 360:6
stirred the heart of every E. — SCOTT 415:19
thorough an E. as ever coveted — KING 297:9
What E. will give his mind — SHAW 496:4
Englishmen: absurd nature of E. — PEPYS 372:7
first to His E. — MILT 351:27
Honest E. — KING 296:21
Mad dogs and E. — COW 163:19
our very name as E. — PITT 374:4
proper drink of E. — BORR 90:8
Englishwoman: This E. is so refined — SMITH 510:27

Englissh: E. and in writyng of oure — CHAU 144:17
E. sweete upon his tonge — CHAU 141:22
engrafted: meekness the e. word — BIBLE 80:10
engross: when he should e. — POPE 376:19
enigma: mystery inside an e. — CHUR 149:28
Resolving the e. — ELIOT 202:21
enjoy: Contented if he might e. — WORD 580:5
e. but half the blessing — GAY 222:9
e. her while she's kind — DRYD 198:17
e. idling thoroughly unless — JER 272:22
e. paradise in the next — BECK 36:20
e. poetry unless we know — THOR 550:25
glorify God and to e. — SHOR 507:7
have to go out and e. it — SMITH 510:23
in due time we may e. them — PRAY 385:21
Let me e. the earth no — HARDY 240:6
most e. contented least — SHAK 493:6
never e. the world aright — TRAH 551:17
that private men e. — SHAK 444:24
to e. it — SMITH 510:11
to e. thy land — SHAK 452:8
enjoy'd: all times I have e. — TENN 543:22
warm and still to be e. — KEATS 291:7
Enjoyed: E. no sooner but despised — SHAK 495:7
e. the gifts of the founder — GIBB 224:8
little to be e. — JOHN 282:8
enjoyment: chief e. of riches consists — SMITH 509:11
e. as the greatest orator — HUME 267:22
Was it done with e. — RUSK 411:20
enjoyments: Fire-side e. — COWP 167:13
it were not for its e. — SURT 525:23
enjoys: now e. his age — DRYD 196:3
Enlarge: E., diminish, interline — SWIFT 527:34
enlargement: stability or e. of the language — JOHN 281:7
enlightened: While on the e. mind — THOM 549:26
enmities: reconciliation where the e. — MAC 323:20
enmity: while covert e. — SHAK 440:30
Enna: fair field Of E. — MILT 347:21
ennemi: Voilà l'e. — CONDE 159:16
ennemies: Les oreilles e. vous écoutent — ANON 9:18
ennemis: Nos amis, les e. — BER 41:15
ennoble: What can e. sots — POPE 379:23
ennobled: which e. whatever it touched — BURKE 111:10
ennui: symétrie, c'est l'e. — HUGO 267:12
ennuyer: Le secret d'e. est...de tout — VOLT 561:21
ennuyeux: sont bons hors le genre e. — VOLT 561:7
Eno: to soar with E. — STEV 521:11
Enoch: E. walked with God — BIBLE 45:30
Enormous: E. through the Sacred Town — BELL 38:28
enough: best is good e. — GOET 230:8
eaten and drunk e. — HOR 259:6
e. for fifty hopes — BROW 99:4
e., for nature's ends — MALL 327:12
E. of science and of art — WORD 582:23
E. that he heard it once — BROW 98:20
had never had e. — GILB 225:9
It is e. — BIBLE 54:46
Once is more than e. — BIRCH 84:11
'tis e., 'twill serve — SHAK 483:3
Was it not e. — SHAW 496:30
When thou hast e. — BIBLE 63:5
enquiries: remote e. — JOHN 281:40
enquiring: My object in e. is to know — HOUS 266:9
enraptur'd: Glorious th' e. main — SMART 509:4
enrich: T'e. unknowing nations — DAN 170:23
enrichment: e. of our native language — DRYD 197:38

ensample: noble e. to his sheep — CHAU 142:1
ense: sit calamus saevior e. — BURT 116:22
Ensham: Above by E. — ARN 15:8
ensign: Th' imperial e. — MILT 345:19
ensky'd: thing e. and sainted — SHAK 463:12
enslave: impossible to e. — BROU 95:6
superstition to e. a philosophy — INGE 270:6
enslaved: All spirits are e. which — SHEL 503:9
ensnare: web as this will I e. — SHAK 474:19
ensue: peace, and e. it — PRAY 391:23
entangled: middle-sized are alone e. — SHEN 505:16
to contemplate an e. bank — DARW 171:28
Entbehren: E. sollst Du — GOET 230:2
entente: Th' e. is al — CHAU 144:16
enter: Abandon all hope, you who e. — DANTE 171:3
e. into the kingdom of heaven — BIBLE 64:11
e. into the kingdom of heaven — BIBLE 67:2
E. not into judgement with — PRAY 399:11
E. these enchanted woods — MER 337:21
e. who does not know geometry — ANON 10:2
King of England cannot e. — PITT 373:20
than for a rich man to e. — BIBLE 67:11
they that have riches e. — BIBLE 70:36
ye cannot e. now — TENN 534:8
entered: are e. into their labours — BIBLE 71:42
iron e. into his soul — PRAY 397:3
enterprise: e. is sick — SHAK 486:23
E. in walking naked — YEATS 584:16
hazard in the glorious e. — MILT 345:1
enterprised: e., nor taken in hand — PRAY 388:25
enterprises: e. of great pith and moment — SHAK 433:8
impediments to great e. — BACON 26:31
enterprising: e. burglar's not a-burgling — GILB 228:20
enterprize: period, pow'r, and e. — SMART 509:1
entertain: Could e. us with no worth — WALL 562:14
e. a cheerful disposition — SHAK 478:22
e. the lag-end of my life — SHAK 440:14
e. With half their forces — SHAK 443:7
forgetful to e. strangers — BIBLE 80:3
There e. him all the saints — MILT 343:18
To e. divine Zenocrate — MARL 330:12
entertained: e. angels unawares — BIBLE 80:3
entertaining: grown very e. to my self — CONG 160:22
entertainment: eligibility of the proffered e. — TROL 553:10
e. this week cost me above — PEPYS 372:20
not dull thy palm with e. — SHAK 430:19
some other custom of e. — SHAK 474:23
entertainments: delightful and most improving e. — ADD 2:9
entertains: e. the harmless day — WOTT 583:13
enthrall: Except you e. me — DONNE 189:9
enthroned: e. in the hearts of kings — SHAK 467:27
enthusiasm: e. I have been cheated — KEATS 294:15
ever achieved without e. — EMER 207:16
enthusiasts: e. can be trusted to speak — BALF 30:4
how to deal with e. — MAC 323:17
Entia: E. non sunt multiplicanda — OCCAM 364:19
entice: e. thee secretly...Thou shalt — BIBLE 48:24
enticing: Mirth can do with her e. — ANON 6:7
Entire: E. and sure the monarch's — PRIOR 401:3
entirely: e. beautiful — AUDEN 19:17
entirety: who would dissipate my e. — MACN 326:13
entrails: In our own proper e. — SHAK 452:8
In the poison'd e. throw — SHAK 462:2

entrañas: y en guerra con mis e. MACH 325:7
entrance: some e. into the language
                                    BACON 27:27
entrances: their exits and their e.
                                    SHAK 425:24
entrap: To e. the wisest   SHAK 467:11
entrusted: e. with arms...should   WIND 575:7
Entschluss: Der christliche E.   NIET 363:8
entsichere: e. ich meinen Browning
                                    JOHST 283:8
Entuned: E. in hir nose ful semely
                                    CHAU 141:15
entwine: Would e. itself verdantly
                                    MOORE 356:4
Enumerat: E. miles vulnera   PROP 401:15
envie: no makyng thow n'e.   CHAU 144:17
envious: e. siege Of watery Neptune
                                    SHAK 478:20
e. Time   MILT 344:17
grows to an e. fever   SHAK 486:25
prudes, your e. railing   BURNS 114:16
To silence e. tongues   SHAK 447:12
environed: e. with a great ditch from
                                    CROM 170:4
envy: attracts the e. of the world
                                    BURKE 109:15
did in e. of great Caesar   SHAK 452:7
do not e. me   DOUG 191:7
E. and wrath shorten   BIBLE 63:13
e. is a kind of praise   GAY 223:15
e. of brilliant men   BEER 37:28
e. of less happier lands   SHAK 478:20
e. of the devil came death   BIBLE 62:12
E.'s a sharper spur than   GAY 223:12
extinguisheth e.   BACON 26:4
from e., hatred, and malice   PRAY 385:16
I e. birds their wings   CLARE 152:7
I e. not in any moods   TENN 536:15
moved with e.   BIBLE 74:8
Pride, E., Malice   LAND 308:17
prisoners of e.   ILL 270:5
Stirr'd up with e. and revenge   MILT 344:23
through e. of thy happy lot   KEATS 291:17
void of e.   THOM 549:9
whom e. never touched   SHEL 505:14
épatés: é., les bourgeois   PRIV 401:12
ephemeral: grave Proves the child e.
                                    AUDEN 19:17
Ephesians: Great is Diana of the E.
                                    BIBLE 74:17
Ephesus: fought with beasts at E.
                                    BIBLE 76:24
Ephraim: E. also is the strength PRAY 393:18
grapes of E. better than the vintage
                                    BIBLE 49:17
epic: legend of an e. hour   CHES 147:8
thundrous E. lilted out   TENN 541:30
epicure: e. would say   SMITH 511:15
Epicuri: Cum ridere voles E. de   HOR 258:16
Epicurus: he was E. owene sone
                                    CHAU 141:27
one of E.' herd of pigs   HOR 258:16
épidermes: et le contact de deux é.
                                    CHAM 139:15
Epigram: What is an E.   COL 156:15
Epigramm: Witz ist das E. auf den Tod
                                    NIET 363:13
epigrams: despotism tempered by e.
                                    CARL 131:21
epilogue: good play needs no e.   SHAK 427:8
epistles: some obscure e. of love SHAK 488:23
epistula: Verbosa et grandis e. venit
                                    JUV 287:27
epitaph: are no e. of that Oak   DONNE 190:23
Believe a woman or an e.   BYRON 124:18
better have a bad e.   SHAK 432:25
e. drear   KIPL 301:18
memorable e.   SELL 420:3
not remember'd in thy e.   SHAK 440:25
surely that may be his e.   STEV 521:5

That's if ye carve my e.   BROW 99:13
Wit is the e. of an emotion   NIET 363:13
epitaphs: nice derangement of e.   SHER 506:14
of worms, and e.   SHAK 479:10
epithet: coined an e. for a knave MAC 323:27
Fair is too foul an e.   MARL 330:10
epithets: To e. like these   BELL 38:29
epitome: all mankind's e.   DRYD 194:13
Eppur: E. si muove   GAL 220:29
equal: admitted to that e. sky   POPE 379:6
all men are created e.   LINC 314:23
All men are e.   FORS 216:26
All shall e. be   GILB 225:23
are more e. than others   ORW 365:9
compel us to be e. upstairs   BARR 34:7
earth the separate and e.   JEFF 272:5
e. are within the Church's   HERB 247:10
e. division of unequal   ELL 206:11
e. in dignity and rights   ANON 4:14
E. in strength   MILT 346:7
e. poise of hope and fear   MILT 341:9
E., unclassed   SHEL 503:12
faith shines e.   BRON 93:18
hast made them e. unto us   BIBLE 67:15
in the dust be e. made   SHIR 507:2
men are created e.   JEFF 272:6
one e. eternity   DONNE 191:3
robbery to be e. with God   BIBLE 78:13
them as if they were e.   FROU 219:18
Though e. to all things   GOLD 231:17
under the rule of e. justice   MILL 339:19
equalises: weight that e. the shepherd
                                    CERV 138:20
equality: e. in fact as corollary BAK 29:25
e. in the servants' hall   BARR 34:7
in a general state of e.   JOHN 277:5
principle of perfect e.   MILL 339:18
true apostles of e.   ARN 15:16
without the idea of e.   HUGH 267:6
equally: Death kicks his way e.   HOR 259:13
henceforth be bestowed e.   SHAK 424:21
It comes e. to us all   DONNE 190:23
equals: disinterested commerce between
e.   GOLD 232:11
least of all between e.   BACON 26:11
equanimity: No man can face with e.
                                    GILB 226:10
equation: e. will come out at last MACN 326:6
Equator: disrespectfully of the E.
                                    SMITH 510:29
they got as far as the E.   THAC 545:32
equi: lente currite noctis e.   MARL 329:11
equinox: who knows when was the e.
                                    BROW 97:20
equipment: shabby e. always deteriorating
                                    ELIOT 202:23
equitem: Post e. sedet atra Cura HOR 260:15
equity: people with e.   PRAY 396:9
equivocate: I will not e.   GARR 221:17
equivocation: e. will undo us   SHAK 436:28
equivocator: here's an e.   SHAK 460:16
Equo: E. ne credite   VIRG 558:1
eradicating: fault without e. the virtue
                                    GOLD 232:8
Erasmus: law-givers are E. and Montaigne
                                    FORS 217:11
Erastian: E. Whig   CHES 146:27
ere: Oon e. it herde, at tothir   CHAU 144:12
erect: e. and manly foe   CANN 130:1
erected: met each other with e.   DRYD 197:30
erecteth: Christ e. his Church   BANC 32:14
erection: rate the cost of the e.   SHAK 441:17
Eremite: sleepless E.   KEATS 292:11
Erickin': to have any beastly E.   KIPL 305:6
Eripuit: E. coelo fulmen   TURG 553:22
err: Better to e. with Pope   BYRON 124:19
e. is human, not to, animal   FROST 219:13
is a people that do e.   PRAY 396:4
most may e. as grossly   DRYD 194:18
reas'ning but to e.   POPE 379:12

To e. is human   POPE 378:27
errand: Blackheath the warlike e. MAC 322:3
e. now to the Antipodes   SHAK 472:9
in thy joyous E. reach   FITZ 213:18
errands: little e. for the Ministers
                                    GILB 225:24
Meet to be sent on e.   SHAK 451:10
erred: have e. exceedingly   BIBLE 50:15
We have e.   PRAY 384:11
erreur: L'e. n'a jamais approché
                                    METT 338:10
erring: e. on ventiferous ripes   HOLM 253:14
error: All men are liable to e.   LOCKE 315:17
charged the troops of e.   BROW 96:5
e. be too highly heap'd   SHAK 427:11
e. by the same example   SHAK 468:3
e. is all in the not done   POUND 382:14
e. is immense   BOL 89:15
fierceness makes E. a fault   HERB 247:6
hateful e.   SHAK 452:2
If this be e.   SHAK 495:5
in endless e. hurl'd   POPE 379:13
Man is in e. throughout   GOET 229:29
man that he is in an e.   LOCKE 315:16
stalking-horse to e.   BOL 89:16
than all the hosts of e.   BRYAN 106:7
ut me malus abstulit e.   VIRG 560:4
very e. of the moon   SHAK 477:8
errors: amusing with numerous e.
                                    GOLD 232:31
e. are volitional and are   JOYCE 286:27
E., like straws   DRYD 195:10
E. look so very ugly   ELIOT 201:23
e. of a wise man   BLAKE 87:9
harmful than reasoned e.   HUXL 269:11
her share some female e.   POPE 380:33
errs: He seldom e.   HOME 253:23
Erst: E. kommt das Fressen   BREC 91:25
erstwhile: my e. dear   MILL 340:1
erthe: This litel spot of e.   CHAU 144:18
erubuit: et e.   CRAS 169:2
erudite: e. Verger translated   BARH 33:7
erump: evade,—e.   HOLM 253:19
erupit: evasit, e.   CIC 151:27
eruption: This bodes some strange e.
                                    SHAK 429:10
es: je te dirai ce que tu e.   BRIL 93:9
Esau: E. my brother is a hairy   BIBLE 46:15
E. selleth his birthright   BIBLE 46:12
E. was a cunning hunter   BIBLE 46:13
hands are the hands of E.   BIBLE 46:16
escadrons: gros e. contre les petits
                                    BUSS 117:7
escalier: L'esprit de l'e.   DID 184:6
escape: Beauty for some provides e.
                                    HUXL 269:1
e. from emotion   ELIOT 205:18
E. me? Never   BROW 101:30
guilty persons e. than one innocent
                                    BLAC 85:6
help those we love to e.   HUGEL 267:5
let me ever e. them   PRAY 399:10
Let no guilty man e.   GRANT 234:3
make our e. into the calm   HUME 268:2
Man may e. from rope   GAY 222:30
What struggle to e.   KEATS 291:3
escaped: e. the shipwreck of time
                                    BACON 24:18
e. with the skin of my   BIBLE 52:29
is e. even as a bird out   PRAY 398:14
that out of battle I e.   OWEN 367:6
through language and e.   BROW 104:8
Eschew: E. evil   PRAY 391:23
escondida: la e. senda   LUIS 320:12
Eseln: Reichtum den grossen E.   LUTH 320:14
Eskdale: E. and Liddesdale   SCOTT 418:24
espaces: ces e. infinis m'effraie PASC 369:7
espagnol: Je parle e. à Dieu   CHAR 140:31
Esperance: E.! Percy   SHAK 440:20
Stands still in e.   SHAK 455:5

espousèd: Methought I saw my late e.
  Saint   MILT 351:12
My fairest, my e.   MILT 348:14
esprit: de l'e. pour être auteur   LA B 306:12
d'e. et les grands n'ont   LA B 306:14
jamais approché de mon e.   METT 338:10
L'e. de l'escalier   DID 184:6
l'e. et dans le coeur comme   LA R 310:17
esprits: favorise que les e. préparés
    PAST 369:16
essays: My e.   BACON 25:17
worse e. prov'd thee my   SHAK 495:3
Esse: E. quam videri bonus malebat
    SALL 413:24
essence: e. of war is violence   MAC 323:8
History is the e. of innumerable   CARL 131:9
purest e. of a human soul   CARL 132:29
uncompounded is their e. pure...   MILT 345:15
Essene: E., Erastian Whig   CHES 146:27
Essentially: E. I integrate the current
    BETJ 42:14
Music is e. useless   SANT 414:3
established: e. injustices are sanctioned
    FRAN 217:25
so sure e.   PRAY 384:8
estate: condescend to men of low e.
    BIBLE 75:17
e. by the same occupation   BUNY 107:13
e. Christ adorned   PRAY 388:25
e. of the Catholick Church   PRAY 385:25
e. o' the world were now   SHAK 463:7
has become a fourth e.   MAC 323:7
low e. of his handmaiden   BIBLE 69:5
mind, body, or e.   PRAY 386:1
order'd their e.   ALEX 3:14
relief of man's e.   BACON 24:17
esteemed: they e. themselves rich MAC 323:26
we e. him not   BIBLE 59:21
esthetic: mystery of e. like that JOYCE 286:18
estimate: enough thou know'st thy e.
    SHAK 494:13
larger than Man can ever e.   AUDEN 18:8
estranging: e. sea   ARN 13:13
estribo: Puesto ya el pie en el e.   CERV 139:2
esuriens: Graeculus e.   JUV 287:16
Esurientes: E. implevit bonis   BIBLE 83:18
esurienti: e. te inferebatur sol et   AUG 21:13
établies: sanction des injustices é.
    FRAN 217:25
État: L'É. c'est moi   LOUI 318:8
ete: appetit hath he to e. a mous   CHAU 142:25
éteint: petite flamme qui ne s'é.   REN 405:13
eternal: draw near to their e. home
    WALL 562:9
e. in the heavens   BIBLE 77:6
E. Passion   ARN 14:3
e. separation which we   STER 520:11
e. silence of these infinite   PASC 369:7
E. summer gilds them yet   BYRON 122:32
e. summer shall not fade   SHAK 492:28
Grant them e. rest   MASS 334:17
Hope springs e.   POPE 379:5
keeps e. whisperings around   KEATS 292:2
lose not the things e.   PRAY 386:16
portion of the E.   SHEL 499:19
swear an e. friendship   CANN 130:4
think ye have e. life   BIBLE 72:3
This way for e. suffering   DANTE 171:3
to be boy e.   SHAK 491:7
eternally: all things abided e.   TRAH 551:19
eternities: on the meeting of two e.
    THOR 550:9
Seasons; not E.   MER 337:9
eternity: ages Of e.   CARN 132:33
day joins the past E.   BYRON 121:4
E. in an hour   BLAKE 85:8
E. is in love with   BLAKE 88:17
E. shut in a span   CRAS 169:8
E.'s too short   ADD 2:20
E.! thou pleasing   ADD 1:24

E. was in that moment   CONG 160:23
E. was in our lips   SHAK 421:26
from here to E.   KIPL 299:10
Heads Were toward E.   DICK 183:16
hid battlements of E.   THOM 548:20
I gave you e. in a single   SHAW 496:29
image of e.   BYRON 121:26
intimates e. to man   ADD 1:24
I saw E. the other night   VAUG 555:22
Lives in E.'s sunrise   BLAKE 86:18
make us heirs of all e.   SHAK 456:14
one equal e.   DONNE 191:3
Passing through nature to e.   SHAK 429:24
same sweet e. of love   HERR 249:9
sells e. to get a toy   SHAK 492:18
Silence is deep as E.   CARL 131:13
Silence is of E.   CARL 132:3
skill'd to sing of Time or E.   TENN 533:12
Some shadows of e.   VAUG 555:15
That opes the palace of E.   MILT 340:24
thievish progress to e.   SHAK 494:10
time without injuring e.   THOR 550:3
white radiance of E.   SHEL 499:26
Who can speak of e. without   BROW 96:10
yet this great wink of e.   CRANE 168:31
eternize: your virtues rare shall e.
    SPEN 515:20
ETERNO: ME SI VA NELL' E. DOLORE
    DANTE 171:3
ether: ampler e.   WORD 578:3
farthest bottle labelled 'E.   BROW 100:7
etherized: Like a patient e. upon
    ELIOT 203:17
ethics: they drew a system of e.   MAC 324:3
Ethiop: Juno but an E. were   SHAK 457:5
Ethiopian: Can the E. change his skin
    BIBLE 60:22
ethnology: e., what not...   BROW 99:9
etiquette: It isn't e. to cut any   CARR 136:10
Where e. prevents me from   SMITH 512:4
étoile: Ma seule é. est morte   NERV 360:26
Eton: during the holidays from E.
    SITW 508:15
playing fields of E.   WELL 567:24
étrange: C'est une é. entreprise   MOL 353:7
étrangers: Plus je vis d'é.   BELL 40:17
étranglés: é. avec les boyaux des   MESL 338:9
Etrurian: where th' E. shades   MILT 345:13
Ettrick: E. and Teviotdale   SCOTT 418:24
Euclid: E. alone has looked   MILL 339:28
fifth proposition of E.   DOYLE 192:28
Eugene: our good Prince E.   SOUT 513:19
Eugene Aram: E., though a thief
    CALV 127:27
Eugenia: Listen, E.   ARN 14:3
eunuch: intellectual e. Castlereagh
    BYRON 122:4
Though Argus were her e.   SHAK 456:27
Time's e.   HOPK 257:3
To be a kind of moral e.   SHEL 502:18
euonymus: Her father's e. shines   BETJ 44:7
Eureka: E.! (I've got it   ARCH 11:23
Euripides: middle-age I preferred E.
    COL 158:6
Europe: are going out all over E.
    GREY 236:19
Better fifty years of E.   TENN 539:9
E. is disclosed as a prone   HARDY 239:13
E. is the less   DONNE 190:20
E. made his woe her own   ARN 13:9
glory of E. is extinguished   BURKE 111:9
noblest river in E.   ADD 2:19
of the community of E.   GLAD 229:18
of the community of E.   SAL 413:19
where will E.'s latter hour   ARN 13:18
Europeans: You are learned E.   MASS 335:15
Eurydice: His half regain'd E.   MILT 343:1
Euston: flushpots of E. and the hanging
    JOYCE 286:5
three in E. waiting-room   CORN 162:20

evade: Fear wist not to e.   THOM 548:11
Evae: clamamus exsules filii E.   ANON 10:19
Evangelist: lips of that E.   TENN 536:18
evangelists: prophets; and some, e.
    BIBLE 77:28
evaporate: making all disagreeables e.
    KEATS 293:18
evasion: admirable e. of whoremaster
  man   SHAK 453:11
evasit: e., erupit   CIC 151:27
Eve: banished children of E.   ANON 10:19
close at the ear of E.   MILT 348:10
E. from his side arose   ANON 8:21
E., with her basket   HODG 252:4
fairest of her daughters E.   MILT 347:24
fallen sons of E.   CHES 147:23
from e. and morning   HOUS 263:16
past E. and Adam's   JOYCE 286:2
pensive E.   COLL 158:17
thro' the land at e. we   TENN 541:28
to E.: Be soon   THOM 548:12
When E. upon the first   HOOD 255:3
eve-jar: spins the brown e.   MER 337:3
Evelyn: E. Hope is dead   BROW 100:25
Even: (E. as you and I)   KIPL 303:3
last pale beam of e.   SHEL 504:7
E. is coming   HOUS 266:4
When the grey-hooded E.   MILT 340:30
Would God it were e.   BIBLE 48:27
evening: autumn e.   ARN 14:8
bright exhalation in the e.   SHAK 447:7
e. and the morning were   BIBLE 45:1
e. full of the linnet's   YEATS 585:11
E. must usher night   SHEL 499:14
e. of my age   ROWE 410:20
e. star is coming   VIRG 560:9
e. withhold not thine hand   BIBLE 56:8
ever went with e. dress   KIPL 303:2
hands be an e. sacrifice   PRAY 399:9
in the e. it is cut down   PRAY 395:18
into the corners of the e.   ELIOT 203:18
It is a beauteous e.   WORD 581:18
Of grateful e. mild   MILT 348:5
undrugged in e. light the decent   CHES 147:12
When e. shuts   BROW 104:6
When it is e.   BIBLE 66:31
When the e. is spread out   ELIOT 203:17
winter e. settles down   ELIOT 204:7
worse at arriving in the e.   CONN 161:14
yet the E. listens   KEATS 292:5
evenings: still recall those e. when
    AUDEN 20:19
evening-star: over there the red e. is
    VIRG 560:11
evensong: e. Of joy illimited   HARDY 239:7
evensong: belles ringeth to e.   HAWES 243:3
event: had over-prepared the e.   POUND 383:20
halves of one august e.   HARDY 239:6
How much the greatest e.   FOX 217:19
hurries to the main e.   HOR 257:20
One e. happeneth to them   BIBLE 55:1
events: coming e. cast their shadows
    CAMP 128:24
e. in the womb of time   SHAK 474:11
that e. have controlled me   LINC 315:1
ever: beauty is a joy for e.   KEATS 288:20
continue thine for e.   FRAY 388:21
e. thus with simple folk   GILB 229:10
e. wilt thou love   KEATS 291:5
hereafter for e. hold his peace   PRAY 389:2
houses shall continue for e.   PRAY 392:28
Is seldom, if e. done   COW 163:20
Mary e. Virgin   MASS 334:15
mercy endureth for e.   PRAY 399:2
not be destroyed for e.   ANON 11:4
punctually come for e. and ever   WHIT 571:4
Round the world for e.   ARN 13:6
that I could last for e.   CONR 161:12
things to last for e.   HOR 261:15
ever-burning: Berenice's e. hair   CHAP 140:4

ever-fixed: it is an e. mark   SHAK 495:5
everlasting: believeth on me hath e. life
   BIBLE 72:7
caught An e. cold   WEBS 567:15
come unto thy e. kingdom   PRAY 388:22
e. watch and moveless   BROW 98:8
e. fire   HOUS 265:4
hath made his e. mansion   SHAK 486:14
have e. life   BIBLE 71:38
life e.   PRAY 384:26
stood from e. to everlasting   TRAH 551:18
Thy e. mercy   MAS 333:26
underneath are the e. arms   BIBLE 48:33
will give them an e. name   BIBLE 60:1
everlastingness: Bright shoots of e.
   VAUG 555:16
evermore: Nameless here for e.   POE 375:5
name liveth for e.   BIBLE 63:26
this time forth for e.   PRAY 398:10
ever-present: e. Deity   BRON 93:19
every: e. blessed thing you hold   GILB 225:30
e. common bush afire   BROW 97:33
e. rood of ground maintain'd   GOLD 230:18
e.—single—one—of—them   KIPL 300:3
e. thing there is a season   BIBLE 55:12
in e. way   COUE 163:8
everybody: e. says I'm such a disagreeable
   GILB 228:26
He who praises e. praises   JOHN 277:18
that e. wants to have read   TWAIN 554:25
Everyman: E., I will go with thee   ANON 5:6
everyone: tombola shakes up e.'s name
   HOR 260:14
Everything: E. has been said   LA B 306:11
e. in the world is good   DRYD 197:28
E. must be like something   FORS 216:23
Greek can do e.   JUV 287:16
make myself laugh at e.   BEAU 35:15
making e. the concern of all   SOLZ 513:1
sans e.   SHAK 425:24
spirit of youth in e.   SHAK 494:17
stronger by e. you see   STER 519:27
They told me I was e.   SHAK 455:15
We can't all do e.   VIRG 560:6
everywhere: his behaviour e.   SHAK 465:24
Out of the e. into here   MACD 325:2
which the centre is e.   ANON 7:27
evidence: e. against their own
  understanding   HAL 237:23
e. of things not seen   BIBLE 79:31
'it's not e.   DICK 182:22
Some circumstantial e.   THOR 550:24
We had e. and no doubt   ELIOT 203:15
evil: afraid to speak e. of dignities BIBLE 81:1
All partial e.   POPE 379:11
all that we are e.   SHAK 453:11
because the days are e.   BIBLE 78:4
because their deeds were e.   BIBLE 71:39
confusion that wish me e.   PRAY 394:15
deliver us from e.   BIBLE 64:24
doeth e. hath not seen God   BIBLE 81:8
done e. to his neighbour   PRAY 390:4
done this e. in thy sight   PRAY 393:4
enslaved which serve things e.   SHEL 503:9
Eschew e.   PRAY 391:23
e. and adulterous generation   BIBLE 66:11
E. be thou my Good   MILT 347:16
E. be to him who evil thinks   ANON 9:6
E. communications corrupt   BIBLE 76:25
e. is wrought by want   HOOD 254:20
e. manners live in brass   SHAK 447:20
e. news rides post   MILT 350:28
e., that good may come   BIBLE 74:37
e. that men do lives after   SHAK 450:17
e. which I would not   BIBLE 75:5
fall'n on e. days   MILT 348:28
Few and e. have the days   BIBLE 46:38
God by curse Created e.   MILT 346:23
it is an unruly e.   BIBLE 80:14
it would be an e. still   MILL 339:9

know all the e. he does   LA R 310:14
knowing good and e.   BIBLE 45:15
knowledge of good and e.   BIBLE 45:8
man's heart is e. from his youth BIBLE 45:36
may know to refuse the e.   BIBLE 58:3
money is the root of all e.   BIBLE 79:18
must return good for e.   VANB 555:4
notorious e. liver   PRAY 387:5
Not rendering evil for e.   BIBLE 80:30
Obscures the show of e.   SHAK 467:10
on the e. and on the good   BIBLE 64:19
overcome e. with good   BIBLE 75:19
predicted e. consequences   TROL 553:5
punishment in itself is e.   BENT 40:27
Resist not e.   BIBLE 64:17
rewarded me e. for good   PRAY 391:24
shall no e. happen unto thee   PRAY 395:22
Shall there be e. in a city   BIBLE 61:19
still to find means of e.   MILT 345:6
Sufficient unto the day is the e. BIBLE 64:32
unto them that call e. good   BIBLE 57:26
what all the blessed E.'s   BROW 99:8
Whenever God prepares e.   ANON 10:1
whose cause this e. is   BIBLE 61:21
withstand in the e. day   BIBLE 78:10
evils: e. and the worst of crimes   SHAW 497:6
e. the lesser is always   THOM 546:15
it the least of all e.   BACON 27:40
let us make imaginary e.   GOLD 232:12
live only by fighting e.   BERL 41:23
only one cure for the e.   MAC 323:24
remedies must expect new e.   BACON 26:28
they are necessary e.   JOHN 282:14
When e. are most free   SHAK 449:7
evil-speaking: my tongue from e.
   PRAY 388:17
evince: always e. its propriety   AUST 23:25
ev'ning: us welcome peaceful e. COWP 167:11
evolution: e. in the mother's shadow
   AUDEN 19:10
E.—a change from an indefinite SPEN 514:29
in the e. of his thought   ARN 16:11
ewe: Is tupping your white e.   SHAK 473:16
Whereof the e. not bites   SHAK 485:23
ewer: safe in a golden e.   BROW 100:4
ewes: My e. breed not   BARN 34:4
ewige: E. Friede ist ein Traum   MOLT 354:4
ewigkeit: Afay in de e.   LEL 313:17
exact: greatness not to be e.   BURKE 109:3
writing an e. man   BACON 27:20
exactitude: L'e. est la politesse des
   LOUI 318:11
exactness: with e. grinds He all LOGAU 316:5
exaggeration: report of my death was
  an e.   TWAIN 554:22
exalt: e. himself shall be abased   BIBLE 67:23
e. us unto the same place   PRAY 386:13
exalted: be e. among the heathen
   PRAY 392:21
Every valley shall be e.   BIBLE 59:5
e. them of low degree   BIBLE 69:6
God hath also highly e.   BIBLE 78:14
Sorrow proud to be e. so   ANON 6:7
exalteth: e. himself shall be abased
   BIBLE 70:9
exalts: how love e. the mind   DRYD 195:33
what man Does which e. him   BROW 105:2
Examinations: E. are formidable even
   COLT 159:9
Examine: E. me   PRAY 391:4
e. my thoughts   PRAY 399:8
e. well your blood   SHAK 469:17
example: don't set us a good e. WILDE 572:25
error by the same e.   SHAK 468:3
E. is always more efficacious JOHN 282:10
E. is the school of mankind   BURKE 112:7
save Europe by her e.   PITT 374:5
examples: History is philosophy from
  e.   DION 184:9
exaudi: e. vocem meam   BIBLE 83:13

exceed: e. all that we can desire   PRAY 386:18
reach should e. his grasp   BROW 98:24
exceedingly: You're e. polite   GILB 228:1
excel: methods different men e.   CHUR 148:23
so great as daring to e.   CHUR 148:21
thou shalt not e.   BIBLE 46:39
'tis useless to e.   LYTT 321:22
excellence: Drear all this e.   POUND 383:19
ne'er will reach an e.   DRYD 197:34
so nearly allied to e.   GOLD 232:8
excellent: e. things are spoken   PRAY 395:16
e. thing in woman   SHAK 456:10
his Name only is e.   PRAY 399:23
is too wonderful and e.   PRAY 399:5
Nature never makes e. things LOCKE 315:14
Then learning is most e.   FOOTE 216:8
excellently: e. bright   JONS 283:24
excelling: preference and distinction of
  e.   CONG 159:29
excels: She e. each mortal thing   SHAK 491:4
Excelsior: strange device, e. !   LONG 316:14
excelsis: Gloria in e. Deo   MASS 334:18
Except: E. the Lord build the house
   PRAY 398:18
e. the present company   OKEE 365:2
excess: carried to e. are wrong   CHUR 149:16
Give me e. of it   SHAK 487:20
Nothing in e.   ANON 9:22
road of e. leads   BLAKE 88:13
so much poverty and e.   PENN 371:14
Such an e. of stupidity   JOHN 275:7
through e. of wisdom is made EMER 207:18
wasteful and ridiculous e.   SHAK 452:25
excessit: e., evasit   CIC 151:27
excessive: right of an e. wrong BROW 104:23
exchange: By just e. one   SIDN 507:16
e. of two fantasies   CHAM 139:15
not e. for the treasures   GIBB 224:6
Exchequer Bond: In a five per cent E.
   ELIOT 202:4
Exciseman: de'il's awa wi' th'E.
   BURNS 113:13
excitability: mischievous e. is the most
   BAG 28:20
excite: actresses e. my amorous JOHN 274:2
fashion must e. your languid GILB 227:23
excitin: too e.' to be pleasant DICK 181:34
exciting: He found it less e.   GILB 225:17
exclamation: Ethelberta breathed a sort
  of e.   HARDY 241:14
excoluere: Inventas aut qui vitam e.
   VIRG 558:23
excommunicate: nor be outlawed, nor
  e.   COKE 154:24
excrement: place of e.   YEATS 584:19
excrucior: sed fieri sentio et e.   CAT 137:14
Excudent: E. alii spirantia mollius
   VIRG 559:1
Excursion: call'd the 'E.'   BYRON 123:6
excursions: consist of e. in my own mind
   COL 157:29
excus'd: e. his devilish deeds   MILT 347:27
excuse: consent began to make e. BIBLE 70:10
denial vain, and coy e.   MILT 343:3
if you'll e. my having   SHAW 498:21
I will not e.   GARR 221:17
knavery and folly to e.   CHUR 149:9
not a single e.   KIPL 300:21
plead that man's e.   ANON 7:24
prove an e. for the glass   SHER 506:31
that with this strange e: AUDEN 19:8
execrable: e. shape   MILT 346:25
execute: hand to e.   JUN 287:5
executing: thought-e. fires   SHAK 454:4
execution: effective as their stringent
  e.   GRANT 233:22
e. confined   SHAK 486:33
e. than for counsel   BACON 27:39
Which smok'd with bloody e.   SHAK 458:3

Executioner: yet I am mine own *E.*
DONNE 190:19

executive: is nominated by the e. GIBB 224:22
executors: Delivering o'er to e. pale
SHAK 443:9
Let's choose e. SHAK 479:10
exegi: Iamque opus e. OVID 366:19
exemplaria: Vos e. Graeca HOR 257:22
exemplars: pages of your Greek e.
HOR 257:22
Exempt: E. from awe SHEL 503:12
exercise: e. myself in great matters
PRAY 398:25
mind what e. is to the body STEE 518:9
on e. depend DRYD 196:5
sad mechanic e. TENN 536:1
exercises: He e. of his brains GILB 226:8
exertions: saved herself by her e. PITT 374:5
exhalation: fall Like a bright e. SHAK 447:7
Rose like an e. MILT 346:2
exhaled: through a pipe and e. in a pun'
LAMB 308:11
exhaust: e. the realm of the possible
PIND 373:15
exhibited: by being publicly e. ALB 3:7
exile: bind your sons to e. KIPL 304:6
journey to endless e. HOR 260:7
Troy came destined an e. VIRG 557:8
exiles: we are e. from our fathers' GALT 221:2
Which none save e. feel AYT 24:5
exist: Art and Science cannot e. BLAKE 86:7
dreamed of good shall e. BROW 98:19
impression that we e. BECK 36:16
She may still e. in undiminished MAC 323:16
should be presumed to e. OCCAM 364:19
we do e. and cease to be SHAK 453:3
Why do you and I e. JOHN 278:5
existence: detail the struggle for e.
DARW 171:26
E. saw him spurn her bounded JOHN 282:25
Let us contemplate e. DICK 179:8
loving longest, when e. AUST 23:10
our e. as a nation PITT 374:4
prefer mere e. to honour JUV 287:25
'Tis woman's whole e. BYRON 122:14
Exit: E., pursued by a bear SHAK 491:16
exits: men to take their e. WEBS 566:26
their e. and their entrances SHAK 425:24
exorciser: No e. harm thee SHAK 428:22
Exoriare: E. aliquis nostris ex ossibus
VIRG 558:15
expands: Work e. so as to fill PARK 369:1
expatiates: Rests and e. in a life POPE 379:5
Expect: E. him not in the just HOUS 265:18
know more of mankind I e. JOHN 279:12
expectancy: e. and rose of the fair
SHAK 433:15
expectation: dream and a folly of e.
BROW 97:21
e. whirls me round SHAK 486:32
indeed better bettered e. SHAK 471:25
now sits E. in the air SHAK 443:12
expectations: worthy ends and e. BACON 26:4
expected: reasonable man could have
e. HERB 246:19
they may reasonably be e. WHAT 569:13
what we least e. generally DISR 186:10
expecto: e. resurrectionem mortuorum
MASS 334:20
expects: e. his evening prey GRAY 234:16
expedient: all things are not e. BIBLE 76:10
consider that it is e. for us BIBLE 72:24
e. for you that I go away BIBLE 72:38
may be most e. for them PRAY 385:8
principle, but an e. DISR 184:15
expéditif: C'est une homme e. MOL 353:21
expedition: abandoning the e. DOUG 191:8
expeditious: He's an e. man MOL 353:21
expellas: Naturam e. furca HOR 258:18
Expende: E. Hannibalem JUV 288:1

expenditure: annual e. nineteen nineteen
DICK 177:4
expense: drinking at somebody else's
e. LEIGH 313:15
e. of spirit in a waste SHAK 495:7
Would be at the e. of two CLOU 153:25
expenses: meet all the e. of living
THOR 550:13
expensive: Everything in Rome is e.
JUV 287:19
love fruit when it's e. PIN 373:17
experience: acquist Of true e. MILT 351:4
are perfected by e. BACON 27:17
contrary to custom and e. HUME 267:21
dirty nurse, E. TENN 534:35
e. find those words mis-plac'd CONG 160:27
E. is the child of Thought DISR 186:41
E. is never limited JAMES 271:11
E. is the name every one WILDE 573:14
E. though noon auctoritee CHAU 143:16
E. teaches slowly FROU 219:19
here can go beyond his e. LOCKE 315:15
I have e. CONG 160:33
knowledge too but recorded e. CARL 131:8
light which e. gives COL 157:20
of trying every e. once ANON 4:24
part of e. BACON 27:27
reality of e. JOYCE 286:19
reporting device for e. WHORF 571:23
sometimes worth a life's e. HOLM 253:21
Then Old Age, and E. ROCH 406:22
Till old e. do attain MILT 342:11
To a great e. one thing BAG 29:14
triumph of hope over e. JOHN 275:36
Yet all e. is an arch wherethro' Gleams
TENN 543:22
experienced: becomes real till it is e.
KEATS 294:18
Experientia: E. does it DICK 177:1
experiment: full tide of successful e.
JEFF 272:7
social and economic e. HOOV 255:24
tried an e. in his life DARW 172:2
expers: Vis consili e. mole ruit HOR 260:23
expert: e. is one who knows more
BUTL 117:13
to those who are e. at it HOR 259:6
Experto: E. credite VIRG 559:10
experts: you never should trust e. SAL 413:18
expiate: death my days should e. SHAK 493:1
expire: I tremble, I e. SHEL 500:13
expires: e., too soon, too soon CONR 161:24
wretched child e. BELL 39:2
expiring: accents of an e. saint STER 520:9
thus e. do foretell SHAK 478:19
explain: e. all the poems that ever
CARR 135:23
'I can't e. *myself* CARR 133:21
Never complain and never e. DISR 185:30
spoil it by trying to e. SHER 506:20
unwilling to e. FROST 218:27
would e. his explanation BYRON 122:3
explaining: e. a passage in the game-act
STEE 517:23
explanations: I do loathe e. BARR 34:12
expletives: While e. their feeble aid
POPE 378:20
exploded: dust of e. beliefs MADAN 326:18
exploding: poets e. like bombs AUDEN 20:16
exploit: dignity compos'd and high e.
MILT 346:9
exploration: shall not cease from e.
ELIOT 203:2
explorers: endeavours are unlucky e.
DOUG 191:8
Explosionsstoff: als einen furchtbaren
E. NIET 363:5
explosive: terrible e. in the presence
NIET 363:5

explosives: You darent handle high e.
SHAW 497:14
export: integrate the current e. BETJ 42:14
exposed: been much e. to authors
WELL 567:29
intellect is improperly e. SMITH 511:5
exposes: e. himself when he is intoxicated
JOHN 278:8
exposition: e. of sleep come upon me
SHAK 471:5
exposure: unseemly e. of the mind
HAZL 243:26
express: e. image of his person BIBLE 79:28
e. our wants as to conceal GOLD 232:5
e. the images of their BACON 27:4
e. train drew up there THOM 547:16
To e. what then I saw WORD 577:4
What I can ne'er e. BYRON 121:22
which a picture cannot e. BACON 25:27
express'd: ne'er so well e. POPE 378:17
expresser: was a most gentle e. of it
HEM 245:2
expresses: 'If this young man e. himself
GILB 227:21
expressible: e. as a sum of two cubes
RAM 404:22
expression: e. of no-encouragement
BRAM 91:19
have not the e. in English ARN 16:4
His e. may often be called ARN 16:7
impassioned e. WORD 583:9
indolent e. and an undulating BELL 40:2
not the e. of personality ELIOT 205:18
vulgar e. of the passion CONG 159:22
expressive: Eyes too e. to be blue ARN 13:4
expressure: e. of his eye SHAK 488:23
expung'd: works to me e. and raz'd
MILT 347:8
exquisite: e. touch SCOTT 418:37
Exsilium: E. impositura cumbae HOR 260:7
extant: be but pyramidally e. BROW 97:15
story is e. SHAK 434:14
extend: let e. thy mind o'er all MILT 350:7
extension: L'e. des privilèges des
FOUR 217:18
extenuate: nothing e. SHAK 477:23
extenuates: e. not wrong SHAK 486:31
extinct: purpose of becoming e. CUPPY 170:15
Extinction: of Character and the E.
DARW 171:28
extinguished: glory of Europe is e.
BURKE 111:9
One e. family waits BETJ 43:9
sometimes overcome, seldom e.
BACON 26:36
extinguishes: wind e. candles LA R 310:15
extirpate: To e. the vipers AYT 24:6
extol: e. Him first, him last MILT 348:16
extracts: e. made of them by others
BACON 27:15
extraordinary: behaving in this e. manner
STOP 523:14
most e. man in Europe STIL 523:14
'this is an e. man JOHN 279:15
extravagance: beautiful does not lead
to e. PER 372:23
extravagancies: undisgraced by those
e. CHES 145:24
extravagant: e. with his own SALL 413:22
e. and irrational which SWIFT 526:8
extreme: e. to mark what is done
PRAY 398:23
where th' e. of vice POPE 379:1
extremes: e. by change more fierce
MILT 346:22
'E. meet' HOOD 255:17
mean between the two e. PRAY 384:7
show his judgement) in e. DRYD 194:14
toil in other men's e. KYD 306:14
two e. appear like man CHUR 149:14

extricate: is unable to e. himself　ADD 2:24
exuitur: cupido gloriae novissima e.
　　　　　　　　　　　　　TAC 531:14
exuletur: utlagetur, aut e.　MAGN 327:2
Exult: E. O shores　WHIT 570:8
　Our souls e.　BLAKE 86:12
exultations: e., agonies, And love
　　　　　　　　　　　　　WORD 582:17
exulting: people all e.　WHIT 570:7
exuvias: redit e. indutus Achilli　VIRG 558:5
eye: apple of his e.　BIBLE 48:30
　auspicious and one dropping e.　SHAK 429:19
　beard and glittering e.　COL 155:5
　bought by judgment of the e.　SHAK 456:20
　brought an e. for all he saw　TENN 537:8
　Cast a cold e.　YEATS 587:10
　custom loathsome to the e.　JAM 271:3
　every e. shall see him　BIBLE 81:10
　e. begins to see　BRON 93:21
　E. for eye　BIBLE 47:25
　e. full of gentle salutations　STER 520:9
　E., gazelle　SPEN 515:14
　e. is not satisfied with　BIBLE 55:7
　e. of heaven to garnish　SHAK 452:25
　e. of man hath not heard　SHAK 471:10
　e. of peninsulas and islands　CAT 136:28
　e. sinks inward　ARN 12:22
　e. the unconquered flame　POUND 382:14
　e. whose bend doth awe　SHAK 448:15
　fettered to her e.　LOV 318:15
　fringed curtains of thine e.　SHAK 485:1
　glass to his sightless e.　NEWB 361:4
　got into this e. of mine　STER 520:10
　great e. of heaven shined　SPEN 516:2
　harvest of a quiet e.　WORD 580:5
　heavenly rhetoric of thine e.　SHAK 457:4
　He had but one e.　DICK 179:35
　he that made the e.　PRAY 396:2
　his e. was backward cast　SPEN 516:6
　hooded e.　THOM 548:2
　hot the e. of heaven　SHAK 492:28
　If thine e. offend thee　BIBLE 67:5
　I have neither e. to see　LENT 313:23
　immortal hand or e.　BLAKE 87:14
　inward e. 'tis an old Man　BLAKE 86:14
　is in thy brother's e.　BIBLE 64:34
　learning more than the fond e.　SHAK 466:19
　Lesbia hath a beaming e.　MOORE 356:11
　Lock'd up from mortal e.　CRAS 169:15
　man has cast a longing e.　JEFF 272:11
　mild and magnificent e.　BROW 102:5
　mine e. may be deceiv'd　SHAK 494:18
　neither a wit in his own e.　CONG 160:11
　not thro', the e.　BLAKE 85:23
　now mine e. seeth thee　BIBLE 53:12
　On it may stay his e.　HERB 247:18
　Russian e. Is underlined　ELIOT 205:14
　saving those that e. thee　SHAK 428:4
　seeing e.　BIBLE 54:18
　sniv'ling and piping your e.　DIBD 175:19
　still-soliciting e.　SHAK 453:6
　Then can I drown an e.　SHAK 493:7
　There's language in her e.　SHAK 487:13
　they shall see eye to e.　BIBLE 59:19
　Thou E. among the blind　WORD 579:7
　thoughts are legible in the e.　ROYD 411:2
　through the e. of a needle　BIBLE 67:11
　turned his blindest e.　CHES 146:21
　twinkling of an e.　BIBLE 76:29
　twinkling of an e.　PRAY 391:4
　Was never e.　ROYD 411:3
　watchful e. and the strong arm　PALM 368:10
　Who sees with equal e.　POPE 379:4
　'with his e. on the object'　ARN 16:12
　with his glittering e.　COL 155:6
　with its soft black e.　MOORE 356:25
eyeball: e. owns the mystic rod　BROW 105:14
　like a coal His e.　SMART 509:3
eye-balls: my e. roll　POPE 376:14

eyebrow: Made to his mistress' e.
　　　　　　　　　　　　　SHAK 425:24
eyelashes: lose our teeth and e.　LEAR 312:24
Eyeless: E. in Gaza　MILT 350:14
eyelids: e. are a little weary　PATER 369:18
　her e. many Graces sate　SPEN 516:11
　marble e. are not wet　BROW 98:8
　Than tir'd e. upon tir'd　TENN 539:13
　wilt weigh mine e. down　SHAK 441:29
　With e. heavy and red　HOOD 255:6
eyes: approach it with e.　YEATS 587:14
　asked him with my e.　JOYCE 286:30
　at times my e. are lenses　DOUG 191:7
　audience look to their e.　SHAK 469:25
　beams from happy human e.　STEV 523:11
　because you'll wear your e.　ZOLA 588:19
　bein' only e.　DICK 182:23
　black e. and lemonade　MOORE 356:3
　Blessed are the e. which　BIBLE 69:29
　bright e. Rain influence　MILT 342:25
　brightness in their failing e.　BLUN 89:2
　brown of her—her e.　MEW 338:12
　Closed his e. in endless　GRAY 235:19
　close your e. with holy　COL 157:1
　cocking their medical e.　DICK 183:11
　cold commemorative e.　ROSS 410:5
　cynosure of neighbouring e.　MILT 342:20
　death bandaged my e.　BROW 103:32
　deep upon her peerless e.　KEATS 291:15
　dry one's e.　BROW 102:1
　electrical skin and glaring e.　SMART 508:22
　e. above him with anxiety　TOCQ 551:8
　e. are quickened so with　GRAV 234:11
　e. did see Olivia first　SHAK 487:21
　e. have they　PRAY 397:18
　e. like lead　BROW 100:35
　E., look your last　SHAK 483:31
　e. of gold and bramble-dew　STEV 523:3
　E. of most unholy blue　MOORE 356:6
　e. purging thick amber　SHAK 432:8
　e. that had lightened　SWIN 529:19
　e., the break of day　SHAK 464:21
　e. the glow-worm lend thee　HERR 249:11
　e. the greenest of things　SWIN 529:16
　E. the shady night has　HOUS 263:2
　e. to behold the sun　BIBLE 56:9
　E. too expressive to be　ARN 13:4
　e. were as a flame of fire　BIBLE 81:14
　e. were blind with stars　HODG 252:8
　fair maidens Quiet e.　STEV 523:2
　four beasts full of e.　BIBLE 81:23
　friend to close his e.　DRYD 195:3
　from star-like e.　CAREW 130:12
　From women's e. this doctrine　SHAK 457:6
　From women's e. this doctrine　SHAK 457:9
　Gasp and Stretch one's E.　BELL 39:7
　gaze not in my e.　HOUS 262:21
　Get thee glass e.　SHAK 455:21
　God be in my e.　ANON 5:9
　greater cats with golden e.　SACK 412:26
　hair the e. of Day　SHEL 505:3
　Hath not a Jew e.　SHAK 467:4
　Have e. to wonder　SHAK 494:20
　Her e. are homes of silent　TENN 536:19
　her e. the gazers strike　POPE 380:32
　her e. were wild　KEATS 290:16
　Her e. were deeper than　ROSS 409:14
　he set her both his e.　LYLY 321:11
　his e. are bright with it　KEATS 294:17
　his e. became so terrible　BECK 36:19
　His e. drop out　LOCK 315:18
　I'd say I had e. again　SHAK 455:7
　I gave her e. my own eyes　BROW 102:2
　in it dazzled their e.　BALL 31:3
　is engender'd in the e.　SHAK 467:9
　is marvellous in our e.　PRAY 398:2
　I was e. to the blind　BIBLE 52:35
　lightened are our e.　SORL 513:10
　Look not in my e.　HOUS 262:21
　Love-darting e.　MILT 341:18

　Love in her sunny e. does　COWL 164:6
　Love looks not with the e.　SHAK 469:22
　lovers' e. are sharp　SCOTT 416:26
　lover's e. will gaze an eagle　SHAK 457:8
　make his e. grow in my brow　SHAK 421:32
　many e. as thou hast wounds　SHAK 450:9
　Men's e. were made to look　SHAK 483:2
　Mine e. are full of tears　SHAK 480:4
　Mine e. do itch　SHAK 477:1
　Mine e. have seen the glory　HOWE 266:19
　mock our e. with air　SHAK 423:7
　My mistress' e. are nothing　SHAK 495:8
　night has a thousand e.　BOUR 90:21
　Night hath a thousand e.　LYLY 321:15
　no eyes but constitutional e.　LINC 315:7
　no e., but fountains　KYD 306:3
　not proud of those two e.　HERR 250:1
　of one whose subdu'd e.　SHAK 477:23
　one, all e.　WORD 580:3
　open The king's e.　SHAK 447:1
　optics of these e. to behold　BROW 96:21
　Our gloom-pleas'd e.　KEATS 292:28
　pair of sparkling e.　GILB 225:26
　pearls that were his e.　SHAK 484:32
　scornful, yet with jealous e.　POPE 376:26
　see nothing with my e.　SAPP 414:6
　shut her wild, wild e.　KEATS 290:20
　Soft e. look'd love　BYRON 120:20
　stars! And all e. else　SHAK 492:10
　stuck in her face for e.　SHAK 456:27
　Suddenly discovering in the e.　POUND 383:14
　that your e. might be shining　LAWR 311:12
　that youth's e. burned　ROSS 410:2
　their e. are burning　AUDEN 20:5
　Their five e. smouldering　DE L 174:4
　therefore want no e.　SHAK 455:6
　they are hid from thy e.　BIBLE 71:3
　They have changed e.　SHAK 485:2
　They strike mine e.　JONS 283:27
　They were full of e. within　BIBLE 81:24
　thine e. like the fishpools　BIBLE 57:9
　things with his half-shut e.　POPE 381:7
　thou hast doves' e. within　BIBLE 56:26
　Thou turn'st mine e.　SHAK 435:9
　through another man's e.　SHAK 426:28
　to me only with thine e.　JONS 284:12
　Two grey e. with lids　SHAK 488:12
　We fix our e. upon his　JOHN 282:16
　what her e. enthral'd　CONG 160:2
　when unto dying e.　TENN 542:4
　wheresoe'er I turn my ravished e.　ADD 2:4
　Whose woollen e. looked　BETJ 44:9
　will trouble their e.　DONNE 190:23
　Will you put out mine e.　SHAK 452:24
　With e. up-rais'd　COLL 158:21
　with fortune and men's e.　SHAK 493:6
　world to turn thine e.　JOHN 282:29
　write the beauty of your e.　SHAK 492:27
　Your e. are lodestars　SHAK 469:21
　You see her e. are open　SHAK 462:19
eyeservice: with e., as menpleasers
　　　　　　　　　　　　　BIBLE 78:8

Faber: F. est suae quisque fortunae
　　　　　　　　　　　　　CLAU 152:26
fabill: that thai be nocht bot f.　BARB 33:3
fables: all the f. in the legend　BACON 25:22
　f., and dangerous deceits　PRAY 400:9
　F. and endless genealogies　BIBLE 79:6
　Hesperian f. true　MILT 347:19
　Than f. yet have feigned　MILT 346:23
fabric: baseless f. of this vision　SHAK 485:20
　out of the earth a f. huge　MILT 346:2
Fabula: F. narratur　HOR 261:22
fac: Dilige et quod vis f.　AUG 21:21
face: Am I in f. to-day　GOLD 232:21
　beautiful f. is a mute　PUBL 402:4
　Beauty's conquest of your f.　AUDEN 20:21
　blubber'd is that pretty f.　PRIOR 400:19
　born with a different f.　BLAKE 86:15
　can hear my Thisby's f.　SHAK 471:18

cheer our soiled f.	PRAY 400:5	owners of their f.	SHAK 494:15	fail'd: flutter'd and f. for breath	ARN 14:6
Communism with a human f.	DUBC 198:24	Private f. in public	AUDEN 20:12	failed: of their bodies have f.	BACON 27:4
construction in the f.	SHAK 458:22	slope of f.	COWP 167:15	tried a little, f. much	STEV 521:5
coolness plays upon his f.	ARN 12:22	so many millions of f.	BROW 96:31	faileth: f. now even dream	THOM 548:17
Cover her f.	WEBS 566:27	that their f. are wrinkled	SHAK 432:8	not when my strength f. me	PRAY 394:17
dew on the f. of the dead	BEERS 38:8	their f. washed	CARR 135:6	failing: she had one f.	BURNS 114:16
disasters in his morning f.	GOLD 231:2	we hid as it were our f.	BIBLE 59:21	failings: He had no f. which were	
dont quite match your f.	ASHF 17:7	facetious: to be f. it is not necessary			BURKE 109:8
everyone has the f. he deserves	ORW 365:18		ROG 407:13	faille: in certein he shal f.	CHAU 142:9
f. Bears a command	SHAK 427:26	faciesve: dices f. Minerva	HOR 258:5	nat o word wol he f.	CHAU 142:31
f. every difficulty except	WILDE 574:1	Facilis: F. descensus Averno	VIRG 558:18	failli: J'ai f. attendre	LOUI 318:10
f. of this congregation	PRAY 388:24	facilité: La vertue refuse la f.	MONT 354:24	fails: if another f.	BROW 105:7
f. that launch'd a thousand	MARL 329:10	facility: fatal f. of the octo-syllabic		life seemed meant for, f.	BROW 101:22
f. the index of a feeling	COWP 168:24		BYRON 121:29	when life f.	AUDEN 19:15
f. with their courtly foreign	TENN 543:4	facilius: f. se abstinent ut non	AUG 21:22	failure: f. of hope	GIBB 224:20
False f. must hide what	SHAK 459:12	Fact: fatal futility of F.	JAMES 271:19	success pays the f. of years	BROW 98:27
fa' your honest sonsie f.	BURNS 115:16	hypothesis by an ugly f.	HUXL 269:5	Women can't forgive f.	CHEK 145:1
flower-like f.	SWIN 530:15	irritable reaching after f.	KEATS 293:19	failures: f. in life arise from pulling	
fyr-reed cherubynnes f.	CHAU 142:4	Matters of f.	TIND 551:5		HARE 242:4
garden of your f.	HERB 246:20	push the logic of a f.	KIPL 299:5	has no conceivable f.	WHIT 571:11
glimpse of His bright f.	VAUG 555:14	story or records a f.	RUSK 411:21	fain: f. see good	PRAY 391:23
glory shineth in this f.	SHAK 480:5	was but A scientific f.	WILDE 572:12	f. wald lie down	BALL 31:5
God hath given you one f.	SHAK 433:13	were judges of f.	PULT 402:9	F. would I climb	RAL 404:14
good f. is a letter	ADD 2:15	when a f. appears opposed	DOYLE 192:5	We are f. of thee still	SWIN 529:8
hide us from the f.	BIBLE 81:30	faction: it made them a f.	MAC 324:17	which I would f. call master	SHAK 453:13
hid the f.	DRYD 196:7	name of a f.	JOHN 281:16	fainéant: f. government is not	TROL 553:4
his f. is all bubukles	SHAK 444:7	that the whisper of a f.	RUSS 412:18	faint: Beginning to f.	TENN 540:9
his natural f. in a glass	BIBLE 80:10	factions: good in canvasses and f.		eating hay when you're f.	CARR 135:31
his prism and silent f.	WORD 580:17		BACON 25:40	f. cold fear thrills through	SHAK 483:21
huge massy f.	MAC 324:7	religious f. are volcanoes	BURKE 111:32	f. heart ne'er wan	BURNS 115:14
languid patience of thy f.	COL 157:16	We cannot revive old f.	ELIOT 202:27	f. praises one another	WYCH 584:2
long wilt thou hide thy f.	PRAY 390:1	factious: would have knocked the f.		F., yet pursuing	BIBLE 49:18
Lord make his f. shine	BIBLE 48:9		JOHN 279:10	reap, if we f. not	BIBLE 77:20
mist in my f.	BROW 103:31	factitious: trout for f. bait	POUND 383:2	so f., so spiritless	SHAK 441:1
Moses hid his f.	BIBLE 47:5	Facts: F. are chiels that winna	BURNS 113:14	thoughts effeminate and f.	MARL 330:11
My f. is pink	ANON 7:2	facts are f. and flinch not	BROW 104:17	watching and with study f.	CHUR 149:1
not recognize me by my f.	TROL 552:11	Facts…F. alone are wanted	DICK 178:15	which the echo is not f.	LAND 309:8
of a plummet-measured f.	YEATS 587:2	F. were never pleasing	BARR 34:11	fainted: should utterly have f.	PRAY 391:9
Pity a human f.	BLAKE 88:7	imagination for his f.	SHER 506:36	we f. Alternately	AUST 22:24
sad swell'd f.	BARH 33:16	intelligent anticipation of f.	CURZ 170:17	Fainting: F. in Coils	CARR 134:11
seen God face to f.	BIBLE 46:25	is free but f. are sacred	SCOTT 415:15	faintly: teaches to deny that f. prays	
see ye have a singing f.	FLET 215:23	will give you all the f.	AUDEN 21:8		QUAR 403:17
seyn somtyme a pale f.	CHAU 142:14	faculties: each according to his f.	BAK 29:25	faints: sense f. picturing them	SHEL 502:10
'She has a lovely f.	TENN 538:12	f., Which sense may reach	DONNE 188:25	fair: anything to show more f.	WORD 581:14
shouldst never see my f. again	TENN 535:26	Hath borne his f. so meek	SHAK 459:6	art f.; thou art goodly	SWIN 528:22
Since first I saw your f.	ANON 7:15	His cogitative f. immers'd	CAREY 130:22	be a black man or a f.	ADD 2:7
sorrows of your changing f.	YEATS 587:12	faculty: creatures by the f. of laughter		brave deserves the f.	DRYD 194:23
spirit passed before my f.	BIBLE 52:15		ADD 2:26	could be f. and yet not fond	OXF 367:14
stamping on a human f.	ORW 365:14	faddling: f. hedonist	STEV 521:20	ever f. and never proud	SHAK 474:18
strong men stand face to f.	KIPL 297:27	fade: f. away into the forest	KEATS 291:18	every f. from fair sometime	SHAK 492:28
taking your f. in your hands	ANON 6:8	F. far away	KEATS 291:18	f. and fatal king	JOHN 273:23
then f. to face	BIBLE 76:14	f. into the light of common	WORD 579:5	f. and floral air	FLEC 214:6
There is a garden in her f.	CAMP 129:22	we all do f. as a leaf	BIBLE 60:12	f. and smell'st so sweet	SHAK 476:19
To prepare a f. to meet	ELIOT 203:19	faded: all his pictures f.	BLAKE 85:7	f. as an Italian sun	BANV 33:1
turn away thy f.	SHAK 452:6	f. away in a wall	BETJ 44:3	f. as the moon	BIBLE 57:5
turning your f. to the light	SASS 414:13	It f. on the crowing	SHAK 429:17	f. days will shine	GILB 228:15
twain he covered his f.	BIBLE 57:28	not hollow cheek or f.	TENN 542:13	f. fat, and forty	SCOTT 418:33
upon the f. of the deep	BIBLE 44:22	fader: carf biforn his f.	CHAU 141:13	F. is foul	SHAK 458:1
Visit her f. too roughly	SHAK 429:28	fades: f. awa' like morning dew	BALL 32:10	F. laughs the morn	GRAY 234:16
Was never f. so pleased	ANON 8:1	F. o'er the waters blue	BYRON 120:5	f. play of the British	DOYLE 192:10
way plain before my f.	PRAY 389:24	f. the glimmering landscape	GRAY 234:18	f. sex is your department	DOYLE 192:9
Where's the f.	KEATS 289:32	Until she f. away	CHES 147:19	F. stood the wind for France	DRAY 193:10
wish I loved its silly f.	RAL 404:20	fading: f. pleasure brings	SIDN 507:28	f. terms and a villain's	SHAK 466:5
with how wan a f.	SIDN 507:18	faece: non tamquam in Romuli f.	CIC 151:16	f. white linen cloth	PRAY 387:6
you find your f. too clear	HOUS 262:21	faenore: Solutus omni f.	HOR 259:7	Fat, f. and forty	OKEE 365:1
Your f., and the God-curst	HARDY 240:10	faery: f.'s child	KEATS 290:16	foul and f. a day	SHAK 458:9
Your f., my thane	SHAK 459:3	in f. lands forlorn	KEATS 291:23	her care was but to be f.	WATS 565:11
Face-flatterer: F. and backbiter are		Of f. damsels met in forest	MILT 350:3	How sweet and f. she seems	WALL 562:31
	TENN 535:14	sing A f.'s song	KEATS 290:17	I have sworn thee f.	SHAK 495:15
faces: Bid them wash their f.	SHAK 427:15	Fail: F. not our feast	SHAK 461:7	in hope of f. advantages	SHAK 466:16
f. are but a gallery	BACON 26:15	heart and voice would f.	CLAR 152:23	Irish are a f. people	JOHN 276:1
gild the f. of the grooms	SHAK 460:11	I f. of my purpose here	BROW 102:1	Is she kind as she is f.	SHAK 491:4
grind the f. of the poor	BIBLE 57:20	I will not f. thee	BIBLE 48:35	Ludlow come in for the f.	HOUS 263:6
I have seen better f.	SHAK 453:23	I would sooner f. than	KEATS 294:6	most divinely f.	TENN 533:6
In nice clean f.	BARH 33:12	Let no man's heart f. because	BIBLE 50:9	Outward be f.	CHUR 148:33
In the f. of men and women	WHIT 571:4	Others must f.	VIDAL 556:20	possession of that f. thou ow'st	SHAK 492:28
know the f. I shall see	ROSS 410:3	Some night you'll f. us	BROW 103:26	receive f. speechless messages	SHAK 465:17
Mild monastic f. in quiet	CLOU 153:12	we'll not f.	SHAK 459:10	she be f.	KEATS 291:5
of these f. in the crowd	POUND 383:11	when ye f.	BIBLE 70:26	She is not f. to outward	COL 154:26
old familiar f.	LAMB 308:6	yet not asham'd to f.	JOHN 282:20	she pitiful as she is f.	GREE 236:10

She was more f. than words	TENN 532:16	
these f. well-spoken days	SHAK 480:19	
this f. defect Of Nature	MILT 349:23	
'This isn't f. dealing	KIPL 301:19	
thou art f.	BIBLE 56:26	
thousand times more f.	SHAK 467:13	
To be f.	LYTT 321:20	
What care I how f. she be	WITH 575:12	
what's right and f.	HUGH 267:7	
where even the old are f.	YEATS 585:18	
will spit on all things f.	CHAP 140:9	
you f. hath made you good	SHAK 464:16	

fairer: f. person lost not Heav'n — MILT 346:9
F. than any wakened eyes — SHEL 503:19
F. than feign'd of old — MILT 350:3
f. than the word — SHAK 465:17
Is f. far in May — JONS 285:8
surely the f. way is not — BACON 25:4
yet far f. than you are — SHAK 421:10
fairest: f. of creation — MILT 349:17
f. shepherd on our green — PEELE 371:6
f. things have fleetest — THOM 547:25
From f. creatures we desire — SHAK 492:22
thou f. among women — BIBLE 56:17
faireste: f. hewed on hir throte — CHAU 142:32
fairies: Do you believe in f. — BARR 34:16
F., black — SHAK 469:16
I don't believe in f. — BARR 34:14
merry world since the f. — SELD 419:24
She is the f.' midwife — SHAK 481:28
There are f. at the bottom — FYL 220:23
was the beginning of f. — BARR 34:13
fairs: f., and bear-baitings — SHAK 491:20
fairy: Come not near our f. queen — SHAK 470:11
die soon, O f.'s son — SPEN 516:9
f. hands their knell is — COLL 158:20
f. kind of writing which — DRYD 196:26
f. tales of science — TENN 538:16
Like f. gifts fading away — MOORE 356:4
Lilly believes it was a f. — AUBR 18:2
'tis almost f. time — SHAK 471:20
fairy-tale: head a f. of olden times — HEINE 244:9
fais: L'amour? Je le f. souvent — PROU 401:22
faisaient: soldats f. la haie — ELIOT 202:8
fait: un seul f. accompli — BOIL 89:11
faite: Je suis f. comme ça — PREV 400:16
faith: aught is want of f. in all — TENN 535:6
break f. with us who die — MCCR 324:31
breastplate of f. and love — BIBLE 79:2
children in whom is no f. — BIBLE 48:31
confidence and f. of the heart — LUTH 320:17
doubt diversified by f. — BROW 99:5
Draw near with f. — PRAY 387:18
f. and fire within us — HARDY 240:8
f. and hope the world will — POPE 379:20
f. and labour of love — BIBLE 78:30
f. as a grain of mustard — BIBLE 67:1
F. consists in believing — VOLT 561:20
f. hath made thee whole — BIBLE 65:26
f., hope, charity — BIBLE 76:14
f. in a nation of sectaries — DISR 186:1
F. is the substance — BIBLE 79:31
F.'s defying — BARN 34:4
f. shines equal — BRON 93:18
f.'s transcendent dower — WORD 581:5
f. that looks through death — WORD 579:13
f.: these ought ye — BIBLE 67:24
f. unfaithful kept him — TENN 534:29
F. which does not doubt — UNAM 554:27
F. without works is dead — BIBLE 80:12
fanatic F. — MOORE 356:28
Fight the good fight of f. — BIBLE 79:19
finisher of our f. — BIBLE 79:35
fought for Queen and F. — TENN 543:4
have not found so great f. — BIBLE 65:16
he hold the Catholick F. — PRAY 385:11
If I break f. — SHAK 456:17
I have kept the f. — BIBLE 79:26

in plain and simple f. — SHAK 451:11
in the unity of the f. — BIBLE 77:28
just shall live by f. — BIBLE 74:31
Kept f. with me — HARDY 239:21
life in thy f. and fear — PRAY 387:16
made of f. and service — SHAK 426:29
more could fright my f. — DRYD 196:13
more f. in honest doubt — TENN 537:11
more strongly have f. — LUTH 320:15
moved by f. to assent to it — HUME 267:21
My staff of f. to walk — RAL 404:12
not for all his f. can see — EMER 206:22
not the dying for a f. — THAC 545:6
purest f. unhappily forsworn — SHAK 494:5
puts me from my f. — SHAK 439:27
sacred dictates of thy f. — ROWE 410:25
scientific f.'s absurd — BROW 100:21
Sea of F. — ARN 12:23
shake a man's f. in himself — SHAW 496:15
should not alter in my f. — JONS 283:25
simple f. than Norman blood — TENN 537:29
Since f. is dead — WYATT 583:20
taking the shield of f. — BIBLE 78:10
that do not have the f. — CHES 147:25
These all died in f. — BIBLE 79:33
this f. I wish to live — VILL 557:6
though I have all f. — BIBLE 76:14
thou of little f. — BIBLE 66:27
vain f., and courage vain — MAC 322:8
which constitutes poetic f. — COL 157:22
with a stronger f. embrace — LOV 318:20
Woman's f. — SCOTT 418:4
faithful: be mentally f. to himself — PAINE 367:20
Be thou f. unto death — BIBLE 81:17
blessed company of all f. — PRAY 388:3
f. and just to me — SHAK 450:18
F. are the wounds — BIBLE 54:38
F., below — DIBD 175:22
f. friend is the medicine — BIBLE 62:25
f. in that which is least — BIBLE 70:27
f. of thy word — GRAH 233:15
f. to thee, Cynara — DOWS 191:12
for the f. are minished — PRAY 389:32
good and f. servant — BIBLE 68:2
him was called F. and True — BIBLE 82:25
O come, all ye f. — ANON 10:4
So f. in love — SCOTT 417:9
words are true and f. — BIBLE 82:31
faithfully: things which we ask f. — PRAY 387:1
faithless: Be not f. — BIBLE 73:11
f. and stubborn generation — PRAY 395:4
F. as the winds or seas — SEDL 419:10
f. was she — ARN 13:7
Human on my f. arm — AUDEN 19:17
faiths: both were f. — ARN 13:8
men's f. are wafer-cakes — SHAK 443:20
old f. loosen and fall — SWIN 530:6
Falcon: dapple-dawn-drawn F. — HOPK 257:4
f. cannot hear the falconer — YEATS 586:15
f., towering in her pride — SHAK 461:5
Gentle as f. or hawk — SKEL 508:16
falconer: f.'s voice — SHAK 482:19
falcons: were rapid f. in a snare — MER 337:17
fall: also say it is good to f. — WHIT 570:20
Another thing to f. — SHAK 463:16
by dividing we f. — DICK 184:5
come and f. on me — MARL 329:12
contemnth small things shall f. — BIBLE 63:7
dew shall weep thy f. to-night — HERB 248:16
diggeth a pit shall f. — BIBLE 56:2
else they will f. — BURKE 108:22
F. and cease — SHAK 456:9
f. backward when thou hast — SHAK 481:27
f. into the ocean — MARL 329:15
F. into the hands of God — TENN 543:3
f. in with the marriage-procession — CLOU 153:10
f. Like a bright exhalation — SHAK 447:7
F. of the Rupee you may — WILDE 573:4

f. on the ground without — BIBLE 65:35
f. upon the thorns of life — SHEL 502:13
fearful thing to f. into — BIBLE 79:30
forts of folly f. — ARN 13:15
great was the f. of it — BIBLE 65:12
haughty spirit before a f. — BIBLE 54:8
Held we f. to rise — BROW 98:32
his f. from power — BURKE 109:5
I meditated on the F. — BETJ 43:1
in this we stand or f. — MILT 348:20
is down needs fear no f. — BUNY 107:32
Is less likely to f. — GAY 223:4
it had a dying f. — SHAK 487:20
laugh at a f. — BROW 102:1
let us worship and f. down — PRAY 396:4
rocks, F. on us — BIBLE 81:30
See that ye f. not out — BIBLE 46:37
shall f. into the ditch — BIBLE 66:29
shall never f. — PRAY 390:5
Soar not too high to f. — MASS 335:16
Something is going to f. — AUDEN 21:10
take warning by the f. — BALL 30:13
that can f. without shaking — MONT 354:7
that elevation and that f. — BURKE 111:9
Then f., Caesar — SHAK 450:1
Therefore f. the people — PRAY 394:22
Things f. apart — YEATS 586:15
thousand shall f. beside — PRAY 395:21
to raise up them that f. — PRAY 385:19
upholdeth all such as f. — PRAY 399:14
was der F. ist — WITT 575:14
Weak men must f. — SHAK 479:25
we should happen to f. — LEAR 312:10
what a f. was there — SHAK 450:28
Why do ye f. so fast — HERR 248:20
will f. into the hands — BIBLE 62:22
yet fear I to f. — RAL 404:14
Fallacy: characterize as the 'Pathetic F. — RUSK 411:11
fallen: All our hope is f. — HOR 261:13
art thou f. from heaven — BIBLE 58:13
Babylon is f. — BIBLE 82:16
F. from his high estate — DRYD 195:3
f. into the midst of it — PRAY 393:15
how are the mighty f. — BIBLE 50:16
How are the mighty f. — BIBLE 50:17
keeps their f. day about — PATER 369:19
lay great and greatly f. — HOMER 254:3
lot is f. unto me — PRAY 390:6
many have f. by the edge of the sword — BIBLE 63:11
say a man is f. in love — STER 520:6
Though f. thyself — WORD 582:17
Fallentis: F. semita vitae — HOR 258:24
fallere: Quis f. possit amantem — VIRG 558:12
falling: by oft f. — LAT 310:20
cruelty To load a f. man — SHAK 447:25
day when heaven was f. — HOUS 265:7
f. out of faithful friends — EDW 200:5
f. with a falling state — POPE 375:12
he hath the f. sickness — SHAK 448:22
my feet from f. — PRAY 397:20
stand secure amidst a f. world — ADD 2:30
Fallings: F. from us — WORD 579:10
fall'n: f. on evil days — MILT 348:28
follow with allegiance a f. — SHAK 422:18
fallow: f. fawns invisible go — THOM 547:20
Falls: F. with the leaf still — FLET 215:8
then he f., as I do — SHAK 447:9
Where he f. short — CHUR 149:15
false: all was f. and hollow — MILT 346:9
betrayed by what is f. — MER 337:14
Beware of f. prophets — BIBLE 65:8
f. creation — SHAK 459:15
F., ere I come — DONNE 190:10
F. face must hide what — SHAK 459:12
f. grief hiding his harmful — SPEN 516:5
f. Idol Honour — WINC 575:4
f. impossible shore — ARN 15:2
f. philosophy — MILT 346:20

f. quantities	DRYD 198:20	F. in his mouth as household	SHAK 445:3	fantastic: horrible, f., incredible	CHAM 139:9
f. teeth and hurling them	DOYLE 191:17	f. with her face	POPE 379:16	In a light f. round	MILT 340:29
f. witness against thy	BIBLE 47:24	mine own f. friend	PRAY 393:11	On the light f. toe	MILT 342:15
Fram'd to make women f.	SHAK 474:12	once f. word	BAYLY 35:10	thinking on f. summer's heat	SHAK 478:17
If she be f.	SHAK 475:22	Familiarity: F. begets boldness	MARM 330:18	fantastical: That it alone is high f.	
men would be f.	LYLY 321:9	familiarly: Talks as f. of John a Gaunt			SHAK 487:20
not then be f. to any man	SHAK 430:19		SHAK 442:11	fantasy: is to be all made of f.	SHAK 426:29
perils among f. brethren	BIBLE 77:12	families: All happy f. resemble one		opinion he held once Of f.	SHAK 449:10
produces a f. impression	WILDE 572:26		TOLS 551:10	vexed not his f. Black	DONNE 190:3
Ring out the f.	TENN 537:14	English county f.	WAUGH 565:29	Far: F. and few	LEAR 312:6
Round numbers are always f.	JOHN 277:19	f. last not three oaks	BROW 97:16	F. be that fate from us	OVID 366:8
save them from f. Sextus	MAC 322:16	Good f. are generally worse	HOPE 256:1	f., far better thing	DICK 183:12
say that I was f. of heart	SHAK 495:2	Great f. of yesterday we	DEFOE 173:14	f. from the lips we love	MOORE 356:19
thou be not f. to others	BACON 27:35	in the best-regulated f.	DICK 177:15	F. from the madding crowd's	GRAY 235:1
wouldst not play f.	SHAK 459:1	Mothers of large f.	BELL 38:31	few and f. between	CAMP 129:10
Falsehood: F. has a perennial spring		of your antediluvian f.	CONG 160:10	He's happy who, f. away	HOR 259:7
	BURKE 109:4	There are secrets in all f.	FARQ 210:7	keep f. from me	OVID 366:9
goodly outside f. hath	SHAK 466:1	famille: au gouvernement d'une f.		keep f. off, you uninitiated	VIRG 558:19
Let her and F. grapple	MILT 352:5		MONT 354:19	more felicity on the f.	SMITH 510:13
strife of Truth with F.	LOW 319:12	family: brought up a large f.	GOLD 232:32	quarrel in a f.-away country	CHAM 139:9
falsely: Anabaptists do f. boast	PRAY 400:12	direction of his f.	WALP 563:14	seems so near and yet so f.	TENN 537:15
prophets prophesy f.	BIBLE 60:18	f. happier for his presence	STEV 521:4	She is f. from the land	MOORE 356:17
Science f. so called	BIBLE 79:21	f. in heaven and earth	BIBLE 77:24	so f. as it goes	DICK 180:11
falseness: f. in all our impressions		f. pride is something in-conceivable		whole is f. from gay	LEAR 312:22
	RUSK 411:11		GILB 226:20	Faraday: remain plain Michael F.	FAR 209:20
falser: f. than vows made in wine		F. Pride	GILB 227:4	farce: la f. est jouée'	RAB 404:1
	SHAK 426:18	his f. was not unworthy	DISR 186:14	second as f.	MARX 333:9
Falstaff: F. shall die of a sweat	SHAK 443:2	I am the f. face	HARDY 240:1	fardels: Who would f. bear	SHAK 433:8
sweet Jack F.	SHAK 439:18	in the running of a f.	MONT 354:19	Fare: F. thee well! and if for ever	
Falter: F., are lost in the storm	ARN 14:9	is the character of a f.	STER 519:20		BYRON 124:33
nor f., nor repent	SHEL 503:15	of a good f.	DEFOE 173:5	showed me his bill of f.	SWIFT 526:17
Who hesitate and f. life	ARN 14:17	One extinguished f. waits	BETJ 43:9	to f. forth on the water	POUND 383:18
faltered: diffidence that f.	POUND 382:14	prolong f. connection	BUTL 118:29	fareweel: Ae f.	BURNS 112:27
If I have f. more or less	STEV 523:11	famine: die by f. die by inches	HENRY 245:20	fare wel: f. al the snow of ferne	CHAU 144:15
fam'd: f. in all great arts	ARN 15:11	f.; from battle and murder	PRAY 385:16	F. my bok, and my devocioun	CHAU 143:29
fame: all my f. for a pot of ale	SHAK 444:4	f. in his face	CHUR 149:5	Farewell: F.! a long farewell	SHAK 447:9
blush to find it f.	POPE 380:18	famous: At every f. victory	SOUT 513:18	f. compliment	SHAK 482:12
damn'd to everlasting f.	POPE 380:1	f. by my sword	GRAH 233:15	f. content	SHAK 475:25
desire of f.	TENN 534:12	f. by their birth	SHAK 478:20	f. goes out sighing	SHAK 487:5
doctor full of phrase and f.	ARN 15:12	f., calm, and dead	BROW 100:34	f. happy fields	MILT 345:10
earth your f. is bright	BRID 92:18	f. men have the whole earth	PER 372:23	f. king	SHAK 479:11
Enough my meed of f.	HOLL 253:4	f. then By wisdom	MILT 350:7	F. night, welcome day	BUNY 107:37
establishment of my f.	GIBB 224:18	found myself f.	BYRON 126:22	F., rewards and Fairies	CORB 162:13
fair f. inspires	POPE 376:26	Let us now praise f. men	BIBLE 63:21	F. to the Highlands	BURNS 114:26
F. and tranquillity can	MONT 354:22	thrice f. deeds she wrought	MAC 321:25	hail, and f. evermore	CAT 137:15
F. is a food that dead	DOBS 187:11	fan: f. spread and streamers	CONG 160:36	life than waving me f.	HOPE 256:4
F. is like a river	BACON 27:5	F. the sinking flame	DICK 180:26	must bid the company f.	RAL 404:19
F. is no plant that grows	MILT 343:9	Fanatics: F. have their dreams	KEATS 289:26	nor bade f. to him	SHAK 458:3
f. is the last thing even	TAC 531:14	fancies: drop your silly f.	CAT 136:27	there be no sadness of f.	TENN 533:4
F. is the spur that	MILT 343:8	f. are more giddy and unfirm	SHAK 489:1	Too-late, F.	ROSS 410:4
f., sete, marcie forzate	GAR 221:10	F. that broke through language	BROW 104:8	with hope f. fear	MILT 347:16
F.'s eternal beadroll	SPEN 516:19	full of f.	KEATS 293:10	farewells: Everlasting f.	DE Q 175:3
f., that all hunt after	SHAK 456:14	Lay your earthly f. down	TENN 541:15	many f. as be stars	SHAK 487:12
foremost shall be damn'd to f.	POPE 375:19	When you set your f. free	BROW 98:31	far-flung: Lord of our f. battle-line	
gives immortal f.	YOUNG 587:9	fancy: Did your f. never stray	GAY 222:21		KIPL 302:7
her f. survives	MILT 350:31	dorgs is some men's f.	DICK 177:9	farm: fields to cross till a f.	BROW 102:14
his f. the ocean sea	BARN 34:5	Ever let the f. roam	KEATS 289:29	keep a f.	SHAK 432:3
immoderate passion for f.	BURKE 109:8	f. cannot cheat so well	KEATS 291:23	snug little f. the earth	COL 156:10
love and f. to nothingness	KEATS 293:2	f. is the sails	KEATS 293:13	farmer: f. that hanged himself	SHAK 460:15
Man dreams of f.	TENN 535:9	f. outwork nature	SHAK 422:2	farmers: f. excessively fortunate	VIRG 560:13
no one shall work for f.	KIPL 304:3	from f. to the heart	POPE 380:4	f., flourish and complain	COWP 168:16
nor yet a fool to f.	POPE 376:23	invention and makes f. lame	COWP 166:20	now the f. swear	KING 297:21
not to purchase f.	DRYD 196:35	keep your f. free	HOUS 262:20	once the embattled f. stood	EMER 206:19
openeth the gate to good f.	BACON 26:4	now the f. passes	HOUS 263:1	Three jolly F.	DE L 174:14
Physicians of the utmost f.	BELL 39:1	odoriferous flowers of f.	SHAK 457:3	farms: pleasant villages and f.	MILT 349:13
Poets' food is love and f.	SHEL 500:14	of most excellent f.	SHAK 436:31	what f. are those	HOUS 263:22
'Rather use than f.	TENN 535:10	of sweet and bitter f.	SHAK 426:26	wi' the weel-stockit f.	BURNS 114:6
selfish hope of a season's f.	NEWB 361:8	So fair a f. few would	HARDY 240:14	far-off: old, unhappy, f. things	WORD 578:14
servants of f.	BACON 26:21	so full of shapes is f.	SHAK 487:20	farrago: discursus nostri f. libelli est	
speaking trump of future f.	BYRON 124:24	Tell me where is f. bred	SHAK 467:9		JUV 287:12
That f. can never heal	AYT 24:5	those by hopeless f. feign'd	TENN 542:4	farrow: old sow that eats her f.	JOYCE 286:16
What is f.	GRAI 233:20	young man's f.	TENN 538:17	farther: f. you go from the church	
while f. elates thee	MOORE 356:8	fancy-free: In maiden meditation, f.			WOTT 583:17
you shall live by f.	SPEN 515:20		SHAK 470:8	know I'm f. off from heav'n	HOOD 254:18
fames: Auri sacra f.	VIRG 558:10	fans: With divers-colour'd f.	SHAK 422:2	Farthest: F. Thule	VIRG 560:10
malesuada F. ac turpis Egestas	VIRG 558:21	Wi' their f. into their	BALL 31:20	farthing: f. less	ADD 2:2
familiar: Be thou f.	SHAK 430:19	fantaisies: f. et le contact de deux		hast paid the uttermost f.	BIBLE 64:14
Don't let us be f. or fond	CONG 161:7		CHAM 139:15	I am a kind of f. dip	STEV 523:13
F. acts are beautiful through	SHEL 503:13	fantasies: Even the linked f.	THOM 548:17	sparrows sold for a f.	BIBLE 65:35
f. friend, whom I trusted	PRAY 392:5	exchange of two f.	CHAM 139:15	Virtue knows to a f. what	WALP 563:22

farthings: sparrows sold for two f.
BIBLE 70:3
fascination: My right elbow has a f.
GILB 227:10
There's a f. frantic GILB 227:18
With f. in his very bow BYRON 123:36
fashion: appear a little out of f. SHAK 444:19
carving the f. of a new SHAK 472:14
f. a gentleman or noble SPEN 515:28
F.—a word which knaves CHUR 149:9
f. of this world passeth BIBLE 76:4
f. of these times SHAK 425:7
f. she detests SHAK 489:17
F., the arbiter STEE 518:4
F., though Folly's child COWP 168:12
garment out of f. SHAK 428:16
glass of f. SHAK 433:15
in my f. DOWS 191:12
in the first style of f. AUST 23:28
'is a highflyer at F. DICK 181:7
laws of markets and f. ALB 3:7
marriage ever out of f. BUTL 118:8
men in shape and f. ASCH 17:3
nothing else holds f. SHAK 487:16
out of the f. CIBB 151:10
tell you the leading f. RUSK 411:5
vegetable f. must excite GILB 227:23
very independent of f. GASK 221:23
will deeply put the f. SHAK 442:24
fashionable: idea ever to be f. is ominous
SANT 414:5
With other f. topics GOLD 232:36
Fashion'd: F. so slenderly HOOD 254:9
Fashioned: F. so purely THOM 548:29
Which day by day were f. PRAY 399:7
fashioneth: clay say to him that f.
BIBLE 59:13
fashions: conscience to fit this year's
f. HELL 244:15
fast: can never be done too f. GOLD 232:17
f. bound in misery PRAY 397:7
f. that I have chosen BIBLE 60:4
fun grew f. and furious BURNS 115:10
he talks it so very f. FARQ 210:6
my heart is f. ANON 7:15
Spare F. MILT 341:27
study and f. SHAK 463:14
then into a f. SHAK 432:2
who will not f. in peace COWP 168:14
Fasten: F. your seatbelts DAVIS 172:18
faster: speed was far f. than light
BULL 106:22
travel f. than a stagecoach GOLD 232:18
fastest: He travels the f. who travels
KIPL 304:11
fastidious: literature is never f. SOUT 514:14
fasting: Apollo turned f. friar MER 337:29
between a fou man and a f. SCOTT 418:26
lives upon hope will die f. FRAN 218:13
nor f., nor birch BLAKE 87:20
thank heaven, f. SHAK 426:17
fasts: that come in f. divine HOPK 256:15
fat: eat the f. of the land BIBLE 46:36
Fair, f., and forty SCOTT 418:33
f. bulls of Basan PRAY 390:18
F., fair and forty OKEE 365:1
f. man a thin one is wildly CONN 161:15
f. of others' works BURT 116:13
f. white woman whom nobody CORN 162:22
find me f. and sleek HOR 258:16
fresher, and more f. DONNE 188:2
grow f. and look young DRYD 196:36
he has nat right f. CHAU 141:23
men about me that are f. SHAK 448:20
oxen should himself be f. JOHN 279:20
seven f. kine BIBLE 46:31
she help'd him to f. BARH 33:6
them is f. and grows old SHAK 438:34
thin man inside every f. ORW 365:11
What is that f. gentleman SHAW 498:26

Who's your f. friend BRUM 106:3
you f. and greasy citizens SHAK 425:2
fatal: fair and f. king JOHN 273:23
f. and perfidious bark MILT 343:10
f. bellman SHAK 460:3
f. facility of the octo-syllabic BYRON 121:29
f. gift of beauty BYRON 121:6
f. to religion as indifference BURKE 111:35
I am a f. man THAC 545:13
Our f. shadows that walk FLET 215:13
So f. to my suit before GARR 221:16
So sweet was ne'er so f. SHAK 477:5
Their f. hands MILT 347:1
fatalistic: Beats like a f. drum ELIOT 204:9
fatality: think there is a f. in it STER 519:9
fate: am the master of my f. HENL 245:5
build that nation's f. BLAKE 85:11
cannot suspend their f. DEFOE 173:2
Far be that f. from us OVID 366:8
f. and metaphysical aid SHAK 459:1
F. cannot harm me SMITH 511:15
f. has torn your living CAT 137:15
F. is not an eagle BOWEN 91:5
F. keeps on happening LOOS 318:2
F. never wounds more deep JOHN 282:23
f. of a nation was riding LONG 316:26
f. of the great wen COBB 154:10
F. so enviously debars MARV 331:19
F.'s Urn shakes HOR 260:7
F., Time, Occasion SHEL 503:10
F. tried to conceal him HOLM 253:7
F. wrote her a most tremendous BEER 37:20
hanging breathless on thy f. LONG 316:7
He either fears his f. GRAH 233:14
how very sad thy f. KEATS 292:23
I feel my f. in what ROET 407:6
I hold f. FORD 216:20
is he that knows not F. CHES 147:4
is no armour against f. SHIR 507:2
I thy f. shall overtake KING 296:11
man and master of his f. TENN 535:2
might read the book of f. SHAK 442:1
now at length my f. I know BROW 101:22
once dead by f. BEAU 36:1
our f. but our business BOWEN 91:6
our folly, or our f. DENH 174:21
profit every day that F. HOR 259:18
shall be the maiden's f. SCOTT 416:12
should they know their f. GRAY 235:13
struggling in the storms of f. POPE 375:12
take a bond of f. SHAK 462:7
that f. and character are NOV 364:9
That Time and F. of all FITZ 212:17
thou and I with F. conspire FITZ 213:16
triumph'd over f. BYRON 124:28
us is over-rul'd by f. MARL 329:18
wayward the decrees of F. are THAC 546:4
what I will is f. MILT 348:30
when f. summons DRYD 196:33
Who can control his f. SHAK 477:19
With the severity of f. FORD 216:12
would F. but mend it PRIOR 401:7
fated: though f. not to die DRYD 196:11
fates: are masters of their f. SHAK 448:17
Father: about my F.'s business BIBLE 69:13
ance his f.'s pride   ‑ BURNS 113:9
are of your f. the devil BIBLE 72:13
because I go to the F. BIBLE 72:40
become the f. of many nations BIBLE 74:40
be happier than your f. SOPH 513:4
believe in God the F. PRAY 384:26
bow my knees unto the F. BIBLE 77:24
brood of Folly without f. MILT 341:23
cannot have God for his f. CYPR 170:19
decrepit f. takes delight SHAK 493:13
did you last see your f. YEAM 584:8
Diogenes struck the f. BURT 116:36
down from the F. of lights BIBLE 80:9
either my f. or my mother STER 519:16
even as your F. which is BIBLE 64:21

everlasting F. BIBLE 58:7
f. answered never a word LONG 317:21
f. compounded with my mother SHAK 453:11
f. had a daughter lov'd SHAK 489:7
f., Harry, to that thought SHAK 442:19
F., I have sinned against BIBLE 70:19
f. is gone wild into his SHAK 442:15
F. is rather vulgar DICK 178:26
F. of his Country ANON 5:7
f. pitieth his own children PRAY 396:11
f.'s helm is far too big FLEM 215:5
F.'s house are many mansions BIBLE 72:31
f.'s joy SCOTT 417:29
F., that I have sinned MASS 334:15
F. which seeth in secret BIBLE 64:22
features of thy f.'s face BYRON 125:13
Glory be to the F. PRAY 384:15
Had it been his f. ANON 5:15
Hath the rain a f. BIBLE 53:4
Have a turnip than his f. JOHN 280:10
He took my f. grossly SHAK 434:30
hired servants of my f.'s BIBLE 70:19
Honour thy f. and thy mother BIBLE 47:24
How many a f. have I seen TENN 536:22
I am thy f.'s spirit SHAK 431:4
I had it from my f. SHAK 446:26
It is a wise f. that knows SHAK 466:9
leave his f. and his mother BIBLE 45:13
lively picture of his f.'s FLET 215:28
man cometh unto the F. BIBLE 72:32
mother on his f. him begot BLAKE 87:2
My f. feeds his flocks HOME 253:22
My f. was an eminent button COLM 159:4
my f. wept BLAKE 87:23
no more like my f. SHAK 429:28
not an angry f. CAMP 129:3
one God the F. Almighty PRAY 387:10
only begotten of the F. BIBLE 71:27
only f. GOLD 232:13
Our F. which art in heaven BIBLE 64:24
Our F. which art in heaven PREV 400:15
resembled My f. SHAK 460:5
She gave her f. forty-one ANON 6:12
son maketh a glad f. BIBLE 53:29
thicker than my f.'s loins BIBLE 51:2
Thy f.'s shame BRET 92:6
'twill come to my f. anon' AUBR 17:26
withered all when my f. died SHAK 436:11
worshipful f. and first founder CAXT 138:2
your F. had an accident POTT 382:1
fathered: Are f. by our heroism ELIOT 203:6
Being so f. and so husbanded SHAK 449:16
fatherless: defendeth the f. and widow
PRAY 399:18
f. children PRAY 385:20
He is a Father of the f. PRAY 394:7
visit the f. and widows BIBLE 80:11
fatherly: thy f. goodness all those PRAY 386:1
fathers: f.-forth whose beauty HOPK 256:23
f. have eaten sour grapes BIBLE 60:34
f., provoke not your children BIBLE 78:7
fet from f. of war-proof SHAK 444:1
healthiest f. stands WHIT 570:15
He slept with his f. BIBLE 51:5
I like to be as my f. were BLUNT 89:5
iniquity of the f. upon BIBLE 47:24
Instead of thy f. PRAY 392:18
Lord God of your f. BIBLE 47:8
our f. have told us PRAY 392:13
past unto the f. by the prophets BIBLE 79:28
sins of your f. HOR 260:25
sojourners, as were all our f. BIBLE 51:39
such as our f. have told us PRAY 395:3
When your f. tempted me PRAY 396:4
which thy f. have set BIBLE 54:23
Father William: You are old, F.
CARR 133:22
You are old, F. SOUT 514:7
fathom: Full f. five SHAK 484:32
Full many a f. deep CAMP 128:16

fathom-line: Where f. could never touch SHAK 438:19
fathoms: 'Tis fifty f. deep BALL 31:20
fatigue: greatest f. in the world VANB 555:5
fatling: young lion and the f. together BIBLE 58:10
fatness: clouds drop f. PRAY 394:3
fatter: he was f. than his cure TENN 533:8
valley sheep are f. PEAC 371:2
Would he were f. SHAK 448:21
Fatti: F. non foste a viver come DANTE 171:13
fatuity: f. of idiots SMITH 511:30
fatuous: what made f. sunbeams toil OWEN 367:5
faucibus: ipsum primisque in f. Orci VIRG 558:21
Faulconbridge: Hadst thou rather be a F. SHAK 452:8
fault: clever to a f. BROW 99:7
Condemn the f. and not SHAK 463:19
f., dear Brutus SHAK 448:17
f. is great in man or woman ANON 7:24
f. was Nature's fault not BYRON 126:3
fault who hath no f. at all TENN 534:26
f. without eradicating GOLD 232:8
fellow f. came to match it SHAK 426:14
fierceness makes Error a f. HERB 247:6
glorious f. of angels POPE 376:8
happy f. MISS 352:20
has no kind of f. or flaw GILB 226:1
it was a grievous f. SHAK 450:17
It was our f. KIPL 300:21
lines together without a f. JOHN 275:27
see thy f. SHAK 443:13
shun the f. I fell BALL 30:13
through my most grievous f. MASS 334:15
To hide the f. I see POPE 381:13
What soul is without f. RIMB 406:8
faultless: Faultily f. TENN 539:27
F. to a fault BROW 104:28
thinks a f. piece to see POPE 378:15
faults: all his f. observ'd SHAK 451:23
All men make f. SHAK 493:12
be buffeted for your f. BIBLE 80:26
Drown all my f. and fears FLET 215:30
f. are such that one loves GOLD 232:9
f. of the age come from BALF 30:5
friend his f. can freely show POPE 378:32
greatest of f. CARL 131:32
Has she no f. then POPE 380:26
his f. lie gently on him SHAK 447:1
I acknowledge my f. PRAY 393:4
men are moulded out of f. SHAK 465:6
Not for thy f. BYRON 121:8
of vile ill-favour'd f. SHAK 469:11
some f. so nearly allied GOLD 232:8
Some f. to make us men SHAK 423:19
those f. it has not strength GOLD 232:38
thou me from my secret f. PRAY 390:14
to her f. a little blind PRIOR 400:23
what f. they commit QUAR 403:20
With all her f. CHUR 148:24
with all thy f. I love BUTL 119:10
with all thy f. COWP 166:33
Faustine: Caressed F. SWIN 529:15
Faustus: F. must be damn'd MARL 329:11
faute: c'est une f. BOUL 90:19
Favete: F. linguis HOR 260:13
favilla: Solvet saeclum in f. CEL 138:5
favour: by f., or by spite POPE 378:32
fear or f. of the crowd KIPL 298:11
Have grace and f. in them SHAK 476:25
in f. with God and man BIBLE 69:14
me of your grace and f. SHAK 453:6
par in f. of the people BURKE 108:18
favourable: attentive and f. hearers HOOK 255:19
f. and gracious unto Sion PRAY 393:8
favoured: firsts in some less f. BETJ 44:11
thou art highly f. BIBLE 69:4

favourites: persuading monarchs to choose f. SWIFT 526:8
favours: bad recommendation to f. FIEL 211:20
in the middle of her f. SHAK 432:11
secret hope for greater f. LA R 310:16
that hangs on princes' f. SHAK 447:9
fav'rite: f. has no friend GRAY 235:7
fawn: f. that flies SWIN 528:19
Unpractis'd he to f. GOLD 230:22
fawning: base spaniel f. SHAK 449:24
like a f. publican he looks SHAK 465:29
fayr: f. as is the rose in May CHAU 143:27
Fe: F. que no duda es fe muerta UNAM 554:27
feáce: noo mwore do zee your f. BARN 33:31
fear: acting and reasoning as f. BURKE 108:9
alike by beauty and by f. WORD 580:8
are the concessions of f. BURKE 109:14
be just, and f. not SHAK 447:12
by means of pity and f. ARIS 12:9
cross'd themselves for f. TENN 538:12
custom, and f. HARDY 240:3
desire and many things to f. BACON 26:8
dread and f. of kings SHAK 467:27
either be fond to live or f. ELIZ 206:3
equal poise of hope and f. MILT 341:9
F. and Hunger that urges VIRG 558:21
F. gave his watch no look AUDEN 20:19
F. God, and keep his commandments BIBLE 56:14
F. God. Honour the king BIBLE 80:25
F. God. Honour the King KITC 305:14
f. in a handful of dust ELIOT 204:10
F. is a flying GAY 222:10
f. is the parent of cruelty FROU 219:20
f. my name shall the Sun BIBLE 62:3
F. no more the heat o' SHAK 428:22
F. not to touch the best RAL 404:10
f. of God before them CROM 169:20
f. of having to weep BEAU 35:15
f. of little men ALL 3:20
f. of some divine and supreme BURT 117:1
f. of the Lord BIBLE 58:9
f. of the Lord is clean PRAY 390:12
f. of the Lord is the beginning PRAY 397:13
f. of tomorrow's dangers DONNE 191:2
F., O Little Hunter KIPL 303:7
f. or favour of the crowd KIPL 298:11
f. that kills WORD 581:2
f. those big words JOYCE 286:22
fear to whom f. BIBLE 75:22
f. usually ends in folly COL 158:3
F. wist not to evade THOM 548:11
fourth is freedom from f. ROOS 407:26
From hope and f. set free SWIN 529:25
given us the spirit of f. BIBLE 79:22
haunts of horror and f. TENN 540:16
have to fear is f. itself ROOS 407:20
hope who never had a f. COWP 167:36
I cannot taint with f. SHAK 462:28
I f. thee, ancient Mariner COL 155:19
if his f. still followed SPEN 516:6
I have a faint cold f. SHAK 483:21
is down needs f. no fall BUNY 107:32
I will f. no evil PRAY 390:22
jelly with the act of f. SHAK 430:8
kings that f. their subjects' SHAK 446:19
Knight without f. and without ANON 9:5
let him be your f. BIBLE 58:4
life in thy faith and f. PRAY 387:16
lives not in f. SHAK 455:5
Men f. death BACON 26:1
name were liable to f. SHAK 448:21
nobility is exempt from f. SHAK 446:9
ocean in the eventide of f. MORR 358:7
O, word of f. SHAK 457:18
Possess them not with f. SHAK 444:26
rather thou dost f. to do SHAK 459:1
salvation with f. and trembling BIBLE 78:15
Severity breedeth f. BACON 26:25

shuddering f. SHAK 467:12
so long as they f. ACC 1:3
so whom shall I f. BIBLE 83:5
suddenly grow gray with f. SHEL 502:11
that which we often f. SHAK 421:25
Thawing cold f. SHAK 444:11
There is no f. in love BIBLE 81:6
there is not a word of f. LAND 308:19
trembled with f. at your frown ENGL 208:19
'Twas only f. first JONS 284:16
whom then shall I f. PRAY 391:7
why f. we to become SHEL 499:25
will eat our meal in f. SHAK 461:12
yet will I f. none ill SCOT 419:5
fear'd: She f. no danger DRYD 196:10
feared: f. nor flattered any flesh DOUG 191:6
nothing to be f. in death LUCR 320:9
fearful: f. thing to fall into BIBLE 79:30
snatch a f. joy GRAY 235:11
To be a lovely and a f. BYRON 122:24
fearfully: I am f. and wonderfully PRAY 399:6
Fear God: F., and take your own BORR 90:10
fearing: so many years of f. death SHAK 450:4
fears: Applying f. to hopes SHAK 495:6
are their griefs and f. BACON 27:2
Drown all my faults and f. FLET 215:30
either f. his fate too much GRAH 233:14
F. of the brave JOHN 283:3
fifty hopes and f. BROW 99:4
forgot the taste of f. SHAK 463:5
have f. that I may cease KEATS 292:30
hopes and f. it heeded SHEL 504:19
I had no human f. WORD 581:10
More pangs and f. than SHAK 447:9
Not mine own f. SHAK 494:21
Our f. do make us traitors SHAK 462:11
past Regrets and Future F. FITZ 212:16
Present f. SHAK 458:20
sum of their f. CHUR 150:16
that any man f. to be dead BACON 27:41
That f. his fellowship SHAK 445:3
tie up thy f. HERB 247:15
To saucy doubts and f. SHAK 461:17
who f. dishonour HOR 261:19
without many f. and distastes BACON 25:20
feast: f. at his earnest wish LEAR 312:21
f. of reason and the flow POPE 380:5
great f. of languages SHAK 457:12
Liberty's a glorious f. BURNS 114:19
nourisher in life's f. SHAK 460:8
people a f. of fat things BIBLE 58:18
perpetual f. of nectared MILT 341:11
sat at any good man's f. SHAK 425:23
scramble at the shearers' f. MILT 343:12
Therefore let us keep the f. BIBLE 75:36
vigil f. his neighbours SHAK 445:3
When I make a f. HAR 242:9
you were going to a f. JONS 283:27
feast-day: upon our solemn f. PRAY 395:9
feasts: uppermost rooms at f. BIBLE 67:22
uppermost rooms at f. BIBLE 68:37
feat: f. on which ourselves BYRON 122:20
feather: f. for each wind that blows SHAK 491:14
friendship never moults a f. DICK 180:5
little ball of f. and bone HARDY 240:20
moulted f. BROW 102:16
Stuck a f. in his cap BANGS 32:16
wit's a f. POPE 379:24
feather'd: f. race with pinions skim FRERE 218:25
feathered: f. glory from her loosening YEATS 586:1
Feather-footed: F. through the plashy fen WAUGH 566:3
feathers: beautified with our f. GREE 236:12
bracelets and bright f. HARDY 240:1
her f. like gold PRAY 394:4
shalt be safe under his f. PRAY 395:21

To wet their silken f. SPEN 516:32
featly: Foot it f. here and there SHAK 484:30
feats: outdares Stokes in azure f. BROW 103:27
to f. of broil and battle SHAK 473:24
''Twas one of my f. BYRON 125:1
What f. he did that day SHAK 445:3
Featur'd: F. like him SHAK 493:6
feature: every f. works AUST 22:9
fed: bite the hand that f. BURKE 112:10
f. and educated RUSK 412:6
f. horses in the morning BIBLE 60:16
f. of the dainties that SHAK 457:1
f. on the fullness of death SWIN 530:5
f. with the same food SHAK 467:4
souls most f. with Shakespeare's CHES 147:17
We both have f. as well SHAK 448:14
you have f. full VIRG 560:9
Federal: F. Union: it must be preserved JACK 270:30
Federation: F. of the world TENN 538:24
fee: bought over God with a f. SWIN 530:23
gorgeous East in f. WORD 582:10
feeble: confirm the f. knees BIBLE 58:33
f. God has stabb'd me GAY 222:6
Most forcible F. SHAK 442:5
not enough to help the f. SHAK 485:27
poor f. sex VICT 556:14
such a f. temper should SHAK 448:16
feebly: His words came f. WORD 581:1
feed: bid thee f. BLAKE 87:26
doth this our Caesar f. SHAK 448:18
f. his flock like a shepherd BIBLE 59:7
F. in the ooze of their ARN 13:6
f. me in a green pasture PRAY 390:21
…F. my lambs BIBLE 73:14
F. the brute PUNCH 403:1
f. thee out of my own vitals CONG 160:6
f. with the rich JOHN 275:23
So shalt thou f. on Death SHAK 495:14
Then f. on thoughts MILT 347:8
feedeth: he f. among the lilies BIBLE 56:24
Feeds: F. beast as man SHAK 421:8
ruin that f. upon COWP 166:10
feel: believe to One does f. KNOX 305:20
can f. that he is dying SUET 524:17
feel a feeling which I f. RIDD 406:3
f. for the common chord BROW 98:22
f. my breasts all perfume JOYCE 286:30
f. not what they inspire SHEL 505:13
f. the earth move HEM 245:3
f. what wretches feel SHAK 454:16
'I f. it more than other DICK 176:28
mean or more than they f. CONN 161:11
must also f. it as a man SHAK 462:18
Of making figments f. HARDY 239:16
Speak what we f. SHAK 456:13
thing that could not f. WORD 581:10
Those who would make us f. CHUR 149:13
to f. so small and sweet PATM 370:5
tragedy to those that f. WALP 563:11
feeling: appeals to diffused f. BAG 28:30
constellations of f. DOUG 191:7
f. that I could last CONR 161:24
f. too falsely disdained SHEL 504:13
f. which I feel you all RIDD 406:3
fellow no f. of his business SHAK 436:26
formal f. comes DICK 183:13
generous and honest f. BURKE 108:24
Had feed the f. of MARL 330:11
I'm not f. very well myself PUNCH 403:2
Love's f. is more soft SHAK 457:8
man is as old as he's f. COLL 158:15
mess of imprecision of f. ELIOT 202:23
petrifies the f. BURNS 113:17
probably is there more true f. JOW 285:23
pulse of f. stirs ARN 12:22
sensible To f. as to sight SHAK 459:15
transmission of f. TOLS 551:14
feelings: on what we call our f. DICK 179:21

out of the f. of humanity BLAC 85:2
overflow of powerful f. WORD 583:10
ultimately determined by the f. SPEN 515:2
fees: hope, but of his f. HERR 250:12
they took their f. BELL 39:1
who straight dream on f. SHAK 481:28
feet: aching hands and bleeding f. ARN 13:24
At her f. he bowed BIBLE 49:11
bathe those beauteous f. FLET 215:29
beat of her unseen f. SHEL 500:6
beautiful are thy f. with shoes BIBLE 57:7
better to die on your f. IBAR 269:16
Came on the following F. THOM 548:14
clothes at a young man's f. BIBLE 73:28
dost thou wash my f. BIBLE 72:27
down Satan under our f. PRAY 385:19
f., and the palms of her BIBLE 51:37
f. are always in the water AMES 4:3
f. have they PRAY 397:18
f. like unto fine brass BIBLE 81:14
f. of him that bringeth BIBLE 59:18
f. of the day and the feet SWIN 528:16
f. of thine high priests SWIN 530:7
f. shall stand in thy gates PRAY 398:11
f. shod with the preparation BIBLE 78:10
f. they hurt in the stocks PRAY 397:3
f. was I to the lame BIBLE 52:35
fell at his f. as dead BIBLE 81:14
great knees and f. SWIN 528:26
hands are a sort of f. TRAH 552:1
Her f. beneath her petticoat SUCK 524:8
Her f. go down to death BIBLE 53:20
Her pretty f. HERR 250:7
is a lantern unto my f. PRAY 398:6
Its f. were tied KEATS 292:10
let my due f. never fail MILT 342:9
moon under her f. BIBLE 82:10
more clothes on his f. SHAK 443:18
my dreams under your f. YEATS 585:9
my f. from falling PRAY 397:20
nations under our f. PRAY 392:23
nearer than hands and f. TENN 533:29
off the dust of your f. BIBLE 65:32
pierced my hands and my f. PRAY 390:20
radical is a man with both f. ROOS 407:24
Scots lords at his f. BALL 31:20
set my f. upon the rock PRAY 392:1
seven f. of English HAR 242:11
slipping underneath our F. FITZ 212:22
splendour and speed of thy f. SWIN 528:16
They hadn't any f. CARR 135:6
those f. in ancient time BLAKE 86:16
Thus I set my printless f. MILT 341:21
thy shoes from off thy f. BIBLE 47:4
to guide our f. into BIBLE 69:7
tremble under her f. TENN 540:12
twain he covered his f. BIBLE 57:28
walk'd those blessed f. SHAK 437:33
wash their f. in soda water ELIOT 204:27
what dread f. BLAKE 87:15
white f. of laughing girls MAC 322:12
world with their f. forward BROW 97:10
Fehlgriff: Erste F. Gottes NIET 363:3
war der zweite F. Gottes NIET 363:4
feigned: Than fables yet have f. MILT 346:23
feigning: f. was called compliment SHAK 489:22
felde: faire f. ful of folke fonde LANG 309:23
fele: tnat thow shalt nat f. CHAU 144:3
felice: ricordarsi del tempo f. DANTE 171:8
felicem: fuisse f. BOET 89:6
Felices: F. ter et amplius HOR 259:21
felicitas: Horatii curiosa f. PETR 373:3
felicite: respect of the pleyn f. CHAU 144:14
felicities: Job than the f. of Solomon BACON 25:19
three fearful f. SIDN 508:4
felicity: Absent thee from f. awhile SHAK 437:25
f. on the far side of baldness SMITH 510:13

none can boast sincere f. DRYD 197:10
Our own f. we make or find JOHN 282:21
possessed approaches f. MER 337:32
shadow of f. WALL 562:15
Their green f. KEATS 293:3
these eyes to behold f. BROW 96:21
throne of human f. JOHN 280:20
What more f. can fall SPEN 515:23
Felix: F. qui potuit rerum cognoscere VIRG 560:14
fell: f. among thieves BIBLE 69:30
f. at his feet as dead BIBLE 81:14
f. before the throne BIBLE 81:32
f. in the weeping brook SHAK 436:19
f. into his anecdotage DISR 186:19
Firefrorefiddle, the Fiend of the F. ELIOT 203:7
From morn To noon he f. MILT 346:3
it f. not BIBLE 65:11
my uncle Toby f. into it STER 520:6
ran to help me when I f. TAYL 531:25
So I f. in love with GILB 229:3
that the wall f. down flat BIBLE 49:2
though the brightest f. SHAK 462:14
We f. out TENN 541:28
where the dead leaf f. KEATS 290:1
fellow: f. that will take rewards SHAK 422:21
himself a most agreeable f. AUST 22:10
His f. traveller ANON 8:4
take a f. eight years old BROW 100:30
touchy, testy, pleasant f. ADD 2:10
want of it, the f. POPE 379:22
'you're a f. DICK 181:32
fellow-citizens: heated passions of his f. HOR 260:18
fellow-creatures: apply that epithet to my f. MILL 339:5
fellow-feeling: f. makes one wond'rous GARR 221:15
fellow-men: one that loves his f. HUNT 268:5
fellow-mortal: earth-born companion
An' f. BURNS 115:21
fellows: fortunate f. that now you HOUS 263:7
hath fram'd strange f. SHAK 465:8
these f. of infinite tongue SHAK 445:13
fellowship: in one communion and f. PRAY 387:4
right hands of f. BIBLE 77:15
simple dues of f. BROW 97:30
felonious: some f. end MILT 341:1
felony: f. to drink small beer SHAK 446:11
felt: darkness which may be f. BIBLE 47:15
f. along the heart WORD 578:4
f. him like the thunder's *ARN 13:16
pity who has f. the woe GAY 223:7
female: despight they cast on f. wits BRAD 91:13
elegance of f. friendship JOHN 282:12
f. atheist talks you dead JOHN 282:22
f. mind is not capable KNOX 305:24
f. of the species is more KIPL 299:4
f. woman is one WARD 564:26
life for the British f. CLOU 153:9
Male and f. created BIBLE 45:5
male and the f. BIBLE 45:34
share some f. errors fall POPE 380:33
unlearned and uninformed f. AUST 24:2
What f. heart can gold GRAY 235:6
Who has a polished f. friend WHURR 572:1
females: with eighty mile o' f. DICK 183:2
femina: Dux f. facti VIRG 557:15
Nemo magis gaudet quam f. JUV 288:6
feminine: Purity is the f. HARE 242:5
she's of the f. gender OKEE 364:23
femme: Cherchons la f. DUMAS 199:2
elle est f. RAC 404:3
femmes: des privilèges des f. FOUR 217:18
fen: through the plashy f. WAUGH 566:3
fences: f. make good neighbours FROST 219:9
Yet all these f. and their HERB 248:11

fennel: f. for you, and columbines
SHAK 436:11
fens: reek o' the rotten f. SHAK 427:23
fera: *cela se f.* CAL 127:9
fercula: *Et illa erant f.* AUG 21:13
feri: *Ita f. ut se mori sentiat* SUET 524:17
feriam: *Sublimi f. sidera vertice* HOR 259:10
Ferments: F. and frets until 'tis BUTL 118:17
fern: sparkle out among the f. TENN 532:20
fern-seed: have the receipt of f. SHAK 438:23
ferocity: whilst it mitigated f. BURKE 111:10
ferrem: *Non ego hoc f.* HOR 261:4
ferry: Crossing alone the nighted f.
HOUS 265:18
fers: *partout il est dans les f.* ROUS 410:17
fertile: such a fix to be so f. NASH 360:4
fervent: f. prayer of a righteous BIBLE 80:19
fessi: *f. venimus larem ad nostrum* CAT 136:28
festal: f. light in Christ-Church ARN 14:16
fester: Lilies that f. smell far SHAK 494:15
Festina: F. lente SUET 524:16
festoon: f. The room with my presence
FRY 219:29
fetch: f. the age of gold MILT 344:11
'We are going to f. you KIPL 298:4
fettered: f. to her eye LOV 318:15
so f. fast we are BROW 98:23
fetters: f., though of gold BACON 27:42
reason Milton wrote in f. BLAKE 88:12
These strong Egyptian f. SHAK 421:17
fettle: f. for the great grey drayhorse
HOPK 256:11
feu: *et allume le f.* LA R 310:15
feud: Fhairshon swore a f. AYT 24:6
feux: *f. qui s'enflamment au* FRAN 218:2
fever: darter es died o' the f. TENN 544:5
f., and the fret KEATS 291:18
f. call'd 'Living' POE 375:3
He had a f. when he was SHAK 448:15
life's fitful f. SHAK 461:12
this her f. might be it DONNE 188:26
feverous: earth Was f. SHAK 460:20
fevers: Time and f. burn away AUDEN 19:17
fever-trees: all set about with f. KIPL 304:21
Février: Generals Janvier and F. NICH 362:23
Few: F. and evil have the days BIBLE 46:38
f. and far between CAMP 129:10
f. are chosen BIBLE 67:18
f. words are the best men SHAK 444:5
Gey f. ANON 5:16
is small potatoes and f. KIPL 304:29
labourers are f. BIBLE 65:29
many for the gain of a f. POPE 381:16
notes are f. BLAKE 88:10
owed by so many to so f. CHUR 150:2
state of mind to have f. BACON 26:8
therefore let thy words be f. BIBLE 55:16
we happy f. SHAK 445:3
Ye are many—they are f. SHEL 502:4
feyned: f. flaterye and japes CHAU 142:7
feyth: yive I f. and ful credence CHAU 143:29
Fhairshon: F. swore a feud AYT 24:6
fiat: bound to say '*f. justitia* MANS 328:16
F. *justitia et pereat* FERD 210:33
F. *justitia et ruant coeli* WATS 565:8
f. *voluntas tua sicut* MASS 335:5
have a bit of F. in my soul BEDD 36:25
fib: Destroy his f. or sophistry POPE 376:22
fickle: f., freckled HOPK 256:23
fierce and f. is the South TENN 542:5
made thee f. as thou art BYRON 126:3
fickleness: f. of the women I love
SHAW 498:9
fico: *Diga ao povo que f.* PEDR 371:4
f. for the phrase SHAK 469:4
fiction: best thing in f. WILDE 573:32
f. lags after truth BURKE 109:16
f. of the truth we think FRY 220:9
in a f., in a dream SHAK 432:27
it as an improbable f. SHAK 490:9

must say to the Muse of f. SCOTT 418:36
Poetry is the supreme f. STEV 520:15
Stranger than f. BYRON 124:7
That is what F. means WILDE 573:3
fiddle: f., sir, and spade SCOTT 418:6
F., we know, is diddle SWIN 529:27
first and I the second f. SPR 517:12
'Fish f. de-dee LEAR 312:17
important beyond all this f. MOORE 355:19
tune played on an old f. BUTL 119:15
fiddled: f. whisper music ELIOT 205:9
fiddler: chemist, f., statesman DRYD 194:13
f.'s old tune MORR 358:12
He was a f. SWIFT 526:16
fiddles: some are fond of f. MAS 333:21
fiddle-strings: Which f. is weakness
DICK 179:31
fide: *Punica f.* SALL 413:25
sed fortius f. et gaude LUTH 320:15
Fidele: To fair F.'s grassy tomb COLL 158:16
fideles: *Adeste,* f. ANON 10:4
fidgety: f. Phil HOFF 252:15
fidus: *f. quae tela gerebat Achates*
VIRG 557:12
fie: f., now would she cry BARN 33:32
field: comes and tills the f. TENN 543:11
Consider the lilies of the f. BIBLE 64:30
corner of a foreign f. BROO 94:30
f. is full of shades THOM 547:24
f. of Golgotha and dead SHAK 479:20
f. of human conflict was CHUR 150:2
From the wet f. ARN 15:5
Man for the f. and woman TENN 542:9
man of the f. BIBLE 46:13
possess the f. CLOU 154:4
sickle in the fruitful f. BLAKE 86:19
that lay field to f. BIBLE 57:24
What though the f. be lost MILT 345:3
fieldmice: f. bawk talk JOYCE 286:8
fields: ancestral f. with his own oxen
HOR 259:7
appeared in football f. PLOM 374:19
Blown f. or flowerful closes SWIN 530:21
f. fall southward SWIN 529:18
f. invested with purpureal WORD 578:3
f. to cross till a farm BROW 102:14
F. to fairness POUND 383:18
flowerless f. of heaven SWIN 528:14
grass returns to the f. and leaves HOR 261:14
I go among the f. and catch KEATS 294:17
me from the f. of sleep WORD 579:2
Poetic f. encompass me ADD 2:4
takes back her folded f. JOYCE 286:9
fiend: dark dominion swung the f. MER 337:5
defy the foul f. SHAK 454:19
F. Walked up and down MILT 347:10
Firefrorefiddle, the F. of the Fell ELIOT 203:7
foul F. coming over BUNY 107:14
hyperbolical f. SHAK 490:19
knows, a frightful f. COL 155:27
Like a f. hid in a cloud BLAKE 87:23
fiends: Beneath is all the f. SHAK 455:17
f. in upper air SCOTT 417:20
f. that plague thee thus COL 155:10
fier: Youk'n hide de f. HARR 242:25
fierce: bright and f. and fickle TENN 542:5
F. as ten furies MILT 346:24
f. blaze of riot cannot SHAK 478:19
f. light which beats upon TENN 533:30
grew more f. and wild HERB 247:15
look not so f. on me MARL 329:15
more f. in its religion NEWM 361:19
were f. and bald and short SASS 414:10
fierceness: f. makes Error a fault HERB 247:6
fiere: my trusty f. BURNS 112:33
fiery: burning f. furnace BIBLE 61:3
f. portal of the east SHAK 479:12
quench all the f. darts BIBLE 78:10
that very f. particle BYRON 123:32
throne was like the f. flame BIBLE 61:8

fife: squealing of the wry-neck'd f.
SHAK 466:13
Thane of F. had a wife SHAK 462:21
That practised on a f. CARR 133:10
tootle-te-tootle the f. BROW 105:31
fifteen: At f. I stopped scowling
POUND 383:16
F. men on the dead man's STEV 521:21
f. wild Decembers BRON 93:22
maiden of bashful f. SHER 506:31
fifth: f. column MOLA 352:29
remember the F. of November ANON 7:10
Fifties: are the tranquillized F. LOW 319:20
fifty: At f. chides his infamous YOUNG 588:5
enough for f. hopes BROW 99:4
F. springs are little room HOUS 262:14
(F. thousand horse KIPL 297:24
Love is lame at f. years HARDY 240:18
fifty-fifty: f. Americanism in this
ROOS 408:6
fig: f. for those by law protected
BURNS 114:19
sewed f. leaves BIBLE 45:16
under his f. tree BIBLE 61:23
We don't care a f. LEAR 312:8
fight: bade me f. had told me so EWER 209:12
better to f. for the good TENN 540:19
cannot f. against the future GLAD 229:12
can we f. with fifty-three TENN 542:21
diminutive of birds, will f. SHAK 462:12
f. begins within himself BROW 99:10
f. for freedom and truth IBSEN 269:19
f. for its King and country ANON 7:19
f. in defence of one's country HOMER 254:2
fighting the lost f. of virtue STEV 521:2
f. like devils SHAK 444:8
Fight the good f. of faith BIBLE 79:19
fought The better f. MILT 348:26
Good at a f. MOORE 357:5
hath no stomach to this f. SHAK 445:3
have not yet begun to f. JONES 283:11
I dare not f. SHAK 443:14
If he f. longer than he SHAK 438:12
I give the f. up BROW 103:6
I have fought a good f. BIBLE 79:26
I purpose to f. it out GRANT 233:21
'Let's f. till six CARR 135:12
man being too proud to f. WILS 574:20
man may f. and no be slain BURNS 115:13
may f. again BUTL 119:15
Our cock won't f. BEAV 36:14
so f. I BIBLE 76:9
then Ile rise and f. againe BALL 31:15
then say it was in f. SHAK 439:7
there is no peril in the f. CORN 162:16
There is only the f. ELIOT 202:24
thought it wrong to f. BELL 39:25
Ulster will f. CHUR 149:18
us must f. on to the end HAIG 237:11
us who will fight and f. GAIT 220:26
We don't want to f. HUNT 268:3
we shall f. on the beaches CHUR 149:31
yourselves like men, and f. BIBLE 49:38
youth that must f. and die HOOV 255:25
fighter: Am I no a bonny f. STEV 521:7
I was ever a f. BROW 103:32
fighters: *Their f. drink the rivers up*
HOUS 265:3
fighting: dies f. has increase GREN 236:15
f. with your land army MONT 355:9
f. with daggers in a hogshead SCOTT 419:2
Football then was f. sorrow HOUS 262:22
live only by f. evils BERL 41:23
wilt thou leave f. o' days SHAK 441:27
fights: captain that knows what he f.
CROM 169:20
that gain'd a hundred f. TENN 541:9
figments: Of making f. feel HARDY 239:12
figs: f. grew upon thorn CHES 146:2
f. of thistles BIBLE 65:9

Green bursting f.   ARN 14:21
long life better than f.   SHAK 421:12
name of the Prophet—f.   SMITH 510:9
fig-tree: Train up a f. in the way   DICK 177:27
Figura: Caballero de la Triste F.
                   CERV 138:12
figure: Behind you swiftly the f.
                   AUDEN 18:18
did come the strangest f.   BROW 103:18
f. in the carpet   JAMES 271:22
f. is easy   AUDEN 18:13
prone and emaciated f.   HARDY 239:13
This f. that thou here   JONS 284:17
Will she make a f.   SWIFT 526:14
figures: might prove anything by f.
                   CARL 131:15
thieves, the nine f.   DICK 178:6
with the drapery of his f.   COL 158:8
filches: f. from me my good name
                  SHAK 475:16
File: nature of an Old F.   DICK 178:27
filed: beadroll worthy to be f.   SPEN 516:19
files: foremost f. of time   TENN 539:7
filia: matre pulchra f. pulchrior   HOR 259:2
filii: clamamus exsules f. Evae   ANON 10:19
Filioque: *qui ex Patre F. procedit*
                 MASS 334:20
Fill: F. ev'ry glass   GAY 222:25
F. high the cup with Samian   BYRON 123:3
f. hup the chinks wi' cheese   SURT 525:8
f. our bowls once more   SHAK 422:22
f. the Cup   FITZ 212:6
f. the Cup   FITZ 212:22
f. the unforgiving minute   KIPL 300:2
it must first f. a pool   BACON 26:33
take our f. of love   BIBLE 53:24
To f. the hour   EMER 207:17
filled: be f. with the Spirit   BIBLE 78:5
f. all the house where   BIBLE 73:22
f. his belly with the husks   BIBLE 70:19
f. the hungry with good   BIBLE 69:6
mouth f. with laughter   PRAY 398:16
nor the ear f. with hearing   BIBLE 55:7
they shall be f.   BIBLE 64:6
fille de chambre: caught hold of the f.'s
                STER 519:14
fillest: f. all things living with   PRAY 399:15
filling: f. the world   SCOTT 418:6
fills: He f. a chair   JOHN 278:26
Fls: F. de Saint Louis   FIRM 212:2
filth: Delights in f. and foul   SPEN 516:14
filthiness: f. and superfluity of naughtiness
                BIBLE 80:10
f., nor foolish talking   BIBLE 78:2
Filths: F. savour but themselves   SHAK 455:11
filthy: fond of her most f. bargain
                SHAK 477:13
righteousnesses are as f. rags   BIBLE 60:12
that is f. and polluted   BIBLE 61:27
upon this f. modern tide   YEATS 587:2
fin: f. in the porphyry font   TENN 542:14
le commencement de la f.   TALL 531:19
Finality: F. is not the language   DISR 184:22
find: can f. information upon it   JOHN 276:28
f. out moonshine   SHAK 470:15
f. the beautiful we must   EMER 207:1
f. the mind's construction   SHAK 458:22
F. thy body by the wall   ARN 13:15
if ye f. my beloved   BIBLE 57:2
not f. anything pleasant   VOLT 560:21
searching f. out God   BIBLE 52:22
see an author and we f.   PASC 369:4
there thou shalt f. me   ANON 7:11
thing could I never f.   BELL 40:10
to f., and not to yield   TENN 544:3
Where shall we f. her   SWIN 528:16
Who fail to f. thee   TENN 539:22
you f. it wond'rous short   GOLD 231:9
findeth: f. his life shall lose   BIBLE 65:40
he that seeketh f.   BIBLE 65:3

finding: fear of f. something worse BELL 39:3
finds: f. too late that men betray GOLD 231:31
Who f. himself   ARN 14:22
Fine: F. art is that in which   RUSK 411:25
F. clothes are good only   JOHN 276:38
f. into an horizontal line   WHEW 569:16
f. writing is next to fine   KEATS 294:23
quite a *disgrace* to be f.   TAYL 531:24
than much f. gold   PRAY 390:12
think is particularly f.   JOHN 276:14
very f. cat indeed   JOHN 279:9
Fine Arts: Considered as One of the F.
                DE Q 175:4
Devil fly away with the f.   CARL 132:5
finem: dabit deus his quoque f.   VIRG 557:13
et respice f.   ANON 10:18
F. di dederint   HOR 259:19
finer: f. investment for any community
                CHUR 150:15
finery: not bedizened with f.   TROL 552:16
fines: sunt certi denique f.   HOR 261:23
finest: 'This was their f. hour'   CHUR 150:1
finger: Better a f. off   SCOTT 418:27
F. do you want on the Trigger   ANON 8:22
F. of birth-strangled babe   SHAK 462:4
God's f. touch'd him   TENN 537:7
his slow and moving f.   SHAK 476:18
little f. shall be thicker   BIBLE 51:2
Moving F. writes   FITZ 213:7
Old Harry's got a f. in it   ELIOT 201:15
once her choppy f. laying   SHAK 458:10
Press'd her cold f. closer   KEATS 290:2
fingernails: paring his f.   JOYCE 286:18
fingers: Contaminate our f. with SHAK 451:13
cool stream thy f. wet   ARN 14:14
dead men's f.   SHAK 436:19
distinguished into joints and f.   TRAH 552:1
drumming with his f.   MAC 324:14
even the works of thy f.   PRAY 389:28
f. of this hand wherewith   BROW 98:12
f. play in skilled unmindfulness
                HARDY 239:12
forth f. of a man's hand   BIBLE 61:5
If she with ivory f. drive   POUND 382:15
Just as my f. on these keys   STEV 520:16
my f. is to my fingers   SHAK 445:5
my f. wandered idly   PROC 401:13
smile upon his f.' ends   SHAK 443:17
terrified vague f.   YEATS 586:1
thrust his icy f. in my maw   SHAK 452:31
with careful f. and benign   KEATS 292:28
With f. weary and worn   HOOD 255:6
finger-stalls: In fitless f.   GILB 227:7
finger-tips: accomplished man to his
f.   HOR 262:4
finis: cuius regni non erit f.   MASS 334:20
finish: logically predicate his f.   KIPL 302:4
we will f. the job   CHUR 150:6
finish'd: f. gentleman from top BYRON 123:37
finished: been f. in half the time WOD 575:21
I have f. my course   BIBLE 79:26
'It is f.   BEDE 37:2
It is f.   BIBLE 73:4
love of f. years   ROSS 408:26
never getting f.   HARDY 241:23
now I have f. the work   OVID 366:19
until it be thoroughly f.   DRAKE 193:1
world where England is f.   MILL 340:2
finisher: author and f. of our faith
                BIBLE 79:35
finishing: Don't keep f. your sentences
                LONS 317:24
finite: f. hearts that yearn   BROW 105:30
quite bury under the F.   CARL 132:19
fio: puto deus f.   VESP 556:12
fi'pun: gen'l'm'n said to the f.' note
                DICK 182:5
fir: f. trees dark and high   HOOD 254:18
thorn shall come up the f.   BIBLE 59:28

fire: adamantine chains and penal f.
                MILT 344:24
anger as the flint bears f.   SHAK 451:24
ashes where once I was f.   BYRON 125:31
at once a gentle f. has   SAPP 414:6
bound Upon a wheel of f.   SHAK 455:25
Bring me my chariot of f.   BLAKE 86:16
broad gate and the great f.   SHAK 421:4
cloven tongues like as of f.   BIBLE 73:22
coals of f.   PRAY 390:9
cosy f. is bright and gay   PAIN 367:15
danger of hell f.   BIBLE 64:12
dropping-wells of f.   TENN 537:6
everlasting f.   HOUS 265:4
every time she shouted 'F.   BELL 39:1
Fell in the f. and was   GRAH 233:13
F. and fleet and candle-lighte   BALL 31:6
F. and hail   PRAY 399:22
F. answers fire   SHAK 444:9
F. burn and cauldron bubble   SHAK 462:2
f. is dying in the grate   MER 337:7
f. is quickly trodden out   SHAK 446:21
f. most pure   DONNE 188:9
f. of my loins   NAB 359:5
f. sall never make thee   BALL 31:7
f. seven times tried this   SHAK 466:22
f. shall heat the deep   TENN 537:25
f. that saith not   BIBLE 54:46
f. that warms cold   CERV 138:20
f. until you see the whites   PUTN 403:6
fretted with golden f.   SHAK 432:15
great a matter a little f. kindleth   BIBLE 80:13
Great F. of London was   DICK 178:19
hand dare seize the f.   BLAKE 87:15
heart of the night with f.   SWIN 530:13
hearts the f.'s centre   SPEN 515:7
heretic that makes the f.   SHAK 491:13
his wheels as burning f.   BIBLE 61:8
I am f. and air   SHAK 424:11
I have seen the f.   BIBLE 59:12
kindles f.   LA R 310:15
knowest Who hast made the F.   KIPL 301:16
Let f. come out   BIBLE 49:19
Lord was not in the f.   BIBLE 51:14
man's heart were as f.   SWIN 528:16
man take f. in his bosom   BIBLE 53:23
martyr in his shirt of f.   SMITH 510:2
men, that are set on f.   PRAY 393:15
ministers a flaming f.   PRAY 396:18
My f.'s extinct   ANON 6:19
neighbour's house is on f.   BURKE 111:1
night in a pillar of f.   BIBLE 47:21
Now stir the f.   COWP 167:11
of glass mingled with f.   BIBLE 82:19
of thee are sword and f.   TENN 534:10
perfect steadiness under f.   KITC 305:14
performs th' effect of f.   MILT 346:21
rain snares, f. and brimstone   PRAY 389:31
right Promethean f.   SHAK 457:3
roast with f.   BIBLE 47:17
set a house on f.   BACON 27:37
shall be found by the f.   BROW 99:18
shalt heap coals of f.   BIBLE 54:29
spark o' Nature's f.   BURNS 113:20
spirit all compact of f.   SHAK 495:19
steep-down gulfs of liquid f.   SHAK 477:21
thorough f.   SHAK 470:2
To Purgatory f. thou com'st   BALL 31:7
to view what f. was near   SOUT 514:19
two irons in the f.   BEAU 36:4
wall next door catches f.   HOR 258:23
What of the faith and f.   HARDY 240:8
You must not take for f.   SHAK 430:21
youth of England are on f.   SHAK 443:12
firebrand: f. plucked out of the burning
                BIBLE 61:20
Fire Brigade: Of London's Noble F.
                BELL 39:8
fired: hand that f. the shot   BALL 31:4
fire-fly: f. wakens   TENN 542:14

fire-folk: look at all the f. sitting HOPK 256:28
Firefrorefiddle: F., the Fiend of the Fell
ELIOT 203:7
fires: arose the answering f. MAC 322:2
Big f. flare up in a wind FRAN 218:2
f. soon burn out themselves SHAK 478:19
Fuel to maintain his f. CAREW 130:12
misled by wandering f. DRYD 196:13
th' assembled f. appear SMART 509:4
thought-executing f. SHAK 454:4
fire-side: adventures were by the f.
GOLD 232:34
glass of wine by his own f. SHER 506:38
no f., howsoe'er defended LONG 317:6
people to leave their own f. AUST 22:10
To make a happy f. clime BURNS 115:15
firing: have what to do after f. REED 405:5
Firm: F. Resolve BURNS 115:14
firmament: f. sheweth his handy-work
PRAY 390:11
is no fellow in the f. SHAK 449:25
spacious f. on high ADD 2:22
there's fury in the f. SASS 415:4
this brave o'erhanging f. SHAK 432:15
Waters that be above the F. PRAY 384:20
Firmly: F. I believe and truly NEWM 362:11
Firmness: *Commodity, F., and Delight*
WOTT 583:16
little objects with like f. BYRON 120:29
Thy f. makes my circle DONNE 190:18
first: beautiful than thy f. love YEATS 584:23
be done for the f. time CORN 162:23
by the clash of the F. HARDY 240:3
certainty are not the f. HOUS 264:21
Ever since afore her F. DICK 179:27
extol Him f., him last MILT 348:16
f. and second class citizens WILL 574:14
f. baby laughed BARR 34:13
f. blow is half the battle GOLD 232:27
f. by whom the new are POPE 378:19
f. casualty when war JOHN 273:18
f. destroys their mind DRYD 196:2
f. duty of a State RUSK 412:6
f. impulse was never CORN 162:18
f. impulses as they are MONT 355:11
f. in a village than second CAES 127:3
f. in war DONNE 187:23
f., last, everlasting BIBLE 76:28
f. of earthly blessings GIBB 224:17
f. of those who know TENN 541:23
f. step that is difficult DU D 198:28
F. time he kissed me BROW 98:12
f. true gentleman that DEKK 173:19
God's f. Creature BACON 28:5
he'd have been here f. CARR 135:32
I am not the f. HOUS 263:13
in the very f. line GOLD 231:19
last shall be f. BIBLE 67:13
loved not at f. sight MARL 329:18
morning were the f. day BIBLE 45:1
Since f. I saw you fresh SHAK 494:18
there is no last nor f. BROW 103:25
Thou know'st the f. time SHAK 455:22
undoubted title to the F. SWIFT 527:1
used by Charles the F. COW 164:4
were the f. that ever burst COL 155:12
when f. your eye I ey'd SHAK 494:18
work is what to put f. PASC 369:3
first-born: against all the f. of Egypt
SHAK 425:17
brought forth her f. son BIBLE 69:9
will smite all the f. BIBLE 47:18
first day: f. of our Jubilee is death
BROW 96:21
firstfruits: f. of them that slept BIBLE 76:22
First-rate: F. School WAUGH 565:30
powers of a f. man BAG 29:16
firsts: f. in some less favoured BETJ 44:11
fish: buttercups fried with f. LEAR 312:21

f. and fishing WALT 564:11
F. is plentiful and cheap LEAR 311:26
f. with the worm that hath SHAK 435:27
have dominion over the f. BIBLE 45:4
in a black and ugly f. HOR 257:9
in the belly of the f. BIBLE 61:22
is a pretty kettle of f. MARY 333:14
It's no f. ye're buying SCOTT 418:2
I was a f. SMITH 510:10
littlest f. may enter BROO 94:13
mind of the skuttle f. ADD 2:24
piece of a broiled f. BIBLE 71:20
said the small 'stute F. KIPL 304:14
seem older than the f. FRY 219:23
St Ives says the smell of f. KILV 296:6
stranded f. gaped among PLOM 374:19
subject to rape like f. DONNE 190:2
that f. would have bright KEATS 289:3
There's a f. that *talks* DE L 173:23
Thou deboshed f. thou SHAK 485:14
Un-dish-cover the f. CARR 136:11
was ever so free as a f. RUSK 412:2
What cat's averse to f. GRAY 235:6
word bites like a f. SPEN 515:15
worms to torture f. COLM 159:6
fished: He f. by obstinate isles POUND 383:3
fishermen: f. that walk upon the beach
SHAK 455:14
Where f. lounge at noon ELIOT 205:4
fishers: Three f. went sailing away
KING 297:2
will make you f. of men BIBLE 64:5
fishes: betray Tawny-finn'd f. SHAK 422:9
Dim moon-eyed f. near HARDY 239:5
f. first to shipping did DRYD 195:22
f. flew and forests walked CHES 146:22
f. leap in silver stream CLARE 152:14
F., that tipple LOV 318:17
how the f. live in the sea SHAK 478:4
little f. of the sea CARR 135:25
Men lived like f. SIDN 507:12
men that f. gnaw'd upon SHAK 480:27
of the loaves and the f. PEAC 370:16
So are the f. CHUR 150:4
uncommunicating muteness of f. LAMB 308:4
welcomes little f. CARR 133:18
fishified: flesh, how art thou f. SHAK 482:22
fishing: angling or float f. I can JOHN 280:28
blow when he goes a-f. WALT 563:34
I go a f. BIBLE 73:13
On f. up the moon PEAC 371:3
was f. in the dull canal ELIOT 204:26
fish-knives: Phone for the f. BETJ 42:19
fish-like: very ancient and f. smell
SHAK 485:7
fishmonger: you are a f. SHAK 432:4
fishpond: That great f. (the sea) DEKK 173:18
fishpools: eyes like the f. in Heshbon
BIBLE 57:9
fishy: f. form and mind BROO 94:13
Fissures: F. appeared in football PLOM 374:19
fist: agin the Secesher's f. WARD 564:27
of f. most valiant SHAK 444:17
fistful: f. of coins ZAP 588:18
fists: groan and shake their f. HOUS 266:8
fit: become f. for this world KEATS 293:14
f. for the kingdom of God BIBLE 69:25
f. to use their freedom MAC 323:25
f. will work on him SHAK 437:9
isn't f. for humans now BETJ 44:4
most senseless and f. man SHAK 472:28
taen the f. o' rhyme BURNS 113:23
they are not f. to live JOHN 276:33
when the f. was on him SHAK 448:15
when the melancholy f. KEATS 291:15
Why then I'll f. you KYD 306:8
fitchew: f. nor the soiled horse SHAK 455:17
fitful: life's f. fever SHAK 461:12
fitless: In f. finger-stalls GILB 227:7
fitly: word f. spoken BIBLE 54:26

fits: wen bein' took with f. DICK 179:27
fitter: Young men are f. to invent
BACON 27:39
Fittest: Survival of the F. is more
DARW 171:27
survival of the f. SPEN 514:30
fitting: f. for a princess SHAK 424:16
It is right and f. MASS 335:3
Fitzgerald: shall hoarse F. bawl
BYRON 124:14
this Edward F. died YEATS 586:19
five: At exactly f. in the afternoon
GARC 221:5
f. days elder than ourselves BROW 96:10
f. minutes too late all COWL 164:21
Full fathom f. SHAK 484:32
Must rise at f. CLAR 152:24
Not f. in five score PORS 381:27
These f. kings did a king THOM 547:4
five-and-twenty: reputation of f.
DRYD 196:36
five per cent: f. is the natural interest
MAC 323:29
five-pound: Wrapped up in a f. note
LEAR 312:11
fix: right to f. the boundary PARN 369:2
such a f. to be so fertile NASH 360:4
fixed: great gulf f. BIBLE 70:29
He f. thee mid this dance BROW 104:11
may surely there be f. PRAY 386:12
You are the one f. point DOYLE 192:23
fizz: sheer necessity of f. BELL 39:31
flabbiness: f. born of the bitch-goddess
JAMES 272:3
flag: death's pale f. is not SHAK 483:30
debt, an' a f. LOW 319:7
f. of all the free CHES 147:3
f. of my disposition WHIT 570:18
out a f. and sign of love SHAK 473:1
spare your country's f. WHIT 571:17
their f. against a power WEBS 566:12
We'll keep the red f. flying CONN 161:10
Whose f. has braved CAMP 129:12
Flag-flapper: Jelly-bellied F. KIPL 305:8
flag-flowers: There grew broad f.
SHEL 503:20
flagitium: Peiusque leto f. timet HOR 261:19
flagons: Stay me with f. BIBLE 56:21
flakes: Some f. have lost their HARDY 240:21
flambeaux: chestnut casts his f. HOUS 264:20
flame: blood and smoke and f. HOUS 266:4
Chloe is my real f. PRIOR 401:1
eye the unconquered f. POUND 382:14
f. of the taper SHAK 428:8
f. out like shining from HOPK 256:12
f.? The Bush is bare BROW 98:29
full of subtil f. BEAU 35:19
hard, gemlike f. PATER 369:21
his eyes were as a f. BIBLE 81:14
in them that little f. REN 405:11
Kindled a f. I still deplore GARR 221:16
one burning f. together TENN 538:9
only change th'expiring f. GAY 223:23
seem'd my f. to qualify SHAK 495:2
so in a shapeless f. DONNE 187:18
Still plays about the f. GAY 222:1
throne was like the fiery f. BIBLE 61:8
Whose f. creeps in at every PEELE 371:7
flamed: f. upon the brazen greaves
TENN 538:8
flames: Commit it then to the f. HUME 267:15
F. in the forehead MILT 343:17
So his f. must waste away CAREW 130:12
thou king of f. CHAP 140:7
warmth of shepherds' f. MARL 330:11
Went by her like thin f. ROSS 409:18
With rich f. BROW 97:8
flaming: ministers a f. fire PRAY 396:18
thou f. minister SHAK 477:5
Wav'd over by that f. brand MILT 350:1

flammantia: *f. moenia mundi* LUCR 320:3
flamme: *f. qui ne s'éteint pas* REN 405:13
flammes: *met le monde entier en f.* VOLT 561:6
Flanders: F. fields the poppies blow MCCR 324:30
F. hath receiv'd our yoke WALL 562:17
had brought him a F. mare HENR 246:2
prodigious armies we had in F. STER 519:26
flanks: silken f. with garlands drest KEATS 291:8
flannel: waistcoat and f. drawers GASK 221:24
flannelled: f. fools at the wicket KIPL 300:4
flap-dragon: easier swallowed than a f. SHAK 457:12
flashes: objects recognised, In f. WORD 580:19
occasional f. of silence SMITH 511:13
Flask: F. of Wine FITZ 212:11
Flat: F. and flexible truths BROW 95:18
half so f. as Walter Scott ANON 7:8
very dangerous f. SHAK 467:2
your life extremely f. GILB 228:29
flaterye: feyned f. and japes CHAU 142:7
flats: different sharps and f. BROW 103:15
flatten: His hide is sure to f. BELL 38:30
flatter: before you f. a man so JOHN 280:29
do but f. with their lips PRAY 389:32
f. beauty's ignorant ear YEATS 586:14
F. the mountain-tops with SHAK 493:9
I am afraid to f. him BURKE 109:5
Regard me as I do not f. SHAK 427:20
flatter'd: Englishman, Being f. CHAP 140:3
I have not f. its rank BYRON 120:38
still contemn'd and f. SHAK 455:5
flattered: being then most f. SHAK 449:11
f. into virtue SURT 525:1
He that loves to be f. SHAK 485:28
who neither feared nor f. DOUG 191:6
flatterer: flattered is worthy o' the f. SHAK 485:28
hypocrite, and f. BLAKE 86:7
flatterers: by f. besieged POPE 376:27
I tell him he hates f. SHAK 449:11
surrounded by sycophants and f. HARD 238:21
flattering: f. unction to your soul SHAK 435:14
Some with a f. word WILDE 572:10
flatters: humours and f. them CHES 145:26
What really f. a man is SHAW 497:4
flattery: Everyone likes f. DISR 185:28
f. is worth his having JOHN 280:29
gained by every sort of f. CHES 146:1
is paid with f. JOHN 281:15
'This is no f. SHAK 424:31
tout for f. COLL 158:14
Was f. lost on poet's ear SCOTT 416:18
Flaubert: His true Penelope was F. POUND 383:3
flavour: from its high celestial f. BYRON 122:26
flaw: no kind of fault or f. GILB 226:1
sans crack or f. SHAK 457:16
flaws: wished the f. were fewer BROW 100:4
flax: smoking f. shall he not quench BIBLE 59:11
flayed: Last week I saw a woman f. SWIFT 527:5
flaying: f. would be fair HOUS 266:8
flea: between a louse and a f. JOHN 279:8
f. Hath smaller fleas SWIFT 528:5
honour the very f. of his dog JONS 284:6
will clog the foot of a f. SHAK 490:1
fleas: dog that praised his f. YEATS 587:4
F. know not whether they LAND 309:15
f. that tease in the high BELL 40:13
o' f. is good fer a dog WEST 569:4
flebilis: *Multis ille bonis f. occidit* HOR 260:1
Flecte: *F. quod est rigidum* LANG 310:1

Flectere: *F. si nequeo superos* VIRG 559:5
fled: earth's foundations f. HOUS 265:7
F. is that music KEATS 291:23
I f. Him THOM 548:8
kissed it and then f. SHEL 503:17
sea saw that, and f. PRAY 397:16
Still as he f. SPEN 516:6
Truth away From you is f. WYATT 583:20
Whence all but he had f. HEM 244:20
world that I am f. SHAK 494:6
flee: death shall f. from them BIBLE 82:7
f. away, and be at rest PRAY 393:10
f. from the wrath to come BIBLE 63:38
sorrow and sighing shall f. BIBLE 59:1
that Fortune list to f. CHAU 142:29
They f. from me WYATT 583:21
wicked f. when no man pursueth BIBLE 54:41
with their armies did f. PRAY 394:8
fleece: forest f. the Wrekin HOUS 263:14
fleeces: Thus you sheep bear f. VIRG 560:20
fleet: All in the Downs the f. GAY 223:28
command of the Channel F. SMITH 512:2
enemy's f. came yonder TENN 539:26
Fire and f. and candle-lighte BALL 31:6
F. in which we serve PRAY 400:2
F. is all lit up WOOD 576:10
f. of stars is anchored FLEC 214:7
F. the time carelessly SHAK 424:20
Spanish f. thou *canst* not SHER 505:27
There's the British F. THAC 546:2
toward the Japanese f. HALS 238:11
we took care of our f. ADD 2:19
fleeth: hireling f. BIBLE 72:19
My soul f. unto the Lord PRAY 398:24
fleets: interested in armies and f. AUDEN 18:15
Fleet Street: who can be dull in F. LAMB 307:23
will take a walk down F. SALA 413:17
flesh: All f. is as grass BIBLE 80:21
All f. is grass BIBLE 59:6
all f. shall see it together BIBLE 59:5
bondwoman was born after the f. BIBLE 77:16
brought him bread and f. BIBLE 51:6
carrion f. than to receive SHAK 467:20
closed up the f. instead BIBLE 45:11
could not all this f. SHAK 440:25
delicate white human f. FIEL 211:25
east wind made f. APPL 11:12
eat bulls' f. PRAY 393:3
eat the f. in that night BIBLE 47:17
fair and unpolluted f. SHAK 437:4
f., alas, is wearied MALL 327:9
f. and blood so cheap HOOD 255:8
f., and the devil PRAY 385:16
f., how art thou fishified SHAK 482:22
f. of my flesh BIBLE 45:12
F. perishes, I live on HARDY 240:1
f. sinks downwards here SHAK 480:16
f. to feel the chain BRON 93:21
From this world-wearied f. SHAK 483:31
he might trust in the f. BIBLE 78:16
if this f. which walls SHAK 479:11
in my f. shall I see God BIBLE 52:31
men are f. and blood SHAK 449:25
mind the things of the f. BIBLE 75:7
more f. than another man SHAK 440:5
my heart and my f. rejoice PRAY 395:11
not against f. and blood BIBLE 78:10
not provision for the f. BIBLE 75:25
reasonable soul and human f. subsisting PRAY 385:14
since f. must live BROW 105:3
sinful lusts of the f. PRAY 388:13
soul to feel the f. BRON 93:21
ta'en out thy heart o' f. BALL 32:3
that look but casual f. YEATS 587:1
these our f. upright DONNE 188:15
they shall be one f. BIBLE 45:13
to me a thorn in the f. BIBLE 77:13

too solid f. would melt SHAK 429:28
unto thee shall all f. come PRAY 393:23
wants to make your f. creep DICK 181:29
willing but the f. is weak BIBLE 68:16
Word was made f. BIBLE 71:27
WORD WAS MADE F. MASS 335:12
would I could subdue the f. BETJ 44:1
yet would God this f. SWIN 530:18
flesh'd: f. Thy maiden sword SHAK 440:26
fleshly: through all this f. dress VAUG 555:16
flesh pots: when we sat by the f. BIBLE 47:23
fletu: *fraterno multum manantia f.* CAT 137:15
fleurs: *amas de f. étrangères* MONT 355:6
flew: f. the web and floated TENN 538:11
sparrows from outside f. BEDE 37:1
flexible: Flat and f. truths BROW 95:18
Flibbertigibbet: This is the foul fiend F. SHAK 454:22
flichterin: wi' f.' noise an' glee BURNS 113:5
flies: Dead f. cause the ointment BIBLE 56:1
f. to wanton boys SHAK 455:9
F., worms, and flowers WATTS 565:24
his skin the swart f. move DOUG 191:10
kisses the Joy as it f. BLAKE 86:18
murmurous haunt of f. KEATS 291:21
shops with large blue f. SMITH 510:7
these summer f. SHAK 457:15
which may catch small f. SWIFT 527:16
flight: alarms of struggle and f. ARN 12:23
His cloister'd f. SHAK 461:13
His f. was madness SHAK 462:11
now wing thy distant f. HADR 237:9
Swift be thy f. SHEL 505:2
that puts the Stars to F. FITZ 212:5
will not take their f. MILT 344:7
flights: f. upon the banks of Thames JONS 284:25
flim-flam: This is a pretty f. BEAU 36:6
flinch: cowards f. and traitors CONN 161:10
facts are facts and f. BROW 104:21
Fling: F. but a stone GREEN 235:28
f. the ringleaders from ARN 16:28
I'll have a f. FLET 215:20
Flinging: F. from his arms I laughed YEATS 585:20
flint: anger as the f. bears fire SHAK 451:24
flirtation: Merely innocent f. BYRON 123:35
flits: bat that f. at close BLAKE 85:11
flittings: Thou tellest my f. PRAY 393:13
float: clouds I'll never f. WORD 579:18
floated: Out flew the web and f. TENN 538:11
floating: f. bulwark of the island BLAC 85:4
flock: feed his f. like a shepherd BIBLE 59:7
f. to gaze the strengthless HOUS 263:3
hair is as a f. of goats BIBLE 56:26
have seen the ravens f. AYT 24:10
keeping watch over their f. BIBLE 69:9
said as we sat in a f. HARDY 240:13
tainted wether of the f. SHAK 467:20
was the f. in woolly fold KEATS 289:9
flocks: My father feeds his f. HOME 253:22
My f. feed not BARN 34:4
shepherds watch'd their f. TATE 531:22
Flodden: F. F.'s fatal field SCOTT 417:25
flog: f. the rank and file ARN 16:28
flogging: habit of f. me constantly TROL 552:11
There is now less f. JOHN 276:32
flood: beached verge of the salt f. SHAK 486:14
f. could not wash away CONG 160:10
f. may bear me far TENN 533:4
F. Of British freedom WORD 582:2
f. unto the world's end PRAY 394:20
giant race before the f. DRYD 196:1
nearly spoiled to F. AYT 24:7
no wave Of a great f. MER 337:10
taken at the f. SHAK 451:27
that were before the f. BIBLE 67:32
Thorough f. SHAK 470:2

687

with me into this angry f.   SHAK 448:14
flood-brim: furthest f. look with me
   ROSS 409:26
Floodgate: F. of the deeper heart FLEC 214:24
Is of so f. and o'bearing   SHAK 473:23
floods: f. are risen   PRAY 396:1
f. came   BIBLE 65:12
haystack in the f.   MORR 358:11
heavily and fell in f.   WORD 580:27
moon, the governess of f.   SHAK 470:6
neither can the f. drown it   BIBLE 57:12
She quells the f. below   CAMP 129:13
flood-ways: On f. to be far departing
   POUND 383:18
floor: fell upon the sanded f.   PAYN 370:9
how the f. of heaven   SHAK 468:15
I could f. them all   DISR 185:31
nicely sanded f.   GOLD 231:4
floors: across the f. of silent seas
   ELIOT 203:21
flop: An' f. round the earth   KIPL 304:10
flopping: must go f. yourself down
   DICK 183:8
Flora: Tasting of F. and the country
   KEATS 291:18
floral: fair and f. air   FLEC 214:6
Florence: F., Elizabethan England
   INGE 270:10
lily of F. blossoming   LONG 316:17
Rode past fair F.   KEATS 290:10
sporting prints of Aunt F.'s   COW 164:2
Flores: F. in the Azores Sir Richard
   TENN 542:21
floribus: aliquid quod in ipsis f. angat
   LUCR 320:11
florid: Let a f. music praise   AUDEN 20:21
flos: Ut f. in saeptis secretus   CAT 137:6
flotte: Elle f.   RAC 404:3
flour: whitter than the lylye f. CHAU 142:32
floures: emperice and flour of f. CHAU 143:41
that passeth soone as f.   CHAU 144:19
that the f. gynnen   CHAU 143:29
thise f. white and rede   CHAU 143:30
flourish: No more doth f.   SPEN 516:13
peculiar f. of his right arm   DICK 181:10
Princes and lords may f.   GOLD 230:18
swoop, a swing, a f.   JAMES 271:34
transfix the f. set on youth   SHAK 493:20
Truth shall f. out   PRAY 395:15
youth of a state arms do f.   BACON 27:34
flourisheth: f. as a flower of a field
   PRAY 396:17
She f. new and new   SKEL 508:18
flourishing: f. like a green bay-tree
   PRAY 391:29
no f. with his sword   REYN 405:20
flours: f. be planted on my grave
   HARDY 241:18
flout: Gild, but to f.   SCOTT 416:13
scout 'em, and f. 'em   SHAK 485:15
Flow: F. gently   BURNS 113:27
foolish tears would f.   CLAR 152:23
I within did f.   TRAH 552:3
rivers of blood must yet f.   JEFF 272:14
salt tides seaward f.   ARN 13:5
Such ebb and f. must ever   WORD 578:8
unus'd to f.   SHAK 493:7
What need you f. so fast   ANON 8:13
Flowed: F. up the hill and down ELIOT 204:21
flower: art the f. of cities all   DUNB 199:10
cometh forth like a f.   BIBLE 52:26
constellated f. that never   SHEL 503:18
creep from flower to f.   SHEL 501:5
die in the f. of their age   BIBLE 49:33
every f. that sad embroidery   MILT 343:15
f. fadeth   BIBLE 59:6
f. grows concealed   CAT 137:6
f. is born to blush unseen   GRAY 234:23
f. of roses in the spring   BIBLE 63:27
F. that once hath blown   FITZ 212:19

f. that shall be mine   WORD 583:2
f. thereof falleth away   BIBLE 80:21
f. with base infection   SHAK 494:15
From every opening f.   WATTS 565:21
glory of man as the f.   BIBLE 80:21
Heaven in a Wild F.   BLAKE 85:8
he flourisheth as a f.   PRAY 396:17
is no stronger than a f.   SHAK 494:4
leaf, the bud, the f.   SPEN 516:13
learning lightly like a f.   TENN 537:21
look like the innocent f.   SHAK 459:3
May prove a beauteous f.   SHAK 482:16
meanest f. that blows   WORD 579:14
of glory in the f.   WORD 579:13
plant and f. of light   JONS 285:8
pluck this f., safety   SHAK 438:29
saw the water-flags in f.   PATM 370:2
simple maiden in her f.   TENN 537:27
summer's f. is to the summer SHAK 494:15
sweetest f. for scent   SHEL 503:24
that a life was but a f.   SHAK 427:2
this is the noble f.   DONNE 190:23
this most goodly f.   SKEL 508:18
this same f. that smiles   HERR 250:5
upon a little western f.   SHAK 470:8
white f. of a blameless life   TENN 533:30
flower-de-luce: f. being one   SHAK 491:26
flowering: About the f. squares TENN 537:18
f. judas   ELIOT 203:4
in the f. of His fields   TENN 535:19
flower-pots: Water your damned f.
   BROW 105:5
flowers: All sorts of f. the which SPEN 515:19
are f. but fading seen   PEELE 371:8
bunch of other men's f.   MONT 355:6
cool-rooted f.   KEATS 292:1
fairest f. o' the season   SHAK 491:23
Flies, worms, and f.   WATTS 565:24
f. and fruits of love   BYRON 125:11
f. appear on the earth   BIBLE 56:22
f. azure, black   SHEL 503:19
f. growing over him   KEATS 295:1
F. I leave you on the grass   TESC 545:2
F. in the garden   STEV 523:7
f. now that frighted thou   SHAK 491:26
F. of all hue   MILT 347:20
f. of the forest are a'   ELL 206:8
f. that bloom in the spring   GILB 227:13
f. were dead   PEAC 371:1
frosts are slain and f.   SWIN 528:17
gathered f. are dead   FLEC 214:13
got me f. to strew Thy way   HERB 247:11
grass break into foam of f.   SWIN 530:18
I have seen f. come   MAS 333:23
it won't be f.   AUDEN 21:10
Larded with sweet f.   SHAK 435:34
Letting a hundred f. blossom   MAO 328:18
No f., by request   AING 3:6
odoriferous f. of fancy   SHAK 457:3
plants and f. Ever sprung   SHAK 447:3
play with f. and smile   SHAK 443:17
Proserpin gathering f.   MILT 347:21
see what f. are at my feet   KEATS 291:20
swath and all its twined f.   KEATS 293:6
That f. would bloom   KEATS 289:3
took the f. to fair   HOUS 264:17
were but as a bed of f.   DONNE 190:26
Where souls do couch on f.   SHAK 423:10
Who gave them f.   OWEN 367:7
with azure moss and f.   SHEL 502:10
You shall pick f.   AUDEN 18:8
flowery: at her f. work doth sing MILT 342:8
f. lap of earth   ARN 13:17
f. way that leads   SHAK 421:4
you walk your f. way   GILB 227:23
flowing: All things are a f. POUND 383:7
land f. with milk   BIBLE 47:6
Robes loosely f.   JONS 283:27
flown: whither f. again   FITZ 213:15
flowret: meanest f. of the vale GRAY 235:15

flow'rs: Insnar'd with f.   MARV 332:3
Time did beckon to the f.   HERB 247:24
flows: Everything f. and nothing stays
   HER 246:5
fluent: f. talkers or most plausible
   HAZL 243:24
flummoxed: Italians call reg'larly f.
   DICK 182:15
flung: f. us on the windy hill   BROO 94:15
flush: f. the man   HOPK 257:7
roses for the f. of youth   ROSS 409:7
flushed: f. print in a poppy there
   THOM 548:27
flushing: constant sound of f. runneth
   BETJ 43:12
flushpots: f. of Euston and the hanging
   JOYCE 286:5
flute: f. and the trumpet   AUDEN 20:21
f., harp   BIBLE 61:3
gauger played the f.   STEV 523:8
his brains upon the f.   BROW 105:4
Shepherds shall f. their   AUDEN 18:8
soft complaining f.   DRYD 197:24
flutes: Of f. and soft recorders MILT 345:21
sound of lyres and f.   PATER 369:19
tune of f. kept stroke   SHAK 422:2
Flutter: F. and bear him up   BETJ 42:11
flutter'd: f. and fail'd for breath   ARN 14:6
fluttered: On f. folk and wild KIPL 304:6
Fluttering: F. and dancing in the breeze
   WORD 577:29
fly: all things f. thee   THOM 548:21
are no longer wings to f.   ELIOT 202:1
'as pigs have to f.   CARR 134:9
blue-bottle f. on a rather large   BARH 33:5
F. fishing may be a very   JOHN 280:28
F., honesty, fly   SMITH 510:5
f. sat upon the axletree   BACON 27:33
f., Sir, may sting   JOHN 274:8
f. that sips treacle is   GAY 222:30
F. to her   TENN 542:5
f. to India for gold   MARL 329:4
fur F. 'bout the ears   BUTL 117:30
I heard a F. buzz   DICK 183:19
I will f. to thee   KEATS 291:20
Like a long-legged f. upon   YEATS 586:3
man is not a f.   POPE 379:8
never f. conceals a hook   BROO 94:13
noise of a f.   DONNE 191:1
Often have seen spiders f.   EDW 200:7
said a spider to a f.   HOW 267:3
small gilded f.   SHAK 455:16
sparks f. upward   BIBLE 52:17
they ever f. by twilight   BACON 27:23
thirsty f.   OLDYS 365:4
those that f.   BUTL 118:12
To f. from   BYRON 120:34
to f. is safe   COWP 167:10
which way shall I f.   MILT 347:10
with the f. in his hand   STER 519:24
with twain he did f.   BIBLE 57:28
You f. them for a moment   TENN 542:21
flyer: no high f.   PEPYS 372:10
fly-fishing: winter f. it is as useful
   WALT 563:32
flyin'-fishes: Where the f. play KIPL 301:5
flying: asleep the snow came f.   BRID 92:12
came f. upon the wings   PRAY 390:8
dear little kangaroos f.   WILDE 573:10
f. and elusive shadow   ARN 12:22
irretrievable time is f.   VIRG 560:17
lead was f.   HOUS 266:4
There is nor f. hence   SHAK 463:7
Foal: F. of an oppressed race COL 157:16
foam: opening on the f.   KEATS 291:23
through sheets of f.   ARN 14:21
was wild and dank with f.   KING 296:25
foam-flowers: f. endure when the
rose-blossoms   SWIN 529:19
foe: commend, A tim'rous f.   POPE 376:27

darkly at the f.   MAC 322:14
erect and manly f.   CANN 130:1
f. but falls before us   DRAKE 193:5
f. of tyrants   CAMP 129:9
f.! they come   BYRON 120:25
f. was folly and his weapon   HOPE 256:2
Forbids the robbing of a f.   CHUR 148:30
friend who never made a f.   TENN 534:31
I was angry with my f.   BLAKE 87:21
like fire he meets the f.   TENN 534:7
met my dearest f. in heaven   SHAK 430:4
nor shuns his f.   DRYD 195:21
not a furnace for your f.   SHAK 446:25
open f. may prove a curse   GAY 223:13
perhaps a jealous f.   SHEL 500:10
praise the merit of a f.   POPE 378:32
redoubled strokes upon the f.   SHAK 458:4
willing f. and sea room   ANON 4:26
wolf far thence that's f.   WEBS 567:9
ye sail to meet the f.   NEWB 361:7
Foeda: F. est in coitu et brevis   PETR 373:5
foeman: it to a soldier and a f.   HOUS 266:4
When the f. bares his steel   GILB 228:18
foes: art in the midst of f.   ELL 206:9
f. nor loving friends can   KIPL 300:2
f. they captive make   CHAN 139:19
Greatly his f. he dreads   CHUR 148:18
his f. pursue him still   SHAK 495:21
Keep far our f.   PRAY 400:5
long inveterate f. saluted   DRYD 197:30
man's f. shall be they   BIBLE 65:39
thrice he routed all his f.   DRYD 195:2
whom we have held as f.   BUTL 119:21
foetus: expeditious extraction of the f.   STER 519:26
fog: brown f. of a winter dawn   ELIOT 204:20
Fear death?—to feel the f.   BROW 103:31
f. comes on little cat   SAND 413:26
f. of the good man's mind   BROW 100:1
f. that rubs its back upon   ELIOT 203:18
London particular…A f.   DICK 176:3
through the f. and filthy air   SHAK 458:1
fog-blathering: You bubble-mouthing, f.   FRY 219:28
fogs: His rising f. prevail upon   DRYD 196:34
foi: *La f. consiste à croire*   VOLT 561:20
foible: omniscience his f.   SMITH 512:11
foie: et le f. du côté droit   MOL 353:17
foil: like shining from shook f.   HOPK 256:12
Than dumb-bell and f.   YEATS 586:20
foil'd: f. circuitous wanderer   ARN 15:1
foining: f. o' nights   SHAK 441:27
fold: f. his legs and have out   JOHN 277:22
f. stands empty   SHAK 470:5
like the wolf on the f.   BYRON 122:1
mill and the f.   HOUS 263:6
Shall f. their tents   LONG 316:10
which are not of this f.   BIBLE 72:20
Folded: F. us round from the dark   SWIN 528:24
Knees and tresses f.   MER 337:1
ocean Is f. and hung   AUDEN 18:9
Quiet takes back her f. fields   JOYCE 286:9
sweetest leaves yet f.   BYRON 124:8
folding: f. of the hands to sleep   BIBLE 53:22
folds: f. shall be full of sheep   PRAY 394:3
tinklings lull the distant f.   GRAY 234:18
foliage: sapless f. of the ocean   SHEL 502:11
folie: C'est une f. à nulle autre Garde bien ta belle f.   MOL 353:19   BANV 33:1
folio: whole volumes in f.   SHAK 456:19
folios: mighty f. first   COWP 168:11
folk: how civil to f. he ne'er   ANST 11:8
Of lusty f.   CHAU 143:20
On fluttered f. and wild   KIPL 304:6
folk-dancing: excepting incest and f.   ANON 4:24
folke: faire felde ful of f. fonde   LANG 309:23
folks: f. git ole en strucken   HARR 242:13
F. *prefer* in fact a hovel   CALV 127:22

folks rail against other f.   FIEL 211:17
was leaving home and my f.   STEV 522:26
follies: f., and misfortunes   GIBB 224:23
f. of the town crept slowly   GOLD 232:18
f. of the wise   JOHN 283:3
No f. to have to repent   TAYL 531:26
Of all human f. there's   MOL 353:19
point out to us our f.   TROL 553:1
pretty f. that themselves   SHAK 466:14
vice and f. of the age   CENT 138:10
vices and f. of human kind   CONG 159:20
Where f. naturally grow   CHUR 148:26
follow: expect to see when I f. you   DOYLE 192:22
f. and find the sun   SWIN 530:13
F. me   BIBLE 64:5
F. The Gleam   TENN 540:21
F. well in order   WHIT 570:10
f. with allegiance a fall'n   SHAK 422:18
F. your Saint   CAMP 129:18
F. your spirit   SHAK 444:3
I f. but myself   SHAK 473:14
I f. the worse   OVID 366:17
Pay, pack, and f.   BURT 116:11
really ought to f. them   LEDR 313:6
their works do f. them   BIBLE 82:18
To f. in their train   HEBER 244:7
to f. mine own teaching   SHAK 465:20
Ye f. wandering fires   TENN 534:22
followed: he arose and f. him   BIBLE 65:21
following: with a mighty f.   MAC 322:13
Follow up: F.! Follow up   BOWEN 90:25
folly: all a too presumptuous f.   HARTE 242:26
Careless f. done and said   HOUS 265:4
dream and a f. of expectation   BROW 97:21
fear usually ends in f.   COL 158:3
foe was f. and his weapon   HOPE 256:2
f.—doctor-like   SHAK 494:5
f. like a stalking-horse   SHAK 427:7
f. of our youth to be   CHES 147:12
f. of the wise   JOHN 280:27
f.'s all they've taught   MOORE 356:18
F.'s at full length   CHES 145:8
fool according to his f.   BIBLE 54:31
fool according to his f.   BIBLE 54:31
fool returneth to his f.   BIBLE 54:32
forts of f. fall   ARN 13:15
from the effects of f.   SPEN 514:27
God calleth preaching f.   HERB 247:12
harmless f. of the time   HERR 248:25
He knew human f. like   AUDEN 18:15
her coral lips such f.   CONG 160:2
knavery and f. to excuse   CHUR 149:9
lovely woman stoops to f.   ELIOT 205:3
lovely woman stoops to f.   GOLD 231:31
of F. without father bred   MILT 341:23
our f., or our fate   DENH 174:21
remember'st not the slightest f.   SHAK 425:10
shoot f. as it flies   POPE 379:2
shunn'st the noise of f.   MILT 342:2
this mad, wicked f.   VICT 556:14
Though age from f. could   SHAK 421:27
'Tis f. to be wise   GRAY 235:13
unworthy piece of f.   BROW 96:33
whirl'd into f. and vice   TENN 539:28
Wisdom excelleth f.   BIBLE 55:10
would be due to human f.   LAW 311:1
would persist in his f.   BLAKE 88:19
folwed: first he f. it hymselve   CHAU 142:3
fond: be fair and yet not f.   OXF 367:14
f. and foolish mind   BALL 30:8
f. of her most filthy bargain   SHAK 477:13
f. of ill-luck that they   JERR 273:8
f. of pets that must be   ELIOT 201:11
f. to live or fear to die   ELIZ 206:3
learning more than the f. eye   SHAK 466:19
let us be familiar or f.   CONG 161:7
men would be f.   LYLY 321:9
over-f. of resisting temptation   BECK 36:21
reason to be f. of grief   SHAK 452:20

too f. to rule alone   POPE 376:26
was probably f. of them   TWAIN 554:14
We are so f. of one another   SWIFT 526:13
When men were f.   SHAK 464:6
fonder: makes the heart grow f.   ANON 4:10
fons: f. Bandusiae splendidior vicinus iugis aquae f.   HOR 261:3   HOR 262:9
font: fin in the porphyry f.   TENN 542:14
portable second-hand f.   KNOX 305:23
Fontarabian: On F. echoes borne   SCOTT 417:23
fonte: Medio de f. leporum   LUCR 320:11
food: Books, and my f.   STEV 523:11
bring f. out of the earth   PRAY 396:20
chief of Scotia's f.   BURNS 113:8
either our cupboard of f.   HERB 248:2
fed with the same f.   SHAK 467:4
f. and not fine words   MOL 353:10
F. enough for a week   MERR 338:8
f. for powder   SHAK 440:12
f. that satisfies hunger   CERV 138:20
gave them f. from heaven   PRAY 395:6
good for f.   BIBLE 45:8
homely was their f.   GARTH 221:20
human nature's daily f.   WORD 581:8
nourishing, and wholesome f.   SWIFT 526:26
with f. convenient for me   BIBLE 54:45
fool: Answer not a f. according   BIBLE 54:31
ass, without being a f.   SURT 525:3
be a f.   POPE 379:14
Better a witty f.   SHAK 488:5
By the f. multitude   SHAK 466:19
'Call me not f. till heaven   SHAK 425:18
clever woman to manage a f.   KIPL 304:35
Dost thou call me f.   SHAK 453:16
every f. in Buxton can be   RUSK 411:13
every f. is not a poet   POPE 376:17
Every f. will be meddling   BIBLE 54:16
f. according to his folly   BIBLE 54:31
F. and his words are soon   SHEN 505:17
f. at forty is a fool indeed   YOUNG 587:15
f. at least in every married   FIEL 211:7
f. can call me friend   YEATS 587:5
f. can play upon the word   SHAK 467:18
f. consistent   POPE 377:13
F. had stuck himself up   BENT 40:26
f. hath said in his heart   PRAY 390:2
f. in the eye of the world   CONG 160:11
f. a man who never   DARW 172:2
f. is happy that he knows   POPE 379:17
f. is love that in your   SHAK 493:18
F. lies here who tried   KIPL 301:18
f. of love   HAZL 243:18
f. returneth to his folly   BIBLE 54:32
f. sees not the same tree   BLAKE 88:16
f. than of the wise   BACON 25:29
f. there was and he made   KIPL 303:29
f., this night thy soul   BIBLE 70:5
f. uttereth all his mind   BIBLE 54:43
f. would persist in his   BLAKE 88:19
greatest f. may ask more than   COLT 159:9
hardly be a beast or a f.   KILV 296:8
haste of a f. is the slowest   SHAD 420:21
heart of the f.   MILT 350:21
he is a Wise man or a F.   BLAKE 86:13
He's a muddle-headed f.   CERV 138:16
he's become the golden f.   BLAKE 87:4
I hate a f.   DICK 178:20
I have played the f.   BIBLE 50:15
I met a f. i' the forest   SHAK 425:18
is the laughter of a f.   BIBLE 55:18
It is better to be a f.   STEV 522:3
knowledgeable f. is a greater   MOL 353:12
life time's f.   SHAK 440:23
longer I live the more f.   ANON 8:19
make a man appear a f.   DRYD 198:11
man suspects himself a f.   YOUNG 588:5
nor yet a f. to fame   POPE 376:23
of wisdom is made a f.   EMER 207:18

only f. in the world BROW 102:20
perfections of a f. BLAKE 87:9
Remains a f. his whole LUTH 321:1
resolv'd to live a f. BEAU 35:19
smarts so little as a f. POPE 376:21
So he is a f. WELL 567:28
stupendous genius! damned f. BYRON 126:17
that's a wise man and a f. SHAK 454:8
There is more hope of a f. BIBLE 54:33
They f. me to the top SHAK 434:23
thou art death's f. SHAK 464:8
Whosoever shall say, Thou f. BIBLE 64:12
wise enough to play the f. SHAK 489:19
wisest f. in Christendom HENR 245:16
worm at one end and a f. JOHN 280:28
You can f. all the people LINC 314:15
foolish: ever did anything very f.
MELB 336:15
exempt from saying a f. thing STER 520:8
fond and f. mind BALL 30:8
f. consistency is the hobgoblin EMER 207:38
f., fond old man SHAK 456:1
f. son is the heaviness BIBLE 53:29
f. tears would flow CLAR 152:23
f. thing to make a long BIBLE 63:29
f. thing was but a toy SHAK 490:27
f. when he had not a pen JOHN 278:19
God hath chosen the f. BIBLE 75:30
He never said a f. thing ROCH 406:18
I cou'd be mighty f. FARQ 210:20
ignorant and f. PRAY 392:28
is a f. thing well done JOHN 276:11
I was young and f. YEATS 584:22
know your own f. business CHES 146:8
shall be likened unto a f. BIBLE 65:12
vain and f. to talk of knowing WOOLF 576:17
foolishest: f. act a wise man commits
BROW 96:33
foolishly: don't *think* f. JOHN 279:11
foolishness: f. of preaching to save
BIBLE 75:29
Mix a little f. with your HOR 261:20
fools: all tongues are called f. SHAK 427:3
coxcombs nature meant but f. POPE 378:11
d—d f. said would happen MELB 336:11
Dreading ev'n f. POPE 376:27
fill the world with f. SPEN 514:27
flannelled f. at the wicket KIPL 300:4
f. admire POPE 378:24
F. are my theme BYRON 124:15
f. by heavenly compulsion SHAK 453:11
f. caught it YEATS 584:16
f. in town on our side TWAIN 554:3
F. may our scorn GAY 223:15
f. rush in where angels POPE 378:31
f. should be so deep-contemplative
SHAK 425:20
f., who came to scoff GOLD 230:24
from children and from f. DRYD 197:20
Hated by f. SWIFT 528:8
have to see these poor f. PEPYS 372:15
house for f. and mad SWIFT 527:25
human bodies are sic f. BURNS 115:27
I am two f. DONNE 190:15
incredulity! the wit of f. CHAP 140:9
leaves 'em still two f. CONG 159:23
most part of f. and knaves BUCH 106:12
Paradise of F. MILT 347:11
prov'd plain f. at last POPE 378:12
scarecrows of f. and the beacons
HUXL 269:10
shoal of f. for tenders CONG 160:36
Silence is the virtue of f. BACON 25:13
Sussex men are noted f. BLAKE 87:1
these deliberate f. SHAK 467:1
they are the money of f. HOBB 251:15
things people make f. SHAW 496:14
this great stage of f. SHAK 455:23
To gaze on Christian f. SHAK 466:13
what f. these mortals be SHAK 470:21

With that which melted f. SHAK 449:24
yesterdays have lighted f. SHAK 463:6
ye suffer f. gladly BIBLE 77:10
foolscap: of f. subjects to be king
BYRON 123:31
Foot: accent of a coming F. DICK 183:18
can f. feel, being shod HOPK 256:12
caught my f. in the mat GROS 237:2
f. already in the stirrup CERV 139:2
f. for foot BIBLE 47:25
f. from thy neighbour's BIBLE 54:28
f. is on my native heath SCOTT 418:32
F. it featly here and there SHAK 484:30
f. less prompt to meet ARN 15:9
f.—slog—slog KIPL 298:6
f. standeth right PRAY 391:6
f. the deformity of which MAC 323:33
Forty-second F. HOOD 254:14
her f. speaks SHAK 487:13
her f. was light KEATS 290:16
Love is swift of f. HERB 247:16
on an 'eathen idol's f. KIPL 301:6
One f. in sea SHAK 472:16
print of a man's naked f. DEFOE 173:7
shining F. shall pass FITZ 213:18
sole of her f. BIBLE 45:35
so light a f. SHAK 482:25
squeeze a right-hand f. CARR 136:7
suffer thy f. to be moved PRAY 398:9
that thou hurt not thy f. PRAY 395:22
football: Fissures appeared in f. fields
PLOM 374:19
F. then was fighting sorrow HOUS 262:22
Footfalls: F. echo in the memory
ELIOT 202:13
f. Of spirits SHEL 502:7
foothills: clearness of the f. CHAN 139:20
footing: yet no f. seen SHAK 495:19
Foot-in-the-grave: F. young man GILB 227:27
Footman: eternal F. hold my coat
ELIOT 203:23
footmen: lowest class is *literary f.*
HAZL 243:29
foot-path: jog on the f. way SHAK 491:21
foot-print: looking for a man's f. BEER 37:27
footprints: 'Because those f. scare me
HOR 258:11
F. on the sands of time LONG 317:4
footsteps: plants his f. in the sea COWP 165:26
footstool: it is his f. BIBLE 64:15
make thine enemies thy f. PRAY 397:11
fop: confess I am a f. in my heart ETH 208:26
six-foot column of f. HOOD 254:24
foppery: excellent f. of the world
SHAK 453:11
sound of shallow f. enter SHAK 466:13
fops: creating a whole tribe of f. SHAK 453:9
for: If I am not f. myself HILL 251:6
know f. whom the *bell* tolls DONNE 190:20
forasmuch: f. as without thee we are
PRAY 386:21
Forbade: F. the rising tear to flow
SCOTT 416:11
forbearance: limit at which f. ceases
BURKE 108:13
forbid: f. them not BIBLE 68:36
God f. BIBLE 71:4
God f. BIBLE 74:43
He shall live a man f. SHAK 458:7
lips are now f. to speak BAYLY 35:10
forbidden: fruit Of that f. tree MILT 344:20
only because it was f. TWAIN 554:19
Forbids: F. the cheating of our CHUR 148:30
Forbode: F. not any severing WORD 579:13
forçats: les f. de la faim POTT 382:3
forc'd: sound is f. BLAKE 88:10
force: achieve more than our f. BURKE 111:24
By verray f. CHAU 143:23
f. alone is but *temporary* BURKE 109:19
f. and beauty of its process JAMES 272:2

F., and fraud HOBB 251:19
f. however great can stretch WHEW 569:16
F., if unassisted by judgement HOR 260:23
F. is not a remedy BRIG 93:7
f. its way IBSEN 270:2
f. that through the green THOM 547:3
know the limitations of f. TROT 553:18
own no argument but f. BROW 97:26
Surprised by unjust f. MILT 341:15
Though the Life F. supplies SHAW 497:1
very f. entangles Itself SHAK 423:10
Who overcomes By f. MILT 345:25
Forced: F. her to do your pleasure
WEBS 567:6
forcibly: f. if we must' CLAY 152:29
ford: baby watched a f. HARDY 240:22
my friend F. WILL 574:11
fore-brain: growth of the f. AUDEN 19:10
forefathers: lords and our f. trod SWIN 530:7
Not to be as their f. PRAY 395:4
rude f. of the hamlet GRAY 234:20
Think of your f. ADAMS 1:8
forefinger: stretch'd f. of all Time
TENN 541:30
forefront: Set ye Uriah in the f. BIBLE 50:19
foregone: denoted a f. conclusion
SHAK 475:27
forehead: burning f. KEATS 291:7
conversing with W.H.'s f. HAZL 243:14
of the godlike f. WORD 577:18
Upon the f. of the age KEATS 292:24
foreheads: With f. villanous low SHAK 485:22
foreign: By f. hands thy dying eyes
POPE 376:10
corner of a f. field BROO 94:30
f. policy of the noble DERBY 175:9
languished in a f. clime MAC 322:9
past is a f. country HART 242:34
ships and the f. faces SWIN 528:15
These f. laws of God HOUS 264:26
wandering on a f. strand SCOTT 416:21
while a f. troop was landed PITT 373:26
foreigner: f. should in any respect
TROL 553:1
foreigners: f. are fools MEYN 338:17
f. are fiends MITF 352:28
f., they are all the same MITF 352:27
more f. I saw BELL 40:17
fore-mast: f. wi' his knee BALL 30:19
foremost: f. fighting BYRON 120:24
f. in battle was Mary Ambree BALL 31:8
you've spoken the f. word BALL 31:1
foresee: Man in portions can f. BYRON 125:19
foresight: mind to aftersight and f.
ELIOT 202:25
forest: All the beasts of the f. PRAY 393:2
all the beasts of the f. PRAY 397:1
clipped hedge is to a f. JOHN 280:8
Dark behind it rose the f. LONG 317:10
f. fleece the Wrekin HOUS 263:19
f. laments in order that CHUR 149:20
thee fade away into the f. KEATS 291:9
This is the f. primeval LONG 316:12
unfathomable deep F. THOM 547:19
forests: f., with their myriad LONG 317:8
green days in f. STEV 522:29
In the f. of the night BLAKE 87:14
When fishes flew and f. CHES 146:22
foresuffered: I Tiresias have f. all
ELIOT 205:2
foretell: could f. this sore distress BRID 92:2
pretences to f. events SWIFT 527:14
for ever: Fare thee well! and if f.
BYRON 124:33
F. and forever and forever POUND 383:16
F.! 'Tis a single word CALV 127:21
Man has F. BROW 100:37
picket's off duty f. BEERS 38:8
safire bracelet lasts f. LOOS 318:3
That is f. England BROO 94:30

forfeit: deadly f. should release — MILT 344:3
f. to a confin'd doom — SHAK 494:21
shall f. fair renown — SCOTT 416:22
forfended: music of f. spheres — PATM 370:7
forgather: f. wi' Sorrow and Care
— BURNS 113:4
forgave: f. th' offence — DRYD 195:35
kindness and f. the theft — BROW 104:25
forge: f. and the mill — HOUS 263:6
f. des Dieux à douzaines — MONT 355:4
man can't f. his own will — GILB 228:35
my f. decayed — ANON 6:19
quick f. and working-house — SHAK 445:6
forget: best sometimes f. — SHAK 475:5
conversing I f. all time — MILT 348:3
do not quite f. — CHES 147:15
do not thou f. me — ASTL 17:20
elephants never f. an injury — SAKI 413:11
f. not all his benefits — PRAY 396:14
F. six counties overhung — MORR 358:10
f. thee, O Jerusalem — PRAY 399:3
f. the human race — BYRON 121:21
f. the source that keeps — MER 337:3
f. us till another year — KIPL 298:13
good and to communicate f. — BIBLE 80:6
Half to f. the wandering — FLEC 214:5
hardest science to f. — POPE 376:12
honour doth f. men's names — SHAK 452:9
How long wilt thou f. — PRAY 390:1
how to f. — KING 296:13
if I f. thee — BRON 93:23
if thou wilt, f. — ROSS 409:8
I sometimes f. — DISR 187:5
knew we should both f. — SWIN 530:10
learn so little and f. — DAV 172:10
Lest we f. — KIPL 302:7
never f. — CARR 134:26
night time I shall not f. — SWIN 529:12
nor worms f. — DICK 179:30
not to f. we are gentlemen — BURKE 108:24
Old men f. — SHAK 445:3
Sun himself cannot f. — ANON 8:4
teach the unforgetful to f. — ROSS 410:6
that I could f. what — SHAK 479:14
thou remember and I f. — SWIN 530:14
we f. because we must — ARN 12:21
with names that men f. — SWIN 529:14
words shall ye f. your tears — MORR 358:3
yet will I not f. thee — BIBLE 59:17
you'll f. 'em all — POPE 380:33
you should f. and smile — ROSS 409:4
forgetful: Earth in f. snow — ELIOT 204:17
f. of their sins — YEATS 586:14
forgetfulness: Not in entire f. — WORD 579:5
steep my senses in f. — SHAK 441:29
who to dumb F. a prey — GRAY 235:2
Forgets: F. the shows of love — SHAK 448:1
forgetteth: f. what manner of man he
— BIBLE 80:10
forgetting: f. the bright speed he — ARN 15:1
F. those things which are — BIBLE 78:18
if f. could be willed — MER 337:3
is but a sleep and a f. — WORD 579:5
I've a grand memory for f. — STEV 521:8
With dark f. of my care — DAN 171:1
world f. — POPE 376:13
forgive: Father, f. them — BIBLE 71:11
f., if I forget thee — BRON 93:23
f. us our debts — BIBLE 64:24
f. us our trespasses — PRAY 384:14
good Lord will f. me — CATH 136:17
I f. him? till seven times — BIBLE 67:7
I'll f. Thy great big one — FROST 219:7
lambs could not f. — DICK 179:30
love nor pity nor f. — KIPL 302:11
mercy to f. — DRYD 196:14
ought to f. our friends — MED 336:8
rarely, if ever, do they f. — WILDE 573:30
To f. enemies H — BLAKE 87:5
to f. them as a christian — AUST 23:19

To f. wrongs darker than — SHEL 503:15
Wilt thou f. those sins — DONNE 189:13
woman can f. another — GAY 222:15
Women can't f. failure — CHEK 145:1
forgiven: f.; for she loved much — BIBLE 69:24
forgiveness: ask of thee f. — SHAK 456:3
F. to the injured does — DRYD 195:30
F. free of evil done — KIPL 298:12
F. of sins — PRAY 384:26
Mutual F. of each vice — BLAKE 85:26
what f. — ELIOT 203:5
forgives: which f. itself anything — SHAW 498:5
forgo: chilly stars I can f. — CORY 163:5
forgot: all the rest f. for which — SHAK 493:4
by the world f. — POPE 376:13
curiosities would be quite f. — AUBR 17:22
f. as soon As done — SHAK 487:3
f. his course — FLEC 214:18
f. the taste of fears — SHAK 463:5
giver is f. — CONG 159:30
God f. me — BROW 99:16
I believe I f. to tell — WELL 567:21
I f. Goschen — CHUR 149:23
I have f. my part — SHAK 428:1
she f. the stars — KEATS 290:11
soul that God f. — HOUS 264:27
unknown propos'd as things f. — POPE 378:29
forgotten: been learnt has been f. — SKIN 508:20
East and west on fields f. — HOUS 263:19
f. nothing and learnt nothing — DUM 199:7
f. nothing — TALL 531:17
God is f. — OWEN 366:28
had f. to say 'When — WOD 575:28
have f. his own sentiments — CLAY 152:29
He hath not f. my age — SOUT 514:9
Homer and Virgil are f. — PORS 381:28
I am all f. — SHAK 421:28
newer object quite f. — SHAK 490:34
of them is f. before God — BIBLE 70:3
ruins of f. times — BROW 97:7
sooner f. than an insult — CHES 145:13
want to be f. even by God — BROW 103:6
foris: ecce intus eras et ego f. — AUG 21:16
forked: f. animal as thou art — SHAK 454:20
forks: pursued it with f. and hope — CARR 133:3
forlorn: cheerless, and f. — HADR 237:9
earth I wait f. — ARN 13:8
F.! the very word is like — KEATS 291:23
in these wild woods f. — MILT 349:18
form: earth was without f. — BIBLE 44:22
ev'ry respect but the f. — GAY 222:31
Fain would I dwell on f. — SHAK 482:12
fishy f. and mind — BROO 94:13
f. of a servant and was — BIBLE 78:13
f. of government rather — JOHN 276:4
f. of sound words — BIBLE 79:23
F. remains — WORD 581:4
F., Riflemen Form — TENN 543:6
hath not f. nor comeliness — BIBLE 59:21
I like definite f. — STEV 521:19
mould of f. — SHAK 433:15
take thy f. from off my — POE 375:6
time to lick it into f. — BURT 116:14
'To every F. of being is — WORD 577:17
what the f. divine — LAND 308:26
formal: f. feeling comes — DICK 183:13
second-best is a f. order — AUDEN 18:13
formed: formed say to him that f. it
— BIBLE 75:14
Man was f. for society — BLAC 85:1
former: again thy f. light restore — SHAK 477:5
f. and the latter rain — PRAY 386:3
f. days were better than — BIBLE 55:20
f. things are passed away — BIBLE 82:31
with those my f. fortunes — SHAK 423:15
formless: f. spawning fury — YEATS 587:2
Formosa: F. facies muta commendatio
— PUBL 402:4
Formosum: F. pastor Corydon ardebat
— VIRG 559:14

forms: f. and substances are circumfused
— WORD 580:19
F. more real than living — SHEL 503:6
f. of government let fools — POPE 379:20
f. of things unknown — SHAK 471:11
mighty f. that do not live — WORD 580:14
formula: f. of that particular emotion
— ELIOT 205:16
Fornication: F., and all uncleanness
— BIBLE 78:2
F. But that was in another — MARL 329:22
From f. — PRAY 385:16
Fors: Quem F. dierum cumque dabit
— HOR 259:18
forsake: f. me not when my strength
— PRAY 394:17
F. not an old friend — BIBLE 62:30
I'll not f. thee — ROWL 411:1
is a woman that you f. — KIPL 299:21
nor f. thee — BIBLE 48:35
forsaken: f. beliefs — ARN 15:25
never the righteous f. — PRAY 391:15
primrose that f. dies — MILT 343:15
why hast thou f. me — BIBLE 68:24
why hast thou f. me — PRAY 390:16
forsaking: f. all other — PRAY 389:3
F. even military men — GILB 228:39
Forsan: F. et haec olim meminisse
— VIRG 557:14
forsook: my true Love has me f. — BALL 32:10
forsworn: That so sweetly were f.
— SHAK 464:21
forsythia: Of prunus and f. across — BETJ 43:12
fort: Hold the f. — BLISS 88:31
La raison du plus f. est — LA F 306:21
fortes: Vixere f. ante Agamemnona
— HOR 261:18
Fortescue: Was Charles Augustus F.
— BELL 38:32
forth: f. I must — HOUS 265:15
Man goeth f. to his work — PRAY 397:1
My road leads me f. — MAS 334:3
Fortis: F. fortuna adiuvat — TER 544:18
fortissimo: Endlich f. — MAHL 327:6
fortiter: Esto peccator et pecca f.
— LUTH 320:15
fortitude: man has of f. and delicacy
— STEV 521:4
What f. the Soul contains — DICK 183:18
fortress: him as his castle and f. — COKE 154:23
This f. built by Nature — SHAK 478:20
fortresses: brambles in the f. thereof
— BIBLE 58:31
forts: f. of folly fall — ARN 13:15
Fortuna: Audentis F. iuvat — VIRG 559:9
Fortis f. adiuvat — TER 544:18
Quandoquidem f. mihi tete — CAT 137:15
fortunae: Faber est suae quisque f.
— CLAU 152:26
fortunatam: f. natam me consule — CIC 152:2
fortunate: better to be f. than wise
— WEBS 567:11
f. fellows that now you — HOUS 263:7
he is at best but f. — SOLON 512:25
fortunatos: f. nimium — VIRG 560:13
fortune: arrows of outrageous f. — SHAK 433:8
be a beauty without a f. — FARQ 210:2
Disdaining f. — SHAK 458:3
disgrace with f. and men's eyes — SHAK 493:6
ere f. made him so — DRYD 196:9
F. aids the brave — TER 544:18
F. is full of fresh variety — BARN 34:3
F. is merry — SHAK 451:7
F.'s a right whore — WEBS 567:1
F., that favours fools — JONS 283:14
good f. where I find it — MOL 354:3
happily upon a plentiful f. — JOHN 275:2
hast Caesar and his f. — CAES 127:2
hath given hostages to f. — BACON 26:31
heaven hath sent me f. — SHAK 425:18

her f. by way of marriage   FIEL 211:29
he's but F.'s knave   SHAK 423:20
he shall see F.   BACON 26:13
how does f. banter us   BOL 89:13
I am F.'s fool   SHAK 483:5
is the mother of good f.   CERV 138:19
leads on to f.   SHAK 451:27
little value of f.   STEE 518:12
made lame by f.'s dearest   SHAK 493:13
maker of his own f.   STEE 518:7
method of making a f.   GRAY 235:21
mock the good housewife F.   SHAK 424:21
mould of a man's f. is   BACON 26:12
one out of suits with f.   SHAK 424:25
On F.'s cap we are not   SHAK 432:11
possession of a good f.   AUST 23:11
secret parts of F.   SHAK 432:11
smith of his own f.   CLAU 152:26
so many men of large f.   AUST 22:26
visit pays Where f. smiles   YOUNG 587:21
whan that F. list to flee   CHAU 142:29
when we are sick in f.   SHAK 453:11
whereas people of f. may   ELIOT 201:23
worky-day f.   SHAK 421:14
You fools of f.   SHAK 486:8
Fortunes: F. tumbling into some men's
                              BACON 25:3
make content with his f.   SHAK 454:12
my f. have Corrupted   SHAK 423:1
of f. sharpe adversitee   CHAU 144:11
with those my former f.   SHAK 423:15
forty: at f., the judgement FRAN 218:10
Fair, fat, and f.   SCOTT 418:33
Fat, fair and f.   OKEE 365:1
fool at f. is a fool indeed   YOUNG 587:15
f. winters shall besiege   SHAK 492:23
F. years long was I grieved   PRAY 396:4
F. years on   BOWEN 90:24
have f. million reasons   KIPL 300:21
hopeful than to be f. years   HOLM 253:14
look young till f.   DRYD 196:36
man over f. is a scoundrel   SHAW 498:4
passing rich with f. pounds   GOLD 230:22
till you come to F. Year   THAC 545:31
forty-three: may very well pass for f.
                              GILB 229:4
forward: f. let us range TENN 539:8
marched breast f.   BROW 98:32
not look f. to posterity   BURKE 111:7
Some men a f. motion love   VAUG 555:17
to hold from this day f.   PRAY 389:4
world with their feet f.   BROW 97:10
Foss: F. is the name of his cat LEAR 311:29
fossil: Language is f. poetry EMER 207:31
foster-child: f. of silence and slow
                              KEATS 291:2
Fostered: F. alike by beauty WORD 580:8
fou: between a f. man and a fasting
                              SCOTT 418:26
f. qui se croyait Victor   COCT 154:13
I wasna f.   BURNS 113:11
There's some are f. o' brandy BURNS 114:9
fought: angels f. against the dragon
                              BIBLE 82:11
better to have f. and lost   CLOU 154:2
courses f. against Sisera   BIBLE 49:9
f. against me from my youth   PRAY 398:21
f. a long hour by Shrewsbury SHAK 440:27
f. at Arques and you were   HENR 245:14
f. the dogs and killed   BROW 103:15
f. with beasts at Ephesus   BIBLE 76:24
He f. upon his stumps   SHEA 498:29
if men f. upon the earth   SCOTT 417:20
I have f. a good fight   BIBLE 79:26
Philip f. men   LEE 313:13
their lives f. for life   SPEN 515:7
what they f. each other   SOUT 513:16
foul: f. and fair a day   SHAK 458:9
f. and midnight murther   GRAY 234:17
f. deed shall smell above   SHAK 450:12

F. deeds will rise   SHAK 430:16
f. is fair   SHAK 458:1
however f. within   CHUR 148:33
I doubt some f. play   SHAK 430:15
Is f. in the ending thereof   PAIN 367:17
less f. profanation   SHAK 464:3
portress f. to see   HOUS 265:5
thank the gods I am f.   SHAK 426:16
too f. an epithet for thee   MARL 330:10
foules: that I here the f. synge CHAU 143:29
foulest: way is commonly the f. BACON 25:4
foully: Thou play'dst most f. for't SHAK 461:6
foul-mouthed: rather a f. nation HAZL 244:1
found: country as good as he had f.
                              COBB 154:9
f. a kingdom   MILT 350:6
f. and lost again and again   ELIOT 202:24
f. in lowly sheds With   MILT 341:6
f. me here   KEATS 290:21
f. myself famous   BYRON 126:22
f. my sheep which was lost   BIBLE 70:16
f. out musical tunes   BIBLE 63:23
f. the Roman nation   VIRG 557:10
Hast thou f. me   BIBLE 51:18
have it f. out by accident   LAMB 308:2
less often sought than f.   BYRON 125:12
lost, and is f.   BIBLE 70:21
not yet f. a role   ACH 1:4
place could no where be f.   PRAY 391:29
shall be f. by the fire   BROW 99:18
They f. no more of her   BIBLE 51:37
When f., make a note   DICK 177:26
when thou mayest be f.   PRAY 391:17
foundation: Good order is the f.
                              BURKE 111:25
laid the f. of the earth   PRAY 396:13
number is the f. of morals   BENT 40:25
foundations: city which hath f. BIBLE 79:32
hour when earth's f. fled   HOUS 265:7
laid the f. of the earth   BIBLE 53:2
laid the f. of the earth   PRAY 396:18
noblest works and f.   BACON 27:4
founded: fixt of old and f. strong HOUS 264:3
founder: father and first f. and embellisher
                              CAXT 138:2
Founding: F. a firm state by proportions
                              MARV 331:20
fount: fresh f.   JONS 283:21
fountain: athirst of the f. of the water
                              BIBLE 82:32
burning f. whence it came   SHEL 499:19
Doth a f. send forth   BIBLE 80:15
f. from the which my current SHAK 476:18
f. is choked up and polluted BURKE 111:15
f. of all goodness   PRAY 385:6
f. of delights rises something LUCR 320:11
'f. of honour'   BAG 28:22
f. sealed   BIBLE 56:28
He is the f. of honour   BACON 27:43
Here at the f.'s sliding   MARV 332:6
hexameter rises the f.'s   COL 157:7
Let the healing f. start   AUDEN 19:5
Like a summer-dried f.   SCOTT 416:5
mighty f. momently was   COL 156:27
perpetual f. of good sense   DRYD 198:9
Rise like a f. for me night   TENN 535:26
woman mov'd is like a f.   SHAK 484:16
fountain'd: many-f. Ida   TENN 541:17
fountains: f. mingle with the river SHEL 502:1
sad f.   ANON 8:13
Shepherding her bright f.   SHEL 500:2
silver f. mud   SHAK 493:12
What objects are the f.   SHEL 504:21
whose f. are within   COL 156:8
founts: f. falling in the courts CHES 146:28
four: f. beasts full of eyes BIBLE 81:23
f. essential human freedoms   ROOS 407:5
F. lagging winters   SHAK 478:13
f. pillars of government   BACON 27:10
F. things greater than   KIPL 297:28

It is f. times as big   LEAR 311:18
four-footed: of f. beasts of the earth
                              BIBLE 73:37
four hundred: f. people in New York
   society   MCAL 321:23
four-in-hand: with the fiery f. COL 158:7
fours: make a simile go on all f. MAC 324:4
fourscore: strong that they come to f.
                              PRAY 395:19
four-square: Which stood f. to all
                              TENN 541:8
fourteen: f. I married My Lord POUND 383:16
F. The good Lord has   CLEM 152:30
fourth: reporters sit has become a f. estate
                              MAC 323:7
fous: *C'étaient des f.* REN 405:13
Le monde est plein de f.   ANON 9:12
foutra: f. for the world   SHAK 442:27
Fove: *F. quod est frigidum* LANG 310:1
foweles: smale f. maken melodye CHAU 141:8
fowl: broiled f. and mushrooms DICK 181:26
Of tame villatic f.   MILT 350:29
over the f. of the air   BIBLE 45:4
Pythagoras concerning wild f. SHAK 490:21
'You elegant f.   LEAR 312:12
fowler: of the snare of the f. PRAY 398:14
fowls: Behold the f. of the air BIBLE 64:28
Beside them shall the f.   PRAY 396:19
creeping things, and f.   BIBLE 73:37
f. came and devoured them   BIBLE 66:16
fowlys: all small f. singis DOUG 191:5
fox: ar'n't that I loves the f. SURT 525:10
daun Russell the f. stirte   CHAU 143:2
f. knows many things   ARCH 11:22
f. said once upon a time   HOR 258:11
from the f. and the lion   MACH 325:8
galloping after a f.   WILDE 573:27
upon F.'s grave the tear   SCOTT 417:3
foxed: ever I was f. it was now PEPYS 372:4
foxes: f. have a sincere interest ELIOT 200:25
f. have holes   BIBLE 65:18
little f.   BIBLE 56:23
may be a portion for f.   PRAY 393:22
fox-hunter: Tell me a man's a f. SURT 525:6
foxlike: f. in the vine   TENN 542:16
foy: *f. je veuil vivre et mourir* VILL 557:6
frabjous: f. day   CARR 134:29
fragile: That nature's f. vessel SHAK 486:13
Fragment: something to this F. of Life
                              STER 519:15
fragments: Death tramples it to f.
                              SHEL 499:26
f. have I shored against   ELIOT 205:12
f. that remained twelve   BIBLE 66:11
Gather up the f. that remain BIBLE 72:5
fragrance: sweetest f. from the herb
                              TROL 552:24
Frail: F. as thy love   PEAC 371:1
F. crowds that a delicate   MOORE 355:23
f. mortality shall trust   BACON 28:16
frailes: *f. y muchos son los caminos*
                              CERV 138:1
frailties: Our f. are invincible STEV 520:26
frailty: but a f. of the mind CONG 161:3
f. of things here   SHEL 501:22
F., thy name is woman   SHAK 429:28
love's the noblest f.   DRYD 196:23
noblest f. of the mind   SHAD 420:20
that by reason of the f.   PRAY 386:8
therefore more f.   SHAK 440:5
frame: Could f. in earth   SPEN 516:20
f. of nature round him   ADD 2:30
f. thy fearful symmetry   BLAKE 87:14
mighty f. of the world   BERK 41:19
sensuous f. Is rack'd   TENN 536:21
shakes this fragile f.   HARDY 240:2
That yarely f. the office   SHAK 422:3
universal f. is without a mind BACON 25:22
Whatever stirs this mortal f. COL 157:2
framed: England is to have it f. WALP 563:8

framework: experience but a defining
  f.   WHORF 571:23
français: *aurait toujours parlé f.* VOLT 561:15
  f. aux hommes et allemand   CHAR 140:31
  F. lève les yeux sans   TOCQ 551:8
  pas clair n'est pas f.   RIV 406:10
  Tout soldat f. porte dans   NAP 359:9
France: baton of a marshal of F.   NAP 359:9
  between F. and England   JERR 273:4
  England the nearer is to F.   CARR 134:15
  Fair stood the wind for F.   DRAY 193:10
  fashion for the maids in F.   SHAK 445:15
  forces the full pride of F.   SHAK 443:7
  F., fam'd in all great   ARN 15:11
  F. has always more or less   BURKE 111:15
  F., mère des arts   DU B 198:25
  F., mother of arts   DU B 198:25
  F. With all her vines   COWP 166:34
  his round hose in F.   SHAK 465:24
  nor the activity of F.   BURKE 109:17
  Our fertile F.   SHAK 445:11
  That sweet enemy, F.   SIDN 507:22
  There lived a singer in F.   SWIN 530:29
  this matter better in F.   STER 518:28
  until F. is adequately   ASQ 17:17
  vasty fields of F.   SHAK 443:4
Frankfort: I went to F.   PORS 381:29
frankincense: branches of the f. tree
   BIBLE 63:27
  f., and myrrh   BIBLE 63:32
frantic: There's a fascination f.   GILB 227:18
frantic-mad: f. with evermore unrest
   SHAK 495:15
frater: *f., ad inferias*   CAT 137:15
  f., ave atque vale   CAT 137:15
Fratresque: *F. tendentes opaco*   HOR 260:22
fratrum: *Par nobile f.*   HOR 262:8
fraud: f., are in war the two   HOBB 251:19
  Grown old in f.   CHUR 149:5
  May is a pious f.   LOW 319:15
  this pious f.   GAY 223:3
fraudatrix: *auellit ab animo f. scientiae*
   JOHN 273:17
frauds: well stored with pious f.
   BURKE 108:14
fray: eager for the f.   CIBB 151:13
freckled: fickle, f.   HOPK 256:23
  f. like a pard   KEATS 290:22
  Of f. Human Nature   DICK 184:3
freckles: f., and doubt   PARK 368:15
  In those f. live their   SHAK 470:2
Fred: Here lies F.   ANON 5:15
Frederick: clustered spires of F. stand
   WHIT 571:15
  Here is cruel F.   HOFF 252:12
fredome: f. is a noble thing   BARB 33:4
free: appal the f.   SHAK 433:1
  assure freedom to the f.   LINC 314:22
  bond nor f.   BIBLE 78:26
  English Church shall be f.   MAGN 327:1
  ever exist in a f. country   BURKE 110:1
  fain have her f.   MER 337:4
  flag of all the f.   CHES 147:3
  f. as nature first made   DRYD 195:29
  f. behave much as the respectable
   AUDEN 19:20
  f. church in a free state   CAV 138:1
  f. have disposition   AUDEN 19:13
  f. land of the grave   HOUS 265:18
  F. love   TENN 534:34
  F. speech, free passes   BETJ 43:6
  f., uncircumscribed   SHEL 503:12
  f. verse is like playing   FROST 219:15
  Greece might still be f.   BYRON 122:33
  half slave and half f.   LINC 314:14
  happy and handsome and f.   AUDEN 18:7
  human beings are born f.   ANON 4:14
  In the country of the f.   BROW 97:36
  I only ask to be f.   DICK 176:6
  Italia shall be f.   MER 338:3

I was born f. as Caesar   SHAK 448:14
I was f. born   BIBLE 74:21
leaves f. to all   MILT 348:7
leaves soul f.   BROW 99:2
let the oppressed go f.   BIBLE 60:4
lines and life are f.   HERB 247:14
Man was born f.   ROUS 410:17
More f. from peril than   SHAK 424:31
naturally were born f.   MILT 352:18
noble that was born most f.   OTWAY 365:27
O'er the land of the f.   KEY 295:14
only less f. Than thou   SHEL 502:12
people let him go f.   PRAY 397:4
perfectly free till all are f.   SPEN 515:3
should themselves be f.   BROO 94:4
So f. we seem   BROW 98:23
Teach the f. man how   AUDEN 19:9
that England should be f.   MAGEE 326:21
Thou art f.   ARN 14:23
truth shall make you f.   BIBLE 72:12
valiant man and f.   TENN 537:15
was ever so f. as a fish   RUSK 412:2
We must be f. or die   WORD 582:3
what a f. government is   BURKE 110:11
When the mind's f.   SHAK 454:13
Who died to make verse f.   PRES 400:14
wholly slaves or wholly f.   DRYD 196:16
whom the truth makes f.   COWP 167:22
Who would be f. themselves   BYRON 120:14
freed: drowsy at that hour which f.
   BROW 95:22
  f. his soul the nearest   JOHN 279:1
  I have f. my soul   BERN 41:24
  thousands He hath f.   CHAN 139:19
freedom: are fit to use their f.   MAC 323:25
  call it the idea of f.   PARK 368:26
  can do for the f. of man   KENN 295:10
  cause of F. is the cause   BOWL 91:7
  desire their Liberty and F.   CHAR 140:19
  du believe in F.'s cause   LOW 319:3
  enemy of truth and f.   IBSEN 269:17
  establishes his true f.   MONT 354:20
  few men talked of f.   CHES 147:13
  fight for f. and truth   IBSEN 269:19
  flame of f. in their souls   SYM 531:3
  Flood Of British f.   WORD 582:2
  f. and curteisie   CHAU 141:9
  F. and not servitude is   BURKE 109:30
  F. and Whisky gang thegither   BURNS 112:35
  F. has a thousand charms   COWP 166:25
  f. of speech   TWAIN 554:7
  F. of the press in Britain   SWAF 525:30
  F. shrieked   CAMP 129:7
  F., the seven pillared   LAWR 311:12
  F. which in no other land   DRYD 197:31
  If I have it in my love   LOV 318:18
  if Man will give up F.   AUDEN 19:11
  I gave my life for f.   EWER 209:12
  In giving f. to the slave   LINC 314:22
  Let f. ring   SMITH 510:24
  newly acquired f. produces   MAC 323:24
  None can love f. heartily   MILT 352:17
  on the principles of f.   BURKE 109:27
  Our f. as free lances   MACN 326:16
  Perfect f. is reserved   COLL 158:13
  Regain'd my f. with a sigh   BYRON 125:17
  service is perfect f.   PRAY 385:2
  speak with the f. of history   BURKE 109:5
  sum obtained I this f.   BIBLE 74:21
  sweet bondage which is f.'s   SHEL 503:16
  That sober f. out of which   TENN 541:11
  this participation of f.   BURKE 110:4
  Thus f. now so seldom wakes   MOORE 356:10
  what is f.   COL 154:25
  What stands if F. fall   KIPL 299:7
  Where F. slowly broadens   TENN 544:11
  With F.'s soil beneath   DRAKE 193:5
freedoms: four essential human f.
   ROOS 407:26
freehold: life is given to none f.   LUCR 320:10

free lances: Our freedom as f.   MACN 326:16
Free-livers: F. on a small scale   IRV 270:23
Freeman: Stubbs butters F.   ROG 407:14
Freemason: F., and an asthmatic
   DOYLE 192:14
freemen: f., are the only slaves   MASS 335:17
  To rule o'er f.   BROO 94:4
freendes: That f. everych oother   CHAU 142:12
freewoman: other by a f.   BIBLE 77:16
freeze: f., thou bitter sky   SHAK 426:1
  f. thy young blood   SHAK 431:5
  To f. the blood I have   WORD 577:22
Freezing: F. persons, recollect   DICK 183:14
  night is f. fast   HOUS 265:1
freezings: What f. have I felt   SHAK 494:16
freight: shall have her earthly f.   WORD 579:8
Freighted: F. with amber grapes   ARN 14:21
French: dislike the F.   WALP 563:21
  F. are wiser than they   BACON 27:14
  F. are with equal advantage   CANN 129:25
  F. army led by an Italian   SHAW 498:7
  F. art, if not sanguinary   SPEN 515:5
  F. novels, French cookery   THAC 545:22
  F., or Turk, or Proosian   GILB 228:10
  F. the empire of the land   JEAN 272:4
  F. truth   ROCH 407:5
  glory of beating the F.   WOLFE 576:7
  half-F., half-English   SHAK 445:14
  how it's improved her F.   GRAH 233:9
  I hate the F. because they   GOLD 232:6
  is not clear is not F.   RIV 406:10
  much all he knew of F.   BLUC 89:1
  not too French F. bean   GILB 227:23
  scrofulous F. novel   BROW 105:8
  some are fond of F.   MAS 333:20
  Speak in F. when you can't   CARR 134:31
  to men F.   CHAR 140:31
  would always have spoken F.   VOLT 561:13
Frenchies: Those F. seek him everywhere
   ORCZY 365:7
Frenchman: F., easy   COWP 166:24
  F. must be always talking   JOHN 278:17
  hate a F.   NELS 360:12
Frenchmen: *Englishman* could beat three
  F.   ADD 2:19
  million F. can't be wrong   GUIN 237:6
Frenssh: F. of Parys was to hire   CHAU 141:15
  F. she spak ful faire   CHAU 141:15
frenzy: in a fine f. rolling   SHAK 471:11
frequent: f. cups prolong the rich   POPE 381:6
  f. hearses shall besiege   POPE 376:9
  f. tears have run   BROW 98:10
  when young did eagerly f.   FITZ 212:20
Frere: F. there was   CHAU 141:19
  mon semblable,—mon f.   BAUD 35:5
  Sois mon f.   CHAM 139:18
Frères: *F. humains qui après nous* VILL 557:4
fresh: both so ancient and so f.   AUG 21:16
  f. lap of the crimson rose   SHAK 470:6
  f. revolving pleasures   GAY 223:23
  f. woods, and pastures   MILT 343:20
  Since first I saw you f.   SHAK 494:18
  So sad, so f.   TENN 542:3
  you've got a nice f. corpse   TWAIN 554:13
fresher: f., and more fat   DONNE 188:2
Fressen: *Erst kommt das F.*   BREC 91:25
fressh: f. as is the month of May
   CHAU 141:11
fret: fever, and the f.   KEATS 291:18
  f. a passage through it   FULL 220:19
  f. not after knowledge   KEATS 292:5
  F. not thyself because   PRAY 391:24
  though you can f. me   SHAK 434:21
Frets: F. doubt the maw-crammed
   BROW 104:3
  f. the saints in heaven   BROW 97:30
  struts and f. his hour   SHAK 463:6
Fretted: F. the pigmy body to decay
   DRYD 194:6
Freude: *F., schöner Götterfunken*   SCH 415:9

friar: Apollo turned fasting f.   MER 337:29
friars: We cannot all be f.   CERV 138:15
while the barefoot f. were   GIBB 224:16
fricassee: will equally serve in a f.   SWIFT 526:26
Friday: F. fil al this meschaunce   CHAU 143:3
takes my man F. with me   DEFOE 173:8
Friede: ewige F. ist ein Traum   MOLT 354:4
friend: are the wounds of a f.   BIBLE 54:38
author as you choose a f.   ROOS 408:10
could not see my little f.   BARH 33:21
countenance of his f.   BIBLE 54:40
country and betraying my f.   FORS 217:12
crack a bottle with a f.   CHES 147:21
equal f.   SURR 524:20
every mess I finds a f.   DIBD 175:18
faithful f. is the medicine   BIBLE 62:25
familiar f., whom I trusted   PRAY 392:5
fav'rite has no f.   GRAY 235:7
Forsake not an old f.   BIBLE 62:30
F. and associate of this   HADR 237:9
F., go up higher   BIBLE 70:8
f. in power is a friend   ADAMS 1:7
friendless name the f.   JOHN 278:35
f. loveth at all times   BIBLE 54:11
f. may spit upon my curious   HERB 248:15
f. may well be reckoned   EMER 207:20
f. of every country   CANN 129:28
f. of Grey   HOLL 253:4
F. of my better days   HALL 238:9
f. or child I speak   ARN 13:8
f. remember'd not   SHAK 426:1
f. should bear his friend's   SHAK 451:22
f. that sticketh closer   BIBLE 54:14
F. to Sir Philip Sidney   GREV 236:18
f. unseen   FLEC 214:23
F., wherefore art thou   BIBLE 68:17
from the candid f.   CANN 130:1
good-natured f. or other   SHER 505:21
handsome house to lodge a f.   SWIFT 527:28
He makes no f.   TENN 514:31
He was my f.   SHAK 450:34
I can merely be your f.   LEAR 312:1
In every f. we lose a part   POPE 381:17
in his life forgave a f.   BLAKE 87:5
in life the firmest f.   BYRON 124:40
I was angry with my f.   BLAKE 87:21
last best f. am   SOUT 513:21
look like a f. on Denmark   SHAK 429:23
marry your old f.'s love   BROW 105:17
mine own familiar f.   PRAY 393:1
never want a f. in need   DICK 177:26
not a fool can call me f.   YEATS 587:5
not a f. to close his eyes   DRYD 195:3
not use a f. as I use Thee   HERB 248:14
of the loss of a dear f.   SOUT 514:17
Over your f. that loves   SHAK 448:10
Patience for our only f.   ARN 14:18
pretended f. is worse   GAY 223:13
religious book, or f.   WOTT 583:13
still a f. in my retreat   COWP 166:21
suspicious f.   POPE 376:27
That love my f.   SHAK 451:1
there is no f. like a sister   ROSS 408:27
Thou art not my f.   EMER 206:20
to have a f. is to be one   EMER 207:1
truest f. to thy lover   MAL 328:8
('twas all he wish'd) a f.   GRAY 235:5
very much his f. indeed   COWP 165:9
what he can find a f. sincere   BULW 107:7
who lost no f.   POPE 378:6
Who's your fat f.   BRUM 106:3
With one chained f.   SHEL 500:10
woman can become a man's f.   CHEK 145:5
world can countervail a f.   GRIM 236:20
world is not thy f. nor   SHAK 483:26
worst f. and enemy   BROO 94:28
yet f. to truth   POPE 378:6
friendless: every f. name the friend   JOHN 278:35

Omnipotent but f. is to reign   SHEL 503:7
friendliness: Of more than common f.   BRID 92:22
friendly: f. seas they softly run   FLEC 214:17
friends: all distresses of our f.   SWIFT 527:22
book is the best of f.   TUPP 553:21
cheating of our f.   CHUR 148:30
choice of f.   COWL 164:14
comes to meet one's f.   BURN 112:22
down his life for his f.   BIBLE 72:36
enter on my list of f.   COWP 167:28
excellent plot, very good f.   SHAK 438:30
faithfullest f. stands   WHIT 570:5
F. and loves we have none   MAS 334:7
f. are lapp'd in lead   BARN 34:1
f. hear no more of him   SHEL 501:19
f. hid in death's dateless   SHAK 493:7
f. of every country save   DISR 185:14
f. of the mammon of unrighteousness   BIBLE 70:26
F., Romans, countrymen   SHAK 450:17
f. thou hast   SHAK 430:19
F. to congratulate their   DRYD 197:30
F. who set forth at our   ARN 14:9
glory was I had such f.   YEATS 586:6
golden f. I had   HOUS 264:10
Good thoughts his only f.   CAMP 129:19
hath f. in the garrison   HAL 237:17
house of God as f.   PRAY 393:11
How few of his f.' houses   JOHN 279:5
I have lost f.   WOOLF 576:20
In spite of all their f.   LEAR 312:7
in the multitude of f.   JONS 283:23
is without three good f.   SHAK 426:3
laughter and the love of f.   BELL 39:15
like him with f. possess'd   SHAK 493:6
matter separateth very f.   BIBLE 54:10
misfortune of our best f.   LA R 310:8
My f. forsake me like   CLARE 152:12
neither foes nor loving f.   KIPL 300:2
old f.   GOLD 232:19
ought to forgive our f.   MED 336:8
Our f., the enemy   BER 41:15
remembering my good f.   SHAK 478:24
shameful to spurn one's f.   LA R 310:10
something left to treat my f.   MALL 327:12
Such men my f. than enemies   SHAK 452:4
Than want of f.   BRET 92:3
they had been f. in youth   COL 156:4
Thy f. are exultations   WORD 582:17
to all thy f.   BIBLE 60:26
to keep f. with himself   STEV 521:4
was the new city of F.   WHIT 570:4
We may live without f.   MER 338:5
when his f. did   BALL 30:8
wretched have no f.   DRYD 195:14
friendship: destitute of sincere f.   BACON 25:14
dupe of f.   HAZL 243:18
elegance of female f.   JOHN 282:12
f. closes its eyes   ANON 9:11
f. from knowledge   BUSS 117:5
F. is Love without his   BYRON 124:37
F. is a disinterested commerce   GOLD 232:11
F. is not always the sequel   JOHN 282:3
F. is constant in all other   SHAK 472:7
f. never moults a feather   DICK 180:25
f. oft has made my heart   BLAKE 87:7
f. recognised by the police   STEV 521:27
F. should be more than   ELIOT 204:3
him to cultivate your f.   JOHN 278:33
honest f. with all nations   JEFF 272:8
let us swear eternal f.   SMITH 511:3
Love, f., charity   SHAK 487:6
Most f. is feigning   SHAK 426:1
of f. with thine enemies   SHAK 450:9
scene where genial f. plays   HOLM 253:6
should keep his f. in constant   JOHN 274:15
swear an eternal f.   CANN 130:4
There is little f.   BACON 26:11

to f. clear   CAREW 130:14
way of f.'s gone   HERB 247:5
woman's f. ever ends   GAY 223:9
Friendships: F. begin with liking   ELIOT 200:23
fright: f. my faith than Three   DRYD 196:13
To f. the souls of fearful   SHAK 480:18
wake in a f.   BARH 33:13
frighted: flowers now that f. thou   SHAK 491:26
F. the reign of Chaos   MILT 345:20
f. with false fire   SHAK 434:15
frighten: street and f. the horses   CAMP 128:8
frightened: It has a f. look in its   SITW 508:14
killed than f. to death   SURT 525:22
upon the stage is not f.   FIEL 211:31
why should you be f.   WEBB 566:6
fringe: movement has a lunatic f.   ROOS 408:5
fringed: f. curtains of thine eye   SHAK 485:1
fringes: f. of a southward-facing   ARN 14:21
frío: f. que templa el ardor   CERV 138:20
Frisch: F. weht der Wind   WAGN 562:1
fritillaries: what purple f.   ARN 15:8
Fritter-my-wig: Fry me!' or 'F.   CARR 133:3
fritters: best f. that ever I eat   PEPYS 372:2
frivolity: chatter of irresponsible f.   DISR 185:18
Frocks: F. and Curls   DICK 184:2
frog: any better'n any other f.   TWAIN 554:5
Expiring f.   DICK 181:31
F. is justly sensitive   BELL 38:29
toe of f.   SHAK 462:3
from: f. here to Eternity   KIPL 299:10
f. the Sublime To the Ridiculous   GRAH 233:11
gamut of the emotions f.   PARK 368:21
fromages: 265 spécialités de f.   DE G 173:17
front: Always show your f.   MOL 353:1
in f. of one's nose   ORW 365:17
which f. these were sent   OWEN 367:7
frontier: f.-grave is far away   NEWB 361:5
where our f. lies to-day   BALD 29:28
frost: forms Of the radiant f.   SHEL 503:27
f. performs its secret   COL 156:21
is able to abide his f.   PRAY 399:21
'it is a f.   SURT 525:16
Terror like a f. shall   AUDEN 19:11
Thaw not the f. which binds   SHEL 499:3
third day comes a f.   SHAK 447:9
though dead with f. ere   GREV 236:17
frosts: f. are slain and flowers   SWIN 528:17
hoary-headed f.   SHAK 470:6
O ye Dews, and F.   PRAY 384:22
frosty: cold, f., windy morning   PEPYS 371:18
F., but kindly   SHAK 425:6
Into the f. starlight   ARN 14:28
froth: f. amid the boundless main   BRON 93:20
Life is mostly f. and bubble   GORD 233:1
Froude: Kingsley goes to F. for history   STUB 524:5
froward: are a very f. generation   BIBLE 48:31
frown: Convey a libel in a f.   SWIFT 527:29
I'll f. and be perverse   SHAK 482:13
more the f. o' the great   SHAK 428:22
Say that she f.   SHAK 484:8
So much as f. on you   SHAK 452:24
trembled with fear at your f.   ENGL 208:19
frown'd: dismal tidings when he f.   GOLD 231:2
frowned: is not true to say I f.   CHES 146:12
Frowns: F. o'er the wide and winding   BYRON 120:31
Her very f. are fairer   COL 155:1
frowst: f. with a book by the fire   KIPL 300:11
frowzy: f. couch in sorrow steep   BURNS 113:22
frozen: Architecture in general is f. music   SCH 415:3
milk comes f. home in pail   SHAK 457:19
pump has f. to-night   GRAV 234:12

Fruchtbarkeit: *F. und den grössten Genuss* NIET 363:9

fruges: *numerus sumus et f. consumere* HOR 258:13

fruit: autumn and the falling f. LAWR 311:8
brought forth f. BIBLE 66:16
eateth not of the f. thereof BIBLE 76:6
forth f. for the use of man PRAY 386:3
Forth reaching to the f. MILT 349:16
forth the f. of good works PRAY 387:2
f. Of that forbidden tree MILT 344:20
f. of the Spirit is love BIBLE 77:18
f. that can fall without MONT 354:7
humid nightblue f. JOYCE 286:29
It bore thy f. and mine KYD 306:7
love f. when it's expensive PIN 373:17
my f. is dreams THOM 548:28
Some f. for Him that dressed HERB 247:20
Sorrow's most detested f. BYRON 120:28
that green f. would swell KEATS 289:3
them f. for their songs ADD 2:25
tree is known by his f. BIBLE 66:8
weakest kind of f. SHAK 467:25
will long for the f. SHER 506:10

fruitful: Be f. BIBLE 45:6
f. ground SURR 524:20
f. vine: upon the walls PRAY 398:20
vineyard in a very f. hill BIBLE 57:21

fruitfulness: of mists and mellow f. KEATS 293:5

fruition: sweet f. of an earthly crown MARL 330:8

fruits: By their f. ye shall know BIBLE 65:10
eat his pleasant f. BIBLE 56:29
flowers and f. of love BYRON 125:11
Like Dead Sea f. MOORE 356:26
Plants f. of life and beauty BLAKE 86:20
to our use the kindly f. PRAY 385:21

fruit-tree: at some f.'s mossy root MARV 332:6

frustra: *f. vigilat qui custodit* BIBLE 83:12

Frustrate: F. their knavish tricks CAREY 130:25
impute to each f. ghost BROW 105:21

Fry: F. me!' or 'Fritter-my-wig CARR 133:3

fubbed: have been f. off SHAK 441:18

fudge: nobler name than f. HOUS 266:16
two-fifths sheer f. LOW 319:8
would cry out 'F. GOLD 232:37

fuego: *f. que calienta el frío* CERV 138:20

Fuel: F. to maintain his fires CAREW 130:12
Gathering f. in vacant lots ELIOT 204:8

fugaces: *Eheu f.* HOR 260:10

fugit: *f. inreparabile tempus* VIRG 560:17

fugitive: f. and cloistered virtue MILT 351:24
f. from th' law of averages MAUL 336:5
What was so f. WORD 579:9

fugues: been f. if he had written f. BUTL 118:32
Of masses and f. and 'ops' GILB 227:6

Fuimus: F. Troes VIRG 558:6

fuisse: *f. felicem* BOET 89:6

Fulfil: F. now, O Lord, the desires PRAY 385:8
not to destroy, but to f. BIBLE 64:10
power faithfully to f. PRAY 386:7
to f. the lusts thereof BIBLE 75:25
universe but to f. it SANT 414:2

fulfilled: f. a long time BIBLE 62:15
our hearts were f. with SWIN 528:24
Willed and f. by high KIPL 300:6

fulfilling: Love is the f. of the law BIBLE 75:23
storm, f. his word PRAY 399:22

fulfils: f. great Nature's plan BURNS 113:21

Full: F. fathom five SHAK 484:32
F. many a fathom deep CAMP 128:16
F. of life now WHIT 570:2
f. of subtil flame BEAU 35:19
F. speed ahead FARR 210:24
f. tide of human existence JOHN 276:21

in a flash, f. HOPK 257:7
now am f. of tears YEATS 584:22
Reading maketh a f. man BACON 27:20
Serenely f. SMITH 511:15
So f. of ugly sights SHAK 480:26
that hath his quiver f. PRAY 398:19
then he's f. of matter SHAK 425:3

full-blown: yet a rose f. HERR 250:16

fuller: f.'s earth for reputations GAY 222:17

fulmen: *Brutum f.* PLINY 374:16
Eripuit coelo f. TURG 553:22
Jovi f. viresque tonandi MAN 328:11

fulness: stature of the f. of Christ BIBLE 77:28

fum: Fy, fa, f. NASHE 360:6

fumble: f. with the sheets SHAK 443:17

fumbles: f. up into a loose adieu SHAK 487:12

fume: stinking f. thereof JAM 271:3

fumitor: Crown'd with rank f. SHAK 455:13

fumo: *sed ex f. dare lucem* HOR 257:19

Fumum: F. et opes strepitumque HOR 261:7

Fun: F. is fun but no girl wants LOOS 318:5
f. to punt than to be punted SAY 415:6
I thought *What Jolly F.* RAL 404:20
I've had my f. o' the Corp'ral's KIPL 298:7
I've taken my f. where KIPL 300:17
people have f. MONT 355:7
There was f. enough BETJ 44:13
We are not here for f. HERB 246:14
will not have the f. CHES 147:25
You have had enough f. HOR 259:6

function: bees each with his own f. VIRG 560:19
f. Is smother'd in surmise SHAK 458:20
F. never dies WORD 581:4

functions: their f. and their offices SHAK 457:8

fundamental: f. brainwork ROSS 410:10

fundamentally: woman was f. sensible JOHN 278:28

funèbre: *mais toute la nuit f.* PROU 401:23

funeral: fancy to see my own f. EDG 199:22
f. bak'd meats SHAK 430:4
F. marches to the grave LONG 317:2
f. sermon (which was long BELL 39:13
f. train which the bridegroom CLOU 153:10
him for the f. expenses JER 272:25
mirth in f. and with dirge SHAK 429:19
misbehaved once at a f. LAMB 307:27
Prepare vault for f. BEER 38:3
seldom seen a costlier f. TENN 533:11
speak in Caesar's f. SHAK 450:17
townspeople how to perform a f. WILL 574:12

funny: Whatever is f. is subversive ORW 365:10

funny-ha-ha: Funny-peculiar or f. HAY 243:6

Funny-peculiar: F. or funny-ha-ha HAY 243:6

fur: f. Fly 'bout the ears BUTL 117:30

furl'd: bright girdle f. ARN 12:23

furnace: burning fiery f. BIBLE 61:3
Heat not a f. for your foe SHAK 446:25
if they burned in a f. BIBLE 81:14
in the f. of affliction BIBLE 59:14
lover, Sighing like f. SHAK 425:24
one great f. flam'd MILT 344:25

furnaces: valley is fatal where f. AUDEN 18:17

furnish: Would f. all we ought KEBLE 295:4

Furnish'd: F. and burnish'd by Aldershot BETJ 44:6

furnished: Cambridge ladies who live in f. CUMM 170:9
know how poorly f. you are PERS 372:29

furniture: choir of heaven and f. BERK 41:19
f. so charming as books SMITH 511:2
of mere church f. at best COWP 167:32

furor: *Ira f. brevis est* HOR 258:15

furriners: (Which is what them f. GILB 228:31

furrow: crush'd beneath the f.'s BURNS 115:19
half-reap'd f. sound asleep KEATS 293:6
I must plough my f. alone ROS 408:16
shining f. TENN 542:14

furrows: made long f. PRAY 398:22
smite The sounding f. TENN 544:3
Thou waterest her f. PRAY 394:3
when in thee time's f. SHAK 493:1

further: Church the f. from God ANDR 4:8
f. us with thy continual PRAY 388:6
I was much f. out than SMITH 510:26
long way f. than Knighton HOUS 264:8
shalt thou go and no f. PARN 369:2

fury: formless spawning f. YEATS 587:2
full of sound and f. SHAK 463:6
f. and the mire of human YEATS 584:12
f. like an ex-wife searching CONN 161:13
f. of a patient man DRYD 194:20
F. slinging flame TENN 536:21
F. with th' abhorred shears MILT 343:8
In her prophetic f. sew'd SHAK 476:4
Nor Hell a f. CONG 160:15
there's f. in the firmament SASS 415:4

fuse: that through the green f. THOM 547:3

fuss: this f. about education MELB 336:21

fust: who gets his blow in f. BILL 84:6

fustian: whose f.'s so sublimely POPE 376:25

futility: f. of our occupation JOHN 273:17

future: cannot fight against the f. GLAD 229:12
Children of the f. age BLAKE 87:17
f., and it works STEF 518:15
f. contained in time past ELIOT 202:12
f. in the slightest HOR 259:20
f. sees BLAKE 87:13
I dipt into the f. TENN 538:24
leave the f. to the divine BACON 24:26
manners of f. generations JOHN 282:7
nursery of f. revolutions BURKE 111:5
plan the f. by the past BURKE 111:31
preparation for the f. DISR 185:37
serve the f. hour WORD 581:15
Time past and time f. ELIOT 202:16
Trust no F. LONG 317:3
want a picture of the f. ORW 365:14
Whose terrible f. may have AUDEN 18:19

futurity: his present is f. HARDY 241:13

futurum: *Quid sit f. cras fuge quaerere* HOR 259:18

Fuzzy-Wuzzy: F., at your 'ome KIPL 299:8

fynde: thou woldest f. an hare CHAU 143:13

fyr-reed: f. cherubynnes face CHAU 142:4

fyve: god that I have wedded f. CHAU 143:17

gabardine: spet upon my Jewish g. SHAK 466:2

Gadarene: 'is *the* G. Swine KIPL 305:7

gadding: thyme and the g. vine MILT 343:6

Gaels: great G. of Ireland CHES 146:17

gai: toujours g., archy MARQ 330:22

gaiety: which has eclipsed the g. JOHN 281:36

gain: comes to him from his g. BROW 100:10
distinct g. to society at large GILB 226:23
For g., not glory POPE 380:12
is but vain hope of g. TICH 551:2
perhaps neither g. nor loss ELIOT 202:24
shall g. the whole world BIBLE 66:35
shall g. the whole world BIBLE 68:34
So might I g. BROW 101:24
soul is competent to g. WORD 577:15
to die is g. BIBLE 78:11
what things were g. to me BIBLE 78:17
Wou'd you g. the tender GAY 222:9

gained: g. in amiability what he BUTL 118:28

greatest misery is a battle g. WELL 567:27

gains: Light g. make heavy purses
BACON 25:35

Gainsboroughs: G. and Lawrences
COW 164:2

gait: forc'd g. of a shuffling nag SHAK 439:26
manner of his g. SHAK 488:23

Galatea: Malo me G. petit VIRG 559:18

Galatians: There's a great text in G.
BROW 105:7

gale: g., it plies the saplings HOUS 263:14
Midland waters with the g. ARN 14:21
note that swells the g. GRAY 235:15

Galeotto: G. was the book and writer
DANTE 171:10

galère: allait-il faire dans cette g. MOL 353:14

Galice: In G. at Seint-Jame CHAU 141:31

Galilean: Pilot of the G. lake MILT 343:11
thou yet take all, G. SWIN 530:4
You have won, G. JUL 286:31

Galilee: rolls nightly on deep G.
BYRON 122:1

Galileo: Blind to G. on his turret
BROW 102:35

gall: take my milk for g. SHAK 459:2
They gave me g. to eat PRAY 394:12
to g. a new-healed wound SHAK 441:9
wormwood and the g. BIBLE 60:29

gallant: died a very g. gentleman ATK 17:21
G. and gay POPE 378:1
He was a braw g. BALL 30:16
We were a g. company BYRON 125:23

gallantry: more to do with g. SHER 506:6
What men call g. BYRON 122:9

galleon: moon was a ghostly g. tossed
NOYES 364:12

galleons: where are the g. of Spain
DOBS 187:10

gallery: faces are but a g. of pictures
BACON 26:15
g. in which the reporters MAC 323:7

galleys: Their g. blaze BYRON 121:32

Gallia: G. est omnis divisa CAES 126:26

galliard: not go to church in a g. SHAK 488:1

galligaskins: Donn'd g. CALV 127:16

gallimaufry: g. or hodgepodge of all
SPEN 517:6

Gallio: G. cared for none of those
BIBLE 74:15

gallop: does he gallop and g. about
STEV 522:18
G. about doing good SMITH 510:25
G. apace SHAK 483:6

galloped: old white horse g. away
ELIOT 203:14
we g. all three BROW 101:12

galloping: Hooves with a g. sound
VIRG 559:7

gallows: complexion is perfect g.
SHAK 484:21
g. fifty cubits high BIBLE 52:4
It grew a g. and did bear KYD 306:7
on the g., or of the pox WILK 574:6
see nothing but the g. BURKE 111:12
Shall there be g. standing SHAK 438:4
statue to him under the g. SMITH 511:24
Under the G.-Tree FLET 215:9

gallows-foot: To the g. KIPL 303:18

gallows-maker: g.; for that frame outlives
SHAK 436:23

gallows-tree: Jack on the g. SCOTT 418:16

galumphing: He went g. back CARR 134:29

gambler: whore and g. BLAKE 85:17

gambling: crew is g. in the forecastle
SHAW 496:33

gambol: Christmas g. oft could SCOTT 417:16

game: Conversation is a g. of circles
EMER 207:14
g. of the few BERK 41:22
g. on these lone heaths HAZL 243:32

g.'s afoot SHAK 444:3
g., That must be lost BEAU 36:10
how you played the g. RICE 405:23
of time to win this g. DRAKE 193:2
once a lady always g. MARQ 330:20
silly g. where nobody wins FULL 220:20
Socratic manner is not a g. BEER 38:4

game-act: explaining a passage in the
g. STEE 517:23

gamecocks: Wits are g. to one another
GAY 223:12

games: their g. should be seen MONT 354:17

gamesome: I am not g. SHAK 448:9

gammon: of g. and spinnage it is DICK 177:12

gamut: g. of the emotions from PARK 368:21

gamyn: of g. and gle WYNT 584:4

Gang: G. aft a-gley BURNS 115:22
he be doing in this g. MOL 353:14
old g. CHUR 149:19
sall we g. and dine the day BALL 32:8
they may g. a kennin wrang BURNS 112:25

Ganges: by the Indian G.' side MARV 332:18

gaol: that we know who lie in g.
WILDE 572:15

world's thy g. DONNE 189:23

gap: made a g. in nature SHAK 422:3
sleep out this great g. SHAK 421:30
That g. is the grave where AUDEN 18:17

gaped: stranded fish g. among PLOM 374:19

gaping: g. wretches of the sea HUNT 268:7

Garda: Lydian laughter of the G.
TENN 533:18

Garde: La G. meurt CAMB 128:2

garden: at the bottom of our g. FYL 220:23
beloved come into his g. BIBLE 56:29
Come into the g. TENN 540:9
concealed in an enclosed g. CAT 137:6
g. and a spring HOR 262:9
g. inclosed is my sister BIBLE 56:28
g. is a lovesome thing BROWN 95:12
g. loves a greenhouse too COWP 167:9
g. of bright images BRAM 91:22
g. of your face HERB 246:20
g. shady this holy lady AUDEN 18:3
g.'s last petals were SWIN 529:19
g., That grows to seed SHAK 429:28
g. with your pen CAMP 128:11
ghost of a g. fronts SWIN 529:17
Glory of the G. lies KIPL 299:12
God Almighty first planted a g. BACON 26:18
God the first g. made COWL 164:9
I have a g. of my own MARV 332:14
I value my g. more ADD 2:25
lodge in a g. of cucumbers BIBLE 57:16
man and a woman in a g. WILDE 573:29
nearer God's Heart in a g. GURN 237:7
Nothing grows in our g. THOM 547:12
Our England is a g. that KIPL 299:12
planted a g. eastward BIBLE 45:7
potter round the g. AUDEN 21:9
rosebud g. of girls TENN 540:11
set to dress this g. SHAK 479:18
summer birdcage in a g. WEBS 567:2
That every Hyacinth the G. FITZ 212:15
There is a g. in her face CAMP 129:22
this best g. of the world SHAK 445:11
through his g. walketh God BROW 105:14
Through this same G. after me FITZ 213:17
walking in the g. in the cool BIBLE 45:16

gardener: Adam was a g. KIPL 299:15
Adam was a g. SHAK 446:13
g. Adam and his wife TENN 537:29
supposing him to be the g. BIBLE 73:8
That half a proper g.'s KIPL 299:15
Will come the G. in white FLEC 214:13

gardeners: ancient gentlemen but g.
SHAK 436:22

gardens: closing time in the g. CONN 161:16
Down by the salley g. YEATS 584:22
g. Of spring and summer THOM 547:7

'imaginary g. with real toads MOORE 355:20
In the g. of the night BRID 92:16
Our bodies are our g. SHAK 474:8
Sowe Carrets in your G. GARD 221:8
sweetest delight of g. BROW 95:21
Thames bordered by its g. MORR 358:10
trim g. takes his pleasure MILT 342:1

garden-state: Such was that happy g.
MARV 332:7

garden-trees: through the vext g. ARN 15:5

gare: say au-dessus de sa g. RATT 405:2

garish: no worship to the g. sun SHAK 483:7

garland: g. briefer than a girl's HOUS 263:3
green willow is my g. HEYW 250:21
rosy g. and a weary head SIDN 507:21
that immortal g. MILT 351:12
wither'd is the g. of the war SHAK 423:16

garlanded: All g. with carven imag'ries
KEATS 289:16

garlands: fantastic g. did she come
SHAK 436:19
g. wither on your brow SHIR 507:3
her silken flanks with g. KEATS 291:8
To her let us g. bring SHAK 491:4
To weave the g. of repose MARV 331:21
you may gather g. there SCOTT 417:30

garleek: Wel loved he g. CHAU 142:5

garlic: cheese and g. in a windmill
SHAK 439:28

garment: deep like as with a g. PRAY 396:18
g. of praise for the spirit BIBLE 60:9
g. was white as snow BIBLE 61:8
know the g. from the man BLAKE 86:1
left his g. in her hand BIBLE 46:30
wax old as doth a g. PRAY 396:13

garments: borders of their g. BIBLE 67:22
dyed in Bozrah BIBLE 60:10
Reasons are not like g. ESSEX 208:24
Stuffs out his vacant g. SHAK 452:20
They part my g. among them PRAY 390:20

garnished: swept, and g. BIBLE 66:13

garret: Born in the g. BYRON 125:24
jewels into a g. four stories BACON 25:7
living in a g. FOOTE 216:6

Garrick: Here lies David G. GOLD 231:18
Our G.'s a salad GOLD 231:16

garrison: hath friends in the g. HAL 237:17

gars: g. ye rin sae still ANON 7:12

Garsington: Here is Hey for G. KETT 295:13

Garter: George and G. dangling POPE 377:33
I like the G. MELB 336:12

garters: thine own heir-apparent g.
SHAK 438:25

gas: All is g. and gaiters DICK 180:21
G. smells awful PARK 368:18
g. was on in the Institute BETJ 44:2

gashouse: evening round behind the g.
ELIOT 204:26

gas-lamps: his g. seven KING 296:20

Gasp: G. and Stretch one's Eyes BELL 39:7
sudden came a g. for breath PAIN 367:18
When he was at the last g. BIBLE 63:30

gat: up to me to my Lord right PRAY 391:14

gate: A-sitting on a g. CARR 136:5
broad g. and the great fire SHAK 421:4
g. is strait SWIN 530:28
G. With dreadful Faces MILT 350:1
into that g. they shall DONNE 191:3
keep the g. of hell SHAK 476:21
latch ter de golden g. HARR 242:17
lead you in at Heaven's g. BLAKE 86:8
matters not how strait the g. HENL 245:5
openeth the g. to good fame BACON 26:4
poor man at his g. ALEX 3:14
their enemies in the g. PRAY 398:19
this is the g. of heaven BIBLE 46:20
which was laid at his g. BIBLE 70:8
Wide is the g. BIBLE 65:6

gate-bars: drops on g. hang in a row
HARDY 241:4

gates: feet shall stand in thy g.	PRAY 398:11
g., and be ye lift up	PRAY 390:24
g. are mine to open	KIPL 301:20
g. of heaven opened against	MAL 328:7
g. of hell shall not prevail	BIBLE 66:33
g. of it shall not be shut	BIBLE 82:34
shut the g. of mercy	GRAY 234:24
stranger that is within thy g.	BIBLE 47:24
temple g. unto my love	SPEN 515:25
There are two g. of Sleep	VIRG 559:3
Gath: Tell it not in G.	BIBLE 50:16
gather: cannot tell who shall g. them	
	PRAY 391:31
g. the lambs with his arm	BIBLE 59:7
G. ye rosebuds while ye	HERR 250:5
gathered: by gloomy Dis Was g.	MILT 347:21
g. from the air a live	POUND 382:14
g. thy children together	BIBLE 67:26
some g. at six	DONNE 190:26
two or three are g.	PRAY 385:8
where two or three are g.	BIBLE 67:6
which cannot be g. up again	BIBLE 50:23
Gathering: G. her brows like gathering	
	BURNS 115:3
g. where thou hast not	BIBLE 68:3
gathers: Who g. all things mortal	
	SWIN 529:22
Gat-tothed: G. I was	CHAU 143:21
Gaudeamus: G. igitur	ANON 10:13
gaudium: quod illud g.	ABEL 1:2
gaudy: g., blabbing	SHAK 446:8
have one other g. night	SHAK 422:28
Neat, but not g.	WESL 568:25
rich, not g.	SHAK 430:19
than this g. melon-flower	BROW 101:7
gauger: g. walked with willing	STEV 523:8
Gaul: G. as a whole is divided	CAES 126:26
I've lost G.	KIPL 302:13
Gaunt: on G.'s embattled pile	MAC 322:4
seige of the city of G.	BALL 31:8
gauntlet: g. with a gift in't	BROW 97:28
gave: g. his only begotten Son	BIBLE 71:38
G. thee life	BLAKE 87:26
g. thee thy renown	CAREW 130:13
I g. you your own soul	SHAW 496:30
Lord g.	BIBLE 52:7
she g. me of the tree	BIBLE 45:17
That we g.	ANON 7:20
then he g. a third	WORD 580:1
What wee g.	ANON 8:17
gawds: consent praise new-born g.	
	SHAK 487:6
gay: g. as innocent	SCOTT 418:15
g. as soft	YOUNG 588:7
I'm a g. deceiver	COLM 159:2
making Gay rich and Rich g.	JOHN 282:1
outward walls so costly g.	SHAK 495:13
second best's a g. goodnight	YEATS 585:6
So g. against the great	AUDEN 18:5
steer From grave to g.	POPE 380:3
whole is far from g.	LEAR 312:22
Gaza: Eyeless in G.	MILT 350:14
gaze: g. not in my eyes	HOUS 262:21
g. on Christian fools with	SHAK 466:13
moveless hands And face and g.	
	HARDY 240:15
Stand fixt in stedfast g.	MILT 344:7
to g. out from the land	LUCR 320:6
gazelle: both Beautiful, one a g.	
	YEATS 585:11
g., delicate wanderer	SPEN 515:14
never nurs'd a dear g.	MOORE 356:25
never nursed a dear G.	DICK 180:29
gazelles: cleaving the grass, g.	MOORE 355:23
gazes: does he see when he g.	HARDY 240:15
gazing: stand ye g. up into heaven	
	BIBLE 73:21
géant: Ses ailes de g. l'empêchent	BAUD 35:6
gear: Gaze at the gilded g.	HARDY 239:5
hate all that Persian g.	HOR 260:4

my ships are out of g.	TENN 542:21
Gebet: ist das vollkommenste G.	LESS 314:1
geck: most notorious g. and gull	SHAK 490:24
Gedanke: Ein einziger dankbarer G.	
	LESS 314:1
'Zwei Seelen und ein G.	HALM 238:10
Geese: G. are swans	ARN 13:14
it for this the wild g.	YEATS 586:19
Like g. about the sky	AUDEN 18:9
still famous for its g.	HOUS 266:15
swans of others are g.	WALP 563:20
Gefahr: vor dem Alles in G. ist	NIET 363:5
gefährlich: g. leben	NIET 363:9
Gefühls: Epigramm auf den Tod eines	
G.	NIET 363:13
Gehazi: Whence comest thou, G.	BIBLE 51:30
Gehenna: to G. or up to the Throne	
	KIPL 304:11
Geist: der G. der stets verneint	GOET 230:1
gem: Full many a g. of purest	GRAY 234:23
Thinking every tear a g.	SHEL 502:3
geminae: Sunt g. Somni portae	VIRG 559:3
gemlike: hard, g. flame	PATER 369:21
gems: prow-promoted g. again	BETJ 42:18
Rich and various g. inlay	MILT 340:25
these the g. of Heav'n	MILT 348:5
Gemüt: Schicksal und G. Namen	NOV 364:9
gender: she's of the feminine g.	OKEE 364:23
genealogies: Fables and endless g.	BIBLE 79:6
general: army led by an Irish g.	SHAW 498:7
country was good for G.	WILS 574:15
feet of the great g.	OVID 366:24
G. Good is the plea	BLAKE 86:7
G. notions are generally	MONT 354:9
g. of our gracious empress	SHAK 445:7
g. Of trotting 'paritors	SHAK 456:26
g.'s disdain'd	SHAK 486:25
good morning!' the g.	SASS 414:18
governed too much by g. maxims	
	BURKE 109:5
'twas caviare to the g.	SHAK 432:23
useless as a g. maxim	MAC 323:28
you find in that great g.	JUV 288:1
generalities: g. of natural right which	
	CHOA 148:14
Glittering g.	EMER 208:14
generally: g. necessary to salvation	
	PRAY 388:19
generals: bite some of my other g.	
	GEOR 223:36
Despite of all your g.	LAND 308:18
Russia has two g. in whom	NICH 362:23
generation: censor of the young g.	
	HOR 257:21
evil and adulterous g.	BIBLE 66:11
faithless and stubborn g.	PRAY 395:4
g. of them that hate me	BIBLE 47:24
g. of vipers	BIBLE 63:38
g. that set not	PRAY 395:4
g. wiser than the children	BIBLE 70:25
Had it been the whole g.	ANON 5:15
I grieved with this g.	PRAY 396:4
leaves is a g. of men	HOMER 253:29
One g. passeth away	BIBLE 55:5
they are a very froward g.	BIBLE 48:31
to a yet more vicious g.	HOR 260:26
ye are a chosen g.	BIBLE 80:23
You're all a lost g.	STEIN 518:18
generations: g. shall call me blessed	
	BIBLE 69:5
G. pass while some tree	BROW 97:16
g. 'from shirt-sleeves	BUTL 117:12
G. have trod	HOPK 256:12
g. of living creatures	LUCR 320:7
No hungry g. tread thee	KEATS 291:23
Ten g. failed to alter	HARDY 241:13
generous: g. and honest feeling that	
	BURKE 108:24
g. and elevated mind	JOHN 282:19
impulses as they are always g.	MONT 355:11

It is the g. spirit	WORD 577:3
My mind as g.	SHAK 453:9
they have more g. sentiments	JOHN 275:4
Genesis: set you square with G.	BROW 99:9
Geneva: grim G. ministers	AYT 24:10
génie: j'ai mis mon g. dans ma vie	
	WILDE 573:35
Le g. n'est qu'une plus	BUFF 106:21
vous croyez un grand g.	BEAU 35:18
Geniumque: G. loci primamque deorum	
	VIRG 559:4
genius: Consult the g. of the place POPE 378:3
'Eccentricities of g.	DICK 182:8
g. and the mortal instruments	SHAK 449:6
g. are the first things	KEATS 293:21
g. does what it must	MER 338:5
G. been defined as a supreme	BUTL 118:34
g. is no more than a girl	POUND 382:15
G. is of no country	CHUR 149:7
G. is one per cent inspiration	EDIS 199:25
G. is only a greater aptitude	BUFF 106:21
g. of the Constitution	PITT 373:28
g. rules is by persuading	STEP 518:20
g. that could cut a Colossus	JOHN 279:18
'G.' (which means transcendent	CARL 131:18
Gives g. a better discerning	GOLD 231:22
good G. presiding over you	KEATS 293:11
have put my g. into my life	WILDE 573:35
If Shakespeare's g. had	CHES 145:24
instantly recognizes g.	DOYLE 192:38
kind of universal g.	DRYD 197:39
man of g. makes no mistakes	JOYCE 286:9
man of g. and his money	SHEN 505:17
models destroy g. and art	HAZL 243:28
only on its heights of g.	HOUS 266:15
Philistine of g. in religion	ARN 16:23
Ramp up my g.	JONS 284:13
she creates a g. to do it	EMER 208:3
sphere for Shelley's g.	ARN 16:2
stupendous g.! damned fool	BYRON 126:17
that is g.	EMER 207:34
Three-fifths of him g.	LOW 319:8
to declare except my g.	WILDE 573:36
To raise the g.	POPE 375:11
true g. is a mind of large	JOHN 281:30
True g. kindles	POPE 376:26
was g. found respectable	BROW 97:31
what a g. I had when	SWIFT 527:9
When a true g. appears	SWIFT 527:8
yourself to be a great g.	BEAU 35:18
Gennesareth: Not of G.	THOM 548:25
genres: Tous les g. sont bons hors	
	VOLT 561:7
gens: g. de qualité savent	MOL 353:23
GENTE: SI VA TRA LA PERDUTA	
G.	DANTE 171:3
genteel: beast to the truly g.	HARDY 241:17
not g. when he gets drunk	BOSW 90:16
gentes: Augescunt aliae g.	LUCR 320:7
gentil: g. that dooth gentil dedis CHAU 143:25
parfit g. knyght	CHAU 141:10
Gentiles: should preach among the G.	
	BIBLE 77:23
gentle: day shall g. his condition	SHAK 445:3
Do not go g. into that	THOM 546:23
G. as falcon or hawk	SKEL 508:16
G. Jesus	WESL 568:17
g. mind by gentle deeds	SPEN 516:23
g. rain from heaven	SHAK 467:27
His life was g.	SHAK 452:7
I have seen them g.	WYATT 583:21
person in vertuous and g.	SPEN 515:28
gentleman: almost a definition of a g.	
	NEWM 362:3
Be a little g.	HOFF 252:14
being g. never is one	SURT 525:2
book is to fashion a g.	SPEN 515:15
died a very gallant g.	ATK 17:21
every Jack became a g.	SHAK 480:24
finish'd g. from top	BYRON 123:37

first true g. that ever — DEKK 173:19
g. has soup at luncheon — CURZ 170:18
g. is not in your books — SHAK 471:27
grand old name of g. — TENN 537:17
he cannot make a g. — BURKE 111:37
I am a g. — SHAK 488:14
I am not quite a g. — ASHF 17:6
kind-hearted g. — COWP 168:3
last g. in Europe — LEV 314:3
Like a fine old English g. — ANON 6:10
little too pedantic for a g. — CONG 160:12
mariner with the g. — DRAKE 193:4
No real English g. — BAG 29:12
not alive so stout a g. — SHAK 440:24
of an officer and a g. — ANON 4:20
Of an old worshipful g. — ANON 4:19
Once a g. — DICK 178:28
perfect g. then neared — HARDY 241:1
prince of darkness is a g. — SHAK 454:24
Shew'd him the g. and scholar — BURNS 115:25
soul of this g.'s way — ANON 10:14
This squash, this g. — SHAK 491:10
unable to describe a g. — TROL 552:15
gentlemanly: g. conduct — ARN 16:26
gives one werry g. ideas — SURT 525:20
sometimes do a very g. thing — STEV 521:15
Gentleman-rankers: G. out on the spree — KIPL 299:10
Gentlemen: Dust was G. and Ladies — DICK 184:2
England since g. came up — SHAK 446:16
g. both — ELIZ 205:23
g. in England — SHAK 445:3
Great-hearted g. — BROW 99:26
Hard-riding country g. — YEATS 587:8
not to forget we are g. — BURKE 108:24
Scholars and g. — WORD 580:20
spoken of themselves as g. — WAUGH 566:2
three g. at once — SHER 506:19
Three jolly g. — DE L 174:6
was not a religion for g. — CHAR 140:25
while the G. go — KIPL 302:22
written by gentlemen for g. — THAC 545:16
You g. of England — PARK 368:25
You g.'s gentlemen are — SHER 506:11
gentleness: from your eyes that g. — SHAK 448:10
Let g. my strong enforcement — SHAK 425:23
gentlest: meekest man and the g. — MAL 328:8
Gentlewomen: Cherubic Creatures—
These G. — DICK 184:3
Gently: G., John, gently down — SMITH 512:3
g. lay my head — BROW 97:6
G. they go — MILL 339:23
his faults lie g. on him — SHAK 447:17
roar you as g. as any sucking — SHAK 469:30
genuine: difference between g. poetry — ARN 16:9
g. spirit of localism — BORR 90:2
place for the g. — MOORE 355:19
genus: Hoc g. omne — HOR 261:24
Genuss: G. vom Dasein einzuernten — NIET 363:9
geographers: g., in Afric-maps — SWIFT 528:2
geographical: Italy is a g. expression — METT 338:11
Geography: G. is about maps — BENT 41:3
g. made up of seas of treacle — MAC 324:21
geological: highly g. home-made cake — DICK 179:3
Geology: G., ethnology — BROW 99:9
geometrical: Great Bear is looking so g. — FRY 220:2
increases in a g. ratio — MALT 328:9
geometricians: we are g. only be chance — JOHN 281:32
geometry: enter who does not know g. — ANON 10:2
G. (which is the only science . — HOBB 251:14
is no 'royal road' to g. — EUCL 209:3

George: Amelia was praying for G. — THAC 545:26
G. and Garter dangling — POPE 377:33
if his name be G. — SHAK 452:9
viler G. the Second — LAND 309:6
George III: G. was a kind of 'consecrated — BAG 29:1
George the Third: G. Ought never — BENT 41:10
geranium: madman shakes a dead g. — ELIOT 204:9
geraniums: cot with a pot of pink g. — MACN 326:8
German: G. tiger with yelps not — CHUR 150:7
is too short to learn G. — PORS 381:30
they just shovel in G. — TWAIN 554:24
to my horse—G. — CHAR 140:31
Germania: G., magni — OVID 366:22
Germans: bomb the G. — BETJ 43:5
G. in Greek — PORS 381:27
let's be beastly to the G. — COW 163:15
to the G. that of the air — JEAN 272:4
Germany: associated against G. — WILS 575:2
his bonnet in G. — SHAK 465:24
wall all G. with brass — MARL 329:5
germens: all g. spill at once — SHAK 454:4
Gesang: Das ist der ewige G. — GOET 230:2
Weib und G. — LUTH 321:1
Gesetz: solle ein allgemeines G. — KANT 288:9
Gestern: G. liebt' ich — LESS 313:26
get: g. into the soup in Ireland — WAUGH 566:1
g. me to England once again — BROO 94:22
g. up for shame — HERR 248:22
they g. on well enough — MELB 336:21
To do nothing and g. something — DISR 186:28
getting: always g. ready to live — EMER 207:43
devotee of the Gospel of G. — SHAW 498:8
G. and spending — WORD 582:19
innate love of g. — VIRG 560:19
gewgaw: This g. world — DRYD 195:13
geyser: From the g. ventilators — BETJ 42:6
Ghastly: G. Good Taste — BETJ 44:15
g. thro' the drizzling — TENN 536:6
We were a g. crew — COL 155:25
Ghost: Come, Holy G. — PRAY 400:5
coming of the Holy G. — PRAY 385:17
conceived by the Holy G. — PRAY 384:26
gave up the g. — BIBLE 74:3
g. of a garden fronts — SWIN 529:17
g. of Roger Casement — YEATS 585:7
G. of the deceased Roman Empire — HOBB 251:21
G. unlaid forbear thee — SHAK 428:22
I'll make a g. of him that — SHAK 431:1
impute to each frustrate g. — BROW 105:21
It is an honest g. — SHAK 431:19
like a g. she glimmers — TENN 542:14
Moves like a g. — SHAK 460:1
of the G. in the machine — RYLE 412:25
poor g. — SHAK 431:3
raise up the g. of a rose — BROW 95:21
That affable familiar g. — SHAK 494:12
There needs no g. — SHAK 431:17
There's the g. of a crazy — COW 164:5
to the bowling of a g. — THOM 547:24
to the Holy G. — PRAY 384:15
Turn thou g. that way — DONNE 188:20
Vex not his g. — SHAK 456:12
We saw the g. of Captain — BETJ 44:3
What beck'ning g. — POPE 376:5
What gentle g. — JONS 285:9
with some old lover's g. — DONNE 189:25
Would brood like a g. — DE L 174:13
Your g. will walk — BROW 100:12
ghosties: From ghoulies and g. — ANON 5:8
ghosts: g. from an enchanter fleeing — SHEL 502:8
g., wandering here — SHAK 470:25
horn and by it real g. — VIRG 559:3
newspaper and I seem to see g. — IBSEN 269:21

sprightly port make the g. — SHAK 423:10
yet a boy I sought for g. — SHEL 501:6
Ghoul: Blimber dug them up like a G. — DICK 177:23
ghoulies: g. and ghosties and long-leggety — ANON 5:8
GHOULS: When I die, the G. — TENN 544:12
giant: are upon the body of a g. — LAND 309:15
arrows in the hand of the g. — PRAY 398:19
baby figure of the g. mass — SHAK 486:27
g. dies — GREEN 235:28
g. race before the flood — DRYD 196:1
g. refreshed with wine — PRAY 395:7
I was the g. great — STEV 522:20
like a g.'s robe — SHAK 462:27
rejoiceth as a g. to run — PRAY 390:11
sees farther than the g. — COL 157:25
To have a g.'s strength — SHAK 464:1
when a g. dies — SHAK 464:11
giants: g. in the earth in those — BIBLE 45:33
on the shoulders of g. — BERN 41:25
on the shoulders of g. — NEWT 362:19
there we saw the g. — BIBLE 48:11
gibber: dead Did squeak and g. — SHAK 429:12
gibbets: cells and g. for 'the man' — ELIZ 162:8
g. keep the lifted hand — YOUNG 587:19
Gibbon: G. moved to flutes — COLM 159:3
Gibeon: stand thou still upon G. — BIBLE 49:4
gibes: g. and flouts and jeers — DISR 185:13
Where be your g. now — SHAK 436:31
giddy: Our fancies are more g. — SHAK 489:1
giddy-paced: most brisk and g. times — SHAK 488:26
Gideon: of the Lord came upon G. — BIBLE 49:15
gier: g.-eagle on his sail — SMART 509:3
gift: gauntlet with a g. in't — BROW 97:28
g. and remembrancer designedly — WHIT 570:18
g. of God may be purchased — BIBLE 73:30
Heaven's last best g. — MILT 348:14
not the g. of martyrdom — DRYD 196:15
perfect g. is from above — BIBLE 80:9
rarest g. To Beauty — MER 337:11
(The deed of g. was many — FROST 219:6
You have a g. — JONS 285:15
gifted: some divinely g. man — TENN 537:1
gift-horse: To look a g. in the mouth — BUTL 117:27
giftie: wad some Pow'r the g. gie — BURNS 115:18
gifts: all the good g. of nature — SHAK 487:24
Bestows her g. on such — JONS 284:10
brilliance of their g. — PATER 369:22
cannot recall their g. — TENN 543:12
contempt of God's good g. — JAM 271:4
Enemies' gifts are no g. — SOPH 513:5
even when they bring g. — VIRG 558:1
g. of God are strown — HEBER 244:6
g. wax poor when givers — SHAK 433:10
He would adore my g. instead — HERB 248:7
Of all the heavenly g. — GRIM 236:20
received g. for men — PRAY 394:10
Saba shall bring g. — PRAY 394:20
supinely enjoyed the g. — GIBB 224:8
there are diversities of g. — BIBLE 76:13
They presented unto him g. — BIBLE 63:32
use the gods' g. wisely — HOR 261:19
us love your goodly g. — SHAK 478:5
Yet take these g. — CAT 137:15
gig: crew of the Captain's g. — CHES 146:27
crew of the captain's g. — GILB 225:16
gigantic: g. smile o' the brown — BROW 101:20
Gilboa: Ye mountains of G. — BIBLE 50:16
Gild: G., but to flout — SCOTT 416:13
g. it with the happiest — SHAK 440:28
g. the faces of the grooms — SHAK 460:11
'To g. refined gold — BYRON 122:31
To g. refined gold — SHAK 452:25
gilded: best-seller is the g. tomb — SMITH 510:20

bug with g. wings POPE 377:1
g. loam or painted clay SHAK 478:8
trim the g. vessel goes GRAY 234:16
Gilding: G. pale streams with heavenly
SHAK 493:9
g. the eastern hemisphere SHER 505:25
Gilead: G. is mine PRAY 393:18
Is there no balm in G. BIBLE 60:21
that appear from mount G. BIBLE 56:26
Gillyflowers: With G. SPEN 517:3
Gilpin: John G. was a citizen COWP 165:15
gilt: dust that is a little g. SHAK 487:6
Gin: G. by pailfuls SCOTT 418:16
G. was mother's milk SHAW 498:15
that I breakfast on g. HERB 246:8
woodcock near the g. SHAK 489:12
ginger: Nutmegs and g. BEAU 36:5
'ot sand an' g. when alive KIPL 299:9
ginger-beer: He cannot abide g. LEAR 311:24
Giotto: G.'s tower LONG 316:17
giovinezza: Quant' è bella g. MED 336:9
Gipfeln: Über allen G. Ist Ruh' GOET 230:11
gipseying: lass that were to go a-g.
LAMB 308:3
Gipsies: same the G. wore ARN 14:13
gipsy: g. by Reynolds to his Majesty's
MAC 324:2
giraffe: Swelling to maculate g. ELIOT 204:14
Giraffes: G.! —a People CAMP 128:10
Gird: G. up now thy loins like BIBLE 53:1
girded: g. himself with strength PRAY 395:24
He g. up his loins BIBLE 51:12
is g. about with power PRAY 394:1
Let your loins be g. about BIBLE 70:6
With your loins g. BIBLE 47:18
girdedst: thou g. thyself BIBLE 73:17
girdeth: g. on his harness boast BIBLE 51:16
girdid: I g. up my Lions & fled WARD 564:24
girdle: bright g. furl'd ARN 12:23
g. do the Gods inherit SHAK 455:17
g. round about the earth SHAK 470:9
leathern g. about his loins BIBLE 63:37
girdled: g. with the gleaming world
TENN 539:16
girl: Above the staggering g. YEATS 586:1
at a g. throwing a ball WOOLF 576:19
Each book that a young g. RUSK 412:13
garland briefer than a g.'s HOUS 263:3
genius is no more than a g. POUND 382:15
g. arose that had red mournful YEATS 586:22
g. like I LOOS 318:1
g.'s lip out of Paris SWIN 531:2
Home is the g.'s prison SHAW 498:3
Is an unlesson'd g. SHAK 467:13
little cottage g. PAIN 367:19
mountainous sports g. BETJ 43:20
no g. wants to laugh all LOOS 318:5
There was a little g. LONG 317:22
to any good g. to be neat TAYL 531:24
touched a broken g. FLEC 214:15
We all love a pretty g. BICK 84:2
You speak like a green g. SHAK 430:20
girl-graduates: sweet g. in their golden
TENN 541:27
girlish: to the brim with g. glee GILB 226:27
girls: Afield for palms the g. HOUS 262:19
All very agreeable g. GILB 226:2
'Always be civil to the g. MITF 352:23
At g. who wear glasses PARK 368:16
Barring drink and the g. LOCK 315:23
before to virgin g. and boys HOR 260:13
Boys and g. tumbling TRAH 551:19
do for pretty g. YEATS 585:16
g. we was all of us ladies we was
MARQ 330:20
lads for the g. HOUS 263:6
My life with g. has ended HOR 261:6
Of all the g. that are CAREY 130:26
pallor of g.' brows OWEN 367:3
prevent girls from being g. HOPE 255:28

process whereby American g. HAMP 238:17
rosebud garden of g. TENN 540:11
rose-lipt g. are sleeping HOUS 264:10
swear to never kiss the g. BROW 100:30
white feet of laughing g. MAC 322:12
girt: loins g. about with truth BIBLE 78:10
git: you've gut to g. up airly LOW 319:1
Gitche Gumee: By the shore of G.
LONG 317:10
Gitche Manito: G., the mighty LONG 317:9
give: All I can g. you I give SWIN 530:22
all other things g. place GAY 223:16
blessed to g. than to receive BIBLE 74:19
did not g. a singel dam FLEM 214:25
freely g. BIBLE 65:31
G. all thou canst WORD 582:16
G., and it shall be given BIBLE 69:23
'G. crowns and pounds HOUS 262:20
G. every man thine ear SHAK 430:19
g. her booby for another GAY 223:11
g. me back my legions AUG 22:4
g. me back my heart BYRON 125:3
g. me back my heart again GRAN 234:4
G. me more love or more CAREW 130:16
G. me,' quoth I SHAK 458:6
G. me your tired LAZ 311:13
g. them a core one time TWAIN 554:17
g. the world the lie RAL 404:10
G. this man place BIBLE 70:7
G. to me the life I love STEV 522:27
g. to the poor BIBLE 67:9
G. us the tools CHUR 150:6
G. us this day our daily BIBLE 64:24
G. what you command AUG 21:17
honourable alike in what we g. LINC 314:22
never g. up their liberties BURKE 110:27
receive but what we g. COL 156:9
such as I have g. I thee BIBLE 73:25
What I desire to g. SHAK 485:12
What will ye g. me BIBLE 68:9
which the world cannot g. PRAY 385:9
given: he would not have g. me WOLS 576:14
one that hath shall be g. BIBLE 68:4
sister is g. to government DICK 178:7
Something g. that way FLET 215:14
unto us a son is g. BIBLE 58:7
giver: author and g. of all good PRAY 386:19
g. is forgot CONG 159:30
Lord and g. of life PRAY 387:11
loveth a cheerful g. BIBLE 77:9
givers: poor when g. prove unkind
SHAK 433:10
gives: g. to airy nothing SHAK 471:11
much good who g. quickly PUBL 402:3
giving: g. and receiving of a Ring PRAY 389:7
Godlike in g. MOORE 357:5
not in the g. vein to-day SHAK 481:6
Stealing and g. odour SHAK 487:20
glacier: g. knocks in the cupboard
AUDEN 18:10
glad: bad g. mad SWIN 529:2
G. did I live and gladly STEV 523:10
gladness when she's g. BARR 34:17
g. of other men's good SHAK 426:4
g. that you won BETJ 44:6
I was g. when they said PRAY 398:11
maketh g. the heart of man PRAY 396:20
moments of g. grace YEATS 587:12
shew ourselves g. in him PRAY 396:3
solitary place shall be g. BIBLE 58:32
son maketh a g. father BIBLE 53:29
To g. me with its soft MOORE 356:25
Trying to be g. HOUS 262:22
was made to make men g. BIBLE 63:15
will rejoice and be g. PRAY 398:2
yea g. with all my heart DRAY 193:21
gladder: My heart is g. than all ROSS 408:23
glade: alone in the bee-loud g. YEATS 585:17
gladiators: What were the g. of Rome
BORR 90:6

gladness: g. of her gladness when BARR 34:17
serve the Lord with g. PRAY 396:11
shall obtain joy and g. BIBLE 59:1
solemn g. even crown'd TENN 536:18
Teach me half the g. SHEL 504:24
thee with the oil of g. PRAY 392:15
Gladstone: G.'s always having LAB 306:10
Glamis: G. hath murder'd sleep SHAK 460:9
G. thou art, and Cawdor SHAK 459:1
glamour: g. Of childish days LAWR 311:7
glance: Doth g. from heaven SHAK 471:11
g. of supernatural hate BYRON 126:7
mutual g. of great politeness BYRON 126:8
whose g. was glum GILB 229:9
glare: from day's detested g. POPE 381:19
strange unheavenly g. BRID 92:13
There is a g. in some men's BAG 28:20
glass: baying for broken g. WAUGH 565:29
dome of many-coloured g. SHEL 499:26
double g. o' the inwariable DICK 182:11
Drink not the third g. HERB 247:1
England is looking in the g. CHES 147:1
Get thee g. eyes SHAK 455:21
g. I drink from is not MUSS 359:2
g. is falling hour by hour MACN 326:8
g. of blessings standing HERB 248:6
g. when I am shrinking ANON 10:14
Grief with a g. that ran SWIN 528:20
He was indeed the g. SHAK 441:24
his natural face in a g. BIBLE 80:10
his own face in the g. WILDE 573:16
it were a sea of g. mingled BIBLE 82:19
like it out of a thin g. PINT 373:18
man that looks on g. HERB 247:18
My g. shall not persuade SHAK 493:1
Over the g.'s edge when BROW 99:2
prove an excuse for the g. SHER 506:31
Satire is a sort of g. SWIFT 525:32
she made mouths in a g. SHAK 454:6
sound of broken g. BELL 40:5
throne there was a sea of g. BIBLE 81:23
through a g., darkly BIBLE 76:14
till I set you up a g. SHAK 434:33
turn down an empty G. FITZ 213:18
when he looked into the g. DISR 186:14
you break the bloody g. MACN 326:8
glasses: At girls who wear g. PARK 368:16
broke our painted g. JORD 285:18
Fill all the g. there COWL 164:8
were two g. and two chairs MACN 326:11
with plenty of looking g. ASHF 17:10
Wiv a ladder and some g. BAT 35:3
gle: of gamyn and g. WYNT 584:4
gleam: add the g. WORD 577:4
Follow The G. TENN 540:21
g. on the years that shall BULW 107:1
spent lights quiver and g. ARN 13:6
gleamed: first she g. upon my sight
WORD 581:7
g. Upon the glassy plain WORD 577:26
gleams: sunbeams with their convex g.
SHEL 500:7
glean: reap thou shouldst but g. HOOD 255:5
world shall g. of me THOM 548:28
glean'd: pen has g. my teeming KEATS 292:30
gleaning: g. of the grapes of Ephraim
BIBLE 49:17
glede: in pursuit the rapid g. SMART 509:3
glee: At their tempestuous g. LONG 317:8
brim with girlish g. GILB 226:27
Piping songs of pleasant g. BLAKE 87:24
glen: Down the rushy g. ALL 3:20
Glenartney: In lone G.'s hazel shade
SCOTT 416:1
Glenlivet: Only half G. AYT 24:7
glib: g. and oily art SHAK 453:5
glides: meadows where it g. ARN 12:22
glimmering: Mere g. and decays VAUG 555:19
glimpse: g. of His bright face VAUG 555:14

glimpses: thus the g. of the moon

SHAK 430:24
glisters: Nor all, that g., gold   GRAY 235:8
glittering: g. and sounding generalities

CHOA 148:14
g. prizes to those who   BIRK 84:14
how that g. taketh me   HERR 250:8
gloat: Hear me g.   KIPL 305:4
global: my wars Were g.   REED 405:7
globe: g. of death and halved   THOM 547:4
great g. itself   SHAK 485:20
rattle of a g. to play   DRYD 195:13
wears the turning g.   HOUS 265:1
globule: primordial atomic g.   GILB 226:20
Glöckchen: Höhr ihr das G. klingeln

HEINE 244:11
gloire: g. et le repos sont choses MONT 354:22
Le jour de g. est arrivé   ROUG 410:16
gloom: Brooding o'er the g.   MER 337:3
g. of earthquake and eclipse   SHEL 503:21
Inspissated g.   JOHN 275:25
Is my g.   THOM 548:23
(Lamps for my g.   SASS 414:19
light to counterfeit a g.   MILT 342:5
Our g.-pleas'd eyes   KEATS 292:28
There g. the dark broad seas   TENN 544:3
tunnel of green g.   BROO 94:17
Upon the growing g.   HARDY 239:7
glooms: Through verdurous g.   KEATS 291:20
Welcome, kindred g.   THOM 549:22
gloomy: g. in England are March

TROL 552:21
way to such g. thoughts   AUST 23:17
Gloria: G. in excelsis Deo   MASS 334:18
G. Patri   MASS 334:14
gloriam: Ad majorem Dei g.   ANON 10:6
sed nomini tuo da g.   BIBLE 83:10
gloried: Jamshyd g. and drank deep

FITZ 212:14
glories: g. and my state depose   SHAK 479:23
G., like glow-worms   WEBS 566:25
g. of our blood and state   SHIR 507:2
in those weaker g. spy   VAUG 555:15
glorify: g. God and to enjoy   SHOR 507:7
glorious: all g. within   PRAY 392:17
g. are those sabbaths which   ABEL 1:1
g. fault of angels   POPE 376:8
G. the sun in mid-career   SMART 509:4
g. thing must be a victory   WELL 567:26
how g.   BETJ 43:3
I'll make thee g. by my pen   GRAH 233:15
reach at the g. gold   SHAK 446:2
shown no g. morning face   STEV 523:11
Sing the g. day's renown   CAMP 128:14
Tam was g.   BURNS 115:6
'tis a g. thing   GILB 225:22
glory: are the days of our g.   BYRON 125:29
Be Thine the g.   DRYD 196:13
brightness of his g.   BIBLE 79:28
brittle g. shineth in this   SHAK 480:5
calls the g. from the grey   BROW 104:6
chief g. of every people   JOHN 281:10
count the g. of my crown   ELIZ 206:5
day of g. has arrived   ROUG 410:16
drown'd my G. in a Shallow Cup FITZ 213:13
duty was the way to g.   TENN 541:14
earth are full of thy g.   PRAY 387:23
earth is full of his g.   BIBLE 57:28
eternal brood of g. excellent   SPEN 516:4
feathered g. from her loosening YEATS 586:1
fierce wretchedness that g.   SHAK 486:10
fill thy breast with g.   HERB 247:3
finished yields the true g.   DRAKE 193:1
from another star in g.   BIBLE 76:26
G. and loveliness have   KEATS 292:26
g. and our absolute boast   WORD 580:16
g. and the nothing   BYRON 121:28
g. and the dream   WORD 579:5
g. as of the only begotten   BIBLE 71:27
G. be to God for dappled   HOPK 256:22

G. be to the Father   PRAY 384:15
g. dropped from their youth   BROW 105:19
g. in the church by Christ Jesus   BIBLE 77:26
g. in the name of Briton   GEOR 224:1
g. is departed from Israel   BIBLE 49:40
g., jest, and riddle   POPE 379:13
G., like the phoenix 'midst   BYRON 124:30
g. of Europe is extinguished   BURKE 111:9
g. of man as the flower   BIBLE 80:21
g. of the Attic stage   ARN 15:10
g. of the Creator   BACON 24:17
G. of the Garden lies   KIPL 299:12
g. of the Lord shall be   BIBLE 59:5
g. of the Lord is risen   BIBLE 60:7
g. of the Lord shone round   BIBLE 69:9
g. of the sun will be dimmed   BALF 30:3
g. of the winning were   MER 337:2
g., or the grave   CAMP 128:22
g. shone around   TATE 531:22
G. to God in the highest   BIBLE 69:11
G. to Man in the highest   SWIN 530:2
g. was I had such friends   YEATS 586:6
g. was not arrayed like   BIBLE 64:30
Go where g. waits thee   MOORE 356:8
has ended and the vast g.   VIRG 558:6
heavens declare the g.   PRAY 390:11
hope of g.   PRAY 386:2
I felt it was g.   BYRON 125:30
infirm g. of the positive   ELIOT 201:33
into g. peep   VAUG 555:21
King of g. shall come   PRAY 390:24
Land of Hope and G.   BENS 40:24
left him alone with his g.   WOLFE 576:5
long hair, it is a g.   BIBLE 76:12
looks on war as all g.   SHER 506:40
madness is the g. of this life   SHAK 486:4
Majesty: of thy G.   PRAY 384:16
much g. and so much shame   MAC 324:11
My gown of g.   RAL 404:12
nothing else but sudden g.   HOBB 251:22
not the g.   GOET 230:5
now my g. smear'd in dust   SHAK 446:22
of being too fond of g.   SMITH 511:37
of g. in the flower   WORD 579:13
of the peacock is the g.   BLAKE 88:21
passed away a g.   WORD 578:22
passes the g. of the world   ANON 11:1
paths of g. lead   GRAY 234:21
quickly the world's g.   THOM 546:7
return the g. of your prime   SHEL 501:14
sea Of g. streams along   BYRON 121:4
short of the g. of God   BIBLE 74:38
solely is the sum of g.   MARL 330:11
that will die in their g.   HOUS 263:8
'There's g. for you   CARR 135:21
'Tis beauty calls and g.   LEE 313:10
'tis to g. we steer'   ROSS 408:25
to crown him with g.   PRAY 389:28
To the g. that was Greece   POE 375:7
To the greater g. of God   ANON 10:6
to thy name give g.   BIBLE 83:10
trailing clouds of g.   WORD 579:5
unspeakable and full of g.   BIBLE 80:20
Vain pomp and g. of this   SHAK 447:9
walked in g. and in joy   WORD 580:28
walked with inward g. crowned SHEL 504:10
walking in an air of g.   VAUG 555:19
what g. is it   BIBLE 80:26
When gout and g. seat me   BROW 100:19
whose g. is their shame   BIBLE 78:19
Why in the name of G. were   KEATS 290:9
with g. not their own   WORD 580:19
glotoun: g. of wordes   LANG 309:24
Gloucester: thy name is G.   SHAK 455:22
Gloucestershire: am a stranger here in

G.   SHAK 478:23
glove: were a g. upon that hand   SHAK 482:7
gloves: complete with hat and g. CALV 127:16
through the fields in g.   CORN 162:22
wore g. in my cap   SHAK 454:18

glow: that g. in the heart that   CONR 161:24
glowing: other g. like the vital   SHEL 500:8
glow-worm: g. shows the matin to be

SHAK 431:14
Her eyes the g. lend thee   HERR 249:11
glow-worms: Glories, like g.   WEBS 566:25
gloz'd: g. but superficially   SHAK 486:30
Glubit: G. magnanimos Remi nepotes

CAT 137:5
Glücklichen: Die Welt des G. ist eine

WITT 575:16
Glückseligkeit: G. nicht ein Ideal der

KANT 288:12
glut: g. thy sorrow on a morning

KEATS 291:15
glutinous: turtle green and g.   BROW 103:16
gluve: he play'd at the g.   BALL 30:17
Glyn: With Elinor G.   ANON 8:23
gnashing: weeping and g. of teeth

BIBLE 65:11
gnat: small grey-coated g.   SHAK 481:28
which strain at a g.   BIBLE 67:24
gnats: wailful choir the small g.   KEATS 293:8
gnaw: g. you so your nether lip   SHAK 477:6
gnaweth: death g. upon them   PRAY 393:1
go: because I g. to the Father   BIBLE 72:40
expedient for you that I g.   BIBLE 72:38
G., and do thou likewise   BIBLE 69:3
G. and find it   KIPL 299:2
G., and he goeth   BIBLE 65:15
G. and look behind   KIPL 299:2
G., and the Lord be with   BIBLE 50:10
g. at once   SHAK 461:23
g. by climbing a birch   FROST 219:1
G., for they call you   ARN 14:10
g. gentle into that good   THOM 546:23
going where I have to g.   ROET 407:6
G., litel bok   CHAU 144:17
G. out into the highways   BIBLE 70:13
G. to the ant thou sluggard   BIBLE 53:21
g. to the devil where he   JOHN 279:31
g. to 't with delight   SHAK 422:24
g. unto the altar of God   PRAY 392:11
g. we know not where   SHAK 464:14
G. West   GREE 235:26
G. ye into all the world   BIBLE 69:2
How you do g. it   BROWN 95:11
I g. on for ever   TENN 532:21
I like to g. by myself   HAZL 243:30
In the name of God, g.   CROM 169:26
I shall g. to him but he   BIBLE 50:22
Is to g. hence unwilling   MILT 349:28
it's no g. the rickshaw   MACN 326:7
I will arise and g. now   YEATS 585:17
I will not let thee g.   BIBLE 46:24
I will not let thee g.   BRID 92:11
Let my people g.   BIBLE 47:13
Let us g. then   ELIOT 203:17
Must you g.   VAUG 555:9
not g., For weariness   DONNE 190:7
therefore pay you cash to g.   KIPL 298:18
There g. the ships   PRAY 397:1
to g. with the man I love   BREC 91:26
to hell I will g.   MILL 339:12
unto Caesar shalt thou g.   BIBLE 74:24
Victoria Station and g.   BEVIN 44:18
we'll g. no more a roving   BYRON 125:25
Whither shall I g. then   PRAY 399:5
will g. into the house   PRAY 398:11
will g. onward the same   HARDY 240:5
Will g. with you along   HERR 249:28
will neither g. nor hang   BIGOD 84:5
goads: words of the wise are as g.

BIBLE 56:12
goal: g. stands up   HOUS 263:10
grave is not its g.   LONG 317:1
stood I to keep the g.   HOUS 262:22
Will be the final g. of ill   TENN 536:24
goals: They live by positive g.   BERL 41:23
goat: Gall of g.   SHAK 462:4

lust of the g. is the bounty	BLAKE 88:21	G. calleth preaching folly	HERB 247:12	G. that after his ymage	CHAU 144:19
luxurious mountain g.	SHAK 445:4	G. cannot change the past	AGAT 3:4	g. that he worships	SWIFT 526:3
sort of fleecy hairy g.	BELL 40:2	G. dawned on Chaos	SHEL 499:11	G. that you took from	KIPL 303:21
goat-footed: This g. bard	KEYN 295:19	G. does not play dice	EINS 200:10	G. the herdsman goads them	YEATS 584:17
goatish: g. disposition to the charge		God, even our own G.	PRAY 394:5	G. this flesh of mine might	SWIN 530:18
	SHAK 453:11	G. exists only for leader-writers	GREE 236:7	G. this, God that	SQUI 517:13
goats: better than sheep or g.	TENN 535:26	G. first maked man	CHAU 143:1	G., thou, and I do know	SHAK 478:12
Cadwallader and all his g.	SHAK 445:9	G. forbid	BIBLE 71:4	G., to me, it seems	FULL 220:10
drink the blood of g.	PRAY 393:3	G. forbid	BIBLE 74:43	G. took him	BIBLE 45:30
G. and monkeys	SHAK 476:15	G. forgot me	BROW 99:16	G. walking in the garden	BIBLE 45:16
g. on the left	BIBLE 68:5	G. for his father who has	CYPR 170:19	G. was very merciful	ANON 8:15
hair is as a flock of g.	BIBLE 56:26	G. fulfils himself in many	TENN 535:25	g. when all our life-breath	ROSS 409:22
refuge for the wild g.	PRAY 397:1	G. gave the increase	BIBLE 75:31	G., who is our home	WORD 579:5
separate me from the g.	CEL 138:8	G. gives us love	TENN 543:14	G. who made thee mighty	BENS 40:24
gobbled: Has g. up the infant child		G. has given you good abilities	ARAB 11:18	G. will grant an end	VIRG 557:13
	HOUS 266:11	G. has written all	BUTL 119:1	G. will pardon me	HEINE 244:13
goblet: me upon a parcel-gilt g.	SHAK 441:20	G. hath also highly exalted	BIBLE 78:14	G. will provide himself	BIBLE 46:10
navel is like a round g.	BIBLE 57:8	G. hath chosen the foolish	BIBLE 75:30	G. will take care of that	SHAW 496:28
goblin: health or g. damn'd	SHAK 430:24	G. hath joined together	BIBLE 67:8	G. will wipe away tears	BIBLE 58:19
goblins: have one of sprites and g.		G. hath joined together	PRAY 389:6	G. within my breast	BRON 93:19
	SHAK 491:12	G. hath joined together	SHAW 496:28	G. would destroy He first	DUP 199:15
		G. hath made them so	WATTS 565:17	G. would make a man miserable	
God: about depth knows about G.	TILL 551:4	G. hath numbered thy kingdom	BIBLE 61:6		CHAR 140:24
acceptable unto G.	BIBLE 75:15	G. help the Minister that	MELB 336:16	good to them that love G.	BIBLE 75:11
Act of G. was defined	HERB 246:19	G., Immortality, Duty	ELIOT 201:30	Grace is given of G.	CLOU 153:18
afraid to look upon G.	BIBLE 47:5	G.-intoxicated man	NOV 364:10	Grace of G. is in Courtesy	BELL 39:14
among the children of G.	BIBLE 62:16	G. is always in the majority	KNOX 305:18	grace of G. I am what I am	BIBLE 76:19
apprehension how like a g.	SHAK 432:15	G. is a Spirit	BIBLE 71:40	grace of G. there goes	BRAD 91:9
are like the peace of G.	JAM 271:6	G. is dead	NIET 363:6	granted scarce to G. above	SPEN 517:2
are the children of G.	BIBLE 75:9	G. is dead	NERV 360:25	greater glory of G.	ANON 10:6
atheist half believes a G.	YOUNG 588:10	G. is his own interpreter	COWP 165:29	grete g. of Loves name	CHAU 143:26
been the same since G. died	MILL 339:25	G. is in the midst of her	PRAY 392:20	Had I but serv'd my G.	SHAK 447:13
be forgotten even by G.	BROW 103:6	G. is love	BIBLE 81:5	Had I but served G.	WOLS 576:14
believe in G. the Father	PRAY 384:26	G. is Love, I dare say	BUTL 119:2	hand into the hand of G.	HASK 243:1
best thing G. invents	BROW 100:29	G. is no respecter of persons	BIBLE 74:2	hands of the living G.	BIBLE 79:30
bitter G. to follow	SWIN 530:3	G. is not a man	BIBLE 48:14	Have G. to be his guide	BUNY 107:32
bought over G. with a fee	SWIN 530:23	G. is not mocked	BIBLE 77:19	Heart within, and G. o'erhead	LONG 317:3
bush afire with G.	BROW 97:33	G. is our hope and strength	PRAY 392:19	He for G. only	MILT 347:22
by Yours faithfully, G.	ANON 4:29	G. is the Judge	PRAY 394:26	he liveth unto G.	BIBLE 75:2
Caesar's self is G.'s	CRAS 169:13	G. is the perfect poet	BROW 103:4	here in the sight of G.	PRAY 388:24
called the children of G.	BIBLE 64:6	G. is Three	NEWM 362:11	He sung of G.	SMART 509:11
cannot serve G. and mammon	BIBLE 64:27	G. is thy law, thou mine	MILT 348:3	he thinks little of G.	PLUT 374:20
caught at G.'s skirts	BROW 101:18	G. is usually on the side	BUSS 117:7	He trusted in G.	PRAY 390:17
chains about the feet of G.	TENN 535:26	G. made the country	COWP 166:31	him know his G. by night	VAUG 555:11
Church the further from G.	ANDR 4:8	G. made the woman	TENN 533:9	honest G. is the noblest	ING 270:17
cometh the wrath of G.	BIBLE 78:3	G. moves in a mysterious	COWP 165:26	honest G.'s the noblest	BUTL 119:7
contempt of G.'s good gifts	JAM 271:4	G. Must think it exceedingly	KNOX 305:22	hope of the City of G.	MAS 334:7
cried out 'God, God, G.	SHAK 443:18	G. never wrought miracle	BACON 25:23	how can he love G. whom	BIBLE 81:7
daughter of the voice of G.	WORD 579:14	G. now accepteth thy works	BIBLE 55:28	how should G. perceive it	PRAY 394:22
dear G. who loveth us	COL 155:30	G. of Bethel	DODD 187:15	I am a G. and cannot find	SHEL 503:3
deny a G. destroy	BACON 25:29	G. of Jacob is our refuge	PRAY 392:20	if a G. there be	SWIN 530:1
Destiny the Commissary of G.	DONNE 189:35	G. of life	BYRON 121:19	If G. be for us	BIBLE 75:12
discussing their duty to G.	WHIT 570:22	G. of love my Shepherd	HERB 248:13	If G. did not exist	VOLT 561:8
doeth evil hath not seen G.	BIBLE 81:8	G. of our fathers	KIPL 302:7	If G. were to take one	ANON 6:2
door-keeper in the house of my G.		G. proved them	BIBLE 62:13	if G. wrote the bill	EMER 207:1
	PRAY 395:13	g. pursuing	SWIN 528:18	I find letters from G.	WHIT 571:4
doth G. respect any person	BIBLE 50:23	G.'s a good man	SHAK 472:35	if there be a G.	ANON 7:5
Doth Job fear G. for naught	BIBLE 52:6	G. save our gracious king	CAREY 130:24	if we were G.'s spies	SHAK 456:3
Enoch walked with G.	BIBLE 45:30	G. save the king	BIBLE 49:42	I press G.'s lamp	BROW 103:8
excellent angler, and now with G.		G. save the king	HOGG 252:24	is forgotten before G.	BIBLE 70:3
	WALT 564:5	G. save the king	SHAK 479:21	is the g. of my idolatry	SHAK 482:15
Fear G., and keep his commandments		G. saw that it was good	BIBLE 45:2	It is an attribute to G.	SHAK 467:27
	BIBLE 56:14	g. self-slain on his own	SWIN 529:20	justify the ways of G. to Men	MILT 344:22
Fear G.. Honour the king	BIBLE 80:25	G.'s finger touch'd him	TENN 537:7	kills the image of G.	MILT 351:22
first the kingdom of G.	BIBLE 64:31	G.'s first Creature	BACON 28:5	knowledge of the Son of G.	BIBLE 77:28
fit for the kingdom of G.	BIBLE 69:25	G.'s great Venite change	DONNE 189:29	laws of G.	HOUS 264:24
Freedom is the cause of G.	BOWL 91:7	G. shall wipe away all	BIBLE 82:4	leaping, and praising G.	BIBLE 73:26
from the heavy wrath of G.	MARL 329:12	G. shall wipe away all	BIBLE 82:31	leave the word of G.	BIBLE 73:27
gifts of G. are strown	HEBER 244:6	G.'s Heart in a garden	GURN 237:7	Let G. arise	PRAY 394:6
glorify G. and to enjoy	SHOR 507:7	G. shed His grace on thee	BATES 35:4	Let G. be true	BIBLE 74:36
Glory to G. in the highest	BIBLE 69:11	G. si Love	FORS 217:9	light but the shadow of G.	BROW 95:17
G. accept him	TENN 541:15	G.'s in his heaven	BROW 103:21	like G.'s own head	COL 155:11
G. all mercy is a God unjust	YOUNG 588:9	G. so commanded	MILT 349:15	Like to a g. he seems	CAT 137:4
G. all things are possible	BIBLE 67:12	G. so loved the world	BIBLE 71:38	lively Oracles of G.	COR 162:25
G. and the doctor we alike	OWEN 366:28	G.'s own name upon a lie	COWP 166:26	Lord G. made them all	ALEX 3:13
G. arranges	THOM 546:10	G. spake all these words	BIBLE 47:24	Lord G. of your fathers	BIBLE 47:8
G. being with thee when	WORD 582:1	G.'s soldier be he	SHAK 463:10	Lord thy G. in vain	BIBLE 48:36
G. be in my head	ANON 5:9	G.'s sons are things	MADD 326:19	love of G. is shed abroad	BIBLE 74:41
'G. be merciful to a soul	ANON 10:14	G.'s thoughts we must	NIGH 363:16	mad all are in G.'s keeping	KIPL 304:25
G. be merciful to me	BIBLE 70:35	G. tempers the wind	STER 519:11	make both G. and an idol	LUTH 320:17
'G. bless us every one	DICK 176:24				

maker and builder is G.	BIBLE 79:32	that G. made the thunder	MAC 323:32	goddesses: wondrously like the immortal	
mammon than a bogus g.	MACN 326:4	that is really your G.	LUTH 320:18	g.	HOMER 253:28
man be more just than G.	BIBLE 52:16	That Man who is from G.	WORD 578:8	godfather: sorry it had so noble a g.	
man hath seen G.	BIBLE 71:28	that would circumvent G.	SHAK 436:27		SHAK 495:17
Man is G.'s image	HERB 247:9	'There is no G.	CLOU 153:22	Godfathers: G. and Godmothers in my	
man Is now become a g.	SHAK 448:14	there is no G.	PRAY 390:2		PRAY 388:12
man sent from G.	BIBLE 71:24	They believe G. to be there	JOHN 275:30	These earthly g. of Heaven's	SHAK 456:15
man's the noblest work of G.	BURNS 113:10	they shall see G.	BIBLE 64:6	Godhead: touching his G.	PRAY 385:14
Man's word is G. in man	TENN 533:31	think I am becoming a g.	VESP 556:12	godheads: …Maidens aspiring to g.	
many are afraid of G.	LOCK 315:20	this g. did shake	SHAK 448:15		STOP 523:15
men as had the fear of G.	CROM 169:20	this is acceptable with G.	BIBLE 80:26	godlike: dictates of his g. mind	
men that G. made mad	CHES 146:17	this is G.'s hill	PRAY 394:9		OTWAY 365:27
mighty G.	BIBLE 58:7	thou being dead art a G.	SWIN 530:7	patient endurance is g.	LONG 316:13
mills of G. grind slowly	LOGAU 316:5	thou city of G.	PRAY 395:16	godliness: Church in continual g.	
morowe longe I to goe to G.	MORE 357:20	thought that the gift of G.	BIBLE 73:30		PRAY 386:23
my duty towards G.	PRAY 388:14	Thou, my G., art in't	HERR 250:15	godly: g. love	PRAY 387:13
my flesh shall I see G.	BIBLE 52:31	Thou shalt have one G. only	CLOU 153:25	may hereafter live a g.	PRAY 384:13
my G.	HOPK 256:8	three person'd G.	DONNE 189:8	ran his g. race	GOLD 230:22
My G., I love Thee	CASW 136:16	thro' darkness up to G.	TENN 536:28	That still a g. race he ran	GOLD 231:10
my G., look upon me	PRAY 390:16	through his garden walketh G.	BROW 105:14	there is not one g. man left	PRAY 389:32
my King and my G.	PRAY 395:11	throws himself on G.	BROW 100:38	Godmothers: Godfathers and G. in my	
nature is the art of G.	BROW 96:13	thy God is a jealous G.	BIBLE 48:21	Baptism	PRAY 388:12
nature of G. is a circle	ANON 7:27	thy God my G.	BIBLE 49:32	Godolphin Horne: G. was nobly born	
Nearer, my G., to thee	ADAMS 1:10	To G. I speak Spanish	CHAR 140:31		BELL 38:33
nearer you are to G.	WOTT 583:17	To justify G.'s ways	HOUS 264:12	Godot: We're waiting for G.	BECK 36:15
neglect G. and his Angels	DONNE 191:1	To see G. only	DONNE 189:12	gods: daughter of the g.	TENN 533:6
not tempt the Lord thy G.	BIBLE 64:2	TO THE UNKNOWN G.	BIBLE 74:12	dish fit for the g.	SHAK 449:9
not the G. of Nature	HERB 248:7	to think there is a G.	CLOU 153:23	first in the world made g.	JONS 284:16
now G. alone knows	KLOP 305:16	trust in G.	AUDEN 21:6	fit love for G.	MILT 349:14
Now G. be praised	WOLFE 576:8	unto the G. of gods appeareth	PRAY 395:12	g. are come down to us	BIBLE 74:4
of the mysteries of G.	BIBLE 75:32	us from the love of G.	BIBLE 75:13	g. love dies young	MEN 336:25
Of what I call G.	BROW 104:29	Verb is G.	HUGO 267:9	gods that made the g.	CHES 146:15
One G., one law, one element	TENN 532:24	Very God of very G.	PRAY 387:10	g. themselves cannot recall	TENN 543:12
one more insult to G.	BROW 102:7	walk humbly with thy G.	BIBLE 61:25	g. thought otherwise	VIRG 558:8
Only G. can tell the saintly	AUDEN 19:20	was G. or Devil	DRYD 194:14	G. who live for ever	MAC 323:2
only…with the idea G. has of you		was the holy Lamb of G.	BLAKE 86:16	he creates G. by the dozen	MONT 355:4
	UNAM 554:28	We give thanks to G. always	BIBLE 78:30	hills like G. together	TENN 539:16
other but the house of G.	BIBLE 46:20	we have a building of G.	BIBLE 77:6	His death concerns the g.	SOPH 513:6
Our G.'s forgotten	QUAR 403:14	were I Lord G.	MACD 325:3	Kings it makes g.	SHAK 481:11
Our sufficiency is of G.	BIBLE 77:4	What G. abandoned	HOUS 265:7	May the g. avert this omen	CIC 151:29
out of the mouth of G.	BIBLE 64:1	What G. hath cleansed	BIBLE 74:1	neither children nor G.	KIPL 298:23
owe G. a death	SHAK 442:7	What g., man, or hero	POUND 383:9	not recognizing the g.	PLATO 374:8
pack and label men for G.	THOM 548:26	What hath G. wrought	BIBLE 48:15	on a par with the g.	SAPP 414:6
peace of G.	BIBLE 78:21	Whenever G. prepares evil	ANON 10:1	people clutching their g.	ELIOT 203:15
people is the voice of G.	ALC 3:9	When G. at first made man	HERB 248:6	shalt have no other g.	BIBLE 47:24
Perfect G.	PRAY 385:14	when G.'s the theme	SMART 509:4	So many g.	WILC 572:6
power belongeth unto G.	PRAY 393:20	when the sons of G. came	BIBLE 45:33	These be thy g., O Israel	BIBLE 48:2
presents the g. unshorn	HERR 248:22	Where is now thy G.	PRAY 392:9	Thinking of his own G.	ARN 13:8
put G. in his statements	WHIT 570:1	Wherever G. erects a house	DEFOE 173:11	to be g. if angels fell	POPE 379:7
put thy trust in G.	PRAY 392:1	Who G. doth late and early	WOTT 583:13	to the girdle do the G.	SHAK 455:17
ranks the same with G.	BROW 103:25	whole armour of G.	BIBLE 78:9	utterance of the early G.	KEATS 290:3
reader of the works of G.	COWP 167:5	whole armour of G.	BIBLE 78:10	Whatever g. may be	SWIN 529:25
reason and the will of G.	ARN 15:15	who saw the face of G.	MARL 329:7	What men or g. are these	KEATS 291:3
reflect that G. is just	JEFF 272:16	Whose G. is their belly	BIBLE 78:19	winning cause pleased the g.	LUCAN 319:22
rejoice and delight in G.	TRAH 551:17	who think not G. at all	MILT 350:1	woman is a dish for the g.	SHAK 424:9
relenting G. Hath placed	ROSS 408:20	Who trusted G. was love	TENN 536:29	Ye are g.	PRAY 395:10
reserved only for G. and angels	BACON 24:24	with Eternal G. for power	TENN 541:12	Ye shall be as g.	BIBLE 45:15
respect of persons with G.	BIBLE 74:34	with the grandeur of G.	HOPK 256:12	God's-Acre: burial-ground G.	LONG 316:18
righteousness of G.	BIBLE 80:10	woman is the work of G.	BLAKE 88:21	goes: grace of God there g.	BRAD 91:9
robbery to be equal with G.	BIBLE 78:13	Woman was G.'s second	NIET 363:4	it g. off at night	SHER 506:28
sacraments to a dying g.	HEINE 244:11	Word was with G.	BIBLE 71:21	goest: whithersoever thou g.	BIBLE 48:36
safe stronghold our G.	LUTH 321:2	worship one G. in Trinity	PRAY 385:12	whither thou g.	BIBLE 49:32
searching find out G.	BIBLE 52:22	Yblessed be g. that I have wedded		goeth: now g. on his way weeping	
seek their meat from G.	PRAY 397:1		CHAU 143:17		PRAY 398:17
seen G. face to face	BIBLE 46:25	ye believe in G.	BIBLE 72:30	whither it g.	BIBLE 71:36
servant of the Living G.	SMART 508:21	Yellow G. forever gazes	HAYES 243:7	Goethe: G. had an aversion to dogs	
she for G. in him	MILT 347:22	yet G. has not said a word	BROW 103:30		NERV 361:1
short of the glory of G.	BIBLE 74:38	you must believe in G.	JOW 286:1	G.'s sage mind and Byron's	ARN 13:18
should not think of G.	SHAK 443:18	you think the laws of G.	SHAW 496:33	open thy G.	CARL 132:20
soul and G. stand sure	BROW 104:9	youth I remembered my G.	SOUT 514:9	going: endure Their g. hence	SHAK 456:2
Spirit of the Lord G. is	BIBLE 60:8	you want to take in G.	LOW 319:1	g. down of the sun	BINY 84:10
spirit shall return unto G.	BIBLE 56:11			g. one knows not where	MAS 334:8
Standeth G. within	LOW 319:13	**God Almighty:** G. first planted a garden		g. to and fro in the earth	BIBLE 52:5
steep and trifid G.	THOM 547:22		BACON 26:18	good both g. and coming	FROST 219:1
Strong Brother in G.	BELL 40:8	Hey for G.	KETT 295:13	knowing to what he was g.	HARDY 240:9
such is the kingdom of G.	BIBLE 68:36	**godamoighty:** Do g. knaw what a's doing		their g. from us to be	BIBLE 62:13
Teach me, my G. and King	HERB 247:18		TENN 541:4	you were g. to a feast	JONS 283:27
thank G. of al	CHAU 144:22	**Goddamm:** Lhude sing G.	POUND 382:4	goings: ordered my g.	PRAY 392:1
that be are ordained of G.	BIBLE 75:20	**goddes:** alle hire g. may availle	CHAU 144:19	gold: apples of g. in pictures	BIBLE 54:26
that G. had put it there	LAB 306:10	**Goddess:** G., excellently bright	JONS 283:24	be prepared g. and amber	JONS 285:14

bow of burning g. — BLAKE 86:16
bringing g. — BIBLE 50:34
burned g. was his colour — CHAU 142:32
buttercup Had blessed with g. — OWEN 367:8
by suicide, a bag of g. — BRAM 91:21
clothing is of wrought g. — PRAY 392:17
cursed craving for g. — VIRG 558:10
desired are they than g. — PRAY 390:12
fetch the age of g. — MILT 344:11
fetters, though of g. — BACON 27:42
fly to India for g. — MARL 329:4
From the red g. keep thy — SCOTT 418:5
given of the g. of Arabia — PRAY 394:21
gleaming in purple and g. — BYRON 122:1
glistering g. but more to shine — BRAD 91:15
g. and flowing serpent — LAWR 311:3
g., and frankincense — BIBLE 63:32
g. and silver becks me — SHAK 452:19
G. a transient — GRAI 233:20
G. is for the mistress — KIPL 298:15
G. kept by a devil till — SHAK 442:15
G. undiscovered (and all — HOR 260:20
g. wes changyd into lede — WYNT 584:4
great deal of g. — JAMES 271:33
hair and harpstring of g. — SWIN 530:3
hands are as g. rings — BIBLE 57:4
hearts of g. and lungs — BELL 39:28
he but litel g. in cofre — CHAU 141:24
her feathers like g. — PRAY 394:8
If g. ruste — CHAU 142:2
Ionian white and g. — ELIOT 205:4
Is she not pure g. — BROW 105:10
jewel of g. in a swine's — BIBLE 53:32
lap to saint-seducing g. — SHAK 481:24
mankind upon a cross of g. — BRYAN 106:8
Nor all, that glisters, g. — GRAY 235:8
over with pillars of g. — BLAKE 86:4
Plate sin with g. — SHAK 455:20
queen in a vesture of g. — PRAY 392:16
reach at the glorious g. — SHAK 446:2
religion of g. — BAG 29:4
sand and ruin and g. — SWIN 530:29
street of the city was pure g. — BIBLE 82:33
streets are paved with g. — COLM 158:25
this foul drain pure g. — TOCQ 551:9
thousands of g. and silver — PRAY 398:5
'To gild refined g. — BYRON 122:31
To gild refined g. — SHAK 452:25
travell'd in the realms of g. — KEATS 292:17
truth with g. she weighs — POPE 375:13
us rarer gifts than g. — BROO 94:7
vine and grapes in g. — FLEC 214:17
with patines of bright g. — SHAK 468:15
Would he have g. — HERB 248:15
gold-dusted: shall we have g. snapdragon — ARN 15:6
golden: after that sweet g. clime —
circle of the g. year — TENN 533:24
days of g. dreams — BRON 93:24
g. apples of the sun — YEATS 586:21
g. bowl be broken — BIBLE 56:11
'g.-calf of Self-love — CARL 131:4
g. days of Saturn's reign — VIRG 559:22
G. lads and girls all must — SHAK 428:22
g. lamps in a green night… — MARV 331:16
G. lie the meadows — MER 337:37
g. locks time hath to silver — PEELE 371:8
g. mind stoops not to shows — SHAK 466:16
G. opinions from all sorts — SHAK 459:7
G. Road to Samarkand — FLEC 214:14
g. vials full of odours — BIBLE 81:27
g. years return — SHEL 500:20
Happy the g. mean — MASS 335:17
Love in a g. bowl — BLAKE 85:19
observ'd a g. rule — BLAKE 87:4
safe in a g. ewer — BROW 100:4
seven g. candlesticks — BIBLE 81:13
Someone who loves the g. mean — HOR 260:9
that there are no g. rules — SHAW 497:35
they did in the g. world — SHAK 424:20

wander in that g. maze — DRYD 197:16
with g. and silver light — YEATS 585:9
you the end of a g. string — BLAKE 86:8
Golden Gate: West to the G. — KIPL 300:24
Goldengrove: Over G. unleaving — HOPK 256:25
Golden Vanity: goes by the name of the G. — BALL 31:2
gold-giving: Nor g. lords like those — POUND 383:19
Goldsmith: Here lies Nolly G. — GARR 221:13
To Oliver G. — JOHN 277:13
golf: When ye come to play g. — MACD 325:1
Golgotha: field of G. and dead men's — SHAK 479:20
memorize another G. — SHAK 458:4
Gomorrah: overthrew Sodom and G. — BIBLE 61:20
gondola: g. of London — DISR 186:18
think you have swam in a g. — SHAK 426:20
What else is like the g. — CLOU 153:20
gone: all are g. — LAMB 308:6
Art thou g. in haste — ROWL 411:1
been and g. and done — GILB 225:12
both are g. — ARN 13:8
from these I would be g. — SHAK 494:5
G. far away into the silent — ROSS 409:3
g. into the world of light — VAUG 555:18
g. over to the majority — CARL 131:11
g. to-morrow — BEHN 38:13
g. to the demnition bow-wows — DICK 180:23
g. up with a merry noise — PRAY 392:24
g. with the wind — DOWS 191:12
great spirit g. — SHAK 421:18
He is g. on the mountain — SCOTT 416:5
I have g. here and there — SHAK 495:3
I would have thee g. — SHAK 482:20
lo, he was g. — PRAY 391:29
Man is very far g. — PRAY 400:7
not dead—but g. before — ROG 407:8
Not lost but g. before — NORT 364:8
not the days that are g. — SOUT 514:8
Now thou art g. — MILT 343:5
of something that is g. — WORD 579:5
prepare not to be g. — SHAK 482:3
She's g. for ever — SHAK 456:8
song of a lad that is g. — STEV 523:4
they are g. — KEATS 289:23
they are g. forever — MANN 328:14
those Lords I had g. so far — MORE 357:12
welcomest when they are g. — SHAK 445:19
what haste I can to be g. — CROM 170:5
What's g. and what's past — SHAK 491:15
Wilt thou be g. — SHAK 483:13
yet now he is g. — LAND 308:24
gong: g. was bombilating — THOM 546:21
that g.-tormented sea — YEATS 586:7
gongs: g. groaning as the guns — CHES 147:2
struck regularly, like g. — COW 163:14
good: All g. things which exist — MILL 339:12
all my g. is but vain hope — TICH 551:2
any g. thing therefore — GREL 236:14
apprehension of the g. — SHAK 478:17
are g. for righting wrongs — LOCK 315:21
are not a terror to g. — BIBLE 75:21
author and giver of all g. — PRAY 386:19
Be g., sweet maid — KING 296:19
Beneath the g. how far — GRAY 235:20
best g. man — ROCH 407:4
better to fight for the g. — TENN 540:19
Blake was no g. — BUTL 118:35
can be g. in the country — WILDE 573:22
captive g. attending captain — SHAK 494:5
choose the g. — BIBLE 58:3
common g. to all — SHAK 452:7
country for our country's g. — BARR 34:23
country was g. for General — WILS 574:15
course only too g. for him — AUST 22:30
creature not too bright or g. — WORD 581:8
crown thy g. with brotherhood — BATES 35:4

do a g. action by stealth — LAMB 308:2
Do all the g. you can — WESL 568:21
doeth g., no not one — PRAY 390:2
dreamed of g. shall exist — BROW 98:19
everything in the world is g. — DRYD 197:28
evil and on the g. — BIBLE 64:19
Evil be thou my G. — MILT 347:16
evil, that g. may come — BIBLE 74:37
for the public g. — COWP 164:28
General G. is the plea — BLAKE 86:7
Ghastly G. Taste — BETJ 44:15
God saw that it was g. — BIBLE 45:2
g. and faithful servant — BIBLE 68:2
g. and increase of the world — TENN 533:9
g. and to communicate forget — BIBLE 80:6
g. as thou art beautiful — TENN 534:19
g. both going and coming — FROST 219:1
G., but not religious-good — HARDY 241:26
g. deed in a naughty — SHAK 468:18
g. deed in all my life — SHAK 486:18
g. die early — DEFOE 173:2
g. die first — WORD 577:11
g. divine that follows — SHAK 465:20
g. ended happily — WILDE 573:3
g. enough to be a clergyman — JOHN 276:7
g. face is a letter — ADD 2:15
g. in canvasses and factions — BACON 25:40
g. income is of no avail — SMITH 510:12
g. Indian is a dead Indian — SHER 505:18
g. in everything — SHAK 424:32
g. is oft interred with — SHAK 450:17
g. man, and did good — HARDY 242:1
g. man is merciful — PRAY 397:14
g. man was ther of religioun — CHAU 141:32
G. men must not obey — EMER 207:32
g. name is rather to be — BIBLE 54:21
g. of one's country — FARQ 210:4
g. of subjects is the end — DEFOE 173:16
g. of the people is — CIC 151:19
g. opinion of a man who — TROL 553:3
g. people's wery scarce — DICK 183:4
g. people were clever — WORD 576:22
g. provoke to harm — SHAK 464:22
g. Shall come of water — BROO 94:11
g. societies say — FORS 217:4
g. that I would I do not — BIBLE 75:5
g. they inculcate — SAKI 413:3
G. Thing — SELL 420:2
g. thing come out of Nazareth — BIBLE 71:31
G. things of day begin — SHAK 461:14
g. to be out on the road — MAS 334:8
G., to forgive — BROW 104:35
g. to them which hate you — BIBLE 69:21
g. unluckily — STOP 523:18
g. want power — SHEL 503:2
g. will toward men — BIBLE 69:11
G. without effort — BYRON 121:20
g. without pretence — POPE 378:9
g. words — SHAK 452:30
g. ye are and bad — TENN 534:17
great who are truly g. — CHAP 140:13
happiness makes them g. — LAND 309:12
have never had it so g. — MACM 325:18
heaviness foreruns the g. — SHAK 442:12
He was a g. man — BIBLE 71:15
He who would do g. to another — BLAKE 86:7
He wos wery g. to me — DICK 176:8
highest g. — CIC 151:21
hold fast that which is g. — BIBLE 79:4
Hold thou the g. — TENN 536:23
if they have a g. thing — SHAK 441:14
in art the best is g. — GOET 230:8
I never saw any g. that — DRYD 195:20
in the common love of g. — TENN 537:15
is the enemy of the g. — VOLT 561:5
is what I call g. company — AUST 23:8
it is for the g. of all — PEDR 371:4
I will be g. — VICT 556:13
kept the g. wine until now — BIBLE 71:34
knowing g. and evil — BIBLE 45:15

knowledge of g. and evil BIBLE 45:8
Know their own g. DRYD 198:18
likes that little g. BUTL 119:8
love, Fool, for the g. PATM 370:1
luxury of doing g. COWP 168:21
mankind does most g. or harm BAG 29:18
man loves what he is g. SHAD 420:22
Men are never so g. or so bad MACK 325:11
motive is the public g. STEE 518:1
must return g. for evil VANB 555:4
never led to g. intention's CERV 138:19
noble type of g. LONG 317:7
nor it cannot come to g. SHAK 430:1
nothing either g. or bad SHAK 432:12
now to call a man *a g. man* JOHN 279:12
only g. thing left to me MUSS 359:3
out of g. still to find MILT 345:6
overcome evil with g. BIBLE 75:19
passions as well as all the g. tunes
SHAW 497:22
perseverance in a g. cause STER 519:19
policy of the g. neighbour ROOS 407:21
rather than to seem g. SALL 413:24
rewarded me evil for g. PRAY 391:24
satisfieth thy mouth with g. PRAY 396:15
scraps are g. deeds past SHAK 487:3
see g. days PRAY 391:23
seek their subjects' g. HERR 249:8
so g. for a Pobble's toes LEAR 312:17
so much too g. for earth JONS 284:2
So the g. has been well ARIS 12:6
sovereign g. of human nature BACON 27:31
success in life is to be a g. animal
SPEN 514:25
that doeth g. is of God BIBLE 81:8
that Thou art g. POPE 381:12
that to the public g. MILT 350:24
their luxury was doing g. GARTH 221:20
them that call evil g. BIBLE 57:26
Then it will be g. night SHEL 500:17
Then the g. minute goes BROW 105:29
There is so much g. ANON 8:2
There's a g. time coming MACK 325:9
They love the G. BROO 94:24
they may see your g. works BIBLE 64:9
they want but what is g. CROM 169:23
things are of g. report BIBLE 78:22
this woman was full of g. BIBLE 73:36
those who go about doing g. CREI 169:17
thyself to be obscurely g. ADD 1:23
to be g. than to be ugly WILDE 573:21
we know the G. AUDEN 19:12
we see but means our g. HERB 248:2
we trust that somehow g. TENN 536:24
what g. came of it SOUT 513:20
when shall all men's g. TENN 533:23
When she was g. LONG 317:22
while g. news baits MILT 350:28
whoso hath this world's g. BIBLE 81:4
will call no being g. MILL 339:5
work for g. to them that love BIBLE 75:11
world has still Much g. HOUS 264:14
worst speaks something g. HERB 247:12
yet don't look too g. KIPL 299:22
you fair hath made you g. SHAK 464:16
Goodbye: G. is not worth while HARDY 241:7
G., moralitee HERB 246:10
G., proud world EMER 206:20
kissed his sad Andromache g. CORN 162:20
nod g. to La Rochefoucauld ELIOT 202:2
goodliest: thou wert the g. person MAL 328:8
goodly: art fair; thou art g. SWIN 528:22
g. fellowship of the Prophets PRAY 384:16
g. to look BIBLE 50:7
I have a g. heritage PRAY 390:6
goodman: g. is not at home BIBLE 53:24
Good morrow: G. to the day so fair
HERR 249:10
I bade g. KEATS 289:5
now g. to our waking souls DONNE 188:30

goodness: delusion that beauty is g.
TOLS 551:11
fountain of all g. PRAY 385:6
G. does not more certainly LAND 309:12
'G. had nothing to do with WEST 568:26
g. never fearful SHAK 464:17
If g. lead him not HERB 248:8
inclination to g. is imprinted BACON 26:19
long-suffering, and of great g. PRAY 396:16
Love, sweetness, g. MILT 351:13
praise the Lord for his g. PRAY 397:7
tell of days in g. spent BYRON 125:22
there is no g. in the worm SHAK 424:8
verily to see the g. PRAY 391:9
Wisdom and g. to the vile SHAK 455:11
Good-night: bid the world G. HERR 249:5
fair g. SCOTT 417:26
gay g. and quickly turn YEATS 585:6
G.; ensured release HOUS 266:5
g., sweet ladies SHAK 436:3
G., sweet prince SHAK 437:28
say g. till it be morrow SHAK 482:20
so, g. DU M 199:6
Which gives the stern'st g. SHAK 460:3
goods: desire other men's g. PRAY 388:18
g. and services can be NOCK 363:18
G. may be most their own CHAR 140:19
his g. are in peace BIBLE 69:36
precious as the G. they sell FITZ 213:14
Riches and G. of Christians PRAY 400:12
worldly g. I thee endow PRAY 389:5
good-sense: reasoning g. CHES 145:25
Goodwins: G., I think they call SHAK 467:2
goose: every g. a swan KING 297:5
g. honking amongst tuneful VIRG 560:7
G., if I had you upon SHAK 453:22
gott'st thou that g. look SHAK 463:1
steals a g. from off a common ANON 7:24
gooseberries: g. which makes my teeth
FLEM 214:28
goost: g. ful blisfully is went CHAU 144:18
Gor'd: G. mine own thoughts SHAK 495:3
gordian: She was a g. shape of dazzling
KEATS 290:22
gore: chequered sides with g. THOM 549:19
Glorious the martyr's g. SMART 509:4
hope it mayn't be human g. DICK 175:25
gored: you tossed and g. several BOSW 90:15
gorge: my g. rises at it SHAK 436:31
gorging: g. Jack and guzzling Jimmy
THAC 545:32
Gorgon: Great G., Prince of darkness
SPEN 516:1
Gorgonised: G. me from head to foot
TENN 540:7
Gorgonzola: Been trotting out the G.
KIPL 305:2
gormandising: Leave g. SHAK 442:31
Gormed: I'm G. DICK 177:21
gory: never shake Thy g. locks SHAK 461:20
Welcome to your g. bed BURNS 114:34
gosling: such a g. to obey instinct
SHAK 427:28
Gospel: devotee of the G. of Getting
SHAW 498:3
Four for the G. makers ANON 6:5
g. according to Jean Jacques CARL 131:24
G. of Silence is now effectively MORL 357:24
G.'s pearls upon our coast MARV 331:16
lineaments of G. books ROYD 411:2
music of the G. leads us FABER 209:14
preach the g. to every BIBLE 69:2
Preferrest thou the g. BUTL 119:20
truth of thy holy G. PRAY 387:3
goss-hawk: well's me o' my gay g.
BALL 30:20
gossip: babbling g. of the air SHAK 488:13
g. from all the nations AUDEN 20:2
G. is a sort of smoke that ELIOT 200:20
g. Report be an honest SHAK 467:2

gost: lat thy g. thee lede CHAU 144:22
Got: G. 'tween asleep and wake SHAK 453:9
I've g. a little list GILB 226:24
Gothic: more than G. ignorance FIEL 211:26
gothiques: *temps barbares et g.* FRAN 217:27
Gott: *G. ist tot* NIET 363:6
G. würfelt nicht EINS 200:10
Nun danket alle G. RINK 406:6
Gotte: *Sakramente einem sterbenden*
G. HEINE 244:11
gotten: he g. himself the victory PRAY 396:7
Gottes: *der zweite Fehlgriff G.* NIET 363:4
Krieg ein Glied in G. Weltordnung
MOLT 354:4
Gottesmühlen: *G. mahlen langsam*
LOGAU 316:3
GOTTINGEN: -NIVERSITY OF G.
CANN 130:5
gout: combined with g. GILB 225:21
g. and glory seat me there BROW 100:19
I say give them the g. MONT 354:11
le bon sens et le bon g. LA B 306:15
that old enemy the g. HOOD 254:21
gouverne: *règne et le peuple se g.* THIE 546:5
gouvernement: *g. d'une famille que d'un*
MONT 354:19
le g. qu'elle mérite MAIS 327:8
Gouverner: *G., c'est choisir* LEVIS 314:5
govern: easy to g. BROU 95:6
G. two millions of men BURKE 109:27
He that would g. others MASS 335:14
I will g. according JAM 271:5
out and g. New South Wales BELL 39:6
people g. themselves THIE 546:5
stars above us, g. SHAK 455:12
such should g. FLET 215:18
To g. is to make choices LEVIS 314:5
governance: charge or rule nor g.
SURR 524:20
peaceably ordered by thy g. PRAY 386:17
governaunce: gentil cok hadde in his
g. CHAU 142:32
governed: England is still g. from
SHAW 498:23
g. by a despot is an inverted JOHN 277:29
g. by thy good Spirit PRAY 385:25
has always been g. CHES 146:6
kings g. their rude age BAG 28:28
nation is not g. BURKE 109:19
well g. as they ought to be HOOK 255:19
wisdom the world is g. OXEN 367:13
governing: right of g. was not property
FOX 217:20
totally incapable of g. CHES 146:6
government: administration of the g.
SWIFT 526:4
all g. is evil OSUL 365:22
any ask me what a free g. BURKE 110:11
become the most corrupt g. JEFF 272:12
best g. is that which OSUL 365:22
called a representative g. DISR 186:34
consequence of cabinet g. BAG 28:23
country has the g. it deserves MAIS 327:8
erected into a system of G. GLAD 229:19
fainéant g. is not TROL 553:4
fit for a nation whose g. SMITH 509:12
forms of g. let fools contest POPE 379:20
four pillars of g. BACON 27:10
giving money to the G. HERB 246:11
G. at Washington lives GARF 221:9
G. and co-operation are RUSK 412:10
G., even in its best state PAINE 367:22
G. is a contrivance BURKE 111:8
G. must have an authority RUSK 412:6
g. of all the people PARK 368:26
g. of men and morning newspapers
PHIL 373:21
g. of the world I live THOR 550:15
G. of the United States WILS 574:23
g. shall be upon his shoulder BIBLE 58:7

g. without a king   BANC 32:13
having share in G. that is nothing
   CHAR 140:19
highest form of g.   SPEN 514:28
How can the G. be carried   WELL 568:3
important thing for G.   KEYN 295:17
increase of his g.   BIBLE 58:7
indispensable duty of g.   PAINE 367:23
is no art which one g.   SMITH 509:15
is the worst form of G.   CHUR 150:19
Is this the g. of Britain's   SHAK 446:3
land of settled g.   TENN 544:11
live under one form of g.   JOHN 276:4
Monarchy is a strong g.   BAG 28:27
No G. can be long secure   DISR 185:35
only an experiment in g.   INGE 270:7
party Parliamentary g.   DISR 185:7
people's g.   WEBS 566:10
rule nations by your g.   VIRG 559:1
still loathe the present G.   HERR 249:16
that g. of the people   LINC 314:23
'That g. is best which   THOR 549:31
there has been no G.   DICK 176:21
Under a g. which imprisons   THOR 550:1
under every form of g.   JOHN 276:6
virtue of paper g.   BURKE 109:13
want of g., is any new   HOBB 251:20
Your sister is given to g.   DICK 178:7
Governments: G. need to have both
   shepherds   VOLT 561:17
   teach g. humanity   PAINE 368:4
Governor: Can't afford them, G.
   SHAW 498:13
G. was strong upon   WILDE 572:12
lord, thy king, thy G.   SHAK 484:15
T'other g.   DICK 181:18
governors: Our supreme g.   WALP 562:19
submit myself to all my g.   PRAY 388:16
governs: g. the passions and resolutions
   HUME 267:22
gowd: g. kames in their hair   BALL 31:20
man's the g. for a' that   BURNS 113:28
Gower: moral G.   CHAU 144:20
gown: loose g. from her shoulders
   WYATT 583:22
My g. of glory   RAL 404:12
sail in amply billowing g.   BELL 39:28
wearing a black g.   CHES 145:11
who preaches in her g.   HOOD 255:12
Goya: one small G. or a Daumier
   AUDEN 19:16
Gracchos: *G. de seditione querentes*
   JUV 287:13
grace: Angels and ministers of g.
   SHAK 430:24
behold such heavenly g.   SPEN 516:2
does it with a better g.   SHAK 488:19
full of g. and truth   BIBLE 71:27
God shed His g. on thee   BATES 35:4
g. before Shakspeare   LAMB 307:5
G. be unto you   BIBLE 81:9
g. did much more abound   BIBLE 74:42
G. is given of God   CLOU 153:18
G. me no grace   SHAK 479:1
G. of God is in Courtesy   BELL 39:14
g. of God I am what I am   BIBLE 76:19
g. of God there goes   BRAD 91:9
g. which followed it was   STER 519:13
grow old with a good g.   STEE 518:2
Have g. and favour in them   SHAK 476:25
heaven such g. did lend her   SHAK 491:4
here's g. and a cod-piece   SHAK 454:8
him was the peculiar g.   BROW 100:36
I ascribe it to Thy g.   WATTS 565:14
In her strong toil of g.   SHAK 424:17
in his mercy lend her g.   TENN 538:12
inward and spiritual g.   PRAY 388:19
means of g.   PRAY 386:2
meek and unaffected g.   GOLD 230:24
me of your g. and favour   SHAK 453:6

moments of glad g.   YEATS 587:12
nothing with a better g.   YOUNG 587:16
serves to g. my measure   PRIOR 401:1
special g. preventing   PRAY 386:10
speech be alway with g.   BIBLE 78:28
sweet attractive g.   MILT 347:22
sweet attractive kind of g.   ROYD 411:2
Take heart of g.   GILB 228:14
Terms like g., new birth   ARN 16:18
their courtly foreign g.   TENN 543:4
then g. us in the disgrace   SHAK 456:14
throne of the heavenly g.   PRAY 384:10
To g. this latter age with   SHAK 440:16
unbought g. of life   BURKE 111:10
Weel are ye wordy o' a g.   BURNS 115:16
what a pretty skipping g.   MARV 332:13
wi' patriarchal g.   BURNS 113:9
with sory g.   CHAU 143:7
womanly discovering g.   DONNE 188:11
Ye are fallen from g.   BIBLE 77:17
graceful: g. air and heavenly mug   FLEM 215:4
Gracehoper: G. was always jigging ajog
   JOYCE 286:13
grace-proud: g. faces   BURNS 115:23
graces: do inherit heaven's g.   SHAK 494:15
g. slighted   COWP 168:5
half-mile g.   BURNS 115:23
of deficiency in *the g.*   JOHN 277:9
that the G. do not seem   CHES 145:27
to sacrifice to the g.   BURKE 111:26
Upon her eyelids many G.   SPEN 516:11
gracilis: *multa g. te puer in rosa*   HOR 259:15
gracious: favourable and g. unto Sion
   PRAY 393:8
g. and courteous to strangers   BACON 26:20
how g. the Lord is   PRAY 391:21
Lord, for he is g.   PRAY 399:2
Remembers me of all his g.   SHAK 452:20
So hallow'd and so g. is   SHAK 429:17
tasted that the Lord is g.   BIBLE 80:22
these are g. drops   SHAK 450:28
gradation: Not by the old g.   SHAK 473:12
gradations: No cold g. of decay   JOHN 279:1
gradient: g.'s against her   AUDEN 20:1
gradual: Was the g. day   SPEN 515:12
gradualness: inevitability of g.   WEBB 566:7
Graeca: *Vos exemplaria G.*   HOR 257:22
Graecia: *G. capta ferum victorem*   HOR 259:2
Graeculus: *G. esuriens*   JUV 287:16
Graft: G. in our hearts the love   PRAY 386:19
grain: chaff well meant for g.   TENN 536:2
faith as a g. of mustard   BIBLE 67:1
goodly g. and the sun-flushed   THOM 548:28
pamphleteer on guano and on g.   TENN 542:20
say which g. will grow   SHAK 458:11
to a g. of mustard seed   BIBLE 66:20
World in a G. of Sand   BLAKE 85:8
Grais: *G. ingenium*   HOR 257:23
gramina: *redeunt iam g. campis*   HOR 261:14
grammar: g., and nonsense, and learning
   GOLD 231:22
Heedless of g.   BARH 33:15
in erecting a g. school   SHAK 446:14
posterity talking bad g.   DISR 187:6
Why care for g. as long   WARD 564:35
grammars: What sairs your g.   BURNS 113:19
Grammatici: *G. certant et adhuc sub*
   HOR 257:15
Grammaticus: *G., rhetor*   JUV 287:16
granary: sitting careless on a g. floor
   KEATS 293:6
grand: g. Perhaps   BROW 99:4
g. style arises in poetry   ARN 16:14
inscrutable and g.   ARN 14:4
It is most g. to die   MAS 334:1
Seul le silence est g.   VIGNY 557:2
that g. old man   NORT 364:7
grandam: ha' been a g. ere she died
   SHAK 457:14
grandes: *des choses g. et hautes*   MONT 354:12

grandest: g. moral attribute   BARR 34:20
grandeur: charged with the g. of God
   HOPK 256:12
g. of the dooms   KEATS 289:1
g. that was Rome   POE 375:7
Scotia's g. springs   BURNS 113:10
with a baldness full of g.   ARN 16:7
grandeurs: g. of his Babylonian heart
   THOM 548:7
grandfather: having an ape for his g.
   HUXL 269:13
he whipped my g.   ADD 2:17
grand-jurymen: g. since before Noah
   was   SHAK 489:26
grandparents: worse than our g.'   HOR 260:26
grands: *g. n'ont point d'âme*   LA B 306:14
grandsire: Church your g. cut his throat
   SWIFT 528:9
his g. cut in alabaster   SHAK 465:11
grange: at the moated g.   SHAK 464:18
Upon the lonely moated g.   TENN 539:23
granites: g. which titanic wars had
   OWEN 367:9
Grantchester: would I were In G.
   BROO 94:20
granted: believe and take for g.   BACON 27:18
Never take anything for g.   DISR 184:28
granting: hold thee but by thy g.
   SHAK 494:13
grants: no go the Government g.   MACN 326:8
grape: burst Joy's g.   KEATS 291:15
G. that can with Logic   FITZ 213:2
g. who will the vine destroy   SHAK 492:18
grapes: chalice of the g. of God   TENN 536:7
fathers have eaten sour g.   BIBLE 60:34
gleaning of the g. of Ephraim   BIBLE 49:17
g. of the wine-press which   MAC 322:6
g. of wrath are stored   HOWE 266:19
it brought forth wild g.   BIBLE 57:22
men gather g. of thorns   BIBLE 65:9
sour g. and ashes   ASHF 17:14
vine and g. in gold   FLEC 214:17
grapeshot: whiff of g.   CARL 131:12
Grapple: G. them to thy soul with
   SHAK 430:19
grapples: g. with his evil star   TENN 537:1
Grasp: G. it like a man of mettle   HILL 251:2
G. not at much   HERB 248:12
reach should exceed his g.   BROW 98:24
grasped: bell-rope and g. it for a tinkle
   BEER 37:14
Grasping: G. at Air   YOUNG 588:8
shadow of an idea without g.   BOWEN 91:1
Grasps: G. in the comer   SHAK 487:5
grass: away suddenly like the g.   PRAY 395:18
blue is the g. about   POUND 382:5
child said *What is the g.*   WHIT 570:18
cleaving the g., gazelles   MOORE 355:23
days of man are but as g.   PRAY 396:17
destroy a blade of g.   BOTT 90:17
Down in the bells and g.   HODG 252:4
eateth g. as an ox   BIBLE 53:8
emerald twinkles in the g.   TENN 540:8
forth g. for the cattle   PRAY 396:9
From the heaps of couch g.   HARDY 240:5
g. below   CLARE 152:13
g. break into foam of flowers   SWIN 530:18
g. grows on the weirs   YEATS 584:22
g. is singing   ELIOT 205:10
g. returns to the fields   HOR 261:3
g. withereth   BIBLE 59:6
g. withereth   BIBLE 80:21
green g. growing over me   BALL 32:11
happy as the g. was green   THOM 547:1
I am the g.   SAND 413:27
I become paler than g.   SAPP 414:6
I fall on g.   MARV 332:3
isn't g. to graze a cow   BETJ 44:4
kissed the lovely g.   BROO 94:15
leaf of g. is no less than   WHIT 570:21

lift me from the g.   SHEL 501:9
Of splendour in the g.   WORD 579:13
seed from the feather'd g.   KEATS 290:1
snake hidden in the g.   VIRG 559:19
Star-scattered on the G.   FITZ 213:18
sturdy steed now goes to g.   BEAU 36:7
That g. is green   STEP 518:22
thinks of winter when the g.   KIPL 302:15
two blades of g. to grow   SWIFT 526:6
Was cut out of the g.   CHES 146:15
grass-bank: g. beyond   ALL 3:21
grasshopper: g. shall be a burden
  BIBLE 56:11
grasshoppers: dozen g. under a fern make
  BURKE 111:16
in our own sight as g.   BIBLE 48:11
of the wings of g.   SHAK 481:28
grassy: G., harvest of the river-fields   ARN 15:8
grate: fire is dying in the g.   MER 337:7
G. on their scrannel pipes   MILT 343:13
which fluttered on the g.   COL 156:22
grateful: g. at last for a little   TENN 540:16
One single g. thought raised   LESS 314:1
spouts the g. liquors   POPE 381:6
that anybody can be g.   CAT 137:8
gratias: Deo g.   MASS 334:19
gratified: lineaments of g. desire
  BLAKE 86:17
gratifying: g. feeling that our duty
  GILB 225:25
gratissima: et dono divum g. *serpit*
  VIRG 558:4
gratitude: begin with liking or g.
  ELIOT 200:23
g. is merely a secret hope   LA R 310:16
inferiority that their g.   JOHN 282:4
Gratuity: taking of a Bribe or G.
  PENN 371:16
gratulations: g. flow in streams unbounded
  CAREY 130:23
gratus: Donec g. *eram tibi*   HOR 260:27
Grau: G., *teurer Freund*   GOET 230:3
grave: arose from the suicide's g.   GILB 227:17
authority ought to be g.   BACON 26:25
Bends to the g. with unperceiv'd
  GOLD 230:20
cold g. she was lain   BALL 32:9
dark and silent g.   RAL 404:15
digs my g. at each remove   HERB 247:23
Dig the g. and let me lie   STEV 523:10
Drop upon Fox's g.   SCOTT 417:3
flours is planted on my g.   HARDY 241:18
foolish tears upon my g.   TENN 533:2
free land of the g.   HOUS 265:18
from the cradle to the g.   SHEL 503:14
Funeral marches to the g.   LONG 317:2
glory lead but to the g.   GRAY 234:21
glory, or the g.   CAMP 128:22
g. and constant in human   JOYCE 286:17
g.; and the barren womb   BIBLE 54:46
g. as little as my bed   KEN 295:9
g. hides all things beautiful   SHEL 503:3
g. is not its goal   LONG 317:1
g. Proves the child ephemeral   AUDEN 19:17
g.'s a fine and private   MARV 332:19
G., thy victoree   ANON 7:4
g., where is thy victory   BIBLE 77:1
hairs with sorrow to the g.   BIBLE 46:35
have made me a g. so rough   TENN 540:15
her heart in his g. is   MOORE 356:17
his vast and wandering g.   TENN 536:4
In ev'ry g. make room   DAV 172:6
in his g. rain'd many   SHAK 436:9
is a kind of healthy g.   SMITH 512:9
is gone wild into his g.   SHAK 442:25
Is that ayont the g.   BURNS 115:24
It sinks me to the g.   FORD 216:15
jealousy is cruel as the g.   BIBLE 57:11
kingdom for a little g.   SHAK 479:15
know the g. doth gape   SHAK 442:31

like Alcestis from the g.   MILT 351:12
mourn all at her g.   BALL 32:9
No g. upon the earth shall   SHAK 424:19
no repentance in the g.   WATTS 565:15
not rest in an English g.   BYRON 126:20
now in his colde g.   CHAU 142:22
pompous in the g.   BROW 97:23
pot of honey on the g.   MER 337:10
quiet, g. man   BAG 29:11
receive no letters in the g.   JOHN 279:29
renowned be thy g.   SHAK 428:22
root is ever in its g.   HERB 248:16
see myself go into my g.   PEPYS 372:21
Shall lead thee to thy g.   WORD 583:4
she is in her g.   WORD 581:6
soldier's g.   BYRON 125:12
steer From g. to gay   POPE 380:3
straight and dusty to the g.   STEV 521:32
thank God for the quiet g.   KEATS 295:2
That gap is the g. where   AUDEN 18:17
that g. where English oak   HARTE 242:26
these graces to the g.   SHAK 488:12
This g. shall have a living   SHAK 437:10
Thy victory, O G.   ROSS 408:20
to your piteous g.   CAT 137:15
travelling toward the g.   WORD 580:6
When my g. is broke up   DONNE 190:5
with O'Leary in the g.   YEATS 586:19
Without a g.   BYRON 121:24
Graved: G. inside of it   BROW 100:14
grave-digger: if I were a g.   JERR 273:6
gravelled: when you were g. for lack
  SHAK 426:22
grave-makers: ditchers and g.   SHAK 436:22
graven: make unto thee any g. image
  BIBLE 47:24
gravender: Wherein I eat my g.   ST L 412:27
graveness: Importing health and g.
  SHAK 436:17
graver: His g. of frost   THOM 549:1
graves: beautiful uncut hair of g.   WHIT 570:18
emblem of untimely g.   COWP 167:16
g. of deceased languages   DICK 177:23
g. of little magazines   PRES 400:14
g. of the martyrs the peewees   STEV 523:5
g. stood tenantless   SHAK 429:12
great persons' g. is speechless   DONNE 190:23
into their voluntarie g.   HERB 248:4
Let's talk of g.   SHAK 479:10
ourselves dishonourable g.   SHAK 448:17
Over the tumbled g.   ELIOT 205:10
They have no g. as yet   CHES 146:24
They have their g. at home...   CHES 146:24
they watch from their g.   BROW 102:5
gravest: luncheon was one of the g. sins
  WAUGH 566:5
gravity: g., profound conceit   SHAK 465:12
reasons find of settled g.   SHAK 493:14
What doth g. out of his   SHAK 439:10
gravy: Davy Abominated g.   BENT 41:6
disliked g. all my life   SMITH 511:3
gray: g. hairs with sorrow   BIBLE 46:35
g. life, and apathetic end   TENN 539:18
Graymalkin: I come, G.   SHAK 458:1
Gray's Elegy: nearly the whole of G.
  WOLFE 576:7
grazed: g. the common of literature
  JOHN 274:28
great: about g. and high things   MONT 354:12
All g. men make mistakes   CHUR 149:23
'because I am the g. world'   FORS 217:4
behind the g. possessions   JAMES 271:23
compare small things with g.   VIRG 560:19
craven fears of being g.   TENN 533:27
creatures g. and small   ALEX 3:13
deep to the g. deep he goes   TENN 534:3
disbelief in g. men   CARL 131:30
dust of g. persons' graves   DONNE 190:23
Ecce, how g. it is   ANDR 4:6
far above the g.   GRAY 235:20

g. a matter a little fire   BIBLE 80:13
g. break through   SHEN 505:16
g. deal of gold   JAMES 271:33
g. empire and little minds   BURKE 110:6
g. gulf fixed   BIBLE 70:29
g. has been done by youth   DISR 185:39
g. have kindness in reserve   POPE 376:29
G. is Diana of the Ephesians   BIBLE 74:17
G. is the hand that holds   THOM 547:5
g. is to be misunderstood   EMER 207:39
g. is truth   BROO 95:2
g. man he grovelled before   THAC 545:23
G. men are not always wise   BIBLE 52:39
G. men are the guide-posts   BURKE 109:7
g. men contending with   BURT 116:24
g. spirit gone   SHAK 421:18
g. things from the valley   CHES 147:30
g. was the fall of it   BIBLE 65:12
g. without a foe   BYRON 121:20
heights by g. men reached   LONG 316:19
he is always g.   DRYD 198:2
Hence no force however g.   WHEW 569:16
he was g.   DRYD 196:9
his weaknesses are g.   KIPL 297:23
its g. scholars great men   HOLM 253:17
lay g. and greatly fallen   HOMER 254:3
Let us bury the G. Duke   TENN 541:5
little seemed to him g.   MAC 324:8
Lives of g. men all remind   LONG 317:4
many people think him g.   JOHN 276:19
name made g. a name   HILL 251:5
No g. man lives in vain   CARL 131:31
Nothing g. was ever achieved   EMER 207:16
no wave Of a g. flood   MER 337:10
our hearts are g.   TENN 535:1
people ever set in a g. place   BAG 29:10
perfum'd chambers of the g.   SHAK 441:29
Rightly to be g.   SHAK 435:31
rudely g.   POPE 379:12
Silence alone is g.   VIGNY 557:2
simple g. ones gone   TENN 540:4
song with the g. and their pride   YEATS 585:8
streets where the g. men   FLEC 214:6
That he is grown so g.   SHAK 448:18
Then must the love be g.   BARN 34:2
there is nothing g. but man   HAM 238:16
those who were truly g.   SPEN 515:7
though fallen, g.   BYRON 120:13
thou wouldst be g.   SHAK 459:1
truly g. who are truly good   CHAP 140:13
truly g. when he acts from   DISR 186:2
very g. man   ADD 2:17
very small the very g.   THAC 546:4
with small men no g. thing   MILL 339:15
would grow g. and stately   STEV 522:23
Great Bear: G. is looking so geometrical
  FRY 220:2
Great Britain: seem to be natives of
G.   CHES 145:27
great-coat: wore a shaggy white g.
  DICK 177:29
greater: behold a g. than themselves
  SHAK 448:21
g. cats with golden eyes   SACK 412:26
g. glory dim the less   SHAK 468:18
G. love hath no man   BIBLE 72:36
g. man, the greater courtesy   TENN 534:36
g. prey upon the less   GREEN 235:27
g. than Solomon is here   BIBLE 66:12
g. than a private citizen   TAC 531:13
half is g. than the whole   HES 250:19
sing of rather g. things   VIRG 559:22
that he is g. than they   RUSK 412:1
that we are g. than we know   WORD 581:5
greatest: g. event it is that ever   FOX 217:19
g. of these is charity   BIBLE 76:14
g. pains to human nature   BAG 29:19
g. prince o' the world   SHAK 423:15
g. thing in the world is   MONT 354:21
happiness of the g. number   BENT 40:25

One of the g.	DRYD 198:6
than not be among the g.	KEATS 294:6
There sunk the g.	BYRON 120:29
time is the g. innovator	BACON 26:28
you the g. of all things	SHAW 496:30
Great-heart: One G.	BUNY 107:31
Great-hearted: G. gentlemen	BROW 99:26
greatly: it's g. to his credit	GILB 228:9
must do so who would g. win	BYRON 125:6
greatness: farewell, to all my g.	SHAK 447:9
far-off touch Of g.	TENN 534:27
G. knows itself	SHAK 440:13
g. of the *British* Nation	ADD 2:19
g. of the world in tears	YEATS 586:22
G., with private men	MASS 335:17
having intended g. for men	ELIOT 201:10
is the nature of all g.	BURKE 109:3
seen the moment of my g.	ELIOT 203:23
some have g. thrust upon	SHAK 489:14
Than g. going off	SHAK 423:6
greaves: flamed upon the brazen g.	
	TENN 538:8
Grecian: merry G. coaster	ARN 14:21
Greece: constitutions of later G.	BAG 28:28
Fair G.	BYRON 120:13
G. a tear	BYRON 123:1
G., could we but approach	YEATS 587:14
G. is fallen and Troy town	COL 155:3
G., once overcome	HOR 259:2
I dream'd that G. might	BYRON 122:33
insolent G. or haughty	JONS 284:22
isles of G.	BYRON 122:32
plague of G. upon thee	SHAK 486:28
To the glory that was G.	POE 375:7
Greedy: G. for the property	SALL 413:22
I am g.	PUNCH 402:29
not g. of filthy lucre	BIBLE 79:12
Greek: 'Because he *was* a G.'	SHEL 505:14
brown G. manuscripts	BROW 99:13
can say a word against G.	SHAW 497:9
carve in Latin or in G.	WALL 562:7
foolish to talk of knowing G.	WOOLF 576:17
Germans in G.	PORS 381:27
G. as a treat	CHUR 150:23
G. can do everything	JUV 287:16
G. was free from rhyme's	JONS 285:6
is not G. in its origin	MAINE 327:7
it was G. to me	SHAK 448:23
mentioned as reading G.	AUST 22:23
me whisky's name in G.	BURNS 112:34
natural, and G.	BYRON 122:23
schoolmasters even today read G.	
	YEATS 587:13
small Latin, and less G.	JONS 284:21
That questioned him in G.	CARR 133:12
there is neither G. nor Jew	BIBLE 78:26
understand G. and Latin	DRYD 198:14
upon you the study of G.	GAIS 220:25
when his wife talks G.	JOHN 280:18
will be paid at the G.	AUG 22:6
your G. exemplars by night	HOR 257:22
Greeks:	BYRON 120:31
G., and to the Barbarians	BIBLE 74:30
G. or the Romans	DISR 185:27
G. who take the beating	HOR 258:12
I fear the G. even when	VIRG 558:1
Let *G.* be *Greeks*	BRAD 91:14
make way, G.	PROP 401:17
To the G. the Muse gave	HOR 257:23
When G. joined Greeks	LEE 313:14
green: actual life springs ever g.	GOET 230:3
blue or the shore-sea g.	FLEC 214:17
children are heard on the g.	BLAKE 88:3
Colourless g. ideas	CHOM 148:15
dry smooth-shaven g.	MILT 342:3
England's g. and pleasant	BLAKE 86:12
England's g. & pleasant Land	BLAKE 86:16
feed me in a g. pasture	PRAY 390:21
force that through the g. fuse	THOM 547:3
g. arms round the bosom	SHEL 503:17

g. banks of Shannon	CAMP 128:20
g. buds they were swellin'	BALL 30:10
g. days in forests	STEV 522:29
G. grow the rushes	ANON 6:5
G. grow the rashes	BURNS 114:1
g. herb for the service	PRAY 396:20
G. I love you green	GARC 221:7
g. lap of the new come	SHAK 480:11
g. mantle of the standing	SHAK 454:23
G. Things upon the Earth	PRAY 384:24
g. thought in a green shade	MARV 332:5
hae laid him on the g.	BALL 30:15
In the morning it is g.	PRAY 395:18
keeps its own wounds g.	BACON 27:9
Learn of the g. world	POUND 382:13
Like golden lamps in a g.	MARV 331:16
Making the g. one red	SHAK 460:13
on a simple village g.	TENN 537:1
out of the hopeful g. stuff	WHIT 570:18
summer's g. all girded	SHAK 492:26
these things in a g. tree	BIBLE 71:10
Time held me g. and dying	THOM 547:2
to look so g. and pale	SHAK 459:8
tunnel of g. gloom	BROO 94:17
turtle g. and glutinous	BROW 103:16
wearin' o' the G.	ANON 6:6
When I was g. in judgment	SHAK 421:33
when the trees were g.	CLARE 152:4
When wheat is g.	SHAK 469:21
Where the g. swell is	HOPK 256:17
green-coat: shoot the sleepy, g.	HOFF 252:21
greenery-yallery: g., Grosvenor Gallery	
	GILB 227:27
greenest: Those eyes the g. of things	
	SWIN 529:16
green-ey'd: g. monster which doth mock	
	SHAK 475:17
greenhouse: loves a garden loves a g.	
	COWP 167:9
greenly: We have done but g.	SHAK 436:5
greenness: Could have recovered g.	
	HERB 247:21
greens: plain water and raw g.	AUDEN 21:6
Greensleeves: G. was all my joy	ANON 5:11
greensward: beech-tree single on the	
g.	MER 337:1
greenwood: I must to the g. go	BALL 31:10
Under the g. tree	SHAK 425:14
Greet: G. the unseen with a cheer	
	BROW 98:33
How should I g. thee	BYRON 126:14
scarely g. me with that	SHAK 493:14
Greise: Ward mancher Kopf zum G.	
	MULL 359:1
grenadier: single Pomeranian g.	BISM 84:22
Grenadiers: talk of Pensions and G.	
	STER 520:1
grene: In a harbour g. aslepe	WEVER 569:7
Grenville: Azores Sir Richard G. lay	
	TENN 542:1
Greta: G. woods are green	SCOTT 417:30
greuaunce: Comparisouns doon ofte	
gret g.	LYDG 321:7
grew: distance g. the Iceberg too	
	HARDY 239:6
g. a gallows and did bear	KYD 306:7
So we g. together	SHAK 470:22
Grex: G. rather than sex	FROST 219:14
grey: calls the glory from the g.	BROW 104:6
eye 'tis an old Man g.	BLAKE 86:14
head grown g. in vain	SHEL 499:21
lend me your g. mare	BALL 32:12
Too lovely to be g.	ARN 13:4
wither'd cheek and tresses g.	SCOTT 416:8
world has grown g. from	SWIN 530:5
grey-grown: g. speechless Christ	SWIN 529:3
greyhound: g., mongrel grim	SHAK 455:1
This fawning g. then did	SHAK 438:20
greyhounds: stand like g. in the slips	
	SHAK 444:3

grief: acquainted with g.	BIBLE 59:21
After long g. and pain	TENN 540:13
are quickened so with g.	GRAV 234:11
bravery of his g. did put	SHAK 437:13
Can I see another's g.	BLAKE 88:8
every one can master a g.	SHAK 472:24
From perfect g. there need	ROSS 410:9
full of g. as age	SHAK 454:1
great As is my g.	SHAK 479:14
Green pleasure or grey g.	SWIN 530:21
G. fills the room up	SHAK 452:20
g. flieth to it	BACON 26:2
G. for awhile is blind	SHEL 502:21
G. for thy dead in silence	BROW 98:8
G. is a species of idleness	JOHN 281:26
G. is itself a med'cine	COWP 164:25
g. itself be mortal	SHEL 499:12
g. never mended no broken	DICK 183:4
g. returns with the revolving	SHEL 499:10
g. that does not speak	SHAK 462:16
g. too much to be told	VIRG 557:20
G. with a glass that ran	SWIN 528:20
hell G. and avenging Cares	VIRG 558:21
hopeless g. is passionless	BROW 98:7
into the bottom of my g.	SHAK 483:18
it was pain and g. to me	PRAY 391:30
Killing care and g.	SHAK 447:3
my faint heart with g.	SHEL 501:15
My particular g.	SHAK 473:23
only time for g.	HOOD 255:9
open his g.	PRAY 387:17
Patch g. with proverbs	SHAK 473:6
Pitched past pitch of g.	HOPK 256:19
plague of sighing and g.	SHAK 439:11
Should be past g.	SHAK 491:15
shows of g.	SHAK 429:25
Silence augmenteth g.	GREV 236:17
silent manliness of g.	GOLD 231:6
Smiling at g.	SHAK 489:7
son of g. at cricket	HOUS 262:22
still sad when others' g.	BYRON 124:35
Thine be the g.	AYT 24:4
thirsty g. in wine we steep	LOV 318:17
Thus g. still treads upon	CONG 160:27
thy mother's g.	BRET 92:6
time remembered is g. forgotten	SWIN 528:17
'tis unmanly g.	SHAK 429:26
To cure this deadly g.	SHAK 462:17
to thee thy mother's g.	BLAKE 85:13
was a journeyman to g.	SHAK 478:15
Was there g. once	NICH 362:24
Which in false g. hiding	SPEN 516:5
within their breasts the g.	AYT 24:5
griefs: all g. which bow	ARN 14:24
cutteth g. in halves	BACON 26:16
Drinking my g.	SHAK 479:22
ere England's g. began	GOLD 230:18
Great g., I see	SHAK 428:19
g. that harrass the distress'd	JOHN 282:23
I am sick of many g.	SHAK 451:25
lion g. loped from	AUDEN 20:19
not my g.	SHAK 479:23
so are their g. and fears	BACON 27:2
solitary g.	JOHN 273:21
Surely he hath borne our g.	BIBLE 59:21
to ease them of their g.	SHAK 486:13
which had soothed the g.	MAC 324:18
grievance: hundred with a g.	LOUI 318:9
grieve: g. his heart	SHAK 462:9
g. or triumph	GOET 230:7
made to g. on account	HARDY 241:18
make the judicious g.	SHAK 433:17
Nor joy nor g. too much	DRYD 197:10
Poor Pope will g. a month	SWIFT 527:23
than a nation g.	DRYD 194:11
Then can I g. at grievances	SHAK 493:7
thou leavest me to g.	SHEL 505:6
what could it g.	KEATS 292:10
grieved: g. with this generation	PRAY 396:4

grieves: aught inanimate e'er g.
    BYRON 120:26
grieving: are you g. HOPK 256:25
grievous: g. crab-tree cudgel BUNY 107:22
  remembrance of them is g. PRAY 387:19
  through my most g. fault MASS 334:15
Griffith: honest chronicler as G. SHAK 447:23
Grill: Let Grill be G. SPEN 516:14
grim: g. grew his countenance BALL 30:18
  g. shape Towered up WORD 580:12
  look g. as hell SHAK 476:18
  Thou hast a g. appearance SHAK 427:26
grimness: what an element of g. ARN 15:27
grin: cheerfully he seems to g. CARR 133:18
  ending with the g. CARR 133:27
  opens on her like a g. ELIOT 204:9
  Relax'd into a universal g. COWP 167:15
  wears one universal g. FIEL 211:13
  woodland g. PAIN 367:19
grind: did g. in the prison house BIBLE 49:27
  g. the faces of the poor BIBLE 57:20
  Laws g. the poor GOLD 231:29
  life is one demd horrid g. DICK 180:22
  mills of God g. slowly LOGAU 316:5
Grinder: G., who serenely grindest
    CALV 127:23
grinders: divided into incisors and g.
    BAG 29:13
  g. cease because they are BIBLE 56:11
grinning: g. honour as Sir Walter
    SHAK 440:21
  to mock your own g. SHAK 436:31
Grishkin: G. is nice ELIOT 205:14
Grisilde: G. is deed CHAU 142:9
gristle: g. and not yet hardened BURKE 109:17
grizzled: His beard was g. SHAK 430:13
groan: Condemn'd alike to g. GRAY 235:13
  depths with bubbling g. BYRON 121:24
  g. of the martyr's woe BLAKE 86:6
  hear each other g. KEATS 291:18
  He gave a g. WORD 580:1
groan'd: My mother g. BLAKE 87:23
groaneth: creation g. and travaileth
    BIBLE 75:10
groaning: g. for burial SHAK 450:12
  I am weary of my g. PRAY 389:26
groans: sovereign of sighs and g.
    SHAK 456:26
  with everlasting g. MILT 346:11
Grocer: God made the wicked G.
    CHES 147:18
Gromboolian: Over the great G. plain
    LEAR 312:2
groom: by his dogs and by his g. COWP 166:6
  that death is but a g. DONNE 189:30
grooms: gild the faces of the g. SHAK 460:15
grooves: In predestinate g. HARE 242:8
  ringing g. of change TENN 539:8
gros: g. escadrons contre les BUSS 117:7
gross: g. as a mountain SHAK 439:4
  lust is g. and brief PETR 373:5
  Not g. to sink SHAK 495:19
  things rank and g. in nature SHAK 429:28
grossen: Volkes...einer g. Lüge HITL 251:9
grossness: Hiding the g. with fair
    SHAK 467:10
  touch of g. in our race ARN 15:26
Grosvenor Galley: greenery-yallery,
  G. GILB 227:27
grotesque: At so g. a blunder BENT 41:10
  from the g. to the horrible DOYLE 192:25
  G. Art in English Poetry BAG 29:20
ground: acre of barren g. SHAK 484:22
  commit his body to the g. PRAY 389:13
  crieth unto me from the g. BIBLE 45:26
  fallen unto me in a fair g. PRAY 390:6
  feet of English g. HAR 242:11
  five miles of fertile g. COL 156:26
  found six feet of g. HOUS 265:6
  gain a little patch of g. SHAK 435:28

g. flew up and hit me WARD 564:28
g., the books, the academes SHAK 457:6
having so little g. SCOTT 419:2
He swalloweth the g. with BIBLE 53:7
In a fair g. KIPL 303:16
In his own g. POPE 380:23
Israelites passed over on dry g. BIBLE 49:1
let us sit upon the g. SHAK 479:11
lose to-morrow the g. won ARN 14:17
man of the dust of the g. BIBLE 45:7
other fell into good g. BIBLE 66:16
seek the g. of my heart PRAY 399:8
stirrup and the g. CAMD 128:5
thou standest is holy g. BIBLE 47:4
tread on classic g. ADD 2:4
upon the g. I see thee stare CHAU 143:13
water spilt on the g. BIBLE 50:23
When every rood of g. maintain'd
    GOLD 230:18
will hardly water the g. BACON 26:33
grounde: that g. is of alle LANG 309:27
olive g. of Academe MILT 350:8
grovelled: he met a great man he g.
    THAC 545:23
groves: g. of their academy BURKE 111:12
  truth in the g. of Academe HOR 259:4
grow: g. every tree that is pleasant BIBLE 45:8
  g. for ever and for ever TENN 542:1
  hand wrought to make it g. FITZ 212:21
  I g. in worth TENN 544:10
  resolved to g. fat DRYD 196:36
  shelter to g. ripe ARN 13:10
  that ye may g. thereby BIBLE 80:22
grow'd: short laugh...'I 'spect I g.
    STOWE 524:1
growing: g., Jock, when ye're sleeping
    SCOTT 418:20
  It is not g. like a tree JONS 285:8
growl: sit and g. JOHN 279:3
grown: I am g. to man's estate STEV 522:19
  When we are g. and take KIPL 298:10
grown-up: hear the g. people's feet
    STEV 522:16
grows: Nothing g. in our garden THOM 547:12
growth: children of a larger g. DRYD 195:15
  g. of the fore-brain AUDEN 19:10
  'G. the only evidence NEWM 361:18
  mushroom of a night's g. DONNE 190:26
  quick a g. to meet decay HERR 249:28
grub: My gravender, or g. ST L 412:27
  old ones, g. SHAW 496:6
grudge: feed fat the ancient g. SHAK 465:29
gruel: Make the g. thick and slab SHAK 462:4
grumble: nothing whatever to g. GILB 228:29
  we g. a little now GOLD 232:30
Grundy: more of Mrs G. LOCK 315:20
  What will Mrs G. think MORT 358:18
gruntled: he was far from being g.
    WOD 575:19
guano: pamphleteer on g. and on grain
    TENN 542:20
guarantee: g. success in war CHUR 151:1
guard: Be on your g. ANON 9:18
  calls not Thee to g. KIPL 302:10
  g. a title that was rich SHAK 452:25
  hate of those ye g. KIPL 304:8
  marrying one of the g. MILNE 340:4
  none but Americans on g. WASH 565:5
  They're changing g. MILNE 340:4
  use its g. staying awake BIBLE 83:12
guarda: g., e passa DANTE 171:4
guarded: ever g. is scarcely worth
    GOLD 232:35
guardian: constitutional g. GILB 226:2
Guards: G. die but do not surrender
    CAMB 128:2
  Lord g. the city BIBLE 83:12
  to guard the g. JUV 287:22

Up G. and at them again WELL 568:9
guardsman: g.'s cut and thrust HUXL 269:3
gude: cog o' g. swats BURNS 113:4
  There's a g. time coming SCOTT 418:31
gudeman: When our g.'s awa' ANON 8:3
gude-willie: We'll tak' a right g. waught
    BURNS 112:31
gudgeon: fool g., this opinion SHAK 465:13
guenille: ma g. m'est chère MOL 353:11
guerdon: fair g. when we hope MILT 343:8
guerra: en g. con mis entrañas MACH 325:7
guerre: g. est l'industrie nationale MIR 352:19
  la g. NAP 359:10
  mais ce n'est pas la g. BOSQ 90:12
guess: first we met we did not g. BRID 92:22
  'G. now who holds thee BROW 98:9
guessing: 'g. what was at the other
    WELL 567:20
guest: at the strange g.'s hand SWIN 529:18
  awaited the expected g. ELIOT 205:1
  away the worthy bidden g. MILT 343:12
  built by the g. DONNE 190:1
  receive an honoured g. AUDEN 19:7
  remembrance of a g. that tarrieth BIBLE 62:18
  shakes his parting g. SHAK 487:5
  some poor nigh-related g. COL 157:17
  Soul, the body's g. RAL 404:10
  speed the going g. POPE 380:6
  your g. tomorrow night' ANON 8:24
guests: hosts and g. BEER 37:17
  I would my g. should praise HAR 242:9
  Unbidden g. SHAK 445:19
guid: g. to be merry and wise BURNS 114:5
guide: being our ruler and g. PRAY 386:16
  great g. of human life HUME 267:14
  g. our feet into the way BIBLE 69:7
  g., philosopher, and friend POPE 380:4
  Have God to be his g. BUNY 107:32
  Who art a light to us g. WORD 579:15
guided: man to be g. by the wiser
    CARL 131:16
Guides: G. cannot master the subtleties
    TWAIN 554:12
  Ye blind g. BIBLE 67:24
guiding-star: he was the g. of a whole
    MOTL 358:20
Guildenstern: That Rosencrantz and
  G. SHAK 437:29
guile: grief hiding his harmful g. SPEN 516:5
  in whom is no g. BIBLE 71:32
  packed with g. BROO 94:23
  that they speak no g. PRAY 391:23
  unfathom'd gulfs of g. BYRON 125:4
  whose spirit there is no g. PRAY 391:16
guilt: art can wash her g. GOLD 231:31
  blood with g. SHEL 503:1
  Calls g., in first confusion CLOU 153:23
  closely connected with g. CONN 161:14
  G. in his heart CHUR 149:5
  g. of dissimulation SCOTT 418:3
  it must seem their g. SHAK 460:11
  no g. to make you turn HOR 258:9
  pens dwell on g. and misery AUST 22:29
  sign of g., or of ill breeding CONG 160:34
  unfortunate circumstance of g. STEV 522:11
  war, without its g. SOM 513:2
  without industry is g. RUSK 411:9
  yet free from g. or pain SHEL 503:12
Guiltier: G. than him they try SHAK 463:14
guiltless: g. that taketh his name BIBLE 47:24
  Some Cromwell g. of his GRAY 234:23
guilts: Close pent-up g. SHAK 454:16
guilty: g., but to me AUDEN 19:17
  g. of our own disasters SHAK 453:11
  g. of such a ballad some SHAK 456:18
  g. party is acquitted PUBL 402:5
  g. persons escape than BLAC 85:6
  In g. splendour COWP 166:37
  Let no g. man escape GRANT 234:3
  like a g. thing suprised WORD 579:10

Lose all their g. stains COWP 165:24
Make mad the g. SHAK 433:1
no g. man is acquitted JUV 288:5
strength of g. kings ARN 13:22
Suspicion always haunts the g. SHAK 446:23
That g. creatures sitting SHAK 433:5
then it started like a g. SHAK 429:16
guinea: fire somewhat like a g. BLAKE 88:29
force of the g. you have RUSK 412:8
jingling of the g. TENN 538:23
rank is but the g.'s stamp BURNS 113:28
sixpences you know to one g. JOHN 280:14
within the compass of a g. IRV 270:23
guinea-pig: lift a g. up by the tail
LOCK 315:18
guineas: crowns and pounds and g.
HOUS 262:20
Guinness: drink G. from a thick mug
PINT 373:18
G., Allsopp, Bass CALV 127:12
guitar: sang to a small g. LEAR 312:11
gulf: great g. fixed BIBLE 70:29
gulfs: g. will wash us down TENN 544:3
steep-down g. of liquid fire SHAK 477:21
gull: g.'s way and the whale's MAS 334:6
most notorious geck and g. SHAK 490:24
gulls: Forgot the cry of g. ELIOT 205:6
g. him with intelligence SHAK 494:12
gulp: he drains his at one g. BROW 105:6
gum: thick amber and plum-tree g.
SHAK 432:8
gums: wept odorous g. and balm MILT 347:19
gun: bare-legg'd beggarly son of a g.
CALV 127:17
escape from rope and g. GAY 222:30
ever lost an English g. TENN 541:9
got The Maxim G. BELL 40:1
out of the barrel of a g. MAO 328:19
through a door with a g. CHAN 139:21
Gunga Din: better man than I am, G.
KIPL 299:20
Gunpowder: G., Printing CARL 131:3
printing, g. and the magnet BACON 28:9
reason why g. treason ANON 7:10
such as g. and sealing-wax CARR 136:4
till the g. ran out FOOTE 216:7
guns: don't get away from the g. KIPL 302:16
gongs groaning as the g. CHES 147:2
G. aren't lawful PARK 368:18
G. will make us powerful GOER 229:25
monstrous anger of the g. OWEN 367:2
these vile g. SHAK 438:16
when the g. begin to shoot KIPL 303:23
gurgite: *Apparent rari nantes in g.*
VIRG 557:11
gurgle: g. he gave GILB 227:17
gurly: g. grew the sea BALL 30:18
gusts: g. shake the door ARN 13:7
gusty: carpets rose along the g. KEATS 289:22
Gute: *ist das G. zu geniessen* GOET 230:8
guts: Are modified in the g. AUDEN 19:4
g. should hale souls SHAK 472:15
his g. in his head SHAK 486:29
I'll lug the g. into SHAK 435:22
strangled in the g. of priests MESL 338:9
Gutta: *G. cavat lapidem* LAT 310:20
G. cavat lapidem OVID 366:27
gutter: We are all in the g. WILDE 573:11
Guy: Ah! County G. SCOTT 418:25
guzzling: was gorging Jack and g.
THAC 545:32
gym: flare was up in the g. BETJ 44:2
gypsy: to the vagrant g. life MAS 334:6
you old g. man HODG 252:9
gyre: g. and gimble in the wabe CARR 134:28
gyves: With g. upon his wrist HOOD 254:12
habendi: *innatus apes amor urget in.*
VIRG 560:19
haberdasher: brother-in-law is h. to Mr
Spurgeon BUTL 119:20

habile: *h. pour connaître tout* LA R 310:14
habileté: *de savoir cacher son h.* LA R 310:13
habit: h. of living indisposeth BROW 97:13
h. rules the unreflecting WORD 581:17
H. with him was all COWP 168:7
How use doth breed a h. SHAK 491:5
I shook the h. off WORD 580:25
Sow a h. READE 405:4
habita: *Tecum h.* PERS 372:29
Habitarunt: *H. di quoque silvas* VIRG 559:16
habitation: even God in his holy h.
PRAY 394:7
h. among the tents of Kedar PRAY 398:7
Let their h. be void PRAY 394:13
local h. and a name SHAK 471:11
of the air have their h. PRAY 396:19
shall be an h. of dragons BIBLE 58:31
habitations: you into everlasting h.
BIBLE 70:26
habiter: *maison est une machine à h.*
LE C 313:5
habits: Of h. devil SHAK 435:18
Small h., well pursued MORE 357:8
Their h. from the Bear BELL 38:26
habitual: live beneath your more h.
WORD 579:13
hack: Do not h. me as you did MONM 354:5
h. my world as in my tyme PARK 368:22
h. my world as in my tyme CHAU 143:19
haedis: *Et ab h. me sequestra* CEL 138:8
haggard: If I do prove her h. SHAK 475:21
Whene'er with h. eyes I view CANN 130:5
Haggards: H. Ride no more STEP 518:24
hag-ridden: h. magic and enchanted
KEYN 295:19
hags: midnight h. SHAK 462:5
haie: *soldats faisaient la h.* ELIOT 202:8
hail: Fire and h. PRAY 399:22
flail of the lashing h. SHEL 500:4
flies no sharp and sided h. HOPK 256:17
h., and farewell evermore CAT 137:15
H. Caesar ANON 10:7
H., fellow, well met SWIFT 527:30
H., glorious edifice SMITH 506:1
H. holy queen ANON 10:19
H. Mary ANON 10:8
H., thou art highly favoured BIBLE 69:4
H. to the Chief who SCOTT 416:4
H. to thee, blithe Spirit SHEL 504:15
indomitable heroes, h. LAND 308:18
Where falls not h. TENN 535:27
Hails: H. me so solemnly to yonder
JONS 285:9
hailstones: h., and coals of fire PRAY 390:9
hair: All her bright golden h. WILDE 572:18
All her h. BROW 103:29
beautiful uncut h. of graves WHIT 570:18
Berenice's ever-burning h. CHAP 140:4
Blind with thine h. the eyes SHEL 505:3
bright h. about the bone DONNE 190:5
colour of his h. HOUS 266:8
down and combed their h. HOUS 265:3
do you pin up your h. with CONG 160:37
draws us with a single h. POPE 381:1
dressing your golden h. HOR 259:15
drew me backward by the h. BROW 98:9
excellent head of h. SHAK 487:26
from his horrid h. MILT 346:26
gowd kames in their h. BALL 31:20
h. as free JONS 283:27
h. did bristle upon his SCOTT 416:11
h. has become very white CARR 133:22
h. is as a flock of goats BIBLE 56:26
h. is mussed on her forehead POUND 382:15
h. of a woman can draw HOW 266:21
h. of his head like BIBLE 61:8
h. of my flesh stood up BIBLE 52:15
h. soft-lifted by the winnowing KEATS 293:6
h. to stand an end SHAK 431:5
has braided her yellow h. BALL 32:1

heart one strangling golden h. ROSS 410:2
her h., her hair MEW 338:12
Her h. that lay along her ROSS 409:15
Her h. was long KEATS 290:16
her h. was so charmingly KING 297:4
his next commodity of h. SHAK 489:18
image doth unfix my h. SHAK 458:20
I must sugar my h. CARR 134:16
lie tangled in her h. LOV 318:15
Like the bright h. uplifted SHEL 502:9
like the h. we breathe SURT 525:4
long black h. out tight ELIOT 205:9
long h., it is a glory BIBLE 76:12
man have long h. BIBLE 76:12
morrow to mine own torn h. HERR 249:10
mother bids me bind my h. HUNT 268:15
My h. is grey BYRON 125:16
my h. is sleek ANON 7:2
never brush their h. BELL 38:26
not your yellow h. YEATS 585:5
of thy amber-dropping h. MILT 341:20
only talks about her h. THOM 549:3
raiment of camel's h. BIBLE 63:37
ruddy limbs and flaming h. BLAKE 86:20
Shall I part my h. behind ELIOT 203:25
She smoothes her h. ELIOT 205:3
stars in her h. were seven ROSS 409:14
strung with his h. SHAK 457:8
That subtle wreath of h. DONNE 188:27
to her *with a single h.* DRYD 198:21
touches a h. of yon gray head WHIT 571:18
wherefore should I kame my h. BALL 32:10
with his long essenced h. MAC 322:7
with long dishevell'd h. SHAK 495:19
with such h. BROW 105:26
With vine leaves in his h. IBSEN 269:23
would make your h. curl GILB 228:34
hairless: white and h. as an egg HERR 249:15
hairs: elf-locks in foul sluttish h.
SHAK 481:28
gray h. with sorrow BIBLE 46:35
h. of your head are all BIBLE 65:36
head and his h. were white BIBLE 81:14
If h. be wires SHAK 495:8
Those set our h. DONNE 188:15
hairy: Esau my brother is a h. BIBLE 46:15
marvellous h. about the face SHAK 471:2
haïssable: *Le moi est h.* PASC 369:12
halcyon: h. days SHAK 445:18
hale: guts should h. souls SHAK 472:15
I should prefer mild h. SURT 525:20
You are h. SOUT 514:7
half: ae h. of the warld thinks SCOTT 418:28
h. a library to make one JOHN 276:24
h. as good as justified BUTL 118:11
H. as sober as a judge LAMB 308:1
H. dead and half alive BETJ 42:10
h. in love with easeful KEATS 291:22
h. is greater than HES 250:19
h. Latin and half Greek SCOTT 415:16
h. of my own life HOR 259:11
H. our days we pass BROW 95:24
H. our days we pass BROW 96:1
h. slave and half free LINC 314:14
h. some sturdy strumpet HARDY 240:7
h. that's got my keys GRAH 233:12
h. the power to do me harm SHAK 477:14
h. to fall POPE 379:13
H. to forget the wandering FLEC 214:5
h. was not told me BIBLE 50:33
have been finished in h. WOD 575:21
of myself and dearer h. MILT 348:15
One h. of the world cannot AUST 22:8
overcome but h. his foe MILT 345:25
temple h. as old as Time ROG 407:9
half-a-dozen: h. of the other MARR 331:7
half-and-half: No h. affair GILB 225:22
half-believers: h. in our casual creeds
ARN 14:17
half-brother: thou h. of the world BAIL 29:22

half-child: Half-devil and h.   KIPL 304:6
Half-devil: H. and half-child   KIPL 304:6
half-human: this h. visitor to our
   KEYN 295:19
half-knowledge: remaining content with
h.   KEATS 293:19
half-light: night and light and the h.
   YEATS 585:9
Half-past: H. one, The street-lamp
   ELIOT 204:9
half-pence: like one another as h.
   SHAK 426:14
half-shut: things with his h. eyes   POPE 381:7
half-way: ill-luck that they run h.   JERR 273:8
hall: decent h. of death   CHES 147:12
equality in the servants' h.   BARR 34:7
H. or Terrace or lofty   LEAR 312:3
Meet her in the h.   COW 164:5
Mr H.'s nay was nay   BENT 41:4
than the pram in the h.   CONN 161:12
vasty h. of death   ARN 14:6
window'd niche of that high h.
   BYRON 120:23
hallow'd: So h. and so gracious is
   SHAK 429:17
Hallowed: H. be thy name   BIBLE 64:24
halls: Amphitrite's destined h.   SHEL 501:23
dwelt in marble h.   BUNN 107:9
In h., in gay attire   SCOTT 416:17
In our h. is hung   WORD 582:3
through those roofless h.   SHEL 502:7
halo: What, after all, Is a h.   FRY 219:27
halt: h., and the blind   BIBLE 70:12
H. by the headstone naming   HOUS 266:2
h. ye between two opinions   BIBLE 51:8
halves: twin h. of one august event
   HARDY 239:6
ham: case when there's h.   DICK 181:8
Shem, H., and Japheth   BIBLE 45:32
hambre: manjar que quita la h.   CERV 138:20
salsa del mundo es el h.   CERV 138:13
hame: It's hame and it's h.   CUNN 170:14
thou must bring her h.   BALL 31:17
Hamelin: H. Town's in Brunswick
   BROW 103:14
Hamlet: announced the tragedy of H.
   SCOTT 418:34
I am not Prince H.   ELIOT 203:24
I'll call thee H.   SHAK 430:24
king drinks to H.   SHAK 437:17
Lord H. is a prince   SHAK 432:1
of H. most of all   HENL 245:12
rude forefathers of the h.   GRAY 234:20
where the kneeling h. drains   TENN 536:7
hamlets: In h., dances on the green
   SCOTT 416:17
Hammer: Amboss oder H. sein   GOET 230:7
be the anvil or the h.   GOET 230:7
His h. of wind   THOM 549:1
little h. under the pillow   DICK 176:11
took an h. in her hand   BIBLE 49:7
hammer'd: Was clash'd and h. from
   TENN 533:22
hammered: h. into line   KIPL 297:26
hammers: busy h. closing rivets up
   SHAK 444:9
hammock: Drake he's in his h. till
   NEWB 361:7
hammock-shroud: His heavy-shotted
h.   TENN 536:4
hams: together with most weak h.
   SHAK 432:8
Ha'nacker Hill: Sally is gone from H.
   BELL 39:26
hand: adorable tennis-girl's h.   BETJ 44:8
Beneath whose awful H. we hold   KIPL 302:7
bite the h. that fed   BURKE 112:10
bloody and invisible h.   SHAK 461:14
bloody h. that drew from   HEINE 244:12
by Time's devouring h.   BRAM 91:23

Clean from my h.   SHAK 460:13
curious engine, your white h.   WEBS 566:21
died by the h. of the Lord   BIBLE 47:23
either h. may rightly clutch   KIPL 298:8
Emprison her soft h.   KEATS 291:15
evening withhold not thine h.   BIBLE 56:8
fingers of this h. wherewith   BROW 98:12
Great is the h. that holds   THOM 547:5
h. and brain went ever   BROW 101:26
h. a needle better fits   BRAD 91:13
h. are all the corners   PRAY 396:4
h. dare seize the fire   BLAKE 87:15
h. for hand   BIBLE 47:25
h. into the hand of God   HASK 243:1
h. is stretched out still   BIBLE 57:27
h. more instrumental   SHAK 429:20
h. of Douglas is his own   SCOTT 417:17
h. of every man's brother   BIBLE 45:38
h. of the physician   BIBLE 63:18
h. on the cockatrice' den   BIBLE 58:11
h. that fired the shot   BALL 31:4
h. that hath made you fair   SHAK 464:16
h. that kings Have lipp'd   SHAK 422:11
h. that rocks the cradle   WALL 562:4
h. that signed the paper   THOM 547:4
H. then of the Potter shake   FITZ 213:10
h. to bless   CHUR 149:3
h. to execute any mischief   CLAR 152:19
h. to execute   GIBB 224:28
h. to execute   JUN 287:5
h. will be against every   BIBLE 46:5
Heaving up my either h.   HERR 250:10
here's my h.   SHAK 485:13
her h., In whose comparison   SHAK 486:19
Her h. on her bosom   SHAK 476:27
him with his skinny h.   COL 155:6
His mind and h. went together   HEM 245:2
his right h. seven stars   BIBLE 81:14
I fear thy skinny h.   COL 155:19
I kiss'd her slender h.   TENN 540:6
immortal h. or eye   BLAKE 87:14
imposition of a mightier h.   MAC 323:26
In a bold determined h.   CAMP 128:14
I put my h. into the bed   SHAK 443:18
it hurts my h.   SHAK 476:11
it will go into his h.   BIBLE 51:38
kingdom of heaven is at h.   BIBLE 63:35
know the sweet Roman h.   SHAK 490:5
lays his h. upon a woman   TOBIN 551:7
led by an invisible h.   SMITH 509:9
left h. is under my head   BIBLE 56:21
left his garment in her h.   BIBLE 46:30
let me kiss that h.   SHAK 455:17
let not thy left h. know   BIBLE 64:22
letters in a big round h.   GILB 228:5
lily in your medieval h.   GILB 227:23
man's h. is not able   SHAK 471:10
mighty h. and by a stretched   BIBLE 48:19
My h. sought hers   BROW 102:2
my knee, my hat, and h.   BROW 96:3
My playfellow, your h.   SHAK 422:21
My times be in Thy h.   BROW 104:13
One lovely h. she stretched   CAMP 129:4
On this side my h.   SHAK 479:22
onward lend thy guiding h.   MILT 350:13
other h. held a weapon   BIBLE 52:1
Our times are in His h.   BROW 104:2
right h. forget her cunning   PRAY 399:3
right h. of the Majesty   BIBLE 79:28
seen by Time's fell h.   SHAK 494:2
Shade of this h.   THOM 548:23
sheep of his h.   PRAY 396:4
she waves her little h.   HARDY 240:16
sitteth on the right h.   PRAY 384:26
soft h., and softer breast   KEATS 292:13
spirit-small h. propping it   BROW 99:19
Sword sleep in my h.   BLAKE 86:9
take the pen out of his h.   ARN 16:8
there's a h.   BURNS 112:33
This living h.   KEATS 290:30

thousand at thy right h.   PRAY 395:21
thrust my h. into his side   BIBLE 73:10
'Tis a good h.   SHAK 476:2
top-mast wi' his h.   BALL 30:19
touch of a vanish'd h.   TENN 532:18
tricks by slight of h.   CONG 160:9
unto you with mine own h.   BIBLE 77:21
waiting for a h.   TENN 536:5
was the h. that wrote it   CRAN 169:1
wav'd her lily h.   GAY 223:30
were a glove upon that h.   SHAK 482:7
Whatsoever thy h. findeth to do   BIBLE 55:29
when I stretched out my h.   STER 519:14
white h. a warm wet cheek   LAND 308:25
whose h. is ever at his   KEATS 291:15
With his own right h.   PRAY 396:7
Your h., your tongue   SHAK 459:3
handbook: it was a constable's h.   KING 297:7
handclasp: Out where the h.'s a little
   CHAP 140:2
handcuffs: young sinner with the h.
   HOUS 266:8
Handel: Compar'd to H.'s a mere
   BYROM 119:24
handful: fear in a h. of dust   ELIOT 204:19
h. of meal in a barrel   BIBLE 51:7
life in the h. of dust   CONR 161:24
handiwork: beyond or above his h.
   JOYCE 286:18
not-incurious in God's h.   BROW 100:24
handkerchief: feels like a damp h.
   MACK 325:10
h. Did an Egyptian   SHAK 476:3
Holding his pocket-h.   CARR 135:10
it is the h. of the Lord   WHIT 570:18
snuffle and sniff and h.   BROO 94:16
handkerchiefs: waistcoats and moral
pocket h.   DICK 182:6
handle: h. not   BIBLE 78:24
I polished up the h.   GILB 228:4
One old jug without a h.   LEAR 311:25
to h. honesty and truth   SHAW 497:14
handles: hath two h.   BURT 116:25
handling: make a slip in h. us   KIPL 302:17
handmaid: nature's h. art   DRYD 195:22
our h. unheeding   PAIN 367:1
Riches are a good h.   BACON 25:9
handmaiden: low estate of his h.   BIBLE 69:5
handmaidens: With her five h.   ROSS 409:19
handmaids: sent me only your h.
   POUND 383:13
hands: accept refreshment at any h.
   GILB 226:22
aching h. and bleeding feet   ARN 13:23
All h. to work   ANON 8:24
are the horny h. of toil   LOW 319:9
Before rude h. have touch'd   JONS 285:4
by joining of h.   PRAY 389:7
caught the world's great h.   HUNT 268:9
clap your h.   BARR 34:16
crag with crooked h.   TENN 533:7
dirty h.   MAC 324:7
Fall into the h. of God   TENN 543:3
folding of the h. to sleep   BIBLE 55:4
Fold our h. round her knees   SWIN 528:16
fortune is in his own h.   BACON 26:12
h., and handle not   PRAY 397:18
h. are as gold rings   BIBLE 57:4
h. are a sort of feet   TRAH 552:1
h. are the hands of Esau   BIBLE 46:16
h. be an evening sacrifice   PRAY 399:9
h. from picking and stealing   PRAY 388:12
h. guiding where I stumble   SASS 414:19
h. I commend my spirit   BIBLE 71:14
h. I commend my spirit   PRAY 391:15
h. of peasants their vile   SHAK 451:21
h. of the living God   BIBLE 79:30
h. that hold the aces which   BETJ 42:13
h. wrought in the work   BIBLE 52:1
hath not a Jew h.   SHAK 467:4

house not made with h.   BIBLE 77:6
house not made with h.   BROW 99:20
in temples made with h.   BIBLE 74:13
into the h. of spoilers   BIBLE 49:6
into the h. of the Lord   BIBLE 62:22
I warmed both h. before   LAND 308:20
Let us hold h. and look   BETJ 43:4
Licence my roving h.   DONNE 188:16
Lift not thy h. to *It*   FITZ 213:8
Made with our h. and our   SWIN 528:24
nearer than h. and feet   TENN 533:29
of those flower-soft h.   SHAK 422:3
Our h. will never meet   HOOD 255:13
Pale h. I loved   HOPE 256:3
pierced my h. and my feet   PRAY 390:20
plunge your h. in water   AUDEN 18:10
right h. of fellowship   BIBLE 77:15
Seem'd washing his h. with   HOOD 254:23
Shake h. for ever   DRAY 193:21
shook h. with time   FORD 216:16
some mischief still for h.   MADAN 326:17
So to'entergraft our h.   DONNE 188:22
Strengthen ye the weak h.   BIBLE 58:33
stretching of the h.   PAIN 367:18
Their fatal h.   MILT 347:1
their h. are blue   LEAR 312:6
Their h. upon their hearts   HOUS 264:23
These h. are not more like   SHAK 430:9
these h. ne'er be clean   SHAK 462:31
they reached out their h.   VIRG 558:22
union of h. and hearts   TAYL 532:6
violent h. upon themselves   PRAY 389:10
washed his h. before   BIBLE 68:21
wash my h. in innocency   PRAY 391:5
Wash your h.   SHAK 462:24
With cold immortal h.   SWIN 529:22
wither'd h. be still stretch'd   YOUNG 588:8
With mine own h. I give   SHAK 480:2
Your little h. were made   BELL 38:24
Your little h. were never   WATTS 565:18
handsaw: I know a hawk from a h.   SHAK 432:18
handshake: h., the cough, the kiss   AUDEN 21:1
handsome: h. in three hundred pounds   SHAK 469:11
h. lad   VIRG 559:15
happy and h. and free   AUDEN 18:7
knave is h.   SHAK 474:21
my h. young man   BALL 31:5
who was once h. and tall   ELIOT 205:7
years to be young and h.   SWIFT 526:22
handy: It'll come in h.   ELIOT 202:8
handy-work: firmament sheweth his
h.   PRAY 390:11
hang: Go h. thyself in thine   SHAK 438:25
h. a calf's-skin on those   SHAK 452:16
h. and brush their bosoms   BROW 105:26
h. a pearl in every cowslip's   SHAK 470:2
H. it all, Robert Browning   POUND 382:6
h. the man over again   BARH 33:9
h. us now in Shrewsbury   HOUS 262:16
h. your hat on a pension   MACN 326:8
H. your husband and be   GAY 222:19
H. yourself   HENR 245:14
Here they h. a man first   MOL 353:22
man as O'Connell is to h.   SMITH 511:24
must indeed all h. together   FRAN 218:14
people h. together artificially   BUTL 118:29
power to h. one another   FARQ 210:9
shall all h. separately   FRAN 218:14
she would h. on him   SHAK 429:28
will neither go nor h.   BIGOD 84:5
will not h. myself to-day   CHES 146:14
hang'd: my poor fool is h.   SHAK 456:11
hanged: being h. in all innocence
  STEV 522:13
h. for stealing horses   HAL 237:22
h. himself   BIBLE 50:25
h. with the Bible under   AUBR 17:23

harps, we h. them up   PRAY 399:3
Here's a farmer that h.   SHAK 460:15
If I were h. on the highest   KIPL 301:14
must they all be h. that   SHAK 462:13
to be h. in a fortnight   JOHN 277:16
hangin: they're h.' men an' women   ANON 6:6
they're h.' Danny Deever   KIPL 298:20
hanging: bare h.   DRYD 198:13
H. and marriage   FARQ 210:19
h. garments of Marylebone   JOYCE 286:5
h. isn't bad enough   HOUS 266:8
H. is too good for him   BUNY 107:17
h.-look to me   CONG 160:4
H. of his cat on Monday   BRAT 91:24
h. prevents a bad marriage   SHAK 488:4
That's cured by h. from   KING 297:20
your silk stocking's h.   SELL 420:3
hangman: even a h.   JERR 273:6
louse for the h.   JONS 284:4
naked to the h.'s noose   HOUS 262:17
Hangs: H. in the uncertain balance
  GREE 236:9
that h. on princes' favours   SHAK 447:9
thereby h. a tale   SHAK 425:19
What h. people…is the unfortunate
  STEV 522:11
hank: rag and a bone and a h.   KIPL 303:29
Hannibalem: Expende H.   JUV 288:1
Hanover: By famous H. city   BROW 103:14
Hans: H.' old Mill his three   DE L 174:4
Hans Breitmann: H. gife a barty   LEL 313:16
Haply: H. I may remember   ROSS 409:9
happen: accidents which started out to h.
  MARQ 331:2
poetry makes nothing h.   AUDEN 19:6
There shall no evil h.   PRAY 395:22
happened: I wonder what h. to him
  COW 163:16
happens: dependent on what h. to her
  ELIOT 201:3
h. anywhere   LARK 310:4
happier: is remembering h. things
  TENN 538:20
seek No h. state   MILT 348:9
that I am h. than I know   MILT 349:5
That Pobbles are h. without   LEAR 312:21
upon the whole a family h.   STEV 521:4
you be h. than your father   SOPH 513:4
happiest: gild it with the h. terms
  SHAK 440:28
h. time of all the glad   TENN 540:20
record of the best and h.   SHEL 505:12
happily: h. upon a plentiful fortune
  JOHN 275:2
happiness: all the h. mankind can
  DRYD 196:25
away you take away his h.   IBSEN 270:4
being too happy in thine h.   KEATS 291:17
Doesn't h. issue from pain   APOL 11:11
general h. of the nation   PEDR 371:4
great spectacle of human h.   SMITH 511:29
H. consists in the multiplicity   JOHN 275:17
h. for the greatest numbers   HUTC 268:20
h. in boats and carriage   HOR 258:19
h. is not an ideal of reason   KANT 288:12
H. is no laughing matter   WHAT 569:12
h. of the greatest number   BENT 40:25
h. of the next world   BROW 97:11
h. of the human race   BURKE 110:7
H.! our being's end   POPE 379:21
h. through another man's   SHAK 426:28
h. too swiftly flies   GRAY 235:13
home-born h.   COWP 167:13
In my great task of h.   STEV 523:11
It is a flaw In h.   KEATS 289:8
lifetime of h.   SHAW 497:17
makes the h. she does not   JOHN 283:6
more right to consume h.   SHAW 496:13
'Our unrivalled h.'   ARN 15:27
pursuit of h.   JEFF 272:6

recall a time of h. in misery   DANTE 171:8
recipe for h. I ever heard   AUST 22:28
secret of h. is to admire   BRAD 91:11
so great my h.   YEATS 587:11
so much h. is produced   JOHN 276:35
than h. makes them good   LAND 309:12
Travelling is the ruin of all h.   BURN 112:17
was the only thing for h.   EDG 199:21
We find our h.   WORD 580:23
Who gain a h. in eyeing   HUXL 269:1
Withdraws into its h.   MARV 332:4
happy: angry and poor and h.   CHES 147:22
Are you all h. now   LAND 308:21
Be h. while y'er leevin   ANON 4:27
Call no man h.   SOLON 512:25
daft and h. hills   THOM 546:22
duty of being h.   STEV 522:4
h. and handsome and free   AUDEN 18:7
h. as birds in the spring   BLAKE 87:20
h. as the grass was green   THOM 547:1
h. could I be with either   GAY 222:35
h. families resemble one   TOLS 551:10
h. he who crowns in shades   GOLD 230:19
H. he who like Ulysses   DU B 198:26
h. in *three wives* as Mr   LAMB 308:13
h. issue out of all their   PRAY 386:1
H. is that city which   ANON 5:12
H. is the man who fears   BIBLE 83:9
H. is the man that hath   PRAY 398:19
h. is the rose distill'd   SHAK 469:17
h. life be these   SURR 524:20
h. low, lie down   SHAK 441:30
h. men that have the power   TENN 543:13
h. noise to hear   HOUS 263:4
h., pair   DRYD 194:23
H. the hare at morning   AUDEN 18:14
H. the man   POPE 380:23
H. the people whose annals   CARL 131:20
H. those early days   VAUG 555:14
He's h. who, far away   HOR 259:7
How h. is he born and taught   WOTT 583:12
How h. some o'er other   SHAK 469:22
how h. you make those   SHAK 493:18
I die h.   FOX 217:22
is h. nature to explore   POPE 379:17
Is that they h. are   WALL 562:16
I've had a h. life   HAZL 244:4
Made h. by compulsion   COL 157:13
make a h. fire-side clime   BURNS 115:15
make two lovers h.   POPE 380:22
making of an old woman h.   FRAN 218:5
me at all h. without you   KEATS 294:30
methinks it were a h. life   SHAK 446:18
More h., if less wise   BYRON 124:42
must be regarded as h.   CAMUS 129:24
myself in nothing else so h.   SHAK 478:24
no chance to be very h.   GAY 223:26
nor as h. as one hopes   LA R 310:18
of us is h. in this world   THAC 545:29
one thing to make men h.   HAZL 243:15
perfectly happy till all are h.   SPEN 515:3
should all be as h. as kings   STEV 522:22
so late their h. seat   MILT 350:1
so long as you're h.   DU M 199:4
splendid and a h. land   GOLD 231:5
that can make a man h.   HOR 258:17
that none should be h.   JOHN 277:5
think no birds so h. as we   LEAR 312:15
This h. breed   SHAK 478:20
Thrice h. he who   MARV 332:22
To keep me h. all the day…   STEV 522:20
To make men h.   POPE 380:10
too h. in thine happiness   KEATS 291:17
'Twere now to be most h.   SHAK 474:20
was most h. and prosperous   GIBB 224:24
was the carver h. while   RUSK 411:20
What makes a nation h.   MILT 350:11
whether you are h.   MILL 338:21
Whoever wants to be h.   MED 336:9
who so h.   LEAR 312:4

world of the h. is quite WITT 575:16
you be right to call h. HOR 261:19
Happy Isles: be we shall touch the H.
  TENN 544:3
haps: neutral-tinted h. and such
  HARDY 239:22
harbor: looking over h. and city SAND 413:26
harbour: h. grene aslepe whereas
  WEVER 569:7
Though the h. bar be moaning KING 290:1
where doth thine h. hold BARN 33:27
Which in life did h. give JONS 284:3
Hard: H. as the palm of ploughman
  SHAK 486:19
  h. dealing teaches th SHAK 466:4
  H.,' replied the Dodger DICK 180:34
  h. sentences of old PRAY 395:3
  h. to catch and conquer MER 337:2
  H. was their lodging GARTH 221:20
  how h. to make a man appear DRYD 198:11
  it was too h. for me PRAY 394:23
  Long is the way And h. MILT 346:17
  never think I have hit h. JOHN 276:20
  Nothing's so h. HERR 249:19
  that thou art an h. man BIBLE 68:3
harden: h. not your hearts PRAY 396:4
  h. Pharaoh's heart BIBLE 47:11
hardened: gristle and not yet h. into the
  bone BURKE 109:17
harder: h. they fall FITZ 214:1
  they would be h. to them TROL 552:20
hard-faced: lot of h. men who look
  BALD 29:26
hardly: He's h. ever sick at sea GILB 227:31
Hardy: H. went down to botanize CHES 148:7
hare: Happy the h. at morning AUDEN 18:14
  h. limp'd trembling through KEATS 289:9
  h. sits snug in leaves HOFF 252:20
  it look'd like h. BARH 33:6
  like the hunting of the h. BLUNT 89:4
  lion than to start a h. SHAK 438:18
  outcry of the hunted h. BLAKE 85:10
  Take your h. when it is GLAS 229:21
  thou woldest fynde an h. CHAU 143:13
  triumph o'er the timid h. THOM 549:18
hare-brained: h. chatter of irresponsible
  DISR 185:18
harelip: makes the h. SHAK 454:22
hares: little hunted h. HODG 252:2
  merry brown h. came leaping KING 296:18
Hark: H., my soul COWP 165:25
  H., the dominant's persistence BROW 105:24
harlot: Every h. was a virgin once
  BLAKE 86:1
  h.'s cry from street BLAKE 85:17
  Portia is Brutus' h. SHAK 449:15
  prerogative of the h. throughout KIPL 305:13
harlots: devoured thy living with h.
  BIBLE 70:22
MOTHER OF H. AND ABOMINATIONS
  BIBLE 82:23
harm: believe that does h. to my wit
  SHAK 487:25
  content with my h. SHAK 426:4
  deceiving, could no longer h. ELIOT 202:20
  I fear we'll come to h. BALL 31:18
  mankind does most good or h. BAG 29:18
  no h. come to the state ANON 10:10
  no h. happen unto me PRAY 389:30
  No people do so much h. CREI 169:17
  prevent h. to others MILL 339:7
  Shall h. Macbeth SHAK 462:6
  to win us to our h. SHAK 458:18
harme: most h. to the mene puple
  LANG 309:26
harmless: Elephant, The only h.
  DONNE 190:3
  h. as doves BIBLE 65:33
  h. necessary cat SHAK 467:22

harmonies: mighty-mouth'd inventor
  of h. TENN 533:12
  tumult of thy mighty h. SHEL 502:13
harmonious: Such h. madness SHEL 504:24
  Uttering such dulcet and h. SHAK 470:7
harmony: best h. in a church MILT 351:26
  from heavenly h. DRYD 197:21
  H. in discord HOR 258:20
  h. is in immortal souls SHAK 468:15
  h. not understood POPE 379:11
  heaven drowsy with the h. SHAK 457:8
  Like h. in music WORD 580:11
  sentimentally I am disposed to h. LAMB 307:2
  their motions h. divine MILT 348:24
  them the other h. of prose DRYD 198:7
  there is a h. In autumn SHEL 501:7
  touches of sweet h. SHAK 468:15
  voice the h. of the world HOOK 255:20
  wherever there is a h. BROW 96:34
  with your ninefold h. MILT 344:10
harms: Ten thousand h. SHAK 421:19
harness: between the joints of the h.
  BIBLE 51:21
  girdeth on his h. boast BIBLE 51:16
  h. and not the horses that CANN 130:7
  hear the h. jingle HOUS 263:9
  least we'll die with h. SHAK 463:7
  My h. piece by piece Thou THOM 548:16
  To wait in heavy h. KIPL 304:6
harp: awake, lute and h. PRAY 393:16
  H. not on that string SHAK 481:10
  h., sackbut BIBLE 61:3
  h. that once through Tara's MOORE 356:9
  h. will I give thanks unto PRAY 392:11
  his wild h. slung behind MOORE 356:13
  merry h. with the lute PRAY 395:9
  No h. like my own could CAMP 128:20
  sing to the h. with a psalm PRAY 396:8
  To one clear h. in divers TENN 535:33
harpers: h. harping with their harps
  BIBLE 82:15
harping: harpers h. with their harps
  BIBLE 82:15
  He hath not heart for h. POUND 383:18
  Still h. on my daughter SHAK 432:6
harps: harpers harping with their h.
  BIBLE 82:15
  h., we hanged them up PRAY 399:3
  having every one of them h. BIBLE 81:27
harp-shaped: whisked past the h. hills
  THOM 546:22
harpy: conference with this h. SHAK 472:9
harrass: all the griefs that h. JOHN 282:23
Harriet: 'treatment of the H. problem'
  FREE 218:24
Harris: 'Bother Mrs H. DICK 179:29
Harrow: H. the house of the dead
  AUDEN 20:7
  toad beneath the h. knows KIPL 302:1
  Would h. up thy soul SHAK 431:5
harrow'd: having h. hell SPEN 515:17
Harry: banish not him thy H.'s SHAK 439:18
  Cry 'God for H. SHAK 444:3
  H., Harry SHAK 442:23
  Jerusalem shall H. die SHAK 442:21
  little touch of H. SHAK 444:12
  Promis'd to H. and his SHAK 443:12
  Such a King H. DRAY 193:11
harshness: enough no h. gives offence
  POPE 378:22
hart: h. desireth the water-brooks PRAY 392:6
  h. ungalled play SHAK 434:16
  lame man leap as an h. BIBLE 58:34
  pants the h. for cooling TATE 531:20
  roe or to a young h. upon BIBLE 57:14
  was I turn'd into a h. SHAK 487:21
harumfrodite: 'E's a kind of a giddy
  h. KIPL 302:23
harvest: according to the joy in h. BIBLE 58:6
  all the H. that I reap'd FITZ 212:21

are white already to h. BIBLE 71:41
grassy h. of the river-fields ARN 15:8
h. is past BIBLE 60:20
h. of a quiet eye WORD 580:5
h. truly is plenteous BIBLE 65:29
Have I no h. but a thorn HERB 247:14
if the h. is over BETJ 43:10
seedtime and h. BIBLE 45:37
Share my h. and my home HOOD 255:5
she laughs with a h. JERR 273:7
Where the thin h. waves COWP 168:26
harvests: Deep h. bury all his pride
  POPE 378:5
  h. of Arretium MAC 322:12
Harwich: about in a steamer from H.
  GILB 226:13
has: 'one of the *h.* beens HONE 254:7
hasard: *de l'observation le h.* PAST 369:16
  jamais n'abolira le h. MALL 327:11
Hasdrubal: of our name lost with H.
  HOR 261:13
Hasdrubale: *Nominis H. interempto*
  HOR 261:13
hässlich: *Welt h. und schlecht* NIET 363:8
Hast: *Ohne H.* GOET 230:15
haste: h. of a fool is the slowest SHAD 420:21
  h., persuade WHIT 571:11
  H. still pays haste SHAK 465:5
  h. to be rich shall not BIBLE 54:42
  I h. me to my bed SHAK 493:5
  I said in my h. PRAY 397:21
  Make h. slowly SUET 524:14
  Men love in h. BYRON 123:38
  Raw h. TENN 539:19
  This sweaty h. SHAK 429:11
  Though I am always in h. WESL 568:20
  Without h. GOET 230:15
  ye shall eat it in h. BIBLE 47:18
hasten: So do our minutes h. SHAK 493:19
hasty: man in his h. days BRID 92:10
hat: A' brushes his h. a mornings
  SHAK 472:25
  Antichrist in that lewd h. JONS 283:15
  away with a h. like that LOOS 318:4
  complete with h. and gloves CALV 127:16
  hang your h. on a pension MACN 326:8
  h. of antique shape ARN 14:13
  himself in a shocking bad h. SURT 525:21
  my knee, my h., and hand BROW 96:3
  No h. upon his head SHAK 431:28
  with my h. upon my head JOHN 280:26
  without pulling off his h. JOHN 274:27
  your h. has got a hole in't CANN 130:7
  your h. upon your brows SHAK 462:16
hatch'd: new-h., unfledg'd comrade
  SHAK 430:19
hatched: an' h. different ELIOT 200:11
hatches: is continually under h. KEATS 293:28
hatchet: did it with my little h. WASH 565:1
hatcheth: h. them not BIBLE 60:25
Hatching: H. vain empires MILT 346:15
hate: away this murdherin' h. OCAS 364:17
  cherish those hearts that h. SHAK 447:12
  do good to them which h. BIBLE 69:21
  English began to h. KIPL 298:1
  generation of them that h. BIBLE 47:24
  glance of supernatural h. BYRON 126:7
  h. a Frenchman NELS 360:12
  h. all Boets and Bainters GEOR 223:34
  h. all that don't love FARQ 210:11
  h. and detest that animal SWIFT 526:23
  h. any one that we know HAZL 243:18
  h. for arts that caus'd HAZL 244:2
  h. him as I do hell-pains POPE 376:20
  h. him for he is a Christian SHAK 473:19
  h. of those ye guard SHAK 465:29
  h. that dreadful hollow KIPL 304:6
  h. the French because they TENN 539:25
  h. the idle pleasures GOLD 232:6
  SHAK 480:19

h. the man you have hurt	TAC 531:8
have seen much to h. here	MILL 340:2
I h. and I love	CAT 137:14
I h. false words	LAND 309:11
I h. the crowd	LAND 309:5
I h. the unholy masses	HOR 260:13
I h. the whole race...There	WELL 568:5
immortal h.)	MILT 345:3
in love, or in h.	STEV 521:26
In time we h. that which	SHAK 421:25
large the h.	AUDEN 18:8
Let them h.	ACC 1:3
must h. and death return	SHEL 501:3
need not be to h.	BYRON 120:34
nought did I in h.	SHAK 477:22
Of a pure impartial h.	THOR 550:28
present day is that men h.	MELB 336:20
religion to make us h.	SWIFT 527:7
roughness breedeth h.	BACON 26:25
sprung from my only h.	SHAK 482:4
Ten men love what I h.	BROW 104:7
that h. him flee before him	PRAY 394:6
There's no h. lost	MIDD 338:20
Those fellows h. us	LAMB 307:34
time to h.	BIBLE 55:12
'tis delicious to h. you	MOORE 356:24
to h. your neighbour	MAC 324:3
hated: being h., don't give way	KIPL 299:22
H. by fools	SWIFT 528:8
H. by one he loves	SHAK 451:23
h. the ruling few than	BENT 41:1
never saw a brute I h.	BROW 99:29
Past reason h.	SHAK 495:7
She might have h.	BROW 101:24
hateful: Must learn the h. art	KING 296:13
shamed life a h.	SHAK 464:14
hater: he was a very good h.	JOHN 280:11
hates: h. dogs and babies	ROST 410:14
He h. our sacred nation	SHAK 465:29
just heaven now h.	ANON 5:14
hateth: h. his brother	BIBLE 81:7
rod h. his son	BIBLE 53:38
hath: one that h. shall be given	BIBLE 68:4
hating: don't give way to h.	KIPL 299:22
in h. all other nations	GASK 222:4
special reason for h. school	BEER 37:21
hatless: young man lands h.	BETJ 42:12
hatred: from envy, h., and malice	PRAY 385:16
h. for the Tory Party	BEVAN 44:16
h. or bitterness toward's	CAV 137:18
like love to h. turn'd	CONG 160:15
stalled ox and h.	BIBLE 54:6
hats: inside men's Sunday h.	BROW 103:15
so many shocking bad h.	WELL 567:22
They wat their h. aboon	BALL 31:19
haughtiness: h. of soul	ADD 1:18
haughty: Greece or h. Rome	JONS 284:22
h. spirit before a fall	BIBLE 54:8
haunches: on silent h.	SAND 413:26
haunt: all the h. be ours	SHAK 423:10
h. of flies on summer eves	KEATS 291:21
h. thy days and chill thy	KEATS 290:30
Haunted: H. for ever by the eternal	WORD 579:7
shape of a woman has h.	KEATS 294:3
summer eves by h. stream	MILT 342:19
That is a h. town to me	LANG 309:17
haunts: Are h. meet for thee	ARN 13:2
h. of coot and hern	TENN 532:30
he h. wakes	SHAK 491:20
mothers and fathers that h. us	IBSEN 269:21
hause-bane: 'Ye'll sit on his white h.	BALL 32:8
haute: h. la tempète et se rit	BAUD 35:6
hautes: des choses grandes et h.	MONT 354:12
have: because other folks h.	FIEL 211:17
h. and to hold from this	PRAY 389:4
H. more than thou showest	SHAK 453:15
if he will h. him	PRAY 390:17

I h. thee not	SHAK 459:15
long as you h. your life	JAMES 271:20
they will not let you h. it	HAZL 243:21
have-his-carcase: h., next to the perpetual	DICK 182:33
haven: their h. under the hill	TENN 532:18
have-nots: haves and the h.	CERV 138:17
haves: h. and the have-nots	CERV 138:17
Havoc: Cry, 'H.!'	SHAK 450:12
hawk: Gentle as falcon or h.	SKEL 508:16
h. at eagles with a dove	HERB 248:9
His h. to fetch the wild-fowl	BALL 32:8
know a h. from a handsaw	SHAK 432:18
hawks: ...Dark h. hear us	JOYCE 286:8
h. favoured an air strike	BART 34:24
Hawkshaw: H., the detective	TAYL 532:7
hawthorn: h. bush a sweeter shade	SHAK 446:19
Stream from the h.	HOUS 264:20
Under the h. in the dale	MILT 342:19
hay: dance an antic h.	MARL 329:17
desire to a bottle of h.	SHAK 471:4
eating h. when you're faint	CARR 135:31
I made h. while the sun	BETJ 43:10
lie tumbling in the h.	SHAK 491:17
that's what h. looks like	MARY 333:16
world is a bundle of h.	BYRON 124:32
haystack: Beside the h. in the floods	MORR 358:11
hazard: h. in the glorious enterprise	MILT 345:1
He has put to h. his ease	BURKE 110:26
Men that h. all	SHAK 466:16
stand the h. of the die	SHAK 481:19
haze: seaward h.	HARDY 240:15
hazel-nut: chariot is an empty h.	SHAK 481:28
Hazlitt: we cannot write like H.	STEV 522:10
he: Art thou h. that should	BIBLE 66:1
H. that hath wife and children	BACON 26:31
poorest h. that is in England	RAIN 404:7
head: bear with a sore h.	MARR 331:4
begins a journey in my h.	SHAK 493:5
body with so old a h.	SHAK 467:26
bowed his comely h.	MARV 332:10
broken h. in Cold Bath	MAC 324:23
cuts the wrong man's h. off	DICK 182:3
dawn many a h. has turned white	MULL 359:1
enjoyed at the h. of a school	WALP 562:18
gently lay my h.	BROW 97:6
God be in my h.	ANON 5:9
good grey h.	TENN 541:7
h. and front of my offending	SHAK 473:24
h. and his hairs were white	BIBLE 81:14
h. and which was the tail	BRIG 93:6
h. could carry all he knew	GOLD 231:3
h. is as full of quarrels	SHAK 483:1
h. is not more native	SHAK 429:20
h. of a family off	DICK 181:23
H. of a traveller	HOUS 266:9
h. off with a golden axe	SHAK 458:10
h. thou dost with oil anoint	SCOT 419:5
h. to contrive	GIBB 224:28
h. upon our battlements	SHAK 458:3
h. which statuaries loved	MAC 323:33
heart or in the h.	SHAK 467:9
heart runs away with his h.	COLM 159:5
He had a h. to contrive	CLAR 152:19
her h. on her knee	SHAK 476:27
Hers is th. upon which	PATER 369:18
hidden her h.	SWIN 530:7
his guts in his h.	SHAK 486:29
If you can keep your h.	KIPL 299:22
I'll hold my h. so high	HOR 259:10
incessantly stand on your h.	CARR 133:22
It shall bruise thy h.	BIBLE 45:20
I've a h. like a concertina	KIPL 298:7
Lay your sleeping h.	AUDEN 19:17
left hand is under my h.	BIBLE 56:21
like God's own h.	COL 155:11
madness was not of the h.	BYRON 125:2

Majesty's h. on a sign-post	MAC 324:2
make you shorter by the h.	ELIZ 205:26
Man with the h.	TENN 542:9
Megrim at her h.	POPE 381:9
My deeds upon my h.	SHAK 468:1
my h. is a map	FIEL 211:21
My h. is bloody	HENL 245:4
My ho h. halls	JOYCE 286:8
never broke any man's h.	SHAK 444:6
not where to lay his h.	BIBLE 65:18
nowhere yet to rest my h.	ARN 13:8
Off with his h.	CIBB 151:12
out of King Charles's h.	DICK 177:7
parboiled h. upon a stake	GRAH 233:16
plateau of Spain forming a h.	HARDY 239:13
poured it on his h.	BIBLE 68:8
repairs his drooping h.	MILT 343:17
rolling his h.	MAC 324:14
seems no bigger than his h.	SHAK 455:14
shadow of her fair vast h.	SWIN 528:26
shake his sapient h.	ARN 15:12
shake of his poor little h.	GILB 227:16
stand. "On my h.	DISR 185:32
star with my exalted h.	HERR 248:19
that by shaking his h.	SHER 505:29
thou bald h.	BIBLE 51:24
Thou wilt show my h.	DANT 171:20
to get one's h. cut off	CARR 135:13
touches a hair of yon gray h.	WHIT 571:18
under my h. a sod	BALL 31:14
Uneasy lies the h. that	SHAK 441:30
what seem'd his h.	MILT 346:24
What though his h. be empty	SWIFT 527:4
which binds so dear a h.	SHEL 499:3
your h. are all numbered	BIBLE 65:36
headache: awake with a dismal h.	GILB 226:12
to-day I happen to have a h.	CARR 135:14
headaches: In h. and in worry	AUDEN 18:10
head-in-air: Johnny h.	PUDN 402:7
headland: naked top Of some bold h.	WORD 577:10
Headlong: H. themselves they threw	MILT 348:27
was h. sent	MILT 346:4
Headmasters: H. have powers at their	CHUR 150:22
Headpiece: H. filled with straw	ELIOT 203:8
Prompt hand and h. clever	HOUS 265:1
heads: had ever very empty h.	BACON 25:7
H. were toward Eternity	DICK 183:16
Hide their diminished h.	MILT 347:13
Hung their h.	SHAK 447:3
lay their h. together	SMITH 511:22
Lift up your h.	PRAY 390:24
stood them on their h.	BARR 34:11
Their h. are green	LEAR 312:6
head-stone: become the h. in the corner	PRAY 398:2
Halt by the h. naming	HOUS 266:2
headstrong: She's as h. as an allegory	SHER 506:15
head-waiter: plump h. at the Cock	TENN 544:9
Heady: H., not strong	POPE 375:20
heal: h. me of my grievous wound	TENN 535:27
That fame can never h.	AYT 24:5
What wound did ever h.	SHAK 475:11
When there is none to h.	KEATS 293:4
heal'd: thy wound be throughly h.	SHAK 490:32
healed: They have h. also the hurt	BIBLE 60:19
with his stripes we are h.	BIBLE 59:22
healer: compassion of the h.'s art	ELIOT 202:21
It is not a great h.	COMP 159:12
healeth: h. those that are broken	PRAY 399:19
healing: arise with h. in his wings	BIBLE 62:3

expected h. wings could see VAUG 555:11
h. of the nations BIBLE 83:1
h. voice of Christian charity BURKE 111:2
no h. has been necessary COMP 159:12
Wordsworth's h. power ARN 13:18
health: art so far from my h. PRAY 390:16
h. and living now begins SHAK 486:1
h., and quiet breathing KEATS 288:20
h. and their complexion AUST 22:17
h. and wealth have missed HUNT 268:10
h. and wealth long to live PRAY 385:5
h. unbought DRYD 196:5
Here's a double h. to thee BYRON 125:32
he that will this h. deny DYER 199:19
horse's h. SHAK 454:28
Importing h. and graveness SHAK 436:17
innocence and h. GOLD 230:18
in sickness and in h. PRAY 389:4
Look to your h. WALT 564:12
overthroweth your h. BACON 26:17
spirit of h. or goblin SHAK 430:24
there is no h. in us PRAY 384:12
thine h. shall spring forth BIBLE 60:5
thy saving h. among all PRAY 394:4
Where h. and plenty cheered GOLD 230:16
healthful: h. Spirit of thy grace PRAY 385:7
Without disease the h. SURR 524:20
healthy: h. bones of a single Pomeranian
                                   BISM 84:22
H. by temp'rance POPE 377:5
h. state of political life MILL 339:10
h. stomach is nothing BUTL 118:31
heap: h. of all your winnings KIPL 300:1
was struck all of a h. SHER 506:5
waters to stand on an h. PRAY 395:5
heap'd: error be too highly h. SHAK 427:17
heapeth: he h. up riches PRAY 391:31
hear: Be swift to h. BIBLE 80:10
ꞏcan h. my Thisby's face SHAK 471:18
child may joy to h. BLAKE 87:5
h. it in the deep heart's YEATS 585:17
H. my law, O my people PRAY 395:3
h. no more at all STEV 523:5
H. not my steps SHAK 460:1
H., O Israel BIBLE 48:20
H. the other side AUG 21:20
h. the word of the Lord BIBLE 61:2
He cannot choose but h. COL 155:6
He that hath ears to h. BIBLE 68:28
houses h. clocks ticking BETJ 42:12
I h. thy shrill delight SHEL 504:18
I h. you HOUS 263:5
in such wise h. them read PRAY 386:5
Lord, ꞏh. our prayers PRAY 388:21
shall he not h. PRAY 396:2
she is sure to h. AUST 22:12
They never would h. SWIFT 527:27
to h. the sins they love SHAK 478:3
to h. those things which BIBLE 69:29
We beseech thee to h. us PRAY 385:18
we can always h. them AUDEN 19:13
we shall h. it BROW 98:20
would h. the mighty crack ADD 2:30
you will h. me DISR 184:10
You will h. more good things HAZL 243:16
heard: after it was h. no more WORD 578:16
Cannot be h. so high SHAK 455:14
Enough that he h. it once BROW 98:20
ever h. Any good LAND 309:6
have ye not h. BIBLE 59:9
h. for their much speaking BIBLE 64:23
H. melodies are sweet KEATS 291:4
H., not regarded SHAK 439:35
I have h. of thee BIBLE 53:12
I will be h. GARR 221:17
more he h. PUNCH 402:25
only tell us what he h. GRAY 235:24
then is h. no more SHAK 463:6
twice I have also h. PRAY 393:20
Which we have h. and known PRAY 395:3

You ain't h. nothin' yet JOLS 283:9
hearers: attentive and favourable h.
                                   HOOK 255:19
edification of the h. BURKE 108:14
not h. only BIBLE 80:10
too deep for his h. GOLD 231:17
heareth: thy servant h. BIBLE 49:36
hearing: Fall asleep, or h. die SHAK 447:3
passionate my sense of h. SHAK 456:25
thought he was within h. JOHN 278:22
hearken: h. than the fat of rams BIBLE 50:4
hearkened: hadst h. to my commandments
                                   BIBLE 59:15
h. not unto the voice PRAY 397:5
hears: h. its winding murmur ARN 12:22
She neither h. nor sees WORD 581:10
hearsay: have formerly lived by h.
                                   BUNY 107:39
walls have h. FONS 216:4
hearse: laureate h. where Lycid lies
                                   MILT 343:15
Underneath this sable h. BROW 97:25
walk before the h. GARR 221:11
hearses: frequent h. shall besiege POPE 376:9
heart: abundance of the h. BIBLE 66:9
abundance weakens his own h. SHAK 493:2
accompany me with a pure h. PRAY 384:10
all's here about my h. SHAK 437:14
Batter my h. DONNE 189:8
beating of man's h. AUDEN 20:6
Blessed are the pure in h. BIBLE 64:6
blind side of the h. CHES 146:18
brains in my head and the h. HOUS 266:7
break, my h. SHAK 430:1
broken h. lies here MAC 322:10
Bury my h. at Wounded Knee BENET 40:20
Calais' lying in my h. MARY 333:13
calm sunshine of the h. CONS 162:4
can no longer tear his h. SWIFT 528:12
consenting language of the h. GAY 223:5
curse with their h. PRAY 393:19
Dear h. how like you WYATT 583:22
deceiveth his own h. BIBLE 80:11
desires of the h. are as crooked AUDEN 18:13
do any man's h. good SHAK 469:29
drops That visit my sad h. SHAK 449:15
education of the h. SCOTT 419:4
Englishman whose h. is BAG 28:31
faint h. ne'er wan BURNS 115:14
faith of the h. alone make both God
                                   LUTH 320:17
Far other aims his h. had GOLD 230:22
felt along the h. WORD 578:4
Floodgate of the deeper h. FLEC 214:24
give me back my h. again GRAN 234:4
God be in my h. ANON 5:9
good Christian at her h. POPE 377:19
great no h. I had to choose LA B 306:14
harden Pharaoh's h. BIBLE 47:11
has stabb'd me to the h. GAY 222:6
hast cleft my h. in twain SHAK 435:17
have garner'd up my h. SHAK 476:18
having war in his h. PRAY 393:12
head and woman with the h. TENN 542:9
hear it in the deep h.'s YEATS 585:17
h. and my flesh rejoice PRAY 395:11
H. and soul do sing SIDN 508:1
h. and stomach of a king ELIZ 206:4
h. and voice would fail CLAR 152:23
h. argues, not the mind ARN 13:20
h. as sound as a bell SHAK 472:23
h. *bleeds for his country* JOHN 274:21
h. cheer thee in the days BIBLE 56:10
h. clings to and confides LUTH 320:18
h. doth need a language COL 157:8
h. fail because of him BIBLE 50:9
h. grows older HOPK 256:26
h. has felt the tender GAY 223:3
h. has its reasons which PASC 369:10
h. hath 'scap'd this sorrow SHAK 494:14

h. high-sorrowful and cloy'd KEATS 291:7
h.—how shall I say BROW 102:22
h. in his grave is lying MOORE 356:17
h. is a small thing QUAR 403:9
h. is deceitful above all BIBLE 60:24
h. is Highland GALT 221:2
h. is inditing of a good PRAY 392:14
h. is like a singing bird ROSS 408:23
h. is on the left MOL 353:17
h. is sick TENN 536:21
h. is strong and the human BAG 28:30
h. keeps empty in thy tomb KING 296:11
h. less bounding at emotion ARN 15:9
h. lies plain ARN 12:22
h. no longer stirred HOUS 266:2
h. of a man is deprest GAY 222:26
h. of a true *Englishman* ADD 2:19
h. of kings is unsearchable BIBLE 54:25
h. of lead POPE 375:18
h. one strangling golden hair ROSS 410:2
h. out of your breast HOUS 264:18
h. runs away with his head COLM 159:5
H.'s denying BARN 34:4
H. speaks to heart NEWM 362:7
h. that has truly lov'd MOORE 356:5
h. the keener ANON 8:9
h. to pity CHUR 149:3
h. unfortified SHAK 429:26
h. untravell'd fondly turns GOLD 231:24
h. were as fire and could SWIN 528:16
h. within blood-tinctured BROW 98:3
H. within, and God o'erhead LONG 317:3
Here's a h. for every fate BYRON 126:1
He sought, For his lost h. SHEL 504:5
he tears out the h. KNOW 305:17
His flaw'd h. SHAK 456:7
home the h. you gave me DRAY 193:16
How the h. listened while THOM 549:26
human h. by which we live WORD 579:14
humble and a contrite h. KIPL 302:7
I am gathered to thy h. MEYN 338:14
I am sick at h. SHAK 429:5
I feel my h. new open'd SHAK 447:9
If thy h. fails thee ELIZ 206:1
I had lock'd my h. BALL 32:11
I had rather coin my h. SHAK 451:21
in the h. or in the head SHAK 467:9
I said to H. BELL 39:17
is the darling of my h. CAREY 130:26
Is your h. at rest FLET 215:19
it be the h. to conceive JUN 287:5
I wish my h. had never ANON 7:15
I would eat his h. SHAK 473:3
Land of H.'s Desire YEATS 585:19
laughter the h. is sorrowful BIBLE 54:1
lent out my h. with usury LAMB 307:24
light h. lives long SHAK 457:14
little body with a mighty h. SHAK 443:13
look in thy h. and write SIDN 507:17
loos'd our h. in tears ARN 13:17
Lord looketh on the h. BIBLE 50:6
make a stone of the h. YEATS 585:2
Make me a clean h. PRAY 393:6
make my seated h. knock SHAK 458:20
Makes my h. go pit-a-pat BROW 103:17
makes the h. grow fonder ANON 4:10
making melody in your h. BIBLE 78:5
man after his own h. BIBLE 50:1
Mercy has a human h. BLAKE 88:7
merry h. doeth good like BIBLE 54:12
merry h. maketh a cheerful BIBLE 54:5
mighty h. is lying still WORD 581:15
My h. aches KEATS 291:16
my h. also in the midst PRAY 390:19
My h. at some noonday BROW 101:15
My h. in hiding HOPK 257:5
My h. is heavy GOET 230:4
My h. is turned to stone SHAK 476:11
My h. leaps up when I behold WORD 578:19
my h. puts forth its pain BROO 94:5

My h.'s in the Highlands   BURNS 114:25
my h. waketh   BIBLE 57:1
My h. was hot within me   PRAY 391:30
My h. would hear her   TENN 540:12
my little h.   SHAK 456:26
my poor h. doth think   LYLY 321:16
naked thinking h.   DONNE 188:1
natural language of the h.   SHAD 420:19
naughtiness of thine h.   BIBLE 50:8
nearer to the H.'s Desire   FITZ 213:16
never a crack in my h.   YEATS 586:5
never has ached with a h.   SWIN 529:7
no man layeth it to h.   BIBLE 60:2
no matter from the h.   SHAK 487:17
nor his h. to report   SHAK 471:10
not more native to the h.   SHAK 429:20
not of the head, but h.   BYRON 125:2
not our h. burn within us   BIBLE 71:18
not your h. be troubled   BIBLE 72:30
not your h. away   HOUS 262:20
now from the h. of joy   BEEC 37:9
no woman's h. So big   SHAK 489:6
of mischief he had a h.   GIBB 224:28
oft has made my h. to ache   BLAKE 87:7
on my h. they tread now   SHAK 479:15
Open my h. and you will   BROW 100:14
Open not thine h. to every   BIBLE 62:28
out my reins and my h.   PRAY 391:4
Out-worn h.   YEATS 585:14
pageant of his bleeding h.   ARN 13:9
Possess thy h.   BRID 92:21
prithee send me back my h.   SUCK 524:12
rag-and-bone shop of the h.   YEATS 584:15
rebuke hath broken my h.   PRAY 394:12
red pavilion of my h.   THOM 547:23
revolting and a rebellious h.   BIBLE 60:17
seal upon thine h.   BIBLE 57:11
Shakespeare unlocked his h.   BROW 101:10
She wants a h.   POPE 377:22
sighing of a contrite h.   PRAY 385:22
since man's h. is small   KIPL 303:16
smoke and flame I lost my h.   HOUS 266:4
softer pillow than my h.   BYRON 126:16
some h. did break   TENN 536:3
some h. indignant breaks   MOORE 356:10
So the h. be right   RAL 404:18
sure of his unspotted h.   PEELE 371:8
Sweeping up the H.   DICK 183:17
sweet concurrence of the h.   HERR 250:11
ta'en out thy h. o' flesh   BALL 32:3
Take any h.   GILB 228:15
Take h. of grace   GILB 228:14
Taming my wild h. to thy   SHAK 472:22
that earth upon thy h.   KIPL 298:8
that had the lion's h.   CHUR 150:21
that maketh glad the h.   PRAY 396:20
that sting my h.   SHAK 475:9
That the bruis'd h. was   SHAK 474:4
That the h. grows old   YEATS 586:20
their captain, the h.   SHAK 442:15
then burst his mighty h.   SHAK 450:28
there will your h. be also   BIBLE 64:26
this h. Shall break   SHAK 454:2
thought my shrivel'd h.   HERB 247:21
thou hast my h.   PRIOR 400:21
thou wilt ease thine h.   BEDD 36:23
thy beak from out my h.   POE 375:6
thy h. lies open   TENN 542:14
thy wine with a merry h.   BIBLE 55:28
tiger's h. wrapp'd   SHAK 446:16
to get your h.'s desire   SHAW 497:33
to mend the h.   POPE 375:11
to my dead h. run them   STEV 523:11
'tween my h. and tongue   SHAK 449:22
twist the sinews of thy h.   BLAKE 87:15
warmth about my h. like a load   KEATS 294:4
wear him In my h.'s core   SHAK 434:2
wear my h. upon my sleeve   SHAK 473:15
well as want of h.   HOOD 254:20
Were not my h. at rest   SEDL 419:13

Were with his h.   BYRON 121:16
where I my h., safe-left   SIDN 507:27
Where my h. lies   BROW 102:34
Whispers the o'er-fraught h.   SHAK 462:16
With a h. for any fate   LONG 317:5
with my h. in't   SHAK 485:13
without the h.   GAY 222:9
With your crooked h.   AUDEN 18:11
would not have such a h.   SHAK 462:23
wouldst wish thine own h.   KEATS 290:30
your h. to a dog to tear   KIPL 302:3
heart-ache: sleep to say we end The h.
    SHAK 433:8
heart-break: h. in the heart of things
    GIBS 225:5
heart-easing: most h. things   KEATS 292:9
heart-throbs: count time by h.   BAIL 29:21
hearth: By this still h.   TENN 543:21
from an unextinguished h.   SHEL 502:14
genial h.   WORD 581:16
Save the cricket on the h.   MILT 342:5
woman for the h.   TENN 542:9
hearth-fire: h. and the home-acre   KIPL 299:21
hearth-stane: His clean h.   BURNS 113:5
heartily: h. rejoice in the strength   PRAY 396:3
heartless: h., witless nature   HOUS 265:10
hearts: cold h. and muddy   BURKE 111:11
Combine your h. in one   SHAK 445:16
day star arise in your h.   BIBLE 80:34
draw H. after them   MILT 350:2
Ensanguin'd h.   COWP 167:16
finite h. that yearn   BROW 105:30
first in the h. of his   LEE 313:7
harden not your h.   PRAY 396:4
h. and intellects like   MILL 339:22
h. are dry as summer dust   WORD 577:11
h. are more than coronets   TENN 537:29
h. beating each to each   BROW 102:14
h. I lost my own   HOUS 265:6
H. just as pure and fair   GILB 226:5
h. of gold and lungs   BELL 39:28
h. that honour could not   BROO 94:27
H. that have lost their   HOUS 265:9
h. That spaniel'd me   SHAK 423:5
h. were fulfilled with   SWIN 528:24
H. wound up with love   SPEN 515:9
hidden in each other's h.   DICK 179:17
is enthroned in the h.   SHAK 467:27
keep your h. and minds   BIBLE 78:21
let not your h. be hardened   VILL 557:4
Lift up your h.   PRAY 387:21
met, but not our h.   HOOD 255:13
opportunity for a jining of h.   DICK 181:1
our h. are great   TENN 535:1
our h., though stout   LONG 317:2
Pluck their h. from them   SHAK 444:26
sleepless children's h. are glad   BETJ 42:8
stout h. and sharp swords   BIRK 84:14
take away our h. o' stone   OCAS 364:17
Their hands upon their h.   HOUS 264:23
their h. are in the right   DISR 186:12
thousand h. beat happily   BYRON 120:20
To live in h. we leave   CAMP 128:19
to place women's h.   WEBS 566:19
to steal away your h.   SHAK 451:1
Two h. that beat as one   HALM 238:10
undeveloped h.   FORS 216:22
union of hands and h.   TAYL 532:6
unto whom all h. be open   PRAY 387:7
When h. have once mingled   SHEL 501:22
Who sing to find your h.   FLEC 214:9
wins more h.   ANON 6:7
You are high in our h.   BETJ 42:15
you hard h.   SHAK 448:6
heart-strings: jesses were my dear h.
    SHAK 475:21
heat: bear the burden and the h.   ARN 13:23
burden and h. of the day   BIBLE 67:15
cold and h.   BIBLE 45:37
Fear no more the h. o'   SHAK 428:22

Giving more light than h.   SHAK 430:21
have neither h. nor light   WEBS 566:25
H. me these irons hot   SHAK 452:22
H. not a furnace for your   SHAK 446:25
h. of life in the handful   CONR 161:24
Lap your loneliness in h.   BETJ 42:7
nor any h.   BIBLE 82:3
not without dust and h.   MILT 351:24
Surprised I was with sudden h.   SOUT 514:19
white h. of this revolution   WILS 574:17
you can't stand the h.   TRUM 553:20
heated: When h. in the chase   TATE 531:20
heath: h., with withering brake   COWP 168:26
h. wore the appearance   HARDY 241:19
said to understand the h.   HARDY 241:20
sword sung on the barren h.   BLAKE 86:19
There's the wind on the h.   BORR 90:5
Upon the h.   SHAK 458:1
Upon this blasted h. you   SHAK 458:13
heathen: be exalted among the h.
    PRAY 392:21
Guard even h. things   CHES 146:19
h. heart that puts her   KIPL 302:10
h. in his blindness   HEBER 244:6
h. make much ado   PRAY 392:20
h. so furiously rage   PRAY 389:15
in perils by the h.   BIBLE 77:12
machine for converting the H.   CARL 131:6
repetitions, as the h. do   BIBLE 64:23
To be avenged of the h.   PRAY 399:24
To break the h.   TENN 534:11
very h. in the carnal part   POPE 377:19
heather: red h. we dance together
    CALV 127:25
heaths: some game on these lone h.
    HAZL 243:32
heat-oppressed: Proceeding from the
    h. brain   SHAK 459:15
heave: angels h. up Sir Launcelot   MAL 328:7
Heaven: All earth can take or H.   SHEL 501:2
All I seek, the h. above   STEV 522:28
all of h. we have below   ADD 2:6
All this and h. too   HENRY 245:22
all to H.   JONES 283:13
appeared a great wonder in h.   BIBLE 82:10
art thou fallen from h.   BIBLE 58:13
ascend to h.   FIRM 212:2
bask in H.'s blue smile   SHEL 500:5
beat on H.'s shore   BLAKE 85:15
Be but the shadow of H.   MILT 348:21
become the hoped-for h.   MILL 339:22
be hell that are not h.   MARL 329:8
betwixt H. and Charing Cross   THOM 548:25
bring all H. before mine   MILT 342:10
bring up the rear in h.   BROW 96:26
by a whirlwind into h.   BIBLE 51:22
call it the Road to H.   BALL 32:5
coming of the King of H.   ANON 9:1
created the h. and the earth   BIBLE 44:22
day when h. was falling   HOUS 265:7
do in h. we are ignorant   SWIFT 527:9
Down from the verge of H.   MILT 348:27
Earth and high h. are fixt   HOUS 264:3
earth breaks up and h.   BROW 99:20
Earth's crammed with h.   BROW 97:33
eleven who went to h.   ANON 6:5
enter into the kingdom of h.   BIBLE 64:11
eye of h. to garnish   SHAK 452:25
family in h. and earth   BIBLE 77:24
Father which art in h.   BIBLE 64:24
flowerless fields of h.   SWIN 528:14
from a high and frosty h.   BRID 92:13
gave them food from h.   PRAY 395:6
Give the jolly h. above   STEV 522:27
God's in his h.   BROW 103:21
God we know the way to h.   ELST 206:11
have sinned against h.   BIBLE 70:19
h. above me and the moral   KANT 288:8
H. and earth shall pass   BIBLE 67:31
H. and Earth are not ruthful   LAO 310:2

H. and Hell   TENN 535:16
H. and Nature seem'd   JONS 284:2
h. be in these lips   MARL 329:10
h. by sea as by land   GILB 225:7
h. commences ere the world   GOLD 230:20
h. drowsy with the harmony   SHAK 457:8
H. in a Wild Flower   BLAKE 85:8
H. in Hell's despair   BLAKE 87:18
H. is above all yet   SHAK 447:4
H. is for thee too high   MILT 349:4
H. itself would stoop   MILT 341:22
H. lies about us in our   WORD 579:5
h. nor earth have been   SHAK 449:17
H. not grim but fair   BROW 98:34
h. peep through the blanket   SHAK 459:2
H. sends us good meat   GARR 221:12
H.'s light forever shines   SHEL 499:26
H. soon sets right   BROW 100:4
H.'s peculiar care   SOM 513:3
H. still guards the right   SHAK 479:5
H. stops the nose at it   SHAK 476:20
h.'s vaults should crack   SHAK 456:8
H. take my soul   SHAK 452:29
h., thou art there   PRAY 399:5
H. to be deluded by him   LEE 313:9
H. vows to keep him   JONS 284:2
H. was in him   WALT 564:16
h. where they would be   PRAY 397:10
h. will help you   LA F 306:17
Hell I suffer seems a H.   MILT 347:15
His blessed part to H.   SHAK 447:16
hot the eye of h.   SHAK 492:28
house as nigh h. as my own   MORE 357:15
how the floor of h.   SHAK 468:15
hurl my soul from h.   SHAK 477:21
I cannot go to h.   NORF 364:1
If h. would make me such   SHAK 477:12
I heard a voice from h.   BIBLE 82:15
I hope for h. thereby   CASW 136:16
in the nurseries of H.   THOM 548:6
I saw h. opened   BIBLE 82:25
it arrive at H.'s vault   MARV 331:17
kindred points of h. and home   WORD 583:1
kingdom of h. is at hand   BIBLE 63:35
Kingdom of H. to all believers   PRAY 384:17
lead you in at H.'s gate   BLAKE 86:8
leave to H. the measure   JOHN 283:5
leaving mercy to h.   FIEL 211:24
less native to high H.   THOM 548:2
Let h. exist   BORG 89:23
look how high the h. is   PRAY 396:17
Lord made h. and earth   BIBLE 47:24
love is h.   SCOTT 416:17
made h. and earth   PRAY 388:20
Made life a h. on earth   KEPP 295:12
maie merily meete in h.   MORE 357:20
met my dearest foe in h.   SHAK 430:4
more than all in h.   BYRON 121:35
mushroom On whom the dew of h.   FORD 216:13
my thirtieth year to h.   THOM 547:6
new h. and a new earth   BIBLE 82:30
new h., new earth   SHAK 421:7
open face of h.   KEATS 292:27
Parting is all we know of h.   DICK 183:20
pavilion of H. is bare   SHEL 500:7
permission of all-ruling H.   MILT 345:8
Puts all H. in a Rage   BLAKE 85:9
quincunx of h. runs low   BROW 95:19
saw h. opened   BIBLE 73:37
serene lights of h.   SHEL 504:7
shalt have treasure in h.   BIBLE 67:9
sings hymns at h.'s gate   SHAK 493:6
stand ye gazing up into h.   BIBLE 73:21
steep and thorny way to h.   SHAK 430:18
summons thee to h. or to hell   SHAK 460:1
symbol of the power of H.   MOORE 355:18
theirs is the kingdom of h.   BIBLE 64:6
then h. mocks itself   SHAK 475:22

then the h. espy   HERB 247:18
There may be h.   BROW 105:23
there was silence in h.   BIBLE 82:5
there was war in h.   BIBLE 82:11
things are the sons of h.   JOHN 281:6
this is the gate of h.   BIBLE 46:20
Those who win h.   BROW 102:27
to be young was very h.   WORD 577:21
top of it reached to h.   BIBLE 46:18
To shun the h. that leads   SHAK 495:7
trouble deaf h. with my   SHAK 493:6
'Twould ring the bells of H.   HODG 252:2
under an English h.   BROO 94:30
unextinguishable laugh in h.   BROW 95:16
waitest for the spark from h.   ARN 14:17
waiting for the spark from h.   ARN 14:15
water'd h. with their tears   BLAKE 87:16
We are all going to H.   GAIN 220:24
weariness Of climbing h.   SHEL 505:5
what's a h.   BROW 98:24
Which we ascribe to h.   SHAK 420:28
who hath made h. and earth   PRAY 398:14
with all the company of h.   PRAY 387:23
without a thought of H.   BROW 96:23
yourselves treasures in h.   BIBLE 64:25
heaven-eyed: h. creature sleeps in earth   WORD 577:18
heavenly: company of the h. host   BLAKE 88:29
fools by h. compulsion   SHAK 453:11
great anger in those h.   VIRG 557:9
H. Hurt, it gives   DICK 184:1
h. touches ne'er touch'd   SHAK 492:27
possession of this h. sight   SHAK 477:21
heavens: are clothed with the h.   TRAH 551:17
create new h. and a new earth   BIBLE 60:14
Distorts the H. from pole   BLAKE 85:23
eternal in the h.   BIBLE 77:6
H., and all the Powers   PRAY 384:16
h. are the work of thy   PRAY 396:13
h. declare the glory   PRAY 390:11
h. dropped at the presence   PRAY 394:7
h.' embroidered cloths   YEATS 585:9
h. fill with commerce   TENN 538:24
h. my wide roof-tree   AYT 24:12
h. themselves blaze forth   SHAK 449:18
h. themselves, the planets   SHAK 486:22
most ancient h.   WORD 579:16
promise h. free from strife   CORY 163:5
starry h. above that plain   THOM 549:28
that rideth upon the h.   PRAY 394:7
heaventree: h. of stars hung with humid   JOYCE 286:29
heavily: they were h. insured   GILB 225:8
why go I thus h.   PRAY 392:9
heaviness: art thou so full of h.   PRAY 392:7
h. foreruns the good event   SHAK 442:12
may endure for a night   PRAY 391:13
I am full of h.   PRAY 394:12
is the h. of his mother   BIBLE 53:29
Lay aside life-harming h.   SHAK 478:22
melody, in our h.   PRAY 399:3
praise for the spirit of h.   BIBLE 60:9
Heav'n: Can make a H. of Hell   MILT 345:10
H. has no rage   CONG 160:15
H.'s great lamps do dive   CAT 136:25
I'm farther off from h.   HOOD 254:18
steep ascent of h.   HEBER 244:7
than serve in h.   MILT 345:11
That we must change for H.   MILT 345:9
these the gems of H.   MILT 348:5
Warring in H. against Heav'n's   MILT 347:14
heav'ns: h. are not too high   HERB 246:26
Heavy: H. as frost   WORD 579:8
h., but no less divine   BYRON 123:5
h. part the music bears   JONS 283:21
h. summons lies like lead   SHAK 459:14
I was h. with the even   THOM 548:15
makes it much more h.   SHAK 486:31
not of the h. batallions   VOLT 561:18

wife doth make a h. husband   SHAK 468:21
he-bear: Himalayan peasant meets the h.   KIPL 299:4
Heber: Jael H.'s wife   BIBLE 49:7
Hebraism: H. and Hellenism   ARN 15:21
Hebrew: This H. will turn Christian   SHAK 466:5
Hebrews: Are they H.   BIBLE 77:11
Hebrew of the H.   BIBLE 78:16
Hebrides: seas colder than the H.   FLEC 214:7
Whether beyond the stormy H.   MILT 343:16
Hecate: mysteries of H. and the night   SHAK 453:3
Pale H.'s offerings   SHAK 460:1
to black H.'s summons   SHAK 461:13
Hector: ago H. took off his plume   CORN 162:20
greatly changed from that H.   VIRG 558:5
H. is dead   SHAK 487:18
Hecuba: What's H. to him or he   SHAK 432:27
hed: up and hit me in the h.   WARD 564:28
hedge: clipped h. is to a forest   JOHN 280:8
divinity doth h. a king   SHAK 436:6
From h. to hedge about   KEATS 292:21
will but look upon the h.   SHAK 492:9
will find by h. or pond   HOUS 262:19
hedgehog: h. one *big* one   ARCH 11:22
When the h. travels furtively   HARDY 239:2
hedge-hogs: Thorny h.   SHAK 470:11
hedges: h. ears   SWIFT 528:6
into the highways and h.   BIBLE 70:13
with filigree h.   WALP 562:21
hedonist: faddling h.   STEV 521:20
heed: h. them not   FITZ 212:9
maugre hir h.   CHAU 143:23
woven with an absent h.   HARDY 239:12
Heedless: H. of grammar   BARH 33:15
heel: near the h. of the courtier   SHAK 436:29
thou shalt bruise his h.   BIBLE 45:20
When plumes were under h.   HOUS 266:4
heels: high h. are most agreeable   SWIFT 526:4
upon the h. of pleasure   CONG 160:27
Heft: H. Of Cathedral Tunes   DICK 184:1
Hegel: Good-bye now, Plato and H.   MACN 326:5
heid: play golf ye maun hae a h.   MACD 325:1
wherefore should I busk my h.   BALL 32:10
heifer: had not plowed with my h.   BIBLE 49:22
Lead'st thou that h. lowing   KEATS 291:8
height: there on that sad h.   THOM 546:24
What pleasure lives in h.   TENN 542:15
years old is half his h.   LEON 313:25
heightening: June for beauty's h.   ARN 15:4
heights: h. by great men reached   LONG 316:19
h. of genius but in its   HOUS 266:15
h., which honest men despise   CHUR 149:5
heill: I that in h. wes and gladnes   DUNB 199:8
Heine: H. for songs   BROW 100:18
heir: appointed h. of all things   BIBLE 79:28
ashes new-create another h.   SHAK 448:3
h. of my invention prove   SHAK 495:17
I the h. of all the ages   TENN 539:7
sole h. of the whole world   TRAH 551:17
heir-apparent: in thine own h. garters   SHAK 438:25
heiresses: All h. are beautiful   DRYD 196:4
heirs: h. of God   BIBLE 75:9
h. through hope of thy   PRAY 388:3
make us h. of all eternity   SHAK 456:14
orphan h. of fixed destiny   SHAK 469:16
to your h. for ever   SHAK 451:4
held: boldest h. his breath   CAMP 128:15
h. the human race in scorn   BELL 38:33
night h. on indignantly   ARN 14:21
Helden: Land, das H. nötig hat   BREC 92:1
Helen: Dust hath closed H.'s eye   NASHE 360:7
first dawn in H.'s arms   YEATS 586:4

H. died   LAND 309:7
H., whose beauty summoned   MARL 330:14
like another H.   DRYD 195:7
Past ruin'd Ilion H. lives   LAND 308:22
wish I were where H. lies   BALL 31:4
Helena: is dross that is not H.   MARL 329:10
Helicon: watered our horses in H.
                                       CHAP 140:10
where H. breaks down   ARN 13:2
hell: agreement with h.   GARR 221:19
all h. broke loose   MILT 348:11
allotted death and h.   MARL 329:13
all we need of h.   DICK 183:20
be h. that are not heaven   MARL 329:8
bells of H. go ting-a-ling-a-ling   ANON 7:4
Better to reign in h.   MILT 345:11
boys, it is all h.   SHER 506:40
Can make a Heav'n of H.   MILT 345:10
characters of h. to trace   GRAY 234:15
come hot from h.   SHAK 450:12
corn and begin raising h.   LEASE 313:4
danger of h. fire   BIBLE 64:12
down to h.   SHAK 446:24
dunnest smoke of h.   SHAK 459:2
gates of h. shall not prevail   BIBLE 66:33
having harrow'd h.   SPEN 515:17
Heaven and H.   TENN 535:16
Heaven in H.'s despair   BLAKE 87:18
He descended into h.   PRAY 384:26
h. for horses   BURT 116:37
h. gat hold upon me   PRAY 397:19
H. is a city much like   SHEL 502:17
H. is full of musical amateurs   SHAW 497:27
H. is murky   SHAK 462:20
h. of a good universe   CUMM 170:12
h. of horses   FLOR 216:1
H. Receive thy new possessor   MILT 345:10
h. they'll roast thee like   BURNS 115:12
h., thou art there also   PRAY 399:5
H. trembled at the hideous   MILT 347:2
her steps take hold on h.   BIBLE 53:20
I'll get a swig in H.   KIPL 299:19
improving his prisons in H.   COL 156:14
Into the mouth of H.   TENN 533:1
I shall move H.   VIRG 559:5
it would be h. on earth   SHAW 497:17
keep the gate of h.   SHAK 476:21
keys of h. and of death   BIBLE 81:15
lead apes in h.   SHAK 484:7
leave my soul in h.   PRAY 390:7
lie in the h. like sheep   PRAY 393:1
make a h. of this world   BECK 36:20
meanest spawn of h.   TENN 538:13
mentions H. to ears polite   POPE 378:4
myself am H.   MILT 347:15
Nor H. a fury   CONG 160:15
opening of the jaws of h.   VIRG 558:21
place is too cold for h.   SHAK 460:17
printing house in H.   BLAKE 88:27
Procuress to the Lords of H.   TENN 536:23
Sent to H.   JOHN 279:17
Sin, Death, and H.   BUNY 107:33
So that's what H. is   SART 414:8
that leads men to this h.   SHAK 495:7
That riches grow in h.   MILT 346:1
that's his h.   BURT 116:23
that there was a way to H.   BUNY 107:26
thee to heaven or to h.   SHAK 460:1
There is a dreadful H.   WATTS 565:16
there must be h.   BROW 105:23
There's h., there's darkness   SHAK 455:17
there's the h.   KYD 306:5
though our estate be h.   BORG 99:23
Thyself to be thy proper H.   BYRON 125:4
to be cast into h. fire   BIBLE 67:5
to h. I will go   MILL 339:5
to make the earth my h.   SHAK 481:9
to quick bosoms is a h.   BYRON 120:30
where we are is H.   MARL 329:8
whose entrance leads to H.   MILT 341:12

Why this is h.   MARL 329:7
wicked as Lord George H.   BEER 37:16
with h. are we at agreement   BIBLE 58:22
hell-broth: Like a h. boil and bubble
                                       SHAK 462:3
helle: eyther hath in hevene or h.
                                       CHAU 143:28
Hellenism: Hebraism and H.   ARN 15:21
Hellespont: have pass'd the H. BYRON 122:20
Hell-fires: dreamin' H. to see   KIPL 300:17
hell-gate: man were porter of h. he
                                       SHAK 460:15
hellhound: h. is always a hellhound
                                       WOD 575:20
hell-kite: O h.   SHAK 462:17
hell-pains: do hate him as I do h.
                                       SHAK 473:19
Helm: *Des grossen Vaters H. ist* FLEM 215:5
mighty father's h. is far   FLEM 215:5
helmet: cowardly put off my h.   SHAK 423:15
h. now shall make a hive   PEELE 371:8
h., the hope of salvation   BIBLE 79:2
helmet-feather: helmet and the h. TENN 538:9
help: cannot h. nor pardon   AUDEN 20:17
comfort of thy h. again   PRAY 393:6
done nothing to h. anybody   TITUS 551:6
enough to h. the feeble up   SHAK 485:27
from whence cometh my h.   PRAY 398:9
God shall h. her   PRAY 392:20
heaven will h. you   LA F 306:17
h. a lame dog over a stile   CHIL 148:13
h. of my countenance   PRAY 392:12
H. of the helpless   LYTE 321:19
h. standeth in the Name   PRAY 398:14
h. the escaping murderer   STEV 521:12
h. those we love to escape   HUGEL 267:5
H. thou mine unbelief   BUTL 119:11
hour that requires such h.   VIRG 558:9
How shall I h. you   HOUS 263:17
make him an h. meet for him   BIBLE 45:10
nor h. for pain   ARN 12:23
Our h. is in the name   PRAY 388:20
place where h. wasn't hired   ANON 5:13
power of ourselves to h.   PRAY 386:9
present h. in time of trouble   ANON 4:18
ran to h. me when I fell   TAYL 531:25
Since there's no h.   DRAY 193:21
there is no h. in them   PRAY 399:16
very present h. in trouble   PRAY 392:19
what is past my h.   FLET 215:12
you can't h. it   BIRK 84:15
your countrymen cannot h.   JOHN 274:20
helped: over, and can't be h.   DICK 182:3
'We shall have h. it   DICK 183:10
helper: Our antagonist is our h.
                                       BURKE 111:23
Thou art my h. and redeemer   PRAY 392:3
Helping: H., when we meet them
                                       KING 296:21
Helpless: H., naked   BLAKE 87:23
h. to hinder that or anything   HARDY 241:16
helps: What h. it now   ARN 13:9
Helter skelter: H., hang sorrow   JONS 284:4
hemispheres: jars two h.   HARDY 239:6
hemlock: though of h. I had drunk
                                       KEATS 291:16
hempen: ever did sing in a h. string
                                       FLET 215:9
h. home-spuns have we swaggering
                                       SHAK 470:16
hen: h. gathereth her chickens   BIBLE 67:26
h. is only an egg's way   BUTL 118:24
of that text a pulled h.   CHAU 141:18
Hence: H., loathed Melancholy   MILT 342:12
H., vain deluding joys   MILT 341:23
that my moving from h.   SOCR 512:20
henceforth: walking from h. in his
                                       PRAY 387:18
hennes: h. for to doon al his plesaunce
                                       CHAU 142:32

hen-peck'd: have they not h. you all
                                       BYRON 122:7
Henri: *Je dirais au roi H.*   ANON 9:17
Henry: H. the 4th ascended   AUST 22:20
Henry King: chief defect of H.   BELL 38:34
Heracleitus: Sage H. says   POUND 383:7
Heraclitus: H., they told me you were
                                       CORY 163:4
herald: death I wish no other h. SHAK 447:23
H. sad and trumpet be   SHAK 492:15
spring the h. of love's   SPEN 515:19
heraldry: boast of h.   GRAY 234:21
herb: from some single h. or tree
                                       MARV 331:21
green h. for the service   PRAY 396:20
h. of grace o' Sundays   SHAK 436:11
sour h. of grace   SHAK 479:19
sweetest fragrance from the h.   TROL 552:24
herbe: *et l'h. qui verdoye*   PERR 372:25
herbs: dinner of h. where love   SHAK 54:6
have it for a garden of h.   BIBLE 51:17
h., and other country   MILT 342:21
is the greatest among h.   BIBLE 66:20
with bitter h. they shall   BIBLE 47:17
Hercules: is not love a H.   SHAK 457:8
Than I to H.   SHAK 429:28
herd: elevates above the vulgar h.
                                       GAIS 220:25
h. of swine ran violently   BIBLE 65:20
lowing h. wind slowly o'er   GRAY 234:18
Herden-Instinkt: *Moralität ist H. in*
Einzehlen   NIET 363:7
herd-instinct: Morality is the h. NIET 363:7
herdman: faithful h.'s art belongs
                                       MILT 343:12
herdsman: God the h. goads them
                                       YEATS 584:17
Here: H. am I   BIBLE 49:35
H. am I, here are you   AUDEN 19:14
H. am I; send me   BIBLE 58:1
H., a sheer hulk   DIBD 175:21
H. continueth to rot   ARB 11:21
H.'s a how-de-doo   GILB 227:2
H.'s tae us   ANON 5:16
H.'s to the widow of fifty   SHER 506:31
H. we go round the prickly   ELIOT 203:9
Lafayette, we are h.   STAN 517:18
nor tarrying h.   SHAK 463:7
though little notic'd h.   COWP 166:4
we are h. to-day   BEHN 38:13
Why are you not h.   THOR 550:27
you are looking for is h.   HOR 258:19
you h., Advocate Brunetto   DANTE 171:11
hereafter: h. for ever hold his peace
                                       PRAY 389:2
She should have died h.   SHAK 463:6
that points out an h.   ADD 1:24
world may talk of h.   COLL 158:12
hereditary: h. monarch was insane BAG 29:9
hereditas: *Damnosa h.*   GAIUS 220:27
heresies: hateful h.   SPEN 515:24
new truths to begin as h.   HUXL 269:12
heresy: Englishman believes be h.
                                       SHAW 498:19
subject of the Arian h.   JOHN 278:21
yet h. signifies no more   HOBB 251:16
heretic: h. that makes the fire   SHAK 491:13
heretics: Poor h. in love there be
                                       DONNE 189:18
heritage: h. unto Israel his people PRAY 399:1
I have a goodly h.   PRAY 390:6
lov'st well is thy true h.   POUND 382:12
Herman: H.'s a German   PORS 381:27
hermit: grievous torment than a h.'s
                                       KEATS 290:24
H. hoar   JOHN 277:14
hermitage: gorgeous palace for a h.
                                       SHAK 479:15
hermits: h. are contented with their
                                       WORD 582:7

h. shall rejoice on every — PRAY 394:3
h. stand about Jerusalem — PRAY 398:15
h., they shall smoke — PRAY 397:2
h. where his life rose — ARN 12:22
hop ye so, ye high h. — PRAY 394:9
immutable as the H. — KIPL 304:32
I to the h. will lift — SCOT 419:6
little h. righteousness — PRAY 394:19
little h. like young sheep — PRAY 397:16
Lord who made the h. — KIPL 303:14
name to the reverberate h. — SHAK 488:13
old brown h. — MAS 334:9
Over the h. and far away — GAY 222:22
'Over the h. and far away' — STEV 523:8
rocks and h. whose heads — SHAK 473:25
strength of the h. is his — PRAY 396:4
though the h. be carried — PRAY 392:19
to be out on the h. alone — KILV 296:8
up mine eyes unto the h. — PRAY 398:9
waters stand in the h. — PRAY 396:18
while the h. remain — TENN 541:26
yon are the h. o' Heaven — BALL 30:18
hill-side: h.'s dew-pearled — BROW 103:21
Him: H. that walked the waves — MILT 343:17
I hid from H. — THOM 548:8
I would remember H. — BEEC 37:9
'That's h. — BARH 33:15
ways with men I find H. — TENN 535:19
Himalayan: H. peasant meets the he-bear — KIPL 299:4
himputation: h. on his morality than — SURT 525:9
himself: end by loving h. better — COL 157:18
'He h. said it' — CIC 151:20
he shall speak for h. — BIBLE 72:15
man for loving h. — BACON 27:8
of a man's actions, h. — BACON 27:36
shake a man's faith in h. — SHAW 496:15
subdue all things to h. — PRAY 389:13
that he has done it all h. — BARR 34:22
when the ado is about h. — TROL 552:18
with h. at war — SHAK 448:11
hinan: Ewig-Weibliche zieht uns h. — GOET 230:6
Hinc: H. illae lacrimae — TER 544:14
hind: h. that would be mated — SHAK 420:26
hinder: all the h. parts — SPEN 516:3
dog's walking on his h. — JOHN 275:10
she's helpless to h. that — HARDY 241:16
Stands on his h. legs with — SHAK 495:21
hindered: sore let and h. — PRAY 386:6
hinders: wickedness that h. loving — BROW 102:31
Hindoo: turns H. — SHEL 501:19
Hindoos: Christianity to the H. — WIS 575:10
hindrance: though it were to his own h. — PRAY 390:5
hindrances: h. to human improvement — MILL 339:18
hinds: h. to bring forth young — PRAY 391:11
Soft maids and village h. — COLL 158:16
hinges: door on its h. — WATTS 565:25
on their h. grate — MILT 347:3
hint: Just h. a fault — POPE 376:26
hip: catch him once upon the h. — SHAK 465:29
I have thee on the h. — SHAK 468:8
smote them h. and thigh — BIBLE 49:23
Hippocrene: blushful H. — KEATS 291:18
Hippopotamus: found it was A H. — CARR 133:13
I shoot the H. — BELL 38:30
hips: We swing ungirded h. — SORL 513:10
whole quire hold their h. — SHAK 470:3
hire: labourer is worthy of his h. — BIBLE 72:15
hired: h. tears — BROW 97:8
I'm sick of the h. women — KIPL 301:10
hireling: h. fleeth — BIBLE 72:19
his: we are h. people — PRAY 396:11
hiss: dismal universal h. — MILT 349:22
hissed: h. along the polished ice — WORD 577:25

histoire: l'h. n'est que le tableau — VOLT 561:10
Peu connu dans l'h. — BER 41:14
historian: h., essentially — JAMES 271:18
H. Imagination is not required — JOHN 274:29
h. of the Roman empire — GIBB 224:15
life of the h. must be — GIBB 224:18
historians: alter the past, h. can — BUTL 118:21
remain a portent to the h. — KEYN 295:16
These gentle h. — BURKE 112:3
Histories: H. make men wise — BACON 27:21
history: Antiquities are h. defaced — BACON 24:18
art is the h. of revivals — BUTL 118:33
below the dignity of h. — MAC 324:15
brutal in the h. of civilisation — BEEC 37:5
fix the period in the h. — GIBB 224:24
great dust-heap called 'h. — BIRR 84:17
great h. of the land — LONG 317:7
have no h. — ELIOT 201:18
H., abounding with kings — MAC 324:21
H. a distillation of rumour — CARL 131:23
H. came — SELL 420:8
H. is a nightmare from — JOYCE 286:23
H. is a pack of lies — STUB 524:5
H. is more or less bunk — FORD 216:11
h. is nothing more than — VOLT 561:10
H. is past politics — SEEL 419:17
H. is philosophy from examples — DION 184:9
H. is the essence of innumerable — CARL 131:9
h. of all hitherto existing — MARX 333:3
h. of England is emphatically — MAC 323:12
h. of the human spirit — ARN 16:17
h. of the world is — CARL 131:31
H. the operator — AUDEN 20:15
h. to produce a little — JAMES 271:8
H. to the defeated — AUDEN 20:17
Human h. becomes more — WELLS 568:16
is a h. of the affections — IRV 270:20
learned anything from h. — HEGEL 244:8
Little known to h. — BER 41:14
maintained the dignity of h. — BOL 89:18
makes rattling good h. — HARDY 239:15
memorable in the h. of our race — CHUR 150:8
men could learn from h. — COL 157:20
no h.; only biography — EMER 207:24
product of h. — CARL 131:8
Real solemn h. — AUST 23:4
serious attention than h. — ARIS 12:10
Thames is liquid h. — BURNS 112:23
There is a h. in all men's — SHAK 442:3
this strange eventful h. — SHAK 425:24
tragedy, comedy, h. — SHAK 432:20
very few Dates in this H. — AUST 22:19
welding of their later h. — HARDY 239:6
When I made h. — ELIOT 203:7
with the freedom of h. — BURKE 109:5
world's h. is the world's — SCH 415:11
history-books: annals are blank in h. — CARL 131:20
hit: can h. from far — HERB 247:16
If you would h. the mark — LONG 316:11
never think I have h. hard — JOHN 276:20
two h. it off as they should — WORD 576:22
up and h. me in the hed — WARD 564:28
very palpable h. — SHAK 437:18
Hitch: H. your wagon to a star — EMER 208:8
hitch'd: then he h. his trousers up — BARH 33:23
hitched: If you mean gettin h. — WARD 564:20
hither: come h. — SHAK 425:14
Hitler: H. has missed the bus — CHAM 139:11
vassal state of H.'s Empire — CHUR 150:7
hive: helmet now shall make a h. — PEELE 371:8
h. for the honey-bee — YEATS 585:17
h. of silvery Bees — LEAR 312:9
ho: music, h. — SHAK 422:8
hoard: Our h. is little — TENN 535:1
hoar-frost: scattereth the h. like ashes — PRAY 399:21
hoarse: Bondage is h. — SHAK 482:19

raven himself is h. — SHAK 459:2
hoary: at best but dull and h. — VAUG 555:19
hob-and-nob: Let us h. with Death — TENN 544:7
Hobbes: H. clearly proves — SWIFT 528:4
hobby-horse: h. is forgot — SHAK 434:8
hobgoblin: consistency is the h. of little minds — EMER 207:38
Hoc: H. erat in votis — HOR 262:9
H. opus — VIRG 558:18
hock: at a weak h. and seltzer — BETJ 42:4
Hock-carts: H., wassails — HERR 248:18
Hockley: Hey H. — KETT 295:13
Hodge: Will H. for ever be — HARDY 239:9
hodgepodge: tongue a gallimaufry or h. — SPEN 517:6
hodmen: unconscious h. of the men — HEINE 244:12
hoe: darned long row to h. — LOW 319:2
h. and she laughs with — JERR 273:7
large h. and a shovel also — KIPL 300:11
hoed: h. and trenched and weeded — HOUS 264:17
hog: all England under a h. — COLL 158:10
hoggish: have his h. mind — SPEN 516:14
hogshead: fighting with daggers in a h. — SCOTT 419:2
Höhere: warte ich…auf H. — NIET 363:2
Höhlen: jahrtausendlang H. geben — NIET 363:6
hoi polloi: h., 'tis no matter what — DRYD 198:4
Hoist: H. with his own petar — SHAK 435:21
Holborn: when I was last in H. — SHAK 481:4
hold: does it h. good measure — BROW 100:4
Earth will h. us — ANON 10:13
hell gat h. upon me — PRAY 397:19
He will h. thee — TENN 538:19
h. a candle to my shames — SHAK 466:15
H., enough! — SHAK 463:9
h. fast that which is good — BIBLE 79:4
H. Infinity in the palm — BLAKE 85:8
H., or cut bow-strings — SHAK 470:1
h. readily in your hand — JOHN 280:17
h. thee but by thy granting — SHAK 494:13
H. the fort — BLISS 88:31
H. thou the good — TENN 536:23
I h. it towards you — KEATS 290:30
It is I you h. — WHIT 570:13
keep a h. of Nurse — BELL 39:3
quire h. their hips and loff — SHAK 470:3
she h. the gorgeous East — WORD 582:10
these should h. their peace — BIBLE 71:2
To cry 'H., hold — SHAK 459:2
to have and to h. from — PRAY 389:4
hold-fast: h. is the only dog — SHAK 443:20
Holding: H. the basin to gowned — MACN 326:9
holds: h. and rolls and throws — REED 405:7
h. him with his skinny — COL 155:6
hole: decayed h. among the mountains — ELIOT 205:10
h. where the tail came — COL 156:11
play on the h. of the asp — BIBLE 58:11
poisoned rat in a h. — SWIFT 526:24
your hat has got a h. in't — CANN 129:26
holes: foxes have h. — BIBLE 65:18
holiday: Being h. — SHAK 483:25
Butcher'd to make a Roman h. — BYRON 121:16
he speaks h. — SHAK 469:10
Is this a h. — SHAK 448:5
it's a regular h. to them — DICK 182:32
Monday is parson's h. — SWIFT 526:19
now I am in a h. humour — SHAK 426:21
On a sunshine h. — MILT 342:22
With many h. and lady terms — SHAK 438:14
holidays: during the h. from Eton — SITW 508:15
h., till we leave school — LEWIS 314:9
year were playing h. — SHAK 438:13
holier: I am h. than thou — BIBLE 60:13
holiest: of the truest and the h. — MAL 327:22
to the H. in the height — NEWM 362:12

holiness: h. becometh thine house PRAY 396:1
h. of the heart's affections KEATS 293:15
'H. rather than peace' NEWM 361:18
Lord in the beauty of h. PRAY 396:5
put off H. BLAKE 86:13
remembrance of his h. PRAY 391:13
Holland: children in H. take pleasure
ANON 7:22
Embosom'd in the deep where H.
GOLD 231:27
H. so low they're only HOOD 255:18
perseverance of H. BURKE 109:17
Hollander: your swag-bellied H. SHAK 475:2
holloa: we'll whoop and we'll h. WHYT 572:2
hollow: all was false and h. MILT 346:9
I hate that dreadful h. TENN 539:25
not h. cheek or faded eye TENN 542:13
We are the h. men ELIOT 203:8
within the h. crown SHAK 479:11
holly: Then heigh-ho! the h. SHAK 426:1
holocaust: lay erewhile a h. MILT 350:30
holsters: h. and cartridge boxes SHAW 496:6
holughnesse: h. of the eighthe spere
CHAU 144:18
holy: All the place is h. ground TENN 541:25
another with an h. kiss BIBLE 75:28
consented together in h. wedlock PRAY 389:7
Hail h. queen ANON 10:19
h., acceptable unto God BIBLE 75:15
h. city of Byzantium YEATS 586:13
H., fair, and wise SHAK 491:4
h. hill, and to thy dwelling PRAY 392:11
H., holy, holy PRAY 387:23
H., Holy PRAY 384:16
h. hush of ancient sacrifice STEV 520:18
h., is the Lord of hosts BIBLE 57:28
h. land Of Walsinghame RAL 404:13
h. nation BIBLE 80:23
h. time is quiet as a nun WORD 581:18
In those h. fields SHAK 437:33
nothing is h. PRAY 386:16
shalt thou suffer thy H. PRAY 390:7
stand in the h. place BIBLE 67:29
stol'n forth of h. writ SHAK 480:25
thou standest is h. ground BIBLE 47:4
to keep it h. BIBLE 47:24
Holy Ghost: Because the H. over
HOPK 256:13
blasphemy against the H. BIBLE 66:7
H. which is given unto BIBLE 74:41
is the temple of the H. BIBLE 76:1
pencil of the H. hath laboured BACON 25:19
revelations and gifts of the H. BUTL 117:11
whether there be any H. BIBLE 74:16
Holy, holy, holy: H., Lord God Almighty
BIBLE 81:24
Holy Spirit: H., and send out from
LANG 309:29
Holze: Aus so krummen H. KANT 288:14
hom: Repeyreth h. fro worldly vanyte
CHAU 144:19
homage: claims the h. of a tear BYRON 120:12
heaven and earth do her h. HOOK 255:20
homards: J'ai le goût des h. NERV 361:1
hombres: vivo en paz con los h. MACH 325:7
home: always come h. to roost SOUT 513:23
beating begins at h. FLET 215:25
confined him h. CLEV 153:4
dream that I am h. again FLEC 214:5
earth is all the h. I have AYT 24:12
give peace at h. PRAY 400:5
goodman is not at h. BIBLE 53:24
Go on h. VIRG 560:9
her princes are come h. SHAK 453:1
h. and beauty BRAH 91:16
h. and rest on the couch CAT 136:28
H. art gone and ta'en thy SHAK 428:22
h. his footsteps he hath SCOTT 416:21
H. is home CLAR 152:25
H. is the girl's prison SHAW 498:3

'H. is the place where FROST 219:2
H. is the sailor STEV 523:10
H. of lost causes ARN 15:25
h. of the brave KEY 295:14
H., Rose CLOU 153:24
home, sweet, sweet h. PAYNE 370:10
h. there's no returning HOUS 265:3
H. they brought her warrior TENN 542:10
h., you idle creatures SHAK 448:5
intruders on his ancient h. ARN 14:21
Irish H. Rule ROS 408:13
I was leaving h. STEV 522:26
joys of h. depend MORE 357:11
Kiss till the cow comes h. BEAU 36:11
knock it never is at h. COWP 165:5
luminous h. of waters ARN 15:1
man goeth to his long h. BIBLE 56:11
much like h. as we can FRY 220:3
never h. came she KING 297:1
of a h. if you are never GROS 236:21
only the wind's h. ELIOT 205:10
points of heaven and h. WORD 583:1
saviours come not h. tonight HOUS 262:13
Share my harvest and my h. HOOD 255:5
straitened circumstances at h. JUV 287:18
that drive one from h. HOOD 254:26
their h. among the dead SHEL 500:10
there's no place like h. PAYNE 370:10
they come h. BACON 25:17
this day and comes safe h. SHAK 445:3
very different from the h. ANON 5:20
who gives a child a h. MAS 333:25
won't go h. till morning BUCK 106:18
home-acre: hearth-fire and the h. KIPL 299:21
Home-keeping: H. youth have ever homely
SHAK 490:28
homeless: those who are h. by choice
SOUT 514:15
homely: Home-keeping youth have ever
h. wits SHAK 490:28
h. was their food GARTH 221:20
It is for h. features MILT 341:18
Their h. joys GRAY 234:21
though it be never so h. CLAR 152:25
Home-made: H. dishes that drive one
HOOD 254:26
Homer: blind H. sing MARL 329:9
Dumb to H. BROW 102:35
H. begged his Bread ANON 7:14
H. invariably composes ARN 16:12
Homer more than H. knew SWIFT 528:1
'H. sometimes sleeps' BYRON 123:7
Seven cities warr'd for H. HEYW 250:22
sometimes even excellent H. nods HOR 258:2
Towns contend for H. Dead ANON 7:14
translator of H. should ARN 16:11
you must not call it H. BENT 41:12
Homeric: unforgotten H. catalogue
GUED 237:4
Homer Lane: H. was killed in action
AUDEN 18:20
homes: h. without a friend CLARE 152:9
Stately H. of England COW 164:3
stately h. of England HEM 244:21
home-spuns: What hempen h. have we
SHAK 470:16
homeward: Austria rides h. with a wreath
CHES 147:6
Look h., Angel MILT 343:16
homewards: Most roads lead men h.
MAS 334:3
hommage: L'hypocrisie est un h. LA R 310:12
homme: et on trouve un h. PASC 369:4
h. comme vous ignore quelque BEAU 35:16
imprescriptibles de l'h. ROB 406:11
le style est l'h. même BUFF 106:20
le vray étude de l'h. CHAR 141:1
L'h. est bien insensé MONT 355:4
L'h. n'est qu'un roseau PASC 369:11

hommes: voulons être h. avant tout
ART 16:29
homo: Ecce h. BIBLE 83:22
ET H. FACTUS EST MASS 334:20
Lupus est h. homini PLAU 374:13
homogeneity: incoherent h. SPEN 514:29
honest: am myself indifferent h. SHAK 433:11
beat the h. men SHAK 462:13
be h., to be kind STEV 521:4
be h. without a thought BROW 96:23
By nature h. POPE 377:5
fa' your h. sonsie face BURNS 115:16
few h. men are better than CROM 169:19
fortunes have Corrupted in SHAK 423:1
gossip Report be an h. woman SHAK 467:2
h., as this world goes SHAK 432:5
h. atheism for my money OTWAY 365:26
h. broker BISM 84:23
h. chronicler as Griffith SHAK 447:23
h. God is the noblest ING 270:17
h. God's the noblest BUTL 119:7
H. labour bears a lovely DEKK 173:20
h. madam's issue SHAK 453:9
h. man's the noblest BURNS 113:10
h. man's the noblest POPE 379:24
h. men and bonnie lasses BURNS 115:4
h. tale speeds best being SHAK 481:9
h. talk and wholesome wine TENN 543:16
h. that but seem to be SHAK 474:12
in a general h. thought SHAK 452:1
It is an h. ghost SHAK 431:19
made h. by an act JONS 283:25
rather an h. woman's son SHAK 466:2
that maxim is not an h. man WHAT 569:14
that the world's grown h. SHAK 432:11
Though I am not naturally h. SHAK 492:8
To be direct and h. is SHAK 475:26
very h. woman SHAK 424:6
whatsoever things are h. BIBLE 78:22
Win us with h. trifles SHAK 458:18
honester: is an old man and no h.
SHAK 472:32
honestly: If possible h. HOR 258:10
honesty: am arm'd so strong in h.
SHAK 451:20
children *capable of h.* RUSK 412:5
Fly, h., fly SMITH 510:5
h. and love doth mince SHAK 475:6
h. is a good thing but MARQ 330:24
H. is praised and left JUV 287:10
H. is the best policy WHAT 569:14
parted so much h. among 'em SHAK 447:24
perilous to a man's h. TROL 553:6
Rich h. dwells like a miser SHAK 427:4
saving of thine h. MORE 357:17
to make thine h. a vice SHAK 475:26
what a fool H. is SHAK 492:7
yet I hold it not h. SHAK 432:8
Your h. must be based RUSK 412:4
honey: Butter and h. shall he eat BIBLE 58:3
citizens kneading up the h. SHAK 443:9
did but taste a little h. BIBLE 50:3
flowing with milk and h. BIBLE 47:6
gather h. from the weed SHAK 444:15
gather h. all the day WATTS 565:21
h. not for yourselves VIRG 560:20
h. of his music vows SHAK 433:15
h. of Hybla SHAK 438:2
h. of poison-flowers TENN 539:29
H., you can cut that right AUDEN 19:14
H., your silk stocking's SELL 420:3
How a bear likes h. MILNE 340:12
is there h. still for tea BROO 94:25
mouth sweet as h. BIBLE 82:9
our hives with h. and wax SWIFT 525:33
pot of h. on the grave MER 337:10
surfeited with h. and began SHAK 439:35
sweeter also than h. PRAY 390:12
They took some h. LEAR 312:11
was locusts and wild h. BIBLE 63:37

honey-bees: so work the h.   SHAK 443:9
honey-coloured: great h. Ramparts
   YEATS 585:4
honeycomb: of an h.   BIBLE 71:20
   strange woman drop as an h.   BIBLE 53:20
   than honey, and the h.   PRAY 390:12
honey'd: h. middle of the night   KEATS 289:12
honey-dew: he on h. hath fed   COL 157:1
honey-heavy: Enjoy the h. dew of slumber
   SHAK 449:12
honeyless: leave them h.   SHAK 451:31
Hongry: H. rooster don't cackle   HARR 242:24
Honi: *H. soit qui mal y pense*   ANON 9:6
honking: to be a goose h. amongst
   VIRG 560:7
honores: contemnere h.   HOR 262:10
honour: air signed with their h.   SPEN 515:8
   all in h.   SHAK 477:22
   cannot be maintained with h.   RUSS 412:19
   did nobody h.   WALP 563:14
   done with Hope and H.   KIPL 299:11
   drowned h. by the locks   SHAK 438:19
   false Idol H.   WINC 575:4
   Fear God. H. the King   KITC 305:14
   'fountain of h.   BAG 28:22
   fount whence h. springs   MARL 330:9
   gilded h. shamefully misplac'd   SHAK 494:5
   Giving h. unto the wife   BIBLE 80:29
   greater share of h.   SHAK 445:1
   hath had some smatch of h.   SHAK 452:6
   hearts that h. could not move   BROO 94:27
   He is the fountain of h.   BACON 27:43
   helps the hurt that H.   TENN 538:23
   his end to be without h.   BIBLE 62:16
   His h. rooted in dishonour   TENN 534:29
   H. all men   BIBLE 80:25
   h. and his quality taken   BLUN 89:3
   h., and keep her in sickness   PRAY 389:3
   h. and life have been spared   FRAN 218:1
   H. a physician with   BIBLE 63:17
   h. aspireth to it   BACON 26:2
   H. be yours   NEWB 361:3
   H. but an empty bubble   DRYD 195:5
   h. doth forget men's names   SHAK 452:9
   h. due unto his Name   PRAY 396:5
   H. hath no skill in surgery   SHAK 440:18
   h. his own word as if his   TENN 534:11
   h. in one eye and death   SHAK 448:12
   h. is the subject of my   SHAK 448:13
   h. Pick'd from the chaff   SHAK 466:20
   H. pricks me   SHAK 440:18
   h. the very flea of his   JONS 284:6
   H. thy father and thy mother   BIBLE 47:24
   honour to whom h.   BIBLE 75:27
   H., without money   RAC 404:6
   idiot race to h.   BURNS 114:29
   I h. him   SHAK 450:15
   In dignitye or h. goeth   DUNB 199:12
   in h. clear   POPE 378:6
   In h. I gained them   NELS 360:18
   Is from the book of h.   SHAK 493:4
   is leisure with h.   CIC 151:33
   Keeps h. bright   SHAK 487:4
   king delighteth to h.   BIBLE 52:3
   learn Latin as an h.   CHUR 150:23
   left hand riches and h.   BIBLE 53:16
   Let us h. if we can   AUDEN 20:11
   like not such grinning h.   SHAK 440:21
   loss of h. was a wrench   GRAH 233:9
   louder he talked of his h.   EMER 207:8
   Lov'd I not h. more   LOV 318:20
   make one vessel unto h.   BIBLE 75:14
   man will not abide in h.   PRAY 392:28
   Mine h. is my life   SHAK 478:8
   not a stain in thine h.   BIBLE 63:16
   peace I hope with h.   DISR 185:15
   peace with h.   CHAM 139:10
   perfect ways of h.   SHAK 448:2
   places where their h. died   POPE 377:26
   post of h. is a private   ADD 1:23

   prefer mere existence to h.   JUV 287:25
   prophet is not without h.   BIBLE 66:23
   republic a roll of h.   CLEV 153:2
   resolved to h. and renown ye   ANON 7:15
   sin to covet h.   SHAK 445:2
   that chastity of h.   BURKE 111:10
   That h. which shall bate   SHAK 456:14
   Thou art a tool of h.   WORD 583:3
   throne *we* h. is the *people's*
   SHER 506:7
   tide is ready her to h.   BEST 42:2
   To keep mine h. from corruption
   SHAK 447:23
   To pluck bright h. from   SHAK 438:19
   to some rag of h.   STEV 521:2
   Trouthe and h.   CHAU 141:9
   Truth the masculine, of H.   HARE 242:5
   When h.'s at the stake   SHAK 435:31
   Ye take mine h. from me   KIPL 300:19
   your quaint h. turn to dust   MARV 332:19
honourable: Brutus is an h. man   SHAK 450:17
   Brutus is an h. man   SHAK 450:18
   daughters were among thy h.   PRAY 392:16
   h. style of a Christian   BROW 96:2
   joss-sticks and h. high-mindedness
   BRAM 91:20
   lest a more h. man than   BIBLE 70:7
   Let us make an h. retreat   SHAK 426:6
   Paul to be h. among all men   PRAY 388:25
honour'd: By strangers h.   POPE 376:10
   He hath h. me of late   SHAK 459:7
   h. of them all   TENN 543:22
   More h. in the breach than   SHAK 430:23
honoured: It has h. us   WEBS 566:14
honouring: Not so much h. thee   JONS 284:12
honours: am stripped of all my h.
   BURKE 112:4
   bears his blushing h. thick   SHAK 447:9
   chase of h. and distinction   BURKE 108:7
   He gave his h. to the world   SHAK 447:16
   held the patent for his h.   BURNS 113:15
   offer you either h. or wages   GAR 221:10
   With all his h.   AUDEN 21:9
honteux: h. de se défier de ses   LA R 310:10
Hood: Here lies bold Robin H.   BALL 31:14
hood-wink'd: h. boy I call'd in aid
   GARR 221:16
hoof: though he divide the h.   BIBLE 48:6
hoofs: h. of a swinish multitude
   BURKE 111:14
   hurry of h. in a village   LONG 316:26
   plunging h. were gone   DE L 174:10
hook: great h. nose like thine   BLAKE 85:21
   my bended h. shall pierce   SHAK 422:9
   never fly conceals a h.   BROO 94:13
   out leviathan with an h.   BIBLE 53:11
   subscribers baits his h.   CHUR 148:30
hookah-mouth: sliding puffs from the
   h.   KIPL 297:28
hook-nosed: with the h. fellow of Rome
   SHAK 442:13
Hooly: H. writ is the scripture   JER 272:31
Hooting: H. and shrieking   SHAK 449:1
   h. at dawn flew away none   BEER 38:2
   h. at the glorious sun   COL 156:19
   life to shunting and h.   BURR 116:10
Hop: H. forty paces through   SHAK 422:4
   h. ye so, ye high hills   PRAY 394:9
hope: Abandon all h., you who enter
   DANTE 171:3
   against hope believed in h.   BIBLE 74:40
   All our h. is fallen   HOR 261:13
   are also heirs through h.   PRAY 388:3
   Can embrace, h.,   HOPK 256:7
   done with H. and Honour   KIPL 299:11
   do not h. to turn again   ELIOT 201:32
   equal h.   MILT 345:1
   equal poise of h. and fear   MILT 341:9
   Evelyn H. is dead   BROW 100:25
   failure of h.   GIBB 224:20
   faith, h., charity   BIBLE 76:14

   From h. and fear set free   SWIN 529:25
   God is our h. and strength   PRAY 392:19
   He that lives upon h. will   FRAN 218:13
   h. again for aught that   MORR 358:8
   H. deferred maketh   BIBLE 53:35
   H., for a season   CAMP 129:7
   h. for the best   SMITH 510:31
   I dreamed of was a dream   ROSS 409:2
   H. is a good breakfast   BACON 25:8
   h. I will be religious   FLEM 214:29
   Hopeless h. hopes   CLARE 152:9
   H. maketh not ashamed   BIBLE 74:41
   H. may vanish   SHEL 500:18
   h. never comes   MILT 344:25
   h. of a fool than of him   BIBLE 54:33
   h. of all the ends   PRAY 394:1
   h. of glory   PRAY 386:2
   h. of the City of God   MAS 334:7
   h. of the ungodly   BIBLE 62:18
   h., once crushed   ARN 15:9
   h. our acquaintance may   DICK 182:5
   H., politeness, the blowing   FORS 217:8
   H. springs eternal   POPE 379:5
   h. that is unwilling   WORD 581:2
   h. that keeps up a wife's   GAY 222:18
   h. who never had a fear   COWP 167:36
   h. without an object cannot   COL 157:15
   I have h. to live   SHAK 464:8
   In faith and h. the world   POPE 379:20
   in sure and certain h.   PRAY 389:13
   Land of H. and Glory   BENS 40:24
   leisure for love or h.   HOOD 255:9
   Let us h. for better things   AUST 23:17
   my h. is better   SHAK 490:12
   Never to h. again   SHAK 447:9
   Nor dread nor h. attend   YEATS 584:20
   not another's h.   WALSH 563:30
   Not to h. for things   HOR 261:15
   nursing the unconquerable h.   ARN 14:20
   only we have h. in Christ   BIBLE 76:21
   patience of h. in our Lord   BIBLE 78:30
   poet's h.   AUDEN 20:14
   reinforcement we may gain from h.
   MILT 345:7
   secret h. for greater favours   LA R 310:16
   Some blessed H.   HARDY 239:7
   strength and my h. is perished   BIBLE 60:29
   tender leaves of h.   SHAK 447:9
   their h. full of immortality   BIBLE 62:13
   Through love, through h.   WORD 581:5
   to hope till H. creates   SHEL 503:15
   to one more rich in h.   SHAK 493:6
   triumph of h. over experience   JOHN 275:36
   True h. is swift   SHAK 481:11
   unsettled is there any h.   EMER 207:15
   Was the h. drunk   SHAK 459:8
   what is h. but deceiving   MER 338:7
   what was dead was H.   WILDE 572:13
   what you can desire or h.   DRYD 197:5
   whence this pleasing h.   ADD 1:24
   when existence or when h.   AUST 23:10
   Where feeble H. could ne'er   MARV 331:18
   wish for what I faintly h.   DRYD 197:16
   with h. farewell fear   MILT 347:16
hoped: getting anything he h.   VIRG 559:14
   never h. can never despair   SHAW 496:11
   substance of things h.   BIBLE 79:31
hoped-for: already become the h. heaven
   MILL 339:22
hopeful: far more cheerful and h.
   HOLM 253:14
   h. green stuff woven   WHIT 570:18
   h. thou'lt recover once   GRAH 233:16
   theirs on the h. past   BROW 101:25
hopefully: To travel h. is a better   STEV 522:9
hopeless: Ages of h. end   MILT 346:11
   either superfluous or h.   NEWM 362:10
   h. grief is passionless   BROW 98:7
   h. passion is my destiny   THAC 545:13
   h. than a scheme of merriment   JOHN 281:21

perennially h.   DICK 176:2
hopes: airy h. my children   WORD 577:14
Applying fears to h.   SHAK 495:6
far-reaching h.   HOR 259:14
fifty h. and fears   BROW 99:4
great h. from Birmingham   AUST 22:18
have no h. but from power   BURKE 110:8
his h. as eager as ours   BURKE 110:21
h. and fears it heeded   SHEL 504:19
H. of high talk with   SHEL 501:6
If h. were dupes   CLOU 181:27
I have set my h. in thee   ANON 11:4
Other desires and other h.   BRON 93:23
without comforts and h.   BACON 25:20
hopeth: h. all things   BIBLE 76:14
hoping: Dreading and h. all   YEATS 584:20
H. it might be so   HARDY 240:14
hoppy: h. on akkant of his joyicity   JOYCE 286:13
hops: h., and women   DICK 176:2
hop-yards: what were h. meant   HOUS 264:12
hora: quae non sperabitur h.   HOR 258:16
Quae rapit h. diem   HOR 261:15
Horace: H.'s precisely lucky strikes   PETR 373:3
H.; whom I hated so   BYRON 121:8
What H. says is   BARH 33:8
Horatio: is H. there   SHAK 429:7
Horatius: Then out spake brave H.   MAC 322:15
well H. kept the bridge   MAC 322:23
höre: Wenn ich Kultur h.   JOHST 283:8
horizon: Drinker of h.'s fluid   SPEN 515:14
h. recedes as we advance   PATT 370:8
h. was clearly marked   HARDY 241:19
horizontal: however fine into an h.   WHEW 569:16
value none But the h.   AUDEN 20:11
horizontale: Vivre est une chute h.   COCT 154:12
horn: blast of that dread h.   SCOTT 417:23
blowing loud his wreathèd h.   SPEN 515:21
His small but sullen h.   COLL 158:18
h. and by it real ghosts   VIRG 559:3
h. of the hunter is heard   CRAW 169:16
lusty h.   SHAK 426:25
mellow h. her pensive soul   COLL 158:21
Put forth a conscious h.   THOM 548:5
South to the blind H.'s   KIPL 300:24
Hornby: my H. and my Barlow   THOM 547:24
hornets: let wasps and h. break   SWIFT 527:16
Hornie: Auld H.   BURNS 112:24
hornpipes: There's h. and strathspeys   BURNS 113:13
horns: h. of Elfland faintly blowing   TENN 541:32
Morning on the silver h.   TENN 542:16
sound of h. and motors   ELIOT 204:27
with crescent h.   MILT 345:16
Horny-handed: H. sons of toil   KEAR 288:18
horreur: l'h. d'une profonde nuit   RAC 404:2
horrible: h., fantastic, incredible   CHAM 139:9
less than h. imaginings   SHAK 458:20
me also out of the h. pit   PRAY 392:1
O, h.! most horrible!   SHAK 431:12
Than reign in this h. place   COWP 167:38
Your h. pleasure   SHAK 454:5
horrid: are they all h.   AUST 23:1
'Mongst h. shapes   MILT 342:12
she was bad she was h.   LONG 317:22
very h. thing   BUTL 117:11
With h. warning gapèd wide   KEATS 290:21
horror: during the h. of a deep night   RAC 404:2
haunts of h. and fear   TENN 540:16
h. and darkness fell upon   BUNY 107:25
h. and its beauty are divine   SHEL 502:5
horror! h.! horror   SHAK 460:21
h. of great darkness fell   BIBLE 46:3
h. of that moment   CARR 134:26

image of that h.   SHAK 456:9
inward h.   ADD 1:24
present h. from the time   SHAK 460:1
scaly h. of his folded tail   MILT 344:12
horrors: Congenial h., hail   THOM 549:22
have supp'd full with h.   SHAK 463:5
scene of h.   SMITH 512:7
hors: was his h. as is a rake   CHAU 141:23
horse: Altogether upon the high h.   BROWN 95:7
behold a pale h.   BIBLE 81:29
behold a white h.   BIBLE 82:25
between a rider and his h.   SURT 525:28
call me h.   SHAK 439:2
cup won by the worst h.   MAS 333:23
dark h.   DISR 187:2
Do not trust the h.   VIRG 558:1
fitchew nor the soiled h.   SHAK 455:17
fit companion is his h.   COWP 165:6
Give a man a h. he can ride   THOM 549:29
good h. in the stable   GOLD 232:7
happy h.   SHAK 421:31
h. back at mine hostess'   SHAK 452:12
h. is counted but a vain   PRAY 391:20
h. is drawn by the cart   KIPL 298:16
h. misus'd upon the road   BLAKE 85:10
h. of that colour   SHAK 488:25
h.'s health   SHAK 454:28
If he were a h.   BAG 28:20
in the strength of an h.   PRAY 399:20
lies about his wooden h.   FLEC 214:18
life and the torturer's h.   AUDEN 19:19
little dearer than his h.   TENN 538:19
man On the sightless h.   WALEY 562:2
my kingdom for a h.   SHAK 481:18
No h.'s cry was that   ARN 14:26
nothing but talk of his h.   SHAK 465:21
not take to h. and mule   PRAY 391:18
O, for a h. with wings   SHAK 428:14
one's h. as he is leaping   HARE 242:4
One stiff blind h.   BROW 99:28
pasture now to buy the h.   SHAK 443:12
something in a flying h.   WORD 579:18
stately h. and make him wince   JOHN 274:8
Strong is the h. upon his   SMART 509:3
teach an old h.   SPEN 516:16
That which is now a h.   SHAK 423:8
to h.   BROW 99:27
to my h.—German   CHAR 140:31
want of a h. the rider   FRAN 218:6
what a h. should have he   SHAK 495:20
where's the bloody h.   CAMP 128:12
white h. galloped away   ELIOT 203:14
White H. of the White Horse   CHES 146:15
will hear the beat of a h.'s   KIPL 304:1
With an old h. that stumbles   HARDY 240:5
youth manages his taxed h.   SMITH 511:38
horseback: On h. after we   COWP 165:16
Horseman: H., pass   YEATS 587:10
horsemanship: world with noble h.   SHAK 440:7
horsemen: h. thereof   BIBLE 51:22
horse-race: h. won at Olympus among   SIDN 508:4
horses: best carriage h.   TROL 553:8
breed of their h. and dogs   PENN 371:15
chariots, and some in h.   PRAY 390:14
drive a coach and six h.   RICE 406:1
entirely by the spade and no h.   MILL 339:16
hanged for stealing h.   HAL 237:22
harness and not the h.   CANN 130:7
hell of h.   FLOR 216:1
horsemen riding upon h.   BIBLE 60:37
H. Heads Were toward Eternity   DICK 183:16
h.' heels Over the paving   ELIOT 202:6
is not best to swap h.   LINC 315:2
Let us take any man's h.   SHAK 442:29
Now the wild white h. play   ARN 13:5
street and frighten the h.   CAMP 128:8
than the h. of instruction   BLAKE 88:22

That plats the manes of h.   SHAK 481:28
They were as fed h.   BIBLE 60:16
us with his panting h.   VIRG 560:11
watered our h. in Helicon   CHAP 140:10
what we spend on our h.   RUSK 411:17
Women and H. and Power   KIPL 297:28
words to trampling h.' feet   SIDN 507:27
Hortus: H. ubi et tecto vicinus   HOR 262:9
hosanna: Glorious h. from the den   SMART 509:4
H. in excelsis   MASS 335:4
hose: tip up bason and a h.   ASHF 17:8
hospes: deferor h.   HOR 258:7
hospitable: on h. thoughts intent   MILT 348:18
hospital: not an inn, but an h.   BROW 97:3
social comfort, in a h.   BROW 97:30
whole earth is our h.   ELIOT 202:22
hospitality: given to h.   BIBLE 79:12
hospitals: rot in h.   SOUT 513:13
host: company of the heavenly h.   BLAKE 88:29
head if you find such a h.   ANST 11:8
h. of Midian was beneath   BIBLE 49:16
h. whatsoever thou spendeth   BIBLE 69:32
h. with someone indistinct   ELIOT 204:16
is like a fashionable h.   SHAK 487:5
play the humble h.   SHAK 461:16
hostages: all of them h. given   LUCAN 319:25
hath given h. to fortune   BACON 26:31
hoste: fas est et ab h. doceri   OVID 366:16
hostess: horse back at mine h.' door   SHAK 452:12
hosts: Even the Lord of h.   PRAY 391:1
h. and guests   BEER 37:17
Lord God of h.   PRAY 387:23
Lord of h. is with us   PRAY 392:20
than all the h. of error   BRYAN 106:7
hot: art neither cold nor h.   BIBLE 81:20
benison of h. water   BROO 94:9
Heat me these irons h.   SHAK 452:22
H. and rebellious liquors   SHAK 425:5
h. for certainties in this   MER 337:18
h. ice and wondrous strange   SHAK 471:13
h. the eye of heaven   SHAK 492:28
iron while it is h.   DRYD 197:37
lull in the h. race   ARN 12:22
My heart was h. within   PRAY 391:30
hot-blooded: I was a h. youth   HOR 261:14
hotch-potch: h. of my little book   JUV 287:12
hotel: back to the Gaierty h.   ASHF 17:15
hotel-keepers: h. continue to give them   TROL 553:2
Hoti: He settled H.'s business   BROW 101:1
Hotspur: H. of the North   SHAK 438:33
Hottentot: him as a respectable H.   CHES 145:32
hound: by the faithful h.   LONG 316:16
footprints of a gigantic h.   DOYLE 192:27
he'll grow into a h.   WHYT 572:2
'His h. is to the hunting   BALL 32:8
H. or spaniel   SHAK 455:1
slepyng h. to wake   CHAU 144:7
houndes: Of smale h. hadde she that   CHAU 141:16
hounds: carcass fit for h.   SHAK 449:9
h. all join in glorious   FIEL 211:36
h. of spring are on winter's   SWIN 528:15
like fell and cruel h.   SHAK 487:21
With h. of Sparta   SHAK 471:7
hour: anguish of a torturing h.   SHAK 471:12
Brahmin strikes the h.   SOUT 513:25
carefully upon your h.   SHAK 429:4
close-companioned inarticulate h.   ROSS 409:24
crowded h. of glorious life   MORD 357:6
dead h. of the night   BALL 32:2
Ere the parting h. go   ARN 13:19
fashion'd to the varying h.   GOLD 230:22
gie me a canny h. at e'en   BURNS 114:2
glory of the positive h.   ELIOT 201:33

have wrought but one h.	BIBLE 67:15
her h. is upon her again	GIBB 225:3
he was but one h. mine	SHAK 493:10
h. is come	SCOTT 418:18
h. that requires such help	VIRG 558:9
h. which freed us from	BROW 95:22
I also had my h.	CHES 146:23
I have had my h.	DRYD 198:16
Improve each shining h.	WATTS 565:21
in the h. of death	PRAY 385:17
its h. come round at last	YEATS 586:16
known as the Children's H.	LONG 316:9
make the h. full complete	SHAK 446:18
matched us with His h.	BROO 94:26
mine h. is not yet come	BIBLE 71:33
nighing his h.	HOUS 264:28
now's the h.	BURNS 114:34
occupation for an idle h.	AUST 23:7
of the superincumbent h.	SHEL 499:17
one bare h. to live	MARL 329:11
So this wing'd h. is dropt	ROSS 409:24
struts and frets his h.	SHAK 463:6
the h. which snatches	HOR 261:15
This is the H. of Lead	DICK 183:14
'This was their finest h.	CHUR 150:1
Time and the h. runs through	SHAK 458:21
'tis the h. of prayer	BYRON 123:8
To fill the h.	EMER 207:17
To one dead deathless h.	ROSS 409:21
What comfortable h. canst	SHAK 481:8
will Europe's latter h.	ARN 13:18
hour-glass: still as the h.	ROSS 409:23
hours: of light return	ARN 13:23
h. will take care of themselves	CHES 145:18
Is to steal a few h. from	MOORE 356:21
keeping company with the h.	WEBS 566:12
lazy leaden-stepping h.	MILT 344:17
Now all strange h.	SWIN 528:26
Seven h. to law	JONES 283:13
Six h. in sleep	COKE 154:22
spent the darksome h.	GOET 230:17
To chase the glowing H.	BYRON 120:21
two golden h.	MANN 328:14
two h.' traffick	SHAK 481:21
Unless h. were cups	SHAK 437:34
weight of h. has chained	SHEL 502:13
housbond: Whan myn h. is fro	CHAU 143:17
Housbondes: H. at chirche dore she	
	CHAU 141:31
house: are of the h. of the Lord	PRAY 398:3
barren woman to keep h.	PRAY 397:15
beat upon that h.	BIBLE 65:11
be mistress of this h.	AUST 23:9
be of one mind in an h.	PRAY 394:7
brawling woman in a wide h.	BIBLE 54:20
built his h. upon the sand	BIBLE 65:12
called the h. of prayer	BIBLE 67:17
Dark h.	TENN 536:5
everything before me in that H.	DISR 185:31
Except the Lord build the h.	PRAY 398:18
Father's h. are many mansions	BIBLE 72:31
go into the h. of the Lord	PRAY 398:11
had a mind to sell his h.	SWIFT 525:34
handsome h. to lodge a friend	SWIFT 527:28
Harrow the h. of the dead	AUDEN 20:7
h. appointed for all living	BIBLE 52:36
h. be divided against itself	BIBLE 68:27
h. built upon another man's	SHAK 469:9
h. for fools and mad	SWIFT 527:25
h. is a living-machine	LE C 313:5
h. is much more to my taste	MORR 358:4
H. is pleased to direct	LENT 313:23
h. not made with hands	BIBLE 77:6
h. not made with hands	BROW 99:20
h. of defence very high	PRAY 395:21
h. of every one is to him	COKE 154:23
H. of Lords as from any	NORF 364:1
h. of the Lord for ever	PRAY 390:22
h. where I was born	HOOD 254:17
h. with deep thatch	BELL 40:11

h. with lawns enclosing	STEV 523:7
in that h. they shall dwell	DONNE 191:3
Is the h. o'ertopping all	BROW 100:7
it filled all the h. where	BIBLE 73:22
little jobs about the h.	AUDEN 21:9
Lord has built the h.	BIBLE 83:12
Lord let the h. of a brute	TENN 532:22
myself in the h. of Rimmon	BIBLE 51:29
no man a h. of good stone	POUND 382:8
now see to thine own h.	BIBLE 51:4
of this h. were dissolved	BIBLE 77:6
other but the h. of God	BIBLE 46:20
palace is more than a h.	COL 158:1
Peace be to this h.	BIBLE 69:26
Peace be to this h.	PRAY 389:8
return no more to his h.	BIBLE 52:19
see the figure of the h.	SHAK 441:17
set a h. on fire	BACON 27:37
Set thine h. in order	BIBLE 59:2
sparrow hath found her an h.	PRAY 395:11
substance of his h. for love	BIBLE 57:12
That this h. will in no	ANON 7:19
them that join house to h.	BIBLE 57:24
There's nae luck about the h.	ANON 8:3
unhouse and h. the Lord	HOPK 256:16
upon the walls of thine h.	PRAY 398:20
water near the h.	HOR 262:9
What! in our h.	SHAK 460:24
When h. and land are gone	FOOTE 216:8
will return into my h.	BIBLE 66:13
You take my h. when you	SHAK 468:10
zeal of thine h. hath even	PRAY 394:11
housed: therein shall be well h.	RUSK 412:6
household: Except that h. virtue	BYRON 126:6
Familiar in his mouth as h.	SHAK 445:3
Her h. motions light	WORD 581:8
h. divided the spoil	PRAY 394:8
h. the Church in continual	PRAY 386:23
put his h. in order	BIBLE 50:25
religion breathing h. laws	WORD 582:9
sacred to the h. gods	THOM 549:23
shall be they of his own h.	BIBLE 65:39
very homely h. savour	BYRON 122:26
house-keepings: jining of houses and h.	
	DICK 181:1
houseless: h. heads and unfed sides	
	SHAK 454:15
housemaids: damp souls of h.	ELIOT 203:27
House of Peers: H. has never been a	
House	BAG 29:5
H., throughout the war	GILB 226:11
we love our H.	GILB 228:23
houses: devour widows' h.	BIBLE 68:37
H. are built to live	BACON 25:34
h. in the night collapsed	PLOM 374:19
h. shall continue for ever	PRAY 392:28
h. that he makes last till	SHAK 436:25
h. thick and sewers annoy	MILT 349:13
h. thunder on your head	JOHN 282:22
Round their golden h.	TENN 539:16
very h. seem asleep	WORD 581:15
housetop: dwell in a corner of the h.	
	BIBLE 54:20
sitteth alone upon the h.	PRAY 396:12
housewife: h. Fortune from her wheel	
	SHAK 424:21
to the h. that's thrifty	SHER 506:31
housewives: h. in your beds	SHAK 474:15
hovel: h. to your dreary marble	CALV 127:22
hovers: Between two worlds life h.	
	BYRON 124:9
How: H. and Where and Who	KIPL 300:12
H. are the mighty fallen	BIBLE 50:17
H. can these things be	BIBLE 71:37
H. can they use such names	SASS 414:19
H. could they tell	PARK 368:23
H. Do I love thee	BROW 98:13
h. do you like *that*	GILB 227:4
H. he will talk	LEE 313:11
H. many things I can do	SOCR 512:22

H. many years a mortal	SHAK 446:18
h. much it is	BROW 99:22
H. NOT TO DO IT	DICK 178:16
H. well I know what I mean	BROW 99:17
that's h. it all began	KIPL 300:22
Howard: Then sware Lord Thomas H.	
	TENN 542:21
Howards: blood of all the H.	POPE 379:23
how-de-doo: Here's a h.	GILB 227:2
Howell & James: H. young man	GILB 227:28
Howl: H., howl, howl, howl	SHAK 456:8
H., ye ships of Tarshish	BIBLE 58:17
howlet: h.'s wing	SHAK 462:3
howling: h. of Irish wolves	SHAK 427:1
Imagine h.	SHAK 464:14
Howls: H. the sublime	DICK 179:22
still h. on for more	SHEL 501:17
Howth Castle: recirculation back to H.	
	JOYCE 286:2
huddled: downward lay the h. suicides	
	PLOM 374:19
h. masses yearning	LAZ 311:13
hue: h. was not the wear	HOUS 264:17
With h. like that when	SHEL 503:21
hues: living h. and odours plain	SHEL 502:8
thee all her lovely h.	DAV 172:16
Hugest: H. of living creatures	MILT 349:1
hugger-mugger: In h. to inter him	
	SHAK 436:5
Hugo: croyait Victor H.	COCT 154:13
H.—hélas	GIDE 225:6
Victor H. madman	COCT 154:13
hugs: don't want any more h.	AUDEN 19:14
h. it to the last	MOORE 356:28
hulk: Here, a sheer h.	DIBD 175:21
Hull: who settled first at H.	DEFOE 173:5
hum: busy h. of men	MILT 342:24
H. half a tune	POPE 377:7
mist and h. of that low	ARN 14:28
pilgrim borne in heedless h.	COLL 158:18
with his surly h.	SHAK 443:9
humains: Frères h. qui après nous	VILL 557:4
human: all that h. hearts endure	GOLD 231:30
all that h. hearts endure	JOHN 282:21
Are all the h. frame requires...'	BELL 39:2
Art's subject is the h.	AUDEN 19:16
bounds of h. Empire	BACON 28:6
breathing h. passion far above	KEATS 291:7
Communism with a h. face	DUBC 198:24
constant in h. sufferings	JOYCE 286:17
contributions to h. development	ARN 15:21
does a H. Form display	BLAKE 85:18
err is h., not to, animal	FROST 219:13
first the h. race began	BURNS 113:21
forget the h. race	BYRON 121:21
happiness of the h. race	BURKE 110:7
held the h. race in scorn	BELL 38:33
highest type of h. nature	SPEN 514:28
history of the h. spirit	ARN 16:17
h. beings are born free	ANON 4:14
h. bodies are sic fools	BURNS 115:27
h. creatures' lives	HOOD 255:7
h. industry springs up	TOCQ 551:9
H. kind Cannot bear	ELIOT 202:14
h. nature is finer	KEATS 293:27
H. on my faithless arm	AUDEN 19:17
I see the lords of h. kind	GOLD 231:28
Larger than h. on the frozen	TENN 535:23
laugh at h. actions	SPIN 517:7
less h. for being devout	MOL 353:25
milk of h. kindness	CHUR 148:22
milk of h. kindness	SHAK 459:1
nothing h. foreign to me	TER 544:17
Peace, the h. dress	BLAKE 88:7
production of h. nature	ADD 2:9
proportioned to the h. constitution	
	BERK 41:21
provide for h. *wants*	BURKE 111:1
purest of h. pleasures	BACON 26:18
sum of h. wretchedness	BYRON 125:18

Terror the h. form divine — BLAKE 88:9
think the full tide of h. — JOHN 276:21
thorough knowledge of h. — AUST 22:31
'Tis a shame to h. nature — HOUS 266:8
To be a soaring h. boy — DICK 176:14
To err is h. — POPE 378:27
To step aside is h. — BURNS 112:25
Treatise of H. Nature — HUME 268:1
When in the course of h. — JEFF 272:5
wisdom of h. contrivances — BURKE 109:18
wish I loved the H. Race — RAL 404:20
would be due to h. folly — LAW 311:1
humani: h. nil a me alienum puto — TER 544:17
Humanities: H. live for ever — NORTH 364:5
humanity: crooked timber of h. — KANT 288:14
h., reason, and justice — BURKE 109:26
H. with all its fears — LONG 316:7
law of h. — BURKE 110:32
out of the feelings of h. — BLAC 85:2
popular h. is treason — ADD 1:21
religion of h. — PAINE 368:7
So act as to treat h. — KANT 288:13
spirit never Did steer h. — SHAK 423:19
still, sad music of h. — WORD 578:7
strait jacket for h. — MER 337:23
teach governments h. — PAINE 368:4
they imitated h. so abominably — SHAK 433:17
wearisome condition of h. — GREV 236:16
human kind: vices and follies of h. — CONG 159:20
human race: h., to which so many — CHES 148:2
humans: It isn't fit for h. now — BETJ 44:4
Humber: Of H. would complain — MARV 332:18
humble: Be it ever so h. — PAYNE 370:10
confess them with an h. — PRAY 384:9
He that is h. ever shall — BUNY 107:32
he that shall h. himself — BIBLE 67:23
h. and a contrite heart — KIPL 302:7
such names and not be h. — SASS 414:19
humbled: maintains that I am h. now — CORN 162:19
humbleness: All h. — SHAK 426:29
whispering h. — SHAK 466:3
humbler: h. heav'n — POPE 379:5
humblest: h. citizen of all the land — BRYAN 106:7
humbleth: he that h. himself shall — BIBLE 70:9
humbly: me to my Lord right h. — PRAY 391:14
walk h. with thy God — BIBLE 61:25
humbug: h. in a Pickwickian point — DICK 181:22
Hume: hand of Mr H. in 1739 — SMITH 511:33
humid: h. nightblue fruit — JOYCE 286:29
Humiliation: valley of H. — BUNY 107:13
humility: 'Had he but the gift of h. — STIL 523:14
H. may clothe an English — COWP 167:35
modest stillness and h. — SHAK 443:21
pride that apes h. — COL 156:13
to visit us in great h. — PRAY 386:4
humour: effusions of wit and h. — AUST 22:31
ever woman in this h. won — SHAK 480:22
H. is odd, grotesque — SWIFT 528:7
h. just, yet new — CHUR 149:12
h. temp'ring virtuous rage — POPE 378:8
most perfect h. and irony — BUTL 118:23
say it is my h. — SHAK 467:20
humoured: must be play'd with and h. — TEMP 532:9
humours: h. and flatters them — CHES 145:26
In all thy h. — ADD 2:10
hump: Camel's h. is an ugly lump — KIPL 300:9
H. that is black and blue — KIPL 300:10
uglier yet is the H. we get — KIPL 300:9
without a positive h. — THAC 545:21
humphed: Camel h. himself — KIPL 304:18
humus: Nos habebit h. — ANON 10:13
Hun: H. is at the gate — KIPL 299:6

Huncamunca: To sun my self in H.'s — FIEL 211:34
hundred: His h.'s soon hit — BROW 100:38
moderate haste might tell a h. — SHAK 430:12
hundreds: h. to Ludlow come — HOUS 263:6
Hundredth: At my door the H. Psalm — CALV 127:23
left him practising the h. — BYRON 126:10
Hung: H. be the heavens with — SHAK 445:17
ocean Is folded and h. — AUDEN 18:9
Hungarian: It's not enough to be H. — KORDA 305:27
Hunger: H. allows no choice — AUDEN 20:9
h. and thirst after righteousness — BIBLE 64:6
H. is the best sauce — CERV 138:13
h. of ambitious minds — SPEN 516:21
H. that urges to wrongdoing — VIRG 558:21
h., thirst, forced marches — GAR 221:10
I perish with h. — BIBLE 70:19
lack, and suffer h. — PRAY 391:22
poverty, h., and dirt — HOOD 255:6
remember the time of h. — BIBLE 63:5
They shall h. no more — BIBLE 82:3
with bodily h. in his eyes — SHAW 497:13
Yet fed your h. like — CRANE 168:30
hungred: I was an h. — BIBLE 68:6
hungry: ate when we were not h. — SWIFT 526:10
Cassius has a lean and h. — SHAK 448:20
fierce, weeping, h. man — CARL 132:24
filleth the h. soul with — PRAY 397:7
have seen the h. ocean gain — SHAK 494:3
He hath filled the h. with — BIBLE 69:6
h. with good things — BIBLE 83:18
I am not h. — PUNCH 402:29
If thine enemy be h. — BIBLE 54:29
is all as h. as the sea — SHAK 489:6
roaming with a h. heart — TENN 543:10
she makes h. — SHAK 422:5
tigers are getting h. — CHUR 151:3
You've time to get h. — MOL 353:16
hunt: can h. a poetaster down — BYRON 124:31
We h. them for the beauty — TENN 542:8
You will see H. — SHEL 501:18
hunted: others by their h. expression — LEWIS 314:8
Past reason h. — SHAK 495:7
hunter: Esau was a cunning h. — BIBLE 46:13
from the snare of the h. — PRAY 395:21
h. home from the hill — STEV 523:10
H. of the East has caught — FITZ 212:5
Nimrod the mighty h. before — BIBLE 46:1
trail'd the h.'s javelin — ARN 14:26
Hunter Dunn: Joan H. — BETJ 44:6
hunters: That seith that h. ben — CHAU 141:18
hunting: discourse was about h. — PEPYS 372:11
ever to call h. one of them — JOHN 280:15
go h. the beautiful deer — AUDEN 18:8
H. he lov'd — SHAK 495:18
I'm weary wi' h. — BALL 31:5
in wet and dirty from h. — SURT 525:26
I went h. wild — OWEN 367:10
like the h. of the hare — BLUNT 89:4
than to h. and shooting — BURR 116:10
There is a passion for h. — DICK 180:35
huntress: Queen and h. — JONS 283:24
hunts: he h. in dreams — TENN 538:21
huntsman: cassock'd h. and a fiddling — COWP 166:7
h. by the bear oppress'd — WALL 562:6
H., rest — SCOTT 416:3
hurl: h. my soul from heaven — SHAK 477:21
hurl'd: Swift to be h. — HOOD 254:10
Hurled: H. headlong flaming from — MILT 344:24
hurly-burly: h. of the chaise-longue — CAMP 128:9
When the h.'s done — SHAK 458:1
hurricanoes: You cataracts and h. — SHAK 454:4

hurried: who was h. hence — CLEV 153:3
hurry: h. of hoofs in a village — LONG 316:26
I am never in a h. — WESL 568:20
old man in a h. — CHUR 149:22
sows h. and reaps — STEV 522:5
hurt: assault and h. the soul — PRAY 386:9
done the lover mortal h. — DOUG 191:10
do nothing for to h. her — THAC 546:3
hate the man you have h. — TAC 531:8
have healed also the h. — BIBLE 60:19
Heavenly H., it gives — DICK 184:1
h. in a state than th — BACON 25:43
h. nor destroy in all my — BIBLE 58:11
h. not thy foot against — PRAY 395:22
h. that Honour feels — TENN 538:23
h. the truest knight — MAL 327:16
h. with the same weapons — SHAK 467:4
I have to be h. — SHAK 477:14
'I'll not h. thee — STER 519:24
it h. too much to laugh — STEV 520:19
shall h. the little wren — BLAKE 85:12
that doth the h. — BACON 27:30
that seek the h. of my soul — PRAY 393:22
that they mayn't h. you — LAMB 307:30
They that have power to h. — SHAK 494:15
Those have most power to h. — BEAU 36:9
hurtig: You are h. be — KIPL 304:22
hurting: once it has stopped h. — BOWEN 91:2
hurts: He h. me most who lavishly — CHUR 148:18
h., and is desir'd — SHAK 424:12
h. the poor creatures — SHAK 454:22
husband: answers till a h. cools — POPE 377:27
bride adorned for her h. — BIBLE 82:30
Chaste to her h. — POPE 377:20
comes my h. from his whist — BROW 100:20
good h., little ant — LOV 318:14
Hang your h. and be dutiful — GAY 222:19
h. a cuckold to make him — SHAK 477:2
h. could have made me like — CONG 160:13
H., I come — SHAK 424:11
h. in these circumstances — GAY 222:31
h. is a whole-time job — BENN 40:22
h. is, the wife is — TENN 538:19
h. nature's riches from — SHAK 494:15
h. of one wife — BIBLE 79:12
h. with a beard on his — SHAK 472:3
ill bred as to love a h. — WYCH 584:1
life her h. makes for her — ELIOT 201:9
man and most indulgent h. — DICK 178:25
monstrous animal a h. and wife — FIEL 211:30
much for one h. to hear — GAY 222:36
My h. then — SHAK 485:13
No worse a h. than — SHAK 422:1
she must have a h. — SHAK 484:7
so in the eyes of a h. — SWIFT 526:22
so may my h. — SHAK 465:6
sways she level in her h.'s — SHAK 489:1
Thy h. is thy lord — SHAK 484:17
unbelieving h. is sanctified — BIBLE 76:3
wife doth make a heavy h. — SHAK 468:21
woman is a crown to her h. — BIBLE 53:33
woman oweth to her h. — SHAK 484:18
husbanded: Being so fathered and so h. — SHAK 449:16
husband-hunting: h. butterfly she ever remembers — MITF 352:22
husbandry: Expresseth his full tilth and h. — SHAK 463:13
There's h. in heaven — SHAK 459:13
husbands: dare not show their h. — SHAK 475:18
divine right of h. — WOLL 576:9
H., love your wives — BIBLE 78:27
reasons for h. to stay at home — ELIOT 201:20
them ask their h. at home — BIBLE 76:17
yourselves to your own h. — BIBLE 78:6
hush: holy h. of ancient sacrifice — STEV 520:18
H.! Here comes the enemy — CONDE 159:16
H., hush, Nobody cares — MORT 358:15

h. with the setting moon · TENN 540:10
H. your tongues · HOR 260:13
old man who said 'H. · LEAR 311:18
There's a breathless h. · NEWB 361:8
hush'd: Now air is h. · COLL 158:18
hushed: h. the shrunken seas · ELIOT 204:15
Hushing: H. the latest traffic · BRID 92:12
husks: come is strew'd with h. · SHAK 487:14
filled his belly with the h. · BIBLE 70:19
hustle: health to h. the Aryan brown · KIPL 301:18
who tried to h. the East · KIPL 301:18
hut: Love in a h. · KEATS 290:24
huts: Love had he found in h. · WORD 581:11
Hyacinth: Children with H.'s temperament · SAKI 413:16
every H. the Garden wears · FITZ 212:15
Hyades: scudding drifts the rainy H. · TENN 543:22
Hybla: rob the H. bees · SHAK 451:31
Hymeneal: Chorus H. · SHEL 504:20
hymns: Chanting faint h. · SHAK 469:17
happy h. of farmers · KING 297:21
Singing h. unbidden · SHEL 504:19
sings h. at heaven's gate · SHAK 493:6
with h. uproarious · BETJ 43:3
yourselves in psalms and h. · BIBLE 78:5
hyperbole: perpetual h. is comely · BACON 26:29
hyperboles: Three-pil'd h · SHAK 457:15
hyperbolical: h. fiend · SHAK 490:19
hypercritical: Constitution or laws by any h. · LINC 314:18
Hyperion: H. to a satyr · SHAK 429:28
Hyphenated: H. Americans · ROOS 408:8
hypocrisie: L'h. est un hommage que le · LA R 310:12
hypocrisy: By thy shut soul's h. · BYRON 125:4
Government is an organized h. · DISR 184:16
h.; from envy · PRAY 385:16
H., the only evil that organized h. · MILT 347:12
That would be h. · BAG 29:8
 · WILDE 573:5
hypocrite: h., and flatterer · BLAKE 86:7
H. lecteur · BAUD 35:5
h. lecteur · ELIOT 204:22
is a h. in his pleasures · JOHN 279:22
hypocrites: h.! for ye pay tithe · BIBLE 67:24
though the cant of h. may · STER 519:30
hypoteneuse: about the square on the h. · GILB 228:17
hypothesis: beautiful h. by an ugly fact · HUXL 269:5
character of a family to an h. · STER 519:23
is the nature of an h. · STER 519:27
hyssop: shalt purge me with h. · PRAY 393:5
will sprinkle me with h. · BIBLE 83:6
hysterics: blind h. of the Celt · TENN 537:16
I: altogether such as I. am · BIBLE 74:28
A noir, E blanc, I. rouge · RIMB 406:9
Here am I., here are you · AUDEN 19:14
I. am fearfully and wonderfully · PRAY 399:6
I. am the batsman · LANG 309:19
'I. am thyself · ROSS 410:3
if I. had not been there · WELL 567:19
'I. is hateful · PASC 369:12
to earth I. · HOUS 265:12
Tush, I. shall never be cast · PRAY 389:30
were I. Lord God · MACD 325:3
Why not I. with thine · SHEL 502:1
iactu: Pulveris exigui i. compressa · VIRG 560:18
Iago: conceiving an I. as an Imogen · KEATS 294:7
Iam: I. redit et virgo · VIRG 559:22
Iambics: I. march from short · COL 157:4
iambos: At non effugies meos i. · CAT 137:16
ianua: dies patet atri i. Ditis · VIRG 558:18
Ibant: I. obscuri sola sub nocte · VIRG 558:20
Iberians: dark I. come · ARN 14:21

ibit: in caelum iusseris i. · JUV 287:16
ice: forth his i. like morsels · PRAY 399:21
hissed along the polished i. · WORD 577:25
his urine is congealed i. · SHAK 464:19
hot i. and wondrous strange · SHAK 471:13
I. formed on the butler's · WOD 575:27
i., mast-high · COL 155:9
In skating over thin i. · EMER 207:33
is good to break the i. · BACON 25:41
penny i. and cold meat · GILB 226:14
To smooth the i. · SHAK 452:25
ye I. and Snow · PRAY 384:22
Iceberg: silent distance grew the I. · HARDY 239:6
ice-cream: emperor is the emperor of i. · STEV 520:14
I., of course · SASS 415:4
iced: three parts i. over · ARN 16:24
Iceland: is not so bad as I. · JOHN 279:23
ices: tea and cakes and i. · ELIOT 203:22
I-chabod: named the child I. · BIBLE 49:40
ichor: perspiration was but i. · BYRON 126:7
icicle: Chaste as the i. · SHAK 428:3
i. on a Dutchman's beard · SHAK 489:28
icicles: hang them up in silent i. · COL 156:23
When i. hang by the wall · SHAK 457:19
icumen: Sumer is i. · ANON 7:18
Ida: There lies a vale in I. · TENN 541:16
Whether on I.'s shady brow · BLAKE 88:10
idea: against invasion by an i. · HUGO 267:11
Between the i. And the reality · ELIOT 203:10
call it the i. of freedom · PARK 368:26
he had only one i. · DISR 186:31
i. ever to be fashionable · SANT 414:5
i. of Death saves · FORS 217:3
is the pain of a new i. · BAG 29:19
me to possess but one i. · JOHN 275:34
politician does get an i. · MARQ 331:1
simplicity of his i. calling · CONR 161:21
young i. how to shoot · THOM 549:10
ideal: happiness is not an i. of reason · KANT 288:12
i. reader suffering from · JOYCE 286:3
it is the i. American who · CHES 148:6
nicht an I. der Vernunft · KANT 288:12
paletot aussi devenait i. · RIMB 406:7
softly sleeps the calm I. · DICK 179:22
idealistic: America is the only i. · WILS 575:3
idealize: they i. love too much · JOW 285:24
ideas: are but the signs of i. · JOHN 281:6
green i. sleep · CHOM 148:15
idées: Elle a des i. au-dessus · RATT 405:2
pas à l'invasion des i. · HUGO 267:11
identity: because he has no i. · KEATS 294:8
equal communion and I. · DONNE 191:3
His i. presses upon me · KEATS 294:2
ides: Beware the i. of March · SHAK 448:7
i. of March are come · SHAK 449:23
idiom: i. of words very little · PRIOR 400:2
idioms: licentious i. · JOHN 282:5
idiosyncrasy: rather i. · BROW 96:27
idiot: blaspheming over the village i. · CHES 148:7
e'er the beauteous i. spoke · CONG 160:2
i. race to honour · BURNS 114:29
i. who praises · GILB 226:25
portrait of a blinking i. · SHAK 466:21
tale Told by an i. · SHAK 463:6
your I. Boy · WORD 577:23
idiots: fatuity of i. · SMITH 511:30
idle: am happiest when I am i. · WARD 564:34
be not i. · BURT 117:3
calling for this i. trade · POPE 376:23
employment for his i. time · WALT 564:3
have not been i.' · ANON 6:9
home, you i. creatures · SHAK 448:5
i. as a painted ship · COL 155:19
i. chatter of a transcendental · GILB 227:21
i. hands to do · WATTS 565:22
i. hill of summer · HOUS 263:18

i. spear and shield · MILT 344:6
idle than when wholly i. · CIC 151:23
i. word that men shall · BIBLE 66:10
most i. and unprofitable · GIBB 224:7
Most 'scruciating i. · KIPL 304:17
Never to be completely i. · THOM 546:11
not learnt how to be i. · MADAN 326:17
solitary, be not i. · JOHN 278:11
whom the world Calls i. · COWP 167:7
would all be i. if we could · JOHN 277:3
ye here all the day i. · BIBLE 67:14
you are i. shallow things · SHAK 490:8
idleness: Conceives by i. · SHAK 445:12
Grief is a species of i. · JOHN 281:26
I. is only the refuge · CHES 145:28
i., its opposite · CERV 138:19
My i. doth hatch · SHAK 421:19
pains and penalties of i. · POPE 375:25
round of strenuous i. · WORD 580:18
idler: Hath been an i. in the land · WORD 580:5
hopes to be, an i. · JOHN 281:17
idling: impossible to enjoy i. · JER 272:22
Idol: false I. Honour · WINC 575:4
make both God and an i. · LUTH 320:17
natural i. of the Anglo-Saxon · BAG 29:4
on an 'eathen i.'s foot · KIPL 301:6
idolaters: i., and whosoever loveth · BIBLE 83:3
idolatries: To its i. a patient knee · BYRON 120:38
idolatry: ancients without i. · CHES 145:20
on this side i. · JONS 285:1
There is no i. in the Mass · JOHN 275:30
Which is the god of my i. · SHAK 482:15
Idols: I. I have loved so long · FITZ 213:13
idoneus: Vixi puellis nuper i. · HOR 261:6
idyll: Will rank as an i. · GILB 227:25
If: I. I am not for myself · HILL 251:6
i. I said so · GOLD 232:4
I. thou must love me · BROW 98:11
i. thou wert there · BURNS 114:31
I. you can keep your head · KIPL 299:22
much virtue in 'i.' · SHAK 427:6
ifs: Talk'st thou to me of 'i.' · SHAK 481:5
ignara: i. mali miseris succurrere · VIRG 557:19
ignoble: base and i. creature · BACON 25:25
end Was not i. · WORD 580:1
soil'd with all i. use · TENN 537:17
ignominy: disgrace and i. of our natures · BROW 96:20
Thy i. sleep with thee · SHAK 440:25
ignorance: Alike in i. · POPE 379:12
child of i. and baseness · BACON 25:31
From i. our comfort flows · PRIOR 401:8
from knowledge i. · BROW 100:10
i. cramps my conversation · HOPE 255:30
I. is not innocence · BROW 101:17
i. of wealth · GOLD 230:18
I. of the law excuses no · SELD 419:21
I pity his i. and despise · DICK 180:10
more than Gothic i. · FIEL 211:26
pure i. · JOHN 274:12
putting us to i. again · BROW 100:5
smallest allowance for i. · HUXL 269:6
there is no sin but i. · MARL 329:19
was distinguished for i. · DISR 186:31
what i. of pain · SHEL 504:21
Where blind and naked I. · TENN 535:11
where i. is bliss · GRAY 235:13
women in a state of i. · KNOX 305:26
ignorant: Be not i. of any thing · BIBLE 62:24
Confound the i. · SHAK 433:1
i. armies clash by night · ARN 12:23
i. of his understanding · COL 157:21
i. of their Mother Tongue · DRYD 198:14
i., unweighing fellow · SHAK 464:20
In language, the i. · DUPPA 199:16
poor, ailing and i. · YEATS 585:3
schoolboy of fourteen is i. · MAC 324:12

they should always be i. AUST 23:5
this right of the i. man CARL 131:16
utterly i. of all moral fear SMITH 512:2
well as the i. and foolish PRAY 392:28
ignorantly: I did it i. in unbelief BIBLE 79:7
therefore ye i. worship BIBLE 74:12
ignore: qu'un homme comme vous i.
BEAU 35:16
ignotique: Urgentur i. longa HOR 261:18
ignotum: omne i. pro magnifico est TAC 531:6
Ignotus: I. *pecori* CAT 137:6
iguala: balanza y peso que i. al pastor
CERV 138:20
île: i. triste et noire BAUD 35:8
Iliad: greater than the I. is born PROP 401:17
Ilium: fuit I. et ingens VIRG 558:6
ill: all the measureless i. TENN 539:29
bad epitaph than their i. SHAK 432:25
he thinks no i. SHAK 493:18
i. all's here about my SHAK 437:14
i. beginning of the night SHAK 451:29
i. bred as to love a husband WYCH 584:1
i. discoverers that think BACON 24:21
I. fares the land GOLD 230:18
i. he cannot cure a name ARN 15:12
i. keeper of promise BACON 25:32
I. met by moonlight SHAK 470:4
let i. tidings tell Themselves SHAK 422:12
much less good than i. HOUS 264:14
no i. can come PRAY 400:5
old and i. and terrified BETJ 44:13
sight of means to do i. SHAK 452:28
than to rail at the i. TENN 540:19
There is some i. a-brewing SHAK 466:11
to do i. our sole delight MILT 345:5
train for i. and not HOUS 264:14
illacrimabiles: sed omnes i. HOR 261:18
ill-bred: so illiberal and so i. CHES 145:10
ill breeding: sign of guilt, or of i.
CONG 160:34
ill-clad: i., ill-nourished ROOS 407:22
ill-contrived: is a singularly i. world
BALF 30:6
ill-doing: doctrine of i. SHAK 491:8
Ille: I. mi par esse deo videtur CAT 137:4
ill-fed: it is i. JOHN 279:16
Ill fortune: I. seldom comes alone
DRYD 195:36
ill-housed: one-third of a nation i.
ROOS 407:22
illiberal: nothing so i. and so ill-bred
CHES 145:10
illiteracy: at the i. of scientists SNOW 512:16
Illiterate: I. him SHER 506:8
ill-luck: fond of i. that they run JERR 273:8
way upon the singular i. CHES 146:6
illness: i. should attend it SHAK 459:1
Living is an i. to which CHAM 139:13
illnesses: i. and dreary old age VIRG 560:16
ill-nourished: ill-clad, i. ROOS 407:22
illogical: doctrine so i. and so dull
KEYN 295:16
ills: climax of all human i. BYRON 122:29
have they of i. to come GRAY 235:12
i. enow To be a woman DONNE 190:4
i. o' life victorious BURNS 115:6
i. the scholar's life assail JOHN 282:29
sure one for all i. RAL 404:17
What i. from beauty spring JOHN 283:4
ill-shapen: creatures at first are i.
BACON 26:27
ill-spent: was a sign of an i. youth SPEN 515:4
ill-tempered: Some think him i. and queer
LEAR 311:20
ill-treated: This is for all i. fellows
HOUS 265:13
illuminate: please thee to i. all Bishops
PRAY 385:18
illuminatio: Dominus i. mea BIBLE 83:5

Illumine: What in me is dark I. MILT 344:22
illumined: i. by flashes of lightning
WILDE 573:37
illumineth: It i. the face SHAK 442:15
ill-usage: complaints of i. contemptible
MELB 336:18
illusion: i. that it is the other GOW 233:7
nothing but sophistry and i. HUME 267:15
only one i. left SMITH 511:6
So thankful for i. CLOU 153:23
illustrate: I the Trinity i. BROW 105:6
Illustrious: I. acts high raptures do
WALL 562:12
less i., goes the clerk COWP 166:1
One of my i. predecessors FIEL 211:9
Illyria: what should I do in I. SHAK 487:22
image: Best i. of myself and dearer
MILT 348:15
compose man's i. and his cry YEATS 586:22
express i. of his person BIBLE 79:28
fleeting i. of a shade SHEL 505:9
God nevertheless his i. FULL 220:15
i. of eternity BYRON 121:26
i. of his Maker SHAK 447:12
I., that flying still WORD 577:26
i. that Nebuchadnezzar BIBLE 61:3
knowledge after the i. BIBLE 78:26
Let us make man in our i. BIBLE 45:4
Man is God's i. HERB 247:9
Save in the constant i. SHAK 488:27
Scatter'd his Maker's i. DRYD 194:2
this i. and superscription BIBLE 67:19
unto thee any graven i. BIBLE 47:24
where name and i. meet AUDEN 20:6
with the i. of the King TENN 534:17
worship the beast and his i. BIBLE 82:17
images: express the i. of their minds
BACON 27:4
garden of bright i. BRAM 91:22
imaginary: Don't let us make i. evils
GOLD 232:12
'i. gardens with real toads MOORE 355:20
i. relish is so sweet SHAK 486:32
imagination: abhorred in my i. it is
SHAK 436:31
affections and the truth of i. KEATS 293:15
Are of i. all compact SHAK 471:11
hunting-grounds for the poetic i. ELIOT 201:7
ideal of reason but of i. KANT 288:12
if i. amend them SHAK 471:19
i. of man's heart is evil BIBLE 45:36
i. cold and barren BURKE 109:16
I. droops her pinion BYRON 123:9
i. of a boy is healthy KEATS 288:19
i. the rudder KEATS 293:13
i. resembled the wings MAC 323:5
i. bodies forth SHAK 471:11
I., which, in truth WORD 580:26
in ages of i. this firm BLAKE 88:26
only upon the force of i. DRYD 196:26
refined play of the i. BURKE 108:7
requisite for an Historian...I. JOHN 274:29
save those that have no i. SHAW 498:20
scattered the proud in the i. BIBLE 69:6
to his i. for his facts SHER 506:36
to sweeten my i. SHAK 455:17
Were it not for i. JOHN 278:4
whispering chambers of I. DICK 179:22
imaginations: my i. are as foul SHAK 434:3
perish through their own i. PRAY 389:25
imagine: buona i. paterna DANTE 171:12
may as well i. the scene COMP 159:13
people i. a vain PRAY 389:15
imagined: i. such a device as they
PRAY 390:15
imaginibus: umbris et i. in veritatem
NEWM 362:6
imaginings: Are less than horrible i.
SHAK 458:20
imbecility: moderation in war is i. MAC 323:8

imitan: pintores i. la naturaleza CERV 139:1
imitate: be obliged to i. himself REYN 405:18
I. him if you dare YEATS 587:3
i. the action of the tiger SHAK 443:21
painters i. nature CERV 139:1
imitated: he who can be i. by none
CHAT 141:5
i. humanity so abominably SHAK 433:17
imitation: not a good i. of Johnson
BURKE 112:14
Were endless i. WORD 579:6
imitator: was a happy i. of Nature HEM 245:2
imitatores: i., servum pecus HOR 259:1
imiter: que personne ne peut i. CHAT 141:5
Immanuel: shall call his name I. BIBLE 58:3
immaturity: that common symptom of
i. WHAR 569:9
immense: error is i. BOL 89:15
immensities: Asiatic vague i. YEATS 587:1
Immensity: I. cloistered in thy dear
DONNE 189:1
swift into the vortex of i. DICK 179:22
imminuit: Damnosa quid non i. dies
HOR 260:26
immonde: De cet égout i. TOCQ 551:9
immoral: people looked on it as i.
GALS 220:30
immorality: i. which involves posing
WEST 569:1
immortal: Being a thing i. as itself
SHAK 430:25
do not seek i. life PIND 373:15
grew i. in his own despite POPE 380:12
i. hand or eye BLAKE 87:14
I. longings in me SHAK 424:10
i. spirit grows WORD 580:11
I., though no more BYRON 120:13
I. youth to mortal maids LAND 308:22
lost the i. part of myself SHAK 475:7
make me i. with a kiss MARL 329:1
pleasures in a long i. dream KEATS 290:23
Sire of an i. strain SHEL 499:4
souls have sight of that i. sea WORD 579:12
when death that is i. has LUCR 320:9
With cold i. hands SWIN 529:22
Immortalia: I. ne speres HOR 261:18
immortalis: Mortalem vitam mors cum
i. LUCR 320:9
immortality: cruel i. Consumes TENN 543:11
earthly i. FORD 216:14
God, I., Duty ELIOT 201:30
heart like a load of i. KEATS 294:4
If I. unveil DICK 183:20
is their hope full of i. BIBLE 62:13
long to believe in i. KEATS 294:29
Nurslings of i. SHEL 503:6
This longing after i. ADD 1:24
this mortal must put on i. BIBLE 76:29
immortalize: mortal thing so to i.
SPEN 515:20
Immortals: President of the I. (in
HARDY 241:25
immured: not alone i. in the brain
SHAK 457:8
Immutable: I. as my regret PEAC 371:1
She was as i. as the Hills KIPL 304:32
Imogen: conceiving an Iago as an I.
KEATS 294:7
imp: i. of fame SHAK 444:17
impairs: All weakness which i. ARN 14:24
Impaling: I. worms to torture COLM 159:6
Imparadised: I. in one another's arms
MILT 348:1
impartial: neutrality of an i. judge
BURKE 111:34
Of a pure i. hate THOR 550:28
security for its i. administration PEEL 371:5
impatience: all patience, and i. SHAK 426:29
impatient: i. of servitude BURKE 109:27
people never so i. PRAY 396:10

Impavidum: *I. ferient ruinae*   HOR 260:19
impeach: I i. him in the name   BURKE 110:33
impeachment: I own the soft i.   SHER 506:23
impedes: All that i. thee from   SHAK 459:1
impediment: cause, or just i.   PRAY 388:23
impediments: i. to great enterprises
                                             BACON 26:31
imperasset: *consensu capax imperii nisi*
  i.   TAC 531:13
Imperativ: *I. ist kategorisch*   KANT 288:10
imperative: i. is Categorical   KANT 288:10
imperator: Sole i. and great general
                                             SHAK 456:26
imperatur: *Naturae enim non i.* BACON 28:10
imperfect: perfect use of an i. medium
                                             WILDE 573:17
  substance, yet being i.   PRAY 399:7
  you i. speakers   SHAK 458:12
imperfections: With all my i. on my
  head   SHAK 431:12
imperial: enslaves you on i. principles
                                             SHAW 498:6
  'I. fiddlestick   CARR 134:27
  Of the i. theme   SHAK 458:19
  We have had an I. lesson   KIPL 300:21
Imperialism: sane I.   ROS 408:14
Imperially: Learn to think I.   CHAM 139:5
imperio: *Tu regere i. populos*   VIRG 559:1
Imperishable: I. peace   HOUS 266:5
Imperium: *I. et Libertas*   DISR 185:19
impertinent: don't ask i. questions
                                             DARW 172:3
  privileg'd to be very i.   FARQ 210:22
imperturbe: Me i.   WHIT 570:6
impious: i. hand to the Crown   BRON 93:14
  i. men bear sway   ADD 1:23
impiously: i. gay   COWP 168:13
implore: we thee i.   ANON 6:17
imponere: *Ter sunt conati i.*   VIRG 560:12
import: works and ones of great i.
                                             HOR 257:11
importance: subject of almost equal i.
                                             BRAM 91:22
important: importunate for being less
  i.   MONT 354:19
  puff and look i. and to say   KIPL 298:18
importantes: *occupations domestiques*
  moins i.   MONT 354:19
importune: I here i. death awhile
                                             SHAK 423:14
  too proud to i.   GRAY 235:21
importunes: *n'en sont pas moins i.*
                                             MONT 354:19
importunity: i. Of business   LAMB 307:33
impose: You i. continency upon us AUG 21:17
imposition: priests by the i. of a mightier
                                             MAC 323:26
impositions: generous beliefs and i.
                                             STEV 521:14
impossibile: *Certum est quia i. est*
                                             TERT 545:1
impossibilities: not i. enough in Religion
                                             BROW 96:8
  Probable i. are to be preferred   ARIS 12:11
impossibility: begotten by despair Upon
  i.   MARV 331:18
impossible: believed as many as six i.
                                             CARR 135:18
  certain because it is i.   TERT 545:1
  false i. shore   ARN 15:2
  have eliminated the i.   DOYLE 192:30
  i.? *cela se fera*   CAL 127:9
  i. loyalties   ARN 15:25
  i. to be silent   BURKE 110:30
  i.? that will be done   CAL 127:9
  In two words: i.   GOLD 232:42
  I wish it were i.   JOHN 280:24
  Patently I. and Vain   KIPL 303:1
  'tis more than i.   CONG 161:6
  With men this is i.   BIBLE 67:12

impostor: let no i. heap   SHEL 504:3
impostors: those two i. just the same
                                             KIPL 299:22
imposuisse: *Pelion i. Olympo*   HOR 260:22
impotently: Rolls i. on as Thou   FITZ 213:8
imprecision: Decay with i.   ELIOT 202:17
  general mess of i. of feeling   ELIOT 202:23
impression: i. of pleasure in itself
                                             BACON 24:14
  us the i. that we exist   BECK 36:16
impressive: i. sights in the world BARR 34:21
impressiveness: i. on what we call our
                                             DICK 179:21
Imprimendi: *Artis nimirum I.*   BACON 28:9
imprint: have done set it in i.   CAXT 138:4
imprison'd: you suffer'd me to be i.
                                             SHAK 490:24
Imprisoned: I. in every fat man a thin
                                             CONN 161:15
  i. in the viewless winds   SHAK 464:14
imprisonetur: *i., aut dissaisiatur* MAGN 327:2
imprisonment: leaves his well belov'd
  i.   DONNE 189:1
improbable: preferred to i. possibilites
                                             ARIS 12:11
improper: only hope it is not i.   GASK 222:2
  proper or i.   FULL 220:10
impropriety: without i.   GILB 226:12
improve: anxious to i. the nick of time
                                             THOR 550:9
  I. each shining hour   WATTS 565:21
  Man can i. himself   AUDEN 19:13
improved: be enormously i. by death
                                             SAKI 413:4
  i. life by the knowledge   VIRG 558:23
improvement: hindrances to human i.
                                             MILL 339:18
  political i. are very laughable   JOHN 275:29
improvements: No great i. in the lot
                                             MILL 338:22
imprudent: Nobody could be so i.
                                             AUST 22:15
impudence: credulity increases his i.
                                             HUME 267:19
  men starve for want of i.   DRYD 195:38
  much of Cockney i. before   RUSK 411:7
impulse: first i. was never a crime
                                             CORN 162:18
  from the i. of the moment   AUST 23:13
  lonely i. of delight   YEATS 585:15
  seas in one i. of your soul   SHAW 496:29
impulses: no truck with first i.   MONT 355:11
impune: *Nemo me i. lacessit*   ANON 10:15
impunity: one provokes me with i.
                                             ANON 10:15
impure: Puritan all things are i.   LAWR 311:2
impurity: we bring i. much rather
                                             MILT 351:24
imputantur: *Qui nobis pereunt et i.*
                                             MART 331:11
impute: sin I i. to each frustrate BROW 105:21
imputeth: whom the Lord i. no sin
                                             PRAY 391:16
in: are out wish to get i.   EMER 208:6
  i. it is merely a bore   WILDE 573:31
  profanation to keep i.   HERR 248:24
  that the one is i.   CHUR 148:20
  Thou, my God, art i.'t   HERR 250:15
  thy coming i.   PRAY 398:10
  who's i., who's out   SHAK 456:3
inaccuracy: hate i.   BUTL 119:5
inactivity: wise and masterly i.   MACK 325:12
inane: along the illimitable i.   TENN 539:20
  Pinnacled dim in the intense i.   SHEL 503:12
inania: *Ditis vacuas et i. regna*   VIRG 558:20
inanimate: if aught i. e'er grieves
                                             BYRON 120:26
  total depravity of i. things   HAM 238:14
Inapprehensible: I., we clutch thee
                                             THOM 548:24

inarticulate: close-companioned i. hour
                                             ROSS 409:24
  conclusions—largely i.   KIPL 302:5
  raid on the i.   ELIOT 202:23
inaudible: Am I i.   FRY 219:29
incantation: by the i. of this verse
                                             SHEL 502:14
incapable: one i. of her own distress
                                             SHAK 436:19
  organically I am i. of a tune   LAMB 307:2
  totally i. of governing   CHES 146:6
incapacity: dark sanctuary of i.   CHES 146:5
incardinate: he's the very devil i.
                                             SHAK 490:23
incarnadine: multitudinous seas i.
                                             SHAK 460:13
  yellow Cheek of hers to i.   FITZ 212:7
Incarnations: glimmering I.   SHEL 499:9
incarnatus: *et i. est de Spiritu Sancto*
                                             MASS 334:20
Incens'd: I. with indignation Satan
                                             MILT 346:26
Incense: blest unfabled I. Tree   DARL 171:21
  call of i.-breathing Morn   GRAY 234:20
  gods themselves throw i.   SHAK 456:4
  i. is an abomination unto   BIBLE 57:17
  Nor what soft i. hangs   KEATS 291:20
  strong thick stupefying i.-smoke BROW 99:14
incertainties: Nothing more certain than
  i.   BARN 34:3
incest: excepting i. and folk-dancing'
                                             ANON 4:24
inch: every i. a king   SHAK 455:16
Inchcape: It is the I. Rock   SOUT 514:2
inches: die by famine die by i.   HENRY 245:20
  when full i. seven   BRID 92:13
incident: curious i. of the dog DOYLE 192:16
  determination of i.   JAMES 271:12
Incipe: *I., parve puer*   VIRG 560:1
incisive: lady of i. features   MER 337:26
incisors: divided into i. and grinders
                                             BAG 29:13
incite: *les couvre, les nourrit, les i.*
                                             MONT 355:1
incivility: to i. and procrastination DE Q 175:5
inclementia: *et durae rapit i. mortis*
                                             VIRG 560:16
inclination: i. to goodness is imprinted
                                             BACON 26:19
  ought to read just as i.   JOHN 274:31
inclin'd: tree's i.   POPE 377:12
Incline: I. our hearts to keep this PRAY 387:8
  i. your ears unto the words   PRAY 395:3
inclined: he i. unto me   PRAY 392:1
  of them i. to the *landed*   ADD 2:14
Include: known for saying 'I. me out'
                                             GOLD 232:44
  You can i. me out   GOLD 232:43
income: Annual i. twenty pounds DICK 177:4
  £40,000 a year a moderate i.   LAMB 308:15
  in which a good i. is   SMITH 510:12
  large i. is the best recipe   AUST 22:28
  organism to live beyond its i.   BUTL 118:27
incommunicable: burden of the i.
                                             DE Q 174:26
incompetent: cursing his staff for i. swine
                                             SASS 414:18
  substitutes election by the i.   SHAW 497:36
incomplete: research is always i.   PATT 370:8
incomprehensible: old, wild, and i.
                                             VICT 556:15
  There are not three i.   PRAY 385:13
in-conceivable: family pride is something
  i.   GILB 226:20
Inconsolable: I. to the minuet in Ariadne
                                             SHER 505:26
inconstancy: Constant in nothing but
  i.   BARN 34:3
  world constant, but i.   SWIFT 527:17
  Yet this i. is such   LOV 318:20

Inconstant: I., childish KEATS 293:10
i. woman GAY 223:26
various world with as i. wing SHEL 501:5
incontinence: Delights in filth and foul
i. SPEN 516:14
on the turpitude of i. SCOTT 418:13
incontinent: else be i. before marriage
SHAK 426:27
incontinently: island descending i.
CHUR 151:4
I will i. drown myself SHAK 474:7
inconvenient: it is confoundedly i.
SMITH 511:27
incorporate: members i. in the mystical
PRAY 388:3
incorruptible: dead shall be raised i.
BIBLE 76:29
seagreen I. CARL 131:26
incorruption: corruptible must put on
i. BIBLE 76:29
is the assurance of i. BIBLE 62:19
it is raised in i. BIBLE 76:27
increase: blessest the i. of it PRAY 394:3
cares were to i. his store HOME 253:22
comforts should i. SHAK 474:20
creatures we desire i. SHAK 492:22
dies fighting has i. GREN 236:15
earth bring forth her i. PRAY 394:5
God gave the i. BIBLE 75:31
good and i. of the world TENN 533:9
I. and multiply upon us PRAY 386:16
i. in thy holy Spirit PRAY 388:22
i. of his government BIBLE 58:7
in her the organs of i. SHAK 453:18
increased: not i. the joy BIBLE 58:6
incredible: horrible, fantastic, i. CHAM 139:9
incredulity: i.! the wit of fools CHAP 140:9
increment: Unearned i. MILL 339:4
indecent: not necessary to be i. ROG 407:13
indefatigable: That i. and unsavoury
engine SPAR 514:23
indemnity: bill of i. raid KRUG 306:1
independence: of earthly blessings, i.
GIBB 224:17
inderpendunt: Ain't to be i. LOW 319:7
index: face the i. of a feeling COWP 168:24
publishes a book without an I. CAMP 128:6
thunders in the i. SHAK 435:5
indexes: He writes i. to perfection
GOLD 232:2
in such i. SHAK 486:27
India: driven out of I. this day BURKE 110:24
final message of I. FORS 217:9
fly to I. for gold MARL 329:4
I.'s spicy shores COWP 164:27
key of I. is London DISR 185:20
my metal of I. SHAK 489:9
treasures of I. GIBB 224:6
Indian: good Indian is a dead I. SHER 505:18
I. Summer of the heart WHIT 571:20
Like the base I. SHAK 477:23
out ten to see a dead I. SHAK 485:8
pith of an I. cane ADD 2:11
poor I.'s sleep KEATS 292:6
poor I. POPE 379:5
Veiling an I. beauty SHAK 467:11
Indicat: I. Motorem Bum... GODL 229:24
indices: are full of i. and surds CARR 134:25
indictment: i. against an whole people
BURKE 109:25
Indies: augmentation of the I. SHAK 490:3
indifference: fatal to religion as i.
BURKE 111:35
i. closely bordering STEV 521:17
me i. and a coach and six COLM 158:24
torpor of our i. JOHN 273:17
indifferent: been delayed till I am i.
JOHN 274:7
coerce an i. and self-indulgent STEP 518:20
i. in a week AUDEN 19:7

It is simply i. HOLM 253:5
to be i. to them SHAW 496:17
indifferently: i. minister justice PRAY 387:14
I will look on both i. SHAK 448:12
indigestion: hurry and reaps i. STEV 522:5
indignantly: day and night held on i.
ARN 14:21
indignatio: facit i. versum JUV 287:11
I. *principis mors* MORE 357:13
indignation: Savage i. there YEATS 587:3
they had i. saying BIBLE 68:8
Where fierce i. can no SWIFT 528:12
indignities: i. men come to dignities
BACON 26:23
indirection: By any i. SHAK 451:21
indirections: By i. find directions out
SHAK 431:27
indiscretion: one blazing i. MORL 358:1
indispensable: eloquence are i. to them
MAC 323:13
indisposeth: living i. us for dying
BROW 97:13
indistinct: host with someone i. ELIOT 204:16
makes it i. SHAK 423:8
inditing: heart is i. of a good matter
PRAY 392:14
individual: common notions in an i.
HOR 257:17
I. is wicked AUDEN 19:11
injustice done to an i. JUN 287:6
liberty of the i. must MILL 339:11
No i. could resent SWIFT 527:24
not the i. JOHN 282:6
individualism: American system of rugged
i. HOOV 255:23
individuals: all my love is towards i.
SWIFT 526:23
worth of the i. composing it MILL 339:14
Indocilis: I. pauperiem pati HOR 259:9
indolent: i. expression and an undulating
BELL 40:2
readers to become more i. GOLD 232:1
you chorus of i. reviewers TENN 533:14
indomitable: Still the i. Irishry YEATS 587:9
indubitably: They so very i. *are* BEER 37:23
inducas: et ne nos i. in tentationem
MASS 335:5
induce: wrong could religion i. LUCR 320:4
indulgence: might expect more i.
GOLD 232:13
others in their turn this i. HOR 257:10
industrie: La guerre est l'i. nationale
MIR 352:19
industrious: i. crew to build in hell
MILT 346:4
industry: birth commonly abateth i.
BACON 27:1
Captains of i. CARL 132:11
greatest river of human i. TOCQ 551:9
i. only, but his judgement BURKE 109:11
i. will improve them REYN 405:16
i. without art is brutality RUSK 411:9
national i. of Prussia MIR 352:19
perilous mode of hard i. BURKE 109:17
spur of i. HUME 267:16
indutus: Hectore qui redit exuvias i.
VIRG 558:5
inebriate: That cheer but not i. COWP 167:11
to cheer but not i. BERK 41:21
ineffectual: beautiful and i. angel ARN 16:10
Remote and i. Don BELL 39:27
inefficiency: efficiency and i. SHAW 497:5
inefficient: efficient and the i. SHAW 497:5
ineptior: Nam risu inepto res i. CAT 137:1
ineptire: desinas i. CAT 136:27
ineptitude: in its abysses of i. HOUS 266:15
inertia: Strenua nos exercet i. HOR 258:19
inestimable: thine i. love in the redemption
PRAY 386:2
inevitability: i. of gradualness WEBB 566:7

inevitable: Awaits alike th' i. hour
GRAY 234:21
in arguing with the i. LOW 319:18
inexactitude: risk of terminological i.
CHUR 149:25
inextinguishable: spark of i. thought
SHEL 505:10
infallible: i. criterion of wisdom
BURKE 111:27
only i. rule we know is SURT 525:2
We are none of us i. THOM 549:5
infâme: écrasez l'i. VOLT 561:11
infamous: quiet, and i. MAC 323:18
infancy: have their i. BOL 89:17
lies about us in our i. WORD 579:5
simpler than the i. SHAK 487:2
wayward was thy i. SHAK 481:8
Infandum: I., regina VIRG 557:20
infans: Non sine dis animosus i. HOR 260:21
infant: At first the i. SHAK 425:24
describe the i. phenomenon DICK 180:16
Has gobbled up the i. child HOUS 266:11
i. crying in the night TENN 536:26
i. prattling on his knee BURNS 113:5
Sooner murder an i. BLAKE 88:24
to a little i. BACON 26:3
Where the noble I. lay CRAS 169:6
Your i. beauty could beget SEDL 419:8
infanticide: is as indefensible as i.
WEST 569:2
infantry: That small i. MILT 345:22
infants: i. question in such wise ROSS 409:20
infect: *milieu de ce cloaque i.* TOCQ 551:9
out briskly to i. a city AUDEN 18:19
infected: All seems i. that th'infected
POPE 378:28
i. minds SHAK 462:26
infection: Against i. and the hand of war
SHAK 478:20
that flower with base i. SHAK 494:15
was free from rhyme's i. JONS 285:6
infects: bad news i. the teller SHAK 421:16
infelicity: i. Seem'd to have years
WEBS 566:27
sense of a constant i. TAYL 532:4
inferias: ad i. CAT 137:15
inferior: knowing myself i. to myself
MILT 352:13
pleasure of pleasing i. CLOU 153:3
inferiority: always conscious of an i.
JOHN 277:6
i. that their gratitude JOHN 282:4
inferiors: English want i. TOCQ 551:8
Infernal: hail I. world MILT 345:10
Inferno: their Dante of the dread I.
BROW 103:1
infidel: infidel as a dog is an i. JOHN 275:26
i., I have thee SHAK 468:8
Wine has play'd the I. FITZ 213:14
infidelity: half i. BURKE 111:35
I. does not consist PAINE 367:20
infierno: nuestro lugar sea el i. BORG 89:23
infini: Malgré moi l'i. me tourmente
MUSS 359:4
Infinite: because there is an I. in him
CARL 132:19
both are i. SHAK 482:15
dark unbottom'd i. abyss MILT 346:16
eternal silence of these i. PASC 369:7
idea of the i. torments MUSS 359:4
speaks an i. deal of nothing SHAK 465:15
that the will is i. SHAK 486:33
Infinity: Hold I. in the palm BLAKE 85:8
shares the nature of i. WORD 577:2
infirm: i. glory of the positive ELIOT 201:33
infirmi: i. est animi exiguique JUV 288:6
infirmitie: feblit with i. DUNB 199:8
infirmities: against the i. of ill health
STER 519:15
sake and thine often i. BIBLE 79:16

should bear his friend's i.   SHAK 451:22
infirmity: comparison with the i.
    HOBB 251:22
  last i. of noble mind   MILT 343:8
  prop To our i.   WORD 580:16
inflame: It will i. you   SHAK 450:25
inflammation: i. of his weekly bills
    BYRON 122:29
inflicted: that pain shall not be i.   SPEN 514:26
inflicts: is one who never i. pain NEWM 362:3
influence: bright eyes Rain i.   MILT 342:25
  Corrupt i.   BURKE 110:16
  i. of the Crown has increased   DUNN 199:14
  i. them till they ask   HUGEL 267:5
  no slight or trivial i.   WORD 578:4
  obedience of planetary i.   SHAK 453:11
  one way their precious i.   MILT 344:7
  Spheres of i.   ANON 7:17
  under the name of I.   BURKE 108:19
influences: bind the sweet i. of Pleiades
    BIBLE 53:5
influenza: 'There was no i. in my BENN 40:21
inform: How all occasions do i.   SHAK 435:29
  i. his princes after his   PRAY 397:4
  I will i. thee   PRAY 391:18
informally: Quite i.   COW 164:4
information: I only ask for i.   DICK 177:10
  knowledge we have lost in i.   ELIOT 202:3
  know where we can find i.   JOHN 276:28
  must resort to other i.   JEFF 272:13
informed: i. by the light of nature
    BACON 24:20
infortune: worst kynde of i. is this
    CHAU 144:11
infrequens: Parcus deorum cultor et i.
    HOR 260:2
infusion: i. of a China plant sweetened
    ADD 2:11
ingeminate: i. the word *Peace*   CLAR 152:20
ingenio: Certare i.   LUCR 320:6
ingenium: Grais i.   HOR 257:23
ingenuas: Adde quod i. didicisse OVID 366:25
ingle: His wee bit i.   BURNS 113:5
Inglese: I. Italianato   ASCH 17:3
Inglissh: Sithe he off I. in makyng
    LYDG 321:6
inglorious: i. period of our dominion
    BURKE 110:24
  mean Our object and i.   WORD 580:10
ingots: take i. with us to market CHAM 139:14
ingrat: cent mécontents et un i.   LOUI 318:9
ingrateful: so i. you deny me   SHAK 452:31
  That make i. man   SHAK 454:4
ingratitude: I hate i. more in a man
    SHAK 490:17
  I., more strong than traitors'   SHAK 450:28
  I., thou marble-hearted   SHAK 453:17
  unkind As man's i.   SHAK 426:1
ingratitudes: great-siz'd monster of i.
    SHAK 487:3
Ingres: I.'s the modern man who
    BROW 100:17
inhabitants: like th' i. o' the earth
    SHAK 458:10
inhearse: thoughts in my brain i.
    SHAK 494:11
inherit: rightly do i. heaven's graces
    SHAK 494:15
  they shall i. the earth   BIBLE 64:6
  To-night it doth i.   ARN 14:6
inheritance: Ruinous i.   GAIUS 220:27
inherited: i. it brick and left it   AUG 22:5
inheritor: i. of the kingdom of heaven
    PRAY 388:12
inhibitions: was to cultivate a few i.
    LOOS 318:6
inhuman: i. shout which hail'd
    BYRON 121:15
inhumanity: Man's i. to man   BURNS 114:23
  that's the essence of i.   SHAW 496:17

iniquities: was bruised for our i.   BIBLE 59:22
iniquity: hand is a right hand of i.
    PRAY 399:12
  I lack i.   SHAK 473:20
  i. of oblivion blindly   BROW 97:18
  Rejoiceth not in i.   BIBLE 76:14
  righteousness, and hated i.   PRAY 392:15
  that grey i.   SHAK 439:16
  visiting the i. of the fathers   BIBLE 47:24
iniuria: Nulla i. est   ULP 554:26
injur'd: I i. neither name   HOLL 253:4
injure: feared it might i. the brain
    CARR 133:22
injured: Forgiveness to the i. does
    DRYD 195:30
  from sense of i. merit   MILT 345:2
  i. lover's hell   MILT 348:19
injuries: is adding insult to i.   MOORE 355:13
injury: efforts to do it a violent i. WOD 575:24
  i. and sullenness against   MILT 352:10
  i. is much sooner forgotten   CHES 145:13
  least i. you can do him   JAMES 271:27
injustice: all the rapine and i.   SMITH 509:8
  conscience with i. is corrupted   SHAK 446:6
  endure an hour and see i.   HOUS 264:5
  him against i. and wrong   PALM 368:10
  i. done to an individual   JUN 287:6
  justice or i. of the cause   JOHN 279:30
  man's inclination to i.   NIEB 362:26
  No i. is done to someone   ULP 554:26
injustices: only to justify their i.   VOLT 561:4
sanction des i. établies   FRAN 217:25
ink: all cough in i.   YEATS 586:14
  all the sea were i.   LYLY 321:16
  comparison all whites are i.   SHAK 486:19
  he hath not drunk i.   SHAK 457:1
  of i. in my pen ran cold   WALP 562:23
  Until his i. were temper'd   SHAK 457:8
inky: 'Tis not alone my i. cloak   SHAK 429:25
inlaid: i. with patines of bright   SHAK 468:15
inland: Though i. far we be   WORD 579:12
  tract Of i. ground   WORD 577:16
inmost: may see the i. part of you
    SHAK 434:33
inn: by a good tavern or i.   JOHN 276:35
  Did this soul's second i.   DONNE 190:1
  Do you remember an I.   BELL 40:12
  earth his sober i.   CAMP 129:19
  find a chamber in the i.   ANON 9:1
  life at best is but an i.   HOW 267:1
  not an i., but an hospital   BROW 97:3
  old i., and the lights   MORR 358:12
  room for them in the i.   BIBLE 69:9
  take mine ease in mine i.   SHAK 440:4
  To gain the timely i.   SHAK 461:15
  warmest welcome, at an i.   SHEN 505:15
  world's an i.   DRYD 197:10
innatus: i. apes amor urget habendi
    VIRG 560:19
inner: Spirit in the i. man   BIBLE 77:24
Innisfree: go to I.   YEATS 585:17
  settle down on I.   NASH 360:3
innkeepers: righteous minds of i.
    CHES 147:21
innocence: being hanged in all i. STEV 522:13
  ceremony of i. is drowned   YEATS 586:15
  dallies with the i. of love   SHAK 489:3
  Ignorance is not i. but sin   BROW 101:17
  i. and health   GOLD 230:18
  I. is closing up his eyes   DRAY 193:21
  I. thy Sister dear   MARV 331:22
  is the badge of lost i.   PAINE 367:22
  our business to lose i.   BOWEN 91:6
  ou; fearful i.   WORD 582:9
  to know we sinn'd is i.   DAV 172:5
  Valour and I.   KIPL 302:6
  Was innocence for i.   SHAK 491:8
innocency: Keep i.   PRAY 391:29
  wash my hands in i.   PRAY 391:5

innocent: another down his i. nose
    SHAK 425:1
  Be i. of the knowledge   SHAK 461:14
  be rich shall not be i.   BIBLE 54:42
  children i. and charming   AUDEN 19:12
  escape than one i. suffer   BLAC 85:6
  gay as i.   SCOTT 418:15
  heart whose love is i.   BYRON 125:22
  i. and quiet mind   STEV 521:28
  i. and the beautiful   YEATS 585:12
  i. as gay   YOUNG 588:7
  i. from the great offence   PRAY 390:13
  i. of the blood of this   BIBLE 68:21
  'Men are not i. as beasts   AUDEN 19:13
  Of the brave and i.   AUDEN 19:7
  shed i. blood   BIBLE 60:6
  source of i. merriment   GILB 227:5
  sweet converse of an i.   KEATS 292:20
  taken reward against the i.   PRAY 390:5
innocuous: lambent but i.   GOUL 233:5
innovate: To i. is not to reform BURKE 112:2
innovations: so are all i.   BACON 26:27
innovator: time is the greatest i.
    BACON 26:28
Inns: all I. have been driven   BELL 40:16
  go to i. to dine   CHES 147:18
innumerable: are creeping things i.
    PRAY 397:1
Inopem: I. me copia fecit   OVID 366:15
inopportune: be magnanimous at an i.
    TROT 553:17
inquest: i. of the nation has begun
    BURKE 110:28
  together like the Coroner's I.   CONG 160:32
inquiète: Ne t'i. donc pas   PASC 369:13
Inquisition: I. dogs and the devildoms
    TENN 542:21
irreparabile: fugit i. tempus   VIRG 560:17
insane: eaten on the i. root   SHAK 458:11
  hereditary monarch was i.   BAG 29:9
  Only the i. take themselves   BEER 38:7
insaniae: tumultuositas vulgi semper i.
    ALC 3:9
inscription: found an altar with this i.
    BIBLE 74:12
inscriptions: In lapidary i. a man is
    JOHN 276:31
inscrutable: Deep and i. singular Name
    ELIOT 204:6
  i. and grand   ARN 14:4
  i. workings of Providence   BIRK 84:16
insect: one is but an i.   JOHN 274:8
  this 'ere 'Tortis' is a i.   PUNCH 402:19
insects: loud and troublesome i.
    BURKE 111:16
insensibility: It argues an i.   LAMB 307:4
  stark i.   JOHN 273:27
insensible: It is i. then   SHAK 440:18
inseparable: i. propriety of time BACON 25:5
  one and i.   WEBS 566:11
insert: correct, i., refine   SWIFT 527:34
inside: mortal blow right i.   AESC 3:2
insight: clearest i.   WORD 580:16
  moment's i. is sometimes   HOLM 253:21
insignificance: sterling i.   AUST 23:28
insignificant: I are now two as i. men
    WALP 563:26
insincerity: mark of i. of purpose BRAM 91:18
insinuating: i. Jacks   SHAK 480:23
  Some busy and i. rogue   SHAK 476:23
insipid: i. and tedious performance
    WALP 562:25
insisted: He i. on people praying JOHN 274:24
insolence: flown with i. and wine MILT 345:18
  i. of wealth will creep   JOHN 277:32
  that i. is not invective   DISR 184:20
  wretch who supports with i.   JOHN 281:15
insolent: i. Greece or haughty   JONS 284:22
insomnia: caelum mittunt i. Manes
    VIRG 559:3

suffering from an ideal i.   JOYCE 286:3
inspiration: Genius is one per cent i.
   EDIS 199:25
is not drawing, but *i.*   CONS 162:3
Sibyl without the i.   BURKE 112:14
inspir'd: one i.   COLL 158:21
inspire: feel not what they i.   SHEL 505:13
our souls i.   PRAY 400:5
inspired: i. by divine revelation BACON 24:20
inspirit: Songs may i. us   BROW 102:6
Inspissated: I. gloom   JOHN 275:25
instability: to dissimulate their i.
   HOUS 266:14
instance: some precious i. of itself
   SHAK 436:8
instances: wise saws and modern i.
   SHAK 425:24
instancy: majestic i.   THOM 548:9
instant: Be i. in season   BIBLE 79:25
wealth of thy wit in an i.   SHAK 467:19
instantaneous: I mean i. courage NAP 359:12
instinct: all healthy i. for it   BUTL 119:3
i. bring back the old names   COL 157:8
i. for being unhappy highly   SAKI 413:6
i. of all great souls   BURKE 109:8
I was a coward on i.   SHAK 439:8
masterful like an i.   CONR 161:23
natural i. to discern   WORD 577:3
such a gosling to obey i.   SHAK 427:28
With whose i. the soul   MARL 330:11
instincts: High i. before which our
   WORD 579:10
true to your animal i.   LAWR 311:4
institooshuns: one of the greatest i.
   WARD 564:26
Institute: I., Legion and Social   BETJ 42:13
institution: i. of the dear love   WHIT 570:5
It's an i.   HUGH 267:8
Toute i. qui ne suppose   ROB 406:12
institutions: him with their dirty i.
   THOR 550:19
these i. were all geniuses   SHAW 498:23
instructing: same time as i. him   HOR 258:1
instruction: I will better the i.   SHAK 467:5
wiser than the horses of i.   BLAKE 88:22
instructions: knows whither awaiting
i.   BEER 38:2
Instructor: grand I.   BURKE 112:1
instrument: Call me what i. you will
   SHAK 434:21
is only the i. of science   JOHN 281:6
instrumental: hand more i. to the brain
   SHAK 429:20
instruments: genius and the mortal i.
   SHAK 449:6
What i. we have agree   AUDEN 19:2
insubstantial: like this i. pageant faded
   SHAK 485:20
insufferable: Oxford that has made me
i.   BEER 37:21
insufficient: conclusions from i. premises
   BUTL 118:26
insularum: Paene i.   CAT 136:28
insult: is adding i. to injuries MOORE 355:13
one more i. to God   BROW 102:7
sooner forgotten than an i.   CHES 145:13
Than when a blockhead's i.   JOHN 282:23
insulted: i. by a very considerable
   GILB 226:26
Insultin: I. the sun   NORTH 364:4
insulting: i. Christmas card   GROS 237:3
insults: i. the victim whom he kills
   COWP 168:28
insured: they were heavily i.   GILB 225:8
insurrection: nature of an i.   SHAK 449:6
intabescant: Virtutem videant i.que
   PERS 372:27
intangible: world i.   THOM 548:24
Integer: I. vitae scelerisque   HOR 259:23

integral: i. and differential calculus
   GILB 228:16
integrate: Essentially I i. the current
   BETJ 42:14
integratio: Amantium irae amoris i.
   TER 544:15
integrity: i. of my intellect   FAR 209:20
knowledge without i. is   JOHN 282:11
virgin white i.   DONNE 187:21
intellect: integrity of my i.   FAR 209:20
i. is improperly exposed   SMITH 511:5
i. not only on its heights   HOUS 266:15
i. of man is forced   YEATS 584:14
'Is it weakness of i.   GILB 227:16
living i. that bred them   MILT 351:21
march of i.   SOUT 514:13
not by the i.   SPEN 515:2
Our meddling i.   WORD 582:23
put on I.   BLAKE 86:13
restless and versatile i.   HUXL 269:13
with the i. of an advocate   BAG 29:17
intellects: few hearts and i. like   MILL 339:22
highest i.   MAC 323:11
intellectual: All i. improvement arises
   JOHN 276:12
being i.   CALV 127:27
I am an i. chap   GILB 226:8
i. life of our century   ARN 15:25
i. ability   ARN 16:26
i. eunuch Castlereagh   BYRON 122:4
i. World   STER 520:2
i. power   WORD 577:13
i. All-in-all   WORD 580:4
moral or i. damage   KRUG 306:1
tear is an i. thing   BLAKE 86:6
this i. being   MILT 346:10
with i. nature is necessary   JOHN 281:32
without some i. intention   RUSK 411:21
word 'I.' suggests straight   AUDEN 20:13
intelligence: glorious work of fine i.
   WORD 582:16
nightly gulls him with i.   SHAK 494:12
people have little i.   LA B 306:14
intelligencies: we are The i.   DONNE 188:24
intelligent: i. anticipation of facts
   CURZ 170:17
i., the witty, the brave   MILL 339:23
Not i.   GILB 228:25
Want it to be i.   SU T 524:19
intelligere: sed i.   SPIN 517:7
intelligible: i. in his own day than COL 158:8
that it is an i. government   BAG 28:27
intemperance: potations excused for
brisk i.   GIBB 224:9
intend: i. to lead a new life   PRAY 387:18
since what I well i.   SHAK 453:5
intended: years damp my i. wing MILT 349:10
intense: i. the agony   BRON 93:21
intensity: Are full of passionate i.
   YEATS 586:15
of every art is its i.   KEATS 293:18
intent: child of glorious great i.   SPEN 516:4
His first avow'd i.   BUNY 107:36
Our true i. is   SHAK 471:16
pier it is my fixed i.   BARH 33:20
prick the sides of my i.   SHAK 459:6
that's told with bad i.   BLAKE 85:14
When on love i.   YEATS 584:19
intention: i. to keep my own counsel
   GLAD 229:16
intentions: firm grasp of his i.   HOR 260:18
intents: Be thy i. wicked or charitable
   SHAK 430:24
inter: In hugger-mugger to i.   SHAK 436:5
intercession: made i. for the transgressors
   BIBLE 59:24
interchange: calm quiet i. of sentiments
   JOHN 276:26
interchanging: pleasing game of i. praise
   HOLM 253:6

intercourse: abject i. between tyrants
   GOLD 232:11
interest: common i. always will prevail
   DRYD 194:17
five per cent is the natural i.   MAC 323:29
I *du* in i.   LOW 319:4
i. to a twice-told tale   BYRON 124:36
i. Unborrowed from the eye   WORD 578:6
O Love, the i.   AUDEN 20:6
unbound by any i. to pay   HOR 259:7
interested: subsequent proceedings i.
   HARTE 242:33
interesting: is that it be i.   JAMES 271:10
person doing i. actions   BAG 28:30
statements was i.   TWAIN 554:1
interference: case of Providential i.
   TEMP 532:8
interfering: in i. with the liberty   MILL 339:6
interfused: something far more deeply
i.   WORD 578:7
Intérieur: 'Vive l'I.   SELL 420:7
interior: Which pries not to the i.
   SHAK 466:19
interline: Enlarge, diminish, i.   SWIFT 527:34
International: I. will encompass the human
   POTT 382:3
interpose: Those who in quarrels i.
   GAY 223:14
interpretation: of bearing some other
i.   DOYLE 192:35
interpreted: i. the world in various
   MARX 333:10
interpreter: God is his own i.   COWP 165:29
I think the i. is the hardest   SHER 505:22
interpreters: in general they need i.
   PIND 373:14
letters, soft i.   PRIOR 400:26
interred: good is oft i. with their
   SHAK 450:1
interstices: with i. between the intersections
   JOHN 281:13
interval: through and make a lucid i.
   DRYD 196:34
intervalos: lleno de lúcidos i.   CERV 138:16
intervals: lucid i. and happy pauses
   BACON 27:44
Not in the lucid i.   WORD 577:5
with frequent lucid i.   CERV 138:16
Intervene: I.. O descend as a dove
   AUDEN 20:15
intervention: No i.   LAND 308:21
interview: first strange and fatal i.
   DONNE 188:10
intervolved: intricate, Eccentric, i.
   MILT 348:24
interwoven: By Bach, i.   GILB 227:6
intestines: product of the smaller i.
   CARL 131:7
intimate: one of my most i. enemies
   ROSS 409:20
into: i. the Dust descend   FITZ 212:18
intolerable: burden of them is i. PRAY 387:19
O vile, I.   SHAK 484:14
intolerant: Time that is i.   AUDEN 19:7
intoxicated: been once i. with power
   BURKE 111:28
exposes himself when he is i.   JOHN 278:8
God-i. man   NOV 364:10
i. with my own eloquence   DISR 186:3
intoxication: best of life is but i.
   BYRON 122:22
Wordsworth's standard of i.   SHOR 507:9
intreasured: weak beginnings lie i.
   SHAK 442:3
Intreat: I. me not to leave thee BIBLE 49:32
intrepid: behaviour was natural and i.
   WALP 562:20
intricate: i., Eccentric, intervolved
   MILT 348:24
intricated: Poor i. soul   DONNE 190:25

intrigue: not the i.	GRAN 234:8
Intrigues: I. half-gather'd	COWP 168:6
intrisicate: knot i. Of life	SHAK 424:14
introduced: any one you've been i.	
	CARR 136:10
when I'm i. to one	RAL 404:20
introduction: one is an i. to any literary	
	JOHN 274:11
Introibo: I. ad altare Dei	MASS 334:13
intrude: I hope I don't i.	POOLE 375:10
intruders: i. on his ancient home	ARN 14:21
intruding: i. eras. farewell	SHAK 435:3
intus: ecce i. eras et ego foris	AUG 21:16
invades: He i. authors like a monarch	
	DRYD 198:3
horrid stillness first i.	DRYD 195:24
invalid: permanent i. called Bunbury	
	WILDE 572:29
invasion: long-promised i.	CHUR 150:4
résiste pas à l'i. des idées	HUGO 267:11
invent: fitter to i. than to judge	BACON 27:39
would be necessary to i. him	VOLT 561:8
would i. some other custom	SHAK 474:23
Inventas: I. aut qui vitam excoluere	
	VIRG 558:23
invented: Accurst be he that first i. war	
	MARL 330:6
England i. the phrase	BAG 28:23
had i. the art of printing	CARL 132:12
poems that ever were i.	CARR 135:23
was that first i. kissing	SWIFT 526:31
Who first i. Work	LAMB 307:33
invention: brightest heaven of i.	SHAK 443:3
heir of my i. prove deformed	SHAK 495:17
I. breeds invention	EMER 208:13
i. is unfruitful	BURKE 109:16
i. of a barbarous age	MILT 344:18
it is a happy i.	ANON 10:3
jerks of i.	SHAK 457:3
Knight said…'It's my own i.	CARR 136:3
'Tis never by i. got	SWIFT 528:7
inventions: have sought out many i.	
	BIBLE 55:24
whoring with their own i.	PRAY 397:6
inventor: mighty-mouth'd i. of harmonies	
	TENN 533:12
return, To plague the i.	SHAK 459:5
inventoried: it shall be i.	SHAK 488:12
invents: about the best thing God i.	
	BROW 100:29
inverted: i. Bowl we call The Sky	FITZ 213:8
investment: There is no finer i.	CHUR 150:15
inveterate: i. foes saluted as they	
	DRYD 197:30
invida: fugerit i. Aetas	HOR 259:20
invincible: dream I saw a city i.	WHIT 570:4
None i. as they	COWP 164:24
inviolable: clutching the i. shade	ARN 14:20
invisible: all things visible and i.	PRAY 387:10
Am I i.	FRY 219:29
I., except to God alone	MILT 347:12
led by an i. hand	SMITH 509:9
musician in that of i. things	LEON 313:24
we walk i.	SHAK 438:23
with thy bloody and i. hand	SHAK 461:14
world i.	THOM 548:24
yet she is not i.	BACON 26:13
invita: i. dices faciesve	HOR 258:5
invitation: much more i. than command	
	STEE 518:6
invitations: Receipted bills and i.	
	AUDEN 20:2
invite: Friendly himself i.	ANON 8:24
Invites: I. my step	POPE 376:5
inviting: think you worth i. to dinner	
	VIRG 560:2
involved: because I am i. in *Mankind*	
	DONNE 190:20
i. with past and future	ELIOT 202:16
invulnerable: air, i.	SHAK 429:15

I. nothings	SHEL 499:20
inward: beam upon my i. view	ARN 13:4
i. and spiritual grace	PRAY 388:19
i. eye 'tis an old Man	BLAKE 86:14
They flash upon that i. eye	WORD 578:1
truth in the i. parts	PRAY 393:5
walked with i. glory crowned	SHEL 504:10
inwardly: i. in our souls	PRAY 386:9
i. they are ravening wolves	BIBLE 65:8
inwariable: double glass o' the i.	DICK 182:11
iocos: Nec ut soles dabis i.	HADR 237:9
Iohannes fac totum: being an absolute	
I.	GREE 236:12
Ionian: isle under I. skies	SHEL 500:13
splendour of I. white	ELIOT 205:4
valleys of I. hills	TENN 541:16
ipsae: veniunt spectentur ut i.	OVID 366:10
Ipse: 'I. dixit	CIC 151:20
Ipswich: I. and Oxford	SHAK 447:22
Ira: I. furor brevis est	HOR 258:15
Sine i. et studio	TAC 531:10
irae: Amantium i. amoris integratio	
	TER 544:15
Dies i.	CEL 138:5
Tantaene animis caelestibus i.	VIRG 557:9
Ireland: from I. coming	SHAK 445:7
get into the soup in I.	WAUGH 566:1
great Gaels of I.	CHES 146:17
'How's poor ould I.	ANON 6:6
inhabitants of I. are not	SMITH 509:16
I. gives England her soldiers	MER 337:24
I. is the old sow that	JOYCE 286:16
I. never was contented…	LAND 308:23
is said to be done in I.	SIDN 508:5
name of I. is mentioned	SMITH 511:30
Now I. has her madness	AUDEN 19:6
Romantic I.'s dead	YEATS 586:19
iridescent: home of i. chitchat	NASH 360:3
Iris: Melted to one vast I.	BYRON 121:4
Spring a livelier i. changes	TENN 538:17
irisch: mein i. Kind	WAGN 562:1
Irish: army led by an I. general	SHAW 498:7
howling of I. wolves	SHAK 427:1
I. are a fair people	JOHN 276:17
I. bull is always pregnant	MAH 327:4
I. Home Rule	ROS 408:13
I. poets	YEATS 587:8
my I. child	WAGN 562:1
now the I. are ashamed	MARV 332:11
symbol of I. art	JOYCE 286:21
That is the I. Question	DISR 184:12
Irishman: Every I., the saying goes	
	HARE 242:6
Irishry: Still the indomitable I.	YEATS 587:9
irked: It i. you	HOUS 266:1
Irks: I. care the crop-full bird	BROW 104:3
iron: beat the i. while it is hot	DRYD 197:37
bound in misery and i.	PRAY 397:7
bruise them with a rod of i.	PRAY 389:18
Cold I.—is master	KIPL 298:15
i. curtain has descended	CHUR 150:18
i. entered into his soul	PRAY 397:3
i. enter into his soul	STER 519:8
i. pokers into true-love	COL 157:6
I. sharpeneth iron	BIBLE 54:40
i. shuts amain	MILT 343:11
i. tears down Pluto's cheek	MILT 342:6
much loft as a light i.	WOD 575:22
my i.'s gone	ANON 6:19
nobles with links of i.	PRAY 399:24
Nor i. bars a cage	LOV 318:18
out through blood and i.	BISM 84:25
painted to look like i.	BISM 84:27
sound of i. on stone	DE L 174:10
strong as links of i.	BURKE 110:2
that meddles with cold i.	BUTL 117:29
Thorough the i. gates of life	MARV 332:9
wink and hold out mine i.	SHAK 443:14
irons: Heat me these i. hot	SHAK 452:22
two i. in the fire	BEAU 36:4

irrational: nothing so extravagant and	
i.	SWIFT 526:8
Irrationally: I. held truths may be more	
	HUXL 269:11
irregular: when most i. they seem	
	MILT 348:24
irrelevant: is the most i. thing	LAMB 307:20
irrepertum: Aurum i. et sic melius	
	HOR 260:20
irresistible: theatre is i.	ARN 16:15
irrevocabile: volat i. verbum	HOR 258:22
irrevocably: out a word takes wing i.	
	HOR 258:22
irritabile: placem genus i. vatum	HOR 259:5
irrt: *Es i. der Mensch*	GOET 229:29
Isaac: God of I.	BIBLE 47:8
thine only son I.	BIBLE 46:9
Iscariot: not I.	BIBLE 72:34
Iser: Of I.	CAMP 128:21
Ishmael: Call me I.	MELV 336:23
Isis: I. and Cam	WORD 582:12
'Till I.' elders reel	POPE 375:21
island: customs of his tribe and i.	SHAW 496:9
floating bulwark of the i.	BLAC 85:4
have cast my lot in an i.	DICK 183:7
i. descending incontinently	CHUR 151:4
make this i. all her own	WALL 562:11
No man is an I.	DONNE 190:20
on a desert i.	BEER 37:27
on this i. now	AUDEN 20:3
some secreted i.	WORD 580:23
Sweet Catullus' all-but-i.	TENN 533:18
'This I. was Blest	DICK 181:12
we shall defend our i.	CHUR 149:31
what a snug little I.	DIBD 175:23
with rocks as an inland i.	SWIN 529:17
Islanded: I. in Severn stream	HOUS 263:12
islands: eye of peninsulas and i.	CAT 136:28
realms and i. were	SHAK 423:22
their favourite i.	AUDEN 18:12
Isle: Fairest I.	DRYD 196:29
i. is full of noises	SHAK 485:17
i. under Ionian skies	SHEL 500:12
natural bravery of your i.	SHAK 428:13
ship, an i.	FLEC 214:21
this scepter'd i.	SHAK 478:20
isles: he taketh up the i.	BIBLE 59:8
i. shall give presents	PRAY 394:20
multitude of the i. may	PRAY 396:6
ships and stars and i.	FLEC 214:9
islets: i. of yellow sand	LEAR 312:16
Islington: bailiff's daughter of I.	BALL 30:9
fields from I. to Marybone	BLAKE 86:4
That lived in I.	BALL 30:7
isn't: as it i., it ain't	CARR 135:2
isolate: art is to limit and i.	GOET 229:27
isolated: Empire stands splendidly i.	
	FOST 217:17
i. verisimilitude caught	KEATS 293:19
isolation: our splendid i.	GOSC 233:3
isolieren: beschränken und zu i.	GOET 229:27
Israel: beauty of I. is slain	BIBLE 50:16
border see I. set	BROW 101:3
chariot of I.	BIBLE 51:22
David…the sweet psalmist of I.	BIBLE 50:28
Deliver I.	PRAY 391:3
even an heritage unto I.	PRAY 399:1
he that keepeth I.	PRAY 398:9
his Name is great in I.	PRAY 395:1
I arose a mother in I.	BIBLE 49:8
I saw all I. scattered	BIBLE 51:19
I., Athens	INGE 270:10
I. loved Joseph	BIBLE 46:26
I. shall be a proverb	BJBLE 50:31
I. smote him with the edge	BIBLE 48:12
I.'s tents do shine so	BLAKE 86:24
may I. now say	PRAY 398:10
neither will I let I. go	BIBLE 47:10
now may I. say	PRAY 398:13
of the stock of I.	BIBLE 78:16

than all the waters of I.   BIBLE 51:28
Then I.'s monarch   DRYD 194:2
Then will I cut off I.   BIBLE 50:31
there is a prophet in I.   BIBLE 51:27
These be thy gods, O I.   BIBLE 48:2
together the out-casts of I.   PRAY 399:19
When I. came out of Egypt   PRAY 397:16
Israelite: Behold an I. indeed   BIBLE 71:32
Israelites: Are they I.   BIBLE 77:11
I. passed over on dry ground   BIBLE 49:1
isst: was er i.   FEUE 210:35
issue: happy i. out of all their   PRAY 386:1
honest madam's i.   SHAK 453:9
ist: Der Mensch i.   FEUE 210:35
isthmus: Plac'd on this i.   POPE 379:12
it: i. shall not come nigh   PRAY 395:21
It's just I.   KIPL 305:9
knew what i. meant once   KLOP 305:16
Italia: I.! oh Italia   BYRON 121:6
I. shall be free   MER 338:3
Italiam: I. fato profugus Laviniaque   VIRG 557:8
Italian: French army led by an I.   SHAW 498:7
good because he learnt I.   BUTL 118:35
No I. priest   SHAK 452:17
perhaps I.   GILB 228:10
roof of blue I. weather   SHEL 501:16
to women I.   CHAR 140:31
writ in very choice I.   SHAK 434:14
Italians: I. call reg'larly flummoxed   DICK 182:15
Italie: Blond comme un soleil d'I.   BANV 33:1
italien: i. aux femmes   CHAR 140:31
Italy: bought his doublet in I.   SHAK 465:24
building here after seeing I.   BURN 112:17
I.. my Italy   BROW 100:14
I. a vassal state of Hitler's   CHUR 150:7
I. from designs by Michael Angelo   TWAIN 554:11
I. is a geographical expression   METT 338:11
Paradise of exiles, I.   SHEL 501:11
proclaim throughout I.   CAV 138:1
shocking collapse of I.   HOR 260:24
Some jay of I.   SHAK 428:16
who has not been in I.   JOHN 277:6
itch: i. of literature comes   LOVER 318:21
poor i. of your opinion   SHAK 427:12
itching: condemn'd to have an i. palm   SHAK 451:12
Ite: I. domum saturae   VIRG 560:9
I. missa est   MASS 335:9
iteration: thou hast damnable i.   SHAK 438:7
itur: sic i. ad astra   VIRG 559:8
Itylus: Is half assuaged for I.   SWIN 528:15
iubeo: Hoc volo, sic i.   JUV 287:21
iubes: Da quod i. et iube quod i. renovare dolorem   AUG 21:17 / VIRG 557:20
Iudaeus: Credat I. Apella   HOR 262:5
iudicat: Securus i. orbis   AUG 21:18
iudice: et adhuc sub i. lis est   HOR 257:15
magno se i. quisque tuetur   LUCAN 319:22
se I. nemo nocens   JUV 288:5
iudicetur: Unde mundus i.   CEL 138:6
iunctura: Reddiderit i. novum   HOR 257:13
Iuppiter: I. ex periuria ridet OVID 366:11
iurare: Nullius addictus i. in verba HOR 258:7
iustis: Quis i. induit arma   LUCAN 319:22
iuvabit: haec olim meminisse i.   VIRG 557:14
iuventa: ego hoc ferrem calidus i.   HOR 261:4
ivoire: Comme en sa tour d'i.   SAIN 413:1
ivory: ebony as if done in i.   FULL 220:15
fashioned of gleaming white i.   VIRG 559:3
his belly is as bright i.   BIBLE 57:4
i., and apes   BIBLE 50:34
i. fingers drive a tune   POUND 382:15
i. on which I work with   AUST 24:3
neck is as a tower of i.   BIBLE 57:9
With a cargo of i.   MAS 333:18
within his i. tower   SAIN 413:1
ivory gate: dreams out of the i.   BROW 95:23

ivy: creeping i. clings to wood   COWP 166:10
pluck an i. branch   ROSS 409:7
yellow bees in the i.-bloom   SHEL 503:6
ivy-mantled: that from yonder i. tow'r   GRAY 234:19

Jabberwock: 'Beware the J.   CARR 134:28
Jack: Damn you, J.   BONE 89:19
every J. became a gentleman   SHAK 480:24
J. shall have Jill   SHAK 471:1
This J., joke   HOPK 257:1
jackal: This whipped j.   CHUR 150:7
Jackals: ...J. piss at their foot   FLAU 214:3
Jackdaw: J. sat on the Cardinal's   BARH 33:11
Jack-daws: some green J.   LEAR 312:9
jacket: could thresh his old J.   COWP 168:1
j. was red and his breeches   COL 156:11
short j. is always worn   EDW 200:2
Jack Ketch: J.'s wife said of his DRYD 198:13
Jack Nastys: J. or fine ladies' maids   HUGH 267:6
Jacks: He calls the knaves, J.   DICK 178:8
Jackson: J. standing like a stone wall   BEE 37:3
Stonewall J. riding ahead   WHIT 571:16
Jacksonian: name for the J. vulgarity   POTT 382:2
Jacky: gorging Jim to guzzling J.   THAC 545:33
Jacob: Angel did with J.   WALT 564:14
God of J.   BIBLE 47:8
God of J. is our refuge   PRAY 392:20
his birthright unto J.   BIBLE 46:14
J. from among the strange   PRAY 397:16
J. served seven years   BIBLE 46:21
J. was a plain man   BIBLE 46:13
Lord will have mercy on J.   BROW 101:3
of J.'s thigh was out   BIBLE 46:23
Talk to him of J.'s ladder   JERR 273:10
They shall awake as J.   DONNE 191:3
traffic of J.'s ladder   THOM 548:25
voice is J.'s voice   BIBLE 46:16
Jacqmar: J. scarf of mauve and green   BETJ 43:14
jade: arrant j. on a journey   GOLD 232:7
let the galled j. wince   SHAK 434:13
jades: hollow pamper'd j. of Asia   SHAK 441:25
ye pampered J. of Asia   MARL 330:16
Jael: J. Heber's wife   BIBLE 49:7
Jaguar: I've never seen a J.   KIPL 300:8
JAH: praise him in his name J.   PRAY 394:7
jail: patron, and the j.   JOHN 282:29
ship is being in a j.   JOHN 274:18
jam: beflagged j. pots   JAMES 271:34
never j. to-day   CARR 135:15
jamais: j. triste archy   MARQ 330:21
mais je n'en parle j.   PROU 401:22
James: J. James Morrison Morrison   MILNE 340:5
work of Henry J. has always   GUED 237:5
James Lee: dead of joy, J.   BROW 101:21
Jameson: indemnity...for raid by Dr J.   KRUG 306:1
Jane: J. Jane Tall as a crane   SITW 508:11
Janus: is the very J. of poets   DRYD 198:5
Janvier: Generals J. and Février   NICH 362:23
Japan: On shining altars of J.   POPE 381:6
Japanese: speed toward the J. fleet   HALS 238:11
jape: Indulge the loud unseemly j. BELL 38:26
japes: feyned flaterye and j.   CHAU 142:7
Japheth: Shem, Ham, and J.   BIBLE 45:32
jargon: j. of their Babylonian   BURKE 111:6
your j. o' your schools   BURNS 113:19
Jarndyce: J. and Jarndyce still drags   DICK 176:2
jasmines: alighted on the j.   LONG 317:13
Jason: Whom J. hath received   BIBLE 74:9
jasper: j. and a sardine stone   BIBLE 81:22
'J. first   BROW 97:34

jaundic'd: looks yellow to the j. eye   POPE 378:28
javelin: trail'd the hunter's j.   ARN 14:26
jaw: j. of an ass have I slain   BIBLE 49:24
jaw-jaw: j. is better than to war-war   CHUR 150:20
jaws: Into the j. of Death   TENN 533:1
j. of darkness do devour   SHAK 469:20
j. that bite   CARR 134:28
opening of the j. of hell   VIRG 558:21
ponderous and marble j.   SHAK 430:24
With gently smiling j.   CARR 133:18
jay: Some j. of Italy   SHAK 428:16
thrush and the j.   SHAK 491:17
jay-bird: j. say ter der squinch-owl   HARR 242:16
jealous: Are to the j. confirmations   SHAK 475:23
Art is a j. mistress   EMER 207:6
jealous for they are j.   SHAK 476:5
J. in honour   SHAK 425:24
Lord thy God am a j. God   BIBLE 47:24
Lord thy God is a j. God   BIBLE 48:21
Of one not easily j.   SHAK 477:23
question with my j. thought   SHAK 493:18
so I am j. now   DONNE 189:10
wit with j. eye surveys   CHUR 148:28
jealousy: beware, my lord, of j.   SHAK 475:17
ear of j. heareth all things   BIBLE 62:10
green-ey'd j.   SHAK 467:12
J. a human face   BLAKE 88:9
j. is cruel as the grave   BIBLE 57:11
mine was j. in love   TENN 534:33
Nor j. Was understood   MILT 348:19
quiet resting from all j.   BEAU 36:10
tyrant J.   DRYD 196:32
Jean Jacques: gospel according to J.   CARL 131:24
jeering: forbear laughing and j.   PEPYS 372:7
jeers: gibes and flouts and j.   DISR 185:13
jeet: j. it shoon   CHAU 142:32
Jeffersonian: Washingtonian dignity for the J.   POTT 382:2
Jehu: like the driving of J.   BIBLE 51:33
jellies: With J. soother than   KEATS 289:20
jelly: j. with the act of fear   SHAK 430:8
Meaty j.   DICK 181:8
pipkin fits this little j.   HERR 249:21
vile j.   SHAK 455:4
Jelly-bellied: J. Flag-flapper   KIPL 305:8
jelofer: j. amiable   SKEL 508:18
Jemmy Grove: J. on his death-bed lay   BALL 30:10
Je-ne-sais-quoi: J. young man   GILB 227:26
Jenny: Betray sweet J.'s unsuspecting   BURNS 113:7
J. kissed me when we met   HUNT 268:10
jeopardy: Went in j. of their lives   BIBLE 50:29
Jericho: down from Jerusalem to J.   BIBLE 69:30
jerks: j. of invention   SHAK 457:3
right to bring me up by j.   DICK 178:9
Jerusalem: Building up of J.   BLAKE 86:10
build thou the walls of J.   PRAY 393:8
Built in J.'s wall   BLAKE 86:8
down from J. to Jericho   BIBLE 69:30
he hath redeemed J.   BIBLE 59:19
hills stand about J.   PRAY 398:15
holy city, new J.   BIBLE 82:30
if I prefer not J. in my   PRAY 399:3
J. is built as a city   PRAY 398:11
J. shall Harry die   SHAK 442:21
J., thou that killest   BIBLE 67:26
J. thy sister calls   BLAKE 86:11
Lord doth build up J.   PRAY 399:19
men from the east to J.   BIBLE 63:31
pray for the peace of J.   PRAY 398:12
Speak ye comfortably to J.   BIBLE 59:4
there J.'s pillars stood   BLAKE 86:4

There's J. and Madagascar		THAC 546:2
thries hadde she been at J.		CHAU 141:31
vow be performed in J.		PRAY 393:23
was J. builded here		BLAKE 86:16
ye daughters of J.		BIBLE 56:16
jessamine: casement j. stirr'd		TENN 540:10
j. faint		SHEL 503:24
Jesse: rod out of the stem of J.		BIBLE 58:9
jesses: j. and restraint		THOM 548:2
j. were my dear heart-strings		SHAK 475:21
jest: bitter is a scornful j.		JOHN 282:23
fellow of infinite j.		SHAK 436:31
glory, j., and riddle		POPE 379:13
good j. for ever		SHAK 438:27
Great men may j. with saints		SHAK 464:3
J. and youthful jollity		MILT 342:14
j.'s prosperity lies		SHAK 457:17
j. without the smile		COL 157:17
Life is a j.		GAY 223:22
poison in j.		SHAK 434:12
To use my self in j.		DONNE 190:7
whole wit in a j.		BEAU 35:19
world's a j.		STEP 518:25
jesters: shallow j. and rash bavin wits
		SHAK 439:34
jesting: nor j.		BIBLE 78:2
jests: He j. at scars		SHAK 482:5
to his memory for his j.		SHER 506:36
Jesu: J., by a nobler deed		CHAN 139:19
J., the very thought		CASW 136:15
Jesuit: tool, a J.		KING 297:16
Jesus: another king, one J.		BIBLE 74:9
Blood of J. whispers		BICK 84:4
bon Sansculotte J.		DESM 175:13
disciple whom J. loved		BIBLE 73:18
Gentle J.		WESL 568:17
J. a pleuré		HUGO 267:13
J. Christ his only Son		PRAY 384:26
J. increased in wisdom		BIBLE 69:14
J. the author and finisher		BIBLE 79:35
J. they run into millions		ROST 410:15
J. wept		BIBLE 72:23
J. wept; Voltaire smiled		HUGO 267:13
J.! with all thy faults		BUTL 119:10
leaning on J.' bosom		BIBLE 72:28
name of J. every knee		BIBLE 78:14
sound of J.' breath		BLAKE 85:24
sure this J. will not do		BLAKE 85:25
sweet reasonableness of J.		ARN 16:22
Jesus Christ: If J. were to come to-day
		CARL 132:26
J. the same yesterday		BIBLE 80:4
jets: j. under his advanced plumes
		SHAK 489:11
Jetty: J., to the milking shed		ING 270:15
jeunesse: *Si j. savoit*		EST 208:25
jeux: *j. d'enfants ne sont pas*		MONT 354:17
Jew: Ebrew J.		SHAK 439:1
Either for Englishman or J.		BLAKE 85:5
Hath not a J. eyes		SHAK 467:4
is neither Greek nor J.		BIBLE 78:26
Liver of blaspheming J.		SHAK 462:4
must the J. be merciful		SHAK 467:27
This is the J.		POPE 381:15
which am a J. of Tarsus		BIBLE 74:20
jewel: immediate j. of their souls
		SHAK 475:16
j. of gold in a swine's		BIBLE 53:32
j. of the just		VAUG 555:20
Lest my j. it should tine		BURNS 113:1
Like a rich j. in an Ethiop's		SHAK 482:2
No j. is like Rosalind		SHAK 426:5
poor j. of their souls		STEV 521:2
precious j. in his head		SHAK 424:32
jewels: are my j.		BURT 116:34
j. five-words long		TENN 541:30
j. into a garret four stories		BACON 25:7
were moving j.		TRAH 551:19
Jewry: In J. is God known		PRAY 395:1
Jews: born King of the J.		BIBLE 63:31

conversion of the J.		MARV 332:18
J., a headstrong		DRYD 194:4
J. stink naturally…is		BROW 95:25
J. which believed not		BIBLE 74:8
like to see the J. coming		BAYL 35:9
Of the J. five times received		BIBLE 77:12
spurn the J.		BROW 95:13
three J.		CAXT 138:3
To choose The J.		EWER 209:13
jig: very walk should be a j.		SHAK 488:1
jilted: Better be courted and j.		CAMP 128:23
Jim: dear brother J.		WORD 583:5
gorging J. to guzzling Jacky		THAC 545:33
they called him Sunny J.		HANFF 238:19
jingle: hear the harness j.		HOUS 263:9
jingo: by j. if we do		HUNT 268:3
jining: j. of hearts and house-keepings
		DICK 181:1
Joan: J. doth keel the pot		SHAK 457:19
Miss J. Hunter Dunn		BETJ 44:8
Job: afflictions of J. than the felicities
		BACON 25:19
blessed the latter end of J.		BIBLE 53:13
Doth J. fear God for naught		BIBLE 52:6
good j. too		GILB 229:6
heard of the patience of J.		BIBLE 80:17
husband is a whole-time j.		BENN 40:22
I am as poor as J.		SHAK 441:8
Living is my j. and my art		MONT 354:23
we will finish the j.		CHUR 150:6
jobs: little j. about the house		AUDEN 21:9
jocund: In such a j. company		WORD 578:1
jocunditie: jasper of j.		DUNB 199:10
jog: j. on the foot-path way		SHAK 491:21
man *might j. on with*		LAMB 308:15
John: back to the shop Mr J.		LOCK 315:22
J. to the seven churches		BIBLE 81:9
to blessed J. the Baptist		MASS 334:15
John-a-dreams: Like J.		SHAK 433:2
John a Gaunt: Talks as familiarly of
J.		SHAK 442:11
John Barleycorn: Inspiring bold J.
		BURNS 115:9
John Bull: greatest of all is J.		BYRON 124:32
John Grubby: J., who was short		CHES 147:9
Johnny: J. head-in-air		PUDN 402:7
Little J. Head-In-Air		HOFF 252:16
John of Gaunt: Old J.		SHAK 478:6
Johnson: good imitation of J.		BURKE 112:14
J. marched to kettle-drums		COLM 159:3
Samuel J.		SMOL 512:14
There is no arguing with J.		GOLD 232:40
joie: *La j. venait toujours après*		APOL 11:11
le peuple a de la j.		MONT 355:7
join: If two lives j.		BROW 99:23
them that j. house to house		BIBLE 57:24
To j. the muster came		MAC 322:13
join'd: third she j. the former two
		DRYD 196:30
joined: persons should not be j.		PRAY 388:23
Those whom God hath j.		PRAY 389:6
What God hath j. together		SHAW 496:28
What therefore God hath j.		BIBLE 67:8
joint: Jacob's thigh was out of j.		BIBLE 46:23
j. and motive of her body		SHAK 487:13
my bones are out of j.		PRAY 390:19
Remove the j.		CARR 136:10
time is out of j.		SHAK 431:26
time was out of j.		STR 524:4
joint-heirs: j. with Christ		BIBLE 75:9
joint-labourer: night j. with the day
		SHAK 429:11
joints: distinguished into j. and fingers
		TRAH 552:1
His square-turn'd j.		SCOTT 417:5
j. that you carve		KIPL 298:5
joke: custard pie… A dirty j.		ORW 365:10
dullness ever loves a j.		POPE 375:17
It's our only j.		BARR 34:22
j.'s a very serious thing		CHUR 148:31

j. well into a Scotch understanding
		SMITH 510:28
Life is a j. that's just		GILB 226:28
many a j. had he		GOLD 231:2
subtleties of the American j.		TWAIN 554:12
This Jack, j.		HOPK 257:1
jokes: difference of taste in j.		ELIOT 200:21
hackney'd j. from Miller		BYRON 124:17
my little j. on Thee		FROST 219:7
Wooden-shoes are standing j.		ADD 2:1
jolitee: on my j.		CHAU 143:19
jollity: Jest and youthful j.		MILT 342:14
needy nothing trimm'd in j.		SHAK 494:5
jolly: '…For he's a j. good fe-el-low
		FARR 210:29
J. boating weather		CORY 163:2
Some credit in being j.		DICK 179:2
There was a j. miller once		BICK 83:28
This life is most j.		SHAK 426:1
Jonadge: wish it was in J.'s belly
		DICK 179:23
Jonah: lot fell upon J.		BIBLE 61:21
Jonathan: must consult Brother J.
		WASH 565:4
Saul and J. were lovely		BIBLE 50:17
Though David had his J.		HERB 247:5
Jones: J.! as from Calais southward
		WORD 582:4
Jonquille: Now the J. o'ercomes		WINC 575:6
jonquils: land-locked pools of j.		BETJ 43:12
Jonson: J. knew the critic's part		COLL 158:23
J.'s learnèd sock be		MILT 342:26
learn'd J.		DRAY 193:15
Jordan: concerning the land of J.		PRAY 392:8
J. was driven back		PRAY 397:16
Joseph: Israel loved J.		BIBLE 46:26
J., who was sold		PRAY 397:3
which knew not J.		BIBLE 46:40
joss-sticks: odour of j. and honourable
		BRAM 91:20
jostle: Philistines may j.		GILB 227:23
jostling: done by j. in the street		BLAKE 87:10
jour: *qu'en un j.*		BOIL 89:11
journalism: from Christianity and j.
		BALF 30:5
journalist: British j.		WOLFE 576:6
of the modern j. may be		CURZ 170:17
Journalists: J. say a thing that they
		BENN 40:23
journey: death the j.'s end		DRYD 197:10
dreariest and the longest j.		SHEL 500:10
he is gone a long j.		BIBLE 53:24
Here is my j.'s end		SHAK 477:20
his j. into a far country		BIBLE 70:18
I have a long j. to take		RAL 404:19
j. to the world below		SOCR 512:19
such a long j.		ELIOT 203:12
then begins a j. in my head		SHAK 493:5
to begin a j. on Sundays		SWIFT 526:33
to take a j.		ANDR 4:7
traveller's j. is done		BLAKE 87:22
when the j.'s over		HOUS 262:15
Will the day's j. take		ROSS 409:11
world is going on a j.		HAZL 243:30
journeying: third-class seat sat the j.
boy		HARDY 240:9
journeyman: that I was a j. to grief
		SHAK 478:15
Journeys: J. end in lovers meeting
		SHAK 488:17
jours: *j. s'en vont je demeure*		APOL 11:11
Jousted: J. in Aspramont or Montalban
		MILT 345:23
Jove: J.'s planet rises		BROW 101:9
lovelier than the Love of J.		MARL 330:3
Nor J. himself when he		SPEN 516:31
whom e'en J. would swear		SHAK 457:5
Jowett: my name is J.		BEEC 37:8
joy: all the j. before death		SWIN 530:4
all the passages of j.		JOHN 283:1

beauty is a j. for ever — KEATS 288:20
Break forth into j. — BIBLE 59:19
Brightened with j. — WORD 577:16
burst J.'s grape — KEATS 291:15
child may j. to hear — BLAKE 87:25
evensong Of j. illimited — HARDY 239:7
ever in j. — BROW 105:1
fed without the aid of j. — BRON 93:24
Gaudium, what j. is in it — ANDR 4:6
Gemme of all j. — DUNB 199:10
good tidings of great j. — BIBLE 69:10
Hath really neither j. — ARN 12:23
headlong j. is ever on the wing — MILT 350:12
He sees it in his j. — WORD 579:5
I should be dead of j. — BROW 101:21
J. and woe are woven fine — BLAKE 85:14
J., beautiful radiance — SCH 415:9
j. cometh in the morning — PRAY 391:13
j. delights in joy — SHAK 492:25
J., Empire and Victory — SHEL 503:15
j. for it worth worlds — HERB 247:1
j. in hevene and peyne — CHAU 143:28
j. in the making — BRID 92:10
j. is but a dish of pain — TICH 551:2
J. is my name — BLAKE 88:1
j. is wisdom — YEATS 585:19
j. nor grieve too much — DRYD 197:10
j. of love is too short — MAL 327:19
j. of the working — KIPL 304:3
j. rul'd the day — DRYD 197:18
j.'s a trinket — STEP 518:25
j.'s soul lies — SHAK 486:21
j. that you can wish — SHAK 467:14
j. unspeakable and full — BIBLE 80:20
j. was never sure — SWIN 529:24
J., whose hand is ever — KEATS 291:15
Labour without j. is base — RUSK 412:3
let j. be unconfined — BYRON 120:21
Like an unbodied j. — SHEL 504:17
My scrip of j. — RAL 404:12
not increased the j. — BIBLE 58:6
now from the heart of j. — BEEC 37:9
oil of j. for mourning — BIBLE 60:9
O j.! that in our embers — WORD 579:9
perfectest herald of j. — SHAK 472:10
purchase pain with all that j. — POPE 377:21
pure and complete j. — TOLS 551:13
Rising in j. over wolds — AUDEN 20:6
shall obtain j. and gladness — BIBLE 59:1
shall reap in j. — PRAY 398:17
snatch a fearful j. — GRAY 235:11
sons of God shouted for j. — BIBLE 53:3
stern j. which warriors feel — SCOTT 416:6
Surprised by j. — WORD 582:15
swift j. and tardy sorrow — THOM 548:3
There is no j. but calm — TENN 539:14
There's not a j. the world — BYRON 125:28
thy bed Of crimson j. — BLAKE 87:12
tumultuous j. — SOUT 514:11
'twere with a defeated j. — SHAK 429:19
Variety's the source of j. — GAY 223:3
walked in glory and in j. — WORD 580:28
Where j. for ever dwells — MILT 345:10
Where's all the j. and mirth — KEPP 295:12
who are capable of j. — SMITH 510:18
who binds to himself a J. — BLAKE 86:18
who for the j. that was — BIBLE 79:35
wish you all j. of the worm — SHAK 424:7
would but apprehend some j. — SHAK 471:11
Writh'd not at passing j. — KEATS 293:4
joyance: With thy clear keen j. — SHEL 504:22
joye: dreme of j. — CHAU 144:1
joyful: be j. in the Lord — PRAY 396:11
day of prosperity be j. — BIBLE 55:21
J. and triumphant — ANON 10:4
j. a thing it is: brethren — PRAY 398:26
j. mother of children — PRAY 397:15
j. rain upon thine inheritance — PRAY 386:3
Let the saints be j. — PRAY 399:24
joyfully: Sing j. to God — BIBLE 83:8

joyicity: hoppy on akkant of his j. — JOYCE 286:13
joyous: j. Errand reach the Spot — FITZ 213:18
rout send forth a j. shout — MAC 322:6
joyously: So j., So maidenly — SKEL 508:17
joys: all our j. are but fantastical — DONNE 188:8
eternal j. of heaven — MARL 329:7
It redoubleth j. — BACON 26:16
J. in another's loss — BLAKE 87:19
j., like griefs, are silent — MARM 330:19
j. of home depend — MORE 357:11
j. of marriage are — FORD 216:14
j. of parents are secret — BACON 27:2
minds me o' departed j. — BURNS 116:7
of Africa and golden j. — SHAK 442:27
present j. are more — DRYD 196:18
season made for j. — GAY 222:28
that's precious in our j. — STER 519:12
Thy j. when shall I see — ANON 5:19
vain deluding j. — MILT 341:23
What lasting j. the man — WHURR 572:1
where time j. are to be — PRAY 386:12
who lived for j. in vain — CLARE 152:8
whom all j. so well agree — SIDN 508:1
Jubilate: *J. Deo* — BIBLE 83:8
Jubilee: first day of our J. is death — BROW 96:21
Judah: J. is my law-giver — PRAY 393:18
J. was his sanctuary — PRAY 397:16
judas: flowering j. — ELIOT 203:4
J. saith unto him — BIBLE 72:34
one thrice worse than J. — SHAK 479:9
judge: after a time they j. them — WILDE 573:30
am no j. of such matters — PRAED 384:5
cause before a great j. — LUCAN 319:22
fitter to invent than to j. — BACON 27:39
Forbear to j. — SHAK 446:7
God is the J. — PRAY 394:26
'I'll be j. — CARR 133:19
j. is condemned when — PUBL 402:5
J. none blessed before — BIBLE 63:1
J. not — BIBLE 69:22
J. not — BIBLE 64:33
J. not the preacher — HERB 247:12
J. not the play before — QUAR 403:15
j. the prize — MILT 342:25
j. the quick and the dead — PRAY 384:26
j. thou my cause — BIBLE 60:32
neutrality of an impartial j. — BURKE 111:34
nor the j.'s robe — SHAK 463:20
now I am a J. — GILB 229:5
own mouth will I j. thee — BIBLE 71:1
righteousness shall he j. — PRAY 396:9
Shall not the J. of all — BIBLE 46:7
Sole j. of truth — POPE 379:13
thee a prince and a j. — BIBLE 47:1
there sits a j. — SHAK 447:4
Th' indifferent j. between — SIDN 507:20
to be decided by the j. — JOHN 279:30
To j. the earth one day — AUDEN 21:7
to make answer to the j. — CEL 138:6
You wags that j. by rote — OTWAY 366:3
judged: guilty man is acquitted if j. — JUV 288:5
they were j. every man — BIBLE 82:29
whereby the world will be j. — CEL 138:6
judgement: at forty, the j. — FRAN 218:10
before we pass j. on others — MOL 353:20
common pursuit of true j. — ELIOT 205:15
His critical j. is so exquisite — FRY 219:24
history is the world's j. — SCH 415:11
if unassisted by j. — HOR 260:23
industry only, but his j. — BURKE 109:11
in the day of j. — PRAY 385:17
into j. with thy servant — PRAY 399:11
Last J. draweth nigh — BLAKE 85:13
people's j. always true — DRYD 194:18
right j. in all things — PRAY 386:14
their j. is a mere lottery — DRYD 198:4
will replace reasoned j. — JUV 287:21

judgements: diff'ring j. serve — COWP 165:14
Give the King thy j. — PRAY 394:18
j. about great and high — MONT 354:12
j. of the Lord are true — PRAY 390:12
judges: hungry j. soon the sentence — POPE 381:4
J. all rang'd (a terrible — GAY 223:1
not my Accuser, but my j. — NEWM 361:15
were j. of fact — PULT 402:9
judgment: be angry with his j. — BROW 96:4
breastplate of j. the Urim — BIBLE 48:1
bring every work into j. — BIBLE 56:14
he looked for j. — BIBLE 57:23
J. drunk — COWP 166:12
j., mercy — BIBLE 67:24
j. of the great whore that — BIBLE 82:22
j. was set — BIBLE 61:8
leaves of the J. Book unfold — TAYL 532:2
O j.! thou art fled — SHAK 450:22
on better j. making — SHAK 494:13
reserve thy j. — SHAK 430:19
thereof in the day of j. — BIBLE 66:10
vulgarize the day of j. — JERR 273:5
waits upon the j. — SHAK 435:8
What j. I had increases — DRYD 198:7
What j. shall I dread — SHAK 467:24
would not give his j. rashly — ADD 2:13
judgments: Delivers brawling j. — TENN 535:11
reasons of state to influence our j. — MANS 328:16
What cause for j. so malign — STUB 524:5
judicious: cannot but make the j. grieve — SHAK 433:17
like a little j. levity — STEV 522:12
Judy O'Grady: Colonel's Lady an' J. — KIPL 300:18
jug: it git loose fum de j. — HARR 242:23
j., jug, tereu — LYLY 321:12
old j. without a handle — LEAR 311:25
juger: j. des choses grandes et — MONT 354:12
juggler: perceive a j.'s sleight — BUTL 118:6
threadbare j. — SHAK 427:9
Jug Jug: 'J.' to dirty ears — ELIOT 204:24
Julia: Whenas in silks my J. goes — HERR 250:8
Julias: J., Maeves and Maureens — BETJ 43:7
Juliet: philosophy can make a J. — SHAK 483:12
Julius Caesar: J.'s ill-erected tower — SHAK 480:6
Jumblies: lands where the J. live — LEAR 312:6
jump: the life to come — SHAK 459:5
j. with common spirits — SHAK 466:19
To j. — BARH 33:20
jumping: finished j. on his mother — GILB 228:21
June: husband J. — WATK 565:7
In the leafy month of J. — COL 155:26
meetings made December J. — TENN 537:12
needs not J. for beauty's — ARN 15:4
serves for the old J. weather — BROW 100:7
When J. is past — CAREW 130:18
Junes: J. that were warmer than — YEATS 586:5
perfumes in three hot J. burn'd — SHAK 494:18
Jungle: keep the J. Law — KIPL 301:13
this is the Law of the J. — KIPL 300:20
juniper: sat down under a j. tree — BIBLE 51:13
Juno: J. but an Ethiop were — SHAK 457:5
J.'s never-forgetting — VIRG 557:8
she's J. when she walks — JONS 285:5
Jupiter: *J. est quodcumque vides* — LUCAN 320:1
J. the Rain-giver — TIB 551:1
Quem J. vult perdere — DUP 199:15
So J. me succour — SKEL 508:18
jurisdiction: Rome hath no j. in this Realm of England — PRAY 400:10
Jurisprudence: gladsome light of J. — COKE 154:19
jury: I'll be j. — CARR 133:19
j. eagerly wrote down all — CARR 134:18
j., passing on the prisoner's — SHAK 463:16

just: all j. works do proceed PRAY 385:9
be j., and fear not SHAK 447:12
Expect him not in the j. HOUS 265:18
faithful and j. to me SHAK 450:18
gods are j. SHAK 456:5
have the interest to be j. AUDEN 19:13
is in its causes j. DRYD 197:4
jewel of the j. VAUG 555:20
j. and lasting peace among LINC 315:3
J. are the ways of God MILT 350:20
J. as I am ELL 206:10
j. man is also a prison THOR 550:1
j. shall live by faith BIBLE 74:31
J. when we're safest BROW 99:4
land of j. and old renown TENN 544:11
meanly j. JOHN 282:29
nothing to do with that j. man BIBLE 68:20
Only the actions of the j. SHIR 507:4
over ninety and nine j. BIBLE 70:17
path of the j. is BIBLE 53:19
rain it raineth on the j. BOWEN 90:22
reflect that God is j. JEFF 272:16
scrupulous and the j. CONR 161:22
sendeth rain on the j. BIBLE 64:19
spirits of j. men BIBLE 80:2
that hath his quarrel j. BILL 84:6
that hath his quarrel j. SHAK 446:6
that some cause was j. AUDEN 20:10
Thou art indeed j., Lord HOPK 257:2
thou art j. TENN 535:30
thou'lt raise me with the j. GRAH 233:16
whatsoever things are j. BIBLE 78:22
With j. enough of learning BYRON 124:17
juster: that I j. am SEDL 419:13
justest: reasoners are not always the j.
thinkers HAZL 243:24
wisest and j. and best PLATO 374:10
justice: has j. enough to accuse GOLD 232:38
humanity, reason, and j. BURKE 109:26
indifferently minister j. PRAY 387:14
j. anywhere and a mind VIRG 557:18
j. est la sanction des FRAN 217:25
j., In fair round belly SHAK 425:24
J. is open to all MATH 336:2
J. is the constant JUST 287:8
J. is truth in action DISR 184:18
j. makes democracy possible NIEB 362:26
j. of my quarrel ANON 6:4
j. or injustice JOHN 279:30
j. should not only be done HEW 250:20
J., though she's painted BUTL 118:14
'J.' was done HARDY 241:25
Let j. be done FERD 210:33
Let j. be done though WATS 565:8
liberty plucks j. by the nose SHAK 463:11
moderator and equal piece of j. BROW 96:19
mystery begins, j. ends BURKE 108:12
Poetic J. POPE 375:13
Revenge is a kind of wild j. BACON 27:7
right or j. MAGN 327:3
sad-ey'd j. SHAK 443:9
strong lance of j. hurtless SHAK 455:20
sword of j. first lay down DEFOE 173:16
talks about j. and right KIPL 301:19
temper so J. with mercy. MILT 349:21
this even-handed j. SHAK 459:5
Thou shalt have j. SHAK 468:7
Thwackum was for doing j. FIEL 211:24
under the rule of equal j. MILL 339:19
what you think j. requires MANS 328:17
When mercy seasons j. SHAK 467:27
Where J. naked is AUDEN 18:10
which is the j. SHAK 455:18
With sword of j. thee ruleth DUNB 199:12
you have ravish'd j. WEBS 567:6
justification: j., in short ARN 16:18
justified: man can only be j. ROS 408:18
shall no man living be j. PRAY 399:11
'Tis half as good as j. BUTL 118:11
Wisdom is j. of her children BIBLE 66:4

justifies: An' j. th' ill opinion BURNS 115:21
end j. the means BUS 117:4
justify: j. the ways of God to Men
MILT 344:22
To j. God's ways to man HOUS 264:12
yet men j. him BIBLE 63:4
justitia: are bound to say '*fiat j.* MANS 328:16
Fiat j. et pereat FERD 210:33
justitian: rectum aut j. MAGN 327:3
justle: When the bells j. HOUS 266:6
justly: fits a man to perform j. MILT 352:8
to do j. BIBLE 61:25
justum: Dignum et j. est MASS 335:3
et nubes pluant J. BIBLE 83:15
Juvenes: J. dum sumus ANON 10:13
juventus: Antiquitas saeculi j. mundi
BACON 25:10
juventutem: Post jucundam j. ANON 10:13

juvescence: in the j. of the year ELIOT 203:4
Juxtaposition: J. his prophet CLOU 153:11
kame: wherefore should I k. my hair
BALL 32:10
Kamerad: exclaiming *Mein lieber K.*
BLUC 89:1
kames: gowd k. in their hair BALL 31:20
Kangaroo: Duck and the K. LEAR 312:4
Old Man K. first KIPL 300:13
kangaroos: dear little k. flying about
WILDE 573:19
kann: Ich k. nicht anders LUTH 320:16
Wovon man nicht sprechen k. WITT 575:17
Kant: K. on the handle-bars BETJ 43:16
Karoo: meaning of the broad K.
HARDY 239:8
Karshish: K., the picker-up of learning's
BROW 100:24
Kaspar: Old K.'s work was done
SOUT 513:14
Kate: K. of my consolation SHAK 484:9
none of us car'd for K. SHAK 485:10
kategorisch: Dieser Imperativ ist k.
KANT 288:10
Keats: dumb to K. BROW 102:35
K., who was kill'd off BYRON 123:32
matter of wonder how K. SHEL 505:14
Prancing Nigger, Blunden, K. BETJ 44:10
What porridge had John K. BROW 103:27
whether Mister John K. KEATS 294:1
Who killed John K. BYRON 125:1
Wordsworth and out-glittering K.
BULW 107:3
Kedar: habitation among the tents of
K. PRAY 398:7
tents of K. BIBLE 56:16
keel: Joan doth k. the pot SHAK 457:19
keen: be swayed by quite as k. GILB 228:13
keener: grows k. with constant use IRV 270:21
with his k. eye MARV 332:9
keep: Except the Lord k. the city PRAY 398:18
He may k. that will HOUS 264:24
If you can k. your head KIPL 299:22
k. a hold of Nurse BELL 39:3
k. her in sickness PRAY 389:3
k. his friendship in constant JOHN 274:15
k. on saying it long enough BENN 40:23
k. the bridge with me MAC 322:17
k. thee in all thy ways PRAY 395:22
k. the gate of hell SHAK 476:21
k. the Jungle Law KIPL 301:13
k. the wolf far thence WEBS 567:9
k. your hearts and minds BIBLE 78:21
many to k. KING 297:3
mercy k. us in the same PRAY 386:19
my own intention to k. GLAD 229:16
need k. the shutters up DICK 179:17
'O k. the Dog far hence ELIOT 204:22
sufficient to k. them together JOHN 276:2
they should k. who can WORD 578:17
to k. Heights WORD 577:15

To k. your head PUDN 402:8
ware that will not k. HOUS 262:15
keeper: Am I my brother's k. BIBLE 45:25
ill k. of promise BACON 25:32
k. Stands up HOUS 263:10
Lord himself is thy k. PRAY 398:9
poacher a k. turned inside KING 297:8
keepers: k. of the walls took away BIBLE 57:2
keepeth: he that k. thee PRAY 398:9
Kempenfelt: When K. went down
COWP 165:31
kenne: Ich k. mich auch nicht GOET 229:28
Kennst: K. du das Land GOET 230:13
K. du es wohl GOET 230:13
kennt: Der k. euch nicht GOET 230:12
Kensal Green: to Paradise by way of
K. CHES 147:12
Kent: everybody knows K. DICK 181:27
talk I'm k. the better BURNS 114:32
Kentish: K. Sir Byng stood for his
BROW 99:26
Kentish Town: Anglo-Norman parish
church of K. BETJ 43:18
dandelions to the courts of K. BETJ 43:19
Pancras and K. repose BLAKE 86:5
Kenton: to the westward over K. BETJ 42:17
kept: I have k. the faith BIBLE 79:26
I k. them in thy name BIBLE 72:42
What wee k. ANON 8:17
kerchief: fetch the county k. HOUS 264:27
kernel: I then was to this k. SHAK 491:10
kettle: always back to the tea-k. DISR 184:17
how agree the k. BIBLE 63:3
I took a k. large and new CARR 135:26
merry k. boils away PAIN 367:15
this is a pretty k. of fish MARY 333:14
Kew: down to K. in lilac-time NOYES 364:11
his Highness' dog at K. POPE 376:16
Richmond and K. Undid me ELIOT 205:5
key: away the k. of knowledge BIBLE 70:2
got the k. of the street DICK 182:37
hands on that golden k. MILT 340:24
k. of India is London DISR 185:20
Turn the k. deftly KEATS 292:29
with an easy k. DRYD 195:17
keys: half that's got my k. GRAH 233:12
k. of all the creeds TENN 536:13
k. of hell and of death BIBLE 81:15
my fingers on these k. STEV 520:16
Over the noisy k. PROC 401:13
Two massy k. he bore MILT 343:11
Khatmandu: idol to the north of K.
HAYES 243:7
Khayyám: come with old K. and leave
FITZ 212:9
come with old K. FITZ 212:19
kiaugh: k. and care beguile BURNS 113:5
kibe: he galls his k. SHAK 436:29
kick: did you k. me downstairs BICK 83:27
I'll k. you downstairs CARR 133:23
scarcely k. to come to the top KEATS 293:31
sportsman wot doesn't k. his wife SURT 525:5
to k. against the pricks BIBLE 73:34
who dies of an ass's k. BROW 102:25
kicked: any k. up stairs before HAL 238:5
cursed and the stairs MILL 339:27
Kicking: K. you seems the common
BROW 106:1
kickshaws: Any pretty little tiny k.
SHAK 442:22
kid: shall lie down with the k. BIBLE 58:10
Thou shalt not seethe a k. BIBLE 47:27
kiddies: k. have crumpled the serviettes
BETJ 42:19
kidneys: blister my k. SURT 525:16
kill: animals never k. for sport FROU 219:17
chap that did not k. me HOUS 266:4
disease and k. the patient BACON 26:17
enough in thee to k. care SHAK 473:9
fain would k. their church TENN 540:14

I k. you — CHAM 139:18
I'll k. you if you quote it — BURG 108:3
I will k. thee — SHAK 477:5
I will k. you — BALL 31:3
k. a king — SHAK 435:2
k. a man as kill a good — MILT 351:22
k. a wife with kindness — SHAK 484:11
K. me to-morrow — SHAK 477:7
K. not the moth nor butterfly — BLAKE 85:13
k. sick people groaning — MARL 329:21
k. thee with much cherishing — SHAK 482:20
k. the poor creature — GASK 221:24
k. with looks — SHAK 479:11
let's k. all the lawyers — SHAK 446:11
nor yet canst thou k. me — DONNE 189:5
Otherwise k. me — MACN 326:13
prepared to k. one another — SHAW 497:15
They k. us for their sport — SHAK 455:9
Thou shalt not k. — BIBLE 47:24
Thou shalt not k. — CLOU 153:26
time to k. — BIBLE 55:12
To k. a human being is — JAMES 271:27
When you have to k. a man — CHUR 151:2
kill'd: I kiss'd thee ere I k. — SHAK 478:1
k. with my own treachery — SHAK 437:19
killed: Better be k. — SURT 525:22
effort very nearly k. her — BELL 39:7
have so many people k. — AUST 24:1
I am the enemy you k. — OWEN 367:12
k. a calf he would do it — AUBR 17:27
k. hisself on principle — DICK 182:35
k. with your hard opinions — SHAK 443:2
killer: here the lover and k. are — DOUG 191:10
killest: thou that k. the prophets — BIBLE 67:26
killeth: letter k. — BIBLE 77:4
killing: k. a cat than choking — KING 297:15
k. Kruger with your mouth — KIPL 297:22
K. myself to die upon — SHAK 478:1
K. no Murder Briefly Discourst — SEXBY 420:17
k. of a mouse on Sunday — BRAT 91:24
kills: man k. the thing he loves — WILDE 572:10
my heart an air that k. — HOUS 263:22
waste remains and k. — EMPS 208:17
kilted: has k. her green kirtle — BALL 32:1
kimonos: Two girls in silk k. — YEATS 585:11
kin: certainly man is of k. — BACON 25:25
If one's own k. and kith — NASH 359:18
k. with kin and kind with — SHAK 479:20
little less than 'k.' — BARH 33:25
little more than k. — SHAK 429:21
makes the whole world k. — SHAK 487:6
kind: beautiful, the tender, the k. — MILL 339:23
be cruel only to be k. — SHAK 435:20
be honest, to be k. — STEV 521:4
coarsely k. — JOHN 278:35
enjoy her while she's k. — DRYD 198:17
Godlike crime was to be k. — BYRON 125:18
grow more cold, more k. — SPAR 514:22
had been k. — JOHN 274:7
he grows k. — SHAK 466:5
Is she k. as she is fair — SHAK 491:4
just the art of being k. — WILC 572:6
just try to be *k.* — FOAK 216:2
K. are her answers — CAMP 129:21
k. of people do they think — CHUR 150:9
k. things done by men with — MAS 333:23
k. William Maginn — LOCK 315:23
k. with kind confound — SHAK 479:20
less than k. — SHAK 429:21
makes one wond'rous k. — GARR 221:15
mein irisch K. — WAGN 562:1
people will always be k. — SASS 414:13
rather more than 'k.' — BARH 33:25
to her virtues very k. — PRIOR 400:23
Too kind—too k. — NIGH 363:15
Yet he was k. — GOLD 231:2
kindest: k. and the best — BURNS 114:24
thou wert the k. man that — MAL 328:8
kindled: k., (yea, but a little — PRAY 389:19

thus musing the fire k. — PRAY 391:30
kindles: k. fire — LA R 310:15
kindleth: matter a little fire k. — BIBLE 80:13
kindliness: cool k. of sheets — BROO 94:8
kindly: k. treat her — GAY 222:9
preserve to our use the k. fruits — PRAY 385:21
kindness: I will some k. do them — SHAK 486:13
kill a wife with k. — SHAK 484:11
k. and consolidates society — JOHN 280:6
K. in another's trouble — GORD 233:1
milk of human k. — CHUR 148:22
milk of human k. — SHAK 459:1
Of k. and of love — WORD 578:4
still the great have k. — POPE 376:29
think it k. to his Majesty — HALL 238:8
value on spontaneous k. — JOHN 278:33
We'll tak a cup o' k. yet — BURNS 112:32
kindnesses: recalling the thought of k. done — CAT 137:9
kindred: haunts two k. spirits flee — KEATS 292:20
to k. dear — CAREW 130:14
kindreds: k. of the earth shall wail — BIBLE 81:10
kine: seven fat k. — BIBLE 46:31
King: a' for our rightfu' K. — BURNS 114:10
against Heav'n's matchless K. — MILT 347:14
ale is a dish for a k. — SHAK 491:17
all were looking for a k. — MACD 325:4
another k., one Jesus — BIBLE 74:9
apples of gold for the k.'s daughter — SWIN 530:17
arose up a new k. over Egypt — BIBLE 46:40
Authority forgets a dying k. — TENN 535:22
banners of the k. advance — VEN 556:5
blessedness alone that makes a K. — TRAH 552:2
born K. of the Jews — BIBLE 63:31
coming of the K. of Heaven — ANON 9:1
conscience as their K. — TENN 534:11
despised, and dying k. — SHEL 504:6
discharge my duties as K. — EDW 200:4
divinity doth hedge a k. — SHAK 436:6
every inch a k. — SHAK 455:16
Fear God. Honour the k. — BIBLE 80:25
fight for its K. and country — ANON 7:19
First Moloch, horrid k. — MILT 345:14
follow the K. — TENN 534:5
Give the K. thy judgements — PRAY 394:18
God bless the K. — BYROM 119:25
God save our gracious k. — CAREY 130:24
God save the k. — BIBLE 49:42
God save the k. — HOGG 252:24
God save the k. — SHAK 479:21
government without a k. — BANC 32:13
hath not offended the k. — MORE 357:18
heart and stomach of a k. — ELIZ 206:4
he might hae been a k. — BALL 30:16
He played the K. as though — FIELD 211:3
herald of love's mighty k. — SPEN 515:19
He that plays the k. shall — SHAK 432:16
I have made unto the K. — PRAY 392:14
I serv'd my k. — SHAK 447:13
I was a K. in Babylon — HENL 245:10
kill a k. — SHAK 435:2
k. and officers of sorts — SHAK 443:9
k. delighteth to honour — BIBLE 52:3
k. drinks to Hamlet — SHAK 437:17
k. for my money — FIEL 211:32
k. is always a king — WOLL 576:10
k. is strongest — BIBLE 62:4
k. may make a nobleman — BURKE 111:37
k. my brother's wreck — ELIOT 204:26
k. never dies — BLAC 85:3
K., observing with judicious — TRAPP 552:5
K. of all these the dead — HOMER 254:6
k. of codpieces — SHAK 456:26
K. of glory shall come — PRAY 390:24
K. of Great Britain is — REED 405:9

K. OF KINGS — BIBLE 82:26
k. of shreds and patches — SHAK 435:12
K. of tremendous majesty — CEL 138:7
k. Over himself — SHEL 503:12
K. over the Water — ANON 7:25
k. reigns — THIE 546:5
k.'s a bawcock — SHAK 444:17
King's a K. — DRAY 193:8
k. sate on the rocky brow — BYRON 122:34
K.'s crown shall fall — SCOTT 415:20
K.'s daughter is all glorious — PRAY 392:17
k.'s English — SHAK 469:5
K.'s First Minister — CHUR 150:12
k. sits in Dunfermline — BALL 31:16
k.'s name is a tower — SHAK 481:12
k.'s name twenty thousand — SHAK 479:7
K. thought mair o' Marie — BALL 31:11
K. to be your servant — SHAK 447:8
K. to have things done — PEPYS 372:6
K. to Oxford sent a troop — BROW 97:26
k. was much moved — BIBLE 50:26
K. with half the East — HOUS 265:3
Lord is K. — PRAY 395:24
lord, thy k., thy governor — SHAK 484:15
My castles are my K.'s — SCOTT 417:21
My dead K. — JOYCE 286:15
My God and K. — HERB 246:26
my K. and my God — PRAY 395:11
my life to make you K. — CHAR 140:29
myself a K. of infinite space — SHAK 432:13
no k. in Israel — BIBLE 49:20
Og the k. of Basan — PRAY 399:1
open The k.'s eyes — SHAK 447:1
Our k. has written a braid — BALL 31:17
our sins lay on the k. — SHAK 444:23
passing brave to be a K. — MARL 330:7
shepherd and the k. — CERV 138:20
shines brightly as a k. — SHAK 468:18
Sir Byng stood for his K. — BROW 99:26
skipping in — SHAK 439:34
so much a k. as a Monarch — SELL 420:5
sort of k. should ever die — BROW 103:23
still am I k. of those — SHAK 479:23
subject's duty is the k.'s — SHAK 444:22
That the k. can do no wrong — BLAC 85:5
That was no more than a k. — SWIN 529:26
There was a k. of Yvetot — BER 41:14
think the k. is but a man — SHAK 444:20
To be a Pirate K. — GILB 228:12
To my true k. I offer'd — MAC 322:8
Under which k. — SHAK 442:28
What a k. — ABEL 1:2
What is a K. — PRIOR 401:6
What must the k. do now — SHAK 479:15
when I am k. — SHAK 446:11
who speaks ill of your k. — NELS 360:12
with the image of the K. — TENN 534:17
worm that hath eat of a k. — SHAK 435:27
Would shake hands with a k. — HALL 238:8
yesterday a K. — BYRON 125:7
King Charles: trouble out of K.'s head — DICK 177:7
Kingcups: K., and loved Lilies — SPEN 517:3
kingdom: Advantage on the k. of the shore — SHAK 494:3
enter into the k. of heaven — BIBLE 64:11
found a k. — MILT 350:6
God hath numbered thy k. — BIBLE 61:6
I never gave you k. — SHAK 454:5
inheritor of the k. — PRAY 388:12
In this k. by the sea — POE 374:22
k. against kingdom — BIBLE 67:28
k. for a stage — SHAK 443:3
k. for it was too small — SHAK 440:24
k. of heaven is at hand — BIBLE 63:35
k. where nobody dies — MILL 339:24
large k. for a little grave — SHAK 479:15
Like to a little k. — SHAK 449:6
man to enter into the k. — BIBLE 67:11
my k. for a horse — SHAK 481:18

My mind to me a k. is	DYER 199:17
of such is the k. of God	BIBLE 68:36
Seek ye first the k. of God	BIBLE 64:31
theirs is the k. of heaven	BIBLE 64:6
thou comest into thy k.	BIBLE 71:12
Thy k. come	BIBLE 64:24
Thy k. is divided	BIBLE 61:6
Yet thy k. shall pass	SWIN 530:7
kingdom of God: k. is within you	
	BIBLE 70:31
riches enter into the k.	BIBLE 70:36
kingdom of heaven: k. is like to a grain	
	BIBLE 66:20
shall not enter into the k.	BIBLE 67:2
kingdoms: all the k. of the world	BIBLE 64:3
hath mus'd of taking k.	SHAK 422:19
K. are clay	SHAK 421:8
many goodly states and k.	KEATS 292:17
King George: In good K.'s glorious	
	GILB 226:11
K. will be able to read	HANC 238:18
Kingly: K. conclaves stern	SHEL 503:1
this k. seal	SHAK 422:21
king of Israel: smote the k. between	
	BIBLE 51:21
King Pandion: K., he is dead	BARN 34:1
kings: abounding with k. thirty	MAC 324:21
All k. shall fall down	PRAY 394:20
all the powerful K.	DONNE 190:26
any madness of their k.	HOR 258:12
are but the breath of k.	BURNS 113:10
bind their k. in chains	PRAY 399:24
cabbages—and k.	CARR 135:7
Captains and the K. depart	KIPL 302:7
come now no K. nor Caesars	POUND 383:19
commonwealths and ruin k.	DRYD 194:5
Conquering k. their titles	CHAN 139:19
divorc'd So many English k.	SHAK 442:18
dread and fear of k.	SHAK 467:27
godly k. had built her	FLEC 214:6
heart of k. is unsearchable	BIBLE 54:25
heart's ease Must k. neglect	SHAK 444:24
it's the sport of k.	SURT 525:4
k. crept out again to feel	BROW 97:35
K.' daughters were among	PRAY 392:16
k. governed their rude	BAG 28:28
k. have cares that wait	GREE 236:11
k. is mostly rapscallions	TWAIN 554:2
k. of the earth: are gathered	PRAY 392:25
k. of the sea	ARN 13:7
K. seek their subjects'	HERR 249:8
k. that fear their subjects'	SHAK 446:19
K. will be tyrants from	BURKE 111:13
K. with their armies did	PRAY 394:8
mad k.	SHAK 452:13
Many k. have sat down upon	BIBLE 62:31
meaner creatures k.	SHAK 481:11
passion for our temperate k.	TENN 541:11
Physicians are like k.	WEBS 566:28
poor and the castles of k.	HOR 259:13
prophets and k. have desired	BIBLE 69:29
ruin'd sides of K.	BEAU 36:1
saddest of all K.	JOHN 273:22
shall be accounted poet k.	KEATS 292:9
should all be as happy as k.	STEV 522:22
sport of k.	SOM 513:2
stories of the death of k.	SHAK 479:11
strength of guilty k.	DEFOE 173:16
subjects is the end of k.	SHAK 422:15
superfluous k. for messengers	GOLD 231:30
That part which laws or k.	JOHN 282:21
That part which laws or k.	THOM 547:4
These five k. did a king	BURNS 114:13
three k. into the east	SHAK 446:20
up and puller down of k.	KIPL 300:2
walk with K.	SHEL 62:31
With k. and counsellors	BIBLE 52:12
Kingsley: Froude believes K. a divine	
	STUB 524:5
kinship: any k. with the stars	MER 337:7

Kipling: Pardoned K. and his views	
	AUDEN 19:8
Rudyards cease from k.	STEP 518:24
kirk: Marie Hamilton's to the k.	BALL 31:11
Kirkconnell: On fair K. lea	BALL 31:4
kirtle: has kilted her green k.	BALL 32:1
kis: k. the steppes	CHAU 144:17
Kismet: is he that saith not 'K.'	CHES 147:4
kiss: add to that k. a score	HERR 249:22
Ae fond k.	BURNS 112:27
another with an holy k.	BIBLE 75:28
Close with her, k. her	SWIN 530:27
Colder thy k.	BYRON 126:13
coughs when you would k.	AUDEN 18:10
coward does it with a k.	WILDE 572:10
drew With one long k.	TENN 533:16
handshake, the cough, the k.	AUDEN 21:1
have felt my soul in a k.	SWIN 530:20
his whole heart in one k.	TENN 543:9
human souls did never k.	KEATS 289:3
I dare not ask a k.	HERR 250:3
I k. his dirty shoe	SHAK 444:17
I'll k. my girl on her	KIPL 301:10
'I saw you take his k.	PATM 370:3
k., a sigh, and so away	CRAS 169:14
k. before they are married	SHAK 445:15
K. her until she be wearied	SHEL 505:3
k. is but a kiss now	MER 337:10
k. Long as my exile	SHAK 428:2
K. me and never no more	MAL 328:4
K. me as if you made believe	BROW 101:15
K. me, Hardy	NELS 360:23
K. me Kate	SHAK 484:10
k. my Julia's dainty leg	HERR 249:15
k. my Lord before I die	MARL 330:13
k. of death	SMITH 510:4
k. on the wrist	STEV 520:20
k. our lady Peace at home	SHAK 441:13
K. the book's outside who	COWP 165:8
k. the place to make it	TAYL 531:25
K. the Son	PRAY 389:19
K. till the cow comes home	BEAU 36:11
leave a k. but in the cup	JONS 284:12
let me k. that hand	SHAK 455:17
make me immortal with a k.	MARL 329:10
man may k. a bonnie lass	BURNS 115:13
many a glowing k. had won	HOOD 255:4
might take occasion to k.	SHAK 426:22
My bluest veins to k.	SHAK 422:11
myself to die upon a k.	SHAK 478:1
Only to k. that air	HERR 250:3
part at last without a k.	MORR 358:11
presently all humbled k. the rod	SHAK 490:31
Quit in a single k.	BRID 92:11
self I needs must k. again	SIDN 507:25
spend that k.	SHAK 424:14
stop his mouth with a k.	SHAK 472:11
swear to never k. the girls	BROW 100:30
Then come k. me	SHAK 488:17
this last lamenting k.	DONNE 188:20
with a single famish'd k.	SHAK 487:12
kiss'd: I k. her slender hand	TENN 540:6
k. again with tears	TENN 541:28
k. thee ere I kill'd thee	SHAK 478:1
kissed: Being k. by a man who didn't	
	KIPL 304:37
First time he k. me	BROW 98:12
first we k. beside the thorn	BRID 92:20
k. by the English dead	OWEN 367:6
k. her once by the pig-sty	THOM 547:11
k. it and then fled	SHEL 503:17
k. the lovely grass	BROO 94:15
laughed and k. his hand	HOUS 266:4
righteousness and peace have k.	PRAY 395:15
said when she k. her cow	SWIFT 526:28
they k. each other's cheek	GILB 228:31
kisses: consign'd k. to them	SHAK 487:12
Give me a thousand k.	CAT 136:26
it rain'd k.	SHAK 422:19
I understand thy k.	SHAK 439:29

Let thy love in k. rain	SHEL 501:9
littered with remembered k.	MACN 326:3
more than k.	DONNE 189:22
my k. bring again	SHAK 464:21
play'd At cards for k.	LYLY 321:10
poor half-k. kill me quite	DRAY 193:17
remembered k. after death	TENN 542:4
Stolen k. much completer	HUNT 268:11
thousand k. the poor last	SHAK 423:14
who k. the Joy as it flies	BLAKE 86:18
who straight on k. dream	SHAK 481:28
With k. four	KEATS 290:20
with the k. of his mouth	BIBLE 56:15
you have forgotten my k.	SWIN 530:11
Kissing: K. don't last: cookery do	MER 338:1
k., kind-hearted gentleman	COWP 168:3
K. with golden face	SHAK 493:9
K. your hand may make you	LOOS 318:3
made For k.	SHAK 480:21
Sweet red splendid k. mouth	SWIN 531:1
that first invented k.	SWIFT 526:31
trembled k.	SHAK 422:11
when the k. had to stop	BROW 105:25
kiss-worthy: thy most k. face	SIDN 507:25
kitchen: anarchy prevails in my k.	
	JOHN 281:1
get out of the k.	TRUM 553:20
in the k. bred	BYRON 125:24
I will make my k.	STEV 522:29
k. and their children	FITZ 213:19
Kitchen-cabals: K., and nursery-mishaps	
	COWP 168:6
Kitchener: if K. was not a great man	
	ASQ 17:19
kitchens: wild cats in your k.	SHAK 474:15
Kite: Ere Chil the K. swoops	KIPL 303:7
kites: fatted all the region k.	SHAK 433:4
kith: If one's own kin and k.	NASH 359:18
kitten: dead k., an egg-shell	WELLS 568:16
My imperial k.	CARR 134:27
rather be a k. and cry mew	SHAK 439:25
kittened: mother's cat had but k.	
	SHAK 439:21
Kitty: K., a fair	GARR 221:16
kleinen: Opfer fällt als einer k.	HITL 251:9
knappeth: k. the spear in sunder	PRAY 392:21
knave: coined an epithet for a k.	MAC 323:27
duteous and knee-crooking k.	SHAK 473:13
he's an arrant k.	SHAK 431:17
he's but Fortune's k.	SHAK 423:20
How absolute the k. is	SHAK 436:28
life a foolish prating k.	SHAK 435:23
neat k. with a smooth tale	WEBS 566:18
petty sneaking k. I knew	BLAKE 87:3
rascally yea-forsooth k.	SHAK 441:4
slipper and subtle k.	SHAK 474:21
To feed the titled k.	BURNS 115:24
knavery: k. and folly to excuse	CHUR 149:5
knaves: call'd them untaught k.	SHAK 438:14
He calls the k., Jacks	DICK 178:8
k. and thieves men shut	SHAK 490:27
most part of fools and k.	BUCH 106:12
We are arrant k.	SHAK 433:11
knavish: are either k. or childish	JOHN 278:9
kneaded: k. by the moon	HARDY 241:21
knee: fore-mast wi' his k.	BALL 30:19
infant prattling on his k.	BURNS 113:5
Jesus every k. should bow	BIBLE 78:14
little abune her k.	BALL 32:1
Lord Primate on bended k.	BARH 33:11
my k., my hat, and hand	BROW 96:3
set upon the nurse's k.	BALL 32:11
sit upon the curate's k.	CHES 147:9
straw under my k.	DONNE 191:2
to the child on thy k.	BRID 92:21
kneel: k. before the Lord our	PRAY 396:4
see the oxen k.	HARDY 240:14
they should k. for peace	SHAK 484:14
wilderness shall k. before him	PRAY 394:20
kneel'd: That k. unto the buds	SHAK 422:17

737

Kneeling: K. ne'er spoil'd silk stocking
    HERB 247:10
meekly k. upon your knees   PRAY 387:18
kneels: Not one k. to another   WHIT 570:22
knees: at the great k. and feet   SWIN 528:26
bow my k. unto the Father   BIBLE 77:24
confirm the feeble k.   BIBLE 58:33
creeps rustling to her k.   KEATS 289:17
K. and tresses folded   MER 337:1
our hands round her k.   SWIN 528:16
Petticoats up to the k.   CLOU 153:15
rest on his k.   DICK 178:24
Richmond I raised my k.   ELIOT 205:5
Sweeney spreads his k.   ELIOT 204:14
than to live on your k.   IBAR 269:16
then I felt to his k.   SHAK 443:18
they are all on their k.   HARDY 240:13
to sit on Sweeney's k.   ELIOT 204:15
work is done upon his k.   KIPL 299:15
knell: By fairy hands their k.   COLL 158:20
it is a k.   SHAK 460:1
Sea-nymphs hourly ring his k.   SHAK 484:32
strikes like a rising k.   BYRON 120:20
knew: George the First k. nothing
    JOHN 276:22
head could carry all he k.   GOLD 231:3
he k. not what to say   BYRON 124:43
I k. all her ways   HOUS 265:8
I k. not all he meant   TENN 534:24
I k. not where   LONG 316:6
I k. that once   STEP 518:25
I k. you once   BROW 105:36
k. it all before you   KIPL 301:11
k. me, and was Ned   HOUS 265:5
much righter than one k.   POUND 383:22
said it that k. it best   BACON 25:30
that he k. nothing yet   BEHN 38:11
that I k. almost as much   JOHN 273:26
that she k. she were   SHAK 482:6
we k. the worst too young   KIPL 299:11
world k. him not   BIBLE 71:26
knife: k. has slit The throat   HOUS 264:9
k. is lost in it   SHEL 501:20
k. see not the wound it   SHAK 459:2
stood there holding the k.   AUDEN 21:7
strike with our spirit's k.   SHEL 499:20
'War even to the k.   BYRON 120:8
War to the k.   PAL 368:8
wind's like a whetted k.   MAS 334:6
Knife-grinder: Needy K.   CANN 129:26
knight: beadsman now that was your
  k.   PEELE 371:8
came a k. to be their wooer   BALL 30:14
gentle k. was pricking   SPEN 515:30
hath no loyal k. and true   TENN 538:6
He is k. dubbed with unhatched   SHAK 490:14
K. at arms   KEATS 290:15
K. of the Doleful Countenance   CERV 138:12
k. shall not be whole   MAL 327:16
K. without fear and without   ANON 9:5
red-cross k. for ever kneel'd   TENN 538:8
Show'd him no carpet k.   SCOTT 417:5
sir priest than sir k.   SHAK 490:15
there lies a new-slain k.   BALL 32:8
There never was k. like   SCOTT 417:9
This k. was indeed a valiant   EVEL 209:6
thy sire was a k.   SCOTT 416:24
knight-errantry: Religion is k.   CERV 138:15
Knightly: ever the K. years were gone
    HENL 245:10
Knighton: long way further than K.
    HOUS 264:8
knights: accomplishing the k.   SHAK 444:9
Armoury of the invincible K.   WORD 582:3
By k. of Logres   MILT 350:3
ladies dead and lovely k.   SHAK 494:19
virtuous deeds that some k.   CAXT 138:4
knit: k. together thine elect   PRAY 387:4
sheet k. at the four corners   BIBLE 73:37
stuff of life to k. me   HOUS 263:16

knits: k. me to thy rugged strand
    SCOTT 416:22
Sleep that k. up the ravell'd   SHAK 460:8
knitter: Like a k. drowsed   HARDY 239:12
knitters: spinsters and the k.   SHAK 489:3
knitting: twisted braids of lilies k.
    MILT 341:20
knob: brains out of a brass k.   DICK 178:23
knobs: k., and flames o' fire   SHAK 444:7
Knochen: Die gesunden K. eines einzigen
    BISM 84:22
knock: k., and it shall be opened   BIBLE 65:2
K. as you please   POPE 376:15
K. at a star with my exalted   HERR 248:19
k. me down with the butt-end   CIBB 151:11
k. on my door in the morning   AUDEN 21:2
right to k. him down for it   JOHN 278:15
stand at the door, and k.   BIBLE 81:21
We should k. him down first   JOHN 277:1
Where k. is open wide   SMART 509:3
knocked: have k. the factious dogs
    JOHN 279:10
k. Mr Toots about the head   DICK 177:29
K. on my sullen heart   STEV 523:11
with decency, k.   POUND 382:14
knocker: Tie up the k.   POPE 376:18
knocketh: voice of my beloved that k.
    BIBLE 57:1
knocking: Here's a k.   SHAK 460:15
k. at Preferment's door   ARN 14:12
K. on the moonlit door   DE L 174:7
Whence is that k.   SHAK 460:12
knocks: k. you down with the butt
    GOLD 232:40
knoll'd: bells have k. to church   SHAK 425:23
knolling: k. a departed friend   SHAK 441:2
knot: k. intrinsicate Of life   SHAK 424:14
So the k. be unknotted   ELIOT 202:10
knot-grass: bunches of k.   KEATS 289:16
knots: pokers into true-love k.   COL 157:6
knotted: Sat and k. all the while   SEDL 419:12
know: 'All that we k. is   BYRON 120:10
all ye need to k.   KEATS 291:11
am he that aspired to k.   BROW 103:3
canvassers whom they do not k.
    HURST 268:17
creditors would hardly k.   FOX 217:24
does not k. himself   LA F 306:20
from what we k.   POPE 379:2
God, thou, and I do k.   SHAK 478:12
God we might k. as much   KIPL 298:17
go we k. not where   SHAK 464:14
hate any one that we k.   HAZL 244:2
have it when they k. it not   SWIFT 528:7
have much ado to k. myself   SHAK 465:7
He will not k. what all   SHAK 469:22
'How shall I k. your true   RAL 404:13
I do not k. myself   GOET 229:28
I k. nothing whatever about   DOYLE 192:14
I k. not the Lord   BIBLE 47:10
I k. not the man   BIBLE 68:19
I k. what I like   BEER 38:5
k. more of mankind I expect   JOHN 279:12
K. most of the rooms   FULL 220:13
k. of England who only   KIPL 298:24
k. so much that ain't so   BILL 84:7
k. that I am God   PRAY 392:21
k. that my redeemer liveth   BIBLE 52:31
k. that which we are   BYRON 124:9
K. the change and feel   KEATS 293:4
k. thee not, old man   SHAK 442:30
K. their own good   DRYD 198:18
K. the man their neighbour   YEATS 586:14
K. then thyself   POPE 379:12
k. the place for the first   ELIOT 203:2
K. thyself   ANON 9:21
'K. thyself'   CARL 132:18
k. to know no more   MILT 348:9
'K. what thou canst work   CARL 132:18
K. ye the land where   BYRON 120:1

K. you the land where   GOET 230:13
let me k. mine end   PRAY 391:30
master of them that k.   DANTE 171:7
more than to k. little   BACON 27:24
neither shall his place k.   BIBLE 52:19
no one to k. what it is   ANON 4:11
now I k. it   GAY 223:22
People of quality k. everything   MOL 353:23
place saying you want to k.   DICK 178:17
searching what we k. not   MILT 351:26
suffer us to k. but little   JOHN 273:17
they k. not what they do   BIBLE 71:11
they merely k. more   SAKI 413:16
To be we k. not what   DRYD 195:26
to k. a thing or two   MOL 353:5
To k. but this   POPE 381:12
to k. that you know not   BACON 26:5
To k. the world   YOUNG 588:11
To k. this only   MILT 350:9
to others that we k. not   SHAK 433:8
unless we k. it to be poetry   THOR 550:25
We k. a subject ourselves   JOHN 276:28
we k. in part   BIBLE 76:14
we k. not anything   TENN 536:26
We k. our will is free   JOHN 275:24
we k. the Good   AUDEN 19:12
What do I k.   MONT 355:3
What they are yet I k. not   SHAK 454:2
when it came to k. me well   MOORE 356:25
which you yourselves do k.   SHAK 451:2
Who k. them best   BURNS 114:29
Know-All: Ole man K. died las' year
    HARR 242:22
knowe: he that kan hymselven k.
    CHAU 142:30
knowed: 'e knew they k.   KIPL 304:5
that there is to be k.   GRAH 233:19
knowest: k. not what a day may bring
    BIBLE 54:36
Speak less than thou k.   SHAK 453:15
thou k. that I love thee   BIBLE 73:16
thou k. my down-sitting   PRAY 399:4
knoweth: He that loveth not k. not
    BIBLE 81:5
knowing: foolish to talk of k. Greek
    WOOLF 576:17
lust of k. what should   FLEC 214:14
misfortune of k. any thing   AUST 23:5
With a k. ignorance   JOHN 273:16
knowledge: After such k.   ELIOT 203:5
all k. to be my province   BACON 28:1
anything be beyond the k.   BEAU 35:16
climbing after k. infinite   MARL 330:8
close the five ports of k.   BROW 95:19
counsel by words without k.   BIBLE 52:41
desire more love and k.   SHAK 424:27
dissemble sometimes your k.   BACON 26:5
finer spirit of all k.   WORD 583:9
first the literature of k.   DE Q 175:6
foundation is the k. of causes   BACON 28:6
fret not after k.   KEATS 292:5
from k. ignorance   BROW 100:10
full of the k. of the Lord   BIBLE 58:11
he would bring home k.   JOHN 277:31
if he wants any k.   COL 158:9
improved life by the k.   VIRG 558:23
increaseth k. increaseth sorrow   BIBLE 55:9
is worth a pound of k.   WESL 568:23
K. advances by steps   MAC 323:3
k. and wonder (which is   BACON 24:14
K. comes   TENN 539:3
K. dwells   COWP 167:23
K. enormous makes a God   KEATS 290:7
K. gained and virtue lost   HOUS 265:4
k. in the making   MILT 352:2
k. is bought in the market   CLOU 153:18
K. is proud that he has   COWP 167:24
K. is of two kinds   JOHN 276:28
k. is, ourselves to know   POPE 380:4
K. itself is power   BACON 28:11

k., it shall vanish   BIBLE 76:14
K. may give weight   CHES 145:31
k. of man is as the waters   BACON 24:20
k. of truth   BACON 27:31
k. of the Son of God   BIBLE 77:28
k. of the ancient languages   BRIG 93:8
k. of the world is only   CHES 145:12
k. of London was extensive   DICK 181:35
k. of nothing   DICK 183:3
k. of a lifetime   WHIS 569:23
K. puffeth up   BIBLE 76:5
k. shall be increased   BIBLE 61:10
k. too but recorded experience   CARL 131:8
k. without integrity is   JOHN 282:11
Let k. grow from more   TENN 535:32
light of k. in their eyes   SYM 531:3
little k. is dangerous   HUXL 269:9
multiplieth words without k.   BIBLE 52:40
No man's k. here can go   LOCKE 315:15
Out-topping k.   ARN 14:23
price for k.   TICK 551:3
province of k. to speak   HOLM 253:20
Pursuit of k. under difficulties   DICK 182:10
renewed in k. after the image   BIBLE 78:26
Science is organized k.   SPEN 514:24
spirit of k. and of the fear   BIBLE 58:9
Such k. is too wonderful   PRAY 399:5
taken away the key of k.   BIBLE 70:2
There is more k.   JOHN 276:8
there k. in the most High   PRAY 394:22
thorough k. of human nature   AUST 22:31
to communicate k.   DE Q 175:7
To follow k. like a sinking   TENN 544:1
to follow virtue and k.   DANTE 171:13
tree of diabolical k.   SHER 506:10
tree of k. of good   BIBLE 45:8
Unto this k. to aspire   DONNE 188:26
What I don't know isn't k.   BEEC 31:9
what is k. but grieving   MER 338:7
What k. can perform   WORD 577:3
which passeth k.   BIBLE 77:25
wisdom we have lost in k.   ELIOT 202:3
With too much k.   POPE 379:12
known: best that is k. and thought ARN 16:1
child is k. by his doings   BIBLE 54:17
devil where he is k.   JOHN 279:31
done and little to be k.   JOHN 280:7
don't choose to have it k.   CHES 146:7
Have ye not k.   BIBLE 59:9
he should have k. no more   HOBB 251:23
If you would be k.   COLT 159:10
In Jewry is God k.   PRAY 395:1
is she k. in all the land   TENN 533:8
know even as also I am k.   BIBLE 76:14
knowing what should not be k.   FLEC 214:14
k. and said in the world   ARN 16:17
k. by the British than   BORR 90:3
k. for his well-knownness   BOOR 89:20
k. of old   KIPL 302:7
k. of them in breaking   BIBLE 71:19
k. too late   SHAK 482:4
life endured and k.   SASS 415:2
light and safer than a k.   HASK 243:1
needs only to be k.   DRYD 196:3
not be k. to do anything   EMER 207:41
So I had nothing k.   SHAK 475:25
Soldier of the Great War K.   KIPL 305:12
That thy way may be k.   PRAY 394:4
then the end is k.   SHAK 451:33
this is all that is k.   NEWM 362:5
till I am k.   JOHN 274:7
Which we have heard and k.   PRAY 395:3
yet hast thou not k. me   BIBLE 72:33
knows: HE k.—HE knows   FITZ 213:6
He k. ye not   GOET 230:12
k. about depth knows about   TILL 551:4
k. even his Bible   ARN 15:22
k. nothing whatever about   KNOX 305:21
k. of a better 'ole   BAIR 29:23
no man truly k. another   BROW 96:32

now God alone k.   KLOP 305:16
'She k. wot's wot   DICK 182:27
that has a mind and k.   SHAW 496:3
knowses: goodness only k.   CHES 147:24
knucklebones: harmless art of k. has
                                    STEV 520:23
knuckle-end: That k. of England
                                    SMITH 510:30
knyf: smylere with the k. under CHAU 142:20
knyght: parfit gentil k.   CHAU 141:10
kotched: sinners'll be k. out late HARR 242:17
Kraken: K. sleepeth   TENN 537:24
Krieg: Der K. ist nichts als eine CLAU 152:27
  K. ein Glied in Gottes   MOLT 354:4
Krorluppia: Nasticreechia K.   LEAR 311:19
Kruger: you've finished killing K.
                                    KIPL 297:22
krummen: Aus so k. Holze   KANT 288:14
Kubla: 'mid this tumult K. heard COL 156:29
Kubla Khan: In Xanadu did K.   COL 156:26
Kultur: Wenn ich K. höre   JOHST 283:8
kummervollen: Wer nie die k. Nächte
                                    GOET 230:12
Kunst: in der K. ist das Beste GOET 230:8
  zuletzt die grösste K.   GOET 229:27
Kurd: say the same about the K. BELL 38:27
Kurtz: Mistah K.—he dead   CONR 161:18
Kyrie: K. eleison   MASS 334:16
label: l. to cover himself with HUXL 269:4
  pack and l. men for God   THOM 548:26
labelled: utensil l. to my will SHAK 488:12
labor: hic l. est   VIRG 558:18
  solely by the l. of my hands   THOR 550:13
laborans: utilitatis pro communi l.
                                    THOM 546:11
laboraverunt: in vanum l. qui aedificant
                                    BIBLE 83:12
labore: dies niti praestante l. LUCR 320:6
labores: Iucundi acti l.   CIC 151:18
laboribus: quod unum est pro l. tantis
                                    CAT 136:28
laborious: perform some very l. duty
                                    SMITH 509:13
labour: all l. Mars what it does SHAK 423:10
  All things are full of l.   BIBLE 55:7
  brow of l. this crown   BRYAN 106:8
  Endless l. to be wrong   JOHN 280:9
  every l. sped   GOLD 231:26
  faith and l. of love   BIBLE 78:30
  forget his l. an' his toil   BURNS 113:5
  Green leaves of thy l.   SWIN 529:28
  had my l. for my travail   SHAK 486:20
  Honest l. bears a lovely   DEKK 173:20
  I l. for peace   PRAY 398:3
  In all l. there is profit   BIBLE 54:2
  l. against our own cure   BROW 97:2
  l. for that which satisfieth   BIBLE 59:25
  l. of doing nothing   STEE 518:8
  l. of your life is to build   MONT 354:15
  l. spread her wholesome   GOLD 230:18
  l. we delight in physics   SHAK 460:19
  l. which he taketh under   BIBLE 55:5
  L. without joy is base   RUSK 412:4
  Learn to l. and to wait   LONG 317:5
  man to l. in his vocation   SHAK 438:10
  many still must l.   BYRON 121:30
  ruined by Chinese cheap l.   HARTE 242:30
  Should life all l. be   TENN 539:15
  should not cease to l.   STEV 521:1
  Six days shalt thou l.   BIBLE 47:24
  sore l.'s bath   SHAK 460:8
  strength then but l. and sorrow   PRAY 395:19
  that l. and are heavy laden   BIBLE 66:5
  their l. is but lost that   PRAY 398:18
  to his l.   PRAY 397:1
  To painful l. both by sea   SHAK 484:17
  true success is to l.   STEV 522:9
  We l. soon   BURNS 115:24
  with difficulty and l.   MILT 347:7
  youth of l. with an age   GOLD 230:19

laboured: builders have l. in vain
                                    BIBLE 83:12
I l. more abundantly than   BIBLE 76:20
labourer: l. is worthy of his hire BIBLE 69:27
  l. to take his possession   RUSK 412:7
labourers: l. are few   BIBLE 65:29
labouring: Albeit l. for a scanty WORD 582:16
  all women l. of child   PRAY 385:20
  l. man, and know but little   HARDY 240:4
  sleep of a l. man is sweet   BIBLE 55:17
labours: are entered into their l. BIBLE 71:42
  Children sweeten l.   BACON 27:3
  completed l. are pleasant   CIC 151:18
  dangers fright him and no l.   JOHN 282:30
  l. of a servile state   BYRON 124:28
  line too l.   POPE 378:23
  may rest from their l.   BIBLE 82:18
  their uncessant l. see   MARV 331:21
Laburnums: L., dropping-wells   TENN 537:6
labyrinth: peopled l. of walls   SHEL 501:23
labyrinthical: l. soul   DONNE 190:25
labyrinthine: l. ways Of my own mind
                                    THOM 548:8
Still more l. buds the rose   BROW 105:13
lac: sine dolo l. concupiscite   BIBLE 83:25
lace: l. my bodice blue   HUNT 268:15
  Through the Nottingham l.   BETJ 42:4
Laces: L. for a lady   KIPL 302:22
lacessit: Nemo me impune l.   ANON 10:15
lachende: l. Löwen müssen kommen
                                    NIET 363:2
lack: accustomed to their l. of breath
                                    YEATS 585:13
I sigh the l. of many   SHAK 493:7
l., and suffer hunger   PRAY 391:22
l. of love from love made   BROW 100:10
should have he did not l.   SHAK 495:20
therefore can I l. nothing   PRAY 390:21
they l. their sacred poet   HOR 261:18
lack'd: If I l. any thing   HERB 247:25
lackey: brisk fond l. to fetch   HOUS 265:18
lacrimae: Hinc illae l.   TER 544:14
  Sunt l. rerum   VIRG 557:17
lad: l. does not care   JOHN 275:19
  l. That I loved bodily   YEATS 585:20
  song of a l. that is gone   STEV 523:4
  was a l. I served a term   GILB 226:29
ladder: are dropping down the l. KIPL 299:11
  he dreamed, and behold a l.   BIBLE 46:18
  is young ambition's l.   SHAK 449:5
  l. out of our vices   AUG 22:3
  l. to all high designs   SHAK 486:23
  Now that my l.'s gone   YEATS 584:15
  Wiv a l. and some glasses   BAT 35:3
laden: labour and are heavy l.   BIBLE 66:5
ladies: Come from a l.' seminary GILB 226:29
  Dust was Gentlemen and L.   DICK 184:2
  girls we was all of us l. we was
                                    MARQ 330:20
  l. dead and lovely knights   SHAK 494:19
  l. most deject and wretched   SHAK 433:15
  l. of St James's   DOBS 187:12
  L. of th' Hesperides   MILT 350:3
  lion among l.   SHAK 470:14
  lords of l. intellectual   BYRON 122:7
  rhyme themselves into l.'   SHAK 445:13
  ribs was sport for l.   SHAK 424:23
  seminaries of young l.   KNOX 305:25
  Store of l.   MILT 342:25
  when he has l. to please   AUST 22:9
  you...I am parshial to l.   ASHF 17:6
  Young l. should take care   AUST 22:17
lads: I lie as l. would choose   HOUS 263:11
  l. in their hundreds   HOUS 263:6
  lightfoot l. are laid   HOUS 264:10
lady: Gaping at the l. in the swing
                                    ELIOT 203:28
He capers nimbly in a l.'s   SHAK 480:18
He keeps a l. in a cage   CHES 147:19
His l.'s ta'en anither   BALL 32:8

I met a l. in the meads — KEATS 290:16
I saw my l. weep — ANON 6:7
l. doth protest too much — SHAK 434:11
L. is as good i' th' dark — HERR 249:12
l. of a 'certain age' — BYRON 123:21
l. of Christ's College — AUBR 17:24
l. of my delight — MEYN 338:15
l.'s lips it was that — FLEM 214:27
L. with a Lamp shall stand — LONG 317:7
l. would be Queen for life — POPE 377:25
l. would not love a shepherd — GREE 236:11
lang will his L. — BALL 30:17
learned in a l.'s eyes — SHAK 457:8
Lord and L. Dalhousie — MCG 325:5
love for any l. — PEELE 371:6
lovely l. — SHEL 505:8
Our L. of Pain — SWIN 529:6
Said our L. of the Snows — KIPL 301:20
There is a l. sweet — ANON 8:1
This l. by the trees — YEATS 584:23
This l. of the West Country — DE L 173:27
Thy mother a l. — SCOTT 416:24
when a l.'s in the case — GAY 223:16
With many holiday and l. — SHAK 438:14
Lady Bountiful: My L. — FARQ 209:24
Lady Fortune: rail'd on L. in good terms — SHAK 425:18
Lady Poltagrue: Went off to tempt my L. — BELL 39:24
lady-smocks: l. all silver-white — SHAK 457:18
laeseris: ingenii est odisse quem l. — TAC 531:8
Lafayette: L., we are here — STAN 517:18
laff'd: dey mus speck ter be l. — HARR 242:13
lag-end: entertain the l. of my life — SHAK 440:14
lager-beer: All goned afay mit de l. — LEL 313:17
laggard: l. in love — SCOTT 417:10
laid: l. end to end — PARK 368:24
l. him in a manger — BIBLE 69:9
l. us as we lay at birth — ARN 13:17
me where thou hast l. him — BIBLE 73:8
not where they have l. him — BIBLE 73:7
Strait side by side were l. — MILT 348:7
These l. the world away — BROO 94:7
when I l. the foundations — BIBLE 53:2
when I'm l. by thee — HERR 249:24
lain: cold grave she was l. — BALL 32:9
l. still and been quiet — BIBLE 52:12
lair: his midnight l. had made — SCOTT 416:1
laisse: On l. un peu de soi-même — HAR 238:20
laisser faire: laisser passer et de l. — QUES 403:22
laissez faire: Faites votre devoir et l. — CORN 162:17
laity: conspiracies against the l. — SHAW 496:21
lake: I hear l. water lapping — YEATS 585:17
into the bosom of the l. — TENN 542:14
waters of the Lydian l. — CAT 136:28
Lake Leman: L. woos me with its crystal — BYRON 120:33
Lalage: I've lost L. — KIPL 302:13
lama: l. sabachthani — BIBLE 68:24
Lamb: Behold the L. of God — BIBLE 71:30
Did he who made the L. — BLAKE 87:16
fell down before the L. — BIBLE 81:27
from the wrath of the L. — BIBLE 81:30
in the blood of the L. — BIBLE 82:2
l. shall be without blemish — BIBLE 47:16
L., the frolic — WORD 577:18
l. to the slaughter — BIBLE 59:22
Little L. — BLAKE 87:26
Mary had a little l. — HALE 237:15
nothing but the L. of God — LAMB 307:25
one dead l. is there — LONG 317:6
'Pipe a song about a L. — BLAKE 87:24
Poor L. — COL 158:9
save one little ewe l. — BIBLE 50:20
shall dwell with the l. — BIBLE 58:10
skin of an innocent l. — SHAK 446:12

That leads me to the L. — COWP 165:23
was the holy L. of God — BLAKE 86:16
will provide himself a l. — BIBLE 46:10
you are yoked with a l. — SHAK 451:24
lambent: l. but innocuous — GOUL 233:5
lambkins: l., we will live — SHAK 443:15
lambs: ...Feed my l. — BIBLE 73:14
gather the l. with his arm — BIBLE 59:7
twinn'd l. that did frisk i' — SHAK 491:8
We're poor little l. who've — KIPL 299:10
lame: feet was I to the l. — BIBLE 52:35
invention and makes fancy l. — COWP 166:20
l. by fortune's dearest — SHAK 493:13
L. dogs over stiles — KING 296:21
l. man leap as an hart — BIBLE 58:34
lament: I may have leave to l. — BURKE 109:5
to l. the past — BURKE 108:17
yet you l. not the days — SOUT 514:8
lamentable: Tell thou the l. tale of me — SHAK 480:8
lamentation: all that l. of the leaves — YEATS 586:22
l., and weeping — BIBLE 63:34
lamented: ye have not l. — BIBLE 66:3
lamenting: he was left l. — CAMP 129:5
Lamentings: L. heard i' the air — SHAK 460:20
lamp: I press God's l. — BROW 103:8
It is a dying l. — SHEL 499:17
Lady with a L. shall stand — LONG 317:7
Slaves of the L. — ARN 12:19
smell too strong of the l. — STER 519:23
unlit l. and the ungirt loin — BROW 105:21
When the l. is shattered — SHEL 501:21
lampada: quasi cursores vitai l. — LUCR 320:7
Lamplough: to sink with L. — STEV 521:11
lamp-posts: MSS as drunkards use l. — HOUS 266:14
lamprey: like the l. — WEBS 566:18
surfeit by eating of a l. — FABY 209:16
lamps: Heav'n's great l. do dive — CAT 136:25
l. are going out all over — GREY 236:19
(L. for my gloom — SASS 414:19
l. of heaven — KING 296:20
old l. for new — ARAB 11:14
Ye living l. — MARV 332:12
lampshell: l. Or the limpet — AUDEN 19:10
Lancaster: time-honour'd L. — SHAK 478:6
lance: l. of justice hurtless — SHAK 455:20
Lancelot: colour which I found In L. — TENN 534:14
day for recreation of L. — DANTE 171:9
was L. wanderingly lewd — TENN 534:20
lancer: 'listed at home for a l. — HOUS 264:19
Lancialotto: Di L. — DANTE 171:9
land: abroad throughout the l. — BRIG 93:1
afternoon they came unto a l. — TENN 539:12
born in the l. of Vainglory — BUNY 107:12
came down and hid the l. — KING 297:1
Ceres re-assume the l. — POPE 378:5
dwell in the l. of the shadow — BIBLE 58:6
eat the fat of the l. — BIBLE 46:36
edge of the long lone l. — SWIN 529:18
England's green & pleasant L. — BLAKE 86:16
even to the l. of darkness — BIBLE 52:20
for a parcel of l. — HOR 262:9
good and bad of every l. — BAIL 29:22
hands prepared the dry l. — PRAY 396:4
heaven by sea as by l. — GILB 225:7
her l. reposed — TENN 543:15
holy l. Of Walsinghame — RAL 404:13
hum of that low l. — ARN 14:28
Ill fares the l. — GOLD 230:18
l. flowing with milk — BIBLE 47:6
l. grows poorer and uglier — CHEK 145:4
l. is bright — CLOU 154:4
l. is scattered with light — BRID 92:8
L. of brown heath and shaggy — SCOTT 415:8
L. of Heart's Desire — YEATS 585:19
L. of Hope and Glory — BENS 40:24
L. of Laundries stood — BETJ 43:17

l. of lost content — HOUS 263:22
L. of our birth — KIPL 298:10
l. of sand and ruin — SWIN 530:29
l. of slaves shall ne'er — BYRON 123:4
l. was ours before we were — FROST 219:5
L. where my fathers died — SMITH 510:24
l. where the Bong-tree — LEAR 312:12
may be long upon the l. — BIBLE 47:24
nakedness of the l. ye — BIBLE 46:34
new people takes the l. — CHES 147:14
O'er the l. of the free — KEY 295:14
off Israel out of the l. — BIBLE 50:31
of the l. of the living — BIBLE 59:23
on this windy sea of l. — MILT 347:10
pleasant l. of counterpane — STEV 522:20
possessed his l. — BIBLE 48:2
presence and no l. beside — SHAK 452:8
ready by water as by l. — ELST 206:15
rock in a weary l. — BIBLE 58:30
scorn of that pleasant l. — PRAY 397:5
seems a moving l. — MILT 349:1
sent to spy out the l. — BIBLE 48:10
splendid and a happy l. — GOLD 231:5
strong man in a blatant l. — TENN 540:4
That makes the promised l. — FRY 219:23
that think there is no l. — BACON 24:21
There shall be no more l. — BROO 94:14
There's the l., or cherry-isle — HERR 248:21
They love their l. because — HALL 238:8
This l. of such dear souls — SHAK 478:20
thro' l. at eve we went — TENN 541:24
to enjoy thy l. — SHAK 452:8
to gaze out from the l. — LUCR 320:6
travel by l. or by water — PRAY 385:20
When house and l. are gone — FOOTE 216:8
Woe to thy l. that's govern'd — SHAK 481:2
landed: them inclined to the l. — ADD 2:14
landlord: had better have a rich l. — SHAW 498:22
I'll marry a l.'s daughter — LAMB 308:7
Sir Roger is l. — ADD 2:12
landmark: Remove not the ancient l. — BIBLE 54:23
removeth his neighbour's l. — BIBLE 48:26
landmarks: l. from the wisdom of our — BURKE 108:21
Landor: With L. and with Donne — YEATS 587:5
lands: broader l. and better days — CHUR 150:3
children who died for our l. — KIPL 298:9
envy of less happier l. — SHAK 478:20
is gone out into all l. — PRAY 390:11
l. after their own names — PRAY 392:28
l. of palm and southern — TENN 533:5
l. were fairly portioned — MAC 322:18
l. where the Jumblies live — LEAR 312:6
other l. beneath another sun — THOM 549:20
young man l. hatless — BETJ 42:12
landscape: fades the glimmering l. — GRAY 234:18
He is but a l.-painter — TENN 539:10
l. but a background — AUDEN 19:16
l. of England in general — AUST 22:22
landscapes: if l. were sold — STEV 521:19
land-thieves: l. and water-thieves — SHAK 465:27
land-travel: In l. or sea-faring — BROW 105:34
lane: In an English l. — BROW 100:12
lanes: streets and l. of the city — BIBLE 70:12
lang: y'er a l. time deid — ANON 4:27
langage: coeur comme dans le l. — LA R 310:17
language: best chosen l. — AUST 22:31
bottom the l. of the unheard — KING 296:14
broke through l. and escaped — BROW 104:8
By that dear l. which — MAC 322:10
conceive you may use any l. — GILB 226:12
consenting l. of the heart — GAY 223:5
enlargement of the l. — JOHN 281:7
enrichment of our native l. — DRYD 197:38
heart doth need a l. — COL 157:8

his strange l. all I know   LAND 308:19
in every l. even deafanddumb   CUMM 170:10
In l., the ignorant   DUPPA 199:16
in our l. should perish   MAC 323:4
is neither speech nor l.   PRAY 390:11
is never the l. of poetry   GRAY 235:22
laboured to refine our l.   JOHN 282:5
l. and ways of behaving   JUV 287:15
l. convey more than they   CONN 161:11
l. he was the lodesterre   LYDG 321:5
l. I have learn'd these   SHAK 478:10
L. is called the garment   CARL 132:15
L. is only the instrument   JOHN 281:6
L. is the dress of thought   JOHN 281:31
language…L. is not simply a reporting
   WHORF 571:23
l. of the heart   POPE 377:5
l. that would make your   GILB 228:34
L. was not powerful enough   DICK 180:16
Learned his great l.   BROW 102:5
literature is simply l.   POUND 384:1
Money speaks sense in a l.   BEHN 38:18
…My l. fails   BELL 39:6
natural l. of the heart   SHAD 420:19
no respect for their l.   SHAW 498:12
persuasive l. of a tear   CHUR 149:17
primitive l. of the law   BURKE 111:6
some entrance into the l.   BACON 27:27
speak a l. of their own   SWIFT 527:29
spoken in their own l.   BIBLE 62:20
sure in l. strange she   KEATS 290:19
There's l. in her eye   SHAK 487:13
they can only speak one l.   DISR 186:21
think anything of that l.   DICK 180:13
Under the tropic is our l.   WALL 562:17
with no l. but a cry   TENN 536:26
Worships l. and forgives   AUDEN 19:7
You taught me l.   SHAK 484:29
languages: ancient l. is mainly a luxury
   BRIG 93:8
at a great feast of l.   SHAK 457:12
because l. are the pedigree   JOHN 280:1
gave l. just as she needed   PRIOR 400:27
graves of deceased l.   DICK 177:23
Playing among the ruined l.   AUDEN 18:5
said will be wit in all l.   DRYD 198:1
'silent in seven l.   BAG 29:11
speaks three or four l.   SHAK 487:24
langueur: une l. Monotone   VERL 556:8
languid: excite your l. spleen   GILB 227:23
l. patience of thy face   COL 157:16
through the music of the l.   LANG 309:18
languish: Relieve my l.   DAN 171:1
languished: l. in a foreign clime   MAC 322:9
Languor: L. cannot be   SHEL 504:22
languors: lilies and l. of virtue   SWIN 529:5
lank: days seem l. and long   GILB 228:29
lantern: gives is a l. on the stern   COL 157:20
word is a l. unto my feet   PRAY 389:6
lap: Carrie to sit on his l.   GROS 237:1
flowery l. of earth   ARN 13:17
fresh l. of the crimson rose   SHAK 470:6
l. to saint-seducing gold   SHAK 481:24
L. your loneliness in heat   BETJ 42:7
That strew the green l.   SHAK 480:11
Uncover, dogs, and l.   SHAK 486:7
lapdogs: when l. breathe their last POPE 381:8
lapidary: l. inscriptions a man is JOHN 276:31
Lapland: lovely as a L. night   WORD 583:4
lapp'd: friends are l. in lead   BARN 34:1
laps: tumbling into some men's l.
   BACON 25:3
lapwing: like a l.   SHAK 472:20
larboard: did swim all to the l.   BALL 31:3
larch: rosy plumelets tuft the l.   TENN 537:9
lard: l. their lean books with   BURT 116:13
lards: l. the lean earth as he   SHAK 438:28
larem: Labore fessi venimus l.   CAT 136:28
large: fly on a rather l. scale   BARH 33:5
It's as l. as life   CARR 136:1

l. a letter I have written   BIBLE 77:21
l., and smooth, and round   SOUT 513:15
l. a trunk before   BELL 38:28
l.-brained woman   BROW 98:15
live in and too l. to hang on a watch-chain
   ANON 8:11
Mothers of l. families   BELL 38:31
Priest writ l.   MILT 351:15
sufficiently l. scale   SPEN 514:33
large-hearted: woman and l. man
   BROW 98:15
largely: drinking l. sobers us again
   POPE 378:13
Larger: L. than human on the frozen
   TENN 535:23
l. than Man can ever estimate   AUDEN 18:8
Lord would use a l. map   SAL 413:20
largess: l. universal   SHAK 444:11
largest: l. lamp is lit   MAC 322:23
lark: l. at break of day   SHAK 493:6
l. at heaven's gate sings   SHAK 428:10
l. becomes a sightless   TENN 537:19
l.-charmèd   HOPK 256:10
l. from her light wing   CRAW 169:16
l. soars   BROW 97:29
l.'s on the wing   BROW 103:21
l., that tirra-lirra chants   SHAK 491:17
late l. twitters from   HENL 245:7
More tuneable than l.   SHAK 469:21
No l. more blithe than he   BICK 83:28
sing as sweetly as the l.   SHAK 468:19
Some late l. singing   HENL 245:9
swallow for the holy l.   BROW 97:27
under the l. full cloud   THOM 547:7
We rise with the l.   BRET 92:2
larke: bisy l.   CHAU 142:18
Larks: Four L. and a Wren   LEAR 311:15
hear the l. so high   HOUS 263:4
larkspur: l. listens, 'I hear   TENN 540:12
larme: l. divine et de ce sourire HUGO 267:13
Lars: L. Porsena of Clusium   MAC 322:11
LASCIATE: L. OGNI SPERANZA VOI
   CH'ENTRATE   DANTE 171:3
lascivious: l. pleasing of a lute SHAK 480:18
lash: delight at once and l.   POPE 378:8
dost thou l. that whore   SHAK 455:19
rum, sodomy and the l.   CHUR 151:7
lass: every l. a queen   KING 297:5
It cam' wi' a l.   JAM 271:7
l. that has acres o' charms   BURNS 114:6
l. that loves a sailor   DIBD 175:20
l. that were to go a-gipseying   LAMB 308:3
l. unparallel'd   SHAK 424:15
lordliest l. of earth   BROO 94:16
Met again, my l.   HOUS 265:5
Sweet l. of Richmond Hill   MACN 326:2
was a lover and his l.   SHAK 427:2
lasse: tout l.   ANON 9:20
lasses: An' then she made the l. BURNS 114:4
He dearly lov'd the l.   BURNS 114:3
lassie: young l. do wi' an auld man
   BURNS 116:3
last: bring a man peace at the l. PRAY 391:29
families l. not three oaks   BROW 97:16
'It will l. my time   CARL 131:10
l. act crowns the play   QUAR 403:15
l. act is bloody   PASC 369:8
l. and best   MILT 349:17
l. breath he drew in   LAMB 308:11
l. enemy that shall be   BIBLE 76:23
l. great Englishman is   TENN 541:6
l. have wrought but one   BIBLE 67:15
L. Judgement draweth nigh   BLAKE 85:13
l. red leaf is whirl'd   TENN 536:8
L. scene of all   SHAK 425:24
l. shall be first   BIBLE 67:13
l. state of that man is   BIBLE 66:14
l. syllable of recorded   SHAK 463:6
l. taste of sweets   SHAK 478:18

l. thing one knows in constructing
   PASC 369:3
l. to lay the old aside   POPE 378:19
L. week in Babylon   HODG 252:10
l. words of Mr Despondency   BUNY 107:37
l. words of Marmion   SCOTT 417:22
l. words which I should   REYN 405:19
lost the l. of England   BELL 40:16
Love of fame is the l.   TAC 531:14
My l. good night   KING 296:11
present were the world's l. night
   DONNE 189:7
that has dawned is your l.   HOR 258:16
that I could l. for ever   CONR 161:24
that's the l. thing I shall   PALM 368:13
there is no l. nor first   BROW 103:25
thief said the l. kind word   BROW 104:25
this day may be the l.   NELS 360:16
Tristram Shandy did not l.   JOHN 276:34
When he was at the l. gasp   BIBLE 63:30
will give unto this l.   BIBLE 67:16
with low l. breath   ROSS 410:3
lasting: memorial longer l. than bronze
   HOR 261:8
latch: no l. ter de golden gate HARR 242:17
latchet: shoe's l. I am not worthy BIBLE 71:29
late: damned fella will be l.   MITF 352:24
It came to them very l.   KIPL 298:1
l. for medicine to be prepared   OVID 366:20
l. or too early for anything   SART 414:9
l. to-morrow to be brave   ARMS 12:17
offering even that too l.   NEV 361:2
of human thought too l.   LA B 306:11
sinners'll be kotched out l.   HARR 242:17
So l. into the night   BYRON 125:25
that leaves him out so l.   FROST 219:11
Too l. came I to love thee   AUG 21:16
Too late, too l.   TENN 534:8
later: It is l. than you think SERV 420:12
there will be sunlight l.   MACN 326:6
Latet: L. anguis in herba   VIRG 559:19
lath: l. of wood painted   BISM 84:27
Latin: carve in L. or in Greek WALL 562:7
half L. and half Greek   SCOTT 415:16
he speaks L.   SHAK 446:11
L., queen of tongues,   JONS 285:6
learn L. as an honour   CHUR 150:23
measures is L. for a whopping   ANST 11:9
small L., and less Greek   JONS 284:21
teach him one word of L.   YEATS 587:13
understand Greek and L.   DRYD 198:14
Your L. names for horns   BURNS 113:19
Latio: artes Intulit agresti L.   HOR 259:2
latitude: Though the l.'s rather PROW 402:2
Latium: arts into rustic L.   HOR 259:2
latoun: croys of l. ful of stones CHAU 142:7
latrone: Cantabit vacuus coram l. viator
   JUV 287:26
Lattenzaun: Es war einmal ein L.
   MORG 357:22
latter: former and the l. rain PRAY 386:3
stand at the l. day   BIBLE 52:31
To carry off the l.   PEAC 371:2
laud: l. and magnify thy glorious
   PRAY 387:23
More l. than gilt o'er-dusted SHAK 487:6
Laudamus: L. te   MASS 334:18
Te Deum l.   ANON 11:3
Laudant: L. illa sed ista legunt MART 331:10
Laudate: L. Dominum   BIBLE 83:11
laudator: l. temporis acti   HOR 257:21
Laudes: L. to their maker early HAWES 243:2
laudi: concedant laurea l.   CIC 151:22
laugh: Anything awful makes me l.
   LAMB 307:27
be dismissed with a l.   HOR 262:7
behind her a meaning l.   EWART 209:11
Democritus would l.   HOR 259:3
do we not l.   SHAK 467:4
his arms hang down to l.   ELIOT 204:14

I did l. sans intermission — SHAK 425:20
if you want a good l. — HOR 258:16
I l. at any mortal thing — BYRON 123:10
I l. to see them whirl — SHEL 500:6
it hurt too much to l. — STEV 520:19
it make the unskilful l. — SHAK 433:17
L. and be well — GREEN 235:28
L. and the world laughs — WILC 572:5
l. as I pass in thunder — SHEL 500:4
l. at a fall — BROW 102:1
L. at all you trembled — COWP 166:14
l. At gilded butterflies — SHAK 456:3
l. at human actions — SPIN 517:7
l. at my own cenotaph — SHEL 500:7
l. at them in our turn — AUST 23:20
L., heart — YEATS 585:14
L. no man to scorn — BIBLE 62:26
l. that spoke the vacant — GOLD 230:21
L. thy girlish laughter — WATS 565:9
l. uproariously in youth — BROO 94:24
L. where we must — POPE 379:2
l. with me, or at me — STER 519:18
make her l. at that — SHAK 436:31
make myself l. at everything — BEAU 35:15
making decent people l. — MOL 353:7
man cannot make him l. — SHAK 442:14
man of quality than to l. — CONG 159:22
must l. By precept only — WORD 582:13
nobody has ever heard me l. — CHES 145:23
no girl wants to l. all — LOOS 318:5
not a thing to l. to scorn — SHAK 426:25
sillier than a silly l. — CAT 137:1
that see me l. me to scorn — PRAY 390:17
that they shall l. and sing — PRAY 394:3
Thy lovely l. — CAT 137:4
unextinguishable l. in heaven — BROW 95:16
Who but must l. — POPE 376:28
laughable: improvement are very l.
— JOHN 275:29
laugh'd: I l. him into patience — SHAK 422:10
l. with counterfeited glee — GOLD 231:2
laughed: first baby l. — BARR 34:13
l. and kissed his hand — HOUS 266:4
L. in the sun — BROO 94:15
l., respectable senators — AUDEN 18:15
l. upon his breast to think — YEATS 585:20
they l. consumedly — FARQ 210:3
laughing: l. and jeering at everything
— PEPYS 372:7
l. devil in his sneer — BYRON 121:31
l. is heard on the hill — BLAKE 88:3
l. lions must come — NIET 363:2
l. queen that caught — HUNT 268:9
L. Water — LONG 317:11
let another half stand l. — SHAK 443:7
only idea of wit…is l. — SMITH 510:28
speaking sweetly and l. sexily — SAPP 414:6
waked herself with l. — SHAK 472:13
laughs: he l. like anything — CHES 145:9
hoe and she l. with a harvest — JERR 273:7
l. at lovers' perjury — DRYD 197:7
l. so sweetly and talks — HOR 259:24
l. the sense of mis'ry — COWP 166:24
more so, when he l. — STER 519:15
while she l. at them — CONG 159:19
laughter: anything that tends to l. — SHAK 441:3
audible l. — CHES 145:10
creatures by the faculty of l. — ADD 2:26
Give me the bonus of l. — BETJ 43:10
His l. at their quaint — MILT 349:3
l. and the love of friends — BELL 39:15
l. and ability and Sighing — DICK 184:2
l. for a month — SHAK 438:27
L. holding both his sides — MILT 342:15
L. is nothing else — HOBB 251:22
l., learnt of friends — BROO 94:30
l. the heart is sorrowful — BIBLE 54:1
l. tinkled among the teacups — ELIOT 203:28
l. you have at your command — CAT 136:28
Lydian l. of the Garda — TENN 533:18

mirth hath present l. — SHAK 488:17
mouth filled with l. — PRAY 398:16
Our sincerest l. — SHEL 504:23
Porter-drinkers' randy l. — YEATS 587:8
so is the l. of a fool — BIBLE 55:18
under running l. — THOM 548:8
weeping and the l. — DOWS 191:13
worst returns to l. — SHAK 455:5
laughters: entwine our arts with l.
— JOYCE 286:10
Launcelot: angels heave up Sir L. — MAL 328:7
Launch: L. your vessel — TENN 540:21
launch'd: Was this the face that l.
— MARL 329:10
Laundries: sunset where the Land of
L. — BETJ 43:17
laundry: it all goes into the l. — KIPL 303:11
Laura: L. had been Petrarch's — BYRON 122:27
Rose-cheeked L. — CAMP 129:16
laurea: concedant l. laudi — CIC 151:22
laurel: burnèd is Apollo's l. — MARL 329:16
Caesar's l. crown — BLAKE 85:16
l. for the perfect prime — ROSS 409:7
L. is green for a season — SWIN 530:5
l., the palms — SWIN 530:4
Only that she might l. grow — MARV 332:2
rose or rue or l. — SWIN 528:25
laurels: Are worth all your l. — BYRON 125:29
l. to paeans — CIC 151:22
lauriers: les l. sont coupés — ANON 9:15
Lava: L. quod est sordidum — LANG 310:1
lavat'ry: l. makes you fear the worst
— COW 164:4
lave: Let the l. go by me — STEV 522:27
lavender: Hot l. — SHAK 491:25
L. water tinged with pink — LEAR 312:17
laver: nous l. de la littérature — ART 16:29
Lavinia: She is L. — SHAK 486:15
law: above me and the moral l. — KANT 288:8
another hath fulfilled the l. — BIBLE 75:22
Any l. which violates — ROB 406:11
army of unalterable l. — MER 337:5
ashamed the l. is such an ass — CHAP 140:12
because they have no l. — TENN 535:18
Born under one l. — GREV 236:16
built with stones of L. — BLAKE 88:20
Bumble…'the l. is a ass — DICK 181:2
Common L. of England — HALE 237:13
determining a point of l. — BURKE 109:28
doctors of l. or divinity — BURKE 108:12
dusty purlieus of the l. — TENN 537:8
egalitarianism of the l. — FRAN 217:26
else but reason…The l. — COKE 154:18
fig for those by l. protected — BURNS 114:19
fugitive from th' l. of averages — MAUL 336:5
fulfilling of the l. — BIBLE 75:23
God is thy l., thou mine — MILT 348:3
Hear my l., O my people — PRAY 395:3
hearts to keep this l. — PRAY 387:8
higher l. than the Constitution — SEW 420:15
himself is a l. rational — CHAP 140:8
I crave the l. — SHAK 468:1
Ignorance of the l. excuses — SELD 419:21
in l.'s grave study six — COKE 154:22
is the L. of the Jungle — KIPL 300:20
it is of no force in l. — COKE 154:17
keep the Jungle L. — KIPL 301:13
Keep ye the l. — KIPL 303:6
known sin, but by the l. — BIBLE 75:4
laid His hand on Moses' l. — BLAKE 85:24
l. and the prophets — BIBLE 65:5
L. by which we live — KIPL 302:17
l. can take a purse — BUTL 118:19
l. doth give it — SHAK 468:6
L. is a bottomless pit — ARB 11:20
L. is the true embodiment — GILB 226:1
L.: It has honoured us — WEBS 566:14
L. of England has been — HERB 246:13
l. of thy mouth is dearer — PRAY 398:5
l.'s delay — SHAK 433:8

l. so general a study — BURKE 109:23
L. to ourselves — MILT 349:15
lay bare the economic l. — MARX 333:8
lesser breeds without the L. — KIPL 302:9
Let them relearn the L. — KIPL 300:6
Lord is an undefiled l. — PRAY 390:12
love Creation's final l. — TENN 536:29
make a scarecrow of the l. — SHAK 463:15
mysterious l. — MILT 348:8
Necessity gives the l. — PUBL 402:6
nine-tenths of the l. of chivalry — SAY 415:6
no l. to make thee rich — SHAK 483:26
Nor l., nor duty — YEATS 585:15
nothing is l. that is not — POW 384:2
Of L. there can be no less — HOOK 255:20
old father antick, the l. — SHAK 438:4
only knew a little of l. — ANON 6:3
ought l. to weed it out — BACON 27:7
people is the chief l. — CIC 151:19
perfection of our l. — ANON 4:13
primitive language of the l. — BURKE 111:6
purlieus of the L. — ETH 208:28
sharp quillets of the l. — SHAK 445:20
should become a universal l. — KANT 288:9
There is but one l. for all — BURKE 110:32
there is not a single l. — PEEL 371:5
These…are a l. unto themselves — BIBLE 74:35
This is the L. of the Yukon — SERV 420:13
touching the l. — BIBLE 78:16
very good l. for all that — SCOTT 418:14
weightier matters of the l. — BIBLE 67:24
where no l. is — BIBLE 74:39
Who to himself is l. — CHAP 140:6
windward of the l. — CHUR 148:29
windy side of the l. — SHAK 490:11
Wrest once the l. to your — SHAK 468:2
lawful: All things are l. for me — BIBLE 76:10
art L. as eating — SHAK 492:12
Is it not l. for me — BIBLE 67:16
is l. prize — GRAY 235:8
seas upon their l. occasions — PRAY 400:3
that which is l. and right — BIBLE 60:35
law-giver: Judah is my l. — PRAY 393:1
law-givers: l. are Erasmus and Montaigne
— FORS 217:11
Lawlands: Ye Highlands and ye L.
— BALL 30:15
lawn: bird-haunted English l. — ARN 14:1
is twice a saint in l. — POPE 377:11
L. as white as driven snow — SHAK 492:2
L. Tennyson — JOYCE 286:24
Out on the l. I lie — AUDEN 20:18
lawns: house with l. enclosing — STEV 523:7
Lawrence: L. was brought down
— AUDEN 18:20
L. was right when he had — GIBB 225:4
Lawrences: Gainsboroughs and L. — COW 164:2
laws: all been produced by l. — DARW 171:28
all things the l. of life — RUSK 412:10
Bad l. are the worst sort — BURKE 110:20
breaking of l. — MORE 357:7
breaking up of l. — TENN 534:10
breathing household l. — WORD 582:9
Government of those L. — CHAR 140:1
Had l. not been — DAV 172:5
her l. is the assurance — BIBLE 62:19
If l. are their enemies — BURKE 110:8
L. are generally found — SHEN 505:16
L. are inoperative in war — CIC 151:31
L. are like spider's webs — SOLON 512:23
L. are like cobwebs — SWIFT 527:16
l. but to obey them — HORS 262:11
L. grind the poor — GOLD 231:29
L., like houses — BURKE 112:11
l. of England are at my — SHAK 442:19
l. of God — HOUS 264:24
l. of God will be suspended — SHAW 496:33
l. of markets and fashion — ALB 3:7
L. were made to be broken — NORTH 364:3
make the l. of a nation — FLET 215:6

never l. me	ANON 5:3
shall l. them in the midst	BIBLE 60:25
thought to l. her far away	KEATS 289:5
under l. of Brutus	SHAK 450:17
which thou must l. ere long	SHAK 494:8
wilt thou l. me thus	WYATT 583:19
with old Khayyám and l.	FITZ 212:9
leaven: l. leaveneth the whole	BIBLE 75:35
l. of malice and wickedness	BIBLE 75:36
l. of malice and wickedness	PRAY 386:11
leaves: bags full of l.	FROST 219:4
burning of the l.	BINY 84:8
Close up these barren l.	WORD 582:23
crowding through the l.	ARN 14:3
Crowned with calm l.	SWIN 529:22
fields and l. to the trees	HOR 261:14
heard the autumnal l.	SHEL 502:7
laughing l. of the tree	SWIN 528:18
l. dead Are driven	SHEL 502:8
l. fall early this autumn	POUND 383:17
l. grow on the tree	YEATS 584:22
l. His shivering mates	THOM 549:23
l. is a generation of men	HOMER 253:29
l. it as fast as they can	LOCK 316:2
l. of the tree were	BIBLE 83:1
l. soul free	BROW 99:2
l. the world to darkness	GRAY 234:18
long l. cover me	SWIN 530:18
noiseless noise among the l.	KEATS 290:13
Of wither'd l.	ARN 14:8
one l. behind a part	HAR 238:20
pond edged with grayish l.	HARDY 240:10
sewed fig l.	BIBLE 45:16
Shatter your l. before	MILT 343:2
tender l. of hope	SHAK 447:9
that lamentation of the l.	YEATS 586:22
Thick as autumnal l.	MILT 345:13
thick on Severn snow the l.	HOUS 263:14
to put l. round his head	DICK 178:27
trees I see barren of l.	SHAK 492:26
What if my l. are falling	SHEL 502:13
When yellow l.	SHAK 494:7
whole deck put on its l.	FLEC 214:19
Wild l. that winds have	SWIN 529:23
leave-taking: It is not worth l.	SHAK 424:13
leaving: Became him like the l. it	
	SHAK 458:22
L. a blacker air	HARDY 240:11
L. his country for his	FITZ 212:4
Lebanon: devour the cedars of L.	
	BIBLE 49:19
his countenance is as L.	BIBLE 57:4
nose is as the tower of L.	BIBLE 57:9
Samarcand to cedar'd L.	KEATS 289:20
leben: gefährlich l.	NIET 363:9
l. wir und nehmen immer	RILKE 406:4
wollt ihr ewig l.	FRED 218:23
Lebens: grün des L. goldner Baum	
	GOET 230:3
lecher: Does l. in my sight	SHAK 455:16
lecherous: follows I am rough and l.	
	SHAK 453:11
he was and l. as a sparwe	CHAU 142:4
Lechery: L., sir, it provokes	SHAK 460:18
wars and l.	SHAK 487:16
lecto: Desideratoque acquiescimus l.	
	CAT 136:28
Lectorem: L. delectando pariterque	
	HOR 258:1
lecture: classic l.	TENN 541:30
lectures: give l. or a little charity	WHIT 571:1
l. in her night-dress	HOOD 255:12
lecturing: I. had convinced me that	
	HUXL 269:7
led: Carlyle has l. us all out	CLOU 154:6
l. his regiment from behind	GILB 225:17
we are most l.	BYRON 126:4
Leda: love of L.	SPEN 516:31
lede: gold wes changyd into l.	WYNT 584:4
lat thy gost thee l.	CHAU 144:22

Lee: swimming down along the L.	
	SPEN 516:31
leef: aspes l. she gan to quake	CHAU 144:9
light as l. on lynde	CHAU 142:11
leek: By this l.	SHAK 445:10
leene: l. was his hors as is	CHAU 141:23
lees: drink Life to the l.	TENN 543:22
feast of wine on the l.	BIBLE 58:18
left: all l. behind on the beach	CARR 133:2
are l. alone with our day	AUDEN 20:17
hath l. you all his walks	SHAK 451:4
have l. a name behind them	BIBLE 63:24
he has l. us there	CLOU 154:6
he l. the thorn wi' me	BURNS 116:8
he was l. lamenting	CAMP 129:5
l. and is now in the centre	MOSL 358:19
l. fair Scotland's strand	BURNS 114:10
l. off before you began	CONG 160:24
of my l. hand	MILT 352:13
other l.	BIBLE 67:33
So far upon the l. side	WEBS 566:19
That we l.	ANON 7:20
thou hast l. thy first love	BIBLE 81:16
Thou hast l. behind	WORD 582:17
'tis better to be l. than	CONG 160:35
We l. our country for our	BARR 34:23
Ye have l. your souls	KEATS 290:31
'You l. us in tatters	HARDY 240:19
left-handed: be termed a l. marriage	
	WOLL 576:12
leg: decreasing l.	SHAK 441:10
here I leave my second l.	HOOD 254:14
kiss my Julia's dainty l.	HERR 249:15
shape of his l.	SHAK 488:23
with a wooden l.	DICK 181:3
legacy: l. from a rich relative	BIRK 84:13
lege: Tolle l.	AUG 21:15
legem: Necessitas dat l. non ipsa	PUBL 402:6
legend: all the fables in the l.	BACON 25:22
l. of an epic hour	CHES 147:8
legens: sed aut l.	THOM 546:11
leges: Silent enim l. inter arma	CIC 151:31
leggemmo: giorno più non vi l. avante	
	DANTE 171:10
legges: were his l. and his toon	CHAU 142:32
leggiavamo: Noi l. un giorno per diletto	
	DANTE 171:9
legible: thoughts are l. in the eye	ROYD 411:2
Legion: My name is L.	BIBLE 68:30
Legion of Honour: cross of the L. has	
been	TWAIN 554:21
legions: give me back my l.	AUG 22:4
legislation: foundation of morals and	
l.	BENT 40:25
legislator: l. of mankind	JOHN 282:7
people is the true l.	BURKE 112:12
legislators: are the unacknowledged l.	
	SHEL 505:13
legislature: l. can manufacture in any	
	BAG 28:21
legitimate: such a thing as l. warfare	
	NEWM 361:14
legs: cannon-ball took off his l.	HOOD 254:13
delighteth he in any man's l.	PRAY 399:20
Four l. good	ORW 365:8
His l. bestrid the ocean	SHAK 423:22
l. are as pillars of marble	BIBLE 57:4
l. when I take my boots	DICK 178:2
losing your l.	SASS 414:13
Matching their lily-white l.	CLOU 153:15
recuvver the use of his l.	DICK 180:8
Taste your l.	SHAK 489:20
thou 'ear my 'erse's l.	TENN 540:24
to lie between maids' l.	SHAK 434:6
vast and trunkless l.	SHEL 502:15
Walk under his huge l.	SHAK 448:17
when his l. were smitten	SHEA 498:29
your l. ungainly huddled	SASS 414:14
legunt: Laudant illa sed ista l.	MART 331:10
Leicester: Here lies the Earl of L.	ANON 5:14

leid: Heute l.' ich	LESS 313:26
Leiden: L. oder triumphieren	GOET 230:7
Leisure: add to these retired L.	MILT 342:1
cometh by opportunity of l.	BIBLE 63:19
conspicuous l. and consumption	VEBL 556:2
I am quite at l.	AUST 23:22
improvement arises from l.	JOHN 276:12
is l. with honour	CIC 151:33
l. answers leisure	SHAK 465:5
l. are the two civilizers	DISR 185:9
l. for love or hope	HOOD 255:9
they detest at l.	BYRON 123:38
we may polish it at l.	DRYD 197:37
What l. to grow wise	ARN 13:10
lekes: oynons, and eek l.	CHAU 142:5
lemon: in the squeezing of a l.	GOLD 232:24
l. is squeezed	GEDD 223:32
lemonade: black eyes and l.	MOORE 356:3
lemon-trees: land where the l. bloom	
	GOET 230:13
lend: I l. it instantly	HERB 248:15
I'll l. you something	SHAK 490:16
I'll l. you thus much moneys	SHAK 466:3
L. less than thou owest	SHAK 453:15
l. me your ears	SHAK 450:17
men who l.	LAMB 307:12
onward l. thy guiding hand	MILT 350:13
lender: borrower, nor a l. be	SHAK 430:19
lenders: thy pen from l.' books	SHAK 454:19
lendeth: merciful, and l.	PRAY 397:14
lendings: you l.	SHAK 454:20
lends: Three things I never l.	SURT 525:17
length: have l. and breadth enough	
	BALL 31:14
l. of days understanding	BIBLE 52:24
L. of days is in her right	BIBLE 53:16
l. of time which is unknowable	BEDE 37:1
words of learned l.	GOLD 231:3
lengthen: To l. our days	MOORE 356:21
lengthening: drags at each remove a l.	
chain	GOLD 231:24
lenses: at times my eyes are l.	DOUG 191:7
lent: l. out my heart with usury	LAMB 307:24
thing only has been l.	ARN 15:13
lente: Festina l.	SUET 524:16
l. currite noctis equi	MARL 329:11
leoni: vulpes aegroto cauta l.	HOR 258:11
Léonie: Weep not for little L.	GRAH 233:9
leopard: l. his spots	BIBLE 60:22
l. shall lie down with	BIBLE 58:10
leporum: Medio de fonte l.	LUCR 320:11
lerne: craft so long to l.	CHAU 143:32
wolde he l. and gladly teche	CHAU 141:25
Lesbia: L. hath a beaming eye	MOORE 356:11
L. let us live and love	CAT 136:25
L. whom Catullus once loved	CAT 137:5
L. with her sparrow	MILL 339:29
mea L.	CAT 136:25
Lesley: saw ye bonnie L.	BURNS 112:23
less: Even l. am	HOPE 256:5
had he pleas'd us l.	ADD 2:3
Is l. likely to fall	GAY 223:4
l. brilliant pen	BEER 37:13
l. often sought than found	BYRON 125:12
L. than a span	BACON 28:15
L. than the dust beneath	HOPE 256:5
Make l. thy body hence	SHAK 442:31
more about less and l.	BUTL 117:13
rather than be l.	MILT 346:7
small Latin, and l. Greek	JONS 284:21
then l. is learned there	JOHN 276:32
lessen: 'because they l. from day	CARR 134:12
lesser: Of the two evils the l.	THOM 546:15
lesson: have had an Imperial l.	KIPL 300:21
still harder l.	PORT 381:33
lessons: reason they're called l.	CARR 134:12
Lest: L. we forget	KIPL 302:7
let: another to l. in the foe	MILT 350:22
before you l. the sun	THOM 547:31
L. her alone	JONS 284:11

L. justice be done	FERD 210:33	
L. my people go	ANON 8:18	
L. there be light	BIBLE 44:22	
l. the sounds of music	SHAK 468:15	
L. the words of my mouth	PRAY 390:13	
L. us make man in our image	BIBLE 45:4	
L. what will be o'er me	STEV 522:28	
sore l. and hindered	PRAY 386:6	
then I will l. you a better	TENN 532:22	
they would but l. it alone	WALP 563:6	
lethargy: kind of l.	SHAK 441:6	
Lethe: Dawn shall over L. break	BELL 39:22	
go not to L.	KEATS 291:13	
itself in ease on L. wharf	SHAK 431:8	
on the wharf of L. waiting	HOUS 265:18	
Lethean: have drunken of things L.	SWIN 530:5	
letrres: nat the l. space	CHAU 144:16	
lets: l. loose a thinker on this	EMER 207:13	
letter: carry a l. to my love	BALL 30:20	
deal by speech than by l.	BACON 26:37	
face is a l. of recommendation	ADD 2:15	
Give 'im a l.	KIPL 302:20	
great art o' l. writin'	DICK 182:14	
has written a braid l.	BALL 31:17	
in one l. of Richardson's	JOHN 276:8	
large a l. I have written	BIBLE 77:21	
l. from his wife	CARR 133:10	
l. killeth	BIBLE 77:4	
that when he wrote a l.	BACON 25:42	
this l. longer than usual	PASC 369:14	
thou unnecessary l.	SHAK 453:21	
till you write your l.	DONNE 190:10	
wordy l. came from Capri	JUV 287:27	
letters: All l., methinks	OSB 365:19	
find l. from God dropt	WHIT 571:4	
generally like women's l.	HAZL 243:8	
his long marvellous l.	AUDEN 21:9	
I am persecuted with l.	CONG 160:37	
l. for a spy	KIPL 302:22	
L. for the rich	AUDEN 20:1	
l. mingle souls	DONNE 189:22	
L. of thanks	AUDEN 20:2	
l., soft interpreters	PRIOR 400:26	
make in the republic of l.	ADD 1:11	
No arts; no l.	HOBB 251:18	
receive no l. in the grave	JOHN 279:29	
than a man of l.	STER 520:8	
your hair with all your l.	CONG 160:37	
letting: then the l. go	DICK 183:14	
levee: l. from a couch in some	CONG 161:4	
level: Are l. now with men	SHAK 423:16	
low life was the l.'s	BROW 100:33	
tones as dry and l.	AUDEN 20:10	
to one dead l. ev'ry mind	POPE 375:24	
level-headed: remember to stay l.	HOR 260:6	
levellers: Your l. wish to level *down*	JOHN 275:5	
leviathan: draw out l. with an hook	BIBLE 53:11	
there is that L.	PRAY 397:1	
There L.	MILT 349:1	
levin: to the burning l.	SCOTT 416:28	
levity: like a little judicious l.	STEV 522:12	
lewd: church l. hirelings climb	MILT 347:18	
Lancelot wanderingly l.	TENN 534:20	
l. fellows of the baser	BIBLE 74:8	
lex: *populi suprema est l.*	CIC 151:17	
Salus populi suprema l.	SELD 419:25	
lexicographer: doomed at last to wake a l.	JOHN 281:8	
L.: a writer of dictionaries	JOHN 274:13	
l. can only hope to escape	JOHN 281:5	
lexicography: am not yet so lost in l.	JOHN 281:6	
lexicon: In the l. of youth	BULW 107:5	
Two men wrote a l.	ANON 8:12	
liaison: l. man and partly P.R.O.	BETJ 42:14	
liar: every man a l.	BIBLE 74:36	
he is a l.	BIBLE 72:13	
often quite picturesque l.	TWAIN 554:15	
only answered 'Little L.	BELL 39:11	
She's like a l. gone	SHAK 477:11	
liars: All men are l.	PRAY 397:21	
do prove the greatest l.	DRAY 193:9	
l. and swearers are fools	SHAK 462:13	
L. ought to have good memories	SIDN 507:11	
Libanus: breaketh the cedars of L.	PRAY 391:10	
even the cedars of L. which	PRAY 396:20	
libation: say about pouring a l.	SOCR 512:20	
libbaty: l.'s a kind o' thing	LOW 319:3	
libel: Convey a l. in a frown	SWIFT 527:29	
libellum: *Cui dono lepidum novum l.*	CAT 136:19	
Liber: *L. scriptus proferetur*	CEL 138:6	
Nullus l. homo capiatur	MAGN 327:2	
libera: *Anglicana ecclesia l.*	MAGN 327:1	
L. Chiesa in libero Stato	CAV 138:1	
Sed l. nos a malo	MASS 335:5	
Liberal: Is either a little L.	GILB 226:8	
learning and a l. education	HENRY 245:21	
panted for a l. profession	COLM 159:4	
phylacteries of the L. Party	ROS 408:17	
When a l. is abused	LENIN 313:19	
you are l. in offers	SHAK 468:12	
Liberator: 'Europe's L.'	BYRON 123:25	
Liberavi: *L. animam meam*	BERN 41:24	
Libertas: *Imperium et L.*	DISR 185:19	
'L. et natale solum'	SWIFT 528:10	
Liberté: *L.! Égalité*	ANON 9:13	
l. et principale retraite	MONT 354:20	
libertee: desiren l.	CHAU 142:12	
liberties: dramatist only wants more l.	JAMES 271:18	
never give up their l.	BURKE 110:27	
libertine: air, a charter'd l.	SHAK 443:6	
puff'd and reckless l.	SHAK 430:18	
liberty: Abstract l.	BURKE 109:21	
all the feelings of l.	PITT 373:21	
Brightest in dungeons, L.	BYRON 125:14	
conceived in l.	LINC 314:23	
consecrate to truth and l.	SHEL 505:6	
desire their l. and Freedom	CHAR 140:19	
distinction between l. and slavery	CAMD 128:4	
eldest Child of L.	WORD 582:11	
give me l.	HENRY 245:27	
Give me the l. to know	MILT 352:4	
he Served human l.	YEATS 587:3	
I am content that l. will	WALP 563:16	
I must have l.	SHAK 425:22	
insolent and L. to be saucy	HAL 237:21	
it certainly destroys l.	JOHN 279:2	
Know no such l.	LOV 318:15	
known rules of ancient l.	MILT 351:7	
l., and of learning	DISR 185:10	
L. and Union	WEBS 566:11	
l. cannot long exist	BURKE 110:14	
l. connected with order	BURKE 109:10	
L. consists in doing what	MILL 339:13	
L. means responsibility	SHAW 497:37	
l. of action of any	MILL 339:6	
l. of the press is	JUN 287:1	
l. of the individual must	MILL 339:11	
l. plucks justice	SHAK 463:11	
L.'s a glorious feast	BURNS 114:19	
l., shall I leave thee	CONG 161:6	
L.'s in every blow	BURNS 115:1	
l. still more	BROW 102:20	
l. to man is eternal vigilance	CURR 170:16	
L., too, must be limited	BURKE 110:12	
life, and l.	JEFF 272:6	
life, l.	ANON 8:14	
light! said L.	SHEL 500:19	
loudest yelps for l. among	JOHN 282:18	
love of l. is the love	HAZL 243:19	
loving-jealous of his l.	SHAK 482:20	
mansion-house of l.	MILT 352:1	
men are to wait for l.	MAC 323:25	
mountain nymph, sweet L.	MILT 342:15	
notion of l. amuses	JOHN 274:21	
O liberty! O l.	ROL 407:15	
On Naples and on l.	CHES 146:21	
People contend for their L.	HAL 237:20	
power and to lose l.	BACON 26:22	
primordial condition of l.	BAK 29:25	
proclaim l. to the captives	BIBLE 60:8	
regulated l. as well	BURKE 110:34	
something to the spirit of l.	BURKE 109:18	
spirit of divinest L.	COL 156:20	
such refreshing airs of l.	BURKE 108:11	
Sweet land of l.	SMITH 510:24	
symptom of constitutional l.	GIBB 224:27	
then shall the voice of l.	CUMM 170:10	
they mean when they cry L.	MILT 351:8	
to enjoy delight with l.	SPEN 515:23	
tree of l. must be refreshed	JEFF 272:10	
utmost bound of civil l.	MILT 351:20	
weight of too much l.	WORD 582:8	
were thy chosen music, L.	WORD 582:18	
woman l. to gad abroad	BIBLE 63:9	
Liberty-Hall: This is L.	GOLD 232:26	
libraries: books out of circulating l.	RUSK 411:19	
spend altogether on our l.	RUSK 411:17	
library: circulating l. in a town	SHER 506:10	
half a l. to make one book	JOHN 276:24	
l. of sixty-two thousand	GIBB 224:25	
l. Was dukedom	SHAK 484:26	
lumber room of his l.	DOYLE 192:1	
take choice of all my l.	SHAK 486:16	
libre: *L'homme est né l.*	ROUS 410:17	
libro: *Galeotto fu il l. e chi*	DANTE 171:10	
licence: apothecary who has paid a l.	SMITH 511:38	
had l. to dare anything	HOR 257:10	
L. they mean when they	MILT 351:8	
l. to print your own money	THOM 549:30	
love not freedom, but l.	MILT 352:17	
universal l. to be good	COL 154:25	
Licences: L. *poétiques. Il n'y en*	BANV 33:2	
Licensed: L., build that nation's	BLAKE 85:17	
licensers: work of twenty l.	MILT 351:25	
licentious: all l. passages are left	GIBB 224:19	
rapacious and l. soldiery	BURKE 110:25	
Licht: *Mehr L.*	GOET 230:14	
lick: enemies shall l. the dust	PRAY 394:20	
time to l. into form	BURT 116:14	
Licked: L. its tongue into	ELIOT 203:14	
l. the soup from the cooks'	BROW 103:15	
moreover the dogs l. his	BIBLE 70:28	
Licker: L. talks mighty loud w'en	HARR 242:23	
with considerbul l. koncealed	WARD 564:29	
Liddell: right part wrote L.	ANON 8:12	
this is Mrs L.	SPR 517:12	
Liddesdale: Eskdale and L.	SCOTT 418:24	
lids: with eternal l. apart	KEATS 292:11	
lie: big l. than to a small	HITL 251:9	
built to comprehend a l.	KIPL 302:17	
Cannot come, l. follows	PROU 401:24	
can rule and dare not l.	TENN 540:4	
compulsion doth in music l.	MILT 340:19	
country folks would l.	SHAK 427:2	
dost thou l. so low	SHAK 450:6	
fain wald l. down	BALL 31:5	
give the world the l.	RAL 404:10	
God's own name upon a l.	COWP 166:26	
He makes me down to l.	SCOT 419:5	
I cannot tell a l.	WASH 565:1	
if a l. may do thee grace	SHAK 440:28	
I l. down alone	HOUS 265:17	
I l. even among the children	PRAY 393:15	
lawn I l. in bed	AUDEN 20:18	
leads you to believe a l.	BLAKE 85:23	
l. as quietly among	EDW 200:6	
l. circumstantial	SHAK 427:5	
l. *diagonally* in his bed	STER 520:7	
l. direct	SHAK 427:5	

little l. Is rounded SHAK 485:20
little l. with dried tubers ELIOT 204:17
living sepulchre of l. CLARE 152:15
Lolita, light of my l. NAB 359:5
London all that l. can afford JOHN 277:17
long as you have your l. JAMES 271:20
long disease, my l. POPE 376:23
long l. will I satisfy PRAY 395:23
long littleness of l. CORN 162:21
Lord and giver of l. PRAY 387:11
low l. was the level's BROW 100:33
Madam L.'s a piece in bloom HENL 245:6
Mad from l.'s history HOOD 254:10
man's l. of any worth is KEATS 294:12
many doors to let out l. FLET 215:11
may here find l. in death COL 156:17
me hath everlasting l. BIBLE 72:7
Men deal with l. as children COWP 165:11
middle of the road of our l. DANTE 171:2
midst of l. we are in death PRAY 389:12
most loathed worldly l. SHAK 464:14
My l. has crept so long TENN 540:16
My l. is run his compass SHAK 452:1
my l. seemed meant BROW 101:22
my l. with coffee spoons ELIOT 203:20
My l. within this band HERB 247:24
name out of the book of l. BIBLE 81:18
nauseous draught of l. ROCH 406:19
need thou hast in l. HOPE 256:5
Nobody can write the l. JOHN 276:3
no l. but the sea-wind SWIN 529:18
No l. that breathes with TENN 543:20
No, no, no l. SHAK 456:11
nostrils the breath of l. BIBLE 45:7
Not so much l. KEATS 290:1
not the l. more than meat BIBLE 64:28
nourisher in l.'s feast SHAK 460:8
now my l. is done TICH 551:2
off twenty years of l. SHAK 450:4
Of his dull l. BEAU 35:19
Of l., of crown, of queen SHAK 431:12
of man's l. a thing apart BYRON 122:14
one l. and one death BROW 101:13
One l. for each to give KIPL 299:7
one l. shall be destroy'd TENN 536:25
one way in to l. SEN 420:9
only evidence of l.' NEWM 361:18
only honour and l. have FRAN 218:1
our l. is very short TAYL 532:3
O world! O l.! O time SHEL 501:14
passion and the l. COL 156:8
pay glad l.'s arrears BROW 104:1
prepared to lay down my l. CLOU 153:9
purpose to a life beyond l. MILT 351:23
put my genius into my l. WILDE 573:35
R..iling at l. CHUR 148:32
receive the crown of l. BIBLE 80:8
regardeth the l. of his beast BIBLE 53:34
Resurrection and the L. AUDEN 21:7
river of water of l. BIBLE 82:35
runners relay the torch of l. LUCR 320:7
run The colours from my l. BROW 98:10
Rushes l. in a race MER 336:26
say that l. is the thing SMITH 510:21
'sech is l. DICK 179:16
selfish being all my l. AUST 23:21
set my l. at a pin's fee SHAK 430:25
set my l. on any chance SHAK 461:10
shade the evening of l. GIBB 224:20
She bid me take l. easy YEATS 584:22
shilling l. will give you AUDEN 21:8
single l. doth well with BACON 26:33
slits the thin-spun l. MILT 343:8
So have I loitered my l. HAZL 243:15
So in my veins red l. might KEATS 290:30
So on the ocean of l. we LONG 317:10
sphere of private l. MELB 336:13
spirit giveth l. BIBLE 77:4
Squat on my l. LARK 310:6
such is L. DICK 178:10

sweet is this human l. CORY 163:5
take my l. and all SHAK 468:10
Tenants of l.'s middle state COWP 167:33
that a l. was but a flower SHAK 427:2
that is l. without theory DISR 186:4
that L. flies FITZ 212:19
That to me gave this l.'s SPEN 517:1
their l. was death ROSS 409:25
their lives fought for l. SPEN 515:7
therefore choose l. that BIBLE 48:29
there is a space of l. KEATS 288:19
There is no l. of a man CARL 131:12
There is no wealth but l. RUSK 412:12
There's the l. for ever STEV 522:27
think ye have eternal l. BIBLE 72:3
this gives l. to thee SHAK 492:28
This is alone L. SHEL 503:15
This l. is most jolly SHAK 426:1
Thorough the iron gates of l. MARV 332:20
those who live Call L. SHEL 504:4
Thou art my l. QUAR 403:13
thousand doors to let out l. MASS 336:1
Three-fourths of l. ARN 16:19
Through l.'s road BYRON 126:15
time of l. is short SHAK 440:19
'Time to taste l. BROW 100:35
'Tisn't l. that matters WALP 563:23
'Tis the sunset of l. gives CAMP 128:24
to this Fragment of L. STER 519:15
travell'd l.'s dull round SHEN 505:15
traveller betwixt l. and death WORD 581:8
tree of l. also BIBLE 45:8
unblemished l. and spotless record
                              HOR 259:23
undying L. BRON 93:19
Vaguely l. leaks away AUDEN 18:10
value of l. lies not MONT 354:16
voyage of their l. SHAK 451:27
walk in newness of l. BIBLE 75:1
well-written L. is almost CARL 131:2
We should show l. neither CHEK 144:26
What a minefield L. is FRY 220:8
What is this l. DAV 172:17
what is your l. BIBLE 80:16
What l. and death is CHAP 140:8
what l. is then to a man BIBLE 63:15
When I consider how my l. NASH 360:1
when l.'s sweet fable CRAS 169:14
Where all l. dies MILT 346:23
which he slew in his l. BIBLE 49:28
which leadeth unto l. BIBLE 65:7
Who saw l. steadily ARN 15:10
will he give for his l. BIBLE 52:8
wine of l. is drawn SHAK 461:1
With seas of l. TRAH 552:3
Women and wine should l. GAY 222:25
worth a l.'s experience HOLM 253:21
yet not come to l. SHAK 442:3
life-blood: book is the precious l. MILT 351:23
LIFE-IN-DEATH: Night-mare L. was
                              COL 155:15
she
Lifeless: L. charms GAY 222:9
life-lie: Take the l. away from IBSEN 270:4
lifetime: knowledge of a l. WHIS 569:23
lift: floods l. up their waves PRAY 396:1
L. her with care HOOD 254:9
l. me as a wave SHEL 502:13
l. mine eyes SCOT 419:6
L. not thy hands to It FITZ 213:8
l. thou up: the light PRAY 389:21
l. up mine eyes PRAY 398:9
L. up your hearts PRAY 387:21
L. up your heads PRAY 390:24
Lifting: L. the cool-hair'd creepers ARN 14:21
l. up of my hands be PRAY 399:9
light: against the dying of the l. THOM 546:23
are the l. of the world BIBLE 64:8
bathe the world in l. WORD 577:10
bear witness of that L. BIBLE 71:25
becometh the children of l. PRAY 388:11

Be near me when my l. is TENN 536:21
blasted with excess of l GRAY 235:19
burning and a shining l BIBLE 72:2
can again thy former l. SHAK 477:5
Casting a dim religious l. MILT 342:10
children of the l. ARN 16:3
come in may see the l. BIBLE 70:1
contend with growing l. SHAK 446:17
darkness have seen a great l. BIBLE 58:6
darkness rather than l. BIBLE 71:39
dusk with a l. behind GILB 229:4
Enable with perpetual l. PRAY 400:5
endeavours are an inward l. WORD 577:3
festal l. in Christ-Church ARN 14:16
garmented in l. SHEL 505:8
give l. to them that sit BIBLE 69:7
giveth l. unto the eyes PRAY 390:12
Give us a l. ELIOT 202:8
Giving more l. than heat SHAK 430:21
God is L. BLAKE 85:18
gone into the world of l. VAUG 555:18
growing or full constant l. DONNE 189:20
Had she been l. SHAK 457:14
happy realms of l. MILT 344:26
have neither heat nor l. WEBS 566:25
have seen a glorious l. SCOT 419:7
heaven the beam of your l. LANG 309:29
he beholds the l. WORD 579:5
here there is no l. KEATS 291:20
He that has l. within his MILT 341:8
hours of l. return ARN 13:23
if bereav'd of l. BLAKE 88:2
if once we lose this l. JONS 285:13
if they fear'd the l. SUCK 524:8
In a l. fantastic round MILT 340:29
infant crying for the l. TENN 536:26
informed by the l. of nature BACON 24:20
It gives a lovely l. MILL 339:26
It is the l. of Terewth DICK 176:16
just is as the shining l. BIBLE 53:19
land is scattered with l. BRID 92:8
land...where the l. is as darkness BIBLE 52:21
leaping l. for you discovers AUDEN 20:3
let me not be l. SHAK 468:21
let perpetual l. shine MASS 334:17
Lets in new l. through WALL 562:9
Let there be l. BIBLE 44:22
'Let there be l.' said God BYRON 123:23
levell'd rule of streaming l. MILT 341:7
lift thou up: the l. PRAY 389:21
l. and leading in England BURKE 111:20
L. and Mrs Humphry Ward CHES 146:12
l., and will aspire SHAK 495:19
l. as leef on lynde CHAU 142:11
l. but the shadow of God BROW 95:17
l. dissolved in star-showers SHEL 504:9
l. emerging from the smoke HOR 257:19
l. excelleth darkness BIBLE 55:10
L. (God's eldest daughter) FULL 220:16
l. heart lives long SHAK 457:14
lighthouse without any l. HOOD 254:24
l. in mine eye DONNE 191:2
l. in the dust lies dead SHEL 501:21
l. of his countenance PRAY 394:4
L. of Lights YEATS 584:18
L. of step and heart was DE L 173:27
l. of thy Holy Spirit PRAY 386:14
l. or leading received MILT 352:7
l.! said Liberty SHEL 500:19
l., shade, and perspective CONS 162:2
l. shineth in darkness BIBLE 71:23
l. such a candle by God's LAT 310:21
l. that I may tread safely HASK 243:1
l. that loses SWIN 528:17
l. that never was WORD 577:4
l. to counterfeit a gloom MILT 342:5
l. to shine upon the road COWP 165:23
l. to thee are both alike PRAY 399:5
l. unto my paths PRAY 398:6
little l. Of love's bestowing DU M 199:6

Lolita, l. of my life — NAB 359:5
mend the Electric L. — BELL 39:29
More l. — GOET 230:14
my l., and my salvation — PRAY 391:7
Of beauty from the l. retir'd — WALL 562:14
Of night and l. — YEATS 585:9
of pure and endless l. — VAUG 555:22
once set is our little l. — CAT 136:25
one equal l. — DONNE 191:3
On the l. fantastic toe — MILT 342:15
out thy l. and thy truth — PRAY 392:11
plant and flower of l. — JONS 285:8
progeny of l. — MILT 348:22
pursuit of sweetness and l. — ARN 15:15
put on the armour of l. — BIBLE 75:24
Put out the l. — SHAK 477:5
Servants of L. — ARN 12:19
severity of perfect l. — TENN 534:14
shadow of l. — SWIN 528:21
shaft of l. across the land — TENN 533:23
shall remember while the l. — SWIN 529:12
shew the l. of thy countenance — PRAY 395:8
should be a place of l. — DISR 185:10
shows sufficient of His l. — BROW 104:27
so l. a foot — SHAK 482:25
source of my l. and my safety — BIBLE 83:5
such glimmerings of l. — BURKE 108:11
than the children of l. — BIBLE 70:25
that celestial l. — MILT 345:9
Then shall thy l. break — BIBLE 60:5
There's a certain Slant of l. — DICK 184:1
third among the sons of l. — SHEL 499:5
Thou art my l. — QUAR 403:13
thy l. is come — BIBLE 60:7
to give them l. — BIBLE 47:21
to noise and blind to l. — SIDN 507:21
took away the l. — MILT 344:16
to shew l. at Calais — JOHN 275:8
Truly the l. is sweet — BIBLE 56:9
turning your face to the l. — SASS 414:13
Turret in a Noose of L. — FITZ 212:5
unclouded blaze of living l. — BYRON 121:37
unveil'd her peerless l. — MILT 348:2
upon us the armour of l. — PRAY 386:4
veil with l. divine — WORD 580:19
want to l. up my own mind — BROW 102:19
was far faster than l. — BULL 106:24
We all *know* what l. is — JOHN 277:7
what l. through yonder — SHAK 482:5
When I consider how my l. — MILT 351:10
Wherefore is l. given — BIBLE 52:14
which are sweetness and l. — SWIFT 525:33
which was L. — BACON 28:5
Yet the l. of a whole life — BOUR 90:21
your l. so shine before men — BIBLE 64:9
Light Brigade: 'Forward the L. — TENN 532:24
lighted: l. rooms Inside your head

— LARK 310:5
lighten: let thy mercy l. upon us — PRAY 384:18
L. our darkness — PRAY 385:10
l. with celestial fire — PRAY 400:5
lighter: altogether l. than vanity itself

— PRAY 393:20
is l. than vanity — BUNY 107:16
Lightfoot: come uppe L. — ING 270:15
many a l. lad — HOUS 264:10
light-headed: l., variable men — STEV 521:30
light-hearted: l. Masters of the waves

— ARN 14:21
light-house: Keeping a l. with his eyes

— CAMP 128:10
l. without any light atop — HOOD 254:24
sitivation at the l. — DICK 182:34
lightless: l. in the quarry — HOUS 264:4
lightly: l. as it comth — CHAU 143:8
l. regarded the counsel — PRAY 397:7
unadvisedly, l., or wantonly — PRAY 388:25
lightness: Thence to a l. — SHAK 432:2
lightning: Brief as the l. — SHAK 469:20
Bring in the bottled l. — DICK 180:20

coruscations of summer l. — GOUL 233:5
Fear no more the l. flash — SHAK 428:22
from Jove the l. — MAN 328:11
From l. and tempest — PRAY 385:16
Have known the l.'s hour — DAY-L 172:22
He snatched the l. shaft — TURG 553:22
I beheld Satan as l. fall — BIBLE 69:28
illumined by flashes of l. — WILDE 573:37
It is to keep the l. out — ISH 270:27
It must be done like l. — JONS 284:8
Shakespeare by flashes of l. — COL 157:31
that the l. made itself — MAC 323:32
Too like the l. — SHAK 482:16
yes O at l. — HOPK 257:6
lights: are but broken l. of thee — TENN 535:31
down from the Father of l. — BIBLE 80:9
Glorious the northern l. — SMART 509:4
God made two great l. — BIBLE 45:3
l. around the shore — ROSS 410:8
l. begin to twinkle from — TENN 544:3
serene l. of heaven — SHEL 504:7
spent l. quiver and gleam — ARN 13:6
Turn up the l. — HENRY 245:24
when all the l. wax dim — HERR 249:23
your l. burning — BIBLE 70:6
ligno: *Regnavit a l. Deus* — VEN 556:6
like: Dear heart how l. you — WYATT 583:22
How I l. to be liked — LAMB 307:32
husband could have made me l. — CONG 160:13
I know what I l. — BEER 38:5
L. as the hart desireth — PRAY 392:6
L. cures like — HAHN 237:10
L. doth quit like — SHAK 465:5
l. my title — STEV 523:6
l. of each thing that — SHAK 456:16
l. one another as half-pence — SHAK 426:14
l. the immortal goddesses — HOMER 253:28
l. to be as my fathers — BLUNT 89:5
l. to something I remember — FORD 216:19
l. unto them that dream — PRAY 398:16
men come to l. a sea-life — JOHN 276:33
my life to l. Scotchmen — LAMB 307:8
none of his friends l. him — WILDE 574:2
shall not look upon his l. — SHAK 430:5
should say you do not l. — WHIS 569:24
sort of thing they l. — LINC 315:4
so what is this l. — FORS 216:23
that l. that sort of place — SHAW 497:23
therefore do as they l. — THUR 550:32
there was nothing *l.* it — CARR 135:31
thou find their l. agen — SCOTT 417:4
Why every one as they l. — SWIFT 526:28
liked: Because I l. you better — HOUS 266:1
l. whate'er She looked — BROW 102:22
that loved and you that l. — ANON 7:15
likely: mighty l. speech — GAY 222:16
likened: be l. unto a foolish man — BIBLE 65:12
likeness: after our l. — BIBLE 45:4
any l. of any thing that — BIBLE 47:24
down to us in the l. of men — BIBLE 74:4
l. of a kingly crown had — MILT 346:24
l. of a fat old man — SHAK 439:15
was made in the l. of men — BIBLE 78:13
likes: She l. her self — CONG 159:19
likewise: Canst thou do l. — DICK 178:3
do thou l. — BIBLE 69:33
liking: Hath lost me in your l. — SHAK 453:6
I have a l. old — CALV 128:1
lilacs: l. last in the dooryard — WHIT 571:12
L. out of the dead land — ELIOT 204:17
lilac-time: Go down to Kew in l.

— NOYES 364:11
lilia: *Manibus date l. plenis* — VIRG 559:2
Lilian: fairy L. — TENN 538:14
lilies: Beauty lives though l. — FLEC 214:9
Consider the l. of the field — BIBLE 64:30
few l. blow — HOPK 256:17
Give me l. in armfuls — VIRG 559:2
had three l. in her hand — ROSS 409:14
he feedeth among the l. — BIBLE 56:24

l. and languors of virtue — SWIN 529:5
l. by the rivers of waters — BIBLE 63:27
l. of all kinds — SHAK 491:26
L. that fester smell far — SHAK 494:15
L. without, roses within — MARV 332:15
Lotos and l. — TENN 541:18
loved L. — SPEN 517:3
pale, lost l. — DOWS 191:12
peacocks and l. for instance — RUSK 411:23
specimens, the l. of ambition — DOUG 191:8
wheat set about with l. — BIBLE 57:8
which feed among the l. — BIBLE 56:26
wringing l. from the acorns — POUND 383:2
Lillabullero: half a dozen bars of L.

— STER 519:21
Lilli Burleno: L. Bullena-la — WHAR 569:10
lily: I see a l. on thy brow — KEATS 290:16
l. of a day — JONS 285:8
l. of Florence blossoming — LONG 316:17
l. of the valleys — BIBLE 56:19
l. whispers, 'I wait — TENN 540:12
morning glows the l. — FLEC 214:11
'My precious L. — CARR 134:27
Now folds the l. all her — TENN 542:14
poppy or a l. in your medieval — GILB 227:23
seen but a bright l. grow — JONS 285:4
to paint the l. — SHAK 452:25
white l. in London — BETJ 42:15
lily-handed: No little l. Baronet he

— TENN 542:20
lily-white: l. boys — ANON 6:5
Lima: curious traveller from L. — WALP 563:9
limb: feels its life in every l. — WORD 583:5
To ease my weary l. — BALL 30:9
limbecks: Distill'd from l. foul — SHAK 495:6
Limbo: Into a L. large and broad — MILT 347:11
limbs: calf's-skin on those recreant l.

— SHAK 452:16
deck your lower l. in pants — NASH 360:5
great smooth marbly l. — BROW 99:13
l. of a poet — HOR 262:2
My l. may issue from your — MARL 329:13
ruddy l. and flaming hair — BLAKE 86:20
slope of mighty l. asleep — SWIN 528:26
Whose l. were made in England — SHAK 444:2
lime: sprinkle the l. like rain — HOUS 265:15
limed: l. soul — SHAK 434:28
limelight: always backing into the l.

— BERN 42:1
lime-tree: l. bower my prison — COL 157:30
limit: act a slave to l. — SHAK 486:33
art is to l. and isolate — GOET 229:27
quiet l. of the world — TENN 543:11
limitary: Proud l. Cherub — MILT 348:12
limitations: to know the l. of force

— TROT 553:18
limited: Liberty, too, must be l.

— BURKE 110:12
limits: Beyond the l. of a vulgar — GRAY 235:20
stony l. cannot hold love — SHAK 482:10
ultimately fixed l. — HOR 261:23
limn: wood ere Thou canst l. — THOM 548:18
limns: l. the water — BACON 28:16
limousine: One perfect l. — PARK 368:17
want is a l. and a ticket — MACN 326:7
limpet: lampshell Or the l. — AUDEN 19:10
Limpopo: greasy L. River — KIPL 304:21
linages: *Dos l. sólos hay en el* — CERV 138:17
Lincoln: L. sped the message — MAC 322:4
Linden: L., when the sun was low

— CAMP 128:21
Linden Lea: Do leän down low in L.

— BARN 33:28
Lindesay: Sir David L. of the Mount

— SCOTT 417:7
Lindsay: While Sandy L. from his BETJ 44:11
line: *active* l. on a walk moving — KLEE 305:5
are six ships of the l. — TENN 542:21
back to cancel half a L. — FITZ 213:7
distant though the last l. be — ROSS 409:26

heroes up the l. to death   SASS 414:10
high aesthetic l.   GILB 227:20
in the very first l.   GOLD 231:19
l. is length without breadth   EUCL 209:2
l. of scarlet thread   BIBLE 48:37
l. too labours   POPE 378:23
l. upon line   BIBLE 58:21
l. will take us hours maybe   YEATS 584:9
lives along the l.   POPE 379:9
oft creep in one dull l.   POPE 378:20
thin red l.   RUSS 412:23
thou whatever suits the l.   COL 157:5
We carved not a l.   WOLFE 576:5
will the l. stretch out   SHAK 462:10
lineage: Poets of the proud old l.   FLEC 214:9
lineaments: l. of gratified desire   BLAKE 86:17
l. of Gospel books   ROYD 411:2
Yet in my l. they trace   BYRON 125:13
linen: clothed in purple and fine l.   BIBLE 70:28
fair white l. cloth   PRAY 387:6
In blanched l.   KEATS 289:20
Love is like l. often chang'd   FLET 215:31
not l. you're wearing   HOOD 255:7
old l. wash whitest   WEBS 566:30
very fine l.   BRUM 106:5
you shall wash your l.   STEV 522:29
lines: consisted of l. like these   CALV 127:10
l. and life are free   HERB 247:14
l. so loves oblique may   MARV 331:19
liquid l. mellifluously bland   BYRON 123:14
Prose is when all the l.   BENT 41:2
smile his face into more l.   SHAK 490:3
town-crier spoke my l.   SHAK 433:16
linger: late rose may yet l.   HOR 260:5
To l. out a purpos'd overthrow   SHAK 494:14
lingered: I l. round them   BRON 94:1
lingering: I alone sit l. here   VAUG 555:18
Something l.   GILB 227:11
lingots: *au marché avec des l.*   CHAM 139:14
lingring: l. and consumptive passion   ETH 208:29
lingua: *l., gloriosi*   THOM 546:16
l., gloriosi   VEN 556:9
linguam: *Et l. et mores*   JUV 287:15
lining: Turn forth her silver l.   MILT 341:2
link: silver l.   SCOTT 416:20
linked: my name too will be l.   OVID 366:12
links: strong as l. of iron   BURKE 110:2
lin-lan-lone: mellow l. of evening bells   TENN 533:15
linnet: evening full of the l.'s   YEATS 585:17
l. born within the cage   TENN 536:15
linnets: pipe but as the l. sing   TENN 536:12
linsy-woolsy: lawless l. brother   BUTL 117:32
lion: from the fox and the l.   MACH 325:8
go upon the l. and adder   PRAY 395:22
is better than a dead l.   BIBLE 55:27
l. among ladies   SHAK 470:14
l. and the fatling together   BIBLE 58:10
L. and the Lizard keep   FITZ 212:14
l. griefs loped from   AUDEN 20:19
l. is the wisdom of God   BLAKE 88:21
l. shall eat straw like   BIBLE 58:11
l. who dies of an ass's   BROW 102:25
Lord L. King-at-arms   SCOTT 417:7
Now the hungry l. roars   SHAK 471:21
pain'd desert l.   ARN 14:26
righteous are bold as a l.   BIBLE 54:41
roaring l.   BIBLE 80:33
Rouse the l. from his lair   SCOTT 418:35
Sporting the l. ramped   MILT 347:26
Strong is the l.   SMART 509:3
that gets the fattest l.   SAKI 413:9
that had the l.'s heart   CHUR 150:21
There is a l. in the way   BIBLE 54:34
Thou wear a l.'s hide   SHAK 452:16
To beard the l. in his   SCOTT 417:18
To rouse a l. than to start   SHAK 438:18
upon a time to the sick l.   HOR 258:11

would be mated with the l.   SHAK 420:26
Lions: I girdid up my L. & fled   WARD 564:24
laughing l. must come   NIET 363:2
Let bears and l. growl   WATTS 565:17
l. do lack   PRAY 391:22
l. of the Daily Telegraph   ARN 15:23
L., or Vanity-Fair he feared not   BUNY 107:33
l. roaring after their   PRAY 397:1
my darling from the l.   PRAY 391:25
my soul is among l.   PRAY 393:15
on the other, l.   PATM 370:7
Rise like L. after slumber   SHEL 502:4
they were stronger than l.   BIBLE 50:17
to have been eaten by l.   CHES 148:3
We are two l. litter'd   SHAK 449:19
lip: girl's l. out of Paris   SWIN 531:2
gnaw you so your nether l.   SHAK 477:6
'Keep a stiff upper l.   CARY 136:14
Teach not thy l. such scorn   SHAK 480:21
Whose l. mature is ever   KEATS 289:31
lipless: Leaned backward with a l.   ELIOT 205:13
lips: Bestow'd his l. on that   SHAK 422:19
Be through my l. to unawakened   SHEL 502:14
coral l. such folly broke   CONG 160:2
far from the l. we love   MOORE 356:19
flatter with their l.   PRAY 389:32
heaven be in these l.   MARL 329:10
Here hung those l. that   SHAK 436:31
Her l. were red   SUCK 524:10
His coward l. did from   SHAK 448:15
In prayer the l. ne'er   HERR 250:11
In the l. that had whispered   SWIN 529:19
keep the door of my l.   PRAY 399:9
Life and these l. have   SHAK 483:22
l. are not yet unsealed   BALD 29:29
l. are now forbid to speak   BAYLY 35:10
l. cannot fail of taking   BURG 108:5
l. of a strange woman drop   BIBLE 53:20
l. of dying men   ARN 14:27
l. of those that are asleep   BIBLE 57:10
l. of those who love you   BRID 92:18
l. once sanctified by Hers   BROW 106:1
l., that they speak no   PRAY 391:23
l. that touch liquor must   YOUNG 588:15
l. to it when I am so dispoged   DICK 179:10
Live l. upon a plummet-measured   YEATS 587:1
mammets and to tilt with l.   SHAK 438:31
meet on l. of living men   BUTL 119:17
On l. that are for others   TENN 542:4
ope my l. let no dog   SHAK 465:12
people of unclean l.   BIBLE 57:29
rain is on our l.   SORL 513:10
Red l. are not so red   OWEN 367:6
round their narrow l.   ROSS 409:25
See my l. tremble   POPE 376:14
soft as l. that laugh   SWIN 528:18
starv'd l. in the gloam   KEATS 290:21
sweet l.   KEATS 292:15
take those l. away   SHAK 464:21
that had red mournful l.   YEATS 586:22
that those l. had language   COWP 166:2
they shoot out their l.   PRAY 390:17
this hath touched thy l.   BIBLE 57:30
Thou shalt open my l.   PRAY 393:8
Thy l. are like a thread   BIBLE 56:26
To part her l.   HERR 249:18
touching of the l.   TENN 538:18
touch lightly with my l.   WHIT 570:11
turn to ashes on the l.   MOORE 356:26
Two l., indifferent red   SHAK 488:12
Upon her perfect l.   TENN 543:9
very good words for the l.   DICK 178:26
When the l. have spoken   SHEL 501:31
Where my Julia's l. do smile   HERR 248:21
winds kiss my parched l.   SHAK 452:31
lipsed: Somwhat he l.   CHAU 141:22
liquefaction: That l. of her clothes   HERR 250:8

liquid: let their l. siftings fall   ELIOT 204:16
l. lines mellifluously   BYRON 123:14
otherwise excellent l.   HERB 246:18
Thames is l. history   BURNS 112:23
liquidation: l. of the British Empire   CHUR 150:12
liquidity: purpose in l.   BROO 94:11
liquor: bowl with atrabilious l.   HUXL 269:2
Good l.   GOLD 231:22
lads for the l.   HOUS 263:6
Life's L. in its Cup   FITZ 212:6
lips that touch l. must   YOUNG 588:15
l. Is quicker   NASH 359:19
Livelier l. than the Muse   HOUS 264:12
such other spiritual l.   BYRON 126:7
which wanteth not l.   BIBLE 57:8
liquors: spouts the grateful l.   POPE 381:6
lisp'd: I l. in numbers   POPE 376:23
list: I've got a little l.   GILB 226:24
list, O, l.!   SHAK 431:5
listed: 'l. at home for a lancer   HOUS 264:19
listen: Darkling I l.   KEATS 291:22
Do you think I can l. all   CARR 133:23
if we care to l.   AUDEN 19:13
L., Eugenia   ARN 14:3
privilege of wisdom to l.   HOLM 253:20
silence is wonderful to l.   HARDY 241:27
world should l. then   SHEL 504:24
Listened: soul L. intensely   WORD 577:16
We l. and looked sideways   COL 155:17
listeners: least stir made the l.   DE L 174:9
listening: Enemy ears are l.   ANON 9:18
is the disease of not l.   SHAK 441:7
listens: who l. to Reason is lost   SHAW 498:2
yet the Evening l.   KEATS 292:5
listeth: wind bloweth where it l.   BIBLE 71:36
listlessness: seek repose In l.   WORD 580:6
lit: Fleet is all l. up   WOOD 576:16
literary: head of the l. profession   DISR 185:29
He lik'd those l. cooks   MORE 357:9
Like an unsuccessful l.   BELL 40:2
l. and scientific opinion   ARN 16:5
l. man   DICK 181:3
lowest class is l. *footmen*   HAZL 243:29
Never l. attempt was more   HUME 268:1
quite disgusted with l.   KEATS 293:12
which with St Paul are l.   ARN 16:18
literature: All that is l. seeks   DE Q 175:7
All the rest is *l.*   VAL 555:1
grazed the common of l.   JOHN 274:28
have failed in l. and art   DISR 186:23
L. flourishes best when   INGE 270:8
l. is a drug   BORR 90:7
L. is news that STAYS news   POUND 383:23
l. is simply language charged   POUND 384:1
l. of *power*   DE Q 175:6
louse in the locks of l.   TENN 544:13
must wash l. off ourselves   ART 16:29
Philistine of genius in l.   ARN 16:23
That great Cham of l.   SMOL 512:14
to produce a little l.   JAMES 271:2
'We cultivate l. upon   SMITH 511:36
When once the itch of l.   LOVER 318:21
Your true lover of l. is   SOUT 514:14
lites: *vos tantas componere l.*   VIRG 559:20
litter: all her l. but one   SHAK 441:3
Like l. that a riot leaves   PLOM 374:19
littérature: *Et tout le reste est l.*   VERL 556:9
faut nous laver de la l.   ART 16:29
littered: l. under Mercury   SHAK 491:18
l. with remembered kisses   MACN 326:3
little: contemptible l. Army   WILH 574:4
done and l. to be known   JOHN 280:7
drink unto one of these l.   BIBLE 65:41
grateful at last for a l.   TENN 540:16
great ones eat up the l.   SHAK 478:4
he only knew a l. of law   ANON 6:3
here a l.   BIBLE 58:21
it was a very l. one   MARR 331:5
l. creep through   SHEN 505:16

l. unto righteousness   PRAY 388:10
L., we fret   BROW 104:35
l. which are yet alive   BIBLE 55:14
man became a l. soul   BIBLE 45:7
men meet on lips of l.   BUTL 119:17
mere l.   BROW 105:1
mother of all l.   BIBLE 45:24
my mother I'm l. in sin   HERB 246:8
noble L. and the noble Dead   WORD 580:24
Of health and l. now begins   SHAK 486:12
out of the book of the l.   PRAY 394:14
out of the land of the l.   BIBLE 59:23
Plain l. and high thinking   WORD 582:9
reasons for l.   JUV 287:25
shadows of the l.   BROW 95:17
shall no man l. be justified   PRAY 399:11
someone's death to get a l.   MOL 353:16
substance with riotous l.   BIBLE 70:18
their preaching and l.   PRAY 385:18
there are no l. people in it   CHEK 144:26
There is no l. with thee   ADD 2:10
things l. with plenteousness   PRAY 399:15
This l. buried man   DONNE 190:1
'tis the l. up to it that   THAC 545:6
truly to get mine own l.   PRAY 388:18
unexamined life is not worth l.   SOCR 511:17
Why seek ye the l. among   BIBLE 71:16
ye are l. poems   LONG 316:8
you to go on l.   SOCR 512:18
living-dead: l. man   SHAK 427:9
living-machine: house is a l.   LE C 313:5
Livingstone: Dr L., I presume   STAN 517:17
livre: métier que de faire un l.   LA B 306:12
livres: et j'ai lu tous les l.   MALL 327:9
Les l. cadrent mal avec   MOL 353:13
Les l. ne se font pas comme   FLAU 214:3
ses l. disposés   PROU 401:23
liv'st: what thou l. Live well   MILT 349:25
Lizard: L.'s leg   SHAK 462:3
say the Lion and the L.   FITZ 212:14
Lizzie Borden: L. took an axe   ANON 6:12
Llama: L. is a woolly sort   BELL 40:2
Lo: L., I come   PRAY 392:2
load: cruelty To l. a falling man   SHAK 447:25
heart like a l. of immortality   KEATS 294:4
him how to l. and bless   KEATS 293:5
l. every rift of your subject   KEATS 294:31
l. would sink a navy   SHAK 447:11
loads: l. of learned lumber   POPE 378:30
loaf: cut l. to steal a shive   SHAK 486:15
quartern l. and Luddites rise   SMITH 510:7
with a L. of Bread beneath   FITZ 212:11
loan: brief l. of his own body   CAB 126:24
l. oft loses both itself   SHAK 430:1
loathe: I do l. explanations   BARR 34:12
I l. the country   CONG 161:5
l. the taste of sweetness   SHAK 439:35
relief Must be to l. her   SHAK 475:21
loathed: performance so l.   SHAK 487:19
loaves: of the l. and the fishes   PEAC 370:16
seven halfpenny l.   SHAK 446:11
lobster: has seen the mailed l.   FRERE 218:26
like a l. boil'd   BUTL 118:3
still the l. held   KING 297:10
'Tis the voice of the l.   CARR 134:16
lobsters: I have a liking for l.   NERV 361:1
local: little l. difficulties   MACM 325:19
l., but prized elsewhere   AUDEN 20:14
l. habitation and a name   SHAK 471:11
not l. prejudices ought   BURKE 109:12
localism: genuine spirit of l.   BORR 90:2
Lochinvar: young L. is come out
                                         SCOTT 417:8
loci: Geniumque l. primamque   VIRG 559:4
lock: it's broken the l.   AUDEN 20:5
why l. him   SHAW 497:32
Wi' ae l. o' his gowden   BALL 32:8
lock'd: Had l. the source of softer
                                         SCOTT 416:11
l. my heart in a case o'   BALL 32:11

locks: combined l. to part   SHAK 431:5
few l. which are left you   SOUT 514:7
l. of the approaching storm   SHEL 502:9
l. up its spoons and packs   SHAW 497:30
louse in the l. of literature   TENN 544:13
never shake Thy gory l.   SHAK 461:20
Open, l.   SHAK 462:5
shaking her invincible l.   MILT 352:3
turn those amber l. to grey   DRAY 193:12
Your l. were like the raven   BURNS 114:12
locust: palmerworm hath left hath the
l.   BIBLE 61:13
locusts: meat was l. and wild honey
                                         BIBLE 63:37
locuta: Roma l. est   AUG 22:2
lodesterre: language he was the l.
                                         LYDG 321:5
lodge: Elephant, Is best to l.   SHAK 490:4
l. in a garden of cucumbers   BIBLE 57:16
still l. Him in the manger   ANON 9:1
lodger: mere l. in my own house
                                         GOLD 232:10
lodgest: where thou l.   BIBLE 49:32
lodging: Hard was their l.   GARTH 221:20
lodgings: poor in their fireless l. AUDEN 20:15
Such as take l. in a head   BUTL 117:21
Lodore: water comes down at L.   SOUT 513:22
lo'ed: l. him like a vera brither   BURNS 115:5
l'offense: monde est ce qui fait l.   MOL 354:1
loft: much l. as a light iron   WOD 575:22
loftier: l. race   SYM 531:3
Loftily: L. lying   BROW 101:2
Lofty: L. and sour to them that   SHAK 447:21
L. designs must close   BROW 101:2
of a l. utterance drest   WORD 581:1
Logic: Common Room stank of L.'
                                         NEWM 361:22
Grape that can with L.   FITZ 213:2
It is the l. of our times   DAY-L 172:23
l. and rhetoric   BACON 27:21
L., of course   CLOU 153:16
overthrow of all his l.   STEV 521:12
push the l. of a fact   KIPL 299:5
That's l.   CARR 135:2
Logical: L. consequences are   HUXL 269:10
logically: l. predicate his finish   KIPL 302:4
logicians: If we may believe our l. ADD 2:26
Logik: Die L. muss für sich selber
                                         WITT 575:15
logs: Tom bears l. into the hall   SHAK 457:19
logyk: That unto l. hadde longe   CHAU 141:23
loi: l. qui viole les droits   ROB 406:11
loin: lamp and the ungirt l.   BROW 105:21
loins: fire of my l.   NAB 359:5
He girded up his l.   BIBLE 51:12
l. girt about with truth   BIBLE 78:10
shudder in the l. engenders   YEATS 586:2
thicker than my father's l.   BIBLE 51:2
up now thy l. like a man   BIBLE 53:1
With your l. girded   BIBLE 47:18
your l. be girded about   BIBLE 70:6
Loire: my Gallic L. more than   DU B 198:27
lois: majestueuse égalité des l.   FRAN 217:26
loiter: do I l. round these chartered
                                         MACN 326:9
loitered: So have I l. my life away
                                         HAZL 243:15
loiterers: Liege of all l. and malecontents
                                         SHAK 456:26
loitering: Alone and palely l.   KEATS 290:15
Lolita: L., light of my life   NAB 359:5
lollipop: lovely Monkey with l. paws
                                         LEAR 312:9
Lombardy: waveless plain of L.   SHEL 501:23
London: Ask the booksellers of L.
                                         BURKE 111:17
chief advantage of L. is   MEYN 338:16
dream of L.   MORR 358:10
in L. only is a trade   DRYD 197:13
is a city much like L.   SHEL 502:17

L.; a nation   DISR 186:17
L. doth pour out her citizens   SHAK 445:6
L. is a fine town   COLM 158:25
L. is a modern Babylon   DISR 186:38
L. is the epitome of our   EMER 207:9
L. particular...A fog   DICK 176:3
L.'s lasting shame   GRAY 234:17
L.'s Noble Fire Brigade   BELL 39:8
L.'s towers   BLAKE 86:12
L. streets the Shropshire   HOUS 263:21
L., that great cesspool   DOYLE 192:3
L., that great sea   SHEL 501:17
L., thou art of townes   DUNB 199:9
L., thou art the flower   DUNB 199:10
lungs of L.   PITT 374:2
Meet me at L.   DONNE 188:2
Of famous L. town   COWP 165:15
One road leads to L.   MAS 334:2
sent him up to fair L.   BALL 30:8
than a rainy Sunday in L.   DE Q 175:1
they all to merry L. came   SPEN 517:1
vilest alleys of L. do   DOYLE 192:1
Weller's knowledge of L.   DICK 181:35
When a man is tired of L.   JOHN 277:17
Where L.'s column   POPE 378:2
London Bridge: broken arch of L.
                                         MAC 323:16
crowd flowed over L.   ELIOT 204:20
that L. was a greater piece   ADD 2:19
lone: 'I am a l. lorn creetur'   DICK 176:27
l. shieling of the misty   GALT 221:2
l. unhaunted place possesst   DONNE 190:1
three l. weirs   ARN 15:3
loneliness: All that bowery l.   TENN 533:13
Lap your l. in heat   BETJ 42:7
lonely: is troubled with her l.   PEPYS 372:8
l. impulse of delight   YEATS 585:15
rapture on the l. shore   BYRON 121:22
to the l. sea and the sky   MAS 334:4
lonesomeness: starlight lit my l.   HARDY 241:5
long: appear most l. and terrible   LEE 313:8
arms l. and small   WYATT 583:22
certified how l. I have to live   PRAY 391:30
craft so l. to lerne   CHAU 143:32
days seem lank and l.   GILB 228:29
feet l. and two feet wide   WORD 582:24
foolish thing to make a l. prologue
                                         BIBLE 63:29
fulfilled a l. time   BIBLE 62:15
has been l. in city pent   KEATS 292:27
How l. a time lies in one   SHAK 478:13
How l. wilt thou forget   PRAY 390:1
I am going a l. way   TENN 535:27
It cannot hold you l.   GOLD 231:9
it hath very l. arms   HAL 238:2
l. as ye both shall live   PRAY 389:3
l. day's task is done   SHAK 423:9
l. for the fruit at last   SHER 506:10
L. is the way And hard   MILT 346:17
l. life will I satisfy   PRAY 395:23
Lord, how l.   BIBLE 58:2
man goeth to his l. home   BIBLE 56:11
many girls l. for it   CAT 137:6
nor that little, l.   YOUNG 588:8
Nor wants that little l.   GOLD 231:7
So l. as men can breathe   SHAK 492:28
that the story need be l.   THOR 550:26
to keep unmarried as l.   SHAW 497:25
week is a l. time in politics   WILS 574:18
witty and it sha'n't be l.   CHES 145:7
words a foot and a half l.   HOR 257:16
You l. for simple pewter   GILB 225:30
long-cramped: l. scroll   BROW 101:24
long'd-for: l. dash of waves is heard
                                         ARN 15:1
longe: day be never so l.   HAWES 243:3
morowe, I to goe to God   MORE 357:20
longer: l. I live the more fool   ANON 8:19
man that was wished l.   JOHN 280:16

longest: dreariest and the l. journey go   SHEL 500:10

longeth: flesh also l. after thee   PRAY 393:21
so l. my soul after thee   PRAY 392:6

longing: has cast a l. eye on them   JEFF 272:11
l. comes upon him to fare   POUND 383:18
l. to be at 'em   ANON 5:10
soul hath a desire and l.   PRAY 395:11
This l. after immortality   ADD 1:24

longings: Immortal l. in me   SHAK 424:10

longitude: l. also is vague   PROW 402:2
L. objected to his theology   SMIL 509:5

long-legged: *l. fly upon the stream*
    YEATS 586:3

Long Melford: then tip them to L.
    BORR 90:11

long-suffering: l., and very pitiful
    BIBLE 62:21
l., and of great goodness   PRAY 396:16

longtemps: *et c'est pour si l.*   MOL 353:8
L. je me suis couché de   PROU 401:20

longue: *l. que parce que je n'ai*   PASC 369:14

look: afraid to l. upon God   BIBLE 47:5
…'Do l. into it'   STER 520:10
do we l. for another   BIBLE 66:1
Hit l. lak sparrer-grass   HARR 242:14
how you l. to other people   UNAM 554:28
I l. at the senators   HALE 237:12
Let him l. to his bond   SHAK 467:3
longing ling'ring l. behind   GRAY 235:2
l., and pass on   DANTE 171:4
l. grim as hell   SHAK 476:18
L. in my face   TRAI 552:4
L. not in my eyes   HOUS 262:21
L. not thou upon the wine   BIBLE 54:24
L. not thou down but up   BROW 104:12
L..not thou on beauty's   SCOTT 418:5
l. no way but downwards   BUNY 107:28
l. on both indifferently   SHAK 448:12
L., stranger   AUDEN 20:3
L. thy last on all things   DE L 174:3
l. to the end   ANON 10:18
L. to the lady   SHAK 461:3
L. to your Moat   HAL 238:4
l. upon myself and curse   SHAK 493:6
l. upon the hedge and follow   SHAK 492:9
L. with thine ears   SHAK 455:18
Men's eyes were made to l.   SHAK 483:2
not l. upon his like again   SHAK 430:5
'O l. at the trees   BRID 92:14
read a nod, a shrug, a l.   SWIFT 527:29
sake l. after our people   SCOTT 415:18
shall tremble at the l.   PRAY 397:2
so l. to thyself   SHAK 490:12
sweet to l. into the fair   KEATS 292:27
that we may l. upon thee   BIBLE 57:6
to l. about us and to die)   POPE 379:1
to l. at things in bloom   HOUS 262:14
We l. before and after   SHEL 504:23
When I do l. on thee   SIDN 508:1

looked: be l. upon by posterity   CLAR 152:22
be so wise as Thurlow l.   FOX 217:21
l. for a city which hath   BIBLE 79:32
l. upon Peter   BIBLE 71:9
wife l. back   BIBLE 46:8

lookers on: God and angels to be l.
    BACON 24:24

looketh: l. on the outward appearance
    BIBLE 50:6

looking: Here's l. at you   BOG 89:8
l. back   BIBLE 69:25
l. for a man's foot-print   BEER 37:27
l. for the sacred Emperor   BRAM 91:18
l. one way   BUNY 107:18
May I be l. at you   TIB 550:34
she was l. all the time   THOM 547:11
They all were l. for a king   MACD 325:4
With l. on his life   SHAK 421:32
would not be l. for Me   PASC 369:13

looking forward: have not been l.
    HOR 258:16

looking-glass: court an amorous l.
    SHAK 480:18
cracked l. of a servant   JOYCE 286:21
dreams and dreams their l.   YEATS 587:1
smiles, As in a l.   SHAK 491:9

looks: full assurance given by l.   ROYD 411:2
her l. went everywhere   BROW 102:22
His l. adorn'd the venerable   GOLD 230:24
I have no proud l.   PRAY 398:25
Stolen l. are nice in chapels   HUNT 268:11
that would those l. reprove   GOLD 230:17
woman as old as she l.   COLL 158:15

loom: she left the l.   TENN 538:11

loomp: poor in a l. is bad   TENN 541:2

looms: passage through these l.   VAUG 555:10

loon: grey-beard l.   COL 155:6
thou cream-faced l.   SHAK 463:1

loo paper: When the l. gets thicker
    MITF 352:25

loopholes: through l. Less than themselves
    TESS 545:3
through the l. of retreat   COWP 167:12

loore: Cristes l. and his apostles   CHAU 142:3

loos'd: l. our heart in tears   ARN 13:17

loose: all hell broke l.   MILT 348:11
l. from every honourable   BURKE 108:23
l. gown from her shoulders   WYATT 583:22
l. the bands of Orion   BIBLE 53:5
l. the bands of wickedness   BIBLE 60:4
L. types of things through   WORD 582:26
Put me into something l.   PIN 373:16
to l. the seals thereof   BIBLE 81:26
wear those things so l.   BARH 33:23

loosen: Until God l. over sea   SWIN 530:19

lops: l. the moulder'd branch   TENN 533:26

loquendi: *est et ius et norma l.*   HOR 257:14

Lord: acceptable year of the L.   BIBLE 60:8
became l. of the ascendant   BURKE 109:6
Because you are a great l.   BEAU 35:18
cometh in the Name of the L.   PRAY 398:3
day of the L. is near   BIBLE 61:17
day which the L. hath made   PRAY 398:2
died by the hand of the L.   BIBLE 47:23
doth the L. require of thee   BIBLE 61:25
earth is the L.'s   BIBLE 76:11
earth is the L.'s   PRAY 390:23
Even the L. of hosts   PRAY 391:1
fear and nurture of the L.   PRAY 389:1
Forgive, O L.   FROST 219:7
glory of the L. shall be   BIBLE 59:5
Good L.   PRAY 385:16
Great l. of all things   POPE 379:13
in the house of the L.   PRAY 390:22
into the hands of the L.   BIBLE 62:22
into the house of the L.   PRAY 398:11
In whom the 'L. of Hosts'   HERB 246:25
kiss my L. before I die   MARL 330:13
knowed the L. was nigher   LOW 319:6
knowledge of the L.   BIBLE 58:11
lesson which the L. us taught   SPEN 515:18
let a l. once own the happy   POPE 378:25
L. and Lady Dalhousie   MCG 325:5
L. Archbishop of Rheims   BARH 33:11
L., art more than they   TENN 535:31
L., behold us with Thy   BUCK 106:16
L. be with thee   BIBLE 50:10
L., dismiss us with Thy   BUCK 106:17
L., dost thou wash my   BIBLE 72:27
L. guards the city   BIBLE 83:12
L. has built the house   BIBLE 83:12
L. hath not spoken by me   BIBLE 51:20
L., have mercy upon us   PRAY 384:18
L., how long   BIBLE 58:2
L. is a man of war   BIBLE 47:22
L. is King   PRAY 395:24
L. is my light   PRAY 391:7
L. is my shepherd   PRAY 390:21
L. is the source of my   BIBLE 83:5
L. let the house of a brute   TENN 532:22
L. looketh on the heart   BIBLE 50:6
L. loveth he chasteneth   BIBLE 80:1
L. make his face shine   BIBLE 48:9
L., make me coy and tender   HERB 248:14
L. mighty in battle   PRAY 390:24
L. No Zoo   DICK 178:29
l. of folded arms   SHAK 456:26
L. of himself   WOTT 583:13
L. OF LORDS   BIBLE 82:26
L. of our far-flung battle-line   KIPL 302:7
L. of thy presence   SHAK 452:8
Lord our God is one L.   BIBLE 48:20
L. prefers common-looking   LINC 315:5
L., remember me when thou   BIBLE 71:12
L. said unto my Lord   PRAY 397:11
L.'s anointed temple   SHAK 460:22
L. set a mark upon Cain   BIBLE 45:28
L. shall bring again Zion   BIBLE 59:19
L.'s my shepherd   SCOT 419:5
l., thy king, thy governor   SHAK 484:15
L. turned   BIBLE 71:9
L. watch between me   BIBLE 46:22
L., what fools these mortals   SHAK 470:21
L. will be there and wait   WHIT 571:2
L., with what care Thou   HERB 248:10
Love is our L.'s meaning   JUL 286:33
married My L. you   POUND 383:16
mouth of the L. hath spoken   BIBLE 59:5
of the coming of the L.   HOWE 266:19
of the mouth of the L.   BIBLE 48:22
of those who love the L.   HUNT 268:4
O L., to what a state   TER 544:20
patience of hope in our L.   BIBLE 78:30
Prepare ye the way of the L.   BIBLE 59:5
Prepare ye the way of the L.   BIBLE 63:36
Rejoice in the L. alway   BIBLE 78:20
remembrance of his dying L.   SPEN 515:31
Sae let the L. be thankit   BURNS 114:14
sapient sutlers of the L.   ELIOT 204:1
Seek ye the L. while he   BIBLE 59:26
servant above his l.   BIBLE 65:34
shall we sing the L.'s song   PRAY 399:3
So love is L. of all   SPEN 515:22
sought the L. aright   BURNS 113:6
soul doth magnify the L.   BIBLE 69:5
Spirit on the L.'s day   BIBLE 81:11
tasted that the L. is gracious   BIBLE 80:22
They have taken away my L.   BIBLE 73:7
'twur the will o' the L.   TENN 544:5
unhouse and house the L.   HOPK 256:16
wait upon the L. shall renew   BIBLE 59:10
Welcum the L. of lycht   DOUG 191:5
we own thee L.   ANON 11:3
what hour your L. doth come   BIBLE 68:1

Lord Jesus: Even so, come, L.   BIBLE 83:4

lordliest: l. lass of earth   BROO 94:16
Whoe'er lived in life most l.   POUND 383:19

Lord Lilac: L. thought it rather rotten
    CHES 147:15

Lord Primate: served the L. on bended
knee   BARH 33:11

Lord Randal: L., my Son   BALL 31:5

lords: About the l. of the creation
    BURNS 115:26
is only a wit among L.   JOHN 274:9
l. and our forefathers   SWIN 530:7
L. are lordliest in their   MILT 350:27
l. have their pleasures   MONT 355:7
L. of Convention 'twas   SCOTT 415:20
l. of human kind pass   GOLD 231:28
L. too are bards   BYRON 124:27
l. who lay you low   SHEL 504:2
l. whose parents were   DEFOE 173:14
Scots l. at his feet   BALL 31:20
They are the l. and owners   SHAK 494:15
thither from the House of L.   NORF 364:1

lordships: good enough for their l.   ANON 8:8

Lord Tomnoddy: my L. went home to
bed   BARH 33:9

lore: all the l. its scholars	KEBLE 295:5	
lose: day you may l. them all'	LEAR 312:17	
findeth his life shall l.	BIBLE 65:40	
hope and nothing to l.	BURKE 110:8	
I love to l. myself	LAMB 307:16	
is nothing much to l.	HOUS 266:3	
l., and start again	KIPL 300:1	
l. a volume to C carries	LAMB 307:15	
l. his own soul	BIBLE 66:35	
l. his own soul	BIBLE 68:34	
l. it that do buy it with	SHAK 465:9	
l. my heart in summer's	HOUS 266:4	
l. myself in dotage	SHAK 421:17	
l. our teeth and eyelashes	LEAR 312:24	
l. our ventures	SHAK 451:27	
l. the name of action	SHAK 433:8	
l., Though full of pain	MILT 346:10	
l. to-morrow the ground	ARN 14:17	
No man can l. what he never	WALT 564:8	
power and to l. liberty	BACON 26:22	
to l. itself in the sky	BROW 98:20	
to l. myself in a mystery	BROW 96:9	
To l. one parent	WILDE 573:1	
to l. thee were to lose	MILT 349:20	
To win or l. it all	GRAH 233:14	
way to l. him	SHAK 421:24	
losers: all are l.	CHAM 139:8	
So both should l. be	HERB 248:7	
loses: l. his misery	ARN 14:22	
Who l., and who wins	SHAK 456:3	
losest: fear thou l. all	HERB 248:12	
losing: conduct of a l. party	BURKE 111:27	
Hath but a l. office	SHAK 441:2	
l. a battle is to gain	WELL 567:25	
L. both beauty and utility	SHAK 445:12	
l. one pleased Cato	LUCAN 319:22	
Still l. when I saw myself	SHAK 495:6	
loss: black as our l.	SITW 508:13	
breathe a word about your l.	KIPL 300:1	
counted l. for Christ	BIBLE 78:17	
deeper sense of her l.	GASK 222:3	
enow To do our country l.	SHAK 445:1	
'Our day is our l.	AUDEN 20:15	
perhaps neither gain nor l.	ELIOT 202:24	
profit and l.	ELIOT 205:6	
upon thy so sore l.	THOM 548:25	
When a man's l. comes	BROW 100:10	
losses: l. are restor'd and sorrows	SHAK 493:7	
lost: All is not l.	MILT 345:3	
are l. in the storm	ARN 14:9	
are paradises we have l.	PROU 402:1	
battles are l. in the same	WHIT 570:20	
better to have fought and l.	CLOU 154:2	
better to have loved and l.	TENN 536:16	
found my sheep which was l.	BIBLE 70:16	
Hath l. me in your liking	SHAK 453:6	
having l. but once your prime	HERR 250:6	
Hearts that have l. their	HOUS 265:9	
He is l. to the forest	SCOTT 106:15	
He sought, For his l. heart	SHEL 504:5	
him was almost l. in Art	COLL 158:23	
Home of l. causes	ARN 15:25	
horse the rider was l.	FRAN 218:6	
I have l. a day	TITUS 551:6	
I have l. all the names	JOHN 278:31	
I long ago l. a hound	THOR 550:8	
Is the year only l.	HERB 247:14	
itself shall not be l.	FRAN 218:20	
Life we have l. in living	ELIOT 202:3	
l., and is found	BIBLE 70:21	
l. an Empire and has not	ACH 1:4	
l. but the son of perdition	BIBLE 72:42	
l. evermore in the main	TENN 543:5	
L. in the quagmire	TENN 534:22	
l. sheep of the house	BIBLE 65:30	
l., that is unsought	CHAU 144:3	
l. the last of England	BELL 40:16	
l. thing could I never	BELL 40:10	
l. to love and truth	BURNS 113:7	
l. to me	BARH 33:8	

l. traveller's dream	BLAKE 86:1	
love it and be l. like	HOUS 262:21	
make wherever we're l.	FRY 220:3	
my bosom and be l. in me	TENN 542:14	
next to a battle l.	WELL 567:27	
Not l. but gone before	NORT 364:8	
Praising what is l.	SHAK 421:5	
recover what has been l.	ELIOT 202:24	
see is lost let it be l.	CAT 136:27	
see your country is l.	WILL 574:8	
Something l. behind	KIPL 299:2	
so that I have l. my edifice	SHAK 469:9	
than never to have l.	BUTL 119:16	
That all was l.	MILT 349:16	
that deliberates is l.	ADD 1:20	
that nothing be l.	BIBLE 72:5	
that Old England is l.	JOHN 277:12	
they're l. to us and counted	MART 331:11	
Though lovers be l. love	THOM 546:19	
treacle is l. in the sweets	GAY 222:30	
we are l. to Love and Truth	KIPL 299:11	
When all is l.	BYRON 125:10	
who have l. their queen	FRY 220:7	
who l. in stormy visions	SHEL 499:20	
who l. the world for love	DRYD 197:8	
whom you so long have l.	WORD 577:23	
yet so l. in lexicography	JOHN 281:6	
You're all a l. generation	STEIN 518:18	
lot: cast my l. in an island	DICK 183:7	
l. has fallen to me	KIPL 303:16	
l. is fallen unto me	PRAY 390:6	
Our loving l. was cast	HOOD 254:8	
policeman's l. is not	GILB 228:19	
Remember L.'s wife	BIBLE 70:32	
Lothario: gay L.	ROWE 410:22	
That false L.	ROWE 410:19	
Lothbury: vapour through L. glide		
	WORD 581:3	
Lotos: L. and lilies	TENN 541:18	
lots: cast l. upon my vesture	PRAY 390:20	
Gathering fuel in vacant l.	ELIOT 204:8	
So they cast l.	BIBLE 61:21	
lotus: like l.-buds that float	HOPE 256:4	
Lou: lady that's known as L.	SERV 420:14	
loud: him upon the l. cymbals	PRAY 400:1	
in the senate l.	CHUR 149:5	
l. and troublesome *insects*	BURKE 111:16	
will and yet was never l.	SHAK 474:18	
louder: l. he talked of his honour	EMER 207:8	
loue: doughterly l. and deere charitie		
	MORE 357:20	
Louis Philippe: L. far better than a		
Napoleon	BAG 28:25	
Lounjun: L. 'roun' en suffer'n'	HARR 242:21	
louse: between a l. and a flea	JOHN 279:8	
l. for the hangman	JONS 284:4	
l. in the locks of literature	TENN 544:13	
louts: oafish l. remember Mum	BETJ 42:8	
lov'd: Had we never l. sae kindly		
	BURNS 112:29	
heart that has truly l.	MOORE 356:5	
He dearly l. the lasses	BURNS 114:3	
I l. Ophelia	SHAK 437:8	
l. not at first sight	SHAK 426:19	
most l., despis'd	SHAK 453:8	
nor no man ever l.	SHAK 495:5	
Shall never be by woman l.	BLAKE 85:12	
She who has never l.	GAY 223:2	
sour to them that l. him	SHAK 447:21	
therefore must be l.	SHAK 486:15	
Thou hast not l.	SHAK 425:10	
till we l.	DONNE 188:29	
We l. the doctrine	DEFOE 173:3	
who never l. before	ANON 10:11	
love: all for l. and a little	DIBD 175:16	
all for l.	SPEN 516:12	
All l. at first	BUTL 118:17	
All l. is lost but upon	DUNB 199:13	
all men all earth to l.	KIPL 303:16	
All who deserve his l.	DRYD 196:3	

ape the magnanimity of l.	MER 337:6	
are beautiful through l.	SHEL 503:13	
are but ministers of L.	COL 157:2	
are l. not a gaping pig	SHAK 467:21	
arms of my true l.	TENN 540:13	
aside a long-cherished l.	CAT 137:10	
As woman's l.	SHAK 434:10	
beautiful than thy first l.	YEATS 584:23	
beauty and l. lay bare	SHEL 503:23	
Because my l. is come	ROSS 408:23	
Because we freely l.	MILT 348:20	
be in l. with his fetters	BACON 27:42	
be my l.	DONNE 187:24	
be my l.	MARL 329:23	
be wroth with one we l.	COL 156:4	
bid me l.	HERR 249:25	
boy's l.	SHAK 454:28	
breastplate of faith and l.	BIBLE 79:2	
bring those who l. Thee	TER 544:20	
can l. freedom heartily	MILT 352:17	
cantons of contemned l.	SHAK 488:13	
carry a letter to my l.	BALL 30:20	
comely in nothing but in l.	BACON 26:29	
compliments and—and l.	AUST 22:27	
constancy of the women who l.	SHAW 498:9	
content with a vegetable l.	GILB 227:23	
corner in the thing I l.	SHAK 475:21	
cruel madness of l.	TENN 539:29	
day and a night L. sang	SWIN 528:24	
Deep as first l.	TENN 542:4	
dinner of herbs where l.	BIBLE 54:6	
do not fall in l. with me	SHAK 426:18	
Dreaming like a l.-adept	SHEL 503:5	
drew them…with bands of l.	BIBLE 61:12	
earth could never living l.	ANON 5:14	
Ends all our month-long l.	BRID 92:11	
Eternity is in l. with	BLAKE 88:17	
ever wilt thou l.	KEATS 291:5	
Except for l.'s sake only	BROW 98:11	
faith and labour of l.	BIBLE 78:30	
far from the lips we l.	MOORE 356:19	
fathom deep I am in l.	SHAK 426:24	
fickleness of the women I l.	SHAW 498:9	
fit l. for Gods	MILT 349:14	
fitter L. for me	DONNE 190:7	
flowers and fruits of l.	BYRON 125:11	
fool of l.	HAZL 243:8	
Forgets the shows of l.	SHAK 448:11	
Frail as thy l.	PEAC 371:1	
Friendship is L. without	BYRON 124:37	
From too much l. of living	SWIN 529:25	
fruit of the Spirit is l.	BIBLE 77:18	
gasp of L.'s latest breath	DRAY 193:21	
Gather the Rose of l.	SPEN 516:13	
gin l. be bonnie	BALL 32:10	
Give to me the life I l.	STEV 522:27	
give up my darling's l.	ANON 9:17	
God gives us l.	TENN 543:14	
godly l.	PRAY 387:13	
God of l. my Shepherd	HERB 248:13	
God si L.	FORS 217:9	
good man's l.	SHAK 426:17	
good to them that l. God	BIBLE 75:11	
Greater l. hath no man	BIBLE 72:36	
greatness on her subjects' l.	PRIOR 401:3	
green and happy in first l.	CLOU 153:23	
Hail wedded l.	MILT 348:8	
hast left thy first l.	BIBLE 81:16	
hate all that don't l.	FARQ 210:11	
hearts such l. toward thee	PRAY 386:18	
help those we l. to escape	HUGEL 267:5	
herald of l.'s mighty king	SPEN 515:19	
herself she will not l.	SUCK 524:7	
hid in the heart of l.	YEATS 586:9	
His banner over me was l.	BIBLE 56:20	
his dark secret l.	BLAKE 87:12	
his for his l.	SHAK 493:8	
honeying and making l.	SHAK 435:10	
How do I l. thee	BROW 98:13	
how I fell in l.	VIRG 560:4	

l. those who love you — VOLT 561:11
L., thou art absolute — CRAS 169:5
l. thy neighbour as thyself — BIBLE 48:8
L. thyself last — SHAK 447:12
l. to all men 'neath — KIPL 298:12
L. warps the mind a little — COWP 168:25
L. was dead — SWIN 529:19
l., was thought a crime — BLAKE 87:17
L. watching Madness with — BYRON 121:7
l. we bear one another — BETJ 43:4
l. were what the rose is — SWIN 530:21
L. what hours were thine — TENN 533:5
l. which consists in this — RILKE 406:5
l. will change in growing — BRID 92:20
l. will yield to business — OVID 366:21
L. wist to pursue — THOM 548:11
l. with a cold climate — SOUT 514:18
l. with handsome Alexis — VIRG 559:14
L. wol nat been constreyned — CHAU 142:12
L. would prove so hard — BRID 92:22
l. you for yourself alone — YEATS 585:5
l. your crooked neighbour — AUDEN 18:11
L. your enemies — BIBLE 69:21
l. your neighbour's wife — MAC 324:3
l. you till the ocean Is — AUDEN 18:9
lyric L. — BROW 104:19
makes thy l. more strong — SHAK 494:8
making l. all year round — BEAU 35:17
making l. is child's play — MITF 352:26
Marriage from l., like vinegar — BYRON 122:26
marry your old friend's l. — BROW 105:17
medicines to make me l. — SHAK 438:24
Men l. in haste — BYRON 123:38
mighty l. — HERB 248:3
mind where people make l. — CAMP 128:8
mischievous devil L. — BUTL 119:2
more l. or more disdain — CAREW 130:16
more of l. than matrimony — GOLD 232:39
more than over shoes in l. — SHAK 490:29
music be the food of l. — SHAK 487:20
My l. and I would lie — HOUS 263:4
My l. for Heathcliff resembles — BRON 93:25
My l. has died for me to-day — BALL 30:12
My l. is of a birth — MARV 331:18
my l. is slain — DONNE 188:12
my l. no whit disdaineth — SHAK 493:10
My l.'s a noble madness — DRYD 196:31
My l. to thee is sound — SHAK 457:16
My only l. sprung from — SHAK 482:4
my part I l. them all — MELB 336:20
Mysterious of connubial l. — MILT 348:7
My true l. hath my heart — SIDN 507:16
my true l. said — PEELE 371:9
My vegetable l. should — MARV 332:18
names of those who l. — HUNT 268:4
Nature is fine in l. — SHAK 436:8
Need we say it was not l. — MILL 340:1
ne'er knew l.'s sad satiety — SHEL 504:22
never doubt I l. — SHAK 431:35
never had but one true l. — BALL 32:9
never taint my l. — SHAK 476:24
new l. may get — WALSH 563:28
Now I know what L. is — VIRG 560:5
Now with his l. — CHAU 142:22
obscure epistles of l. — SHAK 488:23
office and affairs of l. — SHAK 472:7
Of kindness and of l. — WORD 578:4
Of l. and all its smart — BEDD 36:23
O L., the interest — AUDEN 20:6
One of l.'s April-fools — CONG 160:18
Only our l. hath no decay — DONNE 187:23
ounce of l. is worth — WESL 568:23
Our l. shall live — SPEN 515:20
out a flag and sign of l. — SHAK 473:19
oyster may be crossed in l. — SHER 506:4
Pains of l. be sweeter — DRYD 197:36
pangs of disappointed l. — ROWE 410:21
pangs of dispriz'd l. — SHAK 433:8
particular l.'s sake — BROW 104:22
passing the l. of women — BIBLE 50:17

perfect ceremony of l.'s — SHAK 493:2
perfect l. casteth out — BIBLE 81:6
planet of L. is on high — TENN 540:9
Poets' food is l. and fame — SHEL 500:14
Poor heretics in l. there — DONNE 189:18
possible to l. such a man — CHES 145:32
presume too much upon my l. — SHAK 451:19
Prosperity's the very bond of l. — SHAK 492:6
prov'd thee my best of l. — SHAK 495:3
purple light of l. — GRAY 235:17
putting l. away — DICK 183:17
regain L. once possess'd — MILT 350:25
Regent of l. rhymes — SHAK 456:26
remembrance of my former l. — SHAK 490:34
respectful l. — BURKE 111:9
right place for l. — FROST 219:1
right to dissemble your l. — BICK 83:27
right true end of l. — DONNE 188:13
separate us from the l. of God — BIBLE 75:13
service of my l. — SPR 517:10
shackles of an old l. straiten'd — TENN 534:29
She never told her l. — SHAK 489:7
should I your true l. know — SHAK 435:32
show of l. as I was wont — SHAK 448:10
silence was the song of l. — ROSS 409:24
sit down,' says L. — HERB 248:1
soft interpreters of l. — PRIOR 400:26
soft philosopher of l. — DRYD 196:31
some are fou o' l. divine — BURNS 114:9
some l. but little policy — SHAK 480:9
So true a fool is l. that — SHAK 493:18
spirit of l. — SHAK 487:20
sports of l. — JONS 285:12
spring of l. gushed from — COL 155:22
still make l. anew — SEDL 419:14
stony limits cannot hold l. — SHAK 482:10
subject but eternal L. — SHEL 503:10
substance of his house for l. — BIBLE 57:12
swear thou think'st I l. — DONNE 190:14
Sweet L. of youth — BRON 93:23
sweets and the bitters of l. — BYRON 124:38
take our fill of l. — BIBLE 53:24
tell me the truth about l. — AUDEN 21:2
temple gates unto my l. — SPEN 515:25
Than to l. and be loved — POE 374:21
That ever l. did make thee — SHAK 425:10
that I am sick of l. — BIBLE 57:2
'That is l.'s curse — TENN 534:33
That leads me from my l. — HOUS 263:20
That l. had been sae ill — BALL 32:11
that l. lightly may die — SWIN 529:19
That l. my friend — SHAK 451:1
that they l. — WALL 562:16
Then must the l. be great — BARN 34:2
then they dream of l. — SHAK 481:28
there my l. will live — CLARE 152:10
There's beggary in the l. — SHAK 421:7
There shall be no l. lost — JONS 284:9
there's no l. lost between — GOLD 232:30
they idealize l. too much — JOW 285:24
They l. indeed who quake — SIDN 507:23
They l. the Good — BROO 94:24
They l. us for it — TENN 542:8
They sin who tell us l. — SOUT 513:26
think of one's absent l. — TROL 553:9
this youth what 'tis to l. — SHAK 426:29
thou car'st not whom I l. — DONNE 189:10
Through l., through hope — WORD 581:5
through our l. — MAL 328:3
thy l. is better than wine — BIBLE 56:15
thy sweet l. remember'd — SHAK 493:6
till l.'s emulous ardours — ROSS 409:22
time to l. — BIBLE 55:12
'tis the hour of l. — BYRON 123:8
To be wise, and l. — SHAK 487:1
To be wise and eke to l. — SPEN 517:2
To business that we l. — SHAK 422:24
to go with the man I l. — BREC 91:26
To let the warm L. — KEATS 292:4
To live is like to l. — BUTL 119:3

to l. one another — BIBLE 75:22
To l. one maiden only — TENN 534:12
To l. you was pleasant — MOORE 356:24
to make us l. one another — SWIFT 527:7
to manage l. — BUTL 118:15
Too late came I to l. thee — AUG 21:16
To see her is to l. her — BURNS 112:37
to see her was to l. her — BURNS 112:28
To tell the laity our l. — DONNE 190:17
True L. in this differs — SHEL 500:11
Turning mortal for thy l. — SHAK 457:5
turns to thoughts of l. — TENN 538:17
'Twixt women's l. — DONNE 187:22
two from my first l. — VAUG 555:14
us l. your goodly gifts — SHAK 478:5
vanity and l. — CHES 145:29
vanity, sets l. a task — HUNT 268:8
very ecstasy of l. — SHAK 431:29
very few to l. — WORD 581:6
want l.'s majesty — SHAK 480:18
wanton Shrewsbury and l. — POPE 378:1
warrior that is rapt with l. — MARL 330:11
Was there l. once — NICH 362:24
wayward is this foolish l. — SHAK 490:31
We all l. a pretty girl — BICK 84:2
We l. being in love — THAC 545:8
we l. but while we may — TENN 534:34
we l. our House of Peers — GILB 228:23
We l. the precepts — FARQ 210:13
were sooner allured by l. — ASCH 17:1
Werther had a l. for Charlotte — THAC 546:3
We thought that l. could — BRID 92:20
What is commonly called l. — FIEL 211:25
what is l.? I pray thee — RAL 404:8
What is l. — SHAK 488:17
What l. I bore to thee — WORD 577:28
What l. is — HALM 238:10
What l. of thine own kind — SHEL 504:1
What's death? You'll l. — BROW 103:24
What thing is l. for (well — PEELE 371:7
when I l. thee not — SHAK 475:14
when I was in l. with you — HOUS 263:1
when l. and duty clash — TENN 541:29
When l. begins to sicken — SHAK 451:11
When l., converted — SHAK 493:14
When l. grows diseas'd — ETH 208:29
when L. speaks — SHAK 457:8
When L. with unconfined — LOV 318:15
When my l. swears that — SHAK 495:11
where I cannot l. — BEHN 38:14
Where I marry, cannot l. — MOORE 356:22
Where l. is enthron'd — SHAK 488:27
where there is no l. — BACON 26:15
which l. colour the most — RUSK 411:24
who have courage to l. — TROL 552:19
'Whom the gods l. die young' — BYRON 123:11
whose l., never strained — HOR 259:21
wilder shores of l. — BLAN 88:30
will not l. his country — SHAK 450:16
Wilt thou l. her — PRAY 389:3
wise want l. — SHEL 503:2
with the innocence of l. — SHAK 489:3
With which my l. should — SPEN 515:27
woman wakes to l. — TENN 535:9
world and l. were young — RAL 404:9
worst that l. could do — DONNE 189:26
wrapt inflections of our l. — CRANE 168:31
ye love them which l. you — BIBLE 64:20
yet I have not all thy l. — DONNE 189:24
yet I l. her till I die — ANON 8:1
You all did l. him once — SHAK 450:21
You cannot call it l. — SHAK 435:8
your true l.'s coming — SHAK 488:17
loved: better to have l. and lost — TENN 536:16
disciples, whom Jesus l. — BIBLE 72:28
disciple whom Jesus l. — BIBLE 73:18
forgiven; for she l. much — BIBLE 69:24
God so l. the world — BIBLE 71:38
he l. the time too well — CLARE 152:4
himself to be quite l. — TROL 553:6

I l. a lass WITH 575:13
I l. thee once AYT 24:4
I l. you, so I drew LAWR 311:12
Indeed the Idols I have l. FITZ 213:13
I saw and l. GIBB 224:12
Israel l. Joseph BIBLE 46:26
lad That I l. bodily YEATS 585:20
Lesbia whom Catullus once l. CAT 137:5
l. each other beyond belief HEINE 244:10
l. not at first sight MARL 329:18
l. one all together BROW 102:24
l., sir—used to meet BROW 100:8
l. so slight a thing TENN 539:4
l. the bailiff's daughter BALL 30:7
l. Three whole days together SUCK 524:14
men who have l. them TROL 553:10
Might she have l. me BROW 101:24
more I l. my homeland BELL 40:17
no sooner l. but they sighed SHAK 426:27
Not that I l. Caesar less SHAK 450:14
only know we l. in vain BYRON 124:34
our endeavour be so l. SHAK 487:19
Pale hands I l. HOPE 256:3
pressed to say why I l. him MONT 354:18
say the lad that l. you HOUS 266:2
She had been l. WOOLF 576:18
Solomon l. many strange women BIBLE 51:1
so young, I l. him so BROW 99:16
than never to have been l. CONG 160:35
that all we l. of him should SHEL 499:12
that once if I l. you well SWIN 530:20
thrice had I l. thee DONNE 187:18
'Tis better to have l. BUTL 119:16
use him as though you l. WALT 564:9
Wel l. he garleek CHAU 142:5
We that had l. him so BROW 102:5
When you l. me I gave you SHAW 496:29
which he l. passing well SHAK 432:21
Which I have l. long since NEWM 362:15
Whilst loving thou mayst l. SPEN 516:13
love-joy: l., oh! weakness of joy BETJ 44:6
Love-in-idleness: maidens call it, L.
                                                  SHAK 470:8
love-knot: Plaiting a dark red l. NOYES 364:13
loveliest: l. and best FITZ 212:17
l. fairy in the world KING 297:12
L. of trees HOUS 262:14
world the l. and the best BELL 39:30
Love-light: L. of Spain CHES 147:3
loveliness: Enough their simple l. for
me KEATS 292:16
Glory and l. have pass'd KEATS 292:26
Her l. I never knew COL 154:26
I am weak from your l. BETJ 44:6
is a portion of the l. SHEL 499:24
Its l. increases KEATS 288:20
l. and the hour of my death KEATS 294:21
l. Needs not THOM 549:17
They saw a Dream of L. LEL 313:18
woman of so shining l. YEATS 586:17
Lovell: Cat, the Rat, and L. COLL 158:10
love-locks: going with your l. flowing
                                                  ROSS 408:21
lovely: down in l. muck I've lain HOUS 264:13
it's a l. thing MOL 353:5
Lap from some once l. Head FITZ 212:15
l. and a fearful thing BYRON 122:24
l. April of her prime SHAK 492:24
L. are the curves MER 337:3
l. is the rose WORD 578:22
L. lads and dead and rotten HOUS 263:19
l. rice pudding for dinner MILNE 340:10
l. way that led HOUS 265:4
l. woman stoops to folly ELIOT 205:3
l. woman stoops to folly GOLD 231:31
more l. and more temperate SHAK 492:28
whatsoever things are l. BIBLE 78:22
Which once he made more l. SHEL 499:24
you have l. hair CHEK 145:6

love-lyrics: account I write so many l.
                                                  POUND 382:15
love-making: which is the l. BACON 27:31
Love Powders: rogue gives you L.
                                                  LAMB 307:30
Love-quarrels: L. oft in pleasing concord
                                                  MILT 350:26
lover: affliction taught a l. POPE 376:12
days dividing lover and l. SWIN 528:17
give repentance to her l. GOLD 231:31
injured l.'s hell MILT 348:19
Into a L.'s head WORD 582:21
I sighed as a l. GIBB 224:13
It was a l. and his lass SHAK 427:2
lived she was a true l. MAL 328:2
l. and killer are mingled DOUG 191:10
l. and sensualist HENL 245:12
l., and the poet SHAK 471:11
l. of literature is never SOUT 514:14
l.'s eyes will gaze SHAK 457:8
l., Sighing like furnace SHAK 425:24
l. true for whom I pine WHIT 571:2
magnetic, Peripatetic L. GILB 227:24
my fause l. stole my rose BURNS 116:8
one was round her l. CAMP 129:4
passion woman loves her l. BYRON 122:25
propositions of a l. SHAK 426:8
roaming l. CALL 127:7
says to her lusting l. CAT 137:7
searching for a new l. CONN 161:13
since I cannot prove a l. SHAK 480:19
Such a constant l. SUCK 524:14
Suff'ring is the l.'s part GAY 222:9
that is in any manner a l. MAL 328:1
thou wast as true a l. SHAK 425:9
Titan-woman like a l. SWIN 528:26
Who could deceive a l. VIRG 558:12
with some old l.'s ghost DONNE 189:25
you l. of trees BROW 100:12
Your brother and his l. SHAK 463:13
lovers: All but the pieties of l.' CRANE 168:31
Almighty l. in the spring CHES 146:18
At l.' perjuries SHAK 482:13
even l. find their peace FLEC 214:10
I am all true l. are SHAK 488:27
Journeys end in l. meeting SHAK 488:17
laughs at l.' perjury DRYD 197:7
laughs at l.' perjuries OVID 366:11
l.' absent hours SHAK 476:6
l. be lost love shall not THOM 546:19
l. cannot see SHAK 466:14
L. can see to do their SHAK 483:6
l.' ears in hearing SCOTT 416:26
l.' eyes are sharp SCOTT 416:26
l. fled away into the storm KEATS 289:23
l.' hours be full eternity DONNE 189:21
l., just at twelve, awake POPE 380:29
l. must Consign to thee SHAK 428:22
L.' rows make love whole TER 544:15
L., to bed SHAK 471:20
make two l. happy POPE 380:22
motions l.' seasons run DONNE 190:11
old l. are soundest WEBS 566:30
pair of star-cross'd l. SHAK 481:20
Thy l. were all untrue DRYD 197:19
timid l.' declarations AUDEN 20:2
two young l. lately wed TENN 538:7
We that are true l. SHAK 425:11
What need l. wish for more SEDL 419:11
Loves: all the wings of the L. SWIN 530:4
any severing of our l. WORD 579:13
ar'n't that I l. the fox less SURT 525:10
A-waiting for their ain dear l. BALL 31:20
believe the baggage l. CONG 160:17
Fierce wars and faithful l. SPEN 515:29
Friends and l. we have MAS 334:7
girl whom he almost l. TROL 553:6
grete god of L. name CHAU 143:26
Hated by one he l. SHAK 451:23
He l. us not SHAK 462:12

He that l. a rosy cheek CAREW 130:12
hours and all strange l. SWIN 528:26
I l. him at once SURT 525:6
lines so l. oblique may MARV 331:19
l. and comforts should SHAK 474:20
l. him still the better GOLD 232:9
l. into corpses or wives SWIN 529:10
l. of men HOUS 265:4
l. the meat in his youth SHAK 472:18
l. to be flattered is worthy SHAK 485:28
l. to hear himself talk SHAK 482:24
man kills the thing he l. WILDE 572:10
man l. what he is good SHAD 420:22
one l. His world so much BROW 103:22
one that l. his fellow-men HUNT 268:5
others all she l. is love BYRON 122:25
She l. me dearly KEATS 289:5
That l. and saves her soul BROW 99:6
There is no creature l. me SHAK 481:15
truly l. on to the close MOORE 356:5
who l. me must have a touch TENN 534:26
Who l. not woman LUTH 321:1
who l. nothing but himself SOUT 514:15
Love-sick: L. all against our will GILB 227:19
winds were l. with them SHAK 422:2
lovesome: garden is a l. thing BROWN 95:12
lovest: I love all that thou l. SHEL 503:26
l. thou me more that these BIBLE 73:14
What thou l. well POUND 382:12
loveth: He made and l. all COL 155:30
he that l. another hath BIBLE 75:22
Lord l. he correcteth BIBLE 53:15
Lord l. he chasteneth BIBLE 80:1
l. a cheerful giver BIBLE 77:9
l. and maketh a lie BIBLE 83:3
sought him whom my soul l. BIBLE 56:25
that l. not knoweth not God BIBLE 81:5
loving: heart be still as l. BYRON 125:25
in love with l. AUG 21:12
l. himself better than COL 157:18
l. longest, when existence AUST 23:10
l. thou mayst be loved be SPEN 516:13
man for l. himself BACON 27:8
most l. mere folly SHAK 426:1
night was made for l. BYRON 125:26
not stay the siege of l. SHAK 481:24
perfectly sane with l. DICK 178:1
so l. to my mother SHAK 429:28
too much l. you SHAK 475:19
who can help l. the land MOORE 356:2
wickedness that hinders l. BROW 102:31
loving-kindness: thy l. and mercy shall
                                                  PRAY 390:22
lov'st: Because thou l. the one BARN 34:2
low: condescend to men of l. estate
                                                  BIBLE 75:17
dost thou lie so l. SHAK 450:17
exalted them of l. degree BIBLE 69:6
hum of that l. land ARN 14:28
life in l. estate began TENN 537:1
l. estate of his handmaiden BIBLE 69:5
l. life was the level's BROW 100:33
l. on whom assurance sits ELIOT 205:1
Malice is of a l. stature HAL 238:2
Sweet and l. TENN 541:31
That l. man seeks a little BROW 100:38
to cast one's eyes so l. SHAK 455:14
Too l. for envy COWL 164:11
Lowells: L. talk only to Cabots BOSS 90:13
lowely: l., and servysable CHAU 141:13
Löwen: lachende L. müssen kommen
                                                  NIET 363:2
lower: if the l. orders don't WILDE 572:25
madest him l. than the angels PRAY 389:28
lowest: l. and most dejected thing SHAK 455:5
shame to take the l. room BIBLE 70:7
therefore the l. of the arts MOORE 355:17
Low-lands: she sails by the L. low BALL 31:2
lowliness: l. is young ambition's SHAK 449:5
lowly: I am meek and l. in heart BIBLE 66:5

in the l. air   GILB 226:5
low-voiced: ears the l. Best is killed
                                       HARDY 240:3
loyal: fruit Of l. nature   TENN 534:9
L. and neutral, in a moment   SHAK 461:2
loyalties: impossible l.   ARN 15:25
l. which centre upon number one
                                       CHUR 150:27
loyalty: learned body wanted l.   TRAPP 552:5
Lucan: L., and Stace   CHAU 144:17
Lucasta: L. that bright northern   LOV 318:13
Then my L. might I crave   LOV 318:19
lucem: sed ex fumo dare l.   HOR 257:19
lucid: l. intervals and happy   BACON 27:44
l. intervals of life   WORD 577:5
through and make a l. interval   DRYD 196:34
with frequent l. intervals   CERV 138:16
lúcidos: lleno de l. intervalos   CERV 138:16
Lucifer: he falls like L.   SHAK 447:9
L., son of the morning   BIBLE 58:13
L. that often warned them   MILT 344:7
spirits that fell with L.   MARL 329:6
starred night Prince L. uprose   MER 337:5
luck: Has he l.   NAP 359:16
have wished you good l.   PRAY 398:3
light in ragged l.   HENL 245:12
l. of our name lost with   HOR 261:13
L.'s a chance   HOUS 264:14
There's nae l. about the house   ANON 8:3
watching his l. was his   SERV 420:14
luckless: l. man   CAT 137:4
Lucky: L. to touch it   KIPL 302:19
supposed it l. to be born   WHIT 570:19
lucrative: l. business of mystery
                                       BURKE 108:12
lucre: not greedy of filthy l.   BIBLE 79:12
lucro: dierum cumque dabit l.   HOR 259:18
Lucy: 'If L. should be dead   WORD 582:21
When L. ceased to be   WORD 581:6
Luddites: quartern loaf and L. rise
                                       SMITH 510:7
Ludlow: hundreds to L. come   HOUS 263:6
I have been to L. fair   HOUS 264:13
lug: l. the guts into the neighbour
                                       SHAK 435:22
Lüge: Volkes...einer grossen L.   HITL 251:9
lugere: non l., neque detestare   SPIN 517:7
Lugete: L., O Veneres Cupidinesque
                                       CAT 136:22
lugger: forcing her on board the l.   JOHN 283:7
Luke: honour unto L. Evangelist   ROSS 410:1
L., the beloved physician   BIBLE 78:29
lukewarm: then because thou art l.
                                       BIBLE 81:20
Lukewarmness: L. I account a sin
                                       COWL 164:18
lull: l. in the hot race   ARN 12:22
lullaby: dreamy l.   GILB 226:18
I will sing a l.   DEKK 173:22
lull'd: l. with sound of sweetest   SHAK 441:29
Lulled: L. by the singer   MORR 358:9
lumber: loads of learned l.   POPE 378:30
l. of the schools   SWIFT 527:32
lumen: l. de lumine   MASS 334:20
luminous: beating in the void his l. wings
                                       ARN 16:10
l. home of waters   ARN 15:1
lump: leaveneth the whole l.   BIBLE 75:35
l. bred up in darkness   KYD 306:6
luna: te inferebatur sol et l.   AUG 21:13
lunae: celeres reparant caelestia l.
                                       HOR 261:16
Tacitae per amica silentia l.   VIRG 558:3
lunar: l. world securely pry   DRYD 195:23
lunatic: l., the lover   SHAK 471:11
reform movement has a l. fringe   ROOS 408:5
luncheon: dinner, l.   BROW 103:19
gentleman has soup at l.   CURZ 170:18
read a novel before l.   WAUGH 566:5
Lunching: L. with poets   BETJ 44:12

lune: l. ne garde aucune rancune   ELIOT 204:10
lungs: dangerous to the l.   JAM 271:3
even my l. are affected   BEAR 35:11
gold and l. of bronze   BELL 39:28
l. began to crow like chanticleer   SHAK 425:20
l. of London   PITT 374:2
Lupercal: On the L.   SHAK 450:20
Lupus: L. est homo homini   PLAU 374:13
lurcher: half l. and half cur   COWP 167:18
lure: l. it back to cancel half   FITZ 213:7
l. this tassel-gentle back   SHAK 482:19
lurid: It is l. and melodramatic   LAWR 311:11
luscious: now is as l. as locusts   SHAK 474:10
over-canopied with l. woodbine   SHAK 470:10
Lusisti: L. satis   HOR 259:6
lust: commanded l.   KIPL 300:6
Delight of l. is gross   PETR 373:5
horrible that l. and rage   YEATS 586:23
hutch of tasty l.   HOPK 256:15
into ashes all my l.   MARV 332:19
Is l. in action   SHAK 495:7
love is more cruel than l.   SWIN 529:10
L. der Zerstörung ist   BAK 29:24
l. of knowing what should   FLEC 214:14
l. of my mistress's heart   SHAK 454:18
l. of the goat is the bounty   BLAKE 88:21
narrowing l. of gold   TENN 537:15
That own no l. because   TENN 535:18
lusteth: man is he that l. to live   PRAY 391:23
lustily: sing praises l. unto him   PRAY 391:19
lusting: woman says to her l. lover   CAT 137:7
lustre: accomplishments give l.   CHES 145:31
Though changed in outward l.   MILT 345:2
Where is thy l. now   SHAK 455:4
lustres: six l. almost now outwore
                                       DONNE 189:36
lusts: Abstain from fleshly l.   BIBLE 80:24
led away with divers l.   BIBLE 79:24
l. of your father ye will   BIBLE 72:13
sinful l. of the flesh   PRAY 388:13
to fulfil the l. thereof   BIBLE 75:25
lust'st: hotly l. to use her   SHAK 455:19
lusty: flourisheth in l. deeds   MAL 328:1
l. stealth of nature   SHAK 453:9
Of l. folk   CHAU 143:20
young and l. as an eagle   PRAY 396:15
lute: awake, l. and harp   PRAY 393:16
bright Apollo's l.   SHAK 457:8
lascivious pleasing of a l.   SHAK 480:18
little rift within the l.   TENN 535:7
l. its tones   KEATS 289:3
merry harp with the l.   PRAY 395:9
My l., awake   WYATT 583:23
Orpheus with his l. made trees   SHAK 447:3
When the l. is broken   SHEL 501:21
When to her l. Corinna   CAMP 129:17
lutes: to l. of amber   HERR 250:9
Luther: Grand rough old Martin L.
                                       BROW 105:27
L.; the Philistine   ARN 16:23
Lutheran: spleeny L.   SHAK 447:5
luve: he was the Queen's l.   BALL 30:17
L.'s like a red red rose   BURNS 114:27
L. will venture   BURNS 114:33
lux: l. perpetua luceat eis   MASS 334:17
Luxe: L., calme et volupté   BAUD 35:7
luxuries: between l. and necessaries
                                       GALB 220:28
Give us the l. of life   MOTL 358:21
luxurious: damned and l. mountain goat
                                       SHAK 445:4
exquisite sense of the l.   KEATS 293:29
luxury: languages is mainly a l.   BRIG 93:8
Love is like any other l.   TROL 553:15
l., peace   BAUD 35:7
their l. was doing good   GARTH 221:20
They knew l.   MAC 324:6
thinks it l.   ADD 1:17
Lycid: laureate hearse where L.   MILT 343:15
Lycidas: L. is dead   MILT 343:2

So L. sunk low   MILT 343:17
Lydian: Lap me in soft L. airs   MILT 342:26
L. laughter of the Garda   TENN 533:18
waters of the L. lake   CAT 136:28
lye: wenen every thing a l.   CHAU 143:28
lyf: That l. so short   CHAU 143:32
lyght: hath reft the sonne his l.   CHAU 142:13
lying: are to this vice of l.   SHAK 442:9
l., and slandering   PRAY 388:17
l. awake with a dismal   GILB 226:12
not mind l.   BUTL 119:5
One of you is l.   PARK 368:19
this world is given to l.   SHAK 440:27
lym: brach or l.   SHAK 455:1
lynde: light as leef on l.   CHAU 142:11
Lynn: stern-faced men set out from L.
                                       HOOD 254:12
Lyonnesse: When I set out for L.
                                       HARDY 241:5
lyre: drive a tune through the l. POUND 382:15
hang my weapons and my l.   HOR 261:6
Make me thy l.   SHEL 502:13
'Omer smote 'is bloomin' l.   KIPL 304:4
lyres: sound of l. and flutes   PATER 369:19
turn to rhythmic tidal l.   HARDY 239:4
lyric: splendid ecclesiastical l.   DISR 186:7
lyricis: Quodsi me l. vatibus inseres
                                       HOR 259:10
lyve: worthy womman al hir l.   CHAU 141:31
M: N or M   PRAY 388:12
Mab: This is M.   JONS 284:15
Macaroni: called it M.   BANGS 32:16
Macaulay: cocksure of anything as Tom
M.   MELB 336:10
Lord M.   ARN 16:6
M. is well for a while   CARL 132:28
Macavity: there's no one like M.
                                       ELIOT 203:26
Macbeth: Brave M.   SHAK 458:3
M. does murder sleep   SHAK 460:8
M. shall sleep no more   SHAK 460:9
M. shall never vanquish'd   SHAK 462:8
Shall harm M.   SHAK 462:6
There to meet with M.   SHAK 458:1
Macduff: Lay on, M.   SHAK 463:9
M. was from his mother's   SHAK 463:8
mace: that fool's bauble, the m. CROM 169:25
Macedon: There is a river in M.   SHAK 445:5
Macedonia: Come over into M.   BIBLE 74:6
MacGregor: my name is M.   SCOTT 418:32
Machiavel: are much beholden to M.
                                       BACON 24:25
machine: body is a m. for living   TOLS 551:12
less of a taxing m.   LOWE 318:24
m. for converting the Heathen   CARL 131:6
maison est une m. à habiter   LE C 313:5
of the Ghost in the m.   RYLE 412:25
very pulse of the m.   WORD 581:8
you're a m.   SHAW 496:8
Machinery: It is the Age of M.   CARL 131:5
whole m. of the State   BROU 95:4
Mächte: ihr himmlischen M.   GOET 230:12
mackerel: m.-crowded seas   YEATS 586:11
Not so the m.   FRERE 218:25
mackintosh: bit of black m.   WELBY 567:1
mack'rel: blew a m. gale   DRYD 196:20
maculate: Swelling to m. giraffe
                                       ELIOT 204:14
mad: better than when I am m.   KYD 306:5
created the English m.   KIPL 300:14
destroy He first sends m.   DUP 199:15
drive me m. on my deathbed   BYRON 126:20
glad m. brother's   SWIN 529:2
half of the nation is m.   SMOL 512:12
has made me m. all my life   JOHN 279:33
heroically m.   DRYD 194:21
house for fools and m.   SWIFT 527:25
How m. I am   BETJ 44:6
I am but m. north-north-west   SHAK 432:18
I shall go m.   SHAK 454:2

it will make you m.	SHAK 450:25
laid to make the taker m.	SHAK 495:7
learning doth make thee m.	BIBLE 74:25
less m. on one point	KIPL 304:33
let me not be m.	SHAK 453:20
M. about the boy	COW 163:18
m. all are in God's keeping	KIPL 304:25
m. and savage master	SOPH 513:9
m., and sent into England	SHAK 436:30
m. as the vex'd sea	SHAK 455:13
M., bad	LAMB 306:25
M. dogs and Englishmen	COW 163:19
m. that trusts in the tameness	SHAK 454:28
m., 'tis true	SHAK 431:33
M. world	SHAK 452:13
Make m. the guilty	SHAK 433:1
makes men m.	SHAK 477:8
men that God made m.	CHES 146:17
nobly wild, not m.	HERR 249:13
old, m., blind	SHEL 504:6
sad and bad and m.	BROW 100:8
tends the grave of M. Carew	HAYES 243:7
this m., wicked folly	VICT 556:14
tho' some did count him m.	BUNY 107:34
to make poor females m.	SHAK 470:26
Went m. and bit the man	GOLD 231:13
when a heroine goes m.	SHER 506:3
Madagascar: There's Jerusalem and M.	THAC 546:2
Madam: M. I may not call you	ELIZ 205:28
madden: midden whose odours will m.	AUDEN 18:17
now m. to crime	BYRON 120:1
maddest: m. merriest day	TENN 540:20
m. of all mankind	KIPL 300:14
madding: Far from the m. crowd's	GRAY 235:1
made: All things were m. by him	BIBLE 71:22
almost m. for each other	SMITH 511:34
Begotten, not m.	PRAY 387:10
Dost thou know who m. thee	BLAKE 87:26
earth and the world were m.	PRAY 395:17
fearfully and wonderfully m.	PRAY 399:6
He m. and loveth all	COL 155:30
he m. the best of this	BURNS 113:26
In a world I never m.	HOUS 264:25
it is he that hath m. us	PRAY 396:11
knoweth whereof we are m.	PRAY 396:17
m. by the Lord Chancellor	JOHN 276:36
m. heaven and earth	PRAY 388:20
m. honest by an act	JONS 283:25
M. with our hands and our	SWIN 528:24
man was m. to mourn	BURNS 114:22
night was m. for loving	BYRON 125:26
see God m. and eaten	BROW 99:14
thinks he was not m. to die	TENN 535:30
which the Lord hath m.	PRAY 398:2
who m. the Lamb make thee	BLAKE 87:16
Why hast thou m. me thus	BIBLE 75:14
Madeira: M. and a cold capon's leg	SHAK 438:11
Madhouse: I am in a M. and quite	CLARE 152:17
in a m. there exists no	CLARE 152:7
Madhouses: M., prisons, whore-shops	CLARE 152:5
madman: If a m. were to come into	JOHN 277:1
m̀. shakes a dead geranium	ELIOT 204:9
Madmen: M. in authority	KEYN 295:20
of m. is a saint run mad	POPE 380:11
They were m.	REN 405:13
which none but m. know	DRYD 197:26
madness: always very close to m.	ALC 3:9
Anger is a short m.	HOR 258:15
any m. of their kings	HOR 258:12
cure for this sort of m.	BIRK 84:13
end despondency and m.	WORD 580:28
Even to m.	SHAK 474:22
fools accounted his life m.	BIBLE 62:16

from the cruel m. of love	TENN 539:29
Great wits are sure to m.	DRYD 194:6
His flight was m.	SHAK 462:11
His m. was not of the head	BYRON 125:2
it is m.	CONG 160:22
Love watching M. with unalterable	BYRON 121:7
m. and her weather still	AUDEN 19:6
m. is the glory of this	SHAK 486:4
m. of many for the gain	POPE 381:16
m. of the people	PRAY 394:1
m. wherein now he raves	SHAK 432:2
moon-struck m.	MILT 349:24
My love's a noble m.	DRYD 195:11
Such harmonious m.	SHEL 504:24
that any m. I ever yet	SHAK 469:14
that fine m. still he did	DRAY 193:14
that way m. lies	SHAK 454:14
this is very midsummer m.	SHAK 490:6
Though this be m.	SHAK 432:9
Thro' cells of m.	TENN 540:16
To define true m.	SHAK 431:31
work like m. in the brain	COL 156:4
Madoc: M. will be read	PORS 381:28
Madonnas: he only used to draw M.	BROW 102:28
their Rafael of the dear M.	BROW 103:1
madrigal: Sing a merry m.	GILB 227:1
What woeful stuff this m.	POPE 378:25
madrigals: Melodious birds sing m.	MARL 330:1
silence all the airs and m.	MILT 351:25
Maecenas: M. atavis edite regibus	HOR 259:8
Maenad: M. and the Bassarid	SWIN 528:18
Of some fierce M.	SHEL 502:9
Maeonides: old M. the blind	FLEC 214:22
maestro: Il m. di color che sanno	DANTE 171:7
Maeves: Julias, M. and Maureens	BETJ 43:7
magazines: graves of little m.	PRES 400:14
Magdalen: fourteen months at M. College	GIBB 224:7
manufactures of the monks of M.	GIBB 224:8
maggot: m. must be born i'	ELIOT 200:15
me full of m. ostentation	SHAK 457:15
maggot-pies: m. and choughs and rooks	SHAK 461:24
maggots: you not m. in your brains	FLET 215:26
magic: If this be m.	SHAK 492:12
I'm a dealer in m.	GILB 229:2
nothing but a M. Shadow-show	FITZ 213:3
rough m. I here abjure	SHAK 485:24
secret m. of numbers	BROW 96:11
there's m. in the web of it	SHAK 476:4
what mighty m.	SHAK 473:24
With a m. like thee	BYRON 125:27
With m. in my eyes	HARDY 241:6
Maginn: kind William M.	LOCK 315:23
magistrate: m. corruptible	ROB 406:12
magistrates: like m., correct at home	SHAK 443:9
magistri: iurare in verba m.	HOR 258:7
magna: Et quorum pars m. fui	VIRG 557:21
M. est veritas	BIBLE 83:26
Magna Carta: Bible under one arm and M.	AUBR 17:23
Magna Charta: M. is such a fellow	COKE 154:16
magnanimity: In all the m. of thought	- YOUNG 588:5
in victory, m.	CHUR 150:25
M. in politics is not seldom	BURKE 110:6
you might curb your m.	KEATS 294:31
magnanimos: Glubit m. Remi nepotes	CAT 137:5
magnanimous: m. at an inopportune time	TROT 553:17
magnanimously: skilfully and m. all	MILT 352:8

magnet: Can m. ever	GILB 227:24
printing, gunpowder and the m.	BACON 28:9
magnetic: m., Peripatetic Lover	GILB 227:24
magnetism: doubt as to animal m.	COL 157:34
Magnificat: M. anima mea Dominum	BIBLE 83:17
magnificent: It is m.	BOSQ 90:12
mild and m. eye	BROW 102:5
Mute and m.	DRYD 197:29
magnifico: atque omne ignotum pro m.	TAC 531:6
magnifique: C'est m.	BOSQ 90:12
magnify: My soul doth m. the Lord	BIBLE 83:17
praise him, and m.	PRAY 384:21
soul doth m. the Lord	BIBLE 69:5
we laud and m. thy glorious	PRAY 387:23
we m. thee	PRAY 384:18
worthily m. thy holy Name	PRAY 387:7
magnis: parva licet componere m.	VIRG 560:19
Magnus: M. ab integro saeclorum	VIRG 559:22
walls Of M. Martyr	ELIOT 205:4
Magus: M. Zoroaster	SHEL 502:19
Mahomet: M. will go to the hill	BACON 25:33
maid: Bare-footed came the beggar m.	TENN 532:16
dried and a m. not vendible	SHAK 465:14
frozen m.	GARR 221:16
had a m. call'd Barbara	SHAK 476:26
I once was a m.	BURNS 114:17
is the m. ov all maidens	BARN 33:30
lazy finger of a m.	SHAK 481:28
m. forget her ornaments	BIBLE 60:15
m. is not dead, but sleepeth	BIBLE 65:27
M. of Athens	BYRON 125:3
m. sing in the valley	ANON 5:3
m. Subdues me	SHAK 464:6
m. whom there were none	WORD 581:6
She could not live a m.	PEELE 371:9
There was a fair m. dwellin'	BALL 30:10
way of a man with a m.	BIBLE 55:1
way of a man with a m.	KIPL 301:1
Whether a m. so tender	SHAK 473:22
Yonder a m. and her wight	HARDY 240:5
maiden: Else would a m. blush bepaint	SHAK 482:11
flesh'd Thy m. sword	SHAK 440:26
Here's not a modest m. elf	HARDY 240:7
In m. meditation	SHAK 470:8
I pursued a m. and clasped	SHEL 501:4
Is as the m.'s organ	SHAK 488:3
m. hid	SWIN 528:18
m. modesty would float	HUXL 268:23
m. never bold	SHAK 473:24
m. of bashful fifteen	SHER 506:31
rare and radiant m. whom	POE 375:5
shall be the m.'s fate	SCOTT 416:12
simple m. in her flower	TENN 537:27
sweeter m. in a cleaner	KIPL 301:7
This m. she lived with	POE 374:21
undergo such m. pilgrimage	SHAK 469:17
village m. she	TENN 539:10
maidenly: So joyously, So m.	SKEL 508:17
maidens: all the m. pretty	COLM 158:25
Conserv'd of m.' hearts	SHAK 476:4
is the maïd ov all m.	BARN 33:30
...M. aspiring to godheads	STOP 523:15
Twenty love-sick m. we	GILB 227:19
What m. loth	KEATS 291:3
Young men and m.	PRAY 399:23
maids: Immortal youth to mortal m.	LAND 308:22
m. and village hinds shall	COLL 158:16
m. are May when they are	SHAK 426:23
m. strange seraphic pieces	TRAH 551:19
Most incident to m.	SHAK 491:26
seven m. with seven mops	CARR 135:5

Three little m. from school GILB 226:27
when m. lie on their backs SHAK 481:28
maidservant: nor thy m. BIBLE 47:24
Maid-servants: M., I hear people
  complaining CARL 131:38
mail: like a rusty m. SHAK 487:4
This is the Night M. crossing AUDEN 20:1
mailed: seen the m. lobster rise FRERE 218:26
maimed: m., and the halt BIBLE 70:12
main: brook Into the m. SHAK 468:18
flooding in, the m. CLOU 154:4
froth amid the boundless m. BRON 93:20
Glorious th' enraptur'd m. SMART 509:4
lost evermore in the m. TENN 543:5
maintain: m. mine own ways before
  BIBLE 52:25
maintained: I m. myself thus solely
  THOR 550:13
Maior: M. privato visus dum privatus
  TAC 531:13
maiorum: Delicta m. immeritus lues
  HOR 260:25
mair: m. they talk I'm kent BURNS 114:32
Maire: Thy famous M. DUNB 199:12
Maisie: Proud M. is in the wood
  SCOTT 418:21
maison: m. est une machine à habiter
  LE C 313:5
Maister: do not M. or Campbell me
  SCOTT 418:32
That love is m. wher he GOWER 233:6
maistrye: been constreyned by m.
  CHAU 142:12
maîtresses: j'aurai des m. GEOR 223:35
maize: hand with Plenty in the m.
  TENN 542:16
m. and vine TENN 533:5
majestic: m. River floated ARN 14:28
M. though in ruin MILT 346:14
majestical: laid in bed m. SHAK 444:25
majestueue: m. égalité des lois FRAN 217:26
Majesty: appearance of Your M. BIBLE 44:21
his m. is BIBLE 62:22
if his m. our sovereign ANON 8:24
m. of human suffering VIGNY 557:1
M.: of thy Glory PRAY 384:16
Reynolds to his M.'s head MAC 324:2
right hand of the M. BIBLE 79:28
sight so touching in its m. WORD 581:14
This earth of m. SHAK 478:20
want love's m. SHAK 480:18
Major-General: model of a modern M.
  GILB 228:16
majorité: est toujours dans la m.
  KNOX 305:18
majorities: action Wisdom goes by m.
  MER 337:35
majority: ain't that a big enough m.
  TWAIN 554:3
damned, compact, liberal m. IBSEN 269:17
Door— To her divine M. DICK 183:21
has gone over to the m. CARL 131:11
He's gone to join the m. PETR 373:1
indifferent and self-indulgent m. STEP 518:20
joins us to the great m. YOUNG 588:13
m. has the might IBSEN 269:18
m. is always the best repartee DISR 186:35
Majors: with scarlet M. at the Base
  SASS 414:10
make: I could not well m. out SOUT 513:17
I m. it constantly PROU 401:22
I too will something m. BRID 92:10
joint stools to m. faces JOHN 276:30
king may m. a nobleman BURKE 111:37
lest he should m. an end JONS 285:2
m. a better mouse-trap EMER 208:15
m. an end the sooner BACON 26:6
m. both ends meet FULL 220:12
m. his sword to approach BIBLE 53:9
M. me a clean heart PRAY 393:6

M. mouths upon me when SHAK 470:23
m. myself laugh at everything BEAU 35:15
m. the most of what we FITZ 212:18
m. thine own ARN 13:11
M. yourself necessary EMER 207:3
man with m. more opportunities BACON 25:38
not m. a new acquaintance JOHN 279:25
not m. new acquaintance JOHN 274:15
than a Scotsman on the m. BARR 34:21
To m. bad good SHAK 464:22
maked: God first m. man CHAU 143:1
Maker: before the Lord our M. PRAY 396:4
be more pure than his m. BIBLE 52:16
his M.'s image through DRYD 194:2
Laudes to our M. early HAWES 243:2
m. and builder is God BIBLE 79:32
m. buried STEV 523:1
m. is hymself ybeten CHAU 144:2
M. of heaven and earth PRAY 384:26
M. of heaven and earth PRAY 387:10
m. of his own fortune STEE 518:7
meet my M. brow to brow CORN 162:19
that sinneth before his M. BIBLE 63:38
that striveth with his m. BIBLE 59:13
makes: He m. a solitude BYRON 120:4
m. no mistakes does not PHEL 373:7
m. the happiness she does JOHN 283:6
night That either m. me SHAK 477:4
makest: What m. thou BIBLE 59:13
maketh: loveth and m. a lie BIBLE 83:3
making: Holland take pleasure in m.
  ANON 7:22
joy in the m. BRID 92:10
M. peace is harder than STEV 520:21
That I shall be past m. PRIOR 401:7
There came to the m. of man SWIN 528:20
makings: royal m. of a queen SHAK 447:14
Makler: Ehrlicher M. BISM 84:23
mal: connaître tout le m. qu'il fait
  LA R 310:14
mala: Usque ad m. HOR 262:1
malade: sur les bras un homme m.
  NICH 362:22
malades: aime à dépêcher ses m. MOL 353:21
maladie: l'honneur n'est qu'une m.
  RAC 404:6
m. dont le sommeil nous CHAM 139:13
malady: love's a m. without a cure
  DRYD 197:6
m. of not marking SHAK 441:7
medicine worse than the m. FLET 215:16
male: especially the m. of the species
  LAWR 311:6
M. and female created BIBLE 45:5
m. and the female BIBLE 45:34
more deadly than the m. KIPL 299:4
rough m. kiss of blankets BROO 94:8
malecontents: of all loiterers and m.
  SHAK 456:26
malefactions: have proclaim'd their m.
  SHAK 433:5
males: Nothing but m. SHAK 459:11
malesuada: Metus et m. Fames VIRG 558:21
Malfi: Duchess of M. still WEBS 566:24
Malherbe: At last came M. BOIL 89:10
malheur: Tout le m. des hommes vient
  PASC 369:5
malheureux: jamais si m. qu'on croit
  LA R 310:18
malheurs: tableau des crimes et des m.
  VOLT 561:10
mali: Non ignara m. miseris succurrere
  VIRG 557:19
malice: from envy, hatred, and m.
  PRAY 385:16
leaven of m. and wickedness BIBLE 75:36
leaven of m. and wickedness PRAY 386:1
M. is of a low stature HAL 238:2
m., to breed causes JONS 285:15
Much m. mingled with DRYD 196:17

Nor set down aught in m. SHAK 477:23
Pride, Envy, M. LAND 308:17
With m. toward none LINC 315:3
Yet m. never was his aim SWIFT 527:24
malignity: motive-hunting of motiveless
  m. COL 157:28
with a m. truly diabolical BURKE 108:20
Mall: like Mistress M.'s picture SHAK 488:1
mallard: swapping, swapping m. ANON 7:28
mallecho: this is miching m. SHAK 434:9
mallow: slimy m. waves her silky
  COWP 168:26
Malmesey: drowned in a barrel of M.
  FABY 209:17
Malmsey: Of M. and Malvoisie BELL 38:22
Malo: M. me Galatea petit VIRG 559:18
Sed libera nos a m. MASS 335:5
malorum: religio potuit suadere m.
  LUCR 320:4
malt: m. does more than Milton HOUS 264:12
Maluerne: on a May morwenyng on M.
  LANG 309:25
Malvoisie: Of Malmsey and M. BELL 38:22
Mama: M. came and made a scene
  DICK 178:18
m. of dada FAD 209:18
mammets: play with m. SHAK 438:31
mammon: authentic m. than a bogus
  god MACN 326:4
cannot serve God and m. BIBLE 64:27
friends of the m. of unrighteousness
  BIBLE 70:26
M. led them MILT 345:26
man: All know the m. their neighbour
  YEATS 586:14
all that makes a m. TENN 534:12
All that m. is YEATS 584:12
all that may become a m. SHAK 459:9
ambition of a m. RAL 404:16
apparel oft proclaims the m. SHAK 430:19
Arms, and the m. DRYD 198:22
Around the m. bend other LAND 308:17
be a m. ARN 13:1
become a m.'s friend only CHEK 145:5
become the servant of a m. SHAW 496:21
Before M. made us citizens LOW 319:11
be M. and Wife together PRAY 389:7
better angel is a m. right SHAK 495:12
between a m. and a woman GIBB 225:3
Blessed is the m. that PRAY 389:14
Blessed is the m. unto PRAY 391:16
bold bad m. SHAK 447:1
bold bad m. SPEN 516:1
borne me a m. of strife BIBLE 60:23
came to the making of m. SWIN 528:20
Cannot a plain m. live SHAK 480:23
centaur, m. and wife BYRON 123:19
childhood shows the m. MILT 350:7
Child is father of the M. WORD 578:19
coiner the mintage of m. HOUS 263:8
coming of the Son of M. BIBLE 67:32
Cristen m. shall wedde CHAU 143:17
crucify the old m. PRAY 388:10
cruelty To load a falling m. SHAK 447:25
deaf m. to a blind COL 157:19
delighteth he in any m.'s legs PRAY 399:20
detest that animal called m. SWIFT 526:23
dog bites a m. BOG 89:9
Ech m. for hymself CHAU 142:19
encompass'd but one m. SHAK 448:19
end try the m. SHAK 441:23
Eustace is a m. no longer KING 297:16
exclusively for the use of m. PEAC 370:15
eye 'tis an old M. grey BLAKE 86:14
Feeds beast as m. SHAK 421:8
figure of 'The Reasonable M. HERB 246:13
first m. is of the earth BIBLE 76:28
forgetteth what manner of m. BIBLE 80:10
garment from the m. BLAKE 86:1
get out the m. POPE 375:24

God first maked m.   CHAU 143:1
God is not a m.   BIBLE 48:14
good almost kill a m.   MILT 351:22
good m., and did good   HARDY 242:1
grave m.   CLOU 153:14
Greater love hath no m.   BIBLE 72:36
grown m. in the cradle   BURKE 110:13
hang the m. over again   BARH 33:9
Happy is the m. that hath   PRAY 398:19
have put off the old m.   BIBLE 78:26
heart of a m. is deprest   GAY 222:26
He was a good m.   BIBLE 71:15
He was a m.   SHAK 430:5
I am a worm, and no m.   PRAY 390:17
'I am the Son of M.   AUDEN 21:7
I have a m.'s mind   SHAK 449:22
I know myself a m.   DAV 172:11
I love not m. the less   BYRON 121:22
imagination of m.'s heart   BIBLE 45:36
I met an a m. who wasn't there   MEAR 336:7
I not a m. and a brother   WEDG 567:16
is another m. within me   BROW 96:7
is nothing great but m.   HAM 238:16
it is the number of a m.   BIBLE 82:14
lassie do wi' an auld m.   BURNS 116:3
last thing civilized by M.   MER 337:34
laws of m.   HOUS 264:24
Let us make m. in our image   BIBLE 45:4
like a m.'s hand   BIBLE 51:11
looking for a m.'s foot-print   BEER 37:27
made the woman for the m.   TENN 533:9
m. after his own heart   BIBLE 50:1
m. after his deeth moot   CHAU 142:17
m. among a thousand have   BIBLE 55:23
m. and a woman looking   WOOLF 576:19
m. and wife should never   FARQ 210:9
'm. as he is *not* to be   LAMB 308:8
m. becomes aware of his   ARN 12:22
m. be more just than God   BIBLE 52:16
'*M. can have Unity if Man*   AUDEN 19:11
m. clothed in soft raiment   BIBLE 66:2
M. comes and tills   TENN 543:11
M. come through a door   CHAN 139:21
m. delights not me   SHAK 432:15
M. didn't find the animals   NIET 363:3
M. dreams of fame   TENN 535:9
m. for all seasons   WHIT 571:2
m. for loving himself   BACON 27:8
M. for the field and woman   TENN 542:9
m. goes riding   STEV 522:18
M. goeth forth to his work   PRAY 397:1
m. goeth to his long home   BIBLE 56:11
M. has created death   YEATS 584:21
M. has Forever   BROW 100:37
M. has his will   HOLM 253:15
M. has never been the same   MILL 339:25
m. hath no preeminence   BIBLE 55:13
m. hath seen God   BIBLE 71:28
m. he must go with a woman   KIPL 301:9
m. in his hasty days   BRID 92:10
M. is an embodied paradox   COLT 159:11
M. is a noble animal   BROW 97:23
m. is as old as he's feeling   COLL 158:15
M. is but earth   DONNE 190:22
M. is God's image   HERB 247:9
M. is Heaven's masterpiece   QUAR 403:12
M. is in error throughout   GOET 229:29
M. is man's A.B.C.   QUAR 403:18
M. is Nature's sole mistake   GILB 228:28
m. Is now become a god   SHAK 448:14
m. is of kin to the beasts   BACON 25:25
M. is one world   HERB 248:3
M. is only a reed   PASC 369:11
M. is quite insane   MONT 355:4
m. is seldom ashamed   ELIOT 201:10
m. *so* in the way   GASK 221:22
M. is the hunter   TENN 542:8
M. is the master of things   SWIN 530:2
M. is the measure of all   PROT 401:18
M. is the only animal that   TWAIN 554:8

M. is the shuttle   VAUG 555:10
m. may drink and no be   BURNS 115:13
M. may escape from rope   GAY 222:30
m. must be a nonconformist   EMER 207:37
m. of culture rare   GILB 227:20
m. of infinite-resource-and-sagac   KIPL 304:16
m. of sense only trifles   CHES 145:26
m. of the dust of the ground   BIBLE 45:7
m. over forty is a scoundrel   SHAW 498:4
M. partly is and wholly   BROW 100:11
m. plans   THOM 546:10
M., proud man   SHAK 464:2
m. recover'd of the bite   GOLD 231:14
m. remains Sceptreless   SHEL 503:12
m.'s a man for a' that   BURNS 113:29
m.'s desire is   COL 157:33
m. sent from God   BIBLE 71:24
M.'s first disobedience   MILT 344:20
m. shall be as an hiding   BIBLE 58:30
m. shall have his mare   SHAK 471:1
M.'s inhumanity to man   BURNS 114:23
m.'s memory may outlive   SHAK 434:7
m. speaks concerning another   JOHN 278:22
m.'s the gowd for a' that   BURNS 113:28
M.'s word is God in man   TENN 533:31
m. take fire in his bosom   BIBLE 53:23
m. that hath no music   SHAK 468:17
M. that is born of a woman   BIBLE 52:26
M. that is born of a woman   PRAY 389:11
m. that trusteth in him   PRAY 391:21
m. there upon the stage   FIEL 211:31
'M. wants but little here   BUTL 119:8
M. wants but little   GOLD 231:7
M. was formed for society   BLAC 85:1
M. was made for Joy   BLAKE 85:14
m. was made to mourn   BURNS 114:22
man was wolf to the m.   VANZ 555:8
m. who has the power   ANON 8:20
M. who is from God sent   WORD 578:8
m. who is high up loves   BARR 34:22
m. who said 'God Must think   KNOX 305:22
M. who used to notice such   HARDY 239:1
M. will go down into   BALF 30:3
m. with heart   TENN 540:4
m. worth having is true   VANB 555:6
more wonderful than m.   SOPH 513:7
mother's life made me a m.   MAS 333:22
mouth of that wild beast m.   BOL 89:14
must also feel it as a m.   SHAK 462:18
my only study, is m.   BORR 90:1
noblest work of m.   BUTL 119:7
not m. have the upper hand   PRAY 389:29
Not mine, but m.'s   HOUS 265:13
not the m.   SCOTT 418:18
now thy loins like a m.   BIBLE 53:1
of a city and I see a m.   KEATS 294:17
One m. that has a mind   SHAW 496:3
Only a m. harrowing clods   HARDY 240:5
only m. is vile   HEBER 244:6
outward semblance of a m.   DICK 182:18
people arose as one m.   BIBLE 49:31
perfect M.   PRAY 385:14
perilous to a m.'s honesty   TROL 553:6
piece of work is a m.   SHAK 432:15
plain, blunt m.   SHAK 451:1
plead that m.'s excuse   ANON 7:24
posterity as a brave bad m.   CLAR 152:22
presumptuous m.   CANN 130:3
relief of m.'s estate   BACON 24:17
require the life of m.   BIBLE 45:38
right m. in the right place   JEFF 272:18
sabbath was made for m.   BIBLE 68:26
science and study of m.   CHAR 141:1
She knows her m.   DRYD 198:21
she was taken out of M.   BIBLE 45:12
since by m. came death   BIBLE 76:22
single m. in possession   AUST 23:11
sing of arms and the m.   VIRG 557:8
singularly deep young m.   GILB 227:21
smudge and shares m.'s smell   HOPK 256:12

So unto the m. is woman   LONG 317:12
Spirit in the inner m.   BIBLE 77:24
strain of m.'s bred   SHAK 486:1
strange what a m. may do   THAC 545:7
study of mankind is m.   POPE 379:12
style is the m.   BUFF 106:20
substance of men which is m.   SWIN 530:1
Surely m. is a broomstick   SWIFT 526:25
that I was an austere m.   BIBLE 71:1
That make ingrateful m.   SHAK 454:4
that m. with all his noble   DARW 171:24
That the m. I am may cease   TENN 540:4
that the m. should be alone   BIBLE 45:10
that the new m. may be   PRAY 388:9
therefore let him pass for a m.   SHAK 465:22
these last strands of m.   HOPK 256:7
thing but make a m. a woman   PEMB 371:11
this corpse which is m.   SWIN 530:9
This is the state of m.   SHAK 447:9
this M. and this Woman   PRAY 388:24
'This was a m.   SHAK 452:7
Thou art the m.   BIBLE 50:1
To cheat a m. is nothing   GAY 222:29
to do with that just m.   BIBLE 68:20
together let no m. put asunder   PRAY 389:6
tree of m. was never quiet   HOUS 263:15
truly sorry M.'s dominion   BURNS 115:21
Untainted by m.'s misery   SHEL 503:28
vain thing to save a m.   PRAY 391:20
want as an armed m.   BIBLE 53:22
war as is of every m. against   HOBB 251:17
way of a m. with a maid   BIBLE 55:1
way of a m. with a maid   KIPL 301:1
well-shaped m.   AUBR 18:1
were m. But constant   SHAK 491:6
Were not meant for m. alive   HOUS 262:15
What bloody m. is that   SHAK 458:2
What god, m., or hero   POUND 383:9
What is a m.   SHAK 435:29
what is m.   BURNS 115:2
What is m., that thou   PRAY 389:28
What m. has made of man   WORD 578:9
What m. thinks of changing   TROL 553:7
what m. Would do   BROW 105:2
What shall this m. do   BIBLE 73:19
when a m. should marry   BACON 26:35
When God at first made m.   HERB 248:6
When I am grown to m.'s   STEV 522:19
when I became a m.   BIBLE 76:14
when I came to m.'s estate   SHAK 490:27
When is a m. not a man   JOYCE 286:4
Who's master, who's m.   SWIFT 527:30
Whoso sheddeth m.'s blood   BIBLE 45:39
will be against every m.   BIBLE 46:5
wise m. make your rule   BLAKE 87:9
wise m. will make   BACON 25:38
woman and large-hearted m.   BROW 98:15
years a mortal m. may live   SHAK 446:18
yet old enough for a m.   SHAK 488:9
you'll be a M.   KIPL 300:2
Manasses: M. is mine   PRAY 393:18
man-at-arms: m. must now serve on
his   PEELE 371:8
mancipio: Vitaque m.   LUCR 320:10
Mandalay: come you back to M.   KIPL 301:5
Mandarin: M. style...is beloved
   CONN 161:11
mandate: thus the royal m. ran   BURNS 113:21
mandoline: pleasant whining of a m.
   ELIOT 205:4
mandragora: Give me to drink m.
   SHAK 421:30
mandrake: Get with child a m. root
   DONNE 190:8
this quiet m.   DONNE 190:1
mane: Thin m., thick tail   SHAK 495:20
whistling m. of every wind   THOM 548:13
maneat: *Plus uno m. perenne saeclo*
   CAT 136:21
manes: m. of horses in the night SHAK 481:28

manger: laid him in a m.   BIBLE 69:9
m. pour vivre et non pas   MOL 353:2
not too cleanly, m.   CRAS 169:7
One born in a m.   VAUG 555:13
still lodge Him in the m.   ANON 9:1
manges: *Dis-moi que tu m.*   BRIL 93:9
Mangle: immense pecuniary M.   DICK 183:6
mangled: vents In m. forms   SHAK 425:21
mangler: m. in a million million   DICK 181:16
mangrove: m. swamps where the python
  COW 163:20
manhood: ancient customs and its m.
  ENN 208:23
conspiracy against the m.   EMER 207:36
hardened into the bone of m.   BURKE 109:17
M. a struggle   DISR 185:40
M. taken by the Son   NEWM 362:11
sounder piece of British m.   CARL 131:14
strife comes with m.   SCOTT 416:25
touching his M.   PRAY 385:14
manhoods: m. cheap whiles any speaks
  SHAK 445:3
maniac: m. scattering dust   TENN 536:21
manifest: love from love made m.
  BROW 100:10
m. destiny to overspread   OSUL 365:23
manifesto: plain m.   SPEN 515:13
manifold: how m. are thy works   PRAY 397:1
our m. sins and wickedness   PRAY 384:9
sundry and m. changes   PRAY 386:12
man-in-the-street: To the m.   AUDEN 20:13
manjar: m. que quita la hambre   CERV 138:20
mankind: apple damn'd m.   OTWAY 366:2
careless of m.   TENN 539:16
crucify m. upon a cross   BRYAN 106:8
dissensions and animosities of m.
  BURKE 111:3
Ellum she hateth m.   KIPL 303:26
Example is the school of m.   BURKE 112:7
How beauteous m. is   SHAK 485:26
legislator of m.   JOHN 282:7
M. always sets itself on   MARX 333:7
M. is divisible into two   BEER 37:17
misfortunes of m.   GIBB 224:23
need not be to hate, m.   BYRON 120:34
of all m.   BALL 31:9
one giant leap for m.   ARMS 12:18
our countrymen are all m.   GARR 221:18
put m. and posterity most   INGE 270:10
rather as a spectator of m.   ADD 2:8
ride m.   EMER 206:21
superfluities of m.   GAY 222:24
th'original perus'd m.   ARMS 12:15
which m. are warranted   MILL 339:6
willing to love all m.   JOHN 277:30
manliness: silent m. of grief   GOLD 231:6
Manlio: nata mecum consule M.   HOR 261:5
manly: childish valourous than m.
  MARL 330:15
full likely to be a m.   MAL 327:17
man-milliner: respectable architectural
m.   RUSK 411:5
manna: He rained down m. also   PRAY 395:6
his tongue Dropt m.   MILT 346:9
news, the m. of a day   GREEN 235:29
We loathe our m.   DRYD 197:2
manned: m. by Manning and new-manned
  BROW 104:17
manner: in this extraordinary m.   STOP 523:17
m. of his speech   SHAK 421:34
m. rude and wild   BELL 38:25
m. which is my aversion   BYRON 123:6
shall be well and all m.   JUL 286:32
Socratic m. is not a game   BEER 38:4
stolzer M. der Tat   HEINE 244:12
This m. of writing where   MILT 352:13
to the m. born   SHAK 430:23
manners: by his m.   SPEN 516:23
catch the m. living   POPE 379:2
communications corrupt good m. BIBLE 76:25

evil m. live in brass   SHAK 447:20
good m. to mention here   BROWN 95:8
Her m. had not that repose   TENN 537:28
His m. are not so polite   KIPL 301:19
influenced m. in England   BURKE 111:15
Leave off first for m.'   BIBLE 63:14
m. are not idle   TENN 534:9
m. of a dancing master   JOHN 274:10
m. of a Marquis with   GILB 228:33
not men, but m.   FIEL 211:14
Of m. gentle   POPE 378:8
old m.   GOLD 232:19
polish'd m. and fine sense   COWP 167:28
printing thereby to rectify m.   MILT 351:25
take their m. from the Ape   BELL 38:26
talk and Peel has no m.   WELL 567:31
times! Oh, the m.   CIC 151:26
uncouth m.   BURKE 109:15
With sweeter m.   TENN 537:15
Manning: manned by M. and new-manned
  BROW 104:17
Manningtree: M. ox with the pudding
  SHAK 439:16
manque: Un seul être vous m.   LAM 306:24
manservant: thy m.   BIBLE 47:24
mansion: Love has pitched his m.
  YEATS 584:19
made his everlasting m.   SHAK 486:14
m. call the fleeting breath   GRAY 234:22
My m. is   MILT 340:22
upon thy fading m. spend   SHAK 495:13
mansions: Father's house are many m.
  BIBLE 72:31
lasting m. of the dead   COWP 168:10
mantle: cast his m. upon him   BIBLE 51:15
dark her silver m. threw   MILT 348:2
Do cream and m. like   SHAK 465:12
in russet m. clad   SHAK 429:18
m. muffling up his face   SHAK 450:28
You all do know this m.   SHAK 450:26
Mantovano: I salute thee, M.   TENN 543:18
Mantuan: old M.   SHAK 457:2
manufacture: that no legislature can
m.   BAG 28:21
manunkind: busy monster, m.   CUMM 170:11
manure: It is its natural m.   JEFF 272:10
manuscript: m. put away at home HOR 258:6
Youth's sweet-scented M.   FITZ 213:15
manuscripts: brown Greek m.   BROW 99:13
many: 'Complaints is m. and various
  GRAV 234:12
desire and m. things to fear   BACON 26:8
m. are called   BIBLE 67:18
m. for the remission   PRAY 388:1
m. (questionless) canonized   BROW 96:17
m. still must labour   BYRON 121:30
M. things I thought   HOUS 265:4
m. ways out   SEN 420:9
owed by so m. to so few   CHUR 150:2
So m. worlds   TENN 537:2
There's m. a good tune played   BUTL 119:15
we are m.   BIBLE 68:30
What are they among so m.   BIBLE 72:4
What m. men desire   SHAK 466:19
why he makes so m. of them   LINC 315:5
Ye are m.—they are few   SHEL 502:4
many-colour'd: change of m. life he
drew   JOHN 282:25
many-splendoured: That miss the m.
thing   THOM 548:25
map: Lord would use a larger m.   SAL 413:20
M. me no maps   FIEL 211:21
m. with the augmentation   SHAK 490:3
Roll up that m.   PITT 374:6
maps: geographers, in Afric-m.   SWIFT 528:2
Geography is about m.   BENT 41:3
mar: m. all with this starting   SHAK 462:21
Marabar: echo in a M. cave   FORS 217:8
Maran-atha: Let him be Anathema M.
  BIBLE 77:3

Marathon: M. looks on the sea
  BYRON 122:33
marble: dwelt in m. halls   BUNN 107:9
Glowed on the m.   ELIOT 204:23
hovel to your dreary m.   CALV 127:22
I am m.-constant   SHAK 424:4
it brick and left it m.   AUG 22:5
knew that m. bled   FLEC 214:15
legs are as pillars of m.   BIBLE 57:4
m. eyelids are not wet   BROW 98:8
m. index of a mind   WORD 580:17
m. to retain   BYRON 119:31
mould from m. living faces   VIRG 559:1
need of all this m. crust   MARV 332:21
Not m.   SHAK 493:17
slate more than hard m.   DU B 198:27
marbled: Place me on Sunium's m.
  BYRON 123:4
marbly: mistresses with great smooth
m. limbs   BROW 99:13
marbre: Plus que le m. dur me plaist
  DU B 198:27
Marcellus: Tu M. eris   VIRG 559:2
March: ashbuds in the front of M.
  TENN 533:19
Beware the ides of M.   SHAK 448:7
Did m. to the seige   BALL 31:8
dinna ye m. forward in order SCOTT 418:24
droghte of M. hath perced   CHAU 141:7
England are M. and April   TROL 552:21
ides of M. are come   SHAK 449:23
m. of intellect   SOUT 514:13
m. of mind has marched   PEAC 370:13
m. of the human mind is   BURKE 109:29
m. through rapine to disintegration
  GLAD 229:15
Men who m. away   HARDY 240:8
sea-blue bird of M.   TENN 537:9
That highte M.   CHAU 143:1
three hours' m. to dinner   HAZL 243:32
We shall m. prospering   BROW 102:6
winds of M. with beauty   SHAK 491:26
March-bloom: Look! M.   HOPK 256:29
marched: Around the ancient track m.
  MER 337:5
East at heel is m. from   HOUS 265:3
m. breast forward   BROW 98:32
M. into their land   AYT 24:6
M. them along   BROW 99:26
Märchen: Ein M. aus alten Zeiten
  HEINE 244:9
marches: army m. on its stomach   ANON 9:3
Funeral m. to the grave   LONG 317:2
hunger, thirst, forced m.   GAR 221:10
marching: 'Tis the people m.   MORR 358:7
us by m. where it likes   ARN 15:20
marcie: fame, sete, m. forzate   GAR 221:10
mare: animum mutant qui trans m.
  HOR 258:19
brought him a Flanders m.   HENR 246:2
lend me your grey m.   BALL 32:12
man shall have his m. again   SHAK 471:1
Marengo: this is our M.   DOYLE 192:17
Margaret: It is M. you mourn   HOPK 256:27
so kind, As Merry M.   SKEL 508:16
Margate: 'Twas in M. last July   BARH 33:19
marge: page having an ample m.
  TENN 535:12
margin: through a meadow of m.
  SHER 506:26
mari: m. magno turbantibus aequora
  LUCR 320:6
With an *Ave M.*   SKEL 508:19
Maria: Ave M.   ANON 10:8
dulcis virgo M.   ANON 10:19
ex M. Virgine   MASS 334:20
mariage: cadrent mal avec le m. MOL 353:13
speke of wo that is in m.   CHAU 143:16
mariages: Il y a de bons m.   LA R 310:11

Mariana: resides this dejected M.
SHAK 464:18
Marie Hamilton: M.'s to the kirk gane
BALL 31:11
Maries: Yestreen the Queen had four
M. BALL 31:12
Marie Seaton: There was M. BALL 31:12
marigold: m., that goes to bed wi'
SHAK 491:25
marijuana: of m. in his hair LOW 319:20
mariner: haul and draw with the m.
DRAKE 193:4
It is an ancient M. COL 155:5
mariners: My m. TENN 544:3
rest ye, brother m. TENN 539:17
Ye M. of England CAMP 129:12
Marion: M.'s nose looks red SHAK 457:19
marjoram: savory, m. SHAK 491:25
mark: He hath no drowning m.
SHAK 484:21
hundred m. is a long one SHAK 441:18
I press toward the m. BIBLE 78:18
Lord set a m. upon Cain BIBLE 45:28
man's distinctive m. alone BROW 100:11
m., learn PRAY 386:5
m. me how I will undo myself SHAK 480:1
m. of insincerity of purpose BRAM 91:18
M. well her bulwarks PRAY 392:27
not a m. ROST 410:12
That m. our place MCCR 324:30
wilt be extreme to m. what PRAY 398:23
market: knowledge is bought in the m.
CLOU 153:18
love salutations in the m.places BIBLE 68:37
take ingots with us to m. CHAM 139:14
market-place: Antony, Enthron'd i' the
m. SHAK 422:3
Decreed in the m. POUND 383:8
eat his heart in the m. SHAK 473:3
markets: laws of m. and fashion ALB 3:7
When the great m. FLEC 214:10
marking: malady of not m. SHAK 441:7
marks: m. and scars I carry with
BUNY 107:38
terrible m. of the beast HARDY 241:17
marl: to a clod of wayward m. SHAK 472:4
Marlbro: M.'s mighty soul was prov'd
ADD 1:13
praise the Duke of M. won SOUT 513:19
Marlb'rough: M.'s eyes the streams
JOHN 283:3
marle: Over the burning m. MILT 345:22
Marlowe: M.'s mighty line JONS 284:20
marmasyte: Call Tullia's ape a m.
ANON 5:18
Marmion: Were the last words of M.
SCOTT 417:22
Marquis: combines the manners of a
M. GILB 228:33
marred: All that's spoke is m. SHAK 478:1
married is a man that's m. SHAK 421:1
marriage: be incontinent before m.
SHAK 426:27
blessings of m. SHAW 497:32
comedies are ended by a m. BYRON 122:28
Courtship to m. CONG 160:29
curse of m. SHAK 475:21
every m. then is best WATK 565:7
fall in with the m.-procession CLOU 153:10
funeral and with dirge in m. SHAK 429:19
furnish forth the m. tables SHAK 430:4
Hanging and m. FARQ 210:19
hanging prevents a bad m. SHAK 488:4
her fortune by way of m. FIEL 211:29
In m., a man becomes slack STEV 521:24
Is not m. an open question EMER 208:6
joys of m. are the heaven FORD 216:14
long monotony of m. GIBB 225:4
m. and death and division SWIN 529:10
M. from love, like vinegar BYRON 122:26
M. has many pains JOHN 282:9

M. is a step so grave STEV 521:30
M. is like life in this STEV 521:31
M. is nothing but a civil SELD 419:23
M. is popular because it SHAW 497:39
M. is the result CAMP 128:9
M. is the waste-paper basket WEBB 566:8
m. than a ministry BAG 28:29
m. vows As false SHAK 435:4
m. with his brother's wife SHAK 446:28
most happy m. I can picture COL 157:19
My definition of m. SMITH 511:11
nor are given in m. BIBLE 67:21
nor are given in m. SWIFT 527:9
of m. that we find all JOHN 276:2
Second M. in my house FITZ 213:1
termed a *left-handed* m. WOLL 576:12
that is m., Lily thought WOOLF 576:19
think there is any in m. GAY 222:32
Tho' m. makes man and wife CONG 159:23
to the m. of true minds SHAK 495:5
Was m. ever out of fashion BUTL 118:8
woman dictates before m. ELIOT 201:6
marriages: best maker of all m. SHAK 445:16
M. would in general be JOHN 276:36
taste for m. and public executions
DISR 186:25
their m. with other men TROL 553:10
There are good m. LA R 310:11
we will have no more m. SHAK 433:14
why so few m. are happy SWIFT 527:10
marrid: m. man dies in good stile
WARD 564:30
married: Charlotte was a m. lady THAC 546:3
fool at least in every m. FIEL 211:7
fourteen I m. My Lord POUND 383:16
had no taste when you m. SHER 506:27
He's the most m. man WARD 564:32
if ever we had been m. GAY 222:13
if we were not m. at all CONG 161:7
I m. him BRON 93:15
imprudently m. the barber FOOTE 216:7
I'm to be m. to-day GILB 225:33
I would be m. to a single CRAS 169:9
kiss before they are m. SHAK 445:15
let us be m. LEAR 312:12
like to be m. to a poem KEATS 294:20
m. and brought up a large GOLD 232:32
m., charming, chaste BYRON 122:8
m. is a man that's marred SHAK 421:1
m. life three is company WILDE 572:28
m. past redemption DRYD 197:1
M. to immortal verse MILT 342:26
m. with mine uncle SHAK 429:28
M. women are kept women SMITH 510:16
Mocks m. men SHAK 457:18
mostly m. people CLOU 153:23
One was never m. BURT 116:23
Reading goes ill with the m. MOL 353:13
say what delight we m. PEPYS 372:15
she has m. a sot POUND 382:5
should live till I were m. SHAK 472:19
Some were m. KIPL 304:30
so rails against all m. SHAK 469:14
So they were m. MACN 326:12
that are going to be m. GOLD 232:17
They are m. CLOU 153:19
Three daughters m. AUST 23:23
Trade Unionism of the m. SHAW 497:31
Unpleasing to a m. ear SHAK 457:18
wench who is just m. GAY 222:16
Wen you're a man DICK 182:7
woman's business to get m. SHAW 497:25
marries: changed with him who m.
STEV 521:32
much signify whom one m. ROG 407:11
When a man m. SHEL 501:19
marrow: of fat things full of m. BIBLE 58:18
suck out all the m. THOR 550:16
marry: better to m. than to burn BIBLE 76:2
Carlyle and Mrs Carlyle m. BUTL 119:22

'Doänt thou m. for munny TENN 541:1
Every woman should m. DISR 186:22
How can a bishop m. SMITH 511:4
I should m. twenty husbands SHAK 465:23
it in my heart to m. thee CONG 160:28
it was sure to m. a market-gardener
DICK 180:29
Man may not m. his Mother PRAY 400:13
m. a landlord's daughter LAMB 308:7
m. a rich woman as a poor THAC 545:14
M. my body to that dust KING 296:11
m. with his brother SHAK 435:2
m. your old friend's love BROW 105:17
may m. whom she likes THAC 545:21
men that women m. LONG 316:21
never know who they may m. MITF 352:23
persons about to m.—'Don't PUNCH 402:10
quite prepared to m. again GILB 226:3
resurrection they neither m. BIBLE 67:21
that they neither m. SWIFT 527:9
to m. any vun among them DICK 183:2
To m. is to domesticate STEV 521:33
when a man should m. BACON 26:35
Where I m., cannot love MOORE 356:22
while ye may, go m. HERR 250:6
woman should m. a teetotaller STEV 521:29
would advise no man to m. JOHN 280:13
you do *not* m. Mr Collins AUST 23:15
marry'd: At leisure m. CONG 160:27
his throat before he m. SWIFT 528:9
M. in haste CONG 160:27
marrying: Alice is m. one of the guard
MILNE 340:4
m. and giving in marriage BIBLE 67:32
they aren't the m. brand KIPL 301:9
mars: m. creation's plan CANN 130:3
M. to Crab-spawn found GRAV 234:12
Marsala: drinks a good deal of M.
LEAR 311:22
marshal: baton of a m. of France NAP 359:9
We may pick up a m. WELL 567:18
Martha: He lays it on M.'s Sons KIPL 303:10
M. was cumbered about much BIBLE 69:34
martial: ever become valiant and m.
BACON 27:26
have a swashing and a m. SHAK 424:30
his m. cloak around him WOLFE 576:4
Sonorous metal blowing m. MILT 345:20
martinet: I am a perfect m. SMITH 512:4
martlet: like the m. SHAK 466:19
temple-haunting m. SHAK 459:4
Martyr: am the M. of the People
CHAR 140:19
Glorious the m.'s gore SMART 509:4
groan of the m.'s woe BLAKE 86:6
he has the soul of a m. BAG 29:17
if thow deye a m. CHAU 144:13
m. in his shirt of fire SMITH 510:2
Oldcastle died a m. SHAK 443:2
Thou fall'st a blessed m. SHAK 447:12
martyrdom: dreadful m. must run its
course AUDEN 19:19
have not the gift of m. DRYD 196:15
it were a m. to live BROW 97:11
M. is the test JOHN 278:15
martyred: ghosts to be m. over and over
MACN 326:9
martyrs: graves of the m. the peewees
STEV 523:5
noble army of M. PRAY 384:16
stones and clouts make m. BROW 97:5
marvel: m. and a mystery LONG 316:21
m. My birthday Away THOM 547:7
m. save in Eastern clime BURG 108:4
To m. at nothing is just HOR 258:17
marvelled: They m. to see such things
PRAY 392:25
marvelling: She left me m. why my soul
THOM 547:26

marvellous: because he has done m. things
BIBLE 83:7
Chatterton, the m. boy   WORD 580:28
he hath done m. things   PRAY 396:7
it is m. in our eyes   PRAY 398:2
mankind towards the m.   HUME 267:20
marvels: alone workest great m. PRAY 385:7
Marx: M. in the saddlebag   BETJ 43:16
Marxist: know is that I am not a M.
MARX 333:12
Mary: Born of the Virgin M.   PRAY 384:26
Hail M.   ANON 10:8
M. ever Virgin   MASS 334:15
M. had a little lamb   HALE 237:15
M. hath chosen that good   BIBLE 69:35
(M., pity women!)   KIPL 301:11
My M.'s name to give   CLARE 152:10
passion for the name of 'M.'   BYRON 123:15
Philip and M. on a shilling   BUTL 118:7
Where the lady M. is   ROSS 409:19
Mary Ambree: foremost in battle was
M.   BALL 31:8
Marybone: fields from Islington to M.
BLAKE 86:4
Mary-buds: winking M. begin   SHAK 428:10
Mary Jane: What is the matter with M.
MILNE 340:10
Maryland: Green-walled by the hills
of M.   WHIT 571:15
Marylebone: hanging garments of M.
JOYCE 286:5
Mary Magdalene: week cometh M. early
BIBLE 73:5
masculine: Truth the m., of Honour
HARE 242:5
With Spirits m.   MILT 349:23
masculinity: mere contrast for m.
RILKE 406:5
Masefield: To M. something more
BEER 37:15
mask: had a m. like Castlereagh SHEL 502:2
loathsome m. has fallen   SHEL 503:12
m. like open truth to cover   CONG 159:27
m. of night is on my face   SHAK 482:11
To pluck the m. from   BRON 93:14
masons: singing m. building roofs
SHAK 443:9
masquerade: truth in m.   BYRON 123:30
masquerades: Skim milk m. as cream
GILB 228:8
mass: activates the whole m.   VIRG 558:24
between the fields to M.   BETJ 43:7
blessed mutter of the m.   BROW 99:14
is no idolatry in the M.   JOHN 275:30
m. of public wrongs   KYD 306:3
Paris is well worth a m.   HENR 245:15
rough and unordered m.   OVID 366:13
two thousand years of m.   HARDY 239:3
massacre: are not as sudden as a m.
TWAIN 554:6
Masse: breite M. eines Volkes   HITL 251:9
masses: huddled m. yearning   LAZ 311:13
I hate the unholy m.   HOR 260:13
I will back the m. against   GLAD 229:17
m. and fugues and 'ops'   GILB 227:6
sacrifices of M.   PRAY 400:9
massive: m. paws of elder persons
BELL 38:24
mast: m. burst open with a rose FLEC 214:19
m. Of some great ammiral   MILT 345:12
master: ass his m.'s crib   BIBLE 57:15
choice and m. spirits   SHAK 450:8
Cold Iron—is m.   KIPL 298:15
disciple is not above his m.   BIBLE 65:34
eateth your M. with publicans   BIBLE 65:22
great soul of an ancient M.   BROW 102:25
Has a new m.   SHAK 485:11
I am M. of this college   BEEC 37:8
I am the m. of my fate   HENL 245:5
is man and m. of his fate   TENN 535:2

mad and savage m.   SOPH 513:9
Man is the m. of things   SWIN 530:2
m. a grief but he that   SHAK 472:24
m. of himself   MASS 335:14
m. of the house cometh   BIBLE 69:1
m. of them that know   DANTE 171:7
M., we have toiled all   BIBLE 69:18
more subtle m. under heaven   TENN 534:12
only The M. shall praise us   KIPL 304:3
presence of The M.   THAC 545:12
swear allegiance to any m.   HOR 258:7
sweet, just, boyish m.   SANT 414:4
This is our m.   BROW 100:34
Thrice blessed they that m.   SHAK 469:17
'which is to be m.   CARR 135:22
which I would fain call m.   SHAK 453:13
who slew his m.   BIBLE 51:35
Who's m., who's man   SWIFT 527:30
would prove so hard a m.   BRID 92:22
You must be m. and win   GOET 230:7
masterly: wise and m. inactivity
MACK 325:12
masterpiece: Man is Heaven's m.
QUAR 403:12
Nature's great m.   DONNE 190:3
reckoned the m. of Nature   EMER 207:20
masters: ease of the m.   SMITH 509:14
it mates and m. the fear   BACON 26:2
light-hearted M. of the waves   ARN 14:21
noble and approv'd good m.   SHAK 473:24
Old M.   AUDEN 19:18
people are the m.   BURKE 110:18
prevail on our future m.   LOWE 318:23
serve two m.   BIBLE 64:27
spiritual pastors and m.   PRAY 388:16
their Victory but new m.   HAL 237:20
time are m. of their fates   SHAK 448:17
We are the m. at the moment   SHAW 498:25
mastery: achieve of, the m. of HOPK 257:5
voice said in m. while   BROW 98:9
Mastiff: M., greyhound   SHAK 455:1
match: Almighty made 'em to m. the
men   ELIOT 200:19
blue spurt of a lighted m.   BROW 102:14
bread and the big m.   JUV 287:28
dont quite m. your face   ASHF 17:7
love m. was the only thing   EDG 199:21
to make and the m. to win   NEWB 361:8
matched: has m. us with His hour
BROO 94:26
m. of earthly knight's   MAL 328:8
matches: he plays extravagant m. GILB 227:7
m. of the Southron folk   THOM 547:24
Matching: M. their lily-white legs
CLOU 153:15
matchless: now the m. deed's achiev'd
SMART 509:4
matchwood: m., immortal diamond
HOPK 257:1
mate: bold m. of Henry Morgan   MAS 333:21
great artificer Made my m.   STEV 523:3
m. of the Nancy brig   GILB 225:16
shall be the maiden's m.   SCOTT 416:12
there walk'd without a m.   MARV 332:7
mated: thou art m. with a clown TENN 538:19
would be m. with the lion   SHAK 420:26
mater: Magna ista scientiarum m.
BACON 28:8
M. saeva Cupidinum   HOR 261:10
Stabat M. dolorosa   JAC 270:31
Materialismus: Krieg wurde die Welt
in M.   MOLT 354:4
materialistic: Christianity is the most
m.   TEMP 532:11
mates: leaves His shivering m. THOM 549:23
m. and masters the fear   BACON 26:2
mathematics: m., subtile   BACON 27:21
M., rightly viewed   RUSS 412:15
order and mystical m.   BROW 95:20
said to be so like the m.   WALT 563:31

Matilda: M. told such Dreadful Lies
BELL 39:7
matin: glow-worm shows the m.   SHAK 431:14
matre: m. pulchra filia pulchrior HOR 259:22
matrem: ecclesiam non habet m. CYPR 170:19
Matrimonial: M. devotion   GILB 227:3
one cares for m. cooings   BYRON 122:27
matrimony: forms a barrier against m.
KEATS 294:10
in m. is breakfast-time   HERB 246:16
joined together in holy M.   PRAY 388:23
matters of religion and m.   CHES 146:3
more of love than m.   GOLD 232:39
'Tis safest in m. to begin   SHER 506:9
we take m. at its lowest   STEV 521:27
matron: m.'s glance that would GOLD 230:17
Thou sober-suited m.   SHAK 483:6
matter: beginning of any great m.
DRAKE 193:1
Does it m.   SASS 414:13
if it is it doesn't m.   GILB 228:37
is inditing of a good m.   PRAY 392:14
is to take away the m.   BACON 27:11
little 'twill m. to one   HOUS 264:8
m. she drove at succeeded   PRIOR 400:27
More m. with less art   SHAK 431:32
order, said I, this m.   STER 518:28
part nor lot in this m.   BIBLE 73:31
proverb is much m. decocted   FULL 220:11
seeing the root of the m.   BIBLE 52:32
speculations upon m. are voluntary
JOHN 281:32
that the sum of m. remains   BACON 25:15
There is a volume in the m.   POUND 382:15
What is M.   PUNCH 402:15
What is the m. with Mary Jane MILNE 340:10
whose heart is in a m.   BAG 28:31
wretched m. and lame metre   MILT 344:18
mattering: m. once it has stopped
BOWEN 91:2
matters: exercise myself in great m.
PRAY 398:25
m. win great commendation   BACON 25:36
words for little m.   JOHN 275:14
Matthew: M., Mark   ANON 6:15
mature: have in our m. years   TROL 553:11
maturing: bosom-friend of the m. sun
KEATS 293:5
Maud: Come into the garden, M. TENN 540:9
maugree: m. hir heed   CHAU 143:23
Maureens: Julias, Maeves and M. BETJ 43:7
mausoleum: Whose fantastic m.   BETJ 43:9
mavult: enim m. homo verum esse
BACON 28:7
maw: his icy fingers in my m.   SHAK 452:31
maw-crammed: Frets doubt the m. beast
BROW 104:3
mawkish: So sweetly m.   POPE 375:20
mawkishness: thence proceeds m.
KEATS 288:19
maxim: could also will that my m.
KANT 288:9
got The M. Gun   BELL 40:1
useless as a general m.   MAC 323:28
maxima: mea m. culpa   MASS 334:15
Maxime: M. solle ein allgemeines
KANT 288:9
maxims: m. in office ready made
BURKE 108:16
m. preaching down a daughter's TENN 538:22
too much by general m.   BURKE 109:5
maximum: m. of temptation with
SHAW 497:39
May: darling buds of M.   SHAK 492:28
fayr as is the rose in M.   CHAU 143:27
fressh as is the month of M.   CHAU 141:11
fruit and flourish in M.   MAL 328:1
How less what we m. be   BYRON 124:9
In depraved M.   ELIOT 203:4
Is fairer far in M.   JONS 285:8

know not what we m. be   SHAK 436:1
laurel outlives not M.   SWIN 530:5
lawyer tells me I *m*. do   BURKE 109:26
least the seventh of M.   TROL 552:21
maids are M. when they   SHAK 426:23
matter for a M. morning   SHAK 490:10
M. is a pious fraud   LOW 319:15
M. morwenyng on Maluerne   LANG 309:25
may say that M. is come   CLARE 152:14
merry month of M.   BALL 30:10
merry month of M.   BALL 31:13
merry month of M.   BARN 33:32
merry month of M.   BRET 92:5
mid-M.'s eldest child   KEATS 291:21
month of M. Is comen   CHAU 143:29
moonlight-coloured m.   SHEL 503:19
Pink m., double may   BETJ 43:16
Than wish a snow in M.'s   SHAK 456:16
there's an end of M.   HOUS 264:20
Whenas M. was in his pride   BRET 92:5
When that the wife is M.   WATK 565:7
world is white with M.   TENN 534:4
maydenhed: he rafte hire m.   CHAU 143:23
Maying: let's go a-M.   HERR 248:26
May-mess: look: a M.   HOPK 256:29
maypole: organ and the m.   JORD 285:18
where's the M. in the Strand   BRAM 91:23
May-poles: I sing of M.   HERR 248:18
mays: under blanching m.   HOUS 265:8
Maytime: Now in M. to the wicket
   HOUS 262:22
maze: burgeons every m. of quick
   TENN 537:18
mighty m.   POPE 379:1
wander in that golden m.   DRYD 197:16
mazes: in wand'ring m. lost   MILT 346:19
mazily: brooks of Eden m. murmuring
   TENN 533:13
McGregor: Mr M.'s garden   POTT 382:1
McGrew: Dangerous Dan M.   SERV 420:14
me: let m. ever escape them   PRAY 399:10
M. too the Muses made write   VIRG 560:7
no harm happen unto m.   PRAY 389:30
queer save thee and m.   OWEN 366:29
there they died for m.   HOUS 265:6
'This man loved *m*.   LAND 308:25
mead: stream and o'er the m.   BLAKE 87:26
meadow: meander through a m. of margin
   SHER 506:26
painted m.   ADD 2:5
stranger's feet may find the m.   HOUS 265:10
meadows: are no more by-path m.
   STEV 521:32
Do paint the m. with delight   SHAK 457:18
from the m. rich with corn   WHIT 571:15
golden face the m. green   SHAK 493:9
is set in enamelled m.   WALP 562:21
m. runnels   KEATS 289:3
M. trim with daisies pied   MILT 342:20
m. where it glides   ARN 12:22
meadow-sweet: simplest growth of m.
or sorrel   SWIN 528:25
meal: handful of m. in a barrel   BIBLE 51:7
no man gets a full m.   JOHN 276:27
mean: admires m. things is a Snob
   THAC 545:4
careful what they m. thereby   SHAK 486:17
convey more than they m.   CONN 161:11
Down these m. streets   CHAN 139:22
Happy the golden m.   MASS 335:17
if I ever do a m. action   STER 519:3
m. Our object and inglorious   WORD 580:10
no m. of death   SHAK 450:8
nothing common did or m.   MARV 332:9
should say what you m.   CARR 133:29
They m. well   DISR 186:12
Though m. and mighty rotting   SHAK 428:26
to be seated in the m.   SHAK 465:19
what did he m. by that   SHER 505:29
what does it m.   AUDEN 19:14

what I choose it to m.   CARR 135:21
what we m.   ARN 12:22
who loves the golden m.   HOR 260:9
Meander: By slow M.'s margent green
   MILT 341:3
meandering: Meeting those m. down
they   HARDY 240:21
miles m. with a mazy motion   COL 156:28
meaner: because only m. things   ELIOT 201:3
leave all m. things   POPE 379:1
opponent motives m.   BARR 34:9
meanest: m. flowret of the vale   GRAY 235:15
m. of his creatures   BROW 102:36
m. of mankind   POPE 380:1
meaning: another-while m. for meaning
   ALFR 3:17
author to get at his m.   RUSK 411:15
hidden m.—like Basingstoke   GILB 228:36
language charged with m.   POUND 384:1
Love is our Lord's m.   JUL 286:33
m. doesn't matter if it's   GILB 227:21
M., however   CALV 127:24
m. is my meat and drink   BROW 100:31
m. of religion is thus   ARN 16:20
plain man in his plain m.   SHAK 467:19
times when words had a m.   FRAN 227:27
to the m.   CALV 127:11
within the m. of the Act   ANON 4:21
meaningless: polite m. words   YEATS 585:1
meanings: His mind with m. that he
   COWP 167:2
there are two m. packed   CARR 135:21
Where the M., are   DICK 184:1
wrestle With words and m.   ELIOT 202:19
meanly: m. great   SAV 415:5
means: as an end withal, never as m.
   KANT 288:13
best ends by the best m.   HUTC 268:19
By all the m. you can   WESL 568:21
end justifies the m.   BUS 117:4
have to judge beyond my m.   WILDE 574:3
I don't know what it m.   GILB 225:14
in persons of small m.   ELIOT 201:23
knew what England m.   CHES 146:26
live within our m.   WARD 564:36
m. and increased leisure   DISR 185:9
m. in his power which are   KANT 288:11
m. of grace   PRAY 386:2
m. of rising in the world   JOHN 276:29
m. of some change is without   BURKE 111:4
money, m., and content   SHAK 426:3
not live within thy m.   AUDEN 21:6
sight of m. to do ill   SHAK 452:28
take the m. whereby I live   SHAK 468:10
that her hand lacks m.   SHAK 424:25
meant: I knew not all he m.   TENN 534:24
my life seemed m.   BROW 101:22
measels: Did you ever hav the m.
   WARD 564:25
measles: Love is like the m.   JER 272:23
Love's like the m.   JERR 273:3
measure: does it hold good m.   BROW 100:4
fill the m. of the year   KEATS 292:14
good m., pressed down   BIBLE 69:23
in m., like a dancer   ELIOT 202:26
is the m. of the universe   SHEL 503:8
Man is the m. of all things   PROT 401:18
m. of our torment is   KIPL 299:11
M. still for Measure   SHAK 465:5
M. your mind's height   BROW 103:5
narrow m. spans   HOUS 265:13
'Now tread we a m.   SCOTT 417:13
Shrunk to this little m.   SHAK 450:6
Things have their due m.   HOR 261:23
'To lead but one m.   SCOTT 417:12
With what m. ye mete   BIBLE 68:29
measured: dance is a m. pace   BACON 24:23
I've m. it from side   WORD 582:24
m. out my life with coffee spoons
   ELIOT 203:20

m. phrase   WORD 581:1
use in m. language lies   TENN 536:1
Measurement: M. began our might
   YEATS 587:7
Measures: cant of 'M. not men'   CANN 130:7
in short m.   JONS 285:8
system of weights and m.   NAP 359:13
meat: abhorred all manner of m.   PRAY 397:8
benison to fall On our m.   HERR 250:10
can not eat but little m.   ANON 5:21
do seek their m. from God   PRAY 397:1
eater came forth m.   BIBLE 49:21
egg is full of m.   SHAK 483:1
give them m. in due season   PRAY 397:1
Heaven sends us good m.   GARR 221:12
he sent them m. enough   PRAY 395:6
little of solid m. for men   DRYD 198:10
meaning is my m. and drink   BROW 100:31
m. doth this our Caesar   SHAK 448:18
m. in the hall   STEV 523:7
not the life more than m.   BIBLE 64:28
Out-did the m.   HERR 249:16
penny ice and cold m.   GILB 226:14
Some have m. and cannot eat   BURNS 114:14
taste My m.   HERB 248:1
them their m. in due season   PRAY 399:15
They put arsenic in his m.   HOUS 264:15
This dish of m. is too   WALT 564:10
thou gavest m. or drink   BALL 31:7
with cans of poisoned m.   CHES 147:20
ye gave me m.   BIBLE 68:6
meat-fly: Thackeray settled like a m.
   RUSK 411:6
meat-offering: m., thou wouldest not
   PRAY 392:2
meatus: caelique m. Describent radio
   VIRG 559:1
Meccah: some to M. turn to pray FLEC 214:12
mechanic: m. part of wit   ETH 208:30
mechanical: m. arts and merchandise
   BACON 27:34
méchant: Cet animal est très m.   ANON 9:4
un m. animal   MOL 354:2
mécontents: fais cent m. et un ingrat
   LOUI 318:9
meddle: 'm. and muddle'   DERBY 175:9
Not to m. with my toys   STEV 522:19
meddling: Every fool will be m.   BIBLE 54:16
mede: al the floures in the m.   CHAU 143:30
médecine: m. d'une méthode toute
   MOL 353:17
Medes: given to the M. and Persians
   BIBLE 61:6
law of the M. and Persians   BIBLE 61:7
medias: eventum festinat et in m. res
   HOR 257:20
Mediator: our M. and Advocate PRAY 385:23
Medical: M. Crowner's a queer   BARH 33:16
medicina: sero m. paratur   OVID 366:30
medicine: friend is the m. of life BIBLE 62:25
heart doeth good like a m.   BIBLE 54:12
it's late for m. to be   OVID 366:30
m. of our great revenge   SHAK 462:17
m. the less   SHAK 428:19
m. thee to that sweet sleep   SHAK 475:24
m. to heal their sickness   PRAY 399:19
m. worse than the malady   FLET 215:16
miserable have no other m.   SHAK 464:8
My m., work   SHAK 476:8
we now practise m.   MOL 353:17
Medicine Hat: plumed war-bonnet of
M.   BENET 40:19
medicines: me m. to make me love him
   SHAK 438:24
medicus: littera plus sum quam m.
   PLAU 374:15
medieval: lily in your m. hand   GILB 227:23
Medio: M. tutissimus ibis   OVID 366:14
mediocre: tomb of a m. talent   SMITH 510:20

médiocres: L'absence diminue les m.
  passions LA R 310:15
Mediocribus: *M. esse poetis* HOR 258:4
mediocritatem: *Auream quisquis m.*
  HOR 260:9
Mediocrities: over this Cabinet of M.
  DISR 185:36
Mediocrity: M. knows nothing higher
  DOYLE 192:38
  m. of her circumstances SMITH 509:17
meditaris: Silvestrem tenui Musam m.
  avena VIRG 559:11
meditate: matchless songs does m.
  MARV 332:12
  m. the thankless Muse MILT 343:8
meditated: I m. on the Fall BETJ 43:1
meditating: m., or working at something
  THOM 546:11
meditation: disposed to abstracted m.
  JOHN 281:40
  let us all to m. SHAK 446:7
  m. of my heart PRAY 390:13
  notice a cat in profound m. ELIOT 204:6
  sage in m. found SHEL 504:10
  Some happy tone Of m. WORD 582:6
Mediterranean: blue M. SHEL 502:10
  see the shores of the M. JOHN 277:6
medium: m. is the message MCL 325:16
meed: m. of some melodious tear MILT 343:2
meek: am m. and lowly in heart BIBLE 66:5
  believing that the m. shall BIRK 84:12
  Blessed are the m. BIBLE 64:6
  borne his faculties so m. SHAK 459:6
  m. and quiet spirit BIBLE 80:28
  m. and unaffected grace GOLD 230:24
meekest: m. man and the gentlest MAL 328:8
meekly: m. kneeling upon your knees
  PRAY 387:18
meekness: brought salvation down By
  m. SMART 509:4
  m. the engrafted word BIBLE 80:10
meek-spirited: m. shall possess the earth
  PRAY 391:27
meenister: ma doobts aboot the m.
  PUNCH 402:31
meet: brook and river m. LONG 316:20
  comes to m. one's friends BURN 112:22
  'Extremes m. HOOD 255:17
  goeth on to m. the armed men BIBLE 53:6
  If I should m. thee BYRON 126:14
  If we do m. again SHAK 451:32
  It is m. and right so PRAY 387:22
  loved, sir—used to m. BROW 100:8
  make both ends m. FULL 220:12
  M. me at London DONNE 188:2
  m. the raging of the skies CAMP 129:3
  men and mountains m. BLAKE 87:10
  One would m. in every place KEATS 289:32
  shall we three m. again SHAK 458:1
  So I'll m. 'im later KIPL 299:19
  Though infinite can never m. MARV 331:19
  will come out to m. you POUND 383:17
  will make him an help m. BIBLE 45:10
  Yet m. we shall BUTL 119:17
meete: it were a daye very m. MORE 357:20
meeter: therefore deemed it m. PEAC 371:2
meeting: if I was a public m. VICT 556:19
  Journeys end in lovers m. SHAK 488:17
  m. where it likes ARN 15:20
  neither overtaking nor m. CONG 159:25
meets: is meant than m. the ear MILT 342:7
Méfiez-vous: M.! Les oreilles ennemies
  ANON 9:18
Megrim: M. at her head POPE 381:9
melancholic: saturnine, dark, and *m.*
  CONG 159:17
melancholy: black *sun* of *m.* NERV 360:26
  charm can soothe her m. GOLD 231:31
  had this trick of m. SHAK 421:2
  Hail divinest M. MILT 341:25

have a rare recipe for m. LAMB 307:23
loathed M., Of Cerberus MILT 342:12
lovely m. FLET 215:17
m. as an unbrac'd drum CENT 138:11
m. god protect thee SHAK 489:5
m., long, withdrawing ARN 12:23
M. mark'd him for her own GRAY 235:4
m. nor a cynical disposition CHES 145:23
m. of human reflections BAG 29:18
m. out of a song as a weasel SHAK 425:15
m.'s child SHAK 452:2
m. when thou art absent CONG 160:22
moping m. MILT 349:24
most m. MILT 342:2
my cue is villanous m. SHAK 453:12
Naught so sweet as M. BURT 116:12
Pale M. sate retir'd COLL 158:21
sovereign mistress of true m. SHAK 423:4
There's such a charm in m. ROG 407:10
This m. is FORD 216:18
Veil'd M. has her sovran KEATS 291:15
vile m. from my father JOHN 279:33
when the m. fit shall fall KEATS 291:15
wild, m., and elevating BRON 93:17
with a green and yellow m. SHAK 489:7
Young man untroubled by m. BANV 33:1
mélancolie: Jeune homme sans m. BANV 33:1
Melchisedech: ever after the order of
  M. PRAY 397:12
meliora: Video m. OVID 366:17
meliorist: not an optimist but a m.
  ELIOT 201:31
melius: Aurum irrepertum et sic m.
  HOR 260:20
mellificatis: Sic vos non vobis m. apes
  VIRG 560:20
mellow: Indeed is too m. for me MONT 354:7
  m., like good wine PHIL 373:10
mellows: tart temper never m. with
  IRV 270:21
Mellstock: lie in M. churchyard now
  BETJ 42:13
  lie in M. churchyard now HARDY 239:17
melodie: sownes ful of hevenyssh m.
  CHAU 144:18
melodies: Heard m. are sweet KEATS 291:4
  Sweetest m. WORD 579:17
  To ease my breast of m. KEATS 289:25
melodious: divine m. truth KEATS 291:1
  In some m. plot KEATS 291:17
  Melting m. words HERR 250:9
  Move in m. time MILT 344:10
melodramatic: It is lurid and m.
  LAWR 311:11
melody: blund'ring kind of m. DRYD 194:21
  From ancient m. have ceas'd... BLAKE 88:10
  God with the voice of m. PRAY 392:22
  making m. in your heart BIBLE 78:5
  m., in our heaviness PRAY 399:3
  Moved to delight by the m. AUDEN 18:3
  oft than to a chamber m. SIDN 507:27
  pentameter aye falling in m. COL 157:7
  with sound of sweetest m. SHAK 441:29
melodye: smale foweles maken m.
  CHAU 141:8
melon-flower: brighter than this gaudy
  m. BROW 101:7
melons: raiser of huge m. and of pine
  TENN 542:20
  Stumbling on m. MARV 332:3
Melrose: would'st view fair M. aright
  SCOTT 416:13
melt: crown o' the earth doth m. SHAK 423:16
  discandy, m. their sweets SHAK 423:5
  earth shall m. away PRAY 392:20
  I rage, I m., I burn GAY 222:6
  m. itself Into the sea SHAK 442:1
  m. with ruth MILT 343:16
  Now m. into sorrow BYRON 120:1
  So let us m. DONNE 190:17

too solid flesh would m. SHAK 429:28
melted: Are m. into air SHAK 485:20
  M. to one vast Iris BYRON 121:4
  Till he m. like a cloud TENN 542:21
  With that which m. fools SHAK 449:24
melting: body is even like m. wax
  PRAY 390:19
Melting-Pot: great M. where all ZANG 588:17
melts: then m. for ever BURNS 115:7
member: Distinguishable in m. MILT 346:24
  he is a m. of *parliament* BURKE 109:12
  he is not m. of Bristol BURKE 109:12
  is a thing I am not a m. FLEM 215:1
  was made a m. of Christ PRAY 388:12
members: book were all my m. written
  PRAY 399:7
  m. incorporate in the mystical PRAY 388:3
  m. of the common throng GILB 228:22
  m. one of another BIBLE 77:29
membra: disiecti m. poetae HOR 262:2
Membranis: M. intus positis HOR 258:6
meminisse: Forsan et haec olim m. iuvabit
  VIRG 557:14
Nec me m. pigebit Elissae VIRG 558:13
Memling: Emerald findeth no M.
  POUND 382:11
memor: Dum m. ipse mei VIRG 558:13
memorable: m. in the history of our
  CHUR 150:8
memorandum: you don't make a m.
  of it CARR 134:26
memores: m. aliquos fecere merendo
  VIRG 558:23
Memorial: Charles the First out of the
  M. DICK 177:5
  m. longer lasting than HOR 261:8
  Perhaps a frail m. COWP 166:4
  which have no m. BIBLE 63:25
  whole earth as their m. PER 372:23
Memories: M. are hunting horns whose
  APOL 11:10
memorize: m. another Golgotha SHAK 458:4
Memory: Fond M. brings the light
  MOORE 357:2
  Footfalls echo in the m. ELIOT 202:13
  from the m. a rooted sorrow SHAK 463:3
  from the table of my m. SHAK 431:15
  grand m. for forgetting STEV 521:8
  'His m. is going JOHN 279:6
  it comes o'er my m. SHAK 476:7
  M. fades DE L 174:2
  m. of men without distinction BROW 97:18
  m. of yesterday's pleasures DONNE 191:2
  m. that only works backwards CARR 135:16
  Midnight shakes the m. ELIOT 204:9
  mixing M. and desire ELIOT 204:17
  my name and m. BACON 28:14
  Only a m. of the same BROW 101:22
  poetry strays into my m. HOUS 266:17
  Queen *Elizabeth* of most happy m.
  BIBLE 44:20
  Their very m. is fair VAUG 555:18
  there's hope a great man's m. SHAK 434:7
  thy tablets, M. ARN 13:19
  to his m. for his jests SHER 506:36
  while m. holds a seat SHAK 431:15
men: all m. are created equal ANON 8:14
  all things to all m. ANON 6:11
  all things to all m. BIBLE 76:7
  catalogue ye go for m. SHAK 461:9
  clerkes been noght wisest m. CHAU 143:11
  cognizance of m. and things BROW 101:11
  could of m. distinguish SHAK 434:1
  created m. and women different VICT 556:14
  days shall m. seek death BIBLE 82:7
  deals with the memory of m. BROW 97:18
  despised and rejected of m. BIBLE 59:21
  fashions m. with true nobility MARL 330:11
  fear of little m. ALL 3:20
  finds too late that m. betray GOLD 231:31

furnish'd well with m.   SHAK 449:25
great Nature made us m.   LOW 319:11
hell to m.   AESC 3:1
herb for the service of m.   PRAY 396:20
I drew these tides of m.   LAWR 311:12
indignities m. come to dignities
                                         BACON 26:23
I see m. as trees   BIBLE 68:33
it issue not towards m.   BACON 26:19
it's m.'s lives   SCOTT 418:2
justify the ways of God to M.   MILT 344:22
just m. made perfect   BIBLE 80:2
least talked about by m.   PER 372:24
leaves is a generation of m.   HOMER 253:29
life of m. on earth   BEDE 37:1
lips of dying m.   ARN 14:27
make you fishers of m.   BIBLE 64:5
many m.   JOHN 274:22
many m. of large fortune   AUST 22:26
m. all so good for nothing   AUST 23:4
m. and mountains meet   BLAKE 87:10
m. and women with our race   KIPL 298:10
M. are April when they   SHAK 426:23
M. are but children   DRYD 195:15
m. are created equal   JEFF 272:6
m. are everything   CANN 130:7
M. are never so good   MACK 325:11
m. are suspicious   HERR 249:16
m. at most differ as Heaven   TENN 535:16
m. decay   GOLD 230:18
M. don't know women   TROL 552:20
M. fear death   BACON 26:1
m. fought upon the earth   SCOTT 417:20
m. hate one another so   MELB 336:20
M. have precedency   BRAD 91:14
m. in a world of men   KIPL 298:23
M. in great place are thrice   BACON 26:21
m. in shape and fashion   ASCH 17:3
m. in women do require   BLAKE 86:17
M. lived like fishes   SIDN 507:12
M. loved darkness rather   BIBLE 71:39
m. may come and men may   TENN 532:21
M. move unhoming   FRY 220:7
m. must work   KING 297:3
M., my brothers   TENN 538:24
m. naturally were born   MILT 352:18
m. of like passions with   BIBLE 74:5
m. of other minds my fancy   GOLD 231:27
m. only disagree   MILT 346:18
M. seldom make passes   PARK 368:16
m., that are set on fire   PRAY 393:15
m. that were boys when   BELL 40:11
m. that women marry   LONG 316:21
M. were deceivers ever   SHAK 472:16
m. who have loved them   TROL 553:10
M. who march away   HARDY 240:8
m. who will support me   MELB 336:17
m., women, and Herveys   MONT 354:6
m., women, and clergymen   SMITH 511:8
M. would be angels   POPE 379:7
m. would be false   LYLY 321:9
m. would weep upon your   HUXL 268:23
Mocks married m.   SHAK 457:18
need of a world of m.   BROW 103:9
not m., but manners   FIEL 211:14
not stones, but m.   SHAK 450:25
of m. are deceitful upon   PRAY 393:20
proceeded from childless m.   BACON 27:4
proper young m.   BURNS 114:17
punished in the sight of m.   BIBLE 62:13
purgatory of m.   FLOR 216:1
schemes o' mice an' m.   BURNS 115:22
seasons in the mind of m.   KEATS 292:14
sick m.'s dreams   BROW 95:23
Some faults to make us m.   SHAK 423:19
sorts and conditions of m.   PRAY 385:24
stamp is the cant of Not m.   BURKE 108:23
State which dwarfs its m.   MILL 339:15
streets the same as the m.   WHIT 570:15
studied books than m.   BACON 28:13

them to have power over m.   WOLL 576:11
therefore…exceeding tall m.   BACON 25:7
there no way for m. to be   SHAK 428:11
thousand of those m. in England   SHAK 444:27
to form Christian m.   ARN 16:27
tongues of m. and of angels   BIBLE 76:14
trust themselves with m.   SHAK 486:2
unnecessary things are m.   ROCH 406:16
unto the daughters of m.   BIBLE 45:33
us arise and go like m.   STEV 522:35
us in the likeness of m.   BIBLE 74:4
wander in the ways of m.   BURNS 114:15
ways with m. I find Him not   TENN 535:19
What m. or gods are these   KEATS 291:3
When m. were all asleep   BRID 92:12
When m. were fond   SHAK 464:6
Where Destiny with M.   FITZ 213:5
With four-and-twenty m.   AYT 24:6
With m. he can be rational   AUST 22:9
Words are m.'s daughters   MADD 326:19
ye shall die like m.   PRAY 395:10
menace: become a m. to all mankind
                                         NEV 361:2
looks do m. heaven and dare   MARL 330:5
men-children: Bring forth m. only
                                         SHAK 459:11
mend: m. the Electric Light   BELL 39:29
Nor a broken thing m.   BELL 40:10
To m. it or be rid on't   SHAK 461:10
mendacities: Better m.   POUND 383:4
mendacity: only equalled by their m.
                                         TEMP 532:8
mendax: Splendide m. et in omne virgo
                                         HOR 261:2
mended: all is m.   SHAK 471:23
endure what can't be m.   WATTS 565:27
nothing else but to be m.   BUTL 117:22
mendicity: class of clergymen whose
m.   TEMP 532:8
Mendicus: M. es   PLAU 374:15
mendier: de m. dans les rues et   FRAN 217:26
MENE: M.; God hath numbered   BIBLE 61:6
menny: Done because we are too m.
                                         HARDY 241:15
menpleasers: with eyeservice, as m.
                                         BIBLE 78:8
Mens: M. agitat molem et magno   VIRG 558:24
M. cuiusque is est quisque   CIC 151:24
m. sana in corpore sano   JUV 288:4
m. sibi conscia recti   VIRG 557:18
mensa: Nec deus hunc m.   VIRG 560:2
Mensch: Es irrt der M.   GOET 229:29
M. fand die Tiere nicht   NIET 363:3
Menschen: Alle M. werden Brüder   SCH 415:9
verbrennt man am Ende auch M.
                                         HEINE 244:14
mental: m. pursuit for the Building
                                         BLAKE 86:10
m. suffering had been undergone
                                         BUTL 119:12
will not cease from M.   BLAKE 86:16
mention: m. of you in our prayers
                                         BIBLE 78:30
we never m. her   BAYLY 35:10
Without ceasing I make m.   BIBLE 74:29
mentioned: allow their names to be m.
                                         AUST 23:19
mer: savent les secrets de la m.   NERV 361:1
mercenary: Followed their m. calling
                                         HOUS 265:7
merchandise: mechanical arts and m.
                                         BACON 27:34
Mummy is become m.   BROW 97:22
merchant: heaven is like unto a m. man
                                         BIBLE 66:21
m. shall hardly keep himself   BIBLE 63:10
m., to secure his treasure   PRIOR 401:1
merchantman: monarchy is a m. which
                                         AMES 4:3
merchants: like m., venture trade   SHAK 443:9

whose m. are princes   BIBLE 58:16
mercies: tender m. of the wicked   BIBLE 53:34
Thanks for m. past receive   BUCK 106:17
merciful: Blessed are the m.   BIBLE 64:6
'God be m. to a soul   ANON 10:14
God be m. to me a sinner   BIBLE 70:35
God be m. unto us   PRAY 394:4
In a m. eclipse   GILB 225:26
Then must the Jew be m.   SHAK 467:27
was very m. to the birds   ANON 8:15
merciless: black and m. things   JAMES 271:23
mercis: aura plus tost de vous m.   VILL 557:4
Mercuries: English M.   SHAK 443:12
Mercury: ground like feather'd M.
                                         SHAK 440:7
littered under M.   SHAK 491:18
m. sank in the mouth   AUDEN 19:2
To Saturn nor to M.   HOUS 264:26
words of M. are harsh after   SHAK 457:20
Mercy: Charity and M.   DICK 179:6
dimensions of this m. are   CROM 169:22
easy in the m. of his means   THOM 547:2
emboldens sin so much as m.   SHAK 486:6
folks over to God's m.   ELIOT 200:17
full of compassion and m.   BIBLE 62:21
God all m. is a God unjust   YOUNG 588:9
God ha' m. on such as we   KIPL 299:10
God have m. upon one   SHAK 490:12
gracious m. and protection   PRAY 389:9
leaving m. to heaven   FIEL 211:24
likely to have m. on you   VILL 557:4
Lord, have m. upon us   PRAY 384:18
m., and faith   BIBLE 67:24
M. and truth are met   PRAY 395:15
m. does   SHAK 463:20
m. embraceth him on every   PRAY 391:18
m. endureth for ever   PRAY 399:2
M. has a human heart   BLAKE 88:7
M. I asked   CAMD 128:5
m. Of a rude stream   SHAK 447:9
m. to forgive   DRYD 196:14
m. unto thousands of them   BIBLE 47:24
m. upon us miserable sinners   PRAY 385:15
property is ever to have m.   PRAY 385:23
quality of m. is not strain'd   SHAK 467:27
shut the gates of m.   GRAY 234:24
so is his m.   BIBLE 62:22
temper so Justice with m.   MILT 349:21
That m. I to others show   POPE 381:13
they shall obtain m.   BIBLE 64:6
Thy m. on Thy People   KIPL 302:10
to love m.   BIBLE 61:25
When m. seasons justice   SHAK 467:27
will have m. on Jacob yet   BROW 101:3
Meredith: M. is a prose Browning
                                         WILDE 573:37
while M. climbed towards   CHES 148:7
merely: I can m. be your friend   LEAR 312:1
merendo: memores aliquos fecere m.
                                         VIRG 558:23
mereri: quicquam bene velle m.   CAT 137:8
meridian: under any m.   BROW 96:29
merit: by the m. of the wearer   SHAK 466:20
from sense of injured m.   MILT 345:2
his m. handsomely allowed   JOHN 278:32
m. raise the tardy bust   JOHN 282:29
m.'s all his own   CHUR 149:15
m. wins the soul   POPE 381:11
praise the m. of a foe   POPE 378:32
preacher's m. or demerit   BROW 100:4
talk of m. for a bishopric   WEST 569:5
there is no damned m. in it   MELB 336:12
What is m.   PALM 368:12
mérite: gouvernement qu'elle m.   MAIS 327:8
merits: m. of a spotless shirt   TENN 540:23
not weighing our m.   PRAY 388:2
Mermaid: Choicer than the M. Tavern
                                         KEATS 290:28
Done at the M.   BEAU 35:19
M. in the Zodiac   KEATS 290:29

m. on a dolphin's back SHAK 470:7
Which is the M.'s now JONS 284:1
mermaids: have heard the m. singing
ELIOT 203:25
So many m. SHAK 422:3
merrier: m. man SHAK 456:21
merrily: die all, die m. SHAK 440:8
m. hent the stile-a SHAK 491:21
M. sang the monks in Ely CAN 130:9
m. shall I live now SHAK 485:25
Sing we m. unto God our PRAY 395:9
we went m. BYRON 125:23
merriment: hopeless than a scheme of
m. JOHN 281:21
m. of parsons is mighty JOHN 278:25
source of innocent m. GILB 227:5
merry: all went m. as a marriage
BYRON 120:20
be m. BIBLE 70:4
chances men are ever m. SHAK 442:12
even the wise are m. YEATS 585:18
gone up with a m. noise PRAY 392:24
Have they been m. SHAK 483:29
I am not m. SHAK 474:17
It's guid to be m. BURNS 114:5
M. and tragical SHAK 471:1
m. Grecian coaster ARN 14:21
m. heart doeth good like BIBLE 54:12
m. heart goes all the day SHAK 491:21
m. heart maketh a cheerful BIBLE 54:5
m. in hall when beards SHAK 442:26
m. misery BETJ 44:1
m. monarch ROCH 407:2
m. month of May BALL 30:10
m. month of May BALL 31:13
m. month of May BARN 33:32
m. month of May BRET 92:5
m. when I hear sweet music SHAK 468:16
m. world since the fairies SELD 419:24
never m. world in England SHAK 446:10
to be m. BIBLE 55:26
to have such a m. day once PEPYS 372:20
you were born in a m. hour SHAK 472:12
merrygoround: It's no go the m. MACN 326:7
merryman: It's a song of a m. GILB 229:9
Merses: *M. profundo* HOR 261:12
meruit: *Palmam qui m.* JORT 285:19
merye: wantowne and a m. CHAU 141:19
meschaunce: Friday fil al this m. CHAU 143:3
Mesech: constrained to dwell with M.
PRAY 398:7
Meshach: Shadrach, M., and Abed-nego
BIBLE 61:4
mess: birthright for a m. of potage
BIBLE 46:12
birthrite for a m. of potash WARD 564:22
every m. I finds a friend DIBD 175:18
message: give to a gracious m. SHAK 422:12
medium is the m. MCL 325:16
simple m. to the world of man AUDEN 19:11
messager: m. of day CHAU 142:18
messages: receive fair speechless m.
SHAK 465:17
messe: *Paris vaut bien une m.* HENR 245:15
messenger: m. of Satan to buffet me
BIBLE 77:13
other M.'s called Hatta CARR 135:30
messengers: bade his m. ride forth
MAC 322:11
superfluous kings for m. SHAK 422:15
messes: other country m. MILT 342:21
messing: simply m. about in boats
GRAH 233:18
mesures: *système de poids et m.* NAP 359:13
met: day and the way we m. SWIN 530:10
Hail, fellow, well m. SWIFT 527:30
He was m. even now SHAK 455:13
know how first he m. her THAC 546:3
Mercy and truth are m. PRAY 395:15
M. again, my lass HOUS 265:5

m. each other with erected DRYD 197:30
m. my dearest foe in heaven SHAK 430:4
m. them at close of day YEATS 585:1
M. you not with my true RAL 404:13
never be m. with again CARR 133:7
That have m. many one RAL 404:13
When first we m. we did BRID 92:22
metal: Here's m. more attractive SHAK 434:5
my m. of India SHAK 489:9
metaphor: All slang is m. CHES 147:29
to hunt down a tired m. BYRON 124:2
Metaphysic: M. calls for aid on Sense
POPE 375:26
m. wit can fly BUTL 117:20
metaphysical: fate and m. aid SHAK 459:1
métaphysiciens: *dirais volontiers des
m.* CHAM 139:16
metaphysics: of divinity or school m.
HUME 267:15
to circumnavigate the m. STEV 522:2
mete: his hous of m. and drynke CHAU 141:28
With what measure ye m. BIBLE 68:29
metempsychosis: Pythagoras' m.
MARL 329:14
meteor: cloud-encircled m. of the air
SHEL 501:18
Now slides the silent m. TENN 542:14
Shone like a m. streaming MILT 345:19
method: by a completely new m. MOL 353:17
m. and secret and sweet ARN 16:22
m. of making a fortune GRAY 235:21
yet there is m. in't SHAK 432:9
méthode: *d'une m. toute nouvelle* MOL 353:17
methodically: must elope m. GOLD 232:17
Methodist: spiritualized by a M. preacher
WALP 562:27
with the morals of a M. GILB 228:33
methods: different m. different men excel
CHUR 148:23
You know my m. DOYLE 192:8
You know my m. DOYLE 192:31
Methought: M. I heard a voice cry
SHAK 460:8
m. what pain it was SHAK 480:27
Methuselah: all the days of M. were
BIBLE 45:31
métier: *c'est son m.* CATH 136:17
m. et mon art c'est vivre MONT 354:23
m. que de faire un livre LA B 306:12
metre: laws of God and man and m.
LOCK 316:1
m.-making argument EMER 207:29
stretched out of an antique SHAK 492:27
these same m. ballad-mongers SHAK 439:25
understanding what m. is COL 158:4
wretched matter and lame m. MILT 344:18
metropolis: called...'the m. of the empire'
COBB 154:10
mettle: m. in death which commits
SHAK 421:20
m. of your pasture SHAK 444:2
undaunted m. should compose SHAK 459:11
metuant: *dum m.* ACC 1:3
Metus: *M. et malesuada Fames* VIRG 558:21
meum: distinctions of *m.* and *tuum*
LAMB 307:13
M. est propositum ANON 10:14
meurs: *souffre et m. sans parler* VIGNY 557:2
meurt: *m. le bruit parmi le vent* APOL 11:10
On ne m. qu'une fois MOL 353:8
mew: be a kitten and cry m. SHAK 439:25
Let cat's m. rise AUDEN 20:8
Mewling: M. and puking in the nurse's
SHAK 425:24
Mexique Bay: Echo beyond the M.
MARV 331:17
mezzanine: to slip down to the m.
WOD 575:23
mezzo: *m. del cammin di nostra* DANTE 171:2
mice: Appear like m. SHAK 455:14

Like little m. SUCK 524:8
schemes o' m. an' men BURNS 115:22
Michael: M. and his angels fought
BIBLE 82:11
to blessed M. the Archangel MASS 334:15
Michael Angelo: Enter M. BEER 37:25
I believe in M. SHAW 496:22
Italy from designs by M. TWAIN 554:11
M. for breakfast...for luncheon
TWAIN 554:10
might be the name of—M. REYN 405:19
Michelangelo: Talking of M. ELIOT 203:18
micher: m. and eat blackberries SHAK 439:14
miching: this is m. mallecho SHAK 434:9
microscopes: magnifyin' gas m. of hextra
power DICK 182:23
microscopic: Why has not man a m. eye
POPE 379:8
Midas: ass's ears of M. SIDN 508:5
mid-career: Glorious the sun in m.
SMART 509:4
mid-day: more clear, than our m.
DONNE 189:32
midden: m. whose odours will madden
AUDEN 18:17
middle: cannot steer A m. course
MASS 335:18
companions for m. age BACON 26:34
into the m. of things HOR 257:20
me in the m. of my being LAWR 311:3
m. course is the safest OVID 366:14
M. of Next Week CARR 133:12
m. of the road of our life DANTE 171:2
m. state MALL 327:12
someone of the m. class BELL 39:30
Tenants of life's m. state COWP 167:33
Middle Age: enchantments of the M.
Home ARN 15:25
last enchantment of the M. BEER 37:26
m. is to *find out* that POUND 383:22
Restraining reckless m. YEATS 586:8
middle-ageing: With m. care POUND 383:20
Middle Class: M. was quite prepared
BELL 39:6
What is m. morality SHAW 498:14
Middlesex: acre in M. is better than
MAC 324:10
middle-sized: m. are alone entangled
SHEN 505:16
midge: lightly skims the m. BETJ 42:18
Spins like a fretful m. ROSS 409:17
Midian: host of m. was beneath BIBLE 49:16
Midland: M. waters with the gale ARN 14:21
Midlands: When I am living in the M.
BELL 40:9
midnight: at m. speak with the Sun
VAUG 555:11
At the m. in the silence BROW 98:31
blackest M. born MILT 342:12
books consum'd the m. oil GAY 223:10
budding morrow in m. KEATS 292:25
embalmer of the still m. KEATS 292:28
heard the chimes at m. SHAK 442:6
hill during a clear m. HARDY 241:9
iron tongue of m. hath SHAK 471:20
m. never come MARL 329:11
M. shakes the memory ELIOT 204:9
m. shroud the serene lights SHEL 504:7
m. when the noon-heat breathes
HARDY 239:18
mock the m. bell SHAK 422:22
Not to be a-bed after m. SHAK 488:16
Once upon a m. dreary POE 375:4
our m. oil QUAR 403:10
sigh'd upon a m. pillow SHAK 425:9
stroke of m. ceases HOUS 265:17
There m.'s all a-glimmer YEATS 585:17
threshed corn at m. by a tress YEATS 586:17
'Tis the year's m. DONNE 189:27
to hear the chimes at m. STEV 522:2

troubled m. and the noon's ELIOT 202:11
upon the m. with no pain KEATS 291:22
Upon the m. hour KEATS 292:2
visions before m. BROW 95:23
mid-sea: Painted the m. blue FLEC 214:17
midshipmite: bo'sun tight, and a m.
GILB 225:16
midst: God is in the m. of her PRAY 392:20
m. of life we are in death PRAY 389:12
them in the m. of his days BIBLE 60:25
Midsummer: high M. pomps come ARN 15:6
this is very m. madness SHAK 490:6
midwife: She is the fairies' m. SHAK 481:28
mid-winter: In the bleak m. ROSS 409:1
mie: J'aime mieux ma m. ANON 9:17
mien: dark hair and lovesome m.
TENN 532:16
mieux: je vais de mieux en m. COUE 163:8
m. est l'ennemi du bien VOLT 561:5
Tout est pour le m. dans VOLT 561:2
Might: Because the all-enacting M.
HARDY 240:6
do it with thy m. BIBLE 55:29
Exceeds man's m. SHAK 487:1
faith that right makes m. LINC 314:17
'It m. have been HARTE 242:28
'It m. have been WHIT 571:19
Lord of all power and m. PRAY 386:19
majority has the m. IBSEN 269:18
Measurement began our m. YEATS 587:7
m. of Denmark's crown CAMP 128:14
of hearts I feel your m. WORD 579:13
our m. lessens ANON 8:9
spirit of counsel and m. BIBLE 58:9
them mirth us'd all his m. MILT 347:26
woman's m. SHAK 449:22
You m. as well live PARK 368:18
Might-have-been: my name is M. ROSS 410:4
mightier: imposition of a m. hand
MAC 323:26
pen is m. than the sword BULW 107:4
word m. than they in arms MILT 348:26
mightiest: 'Tis m. in the mightiest
SHAK 467:27
mighty: according to the m. working
PRAY 389:13
bringeth m. things to pass PRAY 398:1
God who made thee m. BENS 40:24
how are the m. fallen BIBLE 50:16
How are the m. fallen BIBLE 50:17
Lord m. in battle PRAY 390:24
m. from their seats BIBLE 69:6
m. hand and by a stretched BIBLE 48:19
m. things from small beginnings
DRYD 195:22
same became m. men which BIBLE 45:33
there the shield of the m. BIBLE 50:16
things which are m. BIBLE 75:30
thou art m. yet SHAK 452:3
Though mean and m. rotting SHAK 428:20
migrations: our m. from the blue bed
GOLD 232:34
mild: brought reg'lar and draw'd m.
DICK 179:12
m. and magnificent eye BROW 102:5
m. as she is seeming so GREE 236:10
mildest: He was the m. manner'd
BYRON 122:30
mildews: m. the white wheat SHAK 454:22
mile: compel thee to go a m. BIBLE 64:18
Miles: M. and miles distant though
ROSS 409:26
m. around the wonder grew HOUS 263:1
m. to go before I sleep FROST 219:12
na on the lang Scots m. BURNS 115:3
People come m. to see it GILB 227:10
Sed m., sed pro patria NEWB 361:5
milestones: There's m. on the Dover
Road DICK 178:22
Militant: Poets M. below COWL 164:16

state of Christ's Church m. PRAY 387:12
military: Forsaking even m. men GILB 228:39
m. domination of Prussia ASQ 17:17
m. empires of the shark AUDEN 20:15
order and m. discipline ANON 4:28
thing to be left to the m. CLEM 152:31
When the m. man approaches SHAW 497:30
militavi: Et m. non sine gloria HOR 261:6
milk: are gone to m. the bull JOHN 275:3
buy wine and m. BIBLE 59:25
drunk the m. of Paradise COL 157:1
find a trout in the m. THOR 550:24
flowing with m. and honey BIBLE 47:6
forstre hym wel with m. CHAU 142:25
Gin was mother's m. SHAW 498:15
...Kindly pass the m. PAIN 367:18
little drop of m. PAIN 367:19
M. and then just as it BETJ 42:20
m. comes frozen home SHAK 457:19
m. is more likely to be BUTL 119:4
m. my ewes and weep SHAK 492:5
m. of human kindness BURKE 112:3
m. of human kindness CHUR 148:22
m. of human kindness SHAK 459:1
m. the cow of the world WILB 572:4
m. were scarce out of him SHAK 488:9
she gave him m. BIBLE 49:10
sincere m. of the word BIBLE 80:22
sincere m. of the word BIBLE 83:25
suggestion as a cat laps m. SHAK 485:6
take my m. for gall SHAK 459:2
than putting m. into babies CHUR 150:15
white curd of ass's m. POPE 376:30
milking: to the m. shed ING 270:15
Milk-soup: M. men call domestic bliss
PATM 370:4
milk-white: mounted on her m. steed
BALL 32:4
Mill: In Hans' old M. his three DE L 174:4
John Stuart M. BENT 41:8
m. and the fold HOUS 263:6
m. turns round POPE 381:6
water glideth by the m. SHAK 486:15
mille: Ay clappeth as a m. CHAU 142:10
Da mi basia m. CAT 136:26
Miller: hackney'd jokes from M.
BYRON 124:17
Than wots the m. SHAK 486:15
There was a jolly m. once BICK 83:28
millinery: That jewell'd mass of m.
TENN 540:1
million: Treble that m. HERR 249:22
millionaire: Endowed by the ruined m.
ELIOT 202:22
I am a M. SHAW 497:11
silk hat on a Bradford m. ELIOT 205:1
million-murdering: m. Death ROSS 408:20
millions: among so many m. of faces
BROW 96:31
Jesus they run into m. ROST 410:15
m. of strange shadows SHAK 493:15
mortal m. live *alone* ARN 13:12
our yearly multiplying m. OSUL 365:23
What m. died CAMP 129:8
mills: dark Satanic m. BLAKE 86:16
m. of God grind slowly LOGAU 316:5
millstone: m. were hanged abut his
BIBLE 67:3
m. were hanged about his BIBLE 70:30
mill-stones: Turned to m as they fell
SHEL 502:3
mill-wheel: Except the m.'s sound
SHEL 500:3
Milton: classic M. BRID 92:9
England's M. equals both COWP 167:34
malt does more than M. HOUS 264:12
M. almost requires a solemn LAMB 307:19
M., a name to resound TENN 533:12
M., Death, and Sin YOUNG 588:14
M.'s the prince of poets BYRON 123:5

M.! thou shouldst be living WORD 582:5
M. was for us BROW 102:5
M. wrote in fetters when BLAKE 88:12
morals hold Which M. held WORD 582:3
Some mute inglorious M. GRAY 234:23
mimicked: beggars in the street m.
MAC 323:33
mimsy: All m. were the borogoves
CARR 134:28
mince: honesty and love doth m. SHAK 475:6
They dined on m. LEAR 312:14
mind: am not in my perfect m. SHAK 456:1
amplitude of m. WORD 580:26
autumn in the m. SPAR 514:22
beauty is the m. diseased BYRON 121:13
be of one m. in an house PRAY 394:7
body fill'd and vacant m. SHAK 444:25
calm the troubled m. CONG 159:31
certain unsoundness of m. MAC 323:23
chords in the human m. DICK 176:15
Church and broad of m. BETJ 44:14
Come back into my m. BELL 40:9
complicated state of m. GILB 227:21
conjunction of the m. MARV 331:19
corridors into the m. DOUG 191:7
dagger of the m. SHAK 459:15
depths of his own oceanic m. COL 158:8
dictates of his godlike m. OTWAY 365:27
effectually robs the m. BURKE 108:9
ever by the eternal m. WORD 579:7
excursions in my own m. COL 157:29
feeling which arrests the m. JOYCE 286:17
find the m.'s construction SHAK 458:22
fishy form and m. BROO 94:13
fit of absence of m. SEEL 419:16
fixed m. And high disdain MILT 345:2
fog of the good man's m. BROW 100:1
fond and foolish m. BALL 30:8
fool utterest all his m. BIBLE 54:43
frailty of the m. CONG 161:3
furnish'd with a m. so rare SHAK 428:7
generous and elevated m. JOHN 282:19
golden m. stoops not SHAK 466:16
heart argues, not the m. ARN 13:20
He first damages his m. ANON 10:1
Henceforth my wooing m. SHAK 457:16
her m. grew worse and worse WORD 577:24
his belly will hardly m. JOHN 275:11
His m. his kingdom COWP 167:37
His m. moves upon silence YEATS 586:3
his m. or body to prefer POPE 379:12
how little the m. is actually JOHN 276:23
how love exalts the m. DRYD 195:33
human m. in ruins DAV 172:13
I have a man's m. SHAK 449:22
index of a feeling m. COWP 168:24
in his right m. BIBLE 68:31
Intense irradiation of a m. SHEL 501:18
in the m. of man WORD 578:7
is no passion in the m. BACON 26:2
is nothing great but m. HAM 238:16
labyrinthine ways Of my own m. THOM 548:8
Let this m. be in you BIBLE 78:13
man but chang'd his m. POPE 377:10
man's unconquerable m. WORD 582:17
man that has a m. and knows SHAW 496:3
marble index of a m. WORD 580:17
march of m. has marched PEAC 370:13
Measure your m.'s height BROW 103:5
men agree to be of one m. BACON 25:11
m. and hand went together HEM 245:2
m. and soul, according TENN 535:32
m. be a thoroughfare KEATS 294:26
m., body, or estate PRAY 386:1
m. does not make us soft PER 372:22
m., from pleasure less MARV 332:4
m. has a thousand eyes BOUR 90:21
m. has mountains HOPK 256:20
m. impatient SHAK 429:26
m. in a sound body JUV 288:4

m. instilled throughout — VIRG 558:24
m. is free — DRAY 193:8
m. not to be changed — MILT 345:10
M. of Man — WORD 577:8
m. quite vacant is a mind — COWP 166:19
m. serene for contemplation — GAY 223:17
m. the things of the flesh — BIBLE 75:7
m.; which experienced — SMITH 511:33
minister to a m. diseas'd — SHAK 463:3
moved slowly through the m. — WORD 580:14
my m. baulks at it — COMP 159:13
my m.'s unsworn — EUR 209:4
My m. to me a kingdom is — DYER 199:17
noblest frailty of the m. — SHAD 420:20
not their frame of m. — HOR 258:19
of a sound m. — BIBLE 79:22
of m. to have few things — BACON 26:8
of the human m. is slow — BURKE 109:29
one dead level ev'ry m. — POPE 375:24
out of sight is out of m. — CLOU 154:5
padlock—on her m. — PRIOR 400:23
perfect presence of m. — JAMES 271:29
persuaded in his own m. — BIBLE 79:27
pleased to call your m. — WEST 569:3
raise and erect the m. — BACON 24:19
seasons in the m. of men — KEATS 292:14
serve thee with a quiet m. — PRAY 386:22
She had a frugal m. — COWP 165:17
She undertem her m. afterwards — LAMB 307:9
So let extend thy m. o'er — MILT 350:7
squares of his m. were — AUDEN 19:3
subsistence without a m. — BERK 41:19
that the female m. is not — KNOX 305:24
there's no blemish but the m. — SHAK 490:18
thy m. all virtue — JOHN 274:4
thy m. is a very opal — SHAK 489:5
To cure the m.'s wrong — GREEN 235:28
To work my m. — SHAK 493:5
universal frame is without a m. — BACON 25:22
unseemly exposure of the m. — HAZL 243:26
untrodden region of my m. — KEATS 292:3
want to light up my own m. — BROW 102:19
Was never m. — ROYD 411:3
what a noble m. is here — SHAK 433:15
What is M. — PUNCH 402:15
when the m. lays by its — CAT 136:28
When the m.'s free — SHAK 454:13
whose untutor'd m. — POPE 379:5
Will not go from my m. — SHAK 476:26
with a well-informed m. — AUST 23:5
With profits of the m. — SHAK 463:14
minded: had m. what they were about — STER 519:16
Mindful: M. of th' unhonour'd dead — GRAY 235:3
that thou art m. of him — PRAY 389:28
minds: actions speak great m. — FLET 215:18
cultivated by narrow m. — MILL 339:1
fairly developed m. — FORS 216:22
great empire and little m. — BURKE 110:6
hobgoblin of little m. — EMER 207:18
hunger of ambitious m. — SPEN 516:21
images of their m. where — BACON 27:4
keep your hearts and m. — BIBLE 78:21
marriage of true m. — SHAK 495:5
M. innocent and quiet take — LOV 318:18
only the refuge of weak m. — CHES 145:28
Since wars begin in the m. — ANON 7:16
spur of all great m. — CHAP 140:15
things affect little m. — DISR 186:30
Thou m. me o' departed joys — BURNS 116:7
To men of other m. my fancy — GOLD 231:27
will not weed their own m. — WALP 563:17
mine: be m. the shame — DRYD 196:13
but m. own — SHAK 427:4
he was but one hour m. — SHAK 493:10
Manasses is m. — PRAY 393:18
m. own familiar friend — PRAY 393:11
shall be m. — JONS 284:1
then shouldst thou have m. — SUCK 524:12

'Twas m., 'tis his — SHAK 475:16
would she were m. — LODGE 316:4
minefield: What a m. Life is — FRY 220:8
mineral: animal, and m. — GILB 228:16
miners: rugged m. poured to war — MAC 321:27
Minerva: dices faciesve M. — HOR 258:5
M. when she talks — JONS 285:5
written or created unless M. — HOR 258:5
mines: Like plants in m. which — BROW 103:7
M. reported in the fairway — KIPL 301:12
one yard below their m. — SHAK 435:21
mingle: one another's being m. — SHEL 502:1
To m. with the Universe — BYRON 121:22
mingled: desired my dust to be m. — POUND 383:16
When hearts have once m. — SHEL 501:22
mining-claims: snakeskin-titles of m. — BENET 40:19
minion: Like valour's m. carv'd — SHAK 458:3
this morning morning's m. — HOPK 257:4
minished: for the faithful are m. — PRAY 389:32
Minister: become the King's First M. — CHUR 150:12
discreet and learned M. — PRAY 387:17
God help the M. that meddles — MELB 336:16
m. kiss'd the fiddler's — BURNS 114:28
m. to a mind diseas'd — SHAK 463:3
one fair spirit for my m. — BYRON 121:21
patient Must m. to himself — SHAK 463:3
wisdom of a great m. — JUN 287:3
ministered: Angels came and m. unto — BIBLE 64:4
thousand thousands m. unto him — BIBLE 61:8
ministering: m. angel thou — SCOTT 417:21
m. angel shall my sister — SHAK 437:4
ministers: Angels and m. of grace — SHAK 430:24
Are they m. of Christ — BIBLE 77:11
grim Geneva m. — AYT 24:10
little errands for the M. — GILB 225:24
m. a flaming fire — PRAY 396:18
m. of the new testament — BIBLE 77:4
m. to consult the public — SWIFT 526:8
my actions are my m. — CHAR 140:23
passion-winged M. of thought — SHEL 499:7
you murdering m. — SHAK 459:2
ministrations: m. to one and to all — HARDY 238:22
ministries: Times has made many m. — BAG 28:24
ministry: if the secret m. of frost — COL 156:23
marriage than a m. — BAG 28:29
m. of all the talents — ANON 7:26
work of the m. — BIBLE 77:28
Minnehaha: M., Laughing Water — LONG 317:11
minnows: you this Triton of the m. — SHAK 427:21
minor: spared these m. monuments — BROW 97:12
Minorities: M. almost always — SMITH 511:19
minority: efficient m. to coerce — STEP 518:20
m. is always right — IBSEN 269:18
Minstrel: M. Boy to the war is gone — MOORE 356:13
M. was infirm and old — SCOTT 416:8
ring the fuller m. — TENN 537:15
wandering m. — GILB 226:18
mint: pockets the mark of the m. — CHES 147:22
tithe of m. and anise — BIBLE 67:24
mintage: coiner the m. of man — HOUS 263:8
mints: m., savory — SHAK 491:25
minuet: Inconsolable to the m. in Ariadne — SHER 505:26
minute: Cynthia of this m. — POPE 377:18
do it in M. Particulars — BLAKE 86:7
fill the unforgiving m. — KIPL 300:2
is too m. — GOLD 232:3
m. domestic happiness — KEATS 294:10
m.'s success pays — BROW 98:27

sucker born every m. — BARN 34:6
Then the good m. goes — BROW 105:29
minutes: I have been five m. too — COWL 164:21
m. capons — SHAK 437:34
our m. hasten to their end — SHAK 493:19
see the m. how they run — SHAK 446:18
set with sixty diamond m. — MANN 328:14
think for two m. together — SMITH 511:35
three m. is a long time — HOUS 266:12
to take care of the m. — CHES 145:18
Minx: I am a M., or a Sphinx — DICK 181:14
Mirabeau: Sous le pont M. coule la — APOL 11:11
mirabilia: quia m. fecit — BIBLE 83:7
miracle: any m. attested by a sufficient — HUME 267:18
existence is a mere m. — STEV 522:6
first m. that he wrought — PRAY 388:25
shoulder-blade that is a m. — GILB 227:10
Take the m. of our age — CAREW 130:11
That m. of a youth — EVEL 209:8
would seem a M. — DONNE 190:24
wrought m. to convince atheism — BACON 25:23
miracles: first attended with m. — HUME 267:21
M. do not happen — ARN 16:16
miraculous: With most m. organ — SHAK 433:5
mire: fury and the m. of human — YEATS 584:12
out of the m. and clay — PRAY 392:1
slimepit and the m. — HOUS 265:4
that throw pebbles and m. — WATTS 565:26
mirk: It was m. — BALL 32:6
miroir: et casser son m. — ANON 9:12
mirror: alone and smash his m. — ANON 9:12
Following the m. of all — SHAK 443:12
for fear They m. true — HOUS 262:21
m. crack'd from side — TENN 538:11
m. up to nature — SHAK 433:17
use of a m. — MAC 323:31
mirrors: m. of the sea are strewn — FLEC 214:21
Over the m. meant — HARDY 239:4
Mirth: Bards of Passion and of M. — KEATS 290:31
buys a minute's m. to wail — SHAK 492:18
dim and decorous m. — BROO 94:16
Far from all resort of m. — MILT 342:5
Howe'er in m. most magnified — POUND 383:19
I'll use you for my m. — SHAK 451:16
I love such m. as does — WALT 564:6
In m., that after no repenting — MILT 351:11
limit of becoming m. — SHAK 456:21
M., admit me of thy crew — MILT 342:16
M. can do with her enticing — ANON 6:7
m. hath present laughter — SHAK 488:17
m. in funeral and with — SHAK 429:19
m. that has no bitter springs — KIPL 298:12
them m. us'd all his might — MILT 347:26
Where's all the joy and m. — KEPP 295:12
misbehaved: I m. once at a funeral — LAMB 307:27
misbeliever: You call me m. — SHAK 466:2
miscarriage: success and m. are empty — JOHN 274:14
to be disgraced by m. — JOHN 281:5
miscarriages: pregnancies and at least four m. — BEEC 37:7
Misce: M. stultitiam consiliis — HOR 261:20
miscet: et magno se corpore m. — VIRG 558:24
mischief: All punishment is m. — BENT 40:27
either of virtue or m. — BACON 26:31
From all evil and m. — PRAY 385:16
hand to execute any m. — CLAR 152:19
Have willed more m. than — HOUS 263:13
if m. befell him — BIBLE 46:35
intended m. against thee — PRAY 390:15
it means m. — SHAK 434:9
little knowest the m. — NEWT 362:21
little neglect may breed m. — FRAN 218:6
m. he had a heart to resolve — GIBB 224:28

m. still for hands that　　MADAN 326:17
m., thou art afoot　　SHAK 451:6
Satan finds some m. still　　WATTS 565:22
Spectatress of the m. which　　ROWE 410:23
To m. trained　　CHUR 149:5
mischiefs: I will heap m. upon them
　　BIBLE 48:32
M. feed Like beasts　　JONS 285:16
record the m. he has done　　COWP 166:30
mischievous: m. excitability is　　BAG 28:20
m. devil Love　　BUTL 119:2
miscuit: m. utile dulci　　HOR 258:1
misdoings: sorry for these our m.
　　PRAY 387:19
miserable: are of all men most m.
　　BIBLE 76:21
God would make a man m.　　CHAR 140:24
having made a young girl m.　　FRAN 218:5
I have pass'd a m. night　　SHAK 480:26
make only two people m.　　BUTL 119:22
Me m.　　MILT 347:15
mercy upon us m. sinners　　PRAY 385:15
M. comforters are ye all　　BIBLE 52:27
m. have no other medicine　　SHAK 464:8
m. state of mind to have　　BACON 26:8
most m. things which　　VIRG 557:21
so it is very m.　　TAYL 532:3
miserande: m. puer　　VIRG 559:2
miserere: m. nobis　　MASS 335:7
miseria: Nella m.　　DANTE 171:8
miseries: bound in shallows and in m.
　　SHAK 451:27
heap m. upon us yet entwine　　JOYCE 286:10
whom the m. of the world　　KEATS 289:27
misery: bound in m. and iron　　PRAY 397:7
certain amount of m. which　　LOWE 318:24
departure is taken for m.　　BIBLE 62:13
given to him that is in m.　　BIBLE 52:14
greatest m. is a battle gained　　WELL 567:27
happiness and final m.　　MILT 346:20
is full of m.　　PRAY 389:11
loses his m.　　ARN 14:22
loved in m.　　YEATS 585:20
merry m.　　BETJ 44:1
mine affliction and my m.　　BIBLE 60:29
M. acquaints a man with　　SHAK 485:9
pens dwell on guilt and m.　　AUST 22:29
remember his m. no more　　BIBLE 55:2
result m.　　DICK 177:4
through the vale of m.　　PRAY 395:12
time of happiness in m.　　DANTE 171:8
Untainted by man's m.　　SHEL 503:28
misfortune: alleviate so severe a m.
　　AUST 23:18
m. of our best friends　　LA R 310:8
sort of m. is to have been　　BOET 89:6
writ with me in sour m.'s　　SHAK 483:28
misfortunes: All the m. of men derive
　　PASC 369:5
if a man talks of his m.　　JOHN 278:20
m. and pains of others　　BURKE 108:8
m. hardest to bear are　　LOW 319:17
strong enough to bear the m.　　LA R 310:9
tableau of crimes and m.　　VOLT 561:10
they make m. more bitter　　BACON 27:3
misgivings: Blank m. of a creature
　　WORD 579:10
misgovernment: augur m.　　BURKE 109:23
last refuge of cheap m.　　SHAW 497:12
misleading: words generate m. thoughts
　　SPEN 514:31
misled: education most have been m.
　　DRYD 196:19
long m. by wandering fires　　DRYD 196:13
Mislike: M. me not for my complexion
　　SHAK 466:6
misquote: enough of learning to m.
　　BYRON 124:17
Mis'ry: He gave to M. all he had　　GRAY 235:5
laughs the sense of m.　　COWP 166:24

miss: catching a train is to m.　　CHES 148:11
count and calls her 'M.　　CHES 147:19
m. for pleasure　　GAY 223:31
M. not the discourse　　BIBLE 62:27
so might I m.　　BROW 101:24
missa: Ite m. est　　MASS 335:9
vox m. reverti　　HOR 258:6
missed: No one would have m. her
　　ANON 5:15
who never would be m.　　GILB 226:24
Missing: M. so much and so much
　　CORN 162:22
mission: Never have a m.　　DICK 176:20
missionaries: eaten by m.　　SPOO 517:9
missionary: I would eat a m.　　WILB 572:3
Mississippi: I have seen the M. BURNS 112:23
Mississippi Bay: East all the way into
M.　　KIPL 300:24
Miss T: That whatever M. eats　　DE L 174:11
Missus: M. my Lord　　PUNCH 402:30
mist: broke into a m. with bells BROW 103:11
Faustus like a foggy m.　　MARL 329:13
grey m. on the sea's face　　MAS 334:4
m. and hum of that low　　ARN 14:28
m. in my face　　BROW 103:31
m. is dispell'd when　　GAY 222:26
rolling m. came down　　KING 297:1
mistake: Among all forms of m. ELIOT 201:8
he never overlooks a m.　　HUXL 269:6
it's a m. not　　JAMES 271:20
lie—under a m.　　SWIFT 526:27
Man is Nature's sole m.　　GILB 228:28
m. in the translation　　VANB 555:4
m. to theorize before one　　DOYLE 192:7
There is no m.　　WELL 568:8
We will pardon Thy M.　　BETJ 43:5
when she made any such m.　　DICK 180:5
mistaken: here, unless I am m. DOYLE 192:24
possible you may be m.　　CROM 169:21
To your m. Shrine　　WINC 575:4
mistakes: All great men make m.
　　CHUR 149:23
at the cost of m.　　FROU 219:19
every one gives to their m.　　WILDE 573:14
If he makes m. they must　　CHUR 150:27
I hope will excuse m.　　DICK 180:9
man of genius makes no m.　　JOYCE 286:27
man who makes no m. does　　PHEL 373:7
there are few m. they have　　CHUR 150:17
mistress: Art is a jealous m.　　EMER 207:6
ever be an m. of this house　　AUST 23:17
first an acquaintance, next a m. CHEK 145:5
In ev'ry port a m. find　　GAY 223:29
Like m., like maid　　FARQ 210:15
lordship's principles or your m. WILK 574:6
make me m. to the man　　POPE 376:11
m. I am ashamed to call　　ELIZ 205:28
m. in my own　　KIPL 301:20
m., in the midmost　　POUND 382:5
m. mine　　SHAK 488:17
m. of herself　　POPE 377:28
m. of the months and stars　　SWIN 528:14
m. of the Earl of Craven　　WILS 574:19
m. should be like a little　　WYCH 583:24
m. some rich anger shows　　KEATS 291:15
new m. now I chase　　LOV 318:20
No casual m.　　TENN 536:33
served the lust of my m.'s　　SHAK 454:18
So court a m.　　JONS 284:11
teeming m.　　POPE 377:20
worst m.　　BACON 25:9
mistresses: I shall have m.　　GEOR 223:35
m. with great smooth marbly BROW 99:13
one wife and hardly any m.　　SAKI 413:13
Wives are young men's m.　　BACON 26:34
mists: Season of m. and mellow KEATS 293:5
Those shaken m. a space　　THOM 548:20
When the golden m. are born SHEL 503:26
when the m. in autumn　　KING 297:21
misty: of a ful m. morwe　　CHAU 144:8

misunderstood: To be great is to be m.
　　EMER 207:39
misus'd: m. the king's press damnably
　　SHAK 440:9
misused: m. words generate misleading
　　SPEN 514:31
mites: she threw in two m.　　BIBLE 68:38
Mithras: M., God of the Morning KIPL 303:9
Mithridates: M., he died old　　HOUS 264:16
mitigation: some m. of the criminal law
　　PEEL 371:5
Mittel: Einmischung anderer M. CLAU 152:27
niemals bloss als M. brachest KANT 288:13
unentbehrlich notwendige M. KANT 288:11
mix: I m. them with my brains　　OPIE 365:6
kiss her and m. her with　　SWIN 530:27
M. a little foolishness　　HOR 261:20
winds of heaven m.　　SHEL 502:1
mixing: m. it with other things　　CARR 136:4
mixture: Had the m. peen　　AYT 24:7
m. of a lie doth ever add　　BACON 27:29
Moab: M. is my wash-pot　　PRAY 393:18
moan: Everything did banish m. BARN 33:32
made sweet m.　　KEATS 290:18
m. the expense of many　　SHAK 493:7
That is not paid with m.　　THOM 548:1
virgin-choir to make delicious m.
　　KEATS 292:2
we cast away m.　　SHAK 436:13
moanday: All m̄., tearsday, wailsday
　　JOYCE 286:11
moaning: still he lay m.　　SMITH 510:26
there be no m. of the bar　　TENN 533:3
Moat: Look to your M.　　HAL 238:4
moated: at the m. grange　　SHAK 464:18
mob: amphibious ill-born m.　　DEFOE 173:12
M., Parliament, Rabble　　COBB 154:8
occasions to do what the m. do DICK 181:30
supreme governors, the m.　　WALP 562:19
mobled: who had seen the m. queen
　　SHAK 432:24
mock: augurs m. their own presage
　　SHAK 494:21
How my achievements m.　　SHAK 487:8
if they yet m. what women　　OWEN 367:7
m. on, Voltaire, Rousseau　　BLAKE 86:23
m. our eyes with air　　SHAK 423:7
m. the midnight bell　　SHAK 422:22
m. the riddled corpses　　SASS 414:12
They m. the air with idle　　GRAY 234:14
to m. your own grinning　　SHAK 436:31
When I m. poorness　　JONS 283:18
You smile, and m. me　　SHAK 487:9
mock'd: if he m. himself　　SHAK 448:21
scorn which m. the smart　　ARN 13:9
mocked: God is not m.　　BIBLE 77:19
mocker: Wine is a m.　　BIBLE 54:15
mockeries: things by what their m. be
　　SHAK 444:13
mockery: In monumental m.　　SHAK 487:4
m. is the fume of little　　TENN 534:13
Unreal m., hence　　SHAK 461:12
vain blows malicious m.　　SHAK 429:15
mocking-bird: Out of the m.'s throat
　　WHIT 570:9
Mocks: M. married men　　SHAK 457:18
Which comforts while it m.　　BROW 104:4
model: fellow-countryman is a m. of
a man　　DICK 179:19
m. of a modern Major-General GILB 228:16
when they come to m. Heaven MILT 349:3
models: Rules and m. destroy genius
　　HAZL 243:28
moderate: £40,000 a year a m.
income　　LAMB 308:15
Read that m. man Voltaire　　HARDY 240:17
moderated: absolutism m. by assassination
　　ANON 5:5
moderately: if it be drunk m.　　BIBLE 63:15

moderation: astonished at my own m.   CLIVE 153:5
easier than perfect m.   AUG 21:22
m. in war is imbecility   MAC 323:8
No terms of m. takes place   BACON 25:12
taught to think that m.   BURKE 110:9
There is m. even in excess   DISR 186:42
moderator: without this reasonable m.   BROW 96:19
modern: disease of m. life   ARN 14:19
model of a m. Major-General   GILB 228:16
unsettling element in m. art   WHAR 569:9
What is a m. poet's fate   HOOD 255:14
moderns: Speak of the m. without   CHES 145:20
modest: We should be m. for a modest   LAMB 307:35
modester: People ought to be m.   CARL 132:25
modesty: Enough for m.   BUCH 106:10
in the m. of fearful duty   SHAK 471:15
it is cold m.   SHAK 450:10
ladies of irresistible m.   STEE 518:13
o'erstep not the m. of nature   SHAK 433:17
too much m. is his   GOLD 232:16
Your maiden m. would float   HUXL 268:23
modified: m. in the guts of the living   AUDEN 19:4
M. rapture   GILB 226:30
modus: Est m. in rebus   HOR 261:23
moenia: flammantia m. mundi   LUCR 320:3
Möglichen: Politik ist die Lehre von M.   BISM 84:20
moi: Le m. est haïssable   PASC 369:12
moins: du m. des choses nouvelles   VOLT 560:21
je n'en suis pas m. homme   MOL 353:25
moist: Have you not a m. eye   SHAK 441:10
m., unpleasant body   DICK 180:19
mole: like a bastion's m.   SMART 509:3
m. cinque-spotted   SHAK 428:9
still working like a m.   HERB 247:23
Well said, old m.   SHAK 431:21
wilt thou go ask the M.   BLAKE 85:19
moles: rudis indigestaque m.   OVID 366:13
molis: Tantae m. erat Romanam   VIRG 557:10
Moloch: First M., horrid king   MILT 345:14
mome: m. raths outgrabe   CARR 134:28
moment: Every m. dies a man   BABB 24:13
Every m. dies a man   TENN 544:8
force the m. to its crisis   ELIOT 203:22
from the impulse of the m.   AUST 23:13
m. can so disfigure us   BROW 96:20
m. in the rose-garden   ELIOT 202:16
m. of my greatness flicker   ELIOT 203:23
not seem a m.'s thought   YEATS 584:9
One m. of the mightiest   BYRON 120:29
That m. of mystery   ELIOT 203:7
This little m. mercifully   MER 337:15
moments: m. big as years   KEATS 290:4
m. of glad grace   YEATS 587:12
Wagner has lovely m.   ROSS 410:11
monade: n'avalent pas la m.   NERV 361:1
Monan: danced the moon on M.'s rill   SCOTT 416:1
monarch: cuckold to make him a m.   SHAK 477:2
hereditary m. was insane   BAG 29:9
him down the m. of a shed   GOLD 231:26
I am m. of all I survey   COWP 167:38
merry m.   ROCH 407:2
m. but would give his crown   WALL 562:10
so much a king as a M.   SELL 420:5
throned m. better than   SHAK 467:27
monarchize: To m., be fear'd   SHAK 479:11
monarchs: m. to behold the swelling   SHAK 443:3
m. to choose favourites   SWIFT 526:8
wrote that m. were divine   KIPL 300:5
monarchy: are discontented under m.   HOBB 251:20

characteristic of the English M.   BAG 28:28
constitutional m. such as ours   BAG 29:3
essential to a true m.   BAG 28:21
m. is a merchantman which   AMES 4:3
M. is a strong government   BAG 28:27
monastic: m. faces in quiet collegiate   CLOU 153:12
Monday: classical M. Pops   GILB 227:5
Hanging of his cat on M.   BRAT 91:24
is going to do on M.   YBAR 584:7
M. is parson's holiday   SWIFT 526:19
M., when the sun is hot   MILNE 340:16
monde: Le m. est plein de fous   ANON 9:12
Le scandale du m. est ce   MOL 354:1
moneda: m. general con que todas   CERV 138:20
monedas: por un puñado de m.   ZAP 588:18
monendo: delectando pariterque m.   HOR 258:1
money: blessing that m. cannot buy   WALT 564:12
draining m. from the pockets   SMITH 509:15
employed than in getting m.   JOHN 276:18
except for m.   JOHN 277:4
given his m. upon usury   PRAY 390:5
giving m. to the Government   HERB 246:11
had been corrupted by m.   GREE 236:4
'Hath a dog m.   SHAK 466:3
Her voice is full of m.   FITZ 213:23
he that hath no m.   BIBLE 59:25
I give thee my m.   CONG 160:22
I have spent all the m.   JOHN 278:31
is pretty to see what m.   PEPYS 372:19
licence to print your own m.   THOM 549:30
love of m. is the root   BIBLE 79:18
man of genius and his m.   SHEN 505:17
m. answereth all things   BIBLE 56:4
M. gives me pleasure all   BELL 39:18
m. has a power above   BUTL 118:15
M. has no smell   VESP 556:11
M. is indeed the most important   SHAW 496:34
M. is like muck   BACON 27:12
M. is the most important   SHAW 497:7
M. is the sinews of love   FARQ 210:16
m., means, and content   SHAK 426:3
M. speaks sense in a language   BEHN 38:18
m. the sinews of war   BACON 27:25
mustnt be romantic about m.   SHAW 497:26
No m.   RAC 404:5
no one shall work for m.   KIPL 304:3
Nothing some m. nothing   FONS 216:5
pleasant it is to have m.   CLOU 153:21
plenty of m.   LEAR 312:11
Put m. in thy purse   SHAK 474:9
sinews of war, unlimited m.   CIC 151:30
somehow, make m.   HOR 258:10
so m. comes withal   SHAK 484:5
so much M. as 'twill bring   BUTL 117:26
That's the way the m. goes   MAND 328:10
that time is m.   FRAN 218:3
...there shall be no m.   SHAK 446:11
they are the m. of fools   HOBB 251:15
They hired the m.   COOL 162:12
though we had plenty of m.   KIPL 299:16
Thy m. perish with thee   BIBLE 73:30
We haven't the m.   RUTH 412:24
we have to borrer the m.   WARD 564:36
What m. is better bestowed   THAC 545:11
with m. which they have   HURST 268:17
Moneybag: Aristocracy of the M.   CARL 131:27
money-bags: I did dream of m. to-night   SHAK 466:11
moneye: day he gat hym moore m.   CHAU 142:7
moneys: m. are for values   BACON 24:22
m. is your suit   SHAK 466:3
mongrel: m. grim   SHAK 455:1
thou m. beef-witted lord   SHAK 486:28
monied: other to the m. interest   ADD 2:14

monk: Bernard the m. ne saugh   CHAU 143:28
devil a m. he'd be   MOTT 358:22
M. my son   SOUT 514:10
m. who shook the world   MONT 355:10
Monkey: ere the M. People cry   KIPL 303:7
Into baboon and m.   SHAK 486:1
lovely M. with lollipop paws   LEAR 312:9
never look long upon a m.   CONG 160:3
monkeys: Goats and m.   SHAK 476:15
m. and cats   JAMES 271:24
m. make sorrowful noise   POUND 383:16
wilderness of m.   SHAK 467:7
monks: holiness of m.   YEATS 587:8
manufactures of the m. of Magdalen   GIBB 224:8
Merrily sang the m. in Ely   CAN 130:9
Monmouth: moreover a river at M.   SHAK 445:5
monnaie: l'argent ou de la petite m.   CHAM 139:14
monograph: m. on the ashes of one   DOYLE 191:16
monopoly: shun the temptations of m.   SCOTT 415:15
monosyllabic: nothing so m. as to cheat   FRY 220:6
Monotone: une langueur M.   VERL 556:8
monotonous: it becomes m. after a mile   TROL 553:9
monotony: m. of bearing that it imposed   WOOLF 576:18
to chase m.   GILB 226:8
Which bleats articulate m.   STEP 518:22
monster: fury of the many-headed m.   MASS 335:25
It is the green-ey'd m.   SHAK 475:17
it were a m. unto many   PRAY 394:16
many-headed m. of the pit   POPE 380:17
m. horrendous   VIRG 558:11
m., which the Blatant   SPEN 516:22
That the blunt m. with   SHAK 440:31
were some m. in his thought   SHAK 475:15
monsters: He who fights with m. might   NIET 363:10
Men into m.   FORD 216:18
monstrosity: that numerous piece of m.   BROW 96:30
monstrous: bottom of the m. world   MILT 343:16
m. birth to the world's   SHAK 474:13
m. head and sickening cry   CHES 146:22
M. Regiment of Women   KNOX 305:19
that m. animal a husband   FIEL 211:30
Monstrum: M. horrendum   VIRG 558:11
monstruosity: This is the m. in love   SHAK 486:33
Montaigne: law-givers are Erasmus and M.   FORS 217:11
montent: bas et les bourgeois m.   FLAU 214:3
montes: Parturient m.   HOR 257:18
Montezuma: knows who imprisoned M.   MAC 323:14
month: April is the cruellest m.   ELIOT 204:17
little m.   SHAK 429:28
merry m. of May   BALL 30:10
merry m. of May   BALL 31:13
merry m. of May   BARN 33:32
merry m. of May   BRET 92:5
M. follow month with woe   SHEL 499:14
this first Summer m. that   FITZ 212:10
This is the m.   MILT 344:3
month-long: Ends all our m. love   BRID 92:11
months: mistress of the m. and stars   SWIN 528:14
mother of m. in meadow   SWIN 528:15
twelve m. in all the year   BALL 31:13
Montparnasse: shall not rest quiet in M.   BENET 40:20
Montreal: God! Oh M.   BUTL 119:19

monument: description has left some
m.　BURKE 110:24
'If you ask for his M.　BARH 33:7
If you seek for a m.　ANON 11:2
Levi did from off the M.　BARH 33:20
sat like patience on a m.　SHAK 489:7
shall have a living m.　SHAK 437:10
sonnet is a moment's m.　ROSS 409:21
this shalt find thy m.　SHAK 495:1
Thou art a m.　JONS 284:19
.monumental: Most like a m. statue set
　BROW 98:8
monuments: spared these minor m.
　BROW 97:12
monumentum: m. aere perennius　HOR 261:8
Nisi m. requiris, circumspice　INGE 270:11
Si m. requiris　ANON 11:2
si M. requiris'　BARH 33:7
moon: bay the m.　SHAK 451:14
behold the wandering m.　MILT 342:3
Beneath the visiting m.　SHAK 423:16
blow them at the m.　SHAK 435:21
by the light of the m.　LEAR 312:14
carry the m. in my pocket　BROW 102:13
Come from the dying m.　TENN 541:31
dancing spectre seems the m.　MER 337:13
dwelleth i' the cold o' the m.　BROW 99:24
fair as the m.　BIBLE 57:5
glimpses of the m.　SHAK 430:24
had an affair with the m.　STER 518:29
He appointed the m.　PRAY 397:1
hornèd M.　COL 155:18
hush with the setting m.　TENN 540:10
in the m. the long road　HOUS 263:20
It is the m.　BURNS 116:5
kneaded by the m.　HARDY 241:21
minions of the m.　SHAK 438:1
moment when the m. was blood　CHES 146:22
m. and the stars　PRAY 389:24
m. be still as bright　BYRON 125:25
m. doth with delight　WORD 578:22
m. hath her eclipse endur'd　SHAK 494:21
M., in the valley of Ajalon　BIBLE 49:4
m. is nothing But a circumambulating
　FRY 219:32
m. is under seas　HOUS 265:16
m. No planet is of mine　SHAK 424:4
M. of Heav'n is rising　FITZ 213:17
M. of my Delight who know'st　FITZ 213:17
m. on my left and the dawn　BELL 39:16
m., Rising in clouded majesty　MILT 348:2
m.'s a balloon　CUMM 170:8
m. shines bright　SHAK 468:15
m. shone bright on Mrs　ELIOT 204:27
m. sleeps with Endymion　SHAK 468:19
m., the governess of floods　SHAK 470:6
m. under her feet　BIBLE 82:10
m. Walks the night　DE L 174:16
m. was a ghostly galleon　NOYES 364:12
m. was full　TENN 535:21
moping owl does to the m.　GRAY 234:19
neither the m. by night　PRAY 398:9
new m. late yestreen　BALL 31:18
nose at it and the m. winks　SHAK 476:20
On fishing up the m.　PEAC 371:3
red roses across the m.　MORR 358:13
Regard the m.　ELIOT 204:10
served up the sun and m.　AUG 21:13
Shaped like the crescent m.　WORD 579:18
shines the m. in clouded　TENN 532:16
shining to the quiet m.　COL 156:23
sickle m.　FLEC 214:21
silent as the m.　MILT 350:16
silver apples of the m.　YEATS 586:19
Sliver'd in the m.'s eclipse　SHAK 462:4
slow m. climbs　TENN 544:3
Sun and M. should doubt　BLAKE 85:17
to the cold fruitless m.　SHAK 469:17
unmask her beauty to the m.　SHAK 430:17
very error of the m.　SHAK 477:8

waning m. was haunted　COL 156:27
wan m. sets behind　BURNS 114:30
Whom mortals call the M.　SHEL 500:6
With how sad steps, O M.　SIDN 507:18
yonder blessed m. I swear　SHAK 482:15
you when the m. shall rise　WOTT 583:15
moon-eyed: Dim m. fishes near HARDY 239:5
moonlight: Are as m. unto sunlight
　TENN 539:5
How sweet the m. sleeps　SHAK 468:15
Ill met by m.　SHAK 470:4
In the faint m.　ELIOT 205:10
Look for me by m.　NOYES 364:14
road was a ribbon of m.　NOYES 364:12
silence of the soundless m.　VIRG 558:3
visit it by the pale m.　SCOTT 416:13
moonlit: m. cedar what a burst　ARN 14:2
moonrise: When roses to the m. burst
　HOUS 266:4
moons: m. swiftly wax again after
　HOR 261:16
new m. and sabbaths　BIBLE 57:11
Reason has m.　HODG 252:5
moonshine: consider every thing as m.
　SCOTT 419:4
find out m.　SHAK 470:15
in pallid m.　KEATS 289:15
of the m.'s watery beams　SHAK 481:28
Transcendental m.　CARL 132:7
You m. revellers　SHAK 469:16
moon-struck: m. madness　MILT 349:24
moor: batten on this m.　SHAK 435:7
m. is dark beneath　SHEL 504:7
Moore: before I go, Tom M.　BYRON 125:32
mops: seven maids with seven m. CARR 135:5
moral: All good m. philosophy is
　BACON 24:28
dann kommt die M.　BREC 91:25
Debasing the m. currency　ELIOT 201:26
Englishman thinks he is m.　SHAW 497:28
Everything's got a m.　CARR 134:6
grandest m. attribute　BARR 34:20
heaven above me and the m. law KANT 288:8
His m. pleases　POPE 380:13
Let us be m.　DICK 179:8
m., grave　BACON 27:21
m. life of man forms part　WILDE 573:17
m. man was Werther　THAC 546:3
m. of the devil himself　SHAK 444:15
m. or intellectual damage　KRUG 306:1
perfectly moral till all are m.　SPEN 515:3
religious and m. principles　ARN 16:26
To be a kind of m. eunuch　SHEL 502:18
To point a m.　JOHN 282:31
Unfit to hear m. philosophy　SHAK 486:30
morales: quarts sont des affaires m.
　NAP 359:10
moralists: We are perpetually m. JOHN 281:32
Moralität: M. ist Herden-Instinkt　NIET 363:7
moralitee: Good-bye, m.　HERB 246:10
morality: Absolute m. is the regulation
　SPEN 514:26
Dr Johnson's m. was as English HAWT 243:5
himputation on his m. than　SURT 525:9
its periodical fits of m.　MAC 324:1
Master-m. and slave-morality　NIET 363:12
may be called that of M.　KANT 288:10
m. for morality's sake　COUS 163:9
M. is the herd-instinct　NIET 363:7
m. of art consists　WILDE 573:17
m. touched by emotion　ARN 16:20
personal and national m.　SHAW 496:34
principles of public m.　BURKE 108:16
some people talk of m.　EDG 199:20
then comes m.　BREC 91:25
unawares M. expires　POPE 376:1
What is middle class m.　SHAW 498:14
moralize: loves shall m. my song SPEN 515:29
morals: foundation of m. and legislation
　BENT 40:25

Have you no m.　SHAW 498:13
teach the m. of a whore　JOHN 274:10
with the m. of a Methodist　GILB 228:33
morbo: Venienti occurrite m.　PERS 372:28
Mordre: M. wol out　CHAU 143:4
More: little M. than a little　SHAK 439:35
Lord, art m. than they　TENN 535:31
m. about less and less　BUTL 117:13
m. he heard　PUNCH 402:25
m. of love than matrimony　GOLD 232:39
m. remains to do　BYRON 121:32
m. than ever seems it rich　KEATS 291:22
m.-than-oriental-splendour　KIPL 304:19
M. than somewhat　RUNY 411:4
m. things in heaven　SHAK 431:23
M. to be desired are they　PRAY 390:12
M. will mean worse　AMIS 4:4
M. would be laid at your　SWIN 530:22
no m. of that, Hal　SHAK 439:9
No m.—Oh, never more　SHEL 501:14
No m. o' that　SHAK 462:21
Once is m. than enough　BIRCH 84:11
Romano vivito m.　AMBR 4:2
'she'll vish there wos m.　DICK 182:14
speak as a fool) I am m.　BIBLE 77:11
their language convey m.　CONN 161:11
to take m. than nothing　CARR 134:3
Twist has asked for m.　DICK 180:32
mores: Et linguam et m.　JUV 287:15
tempora, O m.　CIC 151:26
Morgan: old bold mate of Henry M.
　MAS 333:21
morganatic: rumours of a m. alliance
　HARD 238:21
Morgen: M. sterb' ich　LESS 313:26
Morgenlicht: Vom Abendrot zum M.
　MULL 359:1
mori: decorum est pro patria m.　HOR 260:17
In taberna m.　ANON 10:14
laude virum Musa vetat m.　HOR 261:1
Moriamur: M. et in media arma ruamus
　VIRG 558:7
moriar: Non omnis m.　HOR 261:9
Moribus: M. antiquis res stat Romana
　ENN 208:23
Morientis: M. ori　ANON 10:14
morituri: m. te salutant　ANON 10:7
Morn: M. a thousand Roses brings
　FITZ 212:10
m., in russet mantle clad　SHAK 429:18
m. not waking till she　LYLY 321:13
m. went out with sandals　MILT 343:19
new m. she saw not　KEATS 290:11
Son of M. in weary Night's　BLAKE 86:1
Sweet is the breath of m.　MILT 348:4
this the happy m.　MILT 344:3
morning: Almost at odds with m.
　SHAK 461:24
beauty of the m.　WORD 581:14
cold, frosty, windy m.　PEPYS 371:18
comes again in the m.　SHER 506:28
disasters in his m. face　GOLD 231:2
domination over them in the m.　PRAY 393:1
Early one m.　ANON 5:3
evening and the m. were the first BIBLE 45:1
evening than in the m.　CONN 161:1
fares like to the m.'s war　SHAK 446:17
from eve and m.　HOUS 263:16
glorious m. have I seen　SHAK 493:9
God of the M.　KIPL 303:9
great m. of the world when　SHEL 499:11
Happy the hare at m.　AUDEN 18:14
He's for the m.　BROW 100:33
How splendid in the m.　FLEC 214:11
In the m. sow thy seed　BIBLE 56:8
In the m. it is green　PRAY 395:18
I say, before the m.　PRAY 398:24
is the m. to take the air　FRY 219:21
joy cometh in the m.　PRAY 391:13
Lucifer, son of the m.　BIBLE 58:13

methinks I scent the m.	SHAK 431:10
M. in the Bowl of Night	FITZ 212:5
M.'s at seven	BROW 103:21
m. stars sang	BIBLE 53:3
m. well-aired before	BRUM 106:4
Never glad confident m.	BROW 102:8
Never m. wore To evening	TENN 536:3
private view in the m.	EDW 200:2
rise up early in the m.	BIBLE 57:25
shown no glorious m. face	STEV 523:11
started that m. from Devon	GILB 226:14
take the wings of the m.	PRAY 399:5
this morning m.'s minion	HOPK 257:4
three o'clock in the m.	FITZ 213:22
Up in the m. early	BURNS 116:2
vanish in the m.	FRY 219:31
we won't go home till m.	BUCK 106:18
With Death and M.	TENN 542:16
Would God it were m.	BIBLE 48:27

mornings: *always* had m. like this
	MILNE 340:17
Morns: M. abed and daylight	HOUS 262:15
moron: See the happy m.	ANON 7:13
morris: nine men's m. is filled	SHAK 470:5

Morrison's Pill: M. for curing the maladies
	CARL 132:9

morrow: Eagerly I wished the m. POE 375:5
therefore no thought for the m.	BIBLE 64:32
watching for the m.	GOET 230:12

mors: *Indignatio principis m.* MORE 357:13
M. stupebit et natura	CEL 138:6
Nil igitur m. est ad nos	LUCR 320:8
Pallida M. aequo	HOR 259:13

morsel: I found you as a m. SHAK 422:20
m. for a monarch	SHAK 421:32

morsels: casteth forth his ice like m.
	PRAY 399:21

mort: *c'est bâtir la m.* MONT 354:15
Dieu est m.	NERV 360:3
Je veux...que la m. me trouve	MONT 354:14
La m. est le remède	CHAM 139:13
La m., sans phrases	SIEY 508:7
m. ne surprend point le	LA F 306:22
veut abolir la peine de m.	KARR 288:16

mortal: all men m., but themselves
	YOUNG 588:6
chances of this m. life	PRAY 388:5
desperately m.	SHAK 464:21
genius and the m. instruments	SHAK 449:6
'Here came a m.	ARN 13:7
Her last disorder m.	GOLD 231:8
if I laugh at any m. thing	BYRON 123:10
I presume you're m.	SHIR 507:5
M., guilty	AUDEN 19:17
m. millions live *alone*	ARN 13:12
m. mixture of earth's mould	MILT 341:4
m. must put on immortality	BIBLE 76:29
m. thing so to immortalize	SPEN 515:20
rais'd a m. to the skies	DRYD 195:9
shuffled off this m. coil	SHAK 433:8
struck a m. blow right inside	AESC 3:2
time of this m. life	PRAY 386:4
Turning m. for thy love	SHAK 457:5
tush, man, m. men	SHAK 440:12
'twas beyond a m.'s share	MARV 332:8
Who gathers all things m.	SWIN 529:22

Mortalem: *M. vitam mors cum immortalis*
	LUCR 320:9

mortalia: *mentem m. tangunt* VIRG 557:17
mortality: frail m. shall trust BACON 28:16
insensible of m.	SHAK 464:25
it smells of m.	SHAK 455:1
m. touches the heart	VIRG 557:17
M. Weighs heavily	KEATS 292:19
Old m.	BROW 97:7
sad m. o'ersways their	SHAK 494:4
There's nothing serious in m.	SHAK 461:1
urns and sepulchres of m.	CREWE 169:18

mortals: greatest good that m. know ADD 2:6
m. to command success	ADD 1:16

Security Is m.' chiefest	SHAK 462:1
what fools these m. be	SHAK 470:21

morte: *battaglie e m.* GAR 221:10
mortified: m. appetite is never STEV 521:3
mortifying: without very m. reflections
	CONG 160:3

mortis: *etiam opportunitate m.* TAC 531:9
postremo donarem munere m. CAT 137:15
morts: *doit aux m. que la vérité* VOLT 561:19
Il n'y a pas de m. MAET 326:20
mortuus: *Passer m. est meae puellae*
	CAT 136:22

Moscow: If I lived in M. I don't CHEK 145:3
One is don't march on M.	MONT 355:9
Moses: I was with M. BIBLE 48:35
M. hid his face	BIBLE 47:5
was sitting in M.' chair	BLAKE 85:24
which M. sent to spy out	BIBLE 48:10
moss: miles of golden m. AUDEN 18:16
with azure m. and flowers	SHEL 502:10
most: m. material in the postscript
	BACON 25:42
mot: *Le m., c'est le Verbe* HUGO 267:9
mote: Why beholdest thou the m. BIBLE 64:34
motes: m. that people the sunbeams
	MILT 341:24
moth: candle sing'd the m. SHAK 467:1
desire of the m.	SHEL 504:14
Kill not the m. nor butterfly	BLAKE 85:13
like a m.	GAY 222:11
m. and rust doth corrupt	BIBLE 64:25
m. of peace	SHAK 474:6
m.'s kiss	BROW 101:15
mother: and...never called me m.
	WOOD 576:15
back to the great sweet m.	SWIN 530:27
Behold my m. and my brethren	BIBLE 66:15
Behold thy m.	BIBLE 73:2
Christ and his m. and all	HOPK 256:29
'Daughter am I in my m.'s	KIPL 301:20
dearer was the m.	COL 157:9
deceived The m. of mankind	MILT 344:23
either my father or my m.	STER 519:16
finished jumping on his m.	GILB 228:21
gave her m. forty whacks	ANON 6:12
Happy he With such a m.	TENN 542:19
heaviness of his m.	BIBLE 53:29
Honour thy father and thy m.	BIBLE 47:24
I arose a m. in Israel	BIBLE 49:8
ignorant of their M. Tongue	DRYD 198:14
I had No m.	BROW 99:16
is the m.	BIBLE 60:33
is the m. of Parliaments	BRIG 93:4
leave his father and his m.	BIBLE 45:13
mighty M. did unveil	GRAY 235:18
m. bids me bind my hair	HUNT 268:15
m., do not cry	FARM 209:21
m. Ida	TENN 541:17
m. know that you are out	BARH 33:24
m., make my bed	BALL 30:12
m. of all living	BIBLE 45:24
M. OF HARLOTS AND	
ABOMINATIONS	BIBLE 82:23
m. of months in meadow	SWIN 528:15
M. of the Free	BENS 40:24
m. of the lovely Cupids	HOR 261:10
m. o' mine	KIPL 301:14
m. on his father him begot	BLAKE 87:2
m.'s head off	DICK 181:23
m.'s life made me a man	MAS 333:22
m.'s pride	SCOTT 417:29
m. under the dragon's tail	SHAK 453:11
m. who talks about her	DISR 185:11
M., Wife, and Queen	TENN 543:15
m. will be there	HERB 246:7
My M.	TAYL 531:25
my m. cried	SHAK 472:12
My m. groan'd	BLAKE 87:23
'Never had any m.	STOWE 523:19
not the church for his m.	CYPR 170:19

recognize your m. with a smile	VIRG 560:1
standing the sorrowing M.	JAC 270:31
that can so astonish a m.	SHAK 434:17
That great m. of sciences	BACON 28:8
There was their Dacian m.	BYRON 121:16
Thou art thy m.'s glass	SHAK 492:24
thou hast murdered thy m.	MAL 327:17
thy dear m. any courtesy	SHAK 428:5
Thy m. a lady	SCOTT 416:24
thy m.'s grief	BRET 92:6
to be a joyful m. of children	PRAY 397:15
Took great Care of his M.	MILNE 340:5
Upon his m.'s grave	WORD 580:3
What a beautiful m.	HOR 259:22
when the m. that bore you	KIPL 301:11
Whose m. was her painting	SHAK 428:16
yet was ever found a m.	GAY 223:11
Your m. will never see	AUST 23:15

mother-in-law: man said when his m.
died	JER 272:25
mother-naked: m. and ageless-ancient
	DAY-L 172:21
mothers: best-bodied m. stands WHIT 570:15
M. of large families	BELL 38:31
women become like their m.	WILDE 573:2
Younger than she are happy m.	SHAK 481:26
mother-wits: jigging veins of rhyming
m.	MARL 330:2
mothy: m. and warm HARDY 239:2
Yet at m. curfew-tide	HARDY 239:18
motion: Devoid of sense and m. MILT 346:10
God order'd m.	VAUG 555:10
her m. Blush'd	SHAK 473:24
little m. in the air	SHEL 500:3
meandering with a mazy m.	COL 156:28
measured m. like a living	WORD 580:12
m. And the act	ELIOT 203:10
next to the perpetual m.	DICK 182:33
No m. has she now	WORD 581:10
Of time's eternal m.	FORD 216:20
Of undistinguishable m.	WORD 580:9
put them to m.	SHAK 489:20
rolled With visible m.	WORD 577:27
this m. like an angel sings	SHAK 468:15
motions: m. of his spirit are dull SHAK 468:17
secret m. of things	BACON 28:6
two weeping m.	CRAS 169:12
motive: joint and m. of her body SHAK 487:13
m., not the deed	YEATS 584:18
noblest m.	STEE 518:1
motiveless: motive-hunting of m. malignity
	COL 157:28
motives: opponent m. meaner BARR 34:9
reasons and for m. not of State	KIPL 302:5
motley: lived where m. is worn YEATS 585:1
m. fool	SHAK 425:18
M.'s the only wear	SHAK 425:20
myself a m. to the view	SHAK 495:3
Motor Bus: Can it be a M. GODL 229:24
Motoribus: Cincti Bis M. GODL 229:24
motors: sound of horns and m. ELIOT 204:27
mots: m. avaient un sens FRAN 217:27
motto: Be that my m. and my fate
	SWIFT 528:8
With this for m.	TENN 535:10
mottoes: than the m. on sun-dials
	POUND 383:3
those lovely cracker m.	GILB 225:11
motus: *Hi m. animorum atque haec*
	VIRG 560:18
mould: mortal mixture of earth's m.
	MILT 341:4
m. falls close	ROSS 409:25
m. of a man's fortune is	BACON 26:12
then broke the m.	ARIO 12:2
moulded: made and m. of things past
	SHAK 487:6
men are m. out of faults	SHAK 465:6
moulder'd: lops the m. branch TENN 533:26
moulds: Crack nature's m. SHAK 454:4 |

Moulmein: By the old M. Pagoda KIPL 301:5
moulted: m. feather BROW 102:16
mound: From this wave-washed m.
    ROSS 409:26
mount: m., my soul SHAK 480:16
  m. up with wings as eagles BIBLE 59:10
  Singing of M. Abora COL 156:30
mountain: bare m. tops are bald ARN 16:7
  destroy in all my holy m. BIBLE 58:11
  fool alone on a great m. KILV 296:8
  from yonder m. height TENN 542:15
  gross as a m. SHAK 439:4
  He watches from his m. TENN 533:7
  huge m. 'tween my heart SHAK 449:22
  'If the m. will not...') BACON 25:33
  I never see another m. LAMB 307:22
  into an exceeding high m. BIBLE 64:3
  m. and hill shall be made BIBLE 59:5
  m. cradle in Pamere ARN 15:1
  m. sheep are sweeter PEAC 371:2
  M.'s slumbrous voice SHEL 502:7
  shall say unto this m. BIBLE 67:1
  sun looked over the m.'s BROW 103:9
  taking him up into a high m. BIBLE 69:16
  this fair m. leave to feed SHAK 435:7
  tiptoe on the misty m. SHAK 483:14
  Up the airy m. ALL 3:20
mountainous: m. sports girl BETJ 43:20
mountains: Beautiful must be the m.
    BRID 92:17
  Before the m. were brought PRAY 395:17
  came to the Delectable M. BUNY 107:23
  decayed hole among the m. ELIOT 205:10
  heaped-up m. with a thunderbolt VIRG 560:12
  High m. are a feeling BYRON 120:35
  in the rocks of the m. BIBLE 81:30
  Make m. level SHAK 442:1
  men and m. meet BLAKE 87:10
  Molehills seem m. COTT 163:7
  m. also shall bring peace PRAY 394:19
  M. are the beginning RUSK 411:12
  m. by the winter sea TENN 535:20
  m. look on Marathon BYRON 122:33
  m. skipped like rams PRAY 397:16
  M. will heave in childbirth HOR 257:18
  One of the m. WORD 582:18
  paced upon the m. overhead YEATS 587:12
  strength setteth fast the m. PRAY 394:1
  that I could remove m. BIBLE 76:14
  Ye m. of Gilboa BIBLE 50:16
mountain-tops: Flatter the m. with
  sovereign SHAK 493:9
  m. that freeze SHAK 447:3
mountebank: m. who sold pills which
    ADD 2:28
  story of a m. and his zany WALP 563:19
mounted: m. on her milk-white steed
    BALL 32:4
mounts: now he m. above me DRYD 195:12
mourir: et quand on a à m. MOL 353:21
 foy je veuil vivre et m. VILL 557:6
 Partir c'est m. un peu HAR 238:20
mourn: Blessed are they that m. BIBLE 64:6
  countless thousands m. BURNS 114:23
  day be time enough to m. DAN 171:11
  don't m. for me never ANON 5:13
  each will m. her own (she ING 270:16
  I did not m. HOUS 264:4
  I'll sit and m. all BALL 32:9
  I m. for that most lonely YEATS 585:10
  It is Margaret you m. HOPK 256:27
  man was made to m. BURNS 114:22
  M., you powers of Charm CAT 136:22
  No longer m. for me when SHAK 494:6
  now can never m. SHEL 499:21
  time to m. BIBLE 55:12
  to comfort all that m. BIBLE 60:8
  us in summer skies to m. KEATS 289:8
  wherefore should we m. WORD 578:8
  yet shall m. with ever-returning WHIT 571:12

mourn'd: m. the Lord of Burleigh
    TENN 539:11
  Would have m. longer SHAK 429:28
mourned: we have m. unto you BIBLE 66:3
mourner: constant m. o'er the dead
    BYRON 124:35
mourners: Most musical of m. SHEL 499:4
mournful: girl arose that had red m. lips
    YEATS 586:22
  pity and m. awe ARN 13:8
mourning: great m. BIBLE 63:34
  I'm in m. for my life CHEK 144:25
  m. that either his mother AUST 23:29
  oil of joy for m. BIBLE 60:9
  To the noise of the m. TENN 541:5
  widow bird sate m. SHEL 500:3
mourns: England m. for her dead BINY 84:9
  Nature m. her worshipper SCOTT 416:19
mourn'st: who m. the Daisy's fate
    BURNS 115:19
mourra: On m. seul PASC 369:9
mous: appetit hath he to ete a m.
    CHAU 142:25
  if that she saugh a m. CHAU 141:16
mouse: always leave room for the m.
    SAKI 413:15
  Good my m. of virtue SHAK 488:7
  killing of a m. on Sunday BRAT 91:24
  m.'s limp tail hanging MOORE 355:22
  Not a m. Shall disturb SHAK 471:22
  Not a m. stirring SHAK 429:6
  other caught a M. LEAR 312:23
  silly little m. will be born HOR 257:18
  usual to catch a m. or two GRAY 235:23
mouse-trap: baiting a m. with cheese
    SAKI 413:15
Hamlet: The M. SHAK 434:12
  make a better m. EMER 208:15
mousseline: Supplants the m. of Cos
    POUND 383:5
moustache: who didn't wax his m. was
    KIPL 304:37
mouth: body and sweet small m. SWIN 530:13
  book comes into my m. POUND 382:15
  cleave to the roof of my m. PRAY 399:3
  door and bar for thy m. BIBLE 63:12
  Englishman to open his m. SHAW 498:12
  God be in my m. ANON 5:9
  His m. is most sweet BIBLE 57:4
  Keep your m. shut ANON 9:18
  Let the words of my m. PRAY 390:13
  m. filled with laughter PRAY 398:16
  m. is smoother than oil BIBLE 53:20
  m. like an old potato KIPL 298:7
  m. of the Lord doth man BIBLE 48:22
  m. of the Lord hath spoken BIBLE 59:5
  m. of very babes and sucklings PRAY 389:28
  mouths are one with M. BROO 95:1
  m. shall shew thy praise PRAY 393:8
  m. sweet as honey BIBLE 82:9
  m. went a sharp twoedged BIBLE 81:14
  own m. will I judge thee BIBLE 71:1
  pipe for my capacious m. GAY 222:7
  praises of God be in their m. PRAY 399:24
  proceedeth out of the m. of God BIBLE 64:1
  purple-stained m. KEATS 291:18
  red splendid kissing m. SWIN 531:1
  slap-dash down in the m. CONG 160:25
  so he openeth not his m. BIBLE 59:22
  spue thee out of my m. BIBLE 81:20
  which cometh out of the m. BIBLE 66:28
  with the kisses of his m. BIBLE 56:15
  yet he opened not his m. BIBLE 59:22
mouthed: first m. SHAK 435:24
  m. to flesh-burst HOPK 257:7
mouthful: made it out of a m. of air
    YEATS 585:8
mouths: Blind m. MILT 343:12
  enemy in their m. to steal SHAK 475:9
  issue from your smoky m. MARL 329:13

  Make m. upon me when SHAK 470:23
  m., and speak not PRAY 397:18
  m. were made for tankards MAS 333:21
  she made m. in a glass SHAK 454:6
moutons: Revenons à ces m. ANON 9:16
mouvement: Un premier m. ne fut jamais
    CORN 162:18
mouvements: Défiez-vous des premiers
  m. MONT 355:11
Movable: M. Types was disbanding
    CARL 132:12
move: feel the earth m. HEM 245:3
  If I could pray to m. SHAK 449:25
  in him we live, and m. BIBLE 74:14
  I propose to m. immediately GRANT 234:1
  I shall m. Hell VIRG 559:5
  it does m. GAL 220:29
  I will m. the earth ARCH 11:24
  Let's all m. one place CARR 134:4
  M. him into the sun OWEN 367:4
  M. my faint heart with SHEL 501:15
  M. Queen Anne VICT 556:16
  m. with the moving ships SWIN 530:28
  that honour could not m. BROO 94:27
  that it never should m. PRAY 396:18
  this will not m. SUCK 524:7
  whichever way you m. LUCAN 320:1
moved: king was much m. BIBLE 50:26
  M. earth and heaven TENN 544:3
  m. more than with a trumpet SIDN 508:3
  Spirit of God m. upon BIBLE 44:22
  suffer thy foot to be m. PRAY 398:9
  though the earth be m. PRAY 392:10
moveless: m. hands And face and gaze
    HARDY 240:15
  watch and m. woe BROW 98:8
movement: intelligent may begin a m.
    CONR 161:22
  is almost a palpable m. HARDY 241:9
  neither arrest nor m. ELIOT 202:15
movere: Quieta m. magna merces
    SALL 413:23
moveris: quocumque m. LUCAN 320:1
movers: We are the m. and shakers
    OSH 365:20
moves: m. with its own organs SHAK 422:14
  nothing m. in this world MAINE 327:7
moveth: all that m. SPEN 516:25
moving: always m. as the restless
    MARL 330:8
  m. accident is not my trade WORD 577:22
  M. Finger writes FITZ 213:7
  m. from hence to there SOCR 512:20
  m. Toyshop of their heart POPE 380:30
mower: m. whets his scythe MILT 342:19
Mozambic: M., off at sea north-east
    MILT 347:17
MPs: in that House M. divide GILB 226:9
  Of dull M. in close proximity GILB 226:10
Mr Collins: if you do not marry M.
    AUST 23:15
Mr Salteena: M. was an elderly man
    ASHF 17:5
MSS: M. as drunkards use lamp-posts
    HOUS 266:14
M'Tavish: Against the clan M. AYT 24:6
much: do as m. for my true-love BALL 32:9
  just so m., no more BROW 105:28
  M. hath been done BYRON 121:32
  M. have I seen and known TENN 543:22
  M. in our vows SHAK 489:7
  m. is to be done and little JOHN 280:7
  so m. to do TENN 537:2
  tell me how m. SHAK 421:7
  that is too m. in anything BACON 25:37
  'There won't be m. for us CARR 133:13
muchness: Much of a m. VANB 555:3
muck: down in lovely m. I've HOUS 264:13
  Money is like m. BACON 27:12
  when to stop raking the m. ROOS 408:4

cometh in the N. of the Lord — PRAY 398:3
Conveys it in a borrowed n. — PRIOR 401:1
Corsair's n. to other times — BYRON 121:36
coward shame distain his n. — BURNS 114:21
deed without a n. — SHAK 462:5
ev'n for his own n.'s sake — SCOT 419:5
fear my n. shall the Sun — BIBLE 62:3
filches from me my good n. — SHAK 475:16
forget your n. or who you are — CLARE 152:17
ghost of a great n. — LUCAN 319:23
glory in the n. of Briton — GEOR 224:1
good n. is rather to be — BIBLE 54:21
have forgotten your n. — SWIN 530:11
He left the n. — JOHN 282:31
Her n. is never heard — BAYLY 35:10
his N. is great in Israel — PRAY 395:1
I am become a n. — TENN 543:22
I do not like her n. — SHAK 426:12
'I have no n. — BLAKE 88:1
I injur'd neither n. — HOLL 253:4
I kept them in thy n. — BIBLE 72:42
ill he cannot cure a n. — ARN 15:12
in the n. of human nature — BURKE 110:33
is a good travelling n. — FARQ 210:5
Is not the king's n. twenty — SHAK 479:7
king's n. is a tower — SHAK 481:12
leave a living n. behind — WEBS 566:17
Let me not n. it to you — SHAK 477:5
local habitation and a n. — SHAK 471:11
Man by a scribbled n. — THOM 547:5
my n. and memory — BACON 28:14
my n. is Jowett — BEEC 37:8
My n. is Legion — BIBLE 68:30
My n. is Used-to-was — TRAI 552:4
n. Achilles assumed — BROW 97:14
n. in pride and thankfulness — BROW 101:22
n. liveth for evermore — BIBLE 63:26
n. made great is a name — HILL 251:5
n. of Jesus every knee — BIBLE 78:14
N. of the Lord our God — PRAY 390:14
n. of the slough was Despond — BUNY 107:11
n. shall be called Wonderful — BIBLE 58:7
n. to all succeeding ages — DRYD 194:6
n. too will be linked with — OVID 366:12
n. to the reverberate hills — SHAK 488:13
n. was writ in water — KEATS 295:3
n. were not so terrible — SHAK 441:15
nothing but to n. his tools — BUTL 117:16
nothing of a n. — BYRON 121:28
number of his n. — BIBLE 82:13
of the thought of his n. — ELIOT 204:6
'oss, my wife, and my n. — SURT 525:17
Phoebus! what a n. — BYRON 124:24
Poor wounded n. — SHAK 490:32
praise of his holy N. — PRAY 389:1
ready ere I call'd her n. — PRIOR 401:5
refuse thy n. — SHAK 482:8
spared the n. — SWIFT 527:24
talk not to me of a n. — BYRON 125:29
that dare not speak its n. — DOUG 191:4
that have left a n. behind — BIBLE 63:24
that slow sweet n.'s sake — BROW 100:28
that taketh his n. in vain — BIBLE 47:24
them an everlasting n. — BIBLE 60:1
the N. of the Lord — PRAY 398:14
these roarers for the n. — SHAK 484:20
They scratch his n. — BROW 101:27
to see one's n. in print — BYRON 124:16
to thy n. give glory — BIBLE 83:10
unto thy N. give the praise — PRAY 397:17
we worship thy N. — PRAY 384:18
What is your N. — PRAY 388:12
What's in a n. — SHAK 482:9
where n. and image meet — AUDEN 20:2
which is above every n. — BIBLE 78:14
With a n. like yours — CARR 135:19
with the whistling of a n. — POPE 380:1
worth an age without a n. — MORD 357:6
write upon him my new n. — BIBLE 81:19
wrote her n. upon the strand — SPEN 515:20

yet another n. more free — POPE 376:11
yet can't quite n. — LARK 310:5
named: heaven and earth is n. — BIBLE 77:24
n. the child I-chabod — BIBLE 49:40
nameless: n. and abominable colour — HOUS 266:8
N. here for evermore — POE 375:5
n. in worthy deeds — BROW 97:17
n., unremembered, acts — WORD 578:4
Namen: Schicksal und Gemüt N. — NOV 364:9
names: allow their n. to be mentioned — AUST 23:19
calleth them all by their n. — PRAY 399:19
carved n. the rain-drop — HARDY 239:10
commodity of good n. were — SHAK 438:6
have THREE DIFFERENT N. — ELIOT 204:5
hideous n. as Higginbottom — ARN 15:26
honour doth forget men's n. — SHAK 452:9
I have lost all the n. — JOHN 278:31
instinct bring back the old n. — COL 157:8
lands after their own n. — PRAY 392:28
n. in many a mused rhyme — KEATS 291:22
n. of those who love — HUNT 268:4
n. that must not wither — BYRON 120:32
N. that should be on every — CALV 127:12
Not unholy n. — DICK 179:6
of seeing our n. in print — CHES 147:22
sharp n. that never get — BENET 40:19
use such n. and not be humble — SASS 414:19
which grows from common n. — BURKE 110:2
with n. that men remember — SWIN 529:14
worshipp'd by the n. divine — BLAKE 86:1
Naming: N. of Cats is a difficult — ELIOT 204:5
To-day we have n. of parts — REED 405:5
Nan: ever change Kate into N. — BLAKE 86:1
nap: into a short n. at sermon — ADD 2:12
Napier: With Admiral N. — THAC 546:2
Naples: On N. and on liberty — CHES 146:21
Napoleon: He is the N. of crime — DOYLE 192:11
Louis Philippe far better than a N. — BAG 28:25
N. forgot Blücher — CHUR 149:23
N. of the realms of rhyme — BYRON 123:31
N.'s armies always used — SELL 420:7
nappy: we sit bousing at the n. — BURNS 115:3
narcotics: Like dull n. — TENN 536:1
Narr: bleibt ein N. sein Leben lang — LUTH 321:1
narrat: de tauris n. arator — PROP 401:15
narration: n. always going backwards — WALP 562:25
narrative: bald and unconvincing n. — GILB 227:12
narratur: Fabula n. — HOR 261:22
narrow: is cultivated by n. minds — MILL 339:1
make it saft and n. — BALL 30:12
n. is the way — BIBLE 65:7
n. measure spans — HOUS 265:13
narrow-necked: narrow-souled people — as with n. — POPE 381:20
Narrows: N. the world to my neighbour's — MER 337:19
narrow-souled: n. people as with — narrow-necked — POPE 381:20
Nassau: Can Bourbon or N. go higher — PRIOR 400:25
Nasticreechia: N. Krorluppia — LEAR 311:19
nasty: is a n. creature — MOL 354:2
n., brutish, and short — HOBB 251:18
nice man is a man of n. — SWIFT 527:13
Something n. in the woodshed — GIBB 225:2
nata: n. mecum consule Manlio — HOR 261:5
natale: 'Libertas et n. solum' — SWIFT 528:10
natam: fortunatam n. me consule — CIC 152:2
nati: sunt n. — LUCAN 319:25
nation: against the voice of a n. — RUSS 412:18
attention of the n. is — BAG 28:30
build that n.'s fate — BLAKE 85:17
dream that one day this n. — KING 296:15
England is a n. of shopkeepers — NAP 359:15

faith in a n. of sectaries — DISR 186:1
fate of a n. was riding — LONG 316:26
from an ample n. — DICK 183:22
general happiness of the n. — PEDR 371:4
greatest inquest of the n. — BURKE 110:28
hast multiplied the n. — BIBLE 58:6
holy n. — BIBLE 80:23
lift up sword against n. — BIBLE 57:19
mourning of a mighty n. — TENN 541:5
n. is not governed — BURKE 109:19
n. of pure philosophers — BAG 29:2
n. of shop-keepers are — ADAMS 1:9
n. of shopkeepers — SMITH 509:12
n. proud in arms — MILT 340:26
n. shall rise against nation — BIBLE 67:28
N. shall speak peace unto — REND 405:11
N. spoke to a Nation — KIPL 301:20
noble and puissant n. — MILT 352:3
No n. wanted it so much — SWIFT 527:25
our existence as a n. — PITT 374:4
public burden of the n.'s — PRIOR 401:6
publish it to all the n. — PRIOR 400:24
Righteousness exalteth a n. — BIBLE 54:3
Still better for the n. — ANON 5:15
temptation to a rich and lazy n. — KIPL 298:18
Think of what our N. stands — BETJ 43:6
we are a n. of amateurs — ROS 408:15
national: always be above n. prejudices — NORTH 364:2
n. debt — HAM 238:13
N. Debt is a very Good — SELL 420:6
n. repugnances do not touch — BROW 96:28
nationless: tribeless, and n. — SHEL 503:12
nations: all n. shall do him service — PRAY 394:20
are the pedigree of n. — JOHN 280:1
become the father of many n. — BIBLE 74:40
day of small n. has long — CHAM 129:13
friendship with all n. — JEFF 272:8
gossip from all the n. — AUDEN 20:2
healing of the n. — BIBLE 83:1
heard the embattled n. — SQUI 517:13
He smote divers n. — PRAY 399:1
in hating all other n. — GASK 222:4
let fierce contending n. — ADD 1:25
manners of different n. — STEV 522:2
n. are as a drop of a bucket — BIBLE 59:8
n. combine each cry — AUDEN 20:15
N., like men — BOL 89:17
N. touch at their summits — BAG 29:7
n. trek from progress — OWEN 367:11
n. under our feet — PRAY 392:23
n. which have put mankind — INGE 270:10
Of n. beat to dust — KIPL 300:6
People formed Two N. — DISR 186:32
See n. slowly wise — JOHN 282:29
sets all n. by the ears — LAND 308:21
teaching n. how to live — MILT 352:6
that shapes the fate of n. — CONR 161:23
To belong to other n. — GILB 228:10
to foreign n. — BACON 28:14
'Two n. — DISR 186:29
native: considerable in his n. — JOHN 276:1
found him a n. of the rocks — JOHN 274:6
have felt with my n. land — TENN 540:19
My n. land — BYRON 120:6
my n. land — SCOTT 416:21
my n. shore — BYRON 120:5
not more n. to the heart — SHAK 429:20
thunders from her n. oak — CAMP 129:13
Warble his n. wood-notes wild — MILT 342:26
yet my song comes n. with — KEATS 292:5
natives: Educating the n. of Borrioboola-Gha — DICK 176:4
nativity: At my n. — SHAK 439:21
n. was under ursa major — SHAK 453:11
out of love with your n. — SHAK 426:20
stars that reigned at my n. — MARL 329:13
Natur: quite fresh from N.'s mould — DICK 179:19

natura: Mors stupebit et n.   CEL 138:6
N. il fece   ARIO 12:2
N. vacuum abhorret   RAB 403:27
Naturae: N. enim non imperatur
                                                BACON 28:10
natural: behaviour was n. and intrepid
                                                WALP 562:20
five per cent is the n. interest   MAC 323:29
He wants the n. touch   SHAK 462:12
I do it more n.   SHAK 488:19
n. for a man and woman   JOHN 276:2
n. idol of the Anglo-Saxon   BAG 29:4
n. to die as to be born   BACON 26:3
On the stage he was n.   GOLD 231:20
Some n. sorrow   WORD 578:15
something in this more than n.   SHAK 432:17
sorrow enough in the n.   KIPL 302:3
swear her colour is n.   SHER 506:28
term of N. Selection   DARW 171:25
that n. fear in children   BACON 26:1
twice as n.   CARR 136:1
what is n. cannot touch me   ETH 208:26
When we see a n. style   PASC 369:4
naturaleza: pintores imitan la n.   CERV 139:1
naturaliter: testimonium animae n.
  Christianae   TERT 544:21
naturally: poetry comes not as n.
                                               KEATS 293:25
Naturam: N. expellas furca   HOR 258:18
nature: All n. is but art unknown   POPE 379:11
All N. seems at work   COL 157:14
All N. was degraded   BLAKE 85:7
art and n.   SHAK 464:6
be aghast and so will n.   CEL 138:6
Beauty is N.'s brag   MILT 341:18
blind forces of N.   MAINE 327:7
breathless N.'s dark abyss   WORD 578:8
by N. curs'd   CHUR 148:32
constant course of n.   DONNE 190:24
Everything almost Which is N.'s
                                               SHEL 503:28
experiencing n.   BAG 29:14
fancy outwork n.   SHAK 422:2
fault was N.'s fault not   BYRON 126:3
fools call N.   BROW 104:29
force of n. could no farther   DRYD 196:30
frame of n. round him break   ADD 2:30
fulfils great N.'s plan   BURNS 113:21
great N. made us men   LOW 319:11
great n.'s second course   SHAK 460:8
great Secretary of N.   WALT 564:15
happy imitator of N.   HEM 245:2
Has broken N.'s social   BURNS 115:21
Hath read in N.'s mystic   MARV 332:22
Heaven and N. seem'd   JONS 284:2
He is made one with N.   SHEL 499:23
he paid the debt of n.   FABY 209:15
horribly cruel works of n.   DARW 172:1
I am as free as n. first   DRYD 195:29
If honest N. made you fools   BURNS 113:19
informed by the light of n.   BACON 24:20
In N.'s infinite book   SHAK 421:9
In n. there are neither   ING 270:18
interpreter of n.   JOHN 282:7
Is N. felt   WORD 577:5
It can't be N.   CHUR 148:25
lap was N.'s darling laid   GRAY 235:18
law of n.   BURKE 110:32
learn'd is happy n.   POPE 379:17
learned To look on n.   WORD 578:7
life alone does N. live   COL 156:9
looks through N.   POPE 380:2
lusty stealth of n.   SHAK 453:9
made a gap in n.   SHAK 422:3
Man is N.'s sole mistake   GILB 228:28
mere copier of n. can never   REYN 405:17
mirror held up n.'s light   POPE 380:4
mirror up to n.   SHAK 433:17
My n. is subdu'd   SHAK 495:4
N. abhors a vacuum   RAB 403:27

N. admits no lie   CARL 132:3
N. always does contrive   GILB 226:8
N., and Nature's laws   POPE 378:7
N. breeds   MILT 346:23
N. cannot be ordered about   BACON 28:10
N. gave thee   CHUR 149:3
N. hath fram'd strange   SHAK 465:8
n. her custom holds   SHAK 436:20
N. herself seems   ARN 16:8
N. in awe to him   MILT 344:5
N. in him was almost lost   COLL 158:23
N. in you stands   SHAK 453:25
N. is always wise in every   THUR 550:33
N. is but a name   COWP 167:26
N. is creeping up   WHIS 569:22
N. is fine in love   SHAK 436:8
N. is often hidden   BACON 26:36
n. is the art of God   BROW 96:13
N. is tugging at every   EMER 207:4
N. is usually wrong   WHIS 569:20
N. is very consonant   NEWT 362:18
n., kindly bent to ease   SWIFT 527:22
N. made him   ARIO 12:2
N. made her what she is   BURNS 112:37
N. mourns her worshipper   SCOTT 416:19
n. must obey necessity   SHAK 451:28
N. never makes excellent   LOCKE 315:14
n. of all greatness not   BURKE 109:3
n. of God is a circle   ANON 7:27
N., red in tooth and claw   TENN 536:29
N. say one thing and Wisdom   BURKE 112:8
n.'s changing course untrimm'd   SHAK 492:28
N. seems dead   SHAK 460:1
n.'s fragile vessel doth   SHAK 486:13
N.'s great masterpiece   DONNE 190:3
n.'s handmaid art   DRYD 195:22
N. that is above all art   DAN 170:22
n. then   WORD 578:6
n. to advantage dress'd   POPE 378:17
N., we are thine   WORD 577:6
N. wears one universal   FIEL 211:33
necessity...It is a part of n.   SPEN 514:32
new edition of human n.   HAZL 243:12
next to N.   LAND 308:20
nice I suppose it is my n.   ASHF 17:6
One touch of n. makes   SHAK 487:6
out n. with a pitchfork   HOR 258:18
painters imitate n.   CERV 139:1
Passing through n. to eternity   SHAK 429:24
pattern of excelling n.   SHAK 477:5
perfect n. and are perfected   BACON 27:17
priketh hem n. in hir corages)   CHAU 141:8
production of human n.   ADD 2:9
rest in N.   HERB 248:7
rest on N. fix   COKE 154:22
seem'd when N. him began   DRAY 193:7
Since 'tis N.'s law   ROCH 406:15
sovereign good of human n.   BACON 27:31
spark o' N.'s fire   BURNS 113:20
spectacles of books to read N.   DRYD 198:2
standing at ease in N.   WHIT 570:6
still is N.'s priest   WORD 579:5
sullenness against N. not   MILT 352:10
that n. by her mother wit   SPEN 516:20
That n. yet remembers   WORD 579:9
Then n. rul'd   GAY 223:5
'tis N.'s fault alone   CHUR 149:15
'tis their n. too   WATTS 565:17
touched the hem of N.'s shift   SHEL 502:18
Treatise of Human N.   HUME 268:1
weakness of our mortal n.   PRAY 386:15
what n. itselfe cant endure   FLEM 214:26
When N. has work to be done   EMER 208:3
Whose body N. is   POPE 379:10
Wise n. did never put her   BACON 25:7
With N.'s pride   MARL 330:5
witless n.   HOUS 265:10
Yet simple N. to his hope   POPE 379:5
yet to N. true   CHUR 149:12

natures: humane, and devoted n.
                                               CONR 161:22
ignominy of our n.   BROW 96:20
naught: I must have n. beside   THOM 548:10
let it be for n.   BROW 98:11
N. broken save this body   BROO 94:28
n., saith the buyer   BIBLE 54:19
naughtily: if I meant n.   SHAK 487:9
naughtiness: filthiness and superfluity
  of n.   BIBLE 80:10
n. of thine heart   BIBLE 50:8
naughty: amended his former n. life
                                               PRAY 387:5
deed in a n. world   SHAK 468:18
He is a n. child   STEV 522:21
n. night to swim   SHAK 454:21
nauseated: intolerably dull that it n. me
                                               DARW 171:22
nauseous: n. draught of life   ROCH 406:19
Nauticae: et Acus N.   BACON 28:9
naval: his figurative n. manner   DICK 176:10
to me about n. tradition   CHUR 151:7
nave: from the n. to the chaps   SHAK 458:3
navel: n. is like a round goblet   BIBLE 57:8
navibus: n. atque Quadrigis   HOR 258:3
navies: From the nations' airy n.   TENN 538:24
Navita: N. de ventis   PROP 401:15
navy: came the n. of Tharshish   BIBLE 50:34
It is upon the n. under   CHAR 140:21
load would sink a n.   SHAK 447:11
n. nothing but rotten timber   BURKE 110:5
n. of England hath ever   BLAC 85:4
nay: and your n., nay   BIBLE 80:18
say n., for shame   WYATT 583:19
nayles: His n. whitter than   CHAU 142:32
Nazareth: good thing come out of N.
                                               BIBLE 71:31
Nazi: until finally N. Germany   NEV 361:2
né: L'homme est n. libre   ROUS 410:17
Neaera: with the tangles of N.'s   MILT 343:8
near: come not n. to me   BIBLE 60:13
n. in blood   SHAK 461:4
n. me when my light is   TENN 536:21
n. neighbour to Despair   ARN 14:18
seems so n. and yet so far   TENN 537:13
Nearer: N., my God, to thee   ADAMS 1:10
n. than hands and feet   TENN 533:29
n. the Church the further   ANDR 4:8
n. to the Heart's Desire   FITZ 213:16
n. you are to God   WOTT 583:17
near'st: n. and dearest enemy   SHAK 439:36
neat: any good girl to be n.   TAYL 531:24
N., but not gaudy   WESL 568:25
Still to be n.   JONS 283:27
that is not clean and n.   STEV 522:21
Nebuchadnezzar: golden image that
  N.   BIBLE 61:3
necessaries: between luxuries and n.
                                               GALB 220:28
necessary: all things n. to salvation
                                               PRAY 400:6
intellectual nature is n.   JOHN 281:32
is but a n. evil   PAINE 367:21
it is n. not to change   FALK 209:19
Make yourself n. to someone   EMER 207:3
they are n. evils   JOHN 282:1
Necessitas: N. dat legem non ipsa accipit
                                               PUBL 402:6
nécessité: Je n'en vois pas la n.   ARG 12:1
necessities: art of our n. is strange
                                               SHAK 454:11
will dispense with its n.   MOTL 358:21
necessity: am forsworn 'on mere n.'
                                               SHAK 456:11
first n. invented stools   COWP 166:28
I do not see the n.   ARG 12:1
nature must obey n.   SHAK 451:28
N. and chance   MILT 348:30
N. gives the law without   PUBL 402:6
N. hath no law   CROM 170:2

N. is the plea for every | PITT 374:3
N. makes an honest man | DEFOE 173:10
N. never made a good bargain | FRAN 218:8
n. of being *ready* increases | LINC 314:20
n., The tyrant's plea | MILT 347:27
sheer n. of fizz | BELL 39:31
There is no virtue like n. | SHAK 478:16
Thy n. is yet greater than | SIDN 508:6
To grim N. | SHAK 480:7
we were villains by n. | SHAK 453:11
world to see that n. is | FIEL 211:20
neck: his n. brake | BIBLE 49:39
his n. unto a second yoke | HERR 250:4
left his straight n. bent | ROSS 410:2
my n. is very short | MORE 357:17
n. God made for other use | HOUS 262:17
n. is as a tower of ivory | BIBLE 57:9
n. when once broken | WALSH 563:28
Roman people had but one n. | CAL 127:6
Some n. | CHUR 150:10
Thy n. is like the tower | BIBLE 56:26
were hanged abut his n. | BIBLE 67:3
necktie: left my n. God knows where | HOUS 264:13
nectar: hope draws n. in a sieve | COL 157:15
might I of Jove's n. sup | JONS 284:12
they lie beside their n. | TENN 539:16
To comprehend a n. | DICK 183:23
nectarine: n. and curious peach | MARV 332:3
Ned: knew me, and was N. | HOUS 265:5
need: all ye n. to know | KEATS 291:11
living n. charity | ARN 12:20
n. of a world of men | BROW 103:9
n., sickness | PRAY 387:16
n. the other women know | BROW 98:26
n. thou hast in life | HOPE 256:5
seeth his brother have n. | BIBLE 81:4
To suit and serve his n. | HERB 247:15
What can I want or n. | HERB 248:13
When our n. was the sorest | SCOTT 416:5
needed: showing them they were not n. | BELL 39:9
needful: one thing is n. | BIBLE 69:35
needle: blunteth the n. | POUND 382:9
for the n. she | TENN 542:9
Hinders n. and thread | HOOD 255:10
Plying her n. and thread | HOOD 255:6
through the eye of a n. | BIBLE 67:11
Who sayes my hand a n. | BRAD 91:13
needlework: King in raiment of n. | PRAY 392:17
needs: each according to his n. | BAK 29:25
each according to his n. | MARX 333:5
n. not June for beauty's | ARN 15:4
needy: considereth the poor and n. | PRAY 392:4
n. nothing trimm'd in jollity | SHAK 494:5
Ne'er: N. a verse to thee | KING 296:22
nefas: scire n. | HOR 259:19
negabimus: nulli n. aut differemus | MAGN 327:3
negation: This is the n. of God erected | GLAD 229:19
Negative: N. Capability | KEATS 293:19
neglect: little n. may breed mischief | FRAN 218:6
most tender mercy is n. | COWP 168:28
punished for n. these unhappy | JOHN 281:5
Such sweet n. more taketh | JONS 283:27
to the n. of his duties | THOM 549:6
wise and salutary n. | BURKE 109:18
neglected: pleased to have his all n. | JOHN 274:5
negligent: servant's too often a n. elf | BARH 33:10
negotiis: qui procul n. | HOR 259:7
nègres: Le pauvres sont les n. | CHAM 139:17
negro: respecting his n. friend | BECK 36:18
negroes: among the drivers of n. | JOHN 282:18
providing the infant n. | DICK 182:6

nehmen: wir und n. immer Abschied | RILKE 406:4
neiges: où sont les n. d'antan | VILL 557:5
neighbour: guinea in your n.'s pocket | RUSK 412:8
have an accommodating n. | DOYLE 192:12
I am a n. and near bred | SHAK 466:6
know the man their n. | YEATS 586:14
lug the guts into the n. | SHAK 435:22
my duty to my N. | PRAY 388:14
My duty towards my N. | PRAY 388:15
Narrows the world to my n.'s | MER 337:19
near n. to Despair | ARN 14:18
neighed after his n.'s wife | BIBLE 60:16
next-door n. for so many years | SCOTT 418:23
nor done evil to his n. | PRAY 390:4
our n.'s house is on fire | BURKE 111:1
policy of the good n. | ROOS 407:21
removeth his n.'s landmark | BIBLE 48:26
shall love your crooked n. | AUDEN 18:11
shalt not covet thy n.'s | BIBLE 47:24
that he might rob a n. | MAC 323:21
Thou shalt love thy n. | BIBLE 48:8
to hate your n. | MAC 324:3
Withdraw thy foot from thy n.'s | BIBLE 54:28
neighbouring: cynosure of n. eyes | MILT 342:20
neighbours: charity with your n. | PRAY 387:18
From every house the n. met | TENN 536:18
'Good fences make good n. | FROST 219:9
is happening to our n. | CHAM 139:7
songs of peace to all his n. | SHAK 448:1
to make sport for our n. | AUST 23:20
vigil feast his n. | SHAK 445:3
n. after his neighbour's | BIBLE 60:16
neighs: in high and boastful n. | SHAK 444:9
neither: n. children nor Gods | KIPL 298:23
'Tis n. here nor there | SHAK 477:1
nekke: to strecche forth the n. | CHAU 143:5
Nell: Pretty witty N. | PEPYS 372:13
Nelly: Let not poor N. starve | CHAR 140:28
Nelson: death of N. was felt | SOUT 514:17
N. turned his blindest | CHES 146:21
Of N. and the North | CAMP 128:14
To N.'s peerless name | NEWB 361:3
Nelson touch: explain to them the 'N.' | NELS 360:19
keep the N. | NEWB 361:12
Nemo: N. me impune lacessit | ANON 10:15
Nephew: N. of Fox | HOLL 253:4
Neptune: influence N.'s empire stands | SHAK 429:13
N.'s park | SHAK 428:13
nequiores: Nos n. | HOR 260:26
nerve: who am as a n. o'er which | SHEL 501:12
nerves: expredge my n. this night | DICK 179:31
my firm n. | SHAK 461:21
n. prick | TENN 536:21
N. sit ceremonious | DICK 183:13
N. that steeled themselves | AUDEN 21:3
nobody feels for my poor n. | AUST 23:16
to keep the n. at strain | BROW 102:1
with us strengthens our n. | BURKE 111:23
Nervii: day he overcame the N. | SHAK 450:26
nescit: n. vox missa | HOR 258:6
nest: Her soft and chilly n. | KEATS 289:18
her warm n. of renaissance | DAY-L 172:21
leaves the well-built n. | SHEL 501:22
long since my n. is made | TENN 542:6
n. of singing birds | JOHN 273:28
song ye may learn the n. | TENN 535:3
swallow a n. where she | PRAY 395:11
We'll theek our n. when | BALL 32:8
Nestling: N. me everywhere | HOPK 256:6
nests: Birds in their little n. agree | BELL 40:6
birds of the air have n. | BIBLE 65:18
built their n. in my beard | LEAR 311:15
Thus you birds build n. | VIRG 560:20

net: Fain would fling the n. | MER 337:4
have laid a n. for my feet | PRAY 393:15
I will let down the n. | BIBLE 69:18
vain the n. is spread | BIBLE 53:14
Whizzing them over the n. | BETJ 43:20
nets: be n. of such a texture | SHEN 505:16
into their own n. together | PRAY 399:10
n. and stratagems to catch | HERB 248:10
n. of wrong and right | YEATS 585:14
their time in making n. | SWIFT 527:10
them tangled in amorous n. | MILT 350:2
weave but n. to catch | WEBS 566:17
nettle: Out of this n., danger | SHAK 438:29
Tender-handed stroke a n. | HILL 251:2
nettles: apt to be overrun with n. | WALP 563:17
like the dust on the n. | THOM 547:21
n. and brambles | BIBLE 58:31
neutral: Loyal and n., in a moment | SHAK 461:2
studiously n. | WILS 574:21
neutrality: Armed n. | WILS 574:22
for a word—'n.' | BETH 42:3
n. of an impartial judge | BURKE 111:34
neutralize: White shall not n. the black | BROW 104:31
neutral-tinted: n. haps and such | HARDY 239:22
never: be the people n. so impatient | PRAY 396:10
desks and n. go to sea | GILB 228:7
I could n. go back again | MORE 357:12
I n. use a big | GILB 228:2
I n. would lay down my | PITT 373:26
kiss me and n. no more | MAL 328:4
let me n. see | PRIOR 400:28
N. ask me whose | HOUS 263:11
N. do to-day what you can | PUNCH 402:13
n. fly conceals a hook | BROO 94:13
n. home came she | KING 297:1
N., never, never, | SHAK 456:11
n. sad but when she sleeps | SHAK 472:13
n. saw a brute I hated | BROW 99:29
n. see another mountain | LAMB 307:22
n. should move at any time | PRAY 396:18
n. sick at sea | GILB 227:31
n. taste who always drink | PRIOR 401:11
N. the time and the place | BROW 102:24
n. the twain shall meet | KIPL 297:27
n. thought of thinking | GILB 228:6
n. to admit them in your | AUST 23:19
N. to have lived is best | YEATS 585:6
N. trust the artist | LAWR 311:10
n. turned his back | BROW 98:32
N. was born | STOWE 523:19
people have n. had it so good | MACM 325:18
She who has n. lov'd | GAY 223:2
than n. to have lost at all | BUTL 119:16
Which n. were nor no man | SHAK 484:3
who n. would be missed | GILB 226:24
would you had n. seen him | SHAK 476:25
You must n. go down | MILNE 340:6
you n. can tell | SHAW 498:21
Nevermore: 'N.' | POE 375:6
Never-never: your 'N. country' | KIPL 299:3
new: adventure brave and n. | BROW 104:5
against the n. and untried | LINC 314:16
Among n. men | TENN 535:24
blessing of the N. | BACON 25:18
brave n. world | SHAK 485:26
ever reaping something n. | TENN 538:24
first by whom the n. are | POPE 378:19
have put on the n. man | BIBLE 78:26
I make all things n. | BIBLE 82:31
intend to lead a n. life | PRAY 387:18
n. deal for the American | ROOS 407:19
n. friend is as new wine | BIBLE 62:30
n. heaven and a new earth | BIBLE 82:30
n. heaven, new earth | SHAK 421:7
n. man may be raised up | PRAY 388:9

N. nobility is	BACON 26:39
n. people takes the land	CHES 147:14
n. race descends from high	VIRG 559:22
n. song: sing praises lustily	PRAY 391:19
N. styles of architecture	AUDEN 20:7
N. Testament was less	HARDY 241:24
n. wine into old bottles	BIBLE 65:25
n. years ruin and rend	SWIN 530:6
no n. thing under the sun	BIBLE 55:7
offences of affections n.	SHAK 495:3
old lamps for n.	ARAB 11:14
piping songs for ever n.	KEATS 291:6
ring in the n.	TENN 537:14
shall find something n.	VOLT 560:21
sing unto the Lord a n. song	PRAY 396:7
threshold of the n.	WALL 562:9
to hear some n. thing	BIBLE 74:11
Whether it be n. or old	ANON 5:21
write upon him my n. name	BIBLE 81:19
yielding place to n.	TENN 535:25
new-bathed: whose floor the n. stars	
	ARN 15:1
new-born: use of a n. child	FRAN 218:19
Newcastle: sun we have is made of N.	
coal	WALP 563:5
new-comer: blithe n.	WORD 582:25
New England: variety about the N. weather	
	TWAIN 554:23
newer: n. object quite forgotten	SHAK 490:34
n. rite is here	THOM 546:17
newest: oldest sins the n.	SHAK 442:20
new-manned: manned by Manning and	
n.	BROW 104:17
new-moon: up the trumpet in the n.	
	PRAY 395:9
newness: walk in n. of life	BIBLE 75:1
news: bites a dog that is n.	BOG 89:9
bringer of unwelcome n.	SHAK 441:2
evil n. rides post	MILT 350:28
good n. from a far country	BIBLE 54:30
'Have you n. of my boy	KIPL 301:15
Ill n. hath wings	DRAY 193:6
Literature is n. that STAYS	POUND 383:23
master-passion is the love of n.	COWP 168:15
n. and Prince of Peace	FLET 215:29
n. that's fit to print	OCHS 364:20
n., the manna of a day	GREEN 235:29
N. value	RALPH 404:21
was any n. in the paper	AUST 23:26
What n. on the Rialto	SHAK 465:28
newspaper: never to look into a n.	
	SHER 505:20
n. and I seem to see ghosts	IBSEN 269:21
n. is of necessity something	SCOTT 415:15
newspapers: government of men and	
morning in	PHIL 373:12
newt: Eye of n.	SHAK 462:3
Newton: *Let N. be*	POPE 378:7
N. at Peru	WALP 563:9
N., childlike sage	COWP 167:5
statue stood Of N.	WORD 580:17
Newts: N., and blind-worms	SHAK 470:11
New World: I called the N. into existence	
	CANN 130:8
New York: four hundred people in N.	
society	MCAL 321:23
O Carthage! O N.	SASS 415:4
New Yorker: Read *The N.*	AUDEN 21:6
New Zealand: gone to N.	CLOU 153:19
next: n. to a battle lost	WELL 567:27
'n. to of course god america	CUMM 170:10
n. train has gone ten minutes	PUNCH 402:21
next door: wall n. catches fire	HOR 258:23
nexus: sole n. of man to man	CARL 131:17
nez: *Le n. de Cléopâtre*	PASC 369:6
Niagara: wouldn't *live* under N.	CARL 132:28
nice: Cusins is a very n. fellow	SHAW 497:8
'N. but nubbly	KIPL 304:14
n. man is a man of nasty	SWIFT 527:13
n. sort of place, Oxford	SHAW 497:23

N. while it lasted	KIPL 301:11
Too n. for a statesman	GOLD 231:17
nicer: Are wiser and n.	AUDEN 20:12
nicest: n. child I ever knew	BELL 38:32
niche: window'd n. of that high hall	
	BYRON 120:23
Nicholas: St N. soon would be there	
	MOORE 355:12
***nicht:** n. ausrechnen, was es kostet*	
	BREC 91:26
nicht-gown: down stairs in his n.	MILL 340:3
nick: anxious to improve the n.	THOR 550:9
N., or Clootie	BURNS 112:24
nickname: n. is the heaviest stone	
	HAZL 243:27
those who invented the n.	ARN 16:3
nicknamed: n. Adam	CLOU 153:14
Nicodemus: Wise N. saw such light	
	VAUG 555:11
***nidificatis:** Sic vos non vobis n. aves*	
	VIRG 560:20
***niger:** Hic n. est*	HOR 262:3
left bank of the N.	DICK 176:4
niggers: Thet don't agree with n.	LOW 319:3
nigh: shall any plague come n.	PRAY 395:22
they shall not come n. him	PRAY 391:17
nighing: n. his hour	HOUS 264:28
night: acquainted with the n.	FROST 218:27
afraid for any terror by n.	PRAY 395:21
are alternate N. and Day	FITZ 212:13
ask of thee, beloved N.	SHEL 505:4
ate a good supper at n.	ANST 11:7
be by Silvia in the n.	SHAK 491:1
become a borrower of the n.	SHAK 461:7
black bat, in	TENN 540:9
black n. doth take away	SHAK 494:7
blessed candles of the n.	SHAK 468:22
bring in cloudy n. immediately	SHAK 483:6
by n. in a pillar of fire	BIBLE 47:21
City is of N.	THOM 549:27
civil n.	SHAK 483:6
covered by the long n.	HOR 261:18
dangers of this n.	PRAY 385:10
darkness that it may be n.	PRAY 397:1
dark n. of the soul	FITZ 213:22
day and n. shall not cease	BIBLE 45:37
day brought back my n.	MILT 351:14
dead hour of n.	BALL 32:2
Dear N.	VAUG 555:12
drown'd with us in endless n.	HERR 248:26
dusky n. rides down	FIEL 211:36
Evening must usher n.	SHEL 499:14
everlasting n.	DONNE 189:12
Farewell n., welcome day	BUNY 107:37
feet of the n.	SWIN 528:16
fourth watch of the n.	BIBLE 66:25
from this palace of dim n.	SHAK 483:31
hangs upon the cheek of n.	SHAK 482:2
hath n. to do with sleep	MILT 340:28
have toiled all the n.	BIBLE 69:18
heart of the n. with fire	SWIN 530:13
heaviness may endure for a n.	PRAY 391:13
honey'd middle of the n.	KEATS 289:12
horror of a deep n.	RAC 404:2
ignorant armies clash by n.	ARN 12:23
ill beginning of the n.	SHAK 451:29
in death's dateless n.	SHAK 493:7
in endless n.	GRAY 235:19
infant crying in the n.	TENN 536:26
in such a n. as this	SHAK 468:13
In the forests of the n.	BLAKE 87:14
In the gardens of the n.	BRID 92:16
Is it n.	WHIT 570:13
it goes off at n.	SHER 506:28
know'st the mask of n.	SHAK 482:11
last out a n. in Russia	SHAK 463:17
lesser light to rule the n.	BIBLE 45:3
light of the n. on the dew	SWIN 530:13
Long n. succeeds thy little	PEAC 370:20
lovely n. through the shadow	VIRG 558:20

love-performing n.	SHAK 483:6
Love the n.	DRYD 197:18
loving, black-brow'd n.	SHAK 483:7
Making n. hideous	SHAK 430:24
meaner beauties of the n.	WOTT 583:15
middle of the n.	CARR 135:3
Morning in the Bowl of N.	FITZ 212:5
Morn in weary N.'s decline	BLAKE 86:1
mysteries of Hecate and the n.	SHAK 453:3
naughty n. to swim	SHAK 454:21
neither the moon by n.	PRAY 398:9
Never sees horrid n.	SHAK 444:25
n. an atheist half believes	YOUNG 588:10
n. and light and the half-light	YEATS 585:9
N. and silence	SHAK 470:13
n. before Christmas	MOORE 355:12
n. be turned to day	PRAY 399:5
n. cometh	BIBLE 72:14
n. do penance for a day	WORD 580:18
n. has a thousand eyes	BOUR 90:21
N. hath a thousand eyes	LYLY 321:15
n. is crept upon our talk	SHAK 451:28
n. is far spent	BIBLE 75:24
n. is freezing fast	HOUS 265:1
N. is growing gray	HARDY 240:8
n. joint-labourer with	SHAK 429:11
N. Mail crossing the Border	AUDEN 20:1
N. makes no difference	HERR 249:12
n. of memories and of sighs	LAND 308:26
n. of this immortal day	SHEL 503:14
n. of time far surpasseth	BROW 97:20
N., sable goddess	YOUNG 588:1
n.'s black agents	SHAK 461:14
N.'s candles are burnt	SHAK 483:14
n. she'll hae but three	BALL 31:12
N.'s swift dragons cut	SHAK 470:25
n. That either makes me	SHAK 477:4
n. that he was betrayed	PRAY 388:1
n. that wins	SWIN 528:17
N., the shadow of light	SWIN 528:21
n. time I shall not forget	SWIN 529:12
n. to die upon the sand	ARN 14:26
n. was made for loving	BYRON 125:26
N. with her train of stars	HENL 245:8
of an instalment of n.	HARDY 241:19
one n. certifieth another	PRAY 390:11
One the long n. through	HOUS 262:21
only for a n. and away	WYCH 583:24
Out of the n. that covers	HENL 245:4
past as a watch in the n.	PRAY 395:18
perfect day nor n.	SHAK 446:17
poor souls who dwell in N.	BLAKE 85:18
Queen of the silent n.	BEST 42:2
read, much of the n.	ELIOT 204:18
Read out my words at n.	FLEC 214:23
read the Bible day and n.	BLAKE 85:22
reign of Chaos and old N.	MILT 345:20
returned home the previous n.	BULL 106:22
rung n.'s yawning peal	SHAK 461:13
Sable-vested N.	MILT 347:5
sisters Death and N. incessantly	WHIT 570:11
sleep one ever-during n.	CAT 136:25
So late into the n.	BYRON 125:25
sound lovers' tongues by n.	SHAK 482:19
sound of revelry by n.	BYRON 120:20
spend another such a n.	SHAK 480:26
Spirit of N.	SHEL 505:2
Such n. in England ne'er	MAC 321:26
tender is the n.	KEATS 291:20
that go bump in the n.	ANON 5:8
Then it will be *good* n.	SHEL 500:17
there shall be no n. there	BIBLE 82:34
There's n. and day	BORR 90:4
thievish n.	MILT 341:1
This n. methinks is	SHAK 468:20
through the foul womb of n.	SHAK 444:9
thy dangerous brow by n.	SHAK 449:7
'Tis with us perpetual n.	JONS 285:1
toiling upward in the n.	LONG 316:19
trumpets of the n.	SWIN 530:19

vast and middle of the n.   SHAK 430:6
vile contagion of the n.   SHAK 449:13
were the world's last n.   DONNE 189:7
What is the n.   SHAK 461:24
what of the n.   BIBLE 58:14
When the face of n. is   TENN 540:17
womb of uncreated n.   MILT 346:10
Yesterday the bird of n.   SHAK 449:1
yet it is not n.   BYRON 121:4
nightblue: humid n. fruit   JOYCE 286:29
night-cap: give me my n.   MOL 353:3
night-dress: lectures in her n.   HOOD 255:12
nighte: Every n. and alle   BALL 31:6
nighted: cast thy n. colour off   SHAK 429:23
Crossing alone the n. ferry   HOUS 265:14
night-flies: buzzing n. to thy slumber
   SHAK 441:29
night-gown: put on your n.   SHAK 462:24
Nightingale: ah, the N.   ARN 14:2
all but the wakeful n.   MILT 348:2
brown bright n. amorous   SWIN 528:15
Crave the tuneful n.   DRAY 193:19
I the n. all spring through   SWIN 530:13
It was the n.   SHAK 483:13
little brown n. bills his   HARDY 241:2
My n.   SHAK 423:3
n. when May is past   CAREW 130:19
N. cries to the Rose   FITZ 212:7
N. that in the Branches   FITZ 213:15
n. does sit so late   MARV 332:12
n., that on yon bloomy   MILT 351:5
n., if she should sing   SHAK 468:19
n. in the sycamore   STEV 523:7
roar you as 'twere any n.   SHAK 469:30
Save the n. alone   BARN 33:32
sings as sweetly as a n.   SHAK 484:8
spoils the singing of the n.   KEATS 289:8
There is no music in the n.   SHAK 491:1
'tis the ravish'd n.   LYLY 321:12
Where the n. doth sing   KEATS 291:1
nightingales: By Eve's n.   DE L 173:25
n. are singing near   ELIOT 204:16
nightly: its n. roll into darkness
   HARDY 241:20
nightmare: History is a n. from which
   JOYCE 286:23
In the burrows of the N.   AUDEN 18:10
Nights: Chequer-board of N. and Days
   FITZ 213:5
Love not such n. as these   SHAK 454:9
n. are wholesome   SHAK 429:17
open day between the n.   FRY 220:5
O ye N., and Days   PRAY 384:22
night-season: n. also I take no rest
   PRAY 390:16
night-wind: breath Of the n.   ARN 12:23
nihil: Aut Caesar, aut n.   BORG 89:25
Vox et praeterea n.   ANON 11:6
Nil: N. admirari prope res est   HOR 258:17
N. desperandum Teucro duce   HOR 259:16
N. igitur mors est ad nos   LUCR 320:8
N. posse creari De nilo   LUCR 320:5
Nile: N. spills his overflow   HOUS 262:13
on the banks of the N.   SHER 506:15
pour the waters of the N.   CARR 133:17
We live on the N.   LEAR 312:16
'Where's my serpent of old N.   SHAK 421:31
nilo: Nil posse creari De n.   LUCR 320:5
Nilus: N.' mud Lay me stark naked
   SHAK 423:21
nimble: n. and airy servitors trip MILT 351:19
nimbler: it was n. much than hinds
   MARV 332:13
nimini-pimini: pronouncing to yourself
n.   BURG 108:5
Nimrod: N. the mighty hunter before
   BIBLE 46:1
Nimshi: son of N.   BIBLE 51:33
to that of the son of N.   SMITH 512:3
nine: final stroke of n.   ELIOT 204:21

have him n. years a-killing   SHAK 476:10
His choir, the N.   ARN 13:3
n. and sixty ways of constructing KIPL 300:3
N. bean-rows will I have   YEATS 585:17
n. men's morris is filled   SHAK 470:5
not the stroke of n.   HOUS 262:18
there be n. worthy   CAXT 138:3
nine-tenths: n. of the law of chivalry
   SAY 415:6
ninety: n. and nine in the wilderness
   BIBLE 70:15
n. and nine just persons   BIBLE 70:17
That n. lives have been   MCG 325:6
Nineveh: Is one with N. and Tyre KIPL 302:8
ninth: be kept till the n. year   HOR 258:6
Niobe: Like N., all tears   SHAK 429:28
N. of nations   BYRON 121:10
nip: I'll n. him in the bud   ROCHE 406:14
nipping: is a n. and an eager air SHAK 430:22
nipple: plucked my n.   SHAK 459:10
Nisi: N. Dominus aedificaverit   BIBLE 83:12
niti: dies n. praestante labore   LUCR 320:6
nives: Diffugere n.   HOR 261:14
No: Araminta, say 'N.   PRAED 384:4
Blake was n. good   BUTL 118:35
Charybdis of Aye and N.   NEWM 361:21
everlasting N.   CARL 132:17
n. better than you should   BEAU 36:2
n. man gets a full meal   JOHN 276:27
N. money   RAC 404:5
'n. nothing   BYRON 126:19
'N. sense in going further'   KIPL 299:3
N. sun—no moon!   HOOD 254:27
not those men, n.   SOPH 513:6
people cried, 'O N.'   BARH 33:22
There is n. God   PRAY 390:2
there is n. more to say   SHAK 487:18
there is n. such word   BULW 107:5
Noah: before N. was a sailor   SHAK 489:26
cataclysm but one poor N.   HUXL 268:21
N. begat Shem   BIBLE 45:32
N. he often said to his   CHES 147:28
Who married N.'s daughter   AYT 24:7
nobility: ancient n. is the act   BACON 26:39
Betwixt the wind and his n.   SHAK 438:14
fashions men with true n.   MARL 330:11
God destroy man's n.   BACON 25:25
leave us still our old n.   MANN 328:15
New n. is but the act   BACON 26:39
N. is a graceful ornament   BURKE 111:21
N. of birth commonly abateth BACON 27:1
order of n. is of great   BAG 29:4
save N.   BYRON 120:7
True n. is exempt from fear   SHAK 446:9
nobis: Non n.   BIBLE 83:10
noble: be glad to learn of n.   SHAK 451:17
except for a n. purpose   HERB 246:17
fredome is a n. thing   BARB 33:4
grounds for the n. emotions   RUSK 411:10
Here all were n.   BYRON 120:7
Is this the n. nature   SHAK 476:16
Man is a n. animal   BROW 97:23
may see and learn the n.   CAXT 138:4
n. and nude and antique   SWIN 529:4
n. and puissant nation   MILT 352:3
n. ensample to his sheep   CHAU 142:1
N. heart   SPEN 516:4
n. in motive and far-reaching   HOOV 255:24
n. mind is here o'erthrown   SHAK 433:15
not Be n. to myself   SHAK 424:1
not birth that makes us n.   FLET 215:18
pitting their n. birth   LUCR 320:6
quiet us in a death so n.   MILT 351:2
silence is most n. till   SWIN 528:23
Some work of n. note   TENN 544:3
'Tis only n. to be good   TENN 537:29
Was born most n. that was   OTWAY 365:27
What's brave, what's n.   SHAK 423:18
when a n. nature   ARN 16:14
woods the n. savage ran   DRYD 195:29

nobleman: king may make a n. BURKE 111:37
noblemen: all n. who have gone wrong
   GILB 228:22
nobleness: allied with perfect n. ARN 16:13
n. of life Is to do thus   SHAK 421:8
Thy thoughts with n.   SHAK 428:4
nobler: Ring in the n. modes   TENN 537:15
Whether 'tis n.   SHAK 433:8
nobles: n. by the right of an earlier
   MAC 323:26
their n. with links of iron   PRAY 399:24
noblest: amongst the n. of mankind
   CALV 127:27
art the ruins of the n.   SHAK 450:11
Her n. work she classes   BURNS 114:4
honest God is the n.   ING 270:17
honest God's the n.   BUTL 119:7
honest man's the n.   BURNS 113:10
honest man's the n.   POPE 379:24
n. prospect which a Scotchman JOHN 274:30
n. Roman of them all   SHAK 452:7
n. works and foundations   BACON 27:4
Nobly: N., nobly Cape St Vincent
   BROW 101:8
Spurn not the n. born   GILB 226:4
Nobody: Hush, hush, N. cares MORT 358:15
kingdom where n. dies   MILL 339:24
Methinks n. should be sad   SHAK 452:23
N. heard him, the dead man SMITH 510:26
N.; I myself   SHAK 477:10
N. is on my side   AUST 23:16
N. speaks the truth when   BOWEN 91:4
N. tells me anything   GALS 221:1
there's n. at home   POPE 376:15
wants to hear read and n.   TWAIN 554:25
nocens: damnatur ubi n. absolvitur
   PUBL 402:5
Nocturna: N. versate manu   HOR 257:22
nocturnal: private n. terror   AUDEN 20:15
Some n. blackness   HARDY 239:2
Nod: dwelt in the land of N.   BIBLE 45:29
N. with your hand to signify   HOUS 266:9
read a n., a shrug, a look   SWIFT 527:29
noddle: barmie n.'s working prime
   BURNS 113:23
nodosities: n. of the oak without its
   BURKE 112:14
nods: even excellent Homer n.   HOR 258:2
it n. a little   FARQ 210:20
N., and becks   MILT 342:14
Noe: N. entered into the ark   BIBLE 67:32
noes: yeas and honest kersey n. SHAK 457:16
noir: Porte le soleil n. de la   NERV 360:26
noire: île triste et n.   BAUD 35:8
noise: barbarous n. environs me MILT 351:7
chamber deaf to n.   SIDN 507:21
Didst thou not hear a n.   SHAK 460:6
gone up with a merry n.   PRAY 392:24
happy n. to hear   HOUS 263:4
inexplicable dumb-shows and n. SHAK 433:16
make a cheerful n. unto   PRAY 395:9
monkeys make sorrowful n. POUND 383:16
n. in mine ear   DONNE 191:2
n. in the beast's belly   MAL 327:15
n. like that of a water-mill   SWIFT 526:3
n. of battle roll'd   TENN 535:20
n. of the mourning   TENN 541:5
n. of water in mine ears   SHAK 480:27
n. they make in pouring   POPE 381:20
Nursed amid her n.   LAMB 307:24
pleasant n. till noon   COL 155:26
that those who make the n. BURKE 111:16
the n. the people   ANON 7:6
valued till they make a n.   COWP 168:22
was full of foolish n.   TENN 536:22
when every n. appals me   SHAK 460:12
noiseless: n. noise among the leaves
   KEATS 290:13
n. tenor of their way   GRAY 235:1
noises: isle is full of n.   SHAK 485:17

Such labour'd n.   POPE 378:18
Nothink: N. for nothink 'ere   PUNCH 402:20
notice: n. whether it's winter CHEK 145:3
  short n. was her speciality   SAKI 413:5
  was a man who used to n.   HARDY 239:1
nötig: Land, das Helden n. hat   BREC 92:1
not-incurious: n. in God's handiwork
                                     BROW 100:24
notion: Doesn't seem to suit her n.
                                     GILB 227:3
notions: General n. are generally wrong
                                     MONT 354:9
  n. in an individual way   HOR 257:17
notorious: n. evil liver   PRAY 387:5
not quite: n.—so pure as you   BUTL 119:18
Nottingham: N. lace of the curtains BETJ 42:4
nought: n. did I in hate   SHAK 477:22
  n. enters there   SHAK 487:20
  n. shall make us rue   SHAK 453:1
  to do n.   ROSS 410:7
noun: n. at once   SHER 506:1
  verb not a n.   FULL 220:10
Nouns: N. of number   COBB 154:8
nourish: n. all the world   SHAK 457:9
  N. thy children   BIBLE 62:6
  n. us with all goodness   PRAY 386:19
nourisher: n. in life's feast   SHAK 460:8
nourishing: n. a youth sublime TENN 538:16
nourrit: les couvre, les n., les incite
                                     MONT 355:1
nouvelle: d'une méthode toute n. MOL 353:17
nouvelles: du moins des choses n.
                                     VOLT 560:21
novel: advance we may hold a n.
                                     JAMES 271:10
  it is only a n.   AUST 22:31
  last fashionable n.   MAC 324:25
  n. tells a story   FORS 216:24
  n. to be too good to be   SHAW 498:10
  read a n. before luncheon   WAUGH 566:5
  scrofulous French n.   BROW 105:8
  to be given away by a n.   KEATS 294:20
novelty: Novelty, novelty, n.   HOOD 255:15
  This n. on Earth   MILT 349:23
November: no birds,— N.   HOOD 254:28
  N.'s sky is chill   SCOTT 416:27
  remember the Fifth of N.   ANON 7:10
novissima: cupido gloriae n. exuitur
                                     TAC 531:14
Novo: N. cedat ritui   THOM 546:17
novum: Reddiderit iunctura n.   HOR 257:13
now: If it be n.   SHAK 437:15
  If not n. when   HILL 251:6
  N. for dogs and apes   BROW 100:37
  N. I lay me down to sleep   ANON 7:3
  N. is the accepted time   BIBLE 77:7
now-a-days: thing n. men are asham'd
                                     GAY 223:25
nowhere: circumference is n.   ANON 7:27
  N. to fall but off   KING 296:10
  n. yet to rest my head   ARN 13:8
  rest n.   OKEL 365:3
  you are n.   NORT 364:7
Nox: N. est perpetua una dormienda
                                     CAT 136:25
noxious: Of all n. animals   KILV 296:5
nubbly: 'Nice but n.   KIPL 304:14
nuclear: edge of the n. abyss   STEV 520:23
nude: noble and n. and antique SWIN 529:4
nudula: Pallidula rigida n.   HADR 237:9
nugas: esse aliquid putare n.   CAT 136:20
nuisance: himself a n. to other people
                                     MILL 339:11
nuit: l'horreur d'une profonde n. RAC 404:2
Null: is N. an' Void   OCAS 364:18
nulli: n. negabimus aut differemus
                                     MAGN 327:3
Nullius: N. addictus iurare in verba
                                     HOR 258:7
nullum: n. fere scribendi genus   JOHN 277:13

number: Bring out n.   BLAKE 88:18
  count the n. of the beast   BIBLE 82:14
  greatest n. is the foundation   BENT 40:25
  if I Called the Wrong N.   THUR 550:30
  is a very interesting n.   RAM 404:22
  Not on the n.   COWL 164:14
  Nouns of n.   COBB 154:8
  n. of his name   BIBLE 82:13
  n. of my days   PRAY 391:30
  numbers n. all your graces   SHAK 492:27
  teach us to n. our days   PRAY 395:20
  the n. of your years   MONT 354:16
  which no man could n.   BIBLE 81:31
numbered: God hath n. thy kingdom
                                     BIBLE 61:6
  n. with the transgressors   BIBLE 59:24
  of your head are all n.   BIBLE 65:36
numberless: thick and n.   MILT 341:24
number one: loyalties which centre upon
  n.   CHUR 150:27
numbers: divinity in odd n.   SHAK 469:15
  happiness for the greatest n.   HUTC 268:20
  Here are only n. ratified   SHAK 457:3
  in Settle's n.   POPE 375:14
  n. came   POPE 376:23
  secret magic of n.   BROW 96:11
  To add to golden n.   DEKK 173:20
numbness: drowsy n. pains   KEATS 291:16
numeros: n. veniebat ad aptos   OVID 366:23
numerous: n. piece of monstrosity
                                     BROW 96:30
  writers become more n.   GOLD 232:1
numerus: n. sumus et fruges consumere
                                     HOR 258:13
Nun: Come, pensive N.   MILT 341:26
  extremely rowdy N.   COW 164:5
  holy time is quiet as a n.   WORD 581:18
  my daughter the N.   SOUT 514:10
nunc: et n., et semper   MASS 334:14
  N. dimittis servum tuum   BIBLE 83:19
  N. est bibendum   HOR 260:3
Nunc dimittis: sweetest canticle is N.
                                     BACON 26:4
nunnery: Get thee to a n.   SHAK 433:11
  n. Of thy chaste breast   LOV 318:20
Nuns: N. fret not at their convent's
                                     WORD 582:7
nuptials: to any iteration of n. CONG 161:9
nurs'd: never n. a dear gazelle MOORE 356:25
nurse: baby beats the n.   SHAK 463:11
  beggar's n. and Caesar's   SHAK 423:20
  Dear n. of arts   SHAK 445:11
  keep a hold of N.   BELL 39:3
  my most kindly n.   SPEN 517:1
  Nature's soft n.   SHAK 441:29
  N. came in with the tea-things   BETJ 42:9
  n. of manly sentiment   BURKE 111:10
  n. sleeps sweetly   COWP 166:29
  n. unacted desires   BLAKE 88:24
  priest continues what the n.   DRYD 196:19
  Rose a n. of ninety years   TENN 542:11
  set upon the n.'s knee   BALL 32:11
  sucks the n. asleep   SHAK 424:14
  thou good n.   BIBLE 62:6
  will scratch the n.   SHAK 490:31
Nursed: N. amid her noise   LAMB 307:24
  n. upon the self-same hill   MILT 343:4
nurseries: me in the n. of Heaven
                                     THOM 548:6
  n. of all vice and immorality   FIEL 211:16
nursery: n. of future revolutions BURKE 111:5
  n. still leaps out in all   BYRON 119:32
nurses: old men's n.   BACON 26:34
Nursing: N. her wrath to keep it BURNS 115:3
  n. the unconquerable hope   ARN 14:20
nursling: n. of the Sky   SHEL 500:7
nurture: fear and n. of the Lord PRAY 389:1
nuthin: Tar-baby ain't sayin' n. HARR 242:19
Nutmegs: N. and ginger   BEAU 36:5
nuts: Brazil—where the n.   THOM 546:18

like an ape doth n.   SHAK 435:24
nut-shell: could be bounded in a n.
                                     SHAK 432:13
Nye: Old Nicholas N.   DE L 174:13
nyght: muche to seye as it was n.
                                     CHAU 142:13
nyghtyngale: newe abaysed n.   CHAU 144:10
nymph: here's to the n. with but one
                                     SHER 506:32
  n., but for a reed   MARV 332:2
  N., in thy orisons   SHAK 433:9
Nympha: N. pudica Deum vidit   CRAS 169:2
Nymphs: N. and as yet unknown rivers
                                     VIRG 559:4
  N. that reign o'er sewers   COL 156:5
O: But O O O O.   AUDEN 20:20
U vert, O. bleu: voyelles   RIMB 406:9
  Within this wooden O.   SHAK 443:4
oafs: muddied o. at the goals   KIPL 300:4
Oak: ashes of an O. in the Chimney
                                     DONNE 190:23
  nodosities of the o. without   BURKE 112:14
  O., and Ash, and Thorn   KIPL 303:25
  o. and three-ply bronze   HOR 259:12
  standing long an o.   JONS 285:8
  thee the reed is as the o.   SHAK 428:22
  thunders from her native o.   CAMP 129:13
oak-cleaving: Vaunt-couriers to o.
  thunderbolts   SHAK 454:4
oaks: families last not three o. BROW 97:16
  Huge o. and old   KIPL 303:15
  like one of those old o.   BURKE 112:4
  o. from little acorns grow   EVER 209:10
  Tall o.   KEATS 290:5
O altitudo: pursue my reason to an O.
                                     BROW 96:9
oars: o. were silver   SHAK 422:2
oat-cakes: o., and sulphur   SMITH 510:30
oaten: o. stop, or pastoral song COLL 158:17
oath: Cophetua sware a royal o. TENN 532:16
  good mouth-filling o.   SHAK 439:33
  heaven's chancery with the o.   STER 520:5
  He who cheats with an o.   PLUT 374:20
  If ever I utter an o. again   SHAW 498:10
  I have an o. in heaven   SHAK 468:4
  inscriptions a man is not upon o. JOHN 276:31
  they hae sworn a solemn o.   BURNS 114:13
  whore's o.   SHAK 454:28
oaths: God pardon all o. that   SHAK 480:3
  men with o.   LYS 321:8
  O. are but words   BUTL 118:4
  o. are straws   SHAK 443:20
  soldier, Full of strange o.   SHAK 425:24
  vows As false as dicers' o.   SHAK 435:4
oatmeal: literature upon a little o.
                                     SMITH 511:36
Oaxen: rapidum cretae veniemus O.
                                     VIRG 559:13
Obadiah: O. Bind-their-kings   MAC 322:5
obdurate: Lord, if too o. I   STEV 523:11
obeam: tecum o. libens   HOR 261:1
obedience: be swift in all o.   KIPL 303:6
  keeps men in o.   BURT 117:1
  might expect more o.   GOLD 232:13
  o. of distant provinces   MAC 323:9
  o. of planetary influence   SHAK 453:11
  Rebellion to tyrants is o.   BRAD 91:12
obedient: o. heart   PRAY 384:9
  o. to their laws we lie   SIM 508:9
obeisance: made o. to my sheaf BIBLE 46:27
obey: 'E don't o. no orders unless KIPL 298:21
  if anyone is born to o.   COMP 159:14
  love, cherish, and to o.   PRAY 389:4
  not o. the laws too well   EMER 207:32
  o. is better than sacrifice   BIBLE 50:4
  shall in all my best o. you   SHAK 429:27
  with the laws but to o.   HORS 262:11
  woman to o.   TENN 542:9
obeye: everych oother moot o.   CHAU 142:12

obeyed: I o. as a son GIBB 224:13
obeying: except by o. her BACON 28:10
obeys: she o. him LONG 317:12
  when she o. POPE 377:27
object: advertisers don't o. SWAF 525:30
  grand o. of travelling is JOHN 277:6
  hope without an o. cannot COL 157:15
  My o. all sublime GILB 227:5
  o. in enquiring is to know HOUS 266:9
  'with his eye on the o. ARN 16:12
objected: o. to the use of dynamite STEV 521:12
objection: I see no o. to stoutness GILB 225:32
objectionable: many ways extremely
  o. KEYN 295:18
objective: art is by finding an 'o.
  correlative' ELIOT 205:16
objects: What o. are the fountains SHEL 504:21
oblation: o. of himself once offered) PRAY 387:24
oblations: accept our alms and o. PRAY 387:13
  Bring no more vain o. BIBLE 57:17
obligation: always the sequel of o. JOHN 282:3
  because o. is a pain JOHN 282:4
  Possession without o. MER 337:32
  To John I ow'd great o. PRIOR 400:24
oblig'd: that he ne'er o. POPE 376:27
oblivion: commend To cold o. SHEL 500:9
  formless ruin of o. SHAK 487:14
  if I drink o. of a day MER 337:8
  iniquity of o. blindly BROW 97:18
  long journey towards o. LAWR 311:8
  mere o. SHAK 425:24
  my o. is a very Antony SHAK 421:28
  O. is a kind of Annihilation BROW 95:14
  Wherein he puts alms for o. SHAK 487:3
oblivious: with some sweet o. antidote SHAK 463:3
obnoxious: o. to each carping tongue BRAD 91:13
obscene: is usually o. SPEN 515:5
obscure: he who sits o. SHEL 501:18
  I become o. HOR 257:12
  o. nook for me BROW 103:6
  o. sequestered state BROW 104:33
  palpable o. find out MILT 346:16
obscurely: Content thyself to be o. good ADD 1:23
obscuri: *Ibant o. sola sub nocte* VIRG 558:20
obscurity: decent o. of a learned GIBB 224:19
  snatches a man from o. REYN 405:15
Obscurus: *O. fio* HOR 257:12
obsequies: celebrates his o. SCOTT 416:19
  they solemnized their o. BROW 97:8
observance: adoration, duty, and o. SHAK 426:29
observation: bearings of this o. lays DICK 177:31
  common sense and o. BROW 96:18
  Let o. with extensive view JOHN 282:28
  l'o. le hasard ne favorise PAST 369:16
  places cramm'd With o. SHAK 425:21
observations: To o. which ourselves
  we POPE 377:8
observ'd: o. the golden rule BLAKE 87:4
observe: you do not o. DOYLE 192:6
observed: o. of all observers SHAK 433:15
  Since o. by Yours faithfully ANON 4:29
observer: 'An o. of human nature DICK 181:24
  He is a great o. SHAK 448:21
  Is a keen o. of life AUDEN 20:13
observeth: o. the wind shall not sow BIBLE 56:7
obsta: *Principiis o.* OVID 366:20

obstetrical: branches of o. knowledge STER 519:26
Obstinacy: O. in a bad cause BROW 96:15
  of o. in a bad one STER 519:19
obstinate: He fished by o. isles POUND 383:3
obstruction: kind of 'consecrated o. BAG 29:1
obtain: faithfully we may o. effectually PRAY 387:1
Obtruding: O. false rules pranked MILT 341:19
obvious: beyond the o. facts that DOYLE 192:14
occasion: away the o. of all wars FOX 217:23
  Courage mounteth with o. SHAK 452:11
  Fate, Time, O. SHEL 503:10
  on O.'s forelock watchful MILT 350:5
occasions: o. do inform against me SHAK 435:29
  seas upon their lawful o. PRAY 400:3
Occident: worlds in th'yet unformed
  O. DAN 170:23
Occidental Star: setting of that bright BIBLE 44:20
occidit: *ille bonis flebilis o.* HOR 260:1
  o. Spes omnis HOR 261:13
occupation: found o. for an idle hour AUST 23:7
  my estate by the same o. BUNY 107:18
  Othello's o.'s gone SHAK 475:25
  pleasant o. GILB 226:2
  'tis my o. to be plain SHAK 453:23
occupations: let us love our o. DICK 176:23
occupy: o. their business in great PRAY 397:9
ocean: be back on the vast o. HOR 259:17
  Doth cause the O. to attend BEST 42:2
  grateful smell old O. smiles MILT 347:17
  have seen the hungry o. SHAK 494:3
  I have loved thee, O. BYRON 121:27
  In th' o.'s bosom unespied MARV 331:15
  labour in the deep mid-o. TENN 539:17
  mind is tossing on the o. SHAK 465:7
  Neptune's o. wash this blood SHAK 460:13
  o. and the sky together SHEL 501:16
  o. in the eventide of fear MORR 358:7
  o. Is folded and hung AUDEN 18:9
  o. leans against the land GOLD 231:27
  o. of life we pass LONG 317:17
  O.'s child SHEL 501:24
  O.'s nursling, Venice SHEL 501:23
  On one side lay the O. TENN 535:21
  Ransack the o. for orient MARL 329:4
  rivers with the o. SHEL 502:1
  round o. and the living air WORD 578:7
  sapless foliage of the o. SHEL 502:11
  thou deep and dark blue O. BYRON 121:23
  unfathom'd caves of o. GRAY 234:23
  Upon a painted o. COL 155:13
  use the o. as their road WALL 562:8
  Yet for his fame the o. BARN 34:5
oceans: compendious o. CRAS 169:12
  o. crossed HOUS 265:4
ocius: *urna serius o.* HOR 260:7
o'clock: shall be what o. I say it is SHAK 484:13
O'Connell: such a man as O. SMITH 511:24
Octavia: sober eye Of dull O. SHAK 423:21
octavos: light o. fill a spacious COWP 168:11
Octob: twenty third day of O. USSH 554:29
odd: choose the o. AUDEN 21:6
  divinity in o. numbers SHAK 469:15
  How o. Of God EWER 209:13
  It's an o. job MOL 353:7
  It's a very o. thing DE L 174:11
  Nothing o. will do long JOHN 276:34
  not so o. BROW 95:13
  think it exceedingly o. KNOX 305:22
  this was o. CARR 135:3
oddfellow: their desperate o. society THOR 550:19
odds: Almost at o. with morning SHAK 461:24

  o. is gone SHAK 423:16
  Than facing fearful o. MAC 322:15
  what's the o. DU M 199:4
Ode: I intended an O. DOBS 187:14
  O., and elegy JOHN 280:9
Oderint: *O., dum metuant* ACC 1:3
odes: elegies And quoted o. TENN 541:30
  O. to every zephyr KING 296:22
Odi: *O. et amo* CAT 137:14
  O. profanum vulgus et arceo HOR 260:13
odio: *dilectione hominum et o. vitiorum* AUG 22:1
Odious: 'O. POPE 377:15
odisse: *ingenii est o. quem laeseris* TAC 531:8
odoribus: *Perfusus liquidis urget o.* HOR 259:15
odoriferous: o. flowers of fancy SHAK 457:3
odorous: Comparisons are o. SHAK 472:33
odour: o. of joss-sticks and honourable BRAM 91:20
  Stealing and giving o. SHAK 487:20
odours: gentle o. led my steps astray SHEL 503:17
  golden vials full of o. BIBLE 81:27
  heavens rain o. on you SHAK 489:21
  midden whose o. will madden AUDEN 18:17
  O., when sweet violets SHEL 504:12
  Sabean o. from the spicy MILT 347:17
  star-led wizards haste with o. MILT 344:4
  With living hues and o. SHEL 502:8
Odyssey: surge and thunder of the O. LANG 309:18
o'ercargoed: With leaden age o. FLEC 214:16
o'ercome: love o. sae sair BURNS 114:18
o'ertake: I'll o. thee ROWL 411:1
o'ertopping: Is the house o. all BROW 100:7
oeuf: *Voyez-vous cet o.* DID 184:7
Off: 'O. with his head CARR 134:5
  O. with his head SHAK 481:5
  time you were o. HOR 259:6
offal: With this slave's o. SHAK 433:4
offence: conscience void of o. BIBLE 74:22
  forgave th' o. DRYD 195:35
  greatest o. against virtue is HAZL 243:23
  innocent from the great o. PRAY 390:11
  my o. is rank SHAK 434:27
  o. is let the great axe SHAK 436:15
  stumbling and for a rock of o. BIBLE 58:4
  What dire o. from am'rous POPE 380:28
offences: must needs be that o. come BIBLE 67:4
  o. of affections new SHAK 495:3
  sins and o. of my youth PRAY 391:2
  with more o. at my beck SHAK 433:11
offend: coy and tender to o. HERB 248:14
  I'll not willingly o. WATTS 565:27
  we come not to o. SHAK 471:16
  whoso shall o. one of these BIBLE 67:3
offended: him have I o. SHAK 450:14
  If we shadows have o. SHAK 471:23
  This hath not o. the king MORE 357:18
offender: love the o. POPE 376:12
  She hugg'd th' o. DRYD 195:35
offenders: Of society o. who might GILB 226:24
offendeth: can tell how oft he o. PRAY 390:13
offending: am the most o. soul alive SHAK 445:2
  head and front of my o. SHAK 473:24
offense: nat that men yow doon o. CHAU 142:10
offensive: You are extremely o. BIRK 84:1
offer: has seldom an o. of kindness STER 519:1
  nothing to o. but blood CHUR 149:22
  that dare not o. SHAK 485:12
offering: o. too little and asking CANN 129:25
  you the last o. in death CAT 137:15
offerings: nor fields of o. BIBLE 50:16
offers: Life o.—to deny HARDY 241:8

you are liberal in o.   SHAK 468:12
office: find a set of maxims in o.
  BURKE 108:16
insolence of o.   SHAK 433:8
man who has no o. to go   SHAW 497:3
office boys for o. boys   SAL 413:21
o. boy to an Attorney's   GILB 228:4
o. is a matter of right   JEFF 272:15
officer: art thou o.   SHAK 444:16
dashing Swiss o.'   RUSS 412:22
doth fear each bush an o.   SHAK 446:23
o. and a gentleman shall...be   ANON 4:20
officers: They have a king and o.   SHAK 443:9
offices: functions and their o.   SHAK 457:8
officials: that o. are the servants   GOW 233:7
Officious: O., innocent   JOHN 278:35
Officiously: O. to keep alive   CLOU 153:26
offspring: true source Of human o.
  MILT 348:8
oft: o. as ye shall drink it   PRAY 388:1
tell how o. he offendeth   PRAY 390:13
What o. was thought   POPE 378:17
Og: O. the king of Basan   PRAY 399:1
ogled: sighed and pined and o.   THAC 546:3
oil: anointed my head with o.   PRAY 390:22
consum'd the midnight o.   GAY 223:10
head thou dost with o.   SCOT 419:5
little o. in a cruse   BIBLE 51:7
mouth is smoother than o.   BIBLE 53:20
o. of gladness above thy   PRAY 392:15
o. of joy for mourning   BIBLE 60:9
o. out of the tabernacle   BIBLE 50:30
o. to make him a cheerful   PRAY 396:20
O., vinegar   GOLD 231:16
our midnight o.   QUAR 403:10
thine 'incomparable o.'   BYRON 122:6
with boiling o. in it   GILB 227:11
With everlasting o.   MILT 341:1
without the o. and twopence   SMITH 511:7
words were smoother than o.   PRAY 393:12
oily: glib and o. art   SHAK 453:5
ointment: box of very precious o.   BIBLE 68:8
flies cause the o. of the apothecary
  BIBLE 56:1
o. sold for three hundred   BIBLE 72:25
old: Asia and she is too o.   KIPL 304:27
been young, and now am o.   PRAY 391:28
body with so o. a head   SHAK 467:26
comfortless, and worn, and o.   ROSS 409:2
considered the days of o.   PRAY 395:2
crucify the o. man   PRAY 388:10
dressing o. words   SHAK 494:9
first sign of o. age   HICKS 250:23
foolish, fond o. man   SHAK 456:1
growing o. in drawing nothing   COWP 167:4
Grown o. before my time   ROSS 409:7
Grow o. along with me   BROW 104:2
grow o. with a good grace   STEE 518:2
grow virtuous in their o.   POPE 381:21
hard sentences of o.   PRAY 395:3
he died o.   HOUS 264:16
I am too o.   BACON 28:3
I am too o. to fawn upon   SHAK 478:11
I grow o. ever learning   SOLON 512:24
I grow o. grow old...   ELIOT 203:25
I'm not so o.   GILB 226:3
in judgment o.   SHAK 466:17
it is o. and plain   SHAK 489:3
lads that will never be o.   HOUS 263:6
last to lay the o. aside   POPE 378:19
Leaving the o.   WALL 562:9
love every thing that's o.   GOLD 232:19
making of an o. woman happy   FRAN 218:5
man is as o. as he's feeling   COLL 158:15
my folks were growing o.   STEV 522:26
no man would be o.   SWIFT 527:12
not persuade me I am o.   SHAK 493:1
o. Adam in this Child   PRAY 388:9
O. age brings along with   EMER 207:45
O. age hath yet his honour   TENN 544:3

O. age is the most unexpected   TROT 553:16
o. age, serene and bright   WORD 583:4
O. age should burn   THOM 546:23
o. and ill and terrified   BETJ 44:13
O. as I am   DRYD 195:32
o. as we to keep the peace   SHAK 481:25
O. December's bareness   SHAK 494:16
o. faiths loosen and fall   SWIN 530:6
O. friends are best   SELD 419:19
o. is having lighted rooms   LARK 310:5
o. know what they want   SMITH 510:22
o. lamps for new   ARAB 11:14
o. lovers are soundest   WEBS 566:30
o., mad, blind   SHEL 504:6
o. man and no honester   SHAK 472:32
o. man decayed in his intellects   JOHN 279:6
o. man in a dry month   ELIOT 203:3
o. man's wit may wander   TENN 534:2
o. men and children   PRAY 399:23
O. men and comets have   SWIFT 527:14
o. men from the chimney   SIDN 508:2
o. men have grey beards   SHAK 432:8
O. men in country houses   BETJ 42:12
o. men of less truth than   SHAK 492:27
o. men shall dream dreams   BIBLE 61:15
o. men's nurses   BACON 26:34
o. order changeth   TENN 535:25
o. plays began to disgust   EVEL 209:9
o., wild, and incomprehensible   VICT 556:15
o. women (of both sexes)   STER 520:4
read an o. one   ROG 407:12
rebuild it on the o. plan   MILL 339:3
Ring out the o.   TENN 537:14
she is not yet so o.   SHAK 467:13
should accompany o. age   SHAK 463:2
so o., and so profane   SHAK 442:30
sugared about by the o.   KIPL 303:11
teach an o. horse   SPEN 516:16
tell an o. soldier   SHAW 496:6
That is no country for o.   YEATS 586:11
That the heart grows o.   YEATS 586:20
Then O. Age, and Experience   ROCH 406:22
they get to feeling o.   BROO 94:24
They shall grow not o.   BINY 84:10
Though I look o.   SHAK 425:5
times begin to wax o.   BIBLE 62:7
tiresomeness of o. age   ANON 10:13
'Tis well an o. age is out   DRYD 197:19
to make an o. man young   TENN 533:20
Very o. are we men   DE L 173:25
wax o. as doth a garment   PRAY 396:13
Were ruinous and o.   SPEN 516:3
when thou shalt be o.   BIBLE 73:17
When you are o. and gray   YEATS 587:12
When you are very o.   RONS 407:18
where even the o. are fair   YEATS 585:18
Whether it be new or o.   ANON 5:21
will change in growing o.   BRID 92:20
yet o. enough for a man   SHAK 488:9
you are o.   SHAK 453:25
You are o., Father William   CARR 133:22
You are o., Father William   SOUT 514:7
you never can be o.   SHAK 494:18
old age: dance attention upon my o.
  YEATS 586:23
dreary o. and pain sneak up   VIRG 560:16
O., a second child   CHUR 148:32
sad o. you are preparing   TALL 531:18
Oldcastle: O. died a martyr   SHAK 443:2
older: He was o.   LUC 320:2
I grow o. and older   SAY 415:7
O. men declare war   HOOV 255:25
o. than the rocks among   PATER 369:19
richer still the o.   BUTL 118:17
They hurt me. I grow o.   POUND 383:17
oldest: Commit The o. sins   SHAK 442:20
o. hath borne most   SHAK 456:13
When the o. cask is opened   MAC 322:23
old maid: o. courted by Incapacity
  BLAKE 88:14

Old Retainer: O. night and day   BELL 39:4
Old Testament: blessing of the O.
  BACON 25:18
ole: knows of a better 'o.   BAIR 29:23
W'en folks git o. en strucken   HARR 242:13
O'Leary: It's with O. in the grave
  YEATS 586:19
Ole Hundred: when he made O. ring
  LOW 319:6
olet: Pecunia non o.   VESP 556:11
oligarchy: democracy or absolute o.
  ARIS 12:8
olive: o., aloe   TENN 533:5
o.-silvery Sirmio   TENN 533:18
olive-branches: o.: round about thy table
  PRAY 398:20
Olivet: purple brows of O.   TENN 536:18
Olivia: Cry out, 'O.!'   SHAK 488:13
when mine eyes did see O.   SHAK 487:21
ologies: getting instructed in the 'o.'
  CARL 131:38
olores: inter strepere anser o.   VIRG 560:7
Olympian: O. bolts   DISR 184:19
Olympus: horse-race won at O. among
  SIDN 508:4
leafy O. on top of Ossa   VIRG 560:12
Omar: diver O. plucked them from
  LOW 319:10
ombrifuge: o. (Lord love you   CALV 127:16
Omega: 'I am Alpha and O.   AUDEN 21:7
I am Alpha and O.   BIBLE 81:10
omen: Procul o. abesto   OVID 366:8
Quod di o. avertant   CIC 151:29
This is the one best o.   HOMER 254:2
Omer: O., Lucan   CHAU 144:17
'O. smote 'is bloomin' lyre   KIPL 304:4
omitted: have o. the weightier matters
  BIBLE 67:24
O., all the voyage   SHAK 451:27
Omnes: *O. eodem cogimur*   HOR 260:7
omnia: *Amor vincit o.*   CHAU 141:17
non o. possumus omnes   LUC 320:2
Non o. possumus omnes   VIRG 560:6
O. vincit Amor   VIRG 560:8
omnibuses: only ridden more in o.
  HELPS 244:18
Omnipotent: defy th' O. to arms   MILT 344:24
O. but friendless is   SHEL 503:7
omnis: Disce o.   VIRG 558:2
Non o. moriar   HOR 261:9
omniscience: his specialism is o.
  DOYLE 192:21
o. his foible   SMITH 512:11
Omnium: Duke of O.   TROL 552:15
Onan: straight into the sin of O.   VOLT 561:12
Onaway: O.! Awake   LONG 317:13
once: if it were done but o.   DONNE 190:24
I was adored o. too   SHAK 488:24
oblation of himself o.   PRAY 387:24
o. familiar word   BAYLY 35:10
o. in a great while   PEPYS 372:20
O. is more than enough   BIRCH 84:11
O. to every man and nation   LOW 319:12
o. was prodigal before   DRYD 196:2
trying every experience o.   ANON 4:24
was o. handsome and tall   ELIOT 205:7
one: apparel them all in o. livery   SHAK 446:11
doeth good, no not o.   PRAY 390:2
do only o. thing   SMIL 509:6
encompass'd but o. man   SHAK 448:19
had one body and o. heart   DOUG 191:10
heard o. side of the case   BUTL 119:1
he putteth down o.   PRAY 394:26
he sighed for o.   AUDEN 21:9
I am o. with my kind   TENN 540:19
in a procession of o.   DICK 179:20
incorporate and make us o.   SHAK 449:14
is to be o. man picked   SHAK 432:5
Lord our God is o. Lord   BIBLE 48:20
means to make us o.   DONNE 188:22

members o. of another   BIBLE 77:29
mouths are o. with Mouth   BROO 95:1
o. by one back in the Closet   FITZ 213:5
o. damned thing   OMAL 365:5
o. day in thy courts   PRAY 395:13
O. man shall have one vote   CART 136:13
O. man that has a mind   SHAW 496:3
O. more such victory   PYRR 403:7
O. near one is too far   BROW 99:23
o. penny the worse   BARH 33:14
o. small step for a man   ARMS 12:18
o. that was never thought   BIBLE 62:31
O. the long night through   HOUS 262:21
O. to destroy   YOUNG 587:19
o. way in to life   SEN 420:9
stranger to o. of your parents   AUST 23:15
they shall be o. flesh   BIBLE 45:13
To love o. maiden only   TENN 534:12
who but trifles with o.   GAY 223:4
one-and-twenty: Long-expected o.
                                     JOHN 279:28
When I was o.   HOUS 262:20
One-eyed: Country of the Blind the O.
                                     WELLS 568:12
There's a o. yellow idol   HAYES 243:7
onehandled: statue of the o. adulterer
                                     JOYCE 286:25
one-hoss: of the wonderful o. shay
                                     HOLM 253:8
one-third: o. of a nation ill-housed
                                     ROOS 407:22
onion: Let o. atoms lurk within SMITH 511:14
tears live in an o.   SHAK 421:22
onlie: o. begetter of these insuing
                                     SHAK 492:21
only: If o. I could get down   PINT 373:19
keep thee o. unto her   PRAY 389:3
o. begotten of the Father   BIBLE 71:27
O. connect the prose   FORS 217:2
o. to stand high in your   SHAK 467:13
say o. the word   MASS 335:8
only-begotten: o. Son of God   PRAY 387:10
onori: offrirgli nè o. nè stipendi GAR 221:10
onset: Vain thy o.   ARN 13:14
ooth: o. was but by Seinte Loy   CHAU 141:14
ooze: Feed in the o. of their   ARN 13:6
through the o. and slime   SMITH 510:10
oozing: I feel it o. out as it   SHER 506:22
oozy: sea-blooms and the o. woods
                                     SHEL 502:11
opal: thy mind is a very o.   SHAK 489:5
ope: o. my lips let no dog   SHAK 465:12
open: equally o. to the poor   ANON 4:13
light-hearted I take to the o. road WHIT 571:7
o. and notorious evil   PRAY 387:5
O. covenants of peace openly   WILS 575:1
o. his grief   PRAY 387:17
O. not thine heart to every   BIBLE 62:28
O. rebuke is better than   BIBLE 54:37
O. Sesame   ARAB 11:15
o. society and its enemies   POPP 381:24
o. that Pandora's Box you   BEVIN 44:19
o. the Kingdom of Heaven   PRAY 384:17
O. the temple gates   SPEN 515:25
O. the windows   AUST 22:15
O. to me   BIBLE 57:1
o. unto the fields   WORD 581:14
O., ye everlasting gates   MILT 349:2
Secret thoughts and o.   ALB 3:8
Thou shalt o. my lips   PRAY 393:8
You see her eyes are o.   SHAK 462:19
open door: o. for all nations' trade BER 41:16
opened: favourite volume always o.
                                     AUST 23:7
If he were o.   SHAK 490:1
o. the seventh seal   BIBLE 82:5
Towards the door we never o.   ELIOT 202:13
openeth: o. the gate to good fame
                                     BACON 26:4
opening: o. of the prison to them BIBLE 60:8

o. the doors very often   AUST 22:14
openly: engage himself o. and publicly
                                     BLAKE 86:10
himself shall reward you o.   BIBLE 64:22
opera: omnia o. Domini   BIBLE 83:16
operosiores: Divitias o.   HOR 260:16
opes: emergere o. rerumque potiri
                                     LUCR 320:6
Fumum et o. strepitumque   HOR 261:7
golden o.   MILT 343:11
Ophelia: I lov'd O.   SHAK 437:8
opinion: An' justifies th' ill o. BURNS 115:21
Back'd his o. with quotations   PRIOR 401:2
coquetry of public o.   BURKE 110:15
difference of an o.   BROW 96:4
fool gudgeon, this o.   SHAK 465:13
general a man of common o.   BAG 29:15
gross and scope of my o.   SHAK 429:10
In vain o.'s waste   COWP 165:12
Is of his own o. still   BUTL 118:13
literary and scientific o.   ARN 16:5
Nobody holds a good o.   TROL 553:3
north of my lady's o.   SHAK 489:28
o. he held once Of fantasy   SHAK 449:10
o. in good men is but knowledge   MILT 352:2
o. is about a woman   JAMES 271:28
O. is ultimately determined   SPEN 515:2
o. one man entertains   PALM 368:12
o. we are endeavouring   MILL 339:9
o. with the learned   CONG 160:1
our own o. from another   EMER 207:35
plague of o.   SHAK 487:7
poor itch of your o.   SHAK 427:12
reflecting no o. but their own   WILS 574:23
sacrifices it to your o.   BURKE 109:11
scorching world's o.   FLET 215:19
that approve a private o.   HOBB 251:16
thinkest thou of his o.   SHAK 490:21
think the last o. right   POPE 378:26
to admire except his o.   FRY 219:24
were of one o.   MILL 339:8
opinions: don't consult anyone's o.
                                     PERS 372:26
Golden o. from all sorts   SHAK 459:7
good or so bad as their o.   MACK 325:11
halt ye between two o.   BIBLE 51:8
killed with your hard o.   SHAK 443:2
moderate o. they abhor   MAC 323:13
o. are always suspected   LOCKE 315:13
public buys its o.   BUTL 119:4
There are as many o.   TER 544:19
opium: mighty o.   DE Q 175:2
o.-dose for keeping beasts   KING 297:7
Religion…is the o.   MARX 333:6
opponent: o. motives meaner   BARR 34:9
o. of the chosen people   ARN 16:3
opportunitate: sed etiam o. mortis TAC 531:9
opportunities: Devil watches all o.
                                     CONG 160:19
man will make more o.   BACON 25:38
opportunity: cometh by o. of leisure
                                     BIBLE 63:19
had mortal man such o.   BYRON 123:26
man must make his o.   BACON 25:2
O. makes a thief   BACON 28:2
Thou strong seducer, o.   DRYD 195:31
with the maximum of o.   SHAW 497:39
oppose: to o. everything   DERBY 175:8
opposed: o. paths to persevere   PATM 370:6
pretensions need to be bravely o. KEYN 296:1
opposing: by o. end them   SHAK 433:8
Opposition: 'Her Majesty's O.'   BAG 28:23
o. of the stars   MARV 331:19
phrase 'His Majesty's O.'   HOBB 252:1
that the duty of an O.   DERBY 175:8
without a formidable O.   DISR 185:35
oppressed: Foal of an o. race   COL 157:16
He was o.   BIBLE 59:22
to let the o. go free   BIBLE 60:4

oppresseth: while the enemy o. me
                                     PRAY 392:9
oppressing: to the o. city   BIBLE 61:27
oppression: behold o.   BIBLE 57:23
O. makes the wise man mad   BROW 102:10
To make o. bitter   SHAK 433:4
oppressions: else unfelt o. of this
                                     SHEL 501:12
oppressor: common enemy and o.
                                     BURKE 110:33
o.'s wrong   SHAK 433:8
oppugnancy: In mere o.   SHAK 486:24
optabile: o. omnibus sanis et bonis CIC 151:33
optavere: multae o. puellae   CAT 137:6
optics: o. of these eyes to behold BROW 96:21
Optima: O. quaeque dies miseris VIRG 560:16
optimist: not an o. but a meliorist
                                     ELIOT 201:31
o. proclaims that we live   CAB 126:25
opulence: those decisive marks of o.
                                     SMITH 509:11
opulent: To glass the o.   HARDY 239:4
opus: Hoc o.   VIRG 558:18
Iamque o. exegi   OVID 366:19
Orabant: O. causas melius   VIRG 559:1
Oracle: 'I am Sir O.   SHAK 465:12
Oracles: are the lively O. of God COR 162:25
o. are dumb   MILT 344:13
oracular: use of my o. tongue   SHER 506:14
orange: in shades the o. bright MARV 331:16
o. flower perfumes   SCOTT 418:25
orange-blossom: lands of palm, of o.
                                     TENN 533:5
orange-pulp: Drinking watered o.
                                     BROW 105:6
oranges: Coffee and o. in a sunny
                                     STEV 520:18
orange-tree: that I were an o.   HERB 247:20
orantes: Stabant o. primi transmittere
                                     VIRG 558:22
oration: not studied as an o.   OSB 365:19
orator: enjoyment as the greatest o.
                                     HUME 267:22
eyes of men without an o.   SHAK 492:17
I am no o.   SHAK 451:1
orators: swords shall play the o. MARL 330:4
oratory: Chadband style of o. is DICK 176:13
object of o.   MAC 324:20
orb: splendid o. was entirely set BURKE 109:6
orbis: Securus iudicat o.   AUG 21:18
Si fractus illabatur o.   HOR 260:19
orbs: operation of the o.   SHAK 453:3
their glimmering o. did glow   MILT 344:7
orchard: chaffinch sings on the o.
                                     BROW 101:5
Cherry O. is now mine…I've   CHEK 144:24
orchards: new-planted o.   SHAK 451:4
Orci: primisque in faucibus O.   VIRG 558:21
ordained: powers that be are o. BIBLE 75:20
'Tis so o.   PRIOR 401:7
ordainer: o. of order and mystical
                                     BROW 95:20
order: act of o. to a peopled   SHAK 443:9
after the o. of Melchisedech   PRAY 397:12
All things began in o.   BROW 95:20
along with o. and virtue   BURKE 109:10
done decently and in o.   BIBLE 76:18
each in solemn o. followed   WORD 581:1
Good o. is the foundation   BURKE 111:25
he disturbs the o. here   HARDY 240:3
in all line of o.   SHAK 486:22
is simply o. and beauty   BAUD 35:7
liberty connected with o.   BURKE 109:10
old o. changeth   TENN 535:25
ordainer of o. and mystical   BROW 95:20
o. and military discipline   ANON 4:28
o. or proportion   BROW 96:34
O. reigns in Warsaw   ANON 9:14
o., said I, this matter   STER 518:28
party of o. or stability   MILL 339:10

put his household in o. BIBLE 50:25
Set thine house in o. BIBLE 59:2
so I o. it done JUV 287:21
to possess internal o. FORS 217:14
upon the o. of your going SHAK 461:23
order'd: o. their estate ALEX 3:14
ordered: o. my goings PRAY 392:1
orders: Almighty's o. to perform ADD 1:14
ordinance: according to God's holy o.
PRAY 389:4
ordinary: Heaven in o. HERB 248:5
o. one seem original HOR 257:13
such a very o. little woman BETJ 43:4
ordo: integro saeclorum nascitur o.
VIRG 559:22
ordre: ce serait changer l'o. FRAN 217:25
L'o. règne à Varsovie ANON 9:14
tout n'est qu'o. et beauté BAUD 35:7
ore: of your subject with o. KEATS 294:31
with new spangled o. MILT 343:17
oreilles: o. ennemies vous écoutent
ANON 9:18
organ: great o. of public opinion DISR 184:19
Is as the maiden's o. SHAK 488:3
is mellering to the o. DICK 181:8
let the pealing o. blow MILT 342:10
of heav'n's deep o. blow MILT 344:10
o. and the maypole JORD 285:18
o. to enlarge her prayer AUDEN 18:3
Seated one day at the o. PROC 401:13
organise: o. the theatre ARN 16:15
organism: o. to live beyond its income
BUTL 118:27
organized: o. hypocrisy BAG 29:8
organs: his owls was o. DICK 179:27
in her the o. of increase SHAK 453:18
moves with its own o. SHAK 422:14
organ-voice: God-gifted o. of England
TENN 533:12
Oriel: O. Common Room stank NEWM 361:22
Oriens: equis O. adflavit anhelis VIRG 560:1
Oriental: although an O. CHES 147:27
more-than-o.-splendour KIPL 304:19
you are an O. FORS 217:6
origin: indelible stamp of his lowly o.
DARW 171:24
original: Behold the bright o. appear
GAY 223:19
I have nothing o. in me CAMP 129:14
is very far gone from o. PRAY 400:7
L'écrivain o. n'est pas CHAT 141:5
ordinary one seem o. HOR 257:13
o. es infiel a la traducción BORG 89:24
o. is unfaithful BORG 89:24
o. writer is not he who CHAT 141:5
th'o. perus'd mankind ARMS 12:15
originality: exist are the fruits of o.
MILL 339:12
without o. or moral courage SHAW 496:12
originator: Next to the o. of a good
EMER 208:2
origins: Consider your o. DANTE 171:13
Orion: loose the bands of O. BIBLE 53:5
O. and the Dog Are veiled ELIOT 204:15
O. plunges prone HOUS 265:17
orisons: patter out their hasty o. OWEN 367:2
orisonte: th'o. hath reft the sonne
CHAU 142:13
Orlando: Run, run, O. SHAK 426:2
ornament: esteem'st the o. of life SHAK 459:8
grossness with fair o. SHAK 467:10
Nobility is a graceful o. BURKE 111:21
not the foreign aid of o. THOM 549:17
O. is but the guiled shore SHAK 467:11
O. of a meek and quiet BIBLE 80:28
o. of his cheek hath already SHAK 472:26
o. put upon great civic RUSK 411:21
o. to her profession BUNY 107:35
o. which truth doth give SHAK 493:16
respecting all o. RUSK 411:20

still deceived with o. SHAK 467:10
ornaments: Can a maid forget her o.
BIBLE 60:15
hide with o. their want POPE 378:16
made in lieu of many o. SPEN 515:27
ornate: embellisher of o. eloquence
CAXT 138:2
O., and Grotesque Art BAG 29:20
ornavit: Nullum quod tetigit non o.
JOHN 277:13
Orontes: in Tiberim defluxit O. JUV 287:15
Orotunda: "Or Opulent O. Strike
STEV 521:13
orphan-boy: teach the o. to read TENN 538:1
orphans: with wrong'd o.' tears MASS 335:21
Orpheus: Another O. sings again
SHEL 500:21
bid the soul of O. sing MILT 342:6
O. with his lute made trees SHAK 447:3
Orthodoxy: O. is my doxy WARB 564:17
O. or My-doxy and Heterodoxy CARL 131:25
ortolans: Let me die eating o. DISR 187:1
Oscar: You will, O. WHIS 569:25
oss: have them cleanin' his 'o. SURT 525:12
'o., my wife, and my name SURT 525:17
Paid for catching my 'o. SURT 525:13
Ossa: pile O. on Pelion VIRG 560:12
ossmanship: morality than on his 'o.
SURT 525:9
ostentation: blown me full of maggot
o. SHAK 457:15
use rather than for o. GIBB 224:25
ostrich: resembled the wings of an o.
MAC 323:5
tall o. on the ground SMART 509:3
Othello: O.'s occupation's gone SHAK 475:25
other: caitiff smite the o. HOLM 253:11
desire o. men's goods PRAY 388:18
forsaking all o. PRAY 389:3
o. side of the hill' WELL 567:20
strange faces, o. minds TENN 535:24
that I am not as o. men are BIBLE 70:34
their troth either to o. PRAY 389:7
This o. Eden SHAK 478:20
turn to him the o. also BIBLE 64:17
Were t'o. dear charmer away GAY 222:35
others: liberty is the love of o. HAZL 243:19
misfortunes and pains of o. BURKE 108:8
O., I am not the first HOUS 263:13
playtime of the o. BROW 97:36
thou be not false to o. BACON 27:35
we pass judgement on o. MOL 353:20
otherwise: gods thought o. VIRG 558:8
otia: deus nobis haec o. fecit VIRG 559:12
otiosum: Numquam se minus o. esse
CIC 151:23
otiosus: Numquam sis ex toto o. THOM 546:11
otium: cum dignitate o. CIC 151:33
o. et n'ont rien appris TALL 531:17
o. et n'ont rien appris DUM 199:7
ought: hadn't o. to be HARTE 242:28
must believe what you o. NEWM 362:17
not what they o. to do BACON 24:25
O. to be told to come FROST 219:11
tell me I o. to do BURKE 109:26
what things they o. to do PRAY 386:7
which we o. to have done PRAY 384:12
Oun: Properly based O. BROW 101:1
ounce: o. of love is worth a pound
WESL 568:23
ound: that I loves the 'o. more SURT 525:10
Our: O. Father which art BIBLE 64:24
ours: see in Nature that is o. WORD 582:19
They were not o. OWEN 367:7
ourselves: five days elder than o. BROW 96:10
in o., are triumph LONG 316:27
knowledge is, o. to know POPE 380:4
long and carefully at o. MOL 353:20
not we o. PRAY 396:11
of o. to help ourselves PRAY 386:9

Our remedies oft in o. SHAK 420:28
power is the love of o. HAZL 243:19
unsafe to be trusted with o. CONG 159:17
ousel: o. and the throstlecock DRAY 193:19
ousel-cock: o., so black of hue SHAK 470:18
ouses: wasn't for the 'o. in between BAT 35:3
out: down and o. of breath SHAK 440:27
I believe they went o. DISR 186:9
'I can't get o. STER 519:7
I o. of myself AUG 21:16
Lord Coodle would go o. DICK 176:21
many ways o. SEN 420:9
mother know that you are o. BARH 33:24
other o. CHUR 148:20
o., brief candle SHAK 463:6
o. of sight is out of mind CLOU 154:5
O. of the deep have I called PRAY 398:23
O. of this wood do not SHAK 470:19
O. on the lawn I lie AUDEN 20:18
shall preserve thy going o. PRAY 398:10
such as are o. wish to get EMER 208:6
that o. of battle I escaped OWEN 367:9
you will soon be o. of it EMER 207:45
out-argue: out-vote them we will o.
JOHN 277:23
outcast: all alone beweep my o. SHAK 493:6
o. of the people PRAY 390:17
Spiritless o. CANN 129:27
out-casts: together the o. of Israel
PRAY 399:19
outcries: o. pluck me from my naked
KYD 306:2
outcry: Each o. of the hunted hare
BLAKE 85:10
outgrabe: mome raths o. CARR 134:28
outlawed: nor be o., nor excommunicate
COKE 154:24
outlive: shall o. this powerful rime
SHAK 493:17
outlives: He that o. this day SHAK 445:3
laurel o. not May SWIN 530:5
outlook: Could man o. that mark
VAUG 555:20
out-paramoured: woman o. the Turk
SHAK 454:18
outrage: Seal up the mouth of o. SHAK 484:1
outrageously: over-offended ladies the
o. virtuous STEE 518:3
outshine: o. Myriads though bright
MILT 344:26
outside: support it from the o. MELB 336:22
Out-topping: O. knowledge ARN 14:23
out-vote: o. them we will out-argue
JOHN 277:23
outward: hope from o. forms to win
COL 156:8
In all her o. parts Love's COWL 164:6
looketh on the o. appearance BIBLE 50:6
mark of virtue on his o. SHAK 467:10
Of sense and o. things WORD 579:10
o. and visible sign PRAY 388:19
o. shows be least themselves SHAK 467:10
o. show of things SPEN 516:27
taper to the o. room DONNE 189:30
weather on the o. wall SHAK 466:19
outwardly: us both o. in our bodies
PRAY 386:9
outweighs: Which if we find o. ability
SHAK 441:17
outwore: six lustres almost now o.
DONNE 189:36
Out-worn: O. heart YEATS 585:14
rich-proud cost of o. buried age SHAK 494:2
ouvrage: continuel o. de votre vie
MONT 354:15
ouvrages: tranquilles dans les grands
o. VOLT 561:16
ouvres: mon talent dans mes o. WILDE 573:35
over: All this is o. now CAT 136:24
O. hill, over dale SHAK 470:2

O. the hills and far away GAY 222:22
'O. the hills and far away' STEV 523:8
O. the mountains and over AUDEN 18:7
pleasure of having it o. HOOD 254:25
overcame: I came, saw, and o. SHAK 442:13
o. her wild conqueror HOR 259:2
That day he o. the Nervii SHAK 450:26
overcoat: His o. for ever HOUS 265:1
my o. also was entering RIMB 406:7
wind is to put on your o. LOW 319:18
overcome: Be not o. of evil BIBLE 75:19
I have o. the world BIBLE 72:41
sometimes o., seldom extinguished
BACON 26:36
what is else not to be o. MILT 345:3
overcomes: Who o. By force MILT 345:25
overdone: anything so o. is from
SHAK 433:17
overflow: Nile spills his o. HOUS 262:13
overgrown: All o. with azure moss
SHEL 502:10
so with roses o. MARV 332:14
overlaid: people o. with taxes BACON 27:26
over-mastered: o. with a piece of valiant
SHAK 472:4
overmuch: 'I do not promise o.
HARDY 239:22
over-past: until this tyranny be o.
PRAY 393:14
over-prepared: I had o. the event
POUND 383:20
overtake: Till I thy fate shall o. KING 296:11
overtaking: there's neither o. nor meeting
CONG 159:25
overthroweth: o. your health in some
BACON 26:17
overthrown: I have o. some of you
BIBLE 61:20
overwhelm: o. Myself in poesy KEATS 292:7
overwrought: Spirits o. WORD 580:18
over-zealous: mistaken and o. piety
BURKE 110:29
oves: Inter o. locum praesta CEL 138:8
Ovid: O., the soft philosopher DRYD 196:31
Ovide: O., Omer CHAU 144:17
Venus clerk, O. CHAU 143:26
Ovidius: O. Naso was the man SHAK 457:3
ovo: Ab o. HOR 262:1
owe: o. God a death SHAK 442:7
O. no man anything BIBLE 75:22
we o. everything to him JOHN 282:16
You o. me no subscription SHAK 454:5
owed: conflict was so much o. by so many
CHUR 150:2
I have o. to them WORD 578:4
owest: Lend less than thou o. SHAK 453:15
thou o. God a death SHAK 440:17
oweth: woman o. to her husband SHAK 484:18
owl: against the o. SHAK 462:12
blind as any noon-tide o. TENN 534:23
It was the o. that shriek'd SHAK 460:3
nightly sings the staring o. SHAK 457:19
of the white o. sweeping MER 337:3
old o. liv'd in an oak PUNCH 402:25
O. and the Pussy-Cat went LEAR 312:11
O., and the Waverley pen ANON 8:5
o. does to the moon complain GRAY 234:19
o., for all his feathers KEATS 289:9
o. that is in the desert PRAY 396:12
they brought an O. LEAR 312:9
Was by a mousing o. hawk'd SHAK 461:5
white o. in the belfry TENN 543:10
owls: companion to o. BIBLE 52:37
court for o. BIBLE 58:31
eagle among blinking o. SHEL 501:18
last night two black o. BEER 38:2
There I couch when o. do SHAK 485:25
Two O. and a Hen LEAR 311:15
While I live, the o. TENN 544:12
own: at least it is my o. MUSS 359:2

beam that is in thine o. BIBLE 64:34
countries where he came his o. DRYD 195:25
every country but his o. CANN 129:28
his o. received him not BIBLE 71:26
know how to be one's o. MONT 354:21
marked him for his o. WALT 564:14
what I will with mine o. BIBLE 67:16
own-alone: All by my o. self HARR 242:15
owner: ox knoweth his o. BIBLE 57:15
owners: Down went the o. GILB 225:8
owning: demented with the mania of
o. WHIT 570:22
owse: o. and bottom of the sea SHAK 443:8
ox: eateth grass as an o. BIBLE 53:8
Manningtree o. with the pudding
SHAK 439:16
nor his o. BIBLE 47:24
o. goeth to the slaughter BIBLE 53:25
o. knoweth his owner BIBLE 57:15
o. to wrath has mov'd BLAKE 85:12
shall eat straw like the o. BIBLE 58:11
shalt not muzzle the o. BIBLE 48:25
stalled o. and hatred BIBLE 54:6
oxen: fields with his own o. HOR 259:7
Many o. are come about PRAY 390:18
prize-o. and of sheep TENN 542:20
see the o. kneel HARDY 240:14
than a hundred pair of o. HOW 266:21
That our o. may be strong PRAY 399:13
well be 'Who drives fat o. JOHN 279:20
years like great black o. YEATS 584:17
Oxenford: Clerk ther was of O. also
CHAU 141:23
Oxford: At O., as you know JOW 285:21
back at O. or Cambridge BEER 37:22
clever men at O. GRAH 233:19
Half-Way House to Rome, O. PUNCH 402:11
have never seen O. since NEWM 361:23
Ipswich and O. SHAK 447:22
King to O. sent a troop BROW 97:26
nice sort of place, O. SHAW 497:23
noon on O. town FLEC 214:6
O. is on the whole more BAED 28:19
O. that has made me insufferable BEER 37:21
O. to him a dearer name DRYD 197:14
stagecoach from London to O. HAZL 243:16
To O. sent a troop of horse TRAPP 552:5
To the University of O. GIBB 224:7
what a *whole* O. is COL 155:2
which is in O. made DRYD 197:13
Oxford Street: O., stony-hearted
stepmother DE Q 174:27
oxlips: o. and the nodding violet SHAK 470:10
o. and The crown imperial SHAK 491:26
Oxonian: being an O. FARQ 210:22
Oxtail: to the University of O. JOYCE 286:28
Oxus: O., forgetting the bright ARN 15:1
oynons: o., and eek lekes CHAU 142:5
oyster: In an o. shell on top AUDEN 18:3
o. may be crossed in love SHER 506:4
then the world's mine o. SHAK 469:8
your pearl in your foul o. SHAK 427:4
oysters: by no means unlike o. DICK 178:30
four young O. hurried up CARR 135:6
He had often eaten o. GILB 225:9
O. are more beautiful than SAKI 413:7
'that poverty and o. always DICK 182:2
Ozymandias: 'My name is O. SHEL 502:16
pace: Creeps in this petty p. SHAK 463:6
dance is a measured p. BACON 24:23
I don't like the p. SMITH 512:3
not afraid of 'the p. SURT 525:19
Requiescat in p. MASS 335:10
unperturbèd p. THOM 548:9
volonde è nostra p. DANTE 171:16
pacem: dona nobis p. MASS 335:7
Qui desiderat p. VEG 556:3
Solitudinem faciunt p. TAC 531:7
Paces: P. about her room again ELIOT 205:3
three p. thro' the room TENN 538:11

pacience: assaille His wyves p. CHAU 142:9
eek hire p. CHAU 142:9
paciencia: p. y barajar CERV 138:18
Pacific: He star'd at the P. KEATS 292:18
pacings: long mechanic p. to and fro
TENN 539:18
pack: I will p. BROO 94:22
p. and label men for God THOM 548:26
p. the cards and yet cannot BACON 25:40
Pay, p., and follow BURT 116:11
revenged on the whole p. SHAK 490:26
while the growling p. THOM 549:19
packets: like a post with p. SHAK 447:24
pack-horse: rather of the p. on the down
MORR 358:10
that posterity is a p. DISR 184:25
pack-horses: Shall p. SHAK 441:25
packs: p. and sets of great ones SHAK 456:3
pact: p. with you, Walt Whitman
POUND 383:12
pad: I march with bat and p. HOUS 262:22
padded: p. man TENN 540:22
Paddington: Ever-weeping P. BLAKE 86:3
London is to P. CANN 130:2
than at P. CONN 161:14
paddling: p. palms and pinching fingers
SHAK 491:9
Paddock: P. calls SHAK 458:1
paddocks: Cold as p. though they
HERR 250:10
padlock: p.—on her mind PRIOR 400:23
paean: palms and the p. SWIN 530:4
paeans: laurels to p. CIC 151:22
Paene: P. insularum CAT 136:28
pagan: Christian and you find the p.
ZANG 588:16
P. suckled in a creed outworn WORD 582:20
page: character when he was p. CHAR 140:27
I turn the p. BROW 99:18
p. having an ample marge TENN 535:12
Reading this indignant p. BLAKE 87:17
pageant: like this insubstantial p.
SHAK 485:20
p. of his bleeding heart ARN 13:9
pageants: black vesper's p. SHAK 423:7
page-boy: involves posing as a p. WEST 569:1
pages: almost turned down the p.
POUND 383:20
I spring from the p. into WHIT 570:13
paid: nothing a-year, p. quarterly
SURT 525:27
p. a licence of a hundred SMITH 511:38
P. for catching my 'oss SURT 525:13
p. that is well satisfied SHAK 468:11
p. the uttermost farthing BIBLE 64:14
pay as if not p. before SHAK 493:7
That is not p. with moan THOM 548:1
will be p. at the Greek AUG 22:6
pain: After great p. DICK 183:13
After long grief and p. TENN 540:14
almost to amount to p. HUNT 268:14
are born in other's p. THOM 548:1
assuage the unforgotten p. ROSS 410:6
because it gave p. to the bear MAC 324:19
beneath the aromatic p. WINC 575:6
Bring equal ease unto my p. CAREW 130:1
cost Ceres all that p. MILT 347:21
costs worlds of p. MASS 333:24
death who puts an end to p. TENN 534:30
delight in physics p. SHAK 460:19
disinclination to inflict p. MER 338:4
dreary old age and p. sneak VIRG 560:1
Eternal P. ARN 14:3
grievous pleasure and p. SWIN 530:3
groaneth and travaileth in p. BIBLE 75:10
grown with pleasant p. KEATS 292:3
heard a sudden cry of p. STEP 518:26
heart puts forth its p. BROO 94:5
I feel no p. dear mother ANON 6:1
I have no p. FARM 209:21

in rest from p.	DRYD 196:25
intermission of p.	SELD 419:26
it was p. and grief to me	PRAY 391:30
joy is but a dish of p.	TICH 551:2
life's a p. and but a span	DAV 172:11
living thing to suffer p.	SHEL 502:21
lose, Though full of p.	MILT 346:10
methought what p. it was	SHAK 480:27
midnight with no p.	KEATS 291:22
Never p. to tell thy love	BLAKE 86:21
nor help for p.	ARN 12:23
numbing p.	TENN 539:22
Our Lady of P.	SWIN 529:6
P. at her side	POPE 381:9
p. shall not be inflicted	SPEN 514:26
piercing p.	STEV 523:11
pleasure and without one p.	TENN 539:22
pleasures to another's p.	COWP 167:6
pleasure turns to pleasing p.	SPEN 516:17
purchase p. with all that joy	POPE 377:21
quite sure she felt no p.	BROW 103:29
reliev'd their p.	GOLD 230:23
rues et de voler du p.	FRAN 217:26
shall there be any more p.	BIBLE 82:31
Superflux of p.	SWIN 528:13
Sweet is pleasure after p.	DRYD 195:1
tender for another's p.	GRAY 235:13
thou certain p.	GRAN 234:7
thy delight in others' p.	BYRON 125:4
tongueless vigil and all the p.	SWIN 528:15
wandering and the p.	FLEC 214:5
well and she hasn't a p.	MILNE 340:10
what ignorance of p.	SHEL 504:21
what p.	ARN 14:2
what p. it is to part	GAY 222:33
When p. and anguish wring	SCOTT 417:21
wicked to deserve such p.	BROW 99:29
With some p. is fraught	SHEL 504:23
yet free from guilt or p.	SHEL 503:12
pain'd: p. desert lion	ARN 14:26
painful: one is as p. as the other	BACON 26:3
p. pleasure turns to pleasing	SPEN 516:17
pains: His present and your p.	SHAK 443:11
made my p. his prey	SPEN 515:20
men come to greater p.	BACON 26:23
misfortunes and p. of others	BURKE 108:8
One of the greatest p.	BAG 29:19
p. of hell gat hold	PRAY 397:19
P. of love be sweeter far	DRYD 197:36
p. the immortal spirit	ARN 14:24
possessors into p. of all kinds	BUTL 118:34
So double was his p.	SPEN 516:10
stings you for your p.	HILL 251:2
taken great p. to con it	SHAK 488:10
with p. that conquer trust	TENN 536:21
paint: fain would p. a picture	BROW 102:32
let her p. an inch thick	SHAK 436:31
only showed the p.	DRYD 196:7
p. 'em truest praise	ADD 1:15
p. in the public's face	RUSK 411:7
P. me the bold anfractuous	ELIOT 204:11
p. my picture truly like	CROM 169:24
p. the lily	BYRON 122:31
p. the meadows with delight	SHAK 457:18
prepared to p. an angel	BROW 102:30
to p. the lily	SHAK 452:25
painted: are but gilded loam or p.	SHAK 478:8
Duchess p. on the wall	BROW 102:21
idle as a p. ship	COL 155:13
is not to be p. upon	MAC 323:31
lath of wood p.	BISM 84:27
p. cunningly	SPEN 516:3
p. meadow	ADD 2:5
P. the mid-sea blue	FLEC 214:17
p. veil which those who	SHEL 504:4
She p. her face	BIBLE 51:34
so young as they are p.	BEER 34:7
That fears a p. devil	SHAK 460:11
This p. child of dirt	POPE 377:1
was p. on the wall	PETR 372:30

painter: am a p.	CORR 163:1
great p. dips His pencil	SHEL 503:21
great sculptor or p. can	RUSK 411:8
had been the P.'s hand	WORD 577:4
He is but a landscape-p.	TENN 539:10
me a p. and I am grateful	CONS 162:1
painters: know of two p. in the world	WHIS 569:21
'P. and poets alike have	HOR 257:10
p. imitate nature	CERV 139:1
p., poets and builders	MARL 329:2
painting: amateur p. in water-colours	STEV 521:28
knew as much about p.	LAND 309:16
P. thy outward walls so	SHAK 495:13
poem is like that of a p.	HOR 258:3
thoughts on the unreal p.	VIRG 557:17
Whose mother was her p.	SHAK 428:16
paintings: all the allegorical p.	JOHN 280:19
have heard of your p. too	SHAK 433:13
paint-pots: p. and his words a foot	HOR 257:16
paints: Ingres's the modern man who	BROW 100:17
p.	BROW 100:17
want to know a butcher p.	BROW 105:4
pair: been a p. of ragged claws	ELIOT 203:21
of this ever diverse p.	MER 337:17
p. of very strange beasts	SHAK 427:3
p. so famous	SHAK 424:19
resembles a p. of shears	SMITH 511:11
Sleep on, Blest p.	MILT 348:9
Take a p. of sparkling eyes	GILB 225:26
paired: brain went ever p.	BROW 101:26
palace: Be thine own p.	DONNE 189:23
dominions and making his p. desolate	BECK 36:19
from this p. of dim night	SHAK 483:31
gorgeous p. for a hermitage	SHAK 479:15
in the lighted p. near	TENN 538:12
I will make a p. fit	STEV 522:29
leads to the p. of wisdom	BLAKE 88:13
Love in a p. is perhaps	KEATS 290:24
man armed keepeth his p.	BIBLE 69:36
p. and a prison on each	BYRON 121:1
P. in smoky light	POUND 382:7
p. is more than a house	COL 158:1
purple-lined p. of sweet sin	KEATS 290:25
palaces: Dragons in their pleasant p.	BIBLE 58:12
frail p.	ALDR 3:11
gorgeous p.	SHAK 485:20
Mid pleasures and p. though	PAYNE 370:10
plenteousness with thy p.	PRAY 398:12
sleep old p. and towers	SHEL 502:10
paladin: starry p.	BROW 105:12
Palaeozoic: In the P. time	SMITH 510:10
palate: of the liver, but the p.	SHAK 489:6
P., the hutch of tasty	HOPK 256:15
palates: never p. more the dug	SHAK 423:20
palatium: quale p.	ABEL 1:2
pale: behold a p. horse	BIBLE 81:29
bond Which keeps me p.	SHAK 461:14
look not so p.	SHAK 462:24
make p. my cheeks with	WITH 575:12
One p. as the yonder wan	SHEL 500:8
P. as thy smock	SHAK 477:21
P., beyond porch and portal	SWIN 529:22
p. contented sort of discontent	KEATS 290:26
p. from the imagined love	YEATS 587:1
P. grew thy cheek and cold	BYRON 126:13
P. hands I loved	HOPE 256:3
p. prime-roses	SHAK 491:26
p., unripened beauties	ADD 1:19
to look so green and p.	SHAK 459:8
turn not p., beloved snail	CARR 134:15
was a p. young curate then	GILB 229:1
which the world grew p.	JOHN 282:31
Why so p. and wan	SUCK 524:6
paler: I become p. than grass	SAPP 414:6
paletot: p. aussi devenait idéal	RIMB 406:7

paling: p. shuts the spouse Christ	HOPK 256:29
pall: brows shall be their p.	OWEN 367:3
Palladium: of the press is the P.	JUN 287:1
pallescere: nulla p. culpa	HOR 258:9
pallets: cumber Sunlit p.	HOUS 262:15
Upon uneasy p. stretching	SHAK 441:29
palliate: we p. what we cannot cure	JOHN 281:9
Pallida: P. Mors aequo	HOR 259:13
Pallidula: P. rigida nudula	HADR 237:9
Palliser: think that Plantagenet P.	TROL 552:15
Pall Mall: sweet shady side of P.	MORR 358:3
pallor: of girls' brows	OWEN 367:3
palls: everthing p.	ANON 9:20
palm: bear the p. alone	SHAK 448:16
condemn'd to have an itching p.	SHAK 451:12
Hard as the p. of ploughman	SHAK 486:19
has won it bear the p.	JORT 285:19
Hold Infinity in the p.	BLAKE 85:8
In lands of p. and southern	TENN 533:5
Quietly sweating palm to p.	HUXL 268:22
victor's p. without the dust	HOR 258:8
palmae: dulcis sine pulvere p.	HOR 258:8
palmer: votarist in p.'s weed	MILT 340:30
palmerworm: p. hath left hath the locust	BIBLE 61:13
palms: Afield for p. the girls	HOUS 262:19
other p. are won	WORD 579:14
p. and the paean	SWIN 530:4
p. before my feet	CHES 146:23
Palmyra: editions of Balbec and P.	WALP 563:9
palpable: is almost a p. movement	HARDY 241:9
palsey: It hath brought p. to bed	POUND 382:11
palsied: alms Of p. eld	SHAK 464:10
palsy: ole en strucken wid de p.	HARR 242:13
palter'd: Nor p. with Eternal God	TENN 541:12
paltry: aged man is but a p. thing	YEATS 586:12
'Tis p. to be Caesar	SHAK 423:20
Pam: P., you great big mountainous	BETJ 43:20
Pamere: mountain cradle in P.	ARN 15:1
pampered: God's p. people	DRYD 194:4
pamphleteer: p. on guano and on grain	TENN 542:20
Pan: great god P.	BROW 98:6
great P. is dead	BROW 98:2
P. by noon and Bacchus	SWIN 528:18
p. comido y la compañía	CERV 138:14
P. did after Syrinx speed	MARV 332:2
Panachaea: Or P., or Polygony	SPEN 516:15
panache: Cyrano: *Mon p.*	ROST 410:12
Pancras: P. and Kentish Town repose	BLAKE 86:5
Pandoemonium: P., the high capitol	MILT 346:5
Pandora's Box: If you open that P. you	BEVIN 44:19
pane: Lo p. altrui	DANTE 171:17
p. is blind with showers	HOUS 264:20
tap at the p.	BROW 102:14
Panem: P. et circenses	JUV 287:28
p. nostrum quotidianum	MASS 335:5
panes: diamonded with p. of quaint	KEATS 289:16
pang: p. of all the partings	THOM 547:26
sufferance finds a p. as great	SHAK 464:11
Pange: P., lingua	THOM 546:16
P., lingua	VEN 556:4
pangs: In the sweet p. of it remember	SHAK 488:27
p. and fears than wars	SHAK 447:9
Their p. of love	SHAK 486:13
panic: it but p. and emptiness	FORS 216:25

p.'s in thy breastie BURNS 115:20
Panjandrum: grand P. himself FOOTE 216:7
pansies: p., that's for thoughts SHAK 436:10
pansy: p. at my feet WORD 579:5
p. freakt with jet MILT 343:15
pant: I p., I sink SHEL 500:13
pantaloon: lean and slipper'd p. SHAK 425:24
panting: ever p. and for ever young KEATS 291:7
pantoufles: apportez-moi mes p. MOL 353:3
pants: p. the hart for cooling TATE 531:20
your lower limbs in p. NASH 360:5
papa: else his dear p. is poor STEV 522:21
furious p. or a mild engineer AUDEN 20:15
P., potatoes, poultry DICK 178:26
scene of it with my P. DICK 178:18
Papacy: P. is not other than HOBB 251:21
paper: atomic bomb is a p. tiger MAO 328:20
dust upon the p. eye DOUG 191:10
Golly, what a p. STEV 522:14
grey p. with blunt type BROW 105:8
hand that signed the p. THOM 547:4
he hath not eat p. SHAK 457:1
If all the earth were p. LYLY 321:16
just for a scrap of p. BETH 42:3
p. appears dull there is STEE 518:5
That ever blotted p. SHAK 467:15
virtue of p. government BURKE 109:13
was any news in the p. AUST 23:26
paper-mill: thou hast built a p. SHAK 446:14
Papist: P., yet a Calvinist CLEV 153:3
Paquin: P. pull down POUND 382:13
Par: P. nobile fratrum HOR 262:8
parable: will open my mouth in a p. PRAY 395:3
parade: consists in the p. of riches SMITH 509:11
paradis: sont les p. qu'on a perdus PROU 402:1
Paradise: All P. opens DISR 187:1
Beautiful as a wreck of P. SHEL 500:12
drunk the milk of P. COL 157:1
eastern side beheld Of P. MILT 350:1
England is a p. for women BURT 116:37
England is the p. of women FLOR 216:1
enjoy p. in the next BECK 36:20
in P., If we meet BROW 105:36
I was taught in P. KEATS 289:25
Life's p. FORD 216:14
Lost Angel of a ruin'd P. SHEL 499:8
P. by way of Kensal Green CHES 147:12
p. for a sect KEATS 289:26
P. of Fools MILT 347:11
rudiments of P. SOUTH 513:12
shalt thou be with me in p. BIBLE 71:13
Such are the Gates of P. BLAKE 85:26
Thou hast the keys of P. DE Q 175:2
Thou P. of exiles SHEL 501:11
To him are opening p. GRAY 235:15
To live in P. alone MARV 332:8
Upon the trees of P. STEV 523:13
Wilderness is P. enow FITZ 212:11
would destroy their p. GRAY 235:13
paradises: paradises are p. we have lost PROU 402:1
paradox: Man is an embodied p. COLT 159:11
parallel: ours so truly p. MARV 331:19
Parallelograms: Princess of P. BYRON 126:21
parallels: p. in beauty's brow SHAK 493:20
paramours: his sustres and his p. CHAU 142:32
Worn of p. SPEN 517:3
paraphrase: Than the classics in p. POUND 383:4
parcels: she deals it in small p. WEBS 567:1
Parce que: 'P. c'était lui MONT 354:18
Parcere: P. subiectis et debellare VIRG 559:1
parchment: features bound in stale p. MER 337:26

innocent lamb should be made p. SHAK 446:12
rotten p. bonds SHAK 478:20
virtue of wax and p. BURKE 109:24
Parcus: P. deorum cultor et infrequens HOR 260:2
pard: p.-like Spirit SHEL 499:17
pardon: beseech you of your p. SHAK 475:19
cannot help nor p. AUDEN 20:17
faithful people p. and peace PRAY 386:22
God may p. you ELIZ 205:29
God will p. me HEINE 244:13
p. all oaths that are broke SHAK 480:3
they ne'er p. DRYD 195:30
thousand Ta's and P.'s BETJ 43:13
To p. or to bear it COWP 165:9
We cannot beg for p. MACN 326:15
We will p. Thy Mistake BETJ 43:5
pardonable: then it is p. CONG 160:22
Pardoned: P. Kipling and his views AUDEN 19:8
pardoning: p. our offences PRAY 388:2
pardonnera: Et le bon Dieu me p. CATH 136:17
pardoun: Bretful of p. CHAU 142:6
parent: don't object to an aged p. DICK 178:12
Fear is the p. of cruelty FROU 219:20
had a smile for your p. VIRG 560:2
most afflicting to a p.'s AUST 23:18
That would put any p. mad FLEM 214:25
To lose one p. WILDE 573:1
Parentage: P. is a very important SHAW 496:24
'What is your p. SHAK 488:14
parents: begin by loving their p. WILDE 573:30
indiscreetly by most p. STEE 518:10
joys of p. are secret BACON 27:2
lords whose p. were DEFOE 173:14
Of p. good SHAK 444:17
Our p.' age (worse than HOR 260:26
P. first season us HERB 248:10
p.' tears MILT 345:14
stranger to one of your p. AUST 23:15
parentum: Aetas p. peior avis tulit HOR 260:26
parfit: p. gentil knyght CHAU 141:10
paries: Barbiton hic p. habebit HOR 261:6
p. cum proximus ardet HOR 258:23
pariete: in p. erat pictus superque PETR 372:30
Paris: Americans die they go to P. WILDE 573:25
girl's lip out of P. SWIN 531:2
go to P. APPL 11:13
king had given me P. ANON 9:17
P. is well worth a mass HENR 245:15
should go and live in P. ANON 6:2
To mighty P. when he found YEATS 586:4
parish: all the world as my p. WESL 568:18
his pension from his p. RUSK 412:7
p. of rich women AUDEN 19:5
paritors: general Of trotting 'p. SHAK 456:26
parium: judicium p. suorum MAGN 327:2
parle: mais je n'en p. jamais PROU 401:22
parler: souffre et meurs sans p. VIGNY 557:2
Parliament: Bidding the crop-headed P. BROW 99:26
In the P. of man TENN 538:24
p. can do any thing PEMB 371:11
p. is a *deliberative* assembly BURKE 109:12
P. speaking through reporters CARL 132:4
to fun in any Act of P. HERB 246:14
Parliamentary: unhappy Bag of P. Eloquence CARL 132:1
Parliaments: England is the mother of P. BRIG 93:4
we shall have no more P. JONS 284:26
parlour: Is it a party in a p. WORD 580:2

'Will you walk into my p. HOW 267:3
Parnassus: since you my chief P. be SIDN 507:27
Parnell: Poor P. JOYCE 286:15
parochial: Art must be p. in the beginning MOORE 355:16
he was p. JAMES 271:9
parody: devil's walking p. CHES 146:22
parole: Classical quotation is the *p.* JOHN 278:29
paroles: et n'emploient les p. que VOLT 561:4
paronomasia: (You catch the p. CALV 127:15
parritch: halesome p. BURNS 113:8
pars: Et quorum p. magna fui VIRG 557:21
parshial: p. to ladies if they are ASHF 17:6
parson: coughing drowns the p.'s saw SHAK 457:19
If P. lost his senses HODG 252:2
like a p.'s damn HARDY 241:14
Monday is p.'s holiday SWIFT 526:19
parson and the p.'s wife CLOU 153:23
p. knows enough who knows COWP 167:31
P. left conjuring SELD 419:24
p., much bemus'd in beer POPE 376:19
p. own'd his skill GOLD 231:3
Then the P. might preach BLAKE 87:20
There goes the p. COWP 166:1
Tickling a p.'s nose SHAK 481:28
parsons: p. are very like other CHES 145:11
p. do not care for truth STUB 524:5
This merriment of p. is JOHN 278:25
part: come let us kiss and p. DRAY 193:21
death p. thee and me BIBLE 49:32
every man must play a p. SHAK 465:10
ev'ry prudent p. POPE 377:22
forgotten this day we must p. CRAW 169:16
hath chosen that good p. BIBLE 69:35
I am a p. of all TENN 543:22
more willingly p. withal SHAK 432:10
now I know in p. BIBLE 76:14
p. at last without a kiss MORR 358:11
p. my garments among them PRAY 390:20
p. nor lot in this matter BIBLE 73:31
P. steals HARDY 240:2
p. to tear a cat SHAK 469:26
Shall I p. my hair behind ELIOT 203:25
Suff'ring is the lover's p. GAY 222:9
take your own p. BORR 90:10
till death us do p. PRAY 389:4
To p. her time 'twixt reading POPE 377:7
was not p. of their blood KIPL 298:1
We two now p. PATM 370:6
what pain it is to p. GAY 222:23
which I was a major p. VIRG 557:21
you and I must p. SHAK 421:28
partagée: chose du monde la mieux p. DESC 175:11
partakers: p. of the holy Communion PRAY 387:5
parted: a' p. even just between SHAK 443:17
best and worst, and p. BROO 94:6
his words are soon p. SHEN 505:17
Mine never shall be p. MILT 349:19
remember the way we p. SWIN 530:10
though p. then AUDEN 20:19
When we two p. BYRON 126:13
Parthenophil: P. is lost FORD 216:19
Parthians: P., and Medes BIBLE 73:23
partial: p. for th' observer's sake POPE 377:8
participation: have some p. of divineness BACON 24:19
particle: pushing young p. GILB 227:28
Particles: Newtons P. of Light BLAKE 86:24
particular: should love a bright p. star SHAK 420:25
Particulars: must do it in Minute P. BLAKE 86:7
parties: high contracting p. solemnly KELL 295:8
p. against believing their ARB 11:19

P. must ever exist — BURKE 110:1
parting: Ere the p. hour go — ARN 13:19
In every p. there is — ELIOT 201:22
P. is all we know of heaven — DICK 183:20
p. is such sweet sorrow — SHAK 482:20
P.'s well-paid with soon — PATM 370:5
rive not more in p. — SHAK 423:6
stood at the p. of the ways — BIBLE 60:36
Their every p. was to die — TENN 537:12
this p. was well made — SHAK 451:32
partings: pang of all the p. gone — THOM 547:26
Partington: Atlantic Ocean beat Mrs P. — SMITH 511:32
Partir: P. c'est mourir un peu — HAR 238:20
partly: Living and p. living — ELIOT 204:2
p. she was drunk — BURNS 114:18
partner: While his lov'd p. — GOLD 231:26
partridge: Always p. — ANON 9:19
p. sitteth on eggs — BIBLE 60:25
parts: his time plays many p. — SHAK 425:24
P. of it are excellent — PUNCH 403:4
p. of one stupendous whole — POPE 379:10
smaller p.-o'-speech — CALV 127:15
To-day we have naming of p. — REED 405:5
truth in the inward p. — PRAY 393:5
weep upon your hinder p. — HUXL 268:23
Parturient: P. montes — HOR 257:18
party: again to save the p. we love — GAIT 220:26
and...to educate our p. — DISR 185:5
'Collapse of Stout P.' — ANON 8:10
conduct of a losing p. — BURKE 111:27
existence the stupidest p. — MILL 339:2
I always voted at my p.'s — GILB 228:6
Is it a p. in a parlour — WORD 580:2
maintain the p. of the truth — SHAK 445:21
nature of a political p. — TROL 553:8
P. is organized opinion — DISR 185:1
p. of friends — GILB 226:14
p. of order or stability — MILL 339:10
p. Parliamentary government — DISR 185:7
passion and p. blind — COL 157:20
phylacteries of the Liberal P. — ROS 408:17
sooner every p. breaks — AUST 22:13
Stick to your p. — DISR 185:21
Then none was for a p. — MAC 322:18
party-coloured: known by this p. livery — CONG 160:22
Party-spirit: P., which at best is — POPE 381:16
parva: p. licet componere magnis — VIRG 560:19
Parys: Frenssh of P. was to hire — CHAU 141:15
pas: n'y a que le premier p. — DU D 198:28
pasarán: No p. — IBAR 269:15
pascit: atque animum pictura p. — VIRG 557:17
pass: bringeth mighty things to p. — PRAY 398:1
cunning men p. for wise — BACON 25:43
deeds which should not p. — BYRON 120:32
Generations p. while some tree — BROW 97:16
Individuals p. like shadows — BURKE 110:17
I shall not p. this way — GREL 236:14
I will p. nor turn my face — BROW 105:36
let him p. — SHAK 456:12
let this cup p. from me — BIBLE 68:14
let us p. — BURKE 110:19
my words shall not p. away — BIBLE 67:31
p., and turn again — EMER 206:17
p. but the end is not yet — BIBLE 67:27
p. by me as the idle wind — SHAK 451:20
P. into nothingness — KEATS 288:20
p. man's understanding — PRAY 386:18
p. the ammunition — FORGY 216:21
P. the hat for your credit's — KIPL 297:25
p. through things temporal — PRAY 386:16
pay us, p. us — CHES 147:15
shining Foot shall p. — FITZ 213:18
that it may not p. away — KIPL 299:15
therefore let him p. for a man — SHAK 465:22
They shall not p. — IBAR 269:15

thou shalt strangely p. — SHAK 493:14
to p. through this world — GREL 236:14
'Try not the P. — LONG 316:15
well p. for forty-three — GILB 229:4
which they shall not p. — PRAY 396:19
Will she p. in a crowd — SWIFT 526:14
passa: guarda, e p. — DANTE 171:4
passage: desired to fret a p. through — FULL 220:19
Down the p. which we did — ELIOT 202:13
ever you meet with a p. — JOHN 276:14
long black p. up to bed — STEV 522:25
minion carv'd out his p. — SHAK 458:3
North-west p. — STER 520:2
p. is what I call the sublime — COL 158:7
passages: cheated into some fine p. — KEATS 294:15
shuts up all the p. of joy — JOHN 283:1
Time shall not lose our p. — DONNE 188:9
passageways: With smell of steaks in p. — ELIOT 204:7
pass'd: p. the door of Darkness — FITZ 213:4
passe: Tout p. — ANON 9:20
passed: I have p. with a nod — YEATS 585:1
p. by on the other side — BIBLE 69:31
passengers: we the p. — HOW 267:1
Passer: P. mortuus est meae puellae — CAT 136:32
passeront: Ils ne p. pas — NIV 363:17
passes: Everything p. — ANON 9:20
Men seldom make p. — PARK 368:16
p. the glory of the world — ANON 11:1
passeth: fashion of this world p. — BIBLE 76:4
which p. all understanding — BIBLE 78:21
world, that p. — CHAU 144:19
passi: p. graviora — VIRG 557:13
passing: Deign on the p. world — JOHN 282:29
I did but see her p. — ANON 8:1
in the p. of a day — SPEN 516:13
p. the love of women — BIBLE 50:17
So be my p. — HENL 245:9
Writh'd not at p. joy — KEATS 293:4
passing-bells: What p. for these who die — OWEN 367:2
passion: All breathing human p. — KEATS 291:7
All made of p. — SHAK 426:29
all p. spent — MILT 351:4
Bards of P. and of Mirth — KEATS 290:31
betwixt one p. and another — STER 519:3
by thy Cross and P. — PRAY 385:17
commanded By such poor p. — SHAK 423:17
connect the prose and the p. — FORS 217:2
desolate and sick of an old p. — DOWS 191:12
Eternal P. — ARN 14:3
gentleman in such a p. about — SHAW 498:26
has felt the tender p. — GAY 223:3
his p. boiled and bubbled — THAC 546:3
I have no p. for it — JOHN 274:25
immoderate p. for fame — BURKE 109:8
in a dream of p. — SHAK 432:27
Infinite p. — BROW 105:30
Into a towering p. — SHAK 437:13
is so obstinate a p. — HUME 267:16
lingring and consumptive p. — ETH 208:29
maiden p. for a maid — TENN 534:12
Methought it did relieve my p. — SHAK 488:26
One p. doth expel another — CHAP 140:11
p. and party blind — COL 157:20
p. and the life — COL 156:8
p. could bring character — YEATS 587:1
p. for hunting something — DICK 180:35
p. for our temperate kings — TENN 541:11
p. in the mind of man so — BACON 26:2
P., I see, is catching — SHAK 450:13
P. speechless lies — DRAY 193:21
p. that left the ground — BROW 98:20
p. woman loves her lover — BYRON 122:25
periwig-pated fellow tear a p. — SHAK 433:16
Queen was in a furious p. — CARR 134:5
ruling p. — DICK 176:11

ruling p. in man is not — FROST 219:14
ruling p. conquers reason — POPE 377:32
Search then the Ruling P. — POPE 377:13
sentimental p. of a vegetable — GILB 227:23
Some bloody p. shakes your — SHAK 477:6
That is not p.'s slave — SHAK 434:2
To be in a p. you good — BLAKE 85:17
To inspire hopeless p. — THAC 545:13
vulgar expression of the p. — CONG 159:22
well-painted p. — SHAK 476:14
what is p. but pining — MER 338:7
What p. cannot Music raise — DRYD 197:22
when his p. shall have — TENN 538:19
Whom p. could not shake — SHAK 476:16
passionate: Ah beautiful p. body — SWIN 529:7
Are full of p. intensity — YEATS 586:15
discriminate every moment some p. — PATER 369:22
passion-flower: From the p. at the gate — TENN 540:12
passionless: hopeless grief is p. — BROW 98:7
man P.—no — SHEL 503:12
passions: also are men of like p. — BIBLE 74:5
après les instants de p. — VOLT 561:16
Desolate p. — JOHN 273:21
devil to have all the p. — SHAW 497:22
diminue les médiocres p. — LA R 310:15
governs the p. and resolutions — HUME 267:22
his p. which have got — STER 519:25
moderator of p. — WALT 564:3
Oft' shifts her p. — GAY 223:8
other p. fleet to air — SHAK 467:12
p. match'd with mine — TENN 539:5
p. of his fellow-citizens — HOR 260:18
Two master-p. cannot co-exist — CAMP 129:11
we various ruling p. find — POPE 377:24
when he acts from the p. — DISR 186:2
With life all other p. fly — SOUT 513:26
passive: benevolence of the p. order — MER 338:4
p., recording, not thinking — ISH 270:28
passover: Christ our p. is sacrificed — BIBLE 75:36
it is the Lord's p. — BIBLE 47:19
passport: his p. shall be made — SHAK 445:3
past: alter the p., historians can — BUTL 118:21
are p. our dancing days — SHAK 482:1
bitterness of death is p. — BIBLE 50:5
cannot remember the p. — SANT 414:1
future contained in time p. — ELIOT 202:12
give me back my p. years — VIRG 559:6
God cannot change the p. — AGAT 3:4
is the funeral of the p. — CLARE 152:15
itself upon the p. has pow'r — DRYD 198:14
like a child for the p. — LAWR 311:7
Many a woman has a p. — WILDE 573:9
more than things long p. — SHAK 478:18
moulded of things p. — SHAK 487:6
nothing but the p. — KEYN 295:15
p., and future sees — BLAKE 87:13
p. as a watch in the night — PRAY 395:18
P. bury its dead — LONG 317:3
p. is a foreign country — HART 242:34
p. is the only dead thing — THOM 547:17
P. reason hated — SHAK 495:7
p. redress are now with — SHAK 479:3
P. ruin'd Ilion Helen lives — LAND 308:22
plan the future by the p. — BURKE 111:31
rather absurd about the p. — BEER 37:12
remembrance of things p. — SHAK 493:7
remomoring of a cursed p. — VANZ 555:8
scraps are good deeds p. — SHAK 487:3
shall be p. making love — PRIOR 401:7
soul of the whole P. Time — CARL 131:34
they that will times p. — HERR 249:17
thought of our p. years — WORD 579:9
Time p. and time future — ELIOT 202:16
time p. unto the fathers — BIBLE 79:28
to lament the p.   / — BURKE 108:17
to remember what is p. — HAL 238:3

what is p. my help | FLET 215:12
What's p. | SHAK 487:14
What's p. is prologue | SHAK 485:5
world is weary of the p. | SHEL 501:3
years that are p. | PRAY 395:2
pastime: made to take his p. therein
PRAY 397:1
'twas p. to be bound | WORD 582:8
pastor: iguala al p. con el rey | CERV 138:20
Pastoral: Cold P. | KEATS 291:10
p. music on a thin stalk | VIRG 559:11
pastors: some ungracious p. do | SHAK 430:18
spiritual p. and masters | PRAY 388:16
pasture: are the people of his p. | PRAY 396:4
feed me in a green p. | PRAY 390:21
mettle of your p. | SHAK 444:2
sheep of his p. | PRAY 396:11
pasture-ground: in the ooze of their p.
ARN 13:6
pastures: fresh woods, and p. | MILT 343:20
On England's pleasant p. | BLAKE 86:16
Over the green p. there | AUDEN 18:8
pat: Now might I do it p. | SHAK 434:29
P. he comes | SHAK 453:12
Patch: P. grief with proverbs | SHAK 473:6
p., matchwood | HOPK 257:1
p. up thine old body | SHAK 441:27
patches: king of shreds and p. | SHAK 435:12
thing of shreds and p. | GILB 226:18
pate: made by an aged old p. | ANON 4:19
p. of a politician | SHAK 436:27
patent: p. for his honours immediately
BURNS 113:15
so my p. back again is | SHAK 494:13
Pater: P. noster | MASS 335:5
paterna: buona imagine p. | DANTE 171:12
P. rura bubus | HOR 259:7
paternal: dear and kindly p. image
DANTE 171:12
Die of the absolute p. care | ELIOT 202:22
disclaim all my p. care | SHAK 453:3
path: beaten p. to his door | EMER 208:15
ears this p. that wandereth | CHES 147:12
follows the hidden p. down | LUIS 320:12
is the P. of Wickedness | BALL 32:5
Our p. emerges for a while | DOWS 191:3
p. before me leading wherever | WHIT 571:7
p. of the just is | BIBLE 53:19
straight p. along the dusky air | COL 157:11
This downhill p. is easy | ROSS 408:22
was a p. of gold for him | BROW 103:9
Pathetic: characterize as the 'P. Fallacy'
RUSK 411:11
Is not p. | WHIT 571:11
It was too p. for the feelings | AUST 22:24
pathless: heav'n's wide p. way | MILT 342:3
pleasure in the p. woods | BYRON 121:22
pathos: true p. and sublime | BURNS 115:15
paths: all her p. are peace | BIBLE 53:17
bitter p. wherein I stray | KIPL 301:16
leave the trodden p. of men | SHEL 499:11
light unto my p. | PRAY 398:6
make his p. straight | BIBLE 53:36
opposed p. to persevere | PATM 370:6
p. of glory lead | GRAY 234:21
So many p. that wind | WILC 572:6
pathway: p. to the ends of all | KIPL 303:5
patience: all p. | SHAK 426:29
are they that have not p. | SHAK 475:11
be the pattern of all p. | SHAK 454:7
close-lipp'd P. for our only friend | ARN 14:18
drop of p. | SHAK 476:18
grande aptitude à la p. | BUFF 106:21
greater aptitude for p. | BUFF 106:21
habits of peace and p. | WALT 564:3
have heard of the p. of Job | BIBLE 80:17
I laugh'd him into p. | SHAK 422:10
languid p. of thy face | COL 157:16
long will you abuse our p. | CIC 151:25
My p. is now at an end | HITL 251:11

old abusing of God's p. | SHAK 469:5
p., and shuffle the cards | CERV 138:18
p. have her perfect work | BIBLE 80:7
p. of hope in our Lord | BIBLE 78:30
p. possess ye your souls | BIBLE 71:5
P., the beggar's virtue | MASS 335:20
P., thou young and rose-lipp'd | SHAK 476:18
p. under their sufferings | PRAY 386:1
p. will achieve more than | BURKE 111:24
preach'd up p. | PRIOR 401:2
preacheth p. | HERB 247:12
sat like p. on a monument | SHAK 489:7
talk him out of p. | SHAK 475:13
Though with p. He stands | LOGAU 316:5
patient: Beware the fury of a p. | DRYD 194:20
disease and kill the p. | BACON 26:17
not so p. | SHAK 441:8
P. continuance in well | BIBLE 74:33
p. etherized upon a table | ELIOT 203:17
p. Must minister to himself | SHAK 463:3
p., not a brawler | BIBLE 79:12
sit thou a p. looker-on | QUAR 403:15
Thou must be p. | SHAK 455:22
patiently: I waited p. for the Lord | PRAY 392:1
ye shall take it p. | BIBLE 80:26
ye take it p. | BIBLE 80:26
patients: likes to hurry his p. along
MOL 353:21
patines: inlaid with p. of bright gold
SHAK 468:15
patrem: Deum p. qui ecclesiam | CYPR 170:19
patria: decorum est pro p. mori | HOR 260:17
Sed miles, sed pro p. | NEWB 361:5
patriarchal: wi' p. grace | BURNS 113:9
patrician: regular p. | GILB 228:11
This is the P. | DONNE 190:23
patrie: plus j'aimai ma p. | BELL 40:17
patriot: Never was p. yet | DRYD 194:19
soldier and the sunshine p. | PAINE 368:1
steady p. of the world | CANN 129:28
Such is the p.'s boast | GOLD 231:25
patriotic: fights you on p. principles
SHAW 498:6
patriotism: larger p. | ROS 408:14
P. is the last refuge | JOHN 276:25
p. which consists in hating | GASK 222:4
realize that p. is not enough | CAV 137:18
patriots: blood of p. and tyrants | JEFF 272:10
so to be p. | BURKE 108:24
True p. we | BARR 34:23
Patron: Is not a P. | JOHN 274:7
p., and the jail | JOHN 282:29
p. of some thirty charities | TENN 542:20
patronage: public and even private p.
ALB 3:7
Patroness: My celestial P. | MILT 349:9
patronum: tu optimus omnium's p. | CAT 137:3
patter: unintelligible p. | GILB 228:37
pattern: be the p. of all patience | SHAK 454:7
cunning'st p. of excelling nature | SHAK 477:5
In a p. called a war | LOW 318:21
Made him our p. to live | BROW 102:5
which he shewed as a p. | SWIFT 525:34
patterns: Alive like p. a murmuration
AUDEN 20:6
What are p. | LOW 318:25
paucity: p. of human pleasures should
JOHN 280:15
Paul: crush Under P.'s dome | HODG 252:10
holy Apostles Peter and P. | MASS 334:15
once echoed The voice of P. | HARDY 240:4
to pay for collective P. | KIPL 299:16
with the charity of P. | CHUR 148:22
Pauliad: less a Christiad than a P.
HARDY 241:24
pauper: He's only a p. | NOEL 363:19
pauperiem: Duramque callet p. pati
HOR 261:19
Indocilis p. pati | HOR 259:9
paupertas: Nil habet infelix p. | JUV 287:17

pause: Comes a p. in the day's | LONG 316:9
forebear to p. and inquire | WEST 569:1
How dull it is to p. | TENN 543:22
I p. for a reply | SHAK 450:16
p. awhile from letters | JOHN 282:29
pauses: intervals and happy p. | BACON 27:44
pauvre: p. paysan en mon royaume
HENR 245:13
pauvres: p. sont les nègres de | CHAM 139:17
paved: Are each p. with the moon | SHEL 500:6
streets are p. with gold | COLM 158:25
pavement: p. of pearl | ARN 13:7
street and p. mute | HARDY 240:21
pavements: on the p. gray | YEATS 585:17
p. fang'd with murderous | COL 156:5
pavender: That decks the rural p. | ST L 412:27
pavilion: hast the red p. of my heart
THOM 547:23
paving: horses' heels Over the p. | ELIOT 202:6
pavin'-stones: leather on these gritty
p. | KIPL 301:7
paweth: He p. in the valley | BIBLE 53:6
Pawnce: pretty P. | SPEN 517:3
paws: massive p. of elder persons | BELL 38:24
my dear p. | CARR 133:20
pax: et in terra p. hominibus | MASS 334:18
P. Domini sit semper vobiscum | MASS 335:6
P. Vobis | BIBLE 83:20
Pax vobiscum: 'P.' will answer all queries
SCOTT 418:22
pay: called upon to p. the bill | HARD 238:21
devil to p. | MOORE 357:5
even then she had to p. | BELL 39:9
going to p. every penny | GEDD 223:32
I p. thy poverty | SHAK 483:26
make me able to p. for it | PEPYS 371:20
now I must p. for my fun | KIPL 300:17
p. a debt to pleasure | ROCH 406:17
P. every debt | EMER 207:1
p. glad life's arrears | BROW 104:1
P., pack, and follow | BURT 116:11
p.—pay—pay | KIPL 297:25
p. us, pass us | CHES 147:15
Peter to p. for collective Paul | KIPL 299:16
sharper spur than p. | GAY 223:12
sum of things for p. | HOUS 265:7
therefore p. you cash to go away | KIPL 298:18
unbound by any interest to p. | HOR 259:7
wonders what's to p. | HOUS 265:2
ye must p. for one by one | KIPL 303:20
paying: called p. the Dane-geld | KIPL 298:18
payment: p. of half twenty shillings
BURKE 109:2
paynims: That is to wit three p. | CAXT 138:3
Payris: Ez fur away ez P. is | LOW 319:3
pays: I scent wich p. the best | LOW 319:5
p. us but with age | RAL 404:15
p. your money and you takes | ANON 9:2
paz: vivo en p. con los hombres | MACH 325:7
pea: dined on one p. and one bean
LEAR 313:2
nothing left but one split p. | THAC 545:32
peace: all her paths are p. | BIBLE 53:17
alone burns lamps of p. | DE L 174:17
bad p. | FRAN 218:17
bring a man p. at the last | PRAY 391:29
calls it—p. | BYRON 120:4
calm P., and Quiet | MILT 341:27
calm world and a long p. | SHAK 440:10
certain knot of p. | SIDN 507:20
chastisement of our p. | BIBLE 59:22
cherish a just and lasting p. | LINC 315:3
cowardice keeps us in p. | JOHN 278:3
even lovers find their p. | FLEC 214:10
Everlasting p. is a dream | MOLT 354:4
ever was the church for p. | BROW 99:12
faithful people pardon and p. | PRAY 386:22
feet into the way of p. | BIBLE 69:7
first in p. | LEE 313:7
give p. at home | PRAY 400:5

Give p. in our time — PRAY 385:1
give thee p. — BIBLE 48:9
God gave her p. — TENN 543:15
habits of p. and patience — WALT 564:3
had thy p. been as a river — BIBLE 59:15
Had Zimri p. — BIBLE 51:35
hast thou to do with p. — BIBLE 51:32
haunt of ancient P. — TENN 541:22
hereafter for ever hold his p. — PRAY 389:2
his goods are in p. — BIBLE 69:36
I am for 'P. — BRIG 93:2
I came not to send p. — BIBLE 65:38
if only p. of mind doesn't — HOR 258:19
If p. cannot be maintained — RUSS 412:19
I labour for p. — PRAY 398:8
Imperishable p. — HOUS 266:5
I must go where lazy P. — DAV 172:7
ingeminate the word P. — CLAR 152:20
In His will is our p. — DANTE 171:16
in p., goodwill — CHUR 150:25
In p., Love tunes — SCOTT 416:1
interest that keeps p. — CROM 170:1
in the multitude of p. — PRAY 391:27
Let him who desires p. — VEG 556:3
Let us have p. — GRANT 234:2
Let war yield to p. — CIC 151:22
luxury, p. — BAUD 35:7
makes a good p. — HERB 246:21
Making p. is harder than — STEV 520:21
merry songs of p. — SHAK 448:1
mind at p. with all below — BYRON 125:22
moth of p. — SHAK 474:6
mountains also shall bring p. — PRAY 394:19
mountain tops is p. — GOET 230:11
my everlasting p. — HOOD 254:22
My p. is gone — GOET 230:4
my reign is p. — LAND 308:21
Nation shall speak p. unto — REND 405:11
news and Prince of P. — FLET 215:29
nor earth have been at p. — SHAK 449:17
not p. at any price — JERR 273:11
old as we to keep the p. — SHAK 481:25
on earth p. — BIBLE 69:11
p. above all earthly dignities — SHAK 447:10
p. a Christian can die — ADD 2:29
p. among our peoples let — KIPL 303:6
p., and ensue it — PRAY 391:23
p. and propagation are — WALP 563:13
p., and take my rest — PRAY 389:22
p. at the last — NEWM 362:9
P. be to this house — BIBLE 60:26
P. be to this house — PRAY 389:8
P. be unto you — BIBLE 83:20
P.; come away — TENN 536:31
P., comes dropping slow — YEATS 585:17
P., commerce — JEFF 272:8
p. does nothing to relieve — COWP 165:7
p. for our time — CHAM 139:10
p., from him which is — BIBLE 81:9
peaceful sloth, Not p. — MILT 346:12
p. has been broken anywhere — ROOS 407:23
P. hath her victories — MILT 351:17
I hope with honour — DISR 185:15
P. I leave with you — BIBLE 72:35
P.! impudent and shameless — SHAK 446:20
p. in Shelley's mind — SHEL 505:1
P. is a very apoplexy — SHAK 427:27
P. is indivisible — LITV 315:10
P. is in the grave — SHEL 503:3
P. is poor reading — HARDY 239:15
P. its ten thousands — PORT 381:32
p. of God — BIBLE 78:21
p. of Jerusalem — PRAY 398:12
p. of the double bed after — CAMP 128:9
P., perfect peace — BICK 84:4
P. shall go sleep with — SHAK 479:20
P., the human dress — BLAKE 88:7
p. there's nothing so becomes — SHAK 443:21
P. to corrupt no less than — MILT 349:27
P. to him that is far off — BIBLE 60:3

p. to you which were afar — BIBLE 77:22
P. upon earth!' was said — HARDY 239:3
p. within nor calm around — SHEL 504:10
p. with men and at war — MACH 325:7
people the blessing of p. — PRAY 391:12
poor, and mangled P. — SHAK 445:11
potent advocates of p. — GEOR 224:4
practising upon his p. and quiet — SHAK 474:22
preparation of the gospel of p. — BIBLE 78:10
Prince of P. — BIBLE 58:7
righteousness and p. have kissed — PRAY 395:15
right hand carry gentle p. — SHAK 447:12
servant depart in p. — BIBLE 69:12
shall this p. sleep with her — SHAK 448:3
slept in p. — SHAK 447:16
So enamoured on p. that — CLAR 152:21
Sweet P. is crown'd with — VAUG 555:13
that publisheth p. — BIBLE 59:18
that the defences of p. — ANON 7:16
There is no p. — BIBLE 59:16
There is p. from twelve — COW 163:20
There should be p. at home — WATTS 565:19
these voices there is p. — TENN 534:16
they are in p. — BIBLE 62:13
they should kneel for p. — SHAK 484:19
thou return at all in p. — BIBLE 51:20
thousand years of p. — TENN 537:15
thy servants that p. — PRAY 385:9
time of p. — BIBLE 55:12
to gain our p. — SHAK 461:12
To rust in p. — SOUT 513:13
universal P. — TENN 533:23
verses are like the p. of God — JAM 271:6
ways upon a state of p. — VIRG 559:1
weak piping time of p. — SHAK 480:18
What is p.? Is it war? — DICK 176:12
when there is no p. — BIBLE 60:19
which belong unto thy p. — BIBLE 71:3
who art the author of p. — PRAY 385:2
wilderness and call it p. — TAC 531:7
with the soft phrase of p. — SHAK 473:24
work us a perpetual p. — MILT 344:3
Would I were sleep and p. — SHAK 482:20
you that kiss our lady P. — SHAK 441:13
peaceably: 'p. if we can — CLAY 152:29
p. ordered by thy governance — PRAY 386:17
peaceful: made this p. life for us — VIRG 559:12
peacemakers: Blessed are the p. — BIBLE 64:6
peach: Do I dare to eat a p. — ELIOT 203:25
nectarine and curious p. — MARV 332:3
Peacock: Ere Mor the P. flutters — KIPL 303:7
Eyed like a p. — KEATS 290:22
milk-white p. like a ghost — TENN 542:14
p. is the glory of God — BLAKE 88:21
peacocks: apes, and p. — BIBLE 50:34
apes and p. — MAS 333:18
p. and lilies for instance — RUSK 411:23
terraces and p. strutting — KIPL 299:12
pea-green: In a beautiful p. boat — LEAR 312:11
peak: small things from the p. — CHES 147:30
peal: rung night's yawning p. — SHAK 461:13
pear: are on a Catherine p. — SUCK 524:9
go round the prickly p. — ELIOT 203:9
pearl: found one p. of great price — BIBLE 66:21
hang a p. in every cowslip's — SHAK 470:2
ocean for orient p. — MARL 329:4
Of orient p. a double row — CAMP 129:23
pavement of p. — ARN 13:7
threw a p. away — SHAK 477:23
your p. in your foul oyster — SHAK 427:4
pearls: are p. that were his eyes — SHAK 484:32
Give p. away and rubies — HOUS 262:20
p. of thought in Persian — LOW 319:10
search for p. must dive — DRYD 195:10
Some ask'd how p. did grow — HERR 249:18
ye your p. before swine — BIBLE 65:1
pears: our French withered p. — SHAK 420:27
Pearse: P. summoned Cuchulain — YEATS 587:2
peartree: glassy p. leaves and blooms — HOPK 256:24

peas: first green p. — LONG 316:23
peasant: that the toe of the p. — SHAK 436:29
what a rogue and p. slave — SHAK 432:27
peasantry: bold p. — GOLD 230:18
Sing the p. — YEATS 587:8
peasants: hands of p. their vile trash — SHAK 451:21
peascod: squash is before 'tis a p. — SHAK 488:9
pebble: only p. on the beach — BRAI 91:17
pebbles: boys that throw p. and mire — WATTS 565:26
unnumber'd idle p. chafes — SHAK 455:14
peccata: tollis p. mundi — MASS 335:7
peccator: Esto p. et pecca fortiter — LUTH 320:15
Peccavi: P.—I have Sindh — WINK 575:8
P.—I've Scinde — PUNCH 402:16
quia p. nimis cogitatione — MASS 334:15
pécher: p. que pécher en silence — MOL 354:1
peck: p. cautiously at the ball — WOD 575:24
peculiar: in him was the p. grace — BROW 100:36
London was extensive and p. — DICK 181:35
p. people — BIBLE 80:23
Pecunia: P. non olet — VESP 556:11
pecuniam: p. infinitam — CIC 151:30
pecuniary: turning an immense p. Mangle — DICK 183:6
Pedant: precious apothegmaticall P. — NASHE 360:6
pedantic: little too p. for a gentleman — CONG 160:12
pedantical: Figures p. — SHAK 457:15
pedants: Which learned p. much affect — BUTL 117:17
pede: nunc p. libero — HOR 260:3
pedestalled: so be p. in triumph — BROW 104:30
pedigree: languages are the p. of nations — JOHN 280:1
Peel: talk and P. has no manners — WELL 567:31
peep: into glory p. — VAUG 555:21
that would p. and botanize — WORD 580:3
Wizards that p. and that — BIBLE 58:5
peepshow: ticket for the p. — MACN 326:7
Peer: About this unimportant P. — BELL 39:30
hath not left his p. — MILT 343:2
many a p. of England brews — HOUS 264:12
rhyming p. — POPE 376:19
peerage: p., or Westminster Abbey — NELS 360:14
You should study the P. — WILDE 573:32
Peers: My Lord in the P. will — BROU 95:3
praise in p. to write at all — BYRON 124:27
peewees: graves of the martyrs the p. — STEV 523:5
Pegasus: thought it P. — KEATS 292:8
turn and wind a fiery P. — SHAK 440:7
peignoir: Complacencies of the p. — STEV 520:18
peine: donné la p. de naître — BEAU 35:18
la p. d'être dit — BEAU 35:14
pelago: Commisit p. ratem — HOR 259:12
pelf: about what they call p. — CLOU 153:21
I crave no p. — SHAK 486:3
pelican: like a p. in the wilderness — PRAY 396:15
Pluffskin, P. jee — LEAR 312:15
wonderful bird is the p. — MERR 338:8
wouldst thou have me turn p. — CONG 160:6
Pelion: P. imposuisse Olympo — HOR 260:22
pile Ossa on P. — VIRG 560:13
pellucid: more p. streams — WORD 578:3
Pelting: P. each other for the public — COWP 164:28
pen: Biting my truant p. — SIDN 507:17
could use the sword and p. — LAND 308:23
foolish when he had not a p. — JOHN 278:19
forbear To bite his p. — SWIFT 527:23
garden with your p. — CAMP 128:11
he take a p. in his hand — JOHN 274:1

with his sweet p. caught	ROYD 411:3

perfectly: She's p. well and she hasn't MILNE 340:10
that we may p. love thee PRAY 387:7
perfide: *La p. Albion* XTM 584:6
la p. Angleterre BOSS 90:14
perfidious: fatal and p. bark MILT 343:10
her own waters p. Albion XIM 584:6
perform: Almighty's orders to p. ADD 1:14
they are not able to p. PRAY 390:15
performance: All words, And no p. MASS 335:24
her p. keeps no day CAMP 129:21
his p., as he is now SHAK 447:19
it takes away the p. SHAK 460:18
p. so loathed SHAK 487:19
so many years outlive p. SHAK 441:28
that any artistic p. requires JAMES 271:29
performed: vow be p. in Jerusalem PRAY 393:23
perfume: feel my breasts all p. JOYCE 286:30
invisible p. hits the sense SHAK 422:3
p. and most melodious twang AUBR 18:2
throw a p. on the violet SHAK 452:25
perfumes: No p. BRUM 106:5
p. of Arabia will not sweeten SHAK 462:22
P. the chamber thus SHAK 428:8
Perfusus: *P. liquidis urget odoribus* HOR 259:15

Perhaps: grand P. BROW 99:4
seek a great p. RAB 404:1
Peri: P. at the gate Of Eden MOORE 356:27
perii: *ut p.* VIRG 560:4
peril: there is no p. in the fight CORN 162:16
those in p. on the sea WHIT 569:26
vaincre sans p. CORN 162:16
perilous: dim and p. way WORD 577:13
p. mode of hard industry BURKE 109:17
then they knew the p. rock SOUT 514:1
perils: in p. of waters BIBLE 77:12
p. and dangers of this PRAY 385:10
p. Of cheat and charmer HOUS 265:14
what p. do environ BUTL 117:29
What p. past SHAK 442:2
period: belong to the Beardsley p. BEER 37:11
fix the p. in the history GIBB 224:24
inglorious p. of our dominion BURKE 110:24
p., pow'r, and enterprize SMART 509:1
Peripatetic: magnetic, P. Lover GILB 227:24
periphrastic: p. study in a worn-out ELIOT 202:19

perish: all his thoughts will p. BALF 30:3
believeth in him should not p. BIBLE 71:38
day p. wherein I was born BIBLE 52:11
if I p. BIBLE 52:2
I p. with hunger BIBLE 70:19
Must then a Christ p. SHAW 498:20
people p. BIBLE 54:44
p. than to continue schoolmastering CARL 132:27
P. the thought CIBB 151:14
p. through their own imaginations PRAY 389:25
shall p. with the sword BIBLE 68:18
They shall p. PRAY 396:13
though the world p. FERD 210:33
Thy money p. with thee BIBLE 73:30
To p. rather MILT 346:10
whole nation p. not BIBLE 72:24
ye p. from the right way PRAY 389:19
you as well as I P. HOUS 262:21
perished: else p., and he remained BRON 93:25
Just because it p. MILL 340:1
p. in the waters BIBLE 65:20
strength and my hope is p. BIBLE 60:29
weapons of war p. BIBLE 50:17
perishes: cause that p. with them CLOU 153:13
everthing p. ANON 9:20

What's come to perfection p. BROW 102:26
perisheth: righteous p. BIBLE 60:2
peritis: *decede p.* HOR 259:6
periuria: *ex alto p. ridet amantum* OVID 366:11
Perivale: of harbour lights at P. BETJ 42:17
periwig-pated: p. fellow tear a passion SHAK 433:16
perjuries: At lovers' p. SHAK 482:13
high laughs at lovers' p. OVID 366:11
Till p. are common as bad COWP 165:8
perjury: heart to this false p. SHAK 457:4
laughs at lovers' p. DRYD 197:7
Shall I lay p. upon my soul SHAK 468:4
permanence: place had an ancient p. HARDY 241:21
permanent: Nought's p. among the human BYRON 123:33
P. Possibility of Sensation STEV 522:7
Suffering is p. WORD 577:2
permission: p. of all-ruling Heaven MILT 345:8
permitted: not p. unto them to speak BIBLE 76:16
p. to make all the ballads FLET 215:6
pernicious: most p. woman SHAK 431:16
p. race of little odious SWIFT 526:5
p. soul Rot SHAK 477:13
perpetua: *lux p. luceat eis* MASS 334:17
Nox est p. una dormienda CAT 136:25
perpetual: have therefore a p. quarrel BURKE 109:31
let p. light shine on them MASS 334:17
make P. day MARL 329:11
p. hyperbole is comely BACON 26:29
'Tis with us p. night JONS 285:13
perpetually: We are p. moralists JOHN 281:32
which is p. to be conquered BURKE 109:19
perplex: when nae real ills p. them BURNS 115:27
Perplexes: P. monarchs MILT 345:24
Though the dull brain p. KEATS 291:20
perplexity: listlessness from vain p. WORD 580:6
perplexyte: That stad is in p. WYNT 584:4
perquisites: self-respecting scorn of irregular p. WAUGH 566:2
persecute: Why p. we him BIBLE 52:32
persecuted: because I p. the church of God BIBLE 76:19
persecutest: why p. thou me BIBLE 73:33
Persecution: P. is a bad and indirect BROW 96:16
P. produced its natural MAC 324:17
Religious p. may shield BURKE 110:29
some degree of p. SWIFT 527:6
Persephone: Singer of P. WILDE 572:19
Persepolis: ride in triumph through P. MARL 330:7
persever: Ay, do, p. SHAK 470:23
Perseverance: P., dear my lord SHAK 487:4
p. in a good cause STER 519:19
persevere: opposed paths to p. PATM 370:6
Persian: I hate all that P. gear HOR 260:4
P.'s Heaven is easily MOORE 356:3
Persians: given to the Medes and P. BIBLE 61:6
law of the Medes and P. BIBLE 61:7
Persicos: *P. odi* HOR 260:4
persist: fool would p. in his folly BLAKE 88:19
persistence: dominant's p. till it must BROW 105:24
person: adornment of his p. he THOM 549:6
express image of his p. BIBLE 79:28
I am a most superior p. ANON 7:1
p. and the peple his apes CHAU 142:7
p. in the Spanish cape ELIOT 204:15
p. on business from Porlock COL 156:25
purse, my p. SHAK 465:16

personal: No p. considerations GRANT 234:3
P. relations are the important FORS 217:1
personality: escape from p. ELIOT 205:18
personated: himself most feelingly p. SHAK 488:23
persons: God is no respecter of p. BIBLE 74:2
massive paws of elder p. BELL 38:24
Neither confounding the P. PRAY 385:12
p. should not be joined PRAY 388:23
respect of p. with God BIBLE 74:34
perspective: light, shade, and p. CONS 162:2
perspiration: course his p. was but ichor BYRON 126:7
ninety-nine per cent p. EDIS 199:25
perspire: dig till you gently p. KIPL 300:11
that Mr Gladstone may p. CHUR 149:20
persuade: p., threaten WHIT 571:11
persuaded: fully p. in his own mind BIBLE 75:27
were p. of them BIBLE 79:33
persuadest: p. me to be a Christian BIBLE 74:27
persuading: By p. others JUN 287:4
by p. me to it SHAK 486:11
persuasion: alone is not truth, but p. MAC 324:20
firm p. that a thing is so BLAKE 88:26
Persuasions: P. and veiled Destinies SHEL 499:9
persuasive: His gentle reason so p. THOM 549:26
p. language of a tear CHUR 149:17
Pert: P. as a schoolgirl well GILB 226:27
Pertelote: cleped fair damoysele P. CHAU 142:32
Pertness: half P. and half Pout BYRON 119:32
perturbation: polish'd p. SHAK 442:17
perturbations: in new p. and calamities BACON 27:44
perturbed: Rest, rest, p. spirit SHAK 431:25
Peru: from China to P. JOHN 282:28
perus'd: th'original p. mankind ARMS 12:15
perverse: I'll frown and be p. SHAK 482:13
p. creatures in the world ADD 2:18
Perverts: P. the Prophets BYRON 124:23
Peschiera: P., when thy bridge CLOU 154:2
pessimist: p. fears this is true CAB 126:25
pessimus: *Agit p. omnium poeta* CAT 137:3
pest: like a p. in the street CONR 161:21
pester'd: So p. with a popinjay SHAK 438:15
pestilence: breeds p. BLAKE 88:15
from the noisome p. PRAY 395:21
p., and famine PRAY 385:16
p.-stricken multitudes SHEL 502:8
p. that walketh in darkness PRAY 395:21
Shakes p. and war MILT 346:26
she purg'd the air of p. SHAK 487:21
winter, plague and p. NASHE 360:8
pestilences: with wars or p. AUST 23:4
Pests: P. of society BOL 89:14
petal: Now sleeps the crimson p. TENN 542:14
(O filigree p. THOM 548:29
Tip-tilted like the p. TENN 534:7
petals: ever the garden's last p. SWIN 529:19
P., on a wet POUND 383:11
petar: Hoist with his own p. SHAK 435:21
Peter: disciple did outrun P. BIBLE 73:6
first 'twas P.'s drift SHEL 502:18
holy Apostles P. and Paul MASS 334:15
I'll call him P. SHAK 452:9
looked upon P. BIBLE 71:9
P. to pay for collective KIPL 299:16
Simon P. saith unto them BIBLE 73:13
Thou art P. BIBLE 66:33
to see Shock-headed P. HOFF 252:22
Where P. is AMBR 4:1
petis: *Quod p. hic est* HOR 258:19
petitions: desires and p. of thy servants PRAY 385:8
petits: *escadrons contre les p.* BUSS 117:7

Peto: banish P.   SHAK 439:18
Petrarch: if Laura had been P.'s
   BYRON 122:27
petrarchal: would reject a p. coronation
   KEATS 293:32
petrifactions: p. of a plodding brain
   BYRON 124:25
petrifies: p. the feeling   BURNS 113:17
pets: she was not fond of p.   ELIOT 201:11
petticoat: I for one venerate a p.
   BYRON 124:5
p. I were able to live   ELIZ 205:25
petticoatie: She draiglet a' her p.
   BURNS 113:2
Petticoats: P. up to the knees   CLOU 153:15
petty: Creeps in this p. pace   SHAK 463:6
we p. men   SHAK 448:17
petulance: learn that p. is not sarcasm
   DISR 184:20
peuple: je veux être p.   LA B 306:14
ne suppose pas le p. bon   ROB 406:12
règne et le p. se gouverne   THIE 546:5
peur: Chevalier sans p. et sans   ANON 9:5
peut-être: p. Puis il avait expiré   RAB 404:1
pews: Talk about the p. and steeples
   CHES 146:11
pewter: You long for simple p.   GILB 225:30
peyne: beest is deed he hath no p.
   CHAU 142:17
p. I me to strecche forth   CHAU 143:5
ys joy in hevene and p.   CHAU 143:28
phagocytes: Stimulate the p.   SHAW 496:20
phalanx: move In perfect p.   MILT 345:21
Phallic: P. and ambrosial   POUND 383:6
Phantasies: twilight P.   SHEL 499:9
phantasma: p., or a hideous dream
   SHAK 449:6
phantom: She was a p. of delight
   WORD 581:7
phantoms: With p. an unprofitable
   SHEL 499:20
Pharaoh: harden P.'s heart   BIBLE 47:11
Pharisee: touching the law, a P.   BIBLE 78:16
Pharisees: P., hypocrites   BIBLE 67:24
righteousness of the scribes and P.
   BIBLE 64:11
scribes and the P. brought   BIBLE 72:9
Phayrisees: In them infarnal P.   LOW 319:3
pheasant: brake the whirring p. springs
   POPE 381:14
phenomenon: describe the infant p.
   DICK 180:16
Phidias: P. Gave women dreams YEATS 587:1
Phil: fidgety P.   HOFF 252:15
philanthropists: one of those wise p.
who   JERR 273:2
Philip: Appeal from P. drunk   ANON 4:22
hast thou not known me, P.   BIBLE 72:33
Let me see if P. can   HOFF 252:14
P. and Mary on a shilling   BUTL 118:7
P. fought men   LEE 313:13
Philippi: I will see thee at P.   SHAK 451:30
Philistia: P., be thou glad of me PRAY 393:18
Philistine: P. must have originally   ARN 16:3
P. of genius in religion   ARN 16:23
Philistines: daughters of the P. rejoice
   BIBLE 50:16
designation of P.   ARN 15:18
great apostle of the P.   ARN 16:6
P., and Populace   ARN 15:14
P. proper, or middle class   ARN 15:19
P. be upon thee   BIBLE 49:25
Though the P. may jostle   GILB 227:23
Philistinism: P.!—We have not the
expression   ARN 16:4
Philologists: P. who chase   COWP 166:18
Philosophen: Wie ich den P. verstehe
   NIET 363:5
philosopher: any p.-kings in England
   MACN 326:5

guide, p., and friend   POPE 380:4
he was a shrewd p.   BUTL 117:18
nothing so absurd but some p.   CIC 151:17
old p. is still among us   MAC 324:14
P., sir   DICK 181:24
P.!—a fingering slave   WORD 580:3
same time a profound p.   COL 157:24
To a p. no circumstance   GOLD 232:3
too in my time to be a p.   EDW 200:8
What I understand by 'p.'   NIET 363:5
will keep still with my p.   SHAK 454:26
philosophers: nation of pure p.   BAG 29:2
sayings of p.   BUTL 117:31
philosophic: years that bring the p. mind
   WORD 579:13
philosophical: p. and more worthy of
serious   ARIS 12:10
p. doubt as to animal   COL 157:34
philosophie: la p. les éteint   VOLT 561:6
philosophre: al be that he was a p.
   CHAU 141:24
philosophy: Adversity's sweet milk, p.
   SHAK 483:11
All good moral p. is   BACON 24:28
are dreamt of in your p.   SHAK 431:23
Axioms in p. are not axioms KEATS 293:30
bullied into a certain p.   KEATS 293:22
fear divine P.   TENN 536:23
History is p. from examples   DION 184:9
How charming is divine p.   MILT 341:11
if p. could find it out   SHAK 432:17
little p. inclineth man's   BACON 25:24
love for p.   KEATS 293:29
mere P.   BROW 96:24
mere touch of cold p.   KEATS 290:27
natural p., deep   BACON 27:21
new p. calls all in doubt   DONNE 187:19
now-a-days professors of p.   THOR 550:7
P., in its more rigid   STEV 522:7
p. quenches them   VOLT 561:6
P., that lean'd on Heav'n   POPE 375:26
P.! the lumber   SWIFT 527:32
P. will clip an Angel's   KEATS 290:27
regions of p.   HUME 268:2
same p. is a good horse   GOLD 232:7
superstition to enslave a p.   INGE 270:6
This barbarous p.   BURKE 111:11
Unfit to hear moral p.   SHAK 486:30
Unless p. can make a Juliet   SHAK 483:12
phlegm: Spit out thy p.   HERB 247:3
Phoebus: P.' amorous pinches black
   SHAK 421:32
P. Apollo turned fasting   MER 337:29
P., arise   DRUM 193:26
P. 'gins arise   SHAK 428:10
Sweats in the eye of P.   SHAK 444:25
Phoenician: Phlebas the P.   ELIOT 205:6
phoenix: I knew a p. in my youth
   YEATS 585:10
like the p. 'midst her   BYRON 124:30
maiden p.   SHAK 448:3
P. builds her spicy nest   CAREW 130:20
p. moment   DAY-L 172:21
Phone: P. for the fish-knives   BETJ 42:19
Why Did You Answer the P.   THUR 550:30
phrase: doctor full of p. and fame ARN 15:12
England invented the p.   BAG 28:23
fico for the p.   SHAK 469:4
phrases: Certain p. stick in the throat
   RUSS 412:22
La mort, sans p.   SIEY 508:7
p. of your complicated   GILB 227:21
Taffeta p.   SHAK 457:15
phylacteries: p. of the Liberal Party
   ROS 408:17
They make broad their p.   BIBLE 67:22
Phyllis: neat-handed P. dresses   MILT 342:21
P. is my only joy   SEDL 419:10
physic: Take p., pomp   SHAK 454:16
Throw p. to the dogs   SHAK 463:3

physician: beloved p.   BIBLE 78:29
be whole need not a p.   BIBLE 65:23
died last night of my p.   PRIOR 401:4
die when death is our p.   SHAK 474:7
divine than the p.   SHAK 462:26
Every p. almost hath his   FIEL 211:22
Honour a p. with the honour   BIBLE 63:17
if you would call a p.   BACON 26:17
into the hand of the p.   BIBLE 63:18
Pale death, the grand p.   CLARE 152:8
P. art thou   WORD 580:3
P., heal thyself   BIBLE 69:17
Time is the great p.   DISR 186:11
physicians: It is incident to p.   JOHN 273:29
P. are like kings   WEBS 566:28
P. of the utmost fame   BELL 39:1
P. of all men are most   QUAR 403:20
physics: delight in p. pain   SHAK 460:19
physique: To a beautiful p.   AUDEN 19:7
pia: O clemens, o p.   ANON 10:19
pianist: Please do not shoot the p.   ANON 7:9
piano: black p. appassionato   LAWR 311:7
piano-forte: p. is a fine resource   BROW 99:3
pianola: p. 'replaces' Sappho   POUND 383:5
pibble-pabble: no tiddle-taddle nor p.
   SHAK 444:18
Pibroch: P. of Donuil Dhu   SCOTT 417:27
Piccadilly: walk down P. with a poppy
   GILB 227:23
picked: shall have my pocket p.   SHAK 440:4
picker-up: p. of learning's crumbs
   BROW 100:24
picket: p.'s off duty forever   BEERS 38:8
picking: hands from p. and stealing
   PRAY 388:17
Just as I'm p. my nose   AUDEN 21:2
p. dewy apples with your   VIRG 560:4
pick-purse: am no p. of another's wit
   SIDN 507:26
At hand, quoth p.   SHAK 438:22
pickt: not p. from the leaves   BROW 96:18
Pickwick: P., the Owl   ANON 8:5
Pickwickian: used the word in its P.
   DICK 181:22
picnic: to attempt a p. in Eden   BOWEN 91:6
Pictoribus: 'P. atque poetis   HOR 257:10
pictura: atque animum p. pascit inani
   VIRG 557:17
picture: Before my face the p. hangs
   SOUT 514:21
he fain would paint a p.   BROW 102:32
his p., but his book   JONS 284:17
It's no go the p. palace   MACN 326:8
like Mistress Mall's p.   SHAK 488:1
Look here, upon this p.   SHAK 435:6
p. of his father's face   FLET 215:28
p. of somebody reading   KEATS 294:16
p. plac'd the busts between   CHES 145:8
which a p. cannot express   BACON 25:27
your skill to paint my p.   CROM 169:24
pictures: all his p. faded   BLAKE 85:7
dead Are but as p.   SHAK 460:11
gold in p. of silver   BIBLE 54:26
Of cutting all the p. out   BELL 38:23
p. in our eyes to get   DONNE 188:22
they would never buy my p.   LAND 309:16
where the p. for the page   POPE 375:16
'without p. or conversations   CARR 133:14
pie: in a p. by Mrs McGregor   POTT 382:1
p. in the sky when you   HILL 251:3
Puesto ya el p. en el estribo   CERV 139:2
piece: p. of him   SHAK 429:7
surely a p. of divinity in us   BROW 97:4
Piecemeal: P. social engineering POPP 381:25
pieces: Is broken into p.   HOOD 254:22
p. are the phenomena   HUXL 269:6
p. like a potter's vessel   PRAY 389:18
thirty p. of silver   BIBLE 68:9
'Tis all in p.   DONNE 187:19
pied: p. wind-flowers and violets SHEL 503:18

pier: I walk'd upon the p. BARH 33:19
p. it is my fixed intent BARH 33:20
pierce: p. it BIBLE 51:38
pierced: p. my hands and my feet
PRAY 390:20
they also which p. him BIBLE 81:10
Pierian: drunk deep of the P. spring
DRAY 193:15
Pierides: Et me fecere poetam P. VIRG 560:7
pietate: reddite mi hoc pro p. mea CAT 137:12
pietatis: fons p. CEL 138:7
pieties: p. of lovers' hands CRANE 168:31
piety: between p. and poor rhymes
WILDE 573:38
each to each by natural p. WORD 578:10
mistaken and over-zealous p. BURKE 110:29
nor all thy P. nor Wit FITZ 213:7
this in return for my p. CAT 137:12
to p. more prone ALEX 3:15
piffle: are as p. before the wind ASHF 17:11
pig: are love not a gaping p. SHAK 467:21
they brought a P. LEAR 312:9
pigeon: I am p.-liver'd SHAK 433:4
Père, et le Fils, et le P. ANON 9:7
Pigeons: P. on the grass alas STEIN 518:16
pigges: glas he hadde p. bones CHAU 142:7
Piggy-wig: there in a wood a P. stood
LEAR 312:12
pigmy: p.'s straw doth pierce SHAK 455:20
pignora: dedimus tot p. fatis LUCAN 319:25
pigs: 'as p. have to fly CARR 134:9
of Epicurus' herd of p. HOR 258:16
whether p. have wings CARR 135:7
pig-sticking: He took to p. in *quite*
COW 163:16
pig-sty: kissed her once by the p.
THOM 547:11
pike: I'll p. out his bonny blue BALL 32:8
Pilate: P. saith unto him BIBLE 72:44
Suffered under Pontius P. PRAY 384:26
Pilates: gowned and spectacled P.
MACN 326:9
pile: hath made the p. complete TENN 536:25
p. Ossa on Pelion VIRG 560:12
to earn a monumental p. COWP 166:30
pilfering: p., unprotected race CLARE 152:11
pilgrim: loved the p. soul in you
YEATS 587:12
p. borne in heedless hum COLL 158:18
p., forth CHAU 144:22
p.'s limbs affected slumber CAMP 129:20
To be a p. BUNY 107:36
pilgrimage: Ere the days of his p.
LEAR 311:24
quiet p. CAMP 129:19
shall succeed me in my p. BUNY 107:38
thus I'll take my p. RAL 404:12
undergo such maiden p. SHAK 469:17
Who through this weary p. DODD 187:15
with songs beguile your p. FLEC 214:9
pilgrimages: longen folk to goon on p.
CHAU 141:8
pilgrims: Land of the p.' pride SMITH 510:24
strangers and p. on the earth BIBLE 79:33
Robinson Crusoe, and the P. JOHN 280:16
pill: When his potion and his p. HERR 250:12
pillage: Which p. they with merry
SHAK 443:9
pillar: are a well-deserving p. SHAK 468:5
cannot be regarded as a p. MELB 336:22
day in a p. of a cloud BIBLE 47:21
p. of state MILT 346:14
p. of the world transform'd SHAK 421:6
she became a p. of salt BIBLE 46:8
pillared: Freedom, the seven p. LAWR 311:12
pillars: builded over with p. of gold
BLAKE 86:4
four p. of government BACON 27:10
hath hewn out her seven p. BIBLE 53:27
I bear up the p. of it PRAY 394:25

With antique p. massy proof MILT 342:10
Pillicock: P. sat on Pillicock-hill SHAK 454:17
pillow: like a p. on a bed DONNE 188:21
sigh'd upon a midnight p. SHAK 425:9
softer p. than my heart BYRON 126:16
pillow-hill: That sits upon the p. STEV 522:20
pillows: I had two p. at my head STEV 522:20
P. his chin upon an orient MILT 344:11
Take thou of me smooth p. SIDN 507:21
To their deaf p. SHAK 462:26
pills: mountebank who sold p. ADD 2:28
pilot: daring p. in extremity DRYD 194:6
Dropping the p. TENN 532:14
P. of the Galilean lake MILT 343:11
to see my P. face to face TENN 533:4
pilotage: our lives in learning p. MER 337:20
Pilots: P. of the purple twilight TENN 538:24
piminy: miminy, p. GILB 227:26
Pimpernel: demmed, elusive P. ORCZY 365:7
pin: gives the web and the p. SHAK 454:22
little p. Bores through SHAK 479:11
pinn'd it wi' a siller p. BALL 32:11
p. up your hair with all CONG 160:37
set my life at a p.'s fee SHAK 430:25
Stay not for th' other p. HERB 247:11
pinch: death is as a lover's p. SHAK 424:12
They brought one P. SHAK 427:9
pinches: with Phoebus' amorous p.
SHAK 421:32
pinching: be paddling palms and p.
SHAK 491:9
In this our p. cave SHAK 428:15
pin'd: she p. in thought SHAK 489:7
pine: lover true for whom I p. WHIT 571:2
of huge melons and of p. TENN 542:20
of palm and southern p. TENN 533:5
p. within and suffer dearth SHAK 495:13
This spray of Western p. HARTE 242:26
We p. for what is not SHEL 504:23
pine-apple: very p. of politeness SHER 506:12
pined: p. by Arno for my lovelier MAC 322:9
sighed and p. and ogled THAC 546:3
Youth p. away with desire BLAKE 87:22
pines: acquaintance among the p.
THOR 550:50
p. are gossip pines FLEC 214:4
Tall arrowy white p. THOR 550:11
pine-trees: black and gloomy p. LONG 317:10
pinguem: Me p. et nitidum bene curata
HOR 258:16
pinion: Imagination droops her p.
BYRON 123:9
so poor a p. of his wing SHAK 422:15
pinions: race with p. skim the air
FRERE 218:25
Stayed in mid passage his p. SWIN 528:24
Pink: P. and purple Columbine SPEN 517:3
very p. of courtesy SHAK 482:23
very p. of perfection GOLD 232:22
pinkly: p. bursts the spray BETJ 43:12
pinko-gray: white races are really p.
FORS 217:7
pinnacled: There in p. protection BETJ 43:9
pinn'd: p. it wi' a siller pin BALL 32:11
pins: Here files of p. extend POPE 380:31
pintores: p. imitan la naturaleza CERV 139:1
pint-pot: Peace, good p. SHAK 439:13
pints: Love made him weep his p.
AUDEN 21:9
P. and quarts of Ludlow HOUS 264:13
pioneer: Never be a p. SAKI 413:9
Pioneers: P.! O pioneers WHIT 570:10
pios: si qua p. respectant numina VIRG 557:18
pious: p. but Mr Salteena was ASHF 17:9
this p. fraud GAY 223:3
this p. morn KEATS 291:8
well stored with p. frauds BURKE 108:14
pipe: different varieties of p. DOYLE 191:16
my small p. best fits my HERR 249:21
p. a simple song for thinking WORD 577:22

'P. a song about a Lamb BLAKE 87:24
p. but as the linnets sing TENN 536:12
p. for my capacious mouth GAY 222:7
P. me to pastures still HOPK 256:14
P. to the spirit ditties KEATS 291:4
p., with solemn interposing COWP 165:3
quite a three-p. problem DOYLE 192:3
Rumour is a p. SHAK 440:31
So put that in your p. BARH 33:18
thy small p. SHAK 488:3
piped: We have p. unto you BIBLE 66:3
pipers: especially p. BROW 103:20
five-and-thirty p. AYT 24:6
pipes: Grate on their scrannel p. MILT 343:13
Tho' he p. that supply COW 164:4
What p. and timbrels KEATS 291:3
piping: p. loud BLAKE 87:23
P. songs of pleasant glee BLAKE 87:24
sniv'ling and p. your eye DIBD 175:19
weak p. time of peace SHAK 480:18
pipkin: p. fits this little jelly HERR 249:21
Pippa: P. passes BEER 37:25
pippins: old p. toothsomest WEBS 566:30
p. until the p. squeak GEDD 223:32
Pirate: To be a P. King GILB 228:12
pire: C'est p. qu'un crime BOUL 90:19
piscem: Desinat in p. mulier HOR 257:9
pismire: p. is equally perfect WHIT 570:21
pissent: ...Les chacals p. au bas FLAU 214:3
pistol: when his p. misses fire GOLD 232:40
pistols: Have you your p. WHIT 570:10
piston: snorting steam and p. stroke
MORR 358:10
pistons: black statement of p. SPEN 515:13
pit: diggeth a p. shall fall BIBLE 56:2
have beat us to the p. SHAK 452:5
have digged a p. before me PRAY 393:15
know what is in the p. BLAKE 85:19
Law is a bottomless p. ARB 11:20
many-headed monster of the p. POPE 380:17
out of the horrible p. PRAY 392:1
them to the bottomless p. MILT 348:27
there is the sulphurous p. SHAK 455:17
they'll fill a p. as well SHAK 440:12
will go down into the p. BALIF 30:3
pit-a-pat: Makes my heart go p. BROW 103:17
pitch: bumping p. and a blinding NEWB 361:8
Of what validity and p. SHAK 487:20
that when you make p. hot DICK 176:10
toucheth p. shall be defiled BIBLE 63:2
pitch-and-toss: risk it on one turn of
p. KIPL 300:1
pitched: Love has p. his mansion
YEATS 584:19
pitcher: p. be broken at the fountain
BIBLE 56:11
pitchfork: Can't I use my wit as a p.
LARK 310:6
drive out nature with a p. HOR 258:18
thrown on her with a p. SWIFT 526:29
pitee: p. renneth soone in gentil CHAU 142:19
pith: p. is in the postscript HAZL 243:8
p. of an Indian cane ADD 2:11
pitié: se p. de nous povres avez VILL 557:4
pities: He p. the plumage PAINE 368:3
pitieth: father p. his own children
PRAY 396:17
pitiful: 'God be p. BROW 98:1
'twas wondrous p. SHAK 474:1
very p. BIBLE 62:21
were she p. as she is fair GREE 236:10
pitifulness: yet let the p. of thy great
PRAY 385:23
Pitt: O'er P.'s the mournful SCOTT 417:3
P. is to Addington CANN 130:2
pittore: Anch' io sono p. CORR 163:1
pity: by means of p. and fear ARIS 12:9
dint of p. SHAK 450:28
her that she did p. them SHAK 474:1
in myself no p. to myself SHAK 481:15

Is there no p. sitting | SHAK 483:18
It was a p. he couldna | ELIOT 200:11
knows some touch of p. | SHAK 480:20
know what 'tis to p. | SHAK 425:23
love nor p. nor forgive | KIPL 302:17
my childish wave of p. | BETJ 43:19
never a saint took p. | COL 155:20
P. a human face | BLAKE 88:7
p. and mournful awe | ARN 13:8
p. beyond all telling | YEATS 586:9
P. from blust'ring wind | LOV 318:19
p. him afterwards | JOHN 277:1
p. his ignorance and despise | DICK 180:10
P. is the feeling which | JOYCE 286:17
p., like a naked new-born | SHAK 459:6
p. never ceases to be shown | DRYD 194:17
p. of war | OWEN 367:11
p., then embrace | POPE 379:16
p. this busy monster | CUMM 170:11
p. 'tis 'tis true | SHAK 431:33
p. who has felt the woe | GAY 223:7
Poetry is in the p. | OWEN 366:30
some to have p. on me | PRAY 394:12
source of p. | CEL 138:7
Then cherish p. | BLAKE 88:4
yet the p. of it | SHAK 476:13
you should p. me | SHAK 488:13
pium: aliquem fieri posse putare p. | CAT 137:8
place: all in one p. | BOIL 89:11
all other things give p. | GAY 223:16
At the p. where 'e is gone | KIPL 299:19
could have no p. | BIBLE 63:4
degree, priority, and p. | SHAK 486:22
demand our own p. in the sun | BULOW 106:23
earns a p. i' the story | SHAK 422:18
ever set in a great p. | BAG 29:10
exalt us unto the same p. | PRAY 386:13
found p. at the great knees | SWIN 528:26
his p. know him any more | BIBLE 52:19
I go to prepare a p. for you | BIBLE 72:31
in all doth hold his p. | SHAK 449:25
know the p. for the first | ELIOT 203:2
Lord is in this p. | BIBLE 46:19
means get wealth and p. | POPE 380:9
Men in great p. are thrice | BACON 26:21
Never the time and the p. | BROW 102:24
our bourne of Time and P. | TENN 533:4
p. could no where be found | PRAY 391:29
p. for everything | SMIL 509:7
p. for the genuine | MOORE 355:19
p. I set out for | STER 519:9
p., not to live | BROW 97:3
P., that great object | SMITH 509:8
p. thereof shall know it | PRAY 396:17
pride in p. and blood | TENN 537:15
Rabelais dwelling in a dry p. | COL 158:2
right man in the right p. | JEFF 272:18
rising to great p. is by a winding | BACON 26:26
rising unto p. is laborious | BACON 26:23
rivers of water in a dry p. | BIBLE 58:30
spirit of the p. | VIRG 559:4
stand in the holy p. | BIBLE 67:29
suffer A man of his p. | SHAK 447:24
superior to time and p. | JOHN 282:7
that like that sort of p. | SHAW 497:23
till there be no p. | BIBLE 57:24
to keep in the same p. | CARR 134:32
Whigs *not* getting into p. | BYRON 123:33
world I fill up a p. | SHAK 424:24
placem: p. genus irritabile vatum | HOR 259:5
placeo: Quod spiro et p. | HOR 261:11
placere: p. diu nec vivere carmina | HOR 258:25
places: All p. | BROW 96:29
All p. that the eye | SHAK 478:16
Proper words in proper p. | SWIFT 526:20
Quires and P. where they sing | PRAY 385:4
slain in thine high p. | BIBLE 50:17
spiritual wickedness in high p. | BIBLE 78:10

were in their proper p. | TRAH 551:19
which built desolate p. | BIBLE 52:12
place vacante: fois que je donne une p. | LOUI 318:9
plackets: Dread prince of p. | SHAK 456:26
thy hand out of p. | SHAK 454:19
placuisse: Principibus p. viris non | HOR 258:21
plafond: inscrite dans les lignes du p. | ELUA 206:16
plague: from p. | PRAY 385:10
From the fiends that p. | COL 155:10
Make instruments to p. us | SHAK 456:5
p. come nigh thy dwelling | PRAY 395:22
p. o' both your houses | SHAK 483:4
p. of Greece upon thee | SHAK 486:28
return, To p. the inventor | SHAK 459:5
that's his p. | BURT 116:23
winter, p. and pestilence | NASHE 360:8
plagues: of all p. with which mankind | DEFOE 173:15
Of all the p. with which | GRAN 234:5
omit those two main p. | BURT 116:21
p. remain for the ungodly | PRAY 391:18
Plaguy: P. twelvepenny weather | SWIFT 526:11
plain: best p. set | BACON 25:26
common-sense and p. dealing | EMER 207:11
English cooking is that 'p.' | MORP 358:2
entrusted to 'p.' cooks | MORP 358:2
Fanny Kelly's divine p. | LAMB 307:31
great Gromboolian p. | LEAR 312:2
here as on a darkling p. | ARN 12:23
it is old and p. | SHAK 489:3
make it p. upon tables | BIBLE 62:1
my occupation to be p. | SHAK 453:23
not so p. | GILB 226:3
p., blunt man | SHAK 451:1
P. living and high thinking | WORD 582:9
plain man in his p. meaning | SHAK 467:19
p. man live and think no | SHAK 480:23
p. to uninstructed people | HUXL 269:7
remain p. Michael Faraday | FAR 209:20
rough places p. | BIBLE 59:5
shapes of sky or p. | SHEL 504:21
speak p. when counsellors | BACON 25:39
was pricking on the p. | SPEN 515:30
way p. before my face | PRAY 389:24
You are call'd p. Kate | SHAK 484:9
plainness: p. of speech is allied | ARN 16:13
plain-speaking: apology for p. with Mr Snagsby | DICK 176:7
plaintive: Perhaps the p. numbers flow | WORD 578:14
p. treble of the Treasury Bench | DISR 184:19
plaire: règles n'est pas de p. | MOL 353:6
plaisir: c'est que le p. de vivre | TALL 531:16
P. d'amour ne dure qu'un | FLOR 215:34
plaisirs: grands seigneurs ont des p. | MONT 355:7
plaister: candlestick upon the p. | BIBLE 61:5
plaisters: which there are no p. | GARR 221:14
plan: fulfils great Nature's p. | BURNS 113:21
mars creation's p. | CANN 130:3
not without a p. | POPE 379:1
on a new and original p. | GILB 226:6
p. the future by the past | BURKE 111:31
rebuild it on the old p. | MILL 339:3
rest on its original p. | BURKE 110:13
Planco: Consule P. | HOR 261:4
planet: born under a riming p. | SHAK 473:10
every wand'ring p.'s course | MARL 330:8
Jove's p. rises | BROW 101:9
p. of Love is on high | TENN 540:9
When a new p. swims into | KEATS 292:18
planetary: obedience of p. influence | SHAK 453:11
planets: heavens themselves, the p. | SHAK 486:22
other p. circle other suns | POPE 379:3
P. in their stations list'ning | MILT 349:2

then no p. strike | SHAK 429:17
planks: rotten p., slimy posts | CONS 162:1
planned: 'A whole I p. | BROW 104:2
Perfect the cup as p. | BROW 104:13
plans: foolishness with your serious p. | HOR 261:20
hopeful p. to emptiness | HOUS 264:21
plant: green p. groweth | CHES 146:18
p. and flower of light | JONS 285:8
P. thou no roses at my | ROSS 409:8
p. whose virtues have not | EMER 207:42
Sensitive P. in a garden | SHEL 503:22
That busy p. | HERB 247:20
time to p. | BIBLE 55:12
wicked p. | KYD 306:7
Plantagenet: where is P. | CREWE 169:18
planted: God Almighty first p. a garden | BACON 26:18
I have p. | BIBLE 75:31
p. a garden eastward | BIBLE 45:7
planteth: who p. a vineyard | BIBLE 76:6
planting: to find me p. my cabbages | MONT 354:14
plants: grow up as the young p. | PRAY 399:12
ladies are delicate p. | AUST 22:1
p. and flowers Ever sprung | SHAK 447:3
p. in mines which never | BROW 103:7
They are forced p. | JOHN 278:16
Trees did grow and p. did | BARN 33:32
plastic: Of p. circumstance | BROW 104:11
plate: drop a question on your p. | ELIOT 203:19
p. of turtle green | BROW 103:16
P. sin with gold | SHAK 455:20
silver p. on a coffin | OCON 364:22
plates: p. dropp'd from his pocket | SHAK 423:22
platinum: With bullets made of p. | BELL 38:30
Plato: Amicus P. | ARIS 12:12
Good-bye now, to P. and Hegel | MACN 326:5
lend an ear to P. | TENN 539:21
P. for a bashful young | GILB 227:23
P. is dear to me | ARIS 12:12
P. is never sullen | MAC 324:9
P.'s Republic rather than | CIC 151:16
P.'s retirement | MILT 350:8
P. than be correct with | CIC 152:1
P. the wise | TENN 541:23
P., thou reason'st well | ADD 1:24
taught out of the rule of P. | MILT 352:9
platter: cleanly p. on the board | GOLD 231:26
Platz: unseren P. an der Sonne | BULOW 106:23
plaudits: shouts and p. of the throng | LONG 316:21
Plautus: nor P. too light | SHAK 432:20
play: actions that a man might p. | SHAK 429:25
a' the p. was play'd | BALL 31:19
awkward thing to p. with souls | BROW 102:3
better at a p. | MOORE 357:5
Better than a p. | CHAR 140:22
cards and yet cannot p. | BACON 25:40
children with their p. | COWP 165:11
creatures sitting at a p. | SHAK 433:5
discourse than see a p. | BURT 116:30
ended is our brief sweet p. | THOM 548:3
Everything that heard him p. | SHAK 447:3
fool can p. upon the word | SHAK 467:18
good p. needs no epilogue | SHAK 427:8
have written a damned p. | REYN 405:15
I could p. Ercles rarely | SHAK 469:26
I doubt some foul p. | SHAK 430:15
Judge not the p. before | QUAR 403:15
let me not p. a woman | SHAK 469:28
little p. | DU M 199:6
noted that children at p. | MONT 354:17
old come forth to p. | MILT 342:22
our p. is done | SHAK 490:27

our p. is played out	THAC 545:29	'How p. to know Mr Lear
P. all your changes	ING 270:12	life would be very p.
P. it	BOG 89:7	p. sight to see
P. out the play	SHAK 439:19	p. thing it is to be thankful
p.'s the thing	SHAK 433:6	scorn of that p. land
p. the game	NEWB 361:8	so many p. things are
p. the game	NEWB 361:9	**pleasanter:** proves the p. the colder
p. the man	LAT 310:21	
p. the wantons with our	SHAK 479:16	**pleasantness:** Her ways are ways of p.
p. without a woman in it	KYD 306:9	
prologue to a very dull P.	CONG 160:29	p. of an employment does
refined p. of the imagination	BURKE 108:7	**pleas'd:** He more had p. us
rest of the p. may be	PASC 369:8	p. with what he gets
rose up to p.	BIBLE 48:3	**please:** after life does greatly p.
see that Interesting P.	BELL 39:10	are to say what they p.
sheets and p. with flowers	SHAK 443:17	coy, and hard to p.
sun and stars to p. with	SHAW 496:29	I am to do what I p.
that his p. is always fair	HUXL 269:6	Myself alone I seek to p.
They will not let my p. run	DENN 174:25	seeketh only Self to p.
what to say about a p.	SHAW 496:26	some circumstance to p. us
When I p. with my cat	MONT 355:2	strive to p. you every day
wouldst not p. false	SHAK 459:1	to p. thee with my answer
you cannot p. upon me	SHAK 434:21	To tax and to p.
Your p.'s hard to act	CHEK 144:26	Towered cities p. us then
You would p. upon me	SHAK 434:20	'twas natural to p.
play-bills: have no time to read p.		we that live to p.
	BURN 112:22	when he has ladies to p.
playboy: p. of the western world		Yet she never fails to p.
	SYNGE 531:5	**pleased:** All seemed well p.
play'd: be p. with and humoured	TEMP 532:9	apt to be p. as anybody
he p. at the gluve	BALL 30:17	in whom I am well p.
He p. so truly	JONS 284:2	p. not the million
That's sweetly p. in tune	BURNS 114:27	pleasing consists in being p.
play'dst: Thou p. most foully for't		praise to have p. leading men
	SHAK 461:6	**pleases:** Though every prospect p.
played: how you p. the game	RICE 405:23	
I have p. the fool	BIBLE 50:15	**pleaseth:** this age best p. me
p. the King as though under	FIELD 211:3	which it p. him to dwell
she p. it in tights	BEER 37:20	**pleasing:** p. consists in being pleased
Played-out: called P. and Done-to-death		
	TRAI 552:4	pleasure of p. inferior
player: p. on the other side is	HUXL 269:4	pleasure turns to p. pain
poor p., That struts	SHAK 463:6	**Pleasure:** aching P. nigh
There as strikes the P.	FITZ 213:6	because it gave p.
wrapped in a p.'s hide	GREE 236:12	cabinet of p.
players: men and women merely p.		capable of much curious p.
	SHAK 425:24	did p. me in his top-boots
see the p. well bestowed	SHAK 432:25	England take p. in breaking
there be p. that I have	SHAK 433:17	fading p. brings
playfellow: My p., your hand	SHAK 422:21	Forced her to do your p.
playing: from the purpose of p.	SHAK 433:17	general read without p.
on the p. fields of Eton	WELL 567:24	Green p. or grey grief
playmates: I have had p.	LAMB 308:6	grievous p. and pain
plays: he loves no p.	SHAK 448:21	hath no p. in the strength
he p. extravagant matches	GILB 227:7	Holland take p. in making
p. the king shall be welcome	SHAK 432:16	I have no p. in them
p. with them	CHES 145:26	I' the east my p. lies
plaything: child's a p. for an hour		lie doth ever add p.
	LAMB 308:14	little p. out of the way
plaything-house: is a little p. that I got		Love ceases to be a p.
	WALP 562:21	love of p.
playthings: Great princes have great p.		make a bait of p.
	COWP 167:19	make poetry and give p.
playtime: in the p. of the others	BROW 97:36	meant by the p. of life
plea: Good is the p. of the scoundrel		mind, from p. less
	BLAKE 86:7	mixed practicality with p.
necessity, The tyrant's p.	MILT 347:27	Money gives me p. all
Though justice be thy p.	SHAK 467:27	much p. in the reading
what p. so tainted	SHAK 467:10	my p., business
plead: p. that man's excuse	ANON 7:24	necessity of giving p.
which I would not p.	SHAK 463:18	no p. if it were realized
pleasance: Youth is full of p.	SHAK 492:13	no verse can give p.
pleasant: abridgement of all that was		of all weren't to give p.
p.	GOLD 231:18	Of unremembered p.
do not find anything p.	VOLT 560:21	
England's p. pastures seen	BLAKE 86:16	
few think him p. enough	LEAR 311:20	
gets too excitin' to be p.	DICK 181:34	
green and p. bowers	BLAKE 86:12	
How p. it is to have money	CLOU 153:21	

LEAR 311:20	on by their favourite p.
SURT 525:23	painful p. turns to pleasing
KING 296:16	pay a debt to p.
PRAY 399:19	perfect type of a perfect p.
PRAY 397:5	p. afterwards
GASK 222:2	p. and repentance dwell
	p. and without one pain
BUTL 118:17	P. at the helm
	P., blind with tears
BIBLE 53:17	p. in the pathless woods
AUST 23:25	P. is labour too
ADD 2:3	P. is nothing else
SHAK 425:16	P. never is at home
SPEN 516:8	p. of having it over
FRED 218:22	p. of pleasing inferior
SCOTT 417:21	p. of the fleeting year
FRED 218:22	P.'s a sin
GAY 223:18	p. so exquisite as almost
BLAKE 87:19	p. was his business
SWIFT 527:22	public stock of harmless p.
SHAK 490:27	receiv't with p. thine annoy
SHAK 467:23	Refrain from the unholy p.
BURKE 109:9	some to p. take
MILT 342:24	suburbs Of your good p.
DRYD 194:3	Sweet is p. after pain
JOHN 282:27	then my heart with p. fills
AUST 22:9	There is a p. sure
SEDL 419:10	there is no such p. in life
MILT 348:23	Thou doubtful p.
CHES 145:23	though on p. she was bent
BIBLE 63:40	thy most pointed p. take
SHAK 432:23	thy p. they are and were
HAZL 243:22	treads upon the heels of p.
HOR 258:21	trim gardens takes his p.
	turn to p. all they find
HEBER 244:6	Variety is the soul of p.
HERR 249:17	What p. lives in height
PRAY 394:9	when Youth and P. meet
	Your horrible p.
HAZL 243:22	**pleasured:** What lively lad most p. me
CLOU 153:8	
SPEN 516:17	**pleasure-dome:** stately p. decree
KEATS 291:15	**pleasure-house:** built my soul a lordly
MAC 324:19	p.
HERB 248:2	**pleasures:** After the p. of youth
CAB 126:24	coarser p. of my boyish
MARL 329:1	common p.
ANON 7:22	English take their p. sadly
SIDN 507:28	Great lords have their p.
WEBS 567:6	gross and merely sensual p.
JOHN 280:25	has renounced those p.
SWIN 530:21	hate the idle p. of these
SWIN 530:3	In unreproved p. free
PRAY 399:20	is a hypocrite in his p.
ANON 7:22	Look not on p. as they come
BIBLE 56:11	memory of yesterday's p.
LEIGH 313:15	My p. are plenty
PRAY 391:13	other knows what p. man
WEVER 569:7	paucity of human p. should
BACON 24:14	p. and palaces though we
DRYD 196:25	p. are like poppies spread
WILDE 573:20	p. in a long immortal dream
SHAK 422:7	p. of thought surpass eating
BACON 27:29	p. of life is conversation
CHAR 140:24	p. that to verse belong
BEHN 38:12	p. with youth pass away
POPE 377:24	purest of human p.
HERB 246:27	still fresh revolving p.
HOR 261:11	understand the p. of the other
TALL 531:16	we will all the p. prove
MARV 332:4	we will all the p. prove
HOR 258:1	we will some new p. prove
BELL 39:18	with p. too refin'd
QUAR 403:8	**Plebeian:** this the P. bran
WYCH 583:25	
WORD 583:8	**plectuntur:** reges p. Achivi
MILL 339:17	**pledge:** I will p. with mine
HOR 258:25	ne'er refus'd to p. my toast
MOL 353:6	p. our Empire vast across
WORD 578:4	we p. to thee
	pledged: p. their troth either

VIRG 559:17
SPEN 516:17
ROCH 406:17
WILDE 573:20
THAC 545:17
RAL 404:8
TENN 539:22
GRAY 234:16
SHEL 499:9
BYRON 121:22
COWP 165:10
SELD 419:26
KEATS 289:29
HOOD 254:25
CLOU 153:8
SHAK 494:16
BYRON 122:13
HUNT 268:14
EDG 199:24
JOHN 281:36
SHAK 492:25
BELL 38:23
POPE 377:25
SHAK 449:15
DRYD 195:1
WORD 578:1
DRYD 197:26
BROW 105:31
GRAN 234:7
COWP 165:17
STEV 523:11
BIBLE 81:25
CONG 160:27
MILT 342:1
GREEN 236:2
BEHN 38:16
TENN 542:15
BYRON 120:21
SHAK 454:5
YEATS 585:20
COL 156:26
TENN 541:20
ANON 10:13
WORD 578:6
SHAK 451:4
SULLY 524:18
MONT 355:7
BURKE 108:7
SOCR 512:19
SHAK 480:19
MILT 342:16
JOHN 279:22
HERB 247:13
DONNE 191:2
HOUS 266:7
YEATS 585:16
JOHN 280:15
PAYNE 370:10
BURNS 115:7
KEATS 290:23
CLOU 153:21
SMITH 511:28
KEATS 289:27
SOUT 514:8
BACON 26:18
GAY 223:23
AUST 22:8
MARL 329:23
SHAK 495:16
DONNE 187:24
POPE 377:21
DONNE 190:23
HOR 258:12
JONS 284:12
PRIOR 401:10
HUXL 269:2
KIPL 298:10
PRAY 389:7

pledges: Fair p. of a fruitful tree HERR 248:20
Pledging: P. with contented smack
    KEATS 290:29
Pleiades: sweet influences of P. BIBLE 53:5
Pleiads: rainy P. wester HOUS 265:17
  weeping P. wester HOUS 265:16
Plena gratiá: there's Vespers! P. BROW 105:9
Pleni: P. sunt coeli et terra MASS 335:4
plenteous: harvest truly is p. BIBLE 65:29
  thou makest it very p. PRAY 394:2
plenteously: Endue her p. with heavenly
    PRAY 385:5
  p. bringing forth the fruit PRAY 387:2
plenteousness: all things living with p.
    PRAY 399:15
  p. with thy palaces PRAY 399:14
plenties: p., and joyful births SHAK 445:11
plentiful: Fish is p. and cheap LEAR 311:26
plenty: As it is, p. AUDEN 19:1
  delay there lies no p. SHAK 488:17
  hand with P. in the maize TENN 542:16
  just had p. BURNS 113:11
  on the expectation of p. SHAK 460:15
  P. has made me poor OVID 366:15
  p. to get DICK 182:22
  that here is God's p. DRYD 198:8
  Where health and p. cheered GOLD 230:16
plesaunce: hennes for to doon al his p.
    CHAU 142:32
pleuré: d'avoir quelquefois p. MUSS 359:3
  p., Voltaire a souri HUGO 267:13
pleurer: d'être obligé d'en p. BEAU 35:15
pley: Ful craftier to p. she CHAU 141:6
pleyne: deeth moot wepe and p. CHAU 142:17
pli: Quelque chose que sans un p.
    ROST 410:12
plie: fail of taking their p. BURG 108:5
  Je p. et ne romps pas LA F 306:18
plies: it p. the saplings double HOUS 263:14
plight: I p. thee my troth PRAY 389:4
plighter: p. of high hearts SHAK 422:21
plodders: have continual p. ever won
    SHAK 456:15
plods: ploughman homeward p. his
    GRAY 234:18
plot: devil does the p. signify BUCH 106:13
  excellent p., very good friends SHAK 438:30
  Gunpowder Treason and P. ANON 7:10
  Passions spin the p. MER 337:14
  p. for a short story CHEK 145:2
  p. thickens very much upon BUCH 106:14
  This blessed p. SHAK 478:20
  We first survey the p. SHAK 441:17
  women guide the p. SHER 506:24
Plots: P., true or false DRYD 194:5
plotting: p. in the dark COWP 166:30
  p. some new reformation DRYD 197:12
plough: bruised by no p. CAT 137:6
  Following his p. WORD 580:28
  must p. my furrow alone ROS 408:16
  put his hand to the p. BIBLE 69:25
  Speed his p. CHAP 140:5
  this morning held the p. BETJ 42:13
  wherefore p. SHEL 504:2
ploughing: 'Is my team p. HOUS 263:9
ploughman: Hard as the palm of p.
    SHAK 486:19
  p. homeward plods his weary GRAY 234:18
  p. near at hand MILT 342:19
  p. of bulls PROP 401:15
  Whilst the heavy p. snores SHAK 471:21
ploughs: names the rain-drop p.
    HARDY 239:10
ploughshare: Soldiers of the p. as well
    RUSK 412:9
  Stern Ruin's p. drives BURNS 115:19
plowed: had not p. with my heifer
    BIBLE 49:22
plowers: p. plowed upon my back
    PRAY 398:22

plowshares: beat their swords into p.
    BIBLE 57:19
  Beat your p. into swords BIBLE 61:16
pluck: p. it out BIBLE 67:5
  To p. me by the beard SHAK 455:2
  to p. your berries harsh MILT 343:2
pluck'd: p. the ripen'd ears TENN 541:28
plucked: p. my nipple SHAK 459:10
  We p. them as we passed HOOD 254:8
pluckers: which the p. forgot ROSS 409:13
Plucks: P. off my beard and blows
    SHAK 433:3
plum: confectionary p. COWP 166:5
plumage: He pities the p. PAINE 368:3
plume: Hector took off his p. CORN 162:20
  In blast-beruffled p. HARDY 239:7
  Ruffles her pure cold p. TENN 535:28
  saw the helmet and the p. TENN 538:11
plumelets: When rosy p. tuft the larch
    TENN 537:9
plumes: jets under his advanced p.
    SHAK 489:11
  Soil their fair p. with SPEN 516:32
  When p. were under heel HOUS 266:4
plummet: like a leaden p. FORD 216:15
plunder: Let no man stop to p. MAC 323:2
  Take your ill-got p. NEWB 361:11
  Was für p. BLUC 88:32
Plunge: P. it in deep water HOR 261:12
  p. the struggling sheep MAC 322:12
  p. your hands in water AUDEN 18:10
plunged: I p. SHAK 448:14
  p. himself into the billowy GILB 227:17
plunges: Orion p. prone HOUS 265:17
plural: Incorrigibly p. MACN 326:14
plures: Abiit ad p. PETR 373:1
Plus: P. ça change KARR 288:15
  p. royaliste que le roi ANON 9:9
Plush: would as soon assault a P. DICK 184:3
Pluto: won the ear Of P. MILT 343:1
pluvio: p. supplicat herba Iovi TIB 551:1
Plymouth Hoe: dreamin' arl the time
  o' P. NEWB 361:7
pneumatic: Gives promise of p. bliss
    ELIOT 205:14
Po: wandering P. GOLD 231:23
poacher: p. a keeper turned inside KING 297:8
Pobble: P. who has no toes LEAR 312:17
Pobbles: P. are happier without LEAR 312:21
poches: poings dans mes p. crevées
    RIMB 406:7
pocket: carry the moon in my p.
    BROW 102:13
  in your neighbour's p. RUSK 412:8
  in your p. or purse WILS 574:16
  not scruple to pick a p. DENN 174:24
  plates dropp'd from his p. SHAK 423:22
  put it in his p. SHAK 435:11
  shall have my p. picked SHAK 440:4
pockets: hands in holey p. RIMB 406:7
  pension jingle in his p. COWP 168:1
  rare in our p. the mark CHES 147:22
  young man feels his p. HOUS 265:2
Poe: P. with his raven like LOW 319:8
poem: author of that p. WOLFE 576:7
  drowsy frowzy p. BYRON 123:6
  had made one p.'s period MARL 330:11
  he fain would write a p. BROW 102:32
  himself to be a true p. MILT 351:18
  is a heroic p. of its sort CARL 131:12
  It is a pretty p. BENT 41:12
  like to be married to a p. KEATS 294:20
  long p. is a test of invention KEATS 293:13
  p. is like that of a painting HOR 258:3
  p. lovely as a tree KILM 296:3
  P. should be palpable MACL 325:13
  p. should be wordless MACL 325:13
  p. should not mean MACL 325:14
  p. unlimited SHAK 432:20
  p., whose subject is not CHAP 140:14

true ornament of p. MILT 344:18
poems: can explain all the p. CARR 135:23
  most sublime p. which either DRYD 198:6
  P. are made by fools like KILM 296:4
  ye are living p. LONG 316:8
poesy: force of heaven-bred p. SHAK 491:2
  golden cadence of p. SHAK 457:3
  immortal flowers of P. MARL 330:11
  indignation call p. vinum daemonum
    BACON 24:27
  overwhelm Myself in p. KEATS 292:7
  P. was ever thought BACON 24:19
  Sense and wit with p. allied BYRON 124:20
  viewless wings of P. KEATS 291:20
poesye: subgit be to alle p. CHAU 144:17
poet: apothecary than a starved p.
    LOCK 315:22
  because he was a true P. BLAKE 88:12
  better p. than Porson HOUS 266:18
  Buffoon and p. HENL 245:12
  business of a comic p. CONG 159:20
  business of a p. JOHN 282:6
  Byron is only great as a p. GOET 229:26
  consecration, and the P.'s dream WORD 577:4
  driven by a p.'s verses SIDN 508:5
  every fool is not a p. POPE 376:17
  God is the perfect p. BROW 103:4
  good p.'s made JONS 284:24
  Hero can be P. CARL 131:33
  Honour to the greatest p. DANTE 171:6
  I was a p. FLEC 214:23
  Like a P. hidden SHEL 504:19
  limbs of a p. HOR 262:2
  lover, and the p. SHAK 471:11
  Never durst p. touch SHAK 457:8
  Not deep the P. sees ARN 14:7
  On a p.'s lips I slept SHEL 503:5
  passionate heart of the p. TENN 539:28
  Perhaps no person can be a p. MAC 323:23
  p. and not a musician BUTL 118:32
  P. and Saint COWL 164:15
  p. and the dreamer are KEATS 289:28
  p. can do today is to warn OWEN 367:1
  p. could not but be gay WORD 578:1
  P.!—He hath put his heart WORD 582:13
  p. is like the prince BAUD 35:6
  p. is the most unpoetical KEATS 294:8
  p. like a pale candle guttering MACN 326:14
  p. ranks far below LEON 313:24
  p.'s eye SHAK 471:11
  p. sing it with such airs YEATS 584:10
  p.'s inward pride DAY-L 172:22
  P.'s Pen BRAD 91:13
  P. writes under one restriction WORD 583:8
  rights be term'd a p.'s rage SHAK 492:27
  shall be accounted p. kings KEATS 292:9
  shepherds call me also a p. VIRG 560:7
  should possess a p.'s brain DRAY 193:14
  Spare the p. for his subject's COWP 164:29
  that when the P. dies SCOTT 416:19
  They had no p. and they POPE 380:21
  they lack their sacred p. HOR 261:18
  This is truth the p. sings TENN 538:20
  'This p. lies SHAK 492:27
  Thus every p. SWIFT 528:5
  thy once-loved P. sung POPE 377:6
  Thy skill to p. were SHEL 504:24
  true p. that BROW 103:26
  Vex not thou the p.'s TENN 541:20
  was a poor p. named Clough SWIN 529:13
  was ever yet a great p. COL 157:24
  Was flattery lost on p.'s SCOTT 416:18
  were the dreams of a p. JOHN 281:8
  What is a modern p.'s HOOD 255:14
  what is left the p. here BYRON 123:1
  you will never be a p. DRYD 198:23
poeta: Agit pessimus omnium p. CAT 137:3
  Onorate l'altissimo p. DANTE 171:6
poetae: disiecti membra p. HOR 262:2

poetaster: I too can hunt a p. down BYRON 124:31
poete: grete p. of Ytaille CHAU 142:31
Le p. est semblable au BAUD 35:6
poetess: maudlin p. POPE 376:19
poetic: is a pleasure in p. pains COWP 166:35
Meet nurse for a p. child SCOTT 416:22
P. fields encompass me ADD 2:4
P. licence BANV 33:2
putting it was more p. NASH 360:3
which constitutes p. faith COL 157:22
poetical: gods had made thee p. SHAK 426:15
I have heard you are p. FLET 215:14
study in a worn-out p. ELIOT 202:19
to the p. character itself KEATS 294:7
poétiques: Licences p.. Il n'y en BANV 33:4
poetis: Mediocribus esse p. HOR 258:4
'Pictoribus atque p. HOR 257:10
poetrie: Jonson his best piece of p. JONS 283:28
poetry: all metaphor is p. CHES 147:29
Angling is somewhat like p. WALT 564:2
be the Polar star of p. KEATS 293:13
cradled into p. by wrong SHEL 501:13
difference between genuine p. ARN 16:9
friend he drops into p. DICK 181:4
grand style arises in p. ARN 16:14
Grotesque Art in English P. BAG 29:20
has never written any p. CHES 148:4
'I can repeat p. as well CARR 135:24
I didn't read the p. TWAIN 554:1
In p. ARN 16:10
In whining P. DONNE 190:15
It is not p. POPE 376:25
Made p. a mere mechanic COWP 166:27
make p. and give pleasure HOR 261:11
Music and sweet P. agree BARN 34:2
never the language of p. GRAY 235:22
Nothing so much as mincing p. SHAK 439:26
not of p. ARN 16:2
p. almost necessarily declines MAC 323:22
...p. begins to atrophy when POUND 383:21
p. comes not as naturally KEATS 293:25
p. he invented was easy AUDEN 18:15
P. is certainly something COL 158:1
P. is conceived and composed ARN 16:9
P. is in the pity OWEN 366:30
P. is not a turning loose ELIOT 205:18
p. is overheard MILL 339:20
p. is something more philosophical ARIS 12:10
P. is the record SHEL 505:12
P. is the supreme fiction STEV 520:15
P. is the breath and finer WORD 583:9
P. is the spontaneous overflow WORD 583:10
P. is what gets lost FROST 219:16
P. is when some of them BENT 41:2
p. makes nothing happen AUDEN 19:6
p. of earth is never dead KEATS 292:21
p. of Lord Byron they drew MAC 324:3
P.'s a mere drug FARQ 210:17
P. should be great KEATS 293:23
P. should surprise KEATS 293:24
p. sinks and swoons under LAND 309:10
p. strays into my memory HOUS 266:17
P.'s unnat'ral DICK 182:12
p.; the best words COL 157:32
p. women generally write BRON 93:17
p. would be made subsequent MILT 352:9
read a little p. sometimes HOPE 255:30
resuscitate the dead art Of p. POUND 383:1
She that with p. is won BUTL 118:1
smell of burned p. WOD 576:1
So p. DRYD 197:13
then P. and Religion CARL 131:7
unless we know it to be p. THOR 550:25
was trying to say was p. OVID 366:23
We may live without p. MER 338:6
we should drop into p. DICK 181:5
what is p. JOHN 277:7

What is p. RUSK 411:10
will make again, good p. MAC 323:30
word of true p. anywhere JOW 285:23
poets: All p. are mad BURT 116:17
all the pens that ever p. MARL 330:11
he the worst of p. ranks CAT 137:3
include me among the lyric p. HOR 259:10
Irish p. YEATS 587:8
Lunching with p. BETJ 44:12
mighty P. in their misery WORD 581:2
Milton's the prince of p. BYRON 123:5
'Painters and p. alike HOR 257:10
painters, p. and builders MARL 329:2
P. are...the trumpets which SHEL 505:13
p. better prove SHAK 493:8
p. exploding like bombs AUDEN 20:16
P.' food is love and fame SHEL 500:14
P., like painters POPE 378:16
P. Militant below COWL 164:16
P. of the proud old lineage FLEC 214:9
P. that are sown By Nature WORD 577:9
P. that lasting marble WALL 562:7
p., witty BACON 27:21
sensitive race of p. HOR 259:5
Souls of p. dead and gone KEATS 290:28
That the first p. had DRAY 193:13
Three p. DRYD 196:30
Three p. in an age at most SWIFT 527:33
true P. must be truthful OWEN 367:1
We p. in our youth begin WORD 580:28
When amatory p. sing their BYRON 123:14
While pensive p. painful POPE 375:15
with p.' being second-rate HOR 258:4
would be theft in other p. DRYD 198:3
your professional p. WELL 568:5
Pogram: 'To be presented to a P. DICK 179:21
poids: système de p. et mesures NAP 359:13
Poins: banish P. SHAK 439:18
point: Aloof from the entire p. SHAK 453:7
determining a p. of law BURKE 109:28
each to his p. of bliss BROW 105:20
more or less mad on one p. KIPL 304:33
'Not to put too fine a p. DICK 176:7
n'y en a p. de délicieux LA R 310:11
Point against p. SHAK 458:5
P. d'argent RAC 404:5
p. envenom'd too SHAK 437:21
They do not p. on me SHAK 477:6
thus I bore my p. SHAK 439:2
To p. his slow and moving SHAK 476:18
Up to a p., Lord Copper WAUGH 566:4
You've hit the p. PLAU 374:15
poising: p. every weight MARV 331:2
poison: coward's weapon, p. FLET 215:32
He drank the p. and his HOME 253:25
if you p. us SHAK 467:4
I go about and p. wells MARL 329:21
Our Adonais has drunk p. SHEL 499:18
p. England at her roots BOTT 90:17
p. imposed by the authorities PLATO 374:9
p. in jest SHAK 434:12
p. the wells NEWM 361:14
P. while the bee-mouth KEATS 291:15
potent p. quite o'ercrows SHAK 437:26
Slowly the p. the whole EMPS 208:17
strongest p. ever known BLAKE 85:16
sweet p. for the age's SHAK 452:10
poison'd: ingredients of our p. chalice SHAK 459:5
In the p. entrails throw SHAK 462:2
poisoned: crams with cans of p. meat CHES 147:20
p. air and tortured soil KIPL 300:6
p. rat in a hole SWIFT 526:24
poison-flowers: honey of p. and all TENN 539:29
poison-gas: We've got as far as p. HARDY 239:3
poisonous: its p. wine KEATS 291:13
p. damp of night dispunge SHAK 423:4

poisons: p. all the rest WATTS 565:23
poke: heart to p. poor Billy GRAH 233:13
Polar: be the P. star of poetry KEATS 293:13
pole: curses from pole to p. BLAKE 85:24
Heavens from pole to p. BLAKE 85:23
not rapt above the P. MILT 348:28
pole-axed: is no good he must be p. CHUR 150:27
Poles: few virtues that the P. CHUR 150:17
police: friendship recognised by the p. STEV 521:27
'I'll send for the P. CARR 133:11
'Leave Truth to the p. AUDEN 19:12
Policeman: must go back with P. Day KIPL 298:14
p.'s lot is not a happy GILB 228:19
terrorist and the p. both CONR 161:20
policemen: first time how young the p. HICKS 250:23
policies: We cannot restore old p. ELIOT 202:27
policy: either on religion or p. RUSK 412:4
foreign p. of the noble DERBY 175:9
My p. is to be able BEVIN 44:18
p. of the good neighbour ROOS 407:21
rugged brow of careful P. SPEN 516:26
some love but little p. SHAK 480:9
thought contend is the p. MAO 328:18
will be tyrants from p. BURKE 111:13
polis: pas le temps d'être p. MONT 355:8
P. as Polis OCAS 364:18
polish: we may p. it at leisure DRYD 197:37
polish'd: p. perturbation SHAK 442:17
polished: I p. up the handle GILB 228:4
p. and well-rounded HOR 262:10
p. corners of the temple PRAY 399:12
Who has a p. female friend WHURR 572:1
polite: costs nothing to be p. CHUR 150:21⁄2
don't have time to be p. MONT 355:8
His manners are not so p. KIPL 301:19
p. learning and a liberal HENRY 245:21
p. meaningless words YEATS 585:1
till the English grew p. KIPL 299:1
politeness: Hope, p., the blowing FORS 217:8
mutual glance of great p. BYRON 126:8
very pine-apple of p. SHER 506:12
political: accomplice in any species of p. villainy PEAC 370:14
called his p. Cave of Adullam BRIG 93:5
death of a p. economist BAG 29:12
healthy state of p. life MILL 339:10
is by nature a p. animal ARIS 12:7
nature of a p. party TROL 553:8
not regard p. consequences MANS 328:16
off for fear of P. Economy SELL 420:6
p. blank cheque GOSC 233:2
'P. power grows out MAO 328:19
'Principles of P. Economy' BENT 41:8
remembrance of p. affairs MAC 324:22
schemes of p. improvement JOHN 275:29
politician: Every p. ought to sacrifice BURKE 111:26
lief be a Brownist as a p. SHAK 489:29
like a scurvy p. SHAK 455:21
might be the pate of a p. SHAK 436:27
when a p. does get MARQ 331:1
(which makes the p. wise POPE 381:7
politicians: fault of our p. TROL 553:4
Old p. chew on wisdom past POPE 377:14
race of p. put together SWIFT 526:6
politics: Confound their p. CAREY 130:25
everyday p. than a Chatham BAG 28:25
From p. AUST 23:6
gallantry than it has with p. SHER 506:6
give his mind to p. SHAW 496:4
his amusements, like his p. CHUR 149:20
History is past p. SEEL 419:17
holy mistaken zeal in p. JUN 287:4
In p. COL 158:3
Magnanimity in p. is not BURKE 110:6

mule of p. that engenders   DISR 185:41
not the language of p.   DISR 184:22
now in the centre of p.   MOSL 358:19
Philistine of genius in p.   ARN 16:23
P. and the pulpit are terms   BURKE 111:2
p. and little else beside   CAMP 128:13
P. are now nothing more   JOHN 276:29
p. in boil'd and roast   SMITH 512:6
p. in the East may be defined   DISR 186:5
p. in the East is not an exact science   BISM 84:19
P. is not an exact science   BISM 84:19
P. is not a science...but   BISM 84:24
P. is perhaps the only   STEV 521:6
P. we bar   GILB 228:25
That p. go by the weather   GREEN 235:29
They p. like ours profess   GREEN 235:27
They shoved him into p.   BELL 39:5
week is a long time in p.   WILS 574:18
Politik: *P. ist keine exakte Wissenschaft*   BISM 84:19
pollertics: My p., like my religion   WARD 564:21
polluted: fountain is choked up and p.   BURKE 111:15
   her that is filthy and p.   BIBLE 61:27
pollution: unsavoury engine of p.   SPAR 514:23
Polly: Our P. is a sad slut   GAY 222:12
P. put the kettle   DICK 175:26
polly-wog: like a p.'s tail   WARD 564:30
polygamy: Before p. was made a sin   DRYD 194:1
   chaste p.   CAREW 130:15
Polygony: Or Panachaea, or P.   SPEN 516:15
Pomegranate: from Browning some 'P.   BROW 98:3
   of a p. within thy locks   BIBLE 56:26
Pomeranian: bones of a single P. grenadier   BISM 84:22
Pomp: after Sultan with his P.   FITZ 212:13
all our p. of yesterday   KIPL 302:8
grinning at his p.   SHAK 479:11
it has all his p.   BURKE 112:14
nor the tide of p.   SHAK 444:25
p., and circumstance   SHAK 475:25
p. and glory of this world   SHAK 447:9
p. and plenty   JOHN 279:28
P. ascended jubilant   MILT 349:2
p. of a too-credulous day   WORD 582:4
p. of pow'r   GRAY 234:21
possess'd with double p.   SHAK 452:25
slave of p.   SAV 415:5
Take physic, p.   SHAK 454:16
what is p.   SHAK 446:22
'with p. of waters   WORD 582:2
world of p. and state   BEAU 36:1
Pompeii: like a town crier in P.   THOM 546:7
Pompey: base of P.'s statua   SHAK 450:28
great P. Would stand   SHAK 421:32
Knew you not P.   SHAK 448:6
wars of P. the Great   SHAK 444:18
pompous: p. in the grave   BROW 97:23
pomps: p. and vanity of this wicked   PRAY 388:13
will the high Midsummer p.   ARN 15:6
pond: Four ducks on a p.   ALL 3:21
have their stream and p.   BROO 94:10
mantle like a standing p.   SHAK 465:12
p. edged with grayish leaves   HARDY 240:10
will find by hedge or p.   HOUS 262:19
ponies: Five and twenty p.   KIPL 302:22
Her p. have swallowed their   BETJ 42:21
wretched, blind, pit p.   HODG 252:2
pont: *p. Mirabeau coule la Seine*   APOL 11:11
ponts: *de coucher sous les p.*   FRAN 217:26
pool: it must first fill a p.   BACON 26:33
pooled: mussel p. and the heron   THOM 547:6
pools: p. are filled with water   PRAY 395:12
   Where the p. are bright   HOGG 252:23
poop: p. was beaten gold   SHAK 422:2
poor: angry and p. and happy   CHES 147:22

apt the p. are to be proud   SHAK 489:23
Blessed are the p. in spirit   BIBLE 64:6
bring in hither the p.   BIBLE 70:12
congregation of the p.   PRAY 394:24
considereth the p. and needy   PRAY 392:4
cottages of the p.   HOR 259:13
destruction of the p. is   BIBLE 53:30
else his dear papa is p.   STEV 522:21
feel for the p.   LAND 308:16
given to the p.   BIBLE 72:25
give to the p.   BIBLE 67:9
Good to the p.   CAREW 130:14
grind the faces of the p.   BIBLE 57:20
have their p. relations   DICK 176:19
how p. a thing is man   DAN 170:21
I am p. even in thanks   SHAK 432:14
I can dare to be p.   GAY 223:25
I have very p. and unhappy   SHAK 474:23
it inconvenient to be p.   COWP 164:26
Laws grind the p.   GOLD 231:29
letters for the p.   AUDEN 20:1
little more than the p.   SMITH 509:9
makes me p. indeed   SHAK 475:16
marry a rich woman as a p.   THAC 545:14
murmuring p.   COWP 168:14
my goods to feed the p.   BIBLE 76:14
one of the undeserving p.   SHAW 498:14
open to the p. and the rich   ANON 4:13
Plenty has made me p.   OVID 366:15
p., ailing and ignorant   YEATS 585:3
p. always ye have with   BIBLE 72:26
p., And Thou within them   HERB 248:15
p. are Europe's blacks   CHAM 139:17
p. centre of a man's actions   BACON 27:36
p. feeble sex   VICT 556:14
p. have become poorer   SHEL 505:11
p. in a loomp is bad   TENN 541:2
p. in their fireless lodgings   AUDEN 20:15
P. little rich girl   COW 164:1
p. man at his gate   ALEX 3:14
p. man had nothing   BIBLE 50:20
p. man is   HERB 247:9
p. man's dearest friend   BURNS 114:24
p. man slipped   BIBLE 63:4
p. soul sat sighing   SHAK 476:27
P. wandering one   GILB 228:14
Resolve not to be p.   JOHN 279:2
RICH AND THE P.   DISR 186:29
simple annals of the p.   GRAY 234:21
so p. that he is unable   HENR 245:13
specially dangerous man when p.   SHAW 498:22
that the p. have no right   RUSK 412:11
to the play with the p.   SMITH 510:18
train to accept being p.   HOR 259:9
virtuous p.   WILDE 573:23
When that the p. have cried   SHAK 450:19
which forbids rich and p.   FRAN 217:26
your tired, your p.   LAZ 311:13
poorer: richer for p.   PRAY 389:4
   ruined and the land grows p.   CHEK 145:4
poorest: p. he that is in England   RAIN 404:7
   p. man may in his cottage   PITT 373:29
Poorly: P. (poor man) he liv'd   FLET 215:27
poorness: When I mock p.   JONS 283:18
Pop: P. goes the weasel   MAND 328:10
Pope: Better to err with P.   BYRON 124:19
burning of a P.   DRYD 197:5
Poor P. will grieve a month   SWIFT 527:23
P., and all their school   ARN 16:9
P. composes with his eye   ARN 16:12
P.! How many divisions   STAL 517:16
Popery: antiquity inclines a man to P.   FULL 220:14
never be in danger of P.   ADD 2:19
popinjay: So pester'd with a p.   SHAK 438:15
Popish: P. liturgy   PITT 373:25
poppies: Drows'd with the fume of p.   KEATS 293:6
Flanders fields the p.   MCCR 324:30

pleasures are like p. spread   BURNS 115:7
...'p. was nothing to it   DICK 182:31
poppy: flushed print in a p. there   THOM 548:27
Piccadilly with a p. or a lily   GILB 227:23
p., nor mandragora   SHAK 475:24
Pops: classical Monday P.   GILB 227:6
Populace: P.; and America is just   ARN 15:14
propriety give the name of P.   ARN 15:20
popular: base, common and p.   SHAK 444:16
p. humanity is treason   ADD 1:21
popularity: even his darling p.   BURKE 110:26
every difficulty except p.   WILDE 574:1
Population: P., when unchecked   MALT 328:9
single and only talked of p.   GOLD 232:32
populi: *Salus p. suprema*   CIC 151:19
Salus p. suprema lex   SELD 419:25
Vox p.   ALC 3:9
populus: *p. Romanus unam cervicem*   CAL 127:6
porcelain: dainty rogue in p.   MER 337:30
porches: In the p. of mine ears   SHAK 431:11
porcum: *voles Epicuri de grege p.*   HOR 258:16
pores: I pass through the p.   SHEL 500:7
pork: pickled p. they loaded   THAC 545:32
Porlock: person on business from P.   COL 156:25
porpentine: quills upon the fretful p.   SHAK 431:5
porpoise: 'There's a p. close behind   CARR 134:13
porridge: comfort like cold p.   SHAK 485:3
What p. had John Keats   BROW 103:27
porringer: I take my little p.   WORD 583:6
Porson: better poet than P.   HOUS 266:18
port: Alma Mater lie dissolv'd in p.   POPE 375:21
buried him the little p.   TENN 533:11
claret that 'it would be p.   BENT 41:11
every p. he finds a wife   BICK 84:3
ev'ry p. a mistress find   GAY 223:29
Go fetch a pint of p.   TENN 544:9
In every p. a wife   DIBD 175:18
Let him drink p.   HOME 253:25
p. after stormy seas   SPEN 516:3
p. for men   JOHN 278:7
p. is near   WHIT 570:7
Still bent to make some p.   ARN 15:2
There lies the p.   TENN 544:3
with our sprightly p.   SHAK 423:10
portabit: *libenter crucem portas p.*   THOM 546:14
portable: Get hold of p. property   DICK 178:11
P., and compendious oceans   CRAS 169:12
portae: *Sunt geminae Somni p.*   VIRG 559:3
portal: fiery p. of the east   SHAK 479:12
portals: are the p. of discovery   JOYCE 286:27
portcullis: Let the p. fall   SCOTT 417:18
portent: p. to the historians   KEYN 295:16
portents: These are p.   SHAK 477:6
porter: all p. and skittles   DICK 182:32
I'll devil-p. it no further   SHAK 460:17
p. of hell-gate he should   SHAK 460:15
She curs'd Cole P. too   COW 163:22
shone bright on Mrs P.   ELIOT 204:27
porters: poor mechanic p. crowding   SHAK 443:9
Portia: P. is Brutus' harlot   SHAK 449:15
Portion: P. of that around me   BYRON 120:35
p. of that unknown plain   HARDY 239:9
shall be their p. to drink   PRAY 389:31
they may be a p. for foxes   PRAY 393:22
portioned: Then lands were fairly p.   MAC 322:18
portmanteau: You see it's like a p.   CARR 135:28
portrait: p. (in frame) of the Bishop-Elect   KNOX 305:23
p. of a dog that I know   JOHN 280:19

p. of a blinking idiot   SHAK 466:21
two styles of p. painting   DICK 180:6
portraiture: face that left no p. behind
   SASS 415:3
portress: p. foul to see   HOUS 265:5
ports: five p. of knowledge   BROW 95:19
p. of slumber open wide   SHAK 442:17
posing: involves p. as a page-boy   WEST 569:1
position: Every p. must be held   HAIG 237:11
positions: p. of considerable emolument
   GAIS 220:25
positive: p. men are the most credulous
   POPE 381:22
They live by p. goals   BERL 41:23
possédais: chercherais pas si tu ne me
p.   PASC 369:13
possess: meek-spirited shall p. the earth
   PRAY 391:27
patience p. ye your souls   BIBLE 71:5
P. thy heart   BRID 92:21
thou dost p.   SHEL 504:1
possess'd: regain Love once p.   MILT 350:25
possessed: endure what it once p.
   SHEL 501:22
limited in order to be p.   BURKE 110:12
p. all the universe together   SHAW 496:30
p. his land   BIBLE 48:12
Webster was much p. by death   ELIOT 205:13
possessing: art too dear for my p.
   SHAK 494:13
Beauty by constraint, p.   GAY 222:9
yet p. all things   BIBLE 77:8
possession: in p. so   SHAK 495:7
one equal p.   DONNE 191:3
p. of truth as of a city   BROW 96:6
p. of the same   PRAY 400:12
p. of it is intolerable   VANB 555:2
P. without obligation   MER 337:32
single man in p.   AUST 23:11
possessions: are behind the great p.
   JAMES 271:23
he had great p.   BIBLE 67:10
many p. will you be right   HOR 261:19
possessor: Hell Receive thy new p.
   MILT 345:10
possibilites: preferred to improbable p.
   ARIS 12:11
possibilities: To believe only p.   BROW 96:24
Possibility: Permanent P. of Sensation
   STEV 522:7
sceptic to deny the p.   HUXL 269:14
possible: effecting of all things p.
   BACON 28:6
exhaust the realm of the p.   PIND 373:15
if a thing is p.   CAL 127:9
Politics is the art of the p.   BISM 84:20
si c'est p.   CAL 127:9
with God all things are p.   BIBLE 67:12
possidentem: Non p. multa vocaveris
   HOR 261:19
possumus: non omnia p. omnes   LUC 320:2
Non omnia p. omnes   VIRG 560:6
possunt: p., quia posse videntur   VIRG 558:16
post: evil news rides p.   MILT 350:28
like a p. with packets   SHAK 447:24
place with only one p.   SMITH 511:18
P. coitum omne animal   ANON 10:17
p. o'er Land and Ocean   MILT 351:10
p. of honour is a private   ADD 1:23
still as a p.   DE L 174:13
whose p. lay in the rear   ROSS 408:25
postal order: Bringing the cheque and
the p.   AUDEN 20:1
postboy: Never…see…a dead p.   DICK 182:38
post-chaise: driving briskly in a p.
   JOHN 277:15
poster: great p.   ASQ 17:19
posteri: Credite p.   HOR 260:12
posteriors: p. of this day   SHAK 457:13
Posterity: are the trustees of P.   DISR 186:33

have put mankind and p.   INGE 270:10
hope of p.   POWER 384:3
I would fain see P. do   ADD 2:27
looked upon by p. as a brave   CLAR 152:22
not look forward to p.   BURKE 111:7
that p. is a pack-horse   DISR 184:25
Thy p. shall sway   COWP 164:24
Posters: P. of the sea and land   SHAK 458:8
Post Office: stalked through the P.
   YEATS 587:2
post-prandial: sweet p. cigar   BUCH 106:11
postscript: all the pith is in the p.   HAZL 243:8
Here is yet a p.   SHAK 489:16
her Mind but in her P.   STEE 517:24
most material in the p.   BACON 25:42
Postume: P., Postume   BARH 33:8
postures: same our p. were   DONNE 188:23
posy: I made a p. while the day   HERB 247:24
I pluck a p.   BROW 98:34
pot: Another for the p.   PAIN 367:16
crackling of thorns under a p.   BIBLE 55:18
eat our p. of honey   MER 337:10
Joan doth keel the p.   SHAK 457:19
kettle and the earthen p.   BIBLE 63:3
There is death in the p.   BIBLE 51:26
three-hooped p.   SHAK 446:11
treasures from an earthen p.   HERB 247:12
who the P.   FITZ 213:11
potage: birthright for a mess of p.
   BIBLE 46:12
potash: birthrite for a mess of p.
   WARD 564:22
potations: Their dull and deep p.   GIBB 224:9
to forswear thin p.   SHAK 442:16
potato: bashful young p.   GILB 227:23
has a p. in his head   HARE 242:6
mouth like an old p.   KIPL 298:7
potatoes: small p. and few in the hill
   KIPL 304:29
Tired of digging p.   HARDY 240:19
potatori: Huic p.   ANON 10:14
potency: do contain a p. of life   MILT 351:21
potent: Extraordinary how p. cheap music
is   COW 163:12
p., grave, and reverend   SHAK 473:24
they are most p. in potting   SHAK 475:2
potestas: Nam et ipsa scientia p.
   BACON 28:11
potion: When his p. and his pill   HERR 250:12
potions: p. have I drunk of Siren   SHAK 495:6
Potomac: All quiet along the P.   BEERS 38:8
All quiet along the P.   MCCL 324:29
potoribus: Quae scribuntur aquae p.
   HOR 258:25
pots: beflagged jam p.   JAMES 271:34
have lien among the p.   PRAY 394:8
potsherd: Let the p. strive with   BIBLE 59:13
poor p.   HOPK 257:1
p. to scrape himself withal   BIBLE 52:9
Potter: Hand then of the P. shake   FITZ 213:10
pieces like a p.'s vessel   PRAY 389:18
P. and clay endure   BROW 104:10
p. power over the clay   BIBLE 75:14
p. round the garden   AUDEN 21:9
'Who *is* the P.   FITZ 213:11
potting: they are most potent in p.
   SHAK 475:2
pouch: spectacles on nose and p.
   SHAK 425:24
poule: tous les dimanches sa p.   HENR 245:13
poultry: prolonging the lives of the p.
   ELIOT 200:25
pound: love is worth a p. of knowledge
   WESL 568:23
that the p. here in Britain   WILS 574:16
pounding: Hard p. this   WELL 567:32
pounds: About two hundred p. a year
   BUTL 118:10
crowns and p. and guineas   HOUS 262:20
handsome in three hundred p.   SHAK 469:11

how many p. will you find   JUV 288:1
p. will take care of themselves   LOWN 319:21
six hundred p. a-year   SWIFT 527:28
Pour: P. into our hearts such   PRAY 386:18
p. out my spirit upon all   BIBLE 61:15
That I may p. my spirits   SHAK 459:1
poured: been p. into his clothes   WOD 575:28
I am p. out like water   PRAY 390:19
p. it on his head   BIBLE 68:8
pouring: more noise they make in p.
   POPE 381:20
p. forth thy soul abroad   KEATS 291:22
pourpres: p., sang craché   RIMB 406:9
poverty: crime so shameful as p.   FARQ 209:26
drink, and forget his p.   BIBLE 55:2
heart she scorns our p.   SHAK 446:4
In honoured p. thy voice   SHEL 505:6
me neither p. nor riches   BIBLE 54:45
misfortunes of p. carry   JUV 287:17
of the poor is their p.   BIBLE 53:30
p. and oysters always seem   DICK 182:2
p., but not my will   SHAK 483:26
p. come as one that travelleth   BIBLE 53:22
P. has strange bedfellows   BULW 107:6
p., hunger, and dirt   HOOD 255:6
P. is a great enemy   JOHN 279:2
P. is no disgrace   SMITH 511:27
p.'s catching   BEHN 38:17
quiet mind is worse than p.   TRAH 552:2
Slow rises worth by p.   JOHN 282:24
suffer so much p. and excess   PENN 371:14
to put up with rough p.   HOR 261:19
worst of crimes is p.   SHAW 497:6
povre: was a p. Persoun of a Toun
   CHAU 141:32
powder: food for p.   SHAK 440:12
when your p.'s runnin' low   NEWB 361:6
powder-blue: I was wearing my p. suit
   CHAN 139:20
powder'd: Still to be p.   JONS 283:27
powders: p., patches   POPE 380:31
power: absolute p. corrupts   ACTON 1:5
according to the P. of the Sword
   CHAR 140:19
accursed p. which stands   BELL 39:21
another name for absolute p.   WORD 580:26
balance of p.   WALP 563:27
Between his p. and thine   JONS 284:16
certainty of p.   DAY-L 172:22
chief p. in the State   CHUR 150:26
common p. to keep them all   HOBB 251:17
defy P., which seems omnipotent
   SHEL 503:15
depositary of p. is always   DISR 185:43
drunk with sight of p.   KIPL 302:9
every power a double p.   SHAK 457:8
feel all the pride of p.   BURKE 109:18
force of temporal p.   SHAK 467:27
friend in p. is a friend   ADAMS 1:7
from our hands have p.   WORD 581:5
from the p. of our senses   JOHN 281:24
good want p.   SHEL 503:2
greater the p.   BURKE 109:1
have most p. to hurt us   BEAU 36:9
have no hopes but from p.   BURKE 110:8
Him the Almighty P.   MILT 344:24
his fall from p.   BURKE 109:5
Horses and P. and War   KIPL 297:28
If some great P. would   HUXL 269:8
is girded about with p.   PRAY 394:1
Knowledge itself is p.   BACON 28:11
legislative p. is nominated   GIBB 224:22
literature of p.   DE Q 175:6
Lord of all p. and might   PRAY 386:19
nobility is but the act of p.   BACON 26:39
no more than p. in trust   DRYD 194:10
not exempted from her p.   HOOK 255:20
notions about a superior p.   SWIFT 525:31
of the p. of temptation   TROL 553:11
once intoxicated with p.   BURKE 111:28

only purpose for which p.	MILL 339:7
penetrating p.	ARN 16:8
'Political p. grows out	MAO 328:19
p., and the glory	BIBLE 64:24
p. at the top and make	LUCR 320:6
p. breathe forth	SHAK 422:4
p. faithfully to fulfil	PRAY 386:7
p. is passing from	WORD 578:8
P. is so apt to be insolent	HAL 237:21
p. is the love of ourselves	HAZL 243:19
p. of beauty I remember	DRYD 195:32
p. of no calamity while	BROW 96:22
p. of the crown	BURKE 108:19
p. over the spirit to retain	BIBLE 55:25
p. that worketh in us	BIBLE 77:26
p. to hurt and will do	SHAK 494:15
P. without responsibility	KIPL 305:13
ravished me away by a p.	KEATS 294:27
repeat…that all p. is a trust	DISR 186:43
seek for p.	GOLD 230:22
seek p. and to lose	BACON 26:22
seeks to communicate p.	DE Q 175:7
shadow of some unseen P.	SHEL 501:5
supreme p. must be arbitrary	HAL 237:19
symbol of the p. of Heaven	MOORE 355:18
that have the p. to die	TENN 543:13
that p. belongeth unto God	PRAY 393:20
that p. should always be	JONES 283:12
them to have p. over men	WOLL 576:11
though stripp'd of the p.	SCOTT 417:1
Thou hast not half the p.	SHAK 477:14
Unlimited p. is apt to corrupt	PITT 373:23
virtue of that life and p.	FOX 217:23
who has the p. and skill	ANON 8:20
with Eternal God for p.	TENN 541:12
Wordsworth's healing p.	ARN 13:18
world desires to have—P.	BOUL 90:20
powerless: other p. to be born	ARN 13:8
powers: against p.	BIBLE 78:10
Headmasters have p.	CHUR 150:22
p. of a first-rate man	BAG 29:16
p. that be are ordained	BIBLE 75:20
P. that will work for thee	WORD 582:17
principalities, nor p.	BIBLE 75:13
Virtues, P.	MILT 348:22
ye heavenly p.	GOET 230:12
Power-State: conception of the P.	
	TEMP 532:10
pow'r: period, p., and enterprize	
	SMART 509:1
some P. the giftie gie us	BURNS 115:18
pox: on the gallows, or of the p.	WILK 574:6
Practical: P. men	KEYN 295:20
tone of the solid and p.	BURKE 108:16
practicality: has mixed p. with pleasure	
	HOR 258:1
practice: My p. could get along very	
	DOYLE 192:13
My p. is never very absorbing	DOYLE 192:4
not wear them out in p.	BEAU 35:13
P. drives me mad	ANON 6:18
without having good p.	JOHN 280:5
practis'd: he p. what he preach'd	ARMS 12:16
making p. smiles	SHAK 491:9
practise: p. medicine by a completely	
	MOL 353:12
prudence never to p. either	TWAIN 554:7
we shall p. in heaven	BROW 102:26
you would p. this without	SHER 506:2
practised: at seeing it p.	BUTL 119:13
practising: him p. the hundredth psalm	
	BYRON 126:10
praesidium: *et p. et dulce decus meum*	
	HOR 259:8
praeterea: *Vox et p. nihil*	ANON 11:6
praeteritos: *mihi p. referat si Iuppiter*	
	VIRG 559:6
praevalet: *et p.*	BIBLE 83:26
Prague: beautiful city of P.	PROW 402:2
praise: all song of p. is due	SIDN 507:24

alms of thy superfluous p.	DRAY 193:20
author may aspire to p.	JOHN 281:5
can p. too much	JONS 284:18
can stand a wast of p.	SURT 525:11
consent p. new-born gawds	SHAK 487:6
Damn with faint p.	POPE 376:26
dispraised were no small p.	MILT 350:4
envy is a kind of p.	GAY 223:15
free man how to p.	AUDEN 19:9
game of interchanging p.	HOLM 253:6
garment of p. for the spirit	BIBLE 60:9
going for p. to Mount Sion	BUNY 107:12
Hubert Stanley is p. indeed	MORT 358:16
if much of our p. is paid	JOHN 282:16
if there be any p.	BIBLE 78:22
is p.	ASCH 17:2
is the most perfect p.	JONS 283:22
It's not only this we p.	AUDEN 20:8
I will p. any man that	SHAK 422:13
lack tongues to p.	SHAK 494:20
Let a florid music p.	AUDEN 20:21
Let the people p. thee	PRAY 394:4
Let us now p. famous men	BIBLE 63:21
man's self is oblique p.	JOHN 277:33
man worthy of p.	HOR 261:17
mouth shall shew thy p.	PRAY 393:8
Nor named thee but to p.	HALL 238:9
only The Master shall p.	KIPL 304:3
paint 'em truest p.	ADD 1:15
p. him, and magnify	PRAY 384:21
P. is the best diet	SMITH 511:9
p. of his holy Name	PRAY 389:1
p.! praise! praise	WHIT 571:13
p. thee	PRAY 384:16
P. the Lord	BIBLE 83:11
P. the Lord	FORGY 216:21
P. the Lord, O my soul	PRAY 396:14
p. the Lord for his goodness	PRAY 397:7
p. the merit of a foe	POPE 378:32
p. to give	JONS 284:19
pudding against empty p.	POPE 375:13
rest a little from p.	SWIN 530:3
right p. and true perfection	SHAK 468:19
sea Of the deep p.	WORD 582:2
sickens at another's p.	CHUR 148:28
so double be his p.	SPEN 516:10
Some p. at morning what	POPE 378:26
song of thanks and p.	WORD 579:10
stir a little dust of p.	TENN 537:4
they only want p.	MAUG 336:3
They p. those works	MART 331:10
things thou wouldst p.	DE L 174:3
To utter all thy P.	ADD 2:20
unto thy Name give the p.	PRAY 397:17
We p. thee	ANON 11:3
We p. thee	PRAY 384:16
whom all men p.	COWL 164:12
world conspires to p. her	POPE 380:26
praised: 'And everybody p. the Duke	
	SOUT 513:20
be p. than to be pardoned	JONS 285:1
dog that p. his fleas	YEATS 587:4
'God be p.	BROW 98:1
p. him to his face with	TENN 543:4
p. the dead which are already	BIBLE 55:14
praiser: p. of the times that were	HOR 257:21
praises: faint p. one another damn	
	WYCH 584:2
His p. there may grow	HERB 246:26
p. a book becomingly is	LAND 309:9
p. everybody praises nobody	JOHN 277:18
p. from the men	COWL 164:12
Sing p. unto the Lord	PRAY 391:13
Praising: P. all alike	GAY 223:20
P. for oneself is that	BUTL 119:14
P. the lean and sallow	MILT 341:16
P. what is lost	SHAK 421:5
Railing and p. were his	DRYD 194:14
too near the p. of myself	SHAK 467:17
pram: than the p. in the hall	CONN 161:12

prance: man has a mind to *p.*	JOHN 275:22
pranks: do let heaven see the p.	SHAK 475:18
Tell him his p. have been	SHAK 434:32
prata: sat p. biberunt	VIRG 559:21
prate: stones p. of my whereabout	
	SHAK 460:1
prattling: infant p. on his knee	BURNS 113:5
pray: All p. in their distress	BLAKE 88:6
at the senators and I p.	HALE 237:12
doth late and early p.	WOTT 583:13
I am just going to p.	SMITH 511:26
If I could p. to move	SHAK 449:25
Men ought always to p.	BIBLE 70:33
nor p. with you	SHAK 465:28
p., and sing	SHAK 456:3
p. for no man but myself	SHAK 486:3
p. with Kit Smart as any	JOHN 274:24
P. without ceasing	BIBLE 79:3
remain'd to p.	GOLD 230:24
some to Meccah turn to p.	FLEC 214:12
this manner therefore p. ye	BIBLE 64:24
to fold her hands and p.	ROSS 410:1
To p. for her	SHAK 456:27
To whom the Romans p.	MAC 322:21
Watch and p.	BIBLE 68:16
we do p. for mercy	SHAK 467:27
pray'd: having p. together	HERR 249:28
prayed: thrusts the thing we have p.	
	BROW 97:28
prayer: are homes of silent p.	TENN 536:19
called the house of p.	BIBLE 67:17
fervent p. of a righteous	BIBLE 80:19
Four spend in p.	COKE 154:22
home-brewed p.	GREEN 236:1
In p. the lips ne'er act	HERR 250:11
is the most perfect p.	LESS 314:1
let the p. re-echo	LINL 315:8
organ to enlarge her p.	AUDEN 18:3
P. for all who lie beneath…	KIPL 298:8
P. the Church's banquet…	HERB 248:5
rises from p. a better man	MER 337:36
things are wrought by p.	TENN 535:26
Thou that hearest the p.	PRAY 393:23
'tis the hour of p.	BYRON 123:8
troubles me in my p.	DONNE 191:2
prayers: Christopher Robin is saying	
his p.	MILNE 340:11
feed on p.	PEELE 371:8
have the p. of the church	SWIFT 526:33
it for this I uttered p.	MILL 339:27
Knelt down with angry p.	HODG 252:2
Lord, hear our p.	PRAY 388:21
mention of you in our p.	BIBLE 78:30
of you always in my p.	BIBLE 74:29
p. in the hall and some	ASHF 17:9
pretence make long p.	BIBLE 68:37
Their three-mile p.	BURNS 115:23
This was one of my p.	HOR 262:9
which are the p. of saints	BIBLE 81:27
prayeth: He p. best	COL 155:30
He p. well	COL 155:30
praying: Amelia was p. for George	
	THAC 545:26
Nay that's past p.	SHAK 439:2
p., it spoils business	OTWAY 366:5
p., or meditating	THOM 546:11
prays: He p. but faintly and would	
	SHAK 480:12
to deny that faintly p.	QUAR 403:17
preach: An' could na p. for thinkin'	
	BURNS 114:28
p. it long	POPE 375:23
P. not because you have	WHAT 569:11
p. the gospel to every	BIBLE 69:2
should p. among the Gentiles	BIBLE 77:23
Then the Parson might p.	BLAKE 87:20
preach'd: he practis'd what he p.	ARMS 12:16
p. up patience	PRIOR 401:2
preached: p. to death by wild curates	
	SMITH 511:16

when I have p. to others   BIBLE 76:9
preacher: Judge not the p.   HERB 247:12
like the P. found it not   SHEL 504:5
p.'s merit or demerit   BROW 100:4
private advantage of the p.   BURKE 108:14
preachers: was the company of the p.
                                   PRAY 394:8
preaches: wife who p. in her gown
                                   HOOD 255:12
preaching: foolishness of p. to save
                                   BIBLE 75:29
God calleth p. folly   HERB 247:12
p. and living they may   PRAY 385:18
woman's p. is like a dog's   JOHN 275:10
preamble: This is a long p. of a tale
                                   CHAU 143:22
precedency: point of p. between a louse
                                   JOHN 279:8
precedent: From precedent to p. TENN 544:11
is a dangerous p.   CORN 162:23
p. embalms a principle   STOW 524:3
'Twill be recorded for a p.   SHAK 468:3
precedents: well to create good p.
                                   BACON 26:24
precept: more efficacious than p.
                                   JOHN 282:10
p. must be upon precept   BIBLE 58:21
precepts: love the p. for the teacher's
                                   FARQ 210:13
these few p. in thy memory   SHAK 430:19
precincts: Left the warm p.   GRAY 235:2
precious: adds a p. seeing to the eye
                                   SHAK 457:8
all that's p. in our joys   STER 519:12
can make vile things p.   SHAK 454:11
p. apothegmatically Pedant   NASHE 360:6
p. as the Goods they sell   FITZ 213:14
p. stone set in the silver   SHAK 478:20
thy p. Death and Burial   PRAY 385:17
precipice: antagonist over the edge of
a p.   BRAM 91:21
precipices: p. show untrodden green
                                   KEATS 292:25
precisely: thinking too p. on the event
                                   SHAK 435:30
precisian: devil turned p.   MASS 335:19
predecessors: One of my illustrious p.
                                   FIEL 211:9
Predestination: P. in the stride o' yon
                                   KIPL 301:2
predicate: logically p. his finish KIPL 302:4
we all p.   BEER 38:1
predicted: p. evil consequences TROL 553:5
predominance: treachers by spherical
p.   SHAK 453:11
preeminence: hath no p. above a beast
                                   BIBLE 55:13
of the Lord hath the p.   PRAY 398:1
prees: Flee fro the p.   CHAU 144:21
Prefaces: written nothing but his P.
                                   CONG 159:29
prefer: I should p. mild hale   SURT 525:20
p. not Jerusalem in my   PRAY 399:3
preference: p. and distinction of excelling
                                   CONG 159:29
Preferment: knocking at P.'s door ARN 14:12
P. goes by letter and affection   SHAK 473:12
preferred: therefore let use be p.
                                   BACON 25:34
who coming after me is p.   BIBLE 71:29
pregnancies: p. and at least four
miscarriages   BEEC 37:7
pregnant: Irish bull is always p. MAH 327:4
prejudice: Conduct...to the p. of good
order   ANON 4:28
nor do I behold with p.   BROW 96:28
popular p. runs in favour   DICK 179:35
P. of education   STER 520:4
result of PRIDE AND P.   BURN 112:19
To everybody's p. I know   GILB 228:27

prejudices: always be above national
p.   NORTH 364:2
bundle of p.   LAMB 307:7
his personal p. and cranks   ELIOT 205:15
it p. a man so   SMITH 511:17
not local p. ought to guide   BURKE 109:12
print such of the proprietor's p.
                                   SWAF 525:30
prelate: religion without a p. BANC 32:13
Prelatical: Presbyterial, or P. MILT 352:12
prelaty: impertinent yoke of p. MILT 352:15
premier: p. mouvement ne fut jamais
                                   CORN 162:18
que le p. pas qui coûte   DU D 198:28
première: qu'il faut mettre la p. PASC 369:3
premiers: p. mouvements parce qu'ils
                                   MONT 355:11
premises: conclusions from insufficient
p.   BUTL 118:26
prentice: Her p. han' she tried BURNS 114:4
preparation: feet shod with the p.
                                   BIBLE 78:10
Give dreadful note of p.   SHAK 444:9
no p. is thought necessary   STEV 521:6
prepare: good God p. me   PEPYS 372:21
I go to p. a place for you   BIBLE 72:31
p. himself to the battle   BIBLE 76:15
p. to shed them now   SHAK 450:26
P. vault for funeral   BEER 38:3
P. ye the way of the Lord   BIBLE 59:5
P. ye the way of the Lord   BIBLE 63:36
prepared: his hands p. the dry land
                                   PRAY 396:4
who hast p. for them that   PRAY 386:18
préparés: favorise que les esprits p.
                                   PAST 369:16
préparez: vieillesse vous vous p. TALL 531:18
preposterousest: To the p. end BUTL 118:16
Prerogative: almost dead and rotten as
P.   BURKE 108:19
English subject's sole p.   DRYD 197:31
last p.   DRYD 196:14
p. of the harlot throughout   KIPL 305:13
presage: augurs mock their own p.
                                   SHAK 494:21
presagers: dumb p. of my speaking
                                   SHAK 493:3
Presbyter: P. is but old Priest writ
                                   MILT 351:15
Presbyterial: P., or Prelatical MILT 352:12
presence: beautified with his p. PRAY 388:25
before his p. with a song   PRAY 396:11
festoon The room with my p.   FRY 219:29
his p. his clouds removed   PRAY 390:9
his p. with thanksgiving   PRAY 396:3
his p. on the field made   WELL 567:33
made better by their p.   ELIOT 201:27
me not away from thy p.   PRAY 393:6
perfect p. of mind   JAMES 271:29
p. that disturbs me with   WORD 578:7
was conspicuous by its p.   RUSS 412:20
What is better than p.   PUNCH 402:12
Present: act in the living P.   LONG 317:3
All p. and correct   ANON 4:15
ass when thou art p.   CONG 160:22
except the p. company   OKEE 365:2
his p. is futurity   HARDY 241:13
importance only to be p. at it   THOR 550:10
It's God's p. to our nation   KIPL 299:3
know nothing but the p.   KEYN 295:15
many as are here p.   PRAY 384:10
mirth hath p. laughter   SHAK 488:17
No time like the p.   MANL 328:12
offers no redress for the p.   DISR 185:37
p. and your pains we thank   SHAK 443:11
p. help in time of trouble   ANON 4:18
p. in spirit   BIBLE 75:34
p. is the funeral   CLARE 152:11
p. joys are more to flesh   DRYD 196:18
p. were the world's last   DONNE 189:7

Such p. joys therein   DYER 199:17
therefore take the p. time   SHAK 427:2
things which are just in p.   BACON 24:26
un-birthday p.   CARR 135:20
very p. help in trouble   PRAY 392:19
When the P. has latched   HARDY 239:1
presented: 'To be p. to a Pogram DICK 179:21
Présentez: P. toujours le devant au
                                   MOL 353:1
presentiment: she has a p. of it some
                                   STER 519:1
presents: bring p.   PRAY 396:5
Con-found all p. wot eat   SURT 525:14
isles shall give p.   PRAY 394:20
'P.,' I often say, 'endear   LAMB 307:3
preservation: p., and all the blessings
                                   PRAY 386:2
preserve: Lord shall p. thy going out
                                   PRAY 398:10
p. as in a vial the purest   MILT 351:21
P. it as your chiefest   BELL 38:23
p. the unity of the empire   BURKE 110:4
p. the stars from wrong   WORD 579:16
p. to our use the kindly   PRAY 385:21
what we give and what we p.   LINC 314:22
preserved: Federal Union: it must be
p.   JACK 270:30
my life is p.   BIBLE 46:25
Preserver: Creator and P. of all mankind
                                   PRAY 385:24
Destroyer and p.   SHEL 502:8
President: choose to run for P. in 1928
                                   COOL 162:9
P. of the Immortals (in   HARDY 241:25
rather be right than be P.   CLAY 152:28
Press: fell *dead-born from the P.* HUME 268:1
Freedom of the p. in Britain   SWAF 525:30
governs the periodical p.   TROL 553:13
have misus'd the king's p.   SHAK 440:9
I p. toward the mark   BIBLE 78:18
of our idolatry, the p.   COWP 166:13
p. is the *Palladium*   JUN 287:1
P. was squared   BELL 39:6
racket is back in its p.   BETJ 44:6
turned him about in the p.   BIBLE 68:32
pressed: p. at midnight in some YEATS 587:1
p. down my soul   PRAY 393:19
With face and nose p.   YEATS 585:3
Press-men: P.; Slaves of the Lamp ARN 12:19
presume: Let none p.   SHAK 466:20
p. not God to scan   POPE 379:12
P. not that I am the thing   SHAK 443:1
p. to censure I may have   BURKE 109:5
p. too much upon my love   SHAK 451:19
Presumption: You'll be Amused by its
P.   THUR 550:29
presumptuous: p. man   CANN 130:3
servant also from p. sins   PRAY 390:13
prêt: est toujours p. à partir   LA F 306:22
pretence: p. make long prayers BIBLE 68:37
p. of keeping a bawdy-house   JOHN 278:18
some faint meaning make p.   DRYD 196:34
pretend: does p.   BLAKE 87:5
p. to despise Art   BLAKE 86:9
pretended: p. friend is worse   GAY 223:13
Pretender: James II, and the Old P.
                                   GUED 237:5
who P. is   BYROM 119:25
pretending: p. to be wicked and being
                                   WILDE 573:5
pretexts: Tyrants seldom want p.
                                   BURKE 111:30
pretio: Omnia Romae Cum p.   JUV 287:19
pretty: do for p. girls   YEATS 585:16
He is a very p. weoman   FLEM 215:4
It must be so p. with all   WILDE 573:10
p. chickens and their dam   SHAK 462:17
p. follies that themselves   SHAK 466:14
P. fool, it stinted   SHAK 481:27
p. to see what money will   PEPYS 372:19

p. women to deserve them　　AUST 22:26
p. young wards in Chancery　GILB 226:2
Puts on his p. looks　　　SHAK 452:20
Which is p.　　　　　　　GILB 225:14
preudunt: My p. course is steadied
　　　　　　　　　　　　LOW 319:5
prevail: shall p.　　　　BROO 95:2
Should strive and should p.　NEWM 362:13
prevailed: they have not p. against me
　　　　　　　　　　　　PRAY 398:22
prevails: it p.　　　　　BIBLE 83:26
prevarication: in the last dyke of p.
　　　　　　　　　　　　BURKE 110:31
preve: assay ther may no man it p.
　　　　　　　　　　　　CHAU 143:28
prevent: p. harm to others　MILL 339:7
P. us, O Lord　　　　　　PRAY 388:6
way to p. seditions　　　　BACON 27:11
we have a right to p. it　　MILN 340:18
preventing: special grace p.　PRAY 386:10
prevention: p. from evil　MANN 328:13
some p. of abuse　　　　　PEEL 371:5
prevents: p. the rule of wealth　BAG 29:4
p. us everwhere　　　　　ELIOT 202:22
prey: destined p.　　　　SHAW 497:24
down alone bent on his p.　MILT 347:10
greater p. upon the less　　GREEN 235:27
made my pains his p.　　　SPEN 515:20
p. departeth not　　　　　BIBLE 61:26
roaring after their p.　　　PRAY 397:1
takes its p. to privacy　　MOORE 355:22
they not divided the p.　　BIBLE 49:13
thou soon must be his p.　SHEL 501:24
to hast'ning ills a p.　　　GOLD 230:18
whole fastening on her p.　RAC 404:4
yet a p. to all　　　　　　POPE 379:13
Priam: P.'s curtain in the dead　SHAK 441:1
proud as P. murdered with　YEATS 586:22
Priamus: 'En P.　　　　VIRG 557:17
Priapus: of P. in the shrubbery　ELIOT 203:28
price: found one pearl of great p.　BIBLE 66:21
have bought it at any p.　　CLAR 152:21
her p. is far above rubies　BIBLE 55:3
into abatement and low p.　SHAK 487:20
knows the p. of everything　WILDE 573:13
They raised the p.　　　　MAC 323:15
Up goes the p. of shoddy　GILB 225:30
without money and without p.　BIBLE 59:25
prices: contrivance to raise p.　SMITH 509:10
dirty and charging high p.　ELIOT 203:13
prick: If you p. us　　　SHAK 467:4
It is a p.　　　　　　　　PEELE 371:7
p. the sides of my intent　SHAK 459:6
pricking: By the p. of my thumbs SHAK 462:5
knight was p. on the plain　SPEN 515:30
Prickly: P. pear prickly pear　ELIOT 203:9
pricks: although small p.　SHAK 486:27
to kick against the p.　　　BIBLE 73:34
pride: ance his father's p.　BURNS 113:9
burning p. and high disdain　SCOTT 416:11
chief's and sage's p.　　　POPE 380:21
from p.　　　　　　　　　PRAY 385:16
great and their p.　　　　YEATS 585:8
here have P. and Truth　　YEATS 586:8
He that is low no p.　　　BUNY 107:32
I know thy p.　　　　　　BIBLE 50:8
maiden p., adieu　　　　　SHAK 472:22
my family p. is something　GILB 226:20
my high-blown p.　　　　SHAK 447:9
My p. struck out new sparkles　DRYD 196:13
my stronghold and my p.　HOR 259:8
name in p. and thankfulness　BROW 101:22
P. and pleasure　　　　　JOHN 279:28
p., cruelty, and ambition　RAL 404:16
P., Envy, Malice　　　　　LAND 308:17
P. goeth before destruction　BIBLE 54:8
p. in place and blood　　　TENN 537:15
P. in their port　　　　　GOLD 231:28
P. of Life that planned　　HARDY 239:4
p. of power sink and all　BURKE 109:18

p. of the peacock is　　　BLAKE 88:21
P. still is aiming　　　　　POPE 379:7
p. that apes humility　　　COL 156:13
p. that pulls the country　SHAK 475:3
rank p.　　　　　　　　　ADD 1:18
result of P. AND PREJUDICE　BURN 112:19
Shew'd erring p.　　　　　POPE 380:4
Such is our p.　　　　　　DENH 174:21
that perished in his p.　　WORD 580:28
that will her p. deflower　SPEN 516:13
Whenas May was in his p.　BRET 92:5
With Nature's p.　　　　　MARL 330:5
pridie: day that hath no p.　DONNE 190:26
pries: Which p. not to the interior
　　　　　　　　　　　　SHAK 466:19
priest: built to please the p.　BURNS 114:19
Delicate-handed p. intone　TENN 540:3
ghastly p. doth reign　　　MAC 323:1
huntsman and a fiddling p.　COWP 166:7
I will be thy p.　　　　　KEATS 292:3
my religion from the p.　　GOLD 232:41
No Italian p.　　　　　　SHAK 452:17
p. continues what the nurse　DRYD 196:19
P. did offer Christ　　　　PRAY 400:9
P. for ever after the order　PRAY 397:12
P. writ large　　　　　　MILT 351:15
still is Nature's p.　　　　WORD 579:5
sustained from one turbulent p.　HENR 246:1
Than he listen'd to the p.　BALL 31:11
visited by the p.　　　　　SHAK 490:24
with sir p. than sir knight　SHAK 490:15
priestcraft: ere p. did begin　DRYD 194:1
Priested: heron P. shore　THOM 547:6
priesthood: royal p.　　BIBLE 80:23
priestlike: moving waters at their p.
　　　　　　　　　　　　KEATS 292:11
priests: feet of thine high p. tread SWIN 530:7
P., and Deacons　　　　　PRAY 385:18
p. are only men　　　　　BROW 104:18
p. bear rule by their means　BIBLE 60:18
p. by the imposition　　　MAC 323:26
p. in gold and black　　　LAWR 311:5
strangled in the guts of p.　MESL 338:9
treen p. and golden chalices　JEWEL 273:14
with women nor with p.　SOUT 514:5
priez: p. Dieu que tous nous veuille
　　　　　　　　　　　　VILL 557:4
Prig: P., for my life　　　SHAK 491:20
priketh: p. hem nature in hir corages)
　　　　　　　　　　　　CHAU 141:8
prime: barmie noddle's working p.
　　　　　　　　　　　　BURNS 113:23
having lost but once your p.　HERR 250:6
laurel for the perfect p.　　ROSS 409:7
return the glory of your p.　SHEL 501:14
splendour of its p.　　　　SHEL 501:2
Prime Minister: next P. but three　BELL 39:6
Prime Ministers: P. have never yet been
　　　　　　　　　　　　CHUR 150:22
P. and such as they　　　GILB 225:29
prime-roses: pale p.　　SHAK 491:26
primeval: This is the forest p.　LONG 316:12
primitive: p. language of the law
　　　　　　　　　　　　BURKE 111:6
primordial: p. condition of liberty BAK 29:25
protoplasmal p. atomic　　GILB 226:20
primrose: p. by a river's brim　WORD 579:19
P. first born child　　　　FLET 215:21
p. path of dalliance treads　SHAK 430:18
p. that forsaken dies　　　MILT 343:15
Soft silken p. fading timelessly　MILT 344:2
that go the p. way　　　　SHAK 460:17
Primrose Hill: P. and Saint John's Wood
　　　　　　　　　　　　BLAKE 86:4
primroses: p. make a capital salad
　　　　　　　　　　　　DISR 186:15
Wan as p. gather'd at midnight KEATS 289:6
prince: companion a better p.　SHAK 441:1
Dread p. of plackets　　　SHAK 456:26
'God bless the P. of Wales　LINL 315:8

Good-night, sweet p.　　　SHAK 437:2
greatest p. o' the world　　SHAK 423:1
great P. in prison lies　　　DONNE 188:2
news and P. of Peace　　　FLET 215:2
p. and a judge over us　　BIBLE 47:
p. d'Aquitaine à la tour　　NERV 360:26
p. must be able to act　　　MACH 325:
p. of darkness is a gentleman　SHAK 454:2
P. of Denmark being left out　SCOTT 418:3
P. of the Latian name　　MAC 322:1
p., out of thy star　　　　SHAK 432:
Princedoms: P., Virtues　MILT 348:2
Prince-Elective: P. on the modern plan
　　　　　　　　　　　　CHES 146:1
Prince of Wales: nimble-footed madcap
P.　　　　　　　　　　　SHAK 440:6
princerple: I don't believe in p.　LOW 319:
princes: blaze forth the death of p.
　　　　　　　　　　　　SHAK 449:18
fall like one of the p.　　　PRAY 395:10
he might inform his p.　　PRAY 397:4
her p. are come home again　SHAK 453:1
mayest make p. in all lands　PRAY 392:18
of instructing p. to know　SWIFT 526:8
P. and lords may flourish　GOLD 230:18
p. have great playthings　COWP 167:19
p. to act　　　　　　　　SHAK 443:3
p. to the corridors into　　DOUG 191:7
put not your trust in p.　　PRAY 399:16
That sweet aspect of p.　　SHAK 447:9
whose merchants are p.　　BIBLE 58:16
princess: fitting for a p.　SHAK 424:16
P. of Parallelograms　　　BYRON 126:21
Princesse: Et j'aime la P.　ROST 410:13
principal: There were none p.　SHAK 426:14
principalities: against p.　BIBLE 78:10
p., nor powers　　　　　　BIBLE 75:13
principe: femmes est le p. général de
tous progrès　　　　　　FOUR 217:18
Principibus: P. placuisse viris non
　　　　　　　　　　　　HOR 258:21
Principilis: P. obsta　　OVID 366:20
principio: In p. erat Verbum　MASS 335:11
principis: Indignatio p. mors　MORE 357:13
Principle: active P.　　　WORD 577:17
except from some strong p.　MELB 336:15
first human p. I would　　SHAK 442:16
He does everything on p.　SHAW 498:6
killed hisself on p.　　　　DICK 182:35
precedent embalms a p.　　STOW 524:3
p. of the English constitution　BLAC 85:5
p. of beauty in all things　KEATS 294:28
Protection is not a p.　　DISR 184:15
rights is the basic p.　　　FOUR 217:18
something solid like a p.　CONR 161:23
subjects are rebels from p.　BURKE 111:13
That's a p. in life with　　SHAW 498:21
that sensibility of p.　　　BURKE 111:10
principles: Damn your p.　DISR 185:21
Freeport are of different p.　ADD 2:14
invariably from the highest p.　FARR 210:25
lordship's p. or your mistress　WILK 574:6
'P. of Political Economy'　BENT 41:8
p. of public morality　　　BURKE 108:16
p. of a free constitution　GIBB 224:22
religious and moral p.　　ARN 16:26
shews that he has good p.　JOHN 274:27
Their p. are the same　　JOHN 278:34
very sincere in good p.　JOHN 280:5
print: for to p. My book　HERR 250:15
I love a ballad in p.　　　SHAK 492:3
licence to p. your own money　THOM 549:30
news that's fit to p.　　　OCHS 364:20
P. it as it stands　　　　JAMES 271:24
p. of a man's naked foot　DEFOE 173:7
''Sdeath I'll p. it　　　　POPE 376:20
seeing our names in p.　CHES 147:22
still 'tis devils must p.　　MOORE 356:1
wickedness of the world is p.　DICK 179:15

printed: that they were p. in a book
BIBLE 52:30
printers: those books by which the p.
FULL 220:18
printing: hast caused p. to be used
SHAK 446:14
invented the art of p. CARL 132:12
P., and the Protestant CARL 131:3
p., gunpowder and the magnet BACON 28:9
P. has destroyed education DISR 186:21
p. thereby to rectify manners MILT 351:25
was in a p. house in Hell BLAKE 88:27
printless: that on the sands with p.
SHAK 485:23
prints: sporting p. of Aunt Florence's
COW 164:2
priority: degree, p., and place SHAK 486:22
prisca: Ut p. gens mortalium HOR 259:7
Priscian: P. a little scratched SHAK 457:11
prism: with his p. and silent face
WORD 580:17
prison: Came the hero from his p. AYT 24:9
Else a great Prince in p. DONNE 188:25
girl's p. and the woman's SHAW 498:3
He did grind in the p. BIBLE 49:27
In the p. of his days AUDEN 19:9
I was in p. BIBLE 68:6
just man is also a p. THOR 550:1
let's away to p. SHAK 456:3
lime-tree bower my p. COL 157:10
Lord looseth men out of p. PRAY 399:1
opening of the p. to them BIBLE 60:8
palace and a p. on each BYRON 121:1
p. for the colour of his HOUS 266:8
prison in a p. DICK 182:30
Stone walls do not a p. LOV 318:18
This p. where I live unto SHAK 480:13
prisoner: If the p. is happy SHAW 497:32
Like a poor p. in his twisted SHAK 482:20
make each p. pent GILB 227:5
passing on the p.'s life SHAK 463:16
p. of the Lord BIBLE 77:27
p.'s release SIDN 507:20
That takes the reason p. SHAK 458:15
Your p. admits the crimes PETR 373:4
prisoners: addiction and the p. of envy
ILL 270:5
p. out of captivity PRAY 394:7
p. underneath her wings SHAK 445:24
upon all p. and captives PRAY 385:20
Which p. call the sky WILDE 572:8
prison-house: Shades of the p. begin
WORD 579:5
tell the secrets of my p. SHAK 431:5
prisons: improving his p. in Hell COL 156:14
Madhouses, p., whore-shops CLARE 152:5
P. are built with stones BLAKE 88:20
P. of flesh DONNE 189:37
prius: quod non dictum sit p. TER 544:16
Sed haec p. fuere CAT 136:24
privacy: that takes its prey to p.
MOORE 355:22
private: first consult our p. ends
SWIFT 527:22
grave's a fine and p. place MARV 332:19
honour is a p. station ADD 1:23
invade the sphere of p. life MELB 336:13
P. faces in public AUDEN 20:12
p. reason for this AUDEN 21:1
P. respects must yield MILT 350:24
p. station GAY 223:17
p. view in the morning EDW 200:2
that p. men enjoy SHAK 444:24
to serve our p. ends CHUR 148:30
privates: her p., we SHAK 432:11
privato: Maior p. visus dum privatus
TAC 531:13
privileg'd: p. to be very impertinent
FARQ 210:22

privilege: Death is the p. of human
ROWE 410:24
power which stands on P. BELL 39:21
p. I claim for my own sex AUST 23:10
p. of doing as he likes ARN 15:20
p. of wisdom to listen HOLM 253:20
take the p. o' sitting down ELIOT 201:19
privileged: "Cos a coachman's a p.
DICK 183:2
P. and the People formed DISR 186:32
privilèges: L'extension des p. des femmes
FOUR 217:18
stand for your p. we know HEM 245:1
prize: Bound for the p. of all SHAK 494:11
judge the p. MILT 342:25
one receiveth the p. BIBLE 76:8
p.-oxen and of sheep TENN 542:20
p. the thing ungain'd more SHAK 486:21
Timotheus yield the p. DRYD 195:9
We do not run for p. SORL 513:10
prizes: to offer glittering p. BIRK 84:14
which in herself she p. CONG 159:19
prizing: past all p., best SOPH 513:8
P.R.O.: liaison man and partly P. BETJ 42:14
probability: p. is the very guide BUTL 117:9
Probable: P. impossibilities are ARIS 12:11
Probably: of all sits P. Arboreal STEV 521:10
probationary: Eden's dread p. tree
COWP 166:13
Probitas: P. laudatur et alget JUV 287:10
problem: p. must puzzle the devil
BURNS 115:2
problems: of its most difficult p. DICK 181:10
such p. as it can solve MARX 333:7
proboque: Video meliora, p. OVID 366:17
proboscis: sinewy p. did remissly
DONNE 190:3
wreathed His lithe p. MILT 347:26
proceed: all just works do p. PRAY 385:9
p. no further in this business SHAK 459:7
P. to judgment SHAK 468:5
proceedeth: Who p. from the Father
PRAY 387:11
proceedings: p. interested him no more
HARTE 242:33
process: force and beauty of its p.
JAMES 272:2
long p. of getting tired BUTL 118:25
We look at the p. POUND 382:15
procession: in a p. of one DICK 179:20
torchlight p. marching OSUL 365:24
proclaim: p. throughout Italy this CAV 138:1
proclaims: apparel oft p. the man
SHAK 430:19
proclamation: Thou art the p. DONNE 189:33
Proconsul: great P. MAC 323:19
Procrastination: P. is the thief of time
YOUNG 588:4
that to incivility and p. DE Q 175:5
procreant: bed and p. cradle SHAK 459:4
p. urge of the world WHIT 570:17
procreate: that we might p. like trees
BROW 96:33
procreation: ordained for the p. of children
PRAY 389:1
proctors: With prudes for p. TENN 541:27
procul: o p. este, profani VIRG 558:19
P. hinc OVID 366:9
P. omen abesto OVID 366:8
'Qui p. hinc' NEWB 361:5
qui p. negotiis HOR 259:7
Procuress: P. to the Lords of Hell
TENN 536:23
procuring: other means of p. respect
JOHN 276:38
prodigal: chariest maid is p. enough
SHAK 430:17
how p. the soul SHAK 430:21
oppression of their p. weight SHAK 479:17
that but once was p. before DRYD 196:2

who are p. within the compass IRV 270:23
yet p. of ease DRYD 194:7
prodigality: perennial spring of all p.
BURKE 110:16
prodigies: is all Africa and her p.
BROW 96:12
prodigious: p. armies we had in Flanders
STER 519:26
produce: p. it in God's name CARL 132:22
product: infinitesimal fraction of a p.
CARL 132:22
p. of the smaller intestines' CARL 131:7
production: p. of human nature ADD 2:9
productions: love with the p. of time
BLAKE 88:17
These modern p. ELIOT 203:7
Proelium: P. certaminis VEN 556:4
profanation: in the less foul p. SHAK 464:3
p. to keep HERR 248:24
'Twere p. of our joys DONNE 190:17
profane: Coldly p. COWP 168:13
p. one BRAT 91:24
p. the service of the dead SHAK 437:3
so old, and so p. SHAK 442:30
ye p. COWL 164:20
profaned: One word is too often p.
SHEL 504:13
they have desolated and p. GLAD 229:13
profani: o procul este, p. VIRG 558:19
profanum: Odi p. vulgus et arceo HOR 260:13
profess: p. and call themselves PRAY 385:25
p. any religion in name BURKE 111:20
profession: almost charmed me from
SHAK 486:11
my p. SHAK 486:11
ancient p. in the world KIPL 304:36
different branches of a new p. TROL 553:14
discharge of any p. JOHN 276:23
man a debtor to his p. BACON 25:16
ornament to her p. BUNY 107:35
panted for a liberal p. COLM 159:4
Professionally: P. he declines and falls
DICK 181:4
professions: have let in some of all p.
SHAK 460:17
p. are conspiracies against SHAW 496:21
professor: With that more learn'd p.
PORS 381:29
Zarathustra, sometime regius p.
JOYCE 286:28
professors: conscientious p. thereof
PAINE 367:23
P. of the Dismal Science CARL 131:40
p. of philosophy but not THOR 550:7
profit: all labour there is p. BIBLE 54:2
Have no more p. of their SHAK 456:15
in it no p. but the name SHAK 435:28
No p. grows where is no SHAK 484:4
p. and loss ELIOT 205:6
p. every day that Fate HOR 259:18
suffers the soul may not p. MER 337:28
To whose p. CIC 151:32
What p. hath a man of all BIBLE 55:5
what shall it p. a man BIBLE 68:34
When men write for p. WALP 563:15
winds will blow the p. MACN 326:8
profitable: it is not p. MARQ 330:24
profited: What is a man p. BIBLE 66:35
profiteth: it p. me nothing BIBLE 76:14
profits: It little p. that an idle TENN 543:21
nothing p. more Than self-esteem MILT 349:8
With p. of the mind SHAK 463:14
profligate: witty, p., and thin YOUNG 588:14
profonde: l'horreur d'une p. nuit RAC 404:2
profound: thro' the turbulent p. SMART 509:3
turbid look the most p. LAND 309:14
profundis: De p. clamavi ad te BIBLE 83:13
profundo: Merses p. HOR 261:12
profusus: sui p. SALL 413:22
Progeniem: P. vitiosiorem HOR 260:26

progenies: Iam nova p. caelo demittitur
VIRG 559:22
progeny: soul was whose p. they are
MILT 351:21
Prognostics: P. do not always prove
WALP 563:18
progrès: principe général de tous p.
FOUR 217:18
progress: emphatically the history of
p. MAC 323:12
It was no summer p. ANDR 4:7
nations trek from p. OWEN 367:11
party of p. or reform MILL 339:10
p. depends on the unreasonable SHAW 498:1
P., far from consisting SANT 414:1
P. has its drawbacks STEP 518:21
P. is a comfortable disease CUMM 170:11
P., man's distinctive BROW 100:11
p. of a deathless soul DONNE 189:34
p. of human society CARL 132:8
P., therefore SPEN 514:32
spoke of p. spiring round CHES 146:12
thievish p. to eternity SHAK 494:10
To swell a p. ELIOT 203:24
youth, viewing his p. SHAK 442:2
progressive: p. country change is constant
DISR 185:4
proie: entière à sa p. attachée RAC 404:4
projects: p. than for settled business
BACON 27:39
proletarian: substitution of the p.
LENIN 313:21
proletariat: dictatorship of the p.
MARX 333:11
prologue: thing to make a long p.
BIBLE 63:29
What's past is p. SHAK 485:5
witty p. to a very dull Play CONG 160:29
Prologues: P. precede the piece GARR 221:11
p. to the swelling act SHAK 458:19
prolong: Youth to p. YEATS 586:20
Promethean: not where is that P. heat
SHAK 477:5
spring the true P. fire SHAK 457:6
promis'd: I was p. on a time SPEN 516:21
weird women p. SHAK 461:6
promise: freewoman was by p. BIBLE 77:16
he was a young man of p. BALF 30:2
ill keeper of p. BACON 25:32
p.-crammed SHAK 434:4
P., large promise JOHN 281:19
see how truly the P. runs KIPL 303:10
threaten, p. WHIT 571:11
Who broke no p. POPE 378:6
Why didst thou p. such SHAK 493:11
promised: long-p. invasion CHUR 150:4
p. land seem older than FRY 219:23
whom he had p. to defend MAC 323:21
promises: According to thy p. declared
PRAY 384:13
having received the p. BIBLE 79:33
he was a young man of p. BALF 30:2
I have p. to keep FROST 219:12
may obtain thy p. PRAY 386:18
p. as sweet WORD 581:8
p. were, as he then was SHAK 447:19
promontory: like a p. sleeps or swims
MILT 349:1
Since once I sat upon a p. SHAK 470:7
Promoted: P. everybody GILB 225:28
promoting: by p. the wealth BURKE 110:7
promotion: last p. of the blest DRYD 197:32
none will sweat but for p. SHAK 425:7
p. cometh neither from PRAY 394:26
prompt: foot less p. to meet ARN 15:9
P. hand and headpiece clever HOUS 265:1
prone: p. and emaciated figure HARDY 239:13
to piety more p. ALEX 3:15
pronounce: If I p. it chaste GILB 227:25
not frame to p. it right BIBLE 49:20

pronouncing: p. to yourself nimini-pimini
BURG 108:5
proof: bliss in p. SHAK 495:7
lapp'd in p. SHAK 458:5
p. of stupidity than depravity JOHN 275:33
which is incapable of p. LEWES 314:7
proofs: p. of holy writ SHAK 475:23
Prooshans: others may be P. DICK 179:11
Proosian: French, or Turk, or P. GILB 228:10
prooving: method of p. Christianity
WIS 575:10
Prop: P. and Ruin of the State CLEV 153:3
p. To our infirmity WORD 580:16
propagate: learn and p. the best ARN 16:1
likely to p. understanding JOHN 280:13
p., and rot POPE 379:15
propagation: know that peace and p.
WALP 563:13
Was all our p. DONNE 188:22
propensities: excite my amorous p.
JOHN 274:2
side of their natural p. BURKE 112:6
propensity: usual p. of mankind towards
HUME 267:20
proper: always know our p. stations
DICK 176:23
Climb to our p. dark YEATS 587:2
p. man SHAK 469:31
p. or improper FULL 220:10
p. study of mankind is POPE 379:12
p. subject of conversation CHES 146:4
P. words in proper places SWIFT 526:20
p. young men BURNS 114:17
properly: my time has been p. spent
TAYL 531:26
Who never did anything p. LEAR 313:3
property: consider himself as public p.
JEFF 272:17
give me a little snug p. EDG 199:20
Greedy for the p. of others SALL 413:22
P. has its duties as well DRUM 193:24
p. is ever to have mercy PRAY 385:23
P. is theft PROU 401:19
Propinquity and p. of blood SHAK 453:3
right of governing was not p. FOX 217:20
right to the p. of the rich RUSK 412:11
prophecies: p., they shall fail BIBLE 76:14
verification of his own p. TROL 553:5
prophecy: p. is the most gratuitous
ELIOT 201:8
though I have the gift of p. BIBLE 76:14
trumpet of a p.! O, Wind SHEL 502:14
urn Of bitter p. SHEL 501:3
prophesy: eat exceedingly, and p.
JONS 283:16
man may p. SHAK 442:3
p. deceits BIBLE 58:26
we p. in part BIBLE 76:14
your daughters shall p. BIBLE 61:15
prophesying: p. with accents terrible
SHAK 460:20
voices p. war COL 156:29
prophet: I love a p. of the soul EMER 206:22
I'm the P. of the Utterly KIPL 303:1
In the name of the P. SMITH 510:9
Juxtaposition his p. CLOU 153:11
man put off the p. BROW 102:33
Methinks I am a p. new inspir'd SHAK 478:19
more than a p. BIBLE 66:2
p. is not without honour BIBLE 66:23
there arise among you a p. BIBLE 48:23
there is a p. in Israel BIBLE 51:27
What-you-may-call-it is his p. DICK 177:32
prophetic: her p. fury sew'd the work
SHAK 476:4
p. soul! My uncle SHAK 431:9
something like p. strain MILT 342:11
With such p. greeting SHAK 458:13
prophets: at least the wisest p. WALP 563:18
Beware of false p. BIBLE 65:8

goodly fellowship of the P. PRAY 384:16
p. and kings have desired BIBLE 69:29
p. prophesy falsely BIBLE 60:18
Saul also among the p. BIBLE 49:41
this is the law and the p. BIBLE 65:5
thou that killest the p. BIBLE 67:26
unto the fathers by the p. BIBLE 79:28
Who spake by the P. PRAY 387:11
Propinquity: P. and property of blood
SHAK 453:3
'P. does it' WARD 564:37
propitius: 'Sit Deus p. ANON 10:14
proponit: Nam homo p. THOM 546:10
proportion: Every man shouting in p.
SURT 525:18
no p. kept SHAK 480:14
order or p. BROW 96:34
some strangeness in the p. BACON 25:28
proportioned: p. to the human constitution
BERK 41:21
proportions: Founding a firm state by
p. true MARV 331:20
proposal: 'Your p. comes too late
LEAR 311:26
propose: if he do not p. DONNE 188:13
proposed: He p. seven times once
DICK 178:24
proposition: undesirable to believe a
p. RUSS 412:17
propositions: resolve the p. of a lover
SHAK 426:8
propositum: Meum est p. ANON 10:14
propounds: Man p. negotiations KIPL 299:5
propre: moins p. à la société CHAM 139:14
proprie: Difficile est p. communia dicere
HOR 257:17
propriété: La p. c'est le vol PROU 401:19
proprietor: of the p.'s prejudices
SWAF 525:30
propriety: inseparable p. of time BACON 25:5
not always evince its p. AUST 23:25
Study first p. CALV 127:26
propter: Qui p. nos homines MASS 334:20
Proputty: P., proputty TENN 540:24
prose: connect the p. and the passion
FORS 217:2
differs in nothing from p. GRAY 235:22
discourse and nearest p. DRYD 197:15
I love thee in p. PRIOR 400:21
is that p. MOL 353:3
Meredith is a p. Browning WILDE 573:37
only p. BROW 99:18
other harmony of p. DRYD 198:7
pin up my hair with p. CONG 160:37
p. is like a window pane ORW 365:15
P. is when all the lines BENT 41:2
P. on certain occasions LAND 309:10
p. run mad POPE 376:25
p.; words in their best COL 157:32
speaking p. without knowing MOL 353:3
that is not p. is verse MOL 353:4
That p. is verse BYRON 124:21
unattempted yet in p. or rhyme MILT 344:21
Proserpin: where P. gathering flowers
MILT 347:21
prospect: dull p. of a distant good
DRYD 196:18
noblest p. which a Scotchman JOHN 274:30
Though every p. pleases HEBER 244:6
prospects: all his p. bright'ning GOLD 230:20
gilded scenes and shining p. ADD 2:4
prosper: I grow, I p. SHAK 453:10
that shall keep it may p. KIPL 300:20
Why do sinners' ways p. HOPK 257:2
prospering: We shall march p. BROW 102:6
prosperitee: man to han ben in p.
CHAU 144:11
prosperity: day of p. be joyful BIBLE 55:15
I will wish thee p. PRAY 398:12
jest's p. lies in the ear SHAK 457:17

one man who can stand p. CARL 131:36
P. doth best discover vice BACON 25:21
P. doth bewitch men WEBS 567:14
P. is the blessing BACON 25:18
P. is not without many BACON 25:20
P.'s the very bond SHAK 492:6
prosperous: race was most happy and
p. GIBB 224:24
prostitute: I puff the p. away DRYD 198:17
protect: I'll p. it now MORR 358:6
protection: gracious mercy and p.
PRAY 389:9
P. is not a principle DISR 184:15
P. is not only dead DISR 185:22
surrounded with His p. MILT 352:1
use, and p. BACON 25:1
us such strength and p. PRAY 386:8
protector: p. of all that trust PRAY 386:16
protest: lady doth p. too much SHAK 434:11
Protestant: I am the P. whore GWYN 237:8
P. counterpoint BEEC 37:4
protestantism of the P. BURKE 109:22
P., if he wants aid DISR 186:16
P. Religion CARL 131:3
Thy P. to be HERR 249:25
protestantism: p. of the Protestant religion
BURKE 109:22
Protestants: only is the religion of P.
CHIL 148:12
Proteus: Have sight of P. rising WORD 582:20
protoplasmal: p. primordial atomic
GILB 226:20
protracted: That life protracted is p.
JOHN 283:1
proud: apt the poor are to be p. SHAK 489:23
Celia (since thou art so p. CAREW 130:13
ever fair and never p. SHAK 474:18
he hath scattered the p. BIBLE 69:6
he was very stiff and p. CARR 135:27
I have no p. looks PRAY 398:25
I must be p. to see POPE 380:20
know not whether I am p. LAND 309:5
make death p. to take us SHAK 423:18
man being too p. to fight WILS 574:20
might grow p. the while HERR 250:3
nation p. in arms MILT 340:26
nor p. me no prouds SHAK 483:17
not p. of those two eyes HERR 250:1
Poets of the p. old lineage FLEC 214:9
p. and angry dust HOUS 264:22
p. and yet a wretched thing DAV 172:11
p. as Priam murdered with YEATS 586:22
p. full sail of his great SHAK 494:11
p. in heart and mind SHAK 454:18
p. of seeing our names CHES 147:22
P. word you never spoke LAND 308:25
tameless, and swift, and p. SHEL 502:13
too p. for a wit GOLD 231:17
we ain't p. DICK 180:12
Who was so p. ROCH 406:22
Why were they p. KEATS 290:9
woman can be p. and stiff YEATS 584:19
yet not p. to know POPE 378:32
prov'd: Marlbro's mighty soul was p.
ADD 1:13
To have p. most royally SHAK 437:30
prove: Believing where we cannot p.
TENN 535:29
I if thou wouldst p. me CONS 161:25
let us p. JONS 285:12
might p. anything by figures CARL 131:15
P. all things BIBLE 79:4
p. me PRAY 399:8
p. me PRAY 391:4
p. the sweetness of a shower THOM 547:21
since I cannot p. a lover SHAK 480:19
That Love would p. so hard BRID 92:22
proved: God p. them BIBLE 62:13
P. by statistics that some AUDEN 20:10
p. me, and saw my works PRAY 396:4

something or other could be p. FRY 220:2
Which was to be p. EUCL 209:1
whole you have p. to be HARDY 239:21
proven: worthy proving can be p.
TENN 532:15
Provençal: P. song KEATS 291:18
Provence: P. and La Palie CLOU 153:24
Than you found it in P. WILL 574:11
provender: nought but p. SHAK 473:13
proverb: even a p. is no proverb
KEATS 294:18
p. and a byword among all BIBLE 50:31
p. is much matter decocted FULL 220:11
p. is one man's wit RUSS 412:21
p. is something musty SHAK 434:18
Proverbs: King Solomon wrote the P.
NAYL 360:10
Patch grief with p. SHAK 473:6
provide: God will p. himself a lamb
BIBLE 46:10
wisdom to p. for human BURKE 111:8
Provided: 'P. for' DICK 177:16
providence: Behind a frowning p.
COWP 165:28
future to the divine P. BACON 24:26
I go the way that P. dictates HITL 251:10
I may assert eternal P. MILT 344:22
inscrutable workings of P. BIRK 84:16
P. kept it from being any HARDY 241:11
P. their guide MILT 350:1
Providential: case of P. interference
TEMP 532:8
province: all knowledge to be my p.
BACON 28:1
p. of knowledge to speak HOLM 253:20
p. they have desolated GLAD 229:13
provinces: obedience of distant p. MAC 323:9
p. of his body revolted AUDEN 19:3
provincial: was worse than p. JAMES 271:9
proving: worthy p. can be proven
TENN 532:15
provision: Make not p. for the flesh
BIBLE 75:25
provocation: Ask you what p. I have
had POPE 380:19
in the p. PRAY 396:4
provoke: fathers, p. not your children
BIBLE 78:7
voice p. the silent dust GRAY 234:22
provoker: Drink, sir, is a great p.
SHAK 460:18
provokes: one p. me with impunity
ANON 10:15
prow: cove with pushing p. BROW 102:14
sunrise an emerging p. ARN 14:21
proximus: paries cum p. ardet HOR 258:23
Prudence: P. is a rich BLAKE 88:14
p. never to practise either TWAIN 554:7
prudenter: p. agas ANON 10:18
prudes: p., your envious railing
BURNS 114:16
With p. for proctors TENN 541:27
prunella: is all but leather or p. POPE 379:22
prunes: especially p. and prism DICK 178:26
pruninghooks: their spears into p.
BIBLE 57:19
your p. into spears BIBLE 61:16
prunus: p. and forsythia across BETJ 43:12
Prusse: l'industrie nationale de la P.
MIR 352:19
Prussia: military domination of P. ASQ 17:17
national industry of P. MIR 352:19
Prussic acid: She drank P. without any
BARH 33:26
pry: lunar world securely p. DRYD 195:23
psalm: cadence and subtle p. AUDEN 18:3
sing to the harp with a p. PRAY 396:8
Take the p. PRAY 395:9
psalmist: David...the sweet p. of Israel
BIBLE 50:28

psalms: Church with p. must shout
HERB 246:26
David wrote the P. NAYL 360:10
ourselves glad in him with p. PRAY 396:3
p. and hymns and spiritual BIBLE 78:5
sonnets turn'd to holy p. PEELE 371:8
psaltery: p., dulcimer BIBLE 61:3
Psyche: Your mournful P. KEATS 291:14
Psychical: P. Research COW 164:5
ptarmigan: p. that whitens ere his
TENN 534:37
pub: pavender, or p. ST L 412:27
some one take me to a p. CHES 146:12
public: abuse in p. and to read BORR 89:26
complainers for the p. BURKE 108:15
coquetry of p. opinion BURKE 110:15
exempt from p. haunt SHAK 424:32
for the p. good COWP 164:28
man assumes a p. trust JEFF 272:17
ministers to consult the p. SWIFT 526:8
motive is the p. good STEE 518:1
pot of paint in the p.'s RUSK 411:7
principles of p. morality BURKE 108:16
Private faces in p. AUDEN 20:12
p. and merited disgrace STEV 522:13
p. be damned VAND 555:7
p. buys its opinions BUTL 119:4
servants of the p. GOW 233:7
shake the p. ways COWP 166:37
things on which the p. JOHN 281:37
this p. Way Streamed WORD 582:4
three things which the p. HOOD 255:15
Where they enter the p. WHIT 570:15
publican: How like a fawning p. he
SHAK 465:29
publicans: Master with p. and sinners
BIBLE 65:22
not even the p. the same BIBLE 64:20
public executions: taste for marriages
and p. DISR 186:25
publick: p. Prayer in the Church PRAY 400:8
publicly: engage himself openly and p.
BLAKE 86:10
Public schools: P. 'tis public folly feeds
COWP 167:30
P. are the nurseries FIEL 211:16
publish: I'll p., right or wrong BYRON 124:15
P. and be damned WELL 568:10
p. it not in the streets BIBLE 50:16
p. it to all the nation PRIOR 400:24
published: whatever you haven't p.
HOR 258:6
When a new book is p. ROG 407:12
publisher: Now Barabbas was a p.
CAMP 129:15
p. is simply a useful WILDE 573:33
publishing: too good to be worth p.
SHAW 498:10
Puck: just a streak of P. HENL 245:12
pudding: Manningtree ox with the p.
SHAK 439:16
p. against empty praise POPE 375:13
p. as well as translate JOHN 273:31
puellis: Vixi p. nuper idoneus HOR 261:6
puer: Quis multa gracilis te p. HOR 259:15
pueris: p. placeas et declamatio JUV 288:2
puerisque: Virginibus p. canto HOR 260:13
puero: Maxima debetur p. reverentia
JUV 288:7
Se p. HOR 257:21
puff: friends all united to p. SWIN 529:13
I p. the prostitute away DRYD 198:17
with solemn interposing p. COWP 165:3
puffed: get one's self p. TROL 553:14
p. up with this retinue SHAK 442:15
puffeth: Knowledge p. up BIBLE 76:5
puffing: p. is of various sorts SHER 505:23
puffs: p. from the hookah-mouth KIPL 297:28
pug: lovely O most charming p. FLEM 215:4

pugilist: put in the p. (Lord Palmerston)
BAG 28:26
Pugna: P. magna victi sumus LIVY 315:12
puissant: noble and p. nation MILT 352:3
puking: Mewling and p. in the nurse's
SHAK 425:24
pulchrior: matre pulchra filia p. HOR 259:22
p. evenit HOR 261:12
pulchritudo: p. tam antiqua et tam nova
AUG 21:16
Pull: P. down thy vanity POUND 382:13
willing to p. his weight ROOS 408:2
puller: setter up and p. down SHAK 446:20
pulling: p. in one's horse as he HARE 242:4
pulp: p. so bitter THOM 548:19
pulpit: Politics and the p. are BURKE 111:2
pulpits: of their Babylonian p. BURKE 111:6
P. and Sundays HERB 248:16
Pulsanda: P. tellus HOR 260:3
pulse: My p. like a soft drum KING 296:12
Now feel that p. no more MOORE 356:9
people with the one p. MACN 326:11
p. in the eternal mind BROO 94:30
p. of feeling stirs ARN 12:22
secret vigour and a p. EMER 207:10
than feeling a woman's p. STER 519:6
very. p. of the machine WORD 581:8
When the p. begins to throb BRON 93:21
pulses: are proved upon our p. KEATS 293:30
pulvere: dulcis sine p. palmae HOR 258:8
Pulveris: P. exigui iactu compressa
VIRG 560:18
P. Tormentarii, et Acus BACON 28:9
Pulvis: P. et umbra sumus HOR 261:16
pumice: *Arido modo p. expolitum* CAT 136:19
p. isle in Baiae's bay SHEL 502:10
pump: p. has frozen to-night GRAV 234:12
pumpkins: Where the early p. blow
LEAR 311:25
pun: could make so vile a p. DENN 174:24
pipe and exhaled in a p. LAMB 308:11
puñado: por un p. de monedas ZAP 588:18
punch: Some sipping p. WORD 580:2
punctilio: None of your dam p. MER 337:33
Punctuality: P. is the politeness LOUI 318:11
punctually: p. come for ever and ever
WHIT 571:4
punctuate: came in to p. my discourse
COL 158:5
Punica: P. fide SALL 413:25
Punish: P. a body which he could
DRYD 194:7
punished: p. everlastingly JOHN 279:17
p. in the sight of men BIBLE 62:13
should be p. with as severe PENN 371:16
punishment: All p. is mischief BENT 40:27
deserve not p. SHAK 457:4
My p. is greater than BIBLE 45:27
object of p. is MANN 328:13
power of p. is to silence JOHN 282:13
To let the p. fit the crime GILB 227:5
punishments: charged with p. the scroll
HENL 245:5
sanguinary p. which corrupt PAINE 368:4
punt: admit it is more fun to p. SAY 415:6
slow p. swings round ARN 14:14
story got out of the p. JOYCE 286:7
punto: cinco en p. de la tarde GARC 221:5
pupil: in years to be a p. now SHAK 478:11
pupils: Among the dead whose p.
BUTL 119:21
puplis: is the scripture of p. JER 272:21
puppets: shut up the box and the p.
THAC 545:29
whose p. BROW 103:25
puppy: let ev'ry p. drink WHYT 572:2
purchase: it is all a p. HOPK 256:29
p. pain with all that joy POPE 377:21
purchased: gift of God may be p.
BIBLE 73:30

purchasing: I am not worth p. REED 405:9
pure: Because my heart is p. TENN 543:8
be more p. than his maker BIBLE 52:16
Blessed are the p. in heart BIBLE 64:6
If I have led a p. life CAT 137:11
Is she not p. gold BROW 105:10
Live p. TENN 534:5
most particularly p. young GILB 227:23
nation of p. philosophers BAG 29:2
pure all things are p. BIBLE 79:27
p. and eloquent blood DONNE 189:31
P. and ready to mount DANTE 171:15
p. as snow SHAK 433:12
p. mind who refuses apple-dumplings
LAMB 307:6
P., Ornate BAG 29:20
P. religion and undefiled BIBLE 80:11
so p. as you BUTL 119:18
That England was too p. ANON 7:7
what God declares P. MILT 348:7
whatsoever things are p. BIBLE 78:22
working out a p. intent WORD 578:21
pureness: in p. of living and truth
PRAY 386:11
purer: live the p. with the other SHAK 435:17
purest: p. and most thoughtful RUSK 411:24
p. of human pleasures BACON 26:18
purgatory: no other p. but a woman
BEAU 36:12
p. of men FLOR 216:1
To P. fire thou com'st BALL 31:7
purg'd: p. the air of pestilence SHAK 487:21
purge: I'll p., and leave sack SHAK 440:29
Let's p. this choler without SHAK 478:7
shalt p. me with hyssop PRAY 393:5
purged: had by himself p. our sins
BIBLE 79:28
purified: every creature shall be p.
MARL 329:8
purifies: that which p. us is trial MILT 351:24
purify: p. the dialect of the tribe ELIOT 202:25
Puritan: P. all things are impure LAWR 311:2
P. hated bear-baiting MAC 324:19
sometimes he is a kind of p. SHAK 488:22
Puritane-one: Where I saw a P. BRAT 91:24
puriter: *Si vitam p. egi* CAT 137:11
purity: brightness, p., and truth OTWAY 366:4
p., all trial, all obeisance SHAK 426:29
P. is the feminine HARE 242:5
purlieus: dusty p. of the law TENN 537:8
within the p. of the Law ETH 208:28
purling: p. stream ADD 2:5
purloins: p. the Psalms BYRON 124:23
Puro: P. e disposto a salire DANTE 171:15
purple: clothed in p. and fine linen
BIBLE 70:28
desire and p. light of love GRAY 235:1
gleaming in p. and gold BYRON 122:1
I never saw a P. Cow BURG 108:2
now p. with love's wound SHAK 470:8
p. testament of bleeding SHAK 479:13
So cool a p. KEATS 289:4
some p. patch or other HOR 257:11
what p. fritillaries ARN 15:8
purpose: ages one increasing p. runs
TENN 539:2
any p. perverts art CONS 162:5
are the measure of his p. NIGH 363:16
creature hath a p. KEATS 294:17
far-reaching in p. HOOV 255:24
himself except for a noble p. HERB 246:17
his prudent p. to resolve YOUNG 588:5
I embrace the p. of God TENN 540:19
Infirm of p. SHAK 460:11
mark of insincerity of p. BRAM 91:18
My p. is, indeed SHAK 488:25
p. in liquidity BROO 94:11
Shake my fell p. SHAK 459:2
supplies us with its own p. SHAW 497:1
time to every p. under BIBLE 55:12

To speak and p. not SHAK 453:5
unconquerable p. shall be realized
LAMB 307:28
what if I fail of my p. BROW 102:1
with p. of its own WORD 580:12
purposes: Can execute their aery p.
MILT 345:15
purposing: signify A thwarted p.
HARDY 241:8
purpureal: fields invested with p.
WORD 578:3
Purpureus: P., late qui splendeat HOR 257:11
purse: Costly thy habit as thy p. SHAK 430:19
empty p. BRET 92:3
fill thy p. with money SHAK 474:10
law can take a p. in open BUTL 118:19
p., my person SHAK 465:16
Put money in thy p. SHAK 474:9
this consumption of the p. SHAK 441:16
Who steals my p. steals SHAK 475:16
purses: Light gains make heavy p.
BACON 25:35
pursue: hearken if his foes p. SHAK 495:21
it will p. JONS 284:11
knowing it, p. DRYD 198:18
Love wist to p. THOM 548:11
Men must p. things which BACON 24:26
p. my reason to an *O altitudo* BROW 96:9
thing we all p. BEAU 36:10
what shadows we p. BURKE 110:21
who p. Culture in bands WHAR 569:8
will accipitrine to p. THOM 548:2
pursued: it is you who are the p.
SHAW 497:24
p. a maiden and clasped SHEL 501:4
pursues: still the world p. ELIOT 204:24
pursueth: wicked flee when no man p.
BIBLE 54:41
pursuing: god p. SWIN 528:18
Still achieving, still p. LONG 317:5
yet p. BIBLE 49:18
pursuit: common p. of true judgement
ELIOT 205:15
full p. of the uneatable WILDE 573:27
in the p. of the blessing AUST 22:30
liberty and the p. of happiness ANON 8:14
Mad in p. SHAK 495:7
mental p. for the Building BLAKE 86:10
p. of happiness JEFF 272:6
P. of knowledge under difficulties
DICK 182:10
p. of perfection ARN 15:15
Strong in the p. the rapid glede SMART 509:3
What mad p. KEATS 291:3
pursy: fatness of these p. times SHAK 435:16
purtenance: with the p. thereof BIBLE 47:17
purus: vitae scelerisque p. HOR 259:23
push: make one brave p. STEV 522:8
P. off TENN 544:3
p. the logic of a fact KIPL 299:5
Than tarry till they p. us SHAK 452:5
pushing: p. young particle GILB 227:28
pusillanimity: badge of p. and cowardice
SHAK 442:15
Pusset: Used to call his cat P. HARE 242:7
Pussy: What a beautiful P. you are
LEAR 312:11
Pussy-Cat: Owl and the P. went LEAR 312:11
put: by Baptism p. on Christ PRAY 388:11
never be p. out LAT 310:21
p. beneath Thy special BETJ 43:6
p. his hand to the plough BIBLE 69:25
P. it down a we DICK 182:21
P. money in thy purse SHAK 474:9
p. not your trust in princes PRAY 399:16
p. off the old man with BIBLE 78:26
P. off thy shoes from off BIBLE 47:4
P. out the light SHAK 477:5
p. too fine a point upon DICK 176:7
p. upon us the armour PRAY 386:4

p. up with bad things that TROL 553:2
So p. that in your pipe BARH 33:18
with which I will not p. CHUR 151:6
puto: *p. deus fio* VESP 556:12
Puts: P. on his pretty looks SHAK 452:20
putty: p., brass, an' paint KIPL 302:11
puzzle: problem must p. the devil
BURNS 115:2
Rule of three doth p. me ANON 6:18
schoolmasters p. their brain GOLD 231:22
puzzling: This is a p. world ELIOT 201:15
Pym: P., and such carles BROW 99:26
pyramides: *mais comme les p. ça ne*
FLAU 214:3
pyramids: p. they're just as useless
FLAU 214:3
Pyramus: cruel death of P. and Thisby
SHAK 469:23
Pyrenees: P. have ceased to exist LOUI 318:7
that tease in the high P. BELL 40:13
Pythagoras: mystical way of P. BROW 96:11
P. concerning wild fowl SHAK 490:21
P.' metempsychosis MARL 329:14
P. planned it YEATS 587:1
this 'himself' was P. CIC 151:20
python: mangrove swamps where the
p. COW 163:20
Who bought a P. from a man BELL 40:4
Quaäker: I knaw'd a Q. feller TENN 541:1
quack: potent q. COWP 168:28
Quad: always about in the Q. ANON 4:29
no one about in the Q. KNOX 305:22
Quadrigis: *navibus atque Q.* HOR 258:19
Quadripedante: *Q. putrem sonitu quatit*
VIRG 559:7
quadriviis: *Nunc in q. et angiportis*
CAT 137:5
quadruped: hairy q. DARW 171:23
quaesiveris: *Nec te q. extra* PERS 372:26
Quaestio: *Q. subtilissima* RAB 403:29
quaff'd: jested, q., and swore DOYLE 192:39
quaffing: q., and unthinking time
DRYD 197:17
quagmire: Lost in the q. TENN 534:22
quailing: No q., Mrs Gaskell BRON 94:3
quails: we long for q. DRYD 197:2
quake: aspes leef she gan to q. CHAU 144:9
Quaker: out the Q. (Lord Aberdeen)
BAG 28:26
qualify: absence seem'd my flame to
q. SHAK 495:2
qualifying: love admits no q. dross
SHAK 487:10
qualis: *Non sum q. eram bonae* HOR 261:10
qualité: *gens de q. savent* MOL 353:23
qualités: *Des q. trop supérieures*
CHAM 139:14
qualities: Englishman a combination
of q. DICK 181:12
In whom his q. are reigning BYRON 126:6
of four q. of his author ARN 16:11
only two q. in the world SHAW 497:5
Q. too elevated often unfit CHAM 139:14
such q. as would wear well GOLD 232:33
quality: composition and fierce q.
SHAK 453:9
give us a taste of your q. SHAK 432:22
his honour and his q. taken BLUN 89:3
man of q. than to laugh CONG 159:22
People of q. know everything MOL 353:23
q. of his despair CONN 161:16
q. of mercy is not strain'd SHAK 467:27
q. to be exceedingly cheated EVEL 209:7
qualms: Of those cold q. SOUT 514:21
quanta: *q. qualia sunt illa sabbata* ABEL 1:1
Quantula: *Q. sint hominum corpuscula*
JUV 288:3
quantum: I wave the q. o'the sin
BURNS 113:17
Q. mutatus ab illo VIRG 558:5

quarks: Three q. for Muster Mark
JOYCE 286:12
quarrel: arm'd that hath his q. just
SHAK 446:6
armed that hath his q. just BILL 84:6
Beware Of entrance to a q. SHAK 430:19
greatly to find q. in a straw SHAK 435:31
justice of my q. ANON 6:4
q. in a far-away country CHAM 139:9
q. there is no true valour SHAK 473:8
therefore a perpetual q. BURKE 109:31
They quite forgot their q. CARR 134:33
very pretty q. as it stands SHER 506:20
quarrelled: I have q. with my wife
PEAC 370:18
quarrellin: q. wi' the equawtor NORTH 364:4
quarrelling: set them a q. HUME 268:2
quarrels: never strained by nasty q.
HOR 259:21
of q. as an egg is full SHAK 483:1
q. of popes and kings AUST 23:4
quarry: lightless in the q. HOUS 264:4
marked down q. SHAW 497:24
Quarterly: 'I,' says the Q. BYRON 125:1
quartern: q. loaf and Luddites rise
SMITH 510:7
quarters: Sprinkle the q. HOUS 264:28
to the wind's twelve q. HOUS 263:17
quarto: them on a beautiful q. page
SHER 506:26
quartos: Then q. COWP 168:11
quarts: Pints and q. of Ludlow beer
HOUS 264:13
quatit: *Mente q. solida* HOR 260:18
Quatorze: *Q. Le bon Dieu n'a que*
CLEM 152:30
quean: flaunting, extravagant q. SHER 506:31
Queen: am the Ruler of the Q.'s GILB 228:4
Apparent q. unveil'd her MILT 348:2
beggar maid shall be my q. TENN 532:16
enchanting q. break off SHAK 421:19
ev'ry lady would be Q. POPE 377:25
fair q. in a summer's bower SHAK 439:30
had seen the mobled q. SHAK 432:24
Hail holy q. ANON 10:19
he was the Q.'s luve BALL 30:17
I'll q. it no inch further SHAK 492:5
I would not be a q. SHAK 447:2
laughing q. that caught HUNT 268:9
life of our own dear Q. ANON 5:20
Most Gracious Q. ANON 6:17
Mother, Wife, and Q. TENN 543:15
Move Q. Anne VICT 556:16
Of life, of crown, of q. SHAK 431:12
pale Q. of the silent night BEST 42:2
Q. and Faith like a valiant TENN 543:4
Q. and huntress JONS 283:24
q. in a vesture of gold PRAY 392:16
Q. of curds and cream SHAK 492:1
Q. of England is looking CHES 147:1
q. of Scots is this day ELIZ 205:20
Q. so furious that she VICT 556:14
Q. was in a furious passion CARR 134:5
remembrance of a weeping q. SHAK 479:19
right-down regular Royal Q. GILB 225:22
royal makings of a q. SHAK 447:14
since I saw the Q. of France BURKE 111:9
sometime sister, now our q. SHAK 429:19
we love our Q. GILB 228:24
who have lost their q. FRY 220:7
Would grace a summer q. SCOTT 417:30
Yestreen the Q. had four Maries BALL 31:12
Queen Anne: Q. was one of the smallest
BAG 29:10
Queen Elizabeth: No scandal about Q.
SHER 505:24
Q. of most happy memory BIBLE 44:20
Queen Mab: Q. hath been with you...
SHAK 481:28
Queen o' the May: I'm to be Q. TENN 540:20

Queens: beautiful Q. of this world
DONNE 190:26
Q. have died young NASHE 360:7
That all your acts are q. SHAK 491:27
Queensberry: me and the Duchess of
Q. WALP 562:22
queer: him ill-tempered and q. LEAR 311:20
Medical Crowner's a q. BARH 33:16
Q. are the ways of a man HARDY 240:15
q. save thee and me OWEN 366:29
quells: She q. the floods below CAMP 129:13
Quem: *Q. fugis* VIRG 559:16
quench: If I q. thee SHAK 477:5
Many waters cannot q. love BIBLE 57:12
q. all the fiery darts BIBLE 78:10
q. its speed i' the slushy BROW 102:14
smoking flax shall he not q. BIBLE 59:11
quench'd: What hath q. them hath
SHAK 460:2
querimoniis: *Divulsus q.* HOR 259:21
quest: to whose winding q. VAUG 555:10
what thy q. BRID 92:19
questing: fen passes the q. vole WAUGH 566:3
q. beast that had in shape MAL 327:18
question: drop a q. on your plate
ELIOT 203:19
Make that thy q. SHAK 491:11
man with such a silly q. STER 519:17
Others abide our q. ARN 14:23
q. de Swann chez les Verdurin PROU 401:21
q. not to be asked SHAK 439:14
q. with my jealous thought SHAK 493:18
That man may q. SHAK 458:10
that q.'s out of my part SHAK 488:11
what is the q. STEIN 518:19
who but infants q. in such ROSS 409:20
questionable: com'st in such a q. shape
SHAK 430:24
Questioning: Q. is not the mode of
conversation JOHN 276:37
questionings: those obstinate q. WORD 579:10
questions: have answered three q.
CARR 133:23
q. of will or decision CHOM 148:16
q. the distempered part ELIOT 202:21
Them that asks no q. isn't KIPL 302:22
There are innumerable q. JOHN 278:5
qui: *Siete voi q.* DANTE 171:11
quia: *Certum est q. impossibile est*
TERT 545:1
quibble: q. is to Shakespeare what
JOHN 282:15
quick: bitten and pared to the q. MAC 324:7
burgeons every maze of q. TENN 537:18
judge the q. and the dead PRAY 384:26
less q. to spring again ARN 15:9
Q.' and some cry 'Slow' TENN 541:26
q. spirit that is in Antony SHAK 448:9
Touched to the q. BROW 101:16
quicken: turn again, and q. PRAY 395:14
quickened: eyes are q. so with grief
GRAV 234:11
quickeneth: It is the spirit that q. BIBLE 72:8
quickens: faint east q. SWIN 528:16
quickest: that q. in all the world MOL 353:21
quickly: much good who gives q. PUBL 402:3
That thou doest, do q. BIBLE 72:29
quickness: With too much q. ever
POPE 377:21
quick'ning: not look upon the q. sun
DONNE 188:9
quiddities: in thy quips and thy q.
SHAK 438:3
Quidquid: *Q. agas* ANON 10:18
Q. agunt homines JUV 287:12
quiero: *Que no q. verla* GARC 221:6
quies: *prima q. mortalibus aegris* VIRG 558:4
quiet: All q. along the Potomac MCCL 324:29
be q.; and go a-Angling WALT 564:13
by this means cannot q. PRAY 387:17

calm Peace, and Q.   MILT 341:27
Easy live and q. die   SCOTT 418:5
Fair q.   MARV 331:22
'Fie upon this q. life   SHAK 438:33
He sat as q. as a lump   AUDEN 21:7
In q. she reposes   ARN 14:5
lain still and been q.   BIBLE 52:12
Let us have a q. hour   TENN 544:7
lives of q. desperation   THOR 550:4
meek and q. spirit   BIBLE 80:28
my scallop-shell of q.   RAL 404:12
q. along the Potomac to-night   BEERS 38:8
q., grave man   BAG 29:11
q. mind   SURR 524:20
q. mind is worse than poverty   TRAH 552:2
Q. takes back her folded   JOYCE 286:9
Q. to quick bosoms is   BYRON 120:30
q. us in a death so noble   MILT 351:2
serve thee with a q. mind   PRAY 386:22
Study to be q.   BIBLE 79:1
this q.   KEATS 295:2
With q. hours   SHAK 440:14
Quieta: *Q. movere magna merces*
                                      SALL 413:23
quieten: q. down by the throwing
                                      VIRG 560:18
quietest: *q. places Under the sun* HOUS 264:7
quietly: lie as q. among the graves EDW 200:6
Q. they go   MILL 339:23
quietness: q. and in confidence shall
                                      BIBLE 58:27
serve thee in all godly q.   PRAY 386:17
unravish'd bride of q.   KEATS 291:2
quietus: himself might his q. make
                                      SHAK 433:8
quill: through a q.   LAMB 307:11
quillets: nice sharp q. of the law SHAK 445:20
quills: q. upon the fretful porpentine
                                      SHAK 431:5
tender stops of various q.   MILT 343:19
Quinapalus: What says Q.   SHAK 488:5
quince: slices of q.   LEAR 312:14
quincunx: q. of heaven runs low BROW 95:19
Quinquireme: Q. of Nineveh from distant
                                      MAS 333:18
quinta: *La q. columna*   MOLA 352:29
quintessence: heavenly q. they still
                                      MARL 330:11
quip: q. modest   SHAK 427:5
quips: thy q. and thy quiddities SHAK 438:3
quire: full-voiced q. below   MILT 342:10
q. of Saints for evermore   DONNE 189:14
Quires: Q. and Places where they PRAY 385:4
quiring: q. to the young-eyed cherubins
                                      SHAK 468:15
Quis: *Q. rex*   ABEL 1:2
quisque: *Mens cuiusque is est q.* CIC 151:24
quit: age to q. their clogs   MILT 351:7
I are more than q.   PRIOR 400:24
I'll q. the port o' Heaven   NEWB 361:6
Q. in a single kiss   BRID 92:11
q. this mortal frame   POPE 376:3
Q. you like men   BIBLE 77:2
q. your books   WORD 582:22
Q. yourselves like men   BIBLE 49:38
soldiers may not q. the post   TENN 539:21
that dies this year is q.   SHAK 442:8
quiver: man that hath his q. full PRAY 398:19
Quivering: Q. within the wave's intenser
                                      SHEL 502:10
Quo: *Q. vadis*   BIBLE 83:21
quocumque: *q. moveris*   LUCAN 320:1
quodcumque: *Jupiter est q. vides*
                                      LUCAN 320:1
Quot: *Q. homines tot sententiae* TER 544:19
quotation: Every q. contributes something
                                      JOHN 281:7
quotations: Back'd his opinion with q.
                                      PRIOR 401:2
book that furnishes no q.   PEAC 370:12

I hate q.   EMER 207:44
man to read books of q.   CHUR 150:24
quote: I'll kill you if you q.   BURG 108:3
we all q.   EMER 208:1
quoter: sentence is the first q. of it
                                      EMER 208:2
Quoth: Q. the Raven   POE 375:6
quotidianum: *panem nostrum q. da nobis*
                                      MASS 335:5
quotidienne: *que la vie est q.* LAF 306:23
Quoting: Q., for shallow conversational
                                      SASS 414:19
Quousque: *Q. tandem abutere* CIC 151:25
rabbit: There is a r. in a snare STEP 518:26
rabble: army would be a base r. BURKE 110:5
Rabelais: soul of R. dwelling in a dry
                                      COL 158:2
race: All is r.   DISR 186:36
Another r. hath been   WORD 579:14
avails the sceptred r.   LAND 308:26
Foal of an oppressed r.   COL 157:16
forget the human r.   BYRON 121:21
giant r. before the flood   DRYD 196:1
happiness of the human r.   BURKE 110:7
hindered in running the r.   PRAY 386:6
idiot r. to honour   BURNS 114:29
in the history of our r.   CHUR 150:8
like the rest of my r.   BLAKE 86:15
loftier r.   SYM 531:3
longer tolerate the r.   BALF 30:3
lovely ere his r. be run   BYRON 121:37
lull in the hot r.   ARN 12:22
men and women with our r.   KIPL 298:10
most pernicious r. of little   SWIFT 526:5
My r. of glory run   MILT 350:23
now a new r. descends from   VIRG 559:22
of Europe's stone age r.   BETJ 43:8
r. is not to the swift   BIBLE 55:30
r. is run by one and one   KIPL 303:19
r. that is set before us   BIBLE 79:35
r. that long in darkness   SCOT 419:7
ran his godly r.   GOLD 230:22
run the r. with Death   JOHN 279:24
Rushes life in a r.   MER 336:26
That still a godly r. he   GOLD 231:10
they which run in a r.   BIBLE 76:8
till thou run out thy r.   MILT 344:17
tree did end their r.   MARV 332:2
unprotected r.   CLARE 152:11
whose r. is just begun   SHEL 504:17
wish I loved the Human R.   RAL 404:20
races: Some r. increase   LUCR 320:7
Rachel: R. weeping for her children
                                      BIBLE 63:34
seven years for R.   BIBLE 46:21
racial: *r. pride shall tower like* AUDEN 19:11
that makes r. difference   CONR 161:23
rack: Leave not a r. behind   SHAK 485:20
r. dislimns   SHAK 423:8
r. of a too easy chair   POPE 375:25
r. of this tough world   SHAK 456:12
racked: r. with deep despair   MILT 345:4
racket: r. is back in its press   BETJ 44:6
rackets: match'd our r. to these balls
                                      SHAK 443:11
radiance: beautiful r. of the gods SCH 415:9
My r. rare and fathomless   HARDY 241:6
radiant: r. maiden whom the angels
                                      POE 375:5
radical: r. is a man with both feet
                                      ROOS 407:24
radicals: r. have good digestions BUTL 118:31
radio: *caelique meatus Describent r.*
                                      VIRG 559:1
radish: like a forked r.   SHAK 442:10
r. and an egg   COWP 167:14
Rafael: R. made a century of sonnets
                                      BROW 102:28
R. of the dear Madonnas   BROW 103:1
raft: republic is a r. which   AMES 4:3

rafte: he r. hire maydenhed   CHAU 143:2
rafters: lowly sheds With smoky r.
                                      MILT 341:6
stars come down from the r.   AUDEN 18:13
rag: bloomin' old r. over 'ead KIPL 304:10
r. and a bone and a hank KIPL 303:29
rag-and-bone: foul r. shop of the heart
                                      YEATS 584:15
rage: ape an ancient r.   CHES 147:12
captive void of noble r.   TENN 536:15
heathen so furiously r.   PRAY 389:15
Heav'n has no r.   CONG 160:15
horrible that lust and r.   YEATS 586:23
humour temp'ring virtuous r.   POPE 378:8
I r., I melt, I burn   GAY 222:6
nature with hard-favour'd r.   SHAK 443:21
Not die here in a r.   SWIFT 526:24
nothing but a r. to live   POPE 377:21
Puts all Heaven in a R.   BLAKE 85:9
r. against the dying   THOM 546:23
r. of Caliban   WILDE 573:16
replete with too much r.   SHAK 493:2
rights be term'd a poet's r.   SHAK 492:27
this r. shall beauty hold   SHAK 494:4
writing increaseth r.   GREV 236:17
rages: Dog-star r.   POPE 376:18
older that the weight of r.   SPOO 517:8
Sudden she r.   GAY 223:8
raggedness: looped and window'd r.
                                      SHAK 454:15
raging: meet the r. of the skies CAMP 129:3
r. of the sea   PRAY 394:1
strong drink is r.   BIBLE 54:15
ragioniam: *Non r. di lor* DANTE 171:4
rags: Arm it in r.   SHAK 455:20
fond of my r. and tatters   MOL 353:11
righteousnesses are as filthy r. BIBLE 60:12
when in r. and contempt   BUNY 107:19
which are the r. of time   DONNE 190:12
rag-time: Lurching to r. tunes SASS 414:12
raid: indemnity...for r. by Dr Jameson
                                      KRUG 306:1
rail: all night groan on the r.   HOUS 262:16
any body else to r. at me   CONG 160:17
folks r. against other folks   FIEL 211:17
her six young on the r.   BROW 101:19
Say that she r.   SHAK 484:8
than to r. at the ill   TENN 540:19
railing: prudes, your envious r. BURNS 114:16
R. at life   CHUR 148:32
railing for r.   BIBLE 80:30
railroad: You enterprised a r.   RUSK 411:13
rails: purgatorial r.   KEATS 289:10
r. against all married   SHAK 469:14
Star-spiked R. a fiery Smite   THOM 549:2
Railway: Beautiful R. Bridge   MCG 325:6
railway-share: threatened its life with
a r.   CARR 133:8
raiment: body than r.   BIBLE 64:28
King in r. of needlework   PRAY 392:1
man clothed in soft r.   BIBLE 66:2
r. of camel's hair   BIBLE 63:37
rain: able to command the r.   PEPYS 372:5
after the r. when with   SHEL 500:7
again I dissolve it in r.   SHEL 500:4
arbour where the r. beat   ELIOT 202:16
clouds and wind without r.   BIBLE 54:21
clouds return after the r.   BIBLE 56:11
droppeth as the gentle r.   SHAK 467:27
Dull roots with spring r.   ELIOT 204:17
former and the latter r.   PRAY 386:3
Hath the r. a father   BIBLE 53:4
Jupiter the R.-giver   TIB 551:1
look of hard wet r.   CHAN 139:20
more smell the dew and r.   HERB 247:22
neither let there be r.   BIBLE 50:16
r., and sun   TENN 534:2
r. came heavily and fell   WORD 580:30
r. descended   BIBLE 65:20
r. into the little valleys   PRAY 394:3

r. is over and gone | BIBLE 56:22
r. it raineth on the just | BOWEN 90:22
r. it raineth every day | SHAK 490:27
r. set early in to-night | BROW 103:28
sendeth r. on the just | BIBLE 64:19
send my roots r. | HOPK 257:3
small rain down can r. | ANON 8:16
sound of abundance of r. | BIBLE 51:10
Still falls the R. | SITW 508:13
sun and the r. Clash | FRY 219:26
thirsty earth soaks up the r. | COWL 164:7
Though the r. it raineth | SHAK 454:12
thresh of the deep-sea r. | KIPL 300:23
thro' the drizzling r. | TENN 536:6
volleying r. and tossing breeze | ARN 15:5
Weather and r. have undone | KIPL 303:31
with ranging in the r. | GREE 236:8
rainbow: another hue Unto the r.
 | SHAK 452:25
awful r. once in heaven | KEATS 290:27
heart is like a r. shell | ROSS 408:23
It was the R. gave thee | DAV 172:16
on the r. of the salt sand-wave | KEATS 291:15
r. and a cuckoo's song | DAV 172:15
r. comes and goes | WORD 578:22
r. in the sky | TENN 534:2
r. in the sky | WORD 578:19
r. round about the throne | BIBLE 81:22
r.'s glory is shed | SHEL 501:21
rain'd: it r. kisses | SHAK 422:19
rain-drop: names the r. ploughs
 | HARDY 239:10
rained: r. down manna also upon | PRAY 395:6
Raineth: R. drop and staineth slop
 | POUND 382:4
rain it r. on the just | BOWEN 90:22
rainfall: r. at morning and dewfall
 | STEV 522:29
rains: he is dissolving in r. | SHEL 500:5
rainy: not a windy night a r. | SHAK 494:14
r. day and a contentious | BIBLE 54:39
raise: contrivance to r. prices | SMITH 509:10
Lord shall r. me up | RAL 404:15
r. the price of corn | BYRON 119:26
R. the stone | ANON 7:11
to r. the wretched than | GOLD 230:22
what a dust do I r. | BACON 27:33
raised: Behold a man r. up by Christ
 | TENN 536:18
Christ being r. from | BIBLE 75:2
dead shall be r. incorruptible | BIBLE 76:29
it is r. in incorruption | BIBLE 76:27
r. the price of everything | MAC 323:15
raising: r. corn and begin raising | LEASE 313:4
raison: r. du plus fort est toujours
 | LA F 306:21
r. tonne en son cratère | POTT 382:3
tout le monde a r. | LA C 306:16
raisons: Le coeur a ses r. que la | PASC 369:10
rake: thus playing the r. | MOORE 356:29
was his hors as is a r. | CHAU 141:23
woman is at heart a r. | POPE 377:25
rakes: scholar among r. | MAC 324:13
raking: when to stop r. the muck | ROOS 408:4
rallies: voice of the schoolboy r. | NEWB 361:9
Rally: R. behind the Virginians | BEE 37:3
Ralph: Sir R. the Rover tore his | SOUT 514:3
ram: r. caught in a thicket | BIBLE 46:11
Rama: R. was there a voice heard
 | BIBLE 63:34
ramas: Verde r. | GARC 221:7
Rampage: On the R. | DICK 178:10
Ramparts: great honey-coloured R.
 | YEATS 585:4
rams: hearken than the fat of r. | BIBLE 50:4
mountains skipped like r. | PRAY 397:16
My r. speed not | BARN 34:4
ran: It r. a hundred years | HOLM 253:8
r. before Ahab | BIBLE 51:12
r. his godly race | GOLD 230:22

R. purple to the sea | MILT 345:17
So they r. both together | BIBLE 73:6
they r. awa' | MCL 325:15
rancune: lune ne garde aucune r.
 | ELIOT 204:10
random: r. are afterwards confirmed
 | KEATS 293:11
randy: Porter-drinkers' r. laughter
 | YEATS 587:8
rangers: Eight for the eight bold r. | ANON 6:5
Ranges: look behind the R. | KIPL 299:2
Rangoon: chunkin' from R. to Mandalay
 | KIPL 301:5
he can take R. | WELL 567:28
rank: my offence is r. | SHAK 434:27
r. pride | ADD 1:18
r. tongue blossom into | BROW 99:24
that when a man of r. appeared | JOHN 278:32
things r. and gross in nature | SHAK 429:28
unassailable holds on his r. | SHAK 449:25
Will r. as an idyll | GILB 227:25
you will r. as an apostle | GILB 227:23
ranks: even the r. of Tuscany | MAC 322:22
seen in glittering r. | MILT 344:9
service r. the same with God | BROW 103:25
rank-scented: mutable, r. many | SHAK 427:20
Ransack: R. the ocean for orient | MARL 329:4
ransom: Of the world's r. | SHAK 478:20
rap: To r. and knock and enter | BROW 99:4
rapacious: r. and licentious soldiery
 | BURKE 110:25
rape: r.! a rape | WEBS 567:6
subject to r. like fish | DONNE 190:2
Raphaels: they talk'd of their R. | GOLD 231:21
rapid: This particularly r. | GILB 228:37
rapier: dubbed with unhatched r.
 | SHAK 490:14
rapine: all the r. and injustice | SMITH 509:8
march through r. to disintegration
 | GLAD 229:15
R., deceit | DONNE 190:4
rapping: r. at my chamber door | POE 375:4
rapscallions: All kings is mostly r.
 | TWAIN 554:2
rapt: r. one | WORD 577:18
rapture: first fine careless r. | BROW 101:6
Modified r. | GILB 226:30
r. on the lonely shore | BYRON 121:22
raptures: r. and roses of vice | SWIN 529:5
Rara: R. avis in terris nigroque | JUV 287:20
rare: man of culture r. | GILB 227:20
r. in our pockets the mark | CHES 147:22
r. things will | BROW 102:29
Rich and r. were the gems | MOORE 356:16
raree-show: r. of Peter's successor
 | BROW 100:3
rarely: r., comest thou | SHEL 503:25
rarer: made us r. gifts than gold | BROO 94:7
r. spirit never Did steer | SHAK 423:19
rari: r. nantes in gurgite vasto | VIRG 557:11
rascaille: of swich r. | CHAU 144:19
rascal: would rather be called a r. | JOHN 277:9
rascally: r. yea-forsooth knave | SHAK 441:4
Rascals: R., would you live | FRED 218:23
there are r. in all countries | JOHN 278:1
rase: slowly r. she up | BALL 30:11
rash: Her r. hand in evil hour | MILT 349:16
He was not r. | GRAH 233:17
It is too r. | SHAK 482:16
rashes: Green grow the r. | BURNS 114:1
rassembler: On ne peut pas r. à froid
 | DE G 173:17
Rast: aber ohne R. | GOET 230:15
Rat: Cat, the R., and Lovell | COLL 158:10
giant r. of Sumatra | DOYLE 192:26
How now! a r. | SHAK 435:1
it creeps like a r. | BOWEN 91:5
like a r. without a tail | SHAK 458:6
like the sound of a r. | BROW 103:17
poisoned r. in a hole | SWIFT 526:24

r. crept softly through | ELIOT 204:26
ratem: Commisit pelago r. | HOR 259:12
rather: I had r. than forty shillings
 | SHAK 469:3
r. tough worm in your little | GILB 227:16
ratiocination: pay with r. | BUTL 117:14
rationabile: r., sine dolo lac concupiscite
 | BIBLE 83:25
rational: between them and r. converse
 | WOLL 576:10
men he can be r. and unaffected | AUST 22:9
These r. amphibii go | MARV 332:23
rat-riddled: rotten-runged r. stairs
 | BROW 102:13
rats: bins for the thieving r. | DE L 174:4
rattle: hearing 'em r. a little | FARQ 210:1
Pleas'd with r. | POPE 379:18
R. his bones over the stones | NOEL 363:19
r. of a globe to play withal | DRYD 195:13
spoilt his nice new r. | CARR 134:33
Rattlesnake: He thought he saw a R.
 | CARR 133:12
ravage: Any nose May r. | BROW 105:15
rav'd: r. and grew more fierce | HERB 247:15
rave: age should burn and r. | THOM 546:23
soft hand and let her r. | KEATS 291:15
raven: doth the r. o'er the infected
 | SHAK 476:7
locks were like the r. | BURNS 114:12
Quoth the R. | POE 375:6
r. himself is hoarse | SHAK 459:2
There comes Poe with his r. | LOW 319:8
ravening: inwardly they are r. wolves
 | BIBLE 65:8
ravenous: They're a r. horde | GILB 226:14
ravens: obscene r. | SHEL 499:16
r. brought him bread | BIBLE 51:6
three r. sat on a tree | BALL 32:7
you have seen the r. flock | AYT 24:10
raves: madness wherein now he r.
 | SHAK 432:2
To where the Atlantic r. | ARN 14:21
ravish: except you r. me | DONNE 189:9
ravish'd: r. with the whistling | POPE 380:17
you have r. justice | WEBS 567:6
ravished: did not seduce, she r. | MER 337:25
have r. me away by a power | KEATS 294:27
least would have r. her | FIEL 211:11
'tis thou hast r. me | MARL 329:3
ravishment: r. its sweet | KEATS 289:3
such divine enchanting r. | MILT 341:4
raw: Eat not of it r. | BIBLE 47:11
ray: genuine night admits no r. | DRYD 196:34
rayless: In r. majesty | YOUNG 588:1
raz'd: works to me expung'd and r.
 | MILT 347:8
razor: r. ceases to act | HOUS 266:17
to hew blocks with a r. | POPE 381:18
Razors: R. pain you | PARK 368:18
reach: all things above his r. | OVER 366:6
I could r. the brittle | VIRG 560:4
r. should exceed his grasp | BROW 98:24
will r. the bottom first | GRAH 233:10
reached: heights by great men r. | LONG 316:19
top of it r. to heaven | BIBLE 46:18
reaching: r. after fact and reason
 | KEATS 293:19
r. forth unto those things | BIBLE 78:18
reactionaries: All r. are paper tigers
 | MAO 328:20
read: authors whom they never r.
 | CHUR 148:19
be r. but not curiously | BACON 27:19
day therein we r. no more | DANTE 171:10
do *you* r. books *through* | JOHN 276:13
early years I r. very hard | JOHN 273:26
fast as they can r. | HAZL 243:10
general r. without pleasure | JOHN 280:25
have r. and nobody wants | TWAIN 554:4
I cannot r. it | CHES 147:25

I never r. much AUST 23:2
King George will be able to r. HANC 238:18
little I can r. SHAK 421:9
May r. strange matters SHAK 459:3
Much had he r. ARMS 12:15
none can r. the text TENN 535:13
Not that I ever r. them SHER 505:20
public and to r. in secret BORR 89:26
r. a book before reviewing SMITH 511:17
r. and perhaps understand KEATS 293:26
r. a nod, a shrug, a look SWIFT 527:29
r. an old one ROG 407:12
r. a novel before luncheon WAUGH 566:5
r. any thing which I call LAMB 307:17
r. as much as other men HOBB 251:23
R. God aright QUAR 403:28
r. just as inclination JOHN 274:31
r., much of the night ELIOT 204:18
R. no history DISR 186:4
R. not to contradict BACON 27:18
r. Richardson for the story JOHN 276:9
R. somewhat seldomer BROW 99:7
r. the Bible day and night BLAKE 85:22
r. when they're in trouble HOUS 265:13
such wise hear them r. PRAY 386:5
Take up and r. AUG 21:15
teach the orphan-boy to r. TENN 538:1
that they never r. DISR 186:21
they're not the ones they r. MART 331:10
to r., and censure HEM 245:1
to r. a novel I write one DISR 185:26
to write and r. comes SHAK 472:27
Unborn shall r. o'er ocean LAND 309:4
What do you r. SHAK 432:7
Who ever r. him through BURKE 111:17
readable: chief need is that it be r.
TROL 552:14
reader: by delighting the r. HOR 258:1
making the r. breathless KEATS 293:24
R., I married him BRON 93:15
r. seldom peruses a book ADD 2:7
Sagacious r. of the works of God COWP 167:5
said r. to rider AUDEN 18:17
That ideal r. suffering JOYCE 286:3
'Tis the good r. that makes EMER 208:12
readers: common sense of r. uncorrupted
JOHN 281:39
make your r. suffer so much JOHN 281:3
r. to become more indolent GOLD 232:1
so many of my r. belong CHES 148:2
readeth: that he may run that r. BIBLE 62:1
readiness: r. is all SHAK 437:15
reading: distinguish what is worth r.
TREV 552:10
invincible love of r. GIBB 224:6
I prefer r. SMITH 510:21
much pleasure in the r. QUAR 403:8
Peace is poor r. HARDY 239:15
picture of somebody r. KEATS 294:16
R. goes ill with the married MOL 353:13
r. is right which requires JOHN 282:17
R. is sometimes an ingenious HELPS 244:16
r. is to skip judiciously HAM 238:12
R. is to the mind what STEE 518:9
R. maketh a full man BACON 27:20
soul of r. STER 519:22
therefore not worth r. AUST 22:21
There is an art of r. DISP. 187:9
writing's vile hard r. SHER 506:37
your writing and r. SHAK 472:28
reads: He r. much SHAK 448:21
R. verse and thinks she BROW 100:15
Who often r. COWP 168:17
Who r. Incessantly MILT 350:10
read'st: r. the eternal deep WORD 579:7
ready: conference a r. man BACON 27:20
he is always r. to go LA F 306:22
I am r. to depart LAND 308:20
is r. to be thy bride BALL 30:9
most gracious and r. help PRAY 388:5

necessity of being r. increases LINC 314:20
pen: of a r. writer PRAY 392:14
r. ere I call'd her name PRIOR 401:5
R. to be any thing BROW 97:24
r. way to virtue BROW 96:25
real: any less r. and true SHAW 96:14
Forms more r. than living SHEL 503:6
r. till it is experienced KEATS 294:18
realised: about in worlds not r. WORD 579:10
Realism: dislike of R. WILDE 573:16
reality: Between the idea And the r.
ELIOT 203:10
Cannot bear very much r. ELIOT 202:14
may always be another r. FRY 220:9
parts for the time with r. CHUR 150:5
shadows and types to the r. NEWM 362:6
realm: this earth, this r. SHAK 478:20
welfare of this r. do chiefly CHAR 140:21
realms: calls up the r. of fairy BYRON 123:15
Napoleon of the r. of rhyme BYRON 123:31
r. and islands were SHAK 423:22
travell'd in the r. of gold KEATS 292:17
reap: clouds shall not r. BIBLE 56:7
neither do they r. BIBLE 64:28
r. his old reward KIPL 304:8
r., if we faint not BIBLE 77:20
r. thou shouldst but glean HOOD 255:5
shall r. in joy PRAY 398:17
that shall he also r. BIBLE 77:19
they shall r. the whirlwind BIBLE 61:11
you r. a habit READE 405:4
reaped: which never should be r.
TRAH 551:18
reaper: Time the r. THOM 548:28
reapers: Only r. TENN 538:5
reaping: ever r. something new TENN 538:24
r. where thou hast not BIBLE 68:3
That grew the more by r. SHAK 423:22
reaps: hurry and r. indigestion STEV 522:5
seed ye sow, another r. SHEL 504:3
rear: bring up the r. in heaven BROW 96:26
she shall r. my dusky race TENN 539:6
to r. the tender thought THOM 549:10
whose post lay in the r. ROSS 408:25
rearward: r. of a conquer'd woe SHAK 494:14
reason: against the r. of my Love'
KEATS 294:27
all r. is against it BUTL 119:3
Blest with plain r. POPE 378:9
bound To rules of r. HERB 248:1
capability and god-like r. SHAK 435:29
decision or r. or choice CHOM 148:16
Divorced old barren R. FITZ 213:1
false rules pranked in r.'s MILT 341:19
feast of r. and the flow POPE 380:5
gentle r. so persuasive stole THOM 549:26
Give you a r. on compulsion SHAK 439:5
had the full use of my r. CHES 145:23
has been endowed with r. CHEK 145:4
How noble in r. SHAK 432:15
humanity, r., and justice BURKE 109:26
ideal r. but of imagination KANT 288:12
if it be against r. COKE 154:17
in erring r.'s spite POPE 379:11
join compliance with r. BURKE 111:2
kills r. itself MILT 351:22
man who listens to R. is SHAW 498:2
men have lost their r. SHAK 450:22
men that can render a r. BIBLE 54:35
Mere r. is insufficient HUME 267:21
noble and most sovereign r. SHAK 433:15
nothing is law that is not r. POW 384:2
now R. is past care SHAK 495:15
Now tell me the r. SOUT 514:8
other but a woman's r. SHAK 490:30
our r. is our law MILT 349:15
private r. for this AUDEN 21:1
pursue my r. to an O altitudo BROW 96:9
r. abuseth me KYD 306:5
r. and the will of God ARN 15:15

R., an *ignis fatuus* ROCH 406:21
r. can imagine or desire TRAH 552:1
r. doth buckle and bow BACON 24:19
r. firm WORD 581:8
R. has moons HODG 252:5
R. in her most exalted WORD 580:26
r. I should be the same AYT 24:4
R. is not come to repeat SANT 414:2
R. is the life of the law COKE 154:18
R. to rule DRYD 196:14
r. why gunpowder treason ANON 7:10
received nor rhyme nor r. SPEN 516:29
right deed for the wrong r. ELIOT 204:4
strong and the human r. weak BAG 28:30
that great enemy of r. BROW 96:30
That takes the r. prisoner SHAK 458:15
that wants discourse of r. SHAK 429:28
Their's not to r. why TENN 532:24
they do always r. themselves SHAK 445:13
voice of r. is stifled BURKE 110:10
What can we r. POPE 379:2
will not R. and Compare BLAKE 86:2
words clothed in r.'s MILT 346:12
Reasonable: figure of 'The R. Man'
HERB 246:13
r. moderator and equal BROW 96:19
r. man could have expected HERB 246:19
r. man adapts himself SHAW 498:1
r. soul and human flesh PRAY 385:1
reasonableness: secret and sweet r.
ARN 16:22
reasonably: may r. be expected to do
WHAT 569:13
reason'd: r. high Of providence MILT 346:19
reasoned: r. or acted consequentially
CHES 145:25
reasoners: talkers or most plausible r.
HAZL 243:24
reasoning: r. engine lies ROCH 406:22
r., self-sufficing thing WORD 580:4
truth by consecutive r. KEATS 293:16
reasons: five r. we should drink ALDR 3:10
Good r. must SHAK 451:26
His r. are as two grains SHAK 465:15
never give your r. MANS 328:17
R. are not like garments ESSEX 208:24
r. find of settled gravity SHAK 493:14
r. for living JUV 287:25
undemocratic r. and for motives KIPL 302:5
We have forty million r. KIPL 300:21
reasons of state: r. to influence our
judgments MANS 328:16
reason'st: thou r. well ADD 1:24
reave: my two troubles they r. HOUS 266:7
rebel: life, a very r. SHAK 423:4
R. and Atheist too DONNE 189:26
street came the r. tread WHIT 571:16
rebellatrix: r., tandem OVID 366:22
rebelled: Because they r. against PRAY 397:7
rebellion: if r. was the certain consequence
MANS 328:16
little r. now and then JEFF 272:9
r. against the existing SHAW 496:21
r. broached on his sword SHAK 445:7
r. is as the sin of witchcraft BIBLE 50:4
R. lay in his way SHAK 440:15
R. to tyrants is obedience BRAD 91:12
rum, Romanism, and r. BURC 108:1
rebellious: Hot and r. liquors in my
SHAK 425:5
r. arm 'gainst arm SHAK 458:5
revolting and a r. heart BIBLE 60:17
rebels: subjects are r. from principle
BURKE 111:13
rebounds: unless it r. JOHN 276:20
rebuild: r. it on the old plan MILL 339:3
rebuke: Open r. is better than BIBLE 54:37
r. hath broken my heart PRAY 394:1
· to r. the people PRAY 399:2
rebus: *Cedet amor r.* OVID 366:21

recall: greater sorrow than to r. DANTE 171:8
themselves cannot r. their gifts TENN 543:12
recall'd: once spoke can never be r. ROOS 408:9
recalled: anything that could be r. DISR 186:27
recedes: research the horizon r. PATT 370:8
receipt: he had a special r. DU M 199:5
sitting at the r. of custom BIBLE 65:21
receive: blessed to give than to r. BIBLE 74:19
r. one such little child BIBLE 67:3
r. your reward in a certain place BROWN 95:8
Then r. him as best such BYRON 124:41
received: by him best r. MILT 347:23
Freely ye have r. BIBLE 65:3
his own r. him not BIBLE 71:26
receiver: r. is always thought CHES 145:9
receives: heart That watches and r. WORD 582:23
receiveth: Every one that asketh r. BIBLE 65:3
receiving: giving and r. of a Ring PRAY 389:7
recent: pushed by this r. people BURKE 109:17
recettes: r. qui réussissent toujours VAL 555:1
Rechten: seiner R. alle Wahrheit und LESS 314:2
rechtwinklig: die r. gebaut sind ab Leib NIET 363:2
recipe: rare r. for melancholy LAMB 307:23
recipes: aggregate of the r. that VAL 555:1
reciprocal: r. civility of authors JOHN 281:29
recirculation: commodius vicus of r. back JOYCE 286:2
recited: r. verses in writing BIBLE 63:23
reckless: r. what I do to spite SHAK 461:10
Restraining r. middle age YEATS 586:8
reckoned: love that can be r. SHAK 421:7
reckoning: No r. made SHAK 431:12
sense of r. SHAK 444:26
very much at your own r. TROL 553:12
weary r. SHAK 476:6
recks: r. not his own rede SHAK 430:18
recognised: objects r., In flashes WORD 580:19
recognize: did not r. me by my face TROL 552:11
r. virtue and rot PERS 372:27
recognizing: r. the gods that the city PLATO 374:8
recollect: does not r. where he laid JOHN 279:6
recommendation: face is a letter of r. ADD 2:15
face is a mute r. PUBL 402:4
recompense: not because r. is a pleasure JOHN 282:4
reconciles: Custom r. us to everything BURKE 108:10
dinner and feasting r. PEPYS 372:14
r. Discordant elements WORD 580:11
reconciliation: silence and r. where the enmities MAC 323:20
reconnaissance: La r. de la plupart des LA R 310:16
record: Cannot see the r. cut HOUS 263:2
puts a r. on the gramophone ELIOT 205:3
recordanti: r. benefacta priora voluptas CAT 137:9
recorded: knowledge too but r. experience CARL 131:8
recorders: Of flutes and soft r. MILT 345:21
Recording: domesticate the R. Angel STEV 521:33
passive, r., not thinking ISH 270:28
R. Angel, as he wrote STER 520:5
records: away all trivial fond r. SHAK 431:15
recover: it do seldom or never r. SHAK 424:5
r. what has been lost ELIOT 202:24
thou'lt r. once my dust GRAH 233:16
thou might'st him yet r. DRAY 193:21

recreant: calf's-skin on those r. limbs SHAK 452:16
that soldier a mere r. SHAK 486:26
recreate: r. yourselves SHAK 451:4
recreation: purposes of r. he has CHUR 149:20
recte: *Si possis r.* HOR 258:10
Vivere si r. nescis HOR 259:6
recti: *mens sibi conscia r.* VIRG 557:18
rectum: *citraque nequit consistere r.* HOR 261:23
r. aut justitian MAGN 327:3
recurret: *tamen usque r.* HOR 258:18
recuvver: r. the use of his legs DICK 180:8
red: good Tray grew very r. HOFF 252:13
hectic r. SHEL 502:8
In coats of r. DE L 174:6
jolly r. nose BEAU 36:5
Luve's like a r. red rose BURNS 114:27
Making the green one r. SHAK 460:13
more red than her lips' r. SHAK 495:8
Nature, r. in tooth and claw TENN 536:29
pays us poor beggars in r. KIPL 304:9
r. flag flying here CONN 161:10
Red lips are not so r. OWEN 367:6
r. men scalped each other MAC 323:21
r. rose from off this thorn SHAK 445:21
r. wheel barrow WILL 574:10
r. whatso thow be CHAU 144:17
sky is r. BIBLE 66:31
streaks of r. were mingled SUCK 524:9
that never blows so r. FITZ 212:15
thin r. line RUSS 412:23
this cheek a little r. POPE 377:16
vindictive scribble of r. BROW 100:23
your raiment all r. MAC 322:6
redbreast: r., sacred to the household THOM 549:23
r. sit and sing COL 156:23
r. whistles from a garden-croft KEATS 293:9
redder: His coomb was r. than CHAU 142:32
rede: recks not his own r. SHAK 430:18
redeem: down and r. us from virtue SWIN 529:11
redeemed: he hath r. Jerusalem BIBLE 59:19
r. his vices JONS 285:1
which were r. from BIBLE 82:15
redeemer: know that my r. liveth BIBLE 52:31
my strength, and my r. PRAY 390:13
such and so mighty a R. MISS 352:20
Redeeming: R. the time BIBLE 78:4
redemption: married past r. DRYD 197:1
Our great r. from above MILT 344:3
r. of all things by Beauty SHAW 496:22
Redemptorem: *tantum meruit habere R.* MISS 352:20
redeunt: *r. Saturnia regna* VIRG 559:22
red-flannel: birds the colour of r. THOM 546:22
redire: *unde negant r. quemquam* CAT 136:23
redress: Things past r. are now SHAK 479:3
to r. the balance CANN 130:8
redressing: ride abroad r. human wrongs TENN 534:11
redtape: than a r. Talking-machine CARL 132:1
reed: bruised r. shall he not break BIBLE 59:11
he is a thinking r. PASC 369:11
maiden and clasped a r. SHEL 501:4
nymph, but for a r. MARV 332:2
r. shaken with the wind BIBLE 66:2
staff of this bruised r. BIBLE 51:38
thee the r. is as the oak SHAK 428:22
reeds: cottages of strowed r. MARL 330:11
Down in the r. by the river BROW 98:6
hundred r. of decent growth GAY 222:7
My worn r. broken DE L 174:15
reeking: r. into Cadiz Bay BROW 101:8
Reel: R. in a drunkard CHUR 149:1

They r. to and fro PRAY 397:10
reels: There's threesome r. BURNS 113:13
references: always to verify your r. ROUTH 410:18
refin'd: r. with th'accents that DAN 170:23
refine: correct, insert, r. SWIFT 527:34
r. our language to grammatical JOHN 282:5
refined: began to disgust this r. EVEL 209:9
never be r. if I twitch THOM 547:13
r. out of existence JOYCE 286:18
This Englishwoman is so r. SMITH 510:27
refining: unless restored by the r. ELIOT 202:26
Reflection: R., you may come to-morrow SHEL 504:25
reflections: melancholy of human r. BAG 29:18
without very mortifying r. CONG 160:3
reflects: soon as he r. GOET 229:26
reflex: across the r. of a star WORD 577:26
reform: Beginning r. is beginning WELL 568:4
cured by r. or revolution BERL 41:23
party of progress or r. MILL 339:10
r. movement has a lunatic ROOS 408:5
r.', the watchword BRIG 93:2
To innovate is not to r. BURKE 112:2
reformation: be plotting some new r. DRYD 197:12
reforming of R. itself MILT 351:27
reformed: speedily r. MILT 351:20
reformers: All r. are bachelors MOORE 355:15
consolations of middle-aged r. SAKI 413:3
Refrain: R. from the unholy pleasure BELL 38:23
refresh: to r. it when it was dry PRAY 386:3
refreshed: giant r. with wine PRAY 395:7
refreshment: I accept r. at any hands GILB 226:22
reft: th'orisonte hath r. CHAU 142:13
refuge: eternal God is thy r. BIBLE 48:33
God of Jacob is our r. PRAY 392:20
high hills are a r. PRAY 397:1
last weak r. in despair THOM 549:10
they're so easy to take r. IBSEN 270:3
thou hast been our r. PRAY 395:17
refusal: great r. DANTE 171:5
refuse: may know to r. the evil BIBLE 58:3
Which he did thrice r. SHAK 450:20
Refused: R. about the age of three CHES 147:9
stone which the builders r. PRAY 398:2
refuses: Closes nothing, r. nothing WHIT 571:11
refute: this does not r. my general JOHN 275:27
Who can r. a sneer PALEY 368:9
Regain'd: R. my freedom with a sigh BYRON 125:17
regarder: *On doit se r. soi-même* MOL 353:20
regardeth: r. the clouds shall not BIBLE 56:7
regardless: r. of their doom GRAY 235:12
regards: mingled with r. that stand SHAK 453:7
Rege: *R. quod est devium* LANG 310:1
regeneration: madness and despair to the r. CONR 161:21
Regent: God bless the R. SMITH 510:6
R. of love rhymes SHAK 456:26
who revelled with the R. BEER 37:16
reges: *delirant r. plectuntur* HOR 258:12
regibus: *Maecenas atavis edite r.* HOR 259:8
regiment: He led his r. from behind GILB 225:17
Monstrous R. of Women KNOX 305:19
R. an' pokes the 'eathen KIPL 298:21
regina: *r., mater misericordiae* ANON 10:19
region: untrodden r. of my mind KEATS 292:3
register: than the r. of the crimes GIBB 224:23

register'd: r. upon our brazen tombs SHAK 456:14
reg'lar: brought r. and draw'd mild DICK 179:12
règle: r. de toutes les règles MOL 353:6
Regnavit: R. a ligno Deus VEN 556:6
regni: cuius r. non erit finis MASS 334:20
regnum: adveniat r. tuum MASS 335:5
regress: r. is either a downfall BACON 26:23
regret: desire at last and vain r. ROSS 410:6
Immutable as my r. PEAC 371:1
I only r. that I have HALE 237:14
r. can die TENN 537:5
r. the departure of our THOM 549:4
wild with all r. TENN 542:4
Regrets: past R. and Future Fears FITZ 212:16
series of congratulatory r. DISR 185:16
wild r. WILDE 572:14
regular: icily r. TENN 539:27
r. Then most, when most MILT 348:24
right-down r. Royal Queen GILB 225:22
regulate: we must r. all recreations MILT 351:25
Regulations: R. Act WILDE 572:12
Regumque: R. turris HOR 259:13
Reichtum: gemeiniglich R. den grossen Eseln LUTH 320:14
reign: Better to r. in hell MILT 345:11
friendless is to r. SHEL 503:7
had the capacity to r. TAC 531:13
my r. is peace LAND 308:21
Nymphs that r. o'er sewers COL 156:5
of the same sort of r. BENT 40:26
reigned: that I have r. with your ELIZ 206:5
reigneth: Thy God r. BIBLE 59:18
reigns: king r. THIE 546:5
red blood r. in the winter's SHAK 491:17
r. thirty thousand years MAC 324:21
reindeer: Herds of r. move across AUDEN 18:16
R. are coming to drive AUDEN 18:7
reinforcement: r. we may gain from hope MILT 345:7
reins: try out my r. and my heart PRAY 391:4
rejected: despised and r. of men BIBLE 59:21
rejoice: daughters of the Philistines r. BIBLE 50:16
desert shall r. BIBLE 58:32
let us heartily r. PRAY 396:3
Let us then r. ANON 10:13
little hills shall r. PRAY 394:3
Making all the vales r. BLAKE 87:26
men r. when they divide BIBLE 58:6
R. in the Lord alway BIBLE 78:20
r. the heart PRAY 390:12
R. with them that do rejoice BIBLE 75:16
R. ye dead BRID 92:18
thou hast broken may r. PRAY 393:5
will r. and be glad in it PRAY 398:2
rejoiced: my spirit hath r. in God BIBLE 69:5
R. they were na men BURNS 116:1
rejoiceth: r. as a giant to run his PRAY 390:11
r. in his strength BIBLE 53:6
rejoicing: what r. is there ABEL 1:2
relation: just supply and all r. DONNE 187:19
nobody like a r. THAC 545:24
poor r. LAMB 307:20
relations: Augurs and understood r. SHAK 461:24
Bless the squire and his r. DICK 176:23
men have their poor r. DICK 176:19
new stock or to visit r. AUDEN 20:2
personal character and r. NAP 359:10
relationship: r. with beauty and truth KEATS 293:18
relaxes: Bless r. BLAKE 88:23
relearn: Let them r. the Law KIPL 300:6
release: ensured r. HOUS 266:5
relent: make the gods above r. VIRG 559:5
Shall make him once r. BUNY 107:36

relenting: r. God Hath placed ROSS 408:20
relic: cas'd up, like a holy r. WEBS 566:20
sad r. of departed worth BYRON 120:13
relics: hallow'd r. should be hid MILT 344:1
other's hands these r. came DONNE 188:28
unhonour'd his r. are laid MOORE 356:15
relief: Creator and the r. of man's BACON 24:17
death is rather a r. to me FITZ 213:19
not seek for kind r. BLAKE 88:8
r. Must be to loathe her SHAK 475:21
this r. much thanks SHAK 429:5
utterance gave that thought r. WORD 579:1
which sleep provides r. CHAM 139:13
reliev'd: desperate appliances are r. SHAK 435:25
relieve: it did r. my passion much ﹀ SHAK 488:26
thee to comfort and r. them PRAY 386:1
religio: Tantum r. potuit suadere LUCR 320:4
religion: airy subtleties in r. BROW 96:8
are really but of one r. SHAD 420:24
based either on r. or policy RUSK 412:4
brothels with bricks of R. BLAKE 88:20
England but vice and r. SMITH 511:21
enough r. to make us hate SWIFT 527:7
established r. without a prelate BANC 32:13
every thing that regards r. ADD 2:21
fatal to r. as indifference BURKE 111:35
fundamental principle of my r. NEWM 361:20
him about again to our r. FULL 220:14
I cant talk r. to a man SHAW 497:13
I count r. but a childish MARL 329:19
impossibilities enough in R. BROW 96:8
increase in us true r. PRAY 386:19
indirect way to plant r. BROW 96:16
inward tranquillity which r. FORB 216:10
is but an handmaid to r. BACON 24:28
is the r. of Protestants CHIL 148:12
men's minds about to r. BACON 25:24
more beautiful than any r. SAKI 413:7
more fierce in its r. NEWM 361:19
my r. is to do good PAINE 368:5
Notre r. est faite pour MONT 355:1
old r.'s sake HERR 249:6
One r. is as true as another BURT 117:2
Philistine of genius in r. ARN 16:23
r. and matrimony I never CHES 146:3
R. blushing veils her sacred POPE 376:1
r. breathing household WORD 582:9
r. ends BURKE 108:12
R. es la caballería CERV 138:15
r., I hold it to be PAINE 367:23
r. is allowed to invade MELB 336:13
R. is by no means a proper CHES 146:4
R. is knight-errantry CERV 138:15
R. the opium of the people MARX 333:6
r. most prevalent in our BURKE 109:22
r. must still be allowed CHES 145:30
r. of gold BAG 29:4
r. of humanity PAINE 368:7
R.'s in the heart JERR 273:1
r. when in rags and contempt BUNY 107:19
rum and true r. BYRON 122:16
slovenliness is no part of r. WESL 568:22
some of r. EDG 199:20
some other new r. PLATO 374:8
Superstition is the r. BURKE 111:22
suspended the sentiments of r. BURKE 111:29
sweet r. makes A rhapsody SHAK 435:4
take my r. from the priest GOLD 232:41
talks loudly against r. STER 519:25
that a man's r. is CARL 131:28
That is my r. SHAW 497:11
then Poetry and R. CARL 131:4
There is only one r. SHAW 498:11
this man's r. is vain BIBLE 80:11
To become a popular r. INGE 270:6
to profess any r. in name BURKE 111:20

true meaning of r. is thus ARN 16:2﹖
was not a r. for gentlemen CHAR 140:2﹖
We must have r. for religion's COUS 163:﹖
When I mention r. FIEL 211:2﹖
religions: are sixty different r. CAR 130:1﹖
sort of collector of r. SHAW 497:1﹖
religioun: good man was ther of r. CHAU 141:3﹖
religious: among you seem to be r. BIBLE 80:1﹖
constitution a r. animal BURKE 111:1﹖
I hope I will be r. again FLEM 214:2﹖
intellect in r. enquiries NEWM 362:2
not r.-good HARDY 241:2﹖
r. and moral principles ARN 16:2﹖
r. book, or friend WOTT 583:1﹖
R., discountenance every BLAKE 86:﹖
r. factions are volcanoes BURKE 111:3﹖
R. persecution may shield BURKE 110:2﹖
that I suspended my r. GIBB 224:11
troubled with r. doubt CHES 147:﹖
relinquished: only have r. one delight WORD 579:1﹖
relish: r. of the saltness of time SHAK 441:﹖
reluctance: superstitious r. to sit JOHN 278:1﹖
reluctant: with r. feet LONG 316:2﹖
rem: quocumque modo r. HOR 258:1﹖
remain: be amongst you and r. with PRAY 388:4
up the fragments that r. BIBLE 72:5
remained: else perished, and he r. BRON 93:25
while anything r. to be done LUCAN 319:24
remains: look at least on love's r. BROW 103:24
nothing done while aught r. ROG 407:7
One r. SHEL 499:26
Strength in what r. behind... WORD 579:13
remark: Which I wish to r. HARTE 242:29
remarkable: there is nothing left r. SHAK 423:16
remarks: said our r. before DON 187:17
remède: La mort est le r. CHAM 139:13
remedies: encumbering it with r. TOLS 551:12
r. oft in ourselves do SHAK 420:28
that will not apply new r. BACON 26:28
When a lot of r. CHEK 144:23
remedy: Force is not a r. BRIG 93:7
know not how to r. our own KYD 306:4
r. is worse than the disease BACON 27:13
requires a dangerous r. FAWK 210:31
sovereign r. to all diseases BURT 116:29
Things without all r. SHAK 461:12
'Tis a sharp r. RAL 404:17
true r. for superstition BURKE 109:30
remember: can't r. how They go CALV 127:13
don't you r. sweet Alice ENGL 208:19
Do you r. an Inn BELL 40:12
glad to r. even these VIRG 557:14
Half to r. days that have FLEC 214:5
he'll r. with advantages SHAK 445:3
If I do not r. thee PRAY 399:3
if thou wilt, r. ROSS 409:8
I r., I remember HOOD 254:17
I r. the way we parted SWIN 530:10
is to r. what is past HAL 238:3
I would r. Him BEEC 37:9
let not man r. HOUS 264:27
like to something I r. FORD 216:19
Must I r. SHAK 429:28
never r. whether it snowed THOM 546:20
not r. what I must be now SHAK 479:14
oafish louts r. Mum BETJ 42:8
power of beauty I r. DRYD 195:32
r. me when thou comest BIBLE 71:12
R. me when I am dead DOUG 191:9
R. me when I am gone away ROSS 409:3
R. now thy Creator BIBLE 56:11
r. of this unstable world MAL 327:21

r. the Fifth of November	ANON 7:10	loving and a fair r.	SHAK 429:27
R. the sabbath day	BIBLE 47:24	r. churlish	SHAK 427:5
r. the past are condemned	SANT 414:1	Their's not to make r.	TENN 532:24
R. thee	SHAK 431:15	**Report:** R. me and my cause aright	
r. while the light lives	SWIN 529:12		SHAK 437:23
still r. me	MOORE 356:8	whatsoever things are of good r.	BIBLE 78:22
& that no man r. me	HARDY 241:18	Who hath believed our r.	BIBLE 59:20
Till thou r. and I forget	SWIN 530:14	**reporter:** I am a r.	GREE 236:7
To r. with tears	ALL 3:21	**reporters:** gallery in which the r.	MAC 323:7
Well I r. how you smiled	LAND 309:4	through r. to Buncombe	CARL 132:4
We will r. them	BINY 84:10	**reporting:** r. device for experience	
when the iris blooms, R.	COL 155:4		WHORF 571:23
with names that men r.	SWIN 529:14	**reports:** Bring me no more r.	SHAK 462:28
you should r. and be sad	ROSS 409:4	**repos:** demeurer en r. dans une chambre	
remember'd: flowing cups freshly r.			PASC 369:5
	SHAK 445:3	*La gloire et le r. sont*	MONT 354:22
r. for a very long time	MCG 325:6	**repose:** dear r. for limbs with	SHAK 493:5
r. that he once was young	ARMS 12:14	Has earned a night's r.	LONG 317:19
remembered: blue r. hills	HOUS 263:22	Pray for the r. of His soul	ROLFE 407:17
He r. too late on his thorny	PEAC 370:19	r. is taboo'd by anxiety	GILB 226:12
of my youth I r. my God	SOUT 514:9	seek r. In listlessness	WORD 580:6
r. by some for their services	VIRG 558:23	sleep should be his last r.	ANON 8:21
R. on waking	BRID 92:10	weave the garlands of r.	MARV 331:21
r. Perishing be	DE L 174:2	**reposes:** In quiet she r.	ARN 14:5
said anything that was r.	DISR 186:27	**reprehend:** If I r. any thing in this	
would have made myself r.	KEATS 294:28		SHER 506:14
Remembering: R. without ceasing your		**represent:** Unwillingly r.	GILB 227:5
	BIBLE 78:30	**representation:** Taxation and r.	CAMD 128:4
R. him like anything	CHES 147:17	Taxation without r. is	OTIS 365:25
soul r. my good friends	SHAK 478:24	**representative:** expressed by himself	
Remembers: R. me of all his gracious		or r.	CAMD 128:4
	SHAK 452:20	Your r. owes you	BURKE 109:11
remember'st: r. not the slightest folly		**represents:** It r. health	SHAW 497:7
	SHAK 425:10	**repress:** r. the speech they know	
remembrance: appear almost a r.			ELIOT 200:24
	KEATS 293:24	**repress'd:** ardour of my zeal r.	CHUR 148:22
be had in everlasting r.	PRAY 397:14	**reproach:** eternal r. of the divines	
dear r. of his dying Lord	SPEN 515:31		MILT 352:12
Do this in r. of me	PRAY 388:1	It is a r. to religion	PENN 371:14
Makes the r. dear	SHAK 421:5	only hope to escape r.	JOHN 281:5
r. of a guest that tarrieth	BIBLE 62:18	Writing their own r.	SHAK 486:19
r. of them is grievous	PRAY 387:19	**reproche:** *Chevalier sans peur et sans*	
r. of his holiness	PRAY 391:13	*r.*	ANON 9:5
r. of a weeping queen	SHAK 479:19	**reproof:** r. valiant	SHAK 427:5
r. of my former love	SHAK 490:34	**reproofs:** r. from authority ought	
rosemary, that's for r.	SHAK 436:10		BACON 26:25
summon up r. of things past	SHAK 493:7	**reprove:** sager sort our deeds r.	CAT 136:19
Writ in r. more than things	SHAK 478:18	r. all the rest	POPE 377:4
remembrancer: scented gift and r.		**reptile:** first turn myself into a r.	JOHN 274:19
designedly	WHIT 570:18	**republic:** make in the r. of letters	ADD 1:11
remembreth: Crist! whan that it r.		Only Love the Beloved R.	FORS 217:13
	CHAU 143:19	r. a roll of honour	CLEV 153:2
reminiscence: r. sing	WHIT 570:9	r. is a raft which will	AMES 4:3
Reminiscences: R. make one feel so		R. is a government in which	BAG 28:30
deliciously	SHAW 497:2	were living in Plato's R.	CIC 151:16
remission: many for the r. of sins	PRAY 388:1	**republican:** acrimonious and surly r.	
shedding of blood is no r.	BIBLE 79:29		JOHN 281:33
to have r. of pain or guilt	PRAY 400:9	R. form of Government is	SPEN 514:28
remissly: sinewy proboscis did r.		**Republicans:** We are R. and don't propose	
	DONNE 190:3		BURC 108:1
remnant: r. of our Spartan dead BYRON 123:2		**Republics:** R. weak because they appeal	
remnants: some r. of history which			BAG 28:30
	BACON 24:18	**Repudiate:** R. the repudiators	FESS 210:34
remomoring: deem r. of a cursed past		**repugnances:** those national r. do not	
	VANZ 555:8		BROW 96:28
remorse: access and passage to r.	SHAK 459:2	**repugnant:** plainly r. to the Word of	
far rather feel r.	THOM 546:6	God	PRAY 400:8
R., the fatal egg by pleasure	COWP 166:9	**Repugnare:** *R. ut detur vacuum sive*	
remorseful: r. day	SHAK 446:8		DESC 175:12
remorseless: when the r. deep	MILT 343:7	**reputability:** of r. to the gentleman	
Remote: R. and ineffectual Don	BELL 39:27		VEBL 556:1
r. enquiries	JOHN 281:40	**reputation:** At ev'ry word a r. dies	
R. from towns he ran his	GOLD 230:22		POPE 381:21
R., unfriended	GOLD 231:23	Dear for her r. through	SHAK 478:20
remoter: had no need of a r. charm		ever written out of r.	BENT 41:13
	WORD 578:6	I have lost my r.	SHAK 475:7
Remove: R. hence to yonder place BIBLE 67:1		Is spotless r.	SHAK 478:8
R. not the ancient landmark	BIBLE 54:23	made himself of no r.	BIBLE 78:13
remover: bends with the r. to remove		Seeking the bubble r.	SHAK 425:24
	SHAK 495:5	sold my R. for a Song	FITZ 213:13

renaissance: in her warm nest of r.		
	DAY-L 172:21	
renascentur: *Multa r. quae iam cecidere*		
	HOR 257:14	
rend: *mais ne se r. pas*	CAMB 128:2	
render: r. back from out thy breast		
	BYRON 123:2	
r. The deeds of mercy	SHAK 467:27	
R. therefore unto Caesar	BIBLE 67:20	
R. therefore to all their	BIBLE 75:22	
rendezvous: I have a r. with Death		
	SEEG 419:15	
My r. is appointed	WHIT 571:2	
rending: till the r. of the rocks	JOYCE 286:4	
renew: Although a subtler Sphinx r.		
	SHEL 501:1	
Lord shall r. their strength	BIBLE 59:10	
r. a right spirit	PRAY 393:6	
renew'd: wish I were r.	SHAK 495:4	
renewed: is r. in knowledge after BIBLE 78:26		
renewing: r. is of love	EDW 200:5	
renounce: r. the devil and all his PRAY 388:13		
renovare: *iubes r. dolorem*	VIRG 557:20	
renown: land of just and old r.	TENN 544:11	
men of r.	BIBLE 45:33	
Speak no more of his r.	TENN 541:15	
rent: r. the envious Casca made	SHAK 450:27	
That has not been r.	YEATS 584:19	
When I widen the r.	SHEL 500:6	
why? for r.	BYRON 119:27	
repairs: anon r. his drooping head		
	MILT 343:17	
repast: cups prolong the rich r.	POPE 381:6	
repay: I will r.	BIBLE 75:18	
I will r. thee	BIBLE 69:32	
Will find a Tiger well r.	BELL 38:31	
repeal: r. of bad or obnoxious GRANT 233:22		
repeat: come to r. the universe	SANT 414:2	
repeateth: r. a matter separateth BIBLE 54:10		
repeats: r. his words	SHAK 452:20	
repel: retard what we cannot r.	JOHN 281:9	
repent: from their marble caves r.		
	DRUM 193:25	
have no strength to r.	SHAK 440:1	
I do r. it from my very	SHAK 486:18	
I hardly ever r.	NASH 360:1	
It doth r. me	SHEL 502:21	
No follies to have to r.	TAYL 531:26	
nor falter, nor r.	SHEL 503:15	
R. what's past	SHAK 435:15	
R. ye	BIBLE 63:35	
they r. in haste	CONG 160:27	
truly and earnestly r.	PRAY 387:18	
weak alone r.	BYRON 121:33	
we may r. at leisure	CONG 160:27	
repentance: morning cool r. came		
	SCOTT 418:29	
R. is the virtue of weak	DRYD 196:24	
R. is but want of power	DRYD 197:9	
R. is the hire	SCOTT 415:14	
R. on a Sunday	YBAR 584:7	
sinners to r.	BIBLE 65:24	
There's no r. in the grave	WATTS 565:15	
To give r. to her lover	GOLD 231:31	
Where pleasure and r. dwell	RAL 404:8	
repente: *Nemo r. fuit turpissimus* JUV 287:14		
repented: much r.	BYRON 122:11	
repenteth: over one sinner that r. BIBLE 70:17		
repenting: In mirth, that after no r.		
	MILT 351:11	
repetita: *Occidit miseros crambe r.*		
	JUV 287:24	
repetitions: r., as the heathen do BIBLE 64:23		
repine: 'Do not r.	DICK 179:7	
replaces: pianola 'r.' Sappho	POUND 383:5	
replenish: r. the earth	BIBLE 45:6	
replete: thing r. with too much rage		
	SHAK 493:2	
reply: I made r.	HOUS 265:5	
I pause for a r.	SHAK 450:16	

wink a r. down SWIFT 527:29
wrinkle and the r. of five-and-twenty
DRYD 196:36
reputations: large home of ruined r.
ELIOT 201:5
sit upon the murdered r. CONG 160:32
true fuller's earth for r. GAY 222:17
reputed: therefore only are r. wise
SHAK 465:12
request: be ruined at our own r. MORE 357:10
No flowers, by r. AING 3:6
Requiem: R. aeternam dona eis MASS 334:17
thy high r. become a sod KEATS 291:22
To sing a r. SHAK 437:3
Requiescant: R. in pace MASS 335:10
require: men in women do r. BLAKE 86:17
What doth the Lord r. BIBLE 61:25
required: captive r. of us then a song
PRAY 399:3
night thy soul shall be r. BIBLE 70:5
of him can nothing be r. FIEL 211:13
requisite: first r. of a good citizen ROOS 408:2
r. in business than dispatch ADD 1:12
requited: how ill r. SHAK 487:19
rerum: Sunt lacrimae r. VIRG 557:17
res: festinat et in medias r. HOR 257:20
r. age OVID 366:21
R. angusta domi JUV 287:18
rescue: Thus did Apollo r. me HOR 262:6
research: r. is always incomplete PATT 370:8
resemble: we will r. you in that SHAK 467:4
resented: is never r. for an offence
SWIFT 527:3
Who r. it COW 164:5
resentment: difficult to get up r.
NEWM 361:13
reserv'd: Alike r. to blame POPE 376:27
reserve: r. the more weighty voice
BACON 25:41
reserved: life it is r. only for God
BACON 24:24
r. for some end or other CLIVE 153:6
residuum: to this vast r. we may ARN 15:20
resignation: by r. none JEFF 272:15
While r. gently slopes GOLD 230:20
resigned: I am not r. MILL 339:23
resist: fascination that few can r. GILB 227:10
I never r. temptation SHAW 496:5
r. everything except temptation WILDE 573:8
R. not evil BIBLE 64:17
resistance: r. of the Tolbooth-gate
SCOTT 418:19
resisted: know not what's r. BURNS 112:26
resisting: over-fond of r. temptation
BECK 36:21
resistless: r. course was given SCOTT 416:28
resolution: Certain my r. is to die
MILT 349:18
In war, r. CHUR 150:25
r. thus fobbed as it is SHAK 438:4
results of thought and r. TROL 553:11
thus the native hue of r. SHAK 433:8
what r. from despair MILT 345:7
resolutions: governs the passions and
r. HUME 267:22
Of great and mighty r. BUTL 117:28
resolv'd: r. to live a fool BEAU 35:19
when I think I'm best r. SUCK 524:13
Resolve: Firm R. BURNS 115:14
R. not to be poor JOHN 279:2
R. to be thyself ARN 14:22
resolved: r. to grow fat DRYD 196:36
speech they have r. not ELIOT 200:24
Resolves: R.; and re-resolves YOUNG 588:5
To dror r. an' triggers LOW 319:3
resonance: r. of his solitude CONN 161:16
resounding: full-r. line POPE 380:15
resource: infinite-r.-and-sagacity KIPL 304:16
resources: born to consume r. HOR 258:13
r. of civilization are GLAD 229:14

respect: art a fellow of a good r. SHAK 452:6
How I did r. you when you TROL 552:20
Is there no r. of place SHAK 488:20
neither doth God r. any BIBLE 50:23
On both sides more r. SHAK 427:22
other means of procuring r. JOHN 276:38
r. of persons with God BIBLE 74:34
R. was mingled with surprise SCOTT 416:6
too much r. upon the world SHAK 465:9
Which I r. not SHAK 451:20
respectable: consider him as a r. Hottentot
CHES 145:32
devil's most devilish when r. BROW 97:32
more r. he is SHAW 497:19
Not one is r. or unhappy WHIT 570:22
riff-raff apply to what is r. HOPE 255:29
when was genius found r. BROW 97:31
respecter: God is no r. of persons BIBLE 74:2
respects: Private r. must yield MILT 350:24
respice: et r. finem ANON 10:18
respond: start a song and to r. VIRG 560:3
Responsare: R. cupidinibus HOR 262:10
responsibility: Liberty means r. SHAW 497:37
Power without r. KIPL 305:13
r. and to discharge my EDW 200:4
responsible: you know who are r.
PLATO 374:9
Responsive: R. to the cuckoo's note
GRAY 235:16
res publica: consules ne quid r. detrimenti
ANON 10:10
rest: a-brewing towards my r. SHAK 466:11
all the r. were little ELIZ 205:22
because they are at r. PRAY 397:10
choose Their place of r. MILT 350:1
elusive shadow, r. ARN 12:22
far better r. that I go DICK 183:12
flee away, and be at r. PRAY 393:10
From r. and sleep DONNE 189:5
Good r. to all KIPL 301:13
Grant them eternal r. MASS 334:17
have no r. day or night BIBLE 82:17
holy r. NEWM 362:9
home and r. on the couch CAT 136:28
I will give you r. BIBLE 66:5
may r. from their labours BIBLE 82:18
might it die or r. at last SHEL 501:3
needful hours of r. DRYD 194:7
night-season also I take no r. PRAY 390:16
nowhere yet to r. my head ARN 13:8
Now she's at r. DRYD 196:8
one crept silently to R. FITZ 212:17
ordain'd no r. VAUG 555:10
ourselves and never r. MARL 330:8
peace, and take my r. PRAY 389:22
r. a little from praise SWIN 530:3
r. for the sole of her BIBLE 45:35
R. in soft peace JONS 283:28
r. is silence SHAK 437:27
r. may reason and welcome BROW 98:21
r. on its original plan BURKE 110:13
r. quiet in Montparnasse BENET 40:20
R., rest, perturbed spirit SHAK 431:25
r. to his mind WALT 564:3
seeking r. BIBLE 66:13
shall r. upon thy holy hill PRAY 390:4
shortly be with them that r. MILT 350:23
should not enter into my r. PRAY 396:4
sure my bones would not r. BYRON 126:20
that seals up all in r. SHAK 494:7
thenceforth all shall r. eternally SPEN 516:25
then had I been at r. BIBLE 52:12
there did it r. KEATS 290:1
there the weary be at r. BIBLE 52:13
they r. not day and night BIBLE 81:24
who sink to r. COLL 158:19
will not let them r. KEATS 289:27
without r. GOET 230:15
reste: J'y suis, j'y r. MACM 325:17
tout le r. est littérature VERL 556:9

rested: r. the seventh day BIBLE 47:24
restful: r. death I cry SHAK 494:5
restituit: homo nobis cunctando r. ENN 208:22
restless: r. and versatile intellect HUXL 269:13
restlessness: keep them with repining
r. HERB 248:8
Restoration: Church's R. BETJ 43:2
With tranquil r. WORD 578:4
restore: r. the crown to its hereditary
JOHN 276:22
R. thou them that are penitent PRAY 384:13
Time may r. us in his course ARN 13:18
restored: r. by the refining fire ELIOT 202:26
restorer: Tir'd Nature's sweet r.
YOUNG 587:21
restoring: I am r. tranquillity BURKE 109:28
restraint: jesses and r. THOM 548:2
r. with which they write CAMP 128:12
were free from this r. CONG 160:30
resume: to resumption is to r. CHASE 141:4
resurrection: also is the r. of the dead
BIBLE 76:27
also the r. of the dead BIBLE 76:22
certain hope of the R. PRAY 389:13
Church of Ireland r. BETJ 43:9
glorious R. and Ascension PRAY 385:17
'I'm the R. and the Life' AUDEN 21:7
r. they neither marry BIBLE 67:21
r., and the life. BIBLE 72:22
R. of the body PRAY 384:26
symbol of his r. PROU 401:23
resurrectionem: Et expecto r. mortuorum
MASS 334:20
resurrexit: Et r. tertia die MASS 334:20
resuscitate: r. the dead art Of poetry
POUND 383:1
retain: spirit to r. the spirit BIBLE 55:25
retard: r. what we cannot repel JOHN 281:9
retention: they lack r. SHAK 489:6
retentive: r. to the strength of spirit
SHAK 449:3
Reticence: R., in three volumes GLAD 229:20
reticulated: Anything r. or decussated
JOHN 281:13
retinue: puffed up with this r. SHAK 442:15
retire: him to r. from the world DISR 186:19
r. at half-past eight MILL 339:27
Skill'd to r. MILT 350:2
with a blush r. DICK 178:3
Retired: R. to their tea and scandal
CONG 159:21
retirement: short r. urges sweet return
MILT 349:12
retort: r. courteous SHAK 427:5
retrace: Thy steps r. GILB 228:14
retraite: liberté et principale r. MONT 354:20
retreat: conquer or die who've no r.
GAY 223:27
I will not r. a single GARR 221:17
my soul's calm r. VAUG 555:12
through the loopholes of r. COWP 167:12
us make an honourable r. SHAK 426:6
woman's noblest station is r. LYTT 321:21
retreating: Have you seen yourself r.
NASH 360:5
retrench: We r. the superfluities GAY 222:24
retrenchment: r., and reform' BRIG 93:2
retrograde: be not r. JONS 284:13
r. if it does not advance GIBB 224:29
retrorsum: nulla r. HOR 258:11
return: be the day of their r. MAC 324:22
go whence I shall not r. BIBLE 52:20
he shall not r. to me BIBLE 50:52
hours of light r. ARN 13:23
In that state I came, r. VAUG 555:17
I shall r. MAC 321:24
Let us r. to our sheep ANON 9:16
never must r. MILT 343:5
r. into my house from whence BIBLE 66:13
r. no more to his house BIBLE 52:19

r., O Shulamite   BIBLE 57:6
r. Sicilian Muse   MILT 343:14
r. your thanks would pass   BROW 106:1
spirit shall r. unto God   BIBLE 56:11
thou r. at all in peace   BIBLE 51:20
To r. the compliment   GILB 228:1
unto dust shalt thou r.   BIBLE 45:23
returned: r. home the previous night
   BULL 106:22
We r. to our places   ELIOT 203:15
returning: *home there's no r.*   HOUS 265:3
R. were as tedious as go   SHAK 461:25
returns: Not one r. to tell us   FITZ 213:4
not to me r. Day   MILT 347:8
whence they say no one r.   CAT 136:23
reum: Habes confitentem r.   PETR 373:4
re-unite: Your charms r. what common
   SCH 415:9
réussissent: l'ensemble des recettes qui
r.   VAL 555:1
rêve: Vivre sans r., qu'est-ce   ROST 410:13
reveal: What does He then but r.   MILT 351:27
revealed: arm of the Lord r.   BIBLE 59:20
of the Lord shall be r.   BIBLE 59:5
revelation: inspired by divine r.   BACON 24:20
Revelations: It ends with R.   WILDE 573:29
r. and gifts of the Holy Ghost   BUTL 117:11
revelled: all who r. with the Regent
   BEER 37:16
revellers: You moonshine r.   SHAK 469:16
revelry: sound of r. by night   BYRON 120:20
revels: Our r. now are ended   SHAK 485:20
that r. long o' nights   SHAK 449:21
What r. are in hand   SHAK 471:12
revenge: I will most horribly r.   SHAK 445:10
little R. herself went   TENN 543:5
man that studieth r. keeps   BACON 27:9
medicine of our great r.   SHAK 462:17
pleasure in r.   JUV 288:6
ranging for r.   SHAK 450:12
R. his foul and most unnatural   SHAK 431:6
R. is a kind of wild justice   BACON 27:7
R. triumphs over death   BACON 26:2
shall we not r.   SHAK 467:4
spur my dull r.   SHAK 435:29
Stirr'd up with envy and r.   MILT 344:23
study of r.   MILT 345:3
Sweet is r.   BYRON 122:12
sweet r. grows harsh   SHAK 477:9
that a capable and wide r.   SHAK 476:1
revenged: be r. on the whole pack
   SHAK 490:26
revenges: have such r. on you both
   SHAK 454:2
of time brings in his r.   SHAK 490:25
Revenons: R. à ces moutons   ANON 9:16
revenue: Instead of a standing r.
   BURKE 109:31
revenues: She bears a duke's r.   SHAK 446:4
Revere: midnight ride of Paul R.
   LONG 316:25
reverence: more of r. in us dwell
   TENN 535:32
myn herte have hem in r.   CHAU 143:29
mystic r.   BAG 28:21
none so poor to do him r.   SHAK 450:23
r.— That angel   SHAK 428:20
To r. the King   TENN 534:11
reverend: It is a r. thing to see   BACON 26:38
reverent: r. cadence and subtle   AUDEN 18:3
reveries: From r. so airy   COWP 167:4
reversion: no bright r. in the sky   POPE 376:7
reverti: vox missa r.   HOR 258:6
Reviewers: R. are usually people who
   COL 157:26
you chorus of indolent r.   TENN 533:14
reviewing: read a book before r.
   SMITH 511:17
revivals: art is the history of r.   BUTL 118:33

revocare: Sed r. gradum superasque
   VIRG 558:18
revolting: r. and a rebellious heart
   BIBLE 60:17
revolts: It r. me, but I do it   GILB 226:21
revolution: be cured by reform or r.
   BERL 41:23
c'est une grande r.   LA R 310:19
impossible without a violent r.   LENIN 313:21
is…a sort of mental r.   ORW 365:10
not the leaders of a r.   CONR 161:22
reform is beginning r.   WELL 568:4
R., like Saturn   VERG 556:7
see the r. of the times   SHAK 442:1
what a r.   BURKE 111:9
white heat of this r.   WILS 574:17
revolutionary: r. is merely a climber
   ORW 365:16
their r. right to dismember   LINC 314:19
Revolutionists: age fatal to R.   DESM 175:13
revolutions: nursery of future r.   BURKE 111:5
r. are not to be evaded   DISR 185:42
share in two r. is living   PAINE 368:6
that r. never go backward   SEW 420:16
revolve: worlds r. like ancient women
   ELIOT 204:8
reward: himself shall r. you openly
   BIBLE 64:22
in no wise lose his r.   BIBLE 65:41
nothing for r.   SPEN 516:12
only r. of virtue is virtue   EMER 207:21
reap his old r.   KIPL 304:8
receive your r. in a certain place   BROWN 95:8
r. against the innocent   PRAY 390:5
r. of a thing well done   EMER 207:26
what r. have ye   BIBLE 64:20
rewarded: r. me evil for good   PRAY 391:24
thee be plenteously r.   PRAY 387:2
they shall be greatly r.   BIBLE 62:13
rewarder: be my r. he passed over
   BUNY 107:38
rewardest: thou r. every man according
   PRAY 393:20
rewards: are their own r.   FARQ 210:14
fellow that will take r.   SHAK 422:21
r. and Fairies   CORB 162:13
Rex: Ego et R. meus   SHAK 447:8
Quis r.   ABEL 1:2
R. tremendae maiestatis   CEL 138:7
rey: pastor con el r. y al simple   CERV 138:20
Reynolds: gipsy by R. to his Majesty's
   MAC 324:2
When Sir Joshua R. died   BLAKE 85:7
Rheims: Lord Archbishop of R.   BARH 33:11
rhetoric: can't do you love and r.
   STOP 523:16
Death, without r.   SIEY 508:7
heavenly r. of thine eye   SHAK 457:4
logic and r.   BACON 27:21
obscure them by an aimless r.   HUXL 269:13
r. he could not ope   BUTL 117:15
rhetorician: sophistical r.   DISR 185:17
rhetorick: Ornate r. taught out   MILT 352:9
rheum: void your r. upon my beard
   SHAK 466:3
rheumatic: That r. diseases do abound
   SHAK 470:6
rheumatism: to me to complain of r.
   SAKI 413:8
Rhine: henceforth wash the river R.
   COL 156:5
king-like rolls the R.   CALV 127:20
R. circle fair Wertenberg   MARL 329:5
wide and winding R.   BYRON 120:31
You think of the R.   BALD 29:28
rhinoceros: arm'd r. or the Hyrcan tiger
   SHAK 461:21
Rhodope: Brighter than is the silver R.
   MARL 330:3
rhyme: build the lofty r.   MILT 343:2

could not get a r. for roman   FLEM 215:4
free from r.'s infection   JONS 285:6
In a sort of Runic r.   POE 375:1
I r. for fun   BURNS 113:24
me that my murmuring r.   MORR 358:9
names in many a mused r.   KEATS 291:22
Napoleon of the realms of r.   BYRON 123:31
received nor r. nor reason   SPEN 516:29
R. being no necessary adjunct   MILT 344:18
R. is the rock on which   DRYD 194:22
R. thee to good   HERB 246:27
r. themselves into ladies'   SHAK 445:13
r. the rudder is of verses   BUTL 117:25
ruined r.   SWIN 530:25
still more tired of R.   BELL 39:18
taen the fit o' r.   BURNS 113:23
To r. upon a dish   SPEN 515:15
unattempted yet in prose or r.   MILT 344:21
Was never said in r.   KEATS 293:4
rhymed: nor to be r. to death   SIDN 508:5
R. out in love's despair   YEATS 586:14
rhymes: between piety and poor r.
   WILDE 573:38
pair their r. as Venus   BYRON 123:14
Regent of love r.   SHAK 456:26
R. are so scarce in this   CALV 127:25
ring out my mournful r.   TENN 537:15
These r. I've made   CAT 137:16
Rhyming: modern bondage of R.   MILT 344:19
Rialto: What news on the R.   SHAK 465:28
riband: r. in the cap of youth   SHAK 436:17
r. to stick in his coat   BROW 102:4
ribbon: blue r. of the turf   DISR 186:13
road was a r. of moonlight   NOYES 364:12
ribboned: 3lake of a r. coat   NEWB 361:8
ribbons: Tie up my sleeves with r.
   HUNT 268:15
Wi' r. on her breast   BALL 31:11
ribs: breaking of r. was sport   SHAK 424:23
he took one of his r.   BIBLE 45:11
Many a dig in the r.   SURT 525:5
mountain-chains like r.   HARDY 239:13
Ribstone Pippin: 'Right as a R.   BELL 39:17
rice: *it's lovely r. pudding*   MILNE 340:10
pound of R.   LEAR 312:9
rich: am r. beyond the dreams   MOORE 355:14
behave as the r. behave   SMITH 510:19
Eat with the r.   SMITH 510:18
esteemed themselves r.   MAC 323:26
ever by chance grow r.   THOM 547:18
ever seems it r. to die   KEATS 291:22
feed with the r.   JOHN 275:23
from the r. man's table   BIBLE 70:28
He wished all men as r.   GILB 225:28
is not r. enough to do it   REED 405:9
Let him be r. and weary   HERB 248:8
Letters for the r.   AUDEN 20:1
like to one more r. in hope   SHAK 493:6
making Gay r. and Rich gay   JOHN 282:1
marry a r. woman as a poor   THAC 545:14
most r., being poor   SHAK 453:8
no law to make thee r.   SHAK 483:26
no sin, but to be r.   SHAK 452:15
passing r. with forty pounds   GOLD 230:22
Perhaps been poorly r.   SAV 415:5
Poor little r. girl   COW 164:1
property of the r.   RUSK 412:11
r. and poor alike to sleep   FRAN 217:26
R. and rare were the gems   MOORE 356:16
R. AND THE POOR   DISR 186:29
r. have become richer   SHEL 505:11
r. he hath sent empty away   BIBLE 69:6
R. in good works   BIBLE 79:20
R. in the simple worship   KEATS 291:12
r. man in his castle   ALEX 3:14
r. man to enter into   BIBLE 67:11
R. men furnished with ability   BIBLE 63:23
r. men rule the law   GOLD 231:29
r., not gaudy   SHAK 430:19
r. only select from   SMITH 509:9

r., thou'rt poor SHAK 464:9
something r. and strange SHAK 484:32
tell you about the very r. FITZ 213:24
ten thousand times More r. SHAK 467:13
that maketh haste to be r. BIBLE 54:42
There was a certain r. man BIBLE 70:28
to the poor and the r. ANON 4:13
Tullus who was so r. HOR 261:16
When a r. man is fallen BIBLE 63:4
who dies…r. dies disgraced CARN 132:32
wretchedness of being r. SMITH 510:17
Richard: Did scowl on R. SHAK 480:10
R.'s himself again CIBB 151:13
To put down R. SHAK 438:17
Richardson: works of R. are pictures
WALP 562:27
richer: Becomes the f. still the older
BUTL 118:17
r. for poorer PRAY 389:4
R. than all his tribe SHAK 477:23
riches: consists in the parade of r.
SMITH 509:11
earth is full of thy r. PRAY 397:1
he heapeth up r. PRAY 391:31
if r. increase PRAY 393:20
Infinite r. in a little room MARL 329:20
leave their r. for other PRAY 392:28
left hand r. and honour BIBLE 53:16
neither poverty nor r. BIBLE 54:45
R. are a good handmaid BACON 25:9
R. are for spending BACON 26:9
r. enter into the kingdom of God BIBLE 70:36
r. left SURR 524:20
r. of heaven's pavement MILT 345:26
r. to be a valuable thing SWIFT 526:21
r. to those gross asses LUTH 320:14
r., which dispersed lie HERB 248:6
r. which just make more HOR 260:16
so he that getteth r. BIBLE 60:25
That r. grow in hell MILT 346:1
unsearchable r. of Christ BIBLE 77:23
richly: In Belmont is a lady r. SHAK 465:17
Richmond: R. and Kew Undid me
ELIOT 205:5
Richmond Hill: Sweet lass of R. MACN 326:2
richness: Here's r. DICK 180:3
rush With r. HOPK 256:24
ricks: r. stand grey to the sun KIPL 300:23
rickshaw: it's no go the r. MACN 326:7
ricordarsi: Che r. del tempo felice
DANTE 171:8
rid: be r. of one thorn out HOR 259:6
purely to be r. of thee CONG 160:28
To mend it or be r. on't SHAK 461:10
riddance: die and be a r. DICK 176:29
ridden: none the less have r. there
LUTH 321:3
riddle: dishcover the r. CARR 136:11
glory, jest, and r. POPE 379:13
had not found out my r. BIBLE 49:22
read me this r. ANON 8:12
r. wrapped in a mystery CHUR 149:28
Riddles: R. lie here CLEV 153:3
R. of death Thebes SHEL 501:1
ride: As I r. BROW 105:22
ever r. BROW 101:29
r., and speak the truth BYRON 124:10
r. in triumph through Persepolis MARL 330:7
we r. them down TENN 542:8
rideau: en disant 'Tirez le r. RAB 404:1
ridentem: Dulce r. CAT 137:4
Dulce r. Lalagen amabo HOR 259:24
rider: between a r. and his horse SURT 525:28
horse the r. was lost FRAN 218:6
proud r. on so proud a back SHAK 495:20
r.'s back sits dark Anxiety HOR 260:15
said reader to r. AUDEN 18:17
ridere: humanas actiones non r. SPIN 517:7
r. voles Epicuri de grege HOR 258:16
rideret: r. Democritus HOR 259:3

rides: in boats and carriage r. HOR 258:19
Ridete: R. quidquid est domi cachinnorum
CAT 136:28
rideth: that r. upon the heavens PRAY 394:7
ridicule: that it exposes men to r. JUV 287:17
that r. is the best test CHES 145:33
ridiculos: r. homines facit JUV 287:17
ridiculous: from the sublime to the r.
NAP 359:11
Is wasteful and r. excess SHAK 452:25
Made arms r. MILT 350:18
one step above the r. PAINE 367:21
r. as the British public MAC 324:1
Sublime To the R. GRAH 233:11
ridiculus: nascetur r. mus HOR 257:18
riding: man goes r. STEV 522:18
My r. is better BROW 101:27
r. into the bottomless WALEY 562:2
r.'s a joy BROW 101:28
While proudly r. o'er GRAY 234:16
Ridley: good comfort Master R. LAT 310:21
riff-raff: r. apply to what is respectable
HOPE 255:29
rifiuto: Il gran r. DANTE 171:5
rifle: r. all the breathing spring COLL 158:16
Riflemen: R. Form TENN 543:6
rifles: stuttering r.' rapid rattle OWEN 367:2
rift: little r. within the lute TENN 535:7
Riga: R. quod est aridum LANG 310:1
rigged: r. with curses dark MILT 343:10
riggish: Bless her when she is r. SHAK 422:5
right: all goes r. and nothing GILB 228:29
all is r. as right can GILB 226:19
All's r. with the world BROW 103:21
anything but what's r. and fair HUGH 267:7
because not all was r. COWP 168:20
Because r. is right TENN 541:19
been born to set it r. STR 524:4
be r. than be President CLAY 152:28
be secure of private r. DRYD 194:18
convincing myself that I am r. AUST 23:27
defend to the death your r. VOLT 561:24
divine r. of husbands WOLL 576:9
doeth the thing which is r. PRAY 390:4
everyone is r. LA C 306:16
faith that r. makes might LINC 314:17
find out that one WAS r. POUND 383:22
foot standeth r. PRAY 391:6
generalities of natural r. CHOA 148:14
have no r. to the property RUSK 412:11
Heaven soon sets r. BROW 100:4
heaven still guards the r. SHAK 479:5
I'm all r. BONE 89:19
in His r. hand all Truth LESS 314:2
is a r. hand of iniquity PRAY 399:12
laid out just the r. books POUND 383:20
love of truth and r. TENN 537:15
man of the r. MOSL 358:19
minority is always r. IBSEN 269:18
must now and then be r. COWP 164:30
nets of wrong and r. YEATS 585:14
nor blindly r. POPE 378:32
of all the earth do r. BIBLE 46:7
Of r. and wrong he taught ARMS 12:16
our country, r. or wrong DEC 173:1
recognizing in itself what is r. VIRG 557:18
renew a r. spirit PRAY 393:6
reprove her when she's r. SWIFT 527:21
r., and our bounden duty PRAY 387:23
'R. as a Ribstone Pippin BELL 39:17
r. deed for the wrong reason ELIOT 204:4
r. good captain too GILB 227:30
r. hand of the Majesty BIBLE 79:28
r. hand of God the Father PRAY 384:26
r. hands of fellowship BIBLE 77:15
r. little, tight little DIBD 175:23
r. man in the right place JEFF 272:8
r. of an excessive wrong BROW 104:23
r. of the ignorant man CARL 131:16
r. or justice MAGN 327:3

r. side of the blanket ASHF 17:12
r. to a child with SHAW 496:27
r. to be consulted BAG 29:3
r. to dissemble your love BICK 83:27
r. wrong TENN 534:5
rule of r. STEE 518:4
serve him r. BELL 39:29
Sit thou on my r. hand PRAY 397:11
So the heart be r. RAL 404:18
talks about justice and r. KIPL 301:19
that r. early PRAY 392:20
That right was r. COWP 168:19
that was r. HOUS 264:2
To do a great r. SHAK 468:2
took up arms with more r. LUCAN 319:22
true and do what is r. HUXL 269:8
whatever is, is r. POPE 380:4
When r., to be kept right SCH 415:13
which is lawful and r. BIBLE 60:35
which was r. in his own eyes BIBLE 49:29
whose life is in the r. POPE 379:20
with firmness in the r. LINC 315:3
righteous: Be not r. over much BIBLE 55:22
clad in the armor of a r. BRYAN 106:7
fervent prayer of a r. BIBLE 80:19
have seen the r. forsaken BLUN 89:3
I never the r. forsaken PRAY 391:28
not come to call the r. BIBLE 65:24
r., and sober life PRAY 384:13
r. are bold as a lion BIBLE 54:41
r. man regardeth the life BIBLE 53:34
r. minds of innkeepers CHES 147:21
r. perisheth BIBLE 60:2
r. shall be had in everlasting PRAY 397:14
souls of the r. are BIBLE 62:13
When the r. man turneth BUTL 118:28
righteousness: hunger and thirst after r.
BIBLE 64:6
living unto r. PRAY 388:10
on the breastplate of r. BIBLE 78:10
R. exalteth a nation BIBLE 54:3
r., but behold a cry BIBLE 57:23
r. of the scribes and Pharisees BIBLE 64:11
r., and hated iniquity PRAY 392:15
r. and peace have kissed PRAY 395:15
r. shall he judge the world PRAY 396:9
Sun of r. arise with healing BIBLE 62:3
thy r. as the waves BIBLE 59:15
what r. really is ARN 16:22
Within the paths of r. SCOT 419:5
worketh not the r. of God BIBLE 80:10
righteousnesses: r. are as filthy rags
BIBLE 60:12
righter: r. than one knew at say
POUND 383:22
rightfu: was a' for our r.' King BURNS 114:10
right-hand: standing me on the r. side
CEL 138:8
rightly: way of *doing* things r. RUSK 411:26
rights: equal in dignity and r. ANON 4:14
equal in r. and cultivation MILL 339:19
extension of women's r. FOUR 217:18
folly of 'Woman's R.' VICT 556:14
religious r. of an Englishman JUN 287:1
r. inherent and inalienable JEFF 272:6
r. of man is essentially ROB 406:11
whose r. he has trodden BURKE 110:33
rigol: r. hath divorc'd So many SHAK 442:18
rigour: My r. relents BURKE 109:18
riled: no sense In gittin' r. HARTE 242:27
rills: teachers had been woods and r.
WORD 581:11
Rimbauds: he was always chasing R.
PARK 368:20
rime: making beautiful old r. SHAK 494:19
outlive this powerful r. SHAK 493:17
some extemporal god of r. SHAK 456:19
Rime Intrinsica: R., Fontmell Magna
BETJ 42:13
riming: born under a r. planet SHAK 473:10

Rimmon: myself in the house of R.
            BIBLE 51:29
rin: gars ye r. sae still   ANON 7:12
rind: burnished with golden r. MILT 347:19
  how shall taste the r.   THOM 548:19
  sweet as the r.   SWIN 529:8
ring: both the shires they r. HOUS 263:4
  Bright is the r. of words STEV 523:1
  giving and receiving of a R. PRAY 389:7
  he rid at the   BALL 30:16
  only pretty r. time   SHAK 427:2
  r. at the end of his nose LEAR 312:12
  r. on her wand she bore MOORE 356:16
  R. out the false   TENN 537:14
  R. out, wild bells   TENN 537:14
  R. out ye crystal spheres MILT 344:10
  sat unconquered in a r. CHES 147:17
  She heard the bridles r. BALL 32:2
  Sleeps on his luminous r. TENN 541:21
  They now *r.* the bells WALP 563:24
  what shall we do for a r. LEAR 312:12
  With this R. I thee wed PRAY 389:5
Ring-Bo-Ree: forty bottles of R. LEAR 312:9
Ring'd: R. with the azure world TENN 533:7
ring-having: nor in r. POUND 383:18
ringleaders: fling the r. from the Tarpeian
           ARN 16:28
ringlets: do the green sour r. make
           SHAK 485:23
rings: gold r. set with the beryl BIBLE 57:4
Rio: Go rolling down to R. KIPL 300:7
riot: Like litter that a r. leaves PLOM 374:19
  rash fierce blaze of r. SHAK 478:19
  r. is at bottom the language KING 296:14
  winds' and spent waves' r. SWIN 529:21
rioting: r., the old Roman way ARN 16:28
riotous: wasted his substance with r.
  living   BIBLE 70:18
riotousness: r. of the crowd is always
           ALC 3:9
ripe: shelter to grow r. ARN 13:10
  we r. and ripe   SHAK 425:19
Ripeness: R. is all   SHAK 456:2
ripening: His greatness is a-r. SHAK 447:9
riper: chooses Athens in his r. age
           DRYD 197:14
ripes: erring on ventiferous r. HOLM 253:18
ripple: r. under archways HARDY 239:18
rire: *me presse de r. de tout* BEAU 35:15
  r. les honnêtes gens MOL 353:7
rise: Held we fall to r. BROW 98:32
  if the dead r. not   BIBLE 76:24
  may r. on stepping-stones TENN 535:33
  nation shall r. against BIBLE 67:28
  nobody who does not r. JOHN 279:32
  of her should r. herself HARDY 240:7
  populace r. at once against WHIT 570:14
  r. of the United States STEV 520:23
  R., take up thy bed BIBLE 72:1
  r. with the lark and go BRET 92:2
  stoop to r.   MASS 335:16
  That dead men r. up never SWIN 529:25
  to r. out of obscurity JUV 287:18
  us i' the dark to r. BROW 104:27
  Woe unto them that r. up BIBLE 57:25
  wretched than to r. GOLD 230:22
risen: floods are r.   PRAY 396:1
rises: Jove's planet r. BROW 101:9
Rise up: R., my love BIBLE 56:22
risible: authors is one of the most r.
           JOHN 281:29
rising: All r. to great place is BACON 26:26
  Moon of Heav'n is r. once FITZ 213:17
  more than a means of r. JOHN 276:29
  on a plat of r. ground MILT 342:4
  R. and cawing at the gun's SHAK 470:20
  R. in joy over wolds AUDEN 20:6
  r. unto place is laborious BACON 26:23
risk: r. it on one turn of pitch-and-toss
           KIPL 300:1

risu: *r. cognoscere matrem* VIRG 560:1
  r. inepto res ineptior CAT 137:1
  Solventur r. tabulae HOR 262:7
rite: newer r. is here THOM 546:17
  No noble r. nor formal SHAK 436:14
  rites: of payens corsed olde r. CHAU 144:19
  r. for which I love him SHAK 474:6
ritui: *Novo cedat r.* THOM 546:17
Ritz: open to all, like the R. MATH 336:2
rivalry: dead there is no r. MAC 324:9
rivals: Three for the r. ANON 6:5
rive: r. not more in parting SHAK 423:6
riveder: *quindi uscimmo a r. le stelle*
           DANTE 171:14
river: Alph, the sacred r. COL 156:26
  Among the r. sallows KEATS 293:8
  brook and r. meet LONG 316:20
  dale the sacred r. ran COL 156:28
  daughter went through the r. singing
           BUNY 107:37
  Fame is like a r.   BACON 27:5
  fountains mingle with the r. SHEL 502:1
  fruitful r. in the eye SHAK 429:25
  he drinketh up a r. BIBLE 53:10
  House of Parliament upon the r. WELL 567:23
  in the reeds by the r. BROW 98:6
  living r. by the door STEV 523:7
  majestic R. floated ARN 14:28
  nearer to the r.'s trembling SHEL 503:20
  noblest r. in Europe ADD 2:19
  On a tree by a r. a little GILB 227:15
  On either side the r. lie TENN 538:2
  Pentridge by the r. BARN 33:29
  r. at my garden's end SWIFT 527:28
  r. flows on through WORD 581:3
  r. jumps over the mountain AUDEN 18:9
  r. of water of life BIBLE 82:35
  r.-rounded   HOPK 256:10
  Runs not a r. by my palace THAC 545:18
  That even the weariest r. SWIN 529:25
  There is a r. in Macedon SHAK 445:5
  thy peace been as a r. BIBLE 59:15
  Time the refreshing r. AUDEN 20:15
  twice into the same r. HER 246:6
  we'll to the r.   SHAK 422:9
  white flows the r. STEV 522:29
river-fields: grassy harvest of the r. ARN 15:8
rivering: Beside the r. waters of JOYCE 286:8
riverrun: r. past Eve and Adam's,
  from swerve   JOYCE 286:2
rivers: All the r. run into BIBLE 55:6
  By shallow r.   MARL 330:1
  kingdom's r. take their course SHAK 452:31
  lilies by the r. of waters BIBLE 63:27
  love any discourse of r. WALT 564:11
  Nymphs and as yet unknown r. VIRG 559:4
  R. are damp   PARK 368:18
  r. cannot quench SHAK 446:21
  r. in the south   PRAY 398:17
  r. of blood must yet flow JEFF 272:14
  r. of Damascus   BIBLE 51:28
  r. of water in a dry place BIBLE 58:30
  springs into the r. PRAY 396:19
  Their fighters drink the r. HOUS 265:3
rivets: busy hammers closing r. SHAK 444:9
rivulet: r. of text shall meander SHER 506:26
rivulets: Myriads of r. hurrying TENN 542:17
road: along the 'ard 'igh r. PUNCH 402:17
  call it the R. to Heaven BALL 32:5
  free as the r.   HERB 247:14
  goes along the darksome r. CAT 136:23
  good to be out on the r. MAS 334:8
  guide what goes off the r. LANG 310:1
  in the moon the long r. HOUS 263:20
  is a long time on the r. DICK 183:9
  is the high r. that leads JOHN 274:30
  light-hearted I take to the open r. WHIT 571:7
  light to shine upon the r. COWP 165:23
  on a taxed r.   SMITH 511:38
  One r. leads to London MAS 334:2

  On every r. I wandered HOUS 264:1
  On the r. to Mandalay KIPL 301:5
  r. below me   STEV 522:28
  r. is rough and long BRON 93:13
  r. lies long and straight STEV 521:32
  r. of excess leads BLAKE 88:13
  r. through the woods KIPL 303:31
  r. was a ribbon of moonlight NOYES 364:12
  rolling English r. CHES 147:10
  that on a lonesome r. COL 155:27
  who takes no private r. POPE 380:2
  winding r. before me HAZL 243:32
roads: Two r. diverged in a wood
           FROST 219:10
roadway: While I stand on the r.
           YEATS 585:17
roam: soar, but never r. WORD 583:1
  that has been sent to r. COWP 166:11
  Where'er I r.   GOLD 231:24
roaming: where are you r. SHAK 488:17
roar: called upon to give the r. CHUR 150:21
  let him r. again   SHAK 469:29
  most like the r.   ARN 14:26
  r. you as gently as any SHAK 469:30
  Swinging slow with sullen r. MILT 342:4
  they r. their ribs out GILB 229:10
  withdrawing r.   ARN 12:23
roared: ran about the room and r.
           CHES 146:12
roarers: r. for the name of king SHAK 484:20
roareth: What is this that r. thus GODL 229:24
roaring: lions r. after their prey PRAY 393:7
  magnificent r. of the young lions ARN 15:23
  There was a r. in the wind WORD 580:27
roast: In hell they'll r. thee BURNS 115:12
  never strove to rule the r. PRIOR 401:10
  politics in boil'd and r. SMITH 512:6
  r. me in sulphur SHAK 477:21
  r. with fire   BIBLE 47:17
  were but to r. their eggs BACON 27:37
rob: r. a lady of her fortune FIEL 211:29
  r. a neighbour whom he MAC 323:21
  r. the Hybla bees SHAK 451:31
robb'd: r. me of my Robe of Honour
           FITZ 213:14
robbed: that had r. us of immortal
           MER 337:15
robber: can sing in the r.'s face JUV 287:26
  Injurious time now with a r.'s SHAK 487:12
  Now Barabbas was a r. BIBLE 72:45
robbers: in perils of r. BIBLE 77:12
robbery: all full of lies and r. BIBLE 61:26
  end in conquest and r. JOHN 281:25
  In scandal, as in r. CHES 145:9
  r. to be equal with God BIBLE 78:13
  trust not in wrong and r. PRAY 393:20
robbing: Forbids the r. of a foe CHUR 148:30
  r. selected Peter to pay KIPL 299:16
robe: Give me my r. SHAK 424:10
  intertissued r. of gold SHAK 444:25
  like a giant's r.   SHAK 462:27
  nor the judge's r. SHAK 463:20
robes: are arrayed in white r. BIBLE 82:1
  have washed their r. BIBLE 82:2
  R. loosely flowing JONS 283:27
  r. ye weave, another wears SHEL 504:3
  When all her r. are gone ANON 6:20
Robespierre: *R. war nichts als die Hand*
           HEINE 244:12
Robin: bonny sweet R. is all my SHAK 436:11
  R. Redbreast in a Cage BLAKE 85:9
  r.-red-breast   WEBS 567:8
  R.'s not near   KEPP 295:12
  r.'s plucky canton AUDEN 20:15
  Sweet R. sits in the bush SCOTT 418:21
Robinson Crusoe: *R., and the Pilgrim's*
  Progress   JOHN 280:16
Robs: R. not one light seed from KEATS 290:1
  r. the mind of all its BURKE 108:9
robur: *r. et aes triplex* HOR 259:12

821

rock: it was founded upon a r.	BIBLE 65:11	
of a serpent upon a r.	BIBLE 55:1	
pleasant shade of some r.	HOR 259:15	
Rhyme is the r. on which	DRYD 194:22	
r. in a weary land	BIBLE 58:30	
r. I will build my church	BIBLE 66:33	
r. of offence to both	BIBLE 58:4	
sea-wet r. sat down and combed	HOUS 265:3	
set my feet upon the r.	PRAY 392:1	
they knew the perilous r.	SOUT 514:1	
Rocked: R. in the cradle	WILL 574:7	
She r. it, and rated it	EDW 200:5	
rocket: that as he rose like a r.	PAINE 368:2	
rocking horse: sway'd about upon a r.		
	KEATS 292:8	
rocks: hand that r. the cradle	WALL 562:4	
him a native of the r.	JOHN 274:6	
r. and hills whose heads	SHAK 473:25	
r. of the mountains	BIBLE 81:30	
She is older than the r.	PATER 369:19	
stony r. for the conies	PRAY 397:1	
till the rending of the r.	JOYCE 286:4	
With r. unscalable	SHAK 428:13	
rocky: king sate on the r. brow	BYRON 122:34	
rod: Aaron's r. swallowed up	BIBLE 47:12	
all humbled kiss the r.	SHAK 490:31	
bruise them with a r. of iron	PRAY 389:18	
child and spares the r.	HOOD 254:19	
eyeball owns the mystic r.	BROW 105:14	
r. and thy staff comfort	PRAY 390:22	
r. Becomes more mock'd	SHAK 463:11	
r. out of the stem of Jesse	BIBLE 58:9	
r. produces an effect which	JOHN 273:25	
spareth his r. hateth	BIBLE 53:38	
Then spare the r.	BUTL 118:2	
Wisdom be put in a silver r.	BLAKE 85:19	
rode: He r. upon the cherubims	PRAY 390:8	
r. all that day and all	MAL 328:5	
r. madly off in all directions	LEAC 311:14	
that r. sublime	GRAY 235:19	
Roderick: where was R. then	SCOTT 416:7	
rods: Thrice was I beaten with r.	BIBLE 77:12	
roe: r. or to a young hart upon	BIBLE 57:14	
roes: breasts are like two young r.		
	BIBLE 56:26	
Roger: R. is landlord to the whole	ADD 2:12	
rogue: busy and insinuating r.	SHAK 476:23	
consequently a r.	SWIFT 526:16	
dainty r. in porcelain	MER 337:30	
Has he not a r.'s face	CONG 160:4	
r. and peasant slave am	SHAK 432:27	
r. gives you Love Powders	LAMB 307:30	
r. is married to a whore	KIPL 302:18	
smooth-faced snubnosed r.	TENN 539:20	
rogues: r. in buckram let drive	SHAK 439:2	
see the r. flourish	BROW 99:26	
roi: Il était un r. d'Yvetot	BER 41:14	
Si le R. m'avait donné	ANON 9:17	
Roland: R. to the dark tower came		
	SHAK 454:27	
roll: All away began to r.	BLAKE 85:24	
Let it r. on full flood	CHUR 150:3	
r. of the world eastward	HARDY 241:9	
R. on, thou deep and dark	BYRON 121:23	
R. up that map	PITT 374:6	
us r. all our strength	MARV 332:20	
rolling: drunkard made the r. English		
road	CHES 147:10	
Go r. down to Rio	KIPL 300:7	
r. anapaestic	BROW 98:16	
rolls: holds and r. and throws	REED 405:7	
R. impotently on as Thou	FITZ 213:8	
r. it under his tongue	HENRY 245:19	
Roma: R. locuta est	AUG 22:2	
Soldati, io esco da R.	GAR 221:10	
Romae: Si fueris R.	AMBR 4:2	
romain: ni r., ni empire	VOLT 561:9	
Romam: natam me consule R.	CIC 152:2	
Roman: after the high R. fashion		
	SHAK 423:18	
antique R. than a Dane	SHAK 437:24	
at Rome live in the R.	AMBR 4:2	
been a virtue with the R.	KING 297:17	
Butcher'd to make a R. holiday		
	BYRON 121:16	
by a R. Valiantly vanquished	SHAK 423:15	
do know the sweet R. hand	SHAK 490:5	
found the R. nation	VIRG 557:10	
I am a R. citizen	CIC 151:28	
I'm a R. for that	FARQ 210:4	
Make way, you R. writers	PROP 401:17	
noblest R. of them all	SHAK 452:7	
noses cast is of the r.	FLEM 215:4	
R. came to Rye or out	CHES 147:10	
R. Conquest was	SELL 420:2	
R. meal	COWP 167:14	
R. people were the classical	YEATS 587:13	
R.'s life, a Roman's arms	MAC 322:21	
R. thought hath struck	SHAK 421:15	
Than such a R.	SHAK 451:14	
that would not be a R.	SHAK 450:16	
Then 'twas the R.	HOUS 263:15	
you, R., make your task	VIRG 559:1	
Romana: Moribus antiquis res stat R.		
virisque	ENN 208:23	
romance: cloudy symbols of a high r.		
	KEATS 293:1	
not a little given to r.	EVEL 209:6	
R. at short notice was	SAKI 413:5	
you think steam spoils r.	KIPL 301:4	
romances: r. as they would be spiritualized		
	WALP 562:27	
R. paint at full length	BYRON 122:27	
tall woods with high r.	KEATS 292:15	
Roman Empire: Ghost of the deceased		
R.	HOBB 251:21	
Romanism: rum, R., and rebellion		
	BURC 108:1	
Romans: Friends, R., countrymen		
	SHAK 450:17	
Greeks or the R.	DISR 185:27	
R. call it stoicism	ADD 1:18	
R. were like brothers	MAC 322:18	
romantic: In a ruin that's r.	GILB 227:18	
mustnt be r. about money	SHAW 497:26	
Romanus: Civis R. sum	CIC 151:28	
when he could say Civis R.	PALM 368:10	
Rome: At R. she hadde been	CHAU 141:31	
Bishop of R. hath no jurisdiction		
	PRAY 400:10	
Cato is the voice of R.	JONS 283:15	
comen from R. al hoot	CHAU 142:6	
Everything in R. is expensive	JUV 287:19	
Glorious R. hath lost her	COL 155:3	
go from the church of R.	WOTT 583:17	
grandeur that was R.	POE 375:7	
Greece or haughty R.	JONS 284:22	
Half-Way House to R.	PUNCH 402:11	
happy R.	CIC 152:2	
high and palmy state of R.	SHAK 429:12	
hook-nosed fellow of R.	SHAK 442:13	
late comes round by R.	BROW 104:24	
R., believe me	CLOU 153:7	
R. has spoken	AUG 22:2	
R. indeed and room enough	SHAK 448:19	
'R. is above the Nations	KIPL 303:9	
R. live in the Roman style	AMBR 4:2	
R.! my country	BYRON 121:9	
R. of to-day	EMER 207:9	
R., though her eagle through	WALL 562:11	
sires have marched to R.	MAC 322:12	
that I loved R. more	SHAK 450:14	
time will doubt of R.	BYRON 123:13	
varletry Of censuring R.	SHAK 423:21	
village than second at R.'	CAES 127:3	
wealth and din of R.	HOR 261:7	
We burn For R. so near	DAY-L 172:21	
when R. falls	BYRON 121:18	
you cruel men of R.	SHAK 448:6	
Romeo: wherefore art thou R.	SHAK 482:8	
Romuli: tamquam in R. faece sententiam		
	CIC 151:16	
Romulus: than among the dregs of R.		
	CIC 151:16	
Ronsard: 'R. sang of me in the days		
	RONS 407:18	
rood: half a r. Of land	SWIFT 527:28	
roof: cleave to the r. of my mouth PRAY 399:3		
had no r. to shroud his	HEYW 250:22	
He has restored the r.	BETJ 43:3	
humble r. Is weather-proof	HERR 250:14	
r. of blue Italian weather	SHEL 501:16	
shouldest come under my r.	BIBLE 65:14	
shouldst enter under my r.	MASS 335:8	
this majestical r. fretted	SHAK 432:15	
until my r. whirl around	JONS 285:14	
roof-tree: heavens my wide r.	AYT 24:12	
rook: r.-racked	HOPK 256:10	
When the last r.	COL 157:11	
rooks: maggot-pies and choughs and		
r.	SHAK 461:24	
r. are blown about	TENN 536:3	
r. came home in scramble	HODG 252:6	
r. in families homeward	HARDY 241:4	
room: always leave r. for the mouse		
	SAKI 413:15	
coming to that holy r.	DONNE 189:14	
down in the highest r.	BIBLE 70:7	
In ev'ry grave make r.	DAV 172:6	
Infinite riches in a little r.	MARL 329:20	
into a r. full of people	WEBB 566:6	
is always r. at the top	WEBS 566:9	
is it Rome indeed and r.	SHAK 448:19	
no r. for them in the inn	BIBLE 69:9	
r. Do we take up in death	SHIR 507:6	
R. to deny ourselves	KEBLE 295:4	
r. to swing a cat	DICK 177:18	
shame to take the lowest r.	BIBLE 70:7	
shew you a large upper r.	BIBLE 71:6	
sometimes in a smoking r.	KIPL 302:5	
taper to the outward r.	DONNE 189:30	
was not sufficient r.	BARN 34:5	
you shall keep your r.	STEV 522:29	
rooms: Know most of the r.	FULL 220:13	
lighted r. Inside your head	LARK 310:5	
uppermost r. at feasts	BIBLE 67:22	
uppermost r. at feasts	BIBLE 68:37	
roos: r., and sit in hevene	CHAU 144:19	
Rooshan: 'It is R.	DICK 181:9	
Rooshans: Some people...may be R.		
	DICK 179:11	
Roosian: he might have been a R.		
	GILB 228:10	
roost: always come home to r.	SOUT 513:23	
rooster: Hongry r. don't cackle	HARR 242:24	
roosts: Assailant on the perched r.		
	MILT 350:29	
root: because they had no r.	BIBLE 66:16	
eaten on the insane r.	SHAK 458:15	
money is the r. of all evil	BIBLE 79:18	
nips his r.	SHAK 447:9	
r. is ever in its grave	HERB 248:16	
r. of the matter is found	BIBLE 52:32	
square r. of half a number	LONG 317:23	
then the axe to the r.	PAINE 368:4	
unto the r. of the trees	BIBLE 63:39	
roote: me aboute myn herte r.	CHAU 143:19	
roots: broad on the r. of things	BROW 98:17	
poison England at her r.	BOTT 90:17	
r., and ever green	PEELE 371:8	
r. that can be pulled up	ELIOT 200:23	
send my r. rain	HOPK 257:3	
shall grow out of his r.	BIBLE 58:9	
stirring Dull r.	ELIOT 204:17	
rope: escape from r. and gun	GAY 222:30	
to set his hand to a r.	DRAKE 193:4	
Rorate: R., coeli	BIBLE 83:15	
rosa: r. quo locorum	HOR 260:5	
Rosalind: No jewel is like R.	SHAK 426:5	
rose: Against the blown r. may	SHAK 422:17	

blossom as the r.   BIBLE 58:32
brier pluck a white r.   SHAK 445:21
Christmas I no more desire a r.   SHAK 456:16
earthlier happy is the r.   SHAK 469:17
English unofficial r.   BROO 94:18
expectancy and r.   SHAK 433:15
fading r.   CAREW 130:18
Faintly the inimitable r.   WINC 575:5
fause lover stole my r.   BURNS 116:8
fayr as is the r. in May   CHAU 143:27
fresh lap of the crimson r.   SHAK 470:6
Gather therefore the R.   SPEN 516:13
Go, lovely R.   WALL 562:13
hills where his life r.   ARN 12:22
I am the r. of Sharon   BIBLE 56:19
If love were what the r.   SWIN 530:21
I pluck the r.   BROW 105:29
labyrinthine buds the r.   BROW 105:13
late r. may yet linger   HOR 260:5
leaves the R. of Yesterday   FITZ 212:10
lovely is the r.   WORD 578:22
Luve's like a red red r.   BURNS 114:27
mast burst open with a r.   FLEC 214:19
musk of the r. is blown   TENN 540:9
Nightingale cries to the R.   FITZ 212:7
One perfect r.   PARK 368:17
O R., thou art sick   BLAKE 87:12
Pluck a red r. from off   SHAK 445:21
raise up the ghost of a r.   BROW 95:21
ravage with impunity a r.   BROW 105:15
red as any r.   BALL 30:9
R. as where some buried   FITZ 212:15
r. By any other name   SHAK 482:9
R. crossed the road   DOBS 187:14
R. is a rose is a rose   STEIN 518:17
r. like a nymph   SHEL 503:23
R. of all Roses   YEATS 586:10
r. of the rosebud garden   TENN 540:11
r. Of youth   SHAK 422:16
r. o' the wrong side   BROME 93:11
r.'s scent is bitterness   THOM 547:2
r. the wrong way to-day   BEHN 38:20
R., were you not extremely   PRIOR 401:9
r. with all its sweetest   BYRON 124:8
r. without the thorn   HERR 250:13
Roves back the r.   DE L 173:24
sad R. of all my days   YEATS 587:6
secret, and inviolate R.   YEATS 586:18
should vanish with the R.   FITZ 213:15
sorrow on a morning r.   KEATS 291:15
strew on thee r. or rue   SWIN 528:25
supplication to the r.   FLEC 214:11
Sweet r., whose hue   HERB 248:16
That thereby beauty's r.   SHAK 492:22
third day he r. again from   PRAY 384:26
though a r. should shut   KEATS 289:19
tiger sniffs the r.   SASS 415:1
'Tis the last r. of summer   MOORE 356:20
to tell the crooked r.   THOM 547:3
Unceremoniously the r.   WATS 565:12
under the r.   BICK 84:2
When I have pluck'd the r.   SHAK 477:5
when the r. is dead   SHEL 504:12
white r. weeps   TENN 540:12
without thorn the r.   MILT 347:20
yet a r. full-blown   HERR 250:16
roseau: mais c'est un r. pensant   PASC 369:11
Rose Aylmer: R., all were thine   LAND 308:26
rose-blossoms: foam-flowers endure when
the r.   SWIN 529:19
rosebuds: crown ourselves with r.
   BIBLE 62:11
Gather ye r. while ye may   HERR 250:5
like r. fill'd with snow   CAMP 129:23
rose-garden: can the moment in the r.
   ELIOT 202:16
Into the r.   ELIOT 202:13
rose-lipt: many a r. maiden   HOUS 264:10
rosemary: r., that's for remembrance
   SHAK 436:10

you there's r. and rue   SHAK 491:22
Rosencrantz: R. and Guildenstern are
   SHAK 437:29
rose-petals: on a pile of r.   HOR 259:15
rose-red: r. city 'half as old   BURG 108:4
r. sissy half as old   PLOM 374:18
roses: days of wine and r.   DOWS 191:13
Do r. stick like burrs   BROW 105:27
Each Morn a thousand R.   FITZ 212:10
flower of r. in the spring   BIBLE 63:27
In fields where r. fade   HOUS 264:10
It was the time of r.   HOOD 254:8
Lilies without, r. within   MARV 332:15
not a bed of r.   STEV 521:31
own red r. there may blow   THOM 547:24
Plant thou no r. at my   ROSS 409:8
raptures and r. of vice   SWIN 529:5
r., all the way   BROW 103:10
R. at first were white   HERR 249:7
r. for the flush of youth   ROSS 409:7
R. have thorns   SHAK 493:12
r. to the moonrise burst   HOUS 266:4
scent of the r. will hang   MOORE 356:7
Seek r. in December   BYRON 124:18
Strew on her r.   ARN 14:5
'Two red r. across the moon   MORR 358:13
virgins are soft as the r.   BYRON 120:2
wild r., and ivy serpentine   SHEL 503:19
would like my r. to see you   SHER 506:39
rose-water: would pour r. over a toad
   JERR 273:9
rosy: 'Cause another's r. are   WITH 575:12
sent thee late a r. wreath   JONS 284:12
Rosy-fingered: R. dawn   HOMER 254:5
rot: cold obstruction and to r.   SHAK 464:14
go r.   SHAK 491:11
Here continueth to r.   ARB 11:21
I will r.   HOUS 264:27
pernicious soul R.   SHAK 477:13
recognize virtue and r.   PERS 372:27
r. in hospitals   SOUT 513:13
R. inwardly and foul contagion   MILT 343:13
very deep did r.   COL 155:14
we r. and rot   SHAK 425:19
rote: conn'd by r.   SHAK 451:23
Rothschild: are taken by R. and Baring
   GILB 226:16
rots: he sort of r. away   WARD 564:30
rotten: fresh eggs to r. boroughs   MAC 323:15
Lord Lilac thought it rather r.   CHES 147:16
Lovely lads and dead and r.   HOUS 263:19
r. in the state of Denmark   SHAK 431:2
rottenness: r. begins in his conduct
   JEFF 272:11
rotten-runged: r. rat-riddled stairs
   BROW 102:13
rotundity: thick r. o' the world   SHAK 454:4
rotundo: Grais dedit ore r.   HOR 257:23
rotundus: teres, atque r.   HOR 262:10
rough: Because the road is r.   BRON 93:13
follows I am r. and lecherous   SHAK 453:11
from children who were r.   SPEN 515:11
greeting be courteous or r.   AUDEN 21:2
…R. he may be   DICK 179:19
r. magic I here abjure   SHAK 485:24
r. male kiss of blankets   BROO 94:8
r. places plain   BIBLE 59:5
r. than polished diamond   CHES 145:27
R. winds do shake the darling   SHAK 492:28
Rough-hew: R. them how we will
   SHAK 437:11
roughness: r. breedeth hate   BACON 26:25
roughs: among his fellow r.   DOYLE 192:39
Roumania: I am Marie of R.   PARK 368:14
this might be R.   MARY 333:15
round: act of walking r. him   BEER 38:6
himself into the r. hole   SMITH 511:34
large, and smooth, and r.   SOUT 513:15
one was r. her loyer   CAMP 129:4
perfect r.   BROW 98:18

R. numbers are always false   JOHN 277:19
R. the world for ever   ARN 13:6
r. the world away   KING 297:5
r. unvarnish'd tale deliver   SHAK 473:24
r. world so sure   PRAY 395:24
roundabouts: What's lost upon the r.
   CHAL 139:3
rounded: little life Is r.   SHAK 485:20
Round-heads: R. and Wooden-shoes
are   ADD 2:1
R. (Right but Repulsive)   SELL 420:4
rouse: anything might r. him now
   OWEN 367:4
No more shall r. them from   GRAY 234:20
r. a lion than to start   SHAK 438:18
R. the lion from his lair   SCOTT 418:35
roused: r. in many an ancient hall   MAC 322:3
Rousseau: *dessen Seele R. geschaffen*
   HEINE 244:12
mock on, Voltaire, R.   BLAKE 86:23
not ask Jean Jacques R.   COWP 166:5
wild R.   BYRON 120:36
rout: after all their r.   CHUR 148:20
pleasures of having a r.   HOOD 254:25
rove: r. the brakes and thorns   COWP 165:12
rover: blood's a r.   HOUS 262:15
roving: we'll go no more a r.   BYRON 125:25
row: to your Sirmione r.   TENN 533:17
watermen, that r. one way   BURT 116:15
rowing: me r. against the stream
   SCOTT 418:10
r. another   BUNY 107:18
Rowland: Warren's blackin' or R.'s
   DICK 182:12
rows: Lovers' r. make love whole   TER 544:15
royal: Calling a crowned man r.   SWIN 529:26
descended from r. forebears   HOR 259:8
no 'r. road' to geometry   EUCL 209:3
r. captain of this ruin'd   SHAK 444:10
r. priesthood   BIBLE 80:23
R. slice of bread   MILNE 340:7
R. Society desires to confer   FAR 209:20
Tax not the r. Saint   WORD 582:16
This r. throne of kings   SHAK 478:20
royaliste: plus r. que le roi   ANON 9:9
royally: Sorrow so r. in you appears
   SHAK 442:24
To have prov'd most r.   SHAK 437:30
Royalty: R. is a government in which
   BAG 28:30
when you come to R. you   DISR 185:28
ruamus: Moriamur et in media arma
   VIRG 558:7
ruat: r. caelum'   MANS 328:16
rub: there's the r.   SHAK 433:8
What r. or what impediment   SHAK 445:11
rubbish: cast as r. to the void   TENN 536:25
was but the r. of an Adam   SOUTH 513:12
What r.   BLUC 88:32
write such hopeless r.   STEP 518:23
rubens: r. accendit lumina Vesper
   VIRG 560:11
rubies: Give pearls away and r.   HOUS 262:20
her price is far above r.   BIBLE 55:3
price of wisdom is above r.   BIBLE 52:34
R. unparagon'd   SHAK 428:8
Wisdom is better than r.   BIBLE 53:26
rubs: r. nor botches in the work   SHAK 461:11
yellow fog that r. its   ELIOT 203:18
ruby: That r. which you wear   HERR 250:2
rudder: bowsprit got mixed with the
r.   CARR 133:5
rhyme the r. is of verses   BUTL 117:25
snatch'd his r.   ARN 14:21
ruddier: r. than the cherry   GAY 222:8
ruddy: beloved is white and r.   BIBLE 57:3
Now he was r.   BIBLE 50:7
R. Ball has taken flight   THOM 549:2
rude: How r. are the boys that   WATTS 565:26
of which were rather r.   COW 164:2

R. am I in my speech SHAK 473:24
r. forefathers of the hamlet GRAY 234:20
rudest: r. work that tells a story RUSK 411:21
rudiments: r. of education are given
STEE 518:10
Rudyards: R. cease from kipling STEP 518:24
rue: nought shall make us r. SHAK 453:1
rose or r. or laurel SWIN 528:25
R., even for ruth SHAK 479:19
there's rosemary and r. SHAK 491:22
there's r. for you SHAK 436:11
With r. my heart is laden HOUS 264:10
ruff: in antique r. and bonnet JOHN 280:9
ruffian: by the menaces of a r. JOHN 276:16
He's the r. on the stair HENL 245:6
that father s. SHAK 439:16
ruffle: Would r. up your spirits SHAK 451:3
rug: In a r. FRAN 218:16
rugged: Beneath those r. elms GRAY 234:20
harsh cadence of a r. line DRYD 197:33
mere antiquarian is a r. JOHN 277:27
unpolished r. verse I chose DRYD 197:15
rugs: fetch me some r. AUDEN 19:14
Ruh: *Meine R.' ist hin* GOET 230:4
Über allen Gipfeln Ist R.' GOET 230:11
Ruhm: *nicht der R.* GOET 230:5
ruido: *que huye el mundanal r.* LUIS 320:12
ruin: around the dear r. MOORE 356:4
formed for the r. of our sex SMOL 512:13
great deal of *r.* in a nation SMITH 510:1
He bears the seed of r. ARN 13:21
In a r. that's romantic GILB 227:18
Majestic though in r. MILT 346:14
marks the earth with r. BYRON 121:23
Prop and R. of the State CLEV 153:3
Prothero was announcing r. THOM 546:21
Red r. TENN 534:10
r. of all happiness BURN 112:17
r. or to rule the state DRYD 194:8
R. seize thee GRAY 234:14
R.'s ploughshare drives BURNS 115:19
r. that it feeds upon COWP 166:10
sand and r. and gold SWIN 530:29
Spreading r. and scattering BROW 98:6
Thou its r. didst not share DOD 187:16
whom God to r. has design'd DRYD 196:22
With hideous r. and combustion MILT 344:24
yet what r. BYRON 121:17
You will r. no more lives DOYLE 192:18
ruinae: *Impavidum ferient r.* HOR 260:19
ruin'd: from the r. sides of Kings BEAU 36:1
r. piece of nature SHAK 455:17
ruined: be r. at our own request MORE 357:10
nation was ever r. by trade FRAN 218:4
Playing among the r. languages AUDEN 18:5
r. by buying good pennyworths FRAN 218:12
r. by Chinese cheap labour HARTE 242:30
r. Mr Hampden's fortune BURKE 109:2
we dress when we're r. HARDY 240:19
Ruining: R. along the illimitable TENN 539:20
ruinis: *Altior Italiae r.* HOR 260:24
Ruinous: R. inheritance GAIUS 220:27
Were r. and old SPEN 516:3
ruins: description of the r. of St Paul's
WALP 563:9
I shored against my r. ELIOT 205:12
r. of the noblest man SHAK 450:11
sketch the r. of St Paul's MAC 323:16
Ruislip: Gaily into R. Gardens BETJ 43:13
ruit: *consili expers mole r.* HOR 260:23
Ruksh: R., the horse ARN 14:26
rule: bear r. in their kingdoms BIBLE 63:22
Be each man's r. TENN 533:23
broken the second r. of war MONT 355:9
can r. and dare not lie TENN 540:4
charge or r. nor governance SURR 524:20
greater light to the r. the day BIBLE 45:3
greatest r. of all MOL 353:6
Irish Home R. ROS 408:13
levell'd r. of streaming light MILT 341:7

little r. DYER 199:18
monarch's r. must prove PRIOR 401:3
never strove to r. the roast PRIOR 401:10
observ'd the golden r. BLAKE 87:4
oldest r. in the book CARR 134:21
only infallible r. we know SURT 525:2
Only take this r. along SWIFT 527:21
prevents the r. of wealth BAG 29:4
priests bear r. by their BIBLE 60:18
Reason to r. DRYD 196:14
Resolv'd to ruin or to r. DRYD 194:8
rich men r. the law GOLD 231:29
R., Britannia THOM 549:7
R. of three doth puzzle ANON 6:18
Shall all be done by the r. SHAK 422:6
souls of those they r. ARN 13:22
they that r. in England CHES 146:24
too fond to r. alone POPE 376:26
To r. o'er freemen BROO 94:4
wise man make your r. BLAKE 87:9
Rule Britannia: When you've shouted
'R.' KIPL 297:22
ruled: God their severance r. ARN 13:13
ruler: r. of all his substance PRAY 397:4
R. of the Queen's Navee GILB 228:4
that is to be r. in Israel BIBLE 61:24
thee a r. over many things BIBLE 68:2
thou being our r. and guide PRAY 386:16
rulers: captains and r. clothed BIBLE 60:37
r. are not a terror BIBLE 75:21
R. have no authority from MAYH 336:6
rules: hand that r. the world WALL 562:4
known r. of ancient liberty MILT 351:7
Love r. the court SCOTT 416:17
never shows she r. POPE 377:27
Obtruding false r. pranked MILT 341:19
pretences to break known r. CROM 170:2
R. and models destroy genius HAZL 243:28
r. of the game are what HUXL 269:6
there are no golden r. SHAW 497:35
These simple little r. BELL 40:4
truth from r. BUTL 117:34
which the man of genius r. STEP 518:20
ruleth: r. his spirit than he that BIBLE 54:9
ruling: He rather hated the r. BENT 41:1
r. passion in man is not FROST 219:14
r. passion conquers reason POPE 377:32
Search then the R. Passion POPE 377:13
various r. passions find POPE 377:24
rum: r. and true religion BYRON 122:16
r., Romanism, and rebellion BURC 108:1
r., sodomy and the lash CHUR 151:7
what a R. Go everything is WELLS 568:14
Yo-ho-ho, and a bottle of r. STEV 521:21
Rumble: R. thy bellyful SHAK 454:5
Rumbling: R. under blackened girders
BETJ 43:17
Rumoresque: *R. senum severiorum*
CAT 136:25
rumour: History a distillation of r.
CARL 131:23
R. is a pipe SHAK 440:31
sound and r. MORR 358:7
rumours: hear of wars and r. of wars
BIBLE 67:27
run: (Although I run and r.) CHES 147:25
he may r. that readeth it BIBLE 62:1
ill-luck that they r. half-way JERR 273:8
I therefore so r. BIBLE 76:9
Many shall r. to and fro BIBLE 61:10
My race of glory r. MILT 350:23
nearest r. thing WELL 567:19
r. it down SWIFT 528:3
R., run, Orlando SHAK 426:2
r.-stealers flicker THOM 547:24
r. The colours from my BROW 98:10
r. the race with Death JOHN 279:24
r. to and fro like sparks BIBLE 62:14
r. with patience the race BIBLE 79:35
significant than the long r. KEYN 296:2

true love never did r. smooth SHAK 469:18
We do not r. for prize SORL 513:10
which r. in a race run all BIBLE 76:8
While I do r. upon it SHAK 452:6
yet we will make him r. MARV 332:20
runagates: r. continue in scarceness
PRAY 394:7
runcible: He weareth a r. hat LEAR 311:23
R. Cat with crimson whiskers LEAR 312:20
they ate with a r. spoon LEAR 312:14
Runic: Before some fallen R. stone ARN 13:8
In a sort of R. rhyme POE 375:1
runnels: r. pebble-stones KEATS 289:3
running: first sprightly r. could DRYD 195:27
takes all the r. *you* can do CARR 134:32
Whom are you r. away from VIRG 559:16
runs: who r. may read KEBLE 295:5
Run'st: R. thou ne'er so fast ROWL 411:1
run-way: stretched beyond the r. BETJ 42:12
Rupee: chapter on the Fall of the R.
WILDE 573:4
Rupert: R. of Debate BULW 107:2
R. of Parliamentary discussion DISR 184:13
rura: *Paterna r. bubus* HOR 259:7
rural: lovely woman in a r. spot HUNT 268:13
Rural Dean: sly shade of a R. BROO 94:21
Rus: R. in urbe MART 331:14
rush: Who r. to glory CAMP 128:22
Will r. into the state SHAK 468:3
rush'd: He r. into the field BYRON 120:24
rushes: *Green grow the r.* ANON 6:5
Ruskin: Leave to squeamish R. KING 296:15
Russell: R. the fox stirte up atones
CHAU 143:2
russet: r. yeas and honest kersey SHAK 457:16
russet-coated: r. captain that knows what
CROM 169:20
Russia: last out a night in R. SHAK 463:17
R. has two generals NICH 362:23
to you the action of R. CHUR 149:28
Russian: understood that the R. KIPL 304:28
Russians: R. shall not have Constantinople
HUNT 268:3
rust: Less than the r. that never HOPE 256:5
moth and r. doth corrupt BIBLE 64:25
r. of the Barons' Wars WALP 562:24
Tarnished with r. WILDE 572:18
that which never taketh r. SIDN 507:28
To r. in peace SOUT 513:13
To r. unburnish'd TENN 543:22
to wear out than to r. CUMB 170:7
rusteth: r. the craft and the craftsman
POUND 382:10
rustic: r. murmur of their bourg TENN 535:4
rusticity: refined r. WORD 581:16
rustling: dread the r. of the grass
WORD 576:23
rusty: of fighting was grown r. BUTL 117:24
Ruth: Through the sad heart of R.
KEATS 291:23
ruthful: Heaven and Earth are not r.
LAO 310:2
Rye: Before the Roman came to R.
CHES 147:10
Between the acres of the r. SHAK 427:2
Coming through the r. BURNS 113:2
fields of barley and of r. TENN 538:2
r. reach to the chin PEELE 371:9
rymyng: r. is nat worth a toord CHAU 143:15
Saba: kings of Arabia and S. PRAY 394:20
sabachthani: lama s. BIBLE 68:24
Sabaoth: Lord God of S. PRAY 384:16
Sabaoth: grant me that S.'s sight
SPEN 516:25
sabbata: *quanta qualia sunt illa s.* ABEL 1:1
Sabbath: last S. day of 1879 MCG 325:6
Remember the s. day BIBLE 47:24
s. was made for man BIBLE 68:26
sabbaths: glorious are those s. which
ABEL 1:1

new moons and s.   BIBLE 57:17
Sabean: S. odours from the spicy MILT 347:17
saber: Con un no s. sabiendo   JOHN 273:16
Sabidi: Non amo te, S.   MART 331:9
sabiendo: Con un no saber s.   JOHN 273:16
Sabina: Cur valle permutem S.   HOR 260:16
sabios: los pocos s. que en el   LUIS 320:12
sable: s. silver'd   SHAK 430:13
Sable-vested: S. Night   MILT 347:5
sabre: Great Chatham with his s. ANON 5:10
  That took the s. straight   HOUS 266:4
Sabrina: S. fair   MILT 341:20
Sacco: S.'s name will live   VANZ 555:8
sack: I'll purge, and leave s. SHAK 440:29
  intolerable deal of s.   SHAK 439:20
  s. and sugar be a fault   SHAK 439:17
  S. the lot   FISH 212:3
sackbut: s., psaltery   BIBLE 61:3
sacks: s. to sew up wives   THAC 545:18
Sacrament: holy S. to your comfort
    PRAY 387:18
Sacraments: How many S. hath Christ
    PRAY 388:19
  S. in a tongue not understood PRAY 400:8
Sacred: Enormous through the S. Town
    BELL 39:28
  is free but facts are s.   SCOTT 415:15
  s. head of thine   MILT 343:10
  s. rites unfit...   SIDN 507:26
  s. to the household gods THOM 549:23
  two most s. names of earth COWL 164:15
Sacred Heart: convent of the S. ELIOT 204:16
sacrifice: blood Of human s. MILT 345:14
  bodies a living s.   BIBLE 75:15
  Burnt-offerings, and s. for sin PRAY 392:2
  hands be an evening s.   PRAY 399:9
  holy hush of ancient s.   STEV 520:18
  measure of his s.   ROS 408:18
  obey is better than s.   BIBLE 50:4
  ought to s. to the graces BURKE 111:26
  perfect, and sufficient s.   PRAY 387:24
  s. of God is a troubled   PRAY 393:8
  s. to God of the devil's   POPE 381:21
  stands Thine ancient s.   KIPL 302:7
  these coming to the s.   KEATS 291:8
  thou desirest no s.   PRAY 393:8
  Too long a s.   YEATS 585:2
  turn delight into a s.   HERB 246:27
  your prayers one sweet s. SHAK 446:27
sacrificed: Christ our passover is s.
    BIBLE 75:36
  must be s. to conciseness JOHN 281:4
  slain and spent and s.   SWIN 529:3
sacrificers: s., but not butchers SHAK 449:8
sacrifices: he s. it to your opinion
    BURKE 109:11
  he who s. an hundred thousand WALP 563:12
  Upon such s., my Cordelia SHAK 456:4
sacrilege: consecrated s.   DISR 185:6
sacrilegious: s. murder hath broke ope
    SHAK 460:22
sad: All my s. captains   SHAK 422:22
  did seem too solemn s.   SPEN 515:32
  her sadness when she's s. BARR 34:17
  If you find him s.   SHAK 421:23
  know not why I am so s. HEINE 244:9
  know not why I am so s. SHAK 465:7
  like a s. slave   SHAK 493:18
  s. and bad and mad   BROW 100:8
  s. bad glad   SWIN 529:2
  s. I am   BETJ 44:6
  s. mortality o'ersways SHAK 494:4
  s. road lies so clear   PATM 370:6
  s. swell'd face   BARH 33:16
  s. tale's best for winter SHAK 491:12
  s. vicissitude of things   STER 520:13
  s. when others' grief is BYRON 124:35
  She is never s. but when SHAK 472:13
  should remember and be s. ROSS 409:4
  So s., so fresh   TENN 542:3

tell s. stories   SHAK 479:11
there on that s. height   THOM 546:24
would be as s. as night   SHAK 452:23
young are s. and bewildered SMITH 510:22
Your s. tires in a mile-a   SHAK 491:21
sad-coloured: s. sect   HOOD 255:16
saddens: thought which s. while
    BROW 103:13
sadder: s. and a wiser man COL 156:1
saddest: telling the s. tale SHAK 470:3
  that tell of s. thought   SHEL 504:23
saddle: Come s. my horses SCOTT 418:30
  Things are in the s.   EMER 206:21
  up they hang his s.   BEAU 36:7
saddle-leather: Thick-jewell'd shone
  the s.   TENN 538:9
sadly: take their pleasures s. SULLY 524:18
sadness: At all the s. in the sweet
    THOM 547:26
  diverter of s.   WALT 564:3
  Fell into a s.   SHAK 432:2
  Good day s.   ELUA 206:16
  s. of her sadness when BARR 34:17
  shade of s.   WHIT 571:17
  soul shall taste the s. KEATS 291:15
  such a want-wit s. makes SHAK 465:7
  Sweet though in s.   SHEL 502:13
saeclorum: integro s. nascitur ordo
    VIRG 559:22
saeclum: Solvet s. in favilla CEL 138:5
saecula: et in s. saeculorum MASS 334:14
Saepibus: S. in nostris parvam te VIRG 560:4
safe: He give us a s. lodging NEWM 362:9
  s. course for the defeated VIRG 558:7
  s. in a golden ewer   BROW 100:4
  s. I sing with mortal voice MILT 348:28
  see me s. up   MORE 357:16
  us s. under every form   JOHN 276:6
  Winds somewhere s. to sea SWIN 529:25
safeguard: was the s. of the West
    WORD 582:10
safely: I'd toddle s. home SASS 414:11
  to be s. thus   SHAK 461:8
  tread s. into the unknown' HASK 243:1
safer: s. than a known way HASK 243:1
  s. to be in a subordinate THOM 546:9
safest: Just when we're s. BROW 99:4
  middle course is the s. OVID 366:14
safety: every man shall eat in s. SHAK 448:1
  pluck this flower, s.   SHAK 438:29
  source of my light and my s. BIBLE 83:5
  Under the smile of s. wounds SHAK 440:30
safety-catch: s. on my pistol JOHST 283:8
safire: diamond and s. bracelet LOOS 318:3
safliest: s. when with one man mann'd
    DONNE 188:16
saft: make it s. and narrow BALL 30:12
sage: simpleton and the s. CERV 138:20
  When the smiling s. reply'd JOHN 277:14
sager: s. sort our deeds reprove CAT 136:25
said: Everything has been s. LA B 306:11
  fool hath s. in his heart PRAY 390:2
  He s. true things   BROW 99:11
  if I had s. it myself   SWIFT 526:30
  if I s. so   GOLD 232:4
  is a great deal to be s. BENT 41:5
  might be s. on both sides ADD 2:13
  s. anything that was remembered DISR 186:27
  (S. I to myself   GILB 226:6
  s. our remarks before   DON 187:17
  S. the Piggy, 'I will.'   LEAR 312:13
  s. whot a owt to 'a said TENN 541:3
  Seek not to know who s. THOM 546:8
  so very little s.   CHUR 149:10
  that has been known and s. ARN 16:17
  that's not been s. before TER 544:16
  they are carolled and s. STEV 523:1
  thought cannot wisely be s. PEAC 370:19
sail: argosies with portly s. SHAK 465:7
  Never weather-beaten s. CAMP 129:20

s. in amply billowing gown BELL 39:28
sea-mark of my utmost s. SHAK 477:20
shook out more s.   ARN 14:21
sieve I'll thither s.   SHAK 458:6
To s. beyond the sunset TENN 544:3
towers of s. at dawn of day CLOU 154:3
vessel puffs her s.   TENN 544:3
Was it the proud full s. SHAK 494:11
white s.'s shaking   MAS 334:4
sail'd: She hadna s. a league BALL 30:18
sailed: have s. the seas and come
    YEATS 586:13
  Swift has s. into his rest YEATS 587:3
  They s. away for a year LEAR 312:12
  you never s. with *me* before JACK 270:29
sailing: Come s. to the strand BALL 31:20
  failing occurred in the s. CARR 133:6
sailor: Home is the s.   STEV 523:10
  lass that loves a s.   DIBD 175:20
  No man will be a s. who JOHN 274:18
  s. frae the main   BURNS 114:11
  s.'s wife had chestnuts SHAK 458:6
  soldier an' s. too   KIPL 302:23
  take the most gallant s. CHUR 150:16
  there ever s. free to choose KIPL 303:30
Sailor-men: It's very odd that S. should
    BARH 33:23
sailors: s. but men   SHAK 465:27
  s., when away   GAY 223:29
  three s. of Bristol City THAC 545:32
sails: argosies of magic s. TENN 538:24
  Purple the s.   SHAK 422:2
  s. by the Low-lands low BALL 31:2
  To the white dipping s. MAS 334:2
  yet still the s. made   COL 155:26
saint: able to corrupt a s. SHAK 438:7
  accents of an expiring s. STER 520:9
  became a S.   NEWM 362:5
en aucune manière ni s.   VOLT 561:9
  His s. is sure of his unspotted PEELE 371:8
  in vain the s. adore   DRAY 193:16
  little s. best fits a little HERR 249:20
  neither s. nor sophist-led ARN 13:1
  Poet and S.   COWL 164:15
  reel out a s.   CHUR 149:1
  s. in crape is twice   POPE 377:11
  seem a s. when most I play SHAK 480:25
  she cou'd make of me a s. CONG 160:30
  Tax not the royal S.   WORD 582:16
  'twould a s. provoke   POPE 377:15
  with a s.   SHAK 463:12
  worst of madmen is a s. POPE 380:11
sainted: thing ensky'd and s. SHAK 463:12
Saint George: England and S. SHAK 444:3
  S., that swinged the dragon SHAK 452:12
Saint Martin: Expect S.'s summer
    SHAK 445:18
Saints: Communion of S. PRAY 384:26
  follow thy blessed S.   PRAY 387:4
  Great men may jest with s. SHAK 463:3
  his lot is among the s.   BIBLE 62:16
  is the death of his s.   PRAY 397:22
  I think it frets the s. BROW 97:30
  Let the s. be joyful   PRAY 399:24
  perfecting of the s.   BIBLE 77:28
  S. in your injuries   SHAK 474:15
  s. may do the same things BUTL 118:5
  shall never be S. in Heaven BROW 96:17
  than the least of all s. BIBLE 77:23
  thy slaughtered s.   MILT 351:9
  which are the prayers of s. BIBLE 81:27
  With s. dost bait thy hook SHAK 464:5
  with thy quire of S. DONNE 189:14
saint-seducing: lap to s. gold SHAK 481:24
Saint Somebody: Miracles of S.
    BROW 104:15
sair: love o'ercome sae s. BURNS 114:18
saisons: Ô s., ô châteaux   RIMB 406:8
sake: Christ's particular love's s.
    BROW 104:22

country for his country's s. FITZ 212:4
friendship's s. BLAKE 87:7
my s. shall find it BIBLE 65:40
partial for th' observer's s. POPE 377:8
wine for thy stomach's s. BIBLE 79:16
Sal: S. Atticum PLINY 374:17
salad: cheap but wholesome s. COWP 167:27
My s. days SHAK 421:33
Our Garrick's a s. GOLD 231:16
primroses make a capital s. DISR 186:15
s., for which DU M 199:5
salamandrine: Of her s. fires HARDY 239:4
salary: that he had a s. to receive GIBB 224:10
sale: proverai sì come sa di s. DANTE 171:17
Salem: At S. is his tabernacle PRAY 395:1
saleroom: learned babble of the s. CARL 131:19
salire: disposto a s. alle stelle DANTE 171:15
Salisbury: S. makes a great speech MORL 358:1
Salisbury Plain: crossing S. on a bicycle GILB 226:15
salley: Down by the s. gardens YEATS 584:22
sallow: s. waiter brings me beans SASS 415:4
sallows: on mealed-with-yellow s. HOPK 256:29
sally: I make a sudden s. TENN 532:20
S. is gone from Ha'nacker Hill BELL 39:26
There's none like pretty S. CAREY 130:26
salmon: cod's head for the s.'s SHAK 474:18
first s. and the first LONG 316:23
'It was the s. DICK 181:28
s.-falls YEATS 586:11
s. sing in the street AUDEN 18:9
salmons: there is s. in both SHAK 445:5
saloons: Solomon of s. BROW 102:18
salsa: s. del mundo es el hambre CERV 138:13
salt: are the s. of the earth BIBLE 64:7
are the s. of the earth SHEL 501:18
beached verge of the s. flood SHAK 486:14
Distasted with the s. SHAK 487:12
eating an egg without s. KIPL 304:37
s., estranging sea ARN 13:13
s. is the taste of another DANTE 171:17
s. tides seaward flow ARN 13:5
seasoned with s. BIBLE 78:28
she became a pillar of s. BIBLE 46:8
saltness: relish of the s. of time SHAK 441:5
s. agree GOLD 231:16
saltpetre: villainous s. should be digg'd SHAK 438:16
Salus: S. extra ecclesiam non AUG 21:19
S. populi suprema CIC 151:19
S. populi suprema lex SELD 419:25
Una s. victis nullam sperare VIRG 558:7
salut: s. balaiera largement le ROST 410:12
salutant: morituri te s. ANON 10:7
salutations: love s. in the marketplaces BIBLE 68:37
salute: I s. thee, Mantovano TENN 543:18
S. one another with BIBLE 75:28
who are about to die s. ANON 10:7
Who are they you s. WHIT 570:12
Salva: S. me CEL 138:7
salvaged: Our ships have been s. HALS 238:11
salvation: brought s. down By meekness SMART 509:4
generally necessary to s. PRAY 388:19
helmet, the hope of s. BIBLE 79:2
My bottle of s. RAL 404:12
my light, and my s. PRAY 391:7
no s. outside the church AUG 21:19
now is our s. nearer than BIBLE 75:24
s. of our own souls JOHN 275:18
s. of mankind lies only SOLZ 513:1
s. with fear and trembling BIBLE 78:15
shew him my s. PRAY 395:23
Should see s. SHAK 467:27
strength of our s. PRAY 396:3
that publisheth s. BIBLE 59:18

things necessary to s. PRAY 400:6
Salve: S., regina ANON 10:19
Samarcand: silken S. to cedar'd Lebanon KEATS 289:20
Samaritan: ready enough to do the S. SMITH 511:7
Samarkand: take the Golden Road to S. FLEC 214:14
same: he is much the s. ANON 4:17
It all comes to the s. BROW 98:25
it would be all the s. DICK 180:5
Jesus Christ the s. yesterday BIBLE 80:4
more they are the s. KARR 288:15
reason I should be the s. AYT 24:4
s. in thine own act SHAK 459:8
this will go onward the s. HARDY 240:5
thou art the s. PRAY 396:13
we must all say *the s.* MELB 336:14
With the s. cement POPE 375:24
you are the s. you MART 331:13
samite: Clothed in white s. TENN 534:1
samphire: Hangs one that gathers s. SHAK 455:14
sampler: serve to ply The s. MILT 341:18
Samson: carry the buckler unto S. BROW 96:14
S. hath quit himself MILT 351:1
Samuel: Lord called S. BIBLE 49:34
Sana: S. quod est saucium LANG 310:1
sancta: sed s. simplicitas JER 272:20
sanctam: Et unam s. Catholicam et MASS 334:20
sanctified: husband is s. by the wife BIBLE 76:3
lips once s. by Hers BROW 106:1
sanctifies: death canonizes and s. BURKE 109:5
Sanctify: S. the Lord of hosts himself BIBLE 58:4
sanction: s. des injustices établies FRAN 217:25
sanctioned: established injustices are s. FRAN 217:25
sanctities: Round the day's dead s. THOM 548:15
sanctuaries: round these chartered s. MACN 326:9
sanctuarize: indeed should murder s. SHAK 436:18
sanctuary: dark s. of incapacity CHES 146:5
he shall be for a s. BIBLE 58:4
Sanctus: S., sanctus sanctus MASS 335:4
sand: built his house upon the s. BIBLE 65:12
grain of s. WHIT 570:21
islets of yellow s. LEAR 312:16
land of s. and ruin SWIN 530:29
name upon The soft sea-s. LAND 309:4
night to die upon the s. ARN 14:26
plain to be seen in the s. DEFOE 173:7
s. against the wind BLAKE 86:23
S.-strewn caverns ARN 13:6
speed i' the slushy s. BROW 102:14
Such quantities of s. CARR 135:5
tide crept up along the s. KING 297:1
World in a Grain of S. BLAKE 85:8
sandal: bright and battering s. HOPK 256:11
his s. shoon SHAK 435:32
sandals: Bind on thy s. SWIN 528:16
still morn went out with s. MILT 343:16
Sandford: down by S. ARN 15:8
sands: Across the s. of Dee KING 296:25
Footprints on the s. of time LONG 317:4
Here are s. BEAU 36:1
lone and level s. stretch SHEL 502:16
looks at the s. HARDY 240:15
s. with printless foot SHAK 485:23
sang: auld Scotish s. BURNS 113:4
I s. in my chains like THOM 547:2
morning stars s. BIBLE 53:3
Perhaps it may turn out a s. BURNS 113:16

s. themselves to sleep HODG 252:6
s. to a small guitar LEAR 312:11
song the Syrens s. BROW 97:14
Thus s. the uncouth swain MILT 343:19
sanglant: Le dernier acte est s. PASC 369:8
sanglots: Les s. longs VERL 556:4
sanguinary: s. punishments which corrupt PAINE 368:4
sanguis: semen est s. Christianorum TERT 544:22
Sanitas: S. sanitatum et omnia sanitas MEN 336:24
sanitatum: Sanitas s. et omnia sanitas MEN 336:24
sank: s. her in the sea BALL 30:19
she s. by the Low-lands BALL 31:3
sanno: maestro di color che s. DANTE 171:7
sano: mens sana in corpore s. JUV 288:4
sans: s. End FITZ 212:18
S. teeth, sans eyes SHAK 425:24
sanza: e s. alcun sospetto DANTE 171:9
sap: Lord also are full of s. PRAY 396:20
world's whole s. is sunk DONNE 189:24
sapere: s. aude HOR 258:14
sapient: s. sutlers of the Lord ELIOT 204:1
shake his s. head ARN 15:12
sapienti: Dictum s. sat est PLAU 374:14
saplings: it plies the s. double HOUS 263:14
sapphire: 'And second s. BROW 97:34
purer s. melts into the sea TENN 540:8
sapphires: ivory overlaid with s. BIBLE 57:4
Sappho: pianola 'replaces' S. POUND 383:5
Where burning S. loved BYRON 122:32
Whether my S.'s breast HERR 249:7
Sarah: Now Abraham and S. were BIBLE 46:3
Sarcasticul: This is rote S. WARD 564:23
sardine: jasper and a s. stone BIBLE 81:22
Sargent: dangerous to sit to S. ANON 6:8
Sarum: I had you upon S. plain SHAK 453:22
sassy: 'I'm sickly but s. HARR 242:16
sat: Babylon we s. down and wept PRAY 399:3
Dictum sapienti s. est PLAU 374:14
Many kings have s. down BIBLE 62:31
once I s. upon a promontory SHAK 470:7
S. and knotted all SEDL 419:12
s. prata biberunt VIRG 559:21
You have s. too long here CROM 169:26
Satan: beat down S. under our feet PRAY 385:19
capitol Of S. and his peers MILT 346:5
Ev'n S. glowr'd BURNS 115:11
Get thee behind me, S. BIBLE 66:34
Incens'd with indignation S. MILT 346:26
messenger of S. to buffet BIBLE 77:13
my S. BLAKE 86:1
S. as lightning fall from BIBLE 69:28
S. came also among them BIBLE 52:5
S. exalted sat MILT 346:5
S. finds some mischief WATTS 565:22
S. met his ancient friend BYRON 126:9
S., Nick BURNS 112:24
S., so call him now MILT 348:25
Satanic: dark S. mills BLAKE 86:1
satiable: was full of 's. curtiosity KIPL 304:20
satiate: life's cool ev'ning s. POPE 380:7
satiety: another occasion of s. BACON 25:37
ne'er knew love's sad s. SHEL 504:22
satin: always goes into white s. SHER 506:3
satire: It's hard not to write s. JUV 287:9
let s. be my song BYRON 124:15
S., being levelled SWIFT 527:3
S. is a sort of glass SWIFT 525:32
S. or sense POPE 376:30
Verse is. indeed is entirely QUIN 403:25
satiric: by one s. touch SWIFT 527:25
satirical: s. rogue says here that SHAK 432:8
satirist: be the second English s. HALL 238:6

satisfaction: own s. in the year 1399
                               AUST 22:20
  to give you s.   GAY 222:32
satisfied: things that are never s. BIBLE 54:46
  well paid that is well s.   SHAK 468:11
satisfies: Where most she s.   SHAK 422:5
satisfieth: he s. the empty soul   PRAY 397:7
  labour for that which s.   BIBLE 59:25
  s. thy mouth with good   PRAY 396:15
satisfy: long life will I s.   PRAY 395:23
  That poorly s. our eyes   WOTT 583:15
satisfying: s. a voracious appetite FIEL 211:25
Satura: S. quidem tota nostra est QUIN 403:25
saturam: s. non scribere   JUV 287:9
Saturday: S. and Monday   CAREY 130:27
  what he did on S.   YBAR 584:7
Saturn: Sat gray-hair'd S.   KEATS 289:33
  To S. nor to Mercury   HOUS 264:26
  while S. whirls   TENN 541:21
Saturnia: redeunt S. regna   VIRG 559:22
saturnine: s., dark, and melancholic
                         CONG 159:17
satyr: angel s. walks these hills KILV 296:7
sauce: et une seule s.   CAR 130:10
  Hunger is the best s.   CERV 138:13
  only one s.   CAR 130:10
saucefleem: s. he was   CHAU 142:4
saucer: sing the s. and the cup PAIN 367:15
saucy: deep-search'd with s. SHAK 456:15
  s. and audacious eloquence   SHAK 471:15
saugh: if that she s. a mous CHAU 141:16
Saul: S. also among the prophets BIBLE 49:41
  S. and Jonathan were lovely BIBLE 50:17
  S. hath slain his thousands   BIBLE 50:13
  S. was consenting unto   BIBLE 73:29
  S., why persecutest thou   BIBLE 73:33
  weep over S.   BIBLE 50:17
saule: Christe receive thy s.   BALL 31:6
sausage: Don't throw away that s.
                         ELIOT 202:8
savage: mad and s. master   SOPH 513:9
  Unequal laws unto a s.   TENN 543:21
  which a s. wields his club   HUXL 269:3
  wild in woods the noble s.   DRYD 195:29
  will take some s. woman   TENN 539:6
  you with stories of s.   BURKE 109:15
savageness: she will sing the s. out
                        SHAK 476:12
savages: cant in defence of s. JOHN 279:19
save: choose time is to s. time BACON 26:7
  God s. king Solomon   BIBLE 50:30
  God s. the king   HOGG 252:24
  himself he cannot s.   BIBLE 68:23
  matter enough to s. one's own BROW 102:23
  preaching to s. them that believe BIBLE 75:29
  s. my soul   ANON 7:5
  s. them by the barrel-load THOM 548:26
  shall s. his soul alive   BIBLE 60:35
  souls I could not s.   HOUS 265:6
  Themselves they could not s. HOUS 262:13
  vain thing to s. a man   PRAY 391:20
  wilt thou s. the people   ELL 206:12
  you would s. none of me DONNE 188:28
saved: do to be s. in this World HAL 238:4
  He s. others   BIBLE 68:23
  s. herself by her exertions   PITT 374:5
  they only s. the world   CHES 146:25
  we are not s.   BIBLE 60:20
  What must I do to be s.   BIBLE 74:7
  Whosoever will be s.   PRAY 385:11
savent: gens de qualité s.   MOL 353:23
saves: idea of Death s.   FORS 217:3
  who freely s. those who   CEL 138:7
saveth: s. in time of affliction BIBLE 62:21
saving: s. health among all nations
                         PRAY 394:4
  s. those that eye thee   SHAK 428:4
Saviour: Call'd 'S. of the Nations'
                        BYRON 123:25
  it's 'S. of 'is country'   KIPL 303:23

S.'s birth is celebrated   SHAK 429:17
saviours: s. come not home tonight
                        HOUS 262:13
savoir: c'est de s. être à soi MONT 354:21
  que de s. quelque chose   MOL 353:5
savory: s., marjoram   SHAK 491:25
savour: salt have lost his s. BIBLE 64:7
  Seeming and s. all the winter SHAK 491:22
  send forth a stinking s.   BIBLE 56:1
savoury: s. pulp they chew MILT 347:25
saw: drowns the parson's s. SHAK 457:19
  I came, s., and overcame SHAK 442:13
  I just s. Virgil   OVID 366:24
  I s. and loved   GIBB 224:12
  I s. it   BROW 102:23
  I stumbled when I s.   SHAK 455:6
  I who s. the face of God   MARL 329:7
  myself s. and of which I was VIRG 557:21
  Nor do not s. the air too   SHAK 433:16
  s., he sigh'd, he lov'd   GAY 223:6
saws: s. and modern instances SHAK 425:24
Saxon: leave the S. alone   KIPL 301:19
  like that ancient S. phrase LONG 316:18
saxpence: bang—went s. PUNCH 402:18
say: All I can s. is   BROW 102:23
  are to s. what they please FRED 218:22
  Englishman is content to s. JOHN 278:17
  Have something to s.   ARN 16:25
  if I could s. how much   SHAK 472:10
  I s., before the morning PRAY 398:24
  many things to s. unto you BIBLE 72:39
  nothing to what I could s. CARR 134:8
  Poyser 'has her s. out'   ELIOT 200:13
  S. I'm weary   HUNT 268:10
  s. it is my humour   SHAK 467:20
  S. not the struggle naught CLOU 154:4
  s. what you think   TAC 531:12
  should s. what you mean CARR 133:29
  should s. you do not like it WHIS 569:24
  there is no more to s.   SHAK 487:18
  They'l s. it's stolne   BRAD 91:13
  think till I see what I s.   WALL 562:5
  to s. about a play when SHAW 496:26
  To s. as I said then   SHAK 421:33
  to s. the perfectly correct SHAW 496:31
  we must all s. the same   MELB 336:14
  you have nothing to s.   COLT 159:8
  you have something to s. WHAT 569:11
saying: if something is not worth s.
                        BEAU 35:14
  rage for s. something   JOHN 274:17
  s. anything two or three AUST 22:12
  that if they keep on s.   BENN 40:23
  tremble lest a s. learnt   TENN 543:12
sayings: s. are generally like women's
                        HAZL 243:8
  s. of philosophers   BUTL 117:31
Says: S. little   FARQ 209:25
scabbard: he threw away the s. CLAR 152:18
scabbards: have leaped from their s.
                       BURKE 111:9
scabs: Make yourselves s. SHAK 427:12
scaffold: To the s. and the doom AYT 24:9
  Truth forever on the s.   LOW 319:13
scald: mine own tears Do s. SHAK 455:25
scale: e'l salir per l'altrui s. DANTE 171:17
  fly on a rather large s.   BARH 33:5
  sufficiently large s.   SPEN 514:33
  would not sink i' the s.   BROW 104:4
scaled: s. invention or true artistry
                       POUND 382:13
scales: could swear in both the s.
                       SHAK 460:16
Scalinger: S. used to say of the Basques
                     CHAM 139:16
scallop-shell: Give me my s. of quiet
                       RAL 404:12
scaly: s. horror of his folded MILT 344:12
scan: Then gently s. your brother
                       BURNS 112:25

scandal: have no s. while you dine
                       TENN 543:16
  In s., as in robbery   CHES 145:9
  It is public s. that constitutes MOL 354:1
  Love and s. are the best FIEL 211:18
  Retired to their tea and s. CONG 159:21
  s. about Queen Elizabeth SHER 505:24
  there is no s. like rags   FARQ 209:26
scandale: s. du monde est ce qui MOL 354:1
scandalous: s. and poor   ROCH 407:2
scapegoat: Let him go for a s. into
                       BIBLE 48:7
scar: Nor s. that whiter skin SHAK 477:5
scarce: good people's wery s. DICK 183:4
scarcely: I would s. kick to come
                       KEATS 293:31
scarceness: runagates continue in s.
                       PRAY 394:7
scare: 'Because those footprints s.
                       HOR 258:11
  ever s. me with thy tears TENN 543:14
  s. myself with my own desert FROST 219:3
scarecrow: not make a s. of the law
                       SHAK 463:15
scarecrows: s. of fools and the beacons
                       HUXL 269:10
scarely: s. greet me with that sun
                       SHAK 493:14
Scarf: S. up the tender eye SHAK 461:14
scarlet: are like a thread of s. BIBLE 56:26
  Cowards in s. pass   GRAN 234:9
  did not wear his s. coat   WILDE 572:7
  'His sins were s.   BELL 39:19
  In S. town   BALL 30:10
  line of s. thread   BIBLE 48:37
  love that loves a s. coat HOOD 254:15
  Only the s. soldiers   AUDEN 20:4
  though clothed in s.   JONS 284:14
  Though your sins be as s. BIBLE 57:18
  who clothed you in s.   BIBLE 50:17
scars: My marks and s. I carry BUNY 107:38
  seamed with the s. of disease MAC 324:7
  sleeve and show his s.   SHAK 445:3
Scatter: S., as from an unextinguished
                       SHEL 502:14
scatter'd: thousand s. into Clay FITZ 212:8
scattered: land is s. with light BRID 92:8
  let his enemies be s.   PRAY 394:6
  s. the proud in the imagination BIBLE 69:6
  s. the heaped-up mountains VIRG 560:12
scatterest: soon as thou s. them they
                       PRAY 395:18
Scatters: S. the rear of darkness MILT 342:17
scelerisque: vitae s. purus HOR 259:23
scene: behold the swelling s. SHAK 443:3
  highly impossible s.   GILB 225:13
  In life's last s. what   JOHN 283:3
  Last s. of all   SHAK 425:24
  Love gilds the s.   SHER 506:24
  o'er all this s. of man   POPE 379:1
  our lofty s. be acted o'er SHAK 450:5
  s. individable   SHAK 432:20
  s. of it with my Papa   DICK 178:18
  start a s. or two   ELIOT 203:24
  there I laid the s.   COWP 167:17
scenery: end of all natural s. RUSK 411:12
  S. is fine   KEATS 293:27
  s.'s divine   CALV 127:20
scenes: busy s. of crowded life JOHN 282:28
  changing s. of life   TATE 531:21
  no more behind your s. JOHN 274:2
  s. and shining prospects ADD 2:4
scent: dripping with s.   HOR 259:15
  methinks I s. the morning air SHAK 431:10
  s. of the roses will hang MOORE 356:7
  sweetest flower for s.   SHEL 503:24
  Their s. survives their THOM 547:25
  whose s. the fair annoys COWP 165:4
scepter'd: this s. isle   SHAK 478:20

sceptic: s. to deny the possibility
                                    HUXL 269:14
What ever s. could inquire   BUTL 117:19
scepticism: all-dissolving s.   NEWM 362:2
wise s. is the first attribute   LOW 319:16
sceptre: His s. shows the force SHAK 467:27
s. and the ball   SHAK 444:25
s. o'er a slumb'ring world   YOUNG 588:1
sceptred: avails the s. race   LAND 308:26
Sceptreless: man remains S.   SHEL 503:12
sceptrumque: s. tyrannis   TURG 553:22
schaffende: Zerstörung ist zugleich eine
s.   BAK 29:24
Schatten: denen man seinen S. zeigt
                                    NIET 363:6
wollen niemand in den S.   BULOW 106:23
schedules: out divers s. of my beauty
                                    SHAK 488:12
Scheldt: by the lazy S.   GOLD 231:23
scheme: breakfast she'll project a s.
                                    YOUNG 587:18
sorry S. of Things   FITZ 213:16
schemes: s. of political improvement
                                    JOHN 275:29
s. o' mice an' men   BURNS 115:22
Scherzando: S. ma non troppo   GILB 225:15
Schicksal: S. und Gemüt Namen   NOV 364:9
Schlag: Zwei Herzen und ein S.   HALM 238:10
schlecht: Welt hässlich und s.   NIET 363:8
scholar: better s. than Wordsworth
                                    HOUS 266:18
distractions about which, as a s.   LIPP 315:9
He was a s.   SHAK 447:21
s. all Earth's volumes   CHAP 140:16
s. among rakes   MAC 324:13
There mark what ills the s.'s   JOHN 282:29
scholars: nor its great s. great HOLM 253:17
Of white-robed S. only   WORD 582:16
S. and gentlemen   WORD 580:20
S. dispute   HOR 257:15
school: doctrine never was there s.
                                    MILT 350:21
enjoyed at the head of a s.   WALP 562:18
Example is the s. of mankind   BURKE 112:7
hath put his heart to s.   WORD 582:13
he's been to a good s.   SAKI 413:14
in erecting a grammar s.   SHAK 446:14
microcosm of a public s.   DISR 186:39
'S. is pretty bad   WAUGH 565:30
s. nonsense which was knocked   BEER 37:21
special reason for hating s.   BEER 37:21
Than either s. or college   BURNS 114:8
till we leave s.   LEWIS 314:9
Unwillingly to s.   SHAK 425:24
vixen when she went to s.   SHAK 470:24
was whipt at s.   DRYD 198:20
schoolboy: Every s. knows who imprisoned
                                    MAC 323:14
Every s. knows it   TAYL 532:5
I see a s. when I think   YEATS 585:3
s. of fourteen is ignorant   MAC 324:12
s.'s tale   BYRON 120:9
tell what every s. knows   SWIFT 527:20
than that of a s.'s tip   THAC 545:11
then the whining s.   SHAK 425:24
schoolboys: duly to delight s. JUV 288:2
s. from their books   SHAK 482:18
s. playing in the stream   PEELE 371:9
school-days: Thy s. frightful   SHAK 481:8
schoolgirl: Pert as a s. well can be
                                    GILB 226:27
schoolman: he knew no s.'s subtle
                                    POPE 377:5
schoolmaster: s. is abroad   BROU 95:5
schoolmastering: perish than to continue
s.   CARL 132:27
schoolmasters: s. puzzle their brain
                                    GOLD 231:22
s. Deliver us to laws   HERB 248:10
s. even today read Greek   YEATS 587:13

schoolrooms: Better build s. for 'the
boy'   ELIZ 162:8
schools: a' their colleges and s. BURNS 115:27
bewilder'd in the maze of s.   POPE 378:11
lumber of the s.   SWIFT 527:32
public s. with silk   MARL 329:5
rules were not in the s.   BUTL 117:34
s. of thought contend   MAO 328:18
wrangling s.   DONNE 188:26
your jargon o' your s.   BURNS 113:19
Schosse: aus dem S. der Zeit   HEINE 244:12
schuf: er s. alsbald noch andere NIET 363:3
Schumann: S.'s our music-maker now
                                    BROW 100:16
schweigen: darüber muss man s.   WITT 575:17
S. ist golden   CARL 132:23
Sciatica: S.: he cured it   AUBR 17:25
Science: Art and S. cannot exist BLAKE 86:7
commit A social s.   AUDEN 21:5
countenance of all s.   WORD 583:9
despise Art and S.   BLAKE 86:9
everything that relates to s.   LAMB 307:10
Fair S. frown'd not   GRAY 235:4
Geometry (which is the only s.   HOBB 251:14
great tragedy of S.   HUXL 269:5
His soul proud S. never   POPE 379:5
human s. is at a loss   CHOM 148:16
Il faut n'appeler S.   VAL 555:1
La vraye s. et le vray   CHAR 141:1
only applications of s.   PAST 369:17
only the instrument of s.   JOHN 281:6
Politics is not an exact s.   BISM 84:19
Professors of the Dismal S.   CARL 131:40
S. appears   WORD 580:16
S. falsely so called   BIBLE 79:21
S. is his forte   SMITH 512:11
S. is nothing but trained   HUXL 269:3
S. is organized knowledge   SPEN 514:24
S. moves   TENN 539:1
to patient S. dear   WORD 582:12
With the fairy tales of s.   TENN 538:16
sciences: Books must follow s. BACON 25:6
That great mother of s.   BACON 28:8
scientia: et ipsa s. potestas est BACON 28:11
scientiae: ab animo fraudatrix s. JOHN 273:17
scientiarum: Magna ista s. mater
                                    BACON 28:8
scientific: broken open on the most s.
                                    PEAC 370:13
Death was but A s.   WILDE 572:12
if they were s. terms   ARN 16:18
literary and s. opinion   ARN 16:5
s. faith's absurd   BROW 100:21
s. names of beings animalculous   GILB 228:16
scientists: at the illiteracy of s. SNOW 512:16
scintillations: s. of your wit be like
                                    GOUL 233:5
scire: s. nefas   HOR 259:19
scissor-man: red-legged s.   HOFF 252:18
scoff: some that came to s. at him AYT 24:8
who came to s.   GOLD 230:24
scoffer: dull product of a s.'s pen
                                    WORD 577:12
Scoffing: S. his state and grinning
                                    SHAK 479:11
scold: 'amper an' 'inder an' s. men
                                    KIPL 303:11
scole: s. of Stratford atte Bowe CHAU 141:15
scones: buttered s. and crumpets ELIOT 202:5
scooped: thirsted s. the brimming stream
                                    MILT 347:25
scope: that man's s.   SHAK 493:6
scorched: grey wig with the s. foretop
                                    MAC 324:7
they were s.   BIBLE 66:16
Scorer: when the One Great S. comes
                                    RICE 405:23
scorn: deal of s. looks beautiful SHAK 489:24
Disdain and s. ride sparkling   SHAK 472:21
figure for the time of s.   SHAK 476:18

Fools may our s.   GAY 223:15
held the human race in s.   BELL 38:33
little s. is alluring   CONG 161:2
love he laugh'd to s.   SHAK 495:18
S. not the Sonnet   WORD 582:14
s. of irregular perquisites   WAUGH 566:2
s. of that pleasant land   PRAY 397:5
S. the sort now growing   YEATS 587:8
s. to change my state   SHAK 493:6
s. which mock'd the smart   ARN 13:9
sound Of public s.   MILT 349:22
Teach not thy lip such s.   SHAK 480:21
to s. in the bitterness   BIBLE 62:26
treat with virtuous s.   GILB 226:4
very s. of men   PRAY 390:17
We s. their bodies   BAST 35:2
'Where I have had many a s.   BALL 30:9
scorn'd: Not s. in heav'n   COWP 166:4
s. his spirit   SHAK 448:21
was s. and died   GAY 223:6
scorner: thou s. of the ground SHEL 504:24
scornful: dart not s. glances from
                                    SHAK 484:15
sat in the seat of the s.   PRAY 389:14
s., yet with jealous eyes   POPE 376:26
scorning: s. the base degrees   SHAK 449:5
time and nonsense s.   BUCK 106:18
scorpions: will chastise you with s.
                                    BIBLE 51:3
Scot: Had Cain been S.   CLEV 153:4
Scotch: indeed inferior to the S. NORTH 364:2
joke well into a S. understanding
                                    SMITH 510:28
S. civility   ROCH 407:5
that the S. have found   JOHN 277:12
scotch'd: We have s. the snake SHAK 461:12
Scotchman: is that makes a S. happy
                                    JOHN 280:4
Much may be made of a S.   JOHN 276:11
noblest prospect which a S.   JOHN 274:30
one S. but what was a man   LOCK 316:2
Scotchmen: all my life to like S. LAMB 307:8
scot-free: will get off s.   HOR 262:7
Scotia: chief of S.'s food   BURNS 113:8
S.'s grandeur springs   BURNS 113:4
Scotish: swats and an auld S. sang
                                    BURNS 113:4
Scotland: do indeed come from S.
                                    JOHN 274:20
grave Livers do in S. use   WORD 581:1
inferior sort of S.   SMITH 512:5
in S. supports the people   JOHN 281:14
left fair S.'s strand   BURNS 114:10
love S. better than truth   JOHN 281:22
Seeing S.   JOHN 277:24
shiver'd was fair S.'s spear   SCOTT 417:25
Stands S. where it did   SHAK 462:15
That S. led in luve   WYNT 584:4
Scots: dozen of S. at a breakfast SHAK 438:33
S. lords at his feet   BALL 31:20
S., wha hae wi' Wallace   BURNS 114:34
Scotsman: moral attribute of a S. BARR 34:20
S. of your ability let   BARR 34:19
world than a S. on the make   BARR 34:21
Scott: half so flat as Walter S. ANON 7:8
think it was Sir Walter S.   SURT 525:9
wrong part wrote S.   ANON 8:12
Scottish: brave old S. Cavalier AYT 24:11
Froude informs the S. youth   STUB 524:5
scoundrel: given them to such a s.
                                    SWIFT 526:21
Good is the plea of the s.   BLAKE 86:7
last refuge of a s.   JOHN 276:25
man over forty is a s.   SHAW 498:4
scoundrels: healthy hatred of s. CARL 132:2
scoured: with rust than to be s. SHAK 441:15
scourge: made a s. of small cords
                                    BIBLE 71:35
S. of God   MARL 330:17
scout: s. 'em, and flout 'em   SHAK 485:15

scowl: Did s. on Richard SHAK 480:10
With anxious s. drew near AYT 24:10
scowling: At fifteen I stopped s.
POUND 383:16
scramble: s. at the shearers' feast
MILT 343:12
scrap: just for a s. of paper BETH 42:3
scrape: took him a potsherd to s. BIBLE 52:9
scrappy: days when work was s. CHES 147:22
scraps: stolen the s. SHAK 457:12
scratch: quick sharp s. BROW 102:14
s. his name on the Abbey-stones
BROW 101:27
S. the Christian and you ZANG 588:16
will s. the nurse SHAK 490:31
scratched: considerably worried and s.
DICK 178:6
Priscian a little s. SHAK 457:11
Scratches: S. its innocent behind
AUDEN 19:19
scratching: cure it but the s. of a pen
LOVER 318:21
scream: Does not s. WHIT 571:11
like a s. from a crevasse GREE 236:6
mew rise to a s. on the tool-shed AUDEN 20:8
screaming: I am s. out loud all DICK 180:9
screams: strange s. of death SHAK 460:20
screen: s. from seeing and leave SWIN 528:18
screw: s. your courage SHAK 459:10
scribblative: arts babblative and s.
SOUT 514:12
scribble: Always s. GLOU 229:22
fierce vindictive s. of red BROW 100:23
Scribe: At ille inquit 'S. BEDE 37:2
scribendi: Qui nullum fere s. genus
JOHN 277:13
S. cacoethes et aegro JUV 287:23
scribens: aut s. THOM 546:11
scribere: In vento et rapida s. oportet
CAT 137:7
saturam non s. JUV 287:9
scribes: Beware of the s. BIBLE 68:37
of the s. and Pharisees BIBLE 64:11
s., and Pharisees BIBLE 67:24
s. and the Pharisees brought BIBLE 72:9
scrip: My s. of joy RAL 404:12
yet with s. and scrippage SHAK 426:6
scriptores: Cedite Romani s. PROP 401:17
scripturas: Scrutamini s. SELD 419:18
Scripture: devil can cite S. for his
SHAK 466:1
Holy S. containeth PRAY 400:6
I will better it in S. OVER 366:7
S. moveth us in sundry PRAY 384:9
writ is the s. of puplis JER 272:21
Scriptures: hast caused all holy S.
PRAY 386:5
Search the s. BIBLE 72:3
scrivener: notched and cropt s. LAMB 307:11
scrofulous: s. French novel BROW 105:8
scroll: long-cramped s. BROW 101:24
s. of crystal SHEL 500:15
with punishments the s. HENL 245:5
scrotum: s.tightening sea JOYCE 286:20
scruple: Some craven s. SHAK 435:30
scrupulosity: himself with oriental s.
JOHN 282:2
scrupulous: s. and the just CONR 161:22
Scrutamini: S. scripturas SELD 419:18
scullion: Away, you s. SHAK 441:19
sculptor: great s. or painter can be
RUSK 411:8
sculptur'd: s. dead on each side seem
KEATS 289:10
sculpture: like that of s. RUSS 412:15
scum: composed of the s. of the earth
WELL 568:1
scutcheon: honour is a mere s. SHAK 440:18
scuttled: s. ship or cut a throat BYRON 122:30
Scuttling: S. across the floors ELIOT 203:21

Scylla: S. and Charybdis NEWM 361:21
S. and Charybdis SHEL 505:11
scythe: bate his s.'s keen edge SHAK 456:14
mower whets his s. MILT 342:19
poor crooked s. and spade SHIR 507:2
Wanting the s. SHAK 445:12
Scythia: another group to S. VIRG 559:13
Scythian: whitest snow on S. hills
MARL 330:3
se: s., and eek for to be CHAU 143:20
s. Iudice nemo nocens JUV 288:5
sea: all as hungry as the s. SHAK 489:6
all the s. were ink LYLY 321:16
beneath in the abysmal s. TENN 537:24
blow the earth into the s. SHAK 454:3
blue days at s. STEV 522:29
boundless as the s. SHAK 482:17
cold gray stones, O S. TENN 532:17
crown'd with summer s. TENN 535:27
desks and never go to s. GILB 228:7
do be afraid of the s. SYNGE 531:4
dominion of the s. COV 163:10
estranging s. ARN 13:13
far over the summer s. TENN 543:2
frail boat on the rough s. HOR 259:12
From s. to shining sea BATES 35:4
full s. are we now afloat SHAK 451:27
gaping wretches of the s. HUNT 268:7
great and wide s. also PRAY 397:1
gurly grew the s. BALL 30:18
has something of the s. SEDL 419:9
heaven by s. as by land GILB 225:7
he cast into the s. BIBLE 70:30
He divided the s. PRAY 395:5
his footsteps in the s. COWP 165:26
home from s. STEV 523:10
if we gang to s. master BALL 31:18
if Ye take away the s. KIPL 300:19
In a solitude of the s. HARDY 239:4
In cliff to the s. ARN 13:2
in my chains like the s. THOM 547:2
in perils in the s. BIBLE 77:12
in the bottom of the s. SHAK 480:27
in the midst of the s. BIBLE 55:1
in the s. of life enisled ARN 13:12
Into that silent s. COL 155:12
into the midst of the s. PRAY 392:19
is not afraid of the s. SYNGE 531:4
is the sound of the s. ELIOT 204:13
kings of the s. ARN 13:7
little cloud out of the s. BIBLE 51:11
lover of men, the s. SWIN 530:27
mad as the vex'd s. SHAK 455:13
mirrors of the s. are strewn FLEC 214:21
mountains by the winter s. TENN 535:20
never sick at s. GILB 227:31
not having been at s. JOHN 277:26
of a sudden came the s. BROW 103:9
of the swing of the s. HOPK 256:17
one is of the s. WORD 582:18
one s. to the other PRAY 394:20
on this windy s. of land MILT 347:10
owse and bottom of the s. SHAK 443:8
particular s. that it is old HARDY 241:21
Ran purple to the s. MILT 345:17
Receiveth as the s. SHAK 487:20
remain in the broad s. PRAY 394:1
ride swiftly towards the s. CHES 147:14
round me like a bursting s. THOM 548:21
sapphire melts into the s. TENN 540:8
s. for an acre of barren SHAK 484:22
s. gave up the dead which BIBLE 82:29
s. grew civil at her song SHAK 470:7
s. is his PRAY 396:4
S. of Faith ARN 12:23
s. of glass like unto crystal BIBLE 81:23
s. of glass mingled with BIBLE 82:19
s. rises higher CHES 146:16
s. saw that, and fled PRAY 397:16
S. shall give up her dead) PRAY 400:4

s.! the sea XEN 584:5
s. was made his tomb BARN 34:5
s. where it goes ARN 12:22
serpent-haunted s. FLEC 214:8
settle somewhere near the s. KIPL 303:30
sheet and a flowing s. CUNN 170:13
sight of that immortal s. WORD 579:12
snotgreen s. JOYCE 286:20
steady than an ebbing s. FORD 216:20
stillness of the central s. TENN 537:20
stone set in the silver s. SHAK 478:20
summers in a s. of glory SHAK 447:9
sun was shining on the s. CARR 135:3
swaying sound of the s. AUDEN 20:3
that gong-tormented s. YEATS 584:13
that great s. SHEL 501:17
that whirls me to the s. MER 337:10
there was no more s. BIBLE 82:30
they sink through the s. THOM 546:19
those in peril on the s. WHIT 569:26
tideless dolorous midland s. SWIN 530:29
till the s. itself floweth TRAH 551:17
union with its native s. WORD 577:16
uttermost parts of the s. PRAY 399:5
Vext the dim s. TENN 543:22
walking on the s. BIBLE 66:25
water in the rough rude s. SHAK 479:5
waves of the s. BIBLE 59:15
waves of the s. are mighty PRAY 396:1
waves on the great s. LUCR 320:6
Went down into the s. COL 155:7
When I put out to s. TENN 533:3
who rush across the s. HOR 258:19
why the s. is boiling hot CARR 135:7
willing foe and s. room ANON 4:26
Within a walk of the s. BELL 40:11
wrinkled s. beneath him TENN 533:7
yet the s. is not full BIBLE 55:6
sea-beasts: Where the s. rang'd all ARN 13:6
sea-blooms: s. and the oozy woods
SHEL 502:11
sea-change: doth suffer a s. SHAK 484:32
sea-faring: In land-travel or s. BROW 105:34
sea-flower: quiet s. moulded SWIN 528:25
sea-fogs: here the s. lap and cling KIPL 303:13
seagreen: s. Incorruptible CARL 131:26
seagull: Remember you shot a s. CHEK 145:2
seal: opened the seventh s. BIBLE 82:5
S. her sweet eyes weary ROSS 409:5
s. upon thine heart BIBLE 57:11
S. up the mouth of outrage SHAK 484:1
this kingly s. SHAK 422:21
You Heard a S. Bark THUR 550:31
seal'd: Hath s. thee for herself SHAK 434:1
sea-life: When men come to like a s.
JOHN 276:33
sealing wax: shoes—and ships—and
s. CARR 135:7
such as gunpowder and s. CARR 136:4
Seals: S. of love SHAK 464:21
that s. up all in rest SHAK 494:7
to loose the s. thereof BIBLE 81:26
sea-maid: report a s. spawn'd him
SHAK 464:19
seaman: s. tells stories of winds PROP 401:15
sea-mark: Like a great s. SHAK 428:4
very s. of my utmost sail SHAK 477:20
sear: s., the yellow leaf SHAK 463:2
search: active s. for Truth LESS 314:2
s. for pearls must dive DRYD 195:10
S. the scriptures BIBLE 72:3
s. will find it out HERR 249:19
they are not worth the s. SHAK 465:15
where I made s. for thee AUG 21:16
search'd: deep-s. with saucy SHAK 456:15
searched: thou hast s. me out PRAY 399:4
searching: I am s. everywhere STEP 518:27
s. find out God BIBLE 52:22
s. what we know not MILT 351:26

seareth: Earthly glory ageth and s.
 POUND 383:19
seas: floors of silent s. ELIOT 203:21
 gloom the dark broad s. TENN 544:3
 hushed the shrunken s. ELIOT 204:15
 multitudinous s. incarnadine SHAK 460:13
 must down to the s. again MAS 334:4
 now through friendly s. FLEC 214:17
 On the dangers of the s. PARK 368:25
 s. are too long BACON 28:3
 s. colder than the Hebrides FLEC 214:7
 s. do laugh WEBS 567:14
 such as pass on the s. PRAY 400:3
 treacle and s. of butter MAC 324:21
sea-sand: is the ribbed s. COL 155:19
sea-scented: Then a mile of warm s.
 BROW 102:14
sea-shore: boy playing on the s. NEWT 362:20
seasickness: it's as universal as s.
 SHAW 497:29
season: Be instant in s. BIBLE 79:25
 Compels me to disturb your s. MILT 343:2
 due s. we shall reap BIBLE 77:20
 each thing that in s. grows SHAK 456:16
 every thing there is a s. BIBLE 55:12
 give them meat in due s. PRAY 397:1
 in a s. of calm weather WORD 579:12
 it is but for a s. HOUS 264:5
 S. of mists and mellow KEATS 293:5
 s. she hath dressings fit ANON 6:20
 them their meat in due s. PRAY 399:15
 things by s. season'd are SHAK 468:19
 word spoken in due s. BIBLE 54:7
 You lack the s. of all SHAK 461:26
 Youth's the s. made GAY 222:28
season'd: s. with a gracious voice
 SHAK 467:10
seasoned: s. with salt BIBLE 78:28
seasons: From s. such as these SHAK 454:15
 In those vernal s. MILT 352:10
 man for all s. WHIT 571:22
 O s., O castles RIMB 406:8
 s. alter SHAK 470:6
 s.' difference SHAK 424:31
 s. in the mind of men KEATS 292:14
 S.; not Eternities MER 337:9
 S. return MILT 347:8
 Therefore all s. shall COL 156:23
 We've seen the s. through KIPL 300:23
seat: in the s. of the scornful PRAY 389:14
 Not a s. but a springboard CHUR 150:14
 this s. of Mars SHAK 478:20
 with such ease into his s. SHAK 440:7
seatbelts: Fasten your s. DAVIS 172:18
Seated: S. one day at the organ PROC 401:13
seats: chief s. in the synagogues BIBLE 67:22
 chief s. in the synagogues BIBLE 68:37
seaward: woods go s. from the town
 HUNT 268:12
seawards: My road leads me s. MAS 334:2
sea-water: salt s. passes TENN 536:11
sea-wet: Spartans on the s. rock HOUS 265:3
sea-wind: no life but the s. SWIN 529:18
sea-worn: s. crawls HARDY 239:4
seaworms: Battening upon huge s.
 TENN 537:25
second: All things have s. birth WORD 580:21
 beauty faded has no s. spring PHIL 373:9
 everybody allows the s. place SWIFT 527:1
 first and s. class citizens WILL 574:14
 grounds for the s. time PEAC 370:17
 Is s. childishness SHAK 425:24
 loudly against s. marriages FIEL 211:6
 No s. stroke intend MILT 347:1
 s. and sober thoughts HENRY 245:18
 s. best's a gay goodnight YEATS 585:6
 s. eleven sort of chap BARR 34:8
 unto my wife my s. best bed SHAK 496:1
 village than s. at Rome' CAES 127:3

second-best: s. is a formal order
 AUDEN 18:13
second-rate: man and the creed of a s.
 BAG 29:16
 up with poets' being s. HOR 258:4
secrecy: Nature's infinite book of s.
 SHAK 421:9
 s., No lady closer SHAK 438:32
 S. the human dress BLAKE 88:9
secret: At last the s. is out AUDEN 20:22
 bread eaten in s. is pleasant BIBLE 53:28
 cleanse thou me from my s. faults
 PRAY 390:13
 digestion is the great s. SMITH 512:8
 I know that's a s. CONG 160:7
 joys of parents are s. BACON 27:2
 no s. so close SURT 525:28
 public and to read in s. BORR 89:26
 rebuke is better than s. love BIBLE 54:37
 s., and inviolate Rose YEATS 586:18
 s. and sweet reasonableness ARN 16:22
 s. himself shall reward BIBLE 64:22
 s. magic of numbers BROW 96:11
 s. of happiness is to admire BRAD 91:11
 s. parts of Fortune SHAK 432:11
 s. things belong unto BIBLE 48:28
 S. thoughts and open countenance... ALB 3:8
 Seeking His s. deeds ROSS 408:20
 then in s. sin CHUR 148:33
 There is always a wicked s. AUDEN 21:1
 Three may keep a s. FRAN 218:9
 unites it with the s. cause JOYCE 286:17
 when it ceases to be a s. BEHN 38:12
 with every s. thing BIBLE 56:14
Secretary: S. of Nature and all learning
 WALT 564:15
secretly: entice thee s. shalt not BIBLE 48:24
secrets: from whom no s. are hid PRAY 387:7
 s. are edged tools DRYD 197:20
 s. of th' abyss to spy GRAY 235:19
 S. with girls COWP 168:22
 There are s. in all families FARQ 210:7
 They know the s. of the sea NERV 361:1
 will discharge their s. SHAK 462:26
sect: attached to that great s. SHEL 500:9
 It found them a s. MAC 324:17
 paradise for a s. KEATS 289:26
 sad-coloured s. HOOD 255:16
sectaries: faith in a nation of s. DISR 186:1
 Hence jarring s. may learn COWP 165:21
sectes: *Angleterre soixante s.* CAR 130:10
Sects: Two-and-Seventy jarring S. confute
 FITZ 213:2
 whence arise diversity of s. SPEN 515:24
secular: s. bird MILT 350:31
secure: He is s. SHEL 499:21
security: allowed to be a collateral s.
 CHES 145:30
 Our watchword is s. PITT 374:1
 s. for its impartial administration PEEL 371:5
 S. Is mortals' chiefest SHAK 462:1
Securus: S. *iudicat orbis* AUG 21:18
sed: *agua que ahuyenta la s.* CERV 138:20
Sedan chair: flood of tears and a S.
 DICK 182:25
sedens: *Qui s. adversus identidem* CAT 137:4
sedge: river buds among the s. SHEL 503:20
 s. is wither'd from KEATS 290:15
seditione: *tulerit Gracchos de s.* JUV 287:13
seditions: way to prevent s. BACON 27:11
seduce: did not s., she ravished MER 337:25
seducer: Thou strong s. DRYD 195:31
seducing: Giving heed to s. spirits
 BIBLE 79:13
seduction: delusive s. of martial music
 BURN 112:21
Seductive: S. Waltz BYRON 126:11
Sedula: S. *curavi* SPIN 517:7
sedulous: played the s. ape to Hazlitt
 STEV 521:9

see: blind, now I s. BIBLE 72:16
 Can I s. another's woe BLAKE 88:8
 does he s. when he gazes so HARDY 240:15
 fain s. good PRAY 391:23
 I could not see to s. DICK 183:19
 I don't want to s. it GARC 221:6
 'I'm damned if I s. it' NEWB 361:1
 In all things Thee to s. HERB 247:18
 into the wilderness to s. BIBLE 66:2
 I s. a voice SHAK 471:1
 I s. the better way OVID 366:17
 I s. them all so excellently COL 156:7
 "I s. what I eat" is CARR 133:29
 Jupiter is whatever you s. LUCAN 320:1
 kings have desired to s. BIBLE 69:29
 live to s. thee in my touch SHAK 455:7
 Lovers can s. to do their SHAK 483:6
 more I s. of men ROL 407:16
 more people s. than weigh CHES 145:31
 no man s. me more SHAK 447:7
 s. a church by daylight SHAK 472:5
 s. all, nor be afraid BROW 104:2
 s. an author and we find PASC 369:4
 s. better days BEHN 38:15
 s. God made and eaten BROW 99:14
 s. his active child do SHAK 493:13
 seem To s. SHAK 455:21
 s. my own funeral afore EDG 199:22
 S. where she comes apparell'd SHAK 478:2
 shall he not s. PRAY 396:2
 Shall never s. so much SHAK 456:13
 shall no man s. me and live BIBLE 48:5
 taste and s. PRAY 391:21
 then complain we cannot s. BERK 41:18
 Then I shall s. thee again SHAK 451:30
 things which ye s. BIBLE 69:29
 thing that no man never s. DICK 182:38
 To s. and be seen DRYD 198:19
 to s. beyond our bourn KEATS 289:8
 To s. her is to love her BURNS 112:37
 to s. her was to love her BURNS 113:18
 To s. oursels as others BURNS 115:18
 verily to s. the goodness PRAY 391:9
 ye shall not s. me BIBLE 72:40
 yet I s. thee still SHAK 459:15
 you last s. your father YEAM 584:8
seed: Are they the s. of Abraham BIBLE 111:7
 beareth forth good s. PRAY 398:17
 garden, That grows to s. SHAK 429:28
 morning sow thy s. BIBLE 56:8
 Robs not one light s. from KEATS 290:1
 s. its harvest KEATS 289:3
 s. of ruin in himself ARN 13:21
 S. of Wisdom did I sow FITZ 212:21
 s. ye sow, another reaps SHEL 504:3
 wonder (which is the s. BACON 26:14
seeds: I find thy cunning s. ROSS 408:20
 is the least of all s. BIBLE 66:20
 look into the s. of time SHAK 458:11
 some s. fell by the wayside BIBLE 66:16
 winged s. SHEL 502:8
seed-time: Fair s. had my soul WORD 580:8
 s. and harvest BIBLE 45:37
seeing: is not satisfied with s. BIBLE 55:7
 It adds a precious s. SHAK 457:8
 only one way of s. them RUSK 411:26
 only s. a worse England JOHN 277:24
seek: All I s., the heaven above STEV 522:28
 confounded that s. after my soul PRAY 394:15
 If you s. for a monument ANON 11:2
 might'st s. it in My arms THOM 548:22
 Myself alone I s. to please GAY 223:18
 not s. for kind relief BLAKE 88:8
 s., and ye shall find BIBLE 65:2
 S. not to know who said THOM 546:8
 s. power and to lose BACON 26:22
 s. with care LAND 309:11
 s. ye first the kingdom BIBLE 64:31
 s. ye the living among BIBLE 71:16
 S. ye the Lord while he BIBLE 59:26

should I s. farther store	SEDL 419:14
that sometime did me s.	WYATT 583:21
They s. so many new	DONNE 187:19
things I s.	SHEL 504:1
To strive, to s.	TENN 544:3
We s. him here	ORCZY 365:7
where s. is find	SMART 509:3
you shall s. all day ere	SHAK 465:15
seekest: I am He whom thou s.	THOM 548:23
seeketh: he that s. findeth	BIBLE 65:3
seeking: s. asses	MILT 350:6
S. His secret deeds	ROSS 408:20
S. shall find Him	BROW 100:38
S. the food he eats	SHAK 425:16
seeks: one that neither s.	DRYD 195:21
s. her own salvation	SHAK 436:21
Seele: *dessen S. Rousseau geschaffen*	
	HEINE 244:12
Seelen: *'Zwei S. und ein Gedanke*	
	HALM 238:10
Zwei S. wohnen	GOET 229:30
seem: be rather than to s. good	SALL 413:24
men honest that but s.	SHAK 474:12
things are not what they s.	LONG 317:1
seemed: All s. well pleased	MILT 348:23
sweet love s. that April	BRID 92:20
seeming: mild as she is s. so	GREE 236:10
S. and savour all the winter	SHAK 491:22
that most s. virtuous eye	BYRON 125:4
thing I am by s. otherwise	SHAK 474:17
seems: I know not 's.'	SHAK 429:25
seen: evidence of things not s.	BIBLE 79:31
God whom he hath not s.	BIBLE 81:7
have seen what I have s.	SHAK 433:15
If I have s. further it	NEWT 362:19
I have s. dawn and sunset	MAS 333:17
lov'd needs only to be s.	DRYD 196:12
man hath s. God	BIBLE 71:28
Much more had s.	ARMS 12:15
my Lions & fled the S.	WARD 564:24
s., and yet have believed	BIBLE 73:12
s. God face to face	BIBLE 46:25
things a' didn't wish s.	HARDY 241:16
things which I have s.	WORD 578:22
Too early s. unknown	SHAK 482:4
To see and be s.	DRYD 198:19
undoubtedly be s. to be done	HEW 250:20
We have s. thee, O love	SWIN 528:22
What things have we s.	BEAU 35:19
Whom having not s.	BIBLE 80:20
Yet s. too oft	POPE 379:16
sees: draw the Thing as he s.	KIPL 304:3
dwarf s. farther than	COL 157:25
future s.	BLAKE 87:13
She neither hears nor s.	WORD 581:10
Who is it that s. and hears	PUNCH 402:30
Who s. with equal eye	POPE 379:4
seeth: yf himself yt s.	CHAU 143:28
seethe: s. a kid in his mother's	BIBLE 47:27
seethed: spring-tide of blossom s.	BETJ 43:12
segashuate: yo' sym'tums seem ter s.	
	HARR 242:18
seige: Did march to the s.	BALL 31:8
seigneur: *vous êtes un grand s.*	BEAU 35:18
Seinte Loy: gretteste ooth was but by	
S.	CHAU 141:14
seize: hand dare s. the fire	BLAKE 87:15
You s. the flow'r	BURNS 115:7
Selbstmord: *S. ist ein starkes Trostmittel*	
	NIET 363:11
seldom: Is s., if ever done	COW 163:20
Things are s. what they	GILB 228:8
when they s. come	SHAK 438:13
select: that each one should s.	SHEL 500:9
Selection: term of Natural S.	DARW 171:25
self: concentred all in s.	SCOTT 416:22
greater to one than one's s.	WHIT 571:3
never to think of one's s.	CLOU 153:21
seeketh only S. to please	BLAKE 87:19
spirit is the true s.	CIC 151:24

with s. and vain conceit	SHAK 479:11
self-consumer: I am the s. of my woes	
	CLARE 152:12
self-esteem: nothing profits more Than	
s.	MILT 349:8
self-evident: hold these truths to be s.	
	ANON 8:14
luminously s. beings	NEWM 361:17
self-expression: void of s. they confide	
	KIPL 302:5
self-honour'd: s., self-secure	ARN 14:24
self-indulgent: indifferent and s. majority	
	STEP 518:20
selfish: s. being all my life	AUST 23:21
sensible people are s.	EMER 207:4
selfless: s. man and stainless gentle	
	TENN 535:14
self-love: deceiving mirror of s.	MASS 335:22
'golden-calf of S.	CARL 131:4
Sin of s. possesseth all	SHAK 494:1
That true s. and social	POPE 380:4
self-lovers: nature of extreme s.	BACON 27:37
self-protection: is s.	MILL 339:6
Self-reliant: S. like the cat	MOORE 355:22
self-revelation: terrible *fluidity* of s.	
	JAMES 271:16
Self-righteousness: S. is not religion	
	BRON 93:14
self-scann'd: s., self-honour'd	ARN 14:24
Self-school'd: S., self-scann'd	ARN 14:24
self-secure: self-honour'd, s.	ARN 14:24
self-slain: god s. on his own strange	
	SWIN 529:20
self-slaughter: His canon 'gainst s.	
	SHAK 429:28
self-sufficing: reasoning, s. thing WORD 580:4
s. power of Solitude	WORD 580:15
sell: go and s. that thou hast	BIBLE 67:9
had a mind to s. his house	SWIFT 525:34
Most people s. their souls	SMITH 510:14
must poorly s. ourselves	SHAK 487:12
no man might buy or s.	BIBLE 82:13
precious as the Goods they s.	FITZ 213:14
s., or deny, or delay	MAGN 327:3
s. them in the street	CARR 136:6
s. the pasture now to buy	SHAK 443:12
s. with you	SHAK 465:28
there were dreams to s.	BEDD 36:28
will I s. my goodly steed	BALL 30:9
selling: one lives by s. something STEV 520:25
sells: s. eternity to get a toy	SHAK 492:18
seltzer: sipped at a weak hock and s.	
	BETJ 42:4
Selvtion: Wot prawce S. nah	SHAW 497:10
semblable: *mon s.,—mon frère*	BAUD 35:5
semblances: outface it with their s.	
	SHAK 424:30
semen: *s. est sanguis Christianorum*	
	TERT 544:22
semenza: *Considerate la vostra s.*	
	DANTE 171:13
seminaries: large s. of young ladies	
	KNOX 305:25
seminary: Come from a ladies' s.	
	GILB 226:29
semita: *Fallentis s. vitae*	HOR 258:24
semper: *et nunc, et s.*	MASS 334:14
Quod s., quod ubique	VINC 557:7
Sempronius: S.; we'll deserve it	ADD 1:16
senate: give his little s. laws	POPE 376:27
senates: s. hang upon thy tongue	
	THOM 549:16
senators: green-rob'd s. of mighty woods	
	KEATS 290:5
laughed, respectable s.	AUDEN 18:15
look at the s. and I pray	HALE 237:12
teach his s. wisdom	PRAY 397:4
send: Here am I; s. me	BIBLE 58:1
S. me not this	DONNE 190:14
senda: *la escondida s.*	LUIS 320:12

Seneca: S. cannot be too heavy SHAK 432:20
Senectus: *habitant Morbi tristisque S.*	
	VIRG 558:21
senectutem: *Post molestam s.*	ANON 10:13
seniors: earnest advice from my s.	
	THOR 550:6
se'nnights: s. nine times nine	SHAK 458:7
sens: *Le bon s. est la chose*	DESC 175:11
s. et le bon goût il y	LA B 306:15
sensation: Awaiting the s. of a short	
	GILB 226:31
Permanent Possibility of S.	STEV 522:7
s. among us than three	MAC 324:23
sensational: It is somewhat too s.	
	WILDE 573:4
sensations: life of s. rather than KEATS 293:17
s. sweet	WORD 578:4
sense: common s. and observation	
	BROW 96:18
common s. and good taste	SHAW 496:12
deep s. of some deathless	WEBS 567:4
Devoid of s. and motion	MILT 346:10
exquisite s. of the luxurious	KEATS 293:29
it is not s.	CHUR 148:25
light of nature, s.	ROCH 406:21
man of s. only trifles	CHES 145:26
'men of s. never tell it	SHAD 420:24
never deviates into s.	DRYD 196:34
Nor numbed s. to steel it	KEATS 293:4
no s. In gittin' riled	HARTE 242:27
Not when the s. is dim	BEEC 37:9
of decency is want of s.	ROOS 408:11
Of s. and outward things	WORD 579:10
perpetual fountain of good s.	DRYD 198:9
Satire or s.	POPE 376:30
seem an echo to the s.	POPE 378:22
s. and good taste there	LA B 306:15
S. and wit with poesy allied	BYRON 124:20
s. faints picturing them	SHEL 502:10
servilely creeps after s.	DRYD 197:34
some nonsense about s.	STEV 521:13
something more than good s.	COL 158:1
stings and motions of the s.	SHAK 463:14
Take care of the s.	CARR 134:7
That the s. aches at thee	SHAK 476:19
Their s. is with their	MER 337:16
their s. is shut	SHAK 462:19
Through s. and nonsense	DRYD 194:21
what was a man of s.	LOCK 316:2
who all s. doth eat	SHAK 435:18
within the s. they quicken	SHEL 504:12
without one grain of s.	DRYD 195:38
with sober s.	POPE 378:9
senseless: most s. and fit man	SHAK 472:28
you worse than s. things	SHAK 448:6
senses: from the power of our s.	JOHN 281:24
power to touch our s. so)	MILT 344:10
Unto our gentle s.	SHAK 459:14
sensibility: century a dissociation of s.	
	ELIOT 205:17
Dear s.	STER 519:12
it is an immense s.	JAMES 271:14
that s. of principle	BURKE 111:10
sensible: All s. people are selfish EMER 207:4
be bold and be s.	HOR 258:14
which a s. person would	AUST 23:5
woman was *fundamentally* s.	JOHN 278:28
sensibly: things they behave s. about	
	SHAW 496:14
sensitive: Frog is justly s.	BELL 38:29
please the s. race of poets	HOR 259:5
s. being	WORD 580:25
S. Plant in a garden grew	SHEL 503:22
sensual: ascetic rocks and the s.	MER 337:27
merely s. pleasures	BURKE 108:7
Not to the s. ear	KEATS 291:4
s. pleasure without vice	JOHN 280:23
sensualist: lover and s.	HENL 245:12
sent: man s. from God	BIBLE 71:24
say I s. thee thither	SHAK 446:24

s. before my time — SHAK 480:18
s. me only your handmaids — POUND 383:13
sentence: Give s. with me — PRAY 392:10
He mouths a s. — CHUR 149:8
My s. is for open war — MILT 346:8
of the normal British s. — CHUR 150:23
S. first — CARR 134:23
'There is still one s. — BEDE 37:2
sentences: hard s. of old — PRAY 395:3
keep finishing your s. — LONS 317:24
sententia: adhuc una s. non descripta — BEDE 37:2
sententiae: Quot homines tot s. — TER 544:19
sentiat: Ita feri ut se mori s. — SUET 524:17
sentiment: nurse of manly s. and heroic — BURKE 111:10
rich in s. — TENN 541:30
S. is what I am not acquainted — FLEM 215:2
S. was the more dangerous — GREE 236:4
sentimental: s. passion of a vegetable — GILB 227:23
S. Traveller (meaning thereby — STER 518:30
sentimentally: s. I am disposed to harmony — LAMB 307:2
sentiments: have forgotten his own s. — CLAY 152:29
quiet interchange of s. — JOHN 276:26
s. that no legislature — BAG 28:21
suspended the s. of religion — BURKE 111:29
Them's my s. — THAC 545:25
sentinel: s. on Whitehall gate looked — MAC 322:1
sentinels: fix'd s. almost receive — SHAK 444:9
s. to warn th' immortal — MARL 330:12
sentire: s. quae velis — TAC 531:12
sentry: Then the s. turned his — HOUS 265:5
Where stands a wingèd s. — VAUG 555:13
senum: Rumoresque s. severiorum — CAT 136:25
separate: s. and equal station — JEFF 272:5
s. me from the goats — CEL 138:8
to s. us from the love — BIBLE 75:13
separateth: matter s. very friends — BIBLE 54:10
separation: preludes to that eternal s. — STER 520:11
which impel them to the s. — JEFF 272:5
September: Clear in the cool S. morn — WHIT 571:15
In aftermaths of soft S. — HOUS 265:8
Thirty days hath S. — ANON 8:6
sepulchra: Per s. regionum — CEL 138:6
sepulchre: came first to the s. — BIBLE 73:6
man the living s. of life — CLARE 152:15
of his s. unto this day — BIBLE 48:34
s., Wherein we saw thee — SHAK 430:24
shall consume in the s. — PRAY 393:1
sepulchres: are like unto whited s. — BIBLE 67:25
urns and s. of mortality — CREWE 169:18
sequester'd: from her wild s. seat — COLL 158:21
sequestered: obscure s. state — BROW 104:33
sequestra: Et ab haedis me s. — CEL 138:8
sequitur: no more a *s.* than yourself — FIEL 211:27
sequor: Deteriora s. — OVID 366:17
Sera: S. moretur — HOR 260:5
S. nimis vita est crastina — MART 331:8
seram: 'Pone *s.* — JUV 287:22
Seraphim: bright S. in burning row — MILT 340:11
sworded S. — MILT 344:9
seraphims: Above it stood the s. — BIBLE 57:28
flew one of the s. unto me — BIBLE 57:30
Seraphin: S.: continually do cry — PRAY 384:16
serene: becomes more solemn and s. — SHEL 501:7
serf: soil as another man's s. — HOMER 254:6
serfs: With vassals and s. — BUNN 107:9

Sergeant: Cheer for the S.'s weddin' — KIPL 302:18
This fell s., death — SHAK 437:22
Sergeants: There was two-an'-thirty S. — KIPL 302:21
series: great s. of lifetimes starts — VIRG 559:22
sérieuses: comme leurs plus s. actions — MONT 354:17
serious: nothing s. in mortality — SHAK 461:1
severity a s. subject — ARN 16:14
they are too s. — STER 519:10
War is much too s. a thing — CLEM 152:31
seriously: take themselves quite s. — BEER 38:7
serius: urna s. ocius — HOR 260:7
sermon: good honest and painful s. — PEPYS 372:3
Her funeral s. (which was — BELL 39:13
into a short nap at s. — ADD 2:12
Perhaps turn out a s. — BURNS 113:16
verse may find him who a s. — HERB 246:27
Sermons: S. and soda-water the day — BYRON 122:21
S. in stones — SHAK 424:32
years I burn all my s. — WESL 568:19
sero: s. medicina paratur — OVID 366:20
S. te amavi — AUG 21:16
serpent: be the s. under't — SHAK 459:3
cold breast and s. smile — BYRON 125:4
gold and flowing s. is — LAWR 311:3
infernal s. — MILT 344:23
last it biteth like a s. — BIBLE 54:24
s. beguiled me — BIBLE 45:19
s.-haunted sea — FLEC 214:8
s. subtlest beast of all — MILT 349:11
s. was more subtil than — BIBLE 45:14
sharper than a s.'s tooth — SHAK 453:19
that old s. — BIBLE 82:27
'Tis a strange s. — SHAK 422:14
way of a s. upon a rock — BIBLE 55:1
'Where's my s. of old Nile — SHAK 421:31
serpents: Small s. with soft stretching — SWIN 529:15
ye therefore wise as s. — BIBLE 65:33
serpit: dono divum gratissima s. — VIRG 558:4
servant: good and faithful s. — BIBLE 68:2
I'll be your s. — SHAK 485:13
into judgement with thy s. — PRAY 399:11
Is thy s. a dog — BIBLE 51:31
king To be your s. — SHAK 447:8
nor the s. above his lord — BIBLE 65:34
not a brewer's s. — BLAKE 87:8
sends his s. to them — ADD 2:12
s. depart in peace — BIBLE 69:12
s. does not all commands — SHAK 429:1
s. in the land of Egypt — BIBLE 48:19
s. of the Living God — SMART 508:21
s.'s too often a negligent — BARH 33:10
s. to be bred at an University — CONG 160:12
S. to Queen Elizabeth — GREV 236:18
s. with this clause — HERB 247:19
thou thy s. depart in peace — BIBLE 83:19
thy s. heareth — BIBLE 49:36
to become the s. of a man — SHAW 496:27
upon him the form of a s. — BIBLE 78:13
Who was thy s. — HERR 249:23
'Your s.'s cut in half — GRAH 233:12
servants: are the s. of the public — GOW 233:7
equality in the s.' hall — BARR 34:7
S. of Light — ARN 12:19
s. of my father's ha — BIBLE 70:19
s. of the sovereign — BACON 26:21
s. will do that for us — VILL 557:3
To s. kind — CAREW 130:14
When domestic s. are treated — SHAW 497:40
servavit: Sic me s. Apollo — HOR 262:7
serv'd: s. my God with half — SHAK 447:13
serve: began to s. his country — SHAK 427:19
Fleet in which we s. — PRAY 400:2
once to s. our country — ADD 1:22
s. and lose — GOET 230:7

s. God and the King — NEWB 361:12
s. God if the devil bid — SHAK 473:17
S. it right for being so — DICK 180:1
s. thee with a quiet mind — PRAY 386:22
s. the future hour — WORD 581:5
s. the Lord with gladness — PRAY 396:11
s. two masters — BIBLE 64:27
s. who only stand and wait — MILT 351:10
sister hath left me to s. — BIBLE 69:34
than s. in heav'n — MILT 345:11
wear weapons, and s. — PRAY 400:11
served: despised as well as s. — BUTL 116:25
s. God as diligently — WOLS 576:14
they s. the Lord Primate — BARH 33:11
Worshipped and s. the creature — BIBLE 74:32
Youth will be s. — BORR 90:9
serves: s. for the old June weather — BROW 100:7
serveth: among you as he that s. — BIBLE 71:7
That s. not another's will — WOTT 583:12
service: all made of faith and s. — SHAK 426:29
bounden duty and s. — PRAY 388:2
desert in s. — SHAK 487:6
do more essential s. — SWIFT 526:6
done the state some s. — SHAK 477:23
Hack'd hewn with constant s. — SOUT 513:13
He's out on active s. — KIPL 297:23
In s. high — MILT 342:10
no s. — RAC 404:5
s. and conduct of the commonwealth — BURKE 108:24
s. is perfect freedom — PRAY 385:2
s. of my love — SPR 517:10
s. ranks the same with — BROW 103:25
soong the s. dyvyne — CHAU 141:15
Weary and old with s. — SHAK 447:9
When s. sweat for duty — SHAK 425:7
services: hills that goods and s. — NOCK 363:18
remembered by some for their s. — VIRG 558:23
serviettes: kiddies have crumpled the s. — BETJ 42:19
servile: Forsook the labours of a s. — BYRON 124:28
man is freed from s. bands — WOTT 583:13
S. to all the skyey influences — SHAK 464:8
servilely: who s. creeps after sense — DRYD 197:34
serving: cumbered about much s. — BIBLE 69:34
keep six honest s.-men — KIPL 300:12
serving-man: s., proud in heart — SHAK 454:18
serviteurs: les s. feront cela pour — VILL 557:3
servitors: many nimble and airy s. — MILT 351:19
servitude: base laws of s. began — DRYD 195:29
impatient of s. — BURKE 109:27
s. is at once the consequence — CURR 170:16
S. that hugs her chain — GRAY 235:14
servum: s. pecus — HOR 259:1
servysable: lowely, and s. — CHAU 141:15
Sesame: Open S. — ARAB 11:15
sesquipedalia: Proicit ampullas et s. — HOR 257:16
Sesquipedalian: S. blackguard — CLOU 153:17
sessions: s. of sweet silent thought — SHAK 493:7
Sestos: S. and Abydos of her breasts — DONNE 188:14
set: best plain s. — BACON 25:26
border see Israel s. — BROW 101:3
But s. down This — ELIOT 203:15
earth to s. one slip of them — SHAK 491:24
existed a more worthless s. — WELL 568:5
hath he s. our sins from us — PRAY 396:17
have done s. it in imprint — CAXT 138:14
if he will s. himself doggedly — JOHN 274:3
I have s. before you life — BIBLE 48:29
patience the race that is s. — BIBLE 79:35
place I s. out for — STER 519:9
play a s. — SHAK 443:11
s. a house on fire — BACON 27:37

s. my life at a pin's fee | SHAK 430:25
S. up thyself, O God | PRAY 393:15
s. you square with Genesis | BROW 99:9
splendid orb was entirely s. | BURKE 109:6
very thing he'll s. you | BLAKE 87:6
which thy fathers have s. | BIBLE 54:23
sete: fame, s., marcie forzate | GAR 221:10
ets: Heaven soon s. right | BROW 100:4
packs and s. of great ones | SHAK 456:3
etter: s. up and puller down | SHAK 446:20
etting: doors against a s. sun | SHAK 486:5
Hath had elsewhere its s. | WORD 579:5
s. of that bright *Occidental Star* | BIBLE 44:20
time is s. with me | BURNS 114:30
ettle: less will you s. to one | KIPL 300:17
settled: People wish to be s. | EMER 207:15
reasons find of s. gravity | SHAK 493:14
seuil: balaiera largement le s. | ROST 410:12
seven: acts being s. ages | SHAK 425:24
All's set at six and s. | ANON 9:1
devoured the s. good ears | BIBLE 46:32
Freedom, the s. pillared | LAWR 311:12
hewn out her s. pillars | BIBLE 53:27
Jacob served s. years | BIBLE 46:21
Nay, we are s. | WORD 583:7
of the deadly s. it is | SHAK 464:13
s. fat kine | BIBLE 46:31
s. feet of English | HAR 242:11
s. golden candlesticks | BIBLE 81:13
s. maids with seven mops | CARR 135:5
s. other spirits more wicked | BIBLE 66:14
s. stars go squawking | AUDEN 18:9
S. times tried that judgment | SHAK 466:22
S. wealthy Towns contend | ANON 7:14
Until seventy times s. | BIBLE 67:7
when full inches s. | BRID 92:13
Seven Dials: Of S. | GILB 226:5
sevene: world on six and s. | CHAU 144:13
seven-fold: dost thy s. gifts impart | PRAY 400:5
seventeen: Maud is not s. | TENN 540:6
seventeenth: s. century a dissociation | ELIOT 205:17
seventh: opened the s. seal | BIBLE 82:5
s. day is the sabbath | BIBLE 47:24
seventies: gets well into the s. | STEV 522:6
seventy: s. years young | HOLM 253:14
Until s. times seven | BIBLE 67:7
Seventy-five: eighteenth of April in S. | LONG 316:25
seventy-seven: At s. it is time to be | JOHN 281:23
sever: forgotten how soon we must s. | CRAW 169:16
Nothing in life shall s. | CORY 163:3
then we s. | BURNS 112:27
To s. for years | BYRON 126:13
severae: procul este, s. | OVID 366:9
severance: God their s. ruled | ARN 13:13
severe: from lively to s. | POPE 380:3
humanly s. | POPE 378:32
if s. in aught | GOLD 231:2
man s. he was | GOLD 231:2
nothing but herself s. | CAREW 130:14
severing: not any s. of our loves | WORD 579:13
severity: set in with its usual s. | COL 157:27
s. a serious subject | ARN 16:14
S. breedeth fear | BACON 26:25
s. of perfect light | TENN 534:14
Severn: Beside the S.'s dead | HOUS 262:13
came to Rye or out to S. | CHES 147:10
from the S. to the Tyne | KIPL 297:26
Islanded in S. stream | HOUS 263:12
S. breeds worse men than | HOUS 263:21
thick on S. snow the leaves | HOUS 263:14
twice a day the S. fills | TENN 536:11
Seville: bang these dogs of S. | TENN 543:1
sew: sacks to s. up wives | THAC 545:18
teach the orphan-girl to s. | TENN 538:1

sewed: s. fig leaves | BIBLE 45:16
Sewell & Cross: S. young man | GILB 227:28
sewer: midst of this putrid s. | TOCQ 551:9
sewers: Nymphs that reign o'er s. | COL 156:5
Where houses thick and s. | MILT 349:13
sex: all the tyrants of thy s. | CONG 160:22
Can either s. assume | MILT 345:15
Grex rather than s. | FROST 219:14
no stronger than my s. | SHAK 449:16
poor feeble s. | VICT 556:14
ruin of our s. | SMOL 512:13
s. that of loving longest | AUST 23:10
s. whose presence civilizes | COWP 165:4
soft, unhappy s. | BEHN 38:21
subordination of one s. | MILL 339:18
talk on 'S. and Civics | BETJ 43:1
weaker s. | ALEX 3:15
What is your s.'s earliest | LYTT 321:20
'women are a s. by themselves | BEER 37:24
sexes: cleanliness of the s. stands | WHIT 570:15
there are three s. | SMITH 511:8
sexton: s. toll'd the bell | HOOD 254:16
that bald s. | SHAK 452:18
Sextus: save them from false S. | MAC 322:16
seye: eek for to be s. | CHAU 143:20
shabby: tamed and s. tigers | HODG 252:2
shackles: s. of an old love straiten'd | TENN 534:29
their s. fall | COWP 166:32
shade: clutching the inviolable s. | ARN 14:20
Dancing in the chequered s. | MILT 342:22
fleeting image of a s. | SHEL 505:9
gentlemen of the s. | SHAK 438:1
green thought in a green s. | MARV 332:5
his stedfast s. | TENN 541:21
light, s., and perspective | CONS 162:2
old sit under the s. of it | DICK 177:27
S. of His hand | THOM 548:23
Sitting in a pleasant s. | BARN 33:32
sitting in the s. | KIPL 299:14
sly s. of a Rural Dean | BROO 94:21
sweeter s. To shepherds | SHAK 446:19
That anyway trusts her s. | KIPL 303:26
tribute to the passing s. | CAT 137:15
shades: field is full of s. | THOM 547:24
happy he who crowns in s. | GOLD 230:19
Nor those great s. whom | BUTL 119:21
S. of the prison-house | WORD 579:5
shadow: be call'd that s. seem'd | MILT 346:24
darkness and the s. of death | BIBLE 52:20
darkness and in the s. of death | BIBLE 69:7
darkness, and in the s. | PRAY 397:7
dust and a s. | HOR 261:16
earth Be but the s. | MILT 348:21
Falls the S. | ELIOT 203:10
flying and elusive s. | ARN 12:22
Follow a s. | JONS 284:11
he fleeth also as a s. | BIBLE 52:26
horrible s. | SHAK 461:22
land of the s. of death | BIBLE 58:6
Life's but a walking s. | SHAK 463:6
light but the s. of God | BROW 95:17
Like a vast s. mov'd | VAUG 555:22
man walketh in a vain s. | PRAY 391:31
neither s. of turning | BIBLE 80:9
on the earth are as a s. | BIBLE 51:39
pass in the s. of the earth | BROW 95:24
pass in the s. of the earth | BROW 96:1
S. cloak'd from head | TENN 536:13
s. of a great rock | BIBLE 58:30
s. of an idea without grasping | BOWEN 91:1
s. of her even brows | SPEN 516:11
S. of Shadows on the deed | YEATS 584:18
s. of some unseen Power | SHEL 501:5
s. of the Valois is yawning | CHES 147:1
softly flits a s. and a sigh | KIPL 303:7
Swift as a s. | SHAK 469:20
Time watches from the s. | AUDEN 18:10
valley of the s. of death | PRAY 390:22
which his s. will be shown | NIET 363:6

Your s. at morning striding | ELIOT 204:19
shadows: Come like s. | SHAK 462:9
coming events cast their s. | CAMP 128:24
'I am half sick of s. | TENN 538:7
If we s. have offended | SHAK 471:21
in this kind are but s. | SHAK 471:19
millions of strange s. | SHAK 493:15
Our fatal s. that walk | FLET 215:13
s. and types to the reality | NEWM 362:6
s. flee away | BIBLE 56:24
s. now so long do grow | COTT 163:7
s. numberless | KEATS 291:17
s., that showed at noon | LEE 313:8
s. to-night | SHAK 481:16
Some there be that s. kiss | SHAK 466:22
Styl'd but the s. of us men | JONS 284:11
To the dim s. | ROWL 411:1
Types and s. have their | THOM 546:17
very s. of the clouds | WORD 576:23
what s. we are | BURKE 110:21
what s. we pursue | BURKE 110:21
Shadow-show: nothing but a Magic S. | FITZ 213:3
shadowy: with a s. third | BROW 99:23
Shadrach: S., Meshach, and Abed-nego | BIBLE 61:4
shady: In a garden s. this holy | AUDEN 18:3
s. trees cover him with | BIBLE 53:10
shaft: s., at random sent | SCOTT 416:23
shafts: their s. benight the air | HOUS 265:3
shake: also may be used to s. | BELL 38:24
by that s. of the head | SHER 505:29
gusts s. the door | ARN 13:7
Have power to s. me | WORD 576:23
s. a stage | JONS 284:22
s. hands with a king upon | HALL 238:8
s. his sapient head | ARN 15:12
s. off the dust of your | BIBLE 65:32
s. of his poor little head | GILB 227:16
s. their heads | PRAY 390:17
s. their wicked sides | YEATS 586:8
this god did s. | SHAK 448:15
Upon those boughs which s. | SHAK 494:7
shaken: So s. as we are | SHAK 437:32
tempests and is never s. | SHAK 495:5
When taken, To be well s. | COLM 159:7
shakers: We are the movers and s. | OSH 365:20
shakes: s. his parting guest | SHAK 487:5
S. so my single state | SHAK 458:20
s. this fragile frame | HARDY 240:2
Shake-scene: only S. in a country | GREE 236:12
Shakespeare: Corneille is to S. a clipped | JOHN 280:8
entirely as I despise S. | SHAW 496:23
I believe S. was not | COL 158:8
immortal S. rose | JOHN 282:25
It was for gentle S. cut | JONS 284:17
mighty S. | BRID 92:9
Our *myriad-minded* S. | COL 157:23
perhaps understand S. | KEATS 293:26
quibble is to S. what luminous | JOHN 282:15
S., your threefold | BASSE 35:1
S. unlocked his heart' | BROW 101:10
S. was of us | BROW 102:5
S.'s genius had been cultivated | CHES 145:24
S. by flashes of lightning | COL 157:31
S. never had six lines | JOHN 275:27
S. led a life of allegory | KEATS 294:13
S. made use of it first | SHER 505:28
S., undoubtedly wanted | WALP 562:26
S. unlocked his heart | WORD 582:14
souls most fed with S.'s | CHES 147:1
stuff as great part of S. | GEOR 224:2
sweetest S. | MILT 342:26
talk of my being like S. | SCOTT 419:1
That S. should be quite | CHES 147:16
That S. wanted Art | JONS 285:17
to fancy S. this Presider | KEATS 293:11

833

tongue That S. spake — WORD 582:3
To S. gave as much — DRYD 196:2
tried lately to read S. — DARW 171:22
What needs my S. for his — MILT 344:1
Shakespeherian: that S. Rag — ELIOT 204:25
shaking: s., crazy — ROCH 407:3
that can fall without s. — MONT 354:7
to the s. hand of an old — VICT 556:15
shall: His absolute 's.' — SHAK 427:21
shallow: abysses are all so s. — JAMES 271:32
S. brooks murmur most — SIDN 507:14
s. in himself — MILT 350:10
s. streams run dimpling — POPE 377:2
There s. draughts intoxicate — POPE 378:13
you are idle s. things — SHAK 490:8
shallows: bound in s. and in miseries — SHAK 451:27
With his depths and his s. — BURNS 115:2
Shalott: Lady of S. — TENN 538:4
shalt: Thou s. have no other gods — DRYD 196:13
shame: be mine the s. — WHIT 571:17
blush of s. — BIBLE 79:35
despising the s. — SHAK 452:16
doff it for s. — HOUS 263:21
I must keep from s. — SHAK 478:20
is now bound in with s. — MAC 324:11
much glory and so much s. — WEBS 567:4
sense of some deathless s. — BIBLE 76:17
s. for women to speak — BIBLE 70:7
s. to take the lowest room — SHAK 495:7
spirit in a waste of s. — BRET 92:6
Thy father's s. — HOUS 266:8
'Tis a s. to human nature — HOUS 266:3
To live and s. the land — SHAK 428:4
To s. unvulnerable — SHAK 483:8
Upon his brow s. is ashamed — BIBLE 78:19
whose glory is their s. — MAC 322:16
wrought the deed of s. — STEV 522:24
shamed: Ain't you 's., you sleepy-head — TENN 539:4
I am s. thro' all my nature — SHAK 478:20
shameful: s. conquest of itself — LA R 310:10
s. to spurn one's friends — BURKE 111:19
shameless: most s. thing in the world — SHAK 466:15
shames: hold a candle to my s. — SHAK 476:18
s., on my bare head — KIPL 299:9
shammin': generally s. when 'e's dead — MOORE 357:4
shamming: whate'er their gentle s. — SHAK 425:24
shank: his shrunk s. — BURNS 115:17
spindle s. a guid whip-lash — CAMP 128:20
Shannon: On the green banks of S. — ARN 14:13
shape: hat of antique s. — MILT 346:24
If s. it might be call'd — MILT 345:15
in what s. they choose — ASCH 17:3
men in s. and fashion — FITZ 213:12
subtly wrought me into S. — SHAK 430:24
such a questionable s. — SHAK 461:21
Take any s. but that — CARR 135:19
you might be any s. — SHAK 422:14
shaped: It is s., sir, like itself — BROO 94:30
s., made aware — PRAY 393:5
shapen: I was s. in wickedness — SHAK 442:15
shapes: fiery and delectable s. — SHAK 439:21
heaven was full of fiery s. — SHEL 504:21
s. of sky or plain — KIPL 302:10
shard: reeking tube and iron s. — SHAK 445:1
share: greater s. of honour — SHAK 489:4
no one so true Did s. — CHAR 140:19
s. in Government that — PAINE 368:6
s. in two revolutions is — HOOD 255:5
S. my harvest and my home — GOLD 231:1
s. the good man's smile — DOD 187:16
Thou its ruin didst not s. — WORD 582:5
turned to s. the transport — GILB 226:16
shares: s. are a penny — AUDEN 20:15
shark: s. And the tiger

Sharon: I am the rose of S. — BIBLE 56:19
sharp: s. antidote against disgrace — BURKE 111:9
s. as a twoedged sword — BIBLE 53:20
'Somebody's s. — DICK 176:26
so s. the conquerynge — CHAU 143:32
'Tis a s. remedy — RAL 404:17
sharpeneth: s. the countenance of his — BIBLE 54:40
sharper: He'd be s. than a serpent's — DICK 181:17
I returned it s. than — THOR 550:12
s. than a serpent's tooth — SHAK 453:19
sharpest: 'After s. shoures — LANG 309:28
sharpness: overcome the s. of death — PRAY 384:17
sharps: fifty different s. and flats — BROW 103:15
Shatter: S. your leaves before — MILT 343:2
you may s. the vase — MOORE 356:7
shatterday: thumpsday, frightday, s. — JOYCE 286:11
Shattered: S. in shard on shard — THOM 548:21
When the lamp is s. — SHEL 501:21
shaving: when I am s. of a morning — HOUS 266:17
Shaw: Mr S. is (I suspect) — CHES 148:4
shawms: trumpets also, and s. — PRAY 396:8
shay: wonderful one-hoss s. — HOLM 253:8
she: Had it any been but s. — SUCK 524:15
same party was the S. — AUST 23:30
s. shall be called Woman — BIBLE 45:12
S., she is dead — DONNE 187:20
S. that was ever fair — SHAK 474:18
S. who trifles with all — GAY 223:4
That not impossible s. — CRAS 169:15
unexpressive s. — SHAK 426:2
you are the cruell'st s. — SHAK 488:12
sheaf: made obeisance to my s. — BIBLE 46:27
shearers: scramble at the s.' feast — MILT 343:12
sheep before her s. is dumb — BIBLE 59:22
shears: Fury with th' abhorred s. — MILT 343:8
resembles a pair of s. — SMITH 511:11
sheath: sword back in the s. — CHES 147:6
sheath'd: s. their swords for lack — SHAK 444:1
sheaves: bring his s. with him — PRAY 398:11
rode between the barley-s. — TENN 538:8
your s. stood round about — BIBLE 46:27
Sheba: Another S. queen — WITH 575:13
S. had seen all Solomon's — BIBLE 50:32
she-bear: s. thus accosted rends — KIPL 299:4
shed: down the monarch of a s. — GOLD 231:26
man shall his blood be s. — BIBLE 45:39
prepare to s. them now — SHAK 450:26
s. for you and for many — PRAY 388:1
s. his blood for the country — ROOS 408:3
s. innocent blood — BIBLE 60:6
with Burke under a s. — JOHN 279:15
Yet I'll not s. her blood — SHAK 477:5
shedding: s. of blood is no remission — BIBLE 79:29
sheep: better than s. or goats — TENN 535:26
black s. who've gone astray — KIPL 299:10
careth not for the s. — BIBLE 72:19
else their s. — MILT 344:8
Feed my s. — BIBLE 73:15
folds shall be full of s. — PRAY 394:3
found my s. which was lost — BIBLE 70:16
from thy ways like lost s. — PRAY 384:11
giveth his life for the s. — BIBLE 72:18
Go rather to the lost s. — BIBLE 65:30
His silly s. — COWP 166:8
hungry s. look up — MILT 343:13
Let us return to our s. — ANON 9:16
lie in the hell like s. — PRAY 393:1
like s. have gone astray — BIBLE 59:22
little hills like young s. — PRAY 397:16
looking on their silly s. — SHAK 446:19
mountain s. are sweeter — PEAC 371:2

noble ensample to his s. — CHAU 142
of an old half-witted s. — STEP 518:
of s. that are even shorn — BIBLE 56:
One sickly s. infects — WATTS 565:
Other s. I have — BIBLE 72:
plunge the struggling s. — MAC 322:
prize-oxen and of s. — TENN 542:
s. before her shearers — BIBLE 59:
s. bringeth no gain with — POUND 382
s. in sheep's clothing — GOSSE 233
s. may bring forth thousands — PRAY 399:
s. of his hand — PRAY 396
s. on his right hand — BIBLE 68:
s. set me a place and separate — CEL 138:
s. that have not a shepherd — BIBLE 51:1
to you in s.'s clothing — BIBLE 65
were as s. going astray — BIBLE 80:2
you s. bear fleeces not — VIRG 560:
sheep-bells: s. and the ship-bells ring — KIPL 303:1
sheep-hook: know how to hold A s. — MILT 343:
sheer: s., penetrating power — ARN 16:
sheet: although the s. were big — SHAK 489:3
England's winding s. — BLAKE 85:1
s. bleaching on the hedge — SHAK 491:1
s. knit at the four corners — BIBLE 73:3
waters were his winding s. — BARN 34:
wet s. and a flowing sea — CUNN 170:1
sheets: cool kindliness of s. — BROO 94:
fumble with the s. — SHAK 443:1
Sheffield: 'Only Brooks of S. — DICK 176:2
she-goats: go on, my s. — VIRG 560:
shell: convolutions of a smooth-lipped s. — WORD 577:1
Shelley: Burns, S., were with us — BROW 102:
did you once see S. plain — BROW 102:1
peace in S.'s mind — SHEL 505:1
S., whom envy never touched — SHEL 505:1
S. with liquid music — BRID 92:9
sphere for S.'s genius — ARN 16:2
There S. dream'd his white — JOHN 273:19
What S. shrilled — SASS 414:19
shelter: s. to grow ripe — ARN 13:10
To s. me from the cold — BELL 40:1
sheltered: In youth it s. me — MORR 358:6
shelters: 'Naught s. thee — THOM 548:14
Shem: done with the Tents of S. — KIPL 300:23
S., Ham, and Japheth — BIBLE 45:32
Shepherd: call you, S. — ARN 14:10
Dick the s. — SHAK 457:19
equalises the s. and the king — CERV 138:20
every s. tells his tale — MILT 342:19
fairest s. on our green — PEELE 371:6
feed his flock like a s. — BIBLE 59:7
God of love my S. — HERB 248:13
good s. giveth his life — BIBLE 72:1
lady would not love a s. — GREE 236:1
Lord is my s. — PRAY 390:21
sheep that have not a s. — BIBLE 51:19
S. and Bishop of your souls — BIBLE 80:2
s. his sheep — PROP 401:15
slighted, s.'s trade — MILT 343:8
truth in every s.'s tongue — RAL 404:9
weather the s. shuns — HARDY 241:3
What time the s. — SHAK 446:19
Shepherd-boy: thou happy S. — WORD 579:3
shepherdess: s. of sheep — MEYN 338:15
Shepherding: S. her bright fountains — SHEL 500:2
shepherds: have both s. and butchers — VOLT 561:9
s. abiding in the field — BIBLE 69:9
s. call me also a poet — VIRG 560:7
S. shall flute their sweetest — AUDEN 18:8
s. watch'd their flocks — TATE 531:22
That liberal s. give — SHAK 436:19
warmth of s.' flames — MARL 330:11
Sheriffmuir: at S. A battle there was — MCL 325:15

sherris: this valour comes of s. SHAK 442:15
sherris-sack: good s. hath a two-fold
  SHAK 442:15
sherry: s. in the cupboard BETJ 44:10
shew: man can s. any just cause PRAY 389:2
mouth shall s. thy praise PRAY 393:8
s. him my salvation PRAY 395:23
s. ourselves glad in him PRAY 396:3
s. the light of thy countenance PRAY 395:8
we will s. you a thing BIBLE 50:2
sheweth: s. him all the kingdoms BIBLE 64:3
Shibboleth: Say now S. BIBLE 49:20
shield: idle spear and s. MILT 344:6
shall be thy s. and buckler PRAY 395:21
s. of the mighty is vilely BIBLE 50:16
taking the s. of faith BIBLE 78:10
To a lady in his s. TENN 538:8
shieling: From the lone s. GALT 221:2
shift: down let me s. for my self MORE 357:16
then we'll s. our ground SHAK 431:20
shifted: He s. his trumpet GOLD 231:21
shifts: Oft' s. her passions GAY 223:8
shillin: s.' a day KIPL 302:19
shilling: Philip and Mary on a s. BUTL 118:7
s. life will give you all AUDEN 21:8
willing to sell for one s. LEAR 312:13
shillings: payment of half twenty s.
  BURKE 109:2
shimmered: Jeeves s. out and came
  WOD 575:18
shine: anxious for to s. in the high
  GILB 227:20
fire and every one doth s. SHAK 449:25
glistering gold but more to s. BRAD 91:15
Let the hot sun S. on AUDEN 20:21
Let your light so s. before BIBLE 64:9
Lord make his face s. BIBLE 48:9
not to s. in use TENN 543:22
qualified to s. in company SWIFT 527:11
s.; for thy light is come BIBLE 60:7
s. more bright in these SHAK 493:17
S. upon the starry sky BLAKE 86:5
than s. with Pye BYRON 124:19
they s. on all alike POPE 380:32
visitation they shall s. BIBLE 62:14
where the wind's feet s. SWIN 530:18
shined: in her person s. MILT 351:11
them hath the light s. BIBLE 58:6
shiners: nine bright s. ANON 6:5
shines: She s. sae bright to wyle BURNS 116:5
s. the moon in clouded TENN 532:16
substitute s. brightly as a king SHAK 468:18
shineth: light s. in darkness BIBLE 71:23
shingles: naked s. of the world ARN 12:23
shining: Even to s. ones who dwell BETJ 42:8
I see it s. plain HOUS 263:22
s. Foot shall pass FITZ 213:18
s. morning face SHAK 425:24
S. unto no higher end MARV 332:12
will flame out like s. HOPK 256:12
with the sun not s. CHAN 139:20
woman of so s. loveliness YEATS 586:17
shins: own wit till I break my s. SHAK 425:13
ship: all I ask is a tall s. MAS 334:4
build your s. of death LAWR 311:8
idle as a painted s. COL 155:1
is a s.'s upon the sea KIPL 301:1
It was so old a s. FLEC 214:19
My soul, like to a s. WEBS 567:13
One leak will sink a s. BUNY 107:29
s., an isle FLEC 214:21
s. has weather'd every WHIT 570:7
s. I have got in the North BALL 31:2
s. is being in a jail JOHN 274:18
S. of State LONG 316:7
s. that goes DIBD 175:20
s. was still as she could SOUT 513:28
s. would not travel due CARR 133:6
smart s. grew HARDY 239:6
splendid s. BRID 92:19

that gallant s. in twain BALL 30:19
'There was a s. COL 155:6
way of a s. in the midst BIBLE 55:1
What is a s. but a prison BURT 116:27
ship-bells: sheep-bells and the s. KIPL 303:13
Shipman: S. was ther CHAU 141:29
shipping: Thus fishes first to s. DRYD 195:22
ships: beauty and mystery of the s.
  LONG 316:22
go down to the sea in s. PRAY 397:9
Hell to s. AESC 3:1
launch'd a thousand s. MARL 329:10
Like two doomed s. WILDE 572:11
little s. of England brought GUED 237:4
mighty s. ten thousand HODG 252:7
move with the moving s. SWIN 530:28
my s. are out of gear TENN 542:21
Our s. have been salvaged HALS 238:11
s. and stars and isles FLEC 214:9
s. and the foreign faces SWIN 528:15
S. are but boards SHAK 465:27
s., becalmed at eve CLOU 154:3
s., by thousands BYRON 122:34
S., dim-discovered THOM 549:13
s. sail like swans asleep FLEC 214:16
s. that pass in the night LONG 317:17
S., towers, domes WORD 581:14
shoes—and s.—and sealing wax CARR 135:7
'Spanish s. of war TENN 542:21
stately s. go TENN 532:18
storm-beaten s. MAHAN 327:5
There go the s. PRAY 397:1
They crossed in s. the sea HOUS 265:6
thousand s. to Tenedos MARL 330:14
Thou shalt break the s. PRAY 392:26
We are six s. of the line TENN 542:21
When boats or s. came near LEAR 312:19
When stately s. are twirled HODG 252:7
wrong with our bloody s. BEAT 35:12
ye s. of Tarshish BIBLE 58:17
shipwreck: escaped the s. of time
  BACON 24:18
s. of my ill adventured DAN 171:1
thrice I suffered s. BIBLE 77:12
shire: That s. which we the heart
  DRAY 193:18
shires: both the s. they ring them HOUS 263:4
s. have seen it plain HOUS 262:12
shirt: martyr in his s. of fire SMITH 510:2
till he tucks in his s. KIPL 304:28
your s. and your socks GILB 226:15
shirt-sleeves: 'from shirt-sleeves to s.'
  BUTL 117:12
shive: cut loaf to steal a s. SHAK 486:15
shivers: wan west s. SWIN 528:16
shoal: bank and s. of time SHAK 459:5
s. of fools for tenders CONG 160:36
shock: short, sharp s. GILB 226:31
to s. them and keep them SHAW 496:25
we shall s. them SHAK 453:1
shock-headed: my s. victor BETJ 44:6
Than to see S. Peter HOFF 252:22
shocks: thousand natural s. SHAK 433:8
twelve great s. of sound TENN 533:22
withindoors house The s. HOPK 256:29
shod: can foot feel, being s. HOPK 256:12
your feet s. with the preparation BIBLE 78:10
shoddy: Up goes the price of s. GILB 225:30
shoe: Edom will I cast out my s. PRAY 393:18
Finds sixpence in her s. CORB 162:14
I kiss his dirty s. SHAK 444:17
Into a left-hand s. CARR 136:7
s.'s latchet I am not BIBLE 71:29
s. was lost FRAN 218:6
shoelace: tail hanging like a s. MOORE 355:22
shoemaker: take my shoes from the s.
  GOLD 232:41
shoes: adorns my s. HOUS 266:10
beautiful are thy feet with s. BIBLE 57:7
ere those s. were old SHAK 429:28

his s. were far too tight LEAR 312:5
more than over s. in love SHAK 490:29
most of the s. of his soldiers BAG 29:11
Put off thy s. from off BIBLE 47:4
s.—and ships—and sealing wax CARR 135:7
Their s. were clean CARR 135:6
To boil eggs in your s. LEAR 313:3
to call for his old s. SELD 419:19
your s. on your feet BIBLE 47:18
shoe-string: careless s. HERR 249:2
shone: glory of the Lord s. round BIBLE 69:9
S. like a meteor streaming MILT 345:19
that once had s. FLEC 214:10
There s. one woman SWIN 530:29
shook: earth s. PRAY 394:7
monk who s. the world MONT 355:10
s. hands with time FORD 216:16
Ten Days that S. the World REED 405:8
Which ne'er s. hands SHAK 458:3
shoon: night in her silver s. DE L 174:16
wat their cork-heel'd s. BALL 31:19
shoot: Do not hesitate to s. BALF 30:1
I s. the Hippopotamus BELL 38:30
'I will s. you BALL 31:3
Please do not s. the pianist ANON 7:9
s. folly as it flies POPE 379:2
s. the sleepy, green-coat HOFF 252:21
they s. out their lips PRAY 390:17
They up and s. themselves BROO 94:24
young idea how to s. THOM 549:10
shooting: than to hunting and s. BURR 116:10
shooting-stars: s. attend thee HERR 249:11
Shoots: S. higher much than he HERB 247:8
Who s. at the mid-day sun SIDN 507:15
shop: back to the s. Mr John LOCK 315:22
Because a man has s. to mind BROW 105:3
beggar' s. is shut SHAK 483:25
himself a little back s. MONT 354:20
shopkeepers: England is a nation of s.
  NAP 359:15
nation of s. are very seldom ADAMS 1:9
only for a nation of s. SMITH 509:12
shopocracy: hear you abuse the s.
  NORTH 364:6
shops: might shun the awful s. CHES 147:18
shore: after-silence on the s. BYRON 125:10
beat on Heaven's s. BLAKE 85:15
By the s. of Gitche Gumee LONG 317:10
false impossible s. ARN 15:2
high s. of this world SHAK 444:25
lights around the s. ROSS 410:8
longing for the further s. VIRG 558:22
on the kingdom of the s. SHAK 494:3
Over some wide-watered s. MILT 342:4
rapture on the lonely s. BYRON 121:22
Stops with the s. BYRON 121:23
surges lash the sounding s. POPE 378:23
shored: These fragments have I s.
  ELIOT 205:12
shoreless: s. watery wild ARN 13:12
shores: bade betwixt their s. ARN 13:13
s. of darkness there is KEATS 292:25
s. of the Mediterranean JOHN 277:6
wilder s. of love BLAN 88:30
shore-sea: blue or the s. green FLEC 214:17
shoreward: winds s. blow ARN 13:5
shorn: sheep that are even s. BIBLE 56:26
went home s. BROW 102:17
short: being made perfect in a s. BIBLE 62:15
be s. in the story itself BIBLE 63:29
hath but a s. time to live PRAY 389:11
how s. is the longest life KEATS 294:29
Life's s. span forbids HOR 259:14
nasty, brutish, and s. HOBB 251:18
our life is very s. TAYL 532:3
s. jacket is always worn EDW 200:2
s. of the glory of God BIBLE 74:38
take s. views AUDEN 21:6
Take s. views SMITH 510:31
time of life is s. SHAK 440:19

We have as s. a Spring — HERR 249:28
you find it wond'rous s. — GOLD 231:9
shorten: s. I the stature of my — MER 337:8
shorter: make you s. by the head — ELIZ 205:26
s. Poems of Donne — AUDEN 21:3
time to make it s. — PASC 369:14
shortest: s. way is commonly — BACON 25:4
shortness: nothing comparable for s. — BORR 90:11
To spend that s. basely — SHAK 440:19
shot: Am not I s. — LOV 318:12
be s. at for sixpence a-day — DIBD 175:17
bolt is s. back — ARN 12:22
hand that fired the s. — BALL 31:4
have s. mine arrow o'er — SHAK 437:16
s. heard round the world — EMER 206:19
S. so quick — HOUS 264:2
s. to pieces by the shorter — AUDEN 21:3
very long s. — DOYLE 192:15
young Sahib s. divinely — ANON 8:15
shots: of the best s. — VOLT 561:14
shoulder: government shall be upon his s. — BIBLE 58:7
S. the sky — HOUS 264:22
white steam over her s. — AUDEN 20:1
shoulder-blade: left s. that is a miracle — GILB 227:10
Light my touch on your s. — BETJ 43:16
shoulders: Born on our s. — BROW 100:34
dwarfs on the s. of giants — BERN 41:25
lawn about the s. thrown — HERR 249:2
loose gown from her s. — WYATT 583:22
standing on the s. of giants — NEWT 362:19
shout: Ere ceased the inhuman — BYRON 121:15
It's no use raising a s. — AUDEN 19:14
shouted with a great s. — BIBLE 49:2
s. for me — SHAW 498:28
S. round me — WORD 579:3
s. that tore hell's concave — MILT 345:20
s. to him golden shouts — MER 337:37
'S. with the largest — DICK 181:30
There was a s. about my ears — CHES 146:23
Who s. and bang and roar — BELL 39:28
shouted: I went and s. in his ear — CARR 135:27
sons of God s. for joy — BIBLE 53:3
shouting: Every man s. in proportion — SURT 525:18
heavens fill with s. — TENN 538:24
tumult and the s. dies — KIPL 302:7
shouts: cuckoo s. all day at nothing — HOUS 265:9
He s. to scare the monster — KIPL 299:4
shoved: They s. him into politics — BELL 39:5
shovel: limits they just s. in German — TWAIN 554:24
S. your couplets to their — CAMP 128:11
take a large hoe and a s. — KIPL 300:11
Shovelling: S. white steam over her — AUDEN 20:1
show: all rang'd (a terrible s. — GAY 223:1
s. my head to the people — DANT 171:20
s. your front to the world — MOL 353:1
s. you something different — ELIOT 204:19
they come to make a s. — OVID 366:10
thing they most do s. — SHAK 494:15
To s. our simple skill — SHAK 471:16
what they s. to kings — COWP 168:9
shower: falling s. — SHEL 499:17
prove the sweetness of a s. — THOM 547:21
s. of curates has fallen — BRON 93:16
s. your shooting corns — SWIFT 527:26
showers: pane is blind with s. — HOUS 264:20
s. betumble the chestnut — HARDY 241:2
Small s. last long — SHAK 478:19
With true-love s. — SHAK 435:34
ye S. — PRAY 384:21
Showery: S., Flowery — ELLIS 206:13
showest: Have more than thou s. — SHAK 453:15

showing: s. them they were not needed — BELL 39:9
shown: must be s. In courts — MILT 341:18
shows: by submitting the s. — BACON 24:19
mind stoops not to s. of dross — SHAK 466:16
s. sufficient of His light — BROW 104:27
So may the outward s. be — SHAK 467:10
shreds: king of s. and patches — SHAK 435:12
thing of s. and patches — GILB 226:18
shrewishly: he speaks very s. — SHAK 488:9
Shrewsbury: fought a long hour by S. — SHAK 440:27
High the vanes of S. gleam — HOUS 263:12
They hang us now in S. — HOUS 262:16
Shrewsbury School: from S., from Cambridge — SHAW 498:23
shriek: solitary s. — BYRON 122:18
With hollow s. — MILT 344:13
With short shrill s. flits — COLL 158:18
shrieked: s. against his creed — TENN 536:29
shrieking: Hooting and s. — SHAK 449:1
With s. and squeaking — BROW 103:15
shrieks: Not louder s. to pitying — POPE 381:8
shriller: s. than all the music — SHAK 448:7
shrimp: be but a s. of an author — GRAY 235:25
shrine: at the temple's inner s. — WORD 582:1
To your mistaken S. — WINC 575:4
shrines: Curled like vapour over s. — BROW 98:16
shrink: sall never make thee s. — BALL 31:7
shrinking: glass when I am s. — ANON 10:14
wagtail showed no s. — HARDY 240:22
Shropshire: In London streets the S. — HOUS 263:21
S. names are read — HOUS 262:13
shroud: green hill an April s. — KEATS 291:15
My s. of white — SHAK 489:4
stiff dishonoured s. — ELIOT 204:16
White his s. as the mountain — SHAK 435:34
Who ever comes to s. me — DONNE 188:27
shrouded: Virgin in snow — BLAKE 87:22
shrubbery: of Priapus in the s. — ELIOT 203:28
shrug: borne it with a patient s. — SHAK 466:2
read a nod, a s., a look — SWIFT 527:29
Shrunk: S. to this little measure — SHAK 450:6
That s. thy streams — MILT 343:14
shrunken: hushed the s. seas — ELIOT 204:15
shudder: s. in the loins engenders — YEATS 586:2
shuffling: tune and the s. of feet — MORR 358:12
Shulamite: return, O S. — BIBLE 57:6
shun: let me s. that — SHAK 454:14
s. the fault I fell — BALL 30:13
s. the heaven that leads — SHAK 495:7
S. what I follow — BROW 104:7
shunn'st: Sweet bird, that s. — MILT 342:2
shuns: weather the shepherd s. — HARDY 241:3
shunting: to s. and hooting than — BURR 116:10
shut: beggar's shop is s. — SHAK 483:25
gates of it shall not be s. — BIBLE 82:34
shady night has s. — HOUS 263:2
s. her wild, wild eyes — KEATS 290:20
s. the door — POPE 376:18
s. the gates of mercy — GRAY 234:24
s. their doors against — SHAK 486:5
their sense is s. — SHAK 462:19
shuts: none out — WHIT 571:11
shutter: Borne before her on a s. — THAC 546:3
shutters: close the s. fast — COWP 167:11
S., shut your shutters — BETJ 42:5
we'd need keep the s. up — DICK 179:17
shutteth: s. up his bowels of compassion — BIBLE 81:4
shuttle: Man is the s. — VAUG 555:10
musical s. — WHIT 570:9
swifter than a weaver's s. — BIBLE 52:18
shuttlecock: Battledore and s.'s — DICK 181:34
shy: We are not s. — GILB 226:32
Si: S. possis recte — HOR 258:10

Sibyl: contortions of the S. without — BURKE 112:14
S. at Cumae — PETR 373:2
Sibylla: *Teste David cum S.* — CEL 138:5
Sicelides: S. Musae — VIRG 559:22
sich: believe there's no s. a person — DICK 179:29
Sicily: Dost thou remember S. — WILDE 572:19
Syrtes and soft S. — ARN 14:21
sick: all s. persons — PRAY 385:20
cattle then are s. — KING 297:21
enterprise is s. — SHAK 486:23
first pace that is s. — SHAK 486:25
half my men are s. — TENN 542:21
have on our hands a s. man — NICH 362:22
hir'd to watch the s. — COWP 166:29
I am s. of both — JOHN 277:10
I am s. of love — BIBLE 56:21
I am s. of many griefs — SHAK 451:25
I'm more than a little s. — KIPL 298:7
is Brutus s. — SHAK 449:13
is but the daylight s. — SHAK 468:20
I was s. — BIBLE 68:6
kill s. people groaning — MARL 329:21
make any man s. to hear her — PEPYS 372:9
never s. at sea — GILB 227:31
O Rose, thou art s. — BLAKE 87:12
person seldom falls s. — EMER 207:5
report That I am sudden s. — SHAK 421:23
s. men's dreams — BROW 95:23
s. that surfeit with too — SHAK 465:19
they all make me s. — MITF 352:21
They do not make me s. — WHIT 570:22
they that are s. — BIBLE 65:23
to be at when he is s. — JOHN 279:5
Was s. almost to doomsday — SHAK 429:13
were you not extremely s. — PRIOR 401:9
When I was s. and lay a-bed — STEV 522:20
when s. for home — KEATS 291:23
when we are s. in fortune — SHAK 453:11
you s. or are you sullen — JOHN 279:27
sicken: love begins to s. and decay — SHAK 451:11
Will s. soon and die — MILT 344:11
sicken'd: He s. at all triumphs — CHUR 149:4
sickening: monstrous head and s. cry — CHES 146:22
sickens: s. at another's praise — CHUR 148:28
sick-hearted: true, s. slave — HOUS 265:18
sickle: bending s.'s compass come — SHAK 495:5
s. in the fruitful field — BLAKE 86:19
sickly: 'I'm s. but sassy — HARR 242:16
s. sheep infects the flock — WATTS 565:23
smiled a kind of s. smile — HARTE 242:33
sickness: grief, or s. must — KING 296:11
he hath the falling s. — SHAK 448:22
in s. and in health — PRAY 389:4
medicine to heal their s. — PRAY 399:19
My long s. — SHAK 486:12
s., or any other adversity — PRAY 387:21
s. that destroyeth — PRAY 395:21
thy s. shall depart — KIPL 298:8
Sidcup: I could get down to S. — PINT 373:3
side: Are on our s. to-day — MAC 323:2
embraceth him on every s. — PRAY 391:18
Eve from his s. arose — ANON 8:21
had not been on our s. — PRAY 398:13
have only heard one s. — BUTL 119:1
Hear the other s. — AUG 21:20
on the s. of the angels — DISR 185:2
passed by on the other s. — BIBLE 69:31
rose o' the wrong s. — BROME 93:11
she standeth by thy s. — BALL 30:9
shifting his s. — COWP 166:15
s. my hand and on that — SHAK 479:22
s. that's next the sun — SUCK 524:9
thrust my hand into his s. — BIBLE 73:10
Who is on my s. — BIBLE 51:36
side-arms: 'E keeps 'is s. awful — KIPL 298:21

side-long: bashful virgin's s. looks GOLD 230:17
sidera: *Sublimi feriam s. vertice* HOR 259:10
sides: might be said on both s. ADD 2:13
shake their wicked s. YEATS 586:8
There is no woman's s. SHAK 489:6
sidney: Our S. and our perfect man YEATS 585:13
S.'s self BROW 105:12
siècles: *quarante s. vous contemplent* NAP 359:8
siege: envious s. Of watery Neptune SHAK 478:20
stay the s. of loving terms SHAK 481:24
Sieghaftere: *Stärkere, S., Wohlgemutere* NIET 363:2
Siesta: Englishmen detest a S. COW 163:19
Slete: *S. voi qui* DANTE 171:11
sieve: hope draws nectar in a s. COL 157:15
in a s. I'll thither sail SHAK 458:6
they went to sea in a S. LEAR 312:6
sift: to s. those dusts again DONNE 190:23
siftings: let their liquid s. fall ELIOT 204:16
sigh: Here's a s. to those who BYRON 126:1
He took her with a s. BLAKE 86:22
I to s. for her SHAK 456:27
prompts th' eternal s. POPE 379:21
she look'd up to s. SCOTT 417:13
S., heart YEATS 585:14
s. is the sword of an Angel BLAKE 86:6
s. like Tom o' Bedlam SHAK 453:12
S. no more SHAK 472:16
s. the lack of many a thing SHAK 493:7
very s. that silence heaves KEATS 290:13
Sigh'd: S. and look'd DRYD 195:6
s. his soul toward SHAK 468:13
sighed: he s. for one AUDEN 21:9
he s. for the love GILB 229:9
He sobbed and he s. GILB 227:17
I s. as a lover GIBB 224:13
She s. sore EDW 200:5
s. and pined and ogled THAC 546:3
Sighing: laughter and ability and S. DICK 184:2
plague of s. and grief SHAK 439:11
poor soul sat s. by a sycamore SHAK 476:27
s. of a contrite heart PRAY 385:22
sorrow and s. shall flee BIBLE 59:1
sighs: all made of s. and tears SHAK 426:29
my pains a world of s. SHAK 474:1
S. are the natural language SHAD 420:19
s. the strings do break CAMP 129:17
sovereign of s. and groans SHAK 456:26
Spent in star-defeated s. HOUS 262:21
thus advises thee that s. SHAK 489:15
with her family of S. SHEL 499:9
sight: deprived of s. VIRG 558:11
done this evil in thy s. PRAY 393:4
end in s. was a vice BROW 105:2
in thy s. shall no PRAY 399:11
It is not yet in s. SHER 505:27
Lord giveth s. to the blind PRAY 399:17
loved not at first s. MARL 329:18
out of s. is out of mind CLOU 154:5
possession of this heavenly s. SHAK 477:21
punished in the s. of men BIBLE 62:13
right dear in the s. PRAY 397:22
seeing and leave in s. SWIN 528:18
sensible To feeling as to s. SHAK 459:15
s. of means to do ill SHAK 452:28
s. of the unwise they seemed BIBLE 62:13
s. to dream COL 156:3
s. to make an old man young TENN 533:20
spread in the s. of any bird BIBLE 53:14
that is pleasant to the s. BIBLE 45:8
to admit them in your s. AUST 23:19
together here in the s. of God PRAY 388:24
triple s. in blindness keen KEATS 292:25
where I shall live by s. BUNY 107:39
will I cast out of my s. BIBLE 50:31

years in thy s. are but as yesterday PRAY 395:18
sightless: blind man On the s. WALEY 562:2
lark becomes a s. song TENN 537:19
sights: few more impressive s. BARR 34:21
Her s. and sounds BROO 94:30
s. as youthful poets dream MILT 342:26
sign: generation seeketh after a s. BIBLE 66:11
outward and visible s. PRAY 388:19
s. documents which they HURST 268:17
s. you must not touch DONNE 188:27
signal: Only a s. shown and a distant LONG 317:17
really do not see the s. NELS 360:17
signal-elm: s., that looks on Ilsley ARN 15:3
signals: fading s. and grey eternal BEER 37:26
sign'd: one is s. by God's name WHIT 571:4
signed: air s. with their honour SPEN 515:8
hand that s. the paper THOM 547:4
signify: devil does the plot s. BUCH 106:13
does it s. how we dress GASK 221:23
Nod with your hand to s. HOUS 266:9
signiors: Like s. and rich burghers SHAK 465:7
reverend s. SHAK 473:24
signo: *In hoc s. vinces* CONS 162:6
sign-post: Majesty's head on a s. MAC 324:2
signs: are but the s. of ideas JOHN 281:6
dials the s. of leaping-houses SHAK 437:34
discern the s. of the times BIBLE 66:32
Except ye see s. and wonders BIBLE 71:43
multiply my s. and my wonders BIBLE 47:11
S. are taken for wonders ELIOT 203:4
silence: are answered best with s. JONS 285:11
bound the common of s. EMER 207:14
Elected S., sing to me HOPK 256:14
eternal s. of these infinite PASC 369:7
ever widening slowly s. all TENN 535:7
golden Gospel of S. is MORL 357:24
Grief for thy dead in s. BROW 98:8
His mind moves upon s. YEATS 586:3
His s. will sit drooping SHAK 437:9
how the s. surged softly DE L 174:10
in s. with all subjection BIBLE 79:9
in the icy s. of the tomb KEATS 290:30
Let your women keep s. BIBLE 76:16
maintaining the 'conspiracy of s.' COMTE 159:15
makes a s. in the hills TENN 536:11
My gracious s., hail SHAK 427:16
Night and s. SHAK 470:13
occasional flashes of s. SMITH 511:13
of punishment is to s. JOHN 282:13
Of the eternal S. WORD 579:11
of the very sigh that s. KEATS 290:13
pécher que pécher en s. MOL 354:1
rest is s. SHAK 437:27
S. alone is great VIGNY 557:2
s. also does not necessarily ELIOT 201:2
S. and sleep like fields DE L 173:25
S. augmenteth grief GREV 236:17
S. invaded the suburbs AUDEN 19:3
S. is become his mother GOLD 232:15
S. is deep as Eternity CARL 131:13
s. is divine CARL 131:39
S. is golden CARL 132:23
s. is most noble till SWIN 528:23
S. is only commendable SHAK 465:14
S. is the virtue of fools BACON 25:13
S. is the perfectest herald SHAK 472:10
s. is wonderful to listen HARDY 241:27
S. more musical than any ROSS 409:6
s. of the sleep-time BROW 98:31
S. sank COL 155:28
s. sounds no worse than HOUS 263:2
S. that dreadful bell SHAK 475:4
s. that is in the starry WORD 581:11
S.! Voilà l'ennemi CONDE 159:16
S. was pleas'd MILT 348:2
s. was the song of love ROSS 409:24

s. where hath been no sound HOOD 255:11
s., yea, even from good PRAY 391:30
s. yet I pick'd a welcome SHAK 471:15
small change of s. MER 338:2
Sorrow and s. are strong LONG 316:13
Stand shadowless like S. HOOD 255:1
Still-born S. FLEC 214:24
that s. we the tempest fear DRYD 195:24
That temple of s. and reconciliation MAC 323:20
There was s. deep as death CAMP 128:15
Thou foster-child of s. KEATS 291:2
thunders of white s. BROW 98:4
Till a s. fell with TENN 540:10
'Tis visible s. ROSS 409:23
to be in s. BIBLE 79:9
was an easy step to s. AUST 23:6
was s. in heaven about BIBLE 82:5
With s. and tears BYRON 126:14
silences: s. Of dreadful things AUDEN 18:5
silencing: justified in s. mankind MILL 339:8
silent: All s. and all damn'd WORD 580:2
all the s. manliness GOLD 231:6
approached unlocked her s. throat GIBB 225:1
beauty's S. music CAMP 129:16
impossible to be s. BURKE 110:30
joys, like griefs, are s. MARM 330:19
on s. haunches SAND 413:26
S. and amazed even when WHIT 570:1
s. church before the service EMER 207:40
S. enim leges inter arma CIC 151:31
's. in seven languages' BAG 29:11
s. over Africa BROW 101:9
s. touches of time BURKE 111:36
S., upon a peak in Darien KEATS 292:18
s. witnesses to the desolation GEOR 224:4
then s. night MILT 348:5
why art thou s. CRAW 169:16
silentia: *Tacitae per amica s. lunae* VIRG 558:3
Silently: S. and very fast AUDEN 18:16
silk: hallow'd that did breed the s. SHAK 476:4
Kneeling ne'er spoil'd s. stocking HERB 247:10
make his couche of s. CHAU 142:25
public schools with s. MARL 329:5
s. hat on a Bradford millionaire ELIOT 205:1
s. makes the difference FULL 220:21
s. stockings and white JOHN 274:2
s. thread plucks it back SHAK 482:20
that thing of s. POPE 376:30
silken: s. terms precise SHAK 457:15
silks: Whenas in s. my Julia goes HERR 250:8
will in fading s. compose WINC 575:5
silk-worm: Does the s. expend her TOUR 551:16
siller: pinn'd it wi' a s. pin BALL 32:11
sillier: nothing s. than a silly laugh CAT 137:1
silliness: s. to live when to live SHAK 474:7
silly: it's lovely to be s. HOR 261:20
s. game where nobody wins FULL 220:20
s. thoughts so busy keep MILT 344:8
S. women laden with sins BIBLE 79:24
thou s. gentleman SHAK 474:7
'tis very s. BYRON 122:31
Who's S. Billy now GLOU 229:23
wish I loved its s. face RAL 404:20
with such a s. question STER 519:17
You were s. like us AUDEN 19:5
Silurist: Here sleeps the S. SASS 415:3
silvae: *Et paulum s. super his* HOR 262:9
s. sint consule dignae VIRG 559:22
silvas: *Habitarunt di quoque s.* VIRG 559:16
s. Academi quaerere verum HOR 259:4
Silver: Attract a S. Churn GILB 227:24
Between their s. bars FLEC 214:21
Enwrought with golden and s. YEATS 585:9
ever the s. cord be loosed BIBLE 56:11
golden locks time hath to s. PEELE 371:8

gold in pictures of s.	BIBLE 54:26
handful of s. he left us	BROW 102:4
her s. lining on the night	MILT 341:2
is covered with s. wings	PRAY 394:8
Is made of s.	GILB 225:30
night in her s. shoon	DE L 174:16
S. and gold have I none	BIBLE 73:25
s. answer rang...'Not Death	BROW 98:9
s. apples of the moon	YEATS 586:21
s. for the maid	KIPL 298:15
s., ivory	BIBLE 50:34
s. plate on a coffin	OCON 364:22
take s. or small change	CHAM 139:14
thirty pieces of s.	BIBLE 68:9
thousands of gold and s.	PRAY 398:5
watch return'd a s. sound	POPE 380:29
When gold and s. becks	SHAK 452:19
Wisdom be put in a s. rod	BLAKE 85:19

silver'd: sable s. — SHAK 430:13

silver-pointed: Dinted with the s. pencil — BROW 102:28

silver-sweet: How s. sound lovers' tongues — SHAK 482:19

silver-tufted: Her waving s. wand — HOUS 262:19

Silvia: I be by S. in the night — SHAK 491:1

Silv'ry: Bridge of the S. Tay — MCG 325:6

simile: make a s. go on all fours — MAC 324:4

similes: hast the most unsavoury s. — SHAK 438:5

play with s. — WORD 582:26

Similia: S. similibus curantur — HAHN 237:10

Simon: Old S. the Cellarer keeps — BELL 38:22

Simon Pure: real S. — CENT 138:9

simple: asham'd that women are so s. — SHAK 484:19

giveth wisdom unto the s.	PRAY 390:12
rey y al s. con el discreto	CERV 138:20
s. dues of fellowship	BROW 97:30
s. he looks	BURNS 115:2
s. little rules and few	BELL 40:4
s. truth must be abus'd	SHAK 480:23
Teach us delight in s.	KIPL 298:12
'Tis ever thus with s.	GILB 229:10
very s. gentleman	SHAK 492:7

simpleness: When s. and duty tender it — SHAK 471:14

simpler: Make s. daily the beating — AUDEN 20:6

s. than the infancy — SHAK 487:2

Simplex: S. munditiis — HOR 259:15

simplicitas: sancta s. — HUSS 268:18

sed sancta s. — JER 272:20

simplicity: Cultivate s. — LAMB 307:21

holy s.	HUSS 268:18
holy s.	JER 272:20
In his s. sublime	TENN 541:7
Pity my s.	WESL 568:17
simple truth miscall'd s.	SHAK 494:5
s., a child	POPE 378:8
s. or with severity a serious	ARN 16:14
s. of his idea calling	CONR 161:21
s. of the three per cents	DISR 186:8
s. of the three per cents	STOW 524:2
That makes s. a grace	JONS 283:27
true as truth's s.	SHAK 487:2

Simplify: frittered away by detail...S. — THOR 550:17

s. me when I'm dead — DOUG 191:9

simply: s. but with such style — HOR 259:15

simulacrum: itself is but the dark s. — BROW 95:17

sin: abolish the whole body of s. — PRAY 388:10

almost a s. of abstinence	DRYD 195:28
being dead unto s.	PRAY 388:10
Be sure your s. will find	BIBLE 48:17
Be ye angry and s. not	BIBLE 78:1
black and soft as s.	CHES 147:5
bosom s. blows quite away	HERB 248:11

Burnt-offerings, and sacrifice for s. — PRAY 392:2

commit one single venial s.	NEWM 362:4
dark world of s.	BICK 84:4
day we fall into no s.	PRAY 385:3
dreadful record of s.	DOYLE 192:1
emboldens s. so much as mercy	SHAK 486:6
England, full of s.	HERB 247:3
Excepting Original S.	CAMP 129:14
he bare the s. of many	BIBLE 59:24
he died unto s. once	BIBLE 75:2
He that is without s. among	BIBLE 72:10
How shall I lose the s.	POPE 376:12
I'll s. till I blow up	THOM 547:14
in awe, and s. not	PRAY 389:20
I ne'er heard of s.	LOCK 315:23
is not innocence but s.	BROW 101:17
it is no s.	SHAK 464:13
killing s.	STEV 523:11
known s., but by the law	BIBLE 75:4
Lord imputeth no s.	PRAY 391:16
Lukewarmness I account a s.	COWL 164:18
Milton, Death, and S.	YOUNG 588:14
mother I'm living in s.	HERB 246:8
my brother s. against me	BIBLE 67:7
no s., but to be rich	SHAK 452:15
not be a charity in s.	SHAK 464:7
Plate s. with gold	SHAK 455:20
purple-lined palace of sweet s.	KEATS 290:25
say that we have no s.	BIBLE 81:3
Shall we continue in s.	BIBLE 74:43
she knew no s.	DRYD 196:10
s. could blight or sorrow	COL 156:18
S., Death, and Hell	BUNY 107:33
S. I impute to each frustrate	BROW 105:21
S. is behovely	JUL 286:32
S. is ever before me	PRAY 393:4
S. no more	BIBLE 72:11
S. of self-love possesseth	SHAK 494:1
s. of witchcraft	BIBLE 50:4
s. that amends is but patched	SHAK 488:6
s. that was sweet	PAIN 367:17
s. to covet honour	SHAK 445:2
s. to God above	THOR 550:28
s. which doth so easily	BIBLE 79:35
s. who tell us love can	SOUT 513:26
s. will destroy a sinner	BUNY 107:29
s. ye do by two and two	KIPL 303:20
sometimes s.'s a pleasure	BYRON 122:13
sorrow dogging s.	HERB 248:10
that s. fell the angels	SHAK 447:12
then in secret s.	CHUR 148:33
there is no s. but ignorance	MARL 329:19
Thy s.'s not accidental	SHAK 464:15
To go away and s. no more	ANON 6:17
To s. in loving virtue	SHAK 464:6
to s. in secret is not	MOL 354:1
triumph over death and s.	SPEN 515:17
us this day without s.	PRAY 384:18
wages of s. is death	BIBLE 75:3
want of power to s.	DRYD 197:9
wave the quantum o'the s.	BURNS 113:17
We wallow in our s.	ANON 9:1
Where s. abounded	BIBLE 74:42
which taketh away the s.	BIBLE 71:30
Wilt thou forgive that s.	DONNE 189:13
worst s. towards our fellow	SHAW 496:17
Would you like to s.	ANON 8:23

since: s. 'tis so — BROW 101:22

sincere: tho' well-bred, s. — POPE 378:32

very s. in good principles — JOHN 280:5

sincerity: bread of s. and truth — BIBLE 75:36

little s. is a dangerous — WILDE 572:20

Sindh: I have S. — WINK 575:8

sinecure: part of the world is no s. — BYRON 126:18

sinews: money the s. of war — BACON 27:25

S. of concord	FORD 216:14
Stiffen the s.	SHAK 443:21
twist the s. of thy heart	BLAKE 87:15

sinewy: s. proboscis did remissly — DONNE 190:8

sinful: any s. games — HARTE 242:9

sing: blind Homer s. — MARL 329:9

cannot s. the old songs now	CALV 127:1
charmingly sweet you s.	LEAR 312:1
come, let us s.	PRAY 396:9
crow doth s. as sweetly	SHAK 468:1
did s. in a hempen string	FLET 215:9
Elected Silence, s. to me	HOPK 256:14
found in thine heart to s.	SWIN 530:1
her flowery work doth s.	MILT 342:9
how shall we s. to her	SWIN 528:16
I do but s. because I must	TENN 536:12
I know ye s. well	FLET 215:23
I s. of brooks	HERR 248:18
let me s. and die	BYRON 123:4
maid s. in the valley	ANON 5:3
More safe I s. with mortal	MILT 348:28
persons die before they s.	COL 156:16
Places where they s.	PRAY 385:4
poet s. it with such airs	YEATS 584:10
s. A faery's song	KEATS 290:17
S. a merry madrigal	GILB 227:1
s. among the branches	PRAY 396:19
s. like birds i' the cage	SHAK 456:3
S. me your song	GILB 229:8
s. myself	WHIT 570:16
S., my tongue	VEN 556:4
S. no sad songs for me	ROSS 409:8
s. praises unto his name	PRAY 394:7
S., riding's a joy	BROW 101:28
s., that I may seem valiant	DRYD 195:18
S. the peasantry	YEATS 587:8
s. the saucer and the cup	PAIN 367:15
S. thou smoothly with t	CAMP 129:16
s. thy songs of happy cheer	BLAKE 87:8
s. to the child on thy	BRID 92:21
s. to the harp with a psalm	PRAY 396:8
S. to the Lord a new song	BIBLE 83:7
s. unto God with the voice	PRAY 392:22
S. unto the Lord a new	PRAY 391:19
s. unto the Lord a new	PRAY 396:7
S. us one of the songs	PRAY 399:3
S. we merrily unto God	PRAY 395:9
S. whatever is well made	YEATS 587:8
Soul clap its hands and s.	YEATS 586:12
Still wouldst thou s.	KEATS 291:22
suffers little birds to s.	SHAK 486:17
That can s. both high	SHAK 488:17
that they will s. to me	ELIOT 203:25
they shall laugh and s.	PRAY 394:3
tongue of the dumb s.	BIBLE 58:34
used to s. in the water	DICK 178:30
when you s.	SHAK 491:19
Whilst thus I s.	CIBB 151:8
Who s. to find your hearts	FLEC 214:9
Will s. at dawn	BROW 97:27
will s. the savageness out	SHAK 476:12
world in ev'ry corner s.	HERB 246:26
would not s. for Lycidas	MILT 343:2

Singe: S. my white head — SHAK 454:4

That it do s. yourself — SHAK 446:25

singeing: s. of the King of Spain's — DRAKE 193:3

singer: Beside the s. — LAND 309:1

idle s. of an empty day	MORR 358:8
lived a s. in France of old	SWIN 530:29
Lulled by the s.	MORR 358:9
sans S.	FITZ 212:14
s. not the song	ANON 8:7
S. of sweet Colonus	ARN 15:10
Thou the s.	GILB 235:34
When the s. sings them	STEV 523:1

singers: ago he was one of the s. — LEAR 311:21

Singest: S. of summer in full-throated — KEATS 291:17

singeth: milkmaid s. blithe — MILT 342:19

s. with her breast against — HOOD 255:2

singing: angels all were s. out — BYRON 126:5

ear voice suddenly s.	AUDEN 21:1
veryone suddenly burst out s.	SASS 414:16
rass is s.	ELIOT 205:10
ave heard the mermaids s.	ELIOT 203:25
am sick of s.	SWIN 530:3
see ye have a s. face	FLET 215:23
quid waves of thy sweet s.	SHEL 500:16
ove a woman for s.	SHAK 453:14
ne s. in the Wilderness	FITZ 212:11
est of s. birds	JOHN 273:28
ilver waves of thy sweet s.	SHEL 503:11
. and making melody	BIBLE 78:5
. beneath the dome	VERL 556:10
s., 'Here came a mortal	ARN 13:7
. in their glory move	MILT 343:18
. of Mount Abora	COL 156:30
s. so rarely	SCOTT 418:21
. still dost soar	SHEL 504:16
. will never be done	SASS 414:17
There is delight in s.	LAND 309:1
To the Master of all s.	LONG 317:14
went through the river s.	BUNY 107:37
inging-boys: six little S.	BARH 33:12
ngle: in s. blessedness	SHAK 469:17
et a s. completed action	BOIL 89:11
Nothing in the world is s.	SHEL 502:1
s. and only talked of population	GOLD 232:32
. grateful thought raised	LESS 314:1
s. in the field	WORD 578:13
s. life doth well with	BACON 26:33
s. man in possession	AUST 23:11
they come not s. spies	SHAK 436:4
ingles: What strenuous s. we played	
	BETJ 44:6
ings: he s. each song twice over	BROW 101:6
motion like an angel s.	SHAK 468:15
one tell me what she s.	WORD 578:14
ingular: So s. in each particular	SHAK 491:27
ingularity: S. is almost invariably	
	DOYLE 191:15
thyself into the trick of s.	SHAK 489:15
ingularly: s. deep young man	GILB 227:21
inister: that of the strange and s.	
	JAMES 271:15
ink: Help me, Cassius, or I s.	SHAK 448:14
I pant, I s.	SHEL 500:13
load would s. a navy	SHAK 447:11
Not gross to s.	SHAK 495:19
raft which will never s.	AMES 4:3
'S. me the ship	TENN 543:3
s. through the sea they	THOM 546:19
to s. with Lamplough	STEV 521:11
would not s. i' the scale	BROW 104:4
'You may s. by the Low-lands	BALL 31:3
inking: kind of alacrity in s.	SHAK 469:13
when they see me s.	ANON 10:14
inks: He s. into thy depths with	
	BYRON 121:24
It s.	LAND 308:20
So s. the day-star	MILT 343:17
Sinn: kommt mir nicht aus dem S.	
	HEINE 244:9
sinned: all have s.	BIBLE 74:38
I have s. against heaven	BIBLE 70:19
s. against than sinning	SHAK 454:10
sinner: Be a s. and sin strongly	LUTH 320:15
be merciful to me a s.	BIBLE 70:35
I of her a s.	CONG 160:30
over one s. that repenteth	BIBLE 70:17
poor s.	COWP 165:25
sin will destroy a s.	BUNY 107:29
young s. with the handcuffs	HOUS 266:8
sinners: Master with publicans and s.	
	BIBLE 65:22
mercy upon us miserable s.	PRAY 385:15
s.'ll be kotched out late	HARR 242:17
S.; of whom I am chief	BIBLE 79:8
s., plunged beneath their	COWP 165:24
s. to repentance	BIBLE 65:24
stood in the way of s.	PRAY 389:14

There s. must with devils	WATTS 565:16
thou be a breeder of s.	SHAK 433:11
we are s. all	SHAK 446:7
Why do s.' ways prosper	HOPK 257:2
sinning: sinned against than s.	SHAK 454:10
sins: are thinkin' on their s.	BURNS 114:7
Be all my s. remember'd	SHAK 433:9
by himself purged our s.	BIBLE 79:28
by the chain of our s.	PRAY 385:23
Commit The oldest s.	SHAK 442:20
cover the multitude of s.	BIBLE 80:32
dark and weep for their s.	WHIT 570:22
far hath he set our s.	PRAY 396:17
Few love to hear the s.	SHAK 478:3
forgetful of their s.	YEATS 586:14
forgiveth s.	BIBLE 62:21
Her s., which are many	BIBLE 69:24
'His s. were scarlet	BELL 39:19
Silly women laden with s.	BIBLE 79:24
s. and offences of my youth	PRAY 391:2
s. of your fathers	HOR 260:25
s., they are inclin'd	BUTL 117:23
Though your s. be as scarlet	BIBLE 57:18
was one of the gravest s.	WAUGH 566:5
which is the root of all s.	JAM 271:2
yet all s. must bear	DONNE 188:32
Sint: S. ut sunt aut non sint	CLEM 153:1
Sion: again the captivity of S.	PRAY 398:16
favourable and gracious unto S.	PRAY 393:8
God, art praised in S.	PRAY 393:23
his dwelling in S.	PRAY 395:1
one of the songs of S.	PRAY 399:3
praise to Mount S.	BUNY 107:12
Walk about S.	PRAY 392:27
we remembered thee, O S.	PRAY 399:3
sip: can't be tasted in a s.	DICK 180:30
sipped: Who s. no sup	GILB 229:9
Sir-come-spy-see: ask for his Monument,	
S.	BARH 33:7
Sire: S. of an immortal strain	SHEL 499:4
thy s. was a knight	SCOTT 416:24
Siren: potions have I drunk of S. tears	
	SHAK 495:6
Sirens: Blest pair of S.	MILT 340:20
S.! Dear me	DICK 178:30
sires: s. have marched to Rome	MAC 322:12
Sirion: S., like a young unicorn	PRAY 391:10
Sirius: S. pierced the eye with	HARDY 241:9
Sirmio: olive-silvery S.	TENN 533:18
S., bright eye of peninsulas	CAT 136:28
Sisera: courses fought against S.	BIBLE 49:9
S. looked out at a window	BIBLE 49:12
sissy: rose-red s. half as old	PLOM 374:18
sister: azure s. of the spring	SHEL 502:8
Had it been his s.	ANON 5:15
is no friend like a s.	ROSS 408:27
moon is my s.	BELL 39:16
My s. and my sister's child	COWP 165:16
my s., my spouse	BIBLE 56:28
s. Anne replied	PERR 372:25
s. hath left me to serve	BIBLE 69:34
sometime s., now our queen	SHAK 429:19
To live a barren s. all	SHAK 469:17
We have a little s.	BIBLE 57:13
Your brother and my s.	SHAK 426:27
sisterly: fervour of s. animosity	SURT 525:25
sisters: Are s. under their skins	KIPL 300:18
His s. and his cousins	GILB 228:9
Sphere-born harmonious s.	MILT 340:20
weird s.	SHAK 458:8
were twa s. sat in a bour	BALL 30:14
Sisyphus: S. must be regarded	CAMUS 129:24
sit: dangerous to s. to Sargent	ANON 6:8
he cannot s. on it	INGE 270:9
he can't S. still	MILL 339:25
I can s. and look at it	JER 272:26
is a good thing to s.	JOHN 278:14
'I shall s. here	CARR 133:24
let us s. upon the ground	SHAK 479:11
May s. i' th' centre	MILT 341:8

now s. down on my botom	FLEM 215:3
Shall s. and drink with me	BELL 40:11
s. and mourn all at her	BALL 32:9
s. down,' says Love	HERB 248:1
s. him down and die	SHAK 442:2
s. not down in the highest	BIBLE 70:7
S. on your arse for fifty	MACN 326:8
S. thou on my right hand	PRAY 397:11
S. thou still when kings	SCOTT 418:5
superstitious reluctance to s.	JOHN 278:13
Teach us to s. still	ELIOT 202:1
Their strength is to s.	BIBLE 58:24
them that s. in darkness	BIBLE 69:7
Though I s. down now	DISR 184:10
To s. still for once	HOFF 252:14
To s. upon a hill	SHAK 446:18
where men s. and hear each	KEATS 291:18
sittin: of it's s.' and thinkin'	KIPL 300:17
sitting: Are you s. comfortably	LANG 309:20
Lord s. upon a throne	BIBLE 57:28
not soar where he is s.	SHEL 499:19
s. in one place rather	ELIOT 201:13
s. in the shade	KIPL 299:14
take the privilege o' s.	ELIOT 201:19
situation: s. excellente	FOCH 216:3
situations: s. in life that cannot	BRAM 91:21
six: All's set at s. and seven	ANON 9:1
found s. feet of ground	HOUS 265:6
his s. days' work	MILT 349:2
Shakespeare never had s.	JOHN 275:27
S. days shalt thou labour	BIBLE 47:24
S. hours in sleep	COKE 154:22
S. hundred threescore and six	BIBLE 82:14
s. impossible things before	CARR 135:18
s. little Singing-boys	BARH 33:12
s. lustres almost now outwore	DONNE 189:36
S. o'clock	ELIOT 204:7
s. of one and half-a-dozen	MARR 331:7
whether it snowed for s.	THOM 546:20
world on s. and sevene	CHAU 144:13
six foot: content with s.	BROW 97:24
six hundred: Rode the s.	TENN 532:23
sixpence: I give thee s.	CANN 129:27
I only got s.	PUNCH 402:27
precious little for s.	PUNCH 402:20
Whoso has s. is sovereign	CARL 132:14
sixpences: s. you know to one guinea	
	JOHN 280:14
sixte: Welcome the s.	CHAU 143:17
sixteen: At s. you departed	POUND 383:16
sixth: s. age shifts	SHAK 425:24
sixty: s. seconds' worth of distance	
	KIPL 300:2
size: Those of the largest s.	CARR 135:10
skating: In s. over thin ice	EMER 207:33
skelp: I gie them a s.	BURNS 113:4
sketch: s. the ruins of St Paul's	MAC 323:16
Skiddaw: Till S. saw the fire that	MAC 322:4
skies: common people of the s.	WOTT 583:15
exchange thy sullen s.	COWP 166:34
meet the raging of the s.	CAMP 129:3
paint the sable s.	DRUM 193:26
s. are painted with unnumber'd	SHAK 449:25
soaring claim the s.	FRERE 218:26
some watcher of the s.	KEATS 292:18
virgin-daughter of the s.	DRYD 197:32
skilfully: s. and magnanimously all	
	MILT 352:8
skill: All s. to naught	KIPL 301:3
his s. runs on the lees	HERR 250:12
none, or little s.	HERR 250:12
nothing with a deal of s.	COWP 166:23
parson own'd his s.	GOLD 231:3
S. comes so slow	DAV 172:10
s. in antiquity inclines	FULL 220:14
s. in the weapon is nothing	SHAK 442:15
Thy s. to poet were	SHEL 504:24
'Tis God gives s.	ELIOT 201:28
who has the power and s.	ANON 8:20

skilled: fingers play in s. unmindfulness HARDY 239:12

skim: s. away TENN 536:20
S. milk masquerades GILB 228:8

skimble-skamble: such a deal of s. stuff SHAK 439:27

skims: lightly s. the midge BETJ 42:18

skin: Ethiopian change his s. BIBLE 60:22
my s. bristles so that HOUS 266:17
Nor scar that whiter s. SHAK 477:5
s. of an innocent lamb SHAK 446:12
skull beneath the s. ELIOT 205:13
spot on your s. is a shocking AUDEN 18:18
throws her enamell'd s. SHAK 470:10
with the s. of my teeth BIBLE 52:29

skinny: holds him with his s. hand COL 155:6

skins: beauty of their s. TENN 542:8
sisters under their s. KIPL 300:18

skip: art of reading is to s. HAM 238:12
them also to s. like a calf PRAY 391:10

skipped: mountains s. like rams PRAY 397:16

skipper: s. had taken his little LONG 317:20

skipping: s. king SHAK 439:34
With what a pretty s. grace MARV 332:13

skirt: swish of a s. in the dew KIPL 304:1

skirts: caught at God's s. BROW 101:18
grasps the s. of happy chance TENN 537:1

skittish: Unstaid and s. in all motions SHAK 488:27

skittles: all porter and s. DICK 182:32
Life ain't all beer and s. DU M 199:4

Sklaven-Moral: Herren-Moral und S. NIET 363:12

Skugg: Here S. Lies snug FRAN 218:16

skull: more of her than the s. BIBLE 51:37
s. beneath the skin ELIOT 205:13
s. that housed white angels SASS 415:3

skuttle: me in mind of the s. fish ADD 2:24

sky: admitted to that equal s. POPE 379:6
all the blue ethereal s. ADD 2:22
bear him up the Norfolk s. BETJ 42:11
blue s. of spring ALL 3:21
clear blue s. over my head HAZL 243:32
discern the face of the s. BIBLE 66:32
freeze, thou bitter s. SHAK 426:1
inverted Bowl we call The S. FITZ 213:8
Like strips of the s. fallen SHEL 500:6
On a bed of daffodil s. TENN 540:9
shapes of s. or plain SHEL 504:21
Shine upon the starry s. BLAKE 86:5
shoulders held the s. suspended HOUS 265:7
Shoulder the s. HOUS 264:22
s. changes when they are SHAK 426:23
s. grows darker yet CHES 146:16
s. is darkening like AUDEN 21:10
s. is red BIBLE 66:31
stars be blown about the s. YEATS 586:18
to lose itself in the s. BROW 98:20
vaulted s. CLARE 152:13
watched the ocean and the s. SHEL 501:16
Were close against the s. HOOD 254:18
Which prisoners call the s. WILDE 572:8
Who aimeth at the s. HERB 247:8
wide and starry s. STEV 523:10
wrote my will across the s. LAWR 311:12
You'll get pie in the s. HILL 251:3

Skye: Over the sea to S. STEV 523:4

skylark: despise the s.'s song BRON 93:13
s. wounded in the wing BLAKE 85:10

slacks: girls in s. remember Dad BETJ 42:8

slain: am hurt but I am not s. BALL 31:15
beauty of Israel is s. BIBLE 50:16
ere thou hast s. another BROW 97:25
fifty thousand men s. WALP 563:25
I am s. by a fair cruel SHAK 489:4
if the s. think he is slain EMER 206:17
is my most noble lord s. MAL 328:3
jaw of an ass have I s. BIBLE 49:24
law, chance, hath s. DONNE 189:4
many a gallant man was s. ANON 7:8

may fight and no be s. BURNS 115:13
own eyes might see him s. MORR 358:11
Saul hath s. his thousands BIBLE 50:13
shall himself be s. MAC 323:1
s. in thine high places BIBLE 50:17
small s. body SWIN 530:15
That was late s. at Carrow SKEL 508:19
there lies a new-s. knight BALL 32:8
thrice he slew the s. DRYD 195:2

slander: civic s. and the spite TENN 537:15
Fear not s. SHAK 428:22
Have not devis'd this s. SHAK 476:23
S., meanest spawn of Hell TENN 538:13
To speak no s. TENN 534:11
Who's angry at a s. makes JONS 283:20

slandered: hath not s. his neighbour PRAY 390:4

slandering: lying, and s. PRAY 388:17

slang: All s. is metaphor CHES 147:29

Slant: There's a certain S. of light DICK 184:1

slap-dash: am I s. down in the mouth CONG 160:25

slap-up: s. gal in a bang-up chariot DICK 181:15

slashing: s. article THAC 545:15

slate: his thoughts upon a s. HOOD 255:14
wiping something off a s. KIPL 297:23

slates: out the slipping s. BETJ 43:9

slaughter: arrayed for mutual s. WORD 578:21
brought as a lamb to the s. BIBLE 59:22
Forbad to wade through s. GRAY 234:24
out threatenings and s. BIBLE 73:32
ox goeth to the s. BIBLE 53:25
s. will ensue CONG 160:21
steeled themselves for s. AUDEN 21:3

slaughter'd: 'ye have s. and made NEWB 361:11

slaughtered: thy s. saints MILT 351:9

slaughterous: familiar to my s. thoughts SHAK 463:5

slave: Being your s. SHAK 493:18
fingering s. WORD 580:3
giving freedom to the s. LINC 314:22
half s. and half free LINC 314:14
here I stand, your s. SHAK 454:5
like a sad s. SHAK 493:18
No more s. States CHASE 141:2
S. to no sect POPE 380:2
soundly as the wretched s. SHAK 444:25
Till he fac'd the s. SHAK 458:3
true, sick-hearted s. HOUS 265:18
very s. of circumstance BYRON 125:20
What a s. art thou SHAK 439:7
would have made him a s. BURKE 109:2
you were a Christian S. HENL 245:10

slaverie: Chains and s. BURNS 114:34

slavery: between liberty and s. CAMD 128:4
classified as s. CHUR 149:25
cost of the squalor and s. SHAW 498:23
s. of the tea and coffee COBB 154:7
S. they can have anywhere BURKE 110:3
state is a state of S. GILL 229:11
war has saved us from s. WALP 563:16

slaves: because they are all s. GOLD 232:6
Britons never will be s. THOM 549:7
freemen, are the only s. MASS 335:17
grandfather were s. CHEK 144:24
inevitably two kinds of s. ILL 270:5
land of s. shall ne'er BYRON 123:4
S. cannot breathe in England COWP 166:32
s. of some defunct economist KEYN 295:20
S. of the Lamp ARN 12:19
too pure an Air for S. ANON 7:7
voluntarily to submit to be s. PITT 373:21
Which those poor s. with SHEL 500:10
wholly s. or wholly free DRYD 196:16

slavish: you s. herd HOR 259:1

slay: s., and slay, and slay MAC 323:2
Though he s. me BIBLE 52:25

slayer: priest who slew the s. MAC 323:1

red s. think he slays EMER 206:
slayeth: s. the child in the womb POUND 382:
slaying: s. of a beautiful hypothesis HUXL 269
slayn: he was s. in this manere CHAU 144:
slays: red slayer think he s. EMER 206:
s. A thousand LAND 308:
sledge: s. and anvil lie declined ANON 6:
sleek: find me fat and s. HOR 258:
s. and shining creatures TENN 542
Sleek-headed: S. men and such as sleep SHAK 448:
sleekit: s., cow'rin' BURNS 115:
sleep: after-dinner's s. SHAK 464:
Back from the City of S. KIPL 298:
balmy s. YOUNG 587:
By night we s. on the cliffs LEAR 312:
Can s. so soundly SHAK 444:
Care-charmer S. DAN 171
Care-charming S. FLET 215:
Come, S.! O Sleep SIDN 507:
comes with the first s. MEYN 338:
come to the borders of s. THOM 547:
Death and his brother S. SHEL 500
deep s. to fall upon Adam BIBLE 45:
Do I wake or s. KEATS 291:
dreadfully but as a drunken s. SHAK 464:
dreamless, uninvaded s. TENN 537:
drowsy approaches of s. BROW 95:
each day dies with s. HOPK 256:
Entice the dewy-feather'd s. MILT 342:
first sweet s. of night SHEL 501:
folding of the hands to s. BIBLE 53:
From rest and s. DONNE 189:
gray and full of s. YEATS 587:
hath night to do with s. MILT 340:
have an exposition of s. SHAK 471:
her great gift of s. HENL 245:
His s. Was aery light MILT 348:1
How long wilt thou s. BIBLE 53:2
How s. the brave COLL 158:1
I always s. upon ale FARQ 209:2
ideas s. furiously CHOM 148:1
I'll go to s. if I can SHAK 425:1
In s. a king SHAK 494:1
in soot I s. BLAKE 88:
I s. BIBLE 57:
I s. out the thought SHAK 491:19
I s. well MORT 358:1
I wake to s. ROET 407:
keepeth thee will not s. PRAY 398:9
life Is rounded with a s. SHAK 485:2
Macbeth does murder s. SHAK 460:8
Macbeth shall s. no more SHAK 460:9
medicine thee to that sweet s. SHAK 475:24
me from the fields of s. WORD 579:2
might s. out this great gap SHAK 421:30
miles to go before I s. FROST 219:12
nose-painting, s., and urine SHAK 460:18
Now I lay me down to s. ANON 7:3
on him who invented s. CERV 138:20
Only s. BROW 105:35
O sleep! O gentle s. SHAK 441:29
O S.! the friend of Woe SOUT 513:27
season of all natures, s. SHAK 461:26
Shake off this downy s. SHAK 460:23
She looks like s. SHAK 424:17
Silence and s. like fields DE L 173:25
Six hours in s. COKE 154:22
Sleek-headed men and such as s. SHAK 448:20
S. after toil SPEN 516:8
s. an act or two SHAK 448:4
s. and a forgetting WORD 579:5
s. and a sweet dream when MAS 334:6
S.; and if life was bitter SWIN 529:1
s. between term and term SHAK 426:13
sleep, dear, s. BEDD 36:23
s. in Abraham's bosom SHAK 481:7

s. in it besides himself — ADD 2:12
S. is a death — BROW 97:6
S. is sweet to the labouring — BUNY 107:24
S.! it is a gentle thing — COL 155:23
'S. no more — SHAK 460:8
s. not so sound, as sweet — HERR 249:1
s. of a labouring man is — BIBLE 55:17
s. old palaces and towers — SHEL 502:10
s. one ever-during night — CAT 136:25
S. on, my Love — KING 296:11
s. provides relief every — CHAM 139:13
S. shall neither night — SHAK 458:7
S. shall obey me — SOUT 513:24
s. should be his last repose — ANON 8:21
s. that is among the lonely — WORD 581:10
S. to wake — BROW 98:32
S. will come when thou — SHEL 505:4
S. your fill — BELL 39:22
slept an azure-lidded s. — KEATS 289:20
Sword s. in my hand — BLAKE 86:16
them they are even as a s. — PRAY 395:18
There are two gates of S. — VIRG 559:3
There'll be time enough to s. — HOUS 262:15
This s. is sound indeed — SHAK 442:18
thou arise out of thy s. — BIBLE 53:22
thou s. the sleep of death — BLAKE 86:11
time to awake out of s. — BIBLE 75:24
time when first s. begins — VIRG 558:4
To die: to s. — SHAK 433:8
to s. at a bank from ten — JER 272:24
to s. at the root of my — LAWR 311:3
to s. before evening — PATER 369:22
us from everlasting s. — BROW 95:22
waking s. — MONT 355:5
We shall not all s. — BIBLE 76:29
We shall not s. — MCCR 324:31
while some must s. — SHAK 434:16
Would I were s. and peace — SHAK 482:20
would make anyone go to s. — DICK 182:31
would not s. with the brave — HOUS 264:19
yet I would not s. — SHAK 459:14
sleeper: me the s. — THOM 548:28
that was never a quiet s. — TENN 540:15
sleepers: slumbers for the s. in that quiet
earth — BRON 94:1
snorted we in the Seven S. — DONNE 188:29
sleepeth: maid is not dead, but s. — BIBLE 65:27
peradventure he s. — BIBLE 51:9
sleep-flower: s. sways in the wheat its — THOM 548:28
sleeping: growing, Jock, when ye're — SCOTT 418:20
He cursed him in s. — BARH 33:13
kind of s. in the blood — SHAK 441:6
Lay your s. head — AUDEN 19:17
s. and the dead Are — SHAK 460:11
s., by a brother's hand — SHAK 431:12
suddenly he find you s. — BIBLE 69:1
wakened us from s. — BROO 94:26
young love is s. in the shade — MER 337:1
Sleepless: S. as the river under thee — CRANE 168:29
s. soul — WORD 580:28
S. themselves — POPE 375:15
S. with cold commemorative — ROSS 410:5
sleeps: dines he s. — SURT 525:7
heaven-eyed creature s. — WORD 577:18
He wakes or s. with — SHEL 499:19
moon s. with Endymion — SHAK 468:19
Now s. the crimson petal — TENN 542:14
s. feels not the toothache — SHAK 429:2
S. in Elysium — SHAK 444:25
S. on his luminous ring — TENN 541:21
Such s. as may beguile — SURR 524:21
That broods and s. on his — WORD 580:5
Till tir'd, he s. — POPE 379:19
while my pretty one, s. — TENN 541:31
sleep-time: in the silence of the s. — BROW 98:31

sleepwalker: with the assurance of a s. — HITL 251:10
Sleepy: S. with the flow of streams — HOUS 263:18
who in the s. region stay — MORR 358:9
sleepy-head: Ain't you 'shamed, you
s. — STEV 522:24
sleeve: wear my heart upon my s. — SHAK 473:15
sleeves: Tie up my s. with ribbons — HUNT 268:15
sleigh: snow on an ebony s. — AUDEN 18:7
sleight: by the s. of men — BIBLE 77:28
more th' admire his s. — BUTL 118:6
slender: she puts forth a s. hand POUND 382:5
Slept: Edward the Confessor S. under
the dresser — BENT 41:7
firstfruits of them that s. — BIBLE 76:22
He s. with his fathers — BIBLE 51:5
I should have s. — BIBLE 52:12
On a poet's lips I s. — SHEL 503:5
thought he thought I s. — PATM 370:3
while their companions s. — LONG 316:19
Whilst Adam s. — ANON 8:21
slepyng: s. hound to wake — CHAU 144:7
slew: I s. him — SHAK 450:15
s. at his death were more — BIBLE 49:28
s. mighty kings — PRAY 399:1
who s. his master — BIBLE 51:35
Slice: S. him where you like — WOD 575:20
slight: Away, s. man — SHAK 451:15
loved so s. a thing — TENN 539:4
s. all that do — FARQ 210:11
s. what I receive — BROW 104:7
slighted: Doctor s. — OWEN 366:28
slim: Who's the s. boy now — HOR 259:15
slime: daubed it with s. — BIBLE 46:41
slimier s. — BROO 94:12
through the ooze and s. — SMITH 510:10
slimepit: To the s. and the mire — HOUS 265:4
slimier: s. slime — BROO 94:12
slimy: s. things did crawl with — COL 155:14
thousand thousand s. things — COL 155:21
slings: s. and arrows of outrageous — SHAK 433:8
slip: caused his chest to s. — WOD 575:23
in earth to set one s. — SHAK 491:24
make a s. in handling us — KIPL 302:17
Since he gave us all the s. — BROW 105:32
S. into my bosom — TENN 542:14
Then s. I from her bum — SHAK 470:3
then s. out of the world — DRYD 196:36
Under the tension, s. — ELIOT 202:17
slipper: s. and subtle knave — SHAK 474:21
s. knock'd the ground — POPE 380:29
slippered: s. Hesper — BROO 94:19
slippers: bring me my s. — MOL 353:3
walks in his golden s. — BUNY 107:19
slippery: standing is s. — BACON 26:23
Slit: S. your girl's — KING 297:19
slither: in a s. of dyed stuff — POUND 382:15
slits: s. the thin-spun life — MILT 343:8
sliver: envious s. broke — SHAK 436:19
Sloane Square: S. and South Kensington — GILB 226:14
sloe: lush-kept plush-capped s. — HOPK 257:7
slog: foot—s.—slog — KIPL 298:6
slop: Raineth drop and staineth s. — POUND 382:4
slopes: on the butler's upper s. — WOD 575:27
sloth: most of s. — HERB 247:3
much time in studies is s. — BACON 27:16
peaceful s., Not peace — MILT 346:12
s. Finds the down pillow — SHAK 428:18
slothful: s. man saith — BIBLE 54:34
Slouches: S. towards Bethlehem — YEATS 586:16
Slough: bombs, and fall on S. — BETJ 44:5
name of the s. was Despond — BUNY 107:11
was an old person of S. — LEAR 312:26

slovenliness: s. is no part of religion — WESL 568:22
slow: I am s. of speech — BIBLE 47:9
of the human mind is s. — BURKE 109:29
Quick' and some cry 'S. — TENN 541:26
sloeblack, s., black, crowblack — THOM 547:9
s., fresh fount — JONS 283:21
s. to anger is better than — BIBLE 54:9
s. to speak — BIBLE 80:10
slowest: s. thing in the world — SHAD 420:21
slowly: Make haste s. — SUET 524:16
Slug-a-bed: Get up, sweet S. — HERR 248:23
sluggard: foul s.'s comfort — CARL 131:10
Go to the ant thou s. — BIBLE 53:21
s. is wiser in his own — BIBLE 54:35
s.'s cradle — CHAP 140:9
'Tis the voice of the s. — WATTS 565:25
slug-horn: Dauntless the s. to my — BROW 99:30
Slugs: S. leave their lair — COL 157:14
sluices: Close the s. now — VIRG 559:21
sluicing: excellent browsing and s. — WOD 575:26
slum: swear-word in a rustic s. — BEER 37:15
slumber: abed and daylight s. — HOUS 262:15
Ere S.'s chain has bound — MOORE 357:2
honey-heavy dew of s. — SHAK 449:12
keep'st the ports of s. — SHAK 442:17
little sleep, a little s. — BIBLE 53:22
pilgrim's limbs affected s. — CAMP 129:20
shall neither s. not sleep — PRAY 398:9
s. did my spirit seal — WORD 581:10
s. is more sweet than toil — TENN 539:17
will start from her s. — ARN 13:7
slumber'd: That you have but s. here — SHAK 471:23
slumbered: warm between them s. — HOUS 265:11
slumbers: Golden s. kiss your eyes — DEKK 173:22
s. light — SCOTT 417:26
unquiet s. for the sleepers — BRON 94:1
yet hast thou golden s. — DEKK 173:20
slumb'ring: leaden sceptre o'er a s. — YOUNG 588:1
slut: I am not a s. — SHAK 426:16
sluts: now foul s. in dairies — CORB 162:13
sluttish: besmear'd with s. time — SHAK 493:17
elf-locks in foul s. hairs — SHAK 481:28
sly: s., ensnaring art — BURNS 113:7
smack: yet some s. of age in you — SHAK 441:5
small: Almost too s. for sight — SHAK 455:14
arms long and s. — WYATT 583:22
compare s. things with great — VIRG 560:19
creatures great and s. — ALEX 3:13
In s. proportions we just — JONS 285:8
my s. cruse best fits my — HERR 249:20
she deals it in s. parcels — WEBS 567:1
shows how s. the world is — GROS 236:22
S. is beautiful — SCH 415:12
s. Latin, and less Greek — JONS 284:21
s. things from the peak — CHES 147:30
so thoroughly s. and dry — ELIOT 202:1
speaks s. like a woman — SHAK 469:2
squadrons against the s. — BUSS 117:7
still s. voice — BIBLE 51:14
That s. infantry — MILT 345:22
Too s. to live in — ANON 8:11
use of maps on a s. scale — SAL 413:20
very s. the very great are — THAC 546:4
with s. men no great thing — MILL 339:15
smaller: flea Hath s. fleas — SWIFT 528:5
smallest: Queen Anne was one of the
s. people — BAG 29:10
Smart: lief pray with Kit S. — JOHN 274:24
Of love and all its s. — BEDD 36:23
scorn which mock'd the s. — ARN 13:9
smatch: some s. of honour in it — SHAK 452:6
smattering: s. of everything — DICK 183:3

smell: Cheered with the grateful s.
MILT 347:17
even a s. remembered GREE 236:4
I s. a rat ROCHE 406:14
Money has no s. VESP 556:11
s. and hideous hum GODL 229:24
s. of bread and butter BYRON 119:32
s. of burning fills BELL 40:7
s. of burned poetry WOD 576:1
s. of fish there is sometimes KILV 296:6
s. of the blood still SHAK 462:22
s. the blood of a British SHAK 454:27
s. too strong of the lamp STER 519:23
smudge and shares man's s. HOPK 256:12
sweet keen s. ROSS 410:8
this foul deed shall s. SHAK 450:12
this s. of cooped-up angels FRY 220:4
This world would s. like SHEL 501:18
smelleth: he s. the battle afar off BIBLE 53:7
smells: dead thing that s. sweet THOM 547:17
he s. April and May SHAK 469:10
it s. of mortality SHAK 455:17
it s. to heaven SHAK 434:27
smile: bask in Heaven's blue s. SHEL 500:5
betwixt that s. we would SHAK 447:9
Did he s. his work to see BLAKE 87:16
gigantic s. o' the brown BROW 101:20
her own dying s. SHEL 499:9
I dare not beg a s. HERR 250:3
I hear a s. CROSS 170:6
jest without the s. COL 157:17
Let me s. with the wise JOHN 275:23
morn those Angel faces s. NEWM 362:15
Out where the s. dwells CHAP 140:2
recognize your mother with a s. VIRG 560:1
Robert with his watery s. TENN 533:10
share the good man's s. GOLD 231:1
s., and be a villain SHAK 431:16
S. at us CHES 147:15
smiled a kind of sickly s. HARTE 242:33
s. his face into more lines SHAK 490:3
s. of safety wounds SHAK 440:30
s. to those who hate BYRON 126:1
s. upon his fingers' ends SHAK 443:17
vain tribute of a s. SCOTT 416:18
we shall s. SHAK 451:32
When you call me that, s. WIST 575:11
Where my Julia's lips do s. HERR 248:21
you should forget and s. ROSS 409:4
You s., and mock me SHAK 487:9
smiled: At me you s. TENN 537:26
Has s. and said 'Good Night BELL 39:20
Jesus wept; Voltaire s. HUGO 267:13
Until she s. on me COL 154:26
Well I remember how you s. LAND 309:4
smiles: charmed it with s. and soap
CARR 133:8
corner of the world s. HOR 260:8
Seldom he s. SHAK 448:21
She is Venus when she s. JONS 285:5
s., As in a looking-glass SHAK 491:9
S. awake you when you rise DEKK 173:22
S. by his cheerful fire GOLD 231:26
s. his emptiness betray POPE 377:2
s. steals something from SHAK 474:3
s., with sniffles predominating HENRY 245:23
Than s. of other maidens COL 155:1
There's daggers in men's s. SHAK 461:4
thy own sweet s. I see COWP 166:2
welcome ever s. SHAK 487:5
wreathed s. MILT 342:14
smilest: Thou s. and art still ARN 14:23
smiling: He hides a s. face COWP 165:28
like patience on a monument s. at
grief SHAK 489:7
s., destructive man LEE 313:14
S. the boy fell dead BROW 101:16
s. through her tears HOMER 254:1
S., while hurt HARDY 240:16
smil'st: s. upon the stroke that SHAK 483:10

smite: caitiff s. the other HOLM 253:11
s. thee on thy right cheek BIBLE 64:17
Stands ready to s. once MILT 343:13
Star-spiked Rails a fiery S. THOM 549:2
Strength without hands to s. SWIN 528:21
will s. all the firstborn BIBLE 47:18
smiteth: his cheek to him that s. BIBLE 60:31
Smith: conceal him by naming him S.
HOLM 253:7
s., a mighty man is he LONG 317:18
s. of his own fortune CLAU 152:26
s. was the first murd'rer's COWP 167:21
smithy: to forge in the s. of my JOYCE 286:19
smitten: bones are s. asunder PRAY 392:9
s. me to my knee THOM 548:16
smok'd: s. with bloody execution SHAK 458:3
smoke: blood and s. and flame HOUS 266:4
bravery in their rotten s. SHAK 493:11
coaster with a salt-caked s. MAS 333:19
corrupted by this stinking s. JAM 271:4
counties overhung with s. MORR 358:10
her beloved s. LAMB 307:24
hills, they shall s. PRAY 397:2
him full of s. and embers JONS 284:5
horrible Stygian s. JAM 271:3
light emerging from the s. HOR 257:19
man who does not s. STEV 521:29
Only thin s. without flame HARDY 240:5
s. and stir of this dim MILT 340:23
s. and wealth and din HOR 261:7
s. into the smother SHAK 424:28
s. of their torment ascendeth BIBLE 82:17
s. that rubs its muzzle ELIOT 203:18
there's never s. without fire AUDEN 20:22
you gwine do wid de s. HARR 242:25
smoked: Who s. like a chimney BARH 33:17
smokefall: draughty church at s. ELIOT 202:16
smokeless: glittering in the s. air
WORD 581:14
smoking: power of s. at such a rate
LAMB 308:12
s. flax shall he not quench BIBLE 59:11
sometimes in a s. room KIPL 302:5
What a blessing this s. is HELPS 244:17
smoky: Palace in s. light POUND 382:7
Worse than a s. house SHAK 439:28
smooth: I am a s. man BIBLE 46:15
large, and s., and round SOUT 513:15
neat knave with a s. tale WEBS 566:18
person and a s. dispose SHAK 474:12
s. as monumental alabaster SHAK 477:5
Speak unto us s. things BIBLE 58:26
To s. the ice SHAK 452:25
true love never did run s. SHAK 469:18
smoother: his words were s. than oil
PRAY 393:12
mouth is s. than oil BIBLE 53:20
smooth-fac'd: That s. gentleman
SHAK 452:14
smote: He s. divers nations PRAY 399:1
Israel s. him with BIBLE 48:12
s. him thus SHAK 477:23
s. the king of Israel between BIBLE 51:21
s. them hip and thigh BIBLE 49:23
s. the nail into his temples BIBLE 49:7
smother: from the smoke into the s.
SHAK 424:28
smudge: wears man's s. and shares man's
HOPK 256:12
smut-hounds: was brought down by s.
AUDEN 18:20
smylere: s. with the knyf under CHAU 142:20
snaffle: use the s. and the curb CAMP 128:12
snail: church the size of a s. THOM 547:7
creeping like s. SHAK 425:24
is easy paced) this s. DONNE 189:23
said a whiting to a s. CARR 134:13
slug-abed s. upon the thorn THOM 548:5
s.'s on the thorn BROW 103:21
Worm nor s. SHAK 470:12

snails: Like s. did creep HERR 250:7
tender horns of cockled s. SHAK 457:8
snake: earth doth like a s. renew SHEL 500:20
like a wounded s. POPE 378:21
of the eagle or the s. KIPL 301:1
s. hidden in the grass VIRG 559:19
S. is living yet BELL 40:4
there the s. throws her SHAK 470:10
We have scotch'd the s. SHAK 461:12
Snakes: S., in my heart-blood SHAK 479:9
There are no s. to be met JOHN 277:28
You spotted s. with double SHAK 470:11
snap-dragon: s. growing on the walls
NEWM 361:23
we have gold-dusted s. ARN 15:6
snapper-up: s. of unconsidered trifles
SHAK 491:18
snare: delusion, a mockery, and a s.
DENM 174:22
from the s. of the hunter PRAY 395:21
I saw the s. TENN 537:26
of the s. of the fowler PRAY 398:14
There is a rabbit in a s. STEP 518:26
were rapid falcons in a s. MER 337:17
world's great s. uncaught SHAK 423:3
snares: rain s., fire and brimstone
PRAY 389:31
s. of death compassed PRAY 397:19
Snark: If your S. be a Boojum CARR 133:7
S. was a Boojum CARR 133:9
snarled: s. and yelping seas ELIOT 204:11
snatch: s. them straight away SHAK 478:5
snatch'd: s. his rudder ARN 14:21
snatched: s. the lightning shaft TURG 553:22
who has been s. from us BURKE 110:21
snatches: s. a man from obscurity
REYN 405:15
sneaking: petty s. knave I knew BLAKE 87:3
sneer: flinch and traitors s. CONN 161:10
laughing devil in his s. BYRON 121:31
s. at me for leaning all FITZ 213:10
solemn creed with solemn s. BYRON 120:37
teach the rest to s. POPE 376:26
Who can refute a s. PALEY 368:9
witlings sneer, and rivals rail JOHN 282:20
sneering: I was born s. GILB 226:20
sneery: hair and looked very s. ASHF 17:13
sneeze: 'If you s. LEAR 312:16
sneezed: Not to be s. COLM 159:1
sneezes: beat him when he s. CARR 133:26
snicker-snack: vorpal blade went s.
CARR 134:29
snickersnee: I drew my s. GILB 227:8
sniff: snuffle and s. and handkerchief
BROO 94:16
sniffles: with s. predominating HENRY 245:23
sniffs: tiger s. the rose SASS 415:1
Snob: admires mean things is a S.
THAC 545:4
not to be sometimes a S. THAC 545:5
snooze: caribous lie around and s.
COW 163:20
snore: snorer can't hear himself s.
TWAIN 554:18
Weariness Can s. SHAK 428:18
snored: have simply sat and s. CHES 146:12
Snores: S. out the watch of night
SHAK 442:17
snoring: s., she disturbs COWP 166:29
snorted: s. we in the Seven Sleepers
DONNE 188:29
snot: s.green sea JOYCE 286:20
snout: gold in a swine's s. BIBLE 53:32
snow: architecture of the s. EMER 206:24
asleep the s. came flying BRID 92:12
bloodless lay the untrodden s. CAMP 128:21
chaste as unsunn'd s. SHAK 428:12
cherry hung with s. HOUS 262:14
Drifts the appalling s. AUDEN 18:10
Earth in forgetful s. ELIOT 204:17

fall o' the s. JONS 285:4
fare wel al the s. of ferne CHAU 144:15
garment was white as s. BIBLE 61:8
He giveth s. like wool PRAY 399:21
I love s. SHEL 503:27
I, this incessant s. DE L 174:12
last long streak of s. TENN 537:18
Lawn as white as driven s. SHAK 492:2
like the s. falls BURNS 115:7
recollect the S. DICK 183:14
rosebuds fill'd with s. CAMP 129:23
shall be as white as s. BIBLE 57:18
shall be whiter than s. PRAY 393:5
sit brooding in the s. SHAK 457:19
s. and vapours PRAY 399:22
s. disfigured the public AUDEN 19:2
s. in May's new-fangled SHAK 456:16
S. on snow ROSS 409:1
S. which doth the top SPEN 516:31
Virgin shrouded in s. BLAKE 87:22
white as s. BIBLE 81:14
Whiter than new s. SHAK 483:7
wondrous strange s. SHAK 471:13
ye Ice and S. PRAY 384:22
Snowdon: We've the stones of S.
KING 296:20
snowed: s. for six days and six THOM 546:20
snows: are the s. of yesteryear VILL 557:5
From her couch of s. SHEL 500:2
Said our Lady of the S. KIPL 301:20
s. have dispersed HOR 261:14
Snowy: S., Flowy ELLIS 206:13
snub: has a s. nose like to mine BLAKE 85:21
snuff: only took s. GOLD 231:21
s. the approach of tyranny BURKE 109:23
s., tobacker DICK 177:9
You abuse s. COL 157:30
snuff'd: be s. out by an article BYRON 123:32
snuffle: s. and sniff and handkerchief
BROO 94:16
snug: Here Skugg Lies s. FRAN 218:16
what a s. little Island DIBD 175:23
soap: charmed it with smiles and s.
CARR 133:8
hands with invisible s. HOOD 254:23
I used your s. two years PUNCH 402:33
S. and education are not TWAIN 554:6
soap-boiler: I have made a s. costive
WEBS 566:23
soaping: s. her breasts in the bath
EWART 209:11
soar: can creep as well as s. BURKE 112:9
s., but never roam WORD 583:1
S. not too high to fall MASS 335:16
s. where he is sitting SHEL 499:19
that should spur you to s. SWIN 530:22
to s. with Eno STEV 521:11
soared: He has out-s. the shadow SHEL 499:21
soaring: s. ever singest SHEL 504:16
soars: lark s. BROW 97:29
sobbed: He s. and he sighed GILB 227:17
sober: at least not s. JOHN 279:33
Be s., be vigilant BIBLE 80:33
clean, shaved and s. CHAN 139:20
Half as s. as a judge LAMB 308:1
men at whiles are s. HOUS 264:23
once saw Porson s. HOUS 266:14
Philip drunk to Philip s. ANON 4:22
righteous, and s. life PRAY 384:13
second and s. thoughts HENRY 245:18
should be compulsorily s. MAGEE 326:21
s., of good behaviour BIBLE 79:12
that will go to bed s. FLET 215:8
woman s. PEPYS 372:10
sober-suited: s. songstress THOM 549:12
Sobranies: Balkan S. in a wooden box
BETJ 44:10
sobs: Life is made up of s. HENRY 245:23
s. of the violins of aut VERL 556:8
social: commit A s. science AUDEN 21:5

man into the s. masonry WELLS 568:15
Piecemeal s. engineering POPP 381:25
s. and economic experiment HOOV 255:24
s. animal and created DEM 174:19
S. Contract is nothing WELLS 568:15
sociale: ...si s. animal et in commune
DEM 174:19
Socialism: Marxian S. must always
KEYN 295:16
S. can only arrive by bicycle VIER 556:21
socialismo: El s. puede llegar solo
VIER 556:21
socialist: to construct the s. order
LENIN 313:20
société: homme moins propre à la s.
CHAM 139:14
societies: good s. say FORS 217:4
solemn troops and sweet s. MILT 343:18
society: be a distinct gain to s. GILB 226:23
curing the maladies of S. CARL 132:9
first duty to serve s. JOHN 275:18
four hundred people in New York s.
MCAL 321:23
honour which the Royal S. FAR 209:20
in our condition of S. THAC 545:5
In the affluent s. no useful GALB 220:28
kindness and consolidates s. JOHN 280:6
Man seeketh in s. comfort BACON 25:1
Man was formed for s. BLAC 85:1
no s. HOBB 251:18
of motion of modern s. MARX 333:8
often unfit a man for s. CHAM 139:14
One great s. alone on earth WORD 580:24
open s. and its enemies POPP 381:24
Ourself will mingle with s. SHAK 461:16
Our s. distributes itself ARN 15:14
Pests of s. BOL 89:14
S. became my glittering WORD 577:14
S. everywhere is in conspiracy EMER 207:36
S. is all but rude MARV 332:1
solitude sometimes is best s. MILT 349:12
Soul selects her own S. DICK 183:21
such s. As is quiet SHEL 504:1
When s. requires to be MILL 339:3
woman made S. BRAD 91:8
sock: If Jonson's learnèd s. MILT 342:26
socket: Burn to the s. WORD 577:11
sockets: set upon s. of fine gold BIBLE 57:4
socks: when thy s. were JONS 284:22
your shirt and your s. GILB 226:15
Socrates: difficulty contradict S.
PLATO 374:12
S. commits a crime by corrupting
PLATO 374:8
S., I shall not accuse PLATO 374:9
Socratic: S. manner is not a game BEER 38:4
sod: high requiem become a s. KEATS 291:22
under my head a s. BALL 31:14
soda-water: Sermons and s. the day
BYRON 122:21
wash their feet in s. ELIOT 204:27
sodden: nor s. at all with water BIBLE 47:17
That are s. and unkind BELL 40:9
Sodium: Of having discovered S. BENT 41:6
Sodom: overthrew S. and Gomorrah
BIBLE 61:20
sodomy: rum, s. and the lash CHUR 151:7
sods: s. with our bayonets turning
WOLFE 576:3
Sofa: accomplish'd S. last COWP 166:28
wheel the s. round COWP 167:11
soft: black and s. as sin CHES 147:5
mind does not make us s. PER 372:22
seson whan s. was the sonne LANG 309:22
s. answer turneth away BIBLE 54:4
s. as young YOUNG 588:7
S. morning, city JOYCE 286:14
s., unhappy sex BEHN 38:21
so white! O so s. JONS 285:4
with the s. phrase of peace SHAK 473:24

softer: words of his mouth were s.
PRAY 393:12
softly: shall go s. all my years BIBLE 59:3
s. and suddenly vanish CARR 133:7
softness: s. she and sweet attractive
MILT 347:22
that whisper s. in chambers MILT 351:25
soger: s. frae the wars returns BURNS 114:11
Sohne: ist viel zu weit dem S. FLEM 215:5
soi: c'est de savoir être à s. MONT 354:21
soie: Honi s. qui mal y pense SELL 420:3
soil: Before the s. hath smutch'd JONS 285:4
rather be tied to the s. HOMER 254:6
s. Is bare now HOPK 256:12
that grows in every s. BURKE 110:3
this the s., the clime MILT 345:9
soil'd: s. with all ignoble use TENN 537:17
soiled: Anoint and cheer our s. face
PRAY 400:5
sojourners: s., as were all our fathers
BIBLE 51:39
sol: te inferebatur s. et luna AUG 21:13
solace: let us s. ourselves with BIBLE 53:24
Should find some s. there WORD 582:8
sold: book which somehow s. well
BOOR 89:21
guilt is bought and s. SHEL 503:1
I'd not have s. her for it SHAK 477:12
s. a goodly manor SHAK 421:2
s. his birthright unto BIBLE 46:14
s. my Reputation FITZ 213:13
sparrows s. for a farthing BIBLE 65:35
sparrows s. for two farthings BIBLE 70:3
stocks were s. BELL 39:6
Then spoils were fairly s. MAC 322:18
was not this ointment s. BIBLE 72:25
went and s. all that he BIBLE 66:21
Who never s. the truth TENN 541:14
Whose hide he s. WALL 562:6
Soldan: S. of Byzantium is smiling
CHES 146:28
Soldati: S., io esco da Roma GAR 221:10
soldats: capitaine de vingt-quatre s.
ANON 9:8
s. faisaient la haie ELIOT 202:8
soldier: arm our s., Our steed the leg
SHAK 427:11
Ben Battle was a s. bold HOOD 254:13
British s. can stand up SHAW 496:19
death who had the s. singled DOUG 191:10
Drinking is the s.'s pleasure DRYD 195:1
Every French s. carries NAP 359:9
God's s. be he SHAK 463:10
great s. BAG 29:11
himself have been a s. SHAK 438:16
I said an elder s. SHAK 451:18
it to a s. and a foeman HOUS 266:4
majesty the British s. NAP 359:7
most audacious s. CHUR 150:16
never expect a s. to think SHAW 496:18
not having been a s. JOHN 277:26
not tell us what the s. DICK 182:22
s. a mere recreant prove SHAK 486:26
s., and afeard SHAK 462:20
s. an' sailor too KIPL 302:23
s. details his wounds PROP 401:15
s., Full of strange oaths SHAK 425:24
s. I listed DIBD 175:14
s. is better accommodated SHAK 442:4
s. is flat blasphemy SHAK 464:4
S. of the Great War Known KIPL 305:12
s. of the King KITC 305:14
s.'s life is terrible hard MILNE 340:4
s.'s pole is fall'n SHAK 423:16
summer s. and the sunshine PAINE 368:1
tell an old s. SHAW 496:6
soldiers: bid the s. shoot SHAK 437:31
god of s. SHAK 428:4
having s. under me BIBLE 65:15
if you believe the s. SAL 413:18

Ireland gives England her s.	MER 337:24	
Now the s. he smiled	SASS 414:18	
Only the scarlet s.	AUDEN 20:4	
our s. slighted	QUAR 403:14	
s., armed in their stings	SHAK 443:9	
s. bore dead bodies	SHAK 438:14	
s. may not quit the post	TENN 539:21	
S. of the ploughshare	RUSK 412:9	
S. who wish to be a hero	ROST 410:15	
steel my s.' hearts	SHAK 444:26	
substance of ten thousand s.	SHAK 481:16	
They mustered their s.	BALL 31:8	
What is the world, O s.	DE L 174:12	
soldier-saints: s., who row on row		
	BROW 105:20	
soldiery: rapacious and licentious s.		
	BURKE 110:25	
sole: apparition, s. of men	SHEL 502:19	
muove il s. e l'altre stelle	DANTE 171:18	
nothing can be s. or whole	YEATS 584:19	
rest for the s. of her foot	BIBLE 45:35	
solecism: of eternity without a s.	BROW 96:10	
soleil: *Blond comme un s. d'Italie*	BANV 33:1	
rien que le s. qui poudroye	PERR 372:25	
s. *noir de la* mélancholie	NERV 360:26	
solemn: becomes more s. and serene		
	SHEL 501:7	
upon our s. feast-day	PRAY 395:9	
solemnized: they s. their obsequies		
	BROW 97:8	
solemnly: Hails me so s. to yonder yew		
	JONS 285:9	
soles: Nor the s. of her shoe	SHAK 432:11	
S. effugere atque abire	MART 331:11	
S. occidere et redire possunt	CAT 136:25	
Soli: *S. eravamo*	DANTE 171:9	
soliciting: still-s. eye	SHAK 453:6	
This supernatural s.	SHAK 458:20	
solicitor: can only go to his s.	DISR 186:16	
solid: tone of the s. and practical		
	BURKE 108:16	
solitary: Be not s.	BURT 117:3	
How doth the city sit s.	BIBLE 60:27	
s., be not idle	JOHN 278:11	
s. child	WORD 578:10	
spill her s. tea	POPE 377:7	
Through Eden took their s.	MILT 350:1	
till I am s.	JOHN 274:7	
To wander s. there	MARV 332:8	
waste And s. places	SHEL 501:10	
wilderness and the s. place	BIBLE 58:32	
Yon s. Highland lass	WORD 578:13	
solitude: He makes a s.	BYRON 120:4	
I love tranquil s.	SHEL 504:1	
In a s. of the sea	HARDY 239:4	
In s. What happiness	MILT 349:6	
itself is soft like S.'s	SHEL 504:8	
life the s.	YOUNG 588:1	
moment disturbed its s.	BALF 30:3	
Musing in s.	WORD 577:7	
passing sweet, is s.	COWP 166:21	
place of seclusion and s.	MONT 354:20	
seeks to sweet retired s.	MILT 341:8	
self-sufficing power of S.	WORD 580:15	
s. or the quality of his	CONN 161:16	
s. sometimes is best society	MILT 349:12	
s. Through which we go	DE L 174:12	
s.! where are the charms	COWP 167:3	
To this delicious s.	MARV 332:1	
Which is the bliss of s.	WORD 578:1	
'Whosoever is delighted in s.	BACON 26:14	
worst s. is to be destitute	BACON 25:14	
solitudes: misty s.	KIPL 304:1	
that two s. protect	RILKE 406:5	
Solitudinem: *S. faciunt pacem appellant*		
	TAC 531:7	
Solomon: greater than S. is here	BIBLE 66:12	
'in the Proverbs of S.	DICK 177:26	
King S. wrote the Proverbs	NAYL 360:10	
seen all S.'s wisdom	BIBLE 50:32	

S. in all his glory was	BIBLE 64:30	
S. loved many strange women	BIBLE 51:1	
S. of saloons	BROW 102:18	
than the felicities of S.	BACON 25:19	
solum: *nec minus s. quam cum solus*		
	CIC 151:23	
solution: material conditions for its s.		
	MARX 333:7	
people were a kind of s.	CAV 137:17	
solutis: *quid s. est beatius curis*	CAT 136:28	
Solutus: *S. omni faenore*	HOR 259:7	
Solventur: *S. risu tabulae*	HOR 262:7	
somber: decerated dark red as I have		
s.	ASHF 17:8	
some: s. are fond of fiddles	MAS 333:21	
There's s. say that we	MCL 325:15	
somebodee: When every one is s.		
	GILB 225:31	
somebody: spoke a brisk little s.	BROW 99:1	
started out to happen to s. else		
	MARQ 331:2	
someone: morning that it was s. else		
	ROG 407:11	
yourself necessary to s.	EMER 207:3	
somer: s. seson whan soft was	LANG 309:22	
someris: ful ofte a myrie s. day	CHAU 144:8	
Somerset House: aphorism in the records		
of S.	BIRK 84:12	
something: because you have s. to say		
	WHAT 569:11	
Everything must be like s.	FORS 216:23	
of that hidden s.	CONR 161:23	
's. for Posterity	ADD 2:27	
s. in it of divinity more	BROW 97:1	
S. is going to fall like	AUDEN 21:10	
S. must be done	EDW 200:3	
S. nasty in the woodshed	GIBB 225:2	
That s. still which prompts	POPE 379:21	
Time for a little s.	MILNE 340:15	
sometime: that s. did me seek	WYATT 583:21	
somewhat: I have s. against thee	BIBLE 81:16	
More than s.	RUNY 411:4	
somewhere: you want to get s. else		
	CARR 134:32	
sommeil: *une maladie dont le s.*	CHAM 139:13	
sommets: *elle-même vers les s.*	CAMUS 129:24	
Somonour: S. was ther with us	CHAU 142:4	
somwhat: we shall speek of the s.		
	CHAU 144:6	
son: bare-legg'd beggarly s. of a gun		
	CALV 127:17	
bear a s.	BIBLE 58:3	
behold thy s.	BIBLE 73:2	
coming of the S. of Man	BIBLE 67:32	
day leichter of a fair s.	ELIZ 205:20	
far too big for his s.	FLEM 215:5	
Fhairshon had a s.	AYT 24:7	
first murd'rer's s.	COWP 167:21	
forth her firstborn s.	BIBLE 69:9	
gallows and did bear our s.	KYD 306:7	
gave his only begotten S.	BIBLE 71:38	
'I am the S. of Man'	AUDEN 21:7	
Jesus Christ his only S.	PRAY 384:26	
Kiss the S.	PRAY 389:19	
knowledge of the S. of God	BIBLE 77:28	
My s. in tears	GILB 226:7	
My s. is now between nine	YEATS 587:13	
my s., mine own Telemachus	TENN 544:2	
My s. shall not go down	BIBLE 46:35	
only s.	GOLD 232:13	
reputed s. of Coeur-de-Lion	SHAK 452:8	
righteousness unto the King's s.	PRAY 394:18	
rod hateth his s.	BIBLE 53:38	
s. into his bosom creeps	FLET 215:28	
s. of Adam and of Eve	PRIOR 400:25	
s. of a first rate butcher	ASHF 17:12	
s. of a hundred Kings	KIPL 297:24	
S. of man hath not where	BIBLE 65:18	
S. of Morn in weary Night's	BLAKE 86:1	
S. of Saint Louis	FIRM 212:2	

spoken unto us by his S.	BIBLE 79:28	
Take now thy s.	BIBLE 46:9	
This is my beloved S.	BIBLE 63:40	
This my s. was dead	BIBLE 70:21	
this the carpenter's s.	BIBLE 66:22	
thou s. of Belial	BIBLE 50:24	
two-legged thing, a s.	DRYD 194:7	
unto us a s. is given	BIBLE 58:7	
what's a s.	KYD 306:6	
whom if his s. ask bread	BIBLE 65:4	
wise s. maketh a glad	BIBLE 53:29	
wonderful s.	SHAK 434:17	
worthy to be called thy s.	BIBLE 70:19	
younger s. gathered all	BIBLE 70:18	
your s.'s tender years	JUV 288:7	
song: after all an earthly s.	TENN 536:31	
all this for a s.	BURL 112:15	
antique s. we heard last night	SHAK 488:26	
becomes a sightless s.	TENN 537:19	
despise the skylark's s.	BRON 93:13	
Ditto ditto my s.	GILB 226:17	
forth her s. in perfect calm	AUDEN 18:3	
Glorious the s.	SMART 509:4	
goodly manor for a s.	SHAK 421:2	
great *Venite* change the s.	DONNE 189:3	
have I to spur me into s.	YEATS 586:23	
Hear a s. that echoes cheerly	TENN 538:5	
hear but their low lone s.	CARP 132:34	
his presence with a s.	PRAY 396:11	
if such holy s.	MILT 344:11	
I have a s. to sing	GILB 229:8	
I made my s. a coat	YEATS 584:16	
Is the burden of my s.	ANON 6:13	
I the s.	GILB 225:34	
joyful S. I'll raise	ADD 2:20	
let satire be my s.	BYRON 124:15	
loves shall moralize my s.	SPEN 515:29	
main region of my s.	WORD 577:8	
my Reputation for a S.	FITZ 213:13	
my s. comes native with	KEATS 292:5	
oaten stop, or pastoral s.	COLL 158:17	
old s. made by an aged	ANON 4:19	
One grand sweet s.	KING 296:19	
Only in you my s. begins	SIDN 507:24	
'Pipe a s. about a Lamb	BLAKE 87:24	
required of us then a s.	PRAY 399:3	
sans S.	FITZ 212:18	
Short swallow-flights of s.	TENN 536:20	
silence was the s. of love	ROSS 409:24	
sing me a bawdy s.	SHAK 440:3	
s. as a weasel sucks	SHAK 425:15	
s. charms the sense	MILT 346:19	
S. made in lieu of many	SPEN 515:27	
s. of songs	BIBLE 56:15	
S. that should spur you	SWIN 530:22	
s. the Syrens sang	BROW 97:14	
s. too daring	PRIOR 400:22	
s. was wordless	SASS 414:17	
s. well sung	MAS 333:21	
start a s. and to respond	VIRG 560:3	
subject will I frame my s.	CHES 145:7	
suffering what they teach in s.	SHEL 501:11	
sung as it were a new s.	BIBLE 82:15	
swear to the truth of a s.	PRIOR 400:20	
sweetest passage of a s.	MEYN 338:13	
sword he sung a s. of death	BLAKE 86:7	
That is the s. that never	GOET 230:2	
that s. to-night	SHAK 476:26	
that thinks two notes a s.	DAV 172:14	
thee with the breeze of s.	TENN 537:4	
there's ane end of ane old s.	OGIL 364:21	
this s. is consider'd a perfect gem		
	CALV 127:11	
this subject for heroic s.	MILT 349:9	
this the burthen of his s.	BICK 84:1	
Time is our tedious s.	MILT 344:15	
unto the Lord a new s.	PRAY 391:19	
unto the Lord a new s.	PRAY 396:7	
weigh this s. with	YEATS 585:8	
when this s. is sung	WYATT 583:23	

You have heard the s. — KIPL 300:23
songe: apparié notre vie à un s. — MONT 355:5
elles s. — CHAU 144:17
songes: He koude s. make and wel — CHAU 141:12
songs: all their s. are sad — CHES 146:17
Are summer s. for me — SHAK 491:17
Book of S. and Sonnets here — SHAK 469:3
cannot sing the old s. — CALV 127:13
cannot sing the old s. — CLAR 152:23
desires and sombre s. — SWIN 528:26
ever piping s. for ever new — KEATS 291:6
Fair the fall of s. — STEV 523:1
Go, s. — THOM 548:3
harsh after the s. of Apollo — SHAK 457:20
Heine for s. — BROW 100:18
hymns and spiritual s. — BIBLE 78:5
I have s. of my own — VIRG 560:7
I wrote my happy s. — BLAKE 87:25
matchless s. does meditate — MARV 332:12
Our sweetest s. are those — SHEL 504:23
Piping s. of pleasant glee — BLAKE 87:24
Sing no sad s. for me — ROSS 409:8
s. beguile your pilgrimage — FLEC 214:9
S. consecrate to truth — SHEL 505:6
S. may inspirit us — BROW 102:6
s. never heard before — HOR 260:13
s. that I made for thee — BRID 92:21
Sussex s. be sung — BELL 40:11
their dirty and dreary — BROO 94:27
Their lean and flashy s. — MILT 343:13
Their s. were Ave Marys — CORB 162:15
them fruit for their s. — ADD 2:5
to make s. — BELL 40:15
us one of the s. of Sion — PRAY 399:3
Where are the s. of Spring — KEATS 293:7
songstress: sober-suited s. — THOM 549:12
sonitu: s. quatit ungula campum — VIRG 559:7
sonne: brighte s. loste his hewe — CHAU 142:13
'most sheene is the s. — LANG 309:28
seson whan soft was the s. — LANG 309:22
unseren Platz an der S. — BULOW 106:23
Up roos the s. — CHAU 142:21
sonnet: elegy, and s. — JOHN 280:9
it turned to a S. — DOBS 187:14
Scorn not the S. — WORD 582:14
s. is a moment's monument — ROSS 409:21
S.'s scanty plot of ground — WORD 582:8
sonneteer: some starv'd hackney s. — POPE 378:25
sonneter: am sure I shall turn s. — SHAK 456:19
sonnets: Rafael made a century of s. — BROW 102:28
s. turn'd to holy psalms — PEELE 371:8
written s. all his life — BYRON 122:27
Sonorous: S. metal blowing martial — MILT 345:20
sons: God's s. are things — MADD 326:19
Had I as many s. as I have — SHAK 463:10
If I had a thousand s. — SHAK 442:16
patient s. before me stand — GOLD 231:27
s. and your daughters shall — BIBLE 61:15
s. of God came in unto — BIBLE 45:33
s. of God came to present — BIBLE 52:5
s. of God shouted for joy — BIBLE 53:3
that Abraham had two s. — BIBLE 77:16
That our s. may grow up — PRAY 390:19
Their s., they gave — BROO 94:7
things are the s. of heaven — JOHN 281:6
soon: Come s., soon — SHEL 505:4
sooner: make an end the s. — BACON 26:6
no s. looked but they loved — SHAK 426:27
s. every parts breaks up — AUST 22:13
soong: s. the service dyvyne — CHAU 141:15
soot: in s. I sleep — BLAKE 88:5
sooth: charms to s. a savage breast — CONG 160:14
it is silly s. — SHAK 489:3
soothe: s. or wound a heart that's — SCOTT 416:23

to s. thine ear — COLL 158:17
soothed: s. the griefs of forty — MAC 324:18
sooty: guardage to the s. bosom — SHAK 473:22
sophist: Be neither saint nor s.-led — ARN 13:1
Dark-brow'd s. — TENN 541:25
self-torturing s. — BYRON 120:36
sophistry: nothing but s. and illusion — HUME 267:15
wits to s. and affectation — BACON 28:12
Sophocles: that S. is the most perfect — COL 158:6
Sophonisba: S.! Sophonisba — THOM 549:25
Sops: S. in wine — SPEN 517:3
sorcerers: s., and whoremongers — BIBLE 83:3
Sordello: can but be the one 'S.' — POUND 382:6
may hear S.'s story told — BROW 105:11
Who would has heard S.'s — BROW 105:16
sore: bear with a s. head — MARR 331:4
perfectly s. with loving her — DICK 178:1
s. let and hindered — PRAY 386:6
s. throats are always worse — AUST 23:9
sores: full of s. — BIBLE 70:28
sorrel: growth of meadow-sweet or s. — SWIN 528:25
sorrow: ate his bread in s. — GOET 230:12
by the fireside with S. — SHEL 504:25
forgather wi' S. and Care — BURNS 113:4
From the sphere of our s. — SHEL 504:14
Give s. words — SHAK 462:16
hairs with s. to the grave — BIBLE 46:35
heart hath 'scap'd this s. — SHAK 494:14
In s. thou shalt bring — BIBLE 45:21
knowledge increaseth s. — BIBLE 55:9
Labour without s. is base — RUSK 412:3
Lycidas your s. is not dead — MILT 343:17
memory a rooted s. — SHAK 463:3
more in s. than in anger — SHAK 430:11
not be in s. too — BLAKE 88:8
Nought but vast s. was there — DE L 174:5
parting is such sweet s. — SHAK 482:20
Pure and complete s. — TOLS 551:13
Regions of s. — MILT 344:25
Since s. never comes too — GRAY 235:13
sin could blight or s. — COL 156:18
so beguile thy s. — SHAK 486:16
Some natural s. — WORD 578:15
s. and sighing shall flee — BIBLE 59:1
S. and silence are strong — LONG 316:13
s. dogging sin — HERB 248:10
s. enough in the natural — KIPL 302:3
sorrow like unto my s. — BIBLE 60:28
s., need — PRAY 387:16
s. Of each day's growing — DU M 199:6
S. proud to be exalted — ANON 6:7
S.'s most detested fruit — BYRON 120:28
S. so royally in you appears — SHAK 442:24
s.'s tribute to the passing — CAT 137:15
s. than to recall a time — DANTE 171:8
s., wilt thou live — TENN 536:33
S., with her family — SHEL 499:9
swift joy and tardy s. — THOM 548:3
That a s.'s crown of sorrow — TENN 538:20
then but labour and s. — PRAY 395:19
Then glut thy s. on a morning — KEATS 291:15
think is to be full of s. — KEATS 291:19
this s.'s heavenly — SHAK 477:5
thou climbing s. — SHAK 453:24
To S., I bade — KEATS 289:5
'-triumph and s. for angels — BROW 102:7
useless and hopeless s. — JOHN 281:27
We are not sure of s. — SWIN 529:24
Write s. on the bosom — SHAK 479:10
sorrowful: desire of such as be s. — PRAY 385:22
He went away s. — BIBLE 67:10
laughter the heart is s. — BIBLE 54:1
much to say as a s. birth — MAL 327:17
This way for the s. city — DANTE 171:3

sorrowing: was standing the s. Mother — JAC 270:31
sorrows: carried our s. — BIBLE 59:21
costly in our s. — STER 519:12
engluts and swallows other s. — SHAK 473:23
losses are restor'd and s. — SHAK 493:7
man of s. — BIBLE 59:21
shall my s. have an end — ANON 5:19
s. of women would be averted — ELIOT 200:24
s. of your changing face — YEATS 587:12
Then all my s. are — GAY 222:16
There are few s. — SMITH 510:12
transient s., simple wiles — WORD 581:8
When s. come — SHAK 436:4
sorry: may do that I shall be s. — SHAK 451:19
out and I was never s. — HOUS 264:4
s. for these our misdoings — PRAY 387:19
s. Scheme of Things — FITZ 213:16
sort: all the s. of person you — CARL 131:1
is a s. of treason — BURKE 110:9
see a s. of traitors here — SHAK 480:4
sortem: nemo, quam sibi s. — HOR 261:21
sorts: s. and conditions of men — PRAY 385:24
sory: with s. grace — CHAU 143:7
sospetto: e sanza alcun s. — DANTE 171:9
sot: as has married a s. — POUND 382:5
Un s. savant est sot plus — MOL 353:12
sothfastnesse: dwelle with s. — CHAU 144:21
souffrances: majesté des s. humaines — VIGNY 557:1
souffre: s. et meurs sans parler — VIGNY 557:2
souffrons: mais s. sur les cimes — HUGO 267:10
sought: By night on my bed I s. — BIBLE 56:25
Come, long-s. — SHEL 505:3
He s., For his lost heart — SHEL 504:5
I s. them far and found — HOUS 265:6
lack of many a thing I s. — SHAK 493:7
less often s. than found — BYRON 125:12
Love s. is good — SHAK 489:25
never have s. the world — JOHN 279:4
s. the Lord aright — BURNS 113:6
They s. with thimbles — CARR 133:8
to those men that s. him — SHAK 447:21
soul: accomplished is sweet to the s. — BIBLE 53:37
am the captain of my s. — HENL 245:5
art pouring forth thy s. — KEATS 291:22
assault and hurt the s. — PRAY 386:9
Be still, my s. — HOUS 264:3
bit of FIAT in my s. — BEDD 36:25
bitterness of my s. — BIBLE 59:3
bitterness of his s. — BIBLE 62:26
blind his s. with clay — TENN 542:19
Call to the s. when man — VAUG 555:21
call upon my s. within — SHAK 488:13
catch my flying s. — POPE 376:14
chosen thus to fling his s. — HARDY 239:7
city of the s. — BYRON 121:9
clothing for the s. divine — BLAKE 85:14
composed in the s. — ARN 16:9
Conceptions equal to the s.'s — WORD 577:15
confident concerning his s. — SOCR 512:19
Could swell the s. to rage — DRYD 195:8
deep dim s. of a star — SWIN 530:8
Did this s.'s second inn — DONNE 190:1
fancied that I gave a s. — YEATS 585:20
fine point of his s. taken — KEATS 293:14
five windows of the s. — BLAKE 85:23
fool, this night thy s. — BIBLE 70:5
freed his s. the nearest — JOHN 279:1
Full soon thy S. shall — WORD 579:8
God the s. — POPE 379:10
half conceal the S. within — TENN 535:34
half the little s. is dirt — TENN 540:23
haughtiness of s. — ADD 1:18
have felt my s. in a kiss — SWIN 530:21
have given my s. for this — SWIN 530:20
Heart and s. do sing — SIDN 508:1
Heaven take my s. — SHAK 452:29
he had a little S. — MOORE 357:3

Her lips suck forth my s. MARL 329:10
he shall save his s. alive BIBLE 60:35
hides a dark s. MILT 341:8
house of a brute to the s. TENN 532:22
hurl my s. from heaven SHAK 477:21
hushed Casket of my S. KEATS 292:29
if his eager s. FULL 220:19
if I have a s. ANON 7:5
I gave you your own s. SHAW 496:30
I had a s. above buttons COLM 159:4
I have freed my s. BERN 41:24
In books lies the s. CARL 131:34
iron entered into his s. PRAY 397:3
iron enter into his s. STER 519:8
I the stature of my s. MER 337:8
I think nobly of the s. SHAK 490:21
knock and enter in our s. BROW 99:4
lay perjury upon my s. SHAK 468:4
leave my s. in hell PRAY 390:7
leaves s. free BROW 99:2
life unto the bitter in s. BIBLE 52:14
lift my s. to heaven SHAK 446:27
limed s. SHAK 434:28
little s. for a little SWIN 530:9
Lord have mercy on your s. CHAP 140:1
lose his own s. BIBLE 66:35
lose his own s. BIBLE 68:34
loves and saves her s. BROW 99:6
man became a living s. BIBLE 45:7
man loved the pilgrim s. YEATS 587:12
mellow horn her pensive s. COLL 158:21
merciful to a s. of this gentleman's ANON 10:14
Merry of s. he sailed STEV 523:4
mighty s. was prov'd ADD 1:13
mind and s., according TENN 535:32
most comprehensive. was DRYD 198:2
My s. he doth restore again SCOT 419:5
My s. in agony COL 155:20
My s. into the boughs does MARV 332:6
my s. is white BLAKE 88:2
My s., like to a ship WEBS 567:13
My s.'s in arms CIBB 151:13
my unconquerable s. HENL 245:4
night of the s. it is always three o'clock FITZ 213:22
No coward s. is mine BRON 93:18
nor the prophetic s. SHAK 494:21
not thy s. unto a woman BIBLE 62:29
of the sinews of the s. FULL 220:17
Perdition catch my s. SHAK 475:14
Poor intricated s. DONNE 190:25
pray the Lord my s. to keep ANON 7:3
pray the Lord my s. to take ANON 7:3
progress of a deathless s. DONNE 189:34
purest essence of a human s. CARL 132:29
purest s. that e'er was CAREW 130:17
Rest of their bones and s.'s DONNE 189:5
Revolving in his alter'd s. DRYD 195:4
seek the hurt of my s. PRAY 393:22
sigh'd his s. toward SHAK 468:13
Since my dear s. was mistress SHAK 434:1
so longeth my s. after PRAY 392:6
s. and God stand sure BROW 104:9
S. clap its hands and sing YEATS 586:12
s. doth magnify the Lord BIBLE 69:5
s. fleeth unto the Lord PRAY 398:24
s. has to itself decreed KEATS 292:7
s. is an enchanted boat SHEL 503:11
s. is dead that slumbers LONG 317:1
s. is form SPEN 516:28
s. is not more than WHIT 571:3
s. of Adonais SHEL 500:1
s. of a martyr with BAG 29:17
s. of fire JOHN 282:30
s. of her beauty and love SHEL 503:23
s. of our dear brother PRAY 389:13
s. of Philip Sparrow SKEL 508:19
s. of Rabelais dwelling COL 158:2
s. of reading STER 519:22

S. of the Age JONS 284:19
s. of the same stature MONT 354:12
s.'s dark cottage WALL 562:9
S. selects her own Society DICK 183:21
s. shall taste the sadness KEATS 291:15
s. Smoothed itself out BROW 101:24
s. that God forgot HOUS 264:27
S. that rises with us WORD 579:5
S., the body's guest RAL 404:10
S., thou hast much goods BIBLE 70:4
s. to feel the flesh BRON 93:21
s., uneasy POPE 379:5
s. were in my soul's stead BIBLE 52:28
subject's s. is his own SHAK 444:22
suffers the s. may not profit MER 337:28
sweet and virtuous s. HERB 248:17
taught my s. to fancy aught VAUG 555:14
that might create a s. MILT 341:14
This s. should fly from MARL 329:14
Thou art a s. in bliss SHAK 455:25
thou hast delivered my s. PRAY 397:20
'tis my outward s. DONNE 188:27
To wake the s. by tender POPE 375:11
try the s.'s strength BROW 101:14
tumult, of the s. WORD 578:2
two to bear my s. away ANON 6:15
unmakes but to remake the s. BROW 104:33
vale of S.-making KEATS 294:19
Variety is the s. of pleasure BEHN 38:16
Was not spoken of the s. LONG 317:1
waters to a thirsty s. BIBLE 54:30
What fortitude the S. contains DICK 183:18
What s. was his WORD 577:10
which the s. of man is fed MAS 333:26
which war against the s. BIBLE 80:24
whole s. thro' My lips TENN 533:16
whom shall my s. believe BROW 104:7
Whose s. was sad GILB 229:9
Why shrinks the s. ADD 1:24
with her own little s. BETJ 42:9
written three books on the s. BROW 100:5
yet my s. drew back HERB 247:25
soule: to yiue his s. good reste LYDG 321:6
soules: our s. for to beye CHAU 144:19
souls: awkward thing to play with s. BROW 102:3
damp s. of housemaids ELIOT 203:27
depart the s. of the brave CLOU 153:13
division 'tween our s. SHAK 451:29
find rest unto your s. BIBLE 66:5
good morrow to our waking s. DONNE 188:30
guts should hale s. SHAK 472:15
harmony is immortal s. SHAK 468:15
Have ye s. in heaven too KEATS 290:31
instinct of all great s. BURKE 109:8
letters mingle s. DONNE 189:22
Most people sell their s. SMITH 510:14
nor s. to be condemned THUR 550:32
numberless infinities Of s. DONNE 189:3
Our s. exult BLAKE 86:12
patience possess ye your s. BIBLE 71:5
poor jewel of their s. STEV 521:2
poor s. who dwell in Night BLAKE 85:18
Shepherd and Bishop of your s. BIBLE 80:27
s. descend T'affections DONNE 188:25
s. did never kiss and greet KEATS 289:3
s. have sight of that immortal WORD 579:12
s. most fed with Shakespeare's CHES 147:1
s. mounting up to God ROSS 409:18
S. of poets dead and gone KEATS 290:28
s. of the righteous are BIBLE 62:13
s. of women are so small BUTL 118:18
s. with but a single thought HALM 238:10
they have no s. COKE 154:24
Through such s. alone BROW 104:27
times that try men's s. PAINE 368:1
Two s. dwell GOET 229:30
two virtuous s. for life BYRON 123:19
Upon their spotted s. SHAK 479:9
we wish our s. to be SHEL 501:10

When they corrupt the s. ARN 13:22
Where s. do couch on flowers SHAK 423:10
Which sucks two s. DONNE 188:20
whilst our s. negotiate DONNE 188:23
soul-sides: Boasts two s. BROW 102:36
sound: all is not s. JONS 283:27
call him up the S. NEWB 361:7
every s. is sweet TENN 542:17
form of s. words BIBLE 79:23
full of s. and fury SHAK 463:6
hear the s. of the cornet BIBLE 61:3
is the s. of the trumpet BIBLE 53:7
Like the s. of a great Amen PROC 401:14
Making it momentany as a s. SHAK 469:20
measures Of delightful s. SHEL 504:24
mind in a s. body JUV 288:4
My love to thee is s. SHAK 457:16
of a s. mind BIBLE 79:22
other not very s. SMOL 512:12
sighing s. ROSS 410:8
silence where hath been no s. HOOD 255:11
something direful in the s. AUST 22:18
s. and rumour MORR 358:7
s. is dissonant which tells COL 157:12
s. is forc'd BLAKE 88:10
sound is the s. of the sea ELIOT 204:13
s. must seem an echo POPE 378:22
s. of abundance of rain BIBLE 51:10
s. of broken glass BELL 40:5
s. of revelry by night BYRON 120:20
s. of shallow foppery enter SHAK 466:13
that s. awakes my woes BURNS 113:22
Their s. is gone out into PRAY 390:1
though the s. were parted JONS 285:10
tombs a doleful s. WATTS 565:28
trumpet give an uncertain s. BIBLE 76:15
twelve great shocks of s. TENN 533:22
what is that s. which so AUDEN 20:4
will hear the lowest s. SHAK 457:8
With a dead s. on the final ELIOT 204:21
you would s. me from my SHAK 434:20
sounded: trumpets s. for him BUNY 107:38
sounding: I am become as s. brass BIBLE 76:14
Went s. WORD 577:10
soundless: tears on a s.-clapping host THOM 547:24
sounds: concord of well-tuned s. SHAK 492:25
Her sights and s. BROO 94:30
let the s. of music SHAK 468:15
S. and sweet airs SHAK 485:17
s. will take care of themselves CARR 134:7
with concord of sweet s. SHAK 468:15
soup: gentleman has s. at luncheon CURZ 170:18
get into the s. in Ireland WAUGH 566:1
licked the s. from BROW 103:15
S. of the evening CARR 134:17
take the nasty s. away HOFF 252:11
soupe: Je vis de bonne s. MOL 353:10
sour: fathers have eaten s. grapes BIBLE 60:34
How s. sweet music is SHAK 480:15
Lofty and s. to them that SHAK 447:21
s. grapes and ashes ASHF 17:14
s., sober beverage BYRON 122:26
tongue the taste is s. HOUS 266:6
source: Lord is the s. of my light BIBLE 83:5
S. of all things SMART 509:1
s. of innocent merriment GILB 227:5
Tell it to forget the s. MER 337:3
Variety's the s. of joy GAY 223:23
sourest: things turn s. by their deeds SHAK 494:15
souri: pleuré, Voltaire a s. HUGO 267:13
sourire: larme divine et de ce s. HUGO 267:13
South: beaker full of the warm S. KEATS 291:18
fierce and fickle is the S. TENN 542:5
flying S. TENN 542:5
go s. in the winter ELIOT 204:18

long to the sun and the s. SWIN 530:13
nor yet from the s. PRAY 394:26
rivers in the s. PRAY 398:17
S. to the blind Horn's KIPL 300:24
South Africa: S., renowned both far
CAMP 128:13
Southampton: weekly from S. KIPL 300:7
South Country: great hills of the S.
BELL 40:9
southern: bore me in the s. wild BLAKE 88:2
Grow to some S. tree HARDY 239:9
South Kensington: at Sloane Square
and S. GILB 226:14
Southron: matches of the S. folk
THOM 547:24
southward-facing: fringes of a s. brow
ARN 14:21
south-wind: world-wide whisper of the
s. TENN 538:24
souvent: *L'amour? Je le fais s.* PROU 401:22
Sovereign: bandy civilities with my S.
JOHN 275:20
servants of the s. or state BACON 26:21
s. good of human nature BACON 27:31
S. has BAG 29:3
s. of sighs and groans SHAK 456:26
Subject and a S. are clean CHAR 140:19
subject and what to be a s. ELIZ 206:3
that he will have no s. COKE 154:16
Whoso has sixpence is s. CARL 132:14
sovereynetee: 'Wommen desiren to have
s. CHAU 143:24
Soviet: Communism is S. power plus
LENIN 313:22
sow: Ireland is the old s. that JOYCE 286:16
observeth the wind shall not s. BIBLE 56:7
right s. by the ear HENR 246:3
S. an act READE 405:4
sower went forth to s. BIBLE 66:16
s. that hath overwhelm SHAK 441:3
they s. not BIBLE 64:28
They that s. in tears PRAY 398:17
sower: s. went forth to sow BIBLE 66:16
soweth: whatsoever a man s. BIBLE 77:19
sown: It is s. in corruption BIBLE 76:27
nor was ever s. TRAH 551:18
Poets that are s. By Nature WORD 577:9
They have s. the wind BIBLE 61:11
where thou hast not s. BIBLE 68:3
Ye have s. much BIBLE 62:2
sownes: s. ful of hevenyssh melodie
CHAU 144:18
sows: s. hurry and reaps STEV 522:5
space: annihilate but s. and time POPE 380:22
is a s. of life between KEATS 288:19
me more than time and s. LAMB 307:26
myself a king of infinite s. SHAK 432:13
vast s. he fills BURKE 109:5
spaces: great open s. MARQ 330:23
me with their empty s. FROST 219:3
spade: boldly nominate a s. JONS 284:13
cultivated entirely by the s. MILL 339:16
fiddle, sir, and s. SCOTT 418:6
if you don't call me s. SWIFT 526:32
poor crooked scythe and s. SHIR 507:2
s. is never so merely FRY 220:6
S.! with which Wilkinson WORD 583:3
Write with your s. CAMP 128:11
Spades: Let S. be trumps POPE 381:5
S. take up leaves FROST 219:4
s., the emblem of untimely COWP 167:16
Spain: are the galleons of S. DOBS 187:10
like slow old tunes of S. MAS 333:17
plateau of S. forming a head HARDY 239:13
spak: carl s. oo thing CHAU 142:15
Frenssh she s. ful faire CHAU 141:15
spake: God s. all these words BIBLE 47:24
God s. once PRAY 393:20
s. in time past BIBLE 79:28
s. wisely, and could have BIBLE 63:4

span: Contract into a s. HERB 248:6
Less than a s. BACON 28:15
life's a pain and but a s. DAV 172:11
Spaniards: S.' Dispatch ROCH 407:5
S. seem wiser than they BACON 27:14
to thrash the S. too DRAKE 193:2
spaniel: base s. fawning SHAK 449:24
Hound or s. SHAK 455:1
spaniel'd: hearts That s. me SHAK 423:5
Spanish: he cannot speak S. LEAR 311:24
I must learn S. BROW 100:28
person in the S. cape ELIOT 204:15
some are fond of S. wine MAS 333:20
S. sailors with bearded LONG 316:22
'S. ships of war TENN 542:21
taken by a S. Ga-la-lee BALL 31:2
To God I speak S. CHAR 140:31
spans: narrow measure s. HOUS 265:13
spar'd: have better s. a better man
SHAK 440:25
spare: bread enough and to s. BIBLE 70:19
S. all I have FARQ 210:10
s. bed for my friends PEPYS 372:17
s. that tree MORR 358:6
s. the beechen tree CAMP 128:17
s. their women for Thy BETJ 43:5
S. the poet for his subject's COWP 164:29
s. time and in his working GILL 229:11
s. your country's flag WHIT 571:17
to s. those who have submitted VIRG 559:1
spared: honour and life have been s.
FRAN 218:1
s. these minor monuments BROW 97:12
troubles you are yourself s. LUCR 320:6
spares: man that s. these stones SHAK 495:22
spareth: s. his rod hateth BIBLE 53:38
spark: shows a hasty s. SHAK 451:24
s. from heaven to fall ARN 14:15
s. of inextinguishable SHEL 505:10
s. o' Nature's fire BURNS 113:20
Vital s. of heav'nly flame POPE 376:3
waitest for the s. from heaven ARN 14:17
Sparkle: S. for ever TENN 541:30
s. out among the fern TENN 532:20
They s. still the right SHAK 457:9
sparkles: cup but s. near the brim
BYRON 120:19
sparks: like s. among the stubble BIBLE 62:14
painted with unnumber'd s. SHAK 449:25
s. fly upward BIBLE 52:17
sparrer-grass: en I bless ef 'taint s.
HARR 242:14
sparrow: I once had a s. alight THOR 550:21
Lesbia with her s. MILL 339:29
My lady's s. is dead CAT 136:22
providence in the fall of a s. SHAK 437:15
soul of Philip S. SKEL 508:19
s. fall POPE 379:4
s. hath found her an house PRAY 395:11
s.: that sitteth alone PRAY 396:12
sparrows: more value than many s.
BIBLE 65:37
s. from outside flew very BEDE 37:1
s. sold for a farthing BIBLE 65:35
s. sold for two farthings BIBLE 70:3
spars: Under the s. of which HERR 250:14
Spartan: remnant of our S. dead
BYRON 123:2
Spartans: praiseworthy amongst the S.
SPEN 514:33
S. on the sea-wet rock HOUS 265:3
tell the S. SIM 508:9
sparwe: was and lecherous as a s.
CHAU 142:4
spat: you s. on me Wednesday SHAK 466:3
spawn: meanest s. of Hell TENN 538:13
spawn'd: Some report a sea-maid s.
SHAK 464:19
spawning: formless s. fury YEATS 587:2

Spayne: make castels thanne in S.
CHAU 144:1
speak: Books will s. plain BACON 25:39
did he stop and s. to you BROW 102:15
duty to s. one's mind WILDE 573:7
friend or child I s. ARN 13:8
grief that does not s. SHAK 462:16
he shall s. for himself BIBLE 72:15
I also could s. as ye do BIBLE 52:28
if they s. first CONG 160:1
I'll do't before I s. SHAK 453:5
I only s. right SHAK 451:2
let him now s. PRAY 389:2
'Let us not s. BETJ 43:4
Let us not s. of them DANTE 171:4
lips are now forbid to s. BAYLY 35:10
men shall s. well of you BIBLE 69:20
mute and will not s. a word SHAK 484:8
neither s. they through PRAY 397:18
one that can s. so well MASS 335:23
permitted unto them to s. BIBLE 76:16
province of knowledge to s. HOLM 253:20
ride, and s. the truth BYRON 124:10
slow to s. BIBLE 80:10
speak, and to s. well JONS 285:3
s. as the common people ASCH 17:4
s. in Caesar's funeral SHAK 450:17
s. in our tongues the wonderful BIBLE 73:23
S. less than thou knowest SHAK 453:15
S., Lord BIBLE 49:36
S. low, if you speak love SHAK 472:6
S. not when the people SCOTT 418:5
S. now HOUS 263:17
s. of eternity without BROW 96:10
S. of the moderns without CHES 145:20
S. roughly to your little CARR 133:26
'S. softly and carry a big ROOS 408:1
S. the speech SHAK 433:16
S. to Him thou for He hears TENN 533:29
s. to the wise PIND 373:14
S. unto us smooth things BIBLE 58:26
s. very well in the House of Commons
DISR 187:4
S. what we feel SHAK 456:13
s. when he is spoken STEV 522:17
'S. when you're spoken CARR 136:8
S. ye comfortably to Jerusalem BIBLE 59:4
that dare not s. its name DOUG 191:4
they never s. well of one JOHN 276:17
they s. with their enemies PRAY 398:19
those that are asleep to s. BIBLE 57:10
To s. and purpose not SHAK 453:5
unable to s. a word ELIOT 204:4
What should we s. SHAK 428:15
when I s. unto them therof PRAY 398:8
when I think, I must s. SHAK 426:9
When you s. SHAK 491:27
Whereof one cannot s. WITT 575:17
which it is difficult to s. BURKE 110:30
women to s. in the church BIBLE 76:17
word wad ane o' them s. BALL 30:21
would not cease to s. COWP 168:18
You were better s. first SHAK 426:22
speaker: No other s. of my living
SHAK 447:23
speakers: you imperfect s. SHAK 458:12
speaketh: heart the mouth s. BIBLE 66:9
he s. of his own BIBLE 72:13
he s. things not to be BIBLE 63:4
speaking: adepts in the s. trade CHUR 148:27
By drowning their s. BROW 103:15
heard for their much s. BIBLE 64:23
In s. for myself SHAK 473:24
s. in a perpetual hyperbole BACON 26:29
S. to yourselves in psalms BIBLE 78:5
Without s. to me PREV 400:17
speaks: her foot s. SHAK 487:13
He s. to Me as if I was VICT 556:19
he s. very shrewishly SHAK 488:9
No man s. concerning another JOHN 278:22

she never s. well of me   CONG 160:17
She s. poniards   SHAK 472:8
s. small like a woman   SHAK 469:2
When he s.   SHAK 443:6
when Love s.   SHAK 457:8
worst s. something good   HERB 247:12
spear: Bring me my s.   BLAKE 86:16
His s., to equal which   MILT 345:12
idle s. and shield   MILT 344:6
knappeth the s. in sunder   PRAY 392:21
spear-men: stubborn s. still made
                               SCOTT 417:24
spears: stars threw down their s. BLAKE 87:16
teeth are s. and arrows   PRAY 393:15
their s. into pruninghooks   BIBLE 57:19
their s. was like stars   BYRON 122:1
your pruninghooks into s.   BIBLE 61:16
special: s. grace preventing PRAY 386:10
s. receipt of his own   DU M 199:5
specialists: All other men are s.
                               DOYLE 192:21
speciality: short notice was her s. SAKI 413:5
species: female of the s. is more KIPL 299:4
specimen: only s. of Burke is HAZL 243:9
specimens: s., the lilies of ambition
                               DOUG 191:8
spectacle: great s. of human happiness
                               SMITH 511:29
s. unto the world   BIBLE 75:33
spectacles: s. of books to read Nature
                               DRYD 198:2
What a pair of s. is here   SHAK 487:11
without a pair Of s.   HOFF 252:20
With s. on nose and pouch   SHAK 425:24
spectantia: Omnia te adversum s. HOR 258:11
spectare: magnum alterius s. laborem
                               LUCR 320:6
Spectat: S. et audit   CAT 137:4
spectator: s. of mankind than as one ADD 2:8
spectators: actors or s.   SHEL 499:13
Spectatress: S. of the mischief which
                               ROWE 410:23
Spectatum: S. veniunt   OVID 366:10
spectem: Te s.   TIB 550:34
spectre: dancing s. seems the moon
                               MER 337:13
s. of Communism   MARX 333:2
spectre-thin: s., and dies KEATS 291:19
speculations: s. upon matter are voluntary
                               JOHN 281:32
wrung from s. and subtleties   BROW 96:18
speech: aspersion upon my parts of s.
                               SHER 506:13
Consul's s. was low   MAC 322:14
could well itself with S.   TENN 536:14
deal by s. than by letter   BACON 26:37
False are attributes of s.   HOBB 251:13
freedom of s. and expression   ROOS 407:26
freedom of s.   TWAIN 554:7
have strange power of s.   COL 155:29
I am slow of s.   BIBLE 47:9
judgement and the code of s.   HOR 257:14
loath to cast away my s.   SHAK 488:10
make a s.   AUBR 17:27
manner of his s.   SHAK 421:34
neither s. nor language   PRAY 390:11
nor power of s.   SHAK 451:2
Our concern was s.   ELIOT 202:25
perfect plainness of s.   ARN 16:13
Speak the s.   SHAK 433:16
s. created thought   SHEL 503:8
s. in that victorious brow   ARN 14:24
S. is human   CARL 131:39
S. is often barren   ELIOT 201:2
S. is shallow as Time   CARL 131:13
S. is silvern   CARL 132:23
S. is the small change   MER 338:2
s. only to conceal their   VOLT 561:4
s. than to give evidence   HAL 237:23
s. they have resolved not   ELIOT 200:24

stately s.   WORD 581:1
Thy s. bewrayeth thee   BIBLE 68:19
thy s. is comely   BIBLE 56:26
tongue blossom into s.   BROW 99:24
true use of s. is not so   GOLD 232:5
verse is a measured s.   BACON 24:23
your s. be alway with grace   BIBLE 78:28
speeches: to men's charitable s. BACON 28:14
speechless: great persons' graves is s.
                               DONNE 190:23
grey-grown s. Christ   SWIN 529:3
speech-making: subject for practising
s.   JUV 288:2
speed: Deliberate s.   THOM 548:9
forgetting the bright s.   ARN 15:1
our safety is in our s.   EMER 207:33
quench its s. i' the slushy   BROW 102:14
s. the going guest   POPE 380:6
s. the parting guest   POPE 380:25
s. was far faster than   BULL 106:22
time shall teach me s.   SHAK 452:26
speek: shall s. of the somwhat CHAU 144:6
spell: foreigners always s. better TWAIN 554:9
Thy s. through him   ROSS 410:2
Who lies beneath your s.   HOPE 256:3
you s. it with a "V   DICK 182:20
speller: He's the wuss| s. I know
                               WARD 564:31
taste and fancy of the s.   DICK 182:20
spells: seldom talismans and s. COWP 167:25
spem: Vitae summa brevis s. HOR 259:14
Spence: ballad of Sir Patrick S. COL 156:6
spend: most of what we yet may s.
                               FITZ 212:18
s. too much time in studies   BACON 27:16
to s. a little less   STEV 521:4
whatever you have, s. less   JOHN 279:2
spende: so wol we s.   CHAU 143:8
spendeth: whatsoever thou s. more
                               BIBLE 69:32
spending: Getting and s.   WORD 582:19
Riches are for s.   BACON 26:9
S. again what is already   SHAK 494:9
Spens: sent it to Sir Patrick S. BALL 31:17
Spenser: little nearer S. BASSE 35:1
Renowned S.   BASSE 35:1
Thee gentle S. fondly led   LAND 309:2
spent: dollars is unwisely s. CARN 132:31
had s. one whole day well   THOM 546:12
I have s. all the money   JOHN 278:31
s. lights quiver and gleam   ARN 13:6
s. the darksome hours   GOET 230:12
That we s.   ANON 7:20
What wee s.   ANON 8:17
sperabitur: superveniet quae non s. hora
                               HOR 258:16
SPERANZA: LASCIATE OGNI S. VOI
CH'ENTRATE   DANTE 171:3
sperare: salus victis nullam s. VIRG 558:7
speraret: nec quid s. habebat VIRG 559:14
speravi: s.: non confundar in aeternum
                               ANON 11:4
spere: holughnesse of the eighthe s.
                               CHAU 144:18
spermatozoa: million million s. HUXL 268:21
Spes: occidit S. omnis   HOR 261:13
spet: s. upon my Jewish gabardine
                               SHAK 466:2
spewed: Sure the poet...s. up a good
                               DRYD 198:12
sphere: s. for Shelley's genius ARN 16:2
their motion in one s.   SHAK 440:22
Yonder starry s.   MILT 348:24
spheres: all the tuned s. SHAK 423:22
Driv'n by the s.   VAUG 555:22
maintain the music of the s.   BROW 96:34
music of forfended s.   PATM 370:7
seems to shake the s.   DRYD 194:24
S. of action   GRAN 234:10
S. of influence   ANON 7:17

spherical: His body is perfectly s.
                               LEAR 311:23
treachers by s. predominance   SHAK 453:11
Sphinx: Although a subtler S. renew
                               SHEL 501:1
Subtle as S.   SHAK 457:8
Spices: No S. wanting   HERR 249:24
that the s. thereof may   BIBLE 56:29
upon the mountain of s.   BIBLE 57:14
spider: of the smallest s.'s web SHAK 481:28
said a s. to a fly   HOW 267:3
s.'s touch   POPE 379:9
spiders: I saw the s. marching through
                               LOW 319:19
they Often have seen s. fly   EDW 200:7
Weaving s. come not here   SHAK 470:12
spider-web: kind of huge s. JAMES 271:11
spies: if we were God's s. SHAK 456:3
Ye are s.   BIBLE 46:34
spill: stone and let them not s. me
                               MACN 326:13
spilt: water s. on the ground BIBLE 50:23
spin: neither do they s.   BIBLE 64:30
you jade, go s.   SCOTT 418:36
spindle-guide: From coupler-flange to
s.   KIPL 301:2
spinis: iuvat s. de pluribus una HOR 259:6
spinnage: world of gammon and s.
                               DICK 177:12
spinner: stoppeth the s.'s cunning
                               POUND 382:9
Till the S. of the Years   HARDY 239:6
spinners: Hence you long-legg'd s.
                               SHAK 470:12
waggon-spokes made of long s.' legs
                               SHAK 481:28
spinning: candle-light at evening s.
                               RONS 407:12
Spins: S. like a fretful midge ROSS 409:17
spinsters: s. and the knitters SHAK 489:3
spirantia: Excudent alii s. mollius VIRG 559:1
spires: City with her dreaming s. ARN 15:4
from all her reeling s.   MAC 322:2
Ye distant s.   GRAY 235:9
Spirit: be filled with the S. BIBLE 78:5
Blessed are the poor in s.   BIBLE 64:6
Brutus' will start a s.   SHAK 448:18
cabin'd ample S.   ARN 14:6
Curbing his lavish s.   SHAK 458:5
day an unaccustom'd s.   SHAK 483:23
Eternal s. of the chainless   BYRON 125:14
fair s. for my minister   BYRON 121:21
fruit of the S. is love   BIBLE 77:18
genuine s. of localism   BORR 90:2
given us the s. of fear   BIBLE 79:22
God is a S.   BIBLE 71:40
great s. gone   SHAK 421:18
Hail to thee, blithe S.   SHEL 504:15
hands I commend my s.   BIBLE 71:14
hands I commend my s.   PRAY 391:11
haughty s. before a fall   BIBLE 54:8
he that ruleth his s. than   BIBLE 54:9
history of the human s.   ARN 16:17
I go bound in the s. unto   BIBLE 74:18
immortal s. must endure   ARN 14:24
Is a bold s. in a loyal   SHAK 478:8
is the s. that quickeneth   BIBLE 72:8
least erected S. that fell   MILT 345:26
light of thy Holy S.   PRAY 386:24
Love is a s. all compact   SHAK 495:19
meek and quiet s.   BIBLE 80:28
motions of his s. are dull   SHAK 468:17
never approached my s.   METT 338:10
nimble, stirring s.   SHAK 457:14
no more s. in her   BIBLE 50:32
no s. can walk abroad   SHAK 429:17
o'er the s. of my dream   BYRON 124:13
of God is a troubled s.   PRAY 393:8
of kin to God by his s.   BACON 25:25
Of s. so still and quiet   SHAK 473:24

Pipe to the s. ditties KEATS 291:4
praise for the s. of heaviness BIBLE 60:9
present in s. BIBLE 75:34
quick s. that is in Antony SHAK 448:9
received the S. of adoption BIBLE 75:8
renew a right s. PRAY 393:6
retentive to the strength of s. SHAK 449:3
same S. BIBLE 76:13
save the s. of man BYRON 120:2
shall I go then from thy S. PRAY 399:5
slumber did my s. seal WORD 581:10
something to the s. of liberty BURKE 109:18
s. giveth life BIBLE 77:4
s. hath rejoiced in God BIBLE 69:5
s. indeed is willing BIBLE 68:15
S. in the inner man BIBLE 77:24
s. is the true self CIC 151:24
s. like a charmed bark SHEL 500:16
S. of Delight SHEL 503:25
s. of Elijah doth rest BIBLE 51:23
S. of God moved upon BIBLE 44:22
s. of health or goblin SHAK 430:24
s. of the Lord shall rest BIBLE 58:9
S. of the Lord God is upon BIBLE 60:8
s. of the time shall teach SHAK 452:26
s. of youth in everything SHAK 494:17
S. on the Lord's day BIBLE 81:11
s. passed before my face BIBLE 52:15
s. shall return unto God BIBLE 56:11
s. that always denies GOET 230:1
S. that strove For truth SHEL 504:5
Spirit the things of the S. BIBLE 75:7
spirit to retain the s. BIBLE 55:25
s. when her spirit looked ROSS 409:22
s. within nourishes VIRG 558:24
S. with Spirit can meet TENN 533:29
s., yet a woman too WORD 581:8
stablish me with thy free S. PRAY 393:6
stab my s. broad awake STEV 523:11
strength of his s. won through LUCR 320:3
strike with our s.'s knife SHEL 499:20
strongest and the fiercest S. MILT 346:7
take not thy holy S. from PRAY 393:6
that I will pour out my s. BIBLE 61:5
that to break a man's s. SHAW 496:15
there is a s. in the woods WORD 578:20
this body did contain a s. SHAK 440:24
Thy s. walks abroad SHAK 452:3
vanity and vexation of s. BIBLE 55:8
When the unclean s. is BIBLE 66:13
whether a good s. or a bad AUBR 18:2
Wild S., which art moving SHEL 502:8
With too much s. to be POPE 377:21
worship him in s. and in truth BIBLE 71:40
wounded s. who can bear BIBLE 54:13
yet a s. still WORD 581:8
spirits: choice and master s. SHAK 450:8
day of s. VAUG 555:12
drooping s. can raise COWL 164:12
footfalls Of s. SHEL 502:7
Giving heed to seducing s. BIBLE 79:13
He maketh his angels s. PRAY 396:18
her wanton s. look out SHAK 487:13
I can call s. from SHAK 439:23
jump with common s. SHAK 466:19
Other s. there are standing KEATS 292:24
our own s. are we deified WORD 580:28
our s. rush'd together TENN 538:18
seven s. more wicked BIBLE 66:14
s. are enslaved which serve SHEL 503:9
s. of just men BIBLE 80:2
S. overwrought WORD 580:18
s. when they please MILT 345:15
thy haunts two kindred s. KEATS 292:20
Would ruffle up your s. SHAK 451:3
spiritu: Et cum s. tuo MASS 334:11
spiritual: inward and s. grace PRAY 388:19
Millions of s. creatur MILT 348:6
nothing in s. things DONNE 191:2
some such other s. liquor BYRON 126:7

s. wickedness in high places BIBLE 78:10
spirituality: There is a s. about DOYLE 192:20
Spiritum: Et in S. Sanctum MASS 334:20
spiritus: dum s. hos regit artus VIRG 558:13
Sancte S. LANG 309:29
spiro: Quod s. et placeo HOR 261:1
spit: My friend may s. upon my HERB 248:15
s. in my face SHAK 439:2
Surely to s. there glorifies BROW 106:1
spite: beating myself for s. SIDN 507:17
by favour, or by s. POPE 378:32
civic slander and the s. TENN 537:15
may then grow wise for s. SWIFT 527:21
s. of all their friends LEAR 312:7
spits: critic s. on what is done HOOD 255:14
Spitzbübin: S. war sie HEINE 244:10
spleen: excite your languid s. GILB 227:23
mind's wrong biass, s. GREEN 235:28
splendeat: Purpureus, late qui s. HOR 257:11
splendid: our s. isolation GOSC 233:3
s. and a happy land GOLD 231:5
s. in the morning glows FLEC 214:11
s. ship BRID 92:19
Splendide: S. mendax et in omne virgo HOR 261:2
splendidly: Empire stands s. isolated FOST 217:17
splendour: more-than-oriental-s. KIPL 304:19
Not in lone s. hung aloft KEATS 292:11
Of s. in the grass WORD 579:13
s. among shadows SHEL 504:5
s. falls on castle walls TENN 541:32
s. of Ionian white ELIOT 205:4
s. of its prime SHEL 501:2
Stung by the s. of a sudden BROW 100:9
splenetive: though I am not s. and rash SHAK 437:7
split: an' 'E won't s. on a pal KIPL 305:11
downright inhuman to s. it up TWAIN 554:24
s. the ears of the groundlings SHAK 433:16
to make all s. SHAK 469:26
Spohr: With S. and Beethoven GILB 227:6
spoil: company, hath been the s. SHAK 440:2
household divided the s. PRAY 394:8
s. it by trying to explain SHER 506:20
'To come and s. the fun CARR 135:4
when they divide the s. BIBLE 58:6
spoiled: content with what we s. OWEN 367:11
nearly s. ta Flood AYT 24:7
s. the women's chats BROW 103:13
they s. the Egyptians BIBLE 47:20
though s. i' the breeding BROME 93:12
spoilers: them into the hands of s. BIBLE 49:6
spoils: divideth his s. BIBLE 69:36
s. the child and spares HOOD 254:19
s. the singing of the nightingale KEATS 289:8
Stretched out on the s. SWIN 529:20
Then s. were fairly sold MAC 322:18
victor belong the s. MARCY 328:21
spoke: less he s. PUNCH 402:25
S. in her cheeks DONNE 189:31
spoken: days s. unto us by his Son BIBLE 79:28
excellent things are s. PRAY 395:15
Lord hath not s. by me BIBLE 51:20
mouth of the Lord hath s. BIBLE 59:5
possible to the s. one CONN 161:11
Rome has s. AUG 22:2
speak when he is s. STEV 522:17
'Speak when you're s. CARR 136:8
that never have s. yet CHES 147:15
When the lips have s. SHEL 501:21
word fitly s. BIBLE 54:26
you've s. the foremost word BALL 31:1
sponge: city state of the s. AUDEN 20:15
will be married to a s. SHAK 465:25
spongy: s. April at thy hest betrims SHAK 485:19
spoonful: s. for each man of us PAIN 367:16

spoons: faster we counted our s. EMER 207:8
had better count your s. SMITH 510:15
let us count our s. JOHN 275:1
No better than s. FROST 219:4
world locks up its s. SHAW 497:30
sport: animals never kill for s. FROU 219:17
Caesar bleed in s. SHAK 450:5
Detested s. COWP 167:6
had ended his s. with Tess HARDY 241:25
it's the s. of kings SURT 525:4
make s. for our neighbours AUST 23:20
ribs was s. for ladies SHAK 424:23
s. of kings DAV 172:7
s. of kings SOM 513:2
S. that wrinkled Care derides MILT 342:15
They kill us for their s. SHAK 455:9
To s. with Amaryllis MILT 343:8
To s. would be as tedious SHAK 438:13
what sort of s. has Lord ANON 8:15
sported: by him s. on the green SOUT 513:14
sporting: s. prints in the hall AUDEN 21:1
sportive: not shap'd for s. tricks SHAK 480:18
sports: mixt in all our simple s. TENN 537:8
mountainous s. girl BETJ 43:20
play Her cruel s. SPEN 516:24
s. of love JONS 285:12
they excel in athletic s. DISR 186:21
sportsman: fit to be called a s. SURT 525:5
spot: each one s. shall prove KIPL 303:16
It was a sumpshous s. all ASHF 17:10
Out, damned s. SHAK 462:20
s. on your skin is a shocking AUDEN 18:8
s. that's always barred GILB 227:7
there is no s. in thee BIBLE 56:27
Tip me the black s. STEV 521:22
with a s. I damn him SHAK 451:9
spotless: merits of a s. shirt TENN 540:23
unblemished life and s. HOR 259:23
spots: leopard his s. BIBLE 60:22
spotted: s. snakes with double tongue SHAK 470:11
s. souls for this offence SHAK 479:9
wants to have been s. VIRG 559:18
spouse: my sister, my s. BIBLE 56:28
shuts the s. Christ home HOPK 256:29
spout: cataracts and hurricanoes, s. SHAK 454:4
spouts: at his trunk s. out a sea MILT 349:1
s. the grateful liquors POPE 381:6
sprang: I s. to the stirrup BROW 101:12
sprats: open the kegs of salted s. BROW 103:15
sprawled: We s. through the ooze SMITH 510:10
spray: chafe and toss in the s. ARN 13:5
pinkly bursts the s. BETJ 43:12
thy hand a wither'd s. ARN 14:15
spread: I have s. my dreams under YEATS 585:9
I would s. the cloths under YEATS 585:9
net is s. in the sight BIBLE 53:14
not good except it be s. BACON 27:12
s. her conquests farther BURNS 112:37
s. yourselves SHAK 469:24
Spreading: S. ruin and scattering BROW 98:6
Sprechen: S. ist silbern CARL 132:23
Wovon man nicht s. kann WITT 575:17
spree: Gentleman-rankers out on the s. KIPL 299:10
sprightly: s. running could not give DRYD 195:27
spring: Almighty lovers in the s. CHES 146:18
apparell'd like the s. SHAK 478:2
(As if one master-s. controll'd COWP 167:15
azure sister of the s. SHEL 502:8
Blossom by blossom the s. SWIN 528:3
By chilly finger'd s. KEATS 289:6
can S. be far behind SHEL 502:14
Come were but the S. ROSS 409:10
commonly called the s. COWP 168:2

deep of the Pierian s. — DRAY 193:15
every winter change to s. — TENN 536:26
faded has no second s. — PHIL 373:9
Falsehood has a perennial s. — BURKE 109:4
flower of roses in the s. — BIBLE 63:27
flowers that bloom in the s. — GILB 227:13
Fresh s. — SHEL 501:15
garden and a s. — HOR 262:9
happy as birds in the s. — BLAKE 87:20
heart be full of the s. — SWIN 530:12
hounds of s. are on winter's — SWIN 528:15
I been absent in the s. — SHAK 494:17
lap of the new come s. — SHAK 480:11
less quick to s. again — ARN 15:9
messenger of S. — SPEN 515:16
more business in s. — TWAIN 554:23
perennial s. of all prodigality — BURKE 110:16
rifle all the breathing s. — COLL 158:16
smiling face a dream of S. — COL 157:14
S. a young man's fancy lightly — TENN 538:17
S. comes slowly up this — COL 156:2
s. from the pages into — WHIT 570:13
s., full of sweet days — HERB 248:16
S. is come home with her — THOM 548:4
S., nor Summer beauty — DONNE 188:7
s. of Bandusia — HOR 261:3
S. restores balmy warmth — CAT 137:2
s. shut up — BIBLE 56:28
S., sing — ELIOT 203:16
s. the herald of love's — SPEN 515:19
S., the sweet spring — NASHE 360:9
suddenly was changed to S. — SHEL 503:17
Sweet lovers love the s. — SHAK 427:2
that S. should vanish with — FITZ 213:15
There had made a lasting s. — SHAK 447:3
They call it easing the S. — REED 405:6
this s. of love resembleth — SHAK 490:33
through till the s. be done — SWIN 530:13
Treasury is the s. of business — BAG 28:22
We have as short a S. — HERR 249:28
Where are the songs of S. — KEATS 293:7
Where smiling s. its earliest — GOLD 230:16
with ever-returning s. — WHIT 571:12
springboard: Not a seat but a s. — CHUR 150:14
springe: woodcock to mine own s. — SHAK 437:19
springes: s. to catch woodcocks — SHAK 430:21
springs: from seventy s. a score — HOUS 262:14
Red strays of ruined s. — SWIN 529:23
Scotia's grandeur s. — BURNS 113:10
sendeth s. into the rivers — PRAY 396:19
s. o' that countrie — BALL 32:6
Where s. not fail — HOPK 256:17
springtide: brings back her old s. — JOHN 273:20
Springtime: Merry S.'s Harbinger — FLET 215:21
Sprinkle: S. the quarters — HOUS 264:28
s. the lime like rain — HOUS 265:15
You will s. me with hyssop — BIBLE 83:6
sprite: fleeting, wav'ring s. — HADR 237:9
his clear S. — SHEL 499:5
sprites: have one of s. and goblins — SHAK 491:12
Sprouting: S. despondently at area — ELIOT 203:27
spudding: s. up docks — HARDY 240:19
spue: s. thee out of my mouth — BIBLE 81:20
spumantem: Thybrim multo s. sanguine — VIRG 558:17
spur: Fame is the s. that — MILT 343:8
have I to s. me into song — YEATS 586:23
I have no s. — SHAK 459:6
s. of all great minds — CHAP 140:15
Spurgeon: is haberdasher to Mr S. — BUTL 119:20
Spurn: S. not the nobly born — GILB 226:4
s. thee like a cur out — SHAK 449:24
you s. a stranger cur — SHAK 466:3
Spurning: S. of his stirrups like — CHES 147:3

spy: sent to s. out the land — BIBLE 48:10
squad: Don't let the awkward s. — BURNS 116:9
squadrons: big s. against the small — BUSS 117:7
squalor: cost of the s. and slavery — SHAW 498:23
squander: Then do not s. time — FRAN 218:11
squandering: s. wealth was his peculiar — DRYD 194:15
square: given a s. deal afterwards — ROOS 408:3
himself be given a s. deal — ROOS 408:7
I have not kept the s. — SHAK 422:6
set you s. with Genesis — BROW 99:9
slowly grows a glimmering s. — TENN 542:4
s. on the hypoteneuse — GILB 228:17
s. person has squeezed — SMITH 511:34
s. root of half a number — LONG 317:23
you broke a British s. — KIPL 299:8
squared: Press was s. — BELL 39:6
squares: s. of his mind were empty — AUDEN 19:3
squash: s. is before 'tis a peascod — SHAK 488:9
This s., this gentleman — SHAK 491:10
squattin: 'E'll be s.' on the coals — KIPL 299:19
squawking: seven stars go s. — AUDEN 18:9
squeak: dead Did s. and gibber — SHAK 429:12
until the pips s. — GEDD 223:32
squeaking: s. Cleopatra boy — SHAK 424:3
With shrieking and s. — BROW 103:15
squealing: s. of the wry-neck'd fife — SHAK 466:13
squeeze: madly s. a right-hand foot — CARR 136:7
squeezed: they are going to be s. — GEDD 223:32
squeezing: you in the s. of a lemon — GOLD 232:24
squinch-owl: jay-bird say ter der s. — HARR 242:16
squint: gladly banish s. suspicion — MILT 341:9
squints: s. the eye — SHAK 454:22
squire: Bless the s. and his relations — DICK 176:23
squires: hall the gallant s. of Kent — MAC 322:3
s. ride slowly towards — CHES 147:14
stab: s. my spirit broad awake — STEV 523:11
Stabant: *S. orantes primi transmittere* — VIRG 558:22
Stabat: *S. Mater dolorosa* — JAC 270:31
stabb'd: feeble God has s. me — GAY 222:6
stability: party of order or s. — MILL 339:10
to the s. or enlargement — JOHN 281:7
stable: good horse in the s. — GOLD 232:7
stables: That the s. are the real — SHAW 496:32
stablish: s. me with thy free Spirit — PRAY 393:6
stabs: every word s. — SHAK 472:8
Stace: Lucan, and S. — CHAU 144:17
stacher: s. through — BURNS 113:5
stad: That s. is in perplexyte — WYNT 584:4
stadium: it's no go the s. — MACN 326:8
near the S. are trembly — BETJ 42:16
staff: By his cockle hat and s. — SHAK 435:32
I'll break my s. — SHAK 485:24
s. of faith to walk upon — RAL 404:12
s. Which Art hath lodged — WORD 582:13
thy rod and thy s. comfort — PRAY 390:22
trustest upon the s. of this bruised — BIBLE 51:38
was the very s. of my age — SHAK 466:8
your s. in your hand — BIBLE 47:18
stag: runnable s. — DAV 172:8
s. at eve had drunk his — SCOTT 416:1
stage: All the world's a s. — SHAK 425:24
drown the s. with tears — SHAK 433:1
glory of the Attic s. — ARN 15:10
kingdom for a s. — SHAK 443:3
lags the vet'ran on the s. — JOHN 283:2
On the s. he was natural — GOLD 231:20
shake a s. — JONS 284:22

s. is not frightened — FIEL 211:31
s.'s jewel — JONS 284:2
s. where every man must — SHAK 465:10
to the well-trod s. anon — MILT 342:26
To this great s. of fools — SHAK 455:23
well-grac'd actor leaves the s. — SHAK 480:10
were played upon a s. now — SHAK 490:9
wonder of our s. — JONS 284:19
your daughter on the s. — COW 163:21
stage-coach: found in travelling in a s. — IRV 270:25
s. from London to Oxford — HAZL 243:16
travel faster than a s. — GOLD 232:18
stagger: s. like a drunken man — PRAY 397:10
stagnant: fen Of s. waters — WORD 582:5
stain: I offer'd free from s. — MAC 322:8
is darkening like a s. — AUDEN 21:10
Leave not a s. in thine — BIBLE 63:16
of the world's slow s. — SHEL 499:21
To s. the stiff dishonoured — ELIOT 204:16
which felt a s. like a wound — BURKE 111:10
with no s. She faded — SHEL 499:8
stained: s. with their own works — PRAY 397:6
staineth: stain when heaven's sun s. — SHAK 493:10
stainless: s. gentleman — TENN 535:14
stains: of s. and splendid dyes — KEATS 289:16
S. the white radiance — SHEL 499:26
stair: He's the ruffian on the s. — HENL 245:6
I was going up the s. — MEAR 336:7
place is by a winding s. — BACON 26:26
Staircase: S. wit — DID 184:6
stairs: blood ran down the s. — AUDEN 21:7
cursed and kicked the s. — MILL 339:27
down another man's s. — DANTE 171:17
rotten-runged rat-riddled s. — BROW 102:13
they made a pair of s. — SHAK 426:27
stairway: s. which leads to a dark — CHUR 151:4
stake: deep s. they have in such — BURKE 110:5
I am tied to the s. — SHAK 455:3
persons of some substance and s. — WIND 575:7
recollect...what it is we have at s. — PITT 374:4
yonder like another s. — TWAIN 554:24
stal: out of they s. — CHAU 144:22
stale: Poor I am s. — SHAK 428:11
s., not ripe — POPE 375:20
stalked: s. through the Post Office — YEATS 587:2
stalking: s. in my chamber — WYATT 583:21
stalking-horse: truth serve as a s. to error — BOL 89:16
uses his folly like a s. — SHAK 427:7
stall: have gone to s. and bin — FROST 219:11
stalled: s. ox and hatred — BIBLE 54:6
stalls: Tank come down the s. — SASS 414:12
Stamford-town: Burleigh-house by S. — TENN 539:11
stamp: Christ's s. to boot — HERB 247:9
is but the guinea's s. — BURNS 113:28
s. me back to common — FITZ 213:12
stampa: *e poi roppe la s.* — ARIO 12:2
Stamp'd: S. with the image — TENN 534:17
stamping: s. his foot with anger — FARR 210:28
stand: By uniting we s. — DICK 184:5
casement seen her s. — TENN 538:4
feet shall s. in thy gates — PRAY 398:11
Give me somewhere to s. — ARCH 11:24
Here s. — LUTH 320:16
in this we s. or fall — MILT 348:20
I s. at the door — BIBLE 81:21
no time to s. and stare — DAV 172:17
serve who only s. and wait — MILT 351:10
s. at the latter day — BIBLE 52:31
s. at the window — AUDEN 18:11
S. by thyself — BIBLE 60:13
s. in the holy place — BIBLE 67:29
s. me now and ever in good — JOYCE 286:19
s.. "On my head — DISR 185:32
s. out of my sun a little — DIOG 184:8

s. secure amidst a falling ADD 2:30
s. up for bastards SHAK 453:10
s. up for Jesus DUFF 199:1
strengthen such as do s. PRAY 385:19
that men s. upon SHAK 450:3
who shall be able to s. BIBLE 81:30
who will s. on either hand MAC 322:17
Why s. ye here all BIBLE 67:14
standards: With the s. of the peoples TENN 538:24
standeth: foot s. right PRAY 391:6
help s. in the Name PRAY 398:14
Here she s. by thy side BALL 30:9
standing: green mantle of the s. SHAK 454:23
s. for some false impossible ARN 15:2
s. is slippery BACON 26:23
St Andrews: S. by the Northern Sea LANG 309:17
Stands: S. the Church clock BROO 94:25
When he s. like an Ox KIPL 301:19
stand'st: Thou s. unshook amidst POPE 376:21
stane: put in a heart o' s. BALL 32:3
Stanley: how S. scorns BULW 107:2
staple: than the s. of his argument SHAK 457:10
star: across the reflex of a s. WORD 577:26
bright particular s. SHAK 420:25
Bright s. KEATS 292:11
catch a falling s. DONNE 190:8
constant as the northern s. SHAK 449:25
day s. arise in your hearts BIBLE 80:34
deep dim soul of a s. SWIN 530:8
disposition to the charge of a s. SHAK 453:11
Earth is but a s. FLEC 214:10
eastern s. SHAK 424:14
evening s. MILT 349:26
eve's one s. KEATS 289:33
Fair as a s. WORD 581:6
grapples with his evil s. TENN 537:1
great s. early droop'd WHIT 571:12
Hitch your wagon to a s. EMER 208:8
is a tall ship and a s. MAS 334:4
Knock at a s. with my exalted HERR 248:19
loftiest s. of unascended SHEL 503:12
maidenliest s. in the firmament SHAK 453:11
moist s. SHAK 429:13
named a s. BROW 103:26
name to every fixed s. SHAK 456:15
our life's S. WORD 579:5
prince, out of thy s. SHAK 432:1
seen his s. in the east BIBLE 63:31
s. differeth from another BIBLE 76:26
S. for every State WINT 575:9
s. is called Wormwood BIBLE 82:6
S.-scattered on the Grass FITZ 213:18
s. to every wandering bark SHAK 495:5
Sunset and evening s. TENN 533:3
that bright northern s. LOV 318:13
then there was a s. danced SHAK 472:12
Twinkle, twinkle, little s. TAYL 532:1
vague unpunctual s. BROO 94:19
with one bright s. COL 155:18
zenith like a falling s. MILT 346:3
star-captains: anchored and the young s. FLEC 214:7
Star-Chamber: will make a S. matter of it SHAK 469:1
star-cross'd: s. lovers take their life SHAK 481:20
star-defeated: Spent in s. sighs HOUS 262:21
stare: ground I see thee s. CHAU 143:13
no time to stand and s. DAV 172:17
s. in the basin AUDEN 18:10
With a stony British s. TENN 540:7
staring: they stand s. and looking PRAY 390:20
stark: s. insensibility JOHN 273:27
to-day or Molly S.'s a widow STARK 517:20
Stärkere: S., Sieghaftere, Wohlgemutere NIET 363:2

starlight: Into the frosty s. ARN 14:28
s. lit my lonesomeness HARDY 241:5
there was nae s. BALL 32:6
starlings: patterns a murmuration of s. AUDEN 20:6
starlit: s. or a moonlit dome disdains YEATS 584:12
starry: Shine upon the s. sky BLAKE 86:5
silence that is in the s. WORD 581:11
s. night SHEL 503:26
s. paladin BROW 105:12
Where are those s. woods BRID 92:17
stars: all night by troops of s. COL 156:24
any knight with the s. MER 337:7
Blesses his s. ADD 1:17
branch-charmèd by the earnest s. KEATS 290:5
By s. benign HOUS 265:14
certain s. shot madly from SHAK 470:7
chilly s. I can forgo CORY 163:5
companionless Among the s. SHEL 505:5
crowned with the s. TRAH 551:17
cut him out in little s. SHAK 483:7
eyes were blind with s. HODG 252:8
Fast as the s. are slow THOM 547:20
fleet of s. is anchored FLEC 214:7
floor the new-bathed s. ARN 15:1
forth to see the s. again DANTE 171:14
Hard and high to the s. ANON 10:16
head a crown of twelve s. BIBLE 82:10
heaventree of s. hung with humid JOYCE 286:29
he made the s. also BIBLE 45:3
high it'll strike the s. HOR 259:10
his right hand seven s. BIBLE 81:14
in the shining of the s. TENN 535:19
is not in our s. SHAK 448:17
journey-work of the s. WHIT 570:21
lantern thus close up the s. MILT 341:1
Look at the s. HOPK 256:28
looked up to the S. above LEAR 312:11
merely the s.' tennis-balls WEBS 566:29
mistress of the months and s. SWIN 528:14
moon and the s. PRAY 389:28
morning s. sang BIBLE 53:3
Night with her train of s. HENL 245:8
one the s. LANG 309:21
on s. where no human race FROST 219:3
opposition of the s. MARV 331:19
preserve the s. from wrong WORD 579:16
ready to mount to the s. DANTE 171:15
same bright, patient s. KEATS 290:7
seven s. go squawking AUDEN 18:9
seven s. in the sky ANON 6:5
ships and s. and isles FLEC 214:9
s. above us, govern SHAK 455:12
s.! And all eyes else SHAK 492:10
s. and sunbeams know ARN 14:24
s. are dead AUDEN 20:17
s. are old TAYL 532:2
s. are shining bright SHEL 501:8
s. be blown about the sky YEATS 586:18
s. came otherwise BROW 99:24
s. came out far over TENN 543:2
s. come down from the rafters AUDEN 18:13
s. have not dealt me HOUS 266:7
s. in her hair were seven ROSS 409:14
s. in their courses fought BIBLE 49:9
s. peep behind her SHEL 500:6
s. rush out COL 155:16
s. that reigned at my nativity MARL 329:13
s. threw down their spears BLAKE 87:16
s., Which are the brain MER 337:7
s. with deep amaze MILT 344:7
strives to touch the s. SPEN 517:4
sun and the other s. DANTE 171:18
telleth the number of the s. PRAY 399:19
tell the s. as they rise VIRG 559:1
Tempt not the s. FORD 216:12
that puts the S. to Flight FITZ 212:5

that's the way to the s. VIRG 559:8
then I defy you, s. SHAK 483:24
Two s. keep not their motion SHAK 440:22
us are looking at the s. WILDE 573:11
We should be like s. FRY 219:31
what is the s. OCAS 364:15
whose sight all the s. MILT 347:13
with how splendid s. FLEC 214:21
you chaste s. SHAK 477:5
star-shine: bird-song at morning and s. STEV 522:29
star-showers: Like light dissolved in s. SHEL 504:9
star-spangled: 'Tis the s. banner KEY 295:14
start: Brutus' will s. a spirit SHAK 448:18
stand afraid and s. at us BROW 96:20
s. again at your beginnings KIPL 300:1
s. from their spheres SHAK 431:5
s. of the majestic world SHAK 448:16
Stop it at the s. OVID 366:20
will s. from her slumber ARN 13:7
started: be to arrive where we s. ELIOT 203:2
it s. like a guilty thing SHAK 429:16
s. that morning from Devon GILB 226:14
starting: you mar all with this s. SHAK 462:21
startle: s. Composing mortals AUDEN 18:4
startled: burning fills the s. air BELL 40:7
starts: think by fits and s. HOUS 264:23
Was everything by s. DRYD 194:13
starvation: die of s. NEWM 362:4
starve: bury whom he help'd to s. POPE 376:29
hinders our coming you'll s. KIPL 298:5
s. at door HERB 248:15
s. for want of impudence DRYD 195:38
starved: s. apothecary than a starved LOCK 315:22
starving: you have a s. population DISR 184:12
star-y-pointing: Under a s. pyramid MILT 344:1
state: be no assistant for a s. SHAK 432:3
broken with the storms of s. SHAK 447:15
burden on the reeling s. COWP 165:7
by delaying put the s. ENN 208:22
cipher in the s. SAV 415:5
complicated s. of mind GILB 227:21
defrauding of the S. PENN 371:16
disencumber'd Atlas of the s. COWP 166:16
done the s. some service SHAK 477:23
doth more hurt in a s. BACON 25:43
duty in that s. of life PRAY 388:18
everywhere a s. in which much is JOHN 282:8
falling with a falling s. POPE 375:12
first duty of a S. RUSK 412:6
free church in a free S. CAV 138:1
glories and my s. depose SHAK 479:23
great Sun begins his s. MILT 342:18
I am the S. LOUI 318:8
last s. of that man is BIBLE 66:14
middle age of a s. BACON 27:34
motives not of S. KIPL 302:5
no harm come to the s. ANON 10:10
obscure sequestered s. BROW 104:33
of the sovereign or s. BACON 26:21
O Lord, to what a s. TER 544:20
Predicts the ruin of the s. BLAKE 85:10
Prop and Ruin of the S. CLEV 153:3
Scoffing his s. and grinning SHAK 479:11
scorn to change my s. SHAK 493:6
Ship of S. LONG 316:7
Star for every S. WINT 575:9
S. in wonted manner keep JONS 283:24
s. is a state of Slavery GILL 229:11
S. is not 'abolished' ENG 208:18
S. is real AUDEN 18:19
S. which dwarfs its men MILL 339:15
Then all were for the s. MAC 322:18
To the S.'s mellow forms GREEN 236:1
whole machinery of the S. BROU 95:4

world of pomp and s.   BEAU 36:1
worth of a S.   MILL 339:14
wretched s.   SHAK 434:28
stateliest: Wielder of the s. measure
  TENN 543:18
stately: she is tall and s.   TENN 540:6
S. Homes of England   COW 164:3
s. homes of England   HEM 244:21
s. tents of war   MARL 330:2
would grow great and s.   STEV 522:23
statement: black s. of pistons   SPEN 515:13
Englishman unmoved that s.   GILB 228:23
States: composed of indestructible S.
  CHASE 141:3
debt have been small s.   INGE 270:10
goodly s. and kingdoms seen   KEATS 292:17
In s. unborn   SHAK 450:5
No more slave S.   CHASE 141:2
saved the Union of these S.   WHIT 571:10
S., like men   LAND 309:13
statesman: chemist, fiddler, s.   DRYD 194:13
constitutional s. is   BAG 29:15
of a constitutional s.   BAG 29:16
S., yet friend to truth   POPE 378:6
Too nice for a s.   GOLD 231:17
Statesmen: like great S.   GAY 222:33
station: honour is a private s.   ADD 1:23
It isn't that sort of s.   RATT 405:2
walls of that antique s.   BEER 37:26
stationer: s. says   HEM 245:1
stations: always know our proper s.
  DICK 176:23
statisticians: sit With s.   AUDEN 21:5
statistics: damned lies and s.   DISR 187:7
Proved by s. that some   AUDEN 20:10
thoughts we must study s.   NIGH 363:16
We are just s.   HOR 258:13
Stato: Libera Chiesa in libero S.   CAV 138:1
statua: base of Pompey's s.   SHAK 450:28
statuaries: head which s. loved to copy
  MAC 323:33
statue: Most like a monumental s.   BROW 98:8
s. of the onehandled adulterer   JOYCE 286:25
s. to him under the gallows   SMITH 511:24
that *my* s. should be moved   VICT 556:16
statues: disfigured the public s.   AUDEN 19:2
towers and tombs and s.   FLEC 214:6
We like sepulchral s, lay   DONNE 188:23
With s. on the terraces   KIPL 299:12
stature: add one cubit unto his s.   BIBLE 64:29
increased in wisdom and s.   BIBLE 69:14
Malice is of a low s.   HAL 238:2
shorten I the s. of my soul   MER 337:8
s. of the fulness of Christ   BIBLE 77:28
statutes: s. of the Lord are right   PRAY 390:12
stave: will listen to your s.   SHEL 504:25
staves: thou comest to me with s.   BIBLE 50:12
stay: asking peaple to s. with him   ASHF 17:5
behind my tremulous s.   HARDY 239:1
Can't you s.   VAUG 555:9
care to s. than will   SHAK 483:15
earth's foundations s.   HOUS 265:7
Here I am, and here I s.   MACM 325:17
'S. a little   BACON 26:6
S. for me   SHAK 423:10
will not s. in place   ELIOT 202:17
without thee here to s.   MILT 349:28
Stayed: S. in mid passage his pinions
  SWIN 528:24
s. still with her   DONNE 188:2
staying: Tell the people I'm s.   PEDR 371:4
stays: Everything flows and nothing s.
  HER 246:5
that wears the s.   TENN 540:22
stead: now and ever in good s.   JOYCE 286:19
soul were in my soul's s.   BIBLE 52:28
steadfast: would I were s. as thou art
  KEATS 292:11
steadiness: s. under fire but also   KITC 305:14
Steady: S. the Buffs   KIPL 305:1

thought more s. than an ebbing   FORD 216:20
steaks: smell of s. in passageways
  ELIOT 204:7
steal: Blake is damned good to s.   FUS 220:22
Even s. us from ourselves   DRYD 195:17
most cunningly did s. away   HERB 247:24
mouths to s. away their brains   SHAK 475:9
...or s. one poor farthing   NEWM 362:4
silently s. away   LONG 316:10
S. from the world   POPE 380:24
s. my Basil-pot away from   KEATS 290:12
s. out of your company   SHAK 472:31
s. the bags to hold   ISH 270:27
thieves break through and s.   BIBLE 64:25
Thou shalt not s.   BIBLE 47:24
Thou shalt not s.   CLOU 153:28
to s. a few hours from   MOORE 356:21
to s. away your hearts   SHAK 451:1
to s. bread   FRAN 217:26
will s. the very teeth out   ARAB 11:17
stealing: about the country s. ducks
  ARAB 11:18
hands from picking and s.   PRAY 388:17
hanged for s. horses   HAL 237:22
S. and giving odour   SHAK 487:20
steals: robb'd that smiles s. something
  SHAK 474:3
s. a goose from off a common   ANON 7:24
s. my purse steals trash   SHAK 475:16
stealth: do a good action by s.   LAMB 308:2
Do good by s.   POPE 380:18
lusty s. of nature   SHAK 453:9
Steam: exceptin' always S.   KIPL 301:2
fiery s. issued and came   BIBLE 61:8
Shovelling white s. over   AUDEN 20:1
snorting s. and piston stroke   MORR 358:10
s. spoils romance at sea   KIPL 301:4
steam-engine: He traces the s. always
  DISR 184:17
much like a s. in trousers   SMITH 511:10
steamer: about in a s. from Harwich
  GILB 226:13
Steamers: all you Big S.   KIPL 298:4
Great s.   KIPL 300:7
into coffee on board s.   THAC 545:9
steed: Border his s. was the best   SCOTT 417:8
from a s. flying fearless   LONG 316:26
mounted on her milk-white s.   BALL 32:4
Our s. the leg   SHAK 427:11
set her on my pacing s.   KEATS 290:17
Steed threatens s.   SHAK 444:9
sturdy s. now goes to grass   BEAU 36:7
will I sell my goodly s.   BALL 30:9
steeds: instead of mounting barbed s.
  SHAK 480:18
They'll have fleet s. that   SCOTT 417:14
steel: All shod with s.   WORD 577:25
corse again in complete s.   SHAK 430:24
foeman bares his s.   GILB 228:18
foemen worthy of their s.   SCOTT 416:6
Give them the cold s.   ARM 12:13
is clad in complete s.   MILT 341:10
long divorce of s.   SHAK 446:27
with his brandish'd s.   SHAK 458:3
with more than complete s.   ANON 6:4
wounded surgeon plies the s.   ELIOT 202:21
Steel-true: S. and blade-straight   STEV 523:3
steep: hastens to the monstrous s.
  KEATS 292:6
s. and trifid God   THOM 547:22
s. my senses in forgetfulness   SHAK 441:29
When things are s.   HOR 260:6
steeple: church and no s.   SWIFT 528:11
in his lone religious s.   CAMP 128:10
shadow of the s.   CLOU 153:23
stood, and heard the s.   HOUS 264:28
steeples: In s. far and near   HOUS 263:4
Talk about the pews and s.   CHES 146:11
you have drench'd our s.   SHAK 454:4
steer: ships they s. their courses   BUTL 117:25

s. From grave to gay   POPE 380:3
steersmen: grow good s.   MER 337:20
stehe: Hier s. ich   LUTH 320:16
stelle: disposto a salire alle s.   DANTE 171:15
muove il sole e l'altre s.   DANTE 171:18
uscimmo a riveder le s.   DANTE 171:14
Stellenbosch: fear o' S.   KIPL 303:11
stem: rod out of the s. of Jesse   BIBLE 58:9
s. the torrent of a woman's   ANON 8:20
stenches: counted two and seventy s.
  COL 156:5
step: it is only the first s.   DU D 198:28
one s. enough for me   NEWM 362:14
s. should sound or a word   SWIN 529:18
That's one small s.   ARMS 12:18
To s. aside is human   BURNS 112:25
Stephen Sly: S., and old John Naps
  SHAK 484:3
Stepp'd: in blood S. in so far   SHAK 461:25
steppes: kis the s.   CHAU 144:17
stepping: s. where his comrade stood
  SCOTT 417:24
you are s. westward   WORD 578:12
stepping-stones: s. Of their dead selves
  TENN 535:33
steps: countest the s. of the Sun   BLAKE 87:22
Hear not my s.   SHAK 460:1
her s. take hold on hell   BIBLE 53:20
s. Almost as silent   WORD 580:9
s. of virgin liberty   WORD 581:8
with to support uneasy s.   MILT 345:12
stept: She s. to him   BALL 30:9
sterb: Morgen s.' ich   LESS 313:26
sterbenden: Sakramente einem s. Gotte
  HEINE 244:11
sterile: seems to me a s. promontory
  SHAK 432:15
sterility: Into her womb convey s.
  SHAK 453:18
sterling: I myself a s. lad   HOUS 264:13
stern: is a lantern on the s.   COL 157:20
s. to view   GOLD 231:2
sterner: Ambition should be made of
s. stuff   SHAK 450:19
sternest: thou wert the s. knight   MAL 328:8
steward: commended the unjust s.
  BIBLE 70:25
stewards: Others but s. of their   SHAK 494:15
S. of the mysteries   BIBLE 75:32
Stew'd: S. in corruption   SHAK 435:10
St George: streets leading from S.'s
  BUTL 119:12
stick: he fell like the s.   PAINE 368:2
I shall s.   SHAK 465:2
notch it on my s. too   THOR 550:9
softly and carry a big s.   ROOS 408:1
S. close to your desks   GILB 228:7
sticketh: friend that s. closer   BIBLE 54:14
stiff: Bend what is s.   LANG 310:1
'Keep a s. upper lip'   CARY 136:14
stiffnecked: thou art s. people   BIBLE 48:4
stiffness: too much s. in refusing   PRAY 384:17
stifle: to s. is a false opinion   MILL 339:9
Stiggins: S., Bugg   ARN 15:26
still: At the s. point   ELIOT 202:15
best be s.   ARN 13:14
be s.   PRAY 389:20
Be s., my soul   HOUS 264:3
Be s. then   PRAY 392:21
Duchess of Malfi s.   WEBS 566:24
gars ye rin sae s.   ANON 7:12
he can't Sit s.   MILL 339:25
keep s. with my philosopher   SHAK 454:26
mighty heart is lying s.   WORD 581:15
ship was s. as she could   SOUT 513:28
sound of a voice that is s.   TENN 532:18
S. glides the Stream   WORD 581:4
s., sad music of humanity   WORD 578:7
s. small voice   BIBLE 51:14
s. the wonder grew   GOLD 231:3

S. waters run deep — AUDEN 20:22
thou mightest s. the enemy — PRAY 389:28
Thou wouldst s. be ador'd — MOORE 356:4
waves thereof are s. — PRAY 397:10
Will not stay s. — ELIOT 202:17
Still-born: S. Silence — FLEC 214:24
stilleth: s. the raging of the — PRAY 394:1
stillicide: lone cave's s. — HARDY 239:18
stillness: Achieved that s. ultimately — CRANE 168:30
all the air a solemn s. — GRAY 234:18
do a wilful s. entertain — SHAK 465:12
modest s. and humility — SHAK 443:21
s. first invades the ear — DRYD 195:24
s. of the central sea — TENN 537:20
still-vexed: s. Bermoothes — SHAK 484:27
stilly: in the s. night — MOORE 357:2
s. couches she — HARDY 239:4
Stilton: no end of S. Cheese — LEAR 312:9
Stimulate: S. the phagocytes — SHAW 496:20
sting: death, where is thy s. — BIBLE 77:1
Death, where is thy s. — ROSS 408:20
it is a s. — PEELE 371:7
Thy s. is not so sharp — SHAK 426:1
sting-a-ling-a-ling: where is thy s. — ANON 7:4
stingeth: s. like an adder — BIBLE 54:24
stings: soldiers, armed in their s. — SHAK 443:9
that stinks and s. — POPE 377:1
there were s. in their tails — BIBLE 82:8
wanton s. and motions — SHAK 463:14
stink: That the Jews s. naturally…is — BROW 95:25
stinking: apothecary to send forth a s. savour — BIBLE 56:1
stinks: that s. and stings — POPE 377:1
stipendi: *offrirgli nè onori nè s.* — GAR 221:10
stir: Above the smoke and s. — MILT 340:23
How should we s. ourselves — ANON 8:24
Just to s. things up seemed — SALL 413:23
must s. it and stump it — GILB 228:32
No s. in the air — SOUT 513:28
No s. of air was there — KEATS 290:1
S. up — PRAY 387:2
s. without great argument — SHAK 435:31
To s. men's blood — SHAK 451:2
stirbt: er s. ab — ENG 208:18
stirred: night long we have not s. — BROW 103:30
s. the heart of every Englishman — SCOTT 415:19
stirring: s. times we live — HARDY 241:12
stirrup: Betwixt the s. and the ground — CAMD 128:5
foot already in the s. — CERV 139:2
heard his foot upon the s. — DE L 174:10
I sprang to the s. — BROW 101:12
stirrups: Spurning of his s. like — CHES 147:3
stirs: pulse of feeling s. — ARN 12:22
Stitch: S.! stitch — HOOD 255:6
stitching: s. and unstitching has — YEATS 584:9
stithy: Vulcan's s. — SHAK 434:3
St Ives: S. says the smell of fish — KILV 296:6
St Lawrence: I have seen the S. — BURNS 112:23
stock: see how his s. goes — COL 156:10
Stock Exchange: S. and the solicitors' — SHAW 498:23
stocking: Honey, your silk s.'s — SELL 420:3
Kneeling ne'er spoil'd silk s. — HERB 247:10
stockings: come to her in yellow s. — SHAK 489:17
commended thy yellow s. — SHAK 489:15
did you change your s. — AUST 22:17
his s. foul'd — SHAK 431:28
s. were hung by the chimney — MOORE 355:12
stocks: feet they hurt in the s. — PRAY 397:3
s. in fragrant blow — ARN 15:6
worshipped s. and stones — MILT 351:9
Stoeber: Richard Bentley or Elias S. — HOUS 266:15

Stoic: budge doctors of the S. — MILT 341:16
stoicism: think the Romans call it s. — ADD 1:18
stole: precious diadem s. — SHAK 435:11
They knew 'e s. — KIPL 304:5
wonder where you s. 'em — SWIFT 528:10
stolen: s., be your apples — HUNT 268:11
S. sweets are best — CIBB 151:15
s. the scraps — SHAK 457:12
S. waters are sweet — BIBLE 53:28
They have s. his wits away — DE L 173:26
stoles: nice white s. — BARH 33:12
stol'n: had I s. the whole — STEV 523:6
that has s. the treasure — CONG 160:8
stolzer: *s. Männer der Tat* — HEINE 244:12
stomach: army marches on its s. — ANON 9:3
army marches on its s. — NAP 359:17
burst s. like a cave — DOUG 191:10
hath no s. to this fight — SHAK 445:3
healthy s. is nothing — BUTL 118:31
heart and s. of a king — ELIZ 206:4
man Of an unbounded s. — SHAK 447:18
My s. is not good — ANON 5:21
s., gentlemen, a *stomach* — HUNT 268:16
s. sets us to work — ELIOT 201:4
wine for thy s.'s sake — BIBLE 79:16
stomacher: with the red s. — DONNE 188:19
stomachs: used to march on their s. — SELL 420:7
stone: all was as cold as any s. — SHAK 443:18
are themselves as s. — SHAK 494:15
At his heels a s. — SHAK 435:33
Before some fallen Runic s. — ARN 13:8
brass, nor s. — SHAK 494:4
Can make a s. of the heart — YEATS 585:2
conscious s. to beauty — EMER 206:23
Fling but a s. — GREEN 235:28
Florence blossoming in s. — LONG 316:17
give them the s. — MONT 354:11
jasper and a sardine s. — BIBLE 81:22
last to be a precious s. — HERR 250:2
lay s. on stone — ARN 13:23
let him first cast a s. — BIBLE 72:10
maketh a hole in the s. — LAT 310:20
man a house of good s. — POUND 382:8
mighty angel took up a s. — BIBLE 82:24
not a s. — POPE 380:24
not thy foot against a s. — PRAY 395:20
One s. the more swings — KIPL 301:17
operation for the s. — SMITH 512:2
quiet as a s. — KEATS 289:33
Raise the s. — ANON 7:11
seeth the s. taken away — BIBLE 73:5
S., bronze — ELIOT 202:6
s. of stumbling — BIBLE 58:4
s. once echoed The voice — HARDY 240:4
S. that puts the Stars — FITZ 212:5
s. the twenty-first — BROW 99:25
S. walls do not a prison — LOV 318:18
s. which the builders refused — PRAY 398:2
sword of this s. and anvil — MAL 327:14
take away our hearts o' s. — OCAS 364:17
This precious s. set — SHAK 478:20
Virtue is like a rich s. — BACON 25:26
water hollows out a s. — OVID 366:27
we raised not a s. — WOLFE 576:5
will he give him a s. — BIBLE 65:4
Stone Age: Where a S. people breeds — BETJ 43:8
stoned: once was I s. — BIBLE 77:12
stones: Are there no s. in heaven — SHAK 477:16
chose him five smooth s. — BIBLE 50:11
croys of latoun ful of s. — CHAU 142:7
man that spares these s. — SHAK 495:22
not s., but men — SHAK 450:25
s. and clouts make martyrs — BROW 97:9
s. of Rome to rise — SHAK 451:3
s. prate of my whereabout — SHAK 460:1
s. would immediately cry — BIBLE 71:2
threw words like s. — SPEN 515:11
worshipped stocks and s. — MILT 351:9

stonest: s. them which are sent — BIBLE 67:26
stone wall: Jackson standing like a s. — BEE 37:3
stony: Some fell upon s. places — BIBLE 66:16
s. limits cannot hold love — SHAK 482:10
stood: had s. them on their heads — BARR 34:11
Have s. against the world — SHAK 450:23
I've s. upon Achilles' tomb — BYRON 123:13
should have s. that night — SHAK 455:24
since he s. for England — CHES 146:26
s., and heard the steeple — HOUS 264:28
s. there holding the knife — AUDEN 21:7
ten thousand s. before him — BIBLE 61:8
stool: sit upon a s. for some — DICK 178:27
three-foot s. mistaketh me — SHAK 470:3
stools: first necessity invented s. — COWP 166:28
stoop: Do I s. — BROW 98:34
Stooping: S. through a fleecy cloud — MILT 342:3
stop: Anyone can s. a man's life — SEN 420:11
did he s. and speak to you — BROW 102:15
easy and so plain a s. — SHAK 440:31
first cries out s. thief — CONG 160:8
I could not s. for Death — DICK 183:15
Might s. a hole to keep — SHAK 437:2
oaten s., or pastoral song — COLL 158:17
s. his mouth with a kiss — SHAK 472:11
S. it at the start — OVID 366:20
s. my house's ears — SHAK 466:13
S. thine ear against — SCOTT 418:5
s. to busy fools — VAUG 555:12
then s. everyone from doing — HERB 246:9
when the kissing had to s. — BROW 105:25
stopp'd: Nor s. till where he had — COWP 165:19
stopped: clock has s. in the dark — ELIOT 202:9
you've said can't be s. — HOR 258:6
stoppeth: he s. one of three — COL 155:5
stops: tender s. of various quills — MILT 343:19
would seem to know my s. — SHAK 434:20
store: seen thee oft amid thy s. — KEATS 293:6
spread her wholesome s. — GOLD 230:18
were to increase his s. — HOME 253:22
storehouse: rich s. for the glory — BACON 24:17
Storied: S. of old in high immortal — MILT 341:12
stories: jewels into a garret four s. — BACON 25:7
seaman tells s. of winds — PROP 401:15
tell sad s. — SHAK 479:11
to believe of my own s. — IRV 270:24
With dismal s. — BUNY 107:36
you with s. of savage men — BURKE 109:15
storm: are lost in the s. — ARN 14:9
directs the s. — ADD 1:14
he maketh the s. to cease — PRAY 397:10
locks of the approaching s. — SHEL 502:9
lovers fled away into the s. — KEATS 289:23
Now sinks the s. — GAY 223:8
pelting of this pitiless s. — SHAK 454:15
rides upon the s. — COWP 165:26
S. and stress — KAUF 288:17
s., fulfilling his word — PRAY 399:22
s. has gone over me — BURKE 112:4
s. is coming on the Chiltern — CHES 146:13
s. nor in the strife — BYRON 125:10
when the s. is drawing near — MORR 358:7
storms: all thy waves and s. are — PRAY 392:8
sudden s. are short — SHAK 478:19
Where no s. come — HOPK 256:17
storm-troubled: trembler in the world's s. — BRON 93:18
stormy: s. sturdy band — HARDY 240:16
to scape s. days — DONNE 189:12
story: about you, that s. — HOR 261:22
delicious s. is ripe — AUDEN 20:22
earns a place i' the s. — SHAK 422:18
endeth the s. of the Sangreal — MAL 327:22
may hear Sordello's s. — BROW 105:11
novel tells a s. — FORS 216:24

plot for a short s.	CHEK 145:2
read Richardson for the s.	JOHN 276:9
Shuts up the s. of our days	RAL 404:15
Still is the s. told	MAC 322:23
s. always old and always	BROW 104:20
s. for which the world	DOYLE 192:26
s. is extant	SHAK 434:14
s. of Sussex told	BELL 40:11
teach him how to tell my s.	SHAK 474:1
that the s. need be long	THOR 550:26
to be short in the s. itself	BIBLE 63:29
To tell my s.	SHAK 437:25
would some pretty s. tell	TAYL 531:25
Storys: S. to rede ar delitabill	BARB 33:3
story-teller: thought that a s. is born	STEE 517:22
stout: Athenaeum with jugs of s.	HERB 246:15
'Collapse of S. Party'	ANON 8:10
s. Cortez when with eagle	KEATS 292:18
s. hearts and sharp swords	BIRK 84:14
stoutness: see no objection to s.	GILB 225:32
St Patrick: Wearing, by S.'s bounty	LAND 308:23
St Paul: description of the ruins of S.'s	WALP 563:9
Say I am designing S.'s	BENT 41:9
sketch the ruins of S.'s	MAC 323:16
with S. are literary terms	ARN 16:18
Strachan: waiting for Sir Richard S.	ANON 5:10
strack: s. the top-mast wi' his	BALL 30:19
straddled: s. quite over the whole	BUNY 107:15
Stradivari: Antonio S.'s violins	ELIOT 201:28
Strafford: S., who was hurried hence	CLEV 153:3
straight: crooked shall be made s.	BIBLE 59:5
make his paths s.	BIBLE 63:36
might have grown full s.	MARL 329:16
nothing ever ran quite s.	GALS 220:30
s. in the desert a highway	BIBLE 59:5
s., the brave	HOUS 265:6
street which is called S.	BIBLE 73:35
walked s. out of the Ark	SMITH 511:1
straightway: He goeth after her s.	BIBLE 53:25
strain: no, but s.	HOPK 257:3
sages drop the drowsy s.	COWP 165:3
s. of man's bred	SHAK 486:1
That s. again	SHAK 487:20
to keep the nerves at s.	BROW 102:1
which s. at a gnat	BIBLE 67:24
strains: in that might create	MILT 341:14
s. of unpremeditated art	SHEL 504:15
Such s. as would have won	MILT 343:1
strait: Into a desperate s.	MASS 335:18
S. is the gate	BIBLE 65:7
straitened: s. circumstances at home	JUV 287:18
strait jacket: creed a s. for humanity	MER 337:23
Straits: Outside the Western S.	ARN 14:21
With echoing s. between	ARN 13:12
strand: Come sailing to the s.	BALL 31:20
I walk'd along the S.	JOHN 280:26
knits me to thy rugged s.	SCOTT 416:22
left fair Scotland's s.	BURNS 114:10
on some far northern s.	ARN 13:8
where's the Maypole in the S.	BRAM 91:23
wrote her name upon the s.	SPEN 515:20
strands: these last s. of man	HOPK 256:7
strange: All is s.	JOHN 280:9
be very s. and well-bred	CONG 161:7
everything that looks s.	PEPYS 372:7
hand of s. children	PRAY 399:12
have more cunning to be s.	SHAK 482:14
Into something rich and s.	SHAK 484:32
is not that s.	SHAK 473:2
Jacob from among the s.	PRAY 397:16
man with s. bedfellows	SHAK 485:9

millions of s. shadows	SHAK 493:15
Nature hath fram'd s. fellows	SHAK 465:8
owe this s. intelligence	SHAK 458:13
pair of very s. beasts	SHAK 427:3
passing s. and wonderful	SHEL 500:8
Poverty has s. bedfellows	BULW 107:6
song: in a s. land	PRAY 399:3
s. and sinister embroidered	JAMES 271:15
s. and terrible events	SHAK 423:12
s., and unnatural	SHAK 431:7
s., astonished-looking	HUNT 268:7
s. faces, other minds	TENN 535:24
s. hours and all strange	SWIN 528:26
stranger in a s. land	BIBLE 47:2
S. the difference of men's	PEPYS 371:17
this is wondrous s.	SHAK 431:22
too stubborn and too s.	SHAK 448:10
you lisp and wear s. suits	SHAK 426:20
strange-eyed: s. constellations reign	HARDY 239:9
strangeness: some s. in the proportion	BACON 25:28
stranger: entertain Him always like a s.	ANON 9:1
entertain this starry s.	CRAS 169:7
From the wiles of a s.	NASH 359:18
I was a s.	BIBLE 68:6
Look, s.	AUDEN 20:3
On earth I am a s. grown	BURNS 114:15
s. and afraid	HOUS 264:25
s. here in Gloucestershire	SHAK 478:23
s. in a strange land	BIBLE 47:2
s. that is within thy gates	BIBLE 47:24
S. than fiction	BYRON 124:7
s. to my heart and me	SHAK 453:3
s. to one of your parents	AUST 23:15
that is surety for a s.	BIBLE 53:31
What s.'s feet may find	HOUS 265:10
strangers: all the Athenians and s.	BIBLE 74:11
By s. honour'd	POPE 376:10
desire we may be better s.	SHAK 426:10
forgetful to entertain s.	BIBLE 80:3
gracious and courteous to s.	BACON 26:20
Lord careth for the s.	PRAY 399:18
s. of Rome	BIBLE 73:23
they were s. and pilgrims	BIBLE 79:33
we are s. before thee	BIBLE 51:39
strangest: in did come the s. figure	BROW 103:18
strangled: s. her	BROW 103:29
s. illegitimate child	ARN 15:27
s. in the guts of priests	MESL 338:9
strangling: heart one s. golden hair	ROSS 410:2
Than s. in a string	HOUS 262:17
Strapped: S., noosed	HOUS 264:28
Strasbourg: S., a city still famous	HOUS 266:15
stratagem: take her tea without a s.	YOUNG 587:18
stratagems: Fine nets and s. to catch	HERB 248:10
strathspeys: There's hornpipes and s.	BURNS 113:13
straw: Headpiece filled with s.	ELIOT 203:8
Oft stumbles at a s.	SPEN 517:4
pigmy's s. doth pierce	SHAK 455:20
shall eat s. like the ox	BIBLE 58:11
s. under my knee	DONNE 191:2
Take a s. and throw it	SELD 419:22
Things are but as s. dogs	LAO 310:2
strawberries: I saw good s. in your garden	SHAK 481:4
s. at the mouth of their	ELIZ 205:22
S. swimming in the cream	PEELE 371:9
strawed: where thou hast not s.	BIBLE 68:3
straws: oaths are s.	SHAK 443:20
stray: Did your fancy never s.	GAY 222:21
with me you'd fondly s.	GAY 222:22

strayed: s. from thy ways like lost	PRAY 384:11
Though thou hast surely s.	GILB 228:14
strays: Red s. of ruined springs	SWIN 529:23
streaks: glimmers with some s. of day	SHAK 461:15
stream: cool s. thy fingers wet	ARN 14:14
fishes leap in silver s.	CLARE 152:14
little s. best fits a little	HERR 249:21
mercy Of a rude s.	SHAK 447:9
me rowing against the s.	SCOTT 418:10
purling s.	ADD 2:5
salt weed sways in the s.	ARN 13:6
schoolboys playing in the s.	PEELE 371:9
scooped the brimming s.	MILT 347:25
Still glides the S.	WORD 581:4
s. and o'er the mead	BLAKE 87:26
s. will not run long	BURKE 111:11
That even the gentle s.	SPEN 516:32
they have their s. and pond	BROO 94:10
Streamed: this public Way S.	WORD 582:4
streamers: s. waving in the wind	GAY 223:28
with her fan spread and s.	CONG 160:36
streams: coil of his crystalline s.	SHEL 502:10
eyes the s. of dotage flow	JOHN 283:3
Gilding pale s. with heavenly	SHAK 493:9
gratulations flow in s.	CAREY 130:23
hart for cooling s.	TATE 531:20
more pellucid s.	WORD 578:3
Sleepy with the flow of s.	HOUS 263:18
Stillest s.	COWP 167:29
s. in the desert	BIBLE 58:34
S. like the thunder-storm	BYRON 121:11
strength of the s. that	SWIN 528:16
strebt: so lang er s.	GOET 229:29
strecche: Thanne peyne I me to s.	CHAU 143:5
street: done by jostling in the s.	BLAKE 87:10
inability to cross the s.	WOOLF 576:20
in the long unlovely s.	TENN 536:5
looking in the s.	KIPL 302:22
On the bald s.	TENN 536:6
salmon sing in the s.	AUDEN 18:9
s. and pavement mute	HARDY 240:21
s. of the city was pure gold	BIBLE 82:33
s. were time and he	ELIOT 202:2
s. which is called Straight	BIBLE 73:35
where the long s. roars	TENN 537:20
You've got the key of the s.	DICK 182:37
street-lamp: Half-past one, The s.	ELIOT 204:9
streets: Down these mean s.	CHAN 139:22
lion is in the s.	BIBLE 54:34
not in the s. of Askelon	BIBLE 50:16
s. and lanes of the city	BIBLE 70:12
s. are paved with gold	COLM 158:25
s. were fill'd with joyful	TENN 536:18
s. where the great men	FLEC 214:6
ten thousands in our s.	PRAY 399:13
when night Darkens the s.	MILT 345:18
strength: any man by his great s.	PRAY 391:20
confidence shall be your s.	BIBLE 58:27
do unbend your noble s.	SHAK 460:10
girded himself with s.	PRAY 395:24
give s. unto his people	PRAY 391:12
God is our hope and s.	PRAY 392:19
hath shewed s. with his arm	BIBLE 69:6
His s. the more is	BUNY 107:36
hither in thy hour of s.	WORD 580:5
impulse of thy s.	SHEL 502:12
Its s., and struck	HOUS 264:28
length that tower of s.	TENN 541:8
Let us roll all our s.	MARV 332:20
Lord shall renew their s.	BIBLE 59:10
name is a tower of s.	SHAK 481:12
of the Sun in his s.	BIBLE 44:21
On which all s. depends	SMART 509:1
pleasure in the s. of an horse	PRAY 399:20
rejoiceth in his s.	BIBLE 53:6

studying: been s. how I may compare SHAK 480:13

stuff: bosom of that perilous s. SHAK 463:3
I s. my skin ANON 5:21
man might write such s. JOHN 279:7
should be made of sterner s. SHAK 450:19
s. as great part of Shakespeare GEOR 224:2
s. of life to knit me HOUS 263:16
What s. 'tis made SHAK 465:7
written such volumes of s. LEAR 311:20
stuffe: meane and unrefined s. BRAD 91:15
stuffed: We are the s. men ELIOT 203:8
Stuffs: S. out his vacant garments SHAK 452:20
stultitiam: Misce s. consiliis HOR 261:20
stumbled: I s. when I saw SHAK 455:6
stumbles: Oft s. at a straw SPEN 517:4
stumbling: stone of s. and for a rock BIBLE 58:4
stump: You must stir it and s. GILB 228:32
stumps: He fought upon his s. SHEA 498:29
Stung: S. by the splendour BROW 100:9
stunned: like one that hath been s. COL 156:1
stupefying: strong thick s. incense-smoke BROW 99:14
stupid: s. and brutal in the history BEEC 37:5
this is s. stuff HOUS 264:11
stupidest: their existence the s. party MILL 339:2
stupidity: proof of s. than depravity JOHN 275:33
Such an excess of s. JOHN 275:7
There is no sin except s. WILDE 572:23
With s. the gods themselves SCH 415:10
Stupor: First—Chill—then S. DICK 183:14
sturdy: stormy s. band HARDY 240:16
Sturm: S. und Drang KAUF 288:17
sty: No better than a s. SHAK 423:16
Over the nasty s. SHAK 435:10
Stygian: In S. cave forlorn MILT 342:12
S. smoke of the pit that JAM 271:3
style: grand s. arises in poetry ARN 16:14
honourable s. of a Christian BROW 96:2
how the s. refines POPE 378:25
is the only secret of s. ARN 16:25
le s. est l'homme même BUFF 106:20
Mandarin s. beloved CONN 161:11
of his own towering s. CHES 148:8
simply but with such s. HOR 259:15
S. is the dress of thought WESL 568:25
s. is the man BUFF 106:20
Theirs for their s. I'll read SHAK 493:8
to attain an English s. JOHN 281:38
true definition of a s. SWIFT 526:20
When we see a natural s. PASC 369:4
with his eye on his s. ARN 16:12
would do it in a high s. AUBR 17:27
styles: s. are good save the tiresome VOLT 561:7
stynkyng: s. cod Fulfilled CHAU 143:6
stynte: s. of syngyng by the weye CHAU 143:9
stynteth: That s. first whan she CHAU 144:10
suadere: religio potuit s. malorum LUCR 320:4
Suave: S., mari magno turbantibus LUCR 320:6
suavity: such deceitfulness and s. ELIOT 203:26
subdu'd: My nature is s. SHAK 495:4
subdue: He shall s. the people PRAY 392:23
power To chasten and s. WORD 578:7
s. all things to himself PRAY 389:13
s. it BIBLE 45:6
submitted and to s. the arrogant VIRG 559:1
Subdues: maid S. me SHAK 464:6
subduing: thus conceiving and s. MARL 330:11
subeunt: s. morbi tristisque senectus VIRG 560:16

subiectis: Parcere s. et debellare VIRG 559:1
subject: are s. but eternal Love SHEL 503:10
honour is the s. of my SHAK 448:13
human things are s. to decay DRYD 196:33
Lies the s. of all verse BROW 97:25
severity a serious s. ARN 16:14
S. and a Sovereign are CHAR 140:19
s. and what to be a sovereign ELIZ 206:3
s. of almost equal importance BRAM 91:22
s.'s duty is the king's SHAK 444:22
s. unto the higher powers BIBLE 75:20
this s. for heroic song MILT 349:9
We know a s. ourselves JOHN 276:28
subjection: bring it into s. BIBLE 76:9
in silence with all s. BIBLE 79:9
subjects: greatness on her s.' love PRIOR 401:3
Kings seek their s.' good HERR 249:8
Nor sought of foolscap s. BYRON 123:31
s. are rebels from principle BURKE 111:13
S. still loathe the present HERR 249:16
subjugation: foreign conquest and s. WEBS 566:12
sublime: Howls the s. DICK 179:22
maintain the 's. POUND 383:1
One step above the s. PAINE 367:21
passage is what I call the s. COL 158:7
S. To the Ridiculous GRAH 233:11
s. to the ridiculous NAP 359:11
true pathos and s. BURNS 115:15
We can make our lives s. LONG 317:4
Submerged: This S. Tenth BOOTH 89:22
submission: appetite for s. afterwards ELIOT 201:14
Yielded with coy s. MILT 347:23
submit: Must he s. SHAK 479:15
s. myself to all my governors PRAY 388:16
submitting: by s. sways POPE 377:27
s. the shows of things BACON 24:19
subordinate: much safer to be in a s. THOM 546:9
subordination: s. of one sex to the other MILL 339:18
subscription: to the amount of his s. SURT 525:18
You owe me no s. SHAK 454:5
subsequence: mistake s. for consequence JOHN 273:29
subsist: not s. without Dependance STEE 518:14
subsistence: not any s. without a mind BERK 41:19
S. only increases MALT 328:9
subsisting: soul and human flesh s. PRAY 385:14
substance: body and material s. CARL 131:34
nor dividing the S. PRAY 385:12
persons of some s. and stake WIND 575:7
ruler of all his s. PRAY 397:4
S. from the common Earth FITZ 213:12
s. of his house for love BIBLE 57:12
s. of ten thousand soldiers SHAK 481:16
s. of men which is man SWIN 530:1
s., yet being imperfect PRAY 399:7
What is your s. SHAK 493:15
substances: forms and s. are circumfused WORD 580:19
substitute: I know of no s. whatever JAMES 272:2
substitution: s. of the proletarian LENIN 313:21
subterranean: s. fields WORD 580:23
subtil: full of s. flame BEAU 35:19
serpent was more s. than BIBLE 45:14
subtilty: Thy brother came with s. BIBLE 46:17
subtle: cadence and s. psalm AUDEN 18:3
slipper and s. knave SHAK 474:21
s., sly, and bloody SHAK 481:8
subtleties: airy s. in religion BROW 96:8

Destroyed by s. these women MER 337:16
from speculations and s. BROW 96:18
SUBTOPIA: hope that it will stick—S. NAIRN 359:6
suburb: At the new s. stretched BETJ 42:12
suburban: saintly from the s. AUDEN 19:20
suburbs: In the south s. SHAK 490:4
Silence invaded the s. AUDEN 19:3
s. Of your good pleasure SHAK 449:15
subversion: Gracchi complaining about s. JUV 287:13
subversive: Whatever is funny is s. ORW 365:10
succedaneum: s., and a prop To our WORD 580:16
succeed: If at first you don't s. HICK 251:1
It is not enough to s. VIDAL 556:20
Shall life s. in that it BROW 104:4
shall s. me in my pilgrimage BUNY 107:38
s. without any act of betrayal REN 405:12
succeeded: matter she drove at s. PRIOR 400:7
succeeds: Where he s. CHUR 149:13
success: ecstasy, is s. in life PATER 369:21
fore-brain has been a s. AUDEN 19:10
from which s. is banished STEV 521:1
given me earnest of s. SHAK 458:20
guarantee s. in war CHUR 151:1
mortals to command s. ADD 1:16
of the bitch-goddess S. JAMES 272:3
requisite to s. in life SPEN 514:25
s. and miscarriage are JOHN 274:1
S. is counted sweetest DICK 183:23
These s. encourages VIRG 558:16
to vulgar judgments—s. BURKE 111:27
true s. is to labour STEV 522:9
very lively hope of s. SMITH 511:26
successful: full tide of s. experiment JEFF 272:7
S. crimes alone are justified DRYD 197:3
successor: raree-show of Peter's s. BROW 100:3
succour: comfort and s. all them PRAY 387:16
died to s. me BALL 31:4
such: altogether s. as I am BIBLE 74:28
S. as I am SHAK 467:4
s. as she would become FROST 219:6
S. knowledge is too wonderful PRAY 399:5
suck: Doth s. his sweet LODGE 316:3
Her lips s. forth my soul MARL 329:10
I have given s. SHAK 459:10
S. my last breath POPE 376:31
thereout s. they no small PRAY 394:21
Suck-a-Thumb: To naughty little S. HOFF 252:19
suck'd: s. on country pleasures DONNE 188:29
sucker: s. born every minute BARN 34:6
sucking: s. at the bung MAS 333:21
s. child shall play BIBLE 58:11
you as gently as any s. SHAK 469:30
suckle: To s. fools and chronicle SHAK 474:11
sucklings: babes and s. hast thou ordained strength PRAY 389:28
sucks: s. the nurse asleep SHAK 424:14
weasel s. eggs SHAK 425:21
sudden: splendour of a s. thought BROW 100:9
s. glory arising from some HOBB 251:22
S. she rages GAY 223:8
s. storms are short SHAK 478:18
s. thought strikes me CANN 130:4
'That's rather a s. pull up DICK 182:14
unadvis'd, too s. SHAK 482:16
Suddenly: S., as rare things will BROW 102:29
s. cast down PRAY 392:25
sue: used to s. than to command SCOTT 416:2
sueño: haya el que inventó el s. CERV 138:20
sueños: Aún en s. CALD 127:4
los s., sueños son CALD 127:5

Suez: me somewheres east of S.   KIPL 301:8
suffer: Better one s.   DRYD 194:11
  doth s. a sea-change   SHAK 484:32
  escape than one innocent s.   BLAC 85:6
  Hell I s. seems a Heaven   MILT 347:15
  If s. we must   HUGO 267:10
  living thing to s. pain   SHEL 502:21
  should have courage to s.   TROL 552:19
  s. A man of his place   SHAK 447:24
  s. and die   VIGNY 557:2
  s. a witch to live   BIBLE 47:26
  s. for it   BIBLE 80:26
  S. the little children   BIBLE 68:36
  s. thy foot to be moved   PRAY 398:9
  s. thy Holy One to see   PRAY 390:7
  to make your readers s.   JOHN 281:3
  With those that I saw s.   SHAK 484:23
  ye s. fools gladly   BIBLE 77:10
sufferance: s. is the badge of all   SHAK 466:2
suffer'd: have s. greatly   TENN 543:22
Suffered: S. under Pontius Pilate   PRAY 384:26
  well-greaved Achaeans have s.   HOMER 253:28
suffering: About s. they were never   AUDEN 19:18
  learn in s. what they teach   SHEL 501:13
  majesty of human s.   VIGNY 557:1
  mental s. had been undergone   BUTL 119:12
  ruling few than loved the s.   BENT 41:1
  S. is permanent   WORD 577:2
sufferings: constant in human s.   JOYCE 286:17
  myriad s. for the Achaeans   HOMER 253:26
  patience under their s.   PRAY 386:1
suffer'n: Lounjun 'roun' en s.   HARR 242:21
suffers: does, not s. wrong   SHEL 502:20
  nothing the body s.   MER 337:28
suffice: s. for those who belong   WHIT 571:4
sufficeth: it s. me   MAL 327:20
sufficiency: elegant s.   THOM 549:11
  Our s. is of God   BIBLE 77:4
sufficient: he have s. to finish it   BIBLE 70:14
  perfect, and s. sacrifice   PRAY 387:24
  s. conclusions from insufficient   BUTL 118:26
  S. unto the day   BIBLE 64:32
  whole world is not s.   QUAR 403:9
sufficiently: s. degraded in their own   GILB 226:26
  think you are s. decayed   GILB 227:18
sugar: If sack and s. be a fault   SHAK 439:17
  I must s. my hair   CARR 134:16
  s., and saltness agree   GOLD 231:16
  s. o'er The devil himself   SHAK 433:7
sugared: s. about by the old men   KIPL 303:11
suggestion: s. as a cat laps milk   SHAK 485:6
suicide: arose from the s.'s grave   GILB 227:17
  by s., a bag of gold   BRAM 91:21
  thought of s. is a great   NIET 363:11
suicides: downward lay the huddled s.   PLOM 374:19
suis: Je s. comme je suis   PREV 400:16
J'y s., j'y reste   MACM 325:17
Suisse: point de S.   RAC 404:5
suit: Doesn't seem to s. her notion   GILB 227:3
  moneys is your s.   SHAK 466:3
suitable: no s. material to work   COMP 159:14
suitably: s. attired in leather   HOUS 266:9
suitor: think that you are Ann's s.   SHAW 497:24
suits: Than s. a man to say   HOUS 266:1
  thou whatever s. the line   COL 157:5
  trappings and the s. of woe   SHAK 429:25
suivre: il fallait bien les s.   LEDR 313:6
sukebind: when the s. hangs heavy   GIBB 225:3
sullen: Musing full sadly in his s.   SPEN 516:7
  s. from the suppliant crowd   COWP 168:9
  to cope him in these s.   SHAK 425:3
  you sick or are you s.   JOHN 279:27

sullenness: injury and s. against Nature   MILT 352:10
sulphur: oat-cakes, and s.   SMITH 510:30
sulphurous: s. and thought-executing   SHAK 454:4
Sultan: Sultan after S. with his Pomp   FITZ 212:13
sultry: where the climate's s.   BYRON 122:9
sum: ergo s.   DESC 175:10
  Is s. of nothing   SHAK 467:13
  s. obtained I this freedom   BIBLE 74:21
  s. of human wretchedness   BYRON 125:18
  s. of matter remains exactly   BACON 25:15
  s. of things for pay   HOUS 265:7
Sumer: S. is icumen   ANON 7:18
summer: After s. merrily   SHAK 485:25
  bathing of a s.'s day   WORD 580:7
  compare thee to a s.'s day   SHAK 492:28
  Expect Saint Martin's s.   SHAK 445:18
  first S. month that brings   FITZ 212:10
  hollows crown'd with s. sea   TENN 535:27
  idle hill of s.   HOUS 263:18
  if it takes all s.   GRANT 233:21
  Indian S. of the heart   WHIT 571:20
  lose my heart in s.'s even   HOUS 266:4
  murmur of a s.'s day   ARN 14:11
  must have a villa in s.   MORR 358:3
  out far over the s. sea   TENN 543:2
  parting s.'s lingering   GOLD 230:16
  shall see in a s.'s day   SHAK 469:31
  Singest of s. in full-throated   KEATS 291:17
  Spring, nor S. beauty   DONNE 188:7
  S. afternoon   JAMES 271:30
  s. and winter   BIBLE 45:37
  s., and winter hoar   SHEL 501:15
  s. birdcage in a garden   WEBS 567:2
  s. dies the swan   TENN 543:11
  S. has set in with its   COL 157:27
  s. how it ripened   DONNE 188:9
  s. in England is to have   WALP 563:8
  s. is ended   BIBLE 60:20
  s., quite the other way   STEV 522:16
  S. set lip to earth's bosom   THOM 548:27
  s.'s flower is   SHAK 494:15
  s.'s green all girded   SHAK 492:26
  S.'s joys are spoilt   KEATS 289:30
  s.'s lease hath all too   SHAK 492:28
  s. soldier and the sunshine   PAINE 368:1
  S.s pleasures they are   CLARE 152:16
  sweet as s.   SHAK 447:21
  their lordships on a hot s.   ANON 8:8
  thinking on fantastic s.'s   SHAK 478:17
  This guest of s.   SHAK 459:4
  thy eternal s. shall not   SHAK 492:28
  'Tis S. Time on Bredon   KING 297:21
  'Tis the last rose of s.   MOORE 356:20
  tree in the time of s.   BIBLE 63:27
  us in s. skies to mourn   KEATS 289:8
  waken from his s. dreams   SHEL 502:10
  whether it's winter or s.   CHEK 145:3
  Whether he s. clothe   COL 156:23
  your English s.'s done   KIPL 300:23
summer-night: upon a trancèd s.   KEATS 290:5
summers: forests shook three s.'   SHAK 494:18
  s. in a sea of glory   SHAK 447:9
  thousand s. are over   SWIN 530:12
summertime: In s. on Bredon   HOUS 263:4
summerward: He singeth s.   POUND 383:18
summits: Nations touch at their s.   BAG 29:7
  snowy s. old in story   TENN 541:32
summon: To s. his array   MAC 322:11
summoned: Pearse s. Cuchulain   YEATS 587:2
  S. the Immediate Aid   BELL 39:8
summoners: These dreadful s. grace   SHAK 454:10
summons: heavy s. lies like lead   SHAK 459:14
  That s. thee to heaven   SHAK 460:1
  Upon a fearful s.   SHAK 429:16
Summum: S. bonum   CIC 151:21

sums: exact in s.   BAG 29:11
sun: all the beauty of the s.   SHAK 490:33
  are nothing like the s.   SHAK 495:8
  before you let the s.   THOM 547:10
  best s. we have   WALP 563:5
  black s. of melancholy   NERV 360:26
  blushing discontented s.   SHAK 479:12
  Born of the s. they travelled   SPEN 515:8
  bosom-friend of the maturing s.   KEATS 293:5
  Busy old fool, unruly S.   DONNE 190:11
  clear as the s.   BIBLE 57:5
  climbed towards the s.   CHES 148:7
  Close to the s. in lonely   TENN 533:7
  common s.   GRAY 235:15
  countenance was as the s.   BIBLE 81:14
  countest the steps of the S.   BLAKE 87:22
  Distilled by the s.   HARDY 241:21
  doors against a setting s.   SHAK 486:5
  except their s.   BYRON 122:32
  eyes to behold the s.   BIBLE 56:9
  farthing candle to the s.   YOUNG 587:20
  from the s. Take warmth   GREN 236:15
  front the s. climbs slow   CLOU 154:4
  gallant will command the s.   SHAK 484:13
  give me the s.   IBSEN 269:22
  glorious S. uprist   COL 155:11
  Glorious the s. in mid-career   SMART 509:4
  glory of the s. will be   BALF 30:3
  God-curst s.   HARDY 240:10
  going down of the s.   BINY 84:10
  golden apples of the s.   YEATS 586:21
  great S. begins his state   MILT 342:18
  Hath Britain all the s.   SHAK 428:17
  heaven's glorious s.   SHAK 456:15
  he beheld the s.   WORD 577:10
  he taketh under the s.   BIBLE 55:5
  I am too much i' the s.   SHAK 429:22
  Juliet is the s.   SHAK 482:5
  just as the s. was rising   ANON 5:3
  kind old s. will know   OWEN 367:4
  kiss of the s. for pardon   GURN 237:7
  lands beneath another s.   THOM 549:20
  Laughed in the s.   BROO 94:15
  Let the hot s. Shine on   AUDEN 20:21
  light a candle to the s.   SIDN 507:13
  Linden, when the s. was low   CAMP 128:21
  livery of the burnish'd s.   SHAK 466:6
  loves to live i' the s.   SHAK 425:16
  make our s. Stand still   MARV 332:20
  midnight speak with the S.   VAUG 555:11
  Monday, when the s. is hot   MILNE 340:16
  Move him into the s.   OWEN 367:4
  name shall the S. of righteousness   BIBLE 62:3
  never assisted the s.   THOR 550:10
  new thing under the s.   BIBLE 55:7
  Now the s. is laid to sleep   JONS 283:24
  now the s. is rising   WORD 580:27
  of the S. in his strength   BIBLE 44:21
  our own place in the s.   BULOW 106:23
  out again to feel the s.   BROW 97:35
  quietest places Under the s.   HOUS 264:7
  rain, and s.   TENN 534:2
  run to the rime-ringed s.   KIPL 300:24
  sacred radiance of the s.   SHAK 453:3
  scarce could see the s.   ROSS 409:16
  sea-daisies feast on the s.   SWIN 530:2
  self-same s. that shines   SHAK 492:4
  served up the s. and moon   AUG 21:13
  setting s.   SHAK 478:18
  shall the s. light on them   BIBLE 82:3
  shoots at the mid-day s.   SIDN 507:15
  So when the s. in bed   MILT 344:14
  splendid silent s. with   WHIT 570:3
  summer by this s. of York   SHAK 480:17
  S. and Moon should doubt   BLAKE 85:17
  s. and the other stars   DANTE 171:18
  s. and the rain Clash   FRY 219:26
  s. ariseth   PRAY 397:1
  s. came dazzling thro'   TENN 538:8
  s. came up upon the left   COL 155:7

s. go down upon your wrath	BIBLE 78:1	s. on the garden	MACN 326:15	true remedy for s.	BURKE 109:30
s. had long since	BUTL 118:3	there will be s. later	MACN 326:6	**superstitions:** heresies and to end as s.	
s. has gone	SMITH 510:23	**Sunlit:** cumber S. pallets	HOUS 262:15		HUXL 269:12
s. himself a fair hot wench	SHAK 437:34	**sunnier:** to the s. side of doubt	TENN 532:15	It is one of the s.	VOLT 561:15
S. himself cannot forget	ANON 8:4	**Sunny:** then they called him S. Jim		**superstitious:** all things ye are too s.	
s. In dim eclipse	MILT 345:24		HANFF 238:19		BIBLE 74:12
s. is coming down to earth	MER 337:37	**sunrise:** Lives in Eternity's s.	BLAKE 86:18	he is s. grown of late	SHAK 449:10
s. is lost	DONNE 187:19	to see s. in town and country	STEV 522:2	s. reluctance to sit	JOHN 278:13
s. knoweth his going down	PRAY 397:1	**suns:** light of setting s.	WORD 578:7	were it vastly more s.	NEWM 361:19
s. looked over the mountain's	BROW 103:9	million million of s.	TENN 544:4	**supp'd:** have s. full with horrors	SHAK 463:7
s. my self in Huncamunca's	FIEL 211:34	planets circle other s.	POPE 379:3	**supped:** 'Hobson has s.	MILT 344:16
s. not shining and a look	CHAN 139:20	S., that set	JONS 285:13	**supper:** ate a good s. at night	ANST 11:7
s. of heaven prove a micher	SHAK 439:14	with the process of the s.	TENN 539:2	Baptism, and the S.	PRAY 388:19
s. shall not burn thee	PRAY 398:9	**sunset:** after s. fadeth	SHAK 494:7	eat my s. there	WORD 583:6
s. shines warm	WORD 579:4	beliefs may make a fine s.	MADAN 326:18	Hatim Tai cry S.	FITZ 212:9
S.'s rim dips	COL 155:16	Now the s. breezes shiver	NEWB 361:10	If the s. was to my taste	STER 519:13
S., stand thou still upon	BIBLE 49:4	Pentire in a flood of s.	BETJ 42:17	last sad s. with his own	TENN 534:18
s. to me is dark	MILT 350:16	S. and evening star	TENN 533:3	leaned on his breast at s.	BIBLE 73:18
s. to rise on the evil	BIBLE 64:19	S. divides the sky with	BYRON 121:4	s. as a turnpike through	EDW 200:9
s. was shining on the sea	CARR 135:3	s. of life gives me mystical	CAMP 128:24	**suppliant:** not sullen from the s.	COWP 168:9
swear to a touch o' s.	KIPL 302:21	To sail beyond the s.	TENN 544:3	thus the s. prays	JOHN 283:1
sweetheart of the s.	HOOD 255:4	**sunsets:** Autumn s. exquisitely dying		**supplication:** His s. to the rose	FLEC 214:11
tabernacle for the s.	PRAY 390:11		HUXL 269:1	**supplications:** accord to make our common	
there the unregulated s.	BROO 94:19	**sunset-seas:** cloud-continents of s.	ALDR 3:11	s.	PRAY 385:8
There was s. enough	BETJ 44:13	**sunset-touch:** there's a s.	BROW 99:4	**supplied:** which may be better as	SHAK 424:24
Till the s. grows cold	TAYL 532:2	**sunshine:** broad s. of life	JOHN 278:6	**supply:** just s. and all relation	DONNE 187:19
tired the s. with talking	CORY 163:4	calm s. of the heart	CONS 162:4	**support:** I s. it from the outside	MELB 336:22
to be aweary of the s.	SHAK 463:7	made a s. in the shady	SPEN 516:2	May He s. us all the day	NEWM 362:9
to the s. and the south	SWIN 530:13	s. and with applause	BUNY 107:19	may s. us in all dangers	PRAY 386:1
upon the quick'ning s.	DONNE 188:9	s. is a glorious birth	WORD 578:22	s. Caledonia's cause	BURNS 114:5
when heaven's s. staineth	SHAK 493:10	s. to the sunless land	WORD 577:19	to s. him after	SHAK 485:27
when the rising s. has	VIRG 560:11	**sunt:** after s. aut non sint	CLEM 153:1	want is men who will s.	MELB 336:17
'when the s. rises	BLAKE 88:29	S. lacrimae rerum	VIRG 557:17	what is low raise and s.	MILT 344:12
which never saw the s.	BROW 103:7	**Sun-treader:** S., life and light be		**supporter:** pour s. les maux d'autrui	
whose Candle is the S.	FITZ 213:3		BROW 103:12		LA R 310:9
will be ere the set of s.	SHAK 458:1	**sup:** breakfasted with you and shall s.		**supports:** wretch who s. with insolence	
woman clothed with the s.	BIBLE 82:10		BRUCE 106:2		JOHN 281:15
worship to the garish s.	SHAK 483:7	liveth longest doth but s.	HENS 246:4	**suppose:** best way to s. what may	HAL 238:1
yet I saw no s.	TICH 551:2	**supellex:** quam sit tibi curta s.	PERS 372:29	**supposing:** s. him to be the gardener	
you stand out of my s.	DIOG 184:8	**superbos:** subiectis et debellare s.	VIRG 559:1		BIBLE 73:8
sunbeam: s. in a winter's day	DYER 199:18	**superflu:** Le s., chose très nécessaire		**supposuisse:** Triste caput pedibus s.	
sunbeams: didst the stars and s.	ARN 14:24		VOLT 561:14		OVID 366:22
extracting s. out of cucumbers	SWIFT 526:7	**superfluities:** retrench the s. of mankind		**suprema:** populi s. est lex	CIC 151:19
motes that people the s.	MILT 341:24		GAY 222:24	S. citius solvet amor die	HOR 259:21
what made fatuous s. toil	OWEN 367:5	we must have s.	GAY 223:24	**supreme:** in none s.	ARN 15:11
sunburnt: s. mirth	KEATS 291:18	**superfluity:** barren s. of words	GARTH 221:21	Poetry is the s. fiction	STEV 520:15
Sunday: chicken in his pot every s.		filthiness and s. of naughtiness	BIBLE 80:10	s. power must be arbitrary	HAL 237:19
	HENR 245:13	s. comes sooner by white	SHAK 465:19	**supremum:** diem tibi diluxisse s.	HOR 258:16
Here of a S. morning	HOUS 263:4	**superfluous:** is either s. or hopeless		**suprised:** like a guilty thing s.	WORD 579:10
killing of a mouse on S.	BRAT 91:24		NEWM 362:10	**surds:** full of indices and s.	CARR 134:25
Repentance on a S.	YBAR 584:7	It would be s. in me	ADAMS 1:6	**sure:** joy was never s.	SWIN 529:24
sometimes on a S. evening	ELIOT 201:12	S. lags the vet'ran	JOHN 283:2	Most s. in all His ways	NEWM 362:12
than a rainy S. in London	DE Q 175:1	s. kings for messengers	SHAK 422:15	round world so s.	PRAY 395:24
that calm S. that goes	FLEC 214:10	s. is very necessary	VOLT 561:14	soul and God stand s.	BROW 104:9
Sundays: Pulpits and S.	HERB 248:10	**Superflux:** S. of pain	SWIN 528:13	s., the straight	HOUS 265:6
to begin a journey on S.	SWIFT 526:33	**superior:** I am a most s. person	ANON 7:1	What nobody is s. about	BELL 40:3
sundial: I am a s.	BELL 39:23	notions about a s. power	SWIFT 525:31	**surety:** s. for a stranger shall	BIBLE 53:31
sun-dials: than the mottoes on s.		'S. people never make long	MOORE 355:21	**surfeit:** often the s. of our own	SHAK 453:11
	POUND 383:3	s. to time and place	JOHN 282:7	So s.-swell'd	SHAK 442:30
sundown: s. splendid and serene	HENL 245:9	want no-one to be their s.	TOCQ 551:8	s. by eating of a lamprey	FABY 209:16
sundry: s. and manifold changes	PRAY 386:12	**superiority:** s. of one man's opinion		That suffer s.	SHAK 489:6
sun-flower: s. turns on her god	MOORE 356:5		JAMES 271:28	They are as sick that s.	SHAK 465:19
Where my S. wishes to go	BLAKE 87:22	unfounded airs of s.	WALP 563:21	Where no crude s. reigns	MILT 341:11
sung: ever she s. from noon	MORR 358:13	**super-lizards:** not died out like the s.		**surge:** murmuring s.	SHAK 455:14
He s. of God	SMART 509:1		AUDEN 19:10	suface of thine aëry s.	SHEL 502:9
it has s. for three years	WORD 581:3	**superman:** I teach you the s.	NIET 363:1	s. and thunder of the Odyssey	LANG 309:18
s. as it were a new song	BIBLE 82:15	**supernatural:** glance of s. hate	BYRON 126:7	turbulent s. shall cover	SHAK 486:14
s. the dolefull'st ditty	BARN 33:32	nothing mysterious or s.	HUME 267:20	**surgeon:** wounded s. plies the steel	
Sussex songs be s.	BELL 40:11	This s. soliciting	SHAK 458:20		ELIOT 202:21
unseen their dirge is s.	COLL 158:20	**superscription:** Whose is this image and		**surgery:** Honour hath no skill in s.	
Sunium: me on S.'s marbled steep		s.	BIBLE 67:19		SHAK 440:18
	BYRON 123:4	**supersede:** s. the last fashionable	MAC 324:25	**surges:** s. lash the sounding shore	
sunk: All s. beneath the wave	COWP 165:30	**superstition:** fabric of s. has in our			POPE 378:23
So Lycidas s. low	MILT 343:17		BURKE 108:11	**surly:** 'What a s. devil that is	FARR 210:27
s. so low that sacred head	MILT 343:10	species of s. to another	HUME 268:2	**surmise:** each other with a wild s.	
sunless: s. day went down	BYRON 122:17	superstition in avoiding s.	BACON 27:22		KEATS 292:18
sunshine to the s. land	WORD 577:19	S. is the religion of feeble	BURKE 111:22	function Is smother'd in s.	SHAK 458:20
sunlight: Are as moonlight unto s.		S. is the poetry of life	GOET 230:9	**surname:** Out of his s. they have	MAC 323:20
	TENN 539:5	s. to enslave a philosophy	INGE 270:6	**surpass:** nothing earthly could s. her	
s. and the sward	KIPL 303:12	S. sets the whole world	VOLT 561:6		BYRON 122:6

surpassed: Man is something to be s. NIET 363:1
surplice-question: thrilling view of the s. BROW 100:2
surprend: *La mort ne s. point le* LA F 306:22
surprise: His s., therefore, upon TRAV 552:6
Respect was mingled with s. SCOTT 416:6
takes the wise man by s. LA F 306:22
surprised: Not half so s. as I am now WELL 567:30
S. by unjust force MILT 341:15
S. by joy WORD 582:15
surprises: millions of s. HERB 248:10
surrender: daring of a moment's s. ELIOT 205:11
Guards die but do not s. CAMB 128:2
immediate s. can be accepted GRANT 234:1
we shall never s. CHUR 149:31
surrendered: all our enemies having s. CHUR 150:26
Surrey: full S. twilight BETJ 44:8
to that S. homestead BETJ 43:11
Sursum: *S. corda* MASS 335:2
Surtout: *S., Messieurs, point de zèle* TALL 531:15
survey: that takes s. of all SHAK 440:23
We first s. the plot SHAK 441:17
surveyors: there are worse s. EMER 207:7
Survival: S. of the Fittest is more DARW 171:27
s. of the fittest SPEN 514:30
victory there is no s. CHUR 149:30
survived: I s. SIEY 508:8
your gift s. it all AUDEN 19:5
survives: Education is what s. when SKIN 508:20
survivor: ourselves that *I* may be the s. AUST 23:17
Susan: black-ey'd S. came aboard GAY 223:28
Poor S. has passed WORD 581:3
suspect: 'Always s. everybody DICK 180:31
nothing makes a man s. much BACON 27:24
s. The thoughts of others SHAK 466:4
suspected: opinions are always s. LOCKE 315:13
suspended: shoulders held the sky s. HOUS 265:7
s. my religious inquiries GIBB 224:11
s. the sentiments of religion BURKE 111:29
Suspenders: must *not* forget the S. KIPL 304:15
suspension: willing s. of disbelief COL 157:22
suspicion: Caesar's wife must be above s. CAES 127:1
gladly banish squint s. MILT 341:9
S. always haunts the guilty SHAK 446:23
Suspicions: S. amongst thoughts are BACON 27:23
suspicious: Men are s. HERR 249:16
suspiration: Nor windy s. of forc'd SHAK 429:25
Sussex: No more than S. weed KIPL 303:15
S. by the sea KIPL 303:16
S. men are noted fools BLAKE 87:1
S. songs be sung BELL 40:11
sustaining: In our s. corn SHAK 455:13
sustres: his s. and his paramours CHAU 142:32
sutlers: sapient s. of the Lord ELIOT 204:1
swab: only have to s. a plank DICK 176:10
Swaddled: S. with darkness ELIOT 203:4
swaddling: wrapped him in s. clothes BIBLE 69:9
swaddling-clouts: is not yet out of his s. SHAK 432:19
swaggering: By s. could I never thrive SHAK 490:27
swain: better than a homely s. SHAK 446:18
cheered the labouring s. GOLD 230:16
Thus sang the uncouth s. MILT 343:19

swains: That all our s. commend her SHAK 491:4
swallow: chaffering s. for the holy lark BROW 97:27
come before the s. dares SHAK 491:26
sister s. SWIN 530:12
some'll s. tay and stuff MAS 333:20
s. a camel BIBLE 67:24
s. a nest where she may PRAY 395:11
S., flying TENN 542:5
s. has set her six young BROW 101:19
s. twitt'ring from GRAY 234:20
swallowed: easier s. than a flap-dragon SHAK 457:12
others to be s. BACON 27:19
They had s. us up quick PRAY 398:13
to be last s. SHAK 435:24
you be not s. up in books WESL 568:23
swalloweth: s. the ground with fierceness BIBLE 53:7
swallow-flights: Short s. of song TENN 536:20
swallowing: s. his tea in oceans MAC 324:14
swallows: engluts and s. other sorrows SHAK 473:23
gathering s. twitter KEATS 293:9
swam: She s. to the bell-rope BEER 37:14
you have s. in a gondola SHAK 426:20
swamp: down to botanize in the s. CHES 148:7
swan: I will play the s. SHAK 477:18
Leda's goose a s. ANON 5:18
Like a black s. as death AUDEN 18:3
like a sleeping s. SHEL 503:11
Like some full-breasted s. TENN 535:28
now this pale s. in her SHAK 492:20
silver s. GIBB 225:1
so much as a black s. JUV 287:20
summer dies the s. TENN 543:11
s. her downy cygnets save SHAK 445:24
s. sail with her young MER 337:15
Sweet S. of Avon JONS 284:25
swan-bosomed: once more 'neath a s. tree SITW 508:12
swan-like: He makes a s. end SHAK 467:8
Swann: *fut plus question de S.* PROU 401:21
swans: honking amongst tuneful s. VIRG 560:7
in the midst of some s. AUG 21:11
I saw two S. of goodly SPEN 516:31
old ships sail like s. FLEC 214:16
s. are geese ARN 13:14
s. of others are geese WALP 563:20
S. sing before they die COL 156:16
Very like s. DICK 178:30
swap: s. horses while crossing LINC 315:2
swapping: s., swapping mallard ANON 7:28
sware: Unto whom I s. in my wrath PRAY 396:4
Swarm: S. over, Death BETJ 44:4
swarry: friendly s. DICK 182:26
swashing: s. and a martial outside SHAK 424:30
Swat: Is the Akond of S. LEAR 312:25
swath: s. and all its twined flowers KEATS 293:6
swats: cog o' gude s. BURNS 113:4
sway: above this sceptred s. SHAK 467:27
little s. DYER 199:18
love of s. POPE 377:24
swayed: she be s. by quite as keen GILB 228:13
swaying: s. sound of the sea AUDEN 20:3
sways: s. she level in her husband's SHAK 489:1
swear: began he to curse and to s. BIBLE 68:19
s. an eternal friendship CANN 130:4
s. in both the scales against SHAK 460:16
s. like a comfit-maker's SHAK 439:32
S. not at all BIBLE 64:15

s. not by the moon SHAK 482:15
s. thou think'st I love DONNE 190:14
s. to never kiss the girls BROW 100:30
s. to the truth of a song PRIOR 400:20
time I ever heard you s. FARR 210:27
time you s. you're his PARK 368:19
when very angry, s. TWAIN 554:16
swearers: Then the liars and s. are SHAK 462:13
sweareth: He that s. unto his neighbour PRAY 390:5
swearing: let me alone for s. SHAK 490:13
swears: s. with so much grace LEE 313:9
swear-word: s. in a rustic slum BEER 37:15
Sweat: Agony and bloody S. PRAY 385:17
Falstaff shall die of a s. SHAK 443:2
In the s. of thy face shalt BIBLE 45:22
rank s. of an enseamed bed SHAK 435:10
s. and whine about their WHIT 570:22
s. pours down me SAPP 414:6
S. ran and blood sprang HOUS 264:4
tears and s. CHUR 149:29
We spend our midday s. QUAR 403:10
will s. but for promotion SHAK 425:7
sweated: s. through his apostolic BYRON 126:7
sweating: Quietly s. palm to palm HUXL 268:22
sweats: bloody s. WILDE 572:14
Falstaff s. to death SHAK 438:28
S. in the eye of Phoebus SHAK 444:25
Sweeney: Apeneck S. spreads his knees ELIOT 204:14
S. to Mrs Porter ELIOT 204:27
sweep: madly s. the sky SHAK 470:20
So your chimneys I s. BLAKE 88:5
To s. the dust behind SHAK 471:22
Sweeping: S. up the Heart DICK 183:17
sweeps: s. a room as for Thy laws HERB 247:19
sweet: about them if TO-DAY be s. FITZ 212:22
all her task to be s. WATS 565:11
All is not s. JONS 283:27
all s. things BORR 90:4
Beyond a man's saying s. HARDY 238:22
by distance made more s. COLL 158:21
comes in the s. o' the year SHAK 491:17
dead thing that smells s. THOM 547:17
fair and smell'st so s. SHAK 476:19
how it was s. BROW 100:8
How s. and fair she seems WALL 562:13
I mean s. words SHAK 449:24
made this life more s. SHAK 424:31
mouth s. as honey BIBLE 82:9
myself that am so s. to you PATM 370:5
of a labouring man is s. BIBLE 55:17
parting is such s. sorrow SHAK 482:20
passing s., is solitude COWP 166:21
should be buried in so s. SHEL 499:2
sin that was s. PAIN 367:17
Sleep is s. to the labouring BUNY 107:24
so s. is she JONS 285:4
So s. was ne'er so fatal SHAK 477:5
Stolen waters are s. BIBLE 53:28
such s. thunder SHAK 471:7
S. and low TENN 541:31
s. and twenty SHAK 488:17
S. are the uses of adversity SHAK 424:32
s. as summer SHAK 447:21
s. cheat gone DE L 174:5
s. is death who puts TENN 534:30
S. is pleasure after pain DRYD 195:1
S. is revenge BYRON 122:12
S. is the breath of morn MILT 348:4
s. is this human life CORY 163:5
s. love remember'd such SHAK 493:6
s. love seemed that April BRID 92:20
s. poison for the age's SHAK 452:10
s. the moonlight sleeps SHAK 468:15

S. though in sadness	SHEL 502:13	Love is s. of foot	HERB 247:16	s. he sung a song of death	BLAKE 86:19
s. to taste prove in digestion	SHAK 478:14	race is not to the s.	BIBLE 55:30	s. of justice thee ruleth	DUNB 199:12
s. water and bitter	BIBLE 80:15	S. be thine approaching	SHEL 505:4	s. of this stone and anvil	MAL 327:14
S., when the morn is grey	CALV 127:28	S. expires a driv'ler	JOHN 283:3	S. sleep in my hand	BLAKE 86:16
'Tis not so s. now as it	SHAK 487:20	S. has sailed into his	YEATS 587:3	that never stained thy s.	HOPE 256:5
'Tis s. to think	MOORE 356:19	S. was *anima Rabelaisii*	COL 158:2	their tongue a sharp s.	PRAY 393:15
took s. counsel together	PRAY 393:11	tameless, and s., and proud	SHEL 502:13	to hack thy s. as thou	SHAK 439:7
Truly the light is s.	BIBLE 56:9	**swifter:** days are s. than a weaver's		to send peace, but a s.	BIBLE 65:38
under his tongue as a s.	HENRY 245:19		BIBLE 52:18	to the Power of the S.	CHAR 140:19
sweeten: Children s. labours	BACON 27:3	S. than the moone's sphere	SHAK 470:2	two-edged s. in their hands	PRAY 399:24
sweetened: China plant s. with the pith		they were s. than eagles	BIBLE 50:17	upon the edge of the s.	PRAY 393:22
	ADD 2:11	**Swiftly:** S., like an adder to its	PLOM 374:19	went a sharp twoedged s.	BIBLE 81:14
sweeteners: scandal are the best s. of		**swiftness:** swift with s. of the tigress		when he first drew the s.	CLAR 152:18
tea	FIEL 211:18		OWEN 367:11	Who never drew a s.	ANON 5:14
sweeter: mountain sheep are s.	PEAC 371:2	things for s. did I sue	THOM 548:13	with the edge of the s.	BIBLE 48:12
s. also than honey	PRAY 390:12	**swig:** I'll get a s. in Hell	KIPL 299:19	**swords:** beat their s. into plowshares
s. than the berry	GAY 222:8	**swim:** boys that s. on bladders	SHAK 447:9		BIBLE 57:19
s. than the lids of Juno's	SHAK 491:26	naughty night to s.	SHAK 454:21	Keep up your bright s.	SHAK 473:21
world hath not a s. creature	SHAK 476:11	said I could not s.	CARR 134:22	stout hearts and sharp s.	BIRK 84:14
sweetest: make the s. love to frown		So the Cabin-boy did s.	BALL 31:3	s. must have leaped from	BURKE 111:9
	GREE 236:11	s. To thee	GRAH 233:16	s. shall play the orators	MARL 330:4
passing of the s. soul	TENN 536:32	s. to yonder point	SHAK 448:14	turns our s.	SHAK 452:3
Success is counted s.	DICK 183:23	**swimmer:** some strong s. in his agony		yet they be very s.	PRAY 393:12
s. delight of gardens	BROW 95:21		BYRON 122:18	your plowshares into s.	BIBLE 61:16
s. fragrance from the herb	TROL 552:24	**swimming:** Odd figures s. were glimpsed		Your s., made rich	SHAK 450:7
sweet-faced: Pyramus is a s. man			VIRG 557:11	**swore:** By the nine gods he s.	MAC 322:11
	SHAK 469:31	s. in the air…and Others	EDW 200:7	father when the son s.	BURT 116:36
sweetheart: I cheer a dead man's s.		**swine:** gold in a s.'s snout	BIBLE 53:32	My tongue s.	EUR 209:4
	HOUS 263:11	s., though he divide	BIBLE 48:6	not what to say, he s.	BYRON 124:43
Like the s. of the sun	HOOD 255:4	whole herd of s. ran violently	BIBLE 65:20	'Our armies s. terribly	STER 519:28
s., canst thou tell me	BALL 30:9	ye your pearls before s.	BIBLE 65:1	s. as many oaths as I spake	SHAK 454:21
Tray, Blanch, and S.	SHAK 454:29	you s.	BROW 105:9	S. not at all	BENT 41:4
sweeting: Yours are the limbs, my s.		**swing:** Gaping at the lady in the s.		**sworn:** had I so s. as you	SHAK 459:10
	NASH 360:5		ELIOT 203:28	s. twelve have a thief	SHAK 463:16
sweetly: They do but s. chide thee		room to s. a cat	DICK 177:18	**sycamore:** nightingale in the s.	STEV 523:7
	SHAK 492:25	s. for it	KING 297:19	**sycophants:** surrounded by s. and flatterers
who laughs so s. and talks	HOR 259:24	S., swing together	CORY 163:2		HARD 238:1
sweetmeats: Because their breaths with		S. up into the apple-tree	ELIOT 203:16	**syllable:** last s. of recorded time	SHAK 463:6
s.	SHAK 481:28	swoop, a s., a flourish	JAMES 271:34	panting s. through time	COWP 166:18
whole pyramids of s.	DRYD 198:10	'That fellow's got to s.	WILDE 572:9	**syllables:** heroic s. both ways	BYRON 123:24
sweetness: every s. that inspir'd	MARL 330:11	**Swinging:** S. slow with sullen roar		S. govern the world	COKE 154:20
loathe the taste of s.	SHAK 439:35		MILT 342:4	**syllogisms:** Though s. hang not on my
Love, s., goodness	MILT 351:13	**swish:** s. of a skirt in the dew	KIPL 304:1		COWP 164:30
Of linked s. long drawn	MILT 342:26	**Swiss:** dashing S. officer'	RUSS 412:22	**sylph:** She's the only s. I ever saw
prove the s. of a shower	THOM 547:21	some money nothing of S.	FONS 216:5		DICK 180:18
pursuit of s. and light	ARN 15:15	s. cheese would think	MARQ 330:25	**Sylvia:** Who is S.	SHAK 491:4
sea air the s. of Anjou	DU B 198:27	**Switzerland:** I look upon S. as an inferior		**symbol:** s. at your door	ANON 6:5
strong came forth s.	BIBLE 49:21		SMITH 512:5	s. of his resurrection	PROU 401:23
s. in the sad	THOM 547:26	**swoln:** s. with wind and the rank	MILT 343:13	s. of Irish art	JOYCE 286:21
waste its s. on the desert	GRAY 234:23	**swoon:** else s. to death	KEATS 292:12	s. of the power of Heaven	MOORE 355:18
which are s. and light	SWIFT 525:33	**swoop:** At one fell s.	SHAK 462:17	**symbols:** cloudy s. of a high romance
With s. fills the breast	CASW 136:15	s., a swing, a flourish	JAMES 271:34		KEATS 293:1
sweet peas: Here are s.	KEATS 290:14	take away all at one s.	WEBS 567:1	We are s.	EMER 207:30
sweets: all its s. are gone	KEATS 292:13	**sword:** believed he had a s. upstairs		*symétrie:* s., c'est l'ennui	HUGO 267:12
brought'st Thy s. along with Thee			YEATS 584:10	**symmetry:** Could frame thy fearful s.
	HERB 247:17	brave man with a s.	WILDE 572:10		BLAKE 87:14
discandy, melt their s.	SHAK 423:5	could use the s. and pen	LAND 308:23	spoilers of the s. of shelves	LAMB 307:14
I have tasted the s.	BYRON 124:38	fallen by the edge of the s.	BIBLE 63:11	**sympathize:** her great Master so to s.
last taste of s.	SHAK 478:18	famous by my s.	GRAH 233:15		MILT 344:5
Stolen s. are best	CIBB 151:15	flesh'd Thy maiden s.	SHAK 440:26	**Sympathizer:** S. would seem to imply
Stolen s. are always sweeter	HUNT 268:11	flourishing with his s.	REYN 405:20		PEAC 370:14
s. that you suck	KIPL 298:5	hides a s. from hilts unto	SHAK 443:12	**sympathy:** It is the secret s.	SCOTT 416:20
S. to the sweet	SHAK 437:5	His father's s. he has	MOORE 356:13	there were a s. in choice	SHAK 469:20
S. with sweets war not	SHAK 492:25	His s. was in the sheath	COWP 165:31	world is wrought To s.	SHEL 504:19
treacle is lost in the s.	GAY 222:30	Hold then my s.	SHAK 452:6	**symphonies:** Are five sweet s.	ROSS 409:19
wilderness of s.	MILT 348:17	is mightier than the s.	BULW 107:4	**symphony:** consort to th' angelic s.
Sweet-William: S. with his homely		lift up s. against nation	BIBLE 57:19		MILT 344:10
cottage-smell	ARN 15:6	made him can make his s.	BIBLE 53:9	**symptoms:** dying of a hundred good s.
swell: s. the curled waters 'bove	SHAK 454:3	Man for the s.	TENN 542:9		POPE 381:23
swell'd: sad s. face	BARH 33:16	my s., Glued to my scabbard	MASS 335:21	**sym'tums:** yo' s. seem ter segashuate
swellin: green buds they were s.'	BALL 30:10	My s., I give to him	BUNY 107:38		HARR 242:18
She's a s.' wisibly before	DICK 182:16	of thee are s. and fire	TENN 534:10	**synagogues:** chief seats in the s.	BIBLE 67:22
swelling: prologues to the s. act	SHAK 458:19	pen is worse than the s.	BURT 116:22	chief seats in the s.	BIBLE 68:37
swept: cleaned the windows and I s.		puny whipster gets my s.	SHAK 477:17	*synchronize: Violence shall s. your*
	GILB 228:4	Put up thy s. into	BIBLE 72:43		AUDEN 19:11
s., and garnished	BIBLE 66:13	shall never sheathe the s.	ASQ 17:17	**syne:** auld lang s.	BURNS 112:31
S. it for half a year	CARR 135:5	shall perish with the s.	BIBLE 68:18	**synge:** whan she bygynneth to s.	CHAU 144:10
S. with confused alarms	ARN 12:23	sharp as a twoedged s.	BIBLE 53:20	**syngyng:** He kan nat stynte of s.	CHAU 143:9
swift: Be s. to hear	BIBLE 80:10	sigh is the s. of an Angel	BLAKE 86:6	*Synod:* there been a *S. of Cooks*	JOHN 275:13
Cousin S.	DRYD 198:23	s. back in the sheath	CHES 147:6	**synonym:** his Christian name a s.	MAC 323:27

syntax: both in his s. and in his ARN 16:11
Syrens: song the S. sang BROW 97:14
Syrian: allur'd The S. damsels MILT 345:17
S. Orontes has now JUV 287:15
Syrinx: Pan did after S. speed MARV 332:2
syrops: lucent s. KEATS 289:20
Syrtes: Betwixt the S. and soft Sicily
ARN 14:21
system: energies of our s. will decay
BALF 30:3
I must Create a S. BLAKE 86:2
into a s. of Government GLAD 229:19
Observe how s. into system POPE 379:3
to them the decimal s. NAP 359:13
système: s. de poids et mesures NAP 359:13
systems: Atoms or s. into ruin hurl'd
POPE 379:4
Away with S. MER 337:37
Our little s. have their TENN 535:31
T: description the page gave to a T.
FARQ 210:18
Ta: thousand T.'s and Pardon's BETJ 43:13
taäkin: a's doing a-t.' o' meä TENN 541:4
taberna: In t. mori ANON 10:14
tabernacle: At Salem is his t. PRAY 395:1
he set a t. for the sun PRAY 390:11
t. of this house were dissolved BIBLE 77:6
who shall dwell in thy t. PRAY 390:4
tabernas: pulsat pede pauperum t.
HOR 259:13
table: behave mannerly at t. STEV 522:17
from their masters' t. BIBLE 62:1
from the rich man's t. BIBLE 70:28
it before them in a t. BIBLE 58:25
My t. thou hast furnished SCOT 419:5
olive-branches: round about thy t.
PRAY 398:20
T., at the Communion-time PRAY 387:6
though you cannot make a t. JOHN 274:26
Thou shalt prepare a t. PRAY 390:22
to come to the Lord's T. PRAY 387:5
tableau: l'histoire n'est que le t. des crimes
VOLT 561:10
Table Bay: horse and foot going to T.
KIPL 297:24
Table Mountain: I reside at T. HARTE 242:32
tables: make it plain upon t. BIBLE 62:1
serve t. BIBLE 73:27
tablets: thy t., Memory ARN 13:19
taboo: repose is t.'d by anxiety GILB 226:12
tabret: bring hither the t. PRAY 395:9
tabulae: Solventur risu t. HOR 262:7
tache: sans une t. ROST 410:12
tackle: silken t. SHAK 422:3
though thy t.'s torn SHAK 427:26
tactics: master of the art of t. BAG 29:11
tadpole: When you were a t. SMITH 510:10
taedium vitae: helps to keep off the t.
JOHN 274:21
taen: t. the fit o' rhyme BURNS 113:23
taffeta: doublet of changeable s. SHAK 489:5
T. phrases SHAK 457:15
tail: corking-pin stuck through his t.
BARH 33:5
guinea-pig up by the t. LOCK 315:18
head and which was the t. BRIG 93:6
he's treading on my t. CARR 134:13
horror of his folded t. MILT 344:12
Improve his shining t. CARR 133:17
like a rat without a t. SHAK 458:6
mouse's limp t. hanging MOORE 355:22
such a little t. behind BELL 38:28
t. must wag the dog KIPL 298:16
Thin mane, thick t. SHAK 495:20
thy t. hangs down behind KIPL 302:14
was a hole where the t. COL 156:11
tailor: my coat from the t. GOLD 232:41
t. make thy doublet SHAK 489:5
tails: were stings in their t. BIBLE 82:8
taint: I cannot t. with fear SHAK 462:28

never t. my love SHAK 476:24
tainted: t. wether of the flock SHAK 467:25
Taisez-vous: T.! Méfiez-vous ANON 9:18
take: good Lord would t. him AUDEN 20:20
got to t. under my wing GILB 227:14
humbly t. my leave of you SHAK 432:10
Let us t. any man's horses SHAK 442:29
She bid me t. love easy YEATS 584:22
T. any heart GILB 228:15
T. a pair of sparkling GILB 225:26
t. away all at one swoop WEBS 567:1
T. away from English authors TROL 552:12
t. away the matter of them BACON 27:11
T. care of the pence LOWN 319:21
T., eat, this is my Body PRAY 388:1
t. it away PAIN 367:17
T. me, Lieutenant BETJ 43:11
t. my life FARQ 210:10
t. my life and all SHAK 468:10
t. not thy holy Spirit PRAY 393:6
t. our fill of love BIBLE 53:24
t. those lips away SHAK 464:21
T. your hare when it is GLAS 229:21
They have to t. you in' FROST 219:2
thou yet t. all, Galilean SWIN 530:4
which I shall t. with me ROST 410:12
taken: because she was t. out of Man
BIBLE 45:12
day in which he was t. up BIBLE 73:20
Lord hath t. away BIBLE 52:7
One shall be t. BIBLE 67:33
only t. from the French SHER 505:19
They have t. away my Lord BIBLE 73:7
Tho' much is t. TENN 544:3
When t., To be well shaken COLM 159:7
takes: give like that it t. away BYRON 125:28
if it t. all summer GRANT 233:21
money and you t. your choice ANON 9:2
t. a woman must be undone GAY 222:30
t. two to speak the truth THOR 550:23
taketh: that t. from the store MARV 332:17
which t. away the sin BIBLE 71:30
taking-off: deep damnation of his t.
SHAK 459:6
tale: adorn a t. JOHN 282:31
bodies must tell the t. SCOTT 415:19
brings in a several t. SHAK 481:14
Christmas told the merriest t. SCOTT 417:16
honest t. speeds best being SHAK 481:9
how a plain t. shall put SHAK 439:6
I could a t. unfold whose SHAK 431:5
I say the t. as 'twas said SCOTT 416:10
I should have had a t. SCOTT 415:19
I tell the t. that I heard HOUS 264:16
long preamble of a t. CHAU 143:22
mere t. of a tub WEBS 567:3
ower true t. SCOTT 418:8
round unvarnish'd t. deliver SHAK 473:24
t. should be judicious COWP 165:2
t., sir, would cure deafness SHAK 484:25
t. Told by an idiot SHAK 463:6
tedious as a twice-told t. SHAK 452:21
Telling a t. not too importunate MORR 358:9
telling the saddest t. SHAK 470:3
thereby hangs a t. SHAK 425:19
thou the lamentable t. SHAK 480:8
Trust the t. LAWR 311:10
With a t. forsooth he cometh SIDN 508:2
Tale-bearers: T. are as bad as the
tale-makers SHER 506:25
talent: Blest with each t. POPE 376:26
Es bildet ein T. sich GOET 230:10
grand t. pour le silence CARL 131:37
had is just a t. to amuse COW 163:17
into my works is my t. WILDE 573:35
que mon t. dans mes ouvres WILDE 573:35
T. develops in quiet places GOET 230:10
T. does what it can MER 338:5
t. instantly recognizes DOYLE 192:38
t. of our English nation DRYD 197:12

T. which is death to hide MILT 351:10
tomb of a mediocre t. SMITH 510:20
you must have t. too KORDA 305:27
talented: I'm sure he's a t. man PRAED 384:5
talents: career open to t. NAP 359:14
If you have great t. REYN 405:16
ministry of all the t. ANON 7:26
they have tried their t. COL 157:26
tales: children is increased with t.
BACON 26:1
let them tell thee t. SHAK 480:8
marvellous t. FLEC 214:9
tell old t. SHAK 456:3
tali: t. auxilio nec defensoribus VIRG 558:9
talismans: not seldom t. and spells
COWP 167:25
talk: by beginning to t. HAZL 243:13
chance to t. a little wild SHAK 446:26
How he will t. LEE 313:11
I have no small t. WELL 567:31
I never t. about it PROU 401:22
'It's very easy to t. DICK 180:14
It would t. BEAU 36:13
I won't t. of his book JOHN 275:21
legs and have out his t. JOHN 277:22
loves to hear himself t. SHAK 482:24
mair they t. I'm kent BURNS 114:32
night is crept upon our t. SHAK 451:28
nothing but t. of his horse SHAK 465:21
No use to t. to me HOUS 262:20
should t. so very queer BARH 33:23
spent an hour's t. withal SHAK 456:21
T. about the pews and steeples CHES 146:11
t. but a tinkling cymbal BACON 26:15
t. him out of patience SHAK 475:13
t. not to me of a name BYRON 125:29
t. of wills SHAK 479:10
t. six times with the same BYRON 123:34
t. slid north KIPL 297:28
t. too much DRYD 194:12
t. with crowds and keep KIPL 300:2
t. with some old lover's DONNE 189:25
t. with you FLEC 214:20
t. with you SHAK 465:28
They always t. PRIOR 401:11
'Tis the t. GRAN 234:8
to find t. and discourse BACON 27:18
To t. about the rest ANON 8:2
'To t. of many things CARR 135:7
we do not t. of ourselves TROL 552:22
wished him to t. on for ever HAZL 243:17
world may t. of hereafter COLL 158:12
talk'd: So much they t. CHUR 149:10
t. like poor Poll GARR 221:13
they t. of their Raphaels GOLD 231:21
talked: he t. with us by the way BIBLE 71:18
I believe they t. of me FARQ 210:3
least t. about by men PER 372:24
single and only t. of population GOLD 232:32
t. shop like a tenth muse ANON 5:17
worse than being t. about WILDE 573:18
talkers: most fluent t. or most HAZL 243:24
talking: filthiness, nor foolish t. BIBLE 78:2
Frenchman must be always t. JOHN 278:17
T. and eloquence are not JONS 285:3
that you will still be t. SHAK 471:28
tired the sun with t. CORY 163:4
Talking-machine: other than a redtape
T. CARL 132:1
talks: Licker t. mighty loud w'en
HARR 242:23
Minerva when she t. JONS 285:5
She only t. about her hair THOM 549:3
t. it so very fast that FARQ 210:6
t. of Arthur's death SHAK 452:27
t. of darkness at noon-day COWP 166:12
t. of his misfortunes there JOHN 278:20
wish I liked the way it t. RAL 404:20
tall: divinely t. TENN 533:6
He's as t. a man as any's SHAK 487:23

she is t. and stately — TENN 540:6
t. men had ever very empty — BACON 25:7
taller: He is t. by almost — SWIFT 526:1
Tam: T. was glorious — BURNS 115:6
tamarisks: High noon behind the t. — KIPL 298:13
tambourine: play the t. on her other — DICK 180:18
Tamburlaine: T., the Scourge of God — MARL 330:15
tame: Be not too t. neither — SHAK 433:17
hey-day in the blood is t. — SHAK 435:8
tongue can no man t. — BIBLE 80:14
which thou canst not t. — HERB 247:1
tamed: themselves in one year t. — MARV 332:11
tameless: t., and swift, and proud — SHEL 502:13
tameness: trusts in the t. of a wolf — SHAK 454:28
Taming: T. my wild heart to thy — SHAK 472:22
Tam Lin: what I ken this night, T. — BALL 32:3
Tandy: I met wid Napper T. — ANON 6:6
tangere: *Noli me t.* — BAG 28:20
Noli me t. — BIBLE 83:24
tangled: cold Christ and t. Trinities — KIPL 302:2
Hearts after them t. in amorous nets — MILT 350:2
lie t. in her hair — LOV 318:15
tangles: t. of Neaera's hair — MILT 343:8
Tank: T. come down the stalls — SASS 414:12
tankards: mouths were made for t. — MAS 333:21
Tantae: T. molis erat Romanam condere — VIRG 557:10
Tantum: T. ergo sacramentum — THOM 546:17
T. religio potuit suadere — LUCR 320:4
taper: Out went the t. as she — KEATS 289:15
t. to the outward room — DONNE 189:30
with t. light — SHAK 452:25
tapers: she lit her glimmering t. — THOM 548:15
tapestry: wrong side of a Turkey t. — HOW 266:20
tapped: They t. Victor on the shoulder — AUDEN 21:7
tapping: suddenly there came a t. — POE 375:4
tapsalteerie: May a' gae t. — BURNS 114:2
Tara: harp that once through T.'s — MOORE 356:9
when T. rose so high — LAND 308:23
taratantara: tuba terribili sonitu t. — ENN 208:21
Tar-baby: T. ain't sayin' nuthin' — HARR 242:19
tar-barrel: black as a t. — CARR 134:33
tard: dit et l'on vient trop t. — LA B 306:11
Trois heures, c'est toujours trop t. — SART 414:9
tarde: cinco en punto de la t. — GARC 221:5
tare: That t. each other in their — TENN 536:30
tares: amongst the weeds and t. — BROW 96:18
clasping t. cling round — COWP 168:26
corn is but a field of t. — TICH 551:2
enemy came and sowed t. — BIBLE 66:18
t. to which we are all — ELIOT 205:15
tarn: dark t. dry — DE L 174:15
tarnished: is neither t. nor afraid — CHAN 139:22
Tarquin: T.'s ravishing strides — SHAK 460:1
That the great house of T. — MAC 322:11
tarried: too long we have t. — LEAR 312:12
tarrieth: remembrance of a guest that t. — BIBLE 62:18
tarry: do not t. — CAMP 129:1
t. the wheels of his chariots — BIBLE 49:12
will that he t. till I come — BIBLE 73:19
You may for ever t. — HERR 250:6
tarry'd: job too long he t. — SWIFT 528:9
tarrying: make no long t. — PRAY 392:3

nor t. here — SHAK 463:7
Tarshish: ye ships of T. — BIBLE 58:17
Tarsus: man which am a Jew of T. — BIBLE 74:20
Tart: T., cathartic virtue — EMER 207:22
Tartar: T.'s lips — SHAK 462:4
task: all her t. to be sweet — WATS 565:11
All with weary t. fordone — SHAK 471:21
here is a t. for all that — STEV 521:4
long day's t. is done — SHAK 423:9
My t. accomplished — HENL 245:9
There is but one t. for all — VIRG 558:18
thy worldly t. hast done — KIPL 299:7
vanity, sets love a t. — SHAK 428:22
what he reads as a t. will — HUNT 268:8
tasks: Among the t. of real life — JOHN 274:31
tassel-gentle: To lure this t. back again — WORD 577:3
taste: authority on t. — SHAK 482:19
bad t. of the smoker — TAC 531:11
common sense and good t. — ELIOT 200:20
dainty Bacchus gross in t. — SHAW 496:12
difference of t. in jokes — SHAK 457:8
forgot the t. of fears — ELIOT 200:21
Ghastly Good T. — SHAK 463:5
good sense and good t. — BETJ 44:15
last t. of sweets — LA B 306:15
let me t. the whole — SHAK 478:18
must himself create the t. — BROW 104:1
never t. who always drink — WORD 583:11
no t. when you married me — PRIOR 401:11
on my tongue the t. — SHER 506:27
shall t. my *Anno Domini* — HOUS 266:6
supper was to my t. — FARQ 209:22
t. a little honey with — STER 519:13
t. and see — BIBLE 50:3
T. does not come by chance — PRAY 391:21
t. for marriages and public executions — REYN 405:22
DISR 186:25
t. My meat — HERB 248:1
t. not — BIBLE 78:24
t. not the Pierian spring — POPE 378:13
T. not when the wine-cup — SCOTT 418:5
T. your legs — SHAK 489:20
Things sweet to t. prove — SHAK 478:14
undoubtedly wanted t. — WALP 562:26
us a t. of your quality — SHAK 432:22
wild vicissitudes of t. — JOHN 282:26
worse t., than in a churchyard — JOW 285:23
tasted: had t. her sweet body — SHAK 475:25
it can't be t. in a sip — DICK 180:30
Some books are to be t. — BACON 27:19
t. that the Lord is gracious — BIBLE 80:22
t. the sweets and the bitters — BYRON 124:38
tastes: So he that t. woman — GAY 222:30
Their t. may not be — SHAW 497:34
Tasting: T. of Flora and the country — KEATS 291:18
Tat: Die T. ist alles — GOET 230:5
stolzer Männer der T. — HEINE 244:12
tattered: t. coat upon a stick — YEATS 586:12
tatters: fond of my rags and t. — MOL 353:11
'You left us in t. — HARDY 240:19
tattle: have an entertaining t. — CHES 145:25
taught: having been t. anything — MOL 353:23
heeds what we have t. her — GAY 222:12
He t. us little — ARN 13:16
In them is plainest t. — MILT 350:11
right to be t. by the enemy — OVID 366:16
t. Art to fold her hands — ROSS 410:1
taught as if you t. them not — POPE 378:29
t. them as one having authority — BIBLE 65:13
t. to think that moderation — BURKE 110:9
There t. us how to live — TICK 551:3
You t. me first to beg — SHAK 468:12
You t. me language — SHAK 484:29
taughte: afterward he t. — CHAU 142:1
taunting: not t. — BACON 26:25

tavern: creaking couplets in a t. — BYRON 124:14
days in a t. drinking — ANON 10:14
heard a Voice within the T. — FITZ 212:6
not my hostess of the t. — SHAK 438:2
produced as by a good t. or inn — JOHN 276:35
'So is the London T.' — ANON 4:13
t. chair was the throne — JOHN 280:20
that vulgar and t. music — BROW 97:1
tavernes: He knew the t. well — CHAU 141:20
taverns: t. while the tempest hurled — HOUS 264:21
tawdry: t. cheapness Shall outlast — POUND 383:7
tawny: From t. body and sweet — SWIN 530:13
tax: hateful t. levied upon — JOHN 281:12
T. not the royal Saint — WORD 582:16
t. not you, you elements — SHAK 454:5
To t. and to please — BURKE 109:9
Taxation: T. and representation — CAMD 128:4
T. without representation — OTIS 365:25
taxed: schoolboy whips his t. top — SMITH 511:38
world should be t. — BIBLE 69:8
taxes: All t. must — GIBB 224:25
'...as t. is — DICK 177:11
except death and t. — FRAN 218:18
people overlaid with t. — BACON 27:26
T. upon every article which — SMITH 511:37
taxing: less of a t. machine — LOWE 318:24
Tay: Bridge of the Silv'ry T. — MCG 325:6
Te: T. Deum laudamus — ANON 11:3
tea: best sweeteners of t. — FIEL 211:18
her t. without a stratagem — YOUNG 587:18
if this is t. — PUNCH 403:5
Make me some fresh t. — AUDEN 19:14
slavery of the t. and coffee — COBB 154:7
some sipping t. — WORD 580:2
sometimes t. — POPE 381:2
'Take some more t. — CARR 134:3
T., although an Oriental — CHES 147:27
t. and cakes and ices — ELIOT 203:22
t. and comfortable advice — KEATS 294:5
there honey still for t. — BROO 94:25
to their t. and scandal — CONG 159:21
To want my cup of t. — PAIN 367:1
was nothing on it but t. — CARR 133:28
we'll all have t. — DICK 175:26
Why does the t. generally — THAC 545:9
with t. solaces the midnight — JOHN 281:28
teach: apt to t. — BIBLE 79:12
Even while they t. — SEN 420:10
I will t. you my townspeople — WILL 574:12
Let such t. others who — POPE 378:10
She can t. ye how to climb — MILT 341:22
Still pleas'd to t. — POPE 378:32
suffering what they t. in song — SHEL 501:13
t. an old horse — SPEN 516:16
t. Bloody instructions — SHAK 459:5
t. eternal wisdom how — POPE 379:14
T. him how to live — PORT 381:33
t. him how to tell my story — SHAK 474:1
t. him to think for himself — SHEL 499:1
t. his senators wisdom — PRAY 397:4
T. me, my God and King — HERB 247:18
T. me thy way — PRAY 391:8
T. me to feel another's — POPE 381:2
T. me to live — KEN 295:9
t. thee in the way wherein — PRAY 391:18
T. the free man how — AUDEN 19:9
t. the torches to burn — SHAK 482:2
t. the unforgetful to forget — ROSS 410:6
T. us to care and not — ELIOT 202:1
t. you to drink deep ere — SHAK 430:3
Those that do t. young babes — SHAK 476:22
To t. the young idea how — THOM 549:10
what you t. them first — JOHN 275:6
years t. much which — EMER 207:19
teacher: doctrine for the t.'s sake — DEFOE 173:3

precepts for the t.'s	FARQ 210:13	Smiling through her t.	HOMER 254:1	Telemachus: my son, mine own T.
teachers: death of the wretched t.	JUV 287:24	summer tempest came her t.	TENN 542:11		TENN 544:2
t. had been woods and rills	WORD 581:11	t. amid the alien corn	KEATS 291:23	Television: T. The word is half Latin
t., spiritual pastors	PRAY 388:16	t. and sweat'	CHUR 149:29		SCOTT 415:16
teaches: He who cannot t.	SHAW 497:38	t. and toiling breath	ROSS 408:20	tell: How could they t.	PARK 368:23
teachest: Thou t. like a fool	SHAK 421:24	t. fell down	HOUS 264:4	I'll t. thee everything	CARR 136:5
teaching: t. nations how to live	MILT 352:6	T., idle tears	TENN 542:2	I will t. you who you are	CHES 145:15
twenty to follow mine own t.	SHAK 465:20	T. in his eyes	SHAK 432:27	only t. us what he heard	GRAY 235:24
tea-cup: crack in the t. opens	AUDEN 18:10	t. live in an onion	SHAK 421:22	t. a woman's age	GILB 228:27
teacups: laughter tinkled among the t.		T. of eternity	HOUS 265:13	t. her she mustn't	PUNCH 402:23
	ELIOT 203:28	t. of it are wet	SHAK 422:14	T. it not in Gath	BIBLE 50:16
Over the t.	AUDEN 20:22	t. run down his dappled	THOM 549:19	T. me all	JOYCE 286:6
tea-drinker: hardened and shameless		t. scald and start	AUDEN 18:11	T. me more	SHAK 458:12
t.	JOHN 281:28	t. shall drown the wind	SHAK 459:6	T. me not here	HOUS 265:8
team: 'Is my t. ploughing	HOUS 263:9	t. shed for things even	VIRG 557:17	t. me the truth about love	AUDEN 21:2
teapot: fill the t. up	PAIN 367:15	T. wash out a Word	FITZ 213:7	T. me what you eat	BRIL 93:9
tear: dropp'd a t. upon the word	STER 520:5	t. when they would devour	BACON 27:38	T. not as new what ev'ry	COWP 165:2
eye the unanswerable t.	BYRON 121:34	That long drip of human t.	HARDY 240:12	t. sad stories	SHAK 479:11
Forbade the rising t.	SCOTT 416:11	Their wings in t.	TENN 536:20	'T. them I came	DE L 174:8
Greece a t.	BYRON 123:1	therefore I forbid my t.	SHAK 436:20	t. the Spartans	SIM 508:9
has fallen a splendid t.	TENN 540:12	They that sow in t.	PRAY 398:17	t. the towers thereof	PRAY 392:27
meed of some melodious t.	MILT 343:2	through my t.	FLET 215:30	t. you three times is true	CARR 133:1
Mis'ry all he had, a t.	GRAY 235:5	Time with a gift of t.	SWIN 528:20	those who t. us how they	KIPL 298:13
persuasive language of a t.	CHUR 149:17	To remember with a t.	ALL 3:21	You need not t. me what	STER 519:1
repressed the starting t.	JOHN 277:14	water'd heaven with their t.	BLAKE 87:16	you never can t.	SHAW 498:21
shed one English t.	MAC 322:10	water my couch with my t.	PRAY 389:26	telleth: One day t. another	PRAY 390:11
T. him for his bad verses	SHAK 451:8	weeping in this vale of t.	ANON 10:19	t. the number of the stars	PRAY 399:19
t. is an intellectual thing	BLAKE 86:6	Weep thy girlish t.	WATS 565:9	telling: I am t. you	WHIS 569:17
t. our pleasures with rough	MARV 332:20	wipe he t. for ever from	MILT 343:18	pity beyond all t.	YEATS 586:9
T. out your 'eart an' good-bye	KIPL 301:11	With mine own t. I wash	SHAK 480:2	Téméraire: She's the Fighting T.
t. the cave where Echo	SHAK 482:19	With silence and t.	BYRON 126:14		NEWB 361:10
Thinking every t. a gem	SHEL 502:3	with the salt of broken t.	SHAK 487:1	Tempe: ever did in shade of T. sit
To t. each other's eyes	WATTS 565:18	with your fierce t. I pray	THOM 546:24		SIDN 507:26
without a t.	DRYD 197:29	world as a vale of t.	BROW 100:6	temper: could answer for his t.	BAG 28:20
your eyelids wip'd a t.	SHAK 425:23	tease: dost t. us out of thought	KEATS 291:10	He of a t. was so absolute	DRAY 193:7
tearing: t. his meat like a tiger	MAC 324:14	fleas that t. in the high	BELL 40:13	Keep me in t.	SHAK 453:20
tea-rose: t. tea-gown	POUND 383:5	while ye thus t. me together	GAY 222:35	One equal t. of heroic	TENN 544:3
tears: all made of sighs and t.	SHAK 426:29	teases: Because he knows it t.	CARR 133:26	only keep your t.	STER 519:18
big round t.	SHAK 425:1	teashop: In the t.'s ingle-nook	BETJ 43:4	t. and moderate opinions	MAC 323:13
brother's t. have wet them	CAT 137:15	tea-shops: Emperor in the low-class t.		t. never mellows with age	IRV 270:21
Drop t. as fast	SHAK 477:23		BRAM 91:18	temperance: acquire and beget a t.
drowns them all in t.	LAND 308:21	tea-time: creation will expire before t.			SHAK 433:16
dry than women's t.	WEBS 567:7		SMITH 511:18	Meekness, t.	BIBLE 77:18
ever scare me with thy t.	TENN 543:12	teatray: Like a t. in the sky	CARR 134:2	t. would be difficult	JOHN 280:22
foolish t. would flow	CLAR 152:23	teche: he lerne and gladly t.	CHAU 141:25	what availed this t.	MILT 350:22
foolish t. upon my grave	TENN 533:2	Tecum: T. habita	PERS 372:29	temperate: amazed, t., and furious
fountains fraught with t.	KYD 306:3	t. possum vivere nec sine	MART 331:11		SHAK 461:2
frequent t. have run	BROW 98:10	T. vivere amem	HOR 261:1	more lovely and more t.	SHAK 492:28
greatness of the world in t.	YEATS 586:22	Te Deum: Sings its own seablown T.		t. affords me none	CAREW 130:16
have I drunk of Siren t.	SHAK 495:6		BETJ 43:9	t. will	WORD 581:8
Hence all those t. shed	TER 544:14	tedious: insipid and t. performance		tempers: God t. the wind	STER 519:11
Her t. fell with the dews	TENN 539:23		WALP 562:25	tempest: covert from the t.	BIBLE 58:30
he t. out the heart of it	KNOW 305:17	Life is as t. as a twice-told	SHAK 452:21	'Dark lowers the t. overhead	LONG 316:15
hired t.	BROW 97:8	More t. than the dia eight	SHAK 476:6	From lightning and t.	PRAY 385:16
His big t.	SHEL 502:3	t. and brief	SHAK 471:13	in taverns while the t.	HOUS 264:21
If you have t.	SHAK 450:26	t. As a tired horse	SHAK 439:28	stopp'd the t. of the Gods	MARL 330:11
in the mist of t.	THOM 548:8	teeming: glean'd my t. brain	KEATS 292:30	summer t. came her tears	TENN 542:11
iron t. down Pluto's cheek	MILT 342:6	teems: t. with hidden meaning	GILB 228:36	that silence we the t.	DRYD 195:24
keep time with my salt t.	JONS 283:21	Tees: Arno for my lovelier T.	MAC 322:9	tempestas: Quo me cumque rapit t. HOR 258:7
loos'd our heart in t.	ARN 13:11	teeth: children's t. are set on edge		tempests: on t. and is never shaken
Lord God will wipe away t.	BIBLE 58:19		BIBLE 60:34		SHAK 495:5
match with shedding t.	SHAK 479:16	gooseberries which makes my t. watter		On whom Thy t. fell all	HERB 247:22
Mine eyes are full of t.	SHAK 480:4		FLEM 214:28	tempest-tost: Yet it shall be t.	SHAK 458:7
mine eyes from t.	PRAY 397:20	keep their t. clean	SHAK 427:15	tempestuous: At their t. glee	LONG 317:8
mine own t. Do scald	SHAK 455:25	lose our t. and eyelashes	LEAR 312:24	O'er the world's t. sea	EDM 199:26
My son in t.	GILB 226:7	set my t. nothing on edge	SHAK 439:26	tempête: Qui haute la t. et se rit BAUD 35:6
My t. must stop	HOOD 255:10	taking out his false t.	DOYLE 191:17	temple: body is the t. of the Holy Ghost
natural t. they dropped	MILT 350:1	t. are spears and arrows	PRAY 393:15		BIBLE 76:1
Nothing is here for t.	MILT 351:2	Thy t. are like a flock	BIBLE 56:26	his train filled the t.	BIBLE 57:28
now am full of t.	YEATS 584:22	To cast into my t.	SHAK 451:23	in the very t. of delight	KEATS 291:15
of t. and a Sedan chair	DICK 182:25	trouble me cast me in the t.	PRAY 392:9	Lord's anointed t.	SHAK 460:22
often lie too deep for t.	WORD 579:14	weeping and gnashing of t.	BIBLE 65:17	Open the t. gates	SPEN 515:25
put my t. into thy bottle	PRAY 393:13	will steal the very t.	ARAB 11:17	polished corners of the t.	PRAY 399:12
shall wipe away all t.	BIBLE 82:4	with the skin of my t.	BIBLE 52:29	t. of silence and reconciliation	MAC 323:20
shall wipe away all t.	BIBLE 82:31	teetotaller: I'm only a beer t.	SHAW 496:16	that dread T. of Thy worth	KIPL 301:17
shall ye forget your t.	MORR 358:8	woman should marry a t.	STEV 521:29	them all out of the t.	BIBLE 71:35
sheddeth tender t.	SPEN 516:5	Tehee: 'T!' quod she	CHAU 142:28	temple-bells: t. are callin'	KIPL 301:8
shed t. by rule	WORD 582:13	TEKEL: T.; Thou art weighed	BIBLE 61:6	temples: dwelleth not in t. made BIBLE 74:13
sink'st in thine own t.	DEKK 173:21	telegrams: One of those t.	PROU 401:24	Shall now my joyful t. bind	WALL 562:10
slow t.	FLET 215:29	outer life of t. and anger	FORS 217:1	smote the nail into his t.	BIBLE 49:7

solemn t.   SHAK 485:20
t. lie   WORD 581:14
t. of his Gods   MAC 322:15
thy t. are like a piece   BIBLE 56:26
tous les t. de la terre   DID 184:7
Tempora: T. mutantur   ANON 11:5
t., O mores   CIC 151:26
temporal: pass through things t. PRAY 386:16
temporary: of force alone is but *t.*
   BURKE 109:19
tempt: not t. the Lord thy God   BIBLE 64:2
T. me no more   DAY-L 172:22
T. not a desperate man   SHAK 483:27
T. not the stars   FORD 216:12
t. with wand'ring feet   MILT 346:16
to t. my Lady Poltagrue   BELL 39:24
temptabam: quod t. dicere versus
   OVID 366:33
temptation: combines the maximum of
   t.   SHAW 497:39
I never resist t.   SHAW 496:5
insist on their resisting t.   KNOX 305:26
last t.   ELIOT 204:4
lead us not into t.   BIBLE 64:24
man that endureth t.   BIBLE 80:8
of t. is just to yield   GRAH 233:8
of t. in the wilderness   PRAY 396:4
oughtn't to yield to t.   HOPE 255:27
out of the power of t.   TROL 553:11
over-fond of resisting t.   BECK 36:21
resist everything except t.   WILDE 573:8
t. to a rich and lazy nation   KIPL 298:18
that ye enter not into t.   BIBLE 68:16
to t. slow   SHAK 494:15
under t. to it   LOCKE 315:17
Why comes t. but for man   BROW 104:30
temptations: carry us through all t.
   PRAY 386:8
in spite of all t.   GILB 228:10
shun the t. of monopoly   SCOTT 415:15
t. both in wine and women   KITC 305:14
tempted: tempter or the t.   SHAK 464:5
'Tis one thing to be t.   SHAK 463:16
When your fathers t. me   PRAY 396:4
Which other men are t.   BUTL 118:5
tempter: t. or the tempted   SHAK 464:5
tempts: Not all that t. your wand'ring
   GRAY 235:8
tempus: fugit inreparabile t.   VIRG 560:17
T. abire tibi est   HOR 259:6
T. edax rerum   OVID 366:18
ten: Church clock at t. to three   BROO 94:25
good Lord has only t.   CLEM 152:30
T. Days that Shook   REED 405:8
t. thousands in our streets   PRAY 399:13
tenacem: Iustum et t. propositi   HOR 260:18
tenant: She's the t. of the room   HENL 245:6
tenantless: graves stood t.   SHAK 429:12
tend: t. the wounded under fire   KIPL 299:18
Tendebantque: T. manus ripae ulterioris
   VIRG 558:22
tended: however watched and t.   LONG 317:6
tender: beautiful, the t., the kind   MILL 339:23
coy and t. to offend   HERB 248:14
Gave thee such a t. voice   BLAKE 87:26
heart has felt the t. passion   GAY 223:3
t. for another's pain   GRAY 235:13
t. is the night   KEATS 291:20
t. mercies of the wicked   BIBLE 53:34
that are t. and unpleasing   BACON 25:41
true and t. is the North   TENN 542:5
tenderly: Take her up t.   HOOD 254:9
tenderness: Thanks to its t.   WORD 579:14
Want of t. is want of parts   JOHN 275:33
ténébreux: Je suis le t.   NERV 360:26
tenebricosum: Qui nunc it per iter t.
   CAT 136:23
tenement: Into a clayey t.   CAREW 130:17
Like to a t. or pelting   SHAK 478:20
tenir: Doit se t. tout seul   ANON 9:12

son el tenir y el no t.   CERV 138:17
tennis-balls: are merely the stars' t.
   WEBS 566:29
T., my liege   SHAK 443:10
Tennyson: Lawn T.   JOYCE 286:24
T. and Browning   BAG 29:20
T. goes without saying   BUTL 118:35
T. was not Tennysonian   JAMES 271:25
tenor: They kept the noiseless t.   GRAY 235:1
tent: Hosts' did pitch His t.   HERB 246:25
Upon that little t. of blue   WILDE 572:8
woof of my t.'s thin roof   SHEL 500:6
tenth: talked shop like a t. muse   ANON 5:17
This Submerged T.   BOOTH 89:22
ten thousand: t. times More rich
   SHAK 467:13
Tents: done with the T. of Shem KIPL 300:23
dwelling in t.   BIBLE 46:13
habitation among the t. of Kedar PRAY 398:7
in the t. of ungodliness   PRAY 395:13
man to dwell in their t.   PRAY 394:13
murmured in their t.   PRAY 397:5
Shall fold their t.   LONG 316:10
stately t. of war   MARL 330:2
t. of Kedar   BIBLE 56:16
To your t.   BIBLE 51:4
Where Israel's t. do shine   BLAKE 86:24
with thy tribe's black t.   THOM 547:23
tepores: ver egelidos refert t.   CAT 137:2
Ter: T. sunt conati imponere   VIRG 560:12
Terence: T. this is stupid   HOUS 264:11
teres: t., atque rotundus   HOR 262:10
Tereu: Tereu, T.   BARN 33:32
Terewth: It is the light of T.   DICK 176:16
term: sleep between term and t.   SHAK 426:13
t., holidays   LEWIS 314:9
was a lad I served a t.   GILB 228:4
Termagant: whipped for o'erdoing T.
   SHAK 433:16
terminations: were as terrible as her t.
   SHAK 472:8
termini: t. which bound the common
   EMER 207:14
terminological: risk of t. inexactitude
   CHUR 149:25
terms: hard to come to t. with Him
   MOL 353:26
himself in t. too deep for *me*   GILB 227:21
it with the happiest t.   SHAK 440:28
Many t. which have now   HOR 257:14
T. like grace, new birth   ARN 16:18
t. of moderation takes   BACON 25:12
till I come on perfect t.   WHIT 571:2
terra: t. pax hominibus bonae   MASS 334:18
Terrace: Hall or T. or lofty Tower
   LEAR 312:3
t. blackish-brown   BETJ 43:18
t. walk   SWIFT 527:28
terrarum: Ille t. mihi praeter omnis
   HOR 260:8
terre: nous resterons sur la t.   PREV 400:15
tous les temples de la t.   DID 184:7
terrible: All strange and t. events
   SHAK 423:12
being just the t. choice   BROW 104:31
Dark and t. beyond any   MAC 324:22
I the elder and more t.   SHAK 449:19
It would *not* be t.   JOHN 275:14
lend the eye a t. aspect   SHAK 443:21
my name were not so t.   SHAK 441:15
of his eyes became so t.   BECK 36:19
t. as an army with banners   BIBLE 57:5
t. as hell   MILT 346:24
t. as her terminations   SHAK 472:8
t. beauty is born   YEATS 585:1
t. future may have just   AUDEN 18:19
t. in the simplicity   CONR 161:21
which is t.   FIEL 211:5
Which make thee t. and dear   SHEL 505:2
terrified: ill and t. and tight   BETJ 44:13

t. vague fingers   YEATS 586
territorial: last t. claim which I have
   HITL 251:1
Territories: no slave T.   CHASE 141
terror: added a new t. to death   WETH 569
added another t. to death   LYND 321:1
afraid for any t. by night   PRAY 395:2
are not a t. to good works   BIBLE 75:2
For t., not to use   SHAK 463:1
Have struck more t.   SHAK 481:1
make thee a t. to thyself   BIBLE 60:2
perch and not their t.   SHAK 463:1
So full of dismal t. was   SHAK 480:2
T. is the feeling which   JOYCE 286:1
T. like a frost shall halt   AUDEN 19:1
T. of darkness   CHAP 140:
t. of my name   MARL 330:1
T. the human form divine   BLAKE 88:9
There is no t.   SHAK 451:2
Thy t., O Christ   HOPK 257:6
terrorist: t. and the policeman both
   CONR 161:20
terrors: t. of the earth   SHAK 454:2
though t. reign   GOLD 231:30
Tertium: his Wife and a T. Quid KIPL 305:10
test: is the best t. of truth   CHES 145:33
testa: ...pia t.   HOR 261:5
testament: ministers of the new t. BIBLE 77:4
New T. was less a Christiad HARDY 241:24
purple t. of bleeding   SHAK 479:13
testicles: of a tragedy requires t. VOLT 561:2
testify: they are which t. of me   BIBLE 72:3
testimonies: t., O Lord, are very sure
   PRAY 396:1
testimony: t. of the Lord is sure PRAY 390:12
tether: t. time or tide   BURNS 115:8
tied the world in a t.   SWIN 530:23
Tetigisti: T. acu   PLAU 374:15
tetigit: scribendi genus non t.   JOHN 277:13
Teucer: T. shall lead and his star HOR 259:16
Teviotdale: Ettrick and T.   SCOTT 418:24
text: approve it with a t.   SHAK 467:10
ev'ry t. and gloss over   BUTL 117:18
God takes a t.   HERB 247:12
great t. in Galatians   BROW 105:7
square of t. that looks   TENN 535:15
To your t.   ELIZ 205:24
where a neat rivulet of t.   SHER 506:26
Thackeray: T. settled like a meat-fly
   RUSK 411:6
thame: Lat t. say   KEITH 295:7
Thames: brooks are T.'s tributaries ARN 15:8
flights upon the banks of T.   JONS 284:25
of Gennesareth, but T.   THOM 548:25
On banks of T. they must   HOUS 263:21
shall I see the T. again   BETJ 42:18
stripling T. at Bab-lock-hithe   ARN 14:14
Sweet T., run softly   SPEN 516:32
T. bordered by its gardens   MORR 358:10
T. flowed backward to its   PLOM 374:19
T. is between me   WALP 562:22
T. is liquid history   BURNS 112:23
T. was the noblest river   ADD 2:9
'Till T. see Eaton's sons   POPE 375:21
With no allaying T.   LOV 318:16
youthful T.   ARN 15:3
Thammuz: T. came next behind MILT 345:17
Thane: T. of Cawdor lives   SHAK 458:17
T. of Fife had a wife   SHAK 462:21
thank: I t. the goodness   TAYL 531:23
Now t. you all your God   RINK 406:6
say t. you 'most to death   TWAIN 554:17
t. heaven, fasting   SHAK 426:17
T. me no thankings   SHAK 483:17
t. thee, Jew   SHAK 468:9
We t. with brief thanksgiving   SWIN 529:21
thank'd: When I'm not t. at all   FIEL 211:14
thanked: 't. God my wife was dead
   BROW 106:1

thankful: pleasant thing it is to be t.
　PRAY 399:19
thankfulness: name in pride and t.
　BROW 101:22
thankit: Sae let the Lord be t. BURNS 114:14
thankless: To have a t. child SHAK 453:19
Upon a t. arrant RAL 404:10
thanks: angels yield eternal t. SMART 509:2
Catullus gives you warmest t. CAT 137:3
deserves the love and t. PAINE 368:1
give t. unto thee PRAY 387:23
give t. unto the Lord PRAY 399:2
harp will I give t. unto PRAY 392:11
How to return your t. would BROW 106:1
I am poor even in t. SHAK 432:14
I will give t. unto thee PRAY 399:6
Letters of t. AUDEN 20:2
song of t. and praise WORD 579:10
Take the t. of a boy BEEC 37:9
T. for mercies past receive BUCK 106:17
t. to God always for you BIBLE 78:30
T. to the human heart WORD 579:14
to give t. is good SWIN 529:1
wanting to deserve any t. CAT 137:8
when he had given t. PRAY 388:1
thanksgiving: before his presence with
　t. PRAY 396:3
may shew the voice of t. PRAY 391:5
With proud t. BINY 84:9
Tharshish: years came the navy of T.
　BIBLE 50:34
Tharsis: T. and of the isles shall PRAY 394:20
that: I've t. within GARR 221:14
Take t., you hound DOYLE 192:18
thatch: house with deep t. BELL 40:11
worn the ancient t. TENN 539:23
thatch-eaves: vines that round the t.
　KEATS 293:5
thaw'd: That will be t. from SHAK 449:24
Thawing: T. cold fear SHAK 444:11
Theatre: Aunt was off to the T. BELL 39:10
in a t. SHAK 480:10
jusqu'à la fin le t. rempli BOIL 89:11
problems of the modern t. RATT 405:1
t. is irresistible ARN 16:15
t. of man's life it is BACON 24:24
T.'s certainly not what ELIOT 203:7
theatres: t., and temples lie WORD 581:14
Thebes: Riddles of death T. SHEL 501:1
thee: queer save t. and me OWEN 366:29
theek: t. our nest when it grows BALL 32:8
theft: clever t. was praiseworthy SPEN 514:33
kindness and forgave the t. BROW 104:25
Property is t. PROU 401:19
suspicious head of t. is stopp'd SHAK 457:8
would be t. in other poets DRYD 198:3
thegither: had been fou for weeks t.
　BURNS 115:5
them: not of t. BYRON 120:39
theme: Fools are my t. BYRON 124:15
t. For reason DONNE 188:5
t. too great PRIOR 400:22
themselves: should t. be free BROO 94:4
T. they could not save HOUS 262:13
Therein behold t. SHAK 427:20
These…are a law unto t. BIBLE 74:35
violent hands upon t. PRAY 389:10
'women are a sex by t. BEER 37:24
theologians: if you believe the t. SAL 413:18
t. have employed ARN 16:18
théologie: toutes les écoles de t. DID 184:7
theology: golden rule in t. MILT 351:26
objected to his t. SMIL 509:5
Theophilus: thee…most excellent T.
　BIBLE 69:3
T., of all that Jesus BIBLE 73:20
theorems: About binomial t. I'm teeming
　GILB 228:17
Theorie: ist alle T. GOET 230:3
theories: kinds of old defunct t. IBSEN 269:21

theorize: capital mistake to t. before
　DOYLE 192:7
theory: All t. GOET 230:3
there: because he was not t. BARH 33:21
Because it is t. MALL 327:13
cry over me, T., there PRAY 394:15
heaven, thou art t. PRAY 399:5
if I had not been t. WELL 567:19
I shall not be t. SWIN 530:26
T. go the ships PRAY 397:1
t. vor me the apple tree BARN 33:28
thereby: t. hangs a tail SHAK 475:12
therein: all that t. is PRAY 390:23
thereof: place t. shall know it PRAY 396:17
thereout: t. suck they no small advantage
　PRAY 394:22
thereto: t. I give thee my troth PRAY 389:4
Thermodynamics: describe the Second
　Law of T. SNOW 512:16
Thermopylae: There was an old man
　of T. LEAR 313:3
To make a new T. BYRON 123:2
Thersites: T.' body is as good SHAK 428:21
thesis: doctor's t. On education AUDEN 21:4
thews: t. that lie and cumber HOUS 262:15
They: every one else is T. KIPL 304:2
thick: dash'd through t. and thin DRYD 194:21
shall stand so t. with corn PRAY 394:3
t. and numberless MILT 341:24
thickens: now the plot t. very much
　BUCH 106:14
thicker: finger shall be t. than my father's
　BIBLE 51:2
When the loo paper gets t. MITF 352:25
thicket: ram caught in a t. BIBLE 46:11
thief: embrace the impenitent t. STEV 521:12
first cries out stop t. CONG 160:8
he was a t. HEINE 244:10
I come as a t. BIBLE 82:20
if you do take a t. SHAK 472:31
man's apparel fits your t. SHAK 464:24
Opportunity makes a t. BACON 28:2
steals something from the t. SHAK 474:3
subtle t. of youth MILT 351:6
t. doth fear each bush SHAK 446:23
t. said the last kind word BROW 104:25
this first grand t. MILT 347:18
thought as bad as the t. CHES 145:9
which is the t. SHAK 455:18
thievery: Crams his rich t. up SHAK 487:12
thieves: boldest t., be Yank KIPL 302:12
fell among t. BIBLE 69:30
'Gainst knaves and t. men SHAK 490:27
have made it a den of t. BIBLE 67:17
t. break through and steal BIBLE 64:25
t., the nine figures DICK 178:6
Thou best of t. DRYD 195:17
thievish: Time's t. progress SHAK 494:10
thigh: bee with honied t. MILT 342:8
his vesture and on his t. BIBLE 82:26
Jacob's t. was out of joint BIBLE 46:23
smote them hip and t. BIBLE 49:23
thighs: glory from her loosening t.
　YEATS 586:1
thimbles: They sought it with t. CARR 133:8
thin: Imprisoned in every fat man a t.
　CONN 161:15
into t. air SHAK 485:20
it's 'T. red line of 'eroes' KIPL 303:24
like it out of a t. glass PINT 373:18
t. man inside every fat ORW 365:11
t. red line RUSS 412:23
t., yet never clear POPE 375:20
witty, profligate, and t. YOUNG 588:14
Thine: Be T. the glory DRYD 196:13
continue t. for ever PRAY 388:22
not my will, but t. BIBLE 71:8
only call me t. COL 157:5
t. is the kingdom BIBLE 64:24
Why not I with t. SHEL 502:1

thing: do only one t. SMIL 509:6
firm persuasion that a t. BLAKE 88:26
has this t. appear'd again SHAK 429:8
man is not quite the t. AUST 22:14
most unattractive old t. GILB 227:14
nearest run t. WELL 567:19
one damned t. OMAL 365:5
play's the t. SHAK 433:6
reward of a t. well done EMER 207:26
said the t. which was not SWIFT 526:9
t. ensky'd and sainted SHAK 463:12
t. of beauty is a joy KEATS 288:20
t. that ends all other SHAK 423:20
t. they most do show SHAK 494:15
t. wherein we feel there SHEL 504:20
thrusts the t. we have prayed BROW 97:28
very t. he'll set you BLAKE 87:6
we will shew you a t. BIBLE 50:2
When every blessed t. you GILB 225:30
things: all t. to all men BIBLE 76:7
all ye Green T. upon PRAY 384:24
black and merciless t. JAMES 271:23
bright t. come to confusion SHAK 469:20
cognizance of men and t. BROW 101:11
done but earnest of the t. TENN 538:24
excellent t. are spoken PRAY 395:16
God's sons are t. MADD 326:19
How can these t. be BIBLE 71:37
little t. are infinitely DOYLE 191:18
love all beauteous t. BRID 92:10
much for t. beyond our care DRYD 197:10
Of t. to come at large SHAK 486:27
sorry Scheme of T. FITZ 213:16
such t. to be TENN 537:2
there are tears shed for t. VIRG 557:17
These t. shall be SYM 531:3
T. are in the saddle EMER 206:21
t. are not what they seem LONG 317:1
T. are seldom what they GILB 228:8
t. are the sons of heaven JOHN 281:6
T. fall apart YEATS 586:1
t. in boards that moderns LAMB 307:38
T. in books' clothing LAMB 307:18
t. that are not SHAK 452:2
t. that go bump ANON 5:8
t. they have in common BLUN 89:2
t. through Christ which BIBLE 78:23
t. unknown propos'd POPE 378:29
think of t. that would GILB 226:8
think: above all that we ask or t. BIBLE 77:26
because I have time to t. DARW 172:3
because I t. him so SHAK 490:30
because they t. they can VIRG 558:16
Books t. for me LAMB 307:16
comedy to those that t. WALP 563:11
commonly attains to t. right JOHN 281:37
don't t. foolishly JOHN 279:11
expect a soldier to t. SHAW 496:18
Haply I t. on thee SHAK 493:6
How can I know what I t. WALL 562:5
'I am inclined to t. DOYLE 192:36
I can't t. why GILB 228:26
if the while I t. on thee SHAK 493:7
If you can t. KIPL 299:22
infancy to t. all men virtuous BURKE 108:20
I t. continually of those SPEN 515:7
I t. DESC 175:10
It is later than you t. SERV 420:12
never to t. of one's self CLOU 153:21
qualified my mind to t. justly REYN 405:21
She could not t. COWP 168:18
She that could t. and ne'er SHAK 474:18
so we've got to t. RUTH 412:24
swear thou t.'st I love DONNE 190:14
swiss cheese would t. MARQ 330:25
t. by fits and starts HOUS 264:23
t. for two minutes together SMITH 511:35
t. is to be full of sorrow KEATS 291:19
T. no more HOUS 264:6
T. not of them KEATS 293:7

t. of men are widen'd with TENN 539:2
t. of youth are long LONG 316:22
t. that wander through MILT 346:10
t. that arise in me TENN 532:17
T. that do often lie too WORD 579:14
thy t. in me TENN 542:14
to censor one's own t. WALEY 562:2
To understand God's t. NIGH 363:16
United t. and counsels MILT 345:1
Where branched t. KEATS 292:3
With t. beyond the reaches SHAK 430:24
Words without t. never SHAK 434:31
writers expressed t. FRAN 217:27
thousand: cattle upon a t. hills PRAY 393:2
death; a t. doors SEN 420:11
Death has a t. doors MASS 336:1
is better than a t. PRAY 395:13
man picked out of ten t. SHAK 432:5
night has a t. eyes BOUR 90:21
One man among a t. have BIBLE 55:23
t. Blossoms with the Day FITZ 212:8
t. shall fall beside PRAY 395:21
t. times more fair SHAK 467:13
t. years in thy sight PRAY 395:18
'Would he had blotted a t. JONS 285:1
thousands: forth t. and ten thousands PRAY 399:13
Saul hath slain his t. BIBLE 50:13
showing mercy unto t. BIBLE 47:24
t. of gold and silver PRAY 399:5
Where t. equally were meant SWIFT 527:24
Thousandth: T. Man will stand by you KIPL 303:18
Thracian: T. ships and the foreign SWIN 528:15
thral: been constreyned as a t. CHAU 142:12
thraldom: single t. BACON 28:17
thrall: Hath thee in t. KEATS 290:21
thread: can do with a twined t. BURT 116:33
Feels at each t. POPE 379:9
Hinders needle and t. HOOD 255:10
line of scarlet t. BIBLE 48:37
t. of his verbosity finer SHAK 457:10
t. of my own hand's weaving KEATS 292:10
weave their t. with bones SHAK 489:3
with a silk t. plucks it SHAK 482:20
threaded: Time breaks the t. dances AUDEN 18:10
threat: Whiles I t. he lives SHAK 460:1
threaten: t., promise WHIT 571:11
threaten'd: reader's t. POPE 378:21
t., a lion CHAP 140:3
threatened: t. its life with a railway-share CARR 133:8
threatenings: Breathing out t. and slaughter BIBLE 73:32
threats: in your t. SHAK 451:20
three: Every man at t. years old LEON 313:25
married life t. is company WILDE 572:28
rather than hold t. words' SHAK 472:9
shook t. summers' pride SHAK 494:18
There are t. kinds of lies DISR 187:7
thought is irksome and t. minutes HOUS 266:12
t. corners of the world SHAK 453:1
t. gentlemen at once SHER 506:19
T. hours a day will produce TROL 552:13
T. in One KIPL 302:2
T. jolly gentlemen DE L 174:6
t. kings into the east BURNS 114:13
t. little maids from school GILB 226:27
t. lone weirs ARN 15:3
T. may keep a secret FRAN 218:9
t. merry boys are we FLET 215:9
T. o'clock is always too SART 414:9
t. ravens sat on a tree BALL 32:7
t. things which the public HOOD 255:15
t. unspeakably precious TWAIN 554:7
two or t. are gathered PRAY 385:8
whole is divided into t. CAES 126:26

woodspurge has a cup of t. ROSS 410:9
three-and-thirty: I have dragg'd to t. BYRON 126:15
Three Castles: better brand than the T. THAC 545:30
threefold: t. cord is not quickly BIBLE 55:15
three-fourths: Conduct is t. of our life ARN 16:21
three hundred: handsome in t. pounds SHAK 469:11
three o'clock: always t. in the morning FITZ 213:22
t. in the morning courage THOR 550:18
three per cents: elegant simplicity of the t. STOW 524:2
sweet simplicity of the t. DISR 186:8
threescore: age are t. years PRAY 395:19
Now of my t. years HOUS 262:14
thresh: t. his old jacket till COWP 168:1
t. of the deep-sea rain KIPL 300:23
threshold: Across my t. PATM 370:2
goest over the t. thereof FULL 220:13
stand upon the t. of the new WALL 562:9
starry t. of Jove's Court MILT 340:22
sweep across the blue t. ROST 410:12
threw: She t. me in front BETJ 42:22
stars t. down their spears BLAKE 87:16
thrice: thou shalt deny me t. BIBLE 68:12
t. he slew the slain DRYD 195:2
T. is he arm'd that hath SHAK 446:6
T. was I beaten with rods BIBLE 77:12
Weave a circle round him t. COL 157:1
thrid: Cold currents t. HARDY 239:4
thrift: bargains, and my well-won t. SHAK 465:29
t., Horatio SHAK 430:4
thrive: Bold knaves t. without DRYD 195:38
He that would t. CLAR 152:24
throat: Amen' Stuck in my t. SHAK 460:7
down the t. of Old Time DICK 178:4
expression and an undulating t. BELL 40:2
gives me the lie i' the t. SHAK 433:3
if your t. 'tis hard KING 297:19
knife has slit The t. HOUS 264:9
phrases stick in the t. RUSS 412:22
procession marching down your t. OSUL 365:24
rather felt you round my t. HOPE 256:4
thy t. is shut and dried KIPL 303:8
times her little t. around BROW 103:29
To cut his t. before he SWIFT 528:9
to feel the fog in my t. BROW 103:31
unlocked her silent t. GIBB 225:1
your sweet dividing t. CAREW 130:19
throats: My sore t. are always worse AUST 23:9
throb: only t. she gives MOORE 356:10
throbs: with no t. of fiery pain JOHN 279:1
throne: everyone before the t. CEL 138:6
fell before the t. on their BIBLE 81:32
Gehenna or up to the T. KIPL 304:11
High on a t. of royal state MILT 346:6
himself a t. of bayonets INGE 270:9
honour'd for his burning t. SHAK 465:4
I saw a great white t. BIBLE 82:28
it is God's t. BIBLE 64:15
light which beats upon a t. TENN 533:30
Lord sitting upon a t. BIBLE 57:28
rainbow round about the t. BIBLE 81:22
something behind the t. PITT 373:24
stood before the t. BIBLE 81:31
that sitteth upon the t. BIBLE 81:30
This royal t. of kings SHAK 478:20
t. he sits SHAK 444:25
t. of Denmark to thy father SHAK 429:20
t. of human felicity JOHN 280:20
t. of the heavenly grace PRAY 384:10
T. sent word to a Throne KIPL 301:20
t. was like the fiery flame BIBLE 61:8
t. we honour is the people's SHER 506:7

Wrong forever on the t. LOW 319:13
throned: t. on her hundred isles BYRON 121:2
thrones: his stirrups like the t. CHES 147:3
Not t. and crowns ELL 206:12
throng: Leaving the tumultuous t. WORD 577:26
thronum: Coget omnes ante t. CEL 138:6
throstle: t. with his note so true SHAK 470:18
throstlecock: ousel and the t. DRAY 193:19
throte: faireste hewed on hir t. CHAU 142:32
through: he is t. your body REYN 405:20
let them go t. PRAY 395:5
who has gone t. it VIRG 559:10
wind that blows t. me LAWR 311:9
throughly: Wash me t. from my wickedness PRAY 393:4
throw: body I would t. it out of the window BECK 36:17
I t. myself down in my DONNE 191:1
me to dig him up and t. SHAW 496:23
t. away the worser part SHAK 435:17
t. away the dearest thing SHAK 458:22
thrown: then t. out JOHN 280:3
t. on her with a pitchfork SWIFT 526:29
t. upon this filthy modern YEATS 587:2
throws: rolls and t. and breakfalls REED 405:7
t. himself on God BROW 100:38
thrush: aged t. HARDY 239:7
Hangs a T. that sings loud WORD 581:3
rarely pipes the mounted t. TENN 537:9
That's the wise t. BROW 101:6
t. and the jay SHAK 491:17
thrust: guardsman's cut and t. HUXL 269:3
t. my hand into his side BIBLE 73:10
thrusting: by a divine t. SHAK 453:11
Thucydides: be a T. at Boston WALP 563:9
historical works of T. COBD 154:11
Thug: T. and the Druse CHES 146:27
Thule: Ultima T. VIRG 560:10
thumb: Do you bite your t. SHAK 481:22
t. each other's books out RUSK 411:19
thumbs: By the pricking of my t. SHAK 462:5
Leastways if you reckon two t. LEAR 311:21
Thummim: judgment the Urim and the T. BIBLE 48:1
thumping: such a t. crook BETJ 43:4
thunder: dawn comes up like t. outer KIPL 301:5
Glorious the t.'s roar SMART 509:4
Had felt him like the t.'s ARN 13:16
Harsh t. MILT 347:3
Here falling houses t. JOHN 282:22
He was as rattling t. SHAK 423:22
laugh as I pass in t. SHEL 500:4
lightning shaft and power to t. MAN 328:11
such sweet t. SHAK 471:7
surge and t. of the Odyssey LANG 309:18
that God made the t. MAC 323:32
they steal my t. DENN 174:25
t. of the captains BIBLE 53:7
t. of the trumpets SWIN 530:19
voice of a great t. BIBLE 82:15
what serve for the t. SHAK 477:15
thunderbolt: harmless t. PLINY 374:16
heaped-up mountains with a t. VIRG 560:12
like a t. he falls TENN 533:7
thunderbolts: Vaunt-couriers to oak-cleaving t. SHAK 454:4
thunders: t. from her native oak CAMP 129:13
t. in the index SHAK 435:5
t. of white silence BROW 98:4
thunder-stone: Nor the all-dreaded t. SHAK 428:22
thunder-storm: peoples plunging thro' the t. TENN 538:24
Thus: T. have I had thee SHAK 494:13
T., or words to that JOYCE 286:28
'T. thou must do SHAK 459:1
To be t. is nothing SHAK 461:8
thusness: is the reason of this t. WARD 564:33

thwarted: signify A t. purposing
 HARDY 241:8
Thybrim: *T. multo spumantem sanguine*
 VIRG 558:17
Thy-doxy: My-doxy and Heterodoxy
 or T. CARL 131:25
thyme: sweet t. true FLET 215:21
 the wild t. blows SHAK 470:10
 t. and the gadding vine MILT 343:6
thyself: 'And thou t. to all eternity
 ROSS 410:3
 Be so true to t. as thou BACON 27:35
 thou art beside t. BIBLE 74:25
 T. thou gav'st SHAK 494:13
Tiber: drop of allaying T. SHAK 427:14
 Tiber! father T. MAC 322:21
 T. foaming with much blood VIRG 558:17
 troubl'd T. chafing with SHAK 448:14
Tiberim: *Syrus in T. defluxit Orontes*
 JUV 287:15
Tiberius: So T. might have sat ARN 14:4
Ticket: In his hat a Railway-T. LEAR 312:5
 t. at Victoria Station BEVIN 44:18
tickle: if you t. us SHAK 467:4
 I'll t. your catastrophe SHAK 441:19
 t. her with a hoe and she JERR 273:7
tickled: t. with a straw POPE 379:18
 trouts are t. best in muddy BUTL 118:20
tickles: He t. this age that can ANON 5:18
tickling: must be caught with t. SHAK 489:10
 T. a parson's nose as a' SHAK 481:28
 t. Commodity SHAK 452:14
tidal: turn to rhythmic t. lyres HARDY 239:4
tiddle-taddle: no t. nor pibble-pabble
 SHAK 444:18
tide: am drifting with the t. BALL 31:3
 call of the running t. MAS 334:5
 came the t. SPEN 515:20
 'except when the t.'s DICK 177:17
 going out with the t. DICK 177:17
 high t.!' King Alfred CHES 146:20
 Not this t. KIPL 301:15
 perhaps under the whelming t. MILT 343:16
 since written what no t. LAND 309:4
 tether time or t. BURNS 115:8
 t. crept up along the sand KING 297:1
 t. in the affairs of women BYRON 123:20
 t. in the affairs of men SHAK 451:27
 t. is ready her to honour BEST 42:2
 upon this filthy modern t. YEATS 587:2
 veer in the t. SWIN 530:28
tides: salt t. seaward flow ARN 13:5
 t. of men into my hands LAWR 311:12
tidings: him that bringeth good t. BIBLE 59:18
 let ill t. tell Themselves SHAK 422:12
 you good t. of great joy BIBLE 69:10
tie: not fit to t. his brogues SCOTT 419:1
 silken t. SCOTT 416:20
 that love endures no t. DRYD 197:7
 T. up my sleeves with ribbons HUNT 268:15
tied: t. and bound by the chain PRAY 385:23
 t. to the soil as another HOMER 254:6
Tiere: *der Mensch fand die T.* NIET 363:3
Tierra: *desnuda es recordar la T.*
 GARC 221:4
ties: only the string that t. MONT 355:6
tiger: atomic bomb is a paper t. MAO 328:20
 Came Christ the t. ELIOT 203:4
 imitate the action of the t. SHAK 443:21
 master o' the T. SHAK 458:6
 orang-outang or the t. BURKE 110:24
 rhinoceros or the Hyrcan t. SHAK 461:21
 shark And the t. AUDEN 20:15
 side of the German t. with CHUR 150:7
 that with his t.'s heart GREE 236:12
 t.'s heart wrapp'd SHAK 446:16
 t. sniffs the rose SASS 415:1
 t. that hadn't *got* a Christian PUNCH 402:24
 T. well repay the trouble BELL 38:31

tiger-moth: are the t.'s deep-damask'd
 KEATS 289:16
tigers: tamed and shabby t. HODG 252:2
 t. are getting hungry CHUR 151:3
 t. of wrath are wiser than BLAKE 88:22
tiger-skin: On a t. ANON 8:23
tight: his shoes were far too t. LEAR 312:5
 ill and terrified and t. BETJ 44:13
 long black hair out t. ELIOT 205:9
 wearing arm-chairs t. WODJ 575:25
tights: she played it in t. BEER 37:20
tigress: with swiftness of the t. OWEN 367:11
tike: Or bobtail t., or trundle-tail SHAK 455:1
tikleth: t. me aboute myn herte CHAU 143:19
Till: Says Tweed to T. ANON 7:12
tills: Man comes and t. the field TENN 543:11
Tillyvally: T., lady SHAK 488:18
tilt: mammets and to t. with lips SHAK 438:31
tilth: his full t. and husbandry SHAK 463:13
timber: beaten by a piece of t. FRY 219:22
 crooked t. of humanity KANT 288:14
 Like season'd t. HERB 248:17
 navy nothing but rotten t. BURKE 110:5
Timbuctoo: On the plains of T. WILB 572:3
time: abbreviation of t. GIBB 224:20
 aching t. KEATS 290:4
 All of the olden t. ANON 6:10
 All of the olden t. AYT 24:11
 all t. of our tribulation PRAY 385:17
 annihilate but space and t. POPE 380:22
 antique t. would lie unswept SHAK 427:17
 appeareth for a little t. BIBLE 80:16
 backward and abysm of t. SHAK 484:24
 bank and shoal of t. SHAK 459:5
 been a t. for such a word SHAK 463:6
 been so long t. with you BIBLE 72:33
 be more than biting T. ELIOT 204:3
 besmear'd with sluttish t. SHAK 493:17
 bid t. return SHAK 479:6
 but for all t. JONS 284:23
 choose time is to save t. BACON 26:7
 chronicle of wasted t. SHAK 494:19
 city 'half as old as T. BURG 108:4
 conscious is not to be in t. ELIOT 202:16
 conversing I forget all t. MILT 348:3
 cormorant devouring T. SHAK 456:14
 down the throat of Old T. DICK 178:4
 drew from the womb of t. HEINE 244:12
 entertain conjecture of a t. SHAK 444:9
 envious and calumniating t. SHAK 487:6
 envious T. MILT 344:17
 escaped the shipwreck of t. BACON 24:18
 Even such is T. RAL 404:15
 events in the womb of t. SHAK 474:11
 Fate, T., Occasion SHEL 503:10
 first t. of asking PRAY 388:23
 Fleet the t. carelessly SHAK 424:20
 Footprints on the sands of t. LONG 317:4
 foremost files of t. TENN 539:7
 For T., not Corydon ARN 15:7
 Give peace in our t. PRAY 385:1
 God, who as at this t. PRAY 386:14
 grand Instructor, T. BURKE 112:1
 Grown old before my t. ROSS 409:7
 Have no enemy but t. YEATS 585:12
 have not the t. to meet you KIPL 298:18
 he loved the t. too well CLARE 152:4
 him in the t. of trouble PRAY 392:4
 How goes the t. TENN 544:9
 How soon hath T. MILT 351:6
 How T. is slipping underneath FITZ 212:22
 If the street were t. ELIOT 202:2
 in a t. out-worn YEATS 585:14
 in a t. when thou mayest PRAY 391:17
 inseparable propriety of t. BACON 25:5
 irretrievable t. is flying VIRG 560:17
 it also marks the t. SHER 505:25
 It was the t. of roses HOOD 254:8
 Keeping t. POE 375:1
 let not T. deceive you AUDEN 18:10

 lines to t. thou grow'st SHAK 492:2
 long result of T. TENN 538:1
 long t. ago FORD 216:1
 look into the seeds of t. SHAK 458:1
 Look like the t. SHAK 459:
 Love's not T.'s fool SHAK 495:
 me more than t. and space LAMB 307:2
 Men talk of killing t. BOUC 90:1
 my t. has been properly spent TAYL 531:2
 Never the t. and the place BROW 102:2
 night of t. far surpasseth BROW 97:2
 nobility is the act of t. BACON 26:3
 No t. like the present MANL 328:1
 no t. to read play-bills BURN 112:22
 now doth t. waste me SHAK 480:15
 Now is the accepted t. BIBLE 77:7
 Now it is high t. to awake BIBLE 75:24
 Of t.'s eternal motion FORD 216:20
 old common arbitrator, T. SHAK 487:15
 Old T. is still a-flying HERR 250:5
 old T. makes these decay CAREW 130:12
 Old T. the clock-setter SHAK 452:18
 one born out of due t. BIBLE 76:19
 only t. for grief HOOD 255:9
 our bourne of T. and Place TENN 533:4
 O world! O life! O t. SHEL 501:14
 panting T. toil'd after JOHN 282:25
 Perfection is the child of T. HALL 238:7
 precious t. at all to spend SHAK 493:18
 Procrastination is the thief of t. YOUNG 588:4
 ravages of t. not injure HOR 260:26
 Redeeming the t. BIBLE 78:4
 relish of the saltness of t. SHAK 441:5
 remember'd for a very long t. MCG 325:6
 seventy-seven it is t. JOHN 281:23
 shook hands with t. FORD 216:16
 silent touches of t. BURKE 111:36
 spake in t. past BIBLE 79:28
 spare t. and in his working GILL 229:11
 Speech is of T. CARL 132:23
 speech is shallow as T. CARL 131:13
 spirit of the t. shall SHAK 452:26
 stretch'd forefinger of all T. TENN 541:30
 superfluous to demand the t. SHAK 437:34
 superior to t. and place JOHN 282:7
 syllable of recorded t. SHAK 463:6
 temple half as old as T. ROG 407:9
 tether t. or tide BURNS 115:8
 that t. is money FRAN 218:3
 That t. may cease MARL 329:11
 That t. of year thou mayst SHAK 494:7
 thee t.'s furrows I behold SHAK 493:1
 Then do not squander t. FRAN 218:11
 Then while t. serves HERR 248:26
 There's a good t. coming MACK 325:9
 those feet in ancient t. BLAKE 86:16
 three minutes is a long t. HOUS 266:12
 through time t. is conquered ELIOT 202:16
 Thus the whirligig of t. SHAK 490:25
 T., a maniac scattering TENN 536:21
 T. and Fate of all their FITZ 212:17
 T. and fevers burn away AUDEN 19:17
 t. and nonsense scorning BUCK 106:18
 T. and the hour runs through SHAK 458:21
 t. and times are done YEATS 586:21
 T. an endless song YEATS 585:19
 T. did beckon to the flow'rs HERB 247:24
 T. doth transfix the flourish SHAK 493:20
 T. for a little something MILNE 340:15
 t. has come CARR 135:7
 'T. has too much credit COMP 159:12
 T. hath, my lord, a wallet SHAK 487:3
 T. held me green and dying THOM 547:2
 T. hovers o'er JOHN 283:1
 T. in hours VAUG 555:22
 t. is all I lacked DOUG 191:8
 t. is come round SHAK 452:1
 T. is fleeting LONG 317:2
 T. is like a fashionable SHAK 487:5
 T. is on our side GLAD 229:12

T. is our tedious song   MILT 344:15
t. is out of joint   SHAK 431:26
t. is setting with me   BURNS 114:30
t. is the greatest innovator   BACON 26:28
T. is the great physician   DISR 186:11
T. makes ancient good uncouth   LOW 319:14
T. may restore us in his   ARN 13:18
t. now with a robber's   SHAK 487:12
t. of the singing of birds   BIBLE 56:22
T. present and time past   ELIOT 202:12
t. remembered is grief   SWIN 528:17
t. requireth   WHIT 571:22
T.'s eunuch   HOPK 257:3
T.'s fell hand defac'd   SHAK 494:2
t.'s flies   SHAK 486:8
T.'s glory is to calm   SHAK 492:19
T. shall moult away his   SUCK 524:14
T. shall not lose our passages   DONNE 188:9
T. shall throw a dart   BROW 97:25
T.'s noblest offspring   BERK 41:20
T.'s printless torrent   SHEL 500:15
T. stays   DOBS 187:13
T.'s thievish progress   SHAK 494:10
T.'s wheel runs back   BROW 104:10
T.'s wingèd chariot hurrying   MARV 332:19
T. that is intolerant   AUDEN 19:7
t., that takes survey   SHAK 440:23
T. the avenger   BYRON 121:14
T. the devourer of everything   OVID 366:18
T. the reaper   THOM 548:28
T. the refreshing river   AUDEN 20:15
t. to audit The accounts   MACN 326:6
t. to be born   BIBLE 55:12
t. to begin a new   DRYD 197:19
t. to every purpose under   BIBLE 55:12
t. to make it shorter   PASC 369:14
T., to make me grieve   HARDY 240:2
t. to murder and create   ELIOT 203:19
t. to think before I speak   DARW 172:3
T. travels in divers paces   SHAK 426:13
T. was away and somewhere   MACN 326:11
t. was out of joint   STR 524:4
T. watches from the shadow   AUDEN 18:10
T. we may comprehend   BROW 96:10
T., which antiquates antiquities   BROW 97:12
t., which is the author   BACON 24:15
t. will come when you will   DISR 184:10
t. will come   DISR 185:31
T. will doubt of Rome   BYRON 123:13
T. will have his fancy   AUDEN 18:10
t. will have meanly run   HOR 259:20
T. will run back   MILT 344:11
T. with a gift of tears   SWIN 528:20
t. without injuring eternity   THOR 550:3
T. writes no wrinkle   BYRON 121:25
T., you old gypsy man   HODG 252:9
t. you were off   HOR 259:6
'tis but the t.   SHAK 450:3
to sing of T. or Eternity   TENN 533:12
uncertain balance of proud t.   GREE 236:9
unconscionable t. dying   CHAR 140:30
unthinking t.   DRYD 197:17
use your t.   HERR 250:6
waste of t. and effort   VEBL 556:2
Wears out his t.   SHAK 473:13
weary of t.   BLAKE 87:22
We have short t. to stay   HERR 249:28
We take no note of T.   YOUNG 588:2
What's not destroy'd by T.'s   BRAM 91:23
When t. is broke   SHAK 480:14
When T. shall turn those   DRAY 193:12
which are the births of t.   BACON 26:27
which are the rags of t.   DONNE 190:12
whips and scorns of t.   SHAK 433:8
whole length of t. which   BEDE 37:1
With leaden foot t. creeps   JAGO 271:1
with the productions of t.   BLAKE 88:17
yet t. hath his revolution   CREWE 169:18
timebo: quem t.   BIBLE 83:5
timely: t. utterance gave that   WORD 579:1

timendum: nobis nil esse in morte t.
   LUCR 320:9
timeo: t. Danaos et dona   VIRG 558:1
times: brisk and giddy-paced t.   SHAK 488:26
discern the signs of the t.   BIBLE 66:32
It was the best of t.   DICK 183:5
my dear t.' waste   SHAK 493:7
My t. be in Thy hand   BROW 104:13
nature of the t. deceas'd   SHAK 442:3
old t.   GOLD 232:19
Our t. are in His hand   BROW 104:2
praiser of the t. that   HOR 257:21
Praise they that will t. past   HERR 249:17
revolution of the t.   SHAK 442:1
T. are changed with him   STEV 521:32
t. begin to wax old   BIBLE 62:7
T. change   ANON 11:5
T. contains more useful   COBD 154:11
T. go by turns   SOUT 514:20
T. has made many ministries   BAG 28:24
t.! Oh, the manners   CIC 151:26
t. that try men's souls   PAINE 368:1
timet: *Peiusque leto flagitium t.*   HOR 261:19
timing: lucky t. of your death   TAC 531:9
Timor: T. mortis conturbat me   DUNB 198:8
tin: I place a t. wreath upon   POUND 383:9
tine: Lest my jewel it should t.   BURNS 113:1
tinge: t. with a browner shade   GIBB 224:20
tingle: that heareth it shall t.   BIBLE 49:37
tingling: whoreson t.   SHAK 441:6
tinkle: grasped it for a t.   BEER 37:14
tinkling: talk but a t. cymbal   BACON 26:15
t. cymbal   BIBLE 76:14
tinklings. t. lull the distant folds   GRAY 234:18
tins: fish gaped among empty t.   PLOM 374:19
tinsel: vainly flapt its t. wing   MARV 331:18
tip: that of a school-boy's t.   THAC 545:11
t. them to Long Melford   BORR 90:11
t. up bason and a hose   ASHF 17:8
Within the nether t.   COL 155:18
tipple: that t. in the deep   LOV 318:17
tippled: Have ye t. drink more fine
   KEATS 290:28
tippling: His terrible taste for t.   GILB 225:20
tipsy: never gets t. at all   LEAR 311:22
Tip-tilted: T. like the petal   TENN 534:7
tiptoe: on t. for a flight   KEATS 290:14
t. on the misty mountain   SHAK 483:14
Will stand a t. when this   SHAK 445:3
Tir'd: T. with all these   SHAK 494:5
tired: can wait and not be t.   KIPL 299:22
He was so t.   ROLFE 407:17
hunt down a t. metaphor   BYRON 124:2
I'm t. of Love   BELL 39:18
long process of getting t.   BUTL 118:25
one grows t. of the world   WALP 563:2
Thou art t.   ARN 13:14
t. her head   BIBLE 51:34
T. of his dark dominion   MER 337:5
t. the sun with talking   CORY 163:4
t. with labour of far travel   CAT 136:28
When a man is t. of London   JOHN 277:17
who can ever be t. of Bath   AUST 23:3
woman who always was t.   ANON 5:13
your t., your poor   LAZ 311:13
tirent: pour ceux qui t. le mieux   VOLT 561:18
tires: effort nor the failure t.   EMPS 208:17
He t. betimes that spurs   SHAK 478:19
Tiresias: I T.   ELIOT 205:1
T. have foresuffered all   ELIOT 205:2
tiresome: styles are good save the t.
   VOLT 561:7
tiresomeness: t. of old age   ANON 10:13
Tirez: en disant 'T. le rideau   RAB 404:1
Tirra lirra: 'T.   TENN 538:10
Titan: like thy glory, T.   SHEL 503:15
T.-woman like a lover   SWIN 528:26
Tite: T. tute Tati tibi tanta   ENN 208:20
tithe: t. of mint and anise   BIBLE 67:24
t. or toll in our dominions   SHAK 452:17

Titian: much at heart about T.   RUSK 412:1
title: farced t. running 'fore   SHAK 444:25
feel his t. Hang loose   SHAK 462:27
like my t.   STEV 523:6
t., and possession   PRAY 400:12
To guard a t. that was   SHAK 452:25
Who gain'd no t.   POPE 378:6
titles: All thy other t. thou hast   SHAK 453:16
have t. manifold   WORD 582:3
T. are shadows   DEFOE 173:16
t. of veneration to those   BURKE 111:9
titwillow: t., titwillow   GILB 227:15
Tityre: T., tu patulae recubans   VIRG 559:11
toad: Give me your arm, old t.   LARK 310:7
I had rather be a t.   SHAK 475:21
intelligent Mr T.   GRAH 233:19
pour rose-water over a t.   JERR 273:9
should I let the t. *work*   LARK 310:6
Squat like a t.   MILT 348:16
t. beneath the harrow knows   KIPL 302:1
T., that under cold stone   SHAK 462:2
t., ugly and venomous   SHAK 424:32
tree t. is a chef-d'oeuvre   WHIT 570:21
toads: 'imaginary gardens with real t.
   MOORE 355:20
toast: Let the t. pass   SHER 506:31
never had a piece of t.   PAYN 370:9
refus'd to pledge my t.   PRIOR 401:10
standing t. that pleased   DIBD 175:20
Toasted-cheese: enemies 'T.'   CARR 133:4
tobacco: after that tawney weed t.
   JONS 283:17
am going to leave off t.   LAMB 307:28
cigarette t.   DOYLE 191:16
damned t.   BURT 116:29
For thy sake, T.   LAMB 308:5
He who lives without t.   MOL 353:9
superexcellent t.   BURT 116:29
sweeter t. comes from Virginia   THAC 545:30
taking their roguish t.   JONS 284:5
Whether it divine t. were   SPEN 516:15
tobacker: t., and sleep   DICK 177:9
tocsin: t. of the soul   BYRON 123:17
Tod: auf den T. eines Gefühls   NIET 363:13
TO-DAY: about them if T. be sweet
   FITZ 212:22
Be wise t.   YOUNG 588:3
fine day: t.   MALL 327:10
I have lived t.   DRYD 198:15
live t.   MART 331:8
pick t.'s fruits   HOR 259:20
rose the wrong way t.   BEHN 38:20
such a day to-morrow as t.   SHAK 491:7
T. if ye will hear his   PRAY 396:4
t. I suffer   LESS 313:26
t. which the world may   COLL 158:12
we are here t.   BEHN 38:13
toe: printless t.   BROO 94:21
t. of the peasant comes   SHAK 436:29
to t. that line   THOR 550:9
toes: happier without their t.   LEAR 312:21
his t. if his nose is warm   LEAR 312:18
Pobble who has no t.   LEAR 312:17
tread in the bus on my t.   AUDEN 21:2
togae: Cedant arma t.   CIC 151:22
together: all that believed were t.   BIBLE 73:24
Are we here t. alone   WHIT 570:13
comfortably so long t.   GAY 222:13
Father and the Son t. is   PRAY 387:11
Let us remain t. still   SHEL 500:17
makes them cling t.   WORD 580:11
never again so much t.   MACN 326:14
Our lives would grow t.   SWIN 530:21
sufficient to keep them t.   JOHN 276:2
Swing, swing t.   CORY 163:2
they rise or sink T.   TENN 542:18
t. for the sake of strife   CHUR 149:14
toil: are the horny hands of t.   LOW 319:9
day in t.   QUAR 403:10
Death and T.   VIRG 558:21

double t. and trouble | SHAK 462:2
forget his labour an' his t. | BURNS 113:5
Horny-handed sons of t. | KEAR 288:18
In her strong t. of grace | SHAK 424:17
Our love and t. | KIPL 298:10
Remark each anxious t. | JOHN 282:28
slumber is more sweet than t. | TENN 539:17
smeared with t. | HOPK 256:12
some men t. after virtue | LAMB 308:12
they t. not | BIBLE 64:30
T., envy | JOHN 282:29
t. in other men's extremes | KYD 306:4
year with t. of breath | COL 156:17
toil'd: Souls that have t. | TENN 544:3
toiled: we have t. all the night | BIBLE 69:18
toiling: tears and t. breath | ROSS 408:20
Were t. upward in the night | LONG 316:19
toils: alone is worth all these t. | CAT 136:28
token: t. of a covenant between | BIBLE 45:40
tokens: wish there were t. to tell | HOUS 263:7
Words are the t. current | BACON 24:22
Tolbooth-gate: passive resistance of the
T. | SCOTT 418:19
told: grief too much to be t. | VIRG 557:20
I t. my wrath | BLAKE 87:21
'I t. you so | BYRON 124:6
I t. you so | LONG 317:16
Ought to be t. to come | FROST 219:11
our fathers have t. us | PRAY 392:13
They t. me you had been | CARR 134:22
they t. me you were dead | CORY 163:4
t. so as to be understood | BLAKE 88:25
t. you from the beginning | BIBLE 59:9
what we formerly were t. | BLUN 89:3
who bade me right had t. | EWER 209:12
tolerable: Life would be t. | LEWIS 314:10
t. and not to be endured | SHAK 472:30
tolerate: longer t. the race which has
| BALF 30:3
tolerates: that He t. their existence
| BUTL 118:21
toleration: thus t. produced not only
| GIBB 224:21
toll: tithe or t. in our dominions SHAK 452:17
To t. me back from thee | KEATS 291:23
Tolle: T. lege | AUG 21:15
tollis: t. peccata mundi | MASS 335:7
tolls: It t. for *thee* | DONNE 190:20
Tom: Poor T.'s a-cold | SHAK 454:25
so no more of T. | BYRON 123:29
T. will make them weep | SHAK 455:1
Tomata: Chops and T. sauce | DICK 182:19
tomb: blossom on the t. | COWP 168:5
buried in the silent t. | WORD 582:15
dozen of Claret on my T. | KEATS 294:22
fair Fidele's grassy t. | COLL 158:16
fourfold t. | BASSE 35:1
gilded t. of a mediocre | SMITH 510:20
heart keeps empty in thy t. | KING 296:11
icy silence of the t. | KEATS 290:30
In her t. by the side | POE 374:23
in the t. of the Capulets | BURKE 108:6
sea was made his t. | BARN 34:5
smell like what it is—a t. | SHEL 501:18
This side the t. | DAV 172:15
T. hideth trouble | POUND 383:19
t. the womb wherein they | SHAK 494:11
totter towards the t. | SAY 415:7
Tombs: ceremonious, like T. | DICK 183:13
from the t. a doleful sound | WATTS 565:28
register'd upon our brazen t. | SHAK 456:14
Some hang above the t. | COL 155:4
through the t. of all regions | CEL 138:6
towers and t. and statues | FLEC 214:6
tombstone: t. white with the name
| KIPL 301:18
tombstones: t. show | HOUS 262:13
Tom Cobbleigh: Old Uncle T. and all
| BALL 32:12
Tommy: it's T. this | KIPL 303:22

Tomnoddy: My Lord T. is thirty-four
| BROU 95:3
tomorrow: about t. there's no knowing
| MED 336:9
Boast not thyself of t. | BIBLE 54:36
gone t. | BEHN 38:13
late t. to be brave | ARMS 12:17
nor t. shall not drive | DONNE 190:26
question what t. may bring | HOR 259:18
such a day t. as to-day | SHAK 491:7
T., and to-morrow | SHAK 463:6
T. do thy worst | DRYD 198:15
T. for the young | AUDEN 20:16
t. I die | LESS 313:26
T. I may be | FITZ 212:16
t. is another day | MITC 352:21
t.'s life's too late | MART 331:8
t.'s uprising to deeds | MORR 358:12
T. we'll be back | HOR 259:17
t. we shall die | BIBLE 58:15
Unborn T. | FITZ 212:22
you can put off till t. | PUNCH 402:13
Tom Pearse: T., lend me your grey
| BALL 32:12
Tom Thumb: attention and thought about
T. | JOHN 278:12
tom-tit: by a river a little t. | GILB 227:15
tonandi: Jovi fulmen viresque t. | MAN 328:11
tone: deep, autumnal t. | SHEL 502:13
in that t. of voice | PUNCH 402:34
Robert Emmet and Wolfe T. | YEATS 586:19
t. of the company that | CHES 145:16
t. of the solid and practical | BURKE 108:16
tones: Sweet t. are remembered | SHEL 501:21
t. as dry and level | AUDEN 20:10
tonge: Englissh sweete upon his t.
| CHAU 141:22
in writyng of oure t. | CHAU 144:17
Kepe wel they t. | CHAU 142:26
mysmetre for defaute of t. | CHAU 144:17
tongs: have the t. and the bones SHAK 471:3
tongue: administered in the vulgar t.
| PRAY 388:8
bridleth not his t. | BIBLE 80:11
fellows of infinite t. | SHAK 445:13
God's sake hold your t. | DONNE 188:4
Had t. at will and yet | SHAK 474:18
have fallen by the t. | BIBLE 63:11
her t. unbound | CONG 160:2
him whose strenuous t. | KEATS 291:15
his t. as a sweet morsel | HENRY 245:19
his t. Dropt manna | MILT 346:9
his t. is the clapper | SHAK 472:23
his t. to conceive | SHAK 471:10
ignorant of their Mother T. | DRYD 198:14
I held my t. | PRAY 391:30
I mean the t. | WEBS 566:18
I must hold my t. | SHAK 430:1
in a t. not understanded | PRAY 400:8
instead my t. freezes into | SAPP 414:6
is become his mother t. | GOLD 232:15
Keep thy t. from evil | PRAY 391:23
Licked its t. into | ELIOT 203:18
Love's t. is in the eyes | FLET 215:33
men of less truth than t. | SHAK 492:27
my t. from evil-speaking | PRAY 388:17
My t. is the pen | PRAY 392:14
My t. swore | EUR 209:4
nor t. to speak here | LENT 313:23
obnoxious to each carping t. | BRAD 91:13
of a slow t. | BIBLE 47:9
on my t. the taste | HOUS 266:6
our t. with joy | PRAY 398:16
parching t. | KEATS 291:7
senates hang upon thy t. | THOM 549:16
sharp t. is the only edged | IRV 270:21
she had a t. with a tang | SHAK 485:10
Sing, my t. | VEN 556:4
stopp'd his tuneful t. | POPE 377:6
such a t. | SHAK 453:6

their t. a sharp sword | PRAY 393?
t. can no man tame | BIBLE 80?
t. cleave to the roof | PRAY 39?
t. has its desire | AUDEN 20?
t. In every wound of Caesar | SHAK 45?
t. like a button-stick | KIPL 29?
t. of midnight hath told | SHAK 471?
t. of the dumb sing | BIBLE 58?
t. our trumpeter | SHAK 427?
t. proves dainty Bacchus | SHAK 45?
t. to persuade | CLAR 152:?
T.; well that's a wery | DICK 181.?
t., which is the birth | SHAK 442:?
treasure of our t. | DAN 170?
'tween my heart and t. | SHAK 449:?
understanding, but no t. | SHAK 430:?
use of my oracular t. | SHER 506:?
vibrates her eternal t. | YOUNG 587:?
while I held my t. | PRAY 391?
with the valour of my t. | SHAK 45?
would that my t. could utter | TENN 532:?
Your hand, your t. | SHAK 459?
your t.'s sweet air | SHAK 469:?
tongueless: t. vigil and all the pain
| SWIN 528:?
tongues: base sale of chapmen's t.
| SHAK 456:?
bestowed that time in the t. | SHAK 487:?
cloven t. like as of fire | BIBLE 73:?
Finds t. in trees | SHAK 424:?
hath a thousand several t. | SHAK 481:?
lack t. to praise | SHAK 494:?
Latin, queen of t., | JONS 285?
t. of men and of angels | BIBLE 76:?
t., they shall cease | BIBLE 76:?
Walls have t. | SWIFT 528?
whispering t. can poison truth | COL 156?
Wild t. that have not Thee | KIPL 302?
tongue-tied: art made t. by authority
| SHAK 494?
tonight: t. thou shalt have cramps
| SHAK 484:?
world may end t. | BROW 101:?
Too: T. small to live in | ANON 8:?
took: All which I t. from thee | THOM 548:?
'E went an' t. | KIPL 304:?
person you and I t. me | CARL 131:?
They t. him away in a van | AUDEN 21:?
t. the trouble to be born | BEAU 35:?
ye t. me | BIBLE 68.?
tool: Man is a t.-using animal…Without
| CARL 132:1
t. of honour in my hands | WORD 583:?
Too-late: T., Farewell | ROSS 410?
tool-making: Man is a t. animal FRAN 218:?
tools: Give us the t. | CHUR 150:?
secrets are edged t. | DRYD 197:?
t. to work withal | LOW 319:?
tool-shed: rise to a scream on the t.
| AUDEN 20:?
toon: were his legges and his t. CHAU 142:3
toord: rymyng is nat worth a t. | CHAU 143:1
tooth: danger of her former t. | SHAK 461:1
hadde alwey a coltes t. | CHAU 143:2
Nature, red in t. and claw | TENN 536:2?
poison for the age's t. | SHAK 452:1?
set my pugging t. on edge | SHAK 491:1?
sharper than a serpent's t. | SHAK 453:1?
t. for tooth | BIBLE 47:2?
toothache: sleeps feels not the t. SHAK 429:?
That could endure the t. | SHAK 473:?
toothbrush: t. too is airing in this BETJ 43:1?
toothpicks: nothing but a supply of t.
| JERR 273:?
tooth-point: Exactly where each t. goes
| KIPL 302:1
top: beautiful woman on t. | HOR 257:?
is always room at the t. | WEBS 566:?
kick to come to the t. | KEATS 293:31
rise to power at the t. | LUCR 320:6

schoolboy whips his taxed t.   SMITH 511:38
struggle to the t. alone   CAMUS 129:24
t. of it reached to heaven   BIBLE 46:18
t. thing in the world   KEATS 294:23
toper: poor t. whose untutor'd   COWP 168:8
topics: you have but two t.   JOHN 277:10
top-mast: strack the t. wi' his hand
BALL 30:19
topmost: A-top on the t. twig   ROSS 409:13
tops: think their slender t.   HOOD 254:18
torch: bright t.   KEATS 292:4
runners relay the t. of life   LUCR 320:7
t. of her beauty   WOOLF 576:18
torches: our little t. at his fire   COK 154:14
she doth teach the t.   SHAK 482:2
torchlight: t. procession marching
OSUL 365:24
Tories: are T. born wicked   ANON 6:14
T. own no argument   BROW 97:26
unbending T. who follow   MAC 323:13
torment: measure of our t. is   KIPL 299:11
smoke of their t. ascendeth   BIBLE 82:17
there shall no t. touch them   BIBLE 62:13
t. of the night's untruth   DAN 171:1
t. than a hermit's fast   KEATS 290:24
Tormentarii: Pulveris T., et Acus
BACON 28:9
tormented: Am not t. with ten thousand
MARL 329:7
tormenting: criticism is the most t.
STER 519:30
tormentors: words hereafter thy t.
SHAK 478:21
torments: anybody's t. in this world
CHES 146:3
how many t. lie   CIBB 151:9
Our t. also may in length   MILT 346:13
torn: though thy tackle's t.   SHAK 427:26
torpedo: than it becomes a t. to him
JOHN 274:1
torpedoes: Damn the t.   FARR 210:24
torrent: stem the t. of a woman's   ANON 8:20
torrents: t. of her myriad universe
TENN 539:20
torrid: t. or the f.ozen zone   CAREW 130:16
tort: Quand tout le monde a t.   LA C 306:16
Tortis: this 'ere 'T.' is a insect   PUNCH 402:19
torture: Than on the t. of the mind
SHAK 461:12
t. one poor word ten thousand   DRYD 196:35
t. them, into believing   NEWM 362:8
worms to t. fish   COLM 159:6
tortured: poisoned air and t. soil   KIPL 300:6
torturer: life and the t.'s horse   AUDEN 19:19
Tory: hatred for the T. Party   BEVAN 44:16
I may be a T.   PEEL 371:5
T. and Whig in turns shall   SMITH 512:6
T. men and Whig measures   DISR 185:38
wise T. and a wise Whig   JOHN 278:34
toss: chafe and t. in the spray   ARN 13:5
good enough to t.   SHAK 440:12
tossed: t. them down   HOUS 264:28
t. and gored several persons   BOSW 90:15
tossing: mind is t. on the ocean   SHAK 465:7
t. about in a steamer from   GILB 226:13
young men t. on their beds   YEATS 586:14
toss-pots: With t. still had drunken
SHAK 490:27
tot: Gott ist t.   NIET 363:6
toujours trop tard ou trop t.   SART 414:9
total: What's the demd t.   DICK 180:15
totter: charming to t. into vogue   WALP 563:3
t. on in bus'ness   POPE 377:14
t. towards the tomb   SAY 415:7
totters: Who t. forth   SHEL 505:7
totus: et in se ipso t.   HOR 262:10
touch: child beneath her t.   ROSS 409:22
Did but our bodies t.   YEATS 585:20
Do not t. me   BIBLE 83:24
Fear not to t. the best   RAL 404:10

He wants the natural t.   SHAK 462:12
if he do but t. the hills   PRAY 397:2
live to see thee in my t.   SHAK 455:7
nothing, Can t. him further   SHAK 461:12
One t. of nature makes   SHAK 487:6
puts it not unto the t.   GRAH 233:14
To swear to a t. o' sun   KIPL 302:21
t. his weaknesses with   GOLD 232:8
T. me not   BIBLE 73:9
T. not   BIBLE 78:24
T. not the cat but a glove   SCOTT 418:9
t. of earthly years   WORD 581:10
t. of Harry in the night   SHAK 444:12
touched: he t. the hollow of his   BIBLE 46:23
this hath t. thy lips   BIBLE 57:30
t. a broken girl   FLEC 214:15
t. none that he did not   JOHN 277:13
T. to the quick   BROW 101:16
Who t. my clothes   BIBLE 68:32
touches: silent t. of time   BURKE 111:36
Such heavenly t. ne'er   SHAK 492:27
t. a hair of yon gray head   WHIT 571:18
t. of sweet harmony   SHAK 468:15
Who t. this touches a man   WHIT 570:13
toucheth: t. pitch shall be defiled   BIBLE 63:2
Touching: T. all with thine opiate   SHEL 505:3
tough: t. is J.B. Tough   DICK 177:22
was interesting, but t.   TWAIN 554:1
toujours: est t. dans la majorité   KNOX 305:18
tour: Comme en sa t. d'ivoire   SAIN 413:1
d'Aquitaine à la t. abolie   NERV 360:26
tourist: loathsome is the British t.   KILV 296:5
whisper to the t.   BEER 37:26
tourmente: Malgré moi l'infini me t.
MUSS 359:4
tournament: We in the t.   BETJ 44:6
tous: à t. points de vue   COUE 163:8
T. pour un   DUMAS 199:3
tout: Habacuc était capable de t.   VOLT 561:23
t. for flattery   COLL 158:14
tout le monde: Quand t. a tort   LA C 306:16
toves: slithy t.   CARR 134:28
toward: I t. thy bed   FLEC 214:12
tower: Child Roland to the dark t.
SHAK 454:27
clock collected in the t.   HOUS 264:28
intending to build a t.   BIBLE 70:14
Julius Caesar's ill-erected t.   SHAK 480:6
length that t. of strength   TENN 541:8
name is as the t. of strength   SHAK 481:12
nose is as the t. of Lebanon   BIBLE 57:9
Terrace or lofty T.   LEAR 312:3
within his ivory t.   SAIN 413:1
Towered: T. cities please us then   MILT 342:24
towers: branchy between t.   HOPK 256:9
cloud-capp'd t.   SHAK 485:20
London's t.   BLAKE 86:12
sleep old palaces and t.   SHEL 502:10
tell the t. thereof   PRAY 392:27
t. and tombs and statues   FLEC 214:6
Ye t. of Julius   GRAY 234:17
Towery: T. city and branchy between
HOPK 256:9
towing-path: after a mile or two of a
t.   TROL 553:9
town: charms the t. with humour
CHUR 149:12
Country in the t.   MART 331:14
country retreat near the t.   WYCH 583:24
each and every t. or city   HOLM 253:16
Enormous through the Sacred T.   BELL 39:28
gives directions to the t.   SWIFT 528:3
go seaward from the t.   HUNT 268:12
man made the t.   COWP 166:31
sounding through the t.   BALL 30:17
spreading of the hideous t.   MORR 358:10
t. of monks and bones   COL 156:5
What little t. by river   KEATS 291:8
What's this dull t.   KEPP 295:12
when he studies it in t.   COWP 166:17

town-crier: lief the t. spoke my lines
SHAK 433:16
Towns: Seven wealthy T. contend for
HOMER   ANON 7:14
toy: foolish thing was but a t.   SHAK 490:27
sells eternity to get a t.   SHAK 492:18
toys: All is but t.   SHAK 461:1
all my t. beside me lay   STEV 522:20
Deceive boys with t.   LYS 321:18
make you brooches and t.   STEV 522:29
Not to meddle with my t.   STEV 522:19
of t. and things to eat   STEV 522:21
pray'r-books are the t. of age   POPE 379:19
then cast their t. away   COWP 165:11
Toyshop: They shift the moving T.
POPE 380:30
trace: can t. my ancestry back   GILB 226:20
tremblers learn'd to t.   GOLD 231:2
traces: spring are on winter's t.   SWIN 528:15
track: Around the ancient t. marched
MER 337:5
Come flying on our t.   THOM 549:28
tract: left a little t.   WILDE 572:12
trade: adepts in the speaking t.   CHUR 148:27
all is seared with t.   HOPK 256:12
calling for this idle t.   POPE 376:23
craftsman cunning at his t.   KIPL 298:15
dreadful t.   SHAK 455:14
except what t. can give   BROW 105:3
great t. will always be   BURKE 109:3
half a t. and half an art   INGE 270:8
It is His t.   HEINE 244:13
I t. both the living   DRYD 197:38
nation was ever ruined by t.   FRAN 218:4
not accidental, but a t.   SHAK 464:15
not your t. to make tables   JOHN 274:24
that's my t.   CATH 136:17
This t. of mine   BROW 102:19
t. of war I have slain   SHAK 473:20
War is the t. of kings   DRYD 196:28
trader: some grave Tyrian t.   ARN 14:21
trades: It is the best of all t.   BELL 40:15
ugliest of t. have their   JERR 273:6
tradesmen: bow, ye t.   GILB 225:35
Trade Unionism: T. of the married
SHAW 497:31
Trade-Unionists: There are the T.
KEYN 296:1
tradition: America is their oldest t.
WILDE 573:26
from the air a live t.   POUND 382:14
talk to me about naval t.   CHUR 151:7
T. means giving votes   CHES 148:5
traducción: original es infiel a la t.
BORG 89:24
traffic: Hushing the latest t.   BRID 92:12
t. of Jacob's ladder   THOM 548:25
traffick: two hours' t.   SHAK 481:21
traffickers: Shy t.   ARN 14:21
tragedies: There are two t. in life
SHAW 497:33
t. are finish'd by a death   BYRON 122:28
tragedy: be out of it simply a t.   WILDE 573:31
first time as t.   MARX 333:9
greatest t. in the world   WELL 567:26
her a most tremendous t.   BEER 37:20
That is what t. means   STOP 523:18
t. and therefore not worth   AUST 22:21
t., comedy, history   SHAK 432:20
t. is the noblest production   ADD 2:9
T. is thus a representation   ARIS 12:9
t. requires *testicles*   VOLT 561:2
t. to those that feel   WALP 563:11
tragedye: litel myn t.   CHAU 144:17
tragic: In t. life, God wot   MER 337:14
tragical: Merry and t.   SHAK 471:13
trahison: La t. des clercs   BENDA 40:18
Trahit: T. sua quemque voluptas   VIRG 559:17
trail: am still on their t.   THOR 550:8
t. that is always new   KIPL 300:23

trail'd: t. the hunter's javelin ARN 14:26
trailing: t. clouds of glory WORD 579:5
T. in the cool stream thy ARN 14:14
train: catching a t. is to miss CHES 148:11
descending from the t. LEL 313:18
her starry t. MILT 348:5
his t. filled the temple BIBLE 57:28
next t. has gone ten minutes PUNCH 402:21
Of heat the express t. THOM 547:16
take a t. BROO 94:22
t. and tram alternate go BETJ 43:17
t. for ill and not HOUS 264:14
T. up a child in the way BIBLE 54:22
we rush in the t. THOM 549:28
world And all her t. VAUG 555:22
trains: t. all night groan HOUS 262:16
traitor: Do hate the t. DAN 170:20
I find myself a t. with SHAK 480:4
mind by that t. to learning JOHN 273:17
traitors: flinch and t. sneer CONN 161:10
Our fears do make us t. SHAK 462:11
they can see a sort of t. SHAK 480:4
t. and the treason love DRYD 196:21
tram: I'm a t. HARE 242:8
train and t. alternate BETJ 43:17
trample: light doth t. on my days VAUG 555:19
t. the vices themselves AUG 22:3
tramples: Death t. it to fragments SHEL 499:26
Trams: 'T. and dusty trees ELIOT 205:5
trance: He fell into a t. BIBLE 73:37
in mad t. SHEL 499:20
Tränen: Wer nie sein Brot mit T. GOET 230:12
tranquilles: t. dans les grands ouvrages VOLT 561:16
Tranquillity: divine T. TENN 539:22
emotion recollected in t. WORD 583:10
Fame and t. can never be MONT 354:22
I am restoring t. BURKE 109:28
moments of t. in great works VOLT 561:16
t. which religion is powerless FORB 216:10
transcendental: idle chatter of a t. GILB 227:21
T. moonshine CARL 132:7
transform: t. ourselves into beasts SHAK 475:9
transgression: deceived was in the t. BIBLE 79:10
there is no t. BIBLE 74:39
transgressions: was wounded for our t. BIBLE 59:22
transgressors: was numbered with the t. BIBLE 59:24
way of t. is hard BIBLE 53:36
transit: quam cito t. gloria mundi THOM 546:7
Sic t. gloria mundi ANON 11:1
transitory: Action is t. WORD 577:2
this t. life are in trouble PRAY 387:16
translate: pudding as well as t. Epictetus JOHN 273:31
such as cannot write, t. DENH 174:21
translated: thou art t. SHAK 470:17
T. Daughter AUDEN 18:4
t. into another tongue BIBLE 62:20
translation: be a mistake in the t. VANB 555:4
is only a t. of the Bible WHAT 569:15
is unfaithful to the t. BORG 89:24
is what gets lost in t. FROST 219:16
Not a t. SHER 505:19
T.'s thief that addeth MARV 332:17
translations: in a score of bad t. AUDEN 19:11
Some hold t. not unlike HOW 266:20
translator: t. of Homer should above ARN 16:11
translunary: him those brave t. things DRAY 193:13
transmigrates: it t. SHAK 422:14

transport: turned to share the t. WORD 582:15
trappe: Kaught in a t. CHAU 141:16
trappings: t. and the suits of woe SHAK 429:25
trash: peasants their vile t. SHAK 451:21
Traum: ewige Friede ist ein T. MOLT 354:4
traurig: Dass ich so t. bin HEINE 244:9
travail: had my labour for my t. SHAK 486:20
travaileth: groaneth and t. in pain BIBLE 75:10
travaille: fyn and guerdoun for t. CHAU 144:19
travel: Can in a moment t. thither WORD 579:12
discover we must t. too FITZ 213:4
English man does not t. STER 518:31
have discredited your t. SHAK 421:21
heart turns to t. so that POUND 383:15
I t. for travel's sake STEV 521:18
preserve all that t. by land SWIFT 526:33
ship would *not* t. due West CARR 133:6
takes me I t. as a visitor HOR 258:7
tired with labour of far t. CAT 136:28
t. by land or by water PRAY 385:20
t. faster than a stagecoach GOLD 232:18
t. forth without my cloak SHAK 493:11
t. from Dan to Beersheba STER 519:2
t. hopefully is a better STEV 522:9
T., in the younger sort BACON 27:27
T. light and you can sing JUV 287:26
travell'd: t. in the realms of gold KEATS 292:17
travelled: I t. among unknown men WORD 577:28
Traveller: Farewell, Monsieur T. SHAK 426:20
Head of a t. HOUS 266:9
His fellow t. ANON 8:4
lost t.'s dream BLAKE 86:1
misled and lonely t. MILT 341:1
No t. returns SHAK 433:8
Sentimental T. (meaning STER 518:30
spurs the lated t. apace SHAK 461:15
t. betwixt life and death WORD 581:8
t., by the faithful hound LONG 316:16
t. came BLAKE 86:22
t. from an antique land SHEL 502:15
t. from Lima will visit WALP 563:9
t.'s journey is done BLAKE 87:22
World-besotted t. YEATS 587:3
Travellers: outside at 'The T.' Rest' HARDY 241:2
t. must be content SHAK 425:8
traveller's joy: t. beguiles in autumn HOUS 265:9
travelleth: He that t. into a country BACON 27:27
poverty come as one that t. BIBLE 53:22
travelling: Captain is a good t. name FARQ 210:5
grand object of t. is JOHN 277:6
That's fairly worth the t. STEV 523:9
T. is the ruin of all happiness BURN 112:17
travels: t. the fastest who travels KIPL 304:11
T.' will consist of excursions COL 157:29
trawlers: little fleet of t. under sail BETJ 42:17
Tray: good T. grew very red HOFF 252:13
my poor dog T. CAMP 128:20
T., Blanch, and Sweet-heart SHAK 454:29
trays: cheap tin t. MAS 333:19
treachery: fear their subjects' t. SHAK 446:19
justly kill'd with my own t. SHAK 437:19
T.! seek it out SHAK 437:20
which even t. cannot trust JUN 287:7
treacle: fly that sips t. is lost GAY 222:30
tread: because you t. on my dreams YEATS 585:9
face with an undaunted t. STEV 522:25
t. on classic ground ADD 2:4
t. on Earth unguess'd ARN 14:24

t. safely into the unknown' HASK 243:7
Were it ever so airy a t. TENN 540:12
Where'er we t. 'tis haunted BYRON 120:15
wine-press which ye t. MAC 322:6
treason: condoned high t. DISR 185:6
greatest t. ELIOT 204:4
hate traitors and the t. DRYD 196:21
his office t. was no crime DRYD 194:16
If *this* be t. HENRY 245:25
in trust I have found t. ELIZ 206:3
is a sort of t. BURKE 110:9
It were t. to our love THOR 550:28
love grows bitter with t. SWIN 530:5
none dare call it t. HAR 242:10
popular humanity is t. ADD 1:21
reason why gunpowder t. ANON 7:10
That t. can but peep SHAK 436:6
They cannot commit t. COKE 154:24
though they love the t. DAN 170:20
T. has done his worst SHAK 461:12
'Twixt t. and convenience CLEV 153:3
Whilst bloody t. flourish'd SHAK 450:28
who committed t. enough SHAK 460:16
treasonous: prompts 'em their t. parles BROW 99:26
treasons: Is fit for t. SHAK 468:17
treasure: he that has stoln the t. CONG 160:8
it as your chiefest t. BELL 38:23
our delight or as our t. HERB 248:2
purest t. mortal times SHAK 478:8
shalt have t. in heaven BIBLE 67:9
She is your t. SHAK 484:7
this t. in earthen vessels BIBLE 77:5
t. of our tongue DAN 170:23
Where your t. is BIBLE 64:35
treasures: out t. from an earthen pot HERB 247:12
yourselves t. upon earth BIBLE 64:25
yourselves t. in heaven BIBLE 64:25
treasuries: sunken wrack and sumless t. SHAK 443:3
Treasury: T. is the spring of business BAG 28:22
Treasury Bench: plaintive treble of the T. DISR 184:18
wonder sitting on the T. CHUR 149:27
treat: All eager for the t. CARR 135:6
Greek as a t. CHUR 150:23
something left to t. my friends MALL 327:12
t. with virtuous scorn GILB 226:4
who gives a child a t. MAS 333:25
you're giving a t. GILB 226:14
treatise: former t. have I made BIBLE 73:20
T. of Human Nature HUME 268:1
treaty: signed the t. THOM 547:5
treble: again towards childish t. SHAK 425:24
trebled: I would be t. twenty times SHAK 467:13
tree: be ay sticking in a t. SCOTT 418:20
billboard lovely as a t. NASH 360:2
down under a juniper t. BIBLE 51:10
Eden's dread probationary t. COWP 166:13
Generations pass while some t. BROW 97:16
Grow to some Southern t. HARDY 239:9
highly impossible t. GILB 225:13
his own t. of ancestors STEV 521:10
I shall be like that t. SWIFT 527:19
is not growing like a t. JONS 285:8
it is a t. of life BIBLE 53:35
leaves of the t. were BIBLE 83:1
live on this Crumpetty T. LEAR 312:22
Lord God to grow every t. BIBLE 45:8
middle t. and highest there MILT 347:18
more to my taste than a t. MORR 358:4
'neath a swan-bosomed t. SITW 508:12
of the t. of the knowledge BIBLE 45:9
only God can make a t. KILM 296:4
place where the t. falleth BIBLE 56:6
pledges of a fruitful t. HERR 248:20
poem lovely as a t. KILM 296:3

she gave me of the t.   BIBLE 45:17
some single herb or t.   MARV 331:21
that's why the t.   ANON 4:29
there's a t. of many   WORD 579:5
there vor me the apple t.   BARN 33:28
these things in a green t.   BIBLE 71:10
thocht it was a trustie t.   BALL 32:10
three ravens sat on a t.   BALL 32:7
t. by a river a little   GILB 227:15
t. Continues to be   KNOX 305:22
t. did end their race   MARV 332:2
t. is known by his fruit   BIBLE 66:8
t. of actual life springs   GOET 230:3
t. of diabolical knowledge   SHER 506:10
t. of knowledge of good   BIBLE 45:8
t. of liberty must be refreshed   JEFF 272:10
t. of life also   BIBLE 45:8
t. of man was never quiet   HOUS 263:15
t. that a wise man sees   BLAKE 88:16
Under the greenwood t.   SHAK 425:14
was an Old Man in a t.   LEAR 311:16
Was there a t. about which   COWL 164:17
wish I were a t.   HERB 246:23
trees: all the t. are green   KING 297:5
Bosom'd high in tufted t.   MILT 342:20
climbing t. in the Hesperides   SHAK 457:8
did gently kiss the t.   SHAK 468:13
die when the t. were green   CLARE 152:4
fields and leaves to the t.   HOR 261:14
filled the t. and flapped   HODG 252:6
I see men as t.   BIBLE 68:33
might procreate like t.   BROW 96:33
music of its t. at dawn   ARN 14:1
My apple t. will never   FROST 219:9
Of all the t. in England   DE L 174:17
Of all the t. that grow   KIPL 303:25
'O look at the t.   BRID 92:14
Orpheus with his lute made t.   SHAK 447:3
selected the felling of t.   CHUR 149:20
shady t. cover him with   BIBLE 53:10
their tall ancestral t.   HEM 244:21
This lady by the t.   YEATS 584:23
Those t. in whose dim shadow   MAC 323:1
to move and t. to speak   SHAK 461:24
'Trams and dusty t.   ELIOT 205:5
T. did grow and plants   BARN 33:32
t. I see barren of leaves   SHAK 492:26
t. of the Lord also are   PRAY 396:20
T., where you sit   POPE 378:21
unto the root of the t.   BIBLE 63:39
upon the t. that are therein   PRAY 399:3
'whispers through the t.'   POPE 378:21
you lover of t.   BROW 100:12
trek: nations t. from progress   OWEN 367:11
Trelawny: shall T. die   HAWK 243:4
tremble: I t., I expire   SHEL 500:13
Let Sporus t.   POPE 376:30
shall t. at the look of him   PRAY 397:2
start and t. under her feet   TENN 540:12
t. and despoil themselves   SHEL 502:11
t. for my country when   JEFF 272:16
t. like a guilty thing   WORD 579:10
trembled: Laugh at all you t.   COWP 166:14
t. with fear at your frown   ENGL 208:19
tremblers: boding t. learn'd to trace
   GOLD 231:2
trembling: brought the t. woman there
   BLAKE 85:24
salvation with fear and t.   BIBLE 78:15
T., hoping   POPE 376:3
t. seizes all of me   SAPP 414:6
tremendous: This most t. tale of all BETJ 42:8
white t. daybreak   BROO 94:29
trench: Stand in the t., Achilles SHAW 498:28
trenchant: t. blade   BUTL 117:24
trenched: hoed and t. and weeded
   HOUS 264:17
trencher: Dead Caesar's t.   SHAK 422:20
trencher-friends: t., time's flies SHAK 486:8

trencher-man: He is a very valiant t.
   SHAK 471:26
trenches: t. in thy beauty's field SHAK 492:23
Trent: silver T. shall run   SHAK 439:24
was Burton built on T.   HOUS 264:12
trépas: vivre le t. de quelqu'un   MOL 353:16
tres: omnis divisa in partes t.   CAES 126:26
trespass: t. there and go   HOUS 265:10
trespasses: forgive us our t.   PRAY 384:14
tress: corn at midnight by a t. YEATS 586:17
tresses: Knees and t. folded   MER 337:1
t. like the morn   MILT 341:18
trial: is a t. of which you can   SHAW 497:3
purity, all t., all obeisance   SHAK 426:29
T. by jury itself   DENM 174:22
which purifies us is t.   MILT 351:24
triangle: eternal t.   ANON 7:23
tribe: All that t.   HOR 261:24
badge of all our t.   SHAK 466:2
purify the dialect of the t.   ELIOT 202:25
Richer than all his t.   SHAK 477:23
tribeless: t., and nationless   SHEL 503:12
tribes: Form'd of two mighty t. BYRON 124:4
thither the t. go up   PRAY 398:11
tribulation: In all time of our t. PRAY 385:17
which came out of great t.   BIBLE 82:2
world ye shall have t.   BIBLE 72:41
Tribunal: its highest T. will accomplish
   BURKE 110:28
There's a new t. now   BROW 104:32
tributaries: brooks are Thames's t. ARN 15:8
tribute: majesty shall have t. of me
   SHAK 432:16
tribute to whom t. is due   BIBLE 75:22
t. which vice pays to virtue   LA R 310:12
trick: I know a t. worth two   SHAK 438:21
pleasing to t. the trickster   LA F 306:19
win the t.   HOYLE 267:4
trickle: last t. seemed to disappear
   PLOM 374:19
tricks: all t. are either knavish   JOHN 278:9
of the man of many t.   HOMER 254:4
shap'd for sportive t.   SHAK 480:18
There are no t. in plain   SHAK 451:11
t. and all   BROW 102:19
t. that are vain   HARTE 242:29
Women are like t. by slight   CONG 160:9
tried: to be t. before a jury   JOHN 277:2
t. a little, failed much   STEV 521:5
t. their talents at one   COL 157:26
when he is t.   BIBLE 80:8
trifid: steep and t. God   THOM 547:22
trifle: coffee t. with the spoon   POPE 377:7
'twere a careless t.   SHAK 458:22
trifles: man of sense only t.   CHES 145:26
She who t. with all   GAY 223:4
snapper-up of unconsidered t. SHAK 491:18
T. light as air   SHAK 475:23
t. were worth something   CAT 136:20
write t. with dignity   JOHN 278:23
trifling: mother's deafness is very t.
   AUST 22:12
Trigger: Finger do you want on the T.
   ANON 8:22
triggers: To dror resolves an' t.   LOW 319:3
Trimmer: T.' signifies no more HAL 237:18
trimmings: mutton with the usual t.
   DICK 182:26
Trinities: cold Christ and tangled T.
   KIPL 302:2
Trinity: I the T. illustrate   BROW 105:6
T. had never been unkind   NEWM 361:23
we worship one God in T.   PRAY 385:12
trinket: I swung the earth a t.   THOM 548:17
joy's a t.   STEP 518:25
trinkets: ye returned to your t.   KIPL 300:4
triomphe: on t. sans gloire   CORN 162:16
trip: From fearful t. the victor WHIT 570:8
like a fairy t. upon   SHAK 495:19
t. it as ye go   MILT 342:15

triple: There be t. ways to take   KIPL 301:1
t. cord   BURKE 112:5
triplex: robur et aes t.   HOR 259:12
trippingly: t. on the tongue   SHAK 433:16
Triste: Caballero de la T. Figura
   CERV 138:12
coitum omne animal t.   ANON 10:17
île t. et noire   BAUD 35:8
jamais t. archy   MARQ 330:21
La chair est t.   MALL 327:9
t. vieillesse vous vous   TALL 531:18
tristement: anglais s'amusent t. SULLY 524:18
tristesse: Bonjour t.   ELUA 206:16
Tristram: christened let call him T.
   MAL 327:17
Tristram Shandy: Life and Opinions
of T.   WALP 562:25
T. did not last   JOHN 276:34
Triton: hear old T. blow his wreathed
   WORD 582:20
T. blowing loud his wreathed SPEN 515:21
you this T. of the minnows   SHAK 427:21
triumph: devils'-t. and sorrow BROW 102:7
forth in t. from the north   MAC 322:6
in ourselves, are t.   LONG 316:27
lives…We shall not see the t. DICK 183:10
meet with T. and Disaster   KIPL 299:22
of the uncircumcised t.   BIBLE 50:16
Poor is the t.   THOM 549:18
ride in t. through Persepolis MARL 330:7
so be pedestalled in t.   BROW 104:30
there is no glory in the t.   CORN 162:16
t. of hope over experience   JOHN 275:36
t. over death and sin   SPEN 515:17
When learning's t. o'er   JOHN 282:25
triumphant: bound in with the t. sea
   SHAK 478:20
mounts exulting on t. wings   POPE 381:14
triumphantes: Laeti t.   ANON 10:4
triumph'd: t. over fate   BYRON 124:28
triumphs: He sicken'd at all t. CHUR 149:4
trivial: away all t. fond records SHAK 431:15
contests rise from t. things   POPE 380:28
t. and vulgar way of coition BROW 96:33
t. round   KEBLE 295:4
Trochee: T. trips from long to short
   COL 157:3
trod: our forefathers t.   SWIN 530:7
they t. in the wash-tub   CLOU 153:15
t., as on the four winds   MARV 332:13
T. beside me   HOUS 264:1
trodden: little fire is quickly t. SHAK 446:21
t. the winepress alone   BIBLE 60:11
Trois: T. heures, c'est toujours trop tard
   SART 414:9
Trojan: T. 'orses will jump out BEVIN 44:19
Trojans: T. and the well-greaved
   HOMER 253:28
We T. are at an end   VIRG 558:6
Trolley-bus: T. and windy street BETJ 42:7
trolley buses: kissing of the t. hissing
   BETJ 42:16
trompé: amis que d'en être t.   LA R 310:10
tromper: plaisir de t. le trompeur
   LA F 306:19
Troop: T. home to churchyards SHAK 470:25
troops: charged the t. of error BROW 96:5
her Aeneas shall want t.   SHAK 423:10
solemn t. and sweet societies MILT 343:18
tropes: He rang'd his t.   PRIOR 401:2
trophies: among her cloudy t. hung
   KEATS 291:15
Hang their old t. o'er   POPE 380:7
her weedy t. and herself   SHAK 436:16
t. unto the enemies   BROW 96:5
tropic: Under the t. is our language
   WALL 562:17
tropics: nuisance of the t. is   BELL 39:31
Trostmittel: Selbstmord ist ein starkes
T.   NIET 363:11

trot: 'Does it t.   LEAR 313:1
troth: thereto I give thee my t.   PRAY 389:4
Trotting: T. through the dark   KIPL 302:22
trouble: charm of powerful t.   SHAK 462:3
  deliver him in the time of t.   PRAY 392:4
  double toil and t.   SHAK 462:2
  full of t.   BIBLE 52:26
  has t. enough of its own   WILC 572:5
  Man is born unto t.   BIBLE 52:17
  No stranger to t. myself   VIRG 557:19
  present help in time of t.   ANON 4:18
  read when they're in t.   HOUS 265:13
  save t. I wed again   CLARE 152:6
  Today the Roman and his t.   HOUS 263:15
  to have your t. doubl'd   DEFOE 173:9
  took the t. to be born   BEAU 35:18
  transcendent capacity of taking t.   CARL 131:18
  transitory life are in t.   PRAY 387:16
  t. deaf heaven with my   SHAK 493:6
  t. out of King Charles's   DICK 177:7
  t.'s sure   HOUS 264:14
  t. with people is not that   BILL 84:7
  were a t. to my dreams   WORD 580:14
  where all t. seems   SWIN 529:21
  which just make more t.   HOR 260:16
  will t. thine eyes   DONNE 190:23
  women and care and t.   WARD 564:38
  'you ain't see no t. yit   HARR 242:12
troubled: Let not your heart be t.   BIBLE 72:30
  no more was by it t.   THAC 546:3
  see that ye be not t.   BIBLE 67:27
  t. midnight and the noon's   ELIOT 202:11
  t. spirit: a broken   PRAY 393:8
  t. with her lonely life   PEPYS 372:8
troubles: all our t. and adversities   PRAY 385:22
  arms against a sea of t.   SHAK 433:8
  t. of our proud and angry   HOUS 264:22
  t. they reave me of rest   HOUS 266:7
  t. you are yourself spared   LUCR 320:6
  written t. of the brain   SHAK 463:3
  yet nothing t. me less   LAMB 307:26
troublesome: loud and t. *insects*   BURKE 111:16
  very t. to everybody else   CONG 160:22
  women are mostly t. cattle   LOVER 318:22
troubling: wicked cease from t.   BIBLE 52:13
trousers: bottoms of my t. rolled   ELIOT 203:25
  like a steam-engine in t.   SMITH 511:10
  never have your best t.   IBSEN 269:19
  shall wear white flannel t.   ELIOT 203:25
  then he hitch'd his t.   BARH 33:23
trout: gray t. lies asleep   HOGG 252:23
  t. for factitious bait   POUND 383:2
  t. that must be caught   SHAK 489:10
  you find a t. in the milk   THOR 550:24
Trouthe: T. and honour   CHAU 141:9
  T. is the hyest thing that   CHAU 142:14
trouts: t. are tickled best   BUTL 118:20
trovato: è molto ben t.   ANON 10:3
trowel: She lays it on with a t.   CONG 159:24
  should lay it on with a t.   DISR 185:28
trowth: t. thee shal delivere   CHAU 144:22
Troy: fir'd another T.   DRYD 195:7
  half his T. was burn'd   SHAK 441:1
  heard T. doubted   BYRON 123:13
  ringing plains of windy T.   TENN 543:22
  sacked T.'s sacred city   HOMER 254:4
  T. but a heap of smouldering   POUND 382:7
  T. came destined an exile   VIRG 557:8
  Was there another T.   YEATS 586:7
  Where's T.   BRAM 91:23
truant: every t. knew   GOLD 231:2
  have a t. been to chivalry   SHAK 440:16
  t. disposition   SHAK 430:2
truce: t. ought to be allowed   BURKE 111:3
true: any less real and t.   SHAW 496:14
  Arabian Tales were t.   NEWM 361:16

called Faithful and T.   BIBLE 82:25
can the devil speak t.   SHAK 458:16
course of t. love never did run   SHAK 469:18
Dare to be t.   HERB 247:2
dark and t. and tender   TENN 542:5
finished yields the t. glory   DRAKE 193:1
having is t. to his wife   VANB 555:6
heart of a t. *Englishman*   ADD 2:19
if I know what t. love is   TENN 534:28
If it is not t.   ANON 10:3
If t., here only   MILT 347:19
I'll prove more t.   SHAK 482:14
is it t.   BETJ 42:8
it is t.   LAWR 311:11
Let God be t.   BIBLE 74:36
let us be t.   ARN 12:23
lived she was a t. lover   MAL 328:2
long enough it will be t.   BENN 40:23
man would like to be t.   BACON 28:7
Minding t. things by what   SHAK 444:13
my shape as t.   SHAK 453:9
My t. love hath my heart   SIDN 507:16
my t. love said   PEELE 371:9
not necessarily t.   WILDE 573:34
ower t. tale   SCOTT 418:8
people as equally t.   GIBB 224:21
ring in the t.   TENN 537:14
speak t.   TENN 534:5
state by proportions t.   MARV 331:20
tell you three times is t.   CARR 133:1
think what is t. and do   HUXL 269:8
thou wast as t. a lover   SHAK 425:9
'Tis easy to be t.   SEDL 419:14
to itself do rest but t.   SHAK 453:1
to thine own self be t.   SHAK 430:19
t. as truth's simplicity   SHAK 487:2
t. beginning of our end   SHAK 471:16
t. king I offer'd free   MAC 322:8
t. paradises are paradises   PROU 402:1
t. pathos and sublime   BURNS 115:15
T. patriots we   BARR 34:23
t. to thyself as thou be   BACON 27:35
unfaithful kept him falsely t.   TENN 534:29
we are sure they are t.   SHAK 492:3
whatever for supposing it t.   RUSS 412:17
Whatsoever things are t.   BIBLE 78:22
words are t. and faithful   BIBLE 82:31
'You are not t.   WILB 572:4
true-love: do as much for my t.   BALL 32:9
  iron pokers into t. knots   COL 157:6
truer: nothing's t. than them   DICK 177:11
truest: paint 'em t. praise   ADD 1:15
  t. and the holiest that   MAL 327:22
trump: at the last t.   BIBLE 76:29
  speaking t. of future fame   BYRON 124:24
  with the sound of the t.   PRAY 392:24
trumpet: Blow up the t. in the new-moon   PRAY 395:9
  blow your own t.   GILB 228:32
  ever and anon a t. sounds   THOM 548:20
  flute and the t.   AUDEN 20:21
  Glorious the t. and alarm   SMART 509:4
  great voice as of a t.   BIBLE 81:11
  heard the sound of thee t.   BIBLE 49:2
  he blew a t.   BIBLE 49:15
  He shifted his t.   GOLD 231:21
  His t. shrill hath thrice   SPEN 515:16
  is the sound of the t.   BIBLE 53:7
  moved more than with a t.   SIDN 508:3
  shrill t. sounds   CIBB 151:13
  t., at whose voice   DONNE 189:33
  t. give an uncertain sound   BIBLE 76:15
  t. in terrible tones went   ENN 208:21
  t. shall sound   BIBLE 76:29
  t. shall be heard on high   DRYD 197:25
  t.'s loud clangour   DRYD 197:23
  t.'s silver sound is still   SCOTT 417:2
  t. will fling out a wonderful   CEL 138:6
trumpeter: tongue our t.   SHAK 427:11

trumpets: are the eagles and the t.   ELIOT 202
  He saith among the t.   BIBLE 53
  pâtés de foie gras to the sound of t.   SMITH 511:2
  snarling t. 'gan to chide   KEATS 289:
  Sound the t.   DRYD 194:2
  Sound the t.   MOR 357:2
  then the t.   CHES 147:
  thunder of the t. of the night   SWIN 530:
  t. also, and shawms   PRAY 396:
  t. sounded for him   BUNY 107:3
  t. which sing to battle   SHEL 505:1
  up-lifted Angel t. blow   MILT 340:2
  while the t. blow   TENN 542:
trumpits: t. en de bangin' er de   HARR 242:1
trumps: always having the ace of t.   LAB 306:1
  if dirt were t.   LAMB 308:
  Let Spades be t.   POPE 381:
trundle-tail: Or bobtail tike, or t.   SHAK 455:
trunk: large a t. before   BELL 38:2
trunkless: Though t.   GILB 227:
  vast and t. legs   SHEL 502:15
trust: absolute t.   SHAK 458:2
  dare t. themselves with men   SHAK 486:2
  even treachery cannot t.   JUN 287:
  frail mortality shall t.   BACON 28:1
  he might t. in the flesh   BIBLE 78:1
  His t. was with th' Eternal   MILT 346:7
  I can but t. that good   TENN 536:2
  I dare not t. it without   BROW 97:5
  If you can t. yourself   KIPL 299:22
  In the People was my t.   WORD 580:22
  in t. Our youth   RAL 404:15
  man assumes a public t.   JEFF 272:17
  my sure t. is in thee   PRAY 394:16
  never should t. experts   SAL 413:18
  no more than power in t.   DRYD 194:10
  not inclined to t. them   VIRG 560:7
  put not your t. in princes   PRAY 399:16
  put their t. in chariots   PRAY 390:14
  put thy t. in God   PRAY 392:12
  So I t.   MAS 333:23
  that put their t. in him   PRAY 389:1
  T. his sworn brother   SHAK 492:7
  t. I have found treason   ELIZ 206:3
  t. in all things high   TENN 542:19
  t. in God   SMITH 510:31
  t. me not at all or all   TENN 535:8
  T. no Future   LONG 317:3
  T. none   SHAK 443:20
  T. one who has gone through   VIRG 559:10
  T. the tale   LAWR 311:10
  t. thy honest offer'd courtesy   MILT 341:9
  t. to two securities than   CHES 145:30
  was not property but a t.   FOX 217:20
  woman's t.   SCOTT 418:4
  yet will I t. in him   BIBLE 52:25
trusted: armour wherein he t.   BIBLE 69:5
  familiar friend, whom I t.   PRAY 392:5
  few enthusiasts can be t.   BALF 30:4
  He t. in God   PRAY 390:11
  in thee have I t.   PRAY 384:18
  Let no such man be t.   SHAK 468:1
  pays to t. man   THOM 549:21
  to be t. with our selves   CONG 159:17
  unfit to be t.   CHES 146:6
  Who t. God was love indeed   TENN 536:9
trustest: t. upon the staff of this   BIBLE 51:38
trusteth: blessed is the man that t.   PRAY 391:21
trustie: thocht it was a t. tree   BALL 32:10
trusting: There is no t. appearances   SHER 506:35
trusts: He's mad that t.   SHAK 454:28
  nor t. them with   CHES 145:26
trustworthiness: With Carthaginian t.   SALL 413:25

trusty: weapons that t. Achates VIRG 557:12
truth: abode not in the t. BIBLE 72:13
absolute T. belongs LESS 314:2
'Beauty is t. KEATS 291:1
bread of sincerity and t. BIBLE 75:36
bright countenance of t. MILT 352:16
brightness, purity, and t. OTWAY 366:4
bring t. to light SHAK 492:19
casualty when war comes is t. JOHN 273:18
cause Of t. MILT 348:26
Christianity better than T. COL 157:18
closing up truth to t. MILT 351:26
Commencing in a t. SHAK 458:20
Communist must grasp the t. MAO 328:15
consecrate to t. and liberty SHEL 505:6
dared to speak the t. to me TROL 552:20
dead we owe only t. VOLT 561:19
dearer still is t. ARIS 12:12
divine melodious t. KEATS 291:1
does t. sound bitter BROW 102:9
enemy of t. and freedom IBSEN 269:17
fault and t. discourtesy HERB 247:6
feel certain of any t. KEATS 294:11
fiction lags after t. BURKE 109:16
fight for freedom and t. IBSEN 269:19
freeman whom the t. makes free COWP 167:22
full of grace and t. BIBLE 71:27
further to discover t. BACON 24:15
Great is T. BIBLE 62:5
Great is t. BIBLE 83:26
great is t. BROO 95:2
great ocean of t. NEWT 362:20
have not maintained for t. SWIFT 526:8
here have Pride and T. YEATS 586:8
him in possession of t. LOCKE 315:16
him in spirit and in t. BIBLE 71:40
I am the way, the t. BIBLE 72:32
I mean the t. untold OWEN 367:11
inquiry of t. BACON 27:31
is the best test of t. CHES 145:33
'Leave T. to the police AUDEN 19:12
lie which is part a t. TENN 533:25
like open t. to cover lies CONG 159:27
loins girt about with t. BIBLE 78:10
lost to love and t. BURNS 113:7
love of t. TENN 534:12
love of t. and right TENN 537:15
mainly he told the t. TWAIN 553:24
make fiction of the t. FRY 220:9
men of less t. than tongue SHAK 492:27
Mercy and t. are met PRAY 395:15
more to disclose t. BACON 25:5
Nobody speaks the t. when BOWEN 91:4
not t., but things like CHAP 140:14
out thy light and thy t. PRAY 392:11
parsons do not care for t. STUB 524:5
possession of t. as of a city BROW 96:6
rejoiceth in the t. BIBLE 76:14
Scotland better than t. JOHN 281:22
seeming t. which cunning SHAK 467:11
simple t. his utmost skill WOTT 583:12
so T. be in the field MILT 352:5
speaketh the t. from his PRAY 390:4
Spirit that strove For t. SHEL 504:5
Strict Regard for T. BELL 39:7
strife of T. with Falsehood LOW 319:12
swear to the t. of a song PRIOR 400:20
sweet ornament which t. SHAK 493:16
takes two to speak the t. THOR 550:23
tell me the t. about love AUDEN 21:2
that came of telling t. DRYD 195:20
that his simple t. must SHAK 480:23
that I have look'd on t. SHAK 495:3
that she is made of t. SHAK 495:11
that stupendous t. believ'd SMART 509:4
That t. lies somewhere COWP 165:14
there is no other t. DISR 186:36
there *is* such a thing as t. BAG 29:17
they worship T. BROO 94:24

This t. within thy mind TENN 543:19
thy t. then be thy dower SHAK 453:3
to handle honesty and t. SHAW 497:14
true as t.'s simplicity SHAK 487:2
trusted to speak the t. BALF 30:4
t. and untruth together BACON 26:14
T. away From you is fled WYATT 583:20
T. beareth away the victory BIBLE 62:4
T. be veiled SHEL 500:18
t. by consecutive reasoning KEATS 293:16
T. can never be told so BLAKE 88:25
T., ever lovely CAMP 129:9
T., for its own sake KING 297:17
T. from his lips prevail'd GOLD 230:24
t. from rules BUTL 117:34
t. has such a face DRYD 196:12
t. in every shepherd's RAL 404:9
t. in masquerade BYRON 123:30
t. in the groves of Academe HOR 259:4
t. in the inward parts PRAY 393:5
t. is always strange BYRON 124:7
t. is not in us BIBLE 81:3
t. is rarely pure WILDE 572:27
T. is the cry of all BERK 41:22
T. is within ourselves BROW 103:2
t. lies within a little BOL 89:15
T., like a torch HAM 238:15
t. miscall'd simplicity SHAK 494:5
T. never hurts the teller BROW 100:27
t. of imagination KEATS 293:15
t. serve as a stalking-horse BOL 89:16
t. shall be thy warrant RAL 404:10
t. shall make you free BIBLE 72:12
T., Sir, is a cow JOHN 275:3
T. sits upon the lips ARN 14:27
T. stands DONNE 190:6
t. that's told with bad BLAKE 85:14
T. the masculine, of Honour HARE 242:5
T. to her old cavern fled POPE 375:26
t. to o'erpeer SHAK 427:17
t., unity, and concord PRAY 387:13
T., when witty HARE 242:2
t. which you cannot contradict PLATO 374:12
T. will come to light SHAK 466:10
t. with gold she weighs POPE 375:13
unto the enemies of t. BROW 96:5
utter what he thinks t. JOHN 278:15
was all the test of t. COWP 168:7
We'd see t. dawn together BROW 99:2
What is t. BACON 27:28
What is t. BIBLE 72:44
When I tell any T. it is BLAKE 87:11
where deviation from t. JOHN 277:20
Which heavenly t. imparts KEBLE 295:5
whispering tongues can poison t. COL 156:4
would keep abreast of T. LOW 319:14
yet friend to t. POPE 378:6
you have spoken the t. BEDE 37:2
truthful: have disposition to be t. AUDEN 19:13
my name is T. James HARTE 242:32
true Poets must be t. OWEN 367:1
truths: customary fate of new t. HUXL 269:12
Flat and flexible t. BROW 95:18
Irrationally held t. may HUXL 269:11
of darkness tell us t. SHAK 458:18
old verities and t. FAUL 210:30
Some random t. he can impart WORD 580:5
tell him disagreeable t. BULW 107:7
T. as refin'd as ever Athens ARMS 12:16
t. begin as blasphemies SHAW 496:2
t. that wake WORD 579:11
Two t. are told SHAK 458:19
We hold these t. to be ANON 8:14
We hold these t. to be JEFF 272:6
Truth-teller: T. was our England's Alfred TENN 541:13
try: end t. the man SHAK 441:23
Guiltier than him they t. SHAK 463:16
'I'll t. the whole cause CARR 133:19

let us t., try, try MOORE 357:3
times that t. men's souls PAINE 368:1
To t. me with affliction SHAK 476:18
t. him afterwards MOL 353:22
T. me PRAY 399:8
'T. not the Pass LONG 316:15
t. out my reins and my PRAY 391:4
t. the soul's strength BROW 101:14
T., try again HICK 251:1
trying: there is only the t. ELIOT 202:24
T. to be glad HOUS 262:22
us is that I am t. to be BIRK 84:15
trysting: named a t. day MAC 322:11
tu: Et t. CAES 126:28
Et t., Brute SHAK 450:1
T. Marcellus eris VIRG 559:2
T. regere imperio populos VIRG 559:1
tua: Nam t. res agitur HOR 258:23
tub: mere tale of a t. WEBS 567:3
Tuba: T. mirum sparget sonum CEL 138:6
t. terribili sonitu taratantara ENN 208:21
tube: reeking t. and iron shard KIPL 302:10
tuberose: sweet t. SHEL 503:24
tubers: little life with dried t. ELIOT 204:17
tuckets: Then the t. CHES 147:3
tucks: till he t. in his shirt KIPL 304:28
Tucson: T. and Deadwood and Lost BENET 40:19
tue: ou je te t. CHAM 139:18
tuer: t. de temps en temps un VOLT 561:1
tug of war: then was the t. LEE 313:12
tulips: Here t. bloom as they are BROO 94:18
tumbled: Over the t. graves ELIOT 205:10
tumbler: clean t., and a corkscrew DICK 180:20
tumbling: Fortunes...come t. into some BACON 25:3
tumult: of all the t. and bustle SMITH 509:8
to this t. in the clouds YEATS 585:15
t. and the shouting dies KIPL 302:7
t. Kubla heard from far COL 156:29
t., of the soul WORD 578:2
when the t. dwindled BYRON 126:10
tumultuositas: t. vulgi semper insaniae ALC 3:9
tumultuous: t. joy SOUT 514:11
tun: t. of man is thy companion SHAK 439:15
tune: blackbird's t. BROW 100:13
dost thou like this t. SHAK 488:27
from the t. that they play KIPL 304:19
I am incapable of a t. LAMB 307:2
I t. the instrument here DONNE 189:14
out of t. and harsh SHAK 433:15
That's sweetly play'd in t. BURNS 114:27
There's many a good t. BUTL 119:15
t. is catching and will AUDEN 18:13
t. the enchantress plays HOUS 265:8
tuneable: t. than lark to shepherd's SHAK 469:21
tuneful: I turn'd the t. art POPE 380:4
untimely stopp'd his t. tongue POPE 377:6
tunes: chanted snatches of old t. SHAK 436:19
found out musical t. BIBLE 63:23
Heft Of Cathedral T. DICK 184:1
like slow old t. of Spain MAS 333:17
should have all the good t. HILL 251:4
well as all the good t. SHAW 497:22
tunic: all-concealing t. SHEL 502:18
tunnel: Down some profound dull t. OWEN 367:9
t. of green gloom BROO 94:17
tunnies: t. steep'd in brine ARN 14:21
turbid: t. look the most profound LAND 309:14
turbot: price of a large t. for it RUSK 411:18
'T., Sir,' said the waiter WELBY 567:17
way of t.) an archdeacon SMITH 512:10
turbulent: sustained from one t. priest HENR 246:1
turf: Green be the t. above thee HALL 238:9

green t. beneath my feet HAZL 243:32
his head a grass-green t. SHAK 435:33
on the dappled t. at ease WORD 582:26
silent as the t. they trod WORD 580:9
smooth green miles of t. HOUS 265:11
t. that warms the neighbouring COWP 168:26
Turk: French, or T., or Proosian GILB 228:10
Nose of T. SHAK 462:4
take the T. by the beard SHAK 445:14
unspeakable T. should be CARL 132:6
When Man is the T. CHES 146:27
woman out-paramoured the T. SHAK 454:18
turkey: It *was* a t. DICK 176:25
secure all the myrtle and t. AUST 22:28
wrong side of a T. tapestry HOW 266:20
turkey-cock: Contemplation makes a
rare t. SHAK 489:11
Turkish: English, not the T. court
SHAK 442:23
Turks: like those wicked T. DICK 177:32
turmoil: with ceaseless t. seething COL 156:27
turn: Because I do not hope to t.
ELIOT 201:32
going to t. over a new life FLEM 214:28
goodnight and quickly t. YEATS 585:6
high tide and the t. CHES 146:20
It is my t. now NELS 360:11
I t. the page BROW 99:18
'To t. you out KIPL 298:19
t. again, and quicken PRAY 395:14
t. again to cover the earth PRAY 396:19
t. down an empty Glass FITZ 213:18
T. our captivity PRAY 398:17
t. thee behind me BIBLE 51:32
t. the other cheek HOLM 253:11
t. to him the other also BIBLE 64:17
T. us again, O God PRAY 395:8
T. wheresoe'er I may WORD 578:22
you will t. it over once WEST 569:3
turn'd: never t. my back upon Don
TENN 543:1
turned: almost t. down the pages
POUND 383:20
'in case anything t. up DICK 177:2
never t. his back BROW 98:32
night be to t. day PRAY 399:5
this his anger is not t. BIBLE 57:27
t. again the captivity PRAY 398:21
t. aside and wept AYT 24:8
weather t. around THOM 547:7
were t. out of the Realm ELIZ 205:25
turning: gate where they're t. AUDEN 20:5
neither shadow of t. BIBLE 80:9
there's no t. back ROSS 408:22
Turning and t. in widening YEATS 586:15
turnip: getting blood out of a t. MARR 331:3
Have a t. than his father JOHN 280:10
turnips: type your t. down the field
CAMP 128:11
turnpike: consider supper as a t. EDW 200:9
turns: heart untravell'd fondly t. GOLD 231:24
Times go by t. SOUT 514:20
Turpe: siquid T. paras JUV 288:7
turpissimus: Nemo repente fuit t. JUV 287:14
turpitude: on the t. of incontinence
SCOTT 418:13
turrets: half-glimpsèd t. slowly wash
again THOM 548:20
turtle: love of the t. BYRON 120:1
plate of t. green BROW 103:16
straight he t. eats BROW 103:27
think it clever of the t. NASH 360:4
voice of the t. is heard BIBLE 56:22
turtle-dove: the soul of thy t. PRAY 394:24
Tuscany: even the ranks of T. MAC 322:22
Tusculan: T. Mamilius MAC 322:13
Tusculum: T. (beautiful Tusculum)
DICK 177:25
Tush: T., I shall never be cast PRAY 389:30
T., say they PRAY 394:22

tutissimus: Medio t. ibis OVID 366:14
tutus: t. eris OVID 366:21
tuum: distinctions of *meum* and t.
LAMB 307:13
Tu-whit: T., tu-who SHAK 457:19
twa: I droon t. ANON 7:12
t. corbies making a mane BALL 32:8
twain: go with him t. BIBLE 64:18
never the t. shall meet KIPL 297:27
that gallant ship in t. BALL 30:19
t. he covered his face BIBLE 57:28
twang: perfume and most melodious t.
AUBR 18:2
Tweed: Says T. to Till ANON 7:12
Tweedledum: T. and Tweedledee
CARR 134:33
'Twixt T. and Tweedledee BYROM 119:24
twelve: bringing t. good men into a box
BROU 95:4
fragments that remained t. baskets
BIBLE 66:24
just turned t. years old VIRG 560:4
May in the sworn t. have SHAK 463:16
Since t. honest men have PULT 402:9
t. great shocks of sound TENN 533:22
t. months in all the year BALL 31:13
twelvemonth: t. and a day BALL 32:9
twelvepenny: Plaguy t. weather SWIFT 526:11
twelve-winded: yon t. sky HOUS 263:16
twenty: At t. years of age FRAN 218:10
draw but t. miles a day MARL 330:16
first t. years are SOUT 514:16
'Let t. pass BROW 99:25
payment of half t. shillings BURKE 109:2
T. days hence DONNE 188:2
T. love-sick maidens we GILB 227:19
t. more such names SHAK 484:3
t. third day of *Octob* USSH 554:29
twenty-one: Are over the age of t. GILB 226:2
twenty-six: Towards the age of t. BELL 39:5
twenty-three: chaste, and t. BYRON 122:8
twice: it is t. bless'd SHAK 467:27
My life closed t. before DICK 183:20
step t. into the same river HER 246:6
t. as often as any other COKE 154:15
T. a week the winter thorough HOUS 262:22
t. I have also heard PRAY 393:20
twice-told: fresh interest to a t. BYRON 124:36
tedious as a t. tale SHAK 452:21
Twickenham: T. Baptist gang AUDEN 18:20
twig: A-top on the topmost t. ROSS 409:13
Just as the t. is bent POPE 377:12
twilight: dim eclipse disastrous t. MILT 345:24
dreaming through the t. ROSS 409:9
full Surrey t. BETJ 44:8
Pilots of the purple t. TENN 538:24
rises 'midst the t. path COLL 158:18
see'st the t. of such day SHAK 494:7
they ever fly by t. BACON 27:23
When t. was falling TENN 540:5
twilights: Whose t. were more clear
DONNE 189:32
twin: my t. that I breakfast HERB 246:8
twine: Another o' the t. BALL 31:18
twinkle: t., little bat CARR 134:2
T., twinkle, little star TAYL 532:1
with his incomparable t. JAMES 271:32
twinkling: endureth but the t. of an eye
PRAY 391:13
Innumerable t. of the waves AESC 3:3
in the t. of an eye BIBLE 76:29
in the t. of a bed-staff SHAD 420:23
twins: threw the t. she nursed GRAH 233:10
t. of learning that he SHAK 447:2
whereof every one bear t. BIBLE 56:26
twirling: t. in thy hand a wither'd ARN 14:15
twist: to bribe or t. WOLFE 576:6
t. the sinews of thy heart BLAKE 87:15
twitch: *never* be refined if I t. THOM 547:13
twitch'd: t. his mantle blue MILT 343:20

two: be in t. places at once ROCHE 406:1
Can t. walk together BIBLE 61:1
He took out t. pence BIBLE 69:3?
If t. lives join BROW 99:2
I learn t. things PRAY 388:14
In t. words GOLD 232:42
my troubles are t. HOUS 266:?
never by t. and two KIPL 303:19
night t. black owls came BEER 38:2
serve t. masters BIBLE 64:27
takes t. to speak the truth THOR 550:2?
that thinks t. notes a song DAV 172:14
that t. solitudes protect RILKE 406:5?
There went in t. and two BIBLE 45:34
think for t. minutes together SMITH 511:35
T. and two only supreme NEWM 361:17
t. at a time there's no GAY 222:36
t. ears of corn SWIFT 526:6
t. hours' traffick SHAK 481:21
t. irons in the fire BEAU 36:4?
t. legs bad ORW 365:8?
T. master-passions cannot CAMP 129:11
t. meanings packed up into CARR 135:28
T. men look out through LANG 309:21
'T. nations DISR 186:29?
t. or three are gathered BIBLE 67:6
t. or three are gathered PRAY 385:8
t. people miserable instead BUTL 119:22
t. people with the one MACN 326:11
t. strings to my bow FIEL 211:19
T. voices are there STEP 518:22
Wandering between t. worlds ARN 13:8
We t. stood there with BROW 99:21
When t. strong men stand KIPL 297:30
with t. seeming bodies SHAK 470:22
two-and-twenty: myrtle and ivy of sweet
t. BYRON 125:23
twoedged: mouth went a sharp t. sword
BIBLE 81:14
t. sword in their hands PRAY 399:24
two-handed: that t. engine at the door
MILT 343:13
two-legged: that unfeather'd t. thing
DRYD 194:7
twopence: go the length of t. STEV 521:19
I care not t. BEAU 36:3
without the oil and t. SMITH 511:7
Tyburn: me...has a damn'd T.-face
CONG 160:4
Tyger: T.! burning bright BLAKE 87:14
tygre: egre is a t. yond in Ynde CHAU 142:10
tyme: had my world as in my t. CHAU 143:19
t. ylost may nought recovered CHAU 144:14
Tyne: from the Severn to the T. KIPL 297:26
type: grey paper with blunt t. BROW 105:8
highest t. of human nature SPEN 514:28
So careful of the t. she TENN 536:27
t. your turnips down CAMP 128:11
Types: by device of *Movable T.* CARL 132:12
shadows and t. to the reality NEWM 362:6
T. and shadows have their THOM 546:11
typewriter: t. does not generate
DOYLE 192:20
tyranne: Tati tibi tanta t. tulisti ENN 208:20
tyranni: Non vultus instantis t. HOR 260:18
tyrannis: sceptrumque t. TURG 553:22
tyrannous: t. To use it like a giant
SHAK 464:1
tyranny: are the worst sort of t.
BURKE 110:20
Ecclesiastic t.'s DEFOE 173:15
human nature against t. JOHN 276:5
snuff the approach of t. BURKE 109:23
they appeal from t. BYRON 125:15
until this t. be over-past PRAY 393:14
tyrant: art past the t.'s stroke SHAK 428:22
let no t. reap SHEL 504:3
little t. of his fields GRAY 234:32
necessity, The t.'s plea MILT 347:27
nor the face of a t. before HOR 260:18

Thou t. of the mind DRYD 196:32
t. custom SHAK 474:5
t. duke unto a tyrant brother SHAK 424:28
t. laws restrain GOLD 231:30
t.'s vein SHAK 469:27
t. Titus Tatius ENN 208:20
tyrants: Ask all the t. of thy sex CONG 160:22
blood of patriots and t. JEFF 272:10
foe of t. CAMP 129:9
Kings will be t. from policy BURKE 111:13
now the t. KEYN 296:1
Rebellion to t. is obedience BRAD 91:12
sceptre from t. TURG 553:22
'Twixt kings and t. there's HERR 249:8
T. seldom want pretexts BURKE 111:30
When t.' crests and tombs SHAK 495:1
with the barbarity of t. SMITH 511:30
would be t. if they could DEFOE 173:4
Tyrawley: T. and I have been dead CHES 146:7
Tyre: one with Nineveh and T. KIPL 302:8
T., the crowning city BIBLE 58:16
Tyrian: budded T. KEATS 292:1
some grave T. trader ARN 14:21
U: 'U. and 'Non-U' ROSS 408:19
U. vert, O bleu: voyelles RIMB 406:9
Ubi: U. Petrus AMBR 4:1
ubique: Quod semper, quod u. VINC 557:7
ubiquities: They are blazing u. EMER 208:14
uffish: in u. thought he stood CARR 134:29
ugliest: u. of trades have their JERR 273:6
ugly: There is nothing u. CONS 162:2
to be good than to be u. WILDE 573:21
wasn't I born old and u. DICK 176:1
world u. and bad has made NIET 363:8
uita: u. breuis, sensus hebes JOHN 273:17
Ullin: this Lord U.'s daughter CAMP 129:2
Ulpian: U. at the best BROW 99:15
Ulster: U. will fight CHUR 149:18
ulterioris: Tendebantque manus ripae u. VIRG 558:22
Ultima: U. Cumaei venit iam carminis VIRG 559:22
U. Thule VIRG 560:10
ultimate: u. decency of things STEV 522:15
Ultio: voluptas U. JUV 288:6
ultor: aliquis nostris ex ossibus u. VIRG 558:15
ultrices: Luctus et u. posuere cubilia VIRG 558:21
Ulubris: Est U. HOR 258:19
Ulysses: Happy he who like U. has DU B 198:26
U. leaves once more Calypso SHEL 500:21
umbered: Wenlock Edge was u. HOUS 265:11
umble: likewise a very 'u. person DICK 177:6
We are so very 'u. DICK 177:8
umbra: Pulvis et u. sumus HOR 261:16
umbrage: Americans have taken u. PUNCH 402:22
umbrella: u. To keep the scorching FLET 215:19
unjust steals the just's u. BOWEN 90:22
umbrellas: who possess u. FORS 216:26
umbris: u. et imaginibus in veritatem NEWM 362:6
umpire: Chaos u. sits MILT 347:4
Umps: 'U.', said Mr Grewgious DICK 178:5
un: thinking of the old 'u. DICK 176:30
una: iuvat spinis de pluribus u. HOR 259:6
U. salus victis nullam VIRG 558:7
unacceptable: u. face of capitalism HEATH 244:5
unacknowledged: inspire...Poets are the u. legislators SHEL 505:13
unacquainted: is u. with your body BACON 26:17
unadvisedly: u., lightly, or wantonly PRAY 388:25
unaffected: can be rational and u. AUST 22:9

unafraid: ruins would strike him u. HOR 260:19
unalienable: Creator with certain u. rights ANON 8:14
unalterable: watching Madness with u. BYRON 121:7
unam: u. sanctam Catholicam et MASS 334:20
unapt: so u. to perceive how ARN 15:17
Unarm: U., Eros SHAK 423:9
unassailable: That u. holds on his rank SHAK 449:25
unattempted: u. yet in prose or rhyme MILT 344:21
unattractive: most u. old thing GILB 227:14
not against the u. GREE 236:3
unaware: whereof he knew And I was u. HARDY 239:7
unawares: entertained angels u. BIBLE 80:3
unbearable: in victory, u. CHUR 151:5
unbeatable: In defeat, u. CHUR 151:5
unbecoming: u. a man of quality than CONG 159:22
u. men that strove with TENN 544:3
u. the character ANON 4:20
unbegot: Unborn and u. HOUS 265:13
unbelief: Blind u. is sure to err COWP 165:29
did it ignorantly in u. BIBLE 79:7
help thou mine u. BIBLE 68:35
Help thou mine u. BUTL 119:11
help thou my u. FORS 217:10
u. is blind MILT 341:12
unbelieving: u. husband is sanctified BIBLE 76:3
unbelov'd: poor u. ones BETJ 42:7
unbend: u. your noble strength SHAK 460:10
unbends: There is nothing u. GAY 222:27
unbent: like an u. bow DONNE 190:3
She u. her mind afterwards LAMB 307:9
un-birthday: u. present CARR 135:20
unborn: To you yet u. these WHIT 570:2
U. and unbegot HOUS 265:13
Unborrowed: interest U. from the eye WORD 578:6
unbought: u. grace of life BURKE 111:10
unbounded: man Of an u. stomach SHAK 447:18
unbowed: head is bloody, but u. HENL 245:4
unbribed: man will do u. WOLFE 576:6
unbroidered: cramoisi is u. POUND 382:11
unbroken: ties are u. and whose love HOR 259:21
unbuild: I arise and u. it again SHEL 500:7
unburied: friendless bodies of u. WEBS 567:8
unbusy: sole u. thing COL 157:14
unbutton: u. here SHAK 454:20
Uncertain: U., coy SCOTT 417:21
uncertainty: quit a certainty for an u. JOHN 281:20
uncharitableness: from all u. PRAY 385:16
unchaste: No u. action SHAK 453:6
uncircumcised: daughters of the u. triumph BIBLE 50:16
uncircumscribed: u., but man SHEL 503:12
unclassed: u., tribeless SHEL 503:12
uncle: married with mine u. SHAK 429:28
nor u. me no uncle SHAK 479:1
prophetic soul! My u. SHAK 431:9
unclean: he is u. to you BIBLE 48:6
midst of a people of u. lips BIBLE 57:29
u. spirit is gone out BIBLE 66:13
uncleanness: all u., or covetousness BIBLE 78:2
unclouded: u. blaze of living light BYRON 121:37
unclubable: very u. man JOHN 275:16
uncoffin'd: u., and unknown BYRON 121:24
uncomfortable: moral when he is only u. SHAW 497:28
We u. feel GILB 228:18
uncomfortableness: u. of it all BROW 104:26

unconcern'd: Thou u. canst hear POPE 376:21
unconfin'd: Let all her ways be u. PRIOR 400:23
unconfined: let joy be u. BYRON 120:21
unconfused: u., unhurried by emotion JAMES 271:29
unconquerable: man's u. mind WORD 582:17
nursing the u. hope ARN 14:20
th' u. will MILT 345:3
unconquered: eye the u. flame POUND 382:14
unconscious: irony is generally quite u. BUTL 118:23
u. hodmen of the men HEINE 244:12
unconsidered: snapper-up of u. trifles SHAK 491:18
uncontrollable: less free Than thou, O u. SHEL 502:12
unconvincing: bald and u. narrative GILB 227:12
uncorrupt: that leadeth an u. life PRAY 390:4
Uncorseted: U., her friendly bust ELIOT 205:14
uncouth: His u. way MILT 346:16
Time makes ancient good u. LOW 319:14
U. unkist SPEN 517:5
uncouther: better the u. BROW 105:27
Uncover: U., dogs, and lap SHAK 486:7
uncreated: one u. PRAY 385:13
womb of u. night MILT 346:10
uncreating: dies before thy u. word POPE 376:2
unction: not that flattering u. SHAK 435:14
Thy blessed U. from above PRAY 400:5
uncumber'd: u. with a wife DRYD 196:4
undeceived: only u. Of that ELIOT 202:20
undefiled: of the Lord is an u. law PRAY 390:12
Pure religion and u. before BIBLE 80:11
undemocratic: u. reasons and for motives KIPL 302:5
under: they shall go u. the earth PRAY 393:22
u. an English heaven BROO 94:30
U. bare Ben Bulben's head YEATS 587:10
U. his own vine what he SHAK 448:1
under-belly: soft u. of the Axis CHUR 150:13
Undergraduates: U. owe their happiness BEER 37:22
underground: thinking Lays lads u. HOUS 264:6
Till she sunk u. LEAR 311:17
underlings: that we are u. SHAK 448:17
under-peep: would u. her lids SHAK 428:8
undersized: He's a bit u. GILB 226:14
understand: are said to u. one another CHAM 139:16
be understood or to u. GREE 236:7
in the world u. any other BAG 28:27
invented was easy to u. AUDEN 18:15
me to u. wisdom secretly PRAY 393:5
none could u. what she BUNY 107:37
read and perhaps u. Shakespeare KEATS 293:26
some who did not u. them PRAED 384:6
still the less they u. BUTL 118:6
Then thought I to u. this PRAY 394:23
things which others u. WORD 580:5
think I u. people very well FORS 217:6
to u. them SPIN 517:7
u. the heath who had not HARDY 241:20
understanded: tongue not u. of the people PRAY 400:8
understandeth: Who u. thee not SHAK 457:2
understanding: all thy getting get u. BIBLE 53:18
because they appeal to the u. BAG 28:30
evidence against their own u. HAL 237:23
good u. have all they that PRAY 397:13
if thou hast u. BIBLE 53:2
joke well into a Scotch u. SMITH 510:28
length of days u. BIBLE 52:24

likely to propagate u. JOHN 280:13
obliged to find you an u. JOHN 279:21
shall light a candle of u. BIBLE 62:8
spirit of wisdom and u. BIBLE 58:9
they pass all u. JAM 271:6
things as pass man's u. PRAY 386:18
To be totally u. makes STAEL 517:15
u., but no tongue SHAK 430:14
where is the place of u. BIBLE 52:33
which have no u. PRAY 391:18
which passeth all u. BIBLE 78:21
yourself ignorant of his u. COL 157:21
understandings: hearts and muddy u.
BURKE 111:11
understands: she always u. what you
JOHN 278:14
verse and thinks she u. BROW 100:15
understonde: That thow be u. CHAU 144:17
understood: all who u. admired PRAED 384:6
Augurs and u. relations SHAK 461:24
be told so as to be u. BLAKE 88:25
something u. HERB 248:5
those that u. him smiled SHAK 448:23
u. or to understand I would GREE 236:7
undertakers: become of the u. without
it DICK 183:1
u.—walk before the hearse GARR 221:11
Underworld: way down to the U.
VIRG 558:18
undeserving: I'm one of the u. poor
SHAW 498:14
undid: beach u. his corded bales ARN 14:21
what they u. did SHAK 422:2
undiscover'd: u. country from whose
bourn SHAK 433:8
undiscovered: Gold u. (and all the better
HOR 260:20
ocean of truth lay all u. NEWT 362:20
undisgraced: u. by those extravagancies
CHES 145:24
undo: Now mark me how I will u.
SHAK 480:1
should u. a man SHAK 446:12
Some to u. DRYD 198:19
thee does she u. herself TOUR 551:16
to u. the heavy burdens BIBLE 60:4
u. this button SHAK 456:11
undoctored: Against the u. incident
KIPL 298:2
Un-done: Anne Donne, U. DONNE 190:21
I am u. BIBLE 57:29
Is not to leave't u. SHAK 475:18
I was u. by my Auxiliary STEE 518:14
not thought death had u. ELIOT 204:20
'save the u. years OWEN 367:10
some to be u. DRYD 198:19
Than wishest should be u. SHAK 459:1
...thou art u. STER 520:10
u. vast BROW 101:25
We have left u. those things PRAY 384:12
undrugged: see u. in evening light
CHES 147:12
Undulate: U. round the world WHIT 571:13
undulating: expression and an u. throat
BELL 40:2
undurable: delights u. POUND 383:19
undying: u. Life BRON 93:19
Unearned: U. increment MILL 339:4
Uneasy: U. lies the head that wears
SHAK 441:30
You are u. JACK 270:29
uneatable: full pursuit of the u. WILDE 573:27
unequal: equal division of u. earnings
ELL 206:11
Men are made by nature u. FROU 219:18
unexamined: u. life is not worth living
SOCR 512:17
unexpected: Old age is the most u.
TROT 553:16
unexpectedness: which I call *u.* PEAC 370:17

unextinguishable: u. laugh in heaven
BROW 95:16
unfabled: blest u. Incense Tree DARL 171:21
Unfaith: U. in aught is want TENN 535:6
unfathomable: u. depths of his own
oceanic COL 158:8
u. deep Forest THOM 547:19
unfed: houseless heads and u. SHAK 454:15
unfeeling: Th' u. for his own GRAY 235:13
unfeignedly: them that u. love thee
PRAY 387:4
unfit: all things u. GOLD 231:17
often u. a man for society CHAM 139:14
u. to be trusted CHES 146:6
U. to hear moral philosophy SHAK 486:30
unfledg'd: new-hatch'd, u. comrade
SHAK 430:19
unforgetful: teach the u. to forget ROSS 410:6
unforgiving: fill the u. minute KIPL 300:2
unforgotten: assuage the u. pain ROSS 410:6
unfriended: u., melancholy GOLD 231:23
unfriendly: hostile and the towns u.
ELIOT 203:13
U. to the nose and eyes STEV 523:13
Unfrowning: U. caryatides STEV 523:12
unfruitful: he becometh u. BIBLE 66:17
ungain'd: Men prize the thing u.
SHAK 486:21
Ungeheuern: Wer mit U. kämpft NIET 363:10
ungentlemanly: knows how u. he can
look SURT 525:21
unglücklich: u. das Land BREC 92:1
Unglücklichen: eine andere als die des
U. WITT 575:16
ungodliness: dwell in the tents of u.
PRAY 395:13
ungodly: hope of the u. away BIBLE 62:18
in the counsel of the u. PRAY 389:14
plagues remain for the u. PRAY 391:18
seen the u. in great power PRAY 391:29
thyself because of the u. PRAY 391:26
u. he shall rain snares PRAY 389:31
ungrateful: I make one u. person LOUI 318:9
ungratefulness: they call virtue there
u. SIDN 507:19
unguem: Ad u. Factus HOR 262:4
unguess'd: tread on Earth u. ARN 14:24
ungula: putrem sonitu quatit u. VIRG 559:7
Unhand: 'U. it TROL 552:17
unhanged: three good men u. in England
SHAK 438:34
unhappiness: Man's u. CARL 132:19
unhappy: can never be very u. GAY 223:26
dare to be u. ROWE 410:25
each u. family is unhappy TOLS 551:10
instinct for being u. highly SAKI 413:6
is not cannot be made u. LUCR 320:9
learning to care for the u. VIRG 557:19
never as u. as one thinks LA R 310:18
Not one is respectable or u. WHIT 570:22
profession an u. ending JAMES 272:1
that some should be u. JOHN 277:5
u. alternative is before AUST 23:15
u. the land that needs BREC 92:1
which make us so u. JOYCE 286:22
unhaunted: of a lone u. place possesst
DONNE 190:1
unheard: language of the u. KING 296:14
those u. Are sweeter KEATS 291:4
unheavenly: strange u. glare BRID 92:13
unholy: sights u. MILT 342:12
unhoming: Men move u. FRY 220:7
unhonour'd: Mindful of th' u. dead
GRAY 235:3
Unwept, u., and unsung SCOTT 416:22
unhurried: u. by emotion JAMES 271:29
Unhurt: U. people are not much STAR 517:21
unicorn: Sirion, like a young u. PRAY 391:10
uniform: Should be more u. HOOD 254:15
that a good u. must work DICK 182:28

u. 'e wore KIPL 299:17
uniformity: be preferred before u.
BACON 25:34
unigenitum: Christum Filium Dei u.
MASS 334:20
Unimportant: U., of course CARR 134:20
uninformed: u. female who ever dared
AUST 24:2
uninitiated: keep far off, you u. VIRG 558:19
unintelligent: there is anything so u.
ARN 15:17
unintelligible: Of all this u. world
WORD 578:5
u. patter GILB 228:37
Union: Federal U.: it must be preserved
JACK 270:30
Liberty and U. WEBS 566:11
Mysterious u. with its native sea
WORD 577:16
Our u. is perfect DICK 184:4
saved the U. of these States WHIT 571:10
to an indestructible U. CHASE 141:3
u. of a deaf man COL 157:19
u. of hands and hearts TAYL 532:6
u. of this ever diverse MER 337:17
U., strong and great LONG 316:7
u. with Great Britain SMITH 509:16
yet an u. in partition SHAK 470:22
unit: Misses an u. BROW 100:38
unite: Workers of the world, u. MARX 333:4
United: U. Metropolitan Improved
DICK 179:33
United States: British Empire and the
U. CHUR 150:3
great Government of the U. WILS 574:23
rise of the U. STEV 520:23
These U. WHIT 571:14
uniting: By u. we stand DICK 184:5
unity: city: that is at u. PRAY 398:11
come in the u. of the faith BIBLE 77:28
'Man can have U. if Man AUDEN 19:11
preserve the u. of the empire BURKE 110:4
to dwell together in u. PRAY 398:26
Trinity in U. PRAY 385:12
truth, u., and concord PRAY 387:13
universal: maxim should become a u.
law KANT 288:9
Nature wears one u. grin FIEL 211:33
u. dovetailedness with DICK 180:17
u. frame is without a mind BACON 25:22
u. good POPE 379:11
universals: There ain't no u. in this
MACN 326:5
universe: better ordering of the u. ALF 3:16
hell of a good u. CUMM 170:12
I accept the u. CARL 132:30
is the measure of the u. SHEL 503:8
Prais'd be the fathomless u. WHIT 571:13
pretend to understand the U. CARL 132:25
repeat the u. but to fulfil SANT 414:2
richness and variety of the u. HOUS 266:15
To mingle with the U. BYRON 121:22
u. and give me yesterday JONES 283:10
u. is not hostile HOLM 253:5
u. is so vast and so ageless ROS 408:18
We possessed all the u. SHAW 496:30
will turn the u. to ashes CEL 138:5
universities: discipline of colleges and
u. SMITH 509:14
U. incline wits to sophistry BACON 28:12
University: of the U. as a whole COL 155:2
servant to be bred at an U. CONG 160:12
Than his own mother U. DRYD 197:14
true U. of these days is CARL 131:35
U. should be a place DISR 185:10
We are the U. SPR 517:11
unjust: commended the u. steward
BIBLE 70:25
God all mercy is a God u. YOUNG 588:9
just and on the u. BIBLE 64:19

u. steals the just's umbrella   BOWEN 90:22
unkind: call'd deform'd but the u.
     SHAK 490:18
me not (Sweet) I am u.   LOV 318:20
poor when givers prove u.   SHAK 433:10
That are sodden and u.   BELL 40:9
unkindest: u. cut of all   SHAK 450:28
unkindness: his u. may defeat my life
     SHAK 476:24
Men loved u. then   HOUS 264:4
unkist: Uncouth u.   SPEN 517:5
u., and lost   CHAU 144:3
unknit: u. that threatening unkind
     SHAK 484:15
unknowable: length of time which is
u.   BEDE 37:1
world u.   THOM 548:24
Unknowe: U., unkist   CHAU 144:3
unknowing: Alike u. and unknown
     BURNS 114:15
unknown: Alike unknowing and u.
     BURNS 114:15
everything u. is held   TAC 531:6
keep't u.   SHAK 475:18
Of u. modes of being   WORD 580:13
some u. regions preserved   ELIOT 201:7
TO THE U. GOD   BIBLE 74:12
tread safely into the u.'   HASK 243:1
unmourned and u.   HOR 261:18
unseen, u.   POPE 380:24
unlamented: Thus u. let me die   POPE 380:24
unleavened: u. bread of sincerity BIBLE 75:36
unleaving: Over Goldengrove u. HOPK 256:25
unlock'd: Lie all u. to your occasions
     SHAK 465:16
unlocked: Shakespeare u. his heart'
     BROW 101:10
unloose: latchet I am not worthy to u.
     BIBLE 71:29
unlovely: Here in the long u. street
     TENN 536:5
unlucky: who is so u.   MARQ 331:2
unmannerly: them untaught knaves,
u.   SHAK 438:14
unmapped: u. country within us which
     ELIOT 200:22
unmarried: keep u. as long as he can
     SHAW 497:25
unmask: To u. falsehood   SHAK 492:19
u. her beauty to the moon   SHAK 430:17
unmeaning: u. thing they call a thought
     POPE 378:21
unmeritable: This is a slight u. man
     SHAK 451:10
unmindfulness: fingers play in skilled
u.   HARDY 239:12
Unmiss'd: U. but by his dogs   COWP 166:6
unmitigated: ultimate conclusion in u.
     KIPL 299:5
unmixed: Nothing is an u. blessing
     HOR 260:11
unmourned: u. and unknown   HOR 261:18
Unmoved: U., cold   SHAK 494:15
unnatural: cruel, not u.   SHAK 434:26
Do breed u. troubles   SHAK 462:26
Revenge his foul and most u. murder
     SHAK 431:6
thoughts u.   SHAK 475:20
U. vices   ELIOT 203:6
unnecessary: thou u. letter   SHAK 453:21
unnoticed: pathway of a life u.   HOR 258:24
uno: *Crimine ab u.*   VIRG 558:2
unobtrusive: should be great and u.
     KEATS 293:23
unofficial: English u. rose   BROO 94:18
unparagon'd: Rubies u.   SHAK 428:8
unparallel'd: lass u.   SHAK 424:15
unparticular: nice u. man   HARDY 241:10
unpitied: u., unreprieved   MILT 346:11

unpleasant'st: are a few of the u. words
     SHAK 467:15
unpleasing: that are tender and u.
     BACON 25:41
U. to a married ear   SHAK 457:18
unplumb'd: u., salt   ARN 13:13
Unpolicied: Caesar ass U.   SHAK 424:14
unpopular: I was not u. there   BEER 37:21
u. names   ARN 15:25
unpremeditated: strains of u. art SHEL 504:15
u. lay   SCOTT 416:10
unpremeditating: Poured forth his u.
strain   THOM 549:9
unprepared: Magnificently u.   CORN 162:21
unprofitable: flat, and u.   SHAK 429:28
months the most idle and u.   GIBB 224:7
unpropitious: conditions That seem u.
     ELIOT 202:24
unproportion'd: Nor any u. thought
his   SHAK 430:19
unprotected: u. race   CLARE 152:11
unpunctual: vague u. star   BROO 94:19
unquiet: be the earth never so u. PRAY 396:10
sole u. thing   COL 156:22
u. heart and brain   TENN 536:1
u. slumbers for the sleepers   BRON 94:1
unravaged: u. by the fierce intellectual
     ARN 15:25
unreasonable: progress depends on the
u.   SHAW 498:1
unredressed: there is a wrong left u.
     KING 297:18
unrefined: meane and u. stuffe of mine
     BRAD 91:15
unreflecting: habit rules the u. herd
     WORD 581:17
Unregarded: U. age in corners thrown
     SHAK 425:4
unregulated: there the u. sun   BROO 94:19
unremembered: nameless, u., acts
     WORD 578:4
unremembering: She went her u. way
     THOM 547:26
Their u. hearts and heads   YEATS 587:8
unrequited: of what u. affection is
     DICK 178:2
unrest: frantic-mad with evermore u.
     SHAK 495:15
u. which men miscall delight   SHEL 499:21
unreturning: Over the u. brave
     BYRON 120:26
unreveal'd: rest remaineth u.   TENN 536:18
unrighteousness: friends of the mammon
of u.   BIBLE 70:26
unruly: it is an u. evil   BIBLE 80:14
night has been u.   SHAK 460:20
u. wills and affections   PRAY 386:12
unsad: u. and evere untrewe   CHAU 142:8
unsatisfied: it leaves one u.   WILDE 573:20
senses and his heart u.   YEATS 585:3
unsavoury: hast the most u. similes
     SHAK 438:5
unsealed: my lips are not yet u.   BALD 29:29
unseam'd: he u. him from the nave
     SHAK 458:3
unsearchable: heart of kings is u.
     BIBLE 54:25
What th' u. dispose   MILT 351:3
unseemly: how u. is it for my sex
     MARL 330:11
unseen: Floats though u. among us
     SHEL 501:5
Thou art u.   SHEL 504:18
U. before by Gods or wondering
     KEATS 290:6
walk the earth U.   MILT 348:6
unselfishness: sympathetic u. of an oyster
     SAKI 413:7
unsettled: are u. is there any hope
     EMER 207:15

unsex: u. me here   SHAK 459:2
Unshak'd: U. of motion   SHAK 449:25
unshorn: wings presents the god u.
     HERR 248:22
Unsifted: U. in such perilous circumstance
     SHAK 430:20
unsought: lost, that is u.   CHAU 144:3
unsought-for: aye u. slept among his
     KEATS 289:24
unsoundness: without a certain u. of
mind   MAC 323:23
unspeakable: joy u. and full of glory
     BIBLE 80:20
may come to those u. joys   PRAY 387:4
u. Turk should be immediately   CARL 132:6
u. in full pursuit   WILDE 573:27
unspotted: himself u. from the world
     BIBLE 80:11
unstable: remember of this u. world
     MAL 327:21
U. as water   BIBLE 46:39
Unstaid: U. and skittish in all   SHAK 488:27
unstitching: Our stitching and u. has
     YEATS 584:9
unstoried: still u.   FROST 219:6
unstringed: Than an u. viol or a harp
     SHAK 478:10
unsubstantial: dwellings and u. realms
of Dis   VIRG 558:20
unsuccessful: Like an u. literary man
     BELL 40:2
unsung: Unwept, unhonour'd, and u.
     SCOTT 416:22
unswept: antique time would lie u.
     SHAK 427:17
untainted: breastplate than a heart u.
     SHAK 446:6
U. by man's misery   SHEL 503:28
untender: So young, and so u.   SHAK 453:3
unthinking: u. time   DRYD 197:17
untimely: Why came I so u. forth
     WALL 562:15
unting: ain't the 'u. as 'urts 'im
     PUNCH 402:17
'U. fills my thoughts   SURT 525:5
'U. is all that's worth   SURT 525:4
untold: I mean the truth u.   OWEN 367:11
untouched: If thou appear u. by solemn
     WORD 582:1
untravell'd: Gleams that u. world
     TENN 543:22
untrewe: unsad and evere u.   CHAU 142:8
untried: against the new and u. LINC 314:16
left u.   CHES 148:9
untrodden: dwelt among the u. ways
     WORD 581:6
untroubled: Untroubling and u. where
     CLARE 152:13
Untroubling: U. and untroubled where
     CLARE 152:13
untrue: man who's u. to his wife
     AUDEN 20:13
untruth: have put more truth and u.
     BACON 26:14
should tell one wilful u.   NEWM 362:4
torment of the night's u.   DAN 171:1
unused: Albeit u. to the melting SHAK 477:23
unutterable: sighed and looked u. things
     THOM 549:14
unvanquishable: In u. number   SHEL 502:4
unwash'd: Another lean u. artificer
     SHAK 452:27
Unwept: U., unhonour'd, and unsung
     SCOTT 416:22
unwholesome: boiled very soft is not
u.   AUST 22:7
Unwillingly: U. represent   GILB 227:5
unwise: In the sight of the u.   BIBLE 62:13
wise, and to the u.   BIBLE 74:30
unwithered: find u. on its curls HOUS 263:3

unwittingly: u. weave — AUDEN 20:6
unworthiness: At mine u. — SHAK 485:12
  which for our u. we dare not — PRAY 388:7
unworthy: that his family was not u. — DISR 186:14
unwritten: that u. law — DAV 172:4
up: after midnight is to be u. — SHAK 488:16
  be u. and doing — LONG 317:5
  in which he was taken u. — BIBLE 73:20
  Is notwithstanding u. — SHAK 449:21
  levelling u. to themselves — JOHN 275:5
  setteth u. another — PRAY 394:26
  sort of English u. with which — CHUR 151:6
  U. Guards and at them again — WELL 568:9
  U., lad — HOUS 262:15
  U., Lord — PRAY 389:29
  u.! my friend — WORD 582:22
  u. roos Emelye — CHAU 142:21
  U. to a point, Lord Copper — WAUGH 566:4
upbraid: prudently their toils u. — MARV 331:21
UPHARSIN: TEKEL, U. — BIBLE 61:6
up-hill: road wind u. all the way — ROSS 409:11
upmost: once attains the u. round — SHAK 449:5
upon: himself u. his good behaviour — BYRON 123:16
upper: Englishman of our u. class — ARN 15:17
  large u. room furnished — BIBLE 71:6
  let not man have the u. — PRAY 389:29
  Like many of the u. class — BELL 40:5
  men are all u. crust here — HAL 237:16
  To prove the u. classes — COW 164:3
  u. ten thousand — WILL 574:13
uppermost: u. rooms at feasts — BIBLE 68:37
upright: amazed At the u. position — AUDEN 19:10
  cannot always stand u. — PRAY 386:8
  God hath made man u. — BIBLE 55:24
up-rising: down-sitting, and mine u. — PRAY 399:4
uproar: set all the city on an u. — BIBLE 74:8
  u.'s your only music — KEATS 293:20
upside: turneth it u. down — PRAY 399:18
upside down: have turned the world u. — BIBLE 74:9
upstairs: believed he had a sword u. — YEATS 584:10
  compel us to be equal u. — BARR 34:7
  I came u. into the world — CONG 160:5
  never knew any kicked u. — HAL 238:5
upward: Eternal Woman draws us u. — GOET 230:6
Urania: Lament anew, U. — SHEL 499:4
urban: Being u. — BROO 94:23
urbe: Rus in u. — MART 331:14
urge: Always the procreant u. — WHIT 570:17
  u. for destruction is also — BAK 29:24
  U. the flying ball — GRAY 235:10
urgent: bosom of the u. West — BRID 92:19
Uriah: ye U. in the forefront — BIBLE 50:19
Uricon: Are ashes under U. — HOUS 263:15
Urim: judgment the U. and the Thummin — BIBLE 48:1
urine: Cannot contain their u. — SHAK 467:21
  his u. is congealed ice — SHAK 464:19
  nose-painting, sleep, and u. — SHAK 460:18
urn: bubbling and loud-hissing u. — COWP 167:11
  Fate's U. shakes — HOR 260:7
  storied u. or animated bust — GRAY 234:22
  u. Of bitter prophecy — SHEL 501:3
urna: Omne capax movet u. nomen — HOR 260:14
  u. serius ocius — HOR 260:7
urns: u. and sepulchres of mortality — CREWE 169:18
urs: with those dreadful u. — HOLM 253:12
ursa major: my nativity was under u. — SHAK 453:11
us: Not unto u., Lord — BIBLE 83:10
  Not unto u. — PRAY 397:17

usage: if u. so choose — HOR 257:14
use: exclusively for the u. of man — PEAC 370:15
  hotly lust'st to u. her — SHAK 455:19
  How can they u. such names — SASS 414:19
  How could you u. a poor — ANON 5:3
  How u. doth breed a habit — SHAK 491:5
  I'll u. you for my mirth — SHAK 451:16
  'Rather u. than fame' — TENN 535:10
  ring is worn away by u. — OVID 366:27
  u., and protection — BACON 25:1
  u. be preferred before — BACON 25:34
  U. every man after his — SHAK 432:26
  u. him as though you loved — WALT 564:9
  u. of a new-born child — FRAN 218:19
  u. of my body I would throw — BECK 36:17
  u. of speech is not so — GOLD 232:5
  U. ourselves up — FRY 219:31
  u. rather than for ostentation — GIBB 224:25
  u. the gods' gifts wisely — HOR 261:19
used: it will be u. against you — DOYLE 192:10
  like being u. to a thing — SHER 506:21
  then I have u. no other — PUNCH 402:33
  u. by Charles the First — COW 164:4
Used-to-was: My name is U. — TRAI 552:4
useful: ambition mock their u. — GRAY 234:21
  because they can be u. — BUTL 118:21
  be the way to what is u. — COUS 163:9
  working at something u. — THOM 546:11
  you do not know to be u. — MORR 358:14
useless: in u. and hopeless sorrow — JOHN 281:27
  Music is essentially u. — SANT 414:3
  u. as a general maxim — MAC 323:28
  U. each without the other — LONG 317:12
  world are the most u. — RUSK 411:23
uses: all the u. of this world — SHAK 429:28
usquebae: Wi' u. — BURNS 115:9
usu: omnibus u. — LUCR 320:10
Usura: With U. — POUND 382:8
usurp: 'None can u. this height' — KEATS 289:27
  u. authority over the man — BIBLE 79:9
usury: given his money upon u. — PRAY 390:5
  lent out my heart with u. — LAMB 307:24
usus: si volet u. — HOR 257:14
uti: Muneribus sapienter u. — HOR 261:19
utile: être la voie ni de l'u. — COUS 163:9
  miscuit u. dulci — HOR 258:1
utilité: 'L'u. du vivre n'est pas en — MONT 354:16
utility: Losing both beauty and u. — SHAK 445:12
utlagetur: u., aut exuletur — MAGN 327:2
utmost: does the u. that he can — BURNS 115:14
Utopia: Not in U. — WORD 580:23
  than a principality in U. — MAC 324:10
utter: man cannot u. it — BIBLE 55:7
utterance: large u. of the early Gods — KEATS 290:3
utterly: I should u. have fainted — PRAY 391:9
uttermost: u. parts of the sea — PRAY 399:5
V: it with a "V. or a "W — DICK 182:20
vacancies: how are v. to be obtained — JEFF 272:15
vacant: has one v. chair — LONG 317:6
  In v. or in pensive mood — WORD 578:1
  laugh that spoke the v. — GOLD 230:21
  mind quite v. is a mind — COWP 166:19
  Stuffs out his v. garments — SHAK 452:20
  V. heart and hand — SCOTT 418:5
vacations: No extras, no v. — DICK 179:34
vacuum: chimera bombinating in a v. — RAB 403:20
  Nature abhors a v. — RAB 403:27
  say that there is a v. — DESC 175:12
vadis: Quo v. — BIBLE 83:21
vagrom: shall comprehend all v. — SHAK 472:29
vague: Asiatic v. immensities — YEATS 587:1
  terrified v. fingers — YEATS 586:1

v., a dizzy — SOUT 514:1
v. unpunctual star — BROO 94:1
vain: all is v. — ROSS 410:
  amber snuff-box justly v. — POPE 381:1
  builders have laboured in v. — BIBLE 83:1
  deceive you with v. words — BIBLE 78:
  disquieteth himself in v. — PRAY 391:1
  I watched in v. — FLEC 214:1
  No great man lives in v. — CARL 131:3
  only know we loved in v. — BYRON 124:3
  on my sullen heart in v. — STEV 523:1
  people imagine a v. — PRAY 389:1
  seal'd in v. — SHAK 464:2
  that taketh his name in v. — BIBLE 47:2
  this man's religion is v. — BIBLE 80:1
  thou v. world — CANN 130:6
  'tis v. to be a belle — LYTT 321:2
  tricks that are v. — HARTE 242:2
  unsubstantial, v. — COL 155:3
  Use not v. repetitions — BIBLE 64:2
  v. and foolish to talk — WOOLF 576:1
  V. are the thousand creeds — BRON 93:20
  v. the net is spread — BIBLE 53:14
  v. thing to save a man — PRAY 391:20
  v. tribute of a smile — SCOTT 416:18
  v., unnecessary things — ROCH 406:16
  V. wisdom all — MILT 346:20
  watchman waketh but in v. — PRAY 398:1
vaincre: v. sans péril — CORN 162:16
vaingloriousness: 'What does this v. down here — HARDY 239:5
Vainglory: born in the land of V. — BUNY 107:12
  v., and hypocrisy — PRAY 385:16
vainly: v. flapt its tinsel wing — MARV 331:18
  v. men themselves amaze — MARV 331:21
vale: ave atque v. — CAT 137:15
  cool sequester'd v. of life — GRAY 235:1
  Into the v. of years — SHAK 475:21
  shady sadness of a v. — KEATS 289:33
  There lies a v. in Ida — TENN 541:16
  v. of misery use it — PRAY 395:21
  v. of Soul-making — KEATS 294:19
  weeping in this v. of tears — ANON 10:19
  world as a v. of tears — BROW 100:6
Valentine: Bishop V., whose day — DONNE 188:18
  Saint V. is past — SHAK 471:8
valere: sed v. vita est — MART 331:21
vales: Making all the v. rejoice — BLAKE 87:26
valet: his very v. seem'd a hero — BYRON 119:30
  man is a hero to his v. — CORN 162:24
valet de chambre: point de héros pour son v. — CORN 162:24
valiant: ever become v. and martial — BACON 27:24
  Here lies wise and v. dust — CLEV 153:3
  he was v. — SHAK 450:15
  over-mastered with a piece of v. dust — SHAK 472:4
  Ring in the v. man and free — TENN 537:15
  sing, that I may seem v. — DRYD 195:18
  therefore more v. — SHAK 439:18
  v., but not too venturous — LYLY 321:14
  V. in velvet — HENL 245:12
  v. never taste of death — SHAK 449:18
validity: what v. and pitch soe'er — SHAK 487:12
valley: All in the v. of Death — TENN 532:23
  Darker grows the v. — MER 337:3
  Every v. shall be exalted — BIBLE 59:5
  great things from the v. — CHES 147:30
  He paweth in the v. — BIBLE 53:6
  Into many a green v. — AUDEN 18:10
  Love is of the v. — TENN 542:16
  maid sing in the v. — ANON 5:3
  multitudes in the v. of decision — BIBLE 61:3
  To bicker down a v. — TENN 532:20
  v. is fatal where furnaces — AUDEN 18:17

verbosity: exuberance of his own v.
DISR 185:17
out the thread of his v.
SHAK 457:10
revered always not crude v.
JER 272:20
verbrennt: *wo man Bücher v.*
HEINE 244:14
Verbum: *In principio erat V.*
MASS 335:11
V. CARO FACTUM EST
MASS 335:12
volat irrevocabile v.
HOR 258:22
Verde: *V. que te quiero verde*
GARC 221:7
verdict: anticipate the v. of criticism
WILDE 573:33
v. afterwards
CARR 134:23
v. of the world is conclusive
AUG 21:18
verdure: no other v. than its own
KEATS 292:15
Verdurin: *question de Swann chez les*
V.
PROU 401:21
verdurous: v. glooms and winding mossy
KEATS 291:20
Vere-de-Vere: stamps the caste of V.
TENN 537:28
Vereker's: V. secret
JAMES 271:22
Verger: Which an erudite V. translated
BARH 33:7
verification: v. of his own prophecies
TROL 553:5
verify: always to v. your references
ROUTH 410:18
verily: v., I say unto you
BIBLE 72:7
verisimilitude: go by a fine isolated v.
KEATS 293:19
intended to give artistic v.
GILB 227:12
veritas: *Magna est v.*
BIBLE 83:26
sed magis amica v.
ARIS 12:12
v. et praevalebit) great
BROO 95:2
veritatem: *umbris et imaginibus in v.*
NEWM 362:6
v. dixisti
BEDE 37:2
vérité: *doit aux morts que la v.*
VOLT 561:19
verities: v. and truths of the heart
FAUL 210:30
verla: *Que no quiero v.*
GARC 221:6
Verlaine: I'll stay off V. too
PARK 368:20
vermeil-tinctur'd: What need a v. lip
for that
MILT 341:18
vermin: race of little odious v.
SWIFT 526:5
they are lower than v.
BEVAN 44:16
Vermont: Bishop-Elect of V.
KNOX 305:23
vernal: those v. seasons of the year
MILT 352:10
verneint: *der Geist der stets v.*
GOET 230:1
Vernunft: *nicht ein Ideal der V.*
KANT 288:12
vero: *Se non è v.*
ANON 10:3
verre: *mais je bois dans mon v.*
MUSS 359:2
vers: *chantant mes v.*
RONS 407:18
les v. une juste cadence
BOIL 89:10
n'est point prose est v.
MOL 353:4
Versailles: lady at the court of V.
VOLT 561:13
versate: *Nocturna v. manu*
HOR 257:22
versatile: restless and v. intellect
HUXL 269:13
verse: accomplishment of v.
WORD 577:9
Book of V.
FITZ 212:11
bumbast out a blank v.
GREE 236:12
Come, but one v.
SHAK 488:26
Easy my unpremeditated v.
MILT 349:9
full sail of his great v.
SHAK 494:11
Had not my v. extoll'd
CAREW 130:13
himself with ends of v.
BUTL 117:31
I court others in v.
PRIOR 400:21
incantation of this v.
SHEL 502:14
indignation makes me write v.
JUV 287:11
Lies the subject of all v.
BROW 97:25
Married to immortal v.
MILT 342:26
Muses made write v.
VIRG 560:7
My v. again shall gild
DRAY 193:12
Ne'er a v. to thee
KING 296:22
Not v. now
BROW 99:18
no v. can give pleasure
HOR 258:25

of the octo-syllabic v.
BYRON 121:29
Only with those in v.
CONG 160:37
pleasures that to v. belong
KEATS 289:7
proper flow felt in v.
BOIL 89:10
Reads v. and thinks she
BROW 100:15
rough v. should like
POPE 378:23
subject for immortal v.
DAY-L 172:23
that is not prose is v.
MOL 353:4
They say my v. is sad
HOUS 265:13
this unpolished rugged v.
DRYD 197:15
turnings intricate of v.
WORD 580:19
V. calls them forth
LAND 308:22
v. in my sister Emily's
BRON 93:17
v. is a measured speech
BACON 24:23
v. is merely prose
BYRON 124:21
v. may find him who a sermon
HERB 246:27
v. you grave for me
STEV 523:10
v. you make
HOUS 264:11
v. your virtues rare shall
SPEN 515:20
Voice and V.
MILT 340:20
When I a v. shall make
HERR 249:6
Who died to make v. free
PRES 400:14
Writing free v. is like
FROST 219:15
you talk in blank v.
SHAK 426:20
Verser: Hearken unto a V.
HERB 246:27
verses: he has begun to write v.
COL 158:4
How many v. have I thrown
LAND 309:3
recited v. in writing
BIBLE 63:23
some for writing v.
LOCK 315:21
Tear him for his bad v.
SHAK 451:8
write halting v.
STEV 522:2
you murmur my v.
RONS 407:18
versing: relish v.
HERB 247:22
versum: *facit indignatio v.*
JUV 287:11
versus: *quod temptabam dicere v.*
OVID 366:23
vertical: v. man
AUDEN 20:11
vertigo: whirl around With the v.
JONS 285:14
vertu: *une v. traitable*
MOL 353:18
v. du vice de chasteté
VOLT 561:12
virginité pouvait être une v.
VOLT 561:15
vertue: v. refuse la facilité
MONT 354:24
vertuous: v. and gentle discipline
SPEN 515:28
Verulam: large-brow'd V.
TENN 541:23
verum: *Ave v. corpus*
ANON 10:9
Quod enim mavult homo v.
BACON 28:7
silvas Academi quaerere v.
HOR 259:4
very: remember'd for a v. long time
MCG 325:6
V. God of very God
PRAY 387:10
vesper: black v.'s pageants
SHAK 423:7
rubens accendit lumina V.
VIRG 560:11
vespers: friars were singing v.
GIBB 224:16
there's V.
BROW 105:9
vessel: certain v. descending unto
BIBLE 73:37
Let the Irish v. lie
AUDEN 19:7
make one v. unto honour
BIBLE 75:14
pieces like a potter's v.
PRAY 389:18
Some V. of a more ungainly
FITZ 213:10
Thou show'st a noble v.
SHAK 427:26
unto the weaker v.
BIBLE 80:29
vessels: treasure in earthen v.
BIBLE 77:5
vest: Casting the body's v. aside
MARV 332:6
vestals: Acidulous v.
STEV 521:25
vestigia: *'quia me v. terrent*
HOR 258:11
vestry: in the v. after service
SMITH 511:4
vesture: cast lots upon my v.
PRAY 390:20
muddy v. of decay
SHAK 468:15
queen in a v. of gold
PRAY 392:16
v. and on his thigh a name
BIBLE 82:26
v. shalt thou change them
PRAY 396:13
veterans: world its v. rewards
POPE 377:26
vétilles: *tourmenter le peuple par des*
v.
NAP 359:13
vet'ran: lags the v. on the stage
JOHN 283:2
vetustas: *nec edax abolere v.*
OVID 366:19
veuille: *priez Dieu que tous nous v.*
absoudre
VILL 557:4
vex: believe they die to v. me
MELB 336:19

enow themsels to v. them
BURNS 115:27
V. not thou the poet's
TENN 541:24
v. the unhappy dust thou
TENN 533:2
vexation: Multiplication is v.
ANON 6:18
nothing of so infinite v.
WEBS 567:12
vanity and v. of spirit
BIBLE 55:8
vexed: I was not v.
JOHN 279:10
my soul is v. within me
PRAY 392:8
vexes: other v. it
KEATS 289:28
Which v. public men
TENN 544:10
Vexilla: *V. regis prodeunt*
VEN 556:5
Vexing: V. the dull ear of a drowsy
SHAK 452:21
Vhere: V. ish dat barty now
LEL 313:16
viable: basically I'm v. from ten
BETJ 42:14
vial: do preserve as in a v.
MILT 351:21
vials: golden v. full of odours
BIBLE 81:27
viator: *vacuus coram latrone v.*
JUV 287:26
Vibrates: V. in the memory
SHEL 504:12
vibration: That brave v. each way
HERR 250:8
vicar: Evangelical v. in want
KNOX 305:23
vice: apprehend and consider v.
MILT 351:24
bullied out of v.
SURT 525:1
distinction between virtue and v.
JOHN 275:1
end in sight was a v.
BROW 105:21
England but v. and religion
SMITH 511:21
Forgiveness of each v.
BLAKE 85:26
good old-gentlemanly v.
BYRON 122:15
He lash'd the v.
SWIFT 527:24
Hypocrisy is a tribute which v.
LA R 310:12
in a private man a v.
MASS 335:13
in spreading V.'s snares
CHUR 149:6
in the Dust my V. is laid
ANON 6:19
le v. qui est le nôtre
MONT 354:12
lost by not having been v.
WALP 563:22
made of the v. of chastity
VOLT 561:12
make thine honesty a v.
SHAK 475:26
no other v. content you
DONNE 189:15
no v., but beggary
SHAK 452:15
nurseries of all v.
FIEL 211:16
Prosperity doth best discover v.
BACON 25:21
raptures and roses of v.
SWIN 529:5
sensual pleasure without v.
JOHN 280:23
She thought no v. hed sech
LOW 319:6
that reverend v.
SHAK 439:16
There is a v. that most
SHAK 463:18
There is no v. so simple
SHAK 467:10
To sanction V.
BYRON 124:26
under which v. itself lost
BURKE 111:19
v. and follies of the age
CENT 138:10
V. is a monster of so frightful
POPE 379:16
v. whose strong corruption
SHAK 490:17
Virtue itself of v. must
SHAK 435:16
When v. prevails
ADD 1:23
whirl'd into folly and v.
TENN 539:28
vices: dwelt upon her v. too
BELL 39:13
ladder out of our v.
AUG 22:3
made so as to wipe out v.
MONT 355:1
most v. may be committed
BOSW 90:16
of our pleasant v.
SHAK 456:5
redeemed his v.
JONS 285:1
Unnatural v.
ELIOT 203:6
v. and follies of human kind
CONG 159:20
vici: *vidi, v.*
CAES 126:29
vicinity: this well-nightingaled v.
HOUS 266:9
vicious: can't expect a boy to be v.
SAKI 413:14
He was a v. man
JOHN 273:30
vicissitude: This sad v. of things
STER 520:13
vicissitudes: watch the wild v. of taste
JOHN 282:26
Vicisti: *V., Galilaee*
JUL 286:31
victa: *sed v. Catoni*
LUCAN 319:22
victi: *Pugna magna v. sumus*
LIVY 315:12
victim: Any v. demands allegiance
GREE 236:5
Behold the v. of Parthenia's
GAY 223:6
that a v. must be found
GILB 226:24
Who first insults the v.
COWP 168:28

We're w. for Godot — BECK 36:15
waiting-room: now we three in Euston
  w. — CORN 162:20
wak'd: w. in a fright — ANST 11:7
'You have w. me too soon — WATTS 565:25
wake: Do I w. or sleep — KEATS 291:23
Got 'tween asleep and w. — SHAK 453:9
If you w. at midnight — KIPL 302:22
I w. to sleep — ROET 407:6
said 'I'd go and w. them — CARR 135:27
should die before I w. — ANON 7:3
slepyng hound to w. — CHAU 144:7
w. and call me early — TENN 540:20
W.! for the Ruddy Ball — THOM 549:2
w. in a fright — BARH 33:13
w. the soul by tender strokes — POPE 375:11
We w. and whisper awhile — DE L 173:25
we w. eternally — DONNE 189:6
You will w. — BROW 100:26
waked: w. herself with laughing SHAK 472:13
waken: w. thou with me — TENN 542:14
wakened: w. us from sleeping — BROO 94:26
wakes: breed one work that w. — HOPK 257:3
either w. them himself — ADD 2:12
he haunts w. — SHAK 491:20
w. or sleeps with the enduring — SHEL 499:19
wassails, w. — HERR 248:18
waketh: my heart w. — BIBLE 57:1
waking: Remembered on w. — BRID 92:10
w., no such matter — SHAK 494:13
Waldo: W. is one of those people — SAKI 413:4
Wales: bless the Prince of W. — LINL 315:8
good of going to W. — AUDEN 19:15
One road runs to W. — MAS 334:2
Shut the door, W. — BRUM 106:6
walet: His w. lay biforn hym — CHAU 142:6
walk: Can two w. together — BIBLE 61:18
certain term to w. the night — SHAK 431:4
closer w. with God — COWP 165:23
Doth w. in fear and dread — COL 155:27
His morning w. was beneath — SCOTT 418:23
I w. through the valley — PRAY 390:22
may w. uncowed — KIPL 298:11
men must w. at least before — POPE 380:8
me to w. doth make — SCOT 419:5
must try to w. sedately — STEV 522:23
take up thy bed, and w. — BIBLE 72:1
that ye w. circumspectly — BIBLE 78:4
very w. should be a jig — SHAK 488:1
W. about Sion — PRAY 392:27
w. down Piccadilly with — GILB 227:23
w. for a walk's sake — KLEE 305:15
w. humbly with thy God — BIBLE 61:25
w. in newness of life — BIBLE 75:1
w. over the western wave — SHEL 505:2
W. under his huge legs — SHAK 448:17
W. upon England's mountains — BLAKE 86:16
w. with clearer eyes — CHES 147:12
w. with Kings — KIPL 300:2
w. with you — FLEC 214:20
w. with you — SHAK 465:28
w. ye in it — BIBLE 58:29
Where'er you w. — POPE 380:27
'Will you w. a little faster — CARR 134:13
Your ghost will w. — BROW 100:12
you w. your mystic way — GILB 227:21
you w. your flowery way — GILB 227:23
walk'd: I w. upon the pier — BARH 33:19
w. through the wilderness — BUNY 107:10
walked: before him w. very crookedly — SURT 525:29
He w. by himself — KIPL 304:23
w. in darkness have seen — BIBLE 58:6
walkers: Six for the six proud w. — ANON 6:5
walketh: man w. in a vain shadow — PRAY 391:31
w. upon the wings — PRAY 396:18
walking: act of w. round him — BEER 38:6
another one w. beside you — ELIOT 205:8
enterprise In w. naked — YEATS 584:16

from w. up and down — BIBLE 52:5
God w. in the garden — BIBLE 45:16
I nauseate w. — CONG 161:5
men as trees, w. — BIBLE 68:33
that craves wary w. — SHAK 449:4
them w. in an air of glory — VAUG 555:19
W., and leaping — BIBLE 73:26
w. by his wild lone — KIPL 304:24
w. on the sea — BIBLE 66:25
W. so early — SCOTT 418:21
walks: hath left you all his w. — SHAK 451:4
hilly w. — GREEN 235:28
'I'm sure nobody w. much — CARR 135:32
she's Juno when she w. — JONS 285:5
She w. in beauty — BYRON 125:21
these silent w. I tread — COWP 168:10
W. o'er the dew of yon — SHAK 429:18
w. up and down with me — SHAK 452:20
wish I liked the way it w. — RAL 404:20
wall: close the w. up with our — SHAK 443:21
Duchess painted on the w. — BROW 102:21
Find thy body by the w. — ARN 13:15
have I leaped over a w. — BIBLE 50:27
Is that the w. is strong — WILDE 572:15
shall leap over the w. — PRAY 390:10
that doesn't love a w. — FROST 219:8
that the w. fell down flat — BIBLE 49:2
w. all Germany with brass — MARL 329:5
w. will hang my weapons — HOR 261:6
weather on the outward w. — SHAK 466:19
With our backs to the w. — HAIG 237:11
Wallace: wha hae wi' W. bled BURNS 114:34
wallet: Time hath, my lord, a w. — SHAK 487:3
wallow: We w. in our sin — ANON 9:1
wallowed: w. in a score — DONNE 189:13
walls: build thou the w. of Jerusalem — PRAY 393:8
flaming w. of the world — LUCR 320:3
her from thy ancient w. — BLAKE 86:11
it back from w. and leads — HARDY 239:18
keepers of the w. took — BIBLE 57:2
Peace be within thy w. — PRAY 398:12
upon the w. of thine house — PRAY 398:20
w. have hearsay — FONS 216:4
W. have tongues — SWIFT 528:6
w. Of Magnus Martyr — ELIOT 205:4
Washes its w. on the southern — BROW 103:14
wooden w. are the best — COV 163:10
Walrus: W. and the Carpenter — CARR 135:5
Walsingham: holy land Of W. — RAL 404:13
Waltz: Seductive W. — BYRON 126:11
Swoons to a w. — HUXL 268:22
waly, waly: w., up the bank — BALL 32:10
wan: so w. with care — SHAK 437:32
wand: all with thine opiate w. — SHEL 505:3
bright gold ring on her w. — MOORE 356:16
waving silver-tufted w. — HOUS 262:19
were but a w. — MILT 345:12
wander: Forth I w. — HOUS 265:15
I w. in the ways of men — BURNS 114:15
Nor forced him w. — CLEV 153:4
old man's wit may w. — TENN 534:2
Then w. o'er city — SHEL 505:3
Those thoughts that w. — MILT 346:10
to w. unchecked through — BRAM 91:22
w. in that golden maze — DRYD 197:16
we will not w. more — TENN 539:17
whither w. you — SHAK 424:22
whither w. you — SHAK 470:2
wander'd: Here about the beach I w. — TENN 538:16
wandered: I w. lonely as a cloud — WORD 577:29
who w. far and wide after — HOMER 254:4
wanderer: foil'd circuitous w. — ARN 15:1
W., await it too — ARN 14:17
wayworn w. bore — POE 375:7
wandereth: ears this path that w. CHES 147:12
wandering: forget the w. and the pain — FLEC 214:5

Poor w. one — GILB 228:14
W. between two worlds — ARN 13:8
w. minstrel — GILB 226:18
w. voice — WORD 582:25
wand'rer: Himself a w. from the narrow — COWP 166:8
wand'ring: tempt with w. feet — MILT 346:12
wandryng: slepe for weyrynesse of w. — LANG 309:25
waning: Bitter barmaid, w. fast TENN 544:6
wanity: Which is your partickler w. — DICK 182:36
want: articles which they do not w. — HURST 268:17
I'll not w. — SCOT 419:5
must be in w. of a wife — AUST 23:11
Ring out the w. — TENN 537:15
something you probably won't w. — HOPE 255:26
Than w. of friends — BRET 92:3
there is some hidden w. — SHEL 504:20
they w. but what is good — CROM 169:23
third is freedom from w. — ROOS 407:26
those who really w. them — FIEL 211:20
Though much I w. which — DYER 199:17
to get what you w. — SMITH 510:11
to the w. of human wisdom — LAW 310:22
w. as an armed man — BIBLE 53:22
w. no manner of thing — PRAY 391:22
w. of a horse the rider — FRAN 218:6
w. of a thing is perplexing — VANB 555:2
w. of decency is want — ROOS 408:11
W. of tenderness is want — JOHN 275:33
what can Cloe w. — POPE 377:22
What can I w. or need — HERB 248:13
What I shall die to w. — SHAK 485:12
wanted: that have w. everything HAZL 243:15
wanting: balances and art found w. — BIBLE 61:61
world which, w. thee — WALL 562:15
wanton: I do but w. in the South — TENN 542:6
impark the w. mote of dusk — MARV 332:21
that w. in the air — LOV 318:15
to wax w. against Christ — BIBLE 79:15
w. stings and motions — SHAK 463:14
wightly w. with a velvet brow — SHAK 456:27
wanton'd: I w. with thy breakers — BYRON 121:27
wantonly: unadvisedly, lightly, or w. — PRAY 388:25
wantonness: Kindles in clothes a w. — HERR 249:2
Only for w. — SHAK 452:23
wantons: Shall we play the wantons with — SHAK 479:16
wantowne: w. and a merye — CHAU 141:19
wants: Man w. but little — GOLD 231:7
Man w. but little — HOLM 253:13
Man w. but little — YOUNG 588:8
provide for human w. — BURKE 111:8
work does what he w. to do — COLL 158:13
want-wit: w. sadness makes of me — SHAK 465:7
wanwood: Though worlds of w. leafmeal — HOPK 256:26
wap: w. them into our ship's — BALL 31:18
war: able to make w. with him — BIBLE 82:12
All the business of w. — WELL 567:20
all this w. been wrought — MAL 328:3
All whom w. — DONNE 189:4
Austria is going to the w. — CHES 147:2
Beautiful that w. and all — WHIT 570:11
blood-red blossom of w. — TENN 540:18
broken the second rule of w. — MONT 355:9
can wage a pitiless w. — GREE 236:3
casualty when w. comes is truth JOHN 273:18
Come in your w. array — SCOTT 417:27
condemn recourse to w. — KELL 295:8
condition which is called w. — HOBB 251:17
delays are dangerous in w. — DRYD 197:35

endless w. still breed	MILT 351:16	W.'s glorious art	YOUNG 587:19	warr'd: Seven cities w. for Homer	
essence of w. is violence	MAC 323:8	w. should ever come between	LAW 310:22		HEYW 250:22
ever another w. in Europe	BISM 84:26	W. to the knife	PAL 368:8	Warren: W.'s blackin' or Rowland's	
first in w.	LEE 313:7	w., without its guilt	SOM 513:2		DICK 182:12
flinty and steel couch of w.	SHAK 474:5	w. with women nor with	SOUT 514:5	Warring: W. in Heav'n against Heav'n's	
great battle-plans of w.	LUCR 320:6	weapons of w. perished	BIBLE 50:17		MILT 347:14
Grim-visag'd w. hath smooth'd	SHAK 480:18	We've a w.	LOW 319:7	warrior: he lay like a w. taking	WOLFE 576:4
guarantee success in w.	CHUR 151:1	when the blast of w. blows	SHAK 443:21	he mounts the w.'s steed	SCOTT 416:17
having w. in his heart	PRAY 393:12	when the w. is done	SASS 414:11	Here lies a valiant w.	ANON 5:14
Horses and Power and W.	KIPL 297:28	with himself at w.	SHAK 448:11	Home they brought her w.	TENN 542:10
image of w. without its	SURT 525:4	Warble: W., child	SHAK 456:25	painful w. famoused	SHAK 493:4
In a pattern called a w.	LOW 318:25	warbled: w. to the string	MILT 342:6	w. that is rapt with love	MARL 330:11
infection and the hand of w.	SHAK 478:20	warbler: Attic w. pours her throat		Who is the happy W.	WORD 577:3
In w., he mounts	SCOTT 416:17		GRAY 235:16	warriors: stern joy which w. feel	
In w., resolution	CHUR 150:25	ev'ry w. has his tune	COWP 166:27		SCOTT 416:6
In w., three-quarters	NAP 359:10	warbling: thought w. his Doric lay		wars: All skilful in the w.	VAUG 555:13
In w., whichever side	CHAM 139:8		MILT 343:19	all their w. are merry	CHES 146:17
is harder than making w.	STEV 520:21	Warbl'st: W. at eve	MILT 351:5	cluck'd thee to the w.	SHAK 428:5
is the garland of the w.	SHAK 423:16	Ward: Light and Mrs Humphry W.		Fierce w. and faithful loves	SPEN 515:29
it is not w.	BOSQ 90:12		CHES 146:12	granites which titanic w.	OWEN 367:9
Laws are inoperative in w.	CIC 151:31	Thou knowest my old W.	SHAK 439:2	I see w.	VIRG 558:17
Let me have w.	SHAK 427:27	warder: w. silent on the hill	SCOTT 417:2	maketh w. to cease in all	PRAY 392:21
let slip the dogs of w.	SHAK 450:12	wardrobe: silken dalliance in the w.		my w. Were global	REED 405:7
Let w. yield to peace	CIC 151:22		SHAK 443:12	occasion of all w.	FOX 217:23
like to the morning's w.	SHAK 446:17	war-drum: Till the w. throbb'd no		of peace tumultuous w.	SHAK 479:20
looks on w. as all glory	SHER 506:40		TENN 538:24	out the thousand w. of old	TENN 537:15
Lord is a man of w.	BIBLE 47:22	wards: deftly in the oiled w.	KEATS 292:29	rust of the Barons' W.	WALP 562:24
lordship that this is w.	ADAMS 1:6	pretty young w. in Chancery	GILB 226:2	serve in the w.	PRAY 400:11
Love's a man of w.	HERB 247:16	Ware: enough for the bed of W.	SHAK 489:30	Since w. begin in the minds	ANON 7:16
makes a good w.	HERB 246:21	w. of mine own wit	SHAK 425:13	stick i' the w.	SHAK 428:4
midst of a cold w.	BAR 34:25	w. that will not keep	HOUS 262:15	Thy w. brought nothing	DRYD 197:19
Minstrel Boy to the w.	MOORE 356:13	was an old person of W.	LEAR 313:1	w. and lechery	SHAK 487:16
money the sinews of w.	BACON 27:25	warfare: that her w. is accomplished		wars and rumours of w.	BIBLE 67:27
nature of w. consisteth	HOBB 251:17		BIBLE 59:4	with w. or pestilences	AUST 23:4
no discharge in that w.	BIBLE 55:25	Who goeth a w. any time	BIBLE 76:6	Warsaw: Order reigns in W.	ANON 9:14
no less than w. to waste	MILT 349:27	Waring: What's become of W.	BROW 105:32	warts: w., and everything	CROM 169:24
Nor w., nor battle's sound	MILT 344:6	'When I last saw W.	BROW 105:34	war-war: jaw-jaw is better than to w.	
Older men declare w.	HOOV 255:25	warly: An' w. cares	BURNS 114:2		CHUR 150:20
peace with men and at w.	MACH 325:7	warm: Be w., but pure	BYRON 124:22	Warwick: impudent and shameless W.	
pity of w.	OWEN 367:11	I am w.	BIBLE 59:12		SHAK 446:20
prepare for w.	VEG 556:3	now w. and capable	KEATS 290:30	wary: that craves w. walking	SHAK 449:4
ragged infant threaten w.	COWP 168:26	of w. sea-scented beach	BROW 102:14	was: Since I am not what I w.	PRIOR 400:28
sentence is for open w.	MILT 346:8	she's w.	SHAK 492:12	Thinks what ne'er w.	POPE 378:15
Shakes pestilence and w.	MILT 346:26	She winters and keeps w.	CAREW 130:19	W. für plünder	BLUC 88:32
shall they learn w. any more	BIBLE 57:19	This is too w. work	NELS 360:21	wash: art can w. her guilt	GOLD 231:31
sinews of w., unlimited money	CIC 151:30	'Tis very w. weather when	SWIFT 526:12	Bid them w. their faces	SHAK 427:15
'Spanish ships of w.	TENN 542:21	w. and still to be enjoy'd	KEATS 291:7	dost thou w. my feet	BIBLE 72:27
Stand up and take the w.	KIPL 299:6	w. the air in raw inclement	SWIFT 526:7	every night w. I my bed	PRAY 389:26
stately tents of w.	MARL 330:2	w. wind, the west wind	MAS 334:9	flood could not w. away	CONG 160:10
state of w. by nature	SWIFT 528:4	warmed: I w. both hands before	LAND 308:20	gulfs will w. us down	TENN 544:3
subject of it is W.	OWEN 366:30	w. and cooled by the same	SHAK 467:4	henceforth the river Rhine	COL 156:5
tell us all about the w.	SOUT 513:16	warmer: Junes that were w. than		never comes out in the w.	KIPL 303:11
terrible hell make w.	SHAK 479:13		YEATS 586:5	Night incessantly softly w.	WHIT 570:11
testament of bleeding w.	SHAK 479:13	w. than after watery cloudes	LANG 309:28	Tears w. out a Word	FITZ 213:7
That brother should not w.	COWP 165:21	warming-pans: heroes were as good		W. me throughly from my	PRAY 393:4
that first invented w.	MARL 330:8	as w.	MER 337:22	w. my hands in innocency	PRAY 391:5
that made this great w.	LINC 315:6	warms: It w. the very sickness	SHAK 436:16	w. the balm from an anointed	SHAK 479:5
There never was a good w.	FRAN 218:17	light turf that w.	COWP 168:26	w. their feet in soda water	ELIOT 204:27
there was w. in heaven	BIBLE 82:11	warmth: comes native with the w.		W. your hands	SHAK 462:24
they'll start another w.	HERB 246:11		KEATS 292:5	w. your linen and keep	STEV 522:29
Though in the trade of w.	SHAK 473:20	His vigorous w. did	DRYD 194:2	Where air might w.	SWIN 530:18
time of peace thinks of w.	ANON 5:12	Spring restores balmy w.	CAT 137:2	washed: have w. their robes	BIBLE 82:2
time of w.	BIBLE 55:12	w. about my heart like	KEATS 294:4	He w. himself with oriental	JOHN 282:2
To w. and arms I fly	LOV 318:20	w. and colour which I found	TENN 534:14	w. his hands before	BIBLE 68:21
used to w.'s alarms	HOOD 254:13	w. of shepherds' flames	MARL 330:11	Washes: W. its walls on the southern	
very well out of the w.	BALD 29:26	warn: poet can do today is to w.	OWEN 367:1		BROW 103:14
voices prophesying w.	COL 156:29	right to w.	BAG 29:3	washing: Always w.	HARDY 241:23
'W. even to the knife	BYRON 120:8	W. all traffic and detain	KIPL 301:12	country w.	BRUM 106:5
w. has its laws	NEWM 361:14	warned: be w. by me	BELL 39:2	only w.	THOM 547:12
W., he sung	DRYD 195:5	So be w. by my lot (which	KIPL 300:17	taking in one another's w.	ANON 5:4
w. is a necessary part	MOLT 354:4	warning: Give w. to the world that		w. his hands with invisible	HOOD 254:23
W. is much too serious	CLEM 152:31		SHAK 494:6	Where w. ain't done nor	ANON 5:13
w. is regarded as wicked	WILDE 572:22	Henceforth take w. by the fall	BALL 30:13	which came up from the w.	BIBLE 56:26
W. is the national industry	MIR 352:19	will it come without w.	AUDEN 21:2	Washington: Government at W. lives	
W. is the trade of kings	DRYD 196:28	With horrid w. gapèd wide	KEATS 290:21		GARF 221:9
W. its thousands slays	PORT 381:32	warns: w. the heads of parties	ARB 11:19	Washingtonian: W. dignity for the	
W. lays a burden	COWP 165:7	War Office: anything except the British		Jeffersonian	POTT 382:2
W. makes rattling good	HARDY 239:15	W.	SHAW 496:19	wash-pot: Moab is my w.	PRAY 393:12
w.'s a game	COWP 167:20	war-proof: fet from fathers of w.	SHAK 444:1	wash-tub: that they trod in the w.	
W.'s annals will cloud	HARDY 240:5	warrant: truth shall be thy w.	RAL 404:10		CLOU 153:15

watter: which makes my teeth w.
FLEM 214:28
Wattle: ever hear of Captain W. DIBD 175:16
wattles: of clay and w. made YEATS 585:17
they were all out of w. NASH 360:3
waught: right gude-willie w. BURNS 112:31
waul: We w. and cry SHAK 455:22
wav'd: banner w. without a blast
SCOTT 416:14
w. her lily hand GAY 223:30
wave: chin upon an orient w. MILT 344:14
else save the w.'s slash POUND 383:18
great w. that echoes round TENN 535:4
hath seen her w. her hand TENN 538:4
lift me as a w. SHEL 502:13
never a w. of all her waves KIPL 303:3
no w. Of a great flood MER 337:10
Quivering within the w.'s SHEL 502:10
translucent w. MILT 341:20
w. o' the sea SHAK 491:27
w. to pant beneath thy SHEL 502:12
weak as is a breaking w. WORD 580:5
When the blue w. rolls BYRON 122:1
Waverley: W. pen ANON 8:5
waves: came the w. and washed SPEN 515:20
dolphins of kindlier w. MOORE 355:23
floods lift up their w. PRAY 396:1
Him that walked the w. MILT 343:17
Innumerable twinkling of the w. AESC 3:3
I see the w. upon the shore SHEL 504:9
light-hearted Masters of the w. ARN 14:21
Like as the w. make towards SHAK 493:19
long'd-for dash of w. is ARN 15:1
noise of his w. PRAY 394:1
only on the w. behind us COL 157:20
save the w. BYRON 123:4
Though she w. her little hand HARDY 240:16
w. and storms are gone PRAY 392:8
w. bound beneath me BYRON 120:18
w. of thy sweet singing SHEL 500:16
w. of thy sweet singing SHEL 503:11
w. roar and whirl ARN 13:7
w. that beat on Heaven's BLAKE 85:15
w. thereof are still PRAY 397:10
w. were more gay YEATS 586:13
What are the wild w. saying CARP 132:34
wind sang and the same w. SWIN 529:19

waving: not w. but drowning SMITH 510:26
w. his wild tail KIPL 304:24
wax: hives with honey and w. SWIFT 525:33
is even like melting w. PRAY 390:19
Of wyne and w. WYNT 584:4
times begin to w. old BIBLE 62:7
virtue of w. and parchment BURKE 109:24
w. old as doth a garment PRAY 396:13
W. to receive BYRON 119:31
Yet moons swiftly w. again HOR 261:16
wax-works: If you think we're w.
CARR 135:1
way: all gone out of the w. PRAY 390:3
broad is the w. BIBLE 65:6
dangerous w. GOLD 232:25
each thing give him w. SHAK 421:24
every one to his own w. BIBLE 59:22
flowers to strew Thy w. HERB 247:17
gentleman's w. of thinking ANON 10:14
have such a winning w. CONG 160:26
her own w. to perfection BURKE 109:18
I am the w., the truth BIBLE 72:32
I have no w. SHAK 455:4
indirect w. to plant religion BROW 96:16
must have her w. BURKE 110:15
mystical w. of Pythagoras BROW 96:11
of being never *in* the w. CHAR 140:27
one w. in to life SEN 420:9
perish from the right w. PRAY 389:10
Prepare ye the w. of the Lord BIBLE 59:5
Prepare ye the w. of the Lord BIBLE 63:36
ready w. to virtue BROW 96:25
seeking the w. in life LUCR 320:6

shortest w. is commonly BACON 25:4
Something given that w. FLET 215:14
talked with us by the w. BIBLE 71:18
Teach me thy w. PRAY 391:8
teach thee in the w. wherein PRAY 391:18
That's the w. for Billy HOGG 252:23
that's the w. to the stars VIRG 559:8
that there was a w. to Hell BUNY 107:26
This is the w. BIBLE 58:29
this is the w. of them PRAY 392:28
Thou art my w. QUAR 403:13
w. may be known upon earth PRAY 394:4
w. of all the earth BIBLE 49:5
w. of a man with a maid KIPL 301:1
w. of an eagle in the air BIBLE 55:1
w. of transgressors is BIBLE 53:36
w. plain before my face PRAY 389:24
w. that Providence dictates HITL 251:10
w. to dusty death SHAK 463:6
w. to prevent seditions BACON 27:11
w. to the Better there HARDY 240:3
whole breadth of the w. BUNY 107:15
woman has her w. HOLM 253:15
wayfaring: w. men BIBLE 58:35
ways: all her w. be unconfin'd PRIOR 400:23
at the parting of the w. BIBLE 60:36
I knew all her w. HOUS 265:8
is the chief of the w. BIBLE 53:9
keep thee in all thy w. PRAY 395:22
Let me count the w. BROW 98:13
neither are your ways my w. BIBLE 59:27
Queer are the w. of a man HARDY 240:15
That for w. that are dark HARTE 242:29
There are nine and sixty w. KIPL 300:3
vindicate the w. of God POPE 379:2
w. are ways of pleasantness BIBLE 53:17
w. deep and the weather ELIOT 203:12
whose heart are thy w. PRAY 395:12
will maintain mine own w. BIBLE 52:25
world and its w. have BROW 105:18
wayside: some seeds fell by the w.
BIBLE 66:16
wayward: w. is this foolish love SHAK 490:31
What fond and w. thoughts WORD 582:21
we: Even w., Even so MER 336:26
know that which w. are BYRON 124:9
people like us are W. KIPL 304:2
Put it down a w. DICK 182:21
still it is not w. CHES 147:14
W. for a certainty are HOUS 264:21
W. in the tournament BETJ 44:6
weak: concessions of the w. are
BURKE 109:14
earth is w. PRAY 394:25
God hath chosen the w. BIBLE 75:30
he is w. WORD 580:5
How very w. the very wise THAC 546:4
human reason w. BAG 28:30
in the mind of man so w. BACON 26:2
Made w. by time and fate TENN 544:3
Strengthen ye the w. hands BIBLE 58:33
that are otherwise w. men BACON 25:40
to be w. is miserable MILT 345:5
w. alone repent BYRON 121:33
w. as is a breaking wave WORD 580:5
w. from your loveliness BETJ 44:5
w. is their brain-pan BLAKE 87:1
W. men must fall SHAK 479:5
w. one is singled SHEL 501:22
w. piping time of peace SHAK 480:18
willing but the flesh is w. BIBLE 68:16
with w. hands though mighty SHEL 499:15
Weakening: W. the will SPEN 515:12
weaker: Is to the w. side inclin'd
BUTL 118:14
unto the w. vessel BIBLE 80:29
w. sex ALEX 3:15
weakest: w. kind of fruit SHAK 467:25
weak-hearted: comfort and help the w.
PRAY 385:19

weakness: All w. which impairs ARN 14:24
amiable w. FIEL 211:28
Girt round with w. SHEL 499:17
'Is it w. of intellect GILB 227:16
strength is made perfect in w. BIBLE 77:14
Stronger by w. WALL 562:9
thence into a w. SHAK 432:2
w. of our mortal nature PRAY 386:15
With too much w. POPE 379:12
weaknesses: his w. are great KIPL 297:23
We must touch his w. with GOLD 232:8
weal: according to the common w. JAM 271:5
Wealdstone: to the W. turned to waves
BETJ 42:16
wealth: all that w. e'er gave GRAY 234:21
all the w. of Indies THAC 546:3
any means get w. and place POPE 380:9
gave the little w. he had SWIFT 527:25
health and w. long to live PRAY 385:5
His w. a well-spent age CAMP 129:19
in all time of our w. PRAY 385:17
insolence of w. will creep JOHN 277:32
In squandering w. was his DRYD 194:15
love remember'd such w. SHAK 493:6
Outshone the w. of Ormus MILT 346:6
poor man's w. SIDN 507:20
prevents the rule of w. BAG 29:4
Say that health and w. HUNT 263:10
smoke and w. and din HOR 261:7
Swim'st thou in w. DEKK 173:21
their w. increaseth MARL 329:20
There is no w. but life RUSK 412:12
w. of globèd peonies KEATS 291:15
w. of thy wit in an instant SHAK 467:19
w. without producing it SHAW 496:13
w. ye find, another keeps SHEL 504:3
What w. to me the show WORD 578:1
Where w. accumulates GOLD 230:18
wealthy: business of the w. man BELL 39:29
w. and others have nothing ARIS 12:8
w. curled darlings SHAK 473:22
wean'd: were we not w. till then
DONNE 188:29
weaned: w. child shall put his BIBLE 58:11
weapon: folly and his w. wit HOPE 256:2
other hand held a w. BIBLE 52:1
So that skill in the w. SHAK 442:15
weaponless: w. himself MILT 350:18
weapons: get your w. ready WHIT 570:10
let not women's w. SHAK 454:2
w. of war perished BIBLE 50:17
wear w., and serve PRAY 400:11
will hang my w. and my lyre HOR 261:6
wear: have nothing else to w. GILB 227:30
hue was not the w. HOUS 264:17
Should so w. out to nought SHAK 455:17
such qualities as would w. GOLD 232:33
w. an undeserved dignity SHAK 466:20
w. him In my heart's core SHAK 434:2
w. out than to rust out CUMB 170:7
w. the carpet with their YEATS 586:14
w. them out in practice BEAU 35:13
w. your rue with a difference SHAK 436:11
Will us to w. ourselves MARL 330:8
you'll w. your eyes out ZOLA 588:19
wearer: by the merit of the w. SHAK 466:20
weareth: it w. the Christian down KIPL 301:18
wearied: Kiss her until she be w. SHEL 505:3
wearies: you say it w. you SHAK 465:7
weariest: w. and most loathed worldly
SHAK 464:14
wearin: w.' o' the Green ANON 6:6
weariness: In hours of w. WORD 578:4
much study is a w. BIBLE 56:13
W. Can snore SHAK 428:18
w. Of climbing heaven SHEL 505:5
w., the fever KEATS 291:18
w. treads on desire PETR 373:5
wearing: not linen you're w. HOOD 255:7
was w. my powder-blue suit CHAN 139:20

w. arm-chairs tight WOD 575:25
W. not like destruction SPEN 515:6
wearisome: miles and make them w.
SHAK 478:23
wears: She w. her clothes SWIFT 526:29
so w. she to him SHAK 489:1
w. man's smudge and shares HOPK 256:12
w. the turning globe HOUS 265:1
weary: Age shall not w. them BINY 84:10
All with w. task fordone SHAK 471:21
eyelids are a little w. PATER 369:18
I am w. of my groaning PRAY 389:26
I'm w. wi' hunting BALL 31:5
I sae w. fu' o' care BURNS 116:6
I was w. and ill at ease PROC 401:13
Let him be rich and w. HERB 248:6
not be w. in well doing BIBLE 77:20
rock in a w. land BIBLE 58:30
rosy garland and a w. head SIDN 507:21
So w. with disasters SHAK 461:10
there the w. be at rest BIBLE 52:13
weak and w. POE 375:4
w. haunt for me KING 296:17
w. reckoning SHAK 476:6
w., stale, flat SHAK 429:28
W. with toil SHAK 493:5
weasel: Methinks it is like a w. SHAK 434:22
Pop goes the w. MAND 328:10
w. sucks eggs SHAK 425:15
weather: again it was gorgeous w.
CALV 127:25
first talk is of the w. JOHN 281:18
her madness and her w. AUDEN 19:6
If it prove fair w. SUCK 524:14
In sad or singing w. SWIN 530:21
in the blue unclouded w. TENN 538:9
It will be fair w. BIBLE 66:31
Jolly boating w. CORY 163:2
like a change in the w. AUDEN 21:2
no such thing as bad w. RUSK 412:14
not in fine w. CLOU 153:16
Plaguy twelvepenny w. SWIFT 526:11
roof of blue Italian w. SHEL 501:16
serves for the old June w. BROW 100:7
'Tis the hard grey w. KING 296:23
variety about the New England w.
TWAIN 554:23
W. and rain have undone KIPL 303:31
w. on the outward wall SHAK 466:19
w. the cuckoo likes HARDY 241:2
w. the shepherd shuns HARDY 241:3
w. turned around THOM 547:7
winter and rough w. SHAK 425:14
you won't hold up the w. MACN 326:8
weather-beaten: w. sail more willing
bent CAMP 129:20
weather-proof: humble roof Is w.
HERR 250:14
weather-wise: Some are w. FRAN 218:7
weave: unwittingly w. AUDEN 20:6
W. a circle round him thrice COL 157:1
w. but nets to catch WEBS 566:17
w. their thread with bones SHAK 489:3
W. the warp GRAY 234:15
what a tangled web we w. SCOTT 417:19
weaver: swifter than a w.'s shuttle
BIBLE 52:18
weaving: thread of my own hand's w.
KEATS 292:10
web: gives the w. and the pin SHAK 454:22
She left the w. TENN 538:11
there's magic in the w. SHAK 476:4
w. as this will I ensnare SHAK 474:19
what a tangled w. we weave SCOTT 417:19
Webb: Captain W. from Dawley BETJ 44:2
web-foot: Every fork like a white w.
HARDY 240:21
webs: Laws are like spider's w. SOLON 512:23
With swarthy w. TENN 535:28

Webster: Daniel W. struck me much
SMITH 511:10
W. was much possessed ELIOT 205:13
wed: December when they w. SHAK 426:23
save trouble I w. again CLARE 152:6
think to w. it SHAK 420:25
With this Ring I thee w. PRAY 389:5
wedde: Cristen man shall w. CHAU 143:17
wedded: god that I have w. fyve CHAU 143:17
Hail w. love MILT 348:8
this Woman to thy w. wife PRAY 389:3
thou art w. to calamity SHAK 483:9
w. man so hardy be t'assaille CHAU 142:9
wedding: get the w. dresses ready
BYRON 123:34
has bought her w. clothes ADD 2:23
Let's have a w. DICK 178:14
on his w. day GILB 226:7
she did her w. gown GOLD 232:33
Wedding-Guest: W. here beat his breast
COL 155:8
wedding-ring: small circle of a w. CIBB 151:9
wedlock: consented together in holy w.
PRAY 389:7
W., indeed, hath oft compared DAV 172:9
yet w.'s the devil BYRON 124:39
Wednesday: upon W. in Wheeson week
SHAK 441:20
Wee: W., sleekit BURNS 115:20
weed: basest w. outbraves his SHAK 494:15
gather honey from the w. SHAK 444:15
It is a w. that grows BURKE 110:3
Less than the w. that grows HOPE 256:5
more ought law to w. it BACON 27:7
No more than Sussex w. KIPL 303:15
Pernicious w. COWP 165:4
salt w. sways in the stream ARN 13:6
thou be than the fat w. SHAK 431:8
thou w. SHAK 476:19
w. out the fault without GOLD 232:8
What is a w. EMER 207:42
will not w. their own minds WALP 563:17
weeded: hoed and trenched and w.
HOUS 264:17
weeds: all the idle w. that grow SHAK 455:13
At grubbing w. from gravel KIPL 299:14
buy yourself w. GAY 222:34
Long live the w. HOPK 256:18
pendent boughs her coronet SHAK 436:19
rank fumitor and furrow w. SHAK 455:13
Rank w. COWP 168:26
smell far worse than w. SHAK 494:15
w. and tares of mine own BROW 96:18
when we're only burning w. CHES 147:7
Worthless as withered w. BRON 93:20
week: be accomplished in a w. STEV 522:8
keep a w. away SHAK 476:6
mirth to wail a w. SHAK 492:18
w. is a long time in politics WILS 574:18
weeks: been fou for w. thegither BURNS 115:5
weel-stockit: lass wi' the w. farms
BURNS 114:6
weep: Babylon we sit down and w.
WALP 563:10
Bid me to w. HERR 249:26
Doth w. full sore SPEN 516:5
fear of having to w. BEAU 35:15
If it could w., it could BROW 98:8
I saw my lady w. ANON 6:7
I w. for Adonais SHEL 499:3
I w. like a child LAWR 311:7
Love made him w. his pints AUDEN 21:9
make the angels w. SHAK 464:2
men would w. upon your HUXL 268:23
milk my ewes and w. SHAK 492:5
must w. or she will die TENN 542:10
now you w. SHAK 450:28
she would w. to see today DOUG 191:10
should w. for his death HOR 260:1
Some w. in empty rooms COL 155:4

'Tis that I may not w. BYRON 123:10
w. afresh love's long since SHAK 493:7
W., and you weep alone WILC 572:5
w. away the life of care SHEL 504:11
W. for the lives your wishes AUDEN 18:6
w. over Saul BIBLE 50:17
'w.! 'weep BLAKE 88:5
weep with them that w. BIBLE 75:14
W. you no more ANON 8:13
Wherefore w. you SHAK 485:12
Who would not w. POPE 376:28
will make them w. and wail SHAK 455:1
wilt thou w. when I am BYRON 119:28
women must w. KING 297:3
You think I'll w. SHAK 454:2
you *will* w. and know why HOPK 256:26
weepest: why w. thou BIBLE 73:8
weeping: all night in a forest, w. MAL 328:5
are w. in the playtime BROW 97:36
Doth that bode w. SHAK 477:1
Ever-w. Paddington BLAKE 86:3
fierce, w., hungry man CARL 132:24
hearers w. to their beds SHAK 480:8
I have full cause of w. SHAK 454:2
now goeth on his way w. PRAY 398:17
of my w. something have OWEN 367:11
Rachel w. for her children BIBLE 63:34
remembrance of a w. queen SHAK 479:19
w. and gnashing of teeth BIBLE 65:17
w. and the laughter DOWS 191:13
W. and watching GOET 230:12
W. as fast as they stream SHAK 450:9
w. late and early TENN 539:11
w. multitudes ELIOT 202:5
w. Pleiads wester HOUS 265:14
wee-things: Th' expectant w. BURNS 113:5
Wehr: Ein' gute W. und Waffen LUTH 321:2
Weib: W. und Gesang LUTH 321:1
Weibliche: Ewig-W. zieht uns hinan
GOET 230:6
weigh: more people see than w. CHES 145:31
Shall w. your Gods KIPL 304:7
to w. and consider BACON 27:18
w. this song with the great YEATS 585:8
w. thy words in a balance BIBLE 63:12
would w. it down on one side HAL 237:18
weighed: art w. in the balances BIBLE 61:6
weighing: counting votes instead of w.
INGE 270:7
not w. our merits PRAY 388:2
weighs: Which w. upon the heart SHAK 463:3
weight: heavy and the weary w. WORD 578:5
Knowledge may give w. CHES 145:31
let us lay aside every w. BIBLE 79:35
oppression of their prodigal w. SHAK 479:17
w. of hours has chained SHEL 502:13
w. of rages will press SPOO 517:8
whose words are of less w. BACON 25:41
willing to pull his w. ROOS 408:2
weights: are deceitful upon the w.
PRAY 393:20
w. and measures will be NAP 359:13
weighty: reserve the more w. voice
BACON 25:41
weilest: wo w. du WAGN 562:1
Wein: Wer nicht liebt W. LUTH 321:1
weinen: Auf seinem Bette w. sass
GOET 230:12
weird: w. sisters SHAK 458:8
w. women promis'd SHAK 461:6
weirs: three lone w. ARN 15:3
welcome: Advice is seldom w. CHES 145:19
aye be w. back again BURNS 115:13
bear w. in your eye SHAK 459:3
ever with a frolic w. took TENN 544:3
Farewell night, w. day BUNY 107:37
first to w. BYRON 124:40
Freely w. to my cup OLDYS 365:4
hath outstay'd his w. while COL 157:17
I now bid you a w. adoo WARD 564:18

silence yet I pick'd a w.   SHAK 471:15
terrible events are w.   SHAK 423:12
warmest w., at an inn   SHEN 505:15
w. ever smiles   SHAK 487:5
W. the sixte   CHAU 143:17
W. to your gory bed   BURNS 114:34
welcomes: w. at once all the world ANST 11:8
welcomest: w. when they are gone
     SHAK 445:19
welding: w. of their later history
     HARDY 239:6
welfare: most anxious for its w.
     BURKE 108:15
w. of this realm do chiefly   CHAR 140:21
Welfare-State: are led to that of the W.
     TEMP 532:10
welkin: let the w. roar   SHAK 441:25
well: as w. him   JOYCE 286:30
being w.   MART 331:12
do I drink from every w.   CALL 127:7
golden crown like a deep w.   SHAK 479:22
Here lies one who meant w.   STEV 521:5
it is a foolish thing w.   JOHN 276:11
misery use it for a w.   PRAY 395:12
place to make it w.   TAYL 531:25
Sing whatever is w. made   YEATS 587:8
spent one whole day w.   THOM 546:12
that's as w. said   SWIFT 526:30
'tis not so deep as a w.   SHAK 483:3
w. and all manner of thing   JUL 286:32
W. building hath three   WOTT 583:16
We never do anything w.   HAZL 243:25
what thou liv'st Live w.   MILT 349:25
when looking w. can't move   SUCK 524:6
when ye do w.   BIBLE 80:26
who can do all things w.   CHUR 148:23
well-aired: to have the morning w.
     BRUM 106:4
Well-a-way: Made every youth cry W.
     BALL 30:10
wellbeloved: bundle of myrrh is my w.
     BIBLE 56:18
My w. hath a vineyard   BIBLE 57:21
well-born: many a w. and unhappy woman
     ELIOT 201:1
well-bred: be very strange and w.
     CONG 161:7
Tho' learn'd, w.   POPE 378:32
well-conducted: Like a w. person THAC 546:3
well-dressed: sense of being w. gives
     FORB 216:10
well-informed: To come with a w. mind
     AUST 23:5
Wellington: W.! (or 'Villainton')
     BYRON 123:24
well-knownness: who is known for his
w.   BOOR 89:20
well-looking: Is it one of my w. days
     GOLD 232:21
well-nightingaled: To this w. vicinity
     HOUS 266:9
wells: dropping buckets into empty w.
     COWP 167:4
go about and poison w.   MARL 329:21
name is John Wellington W.   GILB 229:2
poison the w.   NEWM 361:14
well-shaped: w. man   AUBR 18:1
well-shot: Spirits of w. woodcock BETJ 42:11
well-spent: almost as rare as a w. one
     CARL 131:2
well-spring: that holds the bubbling w.
     MER 337:3
well-tuned: him upon the w. cymbals
     PRAY 400:1
well-written: w. Life is almost as rare
     CARL 131:2
Welsh: devil understands W.   SHAK 439:31
Makes W. as sweet as ditties   SHAK 439:30
Welshman: care and valour in this W.
     SHAK 444:19

Welt: Die W. ist alles   WITT 575:14
W. des Glücklichen ist   WITT 575:16
W. hässlich und schlecht   NIET 363:8
W. in Materialismus versumpfen MOLT 354:4
welter: w. to the parching wind   MILT 343:2
Weltgeschichte: Die W. ist das Weltgericht
     SCH 415:11
Weltordnung: ein Glied in Gottes W.
     MOLT 354:4
Wembley: melancholy Autumn comes
to W.   BETJ 42:16
wen: fate of the great w.   COBB 154:10
wench: ill-starr'd w.   SHAK 477:21
stuff fit only for a w.   MAS 333:20
sun himself a fair hot w.   SHAK 437:34
w. is dead   MARL 329:22
wenen: not w. every thing a lye CHAU 143:28
Wenlock Edge: W. the wood's in trouble
     HOUS 263:14
W. was umbered   HOUS 265:11
went: he w. among the English   BARR 34:19
they w. to sea in a Sieve   LEAR 312:6
w. to the Bar as a very   GILB 226:6
wentest: when thou w. forth before
     PRAY 394:7
Wenus: young 'ooman a W. or a angel
     DICK 182:13
wepe: deeth moot w. and pleyne CHAU 142:17
wept: Babylon we sat down and w.
     PRAY 399:3
he w. to hear   BLAKE 87:24
I have sometimes w.   MUSS 359:3
I w. as I remembered how   CORY 163:4
Jesus w.   BIBLE 72:23
Jesus w.; Voltaire smiled   HUGO 267:3
my father w.   BLAKE 87:27
turned aside and w.   AYT 24:8
w. odorous gums and balm   MILT 347:19
W. over her   TENN 540:2
w. to see the dolour that   MAL 328:4
wepte: soore w. she if oon   CHAU 141:16
Wertenberg: swift Rhine circle fair W.
     MARL 329:5
Werther: W. had a love for Charlotte
     THAC 546:3
Weser: river W.   BROW 103:14
West: bosom of the urgent W.   BRID 92:19
Cincinnatus of the W.   BYRON 125:9
east is from the w.   PRAY 396:17
east, nor from the w.   PRAY 394:26
gathered to the quiet w.   HENL 245:9
Gigantic daughter of the W.   TENN 533:28
Go W.   GREE 235:26
Go W., young man   SOULE 513:11
in the gardens of the W.   CONN 161:16
look not on the w.   HOUS 264:18
safeguard of the W.   WORD 582:10
sailing away to the w.   KING 297:2
That's where the W. begins   CHAP 140:2
wan w. shivers   SWIN 528:16
W. is West   KIPL 297:27
W. of these out to seas   FLEC 214:7
W. to the Golden Gate   KIPL 300:24
w. yet glimmers with some   SHAK 461:15
without declining W.   DONNE 188:31
would *not* travel due W.   CARR 133:6
West Country: This lady of the W.
     DE L 173:27
wester: weeping Pleiads w.   HOUS 265:16
western: baths Of all the w. stars TENN 544:3
Swiftly walk over the w.   SHEL 505:2
This spray of W. pine   HARTE 242:26
W. custom of one wife   SAKI 413:13
Westminster: 'Till W.'s whole year
     POPE 375:21
Westminster Abbey: peerage, or W.
     NELS 360:14
W. or victory   NELS 360:13
Weston: much of Mr W.'s good wine
     AUST 22:11

westward: land vaguely realizing w.
     FROST 219:6
some w., and all wrong   COWP 165:12
w., look   CLOU 154:4
W. the course of empire   BERK 41:20
you are stepping w.   WORD 578:12
wet: bereft Of w. and wildness HOPK 256:18
wether: tainted w. of the flock SHAK 467:25
wetter: Is w. water   BROO 94:12
weyrynesse: slepe for w. of wandryng
     LANG 309:25
weyveth: Anon he w. milk and flessh
     CHAU 142:25
whacks: gave her mother forty w. ANON 6:12
whale: gull's way and the w.'s   MAS 334:6
prophet with the w.   DICK 179:23
Very like a w.   SHAK 434:22
w. Emerges as he goes   SMART 509:3
whales: Where great w. come sailing
     ARN 13:6
ye W.   PRAY 384:25
whangs: w. along in a world HARDY 240:11
wharf: w. of Lethe waiting   HOUS 265:18
wharfs: sense Of the adjacent w. SHAK 422:3
wharves: black w. and the slips LONG 316:22
what: being for my own self w. am
     HILL 251:6
He knew what's w.   BUTL 117:20
is w. them furriners do)   GILB 228:31
is which and which is w.   MILNE 340:16
not tell us w. the soldier   DICK 182:22
W. and Why and When   KIPL 300:12
w. could she have done   YEATS 586:7
w. has been   DRYD 198:16
w. is here   TENN 538:12
W. *is* the matter with Mary Jane
     MILNE 340:10
W., never   GILB 227:31
w. rough beast   YEATS 586:16
w.'s the odds   DU M 199:4
W. was he doing   BROW 98:6
w. we have been makes us   ELIOT 201:14
Whence and w. art thou   MILT 346:25
whatever: Jupiter is w. you see LUCAN 320:1
W. happens   BELL 40:1
what-is-it: certain w. in his voice WOD 575:19
what-not: w. the afternoon passed
     WOD 575:26
What's-his-name: there is no W. but
Thingummy   DICK 177:32
Whatsoever: W. things are true BIBLE 78:22
wheat: orient and immortal w. TRAH 551:18
That sleep among the w.   CARR 136:6
w. set about with lilies   BIBLE 57:8
When w. is green   SHAK 469:21
wheel: beneath thy chariot w.   HOPE 256:5
ever-whirling w. Of Change   SPEN 516:24
red w. barrow   WILL 574:10
w. broken at the cistern   BIBLE 56:11
w.'s kick and the wind's   MAS 334:4
wheels: all the w. of Being slow TENN 536:21
his w. as burning fire   BIBLE 61:8
tarry the w. of his chariots   BIBLE 49:12
whelks: w., and knobs   SHAK 444:7
When: had forgotten to say 'W. WOD 575:28
If not now w.   HILL 251:6
What and Why and W.   KIPL 300:12
w. a man should marry   BACON 26:35
w. did you last see your   YEAM 584:8
W. first we met we did   BRID 92:22
W. I was a little boy   ANON 8:19
W. the long dark autumn-evenings
     BROW 99:17
w. the sun set where were   BYRON 122:34
W. you are old and gray   YEATS 587:12
whence: canst not tell w. it cometh
     BIBLE 71:36
from w. cometh my help   PRAY 398:2
W. and what art thou   MILT 346:25
W. are we   SHEL 499:13

you know not w. you came FITZ 213:9
where: God knows w. BYRON 123:20
How and W. and Who KIPL 300:12
'O w. are you going AUDEN 18:17
when the sun set w. were BYRON 122:34
W. are the eagles ELIOT 202:5
W. are you now HOPE 256:3
w. but here have Pride YEATS 586:8
W. can we live but days LARK 310:3
W. is Bohun CREWE 169:18
'W. is it COL 156:19
W. is now thy God PRAY 392:9
w. is your comforting HOPK 256:19
W. Peter is AMBR 4:1
w. we are is Hell MARL 329:8
whereabout: stones prate of my w.
SHAK 460:1
whereabouts: to us to conceal our w.
SAKI 413:12
wherefore: every why he had a w.
BUTL 117:19
occasions and causes why and w. SHAK 445:8
w. art thou Romeo SHAK 482:8
w. seeking whom Whence HOUS 266:9
whereof: he knoweth w. we are made
PRAY 396:17
W. one cannot speak WITT 575:17
wheresome'er: w. he is SHAK 443:16
Wherewithal: W. shall a young man
cleanse PRAY 398:4
whetstone: There is no such w. ASCH 17:2
which: is which and w. is what MILNE 340:16
w. of us takes the better SOCR 512:18
whichever: w. way you move LUCAN 320:1
whiffling: w. through the tulgey wood
CARR 134:29
Whig: Erastian W. CHES 146:27
first W. was the Devil JOHN 278:2
perceive you are a vile W. JOHN 276:5
Tory and W. in turns shall SMITH 512:6
Tory men and W. measures DISR 185:38
wise Tory and a wise W. JOHN 278:34
Whigs: Gentleman caught the W. bathing
DISR 184:14
W. admit no force but argument BROW 97:26
W. *not* getting into place BYRON 123:33
while: w. my pretty one TENN 541:31
whim: strangest w. has seized CHES 146:14
tempted by a private w. BELL 39:24
whimper: Not with a bang but a w.
ELIOT 203:11
whimsies: they have my w. PRIOR 400:21
whine: w. about their condition WHIT 570:22
whip: 'Too-slow' will need the w.
TENN 541:26
whip-lash: spindle shank a guid w.
BURNS 115:17
whipp'd: w. the offending Adam out
SHAK 443:5
whipped: child is afraid of being w.
JOHN 273:25
he w. my grandfather ADD 2:17
whippersnapper: Critic and w. BROW 99:1
whipping: ought to get a *good* w. VICT 556:14
who should 'scape w. SHAK 432:26
whips: hath chastised you with w. BIBLE 51:3
w. and scorns of time SHAK 433:8
whipster: Every puny w. gets my sword
SHAK 477:17
whirled: She w. round and round
LEAR 311:17
whirligig: w. of time brings in his
SHAK 490:25
whirls: flood that w. me to the sea
MER 337:10
whirlwind: comfort serves in a w.
HOPK 256:21
Rides in the w. ADD 1:14
sweeping w.'s sway GRAY 234:16
they shall reap the w. BIBLE 61:11

went up by a w. into heaven BIBLE 51:22
w. hath blown the dust DONNE 190:23
whirring: w. pheasant springs POPE 381:14
whisker: educated w. TENN 533:10
whiskers: my fur and w. CARR 133:20
Runcible Cat with crimson w. LEAR 312:20
whiskey: w. afterwards as he was ASHF 17:9
Whisky: Freedom and W. gang thegither
BURNS 112:35
tell me w.'s name in Greek BURNS 112:34
whisper: By all ye cry or w. KIPL 304:7
fiddled w. music ELIOT 205:9
Full well the busy w. GOLD 231:2
His w. came to Me KIPL 299:3
There's a w. down the field KIPL 300:23
We wake and w. awhile DE L 173:25
We w. in her ear WILB 572:4
w. of a faction should RUSS 412:18
w. of the south-wind rushing TENN 538:24
w. softness in chambers MILT 351:25
W. who dares MILNE 340:11
whispered: it's w. every where CONG 160:7
whispering: They've a way of w. to me
HARDY 239:18
...w. from her towers ARN 15:25
w., with white lips BYRON 120:25
whisperings: Foul w. are abroad SHAK 462:26
It keeps eternal w. around KEATS 292:22
whispers: Blood of Jesus w. BICK 84:4
to be drunk Among w. ELIOT 203:4
us whom he w. in the ear BROW 98:21
W. the o'er-fraught heart SHAK 462:16
whist: my husband from his w. BROW 100:20
whist upon w. drive BETJ 42:13
whistle: I'd w. her off and let SHAK 475:21
was hir joly w. wel ywet CHAU 143:12
w., and I'll come to you BURNS 116:4
W. and she'll come to you FLET 215:24
whistled: w. as he went DRYD 195:34
whistles: w. blow forlorn HOUS 262:16
w. in his sound SHAK 425:24
W. o'er the furrowed land MILT 342:19
Whistling: W. to keep myself from
DRYD 195:19
W. to the air SHAK 422:3
white: always goes into w. satin SHER 506:3
are arrayed in w. robes BIBLE 82:1
are w. already to harvest BIBLE 71:41
beloved is w. and ruddy BIBLE 57:3
black ram Is tupping your w. ewe
SHAK 473:16
called the chess-board w. BROW 99:5
clear w., inside KIPL 299:18
curious engine, your w. hand WEBS 566:21
'elp you a lot with the W. KIPL 300:15
garment was w. as snow BIBLE 61:8
hairs were w. like wool BIBLE 81:14
How ill w. hairs become SHAK 442:30
Ionian w. and gold ELIOT 205:4
it here in black and w. JONS 284:7
Lawn as w. as driven snow SHAK 492:2
made them w. in the blood BIBLE 82:2
many a head has turned w. MULL 359:1
my soul is w. BLAKE 88:2
nor w. so very white CANN 129:29
O'er the w. Alps alone DONNE 188:12
pluck a w. rose with me SHAK 445:21
read'st black where I read w. BLAKE 85:22
should be bound in w. vellum RUSK 412:13
So purely w. they were SPEN 516:32
so w.! O so soft JONS 285:4
Take up the W. Man's burden KIPL 304:6
they shall be as w. as snow BIBLE 57:18
thunders of w. silence BROW 98:4
virgin w. integrity DONNE 187:21
Wearing w. for Eastertide HOUS 262:14
w. and hairless as an egg HERR 249:15
w. and small DUNB 199:11
W. as an angel is the English BLAKE 88:2
W. as an orchid she rode AUDEN 18:3

w. dress, her death SPEN 515:6
w. heat of this revolution WILS 574:17
W. his shroud as the mountain SHAK 435:34
W. Horse of the White Horse CHES 146:15
W. in the moon the long HOUS 263:20
w. lies to ice a cake ASQ 17:18
w. races are really pinko-gray FORS 217:7
W. shall not neutralize BROW 104:31
w. tremendous daybreak BROO 94:29
wild w. horses play ARN 13:5
with w. and bristly beard SHAK 492:26
world is w. with May TENN 534:4
whited: like unto w. sepulchres BIBLE 67:25
white-faced: w. and still in the coffin
WHIT 570:11
Whitefoot: W., come uppe Lightfoot
ING 270:15
white-mossed: from under the w. wonder
BRID 92:14
whiten: w. the green plains under SHEL 500:4
whitens: ptarmigan that w. ere his
TENN 534:37
whiter: Did never w. show SPEN 516:31
I shall be w. than snow PRAY 393:5
W. than new snow on a raven's SHAK 483:7
whites: comparison all w. are ink
SHAK 486:19
w. of their eyes PUTN 403:6
white-wash'd: w. wall GOLD 231:4
whitewashed: Guard the decent w. chapel
BETJ 43:7
whither: one knows not w. nor why
MAS 334:8
w. it goeth BIBLE 71:36
W., O splendid ship BRID 92:19
W. shall I go then from PRAY 399:5
whiting: said a w. to a snail CARR 134:13
w. said with its tail HOOD 255:17
Whitman: daintily dressed Walt W.
CHES 148:1
pact with you, Walt W. POUND 383:12
What do you see Walt W. WHIT 570:12
Whizzing: W. them over the net BETJ 43:20
Who: How and Where and W. KIPL 300:12
Who is on my side? w. BIBLE 51:36
W. is this TENN 538:12
W. killed John Keats BYRON 125:1
Whoever: W. it is that leaves him
FROST 219:11
whole: faith hath made thee w. BIBLE 65:26
had I stol'n the w. STEV 523:6
is greater than the w. HES 250:19
nothing can be sole or w. YEATS 584:19
over the measureless w. LUCR 320:3
parts of one stupendous w. POPE 379:10
seeing the w. of them RUSK 411:26
we shall be w. PRAY 395:8
what a *w.* Oxford is COL 155:2
w. breadth of the way BUNY 107:15
w. man in himself HOR 262:10
w. need not a physician BIBLE 65:23
w. wit in a jest BEAU 35:19
wholesome: labour spread her w. store
GOLD 230:18
nights are w. SHAK 449:27
steal out of his w. bed SHAK 449:13
w. salad from the brook COWP 167:27
wholly: some few to be read w. BACON 27:19
Whom: 'W. the gods love die young'
BYRON 123:11
whoop: we'll w. and we'll holloa WHYT 572:2
whooping: out of all w. SHAK 426:7
whopping: measures is Latin for a w.
ANST 11:9
whore: dost thou lash that w. SHAK 455:19
Fortune's a right w. WEBS 567:1
I am the Protestant w. GWYN 237:8
I' the posture of a w. SHAK 424:3
judgment of the great w. BIBLE 82:22
rogue is married to a w. KIPL 302:18

teach the morals of a w.   JOHN 274:10
w. and gambler   BLAKE 85:17
w.'s oath   SHAK 454:28
woman's a w.   JOHN 276:15
you for that cunning w.   SHAK 476:21
young man's w.   JOHN 275:19
whoremaster: admirable evasion of w.
  SHAK 453:11
whoremongers: w., and murderers
  BIBLE 83:3
whores: have brought w. for Eleusis
  POUND 382:11
Out ye w.   PEMB 371:10
whore-shops: Madhouses, prisons, w.
  CLARE 152:5
whoring: w. with their own inventions
  PRAY 397:6
whose: Never ask me w.   HOUS 263:11
Whoso: W. doeth these things   PRAY 390:5
Whosoever: W. will be saved   PRAY 385:11
why: every w. he had a wherefore
  BUTL 117:19
I can't tell you w.   MART 331:9
knows not whither nor w.   MAS 334:8
What and W. and When   KIPL 300:12
w. and wherefore in all   SHAK 445:8
w. are we   SHEL 499:13
W. are you not here   THOR 550:27
W., Edward, tell me why   WORD 577:1
W. in the name of Glory   KEATS 290:9
wibrated: that had better not be w.
  DICK 175:27
wicked: are Tories born w.   ANON 6:14
be equally w. and corrupt   BURKE 108:20
better than one of the w.   SHAK 438:8
desperately w.   BIBLE 60:24
fiery darts of the w.   BIBLE 78:10
from the deceitful and w.   PRAY 392:10
God help the w.   SHAK 439:17
It's worse than w.   PUNCH 402:26
mercies of the w. are cruel   BIBLE 53:34
never wonder to see men w.   SWIFT 527:15
pomps and vanity of this w.   PRAY 388:13
pretending to be w.   WILDE 573:5
seven other spirits more w.   BIBLE 66:14
shake their w. sides   YEATS 586:8
Something is this way comes   SHAK 462:5
so w. as Lord George Hell   BEER 37:16
There is always a w. secret   AUDEN 21:1
this mad, w. folly   VICT 556:14
unto the w.   BIBLE 59:16
war is regarded as w.   WILDE 572:22
w. cease from troubling   BIBLE 52:13
w. flee when no man pursueth   BIBLE 54:41
w. plant   KYD 306:7
w. to deserve such pain   BROW 99:29
wickedness: I was shapen in w.   PRAY 393:5
leaven of malice and w.   BIBLE 75:36
leaven of malice and w.   PRAY 386:11
little to the w. of a woman   BIBLE 63:8
loose the bands of w.   BIBLE 60:4
our manifold sins and w.   PRAY 384:9
spiritual w. in high places   BIBLE 78:10
That is the Path of W.   BALL 32:5
w. of the world is print   DICK 179:15
w. that he hath committed   BIBLE 60:35
w. that hinders loving   BROW 102:31
wicket: flannelled fools at the w.   KIPL 300:4
Now in Maytime to the w.   HOUS 262:22
slow W. of the Night   THOM 549:2
wictim: w. o' connubiality   DICK 182:1
Widdicombe Fair: I want for to go to
W.   BALL 32:12
wide: deep the Poet sees, but w.
  ARN 14:7
feet long and two feet w.   WORD 582:24
nor so w. as a church door   SHAK 483:3
w. also the east is from   PRAY 396:17
W. is the gate   BIBLE 65:6
wider: thee thrice w.   SHAK 442:31
W. still and wider shall   BENS 40:24

widow: came a certain poor w.   BIBLE 68:38
defendeth the fatherless and w.   PRAY 399:18
'eard o' the W. at Windsor   KIPL 304:9
Here's to the w. of fifty   SHER 506:31
to-day or Molly Stark's a w.   STARK 517:20
undone w. sits upon my arm   MASS 335:21
virgin-w. and a *Mourning Bride* DRYD 197:11
w. bird sate mourning   SHEL 500:3
widowhood: comfortable estate of w.
  GAY 222:18
Widow-maker: go with the old grey W.
  KIPL 299:21
widows: defendeth the cause of w.
  PRAY 394:7
devour w.' houses   BIBLE 68:37
must ev'n do as other w.   GAY 222:34
These w.   ADD 2:18
visit the fatherless and w.   BIBLE 80:11
When w. exclaim loudly   FIEL 211:6
w., and all that are desolate   PRAY 385:20
younger w. refuse   BIBLE 79:15
wife: accommodated than with a w.
  SHAK 442:4
account w. and children   BACON 26:32
after his neighbour's w.   BIBLE 60:16
all the world and his w.   ANST 11:8
animal a husband and w.   FIEL 211:30
be 'like Caesar's w.   ANON 6:11
Caesar's w. must be above   CAES 127:1
casual mistress, but a w.   TENN 536:33
centaur, man and w.   BYRON 123:19
chaste w. wise   SURR 524:21
degrees dwindle into a w.   CONG 161:8
every port he finds a w.   BICK 84:3
Giant Despair had a w.   BUNY 107:21
Giving honour unto the w.   BIBLE 80:29
have a w., and so forth   CONG 160:33
have quarrelled with my w.   PEAC 370:18
having is true to his w.   VANB 555:6
Here lies my w.   DRYD 196:8
He that hath w. and children   BACON 26:31
hope that keeps up a w.'s   GAY 222:18
hurling them at his w.   DOYLE 191:17
husband is, the w. is   TENN 538:19
husband of one w.   BIBLE 79:12
I have married a w.   BIBLE 70:11
is no fury like an ex-w.   CONN 161:13
is sanctified by the w.   BIBLE 76:3
Jael Heber's w.   BIBLE 49:7
kick his w. out of bed   SURT 525:5
kill a w. with kindness   SHAK 484:11
lofty character of W.   DICK 177:15
Lord Brutus took to w.   SHAK 449:16
love your neighbour's w.   MAC 324:3
marriage with his brother's w.   SHAK 446:28
Match'd with an aged w.   TENN 543:21
maxim that man and w. should   FARQ 210:9
Mother, W., and Queen   TENN 543:15
must be in want of a w.   AUST 23:11
Nor winsomeness to w.   POUND 383:18
often said to his w.   CHES 147:28
One w. is too much   GAY 222:36
'oss, my w., and my name   SURT 525:17
railing w.   SHAK 439:28
Remember Lot's w.   BIBLE 70:32
roaring of the wind is my w.   KEATS 294:10
sailor's w. had chestnuts   SHAK 458:6
shall cleave unto his w.   BIBLE 45:13
so as to suit his w.   TROL 553:7
Thane of Fife had a w.   SHAK 462:21
'thanked God my w. was dead   BROW 106:1
Than my sonne's w.   ING 270:16
that a man lay down his w.   JOYCE 286:28
that they be Man and W.   PRAY 389:7
then to have or have no w.   BACON 28:17
They took me from my w.   CLARE 152:6
to look after a w.   SURT 525:24
t'other w. would take ill   GAY 222:36
To weans and w.   BURNS 115:15
true and honourable w.   SHAK 449:15

uncumber'd with a w.   DRYD 196:4
upon seeing his w. there   TRAV 552:6
Western custom of one w.   SAKI 413:13
when his w. talks Greek   JOHN 280:18
whose w. shall I take   MOORE 356:29
who's untrue to his w.   AUDEN 20:13
w. for breed   GAY 223:31
w., if you will marry   SHAK 485:13
w. looked back   BIBLE 46:8
w. shall be as the fruitful   PRAY 398:20
w. to be of a studious   JOHN 278:21
w. was pretty   COWP 168:18
w. who preaches in her   HOOD 255:12
Your w. arranges accordingly   JUV 287:12
wig: w. with the scorched foretop   MAC 324:7
wight: Yonder a maid and her w.
  HARDY 240:5
wights: descriptions of the fairest w.
  SHAK 494:19
wigwam: Stood the w. of Nokomis
  LONG 317:10
wild: bore me in the southern w.   BLAKE 88:2
chance to talk a little w.   SHAK 446:26
grew more fierce and w.   HERB 247:15
I went hunting w.   OWEN 367:10
mouth of that w. beast man   BOL 89:14
My father is gone w. into   SHAK 442:25
nobly w., not mad   HERR 249:13
old, w., and incomprehensible   VICT 556:15
Revenge is a kind of w. justice   BACON 27:7
shoreless watery w.   ARN 13:12
this the w. geese spread   YEATS 586:19
three w. lads were we   SCOTT 418:16
W. he may be   DICK 179:19
w., melancholy, and elevating   BRON 93:17
w. with all regret   TENN 542:4
withered, and so w.   SHAK 458:10
wild cats: w. in your kitchens   SHAK 474:15
wilder: w. shores of love   BLAN 88:30
Wilderness: Beside me singing in the
W.   FITZ 212:11
day's journey into the w.   BIBLE 51:13
dwellings of the w.   PRAY 394:3
given it for a w. of monkeys   SHAK 467:7
him that crieth in the w.   BIBLE 59:5
in perils in the w.   BIBLE 77:12
make a w. and call it peace   TAC 531:7
ninety and nine in the w.   BIBLE 70:5
of one crying in the w.   BIBLE 63:36
of temptation in the w.   PRAY 396:4
through the w. of this world   BUNY 107:10
To be a little w.   MARV 332:14
w. and the solitary place   BIBLE 58:32
w. into a glorious empire   BURKE 110:7
w. shall waters break out   BIBLE 58:34
ye out into the w. to see   BIBLE 66:2
wildest: w. beauty in the world   OWEN 367:10
wild-fowl: w. than your lion living
  SHAK 470:14
wildness: bereft Of wet and w.   HOPK 256:18
wile: follow'd with endearing w.   GOLD 231:1
wiles: of w. More unexpert   MILT 346:5
transient sorrows, simple w.   WORD 581:8
wanton w.   MILT 342:14
Wilhelmine: His little grandchild W.
  SOUT 513:14
Wilkinson: Mr W., a clergyman   FITZ 213:21
will: according to the common w.   JAM 271:5
can't forge his own w.   GILB 228:35
care to stay than w.   SHAK 483:15
cause is in my w.   SHAK 449:20
consummated in the General W.
  AUDEN 19:12
even to have had the w.   PROP 401:16
Fix'd fate, free w.   MILT 346:19
his w. his law   COWP 167:37
if she w.   ANON 8:20
Immanent W. and its designs   HARDY 239:11
It shows a w. most incorrect   SHAK 429:26
I w. not let thee go   BRID 92:11

Man has his w.   HOLM 253:15
Michael Henchard's W.   HARDY 241:18
not because we w.   ARN 12:21
not my w., but thine   BIBLE 71:8
questions of w. or decision   CHOM 148:16
reason and the w. of God   ARN 15:15
that the w. is infinite   SHAK 486:33
This is the W. of the Yukon   SERV 420:13
Thy w. be done in earth   BIBLE 64:24
torrent of a woman's w.   ANON 8:20
'twur the w. o' the Lord   TENN 544:5
war 'twixt will and w. not   SHAK 463:18
We *know* our w. is free   JOHN 275:24
we will hear Caesar's w.   SHAK 450:24
w. be what they will be   BUTL 117:10
W. has woven with an absent   HARDY 239:12
W. in over-plus   SHAK 495:10
w. in us is over-rul'd   MARL 329:18
w. most rank   SHAK 475:20
w. reigns   FRAN 218:10
w. replace reasoned judgement   JUV 287:21
w. that my maxim should   KANT 288:9
W. you, won't you   CARR 134:14
wrote my w. across the sky   LAWR 311:12
You w., Oscar   WHIS 569:25
willed: All we have w. or hoped   BROW 98:19
W. and fulfilled by high   KIPL 300:6
w. more mischief than they   HOUS 263:13
William: kind W. Maginn   LOCK 315:23
Willie: Wee W. Winkie rins through
   MILL 340:3
willin: 'When a man says he's w.'
   DICK 176:34
willing: spirit indeed is w. but the flesh
   BIBLE 68:16
w. to sell for one shilling   LEAR 312:13
willingness: w. is to be praised   OVID 366:26
willow: green w. is my garland   HEYW 250:21
Sang 'W.   GILB 227:15
she had a song of 'w.   SHAK 476:26
Sing all a green w.   SHAK 476:27
Stood Dido with a w.   SHAK 468:14
There is a w. grows aslant   SHAK 436:19
willows: runs away into the w.   VIRG 559:18
w. have overfilled   POUND 382:5
w. of the brook compass   BIBLE 53:10
w., old rotten planks   CONS 162:1
W. whiten   TENN 538:3
will-power: possess the w. to be free
   AUDEN 19:13
Wills: such a lot of people's W.   CHES 146:13
talk of w.   SHAK 479:10
which our w. are gardeners   SHAK 474:8
win: can w. the combat of him   BACON 26:2
else had hopes to w. her   CONG 160:30
from outward forms to w.   COL 156:8
hope to w. by't   SHAK 447:12
so who would greatly w.   BYRON 125:6
Those who w. heaven   BROW 102:27
To w. or lose it all   GRAH 233:14
we w.   PHEI 373:6
when I saw myself to w.   SHAK 495:6
yet wouldst wrongly w.   SHAK 459:1
Winchelsea: shall not lie easy at W.
   BENET 40:20
wind: Absence is to love what w.   BUSS 117:6
all aloud the w. doth blow   SHAK 457:19
am a feather for each w.   SHAK 491:14
bay'd the whisp'ring w.   GOLD 230:21
beat of the off-shore w.   KIPL 300:23
blow, thou winter w.   SHAK 426:1
both with w. and stream   SHAK 475:1
breathing of the common w.   WORD 582:17
chiding of the winter's w.   SHAK 424:31
clouds and w. without rain   BIBLE 54:27
east w. made flesh   APPL 11:12
Fair stood the w. for France   DRAY 193:10
fires flare up in a w.   FRAN 218:2
fluttering in the w.   BROW 101:24
Frisch weht der W.   WAGN 562:1

Frosty w. made moan   ROSS 409:1
gentle w. does move   BLAKE 86:21
God tempers the w.   STER 519:11
gone with the w.   DOWS 191:12
hear a voice in every w.   GRAY 235:11
hears him in the w.   POPE 379:5
hiding place from the w.   BIBLE 58:30
impatient as the W.   WORD 582:15
is best to write in w.   CAT 137:7
it were brought forth w.   BIBLE 58:20
large a charter as the w.   SHAK 425:22
let her down the w.   SHAK 475:21
light w. lives or dies   KEATS 293:8
like W. I go'   FITZ 212:21
Loose as the w.   HERB 247:14
Lord was not in the w.   BIBLE 51:14
nets to catch the w.   WEBS 566:17
Nor ever w. blows loudly   TENN 535:27
north w.   BIBLE 56:29
Not with this w. blowing   KIPL 301:15
observeth the w. shall not sow   BIBLE 56:7
of a rushing mighty w.   BIBLE 73:22
only the w.'s home   ELIOT 205:10
Only w. it into a ball   BLAKE 86:8
pass by me as the idle w.   SHAK 451:20
piffle before the w.   ASHF 17:11
reed shaken with the w.   BIBLE 66:2
sand against the w.   BLAKE 86:23
Sits the w. in that corner   SHAK 472:17
soon as the w. goeth over   PRAY 396:17
swoln with w. and the rank   MILT 343:13
tears shall drown the w.   SHAK 459:6
that which way the w. is   SELD 419:22
There's the w. on the heath   BORR 90:5
They have sown the w.   BIBLE 61:11
thunder-storm *against* the w.   BYRON 121:11
trumpet of a prophecy! O, W.   SHEL 502:14
upon the wings of the w.   PRAY 390:8
upon the wings of the w.   PRAY 396:18
warm wind, the west w.   MAS 334:9
welter to the parching w.   MILT 343:2
Western w.   ANON 8:16
western w. was wild   KING 296:25
wheel's kick and the w.'s   MAS 334:4
When the sweet w. did gently   SHAK 468:13
when the w. is southerly   SHAK 432:18
whistling mane of every w.   THOM 548:13
wild West W.   SHEL 502:8
w. and storm   PRAY 399:22
w. and the rain   SHAK 454:12
w. and the rain   SHAK 490:27
w. bloweth where it listeth   BIBLE 71:36
w. blow the earth into   SHAK 454:3
w. doth blow to-day   BALL 32:9
w. extinguishes candles   LA R 310:15
w. is my wife and the stars   KEATS 294:10
w. of change is blowing   MACM 326:1
W. of the western sea   TENN 541:31
w. sang and the same waves   SWIN 529:10
w.'s feet shine along   SWIN 530:18
w.'s in the east   DICK 176:5
w. takes me I travel   HOR 258:7
w. that blows   DIBD 175:20
w. that blows through me   LAWR 311:9
w. that follows fast   CUNN 170:13
w. was a torrent of darkness   NOYES 364:12
with every w. of doctrine   BIBLE 77:28
worn window-sill in the w.   MACN 326:10
winder: w., a casement   DICK 180:4
wind-flowers: pied w. and violets
   SHEL 503:18
winding: England's w. sheet   BLAKE 85:17
hears its w. murmur   ARN 12:22
place is by a w. stair   BACON 26:26
waters were his w. sheet   BARN 34:5
w. up the watch of his   SHAK 485:4
winding-sheet: Her w. is up as high
   SCOTT 418:7
w. of Edward's race   GRAY 234:15

windmill: cheese and garlic in a w.
   SHAK 439:2
window: eating or opening a w.   AUDEN 19:1
little w. where the sun   HOOD 254:1
Sisera looked out at a w.   BIBLE 49:12
stand at the w.   AUDEN 18:1
throw it out of the w.   BECK 36:1
window-glass: Dash the w. to shivers
   SCOTT 418:1
window pane: Good prose is like a w.
   ORW 365:15
window-panes: Drift across the w.
   ELIOT 204:1
windows: By breaking of w.   MORE 357:7
life's five w. of the soul   BLAKE 85:23
not by eastern w. only   CLOU 154:4
Open the w.   AUST 22:15
storied w. richly dight   MILT 342:10
then the W. failed   DICK 183:19
window-sill: On a worn w. in the wind
   MACN 326:10
winds: beteem the w. of heaven   SHAK 429:28
imprisoned in the viewless w.   SHAK 464:1
Let w. unnoticed whistle   BETJ 42:5
seaman tells stories of w.   PROP 401:15
Though all the w. of doctrine   MILT 352:5
when the w. are churning   LUCR 320:6
When the w. are breathing   SHEL 501:8
Where the w. are all asleep   ARN 13:6
will hear the w. howling   ARN 13:7
w., and crack your cheeks   SHAK 454:4
w. blew   BIBLE 65:11
w. blew   BIBLE 65:12
w. come to me from   WORD 579:2
w. kiss my parched lips   SHAK 452:31
w. of heaven mix for ever   SHEL 502:1
w. of March with beauty   SHAK 491:8
W. of the World   KIPL 298:24
w. shoreward blow   ARN 13:5
w. were love-sick with   SHAK 422:2
w. will call the darkness   SHEL 504:7
ye W. of God   PRAY 384:21
Windsmoor: Well-cut W. flapping lightly
   BETJ 43:14
Windsor: 'eard o' the Widow at W.
   KIPL 304:9
wind up: Excepting to w. the sun
   BYRON 126:5
windy: o' the w. side of the law   SHAK 490:11
w. night a rainy morrow   SHAK 494:14
wine: are fond of Spanish w.   MAS 333:20
are lordliest in their w.   MILT 350:27
Be not drunk with w.   BIBLE 78:5
best fits my little w.   HERR 249:20
bin of w.   STEV 523:7
blood and w. are red   WILDE 572:7
buy w. and milk   BIBLE 59:25
Chian w.   ARN 14:21
cup of hot w. with not a drop   SHAK 427:14
days of w. and roses   DOWS 191:13
doesn't get into the w.   CHES 147:28
Drinking the blude-red w.   BALL 31:16
drink one cup of w.   SCOTT 417:12
drink thy w. with a merry   BIBLE 55:28
falser than vows made in w.   SHAK 426:18
feast of w. on the lees   BIBLE 58:18
fetch to me a pint o' w.   BURNS 113:3
Flask of w.   FITZ 212:11
flown with insolence and w.   MILT 345:18
giant refreshed with w.   PRAY 395:7
good w. is a good familiar   SHAK 475:10
he drinks no w.   SHAK 442:14
honest talk and wholesome w.   TENN 543:16
'I don't see any w.   CARR 133:28
I'll not look for w.   JONS 284:12
invisible spirit of w.   SHAK 475:8
'I rather like bad w.   DISR 186:26
Is not old w. wholesomest   WEBS 566:30
'It wasn't the w.   DICK 181:28
last Companion: W.   BELL 40:8

errors of a w. man BLAKE 87:9
fool than of the w. BACON 25:29
Great men are not always w. BIBLE 52:39
Had you been as w. as bold SHAK 466:17
he is a W. man or a Fool BLAKE 86:13
How very weak the very w. THAC 546:4
I heard a w. man say HOUS 262:20
In a bowl to sea went w. PEAC 371:3
leave the W. FITZ 212:19
Let me smile with the w. JOHN 275:23
man w. in his own conceit BIBLE 54:33
may then grow w. for spite SWIFT 527:21
More happy, if less w. BYRON 124:42
more than woman to be w. MOORE 356:23
Nature is always w. THUR 550:33
Nor ever did a w. one ROCH 406:18
nor talk too w. KIPL 299:22
not w. in you own conceits BIBLE 75:17
Obscurely w. JOHN 278:35
only wretched are the w. PRIOR 401:8
same tree that a w. man BLAKE 88:16
so w. as Thurlow looked FOX 217:21
So w. so young SHAK 481:3
so witty and so w. ROCH 406:22
speak to the w. PIND 373:14
teachings of the w. LUCR 320:6
that's a w. man and a fool SHAK 454:8
therefore only are reputed w. SHAK 465:12
therefore w. as serpents BIBLE 65:33
things w. and wonderful ALEX 3:13
'Tis folly to be w. GRAY 235:13
to be fortunate than w. WEBS 567:11
To be w., and love SHAK 487:1
To be w. and eke to love SPEN 517:2
to think as w. men do ASCH 17:4
Virtuous and w. he was ARMS 12:14
What all the w. men promised MELB 336:11
What leisure to grow w. ARN 13:10
wherefore thou be w. TENN 532:15
Who can be w. SHAK 461:2
w. and masterly inactivity MACK 325:12
w., and to the unwise BIBLE 74:30
w. are merry of tongue YEATS 585:18
w. enough to play the fool SHAK 489:19
w. father that knows his SHAK 466:9
w. man will make BACON 25:38
W. men also die PRAY 392:28
w. son maketh a glad BIBLE 53:29
w. want love SHEL 503:2
Words are w. men's counters HOBB 251:15
words of the w. are as goads BIBLE 56:12
world to confound the w. BIBLE 75:30
wisedoom: what is bettre than w.
CHAU 142:27
wisely: Be w. worldly QUAR 403:11
Of one that lov'd not w. SHAK 477:23
spake w., and could have BIBLE 63:4
wise-manned: w. to boot BROW 104:17
wiser: Are w. and nicer AUDEN 20:12
French are w. than they BACON 27:14
generation w. than the children BIBLE 70:25
not the w. grow POMF 375:8
sadder and a w. man COL 156:1
sluggard is w. in his own BIBLE 54:35
that he is w. to-day than POPE 381:19
Thou speakest w. than thou SHAK 425:12
to be guided by the w. CARL 131:16
We are w. than we know EMER 207:27
young man will be w. TENN 534:2
wisest: clerkes been noght w. men
CHAU 143:11
first and w. of them all MILT 350:9
he was the w. bard BEHN 38:11
Only the w. of mankind SMITH 510:11
than the w. man can answer COLT 159:9
w. and justest and best PLATO 374:10
w. fool in Christendom HENR 245:16
w. man the warl' saw BURNS 114:3
W. men MILT 350:19
w., virtuousest, discreetest MILT 349:7

wish: feast at his earnest w. LEAR 312:21
joy that you can w. SHAK 467:14
Thy own wish w. I thee SHAK 456:24
Thy w. was father SHAK 442:19
To w. myself much better SHAK 467:13
Who did not w. to die SHAW 498:27
Whoever hath her w. SHAK 495:10
who would w. to die BORR 90:4
willingly believe what they w. CAES 126:27
w. for what I faintly hope DRYD 197:16
w. I loved the Human Race RAL 404:20
w. thine own heart dry KEATS 290:30
w. 'twere done ARN 13:23
Wish'd: W. to be with them SCOTT 416:9
wished: He whom I w. to see KEPP 295:12
nor w. to change GOLD 230:22
w. all men as rich as he GILB 225:28
W. for to hear KEPP 295:12
w. longer by its readers JOHN 280:16
wishes: all made of w. SHAK 426:29
her little w. and ways HARDY 241:16
there is exact to my w. ANON 5:13
wishest: Than w. should be undone
SHAK 459:1
wision: you see my w.'s limited DICK 182:23
Wissenschaft: Politik ist keine exakte
W. BISM 84:19
wistful: With such a w. eye WILDE 572:8
wit: accepted w. has GILB 229:10
are at their w.'s end PRAY 397:10
attire doth show her w. ANON 6:20
baiting-place of w. SIDN 507:20
Beauty, w., High birth SHAK 487:6
becomes excellent w. SHAK 442:15
Brevity is the soul of w. SHAK 431:30
Devise, w. SHAK 456:19
effusions of w. and humour AUST 22:31
fancy w. will come POPE 376:15
folly and his weapon w. HOPE 256:2
he but have drawn his w. JONS 284:17
His w. invites you by his COWP 165:5
His w. was in his own power JONS 285:1
How the w. brightens POPE 378:25
I had but a little w. ANON 8:19
In w., a man POPE 378:8
is only a w. among Lords JOHN 274:9
mechanic part of w. ETH 208:30
mingled with a little w. DRYD 196:31
Muse gave native w. HOR 257:23
nature by her mother w. SPEN 516:20
neither a w. in his own eye CONG 160:11
no more w. than a Christian SHAK 487:25
nor all thy Piety nor W. FITZ 213:7
of that he shoots his w. SHAK 427:7
of thy w. in an instant SHAK 467:19
old man's w. may wander TENN 534:2
pick-purse of another's w. SIDN 507:26
plays can boast of more w. ETH 208:27
pleasant smooth w. AUBR 18:1
plentiful lack of w. SHAK 432:8
proverb is one man's w. RUSS 412:21
scintillations of your w. GOUL 233:5
Some beams of w. on other DRYD 196:34
spice of w. STEV 523:7
Staircase w. DID 184:6
that has a little tiny w. SHAK 454:12
thirty, the w. FRAN 218:10
too proud for a w. GOLD 231:17
to sharpen a good w. ASCH 17:2
up the watch of his w. SHAK 485:4
use my w. as a pitchfork LARK 310:6
ware of mine own w. SHAK 425:13
wears his w. in his belly SHAK 486:29
well craves a kind of w. SHAK 489:19
whole w. in a jest BEAU 35:19
will be w. in all languages DRYD 198:1
Wisdom and W. are little CHES 145:8
w. I e'er was deafen'd BYRON 124:11
w., if not first GOLD 231:19
w. is nature to advantage POPE 378:17

w. is out BECON 36:22
w. is out SHAK 472:34
W. is the epitaph NIET 363:13
w. its soul COL 156:15
w. Makes such a wound SHEL 501:31
w., nor words, nor worth SHAK 451:2
w. of man to say what dream SHAK 471:9
w.'s a feather POPE 379:24
W.'s an unruly engine HERB 247:4
w.'s false mirror held POPE 380:4
w.'s the noblest frailty SHAD 420:20
W. to persuade DAV 172:12
witty fool than a foolish w. SHAK 488:5
W. will shine DRYD 197:33
w. with dunces POPE 375:22
You have a nimble w. SHAK 426:11
your w. single SHAK 441:10
Your w.'s too hot SHAK 456:23
witch: suffer a w. to live BIBLE 47:26
witchcraft: Nor no w. charm thee
SHAK 428:22
only is the w. I have us'd SHAK 474:1
rebellion is as the sin of w. BIBLE 50:4
w. celebrates SHAK 460:1
witches: think we're burning w. CHES 147:7
witching: very w. time of night SHAK 434:25
with: God knows it I am w. them
WILDE 572:17
Lord of hosts is w. us PRAY 392:20
sort of English up w. which CHUR 151:6
thou art w. me PRAY 390:22
When you see w. BLAKE 85:23
w. you in the squeezing GOLD 232:24
withdraw: (Anthea) must w. from him
HERR 249:23
to w. one's steps VIRG 558:18
withdrew: He departed, he w. CIC 151:27
wither: Age cannot w. her SHAK 422:5
garlands w. on your brow SHIR 507:3
I w. slowly in thine arms TENN 543:11
names that must not w. BYRON 120:32
wither'd: It could not w. be JONS 284:12
w. cheek and tresses grey SCOTT 416:8
w. in my hand HERB 247:24
w. is the garland SHAK 423:16
withered: before they be w. BIBLE 62:11
dried up, and w. PRAY 395:18
they w. away BIBLE 66:16
w., and so wild SHAK 458:10
withereth: Fast w. too KEATS 290:16
Witherington: W. needs must I wail
SHEA 498:29
withers: *it w. away* ENG 208:18
our w. are unwrung SHAK 434:13
withhold: evening w. not thine hand
BIBLE 56:8
Sometimes w. in mercy what MORE 357:10
withholde: man the cours of hire w.
CHAU 142:29
within: he never went w. COWL 164:6
I have that w. SHAK 429:25
kingdom of God is w. you BIBLE 70:31
they that are w. would DAV 172:9
thou wert w. me AUG 21:16
when the fight begins w. BROW 99:10
without: forasmuch as w. thee we
PRAY 386:21
much as w. Thee KNOX 305:21
nor w. you MART 331:13
that are w. would fain go DAV 172:9
that is w. sin among you BIBLE 72:10
those things that are w. BIBLE 77:12
W. ceasing I make mention BIBLE 74:29
w. whose never-failing WOD 575:21
withstand: least we w. Barabbas now
BROW 101:4
w. in the evil day BIBLE 78:10
witless: w. nature HOUS 265:10
witness: shalt not bear false w. BIBLE 47:24
to bear w. of that Light BIBLE 71:25

w. drew her long black — ELIOT 205:9
w. drop as an honeycomb — BIBLE 53:20
w. especially — AUST 23:5
w. forget her sucking child — BIBLE 59:17
w. for the hearth — TENN 542:9
w. has haunted me these — KEATS 294:3
w. has her way — HOLM 253:15
W.! in our hours of ease — SCOTT 417:21
w. is a dish for the gods — SHAK 424:9
w. is his game — TENN 542:8
w. is only a woman — KIPL 298:3
w. is so hard — TENN 542:12
W. is the lesser man — TENN 539:5
w. is the worst — GRAN 234:5
w. learn in silence with — BIBLE 79:9
w., let her be as good — ELIOT 201:9
w. liberty to gad abroad — BIBLE 63:9
w. made Society — BRAD 91:8
w. mov'd is like a fountain — SHAK 484:16
w. of real genius — FITZ 213:19
w. of so shining loveliness — YEATS 586:17
w. out-paramoured the Turk — SHAK 454:18
w., rules us still — MOORE 357:1
W.'s at best a contradiction — POPE 377:29
w. sat, in unwomanly rags — HOOD 255:6
w. says to her lusting — CAT 137:7
w.'s business to get married — SHAW 497:25
w.'s cause is man's — TENN 542:18
w.'s desire is rarely — COL 157:33
w. seldom asks advice before — ADD 2:23
W. seldom Writes her Mind — STEE 517:24
W.'s faith — SCOTT 418:4
w.'s friendship ever ends — GAY 223:9
w. should marry a teetotaller — STEV 521:29
w.'s might — SHAK 449:22
W.'s mind — GAY 223:8
w.'s noblest station is — LYTT 321:21
w. sober — PEPYS 372:10
w.'s preaching is like — JOHN 275:10
w.'s whole life is a history — IRV 270:20
w. take An elder — SHAK 489:1
w. taken in adultery — BIBLE 72:9
w. that deliberates is — ADD 1:20
w. that you forsake her — KIPL 299:21
w., therefore to be won — SHAK 446:1
w. wakes to love — TENN 535:9
w. was full of good works — BIBLE 73:36
W. was God's second blunder — NIET 363:4
W., what have I to do — BIBLE 71:33
W.! when I behold thee — KEATS 293:10
w. which is without discretion — BIBLE 53:32
w. who always was tired — ANON 5:13
w. who, between courses — JAMES 271:21
w. who did not care) — KIPL 303:29
w. whom thou gavest — BIBLE 45:17
w. who wrote the book that — LINC 315:6
W., why weepest thou — BIBLE 73:8
W. will be the last thing — MER 337:34
w. with fair opportunities — THAC 545:21
w. yet think him an angel — THAC 545:7
wrapp'd in a w.'s hide — SHAK 446:16
yet a w. too — WORD 581:8
young W. her name was Dull — BUNY 107:30
woman-head: graves have learnt that
w. — DONNE 190:5
womanhood: Heroic w. — LONG 317:7
W. and childhood fleet — LONG 316:20
womankind: faith in w. — TENN 542:19
spoons and packs off its w. — SHAW 497:30
w. than to suppose they — KEATS 294:1
worst he can of w. — HOME 253:23
womanly: blushing w. discovering grace
— DONNE 188:11
So w., Her demeaning — SKEL 508:17
w. feeling and propriety — VICT 556:14
woman's: is semblative a w. part SHAK 488:3
womb: cloistered in thy dear w. DONNE 189:1
dark w. where I began — MAS 333:22
even so her plenteous w. — SHAK 463:13
events in the w. of time — SHAK 474:11

grave; and the barren w. — BIBLE 54:46
her w. convey sterility — SHAK 453:18
Making their tomb the w. — SHAK 494:11
slayeth the child in the w. — POUND 382:11
this teeming w. of royal — SHAK 478:20
was from his mother's w. — SHAK 463:8
w. of time the body whose — HEINE 244:12
w. of uncreated night — MILT 346:10
wombe: O w.! O bely — CHAU 143:6
women: after the manner of w. — BIBLE 46:6
An' I learned about w. — KIPL 300:16
An' learn about w. from — KIPL 300:17
are not w. truly — JONS 284:11
asham'd that w. are so simple — SHAK 484:19
because w. have cancers — KEATS 293:32
blessed art thou among w. — BIBLE 69:4
by subtleties then — MER 337:16
created men and w. different — VICT 556:14
denyin' the w. are foolish — ELIOT 200:19
dry than w.'s tears — WEBS 567:7
England is the paradise of w. — FLOR 216:1
experience of w. which — DOYLE 192:29
fickleness of the w. I love — SHAW 498:9
Fram'd to make w. false — SHAK 474:12
generally like w.'s letters — HAZL 243:8
girls turn into American w. — HAMP 238:17
Half the sorrows of w. — ELIOT 200:24
happiest w. — ELIOT 201:18
hardly any w. at all — AUST 23:4
he hid himself among w. — BROW 97:14
hops, and w. — DICK 181:27
I must have w. — GAY 222:27
is for w. to keep counsel — SHAK 449:22
let not w.'s weapons — SHAK 454:2
Let us have wine and w. — BYRON 122:21
Let your w. keep silence — BIBLE 76:16
love of w. — BYRON 122:24
many w. — JOHN 274:22
Married w. are kept women — SMITH 510:16
men and w. with our race — KIPL 298:10
Men don't know w. — TROL 552:20
men in w. do require — BLAKE 86:15
men that w. marry — LONG 316:21
men, w., and Herveys — MONT 354:6
men, w., and clergymen — SMITH 511:8
Monstrous Regiment of W. — KNOX 305:19
Most w. are not so young — BEER 37:10
Most w. have no characters — POPE 377:17
Music and w. I cannot — PEPYS 372:16
old w. (of both sexes) — STER 520:4
other w. cloy — SHAK 422:5
passing the love of w. — BIBLE 50:17
Phidias Gave w. dreams — YEATS 587:1
poetry w. generally write — BRON 93:17
pretty w. to deserve them — AUST 22:26
proper function of w. — ELIOT 201:20
room the w. come and go — ELIOT 203:18
shame for w. to speak — BIBLE 76:17
Silly w. laden with sins — BIBLE 79:24
Solomon loved many strange w. — BIBLE 51:1
souls of w. are so small — BUTL 118:18
Spare their w. for Thy — BETJ 43:5
spoiled the w.'s chats — BROW 103:15
stir up the zeal of w. — MILL 339:21
temptations both in wine and w. — KITC 305:14
then God help all w. — CAMP 128:7
Though w. all above — SHAK 455:17
thousand business w. — BETJ 42:6
tide in the affairs of w. — BYRON 123:20
to place w.'s hearts — WEBS 566:19
weird w. promis'd — SHAK 461:5
Were w. never so fair — LYLY 321:9
We wage no war with w. — SOUT 514:5
we w. cannot escape it — GIBB 225:3
Where w. walk in public — WHIT 570:15
which w. don't understand — KIPL 301:9
Why need the other w. know — BROW 98:26
wine and w. — BURT 116:21
With many w. I doubt whether — TROL 552:24
w. and care and trouble — WARD 564:38

W. and Champagne) — BELL 39:2
W. and elephants never — SAKI 413:1
W. and Horses and Power — KIPL 297:2
W. and music should never — GOLD 232:2
W. and wine should life — GAY 222:2
'w. are a sex by themselves — BEER 37:2
w. are in furious secret — SHAW 496:2
W. are like tricks by slight — CONG 160:5
w. are mostly troublesome — LOVER 318:22
W. are much more like each — CHES 145:2
W. are strongest — BIBLE 62:4
w. become like their mothers — WILDE 573:2
W. can't forgive failure — CHEK 145:1
w. guide the plot — SHER 506:24
w. in a state of ignorance — KNOX 305:20
w. like that part which — WEBS 566:18
w. Must be half-workers — SHAK 428:11
w. must weep — KING 297:3
W. never look so well — SURT 525:26
w. of good carriage — SHAK 481:28
W.—one half the human — BAG 28:29
w., physical decay, Yourself — AUDEN 19:5
w.'s eyes this doctrine — SHAK 457:6
w.'s eyes this doctrine — SHAK 457:9
w. should be struck regularly — COW 163:14
w.'s rights is the basic — FOUR 217:18
w. the heart argues — ARN 13:20
W., then, are only children — CHES 145:25
W. what they are — BRAD 91:14
w. with perfect courtesy — KITC 305:14
w., worst and best — TENN 535:16
work its way with the w. — DICK 182:28
would have him about w. — SHAK 443:19
you should be w. — SHAK 458:10
woman: is bettre than a good w.
— CHAU 142:27
love a w. that she woot — CHAU 144:3
worthy w. al hir lyve — CHAU 141:31
Wommen: 'W. desiren to have
sovereynetee — CHAU 143:24
won: Duke of Marlbro' w. — SOUT 513:19
gaily you w. — BETJ 44:6
'is never lost till w. — COWP 168:23
not that you w. or lost — RICE 405:23
our Lord the field is w. — MORE 357:14
prize we sought is w. — WHIT 570:7
'She is w. — SCOTT 417:14
therefore may be w. — SHAK 486:15
Things w. are done — SHAK 486:21
to-morrow the ground w. — ARN 14:17
'Where you will never w. — BALL 30:18
woman in this humour w. — SHAK 480:22
woman, therefore to be w. — SHAK 446:1
wonder: all a w. and a wild desire
— BROW 104:19
all knowledge and w. (which — BACON 24:14
all the w. that would be — TENN 538:24
appeared a great w. in heaven — BIBLE 82:10
Have eyes to w. — SHAK 494:20
I w. any man alive will — GAY 222:19
I w. by my troth — DONNE 188:29
may w. at the workmanship — MILT 341:18
still the w. grew — GOLD 231:3
to see the boneless w. — CHUR 149:27
under the white-mossed w. — BRID 92:14
We w. at ourselves like — WORD 577:2
w. how the Devil they got — POPE 376:24
w. of an hour — BYRON 120:9
w. of our age — GREV 236:17
w. of our stage — JONS 284:19
w. what happened to him — COW 163:16
w. what you've missed — AUDEN 18:10
Worship is transcendent w. — CARL 131:29
wonderful: All things wise and w. ALEX 3:13
knowledge is too w. and excellent
— PRAY 399:5
most w. wonderful — SHAK 426:7
name shall be called W. — BIBLE 58:7
passing strange and w. — SHEL 500:8
speak in our tongues the w. — BIBLE 73:23

There are many w. things   SOPH 513:7
which are too w. for me   BIBLE 55:1
with any thing that is w.   CONG 159:28
w. piece of work which   SHAK 421:21
wonderfully: fearfully and w. made
    PRAY 399:6
wonders: all w. in one sight   CRAS 169:8
carry within us the w.   BROW 96:12
declare the w. that he   PRAY 397:7
Except ye see signs and w.   BIBLE 71:43
his w. in the deep   PRAY 397:9
rich relative work w.   BIRK 84:13
Seven W. of the World   ADD 2:19
signs and my w. in the land of Egypt
    BIBLE 47:11
Signs are taken for w.   ELIOT 203:4
wondrous: tell of all thy w. works
    PRAY 391:5
this is w. strange   SHAK 431:22
What w. life is this   MARV 332:3
won't: if she w.   ANON 8:20
wonynge: w. fer by weste   CHAU 141:29
woo: are April when they w.   SHAK 426:23
Come, w. me   SHAK 426:21
wood: cleave the w. and there   ANON 7:11
God reigned from the w.   VEN 556:6
Heap on more w.   SCOTT 417:15
hewers of w. and drawers   BIBLE 49:3
hollow behind the little w.   TENN 539:25
lath of w. painted   BISM 84:27
must Thou char the w. ere   THOM 548:18
my house in the high w.   BELL 40:11
old w. burn brightest   WEBS 566:30
On Wenlock Edge the w.'s   HOUS 263:14
Out of this w. do not desire   SHAK 470:19
set out to plant a w.   SWIFT 527:20
therefore may be w.   SHAK 486:15
therefore to be w.   SHAK 446:1
whiffling through the tulgey w.   CARR 134:29
You are not w.   SHAK 450:25
you that broke the new w.   POUND 383:12
woodbine: over-canopied with luscious
w.   SHAK 470:10
well-attir'd w.   MILT 343:15
w. spices are wafted abroad   TENN 540:9
woodcock: Now is the w. near the gin
    SHAK 489:12
Spirits of well-shot w.   BETJ 42:11
w. to mine own springe   SHAK 437:19
woodcocks: springes to catch w.   SHAK 430:21
wooden: lies about his w. horse   FLEC 214:18
Sailed off in a w. shoe   FIELD 211:2
this w. O the very casques   SHAK 443:4
wear w. shoes   GOLD 232:6
w. walls are the best walls   COV 163:10
Wooden-shoes: Round-heads and W.
are   ADD 2:1
woodland: a bit of w.   HOR 262:9
stands about the w. ride   HOUS 262:14
woodman: w., spare the beechen
    CAMP 128:17
wood-notes: Warble his native w. wild
    MILT 342:19
woods: Enter these enchanted w.   MER 337:21
green-rob'd senators of mighty w.
    KEATS 290:5
let them be w. of consular   VIRG 559:22
light w. go seaward from   HUNT 268:12
never knew the summer w.   TENN 536:15
pleasure in the pathless w.   BYRON 121:22
road through the w.   KIPL 303:31
sea-blooms and the oozy w.   SHEL 502:11
teachers had been w. and rills   WORD 581:11
there is a spirit in the w.   WORD 578:20
through the Wet Wild W.   KIPL 304:24
too have lived in the w.   VIRG 559:16
when all the w. are still   MILT 351:5
Where are those starry w.   BRID 92:17
w. are lovely   FROST 219:12
w. decay and fall   TENN 543:11

w. with high romances blent   KEATS 292:15
woodshed: Something nasty in the w.
    GIBB 225:2
woodspurge: w. has a cup of three
    ROSS 410:9
wooer: knight to be their w.   BALL 30:14
woof: We know her w.   KEATS 290:27
w. of my tent's thin roof   SHEL 500:6
wooing: w. mind shall be express'd
    SHAK 457:16
w. of it   BACON 27:31
wooings: full length people's w.
    BYRON 122:27
wool: hairs were white like w.   BIBLE 81:14
He giveth snow like w.   PRAY 399:21
his head like the pure w.   BIBLE 61:8
If such as came for w.   BROW 102:17
tease the huswife's w.   MILT 341:18
w. comes not to market   POUND 382:9
woollen: in w.   POPE 377:15
woolly: w., bright   BLAKE 87:26
Woord: W. is but wynd   LYDG 321:4
Woos: W. his own end   TENN 534:37
woot: love a womman that she w.
    CHAU 144:3
Worchyng: W. and wandryng   LANG 309:23
word: been a time for such a w.   SHAK 463:6
before thy uncreating w.   POPE 376:2
beginning was the w.   BIBLE 71:21
beginning was the W.   ELIOT 204:1
be ye doers of the w.   BIBLE 80:10
Bilbo's the w.   CONG 160:15
by every w. that proceedeth   BIBLE 48:22
by every w. that proceedeth   BIBLE 64:1
choke the w.   BIBLE 66:17
comfort of thy holy W.   PRAY 386:5
Every idle w. that men   BIBLE 66:10
father answered never a w.   LONG 317:21
fool can play upon the w.   SHAK 467:18
honour? A w.   SHAK 440:18
in w. mightier than they   MILT 348:26
last kind w. to Christ   BROW 104:25
leave the w. of God   BIBLE 73:27
Lord gave the w.   PRAY 394:8
Man's w. is God in man   TENN 533:31
meanings packed up into one w.   CARR 135:28
meekness the engrafted w.   BIBLE 80:10
nat o w. wol he faille   CHAU 142:31
no w. however sounding   STEV 521:14
once familiar w.   BAYLY 35:10
one Peculiar w.   LAND 309:3
one-while w. for word   ALFR 3:17
plainly repugnant to the W.   PRAY 400:8
Proud w. you never spoke   LAND 308:25
say only the w.   MASS 335:8
sincere milk of the w.   BIBLE 80:22
sincere milk of the w.   BIBLE 83:25
step should sound or a w.   SWIN 529:18
storm, fulfilling his w.   PRAY 399:22
suit the action to the w.   SHAK 433:17
teaching me that w.   SHAK 468:9
Tears wash out a W.   FITZ 213:7
That I kept my w.   DE L 174:8
there is no such w.   BULW 107:5
time lies in one little w.   SHAK 478:13
To-day I pronounced a w.   FLEM 214:27
To honour his own w.   TENN 534:11
torture one poor w. ten   DRYD 196:35
truth of thy holy W.   PRAY 387:13
understanding of thy W.   PRAY 385:18
Was one that kept his w.   HOUS 266:2
We had no w. to say   WILDE 572:11
what the w. did make it   ELIZ 205:19
'When I use a w.   CARR 135:21
w., at random spoken   SCOTT 416:23
w. bites like a fish   SPEN 515:15
w. fitly spoken   BIBLE 54:26
w. in its Pickwickian sense…He   DICK 181:22
w. is a lantern unto my   PRAY 398:6
w. is the Verb   HUGO 267:9

w. is too often profaned   SHEL 504:13
w. spoken in due season   BIBLE 54:7
w. takes wing irrevocably   HOR 258:22
w. wad ane o' them speak   BALL 30:21
W. was made flesh   BIBLE 71:27
W. WAS MADE FLESH   MASS 335:12
w. which in wartime has   BETH 42:3
w. within a word   ELIOT 203:4
yesterday the w. of Caesar might
    SHAK 450:23
yet God has not said a w.   BROW 103:30
wordes: glotoun of w.   LANG 309:24
wordless: poem should be w.   MACL 325:13
song was w.   SASS 414:17
words: all sad w. of tongue   WHIT 571:19
All w., And no performance   MASS 335:24
All w. forgotten   DE L 174:15
arched roof in w. deceiving   MILT 344:13
arrangement of your w.   HOR 257:13
barren superfluity of w.   GARTH 221:21
best w. in the best order   COL 157:32
big w. for little   JOHN 275:14
Bright is the ring of w.   STEV 523:1
coiner of sweet w.   ARN 14:25
common, little, easy w.   WESL 568:24
counsel by w. without knowledge
    BIBLE 52:41
deceive you with vain w.   BIBLE 78:3
dressing old w.   SHAK 494:9
empty w. of a dream   BRID 92:10
even from good w.   PRAY 391:30
experience find those w.   CONG 160:27
fear those big w.   JOYCE 286:22
food and not fine w.   MOL 353:10
Fool and his w. are soon   SHEN 505:17
form of sound w.   BIBLE 79:23
for your w.   SHAK 451:31
Garden it abideth not in w.   KIPL 299:13
Give sorrow w.   SHAK 462:16
God spake all these w.   BIBLE 47:24
good w.   SHAK 452:30
heard w. that have been   BEAU 35:19
Hear what comfortable w.   PRAY 387:20
He w. me, girls   SHAK 424:1
his paint-pots and his w.   HOR 257:16
His w. came feebly   WORD 581:1
How often misused w. generate   SPEN 514:31
idiom of w. very little   PRIOR 400:27
I hate false w.   LAND 309:11
In all his w. most wonderful   NEWM 362:12
last w. of Mr Despondency   BUNY 107:37
Let the w. of my mouth   PRAY 390:13
long w. Bother me   MILNE 340:13
matter decocted into few w.   FULL 220:11
Melting melodious w.   HERR 250:9
Men of few w. are the best   SHAK 444:5
multiplieth w. without knowledge
    BIBLE 52:40
my w. among mankind   SHEL 502:14
my w. are my own   CHAR 140:23
My w. echo Thus   ELIOT 202:13
my w. shall not pass away   BIBLE 67:31
of all w. of tongue   HARTE 242:28
Of every four w. I write   BOIL 89:12
of hard w. like a charm   OSB 365:19
of the unpleasant'st w.   SHAK 467:15
on the alms-basket of w.   SHAK 457:12
polite meaningless w.   YEATS 585:1
Proper w. in proper places   SWIFT 526:20
repeats his w.   SHAK 452:20
Th' artillery of w.   SWIFT 527:31
that my w. were now written   BIBLE 52:30
that w. are the daughters   JOHN 281:6
their large confusing w.   AUDEN 18:5
therefore let thy w. be few   BIBLE 55:16
these are very bitter w.   SHAK 441:26
they give good w.   PRAY 393:19
threw w. like stones   SPEN 515:19
times when w. had a meaning   FRAN 217:27
Uncouth w. in disarray   JOHN 280:9

Our country is the w. GARR 221:18
O w.! O life! O time SHEL 501:14
passes the glory of the w. ANON 11:1
perverse creatures in the w. ADD 2:18
ack of this tough w. SHAK 456:12
remember of this unstable w. MAL 327:21
roll of the w. eastward HARDY 241:9
Rose of all the W. YEATS 586:10
Round the w. for ever ARN 13:6
round w. so sure PRAY 395:24
sea Of the w.'s praise WORD 582:2
secure amidst a falling w. ADD 2:30
see how this w. goes SHAK 455:18
shall gain the whole w. BIBLE 66:35
shall gain the whole w. BIBLE 68:34
shows how small the w. GROS 236:22
singularly ill-contrived w. BALF 30:6
six days' work, a w. MILT 349:2
slowest thing in the w. SHAD 420:21
spectacle unto the w. BIBLE 75:33
start of the majestic w. SHAK 448:16
still the w. pursues ELIOT 204:24
that the w.'s grown honest SHAK 432:11
Then the w. seemed none HOUS 264:13
then the w.'s mine oyster SHAK 469:8
There is a w. elsewhere SHAK 427:24
These laid the w. away BROO 94:7
they only saved the w. CHES 146:25
thick rotundity o' the w. SHAK 454:4
This gewgaw w. DRYD 195:13
This is the way the w. ends ELIOT 203:11
This w.'s no blot for us BROW 100:31
This w. surely is wide STER 519:24
though the w. perish FERD 210:33
Though 'twere to buy a w. SHAK 480:26
Thou seest the w. SHAK 452:5
thrones of all the w. CHES 147:3
tied the w. in a tether SWIN 530:23
To know the w. YOUNG 588:11
to pass through this w. GREL 236:14
to perceive how the w. ARN 15:17
triple pillar of the w. SHAK 421:6
unshook amidst a bursting w. POPE 376:21
warm kind w. is all I know CORY 163:5
were all the w.'s alarms YEATS 586:4
were the youth of the w. BACON 25:10
What a w. SHAW 497:14
What a w. is this BOL 89:13
What is this w. CHAU 142:22
What would the w. be HOPK 256:18
When all the w. is young KING 297:5
whereby the w. will be judged CEL 138:6
where I live unto the w. SHAK 480:13
where the w. is quiet SWIN 529:21
which the w. cannot give PRAY 385:9
whole w. is not sufficient QUAR 403:9
who lost the w. for love DRYD 197:8
whom the w. was not worthy BIBLE 79:34
whoso hath this w.'s good BIBLE 81:4
Why was this w. created JOHN 278:5
wilderness of this w. BUNY 107:10
wish the estate o' the w. SHAK 463:7
w. And all her train VAUG 555:22
w. and I shall ne'er agree COWL 164:11
w. and its ways have BROW 105:18
w. as a vale of tears BROW 100:6
w. be worth thy winning DRYD 195:5
w. forgetting POPE 376:13
w. has grown grey from SWIN 530:5
w. has lost his youth BIBLE 62:7
w. has still Much good HOUS 264:14
w. he finds himself born CARL 131:33
w. holdeth POUND 383:19
w., I count it not BROW 97:3
w. I fill up a place SHAK 424:24
W. in a Grain of Sand BLAKE 85:8
w. invisible THOM 548:24
w. is a comedy to those WALP 563:11
W. is crazier and more MACN 326:14
w. is everything that is WITT 575:14

w. is not thy friend nor SHAK 483:26
w. is so full of a number STEV 522:22
w. is still deceived with SHAK 467:10
w. is too much with us WORD 582:19
w. is weary of the past SHEL 501:3
w. is white with May TENN 534:4
w. knew him not BIBLE 71:26
w. made cunningly Of elements DONNE 189:2
w. may end to-night BROW 101:23
w. may talk of hereafter COLL 158:12
w. must be peopled SHAK 472:19
w. Of all of us WORD 580:23
w. of pomp and state BEAU 36:1
w. of the happy is quite WITT 575:16
w.'s a bubble BACON 28:15
w.'s a jest STEP 518:25
w.'s an inn DRYD 197:10
w.'s as ugly LOCK 315:19
w.'s at an end DAV 172:6
w.'s glory passes away THOM 546:7
w.'s great age begins SHEL 500:20
w. shall end when I forget SWIN 530:16
w. shall glean of me THOM 548:28
w.'s history is the world's SCH 415:11
w.'s storm-troubled sphere BRON 93:18
w.'s whole sap is sunk DONNE 189:8
w., that passeth CHAU 144:19
w. upside down are come BIBLE 74:9
w. will little note LINC 314:23
w. without end BIBLE 77:26
w. without end PRAY 384:15
w. without end PRAY 395:17
w. would go round a deal CARR 133:25
w. would smell like what SHEL 501:18
W., you have kept faith HARDY 239:21
You never enjoy the w. TRAH 551:17
World-besotted: W. traveller YEATS 587:3
worldes: thise wrecched w. appetites
CHAU 144:19
World-losers: W. and world-forsakers
OSH 365:20
worldly: being weary of these w. bars
SHAK 449:3
Be wisely w. QUAR 403:11
breath of w. men cannot SHAK 479:5
which flees the w. clamour LUIS 320:12
w. goods I thee endow PRAY 389:5
worlds: best of all possible w. CAB 126:25
Between two w. life hovers BYRON 124:9
Exhausted w. JOHN 282:25
Wandering between two w. ARN 13:8
what w. away BROW 99:22
w. of wanwood leafmeal HOPK 256:20
world-without-end: w. hour SHAK 493:18
worm: am but as a crushed w. PUNCH 402:30
concealment, like a w. SHAK 489:7
I am a w., and no man PRAY 390:17
invisible w. BLAKE 87:12
is no goodness in the w. SHAK 424:8
man may fish with the w. SHAK 435:27
needlessly sets foot upon a w. COWP 167:28
'Or a rather tough w. GILB 227:16
wish you all joy of the w. SHAK 424:7
w. at one end and a fool JOHN 280:28
W. nor snail SHAK 470:12
w. that never dies BROO 94:14
w., the canker BYRON 125:11
worms: convocation of politic w.
SHAK 435:26
Flies, w., and flowers WATTS 565:24
have made w.' meat of me SHAK 483:4
He was eaten of w. BIBLE 74:3
Impaling w. to torture COLM 159:6
skin w. destroy this body BIBLE 52:31
then w. shall try MARV 332:19
with vilest w. to dwell SHAK 494:6
w. that are thy chambermaids SHAK 483:31
W., wäre ich dennoch eingeritten LUTH 321:3
w. were hallow'd that did SHAK 476:4
wormwood: end is bitter as w. BIBLE 53:20

of the star is called W. BIBLE 82:6
w. and the gall BIBLE 60:29
worn: comfortless, and w., and old
ROSS 409:2
short jacket is always w. EDW 200:2
when we're w. SOUT 513:13
worried: w. and scratched by every
DICK 178:6
worry: In headaches and in w. AUDEN 18:10
worse: bad against the w. DAY-L 172:23
better for w. PRAY 389:4
greater feeling to the w. SHAK 478:17
It is w. than a crime BOUL 90:19
kept it from being any w. HARDY 241:11
medicine w. than the malady FLET 215:16
More will mean w. AMIS 4:4
of finding something w. BELL 39:3
one penny the w. BARH 33:14
other things which were w. KIPL 304:30
remedy is w. than the disease BACON 27:13
state of that man is w. BIBLE 66:14
worst are no w. SHAK 471:19
worser: throw away the w. part SHAK 435:17
worship: All the earth doth w. thee
PRAY 384:16
are come to w. him BIBLE 63:31
him must w. him in spirit BIBLE 71:40
is the only object of w. ANON 7:21
let us w. and fall down PRAY 396:4
Rich in the simple w. KEATS 291:12
therefore ye ignorantly w. BIBLE 74:12
they w. Truth BROO 94:22
to w. God in his own way ROOS 407:26
various modes of w. GIBB 224:21
with my body I thee w. PRAY 389:5
With what deep w. I have COL 156:20
w. her by years of noble TENN 534:12
W. is transcendent wonder CARL 131:29
w. the beast and his image BIBLE 82:17
w. the Lord in the beauty PRAY 396:5
worshipful: w. father and first founder
CAXT 138:2
worshipp'd: w. by the names divine
BLAKE 86:1
Worshipped: W. and served the creature
BIBLE 74:32
w. stocks and stones MILT 351:9
worshipper: Nature mourns her w.
SCOTT 416:19
regular w. of the gods HOR 260:2
worshipp'st: w. at the temple's inner
WORD 582:1
Worships: W. language and forgives
AUDEN 19:7
worst: best and the w. of this SWIN 530:11
best and w., and parted BROO 94:6
best is like the w. KIPL 301:8
be the w. of the company SWIFT 526:15
exacts a full look at the w. HARDY 240:3
His w. is better than any HAZL 243:11
it was the w. of times DICK 183:5
me the w. they could do HOUS 266:7
nor the w. of men BYRON 120:29
No w., there is none HOPK 256:19
that democracy is the w. CHUR 150:19
'This is the w. SHAK 455:8
w. friend and enemy BROO 94:28
w. he can of womankind HOME 253:23
worst inn's w. room POPE 377:33
w. is death SHAK 479:8
w. is yet to come JOHN 273:24
w. of the lot KIPL 302:12
w. returns to laughter SHAK 455:5
w. speaks something good HERB 247:12
w. time of the year ANDR 4:7
worth: alone is w. all these toils CAT 136:28
charter of thy w. gives SHAK 494:13
flattery is w. his having JOHN 280:29
Goodbye is not w. while HARDY 241:7
his worldly w. for this TENN 543:9

I am not w. purchasing — REED 405:9
I do find that I am w. — PEPYS 372:18
If a thing is w. doing — CHES 148:10
in the w. and choice — JONS 283:23
man's w. something — BROW 99:10
not w. going to see — JOHN 278:10
rymyng is nat w. a toord — CHAU 143:15
therefore not w. reading — AUST 22:21
think my trifles were w. — CAT 136:20
thy own w. then not knowing — SHAK 494:13
turned out w. anything — SCOTT 419:3
Were w. a thousand men — SCOTT 416:7
what is W. in anything — BUTL 117:26
Whose w.'s unknown — SHAK 495:5
wit, nor words, nor w. — SHAK 451:2
w. a hundred coats-of-arms — TENN 537:27
w. an age without a name — MORD 357:6
w. by poverty depress'd — JOHN 282:24
W. makes the man — POPE 379:22
w. of a State — MILL 339:14
w. the dust which the rude — SHAK 455:10
worthiness: w. of thy Son Jesus Christ — PRAY 388:7
Worthington: Missis W. — COW 163:21
worthless: more w. still — HOR 260:26
W. as withered weeds — BRON 93:20
w. set than Byron and his — WELL 568:5
worthy: foemen w. of their steel — SCOTT 416:6
found them w. for himself — BIBLE 62:13
labourer is w. of his hire — BIBLE 69:27
latchet I am not w. to unloose — BIBLE 71:29
Lord I am not w. that thou — BIBLE 65:14
Lord, I am not w. — MASS 335:8
nameless in w. deeds — BROW 97:17
philosophical and more w. — ARIS 12:10
there be nine w. — CAXT 138:3
Who is w. to open the book — BIBLE 81:26
whom the world was not w. — BIBLE 79:34
w. ends and expectations — BACON 26:4
w. of the vocation wherewith — BIBLE 77:27
w. to be called thy son — BIBLE 70:19
w. womman al hir lyve — CHAU 141:31
wot: w. not what they are — SHAK 456:15
wotthehell: w. archy wotthehell — MARQ 330:21
would: heaven where they w. be — PRAY 397:10
He w., wouldn't he — RIC 406:2
I w. that you were all — BROW 105:28
I w. they should do — PRAY 388:15
what we w. — ARN 12:22
w. has heard Sordello's — BROW 105:16
W. I were with him — SHAK 443:16
wouldest: meat-offering, thou w. not — PRAY 392:2
thee whither thou w. not — BIBLE 73:17
wouldst: what thou w. highly — SHAK 459:1
wound: Earth felt the w. — MILT 349:16
felt a stain like a w. — BURKE 111:10
first did help to w. itself — SHAK 453:1
heal me of my grievous w. — TENN 535:27
Hearts w. up with love — SPEN 515:9
keen knife see not the w. — SHAK 459:2
long yellow string I w. — BROW 103:29
May soothe or w. a heart — SCOTT 416:23
now purple with love's w. — SHAK 470:8
that never felt a w. — SHAK 482:5
thy w. be throughly heal'd — SHAK 490:32
to gall a new-healed w. — SHAK 441:9
tongue In every w. of Caesar — SHAK 451:3
trickling nonsense heal'd my w. — CONG 160:2
What w. did ever heal — SHAK 475:11
Whose annual w. in Leban — MILT 345:17
Willing to w. — POPE 376:26
wit Makes such a w. — SHEL 501:20
w. for wound — BIBLE 47:25
wounded: 'e went to tend the w. — KIPL 299:18
heal what is w. — LANG 310:1
w. for our transgressions — BIBLE 59:22
w. spirit who can bear — BIBLE 54:13
'You're w. — BROW 101:16

Wounded Knee: Bury my heart at W. — BENET 40:20
wounding: wounded is the w. heart — CRAS 169:3
wounds: bind up the nation's w. — LINC 315:3
Faithful are the w. of a friend — BIBLE 54:38
many eyes as thou hast w. — SHAK 450:9
revenge keeps his own w. green — BACON 27:9
soldier details his w. — PROP 401:15
'These w. I had on Crispin's — SHAK 445:3
to bathe in reeking w. — SHAK 458:4
woven: Has w. a winter robe — HOUS 265:1
them with their w. wings — SHAK 465:7
Wovon: W. man nicht sprechen kann — WITT 575:17
wrack: w. and sumless treasuries — SHAK 443:8
Wragg: W. is in custody — ARN 15:27
wrang: they may gang a kennin w. — BURNS 112:25
wrangle: shall we begin to w. — ANON 7:15
wrapped: w. him in swaddling clothes — BIBLE 69:9
wrapt: All meanly w. in the rude — MILT 344:5
wrath: answer turneth away w. — BIBLE 54:4
between the dragon and his w. — SHAK 453:4
day of w. — CEL 138:5
Envy and w. shorten — BIBLE 63:13
eternal w. Burnt after — MILT 348:27
from the heavy w. of God — MARL 329:12
from the w. of the Lamb — BIBLE 81:30
great day of his w. is — BIBLE 81:30
He who the ox to w. has — BLAKE 85:12
if his w. be kindled — PRAY 389:19
my w. did end — BLAKE 87:21
not your children to w. — BIBLE 78:7
Nursing her w. to keep — BURNS 115:3
slow to w. — BIBLE 80:10
sun go down upon your w. — BIBLE 78:1
tigers of w. are wiser — BLAKE 88:22
Unto whom I sware in my w. — PRAY 396:4
where the grapes of w. — HOWE 266:19
w. endureth but the twinkling — PRAY 391:13
w. of God upon the children — BIBLE 78:3
w. of the lion is the wisdom — BLAKE 88:21
you to flee from the w. — BIBLE 63:38
wreath: rides homeward with a w. — CHES 147:6
sent thee late a rosy w. — JONS 284:12
wreathed: w. the rod of criticism — DISR 187:8
wreaths: laurel w. entwine — HARTE 242:26
wreck: Beautiful as a w. of Paradise — SHEL 500:12
decay Of that colossal w. — SHEL 502:16
king my brother's w. — ELIOT 204:26
wrecks: Vomits its w. — SHEL 501:17
w. of a dissolving dream — SHEL 500:20
Wrekin: forest fleece the W. — HOUS 263:14
Wren: considered Sir Christopher W. — BARH 33:7
I bore this w. — DRYD 195:12
Mr Christopher W. — EVEL 209:8
musician than the w. — SHAK 468:19
poor w. — SHAK 462:12
robin-red-breast and the w. — WEBS 567:8
shall hurt the little w. — BLAKE 85:12
Sir Christopher W. — BENT 41:9
w. goes to't — SHAK 455:16
w. with little quill — SHAK 470:18
youngest w. of nine comes — SHAK 490:2
Wrest: W. once the law to your — SHAK 468:2
wrestle: we w. not against flesh — BIBLE 78:10
w. With words and meanings — ELIOT 202:19
wrestled: There w. a man with him — BIBLE 46:23
w. with him — WALT 564:14
you have w. well — SHAK 424:26
wrestles: w. with us strengthens — BURKE 111:23
wrestling: w. with (my God!) — HOPK 256:8
wretch: sharp-looking w. — SHAK 427:9

shout which hail'd the w. — BYRON 121:
soon the dust of a w. whom — DONNE 190:
w. that dares not die — BURNS 114:
wretched: corruptions made him w. — OTWAY 365:
is a proud and yet a w. — DAV 172:
ladies most deject and w. — SHAK 433:
Most w. men — SHEL 501:
only w. are the wise — PRIOR 401
raise the w. than to rise — GOLD 230:
w. child expires — BELL 39
w. have no friends — DRYD 195:
w. he forsakes — YOUNG 587:
w. in both — SHAK 454
w. state — SHAK 434:2
wretchedness: sum of human w. — BYRON 125:
w. that glory brings us — SHAK 486:
w. of being rich that you — SMITH 510:
wretches: feel what w. feel — SHAK 454:
gaping w. of the sea — HUNT 268:
How shall w. live like — GODL 229:2
Poor naked w. — SHAK 454:
w. hang that jury-men may — POPE 381:
wring: will soon w. their hands — WALP 563:2
wrinkle: first w. and the reputation — DRYD 196:3
Time writes no w. on thine — BYRON 121:2
What stamps the w. deeper — BYRON 120:1
wrinkled: w. deep in time — SHAK 421:3
wrist: kiss on the w. — STEV 520:2
Plunge them in up to the w. — AUDEN 18:1
With gyves upon his w. — HOOD 254:1
writ: censure this mysterious w. — DRYD 196:1
Hooly w. is the scripture — JER 272:2
In all you w. to Rome — SHAK 447:
I never w. — SHAK 495:
name was w. in water — KEATS 295:
Priest w. large — MILT 351:1
w. with me in sour misfortune's — SHAK 483:28
write: baseness to w. fair — SHAK 437:1
can w. the life of a man — JOHN 276:
comfortable I sit down to w. — KEATS 294:2
does not w. himself down — HAZL 243:10
effect men w. in place lite — CHAU 144:16
frustrate of his hope to w. — MILT 351:1
he fain would w. a poem — BROW 102:32
here to w. me down an ass — SHAK 473:5
I always w. of you — SHAK 494:9
I will w. for Antiquity — LAMB 307:37
I w. so many love-lyrics — POUND 382:15
Learn to w. well — BUCH 106:15
little more I have to w. — HERR 249:5
look in thy heart and w. — SIDN 507:17
man may w. at any time — JOHN 274:3
many deaths I live and w. — HERB 247:22
might w. such stuff for ever — JOHN 279:7
much as a man ought to w. — TROL 552:13
never to w. for the sake — KEATS 294:14
not enough for me to w. — LYLY 321:16
Of every four words I w. — BOIL 89:12
restraint with which they w. — CAMP 128:12
sit down to w. — SWIFT 527:34
such as cannot w., translate — DENH 174:21
that w. what men do — BACON 24:25
this hand wherewith I w. — BROW 98:12
Though an angel should w. — MOORE 356:1
To make me w. too much — DAN 170:24
to w. for him with her — ARN 16:8
virtues We w. in water — SHAK 447:3
want to read a novel I w. — DISR 185:26
we cannot w. like Hazlitt — STEV 522:10
When men w. for profit — WALP 563:15
will sometimes wish to w. — COWP 168:17
w. and read comes by nature — SHAK 472:27
W.: for these words are — BIBLE 82:31
w. for the general amusement — SCOTT 418:10
w. in a book — BIBLE 81:30
w. in wind and swift-flowing — CAT 137:7
w. it before them — BIBLE 58:25

y. teach muci which — EMER 207:19
y. that the locust hath — BIBLE 61:14
y. to come seemed waste — YEATS 585:15
yet belie thy happy y. — SHAK 488:3
yeas: In russet y. and honest — SHAK 457:16
Yeats: churchyard Y. is laid — YEATS 587:10
William Y. is laid to rest — AUDEN 19:7
yell: such a y. was there — SCOTT 417:20
Yell'ham: That Y. says — HARDY 241:8
yellow: are already y. with August — POUND 383:17
come to her in y. stockings — SHAK 489:17
Come unto these y. sands — SHAK 484:30
islets of y. sand — LEAR 312:16
learn from the Y. an' Brown — KIPL 300:15
sear, the y. leaf — SHAK 463:2
this square old y. Book — BROW 104:14
Was y. like ripe corn — ROSS 409:15
When y. leaves — SHAK 494:7
Y., and black — SHEL 502:8
Y. God forever gazes down — HAYES 243:7
yelping: Faced by the snarled and y. — ELIOT 204:11
yelps: loudest y. for liberty among — JOHN 282:18
yeoman: It did me y.'s service — SHAK 437:12
yeomanly: this the y. — DONNE 190:23
yerde: 'man maketh ofte a y. — CHAU 144:2
Yes: 'Y.', I answered you — BROW 98:5
yes I said yes I will Y. — JOYCE 286:30
y. O at lightning — HOPK 257:6
yesterday: all our pomp of y. — KIPL 302:8
call back y. — SHAK 479:6
dead Y. — FITZ 212:22
Jesus Christ the same y. — BIBLE 80:4
Myself with Y.'s Sev'n — FITZ 212:16
thy sight are but as y. — PRAY 395:18
universe and give me y. — JONES 283:10
We were saying y. — LUIS 320:13
where leaves the Rose of Y. — FITZ 212:10
y. a King — BYRON 125:7
y. doth not usher it — DONNE 190:26
Y. I loved — LESS 313:26
you'd think it was only y. — MILL 339:25
yesterdays: all our y. have lighted — SHAK 463:6
yesteryear: where are the snows of y. — VILL 557:5
Yestreen: Y. the Queen had four Maries — BALL 31:12
yet: as y. there were none — PRAY 399:7
continency—but not y. — AUG 21:14
young man not y. — BACON 26:35
yeux: *allez vous user les* y. — ZOLA 588:19
Français lève les y. — TOCQ 551:8
yew: never a spray of y. — ARN 14:5
slips of y. — SHAK 462:4
so solemnly to yonder y. — JONS 285:9
stuck all with y. — DOYLE 191:14
true wood, of y.-wood — DE L 174:17
Y. alone burns lamps — DE L 174:17
yew-tree: that y.'s shade — GRAY 234:20
yield: not make the sickle y. — BLAKE 86:19
Private respects must y. — MILT 350:24
temptation is just to y. — GRAH 233:8
to find, and not to y. — TENN 544:3
year has shot her y. — KIPL 300:23
yielded: by her y. — MILT 347:23
yields: craggy mountains y. — SHAK 495:16
ymage: thilke God that after his y. — CHAU 144:19
Ynde: egre is a tygre yond in Y. — CHAU 142:10
Yo-ho-ho: Y., and a bottle of rum — STEV 521:21
yoke: bear the y. in his youth — BIBLE 60:30
bring the inevitable y. — WORD 579:8
Flanders hath receiv'd our y. — WALL 562:17
his neck unto a second y. — HERR 250:4
impertinent y. of prelaty — MILT 352:15
savage bull doth bear the y. — SHAK 472:2

Take my y. upon you — BIBLE 66:5
that ye break every y. — BIBLE 60:4
yoked: you are y. with a lamb — SHAK 451:24
yolk: y. runs down the waistcoat — DICK 180:14
yonge: O y., fressshe folkes — CHAU 144:19
Yorick: Alas, poor Y. — SHAK 436:31
you: Here am I, here are y. — AUDEN 19:14
I cannot live with y. — MART 331:13
married My Lord y. — POUND 383:16
y. against me — BETJ 44:6
y. I should love to live — HOR 261:1
Y., that way — SHAK 457:20
young: all of them desirable y. — BIBLE 60:37
America is a country of y. — EMER 208:11
anchored and the y. star-captains — FLEC 214:7
atrocious crime of being a y. — PITT 373:20
been y., and now am old — PRAY 391:28
believe everything a y. — JOW 285:22
both were y. — BYRON 124:12
care for the y. man's whore — JOHN 275:19
crime by corrupting the y. — PLATO 374:8
embarrassing y. — GAV 222:5
fat and look y. till forty — DRYD 196:36
God guide them—y. — TENN 535:5
gods love dies y. — MEN 336:25
hinds to bring forth y. — PRAY 391:11
how y. the policemen look — HICKS 250:23
I was y. — FLEC 214:23
I was y. and foolish — YEATS 584:22
love's y. dream — MOORE 356:12
made y. with young desires — THOM 548:4
Most women are not so y. — BEER 37:10
nor y. enough for a boy — SHAK 488:9
Not so y. — SHAK 453:14
No y. man believes he shall — HAZL 244:3
panting and for ever y. — KEATS 291:7
proper y. men — BURNS 114:17
remember'd that he once was y. — ARMS 12:14
set her six y. on the rail — BROW 101:19
seventy years y. — HOLM 253:14
she died y. — WEBS 566:27
sight to make an old man y. — TENN 533:20
So wise so y. — SHAK 481:3
So y., and so untender — SHAK 453:3
so y., I loved him so — BROW 99:16
those that are with y. — BIBLE 59:7
to be y. was very heaven — WORD 577:21
To find a y. fellow that — CONG 160:11
Tomorrow for the y. — AUDEN 20:16
we knew the worst too y. — KIPL 299:11
When I was y. — MILNE 340:17
When thou wast y. — BIBLE 73:17
While we are y. — ANON 10:13
Wives are y. men's mistresses — BACON 26:34
world and love were y. — RAL 404:9
years to be y. and handsome — SWIFT 526:22
y. a body with so old — SHAK 467:26
y. and easy under the apple — THOM 547:1
y. and lusty as an eagle — PRAY 396:15
y. and sweating devil here — SHAK 476:2
y. are sad and bewildered — SMITH 510:22
y. as beautiful — YOUNG 588:7
y. can do for the old — SHAW 496:25
y. girl miserable may give — FRAN 218:5
Y. in limbs — SHAK 466:17
y. In one another's arms — YEATS 586:11
y. lassie do wi' an auld — BURNS 116:3
y. man cleanse his way — PRAY 398:4
y. man feels his pockets — HOUS 265:2
y. man lands hatless — BETJ 42:12
y. man not yet — BACON 26:35
y. man's dog with them — BIBLE 62:9
y. man's soul — HOUS 262:22
y. man will be wiser — TENN 534:2
Y. men and maidens — PRAY 399:23
Y. men are fitter to invent — BACON 27:39
y. men glittering and sparkling — TRAH 551:19
Y. men have more virtue — JOHN 275:4
Y. men make great mistakes — JOW 285:24
Y. men shall see visions — BIBLE 61:15

y. men's vision — DRYD 194:
y. men think it is — HOUS 266:
y. to fall asleep for ever — SASS 414:1
you yet call yourself y. — SHAK 441:1
younger: Then let thy love be y. — SHAK 489.
y. son gathered all together — BIBLE 70:1
Y. than she are happy mothers — SHAK 481:2
y. widows refuse — BIBLE 79:1
youngest: not even the y. of us — THOM 549:
y. he was little Billee — THAC 545:3
yours: Have these for y. — HOUS 266:
What I have done is y. — SHAK 492:1
Y. is the Earth and everything — KIPL 300:
y. till the rending — JOYCE 286:
yourself: Could love you for y. alone — YEATS 585:
Keep yourself *to* y. — DICK 182:
Live with y. — PERS 372:2
women, physical decay, Y. — AUDEN 19:
you're not good enough y. — TROL 553:1
yourselves: honey not for y. — VIRG 560:2
youth: After the pleasures of y. — ANON 10:1
banged the y. into dumbness — SHAK 489:2
bear the yoke in his y. — BIBLE 60:3
considered as a debauch of y. — BURKE 108:1
Crabbed age and y. — SHAK 492:13
Creator in the days of thy y. — BIBLE 56:1
days of our y. are — BYRON 125:2
eagle mewing her mighty y. — MILT 352:3
Enjoy'd his y. — DRYD 196:
every y. cry *Well-a-way* — BALL 30:1
flourish set on y. — SHAK 493:20
flower of their y. — VIRG 560:
fought against me from my y. — PRAY 398:21
great has been done by y. — DISR 185:39
green unknowing y. engage — DRYD 197:1
heart is evil from his y. — BIBLE 45:36
How beautiful is y. — MED 336:9
If y. knew — EST 208:25
In flow'r of y. and beauty's — DRYD 194:23
informs the Scottish y. — STUB 524:5
In the lexicon of y. — BULW 107:5
in trust Our y. — RAL 404:15
In y. is pleasure — WEVER 569:7
I remember my y. — CONR 161:2
is the measure of our y. — KIPL 299:1
it is y. that must fight — HOOV 255:25
I was a hot-blooded y. — HOR 261:4
Jenny's unsuspecting y. — BURNS 113:7
laugh uproariously in y. — BROO 94:24
Let age approve of y. — BROW 104:13
loves the meat in his y. — SHAK 472:18
might renew our y. — YEATS 587:14
nourishing a y. sublime — TENN 538:16
of my ill adventured y. — DAN 171:1
riband in the cap of y. — SHAK 436:17
sign of an ill-spent y. — SPEN 515:4
sins and offences of my y. — PRAY 391:2
So long as y. and thou — SHAK 493:1
spirit of y. in everything — SHAK 494:1
stretch the folly of our y. — CHES 147:12
submit to be taught by y. — BURKE 110:23
subtle thief of y. — MILT 351:6
Sweet wine of y. — BROO 94:7
That miracle of a y. — EVEL 209:8
that the April of your y. — HERB 246:20
thee in the days of thy y. — BIBLE 56:10
things Y. needed not — WORD 581:12
thou goodly y. — BALL 30:9
Thou hast nor y. nor age — SHAK 464:10
To y. and age in common — ARN 15:13
traitorously corrupted the y. — SHAK 446:12
well-beloved y. — BALL 30:7
were the y. of the world — BACON 25:10
when Y. and Pleasure meet — BYRON 120:21
Where y. grows pale — KEATS 291:19
Whose y. was full of foolish — TENN 536:22
world has lost his y. — BIBLE 62:7
y. And a little beauty — WEBS 566:20
Y. are boarded — DICK 179:34

GREEK INDEX

γαν: μηδὲν ἄ. ANON: 9:22
γγέλλειν: ὦ ξεῖν', ἀ. Λακεδαιμονίοις SIMO 508:9
γεωμέτρητος: ἀ. μηδεὶς εἰσίτω ANON 10:2
δικεῖν: ἀ. τούς τε νέους διαφθείροντα PLATO 374:8
ἄδωρα: ἐχθρῶν ἄ. δῶρα SOPH 513:5
ἄκρον: ἄ. ἐπ' ἀκροτάτῳ SAPP 414:7
ἄλγεα: πολὺν χρόνον ἄ. πάσχειν HOMER 253:28
ἀλεκτρυόνα: 'Ασκληπιῷ ὀφείλομεν ἀ. SOCR 512:21
ἀληθείᾳ: οὐ μὲν οὖν τῇ ἀ. PLATO 374:12
ἀλώπηξ: πολλ' οἶδ' ἀ. ARCH 11:22
ἀμύνεσθαι: ἀ. περὶ πάτρης HOMER 254:2
ἀνάσσειν: νεκύεσσι καταφθιμένοισιν ἀ. HOMER 254:6
ἄνδρα: ἄ. μοι ἔννεπε, Μοῦσα HOMER 254:4
τίν' ἄ., τίν ἥρωα POUND 383:9
ἄνδρες: ἄ. γὰρ πόλις, καὶ οὐ τείχη NICI 362:25
ἀνεξέταστος: ἀ. βίος οὐ βιωτὸς SOCR 512:17
ἀνήριθμον: κυμάτων ἀ. γέλασμα AESC 3:3
ἀποθανεῖν: ἀ. θέλω PETR 373:2
ἀριστεύειν: ἀ. καὶ ὑπείροχον ἔμμεναι HOMER 253:30
ἄριστον: ἄ. μὲν ὕδωρ PIND 373:13
ἀφροδίσια: πῶς... ἔχεις πρὸς τ. SOPH 513:9
βιβλίον: μέγα β. CALL 127:8
βίος: ὁ β. βραχύς HIPP 251:8
βιωτὸς: ἀνεξέταστος βίος οὐ β. SOCR 512:17
βραδέως: σπεῦδε β. SUET 524:16
βρεκεκεκὲξ: β. κοὰξ κοὰξ ARIS 12:5
γελαίσας: γ. ἱμέροεν SAPP 414:6
γελάσασα: δακρυόεν γ. HOMER 254:1
γέλασμα: κυμάτων ἀνήριθμον γ. AESC 3:3
γενεή: οἵη περ φύλλων γ. HOMER 253:29
γενοίμην: εἴθε.... would I were BROO 94:20
γῆ: ἐπιφανῶν πᾶσα γ. τάφος PERI 372:23
γηράσκω: γ. δ'αἰεὶ πολλὰ διδασκόμενος SOLON 512:24
γλυκύμαλον: οἶον τὸ γ. ἐρεύθεται SAPP 414:7
γλῶσσ': ἡ γ. ὀμώμοχ' EURI 209:4
γνῶθι: γ. σεαυτόν ANON 9:21
δεινά: πολλὰ τὰ δ. SOPH 513:7
δεσπότην: λυττῶντα τινα καὶ ἄργιον δ. SOPH 513:9
δημόσια: σικχαίνω πάντα τὰ δ. CALL 127:7

διδασκόμενος: γηράσκω δ'αἰεὶ πολλὰ δ. SOLON 512:24
δὶς: δ. ἐς τὸν αὐτὸν ποταμὸν HERA 246:6
δῶρα: ἐχθρῶν ἄδωρα δ. SOPH 513:5
εἴθε: εἴ. γενοίμην... would I were BROO 94:20
ἐκκελάθοντ': οὐ μὰν ἐ. SAPP 414:7
ἐλέναυς: ἐ. ἕλανδρος ἑλέπτολις AESC 3:1
ἔν: ἐχῖνος ἔ. μέγα ARCH 11:22
ἐναντιός: ὅττις ἐ. τοι ἰσδάνει SAPP 414:6
ἐπάρουρος: ἐ. ἐὼν θητευέμεν ἄλλῳ HOMER 254:6
ἔπεα: ἔ. πτερόεντα HOMER 253:27
εὐκνήμιδας: Τρῶας καί ἐ. 'Αχαιοὺς HOMER 253:28
εὔκολος: ὁ δ'εὔ. μὲν ἐνθάδ' ARIS 12:4
εὕρηκα ARCH 11:23
εὐτυχέστερος: γένοιο πατρὸς εὐ. SOPH 513:4
ἐχῖνος: ἐ. ἔν μέγα ARCH 11:22
ζῆν: ὅντινα τρόπον χρὴ ζ. PLATO 374:11
ἥρωα: τίν' ἄνδρα, τίν ἥ. POUND 383:9
θάλαττα θάλαττα XENO 584:5
θέλεις: Σίβυλλα, τί θ. PETR 373:2
θεοί: ὃν οἱ θ. φιλοῦσιν MENA 336:25
θητευέμεν: ἐπάρουρος ἐὼν θ. ἄλλῳ HOMER 254:6
ἱμέροεν: γελαίσας ἱ. SAPP 414:6
ἱστορίας: σπουδαιότερον ποίησις ἱ. ARIS 12:10
κάθαρσιν: τοιούτων παθημάτων κ. ARIS 12:9
κακόν: μέγα βιβλίον μέγα κ. CALL 127:8
καλόν: τὸ κ. Decreed in the market POUND 383:8
κεῖτο: κ. μέγας μεγαλωστὶ HOMER 254:3
κῆνος: φαίνεταί μοι κ. ἴσος θέοισιν SAPP 414:6
κλέος: ἐν τοῖς ἄρρεσι κ. ᾖ PERI 372:24
κοὰξ: βρεκεκεκὲξ κ. κ. ARIS 12:5
κυμάτων: κ. ἀνήριθμον γέλασμα AESC 3:3
Λακεδαιμονίοις: ὦ ξεῖν', ἀγγέλλειν Λ. SIMO 508:9
λόγος: περὶ τοῦ ἐπιτυχόντος ὁ λ. PLATO 374:11
λυττῶντα: λ. τινα καὶ ἄργιον δεσπότην SOPH 513:9
μακρή: ἡ δε τέχνη μ. HIPP 251:8
μαλακίας: φιλοσοφοῦμεν ἄνευ μ. PERI 372:22
μέγα: ἐχῖνος ἐν μ. ARCH 11:22
μ. βιβλίον CALL 127:8
μεγαλωστὶ: κεῖτο μέγας μ. HOMER 254:3
μένει: οὐδὲν μ. HERA 246:5
μηδὲν: μ. ἄγαν ANON 9:22
μῆνιν: μ. ἄειδε, θεά HOMER 253:26

μίμησις: τραγῳδία μ. πράξεως σπουδαίας ARIS 12:9
μυριόνους: 'Ανὴρ μ. COLE 157:23
νίκα: τούτῳ ν. CONS 162:6
νικῶμεν: χαίρετε, ν. PHEI 373:6
ξεῖν': ὦ ξ., ἀγγέλλειν Λακεδαιμονίοις SIMO 508:9
ὄλβιον: μηδὲ καλέειν κω ὄ. SOLON 512:25
ὀμώμοχ': ἡ γλῶσσ' ὀ. EURI 209:4
οὗ: οὗτος, οὐ κείνοισιν, οὗ SOPH 513:6
πάντα: π. χωρεῖ HERA 246:5
πέπληγμαι: ὤμοι, π. καιρίαν πληγὴν AESC 3:2
περίφοιτον: μισῶ καὶ π. ἐρώμενον CALL 127:7
πίνω: οὐδ' ἀπὸ κρήνης π. CALL 127:7
ποίησις: σπουδαιότερον π. ἱστορίας ARIS 12:10
πόλις: ἄνδρες γὰρ π. καὶ οὐ τείχη NICI 362:25
πολιτικὸν: ἄνθρωπος φύσει π. ζῷον ARIS 12:7
πολλὰ: π. τὰ δεινὰ SOPH 513:7
πολύτροπον: ἔννεπε, Μοῦσα, π. HOMER 254:4
πορσύνη: δαίμων ἀνδρὶ π. κακά ANON 10:1
πόσων: π. ἐγὼ χρείαν οὐκ ἔχω SOCR 512:22
ποταμὸν: δὶς ἐς τὸν αὐτὸν π. HERA 246:6
πτερόεντα: ἔπεα π. HOMER 253:27
ῥοδοδάκτυλος: ῥ. 'Ηώς HOMER 254:5
Σίβυλλα: Σ., τί θελεις; PETR 373:2
σπεῦδε: σ. βραδέως SUET 524:16
τάφος: ἐπιφανῶν πᾶσα γῆ τ. PERI 372:23
τέθνηκεν: θεοὶς τ. οὗτος SOPH 513:6
τείχη: ἄνδρες γὰρ πόλις καὶ οὐ τ. NICI 362:25
τίν': τ. ἄνδρα, τίν ἥρωα POUND 383:9
ὕδωρ: ἄριστον μεν ὕ. PIND 373:13
φαίνεται: φ. μοι κῆνος ἴσος θέοισιν SAPP 414:6
φιλοκαλοῦμέν: φ. τε γὰρ μετ' εὐτελείας PERI 372:22
φιλοσοφοῦμεν: φ. ἄνευ μαλακίας PERI 372:22
φιλοῦσιν: ὃν οἱ θεοὶ φ. MENA 336:25
φρήν: ἡ δε φ. ἀνώμοτος EURI 209:4
φροντίς: οὐ φ. 'Ιπποκλείδῃ HIPP 251:7
φύλλων: οἵη περ φ. γενεή HOMER 253:29
φῦναι: μὴ φ. τον ἅπαντα νικᾷ λόγον SOPH 513:8
χαίρετε: χ., νικῶμεν PHEI 373:6
χρείαν: πόσων ἐγὼ χ. οὐκ ἔχω SOCR 512:22
χωρεῖ: πάντα χ. HERA 246:5
ὤμοι: ὤ., πέπληγμαι καιρίαν πληγὴν AESC 3:2